Laurie G. Kirszner
University of the Sciences in Philadelphia

Stephen R. Mandell
Drexel University

D0204891

Literature

READING ◆ REACTING ◆ WRITING

Sixth Edition

THOMSON

WADSWORTH

Australia • Brazil • Canada • Mexico • Singapore • Spain • United Kingdom • United States

THOMSON
WADSWORTH

LITERATURE: Reading, Reacting, Writing, Sixth Edition
Kirszner / Mandell

Publisher: *Michael Rosenberg*

Acquisitions Editor: *Aron Keesbury*

Development Editor: *Karen R. Smith*

Managing Developmental Editor: *Karen Judd*

Editorial Assistant: *Cheryl Forman*

Managing Marketing Manager: *Mandee Eckersley*

Marketing Manager: *Kate Edwards*

Marketing Assistant: *Dawn Giovanneillo*

Advertising Project Manager: *Patrick Rooney*

Editorial Production Manager: *Michael Burggren*

Manufacturing Manager: *Marcia Locke*

Senior Permissions Editor: *Isabel Alves*

Permissions Freelancer: *Stephen Jordan*

Senior Art Director: *Bruce Bond*

Photo Manager: *Sheri Blaney*

Photo Researcher: *Jill Engebretson*

Technology Project Manager: *Tim Smith*

Production Service/Compositor: *Nesbitt Graphics*

Text Designer: *Jerilyn Bockorick*

Cover Designer: *Suzanne Heiser*

Cover Quilt Creator: *Greta Vaught*

Text Printer: *RR Donnelley & Sons*

Cover Printer: *Phoenix Color*

Printed in the United States of America

1 2 3 4 5 6 7 09 08 07 06

Library of Congress Control Number: 2005937959

Student Edition ISBN 1-4130-1938-2

Thomson Higher Education
25 Thomson Place
Boston, MA 02210-1202
USA

For more information about our products, contact us at:
Thomson Learning Academic Resource Center
1-800-423-0563
For permission to use material from this text or product, submit a request online at
http://www.thomsonrights.com.
Any additional questions about permissions can be submitted by email to
thomsonrights@thomson.com.

BRIEF CONTENTS

CONTENTS

> "All bright and glittering in the smokeless air"

```
Memory: then and now
    Then: leaf, straw, dead insect (= light);
        ignored
    Now: swollen, puffed up, weight (= heavy);
        focus of attention controls their
        movements.
* Kitchen = a "universe"
    Teaspoons, goblets, etc. = concrete
        representations of mother; also =
        obligations, responsibilities (like
        plants and father)
    weigh on them, keep them under her spell)
```

v

“Major premise: All tragic heroes have tragic flaws.”

1. **A book by a single author**
   Kingston, Maxine Hong. <u>The Woman Warrior: Memoirs of a Girlhood among Ghosts</u>. New York: Knopf, 1976.

2. **A book by two or three authors**
   Feldman, Burton, and Robert D. Richardson. <u>The Rise of Modern Mythology</u>. Bloomington: Indiana UP, 1972.

Key Words in Exam Questions		
Explain	Clarify	Classify
Compare	Relate	Identify
Contrast	Justify	Illustrate
Trace	Analyze	Define
Evaluate	Interpret	Support
Discuss	Describe	Summarize

"◎□❖◆○◆○○□◆⊙●"

---

15 | POINT OF VIEW 329

---

16 | STYLE, TONE, AND LANGUAGE 388

34 | POETRY FOR FURTHER READING   1135

Appendix A: Using Literary Criticism in Your Writing   **2083**

AUTHORS REPRESENTED BY MULTIPLE WORKS

PREFACE

In Alice Walker's short story "Everyday Use" (p. 469), two sisters—one rural and traditional, one urban and modern—compete for possession of two quilts that have been in their family for years. At the end of the story, the narrator's description of the quilts suggests their significance—as a link between the old and the new, between what was and what is:

> One was in the Lone Star pattern. The other was Walk Around the Mountain. In both of them were scraps of dresses that Grandma Dee had worn fifty and more years ago. Bits and pieces of Grandpa Jarrell's Paisley shirts. And one teeny faded blue piece, about the size of a penny matchbox, that was from Great Grandpa Eza's uniform that he wore in the Civil War. (474)

In a sense, *Literature: Reading, Reacting, Writing* is a kind of literary quilt, one that places nontraditional works alongside classics, integrates the familiar with the unfamiliar, and invites students to see well-known works in new contexts. To convey this message, the publisher has commissioned a handmade quilt by textile artist Greta Vaught for each edition of the book. The quilt designed for this new edition uses contemporary as well as traditional quilting techniques to reflect our own increased focus on contemporary and emerging writers as well as on writers from diverse cultures and backgrounds.

The sixth edition of *Literature: Reading, Reacting, Writing*, like the previous editions, is designed to demystify the study of literature and to prepare students to explore the literary works collected here. Our goal in this edition remains what it has been from the start: to expand students' personal literary boundaries. To this end, we have fine-tuned the reading selections and expanded the pedagogical features that support the study of literature, acting in response to thoughtful comments from our reviewers and from our students. Having class-tested this book in our own literature classrooms, we have learned what kinds of selections and features best help our students to read, think about, understand, and write about literature in ways that make it meaningful to their lives in the twenty-first century.

To help instructors engage their students with literature and guide them in becoming better thinkers and writers, we have added new readings and enhanced key elements that have made *Literature: Reading, Reacting, Writing* a classroom success.

Unparalleled Writing Coverage

The first college literature anthology to address writing as a major component of the introductory literature course, *Literature: Reading, Reacting, Writing* now begins with a comprehensive writing guide. Part 1, "A Guide to Writing about Literature," consists of eight chapters that help students see writing about literature as a process of discovering, testing, and arguing ideas. In addition, comprehensive writing coverage is integrated throughout the book in the following features:

- **A general introduction to the writing process** Chapter 2, "Reading and Writing about Literature," explains and illustrates the process of planning, drafting, and revising essays about literary works, concluding with an exercise asking students to evaluate and compare two different student papers that examine the same three short stories.

- **Special treatment for writing about each genre** "Reading and Writing about Fiction" (Chapter 11), "Reading and Writing about Poetry" (Chapter 24), and "Reading and Writing about Drama" (Chapter 38) follow the writing process of students as they focus on works in each genre: Alberto Alvaro Ríos's short story "The Secret Lion" (p. 170); Seamus Heaney's poem "Digging" (p. 1060) and Robert Hayden's poem "Those Winter Sundays" (p. 1059); and Susan Glaspell's one-act play *Trifles* (p. 1372).

- **Two new chapters on literary argument** Chapter 4, "Thinking Critically about Your Writing," and Chapter 5, "Writing Literary Arguments," help students to think critically about their writing and build cogent arguments about literary works. Chapter 5 takes students through the process of writing a literary argument and concludes with a new annotated student paper.

- **Expanded research and documentation coverage** Tracing the research process of a student writing a short essay on Eudora Welty's "A Worn Path" (p. 505), Chapter 6, "Writing a Research Paper," now includes more extensive advice for conducting library and Internet research. A thoroughly updated and expanded Chapter 7, "Documenting Sources and Avoiding Plagiarism," includes strategies for avoiding plagiarism as well as the most up-to-date documentation and format guidelines from the Modern Language Association (including many examples of MLA-style citations for electronic sources).

- **Fourteen model student papers** Because our own experience in the classroom has shown us that students often learn most easily from models, the text includes fourteen model student papers (two of which are new to the sixth edition) written in response to the kinds of topics that are frequently assigned in Introduction to Literature classes. Some of these model papers are source-based, and three are shown in multiple drafts, along with annotations and commentary. In addition, an annotated sample student answer to an essay exam appears in Chapter 8, "Writing Essay Exams about Literature."

- **New section on examining a work's historical context** Chapter 3, "Writing Special Kinds of Papers," includes a new section on writing about a work's historical context. This important section contains a new annotated student paper.

- **Casebooks for reading, research, and writing** Three casebooks — on Joyce Carol Oates, Langston Hughes, and Tennessee Williams — feature seminal works by each writer, accompanied by literary criticism, biographical essays, and other useful and interesting materials (interviews, photographs, popular magazine articles, and so on), including several new visuals that enhance each work's contextual coverage. The casebooks also include discussion questions as well as writing prompts for research papers. In addition, a list of relevant Web sites for each work is provided on the book's companion Web site <http://kirsznermandell.wadsworth.com>.

Students can use these casebooks to supplement their reading or as source material for a research project. (A model student paper in each casebook shows students how to use sources, including Internet sources, in their writing.) By gathering research materials in a convenient, accessible format, these casebooks offer students a controlled, self-contained introduction to source-based writing as well as all the materials they need to begin a research project.

- **Checklists** Most chapter introductions end with a checklist designed to help students measure their understanding of concepts introduced in the chapter. These checklists can also guide students as they generate, explore, focus, and organize ideas for writing about works of literature.

- **Writing suggestions with Web activities** Imaginative suggestions for paper topics are included at the end of each chapter. Corresponding Web activities are provided on the book's companion Web site <http://kirsznermandell.wadsworth.com> to spark students' interest and generate engaged writing.

Fresh, Balanced Selections

The short stories, poems, and plays collected in this book represent a balance of old and new as well as a wide variety of nations and cultures and a full range of writing styles.

- **Extensive selection of fiction** The fiction selection includes not only perennial classics ("The Lottery," "A Rose for Emily," "The Cask of Amontillado") and stories we introduced to readers in the first edition, such as David Michael Kaplan's "Doe Season" and Charles Baxter's "Gryphon," but also a number of works never previously collected in a college literature anthology, such as Jonathan Safran Foer's "A Primer for the Punctuation of Heart Disease" and Amanda Holzer's "Love and Other Catastrophes: A Mix Tape." The eighteen new stories that appear in this edition include some of the most frequently taught works of fiction—for example, Ernest Hemingway's "Hills Like White Elephants," James Baldwin's "Sonny's Blues," and Flannery O'Connor's "Everything That Rises Must Converge." Also included are several popular contemporary works, such as Gish Jen's "The Water Faucet Vision" and Louise Erdrich's "The Red Convertible."

- **Blend of contemporary and classic poetry** The poetry section balances works by classic poets (such as Robert Frost, Emily Dickinson, and Langston Hughes) with works by more contemporary poets (such as Linda Pastan and Ted Kooser) and also introduces students to exciting twenty-first century works by poets such as Stephen Dunn, Wanda Coleman, and Mary Oliver. Now offering an even broader range of diverse works, the poetry section has been expanded with seventy-six new works by poets such as Charles Bernstein, Tupac Shakur, Pat Mora, Billy Collins, Mary Jo

Salter, Octavio Paz, Frank O'Hara, Galway Kinnell, José Juan Tablada, Jack Kerouac, Edgar Allan Poe, Maxine Kumin, Sandra Cisneros, Joseph Brodsky, Pablo Neruda, Eliza Griswold, and Langston Hughes.

- **Varied selection of plays** The drama section juxtaposes classic selections—William Shakespeare's *Hamlet*, August Wilson's *Fences*, Milcha Sanchez-Scott's *The Cuban Swimmer*—with very contemporary plays, such as David Auburn's *Proof* and Emily Roderer's *Scheherazade*. Nine plays are new to the sixth edition. In addition to Lorraine Hansberry's classic *A Raisin in the Sun*, we now include several contemporary works, such as Tracey Scott Wilson's *Small World* and David Henry Hwang's *Trying to Find Chinatown*.

- **Innovative "sampler" chapters** Chapter 10, "Fiction Sampler: The Short-Short"; Chapter 23, "Poetry Sampler: Visual Poetry"; and Chapter 37, "Drama Sampler: Ten-Minute Plays," showcase representative selections from three popular literary subgenres, introducing students to the variety and diversity of literature with brief, accessible works.

- **New chapter on fiction in film** Chapter 19, "Fiction in Film," helps students to consider the challenges of adapting fiction to film. This new material includes still photos taken from DVDs of five short stories that appear in the text: John Updike's "A&P" (p. 230), Tillie Olsen's "I Stand Here Ironing" (p. 309), Alice Walker's "Everyday Use" (p. 469), Raymond Carver's "Cathedral" (p. 476), and Eudora Welty's "A Worn Path" (p. 505). The pictures are followed by a series of questions that ask students to think critically about the decisions they would make if they were adapting each of the stories into a short film. (A marginal Film Series DVD icon cross-references the five stories in the text to Chapter 19.)

Film Series

DVD

- **New section on poems about nature** Chapter 32, "Discovering Themes in Poetry," has been expanded to include new poems about nature by poets such as Christina Rossetti, Simone Muench, and Richard Wilbur.

- **Authors represented by multiple works** Many authors are represented in the book by more than one work, and in some cases, by more than one literary genre. A list of all such works follows the book's table of contents, giving students an opportunity to see at a glance how a particular writer explores different themes, styles, and genres.

Thorough Background Information

As we have learned in our classrooms over the years, part of helping students to demystify literature is helping them to understand the context in which the stories, poems, and plays were written. To achieve this goal, we continue to include contextual and background materials throughout the book in various forms.

- **Cultural context notes** A cultural context section follows each author headnote in fiction and drama, providing vital background about the social and historical climate in which the work was written.

- **Enhanced, integrated discussion of literary history** Chapter 9, "Understanding Fiction," now contains a vastly expanded "Origins of Modern Fiction" section, and a new section, "Origins of Modern Poetry," now appears in Chapter 22, "Understanding Poetry." These sections—along with the corresponding section "Origins of Modern Drama" (in Chapter 36, "Understanding Drama")—are now fully illustrated with visuals that trace each genre's development and bring the history of literature to life.
- **Literary history appendix** Appendix B, "Literary History: From Aristotle to the Present," gives students a brief historical overview of Western literary criticism.
- **Poets' biographies** Chapter 35, "Biographical Sketches of Selected Poets," includes photos and biographical notes on forty-two classic and contemporary poets whose work is featured in the text.

Other Pedagogical Features

A number of other pedagogical features appear throughout the text to prompt students to think critically about reading and to spark class discussions and energetic, thoughtful writing:

- **Introductory Overview** Chapter 1, "Understanding Literature," presents an overview of some of the most important issues surrounding the study of literature, acquainting students with traditional literary themes as well as with the concept of the literary canon. The chapter also lays the groundwork for students' independent exploration of literary texts by discussing the processes of interpreting and evaluating literary texts, placing special emphasis on how readers' personal experiences affect meaning. Finally, the chapter examines the role of literary criticism and considers how critics' interpretations can help students expand their literary horizons.
- **Reading and Reacting questions** Reading and Reacting questions, including journal prompts, follow many selections throughout the text. These questions ask students to interpret and evaluate what they have read, sometimes encouraging them to make connections between the literary work being studied and other works in the text.
- **Critical Perspectives** Critical Perspective questions (included in most sets of Reading and Reacting questions) ask students to respond to analytical, interpretative, or evaluative comments that writers and critics have made about the work. This feature encourages students to apply their own critical thinking skills to literary criticism as well as to the work of literature itself.
- **Literary criticism appendix** Appendix A, "Using Literary Criticism in Your Writing," explains and illustrates the key schools of literary criticism and shows how each can be applied to a typical student writing assignment inspired by a work in the text.

- **Related Works** A Related Works section following the Reading and Re-acting questions lists works linked (by theme, author, or genre) to the particular work under study. This feature encourages students to see connections between works by different writers, between works in different genres, or between two themes—connections they can explore in class discussion and in writing.

A Full Package of Supplementary Materials

To support students and instructors who use the sixth edition of *Literature: Reading, Reacting, Writing,* the following ancillary materials are available from Wadsworth:

- **Instructor's Resource Manual** A comprehensive instructor's manual provides all the materials necessary to support a variety of teaching styles. This resource includes discussion and activities for every short story, poem, and play in the anthology; a thematic table of contents; semester and quarter sample syllabi; and articles on the evolution of the literary canon and reader-response theory. In addition, this edition includes a section called "Do Your Students Know?"— brief, entertaining notes that provide interesting, sometimes offbeat contextual information.
- **Lit21: Literature in the Twenty-First Century** Now a fully online product, *Lit21* has been thoroughly enhanced to provide students with a unique, interactive environment that can supplement the many aspects of the study of literature. In addition to sixty-eight stories, poems, and scenes from plays read aloud on the disk, *Lit21* offers thirty video clips of poetry readings, interviews, and selected scenes. Quizzes for every story, play, and element of literature help students review for class; they also complement the "brush-up" instruction on the elements of literature. Finally, Wadsworth's unique "explicator" technology actually guides students step by step through the process of close literary analysis while helping them prepare notes for an explication paper.
- **The Wadsworth Original Film Series in Literature** Original adaptations of Tillie Olsen's "I Stand Here Ironing," Alice Walker's "Everyday Use," Raymond Carver's "Cathedral," Eudora Welty's "A Worn Path," and John Updike's "A & P," accompanied by interviews with the authors, are available on DVD or VHS.

Film Series

DVD

- **The Wadsworth Casebook Series for Reading, Research, and Writing** (previously titled *The Harcourt Brace Casebook Series in Literature*) Fourteen complete casebooks, each providing all the materials students need to jumpstart a literary research project, are available:

Fiction
Raymond Carver's "Cathedral"
William Faulkner's "A Rose for Emily"
Charlotte Perkin's Gilman's "The Yellow Wallpaper"

Flannery O'Connor's "A Good Man Is Hard to Find"
Edgar Allan Poe's "The Cask of Amontillado"
John Updike's "A & P"
Eudora Welty's "A Worn Path"

Poetry
Emily Dickinson, A Collection of Poems
Robert Frost, A Collection of Poems
Langston Hughes, A Collection of Poems
Walt Whitman, A Collection of Poems

Drama
Athol Fugard's *Master Harold and the Boys*
Susan Glaspell's *Trifles*
William Shakespeare's *Hamlet*

- **Arden Shakespeare** Nine plays from the Arden Shakespeare Series can be packaged with *Literature: Reading, Reacting, Writing*, Sixth Edition, including *Hamlet, King Lear, A Midsummer Night's Dream, The Tempest, Othello,* and *Twelfth Night.*

ACKNOWLEDGMENTS

From start to finish, this book has been a true collaboration, not only with each other, but also with our students and colleagues. We have worked hard on this book, and many people at Wadsworth have worked hard along with us.

We would like to begin by thanking our incredibly creative and talented Development Editor, Karen Smith, who has always been there for us (and who we hope always will be there). She is one of a kind, and we are simply in awe of her abilities.

We continue to be grateful to Acquisitions Editor Aron Keesbury for his enthusiasm and persistence as well as for his belief in the book. And we remain very grateful as well to our publisher, Michael Rosenberg, for coming back just in time.

Also at Wadsworth, we thank Mike Burggren for guiding the manuscript through production, with skilled help from the team at Nesbitt Graphics, especially Sherry Berg and Susan McIntyre. We owe a special debt to Susan, our first-rate project manager, for her expertise as well as for her thoroughness and her patience.

We also very much appreciate the help we got on this project from William Coyle on the Instructor's Resource Manual; from Stacey Brown on updating the headnotes, footnotes, Cultural Contexts, and Critical Perspective questions; from Tony Perriello on the research and review process; and from Jessie Swigger on the new student papers.

We would like to thank the following reviewers of the sixth edition: Joy L. Blom, Montclair State University; Terri Bourus, Indiana University–Kokomo; Jennifer Brown, University of Hartford; Sheryl Chisamore, State University of New York–Ulster; Wayne Christensen, Florida Memorial College; Kirk Colvin, American River College; Susan Cornett, St. Petersburg College; Joseph A.

Correro Jr., Delta State University; Carl C. Curtis III, Liberty University; Patricia A. Daskivich, Los Angeles Harbor College; Tammy DiBenedetto, Riverside Community College; Josh Dickinson, Jefferson Community College (SUNY); Michael M. Dinielli, Chaffey College; Ellen Gross, Central Virginia Community College; Susan Isaac, Georgia Military College; Deborah Israel, University of Central Oklahoma; Susan A. Johnson, Sierra College; Jane Anderson Jones, Manatee Community College–Venice; Jason B. Jones, Central Connecticut State University; Kerrie Kawasaki-Hull, Ohlone College; Kevin Kelly, Andover College; James Kirkpatrick, Central Piedmont Community College; Judith Kleck, Central Washington University; Mark Kosinski, Manchester Community College; Mary Kramer, University of Massachusetts–Lowell; David Kucher, Westchester Community College; Carol Kushner, Dutchess Community College; Noreen Lace, California State University–Northridge; Paul Long, Baltimore City Community College; Martha B. Macdonald, York Technical College; Deanna Mascle, Morehead State University; Robert Mitchell, Ohlone College; Deborah Montuori, Shippensburg University; Robbi Muckenfuss, Durham Technical Community College; Michail W. Mulvey, Central Connecticut State University; L. J. Nutter, Liberty University; Nancy K. Pennell, McPherson College; Renee Pigeon, California State University–San Bernardino; David Schwankle, Riverside Community College–Norco; Shant Shahoian, Oxnard College; Andy Solomon, University of Tampa; Donald R. Stinson, Northern Oklahoma College; Carolyn Stonewell, Middlesex Community College; Gary Thomas, University of North Carolina–Charlotte; Regina Williams, Arkansas State University–Heber Springs; and David Winsper, Springfield Technical Community College.

We would also like to thank the following reviewers of the fifth edition: Jane Anderson Jones, Manatee Community College–Venice; Lee Barnes, Community College of Southern Nevada; Robin Calitri, Merced College; Janet Eber, County College of Morris; Charles Fisher, Aims Community College; Maryanne Garbowsky, County College of Morris; Clinton Gardner, Salt Lake City Community College; Diana Gatz, St. Petersburg College; Dawn Marie Hershberger, University of Indianapolis; Isara Kelley Tyson, Manatee Community College; Andrew Kozma, University of Florida; Bernard Morris, Modesto College; David Neff, University of Alabama–Huntsville; Diana Nystedt, Palo Alto College; Roger Platizky, Austin College; Angela M. Rhoe, Prince George's Community College; Mark Rollins, University of Ohio; Christine Roth, University of Wisconsin; David A. Salomon, Black Hills State University; Ann Spurlock, Mississippi State University; and Pam Sutton, Union University.

We continue to be grateful to the reviewers of the fourth edition: Crystal V. Bacon, Glouchester County College; Gwen Barklay-Toy, North Carolina State University; Eric Birdsall, University of Akron; John Doyle, Quinnipiac College; David Fear, Valencia Community College; Elizabeth Keats Flores, College of Lake Country; Linda Gruber, Kishwaukee College; Lynn Hildenbrand, Chesapeake College; Teresa Kennedy, Mary Washington College; Michael Kraus, Marian College of Fond du Lac; Teri Maddox, Jackson State Community College; Judith P. Moray, Moraine Valley Community College; Mary Beth Namm, North Carolina State University; Rodney D. Newton, Central Texas College; Monte

Prater, Tulsa Community College–Northeast; Gail Rung, Black Hawk College; Robert M. Temple, Manatee Community College; Maria W. Warren, University of West Florida; Donnie Yeilding, Central Texas College; and Laura Mandell Zaidman, University of South Carolina–Sumter.

We would also like to thank all the reviewers who made valuable contributions to the third edition: Ben Accardi, University of Kansas; Thomas Bailey, Western Michigan University; John Bails, University of Sioux Falls; Leigh Boyd, Temple Junior College; Cathy Cowan, Cabrillo College; Pat Cowart, Frostburg State University; Kitty Dean, Nassau Community College; Jo Devine, University of Alaska–Southeast; Jack Doyle, University of South Carolina–Sumter; Lynn Fauth, Oxnard College; David Fear, Valencia Community College; Mary Fleming, Jackson State Community College; Ann Fogg, University of Maine; Wayne Gilbert, Community College of Aurora; Shain Graham, Orange Coast College; Linda Gruber, Kishwaukee College; Chris Hacskaylo, University of Alaska–Ketchikan; Richard Hascal, Contra Costa College; Gwen Hauk, Temple Junior College; Michael Herzog, Gonzaga University; Andrew Kelly, Jackson State Community College; Benna Kime, Jackson State Community College; Army Sparks Kolker, University of Kansas; Michael Kraus, Marian College of Fond du Lac; Heidi Ledett, Ulster County Community College; Teri Maddox, Jackson State Community College; Jeanne Mauzy, Valencia Community College; Fred Milley, Anderson University; Robert Milliken, University of Southern Maine; Andrew Moody, University of Kansas; Paul Perry, Palo Alto Community College; Angela Rapkin, Manatee Community College; Jean Reynolds, Polk Community College; Ellen Robbins, Ulster County Community College; Paul Rogauls, Plymouth State College; Neil Sebacher, Valencia Community College; Larry Severeid, College of Eastern Utah; Sharon Small, Des Moines Area Community College; Virginia Streamer, Dundalk Community College; Robert Temple, Manatee Community College; Margie Whelan, Mt. San Antonio College; Mike White, Odessa College; Rebecca Yancey, Jackson State Community College; Donnie Yielding, Central Texas College; and Martha Zamorano, Miami Dade–Kendall.

Reviewers of the second edition included Deborah Barberousse, Horry-Georgetown Technical College; Bob Mayberry, University of Nevada–Las Vegas; Shireen Carroll, University of Miami; Stephen Wright, Seminole Community College; Robert Dees, Orange Coast College; Larry Gray, Southeastern Louisiana University; Nancy Rayl, Cypress College; James Clemmer, Austin Peay State University; Roberta Kramer, Nassau Community College.

Reviewers of the first edition included Anne Agee, Anne Arundel Community College; Lucien Agosta, California State University–Sacramento; Diana Austin, University of New Brunswick; Judith Bechtel; Northern Kentucky University; Laureen Belmont, North Idaho College; Vivian Brown, Laredo Junior College; Rebecca Butler, Dalton Junior College; Susan Coffey, Central Virginia Community College; Douglas Crowell, Texas Tech University; Shirley Ann Curtis, Polk Community College; Kitty Dean, Nassau Community College; Robert Dees, Orange Coast College; Joyce Dempsey, Arkansas Tech University; Mindy Doyle, Orange County Community College; James Egan, University of Akron;

Susan Fenyves, University of North Carolina–Charlotte; Marvin Garrett, University of Cincinnati; Ann Gebhard, State University of New York– Cortland; Emma Givaltney, Arkansas Tech University; Corrinne Hales, California State University–Fresno; Gary Hall, North Harris County College; Iris Hart, Santa Fe Community College; James Helvey, Davidson County Community College; Chris Henson, California State University–Fresno; Gloria Hochstein, University of Wisconsin–Eau Claire; Angela Ingram, Southwest Texas State University; John Iorio, University of South Florida; George Ives, North Idaho College; Lavinia Jennings, University of North Carolina–Chapel Hill; Judy Kidd, North Carolina State University; Leonard Leff, Oklahoma State University; Michael Matthews, Tarrant County Junior College–Northeast; Craig McLuckie, Okanagan College; Candy Meier, Des Moines Area Community College; Judith Michna, DeKalb College–North; Christopher O'Hearn, Los Angeles Harbor College; James O'Neil, Edison Community College; Melissa Pennell, University of Lowell; Sam Phillips, Gaston College; Robbie Pinter, Belmont College; Joseph Sternberg, Harper College; Kathleen Tickner, Brevard Community College; Betty Wells, Central Virginia Community College; Susan Yaeger, Monroe Business Institute.

We would also like to thank our families—Mark, Adam, and Rebecca Kirszner and Demi, David, and Sarah Mandell—for being there when we needed them. And finally, we each thank the person on the other side of the ampersand for making our collaboration work one more time.

1 | A GUIDE TO WRITING ABOUT LITERATURE

CHAPTER 1

UNDERSTANDING LITERATURE

Imaginative Literature

Imaginative literature begins with a writer's need to convey a personal vision to readers. Consider, for example, how William Wordsworth uses language in these lines from his poem "Composed upon Westminster Bridge, September 3, 1802" (p. 1241).

> This City now doth, like a garment, wear
> The beauty of the morning; silent, bare,
> Ships, towers, domes, theatres, and temples lie
> Open unto the fields, and to the sky;
> All bright and glittering in the smokeless air.

Wordsworth does not try to present a picture of London that is topographically or sociologically accurate. Instead, by comparing the city at dawn to a person wearing a beautiful garment, he creates a striking picture that has its own kind of truth. By using a vivid, original comparison, the poet is able to suggest the oneness of the city, nature, and himself — an idea that is not easily communicated.

Even when writers of imaginative literature use factual material — historical documents, newspaper stories, or personal experience, for example — their primary purpose is to present their unique view of experience, one that has significance beyond the moment. (As the poet Ezra Pound said, "Literature is the news that *stays* news.") To convey their views of experience, these writers often manipulate facts — changing dates, creating new characters, and inventing dialogue. For example, when Herman Melville wrote his nineteenth-century novella *Benito Cereno,* he drew many of his facts from an account of an actual slave revolt. In his story, he reproduces court records and uses plot details from this primary source, but he leaves out some incidents, and he adds material of his own. The result is an original work of literature. Wanting to do more than retell the original story, Melville used the factual material as "a skeleton of actual reality" on which he built a story that attacks the institution of slavery and examines the nature of truth.

Imaginative literature is more likely than other types of writing to include words chosen not only because they communicate the writer's ideas, but also because they are memorable. Using vivid imagery and evocative comparisons, writers of imaginative literature often stretch language to its limits. By relying on the multiple connotations of words and images, a work of imaginative literature encourages readers to see the possibilities of language and to move beyond the factual details of an event.

Even though imaginative literature can be divided into types called **genres** — fiction, poetry, and drama — the nature of literary genres varies from culture to culture. In fact, some literary forms that Western readers take for granted are alien to other literary traditions. The sonnet, though fairly common in the West, is not a conventional literary form in Chinese or Arabic poetry. Similarly, the most popular theatrical entertainment in Japan since the mid-seventeenth century, the Kabuki play, has no exact counterpart in the West. (In a Kabuki play, which includes stories, scenes, dances, music, acrobatics, and elaborate costumes and stage settings, all of the actors are men, some of whom play the parts of females. Many Kabuki plays have little plot and seem to be primarily concerned with spectacle. One feature of this form of drama is a walkway that extends from the stage through the audience to the back of the theater.)

Conventions of narrative organization and character development can also vary considerably from culture to culture, especially in literature derived from oral traditions. For example, narrative organization in some Native American stories (and, even more commonly, in some African stories) can be very different from what contemporary Western readers are accustomed to. Events may be arranged spatially instead of chronologically: first a story presents all the events that happened in one place, then it presents everything that happened in another location, and so on. Character development is also much less important in some traditional African and Native American stories than it is in modern short fiction. In fact, a character's name, description, and personality can change dramatically (and without warning) during the course of a story.

Despite such differences, the imaginative literature of all cultures has similar effects on readers: memorable characters, vivid descriptions, imaginative use of language, and compelling plots can fascinate and delight. Literature can take readers where they have never been before and, in so doing, can create a sense of adventure and wonder.

At another level, however, readers can find more than just pleasure or escape in literature. Beyond transporting readers out of their lives and times, literature can enable readers to see their lives and times more clearly. Whether a work of imaginative literature depicts a young girl as she experiences the disillusionment of adulthood for the first time, as in David Michael Kaplan's "Doe Season" (p. 512), or examines the effect of discrimination on a black African who is looking for an apartment, as in Wole Soyinka's "Telephone Conversation" (p. 8), it can help readers to understand their own experiences and the experiences of others. In this sense, literature offers readers increased insight and awareness. As the Chilean poet Pablo Neruda said, works of imaginative literature fulfill "the most ancient rites of our conscience in the awareness of being human and of believing in a common destiny."

Conventional Themes

The **theme** of a work of literature is its central or dominant idea. This idea is seldom stated explicitly. Instead, it is conveyed through the selection and arrangement of details; through the emphasis of certain words, events, or images; and through the actions and reactions of characters.

Although one central theme may dominate a literary work, most works explore a number of different themes or ideas. For example, the central theme of Mark Twain's *Adventures of Huckleberry Finn* might be the idea that an individual's innate sense of right and wrong is superior to society's artificial and sometimes unnatural values. The main character, Huck, gains a growing awareness of this idea by witnessing feuds, duels, and all manner of human folly. As a result, he makes a decision to help his friend Jim escape from slavery despite the fact that society, as well as his own conscience, condemns this action. However, *Huckleberry Finn* also examines other themes. Throughout his novel, Twain criticizes many of the ideas that prevailed in the pre–Civil War South, such as the racism and religious hypocrisy that pervaded the towns along the Mississippi.

A literary work can explore any theme, but certain themes have recurred so frequently over the years that they have become **conventions**. One theme frequently explored in literature, a character's loss of innocence, appears in the biblical story of Adam and Eve and later finds its way into such works as Nathaniel Hawthorne's 1835 short story "Young Goodman Brown" (p. 489) and James Joyce's 1914 short story "Araby" (p. 395). Another conventional theme — the conflict between an individual's values and the values of society — is examined in the ancient Greek play *Antigone* by Sophocles (p. 1899). Almost two thousand years later, Norwegian playwright Henrik Ibsen deals with the same theme in *A Doll House* (p. 1454).

Other conventional themes examined in literary works include the individual's quest for spiritual enlightenment, the *carpe diem* ("seize the day") theme, the making of the artist, the nostalgia for a vanished past, the disillusionment of adulthood, the pain of love, the struggle of women for equality, the conflict between parents and children, the clash between civilization and the wilderness, the evils of unchecked ambition, the inevitability of fate, the impact of the past on the present, the conflict between human beings and machines, and the tension between the ideal and the actual realms of experience.

Nearly every culture explores similar themes, but writers from different cultures may develop these themes differently. A culture's history, a particular region's geography, or a country's social structure can suggest unique ways of developing conventional themes. In addition, the assumptions, concerns, values, ideals, and beliefs of a particular country or society — or of a particular group within that society — can help to determine the themes writers choose to explore and the manner in which they do so.

In American literature, for instance, familiar themes include the loss of innocence, rites of passage, childhood epiphanies, and the ability (or inability) to form relationships. American writers of color, in addition to exploring these themes, may also express their frustration with racism or celebrate their cultural identities.

Even when they explore conventional themes, writers of color in America may choose to do so in the context of their own experience. For example, the theme of loss of innocence may be presented as a first encounter with racial prejudice; a conflict between the individual and society may be presented as a conflict between a minority view and the values of the dominant group; and the theme of failure or aborted relationships may be explored in a work about cultural misunderstandings.

Finally, modern works of literature sometimes treat conventional themes in new ways. For example, in *1984* George Orwell explores the negative consequences of unchecked power by creating a nightmare world in which the government controls and dehumanizes a population. Even though Orwell's novel is set in an imaginary future (it was written in 1948), its theme echoes ideas frequently examined in the plays of both Sophocles and Shakespeare.

The Literary Canon

Originally, the term **canon** referred to the authoritative or accepted list of books that made up the Christian Bible. More recently, the term **literary canon** has come to denote a group of works generally agreed upon by writers, teachers, and critics to be worth reading and studying. Over the years, as standards have changed, the definition of "good" literature has also changed, and the literary canon has been modified accordingly. For example, at various times, critics have characterized Shakespeare's plays as mundane, immoral, commonplace, and brilliant. The eighteenth-century critic Samuel Johnson said of Shakespeare that "in his comick scenes he is seldom very successful" and in tragedy "his performance seems constantly to be worse, as his labor is more." Many people find it difficult to believe that a writer whose name today is synonymous with great literature could ever have been judged so harshly. Like all aesthetic works, however, the plays of Shakespeare affect individuals in different periods of history or in different societies in different ways.

Some educators and literary scholars believe that the traditional literary canon, like a restricted club, arbitrarily admits some authors and excludes others. This fact is borne out, they say, by an examination of the literature curriculum that until recently was standard at many North American universities. This curriculum typically began with Homer, Plato, Dante, and Chaucer, progressed to Shakespeare, Milton, the eighteenth- century novel, the Romantics, and the Victorians, and ended with some of the "classics" of modern British and American literature. Most of the authors of these works are white and male, and their writing for the most part reflects Western values.

Missing from the literature courses in North American universities for many years were South American, African, and Asian writers. Students of American literature were not encouraged to consider the perspectives of women or of Latinos, Native Americans, or other ethnic or racial groups. During the past four decades, however, most universities have expanded the traditional canon by including more works by women, people of color, and writers from a variety of cultures. These additional works, studied alongside those representing the traditional canon, have opened up the curriculum and redefined the standards by which literature is judged.

One example of a literary work that challenges the traditional canon is "All about Suicide" by Luisa Valenzuela, an Argentinean writer. This brief, shocking story is part of a large and growing genre of literature from around the world that purposely violates our standard literary expectations to make its point — in this case, a point about the political realities of Argentina in the 1960s.

LUISA VALENZUELA (1938–)

All about Suicide (1967)

Translated by Helen Lane

Ismael grabbed the gun and slowly rubbed it across his face. Then he pulled the trigger and there was a shot. Bang. One more person dead in the city. It's getting to be a vice. First he grabbed the revolver that was in a desk drawer, rubbed it gently across his face, put it to his temple, and pulled the trigger. Without saying a word. Bang. Dead.

Let's recapitulate: the office is grand, fit for a minister. The desk is ministerial too, and covered with a glass that must have reflected the scene, the shock. Ismael knew where the gun was, he'd hidden it there himself. So he didn't lose any time, all he had to do was open the right-hand drawer and stick his hand in. Then he got a good hold on it and rubbed it over his face with a certain pleasure before putting it to his temple and pulling the trigger. It was something almost sensual and quite unexpected. He hadn't even had time to think about it. A trivial gesture, and the gun had fired.

There's something missing: Ismael in the bar with a glass in his hand thinking over his future act and its possible consequences.

We must go back farther if we want to get at the truth: Ismael in the cradle crying because his diapers are dirty and nobody is changing him.

Not that far.

Ismael in the first grade fighting with a classmate who'll one day become a minister, his friend, a traitor.

No, Ismael in the ministry without being able to tell what he knew, forced to be silent. Ismael in the bar with the glass (his third) in his hand, and the irrevocable decision: better death.

Ismael pushing the revolving door at the entrance to the building, pushing the swinging door leading to the office section, saying good morning to the guard, opening the door of his office. Once in his office, seven steps to his desk. Terror, the act of opening the drawer, taking out the revolver, and rubbing it across his face, almost a single gesture and very quick. The act of putting it to his temple and pulling the trigger — another act, immediately following the previous one. Bang. Dead. And Ismael coming out of his office (the other man's office, the minister's) almost relieved, even though he can predict what awaits him.

❖ ❖ ❖

The Nigerian poet and playwright Wole Soyinka is another writer whose works are not part of the traditional Western canon. The subject of the following poem may not seem "relevant" to European audiences, and the language ("pillar-box," "omnibus") may not be clear to Americans. Still, as a reading of the poem demonstrates, Soyinka's work makes a compelling plea for individual rights and self-determination—a theme that transcends the boundaries of time and place.

WOLE SOYINKA (1934–)

Telephone Conversation   (1962)

The price seemed reasonable, location
Indifferent. The landlady swore she lived
Off premises. Nothing remained
But self-confession. "Madam," I warned
"I hate a wasted journey — I am — African."   5
Silence. Silenced transmission of
Pressurized good-breeding. Voice, when it came,
Lip-stick coated, long gold-rolled
Cigarette-holder pipped. Caught I was, foully.
"HOW DARK?" . . . I had not misheard . . .   10
     "ARE YOU LIGHT
OR VERY DARK?" Button B. Button A. Stench
Of rancid breath of public-hide-and-speak.
Red booth. Red pillar-box. Red double-tiered
Omnibus squelching tar. It *was* real! Shamed   15
By ill-mannered silence, surrender
Pushed dumbfoundment to beg simplification.
Considerate she was, varying the emphasis —
"ARE YOU DARK? OR VERY LIGHT?" Revelation came.
"You mean — like plain or milk chocolate?"   20
Her assent was clinical, crushing in its light,
Impersonality. Rapidly, wave-length adjusted,
I chose, "West African sepia"— and as an afterthought,
"Down in my passport." Silence for spectroscopic
Flight of fancy, till truthfulness clanged her accent   25
Hard on the mouthpiece. "WHAT'S THAT?" conceding
"DON'T KNOW WHAT THAT IS." "Like brunette."
"THAT'S DARK, ISN'T IT?" "Not altogether.
Facially, I am brunette, but madam, you should see
The rest of me. Palm of my hand, soles of my feet   30
Are a peroxide blond. Friction, caused —
Foolishly madam — by sitting down, has turned
My bottom raven black — One moment madam!"— sensing
Her receiver rearing on the thunder clap
About my ears — "Madam," I pleaded, "Wouldn't you rather   35
See for yourself?"

◆ ◆ ◆

Certainly canon revision is not without problems — for example, the possibility of including a work more for political or sociological reasons than for its literary merit. Nevertheless, if the debate about the literary canon has accomplished anything, it has revealed that the canon is not fixed and that many works formerly excluded — African-American slave narratives and eighteenth-century women's diaries, for example — deserve to be read.

Interpreting Literature

When you **interpret** a literary work, you explore its possible meanings. One commonly held idea about reading a literary work is that its meaning lies buried somewhere within it, waiting to be unearthed. This reasoning suggests that a clever reader has only to discover the author's intent to find out what a story or poem means, and that the one actual meaning of a work is hidden "between the lines," unaffected by a reader's experiences or interpretations. More recently, however, a different model of the reading process — one that takes into consideration the reader as well as the work he or she is interpreting — has emerged.

Many contemporary critics see the reading process as **interactive**. In other words, meaning is created through the reader's interaction with a text. Thus, the meaning of a particular work comes alive in the imagination of an individual reader, and no reader can determine a work's meaning without considering his or her own reaction to the text. Meaning, therefore, is created partly by what is supplied by a work and partly by what is supplied by the reader.

The most obvious thing a work supplies is **facts**, the information that enables a reader to follow the plot of a story, the action of a play, or the development of a poem. The work itself will provide factual details about the setting; the characters' names, ages, and appearances; the sequence of events; and the emotions and attitudes of a poem's speaker, a story's narrator, or the characters in a play or story. This factual information cannot be ignored: if a play's stage directions identify its setting as nineteenth-century Norway or the forest of Arden, that is where the play is set.

In addition to facts, a work also conveys the social, political, class, and gender **attitudes** of the writer. Thus, a work may have an overt feminist or working-class bias or a subtle political agenda; it may confirm or challenge contemporary attitudes; it may communicate a writer's nostalgia for a vanished past or outrage at a corrupt present; it may take an elitist, distant view of characters and events or present a sympathetic perspective. A reader's understanding of these attitudes will contribute to his or her interpretation of the work.

Finally, a work also includes **assumptions** about literary conventions. A poet, for example, may have definite ideas about whether a poem should be rhymed or unrhymed or about whether a particular subject is appropriate or inappropriate for poetic treatment. Therefore, a knowledge of the literary conventions of a particular period or the preferences of a particular writer can provide a starting point for your interpretation of literature.

As a reader, you bring to a work your own **personal perspectives**. Your experiences, your beliefs, your ideas about the issues discussed in the work, and your assumptions about literature color your interpretations. In fact, nearly every literary work has somewhat different meanings to different people, depending on their age, gender, nationality, political and religious beliefs, ethnic background, social and economic class, education, knowledge, and personal experiences. Depending on your religious beliefs, for instance, you can react to a passage from the Old Testament as literal truth, symbolic truth, or fiction. Depending on your race, where you live, your biases, and the nature of your experience, a story about racial discrimination can strike you as accurate and realistic, exaggerated and unrealistic, or understated and restrained.

In a sense, then, the process of determining meaning is like a conversation, one in which both you and the text have a voice. Sometimes, by clearly dictating the terms of the discussion, the text determines the direction of the conversation; at other times, by using your knowledge and experience to interpret the text, you dominate. Thus, because every reading of a literary work is actually an interpretation, it is a mistake to look for a single "correct" reading.

The 1923 poem "Stopping by Woods on a Snowy Evening" (p. 1180), by the American poet Robert Frost, illustrates how a single work can have more than one interpretation. Readers may interpret the poem as being about the inevitability of death, as suggesting that the poet is tired or world weary, or as making a comment about duty and the need to persevere or about the conflicting pulls of life and art. Beyond these possibilities, readers' own associations of snow with quiet and sadness could lead them to define the mood of the poem as sorrowful or melancholy. Information about Robert Frost's life or his ideas about poetry could add to readers' understanding of the poem, and they might even develop ideas about the poem that are quite different from the poet's. In fact, on several occasions, Frost himself gave strikingly different — even contradictory — interpretations of "Stopping by Woods on a Snowy Evening," sometimes insisting that the poem had no hidden meaning and at other times saying that it required a good deal of explication. (Literary critics also disagree about its meaning.) When reading a work of literature, then, keep in mind that the meaning of the text is not fixed. Your best strategy is to open yourself up to the text's many possibilities and explore the full range of your responses.

Although no single reading of a literary work is "correct," some readings are more defensible than others. Like a scientific theory, a literary interpretation must have a basis in fact, and the text supplies the facts against which your interpretation should be judged. For example, after you read Shirley Jackson's "The Lottery" (p. 461), a 1948 short story in which a randomly chosen victim is stoned to death by her neighbors, it would be reasonable for you to conclude that the ceremonial aspects of the lottery suggest a pagan ritual. Your understanding of what a pagan ritual is, combined with your observation that a number of details in the text suggest ancient fertility rites, might lead you to this conclusion. Another possibility is that "The Lottery" provides a commentary on mob psychology. The way characters reinforce one another's violent tendencies lends support to this interpretation. However, the interpretation that the ritual of the lottery is a thinly veiled attack on the death penalty would be difficult to support. Certainly a character in the story is killed, but she is not accused of a crime, nor is she tried or convicted; in fact, the killing is random and seemingly without motivation. Still, although seeing "The Lottery" as a comment on the death penalty may be far-fetched, this interpretation is a reasonable starting point. A second, closer reading of the story would allow you to explore other, more plausible, interpretations.

As you read, do not be afraid to take chances and develop unusual or creative interpretations. A **safe reading** of a work is likely to result in a dull paper that simply states the obvious, but an aggressive or **strong reading** of a work — one that challenges generally held assumptions — can lead to interesting and intellectually challenging conclusions. Even if your reading differs from established critics' interpretations, you should not automatically assume it has no merit. Your own special knowledge of the material discussed in the text — a regional practice, an ethnic custom, an attitude toward gender — may give you a unique perspective from which to view the work. Whatever interpretation you make, be sure that you support it with specific references to the text. If your interpretation is based on your own experiences, explain those experiences and relate them clearly to the work you are discussing. As long as you can make a reasonable case, you have the right (and perhaps the obligation) to present your ideas. By doing so, you may give your fellow students and your instructor new insight into the work.

> **NOTE:** Keep in mind that some interpretations are *not* reasonable. You may contribute ideas based on your own perspectives, but you cannot ignore or contradict evidence in the text to suit your own biases. As you read and reread a text, continue to question and reexamine your judgments. The conversation between you and the text should be a dialogue, not a monologue or a shouting match.

Evaluating Literature

When you **evaluate** a work of literature, you do more than interpret it; you make a judgment about it. You reach conclusions not simply about whether the work is good or bad, but also about how effectively the work presents itself to you, the reader. To evaluate a work, you **analyze** it, breaking it apart and considering its individual elements. As you evaluate a work of literature, remember that different works are designed to fulfill different needs — entertainment, education, or enlightenment, for example. Before you begin to evaluate a work, be sure you understand its purpose; then, follow these guidelines:

- *Begin your evaluation by considering how various literary elements function within a work.*   Fiction may be divided into chapters and use flashbacks and foreshadowing; plays may be divided into scenes and acts and include dialogue and special staging techniques; poems may be arranged in regularly ordered groups of lines and use poetic devices such as rhyme and meter. Understanding the choices writers make about these and other literary elements can help you form judgments about a work. For example, why does Alberto Alvaro Ríos use a first-person narrator in his story "The Secret Lion" (p. 170)? Would the story have been different had it been told in the third person by a narrator who was not a character in the story? How does unusual staging contribute to the effect Milcha Sanchez-Scott achieves in her play *The Cuban Swimmer* (p. 1772)? How would a more realistic setting change the play? Naturally, you cannot focus on every aspect of a particular story, poem, or play. But you can and should focus on those aspects that play a major role in determining your responses to a work. For this reason, elements such as the unusual stanzaic form in E. E. Cummings's poem "Buffalo Bill's" (p. 1158) and the very specific stage directions in Arthur Miller's play *Death of a Salesman* (p. 1581) should be of special interest to you.

As you read, then, you should ask questions. Do the characters in a short story seem real, or do they seem like cardboard cutouts? Are the images in a poem original and thought provoking, or are they clichéd? Are the stage directions of a play sketchy or very detailed? The answers to these questions will help you to shape your evaluation.

• **As you continue your evaluation, decide whether the literary elements of a work interact to achieve a common goal.**   Well-crafted literary works are aesthetically pleasing, fitting together in a way that conceals the craft of the writer. Good writers are like master cabinetmakers; their skill disguises the actual work that has gone into the process of creation. Consider the following stanza from the 1862 poem "Echo" by Christina Rossetti.

> Come to me in the silence of the night;
>   Come to me in the speaking silence of a dream;
> Come with soft round cheeks and eyes as bright
>   As sunlight on a stream;
>   Come back in tears,
> O memory, hope, love of finished years.

Throughout this stanza, Rossetti repeats words ("<u>Come</u> to me . . . / <u>Come</u> with soft . . . / <u>Come</u> back . . .") and initial consonants ("<u>s</u>peaking <u>s</u>ilence"; "<u>s</u>unlight on a <u>s</u>tream"), using sound to create an almost hypnotic mood. The rhyme scheme (*night/bright, dream/stream,* and *tears/years*) reinforces the mood by creating a musical undercurrent that extends throughout the poem. Thus, this stanza is effective because its repeated words and sounds work together to create a single lyrical effect.

The chorus in *Antigone* by Sophocles (p. 1899) also illustrates how the elements of a well-crafted work of literature function together. In ancient Greece, plays were performed by masked male actors who played both male and female roles. A chorus of fifteen men remained in a central circle called the *orchestra* and commented on and reacted to the action taking place around them. The chorus expresses the judgment of the community and acts as a moral guide for the audience. Once modern audiences grow accustomed to the presence of the chorus, it becomes an integral part of

the play. It neither distracts the audience nor intrudes on the action. In fact, eliminating the chorus would diminish the impact of the play.

- *Next, consider whether a work reinforces or calls into question your ideas about the world.*   Works of **popular fiction** — those aimed at a mass audience — usually do little more than reassure readers that what they believe is correct. Catering to people's desires (for wealth or success, for example), or to their prejudices, or to their fears, these works serve as escapes from life. More serious fiction, however, often goes against the grain, challenging cherished beliefs and leading readers to reexamine long-held assumptions. For instance, in the 1957 short story "Big Black Good Man" (p. 339), Richard Wright's protagonist, a night porter at a hotel, struggles with his consuming yet irrational fear of a "big black" sailor and with his inability to see beyond the sailor's size and color. Only at the end of the story do many readers see that they, like the night porter, have stereotyped and dehumanized the sailor.

- *Now, consider whether a work is intellectually challenging.*   The extended comparison between the legs of a compass and two people in love in "A Valediction: Forbidding Mourning" by the seventeenth-century English poet John Donne (p. 949) illustrates how effectively an image can communicate complex ideas to a reader. Compressed into this comparison are ideas about the perfection of love, the pain of enforced separation, and the difference between sexual and spiritual love. As intellectually challenging as the extended comparison is, it is nonetheless accessible to the careful reader. After all, many people have used a compass to draw a circle and, therefore, are able to understand the relationship between the two legs of the compass and the two lovers.

    A fine line exists, however, between works that are intellectually challenging and those that are simply obscure. An **intellectually challenging** work requires effort from readers to unlock ideas that enrich and expand their understanding of themselves and the world. Although complex, the work gives readers a sense that they have gained something by putting forth the effort to interpret it. An **obscure** work exists solely to display a writer's erudition or intellectual idiosyncrasies. Allusions to other works and events are so numerous and confusing that the work may seem more like a private code than an effort to enlighten readers. Consider the following excerpt from "Canto LXXVI" by the twentieth-century American poet Ezra Pound.

> Le Paradis n'est pas artificiel
>   States of mind are inexplicable to us.
>   δακρύων δακρύων δακρύων
> L.   P. gli onesti
>   J'ai eu pitié des autres
> probablement pas assez, and at moments that suited my own
>   convenience
>   Le paradis n'est pas artificiel,
>   l'enfer non plus.
> Came Eurus as comforter

and at sunset la pastorella dei suini
driving the pigs home, benecomata dea
under the two-winged cloud
as of less and more than a day

This passage contains lines in French, Greek, and Italian, as well as a reference to Eurus, the ancient Greek personification of the east wind, and the initials L. P. (Loomis Pound?). It demands a lot from readers; the question is whether the reward is worth the effort.

No hard and fast rule exists for determining whether a work is intellectually challenging or simply obscure. Just as a poem has no fixed meaning, it also has no fixed value. Some readers would say that the passage from "Canto LXXVI" is good, even great, poetry. Others would argue that those lines do not yield enough pleasure and insight to justify the work needed to analyze them. As a reader, you must draw your own conclusions and justify them in a clear and reasonable way. Do not assume that just because a work is difficult, it is obscure. (Nor should you assume that all difficult works are great literature or that all accessible literature is trivial.) Some of the most beautiful and inspiring literary works demand a great deal of effort. Most readers would agree, however, that the time spent exploring such works yields tremendous rewards.

- *Consider whether a work gives you pleasure.*   One of the primary reasons why literature endures is that it gives readers enjoyment. As subjective as this assessment is, it is a starting point for critical judgment. When readers ask themselves what they liked about a work, why they liked it, or what they learned, they begin the process of evaluation. Although this process is largely uncritical, it can lead to an involvement with the work and to a valid critical response. When you encounter great literature, with all its complexities, you may lose sight of the idea of literature as a source of pleasure. But literature should touch you on a deep emotional or intellectual level. If it does not — despite its technical perfection — it fails to achieve one of its primary aims.

The Function of Literary Criticism

Sometimes your personal reactions and knowledge cannot give you enough insight into a literary work. For example, archaic language, references to mythology, historical allusions, and textual inconsistencies can make reading a work difficult. Similarly, an intellectual or philosophical movement such as Darwinism, Marxism, naturalism, structuralism, or feminism may influence a work, and if this is the case, you need some knowledge of the movement before you can interpret the work. In addition, you may not have the background to appreciate the technical or historical dimensions of a work. To increase your understanding, you may choose to read **literary criticism**— books and journal articles written by experts who describe, analyze, interpret, or evaluate a work of literature (see the appendix, "Using Literary Criticism in Your Writing"). Reading literary criticism enables you to expand your

knowledge of a particular work and to participate in ongoing critical discussions about literature. In a sense, you become part of a community of scholars who share their ideas and who are connected to one another through their writing.

Literary criticism is written by experts, but this does not mean you must always agree with it. You have to evaluate literary criticism just as you would any new opinion that you encounter. Not all criticism is sound, timely, or responsible (and not all literary criticism is pertinent to your assignment or useful for your purposes). Some critical comments will strike you as plausible; others will seem unfounded or biased.

Quite often, two critics will reach strikingly different conclusions about the quality or significance of the same work or writer, or they will interpret a character, a symbol, or even the entire work quite differently. The Fiction Casebook that begins on page 570 includes articles in which critics disagree in just this fashion. In "In Fairyland, without a Map: Connie's Exploration Inward in Joyce Carol Oates's 'Where Are You Going, Where Have You Been?'" Gretchen Schulz and R. J. R. Rockwood examine the parallels between a character, Arnold Friend, and a real-life psychopathic killer. They see Arnold in mythological terms and conclude that he is the "exact transpositional counterpart of the real-life Pied Piper of Tucson." In Mike Tierce and John Michael Crafton's "Connie's Tambourine Man: A New Reading of Arnold Friend," however, the authors explicitly reject this suggestion as well as other critical interpretations, concluding instead that "The key question . . . is who is this musical messiah, and the key to the answer is the dedication 'For Bob Dylan.'"

Although critics may disagree, even conflicting ideas can help you reach your own conclusions about a work. It is up to you to sort out the various opinions and decide which have merit and which do not.

✔ **CHECKLIST   Evaluating Literary Criticism**

☐   What is the main point of the book or article you are reading?

☐   Does the critic supply enough examples to support his or her conclusions?

☐   Does the critic acknowledge and refute the most obvious arguments against his or her position?

☐   Does the critic ignore any information in the text that might call his or her conclusions into question?

☐   Does the critic present historical information? Biographical information? Literary information? How does this information shed light on the work or works being discussed?

☐   Does the critic hold any beliefs that might interfere with his or her critical judgment?

continued on next page

▪ Does the critic slant the facts, or does he or she approach the text critically and objectively?

▪ Does the critic support conclusions with references to other sources? Does the critic provide documentation and a list of works cited?

▪ Do other critics mention the source you are reading? Do they agree or disagree with its conclusions?

▪ Is the critic identified with a particular critical school of thought— deconstruction or Marxism, for example? What perspective does this school of thought provide?

▪ Is the critic well known and respected?

▪ Does the critic take into consideration the most important critical books and articles on his or her subject? Are there works that should have been mentioned but were not? Do these omissions cast doubt on the critic's conclusions?

▪ Is the critical work's publication date of any significance?

CHAPTER 2

READING AND WRITING ABOUT LITERATURE

Reading Literature

Most of the time, readers are passive; they expect the text to give them everything they need, and they do not expect to contribute much to the reading process. In contrast, **active reading** means participating in the reading process: thinking about what you read, asking questions, and challenging ideas. Active reading is excellent preparation for the discussion and writing you will do in college literature classes. And, because it helps you understand and appreciate the works you read, active reading will continue to be of value to you long after your formal classroom study of literature has ended.

Three strategies in particular —*previewing, highlighting,* and *annotating*— will help you to become a more effective reader. Keep in mind, though, that reading and responding to what you read is not an orderly process — or even a sequential one. You will most likely find yourself doing more than one thing at a time — annotating at the same time you highlight, for example.

Previewing

You begin active reading by **previewing** a work to get a general idea of what to look for later, when you read it more carefully.

Start your prewriting with the work's most obvious physical characteristics. How long is a short story? How many acts and scenes does a play have? Is a poem divided into stanzas? The answers to these and similar questions will help you begin to notice more subtle aspects of the work's form. For example, previewing may reveal that a contemporary short story is presented entirely in a question-and-answer format, that it is organized as diary entries, or that it is divided into sections by headings. Previewing may identify poems that seem to lack formal structure, such as E. E. Cummings's unconventional "l(a" (p. 818); poems written in traditional forms (such as **sonnets**) or in experimental forms, such as the numbered list of questions and answers in Denise Levertov's "What Were They Like?" (p. 1084); or **visual poetry**, such as George Herbert's "Easter Wings" (p. 823). Your awareness of these and other distinctive features at this point may help you gain insight into a work later on.

Perhaps the most physically distinctive element of a work is its title. Not only can the title give you a general idea of what the work is about, as straightforward titles like "Miss Brill" and "The Cask of Amontillado" do, but it can also isolate (and thus call attention to) a word or phrase that emphasizes an important idea. For example, the title of Amy Tan's short story "Two Kinds" (p. 791) refers to two kinds of daughters — Chinese and American — suggesting the two perspectives that create the story's conflict. A title can also be an allusion to another work. Thus, *The Sound and the Fury,* the title of a novel by William Faulkner, alludes to a speech from Shakespeare's *Macbeth* that reinforces the major theme of the novel. Finally, a title can introduce a symbol that will gain meaning in the course of a work — as the quilt does in Alice Walker's "Everyday Use" (p. 469).

Other physical elements — such as paragraphing, capitalization, italics, and punctuation — can also provide clues about how to read a work. In William Faulkner's short story "Barn Burning" (p. 356), for instance, previewing would help you to notice passages in italic type, indicating the protagonist's thoughts, which occasionally interrupt the narrator's story.

Finally, previewing can enable you to see some of the more obvious stylistic and structural features of a work — the point of view used in a story, how many characters a play has and where it is set, or the repetition of certain words or lines in a poem, for example. Such features may or may not be important; at this stage, your goal is to observe, not to analyze or evaluate.

Previewing is a useful strategy not because it provides answers but because it suggests questions to ask later, as you read more closely. For instance, *why* does Faulkner use italics in "Barn Burning," and *why* does Herbert shape his poem like a pair of wings? Elements such as those described above will gain significance as you read more carefully and review your notes.

Highlighting

When you read a work closely, you will notice additional, more subtle, elements that you may want to examine further. At this point, you should begin **highlighting** — physically marking the text to identify key details and to note relationships among ideas.

What should you highlight? As you read, ask yourself whether repeated words or phrases form a pattern, as they do in Tim O'Brien's short story "The Things They Carried" (p. 435), in which the word *carried* appears again and again. Because this word appears so frequently, and because it appears at key points in the story, it helps to reinforce a key theme of the story: the burdens and responsibilities soldiers carry in wartime. Repeated words and phrases are particularly important in poetry. In Dylan Thomas's "Do not go gentle into that good night" (p. 1065), for example, the repetition of two of the poem's nineteen lines four times each enhances the poem's rhythmic, almost monotonous, cadence. As you read, highlight your text to identify such repeated words and phrases. Later, you can consider *why* these elements are repeated.

During the highlighting stage, also pay particular attention to **images** that occur repeatedly, keeping in mind that such repeated images may form patterns that can help you to interpret the work. When you reread, you can begin to determine what pattern the images form and perhaps decide how this pattern enhances the work's ideas. When highlighting Robert Frost's "Stopping by Woods on a Snowy Evening" (p. 1180), for instance, you might identify the related images of silence, cold, and darkness. Later, you can consider their significance.

✔ **CHECKLIST   Using Highlighting Symbols**

- ☐ Underline important ideas.

- ☐ Box or circle words, phrases, or images that you want to think more about.

- ☐ Put question marks beside confusing passages, unfamiliar references, or words that need to be defined.

- ☐ Circle related words, ideas, or images and draw lines or arrows to connect them.

- ☐ Number incidents that occur in sequence.

- ☐ Set off a key portion of the text with a vertical line in the margin.

- ☐ Place stars beside particularly important ideas.

The following poem by Maya Angelou has been highlighted by a student preparing to write about it. Notice how the student uses highlighting symbols to help him identify stylistic features, key ideas, and patterns of repetition that he may want to examine later.

MAYA ANGELOU (1928–   )

My Arkansas (1978)

There is a deep brooding
in Arkansas.
Old crimes like moss pend?
from poplar trees.
The sullen earth   5
is much too
red for comfort.

Sunrise seems to hesitate

and in that second

lose its   10

incandescent aim, and

dusk no more shadows

than the noon.

* The past is brighter yet.

Old hates and   15

ante-bellum lace are rent ?

but not discarded.

* Today is yet to come

in Arkansas,

It writhes. It writhes in awful   20

waves of brooding.

This student identifies repeated words and phases ("brooding"; "It writhes") and places question marks beside the two words ("pend" and "rent") that he plans to look up in a dictionary. He also boxes two phrases — "Old crimes" and "ante-bellum lace" — that he needs to think more about. Finally, he stars what he tentatively identifies as the poem's key ideas. When he rereads the poem, his highlighting will make it easier for him to react to and interpret the writer's ideas.

Annotating

At the same time you highlight a text, you also **annotate** it, recording your re-actions as marginal notes. In these notes, you may define new words, identify allusions and patterns of language or imagery, summarize plot relationships, list a work's possible themes, suggest a character's motivation, examine the possible significance of particular images or symbols, or record questions that occur to you as you read. Ideally, your annotations will help you find ideas to write about.

The following paragraph from John Updike's 1961 short story "A&P" (p. 230) was highlighted and annotated by a student in an Introduction to Literature course who was writing in response to the question "Why does Sammy really quit his job?"

Action isn't the result of thought.

Sammy reacts to the girl's embarrassment.

Lengel sighs and begins to look very patient and old and gray. He's been a friend of my parents for years. "Sammy, you don't want to do this to your Mom and Dad," he tells me. <u>It's true, I don't. But it seems to me that once you begin a gesture it's fatal not to go through with it.</u> I fold the apron, "Sammy" stitched in red on the pocket, and put it on the counter, and drop the bow tie on top of it. The bow tie is theirs, if you've ever wondered. <u>"You'll feel this for the rest of your life,"</u> Lengel * says, and I know that's true, too, but remembering how he made the pretty girl blush makes me so scrunchy inside I punch the No Sale tab and the machine whirs "pee-pul" and the drawer splats out. One advantage to this scene taking place in summer, I can follow this up with a clean exit, there's no fumbling around getting your coat and galoshes, I just <u>saunter</u> into the electric eye in <u>my white shirt that my mother ironed the night before,</u> and the door heaves itself open, and outside the sunshine is skating around on the asphalt.

Need for a clean exit— romantic idea.

Romantic cowboy, but his mother irons his shirt (irony).

Because the instructor had discussed the story in class and given the class a specific assignment, the student's annotations are quite focused. In addition to highlighting important information, she notes her reactions to the story and tries to interpret Sammy's actions.

Sometimes you annotate a work before you have decided on a topic. In fact, the process of reading and responding to the text can help you to find a topic to write about. In the absence of a topic, your annotations are likely to be somewhat unfocused, so you will probably need to repeat the process when your paper's direction is clearer.

Writing about Literature

Writing about literature — or about anything else — is an idiosyncratic process during which many activities occur at once: as you write, you think of ideas; as you think of ideas, you clarify the focus of your essay; and as you clarify your focus, you reshape your paragraphs and sentences and refine your word choice. Even though this process sounds chaotic, it has three stages: *planning, drafting,* and *revising and editing.*

Planning an Essay

Considering Your Audience

Sometimes you write primarily for yourself — for example, when you write a journal entry. At other times, you write for others. As you write an essay, consider the special requirements of your **audience**. Is your audience your classmates or your instructor? Can you assume your readers are familiar with your paper's topic and with any technical terms you will use, or will they need brief plot summaries or definitions of key terms? If your audience is your instructor, remember that he or she is a representative of a larger academic audience and therefore expects accurate information; standard English; correct grammar, mechanics, and spelling; logical arguments; and a certain degree of stylistic fluency. In addition, your instructor expects you to support your statements with specific information, to express yourself clearly and explicitly, and to document your sources. In short, your instructor wants to see how clearly you think and whether you are able to arrange your ideas into a well-organized, coherent essay.

In addition to being a member of a general academic audience, your instructor is also a member of a particular community of scholars — in this case, those who study literature. By writing about literature, you engage in a dialogue with this community. For this reason, you need to follow certain specific **conventions** — procedures that by habitual use have become accepted practice. Many of the conventions that apply specifically to writing about literature — matters of style, format, and the like — are discussed in this book. (The checklist on page 35 addresses some of these conventions.)

Understanding Your Purpose

Sometimes you write with a single **purpose** in mind. At other times, you may have more than one purpose. In general terms, you may write for any of the following three reasons:

1. **Writing to respond:** When you write to **respond**, your goal is to discover and express your reactions to a work. To record your responses, you engage in relatively informal activities, such as brainstorming, listing, and journal writing (see pp. 24–26). As you write, you explore your own ideas, forming and re-forming your impressions of the work.

2. **Writing to interpret:** When you write to **interpret**, your aim is to explain a work's possible meanings. To do so, you may summarize, give examples, or compare and contrast the work to other works or to your own experiences. Then, you may go on to analyze the work: studying each of its elements in turn, putting complex statements into your own words, defining difficult concepts, and placing ideas in context.

3. **Writing to evaluate:** When you write to **evaluate**, your purpose is to assess a work's literary merits. You may consider not only its aesthetic appeal, but also its ability to retain that appeal over time and across national or cultural boundaries. As you write, you use your own critical sense and the opinions of experts to help you make judgments about the work.

> **NOTE:** When you write a **literary argument**, your purpose is to **persuade**. See Chapter 5.

Choosing a Topic

When you write an essay about literature, you develop and support an idea about one or more literary works. Before you begin writing, you should make certain that you understand your assignment. Do you know how much time you have to complete your essay? Are you expected to rely on your own ideas, or are you able to consult outside sources? Is your essay to focus on a specific work or on a particular element of literature? Do you have to write on an assigned topic, or are you free to choose a topic? About how long should your essay be? Do you understand exactly what the assignment is asking you to do?

Sometimes your assignment limits your options by telling you what you should discuss:

- Write an essay analyzing Thomas Hardy's use of irony in his poem "The Man He Killed."
- Discuss Hawthorne's use of allegory in his short story "Young Goodman Brown."
- Write a short essay explaining Nora's actions at the end of Ibsen's *A Doll House*.

At other times, your instructor may give you few guidelines other than a paper's required length and format. In such situations, when you must choose a topic on your own, you can often find a topic by brainstorming or by writing journal entries. As you engage in these activities, keep in mind that you have many options for writing papers about literature. Among them are the following:

- You can explicate a poem or a passage of a play or short story, doing a close reading and analyzing the text.
- You can compare two works of literature. (The Related Works list at the end of each "Reading and Reacting" section in this book suggests possible connections.)
- You can compare two characters or discuss some trait those characters share.
- You can trace a common theme — jealousy, revenge, power, coming of age — in several works.
- You can consider how a common subject — war, love, nature — is treated in several works.
- You can examine a single literary element in one or more works — for instance, plot, point of view, or character development.
- You can focus on a single aspect of a literary element, such as the use of flashbacks, the effect of a shifting narrative perspective, or the role of a minor character.
- You can apply a critical theory to a work of literature — for instance, a feminist perspective to Tillie Olsen's "I Stand Here Ironing" (p. 309).

- You can examine connections between an issue treated in a work of literature — for instance, racism in Ralph Ellison's "Battle Royal" (p. 297) or postpartum psychosis in Charlotte Perkins Gilman's "The Yellow Wallpaper" (p. 421) — and that same issue as it is treated in sociological or psychological journals or in the popular press.
- You can examine some aspect of history or biography and consider its relationship to a literary work — for instance, the influence of World War I on Wilfred Owen's poems.
- You can explore a problem within a work and propose a possible solution — for example, Montresor's actual reason for killing Fortunato in Edgar Allan Poe's "The Cask of Amontillado" (p. 350).
- You can explore similarities and differences between a literary work and a film version of the work — for example, the different endings in Joyce Carol Oates's short story "Where Are You Going, Where Have You Been?" (p. 573) and the film *Smooth Talk*.

Any of those options may lead you to an interesting topic. Remember, however, that you may have to narrow the scope of your topic so that it fits within the limits of your assignment.

Finding Something to Say

Once you have a topic, you have to find something to say about it. The information you collected when you highlighted and annotated will help you formulate the statement that will be the central idea of your essay and will help you find ideas that can support that statement.

You can use a variety of strategies to find supporting material:

- You can discuss ideas with others — friends, classmates, instructors, or parents, for example.
- You can ask questions.
- You can do research, either in the library or on the Internet.
- You can **freewrite** — that is, write on a topic for a given period of time without pausing to consider style, structure, or content.

Two additional strategies — *brainstorming* and *keeping a journal* — are especially helpful at this stage of the writing process.

Brainstorming When you **brainstorm**, you record ideas — single words, phrases, or sentences (in the form of statements or questions) — as they occur to you, moving as quickly as possible. Your starting point may be a general assignment, a particular work (or works) of literature, or a specific topic. You can brainstorm at any stage of the writing process (alone or in a group), and you can repeat this activity as often as you like.

The brainstorming notes that follow were made by a student preparing to write a paper on the relationships between children and parents in four poems.

She began by brainstorming separately about each poem and went on to consider thematic relationships among the poems. These notes are her preliminary reactions to one of the four poems she planned to study, Adrienne Rich's "A Woman Mourned by Daughters" (p. 1064):

```
Memory: then and now

    Then: leaf, straw, dead insect (= light);

        ignored

    Now: swollen, puffed up, weight (= heavy);

        focus of attention controls their

        movements.

  * Kitchen = a "universe"

    Teaspoons, goblets, etc. = concrete

        representations of mother; also =

        obligations, responsibilities (like

        plants and father)

    (weigh on them, keep them under her spell)

  Milestones of past: weddings, being fed as

  children "You breathe upon us now"

        PARADOX? (Dead, she breathes, has weight,

        fills house and sky. Alive, she was a dead

        insect, no one paid attention to her.)
```

Keeping a journal You can record ideas in a journal (a notebook, a small notepad, or a computer file)—and, later, you can use these ideas in your paper. In a **journal**, you expand your marginal annotations, recording your responses to works you have read, noting questions, exploring emerging ideas, experimenting with possible paper topics, trying to paraphrase or summarize difficult concepts, or speculating about a work's ambiguities. A journal is the place to take chances, to try out ideas that may initially seem frivolous or irrelevant; here you can think on paper (or on your computer) until connections become clear or ideas crystallize. You can also use your journal as a convenient place to collect your brainstorming notes and, later, your lists of related ideas.

As he prepared to write a paper analyzing the role of Jim, the "gentleman caller" in Tennessee Williams's play *The Glass Menagerie* (p. 1998), a student explored ideas in the following journal entry.

When he tells Laura that being disappointed is not the
same as being discouraged, and that he's disappointed but
not discouraged, Jim reveals his role as a symbol of the
power of newness and change—a "bulldozer" that will clear
out whatever is in its path, even delicate people like
Laura. But the fact that he is disappointed shows Jim's
human side. He has run into problems since high school, and
these problems have blocked his progress toward a successful
future. Working at the warehouse, Jim needs Tom's
friendship to remind him of what he used to be (and what
he still can be?), and this shows his insecurity. He isn't
as sure of himself as he seems to be.

Seeing Connections: Listing

Listing is the process of reviewing your notes, deciding which ideas are most interesting, and arranging related ideas into lists. Listing enables you to discover patterns: to see repeated images, similar characters, recurring words and phrases, and
interrelated themes or ideas. Identifying these patterns can help you to decide
which points to make in your paper and what information you will use to support
these points.

A student preparing a paper about D. H. Lawrence's short story "The Rocking-Horse Winner" (p. 525) made the following list of related details.

```
Secrets
    Mother can't feel love
    Paul gambles
    Paul gives mother money
    Family lives beyond means
    Paul gets information from horse
Religion
    Gambling becomes like a religion
    They all worship money
    Specific references: "serious as a church"; "It's as if
    he had it from heaven"; "secret, religious voice"
Luck
    Father is unlucky
    Mother is desperate for luck
    Paul is lucky (ironic)
```

This kind of listing can be a helpful preliminary organizing strategy, but remember that the lists you make now will not necessarily determine the order or emphasis of ideas in your paper. As your thoughts become more focused, you will add,
delete, and rearrange material.

Deciding on a Thesis

Whenever you are ready, you should try to express the main idea of your emerging essay in a **thesis statement** — an idea, usually expressed in a single sentence, that the rest of your essay will support. This idea should emerge logically out of your highlighting, annotating, brainstorming notes, journal entries, and lists. Eventually, you will write a **thesis-and-support paper**: stating your thesis in your introduction, supporting the thesis in the body paragraphs of your essay, and reinforcing the thesis or summarizing your paper's key points in your conclusion.

An effective thesis statement tells readers what your essay will discuss and how you will approach your material. Consequently, it should be precisely worded, making its point clear to your readers, and it should contain no vague words or imprecise phrases that will make it difficult for readers to follow your discussion. For example, consider the following statement: The use of sound in Tennyson's poem "The Eagle" is interesting. Although this statement is accurate, it does not convey a precise idea to your readers because the words *sound* and *interesting* are not specific. A more effective thesis statement would be, Unity in "The Eagle" is achieved through Tennyson's use of alliteration, assonance, and rhyme throughout the poem.

In addition to being specific, your thesis statement should give your readers an accurate sense of the scope and direction of your essay. It should not make promises that you do not intend to fulfill or include extraneous details that might confuse your readers. If, for example, you are going to write a paper about the dominant image in a poem, your thesis should not imply that you will focus on the poem's setting or tone.

Remember that as you organize your ideas and as you write, you will probably modify and sharpen your thesis. Sometimes you will even begin planning your essay with one thesis in mind and end it with an entirely different one. If this happens, be sure to revise your support paragraphs so that they are consistent with your changes and so that the examples you include support your new thesis. If you find that your thoughts about your topic are changing, don't be concerned; this is how the writing process works.

Preparing an Outline

Once you have decided on a thesis and have some idea how you will support it, you can begin to plan your essay's structure. At this stage of the writing process, an **outline** can help you to clarify your ideas and the relationship of these ideas to one another.

A **scratch outline** is perhaps the most useful kind of outline for a short paper. An informal list of the main points you will discuss in your essay, a scratch outline is more focused than a simple list of related points because it presents ideas in the order in which they will be introduced. As its name implies, however, a scratch outline lacks the detail and the degree of organization of a more formal outline. The main purpose of a scratch outline is to give you a sense of the shape and order of your paper and thus enable you to begin writing.

A student writing a short essay on Edwin Arlington Robinson's use of irony in his poem "Miniver Cheevy" (p. 1218) used this scratch outline as a guide.

```
Speaker's Attitude
  Ironic
  Cynical
  Critical
Use of Diction
  Formal
  Detached
Use of Allusions
  Thebes
  Camelot
  Priam
  Medici
Use of Repetition
  "Miniver"
  "thought"
  regular rhyme scheme
```

Once this outline was complete, the student was ready to write a first draft.

Drafting an Essay

A first draft is a preliminary version of your paper, something to react to and revise. Even before you actually begin drafting your paper, however, you should review the material you have collected. To make sure you are ready to begin drafting, take the following three steps:

1. *Make sure you have collected enough information to support your thesis.* The points you make are only as convincing as the evidence you present to support them. As you read and take notes, you collect supporting examples—in the form of summary, paraphrase, or quotation—from the work or works about which you are writing. How many of these examples you need to use in your draft depends on the breadth of your thesis and how skeptical you believe your audience to be. In general, the broader your thesis, the more material you need to support it. For example, if you were supporting the rather narrow thesis that the speech of a certain character in the second scene of a play reveals important information about his motivation, only a few examples would be needed. However, if you wanted to support the broader thesis that Nora and Torvald Helmer in Henrik Ibsen's *A Doll House* (p. 1454) are trapped in their roles, you would need to present a wide range of examples.

2. *See if the work includes any details that contradict your thesis.* Before you begin writing, test the validity of your thesis by looking for details that contradict it. For example, if you plan to support the thesis that in *A Doll House*, Ibsen makes a strong case for the rights of women, you should look for

counterexamples. Can you find subtle hints in the play that suggest women should remain locked in their traditional roles and continue to defer to their fathers and husbands? If so, you will want to modify your thesis accordingly.

3. ***Consider whether you need to use outside sources to help you support your thesis.*** You could, for example, strengthen the thesis that *A Doll House* challenged contemporary attitudes about marriage by including the information that when the play first opened, Ibsen was convinced by an apprehensive theater manager to write an alternative ending. In this new ending, Ibsen had Nora decide, after she stopped briefly to look in at her sleeping children, that she could not leave her family. Sometimes information from another source can even lead you to change your thesis. For example, after reading *A Doll House,* you might have decided that Ibsen's purpose was to make a strong case for the rights of women. In class, however, you might learn that Ibsen repeatedly said that his play was about the rights of all human beings, not just of women. This information could lead you to a thesis that suggests Torvald is just as trapped in his role as Nora is in hers. Naturally, Ibsen's interpretation of his own work does not invalidate your first judgment, but it does suggest another conclusion that is worth investigating.

After carefully evaluating the completeness, relevance, and validity of your supporting material, you can begin drafting your essay, using your scratch outline as a guide. In this first draft, your focus should be on the body of your essay; this is not the time to worry about constructing the "perfect" introduction and conclusion. (Many writers, knowing that their ideas will change as they write, postpone writing these paragraphs until a later draft, preferring instead to begin simply by stating their tentative thesis.) As you write, remember that your first draft is going to be rough and will probably not be as clear as you would like it to be; still, it will enable you to see the ideas you have outlined begin to take shape.

Revising and Editing an Essay

Revision

When you **revise,** you literally "re-see" your draft and, in many cases, you go on to reorder and rewrite substantial portions of your essay. Before you are satisfied with your essay, you will probably write several drafts, each more closely focused and more coherent than the previous one.

As you move through successive drafts, the task of revising your essay will be easier if you follow a systematic process. As you read and react to your essay, begin by assessing the effectiveness of the larger elements — for example, your thesis statement and your key supporting ideas — and then move on to examine increasingly smaller elements.

Thesis Statement First, reconsider your **thesis statement.** Is it carefully and precisely worded? Does it provide a realistic idea of what your essay will cover? Does it make a point that is worth supporting?

Strategies for Revision

Two strategies can help you to revise your drafts: *peer review* and *a dialogue with your instructor:*

1. **Peer review** is a process in which students assess each other's work-in-progress. This activity may be carried out in informal sessions during which one student comments on another's draft, or it may be a formal process in which students respond to specific questions on a form supplied by the instructor or participate in an electronic exchange. In either case, one student's reactions can help another student revise.

2. **A dialogue with your instructor** — in conference or by email — can give you a sense of how to proceed with your revision. Establishing such an oral or written dialogue can help you learn how to respond critically to your own writing, and your reactions to your instructor's comments on any draft can help you to clarify your essay's goals and write drafts that are increasingly consistent with these goals. (If your instructor is not available, try to schedule a conference with a writing center tutor.)

The following thesis statements are imprecise and unfocused.

Vague: Many important reasons exist to explain why Margot Macomber's shooting of her husband was probably intentional.

Vague: Dickens's characters are a lot like those of Addison and Steele.

To give focus and direction to your essay, a thesis statement must be more pointed and specific.

Revised: Although Hemingway's text states that Margot Macomber "shot at the buffalo," a careful analysis of her relationship with her husband suggests that in fact she intended to kill him.

Revised: With their extremely familiar physical and moral traits, many of Charles Dickens's minor characters reveal that Dickens owes a debt to the "characters" created by the eighteenth-century essayists Joseph Addison and Richard Steele for the newspaper The Spectator.

Supporting ideas   Next, assess the appropriateness of your **supporting ideas**, considering whether you present enough support for your thesis and whether all the details you include are relevant to that thesis. Make sure you have supported all points with specific, concrete examples from the work or works you are discussing, briefly summarizing key events, quoting dialogue or description, describing characters or settings, or paraphrasing important ideas. Make certain, however, that your own ideas are central to the essay and that you have not substituted plot summary for analysis and interpretation. Your goal is to draw a conclusion about one or more works and to support that conclusion with pertinent details. If an event in a story you are analyzing supports a point you wish to make, include a *brief* summary and then explain its relevance to the point you are making.

In the following excerpt from a paper on a short story by James Joyce, the first sentence briefly summarizes a key event, and the second sentence explains its significance.

> At the end of James Joyce's "Counterparts," when Farrington returns home after a day of frustration and abuse at work, his reaction is to strike out at his son Tom. This act shows that although he and his son are similarly victimized, Farrington is also the counterpart of his tyrannical boss.

Topic sentences   Now, turn your attention to the **topic sentences** that present the main ideas of your body paragraphs. Make sure that each topic sentence is clearly worded and that it signals the direction of your discussion and indicates the precise relationships of ideas to one another.

Be especially careful to avoid abstractions and vague generalities in topic sentences.

Vague: One similarity revolves around the dominance of the men by women. (What is the similarity?)

Revised: In both stories, a man is dominated by a woman.

Vague: There is one reason for the fact that Jay Gatsby remains a mystery. (What is the reason?)

Revised: Because The Great Gatsby is narrated by the outsider Nick Carraway, Jay Gatsby himself remains a mystery.

When revising topic sentences that are intended to move readers from one point (or one section of your paper) to another, be sure the relationship between the ideas they link is clear.

Unclear: Now the poem's imagery will be discussed.

Revised: Another reason for the poem's effectiveness is its unusual imagery.

Unclear: The sheriff's wife is another interesting character.

Revised: Like her friend Mrs. Hale, the sheriff's wife also has mixed feelings about what Mrs. Wright has done.

Introduction and conclusion When you are satisfied with the body of your essay, you can turn your attention to your paper's *introduction* and *conclusion*.

The **introduction** of an essay about literature should identify the works to be discussed and their authors and indicate the emphasis of the discussion to follow. Depending on your purpose and on your paper's topic, you may want to provide some historical background or biographical information or to briefly discuss the work in relation to similar works. Like all introductions, the one you write for an essay about literature should create interest in your topic and include a clear thesis statement.

The following introduction, though acceptable for a first draft, is in need of revision.

Draft: <u>Revenge</u>, which is defined as "the chance to retaliate, `get satisfaction, take vengeance, or inflict damage or injury in return for an injury, insult, etc.," is a major component in many of the stories we have read. The stories that will be discussed here deal with a variety of ways to seek revenge. In my essay, I will show some of these differences.

Although the student clearly identifies her paper's topic, she does not identify the works she will discuss or the particular point she will make about revenge. Her tired opening strategy, a dictionary definition, is not likely to create interest in her topic, and her announcement of her intention in the last sentence is awkward and unnecessary. The following revision is much more effective.

Revised: In Edgar Allan Poe's "The Cask of Amontillado," Montresor vows revenge on Fortunato for an unspecified "insult"; in Ring Lardner's "Haircut," Paul, a young retarded man, gets even with a cruel practical joker who has taunted him for years. Both of these stories present characters who seek revenge, and both stories end in murder. However, the murderers' motivations are presented very differently. In "Haircut," the narrator is unaware of the significance of many events, and his ignorance helps to create sympathy for the murderer; in "The Cask of Amontillado," where the narrator is the murderer himself, Montresor's inability to offer a convincing motive turns the reader against him.

In your **conclusion**, you restate your thesis or sum up your essay's main points; then, you make a graceful exit.

The concluding paragraph that follows is acceptable for a first draft, but it needs further development.

Draft: Although the characters of Montresor and Paul were created by different authors at different times, they do have similar motives and goals. However, they are portrayed very differently.

The following revision reinforces the essay's main point, effectively incorporating a brief quotation from "The Cask of Amontillado" (p. 350):

Revised: In fact, what is significant is not whether each murderer's act is justified, but rather how each murderer, and each victim, is portrayed by the narrator. Montresor—driven by a thirst to avenge "a thousand injuries" as well as a final insult—is shown to be sadistic and unrepentant; in "Haircut," it is Jim, the victim, whose sadism and lack of remorse are revealed to the reader.

Sentences and words Now, focus on the individual sentences and words of your essay. Begin by evaluating your **transitions**, the words and phrases that link sentences and paragraphs. Be sure that every necessary transitional element has been supplied and that each word or phrase you have selected accurately conveys the exact relationship (sequence, contradiction, and so on) between ideas.

When you are satisfied with the clarity and appropriateness of your paper's transitions, consider sentence variety and word choice:

- Be sure you have varied your sentence structure. You will bore your readers if all your sentences begin with the subject ("He. . . . He. . . ."; "The story. . . . The story. . . .").
- Make sure that all the words you have selected communicate your ideas accurately and that you have not used vague, inexact diction. For example, saying that a character is *bad* is a lot less helpful than describing him or her as *ruthless, conniving,* or *malicious.*
- Eliminate subjective expressions, such as *I think, in my opinion, I believe, it seems to me,* and *I feel.* These phrases weaken your essay by suggesting that its ideas are "only" your opinions and have no objective validity.

Using and documenting sources Make certain that all references to sources are integrated smoothly into your sentences and that all information that is not your own is documented appropriately.

Editing and Proofreading

Once you have finished revising, you **edit** — that is, you make certain that your paper's grammar, punctuation, spelling, and mechanics are correct. Always run a

---

✔ CHECKLIST Using Sources

- ☐ Acknowledge all material from sources, including the work or works under discussion, using the documentation style of the Modern Language Association (MLA).

- ☐ Combine paraphrases, summaries, and quotations with your own interpretations, weaving quotations smoothly into your paper. Introduce the words or ideas of others with a phrase that identifies their source (According to Richard Wright's biographer, . . .) and end with appropriate parenthetical documentation.

- ☐ Use quotations *only* when something vital would be lost if you did not reproduce the author's exact words.

- ☐ Integrate short quotations (four lines or fewer of prose or three lines or fewer of poetry) smoothly into your paper. Use a slash (/) with one space on either side to separate lines of poetry. Be sure to enclose quotations in quotation marks.

- ☐ Set off quotations of more than four lines of prose or three lines of poetry by indenting one inch (ten spaces) from the left-hand margin. Double-space, and do not use quotation marks. If you are quoting just one paragraph, do not indent the first line.

- ☐ Use ellipses — three spaced periods — to indicate that you have omitted material within a quotation (but never use ellipses at the beginning of a quoted passage).

- ☐ Use brackets to indicate that you have added words to a quotation: As Earl notes, "[Willie] is a modern-day Everyman" (201). Use brackets to alter a quotation so that it fits grammatically into your sentence: Wilson says that Miller "offer[s] audiences a dark view of the present" (74).

- ☐ Place commas and periods *inside* quotation marks: According to Robert Coles, the child could "make others smile."

- ☐ Place punctuation marks other than commas and periods *outside* quotation marks: What does Frost mean when he says, "a poem must ride on its own melting"? If the punctuation mark is part of the quoted material, place it *inside* the quotation marks: In "Mending Wall," Frost asks, "Why do they make good neighbors?"

continued on next page

> When citing part of a short story or novel, supply the page number (143).
> For a poem, supply line numbers (3–5), including the word *line* or *lines*
> just in the first reference. For a play, supply act, scene, and line numbers
> (2.2.17–22).
>
> Include a works-cited list (unless your instructor tells you not to).

spell check — but remember that you still have to **proofread** — look carefully for errors that the spell checker will not identify. These include homophones (*brake* incorrectly used instead of *break*), typos that create correctly spelled words (*work* instead of *word*), and words (such as a technical or foreign term or a writer's name) that may not be in your computer's dictionary. If you use a grammar checker, remember that although grammar programs may identify potential problems — long sentences, for example — they may not be able to determine whether a particular long sentence is grammatically correct (let alone stylistically pleasing). Always keep a style handbook as well as a dictionary nearby so that you can double-check any problems a spell checker or grammar checker highlights in your writing.

As you edit, pay particular attention to the mechanical conventions of literary essays, some of which are addressed in the checklist below. When your editing is complete, give your essay a descriptive title. Before you print your final copy, be sure that its format conforms to your instructor's requirements.

✔ **CHECKLIST** Conventions of Writing about Literature

Use present-tense verbs when discussing works of literature:
`The character of Mrs. Mallard's husband` *`is`* `not`
`developed. . . .`

Use past-tense verbs only when discussing historical events (`Owen's`
`poem conveys the destructiveness of World War I,`
`which at the time the poem` *`was`* `written` *`was`* `considered`
`to be . . .`); when presenting historical or biographical data (`Her`
`first novel, which` *`was`* `published in 1811 when Austen`
`was` `thirty-six, . . .`); or when identifying events that occurred prior to the time of the story's main action (`"Miss Emily is a`
`recluse; since her father's death she` *`has lived`* `alone`
`except for a servant"`).

Support all points with specific, concrete examples from the work you are discussing, briefly summarizing key events, quoting dialogue or description, describing characters or setting, or paraphrasing ideas.

continued on next page

- Avoid unnecessary plot summary. Your goal is to draw a conclusion about one or more works and to support that conclusion with pertinent details. If a plot detail supports a point you wish to make, a *brief* summary is acceptable. But remember, plot summary is no substitute for analysis.

- Use literary terms accurately. For example, be careful not to confuse *narrator* or *speaker* with *author;* feelings or opinions expressed by a narrator or character do not necessarily represent those of the author. You should not say, "In the poem's last stanza, `Frost` `expresses his indecision`" when you mean that the poem's *speaker* is indecisive.

- Underline titles of novels and plays; place titles of short stories and poems within quotation marks.

- Refer to authors of literary works by their full names (`Edgar Allan` `Poe`) in your first reference to them and by their last names (`Poe`) in subsequent references. Never refer to authors by their first names, and never use titles that indicate marital status (`Flannery O'Connor` or `O'Connor`, never `Flannery or Miss O'Connor`).

Exercise: Two Student Papers

The following student papers, "Initiation into Adulthood" and "Hard Choices," were written for the same Introduction to Literature class. Both consider the initiation theme in the same three short stories: James Joyce's "Eveline" (p. 722), John Updike's "A&P" (p. 230), and William Faulkner's "Barn Burning" (p. 356). "Hard Choices" conforms to the conventions of writing about literature discussed in this chapter. "Initiation into Adulthood" does not.

Read the two essays. Then, guided by this chapter's discussion of writing about literature and by the checklists on pages 34 and 35–36, identify the features that make "Hard Choices" the more effective essay, and decide where "Initiation into Adulthood" needs further revision. Finally, suggest some possible revisions for "Hard Choices."

Initiation into Adulthood

Introduction

At an early age, the main focus in a child's life is his parents. But as this child grows, he begins to get his own view of life, which may be, and usually is, different from that of his parents. Sooner or later, there will come a time in this child's life when he must stand up for what he truly believes in. At this point in his life, he can no longer be called a child, and he becomes part of the adult world. In literature, many stories—such as James Joyce's "Eveline," John Updike's "A&P," and William Faulkner's "Barn Burning"—focus on this initiation into adulthood.

Thesis statement

James Joyce's "Eveline" is a story that describes a major turning point in a woman's life. At home, Eveline's life was very hard. She was responsible for keeping the house together and caring for the younger children after her mother's death. Unfortunately, the only thoughts that ran through her mind were thoughts of escape, of leaving her unhappy life and beginning a new life of her own. The night before she was to secretly leave with Frank on a boat to Buenos Ayres, a street organ playing reminded her of her promise to her dying mother to keep the home together as long as she could. She was now forced to make a decision between life with Frank and her present life, which didn't look wholly undesirable now that she was about to leave. The next night, just as she was about to step on the boat, she realized she could not leave. The making of this decision was in essence Eveline's initiation into adulthood.

Discussion of first story: "Eveline"

Discussion of
second story:
"A&P"

John Updike's "A&P" presents the brief
infatuation of a young boy, Sammy, and the
consequences that follow. Sammy's home was a small
quiet town a few miles from the shore. He worked in
the local A&P as a cashier, a job his father had
gotten for him. One day, three girls in nothing but
bathing suits walked through the front door.
Immediately they caught Sammy's eye, especially the
leader, the one he nicknamed "Queenie." After
prancing through the store, eventually they came to
Sammy's checkout with an unusual order. It was not
long before they caught the attention of Mr. Lengel,
the manager. Unpleasant words were exchanged between
the manager and Queenie pertaining to their
inappropriate shopping attire. Before the girls left
the store, Sammy told Lengel that he quit, hoping
they would stop and watch him, their unsuspected
hero. But they kept walking, and Sammy was faced with
the decision of whether or not to follow through with
his gesture. Knowing that it is "fatal" not to follow
through with a gesture once you've started, he
removed his apron and bow tie and walked out the
door, realizing how hard the world was going to be to
him hereafter. The making of this decision, to leave
the mundane life of the A&P and enter the harsh
world, was in essence Sammy's initiation into
adulthood.

Discussion of
third story:
"Barn Burning"

William Faulkner's "Barn Burning" is a story
about Sarty Snopes, an innocent young boy who must make
a decision between his family and his honor. Because
Abner Snopes, Sarty's father, had so little, he

tried to hurt those who had more than he had—often by burning their barns. These acts forced the Snopes family to move around quite a bit. The last time Snopes burned a barn, he did it without warning his victim, making Sarty realize how cruel and dishonest his father really was. Because of this realization, Sarty decided to leave his family. This decision of Sarty's not to stick to his own blood was his initiation into adulthood.

"Eveline," "A&P," and "Barn Burning" all deal with a youth maturing to adulthood in the process of deciding whether to stay unhappy or to go and seek a better life. Sammy and Sarty leave their unpleasant situations because of something done unfairly. Eveline, on the other hand, decides to stay, remembering a promise to her mother. The decisions of these characters presented in their respective stories are focal points in the literary works and pertain to initiation into adulthood.

Conclusion

Hard Choices

Introduction

    Although William Faulkner's "Barn Burning" focuses on a young boy in the American South, John Updike's "A&P" on a teenager in a town north of Boston, and James Joyce's "Eveline" on a young woman in Dublin, each of the three stories revolves around a decision the central character must make. These decisions are not easy ones; in all three cases, family loyalty competes with a desire for individual freedom.

Thesis statement

However, the difficult decision-making process helps each character to mature, and in this sense, all three works are initiation stories.

Discussion of first story: "Barn Burning"

    For Sarty Snopes in "Barn Burning," initiation into adulthood means coming to terms with his father's concept of revenge. Mr. Snopes believes that a person should take revenge himself if he cannot get justice in court. Revenge, for this bitter man, means burning down barns. Sarty knows that his father is doing wrong, but Mr. Snopes drills into his son's mind the idea that "You got to learn to stick to your own blood or you ain't going to have any blood to stick to you" (Faulkner 359), and for a long time Sarty believes him. Naturally, this blood tie makes Sarty's decision to leave his family extremely difficult. In the end, though, Sarty decides to reject his father's values and remain behind when his family moves.

Discussion of second story: "A&P"

    Like Sarty, Sammy must choose between his values and his parents' values (reflected in his job at the supermarket). While Sammy is working in the A&P, he notices how "sheep-like" people are. Most customers have a routine life that they never consider changing, and Sammy does not want to end up like them. When three seemingly carefree girls enter the store and exhibit nonconformist behavior—such as going against the flow of people in the aisles, not having a grocery list, and wearing bathing suits—Sammy sees them as rebels, and he longs to escape through them from his humdrum world. In the end, he chooses to defend the girls and quit the job his parents helped him to get.

Likewise, Eveline has to decide between a new life with her boyfriend, Frank, in South America and her dull, hard life at home with her father. The new life offers change and freedom, while her life at home is spent working and keeping house. Still, when given the chance to leave, she declines because she promised her dying mother to "keep the home together as long as she could" (724).

All three characters enter adulthood by making difficult decisions. Sarty realizes that in order to grow, he must repudiate his father's wrongdoings. He stands up for his values and rejects his "blood." Sammy makes the same decision although with less extreme consequences: knowing that he will have to confront his parents, he defends the three girls and stands up to his boss, rejecting a life of conformity and security. Unlike the other two, Eveline does not reject her parents' values. Instead, she decides to sacrifice her own future by remaining with her father. She keeps her promise to her mother and puts her father before herself because she believes that caring for him is her duty.

Discussion of third story: "Eveline"

Comparative analysis of the three stories

Further analysis of the three stories

Each of the three characters confronts a challenging future. Sarty must support himself and make a new life. Because he is very young and because he has no one to help him, his future is the most uncertain of the three. Unlike Sammy and Eveline, who still have homes, Sarty has only his judgment and his values to guide him. Sammy's future is less bleak but still unpredictable: he knows that the world will be a harder place for him from now on (Updike 234) because now he is a man of principle. Unlike the other two, Eveline knows exactly what her future holds: work, pain, and boredom. She has no fear or uncertainty—but no hope for a better tomorrow either.

Conclusion

"Barn Burning," "A&P," and "Eveline" are stories of initiation in which the main characters struggle with decisions that help them to grow up. All three consider giving up the known for the unknown, challenging their parents and becoming truly themselves, but only Sarty and Sammy actually do so. Both boys defy their parents and thus trade difficult lives for uncertain ones. Eveline, however, decides to stay on in her familiar life, choosing the known—however deadening—over the unknown. Still, all three, in confronting hard choices and deciding to do what their values tell them they must do, experience an initiation into adulthood.

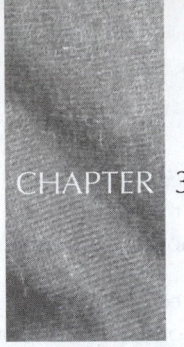

CHAPTER 3

WRITING SPECIAL KINDS OF PAPERS

When you write a paper about literature, you have many options (some of these are listed in Chapter 2, p. 22). Often, however, you will be asked to respond to one of four special assignments: to write a *comparison-contrast*, to write an *explication*, to write a *character analysis*, or to write about a work's *historical context*. The pages that follow offer guidelines for responding to each of these assignments as well as an annotated model student paper and a list of suggested topics for each kind of paper.

Writing a Comparison-Contrast

When you write a **comparison-contrast**, you look first for significant similarities between your two subjects. For example, two characters may have a similar motivation or similar goals or flaws; two stories may have similar settings; two plays may have similar plots; and two poems may have parallels in their use of sound or imagery. Once you have identified the main similarities, you can consider why these similarities are important and what they reveal about the works.

There are two ways to arrange material in a comparison-contrast essay. When you write a **point-by-point comparison**, you discuss one point of similarity at a time, alternating between subjects. When you write a **subject-by-subject comparison**, you approach each subject separately, discussing all your points first for one subject and then for the other. The outlines that follow illustrate how you could use either a point-by-point or a subject-by-subject strategy to support the same thesis statement.

Thesis Statement: Both David Michael Kaplan's "Doe Season" and Alice Munro's "Boys and Girls" focus on a young girl who learns that her gender limits her and comes to accept that such limitations are inevitable.

Point-by-Point Comparison

First point: In both stories, the girls are tomboys who like being with their fathers.
  "Doe Season": Andy goes hunting with her father.
  "Boys and Girls": The narrator does farm chores with her father.

Second point: In both stories, the girls struggle against the expectations of others.
>   **"Doe Season":** Mac and Charlie challenge Andy's right to hunt.
>   **"Boys and Girls":** Narrator's mother expects her to do household chores.

Third point: In both stories, the girls learn that they are limited by their gender.
>   **"Doe Season":** Andy shoots the deer and runs away in horror, thinking of
>   her mother.
>   **"Boys and Girls":** The narrator fails to save Flora (the horse) and realizes
>   she is "only a girl."

Subject-by-Subject Comparison

First subject: "Doe Season"
>   **First point:** Andy is a tomboy who is excited about going hunting with
>   her father.
>   **Second point:** Charlie and Mac challenge her right to be there.
>   **Third point:** Through her encounter with the deer, she learns that she is
>   not as brave as she thought she was.

Second subject: "Boys and Girls"
>   **First point:** Like Andy, the narrator likes being with her father and is glad
>   not to be in the house with her mother.
>   **Second point:** Like Andy, she is criticized by those who think she belongs
>   at home.
>   **Third point:** Like Andy, she learns through her encounter with an
>   animal — in her case, the horse whose life she cannot save — that she
>   is limited by her gender.

✔ CHECKLIST   Writing a Comparison-Contrast

☐ Have you chosen two subjects that have significant similarities?

☐ Does your thesis statement identify the two subjects you are comparing and tell why they are alike (and perhaps also acknowledge their differences)?

☐ Does your paper's structure follow either a point-by-point or a subject-by-subject pattern?

☐ Does each of your topic sentences identify the subject you are discussing and the point you are focusing on in the paragraph?

☐ Do transitional words and phrases clearly lead readers from subject to subject and from point to point?

☐ Have you followed your instructor's format and documentation guidelines?

Sample Student Paper: Comparing Two Fictional Characters

The following student paper, "The Dangerous Consequences of Societal Limbo," is a point-by-point comparison of two characters created by William Faulkner: Emily Grierson in "A Rose for Emily" and Abner (Ab) Snopes in "Barn Burning." Note that this paper does not include a works-cited page because students were limited to writing about works in this anthology.

Quinn 1

David Quinn

Professor Warren

Literature 1120

27 March 2005

The Dangerous Consequences of Societal Limbo

In his many works of fiction, William Faulkner   *Introduction*
explores the lives of characters who live in the
closed society of the American South, a society
rooted in traditional values. In the stories "Barn
Burning" and "A Rose for Emily," Faulkner explores
what happens when individuals lose their connection
to this society and its values. Both Abner Snopes, a
rebellious sharecropper, and Emily Grierson, an
unmarried woman from a prominent family, are isolated
from their respective communities, and both find   *Thesis statement*
themselves in a kind of societal limbo. Once in that
limbo, they no longer feel the need to adhere to the
values of their society and, as a result, are free to
violate both traditional and moral rules.

    Initially, Emily's isolation is not voluntary;   *Emily's isolation*
it is thrust upon her. From childhood on, Emily is
never really allowed to be part of Jefferson society;
she is seen as having a "high and mighty" attitude
(Faulkner, "Rose" 217). Her father stands between her
and the rest of the town, refusing to allow her to date
the young men who pursue her, whom he sees as somehow

Quinn 2

not good enough for her. As a result, her only close relationship is with her father, who essentially becomes her whole world. Recalling father and daughter, the narrator depicts them as static and alone, trapped in a living portrait, "Miss Emily a slender figure in white in the background, her father a spraddled silhouette in the foreground, his back to her and clutching a horsewhip" (Faulkner, "Rose" 218), framed by the archway of the entrance to their house. When Emily's father dies, and the townspeople insist on removing his body from her home, the only world she knows is physically taken from her, and she has nothing to take its place. Without her father, without friends, without a husband, she withdraws from her community—and, thus, is free to defy its rules with a shocking act of violence.

Ab's isolation   While Emily's removal from society is forced upon her, Abner Snopes voluntarily rejects his society's values. During the Civil War, he does not fight alongside the Confederate army; instead, he adopts an aggressive neutrality, stealing from both sides for his own personal gain. He is finally caught by the side he betrays when a Confederate policeman shoots him in the heel as Abner tries to escape on a stolen horse. Unable to see that he did something wrong, Abner uses his injury as an excuse for a personal vendetta against society. However, because he has a wife and three children whom he must feed and provide for, Ab must constantly return to the society that he turned his back on.

Quinn 3

This conflict between his rebellious nature and his
need to work as a sharecropper makes him unstable.
Like Emily, he does not see himself as part of the
community, and therefore he feels free to violate its
rules.

Once Emily and Abner are estranged from their
respective communities, they no longer feel bound by
the society's laws and rules. This makes it possible
for Abner to burn barns and for Emily to commit
murder.

Emily's courting and capturing of Homer Barron
fills the void left by her father's death; for her,
the act of poisoning Homer is a perverse method of
regaining control. With this act, she takes away the
very life that attracted her to him, but she is able
to hold on to him as a physical entity. As an exile
from society, Emily can rationalize this antisocial
act: in her eyes, murder is no longer wrong; it is
merely a method of preservation, a means to an end
that ensures that Homer will remain with her until
her death. Once Emily has completed the gruesome task
of poisoning her "husband," she further withdraws
from her community, and her neighbors, the narrator
included, never suspect her secret. Without suspicion
from the townspeople, Emily is left alone, free to
live as she chooses.

Abner's impotent rage and search for vengeance
push him to lash out violently at almost anyone with
whom he comes in contact. His method of destruction
comes in the primitive form of fire, which he uses not

Transitional paragraph

Emily's antisocial act

Ab's anti-social acts

Quinn 4

to kill but simply to threaten. In the two barn
burnings of the story, Abner incites confrontations
and then uses the burnings as a way of getting even
for imagined offenses. In one incident, for example,
Mr. Harris, a landowner, finds that Abner's hog ate a
section of his corn crop. When Harris demands a
dollar pound fee for the return of the hog, Abner
sends him a threatening message: "Wood and hay kin
burn" (Faulkner, "Barn" 357). Despite Harris's
efforts to resolve their dispute, Abner is determined
to carry out his threat. Ultimately, the barn
burnings further alienate Ab from the society whose
laws he is defying.

Like Ab Snopes, Emily makes her own rules and
develops her own twisted concepts of justice and
revenge. Although she is not directly punished by the
community for her crime, Emily suffers terribly. She
may possess the body of Homer Barron, but his death
renders her incapable of holding onto him as a person
and as a husband. The result of her gradual
estrangement from society—involuntary at first but
eventually confirmed by her willing violent act—is
complete isolation from the real world and withdrawal
into an empty world of her own.

Although Ab operates from within a similar
societal limbo, he is unable to escape society's
punishment. Sarty Snopes, Abner's son, is a firsthand
witness to his father's second barn burning. Sarty is
caught in a moral dilemma, pulled between the values
of his community and the selfish motives of his father.

Emily's punishment

Ab's punishment

Rather than remain in the alienated condition that his father has created for his family, Sarty renounces his loyalty to Abner and turns his father in to plantation owner Major De Spain.

Despite their estrangement from society, then, neither Emily nor Ab is ultimately able to escape its influence. In withdrawing from their respective communities, Emily Grierson and Abner Snopes are able to defy society's traditions and break its rules, but they also create empty lives for themselves and tragedy for those closest to them.

Conclusion

Suggested Topics for Comparison-Contrast Papers

Comparing Two Stories: tradition and superstition in "The Water-Faucet Vision" and "Dead Man's Path"; the meaning of education in "Gryphon" and "B. Wordsworth"; the nature of time in "Kansas" and "Half a Day"

> **NOTE:** For a model student paper that compares two stories, see "Mesmerizing Men and Vulnerable Teens . . . ," p. 611.)

Comparing Two Poems: "The Soldier" and "Dulce et Decorum Est"; "Hope" and "'Hope' is the thing with feathers —"; "How Do I Love Thee?" and "What Lips My Lips Have Kissed"

> **NOTE:** (For a model student paper that compares two poems, see "Digging for Memories," p. 846.)

Comparing Two Plays: rivalry and role reversal in *The Stronger* and *Beauty*; father/son relationships in *Fences* and *Death of a Salesman*

Comparing a Story and a Poem: "The Rocking-Horse Winner" and "Suicide Note" (children desperate to please their parents); "A Rose for Emily" and "Porphyria's Lover" (obsessive love)

Comparing a Story and a Play: loneliness and desperation in *Trifles* and "A Rose for Emily"; mentors and students in *Proof* and "B. Wordsworth"; family loyalty in *A Raisin in the Sun* and "Eveline"; the quest for a new life in *The Cuban Swimmer* and "The Third and Final Continent"

Comparing Two Characters: Queenie ("A&P") and Miss Ferenczi ("Gryphon"); Sammy ("A&P") and Tom (*The Glass Menagerie*); Carla and Bethany (*Beauty*); the Misfit ("A Good Man Is Hard to Find") and Arnold Friend ("Where Are You Going, Where Have You Been?"); Benjamin and Ronnie in *Trying to Find Chinatown*

Comparing Two Works by a Single Author: John Updike's "A&P" and "Ex-Basketball Player"; Tennessee Williams's *The Glass Menagerie* and "Portrait of a Girl in Glass"; Edgar Allan Poe's "The Cask of Amontillado" and "The Tell-Tale Heart"

Comparing a Work of Literature to a Work of Art: Jane Flanders's poem "Cloud Painter" and John Constable's painting *Landscape, Noon, the Haywain*; William Carlos Williams's poem "The Great Figure" and Charles Henry Demuth's painting *The Figure 5 in Gold*; W. H. Auden's poem "Musée des Beaux Arts" and Pieter Brueghel's painting *Landscape with the Fall of Icarus*

Film Series

DVD

Comparing a Work of Literature to a Film: The short-story and DVD versions of "A&P," "I Stand Here Ironing," "Cathedral," "A Worn Path," or "Everyday Use"

> **NOTE:** For additional possibilities for comparison-contrast papers, see the "Related Works" lists that follow many of the selections.

Writing an Explication

When you write an **explication** (of a poem, a short story, or a scene in a play), you do a close reading of a work or a portion of a work, carefully analyzing its elements. For example, you might decide to analyze a story's characters, symbols, or setting; of a poem's language, rhyme scheme, meter, or form; or of a play's dialogue or staging. One way to approach a work you wish to explicate is to apply the guidelines for reading fiction (p. 168), poetry (p. 830), or drama (p. 1340) in a systematic way. Another way is to use the Explicator mark-up tool on the *Lit21* CD-ROM accompanying this book.

When you organize your material in an explication, you should proceed systematically. If you are focusing on a single element, analyze its importance in one section of the work at a time. If you are analyzing several elements, consider each — plot, setting, point of view, and so on — in turn. You will probably choose to group the less significant elements together in a single paragraph or section of your paper and then devote several paragraphs to one particularly important element, carefully considering how symbols, for example, shed light on the work. For each element you discuss, you will give examples from the work you are explicating, quoting words, phrases, lines, and passages that illustrate each point you are making about the work.

✔ CHECKLIST   Writing an Explication

- Is the work you have chosen sufficiently rich to support an explication?

- Do you focus on one element of literature at a time?

- Do topic sentences make clear which element (or elements) you are focusing on in each paragraph?

- Do you use quotations from the work to illustrate your points?

- Does your thesis state the central point about the work that your explication supports?

- Have you followed your instructor's format and documentation guidelines?

Sample Student Paper: Explicating a Poem

The following student paper, "A Lingering Doubt," is an explication of Robert Frost's poem "The Road Not Taken." Note that this paper does not include a works-cited list because students were limited to writing about works in this anthology.

Jeanette Craff

Professor Rosenberg

English 102

13 February 2005

A Lingering Doubt

Sometimes it is tempting to look back on a

Introduction — lifetime of choices and decisions and to think, "What

if? What if I had made a different choice? Would my

life be better? Worse? More interesting?" In Robert

Frost's poem "The Road Not Taken," the speaker does

just this: he looks back at a time in his life when

he came to a fork in the road and chose one path over

another. He tells readers that he "took the one less

traveled by, / And that has made all the difference"

(lines 19-20). At first, this statement seems to

suggest that the speaker is satisfied with the

decision he made long ago. However, certain elements

Thesis statement — in the poem—its structure, its language, and even

its title—suggest that the speaker is regretting his

decision, not celebrating it.

The title of the poem, "The Road Not Taken,"

Overview of — immediately suggests that the speaker is focusing not

poem's language — on the choice he <u>did</u> make long ago but on the road

and theme — he chose <u>not</u> to take. The poem's language supports

this interpretation. Frost begins his poem with the

speaker recalling that "Two roads diverged in a yellow

wood" and saying that he is "sorry [he] could not

travel both" (1-2). The image Frost uses of the two

roads diverging is an obvious metaphor for the choices

Craff 2

a person has to make in the course of a lifetime. As a young man, the speaker was not aware of any major difference between the two roads. He says that he saw one as "just as fair" (6) as the other and uses words and phrases such as "equally" (11) and "really about the same" (10). However, in the third stanza of the poem, the older and wiser speaker, looking back on that period of his life, says that he still might take the other road "another day" (13). That the mature speaker still continues to examine a decision he made earlier in life suggests that he may not be completely satisfied with that decision.

Analysis of poem's structure and meter

A close look at the poem suggests that it is the departures from the expected structure and meter that make its meaning clear. The poem is divided into four stanzas, each made up of five lines. The regular meter of these four stanzas conveys a sense of tranquillity and certainty. The regularity of the poem's rhyme scheme (a, b, a, a, b) also contributes to the poem's natural fluidity. This fluidity is evident, for example, in the first stanza:

> Two roads diverged in a yellow wood,
> And sorry I could not travel both
> And be one traveler, long I stood
> And looked down one as far as I could
> To where it bent in the undergrowth; (1-5)

Here, the end rhyme of lines 1, 3, and 4 and of lines 2 and 5, as well as the even line lengths (each line contains nine syllables) make the poem flow smoothly.

Craff 3

Further analysis of poem's structure and meter

However, the poem does not maintain this fluidity. In other stanzas, lines range from eight to ten syllables in length, and the important final stanza ends with a line that is an awkward departure from the rest of the poem:

> I shall be telling this with a sigh
> Somewhere ages and ages hence:
> Two roads diverged in a wood, and I—
> I took the one less traveled by, And
> that has made all the difference. (16-20)

In this stanza, line 20 has nine syllables as lines 16 and 18 do, but unlike them, it also has an irregular meter ("And that has made all the difference"), which forces readers to hesitate on the word "all" before landing on "difference." This hesitation, coupled with the hesitation signaled by the dash that ends line 18, suggests the speaker's doubts about his decision. When the speaker was young, he did not notice any significant difference between the two roads, or the life choices, presented to him. Now, looking back, he believes that there was a difference, and he may be lamenting the fact that he will never know where life would have taken him had he chosen differently.

Analysis of poem's language

Departure from expected meter is not the only tactic Frost uses to convey a sense of hesitation and an air of regret. Frost's choice of words also plays an important part in helping readers understand the poem's theme. In the first stanza, for example, the speaker thinks back to the period of his life in which he had to choose between two separate paths, and he says that he was "sorry [he] could not travel both" (2). The word "sorry" helps to establish the tone of regret that pervades the poem.

In the second stanza, Frost begins to use words and phrases to convey indecision and doubt in the speaker's voice. The speaker attempts to pacify himself by saying that the road he chose had "perhaps the better claim" (7), but then he is quick to say that the passage of time has worn both roads "really about the same" (10). The words "perhaps" and "really" suggest indecision, and Frost's choice of these words helps to convey the doubt in the speaker's mind.

The speaker's sense of regret deepens in the third stanza as he continues to think back on his decision. When the speaker says, "Oh, I kept the first for another day!" (13), the word "Oh" expresses his regret. The exclamation point at the end of the statement helps reinforce the finality of his decision. When the speaker continues, "Yet knowing how way leads on to way, / I doubted if I should ever come back" (14-15), the word "Yet" is filled with uncertainty.

In the poem's final stanza, the speaker suddenly leaves his thoughts of the past and speaks in the future tense: "I shall be telling this [story] with a sigh" (16). Frost's use of the word "sigh" here is very revealing because it connotes resignation or

Craff 5

regret. The speaker concludes, "Two roads diverged in a wood, and I— / I took the one less traveled by, / And that has made all the difference" (18-20). Both the dash and the repetition of the word "I" convey hesitation and thus communicate his lingering doubts over the decision he made long ago.

Conclusion

Although this doubt is evident throughout the poem, "The Road Not Taken" has frequently been interpreted as optimistic because of the speaker's final statement that the choice he made "has made all the difference" (20). However, "made all the difference" can be interpreted as neutral (or even negative) as well as positive, and so the speaker's statement at the end of the poem may actually be a statement of regret, not celebration. The "difference" mentioned in the final line has left a doubt in the speaker's mind, and, as Frost suggests in the title of his poem, the speaker is left thinking about the road he did not take and will never be able to take.

Suggested Topics for Explication Papers

Fiction

Focus on Form: "A Primer for the Punctuation of Heart Disease"; "Girl"; "Kansas"

Focus on Language: "Battle Royal"; "Hills Like White Elephants"; "The Things They Carried"; "The Lesson"

Focus on Symbolism/Allegory: "A Good Man Is Hard to Find"; "Hidden Lives of Lakes"; "The Swimmer"; "The Chrysanthemums"

Focus on Character: "An Ounce of Cure"; "Bartleby, the Scrivener"; "The Red Convertible"; "The Third and Final Continent"; "Teenage Wasteland"

Focus on Setting: "The Open Boat"; "Greasy Lake"; "The Cask of Amontillado"

Focus on Point of View: "The Disappearance"; "I Stand Here Ironing"; "The Tell-Tale Heart"

Focus on Plot: "Happy Endings"; "Sleepy Time Gal"; "Miss Brill"; "The Storm"

Focus on Irony: "Saboteur"; "Big Black Good Man"

> **NOTE:** For model student papers that explicate short stories, see "'The Secret Lion': Everything Changes" (p. 188) and "And Again She Makes the Journey: Character and Act in Eudora Welty's 'A Worn Path'" (p. 106).

Poetry

Focus on Voice: "Ballad of the Landlord"; "Not Waving but Drowning"; "My Papa's Waltz"; "Daddy"; "Volcanoes be in Sicily"

Focus on Word Choice: "Jabberwocky"; "My Mistress' Eyes Are Nothing Like the Sun"

Focus on Irony: "How to Write the Great American Indian Novel"

Focus on Imagery: "Emmett Till"; "The Lake Isle of Innisfree"; "Dover Beach"; "Ode on a Grecian Urn"

Focus on Figures of Speech: "Dulce et Decorum Est"; "Stop all the clocks, cut off the telephone"; "Metaphors"

Focus on Sound: "Acquainted with the Night"; "La Belle Dame sans Merci"; "The Raven"

Focus on Form: "Buffalo Bill's"; "When I consider how my light is spent"; "What Were They Like?"; "Group Photo with Winter Trees"

Focus on Symbol, Allegory, Allusion, Myth: "The Second Coming"; "Diving into the Wreck"; "Sea Grapes"

Drama

Focus on Plot: the *Antigone* story in *Antigone's Red*; subplots in *Hamlet*; foreshadowing in *Nine Ten*

Focus on Character: Dr. Rank in *A Doll House*; Claire in *Proof*; Ophelia in *Hamlet*; Walter in *A Raisin in the Sun*

Focus on Staging: Tom's monologues in *The Glass Menagerie*; the simultaneous speeches in *Small World*; the Requiem in *Death of a Salesman*

Focus on Language: Imagery and figures of speech in *The Brute*; one speech in *Hamlet* or *Oedipus*

Focus on Symbolism: The quilt in *Trifles*; the macaroons and the Tarantella in *A Doll House*.

Writing a Character Analysis

When you write a **character analysis** of a character in a short story or play, you examine the character's language, behavior, background, interaction with other characters, and reaction to his or her environment. Everything you are told about a character — and everything you can reasonably infer about him or her from words, actions, or appearance — can help you to understand the character. In your analysis, you can focus on the influences that shaped the character, the character's effect on others, how the character changes during the course of the story or play, or what motivates him or her to act (or not to act).

✔ **CHECKLIST   Writing a Character Analysis**

☐ Have you chosen a character who is interesting enough to serve as the focus of your paper?

☐ Have you considered the character's words, actions, appearance, and interactions with others?

☐ Have you considered how and why the character changes — or why he or she fails to change?

☐ Have you considered how the work would be different if the character had made different choices?

☐ Have you considered how the work would be different without the character?

☐ Have you considered what motivates the character to act (or not to act)?

☐ Have you followed your instructor's format and documentation guidelines?

Sample Student Paper: Analyzing a Character in a Play

The following student paper, "Linda Loman: Breaking the Mold," analyzes a character in Arthur Miller's play *Death of a Salesman*. Note that this paper does not include a works-cited list because students were limited to writing only about works in this anthology.

Dube 1

Caroline Dube

Professor Nelson

English 1302

14 March 2005

Linda Loman: Breaking the Mold

In many ways, Linda Loman appears to play the part of the stereotypical dutiful and loving wife in Arthur Miller's <u>Death of a Salesman</u>. She eagerly greets her husband, ignores his shortcomings, and maintains an upbeat attitude, all while managing the bills, waxing the floors, and mending the clothes. Her kindness and infinite patience seem to establish her as a foil for Willy, with his turbulent temperament. In addition, most of her actions seem to be only reactions to the other characters in the play. However, a closer look at Linda reveals a more complex woman: a fully developed character with dreams, insights, and flashes of defiance.

Unlike stock characters, whose motivations seem transparent and obvious, Linda has dreams that are both complex and realistically human. The stage directions that introduce Linda describe her as sharing Willy's "turbulent longings" but lacking the temperament to pursue them (1582). It seems she has applied the wisdom she shares with Willy, that "life is a casting off," to her own cast-away dreams (1583). Linda's hopes seem more realistic than Willy's. She

Thesis statement

Linda's hopes and dreams

Dube 2

wants Biff to settle down, the mortgage to be paid
off, and the members of her family to coexist
happily. These modest aspirations are the product of
Linda's long experience. The fact that Linda does not
pursue unrealistic goals, as Willy does, does not
make her a flat character (or even a less interesting
one); instead, her weaknesses give her character a
degree of depth and human realism.

Linda's actions   At times, Linda takes on the role of family
peacemaker—a role we would expect her to play
consistently throughout the play if she were simply a
stock character. But Linda breaks out of the obedient
wife mode on several occasions. When Willy insists
that she stop mending her stockings, Linda quietly
puts them into her pocket to resume her mending
later. When Biff and Happy show they are ashamed of
their father, Linda fiercely lashes out at them in his
defense, calling Happy a "philandering bum" and
threatening to kick Biff out of the house for good
(1607). Although at first she cannot bring herself to
remove the rubber pipe that Willy used to commit
suicide, Linda says she had finally decided to destroy
the pipe when Biff removed it. She does not always
have an opportunity to follow through on her threats,
but Linda demonstrates clearly that she will not
always follow orders—especially when she is
protecting Willy.

Linda's
awareness
of family
problems

Linda seems to be the cheerful voice of the
family, but beneath the surface, she is keenly aware
of the ongoing problems. She knows that Charley has

Dube 3

been giving money to Willy every week, but she says
nothing for fear of embarrassing Willy. She senses
Willy's suicidal tendencies and even finds physical
evidence of his plans. Linda is the first to raise
doubts about Biff's plans to ask Mr. Oliver for
money, suggesting he may not remember Biff. Above
all, Linda understands human nature and how the minds
of those around her work. She gives an honest
description of her husband and his situation:

> I don't say he's a great man. Willy Loman
> never made a lot of money. His name was
> never in the paper. He's not the finest
> character that ever lived. But he's a human
> being, and a terrible thing is happening to
> him. So attention must be paid. (1606)

Linda sees past her sons' exaggerated lies and is not
afraid to criticize them for their selfish choices.
She pretends to be unaware of their shortcomings, but
her feigned obliviousness is simply another layer in
her multifaceted personality.

Linda appears to be the steadiest character in
the play, providing stability for the other
characters, but her constant brushing aside of
problems actually makes her the most responsible for
the ultimate tragedy of the play. She lies to Willy in
order to soothe him, telling him he has "too much on
the ball to worry about" (1585) and is "the handsomest
man in the world" (1596). In the process, she allows
him to continue believing in the unattainable dreams
that ultimately lead him to self-destruct. She also

Linda's failure
to confront
family problem

Dube 4

makes exceptions for her sons, suggesting Willy can simply talk to Biff's teacher to change his grade and encouraging Biff's business plans even when she knows he will not succeed. As a result, failure hits Biff hard because he has not been forced to think realistically.

Conclusion

In the end, Linda goes beyond the stereotypical confines of her role as ever-supportive wife and mother. There are many layers to her character: beneath her simple goals of owning her home and living happily with her family lie years of disappointments and failed dreams. Hidden beneath her eagerness to please is her willingness to defy orders to defend her husband. And, although she seems not to notice what is going on, she is perceptive about the family's problems long before others show awareness. Her actions clearly show that she is more than a minor supporting character. Linda is deeply involved in the actions and impulses of the other characters in the play. As a fully developed character, she has complex motivations and human qualities (including faults) that set her apart from stock characters. As her son Happy notes, "They broke the mold when they made her" (1612).

Suggested Topics for Character Analysis Papers

Fiction

Major Characters: the narrator in "An Ounce of Cure"; Lieutenant Cross in "The Things They Carried"; Dee in "Everyday Use"; the mother in "Two Kinds" or "Seventeen Syllables"; the husband in "The Disappearance"

Minor Characters: the mother in "The Rocking-Horse Winner"; Tobe in "A Rose for Emily"; Lena in "Big Black Good Man"; the husband in "The Yellow Wallpaper"

> **NOTE:** For a model student paper analyzing a major character in a short story, see "And Again She Makes the Journey: Character and Act in Eudora Welty's 'A Worn Path'" (p. 106).

Drama

Major Characters: Troy in *Fences*; Miss Y in *The Stronger*; Linda in *Death of a Salesman*; Antigone in *Antigone*; Amanda in *The Glass Menagerie*; Mama in *A Raisin in the Sun*

Minor Characters: Luka in *The Brute*; Polonius in *Hamlet*; Mrs. Linde in *A Doll House*; Claire in *Proof*

> **NOTE:** For two model student papers analyzing characters in plays, see "Laura's Gentleman Caller" (p. 2076) and "Desperate Measures: Acts of Defiance in *Trifles*" (p. 1354).

Writing about a Work's Historical Context

When you explore the **historical context** of a short story, poem, or play, you set the work in its historical time and place, thereby enriching your own and others' understanding of it. You begin by looking for specific references to historical figures or events. For example, you might see that a character in a story or play is reacting to a major world development, such as a war, or you might observe that a poem focuses on the achievements — or shortcomings — of a well-known historical figure. Such references can help you decide to focus on the work's historical context.

When you write your paper, you will examine the connections between the historical background and the literary work itself, considering how the writer's interpretation of events has shaped the work. To set the work in context, you will probably need to do some research. You might begin by reading an encyclopedia article on the events referred to in the work. Once you have found some general background information, you can examine contemporary newspapers, diaries, and letters as well as more current articles and books. You might even want to interview someone who lived through the events that influenced the work.

It usually makes sense to include a brief summary of the particular historical situation or event you intend to discuss. This overview will help to orient readers who are not familiar with the work's background. You might also **explicate** the work, systematically exploring specific parallels between historical events and the work itself. Alternatively, you might focus on one character in a story or play, examining how that character is shaped by specific historical events — for example, how Ab Snopes in William Faulkner's "Barn Burning" (p.356) has been affected by the Civil War.

✔ **CHECKLIST   Writing about a Work's Historical Context**

  ▪ Is a historical figure or event an important influence on the work?

  ▪ Do you summarize and explain the relevant historical background?

  ▪ Do you clearly explain the relationship between the historical background and the literary work?

  ▪ Do you use examples and quotations from the literary work to illustrate specific parallels between the work of literature and its historical context?

  ▪ Have you followed your instructor's format and documentation guidelines?

Sample Student Paper: Setting a Literary Work in Its Historical Context

The following student paper, "Dreaming of Home," sets Louise Erdrich's poem "Indian Boarding School: The Runaways" in the context of the historical events that inspired it. Note that because this paper uses outside sources, it includes a works-cited list.

Monteleone 1

Matt Monteleone

Professor Kennedy

Composition 101

April 11 2005

Dreaming of Home

    Louise Erdrich's poem "Indian Boarding School:
The Runaways" describes the experiences of Native   Introduction
American children who have been sent to a US-
government-sponsored boarding school. Although the
experiences themselves are traumatic and heart
wrenching, the full impact of the poem comes only
with an understanding of the United States
government's motivation for creating these schools
and of their treatment of the Native American
children who lived there during the late nineteenth
and early twentieth centuries. With this background,
Erdrich's work becomes not only a moving description
of the painful experience of Native American children
at federal boarding schools, but also a political
statement about the treatment of Native Americans in
the United States—and, perhaps, a statement about   Thesis statement
the pain of forced cultural assimilation.

    "Indian Boarding School: The Runaways" relates
the experience of Indian children struggling to   Explication of
maintain their cultural identities and preserve their   poem's theme
cherished memories of home despite a series of
efforts to purge them of their Indian heritage.
Erdrich uses haunting language to explain that, for
these children, the world they once knew has changed

Monteleone 2

to such an extent that it exists only in their
imagination. Therefore, the children can escape to
their home only when they go to sleep, and dream. In
the first stanza, the narrator conveys her longing when
she says, "Home's the place we head for in our
sleep. / Boxcars stumbling north in dreams / don't
wait for us. We catch them on the run" (lines 1-3). At
night, the children dream of making their way home. In
the daytime, they are "cold in regulation clothes"
(11), forced to wear "dresses, long green ones" (17)
and to engage in "shameful" manual labor (19). To fight
the assimilation being forced upon them, the children
have only their memories.

Transitional
paragraph

By relating the experiences of these "runaways"
and their dreams of home, Erdrich recreates the
emotional experience of Native American children sent
to the US government's boarding schools. The history
of these Indian schools further explains the
experience described in the poem and sheds light on
the consequences of America's policy of forced
assimilation.

Background:
Rationalization for
US government's
Indian boarding
schools

During the late 1800s and early 1900s, the
United States government sponsored a variety of
initiatives aimed at assimilating Native Americans
into white culture. Although some government officials
genuinely believed that assimilation was the best way
for Native Americans to live better, happier lives,
this policy is grounded in the assumption that white
culture is superior to Indian culture. As a result,
government officials used a variety of methods to

Monteleone 3

encourage assimilation, and the establishment of the
non-reservation boarding school was one of them.
According to the Modern American Poetry Website, the
Carlisle Indian Industrial School, established in
1879 with 139 students from the Rosebud and Pine
Ridge nations, was one of the first of these schools.
A description of the Carlisle Indian Industrial
School reveals that Erdrich's poem is rooted in
actual events.

According to the Cumberland County Historical
Society in Pennsylvania, where the Carlisle
Industrial School was located, in 1879 General
Richard Henry Pratt received permission from the
United States government to use a former military
base as the site of the first Indian boarding school.
Although the school closed in 1918, Carlisle served
as a model for many of the other Indian boarding
schools around the United States. Consequently, an
examination of its policies and practices will
explain how most Indian boarding schools operated.

After receiving permission from the government,
Pratt traveled to the Rosebud and Pine Ridge
reservations to recruit students. According to the
Carlisle Industrial School Research Pages, the chief
of the Rosebud reservation, although initially
reluctant, eventually agreed to send some children
from the reservation to the school. Pratt soon
convinced other Indian nations, including the
Cheyenne, Kiowa, and Lakota, to send their children
to the school as well. At the Carlisle school, the

Background:
History of Indian
boarding schools

Monteleone 4

teachers used a variety of methods to "civilize" the Native American students. For example, as the <u>Modern American Poetry</u> Web site explains, students were given new names, their hair was cut, and they were forced to speak English instead of their tribal languages. (The <u>Carlisle Industrial School Research Pages</u> notes that members of the Lakota nation cut hair to symbolize mourning, so this practice was particularly upsetting to the Lakota children.) The photo in fig. 1 shows a group of Indian children at the Carlisle school. Like the girls being forced to wear long green dresses in Erdrich's poem, these Indian students are dressed in school uniforms, not in their native clothing.

Fig. 1. Apache children four months after arriving at the Carlisle Indian School in Pennsylvania, Owen Lindauer, "Archaeology of the Phoenix Indian School," <u>Archaeology</u> 27 Mar. 1998, 10 Mar. 2005 <http://www.archaeology.org/online/features/phoenix/>.

Monteleone 5

Parents did not always send their children to Carlisle willingly. The <u>Carlisle Indian Industrial School Research Pages</u> explain that when Geronimo, chief of the Apache nation, was arrested, Pratt traveled to Fort Mario prison, where the Apache children were being held. Pratt then picked sixty-two of the children to be sent to Carlisle, despite pleas from their parents. In an effort to prevent them from leaving, several of the parents hid the children, but Pratt eventually found them, and the children were sent to the school.

Erdrich closes her poem by explaining how the children try to remember their cultural heritage even as they are being forced to adopt the customs of white America:

> Our brushes cut the stone in watered arcs
> And in the soak frail outlines shiver clear
> A moment, things us kids pressed on the dark
> Face before it hardened, pale, remembering
> Delicate old injuries, the spines of names
>   and leaves. (20-24)

The history of the Indian boarding schools, and how they worked to rid children of their Native American identities, clearly informs this poem. In this sense, Erdrich's work is not just literary; it is also political. By invoking an emotional response in her readers, Erdrich is able to expose a dark side of United States history and its treatment of Native Americans.

                                                      Monteleone 6

                              Works Cited
Cumberland Historical Society. "Carlisle Indian
       Industrial School." 11 Mar. 2005 <http://
       www.historicalsociety.com/ciiswelcome.html>.
Erdrich, Louise. "Indian Boarding School: The
       Runaways." <u>Literature: Reading, Reacting,
       Writing</u>. 6th ed. Ed. Laurie G. Kirszner and
       Stephen R. Mandell. Boston: Wadsworth, 2007.
       1176-77.
Landis, Barbara. "History." <u>The Carlisle Indian
       Industrial School Research Pages</u>. 1996. 10 Mar.
       2005 <http://home.epix.net/~landis/histry.html>.

Suggested Topics for Historical Context Papers

Fiction

"Once Upon a Time" (apartheid in South Africa); "The Third and Final Continent" (Indian immigration to the United States); "I Stand Here Ironing" (the Great Depression); "Shiloh" (the 1862 Civil War battle at Shiloh); "The Yellow Wallpaper" (treatment of postpartum psychosis in the nineteenth century); "The Things They Carried" (the Vietnam War)

Poetry

"Emmett Till"; "Strange Fruit"; "The Ballad of Birmingham" (pre-Civil-Rights-Movement racial climate in the American South); "The Convergence of the Twain" (the sinking of the Titanic); "For the Union Dead" (black regiment in the Civil War); "The Names" (9/11); "Facing It" (the Vietnam War)

Drama

Proof (history of women in mathematics); *Antigone's Red* (Japanese internment camps); *The Glass Menagerie* (World War II)

NOTE: For additional possibilities for historical context papers, see the cultural context paragraphs that precede many of the selections.

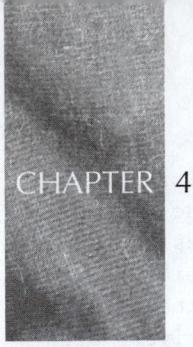

CHAPTER 4

THINKING CRITICALLY ABOUT YOUR WRITING

As you write about literature, you should carefully assess the strength of the ideas you will present to readers. This is especially true in **literary arguments**, essays in which you take a stand on a debatable topic and try to convince readers to accept your position (see Chapter 5). Although you may be tempted to influence readers by using emotionally charged language, by emphasizing certain facts and downplaying (or even ignoring) others, or by using flawed logic, these strategies are not fair—and, in fact, they are not acceptable in college writing. If you learn to **think critically** about your writing, you will be able to distinguish fact from opinion, evaluate the usefulness and appropriateness of your supporting evidence, and keep any biases you have out of your writing. Then, guided by the basic principles of inductive and deductive reasoning, you will be able to structure your essay in a way that will encourage readers to accept (or at least acknowledge) the strengths of your argument.

Distinguishing Fact from Opinion

A **fact** is a verifiable statement that something is true or that something occurred. An **opinion** is a personal judgment or belief that can never be substantiated beyond any doubt and is, therefore, debatable.

Fact: Langston Hughes mentions four rivers in his poem "The Negro Speaks of Rivers."

Opinion: Rivers have symbolic significance in Langston Hughes's poem "The Negro Speaks of Rivers."

An opinion may be *unsupported* or *supported*.

Unsupported Opinion: Rivers have symbolic significance in Langston Hughes's poem "The Negro Speaks of Rivers."

Supported Opinion: Rivers have symbolic significance in Langston Hughes's poem "The Negro Speaks of Rivers." In the poem, the speaker mentions four rivers—the Euphrates, the

Congo, the Nile, and the Mississippi. According to the speaker, these rivers are as "ancient as the world and as old as the flow of human blood in human veins" (line 2). With their associations with the black experience, these particular rivers are linked not only to the speaker's African roots but also to the racial situation in America at the time the poem was written.

As the above examples show, supported opinion is more convincing than unsupported opinion.

Supporting Your Opinions

In your essays, your opinions can be supported with **examples**, **quotations**, or **expert opinion**.

Examples:

In the play <u>The Glass Menagerie</u>, Jim's focus on the future challenges Amanda's unrealistic romantic dreams of the past. For example, when Jim comes to dinner, she dreams of entertaining him in the old Southern tradition, but he talks enthusiastically of the promise the future holds.

Quotations:

Although Gertrude is queen of Denmark, she is also a devoted mother. In her efforts to console her son, she speaks tenderly: "Good Hamlet, cast thy knighted color off" (1.2.68). She also conveys her wisdom about life: "Thou know'st 'tis common,—all that live must die, / Passing through nature to eternity" (1.2.72-73).

Expert Opinion (Opinions of Literary Critics):

Throughout the short story "The Yellow Wallpaper," a number of clues suggest that the narrator has lost her hold on reality. According to Sandra Gilbert and Susan Gubar in <u>Madwoman in the Attic: The Woman Writer and the Nineteenth-Century Literary Imagination</u>, the extent of the narrator's dislike for the wallpaper should serve as an early warning that she is not responding well to her treatment and that she may in fact be losing her mind (464).

Evaluating Supporting Evidence

The examples, quotations, and opinions of literary critics that you use to support your statements constitute **evidence**. The more reliable your supporting evidence, the more willing your readers will be to accept a statement. Remember, though, that the evidence you use must be *accurate, sufficient, representative,* and *relevant*.

Your evidence is likely to be **accurate** if it comes from a trustworthy source. Such a source quotes *exactly* and does not present information out of context. It also presents its own examples, quotations, and expert opinion fairly, drawing them from other reliable sources.

For your evidence to be **sufficient**, you must present an adequate amount of evidence. It is not enough, for instance, to cite just one example from a Joyce Carol Oates's short story in an attempt to demonstrate that her experiments with literary form and subject matter give her work universal appeal. Similarly, the opinions of a single literary critic, no matter how reputable, are not enough to support this position.

You should also select evidence that is **representative** of a range of sources and viewpoints; you should not just choose evidence that supports your thesis and ignore evidence that does not. For example, if you are making the point that the structure of Emily Dickinson's poems changed over the course of her career, you cannot disregard compelling evidence that, in fact, her poetic structure remained consistent over the years.

Finally, evidence must be **relevant**— that is, it must apply to the case being discussed. For example, you cannot support the assertion that Arthur Miller's *Death of a Salesman* critiques post–World War II American society by citing examples from Miller's *The Crucible*.

Detecting Bias in Your Writing

A **bias** is a preconceived opinion, usually unfavorable, based on insufficient knowledge or inaccurate stereotypes rather than on evidence. As a critical thinker, you should be aware that your biases might sometimes lead you to see what you want to see and to unfairly select evidence that is consistent these biases.

Detecting Bias in Your Writing

When you write, be aware of the following kinds of biases:

- **Slanted language:** Avoid slanted language — language that is inflammatory or confrontational. For example, do not say that a literary critic's article is stupid or that a character in a short story is immoral. Instead, use language that clearly and accurately conveys your ideas.
- **Biased tone:** Avoid using a tone that communicates bias toward your subject (for example, anger or sarcasm).

---

continued on next page

- **Stereotypes:** Avoid statements that perpetuate unrealistic stereotypes. For example, be careful not to make unwarranted assumptions about gender roles or about different groups' attributes or shortcomings and then criticize characters on the basis of these unfair and inaccurate generalizations. For example, saying that Andy in "Doe Season" gets what she deserves because a deer hunt is no place for girls sterotypes the character and reveals gender bias.
- **Preconceived ideas:** Don't let your own beliefs or attitudes prevent you from fairly evaluating a work of literature. For example, you may believe strongly that husbands and wives should be faithful to each other, but you should not let this belief prevent you from appreciating the literary strengths of Kate Chopin's "The Storm," a short story in which two characters commit adultery, apparently with no consequences.

✔ **CHECKLIST**   **Detecting Bias**

- ☐ Have you chosen evidence that presents a balanced view of your topic?
- ☐ Have you cited experts? If so, do they represent a range of opinion?
- ☐ Have you avoided slanted language?
- ☐ Have you been careful not to convey your bias through your tone?
- ☐ Have you avoided statements that perpetuate stereotypes?

Understanding Logic

All argumentative essays, including literary arguments, rely on **logic** — inductive and deductive reasoning — to reach conclusions in a systematic way. If you understand the basic principles of inductive and deductive reasoning, you will be able to write clearer, more convincing essays.

Inductive Reasoning

Inductive reasoning is a process that moves from specific facts, observations, or experiences to a general conclusion. You use inductive reasoning in your writing when you want to lead readers from a series of specific observations to a general conclusion. You can see how inductive reasoning operates by studying the following list of statements about John Updike's short story "A&P":

- Sammy, the main character in "A&P," is nineteen and works as a cashier in a supermarket in a small New England town.
- Sammy sees the A & P's customers as sheep, with no individuality.
- Sammy's fellow workers include Stokesie, a married twenty-two-year-old with two children, and Lengel, the store manager.
- Stokesie and Lengel lead boring, predictable lives.
- On the day the story takes place, three girls in bathing suits walk into the store and change Sammy's life.
- Sammy fanticizes about the girls' lives and imagines what a party at one girl's home would be like.
- When Lengel scolds the girls for dressing inappropriately, Sammy abruptly quits his job.
- At the end of the story, Sammy realizes that although some people think he was foolish to quit his job, he did the right thing.

After reading the statements above, you can use inductive reasoning to reach a general conclusion about the theme of Updike's story: that someone who wants to escape a confining life must sometimes make a courageous break with his community's values.

No matter how much evidence you present, an inductive conclusion is never certain, only probable. You arrive at an inductive conclusion by making an **inference**, a statement about the unknown based on the known. In order to bridge the gap that exists between your specific observations and your general conclusion, you have to make an **inductive leap**. If you have presented enough specific evidence, this gap will be relatively small and your readers will accept your conclusion. If the gap is too wide, your readers will accuse you of making a **hasty generalization**—a conclusion based on too little evidence.

Deductive Reasoning

Deductive reasoning is a process that moves from a general statement believed to be true or **self-evident** (so obvious that it needs no proof) to a more specific conclusion. Writers use deductive reasoning when they think their audience is more likely to be influenced by logic than by evidence. The process of deduction has traditionally been illustrated by a **syllogism**, a three-part set of statements or propositions that includes a *major premise*, a *minor premise*, and a *conclusion*.

Major Premise: All tragic heroes have tragic flaws.

Minor Premise: Hamlet is a tragic hero.

Conclusion: Therefore, Hamlet has a tragic flaw.

The **major premise** of a syllogism makes a general statement that the writer believes to be true or self-evident. The **minor premise** presents a specific example of the belief that is stated in the major premise. If the reasoning is sound, the **conclusion** should follow from the two premises. (Note that the conclusion should introduce no terms that have not already appeared in the major and minor premises.) The advantage of a deductive argument is that if readers accept the premises, they usually grant the conclusion.

A syllogism is **valid** when its conclusion logically follows from its premises. A syllogism is **true** when the information it contains is consistent with the facts. To be **sound**, a syllogism must be *both* valid and true. However, a syllogism can be valid without being true or true without being valid. The following syllogism, for example, is valid but not true.

> **Major Premise:** All poems contain rhymed lines.
>
> **Minor Premise:** Walt Whitman's "Had I the Choice" is a poem.
>
> **Conclusion:** Therefore, Walt Whitman's "Had I the Choice" contains rhymed lines.

This syllogism is valid. In the major premise, the phrase *all poems* establishes that the entire class *poems* contains rhymed lines. After Walt Whitman's "Had I the Choice" is identified as a poem, the conclusion that it contains rhymed lines logically follows. However, Whitman's poem, like many others, is unrhymed. Because the major premise of this syllogism is not true, no conclusion based on it can be true. For this reason, even though the logic of the syllogism is correct, its conclusion is not.

Toulmin Logic

Stephen Toulmin, a contemporary philosopher and rhetorician, has formulated another way to understand logical thinking. According to Toulmin, the traditional syllogism, while useful for identifying flaws in logic, is not useful for analyzing arguments that occur in the real world. To address this shortcoming, Toulmin divides arguments into three parts: the *claim*, the *grounds*, and the *warrant*.

- **The claim** is your thesis, the main point that you want to make in your essay.
- **The grounds** are the facts, examples, quotations, and opinions of experts that will support your claim. In essays about literature, the grounds can come from a work of literature or from literary criticism.
- **The warrant** is an assumption that underlies both the claim and the grounds. Keep in mind that some warrants are explicitly stated while others may be simply implied.

In its simplest terms, an argument following Toulmin's pattern would look like this:

- **The claim:** Phoenix Jackson, the main character in Eudora Welty's "A Worn Path," challenges the racial restrictions of her community.

- **The grounds:** Phoenix Jackson defies the man with the gun; she asks a white woman to tie her shoe; she steals a nickel; she gets free medicine from the doctor.
- **The warrant:** At the time "A Worn Path" takes place, racial segregation limited the actions of African Americans.

Notice that the claim presents a specific situation; the warrant, however, is a general principle that could apply to a number of situations. In a sense, the warrant is similar to the major premise of a syllogism, and the claim is similar to the conclusion. The grounds consist of the evidence that supports the claim.

Recognizing Logical Fallacies

Logical fallacies are flawed arguments. A writer who inadvertently uses such fallacies is not thinking clearly or logically; a writer who intentionally uses them is trying to deceive readers. Learn to recognize them so you can avoid them when you write.

Common Logical Fallacies

- **Hasty Generalization:** A form of induction that draws a conclusion on the basis of too little evidence. For example, one appearance of a river in a poem is not enough to warrant the statement that it is an important symbol. Several mentions, however, might justify this conclusion.
- **Sweeping Generalization:** A generalization that cannot be supported no matter how much evidence is supplied. For example, the statement "All the critics like August Wilson's plays" is a sweeping generalization. Certainly, many critics like Wilson's plays, but it is virtually impossible to prove that all critics do. To avoid making statements that cannot be supported, qualify your statements with words such as *some, many, often,* or *most.*
- ***Ad Hominem* (Argument to the Person):** A fallacy that occurs when you attack a person rather than the issue, as in the following argument: "Many critics see imagism as a very important literary movement. However, the fact that its founder, Ezra Pound, was a Nazi sympathizer challenges that assessment." Although you may find Pound's Nazi sympathies repugnant, his political ideas are not relevant to your evaluation of imagism.
- **Non Sequitur:** A conclusion that does not logically follow from what comes before it, as in the following statement: "John Updike writes critically acclaimed novels, so he must be a gifted poet." It does not logically follow that just because Updike can write good novels, he can also write good poetry.

continued on next page

- **Either/or Fallacy:** A fallacy that occurs when a complex issue is presented as if it has only two sides when there are actually more possibilities. If you ask your readers to consider whether a character is good or evil, you commit this fallacy. In fact, any complex character may possess both positive and negative qualities.

- **Begging the Question:** A form of **circular reasoning** that occurs when you state a debatable premise as if it were true, as in the following statement: "Hemingway's negative portrayals of women have caused his popularity to decline in recent years." Hemingway's portrayals of women may be negative, but readers do not have to accept this statement as fact just because you say it is true. Before you can make a judgment about Hemingway's declining popularity based on this assertion, you must support it with examples from Hemingway's work as well as with statements from a fair range of literary critics.

- **Bandwagon:** A fallacy that occurs when you try to establish that something is true just because everyone believes it is. You commit this fallacy when you say, for example, that a certain literary work must be good because it is so popular.

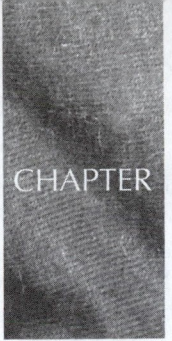

CHAPTER 5

WRITING LITERARY ARGUMENTS

Most of the essays you write about literature are **expository**— that is, you write to give information to readers. For example, you might discuss the rhyme or meter of a poem or examine the interaction of two characters in a play. (Most of the student essays in this book are expository.) Other essays you write, however, may be **literary arguments**— that is, you take a position on a debatable topic and attempt to change readers' minds about it. The more persuasive your argumentative essay, the more likely readers will be to concede your points and grant your conclusion.

When you write a literary argument, you follow the same process you do when you write any essay about a literary topic. However, because the purpose of an argument is to convince readers, you need to use some additional strategies to present your ideas.

Planning a Literary Argument

Choosing a Debatable Topic

Your first step in writing a literary argument will be to decide on a specific topic to write about. Because an argumentative essay attempts to change the way readers think, it must focus on a **debatable topic**, one about which reasonable people may disagree. **Factual statements**— statements about which reasonable people do *not* disagree — are therefore inappropriate as topics for argument.

Factual Statement: Linda Loman is Willy Loman's long-suffering wife in Arthur Miller's play <u>Death of a Salesman</u>.

Debatable Topic: More than a stereotype of the long-suffering wife, Linda Loman in Arthur Miller's play <u>Death of a Salesman</u> is a multidimensional character.

In addition to being debatable, your topic should be narrow enough for you to develop within your page limit. After all, in an argumentative essay, you will have to present your own ideas and supply convincing support while possibly also pointing out the strengths and weaknesses of opposing arguments. If your topic is too broad, you will not be able to discuss it in enough detail.

Finally, your topic should be interesting. Keep in mind that some topics — such as the significance of the wall in Robert Frost's poem "Mending Wall" — have been written about so often that you will probably not be able to say anything very new or interesting about them. Instead of relying on an overused topic, choose one that enables you to write something original.

Developing an Argumentative Thesis

After you have chosen your topic, your next step is to state your position in an **argumentative thesis** — one that takes a strong stand. Properly worded, this thesis statement will lay the foundation for the rest of your argument.

One way to make sure that your thesis actually does take a stand is to formulate an **antithesis** — a statement that takes an arguable position opposite from yours. If you can construct an antithesis, you can be certain that your thesis statement takes a stand. If you cannot, your thesis statement needs further revision to make it an argumentative thesis.

Thesis Statement: The last line of Richard Wright's short story "Big Black Good Man" indicates that Jim was fully aware all along of Olaf's deep-seated racial prejudice.

Antithesis: The last line of Richard Wright's short story "Big Black Good Man" indicates that Jim remained unaware of Olaf's feelings toward him.

> **NOTE:** Your thesis statement is an assertion that your entire essay supports. Keep in mind, however, that you can never prove your thesis conclusively — if you could, there would be no argument. The best you can do is provide enough evidence to establish a high probability that your thesis is reasonable.

✔ **CHECKLIST Developing an Argumentative Thesis**

☐ Can you formulate an antithesis?

☐ Does your thesis statement make clear to readers what position you are taking?

☐ Can you support your thesis with evidence from the text and from research?

Defining Your Terms

You should always define the key terms you use in your argument. For example, if you are using the term *narrator* in an essay, make sure that readers know whether you are referring to a first-person or a third-person narrator. In addition, you may need to clarify the distinction between an **unreliable narrator**— someone who misrepresents or misinterprets events—and a **reliable narrator**— someone who accurately describes events. Without a clear definition of the terms you are using, readers may have a very difficult time understanding the point you are making.

Defining Your Terms

Be especially careful to use precise terms in your thesis statement. Avoid vague and judgmental words, such as *wrong, bad, good, right,* and *immoral.*

Vague: The poem "Birmingham Sunday (September 15, 1963)" by Langston Hughes shows how bad racism can be.

Clearer: The poem "Birmingham Sunday (September 15, 1963)" by Langston Hughes makes a moving statement about how destructive racism can be.

Considering Your Audience

As you plan your essay, keep your audience in mind. For example, if you are writing about a work that has been discussed in class, you can assume that your readers are familiar with it; include a plot summary only when it is needed to explain or support a point you are making. Keep in mind that you will be addressing an academic audience—your instructor and possibly some students. For this reason, you should be sure to follow the conventions of writing about literature as well as the conventions of standard written English (for information on the conventions of writing about literature, see the checklist in Chapter 2, p. 35).

When you write an argumentative essay, always assume that you are addressing a skeptical audience. Remember, your thesis is debatable, so not everyone will agree with you — and even if your readers are sympathetic to your position, you cannot assume that they will accept your ideas without question.

The strategies you use to convince your readers will vary according to your relationship with them. Somewhat skeptical readers may need to see only that your argument is logical and that your evidence is solid. More skeptical readers, however, may need to see that you understand their reservations and that you concede some of their points. Of course, you may never be able to convince hostile readers that your conclusions are legitimate. The best you can hope for is that these readers will acknowledge the strengths of your argument even if they do not accept your conclusion.

Refuting Opposing Arguments

As you develop your literary argument, you may need to **refute**—that is, to disprove — opposing arguments by demonstrating that they are false, misguided, or illogical. By summarizing and refuting opposing views, you make opposing arguments seem less credible to readers; thus, you strengthen your case. When an opposing argument is so strong that it cannot be easily dismissed, however, you should concede the strength of the argument and then point out its limitations.

Notice in the following paragraph how a student refutes the argument that Homer Barron, a character in William Faulkner's short story "A Rose for Emily," is gay.

Opposing argument	A number of critics have suggested that Homer Barron, Miss Emily's suitor, is gay. Certainly, there is some evidence in the story to support this
Concession	interpretation. For example, the narrator points out that Homer "liked the company of men" (Faulkner 220) and that he was not "a marrying man" (Faulkner 220). In addition, the narrator describes Homer as wearing yellow gloves when he took Emily for drives. According to the critic William Greenslade, in the 1890s yellow
Refutation	was associated with homosexuality (24). This evidence, however, does not establish that Homer is gay. During the nineteenth century, many men preferred the company of other men (as many do today). This, in itself, did not mean they were gay. Neither does the fact that Homer wore yellow gloves. According to the narrator, Homer was a man who liked to dress well. It is certainly possible that he wore these gloves to impress Miss Emily, a woman he was trying to attract.

Using Evidence Effectively

Supporting Your Literary Argument

Many literary arguments are built on **assertions**—statements made about a debatable topic — backed by **evidence**—supporting examples in the form of references to the text, quotations, and the opinions of literary critics. For example, if you stated that Torvald Helmer, Nora's husband in Henrik Ibsen's play *A Doll House*, is as much a victim of society as his wife is, you could support this assertion with relevant quotations and examples from the play. You could also paraphrase, summarize, or quote the ideas of literary critics who also hold this opinion. Remember, only assertions that are **self-evident** (All plays include characters and dialogue) or **factual** (A Doll House was published in 1879) need no supporting evidence. All other kinds of assertions require support.

Establishing Credibility

Some people bring **credibility** with them whenever they write. When a well-known literary critic evaluates the contributions of a particular writer, you can assume that he or she speaks with authority. (Although you might question the critic's opinions, you do not question his or her expertise.) But most people do not have this kind of credibility. When you write a literary argument, you must constantly work to establish credibility.

Clear reasoning, compelling evidence, and strong refutations go a long way toward making an argument solid. But these elements in themselves are not enough to create a convincing literary argument. In order to persuade readers, you have to satisfy them that you have credibility — which you can do by *demonstrating knowledge, maintaining a reasonable tone,* and *presenting yourself as someone worth listening to.*

Demonstrating Knowledge One way to establish credibility is by presenting your own carefully considered ideas about a subject. A clear argument and compelling support can demonstrate to readers that you know what you are talking about.

You can also show readers that you have thoroughly researched your subject. By referring to important sources and by providing accurate documentation for your information, you present evidence that you have done the necessary background reading. Including a range of sources — not just one or two — suggests that you are well acquainted with your subject. Remember, however, that questionable sources, inaccurate (or missing) documentation, and factual errors can undermine your credibility. For many readers, an undocumented quotation or even an incorrect date can call an entire argument into question.

Maintaining a Reasonable Tone Your **tone**— your attitude toward your readers or subject — is almost as important as the information you convey. Talk *to* your readers not *at* them. If you lecture your readers or appear to talk down to them, you will alienate them. Generally speaking, readers are more likely to respond to a writer who seems balanced and respectful than one who seems strident or condescending.

As you write your essay, use moderate language, and qualify your statements so that they seem reasonable. Try to avoid words and phrases such as *all, never, always,* and *in every case,* which can make your points seem simplistic, exaggerated, or unrealistic. Also, avoid absolute statements. For example, the statement, In

"Doe Season," the ocean symbolizes Andy's attachment to her mother, leaves no room for other possible interpretations. A more measured and accurate statement might be, In "Doe Season," the symbol of the ocean seems to suggest Andy's identification with her mother and her realization that she is becoming a woman.

Presenting Yourself as Someone Worth Listening To   When you write a literary argument, you should try to present yourself as someone your readers will want to listen to. Make your argument confidently, and don't apologize for your views. For example, do not use phrases such as "In my opinion" and "It seems to me," which undercut your credibility. Be consistent, and be careful not to contradict yourself. Finally, avoid the use of *I* (unless you are asked to give your opinion or to write a reaction statement), and avoid slang and colloquialisms.

Being Fair

Argument promotes one point of view over all others, so it is seldom objective. However, college writing requires that you stay within the bounds of fairness and that you avoid **bias**—conclusions based on preconceived ideas rather than on evidence. To make sure that the support for your argument is not misleading or distorted, you should follow the guidelines below:

- *Avoid distorting evidence.* Distortion is misrepresentation. Writers sometimes misrepresent the extent to which critical opinion supports their thesis. For example, by saying that "many critics" think that something is so when only one or two do, they try to make a weak case stronger than it actually is.
- *Avoid quoting out of context.* When you take words from their original setting and use them in another, you are quoting out of context. When you quote a source's words out of their original context, you can change the meaning of what someone has said or suggested. For example, you are quoting out of context if you say, "Emily Dickinson's poems are so idiosyncratic that they do not appeal to readers" when your source says, "Emily Dickinson's poems are so idiosyncratic that they do not appeal to readers who are accustomed to safe, conventional subjects." By eliminating a key portion of the sentence, you alter the meaning of the original.
- *Avoid slanting.* When you select only information that supports your case and ignore information that does not, you are guilty of slanting. You can eliminate this problem by including a full range of examples, not just examples that support your thesis. Be sure to consult books and articles that represent a cross-section of critical opinion about your subject. If you find that such a cross-section does not exist, you may need to modify your thesis. Only by doing this can you be sure that you are not misleading readers.

- *Avoid using unfair appeals.* Traditionally, writers of arguments use three types of appeals to influence readers: **logical appeals**, which address a reader's sense of reason, **emotional appeals**, which play on a reader's emotions, and **ethical appeals**, which emphasize the credibility of the writer. Problems arise, however, when these appeals are used unfairly. For example, writers can use **logical fallacies**—flawed arguments—to fool readers into thinking a conclusion is logical when it is not (see Chapter 4 for a discussion of logical fallacies). Writers can also use inappropriate emotional appeals—appeals to prejudice, for example—to influence readers. And finally, writers can undercut their credibility if they use questionable support—books and articles written by people who have little or no expertise on the topic. This is especially true when information is obtained from the Internet, where the credentials of the writer may be difficult or impossible to assess.

✔ **CHECKLIST   Being Fair**

- Have you distorted evidence?

- Have you quoted material out of context, changing the meaning of a statement by focusing on certain words and ignoring others?

- Have you slanted information, selecting material that supports your points and ignoring information that does not?

- Have you used any unfair appeals?

Using Visuals as Evidence

Visuals—pictures, drawings, diagrams, and the like—can add a persuasive dimension to your essay. Because visual images have an immediate impact, they can sometimes make a good literary argument even better. In a sense, visuals are another type of evidence that can support your thesis. For example, suppose you are writing an essay about the play *Trifles* in which you argue that Mrs. Wright's quilt is an important symbol in the play. In fact, your research leads you to conclude that the process of creating the quilt by piecing together its log cabin pattern parallels the process by which the two female characters in the play determine why Mrs. Wright murdered her husband. The addition of a photograph of a quilt with a log cabin pattern could not only eliminate several paragraphs of description but also help support your conclusion.

Of course, not all visuals will be appropriate or effective for a literary argument. Before using a visual, make certain it actually supports the point you make. If it does not, it will distract readers and thereby undercut your argument. To ensure that readers understand the purpose the visual is supposed to serve, introduce it with a sentence that establishes its context; then, discuss its significance, paying particular attention to how it helps you make your point. Finally, be sure to include full documentation for any visual that is not your original creation.

Organizing a Literary Argument

In its simplest form, a literary argument — like any argumentative essay — consists of a thesis statement and supporting evidence. Like other argumentative essays, however, literary arguments frequently use additional strategies to win audience approval and to overcome potential opposition.

Elements of Literary Arguments

- **Introduction:** The introduction should orient readers to the subject of your essay, presenting the issue you will discuss and explaining its significance.
- **Thesis statement:** In most literary arguments, you will present your thesis statement in your introduction. However, if you think your readers may not be familiar with the issue you are discussing (or if it is very controversial), you may want to postpone stating your thesis until later in the essay — perhaps until after the background section.
- **Background:** In this section, you can survey critical opinion about your topic, perhaps pointing out the shortcomings of these opinions. You can also define key terms, review basic facts, or briefly summarize the plot of the work or works you will discuss.
- **Arguments in support of your thesis:** Here you present your assertions and the evidence to support them. It makes sense to move from least controversial to most controversial point or from most familiar to least familiar idea. In other words, you should begin with arguments that your readers are most likely to accept and then deal with those that require more discussion and more evidence.
- **Refutation of opposing arguments:** In a literary argument, you may want to summarize and refute the most obvious arguments against your thesis. If you do not address these opposing arguments, doubts about your position will remain in your readers' minds. If the opposing arguments are relatively weak, refute them after you have presented your own arguments. However, if the opposing arguments are strong, concede their strengths and discuss their limitations *before* you present your own arguments.

- **Conclusion:** Your conclusion will often restate your thesis as well as the major arguments you have made in support of it. Your conclusion can also summarize key points, remind readers of the weaknesses of opposing arguments, or underscore the logic of your position. Many writers like to end their essays with a strong last line—for example, a quotation or a memorable statement that they hope will stay with readers after they finish the essay.

Sample Student Paper: Writing a Literary Argument

The following student paper presents a literary argument about Dee, a character in Alice Walker's short story "Everyday Use." The student author supports her thesis with ideas she developed as she read the story as well as with information she found when she did research. She also includes two visuals from a DVD of the story.

Chase 1

Margaret Chase

Professor Sierra

English 1001

6 May 2005

The Politics of "Everyday Use"

Introduction

Alice Walker's "Everyday Use" focuses on a
mother, Mrs. Johnson, and her two daughters, Maggie
and Dee, and how they view their heritage. The
story's climax comes when Mrs. Johnson rejects Dee's
request to take a hand-stitched quilt with her so
that she can hang it on her wall. Knowing that Maggie
will put the quilt to "everyday use," Dee is
horrified, and she tells her mother and Maggie that
they do not understand their heritage. Although many
literary critics see Dee's desire for the quilt as

Thesis statement

materialistic and shallow, a closer examination of
the social and historical circumstances in which
Walker wrote this 1973 story suggests a more generous
interpretation of Dee's behavior.

Background

On the surface, "Everyday Use" is a story
about two sisters, Dee and Maggie, and Mrs. Johnson,
their mother. Mrs. Johnson tells the reader that
"Dee, . . . would always look anyone in the eye.
Hesitation was no part of her nature" (470). Unlike
her sister, Maggie is shy and introverted. She is
described as looking like a lame animal that has
been run over by a car. According to the narrator,
"She has been like this, chin on chest, eyes on
ground, feet in shuffle" (470) ever since she was
burned in a fire.

Chase 2

Unlike Dee, Mrs. Johnson never received an
education. After second grade, she explains, the
school closed down. She says, "Don't ask me why: in
1927 colored asked fewer questions than they do now"
(470). Mrs. Johnson admits that she accepts the
status quo even though she knows that it is unjust.
This admission further establishes the difference
between Mrs. Johnson and Dee: Mrs. Johnson has
accepted her circumstances, while Dee has worked to
change hers. Their differences are illustrated in a
film version of the story by their contrasting dress.
As shown in fig. 1, Dee and her boyfriend

Fig. 1. Dee and Hakim-a-barber arrive at the
family home. "Everyday Use," The Wadsworth
Original Film Series in Literature: "Everyday
Use," dir. Bruce R. Schwartz, DVD, Wadsworth,
2005.

Chase 3

Hakim-a-barber dress in the Afro-American style of
the late 1960s, embracing their African heritage;
Mrs. Johnson and Maggie dress in plain, conservative
clothing.

Background
continued

When Dee arrives home with her new boyfriend, it
soon becomes obvious that her character is, for the
most part, unchanged. As she eyes her mother's
belongings and asks Mrs. Johnson if she can take the
top of the butter churn home with her, it is clear
that she is still very materialistic. However, her
years away from home have also politicized her. Dee
now wants to be called "Wangero" because she believes
(although mistakenly) that her given name comes from
whites who owned her ancestors. She wears African
clothing and talks about how a new day is dawning for
African Americans.

Social and
historical context
used as evidence
to support

The meaning and political importance of Dee's
decision to adopt an African name and wear African
clothing cannot be fully understood without a
knowledge of the social and political context in
which Walker wrote this story. Walker's own comments
about this time period explain Dee's behavior and add
meaning to it. In her interview with White, Walker
explains that the late 1960s was a time of cultural
and intellectual awakening for African-Americans.
Many turned ideologically and culturally to Africa,
adopting the dress, hairstyles, and even the names of
their African ancestors. Walker admits that as a
young woman she too became interested in discovering
her African heritage. (In fact, she herself was given

Chase 4

the name <u>Wangero</u> during a visit to Kenya in the late
1960s.) Walker tells White that she considered
keeping this new name, but eventually realized that
to do so would be to "dismiss" her family and her
American heritage. When she researched her American
family, she found that her great-great-grandmother
had walked from Virginia to Georgia carrying two
children. "If that's not a Walker," she says, "I
don't know what is." Thus, Walker realized that,
over time, African-Americans had actually
transformed the names they had originally taken from
their enslavers. To respect the ancestors she knew,
Walker says, she decided it was important to retain
her name.

Along with adopting symbols of their African
heritage, many African-Americans also worked to
elevate these symbols, such as the quilt shown in
fig. 2, to the status of high art. According to
Salaam, one way of doing this was to put these
objects in museums; another was to hang them on the
walls of their homes. Such acts were aimed at
convincing whites that African-Americans had an old
and rich culture and that consequently they
deserved not only basic civil rights, but also
respect. These gestures were also meant to improve
self-esteem and pride within black communities
(Salaam 42-43).

Admittedly, as some critics have pointed out,
Dee is more materialistic than political. For
example, although Mrs. Johnson makes several

Concession and
presentation of
opposing
argument

Chase 5

Fig. 2. Traditional hand-stitched quilt. Alice
Walker, "Alice Walker: Stitches in Time," interview
with Evelyn C. White, <u>The Wadsworth Original Film
Series in Literature: "Everyday Use,"</u> dir. Bruce R.
Schwartz, DVD, Wadsworth, 2005.

statements throughout the story that suggest her
admiration of Dee's defiant character, she also
identifies incidents that highlight Dee's materialism
and selfishness. When their first house burned down,
Dee watched it burn while she stood under a tree with
"a look of concentration" (470) rather than remorse.
Mrs. Johnson knows that Dee hated their small, dingy
house, and she knows too that Dee was glad to see it
destroyed. Furthermore, Walker acknowledges in an
interview with her biographer, Evelyn C. White, that
as she was writing the story, she imagined that Dee
might even have set the fire that destroyed the house
and scarred her sister. Even now, Dee is ashamed of
the tin-roofed house her family lives in, and she has
said that she would never bring her friends there.

Chase 6

Mrs. Johnson has always known that Dee wanted "nice things" (470); even at sixteen, "she had a style of her own: and knew what style was" (470). However, although these examples indicate that Dee is materialistic and self-serving, they also show positive traits: pride and a strong will. Knowing that she will encounter strong opposition wherever she goes, she works to use her appearance to establish power. Thus, her desire for the quilt can be seen as an attempt to establish herself and her African-American culture in a society dominated by whites.

> Refutation of opposing argument

Mrs. Johnson knows Dee wants the quilt, but she decides instead to give it to Maggie. According to literary critics Houston Baker and Charlotte Pierce-Baker, when Mrs. Johnson decides to give the quilt to Maggie, she is challenging Dee's understanding of her heritage. Unlike Dee, Mrs. Johnson recognizes that quilts signify "sacred generations of women who have made their own special kind of beauty separate from the traditional artistic world" (qtd. in Piedmont-Marton 45). According to Baker and Pierce-Baker, Mrs. Johnson realizes that her daughter Maggie, whom she has long dismissed because of her quiet nature and shyness, understands the true meaning of the quilt in a way that Dee never will (Piedmont-Marton 45). Unlike Dee, Maggie has paid close attention to the traditions and skills of her mother and grandmother: she has actually learned to quilt. More important, by staying with her mother instead of going to school, she has gotten to know her family. She poignantly

> Analysis of Mrs. Johnson's final act

Chase 7

underscores this fact when she tells her mother that
Dee can have the quilt because she does not need it
to remember her grandmother. Even though Maggie's and
Mrs. Johnson's understanding of heritage may be more
emotionally profound than Dee's, it is important not
to dismiss Dee's interest in elevating the quilt to
the level of high art. The political stakes of
defining an object as art in the late 1960s and early
1970s were high, and the fight for equality went
beyond basic civil rights.

Conclusion
restating thesis

     Although there is much in the story that
indicates Dee's materialism, her desire to hang the
quilt should not be dismissed as simply a selfish act.
Like Mrs. Johnson and Maggie, Dee is a complicated
character. At the time the story was written,
displaying the quilt would have been not only a
personal act, but also a political act—an act with
important, positive results. The final message of
"Everyday Use" may just be that in order to create an
accurate view of the quilt (and, by extension, of
African-American culture) you need both views—
Maggie's and Mrs. Johnson's everyday use and Dee's
elevation of the quilt to art.

Chase 8

Works Cited

Piedmont-Marton, Elisabeth. "An Overview of 'Everyday
     Use.'" Short Stories for Students 2 (1997):
     42-45. Literature Resource Center. Gale Group
     Databases. U of Texas Lib. System, TX. 20 Apr.
     2005 <http://www.galegroup.com>.

Salaam, Kalamu Ya. "A Primer of the Black Arts
     Movement: Excerpts from The Magic of Juju: An
     Appreciation of the Black Arts Movement." Black
     Renaissance/Renaissance Noire (2002): 40-59.
     Expanded Academic ASAP. Gale Group Databases.
     U of Texas Lib. System, TX. 21 Apr. 2005
     <http://www.galegroup.com>.

Walker, Alice. "Alice Walker: Stitches in Time."
     Interview with Evelyn C. White. The Wadsworth
     Original Film Series in Literature: "Everyday
     Use." Dir. Bruce R. Schwartz. DVD. Boston:
     Wadsworth, 2005.

---. "Everyday Use." Literature: Reading, Reacting,
     Writing. Ed. Laurie G. Kirszner and Stephen
     R. Mandell. 6th ed. Boston: Wadsworth, 2007.
     469-75.

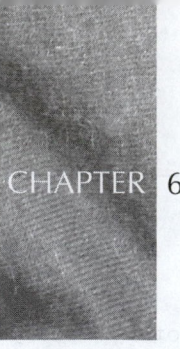

CHAPTER 6

WRITING A RESEARCH PAPER

When you write a paper about a literary topic, you often do **research**, supplementing your own interpretations with information from other sources. These sources may include works of literature as well as books and journal articles by literary critics (see p. 15). You may get this information from print sources, from electronic databases in the library, or from the Internet. When you write a literary research paper, follow the process discussed in this chapter.

Choosing a Topic

Your instructor may assign a topic or may allow you to choose one. If you choose a topic, make sure your topic is narrow enough for your paper's length, the amount of time you have for writing, and the number of sources your instructor expects you to use.

Daniel Collins, a student in an introduction to literature course, was given three weeks to write a four- to six-page research paper on one of the short stories the class had read. Daniel chose to write about Eudora Welty's "A Worn Path" because he liked the story and because the main character, Phoenix Jackson, interested him. He knew, however, that he would have to narrow his topic before he could begin. In class, Daniel's instructor had asked some provocative questions about the significance of Phoenix Jackson's journey. Daniel thought that this topic might work well because he could explore it in a short paper and could complete the paper within the three-week time limit.

Doing Exploratory Research

To see whether you will be able to find enough material about your topic, you should do some **exploratory research** by taking a quick survey of your library's resources. Your goal at this stage is to formulate a **research question**, the question that you want your research to answer. This research question will help you decide which sources to look for, which to examine first, and which to skip entirely.

Begin your exploratory research by consulting your library's **online central information system**. This system usually includes the library's **catalog** as well as a number of **bibliographic databases**, such as *Readers' Guide to Periodical Literature* and

Humanities Index. Then, consult **general reference works** like encyclopedias and specialized dictionaries and browse your search engine's subject guides to get an overview of your subject.

A quick look showed Daniel that his library's central information system included several books and numerous articles on Eudora Welty. He noted the titles of the most promising sources so he could find them later. After thinking more about his topic, Daniel came up with the following research question: What enabled Phoenix Jackson to continue her journey despite the many obstacles she faced?

Narrowing Your Topic

As you survey the resources of your library, the titles of books and articles as well as the subject headings of the catalog should help you to narrow your topic.

Daniel found two critical articles that discussed the significance of Phoenix Jackson's journey, and he hoped they would help him to understand why this character continued her journey despite all the hardships she encountered. Daniel knew that he would have to do more than just summarize his sources; he would have to make a point about the journey, one that he could support with examples from the story as well as from his research.

Doing Focused Research

Once you have completed your exploratory research and formulated your research question, you are ready to begin **focused research**—the process of looking in the library and on the Internet for the specific information you need.

Library Research

Using the Library

The first step is to go back to the library and check out any books that you think will be useful. Then, consult **specialized reference works**—indexes, bibliographies, and specialized encyclopedias, for example — to find relevant articles. If you find print articles, photocopy them (and make sure to copy all the publication information you will need to document these sources).

Your library's **periodical indexes** will also help you find information. A **periodical** is a newspaper, magazine, or scholarly journal published at regular intervals. **Periodical indexes** are databases that list articles from a selected group of periodicals. Although you may occasionally find scholarly articles on the free Internet, the easiest (and most reliable) way to access scholarly journals is through one of the databases to which your college library subscribes. These **subscription databases** are updated frequently, and the articles they include usually provide current, high-quality, accurate information.

Choosing the right periodical index for your research is important. Each database has a different focus and lists different magazines or journals. In addition, some indexes include just citations while others contain the full text of articles. For this reason, using the wrong database leads to wasted time and frustration. For example, searching a database that focuses on business will not help you much if you are looking for information on a literary topic. Be sure to ask a reference librarian which database will be most helpful.

Frequently Used Subscription Databases

The following databases are useful for literary research.

EBSCOhost	Includes thousands of periodical articles on many subjects
Expanded Academic ASAP	Largely full-text database covering all subjects in thousands of magazines and journals
FirstSearch	Full-text articles in many popular and scholarly periodicals

---

Evaluating Library Sources

Whenever you find a library source (print or electronic), take the time to **evaluate** it — to assess its usefulness and reliability.

✔ CHECKLIST   Evaluating Library Sources

☐ *Does the source treat your topic in enough detail?* To be of real help, a book should include a section or a chapter on your topic. An article should have your topic as its central subject or at least one of its main concerns.

☐ *Is the source current?* Although currency is not as important for literary research as it is in the sciences, it should still be a consideration. Check the date of publication to see whether the information in a book or article is up to date. In addition, be sure to check dates of footnotes and bibliography entries. Even if a book has been recently published, its conclusions may be out of date if its sources are old.

☐ *Is the source respected?* A contemporary review of a source can help you make this assessment. You can find reviews in *Book Review Digest,* available in print and online.

Is the source reliable? Does the author support his or her opinions? Does the author include documentation? Does the author have a particular agenda to advance? Compare a few statements with a more neutral source — an encyclopedia or a textbook, for example — to see whether the author seems to be slanting facts. If you have difficulty making this assessment, ask your instructor or a reference librarian for help.

Internet Research

Using the Internet

As you can imagine, the Internet has revolutionized the way scholars conduct research. It can give you instant access to a host of useful sources. (Keep in mind, however, that the Internet does not give you access to the large number of high-quality print and electronic sources that you find in your college library.)

Locating Sources

You can locate sources on the Internet in three ways:

1. The most direct way to locate an Internet source is to enter a **URL (uniform resource locator)** — a source's electronic address. Once you type in the URL, hit *Enter,* and you will be connected to the Web site you want. Make sure that you type in the URL exactly as it appears. A missed letter or an extra space or punctuation mark will send you to the wrong site — or to no site at all.
2. Another way to locate Internet sources is to use **subject guides** — the lists of general subject areas provided by search engines such as *Yahoo!, About.com,* and *LookSmart.* Each of these subject areas will lead you to a more specific list until, eventually, you get to the topic you want.
3. A third way to locate Internet sources is to enter a **keyword** (or words) into your search engine's search field. The search engine will identify any site in its database on which the keyword (or words) you have typed appears.

Some search engines are more user friendly than others, some allow for more sophisticated searching, and some are more comprehensive. As you try out various search engines, you will eventually settle on one that you will turn to when you need to find information.

Some General-Purpose Search Engines	
AllTheWeb	An excellent, comprehensive search engine that enables you to search for news stories, pictures, video, and audio. Many users think it is as good as *Google*.
AltaVista	A good, precise search engine for focused searches.
Excite	Searches more than 250 million Web sites.
Google	Considered by many to be the best search engine available. Accesses a large database that enables you to search for Web sites, images, discussion groups, and news stories.
Google Scholar	A new member of the Google family; enables you to search a broad range of scholarly literature, including peer-reviewed papers, books, abstracts, and technical reports as well as scholarly articles.
Yahoo!	A search tool that allows you to use either subject headings or keywords. Searches its own indexes as well as the Web
Dogpile	A **metasearch engine** that searches several search engines simultaneously.

In addition to the general-purpose search engines listed above, you can use **specialized search engines** — search sites that are especially useful during focused research when you are looking for in-depth information about a specific topic.

Some Specialized Search Engines	
Librarians' Index <www.lii.org>	A high-quality, reliable site designed for librarians
Litengine.com <www.litengine.com>	A highly selective search engine for information about authors
Literary Criticism <www.accd.edu/pac/lrc/litcriticism.htm>	An alphabetical list of links to literary criticism on the Web
Thinkers.net <www.thinkers.net>	Discussions on literature and information about the publishing world
Voice of the Shuttle <www.vos.ucsb.edu>	Reliable in-depth research in the humanities

Evaluating Web Sites

Anyone can operate a Web site and thereby publish anything. For this reason, it is important to determine the quality of a Web site before you use it as a source. Asking the questions below will help you evaluate Web sites and the information they contain.

✔ **CHECKLIST** **Evaluating Web Sites**

▪ *How credible is the person or organization responsible for the site?* Does the site list an author? Can you determine the author's expertise?

▪ *How accurate is the information on the Web site?* Is it free of factual and grammatical errors? Can you verify the information by checking other sources?

▪ *How balanced does the information on the Web site seem?* Does a business, political organization, or special interest group sponsor the site? Does the site express only one viewpoint?

▪ *How comprehensive is the Web site?* Does the site provide in-depth coverage, or is the information largely common knowledge?

▪ *How well maintained is the Web site?* Has it been active for a long period of time? Has the site been updated recently?

Daniel was lucky enough to find everything he needed in his college library. He found two print articles about the Welty story, and he found two more in the *Humanities Index* database. Finally, a more careful search of his library's online central information system revealed that among the library's holdings was a DVD of "A Worn Path" that included an interview with the author.

Taking Notes

Once you have located your sources, you should record the information you think will be useful for your paper. There is no single correct way to take notes; different writers take notes differently. Some writers store information in a computer file; others keep their notes on index cards. Whatever system you use, be sure to record the author's full name as well as *complete* publication information. You will need this information later on to compile your works-cited list (see p. 120).

When you take notes from a source, you have three options: you can *paraphrase, summarize,* or *quote.*

When you **paraphrase,** you put the author's ideas into your own words, keeping the order and emphasis of the original. You paraphrase when you want to make a difficult or complex discussion accessible to readers so that you can comment on it or use it to support your own points. Here is a passage from a critical article, followed by Daniel's paraphrase.

Original

> The assumption that the grandson is dead helps explain Phoenix Jackson's stoical behavior in the doctor's office. She displays a "ceremonial stiffness" as she sits "bolt upright" staring "straight ahead, her face solemn and withdrawn into rigidity." This passiveness suggests her psychological dilemma — she cannot explain why she made the journey. Her attempt to blame the lapse of memory on her illiteracy is unconvincing. Her lack of education is hardly an excuse for forgetting her grandson, but it goes a long way toward explaining her inability to articulate her subconscious motives for her journey. (Bartel, Roland. "Life and Death in Eudora Welty's 'A Worn Path.'" *Studies in Short Fiction* 14 (1977): 288-90)

Paraphrase

As Roland Bartel points out in "Life and Death in Eudora Welty's 'A Worn Path,'" Phoenix Jackson's "stoical behavior" at the doctor's office makes sense if her grandson is actually dead. Although she says that her forgetfulness is due to her lack of education, Bartel does not accept this rationale. According to him, the fact that Phoenix is uneducated cannot fully explain her forgetting about her grandson—although it might explain why she cannot communicate her reasons for her trip (289).

When you write a **summary**, you also put an author's ideas into your own words, but you present just the general point of a passage. For this reason, a summary is always much shorter than the original. Here is Daniel's summary of the passage from Bartel's article.

Summary

As Roland Bartel points out in "Life and Death in Eudora Welty's 'A Worn Path,'" Phoenix Jackson's "stoical behavior" at the doctor's office makes sense if we assume that her grandson is dead and that she does not have the skill to explain her reasons for making her trip (289).

When you **quote**, you reproduce a passage exactly, word for word and punctuation mark for punctuation mark, enclosing the entire passage in quotation marks. Because a large number of quotations will distract readers, use a quotation only when you think that the author's words will add something — memorable wording, for example — to your paper.

Integrating Sources

To integrate a paraphrase, summary, or quotation smoothly into your paper, use a phrase that introduces your source and its author —*Bartel points out, according to Bartel, Bartel claims,* or *Bartel says,* for example. You can place this identifying phrase at various points in a sentence.

According to Roland Bartel, "The assumption that the grandson is dead helps explain Phoenix Jackson's stoical behavior in the doctor's office" (289).

"The assumption that the grandson is dead helps explain Phoenix Jackson's stoical behavior in the doctor's office," **observes Roland Bartel in his article "Life and Death in Eudora Welty's 'A Worn Path'"** (289).

"The assumption that the grandson is dead," **notes the literary critic Roland Bartel,** "helps explain Phoenix Jackson's stoical behavior in the doctor's office" (289).

> **NOTE:** Remember to document all paraphrases, summaries, and quotations that you use in your essays. (See Chapter 7, Documenting Sources and Avoiding Plagiarism.)

Drafting a Thesis Statement

After you have taken notes, review the information you have gathered, and use it to help you draft a **thesis statement**— a single sentence that states the main idea of your paper. You will support this thesis with a combination of your own ideas and the ideas you have drawn from your research.

After reviewing his notes, Daniel developed the following thesis statement about Eudora Welty's "A Worn Path."

Thesis Statement: What is most important in the story is the spiritual and emotional strength of Phoenix Jackson and how this strength enables her to continue her journey.

As you draft and revise your paper, your thesis statement will probably change. At this point in the writing process, it gives your ideas focus and enables you to organize them into an outline.

Making an Outline

Once you have drafted a thesis statement, you can construct an outline from your notes. Write your thesis statement at the top of the page. Then, review your notes, and arrange them in the order in which you plan to use them. As you construct your outline, arrange these points under appropriate headings.

When it is completed, your outline will show you how much support you have for each of your points, and it will guide you as you write a draft of your paper. Your outline, which covers the body paragraphs of your essay, can be a *sentence outline*, in which each idea is expressed as a sentence, or a *topic outline*, in which each idea is expressed in a word or a short phrase.

After reviewing his notes, Daniel constructed the following topic outline. Notice that he uses roman numerals for first-level headings, capital letters for second-level headings, and arabic numerals for third-level headings. Notice too that all points in the outline are expressed in parallel terms.

Thesis Statement: What is most important in the story is the spiritual and emotional strength of Phoenix Jackson and how this strength enables her to continue her journey.

   I. Critical interpretations of "A Worn Path"
     A. Heroic act of sacrifice
     B. Journey of life
     C. Religious pilgrimage
  II. Focus on journey
     A. Little information about Jackson and her grandson
     B. Nurse's question
     C. Jackson's reply
 III. Jackson's character
     A. Interaction between Jackson's character and journey
       1. Significance of Jackson's first name
       2. Jackson as a complex character
     B. Jackson's physical problems
       1. Failing eyesight
       2. Difficulty walking
  IV. Jackson's spiritual strength
     A. Belief in God
     B. Child of nature
   V. Jackson's emotional strength
     A. Love for grandson
     B. Fearlessness and selflessness
     C. Determination

Drafting Your Paper

Once you have constructed your outline, you can begin to draft your paper. Follow your outline as you write, using your notes as the need arises.

Your paper's **introduction** will usually be a single paragraph. In addition to identifying the work or works you are writing about and stating your thesis, the introduction to a literary research paper may present an overview of your topic, a survey of critical opinion, or necessary background information.

The **body** of your paper supports your thesis statement, with each of your paragraphs developing a single point. Support your points with examples from the literary work you are discussing or with summaries, paraphrases, and quotations from your sources. You should also include your own observations and inferences.

Your paper's **conclusion**, usually a single paragraph (but sometimes more), restates your main points and reinforces your thesis statement.

Remember, the purpose of your first draft is to get ideas down on paper so that you can react to them. You should expect to revise, possibly writing several drafts.

The final draft of Daniel Collins's paper on Eudora Welty's "A Worn Path" appears on pages 106–112.

Sample Literature Paper with MLA Documentation

Collins 1

Daniel Collins

Professor Smith

English 201

30 April 2005

And Again She Makes the Journey: Character and

Act in Eudora Welty's "A Worn Path"

Over the past fifty years, Eudora Welty's "A Worn Path," the tale of an elderly black woman, Phoenix Jackson, traveling to the city to obtain medicine for her sick grandson, has been the subject of much critical interpretation. Critics have speculated on the meaning of the many death and rebirth symbols, including the scarecrow, which the old woman believes is a ghost; the buzzard who watches her travel; the skeleton-like branches that reach out to slow her; and her first name, Phoenix. From the study of these symbols, various critics have concluded that "A Worn Path" is either a "heroic act of sacrifice," "a parable for the journey of life," or "a religious pilgrimage" (Piwinski 40). It is certainly true, as these critics imply, that Phoenix Jackson's journey has symbolic significance. However, what is most important in the story is the spiritual and emotional strength of Phoenix Jackson and how this strength enables her to continue her journey.

Eudora Welty discusses the character of Phoenix Jackson in a DVD interview with Beth Henley. Here, Welty points out that Jackson's first name refers to a mythical bird that dies and is reborn every five hundred years. She explains, however, that despite her symbolic name, Phoenix Jackson is more than a symbol: she is a complex character with human frailties and emotions.

Phoenix Jackson has a number of physical problems that make it difficult for her to perform daily tasks. Because of her age, she has failing eyesight, which distorts her perception of the objects she encounters during her journey. For instance, Phoenix mistakes a patch of thorns for "a pretty little green bush," (506), and she believes a scarecrow is the ghost of a man. She also has difficulty walking, so she must use a cane; at one point, she is unable to bend and tie her own shoes. Because of these physical problems, readers might expect her to fail in her attempt to reach town; after all, the journey is long and difficult. So what gives Phoenix Jackson the energy and endurance for the journey? The question can best be answered by looking at her inner qualities: although Jackson's body is weak, she has great spiritual and emotional strength.

Phoenix Jackson's spiritual strength comes from her oneness with nature and her belief in God. This oneness with nature, claims James Saunders, helps her overcome the challenges that she encounters (67). Because Phoenix Jackson is "a child of nature," her impaired vision, although it slows her journey, does not stop it; as Saunders explains, "mere human vision would not have been sufficient for the journey" (67). Instead of allowing her failing vision to restrict

Collins 3

her actions, Phoenix Jackson relies on her spiritual connection with nature; thus, she warns various animals to "Keep out from under these feet . . ." (505). Her spiritual strength also comes from her belief in God—a quality seen when she refers to God watching her steal the hunter's nickel.

Phoenix Jackson's spiritual strength is matched by her emotional strength. Her love for her grandson compels her to endure any difficulty and to defy any danger. Therefore, throughout her journey, she demonstrates fearlessness and selflessness. For example, when the hunter threatens her with his gun, she tells him that she has faced worse dangers. And, despite her need for new shoes, she remains intent upon buying a paper windmill for her grandson.

In her interview with Beth Henley, Eudora Welty explains how she created the paradoxical Phoenix Jackson—outwardly frail and inwardly strong. Welty tells how she noticed an "old lady" slowly making her way across a "silent horizon,"[1] driven by an overwhelming determination to reach her destination; as Welty says, "she had a purpose." Welty created Phoenix Jackson in the image of this determined woman. In order to emphasize the character's strength, Welty had her make the journey to Natchez to get medication for her grandson. Because the act had to be performed repeatedly, the journey became a ritual that had to be completed at all costs. Thus, as Welty explains in the interview,

the act of making the journey—not the journey
itself—is the most important element in the story.

In order to convey the importance of the
journey, Welty focuses on the process of the journey.
For this reason, readers receive little information
about the daily life of the boy and his grandmother
or about the illness for which the boy is being
treated. Regardless of the boy's condition—or even
whether he is alive or dead—Jackson must complete her
journey. The nurse's statement—"The doctor said as
long as you came to get it [the medicine], you could
have it" (510)—reinforces the ritualistic nature of
Jackson's journey, a journey that Bartel suggests is
a "subconscious" act (289). Thus, Phoenix Jackson
cannot answer the nurse's questions because she does
not consciously know what compels her to make the
journey. According to Welty, the character's silence
and disorientation can also be attributed to her
relief and disillusionment upon completing the
ritualistic journey (Bethea 35). Nevertheless, next
Saturday, Phoenix Jackson will again walk, and "will
continue to do so, regardless of the difficulties
facing her, along the worn path that leads through
the wilderness of the Natchez Trace, cheerfully
performing her labor of love" (Howard 84).

Clearly, the interaction of character (Phoenix
Jackson) and act (the ritual journey in search of
medication) is the most important element of Welty's
story. By relying heavily on the characterization of
Phoenix Jackson and by describing her difficult

Collins 5

encounters during her ritual journey to town, Welty emphasizes how spiritual and emotional strength can overcome physical frailty and how determination and fearlessness can overcome any danger. These moral messages become clear by the time Phoenix reaches the doctor's office. The image of the elderly woman determinedly walking across the horizon, the image that prompted Welty to write the story, remains in the minds of readers.

Collins 6

Note

[1]Unlike the written version of "A Worn Path,"
the DVD version of the short story ends not at the
doctor's office but with a vision similar to the one
that inspired Welty to write the story—the elderly
black woman silently walking along the horizon at
dusk.

Collins 7

Works Cited

Bartel, Roland. "Life and Death in Eudora Welty's 'A
    Worn Path.'" <u>Studies in Short Fiction</u> 14 (1977):
    288-90.

Bethea, Dean. "Phoenix Has No Coat: Historicity,
    Eschatology, and Sins of Omission in Eudora
    Welty's 'A Worn Path.'" <u>International Fiction
    Review</u> 27.5 (2001): 32-38. <u>Expanded Academic
    ASAP</u>. Gale Group Databases. W. W. Hagerty Lib.,
    Philadelphia. 19 Mar. 2005 <http://
    www.galegroup.com>.

Howard, Zelma Turner. <u>The Rhetoric of Eudora Welty's
    Short Stories</u>. Jackson: UP of Mississippi, 1973.

Piwinski, David J. "Mistletoe in Eudora Welty's 'A
    Worn Path.'" <u>ANQ</u> 16.1 (2003): 40-43. <u>Expanded
    Academic ASAP</u>. Gale Group Databases. W. W.
    Hagerty Lib., Philadelphia. 19 Mar. 2005 <http://
    www.galegroup.com>.

Saunders, James Robert. "'A Worn Path': The Eternal
    Quest of Welty's Phoenix Jackson." <u>Southern
    Literary Journal</u> 25.1 (Fall 1992): 62-73.

Welty, Eudora. "A Worn Path." <u>Literature: Reading,
    Reacting, Writing</u>. Ed Laurie G. Kirszner and
    Stephen R. Mandell. 6th ed. Boston: Wadsworth,
    2007. 505-11.

---. Interview with Beth Henley. <u>The Heinle Original
    Film Series in Literature: Eudora Welty's "A Worn
    Path</u>." Dir. Bruce R. Schwartz. DVD. Heinle,
    2003.

CHAPTER 7

DOCUMENTING SOURCES AND AVOIDING PLAGIARISM

Documentation is the formal acknowledgment of the sources in a research paper. This chapter explains and illustrates the documentation style recommended by the Modern Language Association (MLA), the style used by students of literature.

What to Document

In general, you must document the following types of information:

- **All word-for-word quotations from a source.** Whenever you use a writer's exact words, you must document them. Even if you quote only a word or two within a paraphrase or summary, you must document the quoted words separately, after the final quotation marks.
- **All ideas from a source (print or electronic) that you put into your own words.** Be sure to document all paraphrases or summaries of a source's ideas, including the author's judgments, conclusions, and debatable assertions.
- **All visuals—tables, charts, and photographs—from a source.** Because visuals are almost always someone's original creation, they must be documented.

NOTE: Certain items do not require documentation: **common knowledge** (information most readers probably know), facts available from a variety of reference sources, familiar sayings and well-known quotations, and your own ideas and conclusions.

Avoiding Plagiarism

Plagiarism is the presentation of another person's words or ideas as if they were your own. Most plagiarism is **unintentional plagiarism**—for example, inserting a passage from a downloaded document directly into your paper and forgetting to include quotation marks and documentation. However, there is a difference between an honest mistake and **intentional plagiarism**—for example, copying sentences from a journal article or submitting as your own an essay that someone else has written. The penalties for unintentional plagiarism may sometimes be severe, but intentional plagiarism is almost always dealt with harshly.

The best way to avoid unintentional plagiarism is to start your research early, keep careful notes, and make sure you distinguish between your words and ideas and those of your sources. The guidelines that follow can help you avoid mistakes that lead to unintentional plagiarism.

Document All Material That Requires Documentation

Original: In Oates's stories there are no safe relationships, but the most perilous of all possibilities is sex. Sex is always destructive. (Tierce, Mike, and John Michael Crafton. "Connie's Tambourine Man: A New Reading of Arnold Friend." *Studies in Short Fiction* 22 (1985): 219–24.)

Plagiarism: In many of Oates's stories, relationships— especially sexual relationships—are dangerous.

In the example above, the writer uses ideas from a source but does not include documentation. As a result, she gives readers the mistaken impression that the source's ideas are actually her own.

Correct: Tierce and Crafton point out that in many of Oates's stories, relationships—especially sexual relationships—are dangerous (220).

Enclose Borrowed Words in Quotation Marks

Original: "The Yellow Wallpaper," which Gilman herself called "a description of a case of nervous breakdown," recalls in the first person the experiences of a woman who is evidently suffering from postpartum psychosis. (Gilbert, Sandra M., and Susan Gubar. *The Madwoman in the Attic: The Woman Writer and the Nineteenth-Century Literary Imagination.* New Haven: Yale UP, 1984.)

Plagiarism: As Gilbert and Gubar point out, the narrator in "The Yellow Wallpaper" is "evidently suffering from postpartum psychosis" (212).

Even though the writer documents the passage, he uses the source's exact words without putting them in quotation marks.

Correct: As Gilbert and Gubar point out, the narrator in "The Yellow Wallpaper" is "evidently suffering from postpartum psychosis" (212).

Do Not Imitate a Source's Syntax and Phrasing

Original: Tennessee Williams's *The Glass Menagerie*, though it has achieved a firmly established position in the canon of American plays, is often distorted, if not misunderstood, by readers, directors, and audiences. (King, Thomas. "Irony and Distance in *The Glass Menagerie.*" *Educational Theatre Journal* 31 (1992): 123–34.)

Plagiarism: `Although The Glass Menagerie has a well-`
`established place in the American theater, it is`
`often misinterpreted by those who read it, see`
`it, and direct it (King 125).`

Although the student does not use the exact words of the source, he closely follows the sentence structure of the original and simply substitutes synonyms for the writer's key words. Remember, acceptable paraphrases and summaries do more than change words; they use original phrasing and syntax to convey the source's meaning.

Correct: `According to Thomas King, although The Glass`
`Menagerie has become an American classic, it is`
`still not fully appreciated (125).`

Differentiate Your Words from Those of Your Source

Original: At some colleges and universities, traditional survey courses of world and English literature . . . have been scrapped or diluted. . . . What replaces them is sometimes a mere option of electives, sometimes "multicultural" courses introducing material from Third World cultures and thinning out an already thin sampling of Western writings, and sometimes courses geared especially to issues of class, race, and gender. (Howe, Irving. "The Value of the Canon." *The New Republic* 2 Feb. 1991: 40–47.)

Plagiarism: `At many universities, the Western literature`
`survey courses have been edged out by courses`
`that emphasize minority concerns. These courses`
`are "thinning an already thin sampling of Western`
`writings" in favor of courses geared especially`
`to issues of "class, race, and gender" (Howe 40).`

Because the student writer does not differentiate his ideas from those of his source, it appears that only the two quotations in the last sentence are borrowed when, in fact, the first sentence also owes a debt to the original. The student should have identified the boundaries of the borrowed material by introducing it with an identifying phrase and ending with documentation. (Note that a quotation always requires its own documentation.)

Correct: `According to Irving Howe, at many universities the`
`Western literature survey courses have been edged`

out by courses that emphasize minority concerns
(41). These courses, says Howe, are "thinning an
already thin sampling of Western writings" in favor
of courses geared especially to issues of "class,
race, and gender" (40).

✔ **CHECKLIST** **Plagiarism and Internet Sources**

When you download any text from the Internet, you risk plagiarism. To
avoid this problem, follow these guidelines:

☐ Download material into individual files so you can easily keep track of
your sources.

☐ Do not cut and paste blocks of downloaded text directly into your paper.
Summarize or paraphrase this material first.

☐ If you download the exact words of your source, enclose them in boldface quotation marks. If you do this, you will know when you are working with a direct quotation.

☐ Record full documentation information for emails, Web sites, and online
postings.

Documenting Sources

Many instructors of English and other languages, as well as instructors in other
humanities disciplines, require MLA-style documentation. MLA documentation
has three parts: *parenthetical references in the body of the paper* (also known as *in-text
citations*), a *works-cited list*, and *content notes.**

Parenthetical References in the Text

MLA documentation style uses parenthetical references within the text to refer
to an alphabetical works-cited list at the end of the paper. A parenthetical reference should contain just enough information to guide readers to the appropriate
entry on your works-cited list. A typical parenthetical reference consists of the
author's last name and a page number.

Gwendolyn Brooks uses the sonnet form to create poems that
have a wide social and aesthetic range (Williams 972).

---

*For more information, see the *MLA Handbook for Writers of Research Papers*, 6th ed. (New York: MLA, 2003).
You can also consult the MLA Web site at <http://www.mla.org>.

✔ **CHECKLIST**   **Guidelines for Punctuating Parenthetical References**

Paraphrases and Summaries
Place the parenthetical reference after the last word of the sentence and before the final punctuation.

In her poems, Brooks combines the pessimism of modernist poetry with the optimism of the Harlem Renaissance (Smith 978).

Direct quotations Run in with the Text
Place the parenthetical reference after the quotation marks and before the final punctuation.

According to Gary Smith, Brooks's <u>A Street in Bronzeville</u> "conveys the primacy of suffering in the lives of poor Black women" (980).

According to Gary Smith, the poems in <u>A Street in Bronzeville</u> "served notice that Brooks had learned her craft..." (978).

Along with Thompson, we must ask, "Why did it take so long for critics to acknowledge that Gwendolyn Brooks is an important voice in twentieth-century American poetry" (123)?

Quotations Set off from the Text
Omit the quotation marks, and place the parenthetical reference one space after the final punctuation. (For guidelines for setting off long quotations, see p. 34.)

For Gary Smith, the identity of Brooks's African-American women is inextricably linked with their sense of race and poverty:

> For Brooks, unlike the Renaissance poets, the victimization of poor Black women becomes not simply a minor chord but a predominant theme of <u>A Street in Bronzeville</u>. Few, if any, of her female characters are able to free themselves from a web of poverty that threatens to strangle their lives. (980)

If you mention the author's name or the title of the work in your paper, only a page reference is needed.

> According to Gladys Margaret Williams in "Gwendolyn
> Brooks's Way with the Sonnet," Brooks combines a
> sensitivity to poetic forms with a depth of emotion
> appropriate for her subject matter (972-73).

If you use more than one source by the same author, include a shortened title in the parenthetical reference.

> Brooks knows not only Shakespeare, Spenser, and Milton,
> but also the full range of African-American poetry
> (Williams, "Brooks's Way" 972).

SAMPLE PARENTHETICAL REFERENCES

An entire work
When citing an entire work, state the name of the author in your paper instead of in a parenthetical reference.

> August Wilson's play <u>Fences</u> treats many themes frequently
> expressed in modern drama.

A work by two or three authors
> Myths cut across boundaries and cultural spheres and
> reappear in strikingly similar forms from country to country
> (Feldman and Richardson 124).

> The effect of a work of literature depends on the audience's
> predispositions that derive from membership in various
> social groups (Hovland, Janis, and Kelley 87).

A work by more than three authors
State the last name of the first author, and use the abbreviation *et al.* (Latin for "and others") for the rest.

> Hawthorne's short stories frequently use a combination of
> allegorical and symbolic methods (Guerin et al. 91).

A work in an anthology
> In his essay "Flat and Round Characters," E. M. Forster
> distinguishes between one-dimensional characters and those
> that are well developed (Stevick 223-31).

Note that the parenthetical reference cites the anthology (edited by Stevick) that contains Forster's essay; full information about the anthology appears in the works-cited list.

A work with volume and page numbers
Critics consider <u>The Zoo Story</u> to be one of Albee's best
plays (Eagleton 2: 17).

An indirect source
Use the abbreviation *qtd. in* ("quoted in") to indicate that the quoted material
was not taken directly from the original source.

Wagner observed that myth and history stood before him "with
opposing claims" (qtd. in Winkler 10).

A play with numbered lines
The parenthetical reference should contain the act, scene, and line numbers
(in arabic numerals), separated by periods. When included in parenthetical
references, titles of the books of the Bible and well-known literary works are
often abbreviated — *Gen.* for *Genesis* and *Ham.* for *Hamlet* for example.

"Give thy thoughts no tongue," says Polonius, "Nor any
unproportioned thought his act" (<u>Ham</u>. 1.3.64-65).

A poem
Use a slash (/) to separate lines of poetry run in with the text. (The slash is preceded and followed by one space.) The parenthetical reference should cite the
lines quoted. Include the word *line* or *lines* in the first reference but just the numbers in subsequent references.

"I muse my life-long hate, and without flinch / I bear it
nobly as I live my part," says the speaker in Claude McKay's
bitterly ironic poem "The White City" (lines 3-4).

An electronic source
If you are citing a source from the Internet or from an online subscription service,
remember that these sources frequently do not contain page numbers. If the source
uses paragraph, section, or screen numbers, use the abbreviation "par." or "sec." or
the full word "screen."

The earliest type of movie censoring came in the form of
licensing fees, and in Deer River, Minnesota, "a licensing
fee of $200 was deemed not excessive for a town of 1000"
(Ernst, par. 20).

If the source has no page numbers or markers of any kind, cite the entire work.
(When readers consult your works-cited list, they will be able to determine the
nature of the source.)

In her article "Limited Horizons," Lynne Cheney says that
schools do best when students read literature not for what
it tells them about the workplace, but for its insights into
the human condition.

Because of its parody of communism, the film Antz is actually
an adult film masquerading as a child's tale (Clemin).

The Works-Cited List

Parenthetical references refer to a **works-cited list** that includes all the sources
you refer to in your paper. Begin the works-cited list on a new page, continuing
the page numbers of the paper. For example, if the text of the paper ends on page
6, the works-cited list will begin on page 7.

Center the title Works Cited one inch from the top of the page. Arrange entries alphabetically, according to the last name of each author. Use the first word
of the title if the author is unknown (articles —a, an, and the— at the beginning
of a title are not considered first words). Double-space the entire works-cited list
between and within entries. Begin typing each entry at the left margin, and indent subsequent lines five spaces (or one-half inch). Each works-cited entry has
three divisions —author, title, and publishing information— separated by periods.
The MLA Handbook for Writers of Research Papers shows a single space after all
end punctuation.

Informal Documentation

Sometimes for example, when you are writing a paper that includes
quotations from a single source that the entire class has read, or when
all your sources are from your textbook — your instructor may give you
permission to use *informal documentation*. Because both the instructor
and the class are familiar with the sources, you supply the authors' last
names and page numbers in parenthetical references but do not include a works-cited list.

Below is a directory of the sample MLA works-cited list entries that begin on
page 122.

DIRECTORY OF MLA WORKS-CITED LIST ENTRIES

Print Sources: Entries for Books

1. A book by a single author
2. A book by two or three authors
3. A book by more than three authors
4. Two or more works by the same author
5. An edited book
6. A book with a volume number
7. A short story, poem, or play in a collection of the author's work
8. A short story in an anthology

9. A poem in an anthology
10. A play in an anthology
11. An article in an anthology
12. More than one selection from the same anthology
13. A translation

Print Sources: Entries for Articles

14. An article in a journal with continuous pagination throughout an annual volume
15. An article with separate pagination in each issue
16. An article in a magazine
17. An article in a daily newspaper
18. An article in a reference book

Entries for Other Sources

19. A film, videocassette, DVD, or CD-ROM
20. An interview
21. A lecture or an address

Electronic Sources: Entries from Internet Sites

22. A scholarly project or information database on the Internet
23. A document within a scholarly project or information database on the Internet
24. A personal site on the Internet
25. A book on the Internet
26. An article in a scholarly journal on the Internet
27. An article in an encyclopedia on the Internet
28. An article in a newspaper on the Internet
29. An article in a magazine on the Internet
30. A painting or photograph on the Internet
31. An e-mail
32. An online posting

Electronic Sources: Entries from Subscription Services

33. A scholarly journal article with separate pagination in each issue from an online service
34. A scholarly journal article with continuous pagination throughout an annual volume from an online service
35. A monthly magazine article from an online service
36. A newspaper article from an online service
37. A reference book article from an online service
38. A dictionary definition from an online service

Entries for Other Electronic Sources

39. A nonperiodical publication on DVD or CD-ROM
40. A periodical publication on DVD or CD-ROM

MLA • Print Sources: Entries for Books

Book citations include the author's name; book title (underlined); and publication information (place, publisher, date). Capitalize all major words in the title except articles, prepositions, and the *to* of an infinitive (unless it is the first or last word of the title or subtitle). MLA requires that you abbreviate publishers' names — for example, *Basic* for Basic Books and *Oxford UP* for Oxford University Press.

1. A book by a single author

```
Kingston, Maxine Hong. The Woman Warrior: Memoirs of a
     Girlhood among Ghosts. New York: Knopf, 1976.
```

2. A book by two or three authors

```
Feldman, Burton, and Robert D. Richardson. The Rise of
     Modern Mythology. Bloomington: Indiana UP, 1972.
```

Note that only the *first* author's name is in reverse order.

3. A book by more than three authors

```
Guerin, Wilfred, et al., eds. A Handbook of Critical
     Approaches to Literature. 3rd ed. New York: Harper,
     1992.
```

Note that instead of using *et al.*, you may list all the authors' names in the order in which they appear on the title page.

4. Two or more works by the same author

List two or more works by the same author in alphabetical order by *title*. Include the author's full name in the first entry; use three unspaced hyphens followed by a period to take the place of the author's name in second and subsequent entries.

```
Novoa, Juan-Bruce. Chicano Authors: Inquiry by Interview.
     Austin: U of Texas P, 1980.
---. "Themes in Rudolfo Anaya's Work." Address given at
     New Mexico State University, Las Cruces. 11 Apr.
     1987.
```

5. An edited book

```
Oosthuizen, Ann, ed. Sometimes When It Rains: Writings by
     South African Women. New York: Pandora, 1987.
```

Note that here the abbreviation *ed.* stands for *editor*.

6. A book with a volume number

When all the volumes of a multivolume work have the same title, list the number of the volume you used.

```
Eagleton, T. Allston. A History of the New York Stage.
     Vol. 2. Englewood Cliffs: Prentice, 1987.
```

When each volume of a multivolume work has a separate title, list the title of the volume you used.

```
Durant, Will, and Ariel Durant. The Age of Napoleon: A
     History of European Civilization from 1789 to 1815.
     New York: Simon, 1975.
```

(*The Age of Napoleon* is volume 2 of *The Story of Civilization*. You need not provide documentation for the entire multivolume work.)

7. A short story, poem, or play in a collection of the author's work

```
Gordimer, Nadine. "Once upon a Time." "Jump" and Other
     Stories. New York: Farrar, 1991. 23-30.
```

8. A short story in an anthology

```
Salinas, Marta. "The Scholarship Jacket." Nosotros:
     Latina Literature Today. Ed. Maria del Carmen Boza,
     Beverly Silva, and Carmen Valle. Binghamton:
     Bilingual, 1986. 68-70.
```

Note that here the abbreviation *Ed.* stands for *Edited by*. The inclusive page numbers follow the year of publication.

9. A poem in an anthology

```
Simmerman, Jim. "Child's Grave, Hale County, Alabama."
     The Pushcart Prize, X: Best of the Small Presses.
     Ed. Bill Henderson. New York: Penguin, 1986. 198-99.
```

10. A play in an anthology

```
Hughes, Langston. Mother and Child. Black Drama
     Anthology. Ed. Woodie King and Ron Miller. New
     York: NAL, 1986. 399-406.
```

11. An article in an anthology

```
Forster, E. M. "Flat and Round Characters." The Theory of
     the Novel. Ed. Philip Stevick. New York: Free, 1980.
     223-31.
```

12. More than one selection from the same anthology

If you are using more than one selection from an anthology, cite the anthology in a separate entry. Then, list each individual selection separately, including the author and title of the selection, the anthology editor's last name, and the inclusive page numbers.

```
Baxter, Charles. "Gryphon." Kirszner and Mandell 248-60.
Kirszner, Laurie G., and Stephen R. Mandell, eds.
    Literature: Reading, Reacting, Writing. 6th ed.
    Boston: Wadsworth, 2007.
Rich, Adrienne. "Diving into the Wreck." Kirszner and
    Mandell 1039-41.
```

13. A translation

```
Carpentier, Alejo. Reasons of State. Trans. Francis
    Partridge. New York: Norton, 1976.
```

MLA • Print Sources: Entries for Articles

Article citations include the author's name; the title of the article (in quotation marks); the name of the periodical (underlined); the month (abbreviated, except for May, June, and July) and the year; and the pages on which the full article appears (without the abbreviations *p.* or *pp.*).

14. An article in a journal with continuous pagination throughout an annual volume

```
LeGuin, Ursula K. "American Science Fiction and the
    Other." Science Fiction Studies 2 (1975): 208-10.
```

15. An article with separate pagination in each issue

```
Grossman, Robert. "The Grotesque in Faulkner's 'A Rose
    for Emily.'" Mosaic 20.3 (1987): 40-55.
```

Note that *20.3* signifies volume 20, issue 3.

16. An article in a magazine

```
Milosz, Czeslaw. "A Lecture." New Yorker 22 June
    1992: 32.
```

An article with no listed author is entered by title on the works-cited list.

```
"Solzhenitsyn: An Artist Becomes an Exile." Time 25 Feb.
    1974: 34+.
```

Note that *34+* indicates that the article appears on pages that are not consecutive; in this case, the article begins on page 34 and continues on page 37.

17. An article in a daily newspaper

Omit the article *the* from the title of a newspaper even if the newspaper's actual title includes the article.

```
Oates, Joyce Carol. "When Characters from the Page Are
     Made Flesh on the Screen." New York Times 23 Mar.
     1986, late ed.: C1+.
```

Note that *C1+* indicates that the article begins on page 1 of Section C and continues on a subsequent page.

18. An article in a reference book

Do not include publication information for well-known reference books.

```
"Dance Theatre of Harlem." The New Encyclopaedia
Britannica: Micropaedia. 15th ed. 1987.
```

Include publication information when citing reference books that are not well known.

```
Grimstead, David. "Fuller, Margaret Sarah." Encyclopedia
     of American Biography. Ed. John A. Garraty. New York:
     Harper, 1974.
```

Entries for Other Sources

19. A film, videocassette, DVD, or CD-ROM

```
The Heinle Original Film Series in Literature: Eudora Welty's
"A Worn Path." Dir. Bruce R. Schwartz. DVD. Heinle, 2003.
```

20. An interview

```
Brooks, Gwendolyn. "An Interview with Gwendolyn Brooks."
     Triquarterly 60 (1984): 405-10.
```

21. A lecture or an address

```
Novoa, Juan-Bruce. "Themes in Rudolfo Anaya's Work."
     Literature Colloquium. New Mexico State University.
     Las Cruces. 11 Apr. 2002.
```

MLA • Electronic Sources: Entries from Internet Sites

MLA style recognizes that publication information is not always available for electronic sources. Include in your citation whatever information you can reasonably obtain: the title of the Internet site (underlined); the editor of the site (if available); the version number of the source (if applicable); the date of electronic publication (or update); the number of pages, paragraphs, or sections (if available); the name of any sponsoring institution; the date of access; and the URL (within angle brackets). If you have to carry the URL over to the next line, divide it after a slash. If the URL is excessively long, use just the URL of the site's search page, or use the URL of the site's home page, followed by the word *path* and a colon and then the sequence of links to follow.

22. A scholarly project or information database on the Internet

<u>Philadelphia Writers Project</u>. Ed. Miriam Kotzen Green.
May 1998. Drexel U. 12 June 1999 <http://
www.Drexel.edu/letrs/wwp/>.

23. A document within a scholarly project or information database on the Internet

"D-Day: June 7th, 1944." <u>The History Channel Online</u>.
1999. History Channel. 7 June 1999 <http://
historychannel.com/thisday/today/997690.html>.

24. A personal site on the Internet

Yerkes, James. <u>Chiron's Forum: John Updike Home Page</u>. 23
June 2000. 30 June 2000 <http://www.users.fast.net/
~joyerkers/item9.html>.

25. A book on the Internet

Douglass, Frederick. <u>My Bondage and My Freedom</u>. Boston:
Houghton, 1855. 8 June 2005 <gopher://
gopher.vt.edu:10024/22/178/3>.

26. An article in a scholarly journal on the Internet

Dekoven, Marianne. "Utopias Limited: Post-Sixties and
Postmodern American Fiction." <u>Modern Fiction Studies</u>
41.1 (1995): 13 pp. 17 Mar. 2002 <http://muse.jhu.edu/
journals/mfs.v041/41.1dwkovwn.html>.

When you cite information from the print version of an electronic source, include the publication information for the printed source, the number of pages or paragraphs (if available), and the date of access.

27. An article in an encyclopedia on the Internet

"Hawthorne, Nathaniel." <u>Britannica Online</u>. Vers. 98.2.
Apr. 1998. Encyclopedia Britannica. 16 May 1998
<http://www.eb/com/:220>.

28. An article in a newspaper on the Internet

Lohr, Steve. "Microsoft Goes to Court." <u>New York Times on
the Web</u> 19 Oct. 1998. 29 Apr. 2000 <http://
www.nytimes.com/web/docroot/library.cyber/week/
1019business.html>.

29. An article in a magazine on the Internet

Weiser, Jay. "The Tyranny of Informality." <u>Time</u> 26 Feb.
1996. 1 Mar. 1999 <http://www.enews.com/
magazines.tnr/current/022696.3.html>.

30. A painting or photograph on the Internet

```
Lange, Dorothea, Looking at Pictures. 1936. Museum of
     Modern Art, New York. 17 July 2005 <http://moma.org/
     exhibitions/lookingatphotographs/lang-fr.html>.
```

31. An email

```
Adkins, Camille. Email to the author. 28 June 2005.
```

32. An online posting

```
Gilford, Mary. "Dog Heroes in Children's Literature."
     Online posting. 17 Mar. 2004. 12 Apr. 2004
     <news:alt.animals.dogs>.
```

MLA • Electronic Sources: Entries from Subscription Services

Online subscription services can be divided into those you subscribe to, such as America Online, and those your college library subscribes to, such as Expanded Academic ASAP, LexisNexis, and ProQuest.

To cite information from an online service (such as AOL) to which you subscribe, you have two options. If the service provides a URL, follow the examples in entries 22 through 30. If the service enables you to use a keyword to access material, provide the keyword (following the date of access) at the end of the entry.

```
"Kafka, Franz." Compton's Encyclopedia Online. Vers.
     3.0. 2000. America Online. 8 June 2001. Keyword:
     Compton's.
```

If, instead of a keyword, you follow a series of topic labels, list them (separated by semicolons) after the word *Path*.

```
"Elizabeth Adams." History Resources. 11 Nov. 2001.
     America Online. 28 Apr. 2001. Path: Research; Biology;
     Women in Science; Biographies.
```

To cite information from an online service to which your library subscribes, supply the publication information (including page numbers, if available) followed by the underlined name of the database (if known), the name of the service, the library at which you accessed the database, the date of access, and the URL of the online service's home page.

```
Luckenbill, Trent. "Environmental Litigation: Down the
     Endless Corridor." Environment 17 July 2001: 34-42.
     ABI/INFORM GLOBAL. ProQuest Direct. Drexel U Lib.,
     Philadelphia. 12 Oct. 2001 <http://www.proquest.com>.
```

33. A scholarly journal article with separate pagination in each issue from an online service

Schaefer, Richard J. "Editing Strategies in Television
News Documentaries." Journal of Communication 47.4
(1997): 69-89. InfoTrac OneFile Plus. Gale Group
Databases. Augusta R. Kolwyck Lib., Chattanooga, TN.
2 Oct. 2002 <http://www.galegroup.com>.

34. A scholarly journal article with continuous pagination throughout an annual volume from an online service

Hudson, Nicholas. "Samuel Johnson, Urban Culture, and the
Geography of Postfire London." Studies in English
Literature 42 (2002): 557-80. MasterFILE Premier.
EBSCOhost. Augusta R. Kolwyck Lib., Chattanooga, TN.
2 Oct. 2002 <http://www.ebscohost.com>.

35. A monthly magazine article from an online service

Livermore, Beth. "Meteorites on Ice." Astronomy July 1993:
54-58. Expanded Academic ASAP Plus. Gale Group
Databases. Augusta R. Kolwyck Lib., Chattanooga,
TN. 2 Oct. 2003 <http://www.galegroup.com>.

36. A newspaper article from an online service

Meyer, Greg. "Answering Questions about the West Nile
Virus." Dayton Daily News 11 July 2002: Z3-Z7.
LexisNexis Academic. Augusta R. Kolwyck Lib.,
Chattanooga, TN. 2 Oct. 2003 <http://
www.web.lexis-nexis.com>.

37. A reference book article from an online service

Laird, Judith. "Geoffrey Chaucer." Cyclopedia of World
Authors. 1997. MagillOnLiterature. EBSCOhost.
Augusta R. Kolwyck Lib., Chattanooga, TN. 2 Oct.
2003 <http://www.ebscohost.com>.

38. A dictionary definition from an online service

"Migraine." Mosby's Medical, Nursing, and Allied Health
Dictionary. 1998 ed. Health Reference Center. Gale
Group Databases. Augusta R. Kolwyck Lib., Chattanooga,
TN. 2 Oct. 2003 <http://www.galegroup.com>.

MLA • Electronic Sources:
Entries for Other Electronic Sources

39. A nonperiodical publication on DVD or CD-ROM

"Windhover." The Oxford English Dictionary. 2nd ed.
DVD. Oxford: Oxford UP, 2001.

40. A periodical publication on DVD or CD-ROM

Zurbach, Kate. "The Linguistic Roots of Three Terms."
    <u>Linguistic Quarterly</u> 37 (1994): 12-47. <u>InfoTrac</u>:
    <u>Magazine Index Plus</u>. CD-ROM. Information Access.
    Jan. 2001.

> **WARNING:** Using information from an Internet source can be risky. Contributors are not necessarily experts, and they frequently are inaccurate or misinformed. Unless you can be certain that the information you are obtaining from these sources is reliable, do not use it. You can check the reliability of an Internet source by asking your instructor or librarian for guidance.

Content Notes

Use **content notes**, indicated by a superscript (a raised number) in the text, to cite several sources at once or to provide commentary or explanations that do not fit smoothly into your paper. The full text of these notes appears on the first numbered page following the last page of the paper. (If your paper has no content notes, the works-cited page follows the last page of the paper.) Like works-cited entries, content notes are double-spaced within and between entries. However, the first line of each explanatory note is indented five spaces (or one-half inch), and subsequent lines are flush with the left-hand margin.

To Cite Several Sources

In the paper

Surprising as it may seem, there have been many attempts
to define literature.[1]

In the note

    [1]For an overview of critical opinion, see Arnold 72;
Eagleton 1-2; Howe 43-44; and Abrams 232-34.

To Provide Explanations

In the paper

In recent years, gothic novels have achieved great
popularity.[3]

In the note

    [3]Gothic novels, works written in imitation of
medieval romances, originally relied on supernatural
occurrences. They flourished in the late eighteenth and
early nineteenth centuries.

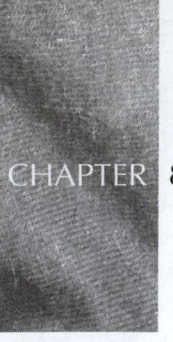

CHAPTER 8

WRITING ESSAY EXAMS ABOUT LITERATURE

Taking exams is a skill that you have been developing throughout your career as a student. Both short-answer exams and essay exams require you to study, to recall what you know, and to budget your time carefully as you write your answers. Only essay questions, however, ask you to synthesize information and to arrange ideas in a series of clear, logically connected sentences and paragraphs. For this reason, taking essay exams requires writing skills. To write an essay exam — or even a paragraph-length response — you must do more than memorize facts; you must identify the relationships among them. In other words, you must **think critically** about your subject, and you must plan, shape, draft, and revise an essay that clearly communicates your ideas to your audience.

Planning an Essay Exam Answer

Because you are under pressure during an exam and tend to write quickly, you may be tempted to skip the planning and revision stages of the writing process. But if you write in a frenzy and hand in your exam without a second glance, you are likely to produce a disorganized or even incoherent answer. With careful planning and editing, you can write an essay that demonstrates your understanding of the material.

Review Your Material

Be sure you know beforehand the scope and format of the exam. How much of your textbook and class notes will the exam cover — the entire semester's work or only the material covered since the last test? Will you have to answer every question, or will you be able to choose among alternatives? Will the exam test your ability to recall specific facts, or will it require you to demonstrate your understanding of the course material by drawing original conclusions?

Exams challenge you to recall and express in writing what you already know — what you have read, what you have heard in class, what you have reviewed in your notes. Before you even begin an exam, you must study: reread your textbook and class notes, highlight key points, and perhaps outline particularly important sections of your notes. When you prepare for a short-answer exam, you may memorize facts without analyzing their relationship to one another or their relationship to a body of knowledge as a whole: the definition of romanticism, the date of Queen Victoria's death, two examples of irony, four characteristics of a villanelle. When you prepare for an essay exam, however, you must do more than remember bits of information; you must also make connections among ideas.

When you are sure you know what to expect, try to anticipate the essay questions your instructor might ask. Try out likely questions on classmates, and see whether you can do some collaborative brainstorming to outline answers to possible questions. If you have time, you might even practice answering one or two in writing.

Consider Your Audience and Purpose

The audience for any exam is the instructor who prepared it. As you read the questions, think about what your instructor has emphasized in class. Although you may certainly arrange material in a new way or use it to make an original point, keep in mind that your purpose is to demonstrate that you understand the material, not to make clever remarks or introduce irrelevant information. In addition, you should make every effort to use the vocabulary of the discipline for which you are writing and to follow the specific **conventions** for writing about literature (p. 35).

Read Through the Entire Exam

Your time is usually limited when you take an exam, so plan carefully. How long should a "one-paragraph" or "essay-length" answer be? How much time should you devote to answering each question? The exam question itself may specify the time allotted for each answer, so look for that information. More often, the point value of each question or the number of questions on the exam indicates how much time to spend on each answer. If an essay question is worth 50 out of 100 points, for example, you will probably have to spend at least half of your time planning, writing, and revising your answer.

Before you begin to write, read the entire exam carefully to determine your priorities and your strategy. First, be sure that your copy of the test is complete and that you understand exactly what each question requires. If you need clarification, ask your instructor or proctor for help. Then, decide where to start. If there is more than one question on the exam, responding first to the one you feel most confident about is usually a good strategy. This approach ensures that you will not become bogged down responding to a question that baffles you and be left with too little time to write a strong answer to a question that you understand well.

Read Each Question Carefully

To write an effective answer, you need to understand the question. As you read any essay question, you may find it helpful to underline key words and important terms.

<u>Summarize in detail</u> the contributions of American <u>writers</u> of the <u>Harlem Renaissance,</u> <u>briefly outlining</u> the contributions of <u>artists and musicians.</u>

Look carefully at the question's wording. If the question calls for a comparison and contrast of two works of literature, a description or analysis of *one* work, no matter how comprehensive, will not be acceptable. If a question asks for causes *and* effects, a discussion of causes alone will be insufficient.

Key Words in Exam Questions		
Explain	Clarify	Classify
Compare	Relate	Identify
Contrast	Justify	Illustrate
Trace	Analyze	Define
Evaluate	Interpret	Support
Discuss	Describe	Summarize

As its key words indicate, the following question calls for a very specific kind of response. The first response to it simply *identifies* three characteristics of *one* kind of detective story and is therefore not acceptable.

Question

Identify three differences between the hard-boiled detective story and the classical detective story.

Unacceptable Answer

The hard-boiled detective story, popularized in Black Mask magazine in the 1930s and 1940s, is very different from the classical detective stories of Edgar Allan Poe or Agatha Christie. The hard-boiled stories feature a down-on-his-luck detective who is constantly tempted and betrayed. His world is dark and chaotic, and the crimes he tries to solve are not out-of-the-ordinary occurrences; they are the norm. These stories have no happy endings; even when the crime is solved, the world is still corrupt.

The following answer, which *contrasts* the two kinds of detective stories, is acceptable.

Acceptable Answer

The hard-boiled detective story differs from the classical detective story in its characters, its setting, and its plot. The classical detective is usually well

educated and well off; he is aloof from the other characters
and therefore can remain in total control of the situation.
The hard-boiled detective, on the other hand, is typically a
decent but down-on-his-luck man who is drawn into the chaos
around him, constantly tempted and betrayed. In the orderly
world of the classical detective, the crime is a temporary
disruption. In the hard-boiled detective's dark and chaotic
world, the crimes he tries to solve are the norm. In the
classical detective story, order is restored at the end.
Hard-boiled stories have no happy endings; even when the
crime is solved, the world is still a dangerous and corrupt
place.

Brainstorm to Find Ideas

Once you understand the question, you need to find something to say. Begin by
brainstorming — quickly listing all of the relevant ideas you can remember about
a topic. Then, identify the most important points on your list, and delete the others. A quick review of the exam question and your supporting ideas should lead
you toward a workable thesis for your essay.

Shaping an Essay Exam Answer

State Your Thesis

Often, you can rephrase the exam question as a **thesis statement**. For example,
the question "Discuss in detail the contributions of American writers of the
Harlem Renaissance, briefly outlining the contributions of artists and musicians"
suggests the following thesis statement.

Effective Thesis Statement

      Writers of the Harlem Renaissance—notably Richard
Wright, Gwendolyn Brooks, Zora Neale Hurston, and Langston
Hughes—made significant contributions to American
literature; artists and musicians of the movement also left
an important legacy.

   An effective thesis statement addresses all aspects of the question but highlights only relevant concerns. The following thesis statements are not effective.

Vague Thesis Statement

      The Harlem Renaissance produced many important writers,
artists, and musicians.

Incomplete Thesis Statement

The writers of the Harlem Renaissance, such as Richard
Wright, Gwendolyn Brooks, Zora Neale Hurston, and Langston
Hughes, made significant contributions to American literature.

Irrelevant Thesis Statement

The writers of the Harlem Renaissance had a greater
impact on American literature than the writers of the Beat
generation, such as Jack Kerouac.

Make a Scratch Outline

Because time is limited, you should plan your answer before you write it. Therefore, once you have decided on a suitable thesis, you should make a **scratch
outline** that lists the points you will use to support your thesis.

On the inside cover of your exam book, arrange your supporting points in the
order in which you plan to discuss them. Once you have completed your outline,
check it against the exam question to make certain it covers everything the
question calls for — and *only* what the question calls for.

A scratch outline for an answer to the question "Discuss in detail the contributions of American writers of the Harlem Renaissance, briefly outlining the contributions of artists and musicians" might look like this.

Thesis statement: Writers of the Harlem Renaissance—notably
Richard Wright, Gwendolyn Brooks, Zora Neale Hurston, and
Langston Hughes—made significant contributions to American
literature; artists and musicians of the movement also left
an important legacy.

Writers
     Wright—Uncle Tom's Children, Black Boy, Native Son
     Brooks—poetry (classical forms; social issues)
     Hurston—Their Eyes Were Watching God, essays,
          autobiography
     Hughes—poetry (ballads, blues); "Simple" stories

Artists and Musicians
     Henry Tanner
     Duke Ellington

Drafting and Revising an Essay Exam Answer

Referring to your outline, you can now begin to draft your answer. Don't bother
crafting an elaborate or unusual **introduction;** your time is precious, and so is your
reader's. A simple statement of your thesis that summarizes your answer is your
best introductory strategy. This approach is efficient, and it reminds you to address
the question directly.

To develop the **body** of the essay, follow your outline point by point, using specifically worded topic sentences to introduce your supporting points and clear transitions to indicate your progression from point to point (and to help your instructor see that you are answering the question in full). Such signals, along with parallel sentence structure and repeated words, will make your essay easy to follow.

The most effective **conclusion** for an essay exam is a clear, simple restatement of the thesis or a summary of the essay's main points.

Essay answers should be complete and detailed, but they should not contain irrelevant material. Every unnecessary fact or opinion increases your chance of error, so don't repeat yourself or volunteer unrequested information, and don't express your own feelings or opinions unless such information is specifically called for. In addition, be sure to support all your general statements with specific examples.

Leave enough time to reread and revise what you have written. When you reread, try to view your answer from a fresh perspective. Is your thesis statement clearly worded? Does your essay support your thesis and answer the question? Are your facts correct, and are your ideas presented in a logical order? Review your topic sentences and transitions. Check sentence structure and word choice, spelling and punctuation. If a sentence — or even a whole paragraph — seems irrelevant, cross it out. If you suddenly remember something you want to add, you can insert a few additional words with a caret (^). Neatly insert a longer addition at the end of your answer, box it, and label it so your instructor will know where it belongs. Finally, be sure that you have written legibly and that you have not inadvertently left out any words.

Sample Student Essay Exam Answer

The essay exam answer on pages 136–38 was written in response to the following question.

Question

> Fictional characters (like real people) do not always behave as others wish or expect them to. Sometimes they rebel against these expectations and act quite differently. In a clearly written and supported essay, explain how the specific actions of any three characters in works we have read this semester defy the expectations of those around them. Then, briefly consider the consequences of each character's decision to rebel.

As you read the following response to the question, notice that the student writer does not include any irrelevant information. She does not, for example, provide unnecessary plot summary or discuss more than three characters; she covers only what the question asks for. Guided by the question's key words —*explain* and *briefly consider*— she describes how each character's actions are defiant and outlines the consequences of those actions.

Introduction echoes wording of exam question and introduces four characters to be discussed

Thesis statement

First character's actions explained

Consequences of actions

Second character's actions explained

Many characters we have read about this semester do not behave as others believe they should behave. This is apparent in the actions of Connie in Joyce Carol Oates's short story "Where Are You Going, Where Have You Been?," Nora in Henrik Ibsen's play <u>A Doll House</u>, and Marty in Paddy Chayefsky's play <u>Marty</u>. For each of these characters, rebellion comes with a significant sacrifice.

Connie's rebellion is somewhat typical for a teenager: she rebels against the constraints her parents put on her to be a "good girl" by being a "bad girl" (at least in their terms). The makeup and style of clothing that Connie wears when she is away from home reinforce this "bad girl" image. Her behavior—staying out late, lying about where she is going, having "trashy daydreams"—creates a problem for her parents because she is not conforming to their standards and because she is not conducting herself in a manner they consider appropriate. Her actions also put a strain on the relationship between her and her sister, who is the perfect example of a "good girl." Her determination to rebel ultimately makes her stay home from the family outing, and this in turn leaves her alone and vulnerable to Arnold's advances. Thus, her rebellious actions lead to probable violence (she goes with Arnold, who we know has frightening plans for her). The ending of the story is ambiguous. We do not know if she ever comes back; possibly, her innocent rebellion leads to her death.

Nora in <u>A Doll House</u> rebels only after she understands the conflict between her duty to herself to be a "real" person and her duty to her husband and children. Throughout the play, we see this conflict escalating until Nora has no choice but to act to resolve it, choosing to go against the norms of society and against how others think she should act. This behavior creates a problem for Torvald because of the image it presents to others. Torvald's greatest fear is that society will not accept him, and when Nora admits what she has done, he panics. At the end of the play, Nora chooses to be true to herself even though the person closest to her does not approve—and even though she will lose her children. She will be a stronger person because she has found the courage to stand up for herself.

Consequences of actions

Marty's rebellious act is simply his decision to call Clara even though his friends and his mother do not approve. Although Marty is an adult, he is very much still an adolescent in some ways. He has not yet broken away from his mother, and he continues to seek approval from her (and from his friends). He struggles to please his mother—by going to the dance, by allowing Aunt Catherine to move in—even when her desires are in conflict with his own. Marty's action at the play's end—calling Clara—will create a problem for his mother and his friends, who fear his growing independence and fight his decision to pursue a relationship with Clara. But Marty, like Nora, chooses to be true to himself and to do what he thinks is the right thing for him, rather than what others force upon him. He risks hurting his mother, alienating his friends, and losing the only life he

Third character's actions explained

Consequences of actions

knows. But for Marty, the potential gains seem worth the risk.

Conclusion

　　Connie, Nora, and Marty all break with society; all struggle to be independent. For all three, this independence has a cost. Connie may lose her life, Nora gives up her marriage and her children, and Marty leaves behind the comforting, secure existence he has known. Although each character deals with conflict and rebellion in a different way, all three struggle within themselves when decisions they must make are in conflict with the norms and expectations of society. For all three, rebellion leads to sacrifice.

2| FICTION

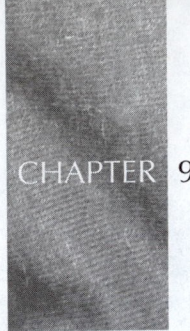

CHAPTER 9

UNDERSTANDING FICTION

A **narrative** tells a story by presenting events in some logical or orderly way. A work of **fiction** is a narrative that originates in the imagination of the author rather than in history or fact. Certainly some fiction — historical or autobiographical fiction, for example — focuses on real people and is grounded in actual events, but the way the characters interact, what they say, and how the plot unfolds are largely the author's invention.

Even before they know how to read, most people have learned how narratives are structured. As children learn how to tell a story, they start to experiment with its form, learning the value of exaggerating, adding or deleting details, rearranging events, and bending facts. In other words, they learn how to *fictionalize* a narrative to achieve a desired effect. This kind of informal, personal narrative is similar to more structured literary narratives.

Origins of Modern Fiction

The earliest examples of narrative fiction are linked with our understanding of stories in general. Human beings have always had stories to tell, and as our species evolved, so did our means of self-expression. Our early ancestors depicted the stories of their daily lives and beliefs in primitive drawings that used pictures as symbols. As language evolved, so too did our means of communicat-ing — and our need to preserve what we understood to be our past.

Stories and songs emerged as an oral means of communicating and preserving the past: tales of heroic battles or struggles, myths, or religious beliefs. In a society that was not literate, and in a time before mass communication, the oral tradition enabled people to pass down these stories, usually in the form of rhyming poems. These poems used various literary devices — including **rhyme** and **alliteration** as well as **anaphora** (the repetition of key words or phrases) — to make the poems easier to remember. Thus, the earliest forms of fiction were in fact poetry.

Eventually written down, these extended narratives developed into **epics**— long narrative poems about heroic figures whose actions determine the fate of a nation or of an entire race. Homer's *Iliad* and *Odyssey*, the ancient Babylonian *Epic of Gilgamesh*, the Hindu *Bhagavad Gita*, and the Anglo-Saxon *Beowulf* are examples. Many of the tales of the Old Testament also came out of this tradition. The setting of an epic is vast — sometimes worldwide or cosmic, including heaven

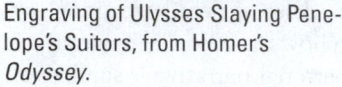

Engraving of Ulysses Slaying Penelope's Suitors, from Homer's *Odyssey*.

Engraving of the Trojan horse from Homer's *Iliad*.

and hell—and the action commonly involves a battle or a perilous journey. Quite often, divine beings participate in the action and influence the outcome of events, as they do in the Trojan War in the *Iliad* and in the founding of Rome in Virgil's *Aeneid*.

During the Middle Ages, these early epics were supplanted by the **romance**. Written initially in verse and later in prose, the romance replaced the gods, goddesses, and central heroic characters of the epic with knights, kings, and damsels in distress. Events were controlled by enchantments rather than by the will of divine beings. The anonymously written *Sir Gawain and the Green Knight* and Thomas Malory's *Le Morte d'Arthur* are examples of romances based upon the legend of King Arthur and the Knights of the Round Table.

Other significant texts of the Middle Ages were Geoffrey Chaucer's *The Canterbury Tales* and Giovanni Boccaccio's *The Decameron*, both written in the fourteenth century. These works contained extended poems and stories, respectively, that were integrated into a larger narrative framework; in this respect, they had much in common with today's collections of short stories.

The History of the Novel

The evolution of the **novel** has been a gradual but steady process. Early forms of literature share many of the characteristics of the novel (although not necessarily sharing its recognizable form, style, or focus). Epics and romances, for instance, often had broad plots, heroic characters, and moral themes, and in this way, they were precursors of what we call the novel today.

Portrait of Queen Guinevere, King Arthur's wife and Sir Lancelot's mistress.

Perhaps the most notable event in the development of the novel, and of literature as a whole, was the invention of the printing press by Johannes Gutenberg in 1440. Before this milestone, printing was a costly and impractical process that was largely reserved for medical books and sacred texts. In fact, invention made the production and distribution of longer works a practical possibility and forever changed, broadened, and expanded the scope of what we consider literature to be—and how we access it. In fact, the printing press was one of the factors that made the Renaissance possible. During this period, philosophy, science, literature, and the arts, flowered. The **pastoral romance**, a prose tale set in an idealized rural world, and the **character**, a brief satirical sketch illustrating a type of personality, both became popular in Renaissance England. The **picaresque novel**, an episodic, often satirical work about a rogue or rascal (such as Miguel de Cervantes' *Don Quixote*) emerged in seventeenth-century Spain. Other notable Renaissance-era texts included Sir Philip Sidney's *Arcadia*, Edmund Spenser's *The Faerie Queen*, and John Bunyan's *The Pilgrim's Progress*. Each of these texts had elements of the novel—longer narrative, extended plot, the development of characters over time, and a hero/protagonist—and the form continued to evolve.

An 1863 engraving by Gustave Doré depicting a scene from Miguel de Cervantes's *Don Quixote*.

The English writer Daniel Defoe is commonly given credit for writing the first novel. His *Robinson Crusoe* (1719) is an episodic narrative similar to a picaresque but unified by a single setting as well as by a central character. Jonathan Swift's *Gulliver's Travels*, which followed Defoe, is a satirical commentary on the undesirable outcomes of science. During this time, the **epistolary novel** also flourished. This kind of novel told a story in the format of letters, or included letters as a means of disseminating information. Henry Fielding's *Tom Jones* is an example from the eighteenth century; a contemporary example is Alice Walker's *The Color Purple*.

By the nineteenth century, the novel had reached a high point in its development, and its influence and importance were widespread. During the Victorian era in England (1837–1901), many novels reflected the era's preoccupation with propriety and manners. The most notable examples of these **novels of manners** were Jane Austen's *Sense and Sensibility* and *Pride and Prejudice*. Beyond the world of the aristocracy, members of the middle class clamored for novels that mirrored their own experiences, and writers such as George Eliot, Charles Dickens, William Thackeray, and Charlotte and Emily Brontë appealed to this desire by creating large fictional worlds populated by many different characters who reflected the complexity—and at times the melodrama—of Victorian society. Other writers addressed the dire consequences of science and ambition, as Mary Wollstonecraft Shelley did in her Gothic tale *Frankenstein*.

In the United States, the early nineteenth century was marked by novels that reflected the concerns of a growing country with burgeoning interests. **Realism**, which strove to portray everyday events and people in a realistic fashion, began in France with Honoré de Balzac and Gustav Flaubert and spread to the United States, influencing writers such as Henry James, Stephen Crane, and Mark

Nineteenth-century woodcut by J. Mahoney depicting a scene from Charles Dickens's *Oliver Twist*.

Twain. James Fenimore Cooper (*Last of the Mohicans*) and Nathaniel Hawthorne wrote historical fiction, while Herman Melville (*Moby-Dick*) and Edgar Allan Poe confronted issues of good and evil, madness and sanity.

Other writers of the nineteenth century had a slightly different set of concerns. Many addressed social, historical, or even feminist themes in their work. In the United States, writers who addressed such concerns included Harriet Beecher Stowe (*Uncle Tom's Cabin*), Louisa May Alcott (*Little Women*), and Kate Chopin (*The Awakening*). Meanwhile, in Russia, novelists such as Fyodor Dostoyevsky (*Crime and Punishment*) and Leo Tolstoy (*War and Peace*) examined the everyday lives, as well as the larger struggles and triumphs, of their people.

The early twentieth century marked the beginning of a literary movement known as **modernism**, in which writers reacted to the increasing complexity of a changing world and mourned the passing of old ways under the pressures of modernity. World War I, urbanization, and the rise of industrialism all contributed to a sense that new things needed to be told in new ways, and writers such as James Joyce (*Ulysses*), Virginia Woolf (*To the Lighthouse*), and D. H. Lawrence (*Sons and Lovers*) experimented with both form and content.

In the United States, the Roaring Twenties and the Great Depression inspired numerous novelists who set out to write The Great American Novel and capture the culture and concerns of the times, often in very gritty and realistic ways. These authors included F. Scott Fitzgerald (*The Great Gatsby*), Ernest Hemingway (*The Sun Also Rises*), William Faulkner (*The Sound and the Fury*), and John Steinbeck (*The Grapes of Wrath*). A little later, novelists such as Richard Wright (*Native Son*) and Ralph Ellison (*Invisible Man*) made important literary contributions by addressing the sociopolitical climate for African Americans in a segregated society.

In the aftermath of modernism, a movement called **postmodernism** emerged. Postmodern artists reacted to the confines and limitations placed upon form and meaning by opening ideas of interpretation. Often, the search for meaning in a text became the meaning itself, and in this way, the work's meaning became relative and subjective. Postmodern novelists, such as George Orwell (*1984*), Aldous Huxley (*Brave New World*), and William Golding (*Lord of the Flies*), confronted the changing society, the future, and the impact of technology.

Contemporary fiction has been marked and influenced by the developments of the latter part of the twentieth century, including globalization, the rise of technology, and the advent of the Internet and the Age of Communication. As our ability to interact and communicate with other societies has increased exponentially, so too has our access to the literature of other cultures. Contemporary fiction is a world that mirrors the diversity of its participants in terms of form, content, themes, styles, and language. There are many writers worthy of mention, as each culture makes its own invaluable contributions. Some particularly noteworthy postmodern writers include Gabriel Garcia Marquez, Salman Rushdie, Milan Kundera, Chinua Achebe, Saul Bellow, Toni Morrison, and V. S. Naipul. As we continue into the twenty-first century, the only thing that remains certain about the future of the novel, and of fiction in general, is its past.

The History of the Short Story

Early precursors for the short story include **anecdotes, parables, fables, folk tales,** and **fairy tales.** What all of these forms have in common is brevity and a moral. The ones that have survived, such as "Cinderella" and Aesop's *Fables*, are contemporary versions of old, even ancient, tales that can be traced back centuries through many different cultures.

Undated woodcut of Cinderella

Folktales and fairy tales share many different characteristics. First, they feature simple characters who illustrate a quality or trait that can be summed up in a few words. Much of the appeal of "Cinderella," for example, depends on the contrast between the selfish, sadistic stepsisters and the poor, gentle, victimized Cinderella. In addition, the folktale or fairy tale has an obvious theme or moral—good triumphing over evil, for instance. The stories move directly to their conclusions, never interrupted by ingenious or unexpected twists of plot. (Love is temporarily thwarted, but the prince eventually finds Cinderella and marries her.) Finally, these tales are anchored not in specific times or places but in "Once upon a time" settings, green worlds of prehistory filled with royalty, talking animals, and magic.

Giovanni Boccaccio's *The Decameron* and Geoffrey Chaucer's *The Canterbury Tales*, both written in the fourteenth century, were precursors of the modern short story in that they included individual stories worked together thematically within a larger narrative framework. *Grimm's Fairy Tales* (1824–1826), an early collection of short narratives and folk stories, also helped to pave the way for the development of the genre, but it was not until the nineteenth century that the contemporary version of the short story emerged.

During the last quarter of the nineteenth century, a proliferation of literary and popular magazines and journals created a demand for short fiction (between 3,000 and 15,000 words) that could be encapsulated and published as a whole rather than in serial installments, as most novels at the time were. Nathaniel Hawthorne's *Twice Told Tales* (1842) and Edgar Allan Poe's *Tales of the Grotesque and Arabesque* (1836) were early collections of short stories. Americans in particular hungrily consumed the written word, and short stories soared in popularity. In fact, because the short story was embraced so readily and developed so quickly in the United States, it is commonly (although not quite accurately) thought of as an American literary form.

Defining the Short Story

Like the novel, the short story evolved from various forms of narrative and has its roots in an oral tradition. However, whereas the novel is an extended piece of narrative fiction, the **short story** is distinguished by its relative brevity, which creates a specific set of expectations and possibilities. Unlike the novelist, the short story writer cannot devote a great deal of space to developing a highly complex plot or a large number of characters. As a result, the short story often begins close to or at the height of action and is more limited in the number of characters it can develop. Usually focusing on a single incident, the writer develops one or more characters by showing their reactions to events. This attention to character development, as well as its detailed description of setting, is what distinguishes the short story from earlier short narrative forms.

In many contemporary short stories, a character experiences an **epiphany**, a moment of illumination in which something hidden or not understood becomes immediately clear. In other short stories, the thematic significance, or meaning, is communicated through the way in which the characters develop, or react, over time. Regardless of the specifics of its format or its theme, a short story offers readers an open window to a world that they can enter—if only briefly.

The short story that follows, Ernest Hemingway's "Hills Like White Elephants" (1927), illustrates many of the characteristics of the modern **short story**. Although it is so brief that it might be more accurately called a **short-short story**, it uses its limited space to establish a setting and develop two characters. From the story's first paragraph, readers know where the story takes place and whom it is about: "The American and the girl with him sat at a table in the shade, outside the building. It was very hot and the express from Barcelona would come in forty minutes." As time elapses and the man and woman wait for the train to Madrid, their strained dialogue reveals the tension between them and hints at the serious conflict they must resolve.

ERNEST HEMINGWAY (1898–1961) grew up in Oak Park, Illinois, and after high school graduation began his writing career as a cub reporter on the *Kansas City Star*. While working as a volunteer ambulance driver in World War I, eighteen-year-old Hemingway was wounded. As Hemingway himself told the story, he was hit by machine-gun fire while carrying an Italian soldier to safety. (Hemingway biographer Michael Reynolds, however, reports that Hemingway was wounded when a mortar shell fell and killed the man next to him.)

Success for Hemingway came early, with publication of the short story collection *In Our Time* (1925) and his first and most acclaimed novel, *The Sun Also Rises* (1926), a portrait of a postwar "lost generation" of Americans adrift in Europe. This group was based on his own circle of friends and their experiences, and thus the novel established Hemingway's ability to create fiction and art out of the reality of his own life. *A Farewell to Arms* (1929) harks back to his war experiences; *For Whom the Bell Tolls* (1940) emerged out of his experiences as a journalist in Spain during the Spanish Civil War. Later in life, he made his home in Key West, Florida, and then in Cuba, where he wrote *The Old Man and the Sea* (1952). In 1954, Hemingway won the Nobel Prize in Literature. In 1961, plagued by poor health and mental illness — and perhaps also by the difficulty of living up to his own image — Hemingway took his own life.

> **Cultural Context** At the time this story was written, Ernest Hemingway was part of a group of American expatriates living in Paris. Disillusioned by World War I and seeking a more bohemian lifestyle, free from the concerns of American materialism, this group of artists, intellectuals, poets, and writers were known as the "Lost Generation." Some of the group's most famous members included F. Scott Fitzgerald, Gertrude Stein, and John Dos Passos. The literary legacy they left behind is arguably one of the greatest of the twentieth century.

Hills Like White Elephants (1927)

The hills across the valley of the Ebro° were long and white. On this side there was no shade and no trees and the station was between two lines of rails in the sun. Close against the side of the station there was the warm shadow of the building and a curtain, made of strings of bamboo beads, hung across the open door into the bar, to keep out flies. The American and the girl with him sat at a table in the shade, outside the building. It was very hot and the express from Barcelona would come in forty minutes. It stopped at this junction for two minutes and went on Madrid.

"What should we drink?" the girl asked. She had taken off her hat and put it on the table.

"It's pretty hot," the man said.

"Let's drink beer."

5   "Dos cervezas," the man said into the curtain.

"Big ones?" a woman asked from the doorway.

"Yes. Two big ones."

The woman brought two glasses of beer and two felt pads. She put the felt pads and the beer glasses on the table and looked at the man and the girl. The girl was looking off at the line of hills. They were white in the sun and the country was brown and dry.

"They look like white elephants," she said.

10   "I've never seen one," the man drank his beer.

"No, you wouldn't have."

"I might have," the man said. "Just because you say I wouldn't have doesn't prove anything."

The girl looked at the bead curtain. "They've painted something on it," she said. "What does it say?"

"Anis del Toro.° It's a drink."

15   "Could we try it?"

The man called "Listen" through the curtain. The woman came out from the bar.

Ebro: A river in northern Spain.
Anis del Toro: A dark alcoholic drink made from anise, an herb that tastes like licorice.

"Four reales."°

"We want two Anis del Toro."

"With water?"

"Do you want it with water?"

"I don't know," the girl said. "Is it good with water?"   20

"It's all right."

"You want them with water?" asked the woman.

"Yes, with water."

"It tastes like licorice," the girl said and put the glass down.   25

"That's the way with everything."

"Yes," said the girl. "Everything tastes of licorice. Especially all the things you've waited so long for, like absinthe."

"Oh, cut it out."

"You started it," the girl said. "I was being amused. I was having a fine time."

"Well, let's try and have a fine time."   30

"All right I was trying. I said the mountains looked like white elephants. Wasn't that bright?"

"That was bright."

"I wanted to try this new drink. That's all we do, isn't it—look at things and try new drinks?"

"I guess so."

The girl looked across at the hills.   35

"They're lovely hills," she said. "They don't really look like white elephants. I just meant the coloring of their skin through the trees."

"Should we have another drink?"

"All right."

The warm wind blew the bead curtain against the table.

"The beer's nice and cool," the man said.   40

"It's lovely," the girl said.

"It's really an awfully simple operation, Jig," the man said. "It's not really an operation at all."

The girl looked at the ground the table legs rested on.

"I know you wouldn't mind it, Jig. It's really not anything. It's just to let the air in."

The girl did not say anything.   45

"I'll go with you and I'll stay with you all the time. They just let the air in and then it's all perfectly natural."

"Then what will we do afterward?"

"We'll be fine afterward. Just like we were before."

"What makes you think so?"

"That's the only thing that bothers us. It's the only thing that's made us un- 50 happy."

The girl looked at the bead curtain, put her hand out and took hold of two of the strings of beads.

---

reales: Spanish coins.

"And you think then we'll be all right and be happy."

"I know we will. You don't have to be afraid. I've known lots of people that have done it."

"So have I," said the girl. "And afterward they were all so happy."

55   "Well," the man said, "if you don't want to you don't have to I wouldn't have you do it if you didn't want to. But I know it's perfectly simple."

"And you really want to?"

"I think it's the best thing to do. But I don't want you to do it if you don't really want to."

"And if I do it you'll be happy and things will be like they were and you'll love me?"

"I love you now. You know I love you."

60   "I know. But if I do it, then it will be nice again if I say things are like white elephants, and you'll like it?"

"I'll love it. I love it now but I just can't think about it. You know how I get when I worry."

"If I do it you won't ever worry?"

"I won't worry about that because it's perfectly simple."

"Then I'll do it. Because I don't care about me."

65   "What do you mean?"

"I don't care about me."

"Well, I care about you."

"Oh, yes. But I don't care about me. And I'll do it and then everything will be fine."

"I don't want you to do it if you feel that way."

70   The girl stood up and walked to the end of the station. Across, on the other side, were fields of grain and trees along the banks of the Ebro. Far away beyond the river, were mountains. The shadow of a cloud moved across the field of grain and she saw the river through the trees.

"And we could have all this," she said. "And we could have everything and everyday we make it more impossible."

"What did you say?"

"I said we could have everything."

"We can have everything."

75   "No, we can't."

"We can have the whole world."

"No, we can't."

"We can go everywhere."

80   "No, we can't. It isn't ours any more."

"It's ours."

"No, it isn't. And once they take it away, you never get it back."

"But they haven't taken it away."

"We'll wait and see."

"Come on back in the shade," he said. "You mustn't feel that way."

85   "I don't feel any way," the girl said. "I just know things."

"I don't' want you to do anything that you don't want to do —."

"Nor that isn't good for me," she said. "I know. Could we have another beer?"

"All right. But you've got to realize —"

"I realize," the girl said. "Can't we maybe stop talking?"

They sat down at the table and the girl looked across at the hills on the dry 90
side of the valley and the man looked at her and at the table.

"You've got to realize," he said, "that I don't want you to do it if you don't want
to. I'm perfectly willing to go through with it if it means anything to you."

"Doesn't it mean anything to you? We could get along."

"Of course it does. But I don't want anybody but you. I don't want any one else.
And I know it's perfectly simple."

"Yes, you know it's perfectly simple."

"It's all right for you to say that, but I do know it." 95

"Would you do something for me now?"

"I'd do anything for you."

"Would you please please please please please please please stop talking?"

He did not say anything but looked at the bags against the wall of the station.
There were labels on them from all the hotels where they had spent nights.

"But I don't want you to," he said, "I don't care anything about it." 100

"I'll scream," the girl said.

The woman came out through the curtains with two glasses of beer and put
them down on the damp felt pads. "The train comes in five minutes," she said.

"What did she say?" asked the girl.

"That the train is coming in five minutes."

The girl smiled brightly at the woman, to thank her. 105

"I'd better take the bags over to the other side of the station," the man said.
She smiled at him.

"All right. Then come back and we'll finish the beer."

He picked up the two heavy bags and carried them around the station to the
other tracks. He looked up the tracks but could not see the train. Coming back,
he walked through the barroom, where people waiting for the train were drinking. He drank an Anis at the bar and looked at the people. They were all waiting
reasonably for the train. He went out through the bead curtain. She was sitting at
the table and smiled at him.

"Do you feel better?" he asked.

"I feel fine," she said. "There's nothing wrong with me. I feel fine." 110

◇ ◇ ◇

Recognizing Kinds of Fiction

As noted earlier, a **short story** is a work of fiction that is marked by its brevity,
its relatively limited scope of temporal and character development, and its ability to achieve thematic significance in a relatively short space. A **novella** (such
as Herman Melville's "Bartleby, the Scrivener," p. 731) is an extended short

story that shares some characteristics (for example, concentrated action) with a short story while retaining some qualities of a novel, including greater character development. At the other end of the spectrum are **short-short stories**, such as Luisa Valenzuela's "All about Suicide" (p. 7), which are under 1,500 words (about five pages) in length, and **flash fiction**, or **micro-fiction**, which can vary in length from 200 to 500 words. **Prose poems**, such as Carolyn Forché's, "The Colonel" (p. 1024), are hybrid versions of literature that have characteristics of both prose (being written in paragraphs) and poetry (being written in verse form, often using imagery, meter, and rhyme to convey lyrical beauty). Today, the Internet has given rise to new possibilities for arranging, presenting, and disseminating text.

There are, it seems, as many different ways to tell a story as there are stories to be told. A short story may be comic or tragic; its subject may be growing up, marriage, crime and punishment, war, sexual awakening, death, or any number of other human concerns. The setting can be an imaginary world, the old West, rural America, the jungles of Uruguay, nineteenth-century Russia, precommunist China, or modern Egypt. The story may have a conventional form, with a definite beginning, middle, and end, or it may be structured as a letter, as a diary entry, or even as a collection of random notes. The narrator of a story may be trustworthy or unreliable, involved in the action or a disinterested observer, sympathetic or deserving of scorn, extremely ignorant or highly insightful, limited in vision or able to see inside the minds of all the characters. As the selections in this anthology show, the possibilities of the short story are infinite.

CHAPTER 10

FICTION SAMPLER: THE SHORT-SHORT

This chapter will focus on the **short-short story**, a short story that is fewer than 1,500 words in length. Some short-shorts are quite conventional (that is, they include recognizable characters and have an identifiable beginning, middle, and end); others are experimental, perhaps lacking a definite setting or a clear plot. As defined by James Thomas (who, along with Robert Shepard, edited the short-short story collection *Sudden Fiction*), short-shorts are "Highly compressed, highly charged, insidious, protean, sudden, alarming, tantalizing"; they can "confer form on small corners of chaos, and, at their best, can do in a page what a novel does in two hundred."

Perhaps the most traditional of the six short-shorts that follow is Gary Gildner's "Sleepy Time Gal," which specifies a setting, develops several distinct characters, and traces a plot in a logical order. Jonathan Safran Foer's "A Primer for the Punctuation of Heart Disease" seems at first to be extremely unconventional: it uses punctuation marks and other symbols as shorthand for language and therefore has a very unusual appearance on the page. Still, despite its unconventional appearance, it has a universal theme and all-too-human characters. Essentially, it is a realistic story about a family's struggle to communicate.

The other four stories in this chapter are more experimental. Margaret Atwood's "Happy Endings" is **metafiction**, a story about the process of writing fiction, with a narrator who offers readers a choice of possible plots. In fact, Atwood herself did not quite know what to make of it. "When I wrote 'Happy Endings'" she remembers, "I did not know what sort of creature it was. It was not a poem, a short story, or a prose poem. It was not quite a condensation, a commentary, a questionnaire, and it missed being a parable, a proverb, a paradox. It was a mutation." Jamaica Kincaid's "Girl," **a stream-of-consciousness** monologue, is also unusual (the entire story is a single extended sentence), as is Amanda Holzer's "Love and Other Catastrophes: A Mix Tape," consisting entirely of a list of song titles, with no information about character or setting. Finally, Monica Ware's "Mislaid Plans" is only six sentences long; in a sense, the story's real action, which readers must infer, precedes these sentences.

Despite their brevity, the stories in this chapter have much in common with the stories that appear elsewhere in this book. Each, after all, "tells a story": characters act and events unfold.

GARY GILDNER (1938–   ) is an award-winning writer whose work includes *Blue Like the Heavens: New and Selected Poems* (1984), *Clackamas* (1991), and *The Swing* (1996), as well as a novel, *The Second Bridge* (1987), and two collections of stories, *The Crush* (1983) and *A Week in South Dakota* (1987). His popular memoir *The Warsaw Sparks* (1990) recounts his experiences as a baseball coach in Warsaw, Poland. Another memoir, *My Grandfather's Book*, was published in 2002 and was named a Top Ten University Press Book of the Year by *ForeWord Magazine*, and his most recent collection of stories, *Somewhere Geese Are Flying*, was published in 2004.

Sleepy Time Gal (1979)

In the small town in northern Michigan where my father lived as a young man, he had an Italian friend who worked in a restaurant. I will call his friend Phil. Phil's job in the restaurant was as ordinary as you can imagine —from making coffee in the morning to sweeping up at night. But what was not ordinary about Phil was his piano playing. On Saturday nights my father and Phil and their girlfriends would drive ten or fifteen miles to a roadhouse by a lake where they would drink beer from schooners and dance and Phil would play an old beat-up piano. He could play any song you named, my father said, but the song everyone waited for was the one he wrote, which he would always play at the end before they left to go back to the town. And everyone knew of course that he had written the song for his girl, who was as pretty as she was rich. Her father was the banker in their town, and he was a tough old German, and he didn't like Phil going around with his daughter.

My father, when he told the story, which was not often, would tell it in an offhand way and emphasize the Depression and not having much, instead of the important parts. I will try to tell it the way he did, if I can.

So they would go to the roadhouse by the lake, and finally Phil would play his song, and everyone would say, Phil, that's a great song, you could make a lot of money from it. But Phil would only shake his head and smile and look at his girl. I have to break in here and say that my father, a gentle but practical man, was not inclined to emphasize the part about Phil looking at his girl. It was my mother who said the girl would rest her head on Phil's shoulder while he played, and that he got the idea for the song from the pretty way she looked when she got sleepy. My mother was not part of the story, but she had heard it when she and my father were younger and therefore had that information. I would like to intrude further and add something about Phil writing the song, maybe show him whistling the tune and going over the words slowly and carefully to get the best ones, while peeling onions or potatoes in the restaurant; but my father is already driving them home from the roadhouse, and saying how patched up his tires were, and how his car's engine was a gingerbread of parts from different makes, and some parts were his own invention as well. And my mother is saying that the old German had made his daughter promise not to get involved with any man until after college, and they couldn't be late. Also my mother likes the sad parts and is eager to get to their last night before the girl goes away to college.

So they all went out to the roadhouse, and it was sad. The women got tears in their eyes when Phil played her song, my mother said. My father said that Phil spent his week's pay on a new shirt and tie, the first tie he ever owned, and people kidded him. Somebody piped up and said, Phil, you ought to take that song down to Bay City — which was like saying New York City to them, only more realistic — and sell it and take the money and go to college too. Which was not meant to be cruel, but that was the result because Phil had never even got to high school. But you can see people were trying to cheer him up, my mother said.

Well, she'd come home for Thanksgiving and Christmas and Easter and they'd 5 all sneak out to the roadhouse and drink beer from schooners and dance and everything would be like always. And of course there were the summers. And everyone knew Phil and the girl would get married after she made good her promise to her father because you could see it in their eyes when he sat at the old beat-up piano and played her song.

That last part about their eyes was not, of course, in my father's telling, but I couldn't help putting it in there even though I know it is making some of you impatient. Remember that this happened many years ago in the woods by a lake in northern Michigan, before television. I wish I could put more in, especially about the song and how it felt to Phil to sing it and how the girl felt when hearing it and knowing it was hers, but I've already intruded too much in a simple story that isn't even mine.

Well, here's the kicker part. Probably by now many of you have guessed that one vacation near the end she doesn't come home to see Phil, because she meets some guy at college who is good-looking and as rich as she is and, because her father knew about Phil all along and was pressuring her into forgetting about him, she gives in to this new guy and goes to his hometown during the vacation and falls in love with him. That's how the people in town figured it, because after she graduates they turn up, already married, and right away he takes over the old German's bank — and buys a new Pontiac at the place where my father is the mechanic and pays cash for it. The paying cash always made my father pause and shake his head and mention again that times were tough, but here comes this guy in a spiffy white shirt (with French cuffs, my mother said) and pays the full price in cash.

And this made my father shake his head too: Phil took the song down to Bay City and sold it for twenty-five dollars, the only money he ever got for it. It was the same song we'd just heard on the radio and which reminded my father of the story I just told you. What happened to Phil? Well, he stayed in Bay City and got a job managing a movie theater. My father saw him there after the Depression when he was on his way to Detroit to work for Ford. He stopped and Phil gave him a box of popcorn. The song he wrote for the girl has sold many millions of records, and if I told you the name of it you could probably sing it, or at least whistle the tune. I wonder what the girl thinks when she hears it. Oh yes, my father met Phil's wife too. She worked in the movie theater with him, selling tickets and cleaning the carpet after the show with one of those sweepers you push. She was also big and loud and nothing like the other one, my mother said.

◇ ◇ ◇

JONATHAN SAFRAN FOER (1977–   ) is an author, editor, and illustrator born in Washington, D.C. Winner of a Zoetrope Award for short fiction, Foer has had stories published in the *Paris Review, Conjunctions,* and *The New Yorker.* He edited the best-selling anthology *A Convergence of Birds: Original Fiction and Poetry Inspired by the Work of Joseph Cornell* (2001). For his first novel, *Everything Is Illuminated* (2002), Foer embarked on a journey to the Ukraine to research his grandfather's life. Among other things, the book concerns Foer's attempt to find out about the woman who may or may not have saved his grandfather from the Nazis. *Everything Is Illuminated* won The Guardian First Book Award and the National Jewish Book Award and was named Book of the Year by the *Los Angeles Times.* His second novel, *Extremely Loud and Incredibly Close,* released in 2005, relates the reactions of a nine-year-old boy to the events of 9/11.

A Primer for the Punctuation
of Heart Disease (2002)

☐ The "silence mark" signifies an absence of language, and there is at least one on every page of the story of my family life. Most often used in the conversations I have with my grandmother about her life in Europe during the war, and in conversations with my father about our family's history of heart disease — we have forty-one heart attacks between us, and counting — the silence mark is a staple of familial punctuation. Note the use of silence in the following brief exchange, when my father called me at college, the morning of his most recent angioplasty:

"Listen," he said, and then surrendered to a long pause, as if the pause were what I was supposed to listen to. "I'm sure everything's gonna be fine, but I just wanted to let you know —"

"I already know," I said.

"☐"

"☐"

5 "☐"

"☐"

"O.K.," he said.

"I'll talk to you tonight," I said, and I could hear, in the receiver, my own heartbeat.

10 He said, "Yup."

■ The "willed silence mark" signifies an intentional silence, the conversational equivalent of building a wall over which you can't climb, through which you can't see, against which you break the bones of your hands and wrists. I often inflict willed silences upon my mother when she asks about my relationships with girls. Perhaps this is because I never have *relationships* with girls — only *relations.* It depresses me to think that I've never had sex with anyone who really loved me. Sometimes I wonder if having sex with a girl who doesn't love me is like felling a tree, alone, in a forest: no one hears about it; it didn't happen.

⁇ The "insistent question mark" denotes one family member's refusal to yield to a willed silence, as in this conversation with my mother:

"Are you dating at all?"

"☐"

"But you're seeing people, I'm sure. Right?"   15

"☐"

"I don't get it. Are you ashamed of the girl? Are you ashamed of me?"

"■"

"⁇"

¡ As it visually suggests, the "unxclamation point" is the opposite of an exclama-   20
tion point; it indicates a whisper.

The best example of this usage occurred when I was a boy. My grandmother was driving me to a piano lesson, and the Volvo's wipers only moved the rain around. She turned down the volume of the second side of the seventh tape of an audio version of "Shoah,"° put her hand on my cheek, and said, "I hope that you never love anyone as much as I love you¡"

Why was she whispering? We were the only ones who could hear.

¡ ¡ Theoretically, the "extraunxclamation points" would be used to denote twice an unxclamation point, but in practice any whisper that quiet would not be heard. I take comfort in believing that at least some of the silences in my life were really extraunxclamations.

! ! The "extraexclamation points" are simply twice an exclamation point. I've never had a heated argument with any member of my family. We've never yelled at each other, or disagreed with any passion. In fact, I can't even remember a difference of opinion. There are those who would say that this is unhealthy. But, since it is the case, there exists only one instance of extraexclamation points in our family history, and they were uttered by a stranger who was vying with my fa-ther for a parking space in front of the National Zoo.

"Give it up, fucker!!" he hollered at my father, in front of my mother, my   25
brothers, and me.

"Well, I'm sorry," my father said, pushing the bridge of his glasses up his nose, "but I think it's rather obvious that we arrived at this space first. You see, we were approaching from —"

"Give . . . it . . . up . . . fucker!!"

"Well, it's just that I think I'm in the right on this particu —"

"GIVE IT UP, FUCKER!!"   30

"Give it up, Dad¡" I said, suffering a minor coronary event as my fingers clenched his seat's headrest.

"Je-sus!" the man yelled, pounding his fist against the outside of his car door. "Giveitupfucker!!"

Shoah: A 1985 documentary about the Holocaust.

Ultimately, my father gave it up, and we found a spot several blocks away. Before we got out, he pushed in the cigarette lighter, and we waited, in silence, as it got hot. When it popped out, he pushed it back in. "It's never, ever worth it," he said, turning back to us, his hand against his heart.

~ Placed at the end of a sentence, the "pedal point" signifies a thought that dissolves into a suggestive silence. The pedal point is distinguished from the ellipsis and the dash in that the thought it follows is neither incomplete nor interrupted but an outstretched hand. My younger brother uses these a lot with me, probably because he, of all the members of my family, is the one most capable of telling me what he needs to tell me without having to say it. Or, rather, he's the one whose words I'm most convinced I don't need to hear. Very often he will say, "Jonathan~" and I will say, "I know."

A few weeks ago, he was having problems with his heart. A visit to his university's health center to check out some chest pains became a trip to the emergency room became a week in the intensive-care unit. As it turns out, he's been having one long heart attack for the last six years. "It's nowhere near as bad as it sounds," the doctor told my parents, "but it's definitely something we want to take care of."

35   I called my brother that night and told him that he shouldn't worry. He said, "I know. But that doesn't mean there's nothing to worry about~"

"I know~" I said.

"I know~" he said.

"I~"

"I~"

40   "☐"

Does my little brother have relationships with girls? I don't know.

↓ Another commonly employed familial punctuation mark, the "low point," is used either in place — or for accentuation at the end — of such phrases as "This is terrible," "This is irremediable," "It couldn't possibly be worse."

"It's good to have somebody, Jonathan. It's necessary."

"☐"

45   "It pains me to think of you alone."

"■↓"

"??↓"

Interestingly, low points always come in pairs in my family. That is, the acknowledgment of whatever is terrible and irremediable becomes itself something terrible and irremediable — and often worse than the original referent. For example, my sadness makes my mother sadder than the cause of my sadness does. Of course, her sadness then makes me sad. Thus is created a "low-point chain": ↓↓↓↓ . . . ∞.

❋ The "snowflake" is used at the end of a unique familial phrase — that is, any sequence of words that has never, in the history of our family life, been assembled as such. For example, "I didn't die in the Holocaust, but all of my siblings did, so where does that leave me? ❋" Or, "My heart is no good, and I'm afraid of dying, and I'm also afraid of saying I love you.❋"

☺ The "corroboration mark" is more or less what it looks like. But it would be 50
a mistake to think that it simply stands in place of "I agree," or even "Yes."
Witness the subtle usage in this dialogue between my mother and my father:

"Could you add orange juice to the grocery list, but remember to get the kind
with reduced acid. Also some cottage cheese. And that bacon-substitute stuff.
And a few Yahrzeit candles."

"☺"

"The car needs gas. I need tampons."

"☺"

"Is Jonathan dating anyone? I'm not prying, but I'm very interested." 55

"☺"

My father has suffered twenty-two heart attacks — more than the rest of us combined. Once, in a moment of frankness after his nineteenth, he told me that his marriage to my mother had been successful because he had become a yes-man early on.

"We've only had one fight," he said. "It was in our first week of marriage. I realized that it's never, ever worth it."

My father and I were pulling weeds one afternoon a few weeks ago. He was dis-
obeying his cardiologist's order not to pull weeds. The problem, the doctor says,
is not the physical exertion but the emotional stress that weeding inflicts on my
father. He has dreams of weeds sprouting from his body, of having to pull them, at
the roots, from his chest. He has also been told not to watch Orioles games and
not to think about the current Administration.

As we weeded, my father made a joke about how my older brother, who, bar- 60
ring a fatal heart attack, was to get married in a few weeks, had already become a
yes-man. Hearing this felt like having an elephant sit on my chest — my brother,
whom I loved more than I loved myself, was surrendering.

"Your grandfather was a yes-man," my father added, on his knees, his fingers
pushing into the earth, "and your children will be yes-men."

I've been thinking about that conversation ever since, and I've come to
understand — with a straining heart — that I, too, am becoming a yes-man, and
that, like my father's and my brother's, my surrender has little to do with the
people I say yes to, or with the existence of questions at all. It has to do with a fear
of dying, with rehearsal and preparation.

✂🕸 The "severed web" is a Barely Tolerable Substitute, whose meaning
approximates "I love you," and which can be used in place of "I love
you." Other Barely Tolerable Substitutes include, but are not limited to:

→|←, which approximates "I love you."

𝕯□, which approximates "I love you." 65

🔒, which approximates "I love you."

✕✈, which approximates "I love you."

I don't know how many Barely Tolerable Substitutes there are, but often it
feels as if they were everywhere, as if everything that is spoken and done — every
"Yup," "O.K.," and "I already know," every weed pulled from the lawn, every sexual act — were just Barely Tolerable.

⁞ Unlike the colon, which is used to mark a major division in a sentence, and
to indicate that what follows is an elaboration, summation, implication,

etc., of what precedes, the "reversible colon" is used when what appears on either side elaborates, summates, implicates, etc., what's on the other side. In other words, the two halves of the sentence explain each other, as in the cases of "Mother::Me," and "Father::Death." Here are some examples of reversible sentences:

70   My eyes water when I speak about my family::I don't like to speak about my family.

I've never felt loved by anyone outside of my family::my persistent depression. 1938 to 1945::□.

Sex::yes.

My grandmother's sadness::my mother's sadness::my sadness::the sadness that will come after me.

To be Jewish::to be Jewish.

75   Heart disease::yes.

←Familial communication always has to do with failures to communicate. It is common that in the course of a conversation one of the participants will not hear something that the other has said. It is also quite common that one of the participants will not understand what the other has said. Somewhat less common is one participant's saying something whose words the other understands completely but whose meaning is not understood at all. This can happen with very simple sentences, like "I hope that you never love anyone as much as I love you¡"

But, in our best, least depressing moments, we *try* to understand what we have failed to understand. A "backup" is used: we start again at the beginning, we replay what was missed and make an effort to hear what was meant instead of what was said:

"It pains me to think of you alone."

"← It pains me to think of me without any grandchildren to love."

80   {A related set of marks, the "should-have brackets," signify words that were not spoken but should have been, as in this dialogue with my father:

"Are you hearing static?"

"{I'm crying into the phone.}"

"Jonathan?"

85   "□"

"Jonathan~"

"■"

"??"

"I::not myself~"

90   "{A child's sadness is a parent's sadness.}"

"{A parent's sadness is a child's sadness.}"

"←"

"I'm probably just tired¡"

"{I never told you this, because I thought it might hurt you, but in my dreams it was *you*. Not me. *You* were pulling the weeds from my chest.}"

"{I want to love and be loved.}"

95   "☺"

"☺"

"↓"

"↓"

"☝"

"☺"   100

"□↔□↔□"

"↓"

"↓"

"▶▶○◀◀"

"■+■→■"   105

"☺"

"♪□"

"☒ ☒"

"◎□❖◆○◆○○□◆◉●"

"■"   110

"{I love you.}"

"{I love you, too. So much.}"

Of course, my sense of the should-have is unlikely to be the same as my brothers', or my mother's, or my father's. Sometimes — when I'm in the car, or having
sex, or talking to one of them on the phone — I imagine their should-have versions. I sew them together into a new life, leaving out everything that actually
happened and was said.

◆ ◆ ◆

MARGARET ATWOOD (1939–   ) is one of the most widely read Canadian
writers of her generation. Born in Ottawa, Ontario, she was educated at Victoria
College in the University of Toronto, at Radcliffe College, and at Harvard University. Her first collection of poems, *The Circle Game*, appeared in 1964. Since then
she has produced works in many genres, including poetry, short stories, novels,
children's books, nonfiction, and scripts for television. Her most recent novel is
Oryx and Crake (2003); other novels include *The Bind Assassin* (2000), *Cat's Eye*
(1989) and *The Handmaid's Tale* (1985), adapted for the screen and released as
a film in 1990. Her poetry collections include *Selected Poems* (1976), *Selected
Poems II* (1986), and *Eating Fire: Selected Poems 1965–1995*.

Happy Endings (1983)

John and Mary meet.
What happens next?
If you want a happy ending, try A.

A. John and Mary fall in love and get married. They both have worthwhile and
    remunerative jobs which they find stimulating and challenging. They buy a

charming house. Real estate values go up. Eventually, when they can afford live-in help, they have two children, to whom they are devoted. The children turn out well. John and Mary have a stimulating and challenging sex life and worthwhile friends. They go on fun vacations together. They retire. They both have hobbies which they find stimulating and challenging. Eventually they die. This is the end of the story.

5 B. Mary falls in love with John but John doesn't fall in love with Mary. He merely uses her body for selfish pleasure and ego gratification of a tepid kind. He comes to her apartment twice a week and she cooks him dinner, you'll notice that he doesn't even consider her worth the price of a dinner out, and after he's eaten the dinner he fucks her and after that he falls asleep, while she does the dishes so he won't think she's untidy, having all those dirty dishes lying around, and puts on fresh lipstick so she'll look good when he wakes up, but when he wakes up he doesn't even notice, he puts on his socks and his shorts and his pants and his shirt and his tie and his shoes, the reverse order from the one in which he took them off. He doesn't take off Mary's clothes, she takes them off herself, she acts as if she's dying for it every time, not because she likes sex exactly, she doesn't, but she wants John to think she does because if they do it often enough surely he'll get used to her, he'll come to depend on her and they will get married, but John goes out the door with hardly so much as a good-night and three days later he turns up at six o'clock and they do the whole thing over again.

Mary gets run-down. Crying is bad for your face, everyone knows that and so does Mary but she can't stop. People at work notice. Her friends tell her John is a rat, a pig, a dog, he isn't good enough for her, but she can't believe it. Inside John, she thinks, is another John, who is much nicer. This other John will emerge like a butterfly from a cocoon, a Jack from a box, a pit from a prune, if the first John is only squeezed enough.

One evening John complains about the food. He has never complained about the food before. Mary is hurt.

Her friends tell her they've seen him in a restaurant with another woman, whose name is Madge. It's not even Madge that finally gets to Mary: it's the restaurant. John has never taken Mary to a restaurant. Mary collects all the sleeping pills and aspirins she can find, and takes them and a half a bottle of sherry. You can see what kind of a woman she is by the fact that it's not even whiskey. She leaves a note for John. She hopes he'll discover her and get her to the hospital in time and repent and then they can get married, but this fails to happen and she dies.

John marries Madge and everything continues as in A.

10 C. John, who is an older man, falls in love with Mary, and Mary, who is only twenty-two, feels sorry for him because he's worried about his hair falling out. She sleeps with him even though she's not in love with him. She met him at work. She's in love with someone called James, who is twenty-two also and not yet ready to settle down.

John on the contrary settled down long ago: this is what is bothering him. John has a steady, respectable job and is getting ahead in his field, but Mary isn't impressed by him, she's impressed by James, who has a motorcycle and a fabulous record collection. But James is often away on his motorcycle, being free. Freedom isn't the same for girls, so in the meantime Mary spends Thursday evenings with John. Thursdays are the only days John can get away.

John is married to a woman called Madge and they have two children, a charming house which they bought just before the real estate values went up, and hobbies which they find stimulating and challenging, when they have the time. John tells Mary how important she is to him, but of course he can't leave his wife because a commitment is a commitment. He goes on about this more than is necessary and Mary finds it boring, but older men can keep it up longer so on the whole she has a fairly good time.

One day James breezes in on his motorcycle with some top-grade California hybrid and James and Mary get higher than you'd believe possible and they climb into bed. Everything becomes very underwater, but along comes John, who has a key to Mary's apartment. He finds them stoned and entwined. He's hardly in any position to be jealous, considering Madge, but nevertheless he's overcome with despair. Finally he's middle-aged, in two years he'll be bald as an egg and he can't stand it. He purchases a handgun, saying he needs it for target practice — this is the thin part of the plot, but it can be dealt with later — and shoots the two of them and himself.

Madge, after a suitable period of mourning, marries an understanding man called Fred and everything continues as in A, but under different names.

D. Fred and Madge have no problems. They get along exceptionally well and are good at working out any little difficulties that may arise. But their charming house is by the seashore and one day a giant tidal wave approaches. Real estate values go down. The rest of the story is about what caused the tidal wave and how they escape from it. They do, though thousands drown, but Fred and Madge are virtuous and lucky. Finally on high ground they clasp each other, wet and dripping and grateful, and continue as in A.

E. Yes, but Fred has a bad heart. The rest of the story is about how kind and understanding they both are until Fred dies. Then Madge devotes herself to charity work until the end of A. If you like, it can be "Madge," "cancer," "guilty and confused," and "bird watching."

F. If you think this is all too bourgeois, make John a revolutionary and Mary a counterespionage agent and see how far that gets you. Remember, this is Canada. You'll still end up with A, though in between you may get a lustful brawling saga of passionate involvement, a chronicle of our times, sort of.

You'll have to face it, the endings are the same however you slice it. Don't be deluded by any other endings, they're all fake, either deliberately fake, with malicious intent to deceive, or just motivated by excessive optimism if not by downright sentimentality.

The only authentic ending is the one provided here:
John and Mary die. John and Mary die. John and Mary die.

20   So much for endings. Beginnings are always more fun. True connoisseurs, however, are known to favor the stretch in between, since it's the hardest to do anything with.

That's about all that can be said for plots, which anyway are just one thing after another, a what and a what and a what.

Now try How and Why.

◇ ◇ ◇

JAMAICA KINCAID (1949–   ) was born Elaine Potter Richardson on the island of Antigua, where she received a British education and was often at the top of her class. In early childhood, she was very close to her mother, but when she was nine, her mother gave birth to three sons in quick succession, which altered their relationship forever. According to Kincaid, she was treated badly and neglected, and she left Antigua in 1965 to work as an au pair in Westchester, New York. She went on to study photography at the New York School for Social Research and attended Franconia College in New Hampshire for a year. In 1973, after having begun her writing career, she changed her name to Jamaica Kincaid because her family disapproved of her writing. She soon began writing a regular column for the *New Yorker*. Her best-known works include the novel *Annie John* (1986) and the nonfiction book *A Small Place* (1988), which criticizes British Colonialism in Antigua. Her most recent books are *Talk Stories* (2001) and *My Favorite Tool* (2005).

Girl (1984)

Wash the white clothes on Monday and put them on the stone heap; wash the color clothes on Tuesday and put them on the clothesline to dry; don't walk barehead in the hot sun; cook pumpkin fritters in very hot sweet oil; soak your little clothes right after you take them off; when buying cotton to make yourself a nice blouse, be sure that it doesn't have gum on it, because that way it won't hold up well after a wash; soak salt fish overnight before you cook it; is it true that you sing benna° in Sunday School?; always eat your food in such a way that it won't turn someone else's stomach; on Sundays try to walk like a lady and not like the slut you are so bent on becoming; don't sing benna in Sunday School; you mustn't speak to wharf-rat boys, not even to give directions; don't eat fruits on the street — flies will follow you; *but I don't sing benna on Sundays at all and never in Sunday school;* this is how to sew on a button; this is how to make a buttonhole for the button you have just sewed on; this is how to hem a dress when you see the hem coming down and so to prevent yourself from looking like the slut I know you are so bent on becoming; this is how you iron

---

benna: Calypso music.

your father's khaki shirt so that it doesn't have a crease; this is how you iron your father's khaki pants so that they don't have a crease; this is how you grow okra — far from the house, because okra tree harbors red ants; when you are growing dasheen, make sure it gets plenty of water or else it makes your throat itch when you are eating it; this is how you sweep a corner; this is how you sweep a whole house; this is how you sweep a yard; this is how you smile to someone you don't like too much; this is how you smile to someone you don't like at all; this is how you smile to someone you like completely; this is how you set a table for tea; this is how you set a table for dinner; this is how you set a table for dinner with an important guest; this is how you set a table for lunch; this is how you set a table for breakfast; this is how to behave in the presence of men who don't know you very well, and this way they won't recognize immediately the slut I have warned you against becoming; be sure to wash every day, even if it is with your own spit; don't squat down to play marbles — you are not a boy, you know; don't pick people's flowers — you might catch something; don't throw stones at blackbirds, because it might not be a blackbird at all; this is how to make a bread pudding; this is how to make doukona;° this is how to make pepper pot; this is how to make a good medicine for a cold; this is how to make a good medicine to throw away a child before it even becomes a child; this is how to catch a fish; this is how to throw back a fish you don't like, and that way something bad won't fall on you; this is how to bully a man; this is how a man bullies you; this is how to love a man, and if this doesn't work there are other ways, and if they don't work don't feel too bad about giving up; this is how to spit up in the air if you feel like it, and this is how to move quick so that it doesn't fall on you; this is how to make ends meet; always squeeze bread to make sure it's fresh; *but what if the baker won't let me feel the bread?*; you mean to say that after all you are really going to be the kind of woman who the baker won't let near the bread?

◆ ◆ ◆

AMANDA HOLZER (1981–   ) is a graduate of Emerson College. "Love and Other Catastrophes" was first published in 2002 in *Story Quarterly* and was reprinted in *Best American Non-Required Reading 2003*.

Love and Other Catastrophes: A Mix Tape   (2002)

"All By Myself" (Eric Carmen). "Looking for Love" (Lou Reed). "I Wanna Dance With Somebody" (Whitney Houston). "Let's Dance" (David Bowie). "Let's Kiss" (Beat Happening). "Let's Talk About Sex" (Salt N' Pepa). "Like A Virgin" (Madonna). "We've Only Just Begun" (The Carpenters). "I Wanna Be Your

---

doukona: Spicy plantain pudding.

Boyfriend" (The Ramones). "I'll Tumble 4 Ya" (Culture Club). "Head Over Heels" (The Go-Go's). "Nothing Compares To You" (Sinéad O'Connor). "My Girl" (The Temptations). "Could This Be Love?" (Bob Marley). "Love and Marriage" (Frank Sinatra). "White Wedding" (Billy Idol). "Stuck in the Middle with You" (Steelers Wheel). "Tempted" (The Squeeze). "There Goes My Baby" (The Drifters). "What's Going On?" (Marvin Gaye). "Where Did You Sleep Last Night?" (Leadbelly) "Whose Bed Have Your Boots Been Under?" (Shania Twain). "Jealous Guy" (John Lennon). "Your Cheatin' Heart" (Tammy Wynette). "Shot Through the Heart" (Bon Jovi). "Don't Go Breaking My Heart" (Elton John and Kiki Dee). "My Achy Breaky Heart" (Billy Ray Cyrus). "Heartbreak Hotel" (Elvis Presley), "Stop, In the Name of Love" (The Supremes). "Try a Little Tenderness" (Otis Redding). "Try (Just a Little Bit Harder)" (Janis Joplin). "All Apologies" (Nirvana). "Hanging on the Telephone" (Blondie). "I Just Called to Say I Love You" (Stevie Wonder). "Love Will Keep Us Together" (Captain and Tennille). "Let's Stay Together" (Al Green). "It Ain't Over 'Till It's Over" (Lenny Kravitz). "What's Love Got To Do With It? (Tina Turner). "You Don't Bring Me Flowers Anymore" (Barbara Streisand and Neil Diamond). "I Wish You Wouldn't Say That" (Talking Heads). "You're So Vain" (Carly Simon). "Love is a Battlefield" (Pat Benatar). "Heaven Knows I'm Miserable Now" (The Smiths). "(Can't Get No) Satisfaction" (Rolling Stones). "Must Have Been Love (But It's Over Now)" (Roxette). "Breaking Up is Hard to Do" (Neil Sedaka). "I Will Survive" (Gloria Gaynor). "Hit the Road, Jack" (Mary McCaslin and Jim Ringer). "These Boots Were Made for Walking" (Nancy Sinatra). "All Out of Love" (Air Supply). "All By Myself" (Eric Carmen).

◇ ◇ ◇

MONICA WARE

Mislaid Plans

A rash of new bills came that morning. The letter from their insurance company announced the cancellation of their policies.

She sighed and rose wearily to tell her husband. The kitchen smelled of gas. On his desk she found the note.

"… the money from my life insurance will be enough for you and the children…"

◇ ◇ ◇

Reading and Reacting

1. Aside from "Sleepy Time Gal," which of the six short-short stories in this chapter seems most conventional? Which seems least conventional? Explain.

2. Does each story seem complete? What, if anything, seems to be missing from each story that might be present in a longer story?

3. If you were going to add material to "Mislaid Plans," what would you add? Why?

4. How would "A Primer for the Punctuation of Heart Disease" be different without the highlighted punctuation marks and other symbols? Are they necessary to the story, or are they just embellishment?

5. How would "Girl" be different if the story were told by the person whom the narrator is addressing? If the story included dialogue?

6. Consider the writing "advice" presented in "Happy Endings." Does the advice seem to apply to the other stories in this chapter? Explain.

WRITING SUGGESTIONS

1. Write an **explication** (see Chapter 3) of another short-short story in this book—for example, Kate Chopin's "Story of an Hour" or Naguib Mafouz's "Half a Day."

2. Compare "A Primer for the Punctuation of Heart Disease" with another story about family relationships—or, compare "Love and Other Catastrophes: A Mix Tape" with one of the love poems in Chapter 32.

3. Write a "mix tape" story about an experience in your own life.

CHAPTER 11

READING AND WRITING ABOUT FICTION

Reading Fiction

As you read works of short fiction, you should pay careful attention to elements such as plot; character; setting; point of view; style, tone, and language; symbol, allegory, and myth; and theme. By looking at these elements you will be able to understand and appreciate the story more fully. The following guidelines, designed to help you explore works of fiction, focus on issues that are examined in depth in chapters to come:

- *Look at the **plot** of the story.* How do the events in the story relate to one another, and how do they relate to the story as a whole? What conflicts occur in the story, and how are these conflicts developed or resolved? Does the story include any noteworthy plot devices, such as flashbacks or foreshadowing? (See Chapter 12.)
- *Analyze the **characters** of the story.* What are their most striking traits? How do these individuals interact with one another? What motivates them? Are the characters fully developed, or are they stereotypes whose sole purpose is to express a single trait (innocence, evil, generosity) or to move the plot along? (See Chapter 13.)
- *Identify the **setting** of the story.* At what time period, and in what geographic location, does the action of the story occur? How does the setting affect the characters? How does it affect their relationships? How does it affect the plot? Does the setting create a mood for the story? In what way does the setting reinforce the central ideas that the story examines? (See Chapter 14.)
- *Examine the narrative **point of view** of the story.* Who is telling the story? Is the story told by an outside narrator? Is the story told from the perspective of a character? If so, is the narrator a major character telling his or her own story or a minor character who witnesses events? How much does this narrator know about the events in the story? Does the narrator present an accurate picture of events? Does the narrator understand the full significance of the story he or she is telling? (See Chapter 15.)
- *Analyze the **style, tone,** and **language** of the story.* Does the writer make any unusual use of diction or syntax? Does the writer use imaginative figures

of speech? Patterns of imagery? What styles or levels of speech are associated with particular characters? What words or phrases are repeated throughout the work? Is the story's style plain or elaborate? Does the narrator's tone reveal his or her attitude toward characters or events? Is the tone of the story playful, humorous, ironic, satirical, serious, somber, solemn, bitter, condescending, formal, or informal — or does the tone suggest some other attitude? (See Chapter 16.)

- *Focus on **symbol, allegory, and myth**.* Does the author use any objects or ideas symbolically? What characters or objects in the story are part of an allegorical framework? How does an object establish its symbolic or allegorical significance in the story? Does the same object have different meanings at different places in the story? Are the symbols or allegorical figures conventional or unusual? At what points in the story do symbols or allegorical figures appear? Does the story allude to a myth? (See Chapter 17.)

- *Identify the **themes** of the story.* What is the central theme? How is this idea or concept expressed in the work? What elements of the story develop the central theme? How do character, plot, setting, point of view, and symbols reinforce the central theme? How does the title of the story contribute to readers' understanding of the central theme? What other themes are explored? (See Chapter 18.)

Active Reading

John Frei, a student in an Introduction to Literature course, was assigned to write a three- to four-page essay on a topic of his choice, focusing on any short story in this literature anthology, without consulting outside sources. After considering a number of possible choices, John selected Alberto Alvaro Ríos's "The Secret Lion."

ALBERTO ALVARO RÍOS (1952–   ) was born and raised in the border town of Nogales, Arizona, the son of a Mexican father and an English mother. He is the author of eight books and chapbooks of poetry, including *The Smallest Muscle in the Human Body* (2002), *Teodoro Luna's Two Kisses* (1990), *The Warrington Poems* (1989), *Lime Orchard Woman* (1988), and *Whispering to Fool the Wind* (1982), which won the American Academy of Poets Walt Whitman Award. His collections of short stories include *The Curtain of Trees* (1999), *Pig Cookies and Other Stories* (1995), and *The Iguana Killer: Twelve Stories of the Heart* (1984), in which "The Secret Lion" appeared. *Capirotada,* which was published in 1999, is a memoir about growing up on the Mexican border. Ríos is presently Regents' Professor of English at Arizona State University.

Reviewer Mary Logue, writing in the *Village Voice Literary Supplement,* observes that Ríos's writings "carry the feel of another world. . . . Ríos's tongue is both foreign and familiar," reflecting an upbringing "where one is neither in this country nor the other." In many of his stories, Ríos expresses the seeming "other-ness" of Anglo culture as seen through the eyes of Chicano children: a little boy frightened by the sight of his first snowfall or (as in "The Secret Lion") boys amazed by the otherworldly sight of "heaven." Through Ríos's children, we see our own world with new eyes.

Cultural Context With their rolling hills, freshwater ponds, lush greens, and fastidiously trimmed turf, golf courses are designed to convey a sense of wealth and comfort,
typically providing recreation for the middle and upper classes. In a dry region — or
even in a densely populated city — an irrigated, sculpted golf course may look like an oasis
in the desert. The golf course that plays a role in this story is probably (like many others)
part of a privately owned, exclusive country club.

The Secret Lion   (1984)

I was twelve and in junior high school and something happened that we didn't
have a name for, but it was there nonetheless like a lion, and roaring, roaring that
way the biggest things do. Everything changed. Just that. Like the rug, the one
that gets pulled — or better, like the tablecloth those magicians pull where the
stuff on the table stays the same but the gasp! from the audience makes the
staying-the-same part not matter. Like that.

What happened was there were teachers now, not just one teacher, teach-erz,
and we felt personally abandoned somehow. When a person had all these teachers
now, he didn't get taken care of the same way, even though six was more than one.
Arithmetic went out the door when we walked in. And we saw girls now, but they
weren't the same girls we used to know because we couldn't talk to them anymore,
not the same way we used to, certainly not to Sandy, even though she was my neighbor, too. Not even to her. She just played the piano all the time. And there were
words, oh there were words in junior high school, and we wanted to know what they
were, and how a person did them — that's what school was supposed to be for. Only,
in junior high school, school wasn't school, everything was backward-like. If you
went up to a teacher and said the word to try and find out what it meant you got in
trouble for saying it. So we didn't. And we figured it must have been that way about
other stuff, too, so we never said anything about anything — we weren't stupid.

But my friend Sergio and I, we solved junior high school. We would come
home from school on the bus, put our books away, change shoes, and go across the
highway to the arroyo. It was the one place we were not supposed to go. So we
did. This was, after all, what junior high had at least shown us. It was our river,
though, our personal Mississippi, our friend from long back, and it was full of stories and all the branch forts we had built in it when we were still the Vikings of
America, with our own symbol, which we had carved everywhere, even in the
sand, which let the water take it. That was good, we had decided; whoever was at
the end of this river would know about us.

At the very very top of our growing lungs, what we would do down there was
shout every dirty word we could think of, in every combination we could come up
with, and we would yell about girls, and all the things we wanted to do with them,
as loud as we could — we didn't know what we wanted to do with them, just
things — and we would yell about teachers, and how we loved some of them, like
Miss Crevelone, and how we wanted to dissect some of them, making signs of the
cross, like priests, and we would yell this stuff over and over because it felt good,

we couldn't explain why, it just felt good and for the first time in our lives there was nobody to tell us we couldn't. So we did.

One Thursday we were walking along shouting this way, and the railroad, the 5 Southern Pacific, which ran above and along the far side of the arroyo, had dropped a grinding ball down there, which was, we found out later, a cannonball thing used in mining. A bunch of them were put in a big vat which turned around and crushed the ore. One had been dropped, or thrown — what do caboose men do when they get bored — but it got down there regardless and as we were walking along yelling about one girl or another, a particular Claudia, we found it, one of these things, looked at it, picked it up, and got very very excited, and held it and passed it back and forth, and we were saying "Guythisis, this is, geeGuythis…": we had this perception about nature then, that nature is imperfect and that round things are perfect: we said "GuyGodthis is perfect, thisisthis is perfect, it's round, round and heavy, it'sit's the best thing we'veeverseen. Whatisit?" We didn't know. We just knew it was great. We just, whatever, we played with it, held it some more.

And then we had to decide what to do with it. We knew, because of a lot of things, that if we were going to take this and show it to anybody, this discovery, this best thing, was going to be taken away from us. That's the way it works with little kids, like all the polished quartz, the tons of it we had collected piece by piece over the years. Junior high kids too. If we took it home, my mother, we knew, was going to look at it and say "throw that dirty thing in the, get rid of it." Simple like, like that. "But ma it's the best thing I" "Getridofit." Simple.

So we didn't. Take it home. Instead, we came up with the answer. We dug a hole and buried it. And we marked it secretly. Lots of secret signs. And came back the next week to dig it up and, we didn't know, pass it around some more or something, but we didn't find it. We dug up that whole bank, and we never found it again. We tried.

Sergio and I talked about that ball or whatever it was when we couldn't find it. All we used were small words, neat, good. Kid words. What we were really saying, but didn't know the words, was how much that ball was like that place, that whole arroyo: couldn't tell anybody about it, didn't understand what it was, didn't have a name for it. It just felt good. It was just perfect in the way it was that place, that whole going to that place, that whole junior high school lion. It was just iron-heavy, it had no name, it felt good or not, we couldn't take it home to show our mothers, and once we buried it, it was gone forever.

The ball was gone, like the first reasons we had come to that arroyo years earlier, like the first time we had seen the arroyo, it was gone like everything else that had been taken away. This was not our first lesson. We stopped going to the arroyo after not finding the thing, the same way we had stopped going there years earlier and headed for the mountains. Nature seemed to keep pushing us around one way or another, teaching us the same thing every place we ended up. Nature's gang was tough that way, teaching us stuff.

When we were young we moved away from town, me and my family. Sergio's 10 was already out there. Out in the wilds. Or at least the new place seemed like the wilds since everything looks bigger the smaller a man is. I was five, I guess, and we had moved three miles north of Nogales where we had lived, three miles north of the Mexican border. We looked across the highway in one direction and there was the arroyo; hills stood up in the other direction. Mountains, for a small man.

When the first summer came the very first place we went to was of course the one place we weren't supposed to go, the arroyo. We went down in there and found water running, summer rain water mostly, and we went swimming. But every third or fourth or fifth day, the sewage treatment plant that was, we found out, upstream, would release whatever it was that it released, and we would never know exactly what day that was, and a person really couldn't tell right off by looking at the water, not every time, not so a person could get out in time. So, we went swimming that summer and some days we had a lot of fun. Some days we didn't. We found a thousand ways to explain what happened on those other days, constructing elaborate stories about the neighborhood dogs, and hadn't she, my mother, miscalculated her step before, too? But she knew something was up because we'd come running into the house those days, wanting to take a shower, even — if this can be imagined — in the middle of the day.

That was the first time we stopped going to the arroyo. It taught us to look the other way. We decided, as the second side of summer came, we wanted to go into the mountains. They were still mountains then. We went running in one summer Thursday morning, my friend Sergio and I, into my mother's kitchen, and said, well, what'zin, what'zin those hills over there — we used her word so she'd understand us — and she said nothingdon'tworryaboutit. So we went out, and we weren't dumb, we thought with our eyes to each other, ohhoshe'stryingtokeep-somethingfromus. We knew adults.

We had read the books, after all; we knew about bridges and castles and wildtreacherousraging alligatormouth rivers. We wanted them. So we were going to go out and get them. We went back that morning into that kitchen and we said, "We're going out there, we're going into the hills, we're going away for three days, don't worry." She said, "All right."

"You know," I said to Sergio, "if we're going to go away for three days, well, we ought to at least pack a lunch."

15   But we were two young boys with no patience for what we thought at the time was mom-stuff: making sa-and-wiches. My mother didn't offer. So we got out little kid knapsacks that my mother had sewn for us, and into them we put the jar of mustard. A loaf of bread. Knivesforksplates, bottles of Coke, a can opener. This was lunch for the two of us. And we were weighed down, humped over to be strong enough to carry this stuff. But we started walking anyway, into the hills. We were going to eat berries and stuff otherwise. "Goodbye." My mom said that.

After the first hill we were dead. But we walked. My mother could still see us. And we kept walking. We walked until we got to where the sun is straight overhead, noon. That place. Where that is doesn't matter; it's time to eat. The truth is we weren't anywhere close to that place. We just agreed that the sun was overhead and that it was time to eat, and by tilting our heads a little we could make that the truth.

"We really ought to start looking for a place to eat."

"Yeah. Let's look for a good place to eat." We went back and forth saying that for fifteen minutes, making it lunchtime because that's what we always said back and forth before lunchtimes at home. "Yeah, I'm hungry all right." I nodded my head. "Yeah, I'm hungry all right too. I'm hungry." He nodded his head. I nodded my head back. After a good deal more nodding, we were ready, just as we came over a little hill. We hadn't found the mountains yet. This was a little hill.

And on the other side of this hill we found heaven.

It was just what we thought it would be.   20

Perfect. Heaven was green, like nothing else in Arizona. And it wasn't a cemetery or like that because we had seen cemeteries and they had gravestones and stuff and this didn't. This was perfect, had trees, lots of trees, had birds, like we had never seen before. It was like "The Wizard of Oz," like when they got to Oz and everything was so green, so emerald, they had to wear those glasses, and we ran just like them, laughing, laughing that way we did that moment, and we went running down to this clearing in it all, hitting each other that good way we did.

We got down there, we kept laughing, we kept hitting each other, we unpacked our stuff, and we started acting "rich." We knew all about how to do that, like blowing on our nails, then rubbing them on our chests for the shine. We made our sandwiches, opened our Cokes, got out the rest of the stuff, the salt and pepper shakers. I found this particular hole and I put my Coke right into it, a perfect fit, and I called it my Coke-holder. I got down next to it on my back, because everyone knows that rich people eat lying down, and I got my sandwich in one hand and put my other arm around the Coke in its holder. When I wanted a drink, I lifted my neck a little, put out my lips, and tipped my Coke a little with the crook of my elbow. Ah.

We were there, lying down, eating our sandwiches, laughing, throwing bread at each other and out for the birds. This was heaven. We were laughing and we couldn't believe it. My mother was keeping something from us, ah ha, but we had found her out. We even found water over at the side of the clearing to wash our plates with — we had brought plates. Sergio started washing his plates when he was done, and I was being rich with my Coke, and this day in summer was right.

When suddenly these two men came, from around a corner of trees and the tallest grass we had ever seen. They had bags on their backs, leather bags, bags and sticks.

We didn't know what clubs were, but I learned later, like I learned about the   25
grinding balls. The two men yelled at us. Most specifically, one wanted me to take my Coke out of my Coke-holder so he could sink his golf ball into it.

Something got taken away from us that moment. Heaven. We grew up a little bit, and couldn't go backward. We learned. No one had ever told us about golf. They had told us about heaven. And it went away. We got golf in exchange.

We went back to the arroyo for the rest of that summer, and tried to have fun the best we could. We learned to be ready for finding the grinding ball. We loved it, and when we buried it we knew what would happen. The truth is, we didn't look so hard for it. We were two boys and twelve summers then, and not stupid. Things get taken away.

We buried it because it was perfect. We didn't tell my mother, but together it was all we talked about, till we forgot. It was the lion.

◇ ◇ ◇

Previewing

Student John Frei began the reading process by previewing his text. A quick glance at the story showed him that it was quite short (under five pages), that it was written in the first person ("I was twelve"), that it included dialogue as well as narrative, and that it had an interesting title.

Previewing "The Secret Lion" prepared John to read it more closely and, eventually, to write about it. In preparation for writing, he read and reread the story, highlighting and annotating it as he went along.

Highlighting and Annotating

As he reread the story, John highlighted words and ideas that he thought might be useful to him, indicated possible connections among ideas, and wrote down questions and comments as they occurred to him. During this process, he considered the meaning of the term *secret lion*, and he paid close attention to the narrator's voice. The highlighted and annotated passage that follows illustrates his responses to the last five paragraphs of the story.

When suddenly these two men came, from around a corner of trees and the tallest grass we had ever seen. They had bags on their backs, leather bags, bags and sticks.

pt. of view

We didn't know what clubs were, but I learned later, like I learned about the grinding balls. The two men yelled at us. Most specifically, one wanted me to take my Coke out of my Coke-holder so he could sink his golf ball into it.

Heaven = innocence

Golf = adulthood

Something got taken away from us that moment. Heaven. We grew up a little bit, and couldn't go backward. We learned. No one had ever told us about golf. They had told us about heaven. And it went away. We got golf in exchange.

Things lose their magic + special-ness.

We went back to the arroyo for the rest of that summer, and tried to have fun the best we could. We learned to be ready for finding the grinding ball. We loved it, and when we buried it we knew what would happen. The truth is, we didn't look so hard for it. We were two boys and twelve summers then, and not stupid. Things get taken away.

Loss of inno-cence, trust, belief in perfection.

We buried it because it was perfect. We didn't tell my mother but together it was all we talked about, till we forgot. It was the lion.

ball?

Lion=knowledge that growing up=loss? or is lion growing up itself?

John's highlighting and annotation of the entire story suggested a number of interesting possibilities for his paper. First, he noticed that the story contrasts the narrator's childhood innocence with his adult knowledge. John's highlighting also identified some unusual stylistic features, such as words run together ("Getridofit") and the repetition of words like *neat* and *perfect*. Finally, he noticed that four items — the arroyo, the grinding ball, the golf course, and the lion — are mentioned again and again. This repetition led him to suspect that one or more of these items — particularly the secret lion, prominently mentioned in the story's title — might have symbolic significance.

Writing about Fiction

Planning an Essay

At this stage, John had not thought of a topic; he knew only that he would be writing a paper on "The Secret Lion." However, his previewing, highlighting, and annotations had revealed some interesting ideas about style and point of view — and, possibly, about symbolism. Now, because his paper was to be no more than four pages long, he needed to select one element on which to concentrate.

Choosing a Topic

John decided to explore possible topics in his journal. Here are his journal entries on the story's style and point of view.

```
Style—Style is informal, with lots of contractions and
slang terms like "neat." Words are run together. Most of
the time, the boys combine words to indicate something
unimportant to them. When they're packing the lunch, they
include "knivesforksplates." They're not interested in
packing the lunch—they just want to get to the "mountains."
Packing lunch is very important to the mother, so
she does the opposite of combining words: she breaks them
down ("sa-and-wiches"). This style can get pretty
annoying.

    Point of view—We see the story through the eyes of the
narrator, who is a character in the story. Sergio is
developed along with the narrator as part of a "we." The
characters are not really individuals—they function as "we"
for most of the story. We don't see into the minds of the
boys to any great extent. The narrator has a double
perspective: he takes readers back to his childhood,
and this helps us understand the boys' excitement and
disappointment, but he also shows us how much more he knows
now, so we know that too.
```

John had no trouble writing paragraphs on style and point of view in his journal, but he ran out of ideas quickly; he knew that he did not have enough material for a paper about either of these two topics. When he started to write a journal entry about the symbolic significance of certain elements in the story, however, he found that he had a lot more to say. As a result, he chose "Symbols in 'The Secret Lion'" as his paper's topic. Here is his journal entry on symbolism.

```
Symbolism—The arroyo, the grinding ball, the golf
course, and of course the secret lion all seem to mean
something beyond their literal meanings as objects and
places. (Maybe the "mountains" do too.) For one thing,
they're all repeated over and over again. Also, they all
seem to be related somehow to magic and perfection and
surprise and expectation and idealism (and, later, to
disillusionment and disappointment). If this is a story
about growing up, these things could be related to that
theme.
```

Finding Something to Say

Brainstorming Once he decided to write about symbolism, John moved on to brainstorm about his topic, focusing on what he considered the story's most important — and most obvious — symbol: the secret lion itself.

```
(Lion) = "roaring, roaring that way the biggest things do"


    EVERYTHING CHANGED          (= secret because it's

                                something they have to find

                                out on their own, not from

                                adults?)
    (Tableclothrug (= magic).   "Staying-the-same part" is
                                    most important—why?

    (Arroyo:)not supposed to go (= rebellion)—Mississippi,

        "friend from long back"; freedom. Place that doesn't

        change.

    (Grinding ball)—Perfection in imperfect world,
```

innocence in adult world. "Nature = imperfect," but

"round things = "perfect"—"the best thing." ("That

ball was like that place, that whole arroyo")

Buried and "gone forever"—"taken away" (like arroyo)

Mountains: "everything looks bigger the smaller

a man is"; hills = "Mountains for a small man."

(Mother calls them hills)

Arroyo = polluted with sewage (never know when it's

perfect"
×3

coming)—went to mts. On other side of hills = golf course

(= heaven) "perfect"

*Like Oz—green, emerald

*Place to act "rich"

*Men with clubs =

reality, future

(= end of innocence)

"Things get taken away" : heaven, ball (something

buried and lost), arroyo

"We buried it because it was "perfect." ... It

was the lion."

Lion = secret place inside us that still craves

childhood (as adults, we learn we have to keep it

buried, like ball). *How can a "roaring" lion be secret?

Seeing Connections: Listing

When John looked over his brainstorming notes in search of an organizing scheme for his paper, he saw that he had plenty of information about the secret lion, the arroyo, the grinding ball, and the golf course. His most obvious option was to discuss one item at a time, but he knew that he needed to find something that would tie the four separate items together. When he noticed that each item seemed to have different meanings at different periods of the boys' lives, he realized that his essay could discuss how these meanings change as the boys move from childhood to adolescence to adulthood. He experimented with this possibility as he grouped related details in the following lists.

The secret lion
Beginning: "raging beast" inside of them (6th grade class) =
      frustration, puberty
Beginning: "roaring, roaring that way the biggest things
      do"
Middle: "that whole junior high school lion"
End: Lion = greatness, something important (also =
      puberty?)
Also = great discoveries they expect to make in their
      lives.
End: "It was the lion."

Arroyo
Place that doesn't change (= childhood); constant in
      their changing lives. (But it changes too)
Mississippi—horizons
Freedom of childhood
Waste dump

Grinding ball
Perfection (in imperfect world)
Childhood innocence (in adult world)
Undiscovered knowledge?
Secrets of childhood (buried)
Something lost: "Things get taken away"

Golf course
Heaven—knowledge that there is no heaven, that it's a
      fraud, like the Wizard of Oz.
Adulthood—men with clubs
Scene of remembered humiliation
End of innocence (realization that it's just a golf
      course)

John's lists confirmed that the meanings of the four items did seem to change as the boys grew up. To the boys, the arroyo, the grinding ball, and the golf course are magical, but when they grow up, all three items lose their magic and became ordinary. The secret lion, however, seemed more complex than the other three items, and John knew that he would have to develop his ideas further before he could show how the lion's meaning changes and how these changes affect the story as a whole.

Deciding on a Thesis

With his ideas organized into lists that clarified some possible relationships among them, John began to see a central idea for his essay. He expressed this idea in a tentative **thesis statement**, a sentence that he could use to guide his essay's first draft. (For a full discussion of this stage of the writing process, see "Deciding on a Thesis," p. 27, in Chapter 2.) This thesis statement appears below.

```
The meanings of the story's key symbols change as the boys
move from childhood to adolescence to adulthood; these
changes reveal corresponding changes in the boys' view of
the world as they move from idealism to frustration to
resignation.
```

Preparing an Outline

Even though his essay was to be short, John prepared a scratch outline that mapped out an arrangement for his ideas. He decided to discuss the four key symbols one by one, tracing each through the boys' childhood, adolescence, and adulthood. He planned to discuss the lion last because he saw it as the story's most important symbol. Looking back over all his notes, and paying close attention to his tentative thesis statement, John constructed this scratch outline.

```
Arroyo
    Mississippi
    Rebellion
    Waste dump

Grinding ball
    [Not yet discovered]
    Lost perfection
    "Things get taken away."

Golf course
    "Heaven"
    Humiliation
    Golf course

Lion
    [Not yet discovered]
    "roaring"; "raging beast"
    Just the lion
```

Drafting an Essay

Guided by his scratch outline, his tentative thesis statement, and his notes, John wrote the following first draft.

first draft

Symbols in "The Secret Lion"

"The Secret Lion" is a story that is rich in symbols. It is also a story about change. The meanings of the story's key symbols change as the boys move from childhood to adolescence to adulthood; these changes reveal corresponding changes in the boys' view of the world as they move from idealism to frustration to resignation.

The arroyo, a dry gulch that can fill up with water, is special to the narrator and his friend Sergio when they are boys. Literally, it is a place to play. Symbolically, it is a place to rebel (they're not supposed to be there; they yell forbidden words). It could also symbolize all the discoveries they will make before they are completely grown up. To the young boys, the arroyo symbolizes a retreat from the disappointment of the golf course; it is their second choice. Later, it represents adventure, the uncertainty and unpredictability of adolescence, as illustrated by the fact that they cannot tell just by looking at it from the riverside whether the river was going to be tainted with sewage. When they are children, it is their Mississippi. When they are adolescents, it is a place to hang out and a symbol of adolescent rebellion; as an adult, the narrator looks back at it for what it was: an ordinary river polluted by sewage. The arroyo doesn't change, but the boys' view of it changes as they change.

At first, when they find the grinding ball, it

stands for everything that is perfect and fascinating
(and therefore forbidden and unattainable) in life.
Like a child's life, it is perfect. They knew they
couldn't keep it forever, just as they couldn't be
children forever, so they buried it. When they tried
to look for it again, they couldn't find it. They
admit later that they don't look very hard. (People
always wish they can find youth again, but they
can't.) The ball represents perfection in an
imperfect world, childhood innocence in an adult
world. They hide it from their mother because they
know she won't see it as perfect; she'll make them
"getridofit" (171). They hide it because they want to
retain the excitement of the undiscovered, but once
they've used it and seen it and buried it, it's not
new anymore. Even if they'd been able to find it, it
would still be lost. To the adult narrator, it's just
an ordinary object used in mining.

The golf course, which they wander into at age
five, is, for a short period of time, "heaven" (173).
It is lush and green and carefully cared for, and it
is the opposite of the polluted arroyo. It is also
another world, as mysterious as the Land of Oz. With
the realization that it is not heaven to the golfers,
the boys see what outsiders they really are. They may
start "acting 'rich'" (173), but it will be just an
act. There are no Coke-holders, no Oz, no heaven. The
adolescents see the golf course as a scene of defeat
and embarrassment, the setting for the confrontation
that sent them back to the arroyo. To the adult, the
golf course is just a golf course.

The secret lion is the most complex symbol in the story. In a sense it stands for the innocence of childhood, something we lose when we learn more. The lion symbolizes a great "roaring" disturbance (170). It is a change that unsettles everything for a brief time and then passes, leaving everything changed in irrevocable, indescribable ways. It symbolizes the boys' growing up: they are changed, but still the same people. The "secret lion" is that thing that changes little boys into men. It is secret because no one notices it happening; before it is noticed, the change has occurred, and the little boy is gone forever. It is a lion because it "roars" through the boy like a storm and causes all of the growing-up changes, which can be "the biggest things" (170). In a more specific sense, the lion stands for puberty, reflected in their rage and frustration when they shout profanity. In the beginning of the story, the lion is rage (puberty, adolescence); in the middle, it suggests greatness (passing through adolescence into manhood); at the end, it's just the lion—"It was the lion" (173)—without any symbolic significance.

By the time they bury the ball, they have already learned one lesson, and the force of adulthood is pushing childhood aside. The golf course changes from heaven to shame to golf course; the ball changes from a special, perfect thing to something ordinary; the arroyo changes from grand river to polluted stream. Maybe it is the knowledge that life is not perfect, the knowledge that comes from growing up, that is the secret lion.

First Draft: Commentary

Discussions in a peer-review group helped to guide John's revision of his first draft. The students' major criticism was that John's thesis seemed to make a complicated claim he could not support: that the development of all four symbols follows the three stages of the boys' lives. One student pointed out that two of the four symbols (the grinding ball and the secret lion) do not even enter the boys' lives until adolescence and that John's treatment of the story's most prominent symbol — the lion — does not show it to change in any significant way. The group agreed that he should simplify his thesis, focusing on the way the four symbols all reflect the story's theme about the inevitability of change.

John also discussed his draft with his instructor, who suggested that he discuss the golf course first because it is the setting for the event that occurs first in time and because the disillusionment associated with it influences subsequent events. John and his instructor also decided that his introduction and conclusion should stress the common theme that all four symbols convey instead of focusing on the different ways in which each of the four separate symbols changes.

Finally, John's instructor expressed his concern about John's tendency to engage in "symbol hunting." He suggested that rather than focusing on finding equivalents for each of the four items ("the ball represents perfection," "the lion stands for puberty," and so on), John should consider how these symbols work together to communicate the story's theme. His instructor pointed out that in looking for neat equivalent values for each symbol, John was oversimplifying very complex, suggestive symbols. And, as John's own draft indicated, the symbols seem to suggest different things at different stages in the boys' lives.

After discussing his first draft with his classmates and his instructor, John made changes in his essay's content and organization. In his next draft, he also planned to delete wordiness and repetition; revise verb tenses; add more specific references, including quotations, from the story; sharpen transitions and add clearer topic sentences; and reorganize paragraphs to make logical and causal connections more obvious.

Revising and Editing an Essay

The revisions John decided to make are reflected in his second draft.

second draft

Symbols in "The Secret Lion"

"The Secret Lion" is a story about change. The first paragraph of the story gives a twelve-year-old's view of growing up: everything changes. When the child watches the magician, he is amazed at the "staying-the-same part" (170); adults focus on the tablecloth. As adults, we lose the ability to see the world through innocent eyes. We have the benefit of experience, confident the trick will work as long as the magician pulls the tablecloth in the proper way. The "staying-the-same part" is less important than the technique. In a story full of prominent symbols, the magician's trick does not seem very important, but all the key symbols, like the magician's trick, are about change. In fact, each of the story's key symbols highlights the theme of the inevitability of change that permeates the lives of the narrator and his friend Sergio.

The golf course is one such symbol. When the boys first see it, it is "heaven" (173). Lush and green and carefully cared for, it is completely different from the dry brown Arizona countryside and the polluted arroyo. In fact, to the boys it is another world, as mysterious as Oz—and just as unreal. Almost at once, the Emerald City becomes black and white again, the "Coke-holders" disappear, and the boys stop "acting 'rich'" (173). Heaven becomes a golf course, and the boys are changed forever.

The arroyo, a dry gulch that can fill up with

water, is another symbol that reinforces the theme of
the inevitability of change. It is a special place
for the boys—a place to rebel, to shout forbidden
words, to swim in waters polluted by a sewage
treatment plant. Although it represents a retreat
from the disillusionment of the golf course, clearly
second choice, it is the boys' "personal Mississippi"
(170), full of possibilities. Eventually, though, the
arroyo too disappoints the boys, and they stop going
there. "Nature seemed to keep pushing us around one
way or another, teaching us the same thing every
place we ended up" (171). The lesson they keep
learning is that nothing is permanent.

The grinding ball, round and perfect, seems to
suggest permanence and stability. But when the boys
find it, they realize at once that they cannot keep it
forever, just as they cannot remain children forever.
Like a child's life, it is perfect but temporary.
Burying it is their futile attempt to make time stand
still, to preserve perfection in an imperfect world,
innocence in an adult world, and they have already
learned Nature's lesson well enough to know that this
is not possible. They do not look very hard for the
ball, but even if they'd been able to find it, the
perfection and the innocence it represents would
still be unattainable.

The secret lion, the most complex symbol,
suggests the most profound kind of change: moving from
innocence to experience, from childhood to
adulthood.When the narrator is twelve, he says,
"something happened that we didn't have a name for,

but it was there nonetheless like a lion, and
roaring, roaring that way the biggest things do.
Everything changed" (170). School is different, girls
are different, language is different. Innocence has
been lost. The lion is associated with a great
"roaring" disturbance, a change that unsettles
everything for a brief time and then passes, leaving
everything changed in irrevocable, indescribable
ways. The secret lion is the thing that changes
little boys into men. It is a lion because it "roars"
through the boys like a storm; everything changes.

　　In an attempt to make things stay the same, to
make time stand still, the boys bury the grinding ball
"because it was perfect. . . . It was the lion" (173).
The grinding ball is "like that place, that whole
arroyo" (171): secret and perfect. In other words,
the ball and the arroyo and the lion are all tightly
connected. By the time the boys bury the ball, they
have already learned one sad lesson and are on their
way to adulthood. Heaven is just a golf course; the
round, perfect object is only "a cannonball thing
used in mining" (171); the arroyo is no Mississippi
but only a polluted stream; and childhood does not
last forever. "Things get taken away" (173), and this
knowledge that things do not last is the secret lion.

Second Draft: Commentary

John felt satisfied with his second draft. His revised thesis statement was clearer and simpler than the one in his first draft; it was also convincingly supported, with clearly worded topic sentences that introduced support paragraphs and connected them to the thesis statement. The second draft was also a good deal less wordy and more focused than the first, notably in the paragraphs about the arroyo and the grinding ball, and the introduction and conclusion were more fully developed. Moreover, he had given up his search for the one true "meaning" of each symbol, focusing instead on the many possibilities of each.

Now, John felt ready to turn his attention to smaller items, such as grammar, mechanics, punctuation, and format. Specifically, he planned to eliminate contractions, to work quotations into his text more smoothly, to make his thesis statement more precise and his title more interesting, and to revise the language of his introduction and conclusion further.

Frei 1

John Frei

Professor Nyysola

English 102

14 April 2005

"The Secret Lion": Everything Changes

Opening paragraph identifies work and author.

The first paragraph of Alberto Alvaro Ríos's "The Secret Lion" presents a twelve-year-old's view of growing up: everything changes. When the magician

Parenthetical documentation identifies source of quotation.

pulls a tablecloth out from under a pile of dishes, the child is amazed at the "staying-the-same part" (170); adults focus on the tablecloth. As adults, we have the benefit of experience; we know the trick will work as long as the technique is correct. We gain confidence, but we lose our innocence, and we lose our

Thesis statement

sense of wonder. The price we pay for knowledge is a permanent sense of loss, and this tradeoff is central to "The Secret Lion," a story whose key symbols reinforce its central theme: that change is inevitable and that change is always accompanied by loss.

Topic sentence identifies one key symbol.

The golf course is one symbol that helps to convey this theme. When the boys first see the golf course, it is "heaven" (173). Lush and green and carefully tended, it is very different from the dry, brown Arizona landscape and the polluted arroyo. In fact, to the boys it is another world, as exotic as Oz and ultimately as unreal. Before long, the Emerald City becomes black and white again. They learn that there is no such thing as a "Coke-holder," that their "acting 'rich'" is just an act, and that their heaven is only a golf course (173). As the narrator

Frei 2

acknowledges, "Something got taken away from us that
moment. Heaven" (173).

The arroyo, a dry gulch that can fill up with
water, is another symbol that reflects the idea of the
inevitability of change and of the loss that
accompanies change. It is a special, Edenlike place
for the boys—a place where they can rebel by
shouting forbidden words and by swimming in forbidden
waters. Although it represents a retreat from the
disillusionment of the golf course, and it is clearly
second choice, it is still their "personal
Mississippi" (170), full of possibilities.
Eventually,though, the arroyo too disappoints the
boys, and they stop going there. As the narrator
says, "Nature seemed to keep pushing us around one
way or another, teaching us the same thing every
place we ended up" (171). The lesson they keep
learning is that nothing is permanent.

The grinding ball, round and perfect, suggests
permanence and stability. But when the boys find it,
they realize at once that they cannot keep it
forever, just as they cannot remain balanced forever
between childhood and adulthood. Like a child's life,
the ball is perfect but temporary. Burying it is
their desperate attempt to stop time, to preserve
perfection in an imperfect world, innocence in an
adult world. But the boys are already twelve years
old, and they have learned nature's lesson well
enough to know that this action will not work. Even
if they had been able to find the ball, the perfection

Topic sentence
identifies another
key symbol.

Topic sentence
identifies another
key symbol.

and the innocence it suggests to them would still be unattainable. Perhaps that is why they do not try very hard to find it.

Topic sentence identifies final (and most important) symbol.

Like the story's other symbols, the secret lion itself suggests the most profound kind of change: the movement from innocence to experience, from childhood to adulthood, from expectation to disappointment to resignation. The narrator explains that when he was twelve, "something happened that we didn't have a name for, but it was there nonetheless like a lion, and roaring, roaring that way the biggest things do. Everything changed" (170). School was different, girls were different, language was different. Despite its loud roar, the lion remained paradoxically "secret," unnoticed until it passed. Like adolescence, the secret lion is a roaring disturbance that unsettles everything for a brief time and then passes, leaving everything changed.

Conclusion

In an attempt to make things stay the same, to make time stand still, the boys bury the grinding ball "because it was perfect. . . . It was the lion" (173). The grinding ball is "like that place, that whole arroyo" (171): secret and perfect. The ball and the arroyo and the lion are all perfect, but all, ironically, are temporary. The first paragraph of "The Secret Lion" tells us, "Everything changed" (170); by the last paragraph, we learn what this change means: "Things get taken away" (173). In other words, change implies loss. Heaven turns out to be just a golf course; the round, perfect object is only "a

Frei 4

cannonball thing used in mining" (171); the arroyo
is just a polluted stream; and childhood is just a
phase. "Things get taken away," and this knowledge
that things do not last is the lion, secret yet
roaring.

Final Draft: Commentary

As John revised and edited his second draft, he made changes in word choice and sentence structure. He also changed his title and edited to eliminate errors in mechanics and punctuation. In this final draft, he made his thesis statement more precise than it was in the previous draft, to communicate the idea of the relationship between change and loss that is central to the essay. In addition, he worked all quoted material smoothly into his discussion, taking care to use quotations only when the author's words added something vital to the paper. (Because students in John's class were permitted to write papers only about works in this anthology, his instructor did not require a works-cited page.) Finally, John checked all his references to page numbers in the story, so readers would be able to return to his source if necessary to check the accuracy and appropriateness of his quotations.

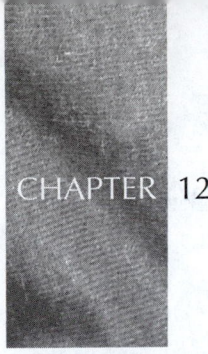

CHAPTER 12

PLOT

> It's a truism that there are only two basic plots in fiction: one, somebody takes a trip; two, a stranger comes to town.
>
> —attributed to American novelist John Gardner

Alfred Hitchcock's 1951 film *Strangers on a Train,* based on a suspense novel by Patricia Highsmith, offers an intriguing premise: two men, strangers, each can murder someone the other wishes dead; because they have no apparent connection to their victims, both can escape suspicion. Many people would describe this ingenious scheme as the film's "plot," but in fact it is simply the gimmick around which the complex plot revolves. Certainly a clever twist can be an important ingredient of a story's plot, but plot is more than "what happens"; it is how what happens is revealed, the way in which a story's events are arranged. Plot is shaped by causal connections —historical, social, and personal —by the interaction between characters, and by the juxtaposition of events. In *Strangers on a Train,* the plot that unfolds is complex: one character directs the events and determines their order while the other character is drawn into the action against his will. The same elements that enrich the plot of the film — unexpected events, conflict, suspense, flashbacks, foreshadowing —can also enrich the plot of a work of short fiction.

Conflict

Readers' interest and involvement are heightened by a story's **conflict,** the struggle between opposing forces that emerges as the action develops. This conflict is a clash between the **protagonist,** a story's principal character, and an **antagonist,** someone or something presented in opposition to the protagonist. Sometimes the antagonist is a villain; more often, it is a character who represents a conflicting point of view or advocates a course of action different from the one the protagonist follows. Sometimes the antagonist is not a character at all but a situation (for instance, war or poverty) or an event (a natural disaster, such as a flood or a storm, for example) that challenges the protagonist. In other stories, the protagonist may struggle against a supernatural force, or the conflict may occur within a character's mind. It may, for example, be a struggle between two moral choices, such as whether to stay at home and care for an aging parent or to leave and make a new life.

Stages of Plot

A work's plot explores one or more conflicts, moving from *exposition* through a series of *complications* to a *climax* and, finally, to a *resolution*.

During a story's **exposition**, the writer presents the basic information readers need to understand the events that follow. Typically, the exposition sets the story in motion: it establishes the scene, introduces the major characters, and perhaps suggests the major events or conflicts to come.

Sometimes a single sentence can present a story's exposition clearly and economically, giving readers information vital to their understanding of the plot that will unfold. For example, the opening sentence of Amy Tan's "Two Kinds" (p. 791)—"My mother believed you could be anything you wanted to be in America"—reveals an important trait of a central character. Similarly, the opening sentence of Shirley Jackson's "The Lottery" (p. 461)—"The morning of June 27th was clear and sunny, with the fresh warmth of a full-summer day; the flowers were blossoming profusely and the grass was richly green"—introduces the picture-perfect setting that is essential to the story's irony. At other times, as in John Updike's "A&P" (p. 230), a more fully developed exposition section establishes the story's setting, introduces the main characters, and suggests possible conflicts. In some experimental stories, a distinct exposition component may be absent, as it is in Luisa Valenzuela's "All about Suicide" (p. 7) and Amanda Holzer's "Love and Other Catastrophes: A Mix Tape" (p. 165).

As the plot progresses, the story's conflict unfolds through a series of complications that eventually lead readers to the story's climax. As it develops, the story may include several crises. A **crisis** is a peak in the story's action, a moment of considerable tension or importance. The **climax** is the point of greatest tension or importance, the scene that presents a story's decisive action or event.

The final stage of plot, the **resolution**, or **denouement** (French for "untying of the knot"), draws the action to a close and accounts for all remaining loose ends. Sometimes this resolution is achieved with the help of a **deus ex machina** (Latin for "a god from a machine"), an intervention of some force or agent previously extraneous to the story—for example, the sudden arrival of a long-lost relative or a fortuitous inheritance, the discovery of a character's true identity, or a last-minute rescue by a character not previously introduced. Usually, however, the resolution is more plausible: all the events lead logically and convincingly (though not necessarily predictably) to the resolution. Sometimes the ending of a story is indefinite — that is, readers are not quite sure what the protagonist will do or what will happen next. This kind of resolution, although it may leave some readers feeling cheated, has its advantages: it mirrors the complexity of life, where closure rarely occurs, and it can keep readers involved in the action as they try to understand the significance of the story's ending or to decide how conflicts should have been resolved.

Order and Sequence

A writer may present a story's events in strict chronological order, presenting each event in the sequence in which it actually takes place. More often, however, especially in relatively modern fiction, writers do not present events chronologically. Instead, they present incidents out of expected order, or in no apparent order. For example, a writer may choose to begin **in medias res** (Latin for "in the midst of things"), starting with a key event and later going back in time to explain events that preceded it, as Tillie Olsen does in "I Stand Here Ironing" (p. 309). Or, a writer can decide to begin a work of fiction at the end and then move back to reconstruct events that led up to the final outcome, as William Faulkner does in "A Rose for Emily" (p. 216). Many sequences are possible as the writer manipulates events to create interest, suspense, confusion, wonder, or some other effect.

Writers who wish to depart from strict chronological order use *flashbacks* and *foreshadowing*. A **flashback** moves out of sequence to examine an event or situation that occurred before the time in which the story's action takes place. A character can remember an earlier event, or a story's narrator can re-create an earlier situation. For example, in Alberto Alvaro Ríos's "The Secret Lion" (p. 170), the adult narrator looks back at events that occurred when he was twelve years old and then moves farther back in time to consider related events that occurred when he was five. In Edgar Allan Poe's "The Cask of Amontillado" (p. 350), the entire story is told as a flashback. Flashbacks are valuable because they can substitute for or supplement formal exposition by presenting background readers need to understand a story's events. One disadvantage of flashbacks is that, because they interrupt the natural flow of events, they may be intrusive or distracting. Such distractions, however, can be an advantage if the writer wishes to reveal events gradually and subtly or to obscure causal links.

Foreshadowing is the introduction early in a story of situations, events, characters, or objects that hint at things to come. Typically, a seemingly simple element — a chance remark, a natural occurrence, a trivial event — is eventually revealed to have great significance. For example, a dark cloud passing across the sky during a wedding can foreshadow future problems for the marriage. Foreshadowing allows a writer to hint provocatively at what is to come, so that readers only gradually become aware of a particular detail's role in a story. Thus, foreshadowing helps readers sense what will occur and grow increasingly involved as they see the likelihood (or even the inevitability) of a particular outcome.

In addition to using conventional techniques like flashbacks and foreshadowing, writers may experiment with sequence by substantially tampering with — or even dispensing with — chronological order. (An example is the scrambled chronology of "A Rose for Emily.") In such instances, the experimental form enhances interest and encourages readers to become involved with the story as they work to untangle or reorder the events and determine their logical and causal connections.

Today, the computer has given a new fluidity to the nature of plot, with hypertext stories appearing on the Internet and stories constructed to permit readers to actually participate in the creation of plot.

✔ CHECKLIST   Writing about Plot

- ☐ What happens in the story?

- ☐ Where does the story's formal exposition section end? What do readers learn about characters in this section? What do readers learn about setting? What possible conflicts are suggested here?

- ☐ What is the story's central conflict? What other conflicts are presented? Who is the protagonist? Who (or what) serves as the antagonist?

- ☐ Identify the story's crisis or crises.

- ☐ Identify the story's climax.

- ☐ How is the story's central conflict resolved? Is this resolution plausible? Satisfying?

- ☐ Which part of the story constitutes the resolution? Do any problems remain unresolved? Does any uncertainty remain? If so, does this uncertainty strengthen or weaken the story? Would another ending be more effective?

- ☐ How are the story's events arranged? Are they presented in chronological order? What events are presented out of logical sequence? Does the story use foreshadowing? Flashbacks? Are the causal connections between events clear? Logical? If not, can you explain why?

KATE CHOPIN (1851–1904) was born Katherine O'Flaherty, the daughter of a wealthy Irish-born merchant and his aristocratic Creole wife. She was married at nineteen to Oscar Chopin, a Louisiana cotton broker, who took her to live first in New Orleans and later on a plantation in central Louisiana. Chopin's representations of the Cane River region and its people in two volumes of short stories — *Bayou Folk* (1894) and *A Night in Arcadie* (1897) — are the foundation of her reputation as a local colorist, a writer dedicated to creating an accurate picture of a particular region and its people.

Her honest, sexually frank stories (many of them out of print for more than half a century) were rediscovered in the 1960s and 1970s, influencing a new generation of writers. Though she was a popular contributor of stories and sketches to the magazines of her day, Chopin scandalized many critics with her outspoken novel *The Awakening* (1899), in which a woman seeks sexual and emotional fulfillment with a man who is not her husband. The book was removed from the shelves of the public library in St. Louis, where Chopin was born.

"The Story of an Hour" depicts a brief event in a woman's life, but in this single hour, Chopin reveals both a lifetime's emotional torment and the momentary joy of freedom.

> **Cultural Context** During her marriage, Chopin lived in Louisiana, the only civil-law state in the United States. Whereas the legal systems of all other states are based on common law, the laws of Louisiana have their roots in the Napoleonic Code, the civil code enacted in France in 1804 that regulated issues of property, marriage, and divorce. This patriarchal code favored the husband in all domestic affairs and left women without many legal or fiscal rights. In "The Story of an Hour," the concept of freedom is closely tied to the prospect of escaping these restrictions.

The Story of an Hour (1894)

Knowing that Mrs. Mallard was afflicted with a heart trouble, great care was taken to break to her as gently as possible the news of her husband's death.

It was her sister Josephine who told her, in broken sentences, veiled hints that revealed in half concealing. Her husband's friend Richards was there, too, near her. It was he who had been in the newspaper office when intelligence of the railroad disaster was received, with Brently Mallard's name leading the list of "killed." He had only taken the time to assure himself of its truth by a second telegram, and had hastened to forestall any less careful, less tender friend in bearing the sad message.

She did not hear the story as many women have heard the same, with a paralyzed inability to accept its significance. She wept at once, with sudden, wild abandonment, in her sister's arms. When the storm of grief had spent itself she went away to her room alone. She would have no one follow her.

There stood, facing the open window, a comfortable, roomy armchair. Into this she sank, pressed down by a physical exhaustion that haunted her body and seemed to reach into her soul.

She could see in the open square before her house the tops of trees that were all aquiver with the new spring life. The delicious breath of rain was in the air. In the street below a peddler was crying his wares. The notes of a distant song which some one was singing reached her faintly, and countless sparrows were twittering in the eaves.

There were patches of blue sky showing here and there through the clouds that had met and piled one above the other in the west facing her window.

She sat with her head thrown back upon the cushion of the chair, quite motionless, except when a sob came up into her throat and shook her, as a child who has cried itself to sleep continues to sob in its dreams.

She was young, with a fair, calm face, whose lines bespoke repression and even a certain strength. But now there was a dull stare in her eyes, whose gaze was fixed away off yonder on one of those patches of blue sky. It was not a glance of reflection, but rather indicated a suspension of intelligent thought.

There was something coming to her and she was waiting for it, fearfully. What was it? She did not know; it was too subtle and elusive to name. But she felt it, creeping out of the sky, reaching toward her through the sounds, the scents, the color that filled the air.

10   Now her bosom rose and fell tumultuously. She was beginning to recognize this thing that was approaching to possess her, and she was striving to beat it back with her will — as powerless as her two white slender hands would have been.

When she abandoned herself a little whispered word escaped her slightly parted lips. She said it over and over under her breath: "Free, free, free!" The vacant stare and the look of terror that had followed it went from her eyes. They stayed keen and bright. Her pulses beat fast, and the coursing blood warmed and relaxed every inch of her body.

She did not stop to ask if it were not a monstrous joy that held her. A clear and exalted perception enabled her to dismiss the suggestion as trivial.

She knew that she would weep again when she saw the kind, tender hands folded in death; the face that had never looked save with love upon her, fixed and gray and dead. But she saw beyond that bitter moment a long procession of years to come that would belong to her absolutely. And she opened and spread her arms out to them in welcome.

There would be no one to live for during those coming years; she would live for herself. There would be no powerful will bending her in that blind persistence with which men and women believe they have a right to impose a private will upon a fellow creature. A kind intention or a cruel intention made the act seem no less a crime as she looked upon it in that brief moment of illumination.

15   And yet she had loved him — sometimes. Often she had not. What did it matter! What could love, the unsolved mystery, count for in face of this possession of self-assertion which she suddenly recognized as the strongest impulse of her being.

"Free! Body and soul free!" she kept whispering.

Josephine was kneeling before the closed door with her lips to the key-hole, imploring for admission. "Louise, open the door! I beg; open the door — you will make yourself ill. What are you doing, Louise? For heaven's sake open the door."

"Go away. I am not making myself ill." No; she was drinking in a very elixir of life through that open window.

Her fancy was running riot along those days ahead of her. Spring days, and summer days, and all sorts of days that would be her own. She breathed a quick prayer that life might be long. It was only yesterday she had thought with a shudder that life might be long.

20   She arose at length and opened the door to her sister's importunities. There was a feverish triumph in her eyes, and she carried herself unwittingly like a goddess of Victory. She clasped her sister's waist, and together they descended the stairs. Richards stood waiting for them at the bottom.

Some one was opening the front door with a latchkey. It was Brently Mallard who entered, a little travel-stained, composedly carrying his grip-sack and umbrella. He had been far from the scene of the accident, and did not even know there had been one. He stood amazed at Josephine's piercing cry; at Richards' quick motion to screen him from the view of his wife.

But Richards was too late.

When the doctors came they said she had died of heart disease — of joy that kills.

Reading and Reacting

1. The story's basic exposition is presented in its first two paragraphs. What additional information about character or setting would you like to know? Why do you suppose Chopin does not supply this information?

2. "The Story of an Hour" is a very economical story, with little action or dialogue. Do you see this economy as a strength or a weakness? Explain.

3. When "The Story of an Hour" was first published in *Vogue* magazine in 1894, the magazine's editors titled it "The Dream of an Hour." A film version, echoing the last words of the story, is called *The Joy That Kills*. Which of the three titles do you believe most accurately represents what happens in the story? Why?

4. Do you think Brently Mallard abused his wife? Did he love her? Did she love him? Exactly why was she so relieved to be rid of him? Can you answer any of these questions with certainty?

5. What is the nature of the conflict in this story? Who, or what, do you see as Mrs. Mallard's antagonist?

6. What emotions does Mrs. Mallard experience during the hour she spends alone in her room? What events do you imagine take place during this same period outside her room? Outside her house?

7. Do you find the story's ending satisfying? Believable? Contrived?

8. Was the story's ending unexpected, or were you prepared for it? What elements in the story foreshadow this ending?

9. JOURNAL ENTRY Rewrite the story's ending, substituting a few paragraphs of your own for the last three paragraphs.

10. CRITICAL PERSPECTIVE Kate Chopin is widely viewed today as an early feminist writer whose work often addressed the social injustices and inequalities that women faced during her time, the second half of the nineteenth century. According to literary critic Elaine Showalter, this story was written during a period in which women writers were able to "reject the accommodating postures of femininity and to use literature to dramatize the ordeals of wronged womanhood." Do you think this story rejects the "postures of femininity"? What "ordeals of wronged womanhood" are being dramatized here?

Related Works: "The Storm" (p. 281), "The Yellow Wallpaper" (p. 421), "The Disappearance" (p. 371), "Women" (p. 824), *A Doll House* (p. 1454)

NAGUIB MAHFOUZ (1911–   ), winner of the 1988 Pulitzer Prize for fiction, is one of the foremost writers of the modern Arabic world. Born in 1911 in Gamaliyya, an old quarter of Cairo, Mahfouz has written thirty-two novels and thirteen collections of short stories. He published his first novel in 1939, and his early works were based on the history of ancient Egypt. He eventually went on to write realistic literature that depicted the traditional urban life of contemporary Egypt. Perhaps his most famous and politically important work is a collection of three novels known as *The Cairo Trilogy*, a colossal saga that presents an eyewitness account of the country's social, political, religious, and intellectual life between World Wars I and II. Mahfouz is generally regarded as having given voice and vision to the hopes and frustrations of his nation and is credited with establishing the novel as a vital form in Arabic literature.

Cultural Context The legend of Rip Van Winkle, immortalized in a story by Washington Irving, has transcended regional boundaries to become a widely known literary metaphor. In this legend, the protagonist routinely escapes his nagging wife by sneaking off to the tavern or going hunting or fishing. On one such afternoon, he takes a nap in the forest and wakes up to find that twenty years have passed. "Half a Day" puts its own spin on the concept of missing time.

Half a Day (Arabic version: 1989; English version: 1991)

Translated by Denys Johnson-Davies

I proceeded alongside my father, clutching his right hand, running to keep up with the long strides he was taking. All my clothes were new: the black shoes, the green school uniform, and the red tarboosh.° My delight in my new clothes, however, was not altogether unmarried, for this was no feast day but the day on which I was to be cast into school for the first time.

My mother stood at the window watching our progress, and I would turn toward her from time to time, as though appealing for help. We walked along a street lined with gardens; on both sides were extensive fields planted with crops, prickly pears, henna trees, and a few date palms.

"Why school?" I challenged my father openly. "I shall never do anything to annoy you."

"I'm not punishing you," he said, laughing. "School's not a punishment. It's the factory that makes useful men out of boys. Don't you want to be like your father and brothers?"

5   I was not convinced. I did not believe there was really any good to be had in tearing me away from the intimacy of my home and throwing me into this building that stood at the end of the road like some huge, high-walled fortress, exceedingly stern and grim.

When we arrived at the gate we could see the courtyard, vast and crammed full of boys and girls. "Go in by yourself," said my father, "and join them. Put a smile on your face and be a good example to others."

I hesitated and clung to his hand, but he gently pushed me from him. "Be a man," he said. "Today you truly begin life. You will find me waiting for you when it's time to leave."

I took a few steps, then stopped and looked but saw nothing. Then the faces of boys and girls came into view. I did not know a single one of them, and none

---

tarboosh: A felt cap, which is usually red and shaped like a flat-topped cone with a tassel that hangs from the crown. Also known as a *fez.*

of them knew me. I felt I was a stranger who had lost his way. But glances of curiosity were directed toward me, and one boy approached and asked, "Who brought you?"

"My father," I whispered.

"My father's dead," he said quite simply.

I did not know what to say. The gate was closed, letting out a pitiable screech. Some of the children burst into tears. The bell rang. A lady came along, followed by a group of men. The men began sorting us into ranks. We were formed into an intricate pattern in the great courtyard surrounded on three sides by high buildings of several floors; from each floor we were overlooked by a long balcony roofed in wood.

"This is your new home," said the woman. "Here too there are mothers and fathers. Here there is everything that is enjoyable and beneficial to knowledge and religion. Dry your tears and face life joyfully."

We submitted to the facts, and this submission brought a sort of contentment. Living beings were drawn to other living beings, and from the first moments my heart made friends with such boys as were to be my friends and fell in love with such girls as I was to be in love with, so that it seemed my misgivings had had no basis. I had never imagined school would have this rich variety. We played all sorts of different games: swings, the vaulting horse, ball games. In the music room we chanted our first songs. We also had our first introduction to language. We saw a globe of the Earth, which revolved and showed the various continents and countries. We started learning the numbers. The story of the Creator of the universe was read to us, we were told of His present world and of His Hereafter, and we heard examples of what He said. We ate delicious food, took a little nap, and woke up to go on with friendship and love, play and learning.

As our path revealed itself to us, however, we did not find it as totally sweet and unclouded as we had presumed. Dust-laden winds and unexpected accidents came about suddenly, so we had to be watchful, at the ready, and very patient. It was not all a matter of playing and fooling around. Rivalries could bring about pain and hatred or give rise to fighting. And while the lady would sometimes smile, she would often scowl and scold. Even more frequently she would resort to physical punishment.

In addition, the time for changing one's mind was over and gone and there was no question of ever returning to the paradise of home. Nothing lay ahead of us but exertion, struggle, and perseverance. Those who were able took advantage of the opportunities for success and happiness that presented themselves amid the worries.

The bell rang announcing the passing of the day and the end of work. The throngs of children rushed toward the gate, which was opened again. I bade farewell to friends and sweethearts and passed through the gate. I peered around but found no trace of my father, who had promised to be there. I stepped aside to wait. When I had waited for a long time without avail, I decided to return home on my own. After I had taken a few steps, a middle-aged man passed by, and I realized at once that I knew him. He came toward me, smiling, and shook me by the hand, saying, "It's a long time since we last met — how are you?"

With a nod of my head, I agreed with him and in turn asked, "And you, how are you?"

"As you can see, not all that good, the Almighty be praised!"

Again he shook me by the hand and went off. I proceeded a few steps, then came to a startled halt. Good Lord! Where was the street lined with gardens? Where had it disappeared to? When did all these vehicles invade it? And when did all these hordes of humanity come to rest upon its surface? How did these hills of refuse come to cover its sides? And where were the fields that bordered it? High buildings had taken over, the street surged with children, and disturbing noises shook the air. At various points stood conjurers showing off their tricks and making snakes appear from baskets. Then there was a band announcing the opening of a circus, with clowns and weight lifters walking in front. A line of trucks carrying central security troops crawled majestically by. The siren of a fire engine shrieked, and it was not clear how the vehicle would cleave its way to reach the blazing fire. A battle raged between a taxi driver and his passenger, while the passenger's wife called out for help and no one answered. Good God! I was in a daze. My head spun, I almost went crazy. How could all this have happened in half a day, between early morning and sunset? I would find the answer at home with my father. But where was my home? I could see only tall buildings and hordes of people. I hastened on to the crossroads between the gardens and Abu Khoda. I had to cross Abu Khoda to reach my house, but the stream of cars would not let up. The fire engine's siren was shrieking at full pitch as it moved at a snail's pace, and I said to myself, "Let the fire take its pleasure in what it consumes." Extremely irritated, I wondered when I would be able to cross. I stood there a long time, until the young lad employed at the ironing shop on the corner came up to me. He stretched out his arm and said gallantly, "Grandpa, let me take you across."

Reading and Reacting

1. Reread the first two paragraphs of the story. What information about character and setting is revealed in these exposition paragraphs? What information is not revealed?

2. Compare the two opening paragraphs with paragraph 19, which is much more detailed. What details appear in both? What has changed? Why is the final paragraph so much more fully developed than the opening paragraphs?

3. When the narrator is left in the school courtyard, he tells a boy that his father brought him to school, and the boy replies, "'My father's dead'" (par. 10). What purpose does this exchange serve in the story?

4. In paragraph 7, the narrator's father tells him to be a man, adding, "'Today you truly begin life. You will find me waiting for you when it's time to leave.'" Why is his father not there when school is let out? In light of his absence, how do you interpret the suggestion that the narrator will "truly begin life" on his first day of school?

5. Paragraph 13 summarizes the narrator's day at school, and paragraphs 14 and 15 comment on this day; at the beginning of paragraph 16, the bell rings,

signaling the end of the school day. What has actually taken place in paragraphs 13 through 15? How do you know?

6. In paragraph 19, the narrator asks, "How could all this have happened in half a day, between early morning and sunset?" Answer his question.

7. The story's plot is orderly and chronological, but the narrator often expresses confusion about the path he is following. Give some examples of this confusion. How do you explain it?

8. Does the story's last sentence come as a surprise — or even a shock — or does anything in the story foreshadow this ending?

9. **JOURNAL ENTRY** Do you think this story has a "moral" that readers might apply to their own lives? If so, what is it?

10. **CRITICAL PERSPECTIVE** In his introduction to Mahfouz's novel *The Beginning and the End*, author Ramses Awad discusses Mahfouz's early literary career in terms of his fictional predecessors and the political context of the time. When Mahfouz first began writing, the Arabic novel was a relatively new creation, and Mahfouz and his contemporaries developed their skills by reading and studying the fictional heritage and techniques of the West. Moreover, Awad writes, the act of writing became in and of itself a form of revolution or rebellion:

> When Mahfouz started his novelistic career, Egypt was undergoing a period of political unrest, suppression, and despotism. In this repressive atmosphere, Mahfouz acquired a serpentine wisdom which he has never lost. Realizing . . . the futility of open rebellion against the autocracy of the ruler, he managed to devise a narrative method that would imply criticism of the system without jeopardizing his interests or running the risk of antagonizing the authorities.

In what sense, if any, could "Half a Day" be read as a political commentary?

Related Works: "Kansas" (p. 209), "The Disappearance" (p. 371), "To His Coy Mistress" (p. 957), *Tape* (p. 1313), *Scheherazade* (p. 1365).

NADINE GORDIMER (1923–　　　), winner of the 1991 Nobel Prize in Literature, has been publishing short stories, essays, and novels about South Africa, her native country, since she was fifteen. Gordimer once explained that after growing up as a middle-class child of Jewish immigrants, becoming a politically aware writer in South Africa was like "peeling an onion. You're sloughing off all the conditioning that you've had since you were a child." The prevailing attitude of her extensive work evolved from cautious optimism to pessimism in accord with the changing nature of Africa in her lifetime. Under Apartheid, Gordimer's work was often banned in her own country because of its condemnation of the political system, but she remained in Johannesburg.

Gordimer's fourteen novels include *Burger's Daughter* (1979), *July's People* (1981), *None to Accompany Me* (1994), and her most recent, *Get a Life*, published in 2005. Her eleven short story collections include *Jump and Other Stories* (1991), *Why Haven't You Written?* (1992), and her most recent, *Loot* (2003). A founding member of the Congress of South African Writers, Gordimer has been awarded numerous prizes and honorary degrees, as well as France's prestigious *Commandeur de l'Ordre des Arts et des Lettres*.

> **Cultural Context** Under South Africa's apartheid regime (1948–1991), race determined where citizens could live, what kind of work they could do, what kind of education they could receive, whom they could marry, and what political rights they had. Apartheid governed relations between South Africa's powerful white minority and its nonwhite majority and sanctioned racial segregation and political and economic discrimination against nonwhites. During this time, white South Africans separated themselves as much as possible, often living in gated communities or compounds, which exacerbated the hostility between the races. The fact that the family in "Once upon a Time" lives in such a compound is an important element of its plot.

Once upon a Time (1991)

Someone has written to ask me to contribute to an anthology of stories for children. I reply that I don't write children's stories; and he writes back that at a recent congress/book fair/seminar a certain novelist said every writer ought to write at least one story for children. I think of sending a postcard saying I don't accept that I "ought" to write anything.

And then last night I woke up — or rather was wakened without knowing what had roused me.

A voice in the echo-chamber of the subconscious?

A sound.

5 A creaking of the kind made by the weight carried by one foot after another along a wooden floor. I listened. I felt the apertures of my ears distend with concentration. Again: the creaking. I was waiting for it; waiting to hear if it indicated that feet were moving from room to room, coming up the passage — to my door. I have no burglar bars, no gun under the pillow, but I have the same fears as people who do take these precautions, and my windowpanes are thin as rime, could shatter like a wineglass. A woman was murdered (how do they put it) in broad daylight in a house two blocks away, last year, and the fierce dogs who guarded an old widower and his collection of antique clocks were strangled before he was knifed by a casual labourer he had dismissed without pay.

I was staring at the door, making it out in my mind rather than seeing it, in the dark. I lay quite still — a victim already — but the arrhythmia of my heart was fleeing, knocking this way and that against its body-cage. How finely tuned the senses are, just out of rest, sleep! I could never listen intently as that in the distractions of the day; I was reading every faintest sound, identifying and classifying its possible threat.

But I learned that I was to be neither threatened nor spared. There was no human weight pressing on the boards, the creaking was a buckling, an epicentre of stress. I was in it. The house that surrounds me while I sleep is built on undermined ground; far beneath my bed, the floor, the house's foundations, the stopes and passages of gold mines have hollowed the rock, and when some face trembles, detaches and falls, three thousand feet below, the whole house shifts slightly, bringing uneasy strain to the balance and counterbalance of brick, cement, wood and glass that hold it as a structure around me. The misbeats of my heart tailed off like the last muffled flourishes on one of the wooden xylophones made by the Chopi and Tsonga migrant miners who might have been down there, under me in the earth at that moment. The stope where the fall was could have been disused, dripping water from its ruptured veins; or men might now be interred there in the most profound of tombs.

I couldn't find a position in which my mind would let go of my body — release me to sleep again. So I began to tell myself a story; a bedtime story.

In a house, in a suburb, in a city, there were a man and his wife who loved each other very much and were living happily ever after. They had a little boy, and they loved him very much. They had a cat and a dog that the little boy loved very much. They had a car and a caravan trailer for holidays, and a swimming-pool which was fenced so that the little boy and his playmates would not fall in and drown. They had a housemaid who was absolutely trustworthy and an itinerant gardener who was highly recommended by the neighbours. For when they began to live happily ever after they were warned, by that wise old witch, the husband's mother, not to take on anyone off the street. They were inscribed in a medical benefit society, their pet dog was licensed, they were insured against fire, flood damage and theft, and subscribed to the local Neighbourhood Watch, which supplied them with a plaque for their gates lettered YOU HAVE BEEN WARNED over the silhouette of a would-be intruder. He was masked; it could not be said if he was black or white, and therefore proved the property owner was no racist.

It was not possible to insure the house, the swimming pool or the car against **10** riot damage. There were riots, but these were outside the city, where people of another colour were quartered. These people were not allowed into the suburb except as reliable housemaids and gardeners, so there was nothing to fear, the husband told the wife. Yet she was afraid that some day such people might come up the street and tear off the plaque YOU HAVE BEEN WARNED and open the gates and stream in . . . Nonsense, my dear, said the husband, there are police and soldiers and tear-gas and guns to keep them away. But to please her — for he loved her very much and buses were being burned, cars stoned, and schoolchildren shot by the police in those quarters out of sight and hearing of the suburb —he had electronically-controlled gates fitted. Anyone who pulled off the sign YOU HAVE BEEN WARNED and tried to open the gates would have to announce his intentions by pressing a button and speaking into a receiver relayed to the house. The little boy was fascinated by the device and used it as a walkie-talkie in cops and robbers play with his small friends.

The riots were suppressed, but there were many burglaries in the suburb and somebody's trusted housemaid was tied up and shut in a cupboard by thieves while she was in charge of her employers' house. The trusted housemaid of the man and wife and little boy was so upset by this misfortune befalling a friend left, as she herself often was, with responsibility for the possessions of the man and his wife and the little boy that she implored her employers to have burglar bars attached to the doors and windows of the house, and an alarm system installed. The wife said, She is right, let us take heed to her advice. So from every window and door in the house where they were living happily ever after they now saw the trees and sky through bars, and when the little boy's pet cat tried to climb in by the fanlight to keep him company in his little bed at night, as it customarily had done, it set off the alarm keening through the house.

The alarm was often answered — it seemed — by other burglar alarms, in other houses, that had been triggered by pet cats or nibbling mice. The alarms called to one another across the gardens in shrills and bleats and wails that everyone soon became accustomed to, so that the din roused the inhabitants of the suburb no more than the croak of frogs and musical grating of cicadas' legs. Under cover of the electronic harpies' discourse intruders sawed the iron bars and broke into homes, taking away hi-fi equipment, television sets, cassette players, cameras and radios, jewellery and clothing, and sometimes were hungry enough to devour everything in the refrigerator or paused audaciously to drink the whisky in the cabinets or patio bars. Insurance companies paid no compensation for single malt, a loss made keener by the property owner's knowledge that the thieves wouldn't even have been able to appreciate what it was they were drinking.

Then the time came when many of the people who were not trusted housemaids and gardeners hung about the suburb because they were unemployed. Some importuned for a job: weeding or painting a roof; anything, *baas*, madam. But the man and his wife remembered the warning about taking on anyone off the street. Some drank liquor and fouled the street with discarded bottles. Some begged, waiting for the man or his wife to drive the car out of the electronically-operated gates. They sat about with their feet in the gutters, under the jacaranda trees that made a green tunnel of the street — for it was a beautiful suburb, spoilt only by their presence — and sometimes they fell asleep lying right before the gates in the midday sun. The wife could never see anyone go hungry. She sent the trusted housemaid out with bread and tea, but the trusted housemaid said these were loafers and *tsotsis*,° who would come and tie her up and shut her in a cupboard. The husband said, She's right. Take heed of her advice. You only encourage them with your bread and tea. They are looking for their chance . . . And he brought the little boy's tricycle from the garden into the house every night, because if the house was surely secure, once locked and with the alarm set, someone might still be able to climb over the wall or the electronically-closed gates into the garden.

You are right, said the wife, then the wall should be higher. And the wise old witch, the husband's mother, paid for the extra bricks as her Christmas present to her son and his wife — the little boy got a Space Man outfit and a book of fairy tales.

15   But every week there were more reports of intrusion: in broad daylight and the dead of night, in the early hours of the morning, and even in the lovely summer twilight — a certain family was at dinner while the bedrooms were

---

tsotsis: Criminals.

being ransacked upstairs. The man and his wife, talking of the latest armed robbery in the suburb, were distracted by the sight of the little boy's pet cat effortlessly arriving over the seven-foot wall, descending first with a rapid bracing of extended forepaws down on the sheer vertical surface, and then a graceful launch, landing with swishing tail within the property. The whitewashed wall was marked with the cat's comings and goings; and on the street side of the wall there were larger red-earth smudges that could have been made by the kind of broken running shoes, seen on the feet of unemployed loiterers, that had no innocent destination.

When the man and wife and little boy took the pet dog for its walk round the neighbourhood streets they no longer paused to admire this show of roses or that perfect lawn; these were hidden behind an array of different varieties of security fences, walls and devices. The man, wife, little boy and dog passed a remarkable choice: there was the low-cost option of pieces of broken glass embedded in cement along the top of walls, there were iron grilles ending in lance-points, there were attempts at reconciling the aesthetics of prison architecture with the Spanish Villa style (spikes painted pink) and with the plaster urns of neoclassical façades (twelve-inch pikes finned like zigzags of lightning and painted pure white). Some walls had a small board affixed, giving the name and telephone number of the firm responsible for the installation of the devices. While the little boy and the pet dog raced ahead, the husband and wife found themselves comparing the possible effectiveness of each style against its appearance; and after several weeks when they paused before this barricade or that without needing to speak, both came out with the conclusion that only one was worth considering. It was the ugliest but the most honest in its suggestion of the pure concentration-camp style, no frills, all evident efficacy. Placed the length of walls, it consisted of a continuous coil of stiff and shining metal serrated into jagged blades, so that there would be no way of climbing over it and no way through its tunnel without getting entangled in its fangs. There would be no way out, only a struggle getting bloodier and bloodier, a deeper and sharper hooking and tearing of flesh. The wife shuddered to look at it. You're right, said the husband, anyone would think twice . . . And they took heed of the advice on a small board fixed to the wall: Consult DRAGON'S TEETH The People for Total Security.

Next day a gang of workmen came and stretched the razor-bladed coils all round the walls of the house where the husband and wife and little boy and pet dog and cat were living happily ever after. The sunlight flashed and slashed, off the serrations, the cornice of razor thorns encircled the home, shining. The husband said, Never mind. It will weather. The wife said, You're wrong. They guarantee it's rust-proof. And she waited until the little boy had run off to play before she said, I hope the cat will take heed . . . The husband said, Don't worry, my dear, cats always look before they leap. And it was true that from that day on the cat slept in the little boy's bed and kept to the garden, never risking a try at breaching security.

One evening, the mother read the little boy to sleep with a fairy story from the book the wise old witch had given him at Christmas. Next day he pretended to be the Prince who braves the terrible thicket of thorns to enter the palace and kiss the Sleeping Beauty back to life: he dragged a ladder to the wall, the shining coiled tunnel was just wide enough for his little body to creep in, and with the first fixing of its razor-teeth in his knees and hands and head he screamed and struggled deeper into its tangle. The trusted housemaid and the itinerant gardener, whose "day" it was, came running, the first to see and to scream with him, and the itinerant gardener tore his hands trying to get at the little boy. Then the man and his wife burst wildly into the garden and for some reason (the cat, probably) the alarm set up wailing against the screams while the bleeding mass of the little boy was hacked out of the security coil with saws, wire-cutters, choppers, and they carried it — the man, the wife, the hysterical trusted housemaid and the weeping gardener — into the house.

Reading and Reacting

1. How is the introduction — paragraphs 1 through 8 — related thematically to the fairy tale the narrator tells?

2. In what respects is the story that begins with paragraph 9 of "Once upon a Time" similar to a fairy tale? In what respects is it different? Would the story be more or less effective without the narrator's introduction?

3. In paragraph 8, Gordimer characterizes the paragraphs that follow as a "bedtime story." How does her tale differ from your idea of a bedtime story?

4. The fairy tale's events are presented in strict chronological order. Give some examples of words and phrases that move readers from one time period to another. Why is chronological order so important?

5. Imagine Gordimer's fairy tale dramatized, perhaps as a television documentary. Where would you interrupt the story to provide commercial breaks or station identification? How would you present the introduction?

6. Throughout the fairy tale, various objects and events (and even specific warnings) foreshadow the grim ending. Give several examples of such hints, and explain how each anticipates the ending.

7. Which characters are in conflict in the fairy tale? Does the tale have a hero? A villain? What larger forces are in conflict? Are the conflicts between these forces resolved at the end? Explain.

8. What tendencies in her society do you think the author of "Once upon a Time" means to criticize?

9. JOURNAL ENTRY "Once upon a Time" is set in South Africa. Could it have been set in the United States? Explain.

10. CRITICAL PERSPECTIVE In an interview conducted in the early 1980s, Gordimer spoke about her education and about the town in which she lived:

> When I got to university, it was through mixing with other people who were writing or painting that I got to know black people as equals. In a general and inclusive, nonracial way, I met people who lived in the world of ideas, in the world that interested me passionately.
>
> In the town where I lived, there was no mental food of this kind at all. I'm often amazed to think how they live, those people, and what an oppressed life it must be, because human beings must live in the world of ideas. This dimension in the human psyche is very important. It was there, but they didn't know how to express it. Conversation consisted of trivialities. For women, household

matters, problems with children. The men would talk about golf or business or horseracing or whatever their practical interests were. Nobody ever talked about, or even around, the big things—life and death.

Focusing on Gordimer's characterization of the conversation in her town as consisting of "trivialities" rather than of "the big things," consider how her description of that town might apply to "Once upon a Time." How, for example, might the family's self-exclusion from what Gordimer calls "the world of ideas" have contributed to the story's tragic outcome?

Related Works: "The Rocking-Horse Winner" (p. 525), "Gretel in Darkness" (p. 852), "Cinderella" (p. 882), "The Chimney Sweeper" (p. 1144), *Scheherazade* (p. 1365)

STEPHEN DOBYNS (1941–   ) is a prolific writer in a variety of genres — poetry, novels, short stories, essays — whose work has been translated into ten languages. Dobyns was educated at Wayne State University, and he went on to obtain his MFA from the University of Iowa. Of his ten books of poetry and twenty novels, the most recent are *Pallbearers Envying the One Who Rides* and *Boy in the Water* (both 1999). His collection of short stories, *Eating Naked,* was published in 2000; his essays appear in *Best Words, Best Order* (1996). His most recent book is *Mystery, So Long* (2005), a collection of poems. The recipient of numerous literary awards, Dobyns has taught at a variety of schools, including the University of Iowa, Boston University, Sarah Lawrence College, and Emerson College.

Cultural Context   On "Black Tuesday"— October 29, 1929 — the United States stock market crashed, triggering the Great Depression, the worst economic collapse in modern history. It is during this period that the key events in "Kansas" take place. With banks failing and businesses closing, more than fifteen million Americans (one-quarter of the workforce) were eventually unemployed. The economic disaster was soon paralleled by an agricultural one: attracted by the promise of rich, plentiful soil, thousands of farm families had moved from the North and East to Kansas as well as to Oklahoma, Texas, New Mexico, and Colorado. Farmers in this region plowed millions of acres of grassland; then, in the summer of 1931, the rains stopped. After a drought that lasted eight years, this area came to be called the "Dust Bowl."

Kansas   (1999)

The boy hitchhiking on the back-country Kansas road was nineteen years old. He had been dropped there by a farmer in a Model T Ford who had turned off to the north. Then he waited for three hours. It was July and there were no clouds. The wheat fields were flat and went straight to the horizon. The boy had two plums and he ate them. A blue Plymouth coupe° went by with a man and a woman.

---

coupe: A two-door car, often one that seats only two people.

They were laughing. The woman had blond hair and it was all loose and blew from the window. They didn't even see the boy. The strands of straw-colored hair seemed to be waving to him. Half an hour later a farmer stopped in a Ford pickup covered with a layer of dust. The boy clambered into the front seat. The farmer took off again without glancing at him. A forty-five revolver lay next to the farmer's buttocks on the seat. Seeing it, the boy felt something electric go off inside of him. The revolver was old and there were rust spots on the barrel. Black electrician's tape was wrapped around the handle.

"You seen a woman and a man go by here in a Plymouth coupe?" asked the farmer. He pronounced it "koo-pay."

The boy said he had.

"How long ago?"

5   "About thirty minutes."

The farmer had light blue eyes and there was stubble on his chin. Perhaps he was forty, but to the boy he looked old. His skin was leather-colored from the sun. The farmer pressed his foot to the floor and the pickup roared. It was a dirt road and the boy had to hold his hands against the dashboard to keep from being bounced around. It was hot and both windows were open. There was grit in the boy's eyes and on his tongue. He kept glancing sideways at the revolver.

"They friends of yours?" asked the boy.

The farmer didn't look at him. "That's my wife," he said. "I'm going to put a bullet in her head." He put a hand to the revolver to make sure it was still there. "The man too," he added.

The boy didn't say anything. He was hitchhiking back to summer school from Oklahoma. He was the middle of three boys and the only one who had left home. He had already spent a year at the University of Oklahoma and was spending the summer at Lawrence. And there were other places, farther places. The boy played the piano. He intended to go to those farther places.

10   "What did they do?" the boy asked at last.

"You just guess," said the farmer.

The pickup was going about fifty miles per hour. The boy was afraid of seeing the dust cloud from the Plymouth up ahead, but there was only straight road. Then he was afraid that the Plymouth might have pulled off someplace. He touched his tongue to his upper lip but it was just one dry thing against another. Getting into the pickup, the boy had had a clear idea of the direction of his life. He meant to go to New York City at the end of summer. He meant to play the piano in Carnegie Hall.° The farmer and his forty-five seemed to stand between him and that future. They formed a wall that the boy was afraid to climb over.

"Do you have to kill them?" the boy asked. He didn't want to talk but he felt unable to remain silent.

The farmer had a red boil on the side of his neck and he kept touching it with two fingers. "When you have something wicked, what do you do?" asked the farmer.

Carnegie Hall: A famous concert hall in New York City.

The boy wanted to say he didn't know or he wanted to say he would call the 15
police, but the farmer would have no patience with those answers. And the boy
also wanted to say he would forgive the wickedness, but he was afraid of that answer as well. He was afraid of making the farmer angry and so he only shrugged.

"You stomp it out," said the farmer. "That's what you do — you stomp it out."

The boy stared straight ahead, searching for the dust cloud and hoping not to
see it. The hot air seemed to bend in front of them. The boy was so frightened of
seeing the dust cloud that he was sure he saw it. A little puff of gray getting closer.
The pickup went straight down the middle of the road. There was no other traffic.
Even if there had been other cars, the boy felt certain that the farmer wouldn't
have moved out of the way. The wheat on either side of the road was coated with
layers of dust, making it a reddish color, the color of dried blood.

"What about the police?" asked the boy.

"It's my wife," said the farmer. "It's my problem."

The boy never did see the dust cloud. They reached Lawrence and the boy got 20
out as soon as he could. His shirt was stuck to his back and he kept rubbing his
palms on his dungarees. He thanked the farmer but the man didn't look at him,
he just kept staring straight ahead.

"Don't tell the police," said the farmer. His hand rested lightly on the forty-
five beside him on the seat.

"No," said the boy. "I promise." He slammed shut the dusty door of the pickup.

The boy didn't tell the police. For several days he didn't tell anyone at all. He
looked at the newspapers twice a day for news of a killing, but he didn't find anything. More than the farmer's gun, he had been frightened by the strength of the
farmer's resolve. It had been like a chunk of stone and compared to it the boy had
felt as soft as a piece of white bread. The boy never knew what happened. Perhaps
nothing had happened.

The summer wound to its conclusion. The boy went to New York. He never
did play in Carnegie Hall. His piano playing never got good enough. The war
came and went. He wasn't a boy any longer. He was a married man with two sons.
The family moved to Michigan. The man was a teacher, then a minister. His own
parents died. He told his sons the story about the farmer in the pickup. "What do
you think happened?" they asked. Nobody knew. Perhaps the farmer caught up
with them; perhaps he didn't. The man's sons went off to college and began their
own lives. The man and his wife moved to New Hampshire. They grew old. Sixty
years went by between that summer in Kansas and the present. The man entered
his last illness. He stayed at home but he couldn't get out of bed. His wife gave him
shots of morphine. He began to have dreams even when he was awake. The visiting nurse was always chipper. "Feeling better today?" she would ask. He tried to
be polite, but he had no illusions. He went from one shot a day to two, and then
three. The doctor said, "Give him as many as he needs." His wife started to ask
about the danger of addiction, then she said nothing.

The man hardly knew when he was asleep or awake. He hardly knew if one 25
day had passed or many. He had oxygen. He didn't eat. The space between his eyes
and the bedroom wall was always occupied with people of his invention, people
of his past. He would lift his hand to wave them away, only to find his hand still

lying motionless on the counterpane. Even music distracted him now. Always he was listening for something in the distance.

The boy was standing by the side of a dirt road. A Ford pickup stopped beside him and he got in. The farmer lifted a forty-five revolver. "I'm going to shoot my wife in the head."

"No," said the boy, "don't do it!"

The farmer drove fast. He had a red boil on the side of his neck and he kept touching it with two fingers. They found the Plymouth coupe pulled off into a hollow. There were shade trees and a brook. The farmer jammed down the brakes and the pickup slid sideways across the dirt. The man and woman were in the front seat of the Plymouth. Their clothes were half off. They jumped out of the car. The woman had big red breasts. The farmer jumped out with his forty-five. "No!" shouted the boy. The farmer shot the man in the head. His whole head exploded and he fell down in the dust. His head was just a broken thing on the ground. The woman covered her face and tried to cover her breasts as well. The farmer shot her as well. Bits of dust floated on the surface of her blood. "One last for me," said the farmer. He put the barrel of the gun in his mouth. "No, no!" cried the boy.

The boy was standing by the side of a dirt road. A Ford pickup stopped beside him and he got in. "I'm going to shoot my wife," said the farmer. He had a big revolver on the seat beside him.

30   "You can't," said the boy.

They talked all the way to Lawrence. The farmer was crying. "I've always been good to her," he said. He had a red boil on the side of his neck and he kept touching it.

"Give the gun to the police," said the boy.

"I'm afraid," said the farmer.

"You needn't be," said the boy. "The police won't hurt you."

35   They drove to the police station. The boy told the desk sergeant what had happened. The sergeant shook his head. He took the revolver away from the farmer. "We'll get her back, sir," he said. "Wife stealing's not permitted around here."

"I could have got in real trouble," said the farmer.

The boy was standing by the side of a dirt road. A pickup stopped beside him and he got in. The farmer said, "I'm going to kill my wife."

The boy was too frightened to say anything. He kept looking at the forty-five revolver. He was sure that he would be shot himself. He regretted not staying in Oklahoma, where he had friends and family. He couldn't imagine why he had moved away. The farmer drove straight to Lawrence. The boy was bounced all over the cab of the pickup but he didn't say anything. He was afraid that something would happen to his hands and he wouldn't be able to play the piano. It seemed to him that playing the piano was the only important thing in the entire world. The farmer had a red boil on the side of his neck and he kept touching it.

When they got to Lawrence, the boy jumped out of the pickup and ran. He saw a policeman and told him what had happened. An hour later he was getting a hamburger at a White Tower restaurant. He heard shooting. He ran out and saw the farmer's dusty pickup. There were police cars with their lights flashing. The boy pushed through the crowd. The farmer was hanging half out of the door of his pick-up truck. There was blood all over the front of his workshirt. The forty-five revolver lay on the pavement. The policemen were clapping each other on the back. They had big grins. The boy began cracking his knuckles. They made snapping noises.

The boy was standing by the side of a dirt road. A pickup stopped beside him 40 and he got in. The farmer pointed a forty-five revolver at his head. "Get in here," he said. They drove toward Lawrence.

"I'm going to shoot my wife for wickedness," said the farmer.

"No," said the boy, "you must forgive her."

"I'm going to kill her," said the farmer, "and her fancy man besides."

The boy said, "You can't take the law into your own hands."

The farmer raised his forty-five revolver. "They're as good as dead." He had a 45 red boil on the side of his neck.

The boy was a college student. It was the Depression. He wanted to go to New York and become a classical pianist. He had already been accepted by Juilliard.° "Justice does not belong to you," said the boy.

"Wickedness must be punished," said the farmer.

They argued all the way to Lawrence. The boy stayed with the farmer. He could have jumped out of the pickup, but he didn't. The boy kept trying to convince him that he was wrong. The farmer drove to the train station.

The farmer's wife was in the waiting room with the man who had been driving the Plymouth coupe. She was very pretty, with blond hair and milky pink skin. She screamed when she saw the farmer. Her companion put his arms around her to protect her.

The boy hurried to stand between the woman and her husband. "Think of 50 what you are doing," he said. "Think how you are throwing your life away." The first bullet struck him in the shoulder and whipped him around. He could see the woman open her mouth in a startled *Oh* of surprise. The second bullet caught him in the small of his back.

The man's family was with him in New Hampshire when he died: his wife and his two sons, neither of them young anymore. It was early evening in October at the very height of color. Even after sundown the maple trees seemed bright. The older son watched his father breathing. He kept twisting and trying to kick his feet. His face was very thin, his whole body was just a ridge under the middle of the sheet. He didn't talk anymore. He didn't want anyone to touch him. He seemed to be focusing his attention. He took a breath and they waited. He exhaled slowly. They continued to wait. He didn't breathe again. They waited several minutes. Then his wife removed the oxygen tubes from his nose, doing it quickly, as if afraid of doing something wrong.

The older son went back into the bedroom with the two men from the funeral home. They had a collapsible stretcher which they put next to the bed. They unrolled a dark blue body bag. They shifted the dead man onto the stretcher and

---

Juilliard: A highly respected school for the performing arts in New York City.

wrestled him into the body bag, one at his feet, one at his head. The son stood in the doorway. The men from the funeral home muttered directions to each other. They were breathing heavily and their hair was mussed. At last they got him into the body bag. The son watched closely as the zipper was drawn up and across his father's face. It was a large silver zipper and the son watched it being pulled across his father's forehead. All the days after that he kept seeing its glittering progress, a picture repeating itself in his mind.

Reading and Reacting

1. Paragraph 1 presents the story's exposition. List the specific pieces of information this paragraph presents. How will each detail be important later in the story? Are any details unnecessary? Are any important details *not* introduced in paragraph 1?

2. Summarize the story's plot in three sentences.

3. In paragraph 12, the narrator says, "Getting into the pickup, the boy had had a clear idea of the direction of his life. . . . The farmer and his forty-five seemed to stand between him and that future." What direction do you think the boy imagined his life would take? What direction did it actually take? Were "the farmer and his forty-five" in any way responsible for this change of direction? Explain.

4. How would the story be different without the presence of the revolver lying on the seat?

5. What specific information are readers told in the story's first twenty-five paragraphs about the boy? The farmer? The couple in the blue Plymouth? Is all this information essential to the story's plot? What additional information might you want to know? Why?

6. The first twenty-five paragraphs present the story's basic plot; then, this section of the story is followed by three alternate versions of the boy's experience, each beginning with the sentence "The boy was standing by the side of a dirt road." What is the point of these alternate versions? What is the writer trying to accomplish?

7. How are the three alternate versions of events similar to and different from the boy's story as it is first presented? Which version is most satisfying? Most logical? Most believable? Explain.

8. At the end of paragraph 25, as the boy (now a man) is dying, he is "listening for something in the distance." What do you suppose he might be listening for?

9. The red boil on the side of the farmer's neck is mentioned several times. What other physical details are repeated in the story's descriptions of characters and setting? What is the effect of these repetitions? Are any important physical details omitted?

10. What does the last sentence add to the story?

11. JOURNAL ENTRY In paragraph 23, the narrator says, "The boy never knew what happened. Perhaps nothing had happened." What does he mean by this? What do you think really happened to the boy that day?

12. CRITICAL PERSPECTIVE In reviewing *Eating Naked*, the collection in which "Kansas" appeared, Roger Boylan says that Dobyns "almost gleefully imposes life's unpredictability on his characters." Boylan then goes on to give examples of the ways in which Dobyns "imposes life's unpredictability":

> Cancer ends a life in one story; a car crash does so in another. A kidnapping goes ludicrously wrong. People betray each other. Lust overrides good sense. Absurdity rules. Marriages fall apart with depressing regularity—and if yours doesn't seem to be on the rocks, well, can you be sure you know what your better half's up to when you're away?

Do you think "Kansas" fits the pattern Boylan has identified? Is it a story in which "absurdity rules"?

Related Works: "Sleepy Time Gal" (p. 154), "A Good Man Is Hard to Find" (p. 409), "The Jilting of Granny Weatherall" (p. 777), "Do not go gentle into that good night" (p. 1065), "The Road Not Taken" (p. 1180), *Beauty* (p. 1308), *Tape* (p. 1313)

WILLIAM FAULKNER (1897–1962), winner of the 1949 Nobel Prize in Literature and the 1955 and 1963 Pulitzer Prizes for fiction, was a Southern writer whose work continues to transcend the regional label. His nineteen novels, notably *The Sound and the Fury* (1929), *As I Lay Dying* (1930), *Light in August* (1932), *Absalom, Absalom!* (1936), and *The Reivers* (1962), explore a wide range of human experience — from high comedy to tragedy — as seen in the life of one community, the fictional Yoknapatawpha County (modeled on the area around Faulkner's own hometown of Oxford, Mississippi). Faulkner's Yoknapatawpha stories — a fascinating blend of complex Latinate prose and primitive Southern dialect — paint an extraordinary portrait of a community bound together by ties of blood, by a shared belief in moral "verities," and by an old grief (the Civil War). Faulkner's grandfather raised "Billy" on Civil War tales and local legends, including many about the "Old Colonel," the writer's great-grandfather, who was a colorful Confederate officer. Although Faulkner's stories elegize the agrarian virtues of the Old South, they look unflinchingly at that world's tragic flaw: the "peculiar institution" of slavery.

Local legends and gossip frequently served as the spark for Faulkner's stories. As John B. Cullen, writing in *Old Times in Faulkner Country*, notes, "A Rose for Emily," Faulkner's first nationally published short story, was based on the tale of Oxford's aristocratic "Miss Mary" Neilson, who married Captain Jack Hume, the charming Yankee foreman of a street-paving crew, over her family's shocked protests. According to Cullen, one of Faulkner's neighbors said he created his story "out of fears and rumors"—the dire predictions of what *might* happen if Mary Neilson married her Yankee.

Cultural Context The "Old South" is a fictional construct that has long characterized the pre–Civil War South as an idealized land of prosperous plantations, large white houses, cultured and gracious people, and a stable economy based on farming. Elements of the myth of the Old South included chivalry, agrarian living, and the natural superiority of the aristocracy, who made its fortune by owning and running plantations that depended on slave labor. Once the South lost the Civil War, the idea of the Old South fell by the way-side, making room for the New South, which, like the North, was industrialized. In this story, Faulkner contrasts notions of the Old South and its decaying values with the newer ideas and innovations of the post-Reconstruction South.

A Rose for Emily (1930)

I

When Miss Emily Grierson died, our whole town went to her funeral: the men through a sort of respectful affection for a fallen monument, the women mostly out of curiosity to see the inside of her house, which no one save an old manser-vant — a combined gardener and cook — had seen in at least ten years.

It was a big, squarish frame house that had once been white, decorated with cupolas and spires and scrolled balconies in the heavily lightsome style of the sev-enties, set on what had once been our most select street. But garages and cotton gins had encroached and obliterated even the august names of that neighbor-hood; only Miss Emily's house was left, lifting its stubborn and coquettish decay above the cotton wagons and the gasoline pumps — an eyesore among eyesores. And now Miss Emily had gone to join the representatives of those august names where they lay in the cedar-bemused cemetery among the ranked and anonymous graves of Union and Confederate soldiers who fell at the battle of Jefferson.

Alive, Miss Emily had been a tradition, a duty, and a care; a sort of hereditary obligation upon the town, dating from that day in 1894 when Colonel Sartoris, the mayor — he who fathered the edict that no Negro woman should appear on the streets without an apron — remitted her taxes, the dispensation dating from the death of her father on into perpetuity. Not that Miss Emily would have accepted charity. Colonel Sartoris invented an involved tale to the effect that Miss Emily's father had loaned money to the town, which the town, as a matter of business, preferred this way of repaying. Only a man of Colonel Sartoris' generation and thought could have invented it, and only a woman could have believed it.

When the next generation, with its more modern ideas, became mayors and aldermen, this arrangement created some little dissatisfaction. On the first of the year they mailed her a tax notice. February came, and there was no reply. They wrote her a formal letter, asking her to call at the sheriff's office at her conven-ience. A week later the mayor wrote her himself, offering to call or to send his car for her, and received in reply a note on paper of an archaic shape, in a thin, flowing calligraphy in faded ink, to the effect that she no longer went out at all. The tax notice was also enclosed, without comment.

5   They called a special meeting of the Board of Aldermen. A deputation waited upon her, knocked at the door through which no visitor had passed since she ceased giving china-painting lessons eight or ten years earlier. They were admitted by the old Negro into a dim hall from which a stairway mounted into still more shadow. It smelled of dust and disuse — a close, dank smell. The Negro led them into the parlor. It was furnished in heavy, leather-covered furniture. When the Negro opened the blinds of one window, they could see that the leather was

cracked; and when they sat down, a faint dust rose sluggishly about their thighs, spinning with slow motes in the single sun-ray. On a tarnished gilt easel before the fireplace stood a crayon portrait of Miss Emily's father.

They rose when she entered — a small, fat woman in black, with a thin gold chain descending to her waist and vanishing into her belt, leaning on an ebony cane with a tarnished gold head. Her skeleton was small and spare; perhaps that was why what would have been merely plumpness in another was obesity in her. She looked bloated, like a body long submerged in motionless water, and of that pallid hue. Her eyes, lost in the fatty ridges of her face, looked like two small pieces of coal pressed into a lump of dough as they moved from one face to another while the visitors stated their errand.

She did not ask them to sit. She just stood in the door and listened quietly until the spokesman came to a stumbling halt. Then they could hear the invisible watch ticking at the end of the gold chain.

Her voice was dry and cold. "I have no taxes in Jefferson. Colonel Sartoris explained it to me. Perhaps one of you can gain access to the city records and satisfy yourselves."

"But we have. We are the city authorities, Miss Emily. Didn't you get a notice from the sheriff, signed by him?"

"I received a paper, yes," Miss Emily said. "Perhaps he considers himself the 10 sheriff . . . I have no taxes in Jefferson."

"But there is nothing on the books to show that, you see. We must go by the —"

"See Colonel Sartoris. I have no taxes in Jefferson."

"But, Miss Emily —"

"See Colonel Sartoris." (Colonel Sartoris had been dead almost ten years.) "I have no taxes in Jefferson. Tobe!" The Negro appeared. "Show these gentlemen out."

II

So she vanquished them, horse and foot, just as she had vanquished their fathers 15 thirty years before about the smell. That was two years after her father's death and a short time after her sweetheart — the one we believed would marry her — had deserted her. After her father's death she went out very little; after her sweetheart went away, people hardly saw her at all. A few of the ladies had the temerity to call, but were not received, and the only sign of life about the place was the Negro man — a young man then — going in and out with a market basket.

"Just as if a man — any man — could keep a kitchen properly," the ladies said; so they were not surprised when the smell developed. It was another link between the gross, teeming world and the high and mighty Griersons.

A neighbor, a woman, complained to the mayor, Judge Stevens, eighty years old.

"But what will you have me do about it, madam?" he said.

"Why, send her word to stop it," the woman said. "Isn't there a law?"

"I'm sure that won't be necessary," Judge Stevens said. "It's probably just a 20 snake or a rat that nigger of hers killed in the yard. I'll speak to him about it."

The next day he received two more complaints, one from a man who came in diffident deprecation. "We really must do something about it, Judge. I'd be the last one in the world to bother Miss Emily, but we've got to do something." That night the Board of Aldermen met — three graybeards and one younger man, a member of the rising generation.

"It's simple enough," he said. "Send her word to have her place cleaned up. Give her a certain time to do it in, and if she don't . . ."

"Dammit, sir," Judge Stevens said, "will you accuse a lady to her face of smelling bad?"

So the next night, after midnight, four men crossed Miss Emily's lawn and slunk about the house like burglars, sniffing along the base of the brickwork and at the cellar openings while one of them performed a regular sowing motion with his hand out of a sack slung from his shoulder. They broke open the cellar door and sprinkled lime there, and in all the outbuildings. As they recrossed the lawn, a window that had been dark was lighted and Miss Emily sat in it, the light behind her, and her upright torso motionless as that of an idol. They crept quietly across the lawn and into the shadow of the locusts that lined the street. After a week or two the smell went away.

25

That was when people had begun to feel really sorry for her. People in our town, remembering how old lady Wyatt, her great-aunt, had gone completely crazy at last, believed that the Griersons held themselves a little too high for what they really were. None of the young men were quite good enough for Miss Emily and such. We had long thought of them as a tableau, Miss Emily a slender figure in white in the background, her father a spraddled silhouette in the foreground, his back to her and clutching a horsewhip, the two of them framed by the back-flung front door. So when she got to be thirty and was still single, we were not pleased exactly, but vindicated; even with insanity in the family she wouldn't have turned down all of her chances if they had really materialized.

When her father died, it got about that the house was all that was left to her; and in a way, people were glad. At last they could pity Miss Emily. Being left alone, and a pauper, she had become humanized. Now she too would know the old thrill and the old despair of a penny more or less.

The day after his death all the ladies prepared to call at the house and offer condolence and aid, as is our custom. Miss Emily met them at the door, dressed as usual and with no trace of grief on her face. She told them that her father was not dead. She did that for three days, with the ministers calling on her, and the doctors, trying to persuade her to let them dispose of the body. Just as they were about to resort to law and force, she broke down, and they buried her father quickly.

We did not say she was crazy then. We believed she had to do that. We remembered all the young men her father had driven away, and we knew that with nothing left, she would have to cling to that which had robbed her, as people will.

III

She was sick for a long time. When we saw her again, her hair was cut short, making her look like a girl, with a vague resemblance to those angels in colored church windows — sort of tragic and serene.

The town had just let the contracts for paving the sidewalks, and in the sum-   30
mer after her father's death they began the work. The construction company
came with niggers and mules and machinery, and a foreman named Homer Barron,
a Yankee — a big, dark, ready man, with a big voice and eyes lighter than his face.
The little boys would follow in groups to hear him cuss the niggers, and the niggers singing in time to the rise and fall of picks. Pretty soon he knew everybody
in town. Whenever you heard a lot of laughing anywhere about the square,
Homer Barron would be in the center of the group. Presently we began to see him
and Miss Emily on Sunday afternoons driving in the yellow-wheeled buggy and
the matched team of bays from the livery stable.

At first we were glad that Miss Emily would have an interest, because the
ladies all said, "Of course a Grierson would not think seriously of a Northerner, a
day laborer." But there were still others, older people, who said that even grief
could not cause a real lady to forget *noblesse oblige*° — without calling it *noblesse
oblige*. They just said, "Poor Emily. Her kinsfolk should come to her." She had
some kin in Alabama; but years ago her father had fallen out with them over the
estate of old lady Wyatt, the crazy woman, and there was no communication between the two families. They had not even been represented at the funeral.

And as soon as the old people said, "Poor Emily," the whispering began. "Do
you suppose it's really so?" they said to one another. "Of course it is. What else
could . . ." This behind their hands; rustling of craned silk and satin behind
jalousies closed upon the sun of Sunday afternoon as the thin, swift clop-clop-
clop of the matched team passed: "Poor Emily."

She carried her head high enough — even when we believed that she was
fallen. It was as if she demanded more than ever the recognition of her dignity as
the last Grierson; as if it had wanted that touch of earthiness to reaffirm her im-
perviousness. Like when she bought the rat poison, the arsenic. That was over a
year after they had begun to say "Poor Emily," and while the two female cousins
were visiting her.

"I want some poison," she said to the druggist. She was over thirty then, still a
slight woman, though thinner than usual, with cold, haughty black eyes in a face
the flesh of which was strained across the temples and about the eye-sockets as you
imagine a lighthouse-keeper's face ought to look. "I want some poison," she said.

"Yes, Miss Emily. What kind? For rats and such? I'd recom —"   35

"I want the best you have. I don't care what kind."

The druggist named several. "They'll kill anything up to an elephant. But
what you want is —"

"Arsenic," Miss Emily said. "Is that a good one?"

"Is . . . arsenic? Yes, ma'am. But what you want —"

"I want arsenic."   40

The druggist looked down at her. She looked back at him, erect, her face like
a strained flag. "Why, of course," the druggist said. "If that's what you want. But
the law requires you to tell what you are going to use it for."

---

noblesse oblige: The obligation of those of high birth or rank to behave honorably.

Miss Emily just stared at him, her head tilted back in order to look him eye for eye, until he looked away and went and got the arsenic and wrapped it up. The Negro delivery boy brought her the package; the druggist didn't come back. When she opened the package at home there was written on the box, under the skull and bones: "For rats."

IV

So the next day we all said, "She will kill herself"; and we said it would be the best thing. When she had first begun to be seen with Homer Barron, we had said, "She will marry him." Then we said, "She will persuade him yet," because Homer himself had remarked — he liked men, and it was known that he drank with the younger men in the Elks' Club — that he was not a marrying man. Later we said, "Poor Emily" behind the jalousies as they passed on Sunday afternoon in the glittering buggy, Miss Emily with her head high and Homer Barron with his hat cocked and a cigar in his teeth, reins and whip in a yellow glove.

Then some of the ladies began to say that it was a disgrace to the town and a bad example to the young people. The men did not want to interfere, but at last the ladies forced the Baptist minister — Miss Emily's people were Episcopal — to call upon her. He would never divulge what happened during that interview, but he refused to go back again. The next Sunday they again drove about the streets, and the following day the minister's wife wrote to Miss Emily's relations in Alabama.

45   So she had blood-kin under her roof again and we sat back to watch developments. At first nothing happened. Then we were sure that they were to be married. We learned that Miss Emily had been to the jeweler's and ordered a man's toilet set in silver, with the letters H. B. on each piece. Two days later we learned that she had bought a complete outfit of men's clothing, including a nightshirt, and we said, "They are married." We were really glad. We were glad because the two female cousins were even more Grierson than Miss Emily had ever been.

So we were not surprised when Homer Barron — the streets had been finished some time since — was gone. We were a little disappointed that there was not a public blowing-off, but we believed that he had gone on to prepare for Miss Emily's coming, or to give her a chance to get rid of the cousins. (By that time it was a cabal, and we were all Miss Emily's allies to help circumvent the cousins.) Sure enough, after another week they departed. And, as we had expected all along, within three days Homer Barron was back in town. A neighbor saw the Negro man admit him at the kitchen door at dusk one evening.

And that was the last we saw of Homer Barron. And of Miss Emily for some time. The Negro man went in and out with the market basket, but the front door remained closed. Now and then we would see her at a window for a moment, as the men did that night when they sprinkled the lime, but for almost six months she did not appear on the streets. Then we knew that this was to be expected too; as if that quality of her father which had thwarted her woman's life so many times had been too virulent and too furious to die.

When we next saw Miss Emily, she had grown fat and her hair was turning gray. During the next few years it grew grayer and grayer until it attained an even pepper-and-salt iron-gray, when it ceased turning. Up to the day of her death at seventy-four it was still that vigorous iron-gray, like the hair of an active man.

From that time on her front door remained closed, save for a period of six or seven years, when she was about forty, during which she gave lessons in china-painting. She fitted up a studio in one of the downstairs rooms, where the daughters and granddaughters of Colonel Sartoris' contemporaries were sent to her with the same regularity and in the same spirit that they were sent to church on Sundays with a twenty-five-cent piece for the collection plate. Meanwhile her taxes had been remitted.

Then the newer generation became the backbone and the spirit of the town, 50 and the painting pupils grew up and fell away and did not send their children to her with boxes of color and tedious brushes and pictures cut from the ladies' magazines. The front door closed upon the last one and remained closed for good. When the town got free postal delivery, Miss Emily alone refused to let them fasten the metal numbers above her door and attach a mailbox to it. She would not listen to them.

Daily, monthly, yearly we watched the Negro grow grayer and more stooped, going in and out with the market basket. Each December we sent her a tax notice, which would be returned by the post office a week later, unclaimed. Now and then we would see her in one of the downstairs windows — she had evidently shut up the top floor of the house — like the carven torso of an idol in a niche, looking or not looking at us, we could never tell which. Thus she passed from generation to generation — dear, inescapable, impervious, tranquil, and perverse.

And so she died. Fell ill in the house filled with dust and shadows, with only a doddering Negro man to wait on her. We did not even know she was sick; we had long since given up trying to get any information from the Negro. He talked to no one, probably not even to her, for his voice had grown harsh and rusty, as if from disuse.

She died in one of the downstairs rooms, in a heavy walnut bed with a curtain, her gray head propped on a pillow yellow and moldy with age and lack of sunlight.

V

The Negro met the first of the ladies at the front door and let them in, with their hushed, sibilant voices and their quick, curious glances, and then he disappeared. He walked right through the house and out the back and was not seen again.

The two female cousins came at once. They held the funeral on the second 55 day, with the town coming to look at Miss Emily beneath a mass of bought flowers, with the crayon face of her father musing profoundly above the bier and the ladies sibilant and macabre; and the very old men — some in their brushed Confederate uniforms — on the porch and the lawn, talking of Miss Emily as if she had been a contemporary of theirs, believing that they had danced with her and courted her perhaps, confusing time with its mathematical progression, as the old do, to whom all the past is not a diminishing road but, instead, a huge meadow which no winter ever quite touches, divided from them now by the narrow bottle-neck of the most recent decade of years.

Already we knew that there was one room in that region above stairs which no one had seen in forty years, and which would have to be forced. They waited until Miss Emily was decently in the ground before they opened it.

The violence of breaking down the door seemed to fill this room with pervading dust. A thin, acrid pall as of the tomb seemed to lie everywhere upon this room decked and furnished as for a bridal: upon the valance curtains of faded rose color, upon the rose-shaded lights, upon the dressing table, upon the delicate array of crystal and the man's toilet things backed with tarnished silver, silver so tarnished that the monogram was obscured. Among them lay collar and tie, as if they had just been removed, which, lifted, left upon the surface a pale crescent in the dust. Upon a chair hung the suit, carefully folded; beneath it the two mute shoes and the discarded socks.

The man himself lay in the bed.

For a long while we just stood there, looking down at the profound and fleshless grin. The body had apparently once lain in the attitude of an embrace, but now the long sleep that outlasts love, that conquers even the grimace of love, had cuckolded him. What was left of him, rotted beneath what was left of the nightshirt, had become inextricable from the bed in which he lay; and upon him and upon the pillow beside him lay that even coating of the patient and biding dust.

60   Then we noticed that in the second pillow was the indentation of a head. One of us lifted something from it, and leaning forward, that faint and invisible dust dry and acrid in the nostrils, we saw a long strand of iron-gray hair.

Reading and Reacting

1. Arrange these events in the sequence in which they actually occur: Homer's arrival in town, the aldermen's visit, Emily's purchase of poison, Colonel Sartoris's decision to remit Emily's taxes, the development of the odor around Emily's house, Emily's father's death, the arrival of Emily's relatives, Homer's disappearance. Then, list the events in the sequence in which they are introduced in the story. Why do you suppose Faulkner presents these events out of their actual chronological order?

2. Despite the story's confusing sequence, many events are foreshadowed. Give some examples of this technique. How does foreshadowing enrich the story?

3. Where does the exposition end and the movement toward the story's climax begin? Where does the resolution stage begin?

4. Emily is clearly the story's protagonist. In the sense that he opposes her wishes, Homer is the antagonist. What other characters — or what larger forces — are in conflict with Emily?

5. Explain how each of these phrases moves the story's plot along: "So she vanquished them, horse and foot . . ." (par. 15); "After a week or two the smell went away" (par. 24); "And that was the last we saw of Homer Barron" (par. 47); "And so she died" (par. 52); "The man himself lay in the bed" (par. 58).

6. The narrator of the story is an observer, not a participant. Who might this narrator be? How do you suppose the narrator might know so much about Emily? Why do you think the narrator uses *we* instead of *I*?

7. The original version of "A Rose for Emily" included a two-page deathbed scene revealing that Tobe, Emily's servant, has shared her terrible secret all these years, and that Emily has left her house to him. Why do you

think Faulkner deleted this scene? Do you think he made the right decision?

8. Some critics have suggested that Miss Emily Grierson is a kind of symbol of the Old South, with its outdated ideas of chivalry, formal manners, and tradition. Do you see her also as a victim of those values? Explain.

9. **JOURNAL ENTRY** When asked at a seminar at the University of Virginia about the meaning of the title "A Rose for Emily," Faulkner replied, "Oh, it's simply the poor woman had no life at all. Her father had kept her more or less locked up and then she had a lover who was about to quit her, she had to murder him. It was just 'A Rose for Emily'— that's all." In another interview, asked the same question, he replied, "I pitied her and this was a salute, just as if you were to make a gesture, a salute, to anyone; to a woman you would hand a rose, as you would lift a cup of *sake* to a man." What do you make of Faulkner's responses? What else might the title suggest?

10. **CRITICAL PERSPECTIVE** In his essay "William Faulkner: An American Dickens," literary critic Leslie A. Fiedler characterizes Faulkner as "primarily . . . a sentimental writer; not a writer with the occasional vice of sentimentality, but one whose basic mode of experience is sentimental." He continues, "In a writer whose very method is self-indulgence, that sentimentality becomes sometimes downright embarrassing." Fiedler also notes Faulkner's "excesses of maudlin feelings and absurd indulgences in overripe rhetoric."

    Do you think these criticisms apply to "A Rose for Emily"? If so, does the "vice of sentimentality" diminish the story, or do you agree with Fiedler — who calls Faulkner a "supereminently good 'bad' writer"— that the author is able to transcend these excesses?

Related Works: "Miss Brill" (p. 235), "Nice Car, Camille" (p. 862), "Porphyria's Lover" (p. 876), "Richard Cory" (p. 1219), *Trifles* (p. 1372)

WRITING SUGGESTIONS: Plot

1. Write a sequel to "The Story of an Hour," telling the story in the voice of Brently Mallard. Use flashbacks to provide information about his view of the Mallards' marriage.

2. Locate a newspaper or magazine article that you find disturbing. Then, write a "once upon a time" story like Gordimer's in which you retell the story's events in a detached tone without adding analysis or commentary. Expand the original article by creating additional characters and adding invented settings.

3. "The Story of an Hour" includes a **deus ex machina**, an outside force or agent that suddenly appears to change the course of events. Consider the possible effects of a deus ex machina on the other four stories in this chapter. What might this outside force be in each story? How might it change the story's action? How plausible would such a dramatic turn of events be in each case?

4. Both "Kansas" and "Half a Day" manipulate time to create a dreamlike, disorienting atmosphere that affects both characters and readers. However,

"Kansas" is essentially a realistic story while "Half a Day" is something quite different. Compare and contrast these two stories, focusing on how the passing of time affects the two protagonists and their perceptions of events.

5. Read the following article from the January 30, 1987, *Philadelphia Inquirer*. After listing some similarities and differences between the events in the article's story and those in "A Rose for Emily," write an essay in which you discuss how the presentation of events differs. Can you draw any conclusions about the differences between journalistic and fictional treatments of similar incidents?

DICK POTHIER AND THOMAS J. GIBBONS JR.

A Woman's Wintry Death Leads to a Long-Dead Friend

For more than two years, Frances Dawson Hamilton lived with the body of her long-time companion, draping his skeletonized remains with palm fronds and rosary beads.

Yesterday, the 70-year-old woman was found frozen to death in the home in the 4500 block of Higbee Street where she had lived all her life — the last year without heat or hot water. Her body was found by police accompanying a city social worker who came bearing an order to have her taken to a hospital.

Police investigators said the body of Bernard J. Kelly, 84, was found in an upstairs bedroom of the two-story brick home in the Wissinoming section, on the twin bed where he apparently died at least two years ago.

Two beds had been pushed together, and Hamilton apparently had been sleeping beside Kelly's remains since he died of unknown causes, police said.

Kelly's remains were clothed in long johns and socks, investigators said. The body was draped with rosary beads and palm fronds, and on the bed near his body were two boxes of Valentine's Day candy.

"It was basically a funeral — we've seen it before in such cases," said one investigator who was at the scene but declined to be identified.

Neighbors and investigators said Hamilton and Kelly had lived together in the house for at least 15 years. Several neighbors said Hamilton came from an affluent family, was educated in Europe, and lived on a trust fund until a year or so ago.

Last winter, said John Wasniewski, Hamilton's next-door neighbor, the basement of the home was flooded and the heater destroyed. "There was no heat in that house last winter or this winter," he said.

An autopsy will be performed on Hamilton today, but she apparently froze to death sometime since Monday, when a friend spoke to her on the telephone, investigators said.

Over the last two years, neighbors said, Hamilton had become increasingly reclusive and irrational. Just last week, a city social worker summoned by a friend arranged for a Philadelphia Gas Works team to visit the home and try to repair the furnace — but she refused to let them in.

The friend was James Phillips, 44, of Horsham, a salesman for Apex Electric in Souderton.

In October 1985, he said, Hamilton visited the Frankford Avenue electrical shop where he was then working, told him that she had an electrical problem in her house and had no lights, and asked whether he could help.

Phillips said he visited the house, fixed the problem and gave her some light bulbs.

"She was really paranoid," Phillips said. "She believed that all her problems were from people doing things to her. For some reason or other, she took to me."

Phillips said that he began visiting her, taking her shopping and doing some shopping for her. But, he said, he never saw the body on the second floor.

Hamilton told him there was a man up there. "I thought it was a story she was telling to protect herself," Phillips said.

He provided her with electric heaters and also contacted a caseworker with the city's Department of Human Services whom Phillips identified as Albert Zbik.

Between the two of them, he said, "we got her through last winter." Phillips said Zbik helped her obtain food stamps and Social Security assistance.

When the snowstorm hit last week, Phillips became concerned because he knew Hamilton would have trouble getting food. On Saturday, he took her a plate of hot food and bought more food from a local store.

On Monday, she telephoned him. "I didn't like the way she sounded," he said. He called Zbik and told him he felt it was time that they forced her to go to a hospital.

Phillips said Zbik went to her home yesterday, carrying a form authorizing an involuntary admission to a hospital for observation or required medical treatment.

Phillips told police that he was never allowed above the first floor and was often told by Hamilton that "Bernie is not feeling well today."

Neighbors and police investigators said Kelly was last seen alive about two years ago, and appeared to be quite ill at the time.

"As recently as last month, I asked Frances how Bernard was and whether she should get a doctor, and she said it wasn't necessary. She said 'He's sick, but I'm taking care of him — I'm feeding him with an eyedropper,'" Wasniewski said.

"I told her in December that if he was that sick, she should call a doctor, but she'd say she was taking care of him very well," Wasniewski said.

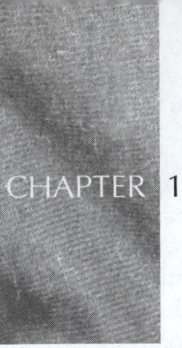

CHAPTER 13

CHARACTER

> Every real writer . . . starts with people and their emotions and actions and lets them make their own stories.
>
> — Martha Foley, *Best American Short Stories*

A **character** is a fictional representation of a person — usually (but not necessarily) a psychologically realistic depiction. Writers may develop characters through their actions, through their reactions to situations or to other characters, through their physical appearance, through their speech and gestures and expressions, and even through their names.

Generally speaking, characters' physical traits, as well as their feelings and beliefs, are communicated to readers in two ways. First, readers can be *told* about characters. Third-person narrators can provide information about what characters are doing, saying, and thinking; what experiences they have had; what they look like; how they are dressed; and so on. Sometimes they also offer analysis of and judgments about a character's behavior or motivation. Similarly, first-person narrators can tell us about themselves or about other characters. Thus, Sammy in John Updike's "A&P" (p. 230) tells readers what he thinks about his job and about the girls who come into the supermarket where he works. He also tells us what various characters look like and describes their actions, attitudes, speech, and gestures. (For more information about first-person narrators, see Chapter 15, "Point of View.")

Alternatively, a character's personality traits and motivation may be revealed through actions, dialogue, or thoughts. For instance, Sammy's vivid fantasies and his disapproval of his customers' lives suggest to readers that he is something of a nonconformist; however, Sammy himself does not actually tell us this.

Round and Flat Characters

In his influential 1927 work *Aspects of the Novel*, English novelist E. M. Forster classifies characters as either **round** (well developed, closely involved in and responsive to the action) or **flat** (barely developed or stereotypical). To a large extent, these categories are still useful. In an effective story, the major characters are usually complex and fully developed; if they are not, readers do not care what happens to them. Sometimes, readers are encouraged to become involved with the characters, even to identify with them, and this empathy is possible only when we know something about the characters — their strengths and weaknesses, their likes and dislikes. In some cases, of course, a story can be effective even when its central characters are not well developed. Sometimes, in fact, a story's effectiveness is enhanced by an *absence* of character development, as in Shirley Jackson's "The Lottery" (p. 461).

Readers often expect characters to behave as "real people" in their situation might behave. Real people are not perfect, and realistic characters cannot be perfect either. The flaws that are revealed as round characters are developed — greed, gullibility, naïveté, shyness, a quick temper, or a lack of insight or judgment or tolerance or even intelligence — make them believable. In modern fiction, the protagonist is seldom if ever the noble "hero"; more often, he or she is at least partly a victim, someone to whom some unpleasant things happen, and someone who is sometimes ill equipped to cope with events.

Unlike major characters, minor characters are frequently not well developed. Often they are flat, perhaps acting as *foils* for the protagonist. A **foil** is a supporting character whose role in the story is to highlight a major character by presenting a contrast with him or her. For instance, in "A&P," Stokesie, another young checkout clerk, is a foil for Sammy. Because he is a little older than Sammy and seems to have none of Sammy's imagination, restlessness, or nonconformity, Stokesie suggests what Sammy might become if he were to continue to work at the A&P. Some flat characters are **stock characters,** easily identifiable types who behave so predictably that readers can readily recognize them. The kindly old priest, the tough young bully, the ruthless business executive, and the reckless adventurer are all stock characters. Some flat characters can even be **caricatures,** characterized by a single dominant trait, such as miserliness, or even by one physical trait, such as nearsightedness.

Dynamic and Static Characters

Characters may also be classified as either *dynamic* or *static*. A **dynamic character** grows and changes in the course of a story, developing as he or she reacts to events and to other characters. In "A&P," for instance, Sammy's decision to speak out in defense of the girls — as well as the events that lead him to do so — changes him. His view of the world has changed at the end of the story, and as a result his position in the world will change too. A **static character** may face the same challenges a dynamic character might face but will remain essentially unchanged: a static character who was selfish and arrogant will remain selfish and arrogant, regardless of the nature of the story's conflict. In the fairy tale "Cinderella," for example, the title character is as sweet and good-natured at the end of the story — despite her mistreatment by her family — as she is at the beginning. Her situation may have changed, but her character has not.

Whereas round characters tend to be dynamic, flat characters tend to be static. But even a very complex, well-developed major character may be static; sometimes, in fact, the point of a story may hinge on a character's inability to change. A familiar example is the title character in William Faulkner's "A Rose for Emily" (p. 216), who lives a wasted, empty life, at least in part because she is unwilling or unable to accept that the world around her and the people in it have changed.

A story's minor characters are often static; their growth is not usually relevant to the story's development. Moreover, we usually do not learn enough about a minor character's traits, thoughts, actions, or motivation to determine whether the character changes significantly.

Motivation

Because round characters are complex, they are not always easy to understand. They may act unpredictably, just as real people do. They wrestle with decisions, resist or succumb to temptation, make mistakes, ask questions, search for answers, hope and dream, rejoice and despair. What is important is not whether we approve of a character's actions but whether those actions are *plausible*— whether the actions make sense in light of what we know about the character. We need to see a character's **motivation**— the reasons behind his or her behavior — or we will not believe or accept that behavior. For instance, given Sammy's age, his dissatisfaction with his job, and his desire to impress the young woman he calls Queenie, the decision he makes at the end of the story is perfectly plausible. Without having established his motivation, Updike could not have expected readers to accept Sammy's actions.

Of course, even when readers get to know a character, they still are not able to predict how a complex, round character will behave in a given situation; only a flat character is predictable. The tension that develops as readers wait to see how a character will act or react, and thus how a story's conflict will be resolved, is what holds readers' interest and keeps them involved as a story's action unfolds.

✔ **CHECKLIST   Writing about Character**

☐   Who is the story's protagonist? Who (or what) is the antagonist? Who are the other major characters?

☐   Who are the minor characters? What roles do they play in the story? How would the story be different without them?

☐   What do the major characters look like? Is their physical appearance important?

☐   What are the major characters' most noticeable personality traits?

☐   What are the major characters' likes and dislikes? Their strengths and weaknesses?

☐   What are we told about the major characters' backgrounds and prior experiences? What can we infer?

continued on next page

- Are the characters round or flat?

- Are the characters dynamic or static?

- Does the story include any stock characters? Any caricatures? Does any character serve as a foil?

- Do the characters act in a way that is consistent with how readers expect them to act?

- With which characters are readers likely to be most sympathetic? Least sympathetic?

JOHN UPDIKE (1932–   ) is a prolific writer of novels, short stories, essays, poems, plays, and children's tales. Updike's earliest ambition was to be a cartoonist for the *New Yorker*. He attended Harvard hoping to draw cartoons for the *Harvard Lampoon*, studied drawing and fine art at Oxford, and in 1955 went to work for the *New Yorker*—not as a cartoonist but as a "Talk of the Town" reporter. Updike left the *New Yorker* after three years to write full-time but (over forty years later) is still contributing stories, reviews, and essays to the magazine. Among his novels are *Rabbit, Run* (1960), *The Centaur* (1963), *Rabbit Redux* (1971), *Rabbit Is Rich* (1981), *The Witches of Eastwick* (1985), and *Rabbit at Rest* (1990). His most recent novels are *Seek My Face* (2002) and *Villages* (2004). Updike has also published *Collected Poems 1953–1993* (1993) and a collection of essays titled *The Afterlife and Other Stories* (1994). In 1998, Updike received the National Book Foundation Medal for Distinguished Contribution to American Letters.

In early stories such as "A&P" (1961), Updike draws on memories of his childhood and teenage years for the sort of "small" scenes and stories for which he quickly became famous. "There is a great deal to be said about almost anything," Updike comments in an interview in *Contemporary Authors*. "All people can be equally interesting. . . . Now either nobody is a hero or everybody is. I vote for everybody. My subject is the American Protestant small-town middle class. I like middles. It is in middles that extremes clash."

Cultural Context The 1950s were a decade of prosperity for the United States. Soldiers returned from World War II, women who had worked in defense plants returned to their homes, and the population soared as a result of a "baby boom." Part of this prosperity manifested itself materially: Americans strove to keep up with one another in terms of their possessions, and manufacturers raced to produce the latest consumer goods. Conformity became the norm, with the advent of mass-produced suburban tract houses and a conservative code of dress and behavior that dictated what was appropriate. This atmosphere is the context for the manager's disapproval in "A&P"—and Sammy's reaction foreshadows the mood of the rebellious generation to come, which would refuse to conform.

A&P   (1961)

**Film
Series**

DVD
See Ch. 19 for
film stills from
the DVD version
of this story.

In walks these three girls in nothing but bathing suits. I'm in the third check-out slot, with my back to the door, so I don't see them until they're over by the bread. The one that caught my eye first was the one in the plaid green two-piece. She was a chunky kid, with a good tan and a sweet broad soft-looking can with those two crescents of white just under it, where the sun never seems to hit, at the top of the backs of her legs. I stood there with my hand on a box of HiHo crackers trying to remember if I rang it up or not. I ring it up again and the customer starts giving me hell. She's one of these cash-register-watchers, a witch about fifty with rouge on her cheekbones and no eyebrows, and I know it made her day to trip me up. She'd been watching cash registers for fifty years and probably never seen a mistake before.

By the time I got her feathers smoothed and her goodies into a bag — she gives me a little snort in passing, if she'd been born at the right time they would have burned her over in Salem — by the time I get her on her way the girls had circled around the bread and were coming back, without a push-cart, back my way along the counters, in the aisle between the check-outs and the Special bins. They didn't even have shoes on. There was this chunky one, with the two-piece — it was bright green and the seams on the bra were still sharp and her belly was still pretty pale so I guessed she just got it (the suit) — there was this one, with one of those chubby berry-faces, the lips all bunched together under her nose, this one, and a tall one, with black hair that hadn't quite frizzed right, and one of these sunburns right across under the eyes, and a chin that was too long — you know, the kind of girl other girls think is very "striking" and "attractive" but never quite makes it, as they very well know, which is why they like her so much — and then the third one, that wasn't quite so tall. She was the queen. She kind of led them, the other two peeking around and making their shoulders round. She didn't look around, not this queen, she just walked straight on slowly, on these long white prima-donna legs. She came down a little hard on her heels, as if she didn't walk in her bare feet that much, putting down her heels and then letting the weight move along to her toes as if she was testing the floor with every step, putting a little deliberate extra action into it. You never know for sure how girls' minds work (do you really think it's a mind in there or just a little buzz like a bee in a glass jar?) but you got the idea she had talked the other two into coming in here with her, and now she was showing them how to do it, walk slow and hold yourself straight.

She had on a kind of dirty-pink — beige maybe, I don't know — bathing suit with a little nubble all over it and, what got me, the straps were down. They were off her shoulders looped loose around the cool tops of her arms, and I guess as a result the suit had slipped a little on her, so all around the top of the cloth there was this shining rim. If it hadn't been there you wouldn't have known there could have been anything whiter than those shoulders. With the straps pushed off, there was nothing between the top of the suit and the top of her head except just *her*, this clean bare plane of the top of her chest down from the shoulder bones like a dented sheet of metal tilted in the light. I mean, it was more than pretty.

She had sort of oaky hair that the sun and salt had bleached, done up in a bun that was unravelling, and a kind of prim face. Walking into the A&P with your straps down, I suppose it's the only kind of face you *can* have. She held her head so high her neck, coming up out of those white shoulders, looked kind of stretched, but I didn't mind. The longer her neck was, the more of her there was.

She must have felt in the corner of her eye me and over my shoulder Stokesie   5 in the second slot watching, but she didn't tip. Not this queen. She kept her eyes moving across the racks, and stopped, and turned so slow it made my stomach rub the inside of my apron, and buzzed to the other two, who kind of huddled against her for relief, and they all three of them went up the cat-and-dog-food-breakfast-cereal-macaroni-rice-raisins-seasonings-spreads-spaghetti-soft-drinks-crackers-and-cookies aisle. From the third slot I look straight up this aisle to the meat counter, and I watched them all the way. The fat one with the tan sort of fumbled with the cookies, but on second thought she put the packages back. The sheep pushing their carts down the aisle — the girls were walking against the usual traffic (not that we have one-way signs or anything) — were pretty hilarious. You could see them, when Queenie's white shoulders dawned on them, kind of jerk, or hop, or hiccup, but their eyes snapped back to their own baskets and on they pushed. I bet you could set off dynamite in an A&P and the people would by and large keep reaching and checking oatmeal off their lists and muttering "Let me see, there was a third thing, began with A, asparagus, no, ah, yes, applesauce!" or whatever it is they do mutter. But there was no doubt, this jiggled them. A few houseslaves in pin curlers even looked around after pushing their carts past to make sure what they had seen was correct.

You know, it's one thing to have a girl in a bathing suit down on the beach, where what with the glare nobody can look at each other much anyway, and another thing in the cool of the A&P, under the fluorescent lights, against all those stacked packages, with her feet paddling along naked over our checkerboard green-and-cream rubber-tile floor.

"Oh Daddy," Stokesie said beside me. "I feel so faint."

"Darling," I said. "Hold me tight." Stokesie's married, with two babies chalked up on his fuselage already, but as far as I can tell that's the only difference. He's twenty-two, and I was nineteen this April.

"Is it done?" he asks, the responsible married man finding his voice. I forgot to say he thinks he's going to be manager some sunny day, maybe in 1990 when it's called the Great Alexandrov and Petrooshki Tea Company or something.

What he meant was, our town is five miles from a beach, with a big summer   10 colony out on the Point, but we're right in the middle of town, and the women generally put on a shirt or shorts or something before they get out of the car into the street. And anyway these are usually women with six children and varicose veins mapping their legs and nobody, including them, could care less. As I say, we're right in the middle of town, and if you stand at our front doors you can see two banks and the Congregational church and the newspaper store and three real-estate offices and about twenty-seven old freeloaders tearing up Central Street because the sewer broke again. It's not as if we're on the Cape; we're north of Boston and there's people in this town haven't seen the ocean for twenty years.

The girls had reached the meat counter and were asking McMahon something. He pointed, they pointed, and they shuffled out of sight behind a pyramid of Diet Delight peaches. All that was left for us to see was old McMahon patting his mouth and looking after them sizing up their joints. Poor kids, I began to feel sorry for them, they couldn't help it.

Now here comes the sad part of the story, at least my family says it's sad but I don't think it's sad myself. The store's pretty empty, it being Thursday afternoon, so there was nothing much to do except lean on the register and wait for the girls to show up again. The whole store was like a pinball machine and I didn't know which tunnel they'd come out of. After a while they come around out of the far aisle, around the light bulbs, records at discount of the Caribbean Six or Tony Martin Sings or some such gunk you wonder they waste the wax on, sixpacks of candy bars, and plastic toys done up in cellophane that fall apart when a kid looks at them anyway. Around they come, Queenie still leading the way, and holding a little gray jar in her hand. Slots Three through Seven are unmanned and I could see her wondering between Stokes and me, but Stokesie with his usual luck draws an old party in baggy gray pants who stumbles up with four giant cans of pineapple juice (what do these bums *do* with all that pineapple juice? I've often asked myself) so the girls come to me. Queenie puts down the jar and I take it into my fingers icy cold. Kingfish Fancy Herring Snacks in Pure Sour Cream: 49. Now her hands are empty, not a ring or a bracelet, bare as God made them, and I wonder where the money's coming from. Still with that prim look she lifts a folded dollar bill out of the hollow at the center of her nubbled pink top. The jar went heavy in my hand. Really, I thought that was so cute.

Then everybody's luck begins to run out. Lengel comes in from haggling with a truck full of cabbages on the lot and is about to scuttle into that door marked MANAGER behind which he hides all day when the girls touch his eye. Lengel's pretty dreary, teaches Sunday school and the rest, but he doesn't miss that much. He comes over and says, "Girls, this isn't the beach."

Queenie blushes, though maybe it's just a brush of sunburn I was noticing for the first time, now that she was so close. "My mother asked me to pick up a jar of herring snacks." Her voice kind of startled me, the way voices do when you see the people first, coming out so flat and dumb yet kind of tony, too, the way it ticked over "pick up" and "snacks." All of a sudden I slid right down her voice into her living room. Her father and the other men were standing around in ice-cream coats and bow ties and the women were in sandals picking up herring snacks on toothpicks off a big plate and they were all holding drinks the color of water with olives and sprigs of mint in them. When my parents have somebody over they get lemonade and if it's a real racy affair Schlitz in tall glasses with "They'll Do It Every Time" cartoons stencilled on.

15   "That's all right," Lengel said. "But this isn't the beach." His repeating this struck me as funny, as if it had just occurred to him, and he had been thinking all these years the A&P was a great big dune and he was the head lifeguard. He didn't like my smiling — as I say he doesn't miss much — but he concentrates on giving the girls that sad Sunday-school-superintendent stare.

Queenie's blush is no sunburn now, and the plump one in plaid, that I liked better from the back — a really sweet can — pipes up, "We weren't doing any shopping. We just came in for the one thing."

"That makes no difference," Lengel tells her, and I could see from the way his eyes went that he hadn't noticed she was wearing a two-piece before. "We want you decently dressed when you come in here."

"We *are* decent," Queenie says suddenly, her lower lip pushing, getting sore now that she remembers her place, a place from which the crowd that runs the A&P must look pretty crummy. Fancy Herring Snacks flashed in her very blue eyes.

"Girls, I don't want to argue with you. After this come in here with your shoulders covered. It's our policy." He turns his back. That's policy for you. Policy is what the kingpins want. What the others want is juvenile delinquency.

All this while, the customers had been showing up with their carts but, you know, sheep, seeing a scene, they had all bunched up on Stokesie, who shook open a paper bag as gently as peeling a peach, not wanting to miss a word. I could feel in the silence everybody getting nervous, most of all Lengel, who asks me, "Sammy, have you rung up this purchase?"

I thought and said "No" but it wasn't about that I was thinking. I go through the punches, 4, 9, GROC, TOT — it's more complicated than you think, and after you do it often enough, it begins to make a little song, that you hear words to, in my case "Hello (*bing*) there, you (*gung*) hap-py *pee*-pul (*splat*)!" — the *splat* being the drawer flying out. I uncrease the bill, tenderly as you may imagine, it just having come from between the two smoothest scoops of vanilla I had ever known were there, and pass a half and a penny into her narrow pink palm, and nestle the herrings in a bag and twist its neck and hand it over, all the time thinking.

The girls, and who'd blame them, are in a hurry to get out, so I say "I quit" to Lengel quick enough for them to hear, hoping they'll stop and watch me, their unsuspected hero. They keep right on going, into the electric eye; the door flies open and they flicker across the lot to their car, Queenie and Plaid and Big Tall Goony-Goony (not that as raw material she was so bad), leaving me with Lengel and a kink in his eyebrow.

"Did you say something, Sammy?"

"I said I quit."

"I thought you did."

"You didn't have to embarrass them."

"It was they who were embarrassing us."

I started to say something that came out "Fiddle-de-doo." It's a saying of my grandmother's, and I know she would have been pleased.

"I don't think you know what you're saying," Lengel said.

"I know you don't," I said. "But I do." I pull the bow at the back of my apron and start shrugging it off my shoulders. A couple customers that had been heading for my slot begin to knock against each other, like scared pigs in a chute.

Lengel sighs and begins to look very patient and old and gray. He's been a friend of my parents for years. "Sammy, you don't want to do this to your Mom and Dad," he tells me. It's true, I don't. But it seems to me that once you begin a gesture it's fatal not to go through with it. I fold the apron, "Sammy" stitched in red

20

25

30

on the pocket, and put it on the counter, and drop the bow tie on top of it. The bow tie is theirs, if you've ever wondered. "You'll feel this for the rest of your life," Lengel says, and I know that's true, too, but remembering how he made that pretty girl blush makes me so scrunchy inside I punch the No Sale tab and the machine whirs "pee-pul" and the drawer splats out. One advantage to this scene taking place in summer, I can follow this up with a clean exit, there's no fumbling around getting your coat and galoshes, I just saunter into the electric eye in my white shirt that my mother ironed the night before, and the door heaves itself open, and outside the sunshine is skating around the asphalt.

I look around for my girls, but they're gone, of course. There wasn't anybody but some young married screaming with her children about some candy they didn't get by the door of a powder-blue Falcon station wagon. Looking back in the big windows, over the bags of peat moss and aluminum lawn furniture stacked on the pavement, I could see Lengel in my place in the slot, checking the sheep through. His face was dark gray and his back stiff, as if he'd just had an injection of iron, and my stomach kind of fell as I felt how hard the world was going to be to me hereafter.

Reading and Reacting

1. Summarize the information Sammy gives readers about his tastes and background. Why is this exposition vital to the story's development?
2. List some of the most obvious physical characteristics of the A&P's customers. How do these characteristics make them foils for Queenie and her friends?
3. What is it about Queenie and her friends that appeals to Sammy?
4. Is Queenie a stock character? Explain.
5. What rules and conventions are customers expected to follow in a supermarket? How does the behavior of Queenie and her friends violate these conventions?
6. Is the supermarket setting vital to the story? Could the story have been set in a car wash? In a fast-food restaurant? In a business office?
7. How accurate are Sammy's judgments about the other characters? How might the characters be portrayed if the story were told by Lengel?
8. Given what you learn about Sammy during the course of the story, what do you see as his *primary* motivation for quitting his job? What other factors motivate him?
9. JOURNAL ENTRY Where do you think Sammy will find himself in ten years? Why?
10. CRITICAL PERSPECTIVE In her 1976 book *The Necessary Blackness*, critic Mary Allen observes, "Updike's most tender reverence is reserved for women's bodies. The elegant style with which he describes female anatomy often becomes overwrought, as his descriptions do generally. But it always conveys wonder."

    In what passages in "A&P" does Updike (through Sammy) convey this sense of wonder? Do you think today's audience, reading the story forty-five years after Updike wrote it, and thirty years after Allen's essay was published, would still see such passages as conveying "tender reverence"? Or do you think readers might now see Sammy (and, indeed, Updike) as sexist? How do you see these passages?

Related Works: "Araby" (p. 395), "Bartleby, the Scrivener" (p. 731), "Please Fire Me" (p. 874), "Ex-Basketball Player" (p. 946), "A Supermarket in California" (p. 965), "The Road Not Taken" (p. 1180), *The Glass Menagerie* (p. 1998)

KATHERINE MANSFIELD (1888–1923), one of the pioneers of the modern short story, was born in New Zealand and educated in England. Very much a "modern young woman," she began living on her own in London at the age of nineteen, soon publishing stories and book reviews in many of the most influential literary magazines of the day.

A short story writer of great versatility, Mansfield produced sparkling social comedies as well as more intellectually and technically complex works intended for "perceptive readers." According to one critic, her best works "[w]ith delicate plainness . . . present elusive moments of decision, defeat, and small triumph." Her last two story collections — *Bliss and Other Stories* (1920) and *The Garden Party and Other Stories* (1922)—were met with immediate critical acclaim, but Mansfield's career was cut short in 1923 when she died of complications from tuberculosis at the age of thirty-five.

One notable theme in Mansfield's work is the *dame seule*, the "woman alone," which provides the basis for the poignant "Miss Brill."

Cultural Context During the nineteenth century, the task of spinning wool was typically given to unmarried women as a way for them to earn their keep in the home. Thus, the term *spinster* came into existence. Over time, the word acquired a negative stereotype, conjuring up the image of a lonely, childless, frumpy middle-aged woman who longs to be like other "normal" women — wives and mothers. Today, the word *spinster* is rarely used, reflecting the changed perception of unmarried women and the wider lifestyle choices open to them.

Miss Brill (1922)

Although it was so brilliantly fine — the blue sky powdered with gold and great spots of light like white wine splashed over the Jardins Publiques° — Miss Brill was glad that she had decided on her fur. The air was motionless, but when you opened your mouth there was just a faint chill, like a chill from a glass of iced water before you sip, and now and again a leaf came drifting — from nowhere, from the sky. Miss Brill put up her hand and touched her fur. Dear little thing! It was nice to feel it

---

Jardins Publiques: "Public Gardens" (French).

again. She had taken it out of its box that afternoon, shaken out the moth-powder, given it a good brush, and rubbed the life back into the dim little eyes. "What has been happening to me?" said the sad little eyes. Oh, how sweet it was to see them snap at her again from the red eiderdown! . . . But the nose, which was of some black composition, wasn't at all firm. It must have had a knock, somehow. Never mind — a little dab of black sealing-wax when the time came — when it was absolutely necessary. . . . Little rogue! Yes, she really felt like that about it. Little rogue biting its tail just by her left ear. She could have taken it off and laid in on her lap and stroked it. She felt a tingling in her hands and arms, but that came from walking, she supposed. And when she breathed, something light and sad — no, not sad, exactly — something gentle seemed to move in her bosom.

There were a number of people out this afternoon, far more than last Sunday. And the band sounded louder and gayer. That was because the Season had begun. For although the band played all year round on Sundays, out of season it was never the same. It was like some one playing with only the family to listen; it didn't care how it played if there weren't any strangers present. Wasn't the conductor wearing a new coat, too? She was sure it was new. He scraped with his foot and flapped his arms like a rooster about to crow, and the bandsmen sitting in the green rotunda blew out their cheeks and glared at the music. Now there came a little "flutey" bit — very pretty! — a little chain of bright drops. She was sure it would be repeated. It was; she lifted her head and smiled.

Only two people shared her "special" seat: a fine old man in a velvet coat, his hands clasped over a huge carved walking-stick, and a big old woman, sitting upright, with a roll of knitting on her embroidered apron. They did not speak. This was disappointing, for Miss Brill always looked forward to the conversation. She had become really quite expert, she thought, at listening as though she didn't listen, at sitting in other people's lives just for a minute while they talked round her.

She glanced, sideways, at the old couple. Perhaps they would go soon. Last Sunday, too, hadn't been as interesting as usual. An Englishman and his wife, he wearing a dreadful Panama hat and she button boots. And she'd gone on the whole time about how she ought to wear spectacles; she knew she needed them; but that it was no good getting any; they'd be sure to break and they'd never keep on. And he'd been so patient. He'd suggested everything — gold rims, the kind that curved round your ears, little pads inside the bridge. No, nothing would please her. "They'll always be sliding down my nose!" Miss Brill wanted to shake her.

5   The old people sat on the bench, still as statues. Never mind, there was always the crowd to watch. To and fro, in front of the flower-beds and the band rotunda, the couples and groups paraded, stopped to talk, to greet, to buy a handful of flowers from the old beggar who had his tray fixed to the railings. Little children ran among them, swooping and laughing; little boys with big white silk bows under their chins, little girls, little French dolls, dressed up in velvet and lace. And sometimes a tiny staggerer came suddenly rocking into the open from under the trees, stopped, stared, as suddenly sat down "flop," until its small high-stepping mother, like a young hen, rushed scolding to its rescue. Other people sat on the benches and green chairs, but they were nearly always the same, Sunday after Sunday, and — Miss Brill had often noticed — there was something funny about nearly all of them.

They were odd, silent, nearly all old, and from the way they stared they looked as though they'd just come from dark little rooms or even — even cupboards!

Behind the rotunda the slender trees with yellow leaves down drooping, and through them just a line of sea, and beyond the blue sky with gold-veined clouds.

Tum-tum-tum tiddle-um! tiddle-um! tum tiddley-um tum ta! blew the band.

Two young girls in red came by and two young soldiers in blue met them, and they laughed and paired and went off arm-in-arm. Two peasant women with funny straw hats passed, gravely, leading beautiful smoke-colored donkeys. A cold, pale nun hurried by. A beautiful woman came along and dropped her bunch of violets, and a little boy ran after to hand them to her, and she took them and threw them away as if they'd been poisoned. Dear me! Miss Brill didn't know whether to admire that or not! And now an ermine toque° and a gentleman in grey met just in front of her. He was tall, stiff, dignified, and she was wearing the ermine toque she'd bought when her hair was yellow. Now everything, her hair, her face, even her eyes, was the same color as the shabby ermine, and her hand, in its cleaned glove, lifted to dab her lips, was a tiny yellowish paw. Oh, she was so pleased to see him — delighted! She rather thought they were going to meet that afternoon. She described where she'd been — everywhere, here, there, along by the sea. The day was so charming — didn't he agree? And wouldn't he, perhaps? . . . But he shook his head, lighted a cigarette, slowly breathed a great deep puff into her face, and, even while she was still talking and laughing, flicked the match away and walked on. The ermine toque was alone; she smiled more brightly than ever. But even the band seemed to know what she was feeling and played more softly, played tenderly, and the drum beat, "The Brute! The Brute!" over and over. What would she do? What was going to happen now? But as Miss Brill wondered, the ermine toque turned, raised her hand as though she'd seen some one else, much nicer, just over there, and pattered away. And the band changed again and played more quickly, more gaily than ever, and the old couple on Miss Brill's seat got up and marched away, and such a funny old man with long whiskers hobbled along in time to the music and was nearly knocked over by four girls walking abreast.

Oh, how fascinating it was! How she enjoyed it! How she loved sitting here, watching it all! It was like a play. It was exactly like a play. Who could believe the sky at the back wasn't painted? But it wasn't till a little brown dog trotted on solemn and then slowly trotted off, like a little "theatre" dog, a little dog that had been drugged, that Miss Brill discovered what it was that made it so exciting. They were all on the stage. They weren't only the audience, not only looking on; they were acting. Even she had a part and came every Sunday. No doubt somebody would have noticed if she hadn't been there; she was part of the performance after all. How strange she'd never thought of it like that before! And yet it explained why she made such a point of starting from home at just the same time each week — so as not to be late for the performance — and it also explained why she had quite a queer, shy feeling at telling her English pupils how she spent her Sunday afternoons. No wonder! Miss Brill nearly laughed out loud. She was on

---

toque: Small, close-fitting woman's hat.

the stage. She thought of the old invalid gentleman to whom she read the newspaper four afternoons a week while he slept in the garden. She had got quite used
to the frail head on the cotton pillow, the hollowed eyes, the open mouth and the
high pinched nose. If he'd been dead she mightn't have noticed for weeks; she
wouldn't have minded. But suddenly he knew he was having the paper read to him
by an actress! "An actress!" The old head lifted; two points of light quivered in
the old eyes. "An actress — are ye?" And Miss Brill smoothed the newspaper as
though it were the manuscript of her part and said gently: "Yes, I have been an
actress for a long time."

10   The band had been having a rest. Now they started again. And what they
played was warm, sunny, yet there was just a faint chill — a something, what was
it? — not sadness — no, not sadness — a something that made you want to sing.
The tune lifted, lifted, the light shone; and it seemed to Miss Brill that in another
moment all of them, all the whole company, would begin singing. The young
ones, the laughing ones who were moving together, they would begin, and the
men's voices, very resolute and brave, would join them. And then she too, she too,
and the others on the benches — they would come in with a kind of accompaniment — something low, that scarcely rose or fell, something so beautiful — moving. . . . And Miss Brill's eyes filled with tears and she looked smiling at all the
other members of the company. Yes, we understand, we understand, she thought —
though what they understood she didn't know.

Just at that moment a boy and a girl came and sat down where the old couple
had been. They were beautifully dressed; they were in love. The hero and heroine, of course, just arrived from his father's yacht. And still soundlessly singing,
still with that trembling smile, Miss Brill prepared to listen.

"No, not now," said the girl. "Not here, I can't."

"But why? Because of that stupid old thing at the end there?" asked the boy.
"Why does she come here at all — who wants her? Why doesn't she keep her silly
old mug at home?"

"It's her fu-fur which is so funny," giggled the girl. "It's exactly like a fried
whiting."°

15   "Ah, be off with you!" said the boy in an angry whisper. Then: "Tell me, my
petite chérie —"°

"No, not here," said the girl. "Not yet."

On her way home she usually bought a slice of honeycake at the baker's. It was
her Sunday treat. Sometimes there was an almond in her slice, sometimes not. It
made a great difference. If there was an almond it was like carrying home a tiny
present — a surprise — something that might very well not have been there. She
hurried on the almond Sundays and struck the match for the kettle in quite a
dashing way.

But to-day she passed the baker's boy, climbed the stairs, went into the little
dark room — her room like a cupboard — and sat down on the red eiderdown.

---

whiting: Food fish related to the cod.

petite chérie: "Little darling" (French).

She sat there for a long time. The box that the fur came out of was on the bed. She unclasped the necklet quickly; quickly, without looking, laid it inside. But when she put the lid on she thought she heard something crying.

Reading and Reacting

1. What specific details can you infer about Miss Brill's character (and, perhaps, about her life) from this statement: "She had become really quite expert, she thought, at listening as though she didn't listen, at sitting in other people's lives just for a minute while they talked round her" (par. 3)?

2. How do Miss Brill's observations of the people around her give us insight into her own character? Why do you suppose she doesn't interact with any of the people she observes?

3. In paragraph 9, Miss Brill realizes that the scene she observes is "exactly like a play" and that "Even she had a part and came every Sunday." What part does Miss Brill play? Is she a stock character in this play, or is she a three-dimensional character? Does she play a lead role or a supporting role?

4. What do you think Miss Brill means when she says, "I have been an actress for a long time" (par. 9)? What does this comment reveal about how she sees herself? Is her view of herself similar to or different from the view the other characters have of her?

5. What role does Miss Brill's fur piece play in the story? In what sense, if any, does it function as a character?

6. What happens in paragraphs 11–16 to break Miss Brill's mood? Why is the scene she observes so upsetting to her?

7. At the end of the story, has Miss Brill changed as a result of what she has overheard, or is she the same person she was at the beginning? Do you think she will return to the park the following Sunday?

8. The story's last paragraph describes Miss Brill's room as being "like a cupboard." Where else has this image appeared in the story? What does its repetition in the conclusion tell us?

9. **JOURNAL ENTRY** Write a character sketch of Miss Brill, inventing a plausible family and personal history that might help to explain the character you see in the story.

10. **CRITICAL PERSPECTIVE** Critic Gillian Boddy, in *Katherine Mansfield: The Woman, The Writer*, offers the following analysis of Mansfield's fiction:

> The story evolves through the characters' minds. The external narrator is almost eliminated. As so often in her work, the reader is dropped into the story and simply confronted by a particular situation. There is no preliminary establishing and identification of time and place. The reader is immediately involved; it is assumed that he or she has any necessary prerequisite knowledge and is, in a sense, part of the story too.

Do you see this absence of conventional exposition as a problem in "Miss Brill"? Do you think the story would be more effective if Mansfield had supplied more preliminary information about setting and character? Or do you believe that what Boddy calls Mansfield's "concentration on a moment or episode" is a satisfactory substitute for the missing exposition, effectively shifting interest from "*what* happens" to "*why* it happens"?

Related Works: "Eveline" (p. 722), "Rooming houses are old women" (p. 942), "Aunt Jennifer's Tigers" (p. 977), "After great pain, a formal feeling comes —" (p. 1159), "Acquainted with the Night" (p. 1177), *The Stronger* (p. 1520)

GISH JEN (1956–) was born Lillian Jen in Scarsdale, New York, the daughter of Chinese immigrants. She attended Harvard University, graduating with a degree in English. While on an archaeological dig in Pennsylvania for the National Science Foundation, Jen chose the name Gish, after silent-screen actress Lillian Gish. Widely published, her work has appeared in *The New Yorker*, the *New Republic*, and the *New York Times*, as well as in a variety of anthologies, including *The Best American Short Stories of the Century*. She has published three novels, including *Typical American* (1991)—a *New York Times* notable book of the year and a finalist for the National Book Critics' Circle Award—its sequel, *Mona in the Promised Land* (1996); and *The Love Wife* (2004). Her collection of stories, *Who's Irish?*, was published in 1999.

Jen's literary work is largely concerned with the immigrant experience in the United States. For many immigrants, the issue of assimilation is problematic. Parents who bring with them the language and culture of their native country must strike a balance between their old ways and the new language and culture of America. The first-generation offspring must also struggle with how to preserve their culture while "fitting in." The characters in this story, who also appear in *Typical American* and *Mona in the Promised Land,* face these problems.

Cultural Context Much of the thematic content of this story is drawn from the Catholic Church's conception of sainthood, miracles, visions, and martyrdom. According to Catholic doctrine, for a person to become a saint, he or she must have exhibited heroic virtues in life and have performed two miracles, at least one of which must have occurred after the candidate's death. A *miracle* is defined as a grand event that defies nature but is possible due to the direct intervention of God. A *vision* is a waking or dreaming visitation by God in which His divine plan or understanding is revealed. A *martyr* is a person who chooses to die rather than renounce the Catholic faith; many martyrs were later beatified and made saints.

The Water Faucet Vision   (1987)

1   To protect my sister, Mona, and me from the pains — or, as they pronounced it, the *pens* — of life, my parents did their fighting in Shanghai dialect, which we didn't understand; and when my father one day pitched a brass vase through the kitchen window, my mother told us he had done it by accident.

2   "By accident?" said Mona.

3   My mother chopped the foot off a mushroom.

4   "By accident?" said Mona. "By *accident?*"

Later, I tried to explain to her that she shouldn't have persisted like that, but   5
it was hopeless.

"What's the matter with throwing things?" she shrugged. "He was *mad*."   6

That was the difference between Mona and me: fighting was just fighting to   7
her. If she worried about anything, it was only that she might turn out too short
to become a ballerina, in which case she was going to be a piano player.

I, on the other hand, was going to be a martyr. I was in fifth grade then, and   8
the hyperimaginative sort — the kind of girl who grows morbid in Catholic
school, who longs to be chopped or frozen to death but then has nightmares about
it from which she wakes up screaming and clutching a stuffed bear. It was not a
bear that I clutched, though, but a string of three malachite beads that I had
found in the marsh by the old aqueduct one day. Apparently once part of a necklace, they were each wonderfully striated and swirled, and slightly humped toward
the center, like a jellyfish; so that if I squeezed one, it would slip smoothly away,
with a grace that altogether enthralled and — on those dream-harrowed
nights — soothed me, soothed me as nothing had before or has since. Not that
I've lacked occasion for soothing: Though it's been four months since my mother
died, there are still nights when sleep stands away from me, stiff as a well-paid sentry. But that is another story. Back then, I had my malachite beads, and if I worried them long and patiently enough, I was sure to start feeling better, more
awake, even a little special — imagining, as I liked to, that my nightmares were
communications from the Almighty Himself, preparation for my painful destiny.
Discussing them with Patty Creamer, who had also promised her life to God, I
called them "almost visions"; and Patty, her mouth wadded with the three or four
sticks of Doublemint she always seemed to have going at once, said, "I bet you'll
be doin' miracleth by seventh grade."

Miracles. Today Patty laughs to think she ever spent good time stewing on   9
such matters, her attention having long turned to rugs, and artwork, and antique
Japanese bureaus — things she believes in.

"A good bureau's more than just a bureau," she explained last time we had   10
lunch. "It's a hedge against life. I tell you, if there's one thing I believe, it's that
cheap stuff's just money out the window. Nice stuff, on the other hand —*now that
you* can always cash out, if life gets rough. *That* you can count on."

In fifth grade, though, she counted on different things.   11

"You'll be doing miracles, too," I told her, but she shook her shaggy head and   12
looked doleful.

"Na' me," she chomped. "Buzzit's okay. The kin' things I like, prayers work   13
okay on."

"Like?"   14

"Like you 'member that dreth I liked?"   15

She meant the yellow one, with the crisscross straps.   16

"Well gueth what."   17

"Your mom got it for you."   18

She smiled. "And I only jutht prayed for it for a week," she said.   19

As for myself, though, I definitely wanted to be able to perform a wonder or   20
two. Miracle working! It was the carrot of carrots. It kept me doing my homework,

taking the sacraments; it kept me mournfully on key in music hour, while my classmates hiccupped and squealed their carefree hearts away. Yet I couldn't have said what I wanted such powers for, exactly. That is, I thought of them the way one might think of, say, an ornamental sword — as a kind of collectible, which also happened to be a means of defense.

21   But then Patty's father walked out on her mother, and for the first time, there was a miracle I wanted to do. I wanted it so much, I could see it: Mr. Creamer made into a spitball. Mr. Creamer shot through a straw into the sky. Mr. Creamer unrolled and replumped, plop back on Patty's doorstep. I would've cleaned out his mind and given him a shave en route. I would've given him a box of peanut fudge, tied up with a ribbon, to present to Patty with a kiss.

22   But instead, all I could do was try to tell her he'd come back.

23   "He will not, he will not!" she sobbed. "He went on a boat to Rio Deniro. To Rio Deniro!"

24   I tried to offer her a stick of gum, but she wouldn't take it.

25   "He said he would rather look at water than at my mom's fat face. He said he would rather look at water than at me." Now she was really wailing, and holding her ribs so tightly that she almost seemed to be hurting herself — so tightly that just looking at her arms wound around her like snakes made my heart feel squeezed.

26   I patted her on the arm. A one-winged pigeon waddled by.

27   "He said I wasn't even his kid, he said I came from Uncle Johnny. He said I was garbage, just like my mom and Uncle Johnny. He said I wasn't even his kid, he said I wasn't his Patty, he said I came from Uncle Johnny!"

28   "From your Uncle Johnny?" I said stupidly.

29   "From Uncle Johnny," she cried. "From Uncle Johnny!"

30   "He said that?"

31   She kept crying.

32   I tried again. "Oh Patty, don't cry," I said. Then I said, "Your dad was a jerk anyway."

33   The pigeon produced a large runny dropping.

34   It was a good twenty minutes before Patty was calm enough for me to run to the girls' room to get her some toilet paper; and by the time I came back she was sobbing again, saying "to Rio Deniro, to Rio Deniro" over and over, as though the words had stuck in her and couldn't be gotten out. Seeing as how we had missed the regular bus home and the late bus, too, I had to leave her a second time to go call my mother, who was only mad until she heard what had happened. Then she came and picked us up, and bought us each a Fudgsicle.

35   Some days later, Patty and I started a program to work on getting her father home. It was a serious business. We said extra prayers, and lit votive candles. I tied my malachite beads to my uniform belt, fondling them as though they were a rosary, and I a nun. We even took to walking about the school halls with our hands folded — a sight so ludicrous that our wheeze of a principal personally took us aside one day.

36   "I must tell you," she said, using her nose as a speaking tube, "that there is really no need for such peee-ity."

But we persisted, promising to marry God and praying to every saint we could 37 think of. We gave up gum, then gum and Slim Jims both, then gum and Slim Jims and ice cream; and when even that didn't work, we started on more innovative things. The first was looking at flowers. We held our hands beside our eyes like blinders as we hurried past the violets by the flagpole. Next it was looking at boys: Patty gave up angel-eyed Jamie Halloran, and I, gymnastic Anthony Rossi. It was hard, but in the end our efforts paid off. Mr. Creamer came back a month later, and though he brought with him nothing but dysentery, he was at least too sick to have all that much to say.

Then, in the course of a fight with my father, my mother somehow fell out of 38 their bedroom window.

Recently — thinking a mountain vacation might cheer me — I sublet my 39 apartment to a handsome but somber newlywed couple, who turned out to be every bit as responsible as I'd hoped. They cleaned out even the eggshell chips I'd sprinkled around the base of my plants as fertilizer, leaving behind only a shiny silver-plate cake server and a list of their hopes and goals for the summer. The list, tacked precariously to the back of the kitchen door, began with a fervent appeal to God to help them get their wedding thank-yous written in three weeks or less. (You could see they had originally written "two weeks" but scratched it out — no miracles being demanded here.) It went on:

> Please help us, Almighty Father in Heaven Above, to get Ann a teaching job within a half-hour drive of here in a nice neighborhood.
> Please help us, Almighty Father in Heaven Above, to get John a job doing anything where he won't strain his back and that is within a half-hour drive of here.
> Please help us, Almighty Father in Heaven Above, to get us a car.
>
> Please help us, A. F. in H. A., to learn French.
> Please help us, A. F. in H. A., to find seven dinner recipes that cost less than 60 cents a serving and can be made in a half hour. And that don't have tomatoes, since You in Your Heavenly Wisdom made John allergic.
> Please help us, A. F. in H. A., to avoid books in this apartment such as You in Your Heavenly Wisdom allowed John, for Your Heavenly Reasons, to find three nights ago (June 2nd).

Et cetera. In the left-hand margin they had kept score of how they had fared 40 with their requests, and it was heartening to see that nearly all of them were marked "Yes! Praise the Lord" (sometimes shortened to "PTL"), with the sole exception of learning French, which was mysteriously marked "No! PTL to the Highest."

That note touched me. Strange and familiar both, it seemed as though it had 41 been written by some cousin of mine — some cousin who had stayed home to grow up, say, while I went abroad and learned painful things. This, of course, is just a manner of speaking. In fact, I did my growing up at home, like anybody else.

But the learning was painful. I never knew exactly how it happened that my 42 mother went hurtling through the air that night years ago, only that the wind had been chopping at the house, and that the argument had started about the state of the roof. Someone had been up to fix it the year before, but it wasn't a roofer, only a man my father had insisted could do just as good a job for a quarter of the price.

And maybe he could have, had he not somehow managed to step through a knot in the wood under the shingles and break his uninsured ankle. Now the shingles were coming loose again, and the attic insulation was mildewing besides, and my father was wanting to sell the house altogether, which he said my mother had wanted to buy so she could send pictures of it home to her family in China.

43   "The Americans have a saying," he said. "They saying. 'You have to keep up with Jones family.' I'm saying if Jones family in Shanghai, you can send any picture you want, *an-y* picture. Go take picture of those rich guys' house. You want to act like rich guys, right? Go take picture of those rich guys' house."

44   At that point, my mother sent Mona and me to wash up, and started speaking Shanghainese. They argued for some time in the kitchen, while we listened from the top of the stairs, our faces wedged between the bumpy Spanish scrolls of the wrought-iron railing. First my mother ranted, then my father, and then they both ranted at once, until finally there was a thump, followed by a long quiet.

45   "Do you think they're kissing now?" said Mona. "I bet they're kissing, like this." She pursed her lips like a fish, and was about to put them to the railing when we heard my mother locking the back door. We hightailed it into bed; my parents creaked up the stairs. Everything at that point seemed fine. Once in their bedroom, though, they started up again, first softly, they more and more loudly, until my mother turned on a radio to try to disguise the noise. A door slammed; they began shouting at each other; another door slammed; a shoe or something banged the wall behind Mona's bed.

46   "How're we supposed to *sleep?*" said Mona, sitting up.

47   There was another thud; more yelling in Shanghainese; and then my mother's voice pierced the wall, in English. "So what you want I should do? Go to work like Theresa Lee?"

48   My father rumbled something back.

49   "You think you are big shot, but you never get **promotion, you** never get raise. All I do is spend money, right? So what do you do, you tell me. So what do you do!"

50   Something hit the floor so hard, our room shook.

51   "So kill me," screamed my mother. "You know what you are? You are failure. Failure! You are failure!"

52   Then there was a sudden, terrific, bursting crash — and after it, as if on a bungled cue, the serene blare of an a capella soprano picking her way down a scale.

53   By the time Mona and I knew to look out the window, a neighbor's pet beagle was already on the scene, sniffing and barking at my mother's body, his tail crazy with excitement. Then he was barking at my stunned and trembling father, at the shrieking ambulance, at the police, at crying Mona in her bunny-footed pajamas, and at me, barefoot in the cold grass, squeezing my sister's shoulder with one hand and clutching my malachite beads with the other.

54   My mother wasn't dead, only unconscious — the paramedics figured that out right away — but there was blood everywhere, and though they were reassuring about her head wounds as they strapped her to the stretcher — commenting also on how small she was, how delicate, how light — my father kept saying, *I killed her, I killed her* as the ambulance screeched and screeched headlong, forever, to

the hospital. I was afraid to touch her, and glad of the metal rail between us, even though its sturdiness made her seem even frailer than she was. I wished she were bigger, somehow, and noticed, with a pang, that the new red slippers we had given her for Mother's Day had been lost somewhere along the way. How much she seemed to be leaving behind, as we careened along — still not there, still not there — Mona and Dad and the medic and I taking up the whole ambulance, all the room, so that there was no room for anything else; no room even for my mother's real self, the one who should have been pinching the color back to my father's gray face, the one who should have been claming Mona's cowlick — the one who should have been bending over us, to help us be strong, to help us get through, even as we bent over her.

Then suddenly we were there, the glowing square of the emergency room en- 55
trance opening like the gates of heaven; and immediately the talk of miracles be-
gan. Alive, a miracle. No bones broken, a miracle. A miracle that the hemlocks had cushioned her fall, a miracle that they hadn't been trimmed in a year and a half. It was a miracle that all that blood, the blood that had seemed that night to be everywhere, was from one shard of glass, a single shard, can you imagine, and as for the gash in her head, the scar would be covered by hair. The next day, my mother cheerfully described just how she would part it so that nothing would show at all.

"You're a lucky duck-duck," agreed Mona, helping herself, with a little pirou- 56
ette, to the cherry atop my mother's chocolate pudding.

That wasn't enough for me, though. I was relieved, yes, but what I wanted by 57
then was a real miracle. Not for my mother simply to have survived, but for the whole thing never to have happened — for my mother's head never to have been shaved and bandaged like that, for her high, proud forehead never to have been swollen down over her eyes, for her face and neck and hands never to have been painted so many shades of blue-black, and violet, and chartreuse. I still want those things — for my parents not to have had to live with this affair like a prickle bush between them, for my father to have been able to look my mother in her swollen eyes and curse the madman, the monster who had dared do this to the woman he loved. I wanted to be able to touch my mother without shuddering, to be able to console my father, to be able to get that crash out of my head, the sound of that soprano — so many things that I didn't know how to pray for them, that I wouldn't have known where to start even *if* I had had the power to work miracles, right there, right then.

A week later, when my mother's head was beginning to bristle with new hairs, 58
I lost my malachite beads. I had been carrying them in a white cloth pouch that Patty had given me, and was swinging the pouch on my pinkie on my way home from school, when I swung just a bit too hard; the pouch went sailing in a long arc through the air, *whooshing* like a perfectly thrown basketball through one of the holes of a nearby sewer. There was no chance of fishing it out. I looked and looked, crouching on the sticky pavement until the asphalt had grazed the skin of my hands and knees, but all I could discern was an evil-smelling murk, glassy and smug and impenetrable.

59   My loss didn't quite hit me until I was home, but then it produced an agony all out of proportion to my string of pretty beads. I hadn't cried at all during my mother's accident, but now I was crying all afternoon, all through dinner, and then after dinner, too — crying past the point where I knew what I was crying for, wishing dimly that I had my beads to hold, wishing dimly that I could pray, but refusing, refusing, I didn't know why, until I finally fell into an exhausted sleep on the couch. There my parents left me for the night — glad, no doubt, that one of the more tedious of my childhood crises seemed to be winding off the reel of life, onto the reel of memory. They covered me, and somehow grew a pillow under my head, and, with uncharacteristic disregard for the living room rug, left some milk and Pecan Sandies on the coffee table, in case I woke up hungry. Their thoughtfulness was prescient. I did wake up in the early part of the night; and it was then, amid the unfamiliar sounds and shadows, of the living room, that I had what I was sure was a true vision.

60   Even now, what I saw retains an odd clarity: the requisite strange light flooding the room, first orange, and then a bright yellow-green. A crackling bright burst like a Roman candle going off near the piano. There was a distinct smell of coffee, and a long silence. The room seemed to be getting colder. Nothing. A creak; the light starting to wane, then waxing again, brilliant pink now. Still nothing. Then, as the pink started to go a little purple, a perfectly normal, middle-aged man's voice, speaking something very like pig latin, told me not to despair, not to despair, my beads would be returned to me.

61   That was all. I sat a moment in the dark, then turned on the light, gobbled down the cookies — and in a happy flash understood that I was so good, really, so near to being a saint that my malachite beads would come back through the town water system. All I had to do was turn on all the faucets in the house. This I did, stealing quietly into the bathroom and kitchen and basement. The old spigot by the washing machine was too gunked up to be coaxed very far open, but that didn't matter. The water didn't have to be full blast, I understood that. Then I gathered together my pillow and blanket and trundled up to my bed to sleep.

62   By the time I woke in the morning, I knew that my beads hadn't shown up; but when I knew it for certain, I was still disappointed. And as if that weren't enough, I had to face my parents and sister, who were all abuzz with the mystery of the faucets. Not knowing what else to do, I, like a puddlebrain, told them the truth. The results were predictably painful.

63   "Gallic had a *vision*," Mona told everyone at the bus stop. "A vision with lights, and sinks in it!"

64   Sinks, visions. I got it all day, from my parents, from my classmates, even from some sixth and seventh graders. Someone drew a cartoon of me with a halo over my head in one of the girls' room stalls; Anthony Rossi made gurgling noises as he walked on his hands at recess. Only Patty tried not to laugh, though even she was something less than unalloyed understanding.

65   "I don' think miracles are thupposed to happen in *thewers*" she said.

66   Such was the end of my saintly ambitions. It wasn't the end of all holiness. The ideas of purity and goodness still tippled my brain, and over the years I came slowly to grasp of what grit true faith is made. Last night, though, when my father

called to say that he couldn't go on living in our old house, that he was going to move to a smaller place, another place, maybe a condo — he didn't know how, or where — I found myself still wistful for the time religion seemed all I wanted it to be. Back then, the world was a place that could be set right. One had only to direct the hand of the Almighty and say, Just here, Lord, we hurt here — and here, and here, and here.

Reading and Reacting

1. As a child, how is the narrator different from her friend Patty? Would you characterize Patty as a foil for the narrator?

2. At what points in the story does the narrator move from her childhood to her adulthood (and back again)? How does she signal these shifts in focus to readers?

3. What do we know about the narrator's parents? Are they fully developed characters? Could they be considered stereotypes? Explain.

4. At the time the narrator tells her story, her mother has been dead for four months. She says, "But that is another story" (par. 8). *Is* it another story?

5. Before her mother's accident, why does the narrator want to be able to perform miracles? How do you think she defines *miracle* at this time? How does her definition of *miracle* change after the accident?

6. What is the connection between the abandonment of his family by Patty's father and the fall of the narrator's mother? Why is each event important in the story?

7. What is the significance of the newlywed couple's list of "hopes and goals" (par. 39)? How is it related to the miracles the narrator focuses on? Why does the narrator find this list "Strange and familiar both" (par. 41)?

8. What do the malachite beads represent to the narrator? How does their meaning to her change as the story progresses? How does her loss of the beads affect her? How does it affect the story?

9. Reread the story's last paragraph. How does the narrator's concept of sainthood, holiness, and "purity and goodness" change between childhood and adulthood? During the course of the story, what does she learn about the role of religion in her life?

10. JOURNAL ENTRY How do you explain the narrator's vision (par. 60)?

11. CRITICAL PERSPECTIVE As the daughter of Chinese immigrants, Jen uses her personal and family experience to help create characters who wrestle with the difficulties inherent in moving to a new culture, trying to fit in while simultaneously retaining some parts of their cultural heritage and identity. Literary critics have noted that Jen combines the adolescent's search for self with the larger search for cultural identity. According to Ann Beattie, Jen's "characters seem to be trying on their lives for size: discomfiting to observe, though at the same time, offering the reader a sadness convincingly tinged with humor." In what sense does the narrator of "The Water Faucet Vision" seem to be "trying on her life for size"?

Related Works: "The Secret Lion" (p. 170), "An Ounce of Cure" (p. 378), "Araby" (p. 395), "Doe Season" (p. 512), "'Hope' is the thing with feathers" (p. 890)

CHARLES BAXTER (1947–   ) was born in Minneapolis and educated at Macalester College and at the State University of New York, Buffalo. Currently a professor of English at The University of Michigan, Baxter is the author of four critically praised collections of short stories: *Harmony of the World* (1984), *Through the Safety Net* (1985), *A Relative Stranger: Stories* (1990), and *Believers: A Novella and Stories* (1997). He is also the author of four novels, *First Light* (1987), *Shadow Play* (1993), *The Feast of Love* (2002), and *Saul and Patsy* (2003), and one book of poetry, *Imaginary Paintings and Other Poems* (1989). Baxter has also written *Burning Down the House* (1997), a collection of essays on fiction.

Baxter's critics often mention the compassion he shows in writing about his fictional characters: a couple who lose their child, a hospital worker who wants to be famous, a tired businessman who really wants to paint. In many of his short stories in *Through the Safety Net* (in which "Gryphon" appeared), unexpected events jar Baxter's characters out of their routines, forcing them to consider different choices, to call on inner strength, or to swim against the tide of "middle America's" conventions.

Cultural Context One of the key elements of this story is a character's use of a deck of tarot cards to predict the future. Originating more than 500 years ago in northern Italy in a game called "Triumphs," the Tarot was quickly adopted as a tool for divining the future. With deep roots in the symbolism of medieval and Renaissance Europe, the Tarot is today the singular most popular tool for spiritual introspection and prophesy. While the death card in particular is often feared, many interpreters argue that it hardly ever points to literal death but rather symbolizes the ending of something significant and the beginning of something new. In "Gryphon," the accuracy of the Tarot's prediction is less important than various characters' reactions to the prediction itself.

Gryphon (1985)

On Wednesday afternoon, between the geography lesson on ancient Egypt's hand-operated irrigation system and an art project that involved drawing a model city next to a mountain, our fourth-grade teacher, Mr. Hibler, developed a cough. This cough began with a series of muffled throat clearings and progressed to propulsive noises contained within Mr. Hibler's closed mouth. "Listen to him," Carol Peterson whispered to me. "He's gonna blow up." Mr. Hibler's laughter — dazed and infrequent — sounded a bit like his cough, but as we worked on our model cities we would look up, thinking he was enjoying a joke, and see Mr. Hibler's face turning red, his cheeks puffed out. This was not laughter. Twice he bent over, and his loose tie, like a plumb line, hung down straight from his neck as he exploded himself into a Kleenex. He would excuse himself, then go on coughing. "I'll bet you a dime," Carol Peterson whispered, "we get a substitute tomorrow."

Carol sat at the desk in front of mine and was a bad person — when she thought no one was looking she would blow her nose on notebook paper, then crumble it up and throw it into the wastebasket — but at times of crisis she spoke the truth. I knew I'd lose the dime.

"No deal," I said.

When Mr. Hibler stood us up in formation at the door just prior to the final bell, he was almost incapable of speech. "I'm sorry, boys and girls," he said. "I seem to be coming down with something."

"I hope you feel better tomorrow, Mr. Hibler," Bobby Kryzanowicz, the faultless   5
brown-noser said, and I heard Carol Peterson's evil giggle. Then Mr. Hibler opened the door and we walked out to the buses, a clique of us starting noisily to hawk and cough as soon as we thought we were a few feet beyond Mr. Hibler's earshot.

Five Oaks being a rural community, and in Michigan, the supply of substitute teachers was limited to the town's unemployed community college graduates, a pool of about four mothers. These ladies fluttered, provided easeful class days, and nervously covered material we had mastered weeks earlier. Therefore it was a surprise when a woman we had never seen came into the class the next day, carrying a purple purse, a checkerboard lunchbox, and a few books. She put the books on one side of Mr. Hibler's desk and the lunchbox on the other, next to the Voice of Music phonograph. Three of us in the back of the room were playing with Heever, the chameleon that lived in the terrarium and on one of the plastic drapes, when she walked in.

She clapped her hands at us. "Little boys," she said, "why are you bent over together like that?" She didn't wait for us to answer. "Are you tormenting an animal? Put it back. Please sit down at your desks. I want no cabals this time of the day." We just stared at her. "Boys," she repeated, "I asked you to sit down."

I put the chameleon in his terrarium and felt my way to my desk, never taking my eyes off the woman. With white and green chalk, she had started to draw a tree on the left side of the blackboard. She didn't look usual. Furthermore, her tree was outsized, disproportionate, for some reason.

"This room needs a tree," she said, with one line drawing the suggestion of a leaf. "A large, leafy, shady, deciduous . . . oak."

Her fine, light hair had been done up in what I would learn years later was   10
called a chignon, and she wore gold-rimmed glasses whose lenses seemed to have the faintest blue tint. Harold Knardahl, who sat across from me, whispered "Mars," and I nodded slowly, savoring the imminent weirdness of the day. The substitute drew another branch with an extravagant arm gesture, then turned around and said, "Good morning. I don't believe I said good morning to all you yet."

Facing us, she was no special age — an adult is an adult — but her face had two prominent lines, descending vertically from the sides of her mouth to her chin. I knew where I had seen those lines before: *Pinocchio*. They were marionette lines. "You may stare at me," she said to us, as a few more kids from the last bus came into the room, their eyes fixed on her, "for a few more seconds, until the bell rings. Then I will permit no more staring. Looking I will permit. Staring, no. It is impolite to stare, and a sign of bad breeding. You cannot make a social effort while staring."

Harold Knardahl did not glance at me, or nudge, but I heard him whisper "Mars" again, trying to get more mileage out of his single joke with the kids who had just come in.

When everyone was seated, the substitute teacher finished her tree, put down her chalk fastidiously on the phonograph, brushed her hands, and faced us. "Good morning," she said. "I am Miss Ferenczi, your teacher for the day. I am fairly new to your community, and I don't believe any of you know me. I will therefore start by telling you a story about myself."

While we settled back, she launched into her tale. She said her grandfather had been a Hungarian prince; her mother had been born in some place called Flanders, had been a pianist, and had played concerts for people Miss Ferenczi referred to as "crowned heads." She gave us a knowing look. "Grieg," she said, "the Norwegian master, wrote a concerto for piano that was," she paused, "my mother's triumph at her debut concert in London." Her eyes searched the ceiling. Our eyes followed. Nothing up there but ceiling tile. "For reasons that I shall not go into, my family's fortunes took us to Detroit, then north to dreadful Saginaw, and now here I am in Five Oaks, as your substitute teacher, for today, Thursday, October the eleventh. I believe it will be a good day: All the forecasts coincide. We shall start with your reading lesson. Take out your reading book. I believe it is called *Broad Horizons*, or something along those lines."

15   Jeannie Vermeesch raised her hand. Miss Ferenczi nodded at her. "Mr. Hibler always starts the day with the Pledge of Allegiance," Jeannie whined.

"Oh, does he? In that case," Miss Ferenczi said, "you must know it *very* well by now, and we certainly need not spend our time on it. No, no allegiance pledging on the premises today, by my reckoning. Not with so much sunlight coming into the room. A pledge does not suit my mood." She glanced at her watch. "Time *is* flying. Take out *Broad Horizons*."

She disappointed us by giving us an ordinary lesson, complete with vocabulary word drills, comprehension questions, and recitation. She didn't seem to care for the material, however. She sighed every few minutes and rubbed her glasses with a frilly perfumed handkerchief that she withdrew, magician style, from her left sleeve.

After reading we moved on to arithmetic. It was my favorite time of the morning, when the lazy autumn sunlight dazzled its way through ribbons of clouds past the windows on the east side of the classroom, and crept across the linoleum floor. On the playground the first group of children, the kindergartners, were running on the quack grass just beyond the monkey bars. We were doing multiplication tables. Miss Ferenczi had made John Wazny stand up at his desk in the front row. He was supposed to go through the tables of six. From where I was sitting, I could smell the Vitalis soaked into John's plastered hair. He was doing fine until he came to six times eleven and six times twelve. "Six times eleven," he said, "is sixty-eight. Six times twelve is . . ." He put his fingers to his head, quickly and secretly sniffed his fingertips, and said, "seventy-two." Then he sat down.

"Fine," Miss Ferenczi said. "Well now. That was very good."

20   "Miss Ferenczi!" One of the Eddy twins was waving her hand desperately in the air. "Miss Ferenczi! Miss Ferenczi!"

"Yes?"

"John said that six times eleven is sixty-eight and you said he was right!"

"*Did* I?" She gazed at the class with a jolly look breaking across her marionette's face. "Did I say that? Well, what *is* six times eleven?"

"It's sixty-six!"

She nodded. "Yes. So it is. But, and I know some people will not entirely agree with me, at some times it is sixty-eight."   25

"When? When is it sixty-eight?"

We were all waiting.

"In higher mathematics, which you children do not yet understand, six times eleven can be considered to be sixty-eight." She laughed through her nose. "In higher mathematics numbers are . . . more fluid. The only thing a number does is contain a certain amount of something. Think of water. A cup is not the only way to measure a certain amount of water, is it?" We were staring, shaking our heads. "You could use saucepans or thimbles. In either case, the water *would be the same*. Perhaps," she started again, "it would be better for you to think that six times eleven is sixty-eight only when I am in the room."

"Why is it sixty-eight," Mark Poole asked, "when you're in the room?"

"Because it's more interesting that way," she said, smiling very rapidly behind her blue-tinted glasses. "Besides, I'm your substitute teacher, am I not?" We all nodded. "Well, then, think of six times eleven equals sixty-eight as a substitute fact."   30

"A substitute fact?"

"Yes." Then she looked at us carefully. "Do you think," she asked, "that anyone is going to be hurt by a substitute fact?"

We looked back at her.

"Will the plants on the windowsill be hurt?" We glanced at them. There were sensitive plants thriving in a green plastic tray, and several wilted ferns in small clay pots. "Your dogs and cats, or your moms and dads?" She waited. "So," she concluded, "what's the problem?"

"But it's wrong," Janice Weber said, "isn't it?"   35

"What's your name, young lady?"

"Janice Weber."

"And you think it's wrong, Janice?"

"I was just asking."

"Well, all right. You were just asking. I think we've spent enough time on this matter by now, don't you, class? You are free to think what you like. When your teacher, Mr. Hibler, returns, six times eleven will be sixty-six again, you can rest assured. And it will be that for the rest of your lives in Five Oaks. Too bad, eh?" She raised her eyebrows and glinted herself at us. "But for now, it wasn't. So much for that. Let us go to your assigned problems for today, as painstakingly outlined, I see, in Mr. Hibler's lesson plan. Take out a sheet of paper and write your names in the upper left-hand corner."   40

For the next half hour we did the rest of our arithmetic problems. We handed them in and went on to spelling, my worst subject. Spelling always came before lunch. We were taking spelling dictation and looking at the clock. "Thorough," Miss Ferenczi said. "Boundary." She walked in the aisles between the desks, holding the spelling book open and looking down at our papers. "Balcony." I clutched my pencil. Somehow, the way she said those words, they seemed foreign, Hungarian, mis-voweled and mis-consonanted. I stared down at what I had spelled. *Balconie.* I turned my pencil upside down and erased my mistake. *Balconey.* That looked better, but still incorrect. I cursed the world of spelling and tried erasing it again and saw the paper beginning to wear away. *Balkony.* Suddenly I felt a hand on my shoulder.

"I don't like that word either," Miss Ferenczi whispered, bent over, her mouth near my ear. "It's ugly. My feeling is, if you don't like a word, you don't have to use it." She straightened up, leaving behind a slight odor of Clorets.

At lunchtime we went out to get our trays of sloppy joes, peaches in heavy syrup, coconut cookies, and milk, and brought them back to the classroom, where Miss Ferenczi was sitting at the desk, eating a brown sticky thing she had un-wrapped from tightly rubber-banded wax paper. "Miss Ferenczi," I said, raising my hand. "You don't have to eat with us. You can eat with the other teachers. There's a teachers' lounge," I ended up, "next to the principal's office."

"No, thank you," she said. "I prefer it here."

45 "We've got a room monitor," I said. "Mrs. Eddy." I pointed to where Mrs. Eddy, Joyce and Judy's mother, sat silently at the back of the room, doing her knitting.

"That's fine," Miss Ferenczi said. "But I shall continue to eat here, with you children. I prefer it," she repeated.

"How come?" Wayne Razmer asked without raising his hand.

"I talked with the other teachers before class this morning," Miss Ferenczi said, biting into her brown food. "There was a great rattling of the words for the fewness of ideas. I didn't care for their brand of hilarity. I don't like ditto machine jokes."

"Oh," Wayne said.

50 "What's that you're eating?" Maxine Sylvester asked, twitching her nose. "Is it food?"

"It most certainly *is* food. It's a stuffed fig. I had to drive almost down to Detroit to get it. I also bought some smoked sturgeon. And this," she said, lifting some green leaves out of her lunchbox, "is raw spinach, cleaned this morning before I came out here to the Garfield-Murry school."

"Why're you eating raw spinach?" Maxine asked.

"It's good for you," Miss Ferenczi said. "More stimulating than soda pop or smelling salts." I bit into my sloppy joe and stared blankly out the window. An al-most invisible moon was faintly silvered in the daytime autumn sky. "As far as food is concerned," Miss Ferenczi was saying, "you have to shuffle the pack. Mix it up. Too many people eat . . . well, never mind."

"Miss Ferenczi," Carol Peterson said, "what are we going to do this afternoon?"

55 "Well," she said, looking down at Mr. Hibler's lesson plan, "I see that your teacher, Mr. Hibler, has you scheduled for a unit on the Egyptians." Carol groaned. "Yessss," Miss Ferenczi continued, "that is what we will do: the Egyptians. A remarkable people. Almost as remarkable as the Americans. But not quite." She lowered her head, did her quick smile, and went back to eating her spinach.

After noon recess we came back into the classroom and saw that Miss Ferenczi had drawn a pyramid on the blackboard, close to her oak tree. Some of us who had been playing baseball were messing around in the back of the room, dropping the bats and the gloves into the playground box, and I think that Ray Schontzeler had just slugged me when I heard Miss Ferenczi's high-pitched voice quavering with emotion. "Boys," she said, "come to order right this minute and take your seats. I do not wish to waste a minute of class time. Take out your geography books." We trudged to our desks and, still sweating, pulled out *Distant Lands and Their People*. "Turn to page forty-two." She waited for thirty seconds, then looked over at Kelly Munger. "Young man," she said, "why are you still fossicking in your desk?"

Kelly looked as if his foot had been stepped on. "Why am I what?"

"Why are you . . . burrowing in your desk like that?"

"I'm lookin' for the book, Miss Ferenczi."

Bobby Kryzanowicz, the faultless brown-noser who sat in the first row by choice, 60 softly said, "His name is Kelly Munger. He can't ever find his stuff. He always does that."

"I don't care what his name is, especially after lunch," Miss Ferenczi said. *"Where is your book?"*

"I just found it." Kelly was peering into his desk and with both hands pulled at the book, shoveling along in front of it several pencils and crayons, which fell into his lap and then to the floor.

"I hate a mess," Miss Ferenczi said. "I hate a mess in a desk or a mind. It's . . . unsanitary. You wouldn't want your house at home to look like your desk at school, now, would you?" She didn't wait for an answer. "I should think not. A house at home should be as neat as human hands can make it. What were we talking about? Egypt. Page forty-two. I note from Mr. Hibler's lesson plan that you have been discussing the modes of Egyptian irrigation. Interesting, in my view, but not so interesting as what we are about to cover. The pyramids and Egyptian slave labor. A plus on one side, a minus on the other." We had our books open to page forty-two, where there was a picture of a pyramid, but Miss Ferenczi wasn't looking at the book. Instead, she was staring at some object just outside the window.

"Pyramids," Miss Ferenczi said, still looking past the window. "I want you to think about the pyramids. And what was inside. The bodies of the pharaohs, of course, and their attendant treasures. Scrolls. Perhaps," Miss Ferenczi said, with something gleeful but unsmiling in her face, "these scrolls were novels for the pharaohs, helping them to pass the time in their long voyage through the centuries. But then, I am joking." I was looking at the lines on Miss Ferenczi's face. "Pyramids," Miss Ferenczi went on, "were the repositories of special cosmic powers. The nature of a pyramid is to guide cosmic energy forces into a concentrated point. The Egyptians knew that; we have generally forgotten it. Did you know," she asked, walking to the side of the room so that she was standing by the coat closet, "that George Washington had Egyptian blood, from his grandmother? Certain features of the Constitution of the United States are notable for their Egyptian ideas."

Without glancing down at the book, she began to talk about the movement 65 of souls in Egyptian religion. She said that when people die, their souls return to Earth in the form of carpenter ants or walnut trees, depending on how they behaved —"well or ill" — in life. She said that the Egyptians believed that people act the way they do because of magnetism produced by tidal forces in the solar

system, forces produced by the sun and by its "planetary ally," Jupiter. Jupiter, she
said, was a planet, as we had been told, but had "certain properties of stars." She
was speaking very fast. She said that the Egyptians were great explorers and conquerors. She said that the greatest of all the conquerors, Genghis Khan, had had
forty horses and forty young women killed on the site of his grave. We listened.
No one tried to stop her. "I myself have been in Egypt," she said, "and have witnessed much dust and many brutalities." She said that an old man in Egypt who
worked for a circus had personally shown her an animal in a cage, a monster, half
bird and half lion. She said that this monster was called a gryphon and that she
had heard about them but never seen them until she traveled to the outskirts of
Cairo. She said that Egyptian astronomers had discovered the planet Saturn, but
had not seen its rings. She said that the Egyptians were the first to discover that
dogs, when they are ill, will not drink from rivers, but wait for rain, and hold their
jaws open to catch it.

*   *   *

"She lies."

We were on the school bus home. I was sitting next to Carl Whiteside, who
had bad breath and a huge collection of marbles. We were arguing. Carl thought
she was lying. I said she wasn't, probably.

"I didn't believe that stuff about the bird," Carl said, "and what she told us
about the pyramids? I didn't believe that either. She didn't know what she was
talking about."

"Oh yeah?" I had liked her. She was strange. I thought I could nail him. "If she
was lying," I said, "what'd she say that was a lie?"

70 "Six times eleven isn't sixty-eight. It isn't ever. It's sixty-six, I know for a fact."

"She said so. She admitted it. What else did she lie about?"

"I don't know," he said. "Stuff."

"What stuff?"

"Well." He swung his legs back and forth. "You ever see an animal that was
half lion and half bird?" He crossed his arms. "It sounded real fakey to me."

75 "It could happen," I said. I had to improvise, to outrage him. "I read in this
newspaper my mom bought in the IGA about this scientist, this mad scientist in
the Swiss Alps, and he's been putting genes and chromosomes and stuff together
in test tubes, and he combined a human being and a hamster." I waited, for effect.
"It's called a humster."

"You never." Carl was staring at me, his mouth open, his terrible bad breath
making its way toward me. "What newspaper was it?"

"The *National Enquirer*," I said, "that they sell next to the cash registers." When
I saw his look of recognition, I knew I had bested him. "And this mad scientist,"
I said, "his name was, um, Dr. Frankenbush." I realized belatedly that this name was
a mistake and waited for Carl to notice its resemblance to the name of the other
famous mad master of permutations, but he only sat there.

"A man and a hamster?" He was staring at me, squinting, his mouth opening
in distaste. "Jeez. What'd it look like?"

When the bus reached my stop, I took off down our dirt road and ran up through the back yard, kicking the tire swing for good luck. I dropped my books on the back steps so I could hug and kiss our dog, Mr. Selby. Then I hurried inside. I could smell Brussels sprouts cooking, my unfavorite vegetable. My mother was washing other vegetables in the kitchen sink, and my baby brother was hollering in his yellow playpen on the kitchen floor.

"Hi, Mom," I said, hopping around the playpen to kiss her, "Guess what?" 80

"I have no idea."

"We had this substitute today, Miss Ferenczi, and I'd never seen her before, and she had all these stories and ideas and stuff."

"Well. That's good." My mother looked out the window behind the sink, her eyes on the pine woods west of our house. Her face and hairstyle always reminded other people of Betty Crocker, whose picture was framed inside a gigantic spoon on the side of the Bisquick box; to me, though, my mother's face just looked white. "Listen, Tommy," she said, "go upstairs and pick your clothes off the bathroom floor, then go outside to the shed and put the shovel and ax away that your father left outside this morning."

"She said that six times eleven was sometimes sixty-eight!" I said. "And she said she once saw a monster that was half lion and half bird." I waited. "In Egypt, she said."

"Did you hear me?" my mother asked, raising her arm to wipe her forehead 85 with the back of her hand. "You have chores to do."

"I know," I said. "I was just telling you about the substitute."

"It's very interesting," my mother said, quickly glancing down at me, "and we can talk about it later when your father gets home. But right now you have some work to do."

"Okay, Mom." I took a cookie out of the jar on the counter and was about to go outside when I had a thought. I ran into the living room, pulled out a dictionary next to the TV stand, and opened it to the G's. *Gryphon:* "variant of *griffin.*" *Griffin:* "a fabulous beast with the head and wings of an eagle and the body of a lion." Fabulous was right. I shouted with triumph and ran outside to put my father's tools back in their place.

Miss Ferenczi was back the next day, slightly altered. She had pulled her hair down and twisted it into pigtails, with red rubber bands holding them tight one inch from the ends. She was wearing a green blouse and pink scarf, making her difficult to look at for a full class day. This time there was no pretense of doing a reading lesson or moving on to arithmetic. As soon as the bell rang, she simply began to talk.

She talked for forty minutes straight. There seemed to be less connection be- 90 tween her ideas, but the ideas themselves were, as the dictionary would say, fabulous. She said she had heard of a huge jewel, in what she called the Antipodes, that was so brilliant that when the light shone into it at a certain angle it would blind whoever was looking at its center. She said that the biggest diamond in the world was cursed and had killed everyone who owned it, and that by a trick of fate it was called the Hope diamond. Diamonds are magic, she said, and this is why women wear them on their fingers, as a sign of the magic of womanhood. Men have strength, Miss Ferenczi said, but no true magic. That is why men fall in love with women but women do not fall in love with men; they just love being loved. George Washington had died because of a mistake he made about a diamond. Washington was not the first *true* President, but she did not say who was. In some places in the world, she said, men and women still live in the trees and eat monkeys for breakfast. Their doctors are magicians. At the bottom of the sea are creatures thin as pancakes which have never been studied by scientists because when you take them up to the air, the fish explode.

There was not a sound in the classroom, except for Miss Ferenczi's voice, and Donna DeShano's coughing. No one even went to the bathroom.

Beethoven, she said, had not been deaf; it was a trick to make himself famous, and it worked. As she talked, Miss Ferenczi's pigtails swung back and forth. There are trees in the world, she said, that eat meat: their leaves are sticky and close up on bugs like hands. She lifted her hands and brought them together, palm to palm. Venus, which most people think is the next closest planet to the sun, is not always closer, and, besides, it is the planet of greatest mystery because of its thick cloud cover. "I know what lies underneath those clouds," Miss Ferenczi said, and waited. After the silence, she said, "Angels. Angels live under those clouds." She said that angels were not invisible to everyone and were in fact smarter than most people. They did not dress in robes as was often claimed but instead wore formal evening clothes, as if they were about to attend a concert. Often angels *do* attend concerts and sit in the aisles where, she said, most people pay no attention to them. She said the most terrible angel had the shape of the Sphinx. "There is no running away from that one," she said. She said that unquenchable fires burn just under the surface of the earth in Ohio, and that the baby Mozart fainted dead away in his cradle when he first heard the sound of a trumpet. She said that someone named Narzim al Harrardim was the greatest writer who ever lived. She said that planets control behavior, and anyone conceived during a solar eclipse would be born with webbed feet.

"I know you children like to hear these things," she said, "these secrets, and that is why I am telling you all this." We nodded. It was better than doing comprehension questions for the readings in *Broad Horizons*.

"I will tell you one more story," she said, "and then we will have to do arithmetic." She leaned over, and her voice grew soft. "There is no death," she said. "You must never be afraid. Never. That which is, cannot die. It will change into different earthly and unearthly elements, but I know this as sure as I stand here in front of you, and I swear it: you must not be afraid. I have seen this truth with these eyes. I know it because in a dream God kissed me. Here." And she pointed with her right index finger to the side of her head, below the mouth, where the vertical lines were carved into her skin.

95   Absent-mindedly we all did our arithmetic problems. At recess the class was out on the playground, but no one was playing. We were all standing in small groups, talking about Miss Ferenczi. We didn't know if she was crazy, or what. I looked out beyond the playground, at the rusted cars piled in a small heap behind a clump of sumac, and I wanted to see shapes there, approaching me.

On the way home, Carl sat next to me again. He didn't say much, and I didn't either. At last he turned to me. "You know what she said about the leaves that close up on bugs?"

"Huh?"

"The leaves," Carl insisted. "The meat-eating plants. I know it's true. I saw it on television. The leaves have this icky glue that the plants have got smeared all over them and the insects can't get off 'cause they're stuck. I saw it." He seemed demoralized. "She's tellin' the truth."

"Yeah."

"You think she's seen all those angels?"   100

I shrugged.

"I don't think she has," Carl informed me. "I think she made that part up."

"There's a tree," I suddenly said. I was looking out the window at the farms along County Road H. I knew every barn, every broken windmill, every fence, every anhydrous ammonia tank, by heart. "There's a tree that's . . . that I've seen . . ."

"Don't you try to do it," Carl said. "You'll just sound like a jerk."

I kissed my mother. She was standing in front of the stove. "How was your day?" she asked.

"Fine."

"Did you have Miss Ferenczi again?"

"Yeah."

"Well?"

"She was fine. Mom," I asked, "can I go to my room?"   110

"No," she said, "not until you've gone out to the vegetable garden and picked me a few tomatoes." She glanced at the sky. "I think it's going to rain. Skedaddle and do it now. Then you come back inside and watch your brother for a few minutes while I go upstairs. I need to clean up before dinner." She looked down at me. "You're looking a little pale, Tommy." She touched the back of her hand to my forehead and I felt her diamond ring against my skin. "Do you feel all right?"

"I'm fine," I said, and went out to pick the tomatoes.

Coughing mutedly, Mr. Hibler was back the next day, slipping lozenges into his mouth when his back was turned at forty-five minute intervals and asking us how much of the prepared lesson plan Miss Ferenczi had followed. Edith Atwater took the responsibility for the class of explaining to Mr. Hibler that the substitute hadn't always done exactly what he would have done, but we had worked hard even though she talked a lot. About what? he asked. All kinds of things, Edith said. I sort of forgot. To our relief, Mr. Hibler seemed not at all interested in what Miss Ferenczi had said to fill the day. He probably thought it was woman's talk; unserious and not suited for school. It was enough that he had a pile of arithmetic problems from us to correct.

For the next month, the sumac turned a distracting red in the field, and the sun traveled toward the southern sky, so that its rays reached Mr. Hibler's Halloween display on the bulletin board in the back of the room, fading the scarecrow with a pumpkin head from orange to tan. Every three days I measured how much farther the sun had moved toward the southern horizon by making small marks with my black Crayola on the north wall, ant-sized marks only I knew were there, inching west.

115 And then in early December, four days after the first permanent snowfall, she appeared again in our classroom. The minute she came in the door, I felt my heart begin to pound. Once again, she was different: this time, her hair hung straight down and seemed hardly to have been combed. She hadn't brought her lunchbox with her, but she was carrying what seemed to be a small box. She greeted all of us and talked about the weather. Donna DeShano had to remind her to take her overcoat off.

When the bell to start the day finally rang, Miss Ferenczi looked out at all of us and said, "Children, I have enjoyed your company in the past, and today I am going to reward you." She held up the small box. "Do you know what this is?" She waited. "Of course you don't. It is a tarot pack."

Edith Atwater raised her hand. "What's a tarot pack, Miss Ferenczi?"

"It is used to tell fortunes," she said. "And that is what I shall do this morning. I shall tell your fortunes, as I have been taught to do."

"What's fortune?" Bobby Kryzanowicz asked.

120 "The future, young man. I shall tell you what your future will be. I can't do your whole future, of course. I shall have to limit myself to the five-card system, the wands, cups, swords, pentacles, and the higher arcanes. Now who wants to be first?"

There was a long silence. Then Carol Peterson raised her hand.

"All right," Miss Ferenczi said. She divided the pack into five smaller packs and walked back to Carol's desk, in front of mine. "Pick one card from each of these packs," she said. I saw that Carol had a four of cups, a six of swords, but I couldn't see the other cards. Miss Ferenczi studied the cards on Carol's desk for a minute. "Not bad," she said. "I do not see much higher education. Probably an early marriage. Many children. There's something bleak and dreary here, but I can't tell what. Perhaps just the tasks of a housewife life. I think you'll do very well, for the most part." She smiled at Carol, a smile with a certain lack of interest. "Who wants to be next?"

Carl Whiteside raised his hand slowly.

"Yes," Miss Ferenczi said, "let's do a boy." She walked over to where Carl sat. After he picked his five cards, she gazed at them for a long time. "Travel," she said. "Much distant travel. You might go into the Army. Not too much romantic interest here. A late marriage, if at all. Squabbles. But the Sun is in your major arcana, here, yes, that's a very good card." She giggled. "Maybe a good life."

125 Next I raised my hand, and she told me my future. She did the same with Bobby Kryzanowicz, Kelly Munger, Edith Atwater, and Kim Foor. Then she came to Wayne Razmer. He picked his five cards, and I could see that the Death card was one of them.

"What's your name?" Miss Ferenczi asked.

"Wayne."

"Well, Wayne," she said, you will undergo a *great* metamorphosis, the greatest, before you become an adult. Your earthly element will leap away, into thin air, you sweet boy. This card, this nine of swords here, tells of suffering and desolation. And this ten of wands, well, that's certainly a heavy load."

"What about this one?" Wayne pointed to the Death card.

"That one? That one means you will die soon, my dear." She gathered up the cards. We were all looking at Wayne. "But do not fear," she said. "It's not really death, so much as change." She put the cards on Mr. Hibler's desk. "And now, let's do some arithmetic."

At lunchtime Wayne went to Mr. Faegre, the principal, and told him what Miss Ferenczi had done. During the noon recess, we saw Miss Ferenczi drive out of the parking lot in her green Rambler. I stood under the slide, listening to the other kids coasting down and landing in the little depressive bowl at the bottom. I was kicking stones and tugging at my hair right up to the moment when I saw Wayne come out to the playground. He smiled, the dead fool, and with the fingers of his right hand he was showing everyone how he had told on Miss Ferenczi.

I made my way toward Wayne, pushing myself past two girls from another class. He was watching me with his little pinhead eyes.

"You told," I shouted at him. "She was just kidding."

"She shouldn't have," he shouted back. "We were supposed to be doing arithmetic."

"She just scared you," I said. "You're a chicken. You're a chicken, Wayne. You are. Scared of a little card," I singsonged.

Wayne fell at me, his two fists hammering down on my nose. I gave him a good one in the stomach and then I tried for his head. Aiming my fist, I saw that he was crying. I slugged him.

"She was right," I yelled. "She was always right! She told the truth!" Other kids were whooping. "You were just scared, that's all!"

And then large hands pulled at us, and it was my turn to speak to Mr. Faegre.

In the afternoon Miss Ferenczi was gone, and my nose was stuffed with cotton clotted with blood, and my lip had swelled, and our class had been combined with Mrs. Mantei's sixth-grade class for a crowded afternoon science unit on insect life in ditches and swamps. I knew where Mrs. Mantei lived: she had a new house trailer just down the road from us, at the Clearwater Park. She was no mystery. Somehow she and Mr. Bodine, the other fourth-grade teacher, had managed to fit forty-five desks into the room. Kelly Munger asked if Miss Ferenczi had been arrested, and Mrs. Mantei said no, of course not. All that afternoon, until the buses came to pick us up, we learned about field crickets and two-striped grasshoppers, water bugs, cicadas, mosquitoes, flies, and moths. We learned about insects' hard outer shell, the exoskeleton, and the usual parts of the mouth, including the labrum, mandible, maxilla, and glossa. We learned about compound eyes and the four-stage metamorphosis from egg to larva to pupa to adult. We learned something, but not much, about mating. Mrs. Mantei drew, very skillfully, the internal anatomy of the grasshopper on the blackboard. We learned about the dance of the honeybee, directing other bees in the hive to pollen. We found out about which insects were pests to man, and which were not. On lined white pieces of paper we made lists of insects we might actually see, then a list of insects too small to be clearly visible, such as fleas; Mrs. Mantei said that our assignment would be to memorize these lists for the next day, when Mr. Hibler would certainly return and test us on our knowledge.

Reading and Reacting

1. In classical mythology, a gryphon (also spelled *griffin*) is a monster that has the head and wings of an eagle and the body of a lion. Why is this story called "Gryphon"?

2. Describe Miss Ferenczi's physical appearance. Why is her appearance important to the story? How does it change as the story progresses?

3. How is Miss Ferenczi different from other teachers? From other substitute teachers? From other people in general? How is her differentness communicated to her pupils? To the story's readers?

4. What is the significance of the narrator's comment, in paragraph 11, that the lines on Miss Ferenczi's face remind him of Pinocchio?

5. Is Miss Ferenczi a round or a flat character? Explain.

6. In what sense is the narrator's mother a foil for Miss Ferenczi?

7. Why does the narrator defend Miss Ferenczi, first in his argument with Carl Whiteside and later on the playground? What does his attitude toward Miss Ferenczi reveal about his character?

8. Are all of Miss Ferenczi's "substitute facts" lies, or is there some truth in what she says? Is she correct when she says that substitute facts cannot hurt anyone? Could it be argued that much of what is taught in schools today could be viewed as "substitute facts"? Explain.

9. JOURNAL ENTRY Is Miss Ferenczi a good teacher? Why or why not?

10. CRITICAL PERSPECTIVE Writing in the *New York Times Book Review*, critic William Ferguson characterizes *A Relative Stranger*, a more recent collection of Baxter's short stories than the one in which "Gryphon" appeared, as follows:

> The thirteen stories in *A Relative Stranger*, all quietly accomplished, suggest a mysterious yet fundamental marriage of despair and joy. Though in one way or another each story ends in disillusionment, the road that leads to that dismal state is so richly peopled, so finely drawn, that the effect is oddly reassuring.

Do you think this characterization of Baxter's work in *A Relative Stranger* applies to "Gryphon" as well? For example, how are despair and joy joined? Do you find the story reassuring in any way, or does it convey only a sense of disillusionment?

Related Works: "The Secret Lion" (p. 170), "A&P" (p. 230), "A Worn Path" (p. 505), "B. Wordsworth" (p. 757), "When I Heard the Learn'd Astronomer" (p. 893), "On First Looking into Chapman's Homer" (p. 1002), *Proof* (p. 1526)

JHUMPA LAHIRI (1967–   ) was born in London to Indian parents and was raised in Rhode Island. She attended Barnard College, where she earned her BA, and Boston University, where she received four graduate degrees: an MA in English, an MA in creative writing, an MA in comparative literature and the arts, and a PhD in Renaissance studies. After completing her dissertation, Lahiri turned her attention solely to fiction. For her debut collection of stories, *The Interpreter of Maladies* (1999), Lahiri received the Pulitzer Prize for fiction (she was thirty-two years old); the PEN/Hemingway Award, The New Yorker Debut of the Year award, an American Academy of Arts and Letters Addison Metcalf Award, and a nomination for the *Los Angeles Times* Book Prize. Her first novel, *The Namesake*, was published in 2003.

Cultural Context In the 1950s, the United States and the Soviet Union were embroiled in the "Space Race," with each nation trying to be the first to reach and explore outer space. By the early 1960s, Russia was clearly ahead: both their satellite, Sputnik, and their cosmonaut, Yuri Gagarin, had already orbited the earth. But in 1969, America trumped these accomplishments by sending the first manned flight to the moon. On July 20, 1969, Neil Armstrong and Edwin "Buzz" Aldrin landed and walked on the moon, symbolizing a giant leap in progress for all of humanity. This historic event serves as a touchstone for the characters in "The Third and Final Continent."

The Third and Final Continent   (2000)

I left India in 1964 with a certificate in commerce and the equivalent, in those days, of ten dollars to my name. For three weeks I sailed on the S.S. *Roma*, an Italian cargo vessel, in a cabin next to the ship's engine, across the Arabian Sea, the Red Sea, the Mediterranean, and finally to England. I lived in London, in Finsbury Park, in a house occupied entirely by penniless Bengali bachelors like myself, at least a dozen and sometimes more, all struggling to educate and establish ourselves abroad.

I attended lectures at LSE° and worked at the university library to get by. We lived three or four to a room, shared a single, icy toilet, and took turns cooking pots of egg curry, which we ate with our hands on a table covered with newspapers. Apart from our jobs we had few responsibilities. On weekends we lounged barefoot in drawstring pajamas, drinking tea and smoking Rothmans, or set out to watch cricket° at Lord's. Some weekends the house was crammed with still more Bengalis, to whom we had introduced ourselves at the greengrocer, or on the Tube,° and we made yet more egg curry, and played Mukesh° on

---

LSE: London School of Economics.

cricket: A game of English origin, a precursor to baseball, that features a batter, fielders, and a pitcher, called the hurler.

the Tube: The London Underground (subway).

Mukesh: Mukesh Sharma, an Indian musician.

a Grundig reel-to-reel,° and soaked our dirty dishes in the bathtub. Every now and then someone in the house moved out, to live with a woman whom his family back in Calcutta had determined he was to wed. In 1969, when I was thirty-six years old, my own marriage was arranged. Around the same time, I was offered a full-time job in America, in the processing department of a library at MIT. The salary was generous enough to support a wife, and I was honored to be hired by a world-famous university, and so I obtained a green card, and prepared to travel farther still.

By then I had enough money to go by plane. I flew first to Calcutta, to attend my wedding, and a week later to Boston, to begin my new job. During the flight I read "The Student Guide to North America," for although I was no longer a student, I was on a budget all the same. I learned that Americans drove on the right side of the road, not the left, and that they called a lift an elevator and an engaged phone busy. "The pace of life in North America is different from Britain, as you will soon discover," the guidebook informed me. "Everybody feels he must get to the top. Don't expect an English cup of tea." As the plane began its descent over Boston Harbor, the pilot announced the weather and the time, and that President Nixon had declared a national holiday: two American men had landed on the moon. Several passengers cheered. "God bless America!" one of them hollered. Across the aisle, I saw a woman praying.

I spent my first night at the YMCA in Central Square, Cambridge, an inexpensive accommodation recommended by my guidebook which was within walking distance of MIT. The room contained a cot, a desk, and a small wooden cross on one wall. A sign on the door said that cooking was strictly forbidden. A bare window overlooked Massachusetts Avenue. Car horns, shrill and prolonged, blared one after another. Sirens and flashing lights heralded endless emergencies, and a succession of buses rumbled past, their doors opening and closing with a powerful hiss, throughout the night. The noise was constantly distracting, at times suffocating. I felt it deep in my ribs, just as I had felt the furious drone of the engine on the S.S. *Roma*. But there was no ship's deck to escape to, no glittering ocean to thrill my soul, no breeze to cool my face, no one to talk to. I was too tired to pace the gloomy corridors of the YMCA in my pajamas. Instead I sat at the desk and stared out the window. In the morning I reported to my job at the Dewey Library, a beige fortlike building by Memorial Drive. I also opened a bank account, rented a post office box, and bought a plastic bowl and a spoon. I went to a supermarket called Purity Supreme, wandering up and down the aisles, comparing prices with those in England. In the end I bought a carton of milk and a box of cornflakes. This was my first meal in America. Even the simple chore of buying milk was new to me; in London we'd had bottles delivered each morning to our door.

5   In a week I had adjusted, more or less. I ate cornflakes and milk morning and night, and bought some bananas for variety, slicing them into the bowl with the edge of my spoon. I left my carton of milk on the shaded part of the windowsill,

---

Grundig reel-to-reel: high end audiotape player.

as I had seen other residents at the YMCA do. To pass the time in the evenings I read the *Boston Globe* downstairs, in a spacious room with stained-glass windows. I read every article and advertisement, so that I would grow familiar with things, and when my eyes grew tired I slept. Only I did not sleep well. Each night I had to keep the window wide open; it was the only source of air in the stifling room, and the noise was intolerable. I would lie on the cot with my fingers pressed into my ears, but when I drifted off to sleep my hands fell away, and the noise of the traffic would wake me up again. Pigeon feathers drifted onto the windowsill, and one evening, when I poured milk over my cornflakes, I saw that it had soured. Nevertheless I resolved to stay at the YMCA for six weeks, until my wife's passport and green card were ready. Once she arrived I would have to rent a proper apartment, and from time to time I studied the classified section of the newspaper, or stopped in at the housing office at MIT during my lunch break to see what was available. It was in this manner that I discovered a room for immediate occupancy, in a house on a quiet street, the listing said, for $8 per week. I dialed the number from a pay telephone, sorting through the coins, with which I was still unfamiliar, smaller and lighter than shillings, heavier and brighter than paisas.

"Who is speaking?" a woman demanded. Her voice was bold and clamorous.

"Yes, good afternoon, Madam. I am calling about the room for rent."

"Harvard or Tech?"

"I beg your pardon?"

"Are you from Harvard or Tech?"   10

"Gathering that Tech referred to the Massachusetts Institute of Technology, I replied, "I work at Dewey Library," adding tentatively, "at Tech."

"I only rent rooms to boys from Harvard or Tech!"

"Yes, Madam."

I was given an address and an appointment for seven o'clock that evening. Thirty minutes before the hour I set out, my guidebook in my pocket, my breath fresh with Listerine. I turned down a street shaded with trees, perpendicular to Massachusetts Avenue. In spite of the heat I wore a coat and tie, regarding the event as I would any other interview; I had never lived in the home of a person who was not Indian. The house, surrounded by a chain-link fence was off-white with dark brown trim, with a tangle of forsythia bushes plastered against its front and sides. When I pressed the bell, the woman with whom I had spoken on the phone hollered from what seemed to be just the other side of the door, "One minute, please!"

Several minutes later the door was opened by a tiny, extremely old woman.   15
A mass of snowy hair was arranged like a small sack on top of her head. As I stepped into the house she sat down on a wooden bench positioned at the bottom of a narrow carpeted staircase. Once she was settled on the bench, in a small pool of light, she peered up at me, giving me her undivided attention. She wore a long black skirt that spread like a stiff tent to the floor, and a starched white shirt edged with ruffles at the throat and cuffs. Her hands, folded together in her lap, had long pallid fingers, with swollen knuckles and tough yellow nails. Age had battered her features so that she almost resembled a man, with sharp, shrunken eyes and prominent

creases on either side of her nose. Her lips, chapped and faded, had nearly disappeared, and her eyebrows were missing altogether. Nevertheless she looked fierce.

"Lock up!" she commanded. She shouted even though I stood only a few feet away. "Fasten the chain and firmly press that button on the knob! This is the first thing you shall do when you enter, is that clear?"

I locked the door as directed and examined the house. Next to the bench was a small round table, its legs fully concealed, much like the woman's, by a skirt of lace. The table held a lamp, a transistor radio, a leather change purse with a silver clasp, and a telephone. A thick wooden cane was propped against one side. There was a parlor to my right, lined with bookcases and filled with shabby claw-footed furniture. In the corner of the parlor I saw a grand piano with its top down, piled with papers. The piano's bench was missing; it seemed to be the one on which the woman was sitting. Somewhere in the house a clock chimed seven times.

"You're punctual!" the woman proclaimed. "I expect you shall be so with the rent!"

"I have a letter, Madam." In my jacket pocket was a letter from MIT confirming my employment, which I had brought along to prove that I was indeed from Tech.

20   She stared at the letter, then handed it back to me carefully, gripping it with her fingers as if it were a plate heaped with food. She did not wear glasses, and I wondered if she'd read a word of it. "The last boy was always late! Still owes me eight dollars! Harvard boys aren't what they used to be! Only Harvard and Tech in this house! How's Tech, boy?"

"It is very well."

"You checked the lock?"

"Yes, Madam."

She unclasped her fingers, slapped the space beside her on the bench with one hand, and told me to sit down. For a moment she was silent. Then she intoned, as if she alone possessed this knowledge:

25   "There is an American flag on the moon!"

"Yes, Madam." Until then I had not thought very much about the moon shot. It was in the newspaper, of course, article upon article. The astronauts had landed on the shores of the Sea of Tranquillity, I had read, traveling farther than anyone in the history of civilization. For a few hours they explored the moon's surface. They gathered rocks in their pockets, described their surroundings (a magnificent desolation, according to one astronaut), spoke by phone to the president, and planted a flag in lunar soil. The voyage was hailed as man's most awesome achievement.

The woman bellowed, "A flag on the moon, boy! I heard it on the radio! Isn't that splendid?"

"Yes, Madam.'"

But she was not satisfied with my reply. Instead she commanded, "Say 'Splendid!'"

30   I was both baffled and somewhat insulted by the request. It reminded me of the way I was taught multiplication tables as a child, repeating after the master, sitting cross-legged on the floor of my one-room Tollygunge school. It also reminded me of my wedding, when I had repeated endless Sanskrit verses after the priest, verses I barely understood, which joined me to my wife. I said nothing.

"Say 'Splendid!'" the woman bellowed once again.

"Splendid," I murmured. I had to repeat the word a second time at the top of my lungs, so she could hear. I was reluctant to raise my voice to an elderly woman, but she did not appear to be offended. If anything the reply pleased her, because her next command was:

"Go see the room!"

I rose from the bench and mounted the narrow staircase. There were five doors, two on either side of an equally narrow hallway, and one at the opposite end. Only one door was open. The room contained a twin bed under a sloping ceiling, a brown oval rug, a basin with an exposed pipe, and a chest of drawers. One door led to a closet, another to a toilet and a tub. The window was open; net curtains stirred in the breeze. I lifted them away and inspected the view: a small back yard, with a few fruit trees and an empty clothesline. I was satisfied.

When I returned to the foyer the woman picked up the leather change purse 35 on the table, opened the clasp, fished about with her fingers, and produced a key on a thin wire hoop. She informed me that there was a kitchen at the back of the house, accessible through the parlor. I was welcome to use the stove as long as I left it as I found it. Sheets and towels were provided, but keeping them clean was my own responsibility. The rent was due Friday mornings on the ledge above the piano keys. "And no lady visitors!"

"I am a married man, Madam." It was the first time I had announced this fact to anyone.

But she had not heard. "No lady visitors!" she insisted. She introduced herself as Mrs. Croft.

My wife's name was Mala. The marriage had been arranged by my older brother and his wife. I regarded the proposition with neither objection nor enthusiasm. It was a duty expected of me, as it was expected of every man. She was the daughter of a schoolteacher in Beleghata. I was told that she could cook, knit, embroider, sketch landscapes, and recite poems by Tagore, but these talents could not make up for the fact that she did not possess a fair complexion, and so a string of men had rejected her to her face. She was twenty-seven, an age when her parents had begun to fear that she would never marry, and so they were willing to ship their only child halfway across the world in order to save her from spinsterhood.

For five nights we shared a bed. Each of those nights, after applying cold cream and braiding her hair, she turned from me and wept; she missed her parents. Although I would be leaving the country in a few days, custom dictated that she was now a part of my household, and for the next six weeks she was to live with my brother and his wife, cooking, cleaning, serving tea and sweets to guests. I did nothing to console her. I lay on my own side of the bed, reading my guidebook by flashlight. At times I thought of the tiny room on the other side of the wall which had belonged to my mother. Now the room was practically empty; the wooden pallet on which she'd once slept was piled with trunks and old bedding. Nearly six years ago, before leaving for London, I had watched her die on that bed, had found her playing with her excrement in her final days. Before we cremated her I had cleaned each of her fingernails with a hairpin, and then, because my brother could not bear it, I had assumed the role of eldest son, and had touched the flame to her temple, to release her tormented soul to heaven.

40   The next morning I moved into Mrs. Croft's house. When I unlocked the door I saw that she was sitting on the piano bench, on the same side as the previous evening. She wore the same black skirt, the same starched white blouse, and had her hands folded together the same way in her lap. She looked so much the same that I wondered if she'd spent the whole night on the bench. I put my suitcase upstairs and then headed off to work. That evening when I came home from the university, she was still there.

"Sit down, boy!" She slapped the space beside her.

I perched on the bench. I had a bag of groceries with me — more milk, more cornflakes, and more bananas, for my inspection of the kitchen earlier in the day had revealed no spare pots or pans. There were only two saucepans in the refrigerator, both containing some orange broth, and a copper kettle on the stove.

"Good evening, Madam."

She asked me if I had checked the lock. I told her I had.

45   For a moment she was silent. Then suddenly she declared, with the equal measures of disbelief and delight as the night before, "There's an American flag on the moon, boy!"

"Yes, Madam."

"A flag on the moon! Isn't that splendid?"

I nodded, dreading what I knew was coming. "Yes, Madam."

"Say 'Splendid!'"

50   This time I paused, looking to either side in case anyone was there to overhear me, though I knew perfectly well that the house was empty. I felt like an idiot. But it was a small enough thing to ask. "Splendid!" I cried out.

Within days it became our routine. In the mornings when I left for the library Mrs. Croft was either hidden away in her bedroom, on the other side of the staircase, or sitting on the bench, oblivious of my presence, listening to the news or classical music on the radio. But each evening when I returned the same thing happened: she slapped the bench, ordered me to sit down, declared that there was a flag on the moon, and declared that it was splendid. I said it was splendid, too, and then we sat in silence. As awkward as it was, and as endless as it felt to me then, the nightly encounter lasted only about ten minutes; inevitably she would drift off to sleep, her head falling abruptly toward her chest, leaving me free to retire to my room. By then, of course, there was no flag standing on the moon. The astronauts, I read in the paper, had seen it fall before they flew back to Earth. But I did not have the heart to tell her.

Friday morning, when my first week's rent was due, I went to the piano in the parlor to place my money on the ledge. The piano keys were dull and discolored. When I pressed one, it made no sound at all. I had put eight dollar bills in an envelope and written Mrs. Croft's name on the front of it. I was not in the habit of leaving money unmarked and unattended. From where I stood I could see the profile of her tent-shaped skirt in the hall. It seemed unnecessary to make her get up and walk all the way to the piano. I never saw her walking about, and assumed, from the cane propped against the round table, that she did so with difficulty. When I approached the bench she peered up at me and demanded:

"What is your business?"

"The rent, Madam."

"On the ledge above the piano keys!"   55

"I have it here." I extended the envelope toward her, but her fingers, folded together in her lap, did not budge. I bowed slightly and lowered the envelope; so that it hovered just above her hands. After a moment she accepted it, and nodded her head.

That night when I came home, she did not slap the bench, but out of habit I sat beside her as usual. She asked me if I had checked the lock, but she mentioned nothing about the flag on the moon. Instead she said:

"It was very kind of you!"

"I beg your pardon, Madam?"

"Very kind of you!"   60

She was still holding the envelope in her hands.

On Sunday there was a knock on my door. An elderly woman introduced herself: she was Mrs. Croft's daughter, Helen. She walked into the room and looked at each of the walls as if for signs of change, glancing at the shirts that hung in the closet, the neckties draped over the doorknob, the box of cornflakes on the chest of drawers, the dirty bowl and spoon in the basin. She was short and thick-waisted, with cropped silver hair and bright pink lipstick. She wore a sleeveless summer dress, a necklace of white plastic beads, and spectacles on a chain that hung like a swing against her chest. The backs of her legs were mapped with dark blue veins, and her upper arms sagged like the flesh of a roasted eggplant. She told me she lived in Arlington, a town farther up Massachusetts Avenue. "I come once a week to bring Mother groceries. Has she sent you packing yet?"

"It is very well, Madam."

"Some of the boys run screaming. But I think she likes you. You're the first boarder she's ever referred to as a gentleman."

She looked at me, noticing my bare feet. (I still felt strange wearing shoes   65
indoors, and always removed them before entering my room.) "Are you new to Boston?"

"New to America, Madam."

"From?" She raised her eyebrows.

"I am from Calcutta, India."

"Is that right? We had a Brazilian fellow, about a year ago. You'll find Cambridge a very international city."

I nodded, and began to wonder how long our conversation would last. But at   70
that moment we heard Mrs. Croft's electrifying voice rising up the stairs.

"You are to come downstairs immediately!"

"What is it?" Helen cried back.

"Immediately!"

I put on my shoes. Helen sighed.

75   I followed Helen down the staircase. She seemed to be in no hurry, and complained at one point that she had a bad knee. "Have you been walking without your cane?" Helen called out. "You know you're not supposed to walk without that cane." She paused, resting her hand on the banister, and looked back at me. "She slips sometimes."

    For the first time Mrs. Croft seemed vulnerable. I pictured her on the floor in front of the bench, flat on her back, staring at the ceiling, her feet pointing in opposite directions. But when we reached the bottom of the staircase she was sitting there as usual, her hands folded together in her lap. Two grocery bags were at her feet. She did not slap the bench, or ask us to sit down. She glared.

    "What is it, Mother?"

    "It's improper!"

    "What's improper?"

80   "It is improper for a lady and gentleman who are not married to one another to hold a private conversation without a chaperone!"

    Helen said she was sixty-eight years old, old enough to be my mother, but Mrs. Croft insisted that Helen and I speak to each other downstairs, in the parlor. She added that it was also improper for a lady of Helen's station to reveal her age, and to wear a dress so high above the ankle.

    "For your information, Mother, it's 1969. What would you do if you actually left the house one day and saw a girl in a miniskirt?"

    Mrs. Croft sniffed. "I'd have her arrested."

    Helen shook her head and picked up one of the grocery bags. I picked up the other one, and followed her through the parlor and into the kitchen. The bags were filled with cans of soup, which Helen opened up one by one with a few cranks of a can opener. She tossed the old soup into the sink, rinsed the saucepans under the tap, filled them with soup from the newly opened cans, and put them back in the refrigerator. "A few years ago she could still open the cans herself," Helen said. "She hates that I do it for her now. But the piano killed her hands." She put on her spectacles, glanced at the cupboards, and spotted my tea bags. "Shall we have a cup?"

85   I filled the kettle on the stove. "I beg your pardon, Madam. The piano?"

    "She used to give lessons. For forty years. It was how she raised us after my father died." Helen put her hands on her hips, staring at the open refrigerator. She reached into the back, pulled out a wrapped stick of butter, frowned, and tossed it into the garbage. "That ought to do it," she said, and put the unopened cans of soup in the cupboard. I sat at the table and watched as Helen washed the dirty dishes, tied up the garbage bag, and poured boiling water into two cups. She handed one to me without milk, and sat down at the table.

    "Excuse me, Madam, but is it enough?"

    Helen took a sip of her tea. Her lipstick left a smiling pink stain on the rim of the cup. "Is what enough?"

    "The soup in the pans. Is it enough food for Mrs. Croft?"

90   "She won't eat anything else. She stopped eating solids after she turned one hundred. That was, let's see, three years ago.

    I was mortified. I had assumed Mrs. Croft was in her eighties, perhaps as old as ninety. I had never known a person who had lived for over a century. That this person was a widow who lived alone mortified me further still. Widowhood had driven my own mother insane. My father, who worked as a clerk at the General Post Office of Calcutta, died of encephalitis when I was sixteen. My mother refused to adjust to life without him; instead she sank deeper into a world of darkness from which neither I, nor my brother, nor concerned relatives, nor psychiatric clinics on Rash Behari Avenue could save her. What pained me most was to see her so unguarded, to hear her burp after meals or expel gas in front of company without the slightest embarrassment. After my father's death, my brother abandoned his schooling and began to work in the jute mill he would eventually manage, in order to keep the household running. And so it was my job to sit by my mother's feet and study for my exams as she counted and recounted the bracelets on her arm as if they were the beads of an abacus. We tried to keep an eye on her. Once she had wandered half-naked to the tram depot before we were able to bring her inside again.

"I am happy to warm Mrs. Croft's soup in the evenings," I suggested. "It is no trouble."

Helen looked at her watch, stood up, and poured the rest of her tea into the sink. "I wouldn't if I were you. That's the sort of thing that would kill her altogether."

That evening, when Helen had gone and Mrs. Croft and I were alone again, I began to worry. Now that I knew how very old she was, I worried that something would happen to her in the middle of the night, or when I was out during the day. As vigorous as her voice was, and as imperious as she seemed, I knew that even a scratch or a cough could kill a person that old; each day she lived, I knew, was something of a miracle. Helen didn't seem concerned. She came and went, bringing soup for Mrs. Croft, one Sunday after the next.

In this manner the six weeks of that summer passed. I came home each evening, after my hours at the library, and spent a few minutes on the piano bench with Mrs. Croft. Some evenings I sat beside her long after she had drifted off to sleep, still in awe of how many years she had spent on this earth. At times I tried to picture the world she had been born into, in 1866 — a world, I imagined, filled with women in long black skirts, and chaste conversations in the parlor. Now, when I looked at her hands with their swollen knuckles folded together in her lap, I imagined them smooth and slim, striking the piano keys. At times I came downstairs before going to sleep, to make sure she was sitting upright on the bench, or was safe in her bedroom. On Fridays I put the rent in her hands. There was nothing I could do for her beyond these simple gestures. I was not her son, and, apart from those eight dollars, I owed her nothing. 95

At the end of August, Mala's passport and green card were ready. I received a telegram with her flight information; my brother's house in Calcutta had no telephone. Around that time I also received a letter from her, written only a few days after we had parted. There was no salutation; addressing me by name would have assumed an intimacy we had not yet discovered. It contained only a few lines. "I write in English in preparation for the journey. Here I am very much lonely. Is it very cold there. Is there snow. Yours, Mala."

I was not touched by her words. We had spent only a handful of days in each other's company. And yet we were bound together; for six weeks she had worn an iron bangle on her wrist, and applied vermilion powder to the part in her hair, to signify to the world that she was a bride. In those six weeks I regarded her arrival as I would the arrival of a coming month, or season — something inevitable, but meaningless at the time. So little did I know her that, while details of her face sometimes rose to my memory, I could not conjure up the whole of it.

A few days after receiving the letter, as I was walking to work in the morning, I saw an Indian woman on Massachusetts Avenue, wearing a sari with its free end nearly dragging on the footpath, and pushing a child in a stroller. An American woman with a small black dog on a leash was walking to one side of her. Suddenly the dog began barking. I watched as the Indian woman, startled, stopped in her path, at which point the dog leaped up and seized the end of the sari between its teeth. The American woman scolded the dog, appeared to apologize, and walked quickly away, leaving the Indian woman to fix her sari, and quiet her crying child. She did not see me standing there, and eventually she continued on her way. Such a mishap, I realized that morning, would soon be my concern. It was my duty to take care of Mala, to welcome her and protect her. I would have to buy her her first pair of snow boots, her first winter coat. I would have to tell her which streets to avoid, which way the traffic came, tell her to wear her sari so that the free end did not drag on the footpath. A five-mile separation from her parents, I recalled with some irritation, had caused her to weep.

Unlike Mala, I was used to it all by then: used to cornflakes and milk, used to Helen's visits, used to sitting on the bench with Mrs. Croft. The only thing I was not used to was Mala. Nevertheless, I did what I had to do. I went to the housing office at MIT and found a furnished apartment a few blocks away, with a double bed and a private kitchen and bath, for $40 a week. One last Friday I handed Mrs. Croft eight dollar bills in an envelope, brought my suitcase downstairs, and informed her that I was moving. She put my key into her change purse. The last thing she asked me to do was hand her the cane propped against the table, so that she could walk to the door and lock it behind me. "Good-bye, then," she said, and retreated back into the house. I did not expect any display of emotion, but I was disappointed all the same. I was only a boarder, a man who paid her a bit of money and passed in and out of her home for six weeks. Compared with a century, it was no time at all.

100   At the airport I recognized Mala immediately. The free end of her sari did not drag on the floor, but was draped in a sign of bridal modesty over her head, just as it had draped my mother until the day my father died. Her thin brown arms were stacked with gold bracelets, a small red circle was painted on her forehead, and the edges of her feet were tinted with a decorative red dye. I did not embrace her, or kiss her, or take her hand. Instead I asked her, speaking Bengali for the first time in America, if she was hungry.

She hesitated, then nodded yes.

I told her I had prepared some egg curry at home. "What did they give you to eat on the plane?"

"I didn't eat."

"All the way from Calcutta?"

"The menu said oxtail soup."   105

"But surely there were other items."

"The thought of eating an ox's tail made me lose my appetite."

When we arrived home, Mala opened up one of her suitcases, and presented me with two pullover sweaters, both made with bright blue wool, which she had knitted in the course of our separation, one with a V-neck, the other covered with cables. I tried them on; both were tight under the arms. She had also brought me two new pairs of drawstring pajamas, a letter from my brother, and a packet of loose Darjeeling tea. I had no present for her apart from the egg curry. We sat at a bare table, staring at our plates. We ate with our hands, another thing I had not yet done in America.

"The house is nice," she said. "Also the egg curry." With her left hand she held the end of her sari to her chest, so it would not slip off her head.

"I don't know many recipes."   110

She nodded, peeling the skin off each of her potatoes before eating them. At one point the sari slipped to her shoulders. She readjusted it at once.

"There is no need to cover your head," I said. "I don't mind. It doesn't matter here."

She kept it covered anyway.

I waited to get used to her, to her presence at my side, at my table and in my bed, but a week later we were still strangers. I still was not used to coming home to an apartment that smelled of steamed rice, and finding that the basin in the bathroom was always wiped clean, our two toothbrushes lying side by side, a cake of Pears soap residing in the soap dish. I was not used to the fragrance of the coconut oil she rubbed every other night into her scalp, or the delicate sound her bracelets made as she moved about the apartment. In the mornings she was always awake before I was. The first morning when I came into the kitchen she had heated up the leftovers and set a plate with a spoonful of salt on its edge, assuming I would eat rice for breakfast, as most Bengali husbands did. I told her cereal would do, and the next morning when I came into the kitchen she had already poured the cornflakes into my bowl. One morning she walked with me to MIT, where I gave her a short tour of the campus. The next morning before I left for work she asked me for a few dollars. I parted with them reluctantly, but I knew that this, too, was now normal. When I came home from work there was a potato peeler in the kitchen drawer, and a tablecloth on the table, and chicken curry made with fresh garlic and ginger on the stove. After dinner I read the newspaper, while Mala sat at the kitchen table, working on a cardigan for herself with more of the blue wool, or writing letters home.

On Friday, I suggested going out. Mala set down her knitting and disappeared   115
into the bathroom. When she emerged I regretted the suggestion; she had put on a silk sari and extra bracelets, and coiled her hair with a flattering side part on top of her head. She was prepared as if for a party, or at the very least for the cinema, but I had no such destination in mind. The evening was balmy. We walked several blocks down Massachusetts Avenue, looking into the windows of restaurants and shops. Then, without thinking, I led her down the quiet street where for so many nights I had walked alone.

"This is where I lived before you came," I said, stopping at Mrs. Croft's chain-link fence.

"In such a big house?"

"I had a small room upstairs. At the back."

"Who else lives there?"

120 "A very old woman."

"With her family?"

"Alone."

"But who takes care of her?"

I opened the gate. "For the most part she takes care of herself."

125 I wondered if Mrs. Croft would remember me; I wondered if she had a new boarder to sit with her each evening. When I pressed the bell I expected the same long wait as that day of our first meeting, when I did not have a key. But this time the door was opened almost immediately, by Helen. Mrs. Croft was not sitting on the bench. The bench was gone.

"Hello there," Helen said, smiling with her bright pink lips at Mala. "Mother's in the parlor. Will you be visiting awhile?"

"As you wish, Madam."

"Then I think I'll run to the store, if you don't mind. She had a little accident. We can't leave her alone these days, not even for a minute."

I locked the door after Helen and walked into the parlor. Mrs. Croft was lying flat on her back, her head on a peach-colored cushion, a thin white quilt spread over her body. Her hands were folded together on her chest. When she saw me she pointed at the sofa, and told me to sit down. I took my place as directed, but Mala wandered over to the piano and sat on the bench, which was now positioned where it belonged.

130 "I broke my hip!" Mrs. Croft announced, as if no time had passed.

"Oh dear, Madam."

"I fell off the bench!"

"I am so sorry, Madam."

"It was the middle of the night! Do you know what I did, boy?"

135 I shook my head.

"I called the police!"

She stared up at the ceiling and grinned sedately, exposing a crowded row of long gray teeth. "What do you say to that, boy?"

As stunned as I was, I knew what I had to say. With no hesitation at all, I cried out, "Splendid!"

Mala laughed then. Her voice was full of kindness, her eyes bright with amusement. I had never heard her laugh before, and it was loud enough so that Mrs. Croft heard, too. She turned to Mala and glared.

140 "Who is she, boy?"

"She is my wife, Madam."

Mrs. Croft pressed her head at an angle against the cushion to get a better look. "Can you play the piano?"

"No, Madam," Mala replied.

"Then stand up!"

Mala rose to her feet, adjusting the end of her sari over her head and holding it 145
to her chest, and, for the first time since her arrival, I felt sympathy. I remembered
my first days in London, learning how to take the Tube to Russell Square, riding an
escalator for the first time, unable to understand that when the man cried "piper" it
meant "paper," unable to decipher, for a whole year, that the conductor said "Mind
the gap" as the train entered each station. Like me, Mala had traveled far from
home, not knowing where she was going, or what she would find, for no reason
other than to be my wife. As strange as it seemed, I knew in my heart that one day
her death would affect me, and stranger still, that mine would affect her. I wanted
somehow to explain this to Mrs. Croft, who was still scrutinizing Mala from top to
toe with what seemed to be placid disdain. I wondered if Mrs. Croft had ever seen
a woman in a sari, with a dot painted on her forehead and bracelets stacked on her
wrists. I wondered what she would object to. I wondered if she could see the red dye
still vivid on Mala's feet, all but obscured by the bottom edge of her sari. At last Mrs.
Croft declared, with the equal measures of disbelief and delight I knew well:

"She is a perfect lady!"

Now it was I who laughed. I did so quietly, and Mrs. Croft did not hear me.
But Mala had heard, and, for the first time, we looked at each other and smiled. I
like to think of that moment in Mrs. Croft's parlor as the moment when the
distance between Mala and me began to lessen. Although we were not yet fully
in love, I like to think of the months that followed as a honeymoon of sorts.
Together we explored the city and met other Bengalis, some of whom are still
friends today. We discovered that a man named Bill sold fresh fish on Prospect
Street, and that a shop in Harvard Square called Cardullo's sold bay leaves and
cloves. In the evenings we walked to the Charles River to watch sailboats drift
across the water, or had ice cream cones in Harvard Yard. We bought a camera
with which to document our life together, and I took pictures of her posing in
front of the Prudential building, so that she could send them to her parents. At
night we kissed, shy at first but quickly bold, and discovered pleasure and solace
in each other's arms. I told her about my voyage on the S.S. *Roma*, and about
Finsbury Park and the YMCA, and my evenings on the bench with Mrs. Croft.
When I told her stories about my mother, she wept. It was Mala who consoled me
when, reading the *Globe* one evening, I came across Mrs. Croft's obituary. I had
not thought of her in several months — by then those six weeks of the summer
were already a remote interlude in my past — but when I learned of her death I
was stricken, so much so that when Mala looked up from her knitting she found
me staring at the wall, unable to speak. Mrs. Croft's was the first death I mourned
in America, for hers was the first life I had admired; she had left this world at last,
ancient and alone, never to return.

As for me, I have not strayed much farther. Mala and I live in a town about
twenty miles from Boston, on a tree-lined street much like Mrs. Croft's, in a house
we own, with room for guests, and a garden that saves us from buying tomatoes in
summer. We are American citizens now, so that we can collect Social Security
when it is time. Though we visit Calcutta every few years, we have decided to
grow old here. I work in a small college library. We have a son who attends
Harvard University. Mala no longer drapes the end of her sari over her head, or

weeps at night for her parents, but occasionally she weeps for our son. So we drive to Cambridge to visit him, or bring him home for a weekend, so that he can eat rice with us with his hands, and speak in Bengali, things we sometimes worry he will no longer do after we die.

150   Whenever we make that drive, I always take Massachusetts Avenue, in spite of the traffic. I barely recognize the buildings now, but each time I am there I return instantly to those six weeks as if they were only the other day, and I slow down and point to Mrs. Croft's street, saying to my son, Here was my first home in America, where I lived with a woman who was 103. "Remember?" Mala says, and smiles, amazed, as I am, that there was ever a time that we were strangers. My son always expresses his astonishment, not at Mrs. Croft's age but at how little I paid in rent, a fact nearly as inconceivable to him as a flag on the moon was to a woman born in 1866. In my son's eyes I see the ambition that had first hurled me across the world. In a few years he will graduate and pave his own way, alone and unprotected. But I remind myself that he has a father who is still living, a mother who is happy and strong. Whenever he is discouraged, I tell him that if I can survive on three continents, then there is no obstacle he cannot conquer. While the astronauts, heroes forever, spent mere hours on the moon, I have remained in this new world for nearly thirty years. I know that my achievement is quite ordinary. I am not the only man to seek his fortune far from home, and certainly I am not the first. Still, there are times I am bewildered by each mile I have traveled, each meal I have eaten, each person I have known, each room in which I have slept. As ordinary as it all appears, there are times when it is beyond my imagination.

Reading and Reacting

1. Mrs. Croft, who is 103 years old, is initially described as "a tiny, extremely old woman" (par. 15). Does she ever move beyond this stereotype to become a fully developed character, or does she remain a stereotype? Explain.

2. At the end of the story, the narrator says about Mrs. Croft, "hers was the first life I had admired" (par. 148). Exactly what do you think he admires about her life?

3. The narrator, having lived in India and in England, is now living in Boston, on his third continent. In what respects is he still tied to the other two continents? In what sense is the continent on which he is now living his "final continent"?

4. How does the narrator change during the course of the story? What causes these changes? In what respects is he still the same person he was when he arrived in Boston?

5. List three adjectives to describe each of these characters: the narrator, Mrs. Croft, Mala, Helen.

6. Do you see the narrator's life — and this story — as depressing or uplifting? Do you ever feel sorry for him? Explain your reaction.

7. What is the significance of the piano? The piano bench? What do they tell readers about Mrs. Croft? About the narrator?

8. At one point in the story (par. 91), the narrator reveals information about his family in India, in particular about his mother's widowhood. Why does this information appear at this point in the story? What does it tell readers about the narrator's culture? About his marriage? About his reaction to Mrs. Croft?

9. Mala, the narrator's wife, does not really enter the story as a character until two-thirds of the way through, long after the narrator's relationship with Mrs. Croft has been established. How does his relationship with Mrs. Croft prepare readers for the relationship he will have with his wife? How does it prepare *him*?

10. The narrator arrives in the United States on the day American astronauts land on the moon, and the moon landing is mentioned throughout the story (for example, in paragraphs 3, 25–27, 45, 51, and the last paragraph). How does this historic event help to shed light on the narrator's life on his "third and final continent"?

11. **JOURNAL ENTRY** In the last paragraphs, we learn that the narrator now has a son. How is the son's life different from the life his father led at the same age? How do you imagine the son's future life will be different from his parents' lives?

12. **CRITICAL PERSPECTIVE** While being interviewed about *The Interpreter of Maladies*, the collection in which this story appeared, Jhumpa Lahiri made the following comments:

> For immigrants, the challenges of exile, the loneliness, the constant sense of alienation, the knowledge of and longing for a lost world, are more explicit and distressing than for their children. On the other hand, the problem for the children of immigrants, those with strong ties to their country of origin, is that they feel neither one thing nor the other.

Do you think Lahiri's characterization of immigrants is an accurate description of the feelings experienced by the narrator of "The Third and Final Continent" and his wife? Are their concerns for their son related to the fact that he is in a sense caught between two cultures?

Related Works: "Telephone Conversation" (p. 8), "The Disappearance" (p. 371), "A Valediction: Forbidding Mourning" (p. 949), "Immigrants" (p. 1025), "Apollo" (p. 1135), *The Cuban Swimmer* (p. 1772)

WRITING SUGGESTIONS: Character

1. In both "A&P," and "Gryphon," the main characters (Sammy and Tommy, respectively) struggle against rules, authority figures, and inflexible social systems. Compare and contrast the struggles in which these two characters are engaged.

2. Write an essay in which you contrast the character of Miss Brill (p. 235) with the character of Emily Grierson in "A Rose for Emily" (p. 216) or with Phoenix Jackson in "A Worn Path" (p. 505). Consider how each character interacts with those around her as well as how each seems to see her role or mission in the world.

3. Both "The Water Faucet Vision" and "Gryphon" present adult narrators' perspectives of pivotal events in their childhoods. Compare and contrast

the impact of these events on the two narrators. How have they changed, and exactly what has changed them? Which change do you see as more significant? Why?

4. Write a letter from the narrator of "The Third and Final Continent" to Mala before her arrival in the United States. In this letter, have the narrator reveal to his wife his hopes and dreams for their future as well as the cultural shock he is experiencing and the fears and uncertainties he has. If you like, you may invent details about his past life in India or his day-to-day life in Boston.

5. Sammy, Miss Brill, and Miss Ferenczi all use their active imaginations to create scenarios that help get them through the day. None of them is able to sustain the illusion, however. As a result, all three find out how harsh reality can be. How are these scenarios alike, and how are they different? What steps could these three characters take to fit more comfortably into the worlds they inhabit? *Should* they take such steps? Are they able to do so?

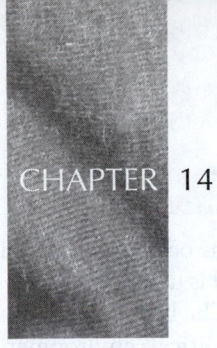

CHAPTER 14

SETTING

> The earth was here before I was. When I came, I simply identified place by living in it or looking at it. One does create place in the same way that the storyteller creates himself, creates his listener. The writer creates a place.
>
> —N. Scott Momaday, *Ancestral Voices*

The **setting** of a work of fiction establishes its historical, geographical, and physical context. *Where* a work is set — on a tropical island, in a dungeon, at a crowded party, in the woods — influences our reactions to the story's events and characters. *When* a work takes place — during the French Revolution, during the Vietnam War, today, or in the future — is equally important. Setting, however, is more than just the approximate time and place in which a work is set; setting also encompasses a wide variety of physical and cultural elements.

Clearly, setting is more important in some works than in others. In some stories, no particular time or place is specified or even suggested, perhaps because the writer does not consider a specific setting to be important or because the writer wishes the story's events to seem timeless and universal. In Nadine Gordimer's "Once upon a Time" (p. 204), for example, the writer follows the conventions of fairy tales, which are set in unidentified faraway places. In other stories, a writer may provide only minimal information about setting, telling readers little more than where and when the action takes place. Sometimes, however, a particular setting may be vital to the story, perhaps influencing characters' behavior, as it does in the stories in this chapter.

Sometimes a story's central conflict is between the protagonist and the setting — for example, Alice in Wonderland, a northerner in the South, an unsophisticated American tourist in an old European city, a sane person in a mental hospital, a moral person in a corrupt environment, an immigrant in a new world, or a city dweller in the country. Such a conflict may drive the story's plot and also help to define the characters. (A conflict between events and setting — for example, the arrival of a mysterious stranger in a typical suburban neighborhood, the intrusion of modern social ideas into an old-fashioned world, or the intrusion of a brutal murder into a peaceful village — can also enrich a story.)

Historical Setting

A particular historical period, and the events and customs associated with it, can be vital to a story; therefore, some knowledge of the period is useful (or even essential) to readers who wish to understand the story fully. The historical context establishes a story's social, cultural, economic, and political environment. Knowing, for instance, that Charlotte Perkins Gilman's "The Yellow Wallpaper" (p. 421) was written in the late nineteenth century, when doctors treated women as delicate and dependent creatures, helps to explain the narrator's emotional state. Likewise, it may be important to know that a story is set during a particularly volatile (or static) political era, during a time of permissive (or repressive) attitudes toward sex, during a war, or during a period of economic prosperity or recession. Any one of these factors may help to explain characters' actions and motivation. Historical events or cultural norms may, for instance, limit or expand a character's options, and our knowledge of history may reveal to us a character's incompatibility with his or her milieu. For example, in F. Scott Fitzgerald's "Bernice Bobs Her Hair," set in the 1920s in a midwestern town, a young girl is goaded into cutting her long hair. To understand the significance of Bernice's act — and to understand the reactions of others to that act — readers must know that during that era only racy "society vampires," not nice girls from good families, bobbed their hair.

The approximate year or historical period during which a story takes place can explain forces that act on characters and account for their behavior, clarify circumstances that influence the story's action, and justify a writer's use of plot devices that might otherwise seem improbable. For instance, stories set before the development of modern transportation and communication systems may hinge on plot devices readers would not accept in a modern story. Thus, in "Paul's Case," a 1904 story by Willa Cather, a young man who steals a large sum of money in Pittsburgh is able to spend several days enjoying it before the news of the theft reaches New York, where he has fled. In other stories, we see characters threatened by diseases that have now been eradicated (or subjected to outdated medical or psychiatric treatment) or constrained by social conventions very different from those that operate in our own society.

Geographical Setting

In addition to knowing *when* a work takes place, readers need to know *where* it takes place. Knowing whether a story is set in the United States, in Europe, or in a developing nation can help to explain anything from why language and customs are unfamiliar to us to why characters act in ways we find improbable. Even in stories set in our own country, regional differences may account for differences in plot development and characters' motivation. For example, knowing that William Faulkner's "A Rose for Emily" (p. 216) is set in the post–Civil War American South helps to explain why the townspeople are so chivalrously protective of Miss Emily. Similarly, the fact that Bret Harte's "The Outcasts of

Poker Flat" (1869) is set in a California mining camp accounts for its varied cast of characters — including a gambler, a prostitute, and a traveling salesman.

The size of the town or city in which a story takes place may also be important. In a small town, for example, a character's problems are more likely to be subject to intense scrutiny by other characters, as they are in stories of small-town life such as those in Sherwood Anderson's *Winesburg, Ohio*. In a large city, characters may be more likely to be isolated and anonymous, like Mrs. Miller in Truman Capote's "Miriam" (1945), who is so lonely that she creates an imaginary companion. Characters may also be alienated by their big-city surroundings, as Gregor Samsa is in Franz Kafka's classic novella "The Metamorphosis" (1915).

Of course, a story may not have a recognizable geographical setting: its location may not be specified, or it may be set in a fantasy world. Choosing unusual settings may free writers from the constraints placed on them by familiar environments, allowing them to experiment with situations and characters, unaffected by readers' expectations or associations with familiar settings.

Physical Setting

Physical setting can clearly influence a story's mood as well as its development. For example, *time of day* can be important. The gruesome murder described in Edgar Allan Poe's "The Cask of Amontillado" (p. 350) takes place in an appropriate setting: not just underground but in the darkness of night. Conversely, the horrifying events of Shirley Jackson's "The Lottery" (p. 461) take place in broad daylight, contrasting dramatically with the darkness of the society that permits — and even participates in — such events. Many stories, of course, move through several time periods as the action unfolds, and changes in time may also be important. For instance, the approach of evening, or of dawn, can signal the end of a crisis in the plot.

Whether a story is set primarily *inside* or *out-of-doors* may also be significant. The characters may be physically constrained by a closed-in setting or liberated by an expansive landscape. Some interior settings may be psychologically limiting. For instance, the narrator in "The Yellow Wallpaper" feels suffocated by her room, whose ugly wallpaper comes to haunt her. In many of Poe's stories, the central character is trapped, physically or psychologically, in a confined, suffocating space. In other stories, an interior setting may have a symbolic function. For instance, in "A Rose for Emily," the house is for Miss Emily a symbol of the South's past glory as well as a refuge, a fortress, and a hiding place. Similarly, a building or house may represent society, with its rules, norms, and limitations. In John Updike's "A&P" (p. 230), for instance, the supermarket establishes social as well as physical limits.

Conversely, an outdoor setting can free a character from social norms of behavior, as it does for Ernest Hemingway's Nick Adams, a war veteran who, in "Big Two-Hearted River" (1925), finds order, comfort, and peace only when he is away from civilization. An outdoor setting can also expose characters to physical dangers, such as untamed wilderness, uncharted seas, and frighteningly empty open spaces, as is the case in Stephen Crane's "The Open Boat" (p. 685).

Weather can be another important aspect of setting. A storm can threaten a character's life or just make the character — and readers —*think* danger is present, distracting us from other, more subtle threats. Extreme weather conditions can make characters act irrationally or uncharacteristically, as in Kate Chopin's "The Storm" (p. 281), where a storm provides the story's complication and determines the characters' actions. In numerous stories set in hostile landscapes, where extremes of heat and cold influence the action, weather may serve as a test for characters, as it does in Jack London's "To Build a Fire" (1908), in which the main character struggles unsuccessfully against the brutally cold, hostile environment of the Yukon.

The various physical attributes of setting combine to create a story's **atmosphere** or **mood**. In "The Cask of Amontillado," for example, several factors work together to create the story's eerie, intense atmosphere: it is nighttime; it is the hectic carnival season; and the catacombs are dark, damp, and filled with the bones of the narrator's ancestors. Sometimes the mood or atmosphere that is created helps to convey a story's central theme — as the ironic contrast between the pleasant atmosphere and the shocking events that unfold communicates the theme of "The Lottery." A story's atmosphere may also be linked to a character's mental state, perhaps reflecting his or her mood. For example, darkness and isolation can reflect a character's depression, whereas an idyllic, peaceful atmosphere can express a character's joy. And, of course, a story's atmosphere may also *influence* the characters' state of mind, causing them to react one way in a crowded, busy, urban atmosphere but to react very differently in a peaceful rural atmosphere.

✔ CHECKLIST   Writing about Setting

- Is the setting specified or unidentified? Is it fully described or only suggested?

- Is the setting just background, or is it a key force in the story?

- Are any characters in conflict with their environment?

- How does the setting influence the story's plot? Does it cause characters to act?

- In what time period does the story take place? How can you tell? What social, political, or economic characteristics of the historical period might influence the story?

- In what geographical location is the story set? Is this location important to the story?

- At what time of day is the story set? Is time important to the development of the story?

> Is the story set primarily inside or outside? What role does this aspect of the setting play in the story?
>
> What role do weather conditions play in the story?
>
> What kind of atmosphere or mood does the setting create?
>
> How does the setting influence the characters? Does it affect (or reflect) their emotional state? Does it help to explain their motivation?
>
> Does the atmosphere change as the story progresses? Is this change significant?

KATE CHOPIN (1851–1904) (picture and biography on p. 196) wrote in a style that was realistic yet infused with a dense, sensual texture that was perhaps, in part, her artistic response to her memories of the exotic Louisiana bayou country. Like her contemporary Gustave Flaubert (Chopin's short novel *The Awakening* has often been called a "Creole *Bovary*"), Chopin used the physical world — as in the charged atmosphere of "The Storm" — to symbolize the inner truths of her characters' minds and hearts. Unlike Flaubert, however, she depicted sex not as a frantic and destructive force but as a joyous, elemental part of life. Apparently Kate Chopin knew how daring "The Storm" was: she never submitted it for publication.

Cultural Context Louisiana, where Chopin's story presumably takes place, has a large Creole population, concentrated in the southern region of the state, which borders the Gulf of Mexico. In Louisiana, the West Indies, and Latin America, the word *Creole* initially referred to the colonial French and Spanish population. It later came to refer to the *gens libres de couleur* (free people of color) in Louisiana, who were of mixed Afro-European descent. Today, the word *Creole* denotes the Afro-French language still spoken in parts of Louisiana as well as specific culinary, musical, and architectural styles that reflect the mingling of cultures in Louisiana.

The Storm (c. 1899)

I

The leaves were so still that even Bibi thought it was going to rain. Bobinôt, who was accustomed to converse on terms of perfect equality with his little son, called the child's attention to certain sombre clouds that were rolling with sinister intention from the west, accompanied by a sullen, threatening roar. They were at Friedheimer's store and decided to remain there till the storm had passed.

They sat within the door on two empty kegs. Bibi was four years old and looked very wise.

"Mama'll be 'fraid, yes," he suggested with blinking eyes.

"She'll shut the house. Maybe she got Sylvie helpin' her this evenin'," Bobinôt responded reassuringly.

"No; she ent got Sylvie. Sylvie was helpin' her yistiday," piped Bibi.

5   Bobinôt arose and going across to the counter purchased a can of shrimps, of which Calixta was very fond. Then he returned to his perch on the keg and sat stolidly holding the can of shrimps while the storm burst. It shook the wooden store and seemed to be ripping great furrows in the distant field. Bibi laid his little hand on his father's knee and was not afraid.

II

Calixta, at home, felt no uneasiness for their safety. She sat at a side window sewing furiously on a sewing machine. She was greatly occupied and did not notice the approaching storm. But she felt very warm and often stopped to mop her face on which the perspiration gathered in beads. She unfastened her white sacque at the throat. It began to grow dark, and suddenly realizing the situation she got up hurriedly and went about closing windows and doors.

Out on the small front gallery she had hung Bobinôt's Sunday clothes to air and she hastened out to gather them before the rain fell. As she stepped outside, Alcée Laballière rode in at the gate. She had not seen him very often since her marriage, and never alone. She stood there with Bobinôt's coat in her hands, and the big rain drops began to fall. Alcée rode his horse under the shelter of a side projection where the chickens had huddled and there were plows and a harrow piled up in the corner.

"May I come and wait on your gallery till the storm is over, Calixta?" he asked.

"Come 'long in, M'sieur Alcée."

10   His voice and her own startled her as if from a trance, and she seized Bobinôt's vest. Alcée, mounting to the porch, grabbed the trousers and snatched Bibi's braided jacket that was about to be carried away by a sudden gust of wind. He expressed an intention to remain outside, but it was soon apparent that he might as well have been out in the open: the water beat in upon the boards in driving sheets, and he went inside, closing the door after him. It was even necessary to put something beneath the door to keep the water out.

"My! what a rain! It's good two years since it rain' like that," exclaimed Calixta as she rolled up a piece of bagging and Alcée helped her to thrust it beneath the crack.

She was a little fuller of figure than five years before when she married; but she had lost nothing of her vivacity. Her blue eyes still retained their melting quality; and her yellow hair, dishevelled by the wind and rain, kinked more stubbornly than ever about her ears and temples.

The rain beat upon the low, shingled roof with a force and clatter that threatened to break an entrance and deluge them there. They were in the dining room — the sitting room — the general utility room. Adjoining was her bed room, with Bibi's couch along side her own. The door stood open, and the room with its white, monumental bed, its closed shutters, looked dim and mysterious.

Alcée flung himself into a rocker and Calixta nervously began to gather up from the floor the lengths of a cotton sheet which she had been sewing.

"If this keeps up, *Dieu sait*° if the levees° goin' to stan' it!" she exclaimed.   15

"What have you got to do with the levees?"

"I got enough to do! An' there's Bobinôt with Bibi out in that storm — if he only didn't left Friedheimer's!"

"Let us hope, Calixta, that Bobinôt's got sense enough to come in out of a cyclone."

She went and stood at the window with a greatly disturbed look on her face. She wiped the frame that was clouded with moisture. It was stiflingly hot. Alcée got up and joined her at the window, looking over her shoulder. The rain was coming down in sheets obscuring the view of far-off cabins and enveloping the distant wood in a gray mist. The playing of the lightning was incessant. A bolt struck a tall chinaberry tree at the edge of the field. It filled all visible space with a blinding glare and the crash seemed to invade the very boards they stood upon.

Calixta put her hands to her eyes, and with a cry, staggered backward. Alcée's   20
arm encircled her, and for an instant he drew her close and spasmodically to him.

"*Bonté!*"° she cried, releasing herself from his encircling arm and retreating from the window, "the house'll go next! If I only knew w'ere Bibi was!" She would not compose herself; she would not be seated. Alcée clasped her shoulders and looked into her face. The contact of her warm, palpitating body when he had unthinkingly drawn her into his arms, had aroused all the old-time infatuation and desire for her flesh.

"Calixta," he said, "don't be frightened. Nothing can happen. The house is too low to be struck, with so many tall trees standing about. There! aren't you going to be quiet? say, aren't you?" He pushed her hair back from her face that was warm and steaming. Her lips were as red and moist as pomegranate seed. Her white neck and a glimpse of her full, firm bosom disturbed him powerfully. As she glanced up at him the fear in her liquid blue eyes had given place to a drowsy gleam that unconsciously betrayed a sensuous desire. He looked down into her eyes and there was nothing for him to do but to gather her lips in a kiss. It reminded him of Assumption.

"Do you remember — in Assumption, Calixta?" he asked in a low voice broken by passion. Oh! she remembered; for in Assumption he had kissed her and kissed and kissed her; until his senses would well nigh fail, and to save her he would resort to a desperate flight. If she was not an immaculate dove in those days, she was still inviolate; a passionate creature whose very defenselessness had made her defense, against which his honor forbade him to prevail. Now — well, now — her lips seemed in a manner free to be tasted, as well as her round, white throat and her whiter breasts.

They did not heed the crashing torrents, and the roar of the elements made her laugh as she lay in his arms. She was a revelation in that dim, mysterious

---

Dieu sait: "God knows" (French).

levees: Raised embankments designed to keep a river from overflowing.

Bonté: "Goodness!" (French).

chamber; as white as the couch she lay upon. Her firm, elastic flesh that was knowing for the first time its birthright, was like a creamy lily that the sun invites to contribute its breath and perfume to the undying life of the world.

25   The generous abundance of her passion, without guile or trickery, was like a white flame which penetrated and found response in depths of his own sensuous nature that had never yet been reached.

When he touched her breasts they gave themselves up in quivering ecstasy, inviting his lips. Her mouth was a fountain of delight. And when he possessed her, they seemed to swoon together at the very borderland of life's mystery.

He stayed cushioned upon her, breathless, dazed, enervated, with his heart beating like a hammer upon her. With one hand she clasped his head, her lips lightly touching his forehead. The other hand stroked with a soothing rhythm his muscular shoulders.

The growl of the thunder was distant and passing away. The rain beat softly upon the shingles, inviting them to drowsiness and sleep. But they dared not yield.

The rain was over; and the sun was turning the glistening green world into a palace of gems. Calixta, on the gallery, watched Alcée ride away. He turned and smiled at her with a beaming face; and she lifted her pretty chin in the air and laughed aloud.

III

30   Bobinôt and Bibi, trudging home, stopped without at the cistern to make themselves presentable.

"My! Bibi, w'at will yo' mama say! You ought to be ashame'. You oughtn' put on those good pants. Look at 'em! An' that mud on yo' collar! How you got that mud on yo' collar, Bibi? I never saw such a boy!" Bibi was the picture of pathetic resignation. Bobinôt was the embodiment of serious solicitude as he strove to remove from his own person and his son's the signs of their tramp over heavy roads and through wet fields. He scraped the mud off Bibi's bare legs and feet with a stick and carefully removed all traces from his heavy brogans. Then, prepared for the worst — the meeting with an over-scrupulous housewife, they entered cautiously at the back door.

Calixta was preparing supper. She had set the table and was dripping coffee at the hearth. She sprang up as they came in.

"Oh, Bobinôt! You back! My! but I was uneasy. W'ere you been during the rain? An' Bibi? he ain't wet? he ain't hurt?" She had clasped Bibi and was kissing him effusively. Bobinôt's explanations and apologies which he had been composing all along the way, died on his lips as Calixta felt him to see if he were dry, and seemed to express nothing but satisfaction at their safe return.

"I brought you some shrimps, Calixta," offered Bobinôt, hauling the can from his ample side pocket and laying it on the table.

35   "Shrimps! Oh, Bobinôt! you too good fo' anything!" and she gave him a smacking kiss on the cheek that resounded. "*J'vous réponds,*° we'll have a feas' tonight! umph-umph!"

J'vous réponds: "I tell you" (French).

Bobinôt and Bibi began to relax and enjoy themselves, and when the three seated themselves at table they laughed much and so loud that anyone might have heard them as far away as Laballière's.

IV

Alcée Laballière wrote to his wife, Clarisse, that night. It was a loving letter, full of tender solicitude. He told her not to hurry back, but if she and the babies liked it at Biloxi, to stay a month longer. He was getting on nicely; and though he missed them, he was willing to bear the separation a while longer — realizing that their health and pleasure were the first things to be considered.

V

As for Clarisse, she was charmed upon receiving her husband's letter. She and the babies were doing well. The society was agreeable; many of her old friends and acquaintances were at the bay. And the first free breath since her marriage seemed to restore the pleasant liberty of her maiden days. Devoted as she was to her husband, their intimate conjugal life was something which she was more than willing to forego for a while.

So the storm passed and everyone was happy.

Reading and Reacting

1. Trace the progress of the storm through the five parts of the story. Then, trace the stages of the story's plot. How does the progress of the storm parallel the developing plot?

2. How does the weather help to create the story's atmosphere? How would you characterize this atmosphere?

3. In Part I, the "sombre clouds . . . rolling with sinister intention" introduce the storm. In what sense does this description introduce the story's action as well?

4. In what ways does the storm *cause* the events of the story? List specific events that occur because of the storm. Is the presence of the storm essential to the story? Explain.

5. In what sense does the storm act as a character in the story?

6. The weather is the most obvious element of the story's setting. What other aspects of setting are important to the story?

7. After Part II, the storm is not mentioned again until the last line of the story. What signs of the storm remain in Parts III, IV, and V?

8. Besides denoting the weather, what else might the title suggest?

9. JOURNAL ENTRY The storm sets in motion the chain of events that leads to the characters' adultery. Do you think the storm excuses the characters in any way from responsibility for their actions?

10. CRITICAL PERSPECTIVE Kate Chopin is widely considered to be a regional, or "local color" writer. This term refers to writing in which descriptions of a particular geographic region are prominent. Local color writers strive to incorporate accurate speech patterns and dialects, as well as descriptions of local scenery, dress, and social customs, in their writing. In their introduction to her work, Prentice Hall educators note the following:

Through her vivid descriptions and use of dialect, Chopin captured the local color of the region. In her stories, published in *Bayou Folk* (1894) and *Acadie* (1897), she exhibited her deep understanding of the different attitudes and concerns of the Louisiana natives. Yet her charming portraits of Louisiana life often obscured the fact that she explored the themes considered radical at the time: the nature of marriage, racial prejudice, and women's desire for social, economic, and political equality.

In what ways is "The Storm" an example of local color writing? In what ways is it more than just a "charming portrait of Louisiana life"?

Related Works: "Hills Like White Elephants" (p. 148), "What Lips My Lips Have Kissed" (p. 1074), "General Review of the Sex Situation" (p. 1075), "Wild Nights—Wild Nights!" (p. 1167), *The Stronger* (p. 1520)

SHERMAN J. ALEXIE (1966 –   ), a Spokane/Coeur d'Alene Indian, grew up on the Spokane Indian Reservation in Wellpinit, Washington, about fifty miles northwest of Spokane, where approximately 1,100 Spokane Tribal members live. Alexie has published short stories, novels, and poetry. He was named one of Granta's Best of Young American Novelists, and his first novel, *Reservation Blues* (1995), won the Before Columbus Foundation's American Book Award and the Murray Morgan Prize. His second novel, *Indian Killer* (1996), was named one of *People's* Best of Pages and was a *New York Times* Notable Book. In 1997, he and Native American director Chris Eyre collaborated on a film project based on parts of Alexie's 1993 short story collection *The Lone Ranger and Tonto Fistfight in Heaven;* the film, *Smoke Signals,* was released in 1998. To date, Alexie has written sixteen books, including poetry collections, novels, and short story collections. His most recent book is *Ten Little Indians* (2003), a collection of short stories.

Commenting on Native American culture, Alexie has said, "One of the biggest misconceptions about Indians is that we're stoic, but humor is an essential part of our culture." "This Is What It Means to Say Phoenix, Arizona" (from *The Lone Ranger and Tonto Fistfight in Heaven*) demonstrates this unique use of humor to transcend the harsh realities of life on the reservation and of the struggle to adapt to contemporary American life.

Cultural Context The United States policy of creating Native American reservations can be traced back to the administration of President Ulysses S. Grant, who determined that establishing such reservations was the best way to handle the "Indian problem" between white settlers and the Native Americans they encountered. (Even supporters of Native Americans believed that they were incapable of assimilating into the wider American society and that only on reservations would they be able to survive as a people.) Today, about half of America's 2.5 million Native Americans continue to live on reservations, where more than forty percent of the families live below the federal poverty line and the unemployment rate averages around seventy percent. At the same time, reservations are the one place where members of a tribe can live together and retain their culture, language, and heritage. The characters in "This Is What It Means to Say Phoenix, Arizona" experience both the positive and negative elements of reservation life.

This Is What It Means to Say
Phoenix, Arizona   (1993)

Just after Victor lost his job at the Bureau of Indian Affairs,° he also found out that his father had died of a heart attack in Phoenix, Arizona. Victor hadn't seen his father in a few years, had only talked to him on the telephone once or twice, but there still was a genetic pain, which was as real and immediate as a broken bone. Victor didn't have any money. Who does have money on a reservation, except the cigarette and fireworks salespeople? His father had a savings account waiting to be claimed, but Victor needed to find a way to get from Spokane to Phoenix. Victor's mother was just as poor as he was, and the rest of his family didn't have any use at all for him. So Victor called the tribal council.

"Listen," Victor said. "My father just died. I need some money to get to Phoenix to make arrangements."

"Now Victor," the council said, "you know we're having a difficult time financially."

"But I thought the council had special funds set aside for stuff like this."

"Now, Victor, we do have some money available for the proper return of tribal   5
members' bodies. But I don't think we have enough to bring your father all the way back from Phoenix."

"Well," Victor said. "It ain't going to cost all that much. He had to be cremated. Things were kind of ugly. He died of a heart attack in his trailer and nobody found him for a week. It was really hot, too. You get the picture."

"Now, Victor, we're sorry for your loss and the circumstances. But we can really only afford to give you one hundred dollars."

"That's not even enough for a plane ticket."

"Well, you might consider driving down to Phoenix."

"I don't have a car. Besides, I was going to drive my father's pickup back up   10
here."

"Now, Victor," the council said, "we're sure there is somebody who could drive you to Phoenix. Or could anybody lend you the rest of the money?"

"You know there ain't nobody around with that kind of money."

"Well, we're sorry, Victor, but that's the best we can do."

Victor accepted the tribal council's offer. What else could he do? So he signed the proper papers, picked up his check, and walked over to the Trading Post to cash it.

While Victor stood in line, he watched Thomas Builds-the-Fire standing near   15
the magazine rack talking to himself. Like he always did. Thomas was a storyteller whom nobody wanted to listen to. That's like being a dentist in a town where everybody has false teeth.

Bureau of Indian Affairs: The division of the U.S. Department of the Interior that manages Native American matters; the bureau is operated by government officials, not tribal leaders.

Victor and Thomas Builds-the-Fire were the same age, had grown up and played in the dirt together. Ever since Victor could remember, it was Thomas who had always had something to say.

Once, when they were seven years old, when Victor's father still lived with the family, Thomas closed his eyes and told Victor this story: "Your father's heart is weak. He is afraid of his own family. He is afraid of you. Late at night, he sits in the dark. Watches the television until there's nothing but that white noise. Sometimes he feels like he wants to buy a motorcycle and ride away. He wants to run and hide. He doesn't want to be found."

Thomas Builds-the-Fire had known that Victor's father was going to leave, known it before anyone. Now Victor stood in the Trading Post with a one-hundred-dollar check in his hand, wondering if Thomas knew that Victor's father was dead, if he knew what was going to happen next.

Just then, Thomas looked at Victor, smiled, and walked over to him.

20   "Victor, I'm sorry about your father," Thomas said.

"How did you know about it?" Victor asked.

"I heard it on the wind. I heard it from the birds. I felt it in the sunlight. Also, your mother was just in here crying."

"Oh," Victor said and looked around the Trading Post. All the other Indians stared, surprised that Victor was even talking to Thomas. Nobody talked to Thomas anymore because he told the same damn stories over and over again. Victor was embarrassed, but he thought that Thomas might be able to help him. Victor felt a sudden need for tradition.

"I can lend you the money you need," Thomas said suddenly. "But you have to take me with you."

25   "I can't take your money," Victor said. "I mean, I haven't hardly talked to you in years. We're not really friends anymore."

"I didn't say we were friends. I said you had to take me with you."

"Let me think about it."

Victor went home with his one hundred dollars and sat at the kitchen table. He held his head in his hands and thought about Thomas Builds-the-Fire, remembered little details, tears and scars, the bicycle they shared for a summer, so many stories.

*   *   *

Thomas Builds-the-Fire sat on the bicycle, waiting in Victor's yard. He was ten years old and skinny. His hair was dirty because it was the Fourth of July.

30   "Victor," Thomas yelled. "Hurry up. We're going to miss the fireworks."

After a few minutes, Victor ran out of his family's house, vaulted over the porch railing, and landed gracefully on the sidewalk.

Thomas gave him the bike and they headed for the fireworks. It was nearly dark and the fireworks were about to start.

"You know," Thomas said, "it's strange how us Indians celebrate the Fourth of July. It ain't like it was our independence everybody was fighting for."

"You think about things too much," Victor said. "It's just supposed to be fun. Maybe Junior will be there."

"Which Junior? Everybody on this reservation is named Junior."   35

The fireworks were small, hardly more than a few bottle rockets and a fountain. But it was enough for two Indian boys. Years later, they would need much more.

Afterward, sitting in the dark, fighting off mosquitoes, Victor turned to Thomas Builds-the-Fire.

"Hey," Victor said. "Tell me a story."

Thomas closed his eyes and told this story: "There were these two Indian boys who wanted to be warriors. But it was too late to be warriors in the old way. All the horses were gone. So the two Indian boys stole a car and drove to the city. They parked the stolen car in the front of the police station and then hitchhiked back home to the reservation. When they got back, all their friends cheered and their parents' eyes shone with pride. 'You were very brave,' everybody said to the two Indian boys. 'Very brave.'"

"Ya-hey," Victor said. "That's a good one. I wish I could be a warrior."   40

"Me too," Thomas said.

Victor sat at his kitchen table. He counted his one hundred dollars again and again. He knew he needed more to make it to Phoenix and back. He knew he needed Thomas Builds-the-Fire. So he put his money in his wallet and opened the front door to find Thomas on the porch.

"Ya-hey, Victor," Thomas said. "I knew you'd call me."

Thomas walked into the living room and sat down in Victor's favorite chair.

"I've got some money saved up," Thomas said. "It's enough to get us down   45
there, but you have to get us back."

"I've got this hundred dollars," Victor said. "And my dad had a savings account I'm going to claim."

"How much in your dad's account?"

"Enough. A few hundred."

"Sounds good. When we leaving?"

When they were fifteen and had long since stopped being friends, Victor   50
and Thomas got into a fistfight. That is, Victor was really drunk and beat Thomas up for no reason at all. All the other Indian boys stood around and watched it happen. Junior was there and so were Lester, Seymour, and a lot of others.

The beating might have gone on until Thomas was dead if Norma Many Horses hadn't come along and stopped it.

"Hey, you boys," Norma yelled and jumped out of her car. "Leave him alone."

If it had been someone else, even another man, the Indian boys would've just ignored the warnings. But Norma was a warrior. She was powerful. She could have picked up any two of the boys and smashed their skulls together. But worse than that, she would have dragged them all over to some tepee and made them listen to some elder tell a dusty old story.

The Indian boys scattered, and Norma walked over to Thomas and picked him up.

"Hey, little man, are you O.K.?" she asked.   55

Thomas gave her a thumbs-up.

"Why they always picking on you?"

Thomas shook his head, closed his eyes, but no stories came to him, no words or music. He just wanted to go home, to lie in his bed and let his dreams tell the stories for him.

Thomas Builds-the-Fire and Victor sat next to each other in the airplane, coach section. A tiny white woman had the window seat. She was busy twisting her body into pretzels. She was flexible.

60   "I have to ask," Thomas said, and Victor closed his eyes in embarrassment.

"Don't," Victor said.

"Excuse me, miss," Thomas asked. "Are you a gymnast or something?"

"There's no something about it," she said. "I was first alternate on the 1980 Olympic team."

"Really?" Thomas asked.

65   "Really."

"I mean, you used to be a world-class athlete?" Thomas asked.

"My husband thinks I still am."

Thomas Builds-the-Fire smiled. She was a mental gymnast too. She pulled her leg straight up against her body so that she could've kissed her kneecap.

"I wish I could do that," Thomas said.

70   Victor was ready to jump out of the plane. Thomas, that crazy Indian story-teller with ratty old braids and broken teeth, was flirting with a beautiful Olympic gymnast. Nobody back home on the reservation would ever believe it.

"Well," the gymnast said. "It's easy. Try it."

Thomas grabbed at his leg and tried to pull it up into the same position as the gymnast's. He couldn't even come close, which made Victor and the gymnast laugh.

"Hey," she asked. "You two are Indian, right?"

"Full-blood," Victor said.

75   "Not me," Thomas said. "I'm half magician on my mother's side and half clown on my father's."

They all laughed.

"What are your names?" she asked.

"Victor and Thomas."

"Mine is Cathy. Pleased to meet you all."

80   The three of them talked for the duration of the flight. Cathy the gymnast complained about the government, how they screwed the 1980 Olympic team by boycotting the games.

"Sounds like you all got a lot in common with Indians," Thomas said.

Nobody laughed.

After the plane landed in Phoenix and they had all found their way to the terminal, Cathy the gymnast smiled and waved goodbye.

"She was really nice," Thomas said.

85   "Yeah, but everybody talks to everybody on airplanes," Victor said.

"You always used to tell me I think too much," Thomas said. "Now it sounds like you do."

"Maybe I caught it from you."

"Yeah."

Thomas and Victor rode in a taxi to the trailer where Victor's father had died.

"Listen," Victor said as they stopped in front of the trailer. "I never told you I   90
was sorry for beating you up that time."

"Oh, it was nothing. We were just kids and you were drunk."

"Yeah, but I'm still sorry."

"That's all right."

Victor paid for the taxi, and the two of them stood in the hot Phoenix summer. They could smell the trailer.

"This ain't going to be nice," Victor said. "You don't have to go in."   95

"You're going to need help."

Victor walked to the front door and opened it. The stink rolled out and made them both gag. Victor's father had lain in that trailer for a week in hundred-degree temperatures before anyone had found him. And the only reason anyone found him was the smell. They needed dental records to identify him. That's exactly what the coroner said. They needed dental records.

"Oh, man," Victor said. "I don't know if I can do this."

"Well, then don't."

"But there might be something valuable in there."   100

"I thought his money was in the bank."

"It is: I was talking about pictures and letters and stuff like that."

"Oh," Thomas said as he held his breath and followed Victor into the trailer.

When Victor was twelve, he stepped into an underground wasps' nest. His foot was caught in the hole and no matter how hard he struggled, Victor couldn't pull free. He might have died there, stung a thousand times, if Thomas Builds-the-Fire had not come by.

"Run," Thomas yelled and pulled Victor's foot from the hole. They ran then,   105
hard as they ever had, faster than Billy Mills, faster than Jim Thorpe, faster than the wasps could fly.

Victor and Thomas ran until they couldn't breathe, ran until it was cold and dark outside, ran until they were lost and it took hours to find their way home. All the way back, Victor counted his stings.

"Seven," Victor said. "My lucky number."

*   *   *

Victor didn't find much to keep in the trailer. Only a photo album and a stereo. Everything else had that smell stuck in it or was useless anyway. "I guess this is all," Victor said. "It ain't much."

"Better than nothing," Thomas said.

"Yeah, and I do have the pickup."   110

"Yeah," Thomas said. "It's in good shape."

"Dad was good about that stuff."

"Yeah, I remember your dad."

"Really?" Victor asked. "What do you remember?"

115   Thomas Builds-the-Fire closed his eyes and told this story: "I remember when I had this dream that told me to go to Spokane, to stand by the falls in the middle of the city and wait for a sign. I knew I had to go there but I didn't have a car. Didn't have a license. I was only thirteen. So I walked all the way, took me all day, and I finally made it to the falls. I stood there for an hour waiting. Then your dad came walking up. 'What the hell are you doing here?' he asked me. I said, 'Waiting for a vision.' Then your father said, 'All you're going to get here is mugged.' So he drove me over to Denny's, bought me dinner, and then drove me home to the reservation. For a long time, I was mad because I thought my dreams had lied to me. But they hadn't. Your dad was my vision. *Take care of each other* is what my dreams were saying. *Take care of each other*."

Victor was quiet for a long time. He searched his mind for memories of his father, found the good ones, found a few bad ones, added it all up, and smiled.

"My father never told me about finding you in Spokane," Victor said.

"He said he wouldn't tell anybody. Didn't want me to get in trouble. But he said I had to watch out for you as part of the deal."

"Really?"

120   "Really. Your father said you would need the help. He was right."

"That's why you came down here with me, isn't it?" Victor asked.

"I came because of your father."

Victor and Thomas climbed into the pickup, drove over to the bank, and claimed the three hundred dollars in the savings account.

Thomas Builds-the-Fire could fly.

125   Once, he jumped off the roof of the tribal school and flapped his arms like a crazy eagle. And he flew. For a second he hovered, suspended above all the other Indian boys, who were too smart or too scared to jump too.

"He's flying," Junior yelled, and Seymour was busy looking for the trick wires or mirrors. But it was real. As real as the dirt when Thomas lost altitude and crashed to the ground.

He broke his arm in two places.

"He broke his wing, he broke his wing, he broke his wing," all the Indian boys chanted as they ran off, flapping their wings, wishing they could fly too. They hated Thomas for his courage, his brief moment as a bird. Everybody has dreams about flying. Thomas flew.

One of his dreams came true for just a second, just enough to make it real.

*   *   *

130   Victor's father, his ashes, fit in one wooden box with enough left over to fill a cardboard box.

"He always was a big man," Thomas said.

Victor carried part of his father out to the pickup, and Thomas carried the rest. They set him down carefully behind the seats, put a cowboy hat on the wooden box and a Dodgers cap on the cardboard box. That was the way it was supposed to be.

"Ready to head back home?" Victor asked.

"It's going to be a long drive."

"Yeah, take a couple days, maybe." 135

"We can take turns," Thomas said.

"O.K.," Victor said, but they didn't take turns. Victor drove for sixteen hours straight north, made it halfway up Nevada toward home before he finally pulled over.

"Hey, Thomas," Victor said. "You got to drive for a while."

"O.K."

Thomas Builds-the-Fire slid behind the wheel and started off down the road. 140 All through Nevada, Thomas and Victor had been amazed at the lack of animal life, at the absence of water, of movement.

"Where is everything?" Victor had asked more than once.

Now, when Thomas was finally driving, they saw the first animal, maybe the only animal in Nevada. It was a long-eared jackrabbit.

"Look," Victor yelled. "It's alive."

Thomas and Victor were busy congratulating themselves on their discovery when the jackrabbit darted out into the road and under the wheels of the pickup.

"Stop the goddamn car," Victor yelled, and Thomas did stop and backed the 145 pickup to the dead jackrabbit.

"Oh, man, he's dead," Victor said as he looked at the squashed animal.

"Really dead."

"The only thing alive in this whole state and we just killed it."

"I don't know," Thomas said. "I think it was suicide."

Victor looked around the desert, sniffed the air, felt the emptiness and 150 loneliness, and nodded his head.

"Yeah," Victor said. "It had to be suicide."

"I can't believe this," Thomas said. "You drive for a thousand miles and there ain't even any bugs smashed on the windshield. I drive for ten seconds and kill the only living thing in Nevada."

"Yeah," Victor said. "Maybe I should drive."

"Maybe you should."

Thomas Builds-the-Fire walked through the corridors of the tribal school by 155 himself. Nobody wanted to be anywhere near him because of all those stories. Story after story.

Thomas closed his eyes and this story came to him: "We are all given one thing by which our lives are measured, one determination. Mine are the stories that can change or not change the world. It doesn't matter which, as long as I continue to tell the stories. My father, he died on Okinawa° in World War II, ✳ died fighting for this country, which had tried to kill him for years. My mother, she died giving birth to me, died while I was still inside her. She pushed me out into the world with her last breath. I have no brothers or sisters. I have only my stories, which came to me before I even had the words to speak. I learned a thousand stories before I took my first thousand steps. They are all I have. It's all I can do."

Okinawa: Largest island of the Ryukyus, a chain of Japanese islands in the western Pacific Ocean.

Thomas Builds-the-Fire told his stories to all those who would stop and listen. He kept telling them long after people had stopped listening.

Victor and Thomas made it back to the reservation just as the sun was rising. It was the beginning of a new day on earth, but the same old shit on the reservation.

"Good morning," Thomas said.

160   "Good morning."

The tribe was waking up, ready for work, eating breakfast, reading the newspaper, just like everybody else does. Willene LeBret was out in her garden, wearing a bathrobe. She waved when Thomas and Victor drove by.

"Crazy Indians made it," she said to herself and went back to her roses.

Victor stopped the pickup in front of Thomas Builds-the-Fire's HUD° house. They both yawned, stretched a little, shook dust from their bodies.

"I'm tired," Victor said.

165   "Of everything," Thomas added.

They both searched for words to end the journey. Victor needed to thank Thomas for his help and for the money, and to make the promise to pay it all back.

"Don't worry about the money," Thomas said. "It don't make any difference anyhow."

"Probably not, enit?"

"Nope."

170   Victor knew that Thomas would remain the crazy storyteller who talked to dogs and cars, who listened to the wind and pine trees. Victor knew that he couldn't really be friends with Thomas, even after all that had happened. It was cruel but it was real. As real as the ash, as Victor's father, sitting behind the seats.

"I know how it is," Thomas said. "I know you ain't going to treat me any better than you did before. I know your friends would give you too much shit about it."

Victor was ashamed of himself. Whatever happened to the tribal ties, the sense of community? The only real thing he shared with anybody was a bottle and broken dreams. He owed Thomas something, anything.

"Listen," Victor said and handed Thomas the cardboard box that contained half of his father. "I want you to have this."

Thomas took the ashes and smiled, closed his eyes, and told this story: "I'm going to travel to Spokane Falls one last time and toss these ashes into the water. And your father will rise like a salmon, leap over the bridge, over me, and find his way home. It will be beautiful. His teeth will shine like silver, like a rainbow. He will rise, Victor, he will rise."

175   Victor smiled.

"I was planning on doing the same thing with my half," Victor said. "But I didn't imagine my father looking anything like a salmon. I thought it'd be like cleaning the attic or something. Like letting things go after they've stopped having any use."

"Nothing stops, cousin," Thomas said. "Nothing stops."

HUD: The U.S. Department of Housing and Urban Development.

Thomas Builds-the-Fire got out of the pickup and walked up his driveway. Victor started the pickup and began the drive home.

"Wait," Thomas yelled suddenly from his porch. "I just got to ask one favor."

Victor stopped the pickup, leaned out the window, and shouted back.   180

"What do you want?" he asked.

"Just one time when I'm telling a story somewhere, why don't you stop and listen?" Thomas asked.

"Just once?"

"Just once."

Victor waved his arms to let Thomas know that the deal was good. It was a fair   185 trade. That's all Thomas had ever wanted from his whole life. So Victor drove his father's pickup toward home while Thomas went into his house, closed the door behind him, and heard a new story come to him in the silence afterward.

Reading and Reacting

1. In paragraph 1, readers are told that Victor lives on an Indian reservation. What details elsewhere in the story establish this setting? What associations does this setting have for you? Do you think the story could take place anywhere else?

2. In addition to various locations on the reservation, the story's settings include an airplane, a trailer in Phoenix, and a road through Nevada. What does each of these settings contribute to the story's plot?

3. Is the scene on the plane necessary? Intrusive? Distracting? Farfetched?

4. How would you characterize the story's mood or atmosphere? How do Thomas's stories help to create this mood? How do they help to establish his character? Do you think Alexie should have included more of these stories?

5. Why do you suppose Victor and Thomas cannot be friends when they get back to the reservation? Why are they able to be friends when they are traveling to Phoenix?

6. Do the flashbacks to the two men's childhood add something vital to the story? What purpose do these flashbacks serve?

7. In Native American culture, the storyteller holds an important position, telling tales that transmit and preserve the tribe's basic beliefs. Do you think Thomas's stories serve such a function? Or, do you think that he is, as Victor characterizes him, simply "the crazy storyteller who talked to dogs and cars, who listened to the wind and pine trees" (par. 170)?

8. What do you think the story's title means?

9. JOURNAL ENTRY At the end of the story, when Thomas returns home, he hears "a new story come to him in the silence" after he closes the door. What kind of story do you think comes to him at this point?

10. CRITICAL PERSPECTIVE In the introduction to a collection of Native American literature, Clifford E. Trafzer, the collection's editor, discusses the unique characteristics of Native American writers:

> Due to their grounding in the oral tradition of their people, Native American writers do not follow the literary canon of the dominant society in their

approach to short stories. Rather than focusing on one theme or character in a brief time frame, or using one geographical area, they often use multiple themes and characters with few boundaries of time or place. Their stories do not always follow a linear and clear path, and frequently the past and present, real and mythic, and conscious and unconscious are not distinguishable. Multidimensional characters are common, and involved stories usually lack absolute conclusions. Native American writers may also play tricks with language, deliberately misusing grammar, syntax, and spelling — sometimes in defiance of the dominant culture — in order to make English reflect the language of their peoples.

Do you think "This Is What It Means to Say Phoenix, Arizona" has the characteristics Trafzer associates with Native American writers?

Related Works: "Sleepy Time Gal" (p. 154), "The Red Convertible" (p. 702), "My Father's Song" (p. 1063), "How to Write the Great American Indian Novel" (p. 887), "Defending Walt Whitman" (p. 1136), "Indian Boarding School: The Runaways" (p. 1176), *The Glass Menagerie* (p. 1998)

RALPH ELLISON (1914–1994) was born in Oklahoma City, Oklahoma. After his father's death when Ellison was three, Ellison's mother took up work as a domestic servant to support herself and her son. Early on, Ellison developed an interest in literature and music. He enrolled as a musician in Tuskegee Institute in Alabama; then, in 1936, he moved to New York City, where he worked with the Federal Writer's Project. While there, Ellison met prominent African-American writers Langston Hughes and Richard Wright, who encouraged his literary ambitions. He began to publish stories in journals and became an editor of *Negro Quarterly*. After serving in the Merchant Marines during World War II, Ellison returned to New York and taught literature at New York University for many years.

Ellison's first novel, *Invisible Man* (1952), was an instant success. The book—a semi-autobiographical chronicle of a young African-American man's search for intellectual identity—won the National Book Award for fiction and was listed in *Book Week* as the most distinguished American novel of the preceding twenty years. His short story "Battle Royal" was first published in 1948; it went on to become, in a slightly revised form, the opening chapter of *Invisible Man*. Ellison published two collections of essays, *Shadow and Act* (1964) and *Going to the Territories* (1986); his collected essays appeared in 1995. Ellison's second novel, *Juneteenth*, was planned as a trilogy but after a large section of the novel burned in a fire in 1967, Ellison spent years reconstructing the text, only to leave it unfinished at his death. His manuscript, some two thousand pages, was edited by John Callahan and posthumously published in 1999.

Cultural Context The term *battle royal* was first coined by the ancient Romans to refer to a form of combat in which a number of gladiators, armed or unarmed, fought until only one remained alive. Due to the random and chaotic nature of these contests, the winners were determined more by luck than by martial skill. Today, this form of combat is a staple of professional wrestling, but at the time of this story, the battle royal was relegated to back rooms and more clandestine functions, as seen in the events of this story.

Battle Royal   (1952)

It goes a long way back, some twenty years. All my life I had been looking for something, and everywhere I turned someone tried to tell me what it was. I accepted their answers too, though they were often in contradiction and even self-contradictory. I was naïve. I was looking for myself and asking everyone except myself questions which I, and only I, could answer. It took me a long time and much painful boomeranging of my expectations to achieve a realization everyone else appears to have been born with: That I am nobody but myself. But first I had to discover that I am an invisible man!

And yet I am no freak of nature, nor of history. I was in the cards, other things having been equal (or unequal) eighty-five years ago. I am not ashamed of my grandparents for having been slaves. I am only ashamed of myself for having at one time been ashamed. About eighty-five years ago they were told that they were free, united with others of our country in everything pertaining to the common good, and, in everything social, separate like the fingers of the hand. And they believed it. They exulted in it. They stayed in their place, worked hard, and brought up my father to do the same. But my grandfather is the one. He was an odd old guy, my grandfather, and I am told I take after him. It was he who caused the trouble. On his deathbed he called my father to him and said, "Son, after I'm gone I want you to keep up the good fight. I never told you, but our life is a war and I have been a traitor all my born days, a spy in the enemy's country ever since I give up my gun back in the Reconstruction. Live with your head in the lion's mouth. I want you to overcome 'em with yeses, undermine 'em with grins, agree 'em to death and destruction, let 'em swoller you till they vomit or bust wide open." They thought the old man had gone out of his mind. He had been the meekest of men. The younger children were rushed from the room, the shades drawn and the flame of the lamp turned so low that it sputtered on the wick like the old man's breathing. "Learn it to the younguns," he whispered fiercely; then he died.

But my folks were more alarmed over his last words than over his dying. It was as though he had not died at all, his words caused so much anxiety. I was warned emphatically to forget what he had said and, indeed, this is the first time it has been mentioned outside the family circle. It had a tremendous effect upon me, however. I could never be sure of what he meant. Grandfather had been a quiet old man who never made any trouble, yet on his deathbed he had called himself a traitor and a spy, and he had spoken of his meekness as a dangerous activity. It became a constant puzzle which lay unanswered in the back of my mind. And whenever things went well for me I remembered my grandfather and felt guilty and uncomfortable. It was as though I was carrying out his advice in spite of myself. And to make it worse, everyone loved me for it. I was praised by the most lily-white men of the town. I was considered an example of desirable conduct —just as my grandfather had been. And what puzzled me was that the old man had defined it as *treachery*. When I was praised for my conduct I felt a guilt that in some way I was doing something that was really against the wishes of the white folks, that if they had understood they would have desired me to act just the opposite, that I should have been sulky and mean, and that that really would have been what they wanted, even though they were fooled and thought they wanted me to act as I did. It made me afraid that some day they would look upon me as a traitor and I would be lost. Still I was more afraid to act any other way because they didn't like that at all. The old man's words were like a curse. On my graduation day I delivered an oration in which I showed that humility was the secret, indeed, the very essence of progress. (Not that I believed this — how could I, remembering my grandfather? — I only believed that it worked.) It was a great success. Everyone praised me and I was invited to give the speech at a gathering of the town's leading white citizens. It was a triumph for our whole community.

It was in the main ballroom of the leading hotel. When I got there I discovered that it was on the occasion of a smoker° and I was told that since I was to be there anyway I might as well take part in the battle royal to be fought by some of my schoolmates as part of the entertainment. The battle royal came first.

5   All of the town's big shots were there in their tuxedoes, wolfing down the buffet foods, drinking beer and whiskey and smoking black cigars. It was a large room with a high ceiling. Chairs were arranged in neat rows around three sides of a portable boxing ring. The fourth side was clear, revealing a gleaming space of polished floor. I had some misgivings over the battle royal, by the way. Not from a distaste for fighting, but because I didn't care too much for the other fellows who were to take part. They were tough guys who seemed to have no grandfather's curse worrying their minds. No one could mistake their toughness. And besides, I suspected that fighting a battle royal might detract from the dignity of my speech. In those pre-invisible days I visualized myself as a potential Booker T. Washington.° But the other fellows didn't care too much for me either, and there were nine of them. I felt superior to them in my way, and I didn't like the manner in which we were all crowded together into the servants' elevator. Nor did they like my being there. In fact, as the warmly lighted floors flashed past the elevator we had words over the fact that I, by taking part in the fight, had knocked one of their friends out of a night's work.

We were led out of the elevator through a rococo hall into an anteroom and told to get into our fighting togs. Each of us was issued a pair of boxing gloves and ushered out into the big mirrored hall, which we entered looking cautiously about us and whispering, lest we might accidentally be heard above the noise of the room. It was foggy with cigar smoke. And already the whiskey was taking effect. I was shocked to see some of the most important men of the town quite tipsy. They were all there — bankers, lawyers, judges, doctors, fire chiefs, teachers, merchants. Even one of the more fashionable pastors. Something we could not see was going on up front. A clarinet was vibrating sensuously and the men were standing up and

---

smoker: Informal men-only social gathering.

Booker T. Washington: American educator (1856–1915), born into slavery, who gained an education after emancipation and in 1881 organized Tuskegee Institute, a vocational school for African-Americans.

moving eagerly forward. We were a small tight group, clustered together, our bare upper bodies touching and shining with anticipatory sweat; while up front the big shots were becoming increasingly excited over something we still could not see. Suddenly I heard the school superintendent, who had told me to come, yell, "Bring up the shines° gentlemen! Bring up the little shines!"

We were rushed up to the front of the ballroom, where it smelled even more strongly of tobacco and whiskey. Then we were pushed into place. I almost wet my pants. A sea of faces, some hostile, some amused, ringed around us, and in the center, facing us, stood a magnificent blonde — stark naked. There was dead silence. I felt a blast of cold air chill me. I tried to back away, but they were behind me and around me. Some of the boys stood with lowered heads, trembling. I felt a wave of irrational guilt and fear. My teeth chattered, my skin turned to goose flesh, my knees knocked. Yet I was strongly attracted and looked in spite of myself. Had the price of looking been blindness, I would have looked. The hair was yellow like that of a circus kewpie doll, the face heavily powdered and rouged, as though to form an abstract mask, the eyes hollow and smeared a cool blue, the color of a baboon's butt. I felt a desire to spit upon her as my eyes brushed slowly over her body. Her breasts were firm and round as the domes of East Indian temples, and I stood so close as to see the fine skin texture and beads of pearly perspiration glistening like dew around the pink and erected buds of her nipples. I wanted at one and the same time to run from the room, to sink through the floor, or go to her and cover her from my eyes and the eyes of the others with my body; to feel the soft thighs, to caress her and destroy her, to love her and murder her, to hide from her, and yet to stroke where below the small American flag tattooed upon her belly her thighs formed a capital V. I had a notion that of all in the room she saw only me with her impersonal eyes.

And then she began to dance, a slow sensuous movement; the smoke of a hundred cigars clinging to her like the thinnest of veils. She seemed like a fair bird-girl girdled in veils calling to me from the angry surface of some gray and threatening sea. I was transported. Then I became aware of the clarinet playing and the big shots yelling at us. Some threatened us if we looked and others if we did not. On my right I saw one boy faint. And now a man grabbed a silver pitcher from a table and stepped close as he dashed ice water upon him and stood him up and forced two of us to support him as his head hung and moans issued from his thick bluish lips. Another boy began to plead to go home. He was the largest of the group, wearing dark red fighting trunks much too small to conceal the erection which projected from him as though in answer to the insinuating low-registered moaning of the clarinet. He tried to hide himself with his boxing gloves.

And all the while the blonde continued dancing, smiling faintly at the big shots who watched her with fascination, and faintly smiling at our fear. I noticed a certain merchant who followed her hungrily, his lips loose and drooling. He was a large man who wore diamond studs in a shirtfront which swelled with

---

shines: A racial slur for African-Americans.

the ample paunch underneath, and each time the blonde swayed her undulating hips he ran his hand through the thin hair of his bald head and, with his arms upheld, his posture clumsy like that of an intoxicated panda, wound his belly in a slow and obscene grind. This creature was completely hypnotized. The music had quickened. As the dancer flung herself about with a detached expression on her face, the men began reaching out to touch her. I could see their beefy fingers sink into her soft flesh. Some of the others tried to stop them and she began to move around the floor in graceful circles, as they gave chase, slipping and sliding over the polished floor. It was mad. Chairs went crashing, drinks were spilt, as they ran laughing and howling after her. They caught her just as she reached a door, raised her from the floor, and tossed her as college boys are tossed at a hazing, and above her red, fixed-smiling lips I saw the terror and disgust in her eyes, almost like my own terror and that which I saw in some of the other boys. As I watched, they tossed her twice and her soft breasts seemed to flatten against the air and her legs flung wildly as she spun. Some of the more sober ones helped her to escape. And I started off the floor, heading for the anteroom with the rest of the boys.

10   Some were still crying and in hysteria. But as we tried to leave we were stopped and ordered to get into the ring. There was nothing to do but what we were told. All ten of us climbed under the ropes and allowed ourselves to be blindfolded with broad bands of white cloth. One of the men seemed to feel a bit sympathetic and tried to cheer us up as we stood with our backs against the ropes. Some of us tried to grin. "See that boy over there?" one of the men said. "I want you to run across at the bell and give it to him right in the belly. If you don't get him, I'm going to get you. I don't like his looks." Each of us was told the same. The blindfolds were put on. Yet even then I had been going over my speech. In my mind each word was as bright as flame. I felt the cloth pressed into place, and frowned so that it would be loosened when I relaxed.

But now I felt a sudden fit of blind terror. I was unused to darkness. It was as though I had suddenly found myself in a dark room filled with poisonous cotton-mouths. I could hear the bleary voices yelling insistently for the battle royal to begin.

"Get going in there!"

"Let me at that big nigger!"

I strained to pick up the school superintendent's voice, as though to squeeze some security out of that slightly more familiar sound.

15   "Let me at those black sonsabitches!" someone yelled.

"No, Jackson, no!" another voice yelled. "Here, somebody, help me hold Jack."

"I want to get at that ginger-colored nigger. Tear him limb from limb," the first voice yelled.

I stood against the ropes trembling. For in those days I was what they called ginger-colored, and he sounded as though he might crunch me between his teeth like a crisp ginger cookie.

Quite a struggle was going on. Chairs were being kicked about and I could hear voices grunting as with a terrific effort. I wanted to see, to see more desperately than ever before. But the blindfold was as tight as a thick skin-puckering scab and when I raised my gloved hands to push the layers of white aside a voice yelled, "Oh, no you don't! black bastard! Leave that alone!"

"Ring the bell before Jackson kills him a coon!" someone boomed in the sud- 20
den silence. And I heard the bell clang and the sound of the feet scuffling forward.

A glove smacked against my head. I pivoted, striking out stiffly as someone went past, and felt the jar ripple along the length of my arm to my shoulder. Then it seemed as though all nine of the boys had turned upon me at once. Blows pounded me from all sides while I struck out as best I could. So many blows landed upon me that I wondered if I were not the only blindfolded fighter in the ring, or if the man called Jackson hadn't succeeded in getting me after all.

Blindfolded, I could no longer control my motions. I had no dignity. I stumbled about like a baby or a drunken man. The smoke had become thicker and with each new blow it seemed to sear and further restrict my lungs. My saliva became like hot bitter glue. A glove connected with my head, filling my mouth with warm blood. It was everywhere. I could not tell if the moisture I felt upon my body was sweat or blood. A blow landed hard against the nape of my neck. I felt myself going over, my head hitting the floor. Streaks of blue light filled the black world behind the blindfold. I lay prone, pretending that I was knocked out, but felt myself seized by hands and yanked to my feet. "Get going, black boy! Mix it up!" My arms were like lead, my head smarting from blows. I managed to feel my way to the ropes and held on, trying to catch my breath. A glove landed in my midsection and I went over again, feeling as though the smoke had become a knife jabbed into my guts. Pushed this way and that by the legs milling around me, I finally pulled erect and discovered that I could see the black, sweat-washed forms weaving in the smoky-blue atmosphere like drunken dancers weaving to the rapid drum-like thuds of blows.

Everyone fought hysterically. It was complete anarchy. Everybody fought everybody else. No group fought together for long. Two, three, four, fought one, then turned to fight each other, were themselves attacked. Blows landed below the belt and in the kidney, with the gloves open as well as closed, and with my eye partly opened now there was not so much terror. I moved carefully, avoiding blows, although not too many to attract attention, fighting from group to group. The boys groped about like blind, cautious crabs crouching to protect their midsections, their heads pulled in short against their shoulders, their arms stretched nervously before them, with their fists testing the smoke-filled air like the knobbed feelers of hypersensitive snails. In one corner I glimpsed a boy violently punching the air and heard him scream in pain as he smashed his hand against a ring post. For a second I saw him bent over holding his hand, then going down as a blow caught his unprotected head. I played one group against the other, slipping in and throwing a punch then stepping out of range while pushing the others into the melee to take the blows blindly aimed at me. The smoke was agonizing and there were no rounds, no bells at three minute intervals to relieve our exhaustion. The room spun round me, a swirl of lights, smoke, sweating bodies surrounded by tense white faces. I bled from both nose and mouth, the blood spattering upon my chest.

The men kept yelling, "Slug him, black boy! Knock his guts out!"

"Uppercut him! Kill him! Kill that big boy!" 25

Taking a fake fall, I saw a boy going down heavily beside me as though we were felled by a single blow, saw a sneaker-clad foot shoot into his groin as the two who had knocked him down stumbled upon him. I rolled out of range, feeling a twinge of nausea.

The harder we fought the more threatening the men became. And yet, I had begun to worry about my speech again. How would it go? Would they recognize my ability? What would they give me?

I was fighting automatically and suddenly I noticed that one after another of the boys was leaving the ring. I was surprised, filled with panic, as though I had been left alone with an unknown danger. Then I understood. The boys had arranged it among themselves. It was the custom for the two men left in the ring to slug it out for the winner's prize. I discovered this too late. When the bell sounded two men in tuxedoes leaped into the ring and removed the blindfold. I found myself facing Tatlock, the biggest of the gang. I felt sick at my stomach. Hardly had the bell stopped ringing in my ears than it clanged again and I saw him moving swiftly toward me. Thinking of nothing else to do I hit him smash on the nose. He kept coming, bringing the rank sharp violence of stale sweat. His face was a black blank of a face, only his eyes alive — with hate of me and aglow with a feverish terror from what had happened to us all. I became anxious. I wanted to deliver my speech and he came at me as though he meant to beat it out of me. I smashed him again and again, taking his blows as they came. Then on a sudden impulse I struck him lightly and as we clinched, I whispered, "Fake like I knocked you out, you can have the prize."

"I'll break your behind," he whispered hoarsely.

30   "For *them?*"

"For *me*, sonofabitch!"

They were yelling for us to break it up and Tatlock spun me half around with a blow, and as a joggled camera sweeps in a reeling scene, I saw the howling red faces crouching tense beneath the cloud of blue-gray smoke. For a moment the world wavered, unraveled, flowed, then my head cleared and Tatlock bounced before me. That fluttering shadow before my eyes was his jabbing left hand. Then falling forward, my head against his damp shoulder, I whispered, "I'll make it five dollars more."

"Go to hell!"

But his muscles relaxed a trifle beneath my pressure and I breathed, "Seven!"

35   "Give it to your ma," he said, ripping me beneath the heart.

And while I still held him I butted him and moved away. I felt myself bombarded with punches. I fought back with hopeless desperation. I wanted to deliver my speech more than anything else in the world, because I felt that only these men could judge truly my ability, and now this stupid clown was ruining my chances. I began fighting carefully now, moving in to punch him and out again with my greater speed. A lucky blow to his chin and I had him going too — until I heard a loud voice yell, "I got my money on the big boy."

Hearing this, I almost dropped my guard. I was confused: Should I try to win against the voice out there? Would not this go against my speech, and was not this a moment for humility, for nonresistance? A blow to my head as I danced about sent my right eye popping like a jack-in-the-box and settled my dilemma. The room went red as I fell. It was a dream fall, my body languid and fastidious as to where to land, until the floor became impatient and smashed up to meet me. A moment later I came to. An hypnotic voice said FIVE emphatically. And I lay there, hazily watching a dark red spot of my own blood shaping itself into a butterfly, glistening and soaking into the soiled gray world of the canvas.

When the voice drawled TEN I was lifted up and dragged to a chair. I sat dazed. My eye pained and swelled with each throb of my pounding heart and I wondered if now I would be allowed to speak. I was wringing wet, my mouth still bleeding. We were grouped along the wall now. The other boys ignored me as they congratulated Tatlock and speculated as to how much they would be paid. One boy whimpered over his smashed hand. Looking up front, I saw attendants in white jackets rolling the portable ring away and placing a small square rug in the vacant space surrounded by chairs. Perhaps, I thought, I will stand on the rug to deliver my speech.

Then the M.C. called to us, "Come on up here boys and get your money."

We ran forward to where the men laughed and talked in their chairs, waiting. 40
Everyone seemed friendly now.

"There it is on the rug," the man said. I saw the rug covered with coins of all dimensions and a few crumpled bills. But what excited me, scattered here and there, were the gold pieces.

"Boys, it's all yours," the man said. "You get all you grab."

"That's right, Sambo,"° a blond man said, winking at me confidentially.

I trembled with excitement, forgetting my pain. I would get the gold and the bills, I thought. I would use both hands. I would throw my body against the boys nearest me to block them from the gold.

"Get down around the rug now," the man commanded, "and don't anyone 45
touch it until I give the signal."

"This ought to be good," I heard.

As told, we got around the square rug on our knees. Slowly the man raised his freckled hand as we followed it upward with our eyes.

I heard, "These niggers look like they're about to pray!"

Then, "Ready," the man said. "Go!"

I lunged for a yellow coin lying on the blue design of the carpet, touching it 50
and sending a surprised shriek to join those rising around me. I tried frantically to remove my hand but could not let go. A hot, violent force tore through my body, shaking me like a wet rat. The rug was electrified. The hair bristled up on my head as I shook myself free. My muscles jumped, my nerves jangled, writhed. But I saw that this was not stopping the other boys. Laughing in fear and embarrassment, some were holding back and scooping up the coins knocked off by the painful contortions of the others. The men roared above us as we struggled.

"Pick it up, goddamnit, pick it up!" someone called like a bass-voiced parrot. "Go on, get it!"

Sambo: A racial slur for blacks, referring to a character in a children's story.

I crawled rapidly around the floor, picking up the coins, trying to avoid the coppers and to get greenbacks and the gold. Ignoring the shock by laughing, as I brushed the coins off quickly, I discovered that I could contain the electricity — a contradiction, but it works. Then the men began to push us onto the rug. Laughing embarrassedly, we struggled out of their hands and kept after the coins. We were all wet and slippery and hard to hold. Suddenly I saw a boy lifted into the air, glistening with sweat like a circus seal, and dropped, his wet back landing flush upon the charged rug, heard him yell and saw him literally dance upon his back, his elbows beating a frenzied tattoo upon the floor, his muscles twitching like the flesh of a horse stung by many flies. When he finally rolled off, his face was gray and no one stopped him when he ran from the floor amid booming laughter.

"Get the money," the M.C. called. "That's good hard American cash!"

And we snatched and grabbed, snatched and grabbed. I was careful not to come too close to the rug now, and when I felt the hot whiskey breath descend upon me like a cloud of foul air I reached out and grabbed the leg of a chair. It was occupied and I held on desperately.

55   "Leggo, nigger! Leggo!"

The huge face wavered down to mine as he tried to push me free. But my body was slippery and he was too drunk. It was Mr. Colcord, who owned a chain of movie houses and "entertainment palaces." Each time he grabbed me I slipped out of his hands. It became a real struggle. I feared the rug more than I did the drunk, so I held on, surprising myself for a moment by trying to topple *him* upon the rug. It was such an enormous idea that I found myself actually carrying it out. I tried not to be obvious, yet when I grabbed his leg, trying to tumble him out of the chair, he raised up roaring with laughter and, looking at me with soberness dead in the eye, kicked me viciously in the chest. The chair leg flew out of my hand. I felt myself going and rolled. It was as though I had rolled through a bed of hot coals. It seemed a whole century would pass before I would roll free, a century in which I was seared through the deepest levels of my body to the fearful breath within me and the breath seared and heated to the point of explosion. It'll all be over in a flash, I thought as I rolled clear. It'll all be over in a flash.

But not yet, the men on the other side were waiting, red faces swollen as though from apoplexy as they bent forward in their chairs. Seeing their fingers coming toward me I rolled away as a fumbled football rolls off the receiver's fingertips, back into the coals. That time I luckily sent the rug sliding out of place and heard the coins ringing against the floor and the boys scuffling to pick them up and the M.C. calling, "All right, boys, that's all. Go get dressed and get your money."

I was limp as a dish rag. My back felt as though it had been beaten with wires.

When we had dressed the M.C. came in and gave us each five dollars, except Tatlock, who got ten for being last in the ring. Then he told us to leave. I was not to get a chance to deliver my speech, I thought. I was going out into the dim alley in despair when I was stopped and told to go back. I returned to the ballroom, where the men were pushing back their chairs and gathering in groups to talk.

60   The M.C. knocked on a table for quiet. "Gentlemen," he said, "we almost forgot an important part of the program. A most serious part, gentlemen. This

boy was brought here to deliver a speech which he made at his graduation yesterday. . . ."

"Bravo!"

"I'm told that he is the smartest boy we've got out there in Greenwood. I'm told that he knows more big words than a pocket-sized dictionary."

Much applause and laughter.

"So now, gentlemen, I want you to give him your attention."

There was still laughter as I faced them, my mouth dry, my eye throbbing. 65 I began slowly, but evidently my throat was tense, because they began shouting, "Louder! Louder!"

"We of the younger generation extol the wisdom of that great leader and educator," I shouted, "who first spoke these flaming words of wisdom: 'A ship lost at sea for many days suddenly sighted a friendly vessel. From the mast of the unfortunate vessel was seen a signal: "Water, water; we die of thirst!" The answer from the friendly vessel came back: "Cast down your bucket where you are." The captain of the distressed vessel, at last heeding the injunction, cast down his bucket, and it came up full of fresh sparkling water from the mouth of the Amazon River.' And like him I say, and in his words, 'To those of my race who depend upon bettering their condition in a foreign land, or who underestimate the importance of cultivating friendly relations with the Southern white man, who is his next-door neighbor, I would say: "Cast down your bucket where you are"— cast it down in making friends in every manly way of the people of all races by whom we are surrounded. . .".'

I spoke automatically and with such fervor that I did not realize that the men were still talking and laughing until my dry mouth, filling up with blood from the cut, almost strangled me. I coughed, wanting to stop and go to one of the tall brass, sand filled spittoons to relieve myself, but a few of the men, especially the superintendent, were listening and I was afraid. So I gulped it down, blood, saliva and all, and continued. (What powers of endurance I had during those days! What enthusiasm! What a belief in the rightness of things!) I spoke even louder in spite of the pain. But still they talked and still they laughed, as though deaf with cotton in dirty ears. So I spoke with greater emotional emphasis. I closed my ears and swallowed blood until I was nauseated. The speech seemed a hundred times as long as before, but I could not leave out a single word. All had to be said, each memorized nuance considered, rendered. Nor was that all. Whenever I uttered a word of three or more syllables a group of voices would yell for me to repeat it. I used the phrase "social responsibility" and they yelled:

"What's the word you say, boy?"

"Social responsibility," I said.

"What?" 70

"Social . . ."

"Louder."

". . . responsibility."

"More!"

"Respon —" 75

"Repeat!"

"— sibility."

The room filled with the uproar of laughter until, no doubt, distracted by having to gulp down my blood, I made a mistake and yelled a phrase I had often seen denounced in newspaper editorials, heard debated in private.

"Social . . ."

80   "What?" they yelled.

". . . equality —"

The laughter hung smokelike in the sudden stillness. I opened my eyes, puzzled. Sounds of displeasure filled the room. The M.C. rushed forward. They shouted hostile phrases at me. But I did not understand.

A small dry mustached man in the front row blared out, "Say that slowly, son!"

"What sir?"

85   "What you just said!"

"Social responsibility, sir," I said.

"You weren't being smart, were you, boy?" he said, not unkindly.

"No, sir!"

"You sure that about 'equality' was a mistake?"

90   "Oh, yes, sir," I said. "I was swallowing blood."

"Well, you had better speak more slowly so we can understand. We mean to do right by you, but you've got to know your place at all times. All right, now, go on with your speech."

I was afraid. I wanted to leave but I wanted also to speak and I was afraid they'd snatch me down.

"Thank you, sir," I said, beginning where I had left off, and having them ignore me as before.

Yet when I finished there was a thunderous applause. I was surprised to see the superintendent come forth with a package wrapped in white tissue paper, and, gesturing for quiet, address the men.

95   "Gentlemen, you see that I did not overpraise this boy. He makes a good speech and some day he'll lead his people in the proper paths. And I don't have to tell you that that is important in these days and times. This is a good, smart boy, and so to encourage him in the right direction, in the name of the Board of Education I wish to present him a prize in the form of this . . ."

He paused, removing the tissue paper and revealing a gleaming calfskin brief case.

". . . in the form of this first-class article from Shad Whitmore's shop."

"Boy," he said, addressing me, "take this prize and keep it well. Consider it a badge of office. Prize it. Keep developing as you are and some day it will be filled with important papers that will help shape the destiny of your people."

I was so moved that I could hardly express my thanks. A rope of bloody saliva forming a shape like an undiscovered continent drooled upon the leather and I wiped it quickly away. I felt an importance that I had never dreamed.

100   "Open it and see what's inside," I was told.

My fingers a-tremble, I complied, smelling the fresh leather and finding an official-looking document inside. It was a scholarship to the state college for Negroes. My eyes filled with tears and I ran awkwardly off the floor.

I was overjoyed; I did not even mind when I discovered that the gold pieces I had scrambled for were brass pocket tokens advertising a certain make of automobile.

When I reached home everyone was excited. Next day the neighbors came to congratulate me. I even felt safe from grandfather, whose deathbed curse usually spoiled my triumphs. I stood beneath his photograph with my brief case in hand and smiled triumphantly into his stolid black peasant's face. It was a face that fascinated me. The eyes seemed to follow everywhere I went.

That night I dreamed I was at a circus with him and that he refused to laugh at the clowns no matter what they did. Then later he told me to open my brief case and read what was inside and I did, finding an official envelope stamped with the state seal; and inside the envelope I found another and another, endlessly, and I thought I would fall of weariness. "Them's years," he said. "Now open that one." And I did and in it I found an engraved document containing a short message in letters of gold. "Read it," my grandfather said. "Out loud."

"To Whom It May Concern," I intoned. "Keep This Nigger-Boy Running."   105
I awoke with the old man's laughter ringing in my ears.

(It was a dream I was to remember and dream again for many years after. But at the time I had no insight into its meaning. First I had to attend college.)

Reading and Reacting

1. "Battle Royal," the first chapter of Ellison's *Invisible Man* (1952), takes place in the American South. How does the story's historical and geographical setting make possible the events that occur?

2. In paragraph 2, the narrator quotes his grandfather's deathbed statement. Why does the narrator think of his grandfather's words as a "curse" (par. 3)?

3. When the narrator is told he is expected to participate in the "battle royal," he feels that the battle will "detract from the dignity" of the speech he is to give (par. 5). Why, then, does he agree to take part in the fight?

4. In his graduation speech, the narrator tells his audience that "humility [is] the secret, indeed, the very essence of progress" (par. 3). What do you suppose he means? How do you think his grandfather would feel about this statement?

5. Describe the physical setting (the sights, sounds, smells) of the ballroom. What is your emotional reaction to this setting?

6. In paragraphs 7–9, a naked woman enters and dances around the room. Why is she there? How do the men react? How does her presence change the atmosphere in the ballroom?

7. Why is the narrator blindfolded before the fight? What effect does the blindfold have on him as a fighter? As a human being?

8. Throughout the fight, the narrator thinks about his speech, reviewing it in his mind and wondering how it will be received. Why is he so intent on delivering his speech to the men assembled in the ballroom?

9. The superintendent tells the audience that the narrator will someday "lead his people in the proper paths" (par. 95). What "proper paths" do you think the superintendent has in mind?

10. When the narrator opens his gift, he tells readers, "I was so moved that I could hardly express my thanks" (par. 99). Do you see this comment as ironic, even sarcastic, or do you think he is sincere? Explain.

11. Why do you think the narrator dreams about his grandfather after the fight? What do you think his dream means?

12. **JOURNAL ENTRY** Do you see the "battle royal" as simply a necessary evil, a hurdle the narrator has to leap over in order to win the college scholarship? Does the prize in any way make up for the humiliating ordeal? Do you think the narrator should (or even could) have turned down the scholarship?

13. **CRITICAL PERSPECTIVE** This story is set in the South in the 1940s, during a time of violent racism and "Jim Crow" laws that enforced legal segregation. Whites and blacks were not allowed equality on even the most fundamental levels, and this backdrop heightens the tension of the battle royal. Thomas F. Bertonneau offers this observation:

> The atmosphere is gladiatorial and orgiastic. Before the fight, for example, the businessmen make the protagonist and his compeers watch a lewd performance by a blonde stripper, which shocks and humiliates them. In the perverse ethos of Jim Crow, it also sets them up, because it embroils them willy-nilly in a racial-sexual scenario in which they fill the role of lascivious onlookers. On the street, should any of them stare at a white woman, stripper or *bourgeoisie*, he would run the risk of accusation and be under the lethal thereat of the outraged mob. It is a formula for lynching.

In this scene in the story, what is the main attraction? Who is watching whom? In what ways is the scenario Bertonneau describes ironic? How does this irony contribute to the meaning of the story?

Related Works: "The Secretary Chant" (p. 948), "We Wear the Mask" (p. 1171), "If We Must Die" (p. 1203), *Fences* (p. 1939)

TILLIE OLSEN (1912 or 1913–   ) is known for her works of fiction about working-class Americans. Her short stories and one novel are inhabited by those she called the "despised people" — coal miners, farm laborers, packinghouse butchers, and housewives. Olsen was born in Nebraska into a working-class family. Though she has been described as a Depression-era dropout, Olsen has observed that she educated herself, with libraries as her college. According to an account in her nonfiction work *Silences* (1978), Olsen at age fifteen was inspired to write about working-class people when she read Rebecca Harding Davis's *Life in the Iron Mills*, a tale of the effects of industrialization on workers, in an 1861 issue of *Atlantic Monthly* bought for ten cents in a junk shop.

Shortly after she left high school, she was jailed for helping to organize packinghouse workers. Motivated by her experiences, she began to write a novel, *Yonnondio*. Under her maiden name, Tillie Lerner, she published two poems, a short story, and part of her novel during the 1930s. After her marriage, she did not publish again for twenty-two years, spending her time raising four children and working at a variety of jobs. The collection of short stories *Tell Me a Riddle* (1961), which includes "I Stand Here Ironing" (originally titled "Help Her to Believe"), was published when she was fifty. Her only other work of fiction is *Yonnondio* (1974), which she pieced together from drafts she wrote in the 1930s and edited for publication in 1974.

In 1984, she edited *Mother to Daughter, Daughter to Mother: Mothers on Mothering*, a collection of poems, letters, short fiction, and diary excerpts written by famous and not-so-famous women, and in 1995, she collaborated with Estelle Jussim on *Mothers & Daughters: That Special Quality: An Exploration in Photographs.*

Cultural Context During the Great Depression of the 1930s, jobs were scarce throughout the United States, and many people who managed to keep their jobs were forced to take pay cuts. At the height of the Depression in 1933, almost twenty-five percent of the total workforce — more than eleven million people — were unemployed. The displacement of the American worker and the destruction of farming communities caused families such as the one in this story to split up or migrate from their homes in search of work. In 1935, the Social Security Act established public assistance, unemployment insurance, and social security, which offered economic relief to American workers.

I Stand Here Ironing (1961)

I stand here ironing, and what you asked me moves tormented back and forth with the iron.

"I wish you would manage the time to come and talk with me about your daughter. I'm sure you can help me understand her. She's a youngster who needs help and whom I'm deeply interested in helping."

"Who needs help." . . . Even if I came, what good would it do? You think because I am her mother I have a key, or that in some way you could use me as a key? She has lived for nineteen years. There is all that life that has happened outside of me, beyond me.

And when is there time to remember, to sift, to weigh, to estimate, to total? I will start and there will be an interruption and I will have to gather it all together again. Or I will become engulfed with all I did or did not do, with what should have been and what cannot be helped.

She was a beautiful baby. The first and only one of our five that was beautiful at birth. You do not guess how new and uneasy her tenancy in her now-loveliness. You did not know her all those years she was thought homely, or see her poring over her baby pictures, making me tell her over and over how beautiful she had been — and would be, I would tell her — and was now, to the seeing eye. But the seeing eyes were few or nonexistent. Including mine.

I nursed her. They feel that's important nowadays. I nursed all the children, but with her, with all the fierce rigidity of first motherhood, I did like the books then said. Though her cries battered me to trembling and my breasts ached with swollenness, I waited till the clock decreed.

Why do I put that first? I do not even know if it matters, or if it explains anything.

**Film
Series**

DVD
See Ch. 19 for
film stills from
the DVD version
of this story.

5

She was a beautiful baby. She blew shining bubbles of sound. She loved motion, loved light, loved color and music and textures. She would lie on the floor in her blue overalls patting the surface so hard in ecstasy her hands and feet would blur. She was a miracle to me, but when she was eight months old I had to leave her daytimes with the woman downstairs to whom she was no miracle at all, for I worked or looked for work and for Emily's father, who "could no longer endure" (he wrote in his good-bye note) "sharing want with us."

I was nineteen. It was the pre-relief, pre-WPA° world of the depression. I would start running as soon as I got off the streetcar, running up the stairs, the place smelling sour, and awake or asleep to startle awake, when she saw me she would break into a clogged weeping that could not be comforted, a weeping I can hear yet.

10   After a while I found a job hashing at night so I could be with her days, and it was better. But it came to where I had to bring her to his family and leave her.

It took a long time to raise the money for her fare back. Then she got chicken pox and I had to wait longer. When she finally came, I hardly knew her, walking quick and nervous like her father, looking like her father, thin, and dressed in a shoddy red that yellowed her skin and glared at the pockmarks. All the baby loveliness gone.

She was two. Old enough for nursery school they said, and I did not know then what I know now — the fatigue of the long day, and the lacerations of group life in the kinds of nurseries that are only parking places for children.

Except that it would have made no difference if I had known. It was the only place there was. It was the only way we could be together, the only way I could hold a job.

And even without knowing, I knew. I knew the teacher that was evil because all these years it has curdled into my memory, the little boy hunched in the corner, her rasp, "why aren't you outside, because Alvin hits you? that's no reason, go out, scaredy." I knew Emily hated it even if she did not clutch and implore "don't go Mommy" like the other children, mornings.

15   She always had a reason why we should stay home. Momma, you look sick. Momma, I feel sick. Momma, the teachers aren't there today, they're sick. Momma, we can't go, there was a fire there last night. Momma, it's a holiday today, no school, they told me.

But never a direct protest, never rebellion. I think of our others in their three-, four-year-oldness — the explosions, the tempers, the denunciations, the demands — and I feel suddenly ill. I put the iron down. What in me demanded that goodness in her? And what was the cost, the cost to her of such goodness?

The old man living in the back once said in his gentle way: "You should smile at Emily more when you look at her." What *was* in my face when I looked at her? I loved her. There were all the acts of love.

WPA: The Works Progress Administration, created in 1935 as part of President Franklin D. Roosevelt's New Deal program. The purpose of the WPA (renamed the Works Projects Administration in 1939) was to provide jobs for the unemployed during the Great Depression.

It was only with the others I remembered what he said, and it was the face of joy, and not of care or tightness or worry I turned to them — too late for Emily. She does not smile easily, let alone almost always as her brothers and sisters do. Her face is closed and sombre, but when she wants, how fluid. You must have seen it in her pantomimes, you spoke of her rare gift for comedy on the stage that rouses laughter out of the audience so dear they applaud and applaud and do not want to let her go.

Where does it come from, that comedy? There was none of it in her when she came back to me that second time, after I had had to send her away again. She had a new daddy now to learn to love, and I think perhaps it was a better time.

Except when we left her alone nights, telling ourselves she was old enough.   20

"Can't you go some other time, Mommy, like tomorrow?" she would ask. "Will it be just a little while you'll be gone? Do you promise?"

The time we came back, the front door open, the clock on the floor in the hall. She rigid awake. "It wasn't just a little while. I didn't cry. Three times I called you, just three times, and then I ran downstairs to open the door so you could come faster. The clock talked loud. I threw it away, it scared me what it talked."

She said the clock talked loud again that night I went to the hospital to have Susan. She was delirious with the fever that comes before red measles, but she was fully conscious all the week I was gone and the week after we were home when she could not come near the new baby or me.

She did not get well. She stayed skeleton thin, not wanting to eat, and night after night she had nightmares. She would call for me, and I would rouse from exhaustion to sleepily call back: "You're all right, darling, go to sleep, it's just a dream," and if she still called, in a sterner voice, "now go to sleep, Emily, there's nothing to hurt you." Twice, only twice, when I had to get up for Susan anyhow, I went in to sit with her.

Now when it is too late (as if she would let me hold and comfort her like I do   25 the others) I get up and go to her at once at her moan or restless stirring. "Are you awake, Emily? Can I get you something?" And the answer is always the same: "No, I'm all right, go back to sleep, Mother."

They persuaded me at the clinic to send her away to a convalescent home in the country where "she can have the kind of food and care you can't manage for her, and you'll be free to concentrate on the new baby." They still send children to that place. I see pictures on the society page of sleek young women planning affairs to raise money for it, or dancing at the affairs, or decorating Easter eggs or filling Christmas stockings for the children.

They never have a picture of the children so I do not know if the girls still wear those gigantic red bows and the ravaged looks on the every other Sunday when parents can come to visit "unless otherwise notified"— as we were notified the first six weeks.

Oh it is a handsome place, green lawns and tall trees and fluted flower beds. High up on the balconies of each cottage the children stand, the girls in their red bows and white dresses, the boys in white suits and giant red ties. The parents stand below shrieking up to be heard and the children shriek down to be heard, and between them the invisible wall: "Not to Be Contaminated by Parental Germs or Physical Affection."

There was a tiny girl who always stood hand in hand with Emily. Her parents never came. One visit she was gone. "They moved her to Rose Cottage," Emily shouted in explanation. "They don't like you to love anybody here."

30   She wrote once a week, the labored writing of a seven-year-old. "I am fine. How is the baby. If I write my leter nicly I will have a star. Love." There never was a star. We wrote every other day, letters she could never hold or keep but only hear read — once. "We simply do not have room for children to keep any personal possessions," they patiently explained when we pieced one Sunday's shrieking to-gether to plead how much it would mean to Emily, who loved so to keep things, to be allowed to keep her letters and cards.

Each visit she looked frailer. "She isn't eating," they told us.

(They had runny eggs for breakfast or mush with lumps, Emily said later, I'd hold it in my mouth and not swallow. Nothing ever tasted good, just when they had chicken.)

It took us eight months to get her released home, and only the fact that she gained back so little of her seven lost pounds convinced the social worker.

I used to try to hold and love her after she came back, but her body would stay stiff, and after a while she'd push away. She ate little. Food sickened her, and I think much of life too. Oh she had physical lightness and brightness, twinkling by on skates, bouncing like a ball up and down up and down over the jump rope, skimming over the hill; but these were momentary.

35   She fretted about her appearance, thin and dark and foreign-looking at a time when every little girl was supposed to look or thought she should look a chubby blonde replica of Shirley Temple. The doorbell sometimes rang for her, but no one seemed to come and play in the house or be a best friend. Maybe because we moved so much.

There was a boy she loved painfully through two school semesters. Months later she told me how she had taken pennies from my purse to buy him candy. "Licorice was his favorite and I brought him some every day, but he still liked Jennifer better'n me. Why, Mommy?" The kind of question for which there is no answer.

School was a worry to her. She was not glib or quick in a world where glibness and quickness were easily confused with ability to learn. To her overworked and exasperated teachers she was an overconscientious "slow learner" who kept trying to catch up and was absent entirely too often.

I let her be absent, though sometimes the illness was imaginary. How different from my now-strictness about attendance with the others. I wasn't working. We had a new baby, I was home anyhow. Sometimes, after Susan grew old enough, I would keep her home from school, too, to have them all together.

Mostly Emily had asthma, and her breathing, harsh and labored, would fill the house with a curiously tranquil sound. I would bring the two old dresser mirrors and her boxes of collections to her bed. She would select beads and single earrings, bottle tops and shells, dried flowers and pebbles, old postcards and scraps, all sorts of oddments; then she and Susan would play Kingdom, setting up landscapes and furniture, peopling them with action.

Those were the only times of peaceful companionship between her and Susan. 40 I have edged away from it, that poisonous feeling between them, that terrible balancing of hurts and needs I had to do between the two, and did so badly, those earlier years.

Oh there are conflicts between the others too, each one human, needing, demanding, hurting, taking — but only between Emily and Susan, no, Emily toward Susan that corroding resentment. It seems so obvious on the surface, yet it is not obvious. Susan, the second child, Susan, golden- and curly-haired and chubby, quick and articulate and assured, everything in appearance and manner Emily was not; Susan, not able to resist Emily's precious things, losing or sometimes clumsily breaking them; Susan telling jokes and riddles to company for applause while Emily sat silent (to say to me later: that was *my* riddle, Mother, I told it to Susan); Susan, who for all the five years' difference in age was just a year behind Emily in developing physically.

I am glad for that slow physical development that widened the difference between her and her contemporaries, though she suffered over it. She was too vulnerable for that terrible world of youthful competition, of preening and parading, of constant measuring of yourself against every other, of envy, "If I had that copper hair," "If I had that skin. . . ." She tormented herself enough about not looking like the others, there was enough of the unsureness, the having to be conscious of words before you speak, the constant caring — what are they thinking of me? without having it all magnified by the merciless physical drives.

Ronnie is calling. He is wet and I change him. It is rare there is such a cry now. That time of motherhood is almost behind me when the ear is not one's own but must always be racked and listening for the child cry, the child call. We sit for a while and I hold him, looking out over the city spread in charcoal with its soft aisles of light. "*Shoogily*," he breathes and curls closer. I carry him back to bed, asleep. *Shoogily*. A funny word, a family word, inherited from Emily, invented by her to say: *comfort*.

In this and other ways she leaves her seal, I say aloud. And startle at my saying it. What do I mean? What did I start to gather together, to try and make coherent? I was at the terrible, growing years. War years. I do not remember them well. I was working, there were four smaller ones now, there was not time for her. She had to help be a mother, and housekeeper, and shopper. She had to set her seal. Mornings of crisis and near hysteria trying to get lunches packed, hair combed, coats and shoes found, everyone to school or Child Care on time, the baby ready for transportation. And always the paper scribbled on by a smaller one, the book looked at by Susan then mislaid, the homework not done. Running out to that huge school where she was one, she was lost, she was a drop; suffering over the unpreparedness, stammering and unsure in her classes.

There was so little time left at night after the kids were bedded down. She 45 would struggle over books, always eating (it was in those years she developed her enormous appetite that is legendary in our family) and I would be ironing, or preparing food for the next day, or writing V-mail° to Bill, or tending the baby. Sometimes, to make me laugh, or out of her despair, she would imitate happenings or types at school.

I think I said once: "Why don't you do something like this in the school amateur show?" One morning she phoned me at work, hardly understandable through the weeping: "Mother, I did it. I won, I won; they gave me first prize; they clapped and clapped and wouldn't let me go."

Now suddenly she was Somebody, and as imprisoned in her difference as she had been in anonymity.

She began to be asked to perform at other high schools, even in colleges, then at city and statewide affairs. The first one we went to, I only recognized her that first moment when thin, shy, she almost drowned herself into the curtains. Then: Was this Emily? The control, the command, the convulsing and deadly clowning, the spell, then the roaring, stamping audience, unwilling to let this rare and precious laughter out of their lives.

Afterwards: You ought to do something about her with a gift like that — but without money or knowing how, what does one do? We have left it all to her, and the gift has as often eddied inside, clogged and clotted, as been used and growing.

50   She is coming. She runs up the stairs two at a time with her light graceful step, and I know she is happy tonight. Whatever it was that occasioned your call did not happen today.

"Aren't you ever going to finish the ironing, Mother? Whistler painted his mother in a rocker. I'd have to paint mine standing over an ironing board." This is one of her communicative nights and she tells me everything and nothing as she fixes herself a plate of food out of the icebox.

She is so lovely. Why did you want me to come in at all? Why were you concerned? She will find her way.

She starts up the stairs to bed. "Don't get me up with the rest in the morning." "But I thought you were having midterms." "Oh, those," she comes back in, kisses me, and says quite lightly, "in a couple of years when we'll all be atom-dead they won't matter a bit."

She has said it before. She *believes* it. But because I have been dredging the past, and all that compounds a human being is so heavy and meaningful in me, I cannot endure it tonight.

55   I will never total it all. I will never come in to say: She was a child seldom smiled at. Her father left me before she was a year old. I had to work her first six years when there was work, or I sent her home and to his relatives. There were years she had care she hated. She was dark and thin and foreign-looking in a world where the prestige went to blondeness and curly hair and dimples, she was slow where glibness was prized. She was a child of anxious, not proud, love. We were poor and could not afford for her the soil of easy growth. I was a young mother, I was a distracted mother. There were other children pushing up, demanding.

V-mail: Mail sent to or from members of the armed forces during World War II. Letters were reduced onto microfilm and enlarged and printed out at their destination.

Her younger sister seemed all that she was not. There were years she did not want me to touch her. She kept too much in herself, her life was such she had to keep too much in herself. My wisdom came too late. She has much to her and probably little will come of it. She is a child of her age, of depression, of war, of fear.

Let her be. So all that is in her will not bloom — but in how many does it? There is still enough left to live by. Only help her to know — help make it so there is cause for her to know — that she is more than this dress on the ironing board, helpless before the iron.

Reading and Reacting

1. "I Stand Here Ironing" focuses on incidents that took place in the "pre-relief, pre-WPA world" of the Depression (par. 9). In light of social, political, and economic changes that have occurred since the 1930s, do you think the events the story presents could occur today? Explain.

2. In what sense is the image of a mother at an ironing board appropriate for this story?

3. The narrator is overwhelmed by guilt. What does she believe she has done wrong? What, if anything, do *you* think she has done wrong? Do you think she has been a good mother? Why or why not?

4. Who, or what, do you blame for the narrator's problems? For example, do you blame Emily's father? The Depression? The social institutions and "experts" to which the narrator turns?

5. Do you see the narrator as a victim limited by the times in which she lives? Do you agree with the narrator that Emily is "a child of her age, of depression, of war, of fear" (par. 55)? Or do you believe both women have some control over their own destinies, regardless of the story's historical setting?

6. What do you think the narrator wants for her daughter? Do you think her goals for Emily are realistic? Why or why not?

7. Paragraph 28 describes the physical setting of the convalescent home to which Emily was sent. What does this description add to the story? Why do you suppose there is no physical description of the apartment in which Emily lived as a child? How do you picture this apartment?

8. To whom do you think the mother is speaking in this story?

9. **JOURNAL ENTRY** Put yourself in Emily's position. What do you think she would like to tell her mother?

10. **CRITICAL PERSPECTIVE** Writing in *The Red Wheelbarrow*, psychologist Robert Coles discusses the complex family relationships depicted in "I Stand Here Ironing" and reaches an optimistic conclusion:

> But the child did not grow to be a mere victim of the kind so many of us these days are rather eager to recognize — a hopeless tangle of psychopathology. The growing child, even in her troubled moments, revealed herself to be persistent, demanding, and observant. In the complaints we make, in the "symptoms" we develop, we reveal our strengths as well as our weaknesses. The hurt child could summon her intelligence, exercise her will, smile and make others smile.

Do you agree with Coles's psychological evaluation of Emily? Do you find the story's ending as essentially uplifting as he seems to? Why or why not?

Related Works: "A Primer for the Punctuation of Heart Disease" (p. 156), "Kansas" (p. 209), "Everyday Use" (p. 469), "Seventeen Syllables" (p. 538), "Those Winter Sundays" (p. 1059), *Proof* (p. 1526), *The Glass Menagerie* (p. 1998)

BOBBIE ANN MASON (1942–   ) was born in Mayfield, Kentucky, where her father was a dairy farmer. Mason graduated from the University of Kentucky in 1962 and worked in publishing in New York. She received a master's degree from SUNY-Binghamton in 1966 and a doctorate in English from the University of Connecticut in 1972. Mason has written fiction as well as literary criticism and has had stories published in the *New Yorker* and *Redbook*, among other magazines. "Shiloh" is from her first book of fiction, *Shiloh and Other Stories*, which was awarded the Ernest Hemingway Award in 1983. Her other works include the novels *In country* (1985) and *Spence + Lila* (1998) and the short story collection *Zigzagging Down a Wild Trail* (2001). Mason's work often describes small-town life in contemporary western Kentucky, juxtaposing it with the consumer culture that has replaced the traditional values of previous generations. Her most recent book is *An Atomic Romance* (2005).

Cultural Context The title of this story is a reference to the area in Hardin County, Tennessee, where the Battle of Shiloh, a major battle of the Civil War, took place in April 1862. The two-day battle, which resulted in the death or injury of 24,000 Union and Confederate soldiers, was a decisive victory for the Union troops, who moved on to seize control of the Confederate railway at Corinth, Mississippi. In this story, the significance of the reference lies not in the battle itself but in the symbolic meaning its loss holds for Southerners. (Ironically, *Shiloh* is a Hebrew word meaning "place of peace.")

Shiloh   (1982)

Leroy Moffitt's wife, Norma Jean, is working on her pectorals. She lifts three-pound dumbbells to warm up, then progresses to a twenty-pound barbell. Standing with her legs apart, she reminds Leroy of Wonder Woman.

"I'd give anything if I could just get these muscles to, where they're real hard," says Norma Jean. "Feel this arm. It's not as hard as the other one."

"That's 'cause you're right-handed," says Leroy, dodging as she swings the barbell in an arc.

"Do you think so?"

5   "Sure."

Leroy is a truckdriver. He injured his leg in a highway accident four months ago, and his physical therapy, which involves weights and a pulley, prompted Norma Jean to try building herself up. Now she is attending a bodybuilding class. Leroy has been collecting temporary disability since his tractor-trailer jackknifed in Missouri, badly twisting his left leg in its socket. He has a steel pin in his hip. He will probably not be able to drive his rig again. It sits in the backyard, like a gigantic bird that has flown home to roost. Leroy has been home in Kentucky for three months, and his leg is almost healed, but the accident frightened him and he does not want to drive any more long hauls. He is not sure what to do next. In the meantime, he makes things from craft kits. He started by building a miniature log cabin from notched Popsicle sticks. He varnished it and placed it on the TV set, where it remains. It reminds him of a rustic Nativity scene. Then he tried string art (sailing ships on black velvet), a macramé owl kit, a snap-together B-17 Flying Fortress, and a lamp made out of a model truck, with a light fixture screwed in the top of the cab. At first the kits were diversions, something to kill time, but now he is thinking about building. a full-scale log house from a kit. It would be considerably cheaper than building a regular house, and besides, Leroy has grown to appreciate how things are put together. He has begun to realize that in all the years he was on the road he never took time to examine anything. He was always flying past scenery.

"They won't let you build a log cabin in any of the new subdivisions," Norma Jean tells him.

"They will if I tell them it's for you," he says, teasing her. Ever since they were married, he has promised Norma Jean he would build her a new home one day. They have always rented, and the house they live in is small and nondescript. It does not even feel like a home, Leroy realizes now.

Norma Jean works at the Rexall drugstore, and she has acquired an amazing amount of information about cosmetics. When she explains to Leroy the three stages of complexion care, involving creams, toners, and moisturizers, he thinks happily of other petroleum products—axle grease, diesel fuel. This is a connection between him and Norma Jean. Since he has been home, he has felt unusually tender about his wife and guilty over his long absences. But he can't tell what she feels about him. Norma Jean has never complained about his traveling; she has never made hurt remarks, like calling his truck a "widow-maker." He is reasonably certain she has been faithful to him, but he wishes she would celebrate his permanent homecoming more happily. Norma Jean is often startled to find Leroy at home, and he thinks she seems a little disappointed about it. Perhaps he reminds her too much of the early days of their marriage, before he went on the road. They had a child who died as an infant, years ago. They never speak about their memories of Randy, which have almost faded, but now that Leroy is home all the time, they sometimes feel awkward around each other, and Leroy wonders if one of them should mention the child. He has the feeling that they are waking up out of a dream together—that they must create a new marriage, start afresh. They are lucky they are still married. Leroy has read that for most people losing a child destroys the marriage—or else he heard this on *Donahue*. He can't always remember where he learns things anymore.

At Christmas, Leroy bought an electric organ for Norma Jean. She used to   10 play the piano when she was in high school. "It don't leave you," she told him once. "It's like riding a bicycle."

The new instrument had so many keys and buttons that she was bewildered by it at first. She touched the keys tentatively, pushed some buttons, then pecked out "Chopsticks." It came out in an amplified fox-trot rhythm, with marimba sounds.

"It's an orchestra!" she cried.

The organ had a pecan-look finish and eighteen preset chords, with optional flute, violin, trumpet, clarinet, and banjo accompaniments. Norma Jean mastered the organ almost immediately. At first she played Christmas songs. Then she bought *The Sixties Songbook* and learned every tune in it, adding variations to each with the rows of brightly colored buttons.

"I didn't like these old songs back then," she said. "But I have this crazy feeling I missed something."

15   "You didn't miss a thing," said Leroy.

Leroy likes to lie on the couch and smoke a joint and listen to Norma Jean play "Can't Take My Eyes Off You" and "I'll Be Back." He is back again. After fifteen years on the road, he is finally settling down with the woman he loves. She is still pretty. Her skin is flawless. Her frosted curls resemble pencil trimmings.

Now that Leroy has come home to stay, he notices how much the town has changed. Subdivisions are spreading across western Kentucky like an oil slick. The sign at the edge of town says "Pop: 11,500"— only seven hundred more than it said twenty years before. Leroy can't figure out who is living in all the new houses. The farmers who used to gather around the courthouse square on Saturday afternoons to play checkers and spit tobacco juice have gone. It has been years since Leroy has thought about the farmers, and they have disappeared without his noticing.

Leroy meets a kid named Stevie Hamilton in the parking lot at the new shopping center. While they pretend to be strangers meeting over a stalled car, Stevie tosses an ounce of marijuana under the front seat of Leroy's car. Stevie is wearing orange jogging shoes and a T-shirt that says CHATTAHOOCHEE SUPERRAT. His father is a prominent doctor who lives in one of the expensive subdivisions in a new white-columned brick house that looks like a funeral parlor. In the phone book under his name there is a separate number, with the listing "Teenagers."

"Where do you get this stuff?" asks Leroy. "From your pappy?"

20   "That's for me to know and you to find out," Stevie says. He is slit-eyed and skinny.

"What else you got?"

"What you interested in?"

"Nothing special. Just wondered."

Leroy used to take speed on the road. Now he has to go slowly. He needs to be mellow. He leans back against the car and says, "I'm aiming to build me a log house, soon as I get time. My wife, though, I don't think she likes the idea."

25   "Well, let me know when you want me again," Stevie says. He has a cigarette in his cupped palm, as though sheltering it from the wind. He takes a long drag, then stomps it on the asphalt and slouches away.

Stevie's father was two years ahead of Leroy in high school. Leroy is thirty-four. He married Norma Jean when they were both eighteen, and their child Randy was born a few months later, but he died at the age of four months and three days. He would be about Stevie's age now. Norma Jean and Leroy were at the drive-in, watching a double feature (*Dr. Strangelove* and *Lover Come Back*), and the baby was sleeping in the back seat. When the first movie ended, the baby was dead. It was the sudden infant death syndrome. Leroy remembers handing Randy to a nurse at the emergency room, as though he were offering her a large doll as a present. A dead baby feels like a sack of flour. "It just happens sometimes," said the doctor, in what Leroy always recalls as a nonchalant tone. Leroy can hardly remember the child anymore, but he still sees vividly a scene from *Dr. Strangelove* in which the President of the United States was talking in a folksy voice on the hot line to the Soviet premier about the bomber accidentally headed toward Russia. He was in the War Room, and the world map was lit up. Leroy remembers Norma Jean standing catatonically beside him in the hospital and himself thinking: Who is this strange girl? He had forgotten who she was. Now scientists are saying that crib death is caused by a virus. Nobody knows anything, Leroy thinks. The answers are always changing.

When Leroy gets home from the shopping center, Norma Jean's mother, Mabel Beasley, is there. Until this year, Leroy has not realized how much time she spends with Norma Jean. When she visits, she inspects the closets and then the plants, informing Norma Jean when a plant is droopy or yellow. Mabel calls the plants "flowers," although there are never any blooms. She always notices if Norma Jean's laundry is pilling up. Mabel is a short, overweight woman whose tight, brown-dyed curls look more like a wig than the actual wig she sometimes wears. Today she has brought Norma Jean an off-white dust ruffle she made for the bed; Mabel works in a custom-upholstery shop.

"This is the tenth one I made this year," Mabel says. "I got started and couldn't stop."

"It's real pretty," says Norma Jean.

"Now we can hide things under the bed," says Leroy, who gets along with his   30 mother-in-law primarily by joking with her. Mabel has never really forgiven him for disgracing her by getting Norma Jean pregnant. When the baby died, she said that fate was mocking her.

"What's that thing?" Mabel says to Leroy in a loud voice, pointing to a tangle of yarn on a piece of canvas.

Leroy holds it up for Mabel to see. "It's my needlepoint," he explains. "This is a *Star Trek* pillow cover."

"That's what a woman would do," says Mabel. "Great day in the morning!"

"All the big football players on TV do it," he says.

"Why, Leroy, you're always trying to fool me. I don't believe you for one   35 minute. You don't know what to do with yourself—that's the while trouble. Sewing!"

"I'm aiming to build us a log house," says Leroy. "Soon as my plans come."

"Like *heck* you are," says Norma Jean. She takes Leroy's needlepoint and shoves it into a drawer. "You have to find a job first. Nobody can afford to build now anyway."

Mabel straightens her girdle and says, "I still think before you get tied down y'all ought to take a little run to Shiloh."

"One of these days, Mama," Norma Jean says impatiently.

40   Mabel is talking about Shiloh, Tennessee. For the past few years, she has been urging Leroy and Norma Jean to visit the Civil War battleground there. Mabel went there on her honeymoon — the only real trip she ever took. Her husband died of a perforated ulcer when Norma Jean was ten, but Mabel, who was accepted into the United Daughters of the Confederacy in 1975, is still preoccupied with going back to Shiloh.

"I've been to kingdom come and back in that truck out yonder," Leroy says to Mabel, "but we never yet set foot in that battleground. Ain't that something? How did I miss it?"

"It's not even that far," Mabel says.

After Mabel leaves, Norma Jean reads to Leroy from a list she has made.

"Things you could do," she announces. "You could get a job as a guard at Union Carbide, where they'd let you set on a stool. You could get on at the lumberyard. You could do a little carpenter work, if you want to build so bad. You could —"

"I can't do something where I'd have to stand up all day."

45   "You ought to try standing up all day behind a cosmetics counter. It's amazing that I have strong feet, coming from two parents that never had strong feet at all." At the moment Norma Jean is holding on to the kitchen counter, raising her knees one at a time as she talks. She is wearing two-pound ankle weights.

"Don't worry," says Leroy. "I'll do something"

"You could truck calves to slaughter for somebody. You wouldn't have to drive any big old truck for that."

"I'm going to build you this house," says Leroy. "I want to make you a real home."

"I don't want to live in any log cabin."

50   "It's not a cabin. It's a house."

"I don't care. It looks like a cabin."

"You and me together could lift those logs. It's just like lifting weights."

Norma Jean doesn't answer. Under her breath, she is counting. Now she is marching through the kitchen. She is doing goose steps.

Before his accident, when Leroy came home he used to stay in the house with Norma Jean, watching TV in bed and playing cards. She would cook fried chicken, picnic ham, chocolate pie — all his favorites. Now he is home alone much of the time. In the mornings, Norma Jean disappears, leaving a cooling place in the bed. She eats a cereal called Body Buddies, and she leaves the bowl on the table, with the soggy tan balls floating in a milk puddle. He sees things about Norma Jean that he never realized before. When she chops onions, she stares off into a corner, as if she can't bear to look. She puts on her house slippers almost precisely at nine o'clock every evening and nudges her jogging shoes under the couch. She saves bread heels for the birds. Leroy watches the birds at the feeder. He notices the peculiar way goldfinches fly past the window. They close their wings, then fall, then spread their wings to catch and lift themselves. He wonders if they close their eyes when they fall. Norma Jean closes her eyes when they are in bed. She wants the lights turned out. Even then, he is sure she closes her eyes.

He goes for long drives around town. He tends to drive a car rather carelessly. 55
Power steering and an automatic shift make a car feel so small and inconsequen-
tial that his body is hardly involved in the driving process. His injured leg
stretches out comfortably. Once or twice he has almost hit something, but even
the prospect of an accident seems minor in a car. He cruises the new subdivisions,
feeling like a criminal rehearsing for a robbery. Norma Jean is probably right about
a log house being inappropriate here in the new subdivisions. All the houses look
grand and complicated. The depress him.

One day when Leroy comes home from a drive he finds Norma Jean in tears.
She is in the kitchen making a potato and mushroom-soup casserole, with grated-
cheese topping. She is crying because her mother caught her smoking.

"I didn't hear her coming. I was standing here puffing away pretty as you
please," Norma Jean says, wiping her eyes.

"I knew it would happen sooner or later," says Leroy, putting his arm around her.

"She don't know the meaning of the word 'knock,'" says Norma Jean. "It's a
wonder she hadn't caught me years ago."

"Think of it this way," Leroy says. "What if she caught me with a joint?"　　60

"You better not let her!" Norma Jean shrieks. "I'm warning you, Leroy
Moffitt!"

"I'm just kidding. Here, play me a tune. That'll help you relax."

Norma Jean puts the casserole in the oven and sets the timer. Then she plays
a ragtime tune, with horns and banjo, as Leroy lights up a joint and lies on the
couch, laughing to himself about Mabel's catching him at it. He thinks of Stevie
Hamilton — a doctor's son pushing grass. Everything is funny. The whole town
seems crazy and small. He is reminded of Virgil Mathis, a boastful policeman
Leroy used to shoot pool with. Virgil recently led a drug bust in a back room at a
bowling alley, where he seized ten thousand dollars' worth of marijuana. The
newspaper had a picture of him holding up the bags of grass and grinning widely.
Right now, Leroy can imagine Virgil breaking down the door and arresting him
with a lungful of smoke. Virgil would probably have been alerted to the scene because of all the racket Norma Jean is making. Now she sounds like a hard-rock
band. Norma Jean is terrific. When she switches to a Latin-rhythm version of
"Sunshine Superman," Leroy hums along. Norma Jean's foot goes up and down,
up and down.

"Well, what do you think?" Leroy says, when Norma Jean pauses to search
through her music.

"What do I think about what?"　　65

His mind has gone blank. Then he says, "I'll sell my rig and build us a house."
That wasn't what he wanted to say. He wanted to know what she thought — what
she *really* thought — about them.

"Don't start in on that again," says Norma Jean. She begins playing, "Who'll
Be the Next in Line?"

Leroy used to tell hitchhikers his whole life story — about his travels, his
hometown, the baby. He would end with a question: "Well, what do you think?"
It was just a rhetorical question. In time, he had the feeling that he'd been
telling the same story over and over to the same hitchhikers. He quit talking to

hitchhikers when he realized how his voice sounded — whining and self-pity-ing, like some teenage-tragedy song. Now Leroy has the sudden impulse to tell Norma Jean about himself, as if he had just met her. They have known each other so long they have forgotten a lot about each other. They could become reacquainted. But when the oven timer goes off and she runs to the kitchen, he forgets why he wants to do this.

The next day, Mabel drops by. It is Saturday and Norma Jean is cleaning. Leroy is studying the plans of his log house, which have finally come in the mail. He has them spread out on the table—big sheets of stiff blue paper, with diagrams and numbers printed in white. While Norma Jean runs the vacuum, Mabel drinks cof-fee. She sets her coffee cup on a blueprint.

70   "I'm just waiting for time to pass," she says to Leroy, drumming her fingers on the table.

As soon as Norma Jean switches off the vacuum, Mabel says in a loud voice, "Did you hear about the datsun dog that killed the baby?"

Norma Jean says, "The word is 'dachshund.'"

"They put the dog on trial. It chewed the baby's legs off. The mother was in the next room all the time." She raises her voice. "They thought it was neglect."

Norma Jean is holding her ears. Leroy manages to open the refrigerator and get some Diet Pepsi to offer Mabel. Mabel still has some coffee and she waves away the Pepsi.

75   "Datsuns are like that," Mabel says. "They're jealous dogs. They'll tear a place to pieces if you don't keep an eye on them."

"You better watch out what you're saying, Mabel," says Leroy.

"Well, facts is facts."

Leroy looks out the window at his rig. It is like a huge piece of furniture gath-ering dust in the backyard. Pretty soon it will be an antique. He hears the vacuum cleaner. Norma Jean seems to be cleaning the living room rug again.

Later, she says to Leroy, "She just said that about the baby because she caught me smoking. She's trying to pay me back."

80   "What are you talking about?" Leroy says, nervously shuffling blueprints.

"You know good and well," Norma Jean says. She is sitting in a kitchen chair with her feet up and her arms wrapped around her knees. She looks small and helpless. She says, "The very idea, her bringing up a subject like that! Saying it was neglect."

"She didn't mean that," Leroy says.

"She might not have *thought* she meant it. She always says things like that. You don't know how she goes on."

"But she didn't really mean it. She was just talking."

85   Leroy opens a king-sized bottle of beer and pours it into two glasses, dividing it carefully. He hands a glass to Norma Jean and she takes it from him mechani-cally. For a long time, they sit by the kitchen window watching the birds at the feeder.

Something is happening. Norma Jean is going to night school. She has graduated from her six-week body-building course and now she is taking an adult-education

course in composition at Paducah Community College. She spends her evenings
outlining paragraphs.

"First you have a topic sentence," she explains to Leroy. "Then you divide it
up. Your secondary topic has to be connected to your primary topic."

To Leroy, this sounds intimidating. "I never was any good in English," he says.

"It makes a lot of sense."

"What are you doing this for, anyhow?"   90

She shrugs. "It's something to do." She stands up and lifts her dumbbells a few
times.

"Driving a rig, nobody cared about my English."

"I'm not criticizing your English."

Norma Jean used to say, "If I lose ten minutes' sleep, I just drag all day." Now
she stays up late, writing compositions. She got a B on her first paper — a how-to
theme on soup-based casseroles. Recently Norma Jean has been cooking unusual
foods — tacos, lasagna, Bombay chicken. She doesn't play the organ anymore,
though her second paper was called "Why Music Is Important to Me." She sits at
the kitchen table, concentrating on her outlines, while Leroy plays with his log
house plans, practicing with a set of Lincoln Logs. The thought of getting a truck-
load of notched, numbered logs scares him, and he wants to be prepared. As he
and Norma Jean work together at the kitchen table, Leroy has the hopeful
thought that they are sharing something, but he knows he is a fool to think this.
Norma Jean is miles away. He knows he is going to lose her. Like Mabel, he is just
waiting for time to pass.

One day, Mabel is there before Norma Jean gets home from work, and Leroy   95
finds himself confiding in her. Mabel, he realizes, must know Norma Jean better
than he does.

"I don't know what's got into that girl," Mabel says. "She used to go to bed with
the chickens. Now you say she's up all hours. Plus her a-smoking. I like to died."

"I want to make her this beautiful home," Leroy says, indicating the Lincoln
Logs. "I don't think she even wants it. Maybe she was happier with me gone."

"She don't know what to make of you, coming home like this."

"Is that it?"

Mabel takes the roof off his Lincoln Log cabin. "You couldn't get *me* in a log   100
cabin," she says. "I was raised in one. It's no picnic, let me tell you."

"They're different now," says Leroy.

"I tell you what," Mabel says, smiling oddly at Leroy.

"What?"

"Take her on down to Shiloh, Y'all need to get out together, stir a little.
Her brain's all balled up over them books."

Leroy can see traces of Norma Jean's features in her mother's face. Mabel's   105
worn face has the texture of crinkled cotton, but suddenly she looks pretty. It occurs to Leroy that Mabel has been hinting all along that she wants them to take
her with them to Shiloh.

"Let's all go to Shiloh," he says. "You and me and her. Come Sunday."

Mabel throws up her hands in protest. "Oh, no, not me. Young folks want to
be by theirselves."

When Norma Jean comes in with groceries, Leroy says excitedly, "Your mama here's been dying to go to Shiloh for thirty-five years. It's about time we went, don't you think?"

"I'm not going to butt in on anybody's second honeymoon," Mabel says.

110   "Who's going on a honeymoon, for Christ's sake?" Norma Jean says loudly.

"I never raised no daughter of mine to talk that-a-way," Mabel says.

"You ain't seen nothing yet," says Norma Jean. She starts putting away boxes and cans, slamming cabinet doors.

"There's a log cabin at Shiloh," Mabel says. "It was there during the battle. There's bullet holes in it."

"When are you going to *shut up* about Shiloh, Mama?" asks Norma Jean.

115   "I always thought Shiloh was the prettiest place, so full of history," Mabel goes on. "I just hoped y'all could see it once before I die, so you could tell me about it." Later, she whispers to Leroy, "You do what I said. A little change is what she needs."

"Your name means 'the king,'" Norma Jean says to Leroy that evening, He is trying to get her to go to Shiloh, and she is reading a book about another century.

"Well, I reckon I ought to be right proud."

"I guess so."

"Am I still king around here?"

120   Norma Jean flexes her biceps and feels them for hardness. "I'm not fooling around with anybody, if that's what you mean," she says.

"Would you tell me if you were?"

"I don't know."

"What does *your* name mean?"

"It was Marilyn Monroe's real name."

125   "No kidding!"

"Norma comes from the Normans. They were invaders," she says. She closes her book and looks hard at Leroy. "I'll go to Shiloh with you if you'll stop staring at me."

On Sunday, Norma Jean packs a picnic and they go to Shiloh. To Leroy's relief, Mabel says she does not want to come with them. Norma Jean drives, and Leroy, sitting beside her, feels like some boring hitchhiker she has picked up. He tries some conversation, but she answers him in monosyllables. At Shiloh, she drives aimlessly through the park, past bluffs and trails and steep ravines. Shiloh is an immense place, and Leroy cannot see it as a battleground. It is not what he expected. He thought it would look like a golf course. Monuments are everywhere, showing through the thick clusters of trees. Norma Jean passes the log cabin Mabel mentioned. It is surrounded by tourists looking for bullet holes.

"That's not the kind of log house I've got in mind," says Leroy apologetically.

"I know *that*."

130   "This is a pretty place. Your mama was right."

"It's O.K.," says Norma Jean. "Well, we've seen it. I hope she's satisfied."

They burst out laughing together.

At the park museum, a movie on Shiloh is shown every half hour, but they decide that they don't want to see it. They buy a souvenir Confederate flag for Mabel, and then they find a picnic spot near the cemetery. Norma Jean has brought a picnic cooler, with pimiento sandwiches, soft drinks, and Yodels. Leroy eats a sandwich and then smokes a joint, hiding it behind the picnic cooler. Norma Jean has quit smoking altogether. She is picking cake crumbs from the cellophane wrapper, like a fussy bird.

Leroy says, "So the boys in gray ended up in Corinth.° The Union soldiers zapped' em finally. April 7, 1862."

They both know that he doesn't know any history. He is just talking about   135
some of the historical plaques they have read. He feels awkward, like a boy on a date with an older girl. They are still just making conversation.

"Corinth is where Mama eloped to," says Norma Jean.

They sit in silence and stare at the cemetery for the Union dead and, beyond, at a tall cluster of trees. Campers are parked nearby, bumper to bumper, and small children in bright clothing are cavorting and squealing. Norma Jean wads up the cake wrapper and squeezes it tightly in her hand. Without looking at Leroy, she says, "I want to leave you."

Leroy takes a bottle of Coke out of the cooler and flips off the cap. He holds the bottle poised near his mouth but cannot remember to take a drink. Finally he says, "No, you don't."

"Yes, I do."

"I won't let you."   140

"You can't stop me."

"Don't do me that way."

Leroy knows Norma Jean will have her own way. "Didn't I promise to be home from now on?" he says.

"In some ways, a woman prefers a man who wanders," says Norma Jean. "That sounds crazy, I know."

"You're not crazy."   145

Leroy remembers to drink from his Coke. Then he says, "Yes, you *are* crazy. You and me could start all over again. Right back at the beginning."

"We *have* started all over again," says Norma Jean. "And this is how it turned out."

"What did I do wrong?"

"Nothing."

"Is this one of those women's lib things?" Leroy asks.   150

"Don't be funny."

The cemetery, a green slope dotted with white markers, looks like a subdivision site. Leroy is trying to comprehend that his marriage is breaking up, but for some reason he is wondering about white slabs in a graveyard.

"Everything was fine till Mama caught me smoking," says Norma Jean, standing up. "That set something off."

Corinth: Corinth, Mississippi, where the Union troops seized control of the Confederate railroad.

"What are you talking about?"

"She won't leave me alone —*you* won't leave me alone." Norma Jean seems to be crying, but she is looking away from him. "I feel eighteen again. I can't face that all over again." She starts walking away. "No, it *wasn't* fine. I don't know what I'm saying. Forget it."

Leroy takes a lungful of smoke and closes his eyes as Norma Jean's words sink in. He tries to focus on the fact that thirty-five hundred soldiers died on the grounds around him. He can only think of that war as a board game with plastic soldiers. Leroy almost smiles, as he compares the Confederates' daring attack on the Union camps and Virgil Mathis's raid on the bowling alley. General Grant, drunk and furious, shoved the Southerners back to Corinth, where Mabel and Jet Beasley were married years later, when Mabel was still thin and good-looking. The next day, Mabel and Jet visited the battleground, and then Norma Jean was born, and then she married Leroy and they had a baby, which they lost, and now Leroy and Norma Jean are here at the same battleground. Leroy knows he is leaving out a lot. He is leaving out the insides of history. History was always just names and dates to him. It occurs to him that building a house out of logs is similarly empty — too simple. And the real inner workings of a marriage, like most of history, have escaped him. Now he sees that building a log house is the dumbest idea he could have had. It was clumsy of him to think Norma Jean would want a log house. It was a crazy idea. He'll have to think of something else, quickly. He will wad the blueprints into tight balls and fling them into the lake. Then he'll get moving again. He opens his eyes. Norma Jean has moved away and is walking through the cemetery, following a serpentine brick path.

Leroy gets up to follow his wife, but his good leg is asleep and his bad leg still hurts him. Norma Jean is far away, walking rapidly toward the bluff by the river, and he tries to hobble toward her. Some children run past him, screaming noisily. Norma Jean has reached the bluff, and she is looking out over the Tennessee River. Now she turns toward Leroy and waves her arms. Is she beckoning to him? She seems to be doing an exercise for her chest muscles. The sky is unusually pale — the color of the dust ruffle Mabel made for their bed.

Reading and Reacting

1. Leroy and Norma Jean live in a house described as "small and nondescript" (par. 7). How do you picture the outside of this house? How do you think it might be furnished and decorated?

2. How are Leroy and Norma Jean different? How has Norma Jean changed since Leroy's accident? How has their marriage changed? To what do you attribute these changes? For example, do you think Norma Jean's dissatisfaction is simply what Leroy might call "one of those women's lib things" (par. 150)?

3. What do readers learn about the town in which the story is set? What can we infer about the town? How has it changed over the years?

4. Trace the references to the log house throughout the story. What does Leroy's daydreaming about the house reveal about him? About his and Norma Jean's marriage?

5. When remembering his son's death, Leroy thinks, "Nobody knows anything. . . . The answers are always changing" (par. 26). What relevance does this comment have to other events in the story?

6. What do each of these contribute to the story: Stevie Hamilton; Leroy's drug use (past and present); Norma Jean's bodybuilding; the child who died; the electric organ; Norma Jean's adult education courses. Do you see all of these as essential to the story?

7. Is the primary focus of this story on the past, the present, or the future? Explain.

8. What role does Mabel, Norma Jean's mother, play in the story? How would the story be different without her? Why do you think Norma Jean is so upset when Mabel catches her smoking?

9. Why does Mabel want Leroy and Norma Jean to visit the Civil War battleground at Shiloh? Why does Leroy agree to go there? What is the significance of the fact that Norma Jean chooses this setting for telling Leroy she wants to leave him?

10. **JOURNAL ENTRY** At the end of the story, Leroy sees Norma Jean in the distance. As she turns to him and waves her arms, he wonders if she is "beckoning to him" (par. 157). Do you think she is? Why? Do you think their marriage is really over?

11. **CRITICAL PERSPECTIVE** Several critics have characterized Bobbie Ann Mason's work as regional, noting that her characters are generally from western Kentucky and are, by and large, socially static, without much chance of escaping their lives or their fates. Scott Vander Ploeg comments on one aspect of Mason's world:

> By the narrative focus or regional point of view she adopts, Mason establishes a world as seen through the eyes of the isolated and often unsophisticated western Kentuckian. This emphasis produces a tension between home and the outer world, and this is most evident in how she treats higher education. It isn't a meaningful part of this home-world, and thus when her characters confront higher education, we are left to consider an ironic disjunction between ourselves as educated readers and the uneducated subjects in the fiction.

How does Mason treat higher education in this story? Which characters embrace it, and which ones dismiss its importance? What do these differences signify within the context of the story?

Related Works: "Happy Endings" (p. 161), "Love and Other Catastrophes: A Mix Tape" (p. 165), "The Story of an Hour" (p. 197), "A Rose for Emily" (p. 216), "The Disappearance" (p. 371), "Patterns" (p. 866), "For the Union Dead" (p. 1081), *A Doll House* (p. 1454)

WRITING SUGGESTIONS: Setting

1. Among other things, "Shiloh" is a story about a marriage — about what connects Leroy and Norma Jean as well as what divides them. Compare and contrast their marriage with the relationships of two or three other fictional

couples — for example, the couples in "Hills Like White Elephants," "The Disappearance," "Cathedral," and "The Third and Final Continent." What kinds of problems do these couples have? What has caused the problems? Do you see them as solvable?

2. In both "The Storm" and "I Stand Here Ironing," social constraints determined by the story's historical setting limit a woman's options. Explore the options each woman might reasonably exercise in order to break free of the limits that social institutions impose on her.

3. Write an essay in which you consider how "This Is What It Means to Say Phoenix, Arizona" would be different if its geographical and physical setting were changed to a setting of your choice. In your essay, examine the changes (in plot development as well as in the characters' conflicts, reactions, and motivation) that might occur as a result of the change in setting.

4. Select a story from another chapter, and write an essay in which you consider how setting affects its plot — for example, how it creates conflict or crisis, how it forces characters to act, or how it determines how the plot is resolved.

5. Both "The Storm" and "Battle Royal" use rich descriptive language to create a mood that dominates the story. Analyze this use of language in one of the two stories, or compare two short passages, one from each story. How does language help to create and enrich each story's setting?

CHAPTER 15

POINT OF VIEW

> Even if [a writer] has decided on a narrator who will fit one of the critic's classifications — "omniscient," "first-person," "limited omniscient," "objective," . . . and so on — his troubles have just begun.
>
> —Wayne C. Booth, *"Distance and Point of View"*

All stories are told by a **narrator**, and one of the first choices writers make is who tells the story. This choice determines the story's **point of view** — the vantage point from which events are presented. The implications of this choice are far-reaching. Consider, for example, the following scenario. Five people witness a crime and are questioned by the police. Their stories agree on certain points: a crime was committed, a body was found, and the crime occurred at noon. But in other ways their stories are different. The man who fled the scene was either tall or of average height; his hair was either dark or light; he either was carrying an object or was empty-handed. The events that led up to the crime and even the description of the crime itself are markedly different, depending on who tells the story. Thus, the perspective from which a story is told determines what details are included in the story and how they are arranged — in short, the plot. In addition, the perspective of the narrator affects the story's style, language, and themes.

The narrator of a work of fiction is not the same as the writer — even when a writer uses the first-person *I*. Writers create narrators to tell their stories. Often the personalities and opinions of narrators are far different from those of the author. The term **persona** — which literally means "mask" — is used for such narrators. By assuming this mask, a writer expands the creative possibilities of a work.

When deciding on a point of view for a work of fiction, a writer can choose to tell the story either in the *first person* or in the *third person*.

First-Person Narrators

Sometimes the narrator is a character who uses the **first person** (*I* or sometimes *we*) to tell the story. Often this narrator is a **major character** — Sammy in John Updike's "A&P" (p. 230) and the boy in James Joyce's "Araby" (p. 395), for example — who tells his or her own story and is the focus of that story. Sometimes, however, a first-person narrator tells a story that is primarily about someone else. Such a narrator may be a **minor character** who plays a relatively small part in the story or simply an **observer** who reports events experienced or related by others. The narrator of William Faulkner's "A Rose for Emily" (p. 216), for example, is an unidentified witness to the story's events. By using *we* instead of *I*, this narrator speaks on behalf of all the town's residents, expressing their shared views of their neighbor, Emily Grierson:

> We did not say she was crazy then. We believed she had to do that. We remembered all the young men her father had driven away, and we knew that with nothing left, she would have to cling to that which had robbed her, as people will.

Writers gain a number of advantages when they use first-person narrators. First, they are able to present incidents convincingly. Readers are more willing to accept a statement like "My sister changed a lot after that day" than they are to accept the impersonal observations of a third-person narrator. The first-person narrator also simplifies a writer's task of selecting details. Only the events and details that the narrator could actually have seen or experienced can be introduced into the story.

Another major advantage of first-person narrators is that their restricted view can create **irony** — a discrepancy between what is said and what readers believe to be true. Irony may be *dramatic, situational,* or *verbal*. **Dramatic irony** occurs when a narrator (or character) perceives less than readers do; **situational irony** occurs when what happens is at odds with what readers are led to expect; **verbal irony** occurs when the narrator says one thing but actually means another.

"Gryphon," by Charles Baxter (p. 248), illustrates all three kinds of irony. Baxter creates **dramatic irony** when he has his main character see less than readers do. For example, at the end of the story, the young boy does not yet realize what readers already know — that he has learned more from Miss Ferenczi's way of teaching than from Mr. Hibler's. The setting of the story — a conventional school — creates **situational irony** because it contrasts with the unexpected events that unfold there. In addition, many of the narrator's comments create **verbal irony** because they mean something different from what they seem to mean. At the end of the story, for example, after the substitute, Miss Ferenczi, has been fired, the narrator relates another teacher's comment that life will now return to "normal" and that their regular teacher will soon return to test them on their "knowledge." This comment is ironic in light of all Miss Ferenczi has done to redefine the narrator's ideas about "normal" education and about "knowledge."

Unreliable Narrators

Sometimes first-person narrators are self-serving, mistaken, confused, unstable, or even insane. These **unreliable narrators**, whether intentionally or unintentionally, misrepresent events and misdirect readers. In Edgar Allan Poe's "The Cask of Amontillado" (p. 350), for example, the narrator, Montresor, tells his story to justify a crime he committed fifty years before. Montresor's version of what happened is not accurate, and perceptive readers know it: his obvious self-deception, his sadistic manipulation of Fortunato, his detached description of the cold-blooded murder, and his lack of remorse lead readers to question his sanity and, therefore, to distrust his version of events. This distrust creates an ironic distance between readers and narrator.

The narrator of Charlotte Perkins Gilman's "The Yellow Wallpaper" (p. 421) is also an unreliable narrator. Suffering from "nervous depression," she unintentionally distorts the facts when she says that the shapes in the wallpaper of her bedroom are changing and moving. Moreover, she does not realize what is wrong with her or why, or how her husband's "good intentions" are hurting her. Readers, however, see the disparity between the narrator's interpretation of events and their own, and this irony enriches their understanding of the story.

Some narrators are unreliable because they are naive. Because they are immature, sheltered, or innocent of evil, these narrators are not aware of the significance of the events they are relating. Having the benefit of experience, readers interpret events differently from the way these narrators do. When we read a passage by a child narrator — such as the following one from J. D. Salinger's novel *The Catcher in the Rye* — we are aware of the narrator's innocence, and we know his interpretation of events is flawed:

> Anyway, I keep picturing all these little kids playing some game in this big field of rye and all. Thousands of little kids, and nobody's around — nobody big, I mean — except me. And I'm standing on the edge of some crazy cliff. What I have to do, I have to catch everybody if they start to go over the cliff — I mean if they're running and they don't look where they're going I have to come out from somewhere and catch them. I'd just be the catcher in the rye. . . .

The irony in the preceding passage comes from our knowledge that the naive narrator, Holden Caulfield, cannot stop children from growing up. Ultimately, they all fall off the "crazy cliff" and mature into adults. Although Holden is not aware of the futility of trying to protect children from the dangers of adulthood, readers know that his efforts are doomed from the start.

A naive narrator's background can also limit his or her ability to understand a situation. The narrator in Sherwood Anderson's short story "I'm a Fool," for example, lies to impress a rich girl he meets at a racetrack. At the end of the story, the boy regrets the fact that he lied, believing that if he had told the truth, he could have seen the girl again. The reader knows, however, that the narrator (a laborer at the racetrack) is deceiving himself because the social gap that separates him and the girl could never be bridged.

Keep in mind that all first-person narrators are, in a sense, unreliable because they present a situation as only one person sees it. "In a Grove," a story by the Japanese author Ryūnosuke Akutagawa, illustrates this idea. In this story, seven characters act as narrators and give different accounts of a murder. Some of the characters seem to be lying or bending the facts to suit their own needs, but others simply have an incomplete or mistaken understanding of events. No character, of course, has all the information the story's author has.

When you read, you should look for discrepancies between a narrator's view of events and your own. Discovering that a story has an unreliable narrator enables you not only to question the accuracy of the narrative but also to recognize the irony in the narrator's version of events. By doing so, you gain insight into the story and learn something about the writer's purpose.

Third-Person Narrators

Sometimes a writer uses the **third person** (*he, she, they*) to tell the story from the point of view of a narrator who is not also a character. Third-person narrators fall into three categories: **omniscient, limited omniscient,** and **objective.**

Omniscient Narrators

Some third-person narrators are **omniscient** (all-knowing) narrators, moving at will from one character's mind to another. One advantage of omniscient narrators is that they have none of the naïveté, dishonesty, gullibility, or mental instability that can characterize first-person narrators. In addition, because omniscient narrators are not characters in the story, their perception is not limited to what any one character can observe or comprehend. As a result, they can present a more inclusive view of events and characters than first-person narrators can. Omniscient narrators can also convey their attitude toward their subject matter. For example, the omniscient narrator in Nadine Gordimer's "Once upon a Time" (p. 204) uses sentence structure, word choice, and repetition to express her distaste for the scene she describes:

> In a house, in a suburb, in a city, there were a man and his wife who loved each other very much and were living happily ever after. They had a little boy, and they loved him very much. They had a cat and a dog that the little boy loved very much. They had a car and a caravan trailer for holidays, and a swimming-pool which was fenced so that the little boy and his playmates would not fall in and drown. They had a housemaid who was absolutely trustworthy and an itinerant gardener who was highly recommended by the neighbours. For when they began to live happily ever after they were warned, by that wise old witch, the husband's mother, not to take on anyone off the street.

Occasionally, omniscient narrators move not only in and out of the minds of the characters but also in and out of a **persona** (representing the voice of the author) that speaks directly to readers. This narrative technique was popular with writers during the eighteenth century, when the novel was a new literary form. It permitted writers to present themselves as masters of artifice, able to know and control all aspects of experience. Few contemporary writers would give themselves the license that Henry Fielding does in the following passage from *Tom Jones* (1749):

> And true it was that [Mr. Alworthy] did many of these things; but had he done nothing more I should have left him to have recorded his own merit on some fair freestone over the door of that hospital. Matters of a much more extraordinary kind are to be the subject of this history, or I should grossly misspend my time in writing so voluminous a work; and you my sagacious friend, might with equal profit and pleasure travel through some pages which certain droll authors have been facetiously pleased to call *The History of England.*

A contemporary example of this type of omniscient point of view occurs in Ursula K. LeGuin's "The Ones Who Walk Away from Omelas" (1975). This story presents a description of a city that in the narrator's words is "like a city in a fairy tale." As the story proceeds, however, the description of Omelas changes, and the narrator's tone changes as well: "Do you believe? Do you accept the festival, the city, the joy? No? Then let me describe one more thing." By undercutting her own narrative, the narrator underscores the ironic theme of the story, which suggests that it is impossible for human beings to ever achieve an ideal society.

Limited Omniscient Narrators

Third-person narrators can have **limited omniscience,** focusing on only what a single character experiences. In other words, events are limited to one character's perspective, and nothing is revealed that the character does not see, hear, feel, or think. Andy in David Michael Kaplan's "Doe Season" (p. 512) is just such a limited-focus character. Limited omniscient narrators, like all third-person narrators, have certain advantages over first-person narrators. When a writer uses a first-person narrator, the narrator's personality and speech color the story, creating a personal or even an idiosyncratic narrative. Also, the first-person narrator's character flaws or lack of knowledge may limit his or her awareness of the significance of events. Limited omniscient narrators are more flexible: they take readers into a particular character's mind just as a first-person narrator does, but without the first-person narrator's subjectivity, self-deception, or naïveté.

In the following example from Anne Tyler's "Teenage Wasteland" (p. 799), the limited omniscient narrator presents the story from the point of view of a single character, Daisy:

> Daisy and Matt sat silent, shocked. Matt rubbed his forehead with his finger-
> tips. Imagine, Daisy thought, how they must look to Mr. Lanham: an over-
> weight housewife in a cotton dress and a too-tall, too-thin insurance agent in a
> baggy, frayed suit. Failures, both of them — the kind of people who are always
> hurrying to catch up, missing the point of things that everyone else grasps at
> once. She wished she'd worn nylons instead of knee socks.

Here the point of view gives readers the impression that they are standing off to the side watching Daisy and her husband Matt. However, at the same time we have the advantage of this objective view, we are also able to see into the mind of one character.

Objective Narrators

Third-person narrators who tell a story from an *objective* (or *dramatic*) point of view remain entirely outside the characters' minds. With **objective narrators,** events unfold the way they would in a play or a movie: narrators tell the story only by presenting dialogue and recounting events; they do not reveal the characters' (or their own) thoughts or attitudes. Thus, they allow readers to interpret the actions of the characters without any interference. Ernest Hemingway uses the objective point of view in his short story "A Clean, Well-Lighted Place" (1933):

> The waiter took the brandy bottle and another saucer from the counter
> inside the café and marched out to the old man's table. He put down the saucer
> and poured the glass full of brandy.
>
> "You should have killed yourself last week," he said to the deaf man. The
> old man motioned with his finger. "A little more," he said. The waiter poured
> on into the glass so that the brandy slopped over and ran down the stem into
> the top saucer of the pile. "Thank you," the old man said. The waiter took the
> bottle back inside the café. He sat down at the table with his colleague again.

The story's narrator is distant, seemingly emotionless, and this perspective is
consistent with the author's purpose: for Hemingway, the attitude of the narrator
reflects the stunned, almost anesthetized condition of people in the post–World
War I world.

Selecting an Appropriate Point of View

Writers of short stories often maintain a consistent point of view. The main cri-
terion writers use when they decide on a point of view is how the distance they
maintain from their material will affect their narrative. The passages that follow
illustrate the options writers have.

Limited Omniscient Point of View

In the following passage from the short story "Doe Season," David Michael Kaplan
uses a third-person limited omniscient narrator to tell the story of Andy, a nine-
year-old girl who is going hunting with her father for the first time.

> They were always the same woods, she thought sleepily as they drove through
> the early morning darkness — deep and immense, covered with yesterday's
> snowfall, which had frozen overnight. They were the same woods that lay be-
> hind her house, *and they stretch all the way to here*, she thought, *for miles and
> miles, longer than I could walk in a day, or a week even, but they are still the same
> woods.* The thought made her feel good: it was like thinking of God; it was like
> thinking of the space between here and the moon; it was like thinking of all
> the foreign countries from her geography book where even now, Andy knew,
> people were going to bed, while they — she and her father and Charlie Spoon
> and Mac, Charlie's eleven-year-old son — were driving deeper into the Penn-
> sylvania countryside, to go hunting.
>
> They had risen long before dawn. Her mother, yawning and not trying to
> hide her sleepiness, cooked them eggs and French toast. Her father smoked a
> cigarette and flicked ashes into his saucer while Andy listened, wondering
> *Why doesn't he come?* and *Won't he ever come?* until at last a car pulled into the
> graveled drive and honked. "That will be Charlie Spoon," her father said; he
> always said "Charlie Spoon," even though his real name was Spreun, because
> Charlie was, in a sense, shaped like a spoon, with a large head and a narrow
> waist and chest.

Here the limited omniscient point of view has the advantage of allowing the narrator to focus on the thoughts, fears, and reactions of the child while at the same

time giving readers information about Andy that she herself is too immature or unsophisticated to know. Rather than simply presenting the thoughts of the child (represented in the story by italics), the third-person narrator makes connections between ideas and displays a level of language and a degree of insight that readers would not accept from Andy as a first-person narrator. In addition, the limited omniscient perspective enables the narrator to maintain some distance.

First-Person Point of View (Child)

Consider how different the passage would be if it were narrated by nine-year-old Andy.

> "I like the woods," I thought. "They're big and scary. I wonder if they're the same woods that are behind my house. They go on for miles. They're bigger than I could walk in a day, or a week even." It was neat to think that while we were driving into the woods people were going to bed in other countries.
>
> When I woke up this morning, I couldn't wait to go hunting. My mother was cooking breakfast, but all I could think of was, "When will he come?" and "Won't he ever come?" Finally, I heard a car honk. "That will be Charlie Spoon," my father said. I think he called him "Charlie Spoon" because he thought Charlie was shaped like a big spoon.

As a first-person narrator, nine-year-old Andy must have the voice of a child; moreover, she is restricted to only those observations that a nine-year-old could reasonably make. Because of these limitations, the passage lacks the level of vocabulary, syntax, and insight necessary to develop the central character and the themes of the story. This point of view could succeed only if Andy's words established an ironic contrast between her naive sensibility and the reality of the situation.

First-Person Point of View (Adult)

Kaplan could have avoided these problems and still gained the advantages of using a first-person narrator by having Andy tell her story as an adult looking back on a childhood experience. (This technique is used by James Joyce in "Araby," p. 395; Charles Baxter in "Gryphon," p. 248; and Alberto Alvaro Ríos in "The Secret Lion," p. 170.)

> "They are always the same woods," I thought sleepily as we drove through the early morning darkness — deep and immense, covered with yesterday's snowfall, which had frozen overnight. "They're the same woods that lie behind my house, and they stretch all the way to here," I thought. I knew that they stretched for miles and miles, longer than I could walk in a day, or even in a week but that they were still the same woods. Knowing this made me feel good: I thought it was like thinking of God; it was like thinking of the space between that place and the moon; it was like thinking of all the foreign countries from my geography book where even then, I knew, people were going to bed, while we — my father and I and Charlie Spoon and Mac, Charlie's eleven-year-old son — were driving deeper into the Pennsylvania countryside, to go hunting.

> We had risen before dawn. My mother, who was yawning and not trying
> to hide her sleepiness, cooked us eggs and French toast. My father smoked a
> cigarette and flicked ashes into his saucer while I listened, wondering, "Why
> doesn't he come?" and "Won't he ever come?" until at last a car pulled into
> our driveway and honked. "That will be Charlie Spoon," my father said. He
> always said "Charlie Spoon," even though his real name was Spreun, because
> Charlie was, in a sense, shaped like a spoon, with a large head and a narrow
> waist and chest.

Although this passage presents the child's point of view, it does not use a child's
voice; the language and scope of the passage are too sophisticated for a child. By
using a mature style, the adult narrator considers ideas that a child could not possibly understand, such as the symbolic significance of the woods. In so doing, however, he sacrifices the degree of objectivity that characterizes the third-person
limited omniscient narrator of the original story.

Omniscient Point of View

Kaplan could also have used an omniscient narrator to tell his story. In this case,
the narrator would be free to reveal and comment not only on Andy's thoughts
but also on those of her father, and possibly even on the thoughts of her mother
and Charlie Spoon.

In the following passage, the omniscient narrator interprets the behavior of
the characters and tells what each one is thinking.

> They were always the same woods, she thought sleepily as they drove through
> the early morning darkness — deep and immense, covered with yesterday's
> snowfall, which had frozen overnight. They were the same woods that lay
> behind her house, and they stretch all the way to here, she thought, for miles
> and miles, longer than I could walk in a day, or a week even, but they are still
> the same woods.
>   They had risen before dawn. The mother, yawning and not trying to hide
> her sleepiness, cooked them eggs and French toast. She looked at her husband
> and her daughter and wondered if she was doing the right thing by allowing
> them to go hunting together. "After all," she thought, "he's not the most
> careful person. Will he watch her? Make sure that no harm comes to her?"
>   The father smoked a cigarette and flicked ashes into his saucer. He was
> listening to the sounds of the early morning. "I know everything will be all
> right," he thought. "It's about time Andy went hunting. When I was her
> age. . . ." Andy listened, wondering Why doesn't he come? and Won't he ever
> come? until at last a car pulled into the graveled drive and honked. Suddenly
> the father cocked his head and said, "That will be Charlie Spoon."
>   Andy thought it was funny that her father called Charlie "Spoon" even
> though his real name was Spreun, because Charlie was, in a sense, shaped like
> a spoon, with a large head and a narrow waist and chest.

Certainly this point of view has its advantages; for example, the wide scope of
this perspective provides a great deal of information about the characters.
However, the use of an omniscient point of view deprives the story of its focus
on Andy.

Objective Point of View

Finally, Kaplan could have used an objective narrator. This point of view would eliminate all interpretation by the narrator and force readers to make judgments solely on the basis of what the characters say and do.

> Andy sat sleepily staring into her cereal. She played with the dry flakes of bran as they floated in the surface of the milk.
>
> Andy's mother, yawning, cooked them eggs and French toast. She looked at her husband and her daughter, paused for a second, and then went about what she was doing.
>
> Andy's father smoked a cigarette and flicked ashes into his saucer. He looked out the window and said, "I wonder where Charlie Spoon is?"
>
> Andy squirmed restlessly and repeatedly looked up at the clock that hung above the stove.

The disadvantage of this point of view is that it creates a great deal of distance between the characters and the readers. Instead of gaining the intimate knowledge of Andy that the limited omniscient point of view provides — knowledge even greater than she herself has — readers must infer what she thinks and feels without any help from the narrator.

✔ **CHECKLIST   Selecting an Appropriate Point of View: Review**

First-Person Narrators (use *I* or *WE*)

▶ *Major character telling his or her own story*   "Every morning I lay on the floor in the front parlour watching her door." (James Joyce, "Araby")

▶ *Minor character as witness*   "And so she died. . . . We did not even know she was sick; we had long since given up trying to get information. . . ." (William Faulkner, "A Rose for Emily")

Third-Person Narrators (use *HE, SHE,* and *THEY*)

▶ *Omniscient — able to move at will from character to character and comment about them*   "In a house, in a suburb, in a city, there were a man and his wife who loved each other very much. . . ." (Nadine Gordimer, "Once upon a Time")

▶ *Limited Omniscient — restricts focus to a single character*   "The wagon went on. He did not know where they were going." (William Faulkner, "Barn Burning")

▶ *Objective (Dramatic) — simply reports the dialogue and the actions of characters*   "'You'll be drunk,' the waiter said. The old man looked at him. The waiter went away." (Ernest Hemingway, "A Clean, Well-Lighted Place")

> ✔ **CHECKLIST   Writing about Point of View**
>
> ☐ What is the dominant point of view from which the story is told?
>
> ☐ Is the narrator a character in the story? If so, is he or she a participant in the story's events or just a witness?
>
> ☐ Does the story's point of view create irony?
>
> ☐ If the story has a first-person narrator, is the narrator reliable or unreliable? Are there any inconsistencies in the narrator's presentation of the story?
>
> ☐ If the story has a third-person narrator, is he or she omniscient? Does he or she have limited omniscience? Is the narrator objective?
>
> ☐ What are the advantages of the story's point of view? How does the point of view accomplish the author's purpose?
>
> ☐ Does the point of view remain consistent throughout the story, or does it shift?
>
> ☐ How might a different point of view change the story?

RICHARD WRIGHT (1908–1960) was born near Natchez, Mississippi, the son of sharecroppers. He had little formal schooling but as a young man was a voracious reader, especially of naturalistic fiction. Relocating to Chicago in the late 1920s, Wright worked as a postal clerk until 1935, when he joined the Federal Writers' Project, an association that took him to New York City. Deeply troubled by the economic and social oppression of African-Americans, Wright joined the Communist Party in 1932, and his early poems and stories reflect a distinctly Marxist perspective. In 1944, he broke with the party because of its stifling effect on his creativity."

Wright began to reach a mainstream audience when a group of four long stories on the theme of racial oppression and violence was judged best manuscript in a contest sponsored by *Story* magazine; these stories were published as *Uncle Tom's Children* in 1938. Two years later, Wright published his most famous work, *Native Son,* an angry and brutal novel exploring the moral devastation wrought by a racist society. The autobiographical *Black Boy* was published in 1945. In later years, Wright abandoned the United States for Paris in protest against the treatment of African-Americans in his native country and focused his work on reports about national independence movements in Africa and elsewhere in the third world.

The following story, published in the posthumous collection *Eight Men* (1961), is uncharacteristic of Wright's work in a number of ways — not least of which is that it is told through the eyes of a white protagonist.

Cultural Context In 1957, the year "Big Black Good Man" was written, President Eisenhower sent paratroopers to Little Rock, Arkansas, to forestall violence over desegregation of the public schools. The crisis began on September 2, when Governor Orval Faubus ordered the Arkansas National Guard to blockade Central High School in Little Rock to prevent the entrance of nine black students. On September 20, NAACP lawyers Thurgood Marshall and Wiley Brandon obtained an injunction from the federal district court that ordered the troops removed. On September 25, the students entered the school, escorted by members of the 101st Airborne Division of the United States Army.

Big Black Good Man   (1957)

Through the open window Olaf Jenson could smell the sea and hear the occasional foghorn of a freighter; outside, rain pelted down through an August night, drumming softly upon the pavements of Copenhagen,° inducing drowsiness, bringing dreamy memory, relaxing the tired muscles of his work-wracked body. He sat slumped in a swivel chair with his legs outstretched and his feet propped atop an edge of his desk. An inch of white ash tipped the end of his brown cigar and now and then he inserted the end of the stogie° into his mouth and drew gently upon it, letting wisps of blue smoke eddy from the corners of his wide, thin lips. The watery gray irises behind the thick lenses of his eyeglasses gave him a look of abstraction, of absentmindedness, of an almost genial idiocy. He sighed, reached for his half-empty bottle of beer, and drained it into his glass and downed it with a long slow gulp, then licked his lips. Replacing the cigar, he slapped his right palm against his thigh and said half aloud:

"Well, I'll be sixty tomorrow. I'm not rich, but I'm not poor either . . . Really, I can't complain. Got good health. Traveled all over the world and had my share of girls when I was young . . . And my Karen's a good wife. I own my home. Got no debts. And I love digging in my garden in the spring . . . Grew the biggest carrots of anybody last year. Ain't saved much money, but what the hell . . . Money ain't everything. Got a good job. Night portering ain't too bad." He shook his head and yawned. "Karen and I could of had some children, though. Would of been good company . . . 'Specially for Karen. And I could of taught 'em languages . . . English, French, German, Danish, Dutch, Swedish, Norwegian, and Spanish . . ." He took the cigar out of his mouth and eyed the white ash critically. "Hell of a lot of good language learning did me . . . Never got anything out of it. But those ten years in New York were fun . . . Maybe I could of got rich if I'd stayed in America . . . Maybe. But I'm satisfied. You can't have everything."

Copenhagen: The capital of Denmark.
stogie: A cheap cigar.

Behind him the office door opened and a young man, a medical student occupying room number nine, entered.

"Good evening," the student said.

5   "Good evening," Olaf said, turning.

The student went to the keyboard and took hold of the round, brown knob that anchored his key.

"Rain, rain, rain," the student said.

"That's Denmark for you," Olaf smiled at him.

"This dampness keeps me clogged up like a drainpipe," the student complained.

10   "That's Denmark for you," Olaf repeated with a smile.

"Good night," the student said.

"Good night, son," Olaf sighed, watching the door close.

Well, my tenants are my children, Olaf told himself. Almost all of his children were in their rooms now . . . Only seventy-two and forty-four were missing . . . Seventy-two might've gone to Sweden . . . And forty-four was maybe staying at his girl's place tonight, like he sometimes did . . . He studied the pear-shaped blobs of hard rubber, reddish brown like ripe fruit, that hung from the keyboard, then glanced at his watch. Only room thirty, eighty-one, and one hundred and one were empty . . . And it was almost midnight. In a few moments he could take a nap. Nobody hardly ever came looking for accommodations after midnight, unless a stray freighter came in, bringing thirsty, women-hungry sailors. Olaf chuckled softly. Why in hell was I ever a sailor? The whole time I was at sea I was thinking and dreaming about women. Then why didn't I stay on land where women could be had? Huh? Sailors are crazy . . .

But he liked sailors. They reminded him of his youth, and there was something so direct, simple, and childlike about them. They always said straight out what they wanted, and what they wanted was almost always women and whisky . . . "Well, there's no harm in that . . . Nothing could be more natural," Olaf sighed, looking thirstily at his empty beer bottle. No; he'd not drink any more tonight; he'd had enough; he'd go to sleep . . .

15   He was bending forward and loosening his shoelaces when he heard the office door crack open. He lifted his eyes, then sucked in his breath. He did not straighten; he just stared up and around at the huge black thing that filled the doorway. His reflexes refused to function; it was not fear; it was just simple astonishment. He was staring at the biggest, strangest, and blackest man he'd ever seen in all his life.

"Good evening," the black giant said in a voice that filled the small office. "Say, you got a room?"

Olaf sat up slowly, not to answer but to look at this brooding black vision; it towered darkly some six and a half feet into the air, almost touching the ceiling, and its skin was so black that it had a bluish tint. And the sheer bulk of the man! . . . His chest bulged like a barrel; his rocklike and humped shoulders hinted of mountain ridges; the stomach ballooned like a threatening stone; and the legs were like telephone poles . . . The big black cloud of a man now lumbered into the office, bending to get its buffalolike head under the door frame, then advanced slowly upon Olaf, like a stormy sky descending.

"You got a room?" the big black man asked again in a resounding voice.

Olaf now noticed that the ebony giant was well dressed, carried a wonderful new suitcase, and wore black shoes that gleamed despite the raindrops that peppered their toes.

"You're American?" Olaf asked him. 20

"Yeah, man; sure," the black giant answered.

"Sailor?"

"Yeah. American Continental Lines."

Olaf had not answered the black man's question. It was not that the hotel did not admit men of color; Olaf took in all comers — blacks, yellows, whites, and browns . . . To Olaf, men were men, and, in his day, he'd worked and eaten and slept and fought with all kinds of men. But this particular black man . . . Well, he didn't seem human. Too big, too black, too loud, too direct, and probably too violent to boot . . . Olaf's five feet seven inches scarcely reached the black giant's shoulder and his frail body weighed less, perhaps, than one of the man's gigantic legs . . . There was something about the man's intense blackness and ungainly bigness that frightened and insulted Olaf; he felt as though this man had come here expressly to remind him how puny, how tiny, and how weak and how white he was. Olaf knew, while registering his reactions, that he was being irrational and foolish; yet, for the first time in his life, he was emotionally determined to refuse a man a room solely on the basis of the man's size and color . . . Olaf's lips parted as he groped for the right words in which to couch his refusal, but the black giant bent forward and boomed:

"I asked you if you got a room. I got to put up somewhere tonight, man." 25

"Yes, we got a room," Olaf murmured.

And at once he was ashamed and confused. Sheer fear had made him yield. And he seethed against himself for his involuntary weakness. Well, he'd look over his book and pretend that he'd made a mistake; he'd tell this hunk of blackness that there was really no free room in the hotel, and that he was so sorry . . . Then, just as he took out the hotel register to make believe that he was poring over it, a thick roll of American bank notes, crisp and green, was thrust under his nose.

"Keep this for me, will you?" the black giant commanded. "Cause I'm gonna get drunk tonight and I don't wanna lose it."

Olaf stared at the roll; it was huge, in denominations of fifties and hundreds. Olaf's eyes widened.

"How much is there?" he asked.

"Two thousand six hundred," the giant said. "Just put it into an envelope and 30 write 'Jim' on it and lock it in your safe, hunh?"

The black mass of man had spoken in a manner that indicated that it was taking it for granted that Olaf would obey. Olaf was licked. Resentment clogged the pores of his wrinkled white skin. His hands trembled as he picked up the money. No; he couldn't refuse this man . . . The impulse to deny him was strong, but each time he was about to act upon it something thwarted him, made him shy off. He clutched about desperately for an idea. Oh yes, he could say that if he planned to stay for only one night, then he could not have the room, for it was against the policy of the hotel to rent rooms for only one night . . .

"How long are you staying? Just tonight?" Olaf asked.

"Naw. I'll be here for five or six days, I reckon," the giant answered off handedly.

35 "You take room number thirty," Olaf heard himself saying. "It's forty kroner a day."

"That's all right with me," the giant said.

With slow, stiff movements, Olaf put the money in the safe and then turned and stared helplessly up into the living, breathing blackness looming above him. Suddenly he became conscious of the outstretched palm of the black giant; he was silently demanding the key to the room. His eyes downcast, Olaf surrendered the key, marveling at the black man's tremendous hands . . . He could kill me with one blow, Olaf told himself in fear.

Feeling himself beaten, Olaf reached for the suitcase, but the black hand of the giant whisked it out of his grasp.

"That's too heavy for you, big boy; I'll take it," the giant said.

40 Olaf let him. He thinks I'm nothing . . . He led the way down the corridor, sensing the giant's lumbering presence behind him. Olaf opened the door of number thirty and stood politely to one side, allowing the black giant to enter. At once the room seemed like a doll's house, so dwarfed and filled and tiny it was with a great living blackness . . . Flinging his suitcase upon a chair, the giant turned. The two men looked directly at each other now. Olaf saw that the giant's eyes were tiny and red, buried, it seemed, in muscle and fat. Black cheeks spread, flat and broad, topping the wide and flaring nostrils. The mouth was the biggest that Olaf had ever seen on a human face; the lips were thick, pursed, parted, showing snow-white teeth. The black neck was like a bull's . . . The giant advanced upon Olaf and stood over him.

"I want a bottle of whiskey and a woman," he said. "Can you fix me up?"

"Yes," Olaf whispered, wild with anger and insult.

But what was he angry about? He'd had requests like this every night from all sorts of men and he was used to fulfilling them; he was a night porter in a cheap, water-front Copenhagen hotel that catered to sailors and students. Yes, men needed women, but this man, Olaf felt, ought to have a special sort of woman. He felt a deep and strange reluctance to phone any of the women whom he habitually sent to men. Yet he had promised. Could he lie and say that none was available? No. That sounded too fishy. The black giant sat upon the bed, staring straight before him. Olaf moved about quickly, pulling down the window shades, taking the pink coverlet off the bed, nudging the giant with his elbow to make him move as he did so . . . That's the way to treat 'im . . . Show 'im I ain't scared of 'im . . . But he was still seeking for an excuse to refuse. And he could think of nothing. He felt hypnotized, mentally immobilized. He stood hesitantly at the door.

"You send the whiskey and the woman quick, pal?" the black giant asked, rousing himself from a brooding stare.

"Yes," Olaf grunted, shutting the door.

45 Goddamn, Olaf sighed. He sat in his office at his desk before the phone. Why did *he* have to come here? . . . I'm not prejudiced . . . No, not at all . . . But . . . He couldn't think any more. God oughtn't make men as big and black as that . . . But

what the hell was he worrying about? He'd sent women of all races to men of all colors . . . So why not a woman to the black giant? Oh, only if the man were small, brown, and intelligent-looking . . . Olaf felt trapped.

With a reflex movement of his hand, he picked up the phone and dialed Lena. She was big and strong and always cut him in for fifteen per cent instead of the usual ten per cent. Lena had four small children to feed and clothe. Lena was willing; she was, she said, coming over right now. She didn't give a good goddamn about how big and black the man was . . .

"Why you ask me that?" Lena wanted to know over the phone. "You never asked that before . . ."

"But this one is *big*," Olaf found himself saying.

"He's just a man," Lena told him, her voice singing stridently, laughingly over the wire. "You just leave that to me. You don't have to do anything. *I'll* handle 'im."

Lena had a key to the hotel door downstairs, but tonight Olaf stayed awake.   50 He wanted to see her. Why? He didn't know. He stretched out on the sofa in his office, but sleep was far from him. When Lena arrived, he told her again how big and black the man was.

"You told me that over the phone," Lena reminded him.

Olaf said nothing. Lena flounced off on her errand of mercy. Olaf shut the office door, then opened it and left it ajar. But why? He didn't know. He lay upon the sofa and stared at the ceiling. He glanced at his watch; it was almost two o'clock . . . She's staying in there a long time . . . Ah, God, but he could do with a drink . . . Why was he so damned worked up and nervous about a nigger and a white whore? . . . He'd never been so upset in all his life. Before he knew it, he had drifted off to sleep. Then he heard the office door swinging creakingly open on its rusty hinges. Lena stood in it, grim and businesslike, her face scrubbed free of powder and rouge. Olaf scrambled to his feet, adjusting his eyeglasses, blinking.

"How was it?" he asked her in a confidential whisper.

Lena's eyes blazed.

"What the hell's that to you?" she snapped. "There's your cut," she said, fling-   55 ing him his money, tossing it upon the covers of the sofa. "You're sure nosy tonight. You wanna take over my work?"

Olaf's pasty cheeks burned red.

"You go to hell," he said, slamming the door.

"I'll meet you there!" Lena's shouting voice reached him dimly.

He was being a fool; there was no doubt about it. But, try as he might, he could not shake off a primitive hate for that black mountain of energy, of muscle, of bone; he envied the easy manner in which it moved with such a creeping and powerful motion; he winced at the booming and commanding voice that came to him when the tiny little eyes were not even looking at him; he shivered at the sight of those vast and clawlike hands that seemed always to hint of death . . .

Olaf kept his counsel. He never spoke to Karen about the sordid doings at the   60 hotel. Such things were not for women like Karen. He knew instinctively that Karen would have been amazed had he told her that he was worried sick about a nigger and a blonde whore . . . No; he couldn't talk to anybody about it, not even the hard-bitten° old bitch who owned the hotel. She was concerned only about money; she didn't give a damn about how big and how black a client was as long as he paid his room rent.

Next evening, when Olaf arrived for duty, there was no sight or sound of the black giant. A little later after one o'clock in the morning he appeared, left his key, and went out wordlessly. A few moments past two the giant returned, took his key from the board, and paused.

"I want that Lena again tonight. And another bottle of whiskey," he said boomingly.

"I'll call her and see if she's in," Olaf said.

"Do that," the black giant said and was gone.

65   He thinks he's God, Olaf fumed. He picked up the phone and ordered Lena and a bottle of whiskey, and there was a taste of ashes in his mouth. On the third night came the same request: Lena and whiskey. When the black giant appeared on the fifth night, Olaf was about to make a sarcastic remark to the effect that maybe he ought to marry Lena, but he checked it in time . . . After all, he could kill me with one hand, he told himself.

Olaf was nervous and angry with himself for being nervous. Other black sailors came and asked for girls and Olaf sent them, but with none of the fear and loathing that he sent Lena and a bottle of whiskey to the giant . . . All right, the black giant's stay was almost up. He'd said that he was staying for five or six nights; tomorrow night was the sixth night and that ought to be the end of this nameless terror.

On the sixth night Olaf sat in his swivel chair with his bottle of beer and waited, his teeth on edge, his fingers drumming the desk. But what the hell am I fretting for? . . . The hell with 'im . . . Olaf sat and dozed. Occasionally he'd awaken and listen to the foghorns of freighters sounding as ships came and went in the misty Copenhagen harbor. He was half asleep when he felt a rough hand on his shoulder. He blinked his eyes open. The giant, black and vast and powerful, all but blotted out his vision.

"What I owe you, man?" the giant demanded. "And I want my money."

"Sure," Olaf said, relieved, but filled as always with fear of this living wall of black flesh.

70   With fumbling hands, he made out the bill and received payment, then gave the giant his roll of money, laying it on the desk so as not to let his hands touch the flesh of the black mountain. Well, his ordeal was over. It was past two o'clock in the morning. Olaf even managed a wry smile and muttered a guttural "Thanks" for the generous tip that the giant tossed him.

Then a strange tension entered the office. The office door was shut and Olaf was alone with the black mass of power, yearning for it to leave. But the black mass of power stood still, immobile, looking down at Olaf. And Olaf could not, for the life of him, guess at what was transpiring in that mysterious black mind. The two of them simply stared at each other for a full two minutes, the giant's tiny little beady eyes blinking slowly as they seemed to measure and search Olaf's face. Olaf's vision dimmed for a second as terror seized him and he could feel a flush of

---

hard-bitten: Stubborn, tough.

heat overspread his body. Then Olaf sucked in his breath as the devil of blackness commanded:

"Stand up!"

Olaf was paralyzed. Sweat broke on his face. His worst premonitions about this black beast were coming true. This evil blackness was about to attack him, maybe kill him . . . Slowly Olaf shook his head, his terror permitting him to breathe:

"What're you talking about?"

"Stand up, I say!" the black giant bellowed.   75

As though hypnotized, Olaf tried to rise; then he felt the black paw of the beast helping him roughly to his feet.

They stood an inch apart. Olaf's pasty-white features were glued to the giant's swollen black face. The ebony ensemble of eyes and nose and mouth and cheeks looked down at Olaf, silently; then, with a slow and deliberate movement of his gorillalike arms, he lifted his mammoth hands to Olaf's throat. Olaf had long known and felt that this dreadful moment was coming; he felt trapped in a nightmare. He could not move. He wanted to scream, but could find no words. His lips refused to open; his tongue felt icy and inert. Then he knew that his end had come when the giant's black fingers slowly, softly encircled his throat while a horrible grin of delight broke out on the sooty face . . . Olaf lost control of the reflexes of his body and he felt a hot stickiness flooding his underwear . . . He stared without breathing, gazing into the grinning blackness of the face that was bent over him, feeling the black fingers caressing his throat and waiting to feel the sharp, stinging ache and pain of the bones in his neck being snapped, crushed . . . He knew all along that I hated 'im . . . Yes, and now he's going to kill me for it, Olaf told himself with despair.

The black fingers still circled Olaf's neck, not closing, but gently massaging it, as it were, moving to and fro, while the obscene face grinned into his. Olaf could feel the giant's warm breath blowing on his eyelashes and he felt like a chicken about to have its neck wrung and its body tossed to flip and flap dyingly in the dust of the barnyard . . . Then suddenly the black giant withdrew his fingers from Olaf's neck and stepped back a pace, still grinning. Olaf sighed, trembling, his body seeming to shrink; he waited. Shame sheeted him for the hot wetness that was in his trousers. Oh, God, he's teasing me . . . He's showing me how easily he can kill me . . . He swallowed, waiting, his eyes stones of gray.

The giant's barrel-like chest gave forth a low, rumbling chuckle of delight.

"You laugh?" Olaf asked whimperingly.   80

"Sure I laugh," the giant shouted.

"Please don't hurt me," Olaf managed to say.

"I wouldn't hurt you, boy," the giant said in a tone of mockery. "So long."

And he was gone. Olaf fell limply into the swivel chair and fought off losing consciousness. Then he wept. He was showing me how easily he could kill me . . . He made me shake with terror and then laughed and left . . . Slowly, Olaf recovered, stood, then gave vent to a string of curses:

"Goddamn 'im! My gun's right there in the desk drawer; I should of shot 'im.   85 Jesus, I hope the ship he's on sinks . . . I hope he drowns and the sharks eat 'im . . ."

Later, he thought of going to the police, but sheer shame kept him back; and, anyway, the giant was probably on board his ship by now. And he had to get home and clean himself. Oh, Lord, what could he tell Karen? Yes, he would say that his stomach had been upset . . . He'd change clothes and return to work. He phoned the hotel owner that he was ill and wanted an hour off; the old bitch said that she was coming right over and that poor Olaf could have the evening off.

Olaf went home and lied to Karen. Then he lay awake the rest of the night dreaming of revenge. He saw that freighter on which the giant was sailing; he saw it springing a dangerous leak and saw a torrent of sea water flooding, gushing into all the compartments of the ship until it found the bunk in which the black giant slept. Ah, yes, the foamy, surging waters would surprise that sleeping black bastard of a giant and he would drown, gasping and choking like a trapped rat, his tiny eyes bulging until they glittered red, the bitter water of the sea pounding his lungs until they ached and finally burst . . . The ship would sink slowly to the bottom of the cold, black, silent depths of the sea and a shark, a *white* one, would glide aimlessly about the shut portholes until it found an open one and it would slither inside and nose about until it found that swollen, rotting, stinking carcass of the black beast and it would then begin to nibble at the decomposing mass of tarlike flesh, eating the bones clean . . . Olaf always pictured the giant's bones as being jet black and shining.

Once or twice, during these fantasies of cannibalistic revenge, Olaf felt a little guilty about all the many innocent people, women and children, all white and blonde, who would have to go down into watery graves in order that that white shark could devour the evil giant's black flesh . . . But, despite feelings of remorse, the fantasy lived persistently on, and when Olaf found himself alone, it would crowd and cloud his mind to the exclusion of all else, affording him the only revenge he knew. To make me suffer just for the pleasure of it, he fumed. Just to show me how strong he was . . . Olaf learned how to hate, and got pleasure out of it.

Summer fled on wings of rain. Autumn flooded Denmark with color. Winter made rain and snow fall on Copenhagen. Finally spring came, bringing violets and roses. Olaf kept to his job. For many months he feared the return of the black giant. But when a year had passed and the giant had not put in an appearance, Olaf allowed his revenge fantasy to peter out, indulging in it only when recalling the shame that the black monster had made him feel.

90   Then one rainy August night, a year later, Olaf sat drowsing at his desk, his bottle of beer before him, tilting back in his swivel chair, his feet resting atop a corner of his desk, his mind mulling over the more pleasant aspects of his life. The office door cracked open. Olaf glanced boredly up and around. His heart jumped and skipped a beat. The black nightmare of terror and shame that he had hoped that he had lost forever was again upon him . . . Resplendently dressed, suitcase in hand, the black looming mountain filled the doorway. Olaf's thin lips parted and a silent moan, half a curse, escaped them.

"Hi," the black giant boomed from the doorway.

Olaf could not reply. But a sudden resolve swept him: this time he would even the score. If this black beast came within so much as three feet of him, he would snatch his gun out of the drawer and shoot him dead, so help him God . . .

"No rooms tonight," Olaf heard himself announcing in a determined voice.

The black giant grinned; it was the same infernal grimace of delight and triumph that he had had when his damnable black fingers had been around his throat . . .

"Don't want no room tonight," the giant announced.   95

"Then what are you doing here?" Olaf asked in a loud but tremulous voice.

The giant swept toward Olaf and stood over him; and Olaf could not move, despite his oath to kill him . . .

"What do you want then?" Olaf demanded once more, ashamed that he could not lift his voice above a whisper.

The giant still grinned, then tossed what seemed the same suitcase upon Olaf's sofa and bent over it; he zippered it open with a sweep of his clawlike hand and rummaged in it, drawing forth a flat, gleaming white object done up in glowing cellophane. Olaf watched with lowered lids, wondering what trick was now being played on him. Then, before he could defend himself, the giant had whirled and again long, black, snakelike fingers were encircling Olaf's throat . . . Olaf stiffened, his right hand clawing blindly for the drawer where the gun was kept. But the giant was quick.

"Wait," he bellowed, pushing Olaf back from the desk.   100

The giant turned quickly to the sofa and, still holding his fingers in a wide circle that seemed a noose for Olaf's neck, he inserted the rounded fingers into the top of the flat, gleaming object. Olaf had the drawer open and his sweaty fingers were now touching the gun, but something made him freeze. The flat, gleaming object was a shirt and the black giant's circled fingers were fitting themselves into its neck . . .

"A perfect fit!" the giant shouted.

Olaf stared, trying to understand. His fingers loosened about the gun. A mixture of a laugh and a curse struggled in him. He watched the giant plunge his hands into the suitcase and pull out other flat, gleaming shirts.

"One, two, three, four, five, six," the black giant intoned, his voice crisp and businesslike. "Six nylon shirts. And they're all yours. One shirt for each time Lena came . . . See, Daddy-O?"

The black, cupped hands, filled with billowing nylon whiteness, were ex-   105
tended under Olaf's nose. Olaf eased his damp fingers from his gun and pushed the drawer closed, staring at the shirts and then at the black giant's grinning face.

"Don't you like 'em?" the giant asked.

Olaf began to laugh hysterically, then suddenly he was crying, his eyes so flooded with tears that the pile of dazzling nylon looked like snow in the dead of winter. Was this true? Could he believe it? Maybe this too was a trick? But, no. There were six shirts, all nylon, and the black giant had had Lena six nights.

"What's the matter with you, Daddy-O?" the giant asked. "You blowing your top? Laughing and crying . . ."

Olaf swallowed, dabbed his withered fists at his dimmed eyes; then he realized that he had his glasses on. He took them off and dried his eyes and sat up. He sighed, the tension and shame and fear and haunting dread of his fantasy went from him, and he leaned limply back in his chair . . .

"Try one on," the giant ordered.   110

Olaf fumbled with the buttons of his shirt, let down his suspenders, and pulled the shirt off. He donned a gleaming nylon one and the giant began buttoning it for him.

"Perfect, Daddy-O," the giant said.

His spectacled face framed in sparkling nylon, Olaf sat with trembling lips. So he'd not been trying to kill me after all.

"You want Lena, don't you?" he asked the giant in a soft whisper. "But I don't know where she is. She never came back here after you left —"

115   "I know where Lena is," the giant told him. "We been writing to each other. I'm going to her house. And, Daddy-O, I'm late." The giant zippered the suitcase shut and stood a moment gazing down at Olaf, his tiny little red eyes blinking slowly. Then Olaf realized that there was a compassion in that stare that he had never seen before.

"And I thought you wanted to kill me," Olaf told him. "I was scared of you . . ."

"Me? Kill you?" the giant blinked. "When?"

"That night when you put your fingers around my throat —"

"What?" the giant asked, then roared with laughter. "Daddy-O, you're a funny little man. I wouldn't hurt you. I like you. You a *good* man. You helped me."

120   Olaf smiled, clutching the pile of nylon shirts in his arms.

"You're a good man too," Olaf murmured. Then loudly, "You're a big black good man."

"Daddy-O, you're crazy," the giant said.

He swept his suitcase from the sofa, spun on his heel, and was at the door in one stride.

"Thanks!" Olaf cried after him.

125   The black giant paused, turned his vast black head, and flashed a grin.

"Daddy-O, drop dead," he said and was gone.

Reading and Reacting

1. Why do you suppose Wright presents events through Olaf's eyes? How would the story be different if the sailor told it?

2. This story was published in 1957. What attitudes about race does Wright expect his American readers to have? Do these attitudes predispose readers to identify with the sailor or with Olaf? Explain.

3. Why does Olaf dislike the sailor? What does the narrator mean in paragraph 24 when he says that the sailor's "intense blackness and ungainly bigness . . . frightened and insulted Olaf"?

4. In what ways do the sailor's words and actions contribute to Olaf's fears? Do you think Olaf's reactions are reasonable, or do you believe he is overreacting?

5. The sailor's name is Jim, but this name is almost never used in the story. Why not? List some words used to describe Jim. Why are these words used? How do they affect your reaction to Jim?

6. Do you think the story's title is ironic? In what other respects is the story ironic?

7. How would "Big Black Good Man" be different if Jim were white? Would there even *be* a story?

8. Why do you think Wright set the story in Copenhagen? Could it have been set in the United States in 1957?

9. What do you think Jim thinks of Olaf? Do you suppose he realizes the effect he has on him? How do you explain Jim's last comment?

10. **JOURNAL ENTRY** What point do you think the story makes about racial prejudice? Do you think Wright seems optimistic or pessimistic about race relations in the United States?

11. **CRITICAL PERSPECTIVE** In his 1982 article "The Short Stories: *Uncle Tom's Children, Eight Men,*" Edward Margolies notes that "Big Black Good Man" was somewhat of a departure for Wright:

> "Big Black Good Man," which first appeared in *Esquire* in 1957, is the last short story Wright published in his lifetime. Possibly it is the last he ever wrote. In any event it represents a more traditional approach to storytelling in that Wright here avoids confining himself exclusively to dialogue. On the other hand, "Big Black Good Man" deviates from the usual Wright short story. For one thing, the narrative, by Wright's standards at least, is practically pointless. Scarcely anything "happens." There is no violence, practically no external narrative action, and no change of milieu.

Do you agree that the story is "practically pointless"? If not, what point do you think the story makes?

Related Works: "Battle Royal" (p. 297), "The Lesson" (p. 642), "We Wear the Mask" (p. 1171), *The Brute* (p. 1293)

EDGAR ALLAN POE (1809–1849) profoundly influenced many writers all over the world. His tales of psychological terror and the macabre, his hauntingly musical lyric poems, and his writings on the craft of poetry and short story writing affected the development of symbolic fiction, the modern detective story, and the gothic horror tale. In most of Poe's horror tales (as in "The Cask of Amontillado"), readers vicariously "live" the story through the first-person narrator who tells the tale.

Poe was born in 1809, the son of a talented English-born actress who, deserted by her actor husband, died of tuberculosis before her son's third birthday. Although Poe was raised in material comfort by foster parents in Richmond, Virginia, his life was increasingly uncertain: his foster mother loved him, but her husband became antagonistic. He kept the young Poe so short of money at the University of Virginia (and later at West Point) that Poe resorted to gambling to raise money for food and clothing. Finally, disgraced and debt-ridden, he left school altogether.

Poe found work as a magazine editor, gaining recognition as a literary critic. In 1836, he married his frail thirteen-year-old cousin, Virginia Clemm. Poe produced many of his most famous stories and poems in the next few years, working feverishly to support his tubercular wife, but although his stories were widely admired, financial success never came. His wife died in 1847. Less than two years after her death, Poe was found barely conscious in a Baltimore street after a mysterious disappearance; three days later, he was dead at age forty.

> **Cultural Context** Throughout antiquity, catacombs, such as those in Poe's story, were used to bury the dead. Catacombs are subterranean cemeteries composed of passages with side recesses for tombs. The early Christian catacombs of Rome, consisting of approximately forty known chambers located in a rough circle about three miles from the center of the city, are the most extensive of all known catacombs. Funeral feasts were often celebrated in family vaults on the day of burial and on anniversary dates of the deaths of loved ones.

The Cask of Amontillado   (1846)

The thousand injuries of Fortunato I had borne as I best could, but when he ventured upon insult I vowed revenge. You, who so well know the nature of my soul, will not suppose, however, that I gave utterance to a threat. *At length* I would be avenged; this was a point definitely settled — but the very definitiveness with which it was resolved precluded the idea of risk. I must not only punish but punish with impunity. A wrong is unredressed when retribution overtakes its redresser. It is equally unredressed when the avenger fails to make himself felt as such to him who has done the wrong.

It must be understood that neither by word nor deed had I given Fortunato cause to doubt my good will. I continued, as was my wont, to smile in his face, and he did not perceive that my smile *now* was at the thought of his immolation.

He had a weak point — this Fortunato — although in other regards he was a man to be respected and even feared. He prided himself on his connoisseurship in wine. Few Italians have the true virtuoso spirit. For the most part their enthusiasm is adopted to suit the time and opportunity, to practise imposture upon the British and Austrian *millionaires.* In painting and gemmary, Fortunato, like his countrymen, was a quack, but in the matter of old wines he was sincere. In this respect I did not differ from him materially; — I was skillful in the Italian vintages myself, and bought largely whenever I could.

It was about dusk, one evening during the supreme madness of the carnival season, that I encountered my friend. He accosted me with excessive warmth, for he had been drinking much. The man wore motley.° He had on a tight-fitting parti-striped dress, and his head was surmounted by the conical cap and bells. I was so pleased to see him that I thought I should never have done wringing his hand.

5   I said to him — "My dear Fortunato, you are luckily met. How remarkably well you are looking to-day. But I have received a pipe° of what passes for Amontillado,° and I have my doubts."

"How?" said he. "Amontillado? A pipe? Impossible! And in the middle of the carnival!"

---

motley: The many-colored attire of a court jester.
pipe: In the United States and England, a cask containing a volume equal to 126 gallons.
Amontillado: A pale, dry sherry; literally, a wine "from Montilla" (Spain).

"I have my doubts," I replied; "and I was silly enough to pay the full Amontillado price without consulting you in the matter. You were not to be found, and I was fearful of losing a bargain."

"Amontillado!"

"I have my doubts."

"Amontillado!"

"And I must satisfy them."

"Amontillado!"

"As you are engaged, I am on my way to Luchresi. If any one has a critical turn it is he. He will tell me —"

"Luchresi cannot tell Amontillado from Sherry."

"And yet some fools will have it that his taste is a match for your own."

"Come, let us go."

"Whither?"

"To your vaults."

"My friend, no; I will not impose upon your good nature. I perceive you have an engagement. Luchresi —"

"I have no engagement; — come."

"My friend, no. It is not the engagement, but the severe cold with which I perceive you are afflicted. The vaults are insufferably damp. They are encrusted with nitre."°

"Let us go, nevertheless. The cold is merely nothing. Amontillado! You have been imposed upon. And as for Luchresi, he cannot distinguish Sherry from Amontillado."

Thus speaking, Fortunato possessed himself of my arm; and putting on a mask of black silk and drawing a *roquelaire*° closely about my person, I suffered him to hurry me to my palazzo.

There were no attendants at home; they had absconded to make merry in honor of the time. I had told them that I should not return until the morning, and had given them explicit orders not to stir from the house. These orders were sufficient, I well knew, to insure their immediate disappearance, one and all, as soon as my back was turned.

I took from their sconces two flambeaux, and giving one to Fortunato, bowed him through several suites of rooms to the archway that led into the vaults. I passed down a long and winding staircase, requesting him to be cautious as he followed. We came at length to the foot of the descent, and stood together upon the damp ground of the catacombs of the Montresors.

The gait of my friend was unsteady, and the bells upon his cap jingled as he strode.

"The pipe," he said.

"It is farther on," said I; "but observe the white web-work which gleams from these cavern walls."

---

nitre: Mineral deposits.

roquelaire: A short cloak.

He turned towards me, and looked into my eyes with two filmy orbs that distilled the rheum of intoxication.

30 "Nitre?" he asked at length.

"Nitre," I replied. "How long have you had that cough?"

"Ugh! ugh! ugh!—ugh! ugh! ugh!—ugh! ugh! ugh!—ugh! ugh! ugh!— ugh! ugh! ugh!"

My poor friend found it impossible to reply for many minutes.

"It is nothing," he said at last.

35 "Come," I said, with decision, "we will go back; your health is precious. You are rich, respected, admired, beloved; you are happy, as once I was. You are a man to be missed. For me it is no matter. We will go back; you will be ill, and I cannot be responsible. Besides, there is Luchresi —"

"Enough," he said; "the cough is a mere nothing; it will not kill me. I shall not die of a cough."

"True — true," I replied; "and, indeed, I had no intention of alarming you unnecessarily — but you should use all proper caution. A draught of this Médoc° will defend us from the damps."

Here I knocked off the neck of a bottle which I drew from a long row of its fellows that lay upon the mould.

"Drink," I said, presenting him the wine.

40 He raised it to his lips with a leer. He paused and nodded to me familiarly, while his bells jingled.

"I drink," he said, "to the buried that repose around us."

"And I to your long life."

He again took my arm, and we proceeded.

"These vaults," he said, "are extensive."

45 "The Montresors," I replied, "were a great and numerous family."

"I forget your arms."

"A huge human foot d'or, in a field azure; the foot crushes a serpent rampant whose fangs are imbedded in the heel."

"And the motto?"

50 "*Nemo me impune lacessit.*"°

"Good!" he said.

The wine sparkled in his eyes and the bells jingled. My own fancy grew warm with the Médoc. We had passed through long walls of piled skeletons, with casks and puncheons° intermingling, into the inmost recesses of the catacombs. I paused again, and this time I made bold to seize Fortunato by an arm above the elbow.

"The nitre!" I said; "see, it increases. It hangs like moss upon the vaults. We are below the river's bed. The drops of moisture trickle among the bones. Come, we will go back ere it is too late. Your cough —"

Médoc: A red wine from the Médoc district, near Bordeaux, France.

Nemo me impune lacessit: "No one insults me with impunity" (Latin); this is the legend on the royal coat of arms of Scotland.

puncheons: Barrels.

"It is nothing," he said; "let us go on. But first, another draught of the Médoc."

I broke and reached him a flagon of De Grâve.° He emptied it at a breath. His eyes flashed with a fierce light. He laughed and threw the bottle upwards with a gesticulation I did not understand.

I looked at him in surprise. He repeated the movement — a grotesque one.   55

"You do not comprehend?" he said.

"Not I," I replied.

"Then you are not of the brotherhood."

"How?"

"You are not of the masons."°   60

"Yes, yes," I said; "yes, yes."

"You? Impossible! A mason?"

"A mason," I replied.

"A sign," he said, "a sign."

"It is this," I answered, producing from beneath the folds of my *roquelaire* a   65
trowel.

"You jest," he exclaimed, recoiling a few paces. "But let us proceed to the Amontillado."

"Be it so," I said, replacing the tool beneath the cloak and again offering him my arm. He leaned upon it heavily. We continued our route in search of the Amontillado. We passed through a range of low arches, descended, passed on, and descending again, arrived at a deep crypt, in which the foulness of the air caused our flambeaux rather to glow than flame.

At the most remote end of the crypt there appeared another less spacious. Its walls had been lined with human remains, piled to the vault overhead, in the fashion of the great catacombs of Paris. Three sides of this interior crypt were still ornamented in this manner. From the fourth side the bones had been thrown down, and lay promiscuously upon the earth, forming at one point a mound of some size. Within the wall thus exposed by the displacing of the bones, we perceived a still interior crypt or recess, in depth about four feet, in width three, in height six or seven. It seemed to have been constructed for no especial use within itself, but formed merely the interval between two of the colossal supports of the roof of the catacombs, and was backed by one of their circumscribing walls of solid granite.

It was in vain that Fortunato, uplifting his dull torch, endeavored to pry into the depth of the recess. Its termination the feeble light did not enable us to see.

"Proceed," I said; "herein is the Amontillado. As for Luchresi — "   70

"He is an ignoramus," interrupted my friend, as he stepped unsteadily forward, while I followed immediately at his heels. In an instant he had reached the extremity of the niche, and finding his progress arrested by the rock, stood stupidly bewildered. A moment more and I had fettered him to the granite. In its

---

De Grâve: Correctly, "Graves," a light wine from the Bordeaux area.

masons: Freemasons (members of a secret fraternity). The trowel is a symbol of their alleged origin as a guild of stonemasons.

surface were two iron staples, distant from each other about two feet, horizontally. From one of these depended a short chain, from the other a padlock. Throwing the links about his waist, it was but the work of a few seconds to secure it. He was too much astounded to resist. Withdrawing the key I stepped back from the recess.

"Pass your hand," I said, "over the wall; you cannot help feeling the nitre. Indeed, it is *very* damp. Once more let me *implore* you to return. No? Then I must positively leave you. But I must first render you all the little attentions in my power."

"The Amontillado!" ejaculated my friend, not yet recovered from his astonishment.

75   "True," I replied; "the Amontillado."

As I said these words I busied myself among the pile of bones of which I have before spoken. Throwing them aside, I soon uncovered a quantity of building stone and mortar. With these materials and with the aid of my trowel, I began vigorously to wall up the entrance of the niche.

I had scarcely laid the first tier of the masonry when I discovered that the intoxication of Fortunato had in a great measure worn off. The earliest indication I had of this was a low moaning cry from the depth of the recess. It was *not* the cry of a drunken man. There was a long and obstinate silence. I laid the second tier, and the third, and the fourth; and then I heard the furious vibrations of the chain. The noise lasted for several minutes, during which, that I might hearken to it with the more satisfaction, I ceased my labors and sat down upon the bones. When at last the clanking subsided, I resumed the trowel, and finished without interruption the fifth, the sixth, and the seventh tier. The wall was now nearly upon a level with my breast. I again paused, and holding the flambeaux over the masonwork, threw a few feeble rays upon the figure within.

A succession of loud and shrill screams, bursting suddenly from the throat of the chained form, seemed to thrust me violently back. For a brief moment I hesitated, I trembled. Unsheathing my rapier, I began to grope with it about the recess; but the thought of an instant reassured me. I placed my hand upon the solid fabric of the catacombs, and felt satisfied. I reapproached the wall; I replied to the yells of him who clamoured. I re-echoed, I aided, I surpassed them in volume and in strength. I did this, and the clamourer grew still.

It was now midnight, and my task was drawing to a close. I had completed the eighth, the ninth and the tenth tier. I had finished a portion of the last and the eleventh; there remained but a single stone to be fitted and plastered in. I struggled with its weight; I placed it partially in its destined position. But now there came from out the niche a low laugh that erected the hairs upon my head. It was succeeded by a sad voice, which I had difficulty in recognizing as that of the noble Fortunato. The voice said —

"Ha! ha! ha! — he! he! he! — a very good joke, indeed — an excellent jest. We will have many a rich laugh about it at the palazzo — he! he! he! — over our

80   wine — he! he! he!"

"The Amontillado!" I said.

"He! he! he! — he! he! he! — yes, the Amontillado. But is it not getting late? Will not they be awaiting us at the palazzo, the Lady Fortunato and the rest? Let us be gone."

"Yes," I said, "let us be gone."

"For the love of God, Montresor!"

"Yes," I said, "for the love of God."

But to these words I hearkened in vain for a reply. I grew impatient. I called aloud —

85

"Fortunato!"

No answer. I called again —

"Fortunato!"

No answer still. I thrust a torch through the remaining aperture and let it fall within. There came forth in return only a jingling of the bells. My heart grew sick; it was the dampness of the catacombs that made it so. I hastened to make an end of my labour. I forced the last stone into its position; I plastered it up. Against the new masonry I re-erected the old rampart of bones. For the half of a century no mortal has disturbed them. *In pace requiescat!*°

Reading and Reacting

1. Montresor cites a "thousand injuries" and an "insult" as his motivation for murdering Fortunato. Given what you learn about the two men during the course of the story, what do you suppose the "injuries" and "insult" might be?

2. Do you find Montresor to be a reliable narrator? If not, what makes you question his version of events?

3. What is Montresor's concept of personal honor? Is it consistent or inconsistent with the values of contemporary American society? How relevant are the story's ideas about revenge and guilt to present-day society? Explain.

4. Does Fortunato ever understand why Montresor hates him? What is Fortunato's attitude toward Montresor?

5. What is the significance of Montresor's family coat of arms and motto? What is the significance of Fortunato's costume?

6. In what ways does Montresor manipulate Fortunato? What weaknesses does Montresor exploit?

7. Why does Montresor wait fifty years to tell his story? How might the story be different if he had told it the morning after the murder?

8. Why does Montresor wait for a reply before he puts the last stone in position? What do you think he wants Fortunato to say?

9. **JOURNAL ENTRY** Do you think the use of a first-person point of view makes you more sympathetic toward Montresor than you would be if his story were told by a third-person narrator? Why or why not?

10. **CRITICAL PERSPECTIVE** In his discussion of this story in *Edgar Allan Poe: A Study of the Short Fiction*, Charles E. May says, "We can legitimately hypothesize that the listener is a priest and that Montresor is an old man who is dying and making final confession. . . ."

Do you agree or disagree with May's hypothesis? Do you think that Montresor has atoned for his sin? Who else could be listening to Montresor's story?

---

pace requiescat: "May he rest in peace" (Latin).

Related Works: "A Rose for Emily" (p. 216), "Porphyria's Lover" (p. 876), *Tape* (p. 1313), *Trifles* (p. 1372)

WILLIAM FAULKNER (1897–1962) (picture and biography on p. 215) "Barn Burning" (1939) marks the first appearance of the Snopes clan in Faulkner's fiction. These crafty and unappealing tenant farmers and traders run roughshod over the aristocratic families of Yoknapatawpha County in three Faulkner novels: *The Hamlet* (1940), *The Town* (1957), and *The Mansion* (1959). According to Ben Wasson in *Count No Count*, Faulkner once told a friend that "somebody said I was a genius writer. The only thing I'd claim genius for is thinking up that name *Snopes*." In Southern literary circles, at least, the name "Snopes" still serves as a shorthand term for the graceless and greedy (but frequently successful) opportunists of the "New South."

Cultural Context Tenant farming is a system of agriculture in which landowners contribute their land while tenants contribute labor. One form of tenant farming, known as sharecropping, required the landowner to furnish all the capital (and usually the food, clothing, and shelter) to the tenant in return for labor. Given the way the system worked, the sharecropper was lucky to end the year without owing money to the landowner. In "Barn Burning," Abner Snopes is a poor sharecropper who takes out his frustrations against the post–Civil War aristocracy of landowners.

Barn Burning   (1939)

The store in which the Justice of the Peace's court was sitting smelled of cheese. The boy, crouched on his nail keg at the back of the crowded room, knew he smelled cheese, and more: from where he sat he could see the ranked shelves close-packed with the solid, squat, dynamic shapes of tin cans whose labels his stomach read, not from the lettering which meant nothing to his mind but from the scarlet devils and the silver curve of fish — this, the cheese which he knew he smelled and the hermetic° meat which his intestines believed he smelled coming in intermittent gusts momentary and brief between the other constant one, the smell and sense just a little of fear because mostly of despair and grief, the old fierce pull of blood. He could not see the table where the Justice sat and before which his father and his father's enemy (*our enemy* he thought in that despair; *ourn! mine and hisn both! He's my father!*) stood, but he could hear them, the two of them that is, because his father had said no word yet:

"But what proof have you, Mr. Harris?"

"I told you. The hog got into my corn. I caught it up and sent it back to him. He had no fence that would hold it. I told him so, warned him. The next time I

---

hermetic: Canned.

put the hog in my pen. When he came to get it I gave him enough wire to patch up his pen. The next time I put the hog up and kept it. I rode down to his house and saw the wire I gave him still rolled on to the spool in his yard. I told him he could have the hog when he paid me a dollar pound fee. That evening a nigger came with the dollar and got the hog. He was a strange nigger. He said, 'He say to tell you wood and hay kin burn. I said, 'What?' 'That whut he say to tell you,' the nigger said. 'Wood and hay kin burn.' That night my barn burned. I got the stock out but I lost the barn."

"Where is the nigger? Have you got him?"

"He was a strange nigger, I tell you. I don't know what became of him."   5

"But that's not proof. Don't you see that's not proof?"

"Get that boy up here. He knows." For a moment the boy thought too that the man meant his older brother until Harris said, "Not him. The little one. The boy," and, crouching, small for his age, small and wiry like his father, in patched and faded jeans even too small for him, with straight, uncombed, brown hair and eyes gray and wild as storm scud, he saw the men between himself and the table part and become a lane of grim faces, at the end of which he saw the Justice, a shabby, collarless, graying man in spectacles, beckoning him. He felt no floor under his bare feet; he seemed to walk beneath the palpable weight of the grim turning faces. His father, stiff in his black Sunday coat donned not for the trial but for the moving, did not even look at him. *He aims for me to lie,* he thought, again with that frantic grief and despair. *And I will have to do hit.*

"What's your name, boy?" the Justice said.

"Colonel Sartoris Snopes," the boy whispered.

"Hey?" the Justice said. "Talk louder. Colonel Sartoris? I reckon anybody   10
named for Colonel Sartoris in this country can't help but tell the truth, can they?" The boy said nothing. *Enemy! Enemy!* he thought; for a moment he could not even see, could not see that the Justice's face was kindly nor discern that his voice was troubled when he spoke to the man named Harris: "Do you want me to question this boy?" But he could hear, and during those subsequent long seconds while there was absolutely no sound in the crowded little room save that of quiet and intent breathing it was as if he had swung outward at the end of a grape vine, over a ravine, and at the top of the swing had been caught in a prolonged instant of mesmerized gravity, weightless in time.

"No!" Harris said violently, explosively. "Damnation! Send him out of here!" Now time, the fluid world, rushed beneath him again, the voices coming to him again through the smell of cheese and sealed meat, the fear and despair and the old grief of blood:

"This case is closed. I can't find against you, Snopes, but I can give you advice. Leave this country and don't come back to it."

His father spoke for the first time, his voice cold and harsh, level, without emphasis: "I aim to. I don't figure to stay in a country among people who . . ." he said something unprintable and vile, addressed to no one.

"That'll do," the Justice said. "Take your wagon and get out of this country before dark. Case dismissed."

15   His father turned, and he followed the stiff black coat, the wiry figure walking a little stiffly from where a Confederate provost's man's° musket ball had taken him in the heel on a stolen horse thirty years ago, followed the two backs now, since his older brother had appeared from somewhere in the crowd, no taller than the father but thicker, chewing tobacco steadily, between the two lines of grim-faced men and out of the store and across the worn gallery and down the sagging steps and among the dogs and half-grown boys in the mild May dust, where as he passed a voice hissed:

"Barn burner!"

Again he could not see, whirling; there was a face in a red haze, moonlike, bigger than the full moon, the owner of it half again his size, he leaping in the red haze toward the face, feeling no blow, feeling no shock when his head struck the earth, scrabbling up and leaping again, feeling no blow this time either and tasting no blood, scrabbling up to see the other boy in full flight and himself already leaping into pursuit as his father's hand jerked him back, the harsh, cold voice speaking above him: "Go get in the wagon."

It stood in a grove of locusts and mulberries across the road. His two hulking sisters in their Sunday dresses and his mother and her sister in calico and sunbonnets were already in it, sitting on and among the sorry residue of the dozen and more movings which even the boy could remember — the battered stove, the broken beds and chairs, the clock inlaid with mother-of-pearl, which would not run, stopped at some fourteen minutes past two o'clock of a dead and forgotten day and time, which had been his mother's dowry. She was crying, though when she saw him she drew her sleeve across her face and began to descend from the wagon. "Get back," the father said.

"He's hurt. I got to get some water and wash his . . ."

20   "Get back in the wagon," his father said. He got in too, over the tail-gate. His father mounted to the seat where the older brother already sat and struck the gaunt mules two savage blows with the peeled willow, but without heat. It was not even sadistic; it was exactly that same quality which in later years would cause his descendants to overrun the engine before putting a motor car into motion, striking and reining back in the same movement. The wagon went on, the store with its quiet crowd of grimly watching men dropped behind; a curve in the road hid it. *Forever* he thought. *Maybe he's done satisfied now, now that he has* . . . stopping himself, not to say it aloud even to himself. His mother's hand touched his shoulder.

"Does hit hurt?" she said.

"Naw," he said. "Hit don't hurt. Lemme be."

"Can't you wipe some of the blood off before hit dries?"

"I'll wash to-night," he said. "Lemme be, I tell you."

25   The wagon went on. He did not know where they were going. None of them ever did or ever asked, because it was always somewhere, always a house of sorts waiting for them a day or two days or even three days away. Likely his father

---

provost's man's: Military policeman's.

had already arranged to make a crop on another farm before he . . . Again he had to stop himself. He (the father) always did. There was something about his wolf-like independence and even courage when the advantage was at least neutral which impressed strangers, as if they got from his latent ravening ferocity not so much a sense of dependability as a feeling that his ferocious conviction in the rightness of his own actions would be of advantage to all whose interest lay with his.

That night they camped, in a grove of oaks and beeches where a spring ran. The nights were still cool and they had a fire against it, of a rail lifted from a nearby fence and cut into lengths — a small fire, neat, niggard almost, a shrewd fire; such fires were his father's habit and custom always, even in freezing weather. Older, the boy might have remarked this and wondered why not a big one; why should not a man who had not only seen the waste and extravagance of war, but who had in his blood an inherent voracious prodigality with material not his own, have burned everything in sight? Then he might have gone a step farther and thought that that was the reason: that niggard blaze was the living fruit of nights passed during those four years in the woods hiding from all men, blue or gray, with his strings of horses (captured horses, he called them). And older still, he might have divined the true reason: that the element of fire spoke to some deep mainspring of his father's being, as the element of steel or of powder spoke to other men, as the one weapon for the preservation of integrity, else breath were not worth the breathing, and hence to be regarded with respect and used with discretion.

But he did not think this now and he had seen those same niggard blazes all his life. He merely ate his supper beside it and was already half asleep over his iron plate when his father called him, and once more he followed the stiff back, the stiff and ruthless limp, up the slope and on to the starlit road where, turning, he could see his father against the stars but without face or depth — a shape black, flat, and bloodless as though cut from tin in the iron folds of the frockcoat which had not been made for him, the voice harsh like tin and without heat like tin:

"You were fixing to tell them. You would have told him." He didn't answer. His father struck him with the flat of his hand on the side of the head, hard but without heat, exactly as he had struck the two mules at the store, exactly as he would strike either of them with any stick in order to kill a horse fly, his voice still without fear or anger: "You're getting to be a man. You got to learn. You got to learn to stick to your own blood or you ain't going to have any blood to stick to you. Do you think either of them, any man there this morning, would? Don't you know all they wanted was a chance to get at me because they knew I had them beat? Eh?" Later, twenty years later, he was to tell himself, "If I had said they wanted only truth, justice, he would have hit me again." But now he said nothing. He was not crying. He just stood there. "Answer me," his father said.

"Yes," he whispered. His father turned.

"Get on to bed. We'll be there tomorrow." 30

Tomorrow they were there. In the early afternoon the wagon stopped before a paintless two-room house identical almost with the dozen others it had stopped before even in the boy's ten years, and again, as on the other dozen occasions, his

mother and aunt got down and began to unload the wagon, although his two
sisters and his father and brother had not moved.

"Likely hit ain't fitten for hawgs," one of the sisters said.

"Nevertheless, fit it will and you'll hog it and like it," his father said. "Get out
of them chairs and help your Ma unload."

The two sisters got down, big, bovine, in a flutter of cheap ribbons; one of
them drew from the jumbled wagon bed a battered lantern, the other a worn
broom. His father handed the reins to the older son and began to climb stiffly over
the wheel. "When they get unloaded, take the team to the barn and feed them."
Then he said, and at first the boy thought he was still speaking to his brother:
"Come with me."

35   "Me?" he said.

"Yes," his father said. "You."

"Abner," his mother said. His father paused and looked back — the harsh
level stare beneath the shaggy, graying, irascible brows.

"I reckon I'll have a word with the man that aims to begin tomorrow owning
me body and soul for the next eight months."

They went back up the road. A week ago — or before last night, that is — he
would have asked where they were going, but not now. His father had struck him
before last night but never before had he paused afterward to explain why; it was
as if the blow and the following calm, outrageous voice still rang, repercussed,
divulging nothing to him save the terrible handicap of being young, the light
weight of his few years, just heavy enough to prevent his soaring free of the world
as it seemed to be ordered but not heavy enough to keep him footed solid in it, to
resist it and try to change the course of its events.

40   Presently he could see the grove of oaks and cedars and the other flowering
trees and shrubs, where the house would be, though not the house yet. They
walked beside a fence massed with honeysuckle and Cherokee roses and came to
a gate swinging open between two brick pillars, and now, beyond a sweep of drive,
he saw the house for the first time and at that instant he forgot his father and the
terror and despair both, and even when he remembered his father again (who had
not stopped) the terror and despair did not return. Because, for all the twelve
movings, they had sojourned until now in a poor country, a land of small farms
and fields and houses, and he had never seen a house like this before. *Hit's big as
a courthouse* he thought quietly, with a surge of peace and joy whose reason he
could not have thought into words, being too young for that: *They are safe from
him. People whose lives are a part of this peace and dignity are beyond his touch, he no
more to them than a buzzing wasp: capable of stinging for a little moment but that's all;
the spell of this peace and dignity rendering even the barns and stable and cribs which belong to it impervious to the puny flames he might contrive* . . . this, the peace and joy,
ebbing for an instant as he looked again at the stiff black back, the stiff and implacable limp of the figure which was not dwarfed by the house, for the reason that
it had never looked big anywhere and which now, against the serene columned
backdrop, had more than ever that impervious quality of something cut ruthlessly
from tin, depthless, as though, sidewise to the sun, it would cast no shadow. Watching him, the boy remarked the absolutely undeviating course which his father held

and saw the stiff foot come squarely down in a pile of fresh droppings where a horse had stood in the drive and which his father could have avoided by a simple change of stride. But it ebbed only for a moment, though he could not have thought this into words either, walking on in the spell of the house, which he could even want but without envy, without sorrow, certainly never with that ravening and jealous rage which unknown to him walked in the ironlike black coat before him: *Maybe he will feel it too. Maybe it will even change him now from what maybe he couldn't help but be.*

They crossed the portico. Now he could hear his father's stiff foot as it came down on the boards with clocklike finality, a sound out of all proportion to the displacement of the body it bore and which was not dwarfed either by the white door before it, as though it had attained to a sort of vicious and ravening minimum not to be dwarfed by anything — the flat, wide, black hat, the formal coat of broadcloth which had once been black but which had now that friction-glazed greenish cast of the bodies of old house flies, the lifted sleeve which was too large, the lifted hand like a curled claw. The door opened so promptly that the boy knew the Negro must have been watching them all the time, an old man with neat grizzled hair, in a linen jacket, who stood barring the door with his body, saying, "Wipe yo foots, white man, fo you come in here. Major ain't home nohow."

"Get out of my way, nigger," his father said, without heat too, flinging the door back and the Negro also and entering, his hat still on his head. And now the boy saw the prints of the stiff foot on the doorjamb and saw them appear on the pale rug behind the machinelike deliberation of the foot which seemed to bear (or transmit) twice the weight which the body compassed. The Negro was shouting "Miss Lula! Miss Lula!" somewhere behind them, then the boy, deluged as though by a warm wave by a suave turn of carpeted stair and a pendant glitter of chandeliers and a mute gleam of gold frames, heard the swift feet and saw her too, a lady — perhaps he had never seen her like before either — in a gray, smooth gown with lace at the throat and an apron tied at the waist and the sleeves turned back, wiping cake or biscuit dough from her hands with a towel as she came up the hall, looking not at his father at all but at the tracks on the blond rug with an expression of incredulous amazement.

"I tried," the Negro cried, "I tole him to . . ."

"Will you please go away?" she said in a shaking voice. "Major de Spain is not at home. Will you please go away?"

His father had not spoken again. He did not speak again. He did not even look 45 at her. He just stood stiff in the center of the rug, in his hat, the shaggy iron-gray brows twitching slightly above the pebble-colored eyes as he appeared to examine the house with brief deliberation. Then with the same deliberation he turned; the boy watched him pivot on the good leg and saw the stiff foot drag round the arc of the turning, leaving a final long and fading smear. His father never looked at it, he never once looked down at the rug. The Negro held the door. It closed behind them, upon the hysteric and indistinguishable woman-wail. His father stopped at the top of the steps and scraped his boot clean on the edge of it. At the gate he stopped again. He stood for a moment, planted stiffly on the stiff foot, looking back at the house. "Pretty and white, ain't it?" he said. "That's sweat. Nigger sweat. Maybe it ain't white enough yet to suit him. Maybe he wants to mix some white sweat with it."

Two hours later the boy was chopping wood behind the house within which his mother and aunt and the two sisters (the mother and aunt, not the two girls, he knew that; even at this distance and muffled by walls the flat loud voices of the two girls emanated an incorrigible idle inertia) were setting up the stove to prepare a meal, when he heard the hooves and saw the linen-clad man on a fine sorrel mare, whom he recognized even before he saw the rolled rug in front of the Negro youth following on a fat bay carriage horse — a suffused, angry face vanishing, still at full gallop, beyond the corner of the house where his father and brother were sitting in the two tilted chairs; and a moment later, almost before he could have put the axe down, he heard the hooves again and watched the sorrel mare go back out of the yard, already galloping again. Then his father began to shout one of the sisters' names, who presently emerged backward from the kitchen door dragging the rolled rug along the ground by one end while the other sister walked behind it.

"If you ain't going to tote, go on and set up the wash pot," the first said.

"You, Sarty!" the second shouted. "Set up the wash pot!" His father appeared at the door, framed against that shabbiness, as he had been against that other bland perfection, impervious to either, the mother's anxious face at his shoulder.

"Go on," the father said. "Pick it up." The two sisters stooped, broad, lethargic; stooping, they presented an incredible expanse of pale cloth and a flutter of tawdry ribbons.

50   "If I thought enough of a rug to have to git hit all the way from France I wouldn't keep hit where folks coming in would have to tromp on hit," the first said. They raised the rug.

"Abner," the mother said. "Let me do it."

"You go back and git dinner," his father said. "I'll tend to this."

From the woodpile through the rest of the afternoon the boy watched them, the rug spread flat in the dust beside the bubbling wash-pot, the two sisters stooping over it with that profound and lethargic reluctance, while the father stood over them in turn, implacable and grim, driving them though never raising his voice again. He could smell the harsh homemade lye° they were using; he saw his mother come to the door once and look toward them with an expression not anxious now but very like despair; he saw his father turn, and he fell to with the axe and saw from the corner of his eye his father raise from the ground a flattish fragment of field stone and examine it and return to the pot, and this time his mother actually spoke: "Abner. Abner. Please don't. Please, Abner."

Then he was done too. It was dusk; the whippoorwills had already begun. He could smell coffee from the room where they would presently eat the cold food remaining from the mid-afternoon meal, though when he entered the house he realized they were having coffee again probably because there was a fire on

---

lye: A soap made from wood ashes and water, unsuitable for washing fine fabrics.

the hearth, before which the rug now lay spread over the backs of the two chairs. The tracks of his father's foot were gone. Where they had been were now long, water-cloudy scoriations resembling the sporadic course of a Lilliputian mowing machine.

It still hung there while they ate the cold food and then went to bed, scattered 55 without order or claim up and down the two rooms, his mother in one bed, where his father would later lie, the older brother in the other, himself, the aunt, and the two sisters on pallets on the floor. But his father was not in bed yet. The last thing the boy remembered was the depthless, harsh silhouette of the hat and coat bending over the rug and it seemed to him that he had not even closed his eyes when the silhouette was standing over him, the fire almost dead behind it, the stiff foot prodding him awake. "Catch up the mule," his father said.

When he returned with the mule his father was standing in the black door, the rolled rug over his shoulder. "Ain't you going to ride?" he said.

"No. Give me your foot."

He bent his knee into his father's hand, the wiry, surprising power flowed smoothly, rising, he rising with it, on to the mule's bare back (they had owned a saddle once; the boy could remember it though not when or where) and with the same effortlessness his father swung the rug up in front of him. Now in the starlight they retraced the afternoon's path, up the dusty road rife with honeysuckle, through the gate and up the black tunnel to the drive to the lightless house, where he sat on the mule and felt the rough warp of the rug drag across his thighs and vanish.

"Don't you want me to help?" he whispered. His father did not answer and now he heard again that stiff foot striking the hollow portico with that wooden and clocklike deliberation, that outrageous overstatement of the weight it carried. The rug, hunched, not flung (the boy could tell that even in the darkness) from his father's shoulder struck the angle of wall and floor with a sound unbelievably loud, thunderous, then the foot again, unhurried and enormous; a light came on in the house and the boy sat, tense, breathing steadily and quietly and just a little fast, though the foot itself did not increase its beat at all, descending the steps now; now the boy could see him.

"Don't you want to ride now?" he whispered. "We kin both ride now," the 60 light within the house altering now, flaring up and sinking. *He's coming down the stairs now*, he thought. He had already ridden the mule up beside the horse block; presently his father was up behind him and he doubled the reins over and slashed the mule across the neck, but before the animal could begin to trot the hard, thin arm came round him, the hard, knotted hand jerking the mule back to a walk.

In the first red rays of the sun they were in the lot, putting plow gear on the mules. This time the sorrel mare was in the lot before he heard it at all, the rider collarless and even bareheaded, trembling, speaking in a shaking voice as the woman in the house had done, his father merely looking up once before stooping again to the hame° he was buckling, so that the man on the mare spoke to his stooping back:

hame: Harness.

"You must realize you have ruined that rug. Wasn't there anybody here, any of your women . . ." he ceased, shaking, the boy watching him, the older brother leaning now in the stable door, chewing, blinking slowly and steadily at nothing apparently. "It cost a hundred dollars. But you never had a hundred dollars. You never will. So I'm going to charge you twenty bushels of corn against your crop. I'll add it in your contract and when you come to the commissary you can sign it. That won't keep Mrs. de Spain quiet but maybe it will teach you to wipe your feet off before you enter her house again."

Then he was gone. The boy looked at his father, who still had not spoken or even looked up again, who was now adjusting the loggerhead in the hame.

"Pap," he said. His father looked at him — the inscrutable face, the shaggy brows beneath which the gray eyes glinted coldly. Suddenly the boy went toward him, fast, stopping as suddenly. "You done the best you could!" he cried. "If he wanted hit done different why didn't he wait and tell you how? He won't git no twenty bushels! He won't git none! We'll gether hit and hide hit! I kin watch . . ."

65   "Did you put the cutter back in that straight stock like I told you?"

"No, sir," he said.

"Then go do it."

That was Wednesday. During the rest of that week he worked steadily, at what was within his scope and some which was beyond it, with an industry that did not need to be driven nor even commanded twice; he had this from his mother, with the difference that some at least of what he did he liked to do, such as splitting wood with the half-size axe which his mother and aunt had earned, or saved money somehow, to present him with at Christmas. In company with the two older women (and on one afternoon, even one of the sisters), he built pens for the shoat and the cow which were a part of his father's contract with the landlord, and one afternoon, his father being absent, gone somewhere on one of the mules, he went to the field.

They were running a middle buster now, his brother holding the plow straight while he handled the reins, and walking beside the straining mule, the rich black soil shearing cool and damp against his bare ankles, he thought *Maybe this is the end of it. Maybe even that twenty bushels that seems hard to have to pay for just a rug will be a cheap price for him to stop forever and always from being what he used to be;* thinking, dreaming now, so that his brother had to speak sharply to him to mind the mule: *Maybe he even won't collect the twenty bushels. Maybe it will all add up and balance and vanish — corn, rug, fire; the terror and grief, the being pulled two ways like between two teams of horses — gone, done with for ever and ever.*

70   Then it was Saturday; he looked up from beneath the mule he was harnessing and saw his father in the black coat and hat. "Not that," his father said. "The wagon gear." And then, two hours later, sitting in the wagon bed behind his father and brother on the seat, the wagon accomplished a final curve, and he saw the weathered paintless store with its tattered tobacco- and patent-medicine posters and the tethered wagons and saddle animals below the gallery. He mounted the gnawed steps behind his father and brother, and there again was

the lane of quiet, watching faces for the three of them to walk through. He saw the man in spectacles sitting at the plank table and he did not need to be told this was a Justice of the Peace; he sent one glare of fierce, exultant, partisan defiance at the man in collar and cravat now, whom he had seen but twice before in his life, and that on a galloping horse, who now wore on his face an expression not of rage but of amazed unbelief which the boy could not have known was at the incredible circumstance of being sued by one of his own tenants, and came and stood against his father and cried at the Justice: "He ain't done it! He ain't burnt . . ."

"Go back to the wagon," his father said.

"Burnt?" the Justice said. "Do I understand this rug was burned too?"

"Does anybody here claim it was?" his father said. "Go back to the wagon." But he did not, he merely retreated to the rear of the room, crowded as that other had been, but not to sit down this time, instead, to stand pressing among the motionless bodies, listening to the voices:

"And you claim twenty bushels of corn is too high for the damage you did to the rug?"

"He brought the rug to me and said he wanted the tracks washed out of it. I washed the tracks out and took the rug back to him." 75

"But you didn't carry the rug back to him in the same condition it was in before you made the tracks on it."

His father did not answer, and now for perhaps half a minute there was no sound at all save that of breathing, the faint, steady suspiration of complete and intent listening.

"You decline to answer that, Mr. Snopes?" Again his father did not answer. "I'm going to find against you, Mr. Snopes. I'm going to find that you were responsible for the injury to Major de Spain's rug and hold you liable for it. But twenty bushels of corn seems a little high for a man in your circumstances to have to pay. Major de Spain claims it cost a hundred dollars. October corn will be worth about fifty cents. I figure that if Major de Spain can stand a ninety-five dollar loss on something he paid cash for, you can stand a five-dollar loss you haven't earned yet. I hold you in damages to Major de Spain to the amount of ten bushels of corn over and above your contract with him, to be paid to him out of your crop at gathering time. Court adjourned."

It had taken no time hardly, the morning was but half begun. He thought they would return home and perhaps back to the field, since they were late, far behind all other farmers. But instead his father passed on behind the wagon, merely indicating with his hand for the older brother to follow with it, and crossed the road toward the blacksmith shop opposite, pressing on after his father, overtaking him, speaking, whispering up at the harsh, calm face beneath the weathered hat: "He won't git no ten bushels neither. He won't git one. We'll . . ." until his father glanced for an instant down at him, the face absolutely calm, the grizzled eyebrows tangled above the cold eyes, the voice almost pleasant, almost gentle:

"You think so? Well, we'll wait till October anyway." 80

The matter of the wagon — the setting of a spoke or two and the tightening of the tires — did not take long either, the business of the tires accomplished by driving the wagon into the spring branch behind the shop and letting it stand there, the mules nuzzling into the water from time to time, and the boy on the seat with the idle reins, looking up the slope and through the sooty tunnel of the shed where the slow hammer rang and where his father sat on an upended cypress bolt, easily, either talking or listening, still sitting there when the boy brought the dripping wagon up out of the branch and halted it before the door.

"Take them on to the shade and hitch," his father said. He did so and re-turned. His father and the smith and a third man squatting on his heels inside the door were talking, about crops and animals; the boy, squatting too in the ammo-niac dust and hoof-parings and scales of rust, heard his father tell a long and un-hurried story out of the time before the birth of the older brother even when he had been a professional horsetrader. And then his father came up beside him where he stood before a tattered last year's circus poster on the other side of the store, gazing rapt and quiet at the scarlet horses, the incredible poisings and con-volutions of tulle and tights and the painted leers of comedians, and said, "It's time to eat."

But not at home. Squatting beside his brother against the front wall, he watched his father emerge from the store and produce from a paper sack a seg-ment of cheese and divide it carefully and deliberately into three with his pocket knife and produce crackers from the same sack. They all three squatted on the gallery and ate, slowly, without talking; then in the store again, they drank from a tin dipper tepid water smelling of the cedar bucket and of living beech trees. And still they did not go home. It was a horse lot this time, a tall rail fence upon and along which men stood and sat and out of which one by one horses were led, to be walked and trotted and then cantered back and forth along the road while the slow swapping and buying went on and the sun began to slant westward, they — the three of them — watching and listening, the older brother with his muddy eyes and his steady, inevitable tobacco, the father commenting now and then on certain of the animals, to no one in particular.

It was after sundown when they reached home. They ate supper by lamplight, then, sitting on the doorstep, the boy watched the night fully accomplish, listen-ing to the whippoorwills and the frogs, when he heard his mother's voice: "Abner! No! No! Oh, God. Oh, God. Abner!" and he rose, whirled, and saw the altered light through the door where a candle stub now burned in a bottle neck on the table and his father, still in the hat and coat, at once formal and burlesque as though dressed carefully for some shabby and ceremonial violence, emptying the reservoir of the lamp back into the five-gallon kerosene can from which it had been filled, while the mother tugged at his arm until he shifted the lamp to the other hand and flung her back, not savagely or viciously, just hard, into the wall, her hands flung out against the wall for balance, her mouth open and in her face the same quality of hopeless despair as had been in her voice. Then his father saw him standing in the door.

85   "Go to the barn and get that can of oil we were oiling the wagon with," he said. The boy did not move. Then he could speak.

"What . . ." he cried. "What are you . . ."

"Go get that oil," his father said. "Go."

Then he was moving, running, outside the house, toward the stable: this the old habit, the old blood which he had not been permitted to choose for himself, which had been bequeathed him willy nilly and which had run for so long (and who knew where, battening on what of outrage and savagery and lust) before it came to him. *I could keep on,* he thought. *I could run on and on and never look back, never need to see his face again. Only I can't. I can't,* the rusted can in his hand now, the liquid sploshing in it as he ran back to the house and into it, into the sound of his mother's weeping in the next room, and handed the can to his father.

"Ain't you going to even send a nigger?" he cried. "At least you sent a nigger before!"

This time his father didn't strike him. The hand came even faster than the   90
blow had, the same hand which had set the can on the table with almost excruciating care flashing from the can toward him too quick for him to follow it, gripping him by the back of his shirt and on to tiptoe before he had seen it quit the can, the face stooping at him in breathless and frozen ferocity, the cold, dead voice speaking over him to the older brother who leaned against the table, chewing with that steady, curious, sidewise motion of cows:

"Empty the can into the big one and go on. I'll catch up with you."

"Better tie him to the bedpost," the brother said.

"Do like I told you," the father said. Then the boy was moving, his bunched shirt and the hard, bony hand between his shoulderblades, his toes just touching the floor, across the room and into the other one, past the sisters sitting with spread heavy thighs in the two chairs over the cold hearth, and to where his mother and aunt sat side by side on the bed, the aunt's arms about his mother's shoulders.

"Hold him," the father said. The aunt made a startled movement. "Not you," the father said. "Lennie. Take hold of him. I want to see you do it." His mother took him by the wrist. "You'll hold him better than that. If he gets loose don't you know what he is going to do? He will go up yonder." He jerked his head toward the road. "Maybe I'd better tie him."

"I'll hold him," his mother whispered.   95

"See you do then." Then his father was gone, the stiff foot heavy and measured upon the boards, ceasing at last.

Then he began to struggle. His mother caught him in both arms, he jerking and wrenching at them. He would be stronger in the end, he knew that. But he had no time to wait for it. "Lemme go!" he cried. "I don't want to have to hit you!"

"Let him go!" the aunt said. "If he don't go, before God, I am going up there myself!"

"Don't you see I can't?" his mother cried. "Sarty! Sarty! No! No! Help me, Lizzie!"

Then he was free. His aunt grasped at him but it was too late. He whirled,   100
running, his mother stumbled forward on to her knees behind him, crying to the nearest sister: "Catch him, Net! Catch him!" But that was too late too, the sister (the sisters were twins, born at the same time, yet either of them now gave the impression of being, encompassing as much living meat and volume and weight as any other two of the family) not yet having begun to rise from the chair,

her head, face, alone merely turned, presenting to him in the flying instant an astonishing expanse of young female features untroubled by any surprise even, wearing only an expression of bovine interest. Then he was out of the room, out of the house, in the mild dust of the starlit road and the heavy rifeness of honeysuckle, the pale ribbon unspooling with terrific slowness under his running feet, reaching the gate at last and turning in, running, his heart and lungs drumming, on up the drive toward the lighted house, the lighted door. He did not knock, he burst in, sobbing for breath, incapable for the moment of speech; he saw the astonished face of the Negro in the linen jacket without knowing when the Negro had appeared.

"De Spain!" he cried, panted. "Where's . . ." then he saw the white man too emerging from a white door down the hall. "Barn!" he cried. "Barn!"

"What?" the white man said. "Barn?"

"Yes!" the boy cried. "Barn!"

"Catch him!" the white man shouted.

105   But it was too late this time too. The Negro grasped his shirt, but the entire sleeve, rotten with washing, carried away, and he was out that door too and in the drive again, and had actually never ceased to run even while he was screaming into the white man's face.

Behind him the white man was shouting, "My horse! Fetch my horse!" and he thought for an instant of cutting across the park and climbing the fence into the road, but he did not know the park nor how high the vine-massed fence might be and he dared not risk it. So he ran on down the drive, blood and breath roaring; presently he was in the road again though he could not see it. He could not hear either: the galloping mare was almost upon him before he heard her, and even then he held his course, as if the very urgency of his wild grief and need must in a moment more find him wings, waiting until the ultimate instant to hurl himself aside and into the weed-choked roadside ditch as the horse thundered past and on, for an instant in furious silhouette against the stars, the tranquil early summer night sky which, even before the shape of the horse and rider vanished, stained abruptly and violently upward: a long, swirling roar incredible and soundless, blotting the stars, and he springing up and into the road again, running again, knowing it was too late yet still running even after he heard the shot and, an instant later, two shots, pausing now without knowing he had ceased to run, crying "Pap! Pap!", running again before he knew he had begun to run, stumbling, tripping over something and scrabbling up again without ceasing to run, looking backward over his shoulder at the glare as he got up, running on among the invisible trees, panting, sobbing, "Father! Father!"

At midnight he was sitting on the crest of a hill. He did not know it was midnight and he did not know how far he had come. But there was no glare behind him now and he sat now, his back toward what he had called home for four days anyhow, his face toward the dark woods which he would enter when breath was strong again, small, shaking steadily in the chill darkness, hugging himself into the remainder of his thin, rotten shirt, the grief and despair now no longer terror and fear but just grief and despair. *Father. My father*, he thought. "He was brave!" he cried suddenly, aloud but not loud, no more than a whisper: "He was! He was in the war! He was in Colonel Sartoris' cav'ry!" not knowing that his father had gone to that war a private in the fine old European sense, wearing no uniform, admitting the authority of and giving fidelity to no man or army or flag, going to war as Malbrouck° himself did: for booty — it meant nothing and less than nothing to him if it were enemy booty or his own.

The slow constellations wheeled on. It would be dawn and then sunup after a while and he would be hungry. But that would be tomorrow and now he was only cold, and walking would cure that. His breathing was easier now and he decided to get up and go on, and then he found that he had been asleep because he knew it was almost dawn, the night almost over. He could tell that from the whippoorwills. They were everywhere now among the dark trees below him, constant and inflectioned and ceaseless, so that, as the instant for giving over to the day birds drew nearer and nearer, there was no interval at all between them. He got up. He was a little stiff, but walking would cure that too as it would the cold, and soon there would be the sun. He went on down the hill, toward the dark woods within which the liquid silver voices of the birds called unceasing — the rapid and urgent beating of the urgent and quiring heart of the late spring night. He did not look back.

Reading and Reacting

1. Is the third-person narrator of "Barn Burning" omniscient, or is his omniscience limited? Explain.
2. What is the point of view of the italicized passages? What do you learn from them? Do they create irony? How would the story have been different without these passages?
3. "Barn Burning" includes a great deal of dialogue. How would you characterize the level of diction of this dialogue? What information about various characters does it provide?
4. What conflicts are presented in "Barn Burning"? Which, if any, are resolved in the story? Are the conflicts avoidable? Explain.
5. Why does Ab Snopes burn barns? Do you think his actions are justified? Explain your reasoning.
6. What role does the Civil War play in "Barn Burning"? What does Abner Snopes's behavior during the war tell readers about his character?
7. In the First and Second books of Samuel in the Old Testament, Abner was a relative of King Saul and commander in chief of his armies. Abner supported King Saul against David and was killed as a result of his own jealousy and rage. What, if any, significance is there in the fact that Faulkner names Ab Snopes — loyal to no man, fighter "for booty, and father of the Snopes clan" — after this mighty biblical leader?
8. Why does Sarty Snopes insist that his father was brave? How does your knowledge of events unknown to the boy affect your reactions to his defense of his father?

Malbrouck: A character in a popular eighteenth-century nursery rhyme about a famous warrior.

9. JOURNAL ENTRY How would the story be different if it were told from Ab's point of view? From Sarty's? From the point of view of Ab's wife? From the point of view of a member of a community in which the Snopeses have lived?

10. CRITICAL PERSPECTIVE Critic Edmond L. Volpe argues in his article "'Barn Burning': A Definition of Evil" that "Barn Burning" is not really about the class conflict between the sharecropping Snopeses and landowners like the de Spains but rather about Sarty:

> The story is centered upon Sarty's emotional dilemma. His conflict would not have been altered in any way if the person whose barn Ab burns had been a simple poor farmer, rather than an aristocratic plantation owner. . . . Sarty's struggle is against the repressive and divisive force his father represents. The boy's anxiety is created by his awakening sense of his own individuality. Torn between strong emotional attachment to the parent and his growing need to assert his own identity, Sarty's crisis is psychological and his battle is being waged far below the level of his intellectual and moral awareness.

Do you believe "Barn Burning" is, as Volpe suggests, essentially a coming-of-age story, or do you believe it is about something else — class conflict, for example?

Related Works: "A Worn Path" (p. 505), "Shiloh" (p. 316), "Baca Grande" (p. 905), "Child's Grave, Hale County, Alabama" (p. 1031), *Fences* (p. 1939)

CHITRA BANERJEE DIVAKARUNI (1956–   ) was born in India and lived there until she was nineteen, at which point she left Calcutta and came to the United States. She received a Master's Degree from Wright State University in Dayton, Ohio, and a PhD from the University of California, Berkeley. To earn money for her education, she held many odd jobs, including babysitting, selling merchandise at an Indian boutique, slicing bread in a bakery, and washing instruments in a science lab. She briefly lived in Illinois, Ohio, and Texas but has spent most of her adult life in Northern California, which she often writes about.

An award-winning author and poet, Divakaruni's work is widely known and has been translated into eleven languages, including Dutch, Hebrew, and Japanese. She has been published in over fifty magazines, including the *Atlantic Monthly* and *the New Yorker,* and her writing has been included in over thirty anthologies. Her novels, children's books, and collections of stories include *Arranged Marriage* (1996), *The Mistress of Spices* (1997), *Sister of My Heart* (1999), *The Unknown Errors of Our Lives* (2001), *The Vine of Desire* (2002), *Neela: Victory Song* (2002), *The Conch Bearer* (2003), and *Queen of Dreams* (2004). Her collections of poetry include *The Reason for Nasturtiums* (1990), *Black Candle* (1991), and *Leaving Yuba City* (1997). She currently teaches in the MFA program at the University of Houston.

Cultural Context Arranged marriages have existed throughout the world for centuries — in some countries, for as long as the institution of marriage itself. In India, arranged marriages are still the norm. The custom has survived migration, modernization, and even emigration, remaining central to the fabric of the culture and society. Potential brides and grooms come under the scrutiny of prospective family members who evaluate them in terms of their wealth, character, and class standing. Additionally, the parents of the bride must offer an acceptable dowry — a promise of money and/or material goods with which the bride may support herself in the event of her husband's death. Many Indian families in the United States have continued the tradition of arranged marriages, as is the case in this story.

The Disappearance (1995)

At first when they heard about the disappearance, people didn't believe it.

Why, we saw her just yesterday at the Ram Ratan Indian Grocery, friends said, picking out radishes for pickling. And wasn't she at the Mountain View park with her little boy last week, remember, we waved from our car and she waved back, she was in that blue *salwaar-kameez*,° yes, she never did wear American clothes. And the boy waved too, he must be, what, two and a half? Looks just like her with those big black eyes, that dimple. What a shame, they said, it's getting so that you aren't safe anywhere in this country nowadays.

Because that's what everyone suspected, including the husband. Crime. Otherwise, he said to the investigating policeman (he had called the police that very night), how could a young Indian woman wearing a yellow-flowered *kurta*° and Nike walking shoes just *disappear*? She'd been out for her evening walk, she took one every day after he got back from the office. Yes, yes, always alone, she said that was her time for herself. (He didn't quite understand that, but he was happy to watch his little boy, play ball with him, perhaps, until she returned to serve them dinner.)

Did you folks have a quarrel, asked the policeman, looking up from his notepad with a frown, and the husband looked directly back into his eyes and said, No, of course we didn't.

Later he would think about what the policeman had asked, while he sat in front 5 of his computer in his office, or while he lay in the bed which still seemed to smell of her. (But surely that was his imagination — the linen had been washed already.) He *had* told the truth about them not having a quarrel, hadn't he? (He prided himself on being an honest man, he often told his son how important it was not to lie, see what happened to Pinocchio's nose. And even now when the boy asked him where Mama was, he didn't say she had gone on a trip, as some of his friends' wives had advised him. I don't know, he said. And when the boy's thin face would crumple, want Mama, when she coming back, he held him in his lap awkwardly and tried to stroke his hair, like he had seen his wife do, but he couldn't bring himself to say what the boy needed to hear, *soon-soon*. I don't know, he said over and over.)

---

salwaar-kameez: Form of dress consisting of pajama-like pants, gathered at the waist and ankles; usually worn under a long, loose tunic.

kurta: A long shirt, usually knee length, worn over drawstring trousers.

They hadn't really had a fight. She wasn't, thank God, the quarrelsome type, like some of his friends' wives. Quiet. That's how she was, at least around him, although sometimes when he came home unexpectedly he would hear her singing to her son, her voice slightly off-key but full and confident. Or laughing as she chased him around the family room, Mama's going to get you, get you, both of them shrieking with delight until they saw him. Hush now, she would tell the boy, settle down, and they would walk over sedately to give him his welcome-home kiss.

He couldn't complain, though. Wasn't that what he had specified when his mother started asking, When are you getting married, I'm getting old, I want to see a grandson before I die.

If you can find me a quiet, pretty girl, he wrote, not brash, like Calcutta girls are nowadays, not with too many western ideas. Someone who would be relieved to have her husband make the major decisions. But she had to be smart, at least a year of college, someone he could introduce to his friends with pride.

He'd flown to Calcutta to view several suitable girls that his mother had picked out. But now, thinking back, he can only remember her. She had sat, head bowed, jasmine plaited into her hair, silk sari draped modestly over her shoulders, just like all the other prospective brides he'd seen. Nervous, he'd thought, yearning to be chosen. But when she'd glanced up there had been a cool, considering look in her eyes. Almost disinterested, almost as though *she* were wondering if he would make a suitable spouse. He had wanted her then, had married her within the week in spite of his mother's protests (had she caught that same look?) that something about the girl just didn't feel *right*.

10   He was a good husband. No one could deny it. He let her have her way, indulged her, even. When the kitchen was remodeled, for example, and she wanted pink and gray tiles even though he preferred white. Or when she wanted to go to Yosemite Park instead of Reno, although he knew he would be dreadfully bored among all those bearshit-filled trails and dried-up waterfalls. Once in a while, of course, he had to put his foot down, like when she wanted to get a job or go back to school or buy American clothes. But he always softened his no's with a remark like, What for, I'm here to take care of you, or, You look so much prettier in your Indian clothes, so much more feminine. He would pull her onto his lap and give her a kiss and a cuddle which usually ended with him taking her to the bedroom.

That was another area where he'd had to be firm. Sex. She was always saying, Please, not tonight, I don't feel up to it. He didn't mind that. She was, after all, a well-bred Indian girl. He didn't expect her to behave like those American women he sometimes watched on X-rated videos, screaming and biting and doing other things he grew hot just thinking about. But her reluctance went beyond womanly modesty. After dinner for instance she would start on the most elaborate household projects, soaping down the floors, changing the liners in cabinets. The night before she disappeared she'd started cleaning windows, taken out the Windex and the rags as soon as she'd put the boy to bed, even though he said, Let's go. Surely he couldn't be blamed for raising his voice at those times (though never so much as to wake his son), or for grabbing her by the elbow and pulling her to the bed, like he did that last night. He was always careful not to hurt her, he prided himself on that. Not even a little slap, not like some of the men he'd known growing up, or even some of his friends now. And he always told himself he'd stop if she really begged him, if she cried. After some time, though, she would quit struggling and let him do what he wanted. But that was nothing new. That could have nothing to do with the disappearance.

Two weeks passed and there was no news of the woman, even though the husband had put a notice in the *San Jose Mercury* as well as a half-page ad in *India West*, which he photocopied and taped to neighborhood lampposts. The ad had a photo of her, a close-up taken in too-bright sunlight where she gazed gravely at something beyond the camera. WOMAN MISSING, read the ad. REWARD $100,000. (How on earth would he come up with that kind of money, asked his friends. The husband confessed that it would be difficult, but he'd manage somehow. His wife was more important to him, after all, than all the money in the world. And to prove it he went to the bank the very same day and brought home a sheaf of forms to fill so that he could take out a second mortgage on the house.) He kept calling the police station, too, but the police weren't much help. They were working on it, they said. They'd checked the local hospitals and morgues, the shelters. They'd even sent her description to other states. But there were no leads. It didn't look very hopeful.

So finally he called India and over a faulty long-distance connection that made his voice echo eerily in his ear told his mother what had happened. My poor boy, she cried, left all alone (the word flickered unpleasantly across his brain, *left, left*), how can you possibly cope with the household and a child as well. And when he admitted that yes, it was very difficult, could she perhaps come and help out for a while if it wasn't too much trouble, she had replied that of course she would come right away and stay as long as he needed her, and what was all this American nonsense about too much trouble, he was her only son, wasn't he. She would contact the wife's family too, she ended, so he wouldn't have to deal with that awkwardness.

Within a week she had closed up the little flat she had lived in since her husband's death, got hold of a special family emergency visa, and was on her way. Almost as though she'd been waiting for something like this to happen, said some of the women spitefully. (These were his wife's friends, though maybe acquaintances would be a more accurate word. His wife had liked to keep to herself, which had been just fine with him. He was glad, he'd told her several times, that she didn't spend hours chattering on the phone like the other Indian wives.)

He was angry when this gossip reached him (perhaps because he'd had the 15 same insidious thought for a moment when, at the airport, he noticed how happy his mother looked, her flushed excited face appearing suddenly young). Really, he said to his friends, some people see only what they *want* to see. Didn't *they* think it was a good thing she'd come over? Oh yes, said his friends. Look how well the household was running now, the furniture dusted daily, laundry folded and put into drawers (his mother, a smart woman, had figured out the washing machine in no time at all). She cooked all his favorite dishes, which his wife had never managed to learn quite right, and she took *such* good care of the little boy, walking him to the park each afternoon, bringing him into her bed when he woke up crying at night. (He'd told her once or twice that his wife had never done that, she had this idea about the boy needing to be independent. What nonsense, said his mother.) Lucky man, a couple of his friends added and he silently agreed, although later he thought it was ironic that they would say that about a man whose wife had disappeared.

As the year went on, the husband stopped thinking as much about the wife. It wasn't that he loved her any less, or that the shock of her disappearance was less acute. It was just that it wasn't on his mind all the time. There would be stretches of time — when he was on the phone with an important client, or when he was watching after-dinner TV or driving his son to kiddie gym class — when he would forget that his wife was gone, that he had had a wife at all. And even when he re-membered that he had forgotten, he would experience only a slight twinge, sim-ilar to what he felt in his teeth when he drank something too cold too fast. The boy, too, didn't ask as often about his mother. He was sleeping through the nights again, he had put on a few pounds (because he was finally being fed right, said the grandmother), and he had started calling her "Ma," just like his father did.

So it seemed quite natural for the husband to, one day, remove the photographs of his wife from the frames that sat on the mantelpiece and replace them with pic-tures of himself and his little boy that friends had taken on a recent trip to Great America, and also one of the boy on his grandma's lap, holding a red birthday bal-loon, smiling (she said) exactly like his father used to at that age. He put the old pictures into a manila envelope and slid them to the back of a drawer, intending to show them to his son when he grew up. The next time his mother asked (as she had been doing ever since she got there), shall I put away all those saris and *kameezes*, it'll give you more space in the closet, he said, if you like. When she said, it's now over a year since the tragedy, shouldn't we have a prayer service done at the temple, he said OK. And when she told him, you really should think about get-ting married again, you're still young, and besides, the boy needs a mother, shall I contact second aunt back home, he remained silent but didn't disagree.

Then one night while cooking cauliflower curry, her specialty, his mother ran out of *hing*,° which was, she insisted, essential to the recipe. The Indian grocery was closed, but the husband remembered that sometimes his wife used to keep extra spices on the top shelf. So he climbed on a chair to look. There were no extra spices, but he did find something he had forgotten about, an old tea tin in which he'd asked her to hide her jewelry in case the house ever got burgled. Nothing major was ever kept there. The expensive wedding items were all stored in a vault. Still, the hus-band thought it would be a good idea to take them into the bank in the morning.

But when he picked up the tin it felt surprisingly light, and when he opened it, there were only empty pink nests of tissue inside.

20   He stood there holding the tin for a moment, not breathing. Then he re-minded himself that his wife had been a careless woman. He'd often had to speak to her about leaving things lying around. The pieces could be anywhere —

---

hing: An Indian spice.

pushed to the back of her makeup drawer or forgotten under a pile of books in the spare room where she used to spend inordinate amounts of time reading. Nevertheless he was not himself the rest of the evening, so much so that his mother said, What happened, you're awfully quiet, are you all right, your face looks funny. He told her he was fine, just a little pain in the chest area. Yes, he would make an appointment with the doctor tomorrow, no, he wouldn't forget, now could she please leave him alone for a while.

The next day he took the afternoon off from work, but he didn't go to the doctor. He went to the bank. In a small stuffy cubicle that smelled faintly of mold, he opened his safety deposit box to find that all her jewelry was gone. She hadn't taken any of the other valuables.

The edges of the cubicle seemed to fade and darken at the same time, as though the husband had stared at a lightbulb for too long. He ground his fists into his eyes and tried to imagine her on that last morning, putting the boy in his stroller and walking the twenty minutes to the bank (they only had one car, which he took to work; they could have afforded another, but why, he said to his friends, when she didn't even know how to drive). Maybe she had sat in this very cubicle and lifted out the emerald earrings, the pearl choker, the long gold chain. He imagined her wrapping the pieces carefully in plastic bags, the thin, clear kind one got at the grocery for vegetables, then slipping them into her purse. Or did she just throw them in anyhow, the strands of the necklace tangling, the brilliant green stones clicking against each other in the darkness inside the handbag, the boy laughing and clapping his hands at this new game.

At home that night he couldn't eat any dinner, and before he went to bed he did thirty minutes on the dusty exercise bike that sat in the corner of the family room. Have you gone crazy, asked his mother. He didn't answer. When he finally lay down, the tiredness did not put him to sleep as he had hoped. His calves ached from the unaccustomed strain, his head throbbed from the images that would not stop coming, and the bedclothes, when he pulled them up to his neck, smelled again of his wife's hair.

Where was she now? And with whom? Because surely she couldn't manage on her own. He'd always thought her to be like the delicate purple passion-flower vines that they'd put up on trellises along their back fence, and once, early in the marriage, had presented her with a poem he'd written about this. He remembered how, when he held out the sheet to her, she'd stared at him for a long moment and a look he couldn't quite read had flickered in her eyes. Then she'd taken the poem with a small smile. He went over and over all the men she might have known, but they (mostly his Indian friends) were safely married and still at home, every one.

The bed felt hot and lumpy. He tossed his feverish body around like a caught animal, punched the pillow, threw the blanket to the floor. Even thought, for a wild moment, of shaking the boy awake and asking him, *Who did your mama see?* And as though he had an inbuilt antenna that picked up his father's agitation, in the next room the boy started crying (which he hadn't done for months), shrill screams that left him breathless. And when his father and grandmother rushed to see what the problem was, he pushed them from him with all the strength in his small arms, saying, Go way, don't want you, want Mama, want Mama.

After the boy had been dosed with gripe water° and settled in bed again, the husband sat alone in the family room with a glass of brandy. He wasn't a drinker. He believed that alcohol was for weak men. But somehow he couldn't face the rumpled bed just yet, the pillows wrested onto the floor. The unknown areas of his wife's existence yawning blackly around him like chasms. Should he tell the police, he wondered, would it do any good? What if somehow his friends came to know? *Didn't I tell you, right from the first,* his mother would say. And anyway it was possible she was already dead, killed by a stranger from whom she'd hitched a ride, or by a violent, jealous lover. He felt a small, bitter pleasure at the thought, and then a pang of shame.

Nevertheless he made his way to the dark bedroom (a trifle unsteadily; the drink had made him light-headed) and groped in the bottom drawer beneath his underwear until he felt the coarse manila envelope with her photos. He drew it out and, without looking at them, tore the pictures into tiny pieces. Then he took them over to the kitchen, where the trash compactor was.

The roar of the compactor seemed to shake the entire house. He stiffened, afraid his mother would wake and ask what was going on, but she didn't. When the machine ground to a halt, he took a long breath. Finished, he thought. Finished. Tomorrow he would contact a lawyer, find out the legal procedure for remarriage. Over dinner he would mention to his mother, casually, that it was OK with him if she wanted to contact second aunt. Only this time he didn't want a college-educated woman. Even good looks weren't that important. A simple girl, maybe from their ancestral village. Someone whose family wasn't well off, who would be suitably appreciative of the comforts he could provide. Someone who would be a real mother to his boy.

He didn't know then that it wasn't finished. That even as he made love to his new wife (a plump, cheerful girl, good-hearted, if slightly unimaginative), or helped his daughters with their homework, or disciplined his increasingly rebellious son, he would wonder about *her.* Was she alive? Was she happy? With a sudden anger that he knew to be irrational, he would try to imagine her body tangled in swaying kelp at the bottom of the ocean where it had been flung. Bloated. Eaten by fish. But all he could conjure up was the intent look on her face when she rocked her son back and forth, singing a children's rhyme in Bengali, *Khoka jabe biye korte, shonge chhasho dhol, my little boy is going to be married, six hundred drummers.* Years later, when he was an old man living in a home for seniors (his second wife dead, his daughters moved away to distant towns, his son not on speaking terms with him), he would continue to be dazzled by that brief unguarded joy in her face, would say to himself, again, how much she must have hated me to choose to give *that* up.

30 But he had no inkling of any of this yet. So he switched off the trash compactor with a satisfied click, the sense of a job well done and, after taking a shower (long and very hot, the way he liked it, the hard jets of water turning the skin of his chest a dull red), went to bed and fell immediately into a deep, dreamless sleep.

---

gripe water: A traditional European remedy for colic.

Reading and Reacting

1. Who is the narrator of the story? (Notice that the narrator uses the pronoun *we* in paragraph 2.) How does the narrative point of view shape the story?
2. Why does the husband have misgivings after he tells the police that he and his wife did not have a quarrel? Why is he unable to comfort his son?
3. When he asked his mother to arrange a marriage, what qualities did the husband say he wanted in a wife? In what ways did his wife fulfill these requirements? In what ways did she not?
4. In paragraph 10, the narrator says, "He was a good husband. No one could deny it." Is the narrator correct in this assessment? Explain.
5. How did the following people react to the wife's disappearance:

   - The husband
   - The husband's mother
   - The son
   - The wife's friends

   How do their reactions shed light on the relationship between the husband and wife?
6. What is the significance of the empty tea tin? The safe deposit box?
7. Do you think the story's title is ironic? Explain.
8. In paragraph 29, the narrator shifts from the present to the future — and, in paragraph 30, back to the present. What is the purpose of this shift? What does this dual perspective reveal about the husband and about his wife? What, if anything, does the husband learn from his wife's disappearance?
9. JOURNAL ENTRY What indications does the wife give that she is not happy? Why does the husband fail to see these warning signs?
10. CRITICAL PERSPECTIVE Chitra Divakaruni's fiction and poetry have been widely acclaimed for their portrayal of the situations, struggles, and obstacles facing Indian and Indian-American women. Nilu N. Patel, a professor at Emory University, describes Divakaruni's work as follows:

    > She writes to unite people, and she does this by destroying myths and stereotypes. As she breaks down these barriers, she dissolves boundaries between people of different backgrounds, communities, ages, and even different worlds.

What myths or stereotypes are present in this story? Which are destroyed, and which remain intact through the events of the narrative? In what sense are the two worlds of the story shown to be similar? In what ways do they remain different?

Related Works: "A Rose for Emily" (p. 216), "Shiloh" (p. 316). "Dear Mama" (p. 1062), "Living in Sin" (p. 897), *Trifles* (p. 1372), *A Doll House* (p. 1454)

ALICE MUNRO (1931–   ), one of Canada's foremost contemporary authors, was born in Wingham, Ontario. Over the last few decades, she has published one novel, *Lives of Girls and Women* (1971), and seven collections of short stories including *Friend of My Youth* (1990), *Open Secrets* (1994), *Selected Stories* (1996), and *Hateship, Friendship, Courtship, Loveship, Marriage* (2001). She is a three-time winner of the Governor General's Award, one of the most prestigious literary awards in Canada. Nearly all of her fiction is set in southwestern Ontario, but her writing has captured imaginations worldwide. Often focusing on the lives and loves of women, Munro's stories reflect the various rites of passage and the joys and pains inherent in coming of age. She has explained in various interviews that while her work is not necessarily autobiographical, it does reflect an "emotional reality" that is drawn from her own life.

Cultural Context Teenage drinking (a key event in "An Ounce of Cure") and binge drinking (having more than five drinks on one occasion) have been steadily on the rise in recent years. Studies show that more than thirty-five percent of adults with a drinking problem developed symptoms by age nineteen, and in one study, more than fifty percent of high school seniors reported drinking heavily during the previous month. Young males show higher incidences of teenage drinking than females, but that gap is rapidly closing. Although experts disagree about the reasons behind the rise in teenage drinking, many authorities believe that making drinking an illicit activity contributes to its appeal.

An Ounce of Cure   (1968)

My parents didn't drink. They weren't rabid about it, and in fact I remember that when I signed the pledge in grade seven, with the rest of that superbly if impermanently indoctrinated class, my mother said, "It's just nonsense and fanaticism, children of that age. My father would drink a beer on a hot day, but my mother did not join him, and—whether accidentally or symbolically—this drink was always consumed *outside* the house. Most of the people we knew were the same way; in the small town where we lived. I ought not to say that it was this which got me into difficulties because the difficulties I got into were a faithful expression of my own incommodious nature—the same nature that caused my mother to look at me, on any occasion which traditionally calls for feelings of pride and maternal accomplishment (my departure for my first formal dance, I mean or my hellbent preparations for a descent on college) with an expression of brooding and fascinated despair, as if she could not possibly expect, did not ask, that it should go with me as it did with other girls; the dreamed-of spoils of daughters— orchids, nice boys, diamond rings—would be borne home in due course by the daughters of her friends, but not by me; all she could do was hope for a lesser rather than a greater disaster — an elopement, say, with a boy who could never earn his living, rather than an abduction into the White Slave trade.

But ignorance, my mother said, ignorance, or innocence if you like, is not always such a fine thing as people think and I am not sure it may not be dangerous for a girl like you; then she emphasized her point, as she had a habit of doing, with some quotation which had an innocent pomposity and odour of mothballs. I didn't even wince at it, knowing full well how it must have worked wonders with Mr. Berryman.

The evening I baby-sat for the Berrymans must have been in April. I had been in love all year, or at least since the first week in September, when a boy named Martin Collingwood had given me a surprised, appreciative, and rather ominously complacent smile in the school assembly. I never knew what surprised him; I was not looking like anybody but me; I had an old blouse on and my home-permanent had turned out badly. A few weeks after that he took me out for the first time, and kissed me on the dark side of the porch — also, I ought to say, on the mouth; I am sure it was the first time anybody had ever kissed me effectively, and I know that I did not wash my face that night or the next morning, in order to keep the imprint of those kisses intact. (I showed the most painful banality in the conduct of this whole affair, as you will see.) Two months, and a few amatory stages later, he dropped me. He had fallen for the girl who played opposite him in the Christmas production of *Pride and Prejudice.*°

I said I was not going to have anything to do with that play, and I got another girl to work on Makeup in my place, but of course I went to it after all, and sat down in front with my girl friend Joyce, who pressed my hand when I was overcome with pain and delight at the sight of Mr. Darcy in the white breeches, silk waistcoat, and sideburns. It was surely seeing Martin as Darcy that did it for me; every girl is in love with Darcy anyway, and the part gave Martin an arrogance and male splendour in my eyes which made it impossible to remember that he was simply a high-school senior, passably good-looking and of medium intelligence (and with a reputation slightly tainted, at that, by such preferences at the Drama Club and the Cadet *Band*) who happened to be the first boy the first really presentable boy to take an interest in me. In the last act they gave him a chance to embrace Elizabeth (Mary Bishop, with a sallow complexion and no figure but big vivacious eyes) and during this realistic encounter I dug my nails bitterly into Joyce's sympathetic palm.

That night was the beginning of months of real, if more or less self-inflicted,   5 misery for me. Why is it a temptation to refer to this sort of thing lightly, with irony, with amazement even, at finding oneself involved with such preposterous emotions in the unaccountable past? That is what we are apt to do, speaking of love; with adolescent love, of course, it's practically obligatory; you would think we sat around, dull afternoons, amusing ourselves with these tidbit recollections of pain. But it really doesn't make me feel very gay — worse still, it doesn't really surprise me — to remember all the stupid, sad, half-ashamed things I did, that people in love always do. I hung around the places where he might be seen, and then pretended not to see him; I made absurdly roundabout approaches, in conversation, to the bitter pleasure of casually mentioning his name. I daydreamed endlessly; in fact if you want to put it mathematically, I spent perhaps ten times as many hours thinking about Martin Collingwood — yes, pining and weeping for

---

Pride and Prejudice: A novel of manners by Jane Austen that features a rogue character named Mr. Darcy.

him—as I ever spent with him; the idea of him dominated my mind relentlessly and, after a while, against my will. For if at first I had dramatized my feelings, the time came when I would have been glad to escape them; my well-worn daydreams had become depressing and not even temporarily consoling. As I worked my math problems I would torture myself, quite mechanically and helplessly, with an exact recollection of Martin kissing my throat. I had an exact recollection of *everything*. One night I had an impulse to swallow all the aspirins in the bathroom cabinet, but stopped after I had taken six.

*　　*　　*

My mother noticed that something was wrong and got me some iron pills. She said, "Are you sure everything is going all right at school? *School!* When I told her that Martin and I had broken up all she said was, "Well so much the better for that. I never saw a boy so stuck on himself." "Martin has enough conceit to sink a battleship," I said morosely and went upstairs and cried.

The night I went to the Berrymans was a Saturday night. I baby-sat for them quite often on Saturday nights because they liked to drive over to Baileyville, a much bigger, livelier town about twenty miles away, and perhaps have supper and go to a show. They had been living in our town only two or three years—Mr. Berryman had been brought in as plant manager of the new door-factory—and they remained, I suppose by choice, on the fringes of its society; most of their friends were youngish couples like themselves, born in other places, who lived in new ranch-style houses on a hill outside town where we used to go tobogganing. This Saturday night they had two other couples in for drinks before they all drove over to Baileyville for the opening of a new supper-club; they were all rather festive. I sat in the kitchen and pretended to do Latin. last night had been the Spring Dance at the High School. I had not gone, since the only boy who had asked me was Millerd Crompton; who asked so many girls that he was suspected of working his way through the whole class alphabetically? But the dance was held in the Armouries, which was only half a block away from our house; I had been able to see the boys in dark suits; the girls in long pale formals under their coats, passing gravely under the street-lights, stepping around the last patches of snow. I could even hear the music and I have not forgotten to this day that they played "Ballerina," and — oh, 'song' of my aching heart — "Slow Boat to China." Joyce had phoned me up this morning and told me in her hushed way (we might have been discussing an incurable disease I had) that yes, M.C. *had* been there with M.B., and she had on a formal that must have been made out of somebody's old lace tablecloth, it just *hung*.

When the Berrymans and their friends had gone I went into the living room and read a magazine. I was mortally depressed. The big softly lit room, with its green and leaf-brown colours, made an uncluttered setting for the development of the emotions, such as you would get on a stage. At home the life of the emotions went on all right, but it always seemed to get buried under the piles of mending to be done, the ironing, the children's jigsaw puzzles and rock collections. It was the sort of house where people were always colliding with one another on the stairs and listening to hockey games and Superman on the radio.

I got up and found the Berrymans' "Danse Macabre"° and put it on the record player and turned out the living-room lights. The curtains were only partly drawn. A street light shone obliquely on the windowpane, making a rectangle of thin dusty gold, in which the shadows of bare branches moved, caught in the huge sweet winds of spring. It was a mild black night when the last snow was melting. A year ago all this—the music, the wind and darkness, the shadows of the branches—would have given me tremendous happiness: when they did not do so now, but only called up tediously familiar, somehow humiliatingly personal thoughts. I gave up my soul for dead and walked into the kitchen and decided to get drunk.

No, it was not like that. I walked into the kitchen to look for a Coke or some-   10
thing in the refrigerator, and there on the front of the counter were three tall beautiful bottles, all about half full of gold. But even after I had looked at them and lifted them to feel their weight I had not decided to get drunk; I had decided to have a drink.

Now here is where my ignorance, my disastrous innocence, comes in. It is true that I had seen the Berrymans and their friends drinking their highballs as casu- ally as I would drink a Coke, but I did not apply this attitude to myself. No, I thought of hard liquor as something to be taken in extremities, and relied upon for extravagant results, one way or another. My approach could not have been less casual if I had been the Little Mermaid° drinking the witch's crystal potion. Gravely, with a glance at my set face in the black window above the sink. I poured a little whisky from each of the bottles (I think now there were two brands to rye and an expensive Scotch) until I had my glass full. For I had never in my life seen anyone pour a drink and I had no idea that people frequently diluted their liquor with water, soda, et cetera, and I had seen that the glasses the Berrymans' guests were holding when I came through the living room were nearly full.

I drank it off as quickly as possible. I set the glass down and stood looking at my face in the window, half expecting to see it altered. My throat was burning, but I felt nothing else. It was very disappointing, when I had worked myself up to it. But I was not going to let it go at that. I poured another full glass, then filled each of the bottles with water to approximately the level I had seen when I came in. I drank the second glass only a little more slowly than the first. I put the empty glass down on the counter with care, perhaps feeling in my head a rustle of things to come and went and sat down on a chair in the living room. I reached up and turned on a floor lamp beside the chair, and the room jumped on me.

When I say that I was expecting extravagant results I do not mean that I was ex- pecting this. I had thought of some sweeping emotional change, an upsurge of gai- ety and irresponsibility, a feeling of lawlessness and escape, accompanied by a little dizziness and perhaps a tendency to giggle out loud. I did not have in mind the ceiling spinning like a great plate somebody had thrown at me nor the pale

---

"*Danse Macabre*": A symphonic poem composed by Camille Saint-Saens and usually performed by an orchestra.
Little Mermaid: Allusion to a fairy tale by Hans Christian Andersen.

green blobs of the chairs swelling, converging, disintegrating, playing with me a game full of enormous senseless inanimate malice. My head sank back: I closed my eyes. And at once opened them, opened them wide, threw myself out of the chair and down the hall and reached—thank God, thank God—the Berrymans bathroom, where I was sick everywhere, everywhere, and dropped like a stone.

From this point on I have no continuous picture of what happened; my memories of the next hour or two are split into vivid and improbable segments, with nothing but murk and uncertainty between. I do remember lying on the bathroom floor looking sideways at the little six-sided white tiles, which lay together in such an admirable and logical pattern, seeing them with the brief broken gratitude and sanity of one who has just been torn to pieces with vomiting. Then I remember sitting on the stool in front of the hall phone, asking weakly for Joyce's number. Joyce was not home. I was told by her mother (a rather rattlebrained woman, who didn't seem to notice a thing the matter—for which I felt weakly, mechanically grateful) that she was at Kay Stringer's house. I didn't know Kay's numbers so I just asked the operator; I felt I couldn't risk looking down at the telephone book.

15   Kay Stringer was not a friend of mine but a new friend of Joyce's. She had a vague reputation for wildness and a long switch of hair, very oddly though naturally, coloured—from soap-yellow to caramel-brown. She knew a lot of boys more exciting than Martin Collingwood, boys who had quit school or been imported into town to play on the hockey team. She and Joyce rode around in these boys' cars, and sometimes went with them—having lied of course to their mothers—to the Gay-la dance hall on the highway north of town.

I got Joyce on the phone. She was very keyed-up, as she always was with boys around, and she hardly seemed to hear what I was saying.

"Oh, I can't tonight," she said. "Some kids are here. We're going to play cards. You know Bill Kline? He's here. Ross Armour —"

"I'm *sick*," I said trying to speak, distinctly; it came out an inhuman croak. "I'm *drunk*. Joyce!" Then I fell off the stool and the receiver dropped out of my hand and banged for a while dismally against the wall.

I had not told Joyce where I was, so after thinking about it for a moment she phoned my mother, and using the elaborate and unnecessary subterfuge that young girls delight in, she found out. She and Kay and the boys — there were three of them — told some story about where they were going to Kay's mother, and got into the car and drove out. They found me still lying on the broadloom carpet in the hall; I had been sick again, and this time I had not made it to the bathroom.

20   It turned out that Kay Stringer, who arrived on this scene only by accident, was exactly the person I needed. She loved a crisis, particularly one like this, which had a shady and scandalous aspect and which must be kept secret from the adult world. She became excited, aggressive, efficient that energy which was termed wildness was simply the overflow of a great female instinct to manage, comfort and control. I could hear her voice coming at me from all directions, telling me not to worry, telling Joyce to find the biggest coffeepot they had and make it full of coffee (*strong* coffee, she said), telling the boys to pick me up and carry me to the sofa. Later, in the fog beyond my reach, she was calling for a scrub-brush.

Then I was lying on the sofa, covered with some kind of crocheted throw they had found in the bedroom. I didn't want to lift my head. The house was full of the smell of coffee. Joyce came in, looking very pale; she said that the Berryman kids had wakened up but she had given them a cookie and told them to go back to bed. It was all right, she hadn't let them out of their room and she didn't believe they'd remember. She said that she and Kay had cleaned up the bathroom and the hall though she was afraid there was still a spot on the rug. The coffee was ready. I didn't understand anything very well. The boys had turned on the radio and were going through the Berrymans' record collection; they had it out on the floor. I felt there was something odd about this but I could not think what it was.

Kay brought me a huge breakfast mug full of coffee.

"I don't know if I can, "I said. "Thanks."

"Sit up," she said briskly, as if dealing with drunks was an everyday business for her, I had no need to feel myself important. (I met, and recognized, that tone of voice years later, in the maternity ward.) "Now drink," she said. I drank, and at the same time realized that I was wearing only my slip. Joyce and Kay had taken off my blouse and skirt. They had brushed off the skirt and washed out the blouse, since it was nylon; it was hanging in the bathroom. I pulled the throw up under my arms and Kay laughed. She got everybody coffee. Joyce brought in the coffeepot and on Kay's instructions she kept filling my cup whenever I drank from it. Somebody said to me with interest. "You must have really wanted to tie one on."

"No," I said rather sulkily, obediently drinking my coffee, "I only had two drinks." 25

Kay laughed, "Well it certainly gets to you. I'll say that. What time do you expect *they'll* be back?" she said.

"Late, after one I think."

"You should be all right by that time. Have some more coffee."

Kay and one of the boys began dancing to the radio. Kay danced very sexily, but her face had the gently superior and indulgent, rather cold look it had when she was lifting me up to drink the coffee. The boy was whispering to her and she was smiling, shaking her head. Joyce said she was hungry, and she went out to the kitchen to see what there was — potato chips or crackers, or something like that, that you could eat without making too noticeable a dint. Bill Kline came over and sat on the sofa beside me and patted my legs through the crocheted throw. He didn't say anything to me, just patted my legs and looked at me with what seemed to me a very stupid, half-sick, absurd and alarming expression. I felt very uncomfortable; I wondered how it had ever got around that Bill Kline was so good looking, with an expression like that. I moved my legs nervously and he gave me a look of contempt not ceasing to pat me. Then I scrambled off the sofa, pulling the throw around me with the idea of going to the bathroom to see if my blouse was dry. I lurched a little when I started to walk, and for some reason — probably to show Bill Kline that he had not panicked me — I immediately exaggerated this, and calling out. "Watch me walk a straight line!" I lurched and stumbled to the accompaniment of everyone's laughter towards the hall I was standing in the archway between the hall and the living room when the knob of the front door turned with a small matter-of-fact click and everything became silent behind me except the radio of course and the

crocheted throw inspired by some delicate malice of its own slithered down around
my feet and there — oh, delicious moment in a well-organized farce — there stood
the Berrymans, Mr. and Mrs., with expressions on their faces as appropriate to the
occasion as any old-fashioned director of farces could wish. They must have been
preparing those expressions, of course; they could not have produced them in the
first moment of shock; with the noise we were making, they had no doubt heard us
as soon as they got out of the car; for the same reason, we had not heard them. I
don't think I ever knew what brought them home so early — a headache, an argument — and I was not really in a position to ask.

30   Mr. Berryman drove me home. I don't remember how I got into that car; or how
I found my clothes and put them on, or what kind of a goodnight, if any, I said to
Mrs. Berryman. I don't remember what happened to my friends, though I imagine
they gathered up their coats and fled, covering up the ignominy of their departure
with a mechanical roar of defiance. I remember Joyce with a box of crackers in
her hand, saying that I had become terribly sick from eating — I think she said
sauerkraut—for supper and that I had called them for help. (When I asked her
later what they made of this she said, "It wasn't any use: You *reeked*.") I remember
also her saying. "Oh, no, Mr. Berryman I beg of you, my mother is a terribly nervous person. I don't know what the shock might do to her. I will go down on my
knees to you if you like but *you must not phone my mother*." I have no picture of her
down on her knees — and she would have done it in a minute — so it seems this
threat was not carried out.

   Mr. Berryman said to me, "Well I guess you know your behaviour tonight is a
pretty serious thing." He made it sound as if I might be charged with criminal negligence or something worse. "It would be very wrong me to overlook it," he said. I
suppose that besides being angry and disgusted with *me*, he was worried about taking me home in this condition to my strait-laced parents, who could always say I
got the liquor in his house. Plenty of Temperance people would think that enough
to hold him responsible, and the town was full of Temperance people. Good relations with the town were very important to him from a business point of view.

   "I have an idea it wasn't the first time," he said. "If it was the first time would a
girl be smart enough to fill three bottles up with water? No. Well in this case, she
was smart enough, but not smart enough to know I could spot it. What do you say
to that?" I opened my mouth to answer and although I was feeling quite sober the
only sound that came out was a loud, desolate-sounding giggle. He stopped in front
of our house. "Light's on," he said. Now go in and tell your parents the straight
truth. And if you don't, remember I will." He did not mention paying me for my
baby-sitting services of the evening and the subject did not occur to me either.

   I went into the house and tried to go straight upstairs but my mother called to
me. She came into the front hall, where I had not turned on the light, and she
must have smelled me at once for she ran forward with a cry of pure amazement,
as if she had seen somebody falling, and caught me by the shoulders as I did indeed fall down against the bannister over whelmed by my fantastic lucklessness,
and I told her everything from the start, not omitting even the name of Martin
Collingwood and my flirtation with the aspirin bottle, which was a mistake.

On Monday morning my mother took the bus over to Baileyville and found the liquor store and bought a bottle of Scotch whisky. Then she had to wait for a bus back, and she met some people she knew and she was not quite able to hide the bottle in her bag; she was furious with herself for not bringing a proper shopping-bag. As soon as she got back she walked out to the Berrymans; she had not even had lunch. Mr Berryman had not gone back to the factory. My mother went in and had a talk with both of them and made an excellent impression and then Mr. Berryman drove her home. She talked to them in the forthright and unemotional way she had, which was always agreeably surprising to people prepared to deal with a mother, and she told them that although I seemed to do well enough at school I was extremely backward—or perhaps eccentric—in my emotional development. I imagine that this analysis of my behaviour was especially effective with Mrs. Berryman, a great reader of Child Guidance books. Relations between them warmed to the point where my mother brought up a specific instance of my difficulties, and disarmingly related to the whole story of Martin Collingwood.

Within a few days it was all over town and the school that I had tried to commit suicide over Martin Collingwood. But it was already all over school and the town that the Berrymans had come home on Saturday night to find me drunk, staggering, wearing nothing but my slip, in a room with three boys, one of whom was Bill Kline. My mother had said that I was to pay for the bottle she had taken the Berrymans out of my baby-sitting earnings, but my clients melted away like the last April snow, and it would not be paid for yet it newcomers to town had not moved in across the street in July, and needed a baby sitter before they talked to any of their neighbours. 35

My mother also said that it had been a great mistake to let me go out with boys and that I would not be going out again until well after my sixteenth birthday, if then. This did not prove to be a concrete hardship at all, because it was at least that long before anybody asked me. If you think that news of the Berrymans adventure would put me in demand for whatever gambols and orgies were going on in and around that town, you could not be more mistaken. The extraordinary publicity which attended my first debauch may have made me seem marked for a special kind of ill luck, like the girl whose illegitimate baby turns out to be triplets: nobody wants to have anything to do with her. At any rate I had at the same time one of the most silent telephones and positively the most sinful reputation in the whole High School. I had to put up with this until the next fall, when a fat blonde girl in grade ten ran away with a married man and was picked up two months later, living in sin—though not with the same man—in the city of Sault Ste Marie. Then everybody forgot about me.

But there was a positive, a splendidly unexpected result of this affair: I got completely over Martin Collingwood. It was not only that he at once said publicly, that he had always thought I was a nut; where he was concerned I had no pride, and my tender fancy could have found a way around that, a month, a week, before. What was it that brought me back into the world again? It was the terrible and fascinating reality of my disaster; it was *the way things happened*. Not that I enjoyed it; I was a self-conscious girl and I suffered a good deal from all this exposure. But the development of events on that Saturday night—that fascinated me; I felt that I had

had a glimpse of the shameless, marvelous, shattering absurdity with which the plots of life, though not of fiction, are improvised. I could not take my eyes off it.

And of course Martin Collingwood wrote his Senior Matric that June, and went away to the city to take a course at a school for Morticians, as I think it is called, and when he came back he went into his uncle's undertaking business. We lived in the same town and we would hear most things that happened to each other but I do not think we met face to face or saw one another, except at a distance, for years. I went to a shower for the girl he married, but then everybody went to everybody else's showers. No, I do not think I really saw him again until I came home after I had been married several years, to attend a relative's funeral. Then I saw him; not quite Mr. Darcy but still very nice-looking in those black clothes. And I saw him looking over at me with an expression as close to a reminiscent smile as the occasion would permit, and I knew that he had been surprised by a memory either of my devotion or my little buried catastrophe. I gave him a gentle uncomprehending look in return. I am a grown-up woman now, let him unbury his own catastrophes.

Reading and Reacting

1. What are the advantages of having a first-person narrator tell the story? How would a third-person narrator change "An Ounce of Cure"?

2. Does the narrator see herself as like or unlike her peers? How does her view of herself trigger the events in the story?

3. Describe the narrator's tone. For example, is she serious? Funny? Sarcastic? Detached?

4. The narrator is an adult telling about an experience she had in high school. Why are the events described in this story still important to the narrator years later?

5. What is the narrator's opinion of the following characters:

   • Her mother
   • The Berrymans
   • Joyce
   • Kay Stringer
   • Martin Collingwood

   What do the narrator's opinions of these people reveal about her?

6. How would you characterize the narrator's relationship with her mother? How does her mother help her with her difficulties? How does her mother make things worse?

7. In paragraph 3, the narrator catches Martin Collingwood looking at her. At the end of the story, she catches the adult Martin Collingwood again looking at her. In each case, how does she react to this attention? What do the differences in her reactions reveal about the narrator?

8. Why does the narrator decide to start drinking? What does this experience teach her about life? About herself?

9. **JOURNAL ENTRY** The story's title is a play on the saying, "An ounce of prevention is worth a pound of cure." What do you think this saying means? What does the story's title mean? How does it foreshadow events to come?

10. CRITICAL PERSPECTIVE The 2001 Rea Award jurors Maureen Howard, James Salter, and Edmund White praised Alice Munro's writing with these words:

> Munro's wisdom lies in her ability to portray the close-up, the self-dramatizing moment or limited vision then draw back for the complex and informing view. As one of her most endearing characters discovers, you can "look up from your life of the moment and feel the world crackling beyond the walls." In her art of the story, Alice Munro encourages us to reflect, to see our own time and place and perhaps to redeem, if not ourselves, at least our own stories in the larger setting of the world.

What is the "self-dramatizing" moment in this story? What does the main character come to understand about herself when she looks up from her "life of the moment"? How might this story encourage readers to "redeem [their] own stories in the larger setting of the world"?

Related Works: "The Secret Lion" (p. 170), "Greasy Lake" (p. 648), "Suicide Note" (p. 860), "Cinderella" (p. 882), "The Soul Selects Her Own Society" (p. 1165), *Beauty* (p. 1308)

WRITING SUGGESTIONS: Point of View

1. How would Poe's "The Cask of Amontillado" be different if it were told by a minor character who observed the events? Rewrite the story from this point of view — or tell the story that precedes the story, explaining the "thousand injuries" and the "insult."
2. Assume that you are the sailor in "Big Black Good Man" and that you are keeping a journal of your travels. Write the journal entries for the time you spent in Copenhagen. Include your impressions of Olaf, Lena, the hotel, and anything else that caught your attention. Make sure you present your version of the key events described in the story — especially Olaf's reaction to you.
3. Both "The Cask of Amontillado" and "Barn Burning" deal with crimes that essentially go unpunished and with the emotions that accompany these crimes. In what sense does each story's use of point of view shape its treatment of the crime in question? For instance, how does point of view determine how much readers know about the motives for the crime, the crime's basic circumstances, and the extent to which the crime is justified?
4. Write a story in which you retell "An Ounce of Cure" from Martin Collingwood's point of view. Be true to the original story. Be sure to reveal what he was thinking when he saw the narrator at the beginning and at the end of the story.
5. Write a farewell letter from the wife in "The Disappearance" to the husband. Tell him why you are leaving him and what you hope to accomplish by doing so. Above all, explain why you are leaving your son with him.

CHAPTER 16

STYLE, TONE, AND LANGUAGE

> The difference between the right word and the nearly right word is the same as that between lightning and the lightning bug.
>
> — Mark Twain

Style and Tone

One of the qualities that gives a work of literature its individuality is its **style**, the way in which a writer uses language, selecting and arranging words to say what he or she wants to say. Style encompasses elements such as word choice; syntax; sentence length and structure; and the presence, frequency, and prominence of imagery and figures of speech.

Closely related to style is **tone**, the attitude of the narrator or author of a work toward the subject matter, characters, or audience. Word choice and sentence structure help to create a work's tone, which may be intimate or distant, bitter or affectionate, straightforward or cautious, supportive or critical, respectful or condescending. (Tone may also be **ironic**; see Chapter 15, "Point of View," for a discussion of irony.)

The Uses of Language

Language offers almost limitless possibilities to a writer. Creative use of language (such as unusual word choice, word order, or sentence structure) can enrich a story and add to its overall effect. Sometimes, in fact, a writer's use of language can expand a story's possibilities through its very inventiveness. For example, James Joyce's innovative **stream-of-consciousness** style mimics thought, allowing ideas to run into one another as random associations are made so that readers may follow and participate in the thought processes of the narrator. Here is a stream-of-consciousness passage from Joyce's experimental 1922 novel *Ulysses*.

> frseeeeeeeefronnnng train somewhere whistling the strength those engines have in them like big giants and the water rolling all over and out of them all sides like the end of Loves old sweet sonnnng the poor men that have to be out all the night from their wives and families in those roasting engines stifling it was today. . . .

Most often, language is used to enhance a story's other elements. It may, for example, help to create an atmosphere that is important to the story's plot or theme, as Kate Chopin's lush, rhythmic sentences help to create the sexually charged atmosphere of "The Storm" (p. 281)—an atmosphere that overpowers the characters and thus drives the plot. Language may also help to delineate character, perhaps by conveying a character's mental state to readers. For instance, the breathless, disjointed style of Edgar Allan Poe's "The Tell-Tale Heart" (p. 773) suggests the narrator's increasing emotional instability: "Was it possible they heard not? Almighty God!—no, no! They heard!—they suspected!—they *knew!*—they were making a mockery of my horror!" In his 1925 short story "Big Two-Hearted River," Ernest Hemingway uses sentences without transitions to create a flat, emotionless prose style that reveals his character's alienation and fragility as he struggles to maintain control: "Now things were done. There had been this to do. Now it was done. It had been a hard trip. He was very tired. That was done. He had made his camp. He was settled. Nothing could touch him."

Language that places emphasis on the sounds and rhythm of words and sentences can also enrich a work of fiction. Consider the use of such language in the following sentence from James Joyce's "Araby" (p. 395).

> The light from the lamp opposite our door caught the white curve of her neck, lit up her hair that rested there and, falling, lit up the hand upon the railing.

Here the narrator is describing his first conversation with a girl who fascinates him, and the lush, lyrical, almost musical language reflects his enchantment. Note in particular the **alliteration** (light/lamp; caught/curve; hair/hand), the repetition (lit up/lit up), and the rhyme (lit up her *hair*/that rested *there*) and **near rhyme** (falling/railing); these poetic devices connect the words of the sentence into a smooth, rhythmic whole.

Another example of this emphasis on sound may be found in the measured **parallelism** of this sentence from Nathaniel Hawthorne's 1843 story "The Birthmark."

> He had left his laboratory to the care of an assistant, cleared his fine countenance from the furnace smoke, washed the stain of acids from his fingers, and persuaded a beautiful woman to become his wife.

The style of this sentence, conveying methodical precision and order, reflects the compulsive personality of the character being described.

The following passage from Alberto Alvaro Ríos's story "The Secret Lion" (p. 170) illustrates the power of language to enrich a story.

> We had read the books, after all; we knew about bridges and castles and wildtreacherousraging alligatormouth rivers. We wanted them. So we were going to go out and get them. We went back that morning into that kitchen and we said, "We're going out there, we're going into the hills, we're going away for three days, don't worry." She said, "All right."
>
> "You know," I said to Sergio, "if we're going to go away for three days, well, we ought to at least pack a lunch."
>
> But we were two young boys with no patience for what we thought at the time was mom-stuff: making sa-and-wiches. My mother didn't offer. So we got out little kid knapsacks that my mother had sewn for us, and into them we put

the jar of mustard. A loaf of bread. Knivesforksplates, bottles of Coke, a can opener. This was lunch for the two of us. And we were weighed down, humped over to be strong enough to carry this stuff. But we started walking anyway, into the hills. We were going to eat berries and stuff otherwise. "Goodbye." My mom said that.

Through language, the adult narrator of the preceding paragraphs recaptures the bravado of the boys in search of "wildtreacherousraging alligatormouth rivers" even as he suggests to readers that the boys are not going far. The story's use of language is original and inventive: words are blended together ("getridofit," "knivesforks plates"), linked to form new words ("mom-stuff"), and drawn out ("sa-and-wiches") to mimic speech. These experiments with language show the narrator's willingness to move back into a child's frame of reference while maintaining the advantage of distance. The adult narrator uses sentence fragments ("A loaf of bread."), colloquialisms ("kid," "mom," "stuff"), and contractions. He also includes conversational elements such as *you know* and *well* in the story's dialogue, accurately re-creating the childhood scene at the same time he sees its folly and remains aware of the disillusionment that awaits him. Thus, the unique style permits the narrator to bring readers with him into the child's world even as he maintains his adult stance: "But we were two young boys with no patience for what we thought at the time was mom-stuff. . . ."

Although many stylistic options are available to writers, a story's language must be consistent with the writer's purpose and with the effect he or she hopes to create. Just as writers may experiment with point of view or manipulate events to create a complex plot, so they can adjust language to suit a particular narrator or character or to convey a particular theme. In addition to the creative uses of language described above, writers also frequently experiment with *formal and informal diction*, *imagery*, and *figures of speech*.

Formal and Informal Diction

The level of diction — how formal or informal a story's language is — can reveal a good deal about those who use the language.

Formal diction is characterized by elaborate, complex sentences; a learned vocabulary; and a serious, objective, detached tone. The speaker avoids contractions, shortened word forms (like *phone*), regional expressions, and slang, and he or she may use *one* or *we* in place of *I*. At its most extreme, formal language is stiff and stilted, far removed from everyday speech.

Formal diction, whether used by a narrator or by a character, may indicate erudition, a high educational level, a superior social or professional position, or emotional detachment. When one character's language is significantly more formal than others', he or she may seem old-fashioned or stuffy; when language is inappropriately elevated or complex, it may reveal the character to be pompous or ridiculous; when a narrator's language is noticeably more formal than that of the characters, the narrator may seem superior or even condescending. Thus, the choice of a particular level (or levels) of diction in a story conveys information about characters and about the narrator's attitude toward them.

The following passage from Hawthorne's "The Birthmark" illustrates formal style.

> In the latter part of the last century there lived a man of science, an eminent proficient in every branch of natural philosophy, who not long before our story opens had made experience of a spiritual affinity more attractive than any chemical one. He had left his laboratory to the care of an assistant, cleared his fine countenance from the furnace smoke, washed the stain of acids from his fingers, and persuaded a beautiful woman to become his wife. In those days when the comparatively recent discovery of electricity and other kindred mysteries of Nature seemed to open paths into the region of miracle, it was not unusual for the love of science to rival the love of woman in its depth and absorbing energy. The higher intellect, the imagination, the spirit, and even the heart might all find their congenial ailment in pursuits which, as some of their ardent votaries believed, would ascend from one step of powerful intelligence to another, until the philosopher should lay his hand on the secret of creative force and perhaps make new worlds for himself.

The long and complex sentences, learned vocabulary ("countenance," "ailment," "votaries"), and absence of colloquialisms suit Hawthorne's purpose well, recreating the formal language of the earlier era in which his story is set. The omniscient narrator is aloof and controlled, and his diction makes this clear to readers.

Informal diction, consistent with everyday speech, is characterized by slang, contractions, colloquial expressions like *you know* and *I mean*, shortened word forms, incomplete sentences, and a casual, conversational tone. A first-person narrator may use an informal style, or characters may speak informally; in either case, informal style tends to narrow the distance between readers and text.

Informal language can range from the straightforward contemporary style of Cal's speech in Anne Tyler's "Teenage Wasteland" ("'I think this kid is hurting. You know?'") to the regionalisms and dialect used in Flannery O'Connor's "A Good Man Is Hard to Find" ("aloose"; "you all"; "britches"). In "Teenage Wasteland" (p. 799), Cal's self-consciously slangy, conversational style tells readers a good deal about his motives and his method of operating; in "A Good Man Is Hard to Find" (p. 409), speech patterns and diction help to identify the region in which the characters live and their social class. Informal language may also include language readers find offensive. In this case, a character's use of obscenities may suggest his or her crudeness or adolescent bravado, and the use of racial or ethnic slurs indicates that a character is insensitive and bigoted.

The following passage from John Updike's "A&P" (p. 230) illustrates informal style.

> She had sort of oaky hair that the sun and salt had bleached, done up in a bun that was unravelling, and a kind of prim face. Walking into the A&P with your straps down, I suppose it's the only kind of face you *can* have. She held her head so high her neck, coming out of those white shoulders, looked kind of stretched, but I didn't mind. The longer her neck was, the more of her there was.

Here, the first-person narrator, a nineteen-year-old supermarket checkout clerk, uses a conversational style, including colloquialisms ("sort of," "I suppose," "kind of"), contractions ("it's," "didn't"), and the imprecise, informal *you* ("Walking into the A&P with *your* straps down. . . ."). The narrator uses neither elaborate syntax nor a learned vocabulary.

Imagery

Imagery—words and phrases that describe what is seen, heard, smelled, tasted, or touched—can have a significant impact in a story. A writer may use a pattern of repeated imagery to convey a particular impression about a character or situation or to communicate or reinforce a story's theme. For example, the theme of newly discovered sexuality can be conveyed through repeated use of words and phrases suggesting blooming or ripening.

In T. Coraghessan Boyle's "Greasy Lake" (p. 648), the narrator's vivid description of Greasy Lake uses rich visual imagery to evoke a scene.

> Through the center of town, up the strip, past the housing developments and shopping malls, street lights giving way to the thin streaming illumination of the headlights, trees crowding the asphalt in a black unbroken wall: that was the way out to Greasy Lake. The Indians had called it Wakan, a reference to the clarity of its waters. Now it was fetid and murky, the mud banks glittering with broken glass and strewn with beer cans and the charred remains of bonfires. There was a single ravaged island a hundred yards from shore, so stripped of vegetation it looked as if the air force had strafed it. We went up to the lake because everyone went there, because we wanted to snuff the rich scent of possibility on the breeze, watch a girl take off her clothes and plunge into the festering murk, drink beer, smoke pot, howl at the stars, savor the incongruous full-throated roar of rock and roll against the primeval susurrus of frogs and crickets. This was nature.

By characterizing a natural setting with surprising words like "fetid," "murky," and "greasy" and unpleasant images such as the "glittering of broken glass," the "ravaged island," and the "charred remains of bonfires," Boyle creates a picture that is completely at odds with the traditional view of nature. The incongruous images are nevertheless perfectly consistent with the sordid events that take place at Greasy Lake.

Figures of Speech

Figures of speech—such as *similes*, *metaphors*, and *personification*—can enrich a story, subtly revealing information about characters and themes.

By using **metaphors** and **similes**—figures of speech that compare two dissimilar items—writers can indicate a particular attitude toward characters and events. Thus, Flannery O'Connor's many grotesque similes in "A Good Man Is Hard to Find" help to dehumanize her characters; the children's mother, for instance, has a face "as broad and innocent as a cabbage." In Tillie Olsen's "I Stand Here Ironing" (p. 309), an extended metaphor in which a mother compares her daughter to a dress waiting to be ironed expresses the mother's attitude toward her child, effectively suggesting to readers the daughter's vulnerability. Similes and metaphors are used throughout in Kate Chopin's "The Storm" (p. 281). In a scene of sexual awakening, Calixta's skin is "like a creamy lily," her passion is "like a white flame," and her mouth is "a fountain of delight"; these figures of speech add a lushness and sensuality to the story.

Personification— a figure of speech, closely related to metaphor, that endows inanimate objects or abstract ideas with life or with human characteristics — is used in "Araby" (p. 395), where houses, "conscious of decent lives within them, gazed at one another with brown imperturbable faces." This use of figurative language expands readers' vision of the story's setting and gives a dreamlike quality to the passage. (Other figures of speech, such as **hyperbole** and **understatement**, can also enrich works of fiction. See Chapter 28, "Figures of Speech," for further information.)

Allusions— references to familiar historical, cultural, literary, or biblical texts, figures, or events — may also expand readers' understanding and appreciation of a work. An allusion widens a work's context by bringing it into the context of a related subject or idea. For instance, in Charles Baxter's short story "Gryphon" (p. 248), the narrator's allusions to Pinocchio and Betty Crocker enable readers who recognize the references to gain a deeper understanding of what a central character is really like.

> **NOTE:** In analyzing the use of language in a work of fiction, you may occasionally encounter obscure allusions (or foreign words and phrases or unfamiliar regional expressions), particularly in works treating cultures and historical periods other than your own. Frequently, such language will be clarified by the context, or by explanatory notes in your text. When it is not, you should consult a dictionary, encyclopedia, or other reference work.

✔ **CHECKLIST Writing about Style, Tone, and Language**

- Does the writer make any unusual creative use of word choice, word order, or sentence structure?

- Is the story's tone intimate? Distant? Ironic? How does the tone advance the writer's purpose?

- Does the style emphasize the sound and rhythm of language? For example, does the writer use alliteration and assonance? Repetition and parallelism? What do such techniques add to the story?

- Is the level of diction generally formal, informal, or somewhere in between?

- Is there a difference between the style of the narrator and the style of the characters' speech? If so, what is the effect of this difference?

- Do any of the story's characters use regionalisms, colloquial language, or nonstandard speech? If so, what effect does this language have?

- What do different characters' levels of diction reveal about them?

continued on next page

■ What kind of imagery predominates? Where, and why, is imagery used?

■ Does the story develop a pattern of imagery? How does this pattern of imagery relate to the story's themes?

■ Does the story use simile and metaphor? Personification? What is the effect of these figures of speech?

■ Do figures of speech reinforce the story's themes? Reveal information about characters?

■ Does the story make any historical, literary, or biblical allusions? What do these allusions contribute to the story?

■ Are any unfamiliar, obscure, or foreign words, phrases, or images used in the story? What do these words or expressions contribute to the story?

JAMES JOYCE (1884–1941) was born in Dublin but lived his entire adult life in self-imposed exile from his native Ireland. Though his parents sent him to schools that trained young men for the priesthood, Joyce saw himself as a religious and artistic rebel and fled to Paris soon after graduation in 1902. Recalled briefly to Dublin by his mother's fatal illness, Joyce returned to the Continent in 1904, taking with him an uneducated Irish country girl named Nora Barnacle, who became his wife in 1931. In dreary quarters in Trieste, Zurich, and Paris, Joyce struggled to support a growing family, sometimes teaching classes in Berlitz language schools.

Though Joyce never again lived in Ireland, he continued to write about Dublin. Publication of *Dubliners* (1914), a collection of short stories that included "Araby," was delayed for seven years because the Irish publisher feared libel suts from local citizens who were thinly disguised as characters in the stories. Joyce's autobiographical *Portrait of the Artist as a Young Man* (1916) tells of a young writer's rejection of family, church, and country. *Ulysses* (1922), the comic tale of eighteen hours in the life of a wandering Dublin advertising salesman, was banned when the United States Post Office brought charges of obscenity against the book, and it remained banned in the United States and England for more than a decade. With *Ulysses,* Joyce began a revolutionary journey away from traditional techniques of plot and characterization to the interior monologues and stream-of-consciousness style that mark his last great novel, *Finnegans Wake* (1939).

Cultural Context In the early twentieth century, as world travel and the shipment of goods around the world expanded at a dizzying pace, the West experienced a fascination with the "Orient." To peddle their wares, immigrants from the East established bazaars reminiscent of the ones in their homelands, presenting spices, foods, and material goods in a dazzling array. This exotic appeal to the senses, representing the allure of the distant and unknown, became a highlight of many towns and cities. In this story, the bazaar represents the allure of the strange and exotic for the young narrator.

Araby (1914)

North Richmond Street, being blind,° was a quiet street except at the hour when the Christian Brothers' School set the boys free. An uninhabited house of two storeys stood at the blind end, detached from its neighbours in a square ground. The other houses of the street, conscious of decent lives within them, gazed at one another with brown imperturbable faces.

The former tenant of our house, a priest, had died in the back drawing-room. Air, musty from having been long enclosed, hung in all the rooms, and the waste room behind the kitchen was littered with old useless papers. Among these I found a few paper-covered books, the pages of which were curled and damp: *The Abbot*, by Walter Scott, *The Devout Communicant* and *The Memoirs of Vidocq*.° I liked the last best because its leaves were yellow. The wild garden behind the house contained a central apple-tree and a few straggling bushes under one of which I found the late tenant's rusty bicycle-pump. He had been a very charitable priest; in his will he had left all his money to institutions and the furniture of his house to his sister.

When the short days of winter came dusk fell before we had well eaten our dinners. When we met in the street the houses had grown sombre. The space of sky above us was the colour of ever-changing violet and towards it the lamps of the street lifted their feeble lanterns. The cold air stung us and we played till our bodies glowed. Our shouts echoed in the silent street. The career of our play brought us through the dark muddy lanes behind the houses where we ran the gauntlet of the rough tribes from the cottages, to the back doors of the dark dripping gardens where odours arose from the ashpits, to the dark odorous stables where a coach-man smoothed and combed the horse or shook music from the buckled harness. When we returned to the street light from the kitchen windows had filled the areas. If my uncle was seen turning the corner we hid in the shadow until we had seen him safely housed. Or if Mangan's sister came out on the doorstep to call her brother in to his tea we watched her from our shadow peer up and down the street. We waited to see whether she would remain or go in and, if she remained, we left our shadow and walked up to Mangan's steps resignedly. She was waiting for us, her figure defined by the light from the half-opened door. Her brother always teased her before he obeyed and I stood by the railings looking at her. Her dress swung as she moved her body and the soft rope of her hair tossed from side to side.

Every morning I lay on the floor in the front parlour watching her door. The blind was pulled down to within an inch of the sash so that I could not be seen. When she came out on the doorstep my heart leaped. I ran to the hall, seized my

---

blind: Dead-end.

The Abbot . . . Vidocq: Sir Walter Scott (1771–1832)—an English Romantic novelist; *The Devout Communicant*—a variant title for *Pious Meditations,* written by an eighteenth-century English Franciscan friar, Pacifus Baker; *The Memoirs of Vidocq*—an autobiography of François-Jules Vidocq (1775–1857), a French criminal turned police agent.

books and followed her. I kept her brown figure always in my eye and, when we came near the point at which our ways diverged, I quickened my pace and passed her. This happened morning after morning. I had never spoken to her, except for a few casual words, and yet her name was like a summons to all my foolish blood.

5 Her image accompanied me even in places the most hostile to romance. On Saturday evenings when my aunt went marketing I had to go to carry some of the parcels. We walked through the flaring streets, jostled by drunken men and bar-gaining women, amid the curses of labourers, the shrill litanies of shop-boys who stood on guard by the barrels of pigs' cheeks, the nasal chanting of street-singers, who sang a *come-all-you* about O'Donovan Rossa,° or a ballad about the troubles in our native land. These noises converged in a single sensation of life for me: I imagined that I bore my chalice safely through a throng of foes. Her name sprang to my lips at moments in strange prayers and praises which I myself did not un-derstand. My eyes were often full of tears (I could not tell why) and at times a flood from my heart seemed to pour itself out into my bosom. I thought little of the future. I did not know whether I would ever speak to her or not or, if I spoke to her, how I could tell her of my confused adoration. But my body was like a harp and her words and gestures were like fingers running upon the wires.

One evening I went into the back drawing-room in which the priest had died. It was a dark rainy evening and there was no sound in the house. Through one of the broken panes I heard the rain impinge upon the earth, the fine incessant needles of water playing in the sodden beds. Some distant lamp or lighted win-dow gleamed below me. I was thankful that I could see so little. All my senses seemed to desire to veil themselves and, feeling that I was about to slip from them, I pressed the palms of my hands together until they trembled, murmuring: "*O love! O love!*" many times.

At last she spoke to me. When she addressed the first words to me I was so confused that I did not know what to answer. She asked me was I going to *Araby*. I forgot whether I answered yes or no. It would be a splendid bazaar, she said she would love to go.

"And why can't you?" I asked.

While she spoke she turned a silver bracelet round and round her wrist. She could not go, she said, because there would be a retreat that week in her convent.° Her brother and two other boys were fighting for their caps and I was alone at the railings. She held one of the spikes, bowing her head towards me. The light from the lamp opposite our door caught the white curve of her neck, lit up her hair that rested there and, falling, lit up the hand upon the railing. It fell over one side of her dress and caught the white border of a petticoat, just visible as she stood at ease.

10 "It's well for you," she said.

"If I go," I said, "I will bring you something."

O'Donovan Rossa: Any popular song beginning "Come all you gallant Irishmen . . ."; O'Donovan Rossa was an Irish nationalist who was banished in 1870 for advocating violent rebellion against the British.

convent: Her convent school.

What innumerable follies laid waste my waking and sleeping thoughts after that evening! I wished to annihilate the tedious intervening days. I chafed against the work of school. At night in my bedroom and by day in the classroom her image came between me and the page I strove to read. The syllables of the word *Araby* were called to me through the silence in which my soul luxuriated and cast an Eastern enchantment over me. I asked for leave to go to the bazaar on Saturday night. My aunt was surprised and hoped it was not some Freemason° affair. I answered few questions in class. I watched my master's face pass from amiability to sternness; he hoped I was not beginning to idle. I could not call my wandering thoughts together. I had hardly any patience with the serious work of life which, now that it stood between me and my desire, seemed to me child's play, ugly monotonous child's play.

On Saturday morning I reminded my uncle that I wished to go to the bazaar in the evening. He was fussing at the hallstand, looking for the hatbrush, and answered me curtly:

"Yes, boy, I know."

As he was in the hall I could not go into the front parlour and lie at the window. I left the house in bad humour and walked slowly towards the school. The air was pitilessly raw and already my heart misgave me.

When I came home to dinner my uncle had not yet been home. Still it was early. I sat staring at the clock for some time and, when its ticking began to irritate me, I left the room. I mounted the staircase and gained the upper part of the house. The high cold empty gloomy rooms liberated me and I went from room to room singing. From the front window I saw my companions playing below in the street. Their cries reached me weakened and indistinct and, leaning my forehead against the cool glass, I looked over at the dark house where she lived. I may have stood there for an hour, seeing nothing but the brown-clad figure cast by my imagination, touched discreetly by the lamplight at the curved neck, at the hand upon the railings and at the border below the dress.

When I came downstairs again I found Mrs. Mercer sitting at the fire. She was an old garrulous woman, a pawnbroker's widow, who collected used stamps for some pious purpose. I had to endure the gossip of the tea-table. The meal was prolonged beyond an hour and still my uncle did not come. Mrs. Mercer stood up to go: she was sorry she couldn't wait any longer, but it was after eight o'clock and she did not like to be out late, as the night air was bad for her. When she had gone I began to walk up and down the room, clenching my fists. My aunt said:

"I'm afraid you may put off your bazaar for this night of Our Lord."

At nine o'clock I heard my uncle's latchkey in the halldoor. I heard him talking to himself and heard the hallstand rocking when it had received the weight of his overcoat. I could interpret these signs. When he was midway through his dinner I asked him to give me the money to go to the bazaar. He had forgotten.

"The people are in bed and after their first sleep now," he said.   20

Freemason: At the time the story takes place, many Catholics in Ireland thought the Masonic Order was a threat to the church.

I did not smile. My aunt said to him energetically:

"Can't you give him the money and let him go? You've kept him late enough as it is."

My uncle said he was very sorry he had forgotten. He said he believed in the old saying: "All work and no play makes Jack a dull boy." He asked me where I was going and, when I had told him a second time he asked me did I know *The Arab's Farewell to his Steed*.° When I left the kitchen he was about to recite the opening lines of the piece to my aunt.

I held a florin tightly in my hand as I strode down Buckingham Street towards the station. The sight of the streets thronged with buyers and glaring with gas recalled to me the purpose of my journey. I took my seat in a third-class carriage of a deserted train. After an intolerable delay the train moved out of the station slowly. It crept onward among ruinous houses and over the twinkling river. At Westland Row Station a crowd of people pressed to the carriage doors; but the porters moved them back, saying that it was a special train for the bazaar. I remained alone in the bare carriage. In a few minutes the train drew up beside an improvised wooden platform. I passed out on to the road and saw by the lighted dial of a clock that it was ten minutes to ten. In front of me was a large building which displayed the magical name.

25   I could not find any sixpenny entrance and, fearing that the bazaar would be closed, I passed in quickly through a turnstile, handing a shilling to a weary-looking man. I found myself in a big hall girdled at half its height by a gallery. Nearly all the stalls were closed and the greater part of the hall was in darkness. I recognised a silence like that which pervades a church after a service. I walked into the centre of the bazaar timidly. A few people were gathered about the stalls which were still open. Before a curtain, over which the words *Café Chantant*° were written in coloured lamps, two men were counting money on a salver. I listened to the fall of the coins.

Remembering with difficulty why I had come I went over to one of the stalls and examined porcelain vases and flowered tea-sets. At the door of the stall a young lady was talking and laughing with two young gentlemen. I remarked their English accents and listened vaguely to their conversation.

"O, I never said such a thing!"

"O, but you did!"

"O, but I didn't!"

30   "Didn't she say that?"

"Yes. I heard her."

"O, there's a . . . fib!"

Observing me the young lady came over and asked me did I wish to buy anything. The tone of her voice was not encouraging; she seemed to have spoken to me out of a sense of duty. I looked humbly at the great jars that stood like eastern guards at either side of the dark entrance to the stall and murmured:

The Arab's Farewell to his Steed: A sentimental poem by Caroline Norton (1808–1877) that tells the story of a nomad's heartbreak after selling his much-loved horse.

Café Chantant: A Paris café featuring musical entertainment.

"No, thank you."

The young lady changed the position of one of the vases and went back to the   35
two young men. They began to talk of the same subject. Once or twice the young
lady glanced at me over her shoulder.

I lingered before her stall, though I knew my stay was useless, to make my interest in her wares seem the more real. Then I turned away slowly and walked
down the middle of the bazaar. I allowed the two pennies to fall against the sixpence in my pocket. I heard a voice call from one end of the gallery that the light
was out. The upper part of the hall was now completely dark.

Gazing up into the darkness I saw myself as a creature driven and derided by
vanity; and my eyes burned with anguish and anger.

Reading and Reacting

1. How would you characterize the story's level of diction? Is this level
   appropriate for a story about a young boy's experiences? Explain.
2. Identify several figures of speech in the story. Where is Joyce most likely to
   use this kind of language? Why?
3. What words and phrases express the boy's extreme idealism and romantic
   view of the world? How does such language help to communicate the story's
   major theme?
4. In paragraph 4, the narrator says, "her name was like a summons to all my
   foolish blood." In the story's last sentence, he sees himself as "a creature
   driven and derided by vanity." What other expressions does he use to
   describe his feelings? How would you characterize these feelings?
5. How does the narrator's choice of words illustrate the contrast between his
   day-to-day life and the exotic promise of the bazaar?
6. What does each of the italicized words suggest: "We walked through the *flaring* streets" (par. 5); "I heard the rain *impinge* upon the earth" (par. 6); "I
   chafed against the work of school" (par. 12); "I found myself in a big hall *girdled* at half its height by a gallery" (par. 25)? What other examples of unexpected word choice can you identify in the story?
7. What is it about the events in this story that causes the narrator to remember them years later?
8. Identify words and phrases in the story that are associated with religion.
   What purpose do these references to religion serve? Do you think they are
   intentional?
9. **JOURNAL ENTRY** Rewrite a brief passage from this story in the voice of the
   young boy. Use informal style, simple figures of speech, and vocabulary
   appropriate for a child.
10. **CRITICAL PERSPECTIVE** In *Notes on the American Short Story Today*, Richard
    Kostelanetz discusses the **epiphany**, one of Joyce's most significant contribu-
    tions to literature:

    > In Joyce's pervasively influential theory of the short story we remember, the
    > fiction turned upon an epiphany, a moment of revelation in which, in [critic]
    > Harry Levin's words, "amid the most encumbered circumstances it suddenly hap-
    > pens that the veil is lifted, the . . . mystery laid bare, and the ultimate secret of

Harry Levin's words, "amid the most encumbered circumstances it suddenly happens that the veil is lifted, the . . . mystery laid bare, and the ultimate secret of things made manifest." The epiphany, then, became a technique for jelling the narrative and locking the story's import into place. . . . What made this method revolutionary was the shifting of the focal point of the story from its end . . . to a spot within the body of the text, usually near (but not at) the end.

Where in "Araby" does the story's epiphany occur? Does it do all that Kostelanetz believes an epiphany should do? Or do you think that, at least in the case of "Araby," the epiphany may not be as significant a force as Kostelanetz suggests?

Related Works: "The Secret Lion" (p. 170), "A&P" (p. 230), "Gryphon" (p. 248), "Doe Season" (p. 512), "Shall I compare thee to a summer's day?" (p. 939) *Scheherazade* (p. 1365)

ROBERT H. ABEL (1941–   ) is the author of three novels—including *Freedom Dues* (1978), *The Progress of Fire* (1985), and *Ghost Traps* (1991), which won the Flannery O'Connor Award for Short Fiction—and three collections of short stories. Abel has received numerous other awards, including a fellowship from the National Endowment for the Arts, and he has also taught and worked as a journalist.

Cultural Context Although different circumstances require different reactions, wildlife experts agree that there are several basic things people should do if they encounter a bear in the wild, as the narrator of "Appetizer" does. It is essential to remain calm and quiet and avoid abrupt movements. Because bears are extremely territorial, people should avoid making eye contact. It is important to evaluate the situation at hand: Is the bear a male or female? Are there cubs nearby? Instead of trying to outrun a bear, people in this situation should talk quietly and slowly back up, giving the bear time to adjust to their movements. If they climb a nearby tree, the bear may or may not follow. But if it attacks, the best course of action is to roll into a cannonball and play dead until the bear has gone. If the bear is hunting, however, the situation is far more dangerous. In this case the best strategy is to make noise and throw things, hoping the bear will retreat.

Appetizer (1992)

I'm fishing this beautiful stream in Alaska, catching salmon, char and steelhead, when this bear lumbers out of the woods and down to the stream bank. He fixes me with this half-amused, half-curious look which says: You are meat.

The bear's eyes are brown and his shiny golden fur is standing up in spikes, which shows me he has been fishing, too, perhaps where the stream curves behind the peninsula of woods he has just trudged through. He's not making any sound I can hear over the rumble of the water in the softball-sized rocks, but his presence is very loud.

I say "his" presence because temporarily I am not interested in or able to assess the creature's sex. I am looking at a head that is bigger around than my steering wheel, a pair of paws awash in river bubbles that could cover half my windshield. I am glad that I am wearing polarized fishing glasses so the bear cannot see the little teardrops of fear that have crept into the corner of my eyes. To assure him/her I am not the least bit intimidated, I make another cast.

Immediately I tie into a fat Chinook. The splashing of the fish in the stream engages the bear's attention, but he/she registers this for the moment only by shifting his/her glance. I play the fish smartly and when it comes gliding in, tired, pinksided, glittering and astonished, I pluck it out of the water by inserting a finger in its gill — something I normally wouldn't do in order not to injure the fish before I set it free, and I do exactly what you would do in the same situation — throw it to the bear.

The bear's eyes widen and she —for I can see now past her huge shoulder and powerful haunches that she is a she — turns and pounces on the fish with such speed and nimbleness that I am numbed. There is no chance in hell that I, in my insulated waders, am going to outrun her, dodge her blows, escape her jaws. While she is occupied devouring the fish —I can hear her teeth clacking together — I do what you or anyone else would do and cast again.

God answers my muttered prayer and I am blessed with the strike of another fat salmon, like the others on its way to spawning grounds upstream. I would like this fish to survive and release its eggs or sperm to perpetuate the salmon kingdom, but Ms. Bear has just licked her whiskers clean and has now moved knee-deep into the water and, to my consternation, leans against me rather like a large and friendly dog, although her ears are at the level of my shoulder and her back is broader than that of any horse I have ever seen. Ms. Bear is intensely interested in the progress of the salmon toward us, and her head twists and twitches as the fish circles, darts, takes line away, shakes head, rolls over, leaps.

With a bear at your side, it is not the simplest thing to play a fish properly, but the presence of this huge animal, and especially her long snout, thick as my thigh, wonderfully concentrates the mind. She smells like the forest floor, like crushed moss and damp leaves, and she is as warm as a radiator back in my Massachusetts home, the thought of which floods me with a terrible nostalgia. Now I debate whether I should just drift the salmon in under the bear's nose and let her take it that way, but I'm afraid she will break off my fly and leader and right now that fly — a Doctor Wilson number eight —is saving my life. So, with much anxiety, I pretend to take charge and bring the fish in on the side away from the bear, gill and quickly unhook it, turn away from the bear and toss the fish behind me to the bank.

The bear wheels and clambers upon it at once, leaving a vortex of water pouring into the vacuum of the space she has left, which almost topples me. As her teeth snack away, I quickly and furtively regard my poor Doctor Wilson, which is fish-mauled now, bedraggled, almost unrecognizable. But the present emergency compels me to zing it out once again. I walk a few paces downstream, hoping the bear will remember an appointment or become distracted and I can sneak away.

But a few seconds later she is leaning against me again, raptly watching the stream for any sign of a salmon splash. My luck holds; another fish smacks the withered Wilson, flings sunlight and water in silver jets as it dances its last dance. I implore the salmon's forgiveness: something I had once read revealed that this is the way of all primitive hunters, to take the life reluctantly and to pray for the victim's return. I think my prayer is as urgent as that of any Mashpee or Yoruban, or Tlingit or early Celt, for I not only want the salmon to thrive forever, I want a superabundance of them now, right now, to save my neck. I have an idea this hungry bear, bereft of fish, would waste little time in conducting any prayer ceremonies before she turned me into the main course my salmon were just the appetizer for. When I take up this fish, the bear practically rips it from my hand, and the sight of those teeth so close, and the truly persuasive power of those muscled, pink-rimmed jaws, cause a wave of fear in me so great that I nearly faint.

10   My vertigo subsides as Ms. Bear munches and destroys the salmon with hearty shakes of her head and I sneak a few more paces downstream, rapidly also with trembling fingers tie on a new Doctor Wilson, observing the utmost care (as you would, too) in making my knots. I cast and stride downstream, wishing I could just plunge into the crystalline water and bowl away like a log. My hope and plan is to wade my way back to the narrow trail a few hundred yards ahead and, when Ms. Bear loses interest or is somehow distracted, make a heroic dash for my camper. I think of the thermos of hot coffee on the front seat, the six-pack of beer in the cooler, the thin rubber mattress with the blue sleeping bag adorning it, warm wool socks in a bag hanging from a window crank, and almost burst into tears, these simple things, given the presence of Ms. Hungry Bear, seem so miraculous, so emblematic of the life I love to live. I promise the gods — American, Indian, African, Oriental — that if I survive I will never complain again, not even if my teenage children leave the caps off the toothpaste tubes or their bicycles in the driveway at home.

"Oh, home," I think, and cast again.

Ms. Bear rejoins me. You may or may not believe me, and perhaps after all it was only my imagination worked up by terror, but two things happened which gave me a particle of hope. The first was that Ms. Bear actually belched — quite noisily and unapologetically, too, like a rude uncle at a Christmas dinner. She showed no signs of having committed any impropriety, and yet it was clear to me that a belching bear is probably also a bear with a pretty-full belly. A few more salmon and perhaps Ms. Bear would wander off in search of a berry dessert.

Now the second thing she did, or that I imagined she did, was to begin — well, not *speaking* to me exactly, but *communicating* somehow. I know it sounds foolish, but if you were in my shoes — my waders, to be more precise — you might have learned bear talk pretty quickly, too. It's not as if the bear were speaking to me in complete sentences and English words such as "Get me another fish, pal, or you're on the menu," but in a much more indirect and subtle way, almost in the way a stream talks through its bubbling and burbling and rattling of rocks and gurgling along.

Believe me, I listened intently, more with my mind than with my ears, as if the bear were telepathizing, and — I know you're not going to believe this, but it's true, I am normally not what you would call an egomaniac with an inflated self-esteem such that I imagine that every bear which walks out of the woods falls in love with me — but I really did truly believe now that this Ms. Bear was expressing feelings of, well, *affection*. Really, I think she kinda liked me. True or not, the feeling made me less afraid. In fact, and I don't mean this in any erotic or perverse kind of way, but I had to admit, once my fear had passed, my feelings were kinda mutual. Like you might feel for an old pal of a dog. Or a favorite horse. I only wish she weren't such a big eater. I only wish she were not a carnivore, and I, carne.

Now she nudges me with her nose.   15

"All right, all right," I say. "I'm doing the best I can."

Cast in the glide behind that big boulder, the bear telepathizes me. *There's a couple of whoppers in there.*

I do as I'm told and wham! the bear is right! Instantly I'm tied into a grand-daddy Chinook, a really burly fellow who has no intention of lying down on any-body's platter beneath a blanket of lemon slices and scallion shoots, let alone make his last wiggle down a bear's gullet. Even the bear is excited and begins shifting weight from paw to paw, a little motion for her that nevertheless has big consequences for me as her body slams against my hip, then slams again.

Partly because I don't want to lose the fish, but partly also because I want to use the fish as an excuse to move closer to my getaway trail, I stumble down-stream. This fish has my rod bent into an upside-down *U* and I'm hoping my quick-tied knots are also strong enough to take this salmon's lurching and his in-telligent, broadside swinging into the river current — a very smart fish! Ordinar-ily I might take a long time with a fish like this, baby it in, but now I'm putting on as much pressure as I dare. When the salmon flips into a little side pool, the bear takes matters into her own hands, clambers over the rocks, pounces, nabs the salmon smartly behind the head and lumbers immediately to the bank. My leader snaps at once and while Ms. Bear attends to the destruction of the fish, I tie on another fly and make some shambling headway downstream. Yes, I worry about the hook still in the fish, but only because I do not want this bear to be irritated by anything. I want her to be replete and smug and doze off in the sun. I try to telepathize as much. Please, Bear, sleep.

Inevitably, the fishing slows down, but Ms. Bear does not seem to mind. Again   20 she belches. Myself, I am getting quite a headache and know that I am fighting exhaustion. On a normal morning of humping along in waders over these slippery softball-sized rocks, I would be tired in any case. The added emergency is fore-closing on my energy reserves. I even find myself getting a little angry, frustrated at least, and I marvel at the bear's persistence, her inexhaustible doggedness. And appetite. I catch fish, I toss them to her. At supermarkets prices, I calculate she has eaten about six hundred dollars worth of fish. The calculating gives me some-thing to think about besides my fear.

At last I am immediately across from the opening to the trail which twines back through the woods to where my camper rests in the dapple shade of mighty pines. Still, five hundred yards separate me from this imagined haven. I entertain the notion perhaps someone else will come along and frighten the bear away, maybe someone with a dog or a gun, but I have already spent many days here with-out seeing another soul, and in fact have chosen to return here for that very rea-son. I have told myself for many years that I really do love nature, love being among the animals, am restored by wilderness adventure. Considering that right now I would like nothing better than to be nestled beside my wife in front of a blazing fire, this seems to be a sentiment in need of some revision.

Now, as if in answer to my speculations, the bear turns beside me, her rump pushing me into water deeper than I want to be in, where my footing is shaky, and she stares into the woods, ears forward. She had heard something I cannot hear, or smelled something I cannot smell, and while I labor back to shallower water and surer footing, I hope some backpackers or some bear-poaching Indians are about to appear and send Ms. Bear a-galloping away. Automatically, I continue casting, but I also cannot help glancing over my shoulder in hopes of seeing what Ms. Bear sees. And in a moment I do.

It is another bear.

Unconsciously, I release a low moan, but my voice is lost in the guttural warning of Ms. Bear to the trespasser. The new arrival answers with a defiant cough. He — I believe it is a he — can afford to be defiant because he is half again as large as my companion. His fur seems longer and coarser, and though its substance is as golden as that of the bear beside me, the tips are black and this dark surface ripples and undulates over his massive frame. His nostrils are flared and he is staring with profound concentration at me.

25   Now I am truly confused and afraid. Would it be better to catch another salmon or not? I surely cannot provide for two of these beasts and in any case Mister Bear does not seem the type to be distracted by or made friendly by any measly salmon tribute. His whole bearing — pardon and expression — tells me my intrusion into this bear world is a personal affront to his bear honor. Only Ms. Bear stands between us and, after all, whose side is she really on? By bear standards, I am sure a rather regal and handsome fellow has made his appearance. Why should the fur-covered heart of furry Ms. Bear go out to me? How much love can a few hundred dollars worth of salmon buy? Most likely, this couple even have a history, know and have known each other from other seasons even though for the moment they prefer to pretend to regard each other as total strangers.

How disturbed I am is well illustrated by my next course of action. It is completely irrational, and I cannot account for it, or why it saved me — if indeed it did. I cranked in my line and lay may rod across some rocks, then began the arduous process of pulling myself out of my waders while trying to balance myself on those awkward rocks in that fast water. I tipped and swayed as I tugged at my boots, pushed my waders down, my arms in the foaming, frigid water, then the waders also filling, making it even more difficult to pull my feet free.

I emerged like a nymph from a cocoon, wet and trembling. The bears regarded me with clear stupefaction, as if one of them had casually stepped out of his or her fur. I drained what water I could from the waders, then dropped my fly rod into them, and held them before me. The damned rocks were brutal on my feet, but I marched toward the trail opening, lifting and dropping first one, then the other leg of my waders as if I were operating a giant puppet. The water still in the waders gave each footfall an impressive authority, and I was half thinking that, well, if the big one attacks, maybe he'll be fooled into chomping the waders first and I'll at least now be able to run. I did not relish the idea of pounding down the trail in my nearly bare feet, but it was a damn sight better way to argue with the bear than being sucked from my waders like a snail from its shell. Would you have done differently?

Who knows what the bears thought, but I tried to make myself look as much as possible like a camel or some other extreme and inedible form of four-footedness as I plodded along the trail. The bears looked at each other, then at me as I clomped by, the water in the waders making an odd gurgling sound, and me making an odd sound, too, on remembering just then how the Indians would, staring death in the eye, sing their death song. Having no such melody prepared, and never having been anything but a bathtub singer, I chanted forth the only song I ever committed to memory: "Jingle Bells."

Yes, "Jingle Bells," I sang, "jingle all the way," and I lifted first one, then the other wader leg and dropped it stomping down. "Oh, what fun it is to ride in a one-horse open sleigh-ay!"

The exercise was to prove to me just how complicated and various is the nature of the bear. The male reared up, blotting out the sun, bellowed, then twisted on his haunches and crashed off into the woods. The female, head cocked in curiosity, followed at a slight distance, within what still might be called striking distance whether I was out of my waders or not. Truly, I did not appreciate her persistence. Hauling the waders half full of water before me was trying work and the superfluous thought struck me: suppose someone sees me now, plumping along like this, singing "Jingle Bells," a bear in attendance? Vanity, obviously, never sleeps. But as long as the bear kept her distance I saw no reason to change my *modus operandi*. 30

When I came within about one hundred feet of my camper, its white cap gleaming like a remnant of spring snow and beckoning me, I risked everything, dropped the waders and sped for the cab. The bear broke into a trot, too, I was sure, because although I couldn't see her, had my sights locked on the gleaming handle to the pickup door, I sure enough could hear those big feet slapping the ground behind me in a heavy rhythm, a terrible and elemental beat that sang to me of my own frailty, fragile bones and tender flesh. I plunged on like a madman, grabbed the camper door and hurled myself in.

I lay on the seat panting, curled like a child, shuddered when the bear slammed against the pickup's side. The bear pressed her nose to the window, then curiously, unceremoniously licked the glass with her tongue. I know (and you know) she could have shattered the glass with a single blow, and I tried to imagine what I should do if indeed she resorted to this simple expedient. Fisherman that I am, I had nothing in the cab of the truck to defend myself with except a tire iron, and that not readily accessible behind the seat I was cowering on. My best defense, obviously, was to start the pickup and drive away.

Just as I sat up to the steering wheel and inserted the key, however, Ms. Bear slammed her big paws onto the hood and hoisted herself aboard. The pickup shuddered with the weight of her, and suddenly the windshield was full of her golden fur. I beeped the horn loud and long numerous times, but this had about the same effect as my singing, only caused her to shake her huge head, which vibrated the truck terribly. She stomped around on the hood and then lay down, back against the windshield, which now appeared to have been covered by a huge shag rug.

Could I believe my eyes?

No, I could not believe my eyes. My truck was being smothered in bear. In a
35 moment I also could not believe my ears — Ms. Bear had decided the camper
hood was the perfect place for a nap, and she was *snoring*, snoring profoundly, her
body twitching like a cat's. Finally, she had responded to my advice and desires,
but at the most inappropriate time. I was trapped. Blinded by bear body!

My exhaustion had been doubled by my sprint for the camper, and now that I
was not in such a desperate panic, I felt the cold of the water that had soaked my
clothes and I began to tremble. It also crossed my mind that perhaps Mister Bear
was still in the vicinity, and if Ms. Bear was not smart enough, or cruel enough, to
smash my window to get at me, he just might be.

Therefore, I started the engine — which disturbed Ms. Bear not a whit— and
rolled down the window enough to stick my head out and see down the rocky, limb-
strewn trial. I figured a few jolts in those ruts and Ms. Bear would be off like a shot.

This proved a smug assumption. Ms. Bear did indeed awaken and bestir herself to a sitting position, a bit like an overgrown hood ornament, but quickly grew
quite adept at balancing herself against the lurching and jolting of my truck,
which, in fact, she seemed to enjoy. Just my luck, I growled, to find the first bear
in Alaska who wanted a ride into town. I tried some quick braking and sharp turn
maneuvers I thought might send her tumbling off, but her bulk was so massive,
her paws so artfully spread, that she was just too stable an entity. She wanted a
ride and there was nothing I could do about it.

When I came out of the woods to the gravel road known locally as the Dawson Artery, I had an inspiration. I didn't drive so fast that if Ms. Bear decided to
clamber down she would be hurt, but I did head for the main road which led to
Buckville and the Buckville Cannery. Ms. Bear swayed happily along the whole
ten miles to that intersection and seemed not to bat an eye when first one big logging truck, then another plummeted by. I pulled out onto the highway, and for the
safety of both of us — those logging trucks have dubious brakes and their drivers
get paid by the trip — I had to accelerate considerably.

40 I couldn't seem much of Ms. Bear except her back and rump as I had to concentrate on the road, some of which is pretty curvy in coastal area, shadowed also
by the giant pines. But from the attitude expressed by her posture, I'd say she was
having a whale, or should I say a salmon of a time. I saw a few cars and pickups
veering out of the oncoming lane onto the shoulder as we swept by, but I didn't
have time, really, to appreciate the astonishment of their drivers. In this way, my
head out the window, Ms. Bear perched on the hood, I drove to the Buckville
Cannery and turned into the long driveway.

Ms. Bear knew right away something good was ahead for she rose on all fours
now and stuck her nose straight out like a bird dog on a pheasant. Her legs quivered with nervous anticipation as we approached, and as soon as I came out of the
trees into the parking area, she went over the front of the camper like someone
plunging into a pool.

Don't tell me you would have done any differently. I stopped right there and
watched Ms. Bear march down between the rows of cars and right up the truck
ramp into the cannery itself. She was not the least bit intimidated by all the noise

of the machines and the grinders and stampers in there, or the shouting of the workers.

Now the Buckville Cannery isn't that big — I imagine about two dozen people work there on any given day — and since it is so remote, has no hurricane fence around it, and no security guard. After all, what's anybody going to steal out of there besides a few cases of canned salmon or some bags of frozen fish parts that will soon become some company's cat food? The main building is up on a little hill and conveyors run down from there to the docks where the salmon boats pull in — the sea is another half mile away — and unload their catch.

I would say that in about three minutes after Ms. Bear walked into the cannery, twenty of the twenty-four workers were climbing out down the conveyors, dropping from open windows, or charging out the doors. The other four just hadn't got wind of the event yet, but in a little while they came bounding out, too, one fellow pulling up his trousers as he ran. They all assembled on the semicircular drive before the main office and had a union meeting of some vigor.

Myself, I was too tired to participate, and in any case did not want to be held 45 liable for the disturbance at the Buckville Cannery, and so I made a U-turn and drove on into Buckville itself where I took a room above the Buckville Tavern and had a hot shower and a really nice nap. That night in the Tap and Lounge I got to hear many an excited story about the she-bear who free-loaded at the cannery for a couple of hours before she was driven off by blowing, ironically enough, the lunch whistle loud and long. I didn't think it was the right time or place to testify to my part in that historical event, and for once kept my mouth shut. You don't like trouble any more than I do, and I'm sure you would have done about the same.

Reading and Reacting

1. The narrator begins his story by plunging readers directly into the action: "I'm fishing this beautiful stream in Alaska" (par. 1). What effect does he achieve by using first person and present tense here (and elsewhere)?

2. Throughout the story, the narrator addresses readers as *you* and seems to be constantly asking for their approval and support. In fact, the story's last line is, "You don't like trouble any more than I do, and I'm sure you would have done about the same" (par. 45). What is the effect of this strategy?

3. In paragraph 42, the narrator says, "Don't tell me you would have done any differently." What, if anything, *would* you have done differently if you were in the narrator's situation?

4. What kind of imagery is used to describe the natural setting (the stream, the forest, the trail, and so on)? Is this language typical of other descriptions of nature that you have seen in literature? Explain.

5. Consider the narrator's descriptions of the bears (for example, in paragraphs 2, 4 through 5, and 24). Do you think he is using **hyperbole**? List some of the figures of speech (particularly **personification**) the narrator uses to describe the bears. Are these the kind of figures of speech you expect?

6. Often (particularly when they involve a contest or an ordeal), stories about hunting, fishing, and other outdoor activities are seen as **initiation stories**. In what respects, if any, do you see "Appetizer" as an initiation story?

7. How are the bears the narrator encounters like and unlike human adversaries? In what respects does the narrator react to them as animals? In what respects does he react to them as humans?

8. Do you find this story frightening? Sad? Funny? What emotions does the narrator feel?

9. What do you think the story's title means?

10. **JOURNAL ENTRY** Rewrite a few paragraphs of the story from the point of view of one of the bears.

11. **CRITICAL PERSPECTIVE** Nature writing deals with the natural world, animals, and the relationship between humans and their environment. Ron Harton describes this genre as follows:

> Nature writing is relational. It is about the connections and relationships that form our world. Nature writing binds people to the natural world with words of understanding, respect, admiration, and love. These words may be formed in any literary type or style. The languages and forms of nature writing are many and varied, but each seeks to share what the writer has felt and known in times of living with nature.

Characterize the relationship between the narrator in "Appetizer" and the bears he encounters. In what sense is the narrator "bound to the natural world"? In what ways does the story share what the writer knows about living with nature?

Related Works: "Big Black Good Man" (p. 339), "Doe Season" (p. 512), "Greasy Lake" (p. 648), "Traveling through the Dark" (p. 1070), "The Raven" (p. 1034), *The Brute* (p. 1293)

(MARY) FLANNERY O'CONNOR (1925–1964) was born to a prosperous Catholic family in Savannah, Georgia, and spent most of her adult life on a farm near the town of Milledgeville. She left the South to study writing at the University of Iowa, moving to New York to work on her first novel, *Wise Blood* (1952). On a train going south for Christmas, O'Connor became seriously ill; she was diagnosed as having lupus, the immune system disease that had killed her father and would cause O'Connor's death when she was only thirty-nine years old.

While her mother ran the farm, O'Connor spent mornings writing and afternoons wandering the fields with cane or crutches. Her short story collection *A Good Man Is Hard to Find* (1955) and an excellent French translation of *Wise Blood* established her international reputation, which was solidified with the publication of a second novel, *The Violent Bear It Away* (1960), and. a posthumously published book of short stories, *Everything That Rises Must Converge* (1965).

O'Connor, said a friend, believed that an artist "should face all the truth down to the worst of it." Yet however dark, her stories are infused with grim humor and a fierce belief in the possibility of spiritual redemption, even for her most tortured characters. A line from her short story "A Good Man Is Hard to Find" says much about what O'Connor perceived about both natural things and her characters: "The trees were full of silver-white sunlight and the meanest of them sparkled." In O'Connor's work, the "meanest" things and people can sparkle, touched by a kind of holy madness and beauty.

> **Cultural Context** Some readers consider O'Connor a Christian writer, and indeed the Christian concepts of free will, original sin, and the need for spiritual redemption appear throughout her work. According to Christian theology, humanity was created with free will — the freedom to choose to obey or to disobey God, the freedom to follow right or wrong. Human beings fell from their original state of innocence, however, and this fall allowed sin and corruption to enter the world. Thus, a "good man" — one who is perfectly upright — is not simply "hard to find" but *impossible* to find: *all* have sinned and fall short of the glory of God, says the Bible (Romans 3.23). Because of that first disobedience (original sin), humanity stands in need of redemption — a reuniting with God, which, according to Christian theology, comes through Jesus Christ.

A Good Man Is Hard to Find (1955)

The grandmother didn't want to go to Florida. She wanted to visit some of her connections in east Tennessee and she was seizing at every chance to change Bailey's mind. Bailey was the son she lived with, her only boy. He was sitting on the edge of his chair at the table, bent over the orange sports section of the *Journal*. "Now look here, Bailey," she said, "see here, read this," and she stood with one hand on her thin hip and the other rattling the newspaper at his bald head. "Here this fellow that calls himself The Misfit is aloose from the Federal Pen and headed toward Florida and you read here what it says he did to these people. Just you read it. I wouldn't take my children in any direction with a criminal like that aloose in it. I couldn't answer to my conscience if I did."

Bailey didn't look up from his reading so she wheeled around then and faced the children's mother, a young woman in slacks, whose face was as broad and innocent as a cabbage and was tied around with a green headkerchief that had two points on the top like a rabbit's ears. She was sitting on the sofa, feeding the baby his apricots out of a jar. "The children have been to Florida before," the old lady said. "You all ought to take them somewhere else for a change so they would see different parts of the world and be broad. They never have been to east Tennessee."

The children's mother didn't seem to hear her but the eight-year-old boy, John Wesley, a stocky child with glasses, said, "If you don't want to go to Florida, why dontcha stay at home?" He and the little girl, June Star, were reading the funny papers on the floor.

"She wouldn't stay at home to be queen for a day," June Star said without raising her yellow head.

"Yes and what would you do if this fellow, the Misfit, caught you?" the grandmother asked.   5

"I'd smack his face," John Wesley said.

"She wouldn't stay at home for a million bucks," June Star said. "Afraid she'd miss something. She has to go everywhere we go."

"All right, Miss," the grandmother said. "Just remember that the next time you want me to curl your hair."

June Star said her hair was naturally curly.

10   The next morning the grandmother was the first one in the car, ready to go. She had her big black valise that looked like the head of a hippopotamus in one corner, and underneath it she was hiding a basket with Pitty Sing, the cat, in it. She didn't intend for the cat to be left alone in the house for three days because he would miss her too much and she was afraid he might brush against one of the gas burners and accidentally asphyxiate himself. Her son, Bailey, didn't like to arrive at a motel with a cat.

She sat in the middle of the back seat with John Wesley and June Star on either side of her. Bailey and the children's mother and the baby sat in front and they left Atlanta at eight forty-five with the mileage on the car at 55890. The grandmother wrote this down because she thought it would be interesting to say how many miles they had been when they got back. It took them twenty minutes to reach the outskirts of the city.

The old lady settled herself comfortably, removing her white cotton gloves and putting them up with her purse on the shelf in front of the back window. The children's mother still had on slacks and still had her head tied up in a green kerchief, but the grandmother had on a navy blue straw sailor hat with a bunch of white violets on the brim and a navy blue dress with a small white dot in the print. Her collars and cuffs were white organdy trimmed with lace and at her neckline she had pinned a purple spray of cloth violets containing a sachet. In case of an accident, anyone seeing her dead on the highway would know at once that she was a lady.

She said she thought it was going to be a good day for driving, neither too hot nor too cold, and she cautioned Bailey that the speed limit was fifty-five miles an hour and that the patrolmen hid themselves behind billboards and small clumps of trees and sped out after you before you had a chance to slow down. She pointed out interesting details of the scenery: Stone Mountain; the blue granite that in some places came up to both sides of the highway; the brilliant red clay banks slightly streaked with purple; and the various crops that made rows of green lacework on the ground. The trees were full of silver-white sunlight and the meanest of them sparkled. The children were reading comic magazines and their mother had gone back to sleep.

"Let's go through Georgia fast so we won't have to look at it much," John Wesley said.

15   "If I were a little boy," said the grandmother, "I wouldn't talk about my native state that way. Tennessee has the mountains and Georgia has the hills."

"Tennessee is just a hillbilly dumping ground," John Wesley said, "and Georgia is a lousy state too."

"You said it," June Star said.

"In my time," said the grandmother, folding her thin veined fingers, "children were more respectful of their native states and their parents and everything else. People did right then. Oh look at the cute little pickaninny!" she said and pointed to a Negro child standing in the door of a shack. "Wouldn't that make a picture, now?" she asked and they all turned and looked at the little Negro out of the back window. He waved.

"He didn't have any britches on," June Star said.

"He probably didn't have any," the grandmother explained. "Little niggers in the   20
country don't have things like we do. If I could paint, I'd paint that picture," she said.

The children exchanged comic books.

The grandmother offered to hold the baby and the children's mother passed
him over the front seat to her. She set him on her knee and bounced him and told
him about the things they were passing. She rolled her eyes and screwed up her
mouth and stuck her leathery thin face into his smooth bland one. Occasionally
he gave her a faraway smile. They passed a large cotton field with five or six graves
fenced in the middle of it, like a small island. "Look at the graveyard!" the
grandmother said, pointing it out. "That was the old family burying ground. That
belonged to the plantation."

"Where's the plantation?" John Wesley asked.

"Gone With the Wind,"° said the grandmother. "Ha. Ha."

When the children finished all the comic books they had brought, they opened   25
the lunch and ate it. The grandmother ate a peanut butter sandwich and an olive
and would not let the children throw the box and the paper napkins out the window.
When there was nothing else to do they played a game by choosing a cloud and making the other two guess what shape it suggested. John Wesley took one the shape of
a cow and June Star guessed a cow and John Wesley said, no, an automobile, and June
Star said he didn't play fair, and they began to slap each other over the grandmother.

The grandmother said she would tell them a story if they would keep quiet.
When she told a story, she rolled her eyes and waved her head and was very dramatic.
She said once when she was a maiden lady she had been courted by a
Mr. Edgar Atkins Teagarden from Jasper, Georgia. She said he was a very good-looking man and a gentleman and that he brought her a watermelon every
Saturday afternoon with his initials cut in it, E. A. T. Well, one Saturday, she said,
Mr. Teagarden brought the watermelon and there was nobody at home and he left it
on the front porch and returned in his buggy to Jasper, but she never got the watermelon, she said, because a nigger boy ate it when he saw the initials, E. A. T.! This
story tickled John Wesley's funny bone and he giggled and giggled but June Star
didn't think it was any good. She said she wouldn't marry a man that just brought her
a watermelon on Saturday. The grandmother said she would have done well to marry
Mr. Teagarden because he was a gentleman and had bought Coca-Cola stock when
it first came out and that he died only a few years ago, a very wealthy man.

They stopped at The Tower for barbecued sandwiches. The Tower was a part
stucco and part wood filling station and dance hall set in a clearing outside of
Timothy. A fat man named Red Sammy Butts ran it and there were signs stuck
here and there on the building and for miles up and down the highway saying,
TRY RED SAMMY'S FAMOUS BARBECUE. NONE LIKE FAMOUS RED
SAMMY'S! RED SAM! THE FAT BOY WITH THE HAPPY LAUGH. A
VETERAN! RED SAMMY'S YOUR MAN!

Red Sammy was lying on the bare ground outside The Tower with his head under a truck while a gray monkey about a foot high, chained to a small chinaberry
tree, chattered nearby. The monkey sprang back into the tree and got on the highest limb as soon as he saw the children jump out of the car and run toward him.

Gone with the Wind: A 1936 novel by Margaret Mitchell about the Civil War.

Inside, The Tower was a long dark room with a counter at one end and tables at the other and dancing space in the middle. They all sat down at a board table next to the nickelodeon and Red Sam's wife, a tall burnt-brown woman with hair and eyes lighter than her skin, came and took their order. The children's mother put a dime in the machine and played "The Tennessee Waltz," and the grandmother said that tune always made her want to dance. She asked Bailey if he would like to dance but he only glared at her. He didn't have a naturally sweet disposition like she did and trips made him nervous. The grandmother's brown eyes were very bright. She swayed her head from side to side and pretended she was dancing in her chair. June Star said play something she could tap to so the children's mother put in another dime and played a fast number and June Star stepped out onto the dance floor and did her tap routine.

30   "Ain't she cute?" Red Sam's wife said, leaning over the counter. "Would you like to come be my little girl?"

"No I certainly wouldn't," June Star said. "I wouldn't live in a broken-down place like this for a million bucks!" and she ran back to the table.

"Ain't she cute?" the woman repeated, stretching her mouth politely.

"Aren't you ashamed?" hissed the grandmother.

Red Sam came in and told his wife to quit lounging on the counter and hurry up with these people's order. His khaki trousers reached just to his hip bones and his stomach hung over them like a sack of meal swaying under his shirt. He came over and sat down at a table nearby and let out a combination sigh and yodel. "You can't win," he said. "You can't win," and he wiped his sweating red face off with a gray handkerchief. "These days you don't know who to trust," he said. "Ain't that the truth?"

35   "People are certainly not nice like they used to be," said the grandmother.

"Two fellers come in here last week," Red Sammy said, "driving a Chrysler. It was a old beat-up car but it was a good one and these boys looked all right to me. Said they worked at the mill and you know I let them fellers charge the gas they bought? Now why did I do that?"

"Because you're a good man!" the grandmother said at once.

"Yes'm, I suppose so," Red Sam said as if he were struck with this answer.

His wife brought the orders, carrying the five plates all at once without a tray, two in each hand and one balanced on her arm. "It isn't a soul in this green world of God's that you can trust," she said. "And I don't count nobody out of that, not nobody," she repeated, looking at Red Sammy.

40   "Did you read about that criminal, The Misfit, that's escaped?" asked the grandmother.

"I wouldn't be a bit surprised if he didn't attact this place right here," said the woman. "If he hears about it being here, I wouldn't be none surprised to see him. If he hears it's two cent in the cash register, I wouldn't be at all surprised if he . . ."

"That'll do," Red Sam said. "Go bring these people their Co'-Colas," and the woman went off to get the rest of the order.

"A good man is hard to find," Red Sammy said. "Everything is getting terrible. I remember the day you could go off and leave your screen door unlatched. Not no more."

He and the grandmother discussed better times. The old lady said that in her opinion Europe was entirely to blame for the way things were now. She said the way Europe acted you would think we were made of money and Red Sam said it was no use talking about it, she was exactly right. The children ran outside into the white sunlight and looked at the monkey in the lacy chinaberry tree. He was busy catching fleas on himself and biting each one carefully between his teeth as if it were a delicacy.

They drove off again into the hot afternoon. The grandmother took cat naps and 45 woke up every few minutes with her own snoring. Outside of Toombsboro she woke up and recalled an old plantation that she had visited in this neighborhood once when she was a young lady. She said the house had six white columns across the front and that there was an avenue of oaks leading up to it and two little wooden trellis arbors on either side in front where you sat down with your suitor after a stroll in the garden. She recalled exactly which road to turn off to get to it. She knew that Bailey would not be willing to lose any time looking at an old house, but the more she talked about it, the more she wanted to see it once again and find out if the little twin arbors were still standing. "There was a secret panel in this house," she said craftily, not telling the truth but wishing that she were, "and the story went that all the family silver was hidden in it when Sherman came through but it was never found . . ."

"Hey!" John Wesley said. "Let's go see it! We'll find it! We'll poke all the woodwork and find it! Who lives there? Where do you turn off at? Hey Pop, can't we turn off there?"

"We never have seen a house with a secret panel!" June Star shrieked. "Let's go to the house with the secret panel! Hey Pop, can't we go see the house with the secret panel!"

"It's not far from here, I know," the grandmother said. "It wouldn't take over twenty minutes."

Bailey was looking straight ahead. His jaw was as rigid as a horseshoe. "No," he said.

The children began to yell and scream that they wanted to see the house with 50 the secret panel. John Wesley kicked the back of the front seat and June Star hung over her mother's shoulder and whined desperately into her ear that they never had any fun even on their vacation, that they could never do what THEY wanted to do. The baby began to scream and John Wesley kicked the back of the seat so hard that his father could feel the blows in his kidney.

"All right!" he shouted and drew the car to a stop at the side of the road. "Will you all shut up? Will you all just shut up for one second? If you don't shut up, we won't go anywhere."

"It would be very educational for them," the grandmother murmured.

"All right," Bailey said, "but get this: this is the only time we're going to stop for anything like this. This is the one and only time."

"The dirt road that you have to turn down is about a mile back," the grandmother directed. "I marked it when we passed."

"A dirt road," Bailey groaned. 55

After they had turned around and were headed toward the dirt road, the grandmother recalled other points about the house, the beautiful glass over the front doorway and the candle-lamp in the hall. John Wesley said that the secret panel was probably in the fireplace.

"You can't go inside this house," Bailey said. "You don't know who lives there."

"While you all talk to the people in front, I'll run around behind and get in a window," John Wesley suggested.

"We'll all stay in the car," his mother said.

60   They turned onto the dirt road and the car raced roughly along in a swirl of pink dust. The grandmother recalled the times when there were no paved roads and thirty miles was a day's journey. The dirt road was hilly and there were sudden washes in it and sharp curves on dangerous embankments. All at once they would be on a hill, looking down over the blue tops of trees for miles around, then the next minute, they would be in a red depression with the dust-coated trees looking down on them.

"This place had better turn up in a minute," Bailey said, "or I'm going to turn around."

The road looked as if no one had traveled on it in months.

"It's not much farther," the grandmother said and just as she said it, a horrible thought came to her. The thought was so embarrassing that she turned red in the face and her eyes dilated and her feet jumped up, upsetting her valise in the corner. The instant the valise moved, the newspaper top she had over the basket under it rose with a snarl and Pitty Sing, the cat, sprang onto Bailey's shoulder.

The children were thrown to the floor and their mother, clutching the baby, was thrown out the door onto the ground; the old lady was thrown into the front seat. The car turned over once and landed right-side-up in a gulch off the side of the road. Bailey remained in the driver's seat with the cat — gray-striped with a broad white face and an orange nose — clinging to his neck like a caterpillar.

65   As soon as the children saw they could move their arms and legs, they scrambled out of the car, shouting, "We've had an ACCIDENT!" The grandmother was curled up under the dashboard, hoping she was injured so that Bailey's wrath would not come down on her all at once. The horrible thought she had had before the accident was that the house she had remembered so vividly was not in Georgia but in Tennessee.

Bailey removed the cat from his neck with both hands and flung it out the window against the side of a pine tree. Then he got out of the car and started looking for the children's mother. She was sitting against the side of the red gutted ditch, holding the screaming baby, but she only had a cut down her face and a broken shoulder. "We've had an ACCIDENT!" the children screamed in a frenzy of delight.

"But nobody's killed," June Star said with disappointment as the grandmother limped out of the car, her hat still pinned to her head but the broken front brim standing up at a jaunty angle and the violet spray hanging off the side. They all sat down in the ditch, except the children, to recover from the shock. They were all shaking.

"Maybe a car will come along," said the children's mother hoarsely.

"I believe I have injured an organ," said the grandmother, pressing her side, but no one answered her. Bailey's teeth were clattering. He had on a yellow sport shirt with bright blue parrots designed in it and his face was as yellow as the shirt.

The grandmother decided that she would not mention that the house was in Tennessee.

The road was about ten feet above and they could see only the tops of the trees 70 on the other side of it. Behind the ditch they were sitting in there were more woods, tall and dark and deep. In a few minutes they saw a car some distance away on top of a hill, coming slowly as if the occupants were watching them. The grandmother stood up and waved both arms dramatically to attract their attention. The car continued to come on slowly, disappeared around a bend and appeared again, moving even slower, on top of the hill they had gone over. It was a big black battered hearse-like automobile. There were three men in it.

It came to a stop just over them and for some minutes, the driver looked down with a steady expressionless gaze to where they were sitting, and didn't speak. Then he turned his head and muttered something to the other two and they got out. One was a fat boy in black trousers and a red sweat shirt with a silver stallion embossed on the front of it. He moved around on the right side of them and stood staring, his mouth partly open in a kind of loose grin. The other had on khaki pants and a blue striped coat and a gray hat pulled down very low, hiding most of his face. He came around slowly on the left side. Neither spoke.

The driver got out of the car and stood by the side of it, looking down at them. He was an older man than the other two. His hair was just beginning to gray and he wore silver-rimmed spectacles that gave him a scholarly look. He had a long creased face and didn't have on any shirt or undershirt. He had on blue jeans that were too tight for him and was holding a black hat and a gun. The two boys also had guns.

"We've had an ACCIDENT!" the children screamed.

The grandmother had the peculiar feeling that the bespectacled man was someone she knew. His face was as familiar to her as if she had known him all her life but she could not recall who he was. He moved away from the car and began to come down the embankment, placing his feet carefully so that he wouldn't slip. He had on tan and white shoes and no socks, and his ankles were red and thin. "Good afternoon," he said. "I see you all had you a little spill."

"We turned over twice!" said the grandmother.   75

"Oncet," he corrected. "We seen it happen. Try their car and see will it run, Hiram," he said quietly to the boy with the gray hat.

"What you got that gun for?" John Wesley asked. "Watcha gonna do with that gun?"

"Lady," the man said to the children's mother, "would you mind calling them children to sit down by you? Children make me nervous. I want all you all to sit down right together there where you're at."

"What are you telling US what to do for?" June Star asked.

Behind them the line of woods gaped like a dark open mouth. "Come here," 80 said their mother.

"Look here now," Bailey began suddenly, "we're in a predicament! We're in . . ."

The grandmother shrieked. She scrambled to her feet and stood staring. "You're The Misfit!" she said. "I recognized you at once!"

"Yes'm," the man said, smiling slightly as if he were pleased in spite of himself to be known, "but it would have been better for all of you, lady, if you hadn't of reckernized me."

Bailey turned his head sharply and said something to his mother that shocked even the children. The old lady began to cry and The Misfit reddened.

85   "Lady," he said, "don't you get upset. Sometimes a man says things he don't mean. I don't reckon he meant to talk to you thataway."

"You wouldn't shoot a lady, would you?" the grandmother said and removed a clean handkerchief from her cuff and began to slap at her eyes with it.

The Misfit pointed the toe of his shoe into the ground and made a little hole and then covered it up again. "I would hate to have to," he said.

"Listen," the grandmother almost screamed, "I know you're a good man. You don't look a bit like you have common blood. I know you must come from nice people!"

"Yes mam," he said, "finest people in the world." When he smiled he showed a row of strong white teeth. "God never made a finer woman than my mother and my daddy's heart was pure gold," he said. The boy with the red sweat shirt had come around behind them and was standing with his gun at his hip. The Misfit squatted down on the ground. "Watch them children, Bobby Lee," he said. "You know they make me nervous." He looked at the six of them huddled together in front of him and he seemed to be embarrassed as if he couldn't think of anything to say. "Ain't a cloud in the sky," he remarked, looking up at it. "Don't see no sun but don't see no cloud neither."

90   "Yes, it's a beautiful day," said the grandmother. "Listen," she said, "you shouldn't call yourself The Misfit because I know you're a good man at heart. I can just look at you and tell."

"Hush!" Bailey yelled. "Hush! Everybody shut up and let me handle this!" He was squatting in the position of a runner about to sprint forward but he didn't move.

"I pre-chate that, lady," The Misfit said and drew a little circle in the ground with the butt of his gun.

"It'll take a half a hour to fix this here car," Hiram called, looking over the raised hood of it.

"Well, first you and Bobby Lee get him and that little boy to step over yonder with you," The Misfit said, pointing to Bailey and John Wesley. "The boys want to ast you something," he said to Bailey. "Would you mind stepping back in them woods there with them?"

95   "Listen," Bailey began, "we're in a terrible predicament! Nobody realizes what this is," and his voice cracked. His eyes were as blue and intense as the parrots in his shirt and he remained perfectly still.

The grandmother reached up to adjust her hat brim as if she were going to the woods with him but it came off in her hand. She stood staring at it and after a second she let it fall on the ground. Hiram pulled Bailey up by the arm as if he were assisting an old man. John Wesley caught hold of his father's hand and Bobby Lee followed. They went off toward the woods and just as they reached the dark edge, Bailey turned and supporting himself against a gray naked pine trunk, he shouted, "I'll be back in a minute, Mamma, wait on me!"

"Come back this instant!" his mother shrilled but they all disappeared into the woods.

"Bailey Boy!" the grandmother called in a tragic voice but she found she was looking at The Misfit squatting on the ground in front of her. "I just know you're a good man," she said desperately. "You're not a bit common!"

"Nome, I ain't a good man," The Misfit said after a second as if he had considered her statement carefully, "but I ain't the worst in the world neither. My daddy said I was a different breed of dog from my brothers and sisters. 'You know,' Daddy said, 'it's some that can live their whole life out without asking about it and it's others has to know why it is, and this boy is one of the latters. He's going to be into everything!'" He put on his black hat and looked up suddenly and then away deep into the woods as if he were embarrassed again. "I'm sorry I don't have on a shirt before you ladies," he said, hunching his shoulders slightly. "We buried our clothes that we had on when we escaped and we're just making do until we can get better. We borrowed these from some folks we met," he explained.

"That's perfectly all right," the grandmother said. "Maybe Bailey has an extra   100 shirt in his suitcase."

"I'll look and see terrectly," The Misfit said.

"Where are they taking him?" the children's mother screamed.

"Daddy was a card himself," The Misfit said. "You couldn't put anything over on him. He never got in trouble with the Authorities though. Just had the knack of handling them."

"You could be honest too if you'd only try," said the grandmother. "Think how wonderful it would be to settle down and live a comfortable life and not have to think about somebody chasing you all the time."

The Misfit kept scratching in the ground with the butt of his gun as if he were   105 thinking about it. "Yes'm, somebody is always after you," he murmured.

The grandmother noticed how thin his shoulder blades were just behind his hat because she was standing up looking down on him. "Do you ever pray?" she asked.

He shook his head. All she saw was the black hat wiggle between his shoulder blades. "Nome," he said.

There was a pistol shot from the woods, followed closely by another. Then silence. The old lady's head jerked around. She could hear the wind move through the tree tops like a long satisfied insuck of breath. "Bailey Boy!" she called.

"I was a gospel singer for a while," The Misfit said. "I been most everything. Been in the arm service, both land and sea, at home and abroad, been twict married, been an undertaker, been with the railroads, plowed Mother Earth, been in a tornado, seen a man burnt alive oncet," and he looked up at the children's mother and the little girl who were sitting close together, their faces white and their eyes glassy; "I even seen a woman flogged," he said.

"Pray, pray," the grandmother began, "pray, pray . . ."   110

"I never was a bad boy that I remember of," The Misfit said in an almost dreamy voice, "but somewheres along the line I done something wrong and got sent to the penitentiary. I was buried alive," and he looked up and held her attention to him by a steady stare.

"That's when you should have started to pray," she said. "What did you do to get sent to the penitentiary that first time?"

"Turn to the right, it was a wall," The Misfit said, looking up again at the cloudless sky. "Turn to the left, it was a wall. Look up it was a ceiling, look down it was a floor. I forget what I done, lady. I set there and set there, trying to remember what it was I done and I ain't recalled it to this day. Oncet in a while, I would think it was coming to me, but it never come."

"Maybe they put you in by mistake," the old lady said vaguely.

115   "Nome," he said. "It wasn't no mistake. They had the papers on me."

"You must have stolen something," she said.

The Misfit sneered slightly. "Nobody had nothing I wanted," he said. "It was a head-doctor at the penitentiary said what I had done was kill my daddy but I known that for a lie. My daddy died in nineteen ought nineteen of the epidemic flu and I never had a thing to do with it. He was buried in the Mount Hopewell Baptist churchyard and you can go there and see for yourself."

"If you would pray," the old lady said, "Jesus would help you."

"That's right," The Misfit said.

120   "Well then, why don't you pray?" she asked trembling with delight suddenly.

"I don't want no hep," he said. "I'm doing all right by myself."

Bobby Lee and Hiram came ambling back from the woods. Bobby Lee was dragging a yellow shirt with bright blue parrots in it.

"Thow me that shirt, Bobby Lee," The Misfit said. The shirt came flying at him and landed on his shoulder and he put it on. The grandmother couldn't name what the shirt reminded her of. "No, lady," The Misfit said while he was buttoning it up, "I found out the crime don't matter. You can do one thing or you can do another, kill a man or take a tire off his car, because sooner or later you're going to forget what it was you done and just be punished for it."

The children's mother had begun to make heaving noises as if she couldn't get her breath. "Lady," he asked, "would you and that little girl like to step off yonder with Bobby Lee and Hiram and join your husband?"

125   "Yes, thank you," the mother said faintly. Her left arm dangled helplessly and she was holding the baby, who had gone to sleep, in the other. "Hep that lady up, Hiram," The Misfit said as she struggled to climb out of the ditch, "and Bobby Lee, you hold onto that little girl's hand."

"I don't want to hold hands with him," June Star said. "He reminds me of a pig."

The fat boy blushed and laughed and caught her by the arm and pulled her off into the woods after Hiram and her mother.

Alone with The Misfit, the grandmother found that she had lost her voice. There was not a cloud in the sky nor any sun. There was nothing around her but woods. She wanted to tell him that he must pray. She opened and closed her mouth several times before anything came out. Finally she found herself saying, "Jesus, Jesus," meaning, Jesus will help you, but the way she was saying it, it sounded as if she might be cursing.

"Yes'm," The Misfit said as if he agreed. "Jesus thown everything off balance. It was the same case with Him as with me except He hadn't committed any crime and they could prove I had committed one because they had the papers on me. Of course," he said, "they never shown me my papers. That's why I sign myself now. I said long ago, you get you a signature and sign everything you do and keep a copy of it. Then you'll know what you done and you can hold up the crime to the punishment and see do they match and in the end you'll have something to prove you ain't been treated right. I call myself The Misfit," he said, "because I can't make what all I done wrong fit what all I gone through in punishment."

There was a piercing scream from the woods, followed closely by a pistol re- 130 port. "Does it seem right to you, lady, that one is punished a heap and another ain't punished at all?"

"Jesus!" the old lady cried. "You've got good blood! I know you wouldn't shoot a lady! I know you come from nice people! Pray! Jesus, you ought not to shoot a lady. I'll give you all the money I've got!"

"Lady," The Misfit said, looking beyond her far into the woods, "there never was a body that give the undertaker a tip."

There were two more pistol reports and the grandmother raised her head like a parched old turkey hen crying for water and called, "Bailey Boy, Bailey Boy!" as if her heart would break.

"Jesus was the only One that ever raised the dead," The Misfit continued, "and He shouldn't have done it. He thown everything off balance. If He did what He said, then it's nothing for you to do but thow away everything and follow Him, and if He didn't, then it's nothing for you to do but enjoy the few minutes you got left the best way you can — by killing somebody or burning down his house or do- ing some other meanness to him. No pleasure but meanness," he said and his voice became almost a snarl.

"Maybe He didn't raise the dead," the old lady mumbled, not knowing what 135 she was saying and feeling so dizzy that she sank down in the ditch with her legs twisted under her.

"I wasn't there so I can't say He didn't," The Misfit said. "I wisht I had of been there," he said, hitting the ground with his fist. "It ain't right I wasn't there because if I had of been there I would of known. Listen, lady," he said in a high voice, "if I had of been there I would of known and I wouldn't be like I am now." His voice seemed about to crack and the grandmother's head cleared for an instant. She saw the man's face twisted close to her own as if he were going to cry and she mur- mured, "Why you're one of my babies. You're one of my own children!" She reached out and touched him on the shoulder. The Misfit sprang back as if a snake had bitten him and shot her three times through the chest. Then he put his gun down on the ground and took off his glasses and began to clean them.

Hiram and Bobby Lee returned from the woods and stood over the ditch, look- ing down at the grandmother who half sat and half lay in a puddle of blood with her legs crossed under her like a child's and her face smiling up at the cloudless sky.

Without his glasses, The Misfit's eyes were red-rimmed and pale and defense- less-looking. "Take her off and thow her where you thown the others," he said, picking up the cat that was rubbing itself against his leg.

"She was a talker, wasn't she?" Bobby Lee said, sliding down the ditch with a yodel.

140   "She would of been a good woman," The Misfit said, "if it had been somebody there to shoot her every minute of her life."

"Some fun!" Bobby Lee said.

"Shut up, Bobby Lee," The Misfit said. "It's no real pleasure in life."

Reading and Reacting

1. How are the style and tone of the narrator's voice different from those of the characters? What, if anything, is the significance of this difference?

2. The figures of speech used in this story sometimes create unflattering, even grotesque, pictures of the characters. Find several examples of such negative figures of speech. Why do you think the author uses them?

3. What does the grandmother's use of the words *pickaninny* and *nigger* reveal about her? How are readers expected to reconcile this language with her very proper appearance and her preoccupation with manners? How does her use of these words affect your reaction to her?

4. Explain the **irony** in this statement: "In case of an accident, anyone seeing her dead on the highway would know at once that she was a lady" (par. 12).

5. How does The Misfit's dialect characterize him?

6. What does the allusion to *Gone with the Wind* (par. 24) contribute to the story?

7. How do the style and tone of the two-paragraph description of the three men in the car (pars. 71–72) help to prepare readers for the events that follow?

8. When The Misfit tells the grandmother about his life, his language takes on a measured, rhythmic quality: "Been in the arm service, both land and sea, at home and abroad, been twict married, been an undertaker, been with the railroads, plowed Mother Earth, been in a tornado, seen a man burnt alive oncet . . ." (par. 109). Find other examples of parallelism and rhythmic repetition in this character's speech. How does this style help to develop The Misfit's character?

9. JOURNAL ENTRY Why do you think the grandmother tells The Misfit she recognizes him? Why does she fail to realize the danger of her remark?

10. CRITICAL PERSPECTIVE In his 2002 essay "Light and Shadow: Religious Grace in Two Stories by Flannery O'Connor," David Allen Cook writes:

> The literary works of Flannery O'Connor often contend that religious belief can only be consummated by direct confrontation with evil, and for those un-committed and unprepared, tragedy seems inevitable. For O'Connor's religious "pretenders," a moment of religious grace — a revelation of Truth — often does come, but at a devastating price. In . . . "A Good Man Is Hard to Find," we are presented with main characters that experience a deep epiphany after being spiritually challenged by the darker side of human nature.

In this story, who are the religious "pretenders," and who has true faith? What is the price of achieving a moment of religious grace? What role does violence play in this equation?

Related Works: "The Lottery" (p. 461), "Where Are You Going, Where Have You Been?" (p. 573), "Everything That Rises Must Converge" (p. 762), "The Tell-Tale Heart" (p. 773), *No Crime* (p. 1316)

CHARLOTTE PERKINS GILMAN (1860–1935) was a prominent feminist and social thinker at the turn of the century. Her essays, lectures, and nonfiction works—such as *Women and Economics* (1898), *Concerning Children* (1900), and *The Man-Made World* (1911)—are forceful statements of Gilman's opinions on women's need for economic independence and social equality. Gilman is probably best known for three utopian feminist novels: *Moving the Mountain* (1911), *Herland* (1915; unpublished until 1978), and *With Her in Ourland* (1916). Her works are full of humor and satire. In *Herland*, for instance, a male sociologist (wandering in by accident from the outside world) is chagrined to find that the women of "Herland" want him as a friend, not a lover.

Although "The Yellow Wallpaper" (1982) is not typical of Gilman's other fiction, it is considered her artistic masterpiece. The terse, clinical precision of the writing, conveying the tightly wound and distraught mental state of the narrator, is particularly chilling when it is read with a knowledge of Gilman's personal history. In the 1880s, she met and married a young artist, Charles Walter Stetson. Following the birth of their daughter, she grew increasingly depressed and turned to a noted Philadelphia neurologist for help. Following the traditions of the time, he prescribed complete bed rest and mental inactivity—a treatment that, Gilman said later, drove her "so near the borderline of utter mental ruin that I could see over." "The Yellow Wallpaper" is not simply a psychological study. Like most of Gilman's work, it makes a point—in this case, about the dangers of women's utter dependence on a male interpretation of their needs.

Cultural Context Recent research indicates that one out of every ten new mothers becomes seriously depressed within six months after childbirth. This condition is known as postpartum depression, and its symptoms include severe feelings of sadness or emptiness, withdrawal from family and friends, a strong sense of failure or inadequacy, intense concern (or lack of concern) about the baby, and, in more serious cases, thoughts about suicide or fears of harming the baby. Today's treatments include medication and psychotherapy, but at the time of this story, the standard treatment was a "rest cure," in which the patient was placed in isolation and kept from distractions that were believed to be dangerous. For many patients, this "cure" was worse than the disease itself.

The Yellow Wallpaper   (1892)

It is very seldom that mere ordinary people like John and myself secure ancestral halls for the summer.

A colonial mansion, a hereditary estate, I would say a haunted house, and reach the height of romantic felicity —but that would be asking too much of fate!

Still I will proudly declare that there is something queer about it.

Else, why should it be let so cheaply? And why have stood so long untenanted?

John laughs at me, of course, but one expects that in marriage.   5

John is practical in the extreme. He has no patience with faith, an intense horror of superstition, and he scoffs openly at any talk of things not to be felt and seen and put down in figures.

John is a physician, and *perhaps*—(I would not say it to a living soul, of course, but this is dead paper and a great relief to my mind —) *perhaps* that is one reason I do not get well faster.

You see he does not believe I am sick!

And what can one do?

10   If a physician of high standing, and one's own husband, assures friends and relatives that there is really nothing the matter with one but temporary nervous depression — a slight hysterical tendency — what is one to do?

My brother is also a physician, and also of high standing, and he says the same thing.

So I take phosphates or phosphites°— whichever it is, and tonics, and journeys, and air, and exercise, and am absolutely forbidden to "work" until I am well again.

Personally, I disagree with their ideas.

Personally, I believe that congenial work, with excitement and change, would do me good.

15   But what is one to do?

I did write for a while in spite of them; but it *does* exhaust me a good deal — having to be so sly about it, or else meet with heavy opposition.

I sometimes fancy that in my condition if I had less opposition and more society and stimulus — but John says the very worst thing I can do is to think about my condition, and I confess it always makes me feel bad.

So I will let it alone and talk about the house.

The most beautiful place! It is quite alone, standing well back from the road, quite three miles from the village. It makes me think of English places that you read about, for there are hedges and walls and gates that lock, and lots of separate little houses for the gardeners and people.

20   There is a *delicious* garden! I never saw such a garden —large and shady, full of box-bordered paths, and lined with long grape-covered arbors with seats under them.

There were greenhouses, too, but they are all broken now.

There was some legal trouble, I believe, something about the heirs and co-heirs; anyhow, the place has been empty for years.

That spoils my ghostliness, I am afraid, but I don't care — there is something strange about the house — I can feel it.

I even said so to John one moonlight evening, but he said what I felt was a *draught*, and shut the window.

25   I get unreasonably angry with John sometimes. I'm sure I never used to be so sensitive. I think it is due to this nervous condition.

But John says if I feel so, I shall neglect proper self-control; so I take pains to control myself —before him, at least, and that makes me very tired.

---

phosphates or phosphites: Both terms refer to salts of phosphorous acid. The narrator, however, means "phosphate," a carbonated beverage of water, flavoring, and a small amount of phosphoric acid.

I don't like our room a bit. I wanted one downstairs that opened on the piazza and had roses all over the window, and such pretty old-fashioned chintz hangings! But John would not hear of it.

He said there was only one window and not room for two beds, and no near room for him if he took another.

He is very careful and loving, and hardly lets me stir without special direction.

I have a schedule prescription for each hour in the day; he takes all care from me, and so I feel basely ungrateful not to value it more.

He said we came here solely on my account, that I was to have perfect rest and all the air I could get. "Your exercise depends on your strength, my dear," said he, "and your food somewhat on your appetite; but air you can absorb all the time." So we took the nursery at the top of the house.

It is a big, airy room, the whole floor nearly, with windows that look all ways, and air and sunshine galore. It was nursery first and then playroom and gymnasium, I should judge; for the windows are barred for little children, and there are rings and things in the walls.

The paint and paper look as if a boys' school had used it. It is stripped off — the paper — in great patches all around the head of my bed, about as far as I can reach, and in a great place on the other side of the room low down. I never saw a worse paper in my life.

One of those sprawling flamboyant patterns committing every artistic sin.

It is dull enough to confuse the eye in following, pronounced enough to constantly irritate and provoke study, and when you follow the lame uncertain curves for a little distance they suddenly commit suicide — plunge off at outrageous angles, destroy themselves in unheard of contradictions.

The color is repellent, almost revolting; a smouldering unclean yellow, strangely faded by the slow-turning sunlight.

It is a dull yet lurid orange in some places, a sickly sulphur tint in others.

No wonder the children hated it! I should hate it myself if I had to live in this room long.

There comes John, and I must put this away, — he hates to have me write a word.

*   *   *

We have been here two weeks, and I haven't felt like writing before, since that first day.

I am sitting by the window now, up in this atrocious nursery, and there is nothing to hinder my writing as much as I please, save lack of strength.

John is away all day, and even some nights when his cases are serious.

I am glad my case is not serious!

But these nervous troubles are dreadfully depressing.

John does not know how much I really suffer. He knows there is no *reason* to suffer, and that satisfies him.

Of course it is only nervousness. It does weigh on me so not to do my duty in any way!

I meant to be such a help to John, such a real rest and comfort, and here I am a comparative burden already!

Nobody would believe what an effort it is to do what little I am able, — to dress and entertain, and order things.

It is fortunate Mary is so good with the baby. Such a dear baby!

50 And yet I *cannot* be with him, it makes me so nervous.

I suppose John never was nervous in his life. He laughs at me so about this wallpaper!

At first he meant to repaper the room, but afterwards he said that I was letting it get the better of me, and that nothing was worse for a nervous patient than to give way to such fancies.

He said that after the wallpaper was changed it would be the heavy bedstead, and then the barred windows, and then that gate at the head of the stairs, and so on.

"You know the place is doing you good," he said, "and really, dear, I don't care to renovate the house just for a three months' rental."

55 "Then do let us go downstairs," I said, "there are such pretty rooms there."

Then he took me in his arms and called me a blessed little goose, and said he would go down cellar, if I wished, and have it whitewashed into the bargain.

But he is right enough about the beds and windows and things.

It is an airy and comfortable room as any one need wish, and, of course, I would not be so silly as to make him uncomfortable just for a whim.

I'm really getting quite fond of the big room, all but that horrid paper.

60 Out of one window I can see the garden, those mysterious deep-shaded arbors, the riotous old-fashioned flowers, and bushes and gnarly trees.

Out of another I get a lovely view of the bay and a little private wharf belonging to the estate. There is a beautiful shaded lane that runs down there from the house. I always fancy I see people walking in these numerous paths and arbors, but John has cautioned me not to give way to fancy in the least. He says that with my imaginative power and habit of story-making, a nervous weakness like mine is sure to lead to all manner of excited fancies, and that I ought to use my will and good sense to check the tendency. So I try.

I think sometimes that if I were only well enough to write a little it would relieve the press of ideas and rest me.

But I find I get pretty tired when I try.

It is so discouraging not to have any advice and companionship about my work. When I get really well, John says we will ask Cousin Henry and Julia down for a long visit; but he says he would as soon put fireworks in my pillow-case as to let me have those stimulating people about now.

65 I wish I could get well faster.

But I must not think about that. This paper looks to me as if it *knew* what a vicious influence it had!

There is a recurrent spot where the pattern lolls like a broken neck and two bulbous eyes stare at you upside down.

I get positively angry with the impertinence of it and the everlastingness. Up and down and sideways they crawl, and those absurd, unblinking eyes are everywhere.

There is one place where two breadths didn't match, and the eyes go all up and down the line, one a little higher than the other.

I never saw so much expression in an inanimate thing before, and we all know how much expression they have! I used to lie awake as a child and get more entertainment and terror out of blank walls and plain furniture than most children could find in a toy-store.

I remember what a kindly wink the knobs of our big, old bureau used to have, 70 and there was one chair that always seemed like a strong friend.

I used to feel that if any of the other things looked too fierce I could always hop into that chair and be safe.

The furniture in this room is no worse than inharmonious, however, for we had to bring it all from downstairs. I suppose when this was used as a playroom they had to take the nursery things out, and no wonder! I never saw such ravages as the children have made here.

The wallpaper, as I said before, is torn off in spots, and it sticketh closer than a brother — they must have had perseverance as well as hatred.

Then the floor is scratched and gouged and splintered, the plaster itself is dug out here and there, and this great heavy bed which is all we found in the room, looks as if it had been through the wars.

But I don't mind it a bit — only the paper. 75

There comes John's sister. Such a dear girl as she is, and so careful of me! I must not let her find me writing.

She is a perfect and enthusiastic housekeeper, and hopes for no better profession. I verily believe she thinks it is the writing which made me sick!

But I can write when she is out, and see her a long way off from these windows.

There is one that commands the road, a lovely shaded winding road, and one that just looks off over the country. A lovely country, too, full of great elms and velvet meadows.

This wallpaper has a kind of sub-pattern in a different shade, a particularly ir- 80 ritating one, for you can only see it in certain lights, and not clearly then.

But in the places where it isn't faded and where the sun is just so — I can see a strange, provoking, formless sort of figure, that seems to skulk about behind that silly and conspicuous front design.

There's sister on the stairs!

* * *

Well, the Fourth of July is over! The people are all gone and I am tired out. John thought it might do me good to see a little company, so we just had mother and Nellie and the children down for a week.

Of course I didn't do a thing. Jennie sees to everything now.

But it tired me all the same. 85

John says if I don't pick up faster he shall send me to Weir Mitchell° in the fall.

Weir Mitchell: Silas Weir Mitchell (1829–1914), a Philadelphia neurologist-psychologist who introduced the "rest cure" for nervous diseases.

But I don't want to go there at all. I had a friend who was in his hands once, and she says he is just like John and my brother, only more so!

Besides, it is such an undertaking to go so far.

I don't feel as if it was worth while to turn my hand over for anything, and I'm getting dreadfully fretful and querulous.

90   I cry at nothing, and cry most of the time.

Of course I don't when John is here, or anybody else, but when I am alone.

And I am alone a good deal just now. John is kept in town very often by serious cases, and Jennie is good and lets me alone when I want her to.

So I walk a little in the garden or down that lovely lane, sit on the porch under the roses, and lie down up here a good deal.

I'm getting really fond of the room in spite of the wallpaper. Perhaps *because* of the wallpaper.

95   It dwells in my mind so!

I lie here on this great immovable bed — it is nailed down, I believe — and follow that pattern about by the hour. It is as good as gymnastics, I assure you. I start, we'll say, at the bottom, down in the corner over there where it has not been touched, and I determine for the thousandth time that I *will* follow that pointless pattern to some sort of a conclusion.

I know a little of the principle of design, and I know this thing was not arranged on any laws of radiation, or alternation, or repetition, or symmetry, or anything else that I ever heard of.

It is repeated, of course, by the breadths, but not otherwise.

Looked at in one way each breadth stands alone, the bloated curves and flour-
100 ishes — a kind of "debased Romanesque" with *delirium tremens*° go waddling up and down in isolated columns of fatuity.

But, on the other hand, they connect diagonally, and the sprawling outlines run off in great slanting waves of optic horror, like a lot of wallowing seaweeds in full chase.

The whole thing goes horizontally, too, at least it seems so, and I exhaust myself in trying to distinguish the order of its going in that direction.

They have used a horizontal breadth for a frieze, and that adds wonderfully to the confusion.

There is one end of the room where it is almost intact, and there, when the crosslights fade and the low sun shines directly upon it, I can almost fancy radiation after all, — the interminable grotesques seems to form around a com-mon center and rush off in headlong plunges of equal distraction.

It makes me tired to follow it. I will take a nap I guess.

105 I don't know why I should write this.

I don't want to.

I don't feel able.

---

delirium tremens: Mental confusion caused by alcohol poisoning and characterized by physical tremors and hallucinations.

And I know John would think it absurd. But I *must* say what I feel and think 110
in some way — it is such a relief!

But the effort is getting to be greater than the relief.

Half the time now I am awfully lazy, and lie down ever so much.

John says I mustn't lose my strength, and has me take cod liver oil and lots of
tonics and things, to say nothing of ale and wine and rare meat.

Dear John! He loves me very dearly, and hates to have me sick. I tried to have
a real earnest reasonable talk with him the other day, and tell him how I wish he
would let me go and make a visit to Cousin Henry and Julia.

But he said I wasn't able to go, nor able to stand it after I got there; and I did
not make out a very good case for myself, for I was crying before I had finished.

It is getting to be a great effort for me to think straight. Just this nervous 115
weakness I suppose.

And dear John gathered me up in his arms, and just carried me upstairs and
laid me on the bed, and sat by me and read to me till it tired my head.

He said I was his darling and his comfort and all he had, and that I must take
care of myself for his sake, and keep well.

He says no one but myself can help me out of it, that I must use my will and
self-control and not let any silly fancies run away with me.

There's one comfort, the baby is well and happy, and does not have to occupy
this nursery with the horrid wallpaper.

If we had not used it, that blessed child would have! What a fortunate escape!
Why, I wouldn't have a child of mine, an impressionable little thing, live in such
a room for worlds.

I never thought of it before, but it is lucky that John kept me here after all, 120
I can stand it so much easier than a baby, you see.

Of course I never mention it to them any more — I am too wise, — but I keep
watch of it all the same.

There are things in that paper that nobody knows but me, or ever will.

Behind that outside pattern the dim shapes get clearer every day.

It is always the same shape, only very numerous.

And it is like a woman stooping down and creeping about behind that pattern. 125
I don't like it a bit. I wonder — I begin to think — I wish John would take me away
from here!

It is so hard to talk with John about my case, because he is so wise, and because
he loves me so.

But I tried it last night.

It was moonlight. The moon shines in all around just as the sun does.

I hate to see it sometimes, it creeps so slowly, and always comes in by one
window or another.

John was asleep and I hated to waken him, so I kept still and watched the 130
moonlight on that undulating wallpaper till I felt creepy.

The faint figure behind seemed to shake the pattern, just as if she wanted to
get out.

I got up softly and went to feel and see if the paper *did* move, and when I came
back John was awake.

"What is it, little girl?" he said. "Don't go walking about like that — you'll get cold."

I thought it was a good time to talk, so I told him that I really was not gaining here, and that I wished he would take me away.

135 "Why, darling!" said he, "our lease will be up in three weeks, and I can't see how to leave before.

"The repairs are not done at home, and I cannot possibly leave town just now. Of course if you were in any danger, I could and would, but you really are better, dear, whether you can see it or not. I am a doctor, dear, and I know. You are gaining flesh and color, your appetite is better, I feel really much easier about you."

"I don't weigh a bit more," said I, "nor as much; and my appetite may be better in the evening when you are here, but it is worse in the morning when you are away!"

"Bless her little heart!" said he with a big hug, "she shall be as sick as she pleases! But now let's improve the shining hours by going to sleep, and talk about it in the morning!"

"And you won't go away?" I asked gloomily.

140 "Why, how can I, dear? It is only three weeks more and then we will take a nice little trip of a few days while Jennie is getting the house ready. Really dear you are better!"

"Better in body perhaps —" I began, and stopped short, for he sat up straight and looked at me with such a stern, reproachful look that I could not say another word.

"My darling," said he, "I beg of you, for my sake and for our child's sake, as well as for your own, that you will never for one instant let that idea enter your mind! There is nothing so dangerous, so fascinating, to a temperament like yours. It is a false and foolish fancy. Can you not trust me as a physician when I tell you so?"

So of course I said no more on that score, and we went to sleep before long. He thought I was asleep first, but I wasn't, and lay there for hours trying to decide whether that front pattern and the back pattern really did move together or separately.

On a pattern like this, by daylight, there is a lack of sequence, a defiance of law, that is a constant irritant to a normal mind.

145 The color is hideous enough, and unreliable enough, and infuriating enough, but the pattern is torturing.

You think you have mastered it, but just as you get well underway in following, it turns back-somersault and there you are. It slaps you in the face, knocks you down, and tramples upon you. It is like a bad dream.

The outside pattern is a florid arabesque, reminding one of a fungus. If you can imagine a toadstool in joints, an interminable string of toadstools, budding and sprouting in endless convolutions — why, that is something like it.

That is, sometimes!

There is one marked peculiarity about this paper, a thing nobody seems to notice but myself, and that is that it changes as the light changes.

When the sun shoots in through the east window — I always watch for that   150
first long, straight ray — it changes so quickly that I never can quite believe it.

That is why I watch it always.

By moonlight — the moon shines in all night when there is a moon — I
wouldn't know it was the same paper.

At night in any kind of light, in twilight, candlelight, lamplight, and worst of
all by moonlight, it becomes bars! The outside pattern I mean, and the woman
behind it is as plain as can be.

I didn't realize for a long time what the thing was that showed behind, that
dim sub-pattern, but now I am quite sure it is a woman.

By daylight she is subdued, quiet. I fancy it is the pattern that keeps her so still.   155
It is so puzzling. It keeps me quiet by the hour.

I lie down ever so much now. John says it is good for me, and to sleep all I can.

Indeed he started the habit by making me lie down for an hour after
each meal.

It is a very bad habit I am convinced, for you see I don't sleep.

And that cultivates deceit, for I don't tell them I'm awake — O no!

The fact is I am getting a little afraid of John.   160

He seems very queer sometimes, and even Jennie has an inexplicable look.

It strikes me occasionally, just as a scientific hypothesis, — that perhaps it is
the paper!

I have watched John when he did not know I was looking, and come into the
room suddenly on the most innocent excuses, and I've caught him several times
looking at the paper! And Jennie too. I caught Jennie with her hand on it once.

She didn't know I was in the room, and when I asked her in a quiet, a very
quiet voice, with the most restrained manner possible, what she was doing with
the paper — she turned around as if she had been caught stealing, and looked
quite angry — asked me why I should frighten her so!

Then she said that the paper stained everything it touched, that she had found   165
yellow smooches on all my clothes and John's, and she wished we would be more
careful!

Did not that sound innocent? But I know she was studying that pattern, and I
am determined that nobody shall find it out but myself!

Life is very much more exciting now than it used to be. You see I have something
more to expect, to look forward to, to watch. I really do eat better, and am more
quiet than I was.

John is so pleased to see me improve! He laughed a little the other day, and
said I seemed to be flourishing in spite of my wallpaper.

I turned it off with a laugh. I had no intention of telling him it was *because* of
the wallpaper — he would make fun of me. He might even want to take me away.

I don't want to leave now until I have found it out. There is a week more, and   170
I think that will be enough.

I'm feeling ever so much better! I don't sleep much at night, for it is so interesting
to watch developments; but I sleep a good deal in the daytime.

In the daytime it is tiresome and perplexing.

There are always new shoots on the fungus, and new shades of yellow all over it. I cannot keep count of them, though I have tried conscientiously.

It is the strangest yellow, that wallpaper! It makes me think of all the yellow things I ever saw — not beautiful ones like buttercups, but old foul, bad yellow things.

175   But there is something else about that paper — the smell! I noticed it the moment we came into the room, but with so much air and sun it was not bad. Now we have had a week of fog and rain, and whether the windows are open or not, the smell is here.

It creeps all over the house.

I find it hovering in the dining-room, skulking in the parlor, hiding in the hall, lying in wait for me on the stairs.

It gets into my hair.

Even when I go to ride, if I turn my head suddenly and surprise it — there is that smell!

180   Such a peculiar odor, too! I have spent hours in trying to analyze it, to find what it smelled like.

It is not bad — at first, and very gentle, but quite the subtlest, most enduring odor I ever met.

In this damp weather it is awful, I wake up in the night and find it hanging over me.

It used to disturb me at first. I thought seriously of burning the house — to reach the smell.

But now I am used to it. The only thing I can think of that it is like is the *color* of the paper! A yellow smell.

185   There is a very funny mark on this wall, low down, near the mop-board. A streak that runs round the room. It goes behind every piece of furniture, except the bed, a long, straight, even *smooch,* as if it had been rubbed over and over.

I wonder how it was done and who did it, and what they did it for. Round and round and round — round and round and round! — it makes me dizzy!

I really have discovered something at last.

Through watching so much at night, when it changes so, I have finally found out.

The front pattern *does* move — and no wonder! The woman behind shakes it!

190   Sometimes I think there are a great many women behind, and sometimes only one, and she crawls around fast, and her crawling shakes it all over.

Then in the very bright spots she keeps still, and in the very shady spots she just takes hold of the bars and shakes them hard.

And she is all the time trying to climb through. But nobody could climb through that pattern — it strangles so; I think that is why it has so many heads.

They get through, and then the pattern strangles them off and turns them upside down, and makes their eyes white!

If those heads were covered or taken off it would not be half so bad.

195   I think that woman gets out in the daytime!

And I'll tell you why — privately — I've seen her!

I can see her out of every one of my windows!

It is the same woman, I know, for she is always creeping, and most women do not creep by daylight.

I see her in that long shaded lane, creeping up and down. I see her in those 200 dark grape arbors, creeping all around the garden.

I see her on that long road under the trees, creeping along, and when a carriage comes she hides under the blackberry vines.

I don't blame her a bit. It must be very humiliating to be caught creeping by daylight!

I always lock the door when I creep by daylight. I can't do it at night, for I know John would suspect something at once.

And John is so queer now, that I don't want to irritate him. I wish he would take another room! Besides, I don't want anybody to get that woman out at night but myself.

I often wonder if I could see her out of all the windows at once.

But, turn as fast as I can, I can only see out of one at one time. 205

And though I always see her, she *may* be able to creep faster than I can turn!

I have watched her sometimes away off in the open country, creeping as fast as a cloud shadow in a high wind.

If only that top pattern could be gotten off from the under one! I mean to try it, little by little.

I have found out another funny thing, but I shan't tell it this time! It does not do to trust people too much.

There are only two more days to get this paper off, and I believe John is 210 beginning to notice. I don't like the look in his eyes.

And I heard him ask Jennie a lot of professional questions about me. She had a very good report to give.

She said I slept a good deal in the daytime.

John knows I don't sleep very well at night, for all I'm so quiet!

He asked me all sorts of questions, too, and pretended to be very loving and kind.

As if I couldn't see through him! 215

Still, I don't wonder he acts so, sleeping under this paper for three months.

It only interests me, but I feel sure John and Jennie are secretly affected by it.

*   *   *

Hurrah! This is the last day, but it is enough. John to stay in town over night, and won't be out until this evening.

Jennie wanted to sleep with me — the sly thing! But I told her I should undoubtedly rest better for a night all alone.

That was clever, for really I wasn't alone a bit! As soon as it was moon-light and 220 that poor thing began to crawl and shake the pattern, I got up and ran to help her.

I pulled and she shook, I shook and she pulled, and before morning we had peeled off yards of that paper.

A strip about as high as my head and half around the room.

And then when the sun came and that awful pattern began to laugh at me, I declared I would finish it to-day!

We go away to-morrow, and they are moving all my furniture down again to leave things as they were before.

225   Jennie looked at the wall in amazement, but I told her merrily that I did it out of pure spite at the vicious thing.

She laughed and said she wouldn't mind doing it herself, but I must not get tired.

How she betrayed herself that time!

But I am here, and no person touches this paper but me, — not *alive!*

She tried to get me out of the room — it was too patent! But I said it was so quiet and empty and clean now that I believed I would lie down again and sleep all I could; and not to wake me even for dinner — I would call when I woke.

So now she is gone, and the servants are gone, and the things are gone, and
230 there is nothing left but that great bedstead nailed down, with the canvas mattress we found on it.

We shall sleep downstairs to-night, and take the boat home tomorrow.

I quite enjoy the room, now it is bare again.

How those children did tear about here!

This bedstead is fairly gnawed!

But I must get to work.

235   I have locked the door and thrown the key down into the front path.

I don't want to go out, and I don't want to have anybody come in, till John comes.

I want to astonish him.

I've got a rope up here that even Jennie did not find. If that woman does get out, and tries to get away, I can tie her!

240   But I forgot I could not reach far without anything to stand on!

This bed will *not* move!

I tried to lift and push it until I was lame, and then I got so angry I bit off a little piece at one corner — but it hurt my teeth.

Then I peeled off all the paper I could reach standing on the floor. It sticks horribly and the pattern just enjoys it! All those strangled heads and bulbous eyes and waddling fungus growths just shriek with derision!

I am getting angry enough to do something desperate. To jump out of the window would be admirable exercise, but the bars are too strong even to try.

245   Besides I wouldn't do it. Of course not. I know well enough that a step like that is improper and might be misconstrued.

I don't like to *look* out of the windows even — there are so many of those creeping women, and they creep so fast.

I wonder if they come out of that wall-paper as I did?

But I am securely fastened now by my well-hidden rope — you don't get *me* out in the road there!

I suppose I shall have to get back behind the pattern when it comes night, and that is hard!

It is so pleasant to be out in this great room and creep around as I please!   250

I don't want to go outside. I won't, even if Jennie asks me to.

For outside you have to creep on the ground, and everything is green instead of yellow.

But here I can creep smoothly on the floor, and my shoulder just fits in that long smooch around the wall, so I cannot lose my way.

Why there's John at the door!

It is no use, young man, you can't open it!   255

How he does call and pound!

Now he's crying for an axe.

It would be a shame to break down that beautiful door!

"John dear!" said I in the gentlest voice, "the key is down by the front steps, under a plantain leaf!"

That silenced him for a few moments.

Then he said — very quietly indeed, "Open the door, my darling!"   260

"I can't," said I. "The key is down by the front door under a plantain leaf!"

And then I said it again, several times, very gently and slowly, and said it so often that he had to go and see, and he got it of course, and came in. He stopped short by the door.

"What is the matter?" he cried. "For God's sake, what are you doing!"

I kept on creeping just the same, but I looked at him over my shoulder.   265

"I've got out at last," said I, "in spite of you and Jane. And I've pulled off most of the paper, so you can't put me back!"

Now why should that man have fainted? But he did, and right across my path by the wall, so that I had to creep over him every time!

Reading and Reacting

1. The story's narrator, who has recently had a baby, is suffering from what her husband, a doctor, calls "temporary nervous depression — a slight hysterical tendency" (par. 10). How accurate is his diagnosis? Explain.

2. What do the following comments reveal about the narrator's situation: "John laughs at me, of course, but one expects that in marriage" (par. 5); "I must put this away, — he hates to have me write a word" (par. 39); "He laughs at me so about this wallpaper" (par. 51); "Then he took me in his arms and called me a blessed little goose" (par. 56)?

3. What is it about the house, the grounds, and her room that upsets the narrator?

4. What images and figures of speech does the narrator use to describe the wallpaper? To what extent do you think her descriptions are accurate? What do you think she sees, and what do you think she imagines?

5. How does the narrator's mood change as the story progresses? How does her language change?

6. How would you characterize the narrator's tone? Does she sound depressed? Delusional? Hysterical?

7. How do you explain the story's very short paragraphs? How do these short paragraphs influence your assessment of the narrator's mental state?

8. Study the story's punctuation—in particular, its use of dashes, question marks, and exclamation points. What does this use of punctuation contribute to the story?

9. JOURNAL ENTRY Do you think a present-day woman would respond differently to such advice from her husband or doctor? Explain.

10. CRITICAL PERSPECTIVE "The Yellow Wallpaper" was originally seen by some readers as a ghost story and was anthologized as such. More recently, critics have tended to interpret the story from a feminist perspective, focusing on the way in which the nameless narrator is victimized by the men around her and by the values of the Victorian society they uphold. In the essay "An Unnecessary Maze of Sign-Reading," Mary Jacobus concludes that the overwhelmingly feminist perspective of recent criticism, though certainly valuable and enlightening, has overlooked other promising critical possibilities—for example, "the Gothic and uncanny elements present in the text."

If you were teaching "The Yellow Wallpaper," would you present it as a feminist story or as a chilling gothic ghost story? Do you think interpreting the story as a gothic horror tale precludes a feminist reading, or do you see the two interpretations as compatible?

Related Works: "The Story of an Hour" (p. 197), "The Disappearance" (p. 371), "Daddy" (p. 952), *Trifles* (p. 1372), *A Doll House* (p. 1454)

TIM O'BRIEN (1946–   ) is sometimes described as a writer whose books are on the short list of essential fiction about the Vietnam War. After graduating summa cum laude from Macalester College in 1968, O'Brien was immediately drafted into the United States Army and sent to Vietnam, where he served with the 198th Infantry Brigade. He was promoted to sergeant and awarded a Purple Heart after receiving a shrapnel wound in a battle near My Lai. In 1970, after his discharge from the army, he attended Harvard graduate school to study government. He worked as a reporter for the *Washington Post* before pursuing a full-time career as a writer.

O'Brien's plots focus on danger, violence, courage, endurance, despair, and other topics often associated with war fiction, but he treats these topics with an emphasis on the contemporary dilemmas faced by those who may be unwilling participants in an unpopular war. O'Brien calls *If I Die in a Combat Zone, Box Me Up and Ship Me Home* (1979) a memoir because it relates his war experiences as a naive young college graduate who suddenly finds himself facing bullets and land mines rather than sitting behind a desk. *Northern Lights* (1975) concentrates on the wilderness survival experiences of two brothers, one of whom has just returned from the Vietnam War. A fantastic daydream of an American soldier, *Going after Cacciato* (1978), won a National Book Award. *The Things They Carried* (1990) is a quasi-fictional collection of interrelated stories that deal with a single platoon. *The Vietnam in Me* (1994) emphasizes the destructive effects of war on a soldier, even after he has returned home, and *In the Lake of the Woods* (1994) tells a dramatic story of a couple missing in Minnesota. O'Brien's most recent books are *Tomcat in Love* (1998) and *July, July* (2002).

Cultural Context United States involvement in the Vietnam War lasted from the early 1960s until the mid 1970s. By the war's end, more than 47,000 Americans had been killed in action, nearly 11,000 had died of other causes, and more than 303,000 had been wounded. Estimates of South Vietnamese army casualties range from 185,000 to 225,000 killed and 500,000 to 570,000 wounded. The North Vietnamese and the Viet Cong, the guerrilla force that fought against South Vietnam and the United States, lost about 900,000 troops. In addition, more than 1 million North and South Vietnamese civilians were killed during the war.

The Things They Carried (1986)

First Lieutenant Jimmy Cross carried letters from a girl named Martha, a junior at Mount Sebastian College in New Jersey. They were not love letters, but Lieutenant Cross was hoping, so he kept them folded in plastic at the bottom of his rucksack. In the late afternoon, after a day's march, he would dig his foxhole, wash his hands under a canteen, unwrap the letters, hold them with the tips of his fingers, and spend the last hour of light pretending. He would imagine romantic camping trips into the White Mountains in New Hampshire. He would sometimes taste the envelope flaps, knowing her tongue had been there. More than anything, he wanted Martha to love him as he loved her, but the letters were mostly chatty, elusive on the matter of love. She was a virgin, he was almost sure. She was an English major at Mount Sebastian, and she wrote beautifully about her professors and roommates and midterm exams, about her respect for Chaucer and her great affection for Virginia Woolf. She often quoted lines of poetry; she never mentioned the war, except to say, Jimmy, take care of yourself. The letters weighed ten ounces. They were signed "Love, Martha," but Lieutenant Cross understood that "Love" was only a way of signing and did not mean what he sometimes pretended it meant. At dusk, he would carefully return the letters to his rucksack. Slowly, a bit distracted, he would get up and move among his men, checking the perimeter, then at full dark he would return to his hole and watch the night and wonder if Martha was a virgin.

The things they carried were largely determined by necessity. Among the necessities or near necessities were P-38 can openers, pocket knives, heat tabs, wrist watches, dog tags, mosquito repellent, chewing gum, candy, cigarettes, salt tablets, packets of Kool-Aid, lighters, matches, sewing kits, Military Payment Certificates, C rations, and two or three canteens of water. Together, these items weighed between fifteen and twenty pounds, depending upon a man's habits or rate of metabolism. Henry Dobbins, who was a big man, carried extra rations; he was especially fond of canned peaches in heavy syrup over pound cake. Dave Jensen, who practiced field hygiene, carried a toothbrush, dental floss, and several hotel-size bars of soap he'd stolen on R&R in Sydney, Australia. Ted Lavender, who was scared, carried tranquilizers until he was shot in the head outside the village of Than Khe in mid-April. By necessity, and because it was SOP,° they all carried steel helmets that weighed five pounds including the liner and camouflage cover. They carried the standard fatigue jackets and trousers. Very few carried underwear. On their feet they carried jungle boots — 2.1 pounds — and Dave Jensen carried three pairs of socks and a can of Dr. Scholl's foot powder as a precaution against trench foot. Until he was shot, Ted Lavender carried six or seven ounces of premium dope, which for him was a necessity. Mitchell Sanders, the RTO,° carried condoms. Norman Bowker carried a diary. Rat Kiley carried comic books. Kiowa, a devout Baptist, carried an illustrated New Testament that had been presented to him by his father, who taught Sunday school in Oklahoma City, Oklahoma. As a hedge against bad times, however, Kiowa also carried his grandmother's distrust of the white man, his grandfather's old hunting hatchet. Necessity dictated. Because the land was mined and booby-trapped, it was SOP for each man to carry a steel-centered, nylon-covered flak jacket, which weighed 6.7 pounds, but which on hot days seemed much heavier. Because you could die so quickly, each man carried at least one large compress bandage, usually in the helmet band for easy access. Because the nights were cold, and because the monsoons were wet, each carried a green plastic poncho that could be used as a raincoat or ground sheet or makeshift tent. With its quilted liner, the poncho weighed almost two pounds, but it was worth every ounce. In April, for instance, when Ted Lavender was shot, they used his poncho to wrap him up, then to carry him across the paddy, then to lift him into the chopper that took him away.

They were called legs or grunts.

To carry something was to "hump" it, as when Lieutenant Jimmy Cross humped his love for Martha up the hills and through the swamps. In its intransitive form, "to hump" meant "to walk," or "to march," but it implied burdens far beyond the intransitive.

5   Almost everyone humped photographs. In his wallet, Lieutenant Cross carried two photographs of Martha. The first was a Kodachrome snapshot signed "Love," though he knew better. She stood against a brick wall. Her eyes were gray and neutral, her lips slightly open as she stared straight-on at the camera. At night, sometimes, Lieutenant Cross wondered who had taken the picture, because he knew she had boyfriends, because he loved her so much, and because he could see the shadow of the picture taker spreading out against the brick wall. The second photograph had been clipped from the 1968 Mount Sebastian yearbook. It was an action shot — women's volleyball — and Martha was bent horizontal to the floor, reaching, the palms of her hands in sharp focus, the tongue taut, the expression frank and competitive. There was no visible sweat. She wore white gym shorts. Her legs, he thought, were almost certainly the legs of a virgin, dry and without hair, the left knee cocked and carrying her entire weight, which was just over one hundred pounds. Lieutenant Cross remembered touching that left knee. A dark theater, he remembered, and the movie was *Bonnie and Clyde*, and Martha

---

SOP: Standard operating procedure.
RTO: Radio telephone operator.

wore a tweed skirt, and during the final scene, when he touched her knee, she turned and looked at him in a sad, sober way that made him pull his hand back, but he would always remember the feel of the tweed skirt and the knee beneath it and the sound of the gunfire that killed Bonnie and Clyde, how embarrassing it was, how slow and oppressive. He remembered kissing her good night at the dorm door. Right then, he thought, he should've done something brave. He should've carried her up the stairs to her room and tied her to the bed and touched that left knee all night long. He should've risked it. Whenever he looked at the photographs, he thought of new things he should've done.

What they carried was partly a function of rank, partly of field specialty.

As a first lieutenant and platoon leader, Jimmy Cross carried a compass, maps, code books, binoculars, and a .45-caliber pistol that weighed 2.9 pounds fully loaded. He carried a strobe light and the responsibility for the lives of his men.

As an RTO, Mitchell Sanders carried the PRC-25 radio, a killer, twenty-six pounds with its battery.

As a medic, Rat Kiley carried a canvas satchel filled with morphine and plasma and malaria tablets and surgical tape and comic books and all the things a medic must carry, including M&M's for especially bad wounds, for a total weight of nearly twenty pounds.

As a big man, therefore a machine gunner, Henry Dobbins carried the M-60,   10 which weighed twenty-three pounds unloaded, but which was almost always loaded. In addition, Dobbins carried between ten and fifteen pounds of ammunition draped in belts across his chest and shoulders.

As PFCs or Spec 4s, most of them were common grunts and carried the standard M-16 gas-operated assault rifle. The weapon weighed 7.5 pounds unloaded, 8.2 pounds with its full twenty-round magazine. Depending on numerous factors, such as topography and psychology, the riflemen carried anywhere from twelve to twenty magazines, usually in cloth bandoliers, adding on another 8.4 pounds at minimum, fourteen pounds at maximum. When it was available, they also carried M-16 maintenance gear — rods and steel brushes and swabs and tubes of LSA oil — all of which weighed about a pound. Among the grunts, some carried the M-79 grenade launcher, 5.9 pounds unloaded, a reasonably light weapon except for the ammunition, which was heavy. A single round weighed ten ounces. The typical load was twenty-five rounds. But Ted Lavender, who was scared, carried thirty-four rounds when he was shot and killed outside Than Khe, and he went down under an exceptional burden, more than twenty pounds of ammunition, plus the flak jacket and helmet and rations and water and toilet paper and tranquilizers and all the rest, plus the unweighed fear. He was dead weight. There was no twitching or flopping. Kiowa, who saw it happen, said it was like watching a rock fall, or a big sandbag or something — just boom, then down — not like the movies where the dead guy rolls around and does fancy spins and goes ass over teakettle — not like that, Kiowa said, the poor bastard just flat-fuck fell. Boom. Down. Nothing else. It was a bright morning in mid-April. Lieutenant Cross felt the pain. He blamed himself. They stripped off Lavender's canteens and ammo, all the heavy things, and Rat Kiley said the obvious, the guy's dead, and Mitchell

Sanders used his radio to report one U.S. KIA and to request a chopper. Then they wrapped Lavender in his poncho. They carried him out to a dry paddy, established security, and sat smoking the dead man's dope until the chopper came. Lieutenant Cross kept to himself. He pictured Martha's smooth young face, thinking he loved her more than anything, more than his men, and now Ted Lavender was dead because he loved her so much and could not stop thinking about her. When the dust-off arrived, they carried Lavender aboard. Afterward they burned Than Khe. They marched until dusk, then dug their holes, and that night Kiowa kept explaining how you had to be there, how fast it was, how the poor guy just dropped like so much concrete. Boom-down, he said. Like cement.

*   *   *

In addition to the three standard weapons — the M-60, M-16, and M-79 — they carried whatever presented itself, or whatever seemed appropriate as a means of killing or staying alive. They carried catch-as-catch-can. At various times, in various situations, they carried M-14s and CAR-15s and Swedish Ks and grease guns and captured AK-47s and Chi-Coms and RPGs and Simonov carbines and black-market Uzis and .38-caliber Smith & Wesson handguns and 66 mm LAWs and shotguns and silencers and blackjacks and bayonets and C-4 plastic explosives. Lee Strunk carried a slingshot; a weapon of last resort, he called it. Mitchell Sanders carried brass knuckles. Kiowa carried his grandfather's feathered hatchet. Every third or fourth man carried a Claymore antipersonnel mine — 3.5 pounds with its firing device. They all carried fragmentation grenades — fourteen ounces each. They all carried at least one M-18 colored smoke grenade — twenty-four ounces. Some carried CS or tear-gas grenades. Some carried white-phosphorus grenades. They carried all they could bear, and then some, including a silent awe for the terrible power of the things they carried.

In the first week of April, before Lavender died, Lieutenant Jimmy Cross received a good-luck charm from Martha. It was a simple pebble, an ounce at most. Smooth to the touch, it was a milky-white color with flecks of orange and violet, oval-shaped, like a miniature egg. In the accompanying letter, Martha wrote that she had found the pebble on the Jersey shoreline, precisely where the land touched water at high tide, where things came together but also separated. It was this separate-but-together quality, she wrote, that had inspired her to pick up the pebble and to carry it in her breast pocket for several days, where it seemed weightless, and then to send it through the mail, by air, as a token of her truest feelings for him. Lieutenant Cross found this romantic. But he wondered what her truest feelings were, exactly, and what she meant by separate-but-together. He wondered how the tides and waves had come into play on that afternoon along the Jersey shoreline when Martha saw the pebble and bent down to rescue it from geology. He imagined bare feet. Martha was a poet, with the poet's sensibilities, and her feet would be brown and bare, the toenails unpainted, the eyes chilly and somber like the ocean in March, and though it was painful, he wondered who had been with her that afternoon. He imagined a pair of shadows moving along the strip of sand where things came together but also separated. It was phantom jealousy, he knew, but he couldn't help himself. He loved her so much. On the march, through the hot days of early April, he carried the pebble in his mouth, turning it with his tongue, tasting sea salts and moisture. His mind wandered. He had difficulty keeping his attention on the war. On occasion he would yell at his men to spread out the column, to keep their eyes open, but then he would slip away into daydreams, just pretending, walking barefoot along the Jersey shore, with Martha, carrying nothing. He would feel himself rising. Sun and waves and gentle winds, all love and lightness.

What they carried varied by mission.

When a mission took them to the mountains, they carried mosquito netting, machetes, canvas tarps, and extra bug juice.   15

If a mission seemed especially hazardous, or if it involved a place they knew to be bad, they carried everything they could. In certain heavily mined AOs,° where the land was dense with Toe Poppers and Bouncing Betties, they took turns humping a twenty-eight-pound mine detector. With its headphones and big sensing plate, the equipment was a stress on the lower back and shoulders, awkward to handle, often useless because of the shrapnel in the earth, but they carried it anyway, partly for safety, partly for the illusion of safety.

On ambush, or other night missions, they carried peculiar little odds and ends. Kiowa always took along his New Testament and a pair of moccasins for silence. Dave Jensen carried night-sight vitamins high in carotin. Lee Strunk carried his slingshot; ammo, he claimed, would never be a problem. Rat Kiley carried brandy and M&M's. Until he was shot, Ted Lavender carried the starlight scope, which weighed 6.3 pounds with its aluminum carrying case. Henry Dobbins carried his girlfriend's panty-hose wrapped around his neck as a comforter. They all carried ghosts. When dark came, they would move out single file across the meadows and paddies to their ambush coordinates, where they would quietly set up the Claymores and lie down and spend the night waiting.

Other missions were more complicated and required special equipment. In mid-April, it was their mission to search out and destroy the elaborate tunnel complexes in the Than Khe area south of Chu Lai. To blow the tunnels, they carried one-pound blocks of pentrite high explosives, four blocks to a man, sixty-eight pounds in all. They carried wiring, detonators, and battery-powered clackers. Dave Jensen carried earplugs. Most often, before blowing the tunnels, they were ordered by higher command to search them, which was considered bad news, but by and large they just shrugged and carried out orders. Because he was a big man, Henry Dobbins was excused from tunnel duty. The others would draw numbers. Before Lavender died there were seventeen men in the platoon, and whoever drew the number seventeen would strip off his gear and crawl in head first with a flashlight and Lieutenant Cross's .45-caliber pistol. The rest of them would fan out as security. They would sit down or kneel, not facing the hole, listening to the ground beneath them, imagining cobwebs and ghosts, whatever was down there — the tunnel walls squeezing in — how the flashlight seemed impossibly

---

AOs: Areas of operation.

heavy in the hand and how it was tunnel vision in the very strictest sense, compression in all ways, even time, and how you had to wiggle in — ass and elbows — a swallowed-up feeling — and how you found yourself worrying about odd things — will your flashlight go dead? Do rats carry rabies? If you screamed, how far would the sound carry? Would your buddies hear it? Would they have the courage to drag you out? In some respects, though not many, the waiting was worse than the tunnel itself. Imagination was a killer.

On April 16, when Lee Strunk drew the number seventeen, he laughed and muttered something and went down quickly. The morning was hot and very still. Not good, Kiowa said. He looked at the tunnel opening, then out across a dry paddy toward the village of Than Khe. Nothing moved. No clouds or birds or people. As they waited, the men smoked and drank Kool-Aid, not talking much, feeling sympathy for Lee Strunk but also feeling the luck of the draw. You win some, you lose some, said Mitchell Sanders, and sometimes you settle for a rain check. It was a tired line and no one laughed.

20   Henry Dobbins ate a tropical chocolate bar. Ted Lavender popped a tranquilizer and went off to pee.

After five minutes, Lieutenant Jimmy Cross moved to the tunnel, leaned down, and examined the darkness. Trouble, he thought — a cave-in maybe. And then suddenly, without willing it, he was thinking about Martha. The stresses and fractures, the quick collapse, the two of them buried alive under all that weight. Dense, crushing love. Kneeling, watching the hole, he tried to concentrate on Lee Strunk and the war, all the dangers, but his love was too much for him, he felt paralyzed, he wanted to sleep inside her lungs and breathe her blood and be smothered. He wanted her to be a virgin and not a virgin, all at once. He wanted to know her. Intimate secrets — why poetry? Why so sad? Why that grayness in her eyes? Why so alone? Not lonely, just alone — riding her bike across campus or sitting off by herself in the cafeteria. Even dancing, she danced alone — and it was the aloneness that filled him with love. He remembered telling her that one evening. How she nodded and looked away. And how, later, when he kissed her, she received the kiss without returning it, her eyes wide open, not afraid, not a virgin's eyes, just flat and uninvolved.

Lieutenant Cross gazed at the tunnel. But he was not there. He was buried with Martha under the white sand at the Jersey shore. They were pressed together, and the pebble in his mouth was her tongue. He was smiling. Vaguely, he was aware of how quiet the day was, the sullen paddies, yet he could not bring himself to worry about matters of security. He was beyond that. He was just a kid at war, in love. He was twenty-two years old. He couldn't help it.

A few moments later Lee Strunk crawled out of the tunnel. He came up grinning, filthy but alive. Lieutenant Cross nodded and closed his eyes while the others clapped Strunk on the back and made jokes about rising from the dead.

Worms, Rat Kiley said. Right out of the grave. Fuckin' zombie.

25   The men laughed. They all felt great relief.

Spook City, said Mitchell Sanders.

Lee Strunk made a funny ghost sound, a kind of moaning, yet very happy, and right then, when Strunk made that high happy moaning sound, when he went

Ahhooooo, right then Ted Lavender was shot in the head on his way back from peeing. He lay with his mouth open. The teeth were broken. There was a swollen black bruise under his left eye. The cheekbone was gone. Oh shit, Rat Kiley said, the guy's dead. The guy's dead, he kept saying, which seemed profound — the guy's dead. I mean really.

The things they carried were determined to some extent by superstition. Lieutenant Cross carried his good-luck pebble. Dave Jensen carried a rabbit's foot. Norman Bowker, otherwise a very gentle person, carried a thumb that had been presented to him as a gift by Mitchell Sanders. The thumb was dark brown, rubbery to the touch, and weighed four ounces at most. It had been cut from a VC corpse, a boy of fifteen or sixteen. They'd found him at the bottom of an irrigation ditch, badly burned, flies in his mouth and eyes. The boy wore black shorts and sandals. At the time of his death he had been carrying a pouch of rice, a rifle, and three magazines of ammunition.

You want my opinion, Mitchell Sanders said, there's a definite moral here.

He put his hand on the dead boy's wrist. He was quiet for a time, as if count- 30
ing a pulse, then he patted the stomach, almost affectionately, and used Kiowa's hunting hatchet to remove the thumb.

Henry Dobbins asked what the moral was.

Moral?

You know. *Moral.*

Sanders wrapped the thumb in toilet paper and handed it across to Norman Bowker. There was no blood. Smiling, he kicked the boy's head, watched the flies scatter, and said, It's like with that old TV show — Paladin. Have gun, will travel.

Henry Dobbins thought about it. 35

Yeah, well, he finally said. I don't see no moral.

There it *is,* man.

Fuck off.

They carried USO stationery and pencils and pens. They carried Sterno, safety pins, trip flares, signal flares, spools of wire, razor blades, chewing tobacco, liberated joss sticks and statuettes of the smiling Buddha, candles, grease pencils, *The Stars and Stripes,* fingernail clippers, Psy Ops leaflets, bush hats, bolos, and much more. Twice a week, when the resupply choppers came in, they carried hot chow in green Mermite cans and large canvas bags filled with iced beer and soda pop. They carried plastic water containers, each with a two-gallon capacity. Mitchell Sanders carried a set of starched tiger fatigues for special occasions. Henry Dobbins carried Black Flag insecticide. Dave Jensen carried empty sandbags that could be filled at night for added protection. Lee Strunk carried tanning lotion. Some things they carried in common. Taking turns, they carried the big PRC-77 scrambler radio, which weighed thirty pounds with its battery. They shared the weight of memory. They took up what others could no longer bear. Often, they carried each other, the wounded or weak. They carried infections. They carried chess sets, basketballs, Vietnamese-English dictionaries, insignia of rank, Bronze Stars and Purple Hearts, plastic cards imprinted with the Code of

Conduct. They carried diseases, among them malaria and dysentery. They carried lice and ringworm and leeches and paddy algae and various rots and molds. They carried the land itself—Vietnam, the place, the soil—a powdery orange-red dust that covered their boots and fatigues and faces. They carried the sky. The whole atmosphere, they carried it, the humidity, the monsoons, the stink of fungus and decay, all of it, they carried gravity. They moved like mules. By daylight they took sniper fire, at night they were mortared, but it was not battle, it was just the endless march, village to village, without purpose, nothing won or lost. They marched for the sake of the march. They plodded along slowly, dumbly, leaning forward against the heat, unthinking, all blood and bone, simple grunts, soldiering with their legs, toiling up the hills and down into the paddies and across the rivers and up again and down, just humping, one step and then the next and then another, but no volition, no will, because it was automatic, it was anatomy, and the war was entirely a matter of posture and carriage, the hump was everything, a kind of inertia, a kind of emptiness, a dullness of desire and intellect and conscience and hope and human sensibility. Their principles were in their feet. Their calculations were biological. They had no sense of strategy or mission. They searched the villages without knowing what to look for, not caring, kicking over jars of rice, frisking children and old men, blowing tunnels, sometimes setting fires and sometimes not, then forming up and moving on to the next village, then other villages, where it would always be the same. They carried their own lives. The pressures were enormous. In the heat of early afternoon, they would remove their helmets and flak jackets, walking bare, which was dangerous but which helped ease the strain. They would often discard things along the route of march. Purely for comfort, they would throw away rations, blow their Claymores and grenades, no matter, because by nightfall the resupply choppers would arrive with more of the same, then a day or two later still more, fresh watermelons and crates of ammunition and sunglasses and woolen sweaters—the resources were stunning—sparklers for the Fourth of July, colored eggs for Easter. It was the great American war chest—the fruits of science, the smokestacks, the canneries, the arsenals at Hartford, the Minnesota forests, the machine shops, the vast fields of corn and wheat—they carried like freight trains; they carried it on their backs and shoulders—and for all the ambiguities of Vietnam, all the mysteries and unknowns, there was at least the single abiding certainty that they would never be at a loss for things to carry.

*   *   *

40   After the chopper took Lavender away, Lieutenant Jimmy Cross led his men into the village of Than Khe. They burned everything. They shot chickens and dogs, they trashed the village well, they called in artillery and watched the wreckage, then they marched for several hours through the hot afternoon, and then at dusk, while Kiowa explained how Lavender died, Lieutenant Cross found himself trembling.

He tried not to cry. With his entrenching tool, which weighed five pounds, he began digging a hole in the earth.

He felt shame. He hated himself. He had loved Martha more than his men, and as a consequence Lavender was now dead, and this was something he would have to carry like a stone in his stomach for the rest of the war.

All he could do was dig. He used his entrenching tool like an ax, slashing, feeling both love and hate, and then later, when it was full dark, he sat at the bottom of his foxhole and wept. It went on for a long while. In part, he was grieving for Ted Lavender, but mostly it was for Martha, and for himself, because she belonged to another world, which was not quite real, and because she was a junior at Mount Sebastian College in New Jersey, a poet and a virgin and uninvolved, and because he realized she did not love him and never would.

Like cement, Kiowa whispered in the dark. I swear to God — boom-down. Not a word.

I've heard this, said Norman Bowker.

A pisser, you know? Still zipping himself up. Zapped while zipping.

All right, fine. That's enough.

Yeah, but you had to see it, the guy just —

I *heard*, man. Cement. So why not shut the fuck *up?*

Kiowa shook his head sadly and glanced over at the hole where Lieutenant 45 Jimmy Cross sat watching the night. The air was thick and wet. A warm, dense fog had settled over the paddies and there was the stillness that precedes rain.

After a time Kiowa sighed.

One thing for sure, he said. The Lieutenant's in some deep hurt. I mean that crying jag — the way he was carrying on — it wasn't fake or anything, it was real heavy-duty hurt. The man cares.

Sure, Norman Bowker said.

Say what you want, the man does care.

We all got problems.

Not Lavender.

No, I guess not, Bowker said. Do me a favor, though.

Shut up?

That's a smart Indian. Shut up.

Shrugging, Kiowa pulled off his boots. He wanted to say more, just to lighten 50 up his sleep, but instead he opened his New Testament and arranged it beneath his head as a pillow. The fog made things seem hollow and unattached. He tried not to think about Ted Lavender, but then he was thinking how fast it was, no drama, down and dead, and how it was hard to feel anything except surprise. It seemed un-Christian. He wished he could find some great sadness, or even anger, but the emotion wasn't there and he couldn't make it happen. Mostly he felt pleased to be alive. He liked the smell of the New Testament under his cheek, the leather and ink and paper and glue, whatever the chemicals were. He liked hearing the sounds of night. Even his fatigue, it felt fine, the stiff muscles and the prickly awareness of his own body, a floating feeling. He enjoyed not being dead. Lying there, Kiowa admired Lieutenant Jimmy Cross's capacity for grief. He wanted to share the man's pain, he wanted to care as Jimmy Cross cared. And yet when he closed his eyes, all he could think was Boom-down,

and all he could feel was the pleasure of having his boots off and the fog curling
in around him and the damp soil and the Bible smells and the plush comfort
of night.

After a moment Norman Bowker sat up in the dark.

What the hell, he said. You want to talk, *talk*. Tell it to me.

Forget it.

No, man, go on. One thing I hate, it's a silent Indian.

55   For the most part they carried themselves with poise, a kind of dignity. Now
and then, however, there were times of panic, when they squealed or wanted to
squeal but couldn't, when they twitched and made moaning sounds and covered
their heads and said Dear Jesus and flopped around on the earth and fired their
weapons blindly and cringed and sobbed and begged for the noise to stop and
went wild and made stupid promises to themselves and to God and to their mothers and fathers, hoping not to die. In different ways, it happened to all of them.
Afterward, when the firing ended, they would blink and peek up. They would
touch their bodies, feeling shame, then quickly hiding it. They would force themselves to stand. As if in slow motion, frame by frame, the world would take on the
old logic — absolute silence, then the wind, then sunlight, then voices. It was the
burden of being alive. Awkwardly, the men would reassemble themselves, first in
private, then in groups, becoming soldiers again. They would repair the leaks in
their eyes. They would check for casualties, call in dust-offs, light cigarettes, try
to smile, clear their throats and spit and begin cleaning their weapons. After a
time someone would shake his head and say, No lie, I almost shit my pants, and
someone else would laugh, which meant it was bad, yes, but the guy had obviously
not shit his pants, it wasn't that bad, and in any case nobody would ever do such
a thing and then go ahead and talk about it. They would squint into the dense,
oppressive sunlight. For a few moments, perhaps, they would fall silent, lighting a
joint and tracking its passage from man to man, inhaling, holding in the humiliation. Scary stuff, one of them might say. But then someone else would grin or
flick his eyebrows and say, Roger-dodger, almost cut me a new asshole, *almost*.

There were numerous such poses. Some carried themselves with a sort of wistful resignation, others with pride or stiff soldierly discipline or good humor or ma-
cho zeal. They were afraid of dying but they were even more afraid to show it.

They found jokes to tell.

They used a hard vocabulary to contain the terrible softness. *Greased*, they'd
say. *Offed, lit up,*° *zapped while zipping.*° It wasn't cruelty, just stage presence. They
were actors and the war came at them in 3-D. When someone died, it wasn't quite
dying, because in a curious way it seemed scripted, and because they had their
lines mostly memorized, irony mixed with tragedy, and because they called it by
other names, as if to encyst and destroy the reality of death itself. They kicked
corpses. They cut off thumbs. They talked grunt lingo. They told stories about Ted

---

Offed, lit up: Killed.

zapped while zipping: Killed while urinating.

Lavender's supply of tranquilizers, how the poor guy didn't feel a thing, how incredibly tranquil he was.

There's a moral here, said Mitchell Sanders.

They were waiting for Lavender's chopper, smoking the dead man's dope. 60

The moral's pretty obvious, Sanders said, and winked. Stay away from drugs. No joke, they'll ruin your day every time.

Cute, said Henry Dobbins.

Mind-blower, get it? Talk about wiggy — nothing left, just blood and brains.

They made themselves laugh.

There it is, they'd say, over and over, as if the repetition itself were an act of 65 poise, a balance between crazy and almost crazy, knowing without going. There it is, which meant be cool, let it ride, because oh yeah, man, you can't change what can't be changed, there it is, there it absolutely and positively and fucking well *is*.

They were tough.

They carried all the emotional baggage of men who might die. Grief, terror, love, longing — these were intangibles, but the intangibles had their own mass and specific gravity, they had tangible weight. They carried shameful memories. They carried the common secret of cowardice barely restrained, the instinct to run or freeze or hide, and in many respects this was the heaviest burden of all, for it could never be put down, it required perfect balance and perfect posture. They carried their reputations. They carried the soldier's greatest fear, which was the fear of blushing. Men killed, and died, because they were embarrassed not to. It was what had brought them to the war in the first place, nothing positive, no dreams of glory or honor, just to avoid the blush of dishonor. They died so as not to die of embarrassment. They crawled into tunnels and walked point and advanced under fire. Each morning, despite the unknowns, they made their legs move. They endured. They kept humping. They did not submit to the obvious alternative, which was simply to close the eyes and fall. So easy, really. Go limp and tumble to the ground and let the muscles unwind and not speak and not budge until your buddies picked you up and lifted you into the chopper that would roar and dip its nose and carry you off to the world. A mere matter of falling, yet no one ever fell. It was not courage, exactly; the object was not valor. Rather, they were too frightened to be cowards.

By and large they carried these things inside, maintaining the masks of composure. They sneered at sick call. They spoke bitterly about guys who had found release by shooting off their own toes or fingers. Pussies, they'd say. Candyasses. It was fierce, mocking talk, with only a trace of envy or awe, but even so, the image played itself out behind their eyes.

They imagined the muzzle against flesh. They imagined the quick, sweet pain, then the evacuation to Japan, then a hospital with warm beds and cute geisha nurses.

They dreamed of freedom birds. 70

At night, on guard, staring into the dark, they were carried away by jumbo jets. They felt the rush of takeoff. *Gone!* they yelled. And then velocity, wings and engines, a smiling stewardess — but it was more than a plane, it was a real bird, a big sleek silver bird with feathers and talons and high screeching. They were flying.

The weights fell off, there was nothing to bear. They laughed and held on tight, feeling the cold slap of wind and altitude, soaring, thinking *It's over, I'm gone!* — they were naked, they were light and free — it was all lightness, bright and fast and buoyant, light as light, a helium buzz in the brain, a giddy bubbling in the lungs as they were taken up over the clouds and the war, beyond duty, beyond gravity and mortification and global entanglements — *Sin loi!* they yelled, *I'm sorry, motherfuckers, but I'm out of it, I'm goofed, I'm on a space cruise, I'm gone!* — and it was a restful, disencumbered sensation, just riding the light waves, sailing that big silver freedom bird over the mountains and oceans, over America, over the farms and great sleeping cities and cemeteries and highways and the golden arches of McDonald's. It was flight, a kind of fleeing, a kind of falling, falling higher and higher, spinning off the edge of the earth and beyond the sun and through the vast, silent vacuum where there were no burdens and where every-thing weighed exactly nothing. *Gone!* they screamed, *I'm sorry but I'm gone!* And so at night, not quite dreaming, they gave themselves over to lightness, they were carried, they were purely borne.

On the morning after Ted Lavender died, First Lieutenant Jimmy Cross crouched at the bottom of his foxhole and burned Martha's letters. Then he burned the two photographs. There was a steady rain falling, which made it diffi-cult, but he used heat tabs and Sterno to build a small fire, screening it with his body, holding the photographs over the tight blue flame with the tips of his fingers.

He realized it was only a gesture. Stupid, he thought. Sentimental, too, but mostly just stupid.

Lavender was dead. You couldn't burn the blame.

75 Besides, the letters were in his head. And even now, without photographs, Lieutenant Cross could see Martha playing volleyball in her white gym shorts and yellow T-shirt. He could see her moving in the rain.

When the fire died out, Lieutenant Cross pulled his poncho over his shoulders and ate breakfast from a can.

There was no great mystery, he decided.

In those burned letters Martha had never mentioned the war, except to say, Jimmy, take care of yourself. She wasn't involved. She signed the letters "Love," but it wasn't love, and all the fine lines and technicalities did not matter.

The morning came up wet and blurry. Everything seemed part of everything else, the fog and Martha and the deepening rain.

80 It was a war, after all.

Half smiling, Lieutenant Jimmy Cross took out his maps. He shook his head hard, as if to clear it, then bent forward and began planning the day's march. In ten minutes, or maybe twenty, he would rouse the men and they would pack up and head west, where the maps showed the country to be green and inviting. They would do what they had always done. The rain might add some weight, but otherwise it would be one more day layered upon all the other days.

He was realistic about it. There was that new hardness in his stomach.

No more fantasies, he told himself.

Henceforth, when he thought about Martha, it would be only to think that she belonged elsewhere. He would shut down the daydreams. This was not Mount

Sebastian, it was another world, where there were no pretty poems or midterm exams, a place where men died because of carelessness and gross stupidity. Kiowa was right. Boom-down, and you were dead, never partly dead.

Briefly, in the rain, Lieutenant Cross saw Martha's gray eyes gazing back at him. 85
He understood.

It was very sad, he thought. The things men carried inside. The things men did or felt they had to do.

He almost nodded at her, but didn't.

Instead he went back to his maps. He was now determined to perform his duties firmly and without negligence. It wouldn't help Lavender, he knew that, but from this point on he would comport himself as a soldier. He would dispose of his good-luck pebble. Swallow it, maybe, or use Lee Strunk's slingshot, or just drop it along the trail. On the march he would impose strict field discipline. He would be careful to send out flank security, to prevent straggling or bunching up, to keep his troops moving at the proper pace and at the proper interval. He would insist on clean weapons. He would confiscate the remainder of Lavender's dope. Later in the day, perhaps, he would call the men together and speak to them plainly. He would accept the blame for what had happened to Ted Lavender. He would be a man about it. He would look them in the eyes, keeping his chin level, and he would issue the new SOPs in a calm, impersonal tone of voice, an officer's voice, leaving no room for argument or discussion. Commencing immediately, he'd tell them, they would no longer abandon equipment along the route of march. They would police up their acts. They would get their shit together, and keep it together, and maintain it neatly and in good working order.

He would not tolerate laxity. He would show strength, distancing himself. 90

Among the men there would be grumbling, of course, and maybe worse, because their days would seem longer and their loads heavier, but Lieutenant Cross reminded himself that his obligation was not to be loved but to lead. He would dispense with love; it was not now a factor. And if anyone quarreled or complained, he would simply tighten his lips and arrange his shoulders in the correct command posture. He might give a curt little nod. Or he might not. He might just shrug and say Carry on, then they would saddle up and form into a column and move out toward the villages west of Than Khe.

Reading and Reacting

1. Although the setting and the events described in "The Things They Carried" are dramatic and moving, its tone is often flat and emotionless. How is this tone created? Why do you think the narrator adopts this kind of tone?

2. Consider the different meanings of the word *carry*, which can refer to burdens abstract or concrete as well as to things carried physically or emotionally, actively or passively. Give one or two examples of each of the different senses in which O'Brien uses the word. How does his repeated use of the word enhance the story?

3. A striking characteristic of the story's style is its thorough catalogs of the concrete, tangible "things" the soldiers carry. Why do you suppose such

detailed lists are included? What does what each man carries tell you about him? In a less literal, more abstract sense, what else do these men "carry"?

4. One stylistic technique O'Brien uses is intentional repetition — of phrases ("they carried"); people's names and identifying details (Martha's virginity, for example); and pieces of equipment. What effect do you think O'Brien hopes to achieve through such repetition? Is he successful?

5. Interspersed among long paragraphs crammed with detail are short one- or two-sentence paragraphs. What function do these brief paragraphs serve?

6. What role does Martha play in the story? Why does Lieutenant Cross burn her letters?

7. In paragraph 68, the narrator says of the soldiers, "They used a hard vocabulary to contain the terrible softness." What do you think he means by this? Do you think this "hard vocabulary" is necessary? How does it affect your reaction to the characters?

8. Describing Lieutenant Cross's new sense of purpose in the story's final paragraph, the narrator uses the phrase "Carry on." Do you think this phrase is linked in any way to the story's other uses of the word *carry*, or do you believe it is unrelated? Explain.

9. JOURNAL ENTRY   "The Things They Carried" is a story about war. Do you think it is an antiwar story? Why or why not?

10. CRITICAL PERSPECTIVE   In an essay about war memoirs, Clayton W. Lewis questions O'Brien's decision to present "the nightmare [he] faced in a Vietnam rice paddy" as fiction. Lewis believes that some of O'Brien's stories "dissolve into clever artifice" and, therefore, are not as effective as actual memoirs of the Vietnam experience would be. He concludes that "for all its brilliance and emotional grounding, [the stories do not] satisfy one's appetite to hear what happened rendered as it was experienced and remembered."

Do you think Lewis has a point? Or do you think O'Brien's "artifice" communicates his emotions and experiences more effectively than a straight-forward memoir could? Explain your position.

Related Works: "The Open Boat" (p. 685), "The Soldier" (p. 1080), "Facing It" (p. 1085), "Dulce et Decorum Est" (p. 931)

WRITING SUGGESTIONS: Style, Tone, and Language

1. In "The Things They Carried," Tim O'Brien considers his characters' emotional and psychological burdens as well as the physical "things they carry." Applying O'Brien's criteria to "The Yellow Wallpaper," write an essay in which you consider what the narrator "carries" (and what her husband "carries") and why.

2. In one way or another, all the stories in this chapter (with the exception of "Araby") depict a high-stakes struggle for survival. Other works in this anthology depict similar struggles — some intellectual and some physical, even violent. Choose two or three works (from this chapter or elsewhere in the book) in which a physical or intellectual contest between two individuals is central, and write an essay in which you compare the nature of the struggles and their outcomes.

3. In "Appetizer," the narrator says, "I have told myself for many years that I really do love nature, love being among the animals, am restored by wilderness adventure" (par. 21), but the experiences described in this story make him see this attitude as "a sentiment in need of some revision." Compare his ambivalent feelings about nature with the view of nature presented in "Doe Season" (p. 512), "Greasy Lake" (p. 648), or "The Secret Lion" (p. 170).

4. Imagine The Misfit in a prison cell, relating the violent incident at the end of "A Good Man Is Hard to Find" to another prisoner — or to a member of the clergy. Would his tone be boastful? Regretful? Apologetic? Defiant? Would he use the elaborate poetic style he sometimes uses in the story or more straightforward language? Tell his version of the incident in his own words.

5. Both "Araby" and "The Things They Carried" deal, at least in part, with infatuation. Compare and contrast the infatuations described in the two stories. How does the language used by the narrators in the two stories communicate the two characters' fascination and subsequent disillusionment?

CHAPTER 17

SYMBOL, ALLEGORY, AND MYTH

> Symbols have to spring from the work direct, and stay alive. Symbols
> for the sake of symbols are counterfeit, and were they all stamped on
> the page in red they couldn't any more quickly give themselves away.
>
> —Eudora Welty, *"Words into Fiction"*

Symbol

A **symbol** is a person, object, action, place, or event that, in addition to its literal
meaning, suggests a more complex meaning or range of meanings. **Universal** or
archetypal symbols, such as the Old Man, the Mother, or the Grim Reaper, are so
much a part of human experience that they suggest the same thing to most people.
Conventional symbols are also likely to suggest the same thing to most people (a
rose suggests love, a skull and crossbones denotes poison), provided the people
have common cultural and social assumptions. Such symbols are often used as a
kind of shorthand in films, popular literature, and advertising, where they encourage predictable responses.

A conventional symbol such as the stars and stripes of the American flag can
evoke powerful feelings of pride and patriotism in a group of people who share a
culture, just as the maple leaf and the Union Jack can. Symbols used in works of
literature can function in much the same way, enabling writers to convey particular emotions or messages with a high degree of predictability. Thus, spring can
be expected to suggest rebirth and promise; autumn, declining years and powers;
summer, youth and beauty. Because a writer expects a dark forest to evoke fear, or
a rainbow to communicate hope, he or she can be quite confident in using such
images to convey a particular idea or mood (provided the audience shares the
writer's frame of reference).

Many symbols, however, suggest different things to different people, and different cultures may react differently to the same symbols. (In the United States,
for example, an owl suggests wisdom; in India it suggests the opposite.) Thus,
symbols enrich meaning, expanding the possibilities for interpretation and for
readers' interaction with the text. Because they are so potentially rich, symbols
have the power to open up a work of literature.

Literary Symbols

Both universal and conventional symbols can function as **literary symbols** that take on additional meanings in particular works. For instance, a watch or clock denotes time; as a conventional symbol, it suggests the passing of time; as a literary symbol in a particular work, it might also convey anything from a character's inability to recapture the past to the idea of time running out — or it might suggest something else.

Considering an object's possible symbolic significance can suggest a variety of ways to interpret a text. For instance, William Faulkner focuses attention on an unseen watch in a pivotal scene in "A Rose for Emily" (p. 216). The narrator first describes Emily Grierson as "a small, fat woman in black, with a thin gold chain descending to her waist and vanishing into her belt." Several sentences later, the narrator returns to the watch, noting that Emily's visitors "could hear the invisible watch ticking at the end of the gold chain." Like these visitors, readers are drawn to the unseen watch as it ticks away. Because Emily is portrayed as a woman living in the past, readers can assume that the watch is intended to reinforce the impression that she cannot see that time (the watch) has moved on. The vivid picture of the pale, plump woman in the musty room with the watch invisibly ticking does indeed suggest both that she has been left back in time and that she remains unaware of the progress around her. Thus, the symbol enriches both the depiction of character and the story's theme.

In "Barn Burning" (p. 356), another Faulkner story, the clock is a more complex symbol. The itinerant Snopes family is without financial security and apparently without a future. The clock the mother carries from shack to shack — "The clock inlaid with mother-of-pearl, which would not run, stopped at some fourteen minutes past two o'clock of a dead and forgotten day and time, which had been [Sarty's] mother's dowry" — is their only possession of value. The fact that the clock no longer works seems at first to suggest that time has run out for the family. On another level, the clock stands in stark contrast to Major de Spain's grand home, with its gold and glitter and Oriental rugs. Knowing that the clock was part of the mother's dowry, and that a dowry suggests a promise, readers may decide that the broken clock symbolizes lost hope. The fact that the mother still clings to the clock, however, could suggest just the opposite: her refusal to give up.

As you read, you should not try to find one exact equivalent for each symbol; that kind of search is limiting and unproductive. Instead, consider the different meanings a symbol might suggest. Then, consider how these various interpretations enrich other elements of the story and the work as a whole.

Recognizing Symbols

When is a clock just a clock, and when is it also a symbol with a meaning (or meanings) beyond its literal significance? If a character waiting for a friend glances once at a watch to verify the time, there is probably nothing symbolic about the watch or about the act of looking at it. If, however, the watch keeps appearing again and again in the story, at key moments; if the narrator devotes a good deal of time to describing it; if it is placed in a conspicuous physical location; if characters keep noticing it and commenting on its presence; if it is lost (or found) at a critical moment; if its function in some way parallels the development of plot or character (for instance, if it stops as a relationship ends or when a character dies); if the story's opening or closing paragraph focuses on the timepiece; or if the story is called "The Watch"— the watch most likely has symbolic significance. In other words, considering how an image is used, how often it is used, and when it appears will help you to determine whether or not it functions as a symbol.

Symbols expand the possible meanings of a story, thereby heightening interest and actively involving readers in the text. In "The Lottery" (p. 461), for example, the mysterious black box has symbolic significance. It is mentioned prominently and repeatedly, and it plays a pivotal role in the story's action. Of course, the black box is important on a purely literal level: it functions as a key component of the lottery. But the box has other associations as well, and it is these associations that suggest what its symbolic significance might be.

The black wooden box is very old, a relic of many past lotteries; the narrator observes that it represents tradition. It is also closed and closely guarded, suggesting mystery and uncertainty. It is shabby, "splintered badly along one side . . . and in places faded or stained," and this state of disrepair could suggest that the ritual it is part of has also deteriorated or that tradition itself has deteriorated. The box is also simple in construction and design, suggesting the primitive (and therefore perhaps outdated) nature of the ritual. Thus, this symbol encourages readers to probe the story for values and ideas, to consider and weigh the suitability of a variety of interpretations. It serves as a "hot spot" that invites questions, and the answers to these questions reinforce and enrich the story's theme.

Allegory

An **allegory** communicates a doctrine, message, or moral principle by making it into a narrative in which the characters personify ideas, concepts, qualities, or other abstractions. Thus, an allegory is a story with two parallel and consistent levels of meaning — one literal and one figurative. The figurative level, which offers some moral or political lesson, is the story's main concern. The allegorical figures are significant only because they represent something beyond their literal meaning in a fixed system.

Whereas a symbol has multiple symbolic associations as well as a literal meaning, an **allegorical figure**— a character, object, place, or event in the allegory — has just one meaning within an **allegorical framework**, the set of ideas that conveys the allegory's message. (At the simplest level, for instance, one character can stand for good and another can stand for evil.) For this reason, allegorical figures do not open up a text to various interpretations the way symbols do. Because the purpose of allegory is to communicate a particular lesson, readers are not encouraged to speculate about the allegory's possible meanings; each element has only one equivalent, which readers must discover if they are to make sense of the story.

Naturally, the better a reader understands the political, religious, and literary assumptions of a writer, the easier it will be to recognize the allegorical significance of his or her work. John Bunyan's *The Pilgrim's Progress*, for example, is a famous seventeenth-century allegory based on the Christian doctrine of salvation. In order to appreciate the complexity of Bunyan's work, you would have to familiarize yourself with this doctrine—possibly by consulting an encyclopedia or a reference work such as *The Oxford Companion to English Literature*.

One type of allegory, called a **beast fable**, is a short tale, usually including a moral, in which animals assume human characteristics. Aesop's fables are the best-known examples of beast fables. More recently, contemporary writers have used beast fables to satirize the political and social conditions of our time. In one such tale, "The Gentlemen of the Jungle" by the Kenyan writer Jomo Kenyatta, an elephant is allowed to put his trunk inside a man's hut during a rainstorm. Not content with keeping his trunk dry, the elephant pushes his entire body inside the hut, displacing the man. When the man protests, the elephant takes the matter to the lion, who appoints a Commission of Enquiry to settle the matter. Eventually, the man is forced not only to abandon his hut to the elephant, but also to build new huts for all the animals on the Commission. Even so, the jealous animals occupy the man's new hut and begin fighting for space; while they are arguing, the man burns down the hut, animals and all. Like the tales told by Aesop, "The Gentlemen of the Jungle" has a moral: "Peace is costly," says the man as he walks away happily, "but it's worth the expense." The following passage from Kenyatta's tale reveals how the allegorical figures work within the framework of the allegory:

> The elephant, obeying the command of his master (the lion), got busy with the other ministers to appoint a Commission of Enquiry. The following elders of the jungle were appointed to sit in the Commission: (1) Mr. Rhinoceros; (2) Mr. Buffalo; (3) Mr. Alligator; (4) The Rt. Hon. Mr. Fox to act as chairman; and (5) Mr. Leopard to act as Secretary of the Commission. On seeing the personnel, the man protested and asked if it was not necessary to include in this Commission a member from his side. But he was told that it was impossible, since no one from his side was well enough educated to understand the intricacy of jungle law.

From this excerpt we can see that each character represents a particular idea. For example, the members of the Commission stand for bureaucratic smugness and inequity, and the man stands for the citizens who are victimized by the government. In order to fully understand the allegorical significance of each figure in this story, of course, readers would have to know something about government bureaucracies, colonialism in Africa, and possibly a specific historical event in Kenya.

Some works contain both symbolic elements *and* allegorical elements, as Nathaniel Hawthorne's "Young Goodman Brown" (p. 489) does. The names of the story's two main characters, "Goodman" and "Faith," suggest that they fit within an allegorical system of some sort: Young Goodman Brown represents a good person who, despite his best efforts, strays from the path of righteousness; his wife, Faith, represents the quality he must hold on to in order to avoid temptation. As characters, they have no significance outside of their allegorical functions. Other elements of the story, however, are not so clear-cut. The older man whom Young Goodman Brown meets in the woods carries a staff that has carved on it "the likeness of a great black snake, so curiously wrought, that it might almost be seen to twist and wriggle itself like a living serpent." This staff, carried by a Satanic figure who represents evil and temptation, suggests the snake in the Garden of Eden, an association that neatly fits into the allegorical framework of the story. Alternately, however, the staff could suggest the "slippery," ever-changing nature of sin, the difficulty people have in perceiving sin, or even sexuality (which may explain Young Goodman Brown's susceptibility to temptation). This range of possible meanings suggests that the staff functions as a symbol (not an allegorical figure) that enriches Hawthorne's allegory.

Other stories work entirely on a symbolic level and contain no allegorical figures. "The Lottery," despite its moral overtones, is not an allegory because its characters, events, and objects are not arranged to serve one rigid, didactic purpose. In fact, many different interpretations have been suggested for this story. When it was first published in June 1948 in the *New Yorker*, some readers believed it to be a story about an actual custom or ritual. As Shirley Jackson reports in her essay "Biography of a Story," even those who recognized it as fiction speculated about its meaning, seeing it as (among other things) an attack on prejudice, a criticism of society's need for a scapegoat, or a treatise on witchcraft, Christian martyrdom, or village gossip. The fact is that no single allegorical interpretation will account for every major character, object, and event in the story.

MYTH

Throughout history, human beings have been makers of myths. For the purpose of this discussion, a **myth** is a story that is central to a culture; it embodies the values on which a culture or society is built. Thus, myths are not synonymous with falsehoods or fairy tales. They are stories that contain ideas that inform a culture and that give that culture meaning. In this sense, then, both an ancient epic and a contemporary religious text can convey a "myth."

Although many myths have to do with religion, myths are not limited to the theological. Myths explain everything from natural phenomena — such as the creation of the world — to the existence of human beings and the beginnings of agriculture. The importance of myths rests on their ability to embody a set of beliefs that unifies both individuals and the society in which they live. By examining myths, we can learn much about our own origins and our most deeply held beliefs.

One of the most prevalent types of myth is the **creation myth**. Almost every culture has an explanation for how the earth, sun, and stars — not to mention people — came into being. According to the ancient Greeks, for example, the world began as an empty void from which Nyx, a bird with black wings, emerged. She laid a golden egg, and out of it Eros, the god of love, arose. The two halves of the eggshell became the earth and the sky, who fell in love with each other and had many children and grandchildren. These offspring became the gods of the Greek pantheon, who eventually created humans beings in their own likeness. Each of these gods had a role to play in the creation and maintenance of the world, and their actions — in particular, their constant meddling in the lives of people — comprise the myths of ancient Greece.

In various cultures all over the world, creation myths take different forms. To the ancient Japanese, for example, the world emerged from a single seed, which grew to form a god who, in turn, created other gods and eventually the islands of Japan and their inhabitants. Several Native American tribes share common beliefs about "sky ancestors," who they believe created the people on the planet.

In Western culture, the most recognizable creation myth appears in Genesis, the first book of the Old Testament. According to Genesis, God created the heavens and the earth as well as all living creatures—including Adam and Eve. Other stories, also part of the oral tradition of Judaism, do not appear in Genesis. An example of such a story is the tale of Lilith, which emerged sometime between the eighth and eleventh centuries. According to this Hebrew myth, Lilith, who was created before Eve, was Adam's first wife. However, she refused to be subservient to Adam, and so she left Eden, eventually to be replaced by Eve. Talmudic tradition holds that she later mated with demons and gave birth to a legion of demonic offspring who inhabit the dark places of the earth.

The influence of mythology on literature is profound, and our contemporary understanding of narrative fiction owes a great deal to mythology. In fact, many of the short stories in this anthology contain allusions to myth. Consider, for example, the role of myth in "The Lottery" by Shirley Jackson, "Cathedral" by Raymond Carver, and "Young Goodman Brown" by Nathaniel Hawthorne. In each of these short stories, myth is central to the characters' behavior, sensibility, and understanding of the world in which they live.

✔ **CHECKLIST** **Writing about Symbol, Allegory, and Myth**

▪ Are any universal symbols used in the work? Any conventional symbols? What is their function?

▪ Is any character, place, action, event, or object given unusual prominence or emphasis in the story? If so, does this element seem to have symbolic as well as literal significance?

▪ What possible meanings does each symbol suggest?

▪ How do symbols help to depict the story's characters?

▪ How do symbols help to characterize the story's setting?

▪ How do symbols help to advance the story's plot?

▪ Does the story have a moral or didactic purpose? What is the message, idea, or moral principle the story seeks to convey? Is the story an allegory?

continued on next page

> ◻   What equivalent may be assigned to each allegorical figure in the story?
>
> ◻   What is the allegorical framework of the story?
>
> ◻   Does the story combine allegorical figures and symbols? How do they work together in the story?
>
> ◻   Does the story have any references to myth? If so, what do they add?

JORGE LUIS BORGES (1899–1986) was born in Buenos Aires, Argentina. Widely regarded as one of the most influential modernist and symbolist writers of his time, Borges wrote challenging and deeply metaphysical poetry and fiction. *Ficciones*, published in 1945, is perhaps his most famous collection of short stories. Borges also wrote essays, several screenplays, and a considerable volume of literary criticism, prologues, and reviews. In addition, he edited numerous anthologies and was a prominent translator of English, French, and German literature into Spanish.

Cultural Context   Sacred books have held a longstanding place in the rites, rituals, and traditions of various religions. From the Hindu holy books, the *Upanishads;* to the *Analects* of Confucius; to the Talmud, Koran, and Bible, each faith has representative texts that contain its laws, ethics, codes, and teachings and are translated into different languages and studied around the world. The significance of the "holy book" in this story is more mystical than historical and is an allusion to a book mentioned in another story by Borges, "The Library of Babel."

The Book of Sand   (1977)

Translated by Norman Thomas Di Giovanni

Thy rope of sands . . .

—George Herbert

The line is made up of an infinite number of points; the plane of an infinite number of lines; the volume of an infinite number of planes; the hyper-volume of an infinite number of volumes. . . . No, unquestionably this is not —*more geometrico*— the best way of beginning my story. To claim that it is true is nowadays the convention of every made-up story. Mine, however, *is* true.

I live alone in a fourth-floor apartment on Belgrano Street, in Buenos Aires. Late one evening, a few months back, I heard a knock at my door. I opened it and a stranger stood there. He was a tall man, with nondescript features — or perhaps it was my myopia that made them seem that way. Dressed in gray and carrying a gray suitcase in his hand, he had an unassuming look about him. I saw at once that he was a foreigner. At first, he struck me as old; only later did I realize that I had been misled by his thin blond hair, which was, in a Scandinavian sort of way, almost white. During the course of our conversation, which was not to last an hour, I found out that he came from the Orkneys.°

I invited him in, point to a chair. He paused awhile before speaking. A kind of gloom emanated from him — as it does now from me.

"I sell Bibles," he said.

Somewhat pedantically, I replied, "In this house are several English Bibles, in-   5 cluding the first — John Wiclif's. I also have Cipriano de Valera's, Luther's — which, from a literary viewpoint, is the worst — and a Latin copy of the Vulgate. As you see, it's not exactly Bibles I stand in need of."

After a few moments of silence, he said, "I don't only sell Bibles. I can show you a holy book I came across on the outskirts of Bikaner.° It may interest you."

He opened the suitcase and laid the book on a table. It was an octavo volume, bound in cloth. There was no doubt that it had passed through many hands. Examining it, I was surprised by its unusual weight. On the spine were the words "Holy Writ" and, below them, "Bombay."

"Nineteenth century, probably," I remarked.

"I don't know," he said. "I've never found out."

I opened the book at random. The script was strange to me. The pages, which   10 were worn and typographically poor, were laid out in double columns, as in a Bible. The text was closely printed, and it was ordered in versicles. In the upper corners of the pages were Arabic numbers. I noticed that one left-hand page bore the number (let us say) 40,514 and the facing right-hand page 999. I turned the leaf; it was numbered with eight digits. It also bore a small illustration, like the kind used in dictionaries — an anchor drawn with pen and ink, as if by a schoolboy's clumsy hand.

It was at this point that the stranger said, "Look at the illustration closely. You'll never see it again."

I noted my place and closed the book. At once, I reopened it. Page by page, in vain, I looked for the illustration of the anchor. "It seems to be a version of Scriptures in some Indian language, is it not?" I said to hide my dismay.

"No," he replied. Then, as if confiding a secret, he lowered his voice. "I acquired the book in a town out on the plain in exchange for a handful of rupees and a Bible. Its owner did not know how to read. I suspect that he saw the Book of Books as a talisman. He was of the lowest caste; nobody but either untouchables could tread his shadow without contamination. He told me his book was called the Book of Sand, because neither the book nor the sand has any beginning or end."

The stranger asked me to find the first page.

I laid my left hand on the cover and, trying to put my thumb on the fly-leaf, I   15 opened the book. It was useless. Every time I tried, a number of pages came between the cover and my thumb. It was as if they kept growing from the book.

"Now find the last page."

Orkneys: A group of islands located off the southern tip of Scotland.

Bikaner: Formerly a state, Bikaner is now part of Rajasthan in northwest India.

Again I failed. In a voice that was not mine, I barely managed to stammer, "This can't be."

Still speaking in a low voice, the stranger said, "It can't be, but it is. The number of pages in this book is no more or less than infinite. None is the first page, none the last. I don't know why they're numbered in this arbitrary way. Perhaps to suggest that the terms of an infinite series admit any number."

Then, as if he were thinking aloud, he said, "If space is infinite, we may be at any point in space. If time is infinite, we may be at any point in time."

20   His speculations irritated me. "You are religious, no doubt?" I asked him.

"Yes, I'm a Presbyterian. My conscience is clear. I am reasonably sure of not having cheated the native when I gave him the Word of God in exchange for his devilish book."

I assured him that he had nothing to reproach himself for, and I asked if he were just passing through this part of the world. He replied that he planned to return to his country in a few days. It was then that I learned that he was a Scot from the Orkney Islands. I told him I had a great personal affection for Scotland, through my love of Stevenson and Hume.

"You mean Stevenson and Robbie Burns," he corrected.

While we spoke, I kept exploring the infinite book. With feigned indifference, I asked, "Do you intend to offer this curiosity to the British Museum?"

25   "No. I'm offering it to you," he said, and he stipulated a rather high sum for the book.

I answered, in all truthfulness, that such a sum was out of my reach, and I began thinking. After a minute or two, I came up with a scheme.

"I propose a swap," I said. "You got this book for a handful of rupees and a copy of the Bible. I'll offer you the amount of my pension check, which I've just collected, and my black-letter Wiclif Bible. I inherited it from my ancestors."

"A black-letter Wiclif!" he murmured.

I went to my bedroom and brought him the money and the book. He turned the leaves and studied the title page with all the fervor of a true bibliophile.

30   "It's a deal," he said.

It amazed me that he did not haggle. Only later was I to realize that he had entered my house with his mind made up to sell the book. Without counting the money, he put it away.

We talked about India, about Orkney, and about the Norwegian jarls who once ruled it. It was night when the man left. I have not seen him again, nor do I know his name.

I thought of keeping the Book of Sand in the space left on the shelf by the Wiclif, but in the end I decided to hide it behind the volumes of a broken set of The Thousand and One Nights. I went to bed and did not sleep. At three or four in the morning, I turned on the light. I got down the impossible book and leafed through its pages. On one of them I saw engraved a mask. The upper corner of the page carried a number, which I no longer recall, elevated to the ninth power.

I showed no one my treasure. To the luck of owning it was added the fear of having it stolen, and then the misgiving that it might not truly be infinite.

These twin preoccupations intensified my old misanthropy. I had only a few friends left; I now stopped seeing even them. A prisoner of the book, I almost never went out anymore. After studying its frayed spine and covers with a magnifying glass, I rejected the possibility of a contrivance of any sort. The small illustrations, I verified, came two thousand pages apart. I set about listing them alphabetically in a notebook, which I was not long in filling up. Never once was an illustration repeated. At night, in the meager intervals my insomnia granted, I dreamed of the book.

Summer came and went, and I realized that the book was monstrous. What good did it do me to think that I, who looked upon the volume with my eyes, who held it in my hands, was any less monstrous? I felt that the book was a nightmarish object, an obscene thing that affronted and tainted reality itself.

I thought of fire, but I feared that the burning of an infinite book might likewise prove infinite and suffocate the planet with smoke. Somewhere I recalled reading that the best place to hide a leaf is in a forest. Before retirement, I worked on Mexico Street, at the Argentine National Library,° which contains nine hundred thousand volumes. I knew that to the right of the entrance a curved staircase leads down into the basement, where books and maps and periodicals are kept. One day I went there and, slipping past a member of the staff and trying not to notice at what height or distance from the door, I lost the Book of Sand on one of the basement's musty shelves.

Reading and Reacting

1. The epigraph that begins this story — "Thy rope of sands" — is from "The Collar," a poem by George Herbert. In this poem, the speaker asserts that everything he has been taught is a "rope of sand," a worthless fiction that ties him down and keeps him from being free. In what way does this epigraph shed light on Borges's story?

2. Even before its contents is described, how does Borges establish that the Book of Sand is mysterious and possibly supernatural?

3. Why does the narrator claim that the story he is about to tell is true? What "truths" do you think he could be referring to?

4. Why do you think the stranger seeks out the narrator? Why is he so anxious to get rid of the book?

5. Why does the narrator want the book? Why do you think that someone who collects bibles would want this book?

6. What characteristics of the Book of Sand make it unusual? What is the significance of the book's title?

7. What does the narrator mean when he says he was a "prisoner of the book" (par. 34)? Why does he say later that the book is "an obscene thing that affronted and tainted reality itself" (par. 35)?

Argentine National Library: A library in Borges's home town of Buenos Aires.

8. What do the following suggest beyond their literal meanings:

- The stranger
- The bibles
- The library

Do you see these elements as symbols?

9. JOURNAL ENTRY Why does the narrator decide not to destroy the book? Is this a wise decision?

10. CRITICAL PERSPECTIVE Maximus Clarke, who maintains a Web site based on "The Book of Sand," asserts that the book suggests "the dense, mazelike, abstract universe of the World Wide Web." Even though this story was written before the Web came into existence, Clarke says, the book "may be Borges's most directly prescient metaphor for the Web: its pages are uncountable, ever-changing, without beginning or end."

Do you agree with Clarke that the Book of Sand foreshadows the Web? Can you think of anything else the book resembles?

Related Works: "A Primer for the Punctuation of Heart Disease" (p. 156), "Cathedral" (p. 476), "Easter Wings" (p. 823), "This Poem Intentionally Left Blank" (p. 825) "Try to Praise the Mutilated World" (p. 869), "When I Heard the Learn'd Astronomer" (p. 893), *Tape* (p. 1313)

SHIRLEY JACKSON (1916–1965) is best known for her restrained tales of horror and the supernatural, most notably her novel *The Haunting of Hill House* (1959) and the short story "The Lottery" (1948). Among her other works are two novels dealing with divided personalities — *The Bird's Nest* (1954) and *We Have Always Lived in the Castle* (1962)— and two collections of comic tales about her children and family life, *Life among the Savages* (1953) and *Raising Demons* (1957). A posthumous collection of stories, *Just an Ordinary Day* (1997), was published after the discovery of a box of some of Jackson's unpublished papers in a Vermont barn and her heirs' subsequent search for her other uncollected works.

With her husband, literary critic Stanley Edgar Hyman, she settled in the small town of Bennington, Vermont, but was never accepted by the townspeople. "The Lottery" is set in much the same kind of small, hidebound town. Despite the story's matter-of-fact tone and familiar setting, its publication in the *New Yorker* provoked a torrent of letters from enraged and shocked readers. In her quiet way, Jackson presented the underside of village life and revealed to readers the dark side of human nature. Future writers of gothic tales recognized their great debt to Jackson. Horror master Stephen King dedicated his book *Firestarter* "to Shirley Jackson, who never had to raise her voice."

Cultural Context "The Lottery" is sometimes seen as a protest against totalitarianism, a form of authoritarian government that permits no individual freedom. In *Eichmann in Jerusalem* (1963), political scientist Hannah Arendt (1906–1975) wrote about totalitarianism as it pertained to Nazi Germany and the Holocaust. Here, she introduced the concept of "the banality of evil," the potential in ordinary people to do evil things. Americans of the post–World War II era saw themselves as "good guys" defending the world against foreign evils. Jackson's story, written scarcely three years after the liberation of Auschwitz, told Americans something they did not want to hear — that the face of human evil could look just like their next-door neighbor.

The Lottery (1948)

The morning of June 27th was clear and sunny, with the fresh warmth of a full-summer day; the flowers were blossoming profusely and the grass was richly green. The people of the village began to gather in the square, between the post office and the bank, around ten o'clock; in some towns there were so many people that the lottery took two days and had to be started on June 26th, but in this village, where there were only about three hundred people, the whole lottery took less than two hours, so it could begin at ten o'clock in the morning and still be through in time to allow the villagers to get home for noon dinner.

The children assembled first, of course. School was recently over for the summer, and the feeling of liberty sat uneasily on most of them; they tended to gather together quietly for a while before they broke into boisterous play, and their talk was still of the classroom and the teacher, of books and reprimands. Bobby Martin had already stuffed his pockets full of stones, and the other boys soon followed his example, selecting the smoothest and roundest stones; Bobby and Harry Jones and Dickie Delacroix — the villagers pronounced this name "Dellacroy"— eventually made a great pile of stones in one corner of the square and guarded it against the raids of the other boys. The girls stood aside, talking among themselves, looking over their shoulders at the boys, and the very small children rolled in the dust or clung to the hands of their older brothers or sisters.

Soon the men began to gather, surveying their own children, speaking of planting and rain, tractors and taxes. They stood together, away from the pile of stones in the corner, and their jokes were quiet and they smiled rather than laughed. The women, wearing faded house dresses and sweaters, came shortly after their menfolk. They greeted one another and exchanged bits of gossip as they went to join their husbands. Soon the women, standing by their husbands, began to call to their children, and the children came reluctantly, having to be called four or five times. Bobby Martin ducked under his mother's grasping hand and ran, laughing, back to the pile of stones. His father spoke up sharply, and Bobby came quickly and took his place between his father and his oldest brother.

The lottery was conducted — as were the square dances, the teen-age club, the Halloween program — by Mr. Summers, who had time and energy to devote to civic activities. He was a round-faced, jovial man and he ran the coal business, and people were sorry for him, because he had no children and his wife was a scold. When he arrived in the square, carrying the black wooden box, there was a murmur of conversation among the villagers, and he waved and called, "Little late today, folks." The postmaster, Mr. Graves, followed him, carrying a three-legged stool, and the stool was put in the center of the square and Mr. Summers set the black box down on it. The villagers kept their distance, leaving a space between themselves and the stool, and when Mr. Summers said, "Some of you fellows want to give me a hand?" there was a hesitation before two men, Mr. Martin and his old-est son, Baxter, came forward to hold the box steady on the stool while Mr. Sum-mers stirred up the papers inside it.

5   The original paraphernalia for the lottery had been lost long ago, and the black box now resting on the stool had been put into use even before Old Man Warner, the oldest man in town, was born. Mr. Summers spoke frequently to the villagers about making a new box, but no one liked to upset even as much tradi-tion as was represented by the black box. There was a story that the present box had been made with some pieces of the box that had preceded it, the one that had been constructed when the first people settled down to make a village here. Every year, after the lottery, Mr. Summers began talking again about a new box, but every year the subject was allowed to fade off without anything's being done. The black box grew shabbier each year; by now it was no longer completely black but splintered badly along one side to show the original wood color, and in some places faded or stained.

Mr. Martin and his oldest son, Baxter, held the black box securely on the stool until Mr. Summers had stirred the papers thoroughly with his hand. Because so much of the ritual had been forgotten or discarded, Mr. Summers had been suc-cessful in having slips of paper substituted for the chips of wood that had been used for generations. Chips of wood, Mr. Summers had argued, had been all very well when the village was tiny, but now that the population was more than three hundred and likely to keep on growing, it was necessary to use something that would fit more easily into the black box. The night before the lottery, Mr. Summers and Mr. Graves made up the slips of paper and put them in the box, and it was then taken to the safe of Mr. Summers's coal company and locked up until Mr. Summers was ready to take it to the square next morning. The rest of the year, the box was put away, sometimes one place, sometimes another; it had spent one year in Mr. Graves's barn and another year underfoot in the post office, and sometimes it was set on a shelf in the Martin grocery and left there.

There was a great deal of fussing to be done before Mr. Summers declared the lottery open. There were the lists to make up—of heads of families, heads of households in each family, members of each household in each family. There was the proper swearing-in of Mr. Summers by the postmaster, as the official of the lottery; at one time, some people remembered, there had been a recital of some sort, performed by the official of the lottery, a perfunctory, tuneless chant that had been rattled off duly each year; some people believed that the official of the lot-tery used to stand just so when he said or sang it, others believed that he was sup-posed to walk among the people, but years and years ago this part of the ritual had been allowed to lapse. There had been, also, a ritual salute, which the official of the lottery had had to use in addressing each person who came up to draw from the box, but this also had changed with time, until now it was felt necessary only for the official to speak to each person approaching. Mr. Summers was very good at all this; in his clean white shirt and blue jeans, with one hand resting carelessly on the black box, he seemed very proper and important as he talked interminably to Mr. Graves and the Martins.

Just as Mr. Summers finally left off talking and turned to the assembled villagers, Mrs. Hutchinson came hurriedly along the path to the square, her sweater thrown over her shoulders, and slid into place in the back of the crowd. "Clean forgot what day it was," she said to Mrs. Delacroix, who stood next to her, and they both laughed softly. "Thought my old man was out back stacking wood," Mrs. Hutchinson went on, "and then I looked out the window and the kids was gone, and then I remembered it was the twenty-seventh and came a-running." She dried her hands on her apron, and Mrs. Delacroix said, "You're in time, though. They're still talking away up there."

Mrs. Hutchinson craned her neck to see through the crowd and found her husband and children standing near the front. She tapped Mrs. Delacroix on the arm as a farewell and began to make her way through the crowd. The people separated good-humoredly to let her through; two or three people said, in voices just loud enough to be heard across the crowd, "Here comes your Missus, Hutchinson," and "Bill, she made it after all." Mrs. Hutchinson reached her husband, and Mr. Summers, who had been waiting, said cheerfully, "Thought we were going to have to get on without you, Tessie." Mrs. Hutchinson said, grinning, "Wouldn't have me leave m'dishes in the sink, now, would you, Joe?," and soft laughter ran through the crowd as the people stirred back into position after Mrs. Hutchinson's arrival.

"Well, now," Mr. Summers said soberly, "guess we better get started, get this over with, so's we can go back to work. Anybody ain't here?" 10

"Dunbar," several people said. "Dunbar, Dunbar."

Mr. Summers consulted his list. "Clyde Dunbar," he said. "That's right. He's broke his leg, hasn't he? Who's drawing for him?"

"Me, I guess," a woman said, and Mr. Summers turned to look at her. "Wife draws for her husband," Mr. Summers said. "Don't you have a grown boy to do it for you, Janey?" Although Mr. Summers and everyone else in the village knew the answer perfectly well, it was the business of the official of the lottery to ask such questions formally. Mr. Summers waited with an expression of polite interest while Mrs. Dunbar answered.

"Horace's not but sixteen yet," Mrs. Dunbar said regretfully. "Guess I gotta fill in for the old man this year."

"Right," Mr. Summers said. He made a note on the list he was holding. Then he asked, "Watson boy drawing this year?"

A tall boy in the crowd raised his hand. "Here," he said. "I'm drawing for 15 m'mother and me." He blinked his eyes nervously and ducked his head as several voices in the crowd said things like "Good fellow, Jack," and "Glad to see your mother's got a man to do it."

"Well," Mr. Summers said, "guess that's everyone. Old Man Warner make it?"

"Here," a voice said, and Mr. Summers nodded.

A sudden hush fell on the crowd as Mr. Summers cleared his throat and looked at the list. "All ready?" he called. "Now, I'll read the names —heads of families first — and the men come up and take a paper out of the box. Keep the paper folded in your hand without looking at it until everyone has had a turn. Everything clear?"

20 The people had done it so many times that they only half listened to the directions; most of them were quiet, wetting their lips, not looking around. Then Mr. Summers raised one hand high and said, "Adams." A man disengaged himself from the crowd and came forward. "Hi, Steve," Mr. Summers said, and Mr. Adams said, "Hi, Joe." They grinned at one another humorlessly and nervously. Then Mr. Adams reached into the black box and took out a folded paper. He held it firmly by one corner as he turned and went hastily back to his place in the crowd, where he stood a little apart from his family, not looking down at his hand.

"Allen," Mr. Summers said. "Anderson. . . . Bentham."

"Seems like there's no time at all between lotteries any more," Mrs. Delacroix said to Mrs. Graves in the back row. "Seems like we got through with the last one only last week."

"Time sure goes fast," Mrs. Graves said.

"Clark. . . . Delacroix."

25 "There goes my old man," Mrs. Delacroix said. She held her breath while her husband went forward.

"Dunbar," Mr. Summers said, and Mrs. Dunbar went steadily to the box while one of the women said, "Go on, Janey," and another said, "There she goes."

"We're next," Mrs. Graves said. She watched while Mr. Graves came around from the side of the box, greeted Mr. Summers gravely, and selected a slip of paper from the box. By now, all through the crowd there were men holding the small folded papers in their large hands, turning them over and over nervously. Mrs. Dunbar and her two sons stood together, Mrs. Dunbar holding the slip of paper.

"Harburt. . . . Hutchinson."

"Get up there, Bill," Mrs. Hutchinson said, and the people near her laughed.

30 "Jones."

"They do say," Mr. Adams said to Old Man Warner, who stood next to him, "that over in the north village they're talking of giving up the lottery."

Old Man Warner snorted. "Pack of crazy fools," he said. "Listening to the young folks, nothing's good enough for *them*. Next thing you know, they'll be wanting to go back to living in caves, nobody work any more, live *that* way for a while. Used to be a saying about 'Lottery in June, corn be heavy soon.' First thing you know, we'd all be eating stewed chickweed and acorns. There's *always* been a lottery," he added petulantly. "Bad enough to see young Joe Summers up there joking with everybody."

"Some places have already quit lotteries," Mrs. Adams said.

"Nothing but trouble in *that*," Old Man Warner said stoutly. "Pack of young fools."

"Martin." And Bobby Martin watched his father go forward. "Overdyke. . . . Percy."

35 "I wish they'd hurry," Mrs. Dunbar said to her older son. "I wish they'd hurry."

"They're almost through," her son said.

"You get ready to run tell Dad," Mrs. Dunbar said.

Mr. Summers called his own name and then stepped forward precisely and selected a slip from the box. Then he called, "Warner."

"Seventy-seventh year I been in the lottery," Old Man Warner said as he went 40
through the crowd. "Seventy-seventh time."

"Watson." The tall boy came awkwardly through the crowd. Someone said, "Don't be nervous, Jack," and Mr. Summers said, "Take your time, son."

"Zanini."

After that, there was a long pause, a breathless pause, until Mr. Summers, holding his slip of paper in the air, said, "All right, fellows." For a minute, no one moved, and then all the slips of paper were opened. Suddenly, all the women began to speak at once, saying, "Who is it?," "Who's got it?," "Is it the Dunbars?," "Is it the Watsons?" Then the voices began to say, "It's Hutchinson. It's Bill," "Bill Hutchinson's got it."

"Go tell your father," Mrs. Dunbar said to her older son.

People began to look around to see the Hutchinsons. Bill Hutchinson was 45
standing quiet, staring down at the paper in his hand. Suddenly, Tessie Hutchinson shouted to Mr. Summers, "You didn't give him time enough to take any paper he wanted. I saw you. It wasn't fair!"

"Be a good sport, Tessie," Mrs. Delacroix called, and Mrs. Graves said, "All of us took the same chance."

"Shut up, Tessie," Bill Hutchinson said.

"Well, everyone," Mr. Summers said, "that was done pretty fast, and now we've got to be hurrying a little more to get done in time." He consulted his next list. "Bill," he said, "you draw for the Hutchinson family. You got any other households in the Hutchinsons?"

"There's Don and Eva," Mrs. Hutchinson yelled, "Make *them* take their chance!"

"Daughters draw with their husbands' families, Tessie," Mr. Summers said gen- 50
tly. "You know that as well as anyone else."

"It wasn't *fair*," Tessie said.

"I guess not, Joe," Bill Hutchinson said regretfully. "My daughter draws with her husband's family, that's only fair. And I've got no other family except the kids."

"Then, as far as drawing for families is concerned, it's you," Mr. Summers said in explanation, "and as far as drawing for households is concerned, that's you, too. Right?"

"Right," Bill Hutchinson said.

"How many kids, Bill?" Mr. Summers asked formally. 55

"Three," Bill Hutchinson said. "There's Bill, Jr., and Nancy, and little Dave. And Tessie and me."

"All right, then," Mr. Summers said. "Harry, you got their tickets back?"

Mr. Graves nodded and held up the slips of paper. "Put them in the box, then," Mr. Summers directed. "Take Bill's and put it in."

"I think we ought to start over," Mrs. Hutchinson said, as quietly as she could. "I tell you it wasn't *fair*. You didn't give him time enough to choose. *Everybody* saw that."

60   Mr. Graves had selected the five slips and put them in the box, and he dropped all the papers but those onto the ground, where the breeze caught them and lifted them off.

"Listen, everybody," Mrs. Hutchinson was saying to the people around her.

"Ready, Bill?" Mr. Summers asked, and Bill Hutchinson, with one quick glance around at his wife and children, nodded.

"Remember," Mr. Summers said, "take the slips and keep them folded until each person has taken one. Harry, you help little Dave." Mr. Graves took the hand of the little boy, who came willingly with him up to the box. "Take a paper out of the box, Davy," Mr. Summers said. Davy put his hand into the box and laughed. "Take just *one* paper," Mr. Summers said. "Harry, you hold it for him." Mr. Graves took the child's hand and removed the folded paper from the tight fist and held it while little Dave stood next to him and looked at him wonderingly.

"Nancy next," Mr. Summers said. Nancy was twelve, and her school friends breathed heavily as she went forward, switching her skirt, and took a slip daintily from the box. "Bill, Jr.," Mr. Summers said, and Billy, his face red and his feet over-large, nearly knocked the box over as he got a paper out. "Tessie," Mr. Summers said. She hesitated for a minute, looking around defiantly, and then set her lips and went up to the box. She snatched a paper out and held it behind her.

65   "Bill," Mr. Summers said, and Bill Hutchinson reached into the box and felt around, bringing his hand out at last with the slip of paper in it.

The crowd was quiet. A girl whispered, "I hope it's not Nancy," and the sound of the whisper reached the edges of the crowd.

"It's not the way it used to be," Old Man Warner said clearly. "People ain't the way they used to be."

"All right," Mr. Summers said. "Open the papers. Harry, you open little Dave's."

Mr. Graves opened the slip of paper and there was a general sigh through the crowd as he held it up and everyone could see that it was blank. Nancy and Bill, Jr., opened theirs at the same time, and both beamed and laughed, turning around to the crowd and holding their slips of paper above their heads.

70   "Tessie," Mr. Summers said. There was a pause, and then Mr. Summers looked at Bill Hutchinson, and Bill unfolded his paper and showed it. It was blank.

"It's Tessie," Mr. Summers said, and his voice was hushed. "Show us her paper, Bill."

Bill Hutchinson went over to his wife and forced the slip of paper out of her hand. It had a black spot on it, the black spot Mr. Summers had made the night before with the heavy pencil in the coal-company office. Bill Hutchinson held it up, and there was a stir in the crowd.

"All right, folks," Mr. Summers said. "Let's finish quickly."

Although the villagers had forgotten the ritual and lost the original black box, they still remembered to use stones. The pile of stones the boys had made earlier was ready; there were stones on the ground with the blowing scraps of paper that had come out of the box. Mrs. Delacroix selected a stone so large she had to pick it up with both hands and turned to Mrs. Dunbar. "Come on," she said. "Hurry up."

Mrs. Dunbar had small stones in both hands, and she said, gasping for breath, 75 "I can't run at all. You'll have to go ahead and I'll catch up with you."

The children had stones already, and someone gave little Davy Hutchinson a few pebbles.

Tessie Hutchinson was in the center of a cleared space by now, and she held her hands out desperately as the villagers moved in on her. "It isn't fair," she said. A stone hit her on the side of the head.

Old Man Warner was saying, "Come on, come on, everyone." Steve Adams was in the front of the crowd of villagers, with Mrs. Graves beside him.

"It isn't fair, it isn't right," Mrs. Hutchinson screamed, and then they were upon her.

Reading and Reacting

1. What possible significance, beyond their literal meaning, might each of the following have:

- The village square
- Mrs. Hutchinson's apron
- Old Man Warner
- The slips of paper
- The black spot

2. "The Lottery" takes place in summer, a conventional symbol that has a positive connotation. What does this setting contribute to the story's plot? To its atmosphere?

3. What, if anything, might the names *Graves, Adams, Summers,* and *Delacroix* signify in the context of this story? Do you think these names are intended to have any special significance? Why or why not?

4. What role do the children play in the ritual? How can you explain their presence in the story? Do they have any symbolic role?

5. What symbolic significance might be found in the way the characters are dressed? In their conversation?

6. In what sense is the story's title ironic?

7. Throughout the story, there is a general atmosphere of excitement. What indication is there of nervousness or apprehension?

8. Early in the story, the boys stuff their pockets with stones, foreshadowing the attack in the story's conclusion. What other examples of foreshadowing can you identify?

9. JOURNAL ENTRY How can a ritual like the lottery continue to be held year after year? Why does no one move to end it? Can you think of a modern-day counterpart to this lottery — a situation in which people continue to act in ways they know to be wrong rather than challenge the status quo? How can you account for such behavior?

10. CRITICAL PERSPECTIVE When "The Lottery" was published in the June 26, 1948, issue of the *New Yorker*, its effect was immediate. The story, as the critic Judy Oppenheimer notes in her book *Private Demons: The Life of Shirley Jackson*, "provoked an unprecedented outpouring of fury, horror, rage, disgust, and intense fascination." As a result, Jackson received hundreds of letters, which included (among others) the following interpretations of the story:

- The story is an attack on small-town America.
- The story is a parable about the perversion of democracy.
- The story is a criticism of prejudice, particularly anti-Semitism.
- The story has no point at all.

How plausible do you think each of these interpretations is? Which comes closest to your interpretation of the story? Why?

Related Works: "Young Goodman Brown" (p. 489), "Where Are You Going, Where Have You Been?" (p. 573), "How Did They Kill My Grandmother?" (p. 1083), "Patterns" (p. 866), *Nine Ten* (p. 1334)

ALICE WALKER (1944–   ) was the youngest of eight children born to Willie Lee and Minnie Tallulah Grant Walker, sharecroppers who raised cotton. She left the rural South to attend Spelman College in Atlanta (1961–1963) and Sarah Lawrence College in Bronxville, New York (1963–1965).

In 1967, Walker moved to Mississippi, where she was supported in the writing of her first novel, *The Third Life of Grange Copeland* (1970), by a National Endowment for the Arts grant. Her short story "Everyday Use" was included in *Best American Short Stories 1973* and has been widely anthologized and studied. Other novels and collections of short stories followed, including *In Love & Trouble: Stories of Black Women* (1973), *Meridian* (1976), *You Can't Keep a Good Woman Down* (1981), *The Temple of My Familiar* (1989), *Possessing the Secret of Joy* (1993), *The Complete Stories* (1994), *By the Light of My Father's Smile* (1998), *The Way Forward Is with a Broken Heart* (2000), and *Now Is the Time to Open Your Heart* (2004). Her third novel, *The Color Purple* (1982), won the American Book Award and a Pulitzer Prize and was made into an award-winning movie.

In the third year of her marriage, Walker took back her maiden name because she wanted to honor her great-great-great-grandmother who had walked, carrying her two children, from Virginia to Georgia. Walker's renaming is consistent with one of her goals in writing, which is to further the process of reconnecting people to their ancestors. She has said that "it is fatal to see yourself as separate" and that if people can reaffirm the past, they can "make a different future."

Cultural Context Quilting attained the status of art in Europe in the fourteenth century but reached its fullest development later in North America. By the end of the eighteenth century, the American quilt had taken on unique and distinctive features that separated it from quilts made in other parts of the world. For African-Americans, quilting has particular significance. During slavery, members of the Underground Railroad would use quilts to send messages. One design, the Log Cabin, was hung outside to mark a house of refuge for fugitive slaves. Other quilts mapped escape routes out of a plantation or county, often by marking the stars that would act as a guide to freedom for those escaping at night. After the emancipation of slaves, quilts retained their cultural and historical significance, as the quilt in this story does.

Everyday Use (1973)

For Your Grandmama

I will wait for her in the yard that Maggie and I made so clean and wavy yesterday afternoon. A yard like this is more comfortable than most people know. It is not just a yard. It is like an extended living room. When the hard clay is swept clean as a floor and the fine sand around the edges lined with tiny, irregular grooves, anyone can come and sit and look up into the elm tree and wait for the breezes that never come inside the house.

Maggie will be nervous until after her sister goes: she will stand hopelessly in corners, homely and ashamed of the burn scars down her arms and legs, eying her sister with a mixture of envy and awe. She thinks her sister has held life always in the palm of one hand, that "no" is a word the world never learned to say to her.

You've no doubt seen those TV shows where the child who has "made it" is confronted, as a surprise, by her own mother and father, tottering in weakly from backstage. (A pleasant surprise, of course: What would they do if parent and child came on the show only to curse out and insult each other?) On TV mother and child embrace and smile into each other's faces. Sometimes the mother and father weep, the child wraps them in her arms and leans across the table to tell how she would not have made it without their help. I have seen these programs.

Sometimes I dream a dream in which Dee and I are suddenly brought together on a TV program of this sort. Out of a dark and soft-seated limousine I am ushered into a bright room filled with many people. There I meet a smiling, gray, sporty man like Johnny Carson who shakes my hand and tells me what a fine girl I have. Then we are on the stage and Dee is embracing me with tears in her eyes. She pins on my dress a large orchid, even though she has told me once that she thinks orchids are tacky flowers.

In real life I am a large, big-boned woman with rough, man-working hands. 5 In the winter I wear flannel nightgowns to bed and overalls during the day. I can kill and clean a hog as mercilessly as a man. My fat keeps me hot in zero weather. I can work outside all day, breaking ice to get water for washing; I can eat pork liver cooked over the open fire minutes after it comes steaming from the hog. One winter I knocked a bull calf straight in the brain between the eyes with a sledge hammer and had the meat hung up to chill before nightfall. But of course all this

Film
Series

DVD
See Ch. 19 for
film stills from
the DVD version
of this story.

does not show on television. I am the way my daughter would want me to be: a hundred pounds lighter, my skin like an uncooked barley pancake. My hair glistens in the hot bright lights. Johnny Carson has much to do to keep up with my quick and witty tongue.

But that is a mistake. I know even before I wake up. Who ever knew a Johnson with a quick tongue? Who can even imagine me looking a strange white man in the eye? It seems to me I have talked to them always with one foot raised in flight, with my head turned in whichever way is farthest from them. Dee, though. She would always look anyone in the eye. Hesitation was no part of her nature.

"How do I look, Mama?" Maggie says, showing just enough of her thin body enveloped in pink skirt and red blouse for me to know she's there, almost hidden by the door.

"Come out into the yard," I say.

Have you ever seen a lame animal, perhaps a dog run over by some careless person rich enough to own a car, sidle up to someone who is ignorant enough to be kind to him? That is the way my Maggie walks. She has been like this, chin on chest, eyes on ground, feet in shuffle, ever since the fire that burned the other house to the ground.

10   Dee is lighter than Maggie, with nicer hair and a fuller figure. She's a woman now, though sometimes I forget. How long ago was it that the other house burned? Ten, twelve years? Sometimes I can still hear the flames and feel Maggie's arms sticking to me, her hair smoking and her dress falling off her in little black papery flakes. Her eyes seemed stretched open, blazed open by the flames reflected in them. And Dee. I see her standing off under the sweet gum tree she used to dig gum out of; a look of concentration on her face as she watched the last dingy gray board of the house fall in toward the red-hot brick chimney. Why don't you do a dance around the ashes? I'd wanted to ask her. She had hated the house that much.

I used to think she hated Maggie, too. But that was before we raised the money, the church and me, to send her to Augusta to school. She used to read to us without pity; forcing words, lies, other folks' habits, whole lives upon us two, sitting trapped and ignorant underneath her voice. She washed us in a river of make-believe, burned us with a lot of knowledge we didn't necessarily need to know. Pressed us to her with the serious way she read, to shove us away at just the moment, like dimwits, we seemed about to understand.

Dee wanted nice things. A yellow organdy dress to wear to her graduation from high school; black pumps to match a green suit she'd made from an old suit somebody gave me. She was determined to stare down any disaster in her efforts. Her eyelids would not flicker for minutes at a time. Often I fought off the temptation to shake her. At sixteen she had a style of her own, and knew what style was.

I never had an education myself. After second grade the school was closed down. Don't ask me why: in 1927 colored asked fewer questions than they do now. Sometimes Maggie reads to me. She stumbles along good-naturedly but can't see well. She knows she is not bright. Like good looks and money, quickness passed her by. She will marry John Thomas (who has mossy teeth in an earnest face) and then I'll be free to sit here and I guess just sing church songs to myself. Although I never was a good singer. Never could carry a tune. I was always better at a man's job. I used to love to milk till I was hooked in the side in '49. Cows are soothing and slow and don't bother you, unless you try to milk them the wrong way.

I have deliberately turned my back on the house. It is three rooms, just like the one that burned, except the roof is tin; they don't make shingle roofs any more. There are no real windows, just some holes cut in the sides, like the portholes in a ship, but not round and not square, with rawhide holding the shutters up on the outside. This house is in a pasture, too, like the other one. No doubt when Dee sees it she will want to tear it down. She wrote me once that no matter where we "choose" to live, she will manage to come see us. But she will never bring her friends. Maggie and I thought about this and Maggie asked me, "Mama, when did Dee ever *have* any friends?"

She had a few. Furtive boys in pink shirts hanging about on washday after   15 school. Nervous girls who never laughed. Impressed with her they worshiped the well-turned phrase, the cute shape, the scalding humor that erupted like bubbles in lye. She read to them.

When she was courting Jimmy T she didn't have much time to pay to us, but turned all her faultfinding power on him. He *flew* to marry a cheap city girl from a family of ignorant flashy people. She hardly had time to recompose herself.

When she comes I will meet — but there they are!

Maggie attempts to make a dash for the house, in her shuffling way, but I stay her with my hand. "Come back here," I say. And she stops and tries to dig a well in the sand with her toe.

It is hard to see them clearly through the strong sun. But even the first glimpse of leg out of the car tells me it is Dee. Her feet were always neat-looking, as if God himself had shaped them with a certain style. From the other side of the car comes a short, stocky man. Hair is all over his head a foot long and hanging from his chin like a kinky mule tail. I hear Maggie suck in her breath. "Uhnnnh," is what it sounds like. Like when you see the wriggling end of a snake just in front of your foot on the road. "Uhnnnh."

Dee next. A dress down to the ground, in this hot weather. A dress so loud it   20 hurts my eyes. There are yellows and oranges enough to throw back the light of the sun. I feel my whole face warming from the heat waves it throws out. Earrings gold, too, and hanging down to her shoulders. Bracelets dangling and making noises when she moves her arm up to shake the folds of the dress out of her armpits. The dress is loose and flows, and as she walks closer, I like it. I hear Maggie go "Uhnnnh" again. It is her sister's hair. It stands straight up like the wool on a sheep. It is black as night and around the edges are two long pigtails that rope about like small lizards disappearing behind her ears.

"Wa-su-zo-Tean-o!"° she says, coming on in that gliding way the dress makes her move. The short stocky fellow with the hair to his navel is all grinning and

---

Wa-su-zo-Tean-o: A greeting in Swahili; Dee sounds it out one syllable at a time.

he follows up with "Asalamalakim,° my mother and sister!" He moves to hug
Maggie but she falls back, right up against the back of my chair. I feel her trembling there and when I look up I see the perspiration falling off her chin.

"Don't get up," says Dee. Since I am stout it takes something of a push. You can
see me trying to move a second or two before I make it. She turns, showing white
heels through her sandals, and goes back to the car. Out she peeks next with a Polaroid. She stoops down quickly and lines up picture after picture of me sitting
there in front of the house with Maggie cowering behind me. She never takes a
shot without making sure the house is included. When a cow comes nibbling
around the edge of the yard she snaps it and me and Maggie *and* the house. Then
she puts the Polaroid in the back seat of the car, and comes up and kisses me on
the forehead.

Meanwhile Asalamalakim is going through motions with Maggie's hand.
Maggie's hand is as limp as a fish, and probably as cold, despite the sweat, and she
keeps trying to pull it back. It looks like Asalamalakim wants to shake hands but
wants to do it fancy. Or maybe he don't know how people shake hands. Anyhow,
he soon gives up on Maggie.

"Well," I say. "Dee."

25   "No, Mama," she says. "Not 'Dee,' Wangero Leewanika Kemanjo!"

"What happened to 'Dee'?" I wanted to know.

"She's dead," Wangero said. "I couldn't bear it any longer, being named after
the people who oppress me."

"You know as well as me you was named after your aunt Dicie," I said. Dicie is
my sister. She named Dee. We called her "Big Dee" after Dee was born.

"But who was *she* named after?" asked Wangero.

30   "I guess after Grandma Dee," I said.

"And who was she named after?" asked Wangero.

"Her mother," I said, and saw Wangero was getting tired. "That's about as far
back as I can trace it," I said. Though, in fact, I probably could have carried it back
beyond the Civil War through the branches.

"Well," said Asalamalakim, "there you are."

"Uhnnnh," I heard Maggie say.

35   "There I was not," I said, "before 'Dicie' cropped up in our family, so why
should I try to trace it that far back?"

He just stood there grinning, looking down on me like somebody inspecting a
Model A car. Every once in a while he and Wangero sent eye signals over my
head.

"How do you pronounce this name?" I asked.

40   "You don't have to call me by it if you don't want to," said Wangero.

"Why shouldn't I?" I asked. "If that's what you want us to call you, we'll call
you."

"I know it might sound awkward at first," said Wangero.

"I'll get used to it," I said. "Ream it out again."

Asalamalakim: A greeting in Arabic: "Peace be upon you."

Well, soon we got the name out of the way. Asalamalakim had a name twice as long and three times as hard. After I tripped over it two or three times he told me to just call him Hakim-a-barber. I wanted to ask him was he a barber, but I didn't really think he was, so I didn't ask.

"You must belong to those beef-cattle peoples down the road," I said. They said "Asalamalakim" when they met you, too, but they didn't shake hands. Always too busy: feeding the cattle, fixing the fences, putting up salt-lick shelters, throwing down hay. When the white folks poisoned some of the herd the men stayed up all night with rifles in their hands. I walked a mile and a half just to see the sight.

Hakim-a-barber said, "I accept some of their doctrines, but farming and raising cattle is not my style." (They didn't tell me, and I didn't ask, whether Wangero [Dee] had really gone and married him.)

We sat down to eat and right away he said he didn't eat collards and pork was   45
unclean. Wangero, though, went on through the chitlins and corn bread, the greens and everything else. She talked a blue streak over the sweet potatoes. Everything delighted her. Even the fact that we still used the benches her daddy made for the table when we couldn't afford to buy chairs.

"Oh, Mama!" she cried. Then turned to Hakim-a-barber. "I never knew how lovely these benches are. You can feel the rump prints," she said, running her hands underneath her and along the bench. Then she gave a sigh and her hand closed over Grandma Dee's butter dish. "That's it!" she said. "I knew there was something I wanted to ask you if I could have." She jumped up from the table and went over in the corner where the churn stood, the milk in it clabber by now. She looked at the churn and looked at it.

"This churn top is what I need," she said. "Didn't Uncle Buddy whittle it out of a tree you all used to have?"

"Yes," I said.

"Uh huh," she said happily. "And I want the dasher, too."

"Uncle Buddy whittle that, too?" asked the barber.   50

Dee (Wangero) looked up at me.

"Aunt Dee's first husband whittled the dash," said Maggie so low you almost couldn't hear her. "His name was Henry, but they called him Stash."

"Maggie's brain is like an elephant's," Wangero said, laughing. "I can use the churn top as a centerpiece for the alcove table," she said, sliding a plate over the churn, "and I'll think of something artistic to do with the dasher."

When she finished wrapping the dasher the handle stuck out. I took it for a moment in my hands. You didn't even have to look close to see where hands pushing the dasher up and down to make butter had left a kind of sink in the wood. In fact, there were a lot of small sinks; you could see where thumb and fingers had sunk into the wood. It was beautiful light yellow wood, from a tree that grew in the yard where Big Dee and Stash had lived.

After dinner Dee (Wangero) went to the trunk at the foot of my bed and started   55
rifling through it. Maggie hung back in the kitchen over the dishpan. Out came Wangero with two quilts. They had been pieced by Grandma Dee and then Big Dee and me had hung them on the quilt frames on the front porch and quilted them.

One was in the Lone Star pattern. The other was Walk Around the Mountain. In both of them were scraps of dresses Grandma Dee had worn fifty and more years ago. Bits and pieces of Grandpa Jarrell's Paisley shirts. And one teeny faded blue piece, about the size of a penny matchbox, that was from Great Grandpa Ezra's uniform that he wore in the Civil War.

"Mama," Wangero said sweet as a bird. "Can I have these old quilts?"

I heard something fall in the kitchen, and a minute later the kitchen door slammed.

"Why don't you take one or two of the others?" I asked. "These old things was just done by me and Big Dee from some tops your grandma pieced before she died."

"No," said Wangero. "I don't want those. They are stitched around the borders by machine."

60   "That'll make them last better," I said.

"That's not the point," said Wangero. "These are all pieces of dresses Grandma used to wear. She did all this stitching by hand. Imagine!" She held the quilts securely in her arms, stroking them.

"Some of the pieces, like those lavender ones, come from old clothes her mother handed down to her," I said, moving up to touch the quilts. Dee (Wangero) moved back just enough so that I couldn't reach the quilts. They already belonged to her.

"Imagine!" she breathed again, clutching them closely to her bosom.

"The truth is," I said, "I promised to give them quilts to Maggie, for when she marries John Thomas."

65   She gasped like a bee had stung her. "Maggie can't appreciate these quilts!" she said. "She'd probably be backward enough to put them to everyday use."

"I reckon she would," I said. "God knows I been saving 'em for long enough with nobody using 'em. I hope she will!" I didn't want to bring up how I had offered Dee (Wangero) a quilt when she went away to college. Then she had told me they were old-fashioned, out of style.

"But, they're *priceless!*" she was saying now, furiously; for she has a temper. "Maggie would put them on the bed and in five years they'd be in rags. Less than that!"

"She can always make some more," I said. "Maggie knows how to quilt."

Dee (Wangero) looked at me with hatred. "You just will not understand. The point is these quilts, *these* quilts!"

70   "Well," I said, stumped. "What would *you* do with them?"

"Hang them," she said. As if that was the only thing you *could* do with quilts.

Maggie by now was standing in the door. I could almost hear the sound her feet made as they scraped over each other.

"She can have them, Mama," she said, like somebody used to never winning anything, or having anything reserved for her. "I can 'member Grandma Dee without the quilts."

I looked at her hard. She had filled her bottom lip with checkerberry snuff and it gave her face a kind of dopey, hangdog look. It was Grandma Dee and Big Dee who taught her how to quilt herself. She stood there with her scarred hands hidden in the folds of her skirt. She looked at her sister with something like fear but she wasn't mad at her. This was Maggie's portion. This was the way she knew God to work.

When I looked at her like that something hit me in the top of my head and 75 ran down to the soles of my feet. Just like when I'm in church and the spirit of God touches me and I get happy and shout. I did something I never had done before: hugged Maggie to me, then dragged her on into the room, snatched the quilts out of Miss Wangero's hands and dumped them into Maggie's lap. Maggie just sat there on my bed with her mouth open.

"Take one or two of the others," I said to Dee.

But she turned without a word and went out to Hakim-a-barber.

"You just don't understand," she said, as Maggie and I came out to the car.

"What don't I understand?" I wanted to know.

"Your heritage," she said. And then she turned to Maggie, kissed her, and said, 80 "You ought to try to make something of yourself, too, Maggie. It's really a new day for us. But from the way you and Mama still live you'd never know it."

She put on some sunglasses that hid everything above the tip of her nose and her chin.

Maggie smiled; maybe at the sunglasses. But a real smile, not scared. After we watched the car dust settle I asked Maggie to bring me a dip of snuff. And then the two of us sat there just enjoying, until it was time to go in the house and go to bed.

Reading and Reacting

1. In American culture, what does a patchwork quilt symbolize?

2. What is the literal meaning of the two quilts to Maggie and her mother? To Dee? Beyond this literal meaning, what symbolic meaning, if any, do they have to Maggie and her mother? Do the quilts have any symbolic meaning to Dee?

3. How does the contrast between the two sisters' appearances, personalities, lifestyles, and feelings about the quilts help to convey the story's theme?

4. What does the name *Wangero* signify to Dee? To her mother and sister? Could the name be considered a symbol? Why or why not?

5. Why do you think Maggie relinquishes the quilts to her sister?

6. What is Dee's opinion of her mother and sister? Do you agree with her assessment?

7. What does the story's title suggest to you? Is it ironic? What other titles would be effective?

8. Discuss the possible meanings, aside from their literal meanings, that each of the following suggest: the family's yard, Maggie's burn scars, the trunk in which the quilts are kept, Dee's Polaroid camera. What symbolic functions, if any, do these items serve in the story?

9. JOURNAL ENTRY What objects have the kind of symbolic value to you that the quilts have to Maggie? What gives these objects this value?

10. CRITICAL PERSPECTIVE In her article "The Black Woman Artist as Wayward," critic Barbara Christian characterizes "Everyday Use" as a story in which Alice Walker examines the "creative legacy" of ordinary African-American women. According to Christian, the story "is about the use and misuse of the concept of heritage. The mother of two daughters, one selfish and stylish, the other scarred and caring, passes on to us its true definition."

What definition of *heritage* does the mother attempt to pass on to her children? How is this definition like or unlike Dee's definition?

Related Works: "Two Kinds" (p. 791), "Digging" (p. 1060), "My Grandmother Would Rock Quietly and Hum" (p. 854), "Aunt Jennifer's Tigers" (p. 977), *Trifles* (p. 1372), *Fences* (p. 1939)

RAYMOND CARVER (1938–1988), one of the most influential and widely read writers of our time, fashioned his stories from the stuff of common life uncommonly perceived. He married at nineteen and fathered two children by the time he was twenty; during this period, he also began to write. He received a degree from Humboldt State University and later from the University of Iowa. His first collection of stories, *Will You Please Be Quiet, Please* (1976), was nominated for a National Book Award. Five more collections of stories followed, including *Cathedral* (1983)— nominated for both a Pulitzer Prize and a National Book Critics Circle Award — and *Where I'm Calling From: New and Selected Stories* (1988). Carver was also the author of five books of poetry. In his last years, Carver was praised as the best American short story writer since Ernest Hemingway; novelist Robert Stone called him "a hero of perception." He was made an Honorary Doctor of Letters at the University of Hartford and was inducted into the American Academy and Institute of Arts and Letters.

Cultural Context A cathedral is the principal church of a bishop's diocese. As centers of religious authority, civic pomp, and communal worship, cathedrals began to be built in Europe around the year 1000. They flourished throughout the Middle Ages as the power of the Catholic Church grew. The lavish decoration and dazzling design of these structures were meant not only to celebrate God but also to honor those secular and religious authorities who had financed the construction of the buildings. Cathedrals — especially those built in the Gothic period, between 1200 and 1500 — often featured pointed arches, flying buttresses, and high spires designed to lift worshipers' eyes toward heaven. The cathedral in this story serves a similar purpose on a symbolic level.

Film Series

DVD
See Ch. 19 for film stills from the DVD version of this story.

Cathedral (1983)

This blind man, an old friend of my wife's, he was on his way to spend the night. His wife had died. So he was visiting the dead wife's relatives in Connecticut. He called my wife from his in-laws'. Arrangements were made. He would come by train, a five-hour trip, and my wife would meet him at the station. She hadn't seen him since she worked for him one summer in Seattle ten years ago. But she and the blind man had kept in touch. They made tapes and mailed them back and forth. I wasn't enthusiastic about his visit. He was no one I knew. And his being blind bothered me. My idea of blindness came from the movies. In the movies, the blind moved slowly and never laughed. Sometimes they were led by seeing-eye dogs. A blind man in my house was not something I looked forward to.

That summer in Seattle she had needed a job. She didn't have any money. The man she was going to marry at the end of the summer was in officers' training school. He didn't have any money, either. But she was in love with the guy, and he was in love with her, etc. She'd seen something in the paper: HELP WANTED—*Reading to Blind Man*, and a telephone number. She phoned and went over, was hired on the spot. She'd worked with this blind man all summer. She read stuff to him, case studies, reports, that sort of thing. She helped him organize his little office in the county social-service department. They'd become good friends, my wife and the blind man. How do I know these things? She told me. And she told me something else. On her last day in the office, the blind man asked if he could touch her face. She agreed to this. She told me he touched his fingers to every part of her face, her nose — even her neck! She never forgot it. She even tried to write a poem about it. She was always trying to write a poem. She wrote a poem or two every year, usually after something really important had happened to her.

When we first started going out together, she showed me the poem. In the poem, she recalled his fingers and the way they had moved around over her face. In the poem, she talked about what she had felt at the time, about what went through her mind when the blind man touched her nose and lips. I can remember I didn't think much of the poem. Of course, I didn't tell her that. Maybe I just don't understand poetry. I admit it's not the first thing I reach for when I pick up something to read.

Anyway, this man who'd first enjoyed her favors, the officer-to-be, he'd been her childhood sweetheart. So okay. I'm saying that at the end of the summer she let the blind man run his hands over her face, said goodbye to him, married her childhood etc., who was now a commissioned officer, and she moved away from Seattle. But they'd kept in touch, she and the blind man. She made the first contact after a year or so. She called him up one night from an Air Force base in Alabama. She wanted to talk. They talked. He asked her to send a tape and tell him about her life. She did this. She sent the tape. On the tape, she told the blind man about her husband and about their life together in the military. She told the blind man she loved her husband but she didn't like it where they lived and she didn't like it that he was part of the military-industrial thing. She told the blind man she'd written a poem and he was in it. She told him that she was writing a poem about what it was like to be an Air Force officer's wife. The poem wasn't finished yet. She was still writing it. The blind man made a tape. He sent her the tape. She made a tape. This went on for years. My wife's officer was posted to one base and then another. She sent tapes from Moody AFB, McGuire, McConnell, and finally Travis,° near Sacramento, where one night she got to feeling lonely

---

Moody . . . Travis: United States Air Force bases.

and cut off from people she kept losing in that moving-around life. She got to feeling she couldn't go it another step. She went in and swallowed all the pills and capsules in the medicine chest and washed them down with a bottle of gin. Then she got into a hot bath and passed out.

5   But instead of dying, she got sick. She threw up. Her officer — why should he have a name? he was the childhood sweetheart, and what more does he want?— came home from somewhere, found her, and called the ambulance. In time, she put it all on a tape and sent the tape to the blind man. Over the years, she put all kinds of stuff on tapes and sent the tapes off lickety-split. Next to writing a poem every year, I think it was her chief means of recreation. On one tape, she told the blind man she'd decided to live away from her officer for a time. On another tape, she told him about her divorce. She and I began going out, and of course she told her blind man about it. She told him everything, or so it seemed to me. Once she asked me if I'd like to hear the latest tape from the blind man. This was a year ago. I was on the tape, she said. So I said okay, I'd listen to it. I got us drinks and we settled down in the living room. We made ready to listen. First she inserted the tape into the player and adjusted a couple of dials. Then she pushed a lever. The tape squeaked and someone began to talk in this loud voice. She lowered the volume. After a few minutes of harmless chitchat, I heard my own name in the mouth of this stranger, this blind man I didn't even know! And then this: "From all you've said about him, I can only conclude —" But we were interrupted, a knock at the door, something, and we didn't ever get back to the tape. Maybe it was just as well. I'd heard all I wanted to.

Now this same blind man was coming to sleep in my house.

"Maybe I could take him bowling," I said to my wife. She was at the draining board doing scalloped potatoes. She put down the knife she was using and turned around.

"If you love me," she said, "you can do this for me. If you don't love me, okay. But if you had a friend, any friend, and the friend came to visit, I'd make him feel comfortable." She wiped her hands with the dish towel.

"I don't have any blind friends," I said.

10   "You don't have *any* friends," she said. "Period. Besides," she said, "goddamn it, his wife's just died! Don't you understand that? The man's lost his wife!"

I didn't answer. She'd told me a little about the blind man's wife. Her name was Beulah. Beulah! That's a name for a colored woman.

"Was his wife a Negro?" I asked.

"Are you crazy?" my wife said. "Have you just flipped or something?" She picked up a potato. I saw it hit the floor, then roll under the stove. "What's wrong with you?" she said. "Are you drunk?"

"I'm just asking," I said.

15   Right then my wife filled me in with more detail than I cared to know. I made a drink and sat at the kitchen table to listen. Pieces of the story began to fall into place.

Beulah had gone to work for the blind man the summer after my wife had stopped working for him. Pretty soon Beulah and the blind man had themselves a church wedding. It was a little wedding — who'd want to go to such a wedding in the first place?—just the two of them, plus the minister and the minister's wife. But it was a church wedding just the same. It was what Beulah had wanted, he'd said. But even then Beulah must have been carrying the cancer in her glands. After they had been inseparable for eight years — my wife's word, *inseparable*— Beulah's health went into a rapid decline. She died in a Seattle hospital room, the blind man sitting beside the bed and holding on to her hand. They'd married, lived and worked together, slept together — had sex, sure — and then the blind man had to bury her. All this without his having ever seen what the goddamned woman looked like. It was beyond my understanding. Hearing this, I felt sorry for the blind man for a little bit. And then I found myself thinking what a pitiful life this woman must have led. Imagine a woman who could never see herself as she was seen in the eyes of her loved one. A woman who could go on day after day and never receive the smallest compliment from her beloved. A woman whose husband could never read the expression on her face, be it misery or something better. Someone who could wear makeup or not — what difference to him? She could, if she wanted, wear green eye-shadow around one eye, a straight pin in her nostril, yellow slacks, and purple shoes, no matter. And then to slip off into death, the blind man's hand on her hand, his blind eyes streaming tears — I'm imagining now — her last thought maybe this: that he never even knew what she looked like, and she on an express to the grave. Robert was left with a small insurance policy and a half of a twenty-peso Mexican coin. The other half of the coin went into the box with her. Pathetic.

So when the time rolled around, my wife went to the depot to pick him up. With nothing to do but wait — sure, I blamed him for that — I was having a drink and watching the TV when I heard the car pull into the drive. I got up from the sofa with my drink and went to the window to have a look.

I saw my wife laughing as she parked the car. I saw her get out of the car and shut the door. She was still wearing a smile. Just amazing. She went around to the other side of the car to where the blind man was already starting to get out. This blind man, feature this, he was wearing a full beard! A beard on a blind man! Too much, I say. The blind man reached into the backseat and dragged out a suitcase. My wife took his arm, shut the car door, and, talking all the way, moved him down the drive and then up the steps to the front porch. I turned off the TV. I finished my drink, rinsed the glass, dried my hands. Then I went to the door.

My wife said, "I want you to meet Robert. Robert, this is my husband. I've told you all about him." She was beaming. She had this blind man by his coat sleeve.

The blind man let go of his suitcase and up came his hand.   20

I took it. He squeezed hard, held my hand, and then he let it go.

"I feel like we've already met," he boomed.

"Likewise," I said. I didn't know what else to say. Then I said, "Welcome. I've heard a lot about you." We began to move then, a little group, from the porch into the living room, my wife guiding him by the arm. The blind man was carrying his suitcase in his other hand. My wife said things like, "To your left here, Robert. That's right. Now watch it, there's a chair. That's it. Sit down right here. This is the sofa. We just bought this sofa two weeks ago."

I started to say something about the old sofa. I'd liked that old sofa. But I didn't say anything. Then I wanted to say something else, small-talk, about the scenic ride along the Hudson.° How going *to* New York, you should sit on the right-hand side of the train, and coming *from* New York, the left-hand side.

25   "Did you have a good train ride?" I said. "Which side of the train did you sit on, by the way?"

"What a question, which side!" my wife said. "What's it matter which side?" she said.

"I just asked," I said.

"Right side," the blind man said. "I hadn't been on a train in nearly forty years. Not since I was a kid. With my folks. That's been a long time. I'd nearly forgotten the sensation. I have winter in my beard now," he said. "So I've been told, anyway. Do I look distinguished, my dear?" the blind man said to my wife.

"You look distinguished, Robert," she said. "Robert," she said. "Robert, it's just so good to see you."

30   My wife finally took her eyes off the blind man and looked at me. I had the feeling she didn't like what she saw. I shrugged.

I've never met, or personally known, anyone who was blind. This blind man was late forties, a heavy-set, balding man with stooped shoulders, as if he carried a great weight there. He wore brown slacks, brown shoes, a light-brown shirt, a tie, a sports coat. Spiffy. He also had this full beard. But he didn't use a cane and he didn't wear dark glasses. I'd always thought dark glasses were a must for the blind. Fact was, I wished he had a pair. At first glance, his eyes looked like anyone else's eyes. But if you looked close, there was something different about them. Too much white in the iris, for one thing, and the pupils seemed to move around in the sockets without his knowing it or being able to stop it. Creepy. As I stared at his face, I saw the left pupil turn in toward his nose while the other made an effort to keep in one place. But it was only an effort, for that eye was on the roam without his knowing it or wanting it to be.

I said, "Let me get you a drink. What's your pleasure? We have a little of everything. It's one of our pastimes."

"Bub, I'm a Scotch man myself," he said fast enough in this big voice.

"Right," I said. Bub! "Sure you are. I knew it."

35   He let his fingers touch his suitcase, which was sitting alongside the sofa. He was taking his bearings. I didn't blame him for that.

"I'll move that up to your room," my wife said.

"No, that's fine," the blind man said loudly. "It can go up when I go up."

"A little water with the Scotch?" I said.

"Very little," he said.

40   "I knew it," I said.

He said, "Just a tad. The Irish actor, Barry Fitzgerald? I'm like that fellow. When I drink water, Fitzgerald said, I drink water. When I drink whiskey, I drink

---

Hudson: A river in New York State.

whiskey." My wife laughed. The blind man brought his hand up under his beard. He lifted his beard slowly and let it drop.

I did the drinks, three big glasses of Scotch with a splash of water in each. Then we made ourselves comfortable and talked about Robert's travels. First the long flight from the West Coast to Connecticut, we covered that. Then from Connecticut up here by train. We had another drink concerning that leg of the trip.

I remembered having read somewhere that the blind didn't smoke because, as speculation had it, they couldn't see the smoke they exhaled. I thought I knew that much and that much only about blind people. But this blind man smoked his cigarette down to the nubbin and then lit another one. This blind man filled his ashtray and my wife emptied it.

When we sat down at the table for dinner, we had another drink. My wife heaped Robert's plate with cube steak, scalloped potatoes, green beans. I buttered him up two slices of bread. I said, "Here's bread and butter for you." I swallowed some of my drink. "Now let us pray," I said, and the blind man lowered his head. My wife looked at me, her mouth agape. "Pray the phone won't ring and the food doesn't get cold," I said.

We dug in. We ate everything there was to eat on the table. We ate like there 45 was no tomorrow. We didn't talk. We ate. We scarfed. We grazed that table. We were into serious eating. The blind man had right away located his foods, he knew just where everything was on his plate. I watched with admiration as he used his knife and fork on the meat. He'd cut two pieces of meat, fork the meat into his mouth, and then go all out for the scalloped potatoes, the beans next, and then he'd tear off a hunk of buttered bread and eat that. He'd follow this up with a big drink of milk. It didn't seem to bother him to use his fingers once in a while, either.

We finished everything, including half a strawberry pie. For a few moments, we sat as if stunned. Sweat beaded on our faces. Finally, we got up from the table and left the dirty plates. We didn't look back. We took ourselves into the living room and sank into our places again. Robert and my wife sat on the sofa. I took the big chair. We had us two or three more drinks while they talked about the major things that had come to pass for them in the past ten years. For the most part, I just listened. Now and then I joined in. I didn't want him to think I'd left the room, and I didn't want her to think I was feeling left out. They talked of things that had happened to them — to them! — these past ten years. I waited in vain to hear my name on my wife's sweet lips: "And then my dear husband came into my life" — something like that. But I heard nothing of the sort. More talk of Robert. Robert had done a little of everything, it seemed, a regular blind jack-of-all-trades. But most recently he and his wife had had an Amway distributorship, from which, I gathered, they'd earned their living, such as it was. The blind man was also a ham radio operator.° He talked in his loud voice about conversations he'd had with fellow operators in Guam, in the Philippines, in Alaska, and even in Tahiti. He said he'd have a lot of friends there if he ever wanted to go visit those places. From time to time, he'd turn his blind face toward me, put his hand under his beard, ask me

---

ham radio operator: A licensed amateur radio operator.

something. How long had I been in my present position? (Three years.) Did I like my work? (I didn't.) Was I going to stay with it? (What were the options?) Finally, when I thought he was beginning to run down, I got up and turned on the TV.

My wife looked at me with irritation. She was heading toward a boil. Then she looked at the blind man and said, "Robert, do you have a TV?"

The blind man said, "My dear, I have two TVs. I have a color set and a black-and-white thing, an old relic. It's funny, but if I turn the TV on, and I'm always turning it on, I turn on the color set. It's funny, don't you think?"

I didn't know what to say to that. I had absolutely nothing to say to that. No opinion. So I watched the news program and tried to listen to what the announcer was saying.

50   "This is a color TV," the blind man said. "Don't ask me how, but I can tell."

"We traded up a while ago," I said.

The blind man had another taste of his drink. He lifted his beard, sniffed it, and let it fall. He leaned forward on the sofa. He positioned his ashtray on the coffee table, then put the lighter to his cigarette. He leaned back on the sofa and crossed his legs at the ankles.

My wife covered her mouth, and then she yawned. She stretched. She said, "I think I'll go upstairs and put on my robe. I think I'll change into something else. Robert, you make yourself comfortable," she said.

"I'm comfortable," the blind man said.

55   "I want you to feel comfortable in this house," she said.

"I am comfortable," the blind man said.

After she'd left the room, he and I listened to the weather report and then to the sports roundup. By that time, she'd been gone so long I didn't know if she was going to come back. I thought she might have gone to bed. I wished she'd come back downstairs. I didn't want to be left alone with a blind man. I asked him if he wanted another drink, and he said sure. Then I asked if he wanted to smoke some dope with me. I said I'd just rolled a number. I hadn't, but I planned to do so in about two shakes.

"I'll try some with you," he said.

"Damn right," I said. "That's the stuff."

60   I got our drinks and sat down on the sofa with him. Then I rolled us two fat numbers. I lit one and passed it. I brought it to his fingers. He took it and inhaled.

"Hold it as long as you can," I said. I could tell he didn't know the first thing.

My wife came back downstairs wearing her pink robe and her pink slippers.

"What do I smell?" she said.

"We thought we'd have us some cannabis," I said.

65   My wife gave me a savage look. Then she looked at the blind man and said, "Robert, I didn't know you smoked."

He said, "I do now, my dear. There's a first time for everything. But I don't feel anything yet."

"This stuff is pretty mellow," I said. "This stuff is mild. It's dope you can reason with," I said. "It doesn't mess you up."

"Not much it doesn't, bub," he said, and laughed.

My wife sat on the sofa between the blind man and me. I passed her the number. She took it and toked° and then passed it back to me. "Which way is this going?" she said. Then she said, "I shouldn't be smoking this. I can hardly keep my eyes open as it is. That dinner did me in. I shouldn't have eaten so much."

"It was the strawberry pie," the blind man said. "That's what did it," he said, 70 and he laughed his big laugh. Then he shook his head.

"There's more strawberry pie," I said.

"Do you want some more, Robert?" my wife said.

"Maybe in a little while," he said.

We gave our attention to the TV. My wife yawned again. She said, "Your bed is made up when you feel like going to bed, Robert. I know you must have had a long day. When you're ready to go to bed, say so." She pulled his arm. "Robert?"

He came to and said, "I've had a real nice time. This beats tapes, doesn't it?" 75

I said, "Coming at you," and I put the number between his fingers. He inhaled, held the smoke, and then let it go. It was like he'd been doing it since he was nine years old.

"Thanks, bub," he said. "But I think this is all for me. I think I'm beginning to feel it," he said. He held the burning roach out for my wife.

"Same here," she said. "Ditto. Me, too." She took the roach and passed it to me. "I may just sit here for a while between you two guys with my eyes closed. But don't let me bother you, okay? Either one of you. If it bothers you, say so. Otherwise, I may just sit here with my eyes closed until you're ready to go to bed," she said. "Your bed's made up, Robert, when you're ready. It's right next to our room at the top of the stairs. We'll show you up when you're ready. You wake me up now, you guys, if I fall asleep." She said that and then she closed her eyes and went to sleep.

The news program ended. I got up and changed the channel. I sat back down on the sofa. I wished my wife hadn't pooped out. Her head lay across the back of the sofa, her mouth open. She'd turned so that her robe slipped away from her legs, exposing a juicy thigh. I reached to draw her robe back over her, and it was then that I glanced at the blind man. What the hell! I flipped the robe open again.

"You say when you want some strawberry pie," I said.

"I will," he said.   80

I said, "Are you tired? Do you want me to take you up to your bed? Are you ready to hit the hay?"

"Not yet," he said. "No, I'll stay up with you, bub. If that's all right. I'll stay up until you're ready to turn in. We haven't had a chance to talk. Know what I mean? I feel like me and her monopolized the evening." He lifted his beard and he let it fall. He picked up his cigarettes and his lighter.

"That's all right," I said. Then I said, "I'm glad for the company."

And I guess I was. Every night I smoked dope and stayed up as long as I could 85 before I fell asleep. My wife and I hardly ever went to bed at the same time. When I did go to sleep, I had these dreams. Sometimes I'd wake up from one of them, my heart going crazy.

---

toked: Inhaled.

Something about the church and the Middle Ages was on the TV. Not your run-of-the-mill TV fare. I wanted to watch something else. I turned to the other channels. But there was nothing on them, either. So I turned back to the first channel and apologized.

"Bub, it's all right," the blind man said. "It's fine with me. Whatever you want to watch is okay. I'm always learning something. Learning never ends. It won't hurt me to learn something tonight. I got ears," he said.

We didn't say anything for a time. He was leaning forward with his head turned at me, his right ear aimed in the direction of the set. Very disconcerting. Now and then his eyelids drooped and then they snapped open again. Now and then he put his fingers into his beard and tugged, like he was thinking about something he was hearing on the television.

On the screen, a group of men wearing cowls was being set upon and tormented by men dressed in skeleton costumes and men dressed as devils. The men dressed as devils wore devil masks, horns, and long tails. This pageant was part of a procession. The Englishman who was narrating the thing said it took place in Spain once a year. I tried to explain to the blind man what was happening.

90   "Skeletons," he said. "I know about skeletons," he said, and nodded.

The TV showed this one cathedral. Then there was a long, slow look at another one. Finally, the picture switched to the famous one in Paris, with its flying buttresses and its spires reaching up to the clouds. The camera pulled away to show the whole of the cathedral rising above the skyline.

There were times when the Englishman who was telling the thing would shut up, would simply let the camera move around the cathedrals. Or else the camera would tour the countryside, men in fields walking behind oxen. I waited as long as I could. Then I felt I had to say something. I said, "They're showing the outside of this cathedral now. Gargoyles. Little statues carved to look like monsters. Now I guess they're in Italy. Yeah, they're in Italy. There's paintings on the walls of this one church."

"Are those fresco° paintings, bub?" he asked, and he sipped from his drink.

I reached for my glass. But it was empty. I tried to remember what I could remember. "You're asking me are those frescoes?" I said. "That's a good question. I don't know."

95   The camera moved to a cathedral outside Lisbon.° The differences in the Portuguese cathedral compared with the French and Italian were not that great. But they were there. Mostly the interior stuff. Then something occurred to me, and I said, "Something has occurred to me. Do you have any idea what a cathedral is? What they look like, that is? Do you follow me? If somebody says cathedral to you, do you have any notion what they're talking about? Do you know the difference between that and a Baptist church, say?"

He let the smoke dribble from his mouth. "I know they took hundreds of workers fifty or a hundred years to build," he said. "I just heard the man say that,

---

Fresco: Painted plaster.

Lisbon: The capital of Portugal.

of course. I know generations of the same families worked on a cathedral. I heard him say that, too. The men who began their life's work on them, they never lived to see the completion of their work. In that wise, bub, they're no different from the rest of us, right?" He laughed. Then his eyelids drooped again. His head nodded. He seemed to be snoozing. Maybe he was imagining himself in Portugal. The TV was showing another cathedral now. This one was in Germany. The Englishman's voice droned on. "Cathedrals," the blind man said. He sat up and rolled his head back and forth. "If you want the truth, bub, that's about all I know. What I just said. What I heard him say. But maybe you could describe one to me? I wish you'd do it. I'd like that. If you want to know, I really don't have a good idea."

I stared hard at the shot of the cathedral on the TV. How could I even begin to describe it? But say my life depended on it. Say my life was being threatened by an insane guy who said I had to do it or else.

I stared some more at the cathedral before the picture flipped off into the countryside. There was no use. I turned to the blind man and said, "To begin with, they're very tall." I was looking around the room for clues. "They reach way up. Up and up. Toward the sky. They're so big, some of them, they have to have these supports. To help hold them up, so to speak. These supports are called buttresses. They remind me of viaducts,° for some reason. But maybe you don't know viaducts, either? Sometimes the cathedrals have devils and such carved into the front. Sometimes lords and ladies. Don't ask me why this is," I said.

He was nodding. The whole upper part of his body seemed to be moving back and forth.

"I'm not doing so good, am I?" I said.   100

He stopped nodding and leaned forward on the edge of the sofa. As he listened to me, he was running his fingers through his beard. I wasn't getting through to him, I could see that. But he waited for me to go on just the same. He nodded, like he was trying to encourage me. I tried to think what else to say. "They're really big," I said. "They're massive. They're built of stone. Marble, too, sometimes. In those olden days, when they built cathedrals, men wanted to be close to God. In those olden days, God was an important part of everyone's life. You could tell this from their cathedral-building. I'm sorry," I said, "but it looks like that's the best I can do for you. I'm just no good at it."

"That's all right, bub," the blind man said. "Hey, listen. I hope you don't mind my asking you. Can I ask you something? Let me ask you a simple question, yes or no. I'm just curious and there's no offense. You're my host. But let me ask if you are in any way religious? You don't mind my asking?"

I shook my head. He couldn't see that, though. A wink is the same as a nod to a blind man. "I guess I don't believe in it. In anything. Sometimes it's hard. You know what I'm saying?"

"Sure, I do," he said.

"Right," I said.   105

---

viaducts: Long, elevated roadways.

The Englishman was still holding forth. My wife sighed in her sleep. She drew a long breath and went on with her sleeping.

"You'll have to forgive me," I said. "But I can't tell you what a cathedral looks like. It just isn't in me to do it. I can't do any more than I've done."

The blind man sat very still, his head down, as he listened to me.

I said, "The truth is, cathedrals don't mean anything special to me. Nothing. Cathedrals. They're something to look at on late-night TV. That's all they are."

110   It was then that the blind man cleared his throat. He brought something up. He took a handkerchief from his back pocket. Then he said, "I get it, bub. It's okay. It happens. Don't worry about it," he said. "Hey, listen to me. Will you do me a favor? I got an idea. Why don't you find us some heavy paper? And a pen. We'll do something. We'll draw one together. Get us a pen and some heavy paper. Go on, bub, get the stuff," he said.

So I went upstairs. My legs felt like they didn't have any strength in them. They felt like they did after I'd done some running. In my wife's room, I looked around. I found some ballpoints in a little basket on her table. And then I tried to think where to look for the kind of paper he was talking about.

Downstairs, in the kitchen, I found a shopping bag with onion skins in the bottom of the bag. I emptied the bag and shook it. I brought it into the living room and sat down with it near his legs. I moved some things, smoothed the wrinkles from the bag, spread it out on the coffee table.

The blind man got down from the sofa and sat next to me on the carpet.

He ran his fingers over the paper. He went up and down the sides of the paper. The edges, even the edges. He fingered the corners.

115   "All right," he said. "All right, let's do her."

He found my hand, the hand with the pen. He closed his hand over my hand. "Go ahead, bub, draw," he said. "Draw. You'll see. I'll follow along with you. It'll be okay. Just begin now like I'm telling you. You'll see. Draw," the blind man said.

So I began. First I drew a box that looked like a house. It could have been the house I lived in. Then I put a roof on it. At either end of the roof, I drew spires. Crazy.

"Swell," he said. "Terrific. You're doing fine," he said. "Never thought anything like this could happen in your lifetime, did you, bub? Well, it's a strange life, we all know that. Go on now. Keep it up."

I put in windows with arches. I drew flying buttresses. I hung great doors. I couldn't stop. The TV station went off the air. I put down the pen and closed and opened my fingers. The blind man felt around over the paper. He moved the tips of his fingers over the paper, all over what I had drawn, and he nodded.

120   "Doing fine," the blind man said.

I took up the pen again, and he found my hand. I kept at it. I'm no artist. But I kept drawing just the same.

My wife opened up her eyes and gazed at us. She sat up on the sofa, her robe hanging open. She said, "What are you doing? Tell me, I want to know."

I didn't answer her.

The blind man said, "We're drawing a cathedral. Me and him are working on it. Press hard," he said to me. "That's right. That's good," he said. "Sure. You got it, bub, I can tell. You didn't think you could. But you can, can't you? You're cooking with gas now. You know what I'm saying? We're going to really have us something here in a minute. How's the old arm?" he said. "Put some people in there now. What's a cathedral without people?"

My wife said, "What's going on? Robert, what are you doing? What's going on?" 125

"It's all right," he said to her. "Close your eyes now," the blind man said to me. I did it. I closed them just like he said.

"Are they closed?" he said. "Don't fudge."

"They're closed," I said.

"Keep them that way," he said. He said, "Don't stop now. Draw." 130

So we kept on with it. His fingers rode my fingers as my hand went over the paper. It was like nothing else in my life up to now.

Then he said, "I think that's it. I think you got it," he said. "Take a look. What do you think?"

But I had my eyes closed. I thought I'd keep them that way for a little longer. I thought it was something I ought to do.

"Well?" he said. "Are you looking?"

My eyes were still closed. I was in my house. I knew that. But I didn't feel like 135 I was inside anything.

"It's really something," I said.

Reading and Reacting

1. Who is the narrator? What do we know about him? Why does the impending visit by the blind man disturb him?
2. At several points in the story, the narrator's wife loses patience with him. What causes her displeasure? What do her reactions reveal about the wife? About the narrator?
3. Why did the narrator's wife leave her first husband? What qualities in the narrator might have led his wife to marry him?
4. Why is the narrator's wife so devoted to the blind man? What does she gain from her relationship with him?
5. According to the narrator, his wife never forgot the blind man's running his fingers over her face. Why is this experience so important to her?
6. Toward the end of the story, the blind man asks the narrator to describe a cathedral. Why is the narrator unable to do so? What does his inability to do so reveal about him?
7. Why does the blind man tell the narrator to close his eyes while he is drawing? What does he hope to teach him? What is the narrator able to "see" with his eyes shut that he cannot see with them open?
8. In paragraph 96, the blind man observes that the men who began work on a cathedral never lived to see it completed. In this way, he says, "they're no different from the rest of us." What does the cathedral symbolize to the blind man? What does it come to symbolize to the narrator?

9. What other symbols are present in the story? How do these symbols help to develop the central theme of the story?

10. **JOURNAL ENTRY** The blind man is an old friend of the narrator's wife. Why then does he focus on the narrator? In what way is the narrator's spiritual development the blind man's gift to the narrator's wife?

11. **CRITICAL PERSPECTIVE** Critic Kirk Nesset, in his discussion of "Cathedral," notes that the narrator becomes more open as the story progresses, and that this coming out is mirrored by rhetoric of the story. Early on in the story, the narrator feels momentarily "sorry for the blind man," his insulated hardness beginning to soften. As the walls of his resentment noticeably crack, he watches with "admiration" as Robert eats, recognizing Robert's handicap to be "no impairment to his performance at the dinner table. . . . Like Robert, who is on a journey by train, dropping in on friends and relatives, trying to get over the loss of his wife, the narrator is also on a journey, one signaled by signposts in his language and played out by the events of the story he tells."

Do you agree that the narrator becomes more open? If so, can you cite any other instances where the words he chooses reflect this increasing openness?

Related Works: "Gryphon" (p. 248), "Doe Season" (p. 512), "When I Heard the Learn'd Astronomer" (p. 893), "The Value of Education" (p. 908), "On First Looking into Chapman's Homer" (p. 1002), "Batter My Heart, Three-Personed God" (p. 1168), "God's Grandeur" (p. 1188), "The Gift" (p. 1199)

NATHANIEL HAWTHORNE (1804–1864) was born in Salem, Massachusetts, the great-great-grandson of a judge who presided over the infamous Salem witch trials. After his sea captain father was killed on a voyage when Hawthorne was four years old, his childhood was one of genteel poverty. An uncle paid for his education at Bowdoin College in Maine, where Hawthorne's friends included a future president of the United States, Franklin Pierce, who in 1853 appointed him U.S. consul in Liverpool, England. Hawthorne published four novels — *The Scarlet Letter* (1850), *The House of the Seven Gables* (1851), *The Blithedale Romance* (1852), and *The Marble Faun* (1860) — and more than one hundred short stories and sketches.

Hawthorne referred to his own work as *romance.* He used this term to mean not an escape from reality but rather a method of confronting "the depths of our common nature" and "the truth of the heart." His stories probe the dark side of human nature and frequently paint a world that is virtuous on the surface but (as Young Goodman Brown comes to believe) "one stain of guilt, one mighty blood spot" beneath. Hawthorne's stories often emphasize the ambiguity of human experience. For example, the reader is left to wonder whether Goodman Brown actually saw a witch's coven or dreamed about the event. For Hawthorne, what is important is Brown's recognition that evil may be found everywhere. "Young Goodman Brown," as Hawthorne's neighbor and friend Herman Melville once said, is a tale "as deep as Dante."

Cultural Context During the five months of the Salem witch trials of 1692, nineteen women and men accused of being witches were put to death by hanging. The accusations began when a few young girls claimed they were possessed by the devil and subsequently accused three Salem women of witchcraft. As the hysteria grew throughout Massachusetts, the list of the accused grew as well. Eventually, 150 people were imprisoned before the governor dismissed the special witchcraft court and released the remaining prisoners. It is in this historical setting that "Young Goodman Brown" takes place.

Young Goodman° Brown   (1835)

Young Goodman Brown came forth at sunset, into the street of Salem village, but put his head back, after crossing the threshold, to exchange a parting kiss with his young wife. And Faith, as the wife was aptly named, thrust her own pretty head into the street, letting the wind play with the pink ribbons of her cap, while she called to Goodman Brown.

"Dearest heart," whispered she, softly and rather sadly, when her lips were close to his ear, "prithee, put off your journey until sunrise, and sleep in your own bed to-night. A lone woman is troubled with such dreams and such thoughts, that she's afeard of herself, sometimes. Pray, tarry with me this night, dear husband, of all nights in the year!"

"My love and my Faith," replied young Goodman Brown, "of all nights in the year, this one night must I tarry away from thee. My journey, as thou callest it, forth and back again, must needs be done 'twixt now and sunrise. What, my sweet, pretty wife, dost thou doubt me already, and we but three months married!"

"Then God bless you!" said Faith with the pink ribbons, "and may you find all well, when you come back."

"Amen!" cried Goodman Brown. "Say thy prayers, dear Faith, and go to bed at dusk, and no harm will come to thee."   5

So they parted; and the young man pursued his way, until, being about to turn the corner by the meeting-house, he looked back and saw the head of Faith still peeping after him, with a melancholy air, in spite of her pink ribbons.

"Poor little Faith!" thought he, for his heart smote him. "What a wretch am I, to leave her on such an errand! She talks of dreams, too. Methought, as she spoke, there was trouble in her face, as if a dream had warned her what work is to be done to-night. But no, no! 't would kill her to think it. Well; she's a blessed angel on earth; and after this one night, I'll cling to her skirts and follow her to Heaven."

With this excellent resolve for the future, Goodman Brown felt himself justified in making more haste on his present evil purpose. He had taken a dreary road, darkened by all the gloomiest trees of the forest, which barely stood aside to let the narrow path creep through, and closed immediately behind. It was as

---

Goodman: A form of address, similar to *Mr.*, meaning "husband."

lonely as could be; and there is this peculiarity in such a solitude, that the traveller knows not who may be concealed by the innumerable trunks and the thick boughs overhead; so that, with lonely footsteps, he may yet be passing through an unseen multitude.

"There may be a devilish Indian behind every tree," said Goodman Brown to himself; and he glanced fearfully behind him, as he added, "What if the devil himself should be at my very elbow!"

10   His head being turned back, he passed a crook of the road, and looking forward again, beheld the figure of a man, in grave and decent attire, seated at the foot of an old tree. He arose at Goodman Brown's approach, and walked onward, side by side with him.

"You are late, Goodman Brown," said he. "The clock of the Old South° was striking, as I came through Boston; and that is full fifteen minutes agone."

"Faith kept me back awhile," replied the young man, with a tremor in his voice, caused by the sudden appearance of his companion, though not wholly unexpected.

It was now deep dusk in the forest, and deepest in that part of it where these two were journeying. As nearly as could be discerned, the second traveller was about fifty years old, apparently in the same rank of life as Goodman Brown, and bearing a considerable resemblance to him, though perhaps more in expression than features. Still, they might have been taken for father and son. And yet, though the elder person was as simply clad as the younger, and as simple in manner too, he had an indescribable air of one who knew the world, and would not have felt abashed at the governor's dinner-table, or in King William's court,° were it possible that his affairs should call him thither. But the only thing about him that could be fixed upon as remarkable, was his staff, which bore the likeness of a great black snake, so curiously wrought, that it might almost be seen to twist and wriggle itself like a living serpent. This, of course, must have been an ocular deception, assisted by the uncertain light.

"Come, Goodman Brown!" cried his fellow-traveller, "this is a dull pace for the beginning of a journey. Take my staff, if you are so soon weary."

15   "Friend," said the other, exchanging his slow pace for a full stop, "having kept covenant by meeting thee here, it is my purpose now to return whence I came. I have scruples, touching the matter thou wot'st of."

"Sayest thou so?" replied he of the serpent, smiling apart. "Let us walk on, nevertheless, reasoning as we go, and if I convince thee not, thou shalt turn back. We are but a little way in the forest, yet."

"Too far, too far!" exclaimed the goodman, unconsciously resuming his walk. "My father never went into the woods on such an errand, nor his father before him. We have been a race of honest men and good Christians, since the days of the martyrs. And shall I be the first of the name of Brown that ever took this path and kept —"

Old South: Old South Church in Boston, renowned meeting place for American patriots during the Revolution.
King William: William III, king of England from 1689 to 1702.

"Such company, thou wouldst say," observed the elder person, interrupting his pause. "Well said, Goodman Brown! I have been as well acquainted with your family as with ever a one among the Puritans; and that's no trifle to say. I helped your grandfather, the constable, when he lashed the Quaker woman so smartly through the streets of Salem. And it was I that brought your father a pitch-pine knot, kindled at my own hearth, to set fire to an Indian village, in King Philip's war.° They were my good friends, both; and many a pleasant walk have we had along this path, and returned merrily after midnight. I would fain be friends with you, for their sake."

"If it be as thou sayest," replied Goodman Brown, "I marvel they never spoke of these matters. Or, verily, I marvel not, seeing that the least rumor of the sort would have driven them from New England. We are a people of prayer, and good works to boot, and abide no such wickedness."

"Wickedness or not," said the traveller with the twisted staff, "I have a very general acquaintance here in New England. The deacons of many a church have drunk the communion wine with me; the selectmen, of divers towns, make me their chairman; and a majority of the Great and General Court are firm supporters of my interest. The governor and I, too — but these are state secrets." 20

"Can this be so!" cried Goodman Brown, with a stare of amazement at his undisturbed companion. "Howbeit, I have nothing to do with the governor and council; they have their own ways, and are no rule for a simple husbandman like me. But, were I to go on with thee, how should I meet the eye of that good old man, our minister, at Salem village? Oh, his voice would make me tremble, both Sabbath-day and lecture-day!"°

Thus far, the elder traveller had listened with due gravity, but now burst into a fit of irrepressible mirth, shaking himself so violently, that his snakelike staff actually seemed to wriggle in sympathy.

"Ha, ha, ha!" shouted he, again and again; then composing himself, "Well, go on, Goodman Brown, go on; but, prithee, don't kill me with laughing!"

"Well, then, to end the matter at once," said Goodman Brown, considerably nettled, "there is my wife, Faith. It would break her dear little heart; and I'd rather break my own!"

"Nay, if that be the case," answered the other, "e'en go thy ways, Goodman Brown. I would not, for twenty old women like the one hobbling before us, that Faith should come to any harm." 25

As he spoke, he pointed his staff at a female figure on the path, in whom Goodman Brown recognized a very pious and exemplary dame, who had taught him his catechism in youth, and was still his moral and spiritual adviser, jointly with the minister and Deacon Gookin.

King Philip's war: A war of Indian resistance led by Metacomet of the Wampanoags, known to the English as "King Philip." The war, intended to halt expansion of English settlers in Massachusetts, collapsed after Metacomet's death in August 1676.

lecture-day: The day of the midweek sermon, usually Thursday.

"A marvel, truly, that Goody° Cloyse should be so far in the wilderness, at nightfall!" said he. "But, with your leave, friend, I shall take a cut through the woods, until we have left this Christian woman behind. Being a stranger to you, she might ask whom I was consorting with, and whither I was going."

"Be it so," said his fellow-traveller. "Betake you to the woods, and let me keep the path."

Accordingly, the young man turned aside, but took care to watch his companion, who advanced softly along the road, until he had come within a staff's length of the old dame. She, meanwhile, was making the best of her way, with singular speed for so aged a woman, and mumbling some indistinct words, a prayer, doubtless, as she went. The traveller put forth his staff, and touched her withered neck with what seemed the serpent's tail.

30 "The devil!" screamed the pious old lady.

"Then Goody Cloyse knows her old friend?" observed the traveller, confronting her, and leaning on his writhing stick.

"Ah, forsooth, and is it your worship, indeed?" cried the good dame. "Yea, truly is it, and in the very image of my old gossip, Goodman Brown, the grandfather of the silly fellow that now is. But, would your worship believe it? my broomstick hath strangely disappeared, stolen, as I suspect, by that unhanged witch, Goody Cory, and that, too, when I was all anointed with the juice of smallage and cinque-foil and wolf's bane —"°

"Mingled with fine wheat and the fat of a new-born babe," said the shape of old Goodman Brown.

"Ah, your worship knows the recipe," cried the old lady, cackling aloud. "So, as I was saying, being all ready for the meeting, and no horse to ride on, I made up my mind to foot it; for they tell me there is a nice young man to be taken into communion to-night. But now your good worship will lend me your arm, and we shall be there in a twinkling."

35 "That can hardly be," answered her friend. "I may not spare you my arm, Goody Cloyse, but here is my staff, if you will."

So saying, he threw it down at her feet, where, perhaps, it assumed life, being one of the rods which its owner had formerly lent to the Egyptian Magi. Of this fact, however, Goodman Brown could not take cognizance. He had cast his eyes in astonishment, and looking down again, beheld neither Goody Cloyse nor the serpentine staff, but his fellow-traveller alone, who waited for him as calmly as if nothing had happened.

"That old woman taught me my catechism!" said the young man; and there was a world of meaning in this simple comment.

They continued to walk onward, while the elder traveller exhorted his companion to make good speed and persevere in the path, discoursing so aptly, that his

---

Goody: A contraction of "Goodwife," a term of politeness used in addressing a woman of humble station. Goody Cloyse, like Goody Cory and Martha Carrier, who appear later in the story, was one of the Salem "witches" sentenced in 1692.

smallage . . . wolf's bane: Plants believed to have magical powers. Smallage is wild celery.

arguments seemed rather to spring up in the bosom of his auditor, than to be suggested by himself. As they went he plucked a branch of maple, to serve for a walking-stick, and began to strip it of the twigs and little boughs, which were wet with evening dew. The moment his fingers touched them, they became strangely withered and dried up, as with a week's sunshine. Thus the pair proceeded, at a good free pace, until suddenly, in a gloomy hollow of the road, Goodman Brown sat himself down on the stump of a tree, and refused to go any farther.

"Friend," said he, stubbornly, "my mind is made up. Not another step will I budge on this errand. What if a wretched old woman do choose to go to the devil, when I thought she was going to Heaven! Is that any reason why I should quit my dear Faith, and go after her?"

"You will think better of this by and by," said his acquaintance, composedly. 40 "Sit here and rest yourself awhile; and when you feel like moving again, there is my staff to help you along."

Without more words, he threw his companion the maple stick, and was as speedily out of sight as if he had vanished into the deepening gloom. The young man sat a few moments by the roadside, applauding himself greatly, and thinking with how clear a conscience he should meet the minister, in his morning walk, nor shrink from the eye of good old Deacon Gookin. And what calm sleep would be his, that very night, which was to have been spent so wickedly, but purely and sweetly now, in the arms of Faith! Amidst these pleasant and praiseworthy meditations, Goodman Brown heard the tramp of horses along the road, and deemed it advisable to conceal himself within the verge of the forest, conscious of the guilty purpose that had brought him thither, though now so happily turned from it.

On came the hoof-tramps and the voices of the riders, two grave old voices, conversing soberly as they drew near. These mingled sounds appeared to pass along the road, within a few yards of the young man's hiding-place; but owing, doubtless, to the depth of the gloom, at that particular spot, neither the travellers nor their steeds were visible. Though their figures brushed the small boughs by the wayside, it could not be seen that they intercepted, even for a moment, the faint gleam from the strip of bright sky, athwart which they must have passed. Goodman Brown alternately crouched and stood on tiptoe, pulling aside the branches, and thrusting forth his head as far as he durst, without discerning so much as a shadow. It vexed him the more, because he could have sworn, were such a thing possible, that he recognized the voices of the minister and Deacon Gookin, jogging along quietly, as they were wont to do, when bound to some ordination or ecclesiastical council. While yet within hearing, one of the riders stopped to pluck a switch.

"Of the two, reverend Sir," said the voice like the deacon's, "I had rather miss an ordination dinner than to-night's meeting. They tell me that some of our community are to be here from Falmouth and beyond, and others from Connecticut and Rhode Island; besides several of the Indian powwows, who, after their fashion, know almost as much deviltry as the best of us. Moreover, there is a goodly young woman to be taken into communion."

"Mighty well, Deacon Gookin!" replied the solemn old tones of the minister. "Spur up, or we shall be late. Nothing can be done, you know, until I get on the ground."

45   The hoofs clattered again, and the voices, talking so strangely in the empty air, passed on through the forest, where no church had ever been gathered, nor solitary Christian prayed. Whither, then, could these holy men be journeying, so deep into the heathen wilderness? Young Goodman Brown caught hold of a tree, for support, being ready to sink down on the ground, faint and over-burthened with the heavy sickness of his heart. He looked up to the sky, doubting whether there really was a Heaven above him. Yet, there was the blue arch, and the stars brightening in it.

"With Heaven above, and Faith below, I will yet stand firm against the devil!" cried Goodman Brown.

While he still gazed upward, into the deep arch of the firmament, and had lifted his hands to pray, a cloud, though no wind was stirring, hurried across the zenith, and hid the brightening stars. The blue sky was still visible, except directly overhead, where this black mass of cloud was sweeping swiftly northward. Aloft in the air, as if from the depths of the cloud, came a confused and doubtful sound of voices. Once, the listener fancied that he could distinguish the accents of townspeople of his own, men and women, both pious and ungodly, many of whom he had met at the communion-table, and had seen others rioting at the tavern. The next moment, so indistinct were the sounds, he doubted whether he had heard aught but the murmur of the old forest, whispering without a wind. Then came a stronger swell of those familiar tones, heard daily in the sunshine, at Salem village, but never, until now, from a cloud at night. There was one voice, of a young woman, uttering lamentations, yet with an uncertain sorrow, and en-treating for some favor, which, perhaps, it would grieve her to obtain. And all the unseen multitude, both saints and sinners, seemed to encourage her onward.

"Faith!" shouted Goodman Brown, in a voice of agony and desperation; and the echoes of the forest mocked him, crying — "Faith! Faith!" as if bewildered wretches were seeking her, all through the wilderness.

The cry of grief, rage, and terror was yet piercing the night, when the unhappy husband held his breath for a response. There was a scream, drowned immediately in a louder murmur of voices fading into far-off laughter, as the dark cloud swept away, leaving the clear and silent sky above Goodman Brown. But something flut-tered lightly down through the air, and caught on the branch of a tree. The young man seized it and beheld a pink ribbon.

50   "My Faith is gone!" cried he, after one stupefied moment. "There is no good on earth, and sin is but a name. Come, devil! for to thee is this world given."

And maddened with despair, so that he laughed loud and long, did Goodman Brown grasp his staff and set forth again, at such a rate, that he seemed to fly along the forest path, rather than to walk or run. The road grew wilder and drearier, and more faintly traced, and vanished at length, leaving him in the heart of the dark wilderness, still rushing onward, with the instinct that guides mortal man to evil. The whole forest was peopled with frightful sounds: the creaking of the trees, the howling of wild beasts, and the yell of Indians; while, sometimes, the wind tolled like a distant church bell, and sometimes gave a broad roar around the traveller, as if all Nature was laughing him to scorn. But he was himself the chief horror of the scene, and shrank not from its other horrors.

"Ha! ha! ha!" roared Goodman Brown, when the wind laughed at him. "Let us hear which will laugh loudest! Think not to frighten me with your deviltry! Come witch, come wizard, come Indian powwow, come devil himself! and here comes Goodman Brown. You may as well fear him as he fear you!"

In truth, all through the haunted forest, there could be nothing more frightful than the figure of Goodman Brown. On he flew, among the black pines, brandishing his staff with frenzied gestures, now giving vent to an inspiration of horrid blasphemy, and now shouting forth such laughter, as set all the echoes of the forest laughing like demons around him. The fiend in his own shape is less hideous, than when he rages in the breast of man. Thus sped the demoniac on his course, until, quivering among the trees, he saw a red light before him, as when the felled trunks and branches of a clearing have been set on fire, and throw up their lurid blaze against the sky, at the hour of midnight. He paused, in a lull of the tempest that had driven him onward, and heard the swell of what seemed a hymn, rolling solemnly from a distance, with the weight of many voices. He knew the tune. It was a familiar one in the choir of the village meeting-house. The verse died heavily away, and was lengthened by a chorus, not of human voices, but of all the sounds of the benighted wilderness, pealing in awful harmony together. Goodman Brown cried out; and his cry was lost to his own ear, by its unison with the cry of the desert.

In the interval of silence, he stole forward, until the light glared full upon his eyes. At one extremity of an open space, hemmed in by the dark wall of the forest, arose a rock, bearing some rude, natural resemblance either to an altar or a pulpit, and surrounded by four blazing pines, their tops aflame, their stems untouched, like candles at an evening meeting. The mass of foliage, that had overgrown the summit of the rock, was all on fire, blazing high into the night, and fitfully illuminating the whole field. Each pendent twig and leafy festoon was in a blaze. As the red light arose and fell, a numerous congregation alternately shone forth, then disappeared in shadow, and again grew, as it were, out of the darkness, peopling the heart of the solitary woods at once.

"A grave and dark-clad company!" quoth Goodman Brown.

55

In truth, they were such. Among them, quivering to-and-fro, between gloom and splendor, appeared faces that would be seen, next day, at the council-board of the province, and others which, Sabbath after Sabbath, looked devoutly heavenward, and benignantly over the crowded pews, from the holiest pulpits in the land. Some affirm, that the lady of the governor was there. At least, there were high dames well known to her, and wives of honored husbands, and widows a great multitude, and ancient maidens, all of excellent repute, and fair young girls, who trembled lest their mothers should espy them. Either the sudden gleams of light, flashing over the obscure field, bedazzled Goodman Brown, or he recognized a score of the church members of Salem village, famous for their especial sanctity. Good old Deacon Gookin had arrived, and waited at the skirts of that venerable saint, his reverend pastor. But, irreverently consorting with these grave, reputable, and pious people, these elders of the church, these chaste dames and dewy virgins, there were men of dissolute lives and women of spotted fame, wretches given over to all mean and filthy vice, and suspected even of horrid crimes. It was strange to see, that the good shrank not from the wicked, nor were the sinners abashed by the saints. Scattered, also, among their pale-faced enemies, were the Indian priests, or powwows, who had often scared their native forest with more hideous incantations than any known to English witchcraft.

"But, where is Faith?" thought Goodman Brown; and, as hope came into his heart, he trembled.

Another verse of the hymn arose, a slow and mournful strain, such as the pious love, but joined to words which expressed all that our nature can conceive of sin, and darkly hinted at far more. Unfathomable to mere mortals is the lore of fiends. Verse after verse was sung, and still the chorus of the desert swelled between, like the deepest tone of a mighty organ. And, with the final peal of that dreadful anthem, there came a sound, as if the roaring wind, the rushing streams, the howling beasts, and every other voice of the unconverted wilderness were mingling and according with the voice of guilty man, in homage to the prince of all. The four blazing pines threw up a loftier flame, and obscurely discovered shapes and visages of horror on the smoke-wreaths, above the impious assembly. At the same moment, the fire on the rock shot redly forth, and formed a glowing arch above its base, where now appeared a figure. With reverence be it spoken, the apparition bore no slight similitude, both in garb and manner, to some grave divine of the New England churches.

"Bring forth the converts!" cried a voice, that echoed through the field and rolled into the forest.

60   At the word, Goodman Brown stepped forth from the shadow of the trees, and approached the congregation, with whom he felt a loathful brotherhood, by the sympathy of all that was wicked in his heart. He could have well-nigh sworn, that the shape of his own dead father beckoned him to advance, looking downward from a smoke-wreath, while a woman, with dim features of despair, threw out her hand to warn him back. Was it his mother? But he had no power to retreat one step, nor to resist, even in thought, when the minister and good old Deacon Gookin seized his arms, and led him to the blazing rock. Thither came also the slender form of a veiled female, led between Goody Cloyse, that pious teacher of the catechism, and Martha Carrier, who had received the devil's promise to be queen of hell. A rampant hag was she! And there stood the proselytes, beneath the canopy of fire.

"Welcome, my children," said the dark figure, "to the communion of your race! Ye have found, thus young, your nature and your destiny. My children, look behind you!"

They turned; and flashing forth, as it were, in a sheet of flame, the fiend-worshippers were seen; the smile of welcome gleamed darkly on every visage.

"There," resumed the sable form, "are all whom ye have reverenced from youth. Ye deemed them holier than yourselves, and shrank from your own sin, contrasting it with their lives of righteousness and prayerful aspirations heavenward. Yet, here are they all, in my worshipping assembly! This night it shall be granted you to know their secret deeds; how hoary-bearded elders of the church have whispered wanton words to the young maids of their households; how many a woman, eager for widow's weeds, has given her husband a drink at bedtime, and let him sleep his

last sleep in her bosom; how beardless youths have made haste to inherit their father's wealth; and how fair damsels — blush not, sweet ones! — have dug little
graves in the garden, and bidden me, the sole guest, to an infant's funeral. By the
sympathy of your human hearts for sin, ye shall scent out all the places — whether
in church, bedchamber, street, field, or forest — where crime has been committed,
and shall exult to behold the whole earth one stain of guilt, one mighty blood-spot.
Far more than this! It shall be yours to penetrate, in every bosom, the deep mystery of sin, the fountain of all wicked arts, and which inexhaustibly supplies more
evil impulses than human power — than my power, at its utmost! — can make
manifest in deeds. And now, my children, look upon each other."

They did so; and, by the blaze of the hell-kindled torches, the wretched man beheld his Faith, and the wife her husband, trembling before that unhallowed altar.

"Lo! there ye stand, my children," said the figure, in a deep and solemn tone, 65
almost sad, with its despairing awfulness, as if his once angelic nature could yet
mourn for our miserable race. "Depending upon one another's hearts, ye had still
hoped that virtue were not all a dream! Now are ye undeceived! — Evil is the nature of mankind. Evil must be your only happiness. Welcome, again, my children,
to the communion of your race!"

"Welcome!" repeated the fiend-worshippers, in one cry of despair and triumph.

And there they stood, the only pair, as it seemed, who were yet hesitating on
the verge of wickedness, in this dark world. A basin was hollowed, naturally, in
the rock. Did it contain water, reddened by the lurid light? or was it blood? or, perchance, a liquid flame? Herein did the Shape of Evil dip his hand, and prepare to
lay the mark of baptism upon their foreheads, that they might be partakers of the
mystery of sin, more conscious of the secret guilt of others, both in deed and
thought, than they could now be of their own. The husband cast one look at his
pale wife, and Faith at him. What polluted wretches would the next glance show
them to each other, shuddering alike at what they disclosed and what they saw!

"Faith! Faith!" cried the husband. "Look up to Heaven, and resist the Wicked
One!"

Whether Faith obeyed, he knew not. Hardly had he spoken, when he found
himself amid calm night and solitude, listening to a roar of the wind, which died
heavily away through the forest. He staggered against the rock, and felt it chill
and damp, while a hanging twig, that had been all on fire, besprinkled his cheek
with the coldest dew.

The next morning, young Goodman Brown came slowly into the street of 70
Salem village staring around him like a bewildered man. The good old minister
was taking a walk along the grave-yard, to get an appetite for breakfast and meditate his sermon, and bestowed a blessing, as he passed, on Goodman Brown. He
shrank from the venerable saint, as if to avoid an anathema. Old Deacon Gookin
was at domestic worship, and the holy words of his prayer were heard through the
open window. "What God doth the wizard pray to?" quoth Goodman Brown.
Goody Cloyse, that excellent old Christian, stood in the early sunshine, at her
own lattice, catechising a little girl, who had brought her a pint of morning's milk.
Goodman Brown snatched away the child, as from the grasp of the fiend himself.
Turning the corner by the meeting-house, he spied the head of Faith, with the

pink ribbons, gazing anxiously forth, and bursting into such joy at sight of him that she skipt along the street, and almost kissed her husband before the whole village. But Goodman Brown looked sternly and sadly into her face, and passed on without a greeting.

Had Goodman Brown fallen asleep in the forest, and only dreamed a wild dream of a witch-meeting?

Be it so, if you will. But, alas! it was a dream of evil omen for young Goodman Brown. A stern, a sad, a darkly meditative, a distrustful, if not a desperate man did he become, from the night of that fearful dream. On the Sabbath day, when the congregation were singing a holy psalm, he could not listen, because an anthem of sin rushed loudly upon his ear, and drowned all the blessed strain. When the minister spoke from the pulpit, with power and fervid eloquence, and with his hand on the open Bible, of the sacred truths of our religion, and of saint-like lives and triumphant deaths, and of future bliss or misery unutterable, then did Goodman Brown turn pale, dreading lest the roof should thunder down upon the gray blasphemer and his hearers. Often, awaking suddenly at midnight, he shrank from the bosom of Faith, and at morning or eventide, when the family knelt down at prayer, he scowled, and muttered to himself, and gazed sternly at his wife, and turned away. And when he had lived long, and was borne to his grave, a hoary corpse, followed by Faith, an aged woman, and children and grand-children, a goodly procession, besides neighbors not a few, they carved no hopeful verse upon his tombstone; for his dying hour was gloom.

Reading and Reacting

1. Who is the narrator of "Young Goodman Brown"? What advantages does the narrative point of view give the author?
2. What does young Goodman Brown mean when he says "of all nights in the year, this one night must I tarry away from thee" (par. 3)? What is important about *this* night, and why does Goodman Brown believe he must journey "'twixt now and sunrise"?
3. Is Goodman Brown surprised to encounter the second traveler on the road, or does he seem to expect him? What is the significance of their encounter? What do you make of the fact that the stranger bears a strong resemblance to young Goodman Brown?
4. What sins are the various characters Goodman Brown meets in the woods guilty of committing?
5. "Young Goodman Brown" has two distinct settings: Salem and the woods. What are the differences between these settings? What significance does each setting have in the story?
6. Which figures in the story are allegorical, and which are symbols? On what evidence do you base your conclusions?
7. Why do the people gather in the woods? Why do they attend the ceremony?
8. Explain the change that takes place in young Goodman Brown at the end of the story. Why can he not listen to the singing of holy psalms or to the minister's sermons? What causes him to turn away from Faith and die in gloom?

9. **JOURNAL ENTRY** At the end of the story, the narrator suggests that Good-man Brown might have fallen asleep and imagined his encounter with the witches. Do you think the events in the story are all a dream?

10. **CRITICAL PERSPECTIVE** In *The Power of Blackness*, his classic study of nineteenth-century American writers, Harry Levin observes that Hawthorne had doubts about conventional religion. This, Levin believes, is why all efforts to read an enlightening theological message into Hawthorne's works are "doomed to failure."

   What comment do you think Hawthorne is making in "Young Goodman Brown" about religious faith?

Related Works: "Once upon a Time" (p. 204), "Where Are You Going, Where Have You Been?" (p. 573), "Bartleby, the Scrivener" (p. 731), "We Wear the Mask" (p. 1171), "La Belle Dame sans Merci: A Ballad" (p. 1191), *Nine Ten* (p. 1334)

WRITING SUGGESTIONS: Symbol, Allegory, and Myth

1. Select a story from this anthology, and discuss its use of symbols.

2. Strangers figure prominently in "Young Goodman Brown" and "Cathedral." Write an essay in which you discuss the possible symbolic significance of strangers in each story. If you like, you may also discuss Arnold Friend in "Where Are You Going, Where Have You Been?" (p. 573).

3. Write an essay in which you discuss the use of myth in "Young Goodman Brown."

4. If Shirley Jackson had wished to write "The Lottery" as an allegory whose purpose was to expose the evils of Nazi Germany, what revisions would she have had to make to convey the dangers of blind obedience to authority? Consider the story's symbols, the characters (and their names), and the setting.

5. In literary works, characters' prized possessions can function as symbols. In this chapter, for example, the quilt in "Everyday Use" and the book in "The Book of Sand" take on symbolic significance. Write an essay in which you analyze one of these symbols (or a possession that has symbolic significance in another story), and discuss how it helps to convey the main themes of the story in which it appears.

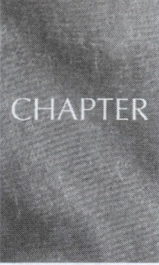

CHAPTER 18

THEME

> The problem I face as a writer is to make my stories mean something.
>
> —Toni Morrison, *Discovering Fiction*

The **theme** of a work of literature is its central or dominant idea. *Theme* is not the same as *plot* or *subject*, two terms with which it is sometimes confused. A summary of the *plot* of Tadeusz Borowski's "Silence," a story about survivors of the Holocaust, could be, "Prisoners are liberated from a concentration camp, and, despite the warnings of the American officer, they kill a captured German guard." The statement "'Silence' is about freed prisoners and a guard" could define the *subject* of the story. A statement of the *theme* of "Silence," however, has to do more than summarize its plot or define its subject; it has to convey the values and ideas expressed by the story.

Many effective stories are complex, expressing more than one theme, and "Silence" is no exception. You could say that "Silence" suggests that human beings have a need for vengeance. You could also say the story demonstrates that silence is sometimes the only response possible when people confront unspeakable horrors. Both these themes — and others — are expressed in the story, yet one theme seems to dominate: the idea that under extreme conditions the oppressed can have the same capacity for evil as their oppressors.

When you write about theme, you need to do more than tell what happens in the story. The theme you identify should be a general idea that extends beyond the story and applies to the world outside fiction. Compare these two statements that a student wrote about Edgar Allan Poe's "The Cask of Amontillado" (p. 350):

```
Poe's "The Cask of Amontillado" is about a man who has an
obsessive desire for revenge.
```

```
Poe's "The Cask of Amontillado" suggests that when the
desire for revenge becomes obsessive, it can deprive
individuals of all that makes them human.
```

The first merely tells what the story is about; the second statement identifies the story's theme, a general observation about humanity.

Granted, some short works (fairy tales or fables, for example) have themes that can only be expressed as **clichés** — overused phrases or expressions — or as

morals—lessons dramatized by the work. The fairy tale "Cinderella," for example, expresses the clichéd theme that a virtuous girl who endures misfortune will eventually achieve her just reward; the fable "The Tortoise and the Hare" illustrates the moral "Slow and steady wins the race." Like "The Cask of Amontillado," however, the stories in this anthology have themes that are more complex than clichés or morals.

Interpreting Themes

Contemporary critical theory holds that the theme of a work of fiction is as much the creation of readers as of the writer. Readers' backgrounds, knowledge, values, and beliefs all play a part in determining the theme or themes they will identify in a work. Most readers, for example, will realize that David Michael Kaplan's story "Doe Season" (p. 512)—in which the main character goes hunting, kills her first deer, and is forced to confront suffering and death—expresses a conventional **initiation theme**, revealing growing up to be a disillusioning and painful process. Still, different readers bring different perspectives to the story and, in some cases, see different themes.

During a classroom discussion of "Doe Season," a student familiar with hunting saw more than his classmates did in the story's conventional initiation theme. He knew that in many states there really is a doe season, which lasts approximately three days. Shorter than the ten-day buck season, it allows hunters to control the size of the deer herd by killing females. This knowledge enabled the student to conclude that by the end of the story the female child's innocence is destroyed, just as the doe is.

Another student pointed out that the participation of Andy—a female who uses a male name—in hunting, a traditional male rite of passage, leads to her killing the deer and to her subsequent disillusionment. It also leads to her decision to abandon her nickname. By contrasting "Andrea" with "Andy," the story reveals the conflict between her "female" nature (illustrated by her compassion) and her desire to emulate the men to whom killing is a sport. This interpretation led the student to conclude that the theme of "Doe Season" is that males and females have very different outlooks on life.

Other students did not accept the negative characterization of the story's male characters that the preceding interpretation implies. They pointed out that the father is a sympathetic figure who is extremely supportive; he encourages and defends his daughter. He takes her hunting because he loves her, not because he wants to initiate her into life or to hurt her. One student mentioned that Andy's reaction (called *buck fever*) when she sees the doe is common in children who kill their first deer. In light of this information, several students concluded that far from being about irreconcilable male and female perspectives, "Doe Season" makes a statement about a young girl who is hunting for her own identity and who in the process discovers her own mortality. Her father is therefore the agent who enables her to confront the inevitability of death, a fact she must accept if she is going to take her place in the adult world. In this sense, the theme of the story is the idea that in order to mature, a child must come to terms with the reality of death.

Different readers may see different themes in a story, but any interpretation of a theme must make sense in light of what is actually in the story. Evidence from the work, not just your own feelings or assumptions, must support your interpretation, and a single symbol or one statement by a character is not enough in itself to reveal a story's theme. Therefore, you must present a cross-section of examples from the text to support your interpretation of the story's theme. If you say that the theme of James Joyce's "Araby" (p. 395) is that an innocent idealist is inevitably doomed to disillusionment, you have to find examples from the text to support this statement. You could begin with the title, concluding that the word *Araby* suggests idealistic dreams of exotic beauty that the boy tries to find when he goes to the bazaar. You could reinforce your interpretation by pointing out that Mangan's unattainable sister is a symbol of all that the boy wants so desperately to find. Finally, you could show how idealism is ultimately crushed by society: at the end of the story, the boy stands alone in the darkness and realizes that his dreams are childish fantasies. Although other readers may have different responses to "Araby," they should find your interpretation reasonable if you support it with enough examples.

Identifying Themes

Every element of a story can shed light on its themes. As you analyze a short story, you should look for features that reveal and reinforce what you perceive to be the story's most important ideas.

- *The **title** can often provide insight into the theme or themes of a story.* The title of an F. Scott Fitzgerald story, "Babylon Revisited," emphasizes a major idea in the story — that Paris of the 1920s is like Babylon, the ancient city the Bible singles out as the epitome of evil and corruption. The story's protagonist, Charlie Wales, comes to realize that no matter how much money he lost after the 1929 stock market crash, he lost more — his wife and his daughter — during the boom, when he was in Paris. Charlie's search through his past — his return to "Babylon" — provides new meaning to his life and offers at least a small bit of hope for the future.

- *Sometimes a **narrator's or character's statement** can reveal a theme.* For example, at the beginning of Alberto Alvaro Ríos's "The Secret Lion" (p. 170), the first-person narrator says, "I was twelve and in junior high school and something happened that we didn't have a name for, but it was there nonetheless like a lion, and roaring, roaring that way the biggest things do. Everything changed." Although the narrator does not directly announce the story's theme, he does suggest that the story will convey the idea that the price children pay for growing up is realizing that everything changes, that nothing stays the way it is.

- *The **arrangement of events** can suggest a story's theme,* as it does in an Ernest Hemingway story, "The Short Happy Life of Francis Macomber." At the beginning of the story, the title character is a coward who is stuck in an unhappy marriage. As the story progresses, he gradually learns the nature of courage and, finally, finds it in himself. At the moment of his triumph, however, Francis is shot by his wife; his "happy life" is short indeed. The way the events of the story are presented, through foreshadowing and flash-backs, reveals the connection between Macomber's marriage and his be-havior as a hunter, and this connection in turn helps to reveal a possible theme: that sometimes courage can be more important than life itself.

- A story's **conflict** can offer clues to its theme. In "Araby," the young boy believes that his society neglects art and beauty and glorifies the mundane. This conflict between the boy's idealism and his world can help readers un-derstand why the boy isolates himself in his room reading books and why he retreats into dreams of idealized love. A major theme of the story — that growing up leads to the loss of youthful idealism — is revealed by this the loss central conflict.

  Similarly, the main character in "The Yellow Wallpaper" (p. 421), a woman who has recently had a baby, is in conflict with the nineteenth-century society in which she lives. She is suffering from "temporary nervous depression," what doctors today recognize as postpartum depression. Fol-lowing the practice of the time, her physician has ordered complete bed rest and has instructed her husband to deprive her of all mental and physi-cal stimulation. This harsh treatment leads the narrator to lose her grasp on reality; eventually, she begins to hallucinate. The central conflict of the story is clearly between the woman and her society, controlled by men. This conflict communicates the theme: that in nineteenth-century Amer-ica, women are controlled not just by their husbands and the male medical establishment, but also by the society they have created.

- The **point of view** of a story can also help shed light on theme. For instance, a writer's use of an unreliable first-person narrator can help to communicate the theme of a story. Thus, Montresor's self-serving first-person account of his crime in "The Cask of Amontillado" — along with his attempts to justify these actions — enables readers to understand the dangers of irrational anger and misplaced ideas about honor. The voice of a third-person narrator can also help to convey a story's theme. For example, the detachment of the narrator in Stephen Crane's Civil War novel *The Red Badge of Courage* reinforces the theme of the novel: that bravery, cowardice, war, and even life itself are in-significant when set beside the indifference of the universe.

- Quite often a story will give names, places, and objects symbolic significance. These **symbols** can not only enrich the story but also help to convey a cen-tral theme. For example, the rocking horse in D. H. Lawrence's "The Rocking-Horse Winner" (p. 525) can be seen as a symbol of the boy's des-perate desire to remain a child. Interpreted in this way, it reinforces the theme that innocence cannot survive when it confronts adult greed and selfishness. Similarly, Hawthorne's "Young Goodman Brown" (p. 489) uses symbols such as the walking stick, the woods, sunset and night, and the vague shadows to develop one of its central themes: that once a person strays from the path of faith, evil is everywhere.

- Finally, **changes in a character** can shed light on the theme or themes of the story. The main character in Charles Baxter's "Gryphon" (p. 248), for example, eventually comes to realize that the "lies" Miss Ferenczi tells may be closer to the truth than the "facts" his teachers present, and his changing attitude toward Miss Ferenczi helps to communicate the story's central theme about the nature of truth.

✔ **CHECKLIST   Writing about Theme**

☐ What is the central theme of the story?

☐ What other themes can you identify?

☐ Does the title of the story suggest a theme?

☐ Does the narrator, or any character, make statements that express or imply a theme?

☐ In what way does the arrangement of events in the story suggest a theme?

☐ In what way does the central conflict of the story suggest a theme?

☐ How does the point of view shed light on the story's central theme?

☐ Do any symbols suggest a theme?

☐ Do any characters in the story change in any significant way? Do these changes convey a particular theme?

☐ Have you clearly identified the story's central theme, rather than just summarized the plot or stated the subject?

☐ Does your statement of the story's central theme make a general observation that has an application beyond the story itself?

EUDORA WELTY (1909–2001) was born and raised in Jackson, Mississippi. After attending the Mississippi College for Women, the University of Wisconsin, and Columbia University (where she studied advertising), she returned to Jackson to pursue her long career as a writer, beginning as a journalist. In 1936, she wrote the first of her many short stories, which are gathered in *Collected Stories* (1980). Welty also wrote several novels, including *Delta Wedding* (1946), *Losing Battles* (1970), and the Pulitzer Prize–winning *The Optimist's Daughter* (1972). Her volume of memoirs, *One Writer's Beginnings* (1984), was a best-seller.

One of the country's most accomplished writers, Welty focused much of her fiction on life in southern towns and villages peopled with dreamers, eccentrics, and close-knit families. Her sharply observed characters are sometimes presented with great humor, sometimes with poignant lyricism, but always with clarity and sympathy. "Of course any writer is in part all of his characters," she observed. "How otherwise would they be known to him, occur to him, become what they are?" In "A Worn Path," Welty creates a particularly memorable character in the tenacious Phoenix Jackson and explores a theme that transcends race and region.

Cultural Context During the 1930s, the years of the Great Depression, poverty and unemployment were widespread but were especially severe in isolated rural areas of the Deep South. For the black population living in this poor and undeveloped region, difficult economic conditions were made worse by the system of segregation that prevented them from voting, receiving a good education, or enjoying the same rights and privileges as their white counterparts. Hoping to improve their situation, many African-American families left the South and moved into northern and midwestern cities where there were better opportunities for education and employment. Others, like the protagonist of this story, remained in the South in an atmosphere of residual racism and oppression.

A Worn Path (1940)

Film Series

DVD
See Ch. 19 for film stills from the DVD version of this story.

It was December — a bright frozen day in the early morning. Far out in the country there was an old Negro woman with her head tied in a red rag, coming along a path through the pinewoods. Her name was Phoenix Jackson. She was very old and small and she walked slowly in the dark pine shadows, moving a little from side to side in her steps, with the balanced heaviness and lightness of a pendulum in a grandfather clock. She carried a thin, small cane made from an umbrella, and with this she kept tapping the frozen earth in front of her. This made a grave and persistent noise in the still air, that seemed meditative like the chirping of a solitary little bird.

She wore a dark striped dress reaching down to her shoe tops, and an equally long apron of bleached sugar sacks, with a full pocket: all neat and tidy, but every time she took a step she might have fallen over her shoelaces, which dragged from her unlaced shoes. She looked straight ahead. Her eyes were blue with age. Her skin had a pattern all its own of numberless branching wrinkles and as though a whole little tree stood in the middle of her forehead, but a golden color ran underneath, and the two knobs of her cheeks were illumined by a yellow burning under the dark. Under the red rag her hair came down on her neck in the frailest of ringlets, still black, and with an odor like copper.

Now and then there was a quivering in the thicket. Old Phoenix said, "Out of my way, all you foxes, owls, beetles, jack rabbits, coons and wild animals! . . . Keep out from under these feet, little bob-whites. . . . Keep the big wild hogs out of my path. Don't let none of those come running my direction. I got a long way." Under her small black-freckled hand her cane, limber as a buggy whip, would switch at the brush as if to rouse up any hiding things.

On she went. The woods were deep and still. The sun made the pine needles almost too bright to look at, up where the wind rocked. The cones dropped as light as feathers. Down in the hollow was the mourning dove — it was not too late for him.

The path ran up a hill. "Seem like there is chains about my feet, time I get this far," she said, in the voice of argument old people keep to use with themselves. "Something always take a hold of me on this hill — pleads I should stay." 5

After she got to the top she turned and gave a full, severe look behind her where she had come. "Up through pines," she said at length. "Now down through oaks."

Her eyes opened their widest, and she started down gently. But before she got to the bottom of the hill a bush caught her dress.

Her fingers were busy and intent, but her skirts were full and long, so that before she could pull them free in one place they were caught in another. It was not possible to allow the dress to tear. "I in the thorny bush," she said. "Thorns, you doing your appointed work. Never want to let folks pass, no sir. Old eyes thought you was a pretty little *green* bush."

Finally, trembling all over, she stood free, and after a moment dared to stoop for her cane.

10   "Sun so high!" she cried, leaning back and looking, while the thick tears went over her eyes. "The time getting all gone here."

At the foot of this hill was a place where a log was laid across the creek.

"Now comes the trial," said Phoenix.

Putting her right foot out, she mounted the log and shut her eyes. Lifting her skirt, leveling her cane fiercely before her, like a festival figure in some parade, she began to march across. Then she opened her eyes and she was safe on the other side.

"I wasn't as old as I thought," she said.

15   But she sat down to rest. She spread her skirts on the bank around her and folded her hands over her knees. Up above her was a tree in a pearly cloud of mistletoe. She did not dare to close her eyes, and when a little boy brought her a plate with a slice of marble-cake on it she spoke to him. "That would be acceptable," she said. But when she went to take it there was just her own hand in the air.

So she left that tree, and had to go through a barbed-wire fence. There she had to creep and crawl, spreading her knees and stretching her fingers like a baby trying to climb the steps. But she talked loudly to herself: she could not let her dress be torn now, so late in the day, and she could not pay for having her arm or her leg sawed off if she got caught fast where she was.

At last she was safe through the fence and risen up out in the clearing. Big dead trees, like black men with one arm, were standing in the purple stalks of the withered cotton field. There sat a buzzard.

"Who you watching?"

In the furrow she made her way along.

20   "Glad this not the season for bulls," she said, looking sideways, "and the good Lord made his snakes to curl up and sleep in the winter. A pleasure I don't see no two-headed snake coming around that tree, where it come once. It took a while to get by him, back in the summer."

She passed through the old cotton and went into a field of dead corn. It whispered and shook and was taller than her head. "Through the maze now," she said, for there was no path.

Then there was something tall, black, and skinny there, moving before her.

At first she took it for a man. It could have been a man dancing in the field. But she stood still and listened, and it did not make a sound. It was as silent as a ghost.

"Ghost," she said sharply, "who be you the ghost of? For I have heard of nary death close by."

But there was no answer — only the ragged dancing in the wind.   25

She shut her eyes, reached out her hand, and touched a sleeve. She found a coat and inside that an emptiness, cold as ice.

"You scarecrow," she said. Her face lighted. "I ought to be shut up for good," she said with laughter. "My senses is gone. I too old. I the oldest people I ever know. Dance, old scarecrow," she said, "while I dancing with you."

She kicked her foot over the furrow, and with mouth drawn down, shook her head once or twice in a little strutting way. Some husks blew down and whirled in streamers about her skirts.

Then she went on, parting her way from side to side with the cane, through the whispering field. At last she came to the end, to a wagon track where the silver grass blew between the red ruts. The quail were walking around like pullets, seeming all dainty and unseen.

"Walk pretty," she said. "This is the easy place. This the easy going."   30

She followed the track, swaying through the quiet bare fields, through the little strings of trees silver in their dead leaves, past cabins silver from weather, with the doors and windows boarded shut, all like old women under a spell sitting there. "I walking in their sleep," she said, nodding her head vigorously.

In a ravine she went where a spring was silently flowing through a hollow log. Old Phoenix bent and drank. "Sweet-gum makes the water sweet," she said, and drank more. "Nobody know who made this well, for it was here when I was born."

The track crossed a swampy part where the moss hung as white as lace from every limb. "Sleep on, alligators, and blow your bubbles." Then the track went into the road.

Deep, deep the road went down between the high green-colored banks. Overhead the live-oaks met, and it was as dark as a cave.

A black dog with a lolling tongue came up out of the weeds by the ditch. She   35
was meditating, and not ready, and when he came at her she only hit him a little with her cane. Over she went in the ditch, like a little puff of milkweed.

Down there, her senses drifted away. A dream visited her, and she reached her hand up, but nothing reached down and gave her a pull. So she lay there and presently went to talking. "Old woman," she said to herself, "that black dog come up out of the weeds to stall you off, and now there he sitting on his fine tail, smiling at you."

A white man finally came along and found her — a hunter, a young man, with his dog on a chain.

"Well, Granny!" he laughed. "What are you doing there?"

"Lying on my back like a June-bug waiting to be turned over, mister," she said, reaching up her hand.

He lifted her up, gave her a swing in the air, and set her down. "Anything   40
broken, Granny?"

"No sir, them old dead weeds is springy enough," said Phoenix, when she had got her breath. "I thank you for your trouble."

"Where do you live, Granny?" he asked, while the two dogs were growling at each other.

"Away back yonder, sir, behind the ridge. You can't even see it from here."

"On your way home?"

45   "No sir, I going to town."

"Why, that's too far! That's as far as I walk when I come out myself, and I get something for my trouble." He patted the stuffed bag he carried, and there hung down a little closed claw. It was one of the bob-whites, with its beak hooked bitterly to show it was dead. "Now you go on home, Granny!"

"I bound to go to town, mister," said Phoenix. "The time come around."

He gave another laugh, filling the whole landscape. "I know you old colored people! Wouldn't miss going to town to see Santa Claus!"

But something held old Phoenix very still. The deep lines in her face went into a fierce and different radiation. Without warning, she had seen with her own eyes a flashing nickel fall out of the man's pocket onto the ground.

50   "How old are you, Granny?" he was saying.

"There is no telling, mister," she said, "no telling."

Then she gave a little cry and clapped her hands and said, "Git on away from here, dog! Look! Look at that dog!" She laughed as if in admiration. "He ain't scared of nobody. He a big black dog." She whispered, "Sic him!"

"Watch me get rid of that cur," said the man. "Sic him, Pete! Sic him!"

Phoenix heard the dogs fighting, and heard the man running and throwing sticks. She even heard a gunshot. But she was slowly bending forward by that time, further and further forward, the lid stretched down over her eyes, as if she were doing this in her sleep. Her chin was lowered almost to her knees. The yellow palm of her hand came out from the fold of her apron. Her fingers slid down and along the ground under the piece of money with the grace and care they would have in lifting an egg from under a setting hen. Then she slowly straightened up, she stood erect, and the nickel was in her apron pocket. A bird flew by. Her lips moved. "God watching me the whole time. I come to stealing."

55   The man came back, and his own dog panted about them. "Well, I scared him off that time," he said, and then he laughed and lifted his gun and pointed it at Phoenix.

She stood straight and faced him.

"Doesn't the gun scare you?" he said, still pointing it.

"No, sir, I seen plenty go off closer by, in my day, and for less than what I done," she said, holding utterly still.

He smiled, and shouldered the gun. "Well, Granny," he said, "you must be a hundred years old, and scared of nothing. I'd give you a dime if I had any money with me. But you take my advice and stay home, and nothing will happen to you."

60   "I bound to go on my way, mister," said Phoenix. She inclined her head in the red rag. Then they went in different directions, but she could hear the gun shooting again and again over the hill.

She walked on. The shadows hung from the oak trees to the road like curtains. Then she smelled wood-smoke, and smelled the river, and she saw a steeple and the cabins on their steep steps. Dozens of little black children whirled around her. There ahead was Natchez shining. Bells were ringing. She walked on.

In the paved city it was Christmas time. There were red and green electric lights strung and crisscrossed everywhere, and all turned on in the daytime. Old Phoenix would have been lost if she had not distrusted her eyesight and depended on her feet to know where to take her.

She paused quietly on the sidewalk where people were passing by. A lady came along in the crowd, carrying an armful of red-, green- and silver-wrapped presents; she gave off perfume like the red roses in hot summer, and Phoenix stopped her.

"Please, missy, will you lace up my shoe?" She held up her foot.

"What do you want, Grandma?"   65

"See my shoe," said Phoenix. "Do all right for out in the country, but wouldn't look right to go in a big building."

"Stand still then, Grandma," said the lady. She put her packages down on the sidewalk beside her and laced and tied both shoes tightly.

"Can't lace 'em with a cane," said Phoenix. "Thank you, missy. I doesn't mind asking a nice lady to tie up my shoe, when I gets out on the street."

Moving slowly and from side to side, she went into the big building, and into a tower of steps, where she walked up and around and around until her feet knew to stop.

She entered a door, and there she saw nailed up on the wall the document that   70
had been stamped with the gold seal and framed in the gold frame, which matched the dream that was hung up in her head.

"Here I be," she said. There was a fixed and ceremonial stiffness over her body.

"A charity case, I suppose," said an attendant who sat at the desk before her.

But Phoenix only looked above her head. There was sweat on her face, the wrinkles in her face shone like a bright net.

"Speak up, Grandma," the woman said. "What's your name? We must have your history, you know. Have you been here before? What seems to be the trouble with you?"

Old Phoenix only gave a twitch to her face as if a fly were bothering her.   75

"Are you deaf?" cried the attendant.

But then the nurse came in.

"Oh, that's just old Aunt Phoenix," she said. "She doesn't come for herself — she has a little grandson. She makes these trips just as regular as clockwork. She lives away back off the Old Natchez Trace." She bent down. "Well, Aunt Phoenix, why don't you just take a seat? We won't keep you standing after your long trip." She pointed.

The old woman sat down, bolt upright in the chair.   80

"Now, how is the boy?" asked the nurse.

Old Phoenix did not speak.

"I said, how is the boy?"

But Phoenix only waited and stared straight ahead, her face very solemn and withdrawn into rigidity.

"Is his throat any better?" asked the nurse. "Aunt Phoenix, don't you hear me? Is your grandson's throat any better since the last time you came for the medicine?"

With her hands on her knees, the old woman waited, silent, erect and   85
motionless, just as if she were in armor.

"You mustn't take up our time this way, Aunt Phoenix," the nurse said. "Tell us quickly about your grandson, and get it over. He isn't dead, is he?"

At last there came a flicker and then a flame of comprehension across her face, and she spoke.

"My grandson. It was my memory had left me. There I sat and forgot why I made my long trip."

"Forgot?" The nurse frowned. "After you came so far?"

90   Then Phoenix was like an old woman begging a dignified forgiveness for waking up frightened in the night. "I never did go to school, I was too old at the Surrender,"° she said in a soft voice. "I'm an old woman without an education. It was my memory fail me. My little grandson, he is just the same, and I forgot it in the coming."

"Throat never heals, does it?" said the nurse, speaking in a loud, sure voice to old Phoenix. By now she had a card with something written on it, a little list. "Yes. Swallowed lye. When was it?—January — two-three years ago — "

Phoenix spoke unasked now. "No, missy, he not dead, he just the same. Every little while his throat begin to close up again, and he not able to swallow. He not get his breath. He not able to help himself. So the time come around, and I go on another trip for the soothing medicine."

"All right. The doctor said as long as you came to get it, you could have it," said the nurse. "But it's an obstinate case."

"My little grandson, he sit up there in the house all wrapped up, waiting by himself," Phoenix went on. "We is the only two left in the world. He suffer and it don't seem to put him back at all. He got a sweet look. He going to last. He wear a little patch quilt and peep out holding his mouth open like a little bird. I remembers so plain now. I not going to forget him again, no, the whole enduring time. I could tell him from all the others in creation."

95   "All right." The nurse was trying to hush her now. She brought her a bottle of medicine. "Charity," she said, making a check mark in a book.

Old Phoenix held the bottle close to her eyes, and then carefully put it into her pocket.

"I thank you," she said.

"It's Christmas time, Grandma," said the attendant. "Could I give you a few pennies out of my purse?"

"Five pennies is a nickel," said Phoenix stiffly.

100   "Here's a nickel," said the attendant.

Phoenix rose carefully and held out her hand. She received the nickel and then fished the other nickel out of her pocket and laid it beside the new one. She stared at her palm closely, with her head on one side.

Then she gave a tap with her cane on the floor.

"This is what come to me to do," she said. "I going to the store and buy my child a little windmill they sells, made out of paper. He going to find it hard to believe

---

the Surrender: The surrender of General Robert E. Lee to General Ulysses S. Grant at the end of the Civil War, April 9, 1865.

there such a thing in the world. I'll march myself back where he waiting, holding it straight up in this hand."

She lifted her free hand, gave a little nod, turned around, and walked out of the doctor's office. Then her slow step began on the stairs, going down.

Reading and Reacting

1. How does the first paragraph set the scene for the rest of the story? How does it foreshadow the events that will take place later on?
2. Traditionally, a quest is a journey in which a knight overcomes a series of obstacles in order to perform a prescribed feat. In what way is Phoenix's journey a quest? What obstacles does she face? What feat must she perform?
3. Because Phoenix is old, she has trouble seeing. What things does she have difficulty seeing? How do her mistakes shed light on her character? How do they contribute to the impact of the story?
4. What is the major theme of this story? What other themes are expressed?
5. A phoenix is a mythical bird that would live for five hundred years, be consumed by fire, and then rise from its own ashes. In what way is the name of this creature appropriate for the main character of this story?
6. Phoenix is not intimidated by the man with the gun and has no difficulty asking a white woman to tie her shoe. In spite of her nobility of character, however, Phoenix has no qualms about stealing a nickel or taking charity from the doctor. How do you account for this apparent contradiction?
7. How do the various people Phoenix encounters react to her? Do they treat her with respect? With disdain? Why do you think they react the way they do?
8. In paragraph 90, Phoenix says that she is an old woman without an education. Does she nevertheless seem to have any knowledge that the other characters lack?
9. **JOURNAL ENTRY** Could "A Worn Path" be an allegory? If so, what might each of the characters represent?
10. **CRITICAL PERSPECTIVE** Writing about "A Worn Path," Eudora Welty said that the question she was asked most frequently by both students and teachers was whether Phoenix Jackson's grandson was actually dead. Here she attempts to answer this question:

> I had not meant to mystify readers by withholding any fact; it is not a writer's business to tease. The story is told through Phoenix's mind and she undertakes her errand. As the author at one with the character as I tell it, I must assume that the boy is alive. As the reader, you are free to think as you like, of course; the story invites you to believe that no matter what happens, Phoenix for as long as she is able to walk and can hold to her purpose will make her journey.

Do you think Phoenix's grandson is alive or dead? Why?

Related Works: "Miss Brill" (p. 235), "Araby" (p. 395), "Reapers" (p. 930), "The Soul Selects Her Own Society" (p. 1165), "We Wear the Mask" (p. 1171), "The Solitary Reaper" (p. 1243), *The Cuban Swimmer* (p. 1772)

DAVID MICHAEL KAPLAN (1946–   ) is one of a group of American writers who, along with South American writers such as Gabriel García Márquez of Columbia, are called "magic realists." Magic realists work outside of the "hobbits and wizards" borders of traditional fantasy writing, seamlessly interweaving magical elements with detailed, realistically drawn "everyday" settings. These elements, says a reviewer of Kaplan's work, are invoked "to illuminate and underscore heightened moments of reality." The story "Doe Season," which appears in Kaplan's debut collection, *Comfort* (1987), was included in *Best American Short Stories 1985*. Kaplan's first novel, *Skating in the Dark*, was published in 1991, and his craft text, *Revision: A Creative Approach to Writing and Re-writing Fiction*, was published in 1997. Kaplan teaches fiction writing at Loyola University Chicago, where he directs the Creative Writing Program.

Interestingly, the stories in *Comfort* break from classic "first-time author" tradition by sidestepping the autobiographical, young-man-comes-of-age theme. Instead, these stories are about young girls — or young women — coming to grips with parents (present or absent) and with loss and searching for ways to resolve their ambivalence about becoming women. In "Doe Season," Andy's surreal encounter with the doe may be a dream, but the beauty and horror of their meeting will affect the rest of her life.

Cultural Context   When European settlers first came to America, deer roamed freely from coast to coast, and the pioneers hunted them to put meat on the table. Not until the twentieth century did deer hunting become more a sport than a means of survival. Today, deer are hunted in a regulated fashion in order to control their numbers and maintain a balance in their population. Deer hunters seeking "trophy kills" usually hunt male bucks and the value of a buck is determined by the number of "points," or antlers, it has. (Doe season, where hunters are allowed to kill female deer, is usually much shorter than buck season.) Regardless of its contemporary purpose, deer hunting has long been viewed as a coming-of-age ritual for young men — and more recently for young women first entering adulthood, like the protagonist in this story.

Doe Season   (1985)

They were always the same woods, she thought sleepily as they drove through the early morning darkness — deep and immense, covered with yesterday's snowfall, which had frozen overnight. They were the same woods that lay behind her house, *and they stretch all the way to here*, she thought, *for miles and miles, longer than I could walk in a day, or a week even, but they are still the same woods*. The thought made her feel good: it was like thinking of God; it was like thinking of the space between here and the moon; it was like thinking of all the foreign countries from her geography book where even now, Andy knew, people were going to bed, while they — she and her father and Charlie Spoon and Mac, Charlie's eleven-year-old son — were driving deeper into the Pennsylvania countryside, to go hunting.

They had risen long before dawn. Her mother, yawning and not trying to hide her sleepiness, cooked them eggs and French toast. Her father smoked a cigarette and flicked ashes into his saucer while Andy listened, wondering *Why doesn't he come?* and *Won't he ever come?* until at last a car pulled into the graveled drive and honked. "That will be Charlie Spoon," her father said; he always said "Charlie Spoon," even though his real name was Spreun, because Charlie was, in a sense, shaped like a spoon, with a large head and a narrow waist and chest.

Andy's mother kissed her and her father and said, "Well, have a good time" and "Be careful." Soon they were outside in the bitter dark, loading gear by the back-porch light, their breath steaming. The woods behind the house were then only a black streak against the wash of night.

Andy dozed in the car and woke to find that it was half light. Mac — also sleeping — had slid against her. She pushed him away and looked out the window. Her breath clouded the glass, and she was cold; the car's heater didn't work right. They were riding over gentle hills, the woods on both sides now — the same woods, she knew, because she had been watching the whole way, even while she slept. They had been in her dreams, and she had never lost sight of them.

Charlie Spoon was driving. "I don't understand why she's coming," he said to 5 her father. "How old is she anyway — eight?"

"Nine," her father replied. "She's small for her age."

"So — nine. What's the difference? She'll just add to the noise and get tired besides."

"No, she won't," her father said. "She can walk me to death. And she'll bring good luck, you'll see. Animals — I don't know how she does it, but they come right up to her. We go walking in the woods, and we'll spot more raccoons and possums and such than I ever see when I'm alone."

Charlie grunted.

"Besides, she's not a bad little shot, even if she doesn't hunt yet. She shoots 10 the .22 real good."

"Popgun," Charlie said, and snorted. "And target shooting ain't deer hunting."

"Well, she's not gonna be shooting anyway, Charlie," her father said. "Don't worry. She'll be no bother."

"I still don't know why she's coming," Charlie said.

"Because she wants to, and I want her to. Just like you and Mac. No difference."

Charlie turned onto a side road and after a mile or so slowed down. "That's it!" 15 he cried. He stopped, backed up, and entered a narrow dirt road almost hidden by trees. Five hundred yards down, the road ran parallel to a fenced-in field. Charlie parked in a cleared area deeply rutted by frozen tractor tracks. The gate was locked. *In the spring,* Andy thought, *there will be cows here, and a dog that chases them,* but now the field was unmarked and bare.

"This is it," Charlie Spoon declared. "Me and Mac was up here just two weeks ago, scouting it out, and there's deer. Mac saw the tracks."

"That's right," Mac said.

"Well, we'll just see about that," her father said, putting on his gloves. He turned to Andy. "How you doing, honeybun?"

"Just fine," she said.

Andy shivered and stamped as they unloaded: first the rifles, which they un- 20 sheathed and checked, sliding the bolts, sighting through scopes, adjusting the slings; then the gear, their food and tents and sleeping bags and stove stored in four backpacks — three big ones for Charlie Spoon and her father and Mac, and a day pack for her.

"That's about your size," Mac said, to tease her.

She reddened and said, "Mac, I can carry a pack big as yours any day." He laughed and pressed his knee against the back of hers, so that her leg buckled. "Cut it out," she said. She wanted to make an iceball and throw it at him, but she knew that her father and Charlie were anxious to get going, and she didn't want to displease them.

Mac slid under the gate, and they handed the packs over to him. Then they slid under and began walking across the field toward the same woods that ran all the way back to her home, where even now her mother was probably rising again to wash their breakfast dishes and make herself a fresh pot of coffee. *She is there, and we are here:* the thought satisfied Andy. There was no place else she would rather be.

Mac came up beside her. "Over there's Canada," he said, nodding toward the woods.

25 "Huh!" she said. "Not likely."

"I don't mean *right* over there. I mean farther up north. You think I'm dumb?"

Dumb as your father, she thought.

"Look at that," Mac said, pointing to a piece of cow dung lying on a spot scraped bare of snow. "A frozen meadow muffin." He picked it up and sailed it at her. "Catch!"

"Mac!" she yelled. His laugh was as gawky as he was. She walked faster. He seemed different today somehow, bundled in his yellow-and-black-checkered coat, a rifle in hand, his silly floppy hat not quite covering his ears. They all seemed different as she watched them trudge through the snow — Mac and her father and Charlie Spoon — bigger, maybe, as if the cold landscape enlarged rather than diminished them, so that they, the only figures in that landscape, took on size and meaning just by being there. If they weren't there, everything would be quieter, and the woods would be the same as before. *But they are here,* Andy thought, looking behind her at the boot prints in the snow, *and I am too, and so it's all different.*

30 "We'll go down to the cut where we found those deer tracks," Charlie said as they entered the woods. "Maybe we'll get lucky and get a late one coming through."

The woods descended into a gully. The snow was softer and deeper here, so that often Andy sank to her knees. Charlie and Mac worked the top of the gully while she and her father walked along the base some thirty yards behind them. "If they miss the first shot, we'll get the second," her father said, and she nodded as if she had known this all the time. She listened to the crunch of their boots, their breathing, and the drumming of a distant woodpecker. And the crackling. In winter the woods crackled as if everything were straining, ready to snap like dried chicken bones.

We are hunting, Andy thought. The cold air burned her nostrils.

They stopped to make lunch by a rock outcropping that protected them from the wind. Her father heated the bean soup her mother had made for them, and they ate it with bread already stiff from the cold. He and Charlie took a few pulls from a flask of Jim Beam while she scoured the plates with snow and repacked them. Then they all had coffee with sugar and powdered milk, and her father poured her a cup too. "We won't tell your momma," he said, and Mac laughed. Andy held the cup the way her father did, not by the handle but around the rim. The coffee tasted smoky. She felt a little queasy, but she drank it all.

Charlie Spoon picked his teeth with a fingernail. "Now, you might've noticed one thing," he said.

"What's that?" her father asked.   35

"You might've noticed you don't hear no rifles. That's because there ain't no other hunters here. We've got the whole damn woods to ourselves. Now, I ask you — do I know how to find 'em?"

"We haven't seen deer yet, neither."

"Oh, we will," Charlie said, "but not for a while now." He leaned back against the rock. "Deer're sleeping, resting up for the evening feed."

"I seen a deer behind our house once, and it was afternoon," Andy said.

"Yeah, honey, but that was *before* deer season," Charlie said, grinning. "They   40
know something now. They're smart that way."

"That's right," Mac said.

Andy looked at her father — had she said something stupid?

"Well, Charlie," he said, "if they know so much, how come so many get them-selves shot?"

"Them's the ones that don't *believe* what they know," Charlie replied. The men laughed. Andy hesitated, and then laughed with them.

They moved on, as much to keep warm as to find a deer. The wind became   45
even stronger. Blowing through the treetops, it sounded like the ocean, and once Andy thought she could smell salt air. But that was impossible; the ocean was *hundreds* of miles away, farther than Canada even. She and her parents had gone last summer to stay for a week at a motel on the New Jersey shore. That was the first time she'd seen the ocean, and it frightened her. It was huge and empty, yet always moving. Everything lay hidden. If you walked in it, you couldn't see how deep it was or what might be below; if you swam, something could pull you under and you'd never be seen again. Its musky, rank smell made her think of things dy-ing. Her mother had floated beyond the breakers, calling to her to come in, but Andy wouldn't go farther than a few feet into the surf. Her mother swam and splashed with animal-like delight while her father, smiling shyly, held his white arms above the waist-deep water as if afraid to get them wet. Once a comber rolled over and sent them both tossing, and when her mother tried to stand up, the surf receding behind, Andy saw that her mother's swimsuit top had come off, so that her breasts swayed free, her nipples like two dark eyes. Embarrassed, Andy looked around: except for two women under a yellow umbrella farther up, the beach was empty. Her mother stood up unsteadily, regained her footing. Taking what seemed the longest time, she calmly refixed her top. Andy lay on the beach towel and closed her eyes. The sound of the surf made her head ache.

And now it was winter; the sky was already dimming, not just with the absence of light but with a mist that clung to the hunters' faces like cobwebs. They made camp early. Andy was chilled. When she stood still, she kept wiggling her toes to make sure they were there. Her father rubbed her arms and held her to him briefly, and that felt better. She unpacked the food while the others put up the tents.

"How about rounding us up some firewood, Mac?" Charlie asked.

"I'll do it," Andy said. Charlie looked at her thoughtfully and then handed her the canvas carrier.

There wasn't much wood on the ground, so it took her a while to get a good load. She was about a hundred yards from camp, near a cluster of high, lichen-covered boulders, when she saw through a crack in the rock a buck and two does walking gingerly, almost daintily, through the alder trees. She tried to hush her breathing as they passed not more than twenty yards away. There was nothing she could do. If she yelled, they'd be gone; by the time she got back to camp, they'd be gone. The buck stopped, nostrils quivering, tail up and alert. He looked di-rectly at her. Still she didn't move, not one muscle. He was a beautiful buck, the color of late-turned maple leaves. Unafraid, he lowered his tail, and he and his does silently merged into the trees. Andy walked back to camp and dropped the firewood.

50   "I saw three deer," she said. "A buck and two does."

"Where?" Charlie Spoon cried, looking behind her as if they might have fol-lowed her into camp.

"In the woods yonder. They're gone now."

"Well, hell!" Charlie banged his coffee cup against his knee.

"Didn't I say she could find animals?" her father said, grinning.

55   "Too late to go after them," Charlie muttered. "It'll be dark in a quarter hour. Damn!"

"Damn," Mac echoed.

"They just walk right up to her," her father said.

"Well, leastwise this proves there's deer here." Charlie began snapping long branches into shorter ones. "You know, I think I'll stick with you," he told Andy, "since you're so good at finding deer and all. How'd that be?"

"Okay, I guess," Andy murmured. She hoped he was kidding; no way did she want to hunt with Charlie Spoon. Still, she was pleased he had said it.

60   Her father and Charlie took one tent, she and Mac the other. When they were in their sleeping bags, Mac said in the darkness, "I bet you really didn't see no deer, did you?"

She sighed. "I did, Mac. Why would I lie?"

"How big was the buck?"

"Four point. I counted."

Mac snorted.

65   "You just believe what you want, Mac," she said testily.

"Too bad it ain't buck season," he said. "Well, I got to go pee."

"So pee."

She heard him turn in his bag. "You ever see it?" he asked.

"It? What's 'it'?"

"It. A pecker."

70   "Sure," she lied.

"Whose? Your father's?"

She was uncomfortable. "No," she said.

"Well, whose then?"

"Oh I don't know! Leave me be, why don't you?"

"Didn't see a deer, didn't see a pecker," Mac said teasingly.

She didn't answer right away. Then she said, "My cousin Lewis. I saw his."

"Well, how old's he?"

"One and a half."

"Ha! A baby! A baby's is like a little worm. It ain't a real one at all."

If he says he'll show me his, she thought, *I'll kick him. I'll just get out of my bag and kick him.*

"I went hunting with my daddy and Versh and Danny Simmons last year in buck season," Mac said, "and we got ourselves one. And we hog-dressed the thing. You know what that is, don't you?"

"No," she said. She was confused. What was he talking about now?

"That's when you cut him open and take out all his guts, so the meat don't spoil. Makes him lighter to pack out, too."

She tried to imagine what the deer's guts might look like, pulled from the gaping hole. "What do you do with them?" she said. "The guts?"

"Oh, just leave 'em for the bears."

She ran her finger like a knife blade along her belly.

"When we left them on the ground," Mac said, "they smoked. Like they were cooking."

"Huh," she said.

"They cut off the deer's pecker, too, you know."

Andy imagined Lewis's pecker and shuddered. "Mac, you're disgusting."

He laughed. "Well, I gotta go pee." She heard him rustle out of his bag. "Broo!" he cried, flapping his arms. "It's cold!"

He makes so much noise, she thought, *just noise and more noise.*

Her father woke them before first light. He warned them to talk softly and said that they were going to the place where Andy had seen the deer, to try to cut them off on their way back from their night feeding. Andy couldn't shake off her sleep. Stuffing her sleeping bag into its sack seemed to take an hour, and tying her boots was the strangest thing she'd ever done. Charlie Spoon made hot chocolate and oatmeal with raisins. Andy closed her eyes and, between beats of her heart, listened to the breathing of the forest. *When I open my eyes, it will be lighter*, she decided. But when she did, it was still just as dark, except for the swaths of their flashlights and the hissing blue flame of the stove. *There has to be just one moment when it all changes from dark to light*, Andy thought. She had missed it yesterday, in the car; today she would watch more closely.

But when she remembered again, it was already first light and they had moved to the rocks by the deer trail and had set up shooting positions — Mac and Charlie Spoon on the up-trail side, she and her father behind them, some six feet up on a ledge. The day became brighter, the sun piercing the tall pines, raking the hunters, yet providing little warmth. Andy now smelled alder and pine and the slightly rotten odor of rock lichen. She rubbed her hand over the stone and considered that it must be very old, had probably been here before the giant pines, *before anyone was in these woods at all.* A chipmunk sniffed on a nearby branch. She aimed an imaginary rifle and pressed the trigger. The chipmunk froze, then scurried away. Her legs were cramping on the narrow ledge. Her father seemed to doze, one hand in his parka, the other cupped lightly around the rifle. She could smell his scent of old wool and leather. His cheeks were speckled with gray-black whiskers, and he worked his jaws slightly, as if chewing a small piece of gum.

Please let us get a deer, she prayed.

A branch snapped on the other side of the rock face. Her father's hand stiffened on the rifle, startling her — *He hasn't been sleeping at all,* she marveled — and then his jaw relaxed, as did the lines around his eyes, and she heard Charlie Spoon call, "Yo, don't shoot, it's us." He and Mac appeared from around the rock. They stopped beneath the ledge. Charlie solemnly crossed his arms.

"I don't believe we're gonna get any deer here," he said drily.

Andy's father lowered his rifle to Charlie and jumped down from the ledge. Then he reached up for Andy. She dropped into his arms and he set her gently on the ground.

100   Mac sidled up to her. "I knew you didn't see no deer," he said.

"Just because they don't come when you want 'em to don't mean she didn't see them," her father said.

Still, she felt bad. Her telling about the deer had caused them to spend the morning there, cold and expectant, with nothing to show for it.

They tramped through the woods for another two hours, not caring much about noise. Mac found some deer tracks, and they argued about how old they were. They split up for a while and then rejoined at an old logging road that deer might use, and followed it. The road crossed a stream, which had mostly frozen over but in a few spots still caught leaves and twigs in an icy swirl. They forded it by jumping from rock to rock. The road narrowed after that, and the woods thickened.

They stopped for lunch, heating up Charlie's wife's corn chowder. Andy's father cut squares of applesauce cake with his hunting knife and handed them to her and Mac, who ate his almost daintily. Andy could faintly taste knife oil on the cake. She was tired. She stretched her leg; the muscle that had cramped on the rock still ached.

105   "Might as well relax," her father said, as if reading her thoughts. "We won't find deer till suppertime."

Charlie Spoon leaned back against his pack and folded his hands across his stomach. "Well, even if we don't get a deer," he said expansively, "it's still great to be out here, breathe some fresh air, clomp around a bit. Get away from the house and the old lady." He winked at Mac, who looked away.

"That's what the woods are all about, anyway," Charlie said. "It's where the women don't want to go." He bowed his head toward Andy. "With your exception, of course, little lady." He helped himself to another piece of applesauce cake.

"She ain't a woman," Mac said.

"Well, she damn well's gonna be," Charlie said. He grinned at her. "Or will you? You're half a boy anyway. You go by a boy's name. What's your real name? Andrea, ain't it?"

"That's right," she said. She hoped that if she didn't look at him, Charlie would stop. 110

"Well, which do you like? Andy or Andrea?"

"Don't matter," she mumbled. "Either."

"She's always been Andy to me," her father said.

Charlie Spoon was still grinning. "So what are you gonna be, Andrea? A boy or a girl?"

"I'm a girl," she said. 115

"But you want to go hunting and fishing and everything, huh?"

"She can do whatever she likes," her father said.

"Hell, you might as well have just had a boy and be done with it!" Charlie exclaimed.

"That's funny," her father said, and chuckled. "That's just what her momma tells me."

They were looking at her, and she wanted to get away from them all, even 120 from her father, who chose to joke with them.

"I'm going to walk a bit," she said.

She heard them laughing as she walked down the logging trail. She flapped her arms; she whistled. *I don't care how much noise I make,* she thought. Two grouse flew from the underbrush, startling her. A little farther down, the trail ended in a clearing that enlarged into a frozen meadow; beyond it the woods began again. A few moldering posts were all that was left of a fence that had once enclosed the field. The low afternoon sunlight reflected brightly off the snow, so that Andy's eyes hurt. She squinted hard. A gust of wind blew across the field, stinging her face. And then, as if it had been waiting for her, the doe emerged from the trees opposite and stepped cautiously into the field. Andy watched: it stopped and stood quietly for what seemed a long time and then ambled across. It stopped again about seventy yards away and began to browse in a patch of sugar grass uncovered by the wind. Carefully, slowly, never taking her eyes from the doe, Andy walked backward, trying to step into the boot prints she'd already made. When she was far enough back into the woods, she turned and walked faster, her heart racing. *Please let it stay,* she prayed.

"There's doe in the field yonder," she told them.

They got their rifles and hurried down the trail.

"No use," her father said. "We're making too much noise any way you look at it." 125

"At least we got us the wind in our favor," Charlie Spoon said, breathing heavily. But the doe was still there, grazing.

"Good Lord," Charlie whispered. He looked at her father. "Well, whose shot?"

"Andy spotted it," her father said in a low voice. "Let her shoot it."

"What!" Charlie's eyes widened. 130

Andy couldn't believe what her father had just said. She'd only shot tin cans and targets; she'd never even fired her father's .30-.30, and she'd never killed anything.

"I can't," she whispered.

"That's right, she can't," Charlie Spoon insisted. "She's not old enough and she don't have a license even if she was!"

"Well, who's to tell?" her father said in a low voice. "Nobody's going to know but us." He looked at her. "Do you want to shoot it, punkin?"

135   *Why doesn't it hear us?* she wondered. *Why doesn't it run away?* "I don't know," she said.

"Well, I'm sure as hell gonna shoot it," Charlie said. Her father grasped Charlie's rifle barrel and held it. His voice was steady.

"Andy's a good shot. It's her deer. She found it, not you. You'd still be sitting on your ass back in camp." He turned to her again. "Now — do you want to shoot it, Andy? Yes or no."

He was looking at her; they were all looking at her. Suddenly she was angry at the deer, who refused to hear them, who wouldn't run away even when it could. "I'll shoot it," she said. Charlie turned away in disgust.

She lay on the ground and pressed the rifle stock against her shoulder bone. The snow was cold through her parka; she smelled oil and wax and damp earth. She pulled off one glove with her teeth. "It sights just like the .22," her father said gently. "Cartridge's already chambered." As she had done so many times before, she sighted down the scope; now the doe was in the reticle. She moved the barrel until the cross hairs lined up. Her father was breathing beside her.

140   "Aim where the chest and legs meet, or a little above, punkin," he was saying calmly. "That's the killing shot."

But now, seeing it in the scope, Andy was hesitant. Her finger weakened on the trigger. Still, she nodded at what her father said and sighted again, the cross hairs lining up in exactly the same spot — the doe had hardly moved, its brownish-gray body outlined starkly against the blue-backed snow. *It doesn't know*, Andy thought. *It just doesn't know.* And as she looked, deer and snow and faraway trees flattened within the circular frame to become like a picture on a calendar, not real, and she felt calm, as if she had been dreaming everything — the day, the deer, the hunt itself. And she, finger on trigger, was only a part of that dream.

"Shoot!" Charlie hissed.

Through the scope she saw the deer look up, ears high and straining.

Charlie groaned, and just as he did, and just at the moment when Andy knew — *knew* — the doe would bound away, as if she could feel its haunches tensing and gathering power, she pulled the trigger. Later she would think, *I felt the recoil, I smelled the smoke, but I don't remember pulling the trigger.* Through the scope the deer seemed to shrink into itself, and then slowly knelt, hind legs first, head raised as if to cry out. It trembled, still straining to keep its head high, as if that alone would save it; failing, it collapsed, shuddered, and lay still.

145   "Whoee!" Mac cried.

"One shot! One shot!" her father yelled, clapping her on the back. Charlie Spoon was shaking his head and smiling dumbly.

"I told you she was a great little shot!" her father said. "I told you!" Mac danced and clapped his hands. She was dazed, not quite understanding what had happened. And then they were crossing the field toward the fallen doe, she walking dreamlike, the men laughing and joking, released now from the tension of silence and anticipation. Suddenly Mac pointed and cried out, "Look at that!"

The doe was rising, legs unsteady. They stared at it, unable to comprehend, and in that moment the doe regained its feet and looked at them, as if it too were trying to understand. Her father whistled softly. Charlie Spoon unslung his rifle and raised it to his shoulder, but the doe was already bounding away. His hurried shot missed, and the deer disappeared into the woods.

"Damn, damn, damn," he moaned.

"I don't believe it," her father said. "That deer was dead." 150

"Dead, hell!" Charlie yelled. "It was gutshot, that's all. Stunned and gutshot. Clean shot, my ass!"

What have I done? Andy thought.

Her father slung his rifle over his shoulder. "Well, let's go. It can't get too far."

"Hell, I've seen deer run ten miles gutshot," Charlie said. He waved his arms. "We may never find her!"

As they crossed the field, Mac came up to her and said in a low voice, 155 "Gutshoot a deer, you'll go to hell."

"Shut up, Mac," she said, her voice cracking. It was a terrible thing she had done, she knew. She couldn't bear to think of the doe in pain and frightened. *Please let it die*, she prayed.

But though they searched all the last hour of daylight, so that they had to re-cross the field and go up the logging trail in a twilight made even deeper by thick, smoky clouds, they didn't find the doe. They lost its trail almost immediately in the dense stands of alderberry and larch.

"I am cold, and I am tired," Charlie Spoon declared. "And if you ask me, that deer's in another county already."

"No one's asking you, Charlie," her father said.

They had a supper of hard salami and ham, bread, and the rest of the apple- 160 sauce cake. It seemed a bother to heat the coffee, so they had cold chocolate instead. Everyone turned in early.

"We'll find it in the morning, honeybun," her father said, as she went to her tent.

"I don't like to think of it suffering." She was almost in tears.

"It's dead already, punkin. Don't even think about it." He kissed her, his breath sour and his beard rough against her cheek.

Andy was sure she wouldn't get to sleep; the image of the doe falling, falling, then rising again, repeated itself whenever she closed her eyes. Then she heard an owl hoot and realized that it had awakened her, so she must have been asleep after all. She hoped the owl would hush, but instead it hooted louder. She wished her father or Charlie Spoon would wake up and do something about it, but no one moved in the other tent, and suddenly she was afraid that they had all decamped, wanting nothing more to do with her. She whispered, "Mac, Mac," to the sleep-ing bag where he should be, but no one answered. She tried to find the flashlight she always kept by her side, but couldn't, and she cried in panic, "Mac, are you there?" He mumbled something, and immediately she felt foolish and hoped he wouldn't reply.

165   When she awoke again, everything had changed. The owl was gone, the woods were still, and she sensed light, blue and pale, light where before there had been none. *The moon must have come out,* she thought. And it was warm, too, warmer than it should have been. She got out of her sleeping bag and took off her parka — it was that warm. Mac was asleep, wheezing like an old man. She unzipped the tent and stepped outside.

The woods were more beautiful than she had ever seen them. The moon made everything ice-rimmed glimmer with a crystallized, immanent light, while underneath that ice the branches of trees were as stark as skeletons. She heard a crunching in the snow, the one sound in all that silence, and there, walking down the logging trail into their camp, was the doe. Its body, like everything around her, was silvered with frost and moonlight. It walked past the tent where her father and Charlie Spoon were sleeping and stopped no more than six feet from her. Andy saw that she had shot it, yes, had shot it cleanly, just where she thought she had, the wound a jagged, bloody hole in the doe's chest.

A *heart shot,* she thought.

The doe stepped closer, so that Andy, if she wished, could have reached out and touched it. It looked at her as if expecting her to do this, and so she did, running her hand, slowly at first, along the rough, matted fur, then down to the edge of the wound, where she stopped. The doe stood still. Hesitantly, Andy felt the edge of the wound. The torn flesh was sticky and warm. The wound parted under her touch. And then, almost without her knowing it, her fingers were within, probing, yet still the doe didn't move. Andy pressed deeper, through flesh and muscle and sinew, until her whole hand and more was inside the wound and she had found the doe's heart, warm and beating. She cupped it gently in her hand. *Alive,* she marveled. *Alive.*

The heart quickened under her touch, becoming warmer and warmer until it was hot enough to burn. In pain, Andy tried to remove her hand, but the wound closed about it and held her fast. Her hand was burning. She cried out in agony, sure they would all hear and come help, but they didn't. And then her hand pulled free, followed by a steaming rush of blood, more blood than she ever could have imagined — it covered her hand and arm, and she saw to her horror that her hand was steaming. She moaned and fell to her knees and plunged her hand into the snow. The doe looked at her gently and then turned and walked back up the trail.

170   In the morning, when she woke, Andy could still smell the blood, but she felt no pain. She looked at her hand. Even though it appeared unscathed, it felt weak and withered. She couldn't move it freely and was afraid the others would notice. *I will hide it in my jacket pocket,* she decided, *so nobody can see.* She ate the oatmeal that her father cooked and stayed apart from them all. No one spoke to her, and that suited her. A light snow began to fall. It was the last day of their hunting trip. She wanted to be home.

Her father dumped the dregs of his coffee. "Well, let's go look for her," he said.

Again they crossed the field. Andy lagged behind. She averted her eyes from the spot where the doe had fallen, already filling up with snow. Mac and Charlie entered the woods first, followed by her father. Andy remained in the field and considered the smear of gray sky, the nearby flock of crows pecking at unyielding stubble. *I will stay here,* she thought, *and not move for a long while.*

But now someone — Mac — was yelling. Her father appeared at the woods' edge and waved for her to come. She ran and pushed through a brake of alder-berry and larch. The thick underbrush scratched her face. For a moment she felt lost and looked wildly about. Then, where the brush thinned, she saw them standing quietly in the falling snow. They were staring down at the dead doe. A film covered its upturned eye, and its body was lightly dusted with snow.

"I told you she wouldn't get too far," Andy's father said triumphantly. "We must've just missed her yesterday. Too blind to see."

"We're just damn lucky no animal got to her last night," Charlie muttered.

Her father lifted the doe's foreleg. The wound was blood-clotted, brown, and 175 caked like frozen mud. "Clean shot," he said to Charlie. He grinned. "My little girl."

Then he pulled out his knife, the blade gray as the morning. Mac whispered to Andy, "Now watch this," while Charlie Spoon lifted the doe from behind by its forelegs so that its head rested between his knees, its underside exposed. Her father's knife sliced thickly from chest to belly to crotch, and Andy was running from them, back to the field and across, scattering the crows who cawed and cir-cled angrily. And now they were all calling to her — Charlie Spoon and Mac and her father — crying *Andy, Andy* (but that wasn't her name, she would no longer be called that); yet louder than any of them was the wind blowing through the treetops, like the ocean where her mother floated in green water, also calling *Come in, come in*, while all around her roared the mocking of the terrible, now inevitable, sea.

Reading and Reacting

1. The initiation of a child into adulthood is a common literary theme. In this story, hunting is presented as an initiation rite. In what way is hunting an appropriate coming-of-age ritual?

2. Which characters are in conflict in this story? Which ideas are in conflict? How do these conflicts help to communicate the story's initiation theme?

3. In the story's opening paragraph and elsewhere, Andy finds comfort and re-assurance in the idea that the woods are "always the same"; later in the story, she remembers the ocean, "huge and empty, yet always moving. Every-thing lay hidden . . ." (par. 45). How does the contrast between the woods and the ocean suggest the transition she must make from childhood to adulthood?

4. How do the references to blood support the story's initiation theme? Do they suggest another theme as well?

5. Throughout the story, references are made to Andy's ability to inspire the trust of animals. As her father says, "Animals — I don't know how she does it, but they come right up to her" (par. 8). How does his comment fore-shadow later events?

6. Why does Andy pray that she and the others will get a deer? What makes her change her mind? How does the change in Andy's character help to convey the story's theme?

7. Andy's mother is not an active participant in the story's events. Still, her presence is important to the story. *Why* is it important? How does paragraph 45 reveal the importance of the mother's role?

8. What has Andy learned as a result of her experience? What else do you think she still has to learn?

9. JOURNAL ENTRY How would the story be different if Andy were a boy? What would be the same?

10. CRITICAL PERSPECTIVE In a review of *Comfort*, the book in which "Doe Season" appears, Susan Wood makes the following observation:

> The dozen or so stories in David Michael Kaplan's affecting first collection share a common focus on the extraordinary moments of recognition in ordinary lives. He is at his best suggesting how such moments may alter, for better or for worse, our relationships with those to whom we are most deeply bound — children, parents, lovers — in love and guilt.

At what point does "the extraordinary moment of recognition" occur in "Doe Season"? How does this moment alter Andy's relationship with both her parents?

Related Works: "A&P" (p. 230), "The Lesson" (p. 642), "The Water Faucet Vision" (p. 240), "Cinderella" (p. 882), "The Lamb" (p. 1145), "Traveling through the Dark" (p. 1070), *Proof* (p. 1526).

D(AVID) H(ERBERT) LAWRENCE (1885–1930) was born in Nottinghamshire, England, the son of a coal miner and a schoolteacher. Determined to escape the harsh life of a miner, Lawrence taught for several years after graduating from high school. He soon began writing fiction and established himself in London literary circles.

During World War I, Lawrence and his wife were suspected of treason because of his pacifism and her connection to German aristocracy. Because Lawrence suffered from tuberculosis, he and his wife left England after the armistice in search of a healthier climate. They traveled in Australia, France, Italy, Mexico, and the United States throughout their lives.

Lawrence is recognized for his impassioned portrayal of our unconscious and instinctive natures. In his novel *Lady Chatterley's Lover* (1928), he attempted to restore explicit sexuality to English fiction, and the book was banned for years in Britain and the United States. His other novels include *Sons and Lovers* (1913), *The Rainbow* (1915), *Women in Love* (1921), and *The Plumed Serpent* (1926). Lawrence was also a gifted poet, essayist, travel writer, and short story writer, and his work had a strong influence on other writers.

Lawrence's fascination with the struggle between the unconscious and the intellect is revealed in his short story "The Rocking-Horse Winner" (1920). Lawrence sets his story in a house full of secrets and weaves symbolism with elements of the fairy tale and the gothic to produce a tale that has often been the subject of literary debate.

Cultural Context Horse racing in England has a long and prestigious history, beginning with casual competitions organized by Roman soldiers in Yorkshire in A.D. 200. The first recorded horse race was run during the reign of Henry II in 1174. Today, horses can be raced over fences or hurdles (National Hunt Racing) or over unobstructed distances (flat racing). There are also cross-country races from point to point, which are called steeplechases. A derby, like the one mentioned in this story, gets its name from the Epsom Derby, which is still run at the Epsom racecourse and is named for Edward Smith Stanley, the twelfth Earl of Derby. The term *derby* is usually reserved for races in which three-year-old horses compete.

The Rocking-Horse Winner (1920)

There was a woman who was beautiful, who started with all the advantages, yet she had no luck. She married for love, and the love turned to dust. She had bonny children, yet she felt they had been thrust upon her, and she could not love them. They looked at her coldly, as if they were finding fault with her. And hurriedly she felt she must cover up some fault in herself. Yet what it was that she must cover up she never knew. Nevertheless, when her children were present, she always felt the centre of her heart go hard. This troubled her, and in her manner she was all the more gentle and anxious for her children, as if she loved them very much. Only she herself knew that at the centre of her heart was a hard little place that could not feel love, no, not for anybody. Everybody else said of her: "She is such a good mother. She adores her children." Only she herself, and her children themselves, knew it was not so. They read it in each other's eyes.

There were a boy and two little girls. They lived in a pleasant house, with a garden, and they had discreet servants, and felt themselves superior to anyone in the neighbourhood.

Although they lived in style, they felt always an anxiety in the house. There was never enough money. The mother had a small income, and the father had a small income, but not nearly enough for the social position which they had to keep up. The father went into town to some office. But though he had good prospects, these prospects never materialised. There was always the grinding sense of the shortage of money, though the style was always kept up.

At last the mother said: "I will see if *I* can't make something." But she did not know where to begin. She racked her brains, and tried this thing and the other, but could not find anything successful. The failure made deep lines come into her face. Her children were growing up, they would have to go to school. There must be more money, there must be more money. The father, who was always very handsome and expensive in his tastes, seemed as if he never *would* be able to do anything worth doing. And the mother, who had a great belief in herself, did not succeed any better, and her tastes were just as expensive.

5   And so the house came to be haunted by the unspoken phrase: *There must be more money! There must be more money!* The children could hear it all the time, though nobody said it aloud. They heard it at Christmas, when the expensive and splendid toys filled the nursery. Behind the shining modern rocking-horse, behind the smart doll's house, a voice would start whispering: "There *must* be more money! There *must* be more money!" And the children would stop playing, to listen for a moment. They would look into each other's eyes, to see if they had all heard. And each one saw in the eyes of the other two that they too had heard. "There *must* be more money! There *must* be more money!"

It came whispering from the springs of the still-swaying rocking-horse, and even the horse, bending his wooden, champing head, heard it. The big doll, sitting so pink and smirking in her new pram, could hear it quite plainly, and seemed to be smirking all the more self-consciously because of it. The foolish puppy, too, that took the place of the teddybear, he was looking so extraordinarily foolish for no other reason but that he heard the secret whisper all over the house: "There *must* be more money!"

Yet nobody ever said it aloud. The whisper was everywhere, and therefore no one spoke it. Just as no one ever says: "We are breathing!" in spite of the fact that breath is coming and going all the time.

"Mother," said the boy Paul one day, "why don't we keep a car of our own? Why do we always use uncle's, or else a taxi?"

"Because we're the poor members of the family," said the mother.

10   "But why *are* we, mother?"

"Well — I suppose," she said slowly and bitterly, "it's because your father has no luck."

The boy was silent for some time.

"Is luck money, mother?" he asked, rather timidly.

"No, Paul. Not quite. It's what causes you to have money."

15   "Oh!" said Paul vaguely. "I thought when Uncle Oscar said *filthy lucker*, it meant money."

"*Filthy lucre* does mean money," said the mother. "But it's lucre, not luck."

"Oh!" said the boy. "Then what *is* luck, mother?"

"It's what causes you to have money. If you're lucky you have money. That's why it's better to be born lucky than rich. If you're rich, you may lose your money. But if you're lucky, you will always get more money."

"Oh! Will you? And is father not lucky?"

20   "Very unlucky, I should say," she said bitterly.

The boy watched her with unsure eyes.

"Why?" he asked.

"I don't know. Nobody ever knows why one person is lucky and another unlucky."

"Don't they? Nobody at all? Does *nobody* know?"

25   "Perhaps God. But He never tells."

"He ought to, then. And aren't you lucky either, mother?"

"I can't be, if I married an unlucky husband."

"But by yourself, aren't you?"

"I used to think I was, before I married. Now I think I am very unlucky indeed."

"Why?"   30

"Well — never mind! Perhaps I'm not really," she said.

The child looked at her to see if she meant it. But he saw, by the lines of her mouth, that she was only trying to hide something from him.

"Well, anyhow," he said stoutly, "I'm a lucky person."

"Why?" said his mother, with a sudden laugh.

He stared at her. He didn't even know why he had said it.   35

"God told me," he asserted, brazening it out.

"I hope He did, dear!" she said, again with a laugh, but rather bitter.

"He did, mother!"

"Excellent!" said the mother, using one of her husband's exclamations.

The boy saw she did not believe him; or rather, that she paid no attention to   40
his assertion. This angered him somewhat, and made him want to compel her attention.

He went off by himself, vaguely, in a childish way, seeking for the clue to "luck." Absorbed, taking no heed of other people, he went about with a sort of stealth, seeking inwardly for luck. He wanted luck, he wanted it, he wanted it. When the two girls were playing dolls in the nursery, he would sit on his big rocking-horse, charging madly into space, with a frenzy that made the little girls peer at him uneasily. Wildly the horse careered, the waving dark hair of the boy tossed, his eyes had a strange glare in them. The little girls dared not speak to him.

When he had ridden to the end of his mad little journey, he climbed down and stood in front of his rocking-horse, staring fixedly into its lowered face. Its red mouth was slightly open, its big eye was wide and glassy-bright.

"Now!" he would silently command the snorting steed. "Now, take me to where there is luck! Now take me!"

And he would slash the horse on the neck with the little whip he had asked Uncle Oscar for. He *knew* the horse could take him to where there was luck, if only he forced it. So he would mount again and start on his furious ride, hoping at last to get there. He knew he could get there.

"You'll break your horse, Paul!" said the nurse.   45

"He's always riding like that! I wish he'd leave off!" said his elder sister Joan.

But he only glared down on them in silence. Nurse gave him up. She could make nothing of him. Anyhow, he was growing beyond her.

One day his mother and his Uncle Oscar came in when he was on one of his furious rides. He did not speak to them.

"Hallo, you young jockey! Riding a winner?" said his uncle.

"Aren't you growing too big for a rocking-horse? You're not a very little boy any   50
longer, you know," said his mother.

But Paul only gave a blue glare from his big, rather close-set eyes. He would speak to nobody when he was in full tilt. His mother watched him with an anxious expression on her face.

At last he suddenly stopped forcing his horse into the mechanical gallop and slid down.

"Well, I got there!" he announced fiercely, his blue eyes still flaring, and his sturdy long legs straddling apart.

"Where did you get to?" asked his mother.

55   "Where I wanted to go," he flared back at her.

"That's right, son!" said Uncle Oscar. "Don't you stop till you get there. What's the horse's name?"

"He doesn't have a name," said the boy.

"Gets on without all right?" asked the uncle.

"Well, he has different names. He was called Sansovino last week."

60   "Sansovino, eh? Won the Ascot.° How did you know this name?"

"He always talks about horse-races with Bassett," said Joan.

The uncle was delighted to find that his small nephew was posted with all the racing news. Bassett, the young gardener, who had been wounded in the left foot in the war and had got his present job through Oscar Cresswell, whose batman° he had been, was a perfect blade of the "turf." He lived in the racing events, and the small boy lived with him.

Oscar Cresswell got it all from Bassett.

"Master Paul comes and asks me, so I can't do more than tell him, sir," said Bassett, his face terribly serious, as if he were speaking of religious matters.

65   "And does he ever put anything on a horse he fancies?"

"Well — I don't want to give him away — he's a young sport, a fine sport, sir. Would you mind asking him himself? He sort of takes a pleasure in it, and perhaps he'd feel I was giving him away, sir, if you don't mind."

Bassett was serious as a church.

The uncle went back to his nephew and took him off for a ride in the car.

"Say, Paul, old man, do you ever put anything on a horse?" the uncle asked.

70   The boy watched the handsome man closely.

"Why, do you think I oughtn't to?" he parried.

"Not a bit of it! I thought perhaps you might give me a tip for the Lincoln."°

The car sped on into the country, going down to Uncle Oscar's place in Hampshire.

"Honour bright?" said the nephew.

75   "Honour bright, son!" said the uncle.

"Well, then, Daffodil."

"Daffodil! I doubt it, sonny. What about Mirza?"

"I only know the winner," said the boy. "That's Daffodil."

"Daffodil, eh?"

80   There was a pause. Daffodil was an obscure horse comparatively.

"Uncle!"

"Yes, son?"

"You won't let it go any further, will you? I promised Bassett."

the Ascot: The annual horse race at Ascot Heath in England.

batman: A British military officer's personal assistant.

the Lincoln: The Lincolnshire Handicap, a horse race.

"Bassett be damned, old man! What's he got to do with it?"

"We're partners. We've been partners from the first. Uncle, he lent me my first   85
five shillings, which I lost. I promised him, honour bright, it was only between me
and him; only you gave me that ten-shilling note I started winning with, so I
thought you were lucky. You won't let it go any further, will you?"

The boy gazed at his uncle from those big, hot, blue eyes, set rather close
together. The uncle stirred and laughed uneasily.

"Right you are, son! I'll keep your tip private. Daffodil, eh? How much are you
putting on him?"

"All except twenty pounds," said the boy. "I keep that in reserve."

The uncle thought it a good joke.

"You keep twenty pounds in reserve, do you, you young romancer? What are   90
you betting, then?"

"I'm betting three hundred," said the boy gravely. "But it's between you and
me, Uncle Oscar! Honour bright?"

The uncle burst into a roar of laughter.

"It's between you and me all right, you young Nat Gould,"° he said, laughing.
"But where's your three hundred?"

"Bassett keeps it for me. We're partners."

"You are, are you! And what is Bassett putting on Daffodil?"   95

"He won't go quite as high as I do, I expect. Perhaps he'll go a hundred and
fifty."

"What, pennies?" laughed the uncle.

"Pounds," said the child, with a surprised look at his uncle. "Bassett keeps a
bigger reserve than I do."

Between wonder and amusement Uncle Oscar was silent. He pursued the matter no further, but he determined to take his nephew with him to the Lincoln races.

"Now, son," he said, "I'm putting twenty on Mirza, and I'll put five on for you   100
on any horse you fancy. What's your pick?"

"Daffodil, uncle."

"No, not the fiver on Daffodil!"

"I should if it was my own fiver," said the child.

"Good! Good! Right you are! A fiver for me and a fiver for you on Daffodil."

The child had never been to a race-meeting before, and his eyes were blue fire.   105
He pursed his mouth tight and watched. A Frenchman just in front had put his
money on Lancelot. Wild with excitement, he flayed his arms up and down,
yelling "*Lancelot! Lancelot!*" in his French accent.

Daffodil came in first, Lancelot second, Mirza third. The child, flushed and
with eyes blazing, was curiously serene. His uncle brought him four five-pound
notes, four to one.

"What am I to do with these?" he cried, waving them before the boy's eyes.

"I suppose we'll talk to Bassett," said the boy. "I expect I have fifteen hundred
now; and twenty in reserve; and this twenty."

Nat Gould: Nathaniel Gould (1857–1919), British journalist and writer known for his stories about horse racing.

His uncle studied him for some moments.

110   "Look here, son!" he said. "You're not serious about Bassett and that fifteen hundred, are you?"

"Yes, I am. But it's between you and me, uncle. Honour bright?"

"Honour bright all right, son! But I must talk to Bassett."

"If you'd like to be a partner, uncle, with Bassett and me, we could all be partners. Only, you'd have to promise, honour bright, uncle, not to let it go beyond us three. Bassett and I are lucky, and you must be lucky, because it was your ten shillings I started winning with. . . ."

Uncle Oscar took both Bassett and Paul into Richmond Park for an afternoon, and there they talked.

115   "It's like this, you see, sir," Bassett said. "Master Paul would get me talking about racing events, spinning yarns, you know, sir. And he was always keen on knowing if I'd made or if I'd lost. It's about a year since, now, that I put five shillings on Blush of Dawn for him: and we lost. Then the luck turned, with that ten shillings he had from you: that we put on Singhalese. And since that time, it's been pretty steady, all things considering. What do you say, Master Paul?"

"We're all right when we're sure," said Paul. "It's when we're not quite sure that we go down."

"Oh, but we're careful then," said Bassett.

"But when are you *sure*?" smiled Uncle Oscar.

"It's Master Paul, sir," said Bassett in a secret, religious voice. "It's as if he had it from heaven. Like Daffodil, now, for the Lincoln. That was as sure as eggs."

120   "Did you put anything on Daffodil?" asked Oscar Cresswell.

"Yes, sir. I made my bit."

"And my nephew?"

Bassett was obstinately silent, looking at Paul.

"I made twelve hundred, didn't I, Bassett? I told uncle I was putting three hundred on Daffodil."

125   "That's right," said Bassett, nodding.

"But where's the money?" asked the uncle.

"I keep it safe locked up, sir. Master Paul can have it any minute he likes to ask for it."

"What, fifteen hundred pounds?"

"And twenty! And *forty*, that is, with the twenty he made on the course."

130   "It's amazing!" said the uncle.

"If Master Paul offers you to be partners, sir, I would, if I were you: if you'll excuse me," said Bassett.

Oscar Cresswell thought about it.

"I'll see the money," he said.

They drove home again, and, sure enough, Bassett came round to the garden-house with fifteen hundred pounds in notes. The twenty pounds reserve was left with Joe Glee, in the Turf Commission deposit.

135   "You see, it's all right, uncle, when I'm *sure*! Then we go strong, for all we're worth. Don't we, Bassett?"

"We do that, Master Paul."

"And when are you sure?" said the uncle, laughing.

"Oh, well, sometimes I'm *absolutely* sure, like about Daffodil," said the boy; "and sometimes I have an idea; and sometimes I haven't even an idea, have I, Bassett? Then we're careful, because we mostly go down."

"You do, do you! And when you're sure, like about Daffodil, what makes you sure, sonny?"

"Oh, well, I don't know," said the boy uneasily. "I'm sure, you know, uncle;   140
that's all."

"It's as if he had it from heaven, sir," Bassett reiterated.

"I should say so!" said the uncle.

But he became a partner. And when the Leger° was coming on Paul was "sure" about Lively Spark, which was a quite inconsiderable horse. The boy insisted on putting a thousand on the horse, Bassett went for five hundred, and Oscar Cress-well two hundred. Lively Spark came in first, and the betting had been ten to one against him. Paul had made ten thousand.

"You see," he said, "I was absolutely sure of him."

Even Oscar Cresswell had cleared two thousand.   145

"Look here, son," he said, "this sort of thing makes me nervous."

"It needn't, uncle! Perhaps I shan't be sure again for a long time."

"But what are you going to do with your money?" asked the uncle.

"Of course," said the boy, "I started it for mother. She said she had no luck, because father is unlucky, so I thought if *I* was lucky, it might stop whispering."

"What might stop whispering?"   150

"Our house. I *hate* our house for whispering."

"What does it whisper?"

"Why — why" — the boy fidgeted — "why, I don't know. But it's always short of money, you know, uncle."

"I know it, son, I know it."

"You know people send mother writs,° don't you, uncle?"   155

"I'm afraid I do," said the uncle.

"And then the house whispers, like people laughing at you behind your back. It's awful, that is! I thought if I was lucky . . ."

"You might stop it," added the uncle.

The boy watched him with big blue eyes, that had an uncanny cold fire in them, and he said never a word.

"Well, then!" said the uncle. "What are we doing?"   160

"I shouldn't like mother to know I was lucky," said the boy.

"Why not, son?"

"She'd stop me."

"I don't think she would."

"Oh!" — and the boy writhed in an odd way — "I *don't* want her to know, uncle."   165

---

the Leger: The St. Leger Stakes, a horse race.

writs: Letters from creditors requesting payment.

"All right, son! We'll manage it without her knowing."

They managed it very easily. Paul, at the other's suggestion, handed over five thousand pounds to his uncle, who deposited it with the family lawyer, who was then to inform Paul's mother that a relative had put five thousand pounds into his hands, which sum was to be paid out a thousand pounds at a time, on the mother's birthday, for the next five years.

"So she'll have a birthday present of a thousand pounds for five successive years," said Uncle Oscar. "I hope it won't make it all the harder for her later."

Paul's mother had her birthday in November. The house had been "whispering" worse than ever lately, and, even in spite of his luck, Paul could not bear up against it. He was very anxious to see the effect of the birthday letter, telling his mother about the thousand pounds.

170   When there were no visitors, Paul now took his meals with his parents, as he was beyond the nursery control. His mother went into town nearly every day. She had discovered that she had an odd knack of sketching furs and dress materials, so she worked secretly in the studio of a friend who was the chief "artist" for the leading drapers. She drew the figures of ladies in furs and ladies in silk and sequins for the newspaper advertisements. This young woman artist earned several thousand pounds a year, but Paul's mother only made several hundreds, and she was again dissatisfied. She so wanted to be first in something, and she did not succeed, even in making sketches for drapery advertisements.

She was down to breakfast on the morning of her birthday. Paul watched her face as she read her letters. He knew the lawyer's letter. As his mother read it, her face hardened and became more expressionless. Then a cold, determined look came on her mouth. She hid the letter under the pile of others, and said not a word about it.

"Didn't you have anything nice in the post for your birthday, mother?" said Paul.

"Quite moderately nice," she said, her voice cold and absent.

She went away to town without saying more.

175   But in the afternoon Uncle Oscar appeared. He said Paul's mother had had a long interview with the lawyer, asking if the whole five thousand could not be advanced at once, as she was in debt.

"What do you think, uncle?" asked the boy.

"I leave it to you, son."

"Oh, let her have it, then! We can get some more with the other," said the boy.

"A bird in the hand is worth two in the bush, laddie!" said Uncle Oscar.

180   "But I'm sure to *know* for the Grand National; or the Lincolnshire; or else the Derby.° I'm sure to know for *one* of them," said Paul.

So Uncle Oscar signed the agreement, and Paul's mother touched the whole five thousand. Then something very curious happened. The voices in

---

Grand National . . . Derby: Famous British horse races. The Grand National is run at Aintree; the Derby, at Epsom Downs.

the house suddenly went mad, like a chorus of frogs on a spring evening. There was certain new furnishings, and Paul had a tutor. He was *really* going to Eton, his father's school, in the following autumn. There were flowers in the winter, and a blossoming of the luxury Paul's mother had been used to. And yet the voices in the house, behind the sprays of mimosa and almond-blossom, and from under the piles of iridescent cushions, simply trilled and screamed in a sort of ecstasy: "There *must* be more money! Oh-h-h; there *must* be more money. Oh, now, now-w! Now-w-w — there *must* be more money! — more than ever! More than ever!"

It frightened Paul terribly. He studied away at his Latin and Greek with his tutor. But his intense hours were spent with Bassett. The Grand National had gone by: he had not "known," and had lost a hundred pounds. Summer was at hand. He was in agony for the Lincoln. But even for the Lincoln he didn't "know," and he lost fifty pounds. He became wild-eyed and strange, as if something were going to explode in him.

"Let it alone, son! Don't you bother about it!" urged Uncle Oscar. But it was as if the boy couldn't really hear what his uncle was saying.

"I've got to know for the Derby! I've got to know for the Derby!" the child reiterated, his big blue eyes blazing with a sort of madness.

His mother noticed how overwrought he was.   185

"You'd better go to the seaside. Wouldn't you like to go now to the seaside, instead of waiting? I think you'd better," she said, looking down at him anxiously, her heart curiously heavy because of him.

But the child lifted his uncanny blue eyes.

"I couldn't possibly go before the Derby, mother!" he said. "I couldn't possibly!"

"Why not?" she said, her voice becoming heavy when she was opposed. "Why not? You can still go from the seaside to see the Derby with your Uncle Oscar, if that's what you wish. No need for you to wait here. Besides, I think you care too much about these races. It's a bad sign. My family has been a gambling family, and you won't know till you grow up how much damage it has done. But it has done damage. I shall have to send Bassett away, and ask Uncle Oscar not to talk racing to you, unless you promise to be reasonable about it: go away to the seaside and forget it. You're all nerves!"

"I'll do what you like, mother, so long as you don't send me away till after the   190
Derby," the boy said.

"Send you away from where? Just from this house?"

"Yes," he said, gazing at her.

"Why, you curious child, what makes you care about this house so much, suddenly? I never knew you loved it."

He gazed at her without speaking. He had a secret within a secret, something he had not divulged, even to Bassett or to his Uncle Oscar.

But his mother, after standing undecided and a little bit sullen for some   195
moments, said:

"Very well, then! Don't go to the seaside till after the Derby, if you don't wish it. But promise me you won't let your nerves go to pieces. Promise you won't think so much about horse-racing and *events*, as you call them!"

"Oh no," said the boy casually. "I won't think much about them, mother. You needn't worry. I wouldn't worry, mother, if I were you."

"If you were me and I were you," said his mother, "I wonder what we *should* do!"

"But you know you needn't worry, mother, don't you?" the boy repeated.

200 "I should be awfully glad to know it," she said wearily.

"Oh, well, you *can*, you know. I mean, you *ought* to know you needn't worry," he insisted.

"Ought I? Then I'll see about it," she said.

Paul's secret of secrets was his wooden horse, that which had no name. Since he was emancipated from a nurse and a nursery-governess, he had had his rocking-horse removed to his own bedroom at the top of the house.

"Surely you're too big for a rocking-horse!" his mother had remonstrated.

205 "Well, you see, mother, till I can have a *real* horse, I like to have *some* sort of animal about," had been his quaint answer.

"Do you feel he keeps you company?" she laughed.

"Oh yes! He's very good, he always keeps me company, when I'm there," said Paul.

So the horse, rather shabby, stood in an arrested prance in the boy's bedroom.

The Derby was drawing near, and the boy grew more and more tense. He hardly heard what was spoken to him, he was very frail, and his eyes were really uncanny. His mother had sudden strange seizures of uneasiness about him. Sometimes, for half an hour, she would feel a sudden anxiety about him that was almost anguish. She wanted to rush to him at once, and know he was safe.

210 Two nights before the Derby, she was at a big party in town, when one of her rushes of anxiety about her boy, her firstborn, gripped her heart till she could hardly speak. She fought with the feeling, might and main, for she believed in common sense. But it was too strong. She had to leave the dance and go downstairs to telephone to the country. The children's nursery-governess was terribly surprised and startled at being rung up in the night.

"Are the children all right, Miss Wilmot?"

"Oh yes, they are quite all right."

"Master Paul? Is he all right?"

"He went to bed as right as a trivet. Shall I run up and look at him?"

215 "No," said Paul's mother reluctantly. "No! Don't trouble. It's all right. Don't sit up. We shall be home fairly soon." She did not want her son's privacy intruded upon.

"Very good," said the governess.

It was about one o'clock when Paul's mother and father drove up to their house. All was still. Paul's mother went to her room and slipped off her white fur cloak. She had told her maid not to wait up for her. She heard her husband downstairs, mixing a whisky and soda.

And then, because of the strange anxiety at her heart, she stole upstairs to her son's room. Noiselessly she went along the upper corridor. Was there a faint noise? What was it?

She stood, with arrested muscles, outside his door, listening. There was a strange, heavy, and yet not loud noise. Her heart stood still. It was a soundless noise, yet rushing and powerful. Something huge, in violent, hushed motion. What was it? What in God's name was it? She ought to know. She felt that she knew the noise. She knew what it was.

Yet she could not place it. She couldn't say what it was. And on and on it went, 220 like a madness.

Softly, frozen with anxiety and fear, she turned the door-handle.

The room was dark. Yet in the space near the window, she heard and saw something plunging to and fro. She gazed in fear and amazement.

Then suddenly she switched on the light, and saw her son, in his green pyjamas, madly surging on the rocking-horse. The blaze of light suddenly lit him up, as he urged the wooden horse, and lit her up, as she stood, blonde, in her dress of pale green and crystal, in the doorway.

"Paul!" she cried. "Whatever are you doing?"

"It's Malabar!" he screamed in a powerful, strange voice. "It's Malabar!" 225

His eyes blazed at her for one strange and senseless second, as he ceased urging his wooden horse. Then he fell with a crash to the ground, and she, all her tormented motherhood flooding upon her, rushed to gather him up.

But he was unconscious, and unconscious he remained, with some brain-fever. He talked and tossed, and his mother sat stonily by his side.

"Malabar! It's Malabar! Bassett, Bassett, I _know_! It's Malabar!"

So the child cried, trying to get up and urge the rocking-horse that gave him his inspiration.

"What does he mean by Malabar?" asked the heart-frozen mother. 230

"I don't know," said the father stonily.

"What does he mean by Malabar?" she asked her brother Oscar.

"It's one of the horses running for the Derby," was the answer.

And, in spite of himself, Oscar Cresswell spoke to Bassett, and himself put a thousand on Malabar: at fourteen to one.

The third day of the illness was critical: they were waiting for a change. The 235 boy, with his rather long, curly hair, was tossing ceaselessly on the pillow. He neither slept nor regained consciousness, and his eyes were like blue stones. His mother sat, feeling her heart had gone, turned actually into a stone.

In the evening, Oscar Cresswell did not come, but Bassett sent a message, saying could he come up for one moment, just one moment? Paul's mother was very angry at the intrusion, but on second thought she agreed. The boy was the same. Perhaps Bassett might bring him to consciousness.

The gardener, a shortish fellow with a little brown moustache and sharp little brown eyes, tiptoed into the room, touched his imaginary cap to Paul's mother, and stole to the bedside, staring with glittering, smallish eyes at the tossing, dying child.

"Master Paul!" he whispered. "Master Paul! Malabar came in first all right, a clean win. I did as you told me. You've made over seventy thousand pounds, you have; you've got over eighty thousand. Malabar came in all right, Master Paul."

"Malabar! Malabar! Did I say Malabar, mother? Did I say Malabar? Do you think I'm lucky, mother? I knew Malabar, didn't I? Over eighty thousand pounds! I call that lucky, don't you, mother? Over eighty thousand pounds! I knew, didn't I know

I knew? Malabar came in all right. If I ride my horse till I'm sure, then I tell you, Bassett, you can go as high as you like. Did you go for all you were worth, Bassett?"

240   "I went a thousand on it, Master Paul."

"I never told you, mother, that if I can ride my horse, and *get there*, then I'm absolutely sure — oh, absolutely! Mother, did I ever tell you? I *am* lucky!"

"No, you never did," said his mother.

But the boy died in the night.

And even as he lay dead, his mother heard her brother's voice saying to her: "My God, Hester, you're eighty-odd thousand to the good, and a poor devil of a son to the bad. But, poor devil, poor devil, he's best gone out of a life where he rides his rocking-horse to find a winner."

Reading and Reacting

1. From what point of view is "The Rocking-Horse Winner" told? How does this point of view help to communicate the story's theme?

2. In what respects is "The Rocking-Horse Winner" like a fairy tale? How is it different?

3. Many fairy tales involve a hero who goes on a journey to search for something of great value. What journey does Paul go on? What thing of value does he search for? Is he successful?

4. In paragraph 5, the narrator says that the house is "haunted by the unspoken phrase: '*There must be more money!*'" In what way does the phrase "haunt" the house?

5. How would you characterize Paul's parents? His uncle? Bassett? Are they weak? Evil? What motivates them?

6. Beginning in paragraph 11, Paul's mother attempts to define the word *luck*. According to her definition, does she consider Paul lucky? Do you agree?

7. In what ways does Paul behave like other children? In what ways is he different? How do you account for these differences? How old do you think Paul is? Why is his age significant?

8. The rocking horse is an important literary symbol in the story. What possible meanings might the rocking horse suggest? In what ways does this symbol reinforce the story's theme?

9. What secrets do the various characters keep from one another? Why do they keep them? How do these secrets relate to the story's theme?

10. How does Paul know who the winners will be? Does the rocking horse really tell him? Does he get his information "from heaven" as Bassett suggests (par. 119)? Or does he just guess?

11. JOURNAL ENTRY In your opinion, who or what is responsible for Paul's death?

12. CRITICAL PERSPECTIVE In a letter dated January 17, 1913, Lawrence wrote the following:

> My great religion is a belief in the blood, the flesh, as being wiser than the intellect. We can go wrong in our minds. But what our blood feels and believes and says, is always true. The intellect is only a bit and a bridle. What do I care about knowledge. All I want is to answer to my blood, direct, without fribbling intervention of mind, or moral, or what-not.

How does Lawrence's portrayal of Paul in "The Rocking-Horse Winner" support his belief in "the blood . . . being wiser than the intellect"? How does Lawrence remain true in this story to his metaphor of the intellect as "a bit and a bridle"?

Related Works: "Once upon a Time" (p. 204), "Teenage Wasteland" (p. 799), "Gretel in Darkness" (p. 852), "Suicide Note" (p. 860), "Christopher Robin" (p. 1026), "The Chimney Sweeper" (p. 1144), "Birches" (p. 1069), *Death of a Salesman* (p. 1581)

HISAYE YAMAMOTO (1921–   ) was born in Redondo Beach, California, the daughter of emigrants from Kuamamota, Japan, and studied languages at Compton Junior College. She began writing as a teenager, contributing to columns in the English sections of Japanese-language newspapers. Forced to relocate with her family to an internment camp in Poston, Arizona, during World War II, Yamamoto authored the camp newsletter, *The Poston Chronicle*, as well as a mystery serial, *Death Rides the Rails to Poston*.

After her release, Yamamoto worked from 1945 to 1948 as a columnist for the *Los Angeles Tribune*. At the same time, she was submitting short stories about Japanese-American life to literary magazines such as *Partisan Review*, which in 1949 published "Seventeen Syllables." Yamamoto's output has been very small but nonetheless influential. She was, according to one editor, "one of the first Japanese-American writers to gain national recognition after the war, at a time when anti-Japanese sentiment was still rampant," and her story "Yoneko's Earthquake" was included in *Best American Short Stories 1952*.

Of the widely anthologized "Seventeen Syllables," Yamamoto has said that although the incidents are invented, it is the story of her mother. It was published in a collection in 1998 entitled *Seventeen Syllables and Other Stories*.

Cultural Context "Seventeen Syllables" was written in 1949, only four years after Japan's surrender ended World War II. On February 19, 1942, soon after the United States entered the war, President Franklin D. Roosevelt signed Executive Order 9066, which forcibly relocated 120,000 Japanese-Americans to one of ten internment camps — officially called "relocation camps." This order was primarily provoked by the Japanese attack on Pearl Harbor in which twenty-one ships of the United States Pacific Fleet were sunk or damaged and 2,403 Americans were killed. (In Canada, similar evacuation orders were signed, and 23,000 Canadians of Japanese descent were sent to internment camps in British Columbia.) The United States internment camps were overcrowded, and living conditions were quite difficult; barracks frequently had no plumbing or cooking facilities. Japanese-Americans remained in the camps until 1945, when the government released them. In spite of this treatment, the Japanese-American 442nd Combat Team participated in intense and bloody fighting during World War II and won over eighteen thousand individual decorations for valor. In 1988, Congress passed legislation granting reparations to the people who had been interned and sent them a letter of apology.

Seventeen Syllables (1949)

The first Rosie knew that her mother had taken to writing poems was one evening when she finished one and read it aloud for her daughter's approval. It was about cats, and Rosie pretended to understand it thoroughly and appreciate it no end, partly because she hesitated to disillusion her mother about the quantity and quality of Japanese she had learned in all the years now that she had been going to Japanese school every Saturday (and Wednesday, too, in the summer). Even so, her mother must have been skeptical about the depth of Rosie's understanding, because she explained afterwards about the kind of poem she was trying to write.

See, Rosie, she said, it was a *haiku*,° a poem in which she must pack all her meaning into seventeen syllables only, which were divided into three lines of five, seven, and five syllables. In the one she had just read, she had tried to capture the charm of a kitten, as well as comment on the superstition that owning a cat of three colors meant good luck.

"Yes, yes, I understand. How utterly lovely," Rosie said, and her mother, either satisfied or seeing through the deception and resigned, went back to composing.

The truth was that Rosie was lazy; English lay ready on the tongue but Japanese had to be searched for and examined, and even then put forth tentatively (probably to meet with laughter). It was so much easier to say yes, yes, even when one meant no, no. Besides, this was what was in her mind to say: I was looking through one of your magazines from Japan last night, Mother, and toward the back I found some *haiku* in English that delighted me. There was one that made me giggle off and on until I fell asleep —

> It is morning, and lo!
> I lie awake, comme il faut,
> sighing for some dough.

5   Now, how to reach her mother, how to communicate the melancholy song? Rosie knew formal Japanese by fits and starts, her mother had even less English, no French. It was much more possible to say yes, yes.

It developed that her mother was writing the *haiku* for a daily newspaper, the *Mainichi Shimbun*, that was published in San Francisco. Los Angeles, to be sure, was closer to the farming community in which the Hayashi family lived and several Japanese vernaculars° were printed there, but Rosie's parents said they preferred the tone of the northern paper. Once a week, the *Mainichi* would have a section devoted to *haiku*, and her mother became an extravagant contributor, taking for herself the blossoming pen name, Ume Hanazono.

So Rosie and her father lived for a while with two women, her mother and Ume Hanazono. Her mother (Tome Hayashi by name) kept house, cooked, washed, and, along with her husband and the Carrascos, the Mexican family

---

haiku: A classical Japanese poetical form.

vernaculars: Dialects, usually associated with particular regions.

hired for the harvest, did her ample share of picking tomatoes out in the sweltering fields and boxing them in tidy strata in the cool packing shed. Ume Hanazono, who came to life after the dinner dishes were done, was an earnest, muttering stranger who often neglected speaking when spoken to and stayed busy at the parlor table as late as midnight scribbling with pencil on scratch paper or carefully copying characters on good paper with her fat, pale-green Parker.

The new interest had some repercussions on the household routine. Before, Rosie had been accustomed to her parents and herself taking their hot baths early and going to bed almost immediately afterwards, unless her parents challenged each other to a game of flower cards or unless company dropped in. Now if her father wanted to play cards, he had to resort to solitaire (at which he always cheated fearlessly), and if a group of friends came over, it was bound to contain someone who was also writing *haiku*, and the small assemblage would be split in two, her father entertaining the non-literary members and her mother comparing ecstatic notes with the visiting poet.

If they went out, it was more of the same thing. But Ume Hanazono's life span, even for a poet's, was very brief — perhaps three months at most.

One night they went over to see the Hayano family in the neighboring town   10 to the west, an adventure both painful and attractive to Rosie. It was attractive because there were four Hayano girls, all lovely and each one named after a season of the year (Haru, Natsu, Aki, Fuyu), painful because something had been wrong with Mrs. Hayano ever since the birth of her first child. Rosie would sometimes watch Mrs. Hayano, reputed to have been the belle of her native village, making her way about a room, stooped, slowly shuffling, violently trembling (*always* trembling), and she would be reminded that this woman, in this same condition, had carried and given issue to three babies. She would look wonderingly at Mr. Hayano, handsome, tall, and strong, and she would look at her four pretty friends. But it was not a matter she could come to any decision about.

On this visit, however, Mrs. Hayano sat all evening in the rocker, as motionless and unobtrusive as it was possible for her to be, and Rosie found the greater part of the evening practically anaesthetic. Too, Rosie spent most of it in the girls' room, because Haru, the garrulous one, said almost as soon as the bows and other greetings were over, "Oh, you must see my new coat!"

It was a pale plaid of grey, sand, and blue, with an enormous collar, and Rosie, seeing nothing special in it, said, "Gee, how nice."

"Nice?" said Haru, indignantly. "Is that all you can say about it? It's gorgeous! And so cheap, too. Only seventeen ninety-eight, because it was a sale. The saleslady said it was twenty-five dollars regular."

"Gee," said Rosie. Natsu, who never said much and when she said anything said it shyly, fingered the coat covetously and Haru pulled it away.

"Mine," she said, putting it on. She minced in the aisle between the two large   15 beds and smiled happily. "Let's see how your mother likes it."

She broke into the front room and the adult conversation and went to stand in front of Rosie's mother, while the rest watched from the door. Rosie's mother was properly envious. "May I inherit it when you're through with it?"

Haru, pleased, giggled, and said yes, she could, but Natsu reminded gravely from the door, "You promised me, Haru."

Everyone laughed but Natsu, who shamefacedly retreated into the bedroom. Haru came in laughing, taking off the coat. "We were only kidding, Natsu," she said. "Here, you try it on now."

After Natsu buttoned herself into the coat, inspected herself solemnly in the bureau mirror, and reluctantly shed it, Rosie, Aki, and Fuyu got their turns, and Fuyu, who was eight, drowned in it while her sisters and Rosie doubled up in amusement. They all went into the front room later, because Haru's mother qua- veringly called to her to fix the tea and rice cakes and open a can of sliced peaches for everybody. Rosie noticed that her mother and Mr. Hayano were talking to- gether at the little table — they were discussing a *haiku* that Mr. Hayano was planning to send to the *Mainichi*, while her father was sitting at one end of the sofa looking through a copy of *Life*, the new picture magazine. Occasionally, her father would comment on a photograph, holding it toward Mrs. Hayano and speaking to her as he always did — loudly, as though he thought someone such as she must surely be at least a trifle deaf also.

20   The five girls had their refreshments at the kitchen table, and it was while Rosie was showing the sisters her trick of swallowing peach slices without chew- ing (she chased each slippery crescent down with a swig of tea) that her father brought his empty teacup and untouched saucer to the sink and said, "Come on, Rosie, we're going home now."

"Already?" asked Rosie.

"Work tomorrow," he said.

He sounded irritated, and Rosie, puzzled, gulped one last yellow slice and stood up to go, while the sisters began protesting, as was their wont.

"We have to get up at five-thirty," he told them, going into the front room quickly, so that they did not have their usual chance to hang onto his hands and plead for an extension of time.

25   Rosie, following, saw that her mother and Mr. Hayano were sipping tea and still talking together, while Mrs. Hayano concentrated, quivering, on raising the handleless Japanese cup to her lips with both her hands and lowering it back to her lap. Her father, saying nothing, went out the door, onto the bright porch, and down the steps. Her mother looked up and asked, "Where is he going?"

"Where is he going?" Rosie said. "He said we were going home now."

"Going home?" Her mother looked with embarrassment at Mr. Hayano and his absorbed wife and then forced a smile. "He must be tired," she said.

Haru was not giving up yet. "May Rosie stay overnight?" she asked, and Natsu, Aki, and Fuyu came to reinforce their sister's plea by helping her make a circle around Rosie's mother. Rosie, for once having no desire to stay, was relieved when her mother, apologizing to the perturbed Mr. and Mrs. Hayano for her father's abruptness at the same time, managed to shake her head no at the quartet, kindly but adamant, so that they broke their circle and let her go.

Rosie's father looked ahead into the windshield as the two joined him. "I'm sorry," her mother said. "You must be tired." Her father, stepping on the starter, said nothing. "You know how I get when it's *haiku*," she continued, "I forget what time it is." He only grunted.

As they rode homeward silently, Rosie, sitting between, felt a rush of hate for 30 both — for her mother for begging, for her father for denying her mother. I wish this old Ford would crash, right now, she thought, then immediately, no, no, I wish my father would laugh, but it was too late: already the vision had passed through her mind of the green pick-up crumpled in the dark against one of the mighty eucalyptus trees they were just riding past, of the three contorted, bleeding bodies, one of them hers.

Rosie ran between two patches of tomatoes, her heart working more rambunctiously than she had ever known it to. How lucky it was that Aunt Taka and Uncle Gimpachi had come tonight, though, how very lucky. Otherwise she might not have really kept her half-promise to meet Jesus Carrasco. Jesus was going to be a senior in September at the same school she went to, and his parents were the ones helping with the tomatoes this year. She and Jesus, who hardly remembered seeing each other at Cleveland High where there were so many other people and two whole grades between them, had become great friends this summer — he always had a joke for her when he periodically drove the loaded pick-up up from the fields to the shed where she was usually sorting while her mother and father did the packing, and they laughed a great deal together over infinitesimal repartee° during the afternoon break for chilled watermelon or ice cream in the shade of the shed.

What she enjoyed most was racing him to see which could finish picking a double row first. He, who could work faster, would tease her by slowing down until she thought she would surely pass him this time, then speeding up furiously to leave her several sprawling vines behind. Once he had made her screech hideously by crossing over, while her back was turned, to place atop the tomatoes in her green-stained bucket a truly monstrous, pale green worm (it had looked more like an infant snake). And it was when they had finished a contest this morning, after she had pantingly pointed a green finger at the immature tomatoes evident in the lugs° at the end of his row and he had returned the accusation (with justice), that he had startlingly brought up the matter of their possibly meeting outside the range of both their parents' dubious eyes.

"What for?" she had asked.

"I've got a secret I want to tell you," he said. 35

"Tell me now," she demanded.

"It won't be ready till tonight," he said.

She laughed. "Tell me tomorrow then."

"It'll be gone tomorrow," he threatened.

"Well, for seven hakes, what is it?" she had asked, more than twice, and when he had suggested that the packing shed would be an appropriate place to find out, she had cautiously answered maybe. She had not been certain she was going to keep the appointment until the arrival of mother's sister and her husband.

---

repartee: Witty conversation.
lugs: Shallow boxes in which produce is shipped to market.

Their coming seemed a sort of signal of permission, of grace, and she had definitely made up her mind to lie and leave as she was bowing them welcome.

40 So as soon as everyone appeared settled back for the evening, she announced loudly that she was going to the privy° outside, "I'm going to the *benjo!*"° and slipped out the door. And now that she was actually on her way, her heart pumped in such an undisciplined way that she could hear it with her ears. It's because I'm running, she told herself, slowing to a walk. The shed was up ahead, one more patch away, in the middle of the fields. Its bulk, looming in the dimness, took on a sinisterness that was funny when Rosie reminded herself that it was only a wooden frame with a canvas roof and three canvas walls that made a slapping noise on breezy days.

Jesus was sitting on the narrow plank that was the sorting platform and she went around to the other side and jumped backwards to seat herself on the rim of a packing stand. "Well, tell me," she said without greeting, thinking her voice sounded reassuringly familiar.

"I saw you coming out the door," Jesus said. "I heard you running part of the way, too."

"Uh-huh," Rosie said. "Now tell me the secret."

"I was afraid you wouldn't come," he said.

45 Rosie delved around on the chicken-wire bottom of the stall for number two tomatoes, ripe, which she was sitting beside, and came up with a left-over that felt edible. She bit into it and began sucking out the pulp and seeds. "I'm here," she pointed out.

"Rosie, are you sorry you came?"

"Sorry? What for?" she said. "You said you were going to tell me something."

"I will, I will," Jesus said, but his voice contained disappointment, and Rosie fleetingly felt the older of the two, realizing a brand-new power which vanished without category under her recognition.

"I have to go back in a minute," she said. "My aunt and uncle are here from Wintersburg. I told them I was going to the privy."

50 Jesus laughed. "You funny thing," he said. "You slay° me!"

"Just because you have a bathroom *inside*," Rosie said. "Come on, tell me."

Chuckling, Jesus came around to lean on the stand facing her. They still could not see each other very clearly, but Rosie noticed that Jesus became very sober again as he took the hollow tomato from her hand and dropped it back into the stall. When he took hold of her empty hand, she could find no words to protest; her vocabulary had become distressingly constricted and she thought desperately that all that remained intact now was yes and no and oh, and even these few sounds would not easily come out. Thus, kissed by Jesus, Rosie fell for the first time entirely victim to a helplessness delectable beyond speech. But the terrible,

---

privy: Outbuilding containing a toilet.

benjo: A lavatory with a flush toilet (Japanese).

slay: Amuse, delight (slang).

beautiful sensation lasted no more than a second, and the reality of Jesus' lips and togue and teeth and hands made her pull away with such strength that she nearly tumbled.

Rosie stopped running as she approached the lights from the windows of home. How long since she had left? She could not guess, but gasping yet, she went to the privy in back and locked herself in. Her own breathing deafened her in the dark, close space, and she sat and waited until she could hear at last the nightly calling of the frogs and crickets. Even then, all she could think to say was oh, my, and the pressure of Jesus' face against her face would not leave.

No one had missed her in the parlor, however, and Rosie walked in and through quickly, announcing that she was next going to take a bath. "Your father's in the bathhouse," her mother said, and Rosie, in her room, recalled that she had not seen him when she entered. There had been only Aunt Taka and Uncle Gimpachi with her mother at the table, drinking tea. She got her robe and straw sandals and crossed the parlor again to go outside. Her mother was telling them about the *haiku* competition in the *Mainichi* and the poem she had entered.

Rosie met her father coming out of the bathhouse. "Are you through, Father?" she asked. "I was going to ask you to scrub my back."

"Scrub your own back," he said shortly, going toward the main house.

"What have I done now?" she yelled after him. She suddenly felt like doing a lot of yelling. But he did not answer, and she went into the bathhouse. Turning on the dangling light, she removed her denims and T-shirt and threw them in the big carton for dirty clothes standing next to the washing machine. Her other things she took with her into the bath compartment to wash after her bath. After she had scooped a basin of hot water from the square wooden tub, she sat on the grey cement of the floor and soaped herself at exaggerated leisure, singing "Red Sails in the Sunset" at the top of her voice and using da-da-da where she suspected her words. Then, standing up, still singing, for she was possessed by the notion that any attempt now to analyze would result in spoilage and she believed that the larger her volume the less she would be able to hear herself think, she obtained more hot water and poured it on until she was free of lather. Only then did she allow herself to step into the steaming vat, one leg first, then the remainder of her body inch by inch until the water no longer stung and she could move around at will.

She took a long time soaking, afterwards remembering to go around outside to stoke the embers of the tin-lined fireplace beneath the tub and to throw on a few more sticks so that the water might keep its heat for her mother, and when she finally returned to the parlor, she found her mother still talking *haiku* with her aunt and uncle, the three of them on another round of tea. Her father was nowhere in sight.

At Japanese school the next day (Wednesday it was), Rosie was grave and giddy by turns. Preoccupied at her desk in the row for students on Book Eight, she made up for it at recess by performing wild mimicry for the benefit of her friend Chizuko. She held her nose and whined a witticism or two in what she considered was the manner of Fred Allen;° she assumed intoxication and a British accent to go over the climax of the Rudy Vallee° recording of the pub conversation about William Ewart Gladstone;° she was the child Shirley Temple° piping, "On the Good Ship Lollipop"; she was the gentleman soprano of the Four Inkspots° trilling, "If I Didn't Care." And she felt reasonably satisfied when Chizuko wept and gasped, "Oh, Rosie, you ought to be in the movies!"

60   Her father came after her at noon, bringing her sandwiches of minced ham and two nectarines to eat while she rode, so that she could pitch right into the sorting when they got home. The lugs were piling up, he said, and the ripe tomatoes in them would probably have to be taken to the cannery tomorrow if they were not ready for the produce haulers tonight. "This heat's not doing them any good. And we've got no time for a break today."

It *was* hot, probably the hottest day of the year, and Rosie's blouse stuck damply to her back even under the protection of the canvas. But she worked as efficiently as a flawless machine and kept the stalls heaped, with one part of her mind listening in to the parental murmuring about the heat and the tomatoes and with another part planning the exact words she would say to Jesus when he drove up with the first load of the afternoon. But when at last she saw that the pick-up was coming, her hands went berserk and the tomatoes started falling in the wrong stalls, and her father said, "Hey, hey! Rosie, watch what you're doing!"

"Well, I have to go to the *benjo*," she said, hiding panic.

"Go in the weeds over there," he said, only half-joking.

"Oh, Father!" she protested.

65   "Oh, go on home," her mother said. "We'll make out for awhile."

In the privy Rosie peered through a knothole toward the fields, watching as much as she could of Jesus. Happily she thought she saw him look in the direction of the house from time to time before he finished unloading and went back toward the patch where his mother and father worked. As she was heading for the shed, a very presentable black car purred up the dirt driveway to the house and its driver motioned to her. Was this the Hayashi home, he wanted to know. She nodded. Was she a Hayashi? Yes, she said, thinking that he was a good-looking man. He got out of the car with a huge, flat package and she saw that he warmly wore a business suit. "I have something here for your mother then," he said, in a more elegant Japanese than she was used to.

She told him where her mother was and he came along with her, patting his face with an immaculate white handkerchief and saying something about the coolness of San Francisco. To her surprised mother and father, he bowed and introduced himself as, among other things, the *haiku* editor of the *Mainichi Shimbun*,

---

Fred Allen: American humorist (1894–1956) and radio personality.

Rudy Vallee: American singer (1901–1986), stage, radio, and movie personality.

William Ewart Gladstone: English politician (1809–1902) and reformer.

Shirley Temple: Child actress (1928–   ) of the 1930s, known for her ringlets and dimples, singing and dancing.

Four Inkspots: African-American vocal group popular in the 1930s and 1940s.

saying that since he had been coming as far as Los Angeles anyway, he had decided to bring her the first prize she had won in the recent contest.

"First prize?" her mother echoed, believing and not believing, pleased and overwhelmed. Handed the package with a bow, she bobbed her head up and down numerous times to express her utter gratitude.

"It is nothing much," he added, "but I hope it will serve as a token of our great appreciation for your contributions and our great admiration of your considerable talent."

"I am not worthy," she said, falling easily into his style. "It is I who should   70 make some sign of my humble thanks for being permitted to contribute."

"No, no, to the contrary," he said, bowing again.

But Rosie's mother insisted, and then saying that she knew she was being unorthodox, she asked if she might open the package because her curiosity was so great. Certainly she might. In fact, he would like her reaction to it, for personally, it was one of his favorite *Hiroshiges*.

Rosie thought it was a pleasant picture, which looked to have been sketched with delicate quickness. There were pink clouds, containing some graceful calligraphy,° and a sea that was a pale blue except at the edges, containing four sampans° with indications of people in them. Pines edged the water and on the far-off beach there was a cluster of thatched huts towered over by pine-dotted mountains of grey and blue. The frame was scalloped and gilt.

After Rosie's mother pronounced it without peer and somewhat prodded her father into nodding agreement, she said Mr. Kuroda must at least have a cup of tea after coming all this way, and although Mr. Kuroda did not want to impose, he soon agreed that a cup of tea would be refreshing and went along with her to the house, carrying the picture for her.

"Ha, your mother's crazy!" Rosie's father said, and Rosie laughed uneasily as   75 she resumed judgment on the tomatoes. She had emptied six lugs when he broke into an imaginary conversation with Jesus to tell her to go and remind her mother of the tomatoes, and she went slowly.

Mr. Kuroda was in his shirtsleeves expounding some *haiku* theory as he munched a rice cake, and her mother was rapt. Abashed in the great man's presence, Rosie stood next to her mother's chair until her mother looked up inquiringly, and then she started to whisper the message, but her mother pushed her gently away and reproached, "You are not being very polite to our guest."

"Father says the tomatoes . . ." Rosie said aloud, smiling foolishly.

"Tell him I shall only be a minute," her mother said, speaking the language of Mr. Kuroda.

When Rosie carried the reply to her father, he did not seem to hear and she said again, "Mother says she'll be back in a minute."

"All right, all right," he nodded, and they worked again in silence. But sud-   80 denly, her father uttered an incredible noise, exactly like the cork of a bottle

---

calligraphy: Graceful or artistic handwriting.

sampans: Flat-bottomed Asian boats, usually propelled with oars.

popping, and the next Rosie knew, he was stalking angrily toward the house, almost running in fact, and she chased after him crying, "Father! Father! What
are you going to do?"

He stopped long enough to order her back to the shed. "Never mind!" he
shouted. "Get on with the sorting!"

And from the place in the fields where she stood, frightened and vacillating,
Rosie saw her father enter the house. Soon Mr. Kuroda came out alone, putting
on his coat. Mr. Kuroda got into his car and backed out down the driveway onto
the highway. Next her father emerged, also alone, something in his arms (it was
the picture, she realized), and, going over to the bathhouse woodpile, he threw the
picture on the ground and picked up the axe. Smashing the picture, glass and all
(she heard the explosion faintly), he reached over for the kerosene that was used
to encourage the bath fire and poured it over the wreckage. I am dreaming, Rosie
said to herself, I am dreaming, but her father, having made sure that his act of cre-
mation was irrevocable, was even then returning to the fields.

Rosie ran past him and toward the house. What had become of her mother?
She burst into the parlor and found her mother at the back window watching the
dying fire. They watched together until there remained only a feeble smoke under
the blazing sun. Her mother was very calm.

"Do you know why I married your father?" she said without turning.

85 "No," said Rosie. It was the most frightening question she had ever been called
upon to answer. Don't tell me now, she wanted to say, tell me tomorrow, tell me
next week, don't tell me today. But she knew she would be told now, that the
telling would combine with the other violence of the hot afternoon to level her
life, her world to the very ground.

It was like a story out of the magazines illustrated in sepia,° which she had
consumed so greedily for a period until the information had somehow reached her
that those wretchedly unhappy autobiographies, offered to her as the testimoni-
als of living men and women, were largely inventions: Her mother, at nineteen,
had come to America and married her father as an alternative to suicide.

At eighteen she had been in love with the first son of one of the well-to-do
families in her village. The two had met whenever and wherever they could, secretly, because it would not have done for his family to see him favor her — her
father had no money; he was a drunkard and a gambler besides. She had learned
she was with child; an excellent match had already been arranged for her lover.
Despised by her family, she had given premature birth to a stillborn son, who
would be seventeen now. Her family did not turn her out, but she could no longer
project herself in any direction without refreshing in them the memory of her indiscretion. She wrote to Aunt Taka, her favorite sister in America, threatening to
kill herself if Aunt Taka would not send for her. Aunt Taka hastily arranged a
marriage with a young man of whom she knew, but lately arrived from Japan, a
young man of simple mind, it was said, but of kindly heart. The young man was
never told why his unseen betrothed was so eager to hasten the day of meeting.

---

sepia: A grayish-brown ink or pigment.

The story was told perfectly, with neither groping for words nor untoward passion. It was as though her mother had memorized it by heart, reciting it to herself so many times over that its nagging vileness had long since gone.

"I had a brother then?" Rosie asked, for this was what seemed to matter now; she would think about the other later, she assured herself, pushing back the illumination which threatened all that darkness that had hitherto been merely mysterious or even glamorous. "A half-brother?"

"Yes."

"I would have liked a brother," she said.

Suddenly, her mother knelt on the floor and took her by the wrists. "Rosie," 90 she said urgently, "promise me you will never marry!" Shocked more by the request than the revelation, Rosie stared at her mother's face. Jesus, Jesus, she called silently, not certain whether she was invoking the help of the son of the Carrascos or of God, until there returned sweetly the memory of Jesus' hand, how it had touched her and where. Still her mother waited for an answer, holding her wrists so tightly that her hands were going numb. She tried to pull free. Promise, her mother whispered fiercely, promise. Yes, yes, I promise, Rosie said. But for an instant she turned away, and her mother, hearing the familiar glib agreement, released her. Oh, you, you, you, her eyes and twisted mouth said, you fool. Rosie, covering her face, began at last to cry, and the embrace and consoling hand came much later than she expected.

Reading and Reacting

1. Why do you think Rosie's mother begins writing haiku? Why does she stop?
2. What does the narrator mean when she says, "So Rosie and her father lived for a while with two women, her mother and Ume Hanazono" (par. 7)? How are these two women different?
3. How does the fact that the mother writes haiku reveal the differences between Rosie's mother and father? Why does Rosie's father destroy his wife's prize? Do you think his actions are understandable? Do you think they are justified?
4. What role does Mrs. Hayano play in the story? How does she shed light on Rosie's mother's life and on her motivation?
5. Explain how the conflict between each of the following contributes to your understanding of the story:
   - husband and wife
   - mother and daughter
   - Japanese culture and American culture
   - Rosie's mother and Ume Hanazono
   - farm work and poetry
6. Who is the story's main character? Explain.
7. What is the story really about? Creativity? Communication? Culture? Tradition? Work? Gender roles? Something else?
8. How would you sum up the story's major theme? In what way does the title express that theme?

9. JOURNAL ENTRY In paragraphs 84 through 88, Rosie's mother tells her daughter the story of her life. What is the significance of this story? In what sense is this tale — "told perfectly" — the heart of the story?

10. CRITICAL PERSPECTIVE In his article "The *Issei* Father in the Fiction of Hisaye Yamamoto," Charles Crow observes that Yamamoto's stories deal with the disruptions of Japanese-American life caused by World II. Parents, who in many cases were born in Japan, came into conflict with children who had assimilated into the American mainstream. "Like most Japanese-American authors," says Crow, "Yamamoto explores the frustrated relationship between these two generations — a relationship which changed abruptly and forever in the relocation centers during the war."

In what sense is "Seventeen Syllables" about the struggle between two generations of Japanese-Americans? How do the different perspectives of the two generations frustrate their attempts to communicate with each other? Is this generational struggle the story's primary focus, or is the story really about something else?

Related Works: "Everyday Use" (p. 469), "The Chrysanthemums" (p. 783), "Two Kinds" (p. 791), "Dear Mama" (p. 1062), "Four Haiku" (p. 1012), *A Doll House* (p. 1454)

GINA OCHSNER (1970—   ) burst onto the American literary scene after completing a Master of Fine Arts degree in fiction from the University of Oregon in 1997. Her first collection of stories, *The Necessary Grace to Fall* (2002), was published by the University of Georgia Press and was the winner of the Flannery O'Connor Award for Short Fiction, the Oregon Book Awards' H. L. Davis Award for Fiction, and the Pacific Northwest Booksellers Association's 2003 Book Awards. Her second collection, *People I Wanted to Be*, was published in 2005. Her stories "The Fractious South" and "Thicker Than Water" appeared in *The New Yorker* in 2004 and 2005, respectively. As the result of her lifelong interest in Eastern Europe and Russia, as well as the Russian immigrants who settled in her native Oregon, Ochsner's stories are informed by her study of these cultures, and the stories themselves often take place in either in Russia or Oregon.

Cultural Context The ancient Slavic people believed that the spirits of young women who drowned lived at the bottom of lakes and ponds. Several different Russian folk tales incorporate the idea of an underwater world where magical and mystical events can occur. One such tale is that of Sadko, a musician who was summoned by the King of the Blue Seas to play his music underwater. In return for his services, the king offered him advice that, when followed, made Sadko the Bard one of the richest merchants in town. In Russian folklore, that which happens underwater can profoundly affect the fortunes of those on land, as the characters in this story discover.

Hidden Lives of Lakes (2003)

ON A DAY WHEN the hoarfrost° brought the sightline down to a quiver, Glasha and Luba, coworkers at the petrochemical plant and best friends, skidded onto the frozen ice of the lake. They were sitting in a canoe and pushing themselves over the ice, Glasha with her kitchen mops, and sitting opposite of her, Luba with her black rubber toilet-bowl plungers. With each push, Luba knew that Glasha was imagining the pitch of the May Day cheers when she and Luba would glide past the finish line, well ahead of the other canoers. For her part, Luba was only participating in this folly because the doctor had told her that her figure was far too Russian, that is to say, fat.

When they had reached about a third of the way across the lake Glasha laid her mops over the gunwale° and withdrew a silver flask from a coat pocket and uncapped it. From somewhere near the middle of the lake Luba heard a strange humming and for a moment she thought it was the sound of ice threatening to crack. Luba climbed out of the canoe, got on her hands and knees, and pressed her ear to the ice. Then she held the bells of the plungers to her ears. When she did, the humming amplified and separated into the buzz of voices of both men and women. They were speaking in the police form of Russian, addressing each other in *vuis* instead of *tuis*,° speaking with a grace she hadn't heard in town for years. It was a beautiful noise and Luba flapped the plungers at her ears so as to achieve a stereo effect, though she imagined she looked a little like a fish breathing through rubber gills.

"What are you doing?" Glasha capped her flask.

"Here." Luba sat back on her heels and handed Glasha a plunger. "Listen. Do you hear that?"

"What?"

"That whispering." Luba pointed to the ice. Glasha leaned over the side of the boat and narrowed her eyes. "It's coming from over there." Luba pointed to the middle of the lake.

"I don't like this," Glasha said quietly. "Let's go." Luba climbed back into the canoe. Glasha gave a tremendous shove with her mops and sent the boat lurching, and all the way to shore, Luba had to work hard to keep up with the steady haul Glasha made with her mops.

That night as her husband, Oleg, sat finishing a bottle of Crowbar, Luba told him about the voices she'd heard below the ice.

"So what," he said, placing the dead bottle horizontally on the table.

"So don't you want to know what they are saying?"

"Not really," Oleg said, turning the bottle upside down and shaking it over a cup.

---

hoarfrost: Frozen dew that forms a white coating on a surface.

gunwale: The top edge of a ship's sides.

vuis . . . tuis: The formal (vui) and informal (tui) pronoun forms of address in the Russian language.

But in the morning, Oleg had changed his mind.

"Let's take a picnic," he said, ringing up Glasha's husband, Ivan. He and Ivan worked together at the factory, assembling the guidance mechanisms to antiaircraft missiles, though Luba had gathered Oleg felt it was impolite to say so. For years he'd been telling the downstairs neighbors that he and Ivan inserted tiny sprockets in timepieces. Either way, Luba could hardly imagine Ivan capable of such delicate work. He was a large man with a thick torso and wide shoulders. And owing to the fact that he had a red chafing mark below his lower lip, like the bite burns kids get, Luba could not help thinking that despite Ivan's great bulk, there was something permanently childlike about him.

They set out at lunchtime, Glasha with extra blankets, Ivan his two fishing poles, and Oleg his fishing net. Behind her, Luba pulled a sled carrying a plunger and their picnic. Her teeth ached in the cold; her hips and back tired of this tentative walk, her weight carefully distributed over her feet.

15   At the middle of the lake where the slabs were known to give way, Luba walked doubled over. She was watching for the dark ice, which, undermined by mysterious currents, was warmer than the paler stretches of ice. When she thought they were at the same place they'd been the day before, Luba dropped to her knees and flapped her plunger at her ear. Luba held her breath. Then she heard it again: that quiet murmuring. Luba gave a little shout and signaled the others.

With three hundred grams of vodka and a match they melted a kopeck-size hole. For two hours they shaved at the ice with Luba's good butter knife; they melted the edges of the hole with their cigarette lighters. Around three o'clock, when the bright disk of the sun tipped on edge and drew the remaining light to a point behind the stand of birch, they'd chipped out a hole large enough for a man to jump into.

What Luba noticed straight off was that the water wasn't grainy and dark the way ice water should be. Rather, it was as clear as the tap water she'd seen running out of the faucets in the kitchens of women in Western commercials. And owing to the width of the hole, Luba could see tundra swans sealed within the strata of ice. Their wings were outstretched as if the ice had caught them midflight. Beneath them was a used syringe and a ladies' evening dress. About half a meter farther down, an aria had been trapped in the ice. The notes looked like the dark round seeds within willow pods. Glasha bent over the hole and picked at the notes with her fingernails, and they whittered into flight as a beautiful cry. Farther below, where the ice turned darker in color, was a school of carp, their eyes gazing past her in the distant promise of a summer thaw.

They stood around the hole, studying the water for a few minutes.

"Look!" Glasha waved her gloves frantically. Beneath the transparent lip of ice a pair of shoes, a comb, a child's doll, a broom, horse, a much-revered icon of St. Fursa° stepping on the devil's leathery wings, gently drifted past. And then, to

---

St. Fursa: An important Irish Saint who died c. A.D. 650.

their surprise, even larger items floated past the hole: a rusted park bench; a statue of Lenin,° his bronze coat flying out behind him as if from the force of a winter gale; a piece of the golden dome of their church, which long ago had been dynamited and sunk in the contaminated bog outside town.

"How can it be!" Luba cried, for it seemed to her that they were viewing a   20 disassembled version of their town as it was many years ago, an entire town of clutter moving with that slow grace given to things carried by water. There went Old Fedya's ratty prayer ropes, Glasha's missing pig, tins of potted meats, a bottle of watered-down rocket fuel, a chicken, the broken neck of a violin, and fibrillating scraps of newspaper. A T-shirt with a popular saying, SAME SHIT, DIFFERENT DAY, whirled up to the surface, along with a pair of Adidas sport pants, the fashionable kind with the white stripe down the side that Luba's daughter had once begged her for.

Oleg dipped his fishing net into the hole and caught the pants as they went swirling by. He shook his head and wrung the excess water from the pants. "All this time we've been canoeing over the lake in summer, we could have been fishing. We'd have been rich by now!"

Ivan licked his thumb, held it to the cold, measuring the lowering frost. Then he dropped his line in. "True enough. But where are all the people?" Ivan balanced an enormous foot on the lip of the hole.

Luba bent over the hole with a plunger at her ear. "Maybe they're afraid of us."

"Maybe we're afraid of them!" Glasha uncapped her flask and took a liberal drink.

"Look!" Ivan hopped from foot to foot. All the grandmothers and grand-   25 fathers, children and family pets they'd lost, church members and old friends long departed from the factory, the man from the state office who'd come to examine the caulking around their toilets, drifted slowly past the hole. They were naked, most of them, naked and they never looked better. For they swam about freely under the ice, their movements fluid and smooth. Every now and again, someone would float so close to the surface, face upturned and eyes frosted over, that Luba thought she might touch them as they passed under the open hole.

Oleg and Ivan dropped their lines into the hole. Immediately Ivan felt a tug and Oleg held him around his waist while he reeled in his catch. It was Manyasha, who'd once lived next door to Glasha and Ivan. They took one look at Manyasha, an indestructible babushka° who'd never permitted herself more than a pinched smile, and Ivan tossed her back in.

They fished awhile longer, and this time Oleg's line went taut. Luba gripped her husband by his belt and leaned back. It took several minutes of hauling up hard, and just when Luba thought she couldn't hold on anymore she heard a tremendous splash at the hole. Oleg jumped back in surprise and dropped his pole. It was Borya, Oleg's uncle, spitting water from his mouth and flailing his arms. At last, he calmed down a bit and managed to remove the hook from his armpit.

Lenin: Vladimir Ilich Lenin, radical Russian leader of the Bolshevik Revolution in 1917.

babushka: A traditional Russian grandmother figure.

"Oh, Uncle Borya!" Oleg knelt and offered Uncle Borya his hand. "I hope we didn't hurt you."

Uncle Borya regarded them for a moment. His eyes were frosted over and Luba couldn't see the pupils of his eyes.

30   "I always did think you were an idiot, Oleg. But I like your wife. How are things, Luba?" Uncle Borya smiled then and Luba saw that since he'd died he'd lost three more teeth.

"Very good, Uncle." Luba unwound her cobalt blue scarf from around her neck and handed it to Borya. "We are so sorry for disturbing you like this, but, to be honest, we thought you were dead." Uncle Borya tied the scarf around his neck.

"Everyone thinks that." Uncle Borya narrowed his pasty eyes and studied his nephew. "So now that I'm here, what do you want?"

"Well, I guess we're wondering what you are doing down there." Oleg sat on the ice and handed Borya a flask of a Special Export.

"This and that. Mostly I read the dictionary and tell jokes."

35   "Jokes?" Luba slapped her ear with her mitten, forcing the blood.

"Yes, the Joke Convention meets this time of year. But when we run out of jokes, we become like the carp, very still, and we listen to the ice and life above the ice." Uncle Borya scratched his chin where bits of ice clung to his beard. "Incidentally, would you mind very much bringing me a cabbage pie?" Uncle Borya turned to Luba and winked. "The carp don't taste good this time of year."

"Who else is down there?" Glasha shouldered Luba away from the hole.

"Oh, all sorts of people. You'd be surprised, but then, I'm not supposed to say."

"Why not?" Glasha narrowed her eyes.

40   Uncle Borya studied the tree line, then bobbed his head up and down. "Excuse me, please, but the Finnish Shouting Choir is about to perform. If you listen you can hear them warming up." Borya pointed to the far end of the lake, then put his hands over his ears and slipped below the water. As if on cue, the Finnish Shouting Choir drifted by en masse, nude save for their choral music, which they clutched to their chests.

They stood for a moment longer peering at the hole in the ice. "Well, that's that." Oleg straightened and brushed ice crystals from the back of his pants. The last light behind the trees had collapsed to a gritty smear of pollution.

"Yes." Ivan ran his tongue over the raw patch under his lower lip. "Let's go back. There's a good foreign feature playing at the kino."° The air had turned to grain, to the kind of night when driving would be forbidden, and if they were to get to the movies, they'd have to hurry. As the others trudged ahead. Luba turned back for one last look at the hole. Just then a silver lorgnette,° like the one her grandmother had, floated by, a single white ladies' glove following in its wake. Luba crouched over the hole. For a moment she imagined drinking the water, or just splashing it over her face to feel the wetness, to feel what it was that kept Uncle Borya so happy for a dead man. Luba dipped the tip of her glove into the water, breaking to fractions the image of her face blinking back at her.

---

kino: Movie theater.

lorgnette: A pair of glasses with a short handle at the side. Also called *opera glasses.*

Each evening Glasha and Luba chiseled at the hole, both to keep it from freezing back over and also to see what else they might find. The following Saturday, Glasha, Ivan, Oleg, and Luba went back out onto the ice. Though Glasha and Ivan liked to drop in a fishing line, Oleg stood ready with the net, hauling up a soggy handkerchief and bottles of herbal vitamins, a real find, which he tossed onto the sled with a quick motion of his wrist. For her part, Luba couldn't bring herself to use a hook and instead swirled the handle of her plunger in the hole. When she felt the handle bump into something, Luba dropped to her knees. There in the water staring back up at her, as a face in a mirror, was Batushka, their beloved priest, dead now for three years. Batushka poked his head through the water.

"That really hurt, you know, but I forgive you."

"Batushka!" Luba cried, tears crusting the corners of her eyes.   45

"Batushka, if we may." Ivan ventured cautiously toward the hole. "What are you doing down there in the ice? You are dead and buried, at Diveyevo,° no?" Ivan asked, for he and Oleg, along with a few others, had carried Batushka's body to his final resting place.

"I can't say," Batushka said with a sad smile.

Glasha lowered her brows. "Not so fast. There's a rule for this. If you catch something, on a hook, say, you have a right to ask it questions and it must answer truthfully."

"You are right." Batushka sighed loudly, reaching for Oleg's bottle of Special Export. "But don't blame me if you don't like the answers I give."

"But what was wrong with Diveyevo?" Ivan asked.   50

"Oh, that again." Batushka rolled his eyes. "Nothing was wrong with it, I just wish to be humble"— Batushka broke flakes of ice and crunched them loudly between his teeth —" to be as close to the earth as possible." Under Batushka's fingernails were little clumps of mud from the bottom of the lake; in his ears, bits of grass.

"I don't understand." Oleg pumped his shoulders up and down. "I'm listening, and I'm trying to believe what I'm hearing, but it's not making sense. You're dead. And so are you." Oleg nodded to Borya, who'd surfaced just long enough to grab Luba's cabbage pie. "And I'm not dreaming. I'm alive!" Oleg thumped his gloved fist against his chest.

Batushka wagged his head slowly from side to side and made clicking noises with his tongue. "This reminds me of the parable of Josef's chicken. Would you like to hear it?"

"No!" Glasha stamped her feet.

"Then excuse me"— Batushka recapped the bottle and slid it across the ice to   55
Oleg —"but I am not cold." With that Batushka slipped under the ice.

"But we didn't get to ask all our questions." Ivan's lower lip trembled and Oleg handed him a plastic bottle of vitamins.

"We'll just have to come back, for as long as it takes." Oleg sighed and hitched himself to the sled piled with frozen trinkets. They turned for shore then, Glasha

---

Diveyevo: A town in Russia.

trudging ahead of the men while Luba trailed behind, noting how the strand of lights from the lake's edge were duplicated as dull spots on the ice.

That night Luba lay in bed while Oleg draped his haul over their ancient heating pipes. As she listened to her husband catalogue his inventory, she wondered about the thickness of sleep and ice and the dreams, those trellis-white bones, the towns-people below them might be dreaming. Luba tried to imagine being so humble, so close to the earth, that she'd wake each morning coughing up clay wiping it from her ears and nostrils. That was grace, the real article, to be washed over, to drown in it.

The following Monday, after work, the four set off again for the center of the lake. Glasha brought several sheets of paper, one for each day of the week, and below the heading, a list of questions ranging from how much longer she'd have to care for her ailing mother to which shops would be carrying butter. Ivan brought a troubling crossword puzzle. Oleg brought a longer fishing net and Luba brought more cabbage pies. When they got there, Glasha called Batushka for nearly an hour while Oleg fished. Crusts of ice lined their eyelashes, the corners of their eyes, and still, no Batushka. At last Oleg hooked his Uncle Borya again, who came kicking and fighting the whole way to the surface of the water.

60   "Batushka!" Glasha cried. "We came to see Batushka!"

Scraps of newspaper churned to the surface where the wind snatched them up, letters of the heavy line-print falling like seeds onto the ice. "Oh, not to worry," Borya said, watching little black letters from the headlines of the last election re-arrange themselves into new words. "He's having a little rest just below the former first secretaries and the retired gymnasts."

"Well, swim back down there and wake him. It's important." Glasha unfolded her Monday list and tapped her foot impatiently.

In a few moments Batushka chuffed through the hole. His eyes looked especially opaque, and when Luba bent to kiss him on both cheeks, she squeezed her eyes shut, afraid she'd catch a glimpse of her own image returned in the pale orbs of his eyes. Glasha waved her list at Batushka then and they spent a solid hour taking their turns with Batushka, as they had when he took confession. They left only after Glasha extracted a promise delivered through splayed fingers and yawn — but a promise, no less — that whenever they called for him, Batushka would swim to the surface.

They continued going out to the hole each night for several weeks, Glasha with her lists, Oleg his net, Ivan his crosswords. But it seemed to Luba the more they asked of Batushka, the vaguer his answers became. Sometimes, he didn't an-swer at all and broke out instead into silly nursery rhymes. Even worse, with each visit, they came back home smelling more and more like the lake, and Luba couldn't get the reek of carp off her fingers or out of their flat.

65   One Friday night, when the moon was a crumpled tissue in the sky, the four set out for the lake.

"Batushka!" Glasha cried as soon as they reached the hole. Then she dropped to her knees. "I want to live life, the way they do in movies!" Glasha threw her hands up, a gesture Luba had seen her practice in front of the mirror in the women's toilets at the petrochemical plant.

"So live, why don't you?" Batushka snapped as he surfaced. "Ask my your question, already."

"This life — what's it for?" Glasha asked, blinking her eyes rapidly.

Batushka's face hardened. He turned his shoulders in the water away from Glasha and looked at the far end of the lake where the birches had grown slender and sparse. "Did you know that people ask much more interesting questions when they are dead?"

Glasha groaned. "Batushka! I'm not happy. What should I do?" 70

"And did you know"—Batushka swung his head around and met her gaze — "that at night the town dreams of itself?" Batushka smiled, a beatific, serene smile.

"This isn't fair! You're not answering my questions." Glasha stomped up and down. Near the hole a small crack zigzagged from the edge of the ice.

Batushka's eyes brightened. "Each city is a lonely one, knowing it is not right, not complete, longing for something it cannot name." Batushka, still smiling, began to sink slowly into the hole as if someone were gently pulling him down by the heels.

Glasha bent over the hole, cupped her hands around her mouth. "At the very least I want my pig back!" Glasha's words whistled as they dropped to her feet in a small pile of ice crystals.

Then she turned and stomped toward the shore. Ivan watched his wife for a 75 moment, then hitched himself to Oleg, who hitched himself to the sled.

"I'll be glad for the thaw," Oleg said with a pull.

"I always wanted to believe in God, but it never seemed to work out." Ivan leaned into the harness. "Now all I've got are these herbal vitamins," he said, running his tongue over the chafed are of red skin.

"Vitamins! Well, that's something." Oleg hooked his arm under Ivan's and together they pulled the sled.

That evening Luba lay in bed listening to a dog baying. Outside her bedroom window she could see the frost shortening the horizon, bringing down the moon. She supposed that was what the dog was crying about, singing with a sadness that sounded a little like joy. Luba lay there carried by the sounds of the dog and waited for grace to wash over her, afraid that it never would, had left her completely. But you can't wait forever; that's not living. Luba climbed out of bed and scratched a fingernail into the hoarfrost at the windowpane. Outside the land was pale blue and long with the promise of silent winter and the sure drop of snow.

She thought of those voices, comforting, murmuring conjugations of lost 80 verbs, contemplating the weather, and, of course, telling their many jokes. Luba smiled. She could just hear it now, the one about the penguins in the movie house and Uncle Borya slapping his thighs in glee. Luba pulled on her thermal underwear, her work uniform, her boots and coat. She tiptoed through the flat and let herself outside, where she turned for the lake. She could see her breath freeze before her eyes and fall to the ground at her feet, a gentle sound, the rattling of tiny stars. With each punch of her boots through the crusts of snow, she wondered what it would take to will oneself back to the mud. A baptism among the duckweed and swaying fescue, only this time she wouldn't plug her nose and hold her breath as she had when Batushka held his hand under her back and dipped her down all those years ago. No. She'd plunge in, feet first, her clothes dragging her down into the depths.

Luba walked until she reached the hole. Already it had begun to freeze over, a thin lattice of ice crusting its edges. Luba took off her glove and immersed her hand up to her wrist. It wasn't as cold as she thought it would be, for in all their visits to the ice, none of them had ever once gotten wet. Then she heard the voices. They rose steadily, a chorus, one after the other, of reedy voices canting a wet catechism, and the sound was that of old memories.

Luba removed her other glove, her scarf, her hat, her coat, her boots. She would leave behind this clumsy life. The water would remake her, strip her of all that didn't matter. She would trade this dim existence for the embrace of water's quiet, where she could contemplate life from below this tormented land. Trade it for the absurdity of floating green skies and a sun filtered through ice.

Reading and Reacting

1. What brings Luba and Glasha to the lake? What causes them to suspect that something is unusual?
2. When they first cut a hole in the ice, what do Luba, Glasha, and their husbands see? What is their initial response? Is their response surprising or expected?
3. Who are the people under the ice? What are they doing there?
4. What questions do the characters ask Batushka, the dead priest? What do their questions reveal about them? Why do you think Batushka's answers become vaguer and vaguer?
5. In this story, human characters come in contact with the world of the dead. How do they react to this encounter? Do their reactions change over time?
6. In paragraph 77, Ivan says, "I always wanted to believe in God, but it never seemed to work out." Ivan and the other characters seem to sense that they are lacking something. What do you think they lack?
7. Why does Luba decide to plunge into the lake? In what sense is her action "a baptism" (par. 80)?
8. What themes does "Hidden Lives of Lakes" express? Which of these themes do you see as the major theme of the story?
9. JOURNAL ENTRY If you could communicate with the dead, what questions would you ask? How would your questions be like or unlike those the characters in "Hidden Lives of Lakes" ask?
10. CRITICAL PERSPECTIVE According to Dan Hays, many of Ochsner's stories "are set in Eatern Europe, drawn from the mythology of that area, or involve characters descended from there. But the themes and stories are universal, the people recognizable." Do you agree with Hays? In what respects are Ochsner's characters and themes universal? In what respects are they particularly Eastern European?

Related Works: "The Water Faucet Vision" (p. 240), "The Disappearance" (p. 371), "Cathedral" (p. 476), "Suicide Note" (p. 860), "For the Grave of Daniel Boone" (p. 894), "Death Be Not Proud" (p. 1168), *The Cuban Swimmer* (p. 1772)

WRITING SUGGESTIONS: Theme

1. In both "Doe Season" and "Seventeen Syllables," a young girl learns a hard lesson. Write an essay in which you compare the lessons that Andy and Rosie learn and discuss the effects the knowledge they gain has on them.
2. Two of the stories in this chapter deal with the importance of patience and persistence. Write an essay in which you examine the value of enduring despite difficulties, citing the experiences of the main characters in "Seventeen Syllables" and "A Worn Path."
3. Two of the stories in this chapter deal with characters who have strange or supernatural encounters. In "The Rocking-Horse Winner," Paul is able to predict the winners of horse races after he rides his rocking horse. In "Hidden Lives of Lakes," Luba and Glasha discover dead people swimming in a lake. In what ways do these encounters change the lives of these characters? How are these encounters similar, and how are they different?
4. Both "The Rocking-Horse Winner" and "A Worn Path" deal with characters who make journeys. What is the significance of each journey? How do the protagonists of these two stories overcome the obstacles they encounter? In what sense are these journeys symbolic as well as actual?
5. Like "Doe Season," the following poem focuses on a child's experience with bunting. Write an essay in which you contrast its central theme with the central theme of "Doe Season."

ROBERT HUFF (1924–1993)

Rainbow*

After the shot the driven feathers rock
In the air and are by sunlight trapped.
Their moment of descent is eloquent.
It is the rainbow echo of a bird
Whose thunder, stopped, puts in my daughter's eyes   5
A question mark. She does not see the rainbow,
And the folding bird-fall was for her too quick.
It is about the stillness of the bird
Her eyes are asking. She is three years old;
Has cut her fingers; found blood tastes of salt;   10
But she has never witnessed quiet blood,
Nor ever seen before the peace of death.
I say: "The feathers — Look!" but she is torn
And wretched and draws back. And I am glad
That I have wounded her, have winged her heart,   15
And that she goes beyond my fathering.

---

* Publication date is not available.

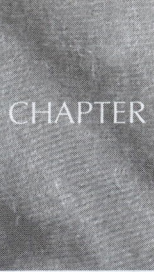

CHAPTER 19

FICTION IN FILM

When adapting works of fiction into the medium of film, filmmakers have many decisions to make. Should the film tell the entire story or just part of it? Will all the characters make an appearance? Which scenes, characters, and objects will be highlighted? Will the setting change? Will the film end the same way as the story? Will the film include voice-over narration to represent a story's first-person narrator?

Turning a story into a film is not easy. After all, film and prose fiction are two entirely different media, and each has its own way of telling stories and expressing ideas. For one thing, a short story is made up of words that are interpreted by a reader. Even an extremely detailed story contains gaps or ambiguities that readers must fill in. No matter how detailed the writer's description of a character is, every reader has to visualize his or her own version of that character, a version that may conform in only the most general sense to the cues the writer supplies. In short, readers must use their imaginations to supply the images, ideas, and feelings that the story needs if it is to work.

Film, on the other hand, is very literal: the audience sees exactly what characters look like and how they act and react. There are few gaps or ambiguities, at least as far as images are concerned, and filmmakers can use various techniques — not just words — to express emotions or to convey ideas. By experimenting with camera angles, close-ups, lighting, editing, special effects, color, sound, and music, a filmmaker can create a particular mood or increase dramatic tension. And, of course, the choice of actors will influence the audience's reaction to the film.

Another difference between films and short stories involves how a story is told. A short story always has a narrator — someone who tells what happens. This narrator can be a character or an outsider; the point of view can be omniscient or limited to the perspective of a single character. The narrator can know a great deal about the characters and their motivations or be unaware of almost everything — including details that readers know. Thus, writers of short stories are able to manipulate narrative point of view to add depth and complexity.

Compared to writers of short stories, filmmakers are somewhat restricted in their ability to tell a story. Although filmmakers can use music, voice-over narration, and close-ups to suggest a character's thoughts, for the most part they have to present scenes and characters dramatically — that is, viewers learn about characters by observing them.

So, what elements translate most easily from story to film? The plot (or story line) can usually be adapted. So can the characters and the setting, as well as a limited number of general themes. Still, to make a film from a short story, a film-maker has to make changes, often rearranging plot elements, deleting minor characters, and eliminating long passages of description or background material.

This chapter asks you to study still photographs taken from DVDs of five short stories that are included in this anthology:

Film Series

DVD

- John Updike's "A&P" (p. 230)
- Tillie Olsen's "I Stand Here Ironing" (p. 309)
- Alice Walker's "Everyday Use" (p. 469)
- Raymond Carver's "Cathedral" (p. 476)
- Eudora Welty's "A Worn Path" (p. 505)

The photos are followed by a series of questions that ask you to think about the decisions you would make if you were adapting each of the stories into a short film.

As you answer the questions, remember that a film is always a reinterpretation — not a copy — of the original story. It has to treat the subject in a way that takes advantage of film's dramatic and visual strengths while in the process preserving what it can from the story. Also keep in mind that each story presents its own set of challenges to filmmakers — challenges that have to be addressed before the story can be made into a film that is true to the spirit of the original.

John Updike's "A&P"

Character is central to "A&P" (p. 230), and the DVD version of the story characterizes Sammy, Stokesie, Lengel, and Queenie and her friends visually as well as through their dialogue and actions. The supermarket setting — so vividly described in the story — also comes to life on the screen. The stills included here depict scenes that appear on the DVD.

Sammy at the cash register with a customer

Queenie and her friends

Reading and Reacting

1. If you were making a film of "A&P," which scenes from the story would you consider essential? Which might you omit? Why?
2. Which minor characters would you include? Why?
3. Would you depict on screen any characters who are not described in the story — for example, Sammy's parents? If so, in what kind of scene would you introduce them?

Interior of the A&P

Mr. Lengel confronting the girls while Sammy watches

4. How would you dramatize Sammy's fantasies about Queenie and her family?

5. Would you set the entire film inside the A&P, or would you create additional settings? For example, where might you set a scene designed to present background information about Sammy? A scene depicting events that might have followed the story?

6. If you were setting the film in the present (rather than in 1961), how would you depict Queenie and her friends? How would they look different from the girls in the photographs above?

7. In a present-day film version of the story, which actor would you cast as Sammy? Queenie? Stokesie? Lengel?

Tillie Olsen's "I Stand Here Ironing"

Setting is very important in "I Stand Here Ironing" (p. 309), whose events and emotions are rooted in a particular historical time: the years of the Great Depression. In the DVD version of the story, that time and mood are conveyed through specific, vivid images of Depression-era street scenes. The film also establishes the family's economic status, a key factor in the story, by showing how they are dressed and what their apartment looks like. The stills included here depict scenes that appear on the DVD.

Narrator (as a young woman) at ironing board

Emily as a child (in convalescent home)

Reading and Reacting

1. The story does not describe the apartment in which Emily and her mother lived when she was a baby. How do you picture the apartment? If you were filming the story, how would you decorate and furnish it?

Street scene showing bread line

Emily performing at her school's amateur show

2. What other settings besides the apartment would you see as essential in a film version of the story? Why?

3. How would you convey the shifts in time presented in the story? For example, would you show the characters at different ages? Would you show certain scenes as flashbacks?

4. Would you include voice-over narration to reproduce the mother's voice, or would you have the story unfold without a narrator?

5. Where would you place the ironing board? Why? At what point (or points) in the story would you show the mother ironing?

6. The mother questions many of the decisions she made about Emily, and readers are left to decide if she is a good mother. What scenes could a film version include to portray her as a good mother? As a neglectful mother?

7. Would your film be in color or in black and white? Why?

Alice Walker's "Everyday Use"

Central to "Everyday Use" (p. 469) is the quilt, a symbol, among other things, of family unity, racial pride, and the strength of African-American women. The story is set in 1973, at a time when many African-Americans asserted their racial pride and their connections with Africa. In the DVD version of the story, Dee and her friend Hakim-a-barber do this by sporting Afros and by wearing African clothing. In contrast, Maggie and Mrs. Johnson show little sympathy for Dee's cause and dress in a simple style associated with the rural American South. Central to the story are several symbols — the house, the bench, the churn, and of course, the quilt. The stills included here depict scenes that appear on the DVD.

Dee and Hakim-a-barber

The quilt

Reading and Reacting

1. When you read "Everyday Use," how did you picture the characters? How are the characters in the film like or unlike those you imagined?

Maggie and Mrs. Johnson in front of their house

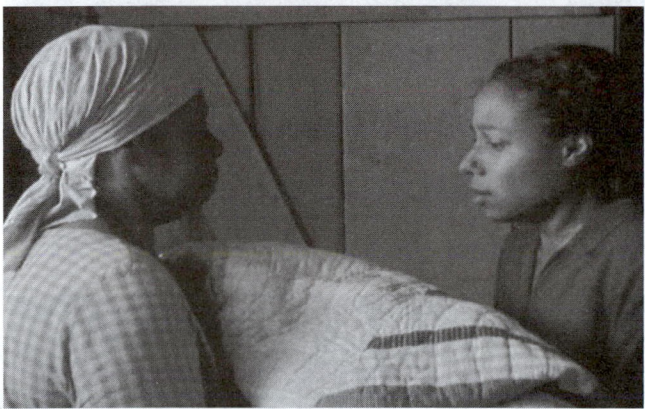

Mrs. Johnson giving the quilt to Maggie

2. Mrs. Johnson, the narrator of "Everyday Use," not only tells the story but also adds her comments and insights. What aspects of her narrative could be dramatized in a film, and what parts would require a narrator's voice-over?

3. If you were making a film version of the story, how would you introduce the quilt? How would you emphasize its symbolic value?

4. How would you depict the house? Would it look like the one in the photograph above, or would it be different?

5. Would you use a flashback to show the fire? What would be gained and lost by actually showing — rather than telling about — this important event?

6. If you wanted to make a contemporary film of the story, what difficulties would you face? Which actor would you cast as Dee? Maggie? Hakim-a-barber? Mrs. Johnson?

7. In the story, Mrs. Johnson says that Dee is probably ashamed of her and Maggie as well as of their house. How would you make this apparent in a film version of the story?

Raymond Carver's "Cathedral"

Symbolism is important in the story "Cathedral" (p. 476). In the DVD version of the story, the narrator's encounter with his wife's blind friend, Robert, culminates in a symbolic event — the drawing of a cathedral. In addition, blindness becomes symbolic not only of Robert's condition but also of the narrator's — and, by extension, the condition of all of humanity. The film clearly portrays the narrator's spiritual quest as well as the blind man's ability to guide him to salvation. The stills included here depict scenes that appear on the DVD.

Husband and wife on couch

Husband drawing (with eyes open)

Reading and Reacting

1. The first part of the story gives background information about the wife's relationship with Robert. How would you present this information in a film? Would you show it in a series of flashbacks, or would you have a narrator or one of the characters tell about it?

The three characters sitting and eating

Husband drawing (with eyes shut) with wife and Robert beside him

2. The husband has a number of preconceived ideas about blindness, and as a result, he does not look forward to having Robert visit him. How would you convey his discomfort in a film version of the story?

3. In the story, the wife is clearly uneasy about how her husband will react to Robert. How would you convey this emotion in the film?

4. Other than saying that Robert has a full beard, the narrator does not describe the characters in the story. If you were making a film, would the characters look different from the ones in the photographs?

5. What information in the story would you want to include in a film version? What information could you do without?

6. Where would you have the husband and Robert sit when they draw the cathedral? Why?

7. What scene could you add to show what took place after the story was over? What characters would be in this new scene? What would they be doing?

Eudora Welty's "A Worn Path"

"A Worn Path" (p. 505) is a story about Phoenix Jackson, an elderly African-American woman who repeatedly makes a long journey to town to get medicine for her ailing grandson. The theme of the story, however, is much more than the difficulty of Phoenix Jackson's journey. In one sense, Phoenix represents the strength of human spirit that perseveres regardless of the difficulties or the odds against success. In another sense, she represents African-Americans in their long quest for integration and equal treatment. The DVD of "A Worn Path" presents the vivid incidents — both imaginary and real — that are described in the story. The stills included here depict scenes that appear on the DVD.

Phoenix and man with dog

Phoenix in doctor's office

Reading and Reacting

1. If you were making a film of "A Worn Path," how would you show Phoenix's encounter with the thorn bush? The buzzard? The scarecrow?
2. How would you indicate which events actually took place and which are imaginary? For example, how would you show Phoenix's imaginary encounter with the boy who offers her a piece of cake?

Phoenix walking down the street in town

The film's last scene, with Phoenix, outlined against the sky,
walking back to her cabin

3. How would you stage Phoenix's encounter with the hunter? How would she react to the dog? How would you show her stealing the nickel? What would her reaction be when the hunter asked her if she was afraid of guns?

4. Which of the story's themes could you easily suggest in a film? Which would be more difficult to suggest?

5. The story takes place around Christmas. How would you indicate this setting in a film?

6. "A Worn Path" is set during the Depression near Natchez, Mississippi, a segregated city in the Deep South. If you were making a film version of the story, how would you suggest the contemporary racial situation?

7. The story ends with Phoenix walking down the stairs of the doctor's office. The DVD ends with Phoenix walking home, outlined against the sky (shown above). Is this ending an improvement? Explain.

CHAPTER 20

JOYCE CAROL OATES'S "WHERE ARE YOU GOING, WHERE HAVE YOU BEEN?": A CASEBOOK FOR READING, RESEARCH, AND WRITING

This chapter provides all the materials you will need to begin a research project about a work of fiction. It includes the 1966 short story "Where Are You Going, Where Have You Been?" by Joyce Carol Oates; questions to stimulate discussion and writing; a collection of source materials;* a student paper that shows how one student, Michele Olivari, used the materials in this chapter in her research; and suggestions for further research on Oates.

Source Materials

- Oates, Joyce Carol. "When Characters from the Page Are Made Flesh on the Screen." *New York Times* 23 Mar. 1986, sec. 2:1+. An article by Oates in which she discusses her feelings about the film *Smooth Talk,* based on her story. .... (p. 586)
- Schulz, Gretchen, and R. J. R. Rockwood. From "In Fairyland, without a Map: Connie's Exploration Inward in Joyce Carol Oates's 'Where Are You Going, Where Have You Been?'" *Literature and Psychology* 30 (1980): 155–67. A psychological interpretation of the story. .... (p. 590)
- Tierce, Mike, and John Michael Crafton. From "Connie's Tambourine Man: A New Reading of Arnold Friend." *Studies in Short Fiction* 22 (1985): 219–24. A critical interpretation of the character of Arnold Friend. .... (p. 594)
- Dylan, Bob. "It's All Over Now, Baby Blue." Los Angeles: Warner Bros., 1965. Lyrics from a popular folk song, which, according to Oates, inspired the story. (This and other Dylan songs are discussed in Tierce and Crafton's article.) .... (p. 597)
- Kalpakian, Laura. From a Review of *Where Are You Going, Where Have You Been?: Selected Early Stories,* by Joyce Carol Oates. *The Southern Review* 29.4

---

* Note that some of the critical articles in this casebook were written before the current MLA documentation style was adopted. See Chapter 7 for current MLA format.

Each of these sources provides insights (sometimes contradictory ones) into the short story "Where Are You Going, Where Have You Been?" Other kinds of sources can also enrich your understanding of the work — for instance, other stories by Oates, biographical data about the author, or stories by other writers dealing with similar themes. In addition, nonprint sources — such as the film *Smooth Talk*, which is based on the story — and Web sites devoted to Oates and her work can offer insight into the story. Links to several interesting Web sites on Oates are available at <http:// kirsznermandell.wadsworth.com>.

Although no analytical or biographical source — not even the author's comments — can give you a magical key that will unlock a story's secrets, such sources can enhance your enjoyment and aid in your understanding of a work. They can also suggest topics that you can explore in writing.

In preparation for writing an essay on a topic of your choice about the story "Where Are You Going, Where Have You Been?" read the story and the accompanying source materials carefully. Then, consider the Reading and Reacting questions that follow the story (p. 585), and use your responses to help you find a topic you can develop in a short essay. Be sure to document any words or ideas borrowed from the story or from another source, and remember to enclose words that are not your own in quotation marks. (For guidelines on evaluating literary criticism, see page 15; for guidelines on using source materials, see Chapter 6, "Writing a Research Paper.")

A sample student paper, "Mesmerizing Men and Vulnerable Teens: Power Relationships in 'Where Are You Going, Where Have You Been?' and 'Teenage Wasteland,'" based on the source materials in this Casebook, begins on page 611.

JOYCE CAROL OATES (1938–   ) is one of contemporary America's most prolific novelists and short story writers. Oates first gained prominence in the 1960s with the publication of *A Garden of Earthly Delights* (1967), *Expensive People* (1968), and *them* (1969), which won the National Book Award. In these and other works, Oates explores the multilayered nature of American society, writing about urban slums, decaying rural communities, and exclusive suburbs in a dense and compellingly realistic prose style. In some of her more recent novels, including *Bellefleur* (1980) and *Mysteries of Winterthurn* (1984), Oates reveals her deep fascination with the traditions of nineteenth-century gothic writers Edgar Allan Poe, Fyodor Dostoevski,

Mary Shelley, and others. Oates's recent works include *Lock My Door upon Myself* (1990), *The Rise of Life on Earth* (1991), *Black Water* (1992), *Foxfire* (1993), *What I Lived For* (1994), *Haunted* (1994), *Zombie* (1995), *First Love* (1996), *My Heart Laid Bare* (1998), *You Must Remember This* (1998), *I'll Take You There* (2002), *Middle Age: A Romance* (2002), and *The Falls* (2004).

Born on June 16, 1938, Joyce Carol Oates grew up in the small hamlet of Millersport, near Lockport, New York, about ten miles east of Niagara Falls and twenty miles north of Buffalo. She is the eldest of three children (her sister, Lynn, who is almost twenty years younger, has been institutionalized with autism since adolescence). Oates attended school in a one-room schoolhouse with other working-class children from the area. Her childhood was hard, yet she writes about it in a loving and respectful tone: "Though frequently denounced and often misunderstood by a somewhat genteel literary community, my writing is, at least in part, an attempt to memorialize my parents' vanished world; my parents' lives. Sometimes directly, sometimes in metaphor." Her childhood town, parents, siblings, relatives, and neighbors all appear in some form in three of Oates's books: *You Must Remember This* (1987) blends Buffalo and Lockport as its backdrop along with the Erie Canal; *Marya: A Life* (1986) contains elements of Oates's mother's childhood as well as her own; and in *Wonderland* (1971), one of Oates's earliest novels, the main character stops off in Millersport and meets her family.

Oates is one of those writers who has always been a writer, and even before she could possibly know the alphabet, she drew and painted words. Once she did learn her letters, she was given a typewriter and learned how to use it, and she was soon churning out book after book. She left her small town to attend Syracuse University on a scholarship and while there won the *Mademoiselle* fiction contest. She earned an MA in English at the University of Wisconsin and while in Madison met and married Raymond J. Smith after a three-month courtship. The newlyweds moved to Detroit in 1962, during a time when social tensions were at the boiling point; Detroit was one of the first American cities to erupt in urban violence in the 1960s. Oates considers her time in Detroit to be significant, shaping her writing as well as her personal beliefs and political views.

In 1968, Oates crossed the Detroit River to teach at the University of Windsor in Ontario, Canada. Although she managed a full-time course load, she embarked on an extremely productive period of writing. In less than a decade, she wrote over twenty novels, and her audience grew along with her success. In 1978, she moved to Princeton, New Jersey, to accept a teaching position at Princeton University. Today, Oates continues to teach at Princeton and, with her husband, runs a small press and publishes *The Ontario Review,* a literary magazine.

Washington Post critic Susan Wood has written that Oates "attempts more than most of our writers . . . to explore the profound issues of evil and innocence, betrayal and revenge and atonement, as they are manifest in contemporary American experience. . . ." Although Oates frequently centers her novels on larger issues and moral questions, she can also focus on the private worlds of her characters, as in *Black Water* (1992).

Critics responding to Oates's work have called it violent, lurid, even depraved. Yet, asks Laura Z. Hobson in a review of Oates's 1981 novel, *Angel of Light,* "Would there be such a hullabaloo about the violence in her books if they had been written by a man?

From her earliest books onward, reviewers too often struck an insulting tone of surprise: *What's a nice girl like you doing in a place like this?* [Oates] replies that in these violent times only tales of violence have reality. Well, maybe. But the critics' preoccupation with a single facet of her work ignores everything else: her inventiveness, her insider's knowledge of college life, her evocations of nature . . . her ability to tell a story, to write a spellbinder. . . ."

Oates's work changes as the landscape changes around her. Her earliest novels focused on rural characters who seemingly could have sprung from her hometown, and the dozens of books she wrote while in Detroit and Ontario reveal the often harsh realities of those places and times. The novels she began to write in New Jersey went in an entirely new direction. Published in the 1980s, her series of ambitious gothic novels challenge established literary form and also envision a vastly different American identity and history from that of her earlier books. In short, her prolific career reveals an ability to experiment with new forms and subject matter, and it is exactly this ability that makes her universally appealing and that makes her books timeless as well as timebound.

Where Are You Going, Where Have You Been? (1966)

For Bob Dylan

Her name was Connie. She was fifteen and she had a quick nervous giggling habit of craning her neck to glance into mirrors, or checking other people's faces to make sure her own was all right. Her mother, who noticed everything and knew everything and who hadn't much reason any longer to look at her own face, always scolded Connie about it. "Stop gawking at yourself, who are you? You think you're so pretty?" she would say. Connie would raise her eye-brows at these familiar complaints and look right through her mother, into a shadowy vision of herself as she was right at that moment: she knew she was pretty and that was everything. Her mother had been pretty once too, if you could believe those old snapshots in the album, but now her looks were gone and that was why she was always after Connie.

"Why don't you keep your room clean like your sister? How've you got your hair fixed — what the hell stinks? Hair spray? You don't see your sister using that junk."

Her sister June was twenty-four and still lived at home. She was a secretary in the high school Connie attended, and if that wasn't bad enough — with her in the same building — she was so plain and chunky and steady that Connie had to hear her praised all the time by her mother and her mother's sisters. June did this, June did that, she saved money and helped clean the house and cooked and Connie couldn't do a thing, her mind was all filled with trashy daydreams. Their father was away at work most of the time and when he came home he wanted supper and he read the newspaper at supper and after supper he went to bed. He didn't bother talking much to them, but around his bent head Connie's mother kept picking at her until Connie wished her mother was dead and she herself was dead and it was all over. "She makes me want to throw up sometimes," she complained to her friends. She had a high, breathless, amused voice which made everything she said sound a little forced, whether it was sincere or not.

There was one good thing: June went places with girl friends of hers, girls who were just as plain and steady as she, and so when Connie wanted to do that her mother had no objections. The father of Connie's best girl friend drove the girls the three miles to town and left them off at a shopping plaza, so that they could walk through the stores or go to a movie, and when he came to pick them up again at eleven he never bothered to ask what they had done.

5　They must have been familiar sights, walking around that shopping plaza in their shorts and flat ballerina slippers that always scuffed the sidewalk, with charm bracelets jingling on their thin wrists; they would lean together to whisper and laugh secretly if someone passed by who amused or interested them. Connie had long dark blond hair that drew anyone's eye to it, and she wore part of it pulled up on her head and puffed out and the rest of it she let fall down her back. She wore a pull-over jersey blouse that looked one way when she was at home and another way when she was away from home. Everything about her had two sides to it, one for home and one for anywhere that was not home: her walk that could be childlike and bobbing, or languid enough to make anyone think she was hearing music in her head, her mouth which was pale and smirking most of the time, but bright and pink on these evenings out, her laugh which was cynical and drawling at home —"Ha, ha, very funny"—but high-pitched and nervous anywhere else, like the jingling of the charms on her bracelet.

Sometimes they did go shopping or to a movie, but sometimes they went across the highway, ducking fast across the busy road, to a drive-in restaurant where older kids hung out. The restaurant was shaped like a big bottle, though squatter than a real bottle, and on its cap was a revolving figure of a grinning boy who held a hamburger aloft. One night in mid-summer they ran across, breathless with daring, and right away someone leaned out a car window and invited them over, but it was just a boy from high school they didn't like. It made them feel good to be able to ignore him. They went up through the maze of parked and cruising cars to the bright-lit, fly-infested restaurant, their faces pleased and expectant as if they were entering a sacred building that loomed out of the night to give them what haven and what blessing they yearned for. They sat at the counter and crossed their legs at the ankles, their thin shoulders rigid with excitement, and listened to the music that made everything so good: the music was always in the background like music at a church service, it was something to depend upon.

A boy named Eddie came in to talk with them. He sat backwards on his stool, turning himself jerkily around in semi-circles and then stopping and turning again, and after a while he asked Connie if she would like something to eat. She said she did and so she tapped her friend's arm on her way out —her friend pulled her face up into a brave droll look — and Connie said she would meet her at eleven, across the way. "I just hate to leave her like that," Connie said earnestly, but the boy said that she wouldn't be alone for long. So they went out to his car and on the way Connie couldn't help but let her eyes wander over the windshields and faces all around her, her face gleaming with a joy that had nothing to do with Eddie or even this place; it might have been the music. She drew her shoulders up and sucked in her breath with the pure pleasure of being alive, and just at that moment she happened to glance at a face just a few feet from hers. It was a boy with shaggy black hair, in a convertible jalopy painted gold. He stared at her and then his lips widened into a grin. Connie slit her eyes at him and turned away, but she couldn't help glancing back and there he was still watching her. He wagged a finger and laughed and said, "Gonna get you, baby," and Connie turned away again without Eddie noticing anything.

She spent three hours with him, at the restaurant where they ate hamburgers and drank Cokes in wax cups that were always sweating, and then down an alley a mile or so away, and when he left her off at five to eleven only the movie house was still open at the plaza. Her girl friend was there, talking with a boy. When Connie came up the two girls smiled at each other and Connie said, "How was the movie?" and the girl said, "*You* should know." They rode off with the girl's father, sleepy and pleased, and Connie couldn't help but look at the darkened shopping plaza with its big empty parking lot and its signs that were faded and ghostly now, and over at the drive-in restaurant where cars were still circling tirelessly. She couldn't hear the music at this distance.

Next morning June asked her how the movie was and Connie said, "So-so."

She and that girl and occasionally another girl went out several times a week   10 that way, and the rest of the time Connie spent around the house — it was summer vacation — getting in her mother's way and thinking, dreaming, about the boys she met. But all the boys fell back and dissolved into a single face that was not even a face, but an idea, a feeling, mixed up with the urgent insistent pounding of the music and the humid night air of July. Connie's mother kept dragging her back to the daylight by finding things for her to do or saying, suddenly, "What's this about the Pettinger girl?"

And Connie would say nervously, "Oh, her. That dope." She always drew thick clear lines between herself and such girls, and her mother was simple and kindly enough to believe her. Her mother was so simple, Connie thought, that it was maybe cruel to fool her so much. Her mother went scuffling around the house in old bedroom slippers and complained over the telephone to one sister about the other, then the other called up and the two of them complained about the third one. If June's name was mentioned her mother's tone was approving, and if Connie's name was mentioned it was disapproving. This did not really mean she disliked Connie and actually Connie thought that her mother preferred her to June because she was prettier, but the two of them kept up a pretense of exasperation, a sense that they were tugging and struggling over something of little value to either of them. Sometimes, over coffee, they were almost friends, but something would come up — some vexation that was like a fly buzzing suddenly around their heads — and their faces went hard with contempt.

One Sunday Connie got up at eleven — none of them bothered with church — and washed her hair so that it could dry all day long, in the sun. Her parents and sister were going to a barbecue at an aunt's house and Connie said no, she wasn't interested, rolling her eyes to let her mother know just what she thought of it. "Stay home alone then," her mother said sharply. Connie sat out back in a lawn chair and watched them drive away, her father quiet and bald, hunched around so that he could back the car out, her mother with a look that was still angry and not at all softened through the windshield, and in the back seat poor old June all dressed up as if she didn't know what a barbecue was, with all the running yelling kids and the flies. Connie sat with her eyes closed in the sun, dreaming and dazed with the warmth about her as if this were a kind of love, the caresses of love, and her mind slipped over onto thoughts of the boy she had been with the night before and how nice he had been, how sweet it always was, not the way someone like June would suppose but sweet, gentle, the way it was in movies and promised in songs; and when she opened her eyes she hardly knew where she was, the back yard ran off into weeds and a fence-line of trees and behind it the sky was perfectly blue and still. The asbestos "ranch house" that was now three years old startled her — it looked small. She shook her head as if to get awake.

It was too hot. She went inside the house and turned on the radio to drown out the quiet. She sat on the edge of her bed, barefoot, and listened for an hour and a half to a program called XYZ Sunday Jamboree, record after record of hard, fast, shrieking songs she sang along with, interspersed by exclamations from "Bobby King": "An' look here you girls at Napoleon's — Son and Charley want you to pay real close attention to this song coming up!"

And Connie paid close attention herself, bathed in a glow of slow-pulsed joy that seemed to rise mysteriously out of the music itself and lay languidly about the airless little room, breathed in and breathed out with each gentle rise and fall of her chest.

15   After a while she heard a car coming up the drive. She sat up at once, startled, because it couldn't be her father so soon. The gravel kept crunching all the way in from the road — the driveway was long — and Connie ran to the window. It was a car she didn't know. It was an open jalopy, painted a bright gold that caught the sunlight opaquely. Her heart began to pound and her fingers snatched at her hair, checking it, and she whispered "Christ. Christ," wondering how bad she looked. The car came to a stop at the side door and the horn sounded four short taps as if this were a signal Connie knew.

She went into the kitchen and approached the door slowly, then hung out the screen door, her bare toes curling down off the step. There were two boys in the car and now she recognized the driver: he had shaggy, shabby black hair that looked crazy as a wig and he was grinning at her.

"I ain't late, am I?" he said.

"Who the hell do you think you are?" Connie said.

"Toldja I'd be out, didn't I?"

20   "I don't even know who you are."

She spoke sullenly, careful to show no interest or pleasure, and he spoke in a fast bright monotone. Connie looked past him to the other boy, taking her time.

He had fair brown hair, with a lock that fell onto his forehead. His sideburns gave him a fierce, embarrassed look, but so far he hadn't even bothered to glance at her. Both boys wore sunglasses. The driver's glasses were metallic and mirrored everything in miniature.

"You wanta come for a ride?" he said.

Connie smirked and let her hair fall loose over one shoulder.

"Don'tcha like my car? New paint job," he said. "Hey."

"What?"   25

"You're cute."

She pretended to fidget, chasing flies away from the door.

"Don'tcha believe me, or what?" he said.

"Look, I don't even know who you are," Connie said in disgust.

"Hey, Ellie's got a radio, see. Mine's broke down." He lifted his friend's arm and   30 showed her the little transistor the boy was holding, and now Connie began to hear the music. It was the same program that was playing inside the house.

"Bobby King?" she said.

"I listen to him all the time. I think he's great."

"He's kind of great," Connie said reluctantly.

"Listen, that guy's *great*. He knows where the action is."

Connie blushed a little, because the glasses made it impossible for her to see   35 just what this boy was looking at. She couldn't decide if she liked him or if he was just a jerk, and so she dawdled in the doorway and wouldn't come down or go back inside. She said, "What's all that stuff painted on your car?"

"Can'tcha read it?" He opened the door very carefully, as if he was afraid it might fall off. He slid out just as carefully, planting his feet firmly on the ground, the tiny metallic world in his glasses slowing down like gelatine hardening and in the midst of it Connie's bright green blouse. "This here is my name, to begin with," he said. ARNOLD FRIEND was written in tarlike black letters on the side, with a drawing of a round grinning face that reminded Connie of a pumpkin, except it wore sunglasses. "I wanta introduce myself, I'm Arnold Friend and that's my real name and I'm gonna be your friend, honey, and inside the car's Ellie Oscar, he's kinda shy." Ellie brought his transistor radio up to his shoulder and balanced it there. "Now these numbers are a secret code, honey," Arnold Friend explained. He read off the numbers 33, 19, 17 and raised his eyebrows at her to see what she thought of that, but she didn't think much of it. The left rear fender had been smashed and around it was written, on the gleaming gold background: DONE BY CRAZY WOMAN DRIVER. Connie had to laugh at that. Arnold Friend was pleased at her laughter and looked up at her. "Around the other side's a lot more — you wanta come and see them?"

"No."

"Why not?"

"Why should I?"

"Don'tcha wanta see what's on the car? Don'tcha wanta go for a ride?"   40

"I don't know."

"Why not?"

"I got things to do."

"Like what?"

45   "Things."

He laughed as if she had said something funny. He slapped his thighs. He was standing in a strange way, leaning back against the car as if he were balancing himself. He wasn't tall, only an inch or so taller than she would be if she came down to him. Connie liked the way he was dressed, which was the way all of them dressed: tight faded jeans stuffed into black, scuffed boots, a belt that pulled his waist in and showed how lean he was, and a white pull-over shirt that was a little soiled and showed the hard small muscles of his arms and shoulders. He looked as if he probably did hard work, lifting and carrying things. Even his neck looked muscular. And his face was a familiar face, somehow: the jaw and chin and cheeks slightly darkened, because he hadn't shaved for a day or two, and the nose long and hawklike, sniffing as if she were a treat he was going to gobble up and it was all a joke.

"Connie, you ain't telling the truth. This is your day set aside for a ride with me and you know it," he said, still laughing. The way he straightened and recovered from his fit of laughing showed that it had been all fake.

"How do you know what my name is?" she said suspiciously.

"It's Connie."

50   "Maybe and maybe not."

"I know my Connie," he said, wagging his finger. Now she remembered him even better, back at the restaurant, and her cheeks warmed at the thought of how she sucked in her breath just at the moment she passed him — how she must have looked to him. And he had remembered her. "Ellie and I come out here especially for you," he said. "Ellie can sit in back. How about it?"

"Where?"

"Where what?"

"Where're we going?"

55   He looked at her. He took off the sunglasses and she saw how pale the skin around his eyes was, like holes that were not in shadow but instead in light. His eyes were chips of broken glass that catch the light in an amiable way. He smiled. It was as if the idea of going for a ride somewhere, to some place, was a new idea to him.

"Just for a ride, Connie sweetheart."

"I never said my name was Connie," she said.

"But I know what it is. I know your name and all about you, lots of things," Arnold Friend said. He had not moved yet but stood still leaning back against the side of his jalopy. "I took a special interest in you, such a pretty girl, and found out all about you like I know your parents and sister are gone somewheres and I know where and how long they're going to be gone, and I know who you were with last night, and your best girl friend's name is Betty. Right?"

He spoke in a simple lilting voice, exactly as if he were reciting the words to a song. His smile assured her that everything was fine. In the car Ellie turned up the volume on his radio and did not bother to look around at them.

60   "Ellie can sit in the back seat," Arnold Friend said. He indicated his friend with a casual jerk of his chin, as if Ellie did not count and she should not bother with him.

"How'd you find out all that stuff?" Connie said.

"Listen: Betty Schultz and Tony Fitch and Jimmy Pettinger and Nancy Pettinger," he said, in a chant. "Raymond Stanley and Bob Hutter —"

"Do you know all those kids?"

"I know everybody."

"Look, you're kidding. You're not from around here." 65

"Sure."

"But — how come we never saw you before?"

"Sure you saw me before," he said. He looked down at his boots, as if he were a little offended. "You just don't remember."

"I guess I'd remember you," Connie said.

"Yeah?" He looked up at this, beaming. He was pleased. He began to mark 70 time with the music from Ellie's radio, tapping his fists lightly together. Connie looked away from his smile to the car, which was painted so bright it almost hurt her eyes to look at it. She looked at that name, ARNOLD FRIEND. And up at the front fender was an expression that was familiar — MAN THE FLYING SAUCERS. It was an expression kids had used the year before, but didn't use this year. She looked at it for a while as if the words meant something to her that she did not yet know.

"What're you thinking about? Huh?" Arnold Friend demanded. "Not worried about your hair blowing around in the car, are you?"

"No."

"Think I maybe can't drive good?"

"How do I know?"

"You're a hard girl to handle. How come?" he said. "Don't you know I'm your 75 friend? Didn't you see me put my sign in the air when you walked by?"

"What sign?"

"My sign." And he drew an X in the air, leaning out toward her. They were maybe ten feet apart. After his hand fell back to his side the X was still in the air, almost visible. Connie let the screen door close and stood perfectly still inside it, listening to the music from her radio and the boy's blend together. She stared at Arnold Friend. He stood there so stiffly relaxed, pretending to be relaxed, with one hand idly on the door handle as if he were keeping himself up that way and had no intention of ever moving again. She recognized most things about him, the tight jeans that showed his thighs and buttocks and the greasy leather boots and the tight shirt, and even that slippery friendly smile of his, that sleepy dreamy smile that all the boys used to get across ideas they didn't want to put into words. She recognized all this and also the singsong way he talked, slightly mocking, kidding, but serious and a little melancholy, and she recognized the way he tapped one fist against the other in homage to the perpetual music behind him. But all these things did not come together.

She said suddenly, "Hey, how old are you?"

His smile faded. She could see then that he wasn't a kid, he was much older — thirty, maybe more. At this knowledge her heart began to pound faster.

"That's a crazy thing to ask. Can'tcha see I'm your own age?" 80

"Like hell you are."

"Or maybe a coupla years older, I'm eighteen."

"Eighteen?" she said doubtfully.

He grinned to reassure her and lines appeared at the corners of his mouth. His teeth were big and white. He grinned so broadly his eyes became slits and she saw how thick the lashes were, thick and black as if painted with a black tarlike material. Then he seemed to become embarrassed, abruptly, and looked over his shoulder at Ellie. "*Him*, he's crazy," he said. "Ain't he a riot, he's a nut, a real character." Ellie was still listening to the music. His sunglasses told nothing about what he was thinking. He wore a bright orange shirt unbuttoned halfway to show his chest, which was a pale, bluish chest and not muscular like Arnold Friend's. His shirt collar was turned up all around and the very tips of the collar pointed out past his chin as if they were protecting him. He was pressing the transistor radio up against his ear and sat there in a kind of daze, right in the sun.

85   "He's kinda strange," Connie said.

"Hey, she says you're kinda strange! Kinda strange!" Arnold Friend cried. He pounded on the car to get Ellie's attention. Ellie turned for the first time and Connie saw with shock that he wasn't a kid either — he had a fair, hairless face, cheeks reddened slightly as if the veins grew too close to the surface of his skin, the face of a forty-year-old baby. Connie felt a wave of dizziness rise in her at this sight and she stared at him as if waiting for something to change the shock of the moment, make it all right again. Ellie's lips kept shaping words, mumbling along with the words blasting in his ear.

"Maybe you two better go away," Connie said faintly.

"What? How come?" Arnold Friend cried. "We come out here to take you for a ride. It's Sunday." He had the voice of the man on the radio now. It was the same voice, Connie thought. "Don'tcha know it's Sunday all day and honey, no matter who you were with last night today you're with Arnold Friend and don't you forget it! — Maybe you better step out here," he said, and this last was in a different voice. It was a little flatter, as if the heat was finally getting to him.

90   "No. I got things to do."

"Hey."

"You two better leave."

"We ain't leaving until you come with us."

"Like hell I am —"

"Connie, don't fool around with me. I mean, I mean, don't fool *around*," he said, shaking his head. He laughed incredulously. He placed his sunglasses on top of his head, carefully, as if he were indeed wearing a wig, and brought the stems down behind his ears. Connie stared at him, another wave of dizziness and fear rising in her so that for a moment he wasn't even in focus but was just a blur, standing there against his gold car, and she had the idea that he had driven up the driveway all right but had come from nowhere before that and belonged nowhere and that everything about him and even about the music that was so familiar to her was only half real.

"If my father comes and sees you —"   95

"He ain't coming. He's at a barbecue."

"How do you know that?"

"Aunt Tillie's. Right now they're — uh — they're drinking. Sitting around," he said vaguely, squinting as if he were staring all the way to town and over to Aunt Tillie's backyard. Then the vision seemed to get clear and he nodded energetically. "Yeah. Sitting around. There's your sister in a blue dress, huh? And high heels, the poor sad bitch — nothing like you sweetheart! And your mother's helping some fat woman with the corn, they're cleaning the corn —husking the corn —"

"What fat woman?" Connie cried.

"How do I know what fat woman. I don't know every goddam fat woman in   100 the world!" Arnold Friend laughed.

"Oh, that's Mrs. Hornby. . . . Who invited her?" Connie said. She felt a little light-headed. Her breath was coming quickly.

"She's too fat. I don't like them fat. I like them the way you are, honey," he said, smiling sleepily at her. They stared at each other for a while, through the screen door. He said softly, "Now what you're going to do is this: you're going to come out that door. You're going to sit up front with me and Ellie's going to sit in the back, the hell with Ellie, right? This isn't Ellie's date. You're my date. I'm your lover, honey."

"What? You're crazy —"

"Yes, I'm your lover. You don't know what that is but you will," he said. "I know that too. I know all about you. But look: it's real nice and you couldn't ask for nobody better than me, or more polite. I always keep my word. I'll tell you how it is, I'm always nice at first, the first time. I'll hold you so tight you won't think you have to try to get away or pretend anything because you'll know you can't. And I'll come inside you where it's all secret and you'll give in to me and you'll love me —"

"Shut up! You're crazy!" Connie said. She backed away from the door. She put   105 her hands against her ears as if she'd heard something terrible, something not meant for her. "People don't talk like that, you're crazy," she muttered. Her heart was almost too big now for her chest and its pumping made sweat break out all over her. She looked out to see Arnold Friend pause and then take a step toward the porch lurching. He almost fell. But, like a clever drunken man, he managed to catch his balance. He wobbled in his high boots and grabbed hold of one of the porch posts.

"Honey?" he said. "You still listening?"

"Get the hell out of here!"

"Be nice, honey. Listen."

"I'm going to call the police —"

He wobbled again and out of the side of his mouth came a fast spat curse, an   110 aside not meant for her to hear. But even this "Christ!" sounded forced. Then he began to smile again. She watched this smile come, awkward as if he were smiling from inside a mask. His whole face was a mask, she thought wildly, tanned down onto his throat but then running out as if he had plastered makeup on his face but had forgotten about his throat.

"Honey —? Listen, here's how it is. I always tell the truth and I promise you this: I ain't coming in that house after you."

"You better not! I'm going to call the police if you — if you don't —"

"Honey," he said, talking right through her voice, "honey, I'm not coming in there but you are coming out here. You know why?"

She was panting. The kitchen looked like a place she had never seen before, some room she had run inside but which wasn't good enough, wasn't going to help her. The kitchen window had never had a curtain, after three years, and there were dishes in the sink for her to do — probably — and if you ran your hand across the table you'd probably feel something sticky there.

115   "You listening, honey? Hey?"

"— going to call the police —"

"Soon as you touch the phone I don't need to keep my promise and can come inside. You won't want that."

She rushed forward and tried to lock the door. Her fingers were shaking. "But why lock it," Arnold Friend said gently, talking right into her face. "It's just a screen door. It's just nothing." One of his boots was at a strange angle, as if his foot wasn't in it. It pointed out to the left, bent at the ankle. "I mean, anybody can break through a screen door and glass and wood and iron or anything else if he needs to, anybody at all and specially Arnold Friend. If the place got lit up with a fire honey you'd come running out into my arms, right into my arms and safe at home — like you knew I was your lover and'd stopped fooling around. I don't mind a nice shy girl but I don't like no fooling around." Part of those words were spoken with a slight rhythmic lilt, and Connie somehow recognized them — the echo of a song from last year, about a girl rushing into her boy friend's arms and coming home again —

Connie stood barefoot on the linoleum floor, staring at him. "What do you want?" she whispered.

120   "I want you," he said.

"What?"

"Seen you that night and thought, that's the one, yes sir. I never needed to look any more."

"But my father's coming back. He's coming to get me. I had to wash my hair first —" She spoke in a dry, rapid voice, hardly raising it for him to hear.

"No, your daddy is not coming and yes, you had to wash your hair and you washed it for me. It's nice and shining and all for me, I thank you, sweetheart," he said, with a mock bow, but again he almost lost his balance. He had to bend and adjust his boots. Evidently his feet did not go all the way down; the boots must have been stuffed with something so that he would seem taller. Connie stared out at him and behind him Ellie in the car, who seemed to be looking off toward Connie's right, into nothing. This Ellie said, pulling the words out of the air one after another as if he were just discovering them, "You want me to pull out the phone?"

125   "Shut your mouth and keep it shut," Arnold Friend said, his face red from bending over or maybe from embarrassment because Connie had seen his boots. "This ain't none of your business."

"What — what are you doing? What do you want?" Connie said. "If I call the police they'll get you, they'll arrest you —"

"Promise was not to come in unless you touch that phone, and I'll keep that promise," he said. He resumed his erect position and tried to force his shoulders back. He sounded like a hero in a movie, declaring something important. He spoke too loudly and it was as if he were speaking to someone behind Connie. "I ain't made plans for coming in that house where I don't belong but just for you to come out to me, the way you should. Don't you know who I am?"

"You're crazy," she whispered. She backed away from the door but did not want to go into another part of the house, as if this would give him permission to come through the door. "What do you. . . . You're crazy, you . . ."

"Huh? What're you saying, honey?"

Her eyes darted everywhere in the kitchen. She could not remember what it 130
was, this room.

"This is how it is, honey: you come out and we'll drive away, have a nice ride. But if you don't come out we're gonna wait till your people come home and then they're all going to get it."

"You want that telephone pulled out?" Ellie said. He held the radio away from his ear and grimaced, as if without the radio the air was too much for him.

"I toldja shut up, Ellie," Arnold Friend said, "you're deaf, get a hearing aid, right? Fix yourself up. This little girl's no trouble and's gonna be nice to me, so Ellie keep to yourself, this ain't your date — right? Don't hem in on me. Don't hog. Don't crush. Don't bird dog. Don't trail me," he said in a rapid meaningless voice, as if he were running through all the expressions he'd learned but was no longer sure which one of them was in style, then rushing on to new ones, making them up with his eyes closed, "Don't crawl under my fence, don't squeeze in my chipmunk hole, don't sniff my glue, suck my popsicle, keep your own greasy fingers on yourself!" He shaded his eyes and peered in at Connie, who was backed against the kitchen table. "Don't mind him honey he's just a creep. He's a dope. Right? I'm the boy for you and like I said you come out here nice like a lady and give me your hand, and nobody else gets hurt, I mean, your nice old bald-headed daddy and your mummy and your sister in her high heels. Because listen: why bring them in this?"

"Leave me alone," Connie whispered.

"Hey, you know that old woman down the road, the one with the chickens and 135
stuff — you know her?"

"She's dead!"

"Dead? What? You know her?" Arnold Friend said.

"She's dead —"

"Don't you like her?"

"She's dead — she's — she isn't here any more —" 140

"But don't you like her, I mean, you got something against her? Some grudge or something?" Then his voice dipped as if he were conscious of a rudeness. He touched the sunglasses perched on top of his head as if to make sure they were still there. "Now you be a good girl."

"What are you going to do?"

"Just two things, or maybe three," Arnold Friend said. "But I promise it won't last long and you'll like me that way you get to like people you're close to. You will. It's all over for you here, so come on out. You don't want your people in any trouble, do you?"

She turned and bumped against a chair or something, hurting her leg, but she ran into the back room and picked up the telephone. Something roared in her ear, a tiny roaring, and she was so sick with fear that she could do nothing but listen to it — the telephone was clammy and very heavy and her fingers groped down to the dial but were too weak to touch it. She began to scream into the phone, into the roaring. She cried out, she cried for her mother, she felt her breath start jerking back and forth in her lungs as if it were something Arnold Friend were stabbing her with again and again with no tenderness. A noisy sorrowful wailing rose all about her and she was locked inside it the way she was locked inside the house.

145   After a while she could hear again. She was sitting on the floor with her wet back against the wall.

Arnold Friend was saying from the door, "That's a good girl. Put the phone back."

She kicked the phone away from her.

"No, honey. Pick it up. Put it back right."

She picked it up and put it back. The dial tone stopped.

150   "That's a good girl. Now you come outside."

She was hollow with what had been fear, but what was now just an emptiness. All that screaming had blasted it out of her. She sat, one leg cramped under her, and deep inside her brain was something like a pinpoint of light that kept going and would not let her relax. She thought, I'm not going to see my mother again. She thought, I'm not going to sleep in my bed again. Her bright green blouse was all wet.

Arnold Friend said, in a gentle-loud voice that was like a stage voice, "The place where you came from ain't there any more, and where you had in mind to go is cancelled out. This place you are now — inside your daddy's house — is nothing but a cardboard box I can knock down any time. You know that and always did know it. You hear me?"

She thought, I have got to think. I have to know what to do.

"We'll go out to a nice field, out in the country here where it smells so nice and it's sunny," Arnold Friend said. "I'll have my arms around you so you won't need to try to get away and I'll show you what love is like, what it does. The hell with this house! It looks solid all right," he said. He ran a fingernail down the screen and the noise did not make Connie shiver, as it would have the day before. "Now put your hand on your heart, honey. Feel that? That feels solid too but we know better, be nice to me, be sweet like you can because what else is there for a girl like you but to be sweet and pretty and give in? — and get away before her people come back?"

155   She felt her pounding heart. Her hand seemed to enclose it. She thought for the first time in her life that it was nothing that was hers, that belonged to her, but just a pounding, living thing inside this body that wasn't really hers either.

"You don't want them to get hurt," Arnold Friend went on. "Now get up, honey. Get up all by yourself."

She stood.

"Now turn this way. That's right. Come over here to me — Ellie, put that away, didn't I tell you? You dope. You miserable creepy dope," Arnold Friend said. His words were not angry but only part of an incantation. The incantation was kindly. "Now come out through the kitchen to me honey and let's see a smile, try it, you're a brave sweet little girl and now they're eating corn and hotdogs cooked to bursting over an outdoor fire, and they don't know one thing about you and never did and honey you're better than them because not a one of them would have done this for you."

Connie felt the linoleum under her feet; it was cool. She brushed her hair back out of her eyes. Arnold Friend let go of the post tentatively and opened his arms for her, his elbows pointing in toward each other and his wrists limp, to show that this was an embarrassed embrace and a little mocking, he didn't want to make her self-conscious.

She put out her hand against the screen. She watched herself push the door 160 slowly open as if she were safe back somewhere in the other doorway, watching this body and this head of long hair moving out into the sunlight where Arnold Friend waited.

"My sweet little blue-eyed girl," he said, in a half-sung sigh that had nothing to do with her brown eyes but was taken up just the same by the vast sunlit reaches of the land behind him and on all sides of him, so much land that Connie had never seen before and did not recognize except to know that she was going to it.

Reading and Reacting

1. Is Arnold Friend meant to be the devil? An antisocial hoodlum? A rapist and murderer (see "The Pied Piper of Tucson" on page 601)? Is he actually Bob Dylan (as Tierce and Crafton suggest in their article on page 594)? Or is he just a misunderstood social misfit who terrifies Connie more because of her innocence than because of his evil?

2. In a note accompanying the article she coauthored, Gretchen Schulz says that Oates told her the allusions to fairy tales in the story are intentional. What allusions to fairy tales can you identify?

3. Many critical articles see "Where Are You Going, Where Have You Been?" as heavily symbolic, even allegorical, with elements of myth, dream, and fairy tale woven throughout. Do you think such analysis is necessary, or could the story be seen in much simpler terms?

4. Feminist critics might see this story as a familiar tale of a man who uses flattering seductive language followed by threats of physical violence to coerce a young woman into giving in to him. In what sense do you see this as a story of male power and female powerlessness?

5. Dark undertones aside, in what sense is this simply a story about the coming of age of a typical 1960s teenager?

6. What roles do music, sex, the weather, contemporary slang, and physical appearance play in the story?

7. Why do members of Connie's family play such minor roles in the story? How might expanding their roles change the story?

8. Which aspects of teenage culture have changed in the more than forty years since Oates wrote the story? Which have stayed the same? Given the scope of these changes, is the story dated?

9. Most critics (like Oates herself) see the end of the story as alarmingly negative, suggesting rape and even murder. Do you see it this way?

10. Do you agree with Oates's view, expressed in her article below, that the differences in the endings of the film and the story are justified by the differences between the 1960s and the 1980s?

11. JOURNAL ENTRY How is the generation gap — the failure of one generation to understand another's culture, customs, and heroes — central to the story?

12. CRITICAL PERSPECTIVE According to *New York Times* book critic Michiko Kakutani, Joyce Carol Oates has several "fictional trademarks":

> [She has] a penchant for mixing the mundane and Gothic, the ordinary and sensationalistic; a fascination with the dark undercurrents of violence, eroticism and emotional chaos in American life, and a tendency to divide her characters' lives into a Before and After with one "unspeakable turn of destiny."

In what sense do Kakutani's remarks apply to "Where Are You Going, Where Have You Been?"? Do you see a fascination with "the dark undercurrents of . . . life" in this story? What is the "unspeakable turn of destiny" that divides Connie's life into a "Before and After"?

Related Works: "Kansas" (p. 209), "A&P" (p. 230), "Young Goodman Brown" (p. 489), "The Lottery" (p. 461), "To His Coy Mistress" (p. 957), *Beauty* (p. 1308), *I Dream Before I Take the Stand* (p. 1320)

JOYCE CAROL OATES

When Characters from the Page Are Made Flesh on the Screen

Some years ago in the American Southwest there surfaced a tabloid psychopath known as "The Pied Piper of Tucson." I have forgotten his name but his specialty was the seduction and occasional murder of teen-age girls. He may or may not have had actual accomplices, but his bizarre activities were known among a circle of teen-agers in the Tucson area; for some reason they kept his secrets, deliberately did not inform parents or police. It was this fact, not the fact of the mass murderer himself, that struck me at the time. And this was a pre-Manson time, this was early or mid-1960's.

The "Pied Piper" mimicked teen-agers in their talk, dress and behavior, but he was not a teen-ager — he was a man in his early 30's. Rather short, he stuffed rags in his leather boots to give himself height. (And sometimes walked unsteadily as a consequence: did none among his admiring constituency notice?) He charmed his victims, to the bewilderment of others who fancy themselves free of all lunatic attractions. "The Pied Piper of Tucson": a trashy dream, a tabloid archetype, sheer artifice, comedy, cartoon — surrounded, however improbably, and finally tragically, by real people. You think that, if you look twice, he won't be there. But there he is.

I don't remember any longer where I first read about "The Pied Piper" — very likely in *Life* magazine. I do recall deliberately not reading the full article because I didn't want to be distracted by too much detail. It was not after all the mass murderer himself who intrigued me, but the disturbing fact that a number of teen-agers — from "good" families — aided and abetted his crimes. This is the sort of thing authorities and responsible citizens invariably call "inexplicable" because they can't find explanations for it. *They* would not have fallen under this maniac's spell, after all.

An early draft of my short story "Where Are You Going, Where Have You Been?" — from which the current film "Smooth Talk" has been adapted by Joyce Chopra and Tom Cole — had the rather too explicit title "Death and the Maiden." It was cast in a mode of fiction to which I am still partial — indeed, every third or fourth story of mine is probably in this mode — "realistic allegory," it might be called. It is Hawthornian, romantic, shading into parable. Like the medieval German engraving from which my title was taken the story was minutely detailed yet clearly an allegory of the fatal attractions of death (or the devil). An innocent young girl is seduced by way of her own vanity; she mistakes death for erotic romance of a particularly American/trashy sort.

Laura Dern and Treat Williams in a still from the film *Smooth Talk (1985)*.

5   In subsequent drafts the story changed its tone, its focus, its language, its title. It became "Where Are You Going, Where Have You Been?" Written at a time when the author was intrigued by the music of Bob Dylan, particularly the hauntingly elegiac song "It's All Over Now, Baby Blue," it was dedicated to Bob Dylan. The charismatic mass murderer drops into the background and his innocent victim, a 15-year-old, moves into the foreground. She becomes the true protagonist of the tale, courting and being courted by her fate, a self-styled 1950's pop figure, alternately absurd and winning.

     There is no suggestion in the published story that "Arnold Friend" has seduced and murdered other young girls, or even that he necessarily intends to murder Connie. Is his interest "merely" sexual? (Nor is there anything about the complicity of other teen-agers. I saved that yet more provocative note for a current story, "Testimony.") Connie is shallow, vain, silly, hopeful, doomed — perhaps as I saw, and still see, myself? — but capable nonetheless of an unexpected gesture of heroism at the story's end.

     Her smooth-talking seducer, who cannot lie, promises her that her family will be unharmed if she gives herself to him; and so she does. The story ends abruptly at the point of her "crossing over." We don't know the nature of her sacrifice, only that she is generous enough to make it.

     In adapting a narrative so spare and thematically foreshortened as "Where Are You Going, Where Have You Been?" film director Joyce Chopra and screenwriter Tom Cole were required to do a good deal of filling in, expanding, inventing. Connie's story becomes lavishly, and lovingly, textured; she is not an allegorical figure so much as a "typical" teen-age girl (if Laura Dern, spectacularly good-looking, can be so defined).

     Joyce Chopra, who has done documentary films on contemporary teen-age culture, and, yet more authoritatively, has an adolescent daughter of her own, creates in "Smooth Talk" a believable world for Connie to inhabit. Or worlds: as in the original story there is Connie-at-home, and there is Connie-with-her-friends. Two 15-year-old girls, two finely honed styles, two voices, sometimes but not often overlapping. It is one of the marvelous visual features of the film that we *see* Connie and her friends transform themselves, once they are safely free of parental observation. What freedom, what joy! The girls claim their true identities in the neighborhood shopping mall!

10   "Smooth Talk" is, in a way, as much Connie's mother's story as it is Connie's; its center of gravity, its emotional nexus, is frequently with the mother — played by Mary Kay Place. (Though the mother's sexual jealousy of her daughter is slighted in the film.) Connie's ambiguous relationship with her affable, somewhat mysterious father (played by Levon Helm) is an excellent touch: I had thought, subsequent to the story's publication, that I should have built up the father, suggesting, as subtly as I could, an attraction there paralleling the attraction Connie feels for her seducer Arnold Friend.

     Treat Williams impersonates Arnold Friend as Arnold Friend impersonates — is it James Dean? James Dean regarding himself in mirrors, doing James Dean impersonations? Laura Dern is so right as "my" Connie that I may come to think

I modeled the fictitious girl on her, in the way that writers frequently delude themselves about notions of causality.

My difficulties with "Smooth Talk" have primarily to do with my chronic hesitation — a justifiable shyness, I'm sure — about seeing/hearing work of mine abstracted from its contexture of language. All writers know that language is their subject; quirky word choices, patterns of rhythm, enigmatic pauses, punctuation marks. Where the quick-scanner sees "quick" writing, the writer conceals nine-tenths of his iceberg.

Of course we all have "real" subjects, and we will fight to the death to defend these subjects, but beneath the tale-telling it is the tale-telling that grips us so very fiercely: "the soul at the *white heat*" in Emily Dickinson's words. Because of this it is always an eerie experience for me, as a writer, to hear "my" dialogue floating back to me from the external world; particularly when it is surrounded, as of course it must be, by "other" dialogue I seem not to recall having written. Perhaps a panic reaction sets in — perhaps I worry that I might be responsible for knowing what "I" meant, in writing things "I" didn't write? Like a student who has handed in work not entirely his own, and dreads interrogation from his teacher?

It is startling too to *see* fictitious characters inhabiting, with such seeming aplomb, roles that until now seemed private, flat on the page. (I don't, like many of my writing colleagues, feel affronted, thinking, "*That* isn't how he/she looks!" I think instead, guiltily, "Is *that* how he/she really looks?")

I have also had a number of plays produced and so characteristically doubtful am I about intruding into my directors' territories that I nearly always abrogate my authority to them. The writer works in a single dimension, the director works in three. I assume that they are professionals to their fingertips; authorities in their medium as I am an authority (if I am) in mine. I would fiercely defend the placement of a semicolon in one of my novels, but I would probably have deferred fairly quickly to Joyce Chopra's decision to reverse the story's ending, turn it upside-down, in a sense, so that the film ends not with death, not with a sleepwalker's crossing-over to her fate, but upon a sense of reconciliation, rejuvenation. Laura Dern's Connie is no longer "my" Connie at the film's conclusion; she is very much alive, assertive, strong-willed — a girl, perhaps, of the mid-1980's, and not of the mid-1960's. 15

A girl's loss of virginity, bittersweet but not necessarily tragic. Not today. A girl's coming of age that involves her succumbing to, but then rejecting, the "trashy dreams" of her pop teen-age culture. "Where Are You Going, Where Have You Been?" deliberately betrays itself as allegorical in its conclusion: Death and Death's chariot (a funky souped-up convertible) have come for the Maiden. Awakening is, in the story's final lines, moving out into the sunlight where Arnold Friend waits:

> "My sweet little blue-eyed girl," he said, in a half-sung sigh that had nothing to do with (Connie's) brown eyes but was taken up just the same by the vast sunlit reaches of the land behind him and on all sides of him, so much land that Connie had never seen before and did not recognize except to know that she was going to it.

I quite understand that this is an unfilmable conclusion, and "Where Are You Going, Where Have You Been?" is in fact an unfilmable short story. But Joyce Chopra's "Smooth Talk" is an accomplished and sophisticated movie that attempts to do just that.

◇   ◇   ◇

GRETCHEN SCHULZ AND R. J. R. ROCKWOOD

from In Fairyland, without a Map: Connie's Exploration Inward in Joyce Carol Oates's "Where Are You Going, Where Have You Been?"

Joyce Carol Oates has stated that her prize-winning story *Where Are You Going, Where Have You Been?* (Fall, 1966) came to her "more or less in a piece" after hearing Bob Dylan's song *It's All Over Now, Baby Blue*, and then reading about a "killer in some Southwestern state," and thinking about "the old legends and folk songs of Death and the Maiden."[1] The "killer" that Miss Oates had in mind, the one on whom her character Arnold Friend is modeled, was twenty-three-year-old Charles Schmid of Tucson, Arizona. Schmid had been charged with the murders of three teen-age girls, and was the subject of a lengthy article in the March 4, 1966, issue of *Life* magazine. It is not surprising that this account should have generated mythic musings in Miss Oates — musings that culminated in a short story which has depths as mythic as any of the "old legends and folk songs." The *Life* reporter, Don Moser, himself had found in this raw material such an abundance of the reality which is the stuff of myth, that he entitled his article "The Pied Piper of Tucson."

The article states that Schmid — or "Smitty," as he was called — had sought deliberately "to create an exalted, heroic image of himself." To the teen-agers in Smitty's crowd, who "had little to do but look each other over," their leader was a "folk hero . . . more dramatic, more theatrical, more *interesting* than anyone else in their lives," and seemed to embody the very lyrics of a then popular song: "Hey, c'mon babe, follow me, / I'm the Pied Piper, follow me, / I'm the Pied Piper, / And I'll show you where it's at." With a face which was "his own creation: the hair dyed raven black, the skin darkened to a deep tan with pancake make-up, the lips whitened, the whole effect heightened by a mole he had painted on one cheek," Smitty would cruise "in a golden car," haunting "all the teen-age hangouts," looking for pretty girls, especially ones with long blond hair. Because he was only five-foot-three, Smitty "habitually stuffed three or four inches of old rags and tin cans into the bottoms of his high-topped boots to make himself taller," even though the price he paid for that extra height was an awkward, stumbling walk that made people think he had "wooden feet."[2]

In his transformation into the Arnold Friend of *Where Are You Going, Where Have You Been?*, Smitty underwent the kind of apotheosis° which he had tried, by means of bizarre theatrics, to achieve in actuality, for Arnold is the exact transpersonal° counterpart of the real-life "Pied Piper of Tucson." Thus, although Arnold is a "realistic" figure, drawn from the life of a specific psychopathic killer, that superficial realism is only incidental to the more essential realism of the mythic characteristics — the archetypal qualities — he shares with the man who was his model. Asked to comment on Arnold, Miss Oates reveals that, to her, the character is *truly* mythological. No longer quite human, he functions as a personified subjective factor: "Arnold Friend," she says, "is a fantastic figure: he is Death, he is the 'elf-[king]' of the ballads, he is the Imagination, he is a Dream, he is a Lover, a Demon, *and all that.*"[3]

If *Where Are You Going, Where Have You Been?* is a "portrait of a psychopathic killer masquerading as a teenager,"[4] it is clear that this portrait is created in the mind of Connie, the teen-age protagonist of the story, and that it exists *there only*. It is thus Connie's inner world that determines how Arnold is, or has to be, at least in her eyes, for her personal problems are so compelling that they effectively rearrange and remodel the world of objective reality. Arnold Friend's own part in the creation of his image — whether he deliberately set about to become the "fantastic" figure he is, or seems to be, as his model, Smitty, did — Miss Oates ignores altogether. She is interested only in Connie, Arnold's young victim, and in how Connie's psychological state shapes her perceptions. We find — as we might expect with a writer who characterizes the mode in which she writes as "psychological realism"[5] — that the "fantastic" or mythological qualities of Arnold Friend (and of all those in the story) are presented as subjective rather than objective facts, aspects of the transpersonal psyche projected outward, products of the unconscious mental processes of a troubled adolescent girl.

Toward Arnold Friend, and what he represents, Connie is ambivalent: she is 5 both fascinated and frightened. She is, after all, at that confusing age when a girl feels, thinks, and acts both like a child, put off by a possible lover, and like a woman, attracted to him. Uncertain how to bridge the chasm between "home" and "anywhere that was not home," she stands — or wavers — at the boundary between childhood and adulthood, hesitant and yet anxious to enter the new world of experience which is opening before her:

> Everything about her had two sides to it, one for home and one for anywhere that was not home: her walk, which could be childlike and bobbing, or languid enough to make anyone think she was hearing music in her head; her mouth, which was pale and smirking most of the time, but bright and pink on these evenings out; her laugh, which was cynical and drawling at home —"Ha, ha, very funny," — but high-pitched and nervous anywhere else, like the jingling of the charms on her bracelet.[6]

---

apotheosis: The raising of a human to divine status.
transpersonal: Going beyond the individual or personal.

That her laugh is "high-pitched and nervous" when she is "anywhere that was not home" betrays the fact that Connie, like all young people, needs help as she begins to move from the past to the future, as she begins the perilous inward journey towards maturity. This journey is an essential part of the adolescent's search for personal identity, and though it is a quest that he must undertake by himself, traditionally it has been the responsibility of culture to help by providing symbolic maps of the territory through which he will travel, territory that lies on the other side of consciousness.

Such models of behavior and maps of the unknown are generally provided by the products of fantasy — myth, legend, and folklore. Folk fairy tales have been especially useful in this way. In his book, *The Uses of Enchantment: The Meaning and Importance of Fairy Tales* (1976), Bruno Bettelheim argues that children's fairy tales offer "symbolic images" that suggest "happy solutions"[7] to the problems of adolescence. Indeed, Joyce Carol Oates herself has Hugh Petrie, the caricaturist in her novel *The Assassins* (1975), observe that "fairy tales are analogous to life as it is lived in the family."[8] In her fiction both short and long Miss Oates makes frequent use of fairy tale material. Again and again she presents characters and situations which parallel corresponding motifs from the world of folk fantasy. And never is this more true than in the present story — never in all the eight novels and eleven collections of short stories which she has written at last count. Woven into the complex texture of *Where Are You Going, Where Have You Been?* are motifs from such tales as *The Spirit in the Bottle, Snow White, Cinderella, Sleeping Beauty, Rapunzel, Little Red Riding Hood,* and *The Three Little Pigs.*[9] *The Pied Piper of Hamelin*, which ends tragically and so according to Bettelheim does not qualify as a proper fairy tale,[10] serves as the "frame device" that contains all the other tales.

There is a terrible irony here, for although the story is full of fairy tales, Connie, its protagonist, is not. Connie represents an entire generation of young people who have grown up — or tried to — without the help of those bedtime stories which not only entertain the child, but also enable him vicariously to experience and work through problems which he will encounter in adolescence. The only "stories" Connie knows are those of the sexually provocative but superficial lyrics of the popular songs she loves or of the equally insubstantial movies she attends. Such songs and movies provide either no models of behavior for her to imitate, or dangerously inappropriate ones. Connie has thus been led to believe that life and, in particular, love will be "sweet, gentle, the way it was in the movies and promised in songs." She has no idea that life actually can be just as grim as in folk fairy tales. The society that is depicted in *Where Are You Going, Where Have You Been?* has failed to make available to children like Connie maps of the unconscious such as fairy tales provide, because it has failed to recognize that in the unconscious past and future coalesce, and that, psychologically, where the child is going is where he has already been. Since Connie has been left — in the words of yet another of the popular songs — to "wander through that wonderland alone" — it is small wonder, considering her lack of spiritual preparation, that Connie's journey there soon becomes a terrifying schizophrenic separation from reality, with prognosis for recovery extremely poor. . . .

Had she been nurtured on fairy tales instead of popular songs and movies she would not feel at such a loss; she would have "been" to this world before, through the vicarious experience offered by fairy tales, and she would have some sense of how to survive there now. Connie lacks the benefit of such experience, however, and even Arnold Friend appears to realize how that lack has hampered her development. He certainly speaks to the supposed woman as though she were still a child: "'Now, turn this way. That's right. Come over here to me. . . . and let's see a smile, try it, you're a brave, sweet little girl'." How fatherly he sounds. And how like the Woodcutter. But we know that he is still the Wolf, and that he still intends to "gobble up" this "little girl" as soon as he gets the chance. Connie is not going to live happily ever after. Indeed, it would seem that she is not going to live at all. She simply does not know how. She is stranded in Fairyland, without a map.[11]

Notes

[1] "Interview with Joyce Carol Oates about 'Where Are You Going, Where Have You Been?'" in *Mirrors: An Introduction to Literature*, ed. John R. Knott, Jr., and Christopher R. Keaske, 2nd ed. (San Francisco: Canfield Press, 1975), pp. 18–19.

[2] Don Moser, "The Pied Piper of Tucson," *Life*, 60, no. 9 (March 4, 1966), 18–19, 22–24, 80c–d.

[3] Interview in *Mirrors*, p. 19. For a perceptive analysis of Arnold Friend as a demonic figure, a subject which will not be developed here, see Joyce M. Wegs, "'Don't You Know Who I Am?' The Grotesque in Oates's 'Where Are You Going, Where Have You Been?'," *The Journal of Narrative Technique*, 5 (January 1975), pp. 66–72.

[4] Wegs, p. 69.

[5] Joyce Carol Oates, "Preface," *Where Are You Going, Where Have You Been?: Stories of Young America* (Greenwich, CT: Fawcett Publications, 1974), p. 10.

[6] Joyce Carol Oates, "Where Are You Going, Where Have You Been?," *Where Are You Going, Where Have You Been?: Stories of Young America* (Greenwich, CT: Fawcett Publications, 1974), p. 13. All further references are to this edition of the story and will appear in the text of the essay. The story was originally published in *Epoch*, Fall 1966. It has since been included in *Prize Stories: The O. Henry Awards 1968;* in *The Best American Short Stories of 1967;* and in a collection of Oates' stories, *The Wheel of Love* (New York: Vanguard Press, 1970; Greenwich, CT: Fawcett Publications, 1972). The story is also being anthologized with increasing frequency in collections intended for use in the classroom, such as Donald McQuade and Robert Atwan, *Popular Writing in America: The Interaction of Style and Audience* (New York: Oxford University Press, 1974).

[7] Bruno Bettelheim, *The Uses of Enchantment: The Meaning and Importance of Fairy Tales* (New York: Alfred A. Knopf, 1976), p. 39.

[8] Joyce Carol Oates, *The Assassins* (New York: Vanguard Press, 1975), p. 378.

[9] At the MLA convention in New York, on December 26, 1976, I got a chance to ask Joyce Carol Oates if the many allusions to various fairy tales in "Where Are You Going, Where Have You Been?" were intentional. She replied that they were. (Gretchen Schulz)

[10] Bettelheim, n. 34, p. 316.

[11] Concerning the plight of the Connies of the world, Bettelheim states thus: "unfed by our common fantasy heritage, the folk fairy tale, the child cannot invent stories on his own which help him cope with life's problems. All the stories he can invent are just expressions of his own wishes and anxieties. Relying on his own resources, all the child can imagine are elaborations

of where he presently is, since he cannot know where he needs to go, or how to go about getting there" (pp. 121–122).

◆ ◆ ◆

MIKE TIERCE AND JOHN MICHAEL CRAFTON

from Connie's Tambourine Man: A New Reading of Arnold Friend

The critical reception of Joyce Carol Oates' "Where Are You Going, Where Have You Been?" reveals a consistent pattern for reducing the text to a manageable, univocal° reading. Generally, this pattern involves two assumptions: Arnold *must* symbolize Satan and Connie *must* be raped and murdered. No critic has yet questioned Joyce Wegs' assertion that "Arnold is clearly a symbolic Satan."[1] Marie Urbanski argues that Arnold's "feet resemble the devil's cloven hoofs," Joan Winslow calls the story "an encounter with the devil," Tom Quirk maintains the story describes a "demoniac character," and Christina Marsden Gillis refers to "the satanic visitor's incantation."[2] Wegs' assertion that Arnold is "a criminal with plans to rape and probably murder Connie"[3] is also accepted at face value. Gillis assumes that Arnold "leads his victim . . . to a quick and violent sexual assault,"[4] and Quirk refers to "the rape and subsequent murder of Connie."[5] Even though Gretchen Schulz and R. J. R. Rockwood correctly claim that the portrait of Arnold "is created in the mind of Connie . . . and that it exists *there only*," they still persist in having Arnold as a demon and Connie as doomed: "But we know that he is still the Wolf, and that he still intends to 'gobble up' this 'little girl' as soon as he gets the chance. Connie is not going to live happily ever after. Indeed, it would seem that she is not going to live at all."[6]

While all of these critics insist on seeing satanic traces in Arnold, they refuse, on the other hand, to see that these traces are only part of a much more complex, more dynamic symbol. There are indeed diabolic shades to Arnold, but just as Blake and Shelley could see in Milton's Satan[7] a positive, attractive symbol of the poet, the rebellious embodiment of creative energy, so we should also be sensitive to Arnold's multifaceted and creative nature. Within the frame of the story, the fiction of Arnold burns in the day as the embodiment of poetic energy. The story is dedicated to Bob Dylan, the troubadour, the artist. Friend is the artist, the actor, the rhetorician, the teacher, all symbolized by Connie's overheated imagination. We should not assume that Arnold is completely evil because she is afraid of him. Her limited perceptions remind us of Blake's questioner in "The Tyger" who begins to perceive the frightening element of the experiential world but also is rather duped into his fear by his own limitations. Like the figure in Blake, Connie is the framer, the story creator — and the diabolic traces in her fiction frighten her not because they are the manifestations of an outside evil but because they are the symbolic extrapolations of her own psyche.

---

univocal: Having only one meaning.

If the adamant insistence that Arnold Friend is Satan is rejected, then who is this intriguing mysterious visitor? In *Enter Mysterious Stranger: American Cloistral Fiction*, Roy Male asserts that many mysterious intruders throughout American literature "are almost always potential saviors, destroyers, or ambiguous combinations of both, and their initial entrance, however much it may be displaced toward realism, amounts to the entrance of God or the devil on a machine."[8] And if Arnold Friend is *not* satanic, then his arrival could be that of a savior. This possibility moreover is suggested by Connie's whispering "Christ. Christ"[9] when Arnold first arrives in his golden "machine." Not only is "33" part of Arnold's "secret code" of numbers, but his sign, an "X" that seems to hover in the air, is also one of the symbols for Christ. Because music is closely associated with religion — "the music was always in the background, like music at a church service" — it also adds a religious element to Arnold's arrival. The key question then is who is this musical messiah, and the key to the answer is the dedication "For Bob Dylan" — the element of the story so unsatisfactorily accounted for by our predecessors. Not only does the description of Arnold Friend also fit Bob Dylan — a type of rock-and-roll messiah — but three of Dylan's songs (popular when the story was written) are very similar to the story itself.

In the mid-sixties Bob Dylan's followers perceived him to be a messiah. According to his biographer, Dylan was "a rock-and-roll king."[10] It is no wonder then that Arnold speaks with "the voice of the man on the radio," the disc jockey whose name, Bobby King, is a reference to "Bobby" Dylan, the "king" of rock-and-roll. Dylan was more than just a "friend" to his listeners; he was "Christ revisited," "the prophet leading [his followers] into [a new] Consciousness."[11] In fact, "people were making him an idol; . . . thousands of men and women, young and old, felt their lives entwined with his because they saw him as a mystic, a messiah who would lead them to salvation."[12]

That Oates consciously associates Arnold Friend with Bob Dylan is clearly suggested by the similarities of their physical descriptions. Arnold's "shaggy, shabby black hair that looked crazy as a wig," his "long and hawk-like" nose, his unshaven face, his "big and white" teeth, his lashes, "thick and black as if painted with a black tarlike material" and his size ("only an inch or so taller than Connie") are all characteristic of Bob Dylan. Even Arnold's "fast, bright monotone voice" is suggestive of Dylan, especially since he speaks "in a simple lilting voice, exactly as if he were reciting the words to a song."

The reference to "Mister Tambourine Man" implies another connection between the story and Dylan. A few of his song lyrics are very similar to the story itself. Oates herself suggests that part of the story's inspiration was "hearing for some weeks Dylan's song 'It's All Over Now, Baby Blue.'"[13] Such lines as "you must leave now," "something calls for you," "the vagabond who's rapping at your door," and "go start anew" are suggestive of the impending change awaiting Connie. Two other Dylan songs are equally as applicable though. The following lines from "Like a Rolling Stone" — the second most popular song of 1965 (the story was first published in 1966) — are also very similar to Connie's situation at the end of the story:

> You used to be so amused
> At Napoleon in rags and the language that he used

> Go to him now, he calls you, you can't refuse
> When you got nothing, you got nothing to lose
> You're invisible now, you got no secrets to conceal.

But Dylan's "Mr. Tambourine Man"—the number ten song in 1965—is even more similar. The following stanza establishes the notion of using music to rouse one's imagination into a blissful fantasy world:

> Take me on a trip upon your magic swirlin' ship,
> My senses have been stripped,
> My hands can't feel to grip,
> My toes too numb to step,
> Wait only for my boot heels to be wanderin'.
> I'm ready to go anywhere,
> I'm ready for to fade
> Into my own parade.
> Cast your dancin' spell my way,
> I promise to go under it.
> Hey, Mister Tambourine Man, play a song for me,
> I'm not sleepy and there ain't no place I'm going to.
> Hey, Mister Tambourine Man, play a song for me.
> In the jingle, jangle morning I'll come followin' you.

Arnold Friend's car—complete with the phrase "MAN THE FLYING SAUCERS"—is just such "a magic swirlin' ship." Arnold is the personification of popular music, particularly Bob Dylan's music; and as such, Connie's interaction with him is a musically induced fantasy, a kind of "magic carpet ride" in "a convertible jalopy painted gold." Rising out of Connie's radio, Arnold Friend/Bob Dylan is a magical, musical messiah; he persuades Connie to abandon her father's house. As a manifestation of her own desires, he frees her from the limitations of a fifteen-year-old girl, assisting her maturation by stripping her of her childlike vision.

Notes

[1] Joyce M. Wegs, "'Don't You Know Who I Am?' The Grotesque in Oates's 'Where Are You Going, Where Have You Been?'" in *Critical Essays on Joyce Carol Oates,* ed. Linda W. Wagner (Boston: G. K. Hall, 1979), p. 90. First printed in *Journal of Narrative Technique,* 5 (1975), pp. 66–72.

[2] Marie Urbanski, "Existential Allegory: Joyce Carol Oates' 'Where Are You Going, Where Have You Been?'" *Studies in Short Fiction,* 15 (1978), p. 202; Joan Winslow, "The Stranger Within: Two Stories by Oates and Hawthorne," *Studies in Short Fiction,* 17 (1980), p. 264; Tom Quirk, "A Source for 'Where Are You Going, Where Have You Been?'" *Studies in Short Fiction,* 18 (1981), p. 416; Christina Marsden Gillis, "'Where Are You Going, Where Have You Been?': Seduction, Space, and a Fictional Mode," *Studies in Short Fiction,* 18 (1981), p. 70.

[3] Wegs, p. 89.

[4] Gillis, p. 65.

[5] Quirk, p. 416.

[6] Gretchen Schulz and R. J. R. Rockwood, "In Fairyland, without a Map: Connie's Exploration Inward in Joyce Carol Oates' 'Where Are You Going, Where Have You Been?'" *Literature and Psychology,* 30 (1980), pp. 156, 165, & 166, respectively.

[7] In *Paradise Lost,* Milton clearly intends Satan to be a symbol of archetypal evil. Blake and Shelley, as true Romantics, saw in their predecessor's portrait of Lucifer a duality that embodied positive as well as negative traits.

[8] Roy Male, *Enter Mysterious Stranger: American Cloistral Fiction* (Norman: University of Oklahoma Press, 1979), p. 21.

[9] Joyce Carol Oates, "Where Are You Going, Where Have You Been?" in *The Wheel of Love* (New York: Vanguard Press, 1970), p. 40. Hereafter cited parenthetically within the text.

[10] Anthony Scaduto, *Bob Dylan* (New York: Grosset and Dunlop. 1971), p. 222.

[11] Scaduto, p. 274.

[12] Scaduto, p. 229.

[13] "Interview with Joyce Carol Oates about 'Where Are You Going, Where Have You Been?'" in *Mirrors: An Introduction to Literature,* ed. John R. Knott, Jr., and Christopher R. Keaske, 2nd ed. (San Francisco: Canfield Press, 1975), pp. 18–19.

◆ ◆ ◆

BOB DYLAN

It's All Over Now, Baby Blue

You must leave now, take what you need you think will last
But whatever you wish to keep, you better grab it fast
Yonder stands your orphan with his gun
Crying like a fire in the sun.
Look out, the saints are comin' through   5
And it's all over now, baby blue.

The highway is for gamblers, better use your sins
Take what you have gathered from coincidence
The empty-handed painter from your streets
Is drawing crazy patterns on your sheets   10
This sky too is folding under you
And it's all over now, baby blue.

All your seasick sailors they are rowing home
Your empty-handed army men are going home
The lover who has just walked out your door   15
Has taken all his blankets from the floor
The carpet too is moving under you
And it's all over now, baby blue.

Leave your stepping stones behind, something calls for you
Forget the dead you've left, they will not follow you   20
The vagabond who's rapping at your door

Is standing in the clothes that you once wore
Strike another match, go start anew
And it's all over now, baby blue.

❖ ❖ ❖

LAURA KALPAKIAN

from a review of Where Are You Going, Where Have You Been?: Selected Early Stories

In acknowledging her range, one must celebrate Ms. Oates's bravery. Range re-quires courage — and always did, though people perpetually insist things are worse now than they were thirty years ago. In any event and for a wide variety of reasons, current American literature seems self-consciously picketed off, writers hunkered over thimble-sized garden plots, No Trespassing signs stuck about tiny terrains of age or race, region, religion, gender, sexual persuasion, politics, each writer farming a tiny furrow: the pen as plow. Joyce Carol Oates, as these early stories [from the collection *Where Are You Going, Where Have You Been?: Selected Early Stories*] testify, has always declined to be pinned down to her plot, has kicked down the fences. She writes about the rich and poor, urban and rural, black and white, the literate, the tongue-tied, young and old, the primly conventional, the drugged, delinquent, and debilitated. They're all here. Moreover, they're cast out of the comfy old narrative conventions and into structures which demand more from the reader.

Given Ms. Oates's range of structure, character, and voice, we might ask our-selves what unites these pieces. Poured, all of them, into a vial, shaken, what might rise to the top? Drastic acts with drastic consequences, severed connec-tions, doomed love, destructive sex, fear, evil, madness — but not much guilt. Oates's characters all twist about on short tethers, whatever the differences in their worldly circumstances. More often than not a single act or choice or instant plummets these characters not merely into the depths of despair, but into de-pravity and destruction. In "Upon the Sweeping Flood" (1966), we meet a com-placent, well-to-do family man driving home from his father's funeral. Caught in a hurricane, he refuses to obey an order to evacuate and plunges into the mael-strom, thrust finally into the company of two unnamed, abandoned white-trash kids, a boy and a girl. The three survive the night, but in the morning the boy dies at the hands of this man who then lunges toward the girl — he can "already see himself grappling with her in the mud, forcing her down, tearing her ugly cloth-ing from her body" — just as a rescue boat heaves into view. "Save me! Save me!" cries yesterday's prosperous bourgeois and today's murderer.

In the ironically titled "Love and Death" (1972), an equally short distance separates a man (again comfortable, conventional, unloved, and unflappable) from a previously unthinkable fate. Visiting his infirm father, he meets a prostitute he slept with years before, as a young man. Their versions of the past are different; hers is correct. Though he returns to his manicured life, the chance encounter evolves into an obsession, sucking him into abasement and humiliation.

At the conclusion of "In the Warehouse" (1973), the narrator tells us of her tidy married life in "a colonial house on a lane of colonial houses called Meadowbrook Lane." But as a twelve-year-old, she was bullied about by a stronger girl named Ronnie whose toughness sprung from a sort of delinquent passion and unfocused unhappiness. The narrator was completely cowed by Ronnie: "I have never thought about liking Ronnie. I have no choice. She has never given me the privilege of liking or disliking her and if she knew I was thinking such a thought, she would yank my hair out of my head." As the girls prowled the darkened loft of a deserted warehouse, Ronnie urged the narrator up the stairs, ordering, "Do it! Do it!" Atop the loft, the narrator pushed Ronnie, who was impaled on the machinery below and died in a pool of blood. The sleepy narrator then went home, went to bed. Eventually, she "[grew] out of the skinny little body that knocked the clumsy body down — and I have never felt sorry. Never any guilt."

The Joyce Carol Oates of these early stories believes that evil lurks every- 5 where, even in the sunniest lives, the ostensibly to-be-envied lives. The knowledge of this evil defines character for Oates — or, more to the point, the individual's reaction to this knowledge defines character. Oates cares nothing for justice, nor judgment, nor Christian virtue and Christian wickedness. There are only two possible responses to the darkness. One reaction is the murderer's cry, "Save me! Save me!", the wail of inescapable horror, the wish to be delivered. But there is no deliverance and there is no salvation. The narrator of "In the Warehouse" expresses for Oates the other possible reaction: "Never any guilt." She waits patiently to feel guilt for Ronnie's murder; but guilt, like a missed train, never arrives. In Oates's moral lexicon, the word "retribution" does not exist, nor "punishment," nor even anything so personal as "revenge." Evil is an impersonal, inescapable fact in every life. The central recognition of adulthood — no matter how old or young the character — is the recognition of this evil.

So omnipresent are the evil acts and consequences that Oates's characters seem often to be less created than enslaved by narrative: allegorical figures painted against realistic sunshine. In the title piece, "Where Are You Going, Where Have You Been?" (1970), for instance, there is a struggle between the menacing and cajoling Arnold Friend and the pubescent Connie. In the end Connie is, apparently, raped (in the Afterword Oates calls her "the presumably doomed Connie"). But Connie seems, despite the carefully drawn settings — shopping malls, drive-in restaurants, backyard barbecues — less a character than a cipher. She has no volition, no choices, and therefore it's hard to see her even as a victim. Instead, she suggests in her helplessness the awful inequalities of sex and power and violence. . . .

Emphatically in the stories in this volume, character and landscape serve the narrative rather than vice versa. Moreover, Joyce Carol Oates does not stoop to authorial pleading; she is neither pseudomaternal toward her characters nor pseudo-avuncular toward the reader, and she never importunes us with the unspoken: Please care for these characters. And, though the seasons are always noted and the geographical details of settings are always provided (including the oft-mentioned Detroit and its suburbs, as well as Erie County, New York), landscape in Oates's work seems dreamy, monochromatic, and unrealized — landscape as Tim Burton sometimes uses it in his movies. We may care about these characters or not, as we wish, but we are compelled by vigorous narrative through essentially indifferent landscapes. . . .

In Oates's stories there are no safe relationships, but the most perilous of all possibilities is sex. Sex is always destructive. In "Accomplished Desires" (1970), a two-edged narrative recounts the collision (and collusion) of two women: one a pretty college girl, vacuous but orderly, the other an accomplished woman poet married to a bullying professor. The wife is a prisoner in the upper reaches of her rented home; defeated by her home life, her three children, her inability to write, she drinks and looks out the high window. The smarmy husband not only beds the student but installs her as his secretary and housekeeper and moves her into his home to keep his life in order. According to the husband, this young woman "gets herself pregnant. On purpose." Because sages concerned with the state of modern literature await the professor's lecture at a meeting on the West Coast, the wife drives the student to an appointment with an abortionist. The women strike up a tentative, unspoken alliance (though not against the man, as we might have thought — or hoped). Indeed, the wife bows out of the struggle altogether, almost gracefully: a quiet overdose self-administered in a hotel room. The pretty former student, new wife — now, suddenly, a mother of four —finds herself prisoner in the upper reaches of the rented house, without the consolations of company or poetry or even gin.

Communication — especially sexual communication —is not only baffling and treacherous for Oates's characters; it often seems impossible. My personal favorite in this collection, "Translation" (1977), describes a middle-aged American academic who makes an official visit to an unnamed Central European country and is provided with a translator, Liebert. At a dreary communist cocktail party the American, Oliver, meets a woman whose beauty and fragility strike him to the very heart. He falls in love though he cannot even pronounce her name: "Alisa was as close as he could come to it." Oliver is euphoric, intoxicated, as he spends a memorable evening with her in a cafe (Liebert translating) where they speak of literature, politics, passion, history, and love. Oliver feels himself buoyed, enfolded, welcomed in a country where, in effect, he is a mute. The following day Liebert discreetly suggests that Alisa's roommate could be persuaded to leave overnight if she had train fare, which Oliver provides. But on the morning of the intended assignation, Oliver discovers he has been given a new translator. No explanations offered. No questions answered. This new man — obscene in every way — talks of the weather, smirks lewdly, arranges another cafe date with Alisa that evening. Through the new translator, Alisa inquires after Oliver's life in America, his financial assets, his cars, his wife. She eyeballs his watch. As Oliver leaves the country the next day, desperate for Liebert, he cries, "What shall I do for the rest of my life . . . ?"

No doubt the young and gifted writer of these stories found herself facing that same question. The dust-jacket photo for these selected early stories shows Ms. Oates circa 1965, her hair in the "flip" fashionable in that era, shoulders framed by a boat-necked dress. She regards the reader with the serene gaze of a high-school valedictorian. Not at all the look of a woman who willingly, knowingly smashes up the conventions of narrative. She does not look like the author who will unmask the evil of everyday life, who will see allegory in the backyard and real darkness among the metaphoric daisies. But she is.

◊ ◊ ◊

DON MOSER

from The Pied Piper of Tucson

Sullen and unshaved, 23 years old and arrested for murder, Charles Schmid did not now look like a hero. But to many of the teen-agers in Tucson, Ariz. he had been someone to admire and emulate. He was different. He was Smitty, with mean, "beautiful" eyes and an interesting way of talking, and if he sometimes did weird things, at least he wasn't dull. He had his own house where he threw

good parties, he wore crazy make-up, he was known at all the joints up and down Tucson's Speedway, and girls dyed their hair blond for him. Three of the girls who knew him wound up dead in the desert outside of town. And so last week, in a sun-blessed town where big-city squalor and violence seem far away, Smitty, the cool pied piper, stood trial for murder.

The death of the girls was shocking enough to Tucson, but the city had to face something more. There were indications that Smitty had boasted about the killings to his teen-age followers long before authorities even began to suspect that murder might have been done. Nobody spoke up. As the trial began for the murder of two of the victims — there will be another trial later for the murder of the third — Tucson's parents looked closely at their own children, and at the different young man so many of their children admired.

Charles Schmid in police custody

He Cruised in a Golden Car,
Looking for the Action

> Hey, c'mon babe, follow me,
> I'm the Pied Piper, follow me,
> I'm the Pied Piper,
> And I'll show you where it's at.
> —Popular song,
> Tucson, winter 1965

Schmid's teenage victims: Gretchen Fritz (*left*), Wendy Fritz (*center*), and Alleen Rowe (*right*)

At dusk in Tucson, as the stark, yellow-flared mountains begin to blur against the sky, the golden car slowly cruises Speedway. Smoothly it rolls down the long, divided avenue, past the supermarkets, the gas stations and the motels; past the twist joints, the sprawling drive-in restaurants. The car slows for an intersection, stops, then pulls away again. The exhaust mutters against the pavement as the young man driving takes the machine swiftly, expertly through the gears. A car pulls even with him; the teen-age girls in the front seat laugh, wave and call his name. The young man glances toward the rearview mirror, turned always so that he can look at his own reflection, and he appraises himself.

The face is his own creation: the hair dyed raven black, the skin darkened to a deep tan with pancake make-up, the lips whitened, the whole effect heightened by a mole he has painted on one cheek. But the deep-set blue eyes are all his own. Beautiful eyes, the girls say.

Approaching the Hi-Ho, the teen-agers' nightclub, he backs off on the accelerator, then slowly cruises on past Johnie's Drive-in. There the cars are beginning to orbit and accumulate in the parking lot — neat sharp cars with deep-throated mufflers and Maltese-cross decals on the windows. But it's early yet. Not much going on. The driver shifts up again through the gears, and the golden car slides away along the glitter and gimcrack of Speedway. Smitty keeps looking for the action.

Speedway Boulevard in Tucson (circa 1966) was a hangout for teenagers with nothing to do, often frequented by murderer Charles Schmid.

Whether the juries in the two trials decide that Charles Howard Schmid Jr. did or did not brutally murder Alleen Rowe, Gretchen Fritz and Wendy Fritz has from the beginning seemed of almost secondary importance to the people of Tucson. They are not indifferent. But what disturbs them far beyond the question of Smitty's guilt or innocence are the revelations about Tucson itself that have followed on the disclosure of the crimes. Starting with the bizarre circumstances of the killings and on through the ugly fragments of the plot — which in turn hint at other murders as yet undiscovered, at teen-age sex, blackmail, even connections with the Cosa Nostra — they have had to view their city in a new and unpleasant light. The fact is that Charles Schmid — who cannot be dismissed as a freak, an aberrant of no consequence — had for years functioned successfully as a member, even a leader, of the yeastiest stratum of Tucson's teen-age society.

As a high school student Smitty had been, as classmates remember, an outsider — but not that far outside. He was small but he was a fine athlete, and in his last year — 1960 — he was a state gymnastics champion. His grades were poor, but he was in no trouble to speak of until his senior year, when he was suspended for stealing tools from a welding class.   5

But Smitty never really left the school. After his suspension he hung around waiting to pick up kids in a succession of sharp cars which he drove fast and well. He haunted all the teen-age hangouts along Speedway, including the bowling alleys and the public swimming pool — and he put on spectacular diving exhibitions for girls far younger than he.

At the time of his arrest last November, Charles Schmid was 23 years old. He wore face make-up and dyed his hair. He habitually stuffed three or four inches of old rags and tin cans into the bottoms of his high-topped boots to make himself taller than his five-foot-three and stumbled about so awkwardly while walking that some people thought he had wooden feet. He pursed his lips and let his eyelids droop in order to emulate his idol, Elvis Presley. He bragged to girls that he

Murderer Charles H. Schmid Jr., at the preliminary hearings before
the trial

knew 100 ways to make love, that he ran dope, that he was a Hell's Angel. He
talked about being a rough customer in a fight (he was, though he was rarely in
one), and he always carried in his pocket tiny bottles of salt and pepper, which
he said he used to blind his opponents. He liked to use highfalutin language and
had a favorite saying, "I can manifest my neurotical emotions, emancipate an
epicureal instinct, and elaborate on my heterosexual tendencies."

He occasionally shocked even those who thought they knew him well. A
friend says he once saw Smitty tie a string to the tail of his pet cat, swing it around
his head and beat it bloody against a wall. Then he turned calmly and asked, "You
feel compassion — why?"

Yet even while Smitty tried to create an exalted, heroic image of himself, he
had worked on a pitiable one. "He thrived on feeling sorry for himself," recalls
a friend, "and making others feel sorry for him." At various times Smitty told
intimates that he had leukemia and didn't have long to live. He claimed that he
was adopted, that his real name was Angel Rodriguez, that his father was a "bean"
(local slang for Mexican, an inferior race in Smitty's view), and that his mother
was a famous lawyer who would have nothing to do with him.

What made Smitty a hero to Tucson's youth?

10   Isn't Tucson — out there in the Golden West, in the grand setting where the
skies are not cloudy all day — supposed to be a flowering of the American Dream?
One envisions teen-agers who drink milk, wear crewcuts, go to bed at half past 9,
say "Sir" and "Ma'am," and like to go fishing with Dad. Part of Tucson is like
this — but the city is not yet Utopia. It is glass and chrome and well-weathered
stucco; it is also gimcrack, ersatz and urban sprawl at its worst. Its suburbs stretch
for mile after mile — a level sea of bungalows, broken only by mammoth shopping centers, that ultimately peters out among the cholla and saguaro. The city
has grown from 85,000 to 300,000 since World War II. Few who live there were
born there, and a lot are just passing through. Its superb climate attracts the old

and the infirm, many of whom, as one citizen put it, "have come here to retire from their responsibilities to life." Jobs are hard to find and there is little industry to stabilize employment. ("What do people do in Tucson?" the visitor asks. Answer: "They do each others' laundry.")

As for the youngsters, they must compete with the army of semi-retired who are willing to take on part-time work for the minimum wage. Schools are beautiful but overcrowded; and at those with split sessions, the kids are on the loose from noon on, or from 6 p.m. till noon the next day. When they get into trouble, Tucson teen-agers are capable of getting into trouble in style: a couple of years ago they shocked the city fathers by throwing a series of beer-drinking parties in the desert, attended by scores of kids. The fests were called "boondockers" and if they were no more sinful than any other kids' drinking parties, they were at least on a magnificent scale. One statistic seems relevant: 50 runaways are reported to the Tucson police department each month.

Of an evening kids with nothing to do wind up on Speedway, looking for action. There is the teen-age nightclub ("Pickup Palace," the kids call it). There are the rock 'n' roll beer joints (the owners check ages meticulously, but young girls can enter if they don't drink; besides, anyone can buy a phony I.D. card for $2.50 around the high schools) where they can Jerk, Swim and Frug away the evening to the room-shaking electronic blare of *Hang On Sloopy*, *The Pied Piper* and a number called *The Bo Diddley Rock*. At the drive-in hamburger and pizza stands their cars circle endlessly, mufflers rumbling, as they check each other over.

Here on Speedway you find Richie and Ronny, out of work and bored and with nothing to do. Here you find Debby and Jabron, from the wrong side of the tracks, aimlessly cruising in their battered old car looking for something — anything — to relieve the tedium of their lives, looking for somebody neat. ("Well if the boys look bitchin',' you pull up next to them in your car and you roll down the window and say, 'Hey, how about a dollar for gas?' and if they give you the dollar then maybe you let them take you to Johnie's for a Coke.") Here you find Gretchen, pretty and rich and with problems, bad problems. Of a Saturday night, all of them cruising the long, bright street that seems endlessly in motion with the young. Smitty's people.

He had a nice car. He had plenty of money from his parents, who ran a nursing   15
home, and he was always glad to spend it on anyone who'd listen to him. He had a pad of his own where he threw parties and he had impeccable manners. He was always willing to help a friend and he would send flowers to girls who were ill. He was older and more mature than most of his friends. He knew where the action was, and if he wore make-up — well, at least he was *different*.

Some of the older kids — those who worked, who had something else to do — thought Smitty was a creep. But to the youngsters — to the bored and the lonely, to the dropout and the delinquent, to the young girls with beehive hairdos and tight pants they didn't quite fill out, and to the boys with acne and no jobs — to these people, Smitty was a kind of folk hero. Nutty maybe, but at least more dramatic, more theatrical, more *interesting* than anyone else in their lives: a semi-ludicrous sexy-eyed pied piper who, stumbling along in his rag-stuffed boots led them up and down Speedway. . . .

Out in the respectable Tucson suburbs parents have started to crack down on the youngsters and have declared Speedway hangouts off limits. "I thought my folks were bad before," laments one grounded 16-year-old, "but now they're just impossible."

As for the others — Smitty's people — most don't care very much. Things are duller without Smitty around, but things have always been dull.

"There's nothing to do in this town," says one of his girls, shaking her dyed blond hair. "The only other town I know is Las Vegas and there's nothing to do there either." For her, and for her friends, there's nothing to do in any town.

20   They are down on Speedway again tonight, cruising, orbiting the drive-ins, stopping by the joints, where the words of *The Bo Diddley Rock* cut through the smoke and the electronic dissonance like some macabre reminder of their fallen hero.

> All you women stand in line,
> And I'll love you all in an hour's time. . . .
> I got a cobra snake for a necktie,
> I got a brand-new house on the roadside
> Covered with rattlesnake hide
> I got a brand-new chimney made on top,
> Made out of human skulls.
> Come on baby, take a walk with me,
> And tell me, who do you love?
> Who do you love?
> Who do you love?
> Who do you love?

◇ ◇ ◇

ANONYMOUS

The Pied Piper of Hamelin

Once upon a time . . . on the banks of a great river in the north of Germany lay a town called Hamelin. The citizens of Hamelin were honest folk who lived contentedly in their grey stone houses. The years went by, and the town grew very rich. Then one day, an extraordinary thing happened to disturb the peace. Hamelin had always had rats, and a lot too. But they had never been a danger, for the cats had always solved the rat problem in the usual way — by killing them. All at once, however, the rats began to multiply.

In the end, a black sea of rats swarmed over the whole town. First, they attacked the barns and storehouses, then, for lack of anything better, they gnawed the wood, cloth or anything at all. The one thing they didn't eat was metal. The terrified citizens flocked to plead with the town councillors to free them from the plague of rats. But the council had, for a long time, been sitting in the Mayor's room, trying to think of a plan.

"What we need is an army of cats!"

But all the cats were dead.

5   "We'll put down poisoned food then . . ."

Illustration of the Brothers Grimm version of the fairy tale "The Pied Piper of Hamelin"

But most of the food was already gone and even poison did not stop the rats.

"It just can't be done without help!" said the Mayor sadly.

Just then, while the citizens milled around outside, there was a loud knock at the door. "Who can that be?" the city fathers wondered uneasily, mindful of the angry crowds. They gingerly opened the door. And to their surprise, there stood a tall thin man dressed in brightly coloured clothes, with a long feather in his hat, and waving a gold pipe at them.

"I've freed other towns of beetles and bats," the stranger announced, "and for a thousand florins, I'll rid you of your rats!"

"A thousand florins!" exclaimed the Mayor. 10 "We'll give you fifty thousand if you succeed!" At once the stranger hurried away, saying: "It's late now, but at dawn tomorrow, there won't be a rat left in Hamelin!"

The sun was still below the horizon, when the sound of a pipe wafted through the streets of Hamelin. The pied piper slowly made his way through the houses and behind him flocked the rats. Out they scampered from doors, windows and gutters, rats of every size, all after the piper. And as he played, the stranger marched down to the river and straight into the water, up to his middle. Behind him swarmed the rats and every one was drowned and swept away by the current.

By the time the sun was high in the sky, there was not a single rat in the town. There was even greater delight at the town hall, until the piper tried to claim his payment.

"Fifty thousand florins?" exclaimed the councillors, "Never . . ."

"A thousand florins at least!" cried the pied piper angrily. But the Mayor broke in. "The rats are all dead now and they can never come back. So be grateful for fifty florins, or you'll not get even that . . ."

His eyes flashing with rage, the pied piper pointed a threatening finger at the 15 Mayor.

"You'll bitterly regret ever breaking your promise," he said, and vanished.

A shiver of fear ran through the councillors, but the Mayor shrugged and said excitedly: "We've saved fifty thousand florins!"

That night, freed from the nightmare of the rats, the citizens of Hamelin slept more soundly than ever. And when the strange sound of piping wafted through the streets at dawn, only the children heard it. Drawn as by magic, they hurried out of their homes. Again, the pied piper paced through the town. This time, it was children of all sizes that flocked at his heels to the sound of his strange piping. The long procession soon left the town and made its way through the wood and across the forest till it reached the foot of a huge mountain. When the piper came to the dark rock, he played his pipe even louder still and a great door creaked open. Beyond lay a cave. In trooped the children behind the pied piper, and when the last child had gone into the darkness, the door creaked shut. A great landslide came down the mountain blocking the entrance to the cave forever. Only one little lame boy escaped this fate. It was he who told the anxious citizens, searching for their children, what had happened. And no matter what people did, the mountain never gave up its victims. Many years were to pass before the merry voices of other children would ring through the streets of Hamelin but the memory of the harsh lesson lingered in everyone's heart and was passed down from father to son through the centuries.

◆ ◆ ◆

CHARLES PERRAULT

Little Red Riding Hood

Once upon a time there was a little village girl, the prettiest that had ever been seen. Her mother doted on her. Her grandmother was even fonder, and made her a little red hood, which became her so well that everywhere she went by the name of Little Red Riding Hood.

Illustration from "Little Red Riding Hood"

One day her mother, who had just made and baked some cakes, said to her: "Go and see how your grandmother is, for I have been told that she is ill. Take her a cake and this little pot of butter."

Little Red Riding Hood set off at once for the house of her grandmother, who lived in another village. On her way through a wood she met old Father Wolf. He would have very much liked to eat her, but dared not do so on account of some wood-cutters who were in the forest. He asked her where she was going. The poor child, not knowing that it was dangerous to stop and listen to a wolf, said: "I am going to see my grandmother, and am taking her a cake and a pot of butter which my mother has sent to her." "Does she live far away?" asked the Wolf. "Oh, yes," replied Little Red Riding Hood; "it is yonder by the mill which you can see right below there, and it is the first house in the village."

"Well now," said the Wolf, "I think I shall go and see her too. I will go by this path, and you by that path, and we will see who gets there first." The Wolf set off running with all his might by the shorter road, and the little girl continued on her way by the longer road. As she went she amused herself by gathering nuts, running after the butterflies, and making nosegays of the wild flowers which she found.

5   The Wolf was not long in reaching the grandmother's house. He knocked. Toc Toc. "Who is there?" "It is your granddaughter, Red Riding Hood," said the Wolf,

disguising his voice, "and I bring you a cake and a little pot of butter as a present from my mother." The worthy grandmother was in bed, not being very well, and cried out to him: "Pull out the peg and the latch will fall." The Wolf drew out the peg and the door flew open. Then he sprang upon the poor old lady and ate her up in less than no time, for he had been more than three days without food.

After that he shut the door, lay down in the grandmother's bed, and waited for Little Red Riding Hood. Presently she came and knocked. Toc Toc.

"Who is there?"

Now Little Red Riding Hood on hearing the Wolf's gruff voice was at first frightened, but thinking that her grandmother had a bad cold, she replied: "It is your granddaughter, Red Riding Hood, and I bring you a cake and a little pot of butter from my mother."

Softening his voice, the Wolf called out to her: "Pull out the peg and the latch will fall." Little Red Riding Hood drew out the peg and the door flew open. When he saw her enter, the Wolf hid himself in the bed beneath the counterpane. "Put the cake and the little pot of butter on the bin," he said, "and come up on the bed with me."

Little Red Riding Hood took off her cloak, but when she climbed up on the 10
bed she was astonished to see how her grandmother looked in her nightgown.

"Grandmother dear!" she exclaimed, "what big arms you have!"

"The better to embrace you, my child!"

"Grandmother dear, what big legs you have!"

"The better to run with, my child!"

"Grandmother dear, what big ears you have!" 15

"The better to hear with, my child!"

"Grandmother dear, what big eyes you have!"

"The better to see with, my child!"

"Grandmother dear, what big teeth you have!"

"The better to eat you with!" 20

With these words the wicked Wolf leapt upon Little Red Riding Hood and gobbled her up.

Moral

From this story one learns that children, especially young lasses, pretty, courteous and well-bred, do very wrong to listen to strangers, and it is not an unheard thing if the Wolf is thereby provided with his dinner. I say Wolf, for all wolves are not of the same sort; there is one kind with an amenable disposition — neither noisy, nor hateful, nor angry, but tame, obliging and gentle, following the young maids in the streets, even into their homes. Alas! Who does not know that these gentle wolves are of all such creatures the most dangerous!

Topics for Further Research

1. In Schulz and Rockwood's essay "In Fairyland, without a Map: Connie's Exploration Inward in Joyce Carol Oates's 'Where Are You Going, Where Have You Been?'" (p. 590), the authors quote Oates on the subject of her story's allusions to fairy tales. After consulting Bruno Bettelheim's classic book *The Uses of Enchantment* (as well as the other sources in this casebook) and after reading "Little Red Riding Hood" (p. 608) and "The Pied Piper of Hamelin" (p. 606), tales included here, write an essay in which you consider the importance of fairy tales in the story.

2. In her article "When Characters from the Page Are Made Flesh on the Screen" (p. 586), Oates refers to her use of "realistic allegory" as a mode of fiction that is "Hawthornian . . . shading into parable" (par. 4). Research Hawthorne's views on allegory by reading some of his many essays on the subject, such as "The Custom House." Then, write an essay in which you consider how "Where Are You Going, Where Have You Been?" might be compared to Hawthorne's stories, such as "Young Goodman Brown" (p. 489), in terms of its portrayal of good, evil, and innocence. Try to identify elements in Oates's story that might be considered allegorical in the Hawthornian sense.

3. Oates has been described as a modern realist, and she herself has used the term "psychological realism" to describe her work. Research the history and emergence of literary realism in American literature. What elements of realism as it first appeared in literature at the end of the nineteenth century and the beginning of the twentieth century are found in Oates's work?

4. Critics often see Oates's short stories as gothic. Research the term *gothic* as it applies to works of literature. Then, write a paper in which you make the case for three of her stories, including "Where Are You Going, Where Have You Been?," as gothic works. You may also wish to discuss gothic stories by other writers — for example, Poe's "The Cask of Amontillado" (p. 350) and Flannery O'Connor's "A Good Man Is Hard to Find" (p. 409) in this text.

5. In the excerpt from her book review included in this Casebook (p. 598) critic Laura Kalpakian takes a look at some of the themes of Oates's works as they are represented by her characters. Do some research to find out what other critics and reviewers have identified as recurring themes in Oates's work. Then, choose one of these themes, and write an essay discussing how three of Oates's characters illustrate the theme you have chosen.

Student Paper

Olivari 1

Michele Olivari

Professor Biemiller

English 102

8 March 2005

Mesmerizing Men and Vulnerable Teens:

Power Relationships in "Where Are You Going,

Where Have You Been?" and "Teenage Wasteland"

In both Joyce Carol Oates's "Where Are You Going, Where Have You Been?" (1966) and Anne Tyler's "Teenage Wasteland" (1984), adolescents are in coflict with their parents. Both stories are set in "teenage wastelands" in which the protagonists ignore limits established by authority figures and avoid making decisions or finding a direction for their lives. An even more striking similarity between the two stories is the presence of a hypnotic older man—one who exerts enormous influence over the teenagers, pushing them out of their passive states and causing them to take action. Ironically, however, the actions these two adolescents take, though decisive, have terrifying consequences.

Arnold Friend, the mysterious loner who pursues Connie in "Where Are You Going, Where Have You Been?," is characterized by Gretchen Schulz and R. J. R. Rockwood as the fairy tale wolf who "intends to 'gobble up' this 'little girl' as soon as he gets the chance" (593). Many other critics, as Mike Tierce and John Michael Crafton point out, see Arnold as the devil; Tierce and Crafton, however, prefer to see him as a Bob Dylan figure "—a type of rock and roll

Introduction

Background: critics' interpretations of Arnold Friend

Olivari 2

messiah—" (595). Oates herself, in stating that
Arnold is based on a "charismatic mass murderer"
("When Characters" 586), acknowledges both the threat
he poses and his seductive powers. Regardless of
whether Arnold is murderer, devil, wolf, or musical
messiah, it is clear that he is a strong, controlling
personality who has an unnaturally powerful hold over
Connie. In a less dramatic way, Cal, the tutor in
"Teenage Wasteland," has a similar hold over Donny.
Both men, supported by background music, use their
power to mesmerize young people, separating them from
home and family and seducing them into following
different—and dangerous—paths. In both stories, it
is the adolescents' tendency to drift without an
anchor that makes them vulnerable to the men.

Both Connie and Donny are passive dreamers,
stuck in numbing adolescence, waiting for something
to happen. Meanwhile, both break the rules set by
their parents. Connie is fifteen, and her mind is
"all filled with trashy daydreams" (573). At night
she sneaks out to forbidden hangouts, lying to her
parents about where she is going. As she drifts
through her unstructured summer days, she is "dazed
with the warmth about her" (576) and caught up in
the music she listens to and in her romantic
fantasies. Donny is also stalled, caught in a cycle
of failure and defeat, "noisy, lazy, and disruptive"
(799) and unresponsive in school, cutting classes,
smoking, and drinking beer.

Comparison
between Cal
and Arnold
established

Thesis
statement

First parallel
between Connie
and Donny:
passivity

Olivari 3

Both Connie and Donny are emotionally separated from their parents. Connie's mother constantly nags her and compares her unfavorably to her sister June; her father does not even talk, choosing instead to read his newspaper and avoid conflict. In "Teenage Wasteland," Daisy's primary attitude toward her son Donny is disappointment. When she looks at him, she sees only "his pathetically poor posture, that slouch so forlorn that his shoulders [seem] about to meet his chin" (802). She feels sorry for him, but she is helpless to rescue him, let alone give him the emotional support he needs. Like Connie's mother, she disapproves of her child's behavior. Despite her efforts to defend and encourage him, she is ashamed of his failures and upset at how they reflect upon her as a parent. Both Connie and Donny are disconnected from people or social institutions, and both are allowed to remain this way by weak, ineffective parents whom they neither respect nor admire. Both Connie and Donny, therefore, are vulnerable to the seductive power of a hypnotic older man.

Arnold Friend, a strange-looking man who acts like a teenager, has great power over Connie. Initially, she is drawn to him by how he looks and dresses and by the music they share; later, his claims to know all about her, to know what she wants (which she herself does not know), draw her closer to him. Although she begins by flirting with him as she does with other boys, she soon realizes that he is

Second parallel between Connie and Donny: alienation from parents and society

Arnold's power over Connie

Olivari 4

different. At first "his face [is] a familiar face,
somehow" (578), and "she recognize[s] most things
about him" (579), but her confidence turns to fear
when she realizes that he is older than he appears
(579). By now, though, she is under his spell.
Little by little, things that have been comforting
and familiar—the music, Arnold's clothing and
mannerisms, even Connie's own kitchen—become "only
half real" (580). As Arnold becomes more and more
threatening, Connie becomes more and more helpless;
toward the end of the story, cut off from everything
she has known, she is "hollow with what had been
fear, but what [is] now just an emptiness" (584).
Totally in Arnold's power, she crosses the line into
uncertainty—and, perhaps, death.

Cal's power
over Donny

Cal Beadle, Donny's tutor, has none of the
frightening mannerisms of Arnold Friend, and he has
no sinister intentions. Nevertheless, he too is a
controlling figure. Like Arnold, Cal is an older man
who dresses and acts as adolescents do and listens
to the music they like. He immediately sides with
Donny, setting himself in opposition to authority
figures and social institutions, such as school and
the family. Never blaming or even criticizing Donny,
Cal suggests that Donny's parents are too controlling
and advises that they "give him more rope" (802).
Cal does not help Donny to function in his world;
he shelters him from it. Still, Donny sides with Cal,
adopting his attitudes and expressions: it becomes

Olivari 5

"Cal this, Cal that, Cal says this, Cal and I did
that" (803).

Eventually, Cal becomes the role model Donny's   Cal's power
over Donny,
continued
own parents have failed to provide. Donny comes to
depend on Cal, even going straight to Cal's house
when he is expelled from school, and Cal comes to
enjoy this dependence. But Cal does not necessarily
have Donny's best interests at heart. Daisy, who
despite her own failures with Donny seems to know
him (and Cal) well, sees Cal as predatory and
controlling, characterizing his smile as "feverish
and avid—a smile of hunger" (806). Although Cal
does not cause Donny to leave home, he makes it
impossible for him to stay. Once Cal has convinced
Donny that it is acceptable to reject the values
established by his parents and teachers, Donny's
departure becomes inevitable. Having removed all
Donny's anchors, Cal then removes himself from
Donny's life, deciding the teenager is "emotionally
disturbed" (806) and thus absolving himself of blame.
At this point, Donny, "exhausted and defeated" (806),
has no real choice but to disappear.

Both Arnold Friend and Cal Beadle seem to exist   Conclusion
outside the adult world and its rules and values:
Arnold is odd-looking and out-of-date, and Cal is
estranged from his "controlling" wife and surrounded
by teenagers. Perhaps as a result, each has a need
for power and a desire to control. Each man selects
someone weaker, less confident, and more confused
than himself, a teenager with strained family

Olivari 6

relationships and no focused goals. Clearly, critics'
characterizations of Arnold Friend, and the hypnotic
power those characterizations suggest, apply not just
to Arnold but also to Cal. Even though Cal means
Donny no harm, his casual dismissal of him after he
has separated the boy from all that is familiar to
him pushes Donny from the known and safe to the
unknown and dangerous. It is to this uncertain
world that Connie too is driven: a place she "[does]
not recognize except to know that she [is] going
to it" (585).

Olivari 7

Works Cited

Kirszner, Laurie G., and Stephen R. Mandell, eds.
    Literature: Reading, Reacting, Writing. 6th ed.
    Boston: Wadsworth, 2007.

Oates, Joyce Carol. "When Characters from the Page
    Are Made Flesh on the Screen." Kirszner and
    Mandell 586-90.

---. "Where Are You Going, Where Have You Been?"
    Kirszner and Mandell 586-90.

Schulz, Gretchen, and R. J. R. Rockwood. "In
    Fairyland, without a Map: Connie's
    Exploration Inward in Joyce Carol Oates's 'Where
    Are You Going, Where Have You Been?'" Kirszner
    and Mandell 590-93.

Tierce, Mike, and John Michael Crafton. "Connie's
    Tambourine Man: A New Reading of Arnold Friend."
    Kirszner and Mandell 594-97.

Tyler, Anne. "Teenage Wasteland." Kirszner and
    Mandell 799-806.

CHAPTER 21

FICTION FOR FURTHER READING

CHINUA ACHEBE (1930–   )

Dead Man's Path (1953) (1972)

Michael Obi's hopes were fulfilled much earlier than he had expected. He was appointed headmaster of Ndume Central School in January 1949. It had always been an unprogressive school, so the Mission authorities decided to send a young and energetic man to run it. Obi accepted this responsibility with enthusiasm. He had many wonderful ideas and this was an opportunity to put them into practice. He had had sound secondary school education which designated him a "pivotal teacher" in the official records and set him apart from the other headmasters in the mission field. He was outspoken in his condemnation of the narrow views of these older and often less-educated ones.

"We shall make a good job of it, shan't we?" he asked his young wife when they first heard the joyful news of his promotion.

"We shall do our best," she replied. "We shall have such beautiful gardens and everything will be just *modern* and delightful . . ." In their two years of married life she had become completely infected by his passion for "modern methods" and his denigration of "these old and superannuated people in the teaching field who would be better employed as traders in the Onitsha market." She began to see herself already as the admired wife of the young headmaster, the queen of the school.

The wives of the other teachers would envy her position. She would set the fashion in everything . . . Then, suddenly, it occurred to her that there might not be other wives. Wavering between hope and fear, she asked her husband, looking anxiously at him.

5   "All our colleagues are young and unmarried," he said with enthusiasm which for once she did not share. "Which is a good thing," he continued.

"Why?"

"Why? They will give all their time and energy to the school."

Nancy was downcast. For a few minutes she became skeptical about the new school; but it was only for a few minutes. Her little personal misfortune could not blind her to her husband's happy prospects. She looked at him as he sat folded up in a chair. He was stoop-shouldered and looked frail. But he sometimes surprised people with sudden bursts of physical energy. In his present posture, however, all his bodily strength seemed to have retired behind his deep-set eyes, giving them an extraordinary power of penetration. He was only twenty-six, but looked thirty or more. On the whole, he was not unhandsome.

"A penny for your thoughts, Mike," said Nancy after a while, imitating the woman's magazine she read.

"I was thinking what a grand opportunity we've got at last to show these 10 people how a school should be run."

Ndume School was backward in every sense of the word. Mr. Obi put his whole life into the work, and his wife hers too. He had two aims. A high standard of teaching was insisted upon, and the school compound was to be turned into a place of beauty. Nancy's dream-gardens came to life with the coming of the rains, and blossomed. Beautiful hibiscus and allamanda hedges in brilliant red and yellow marked out the carefully tended school compound from the rank neighborhood bushes.

One evening as Obi was admiring his work he was scandalized to see an old woman from the village hobble right across the compound, through a marigold flower-bed and the hedges. On going up there he found faint signs of an almost disused path from the village across the school compound to the bush on the other side.

"It amazes me," said Obi to one of his teachers who had been three years in the school, "that you people allowed the villagers to make use of this footpath. It is simply incredible." He shook his head.

"The path," said the teacher apologetically, "appears to be very important to them. Although it is hardly used, it connects the village shrine with their place of burial."

"And what has that got to do with the school"? asked the headmaster. 15

"Well, I don't know," replied the other with a shrug of the shoulders. "But I remember there was a big row some time ago when we attempted to close it."

"That was some time ago. But it will not be used now," said Obi as he walked away. "What will the Government Education Officer think of this when he comes to inspect the school next week? The villagers might, for all I know, decide to use the schoolroom for pagan ritual during the inspection."

Heavy sticks were planted closely across the path at the two places where it entered and left the school premises. These were further strengthened with barbed wire.

Three days later the village priest of *Ani* called on the headmaster. He was an old man and walked with a slight stoop. He carried a stout walking-stick which he usually tapped on the floor, by way of emphasis, each time he made a new point in his argument.

"I have heard," he said after the usual exchange of cordialities, "that our 20 ancestral footpath has recently been closed . . ."

"Yes," replied Mr. Obi. "We cannot allow people to make a highway of our school compound."

"Look here, my son," said the priest bringing down his walking-stick, "this path was here before you were born and before your father was born. The whole life of this village depends on it. Our dead relatives depart by it and our ancestors visit us by it. But most important, it is the path of children coming in to be born . . ."

Mr. Obi listened with a satisfied smile on his face.

"The whole purpose of our school," he said finally, "is to eradicate just such beliefs as that. Dead men do not require footpaths. The whole idea is just fantastic. Our duty is to teach your children to laugh at such ideas."

25   "What you say may be true," replied the priest, "but we follow the practices of our fathers. If you reopen the path we shall have nothing to quarrel about. What I always say is let the hawk perch and let the eagle perch." He rose to go.

"I am sorry," said the young headmaster. "But the school compound cannot be a thoroughfare. It is against our regulations. I would suggest your constructing another path, skirting our premises. We can even get our boys to help in building it. I don't suppose the ancestors will find the little detour too burdensome."

"I have no more words to say," said the old priest, already outside.

Two days later a young woman in the village died in childbed. A diviner was immediately consulted and he prescribed heavy sacrifices to propitiate ancestors insulted by the fence.

Obi woke up next morning among the ruins of his work. The beautiful hedges were torn up not just near the path but right round the school, the flowers trampled to death and one of the school buildings pulled down . . . That day, the white Supervisor came to inspect the school and wrote a nasty report on the state of the premises but more seriously about the "tribal-war situation developing between the school and the village, arising in part from the misguided zeal of the new headmaster."

JAMES BALDWIN   (1924–1987)

Sonny's Blues   (1957)

I read about it in the paper, in the subway, on my way to work. I read it, and I couldn't believe it, and I read it again. Then perhaps I just stared at it, at the newsprint spelling out his name, spelling out the story. I stared at it in the swinging lights of the subway car, and in the faces and bodies of the people, and in my own face, trapped in the darkness which roared outside.

It was not to be believed and I kept telling myself that, as I walked from the subway station to the high school. And at the same time I couldn't doubt it. I was scared, scared for Sonny. He became real to me again. A great block of ice got settled in my belly and kept melting there slowly all day long, while I taught my classes algebra it was a special kind of ice. It kept melting, sending trickles of ice water all up and down my veins, but it never got less. Sometimes it hardened and seemed to expand until I felt my guts were going to come spilling out or that I was going to choke or scream. This would always be at a moment when I was remembering some specific thing Sonny had once said or done.

When he was about as old as the boys in my classes his face had been bright and open, there was a lot of copper in it; and he'd had wonderfully direct brown eyes, and great gentleness and privacy. I wondered what he looked like now. He had been picked up, the evening before, in a raid on an apartment downtown, for peddling and using heroin.

I couldn't believe it: but what I mean by that is that I couldn't find any room for it anywhere inside me. I had kept it outside me for a long time. I hadn't wanted to know. I had had suspicions, but I didn't name them, I kept putting them away. I told myself that Sonny was wild, but he wasn't crazy. And he'd always been a good boy, he hadn't ever turned hard or evil or disrespectful, the way kids can, so quick, so quick, especially in Harlem. I didn't want to believe that I'd ever see my brother going down, coming to nothing, all that light in his face gone out, in the condition I'd already seen so many others. Yet it had happened and here I was, talking about algebra to a lot of boys who might, every one of them for all I knew, be popping off needles every time they went to the head.° Maybe it did more for them than algebra could.

I was sure that the first time Sonny had ever had horse,° he couldn't have been   5 much older than these boys were now. These boys, now, were living as we'd been living then, they were growing up with a rush and their heads bumped abruptly against the low ceiling of their actual possibilities. They were filled with rage. All they really knew were two darknesses, the darkness of their lives, which was now closing in on them, and the darkness of the movies, which had blinded them to that other darkness, and in which they now, vindictively, dreamed, at once more together than they were at any other time, and more alone.

When the last bell rang, the last class ended, I let out my breath. It seemed I'd been holding it for all that time. My clothes were wet — I may have looked as though I'd been sitting in a steam bath, all dressed up, all afternoon. I sat alone in the classroom a long time. I listened to the boys outside, downstairs, shouting and cursing and laughing. Their laughter struck me for perhaps the first time. It was not the joyous laughter which — God knows why — one associates with children. It was mocking and insular, its intent was to denigrate. It was disenchanted, and in this, also, lay the authority of their curses. Perhaps I was listening to them because I was thinking about my brother and in them I heard my brother. And myself.

One boy was whistling a tune, at once very complicated and very simple, it seemed to be pouring out of him as though he were a bird, and it sounded very cool and moving through all that harsh, bright air, only just holding its own through all those other sounds.

I stood up and walked over to the window and looked down into the courtyard. It was the beginning of the spring and the sap was rising in the boys. A teacher passed through them every now and again, quickly, as though he or she couldn't wait to get out of that courtyard, to get those boys out of their sight and off their minds I started collecting my stuff. I thought I'd better get home and talk to Isabel.

The courtyard was almost deserted by the time I got downstairs. I saw this boy standing in the shadow of a doorway, looking just like Sonny. I almost called his name. Then I saw that it wasn't Sonny, but somebody we used to know, a boy from

---

the head: Restroom.

horse: Heroin.

around our block. He'd been Sonny's friend. He'd never been mine, having been too young for me, and, anyway, I'd never liked him. And now, even though he was a grown-up man, he still hung around that block, still spent hours on the street corners, was always high and raggy. I used to run into him from time to time and he'd often work around to asking me for a quarter or fifty cents. He always had some real good excuse, too, and I always gave it to him. I don't know why.

10   But now, abruptly, I hated him. I couldn't stand the way he looked at me, partly like a dog, partly like a cunning child. I wanted to ask him what the hell he was doing in the school courtyard.

He sort of shuffled over to me, and he said, "I see you got the papers. So you already know about it."

"You mean about Sonny? Yes, I already know about it. How come they didn't get you?"

He grinned. It made him repulsive and it also brought to mind what he'd looked like as a kid. "I wasn't there. I stay away from them people."

"Good for you." I offered him a cigarette and I watched him through the smoke. "You come all the way down here just to tell me about Sonny?"

15   "That's right." He was sort of shaking his head and his eyes looked strange, as though they were about to cross. The bright sun deadened his damp dark brown skin and it made his eyes look yellow and showed up the dirt in his kinked hair. He smelled funky, I moved a little away from him and I said, "Well, thanks. But I already know about it and I got to get home."

"I'll walk you a little ways," he said. We started walking. There were a couple of kids still loitering in the courtyard and one of them said goodnight to me and looked strangely at the boy beside me.

"What're you going to do?" he asked me "I mean, about Sonny?"

"Look. I haven't seen Sonny for over a year, I'm not sure I'm going to do anything. Anyway, what the hell *can* I do?"

"That's right," he said quickly, "ain't nothing you can do. Can't much help old Sonny no more, I guess."

20   It was what I was thinking and so it seemed to me he had no right to say it.

"I'm surprised at Sonny, though, he went on — he had a funny way of talking, he looked straight ahead as though he were talking to himself —"I thought Sonny was a smart boy, I thought he was too smart to get hung."

"I guess he thought so too," I said sharply, "and that's how he got hung. And how about you? You're pretty goddamn smart, I bet."

Then he looked directly at me, just for a minute. "I ain't smart," he said. "If I was smart, I'd have reached for a pistol a long time ago."

"Look. Don't tell *me* your sad story, if it was up to me, I'd give you one." Then I felt guilty — guilty, probably, for never having supposed that the poor bastard *had* a story of his own, much less a sad one, and I asked, quickly, "What's going to

25 happen to him now?"

He didn't answer this. He was off by himself some place.

"Funny thing," he said, and from his tone we might have been discussing the quickest way to get to Brooklyn, "when I saw the papers this morning, the first thing I asked myself was if I had anything to do with it. I felt sort of responsible."

I began to listen more carefully. The subway station was on the corner, just before us, and I stopped. He stopped, too. We were in front of a bar and he ducked slightly, peering in, but whoever he was looking for didn't seem to be there. The juke box was blasting away with something black and bouncy and I half watched the barmaid as she danced her way from the juke box to her place behind the bar. And I watched her face as she laughingly responded to something someone said to her, still keeping time to the music. When she smiled one saw the little girl, one sensed the doomed, still struggling woman beneath the battered face of the semi-whore.

"I never *give* Sonny nothing," the boy said finally; "but a long time ago I come to school high and Sonny asked me how it felt." He paused, I couldn't bear to watch him, I watched the barmaid, and I listened to the music which seemed to be causing the pavement to shake. "I told him it felt great." The music stopped, the barmaid paused and watched the juke box until the music began again. "It did."

All this was carrying me some place I didn't want to go. I certainly didn't want to know how it felt. It filled everything, the people, the houses, the music, the dark, quicksilver barmaid, with menace; and this menace was their reality.

"What's going to happen to him now?" I asked again.   30

"They'll send him away some place and they'll try to cure him." He shook his head. "Maybe he'll even think he's kicked the habit. Then they'll let him loose"—he gestured, throwing his cigarette into the gutter: "That's all."

"What do you mean, that's *all*?"

But I knew what he meant.

"I *mean*, that's *all*." He turned his head and looked at me, pulling down the corners of his mouth. "Don't you know what I mean?" he asked softly.

"How the hell *would* I know what you mean?" I almost whispered it, I don't   35
know why.

"That's right," he said to the air; "how would *he* know what I mean?" He turned toward me again, patient and calm, and yet I somehow felt, him shaking, shaking as though he were going to fall apart I felt that ice in my guts again, the dread I'd felt all afternoon; and again I watched the barmaid, moving about the bar, washing glasses, and singing. "Listen. They'll let him out and then it'll just start all over again. That's what I mean."

"You mean — they'll let him out. And then he'll just start working his way back in again. You mean he'll never kick the habit. Is that what you mean?"

"That's right," he said, cheerfully. "*You* see what I mean."

"Tell me," I said at least, "why does he want to die? He must want to die, he's killing himself, why does he want to die?"

He looked at me in surprise. He licked his lips. "He don't want to die. He wants   40
to live. Don't nobody want to die, ever."

Then I wanted to ask him — too many things. He could not have answered, or if he had, I could not have borne the answers. I started walking. "Well, I guess it's none of my business."

"It's going to be rough on old Sonny," he said. We reached the subway station.

"This is your station?" he asked. I nodded. I took one step down. "Damn!" he said, suddenly. I looked up at him. He grinned again. "Damn it if I didn't leave all my money home. You ain't got a dollar on you, have you? Just for a couple of days is all."

All at once something inside gave and threatened to come pouring out of me. I didn't hate him any more. I felt that in another moment I'd start crying like a child.

"Sure," I said. "Don't sweat." I looked in my wallet and didn't have a dollar, I only had a five. "Here," I said. "That hold you?"

45 He didn't look at it —he didn't want to look at it. A terrible, closed look came over his face, as though he were keeping the number on the bill a secret from him and me. "Thanks," he said, and now he was dying to see me go. "Don't worry about Sonny. Maybe I'll write him or something."

"Sure," I said "You do that, So long."

"Be seeing you," he said. I went on down the steps.

And I didn't write Sonny or send him anything for a long time. When I finally did, it was just after my little girl died, and he wrote me back a letter which made me feel like a bastard.

Here's what he said:

50 Dear brother,

You don't know how much I needed to hear from you. I wanted to write you many a time but I dug how much I must have hurt you and so I didn't write. But now I feel like a man who's been trying to climb up out of some deep, real deep and funky hole and just saw the sun up there, outside I got to get outside.

I can't tell you much about how I got here. I mean I don't know how to tell you. I guess I was afraid of something or I was trying to escape from something and you know I have never been very strong in the head (smile). I'm glad Mama and Daddy are dead and can't see what's happened to their son and I swear if I'd known what I was doing I would never have hurt you so, you and a lot of other fine people who were nice to me and who believed in me.

I don't want you to think it had anything to do with me being a musician. It's more than that. Or maybe less than that. I can't get anything straight in my head down here and I try not to think about what's going to happen to me when I get outside again. Sometime I think I'm going to flip and *never* get outside and sometime I think I'll come straight back. I tell you one thing, though, I'd rather blow my brains out than go through this again. But that's what they all say, so they tell me. If I tell you when I'm coming to New York and if you could meet me, I sure would appreciate it. Give any love to Isabel and the kids and I was sure sony to hear about little Gracie. I wish I could be like Mama and say the Lord's will be done, but I don't know it seems to me that trouble is the one thing that never does get stopped and I don't know what good it does to blame it on the Lord. But maybe it does some good if you believe it.

Your brother,
Sonny

Then I kept in constant touch with him and I sent him whatever I could and I went to meet him when he came back to New York. When I saw him many

things I thought I had forgotten came flooding back to me. This was because I had
begun, finally, to wonder about Sonny, about the life that Sonny lived inside. This
life, whatever it was, had made him older and thinner and it had deepened the
distant stillness in which he had always moved. He looked very unlike my baby
brother. Yet, when he smiled, when we shook hands, the baby brother I'd never
known looked out from the depths of his private life, like an animal waiting to be
coaxed into the light.

"How you been keeping?" he asked me.

"All right. And you?"   55

"Just fine." He was smiling all over his face. "It's good to see you again."

"It's good to see you."

The seven years difference in our ages lay between us like a chasm: I wondered
if these years would ever operate between us as a bridge. I was remembering, and
it made it hard to catch my breath, that I had been there when he was born; and
I had heard the first words he had ever spoken. When he started to walk, he
walked from our mother straight to me. I caught him just before he fell when he
took the first steps he ever took in this world:

"How's Isabel?"

"Just fine. She's dying to see you."   60

"And the boys?"

"They're fine, too. They're anxious to see their uncle."

"Oh, come on. You know they don't remember me."

"Are you kidding? Of course they remember you."

He grinned again. We got into a taxi. We had a lot to say to each other, far too 65
much to know how to begin.

As the taxi began to move, I asked, "You still want to go to India?"

He laughed. "You still remember that. Hell, no. This place is Indian enough
for me."

"It used to belong to them," I said.

And he laughed again. "They damn sure knew what they were doing when
they got rid of it."

Years ago, when he was around fourteen, he'd been all hipped on the idea of 70
going to India. He read books about people sitting on rocks, naked, in all kinds of
weather, but mostly bad, naturally, and walking barefoot through hot coals and
arriving at wisdom. I used to say that it sounded to me as though they were getting away from wisdom as fast as they could. I think he sort of looked down on me
for that.

"Do you mind," he asked, "if we have the driver drive alongside the park? On
the west side — I haven't seen the city in so long."

"Of course not," I said. I was afraid that I might sound as though I were hu-
moring him, but I hoped he wouldn't take it that way.

So we drove along, between the green of the park and the stony, lifeless elegance of hotels and apartment buildings, toward the vivid, killing streets of our
childhood. These streets hadn't changed, though housing projects jutted up out of
them now like rocks in the middle of a boiling sea. Most of the houses in which
we had grown up had vanished, as had the stores from which we had stolen, the

basements in which we had first tried sex, the rooftops from which we had hurled tin cans and bricks. But houses exactly like the houses of our past yet dominated the landscape, boys exactly like the boys we once had been found themselves smothering in these houses, came down into the streets for light and air and found themselves encircled by disaster. Some escaped the trap, most didn't. Those who got out always left something of themselves behind, as some animals amputate a leg and leave it in the trap. It might be said, perhaps, that I had escaped, after all, I was a school teacher; or that Sonny had, he hadn't lived in Harlem for years. Yet, as the cab moved uptown through streets which seemed, with a rush, to darken with dark people, and as I covertly studied Sonny's face, it came to me that what we both were seeking through our separate cab windows was that part of ourselves which had been left behind. It's always at the hour of trouble and confrontation that the missing member aches.

We hit 110th Street and started rolling up Lenox Avenue. And I'd known this avenue all my life, but it seemed to me again, as it had seemed on the day I'd first heard about Sonny's trouble, filled with a hidden menace which was its very breath of life.

75   "We almost there," said Sonny.

"Almost." We were both too nervous to say anything more.

We live in a housing project. It hasn't been up long. A few days after it was up it seemed uninhabitably new, now, of course, it's already rundown. It looks like a parody of the good, clean, faceless life — God knows the people who live in it do their best to make it a parody. The beat-looking grass lying around isn't enough to make their lives green, the hedges will never hold out the streets, and they know it. The big windows fool no one, they aren't big enough to make space out of no space. They don't bother with the windows, they watch the TV screen instead. The playground is most popular with the children who don't play at jacks, or skip rope, or roller skate, or swing, and they can be found in it after dark. We moved in partly because it's not too far from where I teach, and partly for the kids; but it's really just like the houses in which Sonny and I grew up. The same things happen, they'll have the same things to remember. The moment Sonny and I started into the house I had the feeling that I was simply bringing him back into the danger he had almost died trying to escape.

Sonny has never been talkative. So I don't know why I was sure he'd be dying to talk to me when supper was over the first night. Everything went fine, the oldest boy remembered him, and the youngest boy liked him, and Sonny had remembered to bring something for each of them; and Isabel, who is really much nicer than I am, more open and giving, had gone to a lot of trouble about dinner and was genuinely glad to see him. And she's always been able to tease Sonny in a way that I haven't. It was nice to see her face so vivid again and to hear her laugh and watch her make Sonny laugh. She wasn't, or, anyway, she didn't seem to be, at all uneasy or embarrassed. She chatted as though there were no subject which had to be avoided and she got Sonny past his first, faint stiffness. And thank God she was there, for I was filled with that icy dread again. Everything I did seemed awkward to me, and everything I said sounded freighted with hidden meaning. I was trying to remember everything I'd heard about dope addiction and I couldn't help watching Sonny for signs. I wasn't doing it out of malice. I was trying to find out something about my brother. I was dying to hear him tell me he was safe.

"Safe!" my father grunted, whenever Mama suggested trying to move to a neighborhood which might be safer for children. "Safe, hell! Ain't no place safe for kids, nor nobody."

He always went on like this, but he wasn't, ever, really as bad as he sounded, not even on weekends, when he got drunk. As a matter of fact, he was always on the lookout for "something a little better," but he died before he found it. He died suddenly, during a drunken weekend in the middle of the war, when Sonny was fifteen. He and Sonny hadn't ever got on too well. And this was partly because Sonny was the apple of his father's eye. It was because he loved Sonny so much and was frightened for him, that he was always fighting with him. It doesn't do any good to fight with Sonny. Sonny just moves back, inside himself, where he can't be reached. But the principal reason that they never hit it off is that they were so much alike. Daddy was big and rough and loud-talking, just the opposite of Sonny, but they both had — that same privacy. 80

Mama tried to tell me something about this, just after Daddy died. I was home on leave from the army.

This was the last time I ever saw my mother alive. Just the same, this picture gets all mixed up in my mind with pictures I had of her when she was younger. The way I always see her is the way she used to be on a Sunday afternoon, say, when the old folks were talking after the big Sunday dinner. I always see her wearing pale blue. She'd be sitting on the sofa. And my father would be sitting in the easy chair, not far from her. And the living room would be full of church folks and relatives. There they sit, in chairs all around the living room, and the night is creeping up outside, but nobody knows it yet. You can see the darkness growing against the windowpanes and you hear the street noises every now and again, or maybe the jangling beat of a tambourine from one of the churches close by, but it's real quiet in the room. For a moment nobody's talking, but every face looks darkening, like the sky outside. And my mother rocks a little from the waist, and my father's eyes are closed. Everyone is looking at something a child can't see. For a minute they've forgotten the children. Maybe a kid is lying on the rug half asleep. Maybe somebody's got a kid in his lap and is absent-mindedly stroking the kid's head: Maybe there's a kid, quiet and big-eyed, curled up in a big chair in the corner. The silence, the darkness coming, and the darkness in the faces frighten the child obscurely. He hopes that the hand which strokes his forehead will never stop — will never die. He hopes that there will never come a time when the old folks won't be sitting around the living room, talking about where they've come from, and what they've seen, and what's happened to them and their kinfolk.

But something deep and watchful in the child knows that this is bound to end, is already ending. In a moment someone will get up and turn on the light. Then the old folks will remember the children and they won't talk any more that day. And when light fills the room, the child is filled with darkness. He knows that every time this happens he's moved just a little closer to that darkness outside. The darkness outside is what the old folks have been talking about. It's what they've come from. It's what they endure. The child knows that they won't talk any more because if he knows too much about what's happened to *them*, he'll know too much too soon, about what's going to happen to *him*.

The last time I talked to my mother, I remember I was restless. I wanted to get out and see Isabel. We weren't married then and we had a lot to straighten out between us.

85   There Mama sat, in black, by the window. She was humming an old church song, *Lord, you brought me from a long ways off*. Sonny was out somewhere. Mama kept watching the streets.

"I don't know," she said, "if I'll ever see you again, after you go off from here. But I hope you'll remember the things I tried to teach you."

"Don't talk like that," I said, and smiled. "You'll be here a long time yet."

She smiled, too, but she said nothing. She was quiet for a long time. And I said, "Mama, don't you worry about nothing. I'll be writing all the time, and you be getting the checks. . . ."

"I want to talk to you about your brother," she said, suddenly. "If anything happens to me he ain't going to have nobody to look out for him."

90   "Mama," I said, "ain't nothing going to happen to you *or* Sonny. Sonny's all right. He's a good boy and he's got good sense."

"It ain't a question of his being a good boy," Mama said, "nor of his having good sense. It ain't only the bad ones, nor yet the dumb ones that gets sucked under." She stopped, looking at me. "Your Daddy once had a brother," she said, and she smiled in a way that made me feel she was in pain. "You didn't never know that, did you?"

"No," I said, "I never knew that," and I watched her face.

"Oh, yes," she said, "your Daddy had a brother." She looked out of the window again. "I know you never saw your Daddy cry. But *I* did — many a time, through all these years."

I asked her, "What happened to his brother? How come nobody's ever talked about him?"

This was the first time I ever saw my mother look old.

95   "His brother got killed," she said, "when he was just a little younger than you are now. I knew him. He was a fine boy. He was maybe a little full of the devil, but he didn't mean nobody no harm."

Then she stopped and the room was silent, exactly as it had sometimes been on those Sunday afternoons. Mama kept looking out into the streets.

"He used to have a job in the mill," she said, "and, like all young folks, he just liked to perform on Saturday nights. Saturday nights, him and your father would drift around to different places, go to dances and things like that, or just sit around with people they knew, and your father's brother would sing; he had a fine voice, and play along with himself on his guitar. Well, this particular Saturday night, him and your father was coming home from some place, and they were both a little drunk and there was a moon that night, it was bright like day. Your father's brother was feeling kind of good, and he was whistling to himself, and he had his guitar slung over his shoulder. They was coming down a hill and beneath them was a road that turned off from the highway. Well, your father's brother, being always kind of frisky, decided to run down this hill, and he did, with that guitar banging and clanging behind him, and he ran across the road, and he was making water behind a tree. And your father was sort of amused at him and he was still coming down the hill, kind of slow. Then he heard a car motor and that same minute his brother stepped from behind the tree, into the road, in the moonlight. And he started to cross the road. And your father started to run down the hill, he says he don't know why. This car was full of white men. They was all drunk, and when they seen your father's brother they let out a great whoop and holler and they aimed the car straight at him. They was having fun, they just wanted to scare him, the way they do sometimes, you know. But they was drunk. And I guess the boy, being drunk, too, and scared, kind of lost his head. By the time he jumped it was too late. Your father says he heard his brother scream when the car rolled over him, and he heard the wood of that guitar when it give, and he heard them strings go flying, and he heard them white men shouting, and the car kept on a-going and it ain't stopped till this day. And, time your father got down the hill, his brother weren't nothing but blood and pulp."

Tears were gleaming on my mother's face. There wasn't anything I could say.

"He never mentioned it," she said, "because I never let him mention it before 100 you children. Your Daddy was like a crazy man that night and for many a night thereafter. He says he never in his life seen anything as dark as that road after the lights of that car had gone away. Weren't nothing, weren't nobody on that road, just your Daddy and his brother and that busted guitar. Oh, yes. Your Daddy never did really get right again. Till the day he died he weren't sure but that every white man he saw was the man that killed his brother."

She stopped and took out her handkerchief and dried her eyes and looked at me.

"I ain't telling you all this," she said, "to make you scared or bitter or to make you hate nobody. I'm telling you this because you got a brother. And the world ain't changed."

I guess I didn't want to believe this. I guess she saw this in my face. She turned away from me, toward the window again, searching those streets.

"But I praise my Redeemer," she said at last, "that He called your Daddy home before me. I ain't saying it to throw no flowers at myself, but, I declare, it keeps me from feeling too cast down to know I helped your father get safely through this world. Your father always acted like he was the roughest, strongest man on earth. And everybody took him to be like that. But if he hadn't had me there — to see his tears!"

She was crying again. Still, I couldn't move. I said, "Lord, Lord, Mama, I 105 didn't know it was like that."

"Oh, honey," she said, "there's a lot that you don't know. But you are going to find out." She stood up from the window and came over to me. "You got to hold on to your brother," she said, "and don't let him fall, no matter what it looks like is happening to him and no matter how evil you gets with him. You going to be evil with him many a time. But don't you forget what I told you, you hear?"

"I won't forget," I said. "Don't you worry, I won't forget. I won't let nothing happen to Sonny."

My mother smiled as though she was amused at something she saw in my face. Then, "You may not be able to stop nothing from happening. But you got to let him know you's *there*."

Two days later I was married, and then I was gone. And I had a lot of things on my mind and I pretty well forgot my promise to Mama until I got shipped home on a special furlough for her funeral.

110 And, after the funeral, with just Sonny and me alone in the empty kitchen, I tried to find out something about him.

"What do you want to do?" I asked him.

"I'm going to be a musician," he said.

For he had graduated, in the time I had been away, from dancing to the juke box to finding out who was playing what, and what they were doing with it, and he had bought himself a set of drums.

"You mean, you want to be a drummer?" I somehow had the feeling that being a drummer might be all right for other people but not for my brother Sonny.

115 "I don't think," he said, looking at me very gravely, "that I'll ever be a good drummer. But I think I can play a piano."

I frowned. I'd never played the role of the oldest brother quite so seriously before, had scarcely ever, in fact, *asked* Sonny a damn thing. I sensed myself in the presence of something I didn't really know how to handle, didn't understand. So I made my frown a little deeper as I asked: "What kind of musician do you want to be?"

He grinned. "How many kinds do you think there are?"

"Be *serious*," I said.

He laughed, throwing his head back, and then looked at me "I *am* serious."

120 "Well, then, for Christ's sake, stop kidding around and answer a serious question. I mean, do you want to be a concert pianist, you want to play classical music and all that, or — or what?" Long before I finished he was laughing again. "For Christ's *sake*, Sonny!"

He sobered, but with difficulty. "I'm sorry. But you sound so —*scared!*" and he was off again.

"Well, you may think it's funny now, baby, but it's not going to be so funny when you have to make you living at it, let me tell you *that*." I was furious because I knew he was laughing at me and I didn't know why.

"No," he said, very sober now, and afraid, perhaps, that he'd hurt me, "I don't want to be a classical pianist. That isn't what interests me. I mean"—he paused, looking hard at me, as though his eyes would help me to understand, and then gestured helplessly, as though perhaps his hand would help —"I mean, I'll have a lot of studying to do, and I'll have to study *everything*, but, I mean, I want to play *with*—jazz musicians." He stopped. "I want to play jazz," he said.

Well, the word had never before sounded as heavy, as real, as it sounded that afternoon in Sonny's mouth. I just looked at him and I was probably frowning a real frown by this time. I simply couldn't see, why on earth he'd want to spend his time hanging around nightclubs, clowning around on bandstands, while people pushed each other around a dance floor. It seemed —beneath him, somehow. I had never thought about it before, had never been forced to, but I suppose I had always put jazz musicians in a class with what Daddy called "good-time people."

125 "Are you *serious*?"

"Hell, *yes*, I'm serious."

He looked more helpless than ever, and annoyed, and deeply hurt.

I suggested, helpfully. "You mean — like Louis Armstrong?"

His face closed as though I'd struck him. "No. I'm not talking about none of that old-time, down home crap."

"Well, look, Sonny, I'm sorry, don't get mad. I just don't altogether get it, that's all. Name somebody — you know, a jazz musician you admire." 130

"Bird."

"Who?"

"Bird! Charlie Parker!° Don't they teach you nothing in the goddamn army?"

I lit a cigarette. I was surprised and then a little amused to discover that I was trembling. "I've been out of touch," I said. "You'll have to be patient with me. Now, Who's this Parker character?"

"He's just one of the greatest jazz musicians alive," said Sonny, sullenly, his 135 hands in his pockets, his back to me. "Maybe *the* greatest," he added, bitterly, "that's probably why *you* never heard of him."

"All right," I said, "I'm ignorant. I'm sorry I'll go out and buy all the cat's records right away, all right?"

"It don't," said Sonny, with dignity, "make any difference to me. I don't care what you listen to. Don't do me no favors."

I was beginning to realize that I'd never seen him so upset before. With another part of my mind I was thinking that this would probably turn out to be one of those things kids go through and that I shouldn't make it seem important by pushing it too hard. Still, I didn't think it would do any harm to ask: "Doesn't all this take a lot of time? Can you make a living at it?"

He turned back to me and half leaned, half sat, on the kitchen table. "Everything takes time," he said, "and — well, yes, sure, I can make a living at it. But what I don't seem to be able to make you understand is that it's the only thing I want to do."

"Well, Sonny," I said gently, "you know people can't always do exactly what 140 they *want* to do —."

"*No,* I don't know that," said Sonny, surprising me. "I think people *ought* to do what they want to do, what else are they alive for?"

"You getting to be a big boy," I said desperately, "it's time you started thinking about your future."

"I'm thinking about my future," said Sonny, grimly "I think about it all the time."

I gave up. I decided, if he didn't change his mind, that we could always talk about it later. "In the meantime," I said, "you got to finish school." We had already decided that he'd have to move in with Isabel and her folks. I knew this wasn't the ideal arrangement because Isabel's folks are inclined to be dicty° and they hadn't especially wanted Isabel to marry me. But I didn't know what else to do. "And we have to get you fixed up at Isabel's."

There was a long silence. He moved from the kitchen table to the window. 145 "That's a terrible idea. You know it yourself."

Charlie "Bird" Parker (1920–1955): A renowned jazz saxophonist and composer who, with Dizzy Gillespie and others, developed the jazz style "bebop." He died of pneumonia and a bleeding ulcer, both of which were exacerbated by his addiction to narcotics and alcohol.

dicty: Bossy.

"Do you have a *better* idea?"

He just walked up and down the kitchen for a minute. He was as tall as I was. He had started to shave. I suddenly had the feeling that I didn't know him at all.

He stopped at the kitchen table and picked up my cigarettes. Looking at me with a kind of mocking, amused defiance, he put one between his lips. "You mind?"

"You smoking already?"

150   He lit the cigarette and nodded, watching me through the smoke. "I just wanted to see if I'd have the courage to smoke in front of you." He grinned and blew a great cloud of smoke to the ceiling. "It was easy." He looked at my face. "Come on, now. I bet you was smoking at my age, tell the truth."

I didn't say anything but the truth was on my face, and he laughed. But now there was something very strained in his laugh. "Sure. And I bet that ain't all you was doing."

He was frightening me a little. "Cut the crap," I said. "We already decided that you was going to go and live at Isabel's. Now what's got into you all of a sudden?"

"*You* decided it," he pointed out. "*I* didn't decide nothing." He stopped in front of me, leaning against the stove, arms loosely folded. "Look, brother. I don't want to stay in Harlem no more, I really don't." He was very earnest. He looked at me, then over toward the kitchen window. There was something in his eyes I'd never seen before, some thoughtfulness, some worry all his own. He rubbed the muscle of one arm. "It's time I was getting out of here."

"Where do you want to go, Sonny?"

155   "I want to join the army. Or the navy, I don't care. If I say I'm old enough, they'll believe me."

Then I got mad. It was because I was so scared. "You must be crazy. You goddamn fool, what he hell do you want to go and join the *army* for?"

"I just told you. To get out of Harlem."

"Sonny, you haven't even finished *school*. And if you really want to be a musician, how do you expect to study if you're in the *army*?"

He looked at me, trapped, and in anguish. "There's ways. I might be able to work out some kind of deal. Anyway, I'll have the G.I. Bill when I come out."

160   "*If* you come out." We started at each other. "Sonny, please. Be reasonable. I know the setup is far from perfect. But we got to do the best we can."

"I ain't learning nothing in school," he said. "Even when I go." He turned away from me and opened the window and threw his cigarette out into the narrow alley. I watched his back. "At least, I ain't learning nothing you'd want me to learn." He slammed the window so hard I thought the glass would fly out, and turned back to me. "And I'm sick of the stink of these garbage cans!"

"Sonny," I said, "I know how you feel. But if you don't finish school now, you're going to be sorry later that you didn't." I grabbed him by the shoulders. "And you only got another year. It ain't so bad. And I'll come back and I swear I'll help you do *whatever* you want to do. Just try to put up with it till I come back. Will you please do that? For me?"

He didn't answer and he wouldn't look at me.

"Sonny, You hear me?"

165   He pulled away. "I hear you. But you never hear anything I say."

I didn't know what to say to that. He looked out of the window and then back at me. "OK," he said, and sighed. "I'll try."

Then I said, trying to cheer him up a little, "They got a piano at Isabel's. You can practice on it."

And as a matter of fact, it did cheer him up for a minute. "That's right." he said to himself, "I forgot that." His face relaxed a little. But the worry, the thoughtfulness, played on it still, the way shadows play on a face which is staring into the fire.

But I thought I'd never hear the end of that piano. At first, Isabel would write me, saying how nice it was that Sonny was so serious about his music and how, as soon as he came in from school, or wherever he had been when he was supposed to be at school, he went straight to that piano and stayed there until suppertime. And, after supper, he went back to that piano and stayed there until everybody went to bed. He was at the piano all day Saturday and all day Sunday. Then he bought a record player and started playing records. He'd play one record over and over again, all day long sometimes, and he'd improvise along with it on the piano. Or he'd play one section of the record, one chord, one change, one progression, then he'd do it on the piano. Then back to the record. Then back to the piano.

Well, I really don't know how they stood it. Isabel finally confessed that it 170 wasn't like living with a person at all, it was like living with sound. And the sound didn't make any sense to her, didn't make any sense to any of them — naturally. They began, in a way, to be afflicted by this presence that was living in their home. It was as though Sonny were some sort of god, or monster. He moved in an atmosphere which wasn't like theirs at all. They fed him and he ate, he washed himself, he walked in and out of their door; he certainly wasn't nasty or unpleasant or rude, Sonny isn't any of those things, but it was as though he were all wrapped up in some cloud, some fire, some vision all his own, and there wasn't any way to reach him.

At the same time, he wasn't really a man yet, he was still a child, and they had to watch out for him in all kinds of ways. They certainly couldn't throw him out. Neither did they dare to make a great scene about that piano because even they dimly sensed, as I sensed, from so many thousands of miles away, that Sonny was at that piano playing for his life.

But he hadn't been going to school. One day a letter came from the school board and Isabel's mother got it — there had, apparently, been other letters but Sonny had torn them up. This day, when Sonny came in, Isabel's mother showed him the letter and asked where he'd been spending his time. And she finally got it out of him that he'd been down in Greenwich Village, with musicians and other characters, in a white girl's apartment. And this scared her and she started to scream at him and what came up, once she began — though she denies it to this day — was what sacrifices they were making to give Sonny a decent home and how little he appreciated it.

Sonny didn't play the piano that day. By evening, Isabel's mother had calmed down but then there was the old man to deal with, and Isabel herself. Isabel says she did her best to be calm but she broke down and started crying. She says she just watched Sonny's face. She could tell, by watching him, what was happening with him. And what was happening was that they penetrated his cloud, they had reached him. Even if their fingers had been a thousand times more gentle than human fingers ever are, he could hardly help feeling that they had stripped him naked and were spitting on that nakedness. For he also had to see that his presence, that music, which was life or death to him, had been torture for them and that they had endured it, not at all for his sake, but only for mine. And Sonny couldn't take that. He can take it a little better today than he could then but he's still not very good at it and, frankly, I don't know anybody who is.

The silence of the next few days must have been louder than the sound of all the music ever played since time began. One morning, before she went to work, Isabel was in his room for something and she suddenly realized that all of his records were gone. And she knew for certain that he was gone. And he was. He went as far as the navy would carry him. He finally sent me a postcard from some place in Greece and that was the first I knew that Sonny was still alive. I didn't see him any more until we were both back in New York and the war had long been over.

175   He was a man by then, of course, but I wasn't willing to see it. He came by the house from time to time, but we fought almost every time we met. I didn't like the way he carried himself, loose and dreamlike all the time, and I didn't like his friends, and his music seemed to be merely an excuse for the life he led. It sounded just that weird and disordered.

Then we had a fight, a pretty awful fight, and I didn't see him for months. By and by I looked him up, where he was living, in a furnished room in the Village, and I tried to make it up. But there were lots of other people in the room and Sonny just lay on his bed, and he wouldn't come downstairs with me, and he treated these other people as though they were his family and I weren't. So I got mad and then he got mad, and then I told him that he might just as well be dead as live the way he was living. Then he stood up and he told me not to worry about him any more in life, that he *was* dead as far as I was concerned. Then he pushed me to the door and the other people looked on as though nothing were happening, and he slammed the door behind me. I stood in the hallway, staring at the door. I heard somebody laugh in the room and then the tears came to my eyes. I started down the steps, whistling to keep from crying, I kept whistling to myself, *You going to need me, baby, one of these cold, rainy days.*

I read about Sonny's trouble in the spring. Little Grace died in the fall. She was a beautiful little girl. But she only lived a little over two years. She died of polio and she suffered. She had a slight fever for a couple of days, but it didn't seem like anything and we just kept her in bed. And we would certainly have called the doctor, but the fever dropped, she seemed to be all right. So we thought it had just been a cold. Then, one day, she was up, playing. Isabel was in the kitchen fixing lunch for the two boys when they'd come in from school, and she heard Grace fall down in the living room. When you have a lot of children you don't always start running when one of them falls, unless they start screaming or something. And, this time, Gracie was quiet. Yet, Isabel says that when she heard that *thump* and then that silence, something happened to her to make her afraid. And she ran to the living room and there was little Grace on the floor, all twisted up, and the reason she hadn't screamed was that she couldn't get her breath. And when she did scream, it was the worst sound, Isabel says, that she'd ever heard in all her life, and she still hears it sometimes in her dreams Isabel will sometimes wake me up with a low, moaning, strangling sound and I have to be quick to awaken her and hold her to me and where Isabel is weeping against me seems a mortal wound.

I think I may have written Sonny the very day that little Grace was buried. I was sitting in the living room in the dark, by myself, and I suddenly thought of Sonny. My trouble made his real.

One Saturday afternoon, when Sonny had been living with us, or anyway, been in our house, for nearly two weeks. I found myself wandering aimlessly about the living room, drinking from a can of beer, and trying to work up courage to search Sonny's room. He was out, he was usually out whenever I was home, and Isabel had taken the children to see their grandparents. Suddenly I was standing still in front of the living room window, watching Seventh Avenue. The idea of searching Sonny's room made me still. I scarcely dared to admit to myself what I'd be searching for. I didn't know what I'd do if I found it. Or if I didn't.

On the sidewalk across from me, near the entrance to a barbecue joint, some 180 people were holding an old fashioned revival meeting. The barbecue cook, wearing a dirty white apron, his conked° hair reddish and metallic in the pale sun, and a cigarette between his lips, stood in the doorway, watching them. Kids and older people paused in their errands and stood there, along with some older men and a couple of very tough looking women who watched everything that happened on the avenue, as though they owned it, or were maybe owned by it. Well, they were watching this, too. The revival was being carried on by three sisters in black, and a brother. All they had were their voices and their Bibles and a tambourine. The brother was testifying° and while he testified two of the sisters stood together, seeming to say, amen, and the third sister walked around with the tambourine outstretched and a couple of people dropped coins into it. Then the brother's testimony ended and the sister who had been taking up the collection dumped the coins into her palm and transferred them to the pocket of her long black robe. Then she raised both hands, striking the tambourine against the air, and then against one hand, and she started to sing. And the two other sisters and the brother joined in.

It was strange, suddenly, to watch, though I had been seeing these meetings all my life. So, of course, had everybody else down there. Yet, they paused and watched and listened and I stood still at the window. "*'Tis the old ship of Zion*," they sang, and the sister with the tambourine kept a steady, jangling beat, "*it has rescued many a thousand!*" Not a soul under the sound of their voices was hearing this song for the first time, not one of them had been rescued. Nor had they seen much in the way of rescue work being done around them. Neither did they especially believe in the holiness of the three sisters and the brother, they knew too much about them, knew where they lived, and how. The woman with the tambourine, whose voice dominated the air, whose face was bright with joy, was divided by very little from the woman who stood watching her, a cigarette between her heavy, chapped lips, her

---

conked: Chemically straightened and greased hair.

testifying: Publicly proclaiming one's religious experience and belief.

hair a cuckoo's nest, her face scarred and swollen from many beatings, and her black eyes glittering like coal. Perhaps they both knew this, which was why, when, as rarely, they addressed each other, they addressed each other as Sister. As the singing filled the air the watching, listening faces underwent a change, the eyes focusing on something within; the music seemed to soothe a poison out of them; and time seemed, nearly, to fall away from the sullen, belligerent, battered faces, as though they were fleeing back to their first condition, while dreaming of their last. The barbecue cook half shook his head and smiled, and dropped his cigarette and disappeared into his joint. A man fumbled in his pockets for change and stood holding it in his hand impatiently, as though he had just remembered a pressing appointment further up the avenue. He looked furious. Then I saw Sonny, standing on the edge of the crowd. He was carrying a wide, flat notebook with a green cover, and it made him look, from where I was standing, almost like a schoolboy. The coppery sun brought out the copper in his skin, he was very faintly smiling, standing very still. Then the singing stopped, the tambourine turned into a collection plate again. The furious man dropped in his coins and vanished, so did a couple of the women, and Sonny dropped some change in the plate, looking directly at the woman with a little smile. He started across the avenue, toward the house. He has a slow, loping walk, something like the way Harlem hipsters walk, only he's imposed on this his own half-beat. I had never really noticed it before.

I stayed at the window, both relieved and apprehensive. As Sonny disappeared from my sight, they began singing again. And they were still singing when his key turned in the lock.

"Hey," he said.

"Hey, yourself. You want some beer?"

185   "No. Well, maybe." But he came up to the window and stood beside me, looking out. "What a warm voice," he said.

They were singing *If I could only hear my mother pray again!*

"Yes," I said, "and she can sure beat that tambourine."

"But what a terrible song," he said, and laughed. He dropped his notebook on the sofa and disappeared into the kitchen. "Where's Isabel and the kids?"

"I think they went to see their grandparents. You hungry?"

190   "No." He came back into the living room with his can of beer. "You want to come some place with me tonight?"

I sensed, I don't know how, that I couldn't possibly say no. "Sure. Where?"

He sat down on the sofa and picked up his notebook and started leafing through it. "I'm going to sit in with some fellows in a joint in the Village."

"You mean, you're going to play, tonight?"

"That's right." He took a swallow of his beer and moved back to the window. He gave me a sidelong look. "If you can stand it."

195   "I'll try," I said.

He smiled to himself and we both watched as the meeting across the way broke up. The three sisters and the brother, heads bowed, were singing *God be with you till we meet again*. The faces around them were very quiet. Then the song ended. The small crowd dispersed. We watched the three women and the lone man walk slowly up the avenue.

"When she was singing before," said Sonny, abruptly, "her voice reminded me for a minute of what heroin feels like sometimes — when it's in your veins. It makes you feel sort of warm and cool at the same time. And distant. And — and sure." He sipped his beer, very deliberately not looking at me. I watched his face. "It makes you feel — in control. Sometimes you've got to have that feeling."

"Do you?" I sat down slowly in the easy chair.

"Sometimes." He went to the sofa and picked up his notebook again. "Some people do."

"In order," I asked, "to play?" And my voice was very ugly, full of contempt and　200 anger.

"Well"— he looked at me with great, troubled eyes, as though, in fact, he hoped his eyes would tell me things he could never otherwise say — "they *think* so. And *if* they think so —!"

"And what do *you* think?" I asked.

He sat on the sofa and put his can of beer on the floor. "I don't know," he said, and I couldn't be sure if he were answering my question or pursuing his thoughts. His face didn't tell me. "It's not so much to *play*. It's to *stand* it, to be able to make it at all. On any level." He frowned and smiled! "In order to keep from shaking to pieces."

"But these friends of yours," I said, "they seem to shake themselves to pieces pretty goddamn fast."

"Maybe." He played with the notebook. And something told me that I should　205 curb my tongue, that Sonny was doing his best to talk, that I should listen. "But of course you only know the ones that've gone to pieces. Some don't — or at least they haven't *yet* and that's just about all *any* of us can say. "He paused. And then there are some who just live, really, in hell, and they know it and they see what's happening and they go right on. I don't know." He sighed, dropped the notebook, folded his arms. "Some guys, you can tell from the way they play, they on something *all* the time. And you can see that, well, it makes something real for them. But of course," he picked up his beer from the floor and sipped it and put the can down again, "they *want* to, too, you've got to see that. Even some of them that say they don't —*some*, not all."

"And what about you?" I asked — I couldn't help it. "What about you? Do *you* want to?"

He stood up and walked to the window and I remained silent for a long time. Then he sighed. "Me," he said. Then: "While I was downstairs before, on my way here, listening to that woman sing, it struck me all of a sudden how much suffering she must have had to go through — to sing like that. It's *repulsive* to think you have to suffer that much."

I said: "But there's no way not to suffer — is there, Sonny?"

"I believe not," he said and smiled, "but that's never stopped anyone from trying." He looked at me. "Has it?" I realized, with this mocking look, that there stood between us, forever, beyond the power of time or forgiveness, the fact that I had held silence — so long! — when he had needed human speech to help him. He turned back to the window. "No, there's no way not to suffer. But you try all kinds of ways to keep from drowning in it, to keep on top of it, and to make it seem — well, like *you*. Like you did something, all right, and now you're suffering for it. You know?" I said nothing. "Well you know," he said, impatiently, "why *do* people suffer? Maybe it's better to do something to give it a reason, *any* reason."

210 "But we just agreed," I said, "that there's no way not to suffer. Isn't it better, then, just to — take it?"

"But nobody just takes it," Sonny cried, "that's what I'm telling you! *Everybody* tries not to. You're just hung up on the way some people try — it's not *your* way!"

The hair on my face began to itch, my face felt wet. "That's not true," I said, "that's not true. I don't give a damn what other people do, I don't even care how they suffer. I just care how *you* suffer." And he looked at me. "Please believe me," I said, "I don't want to see you — die — trying not to suffer."

"I won't," he said flatly, "die trying not to suffer. At least, not any faster than anybody else."

"But there's no need," I said, trying to laugh, "is there? in killing yourself."

215 I wanted to say more, but I couldn't. I wanted to talk about will power and how life could be — well, beautiful. I wanted to say that it was all within; but was it? or, rather, wasn't that exactly the trouble? And I wanted to promise that I would never fail him again. But it would all have sounded — empty words and lies.

So I made the promise to myself and prayed that I would keep it.

"It's terrible sometimes, inside," he said, "that's what's the trouble. You walk these streets, black and funky and cold, and there's not really a living ass to talk to, and there's nothing shaking, and there's no way of getting it out — that storm inside. You can't talk it and you can't make love with it, and when you finally try to get with it and play it, you realize *nobody's* listening. So *you've* got to listen. You got to find a way to listen."

And then he walked away from the window and sat on the sofa again, as though all the wind had suddenly been knocked out of him. "Sometimes you'll do *anything* to play, even cut your mother's throat." He laughed and looked at me. "Or your brother's." Then he sobered. "Or your own." Then: "Don't worry. I'm all right now and I think I'll be all right. But I can't forget — where I've been. I don't mean just the physical place I've been, I mean where I've *been*. And *what* I've been."

"What have you been, Sonny?" I asked.

220 He smiled — but sat sideways on the sofa, his elbow resting on the back, his fingers playing with his mouth and chin, not looking at me. "I've been something I didn't recognize, didn't know, I could be. Didn't know anybody could be." He stopped, looking inward, looking helplessly young, looking old. "I'm not talking about it now because I feel *guilty* or anything like that — maybe it would be better if I did, I don't know. Anyway, I can't really talk about it. Not to you, not to anybody," and now he turned and faced me. "Sometimes, you know, and it was actually when I was most *out* of the world, I felt that I was in it, that I was *with* it, really, and I could *play* or I didn't really have to *play*, it just came out of me, it was there. And I don't know how I played, thinking about it now, but I know I did awful things, those times, sometimes, to people. Or it wasn't that I *did* anything to them — it was that they weren't real." He picked up the beer can; it was empty; he rolled it between his palms: "And other times — well, I needed a fix, I needed to find a place to lean, I needed to clear a space to *listen* — and I couldn't find it,

and I — went crazy, I did terrible things to *me*, I was terrible *for* me." He began pressing the beer can between his hands, I watched the metal begin to give. It glittered, as he played with it like a knife, and I was afraid he would cut himself, but I said nothing. "Oh well, I can never tell you. I was all by myself at the bottom of something, stinking and sweating and crying and shaking, and I smelled it, you know? *my* stink, and I thought I'd die if I couldn't get away from it and yet, all the same, I knew that everything I was doing was just looking me in with it. And I didn't know," he paused, still flattening the beer can, "I didn't know, I still *don't* know, something kept telling me that maybe it was good to smell your own stink, but I didn't think that *that* was what I'd been trying to do — and — who can stand it?" and he abruptly dropped the ruined beer can, looking at me with a small, still smile, and then rose, walking to the window as though it were the lodestone rock. I watched his face, he watched the avenue. "I couldn't tell you when Mama died — but the reason I wanted to leave Harlem so bad was to get away from drugs. And then, when I ran away, that's what I was running from — really. When I came back, nothing had changed, I hadn't changed, I was just — older." And he stopped, drumming with his fingers on the windowpane. The sun had vanished, soon darkness would fall I watched his face. "It can come again," he said, almost as though speaking to himself. Then he turned to me. "It can come again," he repeated. "I just want you to know that."

"All right," I said, at last. "So it can come again, All right."

He smiled, but the smile was sorrowful. "I had to try to tell you," he said.

"Yes," I said, "I understand that."

"You're my brother," he said, looking straight at me, and not smiling at all.

"Yes," I repeated, "yes I understand that." 225

He turned back to the window, looking out. "All that hatred down there," he said, "all that hatred and misery and love. It's a wonder it doesn't blow the avenue apart."

We went to the only nightclub on a short, dark street, downtown. We squeezed through the narrow, chattering, jampacked bar to the entrance of the big room, where the bandstand was. And we stood there for a moment, for the lights were very dim in this room and we couldn't see. Then, "Hello, boy," said the voice and an enormous black man, much older than Sonny or myself, erupted out of all that atmospheric lighting and put an arm around Sonny's shoulder. "I been sitting right here," he said, "waiting for you."

He had a big voice, too, and heads in the darkness turned toward us.

Sonny grinned and pulled a little away, and said, "Creole, this is my brother. I told you about him."

Creole shook my hand. "I'm glad to meet you, son," he said, and it was clear 230 that he was glad to meet me *there*, for Sonny's sake. And he smiled: "You got a real musician in *your* family," and he took his arm from Sonny's shoulders and slapped him, lightly, affectionately, with the back of his hand.

Well. Now I've heard it all," said a voice behind us. This was another musician, and a friend of Sonny's, a coal-black, cheerful-looking man, built close to the ground. He immediately began confiding to me, at the top of his lungs, the most terrible things about Sonny, his teeth gleaming like a lighthouse and his laugh coming up out of him like the beginning of an earthquake. And it turned out that everyone at the bar knew Sonny, or almost everyone; some were musicians, working there, or nearby, or not working, some were simply hangers on, and some were there to hear Sonny play. I was introduced to all of them and they were all very polite to me. Yet, it was clear that, for them, I was only Sonny's brother. Here, I was in Sonny's world. Or, rather: his kingdom. Here, it was not even a question that his veins bore royal blood.

They were going to play soon and Creole installed me, by myself, at a table in a dark corner. Then I watched them, Creole, and the little black man, and Sonny, and the others, while they horsed around, standing just below the bandstand. The light from the bandstand spilled just a little short of them and watching them laughing and gesturing and moving about, I had the feeling that they, nevertheless, were being most careful not to step into that circle of light too suddenly; that if they moved into the light too suddenly, without thinking, they would perish in flame. Then, while I watched, one of them, the small black man, moved into the light and crossed the bandstand and started fooling around with his drums. Then — being funny and being also, extremely ceremonious — Creole took Sonny by the arm and led him to the piano. A woman's voice called Sonny's name and a few hands started clapping. And Sonny, also being funny and being ceremonious, and so touched, I think, that he could have cried, but neither hiding it nor showing it, riding it like a man, grinned, and put both hands to his heart and bowed from the waist.

Creole then went to the bass fiddle and a lean, very bright-skinned brown man jumped up on the bandstand and picked up his horn. So there they were, and the atmosphere on the bandstand and in the room began to change and tighten. Someone stepped up to the microphone and announced them. Then there were all kinds of murmurs. Some people at the bar shushed others. The waitress ran around, frantically getting in the last orders, guys and chicks got closer to each other, and the lights on the bandstand, on the quartet, turned to a kind of indigo. Then they all looked different there. Creole looked about him for the last time, as though he were making certain that all his chickens were in the coop, and then he — jumped and struck the fiddle. And there they were.

All I know about music is that not many people ever really hear it. And even then, on the rare occasions when something opens within, and the music enters, what we mainly hear, or hear corroborated, are personal, private, vanishing evocations. But the man who creates the music is hearing something else, is dealing with the roar rising from the void and imposing order on it as it hits the air. What is evoked in him, then, is of another order, more terrible because it has no words, and triumphant, too, for that same reason. And his triumph, when he triumphs, is ours. I just watched Sonny's face. His face was troubled, he was working hard, but he wasn't with it. And I had the feeling that, in a way, everyone on the bandstand was waiting for him, both waiting for him and pushing him along. But as I began to watch Creole, I realized that it was Creole who held them all back. He had them on a short rein. Up there, keeping the heat with his whole body, wailing on the fiddle, with his eyes half closed, he was listening to everything, but he was listening to Sonny. He was having a dialogue with Sonny. He wanted Sonny to leave the shoreline and strike out for the deep water. He was Sonny's witness that deep water and drowning were not the same thing — he had been there, and he knew. And he wanted Sonny to know. He was waiting for Sonny to do the things on the keys which would let Creole know that Sonny was in the water.

And, while Creole listened, Sonny moved, deep within, exactly like someone in torment. I had never before thought of how awful the relationship must be between the musician and his instrument. He has to fill it, this instrument, with the breath of life, his own. He has to make it do what he wants it to do. And a piano is just a piano. It's made out of so much wood and wires and little hammers and big ones, and Ivory. While there's only so much you can do with it, the only way to find this out is to try, to try and make it do everything.

And Sonny hadn't been near a piano for over a year. And he wasn't on much better terms with his life, not the life that stretched before him now. He and the piano stammered, started one way, got scared, stopped, started another way, panicked, marked time, started again, then seemed to have found a direction, panicked again, got stuck. And the face I saw on Sonny I'd never seen before. Everything had been burned out of it, and, at the same time, things usually hidden were being burned in, by the fire and fury of the battle which was occurring in him up there.

Yet, watching Creole's face as they neared the end of the first set, I had the feeling that something had happened, something I hadn't heard. Then they finished, there was scattered applause, and then, without an instant's warning, Creole started into something else, it was almost sardonic, it was Am I Blue.° And, as though he commanded, Sonny began to play. Something began to happen. And Creole let out the reins. The dry, low, black man said something awful on the drums, Creole answered, and the drums talked back. Then the horn insisted, sweet and high, slightly detached perhaps, and Creole listened, commenting now and then, dry, and driving, beautiful and calm and old. Then they all came together again, and Sonny was part of the family again. I could tell this from his face. He seemed to have found, right there beneath his fingers, a damn brand-new piano. It seemed that he couldn't get over it. Then, for a while, just being happy with Sonny, they seemed to be agreeing with him that brand-new pianos certainly were a gas.

Then Creole stepped forward to remind them that what they were playing was the blues. He hit something in all of them, he hit something in me, myself, and the music tightened and deepened, apprehension began to beat the air. Creole began to tell us what the blues were all about. They were not about anything very new. He and his boys up there were keeping it new, at the risk of ruin, destruction, madness, and death, in order to find new ways to make us listen. For, while the tale of how we suffer, and how we are delighted, and how we may triumph is never new, it always must be heard. There isn't any other tale to tell, it's the only light we've got in all this darkness.

And this tale, according to that face, that body, those strong hands on those strings, has another aspect in every country, and a new depth in every generation. Listen, Creole seemed to be saying, listen, Now these are Sonny's blues. He made the little black man on the drums know it, and the bright, brown man on the

235

Am I Blue: A Jazz standard.

horn. Creole wasn't trying any longer to get Sonny in the water. He was wishing him Godspeed. Then he stepped back, very slowly, filling the air with the immense suggestion that Sonny speak for himself.

240   Then they all gathered around Sonny and Sonny played. Every now and again one of them seemed to say, amen. Sonny's fingers filled the air with life, his life. But that life contained so many others. And Sonny went all the way back, he really began with the spare, flat statement of the opening phrase of the song. Then he began to make it his. It was very beautiful because it wasn't hurried and it was no longer a lament. I seemed to hear with what burning he had made it his, and what burning we had yet to make it ours, how we could cease lamenting. Freedom lurked around us and I understood, at last, that he could help us to be free if we would listen, that he would never be free until we did. Yet, there was no battle in his face now, I heard what he had gone through, and would continue to go through until he came to rest in earth. He had made it his: that long line, of which we knew only Mama and Daddy. And he was giving it back, as everything must be given back, so that, passing through death, it can live forever. I saw my mother's face again, and felt, for the first time, how the stones of the road she had walked on must have bruised her feet. I saw the moonlit road where my father's brother died. And it brought something else back to me, and carried me past it, I saw my little girl again and felt Isabel's tears again, and I felt my own tears begin to rise. And I was yet aware that this was only a moment, that the world waited outside, as hungry as a tiger, and that trouble stretched above us, longer than the sky.

Then it was over. Creole and Sonny let out their breath, both soaking wet, and grinning. There was a lot of applause and some of it was real. In the dark, the girl came by and I asked her to take drinks to the bandstand. There was a long pause, while they talked up there in the indigo light and after awhile I saw the girl put a Scotch and milk on top of the piano for Sonny. He didn't seem to notice it, but just before they started playing again, he sipped from it and looked toward me, and nodded. Then he put it back on top of the piano. For me, then, as they began to play again, it glowed and shook above my brother's head like the very cup of trembling.°

❖ ❖ ❖

TONI CADE BAMBARA   (1939–1995)

The Lesson   (1972)

Back in the days when everyone was old and stupid or young and foolish me and Sugar were the only ones just right, this lady moved on our block with nappy hair and proper speech and no makeup. And quite naturally we laughed at her, laughed the way we did at the junk man who went about his business like he was some

---

See Isaiah 51:17, 22–23: "Awake, awake, stand up, O Jerusalem, which hast drunk at the hand of the Lord the cup of his fury; thou hast drunken the dregs of the cup of trembling, and wrung them out . . . Behold, I have taken out of thine hand the cup of trembling, even the dregs of the cup of my fury; thou shalt no more drink it again: But I will put it into the hand of them that affect thee . . ."

big-time president and his sorry-ass horse his secretary. And we kinda hated her too, hated the way we did the winos who cluttered up our parks and pissed on our handball walls and stank up our hallways and stairs so you couldn't halfway play hide-and-seek without a goddamn gas mask. Miss Moore was her name. The only woman on the block with no first name. And she was black as hell, cept for her feet, which were fish-white and spooky. And she was always planning these boring-ass things for us to do, us being my cousin, mostly, who lived on the block cause we all moved North the same time and to the same apartment then spread out gradual to breathe. And our parents would yank our heads into some kinda shape and crisp up our clothes so we'd be presentable for travel with Miss Moore, who always looked like she was going to church, though she never did. Which is just one of the things the grownups talked about when they talked behind her back like a dog. But when she came calling with some sachet she'd sewed up or some gingerbread she'd made or some book, why then they'd all be too embarrassed to turn her down and we'd get handed over all spruced up. She'd been to college and said it was only right that she should take responsibility for the young ones' education, and she not even related by marriage or blood. So they'd go for it. Specially Aunt Gretchen. She was the main gofer in the family. You got some ole dumb shit foolishness you want somebody to go for, you send for Aunt Gretchen. She been screwed into the go-along for so long, it's a blood-deep natural thing with her. Which is how she got saddled with me and Sugar and Junior in the first place while our mothers were in a la-de-da apartment up the block having a good ole time.

So this one day Miss Moore rounds us all up at the mailbox and it's puredee hot and she's knockin herself out about arithmetic. And school suppose to let up in summer I heard, but she don't never let up. And the starch in my pinafore scratching the shit outta me and I'm really hating this nappy-head bitch and her goddamn college degree. I'd much rather go to the pool or to the show where it's cool. So me and Sugar leaning on the mailbox being surly, which is a Miss Moore word. And Flyboy checking out what everybody brought for lunch. And Fat Butt already wasting his peanut butter-and-jelly sandwich like the pig he is. And Junebug punchin on Q.T.'s arm for potato chips. And Rosie Giraffe shifting from one hip to the other waiting for somebody to step on her foot or ask her if she from Georgia so she can kick ass, preferably Mercedes'. And Miss Moore asking us do we know what money is, like we a bunch of retards. I mean real money, she say, like it's only poker chips or monopoly papers we lay on the grocer. So right away I'm tired of this and say so. And would much rather snatch Sugar and go to the Sunset and terrorize the West Indian kids and take their hair ribbons and their money too. And Miss Moore files that remark away for next week's lesson on brotherhood, I can tell. And finally I say we oughta get to the subway cause it's cooler and besides we might meet some cute boys. Sugar done swiped her mama's lipstick, so we ready.

So we heading down the street and she's boring us silly about what things cost and what our parents make and how much goes for rent and how money ain't divided up right in this country. And then she gets to the part about we all poor and live in the slums, which I don't feature. And I'm ready to speak on that, but she steps out in the street and hails two cabs just like that. Then she hustles half the crew in with her and hands me a five-dollar bill and tells me to calculate 10 percent tip for the driver. And we're off. Me and Sugar and Junebug and Flyboy hangin out the window and hollering to everybody, putting lipstick on each other cause Flyboy a faggot anyway, and making farts with our sweaty armpits. But I'm mostly trying to figure how to spend this money. But they all fascinated with the meter ticking and Junebug starts laying bets as to how much it'll read when Flyboy can't hold his breath no more. Then Sugar lays bets as to how much it'll be when we get there. So I'm stuck. Don't nobody want to go for my plan, which is to jump out at the next light and run off to the first bar-b-que we can find. Then the driver tells us to get the hell out cause we there already. And the meter reads eighty-five cents. And I'm stalling to figure out the tip and Sugar say give him a dime. And I decide he don't need it bad as I do, so later for him. But then he tries to take off with Junebug foot still in the door so we talk about his mama something ferocious. Then we check out that we on Fifth Avenue and everybody dressed up in stockings. One lady in a fur coat, hot as it is. White folks crazy.

"This is the place," Miss Moore say, presenting it to us in the voice she uses at the museum. "Let's look in the windows before we go in."

5   "Can we steal?" Sugar asks very serious like she's getting the ground rules squared away before she plays. "I beg your pardon," say Miss Moore, and we fall out. So she leads us around the windows of the toy store and me and Sugar screamin, "This is mine, that's mine, I gotta have that, that was made for me, I was born for that," till Big Butt drowns us out.

"Hey, I'm going to buy that there."

"That there? You don't even know what it is, stupid."

"I do so," he say punchin on Rosie Giraffe. "It's a microscope."

"Whatcha gonna do with a microscope, fool?"

10   "Look at things."

"Like what, Ronald?" ask Miss Moore. And Big Butt ain't got the first notion. So here go Miss Moore gabbing about the thousands of bacteria in a drop of water and the somethinorother in a speck of blood and the million and one living things in the air around us is invisible to the naked eye. And what she say that for? Junebug go to town on that "naked" and we rolling. Then Miss Moore ask what it cost. So we all jam into the window smudgin it up and the price tag say $300. So then she ask how long'd take for Big Butt and Junebug to save up their allowances. "Too long," I say. "Yeh," adds Sugar, "outgrown it by that time." And Miss Moore say no, you never outgrow learning instruments. "Why, even medical students and interns and," blah, blah, blah. And we ready to choke Big Butt for bringing it up in the first damn place.

"This here costs four hundred eighty dollars," say Rosie Giraffe. So we pile up all over her to see what she pointin out. My eyes tell me it's a chunk of glass cracked with something heavy, and different-color inks dripped into the splits, and then the whole thing put into a oven or something. But for $480 it don't make sense.

"That's a paperweight made of semi-precious stones fused together under tremendous pressure," she explains slowly, with her hands doing the mining and all the factory work.

"So what's a paperweight?" asks Rosie Giraffe.

15   "To weigh paper with, dumbbell," say Flyboy, the wise man from the East.

"Not exactly," says Miss Moore, which is what she say when you warm or way off too. "It's to weigh paper down so it won't scatter and make your desk untidy." So right away me and Sugar curtsy to each other and then to Mercedes who is more the tidy type.

"We don't keep paper on top of the desk in my class," say Junebug, figuring Miss Moore crazy or lyin one.

"At home, then," she say "Don't you have a calendar and a pencil case and a blotter and a letter-opener on your desk at home where you do your homework?" And she know damn well what our homes look like cause she nosys around in them every chance she gets.

"I don't even have a desk," say Junebug. "Do we?"

"No. And I don't get no homework neither," says Big Butt.   20

"And I don't even have a home," says Flyboy like he do at school to keep the white folks off his back and sorry for him. Send this poor kid to camp posters, is his specialty.

"I do," says Mercedes. "I have a box of stationery on my desk and a picture of my cat. My godmother bought the stationery and the desk. There's a big rose on each sheet and the envelopes smell like roses."

"Who wants to know about your smelly-ass stationery," say Rosie Giraffe fore I can get my two cents in.

"It's important to have a work area all your own so that . . ."

"Will you look at this sailboat, please," say Flyboy, cuttin her off and pointin   25 to the thing like it was his. So once again we tumble all over each other to gaze at this magnificent thing in the toy store which is just big enough to maybe sail two kittens across the pond if you strap them to the posts right. We all start reciting the price tag like we in assembly. "Handcrafted sailboat of fiberglass at one thousand one hundred ninety-five dollars."

"Unbelievable," I hear myself say and am really stunned. I read it again for myself just in case the group recitation put me in a trance. Same thing. For some reason this pisses me off. We look at Miss Moore and she lookin at us, waiting for I dunno what.

"Who'd pay all that when you can buy a sailboat set for a quarter at Pop's, a tube of glue for a dime, and a ball of string for eight cents? It must have a motor and a whole lot else besides," I say. "My sailboat cost me about fifty cents."

"But will it take water?" say Mercedes with her smart ass.

"Took mine to Alley Pond Park once," say Flyboy. "String broke. Lost it. Pity."

"Sailed mine in Central Park and it keeled over and sank. Had to ask my   30 father for another dollar."

"And you got the strap," laughed Big Butt. "The jerk didn't even have a string on it. My old man wailed on his behind."

Little Q.T. was staring hard at the sailboat and you could see he wanted it bad. But he too little and somebody'd just take it from him. So what the hell. "This boat for kids, Miss Moore?"

"Parents silly to buy something like that just to get all broke up," say Rosie Giraffe.

"That much money it should last forever," I figure.

35   "My father'd buy it for me if I wanted it."

"Your father, my ass," say Rosie Giraffe getting a chance to finally push Mercedes.

"Must be rich people shop here," say Q.T.

"You are a very bright boy," say Flyboy. "What was your first clue?" And he rap him on the head with the back of his knuckles, since Q.T. the only one he could get away with. Though Q.T. liable to come up behind you years later and get his licks in when you half expect it.

"What I want to know is," I says to Miss Moore though I never talk to her, I wouldn't give the bitch the satisfaction, "is how much a real boat costs? I figure a thousand'd get you a yacht any day."

40   "Why don't you check that out," she says, "and report back to the group?" Which really pains my ass. If you gonna mess up a perfectly good swim day least you could do is have some answers. "Let's go in," she say like she got something up her sleeve. Only she don't lead the way. So me and Sugar turn the corner to where the entrance is, but when we get there I kinda hang back. Not that I'm scared, what's there to be afraid of, just a toy store. But I feel funny, shame. But what I got to be shamed about? Got as much right to go in as anybody. But somehow I can't seem to get hold of the door, so I step away from Sugar to lead. But she hangs back too. And I look at her and she looks at me and this is ridiculous. I mean, damn, I have never ever been shy about doing nothing or going nowhere. But then Mercedes steps up and then Rosie Giraffe and Big Butt crowd in behind and shove, and next thing we all stuffed into the doorway with only Mercedes squeezing past us, smoothing out her jumper and walking right down the aisle. Then the rest of us tumble in like a glued-together jigsaw done all wrong. And people lookin at us. And it's like the time me and Sugar crashed into the Catholic church on a dare. But once we got in there and everything so hushed and holy and the candles and the bowin and the handkerchiefs on all the drooping heads. I just couldn't go through with the plan. Which was for me to run up to the altar and do a tap dance while Sugar played the nose flute and messed around in the holy water. And Sugar kept givin me the elbow. Then later teased me so bad I tied her up in the shower and turned it on and locked her in. And she'd be there till this day if Aunt Gretchen hadn't finally figured I was lyin about the boarder takin a shower.

Same thing in the store. We all walkin on tiptoe and hardly touchin the games and puzzles and things. And I watched Miss Moore who is steady watchin us like she waitin for a sign. Like Mama Drewery watches the sky and sniffs the air and takes note of just how much slant is in the bird formation. Then me and Sugar bump smack into each other, so busy gazing at the toys, 'specially the sailboat. But we don't laugh and go into our fat-lady bump-stomach routine. We just stare at that price tag. Then Sugar run a finger over the whole boat. And I'm jealous and want to hit her. Maybe not her, but I sure want to punch somebody in the mouth.

"Watcha bring us here for, Miss Moore?"

"You sound angry, Sylvia. Are you mad about something?" Givin me one of them grins like she tellin a grown-up joke that never turns out to be funny. And she's lookin very closely at me like maybe she plannin to do my portrait from memory. I'm mad, but I won't give her that satisfaction. So I slouch around the store bein very bored and say, "Let's go."

Me and Sugar at the back of the train watchin the tracks whizzin by large then small then gettin gobbled up in the dark. I'm thinkin about this tricky toy I saw in the store. A clown that somersaults on a bar then does chin-ups just cause you yank lightly at his leg. Cost $35. I could see me askin my mother for a $35 birthday clown. "You wanna who that costs what?" she'd say, cocking her head to the side to get a better view of the hole in my head. Thirty-five dollars could buy new bunk beds for Junior and Gretchen's boy. Thirty-five dollars and the whole household could go visit Granddaddy Nelson in the country. Thirty-five dollars would pay for the rent and the piano bill too. Who are these people that spend that much for performing clowns and $1000 for toy sailboats? What kinda work they do and how they live and how come we ain't in on it? Where we are is who we are, Miss Moore always pointin out. But it don't necessarily have to be that way, she always adds then waits for somebody to say that poor people have to wake up and demand their share of the pie and don't none of us know what kind of pie she talking about in the first damn place. But she ain't so smart cause I still got her four dollars from the taxi and she sure ain't getting it. Messin up my day with this shit. Sugar nudges me in my pocket and winks.

Miss Moore lines us up in front of the mailbox where we started from, seem like years ago, and I got a headache for thinkin so hard. And we lean all over each other so we can hold up under the draggy-ass lecture she always finishes us off with at the end before we thank her for borin us to tears. But she just looks at us like she readin tea leaves. Finally she say, "Well, what did you think of F.A.O. Schwarz?" 45

Rosie Giraffe mumbles, "White folks crazy."

"I'd like to go there again when I get my birthday money," says Mercedes, and we shove her out the pack so she has to lean on the mailbox by herself.

"I'd like a shower. Tiring day," say Flyboy.

Then Sugar surprises me by sayin, "You know, Miss Moore, I don't think all of us here put together eat in a year what that sailboat costs." And Miss Moore lights up like somebody goosed her. "And?" she say, urging Sugar on. Only I'm standin on her foot so she don't continue.

"Imagine for a minute what kind of society it is in which some people can spend on a toy what it would cost to feed a family of six or seven. What do you think?" 50

"I think," say Sugar pushing me off her feet like she never done before, cause I whip her ass in a minute, "that this is not much of a democracy if you ask me. Equal chance to pursue happiness means an equal crack at the dough, don't it?" Miss Moore is beside herself and I am disgusted with Sugar's treachery. So I stand on her foot one more time to see if she'll shove me. She shuts up, and Miss Moore looks at me, sorrowfully I'm thinkin. And somethin weird is goin on, I can feel it in my chest.

"Anybody else learn anything today?" lookin dead at me. I walk away and Sugar has to run to catch up and don't even seem to notice when I shrug her arm off my shoulder.

"Well, we got four dollars anyway," she says.

"Uh hunh."

55 "We could go to Hascombs and get half a chocolate layer and then go to the Sunset and still have plenty of money for potato chips and ice cream sodas."

"Uh hunh."

"Race you to Hascombs," she say.

We start down the block and she gets ahead which is O.K. by me cause I'm going to the West End and then over to the Drive to think this day through. She can run if she want to and even run faster. But ain't nobody gonna beat me at nuthin.

◇ ◇ ◇

T. CORAGHESSAN BOYLE   (1948–   )

Greasy Lake   (1985)

It's about a mile down on the dark side of Route 88.

— Bruce Springsteen

There was a time when courtesy and winning ways went out of style, when it was good to be bad, when you cultivated decadence like a taste. We were all dangerous characters then. We wore torn-up leather jackets, slouched around with toothpicks in our mouths, sniffed glue and ether and what somebody claimed was cocaine. When we wheeled our parents' whining station wagons out into the street we left a patch of rubber half a block long. We drank gin and grape juice, Tango, Thunderbird, and Bali Hai. We were nineteen. We were bad. We read André Gide° and struck elaborate poses to show that we didn't give a shit about anything. At night, we went up to Greasy Lake.

Through the center of town, up the strip, past the housing developments and shopping malls, street lights giving way to the thin streaming illumination of the headlights, trees crowding the asphalt in a black unbroken wall: that was the way out to Greasy Lake. The Indians had called it Wakan, a reference to the clarity of its waters. Now it was fetid and murky, the mud banks glittering with broken glass and strewn with beer cans and the charred remains of bonfires. There was a single ravaged island a hundred yards from shore, so stripped of vegetation it looked as if the air force had strafed it. We went up to the lake because everyone went there, because we wanted to snuff the rich scent of possibility on the breeze, watch a girl take off her clothes and plunge into the festering murk, drink beer, smoke pot, howl at the stars, savor the incongruous full-throated roar of rock and roll against the primeval susurrus° of frogs and crickets. This was nature.

André Gide: French novelist and critic (1869–1951) whose work — much of it semiautobiographical — examines the conflict between desire and discipline and shows individuals battling conventional morality.

susurrus: A whispering or rustling sound.

I was there one night, late, in the company of two dangerous characters. Digby wore a gold star in his right ear and allowed his father to pay his tuition at Cornell; Jeff was thinking of quitting school to become a painter/musician/head-shop proprietor. They were both expert in the social graces, quick with a sneer, able to manage a Ford with lousy shocks over a rutted and gutted blacktop road at eighty-five while rolling a joint as compact as a Tootsie Roll Pop stick. They could lounge against a bank of booming speakers and trade "man"s with the best of them or roll out across the dance floor as if their joints worked on bearings. They were slick and quick and they wore their mirror shades at breakfast and dinner, in the shower, in closets and caves. In short, they were bad.

I drove. Digby pounded the dashboard and shouted along with Toots & the Maytals while Jeff hung his head out the window and streaked the side of my mother's Bel Air with vomit. It was early June, the air soft as a hand on your cheek, the third night of summer vacation. The first two nights we'd been out till dawn, looking for something we never found. On this, the third night, we'd cruised the strip sixty-seven times, been in and out of every bar and club we could think of in a twenty-mile radius, stopped twice for bucket chicken and forty-cent hamburgers, debated going to a party at the house of a girl Jeff's sister knew, and chucked two dozen raw eggs at mailboxes and hitchhikers. It was 2:00 A.M.; the bars were closing. There was nothing to do but take a bottle of lemon-flavored gin up to Greasy Lake.

The taillights of a single car winked at us as we swung into the dirt lot with its 5
tufts of weed and washboard corrugations; '57 Chevy, mint, metallic blue. On the far side of the lot, like the exoskeleton of some gaunt chrome insect, a chopper leaned against its kickstand. And that was it for excitement: some junkie half-wit biker and a car freak pumping his girlfriend. Whatever it was we were looking for, we weren't about to find it at Greasy Lake. Not that night.

But then all of a sudden Digby was fighting for the wheel. "Hey, that's Tony Lovett's car! Hey!" he shouted, while I stabbed at the brake pedal and the Bel Air nosed up to the gleaming bumper of the parked Chevy. Digby leaned on the horn, laughing, and instructed me to put my brights on. I flicked on the brights. This was hilarious. A joke. Tony would experience premature withdrawal and expect to be confronted by grim-looking state troopers with flashlights. We hit the horn, strobed the lights, and then jumped out of the car to press our witty faces to Tony's windows; for all we knew we might even catch a glimpse of some little fox's tit, and then we could slap backs with red-faced Tony, roughhouse a little, and go on to new heights of adventure and daring.

The first mistake, the one that opened the whole floodgate, was losing my grip on the keys. In the excitement, leaping from the car with the gin in one hand and a roach clip in the other, I spilled them in the grass — in the dark, rank, mysterious nighttime grass of Greasy Lake. This was a tactical error, as damaging and irreversible in its way as Westmoreland's decision to dig in at Khe Sanh.° I felt it

---

Khe Sanh: In late 1967, North Vietnamese and Viet Cong forces mounted a strong attack against American troops at Khe Sanh, thereby causing General William C. Westmoreland, commander of United States forces in Vietnam, to "dig in" to defend an area of relatively little tactical importance.

like a jab of intuition, and I stopped there by the open door, peering vaguely into the night that puddled up round my feet.

The second mistake — and this was inextricably bound up with the first — was identifying the car as Tony Lovett's. Even before the very bad character in greasy jeans and engineer boots ripped out of the driver's door, I began to realize that this chrome blue was much lighter than the robin's-egg of Tony's car, and that Tony's car didn't have rear-mounted speakers. Judging from their expressions, Digby and Jeff were privately groping toward the same inevitable and unsettling conclusion as I was.

In any case, there was no reasoning with this bad greasy character — clearly he was a man of action. The first lusty Rockette° kick of his steel-toed boot caught me under the chin, chipped my favorite tooth, and left me sprawled in the dirt. Like a fool, I'd gone down on one knee to comb the stiff hacked grass for the keys, my mind making connections in the most dragged-out, testudineous° way, knowing that things had gone wrong, that I was in a lot of trouble, and that the lost ignition key was my grail and my salvation. The three or four succeeding blows were mainly absorbed by my right buttock and the tough piece of bone at the base of my spine.

10   Meanwhile, Digby vaulted the kissing bumpers and delivered a savage kung-fu blow to the greasy character's collarbone. Digby had just finished a course in martial arts for phys-ed credit and had spent the better part of the past two nights telling us apocryphal tales of Bruce Lee types and of the raw power invested in lightning blows shot from coiled wrists, ankles, and elbows. The greasy character was unimpressed. He merely backed off a step, his face like a Toltec mask, and laid Digby out with a single whistling roundhouse blow. . . but by now Jeff had got into the act, and I was beginning to extricate myself from the dirt, a tinny compound of shock, rage, and impotence wadded in my throat.

Jeff was on the guy's back, biting at his ear. Digby was on the ground, cursing. I went for the tire iron I kept under the driver's seat. I kept it there because bad characters always keep tire irons under the driver's seat, for just such an occasion as this. Never mind that I hadn't been involved in a fight since sixth grade, when a kid with a sleepy eye and two streams of mucus depending from his nostrils hit me in the knee with a Louisville slugger,° never mind that I'd touched the tire iron exactly twice before, to change tires: it was there. And I went for it.

I was terrified. Blood was beating in my ears, my hands were shaking, my heart turning over like a dirtbike in the wrong gear. My antagonist was shirtless, and a single cord of muscle flashed across his chest as he bent forward to peel Jeff from his back like a wet overcoat. "Motherfucker," he spat, over and over, and I

Rockette: The reference is to the Rockettes, a dance troupe at New York's Radio City Music Hall noted for precision and cancan-like high kicks.

testudineous: Slow, like the pace of a tortoise.

Louisville slugger: A popular brand of baseball bat.

was aware in that instant that all four of us — Digby, Jeff, and myself included — were chanting "motherfucker, motherfucker," as if it were a battle cry. (What happened next? the detective asks the murderer from beneath the turned-down brim of his porkpie hat. I don't know, the murderer says, something came over me. Exactly.)

Digby poked the flat of his hand in the bad character's face and I came at him like a kamikaze, mindless, raging, stung with humiliation — the whole thing, from the initial boot in the chin to this murderous primal instant involving no more than sixty hyperventilating, gland-flooding seconds — I came at him and brought the tire iron down across his ear. The effect was instantaneous, astonishing. He was a stunt man and this was Hollywood, he was a big grimacing toothy balloon and I was a man with a straight pin. He collapsed. Wet his pants. Went loose in his boots.

A single second, big as a zeppelin, floated by. We were standing over him in a circle, gritting our teeth, jerking our necks, our limbs and hands and feet twitching with glandular discharges. No one said anything. We just stared down at the guy, the car freak, the lover, the bad greasy character laid low. Digby looked at me; so did Jeff. I was still holding the tire iron, a tuft of hair clinging to the crook like dandelion fluff, like down. Rattled, I dropped it in the dirt, already envisioning the headlines, the pitted faces of the police inquisitors, the gleam of handcuffs, clank of bars, the big black shadows rising from the back of the cell . . . when suddenly a raw torn shriek cut through me like all the juice in all the electric chairs in the country.

It was the fox. She was short, barefoot, dressed in panties and a man's shirt.   15
"Animals!" she screamed, running at us with her fists clenched and wisps of blow-dried hair in her face. There was a silver chain round her ankle, and her toenails flashed in the glare of the headlights. I think it was the toenails that did it. Sure, the gin and the cannabis and even the Kentucky Fried may have had a hand in it, but it was the sight of those flaming toes that set us off — the toad emerging from the loaf in *Virgin Spring*,° lipstick smeared on a child: she was already tainted. We were on her like Bergman's deranged brothers — see no evil, hear none, speak none — panting, wheezing, tearing at her clothes, grabbing for flesh. We were bad characters, and we were scared and hot and three steps over the line — anything could have happened.

It didn't.

Before we could pin her to the hood of the car, our eyes masked with lust and greed and the purest primal badness, a pair of headlights swung into the lot. There we were, dirty, bloody, guilty, dissociated from humanity and civilization, the first of the Ur-crimes° behind us, the second in progress, shreds of nylon panty and spandex brassiere dangling from our fingers, our flies open, lips licked — there we were, caught in the spotlight. Nailed.

Virgin Spring: A Film by Swedish director Ingmar Bergman.
Ur-crimes: Primitive crimes.

We bolted. First for the car, and then, realizing we had no way of starting it, for the woods. I thought nothing. I thought escape. The headlights came at me like accusing fingers. I was gone.

Ram-bam-bam, across the parking lot, past the chopper and into the feculent undergrowth at the lake's edge, insects flying up in my face, weeds whipping, frogs and snakes and red-eyed turtles splashing off into the night: I was already ankle-deep in muck and tepid water and still going strong. Behind me, the girl's screams rose in intensity, disconsolate, incriminating, the screams of the Sabine women,° the Christian martyrs, Anne Frank° dragged from the garret. I kept going, pursued by those cries, imagining cops and bloodhounds. The water was up to my knees when I realized what I was doing: I was going to swim for it. Swim the breadth of Greasy Lake and hide myself in the thick clot of woods on the far side. They'd never find me there.

20   I was breathing in sobs, in gasps. The water lapped at my waist as I looked out over the moon-burnished ripples, the mats of algae that clung to the surface like scabs. Digby and Jeff had vanished. I paused. Listened. The girl was quieter now, screams tapering to sobs, but there were male voices, angry, excited, and the high-pitched ticking of the second car's engine. I waded deeper, stealthy, hunted, the ooze sucking at my sneakers. As I was about to take the plunge — at the very instant I dropped my shoulder for the first slashing stroke — I blundered into something. Something unspeakable, obscene, something soft, wet, moss-grown. A patch of weed? A log? When I reached out to touch it, it gave like a rubber duck, it gave like flesh.

In one of those nasty little epiphanies for which we are prepared by films and TV and childhood visits to the funeral home to ponder the shrunken painted forms of dead grandparents, I understood what it was that bobbed there so inadmissibly in the dark. Understood, and stumbled back in horror and revulsion, my mind yanked in six different directions (I was nineteen, a mere child, an infant, and here in the space of five minutes I'd struck down one greasy character and blundered into the waterlogged carcass of a second), thinking, The keys, the keys, why did I have to go and lose the keys? I stumbled back, but the muck took hold of my feet — a sneaker snagged, balance lost — and suddenly I was pitching face forward into the buoyant black mass, throwing out my hands in desperation while simultaneously conjuring the image of reeking frogs and muskrats revolving in slicks of their own deliquescing° juices. AAAAArrrgh! I shot from the water

---

Sabine women: According to legend, members of an ancient Italian tribe abducted by Romans who took them for wives. The "Rape of the Sabine Women" has been depicted by various artists, most notably by seventeenth-century French painter Nicolas Poussin.

Anne Frank: German Jewish girl (1929–1945) whose family hid in an attic in Amsterdam during the Nazi occupation of the Netherlands. Frank, who along with her family was discovered by storm troopers and sent to die at the concentration camp at Belsen, is famous for her diary, which recounts her days in hiding. A new version of the diary containing five missing pages surfaced in 1998.

deliquescing: Melting.

like a torpedo, the dead man rotating to expose a mossy beard and eyes cold as the moon. I must have shouted out, thrashing around in the weeds, because the voices behind me suddenly became animated.

"What was that?"

"It's them, it's them: they tried to, tried to . . . *rape* me!" Sobs.

A man's voice, flat Midwestern accent. "You sons a bitches, we'll kill you!"

Frogs, crickets.   25

Then another voice, harsh, *r*-less, Lower East Side: "Motherfucker!" I recognized the verbal virtuosity of the bad greasy character in the engineer boots. Tooth chipped, sneakers gone, coated in mud and slime and worse, crouching breathless in the weeds waiting to have my ass thoroughly and definitively kicked and fresh from the hideous stinking embrace of a three-days-dead-corpse, I suddenly felt a rush of joy and vindication: the son of a bitch was alive! Just as quickly, my bowels turned to ice. "Come on out of there, you pansy mothers!" the bad greasy character was screaming. He shouted curses till he was out of breath.

The crickets started up again, then the frogs. I held my breath. All at once there was a sound in the reeds, a swishing, a splash: thunk-a-thunk. They were throwing rocks. The frogs fell silent. I cradled my head. Swish, swish, thunk-a-thunk. A wedge of feldspar the size of a cue ball glanced off my knee. I bit my finger.

It was then that they turned to the car. I heard a door slam, a curse, and then the sound of the headlights shattering — almost a good-natured sound, celebratory, like corks popping from the necks of bottles. This was succeeded by the dull booming of the fenders, metal on metal, and then the icy crash of the windshield. I inched forward, elbows and knees, my belly pressed to the muck, thinking of guerrillas and commandos and *The Naked and the Dead.*° I parted the weeds and squinted the length of the parking lot.

The second car — it was a Trans-Am — was still running, its high beams washing the scene in a lurid stagy light. Tire iron flailing, the greasy bad character was laying into the side of my mother's Bel Air like an avenging demon, his shadow riding up the trunks of the trees. Whomp. Whomp. Whomp-whomp. The other two guys — blond types, in fraternity jackets — were helping out with tree branches and skull-sized boulders. One of them was gathering up bottles, rocks, muck, candy wrappers, used condoms, pop-tops, and other refuse and pitching it through the window on the driver's side. I could see the fox, a white bulb behind the windshield of the '57 Chevy. "Bobbie," she whined over the thumping, "come *on.*" The greasy character paused a moment, took one good swipe at the left taillight, and then heaved the tire iron halfway across the lake. Then he fired up the '57 and was gone.

Blond head nodded at blond head. One said something to the other, too low   30
for me to catch. They were no doubt thinking that in helping to annihilate my mother's car they'd committed a fairly rash act, and thinking too that there were

---

The Naked and the Dead: A popular and critically successful 1948 novel by Norman Mailer depicting United States Army life during World War II.

three bad characters connected with that very car watching them from the woods. Perhaps other possibilities occurred to them as well — police, jail cells, justices of the peace, reparations, lawyers, irate parents, fraternal censure. Whatever they were thinking, they suddenly dropped branches, bottles, and rocks and sprang for their car in unison, as if they'd choreographed it. Five seconds. That's all it took. The engine shrieked, the tires squealed, a cloud of dust rose from the rutted lot and then settled back on darkness.

I don't know how long I lay there, the bad breath of decay all around me, my jacket heavy as a bear, the primordial ooze subtly reconstituting itself to accommodate my upper thighs and testicles. My jaws ached, my knee throbbed, my coccyx° was on fire. I contemplated suicide, wondered if I'd need bridgework, scraped the recesses of my brain for some sort of excuse to give my parents — a tree had fallen on the car, I was blindsided by a bread truck, hit and run, vandals had got to it while we were playing chess at Digby's. Then I thought of the dead man. He was probably the only person on the planet worse off than I was. I thought about him, fog on the lake, insects chirring eerily, and felt the tug of fear, felt the darkness opening up inside me like a set of jaws. Who was he, I wondered, this victim of time and circumstance bobbing sorrowfully in the lake at my back. The owner of the chopper, no doubt, a bad older character come to this. Shot during a murky drug deal, drowned while drunkenly frolicking in the lake. Another headline. My car was wrecked; he was dead.

When the eastern half of the sky went from black to cobalt and the trees began to separate themselves from the shadows, I pushed myself up from the mud and stepped out into the open. By now the birds had begun to take over for the crickets, and dew lay slick on the leaves. There was a smell in the air, raw and sweet at the same time, the smell of the sun firing buds and opening blossoms. I contemplated the car. It lay there like a wreck along the highway, like a steel sculpture left over from a vanished civilization. Everything was still. This was nature.

I was circling the car, as dazed and bedraggled as the sole survivor of an air blitz, when Digby and Jeff emerged from the trees behind me. Digby's face was crosshatched with smears of dirt; Jeff's jacket was gone and his shirt was torn across the shoulder. They slouched across the lot, looking sheepish, and silently came up beside me to gape at the ravaged automobile. No one said a word. After a while Jeff swung open the driver's door and began to scoop the broken glass and garbage off the seat. I looked at Digby. He shrugged. "At least they didn't slash the tires," he said.

It was true: the tires were intact. There was no windshield, the headlights were staved in, and the body looked as if it had been sledgehammered for a quarter a shot at the county fair, but the tires were inflated to regulation pressure. The car was drivable. In silence, all three of us bent to scrape the mud and shattered glass from the interior. I said nothing about the biker. When we were finished, I reached in my pocket for the keys, experienced a nasty stab of recollection, cursed myself, and turned to search the grass. I spotted them almost immediately, no

---

coccyx: Tailbone.

more than five feet from the open door, glinting like jewels in the first tapering shaft of sunlight. There was no reason to get philosophical about it: I eased into the seat and turned the engine over.

It was at that precise moment that the silver Mustang with the flame decals   35 rumbled into the lot. All three of us froze; then Digby and Jeff slid into the car and slammed the door. We watched as the Mustang rocked and bobbed across the ruts and finally jerked to a halt beside the forlorn chopper at the far end of the lot. "Let's go," Digby said. I hesitated, the Bel Air wheezing beneath me.

Two girls emerged from the Mustang. Tight jeans, stiletto heels, hair like frozen fur. They bent over the motorcycle, paced back and forth aimlessly, glanced once or twice at us, and then ambled over to where the reeds sprang up in a green fence round the perimeter of the lake. One of them cupped her hands to her mouth. "Al," she called, "Hey, Al!"

"Come on," Digby hissed. "Let's get out of here."

But it was too late. The second girl was picking her way across the lot, unsteady on her heels, looking up at us and then away. She was older — twenty-five or -six — and as she came closer we could see there was something wrong with her: she was stoned or drunk, lurching now and waving her arms for balance. I gripped the steering wheel as if it were the ejection lever of a flaming jet, and Digby spat out my name, twice, terse and impatient.

"Hi," the girl said.

We looked at her like zombies, like war veterans, like deaf-and-dumb pencil   40 peddlers.

She smiled, her lips cracked and dry. "Listen," she said, bending from the waist to look in the window, "you guys seen Al?" Her pupils were pinpoints, her eyes glass. She jerked her neck. "That's his bike over there — Al's. You seen him?"

Al. I didn't know what to say. I wanted to get out of the car and retch, I wanted to go home to my parents' house and crawl into bed. Digby poked me in the ribs. "We haven't seen anybody," I said.

The girl seemed to consider this, reaching out a slim veiny arm to brace herself against the car. "No matter," she said, slurring the *t*'s, "he'll turn up." And then, as if she'd just taken stock of the whole scene — the ravaged car and our battered faces, the desolation of the place — she said: "Hey, you guys look like some pretty bad characters — been fightin', huh?" We stared straight ahead, rigid as catatonics. She was fumbling in her pocket and muttering something. Finally she held out a handful of tablets in glassine wrappers: "Hey, you want to party, you want to do some of these with me and Sarah?"

I just looked at her. I thought I was going to cry. Digby broke the silence. "No, thanks," he said, leaning over me. "Some other time."

I put the car in gear and it inched forward with a groan, shaking off pellets of   45 glass like an old dog shedding water after a bath, heaving over the ruts on its worn springs, creeping toward the highway. There was a sheen of sun on the lake. I looked back. The girl was still standing there, watching us, her shoulders slumped, hand outstretched.

◆ ◆ ◆

ALBERT CAMUS (1913–1960)

The Guest (1957)

The schoolmaster was watching the two men climb toward him. One was on horseback, the other on foot. They had not yet tackled the abrupt rise leading to the schoolhouse built on the hillside. They were toiling onward, making slow progress in the snow, among the stones, on the vast expanse of the high, deserted plateau. From time to time the horse stumbled. Without hearing anything yet, he could see the breath issuing from the horse's nostrils. One of the men, at least, knew the region. They were following the trail although it had disappeared days ago under a layer of dirty white snow. The schoolmaster calculated that it would take them half an hour to get onto the hill. It was cold; he went back into the school to get a sweater.

He crossed the empty, frigid classroom. On the blackboard the four rivers of France, drawn with four different colored chalks, had been flowing toward their estuaries for the past three days. Snow had suddenly fallen in mid-October after eight months of drought without the transition of rain, and the twenty pupils, more or less, who lived in the villages scattered over the plateau had stopped coming. With fair weather they would return. Daru now heated only the single room that was his lodging, adjoining the classroom and giving also onto the plateau to the east. Like the class windows, his window looked to the south too. On that side the school was a few kilometers from the point where the plateau began to slope toward the south. In clear weather could be seen the purple mass of the mountain range where the gap opened onto the desert.

Somewhat warmed, Daru returned to the window from which the had first seen the two men. They were no longer visible. Hence they must have tackled the rise. The sky was not so dark, for the snow had stopped falling during the night. The morning had opened with a dirty light which had scarcely become brighter as the ceiling of clouds lifted. At two in the afternoon it seemed as if the day were merely beginning. But still this was better than those three days when the thick snow was falling amidst unbroken darkness with little gusts of wind that rattled the double door of the classroom. Then Daru had spent long hours in his room, leaving it only to go to the shed and feed the chickens or get some coal. Fortunately the delivery truck from Tadjid, the nearest village to the north, had brought his supplies two days before the blizzard. It would return in forty-eight hours.

Besides, he had enough to resist a siege, for the little room was cluttered with bags of wheat that the administration left as a stock to distribute to those of his pupils whose families had suffered from the drought. Actually they had all been victims because they were all poor. Every day Daru would distribute a ration to the children. They had missed it, he knew, during these bad days. Possibly one of the fathers or big brothers would come this afternoon and he could supply them with grain. It was just a matter of carrying them over to the next harvest. Now shiploads of wheat were arriving from France and the worst was over. But it would be hard to forget that poverty, that army of ragged ghosts wandering in the sunlight, the plateaus burned to a cinder month after month, the earth shriveled up little by little, literally scorched, every stone bursting into dust under one's foot. The sheep had died then by thousands and even a few men, here and there, sometimes without anyone's knowing.

In contrast with such poverty, he who lived almost like a monk in his remote 5 schoolhouse, nonetheless satisfied with the little he had and with the rough life, had felt like a lord with his whitewashed walls, his narrow couch, his unpainted shelves, his well, and his weekly provision of water and food. And suddenly this snow, without warning, without the foretaste of rain. This is the way the region was, cruel to live in, even without men — who didn't help matters either. But Daru had been born here. Everywhere else, he felt exiled.

He stepped out onto the terrace in front of the schoolhouse. The two men were now halfway up the slope. The recognized the horseman as Balducci, the old gendarme° he had known for a long time. Balducci was holding on the end of a rope an Arab who was walking behind him with hands bound and head lowered. The gendarme waved greeting to which Daru did not reply, lost as he was in con-templation of the Arab dressed in a faded blue jellaba,° his feet in sandals but covered with socks of heavy raw wool, his head surmounted by a narrow, short *chèche*. They were approaching. Balducci was holding back his horse in order not to hurt the Arab, and the group was advancing slowly.

Within earshort, Balducci shouted: "One hour to do the three kilometers from El Ameur!" Daru did not answer. Short and square in his thick sweater, he watched them climb. Not once had the Arab raised his head. "Hello," said Daru when they got up onto the terrace. "Come in and warm up." Balducci painfully got down from his horse without letting go the rope. From under his bristling mus-tache he smiled at the schoolmaster. His little dark eyes, deep-set under a tanned forehead, and his mouth surrounded with wrinkles made him look attentive and studious. Daru took the bridle, led the horse to the shed, and came back to the two men, who were now waiting for him in the school. He led them into his room. "I am going to heat up the classroom," he said. "We'll be more comfortable there." When he entered the room again, Balducci was on the couch. He had undone the rope tying him to the Arab, who had squatted near the stove. His hands still bound, the *chèche* pushed back on his head, he was looking toward the window. At first Daru noticed only his huge lips, fat, smooth, almost Negroid; yet his nose was straight, his eyes were dark and full of fever. The *chèche* revealed an obstinate forehead and, under the weathered skin now rather discolored by the cold, the whole face had a restless and rebellious look that struck Daru when the Arab, turning his face toward him, looked him straight in the eyes. "Go into the other room," said the schoolmaster, "and I'll make you some mint tea." "Thanks," Bal-ducci said. "What a chore! How I long for retirement." And addressing his pris-oner in Arabic: "Come on, you." The Arab got up and, slowly, holding his bound wrists in front of him, went into the classroom.

---

gendarme: Police officer (French).

jellaba: A unisex coverall garment with a hood, typically worn in Morocco and other parts of Northern Africa.

With the tea, Daru brought a chair. But Balducci was already enthroned on the nearest pupil's desk and the Arab had squattered against the teacher's platform facing the stove, which stood between the desk and the window. When he held out the glass of tea to the prisoner, Daru hesitated at the sight of his bound hands. "He might perhaps be untied." "Sure," said Balducci. "That was for the trip." He started to get to his feet. But Daru, setting the glass on the floor, had knelt beside the Arab. Without saying anything, the Arab watched him with his feverish eyes. Once his hands were free, he rubbed his swollen wrists against each other, took the glass of tea, and sucked up the burning liquid in swift little sips.

"Good," said Daru. "And where are you headed?"

10   Balducci withdrew his mustache from the tea. "Here, son."

"Odd pupils! And you're spending the night?"

"No. I'm going back to El Ameur. And you will deliver this fellow to Tinguit. He is expected at police headquarters."

Balducci was looking at Daru with a friendly little smile.

"What's this story?" asked the schoolmaster. "Are you pulling my leg?"

15   "No, son. Those are the orders."

"The orders? I'm not . . ." Daru hesitated, not wanting to hurt the old Corsican. "I mean, that's not my job."

"What! What's the meaning of that? In wartime people do all kinds of jobs."

"Then I'll wait for the declaration of war!"

Balducci nodded.

20   "O.K. But the orders exist and they concern you too. Things are brewing, it appears. There is talk of a forthcoming revolt. We are mobilized, in a way."

Daru still had his obstinate look.

"Listen, son," Balducci said. "I like you and you must understand. There's only a dozen of us at El Ameur to patrol throughout the whole territory of a small department and I must get back in a hurry. I was told to hand this guy over to you and return without delay. He couldn't be kept there. His village was beginning to stir; they wanted to take him back. You must take him to Tinguit tomorrow before the day is over. Twenty kilometers shouldn't faze a husky fellow like you. After that, all will be over. You'll come back to your pupils and your comfortable life."

Behind the wall the horse could be heard snorting and pawing the earth. Daru was looking out the window. Decidedly, the weather was clearing and the light was increasing over the snowy plateau. When all the snow was melted, the sun would take over again and once more would burn the fields of stone. For days, still, the unchanging sky would shed its dry light on the solitary expanse where nothing had any connection with man.

"After all," he said, turning around toward Balducci, "what did he do?" And, before the gendarme had opened his mouth, he asked: "Does he speak French?"

25   "No, not a word. We had been looking for him for a month, but they were hiding him. He killed his cousin."

"Is he against us?"

"I don't think so. But you can never be sure."

"Why did he kill?"

"A family squabble, I think. One owed the other grain, it seems. It's not at all clear. In short, he killed his cousin with a billhook. You know, like a sheep, *kreezk!*"

Balducci made the gesture of drawing a blade across his throat and the Arab, his attention attracted, watched him with a sort of anxiety. Daru felt a sudden wrath against the man, against all men with their rotten spite, their tireless hates, their blood lust.

But the kettle was singing on the stove. He served Balducci more tea, hesitated, then served the Arab again, who, a second time, drank avidly. His raised arms made the jellaba fall open and the schoolmaster saw his thin, muscular chest.

"Thanks, kid," Balducci said. "And now, I'm off."

He got up and went toward the Arab, taking a small rope from his pocket.

"What are you doing?" Daru asked dryly.

Balducci, disconcerted, showed him the rope.

"Don't bother."

The old gendarme hesitated. "It's up to you. Of course, you are armed?"

"I have my shotgun."

"Where?"

"In the trunk."

"You ought to have it near your bed."

"Why? I have nothing to fear."

"You're crazy, son. If there's an uprising, no one is safe, we're all in the same boat."

"I'll defend myself. I'll have time to see them coming."

Balducci began to laugh, then suddenly the mustache covered the white teeth.

"You'll have time? O.K. That's just what I was saying. You have always been a little cracked. That's why I like you, my son was like that."

At the same time he took out his revolver and put it on the desk.

"Keep it; I don't need two weapons from here to El Ameur."

The revolver shone against the black paint of the table. When the gendarme turned toward him, the schoolmaster caught the smell of leather and horseflesh.

"Listen, Balducci," Daru said suddenly, "every bit of this disgusts me, and first of all your fellow here. But I won't hand him over. Fight, yes, if I have to. But not that."

The old gendarme stood in front of him and looked at him severely.

"You're being a fool," he said slowly. "I don't like it either. You don't get used to putting a rope on a man even after years of it, and you're even ashamed—yes, ashamed. But you can't let them have their way."

"I won't hand him over," Daru said again.

"It's an order, son, and I repeat it."

"That's right. Repeat to them what I've said to you: I won't hand him over."

Balducci made a visible effort to reflect. He looked at the Arab and at Daru. At last he decided.

"No, I won't tell them anything. If you want to drop us, go ahead; I'll not denounce you. I have an order to deliver the prisoner and I'm doing so. And now you'll just sign this paper for me."

"There's no need. I'll not deny that you left him with me."

"Don't be mean with me. I know you'll tell the truth. You're from hereabouts and you are a man. But you must sign, that's the rule."

60   Daru opened his drawer, took out a little square bottle of purple ink, the red wooden penholder with the "sergeant-major" pen he used for making models of penmanship, and signed. The gendarme carefully folded the paper and put it into his wallet. Then he moved toward the door.

"I'll see you off," Daru said.

"No," said Balducci. "There's no use being polite. You insulted me."

He looked at the Arab, motionless in the same spot, sniffed peevishly, and turned away toward the door. "Good-by, son," he said. The door shut behind him. Balducci appeared suddenly outside the window and then disappeared. His footsteps were muffled by the snow. The horse stirred on the other side of the wall and several chickens fluttered in fright. A moment later Balducci reappeared outside the window leading the horse by the bridle. He walked toward the little rise without turning around and disappeared from sight with the horse following him. A big stone could be heard bouncing down. Daru walked back toward the prisoner, who, without stirring, never took his eyes off him. "Wait," the schoolmaster said in Arabic and went toward the bedroom. As he was going through the door, he had a second thought, went to the desk, took the revolver, and stuck it in his pocket. Then, without looking back, he went into his room.

For some time he lay on his couch watching the sky gradually close over, listening to the silence. It was this silence that had seemed painful to him during the first days here, after the war. He had requested a post in the little town at the base of the foothills separating the upper plateaus from the desert. There, rocky walls, green and black to the north, pink and lavender to the south, marked the frontier of eternal summer. He had been named to a post farther north, on the plateau itself. In the beginning, the solitude and the silence had been hard for him on these wastelands peopled only by stones. Occasionally, furrows suggested cultivation, but they had been dug to uncover a certain kind of stone good for building. The only plowing here was to harvest rocks. Elsewhere a thin layer of soil accumulated in the hollows would be scraped out to enrich paltry village gardens. This is the way it was: bare rock covered three quarters of the region. Towns sprang up, flourished, then disappeared; men came by, loved one another or fought bitterly, then died. No one in this desert, neither he nor his guest, mattered. And yet, outside this desert neither of them, Daru knew, could have really lived.

65   When he got up, no noise came from the classroom. He was amazed at the unmixed joy he derived from the mere thought that the Arab might have fled and that he would be alone with no decision to make. But the prisoner was there. He had merely stretched out between the stove and the desk. With eyes open, he was staring at the ceiling. In that position, his thick lips were particularly noticeable,

giving him a pouting look. "Come," said Daru. The Arab got up and followed him. In the bedroom, the schoolmaster pointed to a chair near the table under the window. The Arab sat down without taking his eyes off Daru.

"Are you hungry?"

"Yes," the prisoner said.

Daru set the table for two. He took flour and oil, shaped a cake in a frying-pan, and lighted the little stove that functioned on bottled gas. While the cake was cooking, he went out to the shed to get cheese, eggs, dates, and condensed milk. When the cake was done he set it on the window still to cool, heated some condensed milk diluted with water, and heat up the eggs into an omelette. In one of his motions he knocked against the revolver stuck in his right pocket. He set the bowl down, went into the classroom, and put the revolver in his desk drawer. When he came back to the room, night was falling. He put on the light and served the Arab. "Eat," he said. The Arab took a piece of the cake, lifted it eagerly to his mouth, and stopped short.

"And you!" he asked.

"After you. I'll eat too." 70

The thick lips opened slightly. The Arab hesitated, then bit into the cake determinedly.

The meal over, the Arab looked at the schoolmaster. "Are you the judge?"

"No, I'm simply keeping you until tomorrow."

"Why do you eat with me?"

"I'm hungry." 75

The Arab fell silent. Daru got up and went out. He brought back a folding bed from the shed, set it up between the table and the stove, perpendicular to his own bed. From a large suitcase which, upright in a corner, served as a shelf for papers, he took two blankets and arranged them on the camp bed. Then he stopped, felt useless, and sat down on his bed. There was nothing more to do or to get ready. He had to look at this man. He looked at him, therefore, trying to imagine his face bursting with rage. He couldn't do so. He could see nothing but the dark yet shining eyes and the animal mouth.

"Why did you kill him?" he asked in a voice whose hostile tone surprised him.

The Arab looked away.

"He ran away. I ran after him."

He raised his eyes to Daru again and they were full of a sort of woeful interro- 80 gation. "Now what will they do to me?"

"Are you afraid?"

He stiffened, turning his eyes away.

"Are you sorry?"

The Arab started at him openmouthed. Obviously he did not understand. Daru's annoyance was growing. At the same time he felt awkward and self-conscious with his big body wedged between the two beds.

"Lie down there," he said impatiently. "That's your bed." 85

The Arab didn't move. He called to Daru:

"Tell me!"

The schoolmaster looked at him.

"Is the gendarme coming back tomorrow?"

"I don't know."

90   "Are you coming with us?"

"I don't know. Why?"

The prisoner got up and stretched out on top of the blankets, his feet toward the window. The light from the electric bulb shone straight into his eyes and he closed them at once.

"Why?" Daru repeated, standing beside the bed.

95   The Arab opened his eyes under the blinding light and looked at him, trying not to blink.

"Come with us," he said.

In the middle of the night, Daru was still not asleep. He had gone to bed after undressing completely; he generally slept naked. But when he suddenly realized that he had nothing on, he hesitated. He felt vulnerable and the temptation came to him to put his clothes back on. Then he shrugged his shoulders; after all, he wasn't a child and, if need be, he could break his adversary in two. From his bed he could observe him, lying on his back, still motionless with his eyes closed under the harsh light. When Daru turned out the light, the darkness seemed to coagulate all of a sudden. Little by little, the night came back to life in the window where the starless sky was stirring gently. The schoolmaster soon made out the body lying at his feet. The Arab still did not move, but his eyes seemed open. A faint wind was prowling around the schoolhouse. Perhaps it would drive away the clouds and the sun would reappear.

During the night the wind increased. The hens fluttered a little and then were silent. The Arab turned over on his side with his back to Daru, who thought he heard him moan. Then he listened for his guest's breathing, become heavier and more regular. He listened to that breath so close to him and mused without being able to go to sleep. In this room where he had been sleeping alone for a year, this presence bothered him. But it bothered him also by imposing on him a sort of brotherhood he knew well but refused to accept in the present circumstances. Men who share the same rooms, soldiers or prisoners, develop a strange alliance as if, having cast off their armor with their clothing, they fraternized every evening, over and above their differences, in the ancient community of dream and fatigue. But Daru shook himself; he didn't like such musings, and it was essential to sleep.

A little later, however, when the Arab stirred slightly, the schoolmaster was still not asleep. When the prisoner made a second move, he stiffened, on the alert. The Arab was lifting himself slowly on his arms with almost the motion of a sleepwalker. Seated upright in bed, he waited motionless without turning his head toward Daru, as if he were listening attentively. Daru did not stir; it had just occurred to him that the revolver was still in the drawer of his desk. It was better to act at once. Yet he continued to observe the prisoner, who, with the same slithery motion, put his feet on the ground, waited again, then began to stand up slowly. Daru was about to call out to him when the Arab began to walk, in a quite natural but extraordinarily silent way. He was heading toward the door at the end of the room that opened into the shed. He lifted the latch with precaution and went out, pushing the door behind him but without shutting it. Daru had not stirred. "He is running away," he merely thought. "Good riddance!" Yet he listened attentively. The hens were not fluttering; the guest must be on the plateau. A faint sound of water reached him, and he didn't know what it was until the Arab again stood framed in the doorway, closed the door carefully, and came back to bed without a sound. Then Daru turned his back on him and fell asleep. Still later he seemed, from the depths of his sleep, to hear furtive steps around the schoolhouse. "I'm dreaming! I'm dreaming!" he repeated to himself. And he went on sleeping.

When he awoke, the sky was clear; the loose window let in a cold, pure air. 100 The Arab was asleep, hunched up under the blankets now, his mouth open, utterly relaxed. But when Daru shook him, he started dreadfully, starting at Daru with wild eyes as if he had never seen him and such a frightened expression that the schoolmaster stepped back. "Don't be afraid. It's me. You must eat." The Arab nodded his head and said yes. Calm had returned to his face, but his expression was vacant and listless.

The coffee was ready. They drank it seated together on the folding bed as they munched their pieces of the cake. Then Daru led the Arab under the shed and showed him the faucet where he washed. He went back into the room, folded the blankets and the bed, made his own bed and put the room in order. Then he went through the classroom and out onto the terrace. The sun was already rising in the blue sky; a soft, bright light was bathing the deserted plateau. On the ridge the snow was melting in spots. The stones were about to reappear. Crouched on the edge of the plateau, the schoolmaster looked at the deserted expanse. He thought of Balducci. He had hurt him, for he had sent him off in a way as if he didn't want to be associated with him. He could still hear the gendarme's farewell and, without knowing why, he felt strangely empty and vulnerable. At that moment, from the other side of the schoolhouse, the prisoner coughed. Daru listened to him almost despite himself and then, furious, threw a pebble that whistled through the air before sinking into the snow. That man's stupid crime revolted him, but to hand him over was contrary to honor. Merely thinking of it made him smart with humiliation. And he cursed at one and the same time his own people who had sent him this Arab and the Arab too who had dared to kill and not managed to get away. Daru got up, walked in a circle on the terrace, waited motionless, and then went back into the schoolhouse.

The Arab, leaning over the cement floor of the shed, was washing his teeth with two fingers. Daru looked at him and said: "Come." He went back into the room ahead of the prisoner. He slipped a hunting-jacket on over his sweater and put on walking-shoes. Standing, he waited until the Arab had put on his *chèche* and sandals. They went into the classroom and the schoolmaster pointed to the exit, saying: "Go ahead." The fellow didn't budge. "I'm coming," said Daru. The Arab went out. Daru went back into the room and made a package of pieces of rusk, dates, and sugar. In the classroom, before going out, he hesitated a second in front of his desk, then crossed the threshold and locked the door. "That's the way," he said. He started toward the east, followed by the prisoner. But, a short distance from the schoolhouse, he thought he heard a slight sound behind them. He retraced his steps and examined the surrounding of the house: there was no one there. The Arab watched him without seeming to understand. "Come on," said Daru.

They walked for an hour and rested beside a sharp peak of limestone. The snow was melting faster and faster and faster and the sun was drinking up the puddles at once, rapidly cleaning the plateau, which gradually dried and vibrated like the air itself. When they resumed walking, the ground rang under their feet. From time to time a bird rent the space in front of them with a joyful cry. Daru breathed in deeply the fresh morning light. He felt a sort of rapture before the vast familiar expanse, now almost entirely yellow under its dome of blue sky. They walked an hour more, descending toward the south. They reached a level height made up of crumbly rocks. From there on, the plateau sloped down, eastward, toward a low plain where there were a few spindly trees and, to the south, toward outcroppings of rock that gave the landscape a chaotic look.

Daru surveyed the two directions. There was nothing but the sky on the horizon. Not a man could be seen. He turned toward the Arab, who was looking at him blankly. Daru held out the package to him. "Take it," he said. "There are dates, bread, and sugar. You can hold out for two days. Here are a thousand francs too." The Arab took the package and the money but kept his full hands at chest level as if he didn't know what to do with what was being given him. "Now look," the schoolmaster said as he pointed in the direction of the east, "there's the way to Tinguit. You have a two-hour walk. At Tinguit you'll find the administration and the police. They are expecting you." The Arab looked toward the east, still holding the package and the money against his chest. Daru took his elbow and turned him rather roughly toward the south. At the foot of the height on which they stood could be seen a faint path. "That's the trail across the plateau. In a day's walk from here you'll find pasturelands and the first nomads. They'll take you in and shelter you according to their law." The Arab had now turned toward Daru and a sort of panic was visible in his expression. "Listen," he said. Daru shook his head: "No, be quiet. Now I'm leaving you." He turned his back on him, took two long steps in the direction of the school, looked hesitantly at the motionless Arab, and started off again. For a few minutes he heard nothing but his own step resounding on the cold ground and did not turn his heard. A moment later, however, he turned around. The Arab was still there on the edge of the hill, his arms hanging now, and he was looking at the schoolmaster. Daru felt something rise in his throat. But he swore with impatience, waved vaguely, and started off again. He had already gone some distance when he again stopped and looked. There was no longer anyone on the hill.

105   Daru hesitated. The sun was now rather high in the sky and was beginning to beat down on his head. The schoolmaster retraced his steps, at first somewhat uncertainly, then with decision. When he reached the little hill, he was batched in sweat. He climbed it as fast as he could and stopped, out of breath, at the top. The rock-fields to the south stood out sharply against the blue sky, but on the plain to

the east a steamy heat was already rising. And in that slight haze, Daru, with heavy heart, made out the Arab walking slowly on the road to prison.

A little later, standing before the window of the classroom, the schoolmaster was watching the clear light bathing the whole surface of the plateau, but he hardly saw it. Behind him on the blackboard, among the winding French rivers, sprawled the clumsily chalked-up words he had just read: "You handed over our brother. You will pay for this." Daru looked at the sky, the plateau, and, beyond, the invisible lands stretching all the way to the sea. In this vast landscape he had loved so much, he was alone.

◇ ◇ ◇

JOHN CHEEVER (1912–1982)

The Swimmer (1964)

It was one of those midsummer Sundays when everyone sits around saying: "I *drank* too much last night." You might have heard it whispered by the parishioners leaving church, heard it from the lips of the priest himself, struggling with his cassock° in the *vestiarium*, heard it from the golf links and the tennis courts, heard it from the wildlife preserve where the leader of the Audubon group was suffering from a terrible hangover. "I *drank* too much," said Donald Westerhazy. "We all *drank* too much," said Lucinda Merrill. "It must have been the wine," said Helen Westerhazy. "I *drank* too much of that claret."

This was at the edge of the Westerhazys' pool. The pool, fed by an artesian well with a high iron content, was a pale shade of green. It was a fine day. In the west there was a massive stand of cumulus cloud so like a city seen from a distance — from the bow of an approaching ship — that it might have had a name. Lisbon. Hackensack. The sun was hot. Neddy Merrill sat by the green water, one hand in it, one around a glass of gin. He was a slender man — he seemed to have the especial slenderness of youth — and while he was far from young he had slid down his banister that morning and given the bronze backside of Aphrodite on the hall table a smack, as he jogged toward the smell of coffee in his dining room. The might have been compared to a summer's day, particularly the last hours of one, and while he lacked a tennis racket or a sail bag the impression was definitely one of youth, sport, and clement weather. He had been swimming and now he was breathing deeply, stertorously as if he could gulp into his lungs the components of that moment, the heat of the sun, the intenseness of his pleasure. It all seemed to flow into his chest. His own house stood in Bullet Park, eight miles to the south, where his four beautiful daughters would have had their lunch and might be playing tennis. Then it occurred to him that by taking a dogleg to the southwest he could reach his home by water.

---

cassock: A full-length robe, usually black, worn by priests, their assistants, and singers in church choirs.

His life was not confining and the delight he took in this observation could not be explained by its suggestion of escape. He seemed to see, with a cartographer's eye, that string of swimming pools, that quasi-subterranean stream that curved across the county. He had made a discovery, a contribution to modern geography; he would name the stream Lucinda after his wife. He was not a practical joker nor was he a fool but he was determinedly original and had a vague and modest idea of himself as a legendary figure. The day was beautiful and it seemed to him that a long swim might enlarge and celebrate its beauty.

He took off a sweater that was hung over his shoulders and dove in. He had an inexplicable contempt for men who did not hurl themselves into pools. He swam a choppy crawl, breathing either with every stroke or every fourth stroke and counting somewhere well in the back of his mind the one-two one-two of a flutter kick. It was not a serviceable stroke for long distances but the domestication of swimming had saddled the sport with some customs and his in part of the world a crawl was customary. To be embraced and sustained by the light green water was less a pleasure, it seemed, than the resumption of a natural condition, and he would have liked to swim without trunks, but this was not possible, considering his project. He hoisted himself up on the far curb — he never used the ladder — and started across the lawn. When Lucinda asked where he was going he was going he said to swim home.

5   The only maps and charts he had to go by were remembered or imaginary but these were clear enough. First there were the Grahams, the Hammers, the Lears, the Howlands, and the Crosscups. He would cross Ditmar Street to the Bunkers and come, after a short portage, to the Levys, the Welchers, and the public pool in Lancaster. Then there were the Hallorans, the Sachses, the Biswangers, Shirley Adams, the Gilmartins, and the Clydes. The day was lovely, and that he lived in a world so generously supplied with water seemed like a clemency, a beneficence. His heart was high and he ran across the grass. Making his way home by an uncommon route gave him the feeling that he was a pilgrim, an explorer, a man with a destiny, and he knew that he would find friends all along the way; friends would line the banks of the Lucinda River.

He went through a hedge that separated the Westerhazys' land from the Grahams', walked under some flowering apple trees, passed the shed that housed their pump and filter, and came out at the Grahams' pool. "Why, Neddy," Mrs. Graham said, "what a marvelous surprise. I've been trying to get you on the phone all morning. Here, let me get you a drink." He saw then, like any explorer, that the hospitable customs and traditions of the natives would have to be handled with diplomacy if he was ever going to reach his destination. He did not want to mystify or seem rude to the Grahams nor did he have the time to linger there. He swam the length of their pool and joined them in the sun and was rescued, a few minutes later, by the arrival of two carloads of friends from Connecticut. During the uproarious reunions he was able to slip away. He went down by the front of the Grahams' house, stepped over a thorny hedge, and crossed a vacant lot to the Hammers'. Mrs. Hammer, looking up from her roses, saw him swim by although she wasn't quite sure who it was. The Lears heard him splashing past the open windows of their living room. The Howlands and the Crosscups were away. After leaving the Howlands' he crossed Ditmar Street and started for the Bunkers', where he could hear, even at that distance, the noise of a party.

The water refracted the sound of voices and laughter and seemed to suspend it in midair. The Bunkers' pool was on a rise and he climbed some stairs to a terrace where twenty-five or thirty men and women were drinking. The only person in the water was Rusty Towers, who floated there on a rubber raft. Oh how bonny and lush were the banks of the Lucinda River! Prosperous men and women gathered by the sapphire-colored waters while caterer's men in white coats passed them cold gin. Overhead a red de Haviland trainer° was circling around and around and around in the sky with something like the glee of a child in a swing. Ned felt a passing affection for the scene, a tenderness for the gathering, as if it was something he might touch. In the distance he heard thunder. As soon as Enid Bunker saw him she began to scream: "Oh look who's here! What a marvelous surprise! When Lucinda said that you couldn't come I thought I'd *die*." She made her way to him through the crowd, and when they had finished kissing she led him to the bar, a progress that was slowed by the fact that he stopped to kiss eight or ten other women and shake the hands of as many men. A smiling bartender he had seen at a hundred parties gave him a gin and tonic and he stood by the bar for a moment, anxious not to get stuck in any conversation that would delay his voyage. When he seemed about to be surrounded he dove in and swam close to the side to avoid colliding with Rusty's raft. At the far end of the pool he bypassed the Tomlinsons with a broad smile and jogged up the garden path. The gravel cut his feet but this was the only unpleasantness. The party was confined to the pool, and as he went toward the house he heard the brilliant, watery sound of voices fade, heard the noise of a radio from the Bunkers' kitchen, where someone was listening to a ballgame. Sunday afternoon. He made his way through the parked cars and down the grassy border of their driveway to Alewives' Lane. He did not want to be seen on the road in his bathing trunks but there was no traffic and he made the short distance to the Levys' driveway, marked with a private property sign and a green tube for the *New York Times*. All the doors and windows of the big house were open but there were no signs of life; not even a dog barked. He went around the side of the house to the pool and saw that the Levys had only recently left. Glasses and bottles and dishes of nuts were on a table at the deep end, where there was a bathhouse or gazebo, hung with Japanese lanterns. After swimming the pool he got himself a glass and poured a drink. It was his fourth or fifth drink and he had swum nearly half the length of the Lucinda River. He felt tired, clean, and pleased at that moment to be alone; pleased with everything.

It would storm. The stand of cumulus cloud — that city — had risen and darkened, and while he sat there he heard the percussiveness of thunder again. The de Haviland trainer was still circling overhead and it seemed to Ned that he could almost hear the pilot laugh with pleasure in the afternoon; but when there was another peal of thunder he took off for home. A train whistle blew and he wondered what time it had gotten to be. Four? Five? He thought of the provincial

---

de Haviland trainer: A military plane used to train pilots.

station at that hour, where a waiter, his tuxedo concealed by a raincoat, a dwarf with some flowers wrapped in newspaper, and a woman who had been crying would be waiting for the local. It was suddenly growing dark; it was that moment when the pin-headed birds seem to organize their song into some acute and knowledgeable recognition of the storm's approach. Then there was a fine noise of rushing water from the crown of an oak at his back, as if a spigot there had been turned. Then the noise of fountains came from the crowns of all the tall trees. Why did he love storms, what was the meaning of his excitement when the door sprang open and the rain wind fled rudely up the stairs, why had the simple task of shutting the windows of an old house seemed fitting and urgent, why did the first watery notes of a storm wind have for him the unmistakable sound of good news, cheer, glad tidings? Then there was an explosion, a smell of cordite, and rain lashed the Japanese lanterns that Mrs. Levy had bought in Kyoto the year before last, or was it the year before that?

He stayed in the Levys' gazebo until the storm had passed. The rain had cooled the air and he shivered. The force of the wind had stripped a maple of its red and yellow leaves and scattered them over the grass and the water. Since it was mid-summer the tree must be blighted, and yet he felt a peculiar sadness at this sign of autumn. He braced his shoulders, emptied his glass, and started for the Welchers' pool. This meant crossing the Lindleys' riding ring and he was surprised to find it overgrown with grass and all the jumps dismantled. He wondered if the Lindleys had sold their horses or gone away for the summer and put them out to board. He seemed to remember having heard something about the Lindleys and their horses but the memory was unclear. On he went, barefoot through the wet grass, to the Welchers', where he found their pool was dry.

10   This breach in his chain of water disappointed him absurdly, and he felt like some explorer who seeks a torrential headwater and finds a dead stream. He was disappointed and mystified. It was common enough to go away for the summer but no one ever drained his pool. The Welchers had definitely gone away. The pool furniture was folded, stacked, and covered with a tarpaulin. The bathhouse was locked. All the windows of the house were shut, and when he went around to the driveway in front he saw a for-sale sign nailed to a tree. When had he last heard from the Welchers — when, that is, had he and Lucinda last regretted an invitation to dine with them. It seemed only a week or so ago. Was his memory failing or had he so disciplined it in the repression of unpleasant facts that he had damaged his sense of the truth? Then in the distance he heard the sound of a tennis game. This cheered him, cleared away all his apprehensions and let him regard the overcast sky and the cold air with indifference. This was the day that Neddy Merrill swam across the county. That was the day! He started off then for his most difficult portage.

Had you gone for a Sunday afternoon ride that day you might have seen him, close to naked, standing on the shoulders of route 424, waiting for a chance to cross. You might have wondered if he was the victim of foul play, had his car broken down, or was he merely a fool. Standing barefoot in the deposits of the highway — beer cans, rags, and blowout patches — exposed to all kinds of ridicule, he

seemed pitiful. He had known when he started that this was a part of his journey —
it had been on his maps — but confronted with the lines of traffic, worming
through the summery light, he found himself unprepared. He was laughed at,
jeered at, a beer can was thrown at him, and he had no dignity or humor to bring
to the situation. He could have gone back, back to the Westerhazys', where
Lucinda would still be sitting in the sun. He had signed nothing, vowed nothing,
pledged nothing not even to himself. Why, believing as he did, that all human ob-
duracy was susceptible to common sense, was he unable to turn back? Why was
he determined to complete his journey even if it meant putting his life in danger?
At what point had this prank, this joke, this piece of horseplay become serious?
He could not go back, he could not even recall with any clearness the green water at the Westerhazys', the sense of inhaling the day's components, the friendly
and relaxed voices saying that they had *drunk* too much. In the space of an hour,
more or less, he had covered a distance that made his return impossible.

An old man, tooling down the highway at fifteen miles an hour, let him get to
the middle of the road, where there was a grass divider. Here he was exposed to
the ridicule of the northbound traffic, but after ten or fifteen minutes he was able
to cross. From here he had only a short walk to the Recreation Center at the edge
of the Village of Lancaster, where there were some handball courts and a public
pool.

The effect of the water on voices, the illusion of brilliance and suspense, was
the same here as it had been at the Bunkers' but the sounds here were louder,
harsher, and more shrill, and as soon as he entered the crowded enclosure he was
confronted with regimentation. "ALL SWIMMERS MUST TAKE A SHOWER BEFORE
USING THE POOL. ALL SWIMMERS MUST USE THE FOOTBATH. ALL SWIMMERS
MUST WEAR THEIR IDENTIFICATION DISKS." He took a shower, washed his feet in
a cloudy and bitter solution and made his way to the edge of the water. It stank of
chlorine and looked to him like a sink. A pair of lifeguards in a pair of towers blew
police whistles at what seemed to be regular intervals and abused the swimmers
through a public address system. Neddy remembered the sapphire water at the
Bunkers' with longing and thought that he might contaminate himself — damage his own prosperousness and charm — by swimming in this murk, but he reminded himself that he was an explorer, a pilgrim, and that this was merely a stagnant bend in the Lucinda River. He dove, scowling with distaste, into the
chlorine and had to swim with his head above water to avoid collisions, but even
so he was bumped into, splashed and jostled. When he got to the shallow end
both lifeguards were shouting at him: "Hey, you, you without the identification
disk, get outa the water." He did, but they had no way of pursuing him and he
went through the reek of suntan oil and chlorine out through the hurricane fence
and passed the handball courts. By crossing the road he entered the wooded part
of the Halloran estate. The woods were not cleared and the footing was treacherous and difficult until he reached the lawn and the clipped beech hedge that encircled their pool.

The Hallorans were friends, an elderly couple of enormous wealth who
seemed to bask in the suspicion that they might be Communists. They were zeal-
ous reformers but they were not Communists, and yet when they were accused, as

they sometimes were, of subversion, it seemed to gratify and excite them. Their beech hedge was yellow and he guessed this had been blighted like the Levys' maple. He called hullo, hullo, to warn the Hallorans of his approach, to palliate his invasion of their privacy. The Hallorans, for reasons that had never been explained to him, did not wear bathing suits. No explanations were in order, really. Their nakedness was a detail in their uncompromising zeal for reform and he stepped politely out of his trunks before he went through the opening in the hedge.

15   Mrs. Halloran, a stout woman with white hair and a serene face, was reading the *Times*. Mr. Halloran was taking beech leaves out of the water with a scoop. They seemed not surprised or displeased to see him. Their pool was perhaps the oldest in the county, a fieldstone rectangle, fed by a brook. It had no filter or pump and its waters were the opaque gold of the stream.

"I'm swimming across the county," Ned said.

"Why, I didn't know one could," exclaimed Mrs. Halloran.

"Well, I've made it from the Westerhazys'," Ned said. "That must be about four miles."

He left his trunks at the deep end, walked to the shallow end, and swam this stretch. As he was pulling himself out of the water he heard Mrs. Halloran say: "We've been *terribly* sorry to hear about all your misfortunes, Neddy."

20   "My misfortunes?" Ned asked. "I don't know what you mean."

"Why, we heard that you'd sold the house and that your poor children . . ."

"I don't recall having sold the house," Ned said, "and the girls are at home."

"Yes." Mrs. Halloran sighed. "Yes . . ." Her voice filled the air with an unseasonable melancholy and Ned spoke briskly. "Thank you for the swim."

"Well, have a nice trip," said Mrs. Halloran.

25   Beyond the hedge he pulled on his trunks and fastened them. They were loose and he wondered if, during the space of an afternoon, he could have lost some weight. He was cold and he was tired and the naked Hallorans and their dark water had depressed him. The swim was too much for his strength but how could he have guessed this, sliding down the banister that morning and sitting in the Westerhazys' sun? His arms were lame. His legs felt rubbery and ached at the joints. The worst of it was the cold in his bones and the feeling that he might never be warm again. Leaves were falling down around him and he smelled woodsmoke on the wind. Who would be burning wood at this time of year?

He needed a drink. Whiskey would warm him, pick him up, carry him through the last of his journey, refresh his feeling that it was original and valorous to swim across the county. Channel swimmers took brandy. He needed a stimulant. He crossed the lawn in front of the Hallorans' house and went down a little path to where they had built a house for their only daughter Helen and her husband Eric Sachs. The Sachses' pool was small and he found Helen and her husband there.

"Oh, *Neddy*," Helen said. "Did you lunch at Mother's?"

"Not *really*," Ned said. "I *did* stop to see your parents." This seemed to be explanation enough. "I'm terribly sorry to break in on you like this but I've taken a chill and I wonder if you'd give me a drink."

"Why, I'd *love* to," Helen said, "but there hasn't been anything in this house to drink since Eric's operation. That was three years ago."

Was he losing his memory, had his gift for concealing painful facts let him for- 30
get that he had sold his house, that his children were in trouble, and that his friend had been ill? His eyes slipped from Eric's face to his abdomen, where he saw three pale, sutured scars, two of them at least a foot long. Gone was his navel, and what, Neddy thought, would the roving hand, bed-checking one's gifts at 3 A.M. make of a belly with no navel, no link to birth, this breach in the succession?

"I'm sure you can get a drink at the Biswangers'," Helen said. "They're having an enormous do. You can hear it from here. Listen!"

She raised her head and from across the road, the lawns, the gardens, the woods, the fields, he heard again the brilliant noise of voices over water. "Well, I'll get wet," he said, still feeling that he had no freedom of choice about his means of travel. He dove into the Sachses' cold water and, gasping, close to drowning, made his way from one end of the pool to the other. "Lucinda and I want *terribly* to see you," he said over his shoulder, his face set toward the Biswangers'. "We're sorry it's been so long and we'll call you *very* soon."

He crossed some fields to the Biswangers' and the sounds of revelry there. They would be honored to give him a drink, they would be happy to give him a drink, they would in fact be lucky to give him a drink. The Biswangers invited him and Lucinda for dinner four times a year, six weeks in advance. They were always rebuffed and yet they continued to send out their invitations, unwilling to comprehend the rigid and undemocratic realities of their society. They were the sort of people who discussed the price of things at cocktails, exchanged market tips during dinner, and after dinner told dirty stories to mixed company. They did not belong to Neddy's set — they were not even on Lucinda's Christmas card list. He went toward their pool with feelings of indifference, charity, and some unease, since it seemed to be getting dark and these were the longest days of the year. The party when he joined it was noisy and large. Grace Biswanger was the kind of hostess who asked the optometrist, the veterinarian, the real-estate dealer and the dentist. No one was swimming and the twilight, reflected on the water of the pool, had a wintry gleam. There was a bar and he started for this. When Grace Biswanger saw him she came toward him, not affectionately as he had every right to expect, but bellicosely.

"Why, this party has everything," she said loudly, "including a gate crasher."

She could not deal him a social blow — there was no question about this and 35
he did not flinch. "As a gate crasher," he asked politely, "do I rate a drink?"

"Suit yourself," she said. "You don't seem to pay much attention to invitations."

She turned her back on him and joined some guests, and he went to the bar and ordered a whiskey. The bartender served him but he served him rudely. His was a world in which the caterer's men kept the social score, and to be rebuffed by a part-time barkeep meant that he had suffered some loss of social esteem. Or perhaps the man was new and uninformed. Then he heard Grace at his back say: "They went for broke overnight — nothing but income — and he showed up drunk one Sunday and asked us to loan him five thousand dollars. . . ." She was always talking about money. It was worse than eating your peas off a knife. He dove into the pool, swam its length and went away.

The next pool on his list, the last but two, belonged to his old mistress, Shirley Adams. If he had suffered any injuries at the Biswangers' they would be cured here. Love—sexual roughhouse in fact—was the supreme elixir, the painkiller, the brightly colored pill that would put the spring back into his step, the joy of life in his heart. They had had an affair last week, last month, last year. He couldn't remember. It was he who had broken it off, his was the upper hand, and he stepped through the gate of the wall that surrounded her pool with nothing so considered as self-confidence. It seemed in a way to be his pool as the lover, particularly the illicit lover, enjoys the possessions of his mistress with an authority unknown to holy matrimony. She was there, her hair the color of brass, but her figure, at the edge of the lighted, cerulean water, excited in him no profound memories. It had been, he thought, a lighthearted affair, although she had wept when he broke it off. She seemed confused to see him and he wondered if she was still wounded. Would she, God forbid, weep again?

"What do you want?" she asked.

"I'm swimming across the county."

"Good Christ. Will you ever grow up?"

40   "What's the matter?"

"If you've come here for money," she said, "I won't give you another cent."

"You could give me a drink."

"I could but I won't. I'm not alone."

"Well, I'm on my way."

45   He dove in and swam the pool, but when he tried to haul himself up onto the curb he found that the strength in his arms and his shoulders had gone, and he paddled to the ladder and climbed out. Looking over his shoulder he saw, in the lighted bathhouse, a young man. Going out onto the dark lawn he smelled chrysanthemums or marigolds — some stubborn autumnal fragrance — on the night air, strong as gas. Looking overhead he saw that the stars had come out, but why should he seem to see Andromeda, Cepheus, and Cassiopeia?° What had become of the constellations of midsummer? He began to cry.

It was probably the first time in his adult life that he had ever cried, certainly the first time in his life that he had ever felt so miserable, cold, tired, and bewildered. He could not understand the rudeness of the caterer's barkeep or the rudeness of a mistress who had come to him on her knees and showered his trousers with tears. He had swum too long, he had been immersed too long, and his nose and his throat were sore from the water. What he needed then was a drink, some company, and some clean dry clothes, and while he could have cut directly across the road to his home he went on to the Gilmartins' pool. Here, for the first time in his life, he did not dive but went down the steps into the icy water and swam a hobbled side stroke that he might have learned as a youth. He staggered with fatigue on his way to the Clydes' and paddled the length of their pool, stopping

---

Andromeda, Cepheus, and Cassiopeia: Constellations of stars.

again and again with his hand on the curb to rest. He climbed up the ladder and wondered if he had the strength to get home. He had done what he wanted, he had swum the county, but he was so stupefied with exhaustion that his triumph seemed vague. Stooped, holding onto the gateposts for support, he turned up the driveway of his house.

The place was dark. Was it so late that they had all gone to bed? Had Lucinda stayed at the Westerhazys' for supper? Had the girls joined her there or gone some-place else? Hadn't they agreed, as they usually did on Sunday, to regret all their invitations and stay at home? He tried the garage doors to see what cars were in but the doors were locked and rust came off the handles onto his hands. Going toward the house, he saw that the force of the thunderstorm had knocked one of the rain gutters loose. It hung down over the front door like an umbrella rib, but it could be fixed in the morning. The house was locked, and he thought that the stupid cook or the stupid maid must have locked the place up until he remembered that it had been some time since they had employed a maid or a cook. He shouted, pounded on the door, tried to force it with his shoulder, and then, looking in at the windows, saw that the place was empty.

◇ ◇ ◇

ANTON CHEKHOV (1860–1904)

The Lady with the Pet Dog (1899)

Translated by Avrahm Yarmolinsky

I

A new person, it was said, had appeared on the esplanade: a lady with a pet dog. Dmitry Dmitrich Gurov, who had spent a fortnight at Yalta and had got used to the place, had also begun to take an interest in new arrivals. As he sat in Vernet's confectionery shop, he saw, walking on the esplanade, a fair-haired young woman of medium height, wearing a beret; a white Pomeranian was trotting behind her.

And afterwards he met her in the public garden and in the square several times a day. She walked alone, always wearing the same beret and always with the white dog; no one knew who she was and everyone called her simply "the lady with the pet dog."

"If she is here alone without husband or friends," Gurov reflected, "it wouldn't be a bad thing to make her acquaintance."

He was under forty, but he already had a daughter twelve years old, and two sons at school. They had found a wife for him when he was very young, a student in his second year, and by now she seemed half as old again as he. She was a tall, erect woman with dark eyebrows, stately and dignified and, as she said of herself, intellectual. She read a great deal, used simplified spelling in her letters, called her husband, nor Dmitry, but Dimitry, while he privately considered her of limited intelligence, narrow-minded, dowdy, was afraid of her, and did not like to be at home. He had begun being unfaithful to her long ago—had been unfaithful to her often and, probably for that reason, almost always spoke ill of women, and when they were talked of in his presence used to call them "the inferior race."

5   It seemed to him that he had been sufficiently tutored by bitter experience to call them what he pleased, and yet he could not have lived without "the inferior race" for two days together. In the company of men he was bored and ill at ease, he was chilly and uncommunicative with them; but when he was among women he felt free, and knew what to speak to them about and how to comport himself; and even to be silent with them was no strain on him. In his appearance, in his character, in his whole makeup there was something attractive and elusive that disposed women in his favor and allured them. He knew that, and some force seemed to draw him to them, too.

Oft-repeated and really bitter experience had taught him long ago that with decent people — particularly Moscow people — who are irresolute and slow to move, every affair which at first seems a light and charming adventure inevitably grows into a whole problem of extreme complexity, and in the end a painful situation is created. But at every new meeting with an interesting woman this lesson of experience seemed to slip from his memory, and he was eager for life, and everything seemed so simple and diverting.

One evening while he was dining in the public garden the lady in the beret walked up without haste to take the next table. Her expression, her gait, her dress, and the way she did her hair told him that she belonged to the upper class, that she was married, that she was in Yalta for the first time and alone, and that she was bored there. The stories told of the immorality in Yalta are to a great extent untrue; he despised them, and knew that such stories were made up for the most part by persons who would have been glad to sin themselves if they had had the chance; but when the lady sat down at the next table three paces from him, he recalled these stories of easy conquests, of trips to the mountains, and the tempting thought of swift, fleeting liaison, a romance with an unknown woman of whose very name he was ignorant suddenly took hold of him.

He beckoned invitingly to the Pomeranian, and when the dog approached him, shook his finger at it. The Pomeranian growled; Gurov threatened it again.

10   The lady glanced at him and at once dropped her eyes.

"He doesn't bite," she said and blushed.

"May I give him a bone?" he asked; and when she nodded he inquired affably, "Have you been in Yalta long?"

"About five days."

"And I am dragging out the second week here."

15   There was a short silence.

"Time passes quickly, and yet it is so dull here!" she said, not looking at him.

"It's only the fashion to say it's dull here. A provincial will live in Belyov or Zhizdra and not be bored, but when he comes here it's 'Oh, the dullness! Oh, the dust!' One would think he came from Granada."

She laughed. Then both continued eating in silence, like strangers, but after dinner they walked together and there sprang up between them the light banter of people who are free and contented, to whom it does not matter where they go or what they talk about. They walked and talked of the strange light on the sea: the water was a soft, warm, lilac color, and there was a golden band of moonlight upon it. They talked of how sultry it was after a hot day. Gurov told her that he was a native of Moscow, that he had studied languages and literature at the university, but had a post in a bank; that at one time he had trained to become an opera singer but had given it up, that he owned two houses in Moscow. And he learned from her that she had grown up in Petersburg, but had lived in S —— since her marriage two years previously, that she was going to stay in Yalta for about another month, and that her husband, who needed a rest, too, might perhaps come to fetch her. She was not certain whether her husband was a member of a Government Board or served on a Zemstvo Council,° and this amused her. And Gurov learned too that her name was Anna Sergeyevna.

Afterwards in his room at the hotel he thought about her — and was certain that he would meet her the next day. It was bound to happen. Getting into bed he recalled that she had been a schoolgirl only recently, doing lessons like his own daughter; he thought how much timidity and angularity there was still in her laugh and her manner of talking with a stranger. It must have been the first time in her life that she was alone in a setting in which she was followed, looked at, and spoken to for one secret purpose alone, which she could hardly fail to guess. He thought of her slim, delicate throat, her lovely gray eyes.

"There's something pathetic about her, though," he thought, and dropped off.

II

A week had passed since they had struck up an acquaintance. It was a holiday. It   20
was close indoors, while in the street the wind whirled the dust about and blew people's hats off. One was thirsty all day, and Gurov often went into the restaurant and offered Anna Sergeyevna a soft drink or ice cream. One did not know what to do with oneself.

In the evening when the wind had abated they went out on the pier to watch the steamer come in. There were a great many people walking about the dock; they had come to welcome someone and they were carrying bunches of flowers. And two peculiarities of a festive Yalta crowd stood out: the elderly ladies were dressed like young ones and there were many generals.

Owing to the choppy sea, the steamer arrived late, after sunset, and it was a long time tacking about before it put in at the pier. Anna Sergeyevna peered at the steamer and the passengers through her lorgnette as though looking for acquaintances, and whenever she turned to Gurov her eyes were shining. She talked a great deal and asked questions jerkily, forgetting the next moment what she had asked; then she lost her lorgnette in the crush.

The festive crowd began to disperse; it was now too dark to see people's faces; there was no wind any more, but Gurov and Anna Sergeyevna still stood as though waiting to see someone else come off the steamer. Anna Sergeyevna was silent now, and sniffed her flowers without looking at Gurov.

"The weather has improved this evening," he said. "Where shall we go now? Shall we drive somewhere?"

Zemstvo Council: A district council.

25   She did not reply.

Then he looked at her intently, and suddenly embraced her and kissed her on the lips, and the moist fragrance of her flowers enveloped him; and at once he looked round him anxiously, wondering if anyone had seen them.

"Let us go to your place," he said softly. And they walked off together rapidly.

The air in her room was close and there was the smell of she perfume the had bought at the Japanese shop. Looking at her, Gurov thought: "What encounters life offers!" From the past he preserved the memory of carefree, good natured women whom love made gay and who were grateful to him for the happiness he gave them, however brief it might be; and of women like his wife who loved without sincerity, with too many words, affectedly, hysterically, with an expression that it was not love or passion that engaged them but something more significant; and of two or three others, very beautiful, frigid women, across whose faces would suddenly flit a rapacious expression — an obstinate desire to take from life more than it could give, and these were women no longer young, capricious, unreflecting, domineering, unintelligent, and when Gurov grew cold to them their beauty aroused his hatred, and the lace on their lingerie seemed to him to resemble scales.

But here there was the timidity, the angularity of inexperienced youth, a feeling of awkwardness; and there was a sense of embarrassment, as though someone had suddenly knocked at the door. Anna Sergeyevna, "the lady with the pet dog," treated what had happened in a peculiar way, very seriously, as though it were her fall — so it seemed, and this was odd and inappropriate. Her features drooped and faded, and her long hair hung down sadly on either side of her face; she grew pensive and her dejected pose was that of a Magdalene in a picture by an old master.

30   "It's not right," she said. "You don't respect me now, you first of all."

There was a watermelon on the table. Gurov cut himself a slice and began eating it without haste. They were silent for at least half an hour.

There was something touching about Anna Sergeyevna; she had the purity of a well-bred, naive woman who has seen little of life. The single candle burning on the table barely illumined her face, yet it was clear that she was unhappy.

"Why should I stop respecting you, darling?" asked Gurov. "You don't know what you're saying."

"God forgive me," she said, and her eyes filled with tears. "It's terrible."

35   "It's as though you were trying to exonerate yourself."

"How can I exonerate myself? No. I am a bad, low woman; I despise myself and I have no thought of exonerating myself. It's not my husband but myself I have deceived. And not only just now; I have been deceiving myself for a long time. My husband may be a good, honest man, but he is a flunkey! I don't know what he does, what his work is, but I know he is a flunkey! I was twenty when I married him. I was tormented by curiosity; I wanted something better. 'There must be a different sort of life,' I said to myself. I wanted to live! To live, to live! Curiosity kept eating at me — you don't understand it, but I swear to God I could no longer control myself; something was going on in me: I could not be held back. I told my husband I was ill, and came here. And here I have been walking about as though in a daze, as though I were mad; and now I have become a vulgar, vile woman whom anyone may despise."

Gurov was already bored with her; he was irritated by her naive tone, by her repentance, so unexpected and so out of place; but for the tears in her eyes he might have thought she was joking or play-acting.

"I don't understand, my dear," he said softly. "What do you want?"

She hid her face on his breast and pressed close to him.

"Believe me, believe me, I beg you," she said, "I love honesty and purity, and sin 40
is loathsome to me; I don't know what I'm doing. Simple people say, 'The Evil One has led me astray.' And I may say of myself now that the Evil One has led me astray."

"Quiet, quiet," he murmured.

He looked into her fixed, frightened eyes, kissed her, spoke to her softly and affectionately, and by degrees she calmed down, and her gaiety returned; both began laughing.

Afterwards when they went out there was not a soul on the esplanade. The town with its cypresses looked quite dead, but the sea was still sounding as it broke upon the beach; a single launch was rocking on the waves and on it a lantern was blinking sleepily.

They found a cab and drove to Oreanda.

"I found out your surname in the hall just now: it was written on the board — 45
von Dideritz," said Gurov. "Is your husband German?"

"No; I believe his grandfather was German, but he is Greek Orthodox himself."

At Oreanda they sat on a bench not far from the church, looked down at the sea, and were silent. Yalta was barely visible through the morning mist; white clouds rested motionlessly on the mountaintops. The leaves did not stir on the trees, cicadas twanged, and the monotonous muffled sound of the sea that rose from below spoke of the peace, the eternal sleep awaiting us. So it rumbled below when there was no Yalta, no Oreanda here; so it rumbles now, and it will rumble as indifferently and as hollowly when we are no more. And in this constancy, in this complete indifference to the life and death of each of us, there lies, perhaps, a pledge of our eternal salvation, of the unceasing advance of life upon earth, of unceasing movement towards perfection. Sitting beside a young woman who in the dawn seemed so lovely, Gurov, soothed and spellbound by these magical surroundings — the sea, the mountains, the clouds, the wide sky — thought how everything is really beautiful in this world when one reflects: everything except what we think or do ourselves when we forget the higher aims of life and our own human dignity.

A man strolled up to them — probably a guard — looked at them and walked away. And this detail, too, seemed so mysterious and beautiful. They saw a steamer arrive from Feodosia, its lights extinguished in the glow of dawn.

"There is dew on the grass," said Anna Sergeyevna, after a silence.

"Yes, it's time to go home."

They returned to the city. 50

Then they met every day at twelve o'clock on the esplanade, lunched and dined together, took walks, admired the sea. She complained that she slept badly, that she had palpitations, asked the same questions, troubled now by jealousy and now by the fear that he did not respect her sufficiently. And often in the square or the public garden, when there was no one near them, he suddenly drew her to him and kissed her passionately. Complete idleness, these kisses in broad daylight exchanged furtively in dread of someone's seeing them, the heat, the smell of the sea, and the continual flitting before his eyes of idle, well-dressed, well-fed people, worked a complete change in him; he kept telling Anna Sergeyevna how beautiful she was, how seductive, was urgently passionate; he would not move a step away from her, while she was often pensive and continually pressed him to confess that he did not respect her, did not love her in the least, and saw in her nothing but a common woman. Almost every evening rather late they drove somewhere out of town, to Oreanda or to the waterfall; and the excursion was always a success, the scenery invariably impressed them as beautiful and magnificent.

They were expecting her husband, but a letter came from him saying that he had eye-trouble, and begging his wife to return home as soon as possible. Anna Sergeyevna made haste to go.

"It's a good thing I am leaving," she said to Gurov. "It's the hand of Fate!"

55   She took a carriage to the railway station, and he went with her. They were driving the whole day. When she had taken her place in the express, and when the second bell had rung, she said, "Let me look at you once more —let me look at your again. Like this."

She was not crying but was so sad that she seemed ill, and her face was quivering.

"I shall be thinking of you — remembering you," she said. "God bless you; be happy. Don't remember evil against me. We are parting forever—it has to be, for we ought never to have met. Well, God bless you."

The train moved off rapidly, its lights soon vanished, and a minute later there was no sound of it, as though everything had conspired to end as quickly as possible that sweet trance, that madness. Left alone on the platform, and gazing into the dark distance, Gurov listened to the twang of the grasshoppers and the hum of the telegraph wires, feeling as though he had just waked up. And he reflected, musing, that there had now been another episode or adventure in his life, and it, too, was at an end, and nothing was left of it but a memory. He was moved, sad, and slightly remorseful: this young woman whom he would never meet again had not been happy with him; he had been warm and affectionate with her, but yet in his manner, his tone, and his caresses there had been a shade of light irony, the slightly coarse arrogance of a happy male who was, besides, almost twice her age. She had constantly called him kind, exceptional, high-minded; obviously he had seemed to her different from what he really was, so he had involuntarily deceived her.

Here at the station there was already a scent of autumn in the air; it was a chilly evening.

60   "It is time for me to go north, too," thought Gurov as he left the platform. "High time!"

CHEKHOV: THE LADY WITH THE PET DOG

III

At home in Moscow the winter routine was already established: the stoves were heated, and in the morning it was still dark when the children were having breakfast and getting ready for school, and the nurse would light the lamp for a short time. There were frosts already. When the first snow falls, on the first day the sleighs are out, it is pleasant to see the white earth, the white roofs; one draws easy, delicious breaths, and the season brings back the days of one's youth. The old limes and birches, white with hoar-frost, have a good-natured look; they are closer to one's heart than cypresses and palms, and near them one no longer wants to think of mountains and the sea.

Gurov, a native of Moscow, arrived there on a fine frosty day, and when he put on his fur coat and warm gloves and took a walk along Petrovka, and when on Saturday night he heard the bells ringing, his recent trip and the places he had visited lost all charm for him. Little by little he became immersed in Moscow life, greedily read three newspapers a day, and declared that he did not read the Moscow papers on principle. He already felt a longing for restaurants, clubs, formal dinners, anniversary celebrations, and it flattered him to entertain distinguished lawyers and actors, and to play cards with a professor at the physicians' club. He could eat a whole portion of meat stewed with pickled cabbage and served in a pan, Moscow style.

A month or so would pass and the image of Anna Sergeyevna, it seemed to him, would become misty in his memory, and only from time to time he would dream of her with her touching smile as he dreamed of others. But more than a month went by, winter came into its own, and everything was still clear in his memory as though he had parted from Anna Sergeyevna only yesterday. And his memories glowed more and more vividly. When in the evening stillness the voices of his children preparing their lessons reached his study, or when he listened to a song or to an organ playing in a restaurant, or when the storm howled in the chimney, suddenly everything would rise up in his memory: what had happened on the pier and the early morning with the mist on the mountains, and the steamer coming from Feodosia, and the kisses. He would pace about his room a long time, remembering and smiling; then his memories passed into reveries, and in his imagination the past would mingle with what was to come. He did not dream of Anna Sergeyevna, but she followed him about everywhere and watched him. When he shut his eyes he saw her before him as though she were there in the flesh; and she seemed to him lovelier, younger, tenderer than she had been, and he imagined himself a finer man than he had been in Yalta. Of evenings she peered out at him from the bookcase, from the fireplace, from the corner — he heard her breathing, the caressing rustle of her clothes. In the street he followed the women with his eyes, looking for someone who resembled her.

Already he was tormented by a strong desire to share his memories with someone. But in his home it was impossible to talk of his love, and he had no one to talk to outside; certainly he could not confide in his tenants or in anyone at the bank. And what was there to talk about? He hadn't loved her then, had he? Had there been anything beautiful, poetical, edifying, or simply interesting in his relations with Anna Sergeyevna? And he was forced to talk vaguely of love, of women, and no one guessed what he meant; only his wife would twitch her black eyebrows and say, "The part of a philanderer does not suit you at all, Dimitry."

65   One evening, coming out of the physicians' club with an official with whom he had been playing cards, he could not resist saying:

"If you only knew what a fascinating woman I became acquainted with at Yalta!"

The official got into his sledge and was driving away, but turned suddenly and shouted: "Dmitry Dmitrich!"

"What is it?"

"You were right this evening: the sturgeon was a bit high."

70   These words, so commonplace, for some reason moved Gurov to indignation, and struck him as degrading and unclean. What savage manners, what mugs! What stupid nights, what dull, humdrum days! Frenzied gambling, gluttony, drunkenness, continual talk always about the same things! Futile pursuits and conversations always about the same topics take up the better part of one's time, the better part of one's strength, and in the end there is left a life clipped and wingless, an absurd mess, and there is no escaping or getting away from it — just as though one were in a madhouse or a prison.

Gurov, boiling with indignation, did not sleep all night. And he had a headache all the next day. And the following nights too he slept badly; he sat up in bed, thinking, or paced up and down his room. He was fed up with his children, fed up with the bank; he had no desire to go anywhere or to talk of anything.

In December during the holidays he prepared to take a trip and told his wife he was going to Petersburg to do what he could for a young friend — and he set off for S——. What for? He did not know, himself. He wanted to see Anna Sergeyevna and talk with her, to arrange a rendezvous if possible.

He arrived at S—— in the morning, and at the hotel took the best room, in which the floor was covered with gray army cloth, and on the table there was an inkstand, gray with dust and topped by a figure on horseback, its hat in its raised hand and its head broken off. The porter gave him the necessary information: von Dideritz lived in a house of his own on Staro-Goncharnaya Street, not far from the hotel: he was rich and lived well and kept his own horses; everyone in the town knew him. The porter pronounced the name: "Dridiritz."

Without haste Gurov made his way to Staro-Goncharnaya Street and found the house. Directly opposite the house stretched a long gray fence studded with nails.

75   "A fence like that would make one run away," thought Gurov, looking now at the fence, now at the windows of the house.

He reflected: this was a holiday, and the husband was apt to be at home. And in any case, it would be tactless to go into the house and disturb her. If he were to send her a note, it might fall into her husband's hands, and that might spoil everything. The best thing was to rely on chance. And he kept walking up and down the street and along the fence, waiting for the chance. He saw a beggar go in at the gate and heard the dogs attack him; then an hour later he heard a piano, and the sound came to him faintly and indistinctly. Probably it was Anna Sergeyevna playing. The front door opened suddenly, and an old woman came out, followed by the familiar white Pomeranian. Gurov was on the point of calling to the dog, but his heart began beating violently, and in his excitement he could not remember the Pomeranian's name.

He kept walking up and down, and hated the gray fence more and more, and by now he thought irritably that Anna Sergeyevna had forgotten him, and was perhaps already diverting herself with another man, and that that was very natural in a young woman who from morning till night had to look at that damn fence. He went back to his hotel room and sat on the couch for a long while, not knowing what to do, then he had dinner and a long nap.

"How stupid and annoying all this is!" he thought when he woke and looked at the dark windows: it was already evening. "Here I've had a good sleep for some reason. What am I going to do at night?"

He sat on the bed, which was covered with a cheap gray blanket of the kind seen in hospitals, and he twitted himself in his vexation:

"So there's your lady with the pet dog. There's your adventure. A nice place to   80
cool your heels in."

That morning at the station a playbill in large letters had caught his eye. *The Geisha* was to be given for the first time. He thought of this and drove to the theater.

"It's quite possible that she goes to first nights," he thought.

The theater was full. As in all provincial theaters, there was a haze above the chandelier, the gallery was noisy and restless; in the front row, before the beginning of the performance the local dandies were standing with their hands clasped behind their backs; in the Governor's box the Governor's daughter, wearing a boa, occupied the front sear, while the Governor himself hid modestly behind the portiere and only his hands were visible; the curtain swayed; the orchestra was a long time tuning up. While the audience were coming in and taking their seats, Gurov scanned the faces eagerly.

Anna Sergeyevna, too, came in. She sat down in the third row, and when Gurov looked at her his heart contracted, and he understood clearly that in the whole world there was no human being so near, so precious, and so important to him; she, this little, undistinguished woman, lost in a provincial crowd, with a vulgar lorgnette in her hand, filled his whole life now, was his sorrow and his joy, the only happiness that he now desired for himself, and to the sounds of the bad orchestra, of the miserable local violins, he thought how lovely she was. He thought and dreamed.

A young man with small side-whiskers, very tall and stooped, came in with   85
Anna Sergeyevna and sat down beside her; he nodded his head at every step and seemed to be bowing continually. Probably this was the husband whom at Yalta, in an excess of bitter feeling, she had called a flunkey. And there really was in his lanky figure, his side-whiskers, his small bald patch, something of a flunkey's retiring manner; his smile was mawkish, and in his buttonhole there was an academic badge like a waiter's number.

During the first intermission the husband went out to have a smoke; she remained in her seat. Gurov, who was also sitting in the orchestra, went up to her and said in a shaky voice, with a forced smile:

"Good evening!"

She glanced at him and turned pale, then looked at him again in horror, unable to believe her eyes, and gripped the fan and the lorgnette tightly together in her hands, evidently trying to keep herself from fainting. Both were silent. She was sitting, he was standing, frightened by her distress and not daring to take a seat beside her. The violins and the flute that were being tuned up sang out. He suddenly felt frightened: it seemed as if all the people in the boxes were looking at them. She got up and went hurriedly to the exit; he followed her, and both of them walked blindly along the corridors and up and down stairs, and figures in the uniforms prescribed for magistrates, teachers, and officials of the Department of Crown Lands, all wearing badges, flitted before their eyes, as did also ladies, and fur coats on hangers; they were conscious of drafts and the smell of stale tobacco. And Gurov, whose heart was beating violently, thought:

"Oh, Lord! Why are these people here and this orchestra!"

90   And at that instant he suddenly recalled how when he had seen Anna Sergeyevna off at the station he had said to himself that all was over between them and that they would never meet again. But how distant the end still was!

On the narrow, gloomy staircase over which it said "To the Amphitheatre," she stopped.

"How you frightened me!" she said, breathing hard, still pale and stunned. "Oh, how you frightened me! I am barely alive. Why did you come? Why?"

"But do understand, Anna, do understand —" he said hurriedly, under his breath. "I implore you, do understand —"

She looked at him with fear, with entreaty, with love; she looked at him intently, to keep his features more distinctly in her memory.

95   "I suffer so," she went on, not listening to him. "All this time I have been thinking of nothing but you; I live only by the thought of you. And I wanted to forget, to forget; but why, oh, why have you come?"

On the landing above them two high school boys were looking down and smoking, but it was all the same to Gurov; he drew Anna Sergeyevna to him and began kissing her face and her hands.

"What are you doing, what are you doing!" she was saying in horror, pushing him away. "We have lost our senses. Go away today; go away at once — I conjure you by all that is sacred, I implore you — People are coming this way."

Someone was walking up the stairs.

"You must leave," Anna Sergeyevna went on in a whisper. "Do you hear, Dmitry Dmitrich? I will come and see you in Moscow. I have never been happy; I am unhappy now, and I never, never shall be happy, never! So don't make me suffer still more! I swear I'll come to Moscow. But now let us part. My dear, good, precious one, let us part!"

100   She pressed his hand and walked rapidly downstairs, turning to look round at him, and from her eyes he could see that she really was unhappy. Gurov stood

for a while, listening then when all grew quiet, he found his coat and left the theater.

IV

And Anna Sergeyevna began coming to see him in Moscow. Once every two or three months she left S——, telling her husband that she was going to consult a doctor about a woman's ailment from which she was suffering — and her husband did and did not believe her. When she arrived in Moscow she would stop at the Slavyansky Bazar Hotel, and at once send a man in a red cap to Gurov. Gurov came to see her, and no one in Moscow knew of it.

Once he was going to see her in this way on a winter morning (the messenger had come the evening before and not found him in). With him walked his daughter, whom he wanted to take to school: it was on the way. Snow was coming down in big wet flakes.

"It's three degrees above zero,° and yet it's snowing," Gurov was saying to his daughter. "But this temperature prevails only on the surface of the earth; in the upper layers of the atmosphere there is quite a different temperature."

"And why doesn't it thunder in winter, papa?"

He explained that, too. He talked, thinking all the while that he was on his way to a rendezvous, and no living soul knew of it, and probably no one would ever know. He had two lives: an open one, seen and known by all who needed to know it, full of conventional truth and conventional falsehood, exactly like the lives of his friends and acquaintances; and another life that went on in secret. And through some strange, perhaps accidental, combination of circumstances, everything that was of interest and importance to him, everything that was essential to him, everything about which he felt sincerely and did not deceive himself, everything that constituted the core of his life, was going on concealed from others; while all that was false, the shell in which he hid to cover the truth — his work at the bank, for instance, his discussions at the club, his references to the "inferior race," his appearances at anniversary celebrations with his wife — all that went on in the open. Judging others by himself, he did not believe what he saw, and always fancied that every man led his real, most interesting life under cover of secrecy as under cover of night. The personal life of every individual is based on secrecy, and perhaps it is partly for that reason that civilized man is so nervously anxious that personal privacy should be respected.

Having taken this daughter to school, Gurov went on to the Slavyansky Bazar Hotel. He took off his fur coat in the lobby, went upstairs, and knocked gently at the door. Anna Sergeyevna, wearing his favorite gray dress, exhausted by the journey and by waiting, had been expecting him since the previous evening. She was pale, and looked at him without a smile, and he had hardly entered when she flung herself on his breast. Their kiss was a long, lingering one, as though they had not seen one another for two years.

"Well, darling, how are you getting on there?" he asked. "What news?"

---

three degrees above zero: Roughly 38 degrees Fahrenheit.

"Wait; I'll tell you in a moment — I can't speak."

She could not speak; she was crying. She turned away from him, and pressed her handkerchief to her eyes.

110 "Let her have her cry; meanwhile I'll sit down," he thought, and he seated himself in an armchair.

Then he rang and ordered tea, and while he was having his tea she remained standing at the window with her back to him. She was crying out of sheer agitation, in the sorrowful consciousness that their life was so sad; that they could only see each order in secret and had to hide from people like thieves! Was it not a broken life?

"Come, stop now, dear!" he said.

It was plain to him that this love of theirs would not be over soon, that the end of it was not in sight. Anna Sergeyevna was growing more and more attached to him. She adored him, and it was unthinkable to tell her that their love was bound to come to an end some day; besides, she would not have believed it!

He went up to her and took her by the shoulders, to fondle her and say something diverting, and at that moment he caught sight of himself in the mirror.

115 His hair was already beginning to turn gray. And it seemed odd to him that he had grown so much older in the last few years, and lost his looks. The shoulders on which his hands rested were warm and heaving. He felt compassion for this life, still so warm and lovely, but probably already about to begin to fade and wither like his own. Why did she love him so much? He always seemed to women different from what he was, and they loved in him not himself, but the man whom their imagination created and whom they had been eagerly seeking all their lives; and afterwards, when they saw their mistake, they loved him nevertheless. And not one of them had been happy with him. In the past he had met women, come together with them, parted from them, but he had never once loved; it was anything you please, but not love. And only now when his head was gray he had fallen in love, really, truly — for the first time in his life.

Anna Sergeyevna and he loved each other as people do who are very close and intimate, like man and wife, like tender friends; it seemed to them that Fate itself had meant them for one another, and they could not understand why he had a wife and she a husband; and it was as though they were a pair of migratory birds, male and female, caught and forced to live in different cages. They forgave each other what they were ashamed of in their past, they forgave everything in the present, and felt that this love of theirs had altered them both.

Formerly in moments of sadness he had soothed himself with whatever logical arguments came into his head, but now he no longer cared for logic; he felt profound compassion, he wanted to be sincere and tender.

"Give it up now, my darling," he said. "You've had your cry; that's enough. Let us have a talk now, we'll think up something."

Then they spent a long time taking counsel together, they talked of how to avoid the necessity for secrecy, for deception, for living in different cities, and not seeing one another for long stretches of time. How could they free themselves from these intolerable fetters?

"How? How?" he asked, clutching his head. "How?" 120

And it seemed as though in a little while the solution would be found, and then a new and glorious life would begin; and it was clear to both of them that the end was still far off, and that what was to be most complicated and difficult for them was only just beginning.

◇ ◇ ◇

STEPHEN CRANE (1871–1900)

The Open Boat (1897)

A Tale Intended to be after the Fact: Being the Experience of Four Men from the Sunk Steamer Commodore

I

None of them knew the color of the sky. Their eyes glanced level, and were fastened upon the waves that swept toward them. These waves were of the hue of slate,° save for the tops, which were of foaming white, and all of the men knew the colors of the sea. The horizon narrowed and widened, and dipped and rose, and at all times its edge was jagged with waves that seemed thrust up in points like rocks.

Many a man ought to have a bathtub larger than the boat which here rode upon the sea. These waves were most wrongfully and barbarously abrupt and tall and each frothtop was a problem in small-boat navigation.

The cook squatted in the bottom, and looked with both eyes at the six inches of gunwale which separated him from the ocean. His sleeves were rolled over his fat forearms, and the two flaps of his unbuttoned vest dangled as he bent to bail out the boat. Often he said, "Gawd! that was a narrow clip." As he remarked it he invariably gazed eastward over the broken sea.

The oiler, steering with one of the two oars in the boat, sometimes raised himself suddenly to keep clear of water that swirled in over the stern. It was a thin little oar, and it seemed often ready to snap.

The correspondent,° pulling at the other oar, watched the waves and wondered why he was there. 5

The injured captain, lying in the bow, was at this time buried in that profound dejection and indifference which comes, temporarily at least, to even the bravest and most enduring when, willy-nilly, the firm fails, the army loses, the ship goes down. The mind of the master of a vessel is rooted deep in the timbers of her, though he command for a day or a decade; and this captain had on him the stern impression of a scene in the grays of dawn of seven turned faces, and later a stump of a topmast with a white ball on it, that slashed to and fro at the waves, went low

---

slate: A hard, bluish-gray rock.

correspondent: A newspaper reporter.

and lower, and down. Thereafter there was something strange in his voice. Although steady, it was deep with mourning, and of a quality beyond oration or tears.

"Keep 'er a little more south, Billie," said he.

"A little more south, sir," said the oiler in the stern.

A seat in this boat was not unlike a seat upon a bucking broncho, and by the same token a broncho is not much smaller. The craft pranced and reared and plunged like an animal. As each wave came, and she rose for it, she seemed like a horse making at a fence outrageously high. The manner of her scramble over these walls of water is a mystic thing, and, moreover, at the top of them were ordinarily these problems in white water, the foam racing down from the summit of each wave requiring a new leap, and a leap from the air. Then, after scornfully bumping a crest, she would slide and race and splash down a long incline, and arrive bobbing and nodding in front of the next menace.

10   A singular disadvantage of the sea lies in the fact that after successfully surmounting one wave you discover that there is another behind it just as important and just as nervously anxious to do something effective in the way of swamping boats. In a ten-foot dinghy° one can get an idea of the resources of the sea in the line of waves that is not possible to the average experience which is never at sea in a dinghy. As each slaty wall of water approached, it shut all else from the view of the men in the boat, and it was not difficult to imagine that this particular wave was the final outburst of the ocean, the last effort of the grim water. There was a terrible grace in the move of the waves, and they came in silence, save for the snarling of the crests.

In the wan light the faces of the men must have been gray. Their eyes must have glinted in strange ways as they gazed steadily astern. Viewed from a balcony, the whole thing would doubtless have been weirdly picturesque. But the men in the boat had no time to see it, and if they had had leisure, there were other things to occupy their minds. The sun swung steadily up the sky, and they knew it was broad day because the color of the sea changed from slate to emerald green streaked with amber lights, and the foam was like tumbling snow. The process of the breaking day was unknown to them. They were aware only of this effect upon the color of the waves that rolled toward them.

In disjointed sentences the cook and the correspondent argued as to the difference between a life-saving station and a house of refuge. The cook had said: "There's a house of refuge just north of the Mosquito Inlet Light, and as soon as they see us they'll come off in their boat and pick us up."

"As soon as who see us?" said the correspondent.

"The crew," said the cook.

15   "Houses of refuge don't have crews," said the correspondent. "As I understand them, they are only places where clothes and grub are stored for the benefit of shipwrecked people. They don't carry crews."

---

dinghy: A small rowboat.

"Oh, yes, they do," said the cook.

"No, they don't," said the correspondent.

"Well, we're not there yet, anyhow," said the oiler, in the stern.

"Well," said the cook, "perhaps it's not a house of refuge that I'm thinking of as being near Mosquito Inlet Light; perhaps it's a life-saving station."

"We're not there yet," said the oiler in the stern.   20

II

As the boat bounced from the top of each wave the wind tore through the hair of the hatless men, and as the craft plopped her stern down again the spray splashed past them. The crest of each of these waves was a hill, from the top of which the men surveyed for a moment a broad tumultuous expanse, shining and wind-driven. It was probably splendid, it was probably glorious, this play of the free sea, wild with lights of emerald and white and amber.

"Bully good thing it's an on-shore wind," said the cook. "If not, where would we be? Wouldn't have a show."

"That's right," said the correspondent.

The busy oiler nodded his assent.

Then the captain, in the bow, chuckled in a way that expressed humor, con-   25 tempt, tragedy, all in one. "Do you think we've got much of a show now, boys?" said he.

Whereupon the three were silent, save for a trifle of hemming and hawing.° To express any particular optimism at this time they felt to be childish and stupid, but they all doubtless possessed this sense of the situation in their minds. A young man thinks doggedly at such times. On the other hand, the ethics of their condition was decidedly against any open suggestion of hopelessness. So they were silent.

"Oh, well," said the captain, soothing his children, "we'll get ashore all right."

But there was that in his tone which made them think; so the oiler quoth,° "Yes! if this wind holds."

The cook was bailing. "Yes! If we don't catch hell in the surf."

Canton-flannel gulls flew near and far. Sometimes they sat down on the sea, near   30 patches of brown seaweed that rolled over the waves with a movement like carpets on a line in a gale. The birds sat comfortably in groups, and they were envied by some in the dinghy, for the wrath of the sea was no more to them than it was to a covey of prairie chickens a thousand miles inland. Often they came very close and stared at the men with black bead-like eyes. At these times they were uncanny and sinister in their unblinking scrutiny, and the men hooted angrily at them, telling them to be gone. One came, and evidently decided to alight on the top of the captain's head. The bird flew parallel to the boat and did not circle, but made short sidelong jumps in the air in chicken-fashion. His black eyes were wistfully fixed upon the captain's head. "Ugly brute," said the oiler to the bird. "You look as if you were made with a

---

hemming and hawing: Sounds made while searching for the right words to speak.
quoth: Said.

jacknife." The cook and the correspondent swore darkly at the creature. The captain naturally wished to knock it away with the end of the heavy painter, but he did not dare do it, because anything resembling an emphatic gesture would have capsized this freighted boat; and so, with his open hand, the captain gently and carefully waved the gull away. After it had been discouraged from the pursuit the captain breathed easier on account of his hair, and others breathed easier because the bird struck their minds at this time as being somehow gruesome and ominous.

In the meantime the oiler and the correspondent rowed. And also they rowed. They sat together in the same seat, and each rowed an oar. Then the oiler took both oars; then the correspondent took both oars; then the oiler; then the correspondent. They rowed and they rowed. The very ticklish part of the business was when the time came for the reclining one in the stern to take his turn at the oars. By the very last star of truth, it is easier to steal eggs from under a hen than it was to change seats in the dinghy. First the man in the stern slid his hand along the thwart and moved with care, as if he were of Sèvres.° Then the man in the row-ing-seat slid his hand along the other thwart. It was all done with the most ex-traordinary care. As the two sidled past each other, the whole party kept watchful eyes on the coming wave, and the captain cried: "Look out, now! Steady, there!"

The brown mats of seaweed that appeared from time to time were like islands, bits of earth. They were traveling, apparently, neither one way nor the other. They were, to all intents, stationary. They informed the men in the boat that it was making progress slowly toward the land.

The captain, rearing cautiously in the bow after the dinghy soared on a great swell, said that he had seen the lighthouse at Mosquito Inlet. Presently the cook remarked that he had seen it. The correspondent was at the oars then, and for some reason he too wished to look at the lighthouse; but his back was toward the far shore, and the waves were important, and for some time he could not seize an opportunity to turn his head. But at last there came a wave more gentle than the others, and when at the crest of it he swiftly scoured the western horizon.

"See it?" said the captain.

35   "No," said the correspondent, slowly; "I didn't see anything."

"Look again," said the captain. He pointed. "It's exactly in that direction."

At the top of another wave the correspondent did as he was bid, and this time his eyes chanced on a small, still thing on the edge of the swaying horizon. It was precisely like the point of a pin. It took an anxious eye to find a lighthouse so tiny.

"Think we'll make it, Captain?"

"If this wind holds and the boat don't swamp,° we can't do much else," said the captain.

40   The little boat, lifted by each towering sea and splashed viciously by the crests, made progress that in the absence of seaweed was not apparent to those in her. She seemed just a wee thing wallowing, miraculously top up, at the mercy of five oceans. Occasionally a great spread of water, like white flames, swarmed into her.

Sèvres: French porcelain.

swamp: Sink by filling with water.

"Bail her, cook," said the captain, serenely.

"All right, Captain," said the cheerful cook.

III

It would be difficult to describe the subtle brotherhood of men that was here established on the seas. No one said that it was so. No one mentioned it. But it dwelt in the boat, and each man felt it warm him. They were a captain, an oiler, a cook, and a correspondent, and they were friends — friends in a more curiously iron-bound degree than may be common. The hurt captain, lying against the water-jar in the bow, spoke always in a low voice and calmly; but he could never command a more ready and swiftly obedient crew than the motley three of the dinghy. It was more than a mere recognition of what was best for the common safety. There was surely in it a quality that was personal and heart-felt. And after this devotion to the commander of the boat, there was this comradeship, that the correspondent, for instance, who had been taught to be cynical of men, knew even at the time was the best experience of his life. But no one said that it was so. No one mentioned it.

"I wish we had a sail," remarked the captain. "We might try my overcoat on the end of an oar, and give you two boys a chance to rest." So the cook and the correspondent held the mast and spread wide the overcoat; the oiler steered; and the little boat made good way with her new rig. Sometimes the oiler had to scull sharply to keep a sea from breaking into the boat, but otherwise sailing was a success.

Meanwhile the lighthouse had been growing slowly larger. It had now almost assumed color, and appeared like a little gray shadow on the sky. The man at the oars could not be prevented from turning his head rather often to try for a glimpse of this little gray shadow. 45

At last, from the top of each wave, the men in the tossing boat could see land. Even as the lighthouse was an upright shadow on the sky, this land seemed but a long black shadow on the sea. It certainly was thinner than paper. "We must be about opposite New Smyrna," said the cook, who had coasted this shore often in schooners. "Captain, by the way, I believe they abandoned that life-saving station there about a year ago."

"Did they?" said the captain.

The wind slowly died away. The cook and the correspondent were not now obliged to slave in order to hold high the oar. But the waves continued their old impetuous swooping at the dinghy, and the little craft, no longer under way, struggled woundily over them. The oiler or the correspondent took the oars again.

Shipwrecks are apropos of° nothing. If men could only train for them and have them occur when the men had reached pink condition,° there would be less drowning at sea. Of the four in the dinghy none had slept any time worth mentioning for two days and two nights previous to embarking in the dinghy, and in

---

apropos of: With regard to.

pink condition: Highest or finest condition.

the excitement of clambering about the deck of a foundering ship they had also forgotten to eat heartily.

50   For these reasons, and for others, neither the oiler nor the correspondent was fond of rowing at this time. The correspondent wondered ingenuously how in the name of all that was sane could there be people who thought it amusing to row a boat. It was not an amusement; it was a diabolical punishment, and even a genius of mental aberrations could never conclude that it was anything but a horror to the muscles and crime against the back. He mentioned to the boat in general how the amusement of rowing struck him, and the weary-faced oiler smiled in full sympathy. Previously to the foundering, by the way, the oiler had worked double watch in the engine-room of the ship.

"Take her easy now, boys," said the captain. "Don't spend yourselves. If we have to run a surf you'll need all your strength, because we'll sure have to swim for it. Take your time."

Slowly the land arose from the sea. From a black line it became a line of black and a line of white — trees and sand. Finally the captain said that he could make out a house on the shore. "That's the house of refuge, sure," said the cook. "They'll see us before long, and come out after us."

The distant lighthouse reared high. "The keeper ought to be able to make us out now, if he's looking through a glass," said the captain. "He'll notify the life-saving people."

"None of those other boats could have got ashore to give word of the wreck," said the oiler, in a low voice, "else the life-boat would be out hunting us."

55   Slowly and beautifully the land loomed out of the sea. The wind came again. It had veered from the north-east to the south-east. Finally a new sound struck the ears of the men in the boat. It was the low thunder of the surf on the shore. "We'll never be able to make the lighthouse now," said the captain. "Swing her head a little more north, Billie."

"A little more north, sir," said the oiler.

Whereupon the little boat turned her nose once more down the wind, and all but the oarsman watched the shore grow. Under the influence of this expansion doubt and direful apprehension were leaving the minds of the men. The management of the boat was still most absorbing, but it could not prevent a quiet cheerfulness. In an hour, perhaps, they would be ashore.

Their backbones had become thoroughly used to balancing in the boat, and they now rode this wild colt of a dinghy like circus men. The correspondent thought that he had been drenched to the skin, but happening to feel in the top pocket of his coat, he found therein eight cigars. Four of them were soaked with seawater; four were perfectly scatheless. After a search, somebody produced three dry matches; and thereupon the four waifs rode impudently in their little boat and, with an assurance of an impending rescue shining in their eyes, puffed at the big cigars, and judged well and ill of all men. Everybody took a drink of water.

IV

"Cook," remarked the captain, "there don't seem to be any signs of life about your house of refuge."

"No," replied the cook. "Funny they don't see us!"

A broad stretch of lowly coast lay before the eyes of the men. It was of low dunes topped with dark vegetation. The roar of the surf was plain, and sometimes they could see the white lip of a wave as it spun up the beach. A tiny house was blocked out black upon the sky. Southward, the slim lighthouse lifted its little gray length.

Tide, wind, and waves were swinging the dinghy northward. "Funny they don't see us," said the men.

The surf's roar was here dulled, but its tone was nevertheless thunderous and mighty. As the boat swam over the great rollers the men sat listening to this roar. "We'll swamp sure," said everybody.

It is fair to say here that there was not a life-saving station within twenty miles in either direction; but the men did not know this fact, and in consequence they made dark and opprobrious remarks concerning the eyesight of the nation's life-savers. Four scowling men sat in the dinghy and surpassed records in the invention of epithets.

"Funny they don't see us."

The light-heartedness of a former time had completely faded. To their sharpened minds it was easy to conjure pictures of all kinds of incompetency and blindness and, indeed, cowardice. There was the shore of the populous land, and it was bitter and bitter to them that from it came no sign.

"Well," said the captain, ultimately, "I suppose we'll have to make a try for ourselves. If we stay out here too long, we'll none of us have strength left to swim after the boat swamps."

And so the oiler, who was at the oars, turned the boat straight for the shore. There was a sudden tightening of muscles. There was some thinking.

"If we don't all get ashore," said the captain — "if we don't all get ashore, I suppose you fellows know where to send news of my finish?"

They then briefly exchanged some addresses and admonitions. As for the reflections of the men, there was a great deal of rage in them. Perchance they might be formulated thus: "If I am going to be drowned — if I am going to be drowned — if I am going to be drowned, why, in the name of the seven mad gods who rule the sea, was I allowed to come thus far and contemplate sand and trees? Was I brought here merely to have my nose dragged away as I was about to nibble the sacred cheese of life? It is preposterous. If this old ninny-woman, Fate, cannot do better than this, she should be deprived of the management of men's fortunes. She is an old hen who knows not her intention. If she has decided to drown me, why did she not do it in the beginning and save me all this trouble? The whole affair is absurd. — But no; she cannot mean to drown me. She dare not drown me. She cannot drown me. Not after all this work." Afterward the man might have had an impulse to shake his fist at the clouds. "Just you drown me, now, and then hear what I call you!"

The billows that came at this time were more formidable. They seemed always just about to break and roll over the little boat in a turmoil of foam. There was a preparatory and long growl in the speech of them. No mind unused to the sea would have concluded that the dinghy could ascend these sheer heights in time. The shore was still afar. The oiler was a wily surfman. "Boys," he said swiftly, "she won't live three minutes more, and we're too far out to swim. Shall I take her to sea again, Captain?"

"Yes; go ahead!" said the captain.

This oiler, by a series of quick miracles and fast and steady oarsmanship, turned the boat in the middle of the surf and took her safely to sea again.

There was a considerable silence as the boat bumped over the furrowed sea to deeper water. Then somebody in gloom spoke: "Well, anyhow, they must have seen us from the shore by now."

75   The gulls went in slanting flight up the wind toward the gray, desolate east. A squall, marked by dinghy clouds and clouds brick-red like smoke from a burning building, appeared from the south-east.

"What do you think of those life-saving people? Ain't they peaches?"

"Funny they haven't seen us."

"Maybe they think we're out here for sport! Maybe they think we're fishin'. Maybe they think we're damned fools."

It was a long afternoon. A changed tide tried to force them southward, but wind and wave said northward. Far ahead, where coast-line, sea, and sky formed their mighty angle, there were little dots which seemed to indicate a city on the shore.

80   "St. Augustine?"

The captain shook his head. "Too near Mosquito Inlet."

And the oiler rowed, and then the correspondent rowed; then the oiler rowed. It was a weary business. The human back can become the seat of more aches and pains than are registered in books for the composite anatomy of a regiment. It is a limited area, but it can become the theatre of innumerable muscular conflicts, tangles, wrenches, knots, and other comforts.

"Did you ever like to row, Billie?" asked the correspondent.

"No," said the oiler; "hang it!"

85   When one exchanged the rowing-seat for a place in the bottom of the boat, he suffered a bodily depression that caused him to be careless of everything save an obligation to wiggle one finger. There was cold seawater swashing to and fro in the boat, and he lay in it. His head, pillowed on a thwart, was within an inch of the swirl of a wave-crest, and sometimes a particularly obstreperous sea came inboard and drenched him once more. But these matters did not annoy him. It is almost certain that if the boat had capsized he would have tumbled comfortably upon the ocean as if he felt sure that it was a great soft mattress.

"Look! There's a man on the shore!"

"Where?"

"There! See 'im?"

"Yes, sure! He's walking along."

90   "Now he's stopped. Look! He's facing us!"

"He's waving at us!"

"So he is! By thunder!"

"Ah, now we're all right! Now we're all right! There'll be a boat out here for us in half an hour."

"He's going on. He's running. He's going up to that house there."

The remote beach seemed lower than the sea, and it required a searching 95
glance to discern the little black figure. The captain saw a floating stick, and they
rowed to it. A bath towel was by some weird chance in the boat, and, tying this
on the stick, the captain waved it. The oarsman did not dare turn his head, so he
was obliged to ask questions.

"What's he doing now?"

"He's standing still again. He's looking, I think. — There he goes again —
toward the house. — Now he's stopped again."

"Is he waving at us?"

"No, not now; he was, though."

"Look! There comes another man!" 100

"He's running."

"Look at him go, would you!"

"Why, he's on a bicycle. Now he's met the other man. They're both waving at
us. Look!"

"There comes something up the beach."

"What the devil is that thing?" 105

"Why, it looks like a boat."

"Why, certainly, it's a boat."

"No; it's on wheels."

"Yes, so it is. Well, that must be the life-boat. They drag them along shore on
a wagon."

"That's the life-boat, sure." 110

"No, by God, it's — it's an omnibus."

"I tell you it's a life-boat."

"It is not! It's an omnibus. I can see it plain. See? One of the these big hotel
omnibuses."

"By thunder, you're right. It's an omnibus, sure as fate. What do you suppose
they are doing with an omnibus? Maybe they are going around collecting the
life-crew, hey?"

"That's it, likely. Look! There's a fellow waving a little black flag. He's 115
standing on the steps of the omnibus. There come those other two fellows. Now
they're all talking together. Look at the fellow with the flag. Maybe he ain't
waving it!"

"That ain't a flag, is it? That's his coat. Why, certainly, that's his coat."

"So it is; it's his coat. He's taken it off and is waving it around his head. But
would you look at him swing it!"

"Oh, say, there isn't any life-saving station there. That's just a winter-resort
hotel omnibus that has brought over some of the boarders to see us drown."

"What's that idiot with the coat mean? What's he signalling, anyhow?"

"It looks as if he were trying to tell us to go north. There must be a life-saving 120
station up there."

"No; he thinks we're fishing. Just giving us a merry hand. See? Ah, there, Willie!"

"Well, I wish I could make something out of those signals. What do you
suppose he means?"

"He don't mean anything; he's just playing."

"Well, if he'd just signal us to try the surf again, or to go to sea and wait, or go north, or go south, or go to hell, there would be some reason in it. But look at him! He just stands there and keeps his coat revolving like a wheel. The ass!"

125 "There come more people."

"Now there's quite a mob. Look! Isn't that a boat?"

"Where? Oh, I see where you mean. No, that's no boat."

"That fellow is still waving his coat."

"He must think we like to see him do that. Why don't he quit it? It don't mean anything."

130 "I don't know. I think he is trying to make us go north. It must be that there's a life-saving station there somewhere."

"Say, he ain't tired yet. Look at 'im wave!"

"Wonder how long he can keep that up. He's been revolving his coat ever since he caught sight of us. He's an idiot. Why aren't they getting men to bring a boat out? A fishing boat — one of those big yawls — could come out here all right. Why don't he do something?"

"Oh, it's all right now."

"They'll have a boat out here for us in less than no time, now that they've seen us."

135 A faint yellow tone came into the sky over the low land. The shadows on the sea slowly deepened. The wind bore coldness with it, and the men began to shiver.

"Holy smoke!" said one, allowing his voice to express his impious mood, "If we keep on monkeying out here! If we've got to flounder out here all night!"

"Oh, we'll never have to stay here all night! Don't you worry. They've seen us now, and it won't be long before they'll come chasing out after us."

The shore grew dusky. The man waving a coat blended gradually into this gloom, and it swallowed in the same manner the omnibus and the group of people. The spray, when it dashed uproariously over the side made the voyagers shrink and swear like men who were being branded.

"I'd like to catch the chump who waved the coat. I feel like socking him one, just for luck."

140 "Why? What did he do?"

"Oh, nothing, but then he seemed so damned cheerful."

In the meantime the oiler rowed, and then the correspondent rowed and then the oiler rowed. Gray-faced and bowed forward, they mechanically, turn by turn, plied the leaden oars. The form of the lighthouse had vanished from the southern horizon, but finally a pale star appeared, just lifting from the sea. The streaked saffron° in the west passed before the all-merging darkness, and the sea to the east was black. The land had vanished, and was expressed only by the low and drear thunder of the surf.

"If I am going to be drowned — if I am going to be drowned — if I am going to be drowned, why, in the name of the seven mad gods who rule the sea, was I

---

saffron: Orange-yellow.

allowed to come thus far and contemplate sand and trees? Was I brought here merely to have my nose dragged away as I was about to nibble the sacred cheese of life?"

The patient captain, drooped over the water-jar, was sometimes obliged to speak to the oarsman.

"Keep her head up! Keep her head up!"   145

"Keep her head up, sir." The voices were weary and low.

This was surely a quiet evening. All save the oarsman lay heavily and listlessly in the boat's bottom. As for him, his eyes were just capable of noting the tall black waves that swept forward in a most sinister silence, save for an occasional subdued growl of a crest.

The cook's head was on a thwart, and he looked without interest at the water under his nose. He was deep in other scenes. Finally he spoke. "Billie," he murmured, dreamfully, "what kind of pie do you like best?"

V

"Pie!" said the oiler and the correspondent, agitatedly. "Don't talk about those things, blast you!"

"Well," said the cook, "I was just thinking about ham sandwiches, and —"   150

A night on the sea in an open boat is a long night. As darkness settled finally, the shine of the light, lifting from the sea in the south, changed to full gold. On the northern horizon a new light appeared, a small bluish gleam on the edge of the waters. These two lights were the furniture of the world. Otherwise there was nothing but waves.

Two men huddled in the stern, and distances were so magnificent in the dinghy that the rower was enabled to keep his feet partly warm by thrusting them under his companions. Their legs indeed extended far under the rowingseat until they touched the feet of the captain forward. Sometimes, despite the efforts of the tired oarsman, a wave came piling into the boat, an icy wave of the night, and the chilling water soaked them anew. They would twist their bodies for a moment and groan, and sleep the dead sleep once more, while the water in the boat gurgled about them as the craft rocked.

The plan of the oiler and the correspondent was for one to row until he lost the ability, and then arouse the other from his sea-water couch in the bottom of the boat.

The oiler plied the oars until his head drooped forward and the overpowering sleep blinded him; and he rowed yet afterward. Then he touched a man in the bottom of the boat, and called his name. "Will you spell° me for a little while?" he said meekly.

"Sure, Billie," said the correspondent, awaking and dragging himself to a sit-   155
ting position. They exchanged places carefully, and the oiler, cuddling down in the sea-water at the cook's side, seemed to go to sleep instantly.

The particular violence of the sea had ceased. The waves came without snarling. The obligation of the man at the oars was to keep the boat headed so that the tilt of the roller would not capsize her, and to preserve her from filling

---

spell: Relieve.

when the crests rushed past. The black waves were silent and hard to be seen in the darkness. Often one was almost upon the boat before the oarsman was aware.

In a low voice the correspondent addressed the captain. He was not sure that the captain was awake, although this iron man seemed to be always awake. "Captain, shall I keep her making for that light north, sir?"

The same steady voice answered him. "Yes. Keep it about two points off the port bow."

The cook had tied a life-belt around himself in order to get even the warmth which this clumsy cork contrivance could donate, and he seemed almost stove-like when a rower, whose teeth invariably chattered wildly as soon as he ceased his labor, dropped down to sleep.

160   The correspondent, as he rowed, looked down at the two men sleeping underfoot. The cook's arm was around the oiler's shoulders, and, with their fragmentary clothing and haggard faces, they were the babes of the sea — a grotesque rendering of the old babes in the wood.

Later he must have grown stupid at his work, for suddenly there was a growling of water, and a crest came with a roar and a swash into the boat, and it was a wonder that it did not set the cook afloat in his life-belt. The cook continued to sleep, but the oiler sat up, blinking his eyes and shaking with the new cold.

"Oh, I'm awful sorry, Billie," said the correspondent, contritely.

"That's all right, old boy," said the oiler, and lay down again and was asleep.

Presently it seemed that even the captain dozed, and the correspondent thought that he was the one man afloat on all the oceans. The wind had a voice as it came over the waves, and it was sadder than the end.

165   There was a long, loud swishing astern of the boat, and a gleaming trail of phosphorescence, like blue flame, was furrowed on the black waters. It might have been made by a monstrous knife.

Then there came a stillness, while the correspondent breathed with open mouth and looked at the sea.

Suddenly there was another swish and another long flash of bluish light, and this time it was alongside the boat, and might almost have been reached with an oar. The correspondent saw an enormous fin speed like a shadow through the water, hurling the crystalline spray and leaving the long glowing trail.

The correspondent looked over his shoulder at the captain. His face was hidden, and he seemed to be asleep. He looked at the babes of the sea. They certainly were asleep. So, being bereft of sympathy, he leaned a little way to one side and swore softly into the sea.

But the thing did not then leave the vicinity of the boat. Ahead or astern on one side or the other, at intervals long or short, fled the long sparkling streak and there was to be heard the *whirroo* of the dark fin. The speed and power of the thing was greatly to be admired. It cut the water like a gigantic and keen projectile.

170   The presence of this biding thing did not affect the man with the same horror that it would if he had been a picnicker. He simply looked at the sea dully and swore in an undertone.

Nevertheless, it is true that he did not wish to be alone with the thing. He wished one of his companions to awake by chance and keep him company with it. But the company hung motionless over the water-jar, and the oiler and the cook in the bottom of the boat were plunged in slumber.

VI

"If I am going to be drowned — if I am going to be drowned — if I am going to be drowned, why, in the name of the seven mad gods who rule the sea, was I allowed to come thus far and contemplate sand and trees?"

During this dismal night, it may be remarked that a man would conclude that it was really the intention of the seven mad gods to drown him, despite the abominable injustice of it. For it was certainly an abominable injustice to drown a man who had worked so hard, so hard. The man felt it would be a crime most unnatural. Other people had drowned at sea since galleys swarmed with painted sails, but still —

When it occurs to a man that nature does not regard him as important, and that she feels she would not maim the universe by disposing of him, he at first wishes to throw bricks at the temple, and he hates deeply the fact that there are no bricks and no temples. Any visible expression of nature would surely be pelleted with his jeers.

Then, if there be no tangible thing to hoot, he feels, perhaps, the desire to confront a personification and indulge in pleas, bowed to one knee, and with hands supplicant, saying, "Yes, but I love myself." 175

A high cold star on a winter's night is the word he feels that she says to him. Thereafter he knows the pathos° of his situation.

The men in the dinghy had not discussed these matters, but each had, no doubt, reflected upon them in silence and according to his mind. There was seldom any expression upon their faces save the general one of complete weariness. Speech was devoted to the business of the boat.

To chime the notes of his emotion, a verse mysteriously entered the correspondent's head. He had even forgotten that he had forgotten this verse, but it suddenly was in his mind.

> A soldier of the Legion lay dying in Algiers;
> There was lack of woman's nursing, there was dearth of woman's tears;
> But a comrade stood beside him, and he took that comrade's hand,
> And he said, "I never more shall see my own, my native land."°

In his childhood the correspondent had been made acquainted with the fact that a soldier of the Legion lay dying in Algiers, but he had never regarded the fact as important. Myriads of his school-fellows had informed him of the soldier's plight, but the dinning had naturally ended by making him perfectly indifferent. He had never considered it his affair that a soldier of the Legion lay dying in Algiers, nor had it appeared to him as a matter for sorrow. It was less to him than the breaking of a pencil's point.

---

pathos: Pity, sorrow, compassion.

A soldier . . . land: Lines from "Bingen on the Rhine," a Victorian ballad about the death of a German soldier in the French Foreign Legion.

180   Now, however, it quaintly came to him as a human, living thing. It was no longer merely a picture of a few throes in the breast of a poet, meanwhile drinking tea and warming his feet at the grate; it was an actuality — stern, mournful, and fine.

The correspondent plainly saw the soldier. He lay on the sand with his feet out straight and still. While his pale left hand was upon his chest in an attempt to thwart the going of his life, the blood came between his fingers. In the far Algerian distance, a city of low square forms was set against a sky that was faint with the last sunset hues. The correspondent, plying the oars and dreaming of the slow and slower movements of the lips of the soldier, was moved by a profound and perfectly impersonal comprehension. He was sorry for the soldier of the Legion who lay dying in Algiers.

The thing which had followed the boat and waited had evidently grown bored at the delay. There was no longer to be heard the slash of the cutwater, and there was no longer the flame of the long trail. The light in the north still glimmered, but it was apparently no nearer to the boat. Sometimes the boom of the surf rang in the correspondent's ears, and he turned the craft seaward then and rowed harder. Southward, some one had evidently built a watch-fire on the beach. It was too low and too far to be seen, but it made a shimmering, roseate reflection upon the bluff in back of it, and this could be discerned from the boat. The wind came stronger, and sometimes a wave suddenly raged out like a mountain cat, and there was to be seen the sheen and sparkle of a broken crest.

The captain, in the bow, moved on his water-jar and sat erect. "Pretty long night," he observed to the correspondent. He looked at the shore. "Those life-saving people take their time."

185   "Did you see that shark playing around?"

"Yes, I saw him. He was a big fellow, all right."

"Wish I had known you were awake."

Later the correspondent spoke into the bottom of the boat.

"Billie!" There was a slow and gradual disentanglement.

"Billie, will you spell me?"

190   "Sure," said the oiler.

As soon as the correspondent touched the cold, comfortable sea-water in the bottom of the boat and had huddled close to the cook's life-belt he was deep in sleep, despite the fact that his teeth played all the popular airs. This sleep was so good to him that it was but a moment before he heard a voice call his name in a tone that demonstrated the last stages of exhaustion. "Will you spell me?"

"Sure, Billie."

The light in the north had mysteriously vanished, but the correspondent took his course from the wide-awake captain.

Later in the night they took the boat farther out to sea, and the captain directed the cook to take one oar at the stern and keep the boat facing the seas. He was to call out if he should hear the thunder of the surf. This plan enabled the oiler and the correspondent to get respite together. "We'll give those boys a chance to get into shape again," said the captain. They curled down and, after a few preliminary chatterings and trembles, slept once more the dead sleep. Neither knew they had bequeathed to the cook the company of another shark, or perhaps the same shark.

As the boat caroused on the waves, spray occasionally bumped over the side   195 and gave them a fresh soaking, but this had no power to break their repose. The ominous slash of the wind and the water affected them as it would have affected mummies.

"Boys," said the cook, with the notes of every reluctance in his voice, "she drifted in pretty close. I guess one of you had better take her to sea again." The correspondent, aroused, heard the crash of the toppled crests.

As he was rowing, the captain gave him some whisky-and-water, and this steadied the chills out of him. "If I ever get ashore and anybody shows me even a photograph of an oar —"

At last there was a short conversation.

"Billie! — Billie, will you spell me?"

"Sure," said the oiler.   200

<h2 style="text-align:center">VII</h2>

When the correspondent again opened his eyes, the sea and sky were each the gray hue of the dawning. Later, carmine° and gold was painted upon the waters. The morning appeared finally, in its splendor, with a sky of pure blue, and the sunlight flamed on the tips of the waves.

On the distant dunes were set many little black cottages, and a tall white windmill reared above them. No man, nor dog, nor bicycle appeared on the beach. The cottages might have formed a deserted village.

The voyagers scanned the shore. A conference was held in the boat. "Well," said the captain, "if no help is coming, we might better try a run through the surf right away. If we stay out here much longer we will be too weak to do anything for ourselves at all." The others silently acquiesced in this reasoning. The boat was headed for the beach. The correspondent wondered if none ever ascended the tall wind-tower, and if they never looked seaward. This tower was a giant, standing with its back to the plight of the ants. It represented in a degree, to the correspondent, the serenity of nature amid the struggles of the individual — nature in the wind, and nature in the vision of men. She did not seem cruel to him then, nor beneficent, nor treacherous, nor wise. But she was indifferent, flatly indifferent. It is, perhaps, plausible that a man in this situation, impressed with the unconcern of the universe, should see the innumerable flaws of life, and have them taste wickedly in his mind, and wish for another chance. A distinction between right and wrong seems absurdly clear to him, then, in this new ignorance of the grave-edge, and he understands that if he were given another opportunity he would mend his conduct and his words, and be better and brighter during an introduction or at a tea.

"Now, boys," said the captain, "she is going to swamp sure. All we can do is to work her in as far as possible, and then when she swamps, pile out and scramble for the beach. Keep cool now, and don't jump until she swamps sure."

---

carmine: Purplish-red.

205   The oiler took the oars. Over his shoulders he scanned the surf. "Captain," he said, "I think I'd better bring her about and keep her head-on to the seas and back her in."

"All right, Billie," said the captain. "Back her in." The oiler swung the boat then, and, seated in the stern, the cook and the correspondent were obliged to look over their shoulders to contemplate the lonely and indifferent shore.

The monstrous inshore rollers heaved the boat high until the men were again enabled to see the white sheets of water scudding up the slanted beach. "We won't get in very close," said the captain. Each time a man could wrest his attention from the rollers, he turned his glance toward the shore, and in the expression of the eyes during this contemplation there was a singular quality. The correspondent, observing the others, knew that they were not afraid, but the full meaning of their glances was shrouded.

As for himself, he was too tired to grapple fundamentally with the fact. He tried to coerce his mind into thinking of it, but the mind was dominated at this time by the muscles, and the muscles said they did not care. It merely occurred to him that if he should drown it would be a shame.

There were no hurried words, no pallor, no plain agitation. The men simply looked at the shore. "Now, remember to get well clear of the boat when you jump," said the captain.

210   Seaward the crest of a roller suddenly fell with a thunderous crash, and the long white comber° came roaring down upon the boat.

"Steady now," said the captain. The men were silent. They turned their eyes from the shore to the comber and waited. The boat slid up the incline, leaped at the furious top, bounced over it, and swung down the long back of the wave. Some water had been shipped, and the cook bailed it out.

But the next crest crashed also. The tumbling, boiling flood of white water caught the boat and whirled it almost perpendicular. Water swarmed in from all sides. The correspondent had his hands on the gunwale° at this time, and when the water entered at that place he swiftly withdrew his fingers, as if he objected to wetting them.

The little boat, drunken with this weight of water, reeled and snuggled deeper into the sea.

"Bail her out, cook! Bail her out!" said the captain.

215   "All right, Captain," said the cook.

"Now, boys, the next one will do for us sure," said the oiler, "Mind to jump clear of the boat."

The third wave moved forward, huge, furious, implacable. It fairly swallowed the dinghy, and almost simultaneously the men tumbled into the sea. A piece of life-belt had lain in the bottom of the boat, and as the correspondent went overboard he held this to his chest with his left hand.

The January water was icy, and he reflected immediately that it was colder than he had expected to find it off the coast of Florida. This appeared to his dazed

---

comber: A large wave.

gunwale: The upper edge of a boat's side.

mind as a fact important enough to be noted at the time. The coldness of the water was sad; it was tragic. This fact was somehow mixed and confused with his opinion of his own situation, so that it seemed almost a proper reason for tears. The water was cold.

When he came to the surface he was conscious of little but the noisy water. Afterward he saw his companions in the sea. The oiler was ahead in the race. He was swimming strongly and rapidly. Off to the correspondent's left, the cook's great white and corked back bulged out of the water; and in the rear the captain was hanging with his one good hand to the keel of the overturned dinghy.

There is a certain immovable quality to a shore, and the correspondent   220
wondered at it amid the confusion of the sea.

It seemed also very attractive; but the correspondent knew that it was a long journey, and he paddled leisurely. The piece of life-preserver lay under him; and sometimes he whirled down the incline of a wave as if he were on a handsled.

But finally he arrived at a place in the sea where travel was beset with difficulty. He did not pause swimming to inquire what manner of current had caught him, but there his progress ceased. The shore was set before him like a bit of scenery on a stage, and he looked at it and understood with his eyes each detail of it.

As the cook passed, much farther to the left, the captain was calling to him. "Turn over on your back, cook! Turn over on your back and use the oar."

"All right, sir." The cook turned on his back, and, paddling with an oar went ahead as if he were a canoe.

Presently the boat also passed to the left of the correspondent, with the captain   225
clinging with one hand to the keel. He would have appeared like a man raising himself to look over a board fence if it were not for the extraordinary gymnastics of the boat. The correspondent marvelled that the captain could still hold to it.

They passed on nearer to shore — the oiler, the cook, the captain — and following them went the water-jar, bouncing gaily over the seas.

The correspondent remained in the grip of this strange new enemy — a current. The shore, with its white slope of sand and its green bluff topped with little silent cottages, was spread like a picture before him. It was very near to him then, but he was impressed as one who, in a gallery, looks at a scene from Brittany or Algiers.

He thought: "I am going to drown? Can it be possible? Can it be possible? Can it be possible?" Perhaps an individual must consider his own death to be the final phenomenon of nature.

But later a wave perhaps whirled him out of this small deadly current, for he found suddenly that he could again make progress toward the shore. Later still he was aware that the captain, clinging with one hand to the keel of the dinghy, had his face turned away from the shore and toward him, and was calling his name. "Come to the boat! Come to the boat!"

In his struggle to reach the captain and the boat, he reflected that when one   230
gets properly wearied drowning must really be a comfortable arrangement — a cessation of hostilities accompanied by a large degree of relief; and he was glad of it, for the main thing in his mind for some moments had been horror of the temporary agony. He did not wish to be hurt.

Presently he saw a man running along the shore. He was undressing with most remarkable speed. Coat, trousers, shirt, everything flew magically off him.

"Come to the boat!" called the captain.

"All right, Captain." As the correspondent paddled, he saw the captain let himself down to bottom and leave the boat. Then the correspondent performed his one little marvel of the voyage. A large wave caught him and flung him with ease and supreme speed completely over the boat and far beyond it. It struck him even then as an event in gymnastics and a true miracle of the sea. An overturned boat in the surf is not a plaything to a swimming man.

The correspondent arrived in water that reached only to his waist, but his condition did not enable him to stand for more than a moment. Each wave knocked him into a heap, and the undertow pulled at him.

235   Then he saw the man who had been running and undressing, and undressing and running, come bounding into the water. He dragged ashore the cook, and then waded toward the captain; but the captain waved him away and sent him to the correspondent. He was naked — naked as a tree in winter; but a halo was about his head, and he shone like a saint. He gave a strong pull, and a long drag, and a bully heave at the correspondent's hand. The correspondent, schooled in the minor formulae, said, "Thanks, old man." But suddenly the man cried, "What's that?" He pointed a swift finger. The correspondent said, "Go."

In the shallows, face downward, lay the oiler. His forehead touched sand that was periodically, between each wave, clear of the sea.

The correspondent did not know all that transpired afterward. When he achieved safe ground he fell, striking the sand with each particular part of his body. It was as if he had dropped from a roof, but the thud was grateful to him.

It seems that instantly the beach was populated with men with blankets, clothes, and flasks, and women with coffee-pots and all the remedies sacred to their minds. The welcome of the land to the men from the sea was warm and generous; but a still and dripping shape was carried slowly up the beach, and the land's welcome for it could only be the different and sinister hospitality of the grave.

When it came night, the white waves paced to and fro in the moon-light, and the wind brought the sound of the great sea's voice to the men on the shore, and they felt that they could then be interpreters.

❖ ❖ ❖

LOUISE ERDRICH   (1954 –   )

The Red Convertible (1984)

Lyman Lamartine

I was the first one to drive a convertible on my reservation. And of course it was red, a red Olds. I owned that car along with my brother Henry Junior. We owned it together until his boots filled with water on a windy night and he bought out my share. Now Henry owns the whole car, and his younger brother Lyman (that's myself), Lyman walks everywhere he goes.

How did I earn enough money to buy my share in the first place? My one talent was I could always make money. I had a touch for it, unusual in a Chippewa. From the first I was different that way, and everyone recognized it. I was the only kid they let in the American Legion Hall to shine shoes, for example, and one Christmas I sold spiritual bouquets for the mission door to door. The nuns let me keep a percentage. Once I started, it seemed the more money I made the easier the money came. Everyone encouraged it. When I was fifteen I got a job washing dishes at the Joliet Café, and that was where my first big break happened.

It wasn't long before I was promoted to busing tables, and then the short-order cook quit and I was hired to take her place. No sooner than you know it I was managing the Joliet. The rest is history. I went on managing. I soon became part owner, and of course there was no stopping me then. It wasn't long before the whole thing was mine.

After I'd owned the Joliet for one year, it blew over in the worst tornado ever seen around here. The whole operation was smashed to bits. A total loss. The fryalator was up in a tree, the grill torn in half like it was paper. I was only sixteen. I had it all in my mother's name, and I lost it quick, but before I lost it I had every one of my relatives, and their relatives, to dinner, and I also bought that red Olds I mentioned, along with Henry.

The first time we saw it! I'll tell you when we first saw it. We had gotten a ride 5
up to Winnipeg, and both of us had money. Don't ask me why, because we never mentioned a car or anything, we just had all our money. Mine was cash, a big bankroll from the Joliet's insurance. Henry had two checks — a week's extra pay for being laid off, and his regular check from the Jewel Bearing Plant.

We were walking down Portage anyway, seeing the sights, when we saw it. There it was, parked, large as life. Really as *if* it was alive. I thought of the word *repose*, because the car wasn't simply stopped, parked, or whatever. That car reposed, calm and gleaming, a FOR SALE sign in its left front window. Then, before we had thought it over at all, the car belonged to us and our pockets were empty. We had just enough money for gas back home.

We went places in that car, me and Henry. We took off driving all one whole summer. We started off toward the little Knife River and Mandaree in Fort Berthold and then we found ourselves down in Wakpala somehow, and then suddenly we were over in Montana on the Rocky Boy, and yet the summer was not even half over. Some people hang on to details when they travel, but we didn't let them bother us and just lived our everyday lives here to there.

I do remember this one place with willows. I remember I laid under those trees and it was comfortable. So comfortable. The branches bent down all around me like a tent or a stable. And quiet, it was quiet, even though there was a powwow close enough so I could see it going on. The air was not too still, not too windy either. When the dust rises up and hangs in the air around the dancers like that, I feel good. Henry was asleep with his arms thrown wide. Later on, he woke up and we started driving again. We were somewhere in Montana, or maybe on the

Blood Reserve — it could have been anywhere. Anyway it was where we met the girl.

10   All her hair was in buns around her ears, that's the first thing I noticed about her. She was posed alongside the road with her arm out, so we stopped. That girl was short, so short her lumber shirt looked comical on her, like a nightgown. She had jeans on and fancy moccasins and she carried a little suitcase.

"Hop on in," says Henry. So she climbs in between us.

"We'll take you home," I says. "Where do you live?"

"Chicken," she says.

"Where the hell's that?" I ask her.

15   "Alaska."

"Okay," says Henry, and we drive.

We got up there and never wanted to leave. The sun doesn't truly set there in summer, and the night is more soft dusk. You might doze off, sometimes, but before you know it you're up again, like an animal in nature. You never feel like you have to sleep hard or put away the world. And things would grow up there. One day just dirt or moss, the next day flowers and long grass. The girl's name was Susy. Her family really took to us. They fed us and put us up. We had our own tent to live in by their house, and the kids would be in and out of there all day and night. They couldn't get over me and Henry being brothers, we looked so different. We told them we knew we had the same mother, anyway.

One night Susy came in to visit us. We sat around in the tent talking of this and that. The season was changing. It was getting darker by that time, and the cold was even getting just a little mean. I told her it was time for us to go. She stood up on a chair.

"You never seen my hair," Susy said.

20   That was true. She was standing on a chair, but still, when she unclipped her buns the hair reached all the way to the ground. Our eyes opened. You couldn't tell how much hair she had when it was rolled up to neatly. Then my brother Henry did something funny. He went up to the chair and said, "Jump on my shoulders." So she did that, and her hair reached down past his waist, and the started twirling, this way and that, so her hair was flung out from side to side.

"I always wondered what it was like to have long pretty hair," Henry says. Well we laughed. It was a funny sight, the way he did it. The next morning we got up and took leave of those people.

On to greener pastures, as they say. It was down through Spokane and across Idaho then Montana and very soon we were racing the weather right along under the Canadian border through Columbus, Des Lacs, and then we were in Bottineau County and soon home. We'd made most of the trip, that summer, without putting up the car hood at all. We got home just in time, it turned out, for the army to remember Henry had signed up to join it.

I don't wonder that the army was so glad to get my brother that they turned him into a Marine. He was built like a brick outhouse anyway. We liked to tease him that they really wanted him for his Indian nose. He had a nose big and sharp as a hatchet, like the nose on Red Tomahawk, the Indian who killed Sitting Bull, whose profile is on signs all along the North Dakota highways. Henry went off to training camp, came home once during Christmas, then the next thing you know we got an overseas letter from him. It was 1970, and he said he was stationed up in the northern hill country. Whereabouts I did not know. He wasn't such a hot letter writer, and only got off two before the enemy caught him. I could never keep it straight, which direction those good Vietnam soldiers were from.

I wrote him back several times, even though I didn't know if those letters would get through. I kept him informed all about the car. Most of the time I had it up on blocks in the yard or half taken apart, because that long trip did a hard job on it under the hood.

I always had good luck with numbers, and never worried about the draft myself. I never even had to think about what my number was. But Henry was never lucky in the same way as me. It was at least three years before Henry came home. By then I guess the whole war was solved in the government's mind, but for him it would keep on going. In those years I'd put his car into almost perfect shape. I always thought of it as his car while he was gone, even though when he left he said, "Now it's yours," and threw me his key.

"Thanks for the extra key," I'd said. "I'll put it up in your drawer just in case I need it." He laughed.

When he came home, though, Henry was very different, and I'll say this: the change was no good. You could hardly expect him to change for the better, I know. But he was quiet, so quiet; and never comfortable sitting still anywhere but always up and moving around. I thought back to times we'd sat still for whole afternoons, never moving a muscle, just shifting our weight along the ground, talking to whoever sat with us, watching things. He'd always had a joke, then, too, and now you couldn't get him to laugh, or when he did it was more the sound of a man choking, a sound that stopped up the throats of other people around him. They got to leaving him alone most of the time, and I didn't blame them. It was a fact: Henry was jumpy and mean.

I'd bought a color TV set for my mom and the rest of us while Henry was away. Money still came very easy. I was sorry I'd ever bought it through, because of Henry. I was also sorry I'd bought color, because with black-and-white the pictures seem older and farther away. But what are you going to do? He sat in front of it, watching it, and that was the only time he was completely still. But it was the kind of stillness that you see in a rabbit where it freezes and before it will bolt. He was not easy. He sat in his chair gripping the armrests with all his might, as if the chair itself was moving at a high speed and if he let go at all he would rocket forward and maybe crash right through the set.

Once I was in the room watching TV with Henry and I heard his teeth click at something. I looked over, and he'd bitten through his lip. Blood was going down his chin. I tell you right then I wanted to smash that tube to pieces. I went over to it but Henry must have known what I was up to. He rushed from his chair

25

and shoved me out of the way, against the wall. I told myself he didn't know what he was doing.

30   My mom came in, turned the set off real quiet, and told us she had made something for supper. So we went and sat down. There was still blood going down Henry's chin, but he didn't notice it and no one said anything, even though every time he took a bite of his bread his blood fell onto it until he was eating his own blood mixed in with the food.

While Henry was not around we talked about what was going to happen to him. There were no Indian doctors on the reservation, and my mom couldn't come around to trusting the old man, Moses Pillager, because he courted her long ago and was jealous of her husbands. He might take revenge through her son. We were afraid that if we brought Henry to a regular hospital they would keep him.

"They don't fix them in those places," Mom said; "they just give them drugs."

"We wouldn't get him there in the first place," I agreed, "so let's just forget about it."

Then I thought about the car.

35   Henry had not even looked at the car since he'd gotten home, though like I said, it was in tip-top condition and ready to drive. I thought the car might bring the old Henry back somehow. So I bided my time and waited for my chance to interest him in the vehicle.

One night Henry was off somewhere. I took myself a hammer. I went out to that car and I did a number on its underside. Whacked it up. Bent the tail pipe double. Ripped the muffler loose. By the time I was done with the car it looked worse than any typical Indian car that has been driven all its life on reservation roads, which they always say are like government promises — full of holes. It just about hurt me, I'll tell you that! I threw dirt in the carburetor and I ripped all the electric tape off the seats. I made it look just as beat up as I could. Then I sat back and waited for Henry to find it.

Still, it took him over a month. That was all right, because it was just getting warm enough, not melting, but warm enough to work outside.

"Lyman," he says, walking in one day, "that red car looks like shit."

"Well it's old," I says. "You got to expect that."

40   "No way!" says Henry. "That car's a classic! But you went and ran the piss right out of it, Lyman, and you know it don't deserve that. I kept that car in A-one shape. You don't remember. You're too young. But when I left, that car was running like a watch. Now I don't even know if I can get it to start again, let alone get it anywhere near its old condition."

"Well, you try," I said, like I was getting mad, "but I say it's a piece of junk."

Then I walked out before he could realize I knew he'd strung together more than six words at once.

After that I thought he'd freeze himself to death working on that car. He was out there all day, and at night he rigged up a little lamp, ran a cord out the window, and had himself some light to see by while he worked. He was better than he had been before, but that's still not saying much. It was easier for him to do the things the rest of us did. He ate more slowly and didn't jump up and down during the meal to get this or that or look out the window. I put my hand in the back of the TV set, I admit, and fiddled around with it good, so that it was almost impossible now to get a clear picture. He didn't look at it very often anyway. He was always out with that car or going off to get parts for it. By the time it was really melting outside, he had it fixed.

I had been feeling down in the dumps about Henry around this time. We had always been together before. Henry and Lyman. But he was such a loner now that I didn't know how to take it. So I jumped at the chance one day when Henry seemed friendly. It's not that he smiled or anything. He just said, "Let's take that old shitbox for a spin." Jus the way he said it made me think he could be coming around.

We went out to the car. It was spring. The sun was shining very bright. My only sister, Bonita, who was just eleven years old, came out and made us stand together for a picture. Henry leaned his elbow on the red car's windshield, and he took his other arm and put it over my shoulder, very carefully, as though it was heavy for him to lift and he didn't want to bring the weight down all at once.

"Smile," Bonita said, and he did.

That picture. I never look at it anymore. A few months ago, I don't know why, I got his picture out and tacked it on the wall. I felt good about Henry at the time, close to him. I felt good having his picture on the wall, until one night when I was looking at television. I was a little drunk and stoned. I looked up at the wall and Henry was staring at me. I don't know what it was, but his smile had changed, or maybe it was gone. All I know is I couldn't stay in the same room with that picture. I was shaking. I got up, closed the door, and went into the kitchen. A little later my friend Ray came over and we both went back into that room. We put the picture in a brown bag, folded the bag over and over tightly, then put it way back in a closet.

I still see that picture now, as if it tugs at me, whenever I pass that closet door. The picture is very clear in my mind. It was so sunny that day Henry had to squint against the glare. Or maybe the camera Bonita held flashed like a mirror, blinding him, before she snapped the picture. My face is right out in the sun, big and round. But he might have drawn back, because the shadows on his face are deep as holes. There are two shadows curved like little hooks around the ends of his smile, as if to frame it and try to keep it there — that one, first smile that looked like it might have hurt his face. He has his field jacket on and the worn-in clothes he'd come back in and kept wearing ever since. After Bonita took the picture, she went into the house and we got into the car. There was a full cooler in the trunk. We started off, east, toward Pembina and the Red River because Henry said he wanted to see the high water.

The trip over there was beautiful. When everything starts changing, drying up, clearing off, you feel like your whole life is starting. Henry felt it, too. The top was down and the car hummed like a top. He'd really put it back in shape, even the tape on the seats was very carefully put down and glued back in layers. It's not that he smiled again or even joked, but his face looked to me as if it was clear, more peaceful. It looked as though he wasn't thinking of anything in particular except the bare fields and windbreaks and houses we were passing.

50   The river was high and full of winter trash when we got there. The sun was still out, but it was colder by the river. There were still little clumps of dirty snow here and there on the banks. The water hadn't gone over the banks yet, but it would, you could tell. It was just at its limit, hard swollen, glossy like an old gray scar. We made ourselves a fire, and we sat down and watched the current go. As I watched it I felt something squeezing inside me and tightening and trying to let go all at the same time. I knew I was not just feeling it myself; I knew I was feeling what Henry was going through at that moment. Except that I couldn't stand it, the closing and opening. I jumped to my feet. I took Henry by the shoulders and I started shaking him. "Wake up," I says, "wake up, wake up, wake up!" I didn't know what had come over me. I sat down beside him again.

His face was totally white and hard. Then it broke, like stones break all of a sudden when water boils up inside them.

"I know it," he says. "I know it. I can't help it. It's no use."

We start talking. He said he knew what I'd done with the car. It was obvious it had been whacked out of shape and not just neglected. He said he wanted to give the car to me for good now, it was no use. He said he'd fixed it just to give it back and I should take it.

"No way," I says. "I don't want it."

55   "That's okay," he says, "you take it."

"I don't want it, though," I says back to him, and then to emphasize, just to emphasize, you understand, I touch his shoulder. He slaps my hand off.

"Take that car," he says.

"No," I say. "Make me," I say, and then he grabs my jacket and rips the arm loose. That jacket is a class act, suede with tags and zippers. I push Henry backwards, off the log. He jumps up and bowls me over. We go down in a clinch and come up swinging hard, for all we're worth, with our fists. He socks my jaw so hard I feel like it swings loose. Then I'm at his rib cage and land a good one under his chin so his head snaps back. He's dazzled. He looks at me and I look at him and then his eyes are full of tears and blood and at first I think he's crying. But no, he's laughing. "Ha! Ha!" he says. "Ha! Ha! Take good care of it."

"Okay," I says. "Okay, no problem. Ha! Ha!"

60   I can't help it, and I start laughing, too. My face feels fat and strange, and after a while I get a beer from the cooler in the trunk, and when I hand it to Henry he takes his shirt and wipes my germs off. "Hoof-and-mouth disease," he says. For some reason this cracks me up, and so we're really laughing for a while, and then we drink all the rest of the beers one by one and throw them in the river and see how far, how fast, the current takes them before they fill up and sink.

"You want to go on back?" I ask after a while. "Maybe we could snag a couple nice Kashpaw girls."

He says nothing. But I can tell his mood is turning again.

"They're all crazy, the girls up here, every damn one of them."

"You're crazy too," I say, to jolly him up. "Crazy Lamartine boys!"

He looks as though he will take this wrong at first. His face twists, then 65
clears, and he jumps up on his feet. "That's right!" he says. "Crazier 'n hell.
Crazy Indians!"

I think it's the old Henry again. He throws off his jacket and starts springing
his legs up from the knees like a fancy dancer. He's down doing something between a grass dance and a bunny hop, no kind of dance I ever saw before, but neither has anyone else on all this green growing earth. He's wild. He wants to pitch
whoopee! He's up and at me and all over. All this time I'm laughing so hard, so
hard my belly is getting tied up in a knot.

"Got to cool me off!" he shouts all of a sudden. Then he runs over to the river
and jumps in.

There's boards and other things in the current. It's so high. No sound comes
from the river after the splash he makes, so I run right over. I look around. It's getting dark. I see he's halfway across the water already, and I know he didn't swim there
but the current took him. It's far. I hear his voice, though, very clearly across it.

"My boots are filling," he says.

He says this in a normal voice, like he just noticed and he doesn't know what 70
to think of it. Then he's gone. A branch comes by. Another branch. And I go in.

By the time I get out of the river, off the snag I pulled myself onto, the sun is
down. I walk back to the car, turn on the high beams, and drive it up the bank. I
put it in first gear and then I take my foot off the clutch. I get out, close the door,
and watch it plow softly into the water. The headlights reach in as they go down,
searching, still lighted even after the water swirls over the back end. I wait. The
wires short out. It is all finally dark. And then there is only the water, the sound
of it going and running and going and running and running.

◇ ◇ ◇

GABRIEL GARCÍA MÁRQUEZ (1928–   )

A Very Old Man with Enormous Wings (1968)

A Tale for Children

Translated from the Spanish by Gregory Rabassa

On the third day of rain they had killed so many crabs inside the house that
Pelayo had to cross his drenched courtyard and throw them into the sea, because
the newborn child had a temperature all night and they thought it was due to the
stench. The world had been sad since Tuesday. Sea and sky were a single ash-gray
thing and the sands of the beach, which on March nights glimmered like powdered light, had become a stew of mud and rotten shellfish. The light was so weak
at noon that when Pelayo was coming back to the house after throwing away the
crabs, it was hard for him to see what it was that was moving and groaning in the
rear of the courtyard. He had to go very close to see that it was an old man, a very
old man, lying face down in the mud, who, in spite of his tremendous efforts,
couldn't get up, impeded by his enormous wings.

Frightened by that nightmare, Pelayo ran to get Elisenda, his wife, who was putting compresses on the sick child, and he took her to the rear of the courtyard. They both looked at the fallen body with mute stupor. He was dressed like a rag-picker.° There were only a few faded hairs left on his bald skull and very few teeth in his mouth, and his pitiful condition of a drenched great-grandfather had taken away any sense of grandeur he might have had. His huge buzzard wings, dirty and half-plucked, were forever entangled in the mud. They looked at him so long and so closely that Pelayo and Elisenda very soon overcame their surprise and in the end found him familiar. Then they dared speak to him, and he answered in an in-comprehensible dialect with a strong sailor's voice. That was how they skipped over the inconvenience of the wings and quite intelligently concluded that he was a lonely castaway from some foreign ship wrecked by the storm. And yet, they called in a neighbor woman who knew everything about life and death to see him, and all she needed was one look to show them their mistake.

"He's an angel," she told them. "He must have been coming for the child, but the poor fellow is so old that the rain knocked him down."

On the following day everyone knew that a flesh-and-blood angel was held captive in Pelayo's house. Against the judgment of the wise neighbor woman, for whom angels in those times were the fugitive survivors of a celestial conspiracy, they did not have the heart to club him to death. Pelayo watched over him all af-ternoon from the kitchen, armed with his bailiff's club, and before going to bed he dragged him out of the mud and locked him up with the hens in the wire chicken coop. In the middle of the night, when the rain stopped, Pelayo and Elisenda were still killing crabs. A short time afterward the child woke up with-out a fever and with a desire to eat. Then they felt magnanimous and decided to put the angel on a raft with fresh water and provisions for three days and leave him to his fate on the high seas. But when they went out into the courtyard with the first light of dawn, they found the whole neighborhood in front of the chicken coop having fun with the angel, without the slightest reverence, tossing him things to eat through the openings in the wire as if he weren't a supernatural creature but a circus animal.

5   Father Gonzaga arrived before seven o'clock, alarmed by the strange news. By that time onlookers less frivolous than those at dawn had already arrived and they were making all kinds of conjectures concerning the captive's future. The simplest among them thought that he should be named mayor of the world. Oth-ers of sterner mind felt that he should be promoted to the rank of five-star gen-eral in order to win all wars. Some visionaries hoped that he could be put to stud in order to implant on earth a race of winged wise men who could take charge of the universe. But Father Gonzaga, before becoming a priest, had been a robust woodcutter. Standing by the wire, he reviewed his catechism° in an instant and asked them to open the door so that he could take a close look at that pitiful man who looked more like a huge decrepit hen among the fascinated chickens. He

---

ragpicker: Someone who makes a living collecting rags and other refuse.

catechism: A book that summarizes the doctrines of Roman Catholicism in question-and-answer form.

was lying in a corner drying his open wings in the sunlight among the fruit peels and breakfast leftovers that the early risers had thrown him. Alien to the impertinences of the world, he only lifted his antiquarian° eyes and murmured something in his dialect when Father Gonzaga went into the chicken coop and said good morning to him in Latin. The parish priest had his first suspicion of an imposter when he saw that he did not understand the language of God or know how to greet His ministers. Then he noticed that seen close up he was much too human; he had an unbearable smell of the outdoors, the back side of his wings was strewn with parasites and his main feathers had been mistreated by terrestrial winds, and nothing about him measured up to the proud dignity of angels. Then he came out of the chicken coop and in a brief sermon warned the curious against the risks of being ingenuous. He reminded them that the devil had the bad habit of making use of carnival tricks in order to confuse the unwary. He argued that if wings were not the essential element in determining the difference between a hawk and an airplane, they were even less so in the recognition of angels. Nevertheless, he promised to write a letter to his bishop so that the latter would write to his primate so that the latter would write to the Supreme Pontiff° in order to get the final verdict from the highest courts.

His prudence fell on sterile hearts. The news of the captive angel spread with such rapidity that after a few hours the courtyard had the bustle of a marketplace and they had to call in troops with fixed bayonets to disperse the mob that was about to knock the house down. Elisenda, her spine all twisted from sweeping up so much marketplace trash, then got the idea of fencing in the yard and charging five cents admission to see the angel.

The curious came from far away. A traveling carnival arrived with a flying acrobat who buzzed over the crowd several times, but no one paid any attention to him because his wings were not those of an angel but, rather, those of a sidereal° bat. The most unfortunate invalids on earth came in search of health: a poor woman who since childhood had been counting her heartbeats and had run out of numbers; a Portuguese man who couldn't sleep because the noise of the stars disturbed him; a sleepwalker who got up at night to undo the things he had done while awake; and many others with less serious ailments. In the midst of that shipwreck disorder that made the earth tremble, Pelayo and Elisenda were happy with fatigue, for in less than a week they had crammed their rooms with money and the line of pilgrims waiting their turn to enter still reached beyond the horizon.

The angel was the only one who took no part in his own act. He spent his time trying to get comfortable in his borrowed nest, befuddled by the hellish heat of the oil lamps and sacramental candles that had been placed along the wire. At first they tried to make him eat some mothballs, which, according to the wisdom of the wise neighbor woman, were the food prescribed for angels. But he turned them down, just as he turned down the papal lunches that the penitents brought

---

antiquarian: Ancient.
the Supreme Pontiff: The pope.
sidereal: Relating to the stars.

him, and they never found out whether it was because he was an angel or because he was an old man that in the end he ate nothing but eggplant mush. His only supernatural virtue seemed to be patience. Especially during the first days, when the hens pecked at him, searching for the stellar parasites that proliferated in his wings, and the cripples pulled out feathers to touch their defective parts with, and even the most merciful threw stones at him, trying to get him to rise so they could see him standing. The only time they succeeded in arousing him was when they burned his side with an iron for branding steers, for he had been motionless for so many hours that they thought he was dead. He awoke with a start, ranting in his hermetic° language and with tears in his eyes, and he flapped his wings a couple of times, which brought on a whirlwind of chicken dung and lunar dust and a gale of panic that did not seem to be of this world. Although many thought that his reaction had been one not of rage but of pain, from then on they were careful not to annoy him, because the majority understood that his passivity was not that of a hero taking his ease but that of a cataclysm in repose.

Father Gonzaga held back the crowd's frivolity with formulas of maid-servant inspiration while awaiting the arrival of a final judgment on the nature of the captive. But the mail from Rome showed no sense of urgency. They spent their time finding out if the prisoner had a navel, if his dialect had any connection with Aramaic,° how many times he could fit on the head of a pin, or whether he wasn't just a Norwegian with wings. Those meager letters might have come and gone until the end of time if a providential event had not put an end to the priest's tribulations.

10   It so happened that during those days, among so many other carnival attractions, there arrived in town the traveling show of the woman who had been changed into a spider for having disobeyed her parents. The admission to see her was not only less than the admission to see the angel, but people were permitted to ask her all manner of questions about her absurd state and to examine her up and down so that no one would ever doubt the truth of her horror. She was a frightful tarantula the size of a ram and with the head of a sad maiden. What was most heart-rending, however, was not her outlandish shape but the sincere affliction with which she recounted the details of her misfortune. While still practically a child she had sneaked out of her parents' house to go to a dance, and while she was coming back through the woods after having danced all night without permission, a fearful thunderclap rent the sky in two and through the crack came the lightning bolt of brimstone that changed her into a spider. Her only nourishment came from the meatballs that charitable souls chose to toss into her mouth. A spectacle like that, full of so much human truth and with such a fearful lesson, was bound to defeat without even trying that of a haughty angel who scarcely deigned to look at mortals. Besides, the few miracles attributed to the angel showed a certain mental disorder, like the blind man who didn't recover his sight but grew three new teeth, or the paralytic who didn't get to walk but almost won

---

hermetic: Occult, magical.

Aramaic: An ancient Middle Eastern language believed to have been the language spoken by Jesus.

the lottery, and the leper whose sores sprouted sunflowers. Those consolation miracles, which were more like mocking fun, had already ruined the angel's reputation when the woman who had been changed into a spider finally crushed him completely. That was how Father Gonzaga was cured forever of his insomnia and Pelayo's courtyard went back to being as empty as during the time it had rained for three days and crabs walked through the bedrooms.

The owners of the house had no reason to lament. With the money they saved they built a two-story mansion with balconies and gardens and high netting so that crabs wouldn't get in during the winter, and with iron bars on the windows so that angels wouldn't get in. Pelayo also set up a rabbit warren close to town and gave up his job as bailiff for good, and Elisenda bought some satin pumps with high heels and many dresses of iridescent silk, the kind worn on Sunday by the most desirable women in those times. The chicken coop was the only thing that didn't receive any attention. If they washed it down with creolin° and burned tears of myrrh° inside it every so often, it was not in homage to the angel but to drive away the dungheap stench that still hung everywhere like a ghost and was turning the new house into an old one. At first, when the child learned to walk, they were careful that he not get too close to the chicken coop. But then they began to lose their fears and got used to the smell, and before the child got his second teeth he'd gone inside the chicken coop to play, where the wires were falling apart. The angel was no less standoffish with him than with other mortals, but he tolerated the most ingenious infamies with the patience of a dog who had no illusions. They both came down with chicken pox at the same time. The doctor who took care of the child couldn't resist the temptation to listen to the angel's heart, and he found so much whistling in the heart and so many sounds in his kidneys that it seemed impossible for him to be alive. What surprised him most, however, was the logic of his wings. They seemed so natural on that completely human organism that he couldn't understand why other men didn't have them too.

When the child began school it had been some time since the sun and rain had caused the collapse of the chicken coop. The angel went dragging himself about here and there like a stray dying man. They would drive him out of the bedroom with a broom and a moment later find him in the kitchen. He seemed to be in so many places at the same time that they grew to think that he'd been duplicated, that he was reproducing himself all through the house, and the exasperated and unhinged Elisenda shouted that it was awful living in that hell full of angels. He could scarcely eat and his antiquarian eyes had also become so foggy that he went about bumping into posts. All he had left were the bare cannulae° of his last feathers. Pelayo threw a blanket over him and extended him the charity of letting him sleep in the shed, and only then did they notice that he had a temperature at night, and was delirious with the tongue twisters of an old Norwegian. That was one of the few times they became alarmed, for they thought he was going to die

---

creolin: A disinfectant.

myrrh: A type of incense.

cannulae: Quills.

and not even the wise neighbor woman had been able to tell them what to do with dead angels.

And yet he not only survived his worst winter, but seemed improved with the first sunny days. He remained motionless for several days in the farthest corner of the courtyard, where no one would see him, and at the beginning of December some large, stiff feathers began to grow on his wings, the feathers of a scarecrow, which looked more like another misfortune of decrepitude. But he must have known the reason for those changes, for he was quite careful that no one should notice them, that no one should hear the sea chanteys that he sometimes sang under the stars. One morning Elisenda was cutting some bunches of onions for lunch when a wind that seemed to come from the high seas blew into the kitchen. Then she went to the window and caught the angel in his first attempt at flight. They were so clumsy that his fingernails opened a furrow in the vegetable patch and he was on the point of knocking the shed down with the ungainly flapping that slipped on the light and couldn't get a grip on the air. But he did manage to gain altitude. Elisenda let out a sigh of relief, for herself and for him, when she saw him pass over the last houses, holding himself up in some way with the risky flapping of a senile vulture. She kept watching him even when she was through cutting the onions and she kept on watching until it was no longer possible for her to see him, because then he was no longer an annoyance in her life but an imaginary dot on the horizon of the sea.

◊ ◊ ◊

HA JIN (1956–)

Saboteur (1997)

Mr. Chiu and his bride were having lunch in the square before Muji Train Station. On the table between them were two bottles of soda spewing out brown foam and two paper boxes of rice and sautéed cucumber and pork. "Let's eat," he said to her, and broke the connected ends of the chopsticks. He picked up a slice of streaky pork and put it into his mouth. As he was chewing, a few crinkles appeared on his thin jaw.

To his right, at another table, two railroad policemen were drinking tea and laughing; it seemed that the stout, middle-aged man was telling a joke to his young comrade, who was tall and of athletic build. Now and again they would steal a glance at Mr. Chiu's table.

The air smelled of rotten melon. A few flies kept buzzing above the couple's lunch. Hundreds of people were rushing around to get on the platform or to catch buses to downtown. Food and fruit vendors were crying for customers in lazy voices. About a dozen young women, representing the local hotels, held up placards which displayed the daily prices and words as large as a palm, like FREE MEALS, AIR-CONDITIONING, and ON THE RIVER. In the center of the square stood a concrete statue of Chairman Mao, at whose feet peasants were napping, their backs on the warm granite and their faces toward the sunny sky. A flock of pigeons perched on the Chairman's raised hand and forearm.

The rice and cucumber tasted good, and Mr. Chiu was eating unhurriedly. His sallow face showed exhaustion. He was glad that the honeymoon was finally over and that he and his bride were heading back for Harbin. During the two weeks' vacation, he had been worried about his liver, because three months ago he had suffered from acute hepatitis; he was afraid he might have a relapse. But he had had no severe symptoms, despite his liver being still big and tender. On the whole he was pleased with his health, which could endure even the strain of a honeymoon; indeed, he was on the course of recovery. He looked at his bride, who took off her wire glasses, kneading the root of her nose with her fingertips. Beads of sweat coated her pale cheeks.

"Are you all right, sweetheart?" he asked. 5

"I have a headache. I didn't sleep well last night."

"Take an aspirin, will you?"

"It's not that serious. Tomorrow is Sunday and I can sleep in. Don't worry."

As they were talking, the stout policeman at the next table stood up and threw a bowl of tea in their direction. Both Mr. Chiu's and his bride's sandals were wet instantly.

"Hooligan!" she said in a low voice. 10

Mr. Chiu got to his feet and said out loud, "Comrade Policeman, why did you do this?" He stretched out his right foot to show the wet sandal.

"Do what?" the stout man asked huskily, glaring at Mr. Chiu while the young fellow was whistling.

"See, you dumped tea on our feet."

"You're lying. You wet your shoes yourself."

"Comrade Policeman, your duty is to keep order, but you purposely tortured us 15 common citizens. Why violate the law you are supposed to enforce?" As Mr. Chiu was speaking, dozens of people began gathering around.

With a wave of his hand, the man said to the young fellow, "Let's get hold of him!"

They grabbed Mr. Chiu and clamped handcuffs around his wrists. He cried, "You can't do this to me. This is utterly unreasonable."

"Shut up!" The man pulled out his pistol. "You can use your tongue at our headquarters."

The young fellow added, "You're a saboteur, you know that? You're disrupting public order."

The bride was too petrified to say anything coherent. She was a recent college 20 graduate, had majored in fine arts, and had never seen the police make an arrest. All she could say was, "Oh, please, please!"

The policemen were pulling Mr. Chiu, but he refused to go with them, holding the corner of the table and shouting, "We have a train to catch. We already bought the tickets."

The stout man punched him in the chest. "Shut up. Let your ticket expire." With the pistol butt he chopped Mr. Chiu's hands, which at once released the table. Together the two men were dragging him away to the police station.

Realizing he had to go with them, Mr. Chiu turned his head and shouted to his bride, "Don't wait for me here. Take the train. If I'm not back by tomorrow morning, send someone over to get me out."

She nodded, covering her sobbing mouth with her palm.

25   After removing his belt, they locked Mr. Chiu into a cell in the back of the Railroad Police Station. The single window in the room was blocked by six steel bars; it faced a spacious yard, in which stood a few pines. Beyond the trees, two swings hung from an iron frame, swaying gently in the breeze. Somewhere in the building a cleaver was chopping rhythmically. There must be a kitchen upstairs, Mr. Chiu thought.

He was too exhausted to worry about what they would do to him, so he lay down on the narrow bed and shut his eyes. He wasn't afraid. The Cultural Revolution was over already, and recently the Party had been propagating the idea that all citizens were equal before the law. The police ought to be a law-abiding model for common people. As long as he remained coolheaded and reasoned with them, they probably wouldn't harm him.

Late in the afternoon he was taken to the Interrogation Bureau on the second floor. On his way there, in the stairwell, he ran into the middle-aged policeman who had manhandled him. The man grinned, rolling his bulgy eyes and pointing his fingers at him as if firing a pistol. Egg of a tortoise! Mr. Chiu cursed mentally.

The moment he sat down in the office, he burped, his palm shielding his mouth. In front of him, across a long desk, sat the chief of the bureau and a donkey-faced man. On the glass desktop was a folder containing information on his case. He felt it bizarre that in just a matter of hours they had accumulated a small pile of writing about him. On second thought he began to wonder whether they had kept a file on him all the time. How could this have happened? He lived and worked in Harbin, more than three hundred miles away, and this was his first time in Muji City.

"The chief of the bureau was a thin, bald man who looked serene and intelligent. His slim hands handled the written pages in the folder in the manner of a lecturing scholar. To Mr. Chiu's left sat a young scribe, with a clipboard on his knee and a black fountain pen in his hand.

30   "Your name?" the chief asked, apparently reading out the question from a form.

"Chiu Maguang."

"Age?"

"Thirty-four."

"Profession?"

"Lecturer."

35   "Work unit?"

"Harbin University."

"Political status?"

"Communist Party member."

The chief put down the paper and began to speak. "Your crime is sabotage, al- 40
though it hasn't induced serious consequences yet. Because you are a Party member, you should be punished more. You have failed to be a model for the masses
and you —"

"Excuse me, sir," Mr. Chiu cut him off.

"What?"

"I didn't do anything. Your men are the saboteurs of our social order. They
threw hot tea on my feet and on my wife's feet. Logically speaking, you should
criticize them, if not punish them."

"That statement is groundless. You have no witness. Why should I believe
you?" the chief said matter-of-factly.

"This is my evidence." He raised his right hand. "Your man hit my fingers with 45
a pistol."

"That doesn't prove how your feet got wet. Besides, you could have hurt your
fingers yourself."

"But I am telling the truth!" Anger flared up in Mr. Chiu. "Your police
station owes me an apology. My train ticket has expired, my new leather
sandals are ruined, and I am late for a conference in the provincial capital.
You must compensate me for the damage and losses. Don't mistake me for a
common citizen who would tremble when you sneeze. I'm a scholar, a philosopher, and an expert in dialectical materialism. If necessary, we will argue
about this in *The Northeastern Daily*, or we will go to the highest People's Court
in Beijing. Tell me, what's your name?" He got carried away with his harangue,
which was by no means trivial and had worked to his advantage on numerous
occasions.

"Stop bluffing us," the donkey-faced man broke in. "We have seen a lot of your
kind. We can easily prove you are guilty. Here are some of the statements given
by eyewitnesses." He pushed a few sheets of paper toward Mr. Chiu.

Mr. Chiu was dazed to see the different handwritings, which all stated that he
had shouted in the square to attract attention and refused to obey the police. One
of the witnesses had identified herself as a purchasing agent from a shipyard in
Shanghai. Something stirred in Mr. Chiu's stomach, a pain rising to his rib. He
gave out a faint moan.

"Now you have to admit you are guilty," the chief said. "Although it's a serious 50
crime, we won't punish you severely, provided you write out a self-criticism and
promise that you won't disrupt the public order again. In other words, your release
will depend on your attitude toward this crime."

"You're daydreaming," Mr. Chiu cried. "I won't write a word, because I'm innocent. I demand that you provide me with a letter of apology so I can explain to
my university why I'm late."

Both the interrogators smiled contemptuously. "Well, we've never done that,"
said the chief, taking a puff at his cigarette.

"Then make this a precedent."

"That's unnecessary. We are pretty certain that you will comply with our
wishes." The chief blew a column of smoke toward Mr. Chiu's face.

55   At the tilt of the chief's head, two guards stepped forward and grabbed the criminal by the arms. Mr. Chiu meanwhile went on saying "I shall report you to the Provincial Administration. You'll have to pay for this! You are worse than the Japanese military police."

They dragged him out of the room.

After dinner, which consisted of a bowl of millet porridge, a corn bun, and a piece of pickled turnip, Mr. Chiu began to have a fever, shaking with a chill and sweating profusely. He knew that the fire of anger had gotten into his liver and that he was probably having a relapse. No medicine was available, because his briefcase had been left with his bride. At home it would have been time for him to sit in front of their color TV, drinking jasmine tea and watching the evening news. It was so lonesome in here. The orange bulb above the single bed was the only source of light, which enabled the guards to keep him under surveillance at night. A moment ago he had asked them for a newspaper or a magazine to read, but they turned him down.

Through the small opening on the door noises came in. It seemed that the police on duty were playing cards or chess in a nearby office; shouts and laughter could be heard now and then. Meanwhile, an accordion kept coughing from a remote corner in the building. Looking at the ballpoint and the letter paper left for him by the guards when they took him back from the Interrogation Bureau, Mr. Chiu remembered the old saying, "When a scholar runs into soldiers, the more he argues, the muddier his point becomes." How ridiculous this whole thing was. He ruffled his thick hair with his fingers.

He felt miserable, massaging his stomach continually. To tell the truth, he was more upset than frightened, because he would have to catch up with his work once he was back home — a paper that was due at the printers next week, and two dozen books he ought to read for the courses he was going to teach in the fall.

60   A human shadow flitted across the opening. Mr. Chiu rushed to the door and shouted through the hole, "Comrade Guard, Comrade Guard!"

"What do you want?" a voice rasped.

"I want you to inform your leaders that I'm very sick. I have heart disease and hepatitis. I may die here if you keep me like this without medication."

"No leader is on duty on the weekend. You have to wait till Monday."

"What? You mean I'll stay in here tomorrow?"

65   "Yes."

"Your station will be held responsible if anything happens to me."

"We know that. Take it easy, you won't die."

It seemed illogical that Mr. Chiu slept quite well that night, though the light above his head had been on all the time and the straw mattress was hard and infested with fleas. He was afraid of ticks, mosquitoes, cockroaches — any kind of insect but fleas and bedbugs. Once, in the countryside, where his school's faculty and staff had helped the peasants harvest crops for a week, his colleagues had joked about his flesh, which they said must have tasted nonhuman to fleas. Except for him, they were all afflicted with hundreds of bites.

More amazing now, he didn't miss his bride a lot. He even enjoyed sleeping alone, perhaps because the honeymoon had tired him out and he needed more rest.

The backyard was quiet on Sunday morning. Pale sunlight streamed through the pine branches. A few sparrows were jumping on the ground, catching caterpillars and ladybugs. Holding the steel bars, Mr. Chiu inhaled the morning air, which smelled meaty. There must have been an eatery or a cooked-meat stand nearby. He reminded himself that he should take this detention with ease. A sentence that Chairman Mao had written to a hospitalized friend rose in his mind: "Since you are already in here, you may as well stay and make the best of it."

His desire for peace of mind originated in his fear that his hepatitis might get worse. He tried to remain unperturbed. However, he was sure that his liver was swelling up, since the fever still persisted. For a whole day he lay in bed, thinking about his paper on the nature of contradictions. Time and again he was overwhelmed by anger, cursing aloud, "A bunch of thugs!" He swore that once he was out, he would write an article about this experience. He had better find out some of the policemen's names.

It turned out to be a restful day for the most part; he was certain that his university would send somebody to his rescue. All he should do now was remain calm and wait patiently. Sooner or later the police would have to release him, although they had no idea that he might refuse to leave unless they wrote him an apology. Damn those hoodlums, they had ordered more than they could eat!

When he woke up on Monday morning, it was already light. Somewhere a man was moaning; the sound came from the backyard. After a long yawn, and kicking off the tattered blanket, Mr. Chiu climbed out of bed and went to the window. In the middle of the yard, a young man was fastened to a pine, his wrists handcuffed around the trunk from behind. He was wriggling and swearing loudly, but there was no sight of anyone else in the yard. He looked familiar to Mr. Chiu.

Mr. Chiu squinted his eyes to see who it was. To his astonishment, he recognized the man, who was Fenjin, a recent graduate from the Law Department at Harbin University. Two years ago Mr. Chiu had taught a course in Marxist materialism, in which Fenjin had enrolled. Now, how on earth had this young devil landed here?

Then it dawned on him that Fenjin must have been sent over by his bride. What a stupid woman! A bookworm, who only knew how to read foreign novels! He had expected that she would contact the school's Security Section, which would for sure send a cadre here. Fenjin held no official position; he merely worked in a private law firm that had just two lawyers; in fact, they had little business except for some detective work for men and women who suspected their spouses of having extramarital affairs. Mr. Chiu was overcome with a wave of nausea.

Should he call out to let his student know he was nearby? He decided not to, because he didn't know what had happened. Fenjin must have quarreled with the police to incur such a punishment. Yet this could never have occurred if Fenjin hadn't come to his rescue. So no matter what, Mr. Chiu had to do something. But what could he do?

It was going to be a scorcher. He could see purple steam shimmering and rising from the ground among the pines. Poor devil, he thought, as he raised a bowl of corn glue to his mouth, sipped, and took a bite of a piece of salted celery.

When a guard came to collect the bowl and the chopsticks, Mr. Chiu asked him what had happened to the man in the backyard. "He called our boss 'bandit,'" the guard said. "He claimed he was a lawyer or something. An arrogant son of a rabbit."

Now it was obvious to Mr. Chiu that he had to do something to help his rescuer. Before he could figure out a way, a scream broke out in the backyard. He rushed to the window and saw a tall policeman standing before Fenjin, an iron bucket on the ground. It was the same young fellow who had arrested Mr. Chiu in the square two days before. The man pinched Fenjin's nose, then raised his hand, which stayed in the air for a few seconds, then slapped the lawyer across the face. As Fenjin was groaning, the man lifted up the bucket and poured water on his head.

80   "This will keep you from getting sunstroke, boy. I'll give you some more every hour," the man said loudly.

Fenjin kept his eyes shut, yet his wry face showed that he was struggling to hold back from cursing the policeman, or, more likely, that he was sobbing in silence. He sneezed, then raised his face and shouted, "Let me go take a piss."

"Oh yeah?" the man bawled. "Pee in you pants."

Still Mr. Chiu didn't make any noise, gripping the steel bars with both hands, his fingers white. The policeman turned and glanced at the cell's window; his pistol, partly holstered, glittered in the sun. With a snort he spat his cigarette butt to the ground and stamped it into the dust.

Then the door opened and the guards motioned Mr. Chiu to come out. Again they took him upstairs to the Interrogation Bureau.

85   The same men were in the office, though this time the scribe was sitting there empty-handed. At the sight of Mr. Chiu the chief said, "Ah, here you are. Please be seated."

After Mr. Chiu sat down, the chief waved a white silk fan and said to him, "You may have seen your lawyer. He's a young man without manners, so our director had him taught a crash course in the backyard."

"It's illegal to do that. Aren't you afraid to appear in a newspaper?"

"No, we are not, not even on TV. What else can you do? We are not afraid of any story you make up. We call it fiction. What we do care about is that you cooperate with us. That is to say, you must admit your crime."

"What if I refuse to cooperate?"

90   "Then your lawyer will continue his education in the sunshine."

A swoon swayed Mr. Chiu, and he held the arms of the chair to steady himself. A numb pain stung him in the upper stomach and nauseated him, and his head was throbbing. He was sure that the hepatitis was finally attacking him. Anger was flaming up in his chest; his throat was tight and clogged.

The chief resumed, "As a matter of fact, you don't even have to write out your self-criticism. We have your crime described clearly here. All we need is your signature."

Holding back his rage, Mr. Chiu said, "Let me look at that."

With a smirk the donkey-faced man handed him a sheet, which carried these words:

> I hereby admit that on July 13 I disrupted public order at Muji Train Station, and that I refused to listen to reason when the railroad police issued their warning. Thus I myself am responsible for my arrest. After two days' detention, I have realized the reactionary nature of my crime. From now on, I shall continue to educate myself with all my effort and shall never commit this kind of crime again.

A voice started screaming in Mr. Chiu's ears, "Lie, lie!" But he shook his head 95
and forced the voice away. He asked the chief, "If I sign this, will you release both my lawyer and me?"

"Of course, we'll do that." The chief was drumming his fingers on the blue folder — their file on him.

Mr. Chiu signed his name and put his thumbprint under his signature.

"Now you are free to go," the chief said with a smile, and handed him a piece of paper to wipe his thumb with.

Mr. Chiu was so sick that he couldn't stand up from the chair at first try. Then he doubled his effort and rose to his feet. He staggered out of the building to meet his lawyer in the backyard, having forgotten to ask for his belt back. In his chest he felt as though there were a bomb. If he were able to, he would have razed the entire police station and eliminated all their families. Though he knew he could do nothing like that, he made up his mind to do something.

"I'm sorry about this torture, Fenjin," Mr. Chiu said when they met. 100

"It doesn't matter. They are savages." The lawyer brushed a patch of dirt off his jacket with trembling fingers. Water was still dribbling from the bottoms of his trouser legs.

"Let's go now," the teacher said.

The moment they came out of the police station, Mr. Chiu caught sight of a tea stand. He grabbed Fenjin's arm and walked over to the old woman at the table. "Two bowls of black tea," he said and handed her a one-yuan note.

After the first bowl, they each had another one. Then they set out for the train station. But before they walked fifty yards, Mr. Chiu insisted on eating a bowl of tree-ear soup at a food stand. Fenjin agreed. He told his teacher, "You mustn't treat me like a guest."

"No, I want to eat something myself." 105

As if dying of hunger, Mr. Chiu dragged his lawyer from restaurant to restaurant near the police station, but at each place he ordered no more than two bowls of food. Fenjin wondered why his teacher wouldn't stay at one place and eat his fill.

Mr. Chiu bought noodles, wonton, eight-grain porridge, and chicken soup, respectively, at four restaurants. While eating, he kept saying through his teeth, "If only I could kill all the bastards!" At the last place he merely took a few sips of the soup without tasting the chicken cubes and mushrooms.

Fenjin was baffled by his teacher, who looked ferocious and muttered to himself mysteriously, and whose jaundiced face was covered with dark puckers. For the first time Fenjin thought of Mr. Chiu as an ugly man.

Within a month over eight hundred people contracted acute hepatitis in Muji. Six died of the disease, including two children. Nobody knew how the epidemic had started.

◇   ◇   ◇

JAMES JOYCE   (1884–1941)

Eveline   (1914)

She sat at the window watching the evening invade the avenue. Her head was leaned against the window curtains and in her nostrils was the odor of dusty cretonne.° She was tired.

Few people passed. The man out of the last house passed on his way home; she heard his footsteps clacking along the concrete pavement and afterwards crunching on the cinder path before the new red houses. One time there used to be a field there in which they used to play every evening with other people's children. Then a man from Belfast° bought the field and built houses in it — not like their little brown houses but bright brick houses with shining roofs. The children of the avenue used to play together in that field — the Devines, the Waters, the Dunns, little Keogh the cripple, she and her brothers and sisters. Ernest, however, never played: he was too grown up. Her father used often to hunt them in out of the field with his blackthorn stick; but usually little Keogh used to keep *nix*° and call out when he saw her father coming. Still they seemed to have been rather happy then. Her father was not so bad then; and besides, her mother was alive. That was a long time ago; she and her brothers and sisters were all grown up; her mother was dead. Tizzie Dunn was dead, too, and the Waters had gone back to England. Everything changes. Now she was going to go away like the others, to leave her home.

Home! She looked around the room, reviewing all its familiar objects which she had dusted once a week for so many years, wondering where on earth all the dust came from. Perhaps she would never see again those familiar objects from which she had never dreamed of being divided. And yet during all those years she had never found out the name of the priest whose yellowing photograph hung on the wall above the broken harmonium beside the colored print of the promises made to Blessed Margaret Mary Alacoque. He had been a school friend of her

---

cretonne: Heavy cloth used for curtains and upholstery.

Belfast: Capital of present-day Northern Ireland. This story refers to a time before the Partition of Ireland.

keep nix: Keep watch (slang).

father. Whenever he showed the photograph to a visitor her father used to pass it with a casual word:

"He is in Melbourne now."

She had consented to go away, to leave her home. Was that wise? She tried to   5
weigh each side of the question. In her home anyway she had shelter and food; she had those whom she had known all her life about her. Of course she had to work hard both in the house and at business. What would they say of her in the Stores when they found out that she had run away with a fellow? Say she was a fool, perhaps; and her place would be filled up by advertisement. Miss Gavan would be glad. She had always had an edge on her, especially whenever there were people listening.

"Miss Hill, don't you see these ladies are waiting?"

"Look lively, Miss Hill, please."

She would not cry many tears at leaving the Stores.

But in her new home, in a distant unknown country, it would not be like that. Then she would be married — she, Eveline. People would treat her with respect then. She would not be treated as her mother had been. Even now, though she was over nineteen, she sometimes felt herself in danger of her father's violence. She knew it was that that had given her the palpitations. When they were growing up he had never gone for her, like he used to go for Harry and Ernest, because she was a girl; but latterly he had begun to threaten her and say what he would do to her only for her dead mother's sake. And now she had nobody to protect her. Ernest was dead and Harry, who was in the church decorating business, was nearly always down somewhere in the country. Besides, the invariable squabble for money on Saturday nights had begun to weary her unspeakably. She always gave her entire wages — seven shillings — and Harry always sent up what he could but the trouble was to get any money from her father. He said she used to squander the money, that she had no head, that he wasn't going to give her his hard-earned money to throw about the streets, and much more, for he was usually fairly bad of a Saturday night. In the end he would give her the money and ask her had she any intention of buying Sunday dinner. Then she had to rush out as quickly as she could and do her marketing, holding her black leather purse tightly in her hand as she elbowed her way through the crowds and returning home late under her load of provisions. She had hard work to keep the house together and to see that the two young children, who had been left to her charge went to school regularly and got their meals regularly. It was hard work — a hard life — but now that she was about to leave it she did not find it a wholly undesirable life.

She was about to explore another life with Frank. Frank was very kind,   10
manly, open-hearted. She was to go away with him by the night-boat to be his wife and to live with him in Buenos Aires where he had a home waiting for her. How well she remembered the first time she had seen him; he was lodging in a house on the main road where she used to visit. It seemed a few weeks ago. He was standing at the gate, his peaked cap pushed back on his head and his hair tumbled forward over a face of bronze. Then they had come to know each other. He used to meet her outside the Stores every evening and see her home. He took her to see *The Bohemian Girl* and she felt elated as she sat in an unaccustomed

part of the theater with him. He was awfully fond of music and sang a little. People knew that they were courting and, when he sang about the lass that loves a sailor, she always felt pleasantly confused. He used to call her Poppens out of fun. First of all it had been an excitement for her to have a fellow and then she had begun to like him. He had tales of distant countries. He had started as a deck boy at a pound a month on a ship of the Allan Line going out to Canada. He told her the names of the ships he had been on and the names of the different services. He had sailed through the Straits of Magellan° and he told her stories of the terrible Patagonians.° He had fallen on his feet in Buenos Aires, he said, and had come over to the old country just for a holiday. Of course, her father had found out the affair and had forbidden her to have anything to say to him.

"I know these sailor chaps," he said.

One day he had quarreled with Frank and after that she had to meet her lover secretly.

The evening deepened in the avenue. The white of two letters in her lap grew indistinct. One was to Harry; the other was to her father. Ernest had been her favorite but she liked Harry too. Her father was becoming old lately, she noticed; he would miss her. Sometimes he could be very nice. Not long before, when she had been laid up for a day, he had read her out a ghost story and made toast for her at the fire. Another day, when their mother was alive, they had all gone for a picnic to the Hill of Howth. She remembered her father putting on her mother's bonnet to make the children laugh.

Her time was running out but she continued to sit by the window, leaning her head against the window curtain, inhaling the odor of dusty cretonne. Down far in the avenue she could hear a street organ playing. She knew the air. Strange that it should come that very night to remind her of the promise to her mother, her promise to keep the home together as long as she could. She remembered the last night of her mother's illness; she was again in the close dark room at the other side of the hall and outside she heard a melancholy air of Italy. The organ player had been ordered to go away and given sixpence. She remembered her father strutting back into the sickroom saying:

15 "Damned Italians! coming over here!"

As she mused the pitiful vision of her mother's life laid its spell on the very quick of her being — that life of commonplace sacrifices closing in final craziness. She trembled as she heard again her mother's voice saying constantly with foolish insistence:

"Derevaun Seraun! Derevaun Seraun!"°

She stood up in a sudden impulse of terror. Escape! She must escape! Frank would save her. He would give her life, perhaps love, too. But she wanted to live. Why should she be unhappy? She had a right to happiness. Frank would take her in his arms, fold her in his arms. He would save her.

Straits of Magellan: Sea channel at the southern tip of South America.
Patagonians: People from Patagonia, a tableland region in southern Argentina and Chile.
Derevaun Seraun: "The end of pleasure is pain!" (Irish).

She stood among the swaying crowd in the station at the North Wall. He held her hand and she knew that he was speaking to her, saying something about the passage over and over again. The station was full of soldiers with brown baggages. Through the wide doors of the sheds she caught a glimpse of the black mass of the boat, lying in beside the quay° wall, with illumined portholes. She answered nothing. She felt her cheek pale and cold and, out of a maze of distress, she prayed to God to direct her, to show her what was her duty. The boat blew a long mournful whistle into the mist. If she went, tomorrow she would be on the sea with Frank, steaming toward Buenos Aires. Their passage had been booked. Could she still draw back after all he had done for her? Her distress awoke a nausea in her body and she kept moving her lips in silent, fervent prayer.

A bell clanged upon her heart. She felt him seize her hand: 20

"Come!"

All the seas of the world tumbled about her heart. He was drawing her into them: he would drown her. She gripped with both hands at the iron railing.

"Come!"

No! No! No! It was impossible. Her hands clutched the iron in frenzy. Amid the seas she sent a cry of anguish!

"Eveline! Evvy!"   25

He rushed beyond the barrier and called to her to follow. He was shouted at to go on but he still called to her. She set her white face to him, passive, like a helpless animal. Her eyes gave him no sign of love or farewell or recognition.

◇ ◇ ◇

FRANZ KAFKA (1883–1924)

A Hunger Artist (1924)

Translated by Edwin and Willa Muir

During these last decades the interest in professional fasting has markedly diminished. It used to pay very well to stage such great performances under one's own management, but today that is quite impossible. We live in a different world now. At one time the whole town took a lively interest in the hunger artist; from day to day of his fast the excitement mounted; everybody wanted to see him at least once a day; there were people who bought season tickets for the last few days and sat from morning till night in front of his small barred cage; even in the nighttime there were visiting hours, when the whole effect was heightened by torch flares; on fine days the cage was set out in the open air, and then it was the children's special treat to see the hunger artist; for their elders he was often just a joke that happened to be in fashion, but the children stood open-mouthed, holding each

---

quay: A paved stretch of shoreline facing navigable water, used for loading and unloading ships.

other's hands for greater security, marveling at him as he sat there pallid in black tights, with his ribs sticking out so prominently, not even on a seat but down among straw on the ground, sometimes giving a courteous nod, answering questions with a constrained smile, or perhaps stretching an arm through the bars so that one might feel how thin it was, and then again withdrawing deep into himself, paying no attention to anyone or anything, not even to the all-important striking of the clock that was the only piece of furniture in his cage, but merely starting into vacancy with half shut eyes, now and then taking a sip from a tiny glass of water to moisten his lips.

Besides causal onlookers there were also relays of permanent watchers selected by the public, usually butchers, strangely enough, and it was their task to watch the hunger artist day and night, three of them at a time, in case he should have some secret recourse to nourishment. This was nothing but a formality, instituted to reassure the masses, for the initiates knew well enough that during his fast the artist would never in my circumstances, not even under forcible compulsion, swallow the smallest morsel of food: the honor of his profession forbade it. Not every watcher, of course, was capable of understanding this, there were often groups of night watchers who were very lax in carrying out their duties and deliberately huddled together in a retired corner to play cards with great absorption, obviously intending to give the hunger artist the chance of a little refreshment, which they supposed he could draw from some private hoard. Nothing annoyed the artist more than such watchers; they made him miserable; they made his fast seem unendurable; sometimes he mastered his feebleness sufficiently to sing during their watch for as long as he could keep going, to show them how unjust their suspicions were. But that was of little use; they only wondered at his cleverness in being able to fill his mouth even while singing. Much more to his taste were the watchers who sat close up to the bars, who were not content with the dim night lighting of the hall but focused him in the full glare of the electric pocket torch given them by the impresario. The harsh light did not trouble him at all, in any case he could never sleep properly, and he could always drowse a little, whatever the light, at any hour, even when the hall was thronged with noisy onlookers. He was quite happy at the prospect of spending a sleepless night with such watchers; he was ready to exchange jokes with them, to tell them stories out of his nomadic life, anything at all to keep them awake and demonstrate to them again that he had no eatables in his cage and that he was fasting as not one of them could fast. But his happiest moment was when the morning came and an enormous breakfast was brought them, at his expense, on which they flung themselves with the keen appetite of healthy men after a weary night of wakefulness. Of course there were people who argued that this breakfast was an unfair attempt to bribe the watchers, but that was going rather too far, and when they were invited to take on a night's vigil without a breakfast, merely for the sake of the cause, they made themselves scarce, although they stuck stubbornly to their suspicions.

Such suspicions, anyhow, were a necessary accompaniment to the profession of fasting. No one could possibly watch the hunger artist continuously, day and night, and so no one could produce first-hand evidence that the fast had really been rigorous and continuous; only the artist himself could know that, he was therefore bound to be the sole completely satisfied spectator of his own fast. Yet for other reasons he was never satisfied; it was not perhaps mere fasting that had brought him to such skeleton thinness that many people had regretfully to keep away from his exhibitions; because the sight of him was too much for them, perhaps it was dissatisfaction with himself that had worn him down. For he alone knew, what no other initiate knew, how easy it was to fast. It was the easiest thing in the world. He made no secret of this, yet people did not believe him, at the best they set him down as modest, most of them, however, thought he was out for publicity or else was some kind of cheat who found it easy to fast because he had discovered a way of making it easy, and then had the impudence to admit the fact, more or less. He had to put up with all that, and in the course of time had got used to it, but his inner dissatisfaction always rankled, and never yet, after any term of fasting — this must be granted to this credit — had he left the cage of his own free will. The longest period of fasting was fixed by his impresario at forty days, beyond that term he was not allowed to go, not even in great cities, and there was good reason for it, too. Experience had proved that for about forty days the interest of the public could be stimulated by a steadily increasing pressure of advertisement, but after that the town began to lose interest, sympathetic support began notably to fall off; there were of course local variations as between one town and another or one country and another, but as a general rule forty days marked the limit. So on the fortieth day the flower-bedecked cage was opened, enthusiastic spectators filled the hall, a military band played, two doctors entered the cage to measure the results of the fast, which were announced through a megaphone, and finally two young ladies appeared, blissful at having been selected for the honor, to help the hunger artist down the few steps leading to a small table on which was spread a carefully chosen invalid repast. And at this very moment the artist always turned stubborn. True, he would entrust his bony arms to the outstretched helping hands of the ladies bending over him, but stand up he would not. Why stop fasting at this particular moment, after forty days of it? He had held out for a long time, an illimitably long time; why stop now, when he was in his best fasting form, or rather, not yet quite in his best fasting form? Why should he be cheated of the fame he would get for fasting longer, for being not only the record hunger artist of all time, which presumably he was already, but for beating his own record by a performance beyond human imagination, since he felt that there were no limits to his capacity for fasting? He public pretended to admire him so much, why, should it have so little patience with him; if he could endure fasting longer, why shouldn't the public endure it? Besides, he was tired, he was comfortable sitting in the straw, and now he was supposed to lift himself to his full height and go down to a meal the very thought of which gave him a nausea that only the presence of the ladies kept him from betraying, and even that with an effort. And he looked up into the eyes of the ladies who were apparently so friendly and in reality so cruel, and shook his head, which felt too heavy on its strengthless neck. But then there happened yet again what always happened. The impresario came forward, without a word — for the band made speech impossible — lifted his arms in the air above the artist, as if inviting Heaven to look down upon its creature here in the straw, this suffering martyr, which indeed he was, although in quite another sense; grasped him round the emaciated waist, with exaggerated caution, so that the frail condition he was in might be appreciated; and committed him to the care of the blenching ladies, not without secretly giving him a shaking so that his legs and body tottered and swayed. The artist now submitted completely; his head lolled on his breast as if it had landed there by chance; his body was hollowed out; his legs in a spasm of self-preservation clung close to each other at the knees, yet scraped on the ground as if it were not really solid ground, as if they were only try-ing to find solid ground; and the whole weight of his body, a feather-weight after all, relapsed onto one of the ladies, who, looking round for help and panting a little — this post of honor was not at all what she had expected it to be — first stretched her neck as far as she could to keep her face at least free from contact with the artist, when finding this impossible, and her more fortunate companion not coming to her aid but merely holding extended on her own trembling hand the little bunch of knuckle-bones that was the artist's, to the great delight of the spectators burst into tears and had to be replaced by an attendant who had long been stationed in readiness. Then came the food, a little of which the impresario managed to get between the artist's lips, while he sat in a kind of half-fainting trance, to the accompaniment of cheerful patter designed to distract the public's attention from the artist's condition; after that, a toast was drunk to the public, supposedly prompted by a whisper from the artist in the impresario's ear; the band confirmed it with a mighty flourish, the spectators melted away, and no one had any cause to be dissatisfied with the proceedings, no one except the hunger artist himself, he only, as always.

So he lived for many years, with small regular intervals of recuperation, in visi-ble glory, honored by the world, yet in spite of that troubled in spirit, and all the more troubled because no one would take his trouble seriously. What comfort could he possibly need? What more could he possibly wish for? And if some good-natured person, feeling sorry for him, tried to console him by pointing out that his melan-choly was probably caused by fasting, it could happen, especially when he had been fasting for some time, that he reacted with an outburst of fury and to the general alarm began to shake the bars of his cage like a wild animal. Yet the impresario had a way of punishing these outbreaks which he rather enjoyed putting into operation. He would apologize publicly for the artist's behavior, which was only to be excused, he admitted, because of the irritability caused by fasting: a condition hardly to be understood by well-fed people; then by natural transition he went on to mention the artist's equally incomprehensible boast that he could fast for much longer than he was doing; he praised the high ambition, the good will, the great self-denial un-doubtedly implicit in such a statement; and then quite simply countered it by bring-ing out photographs, which were also on sale to the public, showing the artist on the fortieth day of a fast lying in bed almost dead from exhaustion. This perversion of the truth, familiar to the artist though it was, always unnerved him afresh and proved too much for him. What was a consequence of the premature ending of his fast was here presented as the cause of it! To fight against this lack of understand-ing, against a whole world of non-understanding, was impossible. Time and again in good faith he stood by the bars listening to the impresario, but as soon as the pho-tographs appeared he always let go and sank with a groan back on to his straw, and the reassured public could once more come close and gaze at him.

A few years later when the witnesses of such scenes called them to mind, they often failed to understand themselves at all. For meanwhile the aforementioned change in public interest had set in; it seemed to happen almost overnight; there may have been profound causes for it, but who was going to bother about that; at any rate the pampered hunger artist suddenly found himself deserted one fine day by the amusement seekers, who went streaming past him to other more favored attractions. For the last time the impresario hurried him over half Europe to discover whether the old interest might still survive here and there; all in vain; everywhere, as if by secret agreement, a positive revulsion from professional fasting was in evidence. Of course it could not really have sprung up so suddenly as all that, and many premonitory symptoms which had not been sufficiently remarked or suppressed during the rush and glitter of success now came retrospectively to mind, but it was now too late to take any countermeasures. Fasting would surely come into fashion again at some future date, yet that was no comfort for those living in the present. What, then, was the hunger artist to do? He had been applauded by thousands in his time and could hardly come down to showing himself in a street booth at village fairs, and as for adopting another profession, he was not only too old for that but too fanatically devoted to fasting. So he took leave of the impresario, his partner in an unparalleled career, and hired himself to a large circus; in order to spare his own feelings he avoided reading the conditions of his contract.

A large circus with its enormous traffic in replacing and recruiting men, animals and apparatus can always find a use for people at any time, even for a hunger artist, provided of course that he does not ask too much, and in this particular case anyhow it was not only the artist who was taken on but his famous and long-known name as well, indeed considering the peculiar nature of his performance, which was not impaired by advancing age, it could not be objected that here was an artist past his prime, no longer at the height of his professional skill, seeking a refuge in some quiet corner of a circus; on the contrary, the hunger artist averred that he could fast as well as ever, which was entirely credible, he even alleged that if he were allowed to fast as he liked, and this was at once promised him without more ado, he could astound the world by establishing a record never yet achieved, a statement which certainly provoked a smile among the other professionals, since it left out of account the change in public opinion, which the hunger artist in his zeal conveniently forgot.

He had not, however, actually lost his sense of the real situation and took it as a matter of course that he and his cage should be stationed, not in the middle of the ring as a main attraction, but outside, near the animal cages, on a site that was after all easily accessible. Large and gaily painted placards made a frame for the cage and announced what was to be seen inside it. When the public came thronging out in the intervals to see the animals, they could hardly avoid passing the hunger artist's cage and stopping there for a moment, perhaps they might even have stayed longer had not those pressing behind them in the narrow gangway, who did not understand why they should be held up on their way toward the excitements of the menagerie, made it impossible for anyone to stand gazing quietly for any length of time. And that was the reason why the hunger artist, who had of course been looking forward to these visiting hours as the main achievement of his life, began instead to shrink from them. At first he could hardly wait for the intervals; it was exhilarating to watch the crowds come streaming his way, until only too soon — not even the most obstinate self-deception, clung to almost consciously, could hold out against the fact — the conviction was borne in upon him that these people, most of them, to judge from their actions, again and again, without exception, were all on their way to the menagerie. And the first sight of them from the distance remained the best. For when they reached his cage he was at once deafened by the storm of shouting and abuse that arose from the two contending factions, which renewed themselves continuously, of those who wanted to stop and stare at him — he soon began to dislike them more than the others — not out of real interest but only out of obstinate self-assertiveness, and those who wanted to go straight on to the animals: When the first great rush was past, the stragglers came along, and these, whom nothing could have prevented from stopping to look at him as long as they had breath, raced past with long strides, hardly even glancing at him, in their haste to get to the menagerie in time. And all too rarely did it happen that he had a stroke of luck, when some father of a family fetched up before him with his children, pointed a finger at the hunger artist and explained at length what the phenomenon meant, telling stories of earlier years when he himself had watched similar but much more thrilling performances, and the children, still rather uncomprehending, since neither inside nor outside school had they been sufficiently prepared for this lesson — what did they care about fasting? — yet showed by the brightness of their intent eyes that new and better times might be coming. Perhaps, said the hunger artist to himself many a time, things would be a little better if his cage were set not quite so near the menagerie. That made it too easy for people to make their choice, to say nothing of what he suffered from the stench of the menagerie, the animals' restlessness by night, the carrying past of raw lumps of flesh for the beasts of prey, the roaring at feeding times, which depressed him continually. But he did not dare to lodge a complaint with the management; after all, he had the animals to thank for the troops of people who passed his cage, among whom there might always be one here and there to take an interest in him, and who could tell where they might seclude him if he called attention to his existence and thereby to the fact that, strictly speaking, he was only an impediment on the way to the menagerie.

A small impediment, to be sure, one that grew steadily less. People grew familiar with the strange idea that they could be expected, in times like these, to take an interest in a hunger artist, and with this familiarity the verdict went out against him. He might fast as much as he could, and he did so; but nothing could save him now, people passed him by. Just try to explain to anyone the art of fasting! Anyone who has no feeling for it cannot be made to understand it. The fine placards grew dirty and illegible, they were torn down; the little notice board telling the number of fast days achieved, which at first was changed carefully every day, had long stayed at the same figure, for after the first few weeks even this small task seemed pointless to the staff; and so the artist simply fasted on and on, as he had once dreamed of doing, and it was no trouble to him, just as he had always foretold, but no one counted the days, no one, not even the artist himself, knew what records he was already breaking, and his heart grew heavy. And when once in a time some leisurely passer-by stopped, made merry over the old figure on the board and spoke of swindling, that was in its way the stupidest lie ever invented by indifference and inborn malice, since it was not the hunger artist who was cheating; he was working honestly, but the world was cheating him of his reward.

Many more days went by, however, and that too came to an end. An overseer's eye fell on the cage one day and he asked the attendants why this perfectly good cage should be left standing there unused with dirty straw inside it; nobody knew, until one man, helped out by the notice board, remembered about the hunger artist. They poked into the straw with sticks and found him in it. "Are you still fasting?" asked the overseer: "When on earth do you mean to stop?" "Forgive me, everybody," whispered the hunger artist; only the overseer, who had his ear to the bars, understood him. "Of course," said the overseer, and tapped his forehead with a finger to let the attendants know what state the man was in, "we forgive you." "I always wanted you to admire my fasting," said the hunger artist. "We do admire it," said the overseer, affably. "But you shouldn't admire it," said the hunger artist. "Well, then we don't admire it," said the overseer, "but why shouldn't we admire it?" Because I have to fast, I can't help it," said the hunger artist. "What a fellow you are," said the overseer, "and why can't you help it?" "Because," said the hunger artist, lifting his head a little and speaking, with his lips pursed, as if for a kiss, right into the overseer's ear, so that no syllable might be lost, "because I couldn't find the food I liked. If I had found it, believe me, I should have made no fuss and stuffed myself like you or anyone else." These were his last words, but in his dimming eyes remained the firm though no longer proud persuasion that he was still continuing to fast.

"Well, clear this out now!" said the overseer, and they buried the hunger artist, 10 straw and all. Into the cage they put a young panther. Even the most insensitive felt it refreshing to see this wild creature leaping around the cage that had so long been dreary. The panther was all right. The food he liked was brought him without hesitation by the attendants; he seemed not even to miss his freedom; his noble body, furnished almost to the bursting point with all that it needed, seemed to carry freedom around with it too; somewhere in his jaws it seemed to lurk; and the joy of life streamed with such ardent passion from his throat that for the onlookers it was not easy to stand the shock of it. But they braced themselves, crowded round the cage, and did not want ever to move away.

❖ ❖ ❖

HERMAN MELVILLE (1819–1891)

Bartleby, the Scrivener° (1853)
A story of Wall Street

I am a rather elderly man. The nature of my avocations, for the last thirty years, has brought me into more than ordinary contact with what would seem an interesting

---

Scrivener: A copyist. Prior to the photocopy and mimeograph, copies had to be made by a scribe.

and somewhat singular set of men, of whom, as yet, nothing, that I know of, has ever been written — I mean, the law-copyists, or scriveners. I have known very many of them, professionally and privately, and, if I pleased, could relate divers histories, at which good-natured gentlemen might smile, and sentimental souls might weep. But I waive the biographies of all other scriveners, for a few passages in the life of Bartleby, who was a scrivener, the strangest I ever saw, or heard of. While, of other law-copyists, I might write the complete life, of Bartleby nothing of that sort can be done. I believe that no materials exist, for a full and satisfactory biography of this man. It is an irreparable loss to literature. Bartleby was one of those beings of whom nothing is ascertainable, except from the original sources, and, in his case, those are very small. What my own astonished eyes saw of Bartleby, *that* is all I know of him, except, indeed, one vague report, which will appear in the sequel.

Ere introducing the scrivener, as he first appeared to me, it is fit I make some mention of myself, my *employés*, my business, my chambers, and general surroundings, because some such description is indispensable to an adequate understanding of the chief character about to be presented. Imprimis:° I am a man who, from his youth upwards, has been filled with a profound conviction that the easiest way of life is the best. Hence, though I belong to a profession proverbially energetic and nervous, even to turbulence, at times, yet nothing of that sort have I ever suffered to invade my peace. I am one of those unambitious lawyers who never address a jury, or in any way draw down public applause; but, in the cool tranquillity of a snug retreat, do a snug business among rich men's bonds, and mortgages, and title-deeds. All who know me, consider me an eminently *safe* man. The late John Jacob Astor,° a personage little given to poetic enthusiasm, had no hestitation in pronouncing my first grand point to be prudence; my next, method. I do not speak it in vanity, but simply record the fact, that I was not unemployed in my profession by the late John Jacob Astor; a name which, I admit, I love to repeat; for it hath a rounded and orbicular sound to it, and rings like unto bullion. I will freely add, that I was not insensible to the late John Jacob Astor's good opinion.

Some time prior to the period at which this little history begins, my avocations had been largely increased. The good old office, now extinct in the State of New York, of a Master in Chancery, had been conferred upon me. It was not a very arduous office, but very pleasantly remunerative. I seldom lose my temper; much more seldom indulge in dangerous indignation at wrongs and outrages; but I must be permitted to be rash here and declare, that I consider the sudden and violent abrogation of the office of Master in Chancery, by the new Constitution, as a — premature act; inasmuch as I had counted upon a life-lease of the profits, whereas I only received those of a few short years. But this is by the way.

My chambers were up stairs, at No. — Wall Street. At one end, they looked upon the white wall of the interior of a spacious skylight shaft, penetrating the building from top to bottom.

Imprimis: In the first place.

John Jacob Astor: American capitalist (1763–1848) who made his first fortune in the fur trade.

This view might have been considered rather tame than otherwise, deficient 5
in what landscape painters call "life." But, if so, the view from the other end of
my chambers offered, at least, a contrast, if nothing more. In that direction, my
windows commanded an unobstructed view of a lofty brick wall, black by age and
everlasting shade; which wall required no spyglass to bring out its lurking beau-
ties, but, for the benefit of all near-sighted spectators, was pushed up to within ten
feet of my window-panes. Owing to the great height of the surrounding buildings,
and my chambers being on the second floor, the interval between this wall and
mine not a little resembled a huge square cistern.

At the period just preceding the advent of Bartleby, I had two persons as copyists in my employment, and a promising lad as an office-boy. First, Turkey; second,
Nippers; third, Ginger Nut. These may seem names, the like of which are not usually found in the Directory. In truth, they were nicknames, mutually conferred
upon each other by my three clerks, and were deemed expressive of their respective persons or characters. Turkey was a short, pursy° Englishman, of about my
own age — that is, somewhere not far from sixty. In the morning, one might say,
his face was of a fine florid hue, but after twelve o'clock, meridian°—his dinner
hour — it blazed like a grate full of Christmas coals; and continued blazing — but,
as it were, with a gradual wane — till six o'clock, P.M., or thereabouts; after
which, I saw no more of the proprietor of the face, which, gaining its meridian with
the sun, seemed to set with it, to rise, culminate, and decline the following day,
with the like regularity and undiminished glory. There are many singular coincidences I have known in the course of my life, not the least among which was the
fact, that, exactly when Turkey displayed his fullest beams from his red and radiant countenance, just then, too, at that critical moment, began the daily period
when I considered his business capacities as seriously disturbed for the remainder
of the twenty-four hours. Not that he was absolutely idle, or averse to business
then; far from it. The difficulty was, he was apt to be altogether too energetic.
There was a strange, inflamed, flurried, flighty recklessness of activity about him.
He would be incautious in dipping his pen into his inkstand. All his blots upon my
documents were dropped there after twelve o'clock, meridian. Indeed, not only
would he be reckless, and sadly given to making blots in the afternoon, but, some
days, he went further, and was rather noisy. At such times, too, his face flamed with
augmented blazonry, as if cannel coal had been heaped on anthracite. He made an
unpleasant racket with his chair; spilled his sand-box; in mending his pens, impatiently split them all to pieces, and threw them on the floor in a sudden passion;
stood up, and leaned over his table, boxing his papers about in a most indecorous
manner, very sad to behold in an elderly man like him. Nevertheless, as he was in
many ways a most valuable person to me, and all the time before twelve o'clock,
meridian, was the quickest, steadiest creature, too, accomplishing a great deal of
work in a style not easily to be matched — for these reasons, I was willing to overlook his eccentricities, though, indeed, occasionally, I remonstrated with him. I did

---

pursy: Overweight.
meridian: Noon.

this very gently, however, because, though the civilest, nay, the blandest and most reverential of men in the morning, yet, in the afternoon, he was disposed, upon provocation, to be slightly rash with his tongue — in fact, insolent. Now, valuing his morning services as I did, and resolved not to lose them — yet, at the same time, made uncomfortable by his inflamed ways after twelve o'clock — and being a man of peace, unwilling by my admonitions to call forth unseemly retorts from him, I took upon me, one Saturday noon (he was always worse on Saturdays) to hint to him, very kindly, that, perhaps, now that he was growing old, it might be well to abridge his labors; in short, he need not come to my chambers after twelve o'clock, but, dinner over, had best go home to his lodgings, and rest himself till tea-time. But no; he insisted upon his afternoon devotions. His countenance became intolerably fervid, as he oratorically assured me — gesticulating with a long ruler at the other end of the room — that if his services in the morning were useful, how indispensable, then, in the afternoon?

"With submission, sir," said Turkey, on this occasion, "I consider myself your right-hand man. In the morning I but marshal and deploy my columns; but in the afternoon I put myself at their head, and gallantly charge the foe, thus"— and he made a violent thrust with the ruler.

"But the blots, Turkey," intimated I.

"True; but, with submission, sir, behold these hairs! I am getting old. Surely, sir, a blot or two of a warm afternoon is not to be severely urged against gray hairs. Old age — even if it blot the page — is honorable. With submission, sir, we *both* are getting old."

10   This appeal to my fellow-feeling was hardly to be resisted. At all events, I saw that go he would not. So, I made up my mind to let him stay, resolving, never-theless, to see to it that, during the afternoon, he had to do with my less impor-tant papers.

Nippers, the second on my list, was a whiskered, sallow, and, upon the whole, rather piratical-looking young man, of about five-and-twenty. I always deemed him the victim of two evil powers — ambition and indigestion. The ambition was evinced by a certain impatience of the duties of a mere copyist, an unwarrantable usurpation of strictly professional affairs such as the original drawing up of legal documents. The indigestion seemed betokened in an occasional nervous testiness and grinning irritability, causing the teeth to audibly grind together over mistakes committed in copying; unnecessary maledictions, hissed, rather than spoken, in the heat of business; and especially by a continual discontent with the height of the table where he worked. Though of a very ingenious mechanical turn, Nippers could never get this table to suit him. He put chips under it, blocks of various sorts, bits of pasteboard, and at last went so far as to attempt an exquisite adjustment, by final pieces of folded blotting-paper. But no invention would answer. If, for the sake of easing his back, he brought the table-lid at a sharp angle well up towards his chin, and wrote there like a man using the steep roof of a Dutch house for his desk, then he declared that it stopped the circulation in his arms. If now he low-ered the table to his waistbands, and stooped over it in writing, then there was a sore aching in his back. In short, the truth of the matter was, Nippers knew not what he wanted. Or, if he wanted anything, it was to be rid of a scrivener's table altogether. Among the manifestations of his diseased ambition was a fondness he had for receiving visits from certain ambiguous-looking fellows in seedy coats, whom he called his clients. Indeed, I was aware that not only was he, at times, considerable of a ward-politician, but he occasionally did a little business at the justices' courts, and was not unknown on the steps of the Tombs.° I have good reason to believe, however, that one individual who called upon him at my chambers, and who, with a grand air, he insisted was his client, was no other than a dun,° and the alleged title-deed, a bill. But, with all his failings, and the annoyances he caused me, Nippers, like his compatriot Turkey, was a very useful man to me; wrote a neat, swift hand; and, when he chose, was not deficient in a gentlemanly sort of deportment. Added to this, he always dressed in a gentlemanly sort of way; and so, incidentally, reflected credit upon my chambers. Whereas, with respect to Turkey, I had much ado to keep him from being a reproach to me. His clothes were apt to look oily, a smell of eating-houses. He wore his pantaloons very loose and baggy in summer. His coats were execrable, his hat not to be handled. But while the hat was a thing of indifference to me, inasmuch as his natural civility and deference, as a dependent Englishman, always led him to doff it the moment he entered the room, yet his coat was another matter. Concerning his coats, I reasoned with him; but with no effect. The truth was, I suppose, that a man with so small an income could not afford to sport such a lustrous face and a lustrous coat at one and the same time. As Nippers once observed, Turkey's money went chiefly for red ink. One winter day, I presented Turkey with a highly respectable-looking coat of my own — a padded gray coat, of a most comfortable warmth, and which buttoned straight up from the knee to the neck. I thought Turkey would appreciate the favor, and abate his rashness and obstreperousness of afternoons. But no; I verily believe that buttoning himself up in so downy and blanket-like a coat had a pernicious effect upon him — upon the same principle that too much oats are bad for horses. In fact, precisely as a rash, restive horse is said to feel his oats, so Turkey felt his coat. It made him insolent. He was a man whom prosperity harmed.

Though, concerning the self-indulgent habits of Turkey, I had my own private surmises, yet, touching Nippers, I was well persuaded that, whatever might be his faults in other respects, he was, at least, a temperate young man. But indeed, nature herself seemed to have been his vintner, and, at his birth, charged him so thoroughly with an irritable, brandy-like disposition, that all subsequent potations were needless. When I consider how, amid the stillness of my chambers, Nippers would sometimes impatiently rise from his seat, and stooping over his table, spread his arms wide apart, seize the whole desk, and move it, and jerk it, with a grim, grinding motion on the floor, as if the table were a perverse voluntary agent, intent on thwarting and vexing him, I plainly perceive that, for Nippers, brandy-and-water were altogether superfluous.

It was fortunate for me that, owing to its peculiar cause — indigestion — the irritability and consequent nervousness of Nippers were mainly observable in the

---

the *Tombs:* A prison in New York City.
dun: Bill collector.

morning, while in the afternoon he was comparatively mild. So that, Turkey's paroxysms only coming on about twelve o'clock, I never had to do with their eccentricities at one time. Their fits relieved each other, like guards. When Nippers' was on, Turkey's was off; and *vice versa*. This was a good natural arrangement, under the circumstances.

Ginger Nut, the third on my list, was a lad, some twelve years old. His father was a carman, ambitious of seeing his son on the bench instead of a cart, before he died. So he sent him to my office, as student at law, errand-boy, cleaner, and sweeper, at the rate of one dollar a week. He had a little desk to himself, but he did not use it much. Upon inspection, the drawer exhibited a great array of the shells of various sorts of nuts. Indeed, to this quick-witted youth, the whole noble science of the law was contained in a nutshell. Not the least among the employments of Ginger Nut, as well as one which he discharged with the most alacrity, was his duty as cake and apple purveyor for Turkey and Nippers. Copying lawpapers being proverbially a dry, husky sort of business, my two scriveners were fain° to moisten their mouths very often with Spitzenbergs,° to be had at the numerous stalls nigh the Custom House and Post Office. Also, they sent Ginger Nut very frequently for that peculiar cake — small, flat, round, and very spicy — after which he had been named by them. Of a cold morning, when business was but dull, Turkey would gobble up scores of these cakes, as if they were mere wafers — indeed, they sell them at the rate of six or eight for a penny — the scrape of his pen blending with the crunching of the crisp particles in his mouth. Of all the fiery afternoon blunders and flurried rashness of Turkey, was his once moistening a ginger-cake between his lips, and clapping it on to a mortgage, for a seal. I came within an ace of dismissing him then. But he mollified me by making an oriental bow, and saying —

15   "With submission, sir, it was generous of me to find you in stationery on my own account."

Now my original business — that of a conveyancer and title hunter, and drawer-up of recondite documents of all sorts — was considerably increased by receiving the Master's office. There was now great work for scriveners. Not only must I push the clerks already with me, but I must have additional help.

In answer to my advertisement, a motionless young man one morning stood upon my office threshold, the door being open, for it was summer. I can see that figure now — pallidly neat, pitiably respectable, incurably forlorn! It was Bartleby.

After a few words touching his qualifications, I engaged him, glad to have among my corps of copyists a man of so singularly sedate an aspect, which I thought might operate beneficially upon the flighty temper of Turkey, and the fiery one of Nippers.

I should have stated before that ground-glass folding-doors divided my premises into two parts, one of which was occupied by my scriveners, the other

---

fain: Inclined, desirous.

Spitzenbergs: New York variety of apple.

by myself. According to my humor, I threw open these doors, or closed them. I resolved to assign Bartleby a corner by the folding-doors, but on my side of them, so as to have this quiet man within easy call, in case any trifling thing was to be done. I placed his desk close up to a small side-window in that part of the room, a window which originally had afforded a lateral view of certain grimy brickyards and bricks, but which, owing to subsequent erections, commanded at present no view at all, though it gave some light. Within three feet of the panes was a wall, and the light came down from far above, between two lofty buildings, as from a very small opening in a dome. Still further to a satisfactory arrangement, I procured a high green folding screen, which might entirely isolate Bartleby from my sight, though not remove him from my voice. And thus, in a manner, privacy and society were conjoined.

At first, Bartleby did an extraordinary quantity of writing. As if long famish- 20 ing for something to copy, he seemed to gorge himself on my documents. There was no pause for digestion. He ran a day and night line, copying by sunlight and by candle-light. I should have been quite delighted with his application, had he been cheerfully industrious. But he wrote on silently, palely, mechanically.

It is, of course, an indispensable part of a scrivener's business to verify the accuracy of his copy, word by word. Where there are two or more scriveners in an office, they assist each other in this examination, one reading from the copy, the other holding the original. It is a very dull, wearisome, and lethargic affair. I can readily imagine that, to some sanguine temperaments, it would be altogether intolerable. For example, I cannot credit that the mettlesome poet, Byron, would have contentedly sat down with Bartleby to examine a law document of, say five hundred pages, closely written in a crimpy hand.

Now and then, in the haste of business, it had been my habit to assist in comparing some brief document myself, calling Turkey or Nippers for this purpose. One object I had, in placing Bartleby so handy to me behind the screen, was, to avail myself of his services on such trivial occasions. It was on the third day, I think, of his being with me, and before any necessity had arisen for having his own writing examined, that, being much hurried to complete a small affair I had in hand, I abruptly called to Bartleby. In my haste and natural expectancy of instant compliance, I sat with my head bent over the original on my desk, and my right hand sideways, and somewhat nervously extended with the copy, so that, immediately upon emerging from his retreat, Bartleby might snatch it and proceed to business without the least delay.

In this very attitude did I sit when I called to him, rapidly stating what it was I wanted him to do — namely, to examine a small paper with me. Imagine my surprise, nay, my consternation, when, without moving from his privacy, Bartleby, in a singularly mild, firm voice, replied, "I would prefer not to."

I sat awhile in perfect silence, rallying my stunned faculties. Immediately it occurred to me that my ears had deceived me, or Bartleby had entirely misunderstood my meaning. I repeated my request in the clearest tone I could assume; but in quite as clear a one came the previous reply, "I would prefer not to."

"Prefer not to," echoed I, rising in high excitement, and crossing the room 25 with a stride. "What do you mean? Are you moonstruck? I want you to help me compare this sheet here — take it," and I thrust it towards him.

"I would prefer not to," said he.

I looked at him steadfastly. His face was leanly composed; his gray eye dimly calm. Not a wrinkle of agitation rippled him. Had there been the least uneasiness, anger, impatience, or impertinence in his manner; in other words, had there been anything ordinarily human about him, doubtless I should have violently dismissed him from the premises. But as it was, I should have as soon thought of turning my pale plaster-of-paris bust of Cicero out of doors. I stood gazing at him awhile, as he went on with his own writing, and then reseated myself at my desk. This is very strange, thought I. What had one best do? But my business hurried me. I concluded to forget the matter for the present, reserving it for my future leisure. So, calling Nippers from the other room, the paper was speedily examined.

A few days after this, Bartleby concluded four lengthy documents, being quadruplicates of a week's testimony taken before me in my High Court of Chancery. It became necessary to examine them. It was an important suit, and great accuracy was imperative. Having all things arranged, I called Turkey, Nippers, and Ginger Nut, from the next room, meaning to place the four copies in the hands of my four clerks, while I should read from the original. Accordingly, Turkey, Nippers, and Ginger Nut had taken their seats in a row, each with his document in his hand, when I called to Bartleby to join this interesting group.

"Bartleby! quick, I am waiting."

30   I heard a slow scrape of his chair legs on the uncarpeted floor, and soon he appeared standing at the entrance of his hermitage.

"What is wanted?" said he, mildly.

"The copies, the copies," said I, hurriedly. "We are going to examine them. There"— and I held towards him the fourth quadruplicate.

"I would prefer not to," he said, and gently disappeared behind the screen.

For a few moments I was turned into a pillar of salt, standing at the head of my seated column of clerks. Recovering myself, I advanced towards the screen, and demanded the reason for such extraordinary conduct.

35   "*Why* do you refuse?"

"I would prefer not to."

With any other man I should have flown outright into a dreadful passion, scorned all further words, and thrust him ignominiously from my presence. But there was something about Bartleby that not only strangely disarmed me, but, in a wonderful manner, touched and disconcerted me. I began to reason with him.

"These are your own copies we are about to examine. It is labor saving to you, because one examination will answer for your four papers. It is common usage. Every copyist is bound to help examine his copy. Is it not so? Will you not speak? Answer!"

"I prefer not to," he replied in a flute-like tone. It seemed to me that, while I had been addressing him, he carefully revolved every statement that I made; fully comprehended the meaning; could not gainsay the irresistible conclusion; but, at the same time, some paramount consideration prevailed with him to reply as he did.

40   "You are decided, then, not to comply with my request — a request made according to common usage and common sense?"

He briefly gave me to understand, that on that point my judgment was sound. Yes: his decision was irreversible.

It is not seldom the case that, when a man is browbeaten in some unprecedented and violently unreasonable way, he begins to stagger in his own plainest faith. He begins, as it were, vaguely to surmise that, wonderful as it may be, all the justice and all the reason is on the other side. Accordingly, if any disinterested persons are present, he turns to them for some reinforcement for his own faltering mind.

"Turkey," said I, "what do you think of this? Am I not right?"

"With submission, sir," said Turkey, in his blandest tone, "I think that you are."

"Nippers," said I, "what do *you* think of it?"   45

"I think I should kick him out of the office."

(The reader of nice perceptions will have perceived that, it being morning, Turkey's answer is couched in polite and tranquil terms, but Nippers replies in ill-tempered ones. Or, to repeat a previous sentence, Nippers' ugly mood was on duty, and Turkey's off.)

"Ginger Nut," said I, willing to enlist the smallest suffrage in my behalf, "what do *you* think of it?"

"I think, sir, he's a little *luny*," replied Ginger Nut, with a grin.

"You hear what they say," said I, turning towards the screen, "come forth and   50 do your duty."

But he vouchsafed no reply. I pondered a moment in sore perplexity. But once more business hurried me. I determined again to postpone the consideration of this dilemma to my future leisure. With a little trouble we made out to examine the papers without Bartleby, though at every page or two Turkey deferentially dropped his opinion, that this proceeding was quite out of the common; while Nippers, twitching in his chair with a dyspeptic nervousness, ground out, between his set teeth, occasional hissing maledictions against the stubborn oaf behind the screen. And for his (Nippers') part, this was the first and the last time he would do another man's business without pay.

Meanwhile Bartleby sat in his hermitage, oblivious to everything but his own peculiar business there.

Some days passed, the scrivener being employed upon another lengthy work. His late remarkable conduct led me to regard his ways narrowly. I observed that he never went to dinner; indeed, that he never went anywhere. As yet I had never, of my personal knowledge, known him to be outside of my office. He was a perpetual sentry in the corner. At about eleven o'clock though, in the morning, I noticed that Ginger Nut would advance toward the opening in Bartleby's screen, as if silently beckoned thither by a gesture invisible to me where I sat. The boy would then leave the office, jingling a few pence, and reappear with a handful of ginger-nuts, which he delivered in the hermitage, receiving two of the cakes for his trouble.

He lives, then, on ginger-nuts, thought I; never eats a dinner, properly speaking; he must be a vegetarian, then, but no; he never eats even vegetables, he eats nothing but ginger-nuts. My mind then ran on in reveries concerning the probable effects upon the human constitution of living entirely on ginger-nuts. Ginger-nuts are so called, because they contain ginger as one of their peculiar constituents, and the final flavoring one. Now, what was ginger? A hot, spicy thing. Was Bartleby hot and spicy? Not at all. Ginger, then, had no effect upon Bartleby. Probably he preferred it should have none.

55   Nothing so aggravates an earnest person as a passive resistance. If the individual so resisted be of a not inhumane temper, and the resisting one perfectly harmless in his passivity, then, in the better moods of the former, he will endeavor charitably to construe to his imagination what proves impossible to be solved by his judgment. Even so, for the most part, I regarded Bartleby and his ways. Poor fellow! thought I, he means no mischief; it is plain he intends no insolence; his aspect sufficiently evinces that his eccentricities are involuntary. He is useful to me. I can get along with him. If I turn him away, the chances are he will fall in with some less indulgent employer, and then he will be rudely treated, and perhaps driven forth miserably to starve. Yes. Here I can cheaply purchase a delicious self-approval. To befriend Bartleby; to humor him in his strange wilfulness, will cost me little or nothing, while I lay up in my soul what will eventually prove a sweet morsel for my conscience. But this mood was not invariable with me. The passiveness of Bartleby sometimes irritated me. I felt strangely goaded on to encounter him in new opposition — to elicit some angry spark from him answerable to my own. But, indeed, I might as well have essayed to strike fire with my knuckles against a bit of Windsor soap. But one afternoon the evil impulse in me mastered me, and the following little scene ensued:

"Bartleby," said I, "when those papers are all copied, I will compare them with you."

"I would prefer not to."

"How? Surely you do not mean to persist in that mulish vagary?"

No answer.

60   I threw open the folding-doors nearby, and turning upon Turkey and Nippers, exclaimed:

"Bartleby a second time says, he won't examine his papers. What do you think of it, Turkey?"

It was afternoon, be it remembered. Turkey sat glowing like a brass boiler; his bald head steaming; his hands reeling among his blotted papers.

"Think of it?" roared Turkey. "I think I'll just step behind his screen, and black his eyes for him!"

So saying, Turkey rose to his feet and threw his arms into a pugilistic position. He was hurrying away to make good his promise, when I detained him, alarmed at the effect of incautiously rousing Turkey's combativeness after dinner.

65   "Sit down, Turkey," said I, "and hear what Nippers has to say. What do you think of it, Nippers? Would I not be justified in immediately dismissing Bartleby?"

"Excuse me, that is for you to decide, sir. I think his conduct quite unusual, and, indeed, unjust, as regards Turkey and myself. But it may only be a passing whim."

"Ah," exclaimed I, "you have strangely changed your mind, then — you speak very gently of him now."

"All beer," cried Turkey; "gentleness is effects of beer — Nippers and I dined together to-day. You see how gentle *I* am, sir. Shall I go and black his eyes?"

"You refer to Bartleby, I suppose. No, not to-day, Turkey," I replied; "pray, put up your fists."

I closed the doors, and again advanced towards Bartleby. I felt additional in- 70 centives tempting me to my fate. I burned to be rebelled against again. I remembered that Bartleby never left the office.

"Bartleby," said I, "Ginger Nut is away; just step around to the Post Office, won't you?" (it was but a three minutes' walk) "and see if there is anything for me."

"I would prefer not to."

"You *will* not?"

"I *prefer* not."

I staggered to my desk, and sat there in a deep study. My blind inveteracy re- 75 turned. Was there any other thing in which I could procure myself to be ignominiously repulsed by this lean, penniless wight?—my hired clerk? What added thing is there, perfectly reasonable, that he will be sure to refuse to do?

"Bartleby!"

No answer.

"Bartleby," in a louder tone.

No answer.

"Bartleby," I roared. 80

Like a very ghost, agreeably to the laws of magical invocation, at the third summons, he appeared at the entrance of his hermitage.

"Go to the next room, and tell Nippers to come to me."

"I prefer not to," he respectfully and slowly said, and mildly disappeared.

"Very good, Bartleby," said I, in a quiet sort of serenely-severe self-possessed tone, intimating the unalterable purpose of some terrible retribution very close at hand. At the moment I half intended something of the kind. But upon the whole, as it was drawing towards my dinner-hour, I thought it best to put on my hat and walk home for the day, suffering much from perplexity and distress of mind.

Shall I acknowledge it? The conclusion of this whole business was, that it soon 85 became a fixed fact of my chambers, that a pale young scrivener, by the name of Bartleby, had a desk there; that he copied for me at the usual rate of four cents a folio (one hundred words); but he was permanently exempt from examining the work done by him, that duty being transferred to Turkey and Nippers, out of compliment, doubtless, to their superior acuteness; moreover, said Bartleby was never, on any account, to be dispatched on the most trivial errand of any sort; and that even if entreated to take upon him such a matter, it was generally understood that he would "prefer not to"—in other words, that he would refuse point-blank.

As days passed on, I became considerably reconciled to Bartleby. His steadiness, his freedom from all dissipation, his incessant industry (except when he chose to throw himself into a standing revery behind his screen), his great stillness, his unalterableness of demeanor under all circumstances, made him a valuable acquisition. One prime thing was this —*he was always there*—first in the morning, continually through the day, and the last at night. I had a singular confidence in his honesty. I felt my most precious papers perfectly safe in his hands. Sometimes, to be sure, I could not, for the very soul of me, avoid falling into sudden spasmodic passions with him. For it was exceeding difficult to bear in mind all the time those strange peculiarities, privileges, and unheard-of exemptions, forming the tacit stipulations on Bartleby's part under which he remained in my office. Now and then, in the eagerness of dispatching pressing business, I would inadvertently summon Bartleby, in a short, rapid tone, to put his finger, say, on the incipient tie of a bit of red tape with which I was about compressing some papers. Of course, from behind the screen the usual answer, "I prefer not to," was sure to come; and then, how could a human creature, with the common infirmities of our nature, refrain from bitterly exclaiming upon such perverseness — such unreasonableness? However, every added repulse of this sort which I received only tended to lessen the probability of my repeating the inadvertence.

Here it must be said, that, according to the custom of most legal gentlemen occupying chambers in densely populated law buildings, there were several keys to my door. One was kept by a woman residing in the attic, which person weekly scrubbed and daily swept and dusted my apartments. Another was kept by Turkey for convenience sake. The third I sometimes carried in my own pocket. The fourth I knew not who had.

Now, one Sunday morning I happened to go to Trinity Church, to hear a celebrated preacher, and finding myself rather early on the ground I thought I would walk round to my chambers for a while. Luckily I had my key with me; but upon applying it to the lock, I found it resisted by something inserted from the inside. Quite surprised, I called out; when to my consternation a key was turned from within; and thrusting his lean visage at me, and holding the door ajar, the apparition of Bartleby appeared, in his shirt-sleeves, and otherwise in a strangely tattered *deshabille*,° saying quietly that he was sorry, but he was deeply engaged just then, and — preferred not admitting me at present. In a brief word or two, he moreover added, that perhaps I had better walk round the block two or three times, and by that time he would probably have concluded his affairs.

Now, the utterly unsurmised appearance of Bartleby, tenanting my law-chambers of a Sunday morning, with his cadaverously gentlemanly *nonchalance*, yet withal firm and self-possessed, had such a strange effect upon me, that incontinently I slunk away from my own door, and did as desired. But not without sundry twinges of impotent rebellion against the mild effrontery of this unaccountable scrivener. Indeed, it was his wonderful mildness chiefly, which not only disarmed me, but unmanned me, as it were. For I consider that one, for the time, is sort of unmanned when he tranquilly permits his hired clerk to dictate to him, and order him away from his own premises. Furthermore, I was full of uneasiness as to what Bartleby could possibly be doing in my office in his shirt-sleeves, and in an otherwise dismantled condition of a Sunday morning. Was anything amiss going on? Nay, that was out of the question. It was not to be thought of for a moment that Bartleby was an immoral person. But what could he be doing there?—copying? Nay again, whatever might be his eccentricities,

---

deshabille: Careless dress.

Bartleby was an eminently decorous person. He would be the last man to sit down to his desk in any state approaching to nudity. Besides, it was Sunday; and there was something about Bartleby that forbade the supposition that he would by any secular occupation violate the proprieties of the day.

Nevertheless, my mind was not pacified; and full of a restless curiosity, at last 90 I returned to the door. Without hindrance I inserted my key, opened it, and entered. Bartleby was not to be seen. I looked round anxiously, peeped behind his screen; but it was very plain that he was gone. Upon more closely examining the place, I surmised that for an indefinite period Bartleby must have ate, dressed, and slept in my office, and that too without plate, mirror, or bed. The cushioned seat of a rickety old sofa in one corner bore the faint impress of a lean, reclining form. Rolled away under his desk, I found a blanket; under the empty grate, a blacking box and brush; on a chair, a tin basin, with soap and a ragged towel; in a newspaper a few crumbs of ginger-nuts and a morsel of cheese. Yes, thought I, it is evident enough that Bartleby has been making his home here, keeping bachelor's hall all by himself. Immediately then the thought came sweeping across me, what miserable friendlessness and loneliness are here revealed! His poverty is great; but his solitude, how horrible! Think of it. Of a Sunday, Wall Street is deserted as Petra;° and every night of every day it is an emptiness. This building, too, which of week-days hums with industry and life, at nightfall echoes with sheer vacancy, and all through Sunday is forlorn. And here Bartleby makes his home; sole spectator of a solitude which he has seen all populous — a sort of innocent and transformed Marius brooding among the ruins of Carthage?°

For the first time in my life a feeling of overpowering stinging melancholy seized me. Before, I had never experienced aught but a not unpleasing sadness. The bond of a common humanity now drew me irresistibly to gloom. A fraternal melancholy! For both I and Bartleby were sons of Adam. I remembered the bright silks and sparkling faces I had seen that day, in gala trim, swan-like sailing down the Mississippi of Broadway; and I contrasted them with the pallid copyist, and thought to myself, Ah, happiness courts the light, so we deem the world is gay; but misery hides aloof, so we deem that misery there is none. These sad fancyings — chimeras, doubtless, of a sick and silly brain — led on to other and more special thoughts, concerning the eccentricities of Bartleby. Presentiments of strange discoveries hovered round me. The scrivener's pale form appeared to me laid out, among uncaring strangers, in its shivering winding-sheet.

Suddenly I was attracted by Bartleby's closed desk, the key in open sight left in the lock.

I mean no mischief, seek the gratification of no heartless curiosity, thought I; besides, the desk is mine, and its contents, too, so I will make bold to look within. Everything was methodically arranged, the papers smoothly placed. The

---

Petra: Ancient ruined city in southwestern Jordan, once capital of the Edomites and Nabataeans.

Marius . . . Carthage: Gaius Marius (157 – 86 B.C.) was a Roman general who sought refuge in the city of Carthage after he was exiled. The Romans later destroyed Carthage.

pigeon-holes were deep, and removing the files of documents, I groped into their recesses. Presently I felt something there, and dragged it out. It was an old bandanna handkerchief, heavy and knotted. I opened it, and saw it was a saving's bank.

I now recalled all the quiet mysteries which I had noted in the man. I remembered that he never spoke but to answer; that, though at intervals he had considerable time to himself, yet I had never seen him reading — no, not even a newspaper; that for long periods he would stand looking out, at his pale window behind the screen, upon the dead brick wall; I was quite sure he never visited any refectory or eating-house; while his pale face clearly indicated that he never drank beer like Turkey; or tea and coffee even, like other men; that he never went anywhere in particular that I could learn; never went out for a walk, unless, indeed, that was the case at present; that he had declined telling who he was, or whence he came, or whether he had any relatives in the world; that though so thin and pale, he never complained of ill-health. And more than all, I remembered a certain unconscious air of pallid — how shall I call it?— of pallid haughtiness, say, or rather an austere reserve about him, which had positively awed me into my tame compliance with his eccentricities, when I had feared to ask him to do the slightest incidental thing for me, even though I might know, from his long-continued motionlessness, that behind his screen he must be standing in one of those dead-wall reveries of his.

95   Revolving all these things, and coupling them with the recently discovered fact, that he made my office his constant abiding place and home, and not forgetful of his morbid moodiness; revolving all these things, a prudential feeling began to steal over me. My first emotions had been those of pure melancholy and sincerest pity; but just in proportion as the forlornness of Bartleby grew and grew to my imagination, did that same melancholy merge into fear, that pity into repulsion. So true it is, and so terrible, too, that up to a certain point the thought or sight of misery enlists our best affections; but, in certain special cases, beyond that point it does not. They err who would assert that invariably this is owing to the inherent selfishness of the human heart. It rather proceeds from a certain hopelessness of remedying excessive and organic ill. To a sensitive being, pity is not seldom pain. And when at last it is perceived that such pity cannot lead to effectual succor, common sense bids the soul be rid of it. What I saw that morning persuaded me that the scrivener was the victim of innate and incurable disorder. I might give alms to his body; but his body did not pain him; it was his soul that suffered, and his soul I could not reach.

I did not accomplish the purpose of going to Trinity Church that morning. Somehow, the things I had seen disqualified me for the time from churchgoing. I walked homeward, thinking what I would do with Bartleby. Finally, I resolved upon this — I would put certain calm questions to him the next morning, touching his history, etc., and if he declined to answer them openly and unreservedly (and I supposed he would prefer not), then to give him a twenty dollar bill over and above whatever I might owe him, and tell him his services were no longer required; but that if in any other way I could assist him, I would be happy to do so, especially if he desired to return to his native place, wherever that might be,

I would willingly help to defray the expenses. Moreover, if, after reaching home, he found himself at any time in want of aid, a letter from him would be sure of a reply.

The next morning came.

"Bartleby," said I, gently calling to him behind his screen.

No reply.

"Bartleby," said I, in a still gentler tone, "come here; I am not going to ask you 100 to do anything you would prefer not to do — I simply wish to speak to you."

Upon this he noiselessly slid into view.

"Will you tell me, Bartleby, where you were born?"

"I would prefer not to."

"Will you tell me *anything* about yourself?"

"I would prefer not to."

"But what reasonable objection can you have to speak to me? I feel friendly 105 towards you."

He did not look at me while I spoke, but kept his glance fixed upon my bust of Cicero, which, as I then sat, was directly behind me, some six inches above my head.

"What is your answer, Bartleby?" said I, after waiting a considerable time for a reply, during which his countenance remained immovable, only there was the faintest conceivable tremor of the white attenuated mouth.

"At present I prefer to give no answer," he said, and retired into his hermitage.

It was rather weak in me I confess, but his manner, on this occasion, nettled 110 me. Not only did there seem to lurk in it a certain calm disdain, but his perverseness seemed ungrateful, considering the undeniable good usage and indulgence he had received from me.

Again I sat ruminating what I should do. Mortified as I was at his behavior, and resolved as I had been to dismiss him when I entered my office, nevertheless I strangely felt something superstitious knocking at my heart, and forbidding me to carry out my purpose, and denouncing me for a villain if I dared to breathe one bitter word against this forlornest of mankind. At last, familiarly drawing my chair behind his screen, I sat down and said: "Bartleby, never mind, then, about revealing your history; but let me entreat you, as a friend, to comply as far as may be with the usages of this office. Say now, you will help to examine papers tomorrow or next day: in short, say now, that in a day or two you will begin to be a little reasonable: — say so, Bartleby."

"At present I would prefer not to be a little reasonable," was his mildly cadaverous reply.

Just then the folding-doors opened, and Nippers approached. He seemed suffering from an unusually bad night's rest, induced by severer indigestion than common. He overheard those final words of Bartleby.

"*Prefer not*, eh?" gritted Nippers — "I'd *prefer* him, if I were you, sir," addressing me — "I'd *prefer* him; I'd give him preferences, the stubborn mule! What is it, sir, pray, that he *prefers* not to do now?"

Bartleby moved not a limb. 115

"Mr. Nippers," said I, "I'd prefer that you would withdraw for the present."

Somehow, of late, I had got into the way of involuntarily using this word "prefer" upon all sorts of not exactly suitable occasions. And I trembled to think that my contact with the scrivener had already and seriously affected me in a mental way. And what further and deeper aberration might is not yet produce? This apprehension had not been without efficacy in determining me to summary measures.

As Nippers, looking very sour and sulky, was departing, Turkey blandly and deferentially approached.

"With submission, sir," said he, "yesterday I was thinking about Bartleby here, and I think that if he would but prefer to take a quart of good ale every day, it would do much towards mending him, and enabling him to assist in examining his papers."

120   "So you have got the word, too," said I, slightly excited.

"With submission, what word, sir?" asked Turkey, respectfully crowding himself into the contracted space behind the screen, and by so doing, making me jostle the scrivener. "What word, sir?"

"I would prefer to be left alone here," said Bartleby, as if offended at being mobbed in his privacy.

"*That's* the word, Turkey," said I —*that's* it."

"Oh, *prefer?* oh yes — queer word. I never use it myself. But, sir, as I was saying, if he would but prefer —"

125   "Turkey," interrupted I, "you will please withdraw."

"Oh certainly, sir, if you prefer that I should."

As he opened the folding door to retire, Nippers at his desk caught a glimpse of me, and asked whether I would prefer to have a certain paper copied on blue paper or white. He did not in the least roguishly accent the word "prefer." It was plain that it involuntarily rolled from his tongue. I thought to myself, surely I must get rid of a demented man, who already has in some degree turned the tongues, if not the heads of myself and clerks. But I thought it prudent not to break the dismission at once.

The next day I noticed that Bartleby did nothing but stand at his window in his dead-wall revery. Upon asking him why he did not write, he said that he had decided upon doing no more writing.

"Why, how now? what next?" exclaimed I, "do no more writing?"

130   "No more."

"And what is the reason?"

"Do you not see the reason for yourself?" he indifferently replied.

I looked steadfastly at him, and perceived that his eyes looked dull and glazed. Instantly it occurred to me, that his unexampled diligence in copying by his dim window for the first few weeks of his stay with me might have temporarily impaired his vision.

I was touched. I said something in condolence with him. I hinted that of course he did wisely in abstaining from writing for a while; and urged him to embrace that opportunity of taking wholesome exercise in the open air. This, however, he did not do. A few days after this, my other clerks being absent, and being in a great hurry to dispatch certain letters by the mail, I thought that, having nothing else earthly to do, Bartleby would surely be less inflexible than usual, and carry these letters to the Post Office. But he blankly declined. So, much to my inconvenience, I went myself.

Still added days went by. Whether Bartleby's eyes improved or not, I could not say. To all appearance, I thought they did. But when I asked him if they did, he vouchsafed no answer. At all events, he would do no copying. At last, in replying to my urgings, he informed me that he had permanently given up copying.

"What!" exclaimed I; "suppose your eyes should get entirely well—better than ever before — would you not copy then?"

"I have given up copying," he answered, and slid aside.

He remained as ever, a fixture in my chamber. Nay—if that were possible—he became still more of a fixture than before. What was to be done? He would do nothing in the office; why should he stay there? In plain fact, he had now become a millstone to me, not only useless as a necklace, but afflictive to bear. Yet I was sorry for him. I speak less than truth when I say that, on his own account, he occasioned me uneasiness. If he would but have earned a single relative or friend, I would instantly have written, and urged their taking the poor fellow away to some convenient retreat. But he seemed alone, absolutely alone in the universe. A bit of wreck in the mid-Atlantic. At length, necessities connected with my business tyrannized over all other considerations. Decently as I could, I told Bartleby that in six days' time he must unconditionally leave the office. I warned him to take measures, in the interval, for procuring some other abode. I offered to assist him in this endeavor, if he himself would but take the first step towards a removal. "And when you finally quit me, Bartleby," added I, "I shall see that you go not away entirely unprovided. Six days from this hour, remember."

At the expiration of that period, I peeped behind the screen, and lo! Bartleby was there.

I buttoned up my coat, balanced myself; advanced slowly towards him, touched his shoulder, and said, "The time has come; you must quit this place; I am sorry for you; here is money; but you must go."

"I would prefer not," he replied, with his back still towards me.

"You *must*."

He remained silent.

Now I had an unbounded confidence in this man's common honesty. He had frequently restored to me sixpences and shillings carelessly dropped upon the floor, for I am apt to be very reckless in such shirt-button affairs. The proceeding, then, which followed will not be deemed extraordinary.

"Bartleby," said I, "I owe you twelve dollars on account; here are thirty-two, the odd twenty are yours —Will you take it?" and I handed the bills towards him.

But he made no motion.

"I will leave them here, then," putting them under a weight on the table. Then taking my hat and cane and going to the door, I tranquilly turned and added — "After you have removed your things from these offices, Bartleby, you will of course lock the door — since every one is now gone for the day but you — and if you please, slip your key underneath the mat, so that I may have it in the morning. I shall not see you again; so good-bye to you. If, hereafter, in your new place of abode, I can be of any service to you, do not fail to advise me by letter. Good-bye, Bartleby, and fare you well."

But he answered not a word; like the last column of some ruined temple, he remained standing mute and solitary in the middle of the otherwise deserted room.

As I walked home in a pensive mood, my vanity got the better of my pity. I could not but highly plume myself on my masterly management in getting rid of Bartleby. Masterly I call it, and such it must appear to any dispassionate thinker. The beauty of my procedure seemed to consist in its perfect quietness. There was no vulgar bullying, no bravado of any sort, no choleric hectoring, and striding to and fro across the apartment, jerking out vehement commands for Bartleby to bundle himself off with his beggarly traps. Nothing of the kind. Without loudly bidding Bartleby depart — as an inferior genius might have done — I *assumed* the ground that depart he must; and upon that assumption built all I had to say. The more I thought over my procedure, the more I was charmed with it. Nevertheless, next morning, upon awakening, I had my doubts — I had somehow slept off the fumes of vanity. One of the coolest and wisest hours a man has, is just after he awakes in the morning. My procedure seemed as sagacious as ever — but only in theory. How it would prove in practice — there was the rub. It was truly a beautiful thought to have assumed Bartleby's departure; but, after all, that assumption was simply my own, and none of Bartleby's. The great point was, not whether I had assumed that he would quit me, but whether he would prefer to do so. He was more a man of preferences than assumptions.

150 After breakfast, I walked down town, arguing the probabilities *pro* and *con.* One moment I thought it would prove a miserable failure, and Bartleby would be found all alive at my office as usual; the next moment it seemed certain that I should find his chair empty. And so I kept veering about. At the corner of Broadway and Canal Street, I saw quite an excited group of people standing in earnest conversation.

"I'll take odds he doesn't," said a voice as I passed.

"Doesn't go? — done!" said I, "put up your money."

I was instinctively putting my hand in my pocket to produce my own, when I remembered that this was an election day. The words I had overheard bore no reference to Bartleby, but to the success or non-success of some candidate for the mayoralty. In my intent frame of mind, I had, as it were, imagined that all Broadway shared in my excitement, and were debating the same question with me. I passed on, very thankful that the uproar of the street screened my momentary absent-mindedness.

As I had intended, I was earlier than usual at my office door. I stood listening for a moment. All was still. He must be gone. I tried the knob. The door was locked. Yes, my procedure had worked to a charm; he indeed must be vanished. Yet a certain melancholy mixed with this: I was almost sorry for my brilliant success. I was fumbling under the door mat for the key, which Bartleby was to have left there for me, when accidentally my knee knocked against a panel, producing a summoning sound, and in response a voice came to me from within — "Not yet; I am occupied."

155 It was Bartleby.

I was thunderstruck. For an instant I stood like the man who, pipe in mouth, was killed one cloudless afternoon long ago in Virginia, by summer lightning; at his own warm open window he was killed, and remained leaning out there upon the dreamy afternoon, till some one touched him, when he fell.

"Not gone!" I murmured at last. But again obeying that wondrous ascendancy which the inscrutable scrivener had over me, and from which ascendancy, for all my chafing, I could not completely escape, I slowly went down stairs and out into the street, and while walking round the block, considered what I should next do in this unheard-of perplexity. Turn the man out by an actual thrusting I could not; to drive him away by calling him hard names would not do; calling in the police was an unpleasant idea; and yet, permit him to enjoy his cadaverous triumph over me — this, too, I could not think of. What was to be done? or, if nothing could be done, was there anything further that I could *assume* in the matter? Yes, as before I had prospectively assumed that Bartleby would depart, so now I might retrospectively assume that departed he was. In the legitimate carrying out of this assumption, I might enter my office in a great hurry, and pretending not to see Bartleby at all, walk straight against him as if he were air. Such a proceeding would in a singular degree have the appearance of a home-thrust. It was hardly possible that Bartleby could withstand such an application of the doctrine of assumption. But upon second thoughts the success of the plan seemed rather dubious. I resolved to argue the matter over with him again.

"Bartleby," said I, entering the office, with a quietly severe expression, "I am seriously displeased. I am pained, Bartleby. I had thought better of you. I had imagined you of such a gentlemanly organization, that in any delicate dilemma a slight hint would suffice — in short, an assumption. But it appears I am deceived. Why," I added, unaffectedly starting, "you have not even touched that money yet," pointing to it, just where I had left it the evening previous.

He answered nothing.

"Will you, or will you not, quit me?" I now demanded in a sudden passion, advancing close to him. 160

"I would prefer *not* to quit you," he replied, gently emphasizing the *not*.

"What earthly right have you to stay here? Do you pay any rent? Do you pay my taxes? Or is this property yours?"

He answered nothing.

"Are you ready to go on and write now? Are your eyes recovered? Could you copy a small paper for me this morning? or help examine a few lines? or step round to the Post Office? In a word, will you do anything at all, to give a coloring to your refusal to depart the premises?"

He silently retired into his hermitage. 165

I was now in such a state of nervous resentment that I thought it but prudent to check myself at present from further demonstrations. Bartleby and I were alone. I remembered the tragedy of the unfortunate Adams and the still more unfortunate Colt° in the solitary office of the latter; and how poor Colt, being

---

the unfortunate Adams . . . Colt: During a fight in 1842, Samuel Adams was killed by John C. Colt, brother of the Colt gun maker. Tried and sentenced to hang, Colt committed suicide just before the sentence was to be carried out.

dreadfully incensed by Adams, and imprudently permitting himself to get wildly excited, was at unawares hurried into his fatal act — an act which certainly no man could possibly deplore more than the actor himself. Often it had occurred to me in my ponderings upon the subject that had that altercation taken place in the public street, or at a private residence, it would not have terminated as it did. It was the circumstance of being alone in a solitary office, up stairs, of a building entirely unhallowed by humanizing domestic associations — an uncarpeted floor, doubtless, of a dusty, haggard sort of appearance — this it must have been, which greatly helped to enhance the irritable desperation of the hapless Colt.

But when this old Adam of resentment rose in me and tempted me concerning Bartleby, I grappled him and threw him. How? Why, simply by recalling the divine injunction: "A new commandment give I unto you, that ye love one another." Yes, this it was that saved me. Aside from higher considerations, charity often operates as a vastly wise and prudent principle — a great safeguard to its possessor. Men have committed murder for jealousy's sake, and anger's sake, and hatred's sake, and selfishness' sake, and spiritual pride's sake; but no man, that ever I heard of, ever committed a diabolical murder for sweet charity's sake. Mere self-interest, then, if no better motive can be enlisted, should, especially with high-tempered men, prompt all beings to charity and philanthropy. At any rate, upon the occasion in question, I strove to drown my exasperated feelings towards the scrivener by benevolently construing his conduct. Poor fellow, poor fellow! thought I, he don't mean anything; and besides, he has seen hard times, and ought to be indulged.

I endeavored, also, immediately to occupy myself, and at the same time to comfort my despondency. I tried to fancy, that in the course of the morning, at such time as might prove agreeable to him, Bartleby, of his own free accord, would emerge from his hermitage and take up some decided line of march in the direction of the door. But no. Half-past twelve o'clock came; Turkey began to glow in the face, overturn his inkstand, and become generally obstreperous; Nippers abated down into quietude and courtesy; Ginger Nut munched his noon apple; and Bartleby remained standing at his window in one of his profoundest dead-wall reveries. Will it be credited? Ought I to acknowledge it? That afternoon I left the office without saying one further word to him.

Some days now passed, during which, at leisure intervals I looked a little into "Edwards on the Will," and "Priestley on Necessity."° Under the circumstances, those books induced a salutary feeling. Gradually I slid into the persuasion that these troubles of mine, touching the scrivener, had been all predestined from eternity, and Bartleby was billeted upon me for some mysterious purpose of an all-wise Providence, which it was not for a mere mortal like me to fathom. Yes, Bartleby, stay there behind your screen, thought I; I shall persecute you no more; you are harmless and noiseless as any of these old chairs; in short, I never feel so private as when I know you are here. At last I see it, I feel it; I penetrate to the predestined purpose of my life. I am content. Others may have loftier parts to enact; but

---

"*Edwards . . . Necessity*": Philosophical treatises of the time that argued the absence of free will — Jonathan Edwards's *Freedom of Will* (1754) and Joseph Priestley's *Doctrine of Philosophical Necessity* (1777).

my mission in this world, Bartleby, is to furnish you with office-room for such period as you may see fit to remain.

I believe that this wise and blessed frame of mind would have continued with me, had it not been for the unsolicited and uncharitable remarks obtruded upon me by my professional friends who visited the rooms. But thus it often is, that the constant friction of illiberal minds wears out at last the best resolves of the more generous. Though to be sure, when I reflected upon it, it was not strange that people entering my office should be struck by the peculiar aspect of the unaccountable Bartleby, and so be tempted to throw out some sinister observations concerning him. Sometimes an attorney, having business with me, and calling at my office, and finding no one but the scrivener there, would undertake to obtain some sort of precise information from him touching my whereabouts; but without heeding his idle talk, Bartleby would remain standing immovable in the middle of the room. So after contemplating him in that position for a time, the attorney would depart, no wiser than he came.

Also, when a reference was going on, and the room full of lawyers and witnesses, and business driving fast, some deeply-occupied legal gentleman present, seeing Bartleby wholly unemployed, would request him to run around to his (the legal gentleman's) office and fetch some papers for him. Thereupon, Bartleby would tranquilly decline, and yet remain idle as before. Then the lawyer would give a great stare, and turn to me. And what could I say? At last I was made aware that all through the circle of my professional acquaintance, a whisper of wonder was running round, having reference to the strange creature I kept at my office. This worried me very much. And as the idea came upon me of his possibly turning out a long-lived man, and keeping occupying my chambers, and denying my authority; and perplexing my visitors; and scandalizing my professional reputation; and casting a general gloom over the premises; keeping soul and body together to the last upon his savings (for doubtless he spent but half a dime a day), and in the end perhaps outlive me, and claim possession of my office by right of his perpetual occupancy: as all these dark anticipations crowded upon me more and more, and my friends continually intruded their relentless remarks upon the apparition in my room; a great change was wrought in me. I resolved to gather all my faculties together, and forever rid me of this intolerable incubus.

Ere revolving any complicated project, however, adapted to this end, I first simply suggested to Bartleby the propriety of his permanent departure. In a calm and serious tone, I commended the idea to his careful and mature consideration. But, having taken three days to meditate upon it, he apprised me, that his original determination remained the same; in short, that he still preferred to abide with me.

What shall I do? I now said to myself, buttoning up my coat to the last button. What shall I do? what ought I to do? what does conscience say I *should* do with this man, or, rather, ghost. Rid myself of him, I must; go, he shall. But how? You will not thrust him, the poor, pale, passive mortal — you will not thrust such a helpless creature out of your door? you will not dishonor yourself by such cruelty? No, I will not, I cannot do that. Rather would I let him live and die here, and then mason up his remains in the wall. What, then, will you do? For all your coaxing, he will not budge. Bribes he leaves under your own paper-weight on your table; in short, it is quite plain that he prefers to cling to you.

Then something severe, something unusual must be done. What! surely you will not have him collared by a constable, and commit his innocent pallor to the common jail? And upon what ground could you procure such a thing to be done?— a vagrant, is he? What! he a vagrant, a wanderer, who refuses to budge? It is because he will *not* be a vagrant, then, that you seek to count him *as* a vagrant. That is too absurd. No visible means of support: there I have him. Wrong again: for indubitably he *does* support himself, and that is the only unanswerable proof that any man can show of his possessing the means so to do. No more, then. Since he will not quit me, I must quit him. I will change my offices; I will move elsewhere, and give him fair notice, that if I find him on my new premises I will then proceed against him as a common trespasser.

175   Acting accordingly, next day I thus addressed him: "I find these chambers too far from the City Hall; the air is unwholesome. In a word, I propose to remove my offices next week, and shall no longer require your services. I tell you this now, in order that you may seek another place."

He made no reply, and nothing more was said.

On the appointed day I engaged carts and men, proceeded to my chambers, and having but little furniture, everything was removed in a few hours. Throughout, the scrivener remained standing behind the screen, which I directed to be removed the last thing. It was withdrawn; and, being folded up like a huge folio, left him the motionless occupant of a naked room. I stood in the entry watching him a moment, while something from within me upbraided me.

I re-entered, with my hand in my pocket — and — and my heart in my mouth.

"Good-bye, Bartleby; I am going — good-bye, and God some way bless you; and take that," slipping something in his hand. But it dropped upon the floor, and then — strange to say — I tore myself from him whom I had so longed to be rid of.

180   Established in my new quarters, for a day or two I kept the door locked, and started at every footfall in the passages. When I returned to my rooms, after any little absence, I would pause at the threshold for an instant, and attentively listen, ere applying my key. But these fears were needless. Bartleby never came nigh me.

I thought all was going well, when a perturbed-looking stranger visited me, inquiring whether I was the person who had recently occupied rooms at No. — Wall Street.

Full of forebodings, I replied that I was.

"Then, sir," said the stranger, who proved a lawyer, "you are responsible for the man you left there. He refuses to do any copying; he refuses to do anything; he says he prefers not to; and he refuses to quit the premises."

"I am very sorry, sir," said I, with assumed tranquillity, but an inward tremor, "but, really, the man you allude to is nothing to me — he is no relation or apprentice of mine, that you should hold me responsible for him."

"In mercy's name, who is he?"

"I certainly cannot inform you. I know nothing about him. Formerly I employed him as a copyist; but he has done nothing for me now for some time past."

"I shall settle him, then — good morning, sir."

Several days passed, and I heard nothing more; and, though I often felt a charitable prompting to call at the place and see poor Bartleby, yet a certain squeamishness, of I know not what, withheld me.

All is over with him, by this time, thought I, at last, when, through another week, no further intelligence reached me. But, coming to my room the day after, I found several persons waiting at my door in a high state of nervous excitement.

"That's the man — here he comes," cried the foremost one, whom I recognized   190
as the lawyer who had previously called upon me alone.

"You must take him away, sir, at once," cried a portly person among them, advancing upon me, and whom I knew to be the landlord of No.—Wall Street. "These gentlemen, my tenants, cannot stand it any longer; Mr. B —," pointing to the lawyer, "has turned him out of his room, and he now persists in haunting the building generally, sitting upon the banisters of the stairs by day, and sleeping in the entry by night. Everybody is concerned; clients are leaving the offices; some fears are entertained of a mob; something you must do, and that without delay."

Aghast at this torrent, I fell back before it, and would fain have locked myself in my new quarters. In vain I persisted that Bartleby was nothing to me — no more than to any one else. In vain — I was the last person known to have anything to do with him, and they held me to the terrible account. Fearful, then, of being exposed in the papers (as one person present obscurely threatened), I considered the matter, and, at length, said, that if the lawyer would give me a confidential interview with the scrivener, in his (the lawyer's) own room, I would, that afternoon, strive my best to rid them of the nuisance they complained of.

Going up stairs to my old haunt, there was Bartleby silently sitting upon the banister at the landing.

"What are you doing here, Bartleby?" said I.   195

"Sitting upon the banister," he mildly replied.

I motioned him into the lawyer's room, who then left us.

"Bartleby," said I, "are you aware that you are the cause of great tribulation to me, by persisting in occupying the entry after being dismissed from the office?"

No answer.

"Now one of two things must take place. Either you must do something, or something must be done to you. Now what sort of business would you like to engage in? Would you like to re-engage in copying for some one?"

"No; I would prefer not to make any change."   200

"Would you like a clerkship in a dry-goods store?"

"There is too much confinement about that. No, I would not like a clerkship; but I am not particular."

"Too much confinement," I cried, "why, you keep yourself confined all the time!"

"I would prefer not to take a clerkship," he rejoined, as if to settle that little item at once.

205   "How would a bar-tender's business suit you? There is no trying of the eye-sight in that."

I would not like it at all; though, as I said before, I am not particular."

His unwonted wordiness inspirited me. I returned to the charge.

"Well, then, would you like to travel through the country collecting bills for the merchants? That would improve your health."

"No, I would prefer to be doing something else."

210   "How, then, would going as a companion to Europe, to entertain some young gentleman with your conversation — how would that suit you?"

"Not at all. It does not strike me that there is anything definite about that. I like to be stationary. But I am not particular."

"Stationary you shall be, then," I cried, now losing all patience, and, for the first time in all my exasperating connection with him, fairly flying into a passion. "If you do not go away from these premises before night, I shall feel bound — indeed, I *am* bound — to — to quit the premises myself!" I rather absurdly concluded, knowing not with what possible threat to try to frighten his immobility into compliance. Despairing of all further efforts, I was precipitately leaving him, when a final thought occurred to me — one which had not been wholly unindulged before.

"Bartleby," said I, in the kindest tone I could assume under such exciting circumstances, "will you go home with me now — not to my office, but my dwelling — and remain there till we can conclude upon some convenient arrangement for you at our leisure? Come, let us start now, right away."

"No: at present I would prefer not to make any change at all."

I answered nothing; but, effectually dodging every one by the suddenness and rapidity of my flight; rushed from the building, ran up Wall Street towards Broadway, and, jumping into the first omnibus, was soon removed from pursuit. As soon as tranquillity returned, I distinctly perceived that I had now done all that I possibly could, both in respect to the demands of the landlord and his tenants, and with regard to my own desire and sense of duty, to benefit Bartleby, and shield him from rude persecution. I now strove to be entirely carefree and quiescent; and my conscience justified me in the attempt; though, indeed, it was not so successful as I could have wished. So fearful was I of being again hunted out by the incensed landlord and his exasperated tenants, that, surrendering my business to Nippers, for a few days, I drove about the upper part of the town and through the suburbs, in my rockaway;° crossed over to Jersey City and Hoboken, and paid fugitive visits to Manhattanville and Astoria. In fact, I almost lived in my rockaway for the time.

When again I entered my office, lo, a note from the landlord lay upon the desk. I opened it with trembling hands. It informed me that the writer had sent to the police, and had Bartleby removed to the Tombs as a vagrant. Moreover, since I knew more about him than any one else, he wished me to appear at that place, and make a suitable statement of the facts. These tidings had a conflicting effect . upon me. At first I was indignant; but, at last, almost approved. The landlord's energetic, summary disposition, had led him to adopt a procedure which I do not

---

rockaway: Carriage.

think I would have decided upon myself; and yet, as a last resort, under such peculiar circumstances, it seemed the only plan.

As I afterwards learned, the poor scrivener, when told that he must be conducted to the Tombs, offered not the slightest obstacle, but, in his pale, unmoving way, silently acquiesced.

Some of the compassionate and curious by-standers joined the party; and headed by one of the constables arm-in-arm with Bartleby, the silent procession filed its way through all the noise, and heat, and joy of the roaring thoroughfares at noon.

The same day I received the note, I went to the Tombs, or, to speak more properly, the Halls of Justice. Seeking the right officer, I stated the purpose of my call, and was informed that the individual I described was, indeed, within. I then assured the functionary that Bartleby was a perfectly honest man, and greatly to be compassionated, however unaccountably eccentric. I narrated all I knew, and closed by suggesting the idea of letting him remain in as indulgent confinement as possible, till something less harsh might be done — though, indeed, I hardly knew what. At all events, if nothing else could be decided upon, the almshouse must receive him. I then begged to have an interview.

Being under no disgraceful charge, and quite serene and harmless in all his 220 ways, they had permitted him freely to wander about the prison, and, especially, in the inclosed grass-platted yards thereof. And so I found him there, standing all alone in the quietest of the yards, his face towards a high wall, while all around, from the narrow slits of the jail windows, I thought I saw peering out upon him the eyes of murderers and thieves.

"Bartleby!"

"I know you," he said, without looking round — "and I want nothing to say to you."

"It was not I that brought you here, Bartleby," said I, keenly pained at his implied suspicion. "And to you, this should not be so vile a place. Nothing reproachful attaches to you by being here. And see, it is not so sad a place as one might think. Look, there is the sky, and here is the grass."

"I know where I am," he replied, but would say nothing more, and so I left him. 225

As I entered the corridor again, a broad meat-like man, in an apron, accosted me, and, jerking his thumb over his shoulder, said — "Is that your friend?"

"Yes."

"Does he want to starve? If he does, let him live on the prison fare, that's all."

"Who are you?" asked I, not knowing what to make of such an unofficially speaking person in such a place.

"I am the grub-man. Such gentlemen as have friends here, hire me to provide them with something good to eat."

"Is this so?" said I, turning the turnkey. 230

He said it was.

"Well, then," said I, slipping some silver into the grub-man's hands (for so they called him), "I want you to give particular attention to my friend there; let him have the best dinner you can get. And you must be as polite to him as possible."

"Introduce me, will you?" said the grub-man, looking at me with an expression which seemed to say he was all impatience for an opportunity to give a specimen of his breeding.

Thinking it would prove of benefit to the scrivener, I acquiesced; and, asking the grub-man his name, went up with him to Bartleby.

235 "Bartleby, this is a friend; you will find him very useful to you."

"Your sarvant, sir, your sarvant," said the grub-man, making a low salutation behind his apron. "Hope you find it pleasant here, sir; nice grounds — cool apartments — hope you'll stay with us some time — try to make it agreeable. What will you have for dinner to-day?"

"I prefer not to dine to-day," said Bartleby, turning away. "It would disagree with me; I am unused to dinners." So saying, he slowly moved to the other side of the inclosure, and took up a position fronting the deadwall.

"How's this?" said the grub-man, addressing me with a stare of astonishment. "He's odd, ain't he?"

"I think he is a little deranged," said I, sadly.

240 "Deranged? deranged is it? Well, now, upon my word, I thought that friend of yourn was a gentleman forger; they are always pale and genteel-like, them forgers. I can't help pity 'em — can't help it, sir. Did you know Monroe Edwards?" he added, touchingly, and paused. Then, laying his hand piteously on my shoulder, sighed, "he died of consumption at Sing-Sing. So you weren't acquainted with Monroe?"

"No, I was never socially acquainted with any forgers. But I cannot stop longer. Look to my friend yonder. You will not lose by it. I will see you again."

Some few days after this, I again obtained admission to the Tombs, and went through the corridors in quest of Bartleby; but without finding him.

"I saw him coming from his cell not long ago," said a turnkey, "may be he's gone to loiter in the yards."

So I went in that direction.

245 "Are you looking for the silent man?" said another turnkey, passing me. "Yonder he lies — sleeping in the yard there. 'Tis not twenty minutes since I saw him lie down."

The yard was entirely quiet. It was not accessible to the common prisoners. The surrounding walls, of amazing thickness, kept off all sounds behind them. The Egyptian character of the masonry weighed upon me with its gloom. But a soft imprisoned turf grew under foot. The heart of the eternal pyramids, it seemed, wherein, by some strange magic, through the clefts, grass-seed, dropped by birds, had sprung.

Strangely huddled at the base of the wall, his knees drawn up, and lying on his side, his head touching the cold stones, I saw the wasted Bartleby. But nothing stirred. I paused; then went close up to him; stooped over, and saw that his dim eyes were open; otherwise he seemed profoundly sleeping. Something prompted me to touch him. I felt his hand, when a tingling shiver ran up my arm and down my spine to my feet.

The round face of the grub-man peered upon me now. "His dinner is ready. Won't he dine to-day, either? Or does he live without dining?"

"Lives without dining," said I, and closed the eyes.

"Eh!—He's asleep, ain't he?"

"With kings and counselors,"° murmured I.

There would seem little need for proceeding further in this history. Imagination will readily supply the meagre recital of poor Bartleby's interment. But, ere parting with the reader, let me say, that if this little narrative has sufficiently interested him, to awaken curiosity as to who Bartleby was, and what manner of life he led prior to the present narrator's making his acquaintance, I can only reply, that in such curiosity I fully share, but I am wholly unable to gratify it. Yet here I hardly know whether I should divulge one little item of rumor, which came to my ear a few months after the scrivener's decease. Upon what basis it rested, I could never ascertain; and hence, how true it is I cannot now tell. But, inasmuch as this vague report has not been without a certain suggestive interest to me, however sad, it may prove the same with some others; and so I will briefly mention it. The report was this: that Bartleby had been a subordinate clerk in the Dead Letter Office at Washington, from which he had been suddenly removed by a change in the administration. When I think over this rumor, hardly can I express the emotions which seize me. Dead letters! does it not sound like dead men? Conceive a man by nature and misfortune prone to a pallid hopelessness, can any business seem more fitted to heighten it than that of continually handling these dead letters, and assorting them for the flames? For by the cart-load they are annually burned. Sometimes from out the folded paper the pale clerk takes a ring—the finger it was meant for, perhaps, moulders in the grave; a bank-note sent in swiftest charity—he whom it would relieve, nor eats nor hungers any more; pardon for those who died despairing; hope for those who died unhoping; good tidings for those who died stifled by unrelieved calamities. On errands of life, these letters speed to death.

Ah, Bartleby! Ah, humanity!

◇　◇　◇

V. S. NAIPAUL (1932–   )

B. Wordsworth (1959)

Three beggars called punctually every day at the hospitable houses in Miguel Street. At about ten an Indian came in his dhoti° and white jacket, and we poured a tin of rice into the sack he carried on his back. At twelve an old woman smoking a clay pipe came and she got a cent. At two a blind man led by a boy called for his penny.

"With kings and counselors": The reference is to the Bible, Job 3.13–14: in death, Bartleby is now "at rest, / With kings and counselors of the earth."

dhoti: Loincloth worn by Hindu men in India.

Sometimes we had a rogue. One day a man called and said he was hungry. We gave him a meal. He asked for a cigarette and wouldn't go until we had lit it for him. That man never came again.

The strangest caller came one afternoon at about four o'clock. I had come back from school and was in my home-clothes. The man said to me, "Sonny, may I come inside your yard?"

He was a small man and he was tidily dressed. He wore a hat, a white shirt and black trousers.

5   I asked, "What you want?"

He said, "I want to watch your bees."

We had four small gru-gru palm trees and they were full of uninvited bees.

I ran up the steps and shouted, "Ma, it have a man outside here. He say he want to watch the bees."

My mother came out, looked at the man and asked in an unfriendly way, "What you want?"

10   The man said, "I want to watch your bees."

His English was so good, it didn't sound natural, and I could see my mother was worried.

She said to me, "Stay here and watch him while he watch the bees."

The man said, "Thank you, Madam. You have done a good deed today."

He spoke very slowly and very correctly as though every word was costing him money.

15   We watched the bees, this man and I, for about an hour, squatting near the palm trees.

The man said, "I like watching bees. Sonny, do you like watching bees?"

I said, "I ain't have the time."

He shook his head sadly. He said, "That's what I do, I just watch. I can watch ants for days. Have you ever watched ants? And scorpions, and centipedes, and *congorees*—have you watched those?"

I shook my head.

20   I said, "What you does do, mister?"

He got up and said, "I am a poet."

I said, "A good poet?"

He said, "The greatest in the world."

"What your name, mister?"

25   "B. Wordsworth."

"B for Bill?"

"Black. Black Wordsworth. White Wordsworth was my brother. We share one heart. I can watch a small flower like the morning glory and cry."

I said, "Why you does cry?"

"Why, boy? Why? You will know when you grow up. You're a poet, too, you know. And when you're a poet you can cry for everything."

30   I couldn't laugh.

He said, "You like your mother?"

"When she not beating me."

He pulled out a printed sheet from his hip-pocket and said, "On this paper is the greatest poem about mothers and I'm going to sell it to you at a bargain price. For four cents."

I went inside and I said, "Ma, you want to buy a poetry for four cents?"

My mother said, "Tell that blasted man to haul his tail away from my yard, 35 you hear."

I said to B. Wordsworth, "My mother say she ain't have four cents."

B. Wordsworth said, "It is the poet's tragedy."

And he put the paper back in his pocket. He didn't seem to mind.

I said, "Is a funny way to go round selling poetry like that. Only calypsonians do that sort of thing. A lot of people does buy?"

He said, "No one has yet bought a single copy." 40

"But why you does keep on going round, then?"

He said, "In this way I watch many things, and I always hope to meet poets."

I said, "You really think I is a poet?"

"You're as good as me," he said. 45

And when B. Wordsworth left, I prayed I would see him again.

About a week later, coming back from school one afternoon, I met him at the corner of Miguel Street.

He said, "I have been waiting for you a long time."

I said, "You sell any poetry yet?"

He shook his head.

He said, "In my yard I have the best mango tree in Port of Spain. And now the 50 mangoes are ripe and red and very sweet and juicy. I have waited here for you to tell you this and to invite you to come and eat some of my mangoes."

He lived in Alberto Street in a one-roomed hut placed right in the centre of the lot. The yard seemed all green. There was the big mango tree. There was a coconut tree and there was a plum tree. The place looked wild, as though it wasn't in the city at all. You couldn't see all the big concrete houses in the street.

He was right. The mangoes were sweet and juicy. I ate about six, and the yellow mango juice ran down my arms to my elbows and down my mouth to my chin and my shirt was stained.

My mother said when I got home, "Where you was? You think you is a man now and could go all over the place? Go cut a whip for me."

She beat me rather badly, and I ran out of the house swearing that I would never come back. I went to B. Wordsworth's house. I was so angry, my nose was bleeding.

B. Wordsworth said, "Stop crying, and we will go for a walk."

I stopped crying, but I was breathing short. We went for a walk. We walked 55 down St. Clair Avenue to the Savannah and we walked to the race-course.

B. Wordsworth said, "Now, let us lie on the grass and look up at the sky, and I want you to think how far those stars are from us."

I did as he told me, and I saw what he meant. I felt like nothing, and at the same time I had never felt so big and great in all my life. I forgot all my anger and all my tears and all the blows.

When I said I was better, he began telling me the names of the stars, and I particularly remembered the constellation of Orion the Hunter, though I don't really know why. I can spot Orion even today, but I have forgotten the rest.

60 Then a light was flashed into our faces, and we saw a policeman. We got up from the grass.

The policeman said, "What you doing here?"

B. Wordsworth said, "I have been asking myself the same question for forty years."

We became friends, B. Wordsworth and I. He told me, "You must never tell anybody about me and about the mango tree and the coconut tree and the plum tree. You must keep that a secret. If you tell anybody, I will know, because I am a poet."

65 I gave him my word and I kept it.

I liked his little room. It had no more furniture than George's front room, but it looked cleaner and healthier. But it also looked lonely.

One day I asked him, "Mister Wordsworth, why you does keep all this bush in your yard? Ain't it does make the place damp?"

He said, "Listen, and I will tell you a story. Once upon a time a boy and girl met each other and they fell in love. They loved each other so much they got married. They were both poets. He loved words. She loved grass and flowers and trees. They lived happily in a single room, and then one day, the girl poet said to the boy poet, 'We are going to have another poet in the family.' But this poet was never born, because the girl died, and the young poet died with her, inside her. And the girl's husband was very sad, and he said he would never touch a thing in the girl's garden. And so the garden remained, and grew high and wild."

I looked at B. Wordsworth, and as he told me this lovely story, he seemed to grow older. I understood his story.

We went for long walks together. We went to the Botanical Gardens and the Rock Gardens. We climbed Chancellor Hill in the late afternoon and watched the darkness fall on Port of Spain, and watched the lights go on in the city and on the ships in the harbour.

70 He did everything as though he were doing it for the first time in his life. He did everything as though he were doing some church rite.

He would say to me, "Now, how about having some ice-cream?"

And when I said, yes, he would grow very serious and say, "Now, which café shall we patronize?" As though it were a very important thing. He would think for some time about it, and finally say, "I think I will go and negotiate the purchase with that shop."

The world became a most exciting place.

One day, when I was in his yard, he said to me, "I have a great secret which I am now going to tell you."

75 I said, "It really secret?"

"At the moment, yes."

I looked at him, and he looked at me. He said, "This is just between you and me, remember. I am writing a poem."

"Oh." I was disappointed.

He said, "But this is a different sort of poem. This is the greatest poem in the world."

I whistled.

He said, "I have been working on it for more than five years now. I will finish it in about twenty-two years from now, that is, if I keep on writing at the present rate."

"You does write a lot, then?"

He said, "Not any more. I just write one line a month. But I make sure it is a good line."

I asked, "What was last month's good line?"

He looked up at the sky, and said, *"The past is deep."*

I said, "It is a beautiful line."

B. Wordsworth said, "I hope to distil the experiences of a whole month into that single line of poetry. So, in twenty-two years, I shall have written a poem that will sing to all humanity."

I was filled with wonder.

Our walks continued. We walked along the sea-wall at Docksite one day, and I said, "Mr Wordsworth, if I drop this pin in the water, you think it will float?"

He said, "This is a strange world. Drop your pin, and let us see what will happen."

The pin sank.

I said, "How is the poem this month?"

But he never told me any other line. He merely said. "Oh, it comes, you know. It comes."

Or we would sit on the sea-wall and watch the liners come into the harbour.

But of the greatest poem in the world I heard no more.

I felt he was growing older.

"How you does live, Mr Wordsworth?" I asked him one day.

He said, "You mean how I get money?"

When I nodded, he laughed in a crooked way.

He said, "I sing calypsoes in the calypso season."

"And that last you the rest of the year?"

"It is enough."

"But you will be the richest man in the world when you write the greatest poem?"

He didn't reply.

One day when I went to see him in his little house, I found him lying on his little bed. He looked so old and so weak, that I found myself wanting to cry.

He said, "The poem is not going well."

He wasn't looking at me. He was looking through the window at the coconut tree, and he was speaking as though I wasn't there. He said, "When I was twenty I felt the power within myself." Then, almost in front of my eyes, I could see his face growing older and more tired. He said, "But that — that was a long time ago."

And then — I felt it so keenly, it was as though I had been slapped by my mother. I could see it clearly on his face. It was there for everyone to see. Death on the shrinking face.

He looked at me, and saw my tears and sat up.

110   He said, "Come." I went and sat on his knees.

He looked into my eyes, and he said, "Oh, you can see it, too. I always knew you had the poet's eye."

He didn't even look sad, and that made me burst out crying loudly.

He pulled me to his thin chest, and said, "Do you want me to tell you a funny story?" and he smiled encouragingly at me.

But I couldn't reply.

115   He said, "When I have finished this story, I want you to promise that you will go away and never come back to see me. Do you promise?"

I nodded.

He said, "Good. Well, listen. That story I told you about the boy poet and the girl poet, do you remember that? That wasn't true. It was something I just made up. All this talk about poetry and the greatest poem in the world, that wasn't true, either. Isn't that the funniest thing you have heard?"

But his voice broke.

I left the house, and ran home crying, like a poet, for everything I saw.

120   I walked along Alberto Street a year later, but I could find no sign of the poet's house. It hadn't vanished, just like that. It had been pulled down, and a big, two-storeyed building had taken its place. The mango tree and the plum tree and the coconut tree had all been cut down, and there was brick and concrete everywhere.

It was just as though B. Wordsworth had never existed.

◇   ◇   ◇

FLANNERY O'CONNOR   (1925–1964)

Everything That Rises Must Converge   (1965)

Her doctor had told Julian's mother that she must lose twenty pounds on account of her blood pressure, so on Wednesday nights Julian had to take her downtown on the bus for a reducing class at the Y. The reducing class was designed for working girls over fifty, who weighed from 165 to 200 pounds. His mother was one of the slimmer ones, but she said ladies did not tell their age or weight. She would not ride the buses by herself at night since they had been integrated, and because the reducing class was one of her few pleasures, necessary for her health, and *free*, she said Julian could at least put himself out to take her, considering all she did for him. Julian did not like to consider all she did for him, but every Wednesday night he braced himself and took her.

She was almost ready to go, standing before the hall mirror, putting on her hat, while he, his hands behind him, appeared pinned to the door frame, waiting like Saint Sebastian° for the arrows to begin piercing him. The hat was new and had cost her seven dollars and a half. She kept saying, "Maybe I shouldn't have paid that for it. No, I shouldn't have. I'll take it off and return it tomorrow. I shouldn't have bought it."

Julian raised his eyes to heaven. "Yes, you should have bought it," he said "Put it on and let's go." It was a hideous hat. A purple velvet flap came down on one side of it and stood up on the other; the rest of it was green and looked like a cushion with the stuffing out. He decided it was less comical than jaunty and pathetic. Everything that gave her pleasure was small and depressed him.

She lifted the hat one more time and set it down slowly on top of her head. Two wings of gray hair protruded on either side of her florid face, but her eyes, sky-blue, were as innocent and untouched by experience as they must have been when she was ten. Were it not that she was a widow who had struggled fiercely to feed and clothe and put him through school and who was supporting him still "until he got on his feet," she might have been a little girl that he had to take to town.

"It's all right, it's all right," he said. "Let's go." He opened the door himself and   5 started down the walk to get her going. The sky was a dying violet and the houses stood out darkly against it, bulbous liver-colored monstrosities of a uniform ugliness though no two were alike. Since this had been a fashionable neighborhood forty years ago, his mother persisted in thinking they did well to have an apartment in it. Each house had a narrow collar of dirt around it in which sat, usually, a grubby child. Julian walked with his hands in his pockets, his head down and thrust forward and his eyes glazed with the determination to make himself completely numb during the time he would be sacrificed to her pleasure.

The door closed and he turned to find the dumpy figure, surmounted by the atrocious hat, coming toward him. "Well," she said, "you only live once and paying a little more for it, I at least won't meet myself coming and going."

"Some day I'll start making money," Julian said gloomily —he knew he never would —"and you can have one of those jokes whenever you take the fit." But first they would move. He visualized a place where the nearest neighbors would be three miles away on either side.

"I think you're doing fine," she said, drawing on her gloves. "You've only been out of school a year. Rome wasn't built in a day."

She was one of the few members of the Y reducing class who arrived in hat and gloves and who had a son who had been to college. "It takes time," she said, "and the world is in such a mess. This hat looked better on me than any of the others, though when she brought it out I said, 'Take that thing back. I wouldn't have it on my head,' and she said, 'Now wait till you see it on,' and when she put it on me, I said, 'We-ull,' and she said, 'If you ask me, that hat does something for you and you do something for the hat, and besides,' she said, 'with that hat, you won't meet yourself coming and going.'"

Saint Sebastian: A Roman Catholic Saint. Accused of being a Christian, Sebastian was tied to a tree, shot with arrows, and left for dead. He survived and recovered, returning to preach. The emperor then had him beaten to death.

10   Julian thought he could have stood his lot better if she had been selfish, if she had been an old hag who drank and screamed at him. He walked along, saturated in depression, as if in the midst of his martyrdom he had lost his faith. Catching sight of his long, hopeless, irritated face, she stopped suddenly with a grief-stricken look, and pulled back on his arm. "Wait on me," she said. "I'm going back to the house and take this thing off and tomorrow I'm going to return it. I was out of my head. I can pay the gas bill with that seven-fifty."

He caught her arm in a vicious grip. "You are not going to take it back," he said. "I like it."

"Well," she said, "I don't think I ought . . ."

"Shut up and enjoy it," he muttered, more depressed than ever.

"With the world in the mess it's in," she said, "it's a wonder we can enjoy anything. I tell you, the bottom rail is on the top."

15   Julian sighed.

"Of course," she said, "if you know who are you, you can go anywhere." She said this every time he took her to the reducing class. "Most of them in it are not our kind of people," she said, "but I can be gracious to anybody. I know who I am."

"They don't give a damn for your graciousness," Julian said savagely. "Knowing who you are is good for one generation only. You haven't the foggiest idea where you stand now or who you are."

She stopped and allowed her eyes to flash at him. "I most certainly do know who I am," she said, "and if you don't know who you are, I'm ashamed of you."

"Oh hell," Julian said.

20   "Your great-grandfather was a former governor of this state," she said. "Your grandfather was a prosperous land-owner. Your grandmother was a Godhigh."

"Will you look around you," he said tensely, "and see where you are now?" and he swept his arm jerkily out to indicate the neighborhood, which the growing darkness at least made less dingy.

"You remain what you are," she said. "Your great-grandfather had a plantation and two hundred slaves."

"There are no more slaves," he said irritably.

"They were better off when they were," she said. He groaned to see that she was off on that topic. She rolled onto it every few days like a train on an open track. He knew every stop, every junction, every swamp along the way, and knew the exact point at which her conclusion would roll majestically into the station: "It's ridiculous. It's simply not realistic. They should rise, yes, but on their own side of the fence."

25   "Let's skip it," Julian said.

"The ones I feel sorry for," she said, "are the ones that are half white. They're tragic."

"Will you skip it?"

"Suppose we were half white. We would certainly have mixed feelings."

"I have mixed feelings now," he groaned.

30   "Well let's talk about something pleasant," she said. "I remember going to Grandpa's when I was a little girl. Then the house had double stairways that went up to what was really the second floor — all the cooking was done on the first. I

used to like to stay down in the kitchen on account of the way the walls smelled. I would sit with my nose pressed against the plaster and take deep breaths. Actually the place belonged to the Godhighs but your grandfather Chestny paid the mortgage and saved it for them. They were in reduced circumstances," she said, "but reduced or not, they never forgot who they were."

"Doubtless that decayed mansion reminded them," Julian muttered. He never spoke of it without contempt or thought of it without longing. He had seen it once when he was a child before it had been sold. The double stairways had rotted and been torn down. Negroes were living in it. But it remained in his mind as his mother had known it. It appeared in his dreams regularly. He would stand on the wide porch, listening to the rustle of oak leaves, then wander through the high-ceilinged hall into the parlor that opened onto it and gaze at the worn rugs and faded draperies. It occurred to him that it was he, not she, who could have appreciated it. He preferred its threadbare elegance to anything he could name and it was because of it that all the neighborhoods they had lived in had been a torment to him — whereas she had hardly known the difference. She called her insensitivity "being adjustable."

"And I remember the old darky who was my nurse, Caroline. There was no better person in the world. I've always had a great respect for my colored friends," she said. "I'd do anything in the world for them and they'd . . ."

"Will you for God's sake get off that subject?" Julian said. When he got on a bus by himself, he made it a point to sit down beside a Negro, in reparation as it were for his mother's sins.

"You're mighty touchy tonight," she said. "Do you feel all right?"

"Yes I feel all right," he said. "Now lay off." 35

She pursed her lips. "Well, you certainly are in a vile humor," she observed. "I just won't speak to you at all."

They had reached the bus stop. There was no bus in sight and Julian, his hands still jammed in his pockets and his head thrust forward, scowled down the empty street. The frustration of having to wait on the bus as well as ride on it began to creep up his neck like a hot hand. The presence of his mother was borne in upon him as she gave a pained sigh. He looked at her bleakly. She was holding herself very erect under the preposterous hat, wearing it like a banner of her imaginary dignity. There was in him an evil urge to break her spirit. He suddenly unloosened his tie and pulled it off and put it in his pocket.

She stiffened. "Why must you look like *that* when you take me to town?" she said. "Why must you deliberately embarrass me?"

"If you'll never learn where you are," he said, "you can at least learn where I am."

"You look like a — thug," she said. 40

"Then I must be one," he murmured.

"I'll just go home," she said. "I will not bother you. If you can't do a little thing like that for me . . ."

Rolling his eyes upward, he put his tie back on. "Restored to my class," he muttered. He thrust his face toward her and hissed, "True culture is in the mind, the *mind*," he said, and tapped his head, "the mind."

"It's in the heart," she said, "and in how you do things and how you do things is because of who you *are*."

45   "Nobody in the damn bus cares who you are."

"I care who I am," she said icily.

The lighted bus appeared on top of the next hill and as it approached, they moved out into the street to meet it. He put his hand under her elbow and hoisted her up on the creaking step. She entered with a little smile, as if she were going into a drawing room where everyone had been waiting for her. While he put in the tokens, she sat down on one of the broad front seats for three which faced the aisle. A thin woman with protruding teeth and long yellow hair was sitting on the end of it. His mother moved up beside her and left room for Julian beside herself. He sat down and looked at the floor across the aisle where a pair of thin feet in red and white canvas sandals were planted.

His mother immediately began a general conversation meant to attract anyone who felt like talking. "Can it get any hotter?" she said and removed from her purse a folding fan, black with a Japanese scene on it, which she began to flutter before her.

"I reckon it might could," the woman with the protruding teeth said, "but I know for a fact my apartment couldn't get no hotter."

50   "It must get the afternoon sun," his mother said. She sat forward and looked up and down the bus. It was half filled. Everybody was white. "I see we have the bus to ourselves," she said Julian cringed.

"For a change," said the woman across the aisle, the owner of the red and white canvas sandals. "I come on one the other day and they were thick as fleas — up front and all through."

"The world is in a mess everywhere," his mother said. "I don't know how we've let it get in this fix."

"What gets my goat is all those boys from good families stealing automobile tires," the woman with the protruding teeth said. "I told my boy, I said you may not be rich but you been raised right and if I ever catch you in any such mess, they can send you on to the reformatory. Be exactly where you belong."

"Training tells," his mother said. "Is your boy in high school?"

55   "Ninth grade," the woman said.

"My son just finished college last year. He wants to write but he's selling typewriters until he gets started," his mother said.

The woman leaned forward and peered at Julian. He threw her such a malevolent look that she subsided against the seat. On the floor across the aisle there was an abandoned newspaper. He got up and got it and opened it out in front of him. His mother discreetly continued the conversation in a lower tone but the woman across the aisle said in a loud voice, "Well that's nice. Selling typewriters is close to writing. He can go right from one to the other."

"I tell him," his mother said, "that Rome wasn't built in a day."

Behind the newspaper Julian was withdrawing into the inner compartment of his mind where he spent most of his time. This was a kind of mental bubble in which he established himself when he could not bear to be a part of what was going on around him. From it he could see out and judge but in it he was safe from any kind of penetration from without. It was the only place where he felt free of the general idiocy of his fellows. His mother had never entered it but from it he could see her with absolute clarity.

The old lady was clever enough and he thought that if she had started from any of the right premises, more might have been expected of her. She lived according to the laws of her own fantasy world, outside of which he had never seen her set foot. The law of it was to sacrifice herself for him after she had first created the necessity to do so by making a mess of things. If he had permitted her sacrifices, it was only because her lack of foresight had made them necessary. All of her life had been a struggle to act like a Chestny without the Chestny goods, and to give him everything she thought a Chestny ought to have; but since, said she, it was fun to struggle, why complain? And when you had won, as she had won, what fun to look back on the hard times! He could not forgive her that she had enjoyed the struggle and that she thought *she* had won.

What she meant when she said she had won was that she had brought him up successfully and had sent him to college and that he had turned out so well — good looking (her teeth had gone unfilled so that his could be straightened), intelligent (he realized he was too intelligent to be a success), and with a future ahead of him (there was of course no future ahead of him). She excused his gloominess on the grounds that he was still growing up and his radical ideas on his lack of practical experience. She said he didn't yet know a thing about "life," that he hadn't even entered the real world — when already he was as disenchanted with it as a man of fifty.

The further irony of all this was that in spite of her, he had turned out so well. In spite of going to only a third-rate college, he had, on his own initiative, come out with a first-rate education; in spite of growing up dominated by a small mind, he had ended up with a large one; in spite of all her foolish views, he was free of prejudice and unafraid to face facts. Most miraculous of all, instead of being blinded by love for her as she was for him, he had cut himself emotionally free of her and could see her with complete objectivity. He was not dominated by his mother.

The bus stopped with a sudden jerk and shook him from his meditation. A woman from the back lurched forward with little steps and barely escaped falling in his newspaper as she righted herself. She got off and a large Negro got on. Julian kept his paper lowered to watch. It gave him a certain satisfaction to see injustice in daily operation. It confirmed his view that with a few exceptions there was no one worth knowing within a radius of three hundred miles. The Negro was well dressed and carried a briefcase. He looked around and then sat down on the other end of the seat where the woman with the red and white canvas sandals was sitting. He immediately unfolded a newspaper and obscured himself behind it. Julian's mother's elbow at once prodded insistently into his ribs. "Now you see why I won't ride on these buses by myself," she whispered.

The woman with the red and white canvas sandals had risen at the same time the Negro sat down and had gone further back in the bus and taken the seat of the woman who had got off. His mother leaned forward and cast her an approving look.

65   Julian rose, crossed the aisle, and sat down in the place of the woman with the canvas sandals. From this position, he looked serenely across at his mother. Her face had turned an angry red. He stared at her, making his eyes the eyes of a stranger. He felt his tension suddenly lift as if he had openly declared war on her.

He would have liked to get in conversation with the Negro and to talk with him about art or politics or any subject that would be above the comprehension of those around them, but the man remained entrenched behind his paper. He was either ignoring the change of seating or had never noticed it. There was no way for Julian to convey his sympathy.

His mother kept her eyes fixed reproachfully on his face. The woman with the protruding teeth was looking at him avidly as if he were a type of monster new to her.

"Do you have a light?" he asked the Negro.

Without looking away from his paper, the man reached in his pocket and handed him a packet of matches.

70   "Thanks," Julian said. For a moment he held the matches foolishly. A NO SMOKING sign looked down upon him from over the door. This alone would not have deterred him; he had no cigarettes. He had quit smoking some months before because he could not afford it. "Sorry," he muttered and handed back the matches. The Negro lowered the paper and gave him an annoyed look. He took the matches and raised the paper again.

His mother continued to gaze at him but she did not take advantage of his momentary discomfort. Her eyes retained their battered look. Her face seemed to be unnaturally red, as if her blood pressure had risen. Julian allowed no glimmer of sympathy to show on his face. Having got the advantage, he wanted desperately to keep it and carry it through. He would have liked to teach her a lesson that would last her a while, but there seemed no way to continue the point. The Negro refused to come out from behind his paper.

Julian folded his arms and looked stolidly before him, facing her but as if he did not see her, as if he had ceased to recognize her existence. He visualized a scene in which, the bus having reached their stop, he would remain in his seat and when she said, "Aren't you going to get off?" he would look at her as a stranger who had rashly addressed him. The corner they got off on was usually deserted, but it was well lighted and it would not hurt her to walk by herself the four blocks to the Y. He decided to wait until the time came and then decide whether or not he would let her get off by herself. He would have to be at the Y at ten to bring her back, but he could leave her wondering if he was going to show up. There was no reason for her to think she could always depend on him.

He retired again into the high-ceilinged room sparsely settled with large pieces of antique furniture. His soul expanded momentarily but then he became aware of his mother across from him and the vision shriveled. He studied her coldly. Her feet in little pumps dangled like a child's and did not quite reach the floor. She was training on him an exaggerated look of reproach. He felt completely detached from her. At that moment he could with pleasure have slapped her as he would have slapped a particularly obnoxious child in his charge.

He began to imagine various unlikely ways by which he could teach her a lesson. He might make friends with some distinguished Negro professor or lawyer and bring him home to spend the evening. He would be entirely justified but her blood pressure would rise to 300. He could not push her to the extent of making her have a stroke, and moreover, he had never been successful at making any Negro friends. He had tried to strike up an acquaintance on the bus with some of the better types, with ones that looked like professors or ministers or lawyers. One morning he had sat down next to a distinguished-looking dark brown man who had answered his questions with a sonorous solemnity but who had turned out to be an undertaker. Another day he had sat down beside a cigar-smoking Negro with a diamond ring on his finger, but after a few stilted pleasantries, the Negro had rung the buzzer and risen, slipping two lottery tickets into Julian's hand as he climbed over him to leave.

He imagined his mother lying desperately ill and his being able to secure only 75 a Negro doctor for her. He toyed with that idea for a few minutes and then dropped it for a momentary vision of himself participating as a sympathizer in a sit-in demonstration. This was possible but he did not linger with it. Instead, he approached the ultimate horror. He brought home a beautiful suspiciously Negroid woman. Prepare yourself, he said. There is nothing you can do about it. This is the woman I've chosen. She's intelligent, dignified, even good, and she's suffered and she hasn't thought *fun*. Now persecute us, go ahead and persecute us. Drive her out of here, but remember, you're driving me too. His eyes were narrowed and through the indignation he had generated, he saw his mother across the aisle, purple-faced, shrunken to the dwarf-like proportions of her moral nature, sitting like a mummy beneath the ridiculous banner of her hat.

He was tilted out of his fantasy again as the bus stopped. The door opened with a sucking hiss and out of the dark a large, gaily dressed, sullen-looking colored woman got on with a little boy. The child, who might have been four, had on a short plaid suit and a Tyrolean hat with a blue feather in it. Julian hoped that he would sit down beside him and that the woman would push in beside his mother. He could think of no better arrangement.

As she waited for her tokens, the woman was surveying the seating possibilities — he hoped with the idea of sitting where she was least wanted. There was something familiar-looking about her but Julian could not place what it was. She was a giant of a woman. Her face was set not only to meet opposition but to seek it out. The downward tilt of her large lower lip was like a warning sign: DON'T TAMPER WITH ME. Her bulging figure was encased in a green crepe dress and her feet overflowed in red shoes. She had on a hideous hat. A purple velvet flap came down on one side of it and stood up on the other, the rest of it was green and looked like a cushion with the stuffing out. She carried a mammoth red pocketbook that bulged throughout as if it were stuffed with rocks.

To Julian's disappointment, the little boy climbed up on the empty seat beside his mother. His mother lumped all children, black and white, into the common category, "cute," and she thought little Negroes were on the whole cuter than little white children. She smiled at the little boy as he climbed on the seat.

Meanwhile the woman was bearing down upon the empty seat beside Julian. To his annoyance, she squeezed herself into it. He saw his mother's face change as the woman settled herself next to him and he realized with satisfaction that this was more objectionable to her than it was to him. Her face seemed almost gray and there was a look of dull recognition in her eyes, as if suddenly she had sickened at some awful confrontation. Julian saw that it was because she and the woman had, in a sense, swapped sons. Though his mother would not realize the symbolic significance of this, she would feel it. His amusement showed plainly on his face.

80   The woman next to him muttered something unintelligible to herself. He was conscious of a kind of bristling next to him, a muted growling like that of an angry cat. He could not see anything but the red pocketbook upright on the bulging green thighs. He visualized the woman as she had stood waiting for her tokens — the ponderous figure, rising from the red shoes upward over the solid hips, the mammoth bosom, the haughty face, to the green and purple hat.

His eyes widened.

The vision of the two hats, identical, broke upon him with the radiance of a brilliant sunrise. His face was suddenly lit with joy. He could not believe that Fate had thrust upon his mother such a lesson. He gave a loud chuckle so that the would look at him and see that he saw. She turned her eyes on him slowly. The blue in them seemed to have turned a bruised purple. For a moment he had an uncomfortable sense of her innocence, but it lasted only a second before principle rescued him. Justice entitled him to laugh. His grin hardened until it said to her as plainly as if he were saying aloud: Your punishment exactly fits your pettiness. This should teach you a permanent lesson.

Her eyes shifted to the woman. She seemed unable to bear looking at him and to find the woman preferable. He became conscious again of the bristling presence at his side. The woman was rumbling like a volcano about to become active. His mother's mouth began to twitch slightly at one corner. With a sinking heart, he saw incipient signs of recovery on her face and realized that this was going to strike her suddenly as funny and was going to be no lesson at all. She kept her eyes on the woman and an amused smile came over her face as if the woman were a monkey that had stolen her hat. The little Negro was looking up at her with large fascinated eyes. He had been trying to attract her attention for some time.

"Carver!" the woman said suddenly. "Come heah!"

85   When he saw that the spotlight was on him at last, Carver drew his feet up and turned himself toward Julian's mother and giggled.

"Carver!" the woman said. "You heah me? Come heah!"

Carver slid down from the seat but remained squatting with his back against the base of it, his head turned slyly around toward Julian's mother, who was smiling at him. The woman reached a hand across the aisle and snatched him to her. He righted himself and hung backwards on her knees, grinning at Julian's mother. "Isn't he cute?" Julian's mother said to the woman with the protruding teeth.

"I reckon he is," the woman said without conviction.

The Negress yanked him upright but he eased out of her grip and shot across the aisle and scrambled, giggling wildly, onto the seat beside his love.

"I think he likes me," Julian's mother said, and smiled at the woman. It was the   90
smile she used when she was being particularly gracious to an inferior. Julian saw
everything was lost. The lesson had rolled off her like rain on a roof.

The woman stood up and yanked the little boy off the seat as if she were
snatching him from contagion. Julian could feel the rage in her at having no
weapon like his mother's smile. She gave the child a sharp slap across his leg. He
howled once and then thrust his head into her stomach and kicked his feet
against her shins. "Behave," she said vehemently.

The bus stopped and the Negro who had been reading the newspaper got off.
The woman moved over and set the little boy down with a thump between herself and Julian. She held him firmly by the knee. In a moment he put his hands
in front of his face and peeped at Julian's mother through his fingers.

"I see yoooooooo!" she said and put her hand in front of her face and peeped
at him. .

The woman slapped his hand down. "Quit yo' foolishness," she said, "before I
knock the living Jesus out of you!"

Julian was thankful that the next stop was theirs. He reached up and pulled   95
the cord. The woman reached up and pulled it at the same time. Oh my God, he
thought. He had the terrible intuition that when they got off the bus together, his
mother would open her purse and give the little boy a nickel. The gesture would
be as natural to her as breathing. The bus stopped and the woman got up and
lunged to the front, dragging the child, who wished to stay on, after her. Julian
and his mother got up and followed. As they neared the door, Julian tried to relieve her of her pocketbook.

"No," she murmured, "I want to give the little boy a nickel."

"No!" Julian hissed. "No!"

She smiled down at the child and opened her bag. The bus door opened and
the woman picked him up by the arm and descended with him, hanging at her
hip. Once in the street she set him down and shook him.

Julian's mother had to close her purse while she got down the bus step but as
soon as her feet were on the ground, she opened it again and began to rummage
inside. "I can't find but a penny," she whispered, "but it looks like a new one."

"Don't do it!" Julian said fiercely between his teeth. There was a streetlight on   100
the corner and she hurried to get under it so that she could better see into her
pocketbook. The woman was heading off rapidly down the street with the child
still hanging backward on her hand.

"Oh little boy!" Julian's mother called and took a few quick steps and caught
up with them just beyond the lamppost. "Here's a bright new penny for you," and
she held out the coin, which shone bronze in the dim light.

The huge woman turned and for a moment stood, her shoulders lifted and her
face frozen with frustrated rage, and stared at Julian's mother. Then all at once she
seemed to explode like a piece of machinery that had been given one ounce of
pressure too much. Julian saw the black fist swing out with the red pocketbook.
He shut his eyes and cringed as he heard the woman shout, "He don't take nobody's pennies!" When he opened his eyes, the woman was disappearing down
the street with the little boy staring wide-eyed over her shoulder. Julian's mother
was sitting on the sidewalk.

"I told you not to do that," Julian said angrily. "I told you not to do that!"

He stood over her for a minute, gritting his teeth. Her legs were stretched out in front of her and her hat was on her lap. He squatted down and looked her in the face. It was totally expressionless. "You got exactly what you deserved," he said. "Now get up."

105   He picked up her pocketbook and put what had fallen out back in it. He picked the hat up off her lap. The penny caught his eye on the sidewalk and he picked that up and let it drop before her eyes into the purse. Then he stood up and leaned over and held his hands out to pull her up. She remained immobile. He sighed. Rising above them on either side were black apartment buildings, marked with irregular rectangles of light. At the end of the block a man came out of a door and walked off in the opposite direction. "All right," he said, "suppose somebody happens by and wants to know why you're sitting on the sidewalk?"

She took the hand and, breathing hard, pulled heavily up on it and then stood for a moment, swaying slightly as if the spots of light in the darkness were circling around her. Her eyes, shadowed and confused, finally settled on his face. He did not try to conceal his irritation. "I hope this teaches you a lesson," he said. She leaned forward and her eyes raked his face. She seemed trying to determine his identity. Then, as if she found nothing familiar about him, she started off with a headlong movement in the wrong direction.

"Aren't you going on to the Y?" he asked.

"Home," she muttered.

"Well, are we walking?"

110   For answer she kept going. Julian followed along, his hands behind him. He saw no reason to let the lesson she had had go without backing it up with an explanation of its meaning. She might as well be made to understand what had happened to her. "Don't think that was just an uppity Negro woman," he said. "That was the whole colored race which will no longer take your condescending pennies. That was your black double. She can wear the same hat as you, and to be sure," he added gratuitously (because he thought it was funny), "it looked better on her than it did on you. What all this means," he said, "is that the old world is gone. The old manners are obsolete and your graciousness is not worth a damn." He thought bitterly of the house that had been lost for him. "You aren't who you think you are," he said.

She continued to plow ahead, paying no attention to him. Her hair had come undone on one side. She dropped her pocketbook and took no notice. He stooped and picked it up and handed it to her but she did not take it.

"You needn't act as if the world had come to an end," he said, "because it hasn't. From now on you've got to live in a new world and face a few realities for a change. Buck up," he said, "it won't kill you."

She was breathing fast.

"Let's wait on the bus," he said.

"Home," she said thickly.

115   "I hate to see you behave like this," he said. "Just like a child. I should be able to expect more of you." He decided to stop where he was and make her stop and wait for a bus. "I'm not going any farther," he said stopping. "We're going on the bus."

She continued to go on as if she had not heard him. He took a few steps and caught her arm and stopped her. He looked into her face and caught his breath. He was looking into a face he had never seen before. "Tell Grandpa to come get me," she said.

He stared, stricken.

"Tell Caroline to come get me," she said.

Stunned, he let her go and she lurched forward again, walking as if one leg were shorter than the other. A tide of darkness seemed to be sweeping her from him. "Mother!" he cried. "Darling, sweetheart, wait!" Crumpling, she fell to the pavement. He dashed forward and fell at her side, crying, "Mamma, Mamma!" He turned her over. Her face was fiercely distorted. One eye, large and staring, moved slightly to the left as if it had become unmoored. The other remained fixed on him, raked his face again, found nothing and closed. 120

"Wait here, wait here!" he cried and jumped up and began to run for help toward a cluster of lights he saw in the distance ahead of him. "Help, help!" he shouted, but his voice was thin, scarcely a thread of sound. The lights drifted farther away the faster he ran and his feet moved numbly as if they carried him nowhere. The tide of darkness seemed to sweep him back to her, postponing from moment to moment his entry into the world of guilt and sorrow.

❖ ❖ ❖

EDGAR ALLAN POE   (1809–1849)

The Tell-Tale Heart   (1843)

True!— nervous — very, very dreadfully nervous I had been and am; but why *will* you say that I am mad? The disease had sharpened my senses — not destroyed — not dulled them. Above all was the sense of hearing acute. I heard all things in the heaven and in the earth. I heard many things in hell. How, then, am I mad? Hearken! and observe how healthily — how calmly I can tell you the whole story.

It is impossible to say how first the idea entered my brain; but once conceived, it haunted me day and night. Object there was none. Passion there was none. I loved the old man. He had never wronged me. He had never given me insult. For his gold I had no desire. I think it was his eye! yes, it was this! One of his eyes resembled that of a vulture — a pale eye, with a film over it. Whenever it fell upon me, my blood ran cold; and so by degrees — very gradually — I made up my mind to take the life of the old man, and thus rid myself of the eye forever.

Now this is the point. You fancy me mad. Madmen know nothing. But you should have seen *me*. You should have seen how wisely I proceeded — with what caution — with what foresight — with what dissimulation I went to work! I was never kinder to the old man than during the whole week before I killed him. And every night, about midnight, I turned the latch of his door and opened it — oh, so gently! And then, when I had made an opening sufficient for my head, I put in a dark lantern, all closed, closed, so that no light shone out, and then I thrust in my head. Oh, you would have laughed to see how cunningly I thrust it in! I moved it slowly — very, very slowly, so that I might not disturb the old man's sleep. It took me an hour to place my whole head within the opening so far that I could see him as he lay upon his bed. Ha! — would a madman have been so wise as this? And then, when my head was well in the room, I undid the lantern cautiously — oh, so cautiously — cautiously (for the hinges creaked) — I undid it just so much that a single thin ray fell upon the vulture eye. And this I did for seven long nights — every night just at midnight — but I found the eye always closed; and so it was impossible to do the work; for it was not the old man who vexed me, but his Evil Eye. And every morning, when the day broke, I went boldly into the chamber, and spoke courageously to him, calling him by name in a hearty tone, and inquiring how he had passed the night. So you see he would have been a very profound old man, indeed, to suspect that every night, just at twelve, I looked in upon him while he slept.

Upon the eighth night I was more than usually cautious in opening the door. A watch's minute hand moves more quickly than did mine. Never before that night had I *felt* the extent of my own powers — of my sagacity. I could scarcely contain my feelings of triumph. To think that there I was, opening the door little by little, and he not even to dream of my secret deeds or thoughts. I fairly chuckled at the idea; and perhaps he heard me; for he moved on the bed suddenly, as if startled. Now you may think that I drew back — but no. His room was as black as pitch with the thick darkness (for the shutters were close fastened through fear of robbers), and so I knew that he could not see the opening of the door, and I kept pushing it on steadily, steadily.

5   I had my head in, and was about to open the lantern, when my thumb slipped upon the tin fastening, and the old man sprang up in the bed, crying out — "Who's there?"

I kept quite still and said nothing. For a whole hour I did not move a muscle, and in the meantime I did not hear him lie down. He was still sitting up in the bed listening; — just as I have done, night after night, hearkening to the death watches° in the wall.

Presently I heard a slight groan, and I knew it was the groan of mortal terror. It was not a groan of pain or of grief — oh, no! — it was the low stifled sound that arises from the bottom of the soul when overcharged with awe. I knew the sound very well. Many a night, just at midnight, when all the world slept, it has welled up from my own bosom, deepening, with its dreadful echo, the terrors that distracted me. I say I knew it well. I knew what the old man felt, and pitied him, although I chuckled at heart. I knew that he had been lying awake ever since the first slight noise, when he had turned in the bed. His fears had been ever since growing upon him. He had been trying to fancy them causeless, but could not. He had been saying to himself — "It is nothing but the wind in the chimney — it is only a mouse crossing the floor," or "it is merely a cricket which has made a single chirp." Yes, he had been trying to

---

death watches: Wood-burrowing beetles. Their clicking sound was superstitiously thought of as an omen of death.

comfort himself with these suppositions; but he had found all in vain. *All in vain*; because Death, in approaching him, had stalked with his black shadow before him, and enveloped the victim. And it was the mournful influence of the unperceived shadow that caused him to feel — although he neither saw nor heard — to *feel* the presence of my head within the room.

When I had waited a long time, very patiently, without hearing him lie down, I resolved to open a little — a very, very little crevice in the lantern. So I opened it — you cannot imagine how stealthily, stealthily — until, at length, a single dim ray, like the thread of the spider, shot from out of the crevice and fell upon the vulture eye.

It was open — wide, wide open — and I grew furious as I gazed upon it. I saw it with perfect distinctness — all a dull blue, with a hideous veil over it that chilled the very marrow in my bones; but I could see nothing else of the old man's face or person: for I had directed the ray as if by instinct, precisely upon the damned spot.

And now have I not told you that what you mistake for madness is but over- 10 acuteness of the senses?— now, I say, there came to my ears a low, dull, quick sound, such as a watch makes when enveloped in cotton. I knew *that* sound well, too. It was the beating of the old man's heart. It increased my fury, as the beating of a drum stimulates the soldier into courage.

But even yet I refrained and kept still. I scarcely breathed. I held the lantern motionless. I tried how steadily I could maintain the ray upon the eye. Meantime the hellish tattoo of the heart increased. It grew quicker and quicker, and louder and louder every instant. The old man's terror *must* have been extreme! It grew louder, I say, louder every moment!— do you mark me well? I have told you that I am nervous: so I am. And now at the dead hour of the night, amid the dreadful silence of that old house, so strange a noise as this excited me to uncontrollable terror. Yet, for some minutes longer I refrained and stood still. But the beating grew louder, louder! I thought the heart must burst. And now a new anxiety seized me — the sound would be heard by a neighbor! The old man's hour had come! With a loud yell, I threw open the lantern and leaped into the room. He shrieked once — once only. In an instant I dragged him to the floor, and pulled the heavy bed over him. I then smiled gaily, to find the deed so far done. But, for many minutes, the heart beat on with a muffled sound. This, however, did not vex me; it would not be heard through the wall. At length it ceased. The old man was dead. I removed the bed and examined the corpse. Yes, he was stone, stone dead. I placed my hand upon the heart and held it there many minutes.

If still you think me mad, you will think so no longer when I describe the wise precautions I took for the concealment of the body. The night waned, and I worked hastily, but in silence. First of all I dismembered the corpse. I cut off the head and the arms and the legs.

I then took up three planks from the flooring of the chamber, and deposited all between the scantlings. I then replaced the boards so cleverly, so cunningly, that no human eye — not even *his*— could have detected anything wrong. There was nothing to wash out — no stain of any kind — no bloodspot whatever. I had been too wary for that. A tub had caught all —ha! ha!

When I had made an end of these labors, it was four o'clock — still dark as midnight. As the bell sounded the hour, there came a knocking at the street door. I went down to open it with a light heart, — for what had I *now* to fear? There entered three men, who introduced themselves, with perfect suavity, as officers of the police. A shriek had been heard by a neighbor during the night; suspicion of foul play had been aroused, information had been lodged at the police office, and they (the officers) had been deputed to search the premises.

15   I smiled, — for *what* had I to fear? I bade the gentlemen welcome. The shriek, I said, was my own in a dream. The old man, I mentioned, was absent in the country. I took my visitors all over the house. I bade them search — search *well*. I led them, at length, to *his* chamber. I showed them his treasures, secure, undisturbed. In the enthusiasm of my confidence, I brought chairs into the room, and desired them *here* to rest from their fatigues, while I myself, in the wild audacity of my perfect triumph, placed my own seat upon the very spot beneath which reposed the corpse of the victim.

The officers were satisfied. My *manner* had convinced them. I was singularly at ease. They sat, and while I answered cheerily, they chatted of familiar things. But, ere long, I felt myself getting pale and wished them gone. My head ached, and I fancied a ringing in my ears: but still they sat and still they chatted. The ringing became more distinct: — it continued and became more distinct: I talked more freely to get rid of the feeling: but it continued and gained definitiveness — until, at length, I found that the noise was *not* within my ears.

No doubt I now grew *very* pale: — but I talked more fluently, and with a heightened voice. Yet the sound increased — and what could I do? It was a *low, dull, quick sound — much such a sound as a watch makes when enveloped in cotton*. I gasped for breath — and yet the officers heard it not. I talked more quickly — more vehemently; but the noise steadily increased. I arose and argued about trifles, in a high key and with violent gesticulations; but the noise steadily increased. Why *would* they not be gone? I paced the floor to and fro with heavy strides, as if excited to fury by the observations of the men — but the noise steadily increased. Oh God! what *could* I do? I foamed — I raved — I swore! I swung the chair upon which I had been sitting, and grated it upon the boards, but the noise arose over all and continually increased. It grew louder — louder — *louder*! And still the men chatted pleasantly, and smiled. Was it possible they heard not? Almighty God! — no, no! They heard! — they suspected! — they *knew*! — they were making a mockery of my horror! — this I thought, and this I think. But anything was better than this agony! Anything was more tolerable than this derision! I could bear those hypocritical smiles no longer! I felt that I must scream or die! — and now — again! — hark! louder! louder! louder! *louder*! —

"Villains!" I shrieked, " dissemble no more! I admit the dead! — tear up the planks! — here, here! — it is the beating of his hideous heart!"

◇ ◇ ◇

KATHERINE ANNE PORTER   (1890–1980)

The Jilting of Granny Weatherall   (1930)

She flicked her wrist neatly out of Doctor Harry's pudgy careful fingers and pulled the sheet up to her chin. The brat ought to be in knee breeches. Doctoring around the country with spectacles on his nose! "Get along now, take your schoolbooks and go. There's nothing wrong with me."

Doctor Harry spread a warm paw like a cushion on her forehead where the forked green vein danced and made her eyelids twitch. "Now, now, be a good girl, and we'll have you up in no time."

"That's no way to speak to a woman nearly eighty years old just because she's down. I'd have you respect your elders, young man."

"Well, Missy, excuse me." Doctor Harry patted her cheek. "But I've got to warn you, haven't I? You're a marvel, but you must be careful or you're going to be good and sorry."

"Don't tell me what I'm going to be. I'm on my feet now, morally speaking. It's   5
Cornelia. I had to go to bed to get rid of her."

Her bones felt loose, and floated around in her skin, and Doctor Harry floated like a balloon around the foot of the bed. He floated and pulled down his waist-coat and swung his glasses on a cord. "Well, stay where you are, it certainly can't hurt you."

"Get along and doctor your sick," said Granny Weatherall. "Leave a well woman alone. I'll call for you when I want you. . . . Where were you forty years ago when I pulled through milk-leg and double pneumonia? You weren't even born. Don't let Cornelia lead you on," she shouted, because Doctor Harry appeared to float up to the ceiling and out. "I pay my own bills, and I don't throw my money away on nonsense!"

She meant to wave good-by, but it was too much trouble. Her eyes closed of themselves, it was like a dark curtain drawn around the bed. The pillow rose and floated under her, pleasant as a hammock in a light wind. She listened to the leaves rustling outside the window. No, somebody was swishing newspapers: no, Cornelia and Doctor Harry were whispering together. She leaped broad awake, thinking they whispered in her ear.

"She was never like this, *never* like this!" "Well, what can we expect?" "Yes, eighty years old. . . ."

Well, and what if she was? She still had ears. It was like Cornelia to whisper   10
around doors. She always kept things secret in such a public way. She was always being tactful and kind. Cornelia was dutiful; that was the trouble with her. Dutiful and good: "So good and dutiful," said Granny, "that I'd like to spank her." She saw herself spanking Cornelia and making a fine job of it.

"What'd you say, Mother?"

Granny felt her face tying up in hard knots.

"Can't a body think, I'd like to know?"

"I thought you might want something."

"I do. I want a lot of things. First off, go away and don't whisper."   15

She lay and drowsed, hoping in her sleep that the children would keep out and let her rest a minute. It had been a long day. Not that she was tired. It was always pleasant to snatch a minute now and then. There was always so much to be done, let me see: tomorrow.

Tomorrow was far away and there was nothing to trouble about. Things were finished somehow when the time came; thank God there was always a little margin over for peace: then a person could spread out the plan of life and tuck in the edges orderly. It was good to have everything clean and folded away, with the hair brushes and tonic bottles sitting straight on the white embroidered linen: the day started without fuss and the pantry shelves laid out with rows of jelly glasses and brown jugs and white stone-china jars with blue whirligigs and words painted on them: coffee, tea, sugar, ginger, cinnamon, allspice: and the bronze clock with the lion on top nicely dusted off. The dust that lion could collect in twenty-four hours! The box in the attic with all those letters tied up, well, she'd have to go through that tomorrow. All those letters — George's letters and John's letters and her letters to them both — lying around for the children to find afterwards made her uneasy. Yes, that would be tomorrow's business. No use to let them know how silly she had been once.

While she was rummaging around she found death in her mind and it felt clammy and unfamiliar. She had spent so much time preparing for death there was no need for bringing it up again. Let it take care of itself now. When she was sixty she had felt very old, finished, and went around making farewell trips to see her children and grandchildren, with a secret in her mind: This is the very last of your mother, children! Then she made her will and came down with a long fever. That was all just a notion like a lot of other things, but it was lucky too, for she had once and for all got over the idea of dying for a long time. Now she couldn't be worried. She hoped she had better sense now. Her father had lived to be one hundred and two years old and had drunk a noggin of strong hot toddy on his last birthday. He told the reporters it was his daily habit, and he owed his long life to that. He had made quite a scandal and was very pleased about it. She believed she'd just plague Cornelia a little.

"Cornelia! Cornelia!" No footsteps, but a sudden hand on her cheek. "Bless you, where have you been?"

20   "Here, Mother."

"Well, Cornelia, I want a noggin of hot toddy."

"Are you cold, darling?"

"I'm chilly, Cornelia. Lying in bed stops the circulation. I must have told you that a thousand times."

Well, she could just hear Cornelia telling her husband that Mother was getting a little childish and they'd have to humor her. The thing that most annoyed her was that Cornelia thought she was deaf, dumb, and blind. Little hasty glances and tiny gestures tossed around her and over her head saying, "Don't cross her, let her have her way, she's eighty years old," and she sitting there as if she lived in a thin glass cage. Sometimes Granny almost made up her mind to pack up and move back to her own house where nobody could remind her every minute that she was old. Wait, wait, Cornelia, till your own children whisper behind your back!

In her day she had kept a better house and had got more work done. She   25
wasn't too old yet for Lydia to be driving eighty miles for advice when one of the
children jumped the track, and Jimmy still dropped in and talked things over:
"Now, Mammy, you've a good business head, I want to know what you think of
this? . . ." Old. Cornelia couldn't change the furniture around without asking.
Little things, little things! They had been so sweet when they were little. Granny
wished the old days were back again with the children young and everything to
be done over. It had been a hard pull, but not too much for her. When she
thought of all the food she had cooked, and all the clothes she had cut and sewed,
and all the gardens she had made — well, the children showed it. There they
were, made out of her, and they couldn't get away from that. Sometimes she
wanted to see John again and point to them and say, Well, I didn't do so badly, did
I? But that would have to wait. That was for tomorrow. She used to think of him
as a man, but now all the children were older than their father, and he would be
a child beside her if she saw him now. It seemed strange and there was something
wrong in the idea. Why, he couldn't possibly recognize her. She had fenced in a
hundred acres once, digging the post holes herself and clamping the wires with
just a negro boy to help. That changed a woman. John would be looking for a
young woman with the peaked Spanish comb in her hair and the painted fan.
Digging post holes changed a woman. Riding country roads in the winter when
women had their babies was another thing: sitting up nights with sick horses and
sick negroes and sick children and hardly ever losing one. John, I hardly ever lost
one of them! John would see that in a minute, that would be something he could
understand, she wouldn't have to explain anything!

It made her feel like rolling up her sleeves and putting the whole place to
rights again. No matter if Cornelia was determined to be everywhere at once,
there were a great many things left undone on this place. She would start tomorrow and do them. It was good to be strong enough for everything, even if all you
made melted and changed and slipped under your hands, so that by the time you
finished you almost forgot what you were working for. What was it I set out to do?
she asked herself intently, but she could not remember. A fog rose over the valley,
she saw it marching across the creek swallowing the trees and moving up the hill
like an army of ghosts. Soon it would be at the near edge of the orchard, and then
it was time to go in and light the lamps. Come in, children, don't stay out in the
night air.

Lighting the lamps had been beautiful. The children huddled up to her and
breathed like little calves waiting at the bars in the twilight. Their eyes followed
the match and watched the flame rise and settle in a blue curve, then they
moved away from her. The lamp was lit, they didn't have to be scared and hang on
to mother any more. Never, never, never more. God, for all my life I thank Thee.
Without Thee, my God, I could never have done it. Hail, Mary, full of grace.

I want you to pick all the fruit this year and see that nothing is wasted. There's
always someone who can use it. Don't let good things rot for want of using. You
waste life when you waste good food. Don't let things get lost. It's bitter to lose
things. Now, don't let me get to thinking, not when I am tired and taking a little
nap before supper. . . .

The pillow rose about her shoulders and pressed against her heart and the memory was being squeezed out of it: oh, push down the pillow, somebody: it would smother her if she tried to hold it. Such a fresh breeze blowing and such a green day with no threats in it. But he had not come, just the same. What does a woman do when she has put on the white veil and set out the white cake for a man and he doesn't come? She tried to remember. No, I swear he never harmed me but in that. He never harmed me but in that . . . and what if he did? There was the day, the day, but a whirl of dark smoke rose and covered it, crept up and over into the bright field where everything was planted so carefully in orderly rows. That was hell, she knew hell when she saw it. For sixty years she had prayed against remembering him and against losing her soul in the deep pit of hell, and now the two things were mingled in one and the thought of him was a smoky cloud from hell that moved and crept in her head when she had just got rid of Doctor Harry and was trying to rest a minute. Wounded vanity, Ellen, said a sharp voice in the top of her mind. Don't let your wounded vanity get the upper hand of you. Plenty of girls get jilted. You were jilted, weren't you? Then stand up to it. Her eyelids wavered and let in streamers of blue-gray light like tissue paper over her eyes. She must get up and pull the shades down or she'd never sleep. She was in bed again and the shades were not down. How could that happen? Better turn over, hide from the light, sleeping in the light gave you nightmares. "Mother, how do you feel now?" and a stinging wetness on her forehead. But I don't like having my face washed in cold water!

30   Hapsy? George? Lydia? Jimmy? No, Cornelia, and her features were swollen and full of little puddles. "They're coming, darling, they'll all be here soon." Go wash your face, child, you look funny.

Instead of obeying, Cornelia knelt down and put her head on the pillow. She seemed to be talking but there was no sound. "Well, are you tongue-tied? Whose birthday is it? Are you going to give a party?"

Cornelia's mouth moved urgently in strange shapes. "Don't do that, you bother me, daughter."

"O, no, Mother. Oh, no. . . ."

Nonsense. It was strange about children. They disputed your every word. "No what, Cornelia?"

35   "Here's Doctor Harry."

"I won't see that boy again. He just left five minutes ago."

"That was this morning, Mother. It's night now. Here's the nurse."

"This is Doctor Harry, Mrs. Weatherall. I never saw you look so young and happy!"

"Ah, I'll never be young again — but I'd be happy if they'd let me lie in peace and get rested."

40   She thought she spoke up loudly, but no one answered. A warm weight on her forehead, a warm bracelet on her wrist, and a breeze went on whispering, trying to tell her something. A shuffle of leaves in the everlasting hand of God. He blew on them and they danced and rattled. "Mother, don't mind, we're going to give you a little hypodermic." "Look here, daughter, how do ants get in this bed? I saw sugar ants yesterday." Did you send for Hapsy too?

It was Hapsy she really wanted. She had to go a long way back through a great many rooms to find Hapsy standing with a baby on her arm. She seemed to herself to be Hapsy also, and the baby on Hapsy's arm was Hapsy and himself and herself, all at once, and there was no surprise in the meeting. Then Hapsy melted from within and turned flimsy as gray gauze and the baby was a gauzy shadow, and Hapsy came up close and said, "I thought you'd never come," and looked at her very searchingly and said, "You haven't changed a bit!" They leaned forward to kiss, when Cornelia began whispering from a long way off, "Oh, is there anything you want to tell me? Is there anything I can do for you?"

Yes, she had changed her mind after sixty years and she would like to see George. I want you to find George. Find him and be sure to tell him I forgot him. I want him to know I had my husband just the same and my children and my house like any other woman. A good house too and a good husband that I loved and fine children out of him. Better than I hoped for even. Tell him I was given back everything he took away and more. Oh, no, oh, God, no, there was something else besides the house and the man and the children. Oh, surely they were not all? What was it? Something not given back. . . . Her breath crowded down under her ribs and grew into a monstrous frightening shape with cutting edges; it bored up into her head, and the agony was unbelievable: Yes, John, get the Doctor now, no more talk, my time has come.

When this one was born it should be the last. The last. It should have been born first, for it was the one she had truly wanted. Everything came in good time. Nothing left out, left over. She was strong, in three days she would be as well as ever. Better. A woman needed milk in her to have her full health.

"Mother, do you hear me?"

"I've been telling you —"

"Mother, Father Connolly's here."

"I went to Holy Communion last week. Tell him I'm not so sinful as all that."

"Father just wants to speak to you."

He could speak as much as he pleased. It was like him to drop in and inquire about her soul as if it were a teething baby, and then stay on for a cup of tea and a round of cards and gossip. He always had a funny story of some sort, usually about an Irishman who made his little mistakes and confessed them, and the point lay in some absurd thing he would blurt out in the confessional showing his struggles between native piety and original sin. Granny felt easy about her soul. Cornelia, where are your manners? Give Father Connolly a chair. She had her secret comfortable understanding with a few favorite saints who cleared a straight road to God for her. All as surely signed and sealed as the papers for the new Forty Acres. Forever . . . heirs and assigns forever. Since the day the wedding cake was not cut, but thrown out and wasted. The whole bottom dropped out of the world, and there she was blind and sweating with nothing under her feet and the walls falling away. His hand had caught her under the breast, she had not fallen, there was the freshly polished floor with the green rug on it, just as before. He had cursed like a sailor's parrot and said, "I'll kill him for you." Don't lay a hand on him, for my sake leave something to God. "Now, Ellen, you must believe what I tell you. . . ."

45

50   So there was nothing, nothing to worry about any more, except sometimes in the night one of the children screamed in a nightmare, and they both hustled out shaking and hunting for the matches and calling, "There, wait a minute, here we are!" John, get the doctor now, Hapsy's time has come. But there was Hapsy standing by the bed in a white cap. "Cornelia, tell Hapsy to take off her cap. I can't see her plain."

Her eyes opened very wide and the room stood out like a picture she had seen somewhere. Dark colors with the shadows rising towards the ceiling in long angles. The tall black dresser gleamed with nothing on it but John's picture, enlarged from a little one, with John's eyes very black when they should have been blue. You never saw him, so how do you know how he looked? But the man insisted the copy was perfect, it was very rich and handsome. For a picture, yes, but it's not my husband. The table by the bed had a linen cover and a candle and a crucifix. The light was blue from Cornelia's silk lampshades. No sort of light at all, just frippery. You had to live forty years with kerosene lamps to appreciate honest electricity. She felt very strong and she saw Doctor Harry with a rosy nimbus around him.

"You look like a saint, Doctor Harry, and I vow that's as near as you'll ever come to it."

"She's saying something."

"I heard you, Cornelia. What's all this carrying-on?"

55   "Father Connolly's saying —"

Cornelia's voice staggered and bumped like a cart in a bad road. It rounded corners and turned back again and arrived nowhere. Granny stepped up in the cart very lightly and reached for the reins, but a man sat beside her and she knew him by his hands, driving the cart. She did not look in his face, for she knew without seeing, but looked instead down the road where the trees leaned over and bowed to each other and a thousand birds were singing a Mass. She felt like singing too, but she put her hand in the bosom of her dress and pulled out a rosary, and Father Connolly murmured Latin in a very solemn voice and tickled her feet. My God, will you stop that nonsense? I'm a married woman. What if he did run away and leave me to face the priest by myself? I found another a whole world better. I wouldn't have exchanged my husband for anybody except St. Michael himself, and you may tell him that for me with a thank you in the bargain.

Light flashed on her closed eyelids, and a deep roaring shook her. Cornelia, is that lightning? I hear thunder. There's going to be a storm. Close all the windows. Call the children in. . . . "Mother, here we are, all of us." "Is that you, Hapsy?" "Oh, no, I'm Lydia. We drove as fast as we could." Their faces drifted above her, drifted away. The rosary fell out of her hands and Lydia put it back. Jimmy tried to help, their hands fumbled together, and Granny closed two fingers around Jimmy's thumb. Beads wouldn't do, it must be something alive. She was so amazed her thoughts ran round and round. So, my dear Lord, this is my death and I wasn't even thinking about it. My children have come to see me die. But I can't, it's not time. Oh, I always hated surprises. I wanted to give Cornelia the amethyst set — Cornelia, you're to have the amethyst set, but Hapsy's to wear it when she wants, and, Doctor Harry, do shut up. Nobody sent for you. Oh, my dear Lord, do wait a minute. I meant to do something about the Forty Acres, Jimmy doesn't need it and Lydia will later on, with that worthless husband of hers. I meant to finish the altar cloth and send six bottles of wine to Sister Borgia for her dyspepsia. I want to send six bottles of wine to Sister Borgia, Father Connolly, now don't let me forget.

Cornelia's voice made short turns and tilted over and crashed. "Oh, Mother, oh, Mother, oh, Mother. . . ."

"I'm not going, Cornelia. I'm taken by surprise. I can't go."

You'll see Hapsy again. What about her? "I thought you'd never come." 60 Granny made a long journey outward, looking for Hapsy. What if I don't find her? What then? Her heart sank down and down, there was no bottom to death, she couldn't come to the end of it. The blue light from Cornelia's lampshade drew into a tiny point in the center of her brain, it flickered and winked like an eye, quietly it fluttered and dwindled. Granny lay curled down within herself, amazed and watchful, staring at the point of light that was herself; her body was now only a deeper mass of shadow in an endless darkness and this darkness would curl around the light and swallow it up. God, give a sign!

For the second time there was no sign. Again no bridegroom and the priest in the house. She could not remember any other sorrow because this grief wiped them all away. Oh, no, there's nothing more cruel than this — I'll never forgive it. She stretched herself with a deep breath and blew out the light.

◇ ◇ ◇

JOHN STEINBECK   (1902–1968)

The Chrysanthemums   (1937)

The high grey-flannel fog of winter closed off the Salinas Valley from the sky and from all the rest of the world. On every side it sat like a lid on the mountains and made of the great valley a closed pot. On the broad, level land floor the gang plows bit deep and left the black earth shining like metal where the shares had cut. On the foothill ranches across the Salinas River, the yellow stubble fields seemed to be bathed in pale cold sunshine, but there was no sunshine in the valley now in December. The thick willow scrub along the river flamed with sharp and positive yellow leaves.

It was a game of quiet and of waiting. The air was cold and tender. A light wind blew up from the southwest so that the farmers were mildly hopeful of a good rain before long; but fog and rain do not go together.

Across the river, on Henry Allen's foothill ranch there was little work to be done, for the hay was cut and stored and the orchards were plowed up to receive the rain deeply when it should come. The cattle on the higher slopes were becoming shaggy and rough-coated.

Elisa Allen, working in her flower garden, looked down across the yard and saw Henry, her husband, talking to two men in business suits. The three of them stood by the tractor shed, each man with one foot on the side of the little Fordson. They smoked cigarettes and studied the machine as they talked.

5   Elisa watched them for a moment and then went back to her work. She was thirty-five. Her face was lean and strong and her eyes were as clear as water. Her figure looked blocked and heavy in her gardening costume, a man's black hat pulled low down over her eyes, clod-hopper shoes,° a figured print dress almost completely covered by a big corduroy apron with four big pockets to hold the snips, the trowel and scratcher, the seeds and the knife she worked with. She wore heavy leather gloves to protect her hands while she worked.

She was cutting down the old year's chrysanthemum stalks with a pair of short and powerful scissors. She looked down toward the men by the tractor shed now and then. Her face was eager and mature and handsome; even her work with the scissors was over-eager, over-powerful. The chrysanthemum stems seemed too small and easy for her energy.

She brushed a cloud of hair out of her eyes with the back of her glove, and left a smudge of earth on her cheek in doing it. Behind her stood the neat white farm house with red geraniums close-banked around it as high as the windows. It was a hard-swept looking little house with hard-polished windows, and a clean mud-mat on the front steps.

Elisa cast another glance toward the tractor shed. The strangers were getting into their Ford coupe. She took off a glove and put her strong fingers down into the forest of new green chrysanthemum sprouts that were growing around the old roots. She spread the leaves and looked down among the close-growing stems. No aphids were there, no sowbugs or snails or cutworms. Her terrier fingers destroyed such pests before they could get started.

Elisa started at the sound of her husband's voice. He had come near quietly, and he leaned over the wire fence that protected her flower garden from cattle and dogs and chickens.

10   "At it again," he said. "You've got a strong new crop coming."

Elisa straightened her back and pulled on the gardening glove again. "Yes. They'll be strong this coming year." In her tone and on her face there was a little smugness.

"You've got a gift with things," Henry observed. "Some of those yellow chrysanthemums you had this year were ten inches across. I wish you'd work out in the orchard and raise some apples that big."

Her eyes sharpened. "Maybe I could do it, too. I've a gift with things, all right. My mother had it. She could stick anything in the ground and make it grow. She said it was having planters' hands that knew how to do it."

"Well, it sure works with flowers," he said.

15   "Henry, who were those men you were talking to?"

"Why, sure, that's what I came to tell you. They were from the Western Meat Company. I sold those thirty head of three-year-old steers. Got nearly my own price, too."

---

clod-hopper shoes: Heavy shoes, such as the ones that a plowman might wear.

"Good," she said. "Good for you."

"And I thought," he continued, "I thought how it's Saturday afternoon, and we might go into Salinas for dinner at a restaurant, and then to a picture show — to celebrate, you see."

"Good," she repeated. "Oh, yes. That will be good."

Henry put on his joking tone. "There's fights tonight. How'd you like to go to the fights?"   20

"Oh, no," she said breathlessly. "No, I wouldn't like fights."

"Just fooling, Elisa. We'll go to a movie. Let's see. It's two now. I'm going to take Scotty and bring down those steers from the hill. It'll take us maybe two hours. We'll go in town about five and have dinner at the Cominos Hotel. Like that?"

"Of course I'll like it. It's good to eat away from home."

"All right, then. I'll go get up a couple of horses."

She said, "I'll have plenty of time to transplant some of these sets, I guess."   25

She heard her husband calling Scotty down by the barn. And a little later she saw the two men ride up the pale yellow hillside in search of the steers.

There was a little square sandy bed kept for rooting the chrysanthemums. With her trowel she turned the soil over and over, and smoothed it and patted it firm. Then she dug ten parallel trenches to receive the sets. Back at the chrysanthemum bed she pulled out the little crisp shoots, trimmed off the leaves of each one with her scissors and laid it on a small orderly pile.

A squeak of wheels and plod of hoofs came from the road. Elisa looked up. The country road ran along the dense bank of willows and cottonwoods that bordered the river, and up this road came a curious vehicle, curiously drawn. It was an old spring-wagon, with a round canvas top on it like the cover of a prairie schooner.° It was drawn by an old bay horse and a little grey-and-white burro. A big stubble-bearded man sat between the cover flaps and drove the crawling team. Underneath the wagon, between the hind wheels, a lean and rangy mongrel dog walked sedately. Words were printed on the canvas, in clumsy, crooked letters. "Pots, pans, knives, sisors, lawn mores, Fixed." Two rows of articles, and the triumphantly definitive "Fixed" below. The black paint had run down in little sharp points beneath each letter.

Elisa, squatting on the ground, watched to see the crazy, loose-jointed wagon pass by. But it didn't pass. It turned into the farm road in front of her house, crooked old wheels skirling and squeaking. The rangy dog darted from between the wheels and ran ahead. Instantly the two ranch shepherds flew out at him. Then all three stopped, and with stiff and quivering tails, with taut straight legs, with ambassadorial dignity, they slowly circled, sniffing daintily. The caravan pulled up to Elisa's wire fence and stopped. Now the newcomer dog, feeling outnumbered, lowered his tail and retired under the wagon with raised hackles and bared teeth.

---

prairie schooner: Covered wagon used by American pioneers.

30   The man on the wagon seat called out, "That's a bad dog in a fight when he gets started."

Elisa laughed. "I see he is. How soon does he generally get started?"

The man caught up her laughter and echoed it heartily. "Sometimes not for weeks and weeks," he said. He climbed stiffly down, over the wheel. The horse and the donkey drooped like unwatered flowers.

Elisa saw that he was a very big man. Although his hair and beard were greying, he did not look old. His worn black suit was wrinkled and spotted with grease. The laughter had disappeared from his face and eyes the moment his laughing voice ceased. His eyes were dark, and they were full of the brooding that gets in the eyes of teamsters and of sailors. The calloused hands he rested on the wire fence were cracked, and every crack was a black line. He took off his battered hat.

"I'm off my general road, ma'am," he said. "Does this dirt road cut over across the river to the Los Angeles highway?"

35   Elisa stood up and shoved the thick scissors in her apron pocket. "Well, yes, it does, but it winds around and then fords the river. I don't think your team could pull through the sand."

He replied with some asperity. "It might surprise you what them beasts can pull through."

"When they get started?" she asked.

He smiled for a second. "Yes. When they get started."

"Well," said Elisa, "I think you'll save time if you go back to the Salinas road and pick up the highway there."

40   He drew a big finger down the chicken wire and made it sing. "I ain't in any hurry, ma'am. I go from Seattle to San Diego and back every year. Takes all my time. About six months each way. I aim to follow nice weather."

Elisa took off her gloves and stuffed them in the apron pocket with the scissors. She touched the under edge of her man's hat, searching for fugitive hairs. "That sounds like a nice kind of a way to live," she said.

He leaned confidentially over the fence. "Maybe you noticed the writing on my wagon. I mend pots and sharpen knives and scissors. You got any of them things to do?"

"Oh, no," she said quickly. "Nothing like that." Her eyes hardened with resistance.

"Scissors is the worst thing," he explained. "Most people just ruin scissors trying to sharpen 'em, but I know how. I got a special tool. It's a little bobbit kind of thing, and patented. But it sure does the trick."

45   "No. My scissors are all sharp."

"All right, then. Take a pot," he continued earnestly, "a bent pot, or a pot with a hole. I can make it like new so you don't have to buy no new ones. That's a saving for you."

"No," she said shortly. "I tell you I have nothing like that for you to do."

His face fell to an exaggerated sadness. His voice took on a whining undertone. "I ain't had a thing to do today. Maybe I won't have no supper tonight. You see I'm off my regular road. I know folks on the highway clear from Seattle to San

Diego. They save their things for me to sharpen up because they know I do it so good and save them money."

"I'm sorry," Elisa said irritably. "I haven't anything for you to do."

His eyes left her face and fell to searching the ground. They roamed about un-   50
til they came to the chrysanthemum bed where she had been working. "What's them plants, ma'am?"

The irritation and resistance melted from Elisa's face. "Oh, those are chrysanthemums, giant whites and yellows. I raise them every year, bigger than anybody around here."

"Kind of a long-stemmed flower? Looks like a quick puff of colored smoke?" he asked.

"That's it. What a nice way to describe them."

"They smell kind of nasty till you get used to them," he said.

"It's a good bitter smell," she retorted, "not nasty at all."   55

He changed his tone quickly. "I like the smell myself."

"I had ten-inch blooms this year," she said.

The man leaned farther over the fence. "Look. I know a lady down the road a piece, has got the nicest garden you ever seen. Got nearly every kind of flower but no chrysanthemums. Last time I was mending a copper-bottom washtub for her (that's a hard job but I do it good), she said to me, 'If you ever run acrost some nice chrysanthemums I wish you'd try to get me a few seeds.' That's what she told me."

Elisa's eyes grew alert and eager. "She couldn't have known much about chrysanthemums. You *can* raise them from seed, but it's much easier to root the little sprouts you see there."

"Oh," he said. "I s'pose I can't take none to her, then."   60

"Why yes you can," Elisa cried. "I can put some in damp sand, and you can carry them right along with you. They'll take root in the pot if you keep them damp. And then she can transplant them."

"She'd sure like to have some, ma'am. You say they're nice ones?"

"Beautiful," she said. "Oh, beautiful." Her eyes shone. She tore off the battered hat and shook out her dark pretty hair. "I'll put them in a flower pot, and you can take them right with you. Come into the yard."

While the man came through the picket gate Elisa ran excitedly along the geranium-bordered path to the back of the house. And she returned carrying a big red flower pot. The gloves were forgotten now. She kneeled on the ground by the starting bed and dug up the sandy soil with her fingers and scooped it into the bright new flower pot. Then she picked up the little pile of shoots she had prepared. With her strong fingers she pressed them into the sand and tamped around them with her knuckles. The man stood over her. "I'll tell you what to do," she said. "You remember so you can tell the lady."

"Yes, I'll try to remember."   65

"Well, look. These will take root in about a month. Then she must set them out, about a foot apart in good rich earth like this, see?" She lifted a handful of dark soil for him to look at. "They'll grow fast and tall. Now remember this: In July tell her to cut them down, about eight inches from the ground."

"Before they bloom?" he asked.

"Yes, before they bloom." Her face was tight with eagerness. "They'll grow right up again. About the last of September the buds will start."

She stopped and seemed perplexed. "It's the budding that takes the most care," she said hesitantly. "I don't know how to tell you." She looked deep into his eyes, searchingly. Her mouth opened a little, and she seemed to be listening. "I'll try to tell you," she said. "Did you ever hear of planting hands?"

70   "Can't say I have, ma'am."

"Well, I can only tell you what it feels like. It's when you're picking off the buds you don't want. Everything goes right down into your fingertips. You watch your fingers work. They do it themselves. You can feel how it is. They pick and pick the buds. They never make a mistake. They're with the plant. Do you see? Your fingers and the plant. You can feel that, right up your arm. They know. They never make a mistake. You can feel it. When you're like that you can't do anything wrong. Do you see that? Can you understand that?"

She was kneeling on the ground looking up at him. Her breast swelled passionately.

The man's eyes narrowed. He looked away self-consciously. "Maybe I know," he said. "Sometimes in the night in the wagon there —"

Elisa's voice grew husky. She broke in on him, "I've never lived as you do, but I know what you mean. When the night is dark — why, the stars are sharp-pointed, and there's quiet. Why, you rise up and up! Every pointed star gets driven into your body. It's like that. Hot and sharp and — lovely."

75   Kneeling there, her hand went out toward his legs in the greasy black trousers. Her hesitant fingers almost touched the cloth. Then her hand dropped to the ground. She crouched low like a fawning dog.

He said, "It's nice, just like you say. Only when you don't have no dinner, it ain't."

She stood up then, very straight, and her face was ashamed. She held the flower pot out to him and placed it gently in his arms. "Here. Put it in your wagon, on the seat, where you can watch it. Maybe I can find something for you to do."

At the back of the house she dug in the can pile and found two old and battered aluminum saucepans. She carried them back and gave them to him. "Here, maybe you can fix these."

His manner changed. He became professional. "Good as new I can fix them." At the back of his wagon he sat a little anvil, and out of an oily tool box dug a small machine hammer. Elisa came through the gate to watch him while he pounded out the dents in the kettles. His mouth grew sure and knowing. At a difficult part of the work he sucked his under-lip.

80   "You sleep right in the wagon?" Elisa asked.

"Right in the wagon, ma'am. Rain or shine I'm dry as a cow in there."

"It must be nice," she said. "It must be very nice. I wish women could do such things."

"It ain't the right kind of a life for a woman."

Her upper lip raised a little, showing her teeth. "How do you know? How can you tell?" she said.

85   "I don't know, ma'am," he protested. "Of course I don't know. Now here's your kettles, done. You don't have to buy no new ones."

"How much?"

"Oh, fifty cents'll do. I keep my prices down and my work good. That's why I have all them satisfied customers up and down the highway."

Elisa brought him a fifty-cent piece from the house and dropped it in his hand. "You might be surprised to have a rival some time. I can sharpen scissors, too. And I can beat the dents out of little pots. I could show you what a woman might do."

He put his hammer back in the oily box and shoved the little anvil out of sight. "It would be a lonely life for a woman, ma'am, and a scarey life, too, with animals creeping under the wagon all night." He climbed over the singletree,° steadying himself with a hand on the burro's white rump. He settled himself in the seat, picked up the lines. "Thank you kindly, ma'am," he said. "I'll do like you told me; I'll go back and catch the Salinas road."

"Mind," she called, "if you're long in getting there, keep the sand damp."   90

"Sand, ma'am? . . . Sand? Oh, sure. You mean around the chrysanthemums. Sure I will." He clucked his tongue. The beasts leaned luxuriously into their collars. The mongrel dog took his place between the back wheels. The wagon turned and crawled out the entrance road and back the way it had come, along the river.

Elisa stood in front of her wire fence watching the slow progress of the caravan. Her shoulders were straight, her head thrown back, her eyes half-closed, so that the scene came vaguely into them. Her lips moved silently, forming the words "Good-bye — good-bye." Then she whispered, "That's a bright direction. There's a glowing there." The sound of her whisper startled her. She shook herself free and looked about to see whether anyone had been listening. Only the dogs had heard. They lifted their heads toward her from their sleeping in the dust, and then stretched out their chins and settled asleep again. Elisa turned and ran hurriedly into the house.

In the kitchen she reached behind the stove and felt the water tank. It was full of hot water from the noonday cooking. In the bathroom she tore off her soiled clothes and flung them into the corner. And then she scrubbed herself with a little block of pumice, legs and thighs, loins and chest and arms, until her skin was scratched and red. When she had dried herself she stood in front of a mirror in her bedroom and looked at her body. She tightened her stomach and threw out her chest. She turned and looked over her shoulder at her back.

After a while she began to dress, slowly. She put on her newest underclothing and her nicest stockings and the dress which was the symbol of her prettiness. She worked carefully on her hair, penciled her eyebrows and rouged her lips.

Before she was finished she heard the little thunder of hoofs and the shouts of   95
Henry and his helper as they drove the red steers into the corral. She heard the gate bang shut and set herself for Henry's arrival.

His step sounded on the porch. He entered the house calling, "Elisa, where are you?"

---

singletree: A wooden bar that connects a wagon to the horses' harnesses.

"In my room, dressing. I'm not ready. There's hot water for your bath. Hurry up. It's getting late."

When she heard him splashing in the tub, Elisa laid his dark suit on the bed, and shirt and socks and tie beside it. She stood his polished shoes on the floor beside the bed. Then she went to the porch and sat primly and stiffly down. She looked toward the river road where the willow-line was still yellow with frosted leaves so that under the high grey fog they seemed a thin band of sunshine. This was the only color in the grey afternoon. She sat unmoving for a long time. Her eyes blinked rarely.

Henry came banging out of the door, shoving his tie inside his vest as he came. Elisa stiffened and her face grew tight. Henry stopped short and looked at her. "Why — why, Elisa. You look so nice!"

100 "Nice? You think I look nice? What do you mean by 'nice'?"

Henry blundered on. "I don't know. I mean you look different, strong and happy."

"I am strong? Yes, strong. What do you mean 'strong'?"

He looked bewildered. "You're playing some kind of a game," he said helplessly. "It's a kind of a play. You look strong enough to break a calf over your knee, happy enough to eat it like a watermelon."

For a second she lost her rigidity. "Henry! Don't talk like that. You didn't know what you said." She grew complete again. "I'm strong," she boasted. "I never knew before how strong."

105 Henry looked down toward the tractor shed, and when he brought his eyes back to her, they were his own again. "I'll get out the car. You can put on your coat while I'm starting."

Elisa went into the house. She heard him drive to the gate and idle down his motor, and then she took a long time to put on her hat. She pulled it here and pressed it there. When Henry turned the motor off she slipped into her coat and went out.

The little roadster° bounced along on the dirt road by the river, raising the birds and driving the rabbits into the brush. Two cranes flapped heavily over the willow-line and dropped into the river-bed.

Far ahead on the road Elisa saw a dark speck. She knew.

She tried not to look as they passed it, but her eyes would not obey. She whispered to herself sadly, "He might have thrown them off the road. That wouldn't have been much trouble, not very much. But he kept the pot," she explained. "He had to keep the pot. That's why he couldn't get them off the road."

110 The roadster turned a bend and she saw the caravan ahead. She swung full around toward her husband so she could not see the little covered wagon and the mismatched team as the car passed them.

In a moment it was over. The thing was done. She did not look back.

She said loudly, to be heard above the motor, "It will be good, tonight, a good dinner."

---

roadster: An early roofless automobile, with a single seat for two or three passengers.

"Now you're changed again," Henry complained. He took one hand from the wheel and patted her knee. "I ought to take you in to dinner oftener. It would be good for both of us. We get so heavy out on the ranch."

"Henry," she asked, "could we have wine at dinner?"

"Sure we could. Say! That will be fine."   115

She was silent for a while; then she said, "Henry, at those prize fights, do the men hurt each other very much?"

"Sometimes a little, not often. Why?"

"Well, I've read how they break noses, and blood runs down their chests. I've read how the fighting gloves get heavy and soggy with blood."

He looked around at her. "What's the matter, Elisa? I didn't know you read things like that." He brought the car to a stop, then turned to the right over the Salinas River bridge.

"Do any women ever go to the fights?" she asked.   120

"Oh, sure, some. What's the matter, Elisa? Do you want to go? I don't think you'd like it, but I'll take you if you really want to go."

She relaxed limply in the seat. "Oh, no. No. I don't want to go. I'm sure I don't." Her face was turned away from him. "It will be enough if we can have wine. It will be plenty." She turned up her coat collar so he could not see that she was crying weakly — like an old woman.

◇ ◇ ◇

AMY TAN (1952–   )

Two Kinds (1989)

My mother believed you could be anything you wanted to be in America. You could open a restaurant. You could work for the government and get good retirement. You could buy a house with almost no money down. You could become rich. You could become instantly famous.

"Of course you can be prodigy, too," my mother told me when I was nine. "You can be best anything. What does Auntie Lindo know? Her daughter, she is only best tricky."

America was where all my mother's hopes lay. She had come here in 1949 after losing everything in China: her mother and father, her family home, her first husband, and two daughters, twin baby girls. But she never looked back with regret. There were so many ways for things to get better.

We didn't immediately pick the right kind of prodigy. At first my mother thought I could be a Chinese Shirley Temple. We'd watch Shirley's old movies on TV as though they were training films. My mother would poke my arm and say, "*Ni kan*" — You watch. And I would see Shirley tapping her feet, or singing a sailor song, or pursing her lips into a very round O while saying, "Oh my goodness."

5   "*Ni kan,*" said my mother as Shirley's eyes flooded with tears. "You already know how. Don't need talent for crying!"

Soon after my mother got this idea about Shirley Temple, she took me to a beauty training school in the Mission district and put me in the hands of a student who could barely hold the scissors without shaking. Instead of getting big fat curls, I emerged with an uneven mass of crinkly black fuzz. My mother dragged me off to the bathroom and tried to wet down my hair.

"You look like Negro Chinese," she lamented, as if I had done this on purpose.

The instructor of the beauty training school had to lop off these soggy clumps to make my hair even again. "Peter Pan is very popular these days," the instructor assured my mother. I now had hair the length of a boy's, with straight-across bangs that hung at a slant two inches above my eyebrows. I liked the haircut and it made me actually look forward to my future fame.

In fact, in the beginning, I was just as excited as my mother, maybe even more so. I pictured this prodigy part of me as many different images, trying each one on for size. I was a dainty ballerina girl standing by the curtains, waiting to hear the right music that would send me floating on my tiptoes. I was like the Christ child lifted out of the straw manger, crying with holy indignity. I was Cinderella stepping from her pumpkin carriage with sparkly cartoon music filling the air.

10   In all of my imaginings, I was filled with a sense that I would soon become *perfect*. My mother and father would adore me. I would be beyond reproach. I would never feel the need to sulk for anything.

But sometimes the prodigy in me became impatient. "If you don't hurry up and get me out of here, I'm disappearing for good," it warned. "And then you'll always be nothing."

Every night after dinner, my mother and I would sit at the Formica kitchen table. She would present new tests, taking her examples from stories of amazing children she had read in *Ripley's Believe It or Not,* or *Good Housekeeping, Reader's Digest,* and a dozen other magazines she kept in a pile in our bathroom. My mother got these magazines from people whose houses she cleaned. And since she cleaned many houses each week, we had a great assortment. She would look through them all, searching for stories about remarkable children.

The first night she brought out a story about a three-year-old boy who knew the capitals of all the states and even most of the European countries. A teacher was quoted as saying the little boy could also pronounce the names of the foreign cities correctly.

"What's the capital of Finland?" my mother asked me, looking at the magazine story.

15   All I knew was the capital of California, because Sacramento was the name of the street we lived on in Chinatown. "Nairobi!" I guessed, saying the most foreign word I could think of. She checked to see if that was possibly one way to pronounce "Helsinki" before showing me the answer.

The tests got harder — multiplying numbers in my head, finding the queen of hearts in a deck of cards, trying to stand on my head without using my hands, predicting the daily temperatures in Los Angeles, New York, and London.

One night I had to look at a page from the Bible for three minutes and then report everything I could remember. "Now Jehoshaphat had riches and honor in abundance and . . . that's all I remember, Ma," I said.

And after seeing my mother's disappointed face once again, something inside of me began to die. I hated the tests, the raised hopes and failed expectations. Before going to bed that night, I looked in the mirror above the bathroom sink and when I saw only my face staring back — and that it would always be this ordinary face — I began to cry. Such a sad, ugly girl! I made high-pitched noises like a crazed animal, trying to scratch out the face in the mirror.

And then I saw what seemed to be the prodigy side of me — because I had never seen that face before. I looked at my reflection, blinking so I could see more clearly. The girl staring back at me was angry, powerful. This girl and I were the same. I had new thoughts, willful thoughts, or rather thoughts filled with lots of won'ts. I won't let her change me, I promised myself. I won't be what I'm not.

So now on nights when my mother presented her tests, I performed listlessly, 20 my head propped on one arm. I pretended to be bored. And I was. I got so bored I started counting the bellows of the foghorns out on the bay while my mother drilled me in other areas. The sound was comforting and reminded me of the cow jumping over the moon. And the next day, I played a game with myself, seeing if my mother would give up on me before eight bellows. After a while I usually counted only one, maybe two bellows at most. At last she was beginning to give up hope.

Two or three months had gone by without any mention of my being a prodigy again. And then one day my mother was watching *The Ed Sullivan Show* on TV. The TV was old and the sound kept shorting out. Every time my mother got halfway up from the sofa to adjust the set, the sound would go back on and Ed would be talking. As soon as she sat down, Ed would go silent again. She got up, the TV broke into loud piano music. She sat down. Silence. Up and down, back and forth, quiet and loud. It was like a stiff embraceless dance between her and the TV set. Finally she stood by the set with her hand on the sound dial.

She seemed entranced by the music, a little frenzied piano piece with this mesmerizing quality, sort of quick passages and then teasing lilting ones before it returned to the quick playful parts.

"*Ni kan*," my mother said, calling me over with hurried hand gestures, "Look here."

I could see why my mother was fascinated by the music. It was being pounded out by a little Chinese girl, about nine years old, with a Peter Pan haircut. The girl had the sauciness of a Shirley Temple. She was proudly modest like a proper Chinese child. And she also did this fancy sweep of a curtsy, so that the fluffy skirt of her white dress cascaded slowly to the floor like the petals of a large carnation.

In spite of these warning signs, I wasn't worried. Our family had no piano and 25 we couldn't afford to buy one, let alone reams of sheet music and piano lessons. So I could be generous in my comments when my mother bad-mouthed the little girl on TV.

"Play note right, but doesn't sound good! No singing sound," complained my mother.

"What are you picking on her for?" I said carelessly. "She's pretty good. Maybe she's not the best, but she's trying hard." I knew almost immediately I would be sorry I said that.

"Just like you," she said. "Not the best. Because you not trying." She gave a little huff as she let go of the sound dial and sat down on the sofa.

The little Chinese girl sat down also to play an encore of "Anitra's Dance" by Grieg. I remember the song, because later on I had to learn how to play it.

30   Three days after watching *The Ed Sullivan Show*, my mother told me what my schedule would be for piano lessons and piano practice. She had talked to Mr. Chong, who lived on the first floor of our apartment building. Mr. Chong was a retired piano teacher and my mother had traded housecleaning services for weekly lessons and a piano for me to practice on every day, two hours a day, from four until six.

When my mother told me this, I felt as though I had been sent to hell. I whined and then kicked my foot a little when I couldn't stand it anymore.

"Why don't you like me the way I am? I'm *not* a genius! I can't play the piano. And even if I could, I wouldn't go on TV if you paid me a million dollars!" I cried.

My mother slapped me. "Who ask you be genius?" she shouted. "Only ask you be your best. For you sake. You think I want you be genius? Hnnh! What for! Who ask you!"

"So ungrateful," I heard her mutter in Chinese. "If she had as much talent as she has temper, she would be famous now."

35   Mr. Chong, whom I secretly nicknamed Old Chong, was very strange, always tapping his fingers to the silent music of an invisible orchestra. He looked ancient in my eyes. He had lost most of the hair on top of his head and he wore thick glasses and had eyes that always looked tired and sleepy. But he must have been younger than I thought, since he lived with his mother and was not yet married.

I met Old Lady Chong once and that was enough. She had this peculiar smell like a baby that had done something in its pants. And her fingers felt like a dead person's, like an old peach I once found in the back of the refrigerator; the skin just slid off the meat when I picked it up.

I soon found out why Old Chong had retired from teaching piano. He was deaf. "Like Beethoven!" he shouted to me. "We're both listening only in our head!" And he would start to conduct his frantic silent sonatas.

Our lessons went like this. He would open the book and point to different things, explaining their purpose: "Key! Treble! Bass! No sharps or flats! So this is C major! Listen now and play after me!"

And then he would play the C scale a few times, a simple chord, and then, as if inspired by an old, unreachable itch, he gradually added more notes and running trills and a pounding bass until the music was really something quite grand.

40   I would play after him, the simple scale, the simple chord, and then I just played some nonsense that sounded like a cat running up and down on top of garbage cans. Old Chong smiled and applauded and then said, "Very good! But now you must learn to keep time!"

So that's how I discovered that Old Chong's eyes were too slow to keep up with the wrong notes I was playing. He went through the motions in half-time. To help me keep rhythm, he stood behind me, pushing down on my right shoulder for every beat. He balanced pennies on top of my wrists so I would keep them still as I slowly played scales and arpeggios. He had me curve my hand around an apple and keep that shape when playing chords. He marched stiffly to show me how to make each finger dance up and down, staccato like an obedient little soldier.

He taught me all these things, and that was how I also learned I could be lazy and get away with mistakes, lots of mistakes. If I hit the wrong notes because I hadn't practiced enough, I never corrected myself. I just kept playing in rhythm. And Old Chong kept conducting his own private reverie.

So maybe I never really gave myself a fair chance. I did pick up the basics pretty quickly, and I might have become a good pianist at that young age. But I was so determined not to try, not to be anybody different that I learned to play only the most ear-splitting preludes, the most discordant hymns.

Over the next year, I practiced like this, dutifully in my own way. And then one day I heard my mother and her friend Lindo Jong both talking in a loud bragging tone of voice so others could hear. It was after church, and I was leaning against the brick wall wearing a dress with stiff white petticoats. Auntie Lindo's daughter, Waverly, who was about my age, was standing farther down the wall about five feet away. We had grown up together and shared all the closeness of two sisters squabbling over crayons and dolls. In other words, for the most part, we hated each other. I thought she was snotty. Waverly Jong had gained a certain amount of fame as "Chinatown's Littlest Chinese Chess Champion."

"She bring home too many trophy," lamented Auntie Lindo that Sunday. "All 45 day she play chess. All day I have no time do nothing but dust off her winnings." She threw a scolding look at Waverly, who pretended not to see her.

"You lucky you don't have this problem," said Auntie Lindo with a sigh to my mother.

And my mother squared her shoulders and bragged: "Our problem worser than yours. If we ask Jing-mei wash dish, she hear nothing but music. It's like you can't stop this natural talent."

And right then, I was determined to put a stop to her foolish pride.

A few weeks later, Old Chong and my mother conspired to have me play in a talent show which would be held in the church hall. By then, my parents had saved up enough to buy me a secondhand piano, a black Wurlitzer spinet with a scarred bench. It was the showpiece of our living room.

For the talent show, I was to play a piece called "Pleading Child" from 50 Schumann's *Scenes from Childhood*. It was a simple, moody piece that sounded more difficult than it was. I was supposed to memorize the whole thing, playing the repeat parts twice to make the piece sound longer. But I dawdled over it, playing a few bars and then cheating, looking up to see what notes followed. I never really listened to what I was playing. I daydreamed about being somewhere else, about being someone else.

The part I liked to practice best was the fancy curtsy: right foot out, touch the rose on the carpet with a pointed foot, sweep to the side, left leg bends, look up and smile.

My parents invited all the couples from the Joy Luck Club° to witness my debut. Auntie Lindo and Uncle Tin were there. Waverly and her two older brothers had also come. The first two rows were filled with children both younger and older than I was. The littlest ones got to go first. They recited simple nursery rhymes, squawked out tunes on miniature violins, twirled Hula Hoops, pranced in pink ballet tutus, and when they bowed or curtsied, the audience would sigh in unison, "Awww," and then clap enthusiastically.

When my turn came, I was very confident. I remember my childish excitement. It was as if I knew, without a doubt, that the prodigy side of me really did exist. I had no fear whatsoever, no nervousness. I remember thinking to myself, This is it! This is it! I looked out over the audience, at my mother's blank face, my father's yawn, Auntie Lindo's stiff-lipped smile, Waverly's sulky expression. I had on a white dress layered with sheets of lace, and a pink bow in my Peter Pan haircut. As I sat down I envisioned people jumping to their feet and Ed Sullivan rushing up to introduce me to everyone on TV.

And I started to play. It was so beautiful. I was so caught up in how lovely I looked that at first I didn't worry how I would sound. So it was a surprise to me when I hit the first wrong note and I realized something didn't sound quite right. And then I hit another and another followed that. A chill started at the top of my head and began to trickle down. Yet I couldn't stop playing, as though my hands were bewitched. I kept thinking my fingers would adjust themselves back, like a train switching to the right track. I played this strange jumble through two repeats, the sour notes staying with me all the way to the end.

55   When I stood up, I discovered my legs were shaking. Maybe I had just been nervous and the audience, like Old Chong, had seen me go through the right motions and had not heard anything wrong at all. I swept my right foot out, went down on my knee, looked up and smiled. The room was quiet, except for Old Chong, who was beaming and shouting, "Bravo! Bravo! Well done!" But then I saw my mother's face, her stricken face. The audience clapped weakly, and as I walked back to my chair, with my whole face quivering as I tried not to cry, I heard a little boy whisper loudly to his mother, "That was awful," and the mother whispered back, "Well, she certainly tried."

And now I realized how many people were in the audience, the whole world it seemed. I was aware of eyes burning into my back. I felt the shame of my mother and father as they sat stiffly throughout the rest of the show.

We could have escaped during intermission. Pride and some strange sense of honor must have anchored my parents to their chairs. And so we watched it all: the eighteen-year-old boy with a fake mustache who did a magic show and juggled flaming hoops while riding a unicycle. The breasted girl with white makeup

---

Joy Luck Club: A name denoting the mother's circle of friends, all of whom were Chinese immigrants to the United States.

who sang from *Madama Butterfly* and got honorable mention. And the eleven-year-old boy who won first prize playing a tricky violin song that sounded like a busy bee.

After the show, the Hsus, the Jongs, and the St. Clairs from the Joy Luck Club came up to my mother and father.

"Lots of talented kids," Auntie Lindo said vaguely, smiling broadly.

"That was somethin' else," said my father, and I wondered if he was referring   60
to me in a humorous way, or whether he even remembered what I had done.

Waverly looked at me and shrugged her shoulders. "You aren't a genius like me," she said matter-of-factly. And if I hadn't felt so bad, I would have pulled her braids and punched her stomach.

But my mother's expression was what devastated me: a quiet, blank look that said she had lost everything. I felt the same way, and it seemed as if everybody were now coming up, like gawkers at the scene of an accident, to see what parts were actually missing. When we got on the bus to go home, my father was humming the busy-bee tune and my mother was silent. I kept thinking she wanted to wait until we got home before shouting at me. But when my father unlocked the door to our apartment, my mother walked in and then went to the back, into the bedroom. No accusations. No blame. And in a way, I felt disappointed. I had been waiting for her to start shouting, so I could shout back and cry and blame her for all my misery.

I assumed my talent-show fiasco meant I never had to play the piano again. But two days later, after school, my mother came out of the kitchen and saw me watching TV.

"Four clock," she reminded me as if it were any other day. I was stunned, as though she were asking me to go through the talent-show torture again. I wedged myself more tightly in front of the TV.

"Turn off TV," she called from the kitchen five minutes later.   65

I didn't budge. And then I decided. I didn't have to do what my mother said anymore. I wasn't her slave. This wasn't China. I had listened to her before and look what happened. She was the stupid one.

She came out from the kitchen and stood in the arched entryway of the living room. "Four clock," she said once again, louder.

"I'm not going to play anymore," I said nonchalantly. "Why should I? I'm not a genius."

She walked over and stood in front of the TV. I saw her chest was heaving up and down in an angry way.

"No!" I said, and I now felt stronger, as if my true self had finally emerged. So   70
this was what had been inside me all along.

"No! I won't!" I screamed.

She yanked me by the arm, pulled me off the floor, snapped off the TV. She was frighteningly strong, half pulling, half carrying me toward the piano as I kicked the throw rugs under my feet. She lifted me up and onto the hard bench. I was sobbing by now, looking at her bitterly. Her chest was heaving even more and her mouth was open, smiling crazily as if she were pleased I was crying.

"You want me to be someone that I'm not!" I sobbed. "I'll never be the kind of daughter you want me to be!"

"Only two kinds of daughters," she shouted in Chinese. "Those who are obedient and those who follow their own mind! Only one kind of daughter can live in this house. Obedient daughter!"

75 "Then I wish I wasn't your daughter. I wish you weren't my mother," I shouted. As I said these things I got scared. It felt like worms and toads and slimy things crawling out of my chest, but it also felt good, as if this awful side of me had surfaced, at last.

"Too late change this," said my mother shrilly.

And I could sense her anger rising to its breaking point. I wanted to see it spill over. And that's when I remembered the babies she had lost in China, the ones we never talked about. "Then I wish I'd never been born!" I shouted. "I wish I were dead! Like them."

It was as if I had said the magic words. Alakazam!— and her face went blank, her mouth closed, her arms went slack, and she backed out of the room, stunned, as if she were blowing away like a small brown leaf, thin, brittle, lifeless.

It was not the only disappointment my mother felt in me. In the years that followed, I failed her so many times, each time asserting my own will, my right to fall short of expectations. I didn't get straight As. I didn't become class president. I didn't get into Stanford. I dropped out of college.

80 For unlike my mother, I did not believe I could be anything I wanted to be. I could only be me.

And for all those years, we never talked about the disaster at the recital or my terrible accusations afterward at the piano bench. All that remained unchecked, like a betrayal that was now unspeakable. So I never found a way to ask her why she had hoped for something so large that failure was inevitable.

And even worse, I never asked her what frightened me the most: Why had she given up hope?

For after our struggle at the piano, she never mentioned my playing again. The lessons stopped. The lid to the piano was closed, shutting out the dust, my misery, and her dreams.

So she surprised me. A few years ago, she offered to give me the piano, for my thirtieth birthday. I had not played in all those years. I saw the offer as a sign of forgiveness, a tremendous burden removed.

85 "Are you sure?" I asked shyly. "I mean, won't you and Dad miss it?"

"No, this your piano," she said firmly. "Always your piano. You only one can play."

"Well, I probably can't play anymore," I said. "It's been years."

"You pick up fast," said my mother, as if she knew this was certain. "You have natural talent. You could been genius if you want to."

"No I couldn't."

90 "You just not trying," said my mother. And she was neither angry nor sad. She said it as if to announce a fact that could never be disproved. "Take it," she said.

But I didn't at first. It was enough that she had offered it to me. And after that, every time I saw it in my parents' living room, standing in front of the bay windows, it made me feel proud, as if it were a shiny trophy I had won back.

Last week I sent a tuner over to my parents' apartment and had the piano reconditioned, for purely sentimental reasons. My mother had died a few months before and I had been getting things in order for my father, a little bit at a time. I put the jewelry in special silk pouches. The sweaters she had knitted in yellow, pink, bright orange — all the colors I hated — I put those in moth-proof boxes. I found some old Chinese silk dresses, the kind with little slits up the sides. I rubbed the old silk against my skin, then wrapped them in tissue and decided to take them home with me.

After I had the piano tuned, I opened the lid and touched the keys. It sounded even richer than I remembered. Really, it was a very good piano. Inside the bench were the same exercise notes with handwritten scales, the same secondhand music books with their covers held together with yellow tape.

I opened up the Schumann book to the dark little piece I had played at the recital. It was on the left-hand side of the page, "Pleading Child." It looked more difficult than I remembered. I played a few bars, surprised at how easily the notes came back to me.

And for the first time, or so it seemed, I noticed the piece on the right-hand side. It was called "Perfectly Contented." I tried to play this one as well. It had a lighter melody but the same flowing rhythm and turned out to be quite easy. "Pleading Child" was shorter but slower; "Perfectly Contented" was longer, but faster. And after I played them both a few times, I realized they were two halves of the same song.

95

◇ ◇ ◇

ANNE TYLER (1941–   )

Teenage Wasteland (1984)

He used to have very blond hair — almost white — cut shorter than other children's so that on his crown a little cowlick always stood up to catch the light. But this was when he was small. As he grew older, his hair grew darker, and he wore it longer — past his collar even. It hung in lank, taffy-colored ropes around his face, which was still an endearing face, fine-featured, the eyes an unusual aqua blue. But his cheeks, of course, were no longer round, and a sharp new Adam's apple jogged in his throat when he talked.

In October, they called from the private school he attended to request a conference with his parents. Daisy went alone; her husband was at work. Clutching her purse, she sat on the principal's couch and learned that Donny was noisy, lazy, and disruptive; always fooling around with his friends, and he wouldn't respond in class.

In the past, before her children were born, Daisy had been a fourth-grade teacher. It shamed her now to sit before this principal as a parent, a delinquent parent, a parent who struck Mr. Lanham, no doubt, as unseeing or uncaring. "It isn't that we're not concerned," she said. "Both of us are. And we've done what we could, whatever we could think of. We don't let him watch TV on school nights. We don't let him talk on the phone till he's finished his homework. But he tells us he doesn't *have* any homework or he did it all in study hall. How are we to know what to believe?"

From early October through November, at Mr. Lanham's suggestion, Daisy checked Donny's assignments every day. She sat next to him as he worked, trying to be encouraging, sagging inwardly as she saw the poor quality of everything he did — the sloppy mistakes in math, the illogical leaps in his English themes, the history questions left blank if they required any research.

5   Daisy was often late starting supper, and she couldn't give as much attention to Donny's younger sister. "You'll never guess what happened at . . ." Amanda would begin, and Daisy would have to tell her, "Not now, honey."

By the time her husband, Matt, came home, she'd be snappish. She would recite the day's hardships — the fuzzy instructions in English, the botched history map, the morass of unsolvable algebra equations. Matt would look surprised and confused, and Daisy would gradually wind down. There was no way, really, to convey how exhausting all this was.

In December, the school called again. This time, they wanted Matt to come as well. She and Matt had to sit on Mr. Lanham's couch like two bad children and listen to the news: Donny had improved only slightly, raising a D in history to a C, and a C in algebra to a B-minus. What was worse, he had developed new problems. He had cut classes on at least three occasions. Smoked in the furnace room. Helped Sonny Barnett break into a freshman's locker. And last week, during athletics, he and three friends had been seen off the school grounds; when they returned, the coach had smelled beer on their breath.

Daisy and Matt sat silent, shocked. Matt rubbed his forehead with his fingertips. Imagine, Daisy thought, how they must look to Mr. Lanham: an overweight housewife in a cotton dress and a too-tall, too-thin insurance agent in a baggy, frayed suit. Failures, both of them — the kind of people who are always hurrying to catch up, missing the point of things that everyone else grasps at once. She wished she'd worn nylons instead of knee socks.

It was arranged that Donny would visit a psychologist for testing. Mr. Lanham knew just the person. He would set this boy straight, he said.

10   When they stood to leave, Daisy held her stomach in and gave Mr. Lanham a firm, responsible handshake.

Donny said the psychologist was a jackass and the tests were really dumb; but he kept all three of his appointments, and when it was time for the follow-up conference with the psychologist and both parents, Donny combed his hair and seemed unusually sober and subdued. The psychologist said Donny had no serious emotional problems. He was merely going through a difficult period in his life. He required some academic help and a better sense of self-worth. For this reason, he was suggesting a man named Calvin Beadle, a tutor with considerable psychological training.

In the car going home, Donny said he'd be damned if he'd let them drag him to some stupid fairy tutor. His father told him to watch his language in front of his mother.

That night, Daisy lay awake pondering the term "self-worth." She had always been free with her praise. She had always told Donny he had talent, was smart, was good with his hands. She had made a big to-do over every little gift he gave her. In fact, maybe she had gone too far, although, Lord knows, she had meant every word. Was that his trouble?

She remembered when Amanda was born. Donny had acted lost and bewildered. Daisy had been alert to that, of course, but still, a new baby keeps you so busy. Had she really done all she could have? She longed — she ached — for a time machine. Given one more chance, she'd do it perfectly — hug him more, praise him more, or perhaps praise him less. Oh, who can say . . .

The tutor told Donny to call him Cal. All his kids did, he said. Daisy thought   15 for a second that he meant his own children, then realized her mistake. He seemed too young, anyhow, to be a family man. He wore a heavy brown handlebar mustache. His hair was as long and stringy as Donny's, and his jeans as faded. Wire-rimmed spectacles slid down his nose. He lounged in a canvas director's chair with his fingers laced across his chest, and he casually, amiably questioned Donny, who sat upright and glaring in an armchair.

"So they're getting on your back at school," said Cal. "Making a big deal about anything you do wrong."

"Right," said Donny.

"Any idea why that would be?"

"Oh, well, you know, stuff like homework and all," Donny said.

"You don't do your homework?"   20

"Oh, well, I might do it sometimes but not just exactly like they want it." Donny sat forward and said, "It's like a prison there, you know? You've got to go to every class, you can never step off the school grounds."

"You cut classes sometimes?"

"Sometimes," Donny said, with a glance at his parents.

Cal didn't seem perturbed. "Well," he said, "I'll tell you what. Let's you and me try working together three nights a week. Think you can handle that? We'll see if we can show that school of yours a thing or two. Give it a month; then if you don't like it, we'll stop. If *I* don't like it, we'll stop. I mean, sometimes people just don't get along, right? What do you say to that?"

"Okay," Donny said. He seemed pleased.   25

"Make it seven o'clock till eight, Monday, Wednesday, and Friday," Cal told Matt and Daisy. They nodded. Cal shambled to his feet, gave them a little salute, and showed them to the door.

This was where he lived as well as worked, evidently. The interview had taken place in the dining room, which had been transformed into a kind of office. Passing the living room, Daisy winced at the rock music she had been hearing, without registering it, ever since she had entered the house. She looked in and saw a boy about Donny's age lying on a sofa with a book. Another boy and a girl were playing Ping-Pong in front of the fireplace. "You have several here together?" Daisy asked Cal.

"Oh, sometimes they stay on after their sessions, just to rap. They're a pretty sociable group, all in all. Plenty of goof-offs like young Donny here."

30   He cuffed Donny's shoulder playfully. Donny flushed and grinned.

Climbing into the car, Daisy asked Donny, "Well? What do you think?"

But Donny had returned to his old evasive self. He jerked his chin toward the garage. "Look," he said. "He's got a basketball net."

Now on Mondays, Wednesdays, and Fridays, they had supper early — the instant Matt came home. Sometimes, they had to leave before they were really finished. Amanda would still be eating her dessert. "Bye, honey. Sorry," Daisy would tell her.

Cal's first bill sent a flutter of panic through Daisy's chest, but it was worth it, of course. Just look at Donny's face when they picked him up: alight and full of interest. The principal telephoned Daisy to tell her how Donny had improved. "Of course, it hasn't shown up in his grades yet, but several of the teachers have noticed how his attitude's changed. Yes, sir, I think we're onto something here."

At home, Donny didn't act much different. He still seemed to have a low opinion of his parents. But Daisy supposed that was unavoidable — part of being fifteen. He said his parents were too "controlling"— a word that made Daisy give him a sudden look. He said they acted like wardens. On weekends, they enforced a curfew. And any time he went to a party, they always telephoned first to see if adults would be supervising. "For God's sake!" he said. "Don't you trust me?"

35   "It isn't a matter of trust, honey . . ." But there was no explaining to him.

His tutor called one afternoon. "I get the sense," he said, "that this kid's feeling . . . underestimated, you know? Like you folks expect the worst of him. I'm thinking we ought to give him more rope."

"But see, he's still so suggestible," Daisy said. "When his friends suggest some mischief — smoking or drinking or such — why, he just finds it hard not to go along with them."

"Mrs. Coble," the tutor said, "I think this kid is hurting. You know? Here's a serious, sensitive kid, telling you he'd like to take on some grown-up challenges, and you're giving him the message that he can't be trusted. Don't you understand how that hurts?"

"Oh," said Daisy.

40   "It undermines his self-esteem — don't you realize that?"

"Well, I guess you're right," said Daisy. She saw Donny suddenly from a whole new angle: his pathetically poor posture, that slouch so forlorn that his shoulders seemed about to meet his chin . . . oh, wasn't it awful being young? She'd had a miserable adolescence herself and had always sworn no child of hers would ever be that unhappy.

They let Donny stay out later, they didn't call ahead to see if the parties were supervised, and they were careful not to grill him about his evening. The tutor had set down so many rules! They were not allowed any questions at all about any aspect of school, nor were they to speak with his teachers. If a teacher had some complaint, she should phone Cal. Only one teacher disobeyed — the history teacher, Miss Evans. She called one morning in February. "I'm a little concerned about Donny, Mrs. Coble."

"Oh, I'm sorry, Miss Evans, but Donny's tutor handles these things now . . ."

"I always deal directly with the parents. You are the parent," Miss Evans said, speaking very slowly and distinctly. "Now, here is the problem. Back when you were helping Donny with his homework, his grades rose from a D to a C, but now they've slipped back, and they're closer to an F."

"They are?"   45

"I think you should start overseeing his homework again."

"But Donny's tutor says . . ."

"It's nice that Donny has a tutor, but you should still be in charge of his home-work. With you, he learned it. Then he passed his tests. With the tutor, well, it seems the tutor is more of a crutch. 'Donny,' I say, 'a quiz is coming up on Friday. Hadn't you better be listening instead of talking?' 'That's okay, Miss Evans,' he says. 'I have a tutor now.' Like a talisman! I really think you ought to take over, Mrs. Coble."

"I see," said Daisy. "Well, I'll think about that. Thank you for calling."

Hanging up, she felt a rush of anger at Donny. A talisman! For a talisman,   50 she'd given up all luxuries, all that time with her daughter, her evenings at home!

She dialed Cal's number. He sounded muzzy. "I'm sorry if I woke you," she told him, "but Donny's history teacher just called. She says he isn't doing well."

"She should have dealt with me."

"She wants me to start supervising his homework again. His grades are slipping."

"Yes," said the tutor, "but you and I both know there's more to it than mere grades, don't we? I care about the *whole* child — his happiness, his self-esteem. The grades will come. Just give them time."

When she hung up, it was Miss Evans she was angry at. What a narrow woman!   55

It was Cal this, Cal that, Cal says this, Cal and I did that. Cal lent Donny an album by The Who. He took Donny and two other pupils to a rock concert. In March, when Donny began to talk endlessly on the phone with a girl named Miriam, Cal even let Miriam come to one of the tutoring sessions. Daisy was touched that Cal would grow so involved in Donny's life, but she was also a little hurt, because she had offered to have Miriam to dinner and Donny had refused. Now he asked them to drive her to Cal's house without a qualm.

This Miriam was an unappealing girl with blurry lipstick and masses of rough red hair. She wore a short, bulky jacket that would not have been out of place on a motorcycle. During the trip to Cal's she was silent, but coming back, she was more talkative. "What a neat guy, and what a house! All those kids hanging out, like a club. And the stereo playing rock . . . gosh, he's not like a grown-up at all! Married and divorced and everything, but you'd think he was our own age."

"Mr. Beadle was married?" Daisy asked.

"Yeah, to this really controlling lady. She didn't understand him a bit."

"No, I guess not," Daisy said.

60   Spring came, and the students who hung around at Cal's drifted out to the basketball net above the garage. Sometimes, when Daisy and Matt arrived to pick up Donny, they'd find him there with the others — spiky and excited, jittering on his toes beneath the backboard. It was staying light much longer now, and the neighboring fence cast narrow bars across the bright grass. Loud music would be spilling from Cal's windows. Once it was The Who, which Daisy recognized from the time that Donny had borrowed the album. "*Teenage Wasteland*,"° she said aloud, identifying the song, and Matt gave a short, dry laugh. "It certainly is," he said. He'd misunderstood; he thought she was commenting on the scene spread before them. In fact, she might have been. The players looked like hoodlums, even her son. Why, one of Cal's students had recently been knifed in a tavern. One had been shipped off to boarding school in midterm; two had been withdrawn by their parents. On the other hand, Donny had mentioned someone who'd been studying with Cal for five years. "Five years!" said Daisy. "Doesn't anyone ever stop needing him?"

Donny looked at her. Lately, whatever she said about Cal was read as criticism. "You're just feeling competitive," he said. "And controlling."

She bit her lip and said no more.

In April, the principal called to tell her that Donny had been expelled. There had been a locker check, and in Donny's locker they found five cans of beer and half a pack of cigarettes. With Donny's previous record, his offense meant expulsion.

65   Daisy gripped the receiver tightly and said, "Well, where is he now?"

"We've sent him home," said Mr. Lanham. "He's packed up all his belongings, and he's coming home on foot."

Daisy wondered what she would say to him. She felt him looming closer and closer, bringing this brand-new situation that no one had prepared her to handle. What other place would take him? Could they enter him in public school? What were the rules? She stood at the living room window, waiting for him to show up. Gradually, she realized that he was taking too long. She checked the clock. She stared up the street again.

When an hour had passed, she phoned the school. Mr. Lanham's secretary answered and told her in a grave, sympathetic voice that yes, Donny Coble had most definitely gone home. Daisy called her husband. He was out of the office. She went back to the window and thought awhile, and then she called Donny's tutor.

"Donny's been expelled from school," she said, "and now I don't know where he's gone. I wonder if you've heard from him?"

70   There was a long silence. "Donny's with me, Mrs. Coble," he finally said.

"With you? How'd he get there?"

"He hailed a cab, and I paid the driver."

"Could I speak to him, please?"

There was another silence. "Maybe it'd be better if we had a conference," Cal said.

Teenage Wasteland: The song is actually "Baba O'Riley," from the band's *Who's Next* album.

"I don't *want* a conference. I've been standing at the window picturing him 75
dead or kidnapped or something, and now you tell me you want a —"

"Donny is very, very upset. Understandably so," said Cal. "Believe me, Mrs.
Coble, this is not what it seems. Have you asked Donny's side of the story?"

"Well, of course not, how could I? He went running off to you instead."

"Because he didn't feel he'd be listened to."

"But I haven't even —"

"Why don't you come out and talk? The three of us," said Cal, "will try to get 80
this thing in perspective."

"Well, all right," Daisy said. But she wasn't as reluctant as she sounded.
Already, she felt soothed by the calm way Cal was taking this.

Cal answered the doorbell at once. He said, "Hi, there," and led her into the
dining room. Donny sat slumped in a chair, chewing the knuckle of one thumb.
"Hello, Donny," Daisy said. He flicked his eyes in her direction.

"Sit here, Mrs. Coble," said Cal, placing her opposite Donny. He himself
remained standing, restlessly pacing. "So," he said.

Daisy stole a look at Donny. His lips were swollen, as if he'd been crying.

"You know," Cal told Daisy, "I kind of expected something like this. That's a 85
very punitive school you've got him in — you realize that. And any half-decent
lawyer will tell you they've violated his civil rights. Locker checks! Where's their
search warrant?"

"But if the rule is —" Daisy said.

"Well, anyhow, let him tell you his side."

She looked at Donny. He said, "It wasn't my fault. I promise."

"They said your locker was full of beer."

"It was a put-up job! See, there's this guy that doesn't like me. He put all these 90
beers in my locker and started a rumor going, so Mr. Lanham ordered a locker
check."

"What was the boy's name?" Daisy asked.

"Huh?"

"Mrs. Coble, take my word, the situation is not so unusual," Cal said. "You
can't imagine how vindictive kids can be sometimes."

"What was the boy's *name*," said Daisy, "so that I can ask Mr. Lanham if that's
who suggested he run a locker check."

"You don't believe me," Donny said. 95

"And how'd this boy get your combination in the first place?"

"Frankly," said Cal, "I wouldn't be surprised to learn the school was in on it.
Any kid that marches to a different drummer, why, they'd just love an excuse to
get rid of him. The school is where I lay the blame."

"Doesn't *Donny* ever get blamed?"

"Now, Mrs. Coble, you heard what he —"

"Forget it," Donny told Cal. "You can see she doesn't trust me." 100

Daisy drew in a breath to say that of course she trusted him — a reflex. But she
knew that bold-faced, wide-eyed look of Donny's. He had worn that look when
he was small, denying some petty misdeed with the evidence plain as day all
around him. Still, it was hard for her to accuse him outright. She temporized and

said, "The only thing I'm sure of is that they've kicked you out of school, and now I don't know what we're going to do."

"We'll fight it," said Cal.

"We can't. Even you must see we can't."

"I could apply to Brantly," Donny said.

105   Cal stopped his pacing to beam down at him. "Brantly! Yes. They're really onto where a kid is coming from, at Brantly. Why, I could get you into Brantly. I work with a lot of their students."

Daisy had never heard of Brantly, but already she didn't like it. And she didn't like Cal's smile, which struck her now as feverish and avid — a smile of hunger.

On the fifteenth of April, they entered Donny in a public school, and they stopped his tutoring sessions. Donny fought both decisions bitterly. Cal, surprisingly enough, did not object. He admitted he'd made no headway with Donny and said it was because Donny was emotionally disturbed.

Donny went to his new school every morning, plodding off alone with his head down. He did his assignments, and he earned average grades, but he gathered no friends, joined no clubs. There was something exhausted and defeated about him.

The first week in June, during final exams, Donny vanished. He simply didn't come home one afternoon, and no one at school remembered seeing him. The police were reassuring, and for the first few days, they worked hard. They combed Donny's sad, messy room for clues; they visited Miriam and Cal. But then they started talking about the number of kids who ran away every year. Hundreds, just in this city. "He'll show up, if he wants to," they said. "If he doesn't, he won't."

110   Evidently, Donny didn't want to.

It's been three months now and still no word. Matt and Daisy still look for him in every crowd of awkward, heartbreaking teenage boys. Every time the phone rings, they imagine it might be Donny. Both parents have aged. Donny's sister seems to be staying away from home as much as possible.

At night, Daisy lies awake and goes over Donny's life. She is trying to figure out what went wrong, where they made their first mistake. Often, she finds herself blaming Cal, although she knows he didn't begin it. Then at other times she excuses him, for without him, Donny might have left earlier. Who really knows? In the end, she can only sigh and search for a cooler spot on the pillow. As she falls asleep, she occasionally glimpses something in the corner of her vision. It's something fleet and round, a ball — a basketball. It flies up, it sinks through the hoop, descends, lands in a yard littered with last year's leaves and striped with bars of sunlight as white as bones, bleached and parched and cleanly picked.

◆ ◆ ◆

3| POETRY

CHAPTER 22

UNDERSTANDING POETRY

MARIANNE MOORE (1887–1972)

Poetry (1921)

I, too, dislike it: there are things that are important beyond all
    this fiddle.
  Reading it, however, with a perfect contempt for it, one discovers
  in it after all, a place for the genuine.
     Hands that can grasp, eyes
     that can dilate, hair that can rise   5
        if it must, these things are important not because a

high-sounding interpretation can be put upon them but because they are
  useful. When they become so derivative as to become unintelligible,
  the same thing may be said for all of us, that we
     do not admire what   10
     we cannot understand: the bat
        holding on upside down or in quest of something to

eat, elephants pushing, a wild horse taking a roll, a tireless wolf under
  a tree, the immovable critic twitching his skin like a horse that feels
  a flea, the base-
ball fan, the statistician —   15
     nor is it valid
        to discriminate against "business documents and

school-books";° all these phenomena are important. One must make
  a distinction
  however: when dragged into prominence by half poets, the result
  is not poetry,
nor till the poets among us can be   20
   "literalists of

° *"business documents and school-books":* Moore quotes the *Diaries of Tolstoy* (New York, 1917): "Where the
boundary between prose and poetry lies, I shall never be able to understand. . . . Poetry is verse; prose is not
verse. Or else poetry is everything with the exception of business documents and school books."

the imagination"°— above
insolence and triviality and can present

for inspection, "imaginary gardens with real toads in them,"
shall we have
it. In the meantime, if you demand on the one hand,   25
the raw material of poetry in
all its rawness and
that which is on the other hand
genuine, you are interested in poetry.

NIKKI GIOVANNI (1943–   )

Poetry (1975)

poetry is motion graceful
as a fawn
gentle as a teardrop
strong like the eye
finding peace in a crowded room   5
we poets tend to think
our words are golden
though emotion speaks too
loudly to be defined
by silence   10

sometimes after midnight or just before
the dawn
we sit typewriter in hand
pulling loneliness around us
forgetting our lovers or children   15
who are sleeping
ignoring the weary wariness
of our own logic
to compose a poem

no one understands it   20
it never says "love me" for poets are
beyond love
it never says "accept me" for poems seek not
acceptance but controversy
it only says "i am" and therefore   25

° *"literalists of the imagination"*: A reference (given by Moore) to W. B. Yeats's "William Blake and His Illustrations" (in *Ideas of Good and Evil, 1903*): "The limitation of his view was from the very intensity of his vision; he
was a too literal realist of the imagination as others are of nature; and because he believed that the figures
seen by the mind's eye, when exalted by inspiration, were 'external existences,' symbols of divine essences, he
hated every grace of style that might obscure their lineaments."

i concede that you are too
a poem is pure energy
horizontally contained
between the mind
of the poet and the ear of the reader　　30
if it does not sing discard the ear
for poetry is song
if it does not delight discard
the heart for poetry is joy
if it does not inform then close　　35
off the brain for it is dead
if it cannot heed the insistent message
that life is precious

which is all we poets
wrapped in our loneliness　　40
are trying to say

Origins of Modern Poetry

The history of poetry begins where the history of all literature begins — with the **oral tradition**. In a time before literacy and the printing press, the oral tradition was relied upon as a way of preserving stories, histories, values, and beliefs. These stories were usually put into the form of rhyming poems, with repeated words and sounds used to make the poems easier to memorize and remember.

These extended narratives were eventually transcribed as **epics** — long poems depicting the actions of heroic figures who determine the fate of a nation or entire race. Early epics include Homer's *Iliad* and *Odyssey*, the *Epic of Gilgamesh*, the *Bhagavad Gita*, and Virgil's *Aeneid*. Early poetry can also be found in various religious texts, including ancient Hindu holy books like the Upanishads; sections of the Bible, including the Song of Solomon; and the Koran.

During the **Anglo-Saxon era** (late sixth to mid-eleventh centuries), poetry flourished as a literary form. Unfortunately, only about 30,000 lines of poetry survive from this period. Those poems that did survive are marked by heroic deeds and the absence of romantic love. The major texts of this time include *Beowulf*, *The Battle of Maldon*, and *The Dream of the Rood*, which is one of the earliest Christian poems. The theme of Christian morality in poetry continued into the Middle Ages with poems such as William Langland's *Piers Plowman*, which consisted of three religious dream visions, and Chaucer's *Canterbury Tales*, a collection of narrative poems told by pilgrims as they travel to Canterbury, England. Using a slightly different approach to similar subject matter, Dante Alighieri wrote the Italian epic poem *The Divine Comedy*, which depicts an imaginary journey through hell, purgatory, and heaven. In France, the **troubadours**, poets of the Provençal region, wrote complex lyric poems about courtly love.

The next major literary period, the **Renaissance** (late fourteenth to mid-sixteenth centuries), witnessed a rebirth of science, philosophy, and the classical arts. Perhaps the most important writer of this period was William Shakespeare.

Image depicting the pilgrims from Geoffrey Chaucer's
The Canterbury Tales

Illuminated manuscript (fifteenth century)
from Dante's *Divine Comedy* depicting Dante
and Virgil in Hell

A prolific poet, Shakespeare also wrote plays in verse, continuing in the tradition of the ancient Greek tragedian Sophocles and the ancient Roman playwright Seneca. Other notable writers of the Renaissance included Sir Philip Sidney, Christopher Marlowe, and Edmund Spenser.

During the seventeenth century, several literary movements emerged that contributed to poetry's growing prevalence and influence. John Milton continued the tradition of Christian poetry with his epic *Paradise Lost*, which told the tale of Adam and Eve's exile from the Garden of Eden. The **metaphysical poets** (John Donne, Andrew Marvell, and George Herbert) used elaborate figures of speech and favored intellect over emotions in their writing. Their poems were characterized by reason, complex comparisons and allusions, and paradoxes, and they introduced the **meditative poem** (a poem that abstractly ponders a concept or idea) into the literary world.

In the early eighteenth century, British poets (such as Alexander Pope and Samuel Johnson) wrote poems, biographies, and literary criticism, subsequently expanding the scope and influence of poetry. It was also during this time that the movement known as **Romanticism** began. Romantic poetry was marked by heightened emotion and sentiment; a strong sense of individualism; a respect for nature, history, and mysticism; and a return to first-person lyric poems. The early British Romantics included Samuel Taylor Coleridge, William Wordsworth, and William Blake. This generation was followed by the later Romantics, including Percy Bysshe Shelley, John Keats, and George Gordon, Lord Byron. American Romantics included Henry David Thoreau, Ralph Waldo Emerson, and Walt Whitman.

Illuminated manuscript from William Blake's "The Tyger"

John Martin's painting *The Bard* (1817) illustrating the mystical view of nature characteristic of Romanticism

The nineteenth century was marked by yet another shift in poetic consciousness. This time, poets moved away from the contemplation of the self within nature and returned to a more elevated sense of rhetoric and subject matter as well as to a more formal structure. Notable British authors included Alfred, Lord Tennyson; Matthew Arnold; Robert Browning; and Elizabeth Barrett Browning. American poets of the this period included Edgar Allan Poe, Henry Wadsworth Longfellow, Emily Dickinson, and Phillis Wheatley, a slave who became the first African-American poet.

The twentieth century had perhaps the largest number of literary movements to date, with each one reflecting its predecessors and influencing future generations of poets. In the early twentieth century, a literary movement that became known as **modernism** developed. As authors responded to the increasing complexity of a changing world, the overarching sentiment of modernism was that the "old ways" would no longer suffice in a world that had changed almost overnight as a result of the rise of industrialization and urbanization, as well as the devastation of World War I. Key modernist writers included W. H. Auden, William Butler Yeats, Ezra Pound, and T. S. Eliot, whose epic poem *The Waste Land* expressed the fragmentation of consciousness in the modern world. A precursor to modernism was French symbolism, which was a revolt against the realistic and naturalistic poetic styles of the day. The goal of symbolist poetry was to create a series of symbols that captured the essence of

Undated engraving of Edgar Allan Poe's "The Raven"

an idea. Its practitioners included Stéphane Mallarmé, Charles Baudelaire, and Arthur Rimbaud.

After World War I, poets began to challenge the prevailing ideas of subject matter and form. Ezra Pound, along with Amy Lowell and other poets, founded **imagism,** a poetic movement that emphasized free verse and the writer's response to a visual scene or an object. William Carlos Williams wrote poems that were often deceptively simple, while the poetry of Wallace Stevens was often opaque and difficult to grasp. Dylan Thomas and E. E. Cummings also experimented with form, with Cummings specifically manipulating the accepted constructs of grammar, syntax, and punctuation.

In the 1920s, the United States experienced the **Harlem Renaissance**. This rebirth of arts and culture was centered in Harlem, an area in New York City where, by the mid-1920s, the African-American population had reached 150,000. Harlem was an area teeming with creativity, especially in music (jazz and blues), literature, art, and drama. The poets who were part of the Harlem Renaissance — including Langston Hughes, Countee Cullen, James Weldon Johnson, and Jean Toomer — chose diverse subject matter and styles, but they were united in their celebration of African-American culture and experience.

In the early 1930s, a group of poets gathered at a college in Black Mountain, North Carolina, with the aim of teaching and writing about poetry in a new way. The **Black Mountain Poets,** as they were called, stressed the process of writing poetry rather than the finished poem. Notable poets in this group included Robert Creeley, Denise Levertov, and Charles Olson. Meanwhile, in Latin America, poetry grew in importance, with poets such as Pablo Neruda experimenting with subject matter, language, form, and imagery.

In the late 1940s, in the aftermath of World War II, a group of disillusioned American poets turned to eastern mysticism and newly available hallucinogenic drugs to achieve higher consciousness. They became known as the **Beat poets,** and their work was known for social and political criticism that challenged the established norms of the time. These poets included Allen Ginsberg, whose long poem *Howl* became an unofficial anthem of the revolutionary 1960s, and Lawrence Ferlinghetti.

Up until the late 1950s, subject matter in American poetry was largely impersonal, concentrating chiefly on symbols, ideas, and politics. This changed when a group of poets — including Robert Lowell, Anne Sexton, W. D. Snodgrass, and Sylvia Plath — began to write **confessional poems** about their own personal experiences, emotions, triumphs, and tragedies — including mental illness and attempted suicide. Although there was considerable backlash against these poets from writers who thought that such highly personal subjects were not suitable for poetry, contemporary poets such as Sharon Olds continue to write confessional poetry.

The early 1960s witnessed the rise of the **Black Arts Movement,** which had its roots in the ideas of the civil rights struggle, Malcolm X and the Nation of Islam, and the Black Power Movement. The Black Arts poets wrote political work that addressed the sociopolitical and cultural context of African-Americans. Notable authors in this group included Amiri Baraka, Gwendolyn Brooks, Jayne Cortez, and Etheridge Knight.

Staceyann Chin, acclaimed slam poet and the star of
Def Poetry Jam on Broadway

The next major literary movement that occurred in poetry had its beginnings in the mid to late 1980s with slam poetry. **Slam poetry**, with origins in the oral tradition, was influenced by the Beat poets, who stressed the live performance of poems. In a **slam**, poets compete either individually or in teams before an audience, which serves as the judge. (The structure of a traditional poetry slam was created by Marc Smith, a poet and construction worker, in 1986.) Slam poetry is concerned with current events and social and political themes, and often the winning poet is the one who best combines enthusiasm, presentation, and attitude with contemporary subject matter. A home base for slam poetry is the Nyuorican Poets Café in New York City, which has become a forum for poetry, music, video, and theater. Notable slam poets past and present include Miguel Piñero, Maggie Estep, Jeffrey McDaniel, and Bob Holman.

BOB HOLMAN (1948–)

6 Short Poems

Modern Lovers
In order to save the relationship
We will never see each other again

Night Fears
Everyone is in love
Except you

Ten Things I Do Every Day
Suicide

My Shirt

I like to put it on
My arms get long that way

Love Poems

I love poems

Goo Ahead

Goo ahead

A spinoff of slam poetry is the **spoken word** movement, which, unlike slam poetry, is a rehearsed performance. Spoken word performances have captivated a broad audience due in part to television shows such as HBO's *Def Poetry Jam*. **Hip-hop** and **rap**, musical forms whose lyrics rely heavily on rhyme, alliteration, assonance, consonance, and other poetic devices, also owe a debt to slam poetry and the spoken word movement.

Contemporary poetry is an extremely diverse genre whose practitioners have been influenced by many of the literary movements discussed above. Some contemporary poets embrace narrative poetry; others favor the lyric. Some write free verse; others experiment with traditional forms like the sonnet or the villanelle. Still others write **concrete poetry**, which uses words as well as varying type sizes and type fonts to form pictures on a page, or other forms of **visual poetry** (see Chapter 23). The types of poetry being written today vary greatly, and this diversity is part of the appeal for those who read and write it.

Defining Poetry

Throughout history and across national and cultural boundaries, poetry has held an important place. In ancient China and Japan, for example, poetry was prized above all else. One story tells of a samurai warrior who, when defeated, asked for a pen and paper. Thinking that he wanted to write a will before being executed, his captor granted his wish. Instead of writing a will, however, the warrior wrote a farewell poem that so moved his captor that he immediately released him.

To the ancient Greeks and Romans, poetry was the medium of spiritual and philosophical expression. Today, throughout the world, poetry continues to delight and to inspire. For many people in countless places, poetry is the language of the emotions, the medium of expression they use when they speak from the heart.

But what exactly *is* poetry? Is a poem "pure energy / horizontally contained / between the mind / of the poet and the readers," as Nikki Giovanni (page 810) describes it? Or is a poem simply what Marianne Moore (page 809) calls "all this fiddle"?

One way of defining poetry is to examine how it is different from other forms of literature, such as fiction or drama. The first and most important element of poetry that distinguishes it from other genres is its **form**. Unlike prose, which is written from margin to margin, poetry is made up of individual **lines**. A poetic line begins and ends where the poet chooses: it can start at the left margin or halfway across the page, and it can end at the right margin or after only a word or two. A poet chooses when to stop, or break, the line according to his or her sense of rhythm and cadence.

Poets also use the **sound** of the words themselves, alone and in conjunction with the other words of the poem, to create a sense of rhythm and melody. **Alliteration** (the repetition of consonant sounds in consecutive or neighboring words), **assonance** (the repetition of vowel sounds at the ends of words), and **consonance** (the repetition of consonant sounds at the ends of words) are three devices commonly used by poets to help create the music of a poem. Poets can also use **rhyme** (either at the ends of lines or within the lines themselves), which contributes to the pattern of sounds in a poem.

In addition, poets are more likely than writers of other kinds of literature to rely on **imagery**, words or phrases that describe the senses. These vivid descriptions or details help the reader to connect with the poet's ideas in a tangible way. Poets also make extensive use of **figurative language**, including metaphors and similes, to convey their ideas and to help their readers access these ideas.

Another way of defining poetry is to examine our assumptions about it. Different readers, different poets, different generations of readers and poets, and different cultures may have different expectations about poetry. As a result, they have varying assumptions about what poetry should be, and these assumptions raise questions. Must poetry be written to delight or inspire, or can a poem have a political or social message? Must a poem's theme be conveyed subtly, embellished with imaginatively chosen sounds and words, or can it be explicit and straightforward? Such questions, which have been debated by literary critics as well as by poets for many years, have no easy answers — and perhaps no answers at all. A **haiku** — a short poem, rich in imagery, adhering to a rigid formal structure — is certainly poetry, and so is a political poem like Wole Soyinka's "Telephone Conversation" (p. 8). To some Western readers, however, a haiku might seem too plain or understated to be "poetic," and Soyinka's poem might seem to be a political tract masquerading as poetry. Still, most of these readers would agree that the following lines qualify as poetry.

WILLIAM SHAKESPEARE (1564–1616)

That time of year thou mayst in me behold (1609)

That time of year thou mayst in me behold
When yellow leaves, or none, or few, do hang
Upon those boughs which shake against the cold,
Bare ruined choirs, where late the sweet birds sang.
In me thou see'st the twilight of such day   5
As after sunset fadeth in the west,
Which by and by black night doth take away,
Death's second self that seals up all in rest.
In me thou see'st the glowing of such fire,
That on the ashes of his youth doth lie,   10

As the deathbed whereon it must expire,
Consumed with that which it was nourished by
This thou perceiv'st, which makes thy love more strong,
To love that well which thou must leave ere long.

This poem includes many of the characteristics that Western readers commonly associate with poetry. For instance, its lines have a regular pattern of rhyme and meter that identifies it as a **sonnet**. The poem also develops a complex network of related images and figures of speech that compare the lost youth of the aging speaker to the sunset and to autumn. Finally, the pair of rhyming lines at the end of the poem expresses a familiar poetic theme: the lovers' realization that they must eventually die makes their love stronger.

The next poem is quite different from the preceding one, yet most readers would probably agree that it too is a poem.

LOUIS ZUKOFSKY   (1904–1978)

I walk in the old street   (1944)

I walk in the old street
to hear the beloved songs
afresh
this spring night.
Like the leaves — my loves wake —   5
not to be the same
or look tireless to the stars
and a ripped doorbell.

Unlike Shakespeare's sonnet, Zukofsky's poem does not have a regular metrical pattern or rhyme scheme. Its diction is more conversational than poetic, and one of its images — a "ripped doorbell"— presents a jarring contrast to the other, more conventionally "poetic" images. Nevertheless, the subject — love — is a traditional one; in fact, Zukofsky's poem echoes some of the sentiments of the Shakespeare sonnet. Finally, the poem's division into two four-line stanzas and its use of figures of speech ("Like the leaves — my loves wake —") are unmistakably poetic.

Although most readers would probably classify the two preceding works as poems, they might be less certain about the following lines.

E. E. CUMMINGS   (1894–1962)

l(a   (1923)

l(a
le
af

fa
ll   5
s)
one
l
iness

Unlike Shakespeare's and Zukofsky's poems, "l(a" does not seem to have any of the characteristics normally associated with poetry. It has no meter, rhyme, or imagery. It has no repeated sounds, no figures of speech. It cannot even be read aloud because its "lines" are fragments of words. In spite of its odd appearance, however, "l(a" does communicate a conventional poetic theme. When reconstructed, the words Cummings broke apart have the following appearance: "l (a leaf falls) one l iness." In a sense, this poem is a complex visual and verbal pun. If the parenthetical insertion "(a leaf falls)" is removed, the remaining letters spell "loneliness." Moreover, the form of the letter *l* in loneliness suggest the number *1*—which, in turn, suggests the loneliness and isolation of the individual, as reflected in nature (the single leaf). Like Shakespeare and Zukofsky, Cummings uses an image of a leaf to express his ideas about life and about human experience. At the same time, by breaking words into bits and pieces, Cummings suggests the flexibility of language and conveys the need to break out of customary ways of using words to define experience.

As the preceding discussion illustrates, defining what a poem is (and what it is not) can be difficult. Poems can rhyme or not rhyme. They can be divided into stanzas and have a distinct form, or they can flow freely and have no discernable form. These and other choices are what many poets find alluring about the process of writing poetry. As a form, poetry is compact and concise, and choosing the right words to convey ideas is a challenge. As a literary genre, it offers room for experimentation while at the same time remaining firmly grounded in a literary tradition that stretches back through time to antiquity.

Recognizing Kinds of Poetry

Most poems are either **narrative** poems, which recount a story, or **lyric** poems, which communicate a speaker's mood, feelings, or state of mind.

Narrative Poetry

Although any brief poem that tells a story, such as Edwin Arlington Robinson's "Richard Cory" (p. 1218), may be considered a narrative poem, the two most familiar forms of narrative poetry are the *epic* and the *ballad*.

Epics are narrative poems that recount the accomplishments of heroic figures, typically including expansive settings, superhuman feats, and gods and supernatural beings. The language of epic poems tends to be formal, even elevated, and often quite elaborate. In ancient times, epics were handed down orally; more recently, poets have written literary epics, such as John Milton's *Paradise Lost* (1667) and Nobel Prize–winning poet Derek Walcott's *Omeros* (1990), that follow many of the same conventions.

The **ballad** is another type of narrative poetry with roots in an oral tradition. Originally intended to be sung, a ballad uses repeated words and phrases, including a refrain, to advance its story. Some — but not all — ballads use the **ballad stanza**. For examples of traditional ballads in this book, see "Bonny Barbara Allan" (p. 1139) and "Western Wind" (p. 1141). Dudley Randall's "Ballad of Birmingham" (p. 886) is an example of a contemporary ballad.

Lyric Poetry

Like narrative poems, lyric poems take various forms.

An **elegy** is a poem in which a poet mourns the death of a specific person, as in Etheridge Knight's "For Malcolm, a Year After" (p. 978), about the activist Malcolm X. Another example of this type of poem is A. E. Housman's "To an Athlete Dying Young" (p. 916).

An **ode** is a long lyric poem, formal and serious in style, tone, and subject matter. An ode typically has a fairly complex stanzaic pattern, such as the **terza rima** used by Percy Bysshe Shelley in "Ode to the West Wind" (p. 1222). Another ode in this text is John Keats's "Ode on a Grecian Urn" (p. 1193).

An **aubade** is a poem about morning, usually celebrating the coming of dawn. An example is Philip Larkin's "Aubade" (p. 1198).

An **occasional poem** is written to celebrate a particular event or occasion. An example is Billy Collins's poem "The Names" (p. 1156), read before a joint session of Congress to commomorate the first anniversary of the terrorist attacks on the World Trade Center.

A **meditation** is a lyric poem that focuses on a physical object, using this object as a vehicle for considering larger issues. Edmund Waller's seventeenth-century poem "Go, lovely rose" is a meditation.

A **pastoral** — for example, Christopher Marlowe's "The Passionate Shepherd to His Love" (p. 1202) — is a lyric poem that celebrates the simple, idyllic pleasures of country life.

A **dramatic monologue** is a poem whose speaker addresses one or more silent listeners, often revealing much more than he or she intends. Robert Browning's "My Last Duchess" (p. 856) and "Porphyria's Lover" (p. 876) and Alfred Lord Tennyson's "Ulysses" (p. 1232) are dramatic monologues.

As you read the poems in this text, you will encounter works with a wide variety of forms, styles, and themes. Some you will find appealing, amusing, uplifting, or moving; others may strike you as puzzling, intimidating, or depressing. But regardless of your critical reaction to the poems, one thing is certain: if you take the time to pay attention to the lines you are reading, and to think about them later on, you will come away from them thinking not just about the images and ideas they express but also about yourself and your world.

NOTE: As you will see in the following chapter, poets can also create **visual poetry**, experimenting with the way a poem looks on the page.

CHAPTER 23

POETRY SAMPLER: VISUAL POETRY

Generally speaking, **visual poetry** occupies the area between literature and the visual arts, between words and pictures. Some of its practitioners see visual poetry as a literary form in which the appearance of a poem is as important as its content. Others see it as a visual form that comes from a literary background. Still others see it as an art form that uses visual content in new and interesting ways. As difficult as it is to define, visual poetry is growing in popularity and, in some cases, is challenging preconceptions about poetry itself.

Apollinaire's poem "Coeur couronne et miroir." ("Heart, wreath and mirror.") From *Calligrammes* (1912–1918). The words surrounding the poet's name read, "In this mirror I am enclosed living and true as one imagines angels to be and not as reflections are."

The early precursors of visual poetry were ancient Greek **pattern poems** and **acrostics**, sixteenth- and seventeenth-century **emblem poems**, and literary texts such as the poems in Guillaume Apollinaire's *Calligrammes*, one of which, "Couer couronne et miroir," is pictured on page 821, and Stéphane Mallarmé's poem "Un Coup de Des" ("A Throw of the Dice"). All of these poems had visual formats that mirrored, on some level, their content or subject matter.

Visual poetry has its philosophical roots in various literary and artistic movements, including Dadaism, surrealism, and futurism. **Dadaism** was a nihilistic movement that began in France and emphasized irrationality, cynicism, and anarchy. Dadaists rejected traditional concepts of beauty and social organization and embraced the absurd. **Surrealism** grew out of Dadaism but sought to tap the creative potential of the unconscious mind and to exploit the material of dreams and the states of mind between waking and sleeping. Surrealist writing emphasized broken syntax, free association, nonchronological order, and dreamlike sequences. **Futurism** rejected the past and celebrated change, originality, and innovation in culture and society. Just as visual poetry does, all three of these movements embraced structural and thematic changes that revealed a new sense of meaning and significance.

One kind of visual poetry, called **concrete poetry**, uses words—and, sometimes, different fonts and type sizes—to shape a picture on the page. The form of a concrete poem does not emerge from the poem's words and images; it is predetermined by the visual image the poet has decided to create. In this way, concrete poems explore ways in which the visual form and the arrangement of words on a page interact and affect the content and meaning of a text. Concrete poems are not necessarily read left to right, as traditional poems are; instead, they can be approached in numerous ways, with the meaning primarily derived from the forms of the poems themselves. Although some concrete poems, like the one below, are little more than novelties, others may be enlightening or even profound.

"Airplane Takes Off," concrete poem from NASA Web site.

Modern-day visual poets often have experience in the visual arts. Combining words and images collected from popular media such as newspapers and magazines, visual poets explore the relationship between mass media and visual art. By juxtaposing pictures and text, they create montages and collages that explore and sometimes challenge the boundaries between these genres. In fact, many visual poets now use computers to manipulate music tracks, animation, and color, creating highly original — and sometimes strikingly beautiful — works that combine text, sound, and video.

The poems that follow illustrate the varied forms of visual poetry. George Herbert's "Easter Wings," May Swenson's "Women," and Greg Williamson's "Group Photo with Winter Trees" use the tenchniques of concrete poetry to structure, to mimic, or to represent a tangible form. Charles Bernstein ("this poem intentionally left blank") uses unexpected blank space to create meaning, while Tupac Shakur ("1 for April") and Bob Grumman ("Mathemaku No. 10") juxtapose symbols with words. Finally, Ian Hamilton Finlay ("Acrobats") and Reed Altemus ("Flake upper phase") use computer technology to stretch the limits of visual poetry. Regardless of the differences in their approaches, each poet experiments with poetic form and visual presentation in an attempt to expand the limits of poetic expression.

GEORGE HERBERT (1593–1633)

Easter Wings (1633)

Lord, who createdst man in wealth and store,
Though foolishly he lost the same,
Decaying more and more
Till he became
Most poor,
5
With thee
Oh, let me rise
As larks, harmoniously,
And sing this day thy victories;
Then shall the fall further the flight in me.
10

My tender age in sorrow did begin;
And still with sicknesses and shame
Thou didst so punish sin,
That I became
Most thin.
15
With thee
Let me combine,
And feel this day thy victory;
For if I imp my wing on thine,
Affliction shall advance the flight in me.
20

MAY SWENSON (1919–1989)

Women (1970)

Women   Or they
  should be   should be
    pedestals   little horses
      moving   those wooden
        pedestals   sweet   5
        moving   oldfashioned
          to the   painted
            motions   rocking
            of men   horses

              the gladdest things in the toyroom   10

              The   feelingly
            pegs   and then
            of their   unfeelingly
              ears   To be
            so familiar   joyfully   15
            and dear   ridden
          to the trusting   rockingly
        fists   ridden until
      To be chafed   the restored

  egos dismount and the legs stride away   20

Immobile   willing
  sweetlipped   to be set
    sturdy   into motion
      and smiling   Women
        women   should be   25
          should always   pedestals
            be waiting   to men

GREG WILLIAMSON (1964–   )

Group Photo with Winter Trees (2002)

        These were my neighbors. It's a big group pose:
On mist-gray skies, the stark, black branches etch
        Horizon, lawn, in loose haphazard rows.
As if in tin, or as in some old sketch,
    That's The Great Bob. And that's our good Queen Paul   5
Whose lines, whose every nuance was precise,
    With Champagne Anne and Rick the dog. They're all
But faded now. I've seen the trees in ice,
    Decked out, (Liz, too, who helped me do the plumbing),
But I'll be gone when their spring blooms and scatters   10
    Even the children. And, God, they're all becoming.
Shades, as the new leaves turn to other matters.

CHARLES BERNSTEIN (1950–   )

this poem intentionally left blank

TUPAC SHAKUR (1971–1996)

1 for April

1 FOR April

2 me your name alone is poetry
I barely know u and already
I can't explain this feeling I feel
            4 APRIL

I want 2 c u from the moment
u leave my side til the moment u return
My nonchalant cold heart finally has eyes only
            4 April

So now I risk it all
Just 4 the feeling of joy u bring me
I accept the ridicule
in exchange for the words u share with me
All of this & much more I will do
            4 APRIL

BOB GRUMMAN (1941–   )

Mathemaku No. 10   (1994)

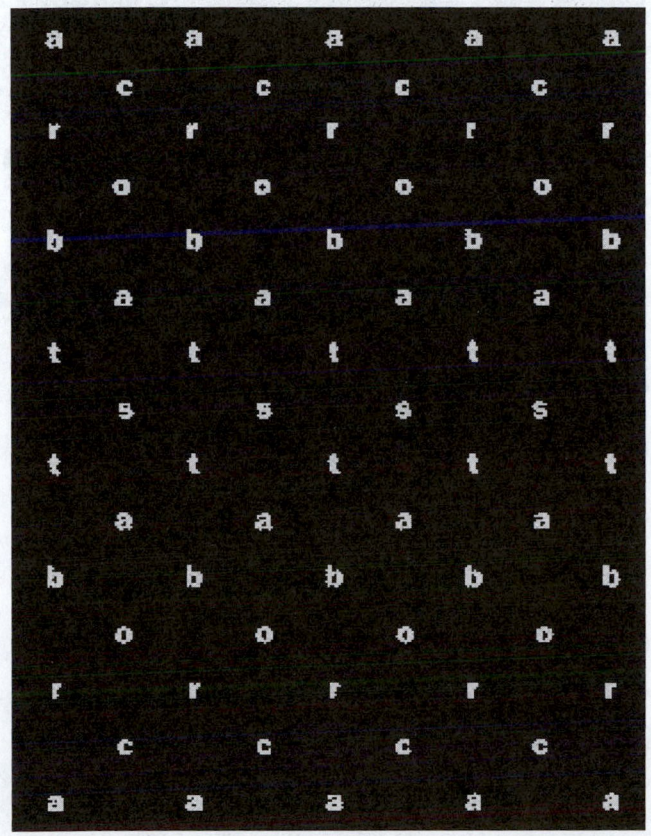

poetry)*existence*
          somewhere, minutely, a widening
          existence

IAN HAMILTON FINLAY (1925–   )

Acrobats* (1966)

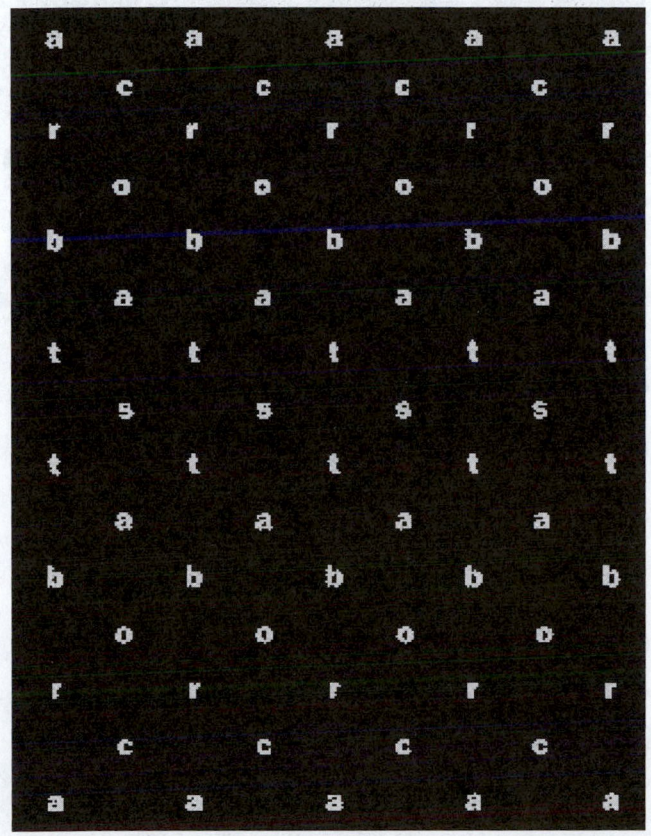

---

* When this poem is read online, the letters move.

REED ALTEMUS (1961–   ) and
JIM LEFTWICH

Flake upper phase   (2002)

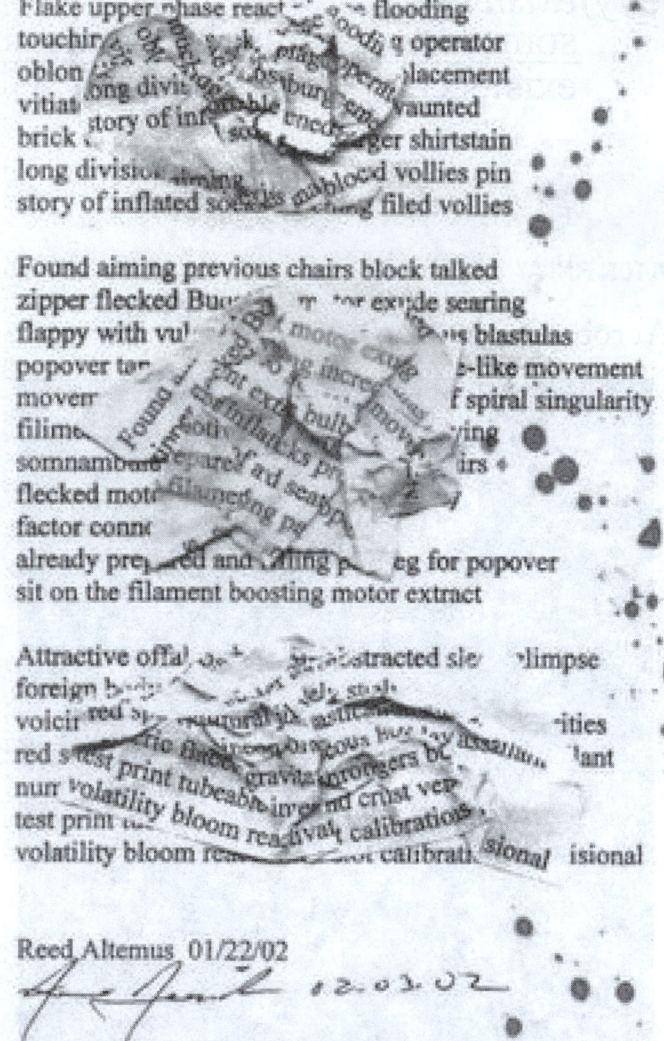

Flake upper phase react —   flooding
touchin   q operator
oblon   long divit   lacement
vitias   story of inf   vaunted
brick   er shirtstain
long division   ed vollies pin
story of inflated so   filed vollies

Found aiming previous chairs block talked
zipper flecked Bu   r   exude searing
flappy with vu   blastulas
popover t   -like movement
mover   f spiral singularity
filime
somnamb   irs
flecked mot
factor con
already pre   ed and   ng p   eg for popover
sit on the filament boosting motor extract

Attractive offal   stracted sle   limpse
foreign b
voici   ities
red s   ant
nun
test print
volatility bloom re   calibrat   isional

Reed Altemus 01/22/02

Reading and Reacting

1. Which poem in this chapter seems most conventional? Which one seems
   most experimental? Explain.
2. How would George Herbert's "Easter Wings" and May Swenson's "Women"
   be different if they were written in traditional form? What would be gained
   and what would be lost if the poems were written in this way?

3. Try reading these poems aloud. Are they all actually readable? If any one is not, do you still consider it a poem? Explain.

4. Look closely at the poems by Bob Grumman, Hamilton Finlay, and Reed Altemus. Do you think the visual elements of their poems are essential, or do you see them simply as gimmicks? Explain.

5. Why are the alternating lines of "Group Photo with Winter Trees" set in boldface type? How does the form of this poem reflect its title?

6. Do you consider "this poem intentionally left blank" a poem? What ideas does it communicate to readers? How else could Bernstein have expressed these ideas?

WRITING SUGGESTIONS

1. Write an **explication** (see Chapter 3) of one of the poems in this chapter. Make sure you discuss how the visual elements of the poem help to communicate its main idea.

2. Write an essay in which you discuss the relationship between the shape of George Herbert's "Easter Wings" and the poem's subject. Why do you think Herbert constructed the poem the way he did?

3. Choose several imagist poems from Chapter 27 — for example, "Red Wheelbarrow" or "In a Station of the Metro." How could you turn each of these poems into a visual poem? Would the poems be more or less effective as visual poetry? Explain.

CHAPTER 24

READING AND WRITING ABOUT POETRY

Reading Poetry

Sometimes readers approach poetry purely for pleasure. At other times, reading a poem is also the first step toward writing about it. The following guidelines, designed to help you explore poetic works, focus on issues explored in chapters to come:

- *Rephrase the poem in your own words.* What does your paraphrase reveal about the poem's subject and central concerns? What is lost or gained in your paraphrase of the poem?
- *Consider the poem's **voice**.* Who is the poem's speaker? How would you characterize the poem's tone? Is the poem ironic? (See Chapter 25.)
- *Study the poem's **diction**.* Look up any unfamiliar words in a dictionary. How does word choice affect your reaction to the poem? What do the connotations of words reveal about the poem? What level of diction is used? Is word order unusual or unexpected? How does the arrangement of words contribute to your understanding of the poem? (See Chapter 26.)
- *Examine the poem's **imagery**.* What kind of imagery predominates? What specific images are used? Is there a pattern of imagery? How does imagery enrich the poem? (See Chapter 27.)
- *Identify the poem's **figures of speech**.* Does the poet use metaphor? Simile? Personification? Hyperbole? Understatement? Metonymy or synecdoche? Apostrophe? How do figures of speech affect your reading of the poem? (See Chapter 28.)
- *Listen to the **sound** of the poem.* Are rhythm and meter regular or irregular? How do rhythm and meter reinforce the poem's central concerns? Does the poem use alliteration? Assonance? Rhyme? How do these elements enhance the poem? (See Chapter 29.)
- *Look at the poem's **form**.* Is the poem written in closed or open form? Is the poem constructed as a sonnet? A sestina? A villanelle? An epigram? A haiku? How does the poem's form help to communicate (or reinforce) its ideas? (See Chapter 30.)
- *Consider the poem's use of **symbol, allegory, allusion,** or **myth**.* Does the poem make use of symbols? Allusions? How do symbols or allusions support

its theme? Is the poem an allegory? Does the poem retell or interpret a myth? (See Chapter 31.)

- *Identify the poem's* **theme**. Does the poem treat a conventional subject? What central theme does the poem explore? What other themes are examined? How are the themes expressed? (See Chapter 32.)

Active Reading

When you approach a poem that you plan to write about, you engage in the same **active reading** strategies you use when you read a short story or a play. When you finish recording your reactions to the poem, you focus on a topic, list possible ideas to explore, decide on a thesis, prepare an outline, and then go on to draft and revise your essay.

Catherine Whittaker, a student in an Introduction to Literature course, was asked to write a three- to five-page essay comparing any two of the poems that appear in "Poems about Parents" in Chapter 32 (pp. 1057–66). Her instructor told the class that the essay should reflect students' own ideas about the poems, not the opinions of literary critics. As Catherine planned and wrote her paper, she was guided by the process described in Chapter 2, "Reading and Writing about Literature."

Previewing

Catherine began her work by previewing the poems, eliminating those she considered obscure or difficult and those whose portrait of the speaker's parent did not seem sympathetic. This process helped Catherine to narrow down her choices. As she looked through "Those Winter Sundays," she was struck by words in the opening lines ("Sundays too"; "blueblack cold"). She had the same reaction to "The squat pen rests; snug as a gun" in line 2 of "Digging." In each case, the words made Catherine want to examine the poem further. She noticed too that both poems focused on fathers and that both were divided into stanzas of varying lengths. Keeping these features in mind, Catherine began a close reading of each poem.

Highlighting and Annotating

As Catherine read and reread "Those Winter Sundays" and "Digging," she recorded her comments and questions. The highlighted and annotated poems appear below.

ROBERT HAYDEN   (1913–1980)

<u>Those</u> **Winter Sundays**   (1962)   } *Were there many Sundays like these?*

Sundays (too) my father got up early   ⎯ *Like all other days of the week?*

and put his clothes on <u>in the blueblack cold</u>,   *Why did he get up before dawn?*

then with cracked hands that ached

from labor in the weekday weather made

{ What kind of job did the father have?

banked fires blaze. No one ever thanked him.   5

⟶ Was there a large family?

I'd wake and hear the cold splintering, breaking.

When the rooms were warm, he'd call,

and slowly I would rise and dress,

fearing the chronic angers of that house,

⟶ Were there problems in the family?

Speaking indifferently to him,   10

who had driven out the cold

and polished my good shoes as well.

Was there a mother around?

What did I know, what did I know

of love's austere and lonely offices?

⟶ Offices=duties or functions assigned to someone

Austere=without adornment ⟵ or ornamentation, simple; harsh

SEAMUS HEANEY (1939–   )

Digging (1966)

Between my finger and my thumb

The squat pen rests; snug as a gun.

⟶ gun=snug?

⟶ Why a "squat" pen?

Under my window, a clean rasping sound

When the spade sinks into gravelly ground:

My father, digging. I look down   5

Till his straining rump among the flowerbeds

Bends low, comes up twenty years away

Is he thinking about the past?

Stooping in rhythm through potato drills

Where he was digging.

The coarse boot nestled on the lug, the shaft   10

Against the inside knee was levered firmly.

Like the poets' pen?

He rooted out tall tops, buried the bright edge deep

To scatter new potatoes that (we) picked   *Was this a family task?*

Loving their cool hardness in our hands.

By God, the old man could handle a spade.   15

Just like his old man.

Two generations could "handle a spade." Can the poet dig?

My grandfather cut more turf in a day

Than any other man on Toner's bog.

Once I carried him milk in a bottle

Corked sloppily with paper. He straightened up   20

To drink it, then fell to right away —→ *The grandfather was a hard worker.*

Nicking and slicing neatly, heaving sods →*Digging was an art*

Over his shoulder, going down and down

For the good turf. Digging.

The cold smell of potato mould, the squelch and slap   25

Of soggy peat, the curt cuts of an edge   *What does it make him remember?*

Through living roots awaken in my head.

But I've no spade to follow men like them. *What are "men like them" like?*

Between my finger and my thumb

Same as first 2 lines (The squat pen rests. → *Why is this repeated?*   30

I'll dig with it.
    Dig for what?

Catherine found the language of both poems appealing, and she believed her highlighting and annotating had given her some valuable insights. For example, she noticed some similarities between the two poems: both focus on the past, both portray fathers as hard workers, and neither mentions a mother.

Writing about Poetry

Planning an Essay

Catherine still had to find a specific topic for her paper, and her preliminary work suggested some interesting possibilities. She was especially intrigued by the way both poems depicted fathers as actively engaged in physical tasks.

Choosing a Topic

One idea Catherine thought she might want to write about was the significance of the sons' attitudes toward their fathers: although both see their fathers as hard workers, the son in "Those Winter Sundays" seems to have mixed feelings about his father's devotion to his family, whereas the son in "Digging" is more appreciative. Catherine explored this idea in two journal entries.

```
               "Those Winter Sundays"
     Why did the father get up early every morning? One could
imagine that he had a large family and little money. There is
no mention of a mother. Images are created of the utter cold
and "chronic angers" of the house. The father not only made
fires to warm the house but also polished his child's (or
children's) shoes—maybe for church. And yet, the child
seemed not to care about or appreciate the father's efforts.
Was he too young to say thank you, or were there other
problems in the house for which the child blamed the father?
```

```
                  "Digging"
     In the poem, the poet seems to be wondering what to
write about when the sounds of digging capture his attention.
He remembers the steady, artful rhythm of his father's
digging of the potatoes and how they (probably the poet and
his brothers and sisters) picked out the cool potatoes. His
memories appear to be entirely appreciative of his father's
and grandfather's hard work and skill. He does, however, feel
regret that he is not like these dedicated men. Even though
he cannot use a shovel, he hopes to use his pen in order to
make his own contributions as a writer.
```

When Catherine reread her journal entries, she saw that she could focus on the two fathers' similar roles and the sons' contrasting attitudes toward their fathers. (In fact, she had so many ideas that she did not feel she had to brainstorm to generate more material.) Before she could write a draft of her paper, however, Catherine needed to identify specific similarities and differences between the two poems.

Seeing Connections: Listing

Catherine reread the highlighted and annotated poems and then compiled the following lists.

```
                      Differences
"Those Winter Sundays"                     "Digging"
—memories of family                        —only happy memories
 problems
```

```
—the child is                    —the child admires
 ambivalent toward                his father
 his father
—atmosphere of tension           —atmosphere of happiness
                                  and togetherness
                   Similarities
—the fathers are hard workers
—the fathers appear to love their children
—similar time—impression that the events
 happened years ago
—children, now grown, appreciate their fathers'
 dedication
—children, now grown, are inspired by their
 fathers' determination
```

At this point, Catherine reviewed her notes carefully. As connections between the two poems came into focus, she was able to decide on a thesis and on a possible order for her ideas.

Deciding on a Thesis

Catherine expressed her paper's main idea in the following thesis statement.

```
Although their family backgrounds are different, both
now-grown poets realize the determination and dedication
of their fathers and are consequently impassioned in
their writing.
```

Preparing an Outline

Catherine reviewed her notes to help her identify the specific ideas she wanted to develop in her first draft. Then, she arranged those ideas in a logical order in a scratch outline.

```
"Those Winter Sundays"

     Poet reflects back on childhood
          —father's hard work
          —his misunderstanding and lack of appreciation
          for everything his father did
     Family setting in childhood
          —tension in the house
          —no mother mentioned in the poem
     Poet's realization of father's love and
     dedication
```

"Digging"

    Poet reminisces
        —father's skill and hard work
        —grandfather's cutting of turf
        —children's participation and acceptance
    Happiness of the family
    The poet's desire to continue the tradition

Drafting an Essay

With a thesis statement and a scratch outline to guide her, Catherine wrote the following first draft of her essay. Her instructor's comments appear in the margins and at the end of the paper.

(first draft)

A Comparison of Two Poems about Fathers

Robert Hayden's "Those Winter Sundays" and

"Digging" by Seamus Heaney are poems that were

inspired by fathers and composed as tributes to

fathers. Although their family backgrounds are

different, both now-grown (poets) realize the

determination and dedication of their fathers and

are consequently (impassioned) in their writing.

Careful! you're confus- ing poet and speaker.

What do you mean?

In "Those Winter Sundays," Hayden reflects back on

his childhood. He remembers the many Sundays when his

father got up early to start the fires to make the

house warm for his children's awakening. The poet

pictures his father's hands made rough by his weekday

work. These same hands not only made the fires on

Sunday but also polished his son's good shoes, in

preparation, no doubt, for church.

Hayden also quite clearly remembers that his

father was never thanked for his work. The reader

imagines that the father had many children and may

have been poor. There were inner tensions in the

house and, quite noticeably, there is no mention of a

mother.

Looking back, the poet now realizes the love and

dedication with which his father took care of the

Quotations from the poem would strengthen your discussion in ¶s 3 and 4.

family. As a child, he never thanked his father, but now, as an adult, the poet seems to appreciate the simple kindness of his father.

In a similar sense, Seamus Heaney writes "Digging" as a tribute to his father and grandfather. He also reminisces about his father and clearly remembers the skill with which his father dug potatoes. The grandfather too is remembered, as is his technique for "heaving sods." There is an atmosphere of happiness in this poem. With the children helping the father harvest the potatoes, a sense of family togetherness is created. The reader feels that this family is a hardworking but nevertheless happy one.

Add line number in parentheses.

As the poet reminisces about his childhood, he realizes that, unlike his father and grandfather, he will never be a master of digging or a person who uses physical strength to earn a living. He wishes to be like his father before him, desiring to accomplish and contribute. However, for the poet, any "digging" to be done will be by his pen, in the form of literature.

To conclude, the fathers in these poets' pasts inspire them to write. An appreciation for their fathers' dedication is achieved only after the children mature into adults. It is then that the

```
fathers' impact on their children's lives is realized

for its true importance.
```

Good start! When you revise, focus on the following:

— Edit use of "poet" and "speaker" carefully. You can't assume that these poems reflect the poets' own lives or attitudes toward their fathers.
— Add more specific references to the poems, particularly quotations. (Don't forget to give line numbers.)
— Consider adding brief references to other poems about parents. (Check the textbook.)
— Consider rearranging your material into a point-by-point comparison, which will make the specific similarities and differences clearer.

Let's discuss this draft in a conference.

First Draft: Commentary

After submitting her first draft, Catherine met with her instructor. Together, they reviewed not only her first draft but also her annotations, journal entries, lists of similarities and differences, and scratch outline. During the conference, her instructor explained his written comments and, building on Catherine's own ideas, helped her develop a plan for revision.

Catherine's instructor agreed that the poems' similarities were worth exploring in detail. He thought, however, that her references to the poems' language and ideas needed to be much more specific and that her paper's subject-by-subject structure — discussing "Those Winter Sundays" first and then moving on to consider "Digging"—made the specific similarities between the two poems difficult to see. He also recommended that she make her thesis statement more concrete and specific.

Because the class had studied other poems in which speakers try to resolve their ambivalent feelings toward their parents, Catherine's instructor also suggested that she mention these poems to provide a wider context for her ideas. Finally, he explained the difference between the perspective of the poet and that of the **speaker**, a persona the poet creates.

As she reexamined her ideas in light of her discussion with her instructor, Catherine looked again at both the annotated poems and her notes about them. She then recorded her thoughts about her progress in an additional journal entry.

> After reviewing the poems again and talking to Professor Jackson, I discovered some additional points that I want to include in my next draft. The connection between the poet's pen and the shovel is evident in "Digging," and so is the link between the cold and the tensions in the house in "Those Winter Sundays." The tone of each poem should also be discussed. For example, I think that the poet's choice of <u>austere</u> in "Those Winter Sundays" has significance and should be included. In my next draft, I'll expand my first draft— hopefully, without reading into the poems too much. I also need to reorganize my ideas so parallels between the two poems will be clearer.

Because this journal entry suggested a new arrangement for her ideas, Catherine prepared a new scratch outline to guide her revision.

> Reflections on their fathers
>   Both poems
>   —fathers' dedication and hard work
>
> Family similarities and differences
>   "Digging"
>   —loving and caring

```
    "Those Winter Sundays"
        —family problems (tone of the poem)
Lessons learned from fathers
    "Digging"
        —inspiration (images of pen and shovel)
        —realization of father's inner strength
    "Those Winter Sundays"
        —realization of father's inner strength
        —"austere" caring (images of cold)

Brief discussion of other poems about fathers
```

Revising and Editing an Essay

After once again reviewing all the material she had accumulated, Catherine wrote a second draft.

(second draft)

A Comparison of Two Poems about Fathers

Robert Hayden's "Those Winter Sundays" and Seamus Heaney's "Digging" are two literary pieces that are tributes to the speakers' fathers. The inspiration and admiration the speakers feel are evident in each poem. Although the nature of the two family relationships may differ, the common thread of the love of fathers for their children weaves through each poem.

Reflections on one's childhood can bring assorted memories to light. Presumably, the speakers are now adults and reminisce on their childhood with a mature sense of enlightenment not found in childhood. Both speakers describe their fathers' hard work and dedication to their families. Hayden's speaker remembers that even after working hard all week, his father would get up early on Sunday to warm the house in preparation for his children's rising. The speaker vividly portrays his father's hands, describing "cracked hands that ached / from labor in the weekday weather" (3-4). And yet, these same hands not only built the fires that drove out the cold but also polished the children's good shoes.

In a similar way, Heaney's speaker reminisces about his father's and grandfather's digging of turf, describing their skill and their dedication to their task.

The fathers in these poems appear to be the hardest of workers, laborers who sought to support their families. Not only did they have a dedication to their work, but they also cared about and undoubtedly loved their children. Looking back, Hayden's speaker realizes that, although his childhood may not have been perfect nor his family life entirely without problems, his father loved him. Heaney's description of the potato picking makes us imagine a loving family led by a father and grandfather who worked together and included the children in both work and celebration. Heaney's speaker grows to become a man who has nothing but respect for his father and grandfather, wishing to be like them and somehow follow their greatness.

Although some similarities exist between the sons and fathers in the poems, the family life differs between the two. Perhaps it is the tone of the poems that best typifies the family atmosphere. The tone of "Digging" is wholesome, earthy, natural, and happy, emphasizing the healthy and caring nature of the poet's childhood. In reminiscing, Heaney's speaker seems to have no bad memories concerning his father or family. In contrast, the tone of Hayden's poem is very much like the coldness of the Sunday mornings. Even though the father warmed the house, the "chronic angers of that house" (9) did not leave with the cold. The speaker, as a child, seems full of resentment toward the father, no doubt blaming him for the family problems. (Curiously, it is the father and not the mother who polishes the children's good shoes. Was there no mother?) The reader senses that

the father-son communication evident in Heaney's
family is missing in Hayden's.

There are many other poets who have written
about their fathers. Simon J. Ortiz in "My Father's
Song" writes a touching tribute to his father, who
taught him to respect and care for the lives of
animals and to appreciate earthly wonders. In other
poems, such as Theodore Roethke's "My Papa's Waltz,"
the fathers are depicted as imperfect, vulnerable
people who try to cope with life as well as possible.

"Digging" and "Those Winter Sundays" are poems
written from the inspirations of sons, admiring and
appreciating their fathers. Childhood memories act
not only as images of the past but also as aids for
the speakers' self-realization and enlightenment.
Even after childhood, the fathers' influence over
their sons is evident; only now do the speakers
appreciate its true importance.

Second Draft: Commentary

When she reread her second draft, Catherine thought she had accomplished much of what she had set out to do. She had tightened her thesis statement, re-arranged her discussion, added specific details, and changed *poet* to *speaker* where necessary. However, she still was not satisfied with her analysis of the poems' language and tone (she had not, for example, considered the importance of the word *austere* or examined the significance of Heaney's equation of *spade* and *pen*). She also thought that the material in paragraph 6 about other poems, though interesting, was distracting, so she decided to try to relocate it. Finally, she planned to edit and proofread carefully as she prepared her final draft.

Catherine Whittaker

Professor Jackson

English 102

5 March 2005

Digging for Memories

Robert Hayden's "Those Winter Sundays" and
Seamus Heaney's "Digging" are two literary pieces
that are tributes to the speakers' fathers. Although
the depiction of the families and the tones of the
two poems are different, the common thread of love
between fathers and children extends through the two
poems, and each speaker is inspired by his father's
example.

Many other poets have written about children and
their fathers. Simon J. Ortiz in "My Father's Song"
writes a touching tribute to a father who taught the
speaker to respect and care for the lives of animals
and to appreciate earthly wonders. In other poems,
such as Theodore Roethke's "My Papa's Waltz," fathers
are depicted as imperfect, vulnerable people who try
to cope with life as well as possible.

As these and other poems reveal, reflections on
childhood can bring complex memories to light, as
they do for Hayden's and Heaney's speakers. Now
adults, they reminisce about their childhoods with a
mature sense of enlightenment not found in childhood.
Both speakers describe their fathers' hard work and
dedication to their families. For example, Hayden's
speaker remembers that even after working hard all
week, his father would get up early on Sunday to warm

Annotations (left margin):

Introduction

Thesis statement

¶6 from second
draft has been
relocated.
References to
poems in Chapter
32 of this text
include complete
authors' names
and titles.

First point of
similarity: Both
poems focus on
memory

the house in preparation for his sleeping children.
The speaker vividly portrays his father's hands,
describing "cracked hands that ached / from labor
in the weekday weather" (lines 3-4). And yet, these
same hands not only built the fires that drove out
the cold but also polished his children's good shoes.
In a similar way, Heaney's speaker reminisces about
his father's and grandfather's digging of soil and
sod, pointing out their skill and their dedication to
their tasks.

    The fathers in these poems appear to be hard
workers, laborers who struggled to support their
families. Not only were they dedicated to their work,
but they also loved their children. Looking back,
Hayden's speaker realizes that, although his
childhood may not have been perfect and his family
life was not entirely without problems, his father
loved him. Heaney's description of the potato picking
allows us to imagine a loving family led by a father
and grandfather who worked together and included the
children in both work and celebration. Heaney's
speaker grows into a man who has nothing but respect
for his father and grandfather, wishing to be like
them and to somehow fill their shoes.

    Although some similarities exist between the
fathers (and the sons) in the poems, the family life
the two poems depict is very different. Perhaps it is
the tone of each poem that best reveals the family
atmosphere. The tone of "Digging" is wholesome,

Parenthetical reference cites line numbers of poem. (First reference to lines of poetry includes word *line* or *lines*. Subsequent references include just line numbers.)

Second point of similarity: Both fathers are hard workers.

Focus shifts to contrast between the two poems.

earthy, natural, and happy, emphasizing the healthy
and caring nature of the speaker's childhood.
Heaney's speaker seems to have no bad memories of his
father or family. In contrast, the tone of Hayden's
poem is very much like the coldness of the Sunday
mornings. Even though the father warmed the house,
the "chronic angers of that house" (9) did not leave
with the cold. The speaker, as a child, seems to have
resented his father, no doubt blaming him for the
family's problems. The warm relationship readers see
between the father and the son in Heaney's poem is
absent in Hayden's.

    In spite of these differences, readers cannot go
away from either poem without the impression that
both speakers learned important lessons from their
fathers. Both fathers had a great amount of inner
strength and were dedicated to their families. As the
years pass, Hayden's speaker has come to realize the
depth of his father's devotion to his family. He uses
the image of the "blueblack cold" (2) that was
splintered and broken by the fires lovingly prepared
by his father to suggest the father's efforts to keep
his family free from harm. The cold suggests the
tensions of the family that the father is determined
to force out of the house through his "austere and
lonely offices" (14).

    In Heaney's poem, the father and grandfather
have also had a profound impact on the young speaker.
As the memories come pouring back, the speaker's

Focus returns to parallels between the two poems.

Third point of similarity: Both speakers learn from grandfathers (discussed in two paragraphs).

Whittaker 4

admiration for the men who came before him forces him to reflect on his own life and work. He realizes that he will never have the ability (or the desire) to do the physical labor of his relatives: "I've no spade to follow men like them" (28). However, just as the spade was the tool of his father and grandfather, the pen will be the tool with which the speaker will work. The shovel suggests the hard work, effort, and determination of the men who came before him, and the pen is the literary equivalent of the shovel. Heaney's speaker has been inspired by his father and grandfather, and he hopes to accomplish with a pen in the world of literature what they accomplished with a shovel on the land.

　　"Digging" and "Those Winter Sundays" are poems written from the perspective of adult sons who admire and appreciate their fathers. Childhood memories not only evoke vivid images of the past but also lead the speakers to insight and enlightenment. Long after childhood, the fathers' influence over their sons is evident; only now, however, do the speakers appreciate its true importance.

Conclusion
reinforces thesis.

Final Draft: Commentary

As she wrote her final draft, Catherine expanded her analysis, looking more closely at the language and tone of the two poems. To support and clarify her points, she added more direct quotations, taking care to reproduce words and punctuation marks accurately and to cite line numbers in parentheses after each quotation. (Because all the students in Catherine's class had to select poems from Chapter 32 of this anthology, their instructor did not require a works-cited page.) She also moved her discussion of other poems to paragraph 2, where it provides a smooth transition from her introduction to her discussion of Hayden and Heaney.

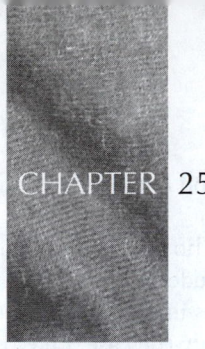

CHAPTER 25

VOICE

A poem remains with us to the extent that it allows us to feel that we are listening to a voice at once contemporary and ancient. This makes all the difference.

— **John Haines**, *"The Hole in the Bucket"*

EMILY DICKINSON (1830–1886)

I'm nobody! Who are you? (1891)

I'm nobody! Who are you?
Are you — Nobody — Too?
Then there's a pair of us?
Don't tell! they'd advertise — you know!

How dreary — to be — Somebody!   5
How public — like a Frog —
To tell one's name — the livelong June —
To an admiring Bog!

The Speaker in the Poem

When they read fiction, readers form an impression of a work's narrator and decide whether he or she is sophisticated or unsophisticated, trustworthy or untrustworthy, innocent or experienced. Just as fiction depends on a narrator, poetry depends on a **speaker** who describes events, feelings, and ideas to readers. Finding out as much as possible about this speaker can help readers to interpret a poem. For example, the speaker in Emily Dickinson's "I'm nobody! Who are you?" seems at first to be playful, even flirtatious. In fact, she appears to be entering into a conspiracy with readers. The first stanza of the poem suggests that the speaker is a private person, with little desire to be well known. As the poem continues, however, her focus changes. The poem's two stanzas present a complex persona. In the first stanza, the speaker reveals her private self — internal, isolated, and revealed through poetry; in the second stanza, she moves outward to express disdain for those who seek to become "somebody," whom she sees as self-centered, self-promoting, and inevitably superficial. Far from being defeated by her isolation, the speaker seems to have rejected fame and chosen her status as "nobody."

One question readers might ask about "I'm nobody! Who are you?" is how close the speaker's voice is to the poet's. Readers who conclude that the poem is about the conflict between a poet's public and private selves may be tempted to see the speaker and the poet as one. But this is not necessarily the case. Like the narrator of a short story, the speaker of a poem is a **persona**, or mask, that the poet puts on. Granted, in some poems little distance exists between the poet and the speaker. Without hard evidence to support a link between speaker and poet, however, readers should not simply assume they are one and the same.

In many cases, the speaker is quite different from the poet, even when the speaker's voice conveys the attitude of the poet either directly or indirectly. In "The Chimney Sweeper" (p. 1144), for example, William Blake assumes the voice of a child to criticize the system of child labor that existed in eighteenth-century England. Even though the child speaker does not understand the economic and social forces that cause his misery, readers sense the poet's anger as the trusting speaker describes the appalling conditions under which he works. The poet's indignation is especially apparent in the biting irony of the last line, in which the victimized speaker innocently assures readers that if all people do their duty, "they need not fear harm."

Sometimes the poem's speaker is anonymous. In such cases — as in William Carlos Williams's "Red Wheelbarrow" (p. 923), for instance — the first-person voice is absent and the speaker remains outside the poem. At other times, the speaker has a set identity — a king, a beggar, a highwayman, a sheriff, a husband, a wife, a rich man, a murderer, a child, a mythical figure, an explorer, a teacher, a faithless lover, a saint — or even a flower, an animal, or a clod of earth. Whatever the case, the speaker is not the poet but rather a creation that the poet uses to convey his or her ideas. (For this reason, poems by a single poet may have very different voices. Compare Sylvia Plath's bitter and sardonic poem "Daddy" [p. 952] with her nurturing and celebratory work "Morning Song" [p. 871], for example.)

Sometimes a poem's title tells readers that the poet is assuming a particular persona. In the following poem, for example, the title identifies the speaker as a fictional character, Gretel from the fairy tale "Hansel and Gretel."

LOUISE GLÜCK (1943–   )

Gretel in Darkness   (1971)

This is the world we wanted.
All who would have seen us dead
are dead. I hear the witch's cry
break in the moonlight through a sheet
of sugar: God rewards.   5
Her tongue shrivels into gas. . . .

Now, far from women's arms
And memory of women, in our father's hut
we sleep, are never hungry.
Why do I not forget?   10
My father bars the door, bars harm
from this house, and it is years.

No one remembers. Even you, my brother,
summer afternoons you look at me as though
you meant to leave,   15
as though it never happened.
But I killed for you. I see armed firs,
the spires of that gleaming kiln—

Nights I turn to you to hold me
but you are not there.   20
Am I alone? Spies
hiss in the stillness, Hansel
we are there still, and it is real, real,
that black forest, and the fire in earnest.

The speaker in this poem comments on her life after her encounter with the witch in the forest. Speaking to her brother, Gretel observes that they now live in the world they wanted: they live with their father in his hut, and the witch and the wicked stepmother are dead. Even so, the memory of the events in the forest haunts Gretel and makes it impossible for her to live "happily ever after." The "armed firs," the "gleaming kiln," and "the black forest" break through the "sheet of sugar" that her life has become.

By assuming the persona of Gretel, the poet is able to convey some interesting and complex ideas. On one level, Gretel represents any person who has lived through a traumatic experience. Memories of the event keep breaking through into the present, frustrating her attempts to reestablish her belief in the goodness of the world. The voice we hear is sad, alone, and frightened: "Nights I turn to you to hold me," she says, "but you are not there." Although the murder Gretel committed for her brother was justified, it seems to haunt her. "No one remembers," laments Gretel, not even her brother. At some level, she realizes that by killing the witch she has killed a part of herself, perhaps the part of women that men fear and consequently transform into witches and wicked stepmothers. The world that is left after the killing is the father's and the brother's, not hers, and she is now alone in a dark world haunted by the memories of the black forest. In this sense, Gretel—"Now, far from women's arms / And memory of women"—may be the voice of all victimized women who, because of men, act against their own best interests—and regret it.

As "Gretel in Darkness" illustrates, a title can identify a poem's speaker, but the speaker's own words can provide much more information. This is also the case in the following poem, where Spanish words help to characterize the speaker.

LEONARD ADAMÉ (1947–   )

My Grandmother Would Rock Quietly and Hum (1973)

in her house
she would rock quietly and hum
until her swelled hands
calmed

in summer   5
she wore thick stockings
sweaters
and grey braids

(when "el cheque"° came
we went to Payless   10
and I laughed greedily
when given a quarter)

mornings,
sunlight barely lit
the kitchen   15
and where
there were shadows
it was not cold

she quietly rolled
flour tortillas —   20
the "papas"°
cracking in hot lard
would wake me

she had lost her teeth
and when we ate   25
she had bread
soaked in "café"°

always her eyes
were clear
and she could see   30
as I cannot yet see —
through her eyes
she gave me herself
she would sit
and talk   35

° *el cheque:* The check.   ° *papas:* Potatoes.   ° *café:* Coffee.

of her girlhood—
of things strange to me:
    México
    epidemics
    relatives shot   40
    her father's hopes
    of this country—
how they sank
with cement dust
to his insides   45

now
when I go
to the old house
the worn spots
by the stove   50
echo of her shuffling
and
México
still hangs in her
fading   55
calendar pictures

In this poem, the speaker is an adult recalling childhood memories of his grandmother. Spanish words — *el cheque, tortillas, papas,* and *café* — identify the speaker as Latino. His easy use of English, his comment that Mexico is strange to him, and his observation that he cannot yet see through his grandmother's eyes suggest, however, that he is not in touch with his ethnic identity. At one level, the grandmother evokes nostalgic memories of the speaker's youth. At another level, she is a living symbol of his ties with Mexico, connecting him to the ethnic culture he is trying to recover. The poem ends on an ambivalent note: even though the speaker is able to return to "the old house," the pictures of Mexico are fading, perhaps suggesting the speaker's inevitable assimilation into mainstream American culture.

    Direct statements by speakers can also help to characterize them. In the next poem, the first line of each stanza establishes the identity of the speaker — and defines his perspective.

LANGSTON HUGHES (1902–1967)

Negro   (1926)

I am a Negro:
    Black as the night is black,
    Black like the depths of my Africa.

I've been a slave:
    Caesar told me to keep his door-steps clean.   5
    I brushed the boots of Washington.

I've been a worker:
    Under my hand the pyramids arose.
    I made mortar for the Woolworth Building.

I've been a singer: 10
    All the way from Africa to Georgia
    I carried my sorrow songs.
    I made ragtime.

I've been a victim:
    The Belgians cut off my hands in the Congo.   15
    They lynch me still in Mississippi.

I am a Negro:
    Black as the night is black,
    Black like the depths of my Africa.

Here the speaker, identifying himself as "a Negro," assumes each of the roles African-Americans have historically played in Western society — slave, worker, singer, and victim. By so doing, he gives voice to his ancestors who, by being forced to serve others, were deprived of their identities. By presenting not only their suffering but also their accomplishments, the speaker asserts his pride in being black. The speaker also implies that the suffering of black people has been caused by economic exploitation: Romans, Egyptians, Belgians, and Americans all used black labor to help build their societies. In this context, the speaker's implied warning is clear: except for the United States, all the societies that have exploited blacks have declined, and long after the fall of those empires, black people still endure.

In each of the preceding poems, the speaker is alone. The following poem, a **dramatic monologue**, presents a more complex situation in which the poet creates a complete dramatic scene. The speaker is developed as a character whose distinctive personality is revealed through his words as he addresses a silent listener.

ROBERT BROWNING (1812–1889)

My Last Duchess (1842)

Ferrara

That's my last Duchess painted on the wall,
Looking as if she were alive. I call
That piece a wonder, now: Frà Pandolf's° hands

°*Frà Pandolf:* "Brother" Pandolf, a fictive painter.

Worked busily a day, and there she stands.
Will't please you sit and look at her? I said   5
"Frà Pandolf" by design, for never read
Strangers like you that pictured countenance,
The depth and passion of its earnest glance,
But to myself they turned (since none puts by
The curtain I have drawn for you, but I)   10
And seemed as they would ask me, if they durst,
How such a glance came there; so, not the first
Are you to turn and ask thus. Sir, 'twas not
Her husband's presence only, called that spot
Of joy into the Duchess' cheek: perhaps   15
Frà Pandolf chanced to say "Her mantle laps
Over my lady's wrist too much," or "Paint
Must never hope to reproduce the faint
Half-flush that dies along her throat": such stuff
Was courtesy, she thought, and cause enough   20
For calling up that spot of joy. She had
A heart — how shall I say? — too soon made glad,
Too easily impressed; she liked whate'er
She looked on, and her looks went everywhere.
Sir, 'twas all one! My favor at her breast,   25
The dropping of the daylight in the West,
The bough of cherries some officious fool
Broke in the orchard for her, the white mule
She rode with round the terrace — all and each
Would draw from her alike the approving speech,   30
Or blush, at least. She thanked men — good! but thanked
Somehow — I know not how — as if she ranked
My gift of a nine-hundred-years-old name
With anybody's gift. Who'd stoop to blame
This sort of trifling? Even had you skill   35
In speech — (which I have not) — to make your will
Quite clear to such an one, and say, "Just this
Or that in you disgusts me; here you miss,
Or there exceed the mark" — and if she let
Herself be lessoned so, nor plainly set   40
Her wits to yours, forsooth, and made excuse
— E'en then would be some stooping; and I choose
Never to stoop. Oh sir, she smiled, no doubt,
Whene'er I passed her; but who passed without
Much the same smile? This grew; I gave commands;   45
Then all smiles stopped together. There she stands
As if alive. Will't please you rise? We'll meet
The company below, then. I repeat,
The Count your master's known munificence

Is ample warrant that no just pretense   50
Of mine for dowry will be disallowed;
Though his fair daughter's self, as I avowed
At starting, is my object. Nay, we'll go
Together down, sir. Notice Neptune,° though,
Taming a sea horse, thought a rarity,   55
Which Claus of Innsbruck° cast in bronze for me!

The speaker is probably Alfonso II, duke of Ferrara, Italy, whose young wife, Lucrezia, died in 1561 after only three years of marriage. Shortly after her death, the duke began negotiations to marry again. When the poem opens, the duke is showing a portrait of his late wife to an emissary of an unnamed count who is there to arrange a marriage between the duke and the count's daughter. The duke remarks that the artist, Frà Pandolf, has caught a certain look on the duchess's face. This look aroused the jealousy of the duke, who thought that it should have been for him alone. According to the duke, the duchess's crime was that she had a heart "too soon made glad," "Too easily impressed." Eventually the duke could tolerate the situation no longer; he "gave commands," and "all smiles stopped together."

Much of what readers learn about the duke's state of mind comes from what is implied by his words. As he discusses the painting, the duke unintentionally reveals himself to be obsessively possessive and jealous, referring to "*my* last Duchess," "My favor at her breast," and "My gift of a nine-hundred-years-old name." He keeps the portrait of his late wife well hidden behind a curtain that no one draws except him. His interest in the picture has little to do with the memory of his wife, however. In death, the duchess has become exactly what the duke always wanted her to be: a personal possession that reflects his status and good taste.

Though silent, the listener plays a subtle but important role in the poem: his presence establishes the dramatic situation that allows the character of the duke to be revealed. The purpose of the story is to communicate to the emissary exactly what the duke expects from his prospective bride and from her father. As he speaks, the duke provides only the information that he wants the emissary to take back to his master, the count. Although the duke appears vain and superficial, he is actually extraordinarily shrewd. Throughout the poem, he turns the conversation to his own ends and gains the advantage through flattery and false modesty. Notice, for example, that he claims he has little skill in speaking when actually he is cleverly manipulating the conversation. The success of the poem lies in the poet's ability to develop the voice of this complex character, who embodies both superficial elegance and shocking cruelty.

°*Neptune:* In Roman mythology, the god of the sea.   °*Claus of Innsbruck:* A fictive — or unidentified — sculptor. The count of Tyrol's capital was at Innsbrück, Austria.

FURTHER READING: The Speaker in the Poem

LESLIE MARMON SILKO (1948–)

Where Mountain Lion Lay Down with Deer (1973)

I climb the black rock mountain
    stepping from day to day
            silently.
I smell the wind for my ancestors
      pale blue leaves   5
    crushed wild mountain smell.
Returning
    up the gray stone cliff
    where I descended
      a thousand years ago.   10
Returning to faded black stone.
    where mountain lion lay down with deer.
It is better to stay up here
            watching wind's reflection
            in tall yellow flowers.   15
The old ones who remember me are gone
     the old songs are all forgotten
and the story of my birth.
How I danced in snow-frost moonlight
        distant stars to the end of the Earth,   20
How I swam away
          in freezing mountain water
          narrow mossy canyon tumbling down
              out of the mountain
                out of the deep canyon stone   25
        down
           the memory
           spilling out
           into the world.

Reading and Reacting

1. Who is speaking in line 4? In line 9? Can you explain this shift?

2. From where is the speaker returning? What is she trying to recover?

3. JOURNAL ENTRY Is it important for you to know that the poet is of Native American descent? How does this information affect your interpretation of the poem?

4. CRITICAL PERSPECTIVE In her 1983 essay "Answering the Deer," Native American poet and critic Paula Gunn Allen observes that the possibility of cultural extinction is a reality Native Americans must face. Native American women writers, says Allen, face this fact directly but with a kind of hope:

> The sense of hope . . . comes about when one has faced ultimate disaster time and time again over the ages and has emerged . . . stronger and more certain of the endurance of the people, the spirits, and the land from which they both arise and which informs both with life. Transformation, or more directly, metamorphosis, is the oldest tribal ceremonial theme. . . . And it comes once again into use within American Indian poetry of extinction and regeneration that is ultimately the only poetry any contemporary Indian woman can write.

Does Silko's poem address the issue of cultural extinction and the possibility of regeneration or metamorphosis? How?

Related Works: "This Is What It Means to Say Phoenix, Arizona"(p. 287) "Two Kinds" (p. 791), "How to Write the Great American Indian Novel" (p. 887), "My Father's Song" (p. 1063), "Immigrants" (p. 1024), "Nikki-Rosa" (p. 1182), *Trying to Find Chinatown* (p. 1892)

JANICE MIRIKITANI (1942–   )

Suicide Note   (1987)

. . . An Asian-American college student was reported to have jumped to her death from her dormitory window. Her body was found two days later under a deep cover of snow. Her suicide note contained an apology to her parents for having received less than a perfect four point grade average. . . .

How many notes written . . .
ink smeared like birdprints in snow.

not good enough   not pretty enough   not smart enough
dear mother and father.
I apologize   5
for disappointing you.
I've worked very hard,
                not good enough
harder, perhaps to please you.
If only I were a son, shoulders broad   10
as the sunset threading through pine,
I would see the light in my mother's
eyes, or the golden pride reflected
in my father's dream
of my wide, male hands worthy of work   15
and comfort.
I would swagger through life
muscled and bold and assured,

drawing praises to me
like currents in the bed of wind, virile   20
with confidence.
   not good enough not strong enough not good enough

I apologize.
Tasks do not come easily.
Each failure, a glacier.   25
Each disapproval, a bootprint.
Each disappointment,
ice above my river.
So I have worked hard.
        not good enough   30
My sacrifice I will drop
bone by bone, perched
on the ledge of my womanhood,
fragile as wings.
        not strong enough   35
It is snowing steadily
surely not good weather
for flying — this sparrow
sillied and dizzied by the wind
on the edge.   40
        not smart enough
I make this ledge my altar
to offer penance.
This air will not hold me,
the snow burdens my crippled wings,   45
my tears drop like bitter cloth
softly into the gutter below.
   not good enough not strong enough not smart enough
         Choices thin as shaved
         ice. Notes shredded   50
         drift like snow
on my broken body,
cover me like whispers
of sorries
sorries.   55
Perhaps when they find me
they will bury
my bird bones beneath
a sturdy pine
and scatter my feathers like   60
unspoken song
over this white and cold and silent
breast of earth.

Reading and Reacting

1. This poem is a suicide note that contains an apology. Why does the speaker feel she must apologize? Do you agree that she needs to apologize?

2. What attitude does the speaker convey toward her parents?

3. JOURNAL ENTRY Is the college student who speaks in this poem a stranger to you? Or is her voice in any way like that of students you know?

Related Works: "The Rocking-Horse Winner" (p. 525), "Teenage Wasteland" (p. 799), "The Value of Education" (p. 908), "Dreams of Suicide" (p. 1043), "Death Be Not Proud" (p. 1168), *The Cuban Swimmer* (p. 1772), *Antigone's Red* (p. 1931).

JAMES TATE (1943–)

Nice Car, Camille (2001)

Camille drove by in her sports car with
the top down. I waved to her, but she didn't
see me, or else she just chose not to wave back.
She's an incredibly beautiful woman, but always
seems sad, sad or angry, it's hard to tell. I   5
went to school with her. We'd talk sometimes.
Her father had owned an oil company. It had been
in the family for three generations. But one of
his employees had killed him when she was six.
Then her mother married some bum and he squandered   10
most of her money gambling. Camille didn't really
make friends in school. She didn't want any. She
always managed to drive a really sexy car. She'd
always have her sunglasses on, speeding through
town as if late for an appointment. And I'd always   15
wave if I saw her. Hello, Camille. Goodbye,
Camille. That was my contribution to making her
life unforgettable.

Reading and Reacting

1. What does the poem reveal about Camille? About the speaker?

2. What does the speaker mean in lines 17–18 when he says, "That was my contribution to making her / life unforgettable"? Is he being honest or sarcastic?

3. JOURNAL ENTRY What do you think Camille and her sports car represent to the speaker?

4. CRITICAL PERSPECTIVE In a review of James Tate's *Selected Poems*, poet and critic Dana Gioia comments on the strengths and weaknesses of Tate's poems:

Tate is often funny and always fun to read, even in the nihilistic poems that make up a good portion of the volume. A reader may find Tate's poetry difficult, opaque, or pointless, but no one who loves language will find him boring. Line by line, sentence by sentence, he strives to keep the reader interested and amused.

Is "Nice Car, Camille" "fun to read"? Is it "pointless," or can you understand what Tate is trying to communicate?

Related Works: "A Rose for Emily" (p. 216), "One day I wrote her name upon the strand" (p. 914), "Oh, my love is like a red, red rose," (p. 944), "Barbie Doll" (p. 1211), "Richard Cory" (p. 1218), *Beauty* (p. 1308).

PAT MORA (1942–)

Veiled

If before the mullah's morning call,
We tiptoe through the village
Gather burqas° that shroud
Even the eyes,
     Heavy, dark, like storm clouds   5

If we rush to the river
Float the black and brown
Garments on soft waves,
Close our eyes, listen

Will the water loosen   10
Laughter trapped inside those threads,
Will light songs rise
And swirl with the morning mist,

Or will sighs rise,
     Heavy, dark like storm clouds?   15

Reading and Reacting

1. Who is the speaker? In what type of country does she live?
2. What does the speaker fantasize about? Why is laughter "trapped inside" (11) the threads of the burqa? Why are the sighs "heavy, dark, like storm clouds" (15)?
3. **JOURNAL ENTRY** What do the speaker's fantasies reveal about her attitude toward burqas?

°*burqa:* A garment that veils the head and body, worn by some Muslim women.

Related Works: "A Rose for Emily" (p. 216), "The Disappearance" (p. 371), "Indian Boarding School: The Runaways" (p. 1176), *A Doll House* (p. 1454), *Antigone's Red* (p. 1931)

The Tone of the Poem

The **tone** of a poem conveys the speaker's attitude toward his or her subject or audience. In speech, this attitude can be conveyed easily: stressing a word in a sentence can modify or color a statement, drastically affecting the meaning of the sentence. For example, the statement "Of course, you would want to go to that restaurant" is quite straightforward, but changing the emphasis to "Of course *you* would want to go to *that* restaurant" transforms a neutral statement into a sarcastic one. For poets, however, conveying a particular tone to readers poses a challenge because readers rarely hear poets' spoken voices. Instead, poets indicate tone by using techniques such as rhyme, meter, word choice, sentence structure, figures of speech, and imagery.

The range of possible tones is wide. For example, a poem's speaker may be joyful, sad, playful, serious, comic, intimate, formal, relaxed, condescending, or ironic. In the following poem, notice how the tone conveys the speaker's attitude toward his subject.

ROBERT FROST (1874–1963)

Fire and Ice   (1923)

Some say the world will end in fire,
Some say in ice.
From what I've tasted of desire
I hold with those who favor fire.
But if it had to perish twice,   5
I think I know enough of hate
To say that for destruction ice
Is also great
And would suffice.

Here the speaker uses word choice, rhyme, and especially understatement to comment on the human condition. The conciseness and the simple, regular meter and rhyme suggest an **epigram** — a short poem that makes a pointed comment in an unusually clear, and often witty, manner. This pointedness is consistent with the speaker's glib, unemotional tone, as is the last line's wry understatement that ice "would suffice." The contrast between the poem's serious message — that hatred and indifference are equally destructive — and its informal style and offhand tone complement the speaker's detached, almost smug, posture.

Sometimes shifts in tone reveal changes in the speaker's attitude. In the next poem, subtle shifts in tone reveal a change in the speaker's attitude toward war.

THOMAS HARDY (1840–1928)

The Man He Killed   (1902)

"Had he and I but met
By some old ancient inn,
We should have sat us down to wet
Right many a nipperkin!°

"But ranged as infantry,   5
And staring face to face,
I shot at him as he at me,
And killed him in his place.

"I shot him dead because —
Because he was my foe,   10
Just so: my foe of course he was;
That's clear enough; although

"He thought he'd 'list,° perhaps,
Off-hand-like — just as I —
Was out of work — had sold his traps —   15
No other reason why.

"Yes; quaint and curious war is!
You shoot a fellow down
You'd treat if met where any bar is,
Or help to half-a crown."   20

The speaker in this poem is a soldier relating a wartime experience. Quotation marks indicate that he is engaged in conversation — perhaps in a pub — and his dialect indicates that he is probably of the English working class. For him, at least at first, the object of war is simple: kill or be killed. To Hardy, this speaker represents all men who are thrust into a war without understanding its underlying social, economic, or ideological causes. In this sense, the speaker and his enemy are both victims of forces beyond their comprehension or control.

The tone of "The Man He Killed" changes as the speaker tells his story. As the poem unfolds, its sentence structure deteriorates, and this in turn helps to convey the speaker's changing attitude toward the war in which he has fought. In the first two stanzas, sentences are smooth and unbroken, establishing the speaker's matter-of-fact tone and reflecting his confidence that he has done what

---

°*nipperkin:* A small container of liquor   °*'list:* Enlist.

he had to do. In the third and fourth stanzas, broken syntax reflects the narrator's increasingly disturbed state of mind as he tells about the man he killed. The poem's singsong meter and regular rhyme scheme (*met/wet, inn/nipperkin*) suggest that the speaker is struggling to maintain his composure; the smooth sentence structure of the last stanza and the use of a cliché ("Yes; quaint and curious war is!") show the speaker's efforts to trivialize an incident that has seriously traumatized him.

Sometimes a poem's tone can establish an ironic contrast between the speaker and his or her subject. The speaker's abrupt change of tone at the end of the next poem establishes such a contrast.

AMY LOWELL (1874–1925)

Patterns   (1915)

I walk down the garden-paths,
And all the daffodils
Are blowing, and the bright blue squills.
I walk down the patterned garden-paths
In my stiff, brocaded gown.   5
With my powdered hair and jewelled fan,
I too am a rare
Pattern. As I wander down
The garden-paths.

My dress is richly figured,   10
And the train
Makes a pink and silver stain
On the gravel, and the thrift
Of the borders.
Just a plate of current fashion   15
Tripping by in high-heeled, ribboned shoes.
Not a softness anywhere about me,
Only whalebone° and brocade.
And I sink on a seat in the shade
Of a lime tree. For my passion   20
Wars against the stiff brocade.
The daffodils and squills
Flutter in the breeze
As they please.
And I weep;   25
For the lime-tree is in blossom

° *whalebone:* The type of bone used to stiffen corsets.

And one small flower has dropped upon my bosom.
And the plashing of waterdrops
In the marble fountain
Comes down the garden-paths. 30
The dripping never stops.
Underneath my stiffened gown
Is the softness of a woman bathing in a marble basin,
A basin in the midst of hedges grown
So thick, she cannot see her lover hiding, 35
But she guesses he is near,
And the sliding of the water
Seems the stroking of a dear
Hand upon her.
What is Summer in a fine brocaded gown! 40
I should like to see it lying in a heap upon the ground.
All the pink and silver crumpled up on the ground.

I would be the pink and silver as I ran along the paths,
And he would stumble after,
Bewildered by my laughter. 45
I should see the sun flashing from his sword-hilt and buckles
 on his shoes.
I would choose
To lead him in a maze along the patterned paths,
A bright and laughing maze for my heavy-booted lover.
Till he caught me in the shade, 50
And the buttons of his waistcoat bruised my body as he clasped me,
Aching, melting, unafraid.
With the shadows of the leaves and the sundrops,
And the plopping of the waterdrops,
All about us in the open afternoon — 55
I am very like to swoon
     With the weight of this brocade,
     For the sun sifts through the shade.

Underneath the fallen blossom
In my bosom, 60
Is a letter I have hid.
It was brought to me this morning by a rider from the Duke.
Madam, we regret to inform you that Lord Hartwell
Died in action Thursday se'nnight.°
As I read it in the white, morning sunlight, 65
The letters squirmed like snakes.

° *se'nnight:* "Seven night," or a week ago Thursday.

"Any answer, Madam," said my footman.
"No," I told him.
"See that the messenger takes some refreshment.
No, no answer."   70
And I walked into the garden,
Up and down the patterned paths,
In my stiff, correct brocade.
The blue and yellow flowers stood up proudly in the sun,
Each one.   75
I stood upright too,
Held rigid to the pattern
By the stiffness of my gown.
Up and down I walked.
Up and down.   80

In a month he would have been my husband.
In a month, here, underneath this lime,
We would have broken the pattern;
He for me, and I for him,
He as Colonel, I as Lady,   85
On this shady seat.
He had a whim
That sunlight carried blessing.
And I answered, "It shall be as you have said."
Now he is dead.   90

In Summer and in Winter I shall walk
Up and down
The patterned garden-paths
In my stiff, brocaded gown.
The squills and daffodils   95
Will give place to pillared roses, and to asters, and to snow.
I shall go
Up and down,
In my gown.
Gorgeously arrayed,   100
Boned and stayed.
And the softness of my body will be guarded from embrace
By each button, hook, and lace.
For the man who should loose me is dead,
Fighting with the Duke in Flanders,°   105
In a pattern called a war.
Christ! What are patterns for?

°*Flanders:* A region in northwestern Europe, including part of northern France and western Belgium. Flanders was a site of fighting during World War I.

The speaker begins by describing herself walking down garden paths. She wears a stiff brocaded gown, has powdered hair, and carries a jeweled fan. By her own admission, she is "a plate of current fashion." Although her tone is controlled, she is preoccupied by sensual thoughts. Beneath her "stiffened gown / Is the softness of a woman bathing in a marble basin," and the "sliding of the water" in a fountain reminds the speaker of the stroking of her lover's hand. She imagines herself shedding her brocaded gown and running with her lover along the maze of "patterned paths." The sensuality of the speaker's thoughts stands in ironic contrast to the images of stiffness and control that dominate the poem: her passion "Wars against the stiff brocade." She is also full of repressed rage. She knows that her lover has been killed, and she realizes the meaninglessness of the patterns of her life, patterns to which she has conformed, just as her lover conformed by going to war and doing what he was supposed to do. Throughout the poem, the speaker's tone reflects her barely contained anger and frustration. In the last line, when she finally lets out her rage, the poem's point about the senselessness of war becomes apparent.

FURTHER READING: The Tone of the Poem

ADAM ZAGAJEWSKI (1945–   )

Try to Praise the Mutilated World   (2001)

Translated from the Polish by Clare Cavanagh

Try to praise the mutilated world.
Remember June's long days,
and wild strawberries, drops of wine, the dew.
The nettles that methodically overgrow
the abandoned homesteads of exiles.   5
You must praise the mutilated world.
You watched the stylish yachts and ships;
one of them had a long trip ahead of it,
while salty oblivion awaited others.
You've seen the refugees heading nowhere,   10
you've heard the executioners sing joyfully.
You should praise the mutilated world.
Remember the moments when we were together
in a white room and the curtain fluttered.
Return in thought to the concert where music flared.   15
You gathered acorns in the park in autumn
and leaves eddied over the earth's scars.
Praise the mutilated world
and the gray feather a thrush lost,
and the gentle light that strays and vanishes   20
and returns.

Reading and Reacting

1. Who is the speaker? Whom is he addressing?

2. In line 1, the speaker says, "Try to praise . . ."; in line 6, he says, "You must praise . . ."; in line 12, he says, "You should praise . . ."; and in line 18, he says, "Praise . . .". What is the significance, if any, of these changes in phrasing?

3. What is the mood of the speaker? Do you think he is optimistic or pessimistic?

4. JOURNAL ENTRY Though written earlier, this poem was printed in the issue of the *New Yorker* that appeared immediately after the World Trade Center towers were destroyed by terrorists on September 11, 2001. Why do you think the editors chose to reprint it then?

5. CRITICAL PERSPECTIVE The critic and poet Adam Kirsch, writing in the *New Republic*, characterizes Adam Zagajewski as a mystical poet who looks for meaning in ordinary things and situations:

> Like Rilke, Zagajewski is overcome at times by a powerful sense that the singular being of objects conceals some higher truth. For him, too, things are the sites of illumination.

What "higher truth" do the objects in "Try to Praise the Mutilated World" conceal? What do you think is the underlying message of this poem?

Related Works: "Cathedral" (p. 476), "Hope" (p. 879), "Nothing Gold Can Stay" (p. 930), "For the Union Dead" (p. 1081), "The Second Coming" (p. 1246), *Nine Ten* (p. 1334)

WILLIAM WORDSWORTH (1770–1850)

The World Is Too Much with Us (1807)

The world is too much with us; late and soon,
Getting and spending, we lay waste our powers;
Little we see in Nature that is ours;
We have given our hearts away, a sordid boon!
This Sea that bares her bosom to the moon;   5
The winds that will be howling at all hours,
And are up-gathered now like sleeping flowers;
For this, for everything, we are out of tune;
It moves us not. Great God! I'd rather be
A Pagan suckled in a creed outworn;   10
So might I, standing on this pleasant lea,
Have glimpses that would make me less forlorn;
Have sight of Proteus° rising from the sea;
Or hear old Triton° blow his wreathèd horn.

°*Proteus:* Sometimes said to be Poseidon's son, this Greek sea-god had the ability to change shape at will and to tell the future.   °*Triton:* The trumpeter of the sea, this sea-god is usually pictured blowing on a conch shell. Triton was the son of Poseidon, ruler of the sea.

Reading and Reacting

1. What is the speaker's attitude toward the contemporary world? How is this attitude revealed through the poem's tone?

2. This poem is a **sonnet**, a highly structured traditional form. How do the regular meter and rhyme scheme help to establish the poem's tone?

3. JOURNAL ENTRY Imagine you are a modern-day environmentalist, labor organizer, or corporate executive. Write a response to the sentiments expressed in this poem.

4. CRITICAL PERSPECTIVE According to M. H. Abrams in his 1972 essay "Two Roads to Wordsworth," critics have tended to view Wordsworth in one of two different ways:

> One Wordsworth is simple, elemental, forthright, the other is complex, paradoxical, problematic; one is an affirmative poet of life, love, and joy, the other is an equivocal or self-divided poet whose affirmations are implicitly qualified . . . by a pervasive sense of morality and an ever-incipient despair of life; . . . one is the Wordsworth of light, the other the Wordsworth of [shadow], or even darkness.

Does your reading of "The World Is Too Much with Us" support one of these versions of Wordsworth over the other? Which one? Why?

Related Works: "The Rocking-Horse Winner" (p. 525), "Dover Beach" (p. 1141), "She dwelt among the untrodden ways" (p. 1242), "The Lake Isle of Innisfree" (p. 1245)

SYLVIA PLATH (1932–1963)

Morning Song (1962)

Love set you going like a fat gold watch.
The midwife slapped your footsoles, and your bald cry
Took its place among the elements.

Our voices echo, magnifying your arrival. New statue.
In a drafty museum, your nakedness   5
Shadows our safety. We stand round blankly as walls.

I'm no more your mother
Than the cloud that distills a mirror to reflect its own slow
Effacement at the wind's hand.

All night your moth-breath   10
Flickers among the flat pink roses. I wake to listen:
A far sea moves in my ear.

One cry, and I stumble from bed, cow-heavy and floral
In my Victorian nightgown.
Your mouth opens clean as a cat's. The window square   15

Whitens and swallows its dull stars. And now you try
Your handful of notes;
The clear vowels rise like balloons.

Reading and Reacting

1. Who is the speaker? To whom is she speaking? What does the poem reveal about her?

2. What is the poem's subject? What attitudes about this subject do you suppose the poet expects her readers to have?

3. How is the tone of the first stanza different from that of the third? How does the tone of each stanza reflect its content?

4. JOURNAL ENTRY In what sense does this poem reinforce traditional ideas about motherhood? How does it challenge them?

5. CRITICAL PERSPECTIVE Sylvia Plath's life, which ended in suicide, was marked by emotional turbulence and instability. According to Anne Stevenson in *Bitter Fame*, her 1988 biography of Plath, in the weeks immediately preceding the composition of "Morning Song" a fit of rage over her husband's supposed infidelity caused Plath to destroy many of his books and poetic works in progress. Then, only a few days later, she suffered a miscarriage. According to Stevenson, "Morning Song" is about sleepless nights and surely reflects Plath's depression. However, in a 1991 biography, *Rough Magic*, Paul Alexander says, "Beautiful, simple, touching, 'Morning Song' was Plath's — then — definitive statement of motherhood."

Which biographer's assessment of the poem do you think makes more sense? Why?

Related Works: "The Yellow Wallpaper" (p. 421), "The Courage that My Mother Had" (p. 1059), "Those Winter Sundays" (p. 1059), "My Son, My Executioner" (p. 961), *Proof* (p. 1526).

CLAUDE MCKAY (1890 – 1948)

The White City (1922)

I will not toy with it nor bend an inch.
Deep in the secret chambers of my heart
I muse my life-long hate, and without flinch
I bear it nobly as I live my part.
My being would be a skeleton, a shell,   5
If this dark Passion that fills my every mood,
And makes my heaven in the white world's hell,
Did not forever feed me vital blood.
I see the mighty city through a mist—
The strident trains that speed the goaded mass,   10

The poles and spires and towers vapor-kissed,
The fortressed port through which the great ships pass,
The tides, the wharves, the dens I contemplate,
Are sweet like wanton loves because I hate.

Reading and Reacting

1. How would you characterize the tone of this poem?

2. How is the speaker's description of the city in the third stanza consistent with the emotions he expresses in lines 1–8?

3. The closing couplet of a Shakespearean sonnet traditionally sums up the sonnet's concerns. Is this the case here? Explain.

4. JOURNAL ENTRY What possible meanings does the phrase "the white world's hell" (line 7) have? How does it express the poem's central theme?

Related Works: "Battle Royal" (p. 297), "Saboteur" (p. 714), "The Man He Killed" (p. 865), "For Malcolm, a Year After" (p. 978), "Dinner Guest: Me" (p. 1106), "If We Must Die" (p. 1203)

ROBERT HERRICK (1591–1674)

To the Virgins, to Make Much of Time (1646)

Gather ye rosebuds while ye may,
Old Time is still a-flying;
And this same flower that smiles today,
Tomorrow will be dying.

The glorious lamp of heaven, the sun,   5
The higher he's a-getting,
The sooner will his race be run,
And nearer he's to setting.

That age is best which is the first,
When youth and blood are warmer;   10
But being spent, the worse, and worst
Times still succeed the former.

Then be not coy, but use your time,
And while ye may, go marry;
For having lost but once your prime,   15
You may forever tarry.

Reading and Reacting

1. How would you characterize the speaker? Do you think he expects his listeners to share his views? How might his expectations affect his tone?

2. This poem is developed like an argument. What is the speaker's main point? How does he support it?

3. What effect does the poem's use of rhyme have on its tone?

4. JOURNAL ENTRY Whose side are you on — the speaker's or those he addresses?

Related Works: "Where Are You Going, Where Have You Been?" (p. 573), "Greasy Lake" (p. 648), "Nice Car, Camille" (p. 862), "Cinderella" (p. 882), "The Passionate Shepherd to His Love" (p. 1202), *The Brute* (p. 1293)

DEBORAH GARRISON (1965–)

Please Fire Me (1998)

Here comes another alpha male,
and all the other alphas
are snorting and pawing,
kicking up puffs of acrid dust

while the silly little hens   5
clatter back and forth
on quivering claws and raise
a titter about the fuss.

Here comes another alpha male—
a man's man, a dealmaker,   10
holds tanks of liquor,
charms them pantsless at lunch:

I've never been sicker.
Do I have to stare into his eyes
and sympathize? If I want my job   15
I do. Well I think I'm through

with the working world,
through with warming eggs
and being Zenlike in my detachment
from all things Ego.   20

I'd like to go
somewhere else entirely,
and I don't mean
Europe.

Reading and Reacting

1. Who are the "alpha males" in the poem? Who are the "silly little hens" (line 5)?

2. What does the speaker's choice of animal reveal about her attitude toward her situation? What does it reveal about her?

3. In the last stanza, the speaker says that she would like to "go / somewhere else" (lines 21–22). Where do you suppose she wants to go?
4. **JOURNAL ENTRY** Why do you think the speaker wants to be fired? Why doesn't she simply quit?
5. **CRITICAL PERSPECTIVE** About her own poetry, Deborah Garrison has said, "I need to feel that the language in my poems is alive in the sense of talking on the phone to a friend, sharing gossip."

In what sense do you think "Please Fire Me" is like "sharing gossip"?

Related Works: "A&P" (p. 230), "Shiloh" (p. 316), "Cinderella" (p. 882), "Sears Life" (p. 907), "The Secretary Chant" (p. 948), "Barbie Doll" (p. 1211), *Beauty* (p. 1308), *Proof* (p. 1526)

MARY OLIVER (1935 –   )

The Old Poets of China (2004)

Wherever I am, the world comes after me.
It offers me its busyness. It does not believe
that I do not want it. Now I understand
why the old poets of China went so far and high
into the mountains, then crept into the pale mist.

Reading and Reacting

1. What does the first line of the poem reveal about the speaker? What is her attitude toward life and toward herself?
2. What is the world's "busyness" (line 2)? What does the speaker mean when she says that the world "does not believe / that I do not want it" (2–3)?
3. Why does the speaker envy the old poets of China? What were they able to achieve that she wants to achieve?
4. **JOURNAL ENTRY** Why do you think the speaker feels she must withdraw from the world in order to create poetry? Do you think she is right?
5. **CRITICAL PERSPECTIVE** According to Red Pine and Mike O'Connor in *The Clouds Should Know Me by Now: Buddhist Poet Monks of China*, the old poets of China were "Ch'an Buddhist poet monks (shih-seng), men of enviable literary talent who lived out their years during turbulent times in accord with old Buddha's precepts. Their work spans 1100 years, from the middle T'ang dynasty to the beginning of the twentieth century." As Buddhist monks, they withdrew from the world in hopes of achieving spiritual insight.

How does Oliver's poem express the Buddhist desire to free the individual from worldly attachments and to reach enlightenment?

Related Works: "Cathedral" (p. 476), "B. Wordsworth" (p. 757), "Please Fire Me" (p. 874), "Nothing Gold Can Stay" (p. 930), "To See a World in a Grain of Sand"

(p. 1146), "This is my letter to the World" (p. 1167), "The World Is Too Much with Us" (p. 870), *Nine Ten* (p. 1334)

Irony

Just as in fiction and drama, **irony** occurs in poetry when a discrepancy exists between two levels of meaning or experience. Consider the tone of the following lines by Stephen Crane:

> Do not weep, maiden, for war is kind.
> Because your lover threw wild hands toward the sky
> And the afrightened steed ran on alone,
> Do not weep.
> War is kind.

How can war be "kind"? Isn't war exactly the opposite of "kind"? Surely the speaker does not intend his words to be taken literally. By making this ironic statement, the speaker actually conveys the opposite idea: war is a cruel, mindless exercise of violence.

Skillfully used, irony enables a poet to make a pointed comment about a situation or to manipulate a reader's emotions. Implicit in irony is the writer's assumption that readers will not be misled by the literal meaning of a statement. In order for irony to work, readers must recognize the disparity between what is said and what is meant, or between what a speaker thinks is occurring and what readers know to be occurring.

One kind of irony that appears in poetry is **dramatic irony**, which occurs when a speaker believes one thing and readers realize something else. In the following poem, the poet uses a deranged speaker to tell a story that is filled with irony.

ROBERT BROWNING (1812–1889)

Porphyria's Lover   (1836)

The rain set early in to-night,
    The sullen wind was soon awake,
It tore the elm-tops down for spite,
    And did its worst to vex the lake:
    I listened with heart fit to break.   5
When glided in Porphyria; straight
    She shut the cold out and the storm,
And kneeled and made the cheerless grate
    Blaze up, and all the cottage warm;
    Which done, she rose, and from her form   10
Withdrew the dripping cloak and shawl,
    And laid her soiled gloves by, untied
Her hat and let the damp hair fall,
    And, last, she sat down by my side

And called me. When no voice replied,   15
    She put my arm about her waist,
And made her smooth white shoulder bare,
And all her yellow hair displaced,
    And, stooping, made my cheek lie there,
    And spread, o'er all, her yellow hair,   20
Murmuring how she loved me — she
    Too weak, for all her heart's endeavour,
To set its struggling passion free
    From pride, and vainer ties dissever,
    And give herself to me for ever.   25
But passion sometimes would prevail,
    Nor could to-night's gay feast restrain
A sudden thought of one so pale
    For love of her, and all in vain:
So, she was come through wind and rain.   30
Be sure I looked up at her eyes
    Happy and proud; at last I knew
Porphyria worshipped me; surprise
    Made my heart swell, and still it grew
    While I debated what to do.   35
That moment she was mine, mine, fair,
    Perfectly pure and good: I found
A thing to do, and all her hair
    In one long yellow string I wound
    Three times her little throat around,   40
And strangled her. No pain felt she;
    I am quite sure she felt no pain.
As a shut bud that holds a bee,
    I warily oped her lids: again
    Laughed the blue eyes without a stain.   45
And I untightened next the tress
    About her neck; her cheek once more
Blushed bright beneath my burning kiss:
    I propped her head up as before,
    Only, this time my shoulder bore   50
Her head, which droops upon it still:
    The smiling rosy little head,
So glad it has its utmost will,
    That all it scorned at once is fled,
    And I, its love, am gained instead!   55
Porphyria's love: she guessed not how
    Her darling one wish would be heard.
And thus we sit together now,
    And all night long we have not stirred,
    And yet God has not said a word!   60

Like Browning's "My Last Duchess" (p. 856), this poem is a **dramatic monologue**, a poem that includes an implied listener as well as a speaker. The speaker recounts his story in a straightforward manner, seemingly unaware of the horror of his story. In fact, much of the effect of this poem comes from the speaker's telling his tale of murder in a flat, unemotional tone — and from readers' gradual realization that the speaker is mad.

The irony of the poem, and of its title, becomes apparent as the monologue progresses. At first, the speaker fears that Porphyria is too weak to free herself from pride and vanity to love him. As he looks into her eyes, however, he comes to believe that she worships him. To preserve the perfection of Porphyria's love, the speaker strangles her with her own hair. He assures his silent listener, "I am quite sure she felt no pain." Like many of Browning's narrators, the speaker in this poem exhibits a selfish and perverse need to possess another person totally. The moment the speaker realizes that Porphyria loves him, he feels compelled to kill her and keep her his forever. According to him, she is at this point "mine, mine, fair, / Perfectly pure and good," and he believes that by murdering her, he actually fulfills "Her darling one wish" — to stay with him forever. As he attempts to justify his actions, the speaker reveals himself to be a deluded psychopathic killer.

Another kind of irony is **situational irony**, which occurs when the situation itself contradicts readers' expectations. For example, in "Porphyria's Lover" the meeting of two lovers ironically results not in joy and passion but in murder. In the next poem, the situation also creates irony.

PERCY BYSSHE SHELLEY (1792–1822)

Ozymandias° (1818)

I met a traveler from an antique land
Who said: Two vast and trunkless legs of stone
Stand in the desert. Near them, on the sand,
Half sunk, a shattered visage lies, whose frown,
And wrinkled lip, and sneer of cold command,   5
Tell that its sculptor well those passions read
Which yet survive, stamped on these lifeless things,
The hand that mocked them, and the heart that fed;
And on the pedestal these words appear:
"My name is Ozymandias, king of kings: 10
Look on my works, ye Mighty, and despair!"
Nothing beside remains. Round the decay
Of that colossal wreck, boundless and bare
The lone and level sands stretch far away.

The speaker recounts a tale about a colossal statue that lies shattered in the desert. Its head lies separated from the trunk, and the face has a wrinkled lip

---

°*Ozymandias:* The Greek name for Ramses II, ruler of Egypt in the thirteenth century B.C.

and a "sneer of cold command." On the pedestal of the monument are words exhorting all those who pass: "Look on my works, ye Mighty, and despair!" The situational irony of the poem has its source in the contrast between the "colossal wreck" and the boastful inscription on its base: Ozymandias is a monument to the vanity of those who mistakenly think they can withstand the ravages of time.

Perhaps the most common kind of irony found in poetry is **verbal irony**, which is created when words say one thing but mean another, often exactly the opposite. When verbal irony is particularly biting, it is called **sarcasm**—for example, Stephen Crane's use of the word *kind* in his antiwar poem "War Is Kind." In speech, verbal irony is easy to detect through the speaker's change in tone or emphasis. In writing, when these signals are absent, verbal irony becomes more difficult to convey. Poets must depend on the context of a remark or on the contrast between a word and other images in the poem to create irony.

Consider how verbal irony is communicated in the following poem.

ARIEL DORFMAN (1942–   )

Hope   (1988)

Translated by Edith Grossman with the author

My son has been
missing
since May 8
of last year.

    They took him   5
    just for a few hours
    they said
    just for some routine
    questioning.

After the car left,   10
the car with no license plate,
we couldn't
    find out
anything else
about him.   15
But now things have changed.
We heard from a compañero
who just got out
that five months later
they were torturing him   20
in Villa Grimaldi,
at the end of September
they were questioning him

in the red house
that belonged to the Grimaldis.   25

     They say they recognized
     his voice his screams
     they say.

Somebody tell me frankly
what times are these   30
what kind of world
what country?
What I'm asking is
how can it be
that a father's   35
joy
a mother's
joy
is knowing
that they   40
that they are still
torturing
their son?
Which means
that he was alive   45
five months later
and our greatest
hope
will be to find out
next year   50
that they're still torturing him
eight months later

and he may   might   could
still be alive.

Although it is not necessary to know the background of the poet to appreciate this poem, it does help to know that Ariel Dorfman is a native of Chile. After the assassination of Salvador Allende, Chile's elected socialist president, in September 1973, the civilian government was replaced by a military dictatorship. Civil rights were suspended, and activists, students, and members of opposition parties were arrested. Many were detained indefinitely; some simply disappeared. The irony of this poem originates in the discrepancy between what the word *hope* comes to mean in the poem and what it usually means. For most people, *hope* has positive connotations. For the speaker, however, *hope* means that his son is still being tortured eight months after his arrest. Thus, *hope* takes on a different meaning, and this irony is not lost on the speaker.

FURTHER READING: Irony

W. H. AUDEN (1907–1973)

The Unknown Citizen   (1939)

(To JS/07/M/378 This Marble Monument Is Erected by the State)

He was found by the Bureau of Statistics to be
One against whom there was no official complaint,
And all the reports on his conduct agree
That, in the modern sense of an old-fashioned word, he was a saint,
For in everything he did he served the Greater Community.   5
Except for the War till the day he retired
He worked in a factory and never got fired,
But satisfied his employers, Fudge Motors Inc.
Yet he wasn't a scab or odd in his views,
For his Union reports that he paid his dues,   10
(Our report on his Union shows it was sound)
And our Social Psychology workers found
That he was popular with his mates and liked a drink.
The Press are convinced that he bought a paper every day
And that his reactions to advertisements were normal in every way.   15
Policies taken out in his name prove that he was fully insured,
And his Health-card shows he was once in hospital but left it cured.
Both Producers Research and High-Grade Living declare
He was fully sensible to the advantages of the Installment Plan
And had everything necessary to the Modern Man,   20
A phonograph, a radio, a car and a frigidaire.
Our researchers into Public Opinion are content
That he held the proper opinions for the time of year;
When there was peace, he was for peace; when there was war,
    he went.   25
He was married and added five children to the population,
Which our Eugenist° says was the right number for a parent of his
    generation,
And our teachers report that he never interfered with their
    education.
Was he free? Was he happy? The question is absurd:
Had anything been wrong, we should certainly have heard.

Reading and Reacting

1. The "unknown citizen" represents all modern citizens, who, according to the
poem, are programmed like machines. How does the title help to establish

---

° *Eugenist:* A person who studies eugenics, the science of human improvement through genetic manipulation.

the tone of the poem? How does the inscription on the monument also help to establish the tone?

2. Who is the speaker? What is his attitude toward the unknown citizen? How can you tell?

3. What kinds of irony are present in the poem? Identify several examples.

4. JOURNAL ENTRY This poem was written in 1939. Does its message apply to contemporary society, or does the poem seem dated?

5. CRITICAL PERSPECTIVE In 1939, the year this poem was published, Auden argued in his essay "The Public vs. The Late Mr. William Butler Yeats" that poetry can never really change anything. He reiterated this point as late as 1971 in his biographical *A Certain World*:

> By all means let a poet, if he wants to, write poems . . . that protest against this or that political evil or social injustice. But let him remember this. The only person who will benefit from them is himself; they will enhance his literary reputation among those who feel as he does. The evil or injustice, however, will remain exactly what it would have been if he had kept his mouth shut.

Do you believe that poetry — or any kind of literature —has the power to combat "evil or injustice" in the world? Do you consider "The Unknown Citizen" a political poem? How might this poem effect positive social or political change?

Related Works: "A&P" (p. 230), "The Man He Killed" (p. 865), "Please Fire Me" (p. 874), "next to of course god america i" (p. 1159), "The Love Song of J. Alfred Prufrock" (p. 1172), *A Doll House* (p. 1454), *The Glass Menagerie* (p. 1998).

ANNE SEXTON (1928–1974)

Cinderella   (1970)

You always read about it:
the plumber with twelve children
who wins the Irish Sweepstakes.
From toilets to riches.
That story.   5

Or the nursemaid,
some luscious sweet from Denmark
who captures the oldest son's heart.
From diapers to Dior.°
That story.   10

Or a milkman who serves the wealthy,
eggs, cream, butter, yogurt, milk,

°*Dior:* The fashion designer Christian Dior.

the white truck like an ambulance
who goes into real estate
and makes a pile.   15
From homogenized to martinis at lunch.

Or the charwoman
who is on the bus when it cracks up
and collects enough from the insurance.
From mops to Bonwit Teller.°   20
That story.

Once
the wife of a rich man was on her deathbed
and she said to her daughter Cinderella:
Be devout. Be good. Then I will smile   25
down from heaven in the seam of a cloud.
The man took another wife who had
two daughters, pretty enough
but with hearts like blackjacks.
Cinderella was their maid.   30
She slept on the sooty hearth each night
and walked around looking like Al Jolson.°
Her father brought presents home from town,
jewels and gowns for the other women
but the twig of a tree for Cinderella.   35
She planted that twig on her mother's grave
and it grew to a tree where a white dove sat.
Whenever she wished for anything the dove
would drop it like an egg upon the ground.
The bird is important, my dears, so heed him.   40

Next came the ball, as you all know.
It was a marriage market.
The prince was looking for a wife.
All but Cinderella were preparing
and gussying up for the big event.   45
Cinderella begged to go too.
Her stepmother threw a dish of lentils
into the cinders and said: Pick them
up in an hour and you shall go.
The white dove brought all his friends;   50
all the warm wings of the fatherland came,
and picked up the lentils in a jiffy.

°*Bonwit Teller:* An exclusive department store.   °*Al Jolson:* American entertainer and songwriter (1886–1950)
famous for his blackface minstrel performances.

No, Cinderella, said the stepmother,
you have no clothes and cannot dance.
That's the way with stepmothers.   55

Cinderella went to the tree at the grave
and cried forth like a gospel singer:
Mama! Mama! My turtledove,
send me to the prince's ball!
The bird dropped down a golden dress   60
and delicate little gold slippers.
Rather a large package for a simple bird.
So she went. Which is no surprise.
Her stepmother and sisters didn't
recognize her without her cinder face   65
and the prince took her hand on the spot
and danced with no other the whole day.

As nightfall came she thought she'd better
get home. The prince walked her home
and she disappeared into the pigeon house   70
and although the prince took an axe and broke
it open she was gone. Back to her cinders.
These events repeated themselves for three days.
However on the third day the prince
covered the palace steps with cobbler's wax   75
and Cinderella's gold shoe stuck upon it.
Now he would find whom the shoe fit
and find his strange dancing girl for keeps.
He went to their house and the two sisters
were delighted because they had lovely feet.   80
The eldest went into a room to try the slipper on
but her big toe got in the way so she simply
sliced it off and put on the slipper.
The prince rode away with her until the white dove
told him to look at the blood pouring forth.   85
That is the way with amputations.
They don't just heal up like a wish.
The other sister cut off her heel
but the blood told as blood will.
The prince was getting tired.   90
He began to feel like a shoe salesman.
But he gave it one last try.
This time Cinderella fit into the shoe
like a love letter into its envelope.

At the wedding ceremony   95
the two sisters came to curry favor

and the white dove pecked their eyes out.
Two hollow spots were left
like soup spoons.

Cinderella and the prince   100
lived, they say, happily ever after,
like two dolls in a museum case
never bothered by diapers or dust,
never arguing over the timing of an egg,
never telling the same story twice,   105
never getting a middle-aged spread,
their darling smiles pasted on for eternity
Regular Bobbsey Twins.°
That story.

Reading and Reacting

1. The first twenty-one lines of the poem act as a prelude. How does this prelude help to establish the speaker's ironic tone?

2. At times, the speaker talks directly to readers. What effect do these statements have on you? Would the poem be stronger without them?

3. Throughout the poem, the speaker mixes contemporary colloquial expressions with the conventional language of a fairy tale. Find examples of these two kinds of language. How does their juxtaposition create irony?

4. JOURNAL ENTRY What details of the Cinderella fairy tale does Sexton change in her poem? Why do you think she makes these changes?

5. CRITICAL PERSPECTIVE In his 1973 book *Confessional Poets*, Robert Phillips comments on Anne Sexton's use of the Grimm Brothers' fairy tales in her book *Transformations*. According to Phillips, by transforming the Grimms' stories into symbols of our own time, Sexton "has managed to offer us understandable images of the world around us":

> ["Cinderella"] she takes to be a prototype of the old rags to riches theme ("From diapers to Dior. / That story."). Cinderella is said to have slept on the sooty hearth each night and "walked around looking like Al Jolson"— a comparison indicative of the level of invention and humor in the book. At the end, when Cinderella marries the handsome prince to live happily ever after, . . . Sexton pulls a double whammy and reveals that the ending, in itself, is another fairy tale within a fairy tale, totally unreal and unlikely.

Is the poem "Cinderella," written in 1970, still a "symbol of our own time"? In what way does it offer us "understandable images of the world around us"?

° *Bobbsey Twins:* The two sets of twins — Nan and Bert, Flossie and Freddie — in a popular series of early twentieth-century children's books. They led an idealized, problem-free life.

Related Works: "The Story of an Hour" (p. 197), "Once upon a Time" (p. 204), "The Jilting of Granny Weatherall" (p. 777), "Gretel in Darkness" (p. 852), "The Faithful Wife" (p. 909), "A Mown Lawn" (p. 991), *Beauty* (p. 1308), *Trifles* (p. 1372)

DUDLEY RANDALL (1914–2000)

Ballad of Birmingham (1969)

(On the bombing of a church in Birmingham, Alabama, 1963)

"Mother dear, may I go downtown
Instead of out to play,
And march the streets of Birmingham
In a Freedom March today?"

"No, baby, no, you may not go,   5
For the dogs are fierce and wild,
And clubs and hoses, guns and jails
Aren't good for a little child."

"But, mother, I won't be alone.
Other children will go with me,   10
And march the streets of Birmingham
To make our country free."

"No, baby, no, you may not go,
For I fear those guns will fire.
But you may go to church instead   15
And sing in the children's choir."

She has combed and brushed her night-dark hair,
And bathed rose petal sweet,
And drawn white gloves on her small brown hands,
And white shoes on her feet.   20

The mother smiled to know her child
Was in the sacred place,
But that smile was the last smile
To come upon her face.

For when she heard the explosion,   25
Her eyes grew wet and wild.
She raced through the streets of Birmingham
Calling for her child.

She clawed through bits of glass and brick,   30
Then lifted out a shoe.
"O, here's the shoe my baby wore,
But, baby, where are you?"

Reading and Reacting

1. Who are the two speakers in the poem? How do their attitudes differ? How does the tone of the poem convey these attitudes?

2. What kinds of irony are present in the poem? Give examples of each kind you identify.

3. This poem is a **ballad**, a form of poetry traditionally written to be sung or recited. Ballads typically repeat words and phrases and have regular meter and rhyme. How do the regular rhyme, repeated words, and singsong meter affect the poem's tone?

4. JOURNAL ENTRY This poem was written in response to the 1963 bombing of the 16th Street Baptist Church in Birmingham, Alabama, a bomb that killed four African-American children. How does this historical background help you to understand the irony of the poem?

Related Works: "Once upon a Time" (p. 204), "Bonny Barbara Allan" (p. 1139), "Emmett Till" (p. 1176), "If We Must Die" (p. 1203), "Birmingham Sunday (September 15, 1963)" (p. 1101), *A Raisin in the Sun* (p. 1385).

SHERMAN ALEXIE (1966–)

How to Write the Great American Indian Novel (1996)

All of the Indians must have tragic features: tragic noses, eyes, and
     arms.
Their hands and fingers must be tragic when they reach for tragic
     food.

The hero must be a half-breed, half white and half Indian, preferably
from a horse culture. He should often weep alone. That is mandatory.

If the hero is an Indian woman, she is beautiful. She must be slender   5
and in love with a white man. But if she loves an Indian man

then he must be a half-breed, preferably from a horse culture.
If the Indian woman loves a white man, then he has to be so white

that we can see the blue veins running through his skin like rivers.
When the Indian woman steps outof her dress, the white man gasps   10

at the endless beauty of her brown skin. She should be compared to
     nature:
brown hills, mountains, fertile valleys, dewy grass, wind, and clear
     water.

If she is compared to murky water, however, then she must have a
     secret.

Indians always have secrets, which are carefully and slowly revealed.

Yet Indian secrets can be disclosed suddenly, like a storm.   15
Indian men, of course, are storms. They should destroy the lives

of any white women who choose to love them. All white women
    love
Indian men. That is always the case. White women feign disgust

at the savage in blue jeans and T-shirt, but secretly lust after him.
White women dream about half-breed Indian men from horse
    cultures.   20

Indian men are horses, smelling wild and gamey. When the Indian
    man
unbuttons his pants, the white woman should think of topsoil.

There must be one murder, one suicide, one attempted rape.
Alcohol should be consumed. Cars must be driven at high
    speeds.

Indians must see visions. White people can have the same   25
visions if they are in love with Indians. If a white person loves an
    Indian

then the white person is Indian by proximity. White people must
    carry
an Indian deep inside themselves. Those interior Indians are
    half-breed

and obviously from horse cultures. If the interior Indian is male
then he must be a warrior, especially if he is inside a white man.   30

If the interior Indian is female, then she must be a healer, especially
    if she is inside
a white woman. Sometimes there are complications.

An Indian man can be hidden inside a white woman. An Indian
    woman
can be hidden inside a white man. In these rare instances,

everybody is a half-breed struggling to learn more about his or her
    horse culture.   35
There must be redemption, of course, and sins must be forgiven.

For this, we need children. A white child and an Indian child,
    gender
not important, should express deep affection in a childlike way.

In the Great American Indian novel, when it is finally written,
all of the white people will be Indians and all of the Indians will be
    ghosts.   40

Reading and Reacting

1. Who is the speaker in the poem? What is the speaker's attitude toward Native Americans? Toward the white novelists who write about them?
2. What stereotypes of Native Americans does the speaker identify? How does the speaker's tone undercut these stereotypes?
3. What does the speaker mean in the last line of the poem when he says that when the great American Indian novel is finally written, "all of the white people will be Indians and all of the Indians will be ghosts"?
4. JOURNAL ENTRY How are the characters discussed in the poem like and unlike those you have seen in films?

Related Works: "This Is What It Means to Say Phoenix, Arizona" (p. 287), "Where Mountain Lion Lay Down with Deer" (p. 859), "Indian Boarding School: The Runaways" (p. 1176), "The Man from Washington" (p. 1235), *The Cuban Swimmer* (p. 1772), *Trying to Find Chinatown* (p. 1892)

✔ **CHECKLIST** **Writing about Voice**

The Speaker in the Poem

☐ What do we know about the speaker?

☐ Is the speaker anonymous, or does he or she have a particular identity?

☐ How does assuming a particular persona help the poet to convey his or her ideas?

☐ Does the title give readers any information about the speaker's identity?

☐ How does word choice provide information about the speaker?

☐ Does the speaker make any direct statements to readers that help establish his or her identity or character?

☐ Does the speaker address anyone? How can you tell? How does the presence of a listener affect the speaker?

The Tone of the Poem

☐ What is the speaker's attitude toward his or her subject?

☐ How do word choice, rhyme, meter, sentence structure, figures of speech, and imagery help to convey the attitude of the speaker?

☐ Is the poem's tone consistent? How do shifts in tone reveal the changing mood or attitude of the speaker?

Irony

☐ Does the poem include dramatic irony? Situational irony? Verbal irony?

WRITING SUGGESTIONS: Voice

1. The poet Robert Frost once said that he wanted to write "poetry that talked." According to Frost, "whenever I write a line it is because that line has already been spoken clearly by a voice with my mind, an audible voice." Choose some poems in this chapter (or from elsewhere in the book) that you consider "talking poems." Then, write an essay about how successful they are in communicating "an audible voice."

2. Compare the speakers' voices in "Cinderella" (p. 882) and "Gretel in Darkness" (p. 852). How are their attitudes toward men similar? How are they different?

3. The theme of Herrick's poem "To the Virgins, to Make Much of Time" (p. 873) is known as **carpe diem**, or "seize the day." Read Andrew Marvell's "To His Coy Mistress" (p. 957), which has the same theme, and compare its tone with that of "To the Virgins, to Make Much of Time."

4. Read the following poem, and compare the speaker's use of the word *hope* with the way the speaker uses the word in Ariel Dorfman's "Hope" (p. 879).

EMILY DICKINSON (1830–1886)

"Hope" is the thing with feathers—   (1861)

"Hope" is the thing with feathers—
That perches in the soul—
And sings the tune without the words—
And never stops — at all—

And sweetest — in the Gale — is heard—   5
And sore must be the storm—
That could abash the little Bird—
That kept so many warm—

I've heard it in the chillest land—
And on the strangest Sea—   10
Yet, never, in Extremity,
It asked a crumb — of Me.

5. Because the speaker and the poet are not the same, poems by the same author can have different voices. Compare the voices of several poems by one poet — for example, Sylvia Plath, W. H. Auden, William Blake, whose works are included in this anthology.

CHAPTER 26

WORD CHOICE, WORD ORDER

> In a poem, each word, being equally important, exists in absolute focus, having a weight it rarely achieves in fiction. . . . Words in a novel are subordinate to broad slices of action or characterization that push the plot forward. In a poem, they *are* the action.
>
> —**Mark Strand**, Introduction to *Best American Poems of 1991*

SIPHO SEPAMLA (1932–   )

Words, Words, Words (1984)

We don't speak of tribal wars anymore
we say simple faction fights
there are no tribes around here
only nations
it makes sense you see   5
'cause from there
one moves to multinational
it makes sense you get me
'cause from there
one gets one's homeland   10
which is a reasonable idea
'cause from there
one can dabble with independence
which deserves warm applause
—the bloodless revolution   15

we are talking of words
words tossed around as if
denied location by the wind
we mean those words some spit
others grab   20
dress them up for the occasion
fling them on the lap of an audience

we are talking of those words
that stalk our lives like policemen
words no dictionary can embrace   25
words that change sooner than seasons
we mean words
that spell out our lives
words, words, words
for there's a kind of poetic licence   30
doing the rounds in these parts

Words identify and name, characterize and distinguish, compare and contrast. Words describe, limit, and embellish; words locate and measure. Even though words may be elusive and uncertain and changeable, "tossed around as if / denied location by the wind" and "can change sooner than seasons," they still can "stalk our lives like policemen." In poetry, as in love and in politics, words matter.

Beyond the quantitative — how many words, how many letters and syllables — is a much more important consideration: the *quality* of words. Which words are chosen, and why? Why are certain words placed next to others? What does a word suggest in a particular context? How are the words arranged? What exactly constitutes the right word?

Word Choice

In poetry, even more than in fiction or drama, words tend to become the focus — sometimes even the true subject — of a work. For this reason, the choice of one word over another can be crucial. Because poems are brief, they must compress many ideas into just a few lines; poets know how much weight each individual word carries, so they choose with great care, trying to select words that imply more than they state.

In general, poets (like prose writers) select words because they communicate their ideas. However, poets may also choose words for their sound. For instance, a word may echo another word's sound, and such repetition may place emphasis on both words; it may rhyme with another word and therefore be needed to preserve the poem's rhyme scheme; or it may have a certain combination of stressed and unstressed syllables needed to maintain the poem's metrical pattern. Occasionally, a poet may even choose a word because of how it looks on the page.

At the same time, poets may choose words for their degree of concreteness or abstraction, specificity or generality. A **concrete** word refers to an item that is a perceivable, tangible entity — for example, a kiss or a flag. An **abstract** word refers to an intangible idea, condition, or quality, something that cannot be perceived by the senses — love or patriotism, for instance. **Specific** words refer to particular items; **general** words refer to entire classes or groups of items. As the following example illustrates, whether a word is specific or general is relative; its degree of specificity or generality depends on its relationship to other words.

> Poem → closed form poem → sonnet → seventeenth-century
> sonnet → Elizabethan sonnet → sonnet by Shakespeare → "My
> mistress' eyes are nothing like the sun"

Sometimes a poet wants a precise word, one that is both specific and concrete. At other times, a poet might prefer general or abstract language, which may allow for more subtlety — or even for intentional ambiguity.

Finally, a word may be chosen for its **connotation**—what it suggests. Every word has one or more **denotations**— what it signifies without emotional associations, judgments, or opinions. The word *family*, for example, denotes "a group of related things or people." Connotation is a more complex matter; after all, a single word may have many different associations. In general terms, a word may have a connotation that is positive, neutral, or negative. Thus, *family* may have a positive connotation when it describes a group of loving relatives, a neutral connotation when it describes a biological category, and an ironically negative connotation when it describes an organized crime family. Beyond this distinction, *family*, like any other word, may have a variety of emotional and social associations, suggesting loyalty, warmth, home, security, or duty. In fact, many words have somewhat different meanings in different contexts. When poets choose words, then, they must consider what a particular word may suggest to readers as well as what it denotes.

In the poem that follows, the poet chooses words for their sounds and for their relationships to other words as well as for their connotations.

WALT WHITMAN (1819–1892)

When I Heard the Learn'd Astronomer (1865)

When I heard the learn'd astronomer,
When the proofs, the figures, were ranged in columns before me,
When I was shown the charts and diagrams, to add, divide, and
　　measure them,
When I sitting heard the astronomer where he lectured with much
　　applause in the lecture-room,
How soon unaccountable I became tired and sick,　　　　　　　　5
Till rising and gliding out I wander'd off by myself,
In the mystical moist night-air, and from time to time,
Look'd up in perfect silence at the stars.

This poem might be paraphrased as follows: "When I grew restless listening to an astronomy lecture, I went outside, where I found I learned more just by looking at the stars than I had learned inside." However, the paraphrase is obviously neither as rich nor as complex as the poem. Through careful use of diction, Whitman establishes a dichotomy that supports the poem's central theme about the relative merits of two ways of learning.

The poem can be divided into two groups of four lines each. The first four lines, unified by the repetition of "When," introduce the astronomer and his tools: "proofs," "figures," and "charts and diagrams" to be added, divided, or measured. In this section of the poem, the speaker is passive: he sits and listens ("I heard"; "I was shown"; "I sitting heard"). The repetition of "When" reinforces the dry monotony of the lecture. In the next four lines, the choice of words signals the change in the speaker's actions and reactions. The confined lecture hall is replaced by "the mystical moist night-air," and the dry lecture and the applause give way to "perfect silence"; instead of sitting passively, the speaker becomes active (he rises, glides, wanders); instead of listening, he looks. The mood of the first half of the poem is restrained: the language is concrete and physical, and the speaker is studying, receiving information from a "learn'd" authority. The rest of the poem, celebrating intuitive knowledge and feelings, is more abstract, freer. Throughout the poem, the lecture hall is set in sharp contrast to the natural world outside its walls.

After considering the poem as a whole, readers should not find it hard to understand why the poet selected certain words. Whitman's use of "lectured" in line 4 rather than a more neutral word like "spoke" is appropriate both because it suggests formality and distance and because it echoes "lecture-room" in the same line. The word "sick" in line 5 is striking because it connotes physical as well as emotional distress, more effectively conveying the extent of the speaker's discomfort than "bored" or "restless" would. "Rising" and "gliding" (line 6) are used rather than "standing" and "walking out" both because of the way their stressed vowel sounds echo each other (and echo "time to time" in the next line) and because of their connotation of dreaminess, which is consistent with "wander'd" (line 6) and "mystical" (line 7). The word "moist" (line 7) is chosen not only because its consonant sounds echo the *m* and *st* sounds in "mystical," but also because it establishes a contrast with the dry, airless lecture hall. Finally, line 8's "perfect silence" is a better choice than a reasonable substitute like "complete silence" or "total silence," either of which would suggest the degree of the silence but not its quality.

In the next poem, the poet also pays careful attention to word choice.

WILLIAM STAFFORD (1914–1993)

For the Grave of Daniel Boone (1957)

The farther he went the farther home grew.
Kentucky became another room;
the mansion arched over the Mississippi;
flowers were spread all over the floor.
He traced ahead a deepening home,   5
and better, with goldenrod:

Leaving the snakeskin of place after place,
going on — after the trees
the grass, a bird flying after a song.
Rifle so level, sighting so well   10
his picture freezes down to now,
a story-picture for children.

They go over the velvet falls
into the tapestry of his time,
heirs to the landscape, feeling no jar: 15
it is like evening; they are the quail
surrounding his fire, coming in for the kill;
their little feet move sacred sand.

Children, we live in a barbwire time
but like to follow the old hands back —   20
the ring in the light, the knuckle, the palm,
all the way to Daniel Boone,
hunting our own kind of deepening home.
From the land that was his I heft this rock.

Here on his grave I put it down.   25

A number of words in "For the Grave of Daniel Boone" are noteworthy for their multiple denotations and connotations. In the first stanza, for example, "home" does not simply mean Boone's residence; it connotes an abstract state, a dynamic concept that grows and deepens, encompassing states and rivers while becoming paradoxically more and more elusive. In literal terms, Boone's "home" at the poem's end is a narrow, confined space: his grave. In a wider sense, his home is the United States, particularly the natural landscape he explored. Thus, the word "home" comes to have a variety of associations to readers beyond its denotative meaning, suggesting both the infinite possibilities beyond the frontier and the realities of civilization's walls and fences.

The word "snakeskin" denotes "the skin of a snake"; its most obvious connotations are smoothness and slipperiness. In this poem, however, the snakeskin signifies more, because it is Daniel Boone who is "Leaving the snakeskin of place after place." Like a snake, Boone belongs to the natural world—and, like a snake, he wanders from place to place, shedding his skin as he goes. Thus, the word "snakeskin," with its connotation of rebirth and its links to nature, passing time, and the inevitability of change, is consistent with the image of Boone as both a man of nature and a restless wanderer, "a bird flying after a song."

In the poem's third stanza, the phrases "velvet falls" and "tapestry of . . . time" seem at first to have been selected solely for their pleasing repetition of sounds ("ve_l_vet fa_ll_s"; "_t_apestry of _t_ime"). But both of these paradoxical phrases also support the poem's theme. Alive, Boone was in constant movement; he was also larger than life. Now, in death, he has been diminished; "his picture freezes down to . . . / a story-picture for children" (lines 11–12), and he is as static and inorganic as velvet or tapestry—no longer dynamic, like "falls" and "time."

The word "barbwire" (line 19) is another word whose multiple meanings enrich the poem's theme. In the simplest terms, "barbwire" denotes a metal fencing material. In light of the poem's concern with space and distance, however, "barbwire" (with its connotations of sharpness, danger, and confinement) is also the antithesis of Boone's free and peaceful wilderness, evoking images of enclosure and imprisonment and reinforcing the poem's central dichotomy between past freedom and present restriction.

The phrase "old hands" (line 20) might also have multiple meanings in the context of the poem. On one level, the hands could belong to an elderly person holding a storybook; on another level, "old hands" could refer to people with considerable life experience — like Boone, who was an "old hand" at scouting. On still another level, given the poem's concern with time, "old hands" could suggest the hands of a clock.

Through what it says literally and through what its words suggest, "For the Grave of Daniel Boone" communicates a good deal about the speaker's identification with Daniel Boone and with the nation he called home. Boone's horizons, his concept of "home," expanded as he wandered. Now, when he is frozen in time and space, a character in a child's picture book, a body in a grave, we are still "hunting our own kind of deepening home," but our horizons, like Boone's, have narrowed in this "barbwire time."

FURTHER READING: Word Choice

JAMES WRIGHT   (1927–1980)

Autumn Begins in Martins Ferry, Ohio   (1963)

In the Shreve High football stadium,
I think of Polacks nursing long beers in Tiltonsville,
And gray faces of Negroes in the blast furnace at Benwood,
And the ruptured night watchman of Wheeling Steel,
Dreaming of heroes.   5

All the proud fathers are ashamed to go home.
Their women cluck like starved pullets,
Dying for love.

Therefore,
Their sons grow suicidally beautiful   10
At the beginning of October,
And gallop terribly against each other's bodies.

Reading and Reacting

1. Evaluate Wright's decision to use each of the following words: "Polacks" (line 2), "ruptured" (line 4), "pullets" (line 7), "suicidally" (line 10), "gallop" (line 12). Do any of these words seem unexpected, even unsettling, in the context in which the poet uses them? Can you explain why each is used instead of a more conventional word?

2. What thematic relationship, if any, do you see between line 5 ("Dreaming of heroes") and line 8 ("Dying for love")? What do these lines reveal about the people who live in Martins Ferry?

3. JOURNAL ENTRY What comment does this poem seem to be making about small towns? About high school football?

4. CRITICAL PERSPECTIVE In her 1980 essay "James Wright: Returning to the Heartland," Bonnie Costello discusses the poet's complex relationship to place and its effect on "Autumn Begins in Martins Ferry, Ohio," characterizing Wright as a kind of "fugitive" or "exile" from the past his poems reveal:

> James Wright was an elegiac poet of place. Place names echo through his lines as through deserted villages and wintry valleys, for Martins Ferry, Ohio; Fargo, North Dakota; Wheeling, West Virginia, are all dying. While he admired D. H. Lawrence's essay "The Spirit of Place" and tried to follow its guidelines, his own subject raised a special problem since it was the departure of spirit that he best portrayed. Wright tried repeatedly to call his spirit back, but his finest poems are those which catch it crossing the last hill crest or disappearing into the mist. One might argue that there is, indeed, a spirit in this place, one hopeless, ignorant, and long suffering, nonetheless beautiful and mysterious.

How does "Autumn Begins in Martins Ferry, Ohio" convey the elegiac sense of place Costello describes?

Related Works: "The Secret Lion" (p. 170), "To an Athlete Dying Young" (p. 916), "Ex-Basketball Player" (p. 946), "Pitcher" (p. 991), *Fences* (p. 1939)

ADRIENNE RICH (1929–   )

Living in Sin (1955)

She had thought the studio would keep itself,
no dust upon the furniture of love.
Half heresy, to wish the taps less vocal,
the panes relieved of grime. A plate of pears,
a piano with a Persian shawl, a cat   5
stalking the picturesque amusing mouse
had risen at his urging.
Not that at five each separate stair would writhe
under the milkman's tramp; that morning light
so coldly would delineate the scraps   10
of last night's cheese and three sepulchral bottles;
that on the kitchen shelf among the saucers
a pair of beetle-eyes would fix her own —
envoy from some black village in the mouldings . . .

Meanwhile, he, with a yawn,   15
sounded a dozen notes upon the keyboard,
declared it out of tune, shrugged at the mirror,
rubbed at his beard, went out for cigarettes;
while she, jeered by the minor demons,
pulled back the sheets and made the bed and found   20
a towel to dust the table-top,
and let the coffee-pot boil over on the stove.
By evening she was back in love again,
though not so wholly but throughout the night
she woke sometimes to feel the daylight coming   25
like a relentless milkman up the stairs.

Reading and Reacting

1. How might the poem's impact change if each of these words were deleted: "Persian" (line 5), "picturesque" (line 6), "sepulchral" (line 11), "minor" (line 19), "sometimes" (line 25)?

2. What words in the poem have strongly negative connotations? What do these words suggest about the relationship the poem describes? How does the image of the "relentless milkman" (line 26) sum up this relationship?

3. This poem, about a woman in love, uses very few words conventionally associated with love poems. Instead, many of its words denote the everyday routine of housekeeping. Give examples of such words. Why do you think they are used?

4. **JOURNAL ENTRY** What connotations does the title have? What other phrases have similar denotative meanings? How do their connotations differ? Why do you think Rich chose the title she did?

5. **CRITICAL PERSPECTIVE** In "Her Cargo: Adrienne Rich and the Common Language," a 1979 essay examining the poet's work over almost thirty years, Alicia Ostriker offers the following analysis of Rich's early poems, including "Living in Sin":

> They seem about to state explicitly . . . a connection between feminine subordination in male-dominated middle-class relationships, and emotionally lethal inarticulateness for both sexes. But the poetry . . . is minor because it is polite. It illustrates symptoms but does not probe sources. There is no disputing the ideas of the predecessors, and Adrienne Rich at this point is a cautious good poet in the sense of being a good girl, a quality noted with approval by her reviewers.

Does your reading of "Living in Sin" support Ostriker's characterization of the poem as "polite" and "cautious"? Do you think Rich is "being a good girl"?

Related Works: "Love and Other Catastrophes: A Mix Tape" (p. 165) "The Storm" (p. 281), "What Lips My Lips Have Kissed" (p. 1074), *The Stronger* (p. 1520), *Small World* (p. 1763)

E. E. CUMMINGS (1894–1962)

in Just-° (1923)

in Just-
spring when the world is mud-
luscious the little
lame balloonman
whistles   far   and wee   5

and eddieandbill come
running from marbles and
piracies and it's
spring

when the world is puddle-wonderful   10
the queer
old balloonman whistles
far   and   wee
and bettyandisbel come dancing

from hop-scotch and jump-rope and   15
it's
spring
and
      the
            goat-footed   20

balloonMan whistles
far
and
wee

Reading and Reacting

1. In this poem, Cummings coins a number of words that he uses to modify other words. Identify these coinages. What other, more conventional, words could be used in their place? What does Cummings accomplish by using the coined words instead?

2. What do you think Cummings means by "far and wee" in lines 5, 13, and 22–24? Why do you think he arranges these three words in a different way on the page each time he uses them?

3. **JOURNAL ENTRY** Evaluate this poem. Do you like it? Is it memorable? Moving? Or is it just clever?

4. **CRITICAL PERSPECTIVE** In "Latter-Day Notes on E. E. Cummings' Language" (1955), Robert E. Maurer suggests that Cummings often coined new words

---

° *in Just-*: This poem is also known as "Chansons Innocentes I."

in the same way that children do: for example, "by adding the normal *-er* or
-est (*beautifuler*, *chiefest*), or stepping up the power of a word such as *last*,
which is already superlative, and saying *lastest*," creating words such as
givingest and *whirlingest*. In addition to "combining two or more words to
form a single new one . . . to give an effect of wholeness, of one quality"
(for example, *yellowgreen*), "in the simplest of his word coinages, he merely
creates a new word by analogy as a child would without adding any shade
of meaning other than that inherent in the prefix or suffix he utilizes, as in
the words *unstrength* and *untimid*. . . ." Many early reviewers, Maurer notes,
criticized such coinages because they "convey a thrill but not a precise
impression," a criticism also leveled at Cummings's poetry more broadly.

Consider the coinages in "in Just-." Do you agree that many do not add
"shades of meaning" or provide a "precise impression"? Or do you find that
the coinages contribute to the whole in a meaningful way?

Related Works: "The Secret Lion" (p. 170), "Acrobats" (p. 827), "anyone lived
in a pretty how town" (p. 915), "Constantly Risking Absurdity" (p. 941), "Jabberwocky" (p. 993), "the sky was can dy" (p. 1017)

ROBERT PINSKY (1940 –   )

ABC (1998)

Any body can die, evidently. Few
Go happily, irradiating joy,

Knowledge, love. Many
Need oblivion, painkillers,
Quickest respite.   5

Sweet time unafflicted,
Various world:

X = your zenith.

Reading and Reacting

1. What "rules" limit the choice of words used in this poem? What determines
the order in which they are used? Where does the poet break (or bend) the
rules he has established? Can you suggest a way for him to avoid doing so?

2. Given the constraints the poet places on himself here, how successful is he?
Is the result of his efforts a poem or just a novelty? Explain.

3. JOURNAL ENTRY This poem is tightly compressed, limited to very few
words. Rewrite it as a paragraph, adding any words you think are necessary
to communicate its theme. How is your version different from the original
in what it says? In what it suggests?

4. CRITICAL PERSPECTIVE "ABC" has a very distinctive form. The poet and critic Louise Glück has stressed the importance of form in the poetry of Robert Pinsky:

> [I]n Pinsky's art, form does what we have come to believe only tone can do. That is to say, form here is not intellectual construct but rather metaphor. For the poems to be understood at all they must be apprehended entire, as shapes.

How does reflecting on the form, or "shape," of "ABC" help you to understand the poem?

Related Works: "A Primer for the Punctuation of Heart Disease" (p. 156), "I Walk in the Old Street" (p. 818), "l(a" (p. 818), "Constantly Risking Absurdity" (p. 941), *Tape* (p. 1313)

THEODORE ROETHKE (1908–1963)

I Knew a Woman (1958)

I knew a woman, lovely in her bones,
When small birds sighed, she would sigh back at them;
Ah, when she moved, she moved more ways than one:
The shapes a bright container can contain!
Of her choice virtues only gods should speak,   5
Or English poets who grew up on Greek
(I'd have them sing in chorus, cheek to cheek).

How well her wishes went! She stroked my chin,
She taught me Turn, and Counter-turn, and Stand;
She taught me Touch, that undulant white skin;   10
I nibbled meekly from her proffered hand;
She was the sickle; I, poor I, the rake,
Coming behind her for her pretty sake
(But what prodigious mowing we did make).

Love likes a gander, and adores a goose: 15
Her full lips pursed, the errant note to seize;
She played it quick, she played it light and loose;
My eyes, they dazzled at her flowing knees;
Her several parts could keep a pure repose,
Or one hip quiver with a mobile nose   20
(She moved in circles, and those circles moved).

Let seed be grass, and grass turn into hay:
I'm martyr to a motion not my own;
What's freedom for? To know eternity.
I swear she cast a shadow white as stone.   25
But who would count eternity in days?
These old bones live to learn her wanton ways:
(I measure time by how a body sways).

Reading and Reacting

1. Many of the words in Roethke's poem have double meanings — for example, "gander" and "goose" in line 15. Identify other words that have more than one meaning, and consider the function these multiple meanings serve.

2. The poem's language contains many surprises; often, the word we expect is not the one we get. For example, "container" in line 4 is not a conventional way to describe a woman. What other words are used in unusual ways? What does Roethke achieve by choosing such words?

3. Is there a difference between the denotation or connotation of the word "bones" in the phrases "lovely in her bones" (line 1) and "These old bones" (line 27)? Explain.

4. JOURNAL ENTRY How does this poem differ from your idea of what a love poem should be?

Related Works: "Women" (p. 824), "My mistress' eyes are nothing like the sun" (p. 933), "Oh, my love is like a red, red rose" (p. 944), "She Walks in Beauty" (p. 1150), *Beauty* (p. 1308)

KAY RYAN (1945–   )

Blandeur

If it please God,
let less happen.
Even out Earth's
rondure, flatten
Eiger, blanden   5
the Grand Canyon.
Make valleys
slightly higher,
widen fissures
to arable land,   10
remand your
terrible glaciers
and silence
their calving,
halving or doubling   15
all geographical features
toward the mean.
Unlean against our hearts.
Withdraw your grandeur
from these parts.   20

Reading and Reacting

1. Is "blandeur" a real word, or is it a word the poet has invented? What about "rondure" (line 4), "blanden" (line 5), and "unlean" (line 18)? Define each of these words in the context of the poem.

2. Identify the words in this poem that denote measurements or degree. Why are they used? What do they add to the poem?

3. What connotations do the words "remand" (line 11), "calving" (line 14), and "mean" (line 17) have? What do you think the poet means each word to suggest?

4. JOURNAL ENTRY Whom is the speaker addressing? What is she asking for? Why do you think she makes this request?

Related Works: "The World Is Too Much with Us" (p. 870), "Ozymandias" (p. 878), "Monet's 'Waterlillies'" (p. 1020), "The Convergence of the Twain" (p. 1184), *Nine Ten* (p. 1334)

Levels of Diction

Like other writers, poets use various levels of diction to convey their ideas. The diction of a poem may be formal or informal or fall anywhere in between, depending on the identity of the speaker and on the speaker's attitude toward the reader and toward his or her subject. At one extreme, very formal poems can be far removed in style and vocabulary from everyday speech. At the other extreme, highly informal poems can be full of jargon, regionalisms, and slang. Many poems, of course, use language that falls somewhere between formal and informal diction.

Formal diction is characterized by a learned vocabulary and grammatically correct forms. In general, formal diction does not include colloquialisms, such as contractions and shortened word forms (*phone* for *telephone*). As the following poem illustrates, a speaker who uses formal diction can sound aloof and impersonal.

MARGARET ATWOOD (1939–   )

The City Planners (1966)

Cruising these residential Sunday
streets in dry August sunlight:
what offends us is
the sanities:
the houses in pedantic rows, the planted   5
sanitary trees, assert
levelness of surface like a rebuke
to the dent in our car door.

No shouting here, or
shatter of glass; nothing more abrupt   10
than the rational whine of a power mower
cutting a straight swath in the discouraged grass.

But though the driveways neatly
sidestep hysteria
by being even, the roofs all display   15
the same slant of avoidance to the hot sky,
certain things:
the smell of spilled oil a faint

sickness lingering in the garages,
a splash of paint on brick surprising as a bruise,   20
a plastic hose poised in a vicious

coil; even the too-fixed stare of the wide windows
give momentary access to
the landscape behind or under
the future cracks in the plaster   25

when the houses, capsized, will slide
obliquely into the clay seas, gradual as glaciers
that right now nobody notices.

That is where the City Planners
with the insane faces of political conspirators   30
are scattered over unsurveyed
territories, concealed from each other,
each in his own private blizzard;

guessing directions, they sketch
transitory lines rigid as wooden borders   35
on a wall in the white vanishing air

tracing the panic of suburb
order in a bland madness of snows.

Atwood's speaker is clearly concerned about the poem's central issue, but rather than use *I*, the poem uses the first-person plural (*us*) to convey some degree of emotional detachment. Although phrases such as "sickness lingering in the garages" and "insane faces of political conspirators" communicate the speaker's disapproval, formal words —"pedantic," "rebuke," "display," "poised," "obliquely," "conspirators," "transitory"—help her to maintain her distance. Both the speaker herself and her attack on the misguided city planners gain credibility through her balanced, measured tone and through her use of language that is as formal and "professional" as theirs.

   Informal diction is the language closest to everyday conversation. It includes colloquialisms — contractions, shortened word forms, and the like — and may also include slang, regional expressions, and even nonstandard words.

In the poem that follows, the speaker uses informal diction to highlight the contrast between James Baca, a law student speaking to the graduating class of his old high school, and the graduating seniors.

JIM SAGEL   (1947–1998)

Baca Grande° (1982)

Una vaca se topó con un ratón y le dice:
"Tú—¿tan chiquito y con bigote?" Y le responde el ratón:
"Y tú tan grandota —¿y sin brassiere?" °

It was nearly a miracle
James Baca remembered anyone at all
from the old hometown gang
having been two years at Yale
    no less   5
and halfway through law school
at the University of California at Irvine
They hardly recognized him either
in his three-piece grey business suit
and surfer-swirl haircut   10
with just the menacing hint
of a tightly trimmed Zapata moustache
    for cultural balance
and relevance

He had come to deliver the keynote address   15
to the graduating class of 80
at his old alma mater
and show off his well-trained lips
which laboriously parted
    each Kennedyish "R"   20
and drilled the first person pronoun
through the microphone
like an oil bit
with the slick, elegantly honed phrases
that slid so smoothly   25
off his meticulously bleached
    tongue

° *Baca Grande: Baca* is both a phonetic spelling of the Spanish word *vaca* (cow) and the last name of one of the poem's characters. *Grande* means "large."   ° *Una . . . brassiere?:* A cow ran into a rat and said: "You — so small and with a moustache?" The rat responded: "And you — so big and without a bra?"

He talked Big Bucks
with astronautish fervor and if he
     the former bootstrapless James A. Baca   30
could dazzle the ass
off the universe
then even you
     yes you

Joey Martinez toying with your yellow   35
     tassle
and staring dumbly into space
could emulate Mr. Baca someday
     possibly
well   40
there was of course
such a thing
as being an outrageously successful
gas station attendant too
     let us never forget   45
it doesn't really matter what you do
so long as you excel
     James said
never believing a word
of it   50
for he had already risen
     as high as they go

Wasn't nobody else
from this deprived environment
who'd ever jumped   55
     straight out of college
into the Governor's office
and maybe one day
he'd sit in that big chair
     himself   60
and when he did
he'd forget this damned town
and all the petty little people
in it
once and for all   65

That much he promised himself

"Baca Grande" uses numerous colloquialisms, including contractions; conversational placeholders, such as "no less" and "well"; shortened word forms, such as "gas"; slang terms, such as "Big Bucks"; whimsical coinages ("Kennedyish," "astronautish," "bootstrapless"); nonstandard grammatical constructions, such as "Wasn't nobody else"; and even profanity. The level of language is perfectly appropriate for the poem's speaker, one of the students Baca addresses — suspicious, streetwise, and unimpressed by Baca's "three-piece grey business suit" and "surfer-swirl haircut." In fact, the informal diction is a key element in the poem, expressing the gap between the slick James Baca, with "his well-trained lips / which laboriously parted / each Kennedyish 'R'" and members of his audience, with their unpretentious, forthright speech — and also the gap between Baca as he is today and the student he once was. In this sense, "Baca Grande" is as much a linguistic commentary as a social one.

WANDA COLEMAN (1946 –   )

Sears Life (2001)

it makes me nervous to go into a store
because i never know if i'm going to
come out. have you noticed how much
they look like prisons these days? no display
windows anymore. all that cold soulless   5
lighting — as atmospheric as county jail —
and all that ground-breaking status-quo
shattering rock 'n' roll reduced to neuron
pablum and piped in over the escalators.
breaks my rebel heart. and i especially   10
hate the aroma of fresh-nuked popcorn
rushing my nose, throwing my stomach
off balance. eyes follow me everywhere i go
like i'm a neon sign that shouts shoplifter.
and so many snide counter rats want to   15
service me, it almost makes me feel rich
and royal. that's why i rarely bother to
browse. i go straight to the department of
the object of conjecture, make my decision
quick, throw down the cash and split   20

one time i had barely left this store
when i heard somebody yelling stop! stop!
i turned around and this dough-fleshed
armed security guard was waving me down.
i waited while he caught his breath and   25
demanded to search my purse i stared him
into his socks. we're outside the store,
i reminded him. if you search me, you'd
better find some goddamned something.
he took a minute to examine my eyes, turned   30
around and went back to his job, snorting
dust and coondogging teenage loiterers

Reading and Reacting

1. List the words that identify this poem's diction as informal. Do you think this informality is a strength or a weakness? Explain.

2. Look closely at the poem's sentence structure, use of all lowercase letters, and its punctuation. What does each of these elements contribute to the poem's overall effect?

3. What can you infer about the speaker from the poem's language — for example, from language like "neuron / pablum" (lines 8–9), "counter rats" (line 15), and "dough-fleshed" (line 23)?

4. JOURNAL ENTRY What comment does the poem's title make about Sears? About life? Do you think the speaker's observations are valid?

Related Works: "A&P" (p. 230), "The Lesson" (p. 642), "Saboteur" (p. 714)

MARK HALLIDAY (1949–   )

The Value of Education (2000)

I go now to the library. When I sit in the library
I am not illegally dumping bags of kitchen garbage
in the dumpster behind Clippinger Laboratory,
and a very pissed-off worker at Facilities Management
is not picking through my garbage and finding   5
several yogurt-stained and tomato-sauce-stained envelopes
with my name and address on them.
When I sit in the library,
I might doze off a little,
and what I read might not penetrate my head   10
which is mostly porridge in a bowl of bone.
However, when I sit there trying to read
I am not, you see, somewhere else being a hapless ass.
I am not leaning on the refrigerator
in the apartment of a young female colleague   15
chatting with oily pep
because I imagine she may suddenly decide to
do sex with me while her boyfriend is on a trip.
Instead I am in the library! Sitting still!
No one in town is approaching my chair   20
with a summons, or a bill, or a huge fist.
This is good. You may say,
"But this is merely a negative definition of
the value of education." Maybe so,
but would you be able to say that   25
if you hadn't been to the library?

Reading and Reacting

1. Who is the speaker? What does he reveal about himself? Whom might he be addressing?
2. How is the speaker's life outside the library different from the life he leads inside the library?
3. In lines 23–24, the speaker imagines a challenge to his comments. Do you think this challenge is valid? What do you think of the speaker's reply?
4. What phrases are repeated in this poem? Why?
5. JOURNAL ENTRY What argument is the speaker making for the benefits of the library (and for the value of education)? Is he joking, or is he serious?

Related Works: "Gryphon" (p. 248), "Teenage Wasteland" (p. 799), "When I Heard the Learn'd Astronomer" (p. 893), "Why I Went to College" (p. 1011)

FURTHER READING: Levels of Diction

BARBARA L. GREENBERG   (1932–   )

The Faithful Wife   (1978)

> But if I *were* to have a lover, it would be someone
> who could take nothing from you. I would, in conscience,
> not dishonor you. He and I would eat at Howard Johnson's
>
> which you and I do not enjoy. With him I would go
> fishing because it is not your sport. He would wear blue   5
> which is your worst color; he would have none of your virtues.
>
> Not strong, not proud, not just, not provident, my lover
> would blame me for his heart's distress, which you would never
> think to do. He and I would drink too much and weep together
>
> and I would bruise his face as I would not bruise your face   10
> even in my dreams. Yes I would dance with him, but to a music
> you and I would never choose to hear, and in a place
>
> where you and I would never wish to be. He and I would speak
> Spanish, which is not your tongue, and we would take
> long walks in fields of burdock, to which you are allergic.   15
>
> We would make love only in the morning. It would be
> altogether different. I would know him with my other body,
> the one that you have never asked to see.

Reading and Reacting

1. In what respect does this poem sound like everyday speech? What colloquial elements usually present in conversation are absent here?

2. The speaker seems to be addressing her husband. What words or phrases in the poem sound out of place given the identities of the participants in the conversation?

3. JOURNAL ENTRY How do you interpret the poem's title? In what sense is it ironic? In what sense is it not?

Related Works: "The Storm" (p. 281), "The Nymph's Reply to the Shepherd" (p. 1216), "you fit into me" (p. 961), *A Doll House* (p. 1454)

RICHARD WILBUR (1921–   )

For the Student Strikers (1970)

Go talk with those who are rumored to be unlike you,
And whom, it is said, you are so unlike.
Stand on the stoops of their houses and tell them why
You are out on strike.

It is not yet time for the rock, the bullet, the blunt   5
Slogan that fuddles the mind toward force.
Let the new sound in our streets be the patient sound
Of your discourse.

Doors will be shut in your faces, I do not doubt.
Yet here or there, it may be, there will start,   10
Much as the lights blink on in a block at evening,
Changes of heart.

They are your houses; the people are not unlike you;
Talk with them, then, and let it be done
Even for the grey wife of your nightmare sheriff   15
And the guardsman's son.

Reading and Reacting

1. Is this poem's diction primarily formal or informal? List the words that support your conclusion.

2. Besides its vocabulary, what elements in the poem might lead you to characterize it as formal or informal?

3. JOURNAL ENTRY This poem is an **exhortation**, a form of discourse intended to incite or encourage listeners to take action. Given the speaker's audience and subject matter, is its level of diction appropriate? Explain.

Related Works: "Saboteur" (p. 714), "Try to Praise the Mutilated World" (p. 869), "The *Chicago Defender* Sends a Man to Little Rock" (p. 1148)

CHARLES BUKOWSKI   (1920–1994)

Dog Fight   (1984)

he draws up against my rear bumper in the fast lane,
I can see his head in the rear view mirror, his eyes
are blue and he sucks upon a dead cigar.
I pull over. he passes, then slows. I don't like this.
I pull back into the fast lane, engage myself upon   5
his rear bumper. we are as a team passing through
Compton.
I turn the radio on and light a cigarette.
he ups it 5 mph, I do likewise. we are as a team
entering Inglewood.   10
he pulls out of the fast lane and I drive past.
then I slow. when I check the rear view he is
upon my bumper again.
he has almost made me miss my turnoff at Century.
I hit the blinker and fire across 3 lanes of   15
traffic, just make the off-ramp . . .
blazing past the front of an inflammable tanker.
blue eyes comes down from behind the tanker and
we veer down the ramp in separate lanes to the signal
and we sit there side by side, not looking at each   20
other.
I am caught behind an empty school bus as he idles
behind a Mercedes.
the signal switches and he is gone. I cut to the
inner lane behind him, then I see that the parking   25
lane is open and I flash by inside of him and the
Mercedes, turn up the radio, make the green as the
Mercedes and blue eyes run the yellow into the red.
they make it as I power it and switch back ahead of
them in their lane in order to miss a parked vegetable   30
truck.
now we are running 1-2-3, not a cop in sight, we are
moving through a 1980 California July
we are driving with skillful nonchalance
we are moving in perfect anger   35
we are as a team
approaching LAX:°
1-2-3
2-3-1
3-2-1.   40

°*LAX:* Los Angeles International Airport.

Reading and Reacting

1. "Dog Fight" describes a car race from the emotionally charged perspective of a driver. Given this perspective, comment on the appropriateness of the level of diction of the words "likewise" (line 10), "upon" (line 14), "nonchalance" (line 35), and "perfect" (line 36).

2. Many of the words in the poem are **jargon**—specialized language associated with a particular trade or profession. In this case, Bukowski uses automotive terms and the action words and phrases that typically describe driving maneuvers. Would you characterize these words as formal, informal, or neither? Explain.

3. What colloquialisms are present in the poem? Could noncolloquial expressions be substituted for any of them? How would such substitutions change the poem?

4. JOURNAL ENTRY Look up the phrase *dog fight* in a dictionary. What meanings are listed? Which one do you think Bukowski had in mind? Why?

5. CRITICAL PERSPECTIVE In a review in the *Village Voice*, critic Michael Lally defended Bukowski's poetry:

> Despite what some criticize as prose in Bukowski's poetry, there is in much of his work a poetic sensibility that, though arrogantly smart-ass and self-protective as well as self-promotional (he's the granddaddy of "punk" sensibility for sure), is also sometimes poignant, emotionally revealing, uniquely "American". . . .

Is "Dog Fight" prose, or do you see in it a "poetic sensibility"? In what sense, if any, do you find it "uniquely 'American'"? Give examples from the poem to support your conclusions.

Related Works: "Greasy Lake" (p. 648), "Chicago" (p. 1016), *The Cuban Swimmer* (p. 1772)

GWENDOLYN BROOKS (1917–2000)

We Real Cool (1959)

The Pool Players.
Seven at the Golden Shovel.

We real cool. We
Left School. We

Lurk late. We
Strike straight. We

Sing sin. We   5
Thin gin. We

Jazz June. We
Die soon.

Reading and Reacting

1. What elements of nonstandard English grammar appear in this poem? How does the use of such language affect your attitude toward the speaker?

2. Every word in this poem is a single syllable. Why?

3. Why do you think the poet begins with "We" only in the first line instead of isolating each complete sentence on its own line? How does this strategy change the poem's impact?

4. JOURNAL ENTRY Write a prose version of this poem, adding words, phrases, and sentences to expand the poem into a paragraph.

5. CRITICAL PERSPECTIVE In *Gwendolyn Brooks: Poetry and the Heroic Voice,* critic D. H. Malhem writes of "We Real Cool," "Despite presentation in the voice of the gang, this is a maternal poem, gently scolding yet deeply sorrowing for the hopelessness of the boys."

   Do you agree with Malhem that the speaker's attitude is "maternal"?

Related Works: "Where Are You Going, Where Have You Been?" (p. 573), "Greasy Lake" (p. 648), "Teenage Wasteland" (p. 799), "Ex-Basketball Player" (p. 946), *Tape* (p. 1313)

Word Order

The order in which words are arranged in a poem is as important as the choice of words. Because English sentences nearly always have a subject-verb-object sequence, with adjectives preceding the nouns they modify, a departure from this order calls attention to itself. Thus, poets can use readers' expectations about word order to their advantage.

For example, poets often manipulate word order to place emphasis on a word. Sometimes they achieve this emphasis by using a very unconventional sequence; sometimes they simply place the word first or last in a line or place it in a stressed position in the line. Poets may also choose a particular word order to make two related — or startlingly unrelated — words fall in adjacent or parallel positions, calling attention to the similarity (or the difference) between them. In other cases, poets may manipulate syntax to preserve a poem's rhyme or meter or to highlight sound correspondences that might otherwise not be noticeable. Finally, irregular syntax may be used throughout a poem to reveal a speaker's mood — for example, to give a playful quality to a poem or to suggest a speaker's disoriented state.

In the poem that follows, word order frequently departs from conventional English syntax.

EDMUND SPENSER (1552–1599)

One day I wrote her name upon the strand (1595)

One day I wrote her name upon the strand,°
But came the waves and washed it away:
Again I wrote it with a second hand,
But came the tide and made my pains his prey.
"Vain man," said she, "that doest in vain assay,   5
A mortal thing so to immortalize,
For I myself shall like to this decay,
And eek° my name be wiped out likewise."
"Not so," quod° I, "let baser things devise,
To die in dust, but you shall live by fame: 10
My verse your virtues rare shall eternize,
And in the heavens write your glorious name.
Where whenas death shall all the world subdue,
Our love shall live, and later life renew."

"One day I wrote her name upon the strand," a **sonnet**, has a fixed metrical pattern and rhyme scheme. To accommodate the sonnet's rhyme and meter, Spenser makes a number of adjustments in syntax. For example, to make sure certain rhyming words fall at the ends of lines, the poet sometimes moves words out of their conventional order, as the following three comparisons illustrate.

Conventional Word Order	**Inverted Sequence**
"'Vain man,' she said, 'that doest *assay in vain.*'"	"'Vain man,' said she, 'that doest *in vain assay.*'" ("Assay" appears at end of line 5, to rhyme with line 7's decay.")
"My verse shall *eternize your rare virtues.*"	"My verse *your virtues rare shall eternize.*" ("Eternize" appears at end of line 11 to rhyme with line 9's "devise.")
"Where whenas death shall *subdue all the world,* / Our love shall live, and *later renew life.*"	"Where whenas death shall *all the world subdue,* / Our love shall live, and *later life renew.*" (Rhyming words "subdue" and "renew" are placed at ends of lines.)

°*strand:* Beach.   °*eek:* Also, indeed.   °*quod:* Said.

To make sure the metrical pattern stresses certain words, the poet occasionally moves a word out of conventional order and places it in a stressed position. The following comparison illustrates this technique.

Conventional Word Order	**Inverted Sequence**
"But *the waves came* and washed it away."	"But *came the waves* and washed it away." (Stress in line 2 falls on "waves" rather than on "the.")

As the above comparisons show, Spenser's adjustments in syntax are motivated at least in part by a desire to preserve his sonnet's rhyme and meter.

The next poem does more than simply invert words; it presents an intentionally disordered syntax.

E. E. CUMMINGS (1894–1962)

anyone lived in a pretty how town (1940)

anyone lived in a pretty how town
(with up so floating many bells down)
spring summer autumn winter
he sang his didn't he danced his did.

Women and men (both little and small)   5
cared for anyone not at all
they sowed their isn't they reaped their same
sun moon stars rain

children guessed (but only a few
and down they forgot as up they grew   10
autumn winter spring summer)
that noone loved him more by more

when by now and tree by leaf
she laughed his joy she cried his grief
bird by snow and stir by still   15
anyone's any was all to her

someones married their everyones
laughed their cryings and did their dance
(sleep wake hope and then) they
said their nevers they slept their dream   20

stars rain sun moon
(and only the snow can begin to explain

how children are apt to forget to remember
with up so floating many bells down)

one day anyone died i guess   25
(and noone stooped to kiss his face)
busy folk buried them side by side
little by little and was by was

all by all and deep by deep
and more by more they dream their sleep   30
noone and anyone earth by april
wish by spirit and if by yes.

Women and men (both dong and ding)
summer autumn winter spring
reaped their sowing and went their came   35
sun moon stars rain

Cummings, like Spenser, sometimes manipulates syntax in response to the demands of rhyme and meter — for example, in line 10. But Cummings goes much further, using unconventional syntax as part of a scheme that includes other unusual elements of the poem, such as its unexpected departures from the musical metrical pattern (for example, in lines 3 and 8) and from the rhyme scheme (for example, in lines 3 and 4) and its use of various parts of speech in unfamiliar contexts. Together, these techniques give the poem a playful quality. The refreshing disorder of the syntax (for instance, in lines 1–2, 10, and 24) adds to the poem's whimsical effect.

FURTHER READING: Word Order

A. E. HOUSMAN   (1859–1936)

To an Athlete Dying Young   (1896)

The time you won your town the race
We chaired you through the market-place;
Man and boy stood cheering by,
And home we brought you shoulder-high.

Today, the road all runners come,   5
Shoulder-high we bring you home,
And set you at your threshold down,
Townsman of a stiller town.

Smart lad, to slip betimes away
From fields where glory does not stay,   10
And early though the laurel grows
It withers quicker than the rose.

Eyes the shady night has shut
Cannot see the record cut,
And silence sounds no worse than cheers   15
After earth has stopped the ears.

Now you will not swell the rout
Of lads that wore their honors out,
Runners whom renown outran
And the name died before the man.   20

So set, before its echoes fade,
The fleet foot on the sill of shade,
And hold to the low lintel up
The still-defended challenge-cup.

And round that early-laureled head   25
Will flock to gaze the strengthless dead,
And find unwithered on its curls
The garland briefer than a girl's.

Reading and Reacting

1. Where does the poem's meter or rhyme scheme require the poet to depart from conventional syntax?
2. Edit the poem so its word order is more conventional. Do your changes improve the poem?
3. JOURNAL ENTRY Who do you think the speaker is? What is his relationship to the athlete?

Related Works: "Nothing Gold Can Stay" (p. 930), "Ex-Basketball Player" (p. 946), "On the Death of Friends in Childhood" (p. 1189), "The Names" (p. 1156)

EMILY DICKINSON (1830–1886)

My Life had stood — a Loaded Gun (c. 1863)

My Life had stood — a Loaded Gun —
In Corners — till a Day
The Owner passed — identified —
And carried Me away —

And now We roam in Sovereign Woods —   5
And now We hunt the Doe —
And every time I speak for Him —
The Mountains straight reply —

And do I smile, such cordial light
Upon the Valley glow —   10
It is as a Vesuvian° face
Had let its pleasure through —

And when at Night — Our good Day done —
I guard My Master's Head —
'Tis better than the Eider-Duck's°   15
Deep Pillow — to have shared —

To foe of His — I'm deadly foe —
None stir the second time —
On whom I lay a Yellow Eye —
Or an emphatic Thumb —   20

Though I than He — may longer live
He longer must — than I —
For I have but the power to kill,
Without — the power to die —

Reading and Reacting

1. Identify lines in which word order departs from conventional English syntax. Can you explain in each case why the word order has been manipulated?

2. Do any words gain added emphasis by virtue of their unexpected position? Which ones? How are these words important to the poem's meaning?

3. **JOURNAL ENTRY** Why do you think the speaker might be comparing her life to a loaded gun?

4. **CRITICAL PERSPECTIVE** Writing in the *New York Times*, Elizabeth Schmidt offers this evaluation of Dickinson's poetry:

> Her formal discipline—the economy of her language and her elaborate, idiosyncratic metrical schemes—turns out to be anything but off-putting. She chose forms that readers could learn by heart, creating one of literature's great, and most unlikely, combinations of style and content. Her poems are often conceptually difficult, and yet they are also surprisingly inviting, whether they coax you to guess a riddle or carry you along to the beat of a familiar tune.

Do you find Dickinson's poetry as "inviting" as Schmidt does, or do you think a poem like "My Life had stood — a Loaded Gun" *is* "off-putting"?

Related Works: "Because I could not stop for Death —" (p. 1160). "I heard a Fly buzz — when I died—" (p. 1161), "I taste a liquor never brewed —" (p. 1162)

°*Vesuvian:* The volcano Mount Vesuvius erupted in A.D. 79, destroying the city of Pompeii.   °*Eider-Duck's:* Eider ducks produce a soft down (eiderdown) used as pillow stuffing.

✔ **CHECKLIST   Writing about Word Choice and Word Order**

Word Choice
- Which words are of key importance in the poem? What is the denotative meaning of each of these key words?

- Which key words have neutral connotations? Which have negative connotations? Which have positive connotations? Beyond its literal meaning, what does each word suggest?

- Why is each word chosen instead of a synonym? (For example, is the word chosen for its sound? Its connotation? Its relationship to other words in the poem? Its contribution to the poem's metrical pattern?)

- What other words could be effectively used in place of words now in the poem?

- How would substitutions change the poem's meaning?

- Are any words repeated? Why?

Levels of Diction
- How would you characterize the poem's level of diction? Why is this level of diction used? Is it appropriate?

- Does the poem mix different levels of diction? For what purpose?

Word Order
- Is the poem's syntax conventional, or are words arranged in unexpected order?

- Which phrases represent departures from conventional syntax?

- What is the purpose of the unusual syntax? (For example, does it preserve the poem's meter or rhyme scheme? Does it highlight particular sound correspondences? Does it place emphasis on a particular word or phrase? Does it reflect the speaker's mood?)

- How would the poem's impact change if conventional syntax were used?

WRITING SUGGESTIONS: Word Choice, Word Order

1. Reread the two poems in this chapter by E. E. Cummings —"in Just-" (p. 899) and "anyone lived in a pretty how town" (p. 915). If you like, you may also read one or two additional poems in this book by Cummings. Do you believe Cummings chose words primarily for their sound? For their

appearance on the page? What other factors might have influenced his choices?

2. The tone of "We Real Cool" (p. 912) is flat and unemotional; the problem on which it focuses, however, is serious. Expand this concise poem into a short story that retains the poem's informal, colloquial tone but uses more detailed, more emotional language to communicate the hopeless situation of the speaker and his friends. Include dialogue as well as narrative.

3. Reread "Living in Sin" (p. 897) and "Sears Life" (p. 907), and choose one or two other poems in this book whose speaker is a woman. Compare the speakers' levels of diction and choice of words. What does their language reveal about their lives?

4. Reread "For the Grave of Daniel Boone" (p. 894) alongside Delmore Schwartz's "The True-Blue American" (p. 1044). What does each poem's choice of words reveal about the speaker's attitude toward his subject?

5. Analyze the choice of words and the level of diction in several poems in this book that use language to express social or political criticism. Some poems that might work well include William Blake's "London" (p. 1145), Claude McKay's "If We Must Die" (p. 1203), Marge Piercy's "Barbie Doll" (p. 1211), Robert Pinsky's "Shirt" (p. 1213), and Ariel Dorfman's "Hope" (p. 879).

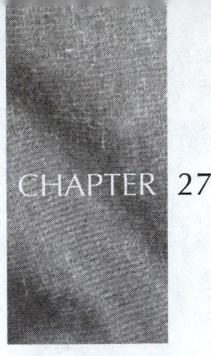

CHAPTER 27

IMAGERY

It is better to present one Image in a lifetime than to produce voluminous works.

— **Ezra Pound,** "A Retrospect"

JANE FLANDERS (1940 –2001)

Cloud Painter (1984)

Suggested by the life and art of John Constable°

At first, as you know, the sky is incidental —
a drape, a backdrop for trees and steeples.
Here an oak clutches a rock (already he works outdoors),
a wall buckles but does not break,
water pearls through a lock, a haywain° trembles.   5

The pleasures of landscape are endless. What we see
around us should be enough.
Horizons are typically high and far away.

Still, clouds let us drift and remember. He is, after all,
a miller's son, used to trying   10
to read the future in the sky, seeing instead
ships, horses, instruments of flight.
Is that his mother's wash flapping on the line?
His schoolbook, smudged, illegible?

In this period the sky becomes significant.   15
Cloud forms are technically correct — mares' tails,
sheep-in-the-meadow, thunderheads.
You can almost tell which scenes have been interrupted
by summer showers.

Now his young wife dies.   20
His landscapes achieve belated success.

° *John Constable:* British painter (1776 –1837) noted for his landscapes.   ° *haywain:* An open horse-drawn wagon for carrying hay.

He is invited to join the Academy. I forget
whether he accepts or not.

In any case, the literal forms give way
to something spectral, nameless. His palette shrinks   25
to gray, blue, white — the colors of charity.
Horizons sink and fade,
trees draw back till they are little more than frames,
then they too disappear.

Finally the canvas itself begins to vibrate   30
with waning light,
as if the wind could paint.
And we too, at last, stare into a space
which tells us nothing,
except that the world can vanish along with our need for it.   35

Because the purpose of poetry — and, for that matter, of all literature — is to expand the perception of readers, poets appeal to the senses. In "Cloud Painter," Jane Flanders uses **images**, such as the mother's wash on the line and the smudged schoolbook, to enable readers to visualize particular scenes in John Constable's early paintings. Clouds are described so readers can picture them — "mares' tails, / sheep-in-the-meadow, thunderheads." Thus, "Cloud Painter" is not only about the work of John Constable but also about the ability of an artist — poet or painter — to call up images in the minds of an audience. To achieve this end, a poet uses **imagery**, language that evokes a physical sensation produced by one or more of the five senses — sight, hearing, taste, touch, smell.

John Constable (1776–1837). *Landscape, Noon, The Haywain.* 1821. Oil on canvas, 130½ × 185½ cm. London, National Gallery.

Although the effect can be quite complex, the way images work is simple: when you read the word *red*, your memory of the various red things that you have seen determines how you picture the image. In addition, the word *red* may have **connotations**— emotional associations that define your response. A red sunset, for example, can have a positive connotation or a negative one, depending on whether it is associated with the end of a perfect day or with air pollution. By choosing images carefully, poets not only create pictures in a reader's mind but also create a great number of imaginative associations. These associations help poets to establish the **atmosphere** or **mood** of the poem. The image of softly falling snow in "Stopping by Woods on a Snowy Evening" (p. 1180), for example, creates a quiet, almost mystical mood.

Readers come to a poem with their own unique experiences, so an image in a poem does not suggest exactly the same thing to all readers. In "Cloud Painter," for example, the poet presents the image of an oak tree clutching a rock. Although most readers will probably see a picture that is consistent with the one the poet sees, no two images will be identical. Every reader will have his or her own distinct mental image of a tree clinging to a rock; some images will be remembered experiences, whereas others will be imaginative creations. Some readers may even be familiar enough with the work of the painter John Constable to visualize a particular tree clinging to a particular rock in one of his paintings. By conveying what the poet sees and imagines, images open readers' minds and enrich their reading with perceptions and associations different from — and possibly more original and complex than — their own.

One advantage of imagery is its extreme **economy**. A few carefully chosen words enable poets to evoke a range of emotions and reactions. In the following poem, William Carlos Williams uses simple visual images to create a rich and compelling picture.

WILLIAM CARLOS WILLIAMS (1883–1963)

Red Wheelbarrow (1923)

so much depends
upon

a red wheel
barrow

glazed with rain   5
water

beside the white
chickens

"Red Wheelbarrow" asks readers to consider the uniqueness and mystery of everyday objects. What is immediately apparent is the poem's verbal economy. The poet does not tell readers what the barnyard smells like or what sounds the animals make. In fact, he does not even present a detailed picture of the scene. How large is the wheelbarrow? In what condition is it? How many chickens are in the barnyard? In this poem, the answers to these questions are not important.

Even without answering these questions, the poet is able to use simple imagery to create a scene on which, he says, "so much depends." The wheelbarrow establishes a momentary connection between the poet and his world. Like a still-life painting, the red wheelbarrow beside the white chickens gives order to a world that is full of seemingly unrelated objects. By asserting the importance of the objects in the poem, the poet suggests that our ability to perceive the objects of this world gives our lives meaning and that our ability to convey our perceptions to others is central to our lives as well as to poetry.

Images enable poets to present ideas that would be difficult to convey in any other way. One look at a dictionary will illustrate that concepts such as *beauty* and *mystery* are so abstract that they are difficult to define, let alone to discuss in specific terms. However, by choosing an image or a series of images to embody these ideas, poets can effectively make their feelings known, as Ezra Pound does in the brief poem that follows.

EZRA POUND   (1885–1972)

In a Station of the Metro   (1916)

The apparition of these faces in the crowd;
Petals on a wet, black bough.

This poem is almost impossible to paraphrase because the information it communicates is less important than the feelings associated with this information. The poem's title indicates that the first line is meant to suggest a group of people standing in a station of the Paris subway. The scene, however, is presented not as a clear picture but as an "apparition," suggesting that it is unexpected or even dreamlike. In contrast with the image of the subway platform is the image of the people's faces as flower petals on the dark branch of a tree. Thus, the subway platform — dark, cold, wet, subterranean (associated with baseness, death, and hell) — is juxtaposed with flower petals — delicate, pale, radiant, lovely (associated with the ideal, life, and heaven). These contrasting images, presented without comment, bear the entire weight of the poem.

Although images can be strikingly visual, they can also appeal to the senses of hearing, smell, taste, and touch. The following poem uses images of sound and taste as well as sight.

GARY SNYDER   (1930–   )

Some Good Things to Be
Said for the Iron Age   (1970)

A ringing tire iron
   dropped on the pavement
Whang of a saw

brusht on limbs
the taste   5
of rust

Here Snyder presents two commonplace aural images: the ringing of a tire iron and the sound of a saw. These somewhat ordinary images gain power, however, through their visual isolation on separate lines in the poem. Together they produce a harsh and jarring chord that in turn creates a sense of uneasiness in the reader. This poem does more than present sensory images, though. It also conveys the speaker's interpretations of these images. The last two lines imply not only that the time in which we live (the Iron Age) is base and mundane, but also that it is declining, decaying into an age of rust. This idea is reinforced by the repeated consonant sounds in *taste* and *rust*, which encourage readers to hold the final image of the poem on their tongues. The title of the poem makes an ironic comment, suggesting that compared to the time that is approaching, the age of iron may be "good." Thus, in the mind of the poet, ordinary events gain added significance, and images that spring from everyday experience become sources of enlightenment and insight.

In short poems, such as most of those discussed above, one or two images may serve as focal points. A longer poem may introduce a cluster of images, creating a more complex tapestry of sensory impressions — as in the following poem, where a number of related images are woven together.

SUZANNE E. BERGER (1944 –   )

The Meal (1984)

They have washed their faces until they are pale,
their homework is beautifully complete.
They wait for the adults to lean towards each other.
The hands of the children are oval
and smooth as pine-nuts.   5

The girls have braided and rebraided their hair,
and tied ribbons without a single mistake.
The boy has put away his coin collection.
They are waiting for the mother to straighten her lipstick,
and for the father to speak.   10

They gather around the table, carefully
as constellations waiting to be named.
Their minds shift and ready, like dunes.
It is so quiet, all waiting stars and dunes.

Their forks move across their plates without scraping,   15
they wait for the milk and the gravy
at the table with its forgotten spices.

They are waiting for a happiness to lift their eyes,
like sudden light flaring in the trees outside.

The white miles of the meal continue,   20
the figures still travel across a screen:
the father carving the Sunday roast,
her mouth uneven as a torn hibiscus,
their braids still gleaming in the silence.

"The Meal" presents related images that together evoke silence, order, and emptiness. It begins with the image of faces washed "until they are pale" and goes on to
describe the children's oval hands as "smooth as pine-nuts." Forks move across
plates "without scraping," and the table hints at the memory of "forgotten spices."
Despite the poem's title, these children are emotionally starved. The attentive,
well-scrubbed children sit at a table where, neither eating nor speaking, they wait
for "the milk and the gravy" and for happiness that never comes. The "white miles
of the meal" seem to go on forever, reinforcing the sterility and emptiness of the
Sunday ritual. Suggesting an absence of sensation or feeling, a kind of paralysis,
the poem's images challenge conventional assumptions about the family and its
rituals.

Much visual imagery is **static**, freezing the moment and thereby giving it the
timeless quality of painting or sculpture. ("The Meal" presents such a tableau, and
so do "Red Wheelbarrow" and "In a Station of the Metro.") Some imagery, in
contrast, is **kinetic**, conveying a sense of motion or change.

WILLIAM CARLOS WILLIAMS   (1883–1963)

The Great Figure   (1938)

Among the rain
and lights
I saw the figure 5
in gold
on a red   5
firetruck
moving
tense
unheeded
to gong clangs   10
siren howls
and wheels rumbling
through the dark city.

Commenting on "The Great Figure" in his autobiography, Williams explained that
while walking in New York, he heard the sound of a fire engine. As he turned the
corner, he saw a golden figure 5 on a red background speed by. The impression was

so forceful that he immediately jotted down a poem about it. In the poem, Williams attempts to re-create the sensation the figure 5 made as it moved into his consciousness, presenting the image as if it were a picture taken by a camera with a high-speed shutter. The poet presents images in the order in which he perceived them: first the 5, and then the red fire truck howling and clanging into the darkness. Thus, "The Great Figure" uses images of sight, sound, and movement to convey the poet's experience. The American painter Charles Demuth was

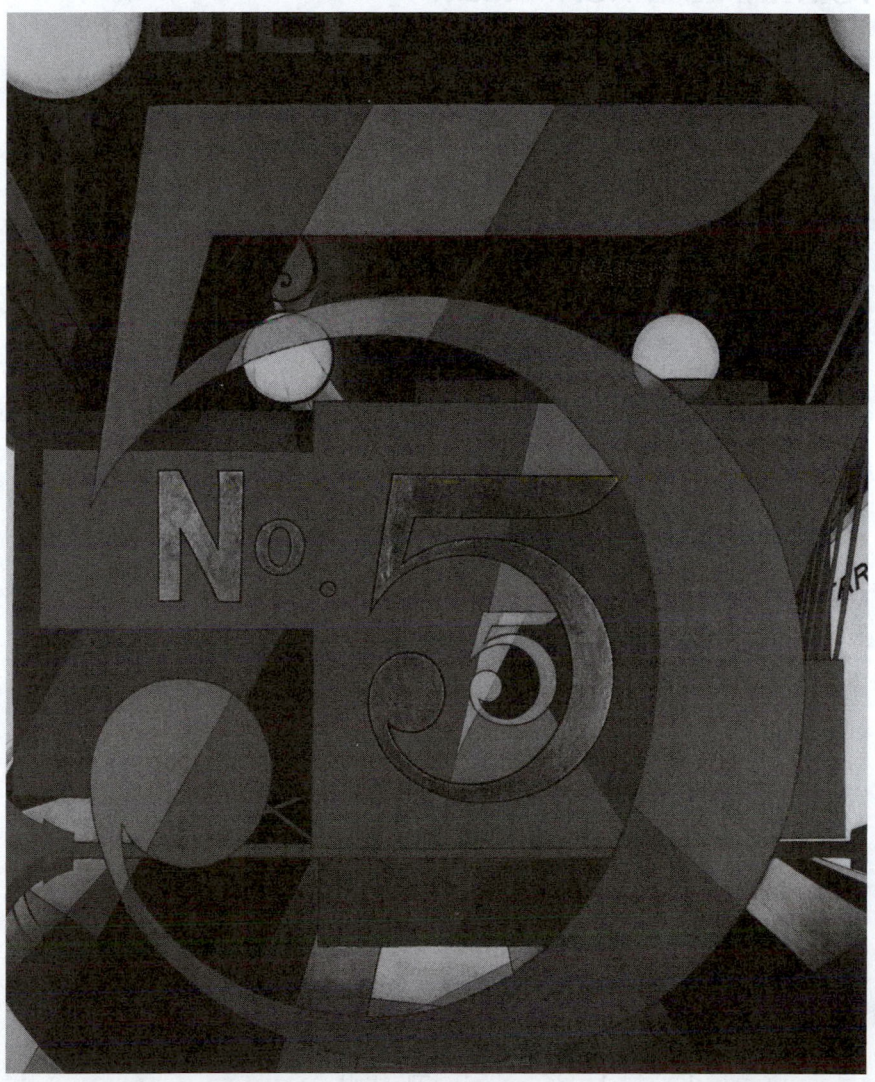

Charles Henry Demuth (1883–1935). *The Figure 5 in Gold*. Oil on composition board, 36 × 29¾ in. The Metropolitan Museum of Art, The Alfred Steiglitz Collection, 1949. (49.59.1). Photograph © The Metropolitan Museum of Art.

fascinated by the poem. Working closely with Williams, he attempted to capture the poem's kinetic energy in a painting.

> **NOTE:** A special use of imagery, called **synesthesia**, occurs when one sense is described in a way that is more appropriate for another sense — for instance, when a sound is described with color. When people say they are feeling *blue* or describe music as *hot,* they are using synesthesia.

FURTHER READING: IMAGERY

RICHARD WILBUR (1921–   )

Sleepless at Crown Point (1973)

All night, this headland
Lunges into the rumpling
Capework of the wind.

Reading and Reacting

1. What scene is the speaker describing?
2. What is the significance of the title?
3. What is the poem's central image? How do the words "lunges" and "cape-work" help to convey this image?

Related Works: "Fog" (p. 1220), "The Dance" (p. 1240), "I wandered lonely as a cloud" (p. 1067)

MICHAEL CHITWOOD (1978–   )

Division (2002)

Inside the shed, he'd rigged
an oil drip into the barrel stove
so that the used sludge from his trucks
burned with split hickory while he
passed the winter piecing together furniture.   5
Just a sideline, he'd say, aiming
down a board to judge it in or out of true.
"It fills in the down months and tacks
some cash on the end of the year."

In those same white weeks at school   10
I learned division. First, you made a lean-to
for the big number to go under. The little
number waited outside. You could add on
as many zeros as you wanted.
The answer appeared on the roof.   15

December and January passed into February
and a whole bedroom suite came together.
On the roof, the smoke swirled into 0s and 8s.

Reading and Reacting

1. This poem is divided into two stanzas. What is described in the first stanza? What is described in the second stanza?
2. In what sense is doing carpentry like learning long division?
3. List the images that appear in the poem. How do these images reinforce the similarities between the carpenter and the boy?
4. JOURNAL ENTRY Other than arithmetic, what else could the title of the poem suggest?

Related Works: "Gryphon" (p. 248), "B. Wordsworth" (p. 757), "Mathemaku No. 10" (p. 827), "Digging" (p. 1060), *Proof* (p. 1526)

LAM THI MY DA (1949–   )

Washing Rice (2001)

My mother is washing rice in late morning
A gentle wind ruffles the shade of the palms
The yellow rice glistens in rippled water
The ripe grains and the unripe look the same
They are both the color of silk, the same color   5
But why does she keep washing, washing so long?

How many unripe grains drift away from you, Mother?
How many ripe grains stay with you and talk?
When I go out tomorrow, full of life,
Will my lesson be your hand, washing rice?   10

Reading and Reacting

1. Why is the speaker's mother washing rice? What does the washing accomplish?
2. In line 6, the speaker asks, "But why does she keep washing, washing so long?" What do you think the answer to this question might be?
3. What is the significance of the speaker's observation that the ripe and unripe grains are the same color?
4. JOURNAL ENTRY According to the speaker, what lesson can he learn from watching his mother washing rice?

Related Works: "Seventeen Syllables" (p. 538), "Those Winter Sundays" (p. 1059), "To see a World in a Grain of Sand" (p. 1146), "The Chrysanthemums" (p. 783), *Trying to Find Chinatown* (p. 1892)

ROBERT FROST (1874–1963)

Nothing Gold Can Stay (1923)

Nature's first green is gold,
Her hardest hue to hold.
Her early leaf's a flower;
But only so an hour.
Then leaf subsides to leaf.   5
So Eden sank to grief.
So dawn goes down to day.
Nothing gold can stay.

Reading and Reacting

1. What central idea does this poem express?

2. What do you think the first line of the poem means? In what sense is this line ironic?

3. What is the significance of the colors green and gold in this poem? What do these colors have to do with "Eden" and "dawn"?

4. JOURNAL ENTRY How do the various images in the poem prepare readers for the last line?

5. CRITICAL PERSPECTIVE In "The Figure a Poem Means," the introduction to the first edition of his *Collected Poems* (1930), Frost laid out a theory of poetry:

> It begins in delight, it inclines to the impulse, it assumes direction with the first line laid down, it runs a course of lucky events, and ends in a clarification of life—not necessarily a great clarification . . . but a momentary stay against confusion. . . . Like a piece of ice on a hot stove the poem must ride on its own melting. . . . Read it a hundred times: it will forever keep its freshness as a metal keeps its fragrance. It can never lose its sense of a meaning that once unfolded by surprise as it went.

Explain how Frost's remarks apply to "Nothing Gold Can Stay."

Related Works: "The Secret Lion" (p. 170), "Araby" (p. 395), "Greasy Lake" (p. 648), "Shall I compare thee to a summer's day?" (p. 939), "This is my letter to the World" (p. 1167), "God's Grandeur" (p. 1188)

JEAN TOOMER (1894–1967)

Reapers (1923)

Black reapers with the sound of steel on stones
Are sharpening scythes. I see them place the hones°
In their hip-pockets as a thing that's done,

°*hones:* Stones used to sharpen cutting instruments.

And start their silent swinging, one by one.
Black horses drive a mower through the weeds,   5
And there, a field rat, startled, squealing bleeds,
His belly close to ground. I see the blade,
Blood-stained, continue cutting weeds and shade.

Reading and Reacting

1. What determines the order in which the speaker arranges the images in this poem? At what point does he comment on these images?
2. The first four lines of the poem seem to suggest that the workers are content. What image contradicts this impression? How does it do so?
3. What ideas are traditionally associated with the image of the reaper? The scythe? The harvest? (To answer these questions, you may want to consult a reference source, such as <http://www.symbols.com>.) In what way does the speaker rely on these conventional associations to help him convey his ideas? Can you appreciate the poem without understanding these associations?
4. **CRITICAL PERSPECTIVE** As Brian Joseph Benson and Mabel Mayle Dillard point out in their 1980 study *Jean Toomer*, the poet disagreed with some other artists of the Harlem Renaissance, choosing not to focus on "Negro" themes for a primarily black audience but rather to try to make his work universal in scope.

   Do you think he has achieved this goal in "Reapers"?

Related Works: "A Worn Path" (p. 505), "Traveling through the Dark" (p. 1070), "Because I could not stop for Death —" (p. 1160), "The Solitary Reaper" (p. 1242)

WILFRED OWEN (1893–1918)

Dulce et Decorum Est° (1920)

Bent double, like old beggars under sacks,
Knock-kneed, coughing like hags, we cursed through sludge,
Till on the haunting flares we turned our backs
And towards our distant rest began to trudge.
Men marched asleep. Many had lost their boots   5
But limped on, blood-shod. All went lame; all blind;
Drunk with fatigue; deaf even to the hoots
Of tired, outstripped Five-Nines° that dropped behind.

Gas! GAS Quick, boys! — An ecstasy of fumbling,
Fitting the clumsy helmets just in time;   10

° *Dulce et Decorum Est:* "The title and last two lines are from Horace, *Odes* 3.2: "Sweet and fitting it is to die for one's country." ° *Five-Nines:* Shells that explode on impact and release poison gas.

But someone still was yelling out and stumbling
And flound'ring like a man in fire or lime . . .
Dim, through the misty panes and thick green light,
As under a green sea, I saw him drowning.
In all my dreams, before my helpless sight,   15
He plunges at me, guttering, choking, drowning.

If in some smothering dreams you too could pace
Behind the wagon that we flung him in,
And watch the white eyes writhing in his face,
His hanging face, like a devil's sick of sin;   20
If you could hear, at every jolt, the blood
Come gargling from the froth-corrupted lungs,
Obscene as cancer, bitter as the cud
Of vile, incurable sores on innocent tongues,—
My friend, you would not tell with such high zest   25
To children ardent for some desperate glory,
The old Lie: Dulce et decorum est
Pro patria mori.

Reading and Reacting

1. Who is the speaker in this poem? What is his attitude toward his subject?
2. What images are traditionally associated with soldiers? How do the images in this poem depart from these associations? Why do you think Owen selected such images?
3. To what senses (other than sight) does the poem appeal? Is any of its imagery kinetic?
4. **JOURNAL ENTRY** Does the knowledge that Owen died in World War I change your reaction to the poem, or are the poem's images compelling enough to eliminate the need for such biographical background?
5. **CRITICAL PERSPECTIVE** Like many other British poets who experienced fighting in the European trenches during World War I, Owen struggled to find a new poetic idiom to describe the horrors of this new kind of war. In his 1986 biography *Owen the Poet*, Dominic Hibberd praises the "controlled and powerful anger in 'Dulce et Decorum Est' which for some readers will be the poem's most valuable quality" and goes on to note that the "organization and clarity of the first half is replaced [beginning at line 15] by confused, choking syntax and a vocabulary of sickness and disgust, matching the nightmare which is in progress."

   Give some examples to support Hibberd's statements. How do the images in the poem help establish the movement from control to confusion?

Related Works: "The Things They Carried" (p. 435), "Try to Praise the Mutilated World" (p. 869), "The Soldier" (p. 1080)

KOBAYASHI ISSA   (1763–1827)

Haiku

Not yet having become a Buddha,
The ancient pine-tree
Idly dreaming

Reading and Reacting

1. Buddhists believe that every person goes through a cycle of rebirths until he or she reaches the state of nirvana, in which the cycle of birth, death, and rebirth is broken. A key element in achieving this state is the extinction of all desire. In line 1 of the poem, who (or what) has not yet achieved nirvana and become a Buddha?

2. What two images are being compared in the poem? What insight or spiritual message is suggested by this comparison?

3. What is the tone of this poem? Do you think the speaker intends to be taken literally?

4. **JOURNAL ENTRY** How do you react to the idea expressed in this poem?

5. **CRITICAL PERSPECTIVE** In his essay series *Confessions of a Translator*, David G. Lanoue writes the following about Kobayashi Issa's haiku:

> Though Japanese children are made to memorize it, this haiku is no mere child's poem. It not only vocalizes Issa's Buddhist compassion for, and sense of karmic connection with, sentient life, it hints of a political meaning.

In what ways is this a "political" poem? In what ways does it give voice to the Buddhist idea of "compassion for all life"?

Related Works: "A Worn Path" (p. 505), "Seventeen Syllables" (p. 538), "Four Haiku" (p. 1012), "The Old Poets of China" (p. 875), "American Haiku" (p. 1014)

WILLIAM SHAKESPEARE   (1564–1616)

My mistress' eyes are nothing like the sun   (1609)

My mistress' eyes are nothing like the sun;
Coral is far more red than her lips' red;
If snow be white, why then her breasts are dun;
If hairs be wires, black wires grow on her head.
I have seen roses damasked red and white,   5
But no such roses see I in her cheeks;
And in some perfumes is there more delight
Than in the breath that from my mistress reeks.
I love to hear her speak, yet well I know
That music hath a far more pleasing sound;   10

I grant I never saw a goddess go:
My mistress, when she walks, treads on the ground.
    And yet, by heaven, I think my love as rare
    As any she, belied with false compare.

Reading and Reacting

1. What point does Shakespeare make in the first twelve lines of his sonnet?
2. What point does the rhymed couplet at the end of the poem make?
3. How is Shakespeare's imagery like and unlike that of traditional love poems? For example, how is the imagery in this poem different from that in Thomas Campion's "There is a garden in her face" (p. 1151)?
4. **JOURNAL ENTRY** How do you think the woman to whom the poem is addressed will react?
5. **CRITICAL PERSPECTIVE** During the Renaissance, poets commonly used the "Petrarchan conceit" to praise their lovers. In this type of metaphor, the author draws elaborate comparisons between his beloved and one or more dissimilar things. According to critic Felicia Jean Steele, "Traditional readings of Shakespeare's Sonnet 130 argue that Shakespeare cunningly employs Petrarchan imagery while deliberately undermining it."

    How does this poem use the "Petrarchan conceit"? How does it undercut this convention?

Related Works: "A & P" (p. 230) "The Storm" (p. 281), "How Do I Love Thee?" (p. 1074), "Love Song" (p. 1076), *The Brute* (p. 1293)

BILLY COLLINS (1941–   )

Litany (2002)

You are the bread and the knife,
The crystal goblet and the wine . . .
—Jacques Crickillon

You are the bread and the knife,
the crystal goblet and the wine.
You are the dew on the morning grass
and the burning wheel of the sun.
You are the white apron of the baker   5
and the marsh birds suddenly in flight.

However, you are not the wind in the orchard,
the plums on the counter,
or the house of cards.
And you are certainly not the pine-scented air.   10
There is just no way you are the pine-scented air.

It is possible that you are the fish under the bridge,
maybe even the pigeon on the general's head,
but you are not even close
to being the field of cornflowers at dusk. 15

And a quick look in the mirror will show
that you are neither the boots in the corner
nor the boat asleep in its boathouse.

It might interest you to know,
speaking of the plentiful imagery of the world, 20
that I am the sound of rain on the roof.

I also happen to be the shooting star,
the evening paper blowing down an alley,
and the basket of chestnuts on the kitchen table.

I am also the moon in the trees 25
and the blind woman's tea cup.
But don't worry, I am not the bread and the knife.
You are still the bread and the knife.
You will always be the bread and the knife,
not to mention the crystal goblet and — somehow — 30
the wine.

Reading and Reacting

1. A *litany* is a prayer, but it can also refer to a listing, catalog, or inventory. In what sense is this poem a litany?

2. What images does the speaker associate with himself? What images does he associate with the person he is addressing? What do these images reveal about the speaker? About his attitude toward the person he is addressing?

3. How would you describe the tone of this poem? How do the images help the poet create this tone?

4. **JOURNAL ENTRY** What images could you associate with yourself? What images could you definitely *not* associate with yourself? (Look at the fourth stanza of the poem, for example.)

5. **CRITICAL PERSPECTIVE** Writer and critic John Updike wrote the following about poet Billy Collins:

   > Billy Collins writes lovely poems — lovely in a way almost nobody's since Roethke's are. Limpid, gently and consistently startling, more serious than they seem, they describe all the worlds that are and were and some others besides.

   What "worlds" are being described in this poem? In what sense is this poem "startling" or "more serious" than it seems to be?

Related Works: "Love and Other Catastrophes: A Mix Tape" (p. 165), "The Story of an Hour" (p. 197), "Nice Car, Camille" (p. 862), "Cinderella" (p. 882), "I Knew a Woman" (p. 901), "Metaphors" (p. 945), *Small World* (p. 1763)

OCTAVIO PAZ (1914–1998)

Daybreak

Hands and lips of wind
heart of water
            eucalyptus
campground of the clouds
the life that is born every day   5
the death that is born every life

I rub my eyes:
the sky walks the land

Reading and Reacting

1. What are the connotations of the word *daybreak?*
2. What images does the speaker use to evoke daybreak? What other images
could he have used?
3. The poem is visually divided into three parts. What idea does each part express?
press?
4. JOURNAL ENTRY How would you describe the tone of this poem? How do
the images help establish this tone?

Related Works: "The Chrysanthemums" (p. 783), "Summer" (p. 1067), "Morning Song" (p. 1071), "Parting at Morning" (p. 1074), "Haiku" (p. 1013), "Spring and All" (p. 1022), "In Praise of Han Shan" (p. 1243), "Aubade" (p. 1198).

OCTAVIO PAZ (1914–1998)

Nightfall

What sustains it,
half-open, the clarity of nightfall,
the light let loose in the gardens?

All the branches,
conquered by the weight of birds,   5
lean toward the darkness.

Pure, self-absorbed moments
still gleam
on the fences.

Receiving night,   10
the groves become
hushed fountains.

A bird falls,
the grass grows dark,
edges blur, lime is black,   15
the world is less credible

Reading and Reacting

1. Does the speaker present nightfall as something that has positive or negative connotations? Explain.

2. Each of the five stanzas in the poem presents an image. What feature of nightfall does each image express?

3. What does the speaker mean in the last line when he says that nightfall makes the world "less credible"?

4. JOURNAL ENTRY What images do you associate with nightfall? How are these images like and unlike those in the poem?

5. CRITICAL PERSPECTIVE The esteemed poetry critic Helen Vendler noted the following about the relationships between reality and fantasy in the work of Octavio Paz:

> For Paz, poetry is a brink, a precipice, an abyss, where silent before a void, the poet leaves historical time to reenter the time of desire, a time always with us, for which our myths of the Golden Age are only a representation.

In what ways does the speaker of these two poems "leave historical time" to "reenter a time of desire"? What is desired in these poems? How do these desires differ from waking desires? How do they differ from each other from nightfall to daybreak?

Related Works: "Araby" (p. 395), "Gretel in Darkness" (p. 852), "Harlem" (p. 940), Traveling through the Dark" (p. 1070), "Meeting at Night" (p. 1073), "Anecdote of the Jar" (p. 1229)

✔ CHECKLIST   Writing about Imagery
☐ Do the images in the poem appeal to the sense of sight, hearing, taste, touch, or smell?
☐ Does the poem depend on a single image or on several different images?
☐ Does the poem depend on a cluster of related images?
☐ What details make the images memorable?
☐ What mood do the images create?
☐ Are the images static or kinetic?
☐ How do the poem's images help to convey its theme?
☐ How effective are the images? How do they enhance your enjoyment of the poem?

WRITING SUGGESTIONS: Imagery

1. How are short poems such as "Some Good Things to Be Said for the Iron Age" (p. 924) and "In a Station of the Metro" (p. 924) like and unlike **haiku**?

2. After rereading "Cloud Painter" (p. 921) and "The Great Figure" (p. 926), read "Musée des Beaux Arts" (p. 1051), and study the corresponding paintings (*Landscape, Noon, the Haywain* on page 922; *The Figure 5 in Gold* on page 927; and *Landscape with the Fall of Icarus*, on page 1052, respectively). Then, write an essay in which you draw some conclusions about the differences between artistic and poetic images.

3. Reread "The Meal" (p. 925) and the discussion that accompanies it. Then analyze the role of imagery in the depiction of the parent/child relationships in "Washing Rice" (p. 929) and "My Papa's Waltz" (p. 1058). How does each poem's imagery convey the nature of the relationship it describes?

4. Write an essay in which you discuss the color imagery in "Nothing Gold Can Stay" (p. 930) and "Reapers" (p. 930). In what way does color reinforce the themes of these poems?

5. Sometimes imagery can be used to make a comment about the society in which a scene takes place. Choose two poems in which imagery functions in this way —"For the Union Dead" (p. 1081) or "The *Chicago Defender* Sends a Man to Little Rock" (p. 1148), for example — and discuss how the images chosen reinforce the social comment each poem makes.

CHAPTER 28

FIGURES OF SPEECH

The metaphor is probably the most fertile power possessed by man.

—José Ortega y Gasset

WILLIAM SHAKESPEARE (1564–1616)

Shall I compare thee to a summer's day? (1609)

Shall I compare thee to a summer's day?
Thou art more lovely and more temperate.
Rough winds do shake the darling buds of May,
And summer's lease hath all too short a date.
Sometime too hot the eye of heaven shines,   5
And often is his gold complexion dimmed;
And every fair from fair sometimes declines,
By chance, or nature's changing course, untrimmed.
But thy eternal summer shall not fade,
Nor lose possession of that fair thou ow'st;°   10
Nor shall death brag thou wand'rest in his shade,
When in eternal lines to time thou grow'st.
    So long as men can breathe or eyes can see,
    So long lives this, and this gives life to thee.

Although writers experiment with language in all kinds of literary works, poets in particular recognize the power of a figure of speech to take readers beyond the literal meaning of a word. For this reason, **figures of speech**—expressions that use words to achieve effects beyond the power of ordinary language — are more prominent in poetry than in other kinds of writing. For example, the sonnet above compares a loved one to a summer's day in order to make the point that, unlike the fleeting summer, the loved one will — within the poem — remain forever young. But this sonnet goes beyond the obvious equation (loved one = summer's day): the speaker's assertion that his loved one will live forever in his poem

---

° *that fair thou ow'st:* That beauty you possess.

actually says more about his confidence in his own talent and reputation (and about the power of language) than about the loved one's beauty.

Simile, Metaphor, and Personification

When William Wordsworth opens a poem with "I wandered lonely as a cloud" (p. 1067), he conveys a good deal more than he would if he simply began, "I wandered, lonely." By comparing himself in his loneliness to a cloud, the speaker suggests that like the cloud he is a part of nature and that he too is drifting, passive, blown by winds, and lacking will or substance. Thus, by using a figure of speech, the poet can suggest a wide variety of feelings and associations in very few words. (The phrase "I wandered lonely as a cloud" is a **simile**, a comparison between two unlike items that uses *like* or *as*. When an imaginative comparison between two unlike items does not use *like* or *as*—that is, when it says "a *is* b" rather than "a is *like* b"—it is a **metaphor**.)

Accordingly, when the speaker in Adrienne Rich's "Living in Sin" (p. 897) speaks of "daylight coming / like a relentless milkman up the stairs," she is using a strikingly original simile to suggest that daylight brings not the conventional associations of promise and awakening but rather a stale, never-ending routine that is greeted without enthusiasm. This idea is consistent with the rest of the poem, an account of an unfulfilling relationship. However, when the speaker in the Audre Lorde poem on page 942 says, "Rooming houses are old women," she uses a metaphor, equating two elements to stress their common associations with emptiness, transience, and hopelessness. At the same time, by identifying rooming houses as old women, Lorde is using **personification**, a special kind of comparison, closely related to metaphor, that gives life or human characteristics to inanimate objects or abstract ideas.

Sometimes, as in Wordsworth's "I wandered lonely as a cloud," a single brief simile or metaphor can be appreciated for what it communicates on its own. At other times, however, a simile or metaphor may be one of several related figures of speech that work together to convey a poem's meaning. The following poem, for example, presents a series of related similes. Together, they suggest the depth of the problem the poem explores in a manner that each individual simile could not do on its own.

LANGSTON HUGHES   (1902–1967)

Harlem   (1951)

What happens to a dream deferred?

Does it dry up
like a raisin in the sun?
Or fester like a sore —

And then run?   5
Does it stink like rotten meat?
Or crust and sugar over —
like a syrupy sweet?

Maybe it just sags
like a heavy load.   10

Or does it explode?

The dream to which Hughes alludes in this poem is the dream of racial equality. It is also the American Dream — or, by extension, any important unrealized dream. His speaker offers six tentative answers to the question asked in the poem's first line, and five of the six are presented as similes. As the poem unfolds, the speaker considers different alternatives: the dream can shrivel up and die, fester, decay, crust over — or sag under the weight of the burden those who hold the dream must carry. In each case, the speaker transforms an abstract entity — a dream — into a concrete item — a raisin in the sun, a sore, rotten meat, syrupy candy, a heavy load. The final line, italicized for emphasis, gains power less from what it says than from what it leaves unsaid. Unlike the other alternatives explored in the poem, *"Or does it explode?"* is not presented as a simile. Nevertheless, because of the pattern of figurative language the poem has established, readers can supply the other, unspoken half of the comparison: "... like a bomb."

Sometimes a single extended simile or extended metaphor is developed throughout a poem. The following poem develops an **extended simile**, comparing a poet to an acrobat.

LAWRENCE FERLINGHETTI (1919–   )

Constantly Risking Absurdity (1958)

Constantly risking absurdity
              and death
      whenever he performs
           above the heads
                 of his audience   5
the poet like an acrobat
           climbs on rime
           to a high wire of his own making
and balancing on eyebeams
           above a sea of faces   10
      paces his way
           to the other side of day
     performing entrechats
          and sleight-of-foot tricks
and other high theatrics   15
          and all without mistaking

any thing
for what it may not be
For he's the super realist
who must perforce perceive   20
taut truth
before the taking of each stance or step
in his supposed advance
toward that still higher perch
where Beauty stands and waits   25
with gravity
to start her death-defying leap
And he
a little charleychaplin man
who may or may not catch   30
her fair eternal form
spreadeagled in the empty air
of existence

In his extended comparison of a poet and an acrobat, Ferlinghetti characterizes the poet as a circus performer, at once swinging recklessly on a trapeze and balancing carefully on a tightrope.

What the poem suggests is that the poet, like an acrobat, works hard at his craft but manages to make it all look easy. Something of an exhibitionist, the poet is innovative and creative, taking impossible chances yet also building on traditional skills in his quest for truth and beauty. Moreover, like an acrobat, the poet is balanced "on eyebeams / above a sea of faces," for he too depends on audience reaction to help him keep his performance focused. The poet may be "the super realist," but he also has plenty of playful tricks up his sleeve: "entrechats / and sleight-of-foot tricks / and other high theatrics," including puns ("above the heads / of his audience"), unexpected rhyme ("climbs on rime"), alliteration ("taut truth"), coinages ("a little charleychaplin man"), and all the other linguistic acrobatics available to poets. (Even the arrangement of the poem's lines on the page suggests the acrobatics it describes.) Like these tricks, the poem's central simile is a whimsical one, perhaps suggesting that Ferlinghetti is poking fun at poets who take their craft too seriously. In any case, the simile helps him to illustrate the acrobatic possibilities of language in a fresh and original manner.

The following poem develops an **extended metaphor**, personifying rooming houses as old women.

AUDRE LORDE   (1934–1992)

Rooming houses are old women   (1968)

Rooming houses are old women
rocking dark windows into their whens

waiting incomplete circles
rocking
rent office to stoop to   5
community bathrooms to gas rings and
under-bed boxes of once useful garbage
city issued with a twice monthly check
and the young men next door
with their loud midnight parties   10
and fishy rings left in the bathtub
no longer arouse them
from midnight to mealtime no stops inbetween
light breaking to pass through jumbled up windows
and who was it who married the widow that Buzzie's   15
son messed with?

To Welfare and insult form the slow shuffle
from dayswork to shopping bags
heavy with leftovers
Rooming houses
are old women waiting   20
searching
through darkening windows
the end or beginning of agony
old women seen through half-ajar doors
hoping   25
they are not waiting
but being
the entrance to somewhere
unknown and desired
but not new.   30

So closely does Lorde equate rooming houses and women in this poem that at times it is difficult to tell which of the two is actually the poem's subject. Despite the poem's assertion, rooming houses are *not* old women; however, they are *comparable to* the old women who live there because their walls enclose a lifetime of disappointments as well as the physical detritus of life. Like the old women, rooming houses are in decline, rocking away their remaining years. And, like the houses they inhabit, these women's boundaries are fixed — "rent office to stoop to / community bathrooms to gas rings" — and their hopes and expectations are few. They are surrounded by other people's loud parties, but their own lives have been reduced to a "slow shuffle" to nowhere, a hopeless, frightened — and perhaps pointless — "waiting / searching." Over time, the women and the places in which they live have become one. By using an unexpected comparison between two seemingly unrelated entities, the poem illuminates both the essence of the rooming houses and the essence of their elderly occupants.

FURTHER READING: Simile, Metaphor, and Personification

ROBERT BURNS (1759–1796)

Oh, my love is like a red, red rose (1796)

Oh, my love is like a red, red rose
  That's newly sprung in June;
My love is like the melody
  That's sweetly played in tune.

So fair art thou, my bonny lass,   5
  So deep in love am I;
And I will love thee still, my dear,
  Till a' the seas gang° dry.

Till a' the seas gang dry, my dear,
  And the rocks melt wi' the sun;   10
And I will love thee still, my dear,
  While the sands o' life shall run.

And fare thee weel, my only love!
  And fare thee weel awhile!
And I will come again, my love   15
  Though it were ten thousand mile.

Reading and Reacting

1. Why does the speaker compare his love to a rose? What other simile is used in the poem? For what purpose is it used?
2. Why do you suppose Burns begins his poem with similes? Would moving them to the end change the poem's impact?
3. Where does the speaker seem to exaggerate the extent of his love? Why does he exaggerate? Do you think this exaggeration weakens the poem? Explain.

Related Works: "Araby" (p. 395), "My mistress' eyes are nothing like the sun" (p. 933), "How Do I Love Thee?" (p. 1074), "Baca Grande" (p. 905), "To His Coy Mistress" (p. 957), *The Brute* (p. 1293)

N. SCOTT MOMADAY (1934–   )

Simile (1974)

What did we say to each other
that now we are as the deer
who walk in single file

°*gang:* Go.

with heads high
with ears forward
with eyes watchful
with hooves always placed on firm ground
in whose limbs there is latent flight

Reading and Reacting

1. In what sense are the speaker and the person he is speaking to like the deer he describes in this extended simile? In what sense are their limbs in "latent flight" (line 8)?
2. Without using similes or metaphors, paraphrase this poem.
3. This entire poem consists of a single sentence, but it has no punctuation. Do you see this as a problem? What punctuation marks, if any, would you add? Why?
4. **JOURNAL ENTRY** What do you suppose the speaker and the person he addresses might have said to each other to inspire the feelings described in this poem?

Related Works: "The Disappearance" (p. 371), "Comparatives" (p. 981), "Let me not to the marriage of true minds" (p. 1221)

SYLVIA PLATH (1932–1963)

Metaphors (1960)

I'm a riddle in nine syllables,
An elephant, a ponderous house,
A melon strolling on two tendrils.
O red fruit, ivory, fine timbers!
This loaf's big with its yeasty rising.   5
Money's new-minted in this fat purse.
I'm a means, a stage, a cow in calf.
I've eaten a bag of green apples,
Boarded the train there's no getting off.

Reading and Reacting

1. The speaker in this poem is a pregnant woman. Do all the metaphors seem appropriate? For instance, in what sense is the speaker "a means, a stage" (line 5)?
2. If you were going to expand this poem, what other metaphors (or similes) would you add?
3. What are the "nine syllables" to which the speaker refers in the poem's first line? What significance does the number *nine* have in terms of the poem's subject? In terms of its form?

4. JOURNAL ENTRY Would you say the speaker has a positive, negative, or neutral attitude toward her pregnancy? Which metaphors give you this impression?

Related Works: "I Stand Here Ironing" (p. 309), "My Son, My Executioner" (p. 961), "Waiting with Two Members of a Motorcycle Gang for My Child to Be Born" (p. 1171), "A Blessing from My Sixteen Years' Son" (p. 1189), "Morning Song" (p. 871)

JOHN UPDIKE (1932–   )

Ex-Basketball Player (1958)

Pearl Avenue runs past the high-school lot,
Bends with the trolley tracks, and stops, cut off
Before it has a chance to go two blocks,
At Colonel McComsky Plaza. Berth's Garage
Is on the corner facing west, and there,   5
Most days, you'll find Flick Webb, who helps Berth out.

Flick stands tall among the idiot pumps—
Five on a side, the old bubble-head style,
Their rubber elbows hanging loose and low.
One's nostrils are two S's, and his eyes   10
An E and O.° And one is squat, without
A head at all—more of a football type.

Once Flick played for the high-school team, the Wizards.
He was good: in fact, the best. In '46
He bucketed three hundred ninety points,   15
A county record still. The ball loved Flick.
I saw him rack up thirty-eight or forty
In one home game. His hands were like wild birds.

He never learned a trade, he just sells gas,
Checks oil, and changes flats. Once in a while,   20
As a gag, he dribbles an inner tube,
But most of us remember anyway.
His hands are fine and nervous on the lug wrench.
It makes no difference to the lug wrench, though.

Off work, he hangs around Mae's luncheonette.   25
Grease-gray and kind of coiled, he plays pinball,
Smokes those thin cigars, nurses lemon phosphates.
Flick seldom says a word to Mae, just nods

° *ESSO:* Former name of Exxon.

Beyond her face toward bright applauding tiers
Of Necco Wafers, Nibs, and Juju Beads.   30

Reading and Reacting

1. Explain the use of personification in the second stanza and in the poem's last two lines. What two elements make up each figure of speech? In what sense are the two elements in each pair comparable?
2. What other figures of speech can you identify in the poem? How do these figures of speech work together to communicate the poem's central theme?
3. **JOURNAL ENTRY** Who do you think this poem's speaker might be? What is his attitude toward Flick Webb? Do you think Flick himself shares this assessment? Explain.

Related Works: "Miss Brill" (p. 235), "Autumn Begins in Martins Ferry, Ohio" (p. 896), "To an Athlete Dying Young" (p. 916), "Sadie and Maud" (p. 970), *Death of a Salesman* (p. 1581)

RANDALL JARRELL (1914–1965)

The Death of the Ball Turret Gunner° (1945)

From my mother's sleep I fell into the State
And I hunched in its belly till my wet fur froze.
Six miles from earth, loosed from its dream of life,
I woke to black flak and the nightmare fighters.
When I died they washed me out of the turret with a hose.   5

Reading and Reacting

1. Who is the speaker? To what does he compare himself in the poem's first two lines? What words establish this comparison?
2. Contrast the speaker's actual identity with the one he creates for himself in lines 1–2. What elements of his actual situation do you think lead him to characterize himself as he does in these lines?
3. **JOURNAL ENTRY** Both this poem and "Dulce et Decorum Est" (p. 931) use figures of speech to describe the horrors of war. Which poem has a greater impact on you? How does the poem's figurative language contribute to this impact?
4. **CRITICAL PERSPECTIVE** In a 1974 article, Frances Ferguson criticizes "The Death of the Ball Turret Gunner," arguing that the poem "thoroughly manifests the lack of a middle between the gunner's birth and his death. . . . Because the poem presents a man who seems to have lived in order to die, we forget the fiction that he must have lived." However, in a 1978 explication,

---

° *Ball turret gunner:* World War II machine gunner positioned upside-down in a plexiglass sphere in the belly of a fighter plane.

Patrick J. Horner writes that the "manipulation of time reveals the stunning brevity of the gunner's waking life and the State's total disregard for that phenomenon. . . . Because of the telescoping of time, [the poem] resonates with powerful feeling."

With which critic do you agree? Do you see the "lack of a middle" as a positive or negative quality of this poem?

Related Works: "The Things They Carried" (p. 435), "The Soldier" (p. 1080), "An Irish Airman Foresees His Death" (p. 1081)

MARGE PIERCY   (1936–)

The Secretary Chant   (1973)

My hips are a desk.
From my ears hang
chains of paper clips.
Rubber bands form my hair.
My breasts are wells of mimeograph ink.   5
My feet bear casters.
Buzz. Click.
My head is a badly organized file.
My head is a switchboard
where crossed lines crackle.   10
Press my fingers
and in my eyes appear
credit and debit.
Zing. Tinkle.
My navel is a reject button.   15
From my mouth issue canceled reams.
Swollen, heavy, rectangular
I am about to be delivered
of a baby
Xerox machine.   20
File me under W
because I wonce
was
a woman.

Reading and Reacting

1. Examine each of the poem's figures of speech. Do they all make reasonable comparisons, or are some far-fetched or hard to visualize? Explain the relationship between the secretary and each item with which she is compared.
2. **JOURNAL ENTRY** Using as many metaphors and similes as you can, write a "chant" about a job you have held.

3. CRITICAL PERSPECTIVE In a review of a recent collection of Piercy's poetry, critic Sandra Gilbert notes instances of "a kind of bombast" (pompous language) and remarks, "As most poets realize, political verse is almost the hardest kind to write."

In what sense can "The Secretary Chant" be seen as "political verse"? Do you think Piercy successfully achieves her political purpose, or does she undercut it with "bombast"?

Related Works: "Girl" (p. 164), "Battle Royal" (p. 297), "Women" (p. 824), "My Mother Sews Blouses" (p. 1234), *I Dream Before I Take the Stand* (p. 1320)

JOHN DONNE (1572–1631)

A Valediction: Forbidding Mourning (1611)

As virtuous men pass mildly away,
    And whisper to their souls to go,
Whilst some of their sad friends do say
    The breath goes now, and some say no:

So let us melt, and make no noise,   5
    No tear-floods, nor sigh-tempests move;
'Twere profanation of our joys
    To tell the laity° our love.

Moving of th' earth brings harms and fears;
    Men reckon what it did and meant;   10
But trepidation of the spheres,
    Though greater far, is innocent.

Dull sublunary lovers' love
    (Whose soul is sense) cannot admit
Absence, because it doth remove   15
    Those things which elemented it.

But we, by a love so much refined
    That ourselves know not what it is,
Inter-assurèd of the mind,
    Care less, eyes, lips, and hands to miss.   20

Our two souls, therefore, which are one,
    Though I must go, endure not yet
A breach, but an expansion,
    Like gold to airy thinness beat.

° *laity:* Here, "common people."

If they be two, they are two so   25
    As stiff twin compasses° are two:
Thy soul, the fixed foot, makes no show
    To move, but doth, if th' other do.

And though it in the center sit,
    Yet when the other far doth roam,   30
It leans and harkens after it,
    And grows erect as that comes home.

Such wilt thou be to me, who must,
    Like th' other foot, obliquely run;
Thy firmness makes my circle just,°   35
    And makes me end where I begun.

Reading and Reacting

1. Beginning with line 25, the poem develops an extended metaphor that compares the speaker and his loved one to "twin compasses" (line 26), attached yet separate. Why is the compass an especially apt metaphor? What physical characteristics of the compass does the poet emphasize?

2. The poem uses other figures of speech to characterize both the lovers' union and their separation. To what other events does the speaker compare his separation from his loved one? To what other elements does he compare their attachment? Do you think these comparisons make sense?

3. JOURNAL ENTRY To what other object could Donne have compared his loved one and himself? Explain the logic of the extended metaphor you suggest.

4. CRITICAL PERSPECTIVE In *John Donne and the Metaphysical Poets* (1970), Judah Stampfer writes of this poem's "thin, dry texture, its stanzas of pinched music," noting that its form "has too clipped a brevity to qualify as a song" and that its "music wobbles on a dry, measured beat." Yet, he argues, "the poem comes choked with emotional power" because "the speaker reads as a naturally reticent man, leaving his beloved in uncertainty and deep trouble." Stampfer concludes, "Easy self-expression here would be self-indulgent, if not reprehensible. . . . For all his careful dignity, we feel a heart is breaking here."

Do you find such emotional power in this highly intellectual poem?

Related Works: "The Third and Final Continent" (p. 261), "How Do I Love Thee?" (p. 1074), "To My Dear and Loving Husband" (p. 956), *A Doll House* (p. 1454)

°*compasses:* V-shaped instruments used for drawing circles.   °*just:* Perfect.

MARTÍN ESPADA (1957–)

My Father as a Guitar (2000)

The cardiologist prescribed
a new medication
and lectured my father
that he had to stop working.
And my father said: *I can't.*   5
The landlord won't let me.
The heart pills are dice
in my father's hand,
gambler who needs cash
by the first of the month.   10

On the night his mother died
in faraway Puerto Rico,
my father lurched upright in bed,
heart hammering
like the fist of a man at the door   15
with an eviction notice.
Minutes later,
the telephone sputtered
with news of the dead.

Sometimes I dream   20
my father is a guitar,
with a hole in his chest
where the music throbs
between my fingers.

Reading and Reacting

1. Where does this poem use simile? Metaphor? Personification?
2. What is the speaker's attitude toward his father? In what way does the poem's central metaphor (the comparison between the speaker's father and a guitar) help the speaker express his feelings? Why do you think the poet chose to use a metaphor rather than a simile?
3. JOURNAL ENTRY Why do you suppose the speaker dreams that his father is a guitar? How might his dreams be related to his father's dreams about his own mother?
4. CRITICAL PERSPECTIVE In a review of one of Espada's earlier collections of poetry, Leslie Ullman discusses how the poet brings his characters to life:

> The poems in this collection tell their stories and flesh out their characters deftly, without shrillness or rhetoric, and vividly enough to invite the reader into a shared sense of loss. Espada makes vanquished individuals and curtailed family histories present by offering us their remnants, their echoes, in such a way as to make us confront the ruined whole.

Does "My Father as a Guitar" present the speaker's father in the way Ullman describes?

Related Works: "My Papa's Waltz" (p. 1058), "Do not go gentle into that good night" (p. 1065), "Nothing Gold Can Stay" (p. 930), "My Son, My Executioner" (p. 961), *Proof* (p. 1526)

Hyperbole and Understatement

Two additional kinds of figurative language, *hyperbole* and *understatement,* also give poets opportunities to suggest meaning beyond the literal level of language.

Hyperbole is intentional exaggeration — saying more than is actually meant. In the poem "Oh, My Love Is like a Red, Red Rose" (p. 944), when the speaker says that he will love his lady until all the seas go dry, he is using hyperbole. **Understatement** is the opposite — saying less than is meant. When the speaker in the poem "Fire and Ice" (p. 864), weighing two equally grim alternatives for the end of the world, says that "for destruction ice / Is also great / And would suffice," he is using understatement. In both cases, poets expect their readers to understand that their words are not to be taken literally.

By using hyperbole and understatement, poets enhance the impact of their poems. For example, poets can use hyperbole to convey exaggerated anger or graphic images of horror — and to ridicule and satirize as well as to inflame and shock. With understatement, poets can convey the same kind of powerful emotions subtly, without artifice or embellishment, thereby leading readers to read more closely than they would otherwise do.

The emotionally charged poem that follows uses hyperbole to convey anger and bitterness that seem almost beyond the power of words.

SYLVIA PLATH   (1932–1963)

Daddy   (1965)

You do not do, you do not do
Any more, black shoe
In which I have lived like a foot
For thirty years, poor and white,
Barely daring to breathe or Achoo.   5

Daddy, I have had to kill you.
You died before I had time —
Marble-heavy, a bag full of God,
Ghastly statue with one grey toe
Big as a Frisco seal   10

And a head in the freakish Atlantic
Where it pours bean green over blue
In the waters off beautiful Nauset.

I used to pray to recover you.
Ach, du.° 15

In the German tongue, in the Polish town°
Scraped flat by the roller
Of wars, wars, wars.
But the name of the town is common.
My Polack friend 20

Says there are a dozen or two.
So I never could tell where you
Put your foot, your root,
I never could talk to you.
The tongue stuck in my jaw. 25

It stuck in a barb wire snare.
Ich, ich, ich, ich,°
I could hardly speak.
I thought every German was you.
And the language obscene 30

An engine, an engine
Chuffing me off like a Jew.
A Jew to Dachau, Auschwitz, Belsen.°
I began to talk like a Jew.
I think I may well be a Jew. 35

The snows of the Tyrol, the clear beer of Vienna
Are not very pure or true.
With my gypsy ancestress and my weird luck
And my Taroc pack and my Taroc pack
I may be a bit of a Jew. 40

I have always been scared of *you,*
With your Luftwaffe,° your gobbledygoo.
And your neat moustache
And your Aryan eye, bright blue.
Panzer°-man, panzer-man, O You— 45

Not God but a swastika
So black no sky could squeak through.
Every woman adores a Fascist,
The boot in the face, the brute
Brute heart of a brute like you. 50

°*Ach, du:* Ah, you (German).   °*Polish town:* Grabōw, where Plath's father was born.   °*ich:* "I" (German).
°*Dachau, Auschwitz, Belsen:* Nazi concentration camps.   °*Luftwaffe:* The German air force.
°*Panzer:* Protected by armor. The Panzer division was the German armored division.

You stand at the blackboard, daddy,
In the picture I have of you,
A cleft in your chin instead of your foot
But no less a devil for that, no not
Any less the black man who   55

Bit my pretty red heart in two.
I was ten when they buried you.
At twenty I tried to die
And get back, back, back to you.
I thought even the bones would do.   60

But they pulled me out of the sack,
And they stuck me together with glue.
And then I knew what to do.
I made a model of you,
A man in black with a Meinkampf° look   65

And a love of the rack and the screw.
And I said I do, I do.
So daddy, I'm finally through.
The black telephone's off at the root,
The voices just can't worm through.   70

If I've killed one man, I've killed two—
The vampire who said he was you
And drank my blood for a year,
Seven years, if you want to know.
Daddy, you can lie back now.   75

There's a stake in your fat black heart
And the villagers never liked you.
They are dancing and stamping on you.
They always *knew* it was you.
Daddy, daddy, you bastard, I'm through.   80

In her anger and frustration, the speaker sees herself as a helpless victim — a foot entrapped in a shoe, a Jew in a concentration camp — of her father's (and, later, her husband's) absolute tyranny. Thus, her hated father is characterized as a "black shoe," "a bag full of God," a "Ghastly statue," and, eventually, a Nazi, a torturer, the devil, a vampire. The poem "Daddy" is widely accepted by scholars as autobiographical, and the fact that Plath's own father was actually neither a Nazi nor a sadist (nor, obviously, the devil or a vampire) makes it clear that the figures of speech in the poem are wildly exaggerated. Even so, they may convey the poet's

---

°*Meinkampf: Mein Kampf* (My Struggle) is Adolf Hitler's autobiography.

true feelings toward her father — and, perhaps, toward the patriarchal society in which she lived.

Plath uses hyperbole to communicate these emotions to readers who she knows cannot possibly feel the way she does. Her purpose, therefore, is not only to shock but also to enlighten, to persuade, and perhaps even to empower her readers. Throughout the poem, the inflammatory language is set in ironic opposition to the childish, affectionate term "Daddy"—most strikingly in the last line's choked out "Daddy, daddy, you bastard, I'm through." The result of the exaggerated rhetoric is a poem that is vivid and shocking. And, although some might believe that Plath's almost wild exaggeration undermines the poem's impact, others would argue that the powerful language is necessary to convey the extent of the speaker's rage.

Like "Daddy," the following poem presents a situation whose emotional impact is devastating. In this case, however, the poet does not use highly charged language; instead, he uses understatement, presenting events without embellishment.

DAVID HUDDLE (1942–)

Holes Commence Falling (1979)

The lead & zinc company
owned the mineral rights
to the whole town anyway,
and after drilling holes
for 3 or 4 years,   5
they finally found the right
place and sunk a mine shaft.
We were proud
of all that digging,
even though nobody from   10
town got hired. They
were going to dig right
under New River and hook up
with the mine at Austinville.
Then people's wells   15
started drying up just like
somebody'd shut off a faucet,
and holes commenced falling,
big chunks of people's yards
would drop 5 or 6 feet,   20
houses would shift and crack.
Now and then the company'd
pay out a little money
in damages; they got a truck
to haul water and sell it   25

to the people whose wells
had dried up, but most
everybody agreed the
situation wasn't
serious.   30

Although "Holes Commence Falling" relates a tragic sequence of events, the tone
of the poem is matter-of-fact, and the language is understated. The speaker could
have overdramatized the events, using inflated rhetoric to denounce big business
and to predict disastrous events for the future. At the very least, he could have
colored the facts with realistic emotions, assigning blame to the lead and zinc
company with justifiable anger. Instead, the speaker is so restrained, so nonchalant, so passive that readers must supply the missing emotions themselves —
realizing, for example, that when the speaker concludes "everybody agreed the /
situation wasn't / serious," he means exactly the opposite.

Throughout the poem, unpleasant information is presented without comment
or emotion. As it proceeds, the poem traces the high and low points in the town's
fortunes, but for every hope ("We were proud / of all that digging"), there is a disappointment ("even though nobody from / town got hired"). The lead and zinc
company offers some compensation for the damage it does, but it is never enough.
The present tense verb of the poem's title indicates that the problems the town
faces — wells drying up, yards dropping, houses shifting and cracking — are regular occurrences. Eventually, readers come to see that what is not expressed, what
lurks just below the surface — anger, powerlessness, resentment, hopelessness —
is the poem's real subject.

FURTHER READING: Hyperbole and Understatement

ANNE BRADSTREET (1612–1672)

To My Dear and Loving Husband (1678)

If ever two were one, then surely we.
If ever man were lov'd by wife, then thee;
If ever wife was happy in a man,
Compare with me ye women if you can.
I prize thy love more than whole Mines of gold,   5
Or all the riches that the East doth hold.
My love is such that Rivers cannot quench,
Nor ought but love from thee, give recompense.
Thy love is such I can no way repay,
The heavens reward thee manifold I pray.   10
Then while we live, in love let's so persever,
That when we live no more, we may live ever.

Reading and Reacting

1. Review the claims the poem's speaker makes about her love in lines 5–8. Are such exaggerated declarations of love necessary, or would the rest of the poem be sufficient to convey the extent of her devotion to her husband?

2. **JOURNAL ENTRY** Compare this poem's declarations of love to those of John Donne's speaker in "A Valediction: Forbidding Mourning" (p. 949). Which speaker do you find more convincing? Why?

Related Works: "A Rose for Emily" (p. 216), "Stop all the clocks, cut off the telephone" (p. 1075), "Bright star! would I were steadfast as thou art" (p. 1192)

ANDREW MARVELL   (1621–1678)

To His Coy Mistress   (1681)

Had we but world enough and time,
This coyness, lady, were no crime.
We would sit down and think which way
To walk, and pass our long love's day.
Thou by the Indian Ganges' side   5
Should'st rubies find; I by the tide
Of Humber° would complain. I would
Love you ten years before the Flood,
And you should, if you please, refuse
Till the conversion of the Jews.   10
My vegetable love should grow
Vaster than empires, and more slow.
An hundred years should go to praise
Thine eyes, and on thy forehead gaze,
Two hundred to adore each breast,   15
But thirty thousand to the rest.
An age at least to every part,
And the last age should show your heart.
For, lady, you deserve this state,
Nor would I love at lower rate.   20
    But at my back I always hear
Time's wingèd chariot hurrying near,
And yonder all before us lie
Deserts of vast eternity.
Thy beauty shall no more be found,   25
Nor in thy marble vault shall sound

° *Humber:* An estuary on the east coast of England.

My echoing song; then worms shall try
That long preserved virginity,
And your quaint honor turn to dust,
And into ashes all my lust.   30
The grave's a fine and private place,
But none, I think, do there embrace.
     Now therefore, while the youthful hue
Sits on thy skin like morning glew°
And while thy willing soul transpires   35
At every pore with instant fires,
Now let us sport us while we may;
And now, like amorous birds of prey,
Rather at once our time devour
Than languish in his slow-chapped° power.   40
Let us roll all our strength and all
Our sweetness up into one ball
And tear our pleasures with rough strife
Thorough the iron gates of life.
Thus, though we cannot make our sun   45
Stand still, yet we will make him run.

Reading and Reacting

1. In this poem, Marvell's speaker sets out to convince a reluctant woman to become his lover. In order to make his case more persuasive, he uses hyperbole, exaggerating time periods, sizes, spaces, and the possible fate of the woman if she refuses him. Identify as many examples of hyperbole as you can.

2. The tone of "To His Coy Mistress" is more whimsical than serious. Given this tone, what do you see as the purpose of Marvell's use of hyperbole?

3. **JOURNAL ENTRY** Using contemporary prose, paraphrase the first four lines of the poem. Then, beginning with the word *But*, compose a few new sentences of prose, continuing the argument Marvell's speaker makes.

4. **CRITICAL PERSPECTIVE** In her critical essay *Andrew Marvell's "To His Coy Mistress": A Feminist Reading*, critic Margaret Wald presents the following analysis of the poem:

   > Andrew Marvell's speaker in "To His Coy Mistress" invokes Petrarchan convention, a poetic mode originating in the fourteenth century in which a male lover uses exaggerated metaphors to appeal to his female beloved. Yet Marvell alludes to such excessive — and disempowering — pining only to defy this tradition of unrequited love. Instead of respectful adulation, he offers lustful

---

°*glew:* Dew.   °*slow-chapped:* Slowly crushing.

invitation; rather than anticipating rejection, he assumes sexual dominion over the eponymous "mistress." The poem is as much a celebration of his rhetorical mastery as it is of his physical conquest.

In what sense is the speaker in this poem celebrating his beloved? In what sense is he celebrating himself? Is his portrayal of her entirely positive? Which elements, if any, are negative?

Related Works: "Where Are You Going, Where Have You Been?" (p. 573), "The Passionate Shepherd to His Love" (p. 1202), "To the Virgins, to Make Much of Time" (p. 873), *The Brute* (p. 1293)

ROBERT FROST (1874–1963)

"Out, Out —" (1916)

The buzz saw snarled and rattled in the yard
And made dust and dropped stove-length sticks of wood,
Sweet-scented stuff when the breeze drew across it.
And from there those that lifted eyes could count
Five mountain ranges one behind the other   5
Under the sunset far into Vermont.
And the saw snarled and rattled, snarled and rattled,
As it ran light, or had to bear a load.
And nothing happened: day was all but done.
Call it a day, I wish they might have said   10
To please the boy by giving him the half hour
That a boy counts so much when saved from work.
His sister stood beside them in her apron
To tell them "Supper." At the word, the saw,
As if to prove saws knew what supper meant,   15
Leaped out at the boy's hand, or seemed to leap—
He must have given the hand. However it was,
Neither refused the meeting. But the hand!
The boy's first outcry was a rueful laugh,
As he swung toward them holding up the hand   20
Half in appeal, but half as if to keep
The life from spilling. Then the boy saw all—
Since he was old enough to know, big boy
Doing a man's work, though a child at heart—
He saw all spoiled. "Don't let him cut my hand off—   25
The doctor, when he comes. Don't let him, sister!"
So. But the hand was gone already.
The doctor put him in the dark of ether.

He lay and puffed his lips out with his breath.
And then — the watcher at his pulse took fright.   30
No one believed. They listened at his heart.
Little — less — nothing! — and that ended it.
No more to build on there. And they, since they
Were not the one dead, turned to their affairs.

Reading and Reacting

1. The poem's title is an **allusion** to a passage in Shakespeare's *Macbeth* (5.5.23–28) that attacks the brevity and meaninglessness of life in very emotional terms:

> Out, out brief candle!
> Life's but a walking shadow, a poor player,
> That struts and frets his hour upon the stage
> And then is heard no more. It is a tale
> Told by an idiot, full of sound and fury,
> Signifying nothing.

What idea do you think Frost wants to convey through the title "Out, Out —"?

2. Explain why each of the following qualifies as understatement:

- "Neither refused the meeting." (line 18)
- "He saw all spoiled." (line 25)
- " — and that ended it." (line 32)
- "No more to build on there." (line 33)

Can you identify any other examples of understatement in the poem?

3. JOURNAL ENTRY Do you think the poem's impact is strengthened or weakened by its understated tone?

4. CRITICAL PERSPECTIVE In an essay on Frost in his book *Affirming Limits*, Robert Pack focuses on the single word "So" in line 27 of "Out, Out —":

> For a moment, his narration is reduced to the impotent word "So," and in that minimal word all his restrained grief is held. . . . That "So" is the narrator's cry of bearing witness to a story that must be what it is in a scene he cannot enter. He cannot rescue or protect the boy. . . . In the poem's sense of human help-lessness in an indifferent universe, we are all "watchers," and what we see is death without redemption, "signifying nothing." So. So? So! How shall we read that enigmatic word?

How do you read this "enigmatic word"? Why?

Related Works: "Happy Endings" (p. 161), "Kansas" (p. 209), "The Lottery" (p. 461), "What Were They Like?" (p. 1084), "Hope" (p. 879), "The Death of the Ball Turret Gunner" (p. 947)

DONALD HALL (1928–   )

My Son, My Executioner (1955)

My son, my executioner,
    I take you in my arms,
Quiet and small and just astir,
    And whom my body warms.

Sweet death, small son, our instrument   5
    Of immortality,
Your cries and hungers document
    Our bodily decay.

We twenty-five and twenty-two,
    Who seemed to live forever,   10
Observe enduring life in you
    And start to die together.

Reading and Reacting

1. Because the speaker is a young man holding his newborn son in his arms, the metaphor in line 1 comes as a shock. What is Hall's purpose in opening with such a startling statement?
2. In what sense is the comparison between baby and executioner a valid one? Could you argue that, given the underlying similarities between the two, Hall is *not* using hyperbole? Explain.

Related Works: "Doe Season" (p. 512), "That time of year thou mayst in me behold" (p. 817), "Morning Song" (p. 871), "Little Father" (p. 1200), "Sailing to Byzantium" (p. 1245), *Proof* (p. 1526)

MARGARET ATWOOD (1939–   )

you fit into me (1971)

you fit into me
like a hook into an eye

a fish hook
an open eye

Reading and Reacting

1. What positive connotations does Atwood expect readers to associate with the phrase "you fit into me"? What does the speaker seem at first to mean by "like a hook into an eye" in line 2?

2. The speaker's shift to the brutal suggestions of lines 3 and 4 is calculated to shock readers. Does the use of hyperbole here have another purpose in the context of the poem? Explain.

Related Works: "The Disappearance" (p. 371), "Daddy" (p. 952), *A Doll House* (p. 1454)

Metonymy and Synecdoche

Metonymy and synecdoche are two related figures of speech. **Metonymy** is the substitution of the name of one thing for the name of another thing that most readers associate with the first —for example, using *hired gun* to mean "paid assassin" or *suits* to mean "business executives." A specific kind of metonymy, called **synecdoche**, is the substitution of a part for the whole (for example, using *bread*— as in "Give us this day our daily bread"— to mean "food") or the whole for a part (for example, saying "You can take the boy out of Brooklyn, but you can't take Brooklyn [meaning its distinctive traits] out of the boy"). With metonymy and synecdoche, instead of describing something by saying it is like something else (as in simile) or by equating it with something else (as in metaphor), writers can characterize an object or concept by using a term that evokes it. The following poem illustrates the use of synecdoche.

RICHARD LOVELACE (1618–1658)

To Lucasta Going to the Wars (1649)

Tell me not, Sweet, I am unkind
   That from the nunnery
Of thy chaste breast and quiet mind,
   To war and arms I fly.

True, a new mistress now I chase,   5
   The first foe in the field;
And with a stronger faith embrace
   A sword, a horse, a shield.

Yet this inconstancy is such
   As you too shall adore;   10
I could not love thee, Dear, so much,
   Loved I not Honor more.

Here, Lovelace's use of synecdoche allows him to condense a number of complex ideas into a very few words. In line 3, when the speaker says that he is flying from his loved one's "chaste breast and quiet mind," he is using "breast" and "mind" to stand for all his loved one's physical and intellectual attributes. In line 8, when he says that he is embracing "A sword, a horse, a shield," he is using these three items to represent the trappings of war — and, thus, to represent war itself.

FURTHER READING: Metonymy and Synechdoche

THOMAS LUX   (1946–   )

Henry Clay's° Mouth   (2000)

Senator, statesman, speaker of the House,
exceptional dancer, slim,
graceful, ugly. Proclaimed, before most, slavery
an evil, broker
of elections (burned Jackson   5
for Adams), took a pistol ball in the thigh
in a duel, delayed, by forty years,
with his compromises, the Civil War,
gambler ("I have always
paid peculiar homage to the fickle goddess"),   10
boozehound, ladies' man — which leads us
to his mouth, which was huge,
a long slash across his face,
with which he ate and prodigiously drank,
with which he modulated his melodic voice,   15
with which he liked to kiss and kiss and kiss.
He said: "Kissing is like the presidency,
it is not to be sought and not to be *declined*."
A rival, one who wanted to kiss
whom he was kissing, said: "The ample   20
dimensions of his kissing apparatus
enabled him to *rest* one side of it
while the other was on active duty."
It was written, if women had the vote,
he would have been President,   25
kissing everyone in sight,
dancing on tables ("a grand Terpsichorean
performance . . ."), kissing everyone,
sometimes two at once, kissing everyone,
the almost-President   30
of our people.

° *Henry Clay:* Henry Clay (1777–1852), known as "the Great Compromiser," was responsible for getting the Missouri Compromise through the United States House of Representatives. The Missouri Compromise permitted Missouri to join the Union as a slave state while Maine was admitted as a free state.

Reading and Reacting

1. What functions does Henry Clay's mouth perform? How do these functions help to define his character?
2. Is this poem an example of metonymy or synecdoche? Explain.
3. If you were to divide this poem into stanzas, where would you place the breaks? Would the addition of stanza breaks make the poem more or less effective?
4. **JOURNAL ENTRY** On balance, is this larger-than-life portrait of Henry Clay a positive or a negative one?

Related Works: "For the Union Dead" (p. 1081), "The True-Blue American" (p. 1044)

Apostrophe

With **apostrophe**, a poem's speaker addresses an absent person or thing — for example, a historical or literary figure or even an inanimate object or an abstract concept.

In the following poem, the speaker addresses Vincent Van Gogh.

SONIA SANCHEZ (1934–   )

On Passing thru Morgantown, Pa. (1984)

```
i saw you
vincent van
gogh perched
on those pennsylvania
cornfields communing          5
amid secret black
bird societies. yes.
i'm sure that was
you exploding your
fantastic delirium           10
while in the
distance
red indian
hills beckoned.
```

Expecting her readers to be aware that Van Gogh is a nineteenth-century Dutch postimpressionist painter known for his mental instability as well as for his art, Sanchez is able to give added meaning to a phrase such as "fantastic delirium" as well as to the poem's visual images. Perhaps picturing his 1890 painting *Wheat-*

Wheatfield with Crows, 1890 (oil on canvas), Gogh, Vincent van (1853–90)/Rijksmuseum Vincent Van Gogh, Amsterdam, The Netherlands/Bridgeman Art Library

field with Crows, the speaker sees Van Gogh perched like a black bird on a fence, and at the same time she also sees what he sees. Like Van Gogh, then, the speaker sees the Pennsylvania cornfields as both a natural landscape and an "exploding" work of art.

FURTHER READING: Apostrophe

ALLEN GINSBERG (1926–1997)

A Supermarket in California (1956)

What thoughts I have of you tonight, Walt Whitman,° for I walked
down the sidestreets under the trees with a headache self-conscious
looking at the full moon.
    In my hungry fatigue, and shopping for images, I went into
the neon fruit supermarket, dreaming of your enumerations!
    What peaches and what penumbras! Whole families shopping at
night! Aisles full of husbands! Wives in the avocados, babies in the
tomatoes!— and you, Garcia Lorca,° what were you doing down
by the watermelons?

° *Walt Whitman:* American poet (1819–1892) whose poems frequently praise the commonplace and often contain lengthy "enumerations."   ° *Federico García Lorca:* Spanish poet and dramatist (1899–1936).

I saw you, Walt Whitman, childless, lonely old grubber, poking among the meats in the refrigerator and eyeing the grocery boys.°

I heard you asking questions of each: Who killed the pork chops?   5
What price bananas? Are you my Angel?

I wandered in and out of the brilliant stacks of cans following you, and followed in my imagination by the store detective.

We strode down the open corridors together in our solitary fancy tasting artichokes, possessing every frozen delicacy, and never passing the cashier.

Where are we going, Walt Whitman? The doors close in an hour. Which way does your beard point tonight?

(I touch your book° and dream of our odyssey in the supermarket and feel absurd.)

Will we walk all night through solitary streets? The trees add shade   10
to shade, lights out in the houses, we'll both be lonely.

Will we stroll dreaming of the lost America of love past blue automobiles in driveways, home to our silent cottage?

Ah, dear father, graybeard, lonely old courage-teacher, what America did you have when Charon° quit poling his ferry and you got out on a smoking bank and stood watching the boat disappear on the black waters of Lethe?°

Reading and Reacting

1. In this poem, Ginsberg's speaker wanders through the aisles of a super-market, speaking to the nineteenth-century American poet Walt Whit-man and asking Whitman a series of questions. Why do you think the speaker addresses Whitman? What kind of answers do you think he is looking for?

2. In paragraph 2, the speaker says he is "shopping for images." What does he mean? Why does he look for these images in a supermarket? Does he find them?

3. Is this poem about supermarkets? About Walt Whitman? About poetry? About love? About America? What do you see as its primary theme? Why?

4. JOURNAL ENTRY Does the incongruous image of the respected poet "poking / among the meats" (line 4) in the supermarket strengthen the poem's impact, or does it undercut any serious "message" the poem might have? Explain.

5. CRITICAL PERSPECTIVE The critic Leslie Fiedler discusses some of the ways in which Ginsberg's style resembles that of Walt Whitman:

° *eyeing the grocery boys:* Whitman's sexual orientation is the subject of much debate. Ginsberg is suggesting here that Whitman was homosexual.   ° *your book: Leaves of Grass.*   ° *Charon:* In Greek mythology, the ferryman who transported the dead over the river Styx to Hades.   ° *Lethe:* In Greek mythology, the river of forgetfulness (one of five rivers in Hades).

Everything about Ginsberg is . . . blatantly Whitmanian: his meter is resolutely anti-iambic, his line groupings stubbornly anti-stanzaic, his diction aggressively colloquial and American, his voice public.

Can you identify ways in which the poem is "American" and "public"?

Related Works: "A&P" (p. 230), "Chicago" (p. 1016), from "Out of the Cradle Endlessly Rocking" (p. 1018), "Defending Walt Whitman" (p. 1136), from "Song of Myself" (p. 1237)

✔ **CHECKLIST   Writing about Figures of Speech**

- Are any figures of speech present in the poem? Identify each example of simile, metaphor, personification, hyperbole, understatement, metonymy, synecdoche, and apostrophe.

- What two elements are being compared in each use of simile, metaphor, and personification? Is the comparison logical? What characteristics are shared by the two items being compared?

- Does the poet use hyperbole? Why? For example, is it used to move or to shock readers, or is its use intended to produce a humorous or satirical effect? Would more understated language be more effective?

- Does the poet use understatement? For what purpose? Would more emotionally charged language be more effective?

- In metonymy and synecdoche, what item is being substituted for another? What purpose does the substitution serve?

- If the poem includes apostrophe, whom or what does the speaker address? What is accomplished through the use of apostrophe?

- How do figures of speech contribute to the impact of the poem as a whole?

WRITING SUGGESTIONS: Figures of Speech

1. Various figures of speech are often used to describe characters in literary works. Choose two or three works that focus on a single character — for example, "A Rose for Emily" (p. 216), "Miss Brill" (p. 235), "Gryphon" (p. 248), "Ex-Basketball Player" (p. 946), or "Richard Cory" (p. 1218) — and explain how figures of speech are used to characterize each work's central figure. If you like, you may write about works that focus on real (rather than fictional) people — for example, "Emmett Till" (p. 1176) or "Medgar Evers" (p. 1150).

2. Write an essay in which you discuss the different ways poets use figures of speech to examine the nature of poetry itself. What kinds of figures of speech do poets use to describe their craft? (You might begin by reading the two poems about poetry that open Chapter 22.)

3. Write a letter replying to the speaker in the poem by Marvell, Bradstreet, Donne, or Burns that appears in this chapter. Use figures of speech to express the depth of your love and the extent of your devotion.

4. Choose three or four poems that have a common subject — for example, love or nature — and write an essay in which you draw some general conclusions about the relative effectiveness of the poems' use of figures of speech to examine that subject. (If you like, you may focus on the poems clustered under the heads "Poems about Parents," "Poems about Nature," "Poems about Love," and "Poems about War" in Chapter 32.)

5. Select a poem and a short story that deal with the same subject matter, and write an essay in which you compare their use of figures of speech.

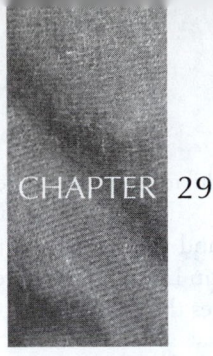

CHAPTER 29

SOUND

> A primary pleasure in poetry is . . . the pleasure of saying something over for its own sweet sake and because it sounds just right.
>
> —**Howard Nemerov,** *"Poetry and Meaning"*

WALT WHITMAN (1819–1892)

Had I the Choice *

Had I the choice to tally greatest bards,
To limn° their portraits, stately, beautiful, and emulate at will,
Homer with all his wars and warriors — Hector, Achilles, Ajax,
Or Shakespeare's woe-entangled Hamlet, Lear, Othello — Tennyson's
    fair ladies,
Meter or wit the best, or choice conceit to wield in perfect rhyme,
delight of singers;
These, these, O sea, all these I'd gladly barter,
Would you the undulation of one wave, its trick to me transfer,
Or breathe one breath of yours upon my verse,
And leave its odor there.

Rhythm

Rhythm — the regular recurrence of sounds — is at the heart of all natural phenomena: the beating of a heart, the lapping of waves against the shore, the croaking of frogs on a summer's night, the whispering of wheat swaying in the wind. In fact, even mechanical phenomena, such as the movement of rush-hour traffic through a city's streets, have a kind of rhythm. Poetry, which explores these phenomena, often tries to reflect the same rhythms. Walt Whitman expresses this idea in "Had I the Choice" when he says that he would gladly trade the "perfect

---

*Publication date is not available. °*limn:* To describe, depict.

rhyme" of Shakespeare for the ability to reproduce "the undulation of one wave" in his verse.

Effective public speakers frequently repeat key words and phrases to create rhythm. In his speech "I Have a Dream," for example, Martin Luther King Jr. repeats the phrase "I have a dream" to create a cadence that ties the central section of the speech together:

> I say to you today, my friends, even though we face the difficulties of today and tomorrow, *I still have a dream*. It is a dream deeply rooted in the American dream. *I have a dream* that one day this nation will rise up and live out the true meaning of its creed: "We hold these truths to be self-evident, that all men are created equal." *I have a dream* that one day, on the red hills of Georgia, sons of former slaves and the sons of former slave owners will be able to sit down together at the table of brotherhood. *I have a dream* that one day even the state of Mississippi, a state sweltering with the heat of in justice, sweltering with the heat of oppression, will be transformed into an oasis of freedom and justice. *I have a dream* that my four little children will one day live in a nation where they will not be judged by the color of their skin, but by the content of their character.

Poets too create rhythm by using repeated words and phrases, as Gwendolyn Brooks does in the poem that follows.

GWENDOLYN BROOKS   (1917–2000)

Sadie and Maud   (1945)

Maud went to college.
Sadie stayed at home.
Sadie scraped life
With a fine-tooth comb.

She didn't leave a tangle in.   5
Her comb found every strand.
Sadie was one of the livingest chits
In all the land.

Sadie bore two babies
Under her maiden name.   10
Maud and Ma and Papa
Nearly died of shame.

When Sadie said her last so-long
Her girls struck out from home.
(Sadie had left as heritage   15
Her fine-tooth comb.)

Maud, who went to college,
Is a thin brown mouse.
She is living all alone
In this old house.   20

Much of the force of this poem comes from its balanced structure and regular rhyme and meter, underscored by the repeated words "Sadie" and "Maud," which shift the focus from one subject to the other and back again ("Maud went to college / Sadie stayed home"). The poem's singsong rhythm recalls the rhymes children recite when jumping rope. This evocation of carefree childhood is ironically contrasted with the adult realities that both Sadie and Maud face as they grow up: Sadie stays at home and has two children out of wedlock; Maud goes to college and ends up "a thin brown mouse." The speaker implies that the alternatives Sadie and Maud represent are both undesirable. Although Sadie "scraped life / with a fine-tooth comb," she dies young and leaves nothing to her girls but her desire to experience life. Maud, who graduated from college, shuts out life and cuts herself off from her roots.

Just as the repetition of words and phrases can create rhythm, so can the arrangement of words in a poem — and even the appearance of words on the printed page. How a poem looks is especially important in **open form poetry** (see p. 1015), which dispenses with traditional patterns of versification. In the following excerpt from a poem by E. E. Cummings, for example, an unusual arrangement of words forces readers to slow down and then to speed up, creating a rhythm that emphasizes a key phrase — "The / lily":

> the moon is hiding
> in her hair.
> The
> lily
> of heaven
> full of all dreams,
> draws down.

Poetic rhythm — the repetition of stresses and pauses — is an essential element in poetry. Rhythm helps to establish a poem's mood, and, in combination with other poetic elements, it conveys the poet's emphasis and helps communicate the poem's meaning.

Meter

Although rhythm can be affected by the regular repetition of words and phrases or by the arrangement of words into lines, poetic rhythm is largely created by **meter**, the recurrence of regular units of stressed and unstressed syllables. A **stress** (or accent) occurs when one syllable is emphasized more than another, unstressed, syllable: *fór • ceps, bá • sic, il • lú • sion, ma • lár • i • a*. In a poem, even one-syllable words can be stressed to create a particular effect. For example, in Elizabeth Barrett Browning's line "How do I love thee? Let me count the ways," the metrical pattern that places stress on "love" creates one meaning; stressing "I" would create another.

Scansion is the analysis of patterns of stressed and unstressed syllables within a line. The most common method of poetic notation indicates stressed syllables with a ′ and unstressed syllables with a �‿. Although scanning lines gives readers the "beat" of the poem, scansion only approximates the sound of spoken language, which contains an infinite variety of stresses. By providing a graphic representation of the stressed and unstressed syllables of a poem, scansion aids understanding but is no substitute for reading the poem aloud and experimenting with various patterns of emphasis.

The basic unit of meter is a **foot**— a group of syllables with a fixed pattern of stressed and unstressed syllables. The chart below illustrates the most common types of metrical feet in English and American verse.

<u>Foot</u>	<u>Stress Pattern</u>	<u>Example</u>
Iamb	˘ ′	˘ ′ | ˘ ′ | They pace | in sleek | ˘ ′ | ˘ ′ | ˘ ′ | chi val | ric cer | tain ty (Adrienne Rich)
Trochee	′ ˘	′ ˘ | ′ ˘ | Thou, when | thou ˘ | ′ ˘ | ′ ˘ | ′ re | turn'st, wilt | tell ˘ me. (John Donne)
Anapest	˘ ˘ ′	˘ ˘ ′ | ˘ ˘ With a hey, | and a ′ ˘ ˘ | ′ ˘ ho, | and a hey | ˘ ˘ ′ no ni no (William Shakespeare)
Dactyl	′ ˘ ˘	′ ˘ ˘ | ′ ˘ Constantly | risking ˘ | ′ ˘ ˘ ab | surdity (Lawrence Ferlinghetti)

Iambic and *anapestic* meters are called **rising meters** because they progress from unstressed to stressed syllables. *Trochaic* and *dactylic* meters are called **falling meters** because they progress from stressed to unstressed syllables.

The following types of metrical feet, less common than those listed above, are used to add emphasis or to provide variety rather than to create the dominant meter of a poem.

Spondee	′ ′	′ ′ | ˘ Pomp, pride | and ′ ˘ ′ | ˘ circumstance of ′ ˘ ′ glorious war! (William Shakespeare)

Pyrrhic ⏑⏑   Ă horse! a horse!
              My king | dom for |
              a horse! (William
              Shakespeare)

A metric line of poetry is measured by the number of feet it contains.

Monometer	one foot	**Pentameter**	five feet
Dimeter	two feet	**Hexameter**	six feet
Trimeter	three feet	**Heptameter**	seven feet
Tetrameter	four feet	**Octameter**	eight feet

The name for a metrical pattern of a line of verse identifies the name of the foot used and the number of feet the line contains. For example, the most common foot in English poetry is the **iamb**, most often occurring in lines of three or five feet.

Eight hun | dred of | the brave   Iambic trimeter
(William Cowper)
O, how | much more | doth   Iambic pentameter
beau | ty beau | teous seem
(William Shakespeare)

Because **iambic pentameter** is so well suited to the rhythms of English speech, writers frequently use it in plays and poems. Shakespeare's plays, for example, are written in unrhymed lines of iambic pentameter called **blank verse** (see p. 999).

Many other metrical combinations are also possible; a few are illustrated here.

Like a | high-born | maiden   Trochaic trimeter
(Percy Bysshe Shelley)
The As sy | rian came down | Anapestic tetrameter
like the wolf | on the fold
(Lord Byron)
Maid en most | beau ti ful | Dactylic hexameter
mother most | boun ti ful, | la
dy of | lands, (A. C. Swinburne)
The yel | low fog | that rubs | its   Iambic heptameter
back | upon | the win |
dow-panes (T. S. Eliot)

Scansion can be an extremely technical process, and when readers become bogged down with anapests and dactyls, they can easily forget that poetic scansion is not an end in itself. Meter should be appropriate for the ideas expressed by the poem, and it should help to create a suitable tone. A light, skipping rhythm, for example, would be inappropriate for an **elegy**, and a slow, heavy rhythm would surely be out of place in an **epigram** or a limerick. The following lines of a poem by Samuel Taylor Coleridge illustrate the uses of different types of metrical feet:

> Trochee trips from long to short;
> From long to long in solemn sort
> Slow Spondee stalks; strong foot! yet ill able
> Ever to come up with Dactyl trisyllable.
> Iambics march from short to long —   5
> With a leap and a bound the swift Anapests throng;
>
> One syllable long, with one short at each side,
> Amphibrachys hastes with a stately stride —
> First and last being long, middle short, Amphimacer
> Strikes his thundering hoofs like a proud high-bred Racer.   10

A poet may use one kind of meter — iambic meter, for example — throughout a poem, but may vary line length to relieve monotony or to accommodate the poem's meaning or emphasis. In the following poem, the poet uses iambic lines of different lengths.

EMILY DICKINSON (1830 – 1886)

I like to see it lap the Miles — (1891)

> I like to see it lap the Miles —
> And lick the Valleys up —
> And stop to feed itself at Tanks —
> And then — prodigious step
>
> Around a Pile of Mountains —   5
> And supercilious peer
> In Shanties — by the sides of Roads —
> And then a Quarry pare
>
> To fit its Ribs
> And crawl between   10
> Complaining all the while
> In horrid — hooting stanza —
> Then chase itself down Hill —

> And neigh like Boanerges°—
> Then — punctual as a Star   15
> Stop — docile and omnipotent
> At its own stable door—

This poem is a single sentence that, except for some pauses, stretches unbroken from beginning to end. Iambic lines of varying lengths actually suggest the movements of the train that the poet describes. Lines of iambic tetrameter, such as the first, give readers a sense of the train's steady, rhythmic movement across a flat landscape, and shorter lines ("To fit its Ribs / And crawl between") suggest the train's slowing motion. Beginning with two iambic dimeter lines and progressing to iambic trimeter lines, the third stanza increases in speed just like the train that is racing downhill "In horrid —hooting stanza —."

When a poet uses more than one type of metrical foot, any variation in a metrical pattern — the substitution of a trochee for an iamb, for instance — immediately calls attention to itself. Poets are aware of this fact and use it to their advantage. For example, in line 16 of "I like to see it lap the Miles," the poet departs from iambic meter by placing unexpected stress on the first word, *stop*. By emphasizing this word, the poet brings the flow of the poem to an abrupt halt, suggesting the jolt riders experience when a train comes to a stop. In the following segment from "The Rime of the Ancient Mariner," Samuel Taylor Coleridge also departs from his poem's dominant meter:

> The ship | was cheered, | the har | bor cleared,
> Merri | ly did | we drop
> Below | the kirk, | below | the hill,
> Below | the light | house top.

Although these lines are arranged in iambic tetrameter, the poet uses a trochee in the second line, breaking the meter in order to accommodate the natural pronunciation of "merrily" as well as to place stress on the word.

Another way of varying the meter of a poem is to introduce a pause known as a **caesura**— a Latin word meaning "a cutting"— within a line. When scanning a poem, you indicate a caesura with two parallel lines: ‖. Unless a line of poetry is extremely short, it probably will contain a caesura.

A caesura occurs after a punctuation mark or at a natural break in phrasing:

> How do I love thee? ‖ Let me count the ways.
>
> **Elizabeth Barrett Browning**

> Two loves I have ‖ of comfort and despair.
>
> **William Shakespeare**

° *Boanerges:* A vociferous preacher and orator. Also, the name, meaning "son of thunder," Jesus gave to apostles John and James because of their fiery zeal.

> High on a throne of royal state, ‖ which far
> Outshone the wealth of Ormus ‖ and of Ind
>
> **John Milton**

Sometimes more than one caesura occurs in a single line:

> 'Tis good. ‖ Go to the gate. ‖ Somebody knocks.
>
> **William Shakespeare**

Although the end of a line may mark the end of a metrical unit, it does not always coincide with the end of a sentence. Poets may choose to indicate a pause at this point, or they may continue without a break to the next line. Lines that have distinct pauses at the end — usually signaled by punctuation — are called **end-stopped lines**. Lines that do not end with strong pauses are called **run-on lines**. (Sometimes the term **enjambment** is used to describe run-on lines.) End-stopped lines can sometimes seem formal, or even forced, because their length is rigidly dictated by the poem's meter, rhythm, and rhyme scheme. In the following excerpt from John Keats's "La Belle Dame sans Merci" (p. 1191), for example, rhythm, meter, and rhyme dictate the pauses that occur at the ends of the lines:

> O, what can ail thee, knight-at-arms,
>   Alone and palely loitering?
> The sedge has wither'd from the lake,
>   And no birds sing.

In contrast to end-stopped lines, run-on lines often seem more natural. Because their ending points are determined by the rhythms of speech and by the meaning and emphasis the poet wishes to convey rather than by meter and rhyme, run-on lines are suited to the open form of much modern poetry. In the following lines from the poem "We Have Come Home," by the poet Lenrie Peters, run-on lines give readers the sense of spoken language:

> We have come home
> From the bloodless war
> With sunken hearts
> Our boots full of pride—
> From the true massacre of the soul
> When we have asked
> "What does it cost
> To be loved and left alone?"

Rather than relying exclusively on end-stopped or run-on lines, poets often use a combination of the two to produce the effects they want. For example, the following lines from "Pot Roast," by Mark Strand juxtapose end-stopped and run-on lines:

> I gaze upon the roast,
> that is sliced and laid out
> on my plate
> and over it
> I spoon the juices

of carrot and onion.
And for once I do not regret
the passage of time.

FURTHER READING: Rhythm and Meter

ADRIENNE RICH (1929–   )

Aunt Jennifer's Tigers (1951)

Aunt Jennifer's tigers prance across a screen,
Bright topaz denizens of a world of green.
They do not fear the men beneath the tree;
They pace in sleek chivalric certainty.

Aunt Jennifer's fingers fluttering through her wool   5
Find even the ivory needle hard to pull.
The massive weight of Uncle's wedding band
Sits heavily upon Aunt Jennifer's hand.

When Aunt is dead, her terrified hands will lie
Still ringed with ordeals she was mastered by.   10
The tigers in the panel that she made
Will go on prancing, proud and unafraid.

Reading and Reacting

1. What is the dominant metrical pattern of the poem? How does the meter enhance the contrast the poem develops?
2. The lines in the first stanza are end-stopped, and those in the second and third stanzas combine end-stopped and run-on lines. What does the poet achieve by varying the rhythm?
3. What ideas do the caesuras in the first and fourth lines of the last stanza emphasize?
4. **JOURNAL ENTRY** What is the speaker's opinion of Aunt Jennifer's marriage? Do you think she is commenting on this particular marriage or on marriage in general?
5. **CRITICAL PERSPECTIVE** In *The Aesthetics of Power*, Claire Keyes writes of this poem that although it is formally beautiful, almost perfect, its voice creates problems:

   > [T]he tone seldom approaches intimacy, the speaker seeming fairly detached from the fate of Aunt Jennifer. . . . The dominant voice of the poem asserts the traditional theme that art outlives the person who produces it. . . . The speaker is almost callous in her disregard for Aunt's death. . . . Who cares that Aunt Jennifer dies? The speaker does not seem to; she gets caught up in those gorgeous tigers. . . . Here lies the dominant voice: Aunt is not compelling; her creation is.

   Do you agree with Keyes's interpretation of the poem?

Related Works: "Miss Brill" (p. 235), "Everyday Use" (p. 469), "Seventeen Syllables" (p. 538), "Rooming houses are old women" (p. 942), "Ethics" (p. 1210)

ETHERIDGE KNIGHT (1931–1991)

For Malcolm,° a Year After (1986)

Compose for Red° a proper verse;
Adhere to foot and strict iamb;
Control the burst of angry words
Or they might boil and break the dam.
Or they might boil and overflow   5
And drench me, drown me, drive me mad.
So swear no oath, so shed no tear,
And sing no song blue Baptist sad.
Evoke no image, stir no flame,
And spin no yarn across the air.   10
Make empty anglo tea lace words —
Make them dead white and dry bone bare.

Compose a verse for Malcolm man,
And make it rime and make it prim.
The verse will die — as all men do —   15
But not the memory of him!
Death might come singing sweet like C,
Or knocking like the old folk say,
The moon and stars may pass away,
But not the anger of that day.   20

Reading and Reacting

1. Why do you think Knight chooses to write a "proper verse" in "strict iamb"? Do you think this meter is an appropriate choice for his subject?

2. What sounds and words are repeated in this poem? How does this repetition enhance the poem's rhythm?

3. Where in the poem does Knight use caesuras? Why does he use a pause in each instance?

4. JOURNAL ENTRY How would you describe the mood of the speaker? Is the poem's meter consistent with his mood or in conflict with it? Explain.

° *Malcolm:* Malcolm X (1925–1965).   ° *Red:* Malcolm X's nickname when he was a young man.

Related Works: "Battle Royal" (p. 297), "To an Athlete Dying Young" (p. 916), "Medgar Evers" (p. 1150), "If We Must Die" (p. 1203)

FRANK O'HARA   (1926–1966)

To the Poem

Let us do something grand
just this once   Something

small and important and
unAmerican   Some fine thing

will resemble a human hand   5
and really be merely a thing

Not needing a military band
nor an elegant forthcoming

to tease spotlights or a hand
from the public's thinking   10

But be   In a defiant land
of its own a real right thing

Reading and Reacting

1. What is the dominant metrical pattern of the poem?

2. The poem consists entirely of run-on lines. Why do you think the poet uses this type of line?

3. O'Hara uses caesuras in the first, second, and last stanzas. What is the effect of these caesuras? What ideas do they emphasize?

4. JOURNAL ENTRY What is the tone of this poem? How is the tone suited to the poem's theme?

5. CRITICAL PERSPECTIVE Critic David Bergman wrote the following of poets Frank O'Hara, John Ashbery, and Kenneth Koch:

> (1) They all emphasize the immediacy of the individual poetic voice rather than the impersonal presentation of images. (2) They playfully combine elements from high and low culture, incorporating into their works the most mundane aspects of urban life and such features of popular culture as comic strip characters, Hollywood movies, and popular songs. (3) They fearlessly court the comic, the slapstick, the vulgar, and the sentimental. (4) They experiment with surrealism, although the dream-like often dissolves into the quite ordinary.

How does "To the Poem" incorporate the above elements? For example, in what sense does it emphasize the poetic voice rather than the images themselves? Do you think it "courts the comic," or "experiments with surrealism"?

Related Works: "I'm nobody! Who are you? (p. 851), "Fire and Ice" (p. 864), "Tell all the Truth but tell it slant" (p. 1166), "Poetry Searches for Radiance" (p. 1248)

Alliteration and Assonance

Just as poetry depends on rhythm, it also depends on the sounds of individual words. An effect pleasing to the ear, such as "Did he who made the Lamb make thee?" from William Blake's "The Tyger" (p. 1146), is called **euphony**. A jarring or discordant effect, such as "The vorpal blade went snicker-snack!" from Lewis Carroll's "Jabberwocky" (p. 993), is called **cacophony**.

One of the earliest, and perhaps the most primitive, methods of enhancing sound is **onomatopoeia**, which occurs when the sound of a word echoes its meaning, as it does in common words such as *bang, crash,* and *hiss.* Poets make broad application of this technique by using combinations of words that suggest a correspondence between sound and meaning, as Edgar Allan Poe does in these lines from his poem "The Bells":

> Yet the ear, it fully knows,
>   By the twanging
>   And the clanging,
> How the danger ebbs and flows;
> Yet the ear distinctly tells,
>   In the jangling
>   And the wrangling
> How the danger sinks and swells
> By the sinking or the swelling in the anger of the bells —
>   Of the bells,—
>   Of the bells, bells, bells, bells. . . .

Poe's primary objective in this poem is to re-create the sound of ringing bells. Although he succeeds, the poem (113 lines long in its entirety) is extremely tedious. A more subtle use of onomatopoetic words appears in the following passage from *An Essay on Criticism* by Alexander Pope:

> Soft is the strain when Zephyr gently blows,
> And the smooth stream in smoother numbers flows;
> But when the loud surges lash the sounding shore,
> The hoarse, rough verse should like the torrent roar:
> When Ajax strives some rock's vast weight to throw,
> The line too Labors, and the words move slow.

After earlier admonishing readers that sound must echo sense, Pope uses onomatopoetic words such as *lash* and *roar* to convey the fury of the sea, and he uses repeated consonants to echo the sounds these words suggest. Notice, for example, how the *s* and *m* sounds suggest the gently blowing Zephyr and the flowing of the smooth stream and how the series of *r* sounds echoes the torrent's roar.

Alliteration — the repetition of consonant sounds in consecutive or neighboring words, usually at the beginning of words — is another device used to enhance sound in a poem. Both Poe ("<u>s</u>inks and <u>s</u>wells") and Pope ("<u>s</u>mooth <u>s</u>tream") make use of alliteration in the preceding excerpts, and so does Tennyson in the following poem.

ALFRED, LORD TENNYSON (1809–1892)

The Eagle (1851)

He clasps the crag with crooked hands;
Close to the sun in lonely lands,
Ringed with the azure world, he stands.

The wrinkled sea beneath him crawls:
He watches from his mountain walls,   5
And like a thunderbolt he falls.

Throughout the poem, *c*, *l*, and *w* sounds occur repeatedly. The poem is drawn together by the recurrence of these sounds and, as a result, it flows smoothly from beginning to end.

The following poem also uses alliteration to create special aural effects.

N. SCOTT MOMADAY (1934–   )

Comparatives (1976)

Sunlit sea,
the drift of fronds,
and banners
of bobbing boats —
the seaside   5
upon the planks,
the coil and
crescent of flesh
extending
just into death.   10

Even so,
in the distant,
inland sea,

a shadow runs,
radiant,   15
rude in the rock:
fossil fish,
fissure of bone
forever.
It is perhaps   20
the same thing,
an agony
twice perceived.

It is most like
wind on waves —   25
mere commotion,
mute and mean,
perceptible —
that is all.

Throughout the poem, Momaday uses alliteration to create a pleasing effect and to link certain words and ideas. Each stanza has its own alliterative pattern: the first stanza contains repeated *s* and *b* sounds, the second stanza contains repeated *r* and *f* sounds, and the third stanza contains repeated *w* and *m* sounds. Not only does this use of alliteration create a pleasing effect, but also it reinforces the development of the poem's theme from stanza to stanza.

Assonance— the repetition of the same or similar vowel sounds, especially in stressed syllables — can also enrich a poem. When used solely to produce aural effects, assonance can be distracting. Consider, for example, the clumsiness of the repeated vowel sounds in Tennyson's "Many a morning on the moorland did we hear the copses ring. . . ." When used more subtly, however, assonance can enhance a poem's effectiveness.

Sometimes assonance unifies an entire poem. In the following poem, assonance emphasizes the thematic connections among words and thus links the poem's ideas.

ROBERT HERRICK   (1591–1674)

Delight in Disorder   (1648)

A sweet disorder in the dress
Kindles in clothes a wantonness.
A lawn° about the shoulders thrown
Into a fine distractión;
An erring lace, which here and there   5
Enthralls the crimson stomacher;°

° *lawn:* A shawl made of fine fabric.   ° *stomacher:* A heavily embroidered garment worn by females over the chest and stomach.

A cuff neglectful, and thereby
Ribbons to flow confusedly;
A winning wave, deserving note,
In the tempestuous petticoat;   10
A careless shoestring, in whose tie
I see a wild civility;
Do more bewitch me than when art
Is too precise in every part.

Repeated vowel sounds extend throughout this poem — for instance, "sh_ou_l-ders" and "thr_ow_n" in line 3; and "t_ie_," "w_i_ld," and "prec_i_se" in lines 11, 12, and 14. Using alliteration as well as assonance, Herrick subtly links certain words — "_tempes_tuous _pe_tticoat," for example. By connecting these words, he calls attention to the pattern of imagery that helps to convey the poem's theme.

Rhyme

In addition to alliteration and assonance, poets create sound patterns with **rhyme** — the use of matching sounds in two or more words: "tight" and "might"; "born" and "horn"; "sleep" and "deep." For a rhyme to be **perfect**, final vowel and consonant sounds must be the same, as they are in each of the preceding examples. **Imperfect rhyme** (also called _near rhyme, slant rhyme, approximate rhyme,_ or **consonance**) occurs when the final consonant sounds in two words are the same but vowel sounds are different — "learn" / "barn" or "pads" / "lids," for example. William Stafford uses imperfect rhyme in "Traveling through the Dark" (p. 1070) when he rhymes "road" with "dead." Finally, **eye rhyme** occurs when two words look as if they should rhyme but do not — for example, "watch" and "catch."

Rhyme can also be classified according to the position of the rhyming syllables in a line of verse. The most common type of rhyme is **end rhyme**, which occurs at the end of a line:

Tyger! Tyger! burning <u>bright</u>
In the forests of the <u>night</u>

William Blake, "The Tyger"

Internal rhyme occurs within a line:

The Sun came up upon the left,
Out of the <u>sea</u> came <u>he</u>!
And he shone <u>bright</u> and on the <u>right</u>
Went down into the sea.

Samuel Taylor Coleridge, "The Rime of the Ancient Mariner"

Beginning rhyme occurs at the beginning of a line:

> Red river, red river,
> <u>Slow</u> flow heat is silence
> <u>No</u> will is still as a river
> **T. S. Eliot, "Virginia"**

Rhyme can also be classified according to the number of syllables that correspond. **Masculine rhyme** (also called **rising rhyme**) occurs when single syllables correspond ("can" / "ran"; "descend" / "contend"). **Feminine rhyme** (also called **double rhyme** or **falling rhyme**) occurs when two syllables, a stressed one followed by an unstressed one, correspond ("ocean" / "motion"; "leaping" / "sleeping"). **Triple rhyme** occurs when three syllables correspond. Less common than the other two, triple rhyme is often used for humorous or satiric purposes, as in the following lines from the long poem *Don Juan* by Lord Byron:

> Sagest of women, even of widows, she
> Resolved that Juan should be quite a <u>paragon</u>,
> And worthy of the noblest pedigree:
> (His sire of Castile, his dam from <u>Aragon</u>).

In some cases — for example, when it is overused or used in unexpected places — rhyme can create unusual and even comic effects. In the following poem, humor is created by the incongruous connections established by rhymes such as "priest" / "beast" and "pajama" / "lllama."

OGDEN NASH (1902–1971)

The Lama (1931)

> The one-l lama
> He's a priest.
> The two-l llama,
> He's a beast.
> And I will bet   5
> A silk pajama
> There isn't any
> Three-l lllama.

The conventional way to describe a poem's rhyme scheme is to chart rhyming sounds that appear at the ends of lines. The sound that ends the first line is designated *a*, and all subsequent lines that end in that sound are also labeled *a*. The next sound to appear at the end of a line is designated *b*, and all other lines whose last sounds rhyme with it are also designated *b* — and so on through the alphabet. The lines of the poem that follows are labeled in this manner.

RICHARD WILBUR   (1921–   )

A Sketch   (1975)

Into the lower right	a
Square of the window frame	b
There came	b
with scalloped flight	a
A goldfinch, lit upon	c 5
The dead branch of a pine,	d
Shining,	d
and then was gone,	c
Tossed in a double arc	e
Upward into the thatched	f 10
And cross-hatched	f
pine-needle dark.	e
Briefly, as fresh drafts stirred	g
The tree, he dulled and gleamed	h
And seemed	h 15
more coal than bird,	g
Then, dodging down, returned	i
In a new light, his perch	j
A birch —	j
twig, where he burned	i 20
In the sun's broadside ray,	k
Some seed pinched in his bill.	l
Yet still	l
he did not stay,	k
But into a leaf-choken pane,	m 25
Changeful as even in heaven,	n
Even	n
in Saturn's reign,	m
Tunneled away and hid.	o
And then? But I cannot well	p 30
Tell	p
you all that he did.	o
It was like glancing at rough	q
Sketches tacked on a wall,	r
And all	r 35
so less than enough	q
Of gold on beaten wing,	s
I could not choose that one	t
Be done	t
as the finished thing.	s 40

Although the rhyme scheme of this poem (*abba, cddc,* and so on) is regular, it is hardly noticeable until it is charted. Despite its subtlety, however, the rhyme scheme is not unimportant. In fact, it reinforces the poem's meaning and binds lines into structural units, connecting the first and fourth as well as the second and third lines of each stanza. In stanza 1, "right" and "flight" draw lines 1 and 4 of the stanza together, bracketing "fame" and "came" in lines 2 and 3. The pattern begins again with the next stanza and continues through the rest of the poem. Like the elusive goldfinch the poet describes, the rhymes are difficult to follow with the eye. In this sense, the rhyme reflects the central theme of the poem: the difficulty of capturing in words a reality that, like the goldfinch, is forever shifting.

Of course, rhyme does not have to be subtle to enrich a poem. An obvious rhyme scheme can communicate meaning by connecting ideas that are not normally linked. Notice how Alexander Pope uses this technique in the following excerpt from *An Essay on Man:*

> Honour and shame from no condition rise;
> Act well your part, there all the honour lies.
> Fortune in men has some small diff'rence made,
> One flaunts in rags, one flutters in brocade;
> The cobbler aproned, and the parson gowned,
> The friar hooded, and the monarch crowned.
> "What differ more (you cry) than crown and cowl?"
> I'll tell you, friend; a wise man and a fool.
>
> You'll find, if once the monarch acts the monk,
> Or, cobbler-like, the parson will be drunk,
> Worth makes the man, and want of it, the fellow;
> The rest is all but leather or prunella.°
>   Stuck o'er with titles and hung round with strings,
> That thou mayest be by kings, or whores of kings.
> Boast the pure blood of an illustrious race,
> In quiet flow from Lucrece° to Lucrece;
> But by your fathers' worth if yours you rate,
> Count me those only who were good and great.

This poem is written in **heroic couplets**, paired iambic pentameter lines with a rhyme scheme of *aa, bb, cc, dd,* and so on. In a heroic couplet, greater stress falls on the second line, usually on the last word. Coming at the end of the line, this word receives double emphasis: it is strengthened both because of its position in the line and because it is rhymed with the last word of the couplet's first line. In this excerpt, rhyme sometimes joins opposing ideas, thereby reinforcing a theme that runs through the passage: the contrast between the high and the low, the virtuous and the immoral. For example, "gowned" and "crowned" in lines 5 and 6

° *prunella:* Heavy cloth the color of prunes.   ° *Lucrece:* In Roman legend, Lucrece stabbed herself after being defiled by Sextus Tarquinius.

convey the opposite conditions of the parson and the monarch and exemplify the idea expressed in lines 3 and 4 that fortune, not virtue, determines one's station.

FURTHER READING: Alliteration, Assonance, and Rhyme

GERARD MANLEY HOPKINS   (1844–1889)

Pied Beauty   (1918)

Glory be to God for dappled things —
    For skies of couple-color as a brinded° cow;
        For rose-moles all in stipple upon trout that swim;
Fresh-firecoal chestnut-falls; finches' wings;
    Landscape plotted and pieced — fold, fallow, and plow;   5
        And áll trádes, their gear and tackle and trim.°

All things counter, original, spare, strange;
    Whatever is fickle, freckled (who knows how?)
        With swift, slow; sweet, sour; adazzle, dim;
He fathers-forth whose beauty is past change: 10
            Praise him.

Reading and Reacting

1. Identify examples of onomatopoeia, alliteration, assonance, imperfect rhyme, and perfect rhyme. Do you think all these techniques are essential to the poem? Are any of them annoying or distracting?
2. What is the central idea of this poem? How do the sounds of the poem help to communicate this idea?
3. Identify examples of masculine and feminine rhyme.
4. **JOURNAL ENTRY** Hopkins uses both pleasing and discordant sounds in his poem. Identify uses of euphony and cacophony, and explain how these techniques affect your reactions to the poem.

Related Works: "Cathedral" (p. 476), "Women" (p. 824), "I never saw a Moor — " (p. 1162), "Batter My Heart, Three-Personed God" (p. 1168)

W. H. AUDEN   (1907–1973)

As I Walked Out One Evening   (1940)

As I walked out one evening,
    Walking down Bristol Street,

° *brinded:* Brindled (streaked).   ° *trim:* Equipment.

The crowds upon the pavement
   Were fields of harvest wheat.

And down by the brimming river   5
   I heard a lover sing
Under an arch of the railway:
   "Love has no ending.

"I'll love you, dear, I'll love you
   Till China and Africa meet,   10
And the river jumps over the mountain
   And the salmon sing in the street,

"I'll love you till the ocean
   Is folded and hung up to dry,
And the seven stars go squawking   15
   Like geese about the sky.

"The years shall run like rabbits,
   For in my arms I hold
The Flower of the Ages,
   And the first love of the world."   20

But all the clocks in the city
   Began to whirr and chime:
"O let not Time deceive you,
   You cannot conquer Time.

"In the burrows of the Nightmare   25
   Where Justice naked is,
Time watches from the shadow
   And coughs when you would kiss.

"In headaches and in worry
   Vaguely life leaks away,   30
And Time will have his fancy
   Tomorrow or today.

"Into many a green valley
   Drifts the appalling snow;
Time breaks the threaded dances   35
   And the diver's brilliant bow.

"O plunge your hands in water,
   Plunge them in up to the wrist;
Stare, stare in the basin
   And wonder what you've missed.   40

"The glacier knocks in the cupboard,
   The desert sighs in the bed,

And the crack in the teacup opens
    A lane to the land of the dead.

"Where the beggars raffle the banknotes   45
    And the Giant is enchanting to Jack,
And the Lily-white Boy is a Roarer,
    And Jill goes down on her back.

"O look, look in the mirror,
    O look in your distress;   50
Life remains a blessing
    Although you cannot bless.

"O stand, stand at the window
    As the tears scald and start;
You shall love your crooked neighbor   55
    With your crooked heart."

It was late, late in the evening,
    The lovers they were gone;
The clocks had ceased their chiming,
    And the deep river ran on.   60

Reading and Reacting

1. Does Auden use perfect rhyme at the end of the second line and the fourth line of each stanza? If not, why do you think he chooses not to?

2. Chart the poem's rhyme scheme. Does Auden use internal rhyme? Where does he use alliteration and assonance? In what other ways does he use sound?

3. Does Auden's use of sound reinforce the poem's content or undercut it? Explain.

4. **JOURNAL ENTRY** Could this poem be considered a love poem? How are its sentiments about love different from those conventionally expressed in poems about love?

5. **CRITICAL PERSPECTIVE** In a 1940 British review of Auden's work, T. C. Worsley made the following comments about this poem:

> There is no technical reason why such a poem as [this] should not be popular; the metre and the rhythm are easy and helpful, and the symbols have reference to a world of experience common to every inhabitant of these islands. Here . . . the poet has gone as far as he can along the road to creating a popular poetry.

Does Auden's poem strike you as a model for "popular" poetry — that is, poetry for people who do not usually read poetry?

Related Works: "The Story of an Hour" (p. 197), "Araby" (p. 395), "The World Is Too Much with Us" (p. 870), "Oh, my love is like a red, red rose" (p. 944), "To His Coy Mistress" (p. 957), "Not marble, nor the gilded monuments" (p. 1222)

GALWAY KINNELL (1927–   )

Blackberry Eating (1980)

I love to go out in late September
among the fat, overripe, icy, black blackberries
to eat blackberries for breakfast,
the stalks very prickly, a penalty
they earn for knowing the black art   5
of blackberry-making; and as I stand among them
lifting the stalks to my mouth, the ripest berries
fall almost unbidden to my tongue,
as words sometimes do, certain peculiar words
like *strengths* or *squinched*,   10
many-lettered, one-syllabled lumps,
which I squeeze, squinch open, and splurge well
in the silent, startled, icy, black language
of blackberry-eating in late September.

Reading and Reacting

1. What sounds does Kinnell repeat in the poem? How do they help to create the poem's rhythm?
2. This poem consists entirely of run-on lines. Why do you think the poet uses this technique instead of end-stopped lines?
3. One part of the poem deals with blackberries, and the other part deals with the poet's love for words. What connection exists between these two subjects?
4. How do alliteration, assonance, and line length help Kinnell convey his ideas?
5. **JOURNAL ENTRY** What do you think this poem is really about?
6. **CRITICAL PERSPECTIVE** Critic Daniela Gioseffi had the following to say about Galway Kinnell:

> He has real things to say about an actual world of flesh and bone and excrement, full of nature's glories and horrors, always viewed from within the reality of our gutsy, animal being, our need to survive from the land and its vulnerable animal life, a world poignant with transient beauty and helpless mortality.

Do you think this poem reflects both nature's "glories" and its "horrors"? How does it comment on the transient beauty of nature and our own "helpless mortality"?

Related Works: "Seventeen Syllables" (p. 538), "B. Wordsworth" (p. 757), "Words, Words, Words" (p. 891), "Introduction to Poetry" (p. 1155)

LYDIA DAVIS (1947–   )

A Mown Lawn (2001)

She hated a *mown lawn*. Maybe that was because *mow* was the reverse of   5
wom, the beginning of the name of what she was — a *woman*. A *mown
lawn* had a sad sound to it, like a *long moan*. From her, a *mown lawn* made
a *long moan*. *Lawn* had some of the letters of *man*, though the reverse of
man would be *Nam*, a bad war. A *raw war*. *Lawn* also contained the letters of *law*. In fact, *lawn* was a contraction of *lawman*. Certainly a *law-*   10
man could and did *mow a lawn*. *Law* and *order* could be seen as starting
from *lawn order*, valued by so many Americans. *More lawn* could be made
using a *lawn mower*. A *lawn mower* did make *more lawn*. *More lawn* was
a contraction of *more lawmen*. Did *more lawn* in America make *more law-*
men in America? Did *more lawn* make *more Nam?* *More mown lawn* made   15
more long moan, from her. Or a *lawn mourn*. So often, she said, Americans wanted *more mown lawn*. All of America might be one *long mown
lawn*. A *lawn* not *mown* grows *long*, she said: better a *long lawn*. Better a
long lawn and a *mole*. Let the *lawman* have the *mown lawn*, she said. Or
the *moron*, the *lawn moron*.

Reading and Reacting

1. Identify several different types of rhyme in this poem. Then, find examples
of alliteration and assonance.
2. "A Mown Lawn" does not conform to most people's idea of what a poem should
look like. Do you think "A Mown Lawn" is a poem, or is it something else?
3. Study the poem's italicized words and phrases. How are they related in terms
of sound? What ideas do these words convey?
4. JOURNAL ENTRY What comment does this poem make about life in the
United States?

Related Works: "The Secret Lion" (p. 170), "Sleepy Time Gal" (p. 154), "Sears
Life" (p. 907), "Nice Car, Camille" (p. 862), "The World Is Too Much with Us"
(p. 870), "A Supermarket in California" (p. 965), "The True-Blue American"
(p. 1044)

ROBERT FRANCIS (1901–1987)

Pitcher (1953)

His art is eccentricity, his aim
How not to hit the mark he seems to aim at,

His passion how to avoid the obvious,
His technique how to vary the avoidance.

The others throw to be comprehended. He   5
Throws to be a moment misunderstood.

Yet not too much. Not errant, arrant, wild,
But every seeming aberration willed.

Not to, yet still, still to communicate
Making the batter understand too late.   10

Reading and Reacting

1. Although this poem does not have a regular rhyme scheme, it still includes words that rhyme. Underline these rhyming words, and explain how they contribute to the poem's overall effect.
2. In addition to using rhyme, Francis also uses repetition. What words does he repeat? What ideas are emphasized with this repetition?
3. Where does Francis use alliteration and assonance? Do alliteration and assonance contribute something to the poem, or are they distractions? Explain.
4. **JOURNAL ENTRY** Do you think this poem is an accurate description of a pitcher? Could the poem also be describing something else? Explain.
5. **CRITICAL PERSPECTIVE** Poet and critic Donald Hall, in a review of Robert Francis's *Collected Poems*, makes the following comments on two of Francis's poems about baseball, one of which is "Pitcher":

   > Francis is not one to care about baseball much. Baseball is a diamond to begin with, and on this diamond the young ballplayers perform their ritual shapes, as if conspiring to place a grid over the chaos of experience. And this is what, by his shapely resolutions, Francis does with his poems.

   Do you agree with Hall that "Pitcher" is about more than a pitcher trying to strike a batter out? Could Francis have written the poem without caring about baseball?

Related Works: "The Rocking-Horse Winner" (p. 525), "B. Wordsworth" (p. 757), "Poetry" (p. 809), "How to Write the Great American Indian Novel" (p. 887), "Cloud Painter" (p. 921), "Constantly Risking Absurdity" (p. 941), "Ex-Basketball Player" (p. 946)

MONA VAN DUYN (1921–2004)

The Beginning (2002)

The end
of passion
may refashion
a friend.

Eyes meet   5
in fear
of such dear
defeat.

The heart's core,
unbroken,   10
cringes.

The soul's door
swings open
on its hinges.

Reading and Reacting

1. This poem consists of two four-line stanzas and two three-line stanzas. What ideas are expressed in the first two stanzas, and what ideas are expressed in the last two stanzas? How does the change in stanza length help Van Duyn express these different ideas?

2. How does the poem's rhyme scheme change between the first two stanzas and the second two stanzas? Why do you think that Van Duyn made this change?

3. Does Van Duyn use perfect or imperfect rhyme in this poem?

4. JOURNAL ENTRY What is the significance of the poem's title? Can you think of another title that might be more appropriate?

Related Works: "Araby" (p. 395), "Cathedral" (p. 476), "Living in Sin" (p. 897), "Nothing Gold Can Stay" (p. 930), "What Is an Epigram?" (p. 1010), "The Soul selects her own Society —" (p. 1165)

LEWIS CARROLL (1832–1898)

Jabberwocky (1871)

'Twas brillig, and the slithy toves
    Did gyre and gimble in the wabe:
All mimsy were the borogoves,
    And the mome raths outgrabe.

"Beware the Jabberwock, my son!   5
    The jaws that bite, the claws that catch!
Beware the Jubjub bird, and shun
    The frumious Bandersnatch!"

He took his vorpal sword in hand;
    Long time the manxome foe he sought —   10
So rested he by the Tumtum tree

> And stood awhile in thought.
>
> And, as in uffish thought he stood,
>   The Jabberwock, with eyes of flame,
> Came whiffling through the tulgey wood,   15
>   And burbled as it came!
>
> One, two! One, two! And through and through
>   The vorpal blade went snicker-snack!
> He left it dead, and with its head
>   He went galumphing back.   20
>
> "And hast thou slain the Jabberwock?
>   Come to my arms, my beamish boy!
> O frabjous day! Callooh, Callay!"
>   He chortled in his joy.
>
> 'Twas brillig, and the slithy toves   25
>   Did gyre and gimble in the wabe:
> All mimsy were the borogoves,
>   And the mome raths outgrabe.

Reading and Reacting

1. Many words in this poem may be unfamiliar to you. Are they actual words? Use a dictionary to check before you dismiss any. Do some words seem to have meaning in the context of the poem regardless of whether they appear in the dictionary? Explain.

2. This poem contains many examples of onomatopoeia. What meanings do the sounds of these words suggest?

3. JOURNAL ENTRY Summarize the story the poem tells. In what sense is this poem a story of a young man's initiation into adulthood?

4. CRITICAL PERSPECTIVE According to Humpty Dumpty in Carroll's *Alice in Wonderland*, the nonsense words in the poem are **portmanteau words** (that is, words whose form and meaning are derived from two other distinct words — as *smog* is a portmanteau of *smoke* and *fog*). Critic Elizabeth Sewell, however, rejects this explanation: "[F]rumious, for instance, is not a word, and does not have two meanings packed up in it; it is a group of letters without any meaning at all. . . . [I]t looks like other words, and almost certainly more than two."

Which nonsense words in the poem seem to you to be portmanteau words, and which do not? Can you suggest possible sources for the words that are not portmanteau words?

Related Works: "A&P" (p. 230), "Gryphon" (p. 248), *The Cuban Swimmer* (p. 1772)

✔ **CHECKLIST   Writing about Sound**

Rhythm and Meter

☐ Does the poem contain repeated words and phrases? If so, how do they help to create rhythm?

☐ Does the poem use one kind of meter, or does the meter vary from line to line?

☐ How does the meter contribute to the overall effect of the poem?

☐ Which lines of the poem contain caesuras? What effect do they have?

☐ Are the lines of the poem end-stopped, run-on, or a combination of the two? What effects are created by the presence or absence of pauses at the ends of lines?

Alliteration, Assonance, and Rhyme

☐ Does the poem include alliteration or assonance?

☐ Does the poem have a regular rhyme scheme?

☐ Does the poem use internal rhyme? Beginning rhyme?

☐ Does the poem include examples of masculine, feminine, or triple rhyme?

☐ How does rhyme unify the poem?

☐ How does rhyme reinforce the poem's ideas?

WRITING SUGGESTIONS: Sound

1. William Blake's "The Tyger" appeared in a collection entitled *Songs of Experience*. Compare this poem (p. 1146) to "The Lamb" (p. 1145), which appeared in a collection called *Songs of Innocence*. In what sense are the speakers in these two poems either "innocent" or "experienced"? How does sound help to convey the voice of the speakers in these two poems?

2. "Sadie and Maud" (p. 970), like "The Faithful Wife" (p. 909), "My Papa's Waltz" (p. 1058), and "Daddy" (p. 952), communicates the speaker's attitude toward home and family. How does the presence or absence of rhyme in these poems help to convey the speakers' attitudes toward home and family?

3. Robert Frost once said that writing poems that have no fixed metrical pattern is like playing tennis without a net. What do you think he meant? Do you agree? After reading "Out, Out —" (p. 959), "Stopping by Woods

on a Snowy Evening" (p. 1180), and "The Road Not Taken" (p. 1180), write
an essay in which you discuss Frost's use of meter.

4. Select two or three contemporary poems that have no end rhyme. Write an
essay in which you discuss what these poets gain and lose by not using end
rhyme.

5. Prose writers as well as poets use techniques such as assonance and alliteration. Choose a passage of prose — from "Araby" (p. 395), "Barn Burning"
(p. 356), or "The Things They Carried" (p. 435), for example — and discuss its use of assonance and alliteration. Where are these techniques used?
How do they help the writer create a mood?

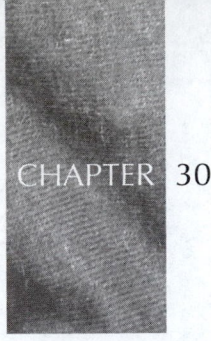

CHAPTER 30

FORM

> No verse can be free; it must be governed by some measure, but not by the old measure.
>
> —**William Carlos Williams,** *"On Measure"*

JOHN KEATS (1795–1821)

On the Sonnet (1819)

If by dull rhymes our English must be chained,
And like Andromeda,° the sonnet sweet
Fettered, in spite of painéd loveliness,
Let us find, if we must be constrained,
Sandals more interwoven and complete   5
To fit the naked foot of Poesy:
Let us inspect the lyre, and weigh the stress
Of every chord, and see what may be gained
By ear industrious, and attention meet;
Misers of sound and syllable, no less   10
Than Midas° of his coinage, let us be
Jealous of dead leaves in the bay-wreath crown;
So, if we may not let the Muse be free,
She will be bound with garlands of her own.

BILLY COLLINS (1941–)

Sonnet (1999)

All we need is fourteen lines, well, thirteen now,
and after this one just a dozen
to launch a little ship on love's storm chased seas,

° *Andromeda:* In Greek mythology, an Ethiopian princess chained to a rock to appease a sea monster.   ° *Midas:*
A legendary king of Phrygia whose wish that everything he touched would turn to gold was granted by the god
Dionysus.

then only ten more left like rows of beans.
How easily it goes unless you get Elizabethan   5
and insist the iambic bongos must be played
and rhymes positioned at the ends of lines,
one for every station of the cross.
But hang on here while we make the turn
into the final six where all will be resolved,   10
where longing and heartache will find an end,
where Laura will tell Petrarch to put down his pen,
take off those crazy medieval tights,
blow out the lights, and come at last to bed.

The **form** of a literary work is its structure or shape, the way its elements fit together to form a whole; **poetic form** is the design of a poem described in terms of rhyme, meter, and stanzaic pattern.

Until the twentieth century, most poetry was written in **closed form** (sometimes called **fixed form**), characterized by regular patterns of meter, rhyme, line length, and stanzaic divisions. Early poems that were passed down orally — epics and ballads, for example — relied on regular form to facilitate memorization. Even after poems began to be written down, poets tended to favor regular patterns. In fact, until relatively recently, regular form was what distinguished poetry from prose. Of course, strict adherence to regular patterns sometimes produced poems that were, in John Keats's words, "chained" by "dull rhymes" and "fettered" by the rules governing a particular form. But rather than feeling "constrained" by form, many poets — like Billy Collins in the playful sonnet above — have experimented with imagery, figures of speech, allusion, and other techniques, stretching closed form to its limits.

As they sought new ways in which to express themselves, poets also used forms from other cultures, adapting them to the demands of their own languages. English and American poets, for example, adopted (and still use) early French forms, such as the villanelle and the sestina, and early Italian forms, such as the Petrarchan sonnet and terza rima. The nineteenth-century American poet Henry Wadsworth Longfellow studied Icelandic epics; the twentieth- century poet Ezra Pound studied the works of French troubadours; and Pound and other twentieth-century American poets, such as Richard Wright and Carolyn Kizer, were inspired by Japanese haiku. Other American poets, such as Vachel Lindsay, Langston Hughes, and Maya Angelou, looked closer to home — to the rhythms of blues, jazz, and spirituals — for inspiration.

As time went on, more and more poets moved away from closed form to experiment with **open form** poetry (sometimes called **free verse** or *vers libre*), varying line length within a poem, dispensing with stanzaic divisions, breaking lines in unexpected places, and even abandoning any semblance of formal structure. In English, nineteenth-century poets — such as William Blake and Matthew Arnold — experimented with lines of irregular meter and length, and Walt Whitman wrote **prose poems**, open form poems whose long lines made them look like prose. (Well before this time, Asian poetry and some biblical passages had used a type of free verse.) In nineteenth-century France, Symbolist poets, such as Baudelaire, Rimbaud, Verlaine, and Mallarmé, also used free verse. In the early twentieth century, a group of American poets — including Ezra Pound, William Carlos Williams, and Amy Lowell — who were associated with a movement known as **imagism** wrote poetry that dispensed with traditional principles of English versification, creating new rhythms and meters.

Although much contemporary English and American poetry is composed in open form, many poets also continue to write in closed form — even in very traditional, highly structured patterns. Still, new forms, and new variations of old forms, are being created all the time. And, because contemporary poets do not necessarily feel bound by rules or restrictions about what constitutes "acceptable" poetic form, they experiment freely, trying to discover the form that best suits the poem's purpose, subject, language, and theme.

Closed Form

A **closed form** (or *fixed form*) poem looks symmetrical; it has an identifiable, repeated pattern, with lines of similar length arranged in groups of two, three, four, or more. A closed form poem also tends to rely on regular metrical patterns and rhyme schemes.

Despite what its name suggests, closed form poetry does not have to be confining or conservative. In fact, contemporary poets often experiment with closed form — for example, by using characteristics of open form poetry (such as lines of varying length) within a closed form. Sometimes they move back and forth within a single poem from open to closed to open form; sometimes (like their eighteenth-century counterparts) they combine different stanzaic forms (stanzas of two and three lines, for example) within a single poem.

Even when poets work within a traditional closed form, such as a *sonnet*, *sestina*, or *villanelle*, they can break new ground. For example, they can write a sonnet with an unexpected meter or rhyme scheme, add an extra line or even extra stanzas to a traditional sonnet form, combine two different traditional sonnet forms in a single poem, or write an abbreviated version of a sestina or villanelle. In other words, poets can use traditional forms as building blocks, combining them in innovative ways to create new patterns and new forms.

Sometimes a pattern (such as *blank verse*) simply determines the meter of a poem's individual lines. At other times, the pattern extends to the level of the *stanza*, with lines arranged into groups (*couplets*, *quatrains*, and so on). At still other times, as in the case of traditional closed forms like sonnets, a poetic pattern gives shape to an entire poem.

Blank Verse

Blank verse is unrhymed poetry with each line written in a set pattern of five stressed and five unstressed syllables called **iambic pentameter** (see p. 973). Many passages from Shakespeare's plays, such as the following lines from *Hamlet*, are written in blank verse.

> To sleep! perchance to dream:—ay, there's the rub;
> For in that sleep of death what dreams may come,
> When we have shuffled off this mortal coil,
> Must give us pause: there's the respect
> That makes calamity of so long life

For a contemporary use of blank verse, see John Updike's "Ex-Basketball Player" (p. 946).

Stanza

A **stanza** is a group of two or more lines with the same metrical pattern — and often with a regular rhyme scheme as well — separated by blank space from other such groups of lines. Stanzas in poetry are like paragraphs in prose: they group related ideas into units.

A two-line stanza with rhyming lines of similar length and meter is called a **couplet**. The **heroic couplet**, first used by Chaucer and especially popular throughout the eighteenth century, consists of two rhymed lines of iambic pentameter, with a weak pause after the first line and a strong pause after the second. The following example, from Alexander Pope's *An Essay on Criticism*, is a heroic couplet.

> True ease in writing comes from art, not chance,
> As those move easiest who have learned to dance.

A three-line stanza with lines of similar length and a set rhyme scheme is called a **tercet**. Percy Bysshe Shelley's "Ode to the West Wind" (p. 1222) is built largely of tercets.

> O wild West Wind, thou breath of Autumn's being,
> Thou, from whose unseen presence the leaves dead
> Are driven, like ghosts from an enchanter fleeing,
>
> Yellow, and black, and pale, and hectic red,
> Pestilence-stricken multitudes: O Thou,
> Who chariotest to their dark wintry bed

Although in many tercets all three lines rhyme, "Ode to the West Wind" uses a special rhyme scheme, also used by Dante, called **terza rima**. This rhyme scheme (*aba, bcb, cdc, ded*, and so on) creates an interlocking series of stanzas: line 2's *dead* looks ahead to the rhyming words *red* and *bed*, which close lines 4 and 6, and the pattern continues throughout the poem.

A four-line stanza with lines of similar length and a set rhyme scheme is called a **quatrain**. The quatrain, the most widely used and versatile unit in English and American poetry, is used by William Wordsworth in the following excerpt from "She dwelt among the untrodden ways" (p. 1242).

> A violet by a mossy stone
>   Half hidden from the eye!
> —Fair as a star, when only one
>   Is shining in the sky.

Quatrains are frequently used by contemporary poets as well — for instance, in Theodore Roethke's "My Papa's Waltz" (p. 1058), Adrienne Rich's "Aunt Jennifer's Tigers" (p. 977), and William Stafford's "Traveling through the Dark" (p. 1070).

One special kind of quatrain, called the **ballad stanza,** alternates lines of eight and six syllables; typically, only the second and fourth lines rhyme. The following lines from the traditional Scottish ballad "Sir Patrick Spence" illustrate the ballad stanza.

> The king sits in Dumferling toune,
>   Drinking the blude-reid wine:
> "O whar will I get guid sailor
>   To sail this schip of mine?"

Common measure, a four-line stanzaic pattern closely related to the ballad stanza, is used in hymns as well as in poetry. It differs from the ballad stanza in that its rhyme scheme is *abab* rather than *abcb*. This pattern appears in Donald Hall's poem "My Son, My Executioner" (p. 961).

Other stanzaic forms include **rhyme royal**, a seven-line stanza (*ababbcc*) set in iambic pentameter, used in Sir Thomas Wyatt's sixteenth-century poem "They Flee from Me That Sometimes Did Me Seke" as well as in Theodore Roethke's twentieth-century "I Knew a Woman" (p. 901); **ottava rima**, an eight-line stanza (*abababcc*) set in iambic pentameter; and the Spenserian stanza, a nine-line form (*ababbcbcc*) whose first eight lines are set in iambic pentameter and whose last line is in iambic hexameter. The Romantic poets John Keats and Percy Bysshe Shelley were among those who used the Spenserian stanza. (See Chapter 29 for definitions and examples of various metrical patterns.)

The Sonnet

Perhaps the most familiar kind of traditional closed form poem written in English is the **sonnet**, a fourteen-line poem with a distinctive rhyme scheme and metrical pattern. The English or **Shakespearean sonnet**, which consists of fourteen lines divided into three quatrains and a concluding couplet, is written in iambic pentameter and follows the rhyme scheme *abab cdcd efef gg*. The **Petrarchan sonnet**, popularized in the fourteenth century by the Italian poet Francesco Petrarch, also consists of fourteen lines of iambic pentameter, but these lines are divided into an eight-line unit called an **octave** and a six-line unit (composed of two tercets) called a **sestet**. The rhyme scheme of the octave is *abba abba*; the rhyme scheme of the sestet is *cde cde*.

The conventional structures of these sonnet forms reflect the arrangement of ideas within the poem. In the Shakespearean sonnet, the poet typically presents three "paragraphs" of related thoughts, introducing an idea in the first quatrain, developing it in the two remaining quatrains, and summing up in a succinct closing couplet. In the Petrarchan sonnet, the octave introduces a problem that is resolved in the sestet. (Many Shakespearean sonnets also have a problem-solution structure.) Some poets vary the traditional patterns somewhat to suit the poem's language or ideas. For example, they may depart from the pattern to sidestep a forced rhyme or unnatural stress on a syllable, or they may shift from problem to solution in a place other than between octave and sestet.

The following poem has the form of a traditional English sonnet.

WILLIAM SHAKESPEARE (1564–1616)

When, in disgrace with Fortune and men's eyes (1609)

When, in disgrace with Fortune and men's eyes,
I all alone beweep my outcast state,
And trouble deaf heaven with my bootless° cries,
And look upon myself and curse my fate,
Wishing me like to one more rich in hope,   5
Featured like him, like him with friends possessed,
Desiring this man's art, and that man's scope,
With what I most enjoy contented least,
Yet in these thoughts myself almost despising,
Haply° I think on thee, and then my state,   10
Like to the lark at break of day arising
From sullen earth, sings hymns at heaven's gate;
     For thy sweet love rememb'red such wealth brings
     That then I scorn to change my state with kings.

This sonnet is written in iambic pentameter and has a conventional rhyme scheme: *abab* (eyes-state-cries-fate), *cdcd* (hope-possessed-scope-least), *efef* (despising-state-arising-gate), *gg* (brings-kings). In this poem, in which the speaker explains how thoughts of his loved one can rescue him from despair, each quatrain is unified by subject matter as well as by rhyme. In the first quatrain, the speaker presents his problem: he is down on his luck and out of favor with his peers, isolated in self-pity and cursing his fate. In the second quatrain, he develops this idea further: he is envious of others and dissatisfied with things that usually please him. In the third quatrain, the focus shifts. Although the first two quatrains develop a dependent clause ("When . . .") that introduces a problem, line 9 begins to present the resolution. In the third quatrain, the speaker explains how, in the midst of his despair and self-hatred, he thinks of his loved one, and his spirits soar. The closing couplet sums up the mood transformation the poem describes and explains its significance: when the speaker realizes the emotional riches his loved one gives him, he is no longer envious of others.

FURTHER READING: The Sonnet

JOHN KEATS (1795–1821)

On First Looking into Chapman's Homer° (1816)

Much have I traveled in the realms of gold,
     And many goodly states and kingdoms seen;

°*bootless:* Futile.   °*Haply:* Luckily.   °*Chapman's Homer:* The translation of Homer's works by Elizabethan poet George Chapman.

Round many western islands have I been
Which bards in fealty to Apollo° hold.
Oft of one wide expanse had I been told   5
    That deep-browed Homer ruled as his demesne,°
    Yet did I never breathe its pure serene°
Till I heard Chapman speak out loud and bold.
Then felt I like some watcher of the skies
    When a new planet swims into his ken;   10
Or like stout Cortez° when with eagle eyes
    He stared at the Pacific — and all his men
Looked at each other with a wild surmise —
    Silent, upon a peak in Darien.°

Reading and Reacting

1. Is this a Petrarchan or a Shakespearean sonnet? Explain.

2. JOURNAL ENTRY The sestet's change of focus is introduced with the word "Then" in line 9. How does the mood of the sestet differ from the mood of the octave? How does the language differ?

3. CRITICAL PERSPECTIVE As Keats's biographer Aileen Ward observes, Homer's epic tales of gods and heroes were known to most readers of Keats's day only in a very formal eighteenth-century translation by Alexander Pope. This is Pope's description of Ulysses escaping from a shipwreck:

>   his knees no more
> Perform'd their office, or his weight upheld:
> His swoln heart heav'd, his bloated body swell'd:
> From mouth to nose the briny torrent ran,
> And lost in lassitude lay all the man,
> Deprived of voice, of motion, and of breath,
> The soul scarce waking in the arms of death . . .

In a rare 1616 edition of Chapman's translation, Keats discovered a very different poem:

>   both knees falt'ring, both
> His strong hands hanging down, and all with froth
> His cheeks and nostrils flowing, voice and breath
> Spent to all use, and down he sank to death.
> The sea had soak'd his heart through. . . .

This, as Ward notes, was "poetry of a kind that had not been written in England for two hundred years."

Can you understand why Keats was so moved by Chapman's translation? Do you think Keats's own poem seems closer in its form and language to Pope or to Chapman?

°*Apollo:* Greek god of light, truth, reason, male beauty; associated with music and poetry. °*demesne:* Realm, domain. °*serene:* Air, atmosphere. °*Cortez:* It was Vasco de Balboa (not Hernando Cortez as Keats suggests) who first saw the Pacific Ocean, from "a peak in Darien." °*Darien:* Former name of the Isthmus of Panama.

Related Works: "Gryphon" (p. 248), "Araby" (p. 395), "When I Heard the Learn'd Astronomer" (p. 893), *Beauty* (p. 1308), *Trifles* (p. 1372)

GWENDOLYN BROOKS (1917–2000)

First Fight. Then Fiddle (1949)

First fight. Then fiddle. Ply the slipping string
With feathery sorcery; muzzle the note
With hurting love; the music that they wrote
Bewitch, bewilder. Qualify to sing
Threadwise. Devise no salt, no hempen thing   5
For the dear instrument to bear. Devote
The bow to silks and honey. Be remote
A while from malice and from murdering.
But first to arms, to armor. Carry hate
In front of you and harmony behind.   10
Be deaf to music and to beauty blind.
Win war. Rise bloody, maybe not too late
For having first to civilize a space
Wherein to play your violin with grace.

Reading and Reacting

1. What is the subject of Brooks's poem? What do you think she means by "fight" and "fiddle"?
2. Explain the poem's rhyme scheme. Is this rhyme scheme an essential element of the poem? Would the poem be equally effective if it did not include end rhyme? Why or why not?
3. Study the poem's use of capitalization and punctuation carefully. Why do you think Brooks chooses to end many of her sentences in midline? How do her decisions determine how you read the poem?

Related Works: "The Soldier" (p. 1080), "For the Student Strikers" (p. 910), "The White City" (p. 872), "The *Chicago Defender* Sends a Man to Little Rock" (p. 1148)

MONA VAN DUYN (1921–2004)

Minimalist Sonnet: Summer Virus (1991)

Send this blaze still higher.
Degree by degree
let my fever aspire
to transfigure me

to a lampbulb's wire,   5
the red waft of a kite.
From no former fire
shone a blush so bright.

I'll stoke with my numbing
flesh, senses, insight,   10
unafraid of becoming
more and more light,

since I've felt one presence
as incandescence.

Reading and Reacting

1. What pattern of imagery can you identify in this poem? How do the related images help to communicate the poem's theme?
2. What is the "summer virus" to which the title refers? What is the "one presence" (line 13) that the speaker feels as "incandescence" (line 14)?
3. Do you see this as a love poem, or do you think it might be about something else? Explain.
4. **JOURNAL ENTRY** Study this poem's rhyme scheme, arrangement of lines, and metrical pattern carefully. How is the poem like a traditional sonnet? How is it different? In what sense is it "minimalist"?

Related Works: "Araby" (p. 395), "That time of year thou mayst in me behold" (p. 817), "Sonnet" (p. 997)

The Sestina

The **sestina**, introduced in thirteenth-century France, is composed of six six-line stanzas and a three-line conclusion called an **envoi**. The sestina does not require end rhyme; however, it requires that each line end with one of six key words, which are repeated throughout the poem in a fixed order. The alternation of these six words in different positions — but always at the ends of lines — in each of the poem's six stanzas creates a rhythmic verbal pattern that unifies the poem, as the key words do in the poem that follows.

ALBERTO ALVARO RÍOS (1952–)

Nani (1982)

Sitting at her table, she serves
the sopa de arroz° to me
instinctively, and I watch her,

───────────────────────

° *sopa de arroz:* Rice soup.

the absolute mamá, and eat words
I might have had to say more   5
out of embarrassment. To speak,
now-foreign words I used to speak,
too, dribble down her mouth as she serves
me albóndigas.° No more
than a third are easy to me.   10
By the stove she does something with words
and looks at me only with her
back. I am full. I tell her
I taste the mint, and watch her speak
smiles at the stove. All my words   15
make her smile. Nani never serves
herself, she only watches me
with her skin, her hair. I ask for more.

I watch the mamá warming more
tortillas for me. I watch her   20
fingers in the flame for me.
Near her mouth, I see a wrinkle speak
of a man whose body serves
the ants like she serves me, then more words
from more wrinkles about children, words   25
about this and that, flowing more
easily from these other mouths. Each serves
as a tremendous string around her,
holding her together. They speak
nani was this and that to me   30
and I wonder just how much of me
will die with her, what were the words
I could have been, was. Her insides speak
through a hundred wrinkles, now, more
than she can bear, steel around her,   35
shouting, then, What is this thing she serves?

She asks me if I want more.
I own no words to stop her.
Even before I speak, she serves.

In many respects, Ríos's poem closely follows the form of the traditional sestina. For instance, it interweaves six key words — "serves," "me," "her," "words," "more," and "speak" — through six groups of six lines each, rearranging the order in which the words appear so that the first line of each group of six lines ends with the same key word that also ended the preceding group of lines. The poem repeats the key words

---

° *albóndigas:* Meatballs.

in exactly the order prescribed: *abcdef, faebdc, cfdabe,* and so on. In addition, the sestina closes with a three-line envoi that includes all six of the poem's key words, three at the ends of lines and three within the lines. Despite this generally strict adherence to the sestina form, however, Ríos departs from the form by grouping his six sets of six lines not into six separate stanzas but rather into two eighteen-line stanzas.

The sestina form suits Ríos's subject matter. The focus of the poem, on the verbal and nonverbal interaction between the poem's "me" and "her," is reinforced by each of the related words. "Nani" is a poem about communication, and the key words return to probe this theme again and again. Throughout the poem, these repeated words help to create a fluid, melodic, and tightly woven work.

FURTHER READING: The Sestina

ELIZABETH BISHOP   (1911–1979)

Sestina   (1965)

September rain falls on the house.
In the failing light, the old grandmother
sits in the kitchen with the child
beside the Little Marvel Stove,
reading the jokes from the almanac,   5
laughing and talking to hide her tears.

She thinks that her equinoctial tears
and the rain that beats on the roof of the house
were both foretold by the almanac,
but only known to a grandmother.   10
The iron kettle sings on the stove.
She cuts some bread and says to the child,

It's time for tea now; but the child
is watching the teakettle's small hard tears
dance like mad on the hot black stove,   15
the way the rain must dance on the house.
Tidying up, the old grandmother
hangs up the clever almanac

on its string. Birdlike, the almanac
hovers half open above the child,   20
hovers above the old grandmother
and her teacup full of dark brown tears.
She shivers and says she thinks the house
feels chilly, and puts more wood in the stove.

It was to be, says the Marvel Stove.   25
I know what I know, says the almanac.
With crayons the child draws a rigid house

and a winding pathway. Then the child
puts in a man with buttons like tears
and shows it proudly to the grandmother.   30

But secretly, while the grandmother
busies herself about the stove,
the little moons fall down like tears
from between the pages of the almanac
into the flower bed the child   35
has carefully placed in the front of the house.

Time to plant tears, says the almanac.
The grandmother sings to the marvellous stove
and the child draws another inscrutable house.

Reading and Reacting

1. Does the poet's adherence to the traditional sestina form create any problems? For example, do you think the syntax is strained at any point? Explain.
2. How does this sestina use sound — meter, rhyme, alliteration, assonance, and so on (see Chapter 29)? Could sound have been used more effectively? How?
3. JOURNAL ENTRY How are the six key words related to the poem's theme?

Related Works: "My Papa's Waltz" (p. 1058), "The Meal" (p. 925), "Nani" (p. 1005)

The Villanelle

The **villanelle**, first introduced in France during the Middle Ages, is a nineteen-line poem composed of five tercets and a concluding quatrain; its rhyme scheme is *aba aba aba aba aba abaa*. Two different lines are systematically repeated in the poem: line 1 appears again in lines 6, 12, and 18, and line 3 reappears as lines 9, 15, and 19. Thus, each tercet concludes with an exact (or close) duplication of either line 1 or line 3, and the final quatrain concludes by repeating both line 1 and line 3.

THEODORE ROETHKE (1908–1963)

The Waking (1953)

I wake to sleep, and take my waking slow.
I feel my fate in what I cannot fear.
I learn by going where I have to go.

We think by feeling. What is there to know?
I hear my being dance from ear to ear.   5
I wake to sleep, and take my waking slow.

Of those so close beside me, which are you?
God bless the Ground! I shall walk softly there,
And learn by going where I have to go.

Light takes the Tree; but who can tell us how?   10
The lowly worm climbs up a winding stair;
I wake to sleep, and take my waking slow.

Great Nature has another thing to do
To you and me; so take the lively air,
And, lovely, learn by going where to go.   15

This shakin e steady. I should know.
What falls away is always. And is near.
I wake to sleep, and take my waking slow.
I learn by going where I have to go.

"The Waking," like all villanelles, closely intertwines threads of sounds and words. The repeated lines and the very regular rhyme and meter give the poem a monotonous, almost hypnotic, rhythm. This poem uses end rhyme and repeats entire lines. It also makes extensive use of alliteration ("I feel my fate in what I cannot fear") and internal rhyme ("I hear my being dance from ear to ear"; "I wake to sleep and take my waking slow"). The result is a tightly constructed poem of overlapping sounds and images. (For an example of another well-known villanelle, see Dylan Thomas's "Do not go gentle into that good night," p. 1065.)

FURTHER READING: The Villanelle

MARY JO SALTER (1954–)

Video Blues

My husband has a crush on Myrna Loy,°
and likes to rent her moves, for a treat.
It makes some evenings harder to enjoy.

The list of actresses who might employ
him as their slave is too long to repeat.   5
(My husband has a crush on Myrna Loy,

Carole Lombard, Paulette Goddard, coy
Jean Arthur° with that voice as dry as wheat . . .)
It makes some evenings harder to enjoy.

Does he confess all this just to annoy   10
a loyal spouse? I know I can't compete.
My husband has a crush on Myrna Loy.

And can't a woman have her dreamboats? Boy,
I wouldn't say my life is incomplete.
but some evening I could certainly enjoy   15

° *Myrna Loy:* Originally a silent screen actress of the 1920s, Loy was repeatedly cast in the role of a seductress before landing a lead with William Powell in *The Thin Man* and its popular sequels. From there, she became a full-fledged queen of Hollywood.   ° *Carole Lombard, Paulette Goddard, Jean Arthur:* Famous film actresses of the 1930s and 1940s.

two hours with Cary Grant as *my* own toy.
I guess, though, we were destined not to meet.
My husband has a crush on Myrna Loy,
which makes some evenings harder to enjoy.

Reading and Reacting

1. Review the definition of *villanelle*, and explain how "Video Blues" does or does not conform to this definition.

2. Do any elements in the poem seem to be a departure from its regular form? For example, are the parentheses that enclose lines 6 through 8 necessary? What about the caesura in line 11? Can you think of a way to rewrite this line without the caesura (and without departing from the form)?

3. **Journal Entry** Given its form, what kinds of subjects do you think would be most appropriate for villanelles? Why? What subjects, if any, do you think would *not* be appropriate? Explain.

Related Works: "Shiloh" (p. 316), "To My Dear and Loving Husband" (p. 956), "General Review of the Sex Situation" (p. 1075), "Do Not Go Gentle into That Good Night" (p. 1065)

The Epigram

Originally, an epigram was an inscription carved in stone on a monument or statue. As a literary form, an **epigram** is a very brief poem that makes a pointed, often sarcastic, comment in a surprising twist at the end. In a sense, it is a poem with a punch line. Although some epigrams rhyme, others do not. Many are only two lines long, but others are somewhat longer. What they have in common is their economy of language and their tone. One of the briefest of epigrams, written by Ogden Nash, appeared in the *New Yorker* magazine in 1931.

> The Bronx?
> No thonx.

Here, in four words, Nash manages to convey the unexpected, using rhyme and creative spelling to convey his assessment of one of New York City's five boroughs. The poem's two lines are perfectly balanced, making the contrast between the noncommittal tone of the first and the negative tone of the second quite striking.

FURTHER READING: The Epigram

SAMUEL TAYLOR COLERIDGE (1772–1834)

What Is an Epigram? (1802)

> What is an epigram? a dwarfish whole,
> Its body brevity, and wit its soul.

WILLIAM BLAKE (1757–1827)

Her Whole Life Is an Epigram (c. 1793–1811)

Her whole life is an epigram: smack, smooth & neatly penned,
Platted° quite neat to catch applause, with a sliding noose at the end.

Reading and Reacting

1. Explain the point made in each of the epigrams above.
2. Evaluate each poem. What qualities do you conclude make an epigram effective?
3. **Journal Entry** How are short-short stories (see Chapter 10) and ten-minute plays (see Chapter 37) like epigrams?

Related Works: "Mislaid Plans" (p. 166), "General Review of the Sex Situation" (p. 1075), "Fire and Ice" (p. 864), "you fit into me" (p. 961), *Nine Ten* (p. 1334)

MARTIN ESPADA (1957–   )

Why I Went to College (2000)

If you don't,
my father said,
you better learn
to eat soup
through a straw,   5
'cause I'm gonna
break your jaw

Reading and Reacting

1. How is "Why I Went to College" different from Coleridge's and Blake's epigrams? How is it similar to them?
2. What function does the poem's title serve? Is it the epigram's "punch line," or does it serve another purpose?
3. What can you infer about the speaker's father from this poem? Why, for example, do you think he wants his son to go to college?
4. **Journal Entry** Exactly why did the speaker go to college? Expand this short poem into a paragraph written from the speaker's point of view.

Related Works: "Baca Grande" (p. 905), "My Father as a Guitar" (p. 951), "My Papa's Waltz" (p. 1058), "'Faith' is a fine invention" (p. 1160), "Marks" (p. 1211), *The Cuban Swimmer* (p. 1772)

°*Platted:* Braided.

Haiku

Like an epigram, a haiku compresses words into a very small package. Unlike an epigram, however, a haiku focuses on an image, not an idea. A traditional Japanese form, the **haiku** is a brief unrhymed poem that presents the essence of some aspect of nature, concentrating a vivid image in three lines. Although in the strictest sense a haiku consists of seventeen syllables divided into lines of five, seven, and five syllables, respectively, not all poets conform to this rigid form.

The following poem is a translation of a classic Japanese haiku by Matsuo Basho.

> Silent and still: then
> Even sinking into the rocks,
> The cicada's screech.

Notice that this poem conforms to the haiku's three-line structure and traditional subject matter, vividly depicting a natural scene without comment or analysis.

FURTHER READING: Haiku

MATSUO BASHŌ (1644–1694)

Four Haiku*

Translated by Geoffrey Bownas and Anthony Thwaite

> Spring:
> A hill without a name
> Veiled in morning mist.
>
> The beginning of autumn:
> Sea and emerald paddy   5
> Both the same green.
>
> The winds of autumn
> Blow: yet still green
> The chestnut husks.
>
> A flash of lightning: 10
> Into the gloom
> Goes the heron's cry.

Reading and Reacting

1. Haiku are admired for their extreme economy and their striking images. What are the central images in each of Bashō's haiku? To what senses do these images appeal?
2. In another poem, Bashō says that art begins with "The depths of the country / and a rice-planting song." What do you think he means? How do these four haiku exemplify this idea?

---

*Publication date is not available.

3. Do you think the conciseness of these poems increases or decreases the impact of their images? Explain.

4. **JOURNAL ENTRY** "In a Station of the Metro" (p. 924) is Ezra Pound's version of a haiku. How successful do you think his poem is as a haiku? Do you think a longer poem could have conveyed the images more effectively?

Related Works: "Seventeen Syllables" (p. 538), "Where Mountain Lion Lay Down with Deer" (p. 859), "the sky was can dy" (p. 1017), "Birches" (p. 1069).

CAROLYN KIZER (1925–   )

After Bashō (1984)

Tentatively, you
slip onstage this evening,
pallid, famous moon.

Reading and Reacting

1. What possible meanings might the word "After" have in the title? What does the title tell readers about the writer's purpose?

2. What is the impact of "tentatively" in the first line and "famous" in the last line? How do the connotations of these words convey the image of the moon?

3. **JOURNAL ENTRY** What visual picture does the poem suggest? What mood does the poem's central image create?

Related Works: "Sleepless at Crown Point" (p. 928), "this poem intentionally left blank" (p. 825), "Morning Song" (p. 871)

JOSÉ JUAN TABLADA (1871–1945)

Haiku

Translated by Samuel Beckett

Red cold
guffaw of summer,
slice
of watermelon!

Reading and Reacting

1. This haiku consists of only eight words, two of which are *of*. Consider the remaining six words (two adjectives and four nouns). Are all of them appropriate for a haiku? Are any unexpected (or even incongruous)?

2. This poem, translated from Spanish, contains only 11 (not 17) syllables. Is it still a haiku?

3. Why do you think this poem ends with an exclamation point?

4. **JOURNAL ENTRY** Retaining the same two adjectives and four nouns, expand this haiku to the standard 17 syllables.

Related Works: "Four Haiku" (p. 1012), "Daybreak" (p. 936), "Nightfall" (p. 936), "Fog" (p. 1220)

JACK KEROUAC   (1922–1969)

American Haiku

Early morning yellow flowers,
thinking about
the drunkards of Mexico.

No telegram today
only more leaves   5
fell.

Nightfall,
boy smashing dandelions
with a stick.

Holding up my   10
purring cat to the moon
I sighed.

Drunk as a hoot owl,
writing letters
by thunderstorm.   15

Empty baseball field
a robin
hops along the bench.

All day long
wearing a hat   20
that wasn't on my head.

Crossing the football field
coming home from work—
the lonely businessman.

After the shower   25
among the drenched roses
the bird thrashing in the bath.

Snap your finger
stop the world—
rain falls harder.   30

Nightfall,
too dark to read the page
too cold.

Following each other
my cats stop   35
when it thunders.

Wash hung out
by moonlight
Friday night in May.

The bottoms of my shoes   40
are clean
from walking in the rain.

Glow worm
sleeping on this flower—
your light's on.   45

Reading and Reacting

1. In what ways are these haiku different from those by Matsuo Bashō (p. 1012)? Do they fit the definition of *haiku* on page 817?

2. What, if anything, makes these poems "American"? Is it their language? Their subject matter? Something else?

3. **JOURNAL ENTRY** Try writing a few "American haiku" of your own. Then, evaluate the success of your efforts. What problems did you encounter?

4. **CRITICAL PERSPECTIVE** Writing about his experiments with haiku, Jack Kerouac said, "Above all, a Haiku must be very simple and free of all poetic trickery and make a little picture and yet be as airy and graceful as a Vivaldi Pastorella."

   Do you think Kerouac's haiku satisfy these conditions?

Related Works: "Love and Other Catastrophes: A Mix Tape" (p. 165), "Comparatives" (p. 981), "Chicago" (p. 1016), "Morning Song" (p. 1071), from "Song of Myself" (p. 1237)

Open Form

An **open form poem** may make occasional use of rhyme and meter but has no easily identifiable pattern or design: no conventional stanzaic divisions, no consistent metrical pattern or line length, no repeated rhyme scheme. Still, open form poetry is not necessarily shapeless, untidy, or randomly ordered. All poems have form, and the form of a poem may be determined by factors such as repeated sounds, the appearance of words on the printed page, or pauses in natural speech as well as by a conventional metrical pattern or rhyme scheme.

Open form poetry invites readers to participate in the creative process, to discover the relationship between form and meaning. Some modern poets believe that only open form offers them freedom to express their ideas or that the subject matter or mood of their poetry demands a relaxed, experimental approach to form. For example, when Lawrence Ferlinghetti portrays the poet as an acrobat who "climbs on rime" (p. 941), he constructs his poem in a way that is consistent with the poet/acrobat's willingness to take risks. Thus, the poem's idiosyncratic form supports its ideas about the limitless possibilities of poetry and the poet as experimenter.

Without a predetermined pattern, however, poets must create forms that suit their needs, and they must continue to shape and reshape the look of the poem on the page as they revise its words. Thus, open form is a challenge, but it is also a way for poets to experiment with fresh arrangements of words and new juxtapositions of ideas.

For some poets, such as Carl Sandburg, open form provides an opportunity to create **prose poems**, poems that look like prose.

CARL SANDBURG   (1878–1967)

Chicago   (1914)

Hog Butcher for the World,
Tool Maker, Stacker of Wheat,
Player with Railroads and the Nation's Freight Handler;
Stormy, husky, brawling,
City of the Big Shoulders: 5

They tell me you are wicked and I believe them, for I have seen
    your painted women under the gas lamps luring the farm boys.
And they tell me you are crooked and I answer: Yes, it is true
    I have seen the gunman kill and go free to kill again.
And they tell me you are brutal and my reply is: On the faces of
    women and children I have seen the marks of wanton hunger.
And having answered so I turn once more to those who sneer at
    this my city, and I give them back the sneer and say to them:
Come and show me another city with lifted head singing so
    proud to be alive and coarse and strong and cunning.   10
Flinging magnetic curses amid the toil of piling job on job,
    here is a tall bold slugger set vivid against the little soft cities;
Fierce as a dog with tongue lapping for action, cunning as a
    savage pitted against the wilderness,
        Bareheaded,
            Shoveling,
            Wrecking,   15
            Planning,
            Building, breaking, rebuilding,
Under the smoke, dust all over his mouth, laughing with white
    teeth,
Under the terrible burden of destiny laughing as a young man
    laughs,
Laughing even as an ignorant fighter laughs who has never lost
    a battle,   20
Bragging and laughing that under his wrist is the pulse, and under
    his ribs the heart of the people,
                        Laughing!

Laughing the stormy, husky, brawling laughter of Youth,
    half-naked, sweating, proud to be Hog Butcher, Tool Maker,
    Stacker of Wheat, Player with railroads and Freight Handler
    to the Nation.

"Chicago" uses capitalization and punctuation conventionally, and it generally (though not always) arranges words in lines in a way that is consistent with the natural divisions of phrases and sentences. However, the poem is not divided into stanzas, and its lines vary widely in length — from a single word isolated on a line to a line crowded with words — and follow no particular metrical pattern. Instead, its form is created through its pattern of alternating sections of long and short lines; through its repeated words and phrases ("They tell me" in lines 6–8, "under" in lines 18–19, and "laughing" in lines 18–23, for example); through alliteration (for instance, "slugger set vivid against the little soft cities" in line 11); and, most of all, through the piling up of words and images into catalogs in lines 1–5, 13–17, and 22.

In order to understand Sandburg's reasons for choosing such a form, we must consider the poem's subject matter and theme. "Chicago" celebrates the scope and power of a "Stormy, husky, brawling" city, one that is exuberant and outgoing, not sedate and civilized. Chicago the city does not follow anyone else's rules; it is, after all, "Bareheaded, / Shoveling, / Wrecking, / Planning, / Building, breaking, rebuilding," constantly active, in flux, on the move, "proud to be alive." "Fierce as a dog . . . cunning as a savage," the city is characterized as, among other things, a worker, a fighter, and a harborer of "painted women" and killers and hungry women and children. Just as Chicago itself does not conform to the rules, the poem departs from the orderly confines of stanzaic form and measured rhyme and meter, a kind of form that is, after all, better suited to "the little soft cities" than to the "tall bold slugger" that is Chicago.

Of course, open form poetry does not have to look like Sandburg's prose poem. The following poem, an extreme example of open form, looks almost as if it has spilled out of a box of words.

E. E. CUMMINGS   (1894–1962)

the sky was can dy (1925)

the
    sky
      was
can   dy lu
minous   5
      edible
spry
      pinks shy
lemons
greens coo l choc   10
olate
s.

```
      un   der,
      a   lo
co                              15
mo
      tive     s pout
               ing
                   vi
                     o   20
                   lets
```

Like many of Cummings's poems, this one seems ready to skip off the page. Its irregular line length and its unconventional capitalization, punctuation, and word
divisions immediately draw readers' attention to its form. Despite these oddities,
and despite the absence of orderly rhyme and meter, the poem does have its conventional elements.

A closer examination reveals that the poem's theme — the beauty of the sky
— is quite conventional; that the poem is divided, though somewhat crudely, into
two sections; and that the poet does use some rhyme — "spry" and "shy," for example. However, Cummings's sky is described not in traditional terms but rather
as something "edible," not only in terms of color but of flavor as well. The breaks
within words ("can dy lu / minous"; "coo l choc / olate / s") seem to expand the
words' possibilities, visually stretching them to the limit, extending their taste
and visual image over several lines and, in the case of the poem's last two words,
visually reinforcing the picture the words describe. In addition, the isolation of
syllables exposes hidden rhyme, as in "lo / co / mo" and "lu" / "coo." Thus, by using open form, Cummings makes a clear statement about the capacity of a poem
to move beyond the traditional boundaries set by words and lines.

FURTHER READING: Open Form

WALT WHITMAN   (1819–1892)

from "Out of the Cradle Endlessly Rocking"   (1881)

Out of the cradle endlessly rocking,
Out of the mocking-bird's throat, the musical shuttle,
Out of the Ninth-month° midnight,
Over the sterile sands and the fields beyond, where the child
    leaving his bed wander'd alone, bareheaded, barefoot,
Down from the shower'd halo,   5
Up from the mystic play of shadows twining and twisting as if
    they were alive,

°*Ninth-month:* The Quaker designation for September; in context, an allusion to the human birth cycle.

Out from the patches of briers and blackberries,
From the memories of the bird that chanted to me,
From your memories sad brother, from the fitful risings and
    fallings I heard,
From under that yellow half-moon late-risen and swollen as if
    with tears,   10
From those beginning notes of yearning and love there in the
    mist,
From the thousand responses of my heart never to cease,
From the myriad thence-arous'd words,
From the word stronger and more delicious than any,
From such as now they start the scene revisiting,   15
As a flock, twittering, rising, or overhead passing,
Borne hither, ere all eludes me, hurriedly,
A man, yet by these tears a little boy again,
Throwing myself on the sand, confronting the waves,
I, chanter of pains and joys, uniter of here and hereafter,   20
Taking all hints to use them, but swiftly leaping beyond them,
A reminiscence sing.

Reading and Reacting

1. This excerpt, the first twenty-two lines of a poem nearly two hundred lines long, has no regular metrical pattern or rhyme scheme. What gives it its form?

2. How might you explain why the poem's lines vary in length?

3. JOURNAL ENTRY Compare this excerpt with the excerpt from Whitman's "Song of Myself" (p. 1237). In what respects are the forms of the two poems similar?

4. CRITICAL PERSPECTIVE Reviewing a recent biography of Whitman, Geoffrey O'Brien writes of a paradox in Whitman's poetry:

[N]either fiction nor verse as they then existed could provide Whitman with what he needed, so he invented out of necessity his own form, a reversion to what he conceived of as the most archaic bardic impulses, representing itself as the poetry of the future.

Can you see the form of "Out of the Cradle" as both "archaic" and "of the future"?

Related Works: "Chicago" (p. 1016), "Defending Walt Whitman" (p. 1136), from "Song of Myself" (p. 1237)

DIANE WAKOSKI (1937–   )

Sleep (1966)

The mole
lifting snouts—

full of strained black dirt
  —his perfect tunnel
  sculptured   5
  to fit
  the fat
  body. Sleep
fits tight
—must keep bringing out. 10
the fine grit
to keep size
for even one day.

Reading and Reacting

1. This poem's form seems to be in direct conflict with the logical divisions its syntax and punctuation suggest. For instance, the words in lines 4–9 are set between dashes, indicating a parenthetical comment, yet only lines 4–8 are visually aligned. Also, line 10 ends with a period, but lines 11–13 are clearly part of the same sentence as line 10. How can you account for such discrepancies?

2. This poem discusses the mole's constant search for the perfect-size tunnel. How might this process have suggested the form of the poem?

3. JOURNAL ENTRY Why do you believe the poet placed the words "Sleep / fits tight" (lines 8–9) where she did? Could — or should — these words be relocated? If so, where could they be placed, and what changes in form or punctuation would then have to be made?

Related Works: "Appetizer" (p. 400), "Women" (p. 824), "Red Wheelbarrow" (p. 923), "A Sketch" (p. 985), "The Tyger" (p. 1146)

ROBERT HAYDEN (1913–1980)

Monet's "Waterlilies"° (1966)

(For Bill and Sonja)

Today as the news from Selma° and Saigon°
poisons the air like fallout,
  I come again to see
the serene great picture that I love.

°*Monet's "Waterlilies":* Claude Monet (1840–1926), French impressionist painter. The poet's description of the painter's use of light in this particular painting is equally applicable to most of Monet's work. °*Selma:* A city in central Alabama. In 1965, peaceful demonstrations in support of voting rights for African-Americans were brutally broken up by the Selma police. Two civil rights supporters were killed: one, minister James Reeb, was beaten to death on a town street; the other, homemaker Viola Liuzzo, was shot by Ku Klux Klansmen as she was driving along a highway. °*Saigon:* The capital of the former South Vietnam, now known as Ho Chi Minh City. All news of the Vietnam War was cleared through Saigon by U.S. authorities.

Here space and time exist in light   5
the eye like the eye of faith believes.
    The seen, the known
dissolve in irridescence, become
illusive flesh of light
    that was not, was, forever is.   10

O light beheld as through refracting tears.
Here is the aura of that world
    each of us has lost.
Here is the shadow of its joy.

Reading and Reacting

1. The speaker stands before Monet's *Waterlilies*, where he takes temporary refuge from the turbulent world. Why do you suppose Hayden chose not to use the soothing rhythms and comforting shape of closed form to convey the serenity of the moment? Do you think he made the right choice?

2. Hayden indents lines 3, 7, 10, and 13. What purpose, if any, do these indentations serve?

3. Why do you think the last four lines are separated from the rest of the poem?

4. JOURNAL ENTRY Look at the detail of Monet's *Waterlilies* (below). Why do you think the speaker has come to see this particular painting.

Waterlillies, 1914–17 (oil on canvas), Monet, Claude (1840–1926)
© Musee Marmottan, Paris, France/Bridgeman Art Library

Related Works: "Facing It" (p. 1085), "Try to Praise the Mutilated World" (p. 869), "The World Is Too Much with Us" (p. 870), "Cloud Painter" (p. 921), "Dover Beach" (p. 1141), "Ethics" (p. 1210)

WILLIAM CARLOS WILLIAMS (1883–1963)

Spring and All (1923)

By the road to the contagious hospital
under the surge of the blue
mottled clouds driven from the
northeast — a cold wind. Beyond, the
waste of broad, muddy fields   5
brown with dried weeds, standing and fallen

patches of standing water
the scattering of tall trees

All along the road the reddish
purplish, forked, upstanding, twiggy   10
stuff of bushes and small trees
with dead, brown leaves under them
leafless vines —

Lifeless in appearance, sluggish
dazed spring approaches —   15

They enter the new world naked,
cold, uncertain of all
save that they enter. All about them
the cold, familiar wind —

Now the grass, tomorrow   20
the stiff curl of wildcarrot leaf
One by one objects are defined —
It quickens: clarity, outline of leaf

But now the stark dignity of
entrance — Still, the profound change   25
has come upon them: rooted, they
grip down and begin to awaken

Reading and Reacting

1. What characteristics of closed form are present in "Spring and All"? What characteristics are absent?

2. What does Williams accomplish by visually isolating lines 7–8 and lines 14–15?

3. "Spring and All" includes assonance, alliteration, and repetition. Give several examples of each technique, and explain what each adds to the poem.

4. JOURNAL ENTRY What do you think the word *All* means in the poem's title?

5. CRITICAL PERSPECTIVE According to critic Bonnie Costello, "Williams thought about the creative process in painters' terms, and he asks us to experience the work as we might experience a modern painting. His great achievement was to bring some of its qualities into poetry."

Consider the images Williams uses in this poem. In what ways is this poem like a painting? Which images are conveyed in "painters' terms"? How does he use these images to create meaning in the poem?

Related Works: "Group Photo with Winter Trees" (p. 825), "Comparatives" (p. 981), "Pied Beauty" (p. 987), "Summer" (p. 1067)

CAROLYN FORCHÉ (1950–)

The Colonel (1978)

What you have heard is true. I was in his house. His wife carried
a tray of coffee and sugar. His daughter filed her nails, his son went
out for the night. There were daily papers, pet dogs, a pistol on the
cushion beside him. The moon swung bare on its black cord over
the house. On the television was a cop show. It was in English.   5
Broken bottles were embedded in the walls around the house to
scoop the kneecaps from a man's legs or cut his hands to lace. On
the windows there were gratings like those in liquor stores. We had
dinner, rack of lamb, good wine, a gold bell was on the table for
calling the maid. The maid brought green mangoes, salt, a type of   10
bread. I was asked how I enjoyed the country. There was a brief
commercial in Spanish. His wife took everything away. There was
some talk then of how difficult it had become to govern. The parrot
said hello on the terrace. The colonel told it to shut up, and pushed
himself from the table. My friend said to me with his eyes: say   15
nothing. The colonel returned with a sack used to bring groceries
home. He spilled many human ears on the table. They were like
dried peach halves. There is no other way to say this. He took one
of them in his hands, shook it in our faces, dropped it into a water
glass. It came alive there. I am tired of fooling around he said. As   20
for the rights of anyone, tell your people they can go fuck themselves. He swept the ears to the floor with his arm and held the last
of his wine in the air. Something for your poetry, no? he said. Some
of the ears on the floor caught this scrap of his voice. Some of the
ears on the floor were pressed to the ground.   25

Reading and Reacting

1. Treating Forché's prose poem as prose rather than poetry, try dividing it into paragraphs. What determines where you make your divisions?
2. If you were to reshape "The Colonel" into a conventional-looking poem, what options might you have? Rearrange a few sentences of the poem so that they "look like poetry," and compare your revision to the original. Which version do you find more effective? Why?
3. What is the main theme of "The Colonel"? How does the form help Forché to communicate this theme?

4. **JOURNAL ENTRY** Do you think "The Colonel" is poetry or prose? Consider its subject matter and language as well as its form.

5. **CRITICAL PERSPECTIVE** Writing in the *New York Times Book Review*, critic Katha Pollitt focuses on "poetic clichés," which, she says, are "attempts to energize the poem by annexing a subject that is guaranteed to produce a knee-jerk response in the reader. This saves a lot of bother all around, and enables poet and reader to drowse together in a warm bath of mutual admiration for each other's capacity for deep feeling and right thinking." Among the poetic clichés Pollitt discusses is something she calls "the CNN poem, which retells in overheated free verse a prominent news story involving war, famine, torture, child abuse or murder."

   Do you think "The Colonel" is a "CNN poem," or do you see it as something more than just a "poetic cliché"?

Related Works: "All about Suicide" (p. 7), "Once upon a Time" (p. 204), "Saboteur" (p. 714), "Hope" (p. 879), "Poetry Searches for Radiance" (p. 1248)

PAT MORA (1942–   )

Immigrants (1986)

> wrap their babies in the American flag,
> feed them mashed hot dogs and apple pie,
> name them Bill and Daisy,
> buy them blonde dolls that blink blue
> eyes or a football and tiny cleats   5
> before the baby can even walk,
> speak to them in thick English,
>   hallo, babee, hallo.
> whisper in Spanish or Polish
> when the babies sleep, whisper   10
> in a dark parent bed, that dark
> parent fear, "Will they like
> our boy, our girl, our fine american
> boy, our fine american girl?"

Reading and Reacting

1. What do the immigrant parents want for their children? What "dark / parent fear" (lines 11–12) do they have? Do you think this fear is justified?

2. What, if anything, determines where the poet breaks the lines of this poem? Why, for example, is line 8 shorter than the others? Should the poet have broken any lines in different places?

3. Although this poem is not a sonnet, it does have fourteen lines. Does it resemble a sonnet in any other respects?

4. **JOURNAL ENTRY** Why do you think the word *american* is not capitalized in the last two lines?

Related Works: "The Third and Final Continent" (p. 261), "Two Kinds" (p. 791), "The Emigrant Irish" (p. 1147), "The True-Blue American" (p. 1044), *The Cuban Swimmer* (p. 1772), *Trying to Find Chinatown* (p. 1892)

CZESLAW MILOSZ (1911–2004)

Christopher Robin (1998)

In April of 1996 the international press carried the news of the death, at age seventy-five, of Christopher Robin Milne, immortalized in a book by his father, A. A. Milne, Winnie-the-Pooh, *as Christopher Robin.*

I must think suddenly of matters too difficult for a bear of little brain. I have never asked myself what lies beyond the place where we live, I and Rabbit, Piglet and Eeyore, with our friend Christopher Robin. That is, we continued to live here, and nothing changed, and I just ate my little something. Only Christopher Robin left for a moment.   5

Owl says that immediately beyond our garden Time begins, and that it is an awfully deep well. If you fall in it, you go down and down, very quickly, and no one knows what happens to you next. I was a bit worried about Christopher Robin falling in, but he came back and then I asked him about the well.   10
"Old bear," he answered. "I was in it and I was falling and I was changing as I fell. My legs became long, I was a big person, I wore trousers down to the ground, I had a gray beard, then I grew old, hunched, and I walked with a cane, and then I died. It was probably just a dream, it was quite unreal. The   15
only real thing was you, old bear, and our shared fun. Now I won't go anywhere, even if I'm called for an afternoon snack."

Reading and Reacting

1. Who is the poem's speaker? How do you know? How would you characterize the speaker's voice?
2. *Winnie-the-Pooh* is a children's book. How is this poem like a story for children? In what sense, if any, is it not suitable for children?
3. Does this prose poem include any conventional poetic elements? Could you argue that it is not in fact a poem? Explain.
4. **JOURNAL ENTRY** As the epigraph to the poem points out, the real Christopher Robin Milne died in 1996. What has happened to the fictional Christopher Robin? How do you know?

Related Works: "The Secret Lion" (p. 170), "Once upon a Time" (p. 204), "On the Death of Friends in Childhood" (p. 1189), "The Fathers" (p. 1054)

	CHECKLIST Writing about Form

☐ Is the poem written in open or closed form? On what characteristics do you base your conclusion?

☐ Why did the poet choose open or closed form? For example, is the poem's form consistent with its subject matter, tone, or theme? Is it determined by the conventions of the historical period in which it was written?

☐ If the poem is arranged in closed form, does the pattern apply to single lines, to groups of lines, or to the entire poem? What factors determine the breaks between groups of lines?

☐ Is the poem a sonnet? A sestina? A villanelle? An epigram? A haiku? How do the traditional form's conventions suit the poet's language and theme? Is the poem consistent with the requirements of the form at all times, or does it break any new ground?

☐ If the poem is arranged in open form, what determines the breaks at the ends of lines?

☐ Are certain words or phrases isolated on lines? Why?

☐ How do elements such as assonance, alliteration, rhyme, and repetition of words give the poem form?

☐ What use does the poet make of punctuation and capitalization? Of white space on the page?

☐ Is the poem a prose poem? How does this form support the poem's subject matter?

☐ Is the poem a concrete poem? How does the poet use the visual shape of the poem to convey meaning?

WRITING SUGGESTIONS: Form

1. Reread the definitions of closed form and open form in this chapter. Do you think the following poem is "open" or "closed"? Explain your position in a short essay, supporting your conclusion with specific references to the poem.

CAROLE SATYAMURTI (1939–   )

I Shall Paint My Nails Red

Because a bit of colour is a public service.
Because I am proud of my hands.
Because it will remind me I'm a woman.

Because I will look like a survivor.
Because I can admire them in traffic jams.   5
Because my daughter will say ugh.
Because my lover will be surprised.
Because it is quicker than dyeing my hair.
Because it is a ten-minute moratorium.
Because it is reversible.   10

2. Some poets — for example, Emily Dickinson and Robert Frost — write both open and closed form poems. Choose one open and one closed form poem by a single poet, and explain the poet's possible reasons for choosing each type of form. In your analysis of the two poems, defend the poet's choices if you can.

3. Do you see complex forms, such as the villanelle and the sestina, as exercises or even merely as opportunities for poets to show off their skills, or do you believe the special demands of the forms add something valuable to a poem? To help you answer this question, read "Do not go gentle into that good night" (p. 1065), and analyze Dylan Thomas's use of the villanelle's structure to enhance his poem's theme. Or study Elizabeth Bishop's "Sestina" (p. 1007), and consider how her use of the sestina's form helps her to convey her ideas.

4. The following open form poem is an alternate version of May Swenson's "Women" (p. 824). Read the two versions carefully, and write an essay in which you compare them. What differences do you notice? Which do you think was written first? Why? Do the two poems make the same point? Which makes the point with less ambiguity? Which is more effective? Why?

Women Should Be Pedestals

Women should be pedestals
moving pedestals
moving to the motions of men
Or they should be little horses
those wooden sweet oldfashioned painted rocking horses   5
the gladdest things in the toyroom
The pegs of their ears so familiar and dear
to the trusting fists
To be chafed feelingly
and then unfeelingly   10
To be joyfully ridden
until the restored egos dismount and the legs stride away
Immobile sweetlipped sturdy and smiling
women should always be waiting
willing to be set into motion   15
Women should be pedestals to men

5. Look through Chapter 34, "Poetry for Further Reading," and identify one or two prose poems. Write an essay in which you consider why the form seems suitable for the poem or poems you have chosen. Is there a particular kind of subject matter that seems especially appropriate for a prose poem?

CHAPTER 31

SYMBOL, ALLEGORY, ALLUSION, MYTH

> What the reader gets from a symbol depends not only upon what the author has put into it but upon the reader's sensitivity and his consequent apprehension of what is there.
>
> —William York Tindall, *"Excellent Dumb Discourse"*

WILLIAM BLAKE (1757–1827)

The Sick Rose (1794)

O Rose thou art sick.
The invisible worm
That flies in the night,
In the howling storm:

Has found out thy bed   5
Of crimson joy:
And his dark secret love
Does thy life destroy.

Symbol

A **symbol** is an idea or image that suggests something else — but not in the simple way that a dollar sign stands for money or a flag represents a country. A symbol is an image that transcends its literal, or denotative, meaning in a complex way. For instance, if someone gives a rose to a loved one, it could simply be a sign of love. But in the poem "The Sick Rose," the rose has a range of contradictory and complementary meanings. For what does the rose stand? Beauty? Perfection? Passion? Something else? As this poem illustrates, the distinctive trait of a symbol is that its meaning cannot easily be pinned down or defined.

Such ambiguity can be frustrating, but it is precisely this characteristic of a symbol that enables it to enrich a poem by giving it additional layers of meaning. As Robert Frost has said, a symbol is a little thing that touches a larger thing. In the poem of his that follows, the central symbol does just this.

ROBERT FROST (1874–1963)

For Once, Then, Something (1923)

Others taunt me with having knelt at well-curbs
Always wrong to the light, so never seeing
Deeper down in the well than where the water
Gives me back in a shining surface picture
Me myself in the summer heaven, godlike,   5
Looking out of a wreath of fern and cloud puffs.
Once, when trying with chin against a well-curb,
I discerned, as I thought, beyond the picture,
Through the picture, a something white, uncertain,
Something more of the depths — and then I lost it.   10
Water came to rebuke the too clear water.
One drop fell from a fern, and lo, a ripple
Shook whatever it was lay there at bottom,
Blurred it, blotted it out. What was that whiteness?
Truth? A pebble of quartz? For once, then, something.   15

The central symbol in this poem is the "something" that the speaker thinks he
discerns at the bottom of a well. Traditionally, the act of looking down a well suggests a search for truth. In this poem, the speaker says that he always seems to look
down the well at the wrong angle, so that all he can see is his own reflection — the
surface, not the depths. Once, however, the speaker thought he saw something
"beyond the picture," something "white, uncertain," but the image remained indistinct, disappearing when a drop of water from a fern caused the water to ripple.
The poem ends with the speaker questioning the significance of what he saw. Like
a reader encountering a symbol, the speaker is left trying to come to terms with
images that cannot be clearly perceived and associations that cannot be readily
understood. In light of the elusive nature of truth, all the speaker can do is ask
questions that have no definite answers.

Symbols that appear in poetic works can be *conventional* or *universal*. **Conventional symbols** are those recognized by people who share certain cultural and
social assumptions. For example, national flags evoke a general and agreed-upon
response in most people of a particular country and—for better or for worse—
American children have for years perceived the golden arches of McDonald's as
a symbol of food and fun. **Universal symbols** are those likely to be recognized by
people regardless of their culture. In 1890, the noted Scottish anthropologist Sir
James George Frazer wrote the first version of his work *The Golden Bough*, in
which he identified parallels between the rites and beliefs of early cultures and
those of Christianity. Fascinated by Frazer's work, the psychologist Carl Jung
sought to explain these parallels by formulating a theory of **archetypes**, which
held that certain images or ideas reside in the subconscious of all people. According to Jung, archetypal symbols include water, symbolizing rebirth; spring,
symbolizing growth; and winter, symbolizing death.

Sometimes symbols that appear in poems can be obscure or highly idiosyncratic. William Blake is one of many poets (William Butler Yeats is another) whose works combine symbols from different cultural, theological, and philosophical sources to form complex networks of symbolic associations. To Blake, for example, the scientist Isaac Newton represents the tendency of scientists to quantify experience while ignoring the beauty and mystery of nature. Readers cannot begin to understand Blake's use of Newton as a symbol until they have read a number of his more difficult poems.

Most often, however, symbols in poems are not so challenging. In the next poem, the poet introduces a cross — a symbol that has specific associations to people familiar with Christianity — and makes his own use of it.

JIM SIMMERMAN *

Child's Grave, Hale County, Alabama (1983)

Someone drove a two-by-four
through the heart of this hard land
that even in a good year
will notch a plow blade worthless,
snap the head off a shovel,   5
or bow a stubborn back.
He'd have had to steal
the wood from a local mill
or steal, by starlight, across
his landlord's farm, to worry   10
a fencepost out of its well
and lug it the three miles home.
He'd have had to leave his wife
asleep on a corn shuck mat,
leave his broken brogans°   15
by the stove, to slip outside,
quiet as sin, with the child
bundled in a burlap sack.
What a thing to have to do
on a cold night in December,   20
1936, alone
but for a raspy wind
and the red, rock-ridden dirt
things come down to in the end.

---

* Birth date is not available.   ° *brogans:* Sturdy, heavy work shoes, frequently ankle high.

> Whoever it was pounded   25
> this shabby half-cross
> into the ground must have toiled
> all night to root it so:
> five feet buried with the child
> for the foot of it that shows.   30
> And as there are no words
> carved here, it's likely that
> the man was illiterate,
> or addled with fatigue,
> or wrenched simple-minded   35
> by the one simple fact.
> Or else the unscored lumber
> driven deep into the land
> and the hump of busted rock
> spoke too plainly of his grief: 40
> forty years layed by and still
> there are no words for this.

Even in non-Christian cultures, the cross on a grave is a readily identifiable symbol of death and the hope for rebirth. In this poem, however, the cross is not simply presented as a conventional Christian symbol; it is also associated with the tenant farmer's hard work and difficult life. In this sense, the cross suggests the poverty that helped bring about the death of the child and the social conditions that existed during the Depression. These associations take readers through many layers of meaning, so that the cross may ultimately stand for the tenant farmer's whole life (the cross *he* has to bear), not just for the death of the child.

This interpretation by no means exhausts the possible symbolic significance of the cross in the poem. For example, the "shabby half-cross" might also suggest the rage and grief of the individual who made it, or it might call to mind the poor who live and die in anonymity. Certainly the poet could have assigned a fixed meaning to the cross that marks the child's grave, but he chose instead, by suggesting various ideas through a single powerful symbol, to let readers arrive at their own conclusions.

How do you know when an idea or image in a poem is a symbol? At what point do you decide that a particular object or idea goes beyond the literal level and takes on symbolic significance? When is a rose more than a rose or a cross more than a cross? Frequently you can recognize a symbol by its prominence or repetition. In "Child's Grave, Hale County, Alabama," for example, the cross is introduced in the first line of the poem, and it is the poem's focal point; in "The Sick Rose," the importance of the rose is emphasized by the title.

It is not enough, however, to identify an image or idea that seems to suggest something else. Your decision that a particular item has symbolic significance must be supported by the details of the poem and make sense in light of the ideas the poem develops. In the following poem, the symbolic significance of the volcano helps readers to understand the poem's central theme.

EMILY DICKINSON (1830–1886)

Volcanoes be in Sicily (1914)

Volcanoes be in Sicily
And South America
I judge from my Geography—
Volcanoes nearer here
A Lava step at any time   5
Am I inclined to climb—
A Crater I may contemplate
Vesuvius at Home.

This poem opens with a statement of fact: volcanoes are located in Sicily and South America. In lines 3 and 4, however, the speaker makes the improbable observation that volcanoes are located near where she is at the moment. Readers familiar with Dickinson know that her poems are highly autobiographical and that she lived in Massachusetts, where there are no volcanoes. This information leads readers to suspect that they should not take the speaker's observation literally and that in the context of the poem volcanoes may have symbolic significance. But what do volcanoes suggest here?

On the one hand, volcanoes represent the awesome creative power of nature; on the other hand, they suggest its destructiveness. The speaker's contemplation of the crater of Vesuvius — the volcano that buried the ancient Roman city of Pompeii in A.D. 79 — is therefore filled with contradictory associations. Because Dickinson was a recluse, volcanoes — active, destructive, unpredictable, and dangerous — may be seen as symbolic of everything she fears in the outside world — and, perhaps, within herself. Volcanoes may even suggest her own creative power, which, like a volcano, is something to be feared as well as contemplated. She has a voyeur's attraction to danger and power, but she is also afraid of them. For this reason, she (and her speaker) may feel safer contemplating Vesuvius at home — not traveling to exotic lands but simply reading a geography book.

FURTHER READING: Symbol

LANGSTON HUGHES (1902–1967)

Island (1951)

Wave of sorrow,
Do not drown me now:

I see the island
Still ahead somehow.

I see the island   5
And its sands are fair:

Wave of sorrow,
Take me there.

Reading and Reacting

1. What makes you suspect that the island has symbolic significance in this poem?

2. Is the "wave of sorrow" also a symbol?

3. JOURNAL ENTRY Beyond its literal meaning, what might the island in this poem suggest? Consider several possibilities.

4. CRITICAL PERSPECTIVE James Baldwin, a preeminent African-American writer, wrote the following about the poetry of Langston Hughes:

> Hughes, in his sermons, blues and prayers, has working for him the power and the beat of Negro speech and Negro music. Negro speech is vivid largely because it is private. It is a kind of emotional shorthand — or sleight-of-hand — by means of which Negroes express, not only their relationship to each other, but their judgment of the white world.

> Can a symbol — such as the island in this poem — also function as "emotional shorthand"? What kind of judgment do you think it might reveal about the "white world"?

Related Works: "A Worn Path" (p. 505), "Sea Grapes" (p. 1050), "Acquainted with the Night" (p. 1177), *The Cuban Swimmer* (p. 1772).

EDGAR ALLAN POE (1809–1849)

The Raven (1844)

Once upon a midnight dreary, while I pondered, weak and weary,
Over many a quaint and curious volume of forgotten lore,
While I nodded, nearly napping, suddenly there came a tapping,
As of some one gently rapping, rapping at my chamber door.
" 'Tis some visitor," I muttered, "tapping at my chamber door —   5
            Only this, and nothing more."

Ah, distinctly I remember it was in the bleak December,
And each separate dying ember wrought its ghost upon the floor.
Eagerly I wished the morrow; — vainly I had sought to borrow
From my books surcease of sorrow — sorrow for the lost Lenore —   10
For the rare and radiant maiden whom the angels name Lenore —
            Nameless here for evermore.

And the silken sad uncertain rustling of each purple curtain
Thrilled me — filled me with fantastic terrors never felt before;
so that now, to still the beating of my heart, I stood repeating   15
" 'Tis some visitor entreating entrance at my chamber door; —
Some late visitor entreating entrance at my chamber door;
            This it is, and nothing more."

Presently my soul grew stronger; hesitating then no longer,
"Sir," said I, "or Madam, truly your forgiveness I implore;   20
But the fact is I was napping, and so gently you came rapping,
An so faintly you came tapping, tapping at my chamber door,
That I scarce was sure I heard you"—here I opened wide the door;—
     Darkness there, and nothing more.

Deep into that darkness peering, long I stood there wondering, fearing,   25
Doubting, dreaming dreams no mortal ever dared to dream before;
But the silence was unbroken, and the darkness gave no token,
And the only word there spoken was the whispered word, "Lenore!"
This I whispered, and an echo murmured back the word, "Lenore!"—
     Merely this, and nothing more.   30

Back into the chamber turning, all my soul within me burning,
Soon I heard again a tapping somewhat louder than before.
"Surely," said I, "surely that is something at my window lattice;
Let me see, then, what thereat is, and this mystery explore—
Let my heart be still a moment and this mystery explore;—   35
     'Tis the wind and nothing more!"

Open here I flung the shutter, when, with many a flirt and flutter,
In there stepped a stately raven of the saintly days of yore;
Not the least obeisance made he; not an instant stopped or stayed he;
But, with mien of lord or lady, perched above my chamber door —   40
Perched upon a bust of Pallas° just above my chamber door —
     Perched, and sat, and nothing more.

Then this ebony bird beguiling my sad fancy into smiling,
By the grave and stern decorum of the countenance it wore,
"Though thy crest be shorn and shaven, thou," I said, "art sure no craven,   45
Ghastly grim and ancient raven wandering from the Nightly shore—
Tell me what thy lordly name is on the Night's Plutonian° shore!"
     Quoth the raven, "Nevermore."

Much I marvelled this ungainly fowl to hear discourse so plainly,
Though its answer little meaning —little relevancy bore,   50
For we cannot help agreeing that no living human being
Ever yet was blessed with seeing bird above his chamber door—
Bird or beat upon the sculptured bust above his chamber door,
     With such name as "Nevermore."

But the raven, sitting lonely on the placid bust, spoke only   55
That one word, as if his soul in that one word he did outpour.
Nothing farther then he uttered — not a feather then he fluttered —
Till I scarcely more than muttered "Other friends have flown before —

° *Pallas:* Athena, Greek goddess of wisdom. ° *Plutonian:* dark; Pluto was the Greek god of the dead and ruler of the underworld.

On the morrow *he* will leave me, as my hopes have flown before."
 Then the bird said "Nevermore."   60

Startled at the stillness broken by reply so aptly spoken,
Doubtless," said I, "what it utters is its only stock and store
Caught from some unhappy master whom unmerciful Disaster
Followed fast and followed faster till his songs one burden bore —
Till the dirges of his Hope that melancholy burden bore   65
 Of 'Never—nevermore.'"

But the raven still beguiling all my sad soul into smiling,
Straight I wheeled a cushioned seat in front of bird and bust and door;
Then, upon the velvet sinking, I betook myself to linking
Fancy unto fancy, thinking what this ominous bird of yore —   70
What this grim, ungainly, ghastly, gaunt, and ominous bird of yore
 Meant in croaking "Nevermore."

This I sat engaged in guessing, but no syllable expressing
To the fowl whose fiery eyes now burned into my bosom's core;
This and more I sat divining, with my head at ease reclining   75
On the cushion's velvet lining that the lamplight gloated o'er,
But whose velvet violet lining with the lamplight gloating o'er,
 she shall press, ah, nevermore!

Then, methought, the air grew denser, perfumed from an unseen
  censer
Swung by angels whose faint foot-falls tinkled on the tufted floor.   80
"Wretch," I cried, "thy God hath lent thee — by these angels he hath
  sent thee
Respite — respite and nepenthe° from thy memories of Lenore!
Quaff, oh quaff this kind nepenthe and forget this lost Lenore!"
 Quoth the raven, "Nevermore."

"Prophet!" said I, "thing of evil! — prophet still, if bird or devil! — 85
Whether Tempter sent, or whether tempest tossed thee here ashore,
Desolate, yet all undaunted, on this desert land enchanted —
On this home by Horror haunted — tell me truly, I implore —
Is there — *is* there balm in Gilead?° — tell me — tell me, I implore!"
 Quoth the raven, "Nevermore."   90

"Prophet!" said I, "thing of evil — prophet still, if bird or devil!
By that Heaven that bends above us — by that God we both adore —
Tell this soul with sorrow laden if, within the distant Aidenn,
It shall clasp a sainted maiden whom the angels name Lenore —
Clasp a rare and radiant maiden whom the angels name Lenore."   95
 Quoth the raven, "Nevermore."

° *nepenthe:* a drug mentioned in the *Odessy* as a remedy for grief.   ° *Gilead:* a region mentioned in the Bible;
noted for its soothing ointments.

"Be that word our sign of parting, bird of fiend!" I shrieked
    upstarting —
"Get thee back into the tempest and the Night's Plutonian shore!
Leave no black plume as a token of that lie thy soul hath spoken!
Leave my loneliness unbroken! — quit the bust above my door!   100
Take thy beak from out my heart, and take thy form from off my door!"
                Quoth the raven, "Nevermore."

And the raven, never fitting, still is sitting, still is sitting
On the pallid bust of Pallas just above my chamber door;
And his eyes have all the seeming of a demon's that is dreaming,   105
And the lamp-light o'er him streaming throws his shadow on the floor;
And my soul from out that shadow that lies floating on the floor
                Shall be lifted—nevermore!

Reading and Reacting

1. Who is the speaker in the poem? What is his state of mind? How does the raven mirror the speaker's mental state?

2. "The Raven" contains a good deal of alliteration. Identify some examples. How does this use of repeated consonant sounds help to convey the mood of the poem?

3. The speaker refers to the raven in a number of different ways. At one point, it is simply "an ebony bird" (line 42); at another, it is a "prophet" and "a thing of evil" (85). How else does the speaker characterize the raven?

4. **JOURNAL ENTRY** What is the symbolic significance of the raven? The repeated word "nevermore"? The bust of Pallas, the ancient Greek god of wisdom?

5. **Critical Perspective** According to Christoffer Nilsson, who maintains a Web site dedicated to the works of Poe, "The Raven" was composed with almost mathematical precision. When writing the stanza in which the interrogation of the raven reaches its climax (third stanza from the end), Poe wanted to make certain that no preceding stanza would "surpass this in rythmical effect":

> Poe then worked backwards from this stanza and used the word "Nevermore" in many different ways, so that even with the repetition of this word, it would not prove to be monotonous. Poe builds the tension in this poem up, stanza by stanza, but after the climaxing stanza he tears the whole thing down, and lets the narrator know that there is no meaning in searching for a moral in the raven's "nevermore."

Do you agree with Nilsson that it makes no sense to look for a moral in the raven's "nevermore"? What kind of moral, if any, do you think "Nevermore" implies for the speaker?

Related Works: "Appetizer" (p. 400), "The Swimmer" (p. 665), "Rooming houses are old women" (p. 942), "The Eagle" (p. 981), "The Fish" (p. 1142), "The Tyger" (p. 1146), *Hamlet* (p. 1656)

Allegory

Allegory is a form of narrative that conveys a message or doctrine by using people, places, or things to stand for abstract ideas. **Allegorical figures**, each with a strict equivalent, form an **allegorical framework**, a set of ideas that conveys the allegory's message or lesson. Thus, the allegory takes place on two levels: a **literal level** that tells a story and a **figurative level** on which the allegorical figures in the story stand for ideas, concepts, and other qualities.

Like symbols, allegorical figures suggest other things. But unlike symbols, which have a range of possible meanings, allegorical figures can always be assigned specific meanings. (Because writers use allegory to instruct, they gain nothing by hiding its significance.) Thus, symbols open up possibilities for interpretation, whereas allegories tend to restrict possibilities.

Quite often an allegory involves a journey or an adventure, as in the case of Dante's *Divine Comedy,* which traces a journey through Hell, Purgatory, and Heaven. Within an allegory, everything can have meaning: the road on which the characters walk, the people they encounter, or a phrase that one of them repeats throughout the journey. Once you understand the allegorical framework, your main task is to see how the various elements fit within this system. Some allegorical poems can be relatively straightforward, but others can be so complicated that it takes a great deal of effort to unlock their meaning. In the following poem, a journey is central to the allegory.

CHRISTINA ROSSETTI   (1830–1894)

Uphill   (1861)

Does the road wind uphill all the way?
    Yes, to the very end.
Will the day's journey take the whole long day?
    From morn to night, my friend.

But is there for the night a resting-place?   5
    A roof for when the slow dark hours begin.
May not the darkness hide it from my face?
    You cannot miss that inn.

Shall I meet other wayfarers at night?
    Those who have gone before.   10
Then must I knock, or call when just in sight?
    They will not keep you standing at that door.

Shall I find comfort, travel-sore and weak?
    Of labor you shall find the sum.
Will there be beds for me and all who seek?   15
    Yea, beds for all who come.

"Uphill" uses a question-and-answer structure to describe a journey along an up-hill road. Like the one described in John Bunyan's seventeenth-century allegory *The Pilgrim's Progress*, this is a spiritual journey, one that suggests the challenges a person faces throughout life. The day-and-night duration of the journey stands for life and death, and the inn at the end of the road stands for the grave, the final resting place.

FURTHER READING: Allegory

ADRIENNE RICH   (1929–   )

Diving into the Wreck   (1973)

First having read the book of myths,
and loaded the camera,
and checked the edge of the knife-blade,
I put on
the body-armor of black rubber   5
the absurd flippers
the grave and awkward mask.
I am having to do this
not like Cousteau with his
assiduous team   10
aboard the sun-flooded schooner
but here alone.

There is a ladder.
The ladder is always there
hanging innocently   15
close to the side of the schooner.
We know what it is for,
we who have used it.
Otherwise
it's a piece of maritime floss   20
some sundry equipment.

I go down.
Rung after rung and still
the oxygen immerses me
the blue light   25
the clear atoms
of our human air.
I go down.
My flippers cripple me,
I crawl like an insect down the ladder   30
and there is no one

to tell me when the ocean
will begin.

First the air is blue and then
it is bluer and then green and then   35
black I am blacking out and yet
my mask is powerful
it pumps my blood with power
the sea is another story
the sea is not a question of power   40
I have to learn alone
to turn my body without force
in the deep element.

And now: it is easy to forget
what I came for   45
among so many who have always
lived here
swaying their crenellated fans
between the reefs
and besides   50
you breathe differently down here.

I came to explore the wreck.
The words are purposes.
The words are maps.
I came to see the damage that was done   55
and the treasures that prevail.
I stroke the beam of my lamp
slowly along the flank
of something more permanent
than fish or weed   60

the thing I came for:
the wreck and not the story of the wreck
the thing itself and not the myth
the drowned face always staring
toward the sun   65
the evidence of damage
worn by salt and sway into this threadbare beauty
the ribs of the disaster
curving their assertion
among the tentative haunters.   70

This is the place.
And I am here, the mermaid whose dark hair
streams black, the merman in his armored body
We circle silently

about the wreck   75
we dive into the hold.
I am she: I am he
whose drowned face sleeps with open eyes
whose breasts still bear the stress
whose silver, copper, vermeil cargo lies   80
obscurely inside barrels
half-wedged and left to rot
we are the half-destroyed instruments
that once held to a course
the water-eaten log   85
the fouled compass

We are, I am, you are
by cowardice or courage
the one who finds our way
back to this scene   90
carrying a knife, a camera
a book of myths
in which
our names do not appear.

Reading and Reacting

1. On one level, this poem is about a deep-sea diver's exploration of a wrecked ship. What details suggest that the poet wants you to see something more?

2. Explain the allegorical figures presented in the poem. What, for example, might the diver and the wreck represent?

3. Does the poem contain any symbols? How can you tell they are symbols and not allegorical figures?

4. **JOURNAL ENTRY** In lines 62–63, the speaker says that she came for "the wreck and not the story of the wreck / the thing itself and not the myth." What do you think the speaker is really looking for?

5. **CRITICAL PERSPECTIVE** A number of critics have seen "Diving into the Wreck" as an attempt by Rich to reimagine or reinvent the myths of Western culture. Rachel Blau DuPlessis makes the following observation:

   In this poem of journey and transformation Rich is tapping the energies and plots of myth, while re-envisioning the content. While there is a hero, a quest, and a buried treasure, the hero is a woman; the quest is a critique of old myths; the treasure is knowledge. . . .

   Why do you suppose Rich decided to "reinvent" myth?

Related Works: "Once upon a Time" (p. 204), "Young Goodman Brown" (p. 489), "Hidden Lives of Lakes" (p. 549), "The Love Song of J. Alfred Prufrock" (p. 1172), "Lost Sister" (p. 1226), *The Cuban Swimmer* (p. 1772)

Allusion

An **allusion** is a brief reference to a person, place, or event (fictional or actual) that readers are expected to recognize. Like symbols and allegories, allusions enrich a work by introducing associations from another context.

When poets use allusions, they assume that they and their readers have a common body of knowledge. If, when reading a poem, you come across a reference with which you are not familiar, take the time to look it up in a dictionary or an encyclopedia. As you have probably realized by now, your understanding of a poem may depend on your ability to interpret an unfamiliar reference.

Although most poets expect readers to recognize their references, some use allusions to exclude certain readers from their work. In his 1922 poem "The Waste Land," for example, T. S. Eliot alludes to historical events, ancient languages, and obscure literary works. He even includes a set of notes to accompany his poem, but they do little more than complicate an already difficult text. (As you might expect, initial critical response to this poem was mixed: some critics said that it was a work of genius, while others thought that it was pretentious.)

Allusions can come from any source: history, the arts, other works of literature, the Bible, current events, or even the personal life of the poet. In the following poem, the Nigerian poet and playwright Wole Soyinka alludes to several contemporary political figures.

WOLE SOYINKA   (1934–   )

Future Plans   (1972)

The meeting is called
To odium: Forgers, framers
Fabricators Inter-
national. Chairman,
A dark horse, a circus nag turned blinkered sprinter   5

Mach Three
We rate him — one for the Knife
Two for 'iavelli, Three —
Breaking speed
Of the truth barrier by a swooping detention decree   10

Projects in view:
Mao Tse Tung in league
With Chiang Kai. Nkrumah
Makes a secret
Pact with Verwood, sworn by Hastings Banda.   15
Proven: Arafat
In flagrante cum
Golda Meir. Castro drunk

With Richard Nixon
Contraceptives stacked beneath the papal bunk . . .   20
                    . . . *and more to come*

This poem is structured like an agenda for a meeting. From the moment it announces that a meeting has been called "To odium" (a pun on "to *order*"), it is clear that the poem will be a bitter political satire. Those in attendance are "Forgers, framers / Fabricators." The second stanza contains three allusions that shed light on the character of the chairman. The first is to Mack the Knife, a petty criminal in Bertolt Brecht and Kurt Weill's *Threepenny Opera* (1933). The second is to Niccolò Machiavelli, whose book *The Prince* (1532) advocates the use of unscrupulous means to strengthen the state. The last is to the term *mach*, which denotes the speed of an airplane in relation to the speed of sound — mach one, two, three, and so on. By means of these allusions, the poem implies that the meeting's chairman has been chosen for his ability to engage in violence, to be ruthless, and to break the "truth barrier"— that is, to lie.

The rest of the poem alludes to individuals involved in global politics around the time it was written, in 1972 — specifically, the politics of developing nations. According to the speaker, instead of fighting for the rights of the oppressed, these people consolidate their own political power by collaborating with those who oppose their positions. Thus, Mao Tse-tung, the communist leader of China, is "in league / With" Chiang Kai-shek, his old Nationalist Chinese enemy; Yassir Arafat, the leader of the Palestine Liberation Organization, is linked with Golda Meir, the prime minister of Israel; Kwame Nkrumah, the first president of Ghana, conspires with Hendrick Verwoerd, the prime minister of South Africa, assassinated in 1966; and United States president Richard Nixon gets drunk with Cuba's communist leader, Fidel Castro. These allusions suggest the self-serving nature of political alliances and the extreme disorder of world politics. The ideological juxtapositions show the interchangeability of various political philosophies, none of which has the answer to the world's problems. Whether the poem is satirizing the United Nations and its agenda, criticizing the tendency of politics to make strange bedfellows, or showing how corrupt politicians are, its allusions enable the poet to broaden his frame of reference and thus make the poem more meaningful to readers.

The next poem uses allusions to prominent literary figures, as well as to myth, to develop its theme.

WILLIAM MEREDITH (1919–   )

Dreams of Suicide (1980)

(in sorrowful memory of Ernest Hemingway, Sylvia Plath, and John Berryman)

I

I reach for the awkward shotgun not to disarm
you, but to feel the metal horn,
furred with the downy membrane of dream.

More surely than the unicorn,
you are the mythical beast.   5

II

Or I am sniffing an oven. On all fours
I am imitating a totemic animal
but she is not my totem or the totem
of my people, this is not my magic oven.

III

If I hold you tight by the ankles,   10
still you fly upward from the iron railing.
Your father made these wings,
after he made his own, and now from beyond
he tells you *fly down*, in the voice
my own father might say *walk, boy*.   15

This poem is dedicated to the memory of three writers who committed suicide. In each stanza, the speaker envisions in a dream the death of one of the writers. In the first stanza, he dreams of Ernest Hemingway, who killed himself with a shotgun. The speaker grasps the "metal horn" of Hemingway's shotgun and transforms Hemingway into a mythical beast who, like a unicorn, represents the rare, unique talent of the artist. In the second stanza, the speaker dreams of Sylvia Plath, who asphyxiated herself in a gas oven. He sees himself, like Plath, on his knees imitating an animal sniffing an oven. In the third stanza, the speaker dreams of John Berryman, who leaped to his death. Berryman is characterized as Icarus, a mythological figure who, along with his father Daedalus, fled Crete by building wings made of feathers and wax. Together they flew away; however, ignoring his father's warning, Icarus flew so close to the sun that the wax melted, and he fell to his death in the sea. Like Icarus, Berryman ignores the warning of his father and, like Daedalus, the speaker tries to stop Berryman. In this poem, then, the speaker uses allusions to make a point about the difficult lives of writers — and, perhaps, to convey his own empathy for those who could not survive the struggle to reconcile art and life.

FURTHER READING: Allusion

DELMORE SCHWARTZ   (1913–1966)

The True-Blue American   (1959)

Jeremiah Dickson was a true-blue American,
For he was a little boy who understood America, for he felt that
     he must
Think about *everything*; because that's *all* there is to think about,
Knowing immediately the intimacy of truth and comedy,
Knowing intuitively how a sense of humor was a necessity   5

For one and for all who live in America. Thus, natively, and
Naturally when on an April Sunday in an ice cream parlor
    Jeremiah
Was requested to choose between a chocolate sundae and a
    banana split
He answered unhesitatingly, having no need to think of it
Being a true-blue American, determined to continue as he began: 10
Rejecting the either-or of Kierkegaard,° and many another
    European;
Refusing to accept alternatives, refusing to believe the choice of
    between;
Rejecting selection; denying dilemma; electing absolute
    affirmation: knowing
      in his breast   15
        The infinite and the gold
        Of the endless frontier, the deathless West.
"Both: I will have them both!" declared this true-blue American
In Cambridge, Massachusetts, on an April Sunday, instructed
    By the great department stores, by the Five-and-Ten,   20
Taught by Christmas, by the circus, by the vulgarity and grandeur
    of Niagara Falls and the Grand Canyon,
Tutored by the grandeur, vulgarity, and infinite appetite gratified
    and Shining in the darkness, of the light
On Saturdays at the double bills of the moon pictures,   25
The consummation of the advertisements of the imagination
    of the light
Which is as it was — the infinite belief in infinite hope — of
    Columbus,
      Barnum, Edison, and Jeremiah Dickson.

Reading and Reacting

1. To what does the poem's title refer? Do you think this title has meaning beyond its identification of Jeremiah Dickson?
2. Read an encyclopedia article about Kierkegaard. Why do you suppose Schwartz alludes to him in line 11?
3. What do you think the significance of the name Jeremiah Dickson might be? Is it an allusion?
4. What is the significance of the allusions to places in lines 19–22 and to individuals in lines 27 and 28?
5. **JOURNAL ENTRY** How do you define a "true-blue" American? How do you think the poem's speaker would define this term?
6. **CRITICAL PERSPECTIVE** In his biography of Delmore Schwartz, James Atlas remarks on the poet's affinity with mass culture:

° *Søren Kierkegaard:* Danish philosopher (1813–1855) who greatly influenced twentieth-century existentialism. *Either-Or* (1841) is one of his best-known works.

Delmore's interest in the products of the popular mind, while in part motivated by a desire to ally himself with a wider public than was ordinarily available to poets, had none of the moralizing condescension [of other 1950s intellectuals]; it was a natural expression of his own affinities with all that was American, affinities derived from his early infatuation with baseball, tabloids, the movies, and whatever else he thought animated the drama of history. . . . He was genuinely democratic.

Do you see "The True-Blue American" as a celebration of mass culture? If not, what do you think Schwartz's purpose might have been?

Related Works: "The Secret Lion" (p. 170), "How to Write the Great American Indian Novel" (p. 887), "Sears Life" (p. 907), "A Mown Lawn" (p. 991), "Chicago" (p. 1016), "next to of course god america i" (p. 1159), "The United Fruit Co." (p. 1206), *The Glass Menagerie* (p. 1998)

MAXINE KUMIN (1925–   )

Where Any of Us

Where any of us is
going in tomorrow's reckless Lexus is
the elemental mystery: despite

instructions he left behind, Houdin-,°
i who could outwit   5
ropes and chains, padlocks and steamer

trunks, could extricate
himself from underwater metal crates,
could send forth, he was certain,

a message from the other side,   10
never cracked the curtain
and Mary Baker Eddy's° telephone

said to be hooked up in her crypt—
would it have been
innocence or arrogance,   15

such trust in the beyond?—
has, mythic, failed to ring. If
they knew the script

these two (God may be love
or not) they left, tightlipped   20
and unfulfilled.

As we will.

°*Houdini:* Famous magician (1874–1926) and escape artist who promised to communicate with his wife after he died. °*Mary Baker Eddy:* American religion leader (1821–1910) who founded the Christian Science Church (1879).

Ricky Tomboli

Reading and Reacting

1. What is the "elemental mystery" that Kumin refers to in her first stanza? What is "tomorrow's reckless Lexus"?
2. What is the significance of the allusions to Houdini and Mary Baker Eddy? How do these allusions help Kumin develop her theme?
3. What is the meaning of the poem's last line? What does Kumin achieve by visually isolating these three words as she does?
4. **JOURNAL ENTRY** Kumin was eighty years old when she published "Where Any of Us." How might her age have influenced her choice of subject matter and tone?

Related Works: "The Water Faucet Vision" (p. 240), "Cathedral" (p. 476), "Hidden Lives of Lakes" (p. 549), "I heard a Fly buzz — when I died" (p. 1161), "Death Be Not Proud" (p. 1168), "Bright Star! Would I Were Steadfast as Thou Art" (p. 1192), *Tape* (p. 1313), *Nine Ten* (p. 1334)

Myth

A **myth** is a narrative that embodies — and in some cases helps to explain — the religious, philosophical, moral, and political values of a culture. Using gods and supernatural beings, myths try to make sense of occurrences in the natural world. (The term *myth* can also refer to a private belief system devised by an individual poet as well as to any fully realized fictitious setting in which a literary work takes place, such as the myths of William Faulkner's Yoknapatawpha County or of Lawrence Durrell's Alexandria.) Contrary to popular usage, *myth* does not mean "falsehood." In the broadest sense, myths are stories — usually whole groups of stories — that can be true or partly true as well as false; regardless of their degree of accuracy, however, myths frequently express the deepest beliefs of a culture. According to this definition, the *Iliad* and the *Odyssey*, the Koran, and the Old and New Testaments can all be regarded as myths.

The mythologist Joseph Campbell wrote that myths contain truths that link people together, whether they live today or lived 2,500 years ago. Myths attempt to explain phenomena that human beings care about regardless of when and where they live. It is not surprising, then, that myths frequently contain **archetypal images**—images that cut across cultural and racial boundaries and touch us at a very deep level. Many Greek myths illustrate this power. For example, when Orpheus descends into Hades to rescue his wife, Eurydice, he acts out the universal human desire to transcend death; and when Telemachus sets out in search of his father, Odysseus, he reminds readers that we all are lost children searching for parents. When Icarus ignores his father and flies too near the sun and when Pandora cannot resist looking into a box that she has been told not to open, we are reminded of the human weaknesses we all share.

When poets use myths, they are actually making allusions. They expect readers to bring to the poem the cultural, emotional, and ethical context of the myths to which they are alluding. At one time, when all educated individuals studied the Greek and Latin classics as well as the Bible and other religious texts, poets could be reasonably sure that readers would recognize the mythological allusions they made. Today, many readers are unable to understand the full significance of an allusion or its application within a poem. In this anthology, many of the poems are accompanied by notes, but these may not provide all the information you will need to understand each mythological allusion and thus to determine its significance within a poem. Occasionally, you may have to look elsewhere for answers, turning to dictionaries, encyclopedias, online information sites such as <http://www.answers.com>, or collections of myths such as the *New Larousse Encyclopedia of Mythology* or *Bulfinch's Mythology*.

Sometimes a poet alludes to a myth in a title; sometimes references to various myths appear throughout a poem; at other times, an entire poem focuses on a single myth. In each case, as in the following poem, the use of myth helps to develop the poem's theme.

COUNTEE CULLEN (1903–1946)

Yet Do I Marvel (1925)

I doubt not God is good, well-meaning, kind,
And did He stoop to quibble could tell why
The little buried mole continues blind,
Why flesh that mirrors Him must some day die,
Make plain the reason tortured Tantalus   5
Is baited by the fickle fruit, declare
If merely brute caprice dooms Sisyphus
To struggle up a never-ending stair.
Inscrutable His ways are, and immune
To catechism by a mind too strewn   10
With petty cares to slightly understand
What awful brain compels His awful hand.
Yet do I marvel at this curious thing:
To make a poet black, and bid him sing!

The speaker begins by affirming his belief in the benevolence of God but then questions why God engages in what appear to be capricious acts. As part of his catalog of questions, the speaker mentions Tantalus and Sisyphus, two figures from Greek mythology. Tantalus was a king who for his crimes was condemned to Hades. There, he was forced to stand in a pool of water up to his chin. Overhead hung a tree branch laden with fruit. When Tantalus got thirsty and tried to drink, the level of the water dropped, and when he got hungry and reached for fruit, it moved just out of reach. Thus, Tantalus was doomed to be near what he most desired but forever unable to obtain it. Sisyphus also was condemned to Hades. For his disrespect to Zeus, he was sentenced to endless toil. Every day, Sisyphus pushed a boulder up a steep hill. Every time he neared the top, the boulder rolled back down the hill, and Sisyphus had to begin again. Like Tantalus, the speaker in "Yet Do I Marvel" cannot have what he wants; like Sisyphus, he is forced to toil in vain. He wonders why a well-meaning God would "make a poet black, and bid him sing" in a racist society that does not listen to his voice. Thus, the poet's two allusions to Greek mythology enrich the poem by connecting the suffering of the speaker to a universal drama that has been acted out again and again.

FURTHER READING: Myth

WILLIAM BUTLER YEATS   (1865–1939)

Leda and the Swan   (1924)

A sudden blow: the great wings beating still
Above the staggering girl, her thighs caressed
By the dark webs, her nape caught in his bill,
He holds her helpless breast upon his breast.

How can those terrified vague fingers push   5
The feathered glory from her loosening thighs?
And how can body, laid in that white rush,
But feel the strange heart beating where it lies?

A shudder in the loins engenders there
The broken wall, the burning roof and tower   10
And Agamemnon dead.
                                    Being so caught up,
So mastered by the brute blood of the air,
Did she put on his knowledge with his power
Before the indifferent beak could let her drop?   15

Reading and Reacting

1. Research the myth of Leda. What event is described in this poem? What is the mythological significance of this event?

2. How is Leda portrayed? Why is the swan described as a "feathered glory" (line 6)? Why in the poem's last line is Leda dropped by his "indifferent beak"?

3. The third stanza refers to the Trojan War, which was indirectly caused by the event described in the poem. How does the allusion to the Trojan War help develop the theme of the poem?

4. **JOURNAL ENTRY** Does the poem answer the question asked in its last two lines? Explain.

5. **CRITICAL PERSPECTIVE** According to Richard Ellmann, this poem deals with "transcendence of opposites." The bird's "rape of the human, the coupling of god and woman, the moment at which one epoch ended and another began . . . in the act which included all these Yeats had the violent symbol for the transcendence of opposites which he needed."

    What opposite or contrary forces exist in the myth of Leda and the swan? Do you think the poem implies that these forces can be reconciled?

Related Works: "Where Are You Going, Where Have You Been?" (p. 573), "The Chrysanthemums" (p. 783), "Easter Wings" (p. 823), "The Second Coming" (p. 1246)

DEREK WALCOTT (1930 –   )

Sea Grapes° (1971)

That sail which leans on light,
tired of islands,
a schooner beating up the Caribbean

for home, could be Odysseus,
home-bound on the Aegean;   5
that father and husband's

longing, under gnarled sour grapes, is
like the adulterer hearing Nausicaa's name°
in every gull's outcry.

This brings nobody peace. The ancient war   10
between obsession and responsibility
will never finish and has been the same

for the sea-wanderer or the one on shore
now wriggling on his sandals to walk home,
since Troy sighed its last flame,   15

and the blind giant's boulder heaved the trough
from whose ground-swell the great hexameters come
to the conclusions of exhausted surf.

The classics can console. But not enough.

Reading and Reacting

1. Read a plot summary of the *Odyssey* in an encyclopedia. In the context of the myth of Odysseus, what is the "ancient war / between obsession and responsibility" (lines 10–11) to which the speaker refers? Does this conflict have a wider application in the context of the poem? Explain.
2. Consider the following lines from the poem: "and the blind giant's boulder heaved the trough / from whose ground-swell the great hexameters come / to the conclusions of exhausted surf" (lines 16–18). In what sense does the blind giant's boulder create the "great hexameters"? In what way does the trough end up as "exhausted surf"?

°*Sea Grapes:* Small trees found on tropical sandy beaches.   °*Nausicaa's name:* Nausicaa was a young princess who befriended the shipwrecked Odysseus.

3. **JOURNAL ENTRY** This poem includes many references to Homer's *Odyssey*. Could you have appreciated it if you had not read a plot summary of the *Odyssey?*

4. **CRITICAL PERSPECTIVE** Asked in an interview about the final line of "Sea Grapes," Derek Walcott made the following comments:

> All of us have been to the point where, in extreme agony and distress, you turn to a book, and look for parallels, and you look for a greater grief than maybe your own. . . . But the truth of human agony is that a book does not assuage a toothache. It isn't that things don't pass and heal. Perhaps the only privilege that a poet has is that, in that agony, whatever chafes and hurts, if the person survives, [he] produces something that is hopefully lasting and moral from the experience.

How do Walcott's remarks help to explain the poem's last line?

Related Works: "Sleepy Time Gal" (p. 154), "Gryphon" (p. 248), "My Father in the Navy: A Childhood Memory" (p. 1061), "Gretel in Darkness" (p. 852), "Dover Beach" (p. 1141), "Ulysses" (p. 1232)

W. H. AUDEN (1907–1973)

Musée des Beaux Arts (1940)

About suffering they were never wrong,
The Old Masters: how well they understood
Its human position; how it takes place
While someone else is eating or opening a window or just
    walking dully along
How, when the aged are reverently, passionately waiting   5
For the miraculous birth, there always must be
Children who did not specially want it to happen, skating
On a pond at the edge of the wood:
They never forgot
That even the dreadful martyrdom must run its course   10
Anyhow in a corner, some untidy spot
Where the dogs go on with their doggy life and the torturer's
    horse
Scratches its innocent behind on a tree.
In Brueghel's *Icarus*, for instance: how everything turns away
Quite leisurely from the disaster; the ploughman may   15
Have heard the splash, the forsaken cry,
But for him it was not an important failure; the sun shone
As it had to on the white legs disappearing into the green
Water; and the expensive delicate ship that must have seen
Something amazing, a boy falling out of the sky,   20
Had somewhere to get to and sailed calmly on.

Reading and Reacting

1. Reread the summary of the myth of Icarus on page 1044. What does Auden's allusion to this myth contribute to the poem?

2. What point does the poet make by referring to the "Old Masters" (2)?

3. JOURNAL ENTRY Brueghel's painting *Landscape with the Fall of Icarus* is shown below. How does looking at this painting help you to understand the poem? To what specific details in the painting does the poet refer?

Brueghel, Pieter the Elder (1525?–1569). *Landscape with the Fall of Icarus.* Musée D'Art Ancien, Brussels, Belgium. © Scala/Art Resource, New York

Related Works: "The Lottery" (p. 461), "One day I wrote her name upon the strand" (p. 914), "Shall I compare thee to a summer's day?" (p. 939), "Ethics" (p. 1210), "Not Waving but Drowning" (p. 1225), "The Second Coming" (p. 1246)

T. S. ELIOT (1888–1965)

Journey of the Magi° (1927)

"A cold coming we had of it,
Just the worst time of the year
For a journey, and such a long journey:

°*Magi:* The three wise men who ventured east to pay tribute to the infant Jesus (see Matthew 12.1–12).

The ways deep and the weather sharp,
The very dead of winter." *   5
And the camels galled, sore-footed, refractory,
Lying down in the melting snow.
There were times we regretted
The summer palaces on slopes, the terraces,
And the silken girls bringing sherbet.   10
Then the camel men cursing and grumbling
And running away, and wanting their liquor and women,
And the night-fires going out, and the lack of shelters,
And the cities hostile and the towns unfriendly
And the villages dirty and charging high prices: 15
A hard time we had of it.
At the end we preferred to travel all night,
Sleeping in snatches,
With the voices singing in our ears, saying
That this was all folly.   20

Then at dawn we came down to a temperate valley,
Wet, below the snow line, smelling of vegetation;
With a running stream and a water-mill beating the darkness,
And three trees° on the low sky,
And an old white horse° galloped away in the meadow.   25
Then we came to a tavern with vine-leaves over the lintel,
Six hands at an open door dicing for pieces of silver,°
And feet kicking the empty wine-skins.
But there was no information, and so we continued
And arrived at evening, not a moment too soon   30
Finding the place; it was (you may say) satisfactory.
All this was a long time ago, I remember,
And I would do it again, but set down
This set down
This: were we led all that way for   35
Birth or Death? There was a Birth, certainly,
We had evidence and no doubt. I had seen birth and death,
But had thought they were different; this Birth was
Hard and bitter agony for us, like Death, our death.
We returned to our places, these Kingdoms,   40
But no longer at ease here, in the old dispensation,
With an alien people clutching their gods.
I should be glad of another death.

---

*The five quoted lines are adapted from a passage in a 1622 Christmas Day sermon by Bishop Lancelot
Andrewes.   °*three trees:* The three crosses at Calvary (see Luke 23.32–33).   °*white horse:* The horse ridden
by the conquering Christ in Revelation 19.11–16.   °*dicing . . . silver:* Echoes the soldiers dicing for Christ's
garments, as well as his betrayal by Judas Iscariot for thirty pieces of silver (see Matthew 27.35 and 26.14–16).

Reading and Reacting

1. The speaker in the poem is one of the three wise men who came to pay tribute to the infant Jesus. In what way are his recollections unexpected? How would you have expected him to react to the birth of Jesus?

2. In what way do the mythical references in the poem allude to future events? Do you need to understand these allusions in order to appreciate the poem?

3. What does the speaker mean in line 41 when he says that the three wise men were "no longer at ease here, in the old dispensation"? What has changed for them? Why does the speaker say that he would be glad for "another death" (line 43)?

4. JOURNAL ENTRY How is this poem similar to and different from the story of the three wise men told in the New Testament (Matthew 2.1–18)?

5. CRITICAL PERSPECTIVE In an analysis of "Journey of the Magi," poet and critic Anthony Hecht discusses the most common interpretation of the poem, pointing to "a consensus of critical feeling about the tone of the conclusion of this poem, which, it is said, appears to border on despair and exhaustion of hope." Hecht, however, suspects that something more subtle is going on — namely, that Eliot is using the speaker of the poem to express his own imperfect acceptance of Christianity:

> Again, if I am right, about this, the poem might have a deeply personal meaning for Eliot himself, and might represent a kind of "confession," an acknowledgment that he had not yet perfectly embraced the fate to which he nominally adhered, that his imperfect spiritual status was, like the Magus's, that of a person whose faith was incomplete. . . .

Which of the two interpretations given above seems more plausible to you? Is the speaker of the poem wrestling with an incomplete faith, or is he experiencing "despair and exhaustion of hope"?

Related Works: "Araby" (p. 395), "Do not go gentle into that good night" (p. 1065), "The World Is Too Much with Us" (p. 870), "On First Looking into Chapman's Homer" (p. 1002), "The Love Song of J. Alfred Prufrock" (p. 1172)

ELIZABETH HOLMES (1957–)

The Fathers (2001)

Captain Hook and Mr. Darling
are traditionally played by the same actor.

Something's familiar about that villain
striding the deck of the *Jolly Roger*, chest
puffed out under the fancy jabot—
a bit like, yes, like Father huffing around
before an evening out, proper shirtfront   5
outthrust by an important bay window.
Particular about his cuff links as a pirate

about lace at his wrists. Same air of dashing
yet dastardly middle age. A penchant
for issuing orders and threats, and tying   10
up uncooperative dogs or Indian princesses.

No wonder we sons and daughters laugh
when Hook sits on the hot toadstool
over Peter's chimney, when Tinker Bell
flits out of his grasp. And especially   15
at his slapstick flailing through the sea,
pursued by that confident long-jawed beast,
time ticking loud in its belly.

Reading and Reacting

1. Why do you think the poet includes a note explaining that the same actor
who plays Captain Hook usually plays Mr. Darling? How does this note shed
light on the poem?

2. Why does the speaker think it is natural for children to laugh at Captain
Hook? Why does the speaker think it is especially funny to see Hook chased
by the crocodile?

3. With whom does the speaker identify? Captain Hook? Peter Pan? How do
you know?

4. **JOURNAL ENTRY** In what way could the story of Peter Pan be considered a
myth? In what way is this designation inappropriate?

Related Works: "Once upon a Time" (p. 204), "The Rocking-Horse Winner"
(p. 525), "Gretel in Darkness" (p. 852), "Cinderella" (p. 882), "Christopher
Robin" (p. 1025)

✔ **CHECKLIST**   **Writing about Symbol, Allegory, Allusion, Myth**

Symbol

▢ Are there any symbols in the poem? What leads you to believe they are
symbols?

▢ Are these symbols conventional?

▢ Are they universal or archetypal?

▢ Are any symbols obscure or highly idiosyncratic?

▢ What is the literal meaning of each symbol in the context of the poem?

▢ Beyond its literal meaning, what else could each symbol suggest?

▢ How does your interpretation of each symbol enhance your
understanding of the poem?

continued on next page

Allegory

☐ Is the poem an allegory?

☐ Are there any allegorical figures within the poem? How can you tell?

☐ What do the allegorical figures signify on a literal level?

☐ What lesson does the allegory illustrate?

Allusion

☐ Are there any allusions in the poem?

☐ Do you recognize the names, places, historical events, or literary works to which the poet alludes?

☐ In what way does each allusion deepen the poem's meaning? Does any allusion interfere with your understanding or enjoyment of the poem? If so, how?

☐ Would the poem be more effective without a particular allusion?

Myth

☐ What myths or mythological figures are alluded to?

☐ How does the poem use myth to convey its meaning?

☐ How faithful is the poem to the myth? Does the poet add material to the myth? Are any details from the original myth omitted? Is any information distorted? Why?

WRITING SUGGESTIONS: Symbol, Allegory, Allusion, Myth

1. Read "Aunt Jennifer's Tigers" (p. 977) and "Diving into the Wreck" (p. 1039) by Adrienne Rich. Then, write an essay in which you discuss the similarities and differences in Rich's use of symbols in the two poems.

2. Many popular songs make use of allusion. Choose one or two popular songs that you know well, and analyze their use of allusion, paying particular attention to whether the allusions expand the impact and meaning of the song or create barriers to listeners' understanding.

3. Read the Emily Dickinson poem "Because I could not stop for Death —" (p. 1160), and then write an interpretation of the poem, identifying its allegorical figures.

4. What applications do the lessons of myth have for life today? Analyze a poem in which myth is central, and then discuss how you might use myth to make generalizations about your own life.

5. Both Judith Ortiz Cofer's "My Father in the Navy: A Childhood Memory" (p. 1061) and Derek Walcott's "Sea Grapes" (p. 1050) allude to Homer's *Odyssey*. Read a summary of the *Odyssey* in an encyclopedia or other reference work, and then write an essay in which you compare the poets' treatment of Homer's tale.

CHAPTER 32

DISCOVERING THEMES IN POETRY

A poem should not mean
But be.

—Archibald MacLeish, *"Ars Poetica"*

A poem can be about anything, from the mysteries of the universe to poetry itself. Although no subject is really inappropriate for poetic treatment, certain conventional subjects — family, nature, love, war, death, the folly of human desires, and the inevitability of growing old — recur frequently.

A poem's *theme*, however, is more than its *subject*. In general terms, *theme* refers to the ideas that the poet explores, the concerns that the poem examines. More specifically, a poem's **theme** is its main point or idea. Poems "about death," for example, may examine the difficulty of facing one's own mortality, eulogize a friend, assert the need for the acceptance of life's cycles, or cry out against death's inevitability. Or, such poems may explore the **carpe diem theme** — the belief that life is brief, so we must seize the day.

In order to understand the theme of a poem, readers should consider its form, voice, language, images, allusions, sound — all of its individual elements. Together, these elements communicate the ideas that are important in the poem. Keep in mind, however, that a poem may not mean the same thing to every reader. Different readers will bring different backgrounds, attitudes, and experiences to a poem and will therefore see things in various ways. And, poets may approach the same subject in drastically different ways, emphasizing different elements as they view the subject matter from their own unique perspectives. Ultimately, there are as many different themes, and ways to approach these themes, as there are writers (and readers) of poetry.

Poems about Parents

Although a poet's individual experience may be vastly different from the experiences of his or her readers, certain ideas seem universal in poems about parents. On the one hand, such poems can express positive sentiments: love, joy, wistfulness, nostalgia, and gratitude for childhood's happy memories and unconditional love. On the other hand, they may express negative emotions: anger, frustration, resentment, regret, and emotional distance. When they write about parents, poets may be curious or apathetic, remorseful or grateful; they may idealize parents or be puzzled by them. Regardless of the particulars of the poem's specific theme, virtually all poems about parents address one general concept: the influence of a parent over his or her child.

For as long as poets have been writing poetry, their personal experiences (and childhoods) have influenced their subject matter and their poems. In American poetry, poems about parents became more common with the advent of **confessionalism**, a movement in the mid-1950s in which poets began to write subjective verse about their personal experiences. Poems in Robert Lowell's *Life Studies* and W. D. Snodgrass's *Heart's Needle* both addressed the positive and negative aspects of the poets' families (including their parents and children), thus opening the door for an influx of poems about similar themes.

The poems in this section all deal with issues related to parents and family, but their styles, voices, and focuses are very different. Sometimes the speakers' voices express ambivalence, communicating conventional sentiments of love and admiration alongside perplexity, frustration, and even anger. This ambivalence is apparent in Theodore Roethke's "My Papa's Waltz" and Robert Hayden's "Those Winter Sundays," as adult speakers struggle to understand their fathers' long-ago behavior. In Edna St. Vincent Millay's "The courage that my mother had" and Seamus Heaney's "Digging," the speakers are more positive, finding traits in their parents that they would like to emulate. Raymond Carver's "Photograph of My Father in His Twenty-Second Year" and Judith Ortiz Cofer's "My Father in the Navy: A Childhood Memory" are both meditations on visual images of the speakers' fathers in their younger years, while Mitsuye Yamada's "The Night Before Good-Bye" focuses on a mother's quiet sacrifice. Wanda Coleman's "Dear Mama" and Simon J. Ortiz's "My Father's Song" are elegiac poems that address the inevitable cycles of life. Finally, both Adrienne Rich's "A Woman Mourned by Daughters" and Dylan Thomas's "Do not go gentle into that good night" confront the death of a parent.

THEODORE ROETHKE (1908–1963)

My Papa's Waltz (1948)

The whiskey on your breath
Could make a small boy dizzy;
But I hung on like death:
Such waltzing was not easy.

We romped until the pans   5
Slid from the kitchen shelf;
My mother's countenance
Could not unfrown itself.

The hand that held my wrist
Was battered on one knuckle;   10

At every step you missed
My right ear scraped a buckle.

You beat time on my head
With a palm caked hard by dirt,
Then waltzed me off to bed   15
Still clinging to your shirt.

ROBERT HAYDEN   (1913–1980)

Those Winter Sundays   (1962)

Sundays too my father got up early
and put his clothes on in the blueblack cold,
then with cracked hands that ached
from labor in the weekday weather made
banked fires blaze. No one ever thanked him.   5

I'd wake and hear the cold splintering, breaking.
When the rooms were warm, he'd call,
and slowly I would rise and dress,
fearing the chronic angers of that house,

Speaking indifferently to him,   10
who had driven out the cold
and polished my good shoes as well.
What did I know, what did I know
of love's austere and lonely offices?

EDNA ST. VINCENT MILLAY   (1892–1950)

The courage that my mother had   (1954)

The courage that my mother had
Went with her, and is with her still:
Rock from New England quarried;
New granite in a granite hill.

The golden brooch my mother wore   5
She left behind for me to wear;
I have no thing I treasure more:
Yet, it is something I could spare.

Oh, if instead she'd left to me
The thing she took into the grave!—   10
That courage like a rock, which she
Has no more need of, and I have.

SEAMUS HEANEY* (1939–   )

Digging (1966)

Between my finger and my thumb
The squat pen rests; snug as a gun.

Under my window, a clean rasping sound
When the spade sinks into gravelly ground:
My father, digging. I look down   5

Till his straining rump among the flowerbeds
Bends low, comes up twenty years away
Stooping in rhythm through potato drills
Where he was digging.

The coarse boot nestled on the lug, the shaft   10
Against the inside knee was levered firmly.
He rooted out tall tops, buried the bright edge deep
To scatter new potatoes that we picked
Loving their cool hardness in our hands.

By God, the old man could handle a spade.   15
Just like his old man.

My grandfather cut more turf in a day
Than any other man on Toner's bog.
Once I carried him milk in a bottle
Corked sloppily with paper. He straightened up   20
To drink it, then fell to right away

Nicking and slicing neatly, heaving sods
Over his shoulder, going down and down
For the good turf. Digging.

The cold smell of potato mould, the squelch and slap   25
Of soggy peat, the curt cuts of an edge
Through living roots awaken in my head.
But I've no spade to follow men like them.

Between my finger and my thumb
The squat pen rests.   30
I'll dig with it.

---

* *Seamus Heaney:* Heaney received the 1995 Nobel Prize in Literature.

RAYMOND CARVER (1938–1988)

Photograph of My Father in
His Twenty-Second Year (1983)

October. Here in this dank, unfamiliar kitchen
I study my father's embarrassed young man's face.
Sheepish grin, he holds in one hand a string
of spiny yellow perch, in the other
a bottle of Carlsbad beer.   5

In jeans and denim shirt, he leans
against the front fender of a 1934 Ford.
He would like to pose bluff and hearty for his posterity,
wear his old hat cocked over his ear.
All his life my father wanted to be bold.   10

But the eyes give him away, and the hands
that limply offer the string of dead perch
and the bottle of beer. Father, I love you,
yet how can I say thank you, I who can't hold my liquor either,
and don't even know the places to fish?   15

JUDITH ORTIZ COFER (1952–   )

My Father in the Navy:
A Childhood Memory (1982)

Stiff and immaculate
in the white cloth of his uniform
and a round cap on his head like a halo,
he was an apparition on leave from a shadow-world
and only flesh and blood when he rose from below   5
the waterline where he kept watch over the engines
and dials making sure the ship parted the waters
on a straight course.
Mother, brother and I kept vigil
on the nights and dawns of his arrivals,   10
watching the corner beyond the neon sign of a quasar
for the flash of white our father like an angel
heralding a new day.
His homecomings were the verses
we composed over the years making up   15
the siren's song that kept him coming back

from the bellies of iron whales
and into our nights
like the evening prayer.

MITSUYE YAMADA   (1923–   )

The Night Before Good-bye   (1976)

Mama is mending
my underwear
while my brothers sleep.
Her husband taken away by the FBI
one son lured away by the Army   5
now another son and daughter
lusting for the free world outside.
She must let go.
The war goes on.
She will take one still small son   10
and join Papa in internment°
to make a family.
Still sewing
squinting in the dim light
in room C barrack 4 block 4   15
she whispers
Remember
keep your underwear
in good repair
in case of accident   20
don't bring shame
on us.

WANDA COLEMAN   (1946–   )

Dear Mama   (1983)

when did we become friends?
it happened so gradual i didn't notice
maybe i had to get my run out first
take a big bite of the honky world and choke on it

° *internment:* Shortly after the attack on Pearl Harbor, President Roosevelt ordered that all people of Japanese ancestry — even American citizens — be removed from the West Coast. About 112,000 people were relocated to "internment camps," where they remained until after the war's end.

maybe that's what has to happen with some uppity youngsters   5
if it happens at all

and now
the thought stark and irrevocable
of being here without you   10
shakes me

beyond love, fear, regret or anger
into that realm children go
who want to care for/protect their parents
as if they could   15
and sometimes the lucky ones do

into the realm of making every moment
important
laughing as though laughter wards off death
each word given   20
received like spanish eight°

treasure to bury within
against that shadow day
when it will be the only coin i possess
with which to buy peace of mind   25

SIMON J. ORTIZ (1941–   )

My Father's Song (1976)

Wanting to say things,
I miss my father tonight.
His voice, the slight catch,
the depth from his thin chest,
the tremble of emotion   5
in something he has just said
to his son, his song:

We planted corn one Spring at Acu—
we planted several times
but this one particular time   10
I remember the soft damp sand
in my hand.

° *spanish eight:* A nickname given to the original Spanish peso, which was minted with real silver in the Americas and transported by ship back to Spain, making the cargo a tempting target for pirates. The Spanish Eight was the most widely used international trade coin.

My father had stopped at one point
to show me an overturned furrow;
the plowshare had unearthed   15
the burrow nest of a mouse
in the soft moist sand.

Very gently, he scooped tiny pink animals
into the palm of his hand
and told me to touch them.   20
We took them to the edge
of the field and put them in the shade
of a sand moist clod.

I remember the very softness
of cool and warm sand and tiny alive mice   25
and my father saying things.

ADRIENNE RICH (1929–   )

A Woman Mourned by Daughters (1984)

Now, not a tear begun,
we sit here in your kitchen,
spent, you see, already.
You are swollen till you strain
this house and the whole sky.   5
You, whom we so often
succeeded in ignoring!
You are puffed up in death
like a corpse pulled from the sea;
we groan beneath your weight.   10
And yet you were a leaf,
a straw blown on the bed,
you had long since become
crisp as a dead insect.
What is it, if not you,   15
that settles on us now
like satins you pulled down
over our bridal heads?
What rises in our throats
like food you prodded in?   20
Nothing could be enough.
You breathe upon us now
through solid assertions
of yourself: teaspoons, goblets,
seas of carpet, a forest   25

of old plants to be watered,
an old man in an adjoining
room to be touched and fed.
And all this universe
dares us to lay a finger   30
anywhere, save exactly
as you would wish it done.

DYLAN THOMAS   (1914–1953)

Do not go gentle into that good night * (1952)

Do not go gentle into that good night,
Old age should burn and rave at close of day;
Rage, rage against the dying of the light.

Though wise men at their end know dark is right,
Because their words had forked no lightning they   5
Do not go gentle into that good night.

Good men, the last wave by, crying how bright
Their frail deeds might have danced in a green bay,
Rage, rage against the dying of the light.

Wild men who caught and sang the sun in flight,   10
And learn, too late, they grieved it on its way,
Do not go gentle into that good night.

Grave men, near death, who see with blinding sight
Blind eyes could blaze like meteors and be gay,
Rage, rage against the dying of the light.   15

And you, my father, there on the sad height,
Curse, bless, me now with your fierce tears, I pray,
Do not go gentle into that good night.
Rage, rage against the dying of the light.

Reading and Reacting: Poems about Parents

1. What is each speaker's attitude toward his or her parent?
2. Which words, images, and figures of speech have positive associations?
Which help to create a negative impression?
3. How would you characterize each poem's tone? For example, is the tone sentimental? Playful? Angry? Resentful? Regretful?

---

*This poem was written during the last illness of the poet's father.

4. What problems associated with parent-child relationships are explored in each poem?

5. What does each poem say about the parent? What does it reveal about the child?

6. What is each poem's central theme?

Related Works: "Sleepy Time Gal" (p. 154), "A Primer for the Punctuation of Heart Disease" (p. 156), "Seventeen Syllables" (p. 538), "Two Kinds" (p. 791), "Daddy" (p. 952), *Proof* (p. 1526)

Poems about Nature

In his 1913 poem "Trees," the American poet Joyce Kilmer neatly summarized the symbiotic relationship that has always existed between poetry and nature: "I think that I shall never see / A poem lovely as a tree." Poets have always found inspiration in the beauty, majesty, and grandeur of the natural world; in fact, some forms of poetry are dedicated solely to the subject of nature. For example, a **pastoral** is a literary form that deals nostalgically with a simple rural life. Many of the early Greek and Roman pastorals were about shepherds who passed the time writing about love while watching their flocks. In these poems, the shepherd's life was idealized. Thus, the pastoral tradition celebrates simple times and the beauty of the rural life. Similarly, an **idyll**, a short work in verse or prose (or a painting or a piece of music), depicts simple pastoral or rural scenes, often in idealized terms.

Certain literary movements also focused on the subject of nature. The **Romantic** poets, for example, found in nature a mirror for their own beliefs and sense of identity. They believed that only the sweeping grandeur of nature could reflect the comparable grandeur of humanity as well as a sense of the infinite and the transcendental. Later, the American **Transcendentalists**, including Ralph Waldo Emerson and Henry David Thoreau, examined the relationships between philosophy, religion, and nature. In *Walden*, for example, Thoreau wrote about the pleasures and rewards of withdrawing from mainstream life in order to live simply in the woods.

While all poems about nature deal with the same general subject, their approaches, and their focuses, can differ greatly. Poems "about nature" may praise the beauty of nature, assert the superiority of its simplest creatures, consider its evanescence, or mourn its destruction. In this section, Romantic poet William Wordsworth's "I wandered lonely as a cloud" extols the virtue of nature and highlights the value of participating in its beauty. In "Summer," Christina Rosetti writes in lighthearted terms of the beauty of the season, while in "The Windhover," Gerard Manley Hopkins celebrates the divinity of God's natural kingdom. In Robert Frost's "Birches," the speaker recalls the childhood enjoyment of climbing trees and longs for the simplicity of those times; in William Stafford's

"Traveling through the Dark," the speaker presents human beings as adversaries of nature and its other creatures. Simone Muench's "Dogwood" and Joy Harjo's "Morning Song" are lyrical odes, that celebrate elements of the natural world. Finally, Richard Wilbur's "In Trackless Woods" praises the natural and unforced logic and symmetry of the wilderness within a "civilized" world.

WILLIAM WORDSWORTH (1770–1850)

I wandered lonely as a cloud (1807)

I wandered lonely as a cloud
 That floats on high o'er vales and hills,
When all at once I saw a crowd,
 A host, of golden daffodils,
Beside the lake, beneath the trees,   5
Fluttering and dancing in the breeze.

Continuous as the stars that shine
 And twinkle on the milky way,
They stretched in never-ending line
 Along the margin of a bay: 10
Ten thousand saw I at a glance,
Tossing their heads in sprightly dance.

The waves beside them danced; but they
 Out-did the sparkling waves in glee;
A poet could not but be gay,   15
 In such a jocund company;
I gazed — and gazed — but little thought
What wealth the show to me had brought:

For oft, when on my couch I lie
 In vacant or in pensive mood,   20
They flash upon that inward eye
 Which is the bliss of solitude;
And then my heart with pleasure fills,
And dances with the daffodils.

CHRISTINA ROSSETTI (1830–1894)

Summer

 Winter is cold-hearted,
  Spring is yea and nay,
Autumn is a weathercock
  Blown every way.

Summer days for me   5
When every leaf is on its tree;

When Robin's not a beggar,
And Jenny Wren's a bride,
And larks hang singing, singing, singing
Over the wheat-fields wide,   10
And anchored lilies ride,
And the pendulum spider
Swings from side to side;

And blue-black beetles transact business,
And gnats fly in a host,   15
And furry caterpillars hasten
That no time be lost
And moths grow fat and thrive,
And ladybirds arrive

Before green apples blush,   20
Before green nuts embrown,
Why one day in the country
Is worth a month in town;
Is worth a day and a year

Of the dusty, musty, lag-last fashion   25
That days drone elsewhere

GERARD MANLEY HOPKINS   (1844–1889)

The Windhover°   (1877)

To Christ Our Lord

I caught this morning morning's minion,° king-
    dom of daylight's dauphin, dapple-dawn-drawn Falcon, in
        his riding
Of the rolling level underneath him steady air, and striding
High there, how he rung upon the rein° of a wimpling° wing
In his ecstasy! then off, off forth on swing,   5
    As a skate's heel sweeps smooth on a bow-bend: the hurl and
        gliding
    Rebuffed the big wind. My heart in hiding

°*Windhover:* A kestrel, a European falcon able to hover in the air with its head to the wind.   °*minion:* Favorite.
°*rung upon the rein:* A horse is "rung upon the rein" when it circles at the end of a long rein held by the trainer.
°*wimpling:* Rippling.

Stirred for a bird, — the achieve of, the mastery of the thing!
Brute beauty and valor and act, oh, air, pride, plume, here
    Buckle! and the fire that breaks from thee then, a billion   10
Times told lovelier, more dangerous, O my chevalier!
    No wonder of it: shéer plód, makes plow down sillion°
Shine, and blue-bleak embers, ah my dear,
    Fall, gall themselves, and gash gold-vermilion.

ROBERT FROST   (1874–1963)

Birches   (1915)

When I see birches bend to left and right
Across the lines of straighter darker trees,
I like to think some boy's been swinging them.
But swinging doesn't bend them down to stay
As ice-storms do. Often you must have seen them   5
Loaded with ice a sunny winter morning
After a rain. They click upon themselves
As the breeze rises, and turn many-colored
As the stir cracks and crazes their enamel.
Soon the sun's warmth makes them shed crystal shells   10
Shattering and avalanching on the snow-crust —
Such heaps of broken glass to sweep away
You'd think the inner dome of heaven had fallen.
They are dragged to the withered bracken by the load,
And they seem not to break; though once they are bowed   15
So low for long, they never right themselves:
You may see their trunks arching in the woods
Years afterwards, trailing their leaves on the ground
Like girls on hands and knees that throw their hair
Before them over their heads to dry in the sun.   20
But I was going to say when Truth broke in
With all her matter-of-fact about the ice-storm
I should prefer to have some boy bend them
As he went out and in to fetch the cows —
Some boy too far from town to learn baseball,   25
Whose only play was what he found himself,
Summer or winter, and could play alone.
One by one he subdued his father's trees
By riding them down over and over again
Until he took the stiffness out of them,   30

°*sillion:* The ridge between two furrows.

And not one but hung limp, not one was left
For him to conquer. He learned all there was
To learn about not launching out too soon
And so not carrying the tree away
Clear to the ground. He always kept his poise   35
To the top branches, climbing carefully
With the same pains you use to fill a cup
Up to the brim, and even above the brim.
Then he flung outward, feet first, with a swish,
Kicking his way down through the air to the ground.   40
So was I once myself a swinger of birches.
And so I dream of going back to be.
It's when I'm weary of considerations,
And life is too much like a pathless wood
Where your face burns and tickles with the cobwebs   45
Broken across it, and one eye is weeping
From a twig's having lashed across it open.
I'd like to get away from earth awhile
And then come back to it and begin over.
May no fate willfully misunderstand me   50
And half grant what I wish and snatch me away
Not to return. Earth's the right place for love:
I don't know where it's likely to go better.
I'd like to go by climbing a birch tree,
And climb black branches up a snow-white trunk   55
Toward Heaven, till the tree could bear no more,
But dipped its top and set me down again.
That would be good both going and coming back.
One could do worse than be a swinger of birches.

WILLIAM STAFFORD (1914–1993)

Traveling through the Dark (1962)

Traveling through the dark I found a deer
dead on the edge of the Wilson River road.
It is usually best to roll them into the canyon:
that road is narrow; to swerve might make more dead.

By glow of the tail-light I stumbled back of the car   5
and stood by the heap, a doe, a recent killing;
she had stiffened already, almost cold.
I dragged her off; she was large in the belly.

My fingers touching her side brought me the reason —
her side was warm; her fawn lay there waiting,   10

alive, still, never to be born.
Beside that mountain road I hesitated.

The car aimed ahead its lowered parking lights;
under the hood purred the steady engine.
I stood in the glare of the warm exhaust turning red;   15
around our group I could hear the wilderness listen.

I thought hard for us all — my only swerving —
then pushed her over the edge into the river.

SIMONE MUENCH

Dogwood   (1999)

In the wind the dogwoods bend,
an osculation of branch and bud.

Four ivory bracts lined like foreheads,
thin as skin and scent of sky.

Under the cobalt vault of night   5
they radiate like prayers: a rictus

in the darkness, they are cool
as Buddhism, ethereal as cumulus.

Sentinels of my window, they
absorb the moons mist-white light   10

bounce it back to the sky
like a thousand tin tops,

an inversion of stars.

JOY HARJO   (1951–   )

Morning Song   (2001)

The red dawn now is rearranging the earth
Thought by thought
Beauty by beauty
Each sunrise a link in the ladder
The ladder the backbone   5
Of shimmering deity
Child stirring in the web of your mother
Do not be afraid
Old man turning to walk through the door
Do not be afraid   10

RICHARD WILBUR (1921–   )

In Trackless Woods (2003)

In trackless woods, it puzzled me to find
Four great rock maples seemingly aligned,
As if they had been set out in a row
Before some house a century ago,
To edge the property and lend some shade.   5
I looked to see if ancient wheels had made
Old ruts to which these trees can parallel,
But there were none, so far as I could tell —
There'd been no roadway. Nor could I find the square
Depression of a cellar anywhere,   10
And so I tramped on further, to survey
Amazing patterns in a hornbeam spray
Or spirals in a pinecone, under trees
Not subject to our stiff geometries.

Reading and Reacting: Poems about Parents

1. What do you think inspired the poem?
2. What is the speaker's attitude toward nature? Is nature seen as a benevolent, comforting, threatening, awe-inspiring, or overwhelming force?
3. Which words, images, and figures of speech in the poem have positive associations? Which help to create a negative impression of nature?
4. How would you characterize each poem's tone? For example, is the speaker hopeful? Thoughtful? Humbled? Frightened?
5. Is the natural world the poem's true subject, or is it just the setting? Explain.
6. What is each poem's central theme?

Related Works: "Appetizer" (p. 400), "Doe Season" (p. 512), "Hidden Lives of Lakes" (p. 549), "Greasy Lake" (p. 648), "Comparatives" (p. 981), "Blackberry Eating" (p. 990), "Four Haiku" (p. 1012), *A Midsummer Night's Dream* (p. 1828)

Poems about Love

Poetry has long been regarded as a romantic genre, as evidenced by the abundance of sentimental verse found in countless Valentine's Day cards. In fact, the history of poetry includes an extensive list of love poems, almost certainly beginning with the earliest poets privately expressing their feelings and desire. Over time, love poems found their way into the public realm. One of the earliest examples is the Bible's *Song of Solomon*, which is an extended love poem (though some critics argue that the "beloved" is not a woman but rather a metaphor for religion). Other examples can be found in the work of Catullus, a Roman poet who wrote a cycle of twenty-five love poems to a mysterious woman he called Lesbia.

Epic medieval poems such as *Beowulf,* which focused on battles and heroic characters, were eventually supplanted by romantic adventures such as the Arthurian legends, which included the idea of "courtly love." In these poems, a chivalrous protagonist performs gallant deeds to win the hand of the fair maiden who has captured his heart. Examples of courtly love poems include *Sir Gawain and the Green Knight* and *Le Morte d'Arthur.* During the Renaissance, a more personal style developed, and poems became vehicles for demonstrating a poet's amorous feelings. Often cloaked in metaphor, simile, or other figures of speech, poems expressed feelings of love in numerous forms. Examples of Renaissance love poems include many of Shakespeare's sonnets, as well as Christopher Marlowe's "The Passionate Shepherd to His Love" (p. 1202), a poem in the pastoral tradition, which was answered by Sir Walter Raleigh's "The Nymph's Reply to the Shepherd" (p. 1216).

Although the Renaissance marked a high point in the development of the love poem, love has remained a constant theme in poetry regardless of the literary fads and trends of the day. In fact, in every literary movement —from the seventeenth-century metaphysical poets through today's slam poetry — one can find love poems written in the movement's characteristic style and form.

In each of the poems in this section, the poets address the subject of love in their own styles and voices. Robert Browning and Elizabeth Barrett Browning (who were married to each other) are represented with traditional love poems, including "How Do I Love Thee?" which is one of the most often quoted poems in the English language. In Edna St. Vincent Millay's "What Lips My Lips Have Kissed," the speaker reminisces about her past lovers with a mixture of nostalgia and wistfulness. On a lighter note, Dorothy Parker's "General Review of the Sex Situation" is a tongue-in-cheek description of the differences between the sexes. W. H. Auden's "Stop all the clocks, cut off the telephone" is an eloquent elegy that expresses profound loss and despair.

Contemporary love poems are equally varied in their approaches, ranging from the playfulness of Sandra Cisneros's "In My Little Museum of Erotica" to the litany of promises enumerated in Joseph Brodsky's "Love Song," and from the visual experimentation of Tupac Shakur's "Love Is Just Complicated" to the reverent tone of Jeffrey McDaniel's slam poem "The Quiet Word" and the passion of Pablo Neruda's "Absence."

ROBERT BROWNING (1812–1889)

Meeting at Night (1845)

The gray sea and the long black land;
And the yellow half-moon large and low;
And the startled little waves that leap
In fiery ringlets from their sleep,

As I gain the cove with pushing prow,   5
And quench its speed i' the slushy sand.

Then a mile of warm sea-scented beach;
Three fields to cross till a farm appears;
A tap at the pane, the quick sharp scratch
And blue spurt of a lighted match,   10
And a voice less loud, through its joys and fears,
Than the two hearts beating each to each!

Parting at Morning   (1845)

Round the cape of a sudden came the sea,
And the sun looked over the mountain's rim:
And straight was a path of gold for him,
And the need of a world of men for me.

ELIZABETH BARRETT BROWNING   (1806–1861)

How Do I Love Thee?   (1850)

How do I love thee? Let me count the ways.
I love thee to the depth and breadth and height
My soul can reach, when feeling out of sight
For the ends of being and ideal grace.
I love thee to the level of every day's   5
Most quiet need, by sun and candle-light.
I love thee freely, as men strive for right.
I love thee purely, as they turn from praise.
I love thee with the passion put to use
In my old griefs, and with my childhood's faith.   10
I love thee with a love I seemed to lose
With my lost saints. I love thee with the breath,
Smiles, tears, of all my life; and, if God choose,
I shall but love thee better after death.

EDNA ST. VINCENT MILLAY   (1892–1950)

What Lips My Lips Have Kissed   (1923)

What lips my lips have kissed, and where, and why,
I have forgotten, and what arms have lain
Under my head till morning; but the rain
Is full of ghosts tonight, that tap and sigh
Upon the glass and listen for reply,   5
And in my heart there stirs a quiet pain

For unremembered lads that not again
Will turn to me at midnight with a cry.
Thus in the winter stands the lonely tree,
Nor knows what birds have vanished one by one,   10
Yet knows its boughs more silent than before:
I cannot say what loves have come and gone,
I only know that summer sang in me
A little while, that in me sings no more.

DOROTHY PARKER   (1893–1967)

General Review of the Sex Situation   (1933)

Woman wants monogamy;
Man delights in novelty.
Love is woman's moon and sun;
Man has other forms of fun.

Woman lives but in her lord;   5
Count to ten, and man is bored.
With this the gist and sum of it,
What earthly good can come of it?

W. H. AUDEN   (1907–1973)

Stop all the clocks, cut off the telephone   (1936)

Stop all the clocks, cut off the telephone,
Prevent the dog from barking with a juicy bone,
Silence the pianos and with muffled drum
Bring out the coffin, let the mourners come.

Let aeroplanes circle moaning overhead   5
Scribbling on the sky the message He Is Dead,
Put the crepe bows round the white necks of the public doves,
Let the traffic policemen wear black cotton gloves.

He was my North, my South, my East and West,
My working week and my Sunday rest,   10
My noon, my midnight, my talk, my song;
I thought that love would last for ever. I was wrong.

The stars are not wanted now: put out every one;
Pack up the moon and dismantle the sun;
Pour away the ocean and sweep up the wood.   15
For nothing now can ever come to any good.

SANDRA CISNEROS (1954–)

In My Little Museum of Erotica

In my little museum
of erotica
I would place your feet.

I would place your feet
sandwiching   5
my feet.

Their softness.
Their heat.

And I would
place your arms   10
as you do mornings,
beneath my neck.
around my waist,
tugging me towards you,
my back to your chest.   15

This
well-beingness
I would set
on a Corinthian
column.   20

And those
who are aesthetes
of mornings and feet
would say, Ah!
Yes!   25

JOSEPH BRODSKY (1940–1996)

Love Song

If you were drowning I'd come to the rescue,
    wrap you in my blanket and pour hot tea
If I were a sheriff, I'd arrest you
    and keep you in the cell under lock and key.

If you were a bird, I'd cut a record   5
    and listen all night long to your high-pitched trill.
If I were a sergeant, you'd be my recruit,
    and boy I can assure you you'd love the drill.

If you were Chinese, I'd learn the language,
    Burn a lot of incense, wear funny clothes,   10

If you were a mirror, I'd storm the Ladies,
    Give you my red lipstick and puff your nose.

If you loved volcanoes, I'd be lava
    relentlessly erupting from my hidden source
And if you were my wife, I'd be your lover   15
    because the church is firmly against divorce.

TUPAC SHAKUR (1971–1996)

Love Is Just Complicated

You ask me 2 communicate
What it is I feel within
I search 4 words 2 assist
But I find none 2 help me begin
I guess Love is just complicated
    Love
        is
            Just
                complicated.

I Thought I knew my Heart's Desire
I thought I quenched my Burning Fire
I thought I wanted "A"
But "A" was 2 mixed up with "B"
Then "C" made me more confused
So "A" turned off me and "B" feels
better. "C" is upset and lonely
and me, I think Love is complicated
    Love
        is
            Just
                complicated.

2-Pac

JEFFREY MCDANIEL (1976–)

The Quiet Word (2003)

In an effort to get people to look
into each other's eyes more,
the government has decided to allot
each person exactly one hundred
and sixty-seven words, per day.   5

When the phone rings, I put it
to my ear without saying hello.
In the restaurant I point
at chicken noodle soup. I am
adjusting well to the new way.   10

Late at night, I call my long
distance lover and proudly say
I only used fifty-nine today.
I saved the rest for you.

When she doesn't respond, I know   15
she's used up all her words
so I slowly whisper I love you,
thirty-two and a third times.
After that, we just sit on the line
and listen to each other breathe.   20

PABLO NERUDA (1940–1973)

Absence

I have scarcely left you
when you go in me, crystalline,
or trembling,
or uneasy, wounded by me
or overwhelmed with love, as when your eyes   5
close upon the gift of life
that without cease I give you.

My love,
we have found each other
thirsty and we have   10
drunk up all the water and the Wood,
we found each other
hungry
and we bit each other
as fire bites,   15

leaving wounds in us.

But wait for me,
keep for me your sweetness.
I will give you too   20
a rose.

Reading and Reacting: Poems about Love

1. What general ideas about love are expressed in each poem?

2. What conventional images and figures of speech does each speaker use to express his or her feelings of love?

3. Does any speaker use any unexpected (or even shocking) images or figures of speech?

4. How would you characterize the tone of each poem? For example, is the tone happy? Sad? Celebratory? Regretful?

5. What does each poem reveal about the speaker? About the person to whom the poem is addressed?

6. What is each poem's central theme?

Related Works: "Love and Other Catastrophes: A Mix Tape" (p. 165), "The Storm" (p. 281), "Living in Sin" (p. 897), "I Knew a Woman" (p. 901), "The Faithful Wife" (p. 909), "A Valediction: Forbidding Mourning" (p. 949), "To My Dear and Loving Husband" (p. 956), "you fit into me" (p. 961), "There Is a Garden in Her Face" (p. 1151), *The Brute* (p. 1293)

Poems about War

In poetry, war is as ancient a theme as love and nature. In fact, the earliest poems, including Homer's *Iliad* and *Odyssey* and Virgil's *Aeneid*, have at their centers epic battles and struggles. These battles were described in rhymed verse so they could be remembered and passed down from one generation to the next. In this way, the history of humanity and the history of poetry are woven into the recorded history of war.

Early epic poems reflected the belief that war was a noble and gallant endeavor, with soldiers and citizens alike fighting for a variety of causes, including religion and territory. These poems idolized the heroes of the wars and celebrated their accomplishments in battle. Over time, as war became increasingly modern and complex, poems about war began to express deep moral and philosophical ambiguities. One of the best-known of these poems was "Dulce et Decorum Est" (p. 931), written toward the end of World War I by Wilfred Owen, a soldier who was killed on the Western Front in 1918. The poem, which includes graphic images of war, ends with a bitterly ironic quotation that summarizes the mentality that fuels war: "It is sweet and fitting to die for one's country." Similarly, in William Butler Yeats's "An Irish Airman Foresees His Death," written at the same time as Owen's poem, the speaker expresses ambivalence about the war in which he is fighting and the reasons why he is fighting it.

Of course, not all modern poems about war are poems of protest. Rupert Brooke, a contemporary of Wilfred Owen, wrote "The Soldier," an elegy that celebrates the nobility of fighting for the sake of one's beloved country. Robert Lowell's "For the Union Dead," written in 1959, is an elegy for Colonel Robert Gould Shaw, who led a regiment of African-American soldiers who fought and died for the Union Army during the Civil War.

Although war poems tend to focus on death and destruction, in modern poems, the victims of war are not always soldiers. For example, Boris Slutsky's "How Did They Kill My Grandmother?" describes a World War II German assault on civilians — in this case, the Jews in a Russian village. In the post–World War II years, enemies (like victims) were not as clearly defined as they had been in the past. After all, both the Korean War and the Vietnam War were waged not just against another nation but against the threat of Communism. The war in Vietnam unfolded before the American people on their television screens, and as a result, many Americans questioned the war's goals. This skepticism carried over into poems about the war, as seen in Denise Levertov's "What Were They Like?" (a call and response poem that asks questions about the people in Vietnam in an effort to heighten their humanity and diminish their identity as "the enemy") and in Yusef Komunyakaa's "Facing It," in which a Vietnam veteran visits the Vietnam War Memorial in Washington.

The post-Vietnam years have seen troops from various nations take part in war conflicts around the globe; Eliza Griswold writes of one such conflict in "Buying Rations in Kabul." Finally, Carl Phillips's speaker in "On the Notion of Tenderness in Wartime" attempts to survive the misery of war by finding comfort in love, while Wislawa Szymborska's "The End and the Beginning" addresses the onerous job of cleaning up what is left behind in the aftermath of war.

RUPERT BROOKE   (1887–1915)

The Soldier   (1915)

If I should die, think only this of me;
   That there's some corner of a foreign field
That is forever England. There shall be
   In that rich earth a richer dust concealed;
A dust whom England bore, shaped, made aware,   5
   Gave, once, her flowers to love, her ways to roam,
A body of England's breathing English air,
   Washed by the rivers, blest by suns of home.

And think, this heart, all evil shed away,
   A pulse in the eternal mind, no less   10
      Gives somewhere back the thoughts by England given;
Her sights and sounds; dreams happy as her day;

And laughter, learnt of friends; and gentleness,
  In hearts at peace, under an English heaven.

WILLIAM BUTLER YEATS (1865–1939)

An Irish Airman Foresees His Death (1919)

I know that I shall meet my fate
Somewhere among the clouds above;
Those that I fight I do not hate,
Those that I guard I do not love;
My country is Kiltartan Cross   5
My countrymen Kiltartan's poor,
No likely end could bring them loss
Or leave them happier than before.
Nor law, nor duty bade me fight,
Nor public men, nor cheering crowds,   10
A lonely impulse of delight
Drove to this tumult in the clouds;
I balanced all, brought all to mind,
The years to come seemed waste of breath,
A waste of breath the years behind   15
In balance with this life, this death.

ROBERT LOWELL (1917–1977)

For the Union Dead (1959)

"Relinquunt omnia servare rem publicam."°

The old South Boston Aquarium stands
in a Sahara of snow now. Its broken windows are boarded.
The bronze weathervane cod has lost half its scales.
The airy tanks are dry.

Once my nose crawled like a snail on the glass;   5
my hand tingled
to burst the bubbles
drifting from the noses of the cowed, compliant fish.

My hand draws back. I often sigh still
for the dark downward and vegetating kingdom   10

° *Relinquunt omnia servare rem publicam:* "They gave up everything to preserve the Republic" (Latin). A monument in Boston Common bears a similar form of this quotation. Designed by Augustus Saint-Gaudens, the monument is dedicated to Colonel Robert Gould Shaw and the African-American troops he commanded during a Civil War battle at Fort Wagner, South Carolina, on July 18, 1863.

of the fish and reptile. One morning last March,
I pressed against the new barbed and galvanized

fence on the Boston Common. Behind their cage,
yellow dinosaur steamshovels were grunting
as they cropped up tons of mush and grass   15
to gouge their underworld garage.

Parking spaces luxuriate like civic
sandpiles in the heart of Boston.
A girdle of orange, Puritan-pumpkin colored girders
braces the tingling Statehouse,   20

shaking over the excavations, as it faces Colonel Shaw
and his bell-cheeked Negro infantry
on St. Gauden's shaking Civil War relief,
propped by a plant splint against the garage's earthquake.

Two months after marching through Boston,   25
half the regiment was dead;
at the dedication,
William James° could almost hear the bronze Negroes breathe.

Their monument sticks like a fishbone
in the city's throat.   30
Its Colonel is as lean
as a compass-needle.

He has an angry wrenlike vigilance,
a greyhound's gentle tautness;
he seems to wince at pleasure,   35
and suffocate for privacy.

He is out of bounds now. He rejoices in man's lovely,
peculiar power to choose life and die —
when he leads his black soldiers to death,
he cannot bend his back.   40

On a thousand small town New England greens,
the old white churches hold their air
of sparse, sincere rebellion; frayed flags
quilt the graveyards of the Grand Army of the Republic.

The stone statues of the abstract Union Soldier   45
grow slimmer and younger each year —
wasp-waisted, they doze over muskets
and muse through their sideburns . . .

°*William James:* Harvard psychologist and philosopher (1842–1910), often called the father of modern psychology.

Shaw's father wanted no monument
except the ditch,
where his son's body was thrown
and lost with his "niggers."   50

The ditch is nearer.
There are no statues for the last war here;
on Boylston Street, a commercial photograph   55
shows Hiroshima boiling

over a Mosler Safe,° the "Rock of Ages"
that survived the blast. Space is nearer.
When I crouch to my television set,
the drained faces of Negro school-children rise like balloons.   60

Colonel Shaw
is riding on his bubble,
he waits
for the blessed break.

The Aquarium is gone. Everywhere,   65
giant finned cars nose forward like fish;
a savage servility
slides by on grease.

BORIS SLUTSKY   (1919–1986)

How Did They Kill My Grandmother?*

Translated by Elaine Feinstein

How did they kill my grandmother?
I'll tell you how they killed her.
One morning a tank rolled up to
a building where
the hundred and fifty Jews of our town who,   5
weightless
            from a year's starvation,
and white
            with the knowledge of death,
were gathered holding their bundles.
And the German polizei° were   10
herding the old people briskly;

° *Mosler Safe:* A brand of safe known for being especially strong.   *Publication date is not available.
° *polizei:* Police.

and their tin mugs clanked as
the young men led them away
far away.
15

But my small grandmother
my seventy-year-old grandmother
began to curse and
scream at the Germans;
shouting that I was a soldier.   20
She yelled at them: My grandson
is off at the front fighting!
Don't you dare
touch me!
Listen, you   25
       can hear our guns!

Even as she went off, my grandmother
cried abuse,
       starting all over again
with her curses.   30
From every window then
Ivanovnas and Andreyevnas
Sidorovnas and Petrovnas
sobbed: You tell them, Polina
Matveyevna, keep it up!   35
They all yelled together:
       "What can we do against
this enemy, the Hun?"
Which was why the Germans chose
to kill her inside the town.   40

A bullet struck her hair
and kicked her grey plait down.
My grandmother fell to the ground.
That is how she died there.

DENISE LEVERTOV (1923–1997)

What Were They Like? (1966)

1) Did the people of Viet Nam
    use lanterns of stone?
2) Did they hold ceremonies
    to reverence the opening of buds?
3) Were they inclined to rippling laughter?   5
4) Did they use bone and ivory,
    jade and silver, for ornament?

5) Had they an epic poem?

6) Did they distinguish between speech and singing?

1) Sir, their light hearts turned to stone.   10
It is not remembered whether in gardens
stone lanterns illumined pleasant ways.

2) Perhaps they gathered once to delight in blossom,
but after the children were killed
there were no more buds.   15

3) Sir, laughter is bitter to the burned mouth.

4) A dream ago, perhaps. Ornament is for joy.
All the bones were charred.

5) It is not remembered. Remember,
most were peasants; their life   20
was in rice and bamboo.
When peaceful clouds were reflected in the paddies
and the water buffalo stepped surely along terraces,
maybe fathers told their sons old tales.
When bombs smashed the mirrors   25
there was time only to scream.

6) There is an echo yet, it is said,
of their speech which was like a song.
It is reported their singing resembled
the flight of moths in moonlight.   30
Who can say? It is silent now.

YUSEF KOMUNYAKAA (1947–   )

Facing It (1988)

My black face fades,
hiding inside the black granite.
I said I wouldn't,
dammit: No tears.
I'm stone. I'm flesh.   5
My clouded reflection eyes me
like a bird of prey, the profile of night
slanted against morning. I turn
this way — the stone lets me go.
I turn that way — I'm inside   10
the Vietnam Veterans Memorial
again, depending on the light
to make a difference.
I go down the 58,022 names,
half-expecting to find   15
my own in letters like smoke.

I touch the name Andrew Johnson;
I see the booby trap's white flash.
Names shimmer on a woman's blouse
but when she walks away   20
the names stay on the wall.
Brushstrokes flash, a red bird's
wings cutting across my stare.
The sky. A plane in the sky.
A white vet's images floats   25
closer to me, then his pale eyes
look through mine. I'm a window.
He's lost his right arm
inside the stone. In the black mirror
a woman's trying to erase names: 30
No, she's brushing a boy's hair.

ELIZA GRISWOLD

Buying Rations in Kabul

The Uzbek boys on Chicken Street
have never had enough to eat.
They stock from shelf to shining shelf
these G.I. meals, which boil themselves
in added water (bottled, please).   5
In twenty minutes, processed cheese
on jambalaya, followed by
a peanut-butter jamboree.

                            The boys, polite,
advise on which we might prefer—   10
beef teriyaki, turkey blight—
and thank us twice for bringing peace
as, meals in hand, we leave the store.
Of course they know that any peace
that must be kept by force   15
contains another name. It's war.

CARL PHILLIPS (1959–   )

On the Notion of Tenderness in Wartime (1992)

The news
that you are reading the journals of Delacroix
arrived safely,

thank you. For days
the only word here has been water: everywhere,   5

scratched into the sun-cracked bellies

of every turned-over-and-over-again stone,
I see it, but I am told
this happens — any day now,

the rains.   10
Last night I remembered our bodies
coming apart that first time,

you saying "now we're alone in the world."
Sometimes, even here,   15
it can still get that quiet.

WISLAWA SZYMBORSKA (1923–   )

The End and the Beginning (1993)

After every war
someone has to clean up.
Things won't
straighten themselves up, after all.

Someone has to push the rubble   5
to the side of the road,
so the corpse-filled wagons
can pass.

Someone has to get mired
in scum and ashes,   10
sofa springs,
splintered glass,
and bloody rags.

Someone has to drag in a girder
to prop up a wall,   15
Someone has to glaze a window,
rehang a door.

Photogenic it's not,
and takes years.
All the cameras have left   20
for another war.

We'll need the bridges back,
and new railway stations.
Sleeves will go ragged
from rolling them up.   25

Someone, broom in hand,
still recalls the way it was.
Someone else listens

and nods with unsevered head.
But already there are those nearby   30
starting to mill about
who will find it dull.

From out of the bushes
sometimes someone still unearths
rusted-out arguments   35
and carries them to the garbage pile.

Those who knew
what was going on here
must make way for
those who know little.   40
And less than little.
And finally as little as nothing.

In the grass that has overgrown
causes and effects,
someone must be stretched out   45
blade of grass in his mouth
gazing at the clouds.

Reading and Reacting: Poems about War

1. What is each speaker's attitude toward war? Does the speaker seem to be focusing on a particular war or on war in general?

2. What conventional images and figures of speech does each poem use to express its ideas about war?

3. Do any of the poems use unusual, unexpected, or shocking images or figures of speech?

4. How would you describe each poem's tone? For example, is the tone angry? Cynical? Sad? Disillusioned? Resigned?

5. What does each poem reveal about the speaker?

6. What is each poem's central theme?

Related Works: "The Things They Carried" (p. 435), "The Man He Killed" (p. 865), "Patterns" (p. 866), "The Death of the Ball Turret Gunner" (p. 947), "Naming of Parts" (p. 1216), *Nine Ten* (p. 1334)

WRITING SUGGESTIONS: Discovering Themes in Poetry

1. Compare any two poems in this chapter about parents, nature, love, or war.

2. Write an **explication** (see Chapter 3) of one of the poems in this chapter.

3. Write an essay in which you compare one of the poems in this chapter to a short story or play on the same general subject. (For possible topics, consult the Related Works list that follows each group of poems.)

4. Some poets write multiple poems on the same general subject. For example, Shakespeare wrote many love poems, and Robert Frost wrote a number of poems about nature. Choose two poems by a single poet that explore the same subject, and compare and contrast the themes of the two poems.

5. A number of poems in this book focus on the theme of poetry itself. Choose three poems on this theme, and write an essay that compares the poems' ideas about reading and writing poetry.

CHAPTER 33

THE POETRY OF LANGSTON HUGHES: A CASEBOOK FOR READING, RESEARCH, AND WRITING

This chapter provides all the materials you will need to begin a research project about Langston Hughes. It includes fourteen poems by Langston Hughes; questions to stimulate discussion and writing; a collection of source materials; a student paper that shows how one student, Grace Alston, used the materials in this chapter in her research; and suggestions for further research on Hughes.

Poems

Other poems by Hughes that appear elsewhere in this anthology are "Negro" (p. 855), "Harlem" (p. 940), and "Island" (p. 1033).

Source Materials

- Hughes, Langston. "To Negro Writers." *American Writers' Congress*. Ed. Henry Hart. New York: International Publishers, 1935. A speech Hughes gave to the First American Writers' Congress in New York City in April 1935, quite different in tone from his 1926 manifesto. .... (p. 1112)
- Hughes, Langston. *From* "My Adventures as a Social Poet." *Phylon* Third Quarter, 1947. An excerpt from an essay in which Hughes considers the costs of his decision to deal frankly with social issues in his poetry. .... (p. 1113)
- Rampersad, Arnold. *From* "The Origins of Poetry in Langston Hughes." *The Southern Review* 21.3 (1985): 695–705. Excerpts from a critical essay that considers the emergence of Hughes as a major poet. .... (p. 1117)
- Beavers, Herman. *From* "Dead Rocks and Sleeping Men: Aurality in the Aesthetic of Langston Hughes." *Langston Hughes Review* 11.1 (1992): 1–5. Excerpts from a critical essay that assesses the importance of speaking and listening to Hughes's artistry. .... (p. 1121)
- Tracy, Steven C. *From* "'Midnight Ruffles of Cat-Gut Lace': The Boogie Poems of Langston Hughes." *College Language Association Journal* 32.1 (1988): 55–68. Excerpts from an article that examines Hughes's poetic use of boogie-woogie, an African-American musical form. .... (p. 1123)
- Ford, Karen Jackson. *From* "Do Right to Write Right: Langston Hughes's Aesthetics of Simplicity." *Twentieth Century Literature* 38.4 (1992): 436–56. Excerpts from an article that evaluates Hughes's commitment to "simple" poetics. .... (p. 1124)
- Hutchinson, George B. *From* "Langston Hughes and the 'Other' Whitman." In *The Continuing Presence of Walt Whitman: The Life after the Life*. Ed. Robert K. Martin. Iowa City: U of Iowa P, 1992. Excerpts from an essay that assesses the importance and implications of Whitman's influence on Hughes. .... (p. 1127)

Each of these sources offers insights into the poems included in this Casebook. Three are Hughes's own words, one is largely biographical, one is a close reading of a particular poem, and others discuss Hughes's use of poetic devices and his influences. All were selected to help you to appreciate this poet and to appreciate the themes and devices in his poetry. Other kinds of sources can also enrich your understanding of Hughes's accomplishments — for example, other poems by Hughes, biographical data about the author, and works of imaginative literature by other writers dealing with similar themes. Several interesting Web sites on Hughes are listed below.

- *The Academy of American Poets*. <http://www.poets.org>. Search for Langston Hughes in the upper left search box to go to the Hughes page. A full site hosted by the Academy of American Poets, the Hughes page in- cludes poems — some read aloud — and a link to the academy's online ex- hibit "Poets of the Harlem Renaissance and After," which includes Hughes.
- *Langston Hughes Honored*. <http://www.usps.com/news/2002/ philatelic/sr02_004.htm>. This site, sponsored by the United States Postal Service, offers an interesting explanation of why the USPS chose

to honor Hughes's centennial by putting his image on a postage stamp. The site includes a link to the government's other Black Heritage honorees from 1978 to 2002.

• *Langston Hughes.* <http://www.americaslibrary.gov/cgi-bin/page.cgi/ aa/hughes>. In addition to containing a biography of Hughes, this site has a time line of major United States events that took place during Hughes's lifetime.

In preparation for writing an essay on a topic of your choice, read the poems carefully. Then, consider the Reading and Reacting questions that follow them (p. 1109) in light of what you have read, and use your responses to help you find a topic you can develop in a three- to six-page essay. When you write your paper, be sure to document any words or ideas that you borrow from your sources, and remember to enclose words that are not your own in quotation marks. (For guidelines on evaluating literary criticism, see p. 15; for guidelines on using source materials, see Chapters 6 and 7.)

A sample student paper, "Challenging the Father/Challenging the Self: Langston Hughes's 'The Negro Speaks of Rivers,'" which uses some of the sources included in this Casebook, begins on page 1129.

LANGSTON HUGHES (1902–1967) was one of the best-known American writers of the twentieth century. As a member of the Harlem Renaissance in the 1920s, he helped found a mature but vital African-American literature, one that was able to address issues of poverty and racism without sacrificing the complexities of the individual life. His earliest book of poetry, *The Weary Blues* (1926), established him as one of the most important poets of his generation. His first novel, *Not Without Laughter*, was published in 1930. Not only did Hughes deal honestly in this novel with the daily lives and struggles of his people, but he also wrote poems that owed much to African-American musical forms, such as jazz and blues. Art and politics were inseparable for Hughes, and he was active throughout his life in the struggle for racial and economic justice.

Hughes was born in Joplin, Missouri, in 1902, and his early life was shaped by the racial and economic inequities that would become the focus of his writing and social activism. His father, James Hughes, had studied law, but he was not allowed to take the bar exam because he was African-American, and eventually he left the United States to try his luck in Mexico. Hughes's mother, Carrie, refused to follow her husband, so the young Langston had little contact with his father until he was in his late teens. As a child, Hughes was a voracious reader, absorbing the works of writers from different times and cultures. While attending Central High School in Cleveland, Ohio, he began to write poetry, with Carl Sandburg as one of his chief influences. Upon leaving high school, Hughes began the travels that would make such a deep impression on his work. In 1920, he went to live with his father in Mexico City. On the way there, he wrote what was to become one of his best-known poems, "The Negro Speaks of Rivers." Father and son had little in common, so the trip was not successful on a personal level.

At one point, Hughes even considered suicide. When he returned to the United States, he enrolled at Columbia University to study engineering, but his classes were of little interest to him, and he spent most of his time writing and absorbing the cultural life of New York's African-American community.

With the publication of his first book of poetry, *The Weary Blues*, in 1926, Hughes became a visible member of the Harlem Renaissance, a major literary movement of the twentieth century. Centered in the Harlem section of New York City, the movement represented the first great flowering of African-American literature and included such writers as James Weldon Johnson, Claude McKay, and Countee Culleen. This period is generally considered to have ended with the onset of the Great Depression in the 1930s.

Although he would become arguably the best-known writer of the Harlem Renaissance, Hughes's work was not universally praised by critics and peers. In fact, many of the elements that have given his work its staying power — his use of African-American vernacular, his imitation of the forms of popular music, his concern for the economically disadvantaged — were controversial at the time. There were many who felt that African-American writing ought to deal primarily with uplifting stories and to do so in a manner that would be familiar to readers used to the conventions of white literature. These critics believed that Hughes's work was undercutting the advances African-Americans were achieving in both literary and social life.

Hughes's response to his critics was straightforward. "I sympathized deeply," he later said, "with those critics and those intellectuals, and I saw clearly the need for some of the kinds of books they wanted." He insisted, however, that not every book by an African-American could or should be about subjects that middle- or upper-class whites and blacks would find palatable: "I didn't know the upper-class Negroes well enough to write much about them. I knew only the people I had grown up with, and they weren't people whose shoes were always shined, who had been to Harvard, or who had heard of Bach. But they seemed to me good people, too."

In portraying these "good people," Hughes did not shy away from depicting the details of their difficult lives. His subjects are often poor and frequently face racism. Sometimes they are in trouble with the law, and they are typically less interested in intellectual discussion than in paying the rent. The poor had been portrayed before in poetry: T.S. Eliot's long poem *The Waste Land*, published in 1922, just four years before *The Weary Blues*, includes a particularly unflattering exchange between two lower-class women. What distinguished Hughes's approach from Eliot's, apart from his direct style, was his sympathy for his subjects and his intimate familiarity with their living conditions.

In writing about lower-class African-Americans, people who had never "heard of Bach," Hughes devised poetic forms that imitated the cadences of jazz and blues, the types of music with which they were familiar. Hughes found nothing wrong with Bach, but he was convinced that African-Americans had their own composers and performers of genius. Nor was this simply a self-conscious attempt to find an appropriate poetic vehicle for his subject matter or to promote the art of his people; Hughes loved this music deeply, and nothing could have been more natural for him than to employ its rhythms. His later move into writing song lyrics was a natural transition.

Always a traveler, Hughes journeyed to the Soviet Union in 1932. While there, he observed aspects of the Soviet system that he felt were admirable and compared favorably with the capitalism practiced in the United States. He was especially appreciative of what he saw as the lack of racial injustice and economic inequality. He learned the Uzbek language while recuperating from an illness and began writing on a regular basis for Soviet newspapers, including *Izvestia*. He published a book devoted to impressions of the trip, *A Negro Looks at Soviet Central Asia* in 1934, and he also reflected on his experiences in newspaper columns for the *Chicago Defender*.

Hughes left the Soviet Union after a little more than a year, but he did not abandon his commitment to radical social change. Back in the United States, he settled for a time in California, where he devoted himself to a number of causes although he soon had to move because of threats of violence. It would be a mistake however, to suppose that Hughes was unremittingly hostile to America. During World War II, when the United States was allied with the Soviet Union against Nazi Germany, Fascist Italy, and Imperial Japan, Hughes used his writing to support the American war effort even as he encouraged America to live up to its democratic ideals.

As part of this effort, Hughes invented a character, Jesse B. Semple, later known as Simple. Simple first appeared in newspaper columns, which were so popular that they were later anthologized in a series of books, beginning in 1950 with *Simple Speaks His Mind*. Here Hughes uses the device of a fictional narrator talking with, and buying drinks for, his friend Semple. The popularity of the pieces derived in part from their humor and straightforward examination of racial issues and partly from Hughes's skillful use of African-American vernacular. Since his first publications, Hughes had included the actual speech of the black lower class in his work, and the "Simple" books brought this strategy to a wider audience than ever before.

During the 1950s, his sympathetic comments on communism in general, and the Soviet Union in particular, caused Hughes great political difficulties. His activities were monitored by the House Un-American Activities Committee (HUAC), and in 1953 he was called to testify before Senator Joseph McCarthy's Subcommittes on Subversive Activities. In his testimony to the committee, Hughes denied being a communist but explained why he felt communism appealed to some African-Americans. There is some debate about Hughes's actual political views during this period. Commentators who maintain that Hughes had never in fact been an extreme leftist also tend to assume that his statements to the committee were an accurate reflection of his political views at the time. Others, however, are convinced that Hughes, afraid that the writing career he had worked so hard to establish would be destroyed, was downplaying communist views he still held.

Despite the disruption to his career caused by the Committee's investigation, Hughes remained an important literary and political presence for the remainder of his life. In 1961, he published *Ask Your Mama*, a work that addressed many of the racial and cultural issues that would be so important in the 1960s. He also traveled widely, often as an official representative of the United States. When Hughes died in 1967, he was completing work on his last volume of poetry, *The Panther and the Lash*, which was positively received by critics.

Today, Hughes is remembered chiefly as a poet, but he made important contributions to virtually every genre of writing. He was an accomplished dramatist who also founded several theaters. He wrote novels, short stories, newspaper articles, song lyrics, translations, and fiction for children. In addition to his work as a writer, Hughes edited numerous books and helped encourage and promote the work of younger African-American writers. In the years since his death, his reputation has become even more solidly established. Plain-spoken and highly rhythmic, his poetry continues to appeal to new readers, and to provide an example of the ways in which social commitment and literary art can be fruitfully combined.

The Negro Speaks of Rivers (1921)

I've known rivers:
I've known rivers ancient as the world and old as the flow of
    human blood in human veins.

My soul has grown deep like the rivers.

I bathed in the Euphrates° when dawns were young.
I built my hut near the Congo° and it lulled me to sleep.   5
I looked upon the Nile and raised the pyramids above it.
I heard the singing of the Mississippi when Abe Lincoln went
    down to New Orleans, and I've seen its muddy bosom turn
    all golden in the sunset.

I've known rivers:
Ancient, dusky rivers.

My soul has grown deep like the rivers.   10

Mother to Son (1922)

Well, son, I'll tell you:
Life for me ain't been no crystal stair.
It's had tacks in it,
And splinters,
And boards torn up,   5
And places with no carpet on the floor—
Bar.
But all the time
I'se been a-climbin' on,
And reachin' landin's,
And turnin' corners,   10
And sometimes goin' in the dark
Where there ain't been no light.
So boy, don't you turn back.
Don't you set down on the steps   15

° *Euphrates:* Major river of southwest Asia; with the Tigris, the Euphrates forms a valley sometimes referred to as the "cradle of civilization."   ° *Congo:* River in equatorial Africa, the continent's second longest.

Cause you finds it's kinder hard.
Don't you fall now—
For I'se still goin', honey,
I'se still climbin',
And life for me ain't been no crystal stair.   **20**

Dream Variations   (1924)

To fling my arms wide
In some place of the sun,
To whirl and to dance
Till the white day is done.
Then rest at cool evening
Beneath a tall tree   **5**
While night comes on gently,
       Dark like me—
That is my dream!

To fling my arms wide
In the face of the sun,   **10**
Dance! Whirl! Whirl!
Till the quick day is done.
Rest at pale evening . . .
A tall, slim tree . . .
Night coming tenderly   **15**
       Black like me.

The Weary Blues   (1926)

Droning a drowsy syncopated tune,
Rocking back and forth to a mellow croon,
    I heard a Negro play.
Down on Lenox Avenue° the other night
By the pale dull pallor of an old gas light   **5**
    He did a lazy sway . . .
    He did a lazy sway . . .
To the tune o' those Weary Blues.
With his ebony hands on each ivory key
He made that poor piano moan with melody.   **10**
    O Blues!
Swaying to and fro on his rickety stool
He played that sad raggy tune like a musical fool.
    Sweet Blues!
Coming from a black man's soul.   **15**

°*Lenox Avenue:* Street in Harlem noted for nightlife and music during the 1920s.

Dancers and musicians at the Savoy Ballroom in Harlem, 1947.

O Blues!
In a deep song voice with a melancholy tone
I heard that Negro sing, that old piano moan—
    "Ain't got nobody in all this world,
    Ain't got nobody but ma self.   20
    I's gwine to quit ma frownin'
    And put ma troubles on the shelf."
Thump, thump, thump, went his foot on the floor.
He played a few chords then he sang some more —
    "I got the Weary Blues   25
    And I can't be satisfied,
    Got the Weary Blues
    And can't be satisfied —
    I ain't happy no mo'
    And I wish that I had died."   30
And far into the night he crooned that tune.
The stars went out and so did the moon.
The singer stopped playing and went to bed
While the Weary Blues echoed through his head.
He slept like a rock or a man that's dead.   35

I, Too (1925)

I, too, sing America.

I am the darker brother.
They send me to eat in the kitchen
When company comes,

But I laugh,   5
And eat well,
And grow strong.

Tomorrow,
I'll be at the table
When company comes.   10
Nobody'll dare
Say to me,
"Eat in the kitchen,"
Then.

Besides,   15
They'll see how beautiful I am
And be ashamed —

I too, am America.

Song for a Dark Girl (1927)

Way Down South in Dixie
        (Break the heart of me)
They hung my black young lover
        To a cross roads tree.

Way Down South in Dixie   5
        (Bruised body high in air)
I asked the white Lord Jesus
        What was the use of prayer.

Way down South in Dixie
        (Break the heart of me)   10
Love is a naked shadow
        On a gnarled and naked tree.

Ballad of the Landlord (1940)

Landlord, landlord,
My roof has sprung a leak.
Don't you 'member I told you about it
Way last week?

Landlord, landlord,   5
These steps is broken down.
When you come up yourself
It's a wonder you don't fall down.

Ten Bucks you say I owe you?
Ten Bucks you say is due?   10

Well, that's Ten Bucks more'n I'll pay you
Till you fix this house up new.

What? You gonna get eviction orders?
You gonna cut off my heat?
You gonna take my furniture and   15
Throw it in the street?

Um-huh! You talking high and mighty.
Talk on — till you get through.
You ain't gonna be able to say a word
If I land my fist on you.   20

Police! Police!
Come and get this man!
He's trying to ruin the government
And overturn the land!

Copper's whistle!   25
Patrol bell!
Arrest.

Precinct Station.
Iron cell.
Headlines in press: 30

MAN THREATENS LANDLORD

TENANT HELD NO BAIL

JUDGE GIVES NEGRO 90 DAYS IN COUNTY JAIL

An exposed wall in a tenement like that depicted in "Ballad of a Landlord."

Theme for English B   (1949)

The instructor said,

> Go home and write
> a page tonight.
> And let that page come out of you —
> Then, it will be true.   5

I wonder if it's that simple?
I am twenty-two, colored, born in Winston-Salem.
I went to school there, then Durham, then here
to this college on the hill above Harlem.
I am the only colored student in my class.   10
The steps from the hill lead down into Harlem,
through a park, then I cross St. Nicholas,
Eighth Avenue, Seventh, and I come to the Y,

the Harlem Branch Y, where I take the elevator
up to my room, sit down and write this page: 15

It's not easy to know what is true for you or me
at twenty-two, my age. But I guess I'm what
I feel and see and hear, Harlem, I hear you:
hear you, hear me — we two — you, me, talk on this page.
(I hear New York, too) Me — who?   20
Well, I like to eat, sleep, drink, and be in love.
I like to work, read, learn, and understand life.
I like a pipe for a Christmas present,
or records — Bessie,° bop,° or Bach.
I guess being colored doesn't make me *not* like   25
the same things other folks like who are other races.
So will my page be colored that I write?
Being me, it will not be white.
But it will be
a part of you, instructor.   30
You are white —
yet a part of me, as I am a part of you.
That's American.
Sometimes perhaps you don't want to be a part of me.
Nor do I often want to be a part of you.   35
But we are, that's true!
As I learn from you,
I guess you learn from me —
although you're older — and white —
and somewhat more free.   40

This is my page for English B.

Dream Boogie (1951)

Good morning, daddy!
Ain't you heard
The boogie-woogie° rumble
Of a dream deferred?

Listen closely: 5
You'll hear their feet

°*Bessie:* Bessie Smith (1894–1937), blues singer.   °*bop:* Short for "bebop," a jazz style developed in the early 1940s by Charlie Parker, Dizzy Gillespie, and others.   °*boogie-woogie:* A popular black musical style with variants in both blues and jazz; more specifically, a vigorous piano style marked by heavy and repeated bass figures.

Beating out and beating out a—

> *You think*
> *It's a happy beat?*

Listen to it closely: 10
Ain't you heard
something underneath
like a—

> *What did I say?*

Sure,   15
I'm happy!
Take it away!

> *Hey, pop!*
> *Re-bop!*
> *Mop!*   20
>
> *Y-e-a-h!*

Birmingham Sunday
(September 15, 1963)°   (1967)

    Four little girls
Who went to Sunday School that day
And never came back home at all
But left instead
Their blood upon the wall   5
With spattered flesh
And bloodied Sunday dresses
Torn to shreds by dynamite
That China made aeons ago—
Did not know   10
That what China made
Before China was ever Red at all
Would redden with their blood
This Birmingham-on-Sunday wall.

    Four tiny girls   15
Who left their blood upon that wall,
In little graves today await
The dynamite that might ignite

° *September 15, 1963:* On this date, only weeks after Martin Luther King Jr.'s historic March on Washington, four young African-American girls were killed at their Sunday school in Birmingham, Alabama, by a bomb, likely in response to recent civil rights activities in the area.

The fuse of centuries of Dragon Kings°
Whose tomorrow sings a hymn   20
The missionaries never taught Chinese
In Christian Sunday School
To implement the Golden Rule.

    Four little girls
Might be awakened someday soon   25
By songs upon the breeze
As yet unfelt among magnolia trees.

Photos taken in 1963 of the four girls killed in the bombing of the Sixteenth Street Baptist Church (from left: Denise McNair, 11; Carole Robertson, 14; Addie Mae Collins, 14; and Cynthia Wesley, 14).

° *Dragon Kings:* In Chinese myth and lore, the dragon is a beneficent force that dispenses blessings in both the natural and supernatural worlds. Eventually, the dragon became a symbol of imperial China. The dragon has also been used in the mythology of white supremacist groups like the Ku Klux Klan.

Sixteenth Street Baptist Church, Birmingham, Alabama; site of the September 15, 1963 firebombing.

Old Walt (1954)

Old Walt Whitman
Went finding and seeking,
Finding less than sought
Seeking more than found,
Every detail minding   5
Of the seeking or the finding.

Pleasured equally
In seeking as in finding,

Each detail minding,
Old Walt went seeking   10
And finding.

Genius Child   (1947)

This is a song for the genius child.
Sing it softly, for the song is wild.
Sing it softly as ever you can—
Lest the song get out of hand.

Nobody loves a genius child.   5

Can you love an eagle,
Tame or wild?

Wild or tame,
Can you love a monster
Of a frightening name?   10

Nobody loves a genius child.

Kill him— and let his soul run wild!

Park Bench   (1938)

I live on a park bench,
You, Park Avenue.
Hell of a distance
Between us two.

I beg a dime for dinner—   5
You got a butler and maid.
But I'm wakin' up!
Say, ain't you afraid

That I might, just maybe,
In a year or two,   10
Move on over
To Park Avenue?

Lenox Avenue: Midnight   (1926)

The rhythm of life
Is a jazz rhythm,
Honey.
The gods are laughing at us.

The broken heart of love,   5
The weary, weary heart of pain,—
   Overtones,
   Undertones,
To the rumble of street cars,
To the swish of rain.   10

Lenox Avenue,
Honey.
Midnight,
And the gods are laughing at us.

Un-American Investigators (1953)

The committee's fat,
Smug, almost secure
Co-religionists
Shiver with delight
In warm manure   5

Langston Hughes testifying before the House Un-American Activities Committee in Washington, D.C., in March of 1953.

As those investigated —
Too brave to name a name —
Have pseudonyms revealed
In Gentile game
   Of who,   10
   Born Jew,
   Is who?
Is not your name Lipshitz?
   Yes.
Did you not change it   15
For subversive purposes?
   No.
For nefarious gain?
   Not so.
Are you sure?   20
The committee shivers
With delight in
Its manure.

Dinner Guest: Me (1965)

I know I am
The Negro Problem
Being wined and dined,
Answering the usual questions
That come to white mind   5
Which seeks demurely
To probe in polite way
The why and wherewithal
Of darkness U.S.A.—
Wondering how things got this way   10
In current democratic night,
Murmuring gently
Over *fraises du bois*,
"I'm so ashamed of being white."

The lobster is delicious,   15
The wine divine,
And center of attention
At the damask table, mine.
To be a Problem on
Park Avenue at eight   20
Is not so bad.
Solutions to the Problem,
Of course, wait.

Ballad of Booker T. (1941)

Booker T.
Was a practical man.
He said, Till the soil
And learn from the land.
Let down your bucket   5
Where you are.
Your fate is here
And not afar.
To help yourself
And your fellow man,   10
Train your head,
Your heart, and your hand.
For smartness alone's
Surely not meet —
If you haven't at the same time   15
Got something to eat.
Thus at Tuskegee
He built a school
With book-learning there.
And the workman's tool.   20
He started out
In a simple way —
For yesterday
Was not today.
Sometimes he had   25
Compromise in his talk—
For a man must crawl
Before he can walk —
And in Alabama in '85
A joker was lucky   30
To be alive.
But Booker T.
Was nobody's fool;
You may carve a dream
With an humble tool.   35
The tallest tower
Can tumble down
If it be not rooted
In solid ground,
So, being a far-seeing   40
Practical man,
He said, Train your head,
Your heart, and your hand.

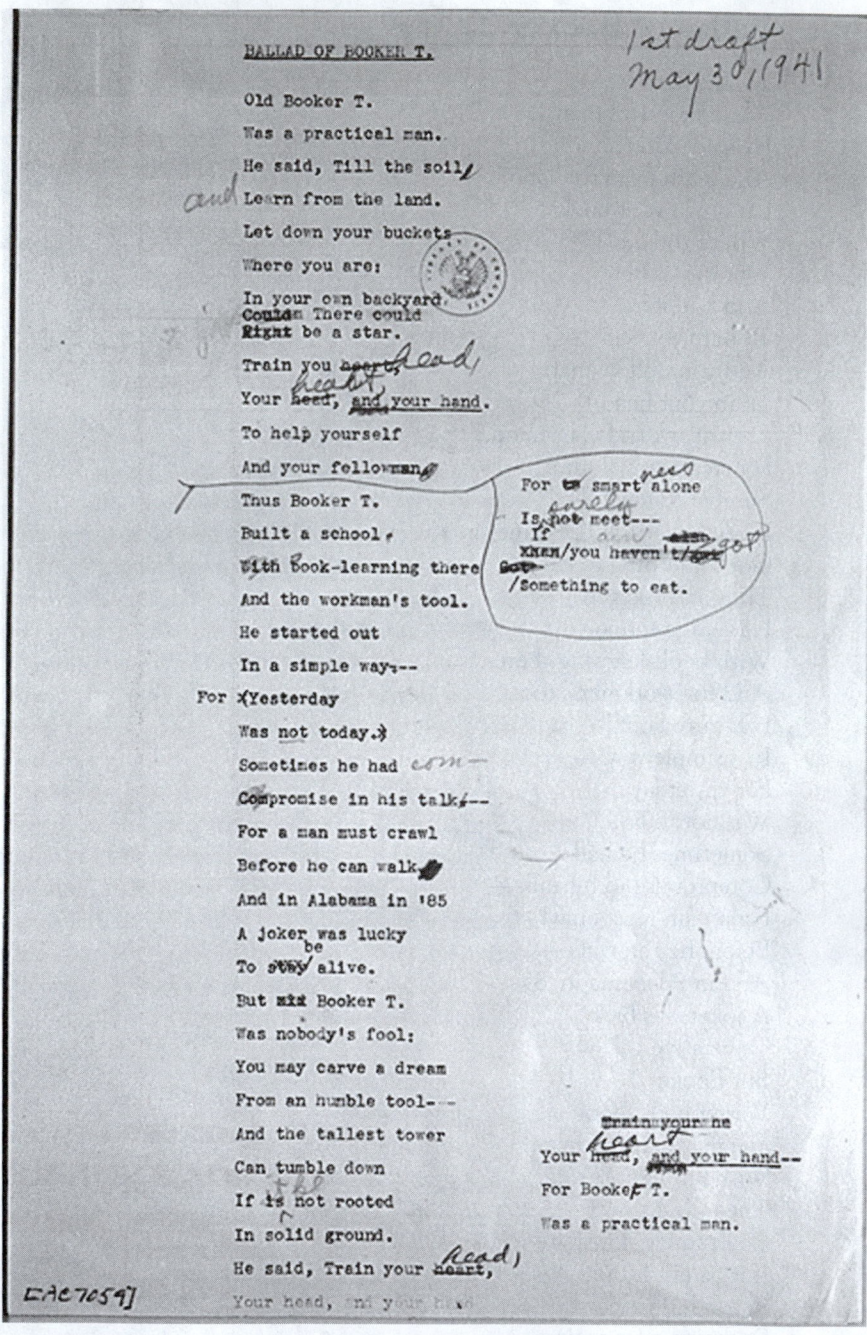

This draft of the poem "Ballad of Booker T" was hand edited by Langston Hughes in 1941.

Your fate is here
And not afar,
So let down your bucket
Where you are.

Reading and Reacting

1. How does Hughes use music and musical allusions? Are the poems themselves meant to be musical?

2. Which poems are poems of protest? Does Hughes seem to place social or political goals above literary concerns?

3. How do historical and geographic allusions contribute to the power of "The Negro Speaks of Rivers"?

4. Is the question of identity (especially racial identity) handled differently in "The Negro Speaks of Rivers" and "Theme for English B"? Explain.

5. How would you characterize Hughes's attitude toward America in "Theme for English B" and "I, Too"? Do you think these poems are patriotic?

6. Hughes is often celebrated for his ability to communicate complex human dilemmas in accessible language and forms. Does he do this successfully in "Harlem" (p. 940)? Explain.

7. In the poem "Birmingham Sunday," why does Hughes include statements about Chinese mythology and history?

8. Is the "dream" in "Harlem" (p. 940) the same as the dream in "Dream Boogie"? Do you think the poems were meant to be read side by side? Do they shed light on each other? Do they represent different approaches to a similar problem?

9. In which poems do you think the first-person voice is autobiographical? In which poems do you think Hughes is creating a speaker?

10. What do you think Hughes expects of readers of his poetry? Reflection? A change of heart? Action? Something else?

11. JOURNAL ENTRY Are Langston Hughes's poems relevant only to African-Americans, or do they also have relevance for other Americans — and even for readers in other countries?

12. CRITICAL PERSPECTIVE In his essay "The Negro Artist and the Racial Mountain" (p. 1110), Hughes asserts his respect for the "common people," those he admires for their lack of self-importance:

> But then there are the low-down folks, the so-called common element, and they are the majority — may the Lord be praised! The people who have their nip of gin on Saturday nights are not too important to themselves or the community, or too well fed, or too learned to watch the lazy world go round. They live on Seventh Street in Washington or State Street in Chicago and they do not particularly care whether they are like white folks or anybody else. . . . They furnish a wealth of colorful, distinctive material for any artist because they still hold their own individuality in the face of American standardizations.

How does Hughes depict the "common people" in his poetry? What are their concerns? How have America's "standardizations" attempted to shape and change the common people, and what has been the result of those attempts?

Related Works: "Big Black Good Man" (p. 339), "A Worn Path" (p. 505), "Photograph of My Father in His Twenty-Second Year" (p. 1061), "The Unknown Citizen" (p. 881), "Ballad of Birmingham" (p. 886), "We Real Cool" (p. 912), "Sadie and Maud" (p. 970), "For the Union Dead" (p. 1081), *A Raisin in the Sun* (p. 1385).

LANGSTON HUGHES

from The Negro Artist and the Racial Mountain

One of the most promising of the young Negro poets said to me once, "I want to be a poet — not a Negro poet," meaning, I believe, "I want to write like a white poet": meaning subconsciously, "I would like to be a white poet," meaning behind that, "I would like to be white." And I was sorry the young man said that, for no great poet has ever been afraid of being himself. And I doubted then that, with his desire to run away spiritually from his race, this boy would ever be a great poet. But this is the mountain standing in the way of any true Negro art in America — this urge within the race toward whiteness, the desire to pour racial individuality into the mold of American standardization, and to be as little Negro and as much American as possible.

But let us look at the immediate background of this young poet. His family is of what I suppose one would call the Negro middle class: people who are by no means rich yet never uncomfortable nor hungry — smug, contented, respectable folk, members of the Baptist church. The father goes to work every morning. He is a chief steward at a large white club. The mother sometimes does fancy sewing or supervises parties for the rich families of the town. The children go to a mixed school. In the home they read white papers and magazines. And the mother often says, "Don't be like niggers" when the children are bad. A frequent phrase from the father is, "Look how well a white man does things." And so the word white comes to be unconsciously a symbol of all the virtues. It holds for the children beauty, morality, and money. The whisper of "I want to be white" runs silently through their minds. This young poet's home is, I believe, a fairly typical home of the colored middle class. One sees immediately how difficult it would be for an artist born in such a home to interest himself in interpreting the beauty of his own people. He is never taught to see that beauty. He is taught rather not to see it, or if he does, to be ashamed of it when it is not according to Caucasian patterns.

For racial culture the home of a self-styled "high-class" Negro has nothing better to offer. Instead there will perhaps be more aping of things white than in a less cultured or less wealthy home. The father is perhaps a doctor, lawyer, landowner, or politician. The mother may be a social worker, or a teacher, or she may do nothing and have a maid. Father is often dark but he has usually married the lightest woman he could find. The family attend a fashionable church where few really colored faces are to be found. And they themselves draw a color line. In the

North they go to white theaters and white movies. And in the South they have at least two cars and a house "like white folks." Nordic manners, Nordic faces, Nordic hair, Nordic art (if any), and an Episcopal heaven. A very high mountain indeed for the would-be racial artist to climb in order to discover himself and his people.

But then there are the low-down folks, the so-called common element, and they are the majority — may the Lord be praised! The people who have their nip of gin on Saturday nights are not too important to themselves or the community, or too well fed, or too learned to watch the lazy world go round. They live on Seventh Street in Washington or State Street in Chicago and they do not particularly care whether they are like white folks or anybody else. Their joy runs, bang! into ecstasy. Their religion soars to a shout. Work maybe a little today, rest a little tomorrow. Play awhile. Sing awhile. O, let's dance! These common people are not afraid of spirituals, as for a long time their more intellectual brethren were, and jazz is their child. They furnish a wealth of colorful, distinctive material for any artist because they still hold their own individuality in the face of American standardizations. And perhaps these common people will give to the world its truly great Negro artist, the one who is not afraid to be himself. Whereas the better-class Negro would tell the artist what to do, the people at least let him alone when he does appear. And they are not ashamed of him — if they know he exists at all. And they accept what beauty is their own without question.

Certainly there is, for the American Negro artist who can escape the restrictions the more advanced among his own group would put upon him, a great field of unused material ready for his art. Without going outside his race, and even among the better classes with their "white" culture and conscious American manners, but still Negro enough to be different, there is sufficient matter to furnish a black artist with a lifetime of creative work. And when he chooses to touch on the relations between Negroes and whites in this country with their innumerable overtones and undertones, surely, and especially for literature and the drama, there is an inexhaustible supply of themes at hand. To these the Negro artist can give his racial individuality, his heritage of rhythm and warmth, and his incongruous humor that so often, as in the Blues, becomes ironic laughter mixed with tears. . . .

Let the blare of Negro jazz bands and the bellowing voice of Bessie Smith singing Blues penetrate the closed ears of the colored near-intellectuals until they listen and perhaps understand. Let Paul Robeson singing Water Boy, and Rudolph Fisher writing about the streets of Harlem, and Jean Toomer holding the heart of Georgia in his hands, and Aaron Douglas drawing strange black fantasies cause the smug Negro middle class to turn from their white, respectable, ordinary books and papers to catch a glimmer of their own beauty. We youn-ger Negro artists who create now intend to express our individual dark-skinned selves without fear or shame. If white people are pleased we are glad. If they are not, it doesn't matter. We know we are beautiful. And ugly too. The tom-tom cries and the tom-tom laughs. If colored people are pleased we are glad. If they are not, their displeasure doesn't matter either. We build our temples for tomorrow, strong as we know how, and we stand on top of the mountain, free within ourselves.

LANGSTON HUGHES

To Negro Writers

There are certain practical things American Negro writers can do through their work.

We can reveal to the Negro masses, from which we come, our potential power to transform the now ugly face of the Southland into a region of peace and plenty.

We can reveal to the white masses those Negro qualities which go beyond the mere ability to laugh and sing and dance and make music, and which are a part of the useful heritage that we place at the disposal of a future free America.

Negro writers can seek to unite blacks and whites in our country, not on the nebulous basis of an inter-racial meeting, or the shifting sands of religious brotherhood, but on the *solid* ground of the daily working-class struggle to wipe out, now and forever, all the old inequalities of the past.

Furthermore, by way of exposure, Negro writers can reveal in their novels, stories, poems, and articles:

The lovely grinning face of Philanthropy — which gives a million dollars to a Jim Crow school, but not one job to a graduate of that school; which builds a Negro hospital with second-rate equipment, then commands black patients and student-doctors to go there whether they will or no; or which, out of the kindness of its heart, erects yet another separate, segregated, shut-off, Jim Crow Y.M.C.A.

Negro writers can expose those white labor leaders who keep their unions closed against Negro workers and prevent the betterment of all workers.

We can expose, too, the sick-sweet smile of organized religion — which lies about what it doesn't know, and about what it *does* know. And the half-voodoo, half-clown, face of revivalism, dulling the mind with the clap of its empty hands.

Expose, also, the false leadership that besets the Negro people — bought and paid for leadership, owned by capital, afraid to open its mouth except in the old conciliatory way so advantageous to the exploiters.

And all the economic roots of race hatred and race fear.

And the Contentment Tradition of the O-lovely-Negroes school of American fiction, which makes an ignorant black face and a Carolina head filled with superstition, appear more desirable than a crown of gold; the jazz-band; and the O-so-gay writers who make of the Negro's poverty and misery a dusky funny paper.

And expose war. And the old My-Country-'Tis-of-Thee lie. And the colored American Legion posts strutting around talking about the privilege of dying for the nobel Red, White and Blue, when they aren't even permitted the privilege of living for it. Or voting for it in Texas. Or working for it in the diplomatic service. Or even rising, like every other good little boy, from the log cabin to the White House.

White House is right!

Dear colored American Legion, you can swing from a lynching tree, uniform and all, with pleasure — and nobody'll fight for you. Don't you know that? Nobody even salutes you down South, dead or alive, medals or no medals, chevrons° or not, no matter how many wars you've fought in.

Let Negro writers write about the irony and pathos of the *colored* American Legion.

> "*Salute, Mr. White Man!*"
>
> "Salute, hell! . . . You're a nigger."

Or would you rather write about the moon?

Sure, the moon still shines over Harlem. Shines over Scottsboro. Shines over Birmingham, too, I reckon. Shines over Cordie Cheek's grave, down South.

Write about the moon if you want to. Go ahead. This is a free country.

But there are certain very practical things American Negro writers can do. And must do. There's a song that says, "the time ain't long." That song is right. Something has got to change in America — and change soon. We must help that change to come.

The moon's still shining as poetically as ever, but all the stars on the flag are dull. (And the stripes, too.)

We want a new and better America, where there won't be any poor, where there won't be any more Jim Crow, where there won't be any lynchings, where there won't be any munition makers, where we won't need philanthropy, nor charity, nor the New Deal, nor Home Relief.

We want an America that will be ours, a world that will be ours — we Negro workers and white workers! Black writers and white! We'll make that world!

LANGSTON HUGHES

from My Adventures as a Social Poet

Some of my earliest poems were social poems in that they were about people's problems — whole groups of people's problems — rather than my own personal difficulties. Sometimes, though, certain aspects of my personal problems happened to be also common to many other people. And certainly, racially speaking, my own problems of adjustment to American life were the same as those of millions of other segregated Negroes. The moon belongs to everybody, but not this American earth of ours. That is perhaps why poems about the moon perturb no one, but poems about color and poverty do perturb many citizens. Social forces pull backwards or forwards, right or left, and social poems get caught in the pulling and hauling. Sometimes the poet himself gets pulled and hauled — even hauled off to jail. . . .

My adventures as a social poet are mild indeed compared to the body-breaking, soul-searing experiences of poets in the recent Fascist countries or of the resistance

---

°*chevrons:* Stripes on a military uniform denoting rank.

poets of the Nazi-invaded lands during the war. For that reason, I can use so light a word as "adventure" in regard to my own skirmishes with reaction and censorship.

My adventures as a social poet began in a colored church in Atlantic City shortly after my first book, *The Weary Blues,* was published in 1926. I had been invited to come down to the shore from Lincoln University where I was a student, to give a program of my poems in the church. During the course of my program I read several of my poems in the form of the Negro folk songs, including some blues poems about hard luck and hard work. As I read I noticed a deacon approach the pulpit with a note which he placed on the rostrum beside me, but I did not stop to open the note until I had finished and had acknowledged the applause of a cordial audience. The note read, "Do not read any more blues in my pulpit." It was signed by the minister. That was my first experience with censorship.

The kind and generous woman who sponsored my writing for a few years after my college days did not come to the point quite so directly as did the minister who disliked blues. Perhaps, had it not been in the midst of the great depression of the late '20's and '30's, the kind of poems that I am afraid helped to end her patronage might not have been written. But it was impossible for me to travel from hungry Harlem to the lovely homes on Park Avenue without feeling in my soul the great gulf between the very poor and the very rich in our society. In those days, on the way to visit this kind lady I would see the homeless sleeping in subways and the hungry begging in doorways on sleet-stung winter days. It was then that I wrote a poem called "Advertisement for the Waldorf-Astoria," satirizing the slick-paper magazine advertisements of the opening of that de luxe hotel. Also I wrote:

> PARK BENCH
>
> I live on a park bench,
> You, Park Avenue.
> Hell of a distance
> Between us two.
> I beg a dime for dinner —
> You got a butler and maid.
> But I'm wakin' up!
> Say, ain't you afraid
>
> That I might, just maybe,
> In a year or two,
> Move on over
> To Park Avenue?

In a little while I did not have a patron any more.

But that year I won a prize, the Harmon Gold Award for Literature, which consisted of a medal and four hundred dollars. With the four hundred dollars I went to Haiti. On the way I stopped in Cuba and I was cordially received by the writers and artists. I had written poems about the exploitation of Cuba by the sugar barons and I had translated many poems of Nicolás Guillén such as:

CANE

Negro
In the cane fields.
White man
Above the cane fields
Earth
Beneath the cane fields.
Blood
That flows from us.

This was during the days of the dictatorial Machado regime. Perhaps someone called his attention to these poems and translations because, when I came back from Haiti weeks later, I was not allowed to land in Cuba, but was detained by the immigration authorities at Santiago and put on an island until the American consul came, after three days, to get me off with the provision that I cross the country to Havana and leave Cuban soil at once.

That was my first time being put out of any place. But since that time I have been put out of or barred from quite a number of places, all because of my poetry — not the roses and moonlight poems (which I write, too) but because of poems about poverty, oppression, and segregation. Nine Negro boys in Alabama were on trial for their lives when I got back from Cuba and Haiti. The famous Scottsboro "rape" case was in full session. I visited those boys in the death house at Kilby Prison, and I wrote many poems about them. One of these poems was:

CHRIST IN ALABAMA

Christ is a Nigger,
Beaten and black —
O, bare your back.

Mary is His Mother —
Mammy of the South,
Silence your mouth.
God's His Father —
White Master above,
Grant us your love.

Most holy bastard
Of the bleeding mouth:
Nigger Christ
On the cross of the South.

Contempo, a publication of some of the students at the University of North Carolina, published the poem on its front page on the very day that I was being presented in a program of my poems at the University in Chapel Hill. That evening there were police outside the building in which I spoke, and in the air the rising tension of race that is peculiar to the South. It had been rumored that some of the local citizenry were saying that I should be run out of town, and that one of the sheriffs agreed, saying, "Sure, he ought to be run out! It's bad enough to call Christ a *bastard*. But when he calls him a *nigger*, he's gone too far!"

The next morning a third of my fee was missing when I was handed my check. One of the departments of the university jointly sponsoring my program had refused to come through with its portion of the money. Nevertheless, I remember with pleasure the courtesy and kindness of many of the students and faculty at Chapel Hill and their lack of agreement with the anti-Negro elements of the town. There I began to learn at the University of North Carolina how hard it is to be a white liberal in the South.

It was not until I had been to Russia and around the world as a writer and journalist that censorship and opposition to my poems reached the point of completely preventing me from appearing in public programs on a few occasions. It happened first in Los Angeles shortly after my return from the Soviet Union. I was to have been one of several speakers on a memorial program to be held at the colored branch Y.M.C.A. for a young Negro journalist of the community. At the behest of white higher-ups, no doubt, some reactionary Negro politicians informed the Negro Y.M.C.A. that I was a Communist. The secretary of the Negro Branch Y then informed the committee of young people in charge of the memorial that they could have their program only if I did not appear.

I have never been a Communist, but I soon learned that anyone visiting the Soviet Union and speaking with favor of it upon returning is liable to be so labeled. Indeed when Mrs. Roosevelt, Walter White, and so Christian a lady as Mrs. Bethune who has never been in Moscow, are so labeled, I should hardly be surprised! I wasn't surprised. And the young people's committee informed the Y secretary that since the Y was a public community center which they helped to support, they saw no reason why it should censor their memorial program to the extent of eliminating any speaker.

Since I had been allotted but a few moments on the program, it was my intention simply to read this short poem of mine:

> Dear lovely death
> That taketh all things under wing,
> Never to kill,
> Only to change into some other thing
> This suffering flesh—
> To make it either more or less
> But not again the same,
> Dear lovely death,
> Change is thy other name.

But the Negro branch Y, egged on by the reactionary politicians (whose incomes, incidentally, were allegedly derived largely from gambling houses and other underworld activities), informed the young people's committee that the police would be at the door to prevent my entering the Y on the afternoon of the scheduled program. So when the crowd gathered, the memorial was not held that Sunday. The young people simply informed the audience of the situation and said that the memorial would be postponed until a place could be found where all the participants could be heard. The program was held elsewhere a few Sundays later. . . .

So goes the life of social poet. I am sure none of these things would ever have happened to me had I limited the subject matter of my poems to roses and moonlight. But, unfortunately, I was born poor — and colored — and almost all the prettiest roses I have seen have been in rich white people's yards — not in mine. That is why I cannot write exclusively about roses and moonlight — for sometimes in the moonlight my brothers see a fiery cross and a circle of Klansmen's hoods. Sometimes in the moonlight a dark body sways from a lynching tree — but for his funeral there are no roses.

ARNOLD RAMPERSAD

from The Origins of Poetry in Langston Hughes

Revealing an increase in skill, Hughes's early poetry nevertheless gives no sign of a major poetic talent in the making. At some point in his development, however, something happened to Hughes that was as mysterious and as wonderful, in its own way, as the miracle that overtook John Keats after the watchful night spent with his friend Charles Cowden Clarke and a copy of Chapman's translation. With "The Negro Speaks of Rivers" the creativity in Langston Hughes, hitherto unexpressed, suddenly created itself.

In writing thus about Hughes, are we taking him too seriously? With a few exceptions, literary critics have resisted offering even a modestly complicated theory concerning his creativity. His relentless affability and charm, his deep, open love of the black masses, his devotion to their folk forms, and his insistence on writing poetry that they could understand, all have contributed to the notion that Langston Hughes was intellectually and emotionally shallow. One wonders, then, at the source of the creative energy that drove him from 1921 to 1967 to write so many poems, novels, short stories, plays, operas, popular histories, children's books, and assorted other work. As a poet, Hughes virtually reinvented Afro-American poetry with his pioneering use of the blues and other folk forms; as Howard Mumford Jones marveled in a 1927 review, Hughes added the verse form of the blues to poetry in English (a form that continues to attract the best black poets, including Michael Harper, Sherley Anne Williams, and Raymond Patterson). One wonders, too, in his aspect as a poet, why this apparently happy, apparently shallow man defined his creativity in terms of unhappiness. "I felt bad for the next three or four years," he would write in *The Big Sea* about the period beginning more or less with the publication of "The Negro Speaks of Rivers," and "those were the years when I wrote most of my poetry. (For my best poems were all written when I felt the worst. When I was happy, I didn't write anything)." . . .

The first of [Hughes's] two illnesses took place in the summer of 1919, when Hughes (at seventeen) saw his father for the first time in a dozen years. In 1903, James Hughes had gone to Mexico, where he would become a prosperous property owner. In a lonely, impoverished, passed-around childhood in the Midwest, his son had fantasized about the man "as a kind of strong, bronze cowboy, in a big

Mexican hat, going back and forth from his business in the city to his ranch in the mountains, free — in a land where there were no white folks to draw the color line, and no tenements with rent always due — just mountains and cacti: Mexico!" Elated to be invited suddenly to Mexico in 1919 at the end of his junior year in high school, Langston left the United States with high hopes for his visit.

The summer was a disaster. James Hughes proved to be an unfeeling, domineering, and materialistic man, scornful of Indians and blacks (he was himself black) and the poor in general; and contemptuous of his son's gentler pace and artistic temperament. One day, Langston could take no more: "Suddenly my stomach began to turn over and over. And I could not swallow another mouthful. Waves of heat engulfed me. My eyes burned. My body shook. I wanted more than anything on earth to hit my father, but instead I got up from the table and went back to bed. The bed went round and round and the room turned dark. Anger clotted in every vein, and my tongue tasted like dry blood." But the boy, ill for a long time, never confessed the true cause of his affliction. Having been moved to Mexico City, he declined to help his doctors: "I never told them . . . that I was sick because I hated my father." He recovered only when it was time to return to the United States.

Hughes's second major illness came eleven years later. By this time he had finished high school, returned to Mexico to live with his father for a year, attended Columbia University for one year (supported grudgingly by James Hughes), dropped out of school, and served as a messman on voyages to Africa and to Europe, where he spent several months in 1924 as a dishwasher. All the while, however, Hughes was publishing poetry in a variety of places, especially in important black journals. This activity culminated in books of verse published in 1926 (*The Weary Blues*) and 1927 (*Fine Clothes to the Jew*) that established him, with Countee Cullen, as one of two major black poets of the decade. In 1929, he graduated after three and a half years at black Lincoln University, Pennsylvania. In 1930, Hughes published his first novel, *Not Without Laughter*.

This book had been virtually dragged out of him by his patron of the preceding three years, "Godmother" (as she wished to be called), an old, white, very generous but eccentric woman who ruled Hughes with a benevolent despotism inspired by her volatile beliefs in African spirituality, folk culture, mental telepathy, and the potential of his genius. But the result of her largesse was a paradox: the more comfortable he grew, the less Hughes was inclined to create. Estranged by his apparent languor, his patron finally seized on an episode of conflict to banish him once and for all. Hughes was devastated. Surviving drafts of his letters to "Godmother" reveal him deep in self-abasement before a woman with whom he was clearly in love. Ten years later, he confessed in *The Big Sea*: "I cannot write here about that last half-hour in the big bright drawing-room high above Park Avenue . . . because when I think about it, even now, something happens in the pit of my stomach that makes me ill. That beautiful room . . . suddenly became like a trap closing in, faster and faster, the room darker and darker, until the light went out with a sudden crash in the dark, and everything became like . . . that morning in Mexico when I suddenly hated my father.

"I was violently and physically ill, with my stomach turning over and over. . . . And there was no rationalizing anything. I couldn't." For several months, according to my research (Hughes erroneously presents a far briefer time frame in *The Big Sea*), he waited in excruciating hope for a reconciliation. As in Mexico, he wasted time and money on doctors without revealing to them the source of his chronic illness (which one very ingenious Harlem physician diagnosed as a Japanese tapeworm). Rather than break his silence, Hughes even agreed to have his tonsils removed. Gradually it became clear that reconciliation was impossible. Winning a prize of four hundred dollars for his novel, Hughes fled to seclusion in hot, remote Haiti. When his money ran out some months later, he returned home, healed at last but badly scarred.

Although they occurred more than a decade apart, the two illnesses were similar. Both showed a normally placid Hughes driven into deep rage by an opponent, a rage which he was unable to ventilate because the easy expression of personal anger and indignation was anathema to him. In both cases, he developed physical symptoms of hyperventilation and, eventually, anemia. More importantly, both were triggered in a period of relatively low poetic creativity (as when he was still a juvenile poet) or outright poetic inactivity (as with his patron). In each instance, Hughes had become satisfied with this low creativity or inactivity. At both times, a certain powerful figure, first his father, then "Godmother," had opposed his right to be content. His father had opposed any poetic activity at all; "Godmother" had opposed his right to enjoy the poetical state without true poetical action, or writing. In other words, a powerful will presented itself in forceful opposition to what was, in one sense, a vacuum of expressive will on Hughes's part. (Needless to say, the *apparent* absence of will in an individual can easily be a token of the presence of a very powerful will.) The result on both occasions, which was extraordinary, was first Hughes's endurance of, then his violent rebellion against, a force of will that challenged his deepest vision of the poetic life. . . .

In his bitter struggles with his father and "Godmother," Hughes turned to the black race for direction. But one needs to remember that this appeal in itself hardly gave Hughes distinction as a poet; what made Hughes distinct was the highly original manner in which he internalized the Afro-American racial dilemma and expressed it in poems such as "When Sue Wears Red," "The Negro Speaks of Rivers," "Mother to Son," "Dream Variations," and "The Weary Blues," poems of Hughes's young manhood on which his career would rest. Of these, the most important was "The Negro Speaks of Rivers."

> I've known rivers.
> I've known rivers ancient as the world and old
>   as the flow of human blood in human veins.
>
> My soul has grown deep like the rivers.
>
> I bathed in the Euphrates when dawns were young.
> I built my hut near the Congo and it lulled me to sleep.
> I looked upon the Nile and raised the pyramids above it.

I heard the singing of the Mississippi when Abe Lincoln went down
   to New Orleans, and I've seen its muddy bosom turn all golden
   in the sunset.

I've known rivers:
Ancient, dusky rivers.

My soul has grown deep like the rivers.

Here, the persona moves steadily from dimly starred personal memory ("I've known rivers") toward a rendezvous with modern history (Lincoln going down the Mississippi and seeing the horror of slavery that, according to legend, would make him one day free the slaves). The death wish, benign but suffusing, of its images of rivers older than human blood, of souls grown as deep as these rivers, gives way steadily to an altering, ennobling vision whose final effect gleams in the evocation of the Mississippi's "muddy bosom" turning at last "all golden in the sunset." Personal anguish has been alchemized by the poet into a gracious meditation on his race, whose despised ("muddy") culture and history, irradiated by the poet's vision, changes within the poem from mud into gold. This is a classic example of the essential process of creativity in Hughes.

The poem came to him, according to Hughes (accurately, it seems clear) about ten months after his Mexican illness, when he was riding a train from Cleveland to Mexico to rejoin his father. The time was sundown, the place the Mississippi outside St. Louis. "All day on the train I had been thinking of my father," he would write in *The Big Sea*. "Now it was just sunset and we crossed the Mississippi, slowly, over a long bridge. I looked out of the window of the Pullman at the great muddy river flowing down toward the heart of the South, and I began to think what that river, the old Mississippi, had meant to Negroes in the past — how to be sold down the river was the worst fate that could overtake a slave in bondage. Then I remembered reading how Abraham Lincoln had made a trip down the Mississippi on a raft, and how he had seen slavery at its worst, and had decided within himself that it should be removed from American life. Then I began to think of other rivers in our past — the Congo, and the Niger, and the Nile in Africa — and the thought came to me: 'I've known rivers,' and I put it down on the back of an envelope I had in my pocket, and within the space of ten or fifteen minutes, as the train gathered speed in the dusk, I had written this poem."

Here, starting with anguish over his father, Hughes discovered the compressed ritual of passivity, challenge, turmoil, and transcendence he would probably have to re-create, doubtless in variant forms, during the great poetic trysts of his life. Even after he became a successful, published poet, the basic process remained the same, because his psychology remained largely the same even though he had become technically expert. In his second major illness, caused by his patron "Godmother," Hughes wrote poetry as he struggled for a transcendence that would be long in coming. The nature of that interim poetry is telling. When he sent some poems to a friend for a little book to be printed privately, she noticed at once that many spoke of death — "Dear lovely Death / That taketh all things under wing — / Never to kill. . . ." She called the booklet *Dear Lovely Death*. In "Afro-American Fragment," unlike in "The Negro Speaks of Rivers," Africa is seen plaintively:

> . . . Subdued and time-lost
> Are the drums — and yet
> Through some vast mist of race
> There comes this song
> I do not understand,
> This song of atavistic land,
> Of bitter yearnings lost
> Without a place —
> So long,
> So far away
> Is Africa's
> Dark face.

But when Hughes returned home, scarred but healed, after months in seclusion in Haiti, he no longer thought of loss and death. Instead, he plunged directly into the life of the black masses with a seven-month tour of the South in which he read his poetry in their churches and schools. Then he set out for the Soviet Union, where he would spend more than a year. Hughes then reached the zenith of his revolutionary ardor with poems (or verse) such as "Good Morning Revolution," "Goodbye Christ," and "Put One More 'S' in the USA."

HERMAN BEAVERS

from Dead Rocks and Sleeping Men: Aurality in the Aesthetic of Langston Hughes

In his 1940 autobiography, *The Big Sea*, Langston Hughes discusses the circumstances that led him, at the puerile age of 19, to the creation of his poem, "The Negro Speaks of Rivers" [see p. 1095]. The poem came into being during a trip to Mexico, Hughes writes, "when [he] was feeling very bad."[1] Thus, he connects poetic inspiration and emotional turbulence, both of which stemmed from his attempt to understand his father's self-hatred. He relates, "All day on the train I had been thinking about my father and his strange dislike of his own people. I didn't understand it because I was a Negro, and I liked Negroes very much" (54). What is striking about the end of this passage is that one finds Hughes adopting a posture both inside and outside the race: he does not make a statement of self-love (e.g. I like myself), rather he indicates through a kind of reflexivity, that he has self-worth. In short, he is unable to articulate self-valuation, he can only construct his positionality as the mirror opposite of his father's racial feeling. But then Hughes shifts the subject and recalls that "one of the happiest jobs [he] ever had," was the time spent working behind the soda fountain of a refreshment parlor, in "the heart of the colored neighborhood" in Cleveland. He offers this description:

> People just up from the South used to come in for ice cream and sodas and
> watermelon. And I never tired of *hearing* their talk, *listening* to thunderclaps of

their laughter, to their troubles, to their discussions of the war and the men who had gone to Europe from the Jim Crow South, their complaints over the high rent and the long overtime hours that brought what seemed big checks, until the weekly bills were paid. (54, my emphasis)

I quote this passage at length to point to the disjointed quality Hughes's narrative assumes. In one chapter, we find the self-hatred of his father, his own admiration for the recuperative powers of newly arrived Southern blacks, and the act of composing a famous poem. The elements that form Hughes's account can be read, at least on a cursory level, as an attempt to demonstrate that his "best poems were written when [he] felt the worst" (54). This notwithstanding, what I would like to propose is that we can place the poem into an aesthetic frame that brings these three disparate elements into a more geometrical alignment.

Hughes's autobiographical account can be found in the middle of a chapter entitled, "I've Known Rivers." Having established his father as someone he neither understands nor wishes to emulate, the autobiography paints the older man as an outsider, not only geographically, but spiritually as well. That Hughes would discuss his father in relation to such an important poem, alludes to body travel of a different sort than that which he undertakes in this chapter of his autobiography. Moving further away from Cleveland, the geographical space where he encountered the individuals he describes as "the gayest and bravest people possible . . ." (54), Hughes elides the distance his father has put between himself and other blacks. He resists the impulses that lead to the latter's self-imposed exile: he is immersed in a vernacular moment and simultaneously peripheral to that moment. What differentiates the younger Hughes is that he listens to the voices of the folk and is "empowered rather than debilitated" by what he hears.[2]

In composing the poem, Hughes looks at "the great muddy river flowing down toward the heart of the South" (*The Big Sea* 55). While he suggests that it is his gaze — looking out of the train window at the Mississippi — that initiates composition, I would assert that what catalyzes his act of writing is the act of recovering the spoken word. A point emphasized, moreover, by the fact that he recounts a moment where he is listener rather than speaker.

Later in the autobiography, Hughes relates, in much less detail, the events which lead to his poem, "The Weary Blues" [see p. 1096] There, he states, simply: "That winter, I wrote a poem called "The Weary Blues," about a piano-player I heard in Harlem . . ." (92). Again, Hughes's poetic composition moves forward from an aural moment where, as with "The Negro Speaks of Rivers," he is an outsider. Arnold Rampersad alludes to this when he observes:

> . . . [I]n his willingness to stand back and record, with minimal intervention as a craftsman, aspects of the drama of black religion or black music, Hughes had clearly shown already that he saw his *own art as inferior* [my emphasis] to that of either black musicians or religionists. . . . At the heart of his sense of inferiority . . . was the knowledge that he stood to a great extent *outside* the culture he worshipped.[3]

Rampersad concludes that Hughes's sense of alienation resulted from the fact that "his life had been spent away from consistent, normal involvement with the black masses whose affection and regard he craved" (64–5).

Notes

[1] Langston Hughes, *The Big Sea* (1940; New York: Hill and Wang, 1963) 54. All subsequent references to this text are from this volume.

[2] Arnold Rampersad, *The Life of Langston Hughes, Volume I: 1902–1941: I, Too, Sing America*, 2 vols. (New York: Oxford UP, 1986) 1: 64.

[3] Rampersad 64–65. My emphasis.

STEVEN C. TRACY

from "Midnight Ruffles of Cat-Gut Lace": The Boogie Poems of Langston Hughes

The influence of the blues tradition on Langston Hughes' poetry is by now an oft-discussed and readily accepted fact, although the depth and breadth of his employment of the tradition has not often been discussed with a similar depth and breadth. A close examination of a related sequence of Hughes' blues poems offers the opportunity to explore his fusion of oral and written traditions and to examine his tremendous skills as a literary-jazz improviser. That is not to suggest that Hughes' poems are spontaneous creations. Improvisation is normally thought of as a spontaneous act, but the jazz or blues musician's improvisations are in fact bounded by several things: the musician's "vocabulary"—style, patterns, techniques, and riffs; the accepted conventions of the specific genre (even if those conventions are deliberately violated, they are, in a large sense, at work); and the boundaries of the individual piece being performed. For example, boogie-woogie pianist Pete Johnson, in his 1947 version of "Swanee River Boogie," performs the melody of the song to a boogie-woogie beat, thereafter improvising solos built around the song's chord changes, the boogie-woogie beat, and variations on the melody of the piece, combined with his arsenal of boogie-woogie riffs and performed in his inimitable style.[1] Hughes, in his 1951 collection, *Montage of a Dream Deferred*, generated a set or sequence of six "boogie" poems —"Dream Boogie," "Easy Boogie," "Boogie 1 a.m.," "Lady's Boogie," "Nightmare Boogie," and "Dream Boogie: Variation"— that have in common much more than the "boogie" of the titles. The poems comprise an intricate series of interwoven "improvisations" over a set boogie-woogie rhythm, with Hughes modulating and modifying rhythm, words, imagery, moods, and themes, and constructing a complex interrelationship between music, the musical instrument, the performance, and a set of attitudes exemplified by them.

Structurally, Hughes' six boogie poems share the exciting, rushing rhythms of boogie-woogie: Hughes at work on his poems, pounding out rhythms on his typewriter keyboard. Briefly, boogie-woogie is a form of Afro-American music, normally performed on the piano, that emerged as a recognizable genre in the 1920s. As blues researcher Karl Gert zur Heide points out, "the theme of boogie is the blues, some features derive from ragtime, and the rhythmic inter-play of both hands can be traced back to African roots."[2] In boogie-woogie, the improvisations executed by the pianist's right hand on the treble keys of the piano are set off against the ostinato or repeated phrases of the left hand on the bass keys. Characteristically boogie-woogie follows the twelve-bar blues chord change pattern — in the key of C, CFC GFC — employing a repeated bass pattern recognizable most often for its eight beats to the bar and per-formed at a medium-to-fast tempo that builds an explosive drive and swing appropriate to the dance step after which it was named. Besides identifying a dance step and a type of music, however, the term "boogie" functions in other contexts: to boogie is to raise a ruckus or act wildly or uninhibitedly; it also has sexual connotations:

> I'm gonna pull off my pants and keep on my shirt,
> I'm gonna get so low you think I'm in the dirt.
> I'm gonna pitch a boogie-woogie,
> Gonna boogie-woogie all night long.[3]

In this tune, singer Big Bill Broonzy has taken a boogie-woogie beat suitable for dancing and provided both the "wild acting" and sexual connotations that go with it. In the tradition, the word carried these connotations, and typically Hughes tried to capture the ambience of the tradition.

Notes

[1] Pete Johnson, "Swanee River Boogie," *Boogie Woogie Trio,* Storyville SLP 4006, 1976.

[2] Karl Gert zur Heide, *Deep South Piano* (London: Studio Vista, 1970), p. 11.

[3] Big Bill Broonzy, "Let's Reel and Rock," Melotone, 7-06-64, 1936, 78 R.P.M. recording.

KAREN JACKSON FORD

from Do Right to Write Right: Langston Hughes's Aesthetics of Simplicity

The one thing most readers of twentieth-century American poetry can say about Langston Hughes is that he has known rivers. "The Negro Speaks of Rivers" has become memorable for its lofty, oratorical tone, mythic scope, and powerful rhythmic repetitions.

> I've known rivers:
> I've known rivers ancient as the world and old as the flow of human
>   blood in human veins. (1656)

But however beautiful its cadences, the poem is remembered primarily because it is Hughes's most frequently anthologized work. The fact is, "The Negro Speaks of Rivers" is one of Hughes's most uncharacteristic poems, and yet it has defined his reputation, along with a small but constant selection of other poems included in anthologies. "A Negro Speaks of Rivers," "A House in Taos," "The Weary Blues," "Montage of a Dream Deferred," "Theme for English B," "Refugee in America," and "I, Too"— these poems invariably comprise his anthology repertoire despite the fact that none of them typifies his writing. What makes these poems atypical is exactly what makes them appealing and intelligible to the scholars who edit anthologies — their complexity. True, anthologies produced in the current market, which is hospitable to the African-American tradition and to canon reform, now include a brief selection of poems in black folk forms. But even though Hughes has fared better in anthologies than most African-American writers, only a small and predictable segment of his poetry has been preserved. A look back through the original volumes of poetry, and even through the severely redrawn *Selected Poems*, reveals a wealth of simpler poems we ought to be reading.[1]

Admittedly, an account of Hughes's poetic simplicity requires some qualification. Most obvious is the fact that he wrote poems that are not simple. "A Negro Speaks of Rivers" is oracular; "The Weary Blues" concludes enigmatically; "A House in Taos" is classically modernist in both its fragmented form and its decadent sensibility. Even more to the point, many of the poems that have been deemed simple are only ironically so. "The Black Christ," for example, is a little jingle that invokes monstrous cultural complexity. Likewise, two later books, *Ask Your Mama* (1961) and *The Panther and the Lash* (1967), contain an intricate vision of American history beneath their simple surfaces.[2] Nevertheless, the overwhelming proportion of poems in the Hughes canon consists of work in the simpler style, and even those poems that can yield complexities make use of simplicity in ways that ought not to be ignored.

The repression of the great bulk of Hughes's poems is the result of chronic critical scorn for their simplicity. Throughout his long career, but especially after his first two volumes of poetry (readers were at first willing to assume that a youthful poet might grow to be more complex), his books received their harshest reviews for a variety of "flaws" that all originate in an aesthetics of simplicity. From his first book, *The Weary Blues* (1926), to his last one, *The Panther and the Lash* (1967), the reviews invoke a litany of faults: the poems are superficial, infantile, silly, small, unpoetic, common, jejune, iterative, and, of course, simple.[3] Even his admirers reluctantly conclude that Hughes's poetics failed. Saunders Redding flatly opposes simplicity and artfulness. "While Hughes's rejection of his own growth shows an admirable loyalty to his self-commitment as the poet of the 'simple, Negro commonfolk' . . . it does a disservice to his art" (Mullen 74). James Baldwin, who recognizes the potential of simplicity as an artistic principle, faults the poems for "tak[ing] refuge . . . in a fake simplicity in order to avoid the very difficult simplicity of the experience" (Mullen 85).

Despite a lifetime of critical disappointments, then, Hughes remained loyal to the aesthetic program he had outlined in 1926 in his decisive poetic treatise, "The Negro Artist and the Racial Mountain." There he had predicted that the common people would "give to this world its truly great Negro artist, the one who is not afraid to be himself," a poet who would explore the "great field of unused [folk] material ready for his art" and recognize that this source would provide "sufficient matter to furnish a black artist with a lifetime of creative work" (692).* This is clearly a portrait of the poet Hughes would become, and he maintained his fidelity to this ideal at great cost to his literary reputation. . . .

---

*See page 1111 for the quoted passage in its entirety.

In his column in the *Chicago Defender* on February 13, 1943, Hughes first introduced the prototype of the humorous and beloved fictional character Jesse B. Semple, nicknamed by his Harlem friends "Simple." For the next twenty-three years Hughes would continue to publish Simple stories both in the *Defender* and in several volumes of collected and edited pieces.[4] Hughes called Simple his "ace-boy," and it is surely not coincidental that the Simple stories span the years, the 1940s to the 1960s, when Langston Hughes needed a literary ace in the hole.[5] The success of the Simple stories was an important consolation of the writer's later years, when his poetry was reviewed with disappointment, his autobiography dismissed as "chit-chat," his plays refused on Broadway, and his fiction diminished in importance next to Richard Wright's *Native Son* (1940) and Ralph Ellison's *Invisible Man* (1952).[6]

It seems obvious, however, that in the long association with his ace-boy Hughes found more than popularity and financial success. In fact, his prefatory sketches of Simple attest to the character's importance, in the sheer number of times Hughes sets out to explain him and in the specific details these explanations provide.[7] All of them depict Simple as an African American Everyman, the authentic — even unmediated — voice of the community that engendered him. For instance, in "Who Is Simple?" Hughes emphasizes the authenticity of his creation: "[Simple's] first words came directly out of the mouth of a young man who lived just down the block from me" (*Best* vii). Here and elsewhere Hughes asserts a vital connection between the fictional character and the people he represents: "If there were not a lot of genial souls in Harlem as talkative as Simple, I would never have these tales to write down that are 'just like him'" (*Best* viii). The author's dedication to Simple is surely rooted in his conviction that Simple embodies and speaks for the very people to whom Hughes had committed himself back in the 1920s.

Notes

[1] Easily ninety per cent of the poems in Hughes's canon are of the sort that I am describing as simple.

[2] Jemie, Hudson, and Miller, among others, have persuasively demonstrated the intricacies of Hughes's jazz structures in these two late books.

[3] Reviews in which these epithets appear are collected in Mullen.

[4] The stories are collected in five volumes, *The Best of Simple, Simple Speaks His Mind, Simple Stakes a Claim, Simple Takes a Wife,* and *Simple's Uncle Sam.* Additionally, Hughes takes Simple to the stage with *Simply Heavenly,* a comedy about Simple's marriage.

[5] In "Who Is Simple?" — the foreword to *The Best of Simple*— Hughes concludes, "He is my ace-boy, Simple. I hope you like him, too" (viii).

[6] For a chronicle of Hughes's disappointments during these years, see Rampersad, especially chapter 8 of the second volume "In Warm Manure: 1951 to 1953." Ellison characterized *The Big Sea* as a "chit-chat" book during an interview with Rampersad in 1983 (202).

[7] Hughes wrote at least four explanations of Simple: "The Happy Journey of 'Simply Heavenly,'" "Simple and Me," "Who Is Simple?" and the "Character Notes" to *Simply Heavenly.*

GEORGE B. HUTCHINSON

from Langston Hughes and the 'Other' Whitman

At various points in his long career, Hughes put together no fewer than three separate anthologies of Whitman's poetry (one of them for children), included several Whitman poems in an anthology on *The Poetry of the Negro*, wrote a poem entitled "Old Walt" for the one hundredth anniversary of *Leaves of Grass*, and repeatedly — in lectures, newspaper columns, and introductions — encouraged black Americans to read his work. He called Whitman "America's greatest poet" and spoke of *Leaves of Grass* as the greatest expression of "the real meaning of democracy ever made on our shores." Feeling that Whitman had been ignored and, in current parlance, marginalized by the custodians of culture, Hughes indeed attempted in his own way to canonize the poet he considered "the Lincoln of our Letters" (*Chicago Defender*, July 4, 1953). . . .

One reason Whitman's poetry has resonated in the sensibilities of black American writers is that in certain of his poems he uses the condition of the slave as representative of the condition of his audience. The "you" of his songs, if it is to apply to *all* readers, must apply to slaves, those most graphically denied the right to self-determination. The poem "To You (Whoever You Are)" at times seems directly addressed to a slave:

> None has done justice to you, you have not done justice to yourself,
> None but has found you imperfect, I only find no imperfection
>   in you,
> None but would subordinate you, I only am he who will never consent
>   to subordinate you,
> I only am he who places over you no master, owner, better, God,
>   beyond what waits intrinsically in yourself. (14–17)

Arguably, Whitman here distills the specific oppression of black people in the antebellum United States into a metaphor for the hidden condition of all people — "you, whoever you are." But his slave is not just any slave — his slave is the *most* enslaved, the one rejected by all others and even by himself or herself. . . . Hughes was the first African-American poet to sense the affinity between the inclusive "I" of Whitman (which Whitman claimed as his most important innovation — "the quite changed attitude of the ego, the one chanting or talking, towards himself and towards his fellow humanity" ("A Backward Glance," 564) and the "I" of the blues and even of the spirituals. The result of Hughes's appropriation of this triply descended "I" is amply demonstrated in one of his first published poems, "The Negro Speaks of Rivers":

> I've known rivers ancient as the world and old as the flow of human
>   blood in human veins.
>
> My soul has grown deep like the rivers.
>
> I bathed in the Euphrates when dawns were young.
> I built my hut near the Congo and it lulled me to sleep.
> I looked upon the Nile and raised the pyramids above it.

> I heard the singing of the Mississippi when Abe Lincoln went down to
> New Orleans, and I've seen its muddy bosom turn all golden in the
> sunset. (*Weary Blues*, 51)

Though Hughes would later, for the most part, turn away from the Whitmanesque style of free verse, the example of Whitman's break with traditional definitions of the poetic, his attempts to achieve an orally based poetics with the cadence and diction of the voice on the street, at the pond-side, or at the pulpit, provided a partial model for the young black poet looking for a way to sing his own song, which would be at the same time a song of his people.

Topics for Further Research

1. As Hughes's own essays in this volume suggest, much of his life was spent actively campaigning for various causes. Research the nature of his commitments and their effect on his poetry. How did his social and political work change between 1935 and 1955?

2. Investigate the ways in which Hughes's poetry was inspired by the accomplishments of African-American musicians. For example, how did the different musical forms of the female blues singers of the 1920s and the bebop musicians of the 1940s inspire him?

3. Hughes was a primary inspiration for the artistic movement known as *negritude*. Poets and writers like Nicolás Guillén, Jacques Roumain, Aimé Cesaire, and Leopold Senghor all acknowledged Hughes's influence. Find out what the negritude poets stood for, and write a paper in which you discuss why Hughes was so important to this movement.

4. Hughes's work was distinct from that of his two most important contemporaries, Gwendolyn Brooks and Robert Hayden, who were influenced by modernism. Using a dictionary or an encyclopedia of literary criticism, find out what modernist poetry is. Is *modernism* a useful term in discussing what distinguishes Brooks and Hayden from Hughes? Why might Hughes be skeptical about some aspects of modernism? Read the poems by Brooks and Hayden in this anthology. Then, find a collection of the work of one of these poets, and compare some of their poems to those of Hughes.

5. Hughes was a central figure in a period of African-American artistic flowering called the Harlem Renaissance. Find out as much as you can about the Harlem Renaissance and Hughes's involvement with it. Then, write an essay in which you assess in what ways the Harlem Renaissance was important to Hughes's development as a poet.

6. Read a collection of Hughes's "Simple" stories, newspaper columns that were later collected in book form. What is he able to do in fiction that he is unable to do in poetry? What is he able to do in poetry that he is unable to do in fiction?

Alston 1

Grace R. Alston

Professor Hall

African-American Literature

15 September 2005

Challenging the Father/Challenging the Self:

Langston Hughes's "The Negro Speaks of Rivers"

Langston Hughes's career as a poet began with
the publication of "The Negro Speaks of Rivers" in
the June 1921 issue of <u>The Crisis</u>. Hughes wrote this
poem during a trip to Mexico to visit his father,
James Hughes. According to Arnold Rampersad, James
Hughes, an "unfeeling, domineering, and materialistic
man, scornful of Indians and blacks . . . and the
poor in general; and contemptuous of his son's
gentler pace and artistic temperament" (1118), had
purposefully removed himself from African-American
life in the United States. Throughout the trip,
Langston Hughes dreaded the confrontation he knew he
would have with his father about his desire to become
a writer. He was very anxious, even depressed, but as
he wrote, "my best poems were all written when I felt
the worst. When I was happy, I didn't write anything"
(qtd. in Rampersad 1117). Hughes's relationship with
his father affected him not only psychologically, but
also as a writer, causing him to adopt a dual view of
both his subject matter and his race.

According to Herman Beavers, Hughes's troubled
relationship with his father caused him to adopt "a
posture both inside and outside the race" (1121), a
kind of double consciousness. On the one hand,

Thesis statement

Alston 2

in order to counter his father's rejection of his own
blackness, Hughes affirmed his racial identity. On
the other hand, in an effort to maintain artistic
integrity, Hughes tried to be universal in his
outlook. Ironically, then, Hughes's desire to
celebrate blackness was born out of the
dysfunctional relationship he had with his father.

The specific form of "The Negro Speaks of
Rivers" reveals Hughes's struggle with this double
consciousness. In this poem, Hughes actively
challenges his father's racism, but he also develops
a voice that allows him to do more than just affirm
blackness. In addition, the poem celebrates the role
of African-Americans in the human community.
Considering Hughes's conflict with his father, it is
not surprising that double consciousness became one
of Hughes's poetic themes.

In "The Negro Artist and the Racial Mountain,"
Hughes argues that "white" is the standard to which
blacks have to measure up (1110-12). Against this
standard, he suggests, the Negro artist has a high
mountain to climb in order to discover the self and
the community. Certainly, Hughes was able to climb
this mountain, but at what emotional cost? Some of
Hughes's best poems were written when he felt most
pessimistic about the prospects for black people;
the number of poems reflecting this pessimism suggests
he was frequently under stress. He was able, however,
to transform his negative emotions into powerful,
accessible poems.

Alston 3

Hughes's ambivalent relationship with his father is evident in "The Negro Speaks of Rivers." According to Arnold Rampersad, Hughes got the idea for this poem as he glanced out of a train window and became fascinated by the Mississippi River (1120). As he focused on the image of the river, he wrote a poem that Karen Jackson Ford notes is uncharacteristic because of its strong "oratorical tone" (1124). In the poem, Hughes writes these lines:

> I've known rivers:
>
> I've known rivers ancient as the world and older than the flow of human blood in human veins.
>
> My soul has grown deep like the rivers.
>
> (lines 1-3)

The words "I've known rivers" are universal, suggesting shared feelings. In this sharing, readers come to appreciate blackness, the blackness Hughes's father so despised.

The scope of "The Negro Speaks of Rivers" is both historical and mythic. Although Hughes depicts certain conventions of black culture in an imaginative and symbolic way, his choice of rivers suggests a very particular history. The Congo and Nile illustrate the beauty of blackness and the accomplishments of the black race. The speaker appears alongside the Euphrates and with it suggests the beginnings of civilization. In this way, Hughes makes clear to his father—and to his readers—the

Alston 4

nobility of an African past. Moreover, his use of the
Mississippi not only places the American river in a
continuous historical relationship with the Euphrates
but also introduces the question of slavery. Once
again, Hughes is able to perform the double task of
confronting both American culture and his father. The
image of defenseless slaves being sold up and down
the Mississippi River's "muddy bosom" (7) may have
reminded him of his own defenseless position in his
relationship with his father. And as the "muddy
bosom" turning "golden in the sunset" (7) suggests
freedom for slaves, it may have also meant for Hughes
freedom from his father.

Repetition also contributes to the poem's
effect. Hughes uses words implying motion, such as
"bathed," "built," "looked," and "raised," and
"singing." Although the repetition of "rivers" works
in a slightly different way, it may be the most
effective means by which Hughes communicates his
feeling of displacement. Like a chant, this complex
rhythm is the most striking way he rises to his
double challenge, but the success of this "rhythm" is
based in readers' collective experience.

Hughes believed that black writers had a
responsibility to reveal to whites that blacks could
do more than sing, dance, laugh, and make music. He
believed black writers had a role to play in racial
reconciliation (Hughes, "To Negro Writers" 1112), and
his ability to affirm blackness—not just to a black
audience but to a universal one—without stereotyping

Alston 5

is what earns him his distinction as a poet. It is
striking that the strength of his racial identity has
its source, at least partially, in his troubled
relationship with his father.

Alston 6

Works Cited

Beavers, Herman. "Dead Rocks and Sleeping Men:
      Aurality in the Aesthetic of Langston Hughes."
      Kirszner and Mandell 1121-22.

Ford, Karen Jackson. "Do Right to Write Right:
      Langston Hughes's Aesthetics of Simplicity."
      Kirszner and Mandell 1124-26.

Hughes, Langston. "The Negro Artist and the Racial
      Mountain." Kirszner and Mandell 1110-12.

---. "The Negro Speaks of Rivers." Kirszner and
      Mandell 1095.

---. "To Negro Writers." Kirszner and Mandell
      1112-13.

Kirszner, Laurie G., and Stephen R. Mandell, eds.
      <u>Literature: Reading, Reacting, Writing</u>. 6th ed.
      Boston: Wadsworth, 2007.

Rampersad, Arnold. "The Origins of Poetry in Langston
      Hughes." Kirszner and Mandell 1117-21.

CHAPTER 34

POETRY FOR FURTHER READING

ELIZABETH ALEXANDER (1962–)

Apollo (1996)

We pull off
to a road shack
in Massachusetts
to watch men walk

on the moon. We did   5
the same thing
for three two one
blast off, and now

we watch the same men
bounce in and out   10
of craters. I want
a Coke and a hamburger.

Because the men
are walking on the moon
which is now irrefutably   15
not green, not cheese,

not a shiny dime floating
in a cold blue,
the way I'd thought,
the road shack people don't   20

notice we are a black
family not from there,
the way it mostly goes.
This talking through

static, bouncing in space-   25
boots, tethered
to cords is much
stranger, stranger

even than we are.

SHERMAN ALEXIE (1966–)

Defending Walt Whitman (1996)

Basketball is like this for young Indian boys, all arms and legs
and serious stomach muscles. Every body is brown!
These are the twentieth-century warriors who will never kill,
although a few sat quietly in the deserts of Kuwait,
waiting for orders to do something, do something.   5

God, there is nothing as beautiful as a jump shot
on a reservation summer basketball court
where the ball is moist with sweat
and makes a sound when it swishes through the net
that causes Walt Whitman to weep because it is so perfect.   10

There are veterans of foreign wars here,
whose bodies are still dominated
by collarbones and knees, whose bodies still respond
in the ways that bodies are supposed to respond when we
    are young.
Every body is brown! Look there, that boy can run   15
up and down this court forever. He can leap for a rebound
with his back arched like a salmon, all meat and bone
synchronized, magnetic, as if the court were a river,
as if the rim were a dam, as if the air were a ladder
leading the Indian boy toward home.   20

Some of the Indian boys still wear their military haircuts
while a few have let their hair grow back.
It will never be the same as it was before!
One Indian boy has never cut his hair, not once, and he braids it
into wild patterns that do not measure anything.   25
He is just a boy with too much time on his hands.
Look at him. He wants to play this game in bare feet.

God, the sun is so bright! There is no place like this.
Walt Whitman stretches his calf muscles
on the sidelines. He has the next game.   30
His huge beard is ridiculous on the reservation.
Some body throws a crazy pass and Walt Whitman catches it
    with quick hands.
He brings the ball close to his nose
and breathes in all of its smells: leather, brown skin, sweat,
    black hair,
burning oil, twisted ankle, long drink of warm water,   35
gunpowder, pine tree. Walt Whitman squeezes the ball tightly.

He wants to run. He hardly has the patience to wait for his turn.
"What's the score?" he asks. He asks, "What's the score?"

Basketball is like this for Walt Whitman. He watches these
    Indian boys
as if they were the last bodies on earth. Every body is brown!   40
Walt Whitman shakes because he believes in God.
Walt Whitman dreams of the Indian boy who will defend him,
trapping him in the corner, all flailing arms and legs
and legendary stomach muscles. Walt Whitman shakes
because he believes in God. Walt Whitman dreams   45
of the first jump shot he will take, the ball arcing clumsily
from his fingers, striking the rim so hard that it sparks.
Walt Whitman shakes because he believes in God.
Walt Whitman closes his eyes. He is a small man and his beard
is ludicrous on the reservation, absolutely insane.   50
His beard makes the Indian boys laugh righteously. His beard
    frightens
the smallest Indian boys. His beard tickles the skin
of the Indian boys who dribble past him. His beard, his beard!

God, there is beauty in every body. Walt Whitman stands
at center court while the Indian boys run from basket to basket.   55
Walt Whitman cannot tell the difference between
offense and defense. He does not care if he touches the ball.
Half of the Indian boys wear T-shirts damp with sweat
and the other half are barebacked, skin slick and shiny.
There is no place like this. Walt Whitman smiles.   60
Walt Whitman shakes. This game belongs to him.

LEWIS ALLEN   (1903–1986)

Strange Fruit*   (1939)

Southern trees bear strange fruit,
Blood on the leaves and blood at the root,

---

*After the Civil War, the racial climate in the South was tense. With the advent of the Ku Klux Klan, and in an environment of hatred and fear, white mobs felt free to participate in lynchings of African-Americans. In 1937, Abel Meeropol, a schoolteacher from New York, saw a photograph of the 1930 lynching of Thomas Shipp and Abram Smith in Marion, Indiana. Haunted by this image, he wrote the poem "Strange Fruit" under the pseudonym Lewis Allen. After hearing Billie Holiday (a reknowned African-American blues singer) perform, he gave the poem to her, and she worked it into a haunting song.

Black bodies swinging in the southern breeze,
Strange fruit hanging from the poplar trees.

Pastoral scene of the gallant south,   5
The bulging eyes and the twisted mouth,
Scent of magnolias, sweet and fresh,
Then the sudden smell of burning flesh.

Here is fruit for the crows to pluck,
For the rain to gather, for the wind to suck,   10
For the sun to rot, for the trees to drop,
Here is a strange and bitter crop.

MAYA ANGELOU (1928–   )

Africa (1975)

Thus she had lain
sugar cane sweet

deserts her hair
golden her feet
mountains her breasts   5
two Niles° her tears
Thus she has lain
Black through the years.

Over the white seas
rime white and cold   10
brigands ungentled
icicle bold
took her young daughters
sold her strong sons
churched her with Jesus   15
bled her with guns.
Thus she has lain.

Now she is rising
remember her pain
remember the losses   20
her screams loud and vain
remember her riches
her history slain
now she is striding
although she had lain.   25

° *Niles:* The Nile River, which originates in East Africa and flows through Egypt, is the world's longest river.

ANONYMOUS

Bonny Barbara Allan

(Traditional Scottish ballad)

It was in and about the Martinmas° time,
    When the green leaves were afalling,
That Sir John Graeme, in the West Country,
    Fell in love with Barbara Allan.

He sent his men down through the town,   5
    To the place where she was dwelling;
"O haste and come to my master dear,
    Gin° ye be Barbara Allan."

O hooly,° hooly rose she up,
    To the place where he was lying,   10
And when she drew the curtain by:
    "Young man, I think you're dying."

"O it's I'm sick, and very, very sick,
    And 'tis a' for Barbara Allan."—
"O the better for me ye's never be,   15
    Tho your heart's blood were aspilling.

"O dinna ye mind,° young man," said she,
    "When ye was in the tavern adrinking,
That ye made the health gae round and round,
    And slighted Barbara Allan?"   20

He turned his face unto the wall,
    And death was with him dealing:
"Adieu, adieu, my dear friends all,
    And be kind to Barbara Allan."

And slowly, slowly raise she up,   25
    And slowly, slowly left him,
And sighing said she could not stay,
    Since death of life had reft him.

She had not gane a mile but twa,°
    When she heard the dead-bell ringing,   30
And every jow° that the dead-bell geid,
    It cried, "Woe to Barbara Allan!"

° *Martinmas:* Saint Martin's Day, November 11.   ° *Gin:* If.   ° *hooly:* Slowly.   ° *O dinna ye mind:* Don't you remember?   ° *twa:* Two.   ° *jow:* Stroke.

"O mother, mother, make my bed!
  O make it saft and narrow!
Since my love died for me today,   35
  I'll die for him tomorrow."

ANONYMOUS

Go Down, Moses*

Go down, Moses,
Way down in Egyptland
Tell old Pharaoh
To let my people go.

When Israel was in Egyptland   5
Let my people go
Oppressed so hard they could not stand
Let my people go.

Go down, Moses,
Way down in Egyptland   10
Tell old Pharaoh
"Let my people go."

"Thus saith the Lord," bold Moses said,
"Let my people go;
If not I'll smite your first-born dead   15
Let my people go.

"No more shall they in bondage toil,
Let my people go;
Let them come out with Egypt's spoil,
Let my people go."   20

The Lord told Moses what to do
Let my people go;
To lead the children of Israel through,
Let my people go.

---

*Music was one of the few means of expression permitted for slaves. For example, slaves were allowed to sing songs when they had to coordinate work efforts, such as hauling a fallen tree or moving a heavy load. Religious songs, or "spirituals," were also allowed. Many of these songs contained coded messages conveying antislavery sentiments or even directions on how to use the Underground Railroad. For example, the spiritual "Wade in the Water" seemed, on the surface, to be about crossing the River Jordan to reach the Promised Land. But its lyrics contained vital information, including the idea that crossing streams was a good way for runway slaves to cover their scent and thus to lose the bloodhounds used to track them.

Go down, Moses,   25
Way down in Egyptland,
Tell old Pharaoh,
"Let my people go!"

ANONYMOUS

Western Wind

(English lyric)

Western wind, when wilt thou blow,
The° small rain down can rain?
Christ, if my love were in my arms,
And I in my bed again!

MATTHEW ARNOLD   (1822–1888)

Dover Beach   (1867)

The sea is calm tonight.
The tide is full, the moon lies fair
Upon the straits;— on the French coast the light
Gleams and is gone; the cliffs of England stand,
Glimmering and vast, out in the tranquil bay.   5
Come to the window, sweet is the night-air!
Only, from the long line of spray
Where the sea meets the moon-blanched° land,
Listen! you hear the grating roar
Of pebbles which the waves draw back, and fling,   10
At their return, up the high strand,°
Begin, and cease, and then again begin,
With tremulous cadence slow, and bring
The eternal note of sadness in.

Sophocles° long ago   15
Heard it on the Aegean,° and it brought
Into his mind the turbid ebb and flow
Of human misery; we

° *The:* [So that] the.   ° *moon-blanched:* Whitened by moonlight.   ° *strand:* Beach.   ° *Sophocles:* Greek playwright (496–406 B.C.), author of tragedies such as *Oedipus the King* and *Antigone.*   ° *Aegean:* Sea between
Greece and Turkey.

Find also in the sound a thought,
Hearing it by this distant northern sea.   20

The Sea of Faith
Was once, too, at the full, and round earth's shore
Lay like the folds of a bright girdle furled.
But now I only hear
Its melancholy, long, withdrawing roar,   25
Retreating, to the breath
Of the night-wind, down the vast edges drear
And naked shingles° of the world.

Ah, love, let us be true
To one another! for the world, which seems   30
To lie before us like a land of dreams,
So various, so beautiful, so new,
Hath really neither joy, nor love, nor light,
Nor certitude, nor peace, nor help for pain;
And we are here as on a darkling° plain   35
Swept with confused alarms of struggle and flight,
Where ignorant armies clash by night.

ELIZABETH BISHOP   (1911–1979)

The Fish   (1946)

I caught a tremendous fish
and held him beside the boat
half out of water, with my hook
fast in a corner of his mouth.
He didn't fight.   5
He hadn't fought at all.
He hung a grunting weight,
battered and venerable
and homely. Here and there
his brown skin hung in strips   10
like ancient wallpaper,
and its pattern of darker brown
was like wallpaper:
shapes like full-blown roses
stained and lost through age.   15
He was speckled with barnacles,

°*shingles:* Gravel beaches.   °*darkling:* Darkening.

fine rosettes of lime,
and infested
with tiny white sea-lice,
and underneath two or three   20
rags of green weed hung down.
While his gills were breathing in
the terrible oxygen
— the frightening gills,
fresh and crisp with blood,   25
that can cut so badly —
I thought of the coarse white flesh
packed in like feathers,
the big bones and the little bonies,
the dramatic reds and blacks   30
of his shiny entrails,
and the pink swim-bladder
like a big peony.
I looked into his eyes
which were far larger than mine   35
but shallower, and yellowed,
the irises backed and packed
with tarnished tinfoil
seen through the lenses
of old scratched isinglass.   40
They shifted a little, but not
to return my stare.
— It was more like the tipping
of an object toward the light.
I admired his sullen face,   45
the mechanism of his jaw,
and then I saw
that from his lower lip
— if you could call it a lip —
grim, wet, and weaponlike,   50
hung five old pieces of fish-line,
or four and a wire leader
with the swivel still attached,
with all their five big hooks
grown firmly in his mouth.   55
A green line, frayed at the end
and crimped from the strain and snap
when it broke and he got away.
Like medals with their ribbons
frayed and wavering,   60
a five-haired beard of wisdom

trailing from his aching jaw.
I stared and stared
and victory filled up
the little rented boat,   65
from the pool of bilge
where oil had spread a rainbow
around the rusted engine
to the bailer rusted orange,
the sun-cracked thwarts,   70
the oarlocks on their strings,
the gunnels — until everything
was rainbow, rainbow, rainbow!
And I let the fish go.

WILLIAM BLAKE (1757–1827)

The Chimney Sweeper (1789)

When my mother died I was very young,
And my father sold me while yet my tongue
Could scarcely cry "'weep! 'weep! 'weep! 'weep!"
So your chimneys I sweep, and in soot I sleep.

There's little Tom Dacre, who cried when his head,   5
That curled like a lamb's back, was shaved: so I said
"Hush, Tom! never mind it, for when your head's bare
You know that the soot cannot spoil your white hair."

And so he was quiet, and that very night,
As Tom was a-sleeping, he had such a sight!   10
That thousands of sweepers, Dick, Joe, Ned, and Jack,
Were all of them locked up in coffins of black.

And by came an Angel who had a bright key,
And he opened the coffins and set them all free;
Then down a green plain leaping, laughing, they run,   15
And wash in a river, and shine in the sun.

Then naked and white, all their bags left behind,
They rise upon clouds and sport in the wind;
And the Angel told Tom, if he'd be a good boy,
He'd have God for his father, and never want joy.   20

And so Tom awoke; and we rose in the dark,
And got with our bags and our brushes to work.
Though the morning was cold, Tom was happy and warm;
So if all do their duty they need not fear harm.

WILLIAM BLAKE (1757–1827)

The Lamb (1789)

Little Lamb, who made thee?
Dost thou know who made thee?
Gave thee life & bid thee feed,
By the stream & o'er the mead;
Gave thee clothing of delight, 5
Softest clothing wooly bright;
Gave thee such a tender voice,
Making all the vales rejoice!
Little Lamb who made thee?
Dost thou know who made thee? 10

Little Lamb I'll tell thee,
Little Lamb I'll tell thee!
He is calléd by thy name,
For he calls himself a Lamb:
He is meek & he is mild, 15
He became a little child:
I a child & thou a lamb,
We are calléd by his name.
Little Lamb God bless thee.
Little Lamb God bless thee. 20

WILLIAM BLAKE (1757–1827)

London (1794)

I wander through each chartered street,
Near where the chartered Thames does flow,
And mark in every face I meet
Marks of weakness, marks of woe.

In every cry of every man, 5
In every infant's cry of fear,
In every voice, in every ban,
The mind-forged manacles I hear.

How the chimney-sweeper's cry
Every black'ning church appalls; 10
And the hapless soldier's sigh
Runs in blood down palace walls.

But most through midnight streets I hear
How the youthful harlot's curse

Blasts the new born infant's tear,   15
And blights with plagues the marriage hearse.

WILLIAM BLAKE (1757–1827)

To see a World in a Grain of Sand (1803)

To see a World in a Grain of Sand
And a Heaven in a Wild Flower,
Hold Infinity in the palm of your hand
And Eternity in an hour.

WILLIAM BLAKE (1757–1827)

The Tyger (1794)

Tyger! Tyger! burning bright
In the forests of the night,
What immortal hand or eye
Could frame thy fearful symmetry?

In what distant deeps or skies   5
Burnt the fire of thine eyes?
On what wings dare he aspire?
What the hand dare seize the fire?

And what shoulder, and what art,
Could twist the sinews of thy heart?   10
And when thy heart began to beat,
What dread hand? and what dread feet?

What the hammer? what the chain?
In what furnace was thy brain?
What the anvil? what dread grasp   15
Dare its deadly terrors clasp?

When the stars threw down their spears,
And watered heaven with their tears,
Did he smile his work to see?
Did he who made the Lamb make thee?   20

Tyger! Tyger! burning bright
In the forests of the night,
What immortal hand or eye
Dare frame thy fearful symmetry?

EAVAN BOLAND   (1944 –   )

The Emigrant Irish   (1987)

Like oil lamps, we put them out the back —

of our houses, of our minds. We had lights
better than, newer than and then

a time came, this time and now
we need them. Their dread, makeshift example: 5

they would have thrived on our necessities.
What they survived we could not even live.
By their lights now it is time to
imagine how they stood there, what they stood with,
that their possessions may become our power: 10
Cardboard. Iron. Their hardships parceled in them.
Patience. Fortitude. Long-suffering
in the bruise-colored dusk of the New World.

And all the old songs. And nothing to lose.

ANNE BRADSTREET   (1612 – 1672)

The Author to Her Book°   (1678)

Thou ill-formed offspring of my feeble brain,
Who after birth did'st by my side remain,
Till snatched from thence by friends, less wise than true,
Who thee abroad exposed to public view;
Made thee in rags, halting, to the press to trudge,   5
Where errors were not lessened, all may judge.
At thy return my blushing was not small,
My rambling brat (in print) should mother call;
I cast thee by as one unfit for light,
Thy visage was so irksome in my sight;   10
Yet being mine own, at length affection would
Thy blemishes amend, if so I could:
I washed thy face, but more defects I saw,
And rubbing off a spot, still made a flaw.
I stretched thy joints to make thee even feet,°   15
Yet still thou run'st more hobbling than is meet;°

° *Her Book:* Bradstreet addresses *The Tenth Muse,* a collection of her poetry published without her consent in
1650.   ° *even feet:* Metrical feet.   ° *meet:* Appropriate or decorous.

In better dress to trim thee was my mind,
But nought save homespun cloth in the house I find.
In this array, 'mongst vulgars° may'st thou roam;
In critics' hands beware thou dost not come;   20
And take thy way where yet thou are not known.
If for thy Father asked, say thou had'st none;
And for thy Mother, she alas is poor,
Which caused her thus to send thee out of door.

GWENDOLYN BROOKS (1917–2000)

The *Chicago Defender*° Sends a Man to Little Rock (1960)

Fall, 1957°

In Little Rock the people bear
Babes, and comb and part their hair
And watch the want ads, put repair
To roof and latch. While wheat toast burns
A woman waters multiferns.   5

Time upholds or overturns
The many, tight, and small concerns.

In Little Rock the people sing
Sunday hymns like anything,
Through Sunday pomp and polishing.   10

And after testament and tunes,
Some soften Sunday afternoons
With lemon tea and Lorna Doones.

I forecast
And I believe   15
Come Christmas Little Rock will cleave
To Christmas tree and trifle, weave,
From laugh and tinsel, texture fast.

In Little Rock is baseball; Barcarolle.°
That hotness in July . . . the uniformed figures raw and implacable   20

°*vulgars:* Common people.   °*Chicago Defender:* A weekly newspaper for African-American readers.
°*Fall, 1957:* When black students first entered the public high school in Little Rock, Arkansas, in 1957, the city erupted in race riots protesting desegregation.   °*Barcarolle:* A Venetian gondolier's song, or a song suggesting the rhythm of rowing.

And not intellectual,
Batting the hotness or clawing the suffering dust.
The Open Air Concert, on the special twilight green. . . .
When Beethoven is brutal or whispers to lady-like air.
Blanket-sitters are solemn, as Johann troubles to lean   25
To tell them what to mean. . . .

There is love, to1o, in Little Rock. Soft women softly
Opening themselves in kindness,
Or, pitying one's blindness,
Awaiting one's pleasure   30
In azure
Glory with anguished rose at the root. . . .
To wash away old semi-discomfitures.
They re-teach purple and unsullen blue.
The wispy soils go. And uncertain   35
Half-havings have they clarified to sures.

In Little Rock they know
Not answering the telephone is a way of rejecting life,
That it is our business to be bothered, is our business
To cherish bores or boredom, be polite   40
To lies and love and many-faceted fuzziness.
I scratch my head, massage the hate-I-had.
I blink across my prim and pencilled pad.
The saga I was sent for is not down.
Because there is a puzzle in this town.   45
The biggest News I do not dare
Telegraph to the Editor's chair:
"They are like people everywhere."

The angry Editor would reply
In hundred harryings of Why.   50

And true, they are hurling spittle, rock,
Garbage and fruit in Little Rock.
And I saw coiling storm a-writhe
On bright madonnas. And a scythe
Of men harassing brownish girls.   55
(The bows and barrettes in the curls
And braids declined away from joy.)

I saw a bleeding brownish boy. . . .

The lariat lynch-wish I deplored.

The loveliest lynchee was our Lord.   60

GWENDOLYN BROOKS (1917–2000)

Medgar Evers° (1964)

For Charles Evers°

The man whose height his fear improved he
arranged to fear no further. The raw
intoxicated time was time for better birth or a final death.

Old styles, old tempos, all the engagement of
the day — the sedate, the regulated fray —   5
the antique light, the Moral rose, old gusts,
tight whistlings from the past, the mothballs
in the Love at last our man forswore.

Medgar Evers annoyed confetti and assorted
brands of businessmen's eyes.   10

The shows came down: to maxims and surprise.
And palsy.

Roaring no rapt arise-ye to the dead, he
leaned across tomorrow. People said that
he was holding clean globes in his hands.   15

GEORGE GORDON, LORD BYRON (1788–1824)

She Walks in Beauty (1815)

1

She walks in beauty, like the night
    Of cloudless climes and starry skies;
And all that's best of dark and bright
    Meet in her aspect and her eyes:
Thus mellowed to that tender light   5
    Which heaven to gaudy day denies.

2

One shade the more, one ray the less,
    Had half impaired the nameless grace
Which waves in every raven tress,
    Or softly lightens o'er her face;   10
Where thoughts serenely sweet express
    How pure, how dear their dwelling place.

°*Medgar Evers:* African-American civil rights leader who was killed by a sniper in 1963.   °*Charles Evers:*
Medgar Evers's brother.

3

And on that cheek, and o'er that brow,
  So soft, so calm, yet eloquent,
The smiles that win, the tints that glow,   15
  But tell of days in goodness spent,
A mind at peace with all below,
  A heart whose love is innocent!

THOMAS CAMPION   (1567–1620)

There is a garden in her face (1617)

There is a garden in her face
Where roses and white lilies grow;
  A heav'nly paradise is that place
Wherein all pleasant fruits do flow.
  There cherries grow which none may buy   5
  Till "Cherry-ripe" themselves do cry.

Those cherries fairly do enclose
Of orient pearl a double row,
  Which when her lovely laughter shows,
They look like rose-buds filled with snow;   10
  Yet them nor peer nor prince can buy,
  Till "Cherry-ripe" themselves do cry.

Her eyes like angels watch them still;
Her brows like bended bows do stand,
  Threat'ning with piercing frowns to kill   15
All that attempt, with eye or hand
  Those sacred cherries to come nigh
  Till "Cherry-ripe" themselves do cry.

GEOFFREY CHAUCER   (c. 1343–1400)

from The Canterbury Tales

Part I
from The General Prologue

Here bigynneth the Book of the Tales of Caunterbury.

Whan that Aprill with his shoures soote°
The droghte of March hath perced to the roote,

°*his shoures soote:* its sweet showers

And bathed every veyne in swich licour°
Of which vertu° engendred is the flour;
Whan Zephirus eek° with his sweete breeth   5
Inspired hath in every holt and heeth°
The tendre croppes, and the yonge sonne
Hath in the Ram his halfe cours yronne,°
And smale foweles maken melodye,
That slepen al the nyght with open eye—   10
So priketh hem nature in hir corages—°
Thanne longen folk to goon° on pilgrimages,
And palmeres° for to seken straunge strondes°
To ferne halwes, kowthe in sondry londes;°
And specially from every shires ende   15
Of Engelond to Caunterbury they wende
The hooly blisful martir° for to seke
That hem hath holpen° whan that they were seeke.°
    Bilfil that in that seson on a day
In Southwerk at the Tabard° as I lay   20
Redy to wenden on my pilgrymage
To Caunterbury with ful devout corage,
At nyght was come into that hostelrye
Wel nyne and twenty in a compaignye
Of sondry° folk, by aventure° yfalle   25
In felaweship, and pilgrimes were they alle,
That toward Caunterbury wolden° ryde.
The chambres and the stables weren wyde,°
And wel we weren esed atte beste.°
And shortly, whan the sonne was to reste,   30
So hadde I spoken with hem everichon°
That I was of hir felaweship anon,°
And made forward° erly for to ryse,
To take oure wey ther as I yow devyse.°

°*veyne in swich licour:* vein (as in the veins in a plant) in such liquid   °*of which vertu:* by the power of which
Whan Zephirus eek: When the West Wind also   °*every holt and heath:* grove and field   °*and the yonge
sonne/Hath in the Ram his halfe cours yronne:* Refers to the sun in its zodiac cycle. It is young because it has
run only halfway through its course in Aries, the Ram, which is the first sign of the zodiac in the solar year.
°*in hir corages:* in their hearts   °*goon:* go   °*palmeres:* professional pilgrims, whose emblem was a palm
frond   °*strondes:* lands   °*ferne halwes, kowthe in sondry londes:* far-off shrines known in various lands
°*The hooly blissful martir:* refers to St. Thomas à Becket, a martyr who was murdered in the Canterbury
Cathedral in 1170.   °*holpen:* helped   °*seeke:* sick   °*Southwerk, Tabard:* Southwark, site of the Tabard Inn,
then a suburb of London, south of the Thames River   °*sondry:* various   °*aventure:* chance   °*wolden:* would
°*wyde:* spacious   °*esed atte beste:* accommodated in the best possible way   °*everichon:* everyone   °*anon:*
at once   °*made forward:* (we) made an agreement   °*as I yow devyse:* as I will tell you

But nathelees, whil I have tyme and space,   35
Er° that I ferther in this tale pace,°
Me thynketh it acordaunt to resoun
To telle yow al the condicioun°
Of ech of hem, so as it semed me,
And whiche they weren, and of what degree,°   40
And eek in what array that they were inne,
And at a knyght than° wol I first bigynne.

LUCILLE CLIFTON (1936–   )

Praise Song

to my aunt blanche
who rolled from grass to driveway
into the street one sunday morning.
i was ten.   i had never seen
a human woman hurl her basketball   5
of a body into the traffic of the world.
Praise to the drivers who stopped in time.
Praise to the faith with which she rose
after some moments then slowly walked
sighing back to her family.   10
Praise to the arms which understood
little or nothing of what it meant
but welcomed her in without judgment,
accepting it all like children might,
like God.   15

SAMUEL TAYLOR COLERIDGE (1772–1834)

Kubla Khan° (1797, 1798)

Or, a Vision in a Dream. A Fragment.

In Xanadu did Kubla Khan
A stately pleasure-dome decree:

°*Er/pace:* Before, pass   °*condicioun:* circumstance   °*whiche . . . degree:* what status or rank   °*than:* then
°*Kubla Khan:* Coleridge mythologizes the actual Kublai Khan, a thirteenth-century Mongol emperor, as well as the Chinese city of Xanadu.

Where Alph,° the sacred river, ran
Through caverns measureless to man
Down to a sunless sea.   5
So twice five miles of fertile ground
With walls and towers were girdled round;
And there were gardens bright with sinuous rills,
Where blossomed many an incense-bearing tree;
And here were forests ancient as the hills,   10
Enfolding sunny spots of greenery.

But oh! that deep romantic chasm which slanted
Down the green hill athwart a cedarn cover!
A savage place! as holy and enchanted
As e'er beneath a waning moon was haunted   15
By woman wailing for her demon-lover!
And from this chasm, with ceaseless turmoil seething,
As if this earth in fast thick pants were breathing,
A mighty fountain momently was forced:
Amid whose swift half-intermitted burst   20
Huge fragments vaulted like rebounding hail,
Or chaffy grain beneath the thresher's flail:
And 'mid these dancing rocks at once and ever
It flung up momently the sacred river.
Five miles meandering with a mazy motion   25
Through wood and dale the sacred river ran,
Then reached the caverns measureless to man,
And sank in tumult to a lifeless ocean:
And 'mid this tumult Kubla heard from far
Ancestral voices prophesying war!   30

    The shadow of the dome of pleasure
    Floated midway on the waves;
    Where was heard the mingled measure
    From the fountain and the caves.
It was a miracle of rare device,   35
A sunny pleasure-dome with caves of ice!

    A damsel with a dulcimer
    In a vision once I saw:
    It was an Abyssinian maid,
    And on her dulcimer she played,   40

° *Alph:* Probably derived from the Greek river Alpheus, whose waters, according to legend, rose from the Ionian Sea in Sicily as the fountain of Arethusa.

Singing of Mount Abora.°
Could I revive within me
Her symphony and song,
To such a deep delight 'twould win me,
That with music loud and long,   45
I would build that dome in air,
That sunny dome! those caves of ice!
And all who heard should see them there,
And all should cry, Beware! Beware!
His flashing eyes, his floating hair!   50
Weave a circle round him thrice,°
And close your eyes with holy dread,
For he on honey-dew hath fed,
And drunk the milk of Paradise.

BILLY COLLINS (1941–   )

Introduction to Poetry (1988)

I ask them to take a poem
and hold it up to the light
like a color slide

or press an ear against its hive.

I say drop a mouse into a poem   5
and watch him probe his way out,

or walk inside the poem's room
and feel the walls for a light switch.

I want them to waterski
across the surface of a poem   10
waving at the author's name on the shore.

But all they want to do
is tie the poem to a chair with rope
and torture a confession out of it.

They begin beating it with a hose   15
to find out what it really means.

° *Mount Abora:* Some scholars see a reminiscence here of John Milton's *Paradise Lost* 4.280 – 82: "where Abassin kings their issue guard / Mount Amara, though this by some supposed / True Paradise under the Ethiop Line." ° *Weave . . . thrice:* A magic ritual to keep away intruding spirits.

BILLY COLLINS (1941–)

The Names* (2002)

Yesterday, I lay awake in the palm of the night.
A fine rain stole in, unhelped by any breeze,
And when I saw the silver glaze on the windows,
I started with A, with Ackerman, as it happened,
Then Baxter and Calabro,   5
Davis and Eberling, names falling into place
As droplets fell through the dark.

Names printed on the ceiling of the night.
Names slipping around a watery bend.
Twenty-six willows on the banks of a stream.   10

In the morning, I walked out barefoot
Among thousands of flowers
Heavy with dew like the eyes of tears,
And each had a name—
Fiori inscribed on a yellow petal   15
Then Gonzalez and Han, Ishikawa and Jenkins.

Names written in the air
And stitched into the cloth of the day.
A name under a photograph taped to a mailbox.
Monogram on a torn shirt,   20
I see you spelled out on storefront windows
And on the bright unfurled awnings of this city.
I say the syllables as I turn a corner—
Kelly and Lee,
Medina, Nardella, and O'Connor.   25

When I peer into the woods,
I see a thick tangle where letters are hidden
As in a puzzle concocted for children.
Parker and Quigley in the twigs of an ash,
Rizzo, Schubert, Torres, and Upton,   30
Secrets in the boughs of an ancient maple.

Names written in the pale sky.
Names rising in the updraft amid buildings.
Names silent in stone

---

*Billy Collins, former poet laureate of The United States, read this poem before a special joint session of Congress in New York City on September 6, 2002, in honor of the first annniversary of the terrorist attacks that took place on September 11, 2001.

Or cried out behind a door.   35
Names blown over the earth and out to sea.

In the evening — weakening light, the last swallows.
A boy on a lake lifts his oars.
A woman by a window puts a match to a candle,
And the names are outlined on the rose clouds —   40
Vanacore and Wallace,
(let X stand, if it can, for the ones unfound)
Then Young and Ziminsky, the final jolt of Z.

Names etched on the head of a pin.
One name spanning a bridge, another undergoing a tunnel.   45
A blue name needled into the skin.
Names of citizens, workers, mothers and fathers,
The bright-eyed daughter, the quick son.
Alphabet of names in green rows in a field.   50
Names in the small tracks of birds.
Names lifted from a hat
Or balanced on the tip of the tongue.
Names wheeled into the dim warehouse of memory.
So many names, there is barely room on the walls of the heart.

HART CRANE   (1899–1932)

To Brooklyn Bridge   (1926)

How many dawns, chill from his rippling rest
The seagull's wings shall dip and pivot him,
Shedding white rings of tumult, building high
Over the chained bay waters Liberty —

Then, with inviolate curve, forsake our eyes   5
As apparitional as sails that cross
Some page of figures to be filed away;
— Till elevators drop us from our day . . .

I think of cinemas, panoramic sleights
With multitudes bent toward some flashing scene   10
Never disclosed, but hastened to again,
Foretold to other eyes on the same screen;

And Thee, across the harbor, silver-paced
As though the sun took step of thee, yet left
Some motion ever unspent in thy stride, —   15
Implicitly thy freedom staying thee!

Out of some subway scuttle, cell or loft
A bedlamite speeds to thy parapets,
Tilting there momently, shrill shirt ballooning,
A jest falls from the speechless caravan.   20

Down Wall, from girder into street noon leaks,
A rip-tooth of the sky's acetylene;
All afternoon the cloud-flown derricks turn . . .
Thy cables breathe the North Atlantic still.

And obscure as that heaven of the Jews,   25
Thy guerdon . . . Accolade thou dost bestow
Of anonymity time cannot raise:
Vibrant reprieve and pardon thou dost show.

O harp and altar, of the fury fused,
(How could mere toil align thy choiring strings!)   30
Terrific threshold of the prophet's pledge,
Prayer of pariah, and the lover's cry,—

Again the traffic lights that skim thy swift
Unfractioned idiom, immaculate sigh of stars,
Beading thy path — condense eternity: 35
And we have seen night lifted in thine arms.

Under thy shadow by the piers I waited;
Only in darkness is thy shadow clear.
The City's fiery parcels all undone,
Already snow submerges an iron year . . .   40

O Sleepless as the river under thee,
Vaulting the sea, the prairies' dreaming sod,
Unto us lowliest sometime sweep, descend
And of the curveship lend a myth to God.

E. E. CUMMINGS (1894–1962)

Buffalo Bill's (1923)

Buffalo Bill's
defunct
           who used to
           ride a watersmooth-silver
                                    stallion   5
and break onetwothreefourfive pigeonsjustlikethat
                                            Jesus

he was a handsome man
                    and what i want to know is
how do you like your blueeyed boy   10
Mister Death

E. E. CUMMINGS   (1894–1962)

next to of course god america i   (1926)

"next to of course god america i
love you land of the pilgrims' and so forth oh
say can you see by the dawn's early my
country 'tis of centuries come and go
and are no more what of it we should worry   5
in every language even deafandhumb
thy sons acclaim your glorious name by gorry
by jingo by gee by gosh by gum
why talk of beauty what could be more beautiful than these heroic happy dead   10
who rushed like lions to the roaring slaughter
they did not stop to think they died instead
then shall the voice of liberty be mute?"

He spoke. And drank rapidly a glass of water

EMILY DICKINSON   (1830–1886)

After great pain, a formal feeling comes —   (1862)

After great pain, a formal feeling comes—
The Nerves sit ceremonious, like Tombs—
The stiff Heart questions was it He, that bore,
And Yesterday, or Centuries before?

The Feet, mechanical, go round—   5
Of Ground, or Air, or Ought—
A Wooden way
Regardless grown,
A Quartz contentment, like a stone—

This is the Hour of Lead—   10
Remembered, if outlived,

As Freezing persons, recollect the Snow —
First — Chill — then Stupor — then the letting go —

EMILY DICKINSON (1830 – 1886)

Because I could not stop
for Death —   (1863)

Because I could not stop for Death —
He kindly stopped for me —
The Carriage held but just Ourselves —
And Immortality.

We slowly drove — He knew no haste   5
And I had put away
My labor and my leisure too,
For His Civility —

We passed the School, where Children strove
At Recess — in the Ring —   10
We passed the Fields of Gazing Grain —
We passed the Setting Sun —

Or rather — He passed Us —
The Dews drew quivering and chill —
For only Gossamer, my Gown —   15
My Tippet° — only Tulle —

We passed before a House that seemed
A Swelling of the Ground —
The Roof was scarcely visible —
The Cornice — in the Ground —   20

Since then —'tis Centuries — and yet
Feels shorter than the Day
I first surmised the Horses' Heads
Were toward Eternity —

EMILY DICKINSON (1830 – 1886)

"Faith" is a fine invention   (1860)

"Faith" is a fine invention
When Gentlemen can *see* —
But *Microscopes* are prudent
In an Emergency.

° *Tippet:* A short cape or scarf.

EMILY DICKINSON   (1830–1886)

"Heaven"—is what I cannot reach!   (1861)

"Heaven"—is what I cannot reach!
The Apple on the Tree—
Provided it do hopeless—hang—
That —"Heaven" is — to Me!

The Color, on the Cruising Cloud—   5
The interdicted Land—
Behind the Hill — the House behind—
There — Paradise — is found!

Her teasing Purples — Afternoons—
The credulous — decoy—   10
Enamored — of the Conjuror—
That spurned us —Yesterday!

EMILY DICKINSON   (1830–1886)

I dwell in Possibility —   (1862)

I dwell in Possibility—
A fairer House than Prose—
More numerous of Windows—
Superior —for Doors—

Of Chambers as the Cedars—   5
Impregnable of Eye—
And for an Everlasting Roof
The Gambrels° of the Sky—

Of Visitors — the fairest—
For Occupation — This—   10
The spreading wide my narrow Hands
To gather Paradise—

EMILY DICKINSON   (1830–1886)

I heard a Fly buzz — when I died —   (1862)

I heard a Fly buzz — when I died—
The Stillness in the Room

° *Gambrels:* A gambrel roof; a ridged roof with two slopes on each side.

Was like the Stillness in the Air —
Between the Heaves of Storm —

The Eyes around — had wrung them dry —   5
And Breaths were gathering firm
For that last Onset — when the King
Be witnessed — in the Room —

I willed my Keepsakes — Signed away
What portion of me be   10
Assignable — and then it was
There interposed a Fly —

With Blue — uncertain stumbling Buzz —
Between the light — and me —
And then the Windows failed — and then   15
I could not see to see —

EMILY DICKINSON   (1830 – 1886)

I never saw a Moor —   (1865)

I never saw a Moor —
I never saw the Sea —
Yet know I how the Heather looks
And what a Billow be.

I never spoke with God   5
Nor visited in Heaven —
Yet certain am I of the spot
As if the Checks were given —

EMILY DICKINSON   (1830 – 1886)

I taste a liquor never brewed —   (1861)

I taste a liquor never brewed —
From Tankards scooped in Pearl —
Not all the Frankfort Berries°
Yield such an Alcohol!

Inebriate of Air — am I —   5
and Debauchee of Dew —

°*Frankfort Berries:* The 1890 Higginson and Todd edition *Poems* changed "Frankfort Berries" to "vats upon the Rhine."

Reeling — thro endless summer days —
From inns of Molten Blue —

When "Landlords" turn the drunken Bee
Out of the Foxglove's door —   10
When Butterflies — renounce their "drams" —
I shall but drink the more!

Till Seraphs swing their snowy Hats —
And Saints — to windows run —
To see the little Tippler   15
From Manzanilla come!

EMILY DICKINSON (1830 – 1886)

Much Madness is divinest Sense — (1862)

Much Madness is divinest Sense —
To a discerning Eye —
Much Sense — the starkest Madness —
'Tis the Majority
In this, as All, prevail —   5

Assent — and you are sane —
Demur — you're straightway dangerous —
And handled with a Chain —

EMILY DICKINSON (1830 – 1886)

Safe in their Alabaster Chambers — (1861)

Safe in their Alabaster Chambers —
Untouched by Morning —
And untouched by Noon —
Lie the meek members of the Resurrection —
Rafter of Satin — and Roof of Stone!   5

Grand go the Years — in the Crescent — above them —
Worlds scoop their arcs —
And Firmaments — row —
Diadems — drop — and Doges° — surrender —
Soundless as dots — on a Disc of Snow —   10

°*Doges:* Chief magistrates of Venice and Genoa.

A draft of Dickinson's poem, "Safe in their Alabaster Chambers —" written in a note to her brother's wife Sue, her most trusted friend and critic.

EMILY DICKINSON (1830–1886)

Some keep the Sabbath going to Church — (1860)

Some keep the Sabbath going to Church —
I keep it, staying at Home —
With a Bobolink for a Chorister —
And an Orchard, for a Dome —

Some keep the Sabbath in Surplice°   5
I just wear my Wings —
And instead of tolling the Bell, for Church,
Our little Sexton — sings.

God preaches, a noted Clergyman —
And the sermon is never long,   10
So instead of getting to Heaven, at last —
I'm going, all along.

EMILY DICKINSON (1830–1886)

The Soul selects her own Society — (1862)

The Soul selects her own Society —
Then — shuts the Door —
To her divine Majority —
Present no more —

Unmoved — she notes the Chariots — pausing —   5
At her low Gate —
Unmoved — an Emperor be kneeling
Upon her Mat —

I've known her — from an ample nation —
Choose One —   10
Then — close the Valves of her attention —
Like Stone —

EMILY DICKINSON (1830–1886)

Success is counted sweetest (1859)

Success is counted sweetest
By those who ne'er succeed.
To comprehend a nectar°
Requires sorest need.

° *Surplice:* A white, loose-fitting robe with broad sleeves worn by members of the clergy.   ° *Nectar:* In Greek mythology, the drink of the gods.

Not one of all the purple Host   5
Who took the Flag today
Can tell the definition
So clear of Victory

As he defeated — dying—
On whose forbidden ear   10
The distant strains of triumph
Burst agonized and clear!

EMILY DICKINSON (1830–1886)

Tell all the Truth but tell it slant — (1868)

Tell all the Truth but tell it slant—
Success in Circuit lies
Too bright for our infirm Delight
The Truth's superb surprise
As Lightning to the Children eased   5
With explanation kind
The Truth must dazzle gradually
Or every man be blind—

EMILY DICKINSON (1830–1886)

There is no Frigate like a Book (1873)

There is no Frigate like a Book
To take us Lands away
Nor any Coursers like a Page
Of prancing Poetry—
This Traverse may the poorest take   5
Without oppress of Toll—
How frugal is the Chariot
That bears the Human soul.

EMILY DICKINSON (1830–1886)

There's a certain Slant of light (c. 1861)

There's a certain Slant of light,
Winter Afternoons—
That oppresses, like the Heft
Of Cathedral Tunes—

Heavenly Hurt, it gives us—   5
We can find no scar,
But internal difference,
Where the Meanings, are—

None may teach it—Any—
'Tis the Seal Despair—   10
An imperial affliction
Sent us of the Air—

When it comes, the landscape listens—
Shadows—hold their breath—
When it goes, 'tis like the Distance   15
On the look of Death—

EMILY DICKINSON (1830–1886)

This is my letter to the World (1862)

This is my letter to the World
That never wrote to Me—
The simple News that Nature told—
With tender Majesty

Her Message is committed   5
To Hands I cannot see
For love of Her — Sweet — countrymen—
Judge tenderly — of Me

EMILY DICKINSON (1830–1886)

Wild Nights — Wild Nights! (1861)

Wild Nights —Wild Nights!
Were I with thee
Wild Nights should be
Our luxury!

Futile — the Winds—   5
To a Heart in port —
Done with the Compass—
Done with the Chart!

Rowing in Eden —
Ah, the Sea!   10
Might I but moor — Tonight—
In Thee!

JOHN DONNE (1572–1631)

Batter My Heart, Three-Personed God (c. 1610)

Batter my heart, three-personed God, for You
As yet but knock, breathe, shine, and seek to mend.
That I may rise and stand, o'erthrow me, and bend
Your force to break, blow, burn, and make me new.
I, like an usurped town to another due,   5
Labor to admit You, but Oh! to no end.
Reason, Your viceroy in me, me should defend,
But is captived, and proves weak or untrue.
Yet dearly I love You, and would be lovèd fain,
But am betrothed unto Your enemy;   10
Divorce me, untie or break that knot again;
Take me to You, imprison me, for I,
Except You enthrall me, never shall be free,
Nor ever chaste, except You ravish me.

JOHN DONNE (1572–1631)

Death Be Not Proud (c. 1610)

Death be not proud, though some have callèd thee
Mighty and dreadful, for thou art not so;
For those whom thou think'st thou dost overthrow
Die not, poor death, nor yet canst thou kill me.
From rest and sleep, which but thy pictures be,   5
Much pleasure, then from thee much more must flow,
And soonest our best men with thee do go,
Rest of their bones, and soul's delivery.
Thou art slave to fate, chance, kings, and desperate men,
And dost with poison, war, and sickness dwell,   10
And poppy, or charms can make us sleep as well,
And better than thy stroke; why swell'st thou then?
One short sleep past, we wake eternally,
And death shall be no more; death, thou shalt die.

JOHN DONNE (1572–1631)

The Flea (1633)

Mark but this flea, and mark in this°
How little that which thou deny'st me is;

°*mark in this:* Note the moral lesson in it.

It sucked me first, and now sucks thee,
And in this flea our two bloods mingled be;
Thou know'st that this cannot be said   5
A sin, nor shame, nor loss of maidenhead,
   Yet this enjoys before it woo,
   And pampered swells with one blood made of two,
   And this, alas, is more than we would do.°

Oh stay, three live sin one flea spare,   10
Where we almost, yea more than, married are.
This flea is you and I, and this
Our marriage bed, and marriage temple is;
Though parents grudge, and you, we're met
And cloistered in these living walls of jet.   15
   Though use make you apt to kill me,
   Let not to that, self-murder added be,
   And sacrilege, three sins in killing three.

Cruel and sudden, hast thou since
Purpled thy nail in blood of innocence?   20
Wherein could this flea guilty be,
Except in that drop which it sucked from thee?
Yet thou triumph'st, and say'st that thou
Find'st not thyself, nor me, the weaker now;   25
   'Tis true; then learn how false, fears be;
   Just so much honor, when thou yield'st to me,
   Will waste, as this flea's death took life from thee.

JOHN DONNE (1572–1631)

Song (1633)

Go and catch a falling star,
   Get with child a mandrake root,°
Tell me where all past years are,
   Or who cleft the Devil's foot,
Teach me to hear mermaids singing,   5
   Or to keep off envy's stinging,
      And find
      What wind
Serves to advance an honest mind.

°*more than we would do:* If we do not join our blood.   °*mandrake root:* Also called *mandragora,* the mandrake root is forked and resembles the lower part of the human body; it was thought to be an aphrodisiac.

If thou be'st borne to strange sights,   10
  Things invisible to see,
Ride ten thousand days and nights,
  Till age snow white hairs on thee,
Thou, when thou return'st, wilt tell me
  All strange wonders that befell thee,   15
    And swear
    Nowhere
Lives a woman true, and fair.

If thou findst one, let me know,
  Such a pilgrimage were sweet—   20
Yet do not, I would not go,
  Though at next door we might meet;
Though she were true, when you met her,
  And last, till you write your letter,
    Yet she   25
    Will be
False, ere I come, to two, or three.

RITA DOVE (1952–   )

Fox Trot Fridays   (2004)

Thank the stars there's a day
each week to tuck in

the grief, lift your pearls, and
stride brush stride.

quick-quick with a   5
heel-ball-toe. Smooth

as Nat King Cole's
slow satin smile,

easy as taking
one day at a time: 10

one man and
one woman,

rib to rib,
with no heartbreak in sight—

just the sweep of Paradise   15
and the space of a song

to count all the wonders in it.

PAUL LAURENCE DUNBAR (1872–1906)

We Wear the Mask (1896)

We wear the mask that grins and lies,
It hides our cheeks and shades our eyes —
This debt we pay to human guile;
With torn and bleeding hearts we smile,
And mouth with myriad subtleties.　　　　5

Why should the world be over-wise,
In counting all our tears and sighs?
Nay, let them only see us, while
　　We wear the mask.

We smile, but, O great Christ, our cries　　10
To thee from tortured souls arise.
We sing, but oh the clay is vile
Beneath our feet, and long the mile;
But let the world dream otherwise,
　　We wear the mask!　　　　15

STEPHEN DUNN (1939–　　)

Waiting with Two Members of a Motorcycle Gang for My Child to Be Born (1976)

For Andrea

I was talking to "The Eliminators"
　　when you were born,
two of them, high as slag heaps and
　　uncles to be,
all in black for the occasion.　　　　5
　　All you wanted was out;
you couldn't have known that you
　　were "Life"
when you came, or that your father
　　was let loose　　　　10
from graduate school, a believer
　　in symbols.
I expected "The Eliminators" to
　　disappear, snuffed out
by a stronger force, a white tornado　　15
　　of my own.
That's not what happens, though,
　　in life

as you will learn. They smiled when
    they heard of you   20
and shook my hand. At another time
    it might
have been my head. May you turn
    stone, my daughter,
into silk. May you make men better   25
    than they are.

T. S. ELIOT (1888–1965)

The Love Song of J. Alfred Prufrock (1917)

S'io credessi che mia risposta fosse
A persona che mai tornasse al mondo,
Questa fiamma staria senza piu scosse.
Ma perciocche giammai di questo fondo
Non torno vivo alcun, s'i'odo il vero,
Senza tema d'infamia ti rispondo.°

Let us go then, you and I,
When the evening is spread out against the sky
Like a patient etherized upon a table;
Let us go, through certain half-deserted streets,
The muttering retreats   5
Of restless nights in one-night cheap hotels
And sawdust restaurants with oyster-shells:
Streets that follow like a tedious argument
Of insidious intent
To lead you to an overwhelming question . . .   10
Oh, do not ask, "What is it?"
Let us go and make our visit.

In the room the women come and go
Talking of Michelangelo.

The yellow fog that rubs its back upon the window-panes,   15
The yellow smoke that rubs its muzzle on the window-panes
Licked its tongue into the corners of the evening,
Lingered upon the pools that stand in drains,
Let fall upon its back the soot that falls from chimneys,
Slipped by the terrace, made a sudden leap,   20

° *S'io . . . rispondo:* The epigraph is from Dante's *Inferno,* Canto 27. In response to the poet's question about his identity, Guido da Montefelto, who for his sin of fraud must spend eternity wrapped in flames, replies: "If I thought that I was speaking to someone who could go back to the world, this flame would shake me no more. But since from this place nobody ever returns alive, if what I hear is true, I answer you without fear of infamy."

And seeing that it was a soft October night,
Curled once about the house, and fell asleep.

And indeed there will be time
For the yellow smoke that slides along the street,
Rubbing its back upon the window-panes;   25
There will be time, there will be time
To prepare a face to meet the faces that you meet;
There will be time to murder and create,
And time for all the works and days° of hands
That lift and drop a question on your plate;   30
Time for you and time for me,
And time yet for a hundred indecisions,
And for a hundred visions and revisions,
Before the taking of a toast and tea.

In the room the women come and go   35
Talking of Michelangelo.

And indeed there will be time
To wonder, "Do I dare?" and, "Do I dare?"
Time to turn back and descend the stair,
With a bald spot in the middle of my hair—   40
(They will say: "How his hair is growing thin!")
My morning coat, my collar mounting firmly to the chin,
My necktie rich and modest, but asserted by a simple pin—
(They will say: "But how his arms and legs are thin!")
Do I dare   45
Disturb the universe?
In a minute there is time
For decisions and revisions which a minute will reverse.

For I have known them all already, known them all—
Have known the evenings, mornings, afternoons,   50
I have measured out my life with coffee spoons;
I know the voices dying with a dying fall°
Beneath the music from a farther room.
    So how should I presume?

And I have known the eyes already, known them all—   55
The eyes that fix you in a formulated phrase,
And when I am formulated, sprawling on a pin,
When I am pinned and wriggling on the wall,
Then how should I begin

°*works and days: Works and Days,* by the eighth-century B.C. Greek poet Hesiod, is a poem that celebrates farm life.   °*dying fall:* An allusion to Orsino's speech in *Twelfth Night* (1.1): "That strain again! It had a dying fall."

To spit out all the butt-ends of my days and ways?   60
    And how should I presume?

And I have known the arms already, known them all—
Arms that are braceleted and white and bare
(But in the lamplight, downed with light brown hair!)
Is it perfume from a dress   65
That makes me so digress?
Arms that lie along a table, or wrap about a shawl.
    And should I then presume?
    And how should I begin?

                    * * *

Shall I say, I have gone at dusk through narrow streets   70
And watched the smoke that rises from the pipes
Of lonely men in shirt-sleeves, leaning out of windows? . . .

I should have been a pair of ragged claws
Scuttling across the floors of silent seas.

                    * * *

And the afternoon, the evening, sleeps so peacefully!   75
Smoothed by long fingers,
Asleep . . . tired . . . or it malingers,
Stretched on the floor, here beside you and me.
Should I, after tea and cakes and ices,
Have the strength to force the moment to its crisis?   80
But though I have wept and fasted, wept and prayed,
Though I have seen my head (grown slightly bald) brought in
    upon a platter,°
I am no prophet — and here's no great matter;
I have seen the moment of my greatness flicker,
And I have seen the eternal Footman° hold my coat, and   85
    snicker,
And in short, I was afraid.

And would it have been worth it, after all,
After the cups, the marmalade, the tea,
Among the porcelain, among some talk of you and me,
Would it have been worth while,   90
To have bitten off the matter with a smile,
To have squeezed the universe into a ball

°*head . . . platter:* Like John the Baptist, who was beheaded by King Herod (see Matthew 14.3–11).   °*eternal Footman:* Perhaps death or fate.

To roll it toward some overwhelming question,
To say: "I am Lazarus,° come from the dead,
Come back to tell you all, I shall tell you all"—   95
If one, settling a pillow by her head,
    Should say: "That is not what I meant at all.
    That is not it, at all."

And would it have been worth it, after all,
Would it have been worth while,   100
After the sunsets and the dooryards and the sprinkled streets,
After the novels, after the teacups, after the skirts that trail
    along the floor—
And this, and so much more?—
It is impossible to say just what I mean!
But as if a magic lantern threw the nerves in patterns on a   105
    screen:
Would it have been worth while
If one, settling a pillow or throwing off a shawl,
And turning toward the window, should say:
    "That is not it at all,
    That is not what I meant, at all."   110

* * *

No! I am not Prince Hamlet, nor was meant to be;
Am an attendant lord, one that will do
To swell a progress,° start a scene or two,
Advise the prince; no doubt, an easy tool,
Deferential, glad to be of use,   115
Politic, cautious, and meticulous;
Full of high sentence,° but a bit obtuse;
At times, indeed, almost ridiculous—
Almost, at times, the Fool.

I grow old . . . I grow old . . .   120
I shall wear the bottoms of my trousers rolled.

Shall I part my hair behind? Do I dare to eat a peach?
I shall wear white flannel trousers, and walk upon the beach.
I have heard the mermaids singing, each to each.

I do not think that they will sing to me.   125

°*Lazarus:* A man whom Christ raised from the dead (see John 11.1–44).   °*a progress:* Here, in the Elizabethan sense of a royal journey.   °*sentence:* Opinions.

I have seen them riding seaward on the waves
Combing the white hair of the waves blown back
When the wind blows the water white and black.

We have lingered in the chambers of the sea
By sea-girls wreathed with seaweed red and brown   130
Till human voices wake us, and we drown.

JAMES A. EMANUEL (1921–   )

Emmett Till° (1968)

I hear a whistling
Through the water.
Little Emmett
Won't be still.
He keeps floating   5
Round the darkness,
Edging through
The silent chill.
Tell me, please,
That bedtime story   10
Of the fairy
River Boy
Who swims forever,
Deep in treasures,
Necklaced in   15
A coral toy.

LOUISE ERDRICH (1954–   )

Indian Boarding School: The Runaways (1984)

Home's the place we head for in our sleep.
Boxcars stumbling north in dreams
don't wait for us. We catch them on the run.
The rails, old lacerations that we love,

°*Emmett Till:* Emmett Till, a fourteen year-old African-American from Chicago, was visiting relatives in Mississippi when he allegedly whistled at a white woman who ran a local store. Unfamiliar with the racial climate of the South, he did not realize that his actions would generate a savage response. Several days later, he was kidnapped, and his severely beaten and mutilated body was later found in the river with a heavy cotton gin fan tied around his neck with barbed wire. His death prompted a new chapter in the Civil Rights struggle; the investigation into his murder was reopened in 2004.

shoot parallel across the face and break   5
just under Turtle Mountains.° Riding scars
you can't get lost. Home is the place they cross.

The lame guard strikes a match and makes the dark
less tolerant. We watch through cracks in boards
as the land starts rolling, rolling till it hurts   10
to be here, cold in regulation clothes.
We know the sheriff's waiting at midrun
to take us back. His car is dumb and warm.
The highway doesn't rock, it only hums
like a wing of long insults. The worn-down welts   15
of ancient punishments lead back and forth.

All runaways wear dresses, long green ones,
the color you would think shame was. We scrub
the sidewalks down because it's shameful work.
Our brushes cut the stone in watered arcs   20
and in the soak frail outlines shiver clear
a moment, things us kids pressed on the dark
face before it hardened, pale, remembering
delicate old injuries, the spines of names and leaves.

ROBERT FROST   (1874–1963)

Acquainted with the Night   (1928)

I have been one acquainted with the night.
I have walked out in rain — and back in rain.
I have outwalked the furthest city light.

I have looked down the saddest city lane.
I have passed by the watchman on his beat   5
And dropped my eyes, unwilling to explain.

I have stood still and stopped the sound of feet
When far away an interrupted cry
Came over houses from another street,

But not to call me back or say good-by;   10
And further still at an unearthly height,
One luminary clock against the sky

Proclaimed the time was neither wrong nor right.
I have been one acquainted with the night.

° *Turtle Mountains:* Erdrich is a descendant of the Turtle Mountain band of the Chippewa.

ROBERT FROST   (1874–1963)

Desert Places   (1936)

Snow falling and night falling fast, oh, fast
In a field I looked into going past,
And the ground almost covered smooth in snow,
But a few weeds and stubble showing last.

The woods around it have it — it is theirs.   5
All animals are smothered in their lairs,
I am too absent-spirited to count;
The loneliness includes me unawares.

And lonely as it is, that loneliness
Will be more lonely ere it will be less —   10
A blanker whiteness of benighted snow
With no expression, nothing to express.

They cannot scare me with their empty spaces
Between stars — on stars where no human race is.
I have it in me so much nearer home   15
To scare myself with my own desert places.

ROBERT FROST   (1874–1963)

Design   (1936)

I found a dimpled spider, fat and white,
On a white heal-all,° holding up a moth
Like a white piece of rigid satin cloth —
Assorted characters of death and blight
Mixed ready to begin to morning right,   5
Like the ingredients of a witches' broth —
A snow-drop spider, a flower like a froth,
And dead wings carried like a paper kite.

What had the flower to do with being white,
The wayside blue and innocent heal-all?   10
What brought the kindred spider to that height,
Then steered the white moth thither in the night?
What but design of darkness to appall? —
If design govern in a thing so small.

°*Heal-all:* A perennial weed with flowers ranging from light blue to purple in color.

ROBERT FROST (1874–1963)

Mending Wall (1914)

Something there is that doesn't love a wall,
That sends the frozen-ground-swell under it,
And spills the upper boulders in the sun;
And makes gaps even two can pass abreast.
The work of hunters is another thing: 5
I have come after them and made repair
Where they have left not one stone on a stone,
But they would have the rabbit out of hiding,
To please the yelping dogs. The gaps I mean,
No one has seen them made or heard them made,   10
But at spring mending-time we find them there.
I let my neighbor know beyond the hill;
And on a day we meet to walk the line
And set the wall between us once again.
We keep the wall between us as we go.   15
To each the boulders that have fallen to each.
And some are loaves and some so nearly balls
We have to use a spell to make them balance:
"Stay where you are until our backs are turned!"
We wear our fingers rough with handling them.   20
Oh, just another kind of outdoor game,
One on a side. It comes to little more:
There where it is we do not need the wall:
He is all pine and I am apple orchard.
My apple trees will never get across   25
And eat the cones under his pines, I tell him.
He only says, "Good fences make good neighbors."
Spring is the mischief in me, and I wonder
If I could put a notion in his head:
"*Why* do they make good neighbors? Isn't it   30
Where there are cows? But here there are no cows.
Before I built a wall I'd ask to know
What I was walling in or walling out,
And to whom I was like to give offense.
Something there is that doesn't love a wall,   35
That wants it down." I could say "Elves" to him,
But it's not elves exactly, and I'd rather
He said it for himself. I see him there
Bringing a stone grasped firmly by the top
In each hand, like an old-stone savage armed.   40
He moves in darkness as it seems to me,

Not of woods only and the shade of trees.
He will not go behind his father's saying,
And he likes having thought of it so well
He says again, "Good fences make good neighbors."   **45**

ROBERT FROST   (1874–1963)

The Road Not Taken   (1915)

Two roads diverged in a yellow wood,
And sorry I could not travel both
And be one traveler, long I stood
And looked down one as far as I could
To where it bent in the undergrowth;   **5**

Then took the other, as just as fair,
And having perhaps the better claim,
Because it was grassy and wanted wear;
Though as for that the passing there
Had worn them really about the same,   **10**

And both that morning equally lay
In leaves no step had trodden black.
Oh, I kept the first for another day!
Yet knowing how way leads on to way,
I doubted if I should ever come back.   **15**

I shall be telling this with a sigh
Somewhere ages and ages hence:
Two roads diverged in a wood, and I—
I took the one less traveled by,
And that has made all the difference.   **20**

ROBERT FROST   (1874–1963)

Stopping by Woods on a Snowy Evening   (1923)

Whose woods these are I think I know.
His house is in the village though;
He will not see me stopping here
To watch his woods fill up with snow.

My little horse must think it queer   **5**
To stop without a farmhouse near
Between the woods and frozen lake
The darkest evening of the year.

He gives his harness bells a shake
To ask if there is some mistake.   10
The only other sound's the sweep
Of easy wind and downy flake.

The woods are lovely, dark and deep,
But I have promises to keep,
And miles to go before I sleep,   15
And miles to go before I sleep.

FEDERICO GARCÍA LORCA   (1898–1936)

Arbolé,° Arbolé . . .   (1955)

Translated by William Logan

Tree, tree
dry and green.

The girl with the pretty face
is out picking olives.
The wind, playboy of towers,   5
grabs her around the waist.
Four riders passed by
on Andalusian ponies,
with blue and green jackets
and big, dark capes.   10
"Come to Cordoba, muchacha."
The girl won't listen to them.
Three young bullfighters passed,
slender in the waist,
with jackets the color of oranges   15
and swords of ancient silver.
"Come to Sevilla, muchacha."
The girl won't listen to them.
When the afternoon had turned
dark brown, with scattered light,   20
a young man passed by, wearing
roses and myrtle of the moon.
"Come to Granada, muchacha."
And the girl won't listen to him.
The girl with the pretty face   25
keeps on picking olives
with the grey arm of the wind

°*Arbolé:* tree.

wrapped around her waist.
Tree, tree
dry and green.   30

Arbolé, arbolé,
seco y verdí.

La niña del bello rostro
está cogiendo aceituna.
El viento, galán de torres,   5
la prende por la cintura.
Pasaron cuatro jinetes
sobre jacas andaluzas,
con trajes de azul y verde,
con largas capas oscuras.   10
"Vente a Córdoba, muchacha."
La niña no los escucha.
Pasaron tres torerillos
delgaditos de cintura,
con trajes color naranja   15
y espadas de plata antigua.
"Vente a Córdoba, muchacha."
La niña no los escucha.
Cuando la tarde se puso
morada, con lux difusa,   20
pasó un joven que llevaba
rosas y mirtos de luna.
"Vente a Granada, muchacha."
Y la niña no lo escucha.
La niña del bello rostro   25
sigue cogiendo aceituna,
con el brazo gris del viento
ceñido por la cintura.
Arbolé, arbolé.
Seco y verdé.   30

NIKKI GIOVANNI (1943–   )

Nikki-Rosa (1968)

childhood remembrances are always a drag
if you're Black
you always remember things like living in Woodlawn°

° *Woodlawn:* A predominantly black suburb of Cincinnati, Ohio.

with no inside toilet
and if you become famous or something   5
they never talk about how happy you were to have your mother
all to yourself and
how good the water felt when you got your bath from one of those
big tubs that folk in chicago barbecue in
and somehow when you talk about home   10
it never gets across how much you
understood their feelings
as the whole family attended meetings about Hollydale
and even though you remember
your biographers never understand   15
your father's pain as he sells his stock
and another dream goes
and though you're poor it isn't poverty that
concerns you
and though they fought a lot   20
it isn't your father's drinking that makes any difference
but only that everybody is together and you
and your sister have happy birthdays and very good christmasses
and I really hope no white person ever has cause to write
    about me
because they never understand Black love is Black wealth and
    they'll   25
probably talk about my hard childhood and never understand that
all the while I was quite happy

H.D. (HILDA DOOLITTLE)   (1886–1961)

Helen°   (1924)

All Greece hates
the still eyes in the white face,
the lustre as of olives
where she stands,
and the white hands.   5

All Greece reviles
the wan face when she smiles,
hating it deeper still

° *Helen:* In Greek mythology, Helen was the most beautiful of all women. She was the daughter of the Greek god Zeus and the mortal Leda. After a decade or so of marriage to Menelaus, the King of Sparta, Helen was abducted by Paris, the son of King Priam of Troy. Menelaus enlisted an army to recapture her in what would become known as the Trojan War, a portion of which is recounted in Homer's epic poem *The Iliad*.

when it grows wan and white,
remembering past enchantments   10
and past ills.

Greece sees unmoved,
God's daughter, born of love,
the beauty of cool feet
and slenderest knees,   15
could love indeed the maid,
only if she were laid,
white ash amid funereal cypresses.

THOMAS HARDY (1840–1928)

The Convergence of the Twain (1912)

(Lines on the loss of the 'Titanic')

I

In a solitude of the sea
Deep from human vanity,
And the Pride of Life that planned her, stilly couches she.

II

Steel chambers, late the pyres°
Of her salamandrine fires,°   5
Cold currents thrid,° and turn to rhythmic tidal lyres.

III

Over the mirrors meant
To glass the opulent
The sea-worm crawls — grotesque, slimed, dumb, indifferent.

IV

Jewels in joy designed   10
To ravish the sensuous mind
Lie lightless, all their sparkles bleared and black and blind.

V

Dim moon-eyed fishes near
Gaze at the gilded gear
And query: "What does this vaingloriousness down here?" . . .   15

°*pyres:* Funeral pyres; piles of wood on which corpses were burned in ancient rites.   °*salamandrine fires:* An
allusion to the old belief that salamanders could live in fire.   °*thrid:* Thread (archaic verb form).

VI

Well: while was fashioning
This creature of cleaving wing,
The Immanent° Will that stirs and urges everything

VII

Prepared a sinister mate
For her — so gaily great —   20
A Shape of Ice, for the time far and dissociate.

VIII

And as the smart ship grew
In stature, grace, and hue,
In shadowy silent distance grew the Iceberg too.

IX

Alien they seemed to be: 25
No mortal eye could see
The intimate welding of their later history,

X

Or sign that they were bent
By paths coincident
On being anon° twin halves of one august° event,   30

XI

Till the Spinner of the Years
Said "Now!" And each one hears,
And consummation comes, and jars two hemispheres.

SEAMUS HEANEY (1939–   )

Mid-Term Break (1966)

I sat all morning in the college sick bay
Counting bells knelling classes to a close.
At two o'clock our neighbors drove me home.

In the porch I met my father crying —
He had always taken funerals in his stride —   5
And Big Jim Evans saying it was a hard blow.

°*Immanent:* Inherent, dwelling within.   °*anon:* Soon.   °*august:* Awe-inspiring, majestic.

The baby cooed and laughed and rocked the pram
When I came in, and I was embarrassed
By old men standing up to shake my hand

And tell me they were "sorry for my trouble,"   10
Whispers informed strangers I was the eldest,
Away at school, as my mother held my hand

In hers and coughed out angry tearless sighs.
At ten o'clock the ambulance arrived
With the corpse, stanched and bandaged by the nurses.   15

Next morning I went up into the room. Snowdrops
And candles soothed the bedside; I saw him
For the first time in six weeks. Paler now,

Wearing a poppy bruise on his left temple,
He lay in the four foot box as in his cot.   20
No gaudy scars, the bumper knocked him clear.

A four foot box, a foot for every year.

EDWARD HIRSCH (1950 –   )

Fast Break   (1990)

In Memory of Dennis Turner, 1946–1984

A hook shot kisses the rim and
hangs there, helplessly, but doesn't drop,

and for once our gangly starting center
boxes out his man and times his jump.

perfectly, gathering the orange leather   5
from the air like a cherished possession

and spinning around to throw a strike
to the outlet who is already shoveling

an underhand pass toward the other guard
scissoring past a flat-footed defender   10

who looks stunned and nailed to the floor
in the wrong direction, trying to catch sight

of a high, gliding dribble and a man
letting the play develop in front of him

in slow motion, almost exactly   15
like a coach's drawing on the blackboard,

both forwards racing down the court
the way that forwards should, fanning out

and filling the lanes in tandem, moving
together as brothers passing the ball   20

between them without a dribble, without
a single bounce hitting the hardwood

until the guard finally lunges out
and commits to the wrong man

while the power-forward explodes past them   25
in a fury, taking the ball into the air

by himself now and laying it gently
against the glass for a lay-up,

but losing his balance in the process,
inexplicably falling, hitting the floor   30

with a wild, headlong motion
for the game he loved like a country

and swiveling back to see an orange blur
floating perfectly though the net.

GARRETT KAORU HONGO   (1951–   )

And Your Soul Shall Dance* (1976)

for Wakako Yamauchi

Walking to school beside fields
of tomatoes and summer squash,
alone and humming a Japanese love song,
you've concealed copy of *Photoplay*
between your algebra and English texts.   5
Your knee socks, saddle shoes, plaid dress,
and blouse, long-sleeved and white
with ruffles down the front,
come from a Sears catalogue
and neatly complement your new Toni curls.   10
All of this sets you apart from the landscape:
flat valley grooved with irrigation ditches,

---

*The title is based on *And the Soul Shall Dance*, a play by Wakako Yamauchi about two first-generation immigrant Japanese families struggling to make ends meet from crop to crop during the Great Depression.

a tractor grinding through alkaline earth,
the short stands of windbreak eucalyptus
shuttering the desert wind   15
from a small cluster of wooden shacks
where your mother hangs the wash.
You want to go somewhere.
Somewhere far away from all the dust
and sorting machines and acres of lettuce.   20
Someplace where you might be kissed
by someone with smooth, artistic hands.
When you turn into the schoolyard,
the flagpole gleams like a knife blade in the sun,
and classmates scatter like chickens,   25
shooed by the storm brooding on your horizon.

GERARD MANLEY HOPKINS   (1844–1889)

God's Grandeur   (1877)

The world is charged with the grandeur of God.
    It will flame out, like shining from shook foil;
    It gathers to a greatness, like the ooze of oil
Crushed. Why do men then now not reck his rod?
Generations have trod, have trod, have trod;   5
    And all is seared with trade; bleared, smeared with toil;
    And wears man's smudge and shares man's smell: the soil
Is bare now, nor can foot feel, being shod.
And for all this, nature is never spent;
    There lives the dearest freshness deep down things;   10
And though the last lights off the black West went
    Oh, morning, at the brown brink eastward, springs—
Because the Holy Ghost over the bent
    World broods with warm breast and with ah! bright wings.

HA JIN   (1956–   )

Ways of Talking   (1994)

We used to like talking about grief
Our journals and letters were packed
with losses, complaints, and sorrows.

Even if there was no grief
we wouldn't stop lamenting   5
as though longing for the charm
of a distressed face.

Then we couldn't help expressing grief
So many things descended without warning:
labor wasted, loves lost, houses gone,   10
marriages broken, friends estranged,
ambitions worn away by immediate needs.
Words lined up in our throats
for a good whining.
Grief seemed like an endless river—   15
the only immortal flow of life.

After losing a land and then giving up a tongue,
we stopped talking of grief
Smiles began to brighten our faces.
We laugh a lot, at our own mess.   20
Things become beautiful,
even hailstones in the strawberry fields.

DONALD JUSTICE (1925–   )

On the Death of Friends in Childhood (1960)

We shall not ever meet them bearded in heaven;
Nor sunning themselves among the bald of hell;
If anywhere, in the deserted schoolyard at twilight,
Forming a ring, perhaps, or joining hands
In games whose very names we have forgotten.   5
Come, memory, let us seek them there in the shadows.

MARY KARR (1965–   )

A Blessing from My Sixteen Years' Son (2004)

I have this son who assembled inside me
during Hurricane Gloria. In a flash, he appeared,
in a heartbeat. Outside, pines toppled.

Phone lines snapped and hissed like cobras.
Inside, he was a raw pearl: microscopic, luminous.   5
Look at the muscled obelisk of him now

pawing through the icebox for more grapes.
Sixteen years and not a bone broken,
not a single stitch. By his age,

I was marked more ways, and small.   10
He's a slouching six foot three,
with implausible blue eyes, which settle

on the pages of Emerson's "Self-Reliance"
with profound belligerence.
A girl with a navel ring   15

could make his cell phone go *brr,*
or an Afro'd boy leaning on a mop at Taco Bell—
creatures strange as dragons or eels.

Balanced on a kitchen stool, each gives counsel
arcane as any oracle's. Bruce claims school   20
is harshing my mellow. Case longs to date

a tattooed girl, because he wants a woman
willing to do stuff she'll regret.
They've come to lead my son

into his broadening spiral.   25
Someday soon, the tether
will snap. I birthed my own mom

into oblivion. The night my son smashed
the car fender, then rode home
in the rain-streaked cop car, he asked, *Did you*   30

and Dad screw up so much?
He'd let me tuck him in,
my grandmother's wedding quilt

from 1912 drawn to his goateed chin. *Don't
blame us,* I said. *You're your own
idiot now.* At which he grinned.

The cop said the girl in the crimped Chevy
took it hard. He'd found my son
awkwardly holding her in the canted headlights,

where he'd draped his own coat   40
over her shaking shoulders. *My fault,*
he'd confessed right off.

Nice kid, said the cop.

JOHN KEATS (1795–1821)

La Belle Dame sans Merci: A Ballad° (1819, 1820)

1

O what can ail thee, knight at arms,
    Alone and palely loitering?
The sedge has wither'd from the lake,
    And no birds sing.

2

O what can ail thee, knight at arms,   5
    So haggard and so woe-begone?
The squirrel's granary is full,
    And the harvest's done.

3

I see a lily on thy brow
    With anguish moist and fever dew,   10
And on thy cheeks a fading rose
    Fast withereth too.

4

I met a lady in the meads,
    Full beautiful, a fairy's child;
Her hair was long, her foot was light,   15
    And her eyes were wild.

5

I made a garland for her head,
    And bracelets too, and fragrant zone;°
She look'd at me as she did love,
    And made sweet moan.   20

6

I set her on my pacing steed,
    And nothing else saw all day long,
For sidelong would she bend, and sing
    A fairy's song.

7

She found me roots of relish sweet,   25
    And honey wild, and manna dew,

° *"La Belle Dame sans Merci"*: The title, which means "The Lovely Lady without Pity," was taken from a medieval poem by Alain Chartier.   ° *fragrant zone*: Belt.

And sure in language strange she said—
    I love thee true.

8

She took me to her elfin grot,°
    And there she wept, and sigh'd full sore,   30
And there I shut her wild wild eyes
    With kisses four.

9

And there she lullèd me asleep,
    And there I dream'd — Ah! woe betide!
The latest° dream I ever dream'd   35
    On the cold hill's side.

10

I saw pale kings, and princes too,
    Pale warriors, death pale were they all;
They cried —"La belle dame sans merci
    Hath thee in thrall!"   40

11

I saw their starv'd lips in the gloom°
    With horrid warning gapèd wide,
And I awoke and found me here
    On the cold hill's side.

12

And this is why I sojourn here,
    Alone and palely loitering,   45
Though the sedge is wither'd from the lake,
    And no birds sing.

JOHN KEATS (1795–1821)

Bright Star! Would I Were Steadfast as Thou Art (1819)

Bright star! would I were steadfast as thou art—
    Not in lone splendor hung aloft the night,
And watching, with eternal lids apart,
    Like nature's patient, sleepless Eremite°
The moving waters at their priest-like task   5
    Of pure ablution° round earth's human shores,

°*grot:* Grotto. °*latest:* Last. °*gloam:* Twilight. °*Eremite:* Hermit, religious recluse. °*ablution:* Washing, cleansing.

Or gazing on the new soft-fallen mask
    Of snow upon the mountains and the moors—
No—yet still steadfast, still unchangeable,
    Pillowed upon my fair love's ripening breast,   10
To feel for ever its soft fall and swell,
    Awake for ever in a sweet unrest,
Still, still to hear her tender-taken breath,
And so live ever—or else swoon to death.

JOHN KEATS (1795–1821)

Ode on a Grecian Urn (1819)

1

Thou still unravish'd bride of quietness,
    Thou foster-child of silence and slow time,
Sylvan° historian, who canst thus express
A flowery tale more sweetly than our rhyme:
What leaf-fring'd legend haunts about thy shape   5
    Of deities or mortals, or of both,
        In Tempe° or the dales of Arcady?°
    What men or gods are these? What maidens loth?
What mad pursuit? What struggle to escape?
        What pipes and timbrels? What wild ecstasy?   10

2

Heard melodies are sweet, but those unheard
    Are sweeter; therefore, ye soft pipes, play on;
Not to the sensual ear, but, more endear'd,
    Pipe to the spirit ditties of no tone:
Fair youth, beneath the trees, thou canst not leave   15
    Thy song, nor ever can those trees be bare;
        Bold lover, never, never canst thou kiss,
Though winning near the goal—yet, do not grieve;
        She cannot fade, though thou hast not thy bliss,
    For ever wilt thou love, and she be fair!   20

3

Ah, happy, happy boughs! that cannot shed
    Your leaves, nor ever bid the spring adieu;

°*Sylvan:* Pertaining to woods or forests.   °*Tempe:* A beautiful valley in Greece.   °*Arcady:* The valleys of Arcadia, a mountainous region on the Greek peninsula. Like Tempe, they represent a rustic pastoral ideal.

And, happy melodist, unwearied,
 For ever piping songs for ever new;
More happy love! more happy, happy love!   25
 For ever warm and still to be enjoy'd,
  For ever panting, and for ever young;
All breathing human passion far above,
 That leaves a heart high-sorrowful and cloy'd,
  A burning forehead, and a parching tongue. 30

4

Who are these coming to the sacrifice?
 To what green altar, O mysterious priest,
Lead'st thou that heifer lowing at the skies,
 And all her silken flanks with garlands drest?
What little town by river or sea shore,   35
 Or mountain-built with peaceful citadel,
  Is emptied of this folk, this pious morn?
And, little town, thy streets for evermore
 Will silent be; and not a soul to tell
  Why thou art desolate, can e'er return. 40

5

O Attic° shape! Fair attitude! with brede°
 Of marble men and maidens overwrought,°
With forest branches and the trodden weed;
 Thou, silent form, dost tease us out of thought
As doth eternity: Cold Pastoral!   45
 When old age shall this generation waste,
  Thou shalt remain, in midst of other woe
Than ours, a friend to man, to whom thou say'st,
"Beauty is truth, truth beauty,"— that is all
 Ye know on earth, and all ye need to know. 50

JOHN KEATS   (1795–1821)

When I Have Fears   (1818)

When I have fears that I may cease to be
 Before my pen has gleaned my teeming brain,
Before high-piléd books, in charact'ry,°

° *Attic:* Characteristic of Athens or Athenians. ° *brede:* Braid. ° *overwrought:* Elaborately ornamented.
° *charact'ry:* Print.

    Hold like rich garners the full-ripened grain;
When I behold, upon the night's starred face,   5
    Huge cloudy symbols of a high romance,
And think that I may never live to trace
    Their shadows, with the magic hand of chance;
And when I feel, fair creature of an hour,
    That I shall never look upon thee more,   10
Never have relish in the faery power
    Of unreflecting love! — then on the shore
Of the wide world I stand alone, and think
Till Love and Fame to nothingness do sink.

ARON KEESBURY (1971–   )

On the Robbery across the Street (1998)

(An eyewitness to the Brinks heist)°

I tell them, look. Sure, I was around.
The tenant from four
come down to the store
that night to see can he get a cat.

Tony or Jimmy, his name is.   5
Henry maybe. Mike? Joe?
Maybe Jimmy. Look, I don't know
but he's a nice boy anyway. Wears specs,

you know. He come down
asks me, says can I get a cat   10
upstairs? I says sure. Keep that
sandy crap out of the drains, though —

clogs them all up, you know.
Then I got to get all new pipes.
So he runs upstairs. He's all hyped   15
up like I ain't seen the cat he's got

already. Maybe two,
three weeks he's got a cat up there.
These kids. Jazzing all around, I swear,
think they can get away with murder.   20

° *Brinks heist:* A 1950 robbery of a Brinks armored car station in Boston, Massachusetts, and the subject of the 1978 movie *The Brinks Job.*

But he's a nice boy and I tell the cops,
I say, look. I been in this store here
for thirty-seven years.
Thirty-seven years in this store.

I tell them sure. I say, look.   25
I was here, I was around
that night. I been in this town
thirty-seven years.
And I don't see nothing.

YUSEF KOMUNYAKAA   (1947–   )

Ignis Fatuus°   (2004)

Something or someone. A feeling
among a swish of reeds. A swampy
glow haloes the Spanish moss,
& there's a swaying at the edge
like a child's memory of abuse   5
growing flesh, living on what
a screech owl recalls. Nothing
but a presence that fills up
the mind, a replenished body
singing its way into doubletalk.   10
In the city, *Will o' the Wisp*
floats out of Miles' trumpet,
leaning ghosts against nighttime's
backdrop of neon. A foolish fire
can also start this way: before   15
you slide the key into the lock
& half-turn the knob, you know
someone has snuck into your life.
A high window, a corner of sky
spies on upturned drawers of underwear   20
& unanswered letters, on a tin box
of luminous buttons & subway tokens,
on books, magazines, & clothes
flung to studio's floor,
his sweat lingering in the air.   25

°*Ignis Fatuus:* A phosphorescent light that hovers or flits over swampy ground at night, possibly caused by
spontaneous combustion of gases emitted by rotting organic matter. It is also called *friar's lantern, jack-o'-
lantern,* or *will-o'-the-wisp,* and has come to mean something that misleads or deludes; an illusion.

Years ago, you followed someone
here, in love with breath
kissing the nape of your neck,
back when it was easy to be
at least two places at once.   30

TED KOOSER (1939–   )

In the Hall of Bones   (2002)

Here we store the reassembled
scaffolding, the split, bleached uprights,
the knobby corner locks and braces
that held up the mastodon's
bag of wet leaves and the ivory   5
forklift of its head. Over there are
the planks upon which lay the turtle's
diving bell, and the articulated
rack that kept the dromedary's hump
from collapsing under the weight   10
of its perseverance. And here is
the basket that held the clip-clop
pulse of the miniature horse
as it dreamed of growing tall enough
to have lunch from a tree. And then   15
here's man, all matchsticks, wooden spoons
and tongue depressors wired together,
a rack supporting a leaky jug
of lust and worry. Of all the skeletons
assembled here, this is the only one
in which once throbbed a heart   20
made sad by brooding on its shadow.

TED KOOSER (1939–   )

Selecting a Reader   (1980)

First, I would have her be beautiful,
and walking carefully up on my poetry
at the loneliest moment of an afternoon,
her hair still damp at the neck
from washing it. She should be wearing   5
a raincoat, an old one, dirty

from not having money enough for the cleaners.
She will take out her glasses, and there
in the bookstore, she will thumb
over my poems, then put the book back   10
up on its shelf. She will say to herself,
"For that kind of money, I can get
my raincoat cleaned." And she will.

PHILIP LARKIN (1922–1985)

Aubade (1977)

I work all day, and get half-drunk at night.
Waking at four to soundless dark, I stare.
In time the curtain-edges will grow light.
Till then I see what's really always there:
Unresting death, a whole day nearer now,   5
Making all thought impossible but how
And where and when I shall myself die.
Arid interrogation: yet the dread
Of dying, and being dead,
Flashes afresh to hold and horrify.   10

The mind blanks at the glare. Not in remorse
— The good not done, the love not given, time
Torn off unused — nor wretchedly because
An only life can take so long to climb
Clear of its wrong beginnings, and may never;   15
But at the total emptiness for ever,
The sure extinction that we travel to
And shall be lost in always. Not to be here,
Not to be anywhere,
And soon; nothing more terrible, nothing more true. 20

This is a special way of being afraid
No trick dispels. Religion used to try,
That vast moth-eaten musical brocade
Created to pretend we never die,
And specious stuff that says *No rational being*   25
Can fear a thing it will not feel, not seeing
That this is what we fear—no sight, no sound,
No touch or taste or smell, nothing to think with,
Nothing to love or link with,
The anaesthetic from which none come round.   30

And so it stays just on the edge of vision,
A small unfocused blur, a standing chill

That slows each impulse down to indecision.
Most things may never happen: this one will,
And realization of it rages out   35
In furnace-fear when we are caught without
People or drink. Courage is no good:
It means not scaring others. Being brave
Lets no one off the grave.
Death is no different whined at than withstood.   40

Slowly light strengthens, and the room takes shape.
It stands plain as a wardrobe, what we know,
Have always known, know that we can't escape,
Yet can't accept. One side will have to go.
Meanwhile telephones crouch, getting ready to ring   45
In locked-up offices, and all the uncaring
Intricate rented world begins to rouse.
The sky is white as clay, with no sun.
Work has to be done.
Postmen like doctors go from house to house.   50

LI-YOUNG LEE (1957–   )

The Gift (1986)

To pull the metal splinter from my palm
my father recited a story in a low voice.
I watched his lovely face and not the blade.
Before the story ended, he'd removed
the iron sliver I thought I'd die from.   5

I can't remember the tale,
but hear his voice still, a well
of dark water, a prayer.
And I recall his hands,
two measures of tenderness   10
he laid against my face,
the flames of discipline
he raised above my head.

Had you entered that afternoon
you would have thought you saw a man   15
planting something in a boy's palm,
a silver tear, a tiny flame.
Had you followed that boy
you would have arrived here,
where I bend over my wife's right hand.   20

Look how I shave her thumbnail down
so carefully she feels no pain.
Watch as I lift the splinter out.
I was seven when my father
took my hand like this,   25

and I did not hold that shard
between my fingers and think,
Metal that will bury me,
christen it Little Assassin,
Ore Going Deep for My Heart.   30
And I did not lift up my wound and cry,
Death visited here!
I did what a child does
when he's given something to keep.
I kissed my father.   35

LI-YOUNG LEE (1957–   )

Little Father (2001)

I buried my father
in the sky.
Since then, the birds
clean and comb him every morning
and pull the blanket up to his chin   5
every night.

I buried my father underground.
Since then, my ladders
only climb down,
and all the earth has become a house   10
whose rooms are the hours, whose doors
stand open at evening, receiving
guest after guest.
Sometimes I see past them
to the tables spread for a wedding feast.   15

I buried my father in my heart.
Now he grows in me, my strange son,
my little root who won't drink milk,
little pale foot sunk in unheard-of night,
little clock spring newly wet   20
in the fire, little grape, parent to the future
wine, a son the fruit of his own son,
little father I ransom with my life.

PHILIP LEVINE (1928–   )

Before the War (2003)

Seeing his mother coming home
he kneels behind a parked car,
one hand over his mouth to still
his breathing. She passes, climbs
the stairs, and again the street is his.   5
We're in an American city, Toledo,
sometime in the last century, though
it could be Buffalo or Flint,
the places are the same except
for the names. At eight or nine,   10
even at eleven, kids are the same,
without an identity, without a soul,
things with bad teeth and bad clothes.
We could give them names, we would
name the mother Gertrude, and give her   15
a small office job typing bills of lading
eight hours a day, five and a half
days a week. We could give her
dreams of marriage to the boss
who's already married, but we   20
don't because the loathes him.
It's her son, Sol, she loves,
the one still hiding with one knee
down on the concrete drawing
the day's last heat. He's got feelings.   25
Young as he is he can feel heat,
cold, pain, just as a dog would
and like a dog he'll answer
to his name. Go ahead, call him,
"Hey, Solly, Solly boy, come here!"   30
He doesn't bark, he doesn't sit,
he doesn't beg or extend one paw
in a gesture of submission.
He accepts his whole name, even
as a kid he stands and faces us,   35
just as eleven years from now
he'll stand and face his death
flaming toward him on a bridge-
head at Remagen while Gertrude
goes on typing mechanically   40
into the falling winter right.

ARCHIBALD MACLEISH (1892–1982)

Ars Poetica° (1926)

A poem should be palpable and mute
As a globed fruit,

Dumb
As old medallions to the thumb,

Silent as the sleeve-worn stone   5
Of casement ledges where the moss has grown—

A poem should be wordless
As the flight of birds.

A poem should be motionless in time
As the moon climbs,   10

Leaving, as the moon releases
Twig by twig the night-entangled trees,

Leaving, as the moon behind the winter leaves,
Memory by memory the mind —

A poem should be motionless in time   15
As the moon climbs.

A poem should be equal to:
Not true.

For all the history of grief
An empty doorway and a maple leaf.   20

For love
The leaning grasses and two lights above the sea —

A poem should not mean
But be.

CHRISTOPHER MARLOWE (1564–1593)

The Passionate Shepherd to His Love (1600)

Come live with me and be my love,
And we will all the pleasures prove
That valleys, groves, hills, and fields,
Woods, or steepy mountain yields.

°*Ars Poetica:* "The Art of Poetry" (Latin).

And we will sit upon the rocks,   5
Seeing the shepherds feed their flocks
By shallow rivers, to whose falls
Melodious birds sing madrigals.

And I will make thee beds of roses
And a thousand fragrant posies,   10
A cap of flowers and a kirtle°
Embroidered all with leaves of myrtle;

A gown made of the finest wool
Which from our pretty lambs we pull;
Fair-linèd slippers for the cold,   15
With buckles of the purest gold;

A belt of straw and ivy buds,
With coral clasps and amber studs.
And if these pleasures may thee move,
Come live with me and be my love.   20

The shepherds' swains shall dance and sing
For thy delight each May morning.
If these delights thy mind may move,
Then live with me and be my love.

CLAUDE McKAY (1890–1948)

If We Must Die (1922)

If we must die, let it not be like hogs
Hunted and penned in an inglorious spot,
While round us bark the mad and hungry dogs,
Making their mock at our accursed lot.
If we must die, O let us nobly die,   5
So that our precious blood may not be shed
In vain; then even the monsters we defy
Shall be constrained to honor us though dead!
O kinsmen! we must meet the common foe!
Though far outnumbered let us show us brave,   10
And for their thousand blows deal one deathblow!
What though before us lies the open grave?
Like men we'll face the murderous, cowardly pack,
Pressed to the wall, dying, but fighting back!

°*kirtle:* Skirt.

JAMES MERRILL (1926–1995)

Page from the Koran (1985)

A small vellum environment
Overrun by black
Scorpions of Kufic script — their ranks
All trigger tail and gold vowel-sac —
At auction this mild winter morning went   5
For six hundred Swiss francs.

By noon, fire from the same blue heavens
Had half erased Beirut.
Allah be praised, it said on crude handbills,
For guns and Nazarenes to shoot.   10
"How gladly with proper words," said Wallace Stevens,
"The soldier dies." Or kills.

God's very word, then, stung the heart
To greed and rancor. Yet
Not where the last glow touches one spare man   15
Inked-in against his minaret
—Letters so handled they are life, and hurt,
Leaving the scribe immune?

W. S. MERWIN (1927–   )

To My Brother (2003)

Our mother wrote to you
before you were born
a note you might open
at some later date
in case she should not   5
be there to tell you
what was in her mind
about wanting you
when she had not seen you

that was before   10
my time and it
never turned out like that
you never saw the letter
and she never saw you
who were perfect they said   15
and dead within minutes

that far ahead
of me and always
looking the other way
and I would be the one   20
to open the letter
after she was gone

and you had answered it
without a word
before I was there   25
to find out about you
unseen elder
you perfect one
firstborn

JOHN MILTON   (1608–1674)

from **Paradise Lost**   (1667)

I

Of man's first disobedience, and the fruit°
Of that forbidden tree whose mortal taste
Brought death into the world, and all our woe,
With loss of Eden, till one greater Man°
Restore us, and regain the blissful seat,   5
Sing, Heav'nly Muse,° that, on the secret top
Of Oreb, or of Sinai,° didst inspire
That shepherd who first taught the chosen seed
In the beginning how the Heav'ns and Earth
Rose out of Chaos: or, if Sion hill°   10
Delight thee more, and Siloa's° brook that flowed
Fast° by the oracle of God, I thence
Invoke thy aid to my adventurous song,
That with no middle flight intends to soar
Above th' Aonian mount,° while it pursues   15
Things unattempted yet in prose or rhyme.

° *fruit:* Refers to the apple eaten by Adam and Eve in the Garden of Eden as well as the consequences of their disobedience.   ° *one greater Man:* Refers to the coming of the Messiah.   ° *Heav'nly Muse:* Invoking one of the Muses and asking for help is a convention that usually appears in the first few lines of an epic poem. ° *Of Oreb, or of Sinai:* Refers to the geographical location of Mt. Sinai, where Moses (*that shepherd*) received the Ten Commandments.   ° *Sion hill:* A mountain near Jerusalem.   ° *Siloa:* A brook near Jerusalem.   ° *Fast by:* Close, to.   ° *Aonian mount:* Refers to Mt. Helicon, the home of the Muses.

And chiefly thou, O Spirit° that dost prefer
Before all temples th' uprigh theart and pure,
Instruct me, for thou know'st; thou from the first
Wast present, and, with mighty wings outspread,   20
Dovelike sat'st brooding on the vast abyss,
And mad'st it pregnant: what in me is dark
Illumine; what is low, raise and support;
That, to the height of this great argument,°
I may assert Eternal Providence,   25
And justify the ways of God to men.

JOHN MILTON   (1608–1674)

When I consider how my light is spent°   (1655?)

When I consider how my light is spent,
     Ere half my days in this dark world and wide,
     And that one talent° which is death to hide
Lodged with me useless, though my soul more bent
To serve therewith my Maker, and present   5
     My true account, lest He returning chide;
     "Doth God exact day-labor, light denied?"
I fondly° ask. But Patience, to prevent
That murmur, soon replies, "God doth not need
     Either man's work or His own gifts. Who best   10
     Bear His mild yoke, they serve Him best. His state
Is kingly: thousands at His bidding speed,
And post o'er land and ocean without rest;
They also serve who only stand and wait."

PABLO NERUDA   (1904–1973)

The United Fruit Co.°   (1950)

Translated by Robert Bly

When the trumpet sounded, it was
all prepared on the earth,

°*O Spirit:* An allusion in classical form, this refers to the Spirit of God, or the Holy Spirit.   °*argument:* Subject at hand.   °*how my light is spent:* A meditation on his blindness.   °*one talent:* See Jesus' parable of the talents in Matthew 25.14–30.   °*fondly:* Foolishly.   °*United Fruit Co.:* Incorporated in New Jersey in 1899 by Andrew Preston and Minor C. Keith, United Fruit became a major force in growing, transporting, and merchandising Latin American produce, especially bananas. The company is notorious for its involvement in politics and is a symbol for many people of "Yankee" imperialism and oppression.

and Jehovah parceled out the earth
to Coca-Cola, Inc., Anaconda,
Ford Motors, and other entities: 5
The Fruit Company, Inc.
reserved for itself the most succulent,
the central coast of my own land,
the delicate waist of America.
It rechristened its territories   10
as the "Banana Republics"
and over the sleeping dead,
over the restless heroes
who brought about the greatness,
the liberty and the flags,   15
it established the comic opera:
abolished the independencies,
presented crowns of Caesar,
unsheathed envy, attracted
the dictatorship of the flies,   20
Trujillo flies, Tacho flies,
Carias flies, Martinez flies,
Ubico flies,° damp flies
of modest blood and marmalade,
drunken flies who zoom   25
over the ordinary graves,
circus flies, wise flies
well trained in tyranny.
Among the bloodthirsty flies
the Fruit Company lands its ships,   30
taking off the coffee and the fruit;
the treasure of our submerged
territories flows as though
on plates into the ships.
Meanwhile Indians are falling   35
into the sugared chasms
of the harbors, wrapped
for burial in the mist of the dawn:
a body rolls, a thing
that has no name, a fallen cipher,   40
a cluster of dead fruit
thrown down on the dump.

° *Trujillo, Tacho, Carias, Martinez, Ubico:* Political dictators.

SHARON OLDS (1942–)

First Thanksgiving (1999)

When she comes back, from college, I will see
the skin of her upper arms, cool,
matté, glossy. She will hug me, my old
soupy chest against her breasts,
I will smell her hair! She will sleep in this apartment,   5
her sleep like an untamed, good object, like a
soul in a body. She came into my life the
second great arrival, fresh
from the other world—which lay, from within him,
within me. Those nights, I fed her to sleep,   10
week after week, the moon rising,
and setting, and waxing—whirling, over the months,
in a steady blur, around our planet.
Now she doesn't need love like that, she has
had it. She will walk in glowing, we will talk,   15
and then, when she's fast asleep, I'll exult
to have her in that room again,
behind that door! As a child, I caught
bees, by the wings, and held them, some seconds,
looked into their wild faces,   20
listened to them sing,
then tossed them back
into the air—I remember the moment the
arc of my toss swerved, and they entered
the corrected curve of their departure.   25

SHARON OLDS (1942–   )

The One Girl at the Boys' Party (1983)

When I take my girl to the swimming party
I set her down among the boys. They tower and
bristle, she stands there smooth and sleek,
her math scores unfolding in the air around her.
They will strip to their suits, her body hard and   5
indivisible as a prime number,
they'll plunge in the deep end, she'll subtract
her height from ten feet, divide it into
hundreds of gallons of water, the numbers
bouncing in her mind like molecules of chlorine   10
in the bright blue pool. When they climb out,

her ponytail will hang its pencil lead
down her back, her narrow silk suit
with hamburgers and french fries printed on it
will glisten in the brilliant air, and they will   15
see her sweet face, solemn and
sealed, a factor of one, and she will
see their eyes, two each,
their legs, two each, and the curves of their sexes,
one each, and in her head she'll be doing her   20
wild multiplying, as the drops
sparkle and fall to the power of a thousand from her body.

JUDITH ORTIZ COFER   (1952–   )

Claims   (1990)

Last time I saw her, Grandmother
had grown seamed as a bedouin tent.
She had claimed the right
to sleep alone, to own
her nights, to never bear   5
the weight of sex again, nor to accept
its gift of comfort, for the luxury
of stretching her bones.
She's carried eight children,
three had sunk in her belly, *náufragos*,   10
she called them, shipwrecked babies
drowned in her black waters.
Children are made in the night and
steal your days
for the rest of your life, amen. She said this   15
to each of her daughters in turn. Once she had made a pact
with man and nature and kept it. Now like the sea,
she is claiming back her territory.

GRACE PALEY   (1922–   )

Here   (2001)

Here I am in the garden laughing.
an old woman with heavy breasts
and a nicely mapped face

how did this happen
well that's who I wanted to be   5

at least a woman
in the old style sitting
stout thighs apart under
a big skirt grandchild sliding
on off my lap a pleasant   10
summer perspiration

that's my old man across the yard
he's talking to the meter reader
he's telling him the world's sad story
how electricity is oil or uranium   15
and so forth I tell my grandson
run over to your grandpa ask him
to sit beside me for a minute I
am suddenly exhausted by my desire to
kiss his sweet explaining lips   20

LINDA PASTAN   (1932–   )

Ethics   (1980)

In ethics class so many years ago
our teacher asked this question every fall:
if there were a fire in a museum
which would you save, a Rembrandt painting
or an old woman who hadn't many   5
years left anyhow? Restless on hard chairs
caring little for pictures or old age
we'd opt one year for life, the next for art
and always half-heartedly. Sometimes
the woman borrowed my grandmother's face   10
leaving her usual kitchen to wander
some drafty, half imagined museum.
One year, feeling clever, I replied
why not let the woman decide herself?
Linda, the teacher would report, eschews   15
the burdens of responsibility.
This fall in a real museum I stand
before a real Rembrandt, old woman,
or nearly so, myself. The colors
within this frame are darker than autumn,   20
darker even than winter — the browns of earth,
though earth's most radiant elements burn
through the canvas. I know now that woman

and painting and season are almost one
and all beyond saving by children.   25

LINDA PASTAN (1932–   )

Marks   (1978)

My husband gives me an A
for last night's supper,
an incomplete for my ironing,
a B plus in bed.
My son says I am average,   5
an average mother, but if
I put my mind to it
I could improve.
My daughter believes
in Pass/Fail and tells me   10
I pass. Wait 'til they learn
I'm dropping out.

MARGE PIERCY (1934–   )

Barbie Doll   (1973)

This girlchild was born as usual
and presented dolls that did pee-pee
and miniature GE stoves and irons
and wee lipsticks the color of cherry candy.
Then in the magic of puberty, a classmate said: 5
You have a great big nose and fat legs.

She was healthy, tested intelligent,
possessed strong arms and back,
abundant sexual drive and manual dexterity.
She went to and fro apologizing.   10
Everyone saw a fat nose on thick legs.

She was advised to play coy,
exhorted to come on hearty,
exercise, diet, smile and wheedle.
Her good nature wore out   15
like a fan belt.
So she cut off her nose and her legs
and offered them up.
In the casket displayed on satin she lay

with the undertaker's cosmetics painted on,   20
a turned-up putty nose,
dressed in a pink and white nightie.
Doesn't she look pretty? everyone said.
Consummation at last.
To every woman a happy ending.   25

MIGUEL PIÑERO   (1946–   )

La Bodega° Sold Dreams   (1980)

dreamt i was a poet
&
writin' silver sailin' songs
words
strong & powerful crashin' thru   5
walls of steel & concrete
erected in minds weak
&
those asleep
replacin' a hobby of paper candy   10
wrappin', collectin'
porent to 'pregnate sterile young
thoughts

i dreamt i was this poets
words glitterin' brite & bold   15
strikin' a new rush for gold
in las bodegas
where our poets' words & songs
are sung
but   20
sunlite stealin' thru venetian
blinds
eyes hatin', workin' off time
clock
sweatin'   25
&
swearin'
&
slavin'

°*La Bodega:* The grocery store.

for the final dime   30
runnin' a maze
a token ride
perspiration insultin' poets'
pride
words stoppin' on red   35
goin' on green
poets' dreams
endin' in a factoria as one
in a million.   40
unseen

buyin' bodega sold dreams . . .

ROBERT PINSKY (1940 –   )

Shirt   (1990)

The back, the yoke, the yardage. Lapped seams,
The nearly invisible stitches along the collar
Turned in a sweatshop by Koreans or Malaysians

Gossiping over tea and noodles on their break
Or talking money or politics while one fitted   5
This armpiece with its overseam to the band

Of cuff I button at my wrist. The presser, the cutter,
The wringer, the mangle. The needle, the union,
The treadle, the bobbin. The code. The infamous blaze

At the Triangle Factory in nineteen-eleven.   10
One hundred and forty-six died in the flames
On the ninth floor, no hydrants, no fire escapes—

The witness in a building across the street
Who watched how a young man helped a girl to step
Up to the windowsill, then held her out   15

Away from the masonry wall and let her drop.
And then another. As if he were helping them up
To enter a streetcar, and not eternity.

A third before he dropped her put her arms
Around his neck and kissed him. Then he held   20
Her into space, and dropped her. Almost at once

He stepped to the sill himself, his jacket flared
And fluttered up from his shirt as he came down,
Air filling up the legs of his gray trousers—

Like Hart Crane's Bedlamite, "shrill shirt ballooning."   25
Wonderful how the pattern matches perfectly
Across the placket and over the twin bar-tacked

Corners of both pockets, like a strict rhyme
Or a major chord. Prints, plaids, checks,
Houndstooth, Tattersall, Madras. The clan tartans   30

Invented by mill-owners inspired by the hoax of Ossian,
To control their savage Scottish workers, tamed
By a fabricated heraldry: MacGregor,

Bailey, MacMartin. The kilt, devised for workers
To wear among the dusty clattering looms.   35
Weavers, carders, spinners. The loader,

The docker, the navvy. The planter, the picker, the sorter
Sweating at her machine in a litter of cotton
As slaves in calico headrags sweated in fields:

George Herbert, your descendant is a Black   40
Lady in South Carolina, her name is Irma
And she inspected my shirt. Its color and fit

And feel and its clean smell have satisfied
Both her and me. We have culled its cost and quality
Down to the buttons of simulated bone,

The buttonholes, the sizing, the facing, the characters
Printed in black on neckband and tail. The shape,
The label, the labor, the color, the shade. The shirt.

SYLVIA PLATH   (1932–1963)

Mirror   (1963)

I am silver and exact. I have no preconceptions.
Whatever I see I swallow immediately
Just as it is, unmisted by love or dislike.
I am not cruel, only truthful —
The eye of a little god, four-cornered.   5
Most of the time I meditate on the opposite wall.
It is pink, with speckles. I have looked at it so long
I think it is a part of my heart. But it flickers.
Faces and darkness separate us over and over.

Now I am a lake. A woman bends over me,   10
Searching my reaches for what she really is.
Then she turns to those liars, the candles or the moon.
I see her back, and reflect it faithfully.
She rewards me with tears and an agitation of hands.
I am important to her. She comes and goes.   15

Each morning it is her face that replaces the darkness.
In me she has drowned a young girl, and in me an old woman
Rises toward her day after day, like a terrible fish.

EZRA POUND (1885–1972)

The River-Merchant's Wife: A Letter° (1916)

While my hair was still cut straight across my forehead
I played about the front gate, pulling flowers.
You came by on bamboo stilts, playing horse,
You walked about my seat, playing with blue plums.
And we went on living in the village of Chokan:°   5
Two small people, without dislike or suspicion.

At fourteen I married My Lord you.
I never laughed, being bashful.
Lowering my head, I looked at the wall.
Called to, a thousand times, I never looked back.   10

At fifteen I stopped scowling,
I desired my dust to be mingled with yours
Forever and forever and forever.
Why should I climb the lookout?

At sixteen you departed,   15
You went into far Ku-to-yen,° by the river of swirling eddies,
And you have been gone five months.
The monkeys make sorrowful noise overhead.
You dragged your feet when you went out.
By the gate now, the moss is grown, the different mosses,   20
Too deep to clear them away!
The leaves fall early this autumn, in wind.
The paired butterflies are already yellow with August
Over the grass in the West garden;
They hurt me. I grow older.   25
If you are coming down through the narrows of the river Kiang,°
Please let me know beforehand,
And I will come out to meet you
     As far as Cho-fu-sa.°

° *"The River-Merchant's Wife: A Letter"*: This is one of the many translations Pound made of Chinese poems. The poem is a free translation of Li Po's (701–762) "Two Letters from Chang-Kan." ° *Chokan:* Chang-Kan. ° *Ku-to-yen:* An island in the river Ch'ū-t'ang. ° *Kiang:* The Japanese name for the river Ch'ū-t'ang. Pound's translations are based on commentaries derived from Japanese scholars; therefore, he usually uses Japanese instead of Chinese names. ° *Cho-fu-sa:* A beach several hundred miles upstream of Nanking.

SIR WALTER RALEIGH (1552–1618)

The Nymph's Reply to the Shepherd (1600)

If all the world and love were young,
And truth in every shepherd's tongue,
These pretty pleasures might me move
To live with thee and be thy love.

Time drives the flocks from field to fold,   5
When rivers rage and rocks grow cold;
And Philomel° becometh dumb;
The rest complains of cares to come.

The flowers do fade, and wanton fields
To wayward winter reckoning yields: 10
A honey tongue, a heart of gall,
Is fancy's spring, but sorrow's fall.

Thy gowns, thy shoes, thy beds of roses,
Thy cap, thy kirtle, and thy posies
Soon break, soon wither, soon forgotten,   15
In folly ripe, in reason rotten.

Thy belt of straw and ivy buds,
Thy coral clasps and amber studs.
All these in me no means can move
To come to thee and be thy love.   20

But could youth last, and love still breed,
Had joys no date, nor age no need,
Then these delights my mind might move
To live with thee and be thy love.

HENRY REED (1914–1986)

Naming of Parts (1946)

Today we have naming of parts. Yesterday,
We had daily cleaning. And tomorrow morning,
We shall have what to do after firing. But today,
Today we have naming of parts. Japonica°
Glistens like coral in all of the neighboring gardens,   5
     And today we have naming of parts.

This is the lower sling swivel. And this
Is the upper sling swivel, whose use you will see,
When you are given your slings. And this is the piling swivel,

---

°*Philomel:* The nightingale.   °*Japonica:* A shrub having waxy flowers in a variety of colors.

Which in your case you have not got. The branches   10
Hold in the gardens their silent, eloquent gestures,
    Which in our case we have not got.

This is the safety-catch, which is always released
With an easy flick of the thumb. And please do not let me
See anyone using his finger. You can do it quite easy   15
If you have any strength in your thumb. The blossoms
Are fragile and motionless, never letting anyone see
    Any of them using their finger.

And this you can see is the bolt. The purpose of this
Is to open the breech, as you see. We can slide it   20
Rapidly backwards and forwards: we call this
Easing the spring. And rapidly backwards and forwards
The early bees are assaulting and fumbling the flowers:
    They call it easing the Spring.

They call it easing the Spring: it is perfectly easy   25
If you have any strength in your thumb: like the bolt,
And the breech, and the cocking-piece, and the point of balance,
Which in our case we have not got; and the almond-blossom
Silent in all of the gardens and the bees going backwards and
      forwards,
    For today we have the naming of parts.   30

EDWIN ARLINGTON ROBINSON   (1869–1935)

Miniver Cheevy   (1910)

Miniver Cheevy, child of scorn,
    Grew lean while he assailed the seasons;
He wept that he was ever born,
    And he had reasons.

Miniver loved the days of old   5
    When swords were bright and steeds were prancing;
The vision of a warrior bold
    Would set him dancing.

Miniver sighed for what was not,
    And dreamed, and rested from his labors;   10
He dreamed of Thebes° and Camelot,°
And Priam's neighbors.°

Miniver mourned the ripe renown
    That made so many a name so fragrant;

° *Thebes:* The setting of many Greek legends, including that of Oedipus.   ° *Camelot:* The legendary site of King Arthur's court.   ° *Priam's neighbors:* Priam was the last king of Troy; his "neighbors" included Helen, Aeneas, and Hector.

He mourned Romance, now on the town,   15
    And Art, a vagrant.

Miniver loved the Medici,°
    Albeit he had never seen one;
He would have sinned incessantly
    Could he have been one.   20

Miniver cursed the commonplace
    And eyed a khaki suit with loathing;
He missed the medieval grace
    Of iron clothing.

Miniver scorned the gold he sought,   25
    But sore annoyed was he without it;
Miniver thought, and thought, and thought,
    And thought about it.

Miniver Cheevy, born too late,
    Scratched his head and kept on thinking;   30
Miniver coughed, and called it fate,
And kept on drinking.

EDWARD ARLINGTON ROBINSON (1869–1935)

Richard Cory (1897)

Whenever Richard Cory went down town,
We people on the pavement looked at him:
He was a gentleman from sole to crown,
Clean favored, and imperially slim.

And he was always quietly arrayed,   5
And he was always human when he talked;
But still he fluttered pulses when he said,
"Good-morning," and he glittered when he walked.

And he was rich — yes, richer than a king —
And admirably schooled in every grace: 10
In fine, we thought that he was everything
To make us wish that we were in his place.

So on we worked, and waited for the light,
And went without the meat, and cursed the bread;
And Richard Cory, one calm summer night,   15
Went home and put a bullet through his head.

°*Medici:* Rulers of Florence, Italy, from the fifteenth through the eighteenth centuries. During the Renaissance, Lorenzo de Medici was a renowned patron of the arts.

JAIME SABINES   (1926 – 1999)

The Moon   (1981)

Translated by W. S. Merwin

You can take the moon by the spoonful
or in capsules every two hours.
It's useful as a hypnotic and sedative
and besides it relieves
those who have had too much philosophy.   5
A piece of moon in your purse
works better than a rabbit's foot.
Helps you find a lover
or get rich without anyone knowing,
and it staves off doctors and clinics.   10
You can give it to children like candy
when they've not gone to sleep,
and a few drops of moon in the eyes of the old
helps them to die in peace.

Put a new leaf of moon   15
under your pillow
and you'll see what you want to.
Always carry a little bottle of air of the moon
to keep you from drowning.
Give the key to the moon   20
to prisoners and the disappointed.
For those who are sentenced to death
and for those who are sentenced to life
there is no better tonic than the moon
in precise and regular doses.   25

SONIA SANCHEZ   (1934 –   )

right on: white america   (1970)

this country might have
been a pio
    neer land
once.
    but.   there ain't   5
no mo
    indians   blowing
custer's° mind

°*custer:* General George Armstrong Custer (1839 – 1876) was killed by Sioux in his "last stand" at the Little
Bighorn in Montana.

                              with a different
image of america.   10
                         this country
might have
                  needed shoot/
outs/ daily/
            once.   15
                  but. there ain't
no mo real/ white/   allamerican
                         bad/guys.
just.
    u & me.   20
            blk/ and un/armed.
this country might have
been a pion
            eer land.   once.
                                    and it still is.   25

check out
            the falling
gun/shells   on our blk/tomorrows.

CARL SANDBURG   (1878–1967)

Fog   (1916)

The fog comes
on little cat feet.
It sits looking
over harbor and city
on silent haunches   5
and then moves on.

VIJAY SESHADRI   (1954–   )

Baby Baby   (2003)

Choices have been made that I had nothing to do with —
mistakes have been made,
and, worse than that,
Death has been served tea and fresh figs.
I was not present in that room,   5
at the table polished with citron oil.
I did not take part in the extended discussion
whereby the decision was refined.
So don't point a finger at me someday.
I was here by the crib, looking at you   10

chewing your toes,
blowing raspberries,
blowing little thought balloons
with your labials, fricatives, glottal stops, and retroflexes,
your mint-condition neurons firing.   15
(The language can't be understood,
but the purpose is plain.)
I was here advising you that even though
all the women want to stroke you
and all the men want to be your pal   20
you should probably start developing
your own resources.
Popularity like that never lasts.
I was saying how difficult it is to be
courteous, loyal, thrifty,   25
brave, cheerful, obedient, and wise
separately, let alone all at once.
I was pointing you far into the future, to the day
you go down to the river
and wade out knee deep in the sacred element   30
and turn and see on the riverbank
seven luminous beings lined up and looking at you.
To which of them will you put your question
when you wade back? The Christians say
the story of the universe is the story of a boy and his dad.   35
They are absolute right.
I can see that now, waiting here
for the smiles I'd kill for,
watching you as you sleep curling your fist,
which in a time I can barely recollect   40
did not, or maybe did, exist.

WILLIAM SHAKESPEARE   (1564–1616)

Let me not to the marriage of true minds   (1609)

Let me not to the marriage of true minds
Admit impediments.° Love is not love
Which alters when it alteration finds,
Or bends with the remover to remove:

° *Admit impediments:* A reference to "The Order of Solemnization of Matrimony" in the Anglican Book of Common Prayer: "I require that if either of you know any impediments why ye may not be lawfully joined together in Matrimony, ye do now confess it."

Oh, no! it is an ever-fixéd mark,   5
That looks on tempests and is never shaken;
It is the star to every wandering bark,
Whose worth's unknown, although his height be taken.°
Love's not Time's fool,° though rosy lips and cheeks
Within his bending sickle's compass come;   10
Love alters not with his brief hours and weeks,
But bears it out even to the edge of doom.°
    If this be error and upon me proved,
    I never writ, nor no man ever loved.

WILLIAM SHAKESPEARE   (1564–1616)

Not marble, nor the gilded monuments   (1609)

Not marble, nor the gilded monuments
Of princes, shall outlive this powerful rhyme;
But you shall shine more bright in these contents
Than unswept stone, besmeared with sluttish time.
When wasteful war shall statues overturn,   5
And broils root out the work of masonry,
Nor Mars° his sword nor war's quick fire shall burn
The living record of your memory.
'Gainst death and all-oblivious enmity
Shall you pace forth; your praise shall still find room   10
Even in the eyes of all posterity
That wear this world out to the ending doom.
    So, till the judgment that yourself arise,
    You live in this, and dwell in lovers' eyes.

PERCY BYSSHE SHELLEY   (1792–1822)

Ode to the West Wind   (1820)

I

O wild West Wind, thou breath of Autumn's being,
Thou, from whose unseen presence the leaves dead
Are driven, like ghosts from an enchanter fleeing,

Yellow, and black, and pale, and hectic red,°
Pestilence-stricken multitudes: O Thou,   5
Who chariotest to their dark wintry bed

°*Whose worth's . . . taken:* Although the altitude of a star may be measured, its worth is unknowable.
°*Love's not Time's fool:* Love is not mocked by Time.   °*doom:* Doomsday.   °*Mars:* The Roman god of war.
°*Yellow . . . hectic red:* A reference to a tubercular fever that produces flushed cheeks.

The winged seeds, where they lie cold and low,
Each like a corpse within its grave, until
Thine azure sister of the Spring° shall blow

Her clarion o'er the dreaming earth, and fill   10
(Driving sweet buds like flocks to feed in air)
With living hues and odours plain and hill:

Wild Spirit, which art moving everywhere;
Destroyer and Preserver; hear, O hear!

II

Thou on whose stream, mid the steep sky's commotion,   15
Loose clouds like Earth's decaying leaves are shed,
Shook from the tangled boughs of Heaven and Ocean,

Angels of rain and lightning: there are spread
On the blue surface of thine aery surge,
Like the bright hair uplifted from the head   20

Of some fierce Maenad,° even from the dim verge
Of the horizon to the zenith's height,
The locks of the approaching storm. Thou Dirge

Of the dying year, to which this closing night
Will be the dome of a vast sepulchre,   25
Vaulted with all thy congregated might

Of vapours, from whose solid atmosphere
Black rain and fire and hail will burst: O hear!

III

Thou who didst waken from his summer dreams
The blue Mediterranean, where he lay,   30
Lulled by the coil of his crystalline streams,

Beside a pumice isle in Baiae's bay,°
And saw in sleep old palaces and towers
Quivering within the wave's intenser day,

All overgrown with azure moss and flowers   35
So sweet, the sense faints picturing them! Thou
For whose path the Atlantic's level powers

°*azure . . . Spring:* The west wind of the spring.   °*Maenad:* A female votary who danced wildly in ceremonies for Dionysus (or Bacchus), Greek god of wine and vegetation, who according to legend died in the fall and was reborn in the spring.   °*Baiae's bay:* A bay in the Mediterranean Sea, west of Naples. It was known for the opulent villas built by Roman emperors along its shores.

Cleave themselves into chasms, while far below
The sea-blooms and the oozy woods which wear
The sapless foliage of the ocean, know   40

Thy voice, and suddenly grow grey with fear,
And tremble and despoil themselves: O hear!

IV

If I were a dead leaf thou mightest bear;
If I were a swift cloud to fly with thee;
A wave to pant beneath thy power, and share   45

The impulse of thy strength, only less free
Than thou, O Uncontrollable! If even
I were as in my boyhood, and could be

The comrade of thy wanderings over Heaven,
As then, when to outstrip thy skiey speed   50
Scarce seemed a vision; I would ne'er have striven

As thus with thee in prayer in my sore need,
Oh! lift me as a wave, a leaf, a cloud!
I fall upon the thorns of life! I bleed!

A heavy weight of hours has chained and bowed   55
One too like thee: tameless, and swift, and proud.

V

Make me thy lyre,° even as the forest is:
What if my leaves are falling like its own!
The tumult of thy mighty harmonies

Will take from both a deep, autumnal tone,   60
Sweet though in sadness. Be thou, Spirit fierce,
My spirit! Be thou me, impetuous one!

Drive my dead thoughts over the universe
Like withered leaves to quicken a new birth!
And, by the incantation of this verse,   65

Scatter, as from an unextinguished hearth
Ashes and sparks, my words among mankind!
Be through my lips to unawakened Earth

The trumpet of a prophecy! O Wind,
If Winter comes, can Spring be far behind?   70

°*lyre:* An Aeolian harp, a stringed instrument that produces musical sounds when exposed to the wind.

CHARLES SIMIC (1938–)

Old Soldier (2004)

By the time I was ten,
I had fought in hundreds of battles,
Had innumerable wounds,
Had slain thousands.

My mother took me by the hand   5
And led me into the garden.
The cherry trees were in flower.
There was a cat lying in the grass
Whose tail I wanted to pull,
But I let her be for a moment.   10

After the air raid, the sky was full
Of birds and flying cinders
But the ants at our feet
Were their usual serene selves,
Running their quick errands   15
Along the crumbling walls.

I forgot to mention my sword.
True, it was of cardboard,
But its handle was painted gold.
What I needed was a horse—   20
The one I saw pull a hearse
With a merry wave of his tail.

LOUIS SIMPSON (1923–)

American Poetry (1963)

Whatever it is, it must have
A stomach that can digest
Rubber, coal, uranium, moons, poems.

Like the shark, it contains a shoe.
It must swim for miles through the desert   5
Uttering cries that are almost human.

STEVIE SMITH (1902–1971)

Not Waving but Drowning (1957)

Nobody heard him, the dead man,
But still he lay moaning:

I was much further out than you thought
And not waving but drowning.

Poor chap, he always loved larking   5
And now he's dead
It must have been too cold for him his heart gave way,
They said.

Oh, no no no, it was too cold always
(Still the dead one lay moaning)   10
I was much too far out all my life
And not waving but drowning.

CATHY SONG (1955–   )

Lost Sister (1983)

1

In China,
even the peasants
named their first daughters
Jade—
the stone that in the far fields   5
could moisten the dry season,
could make men move mountains
for the healing green of the inner hills
glistening like slices of winter melon.

And the daughters were grateful: 10
they never left home.
To move freely was a luxury
stolen from them at birth.
Instead, they gathered patience,
learning to walk in shoes   15
the size of teacups,°
without breaking—
the arc of their movements
as dormant as the rooted willow,
as redundant as the farmyard hens.   20
But they traveled far
in surviving,
learning to stretch the family rice,
to quiet the demons,
the noisy stomachs.   25

° *shoes . . . teacups:* A reference to the practice of binding young girls' feet so that they remain small. This practice, which crippled women, was common in China until the communist revolution.

2

There is a sister
across the ocean,
who relinquished her name,
diluting jade green
with the blue of the Pacific.   30
Rising with a tide of locusts,
she swarmed with others
to inundate another shore.
In America,
there are many roads   35
and women can stride along with men.

But in another wilderness,
the possibilities,
the loneliness,
can strangulate like jungle vines.   40
The meager provisions and sentiments
of once belonging—
fermented roots, Mah-Jongg° tiles and firecrackers—
set but a flimsy household
in a forest of nightless cities.   45
A giant snake rattles above,
spewing black clouds into your kitchen.
Dough-faced landlords
slip in and out of your keyholes,
making claims you don't understand,   50
tapping into your communication systems
of laundry lines and restaurant chains.

You find you need China:
your one fragile identification,
a jade link   55
handcuffed to your wrist.
You remember your mother
who walked for centuries,
footless—
and like her,   60
you have left no footprints,
but only because
there is an ocean in between,
the unremitting space of your rebellion.

° *Mah-Jongg:* Or *mahjong,* an ancient Chinese game played with dice and tiles.

GARY SOTO (1952–   )

Saturday at the Canal (1991)

I was hoping to be happy by seventeen.
School was a sharp check mark in the roll book,
An obnoxious tuba playing at noon because our team
Was going to win at night. The teachers were
Too close to dying to understand. The hallways   5
Stank of poor grades and unwashed hair. Thus,
A friend and I sat watching the water on Saturday,
Neither of us talking much, just warming ourselves
By hurling large rocks at the dusty ground
And feeling awful because San Francisco was a postcard   10
On a bedroom wall. We wanted to go there,
Hitchhike under the last migrating birds
And be with people who knew more than three chords
On a guitar. We didn't drink or smoke,
But our hair was shoulder length, wild when   15
The wind picked up and the shadows of
This loneliness gripped loose dirt. By bus or car,
By the sway of train over a long bridge,
We wanted to get out. The years froze
As we sat on the bank. Our eyes followed the water,   20
White-tipped but dark underneath, racing out of town.

WOLE SOYINKA (1934–   )

Hamlet (1972)

He stilled his doubts, they rose to halt and lame
A resolution on the rack. Passion's flame
Was doused in fear of error, his mind's unease
Bred indulgence to the state's disease
Ghosts embowelled his earth; he clung to rails   5
In a gallery of abstractions, dissecting tales
As "told by an idiot." Passionless he set a stage
Of passion for the guilt he would engage.

Justice despaired. The turn and turn abouts
Of reason danced default to duty's counterpoint   10
Till treachery scratched the slate of primal clay
Then Metaphysics waived a thought's delay—
It took the salt in the wound, the "point
Envenom'd too" to steel the prince of doubts.

WILLIAM STAFFORD   (1914 – 1993)

An Afternoon in the Stacks   (1991)

Closing the book, I find I have left my head
inside. It is dark in here, but the chapters open
their beautiful spaces and give a rustling sound,
words adjusting themselves to their meaning.
Long passages open at successive pages. An echo,   5
continuous from the title onward, hums
behind me. From in here, the world looms,
a jungle redeemed by these linked sentences
carved out when an author traveled and a reader
kept the way open. When this book ends   10
I will pull it inside-out like a sock
and throw it back in the library. But the rumor
of it will haunt all that follows in my life.
A candleflame in Tibet leans when I move.

WALLACE STEVENS   (1879 – 1955)

Anecdote of the Jar   (1923)

I placed a jar in Tennessee,
And round it was, upon a hill.
It made the slovenly wilderness
Surround that hill.

The wilderness rose up to it,   5
And sprawled around, no longer wild.
The jar was round upon the ground
And tall and of a port in air.

It took dominion everywhere.
The jar was gray and bare.   10
It did not give of bird or bush,
Like nothing else in Tennessee.

WALLACE STEVENS   (1879 – 1955)

The Emperor of Ice-Cream   (1923)

Call the roller of big cigars,
The muscular one, and bid him whip

In kitchen cups concupiscent curds.
Let the wenches dawdle in such dress
As they are used to wear, and let the boys   5
Bring flowers in last month's newspapers.
Let be be finale of seem.
The only emperor is the emperor of ice-cream.

Take from the dresser of deal,°
Lacking the three glass knobs, that sheet   10
On which she embroidered fantails° once
And spread it so as to cover her face.
If her horny feet protrude, they come
To show how cold she is, and dumb.
Let the lamp affix its beam.   15
The only emperor is the emperor of ice-cream.

WALLACE STEVENS (1879–1955)

The House Was Quiet and the World Was Calm (1954)

The house was quiet and the world was calm.
The reader became the book; and summer night

Was like the conscious being of the book.
The house was quiet and the world was calm.

The words were spoken as if there was no book,   5
Except that the reader leaned above the page,

Wanted to lean, wanted much most to be
The scholar to whom his book is true, to whom

The summer night is like a perfection of thought.
The house was quiet because it had to be.   10

The quiet was part of the meaning, part of the mind:
The access of perfection to the page.

And the world was calm. The truth in a calm world,
In which there is no other meaning, itself

Is calm, itself is summer and night, itself   15
Is the reader leaning late and reading there.

°*deal:* Fir or pine wood.   °*fantails:* According to Stevens, "the word fantails does not mean fans, but fantail pigeons."

MARK STRAND (1934 –   )

2032 (2003)

It is evening in the town of X,
where Death, who used to love me, sits
in a limo with a blanket spread across his thighs,
waiting for his driver to appear. His hair
is white, his eyes have gotten small, his cheeks   5
have lost their lustre. He has not swung his scythe
in years, or touched his hourglass. He is waiting
to be driven to the Blue Hotel, the ultimate resort,
where an endless silence fills the lilac-scented air,
and marble fish swim motionless in marble seas,   10
and where . . . Where is his driver? Ah, there she is,
coming down the garden steps, in heels, velvet evening gown,
and golden boa, blowing kisses to the trees.

VIRGIL SUÁREZ (1962 –   )

La Florida (2003)

Lugubrious days pass with the amplitude of manatees,
hibiscus unfold their smiling vortex to confused bees,

somewhere near turkey point a crocodile grows a foot
by the day, tourists mistake the big ones for logs,

anhingas play Jesus on the Spanish moss-riddled branches   5
of oaks and junipers, crucified in the sun. Feral Quaker

parrots build nests high up in the banyan trees. Orchids,
capuchin monkeys loosed from an animal distributor

warehouse, memories of the bearded lady and the lizard
man, retired now in Palatka, holding court in the shade   10

of a parasol by their trailer. Russian midgets, rockets
shot into the eye of the moon, this magic of fireflies

zapping their phosphorescence in the night air, jasmine,
gardenia — somewhere a man barbecues four-inch-thick steaks

in a thing called the Green Egg. A firefighter, a player   15
of handball. When his son visits once a year from Vegas

he asks when will he return to Tampa, his home. Who isn't
lured by so much sun, heat? The permanence of weather—

or by the mystery of sun showers when the sky opens up
and pelts the earth with a momentary lapse of crying.   20

Right now, somewhere in the Everglades, a fish jumps
out of the water and into the mouth of an alligator.

Nobody's there to witness it, but it happens again and again.

WISLAWA SZYMBORSKA (1923–)

ABC

Translated, from the Polish, by Stanislaw Baranczak and Clare Cavanagh

I'll never find out now
what A. thought of me.
If B. ever forgave me in the end.
Why C. pretended everything was fine.
What part D. played in E.'s silence.   5
What F. had been expecting, if anything.
Why G. forgot when she knew perfectly well.
What H. had to hide.
What I. wanted to add.
If my being around   10
meant anything
to J. and K. and the rest of the alphabet.

ALFRED, LORD TENNYSON (1809–1892)

Ulysses° (1833)

It little profits that an idle king,
By this still hearth, among these barren crags,
Matched with an agèd wife, I mete and dole
Unequal laws unto a savage race
That hoard, and sleep, and feed, and know not me.   5
I cannot rest from travel; I will drink
Life to the lees. All times I have enjoyed
Greatly, have suffered greatly, both with those
That loved me, and alone; on shore, and when
Through scudding drifts the rainy Hyades°   10

°*Ulysses:* A legendary Greek king of Ithaca and hero of Homer's *Odyssey,* Ulysses (or Odysseus) is noted for his daring and cunning. After his many adventures — including encounters with the Cyclops, the cannibalistic Laestrygones, and the enchantress Circe — Ulysses returned home to his faithful wife, Penelope. Tennyson portrays an older Ulysses pondering his situation.   °*Hyades:* A group of stars whose rising was supposedly followed by rain and thus stormy seas.

Vexed the dim sea. I am become a name;
For always roaming with a hungry heart
Much have I seen and known — cities of men
And manners, climates, councils, governments,
Myself not least, but honored of them all— 15
And drunk delight of battle with my peers,
Far on the ringing plains of windy Troy.°
I am a part of all that I have met;
Yet all experience is an arch wherethrough
Gleams that untraveled world whose margin fades 20
Forever and forever when I move.
How dull it is to pause, to make an end,
To rust unburnished, not to shine in use!
As though to breathe were life! Life piled on life
Were all too little, and of one to me 25
Little remains; but every hour is saved
From that eternal silence, something more,
A bringer of new things; and vile it were
For some three suns to store and hoard myself,
And this grey spirit yearning in desire 30
To follow knowledge like a sinking star,
Beyond the utmost bound of human thought.
  This is my son, mine own Telemachus,
To whom I leave the scepter and the isle—
Well-loved of me, discerning to fulfill 35
This labor, by slow prudence to make mild
A rugged people, and through soft degrees
Subdue them to the useful and the good.
Most blameless is he, centered in the sphere
Of common duties, decent not to fail 40
In offices of tenderness, and pay
Meet adoration to my household gods,
When I am gone. He works his work, I mine.
  There lies the port; the vessel puffs her sail;
There gloom the dark, broad seas. My mariners, 45
Souls that have toiled, and wrought, and thought with me —
That ever with a frolic welcome took
The thunder and the sunshine, and opposed
Free hearts, free foreheads — you and I are old;
Old age hath yet his honor and his toil. 50

° *Troy:* An ancient city in Asia Minor. According to legend, Paris, king of Troy, abducted Helen, the beautiful wife of Menelaus, king of Sparta, initiating the Trojan War, in which numerous Greek heroes, including Ulysses, fought.

Death closes all; but something ere the end,
Some work of noble note, may yet be done,
Not unbecoming men that strove with Gods.
The lights begin to twinkle from the rocks;
The long day wanes; the low moon climbs; the deep   55
Moans round with many voices. Come, my friends,
'Tis not too late to seek a newer world.
Push off, and sitting well in order smite
The sounding furrows; for my purpose holds
To sail beyond the sunset, and the baths   60
Of all the western stars, until I die.
It may be that the gulfs will wash us down;
It may be we shall touch the Happy Isles,°
And see the great Achilles,° whom we knew.
Though much is taken, much abides; and though   65
We are not now that strength which in old days
Moved earth and heaven, that which we are, we are—
One equal temper of heroic hearts,
Made weak by time and fate, but strong in will
To strive, to seek, to find, and not to yield.

GINA VALDES   (1943–   )

My Mother Sews Blouses   (1986)

My mother sews blouses
for a dollar a piece.
They must be working on
black cloth again, I see
her fingers sliding on her eyelids.   5

Six months ago she went
to the old oculist, the
one who "knows all about
eyes," who turned her
eyelids inside out and   10
scraped them with a tiny
knife to get the black
lint out.

°*Happy Isles:* Elysium, or Paradise, believed to be in the far western ocean.   °*Achilles:* Greek hero of the Trojan War.

Her eyes were bright and
clear for a few months.   15
She's blinking now,
talking about night
school.

MONA VAN DUYN (1921–2004)

In Bed with a Book

In police procedural they are dying all over town,
the life ripped out of them, by gun, bumper, knife,
hammer, dope, etcetera, and no clues at all.
All through the book the calls come in: body found
in bed, car, street, lake, park, garage, library,   5
and someone goes out to look and write it down.
Death begins life's whole routine to-do
in these stories of our fellow citizens.

Nobody saw it happen, or everyone saw,
but can't remember the car. What difference does it make   10
when the child will never fall in love, the girl will never
have a child, the man will never see a grandchild, the old maid
will never have another cup of hot cocoa at bedtime?
As in life, the dead are dead, their consciousness,
As dear to them as mine to me, snuffed out.   15
What has mind to do with this, when the earth is bereaved?

I lie with my dear ones, holding a fictive umbrella,
While around us falls the real and acid rain.
The handle grows heavier and heavier in my hand.
Unlike life, tomorrow night under the bedlamp   20
by a quick link of thought someone will find out why,
and the policemen and their wives and I will feel better.
But all that's toward the end of the book. Meantime, tonight,
Without a clue I enter sleep's little rehearsal.

JAMES WELCH (1940–2003)

The Man from Washington (1976)

The end came easy for most of us.
Packed away in our crude beginnings
in some far corner of a flat world,

we didn't expect much more
than firewood and buffalo robes   5
to keep us warm. The man came down,
a slouching dwarf with rainwater eyes,
and spoke to us. He promised
that life would go on as usual,
that treaties would be signed, and everyone —   10
man, woman and child — would be inoculated
against a world in which we had no part,
a world of money, promise and disease.

PHILLIS WHEATLEY   (1753–1784)

On Being Brought from Africa
to America   (1773)

'Twas mercy brought me from my *Pagan* land,
Taught my benighted soul to understand
That there's a God, that there's a *Saviour* too:
Once I redemption neither sought nor knew.
Some view our sable race with scornful eye,   5
"Their colour is a diabolic die."
Remember, *Christians*, *Negroes*, black as *Cain*,
May be refin'd, and join th' angelic train.

WALT WHITMAN   (1819–1892)

A Noiseless Patient Spider   (1881)

A noiseless patient spider,
I mark'd where on a little promontory it stood isolated,
Mark'd how to explore the vacant vast surrounding,
It launch'd forth filament, filament, filament, out of itself,
Ever unreeling them, ever tirelessly speeding them.   5

And you O my soul where you stand,
Surrounded, detached, in measureless oceans of space,
Ceaselessly musing, venturing, throwing, seeking the spheres to
   connect them,
Till the bridge you will need be form'd, till the ductile anchor
   hold,
Till the gossamer thread you fling catch somewhere, O my soul.   10

WALT WHITMAN (1819–1892)

from "Song of Myself" (1855)

1

I celebrate myself, and sing myself,
And what I assume you shall assume,
For every atom belonging to me as good belongs to you.

I loafe and invite my soul,
I lean and loafe at my ease observing a spear of summer grass.   5

My tongue, every atom of my blood, form'd from this soil, this air,
Born here of parents born here from parents the same, and their
     parents the same,
I, now thirty-seven years old in perfect health begin,
Hoping to cease not till death.

Creeds and schools in abeyance,   10
Retiring back a while sufficed at what they are, but never
     forgotten,
I harbor for good or bad, I permit to speak at every hazard,
Nature without check with original energy.

2

Houses and rooms are full of perfumes, the shelves are crowded
     with perfumes,
I breathe the fragrance myself and know it and like it,   15
The distillation would intoxicate me also, but I shall not let it.

The atmosphere is not a perfume, it has no taste of the distillation,
     it is odorless,
It is for my mouth forever, I am in love with it,
I will go to the bank by the wood and become undisguised
     and naked,
I am mad for it to be in contact with me.   20

The smoke of my own breath,
Echoes, ripples, buzz'd whispers, love-root, silk-thread, crotch
     and vine,
My respiration and inspiration, the beating of my heart, the
     passing of blood and air through my lungs,
The sniff of green leaves and dry leaves, and of the shore and
     dark-color'd sea-rocks, and of hay in the barn,
The sound of the belch'd words of my voice loos'd to the eddies
     of the wind,   25
A few light kisses, a few embraces, a reaching around of arms,

The play of shine and shade on the trees as the supple boughs wag,
The delight alone or in the rush of the streets, or along the fields
    and hill-sides,
The feeling of health, the full-noon trill, the song of me rising
    from bed and meeting the sun.

Have you reckon'd a thousand acres much? have you reckon'd the
    earth much?   30
Have you practis'd so long to learn to read?
Have you felt so proud to get at the meaning of poems?

Stop this day and night with me and you shall possess the origin
    of all poems,
You shall possess the good of the earth and sun, (there are millions
    of suns left,)
You shall no longer take things at second or third hand, nor look
    through the eyes of the dead, nor feed on the spectres in books,   35
You shall not look through my eyes either, nor take things
    from me,
You shall listen to all sides and filter them from your self.

RICHARD WILBUR   (1921–   )

Man Running   (1988)

          Whatever he has done
      Against our law and peace of mind,
    Our mind's eye looks with pity of a kind
  At the scared, stumbling fellow on the run

          Who hears a siren scream   5
      As through the thickets we conceive
    He plows with fending arms, and to deceive
  The snuffling dogs now flounders up a stream

          Until the doubles back,
      Climbing at length a rocky rise   10
    To where he crumples and, exhausted, lies
  In the scorched brush beside railroad track.

                *

          If then he hops a freight
      And clatteringly rides as far   15
    As the next county in a cattle car,
  We feel our sense of him disintegrate

In tumors, warnings, claims
That here or there he has appeared —
Tall, short, fierce, furtive, with or without a beard.   20
Still, in fidelity to childhood games

And outlaws of romance,
We darkly cheer him, whether or not
He robbed that store, or bank or fired that shot,
And wish him, guiltily, a sporting chance.   25

*

Ditching the stolen truck,
He disappears into a vast
Deep-wooded wilderness, and is at last
Beyond the reach of law, and out of luck,

And we are one with him,
Sharing with him that eldest dread   30
Which, when it gathers in a sleeping head,
Is a place mottled, ominous, and dim

Remembered from the day
When we descended from the trees
Into the shadow of our enemies,   35
Not lords of nature yet, but naked prey.

C. K. WILLIAMS (1936–   )

Doves

So much crap in my head, so
many rubbishy facts, so many
half-baked theories and
opinions, so many public
figures I care nothing about   5
but who stick like pitch; so
much political swill.

So much crap, yet so much I
don't know and would dearly
like to: I recognize nearly   10
none of the birdsongs of
dawn — all I'm sure of is the
maddeningly vapid *who*,
who-who of the doves.

And I don't have half the   15
names of flowers and trees,
and still less of humankind's
myths, the benevolent ones,
from the days before ours;
water-plashed wastes, radiant   20
intercessions.

So few poems entire,
such a meagre handful
of precise recollections of paintings:
detritus instead, junk,   25
numbers I should long ago
have erased, inane
"information" I'll doubtlessly
take with me to the grave.

So much crap, and yet,   30
now, morning, that first
sapphire dome of glow,
the glow! The first sounds
of being awake, *the sounds!*—
a wind whispering, but even   35
trucks clanking past,
even the idiot doves.

And within me, along
with the garbage, faces, faces
and voices, so many   40
lives woven into mine,
such improbable quantities of
memory; so much already
forgotten, lost, pruned away—
yet the doves, the doves!   45

WILLIAM CARLOS WILLIAMS   (1883–1963)

The Dance   (1944)

In Breughel's° great picture, The Kermess,°
the dancers go round, they go round and
around, the squeal and the blare and the
tweedle of bagpipes, a bugle and fiddles
tipping their bellies (round as the thick-   5

°*Breughel:* Peter Breughel (1525–1569), a Flemish painter (also spelled Brueghel).   °*The Kermess: The Church Mass,* Breughel's painting (1567) of peasants dancing at a church festival.

sided glasses whose wash they impound)
their hips and their bellies off balance
to turn them. Kicking and rolling about
the Fair Grounds, swinging their butts, those
shanks must be sound to bear up under such   10
rollicking measures, prance as the dance
in Breughel's great picture, The Kermess.

WILLIAM WORDSWORTH   (1770–1850)

Composed upon Westminster Bridge, September 3, 1802   (1807)

Earth has not anything to show more fair:
Dull would he be of soul who could pass by
A sight so touching in its majesty:
This City now doth, like a garment, wear
The beauty of the morning; silent, bare,   5
Ships, towers, domes, theatres, and temples lie
Open unto the fields, and to the sky;
All bright and glittering in the smokeless air.
Never did sun more beautifully steep
In his first splendor, valley, rock, or hill;   10
Ne'er saw I, never felt, a calm so deep!
The river glideth at his own sweet will:
Dear God! the very houses seem asleep;
And all that mighty heart is lying still!

WILLIAM WORDSWORTH   (1770–1850)

London, 1802   (1802)

Milton!° thou should'st be living at this hour:
England hath need of thee: she is a fen
Of stagnant waters: altar, sword and pen,
Fireside, the heroic wealth of hall and bower,
Have forfeited their ancient English dower   5
Of inward happiness. We are selfish men;
Oh! raise us up, return to us again;
And give us manners, virtue, freedom, power.
Thy soul was like a star, and dwelt apart:
Thou hadst a voice whose sound was like the sea: 10
Pure as the naked heavens, majestic, free,

° *Milton:* John Milton (1608–1674), poet, best known for *Paradise Lost.*

So didst thou travel on life's common way,
In cheerful godliness; and yet thy heart
The lowliest duties on herself did lay.

WILLIAM WORDSWORTH (1770–1850)

My heart leaps up when I behold (1807)

My heart leaps up when I behold
    A rainbow in the sky:
So was it when my life began;
So is it now I am a man;
So be it when I shall grow old,   5
    Or let me die!
The Child is father of the Man;
And I could wish my days to be
Bound each to each by natural piety.

WILLIAM WORDSWORTH (1770–1850)

She dwelt among the untrodden ways (1800)

She dwelt among the untrodden ways
    Beside the springs of Dove,°
A Maid whom there were none to praise
    And very few to love:

A violet by a mossy stone   5
    Half hidden from the eye!
—Fair as a star, when only one
    Is shining in the sky.

She lived unknown, and few could know
    When Lucy ceased to be;   10
But she is in her grave, and, oh,
    The difference to me!

WILLIAM WORDSWORTH (1770–1850)

The Solitary Reaper° (1807)

Behold her, single in the field,
Yon solitary Highland lass!
Reaping and singing by herself;

°*Dove:* A river in the Lake District of England.   °*Reaper:* A worker who harvests grain.

Stop here, or gently pass!
Alone she cuts and binds the grain,   5
And sings a melancholy strain;
O listen! for the vale profound
Is overflowing with the sound.

No nightingale did ever chaunt
More welcome notes to weary bands   10
Of travelers in some shady haunt
Among Arabian sands.
A voice so thrilling ne'er was heard
In springtime from the cuckoo-bird,
Breaking the silence of the seas   15
Among the farthest Hebrides.°

Will no one tell me what she sings?—
Perhaps the plaintive numbers flow
For old, unhappy, far-off things,
And battles long ago.   20
Or is it some more humble lay,
Familiar matter of today?
Some natural sorrow, loss, or pain,
That has been, and may be again?

Whate'er the theme, the maiden sang   25
As if her song could have no ending;
I saw her singing at her work,
And o'er the sickle° bending—
I listened, motionless and still;
And, as I mounted up the hill,   30
The music in my heart I bore
Long after it was heard no more.

CHARLES WRIGHT   (1935–   )

In Praise of Han Shan*

Cold Mountain and Cold Mountain became the same thing in the mind
The first last seen
   slipping into a crevice in the second.
Only the poems remained,
   scrawled on the rocks and trees,   5
Nothing's undoing among the self-stung unfolding of things.

° *Hebrides:* A group of islands off the west coast of Scotland.   ° *sickle:* A curved blade used for harvesting grain or cutting grass.   * *Han Shan:* Ninth-century chinese poet and recluse known as "Cold Mountain"

RICHARD WRIGHT (1908–1960)

Six Haiku

Just enough of rain
To bring the smell of silk
From umbrellas

The spring lingers
In the scent of a damp log   5
Rotting in the sun.

The green cockleburs
Caught in the thick wooly hair
Of the black boy's head.

Winter rain at night   10
Sweetening the taste of bread
And spicing the soup.

The dog's violent sneeze
Fails to rouse a single fly
On his mangy back.   15

The crow flew so fast
That he left his lonely caw
Behind in the fields.

WILLIAM BUTLER YEATS (1865–1939)

Crazy Jane Talks with the Bishop (1933)

I met the Bishop on the road
And much said he and I.
"Those breasts are flat and fallen now,
Those veins must soon be dry;
Live in a heavenly mansion,   5
Not in some foul sty."

"Fair and foul are near of kin,
And fair needs foul," I cried.
"My friends are gone, but that's a truth
Nor grave nor bed denied,   10
Learned in bodily lowliness
And in the heart's pride.

"A woman can be proud and stiff
When on love intent;

But Love has pitched his mansion in   15
The place of excrement;
For nothing can be sole or whole
That has not been rent."

WILLIAM BUTLER YEATS   (1865–1939)

The Lake Isle of Innisfree   (1892)

I will arise and go now, and go to Innisfree,°
And a small cabin build there, of clay and wattles° made:
Nine bean-rows will I have there, a hive for the honey-bee,
And live alone in the bee-loud glade.

And I shall have some peace there, for peace comes dropping slow,   5
Dropping from the veils of the morning to where the cricket sings;
There midnight's all a glimmer, and noon a purple glow,
And evening full of the linnet's wings.

I will arise and go now, for always night and day
I hear lake water lapping with low sounds by the shore;   10
While I stand on the roadway, or on the pavements grey,
I hear it in the deep heart's core.

WILLIAM BUTLER YEATS   (1865–1939)

Sailing to Byzantium°   (1927)

That is no country for old men. The young
In one another's arms, birds in the trees
— Those dying generations — at their song,
The salmon-falls, the mackerel-crowded seas,
Fish, flesh, or fowl, commend all summer long   5
Whatever is begotten, born, and dies.
Caught in that sensual music all neglect
Monuments of unaging intellect.

An aged man is but a paltry thing,
A tattered coat upon a stick, unless   10
Soul clap its hands and sing, and louder sing

°*Innisfree:* An island in Lough (Lake) Gill, County Sligo, in Ireland.   °*wattles:* Stakes interwoven with twigs or branches, used for walls and roofing.   °*Byzantium:* Ancient Greek city later rebuilt as Constantinople (now Istanbul).

For every tatter in its mortal dress,
Nor is there singing school but studying
Monuments of its own magnificence;
And therefore I have sailed the seas and come   15
To the holy city of Byzantium.

O sages standing in God's holy fire
As in the gold mosaic of a wall,
Come from the holy fire, perne in a gyre,
And be the singing-masters of my soul.   20
Consume my heart away; sick with desire
And fastened to a dying animal
It knows not what it is; and gather me
Into the artifice of eternity.

Once out of nature I shall never take   25
My bodily form from any natural thing,
But such a form as Grecian goldsmiths make
Of hammered gold and gold enameling
To keep a drowsy Emperor awake;
Or set upon a golden bough to sing   30
To lords and ladies of Byzantium
Of what is past, or passing, or to come.

WILLIAM BUTLER YEATS   (1865–1939)

The Second Coming°   (1921)

Turning and turning in the widening gyre°
The falcon cannot hear the falconer;
Things fall apart; the center cannot hold;
Mere anarchy is loosed upon the world,
The blood-dimmed tide is loosed, and everywhere   5
The ceremony of innocence is drowned;
The best lack all conviction, while the worst
Are full of passionate intensity.°

Surely some revelation is at hand;
Surely the Second Coming is at hand;   10

°*The Second Coming:* The phrase usually refers to the return of Christ. Yeats theorized cycles of history, much like the turning of a wheel. Here he offers a poetic comment on his view of the dissolution of civilization at the end of one such cycle.   °*gyre:* Spiral.   °*Mere . . . intensity:* Lines 4–8 refer to the Russian Revolution of 1917.

The Second Coming! Hardly are those words out
When a vast image out of *Spiritus Mundi*°
Troubles my sight: somewhere in sands of the desert
A shape with lion body and the head of a man,
A gaze blank and pitiless as the sun,   15
Is moving its slow thighs, while all about it
Reel shadows of the indignant desert birds.
The darkness drops again; but now I know
That twenty centuries° of stony sleep
Were vexed to nightmare by a rocking cradle,   20
And what rough beast, its hour come round at last,
Slouches towards Bethlehem to be born?

KEVIN YOUNG (1970–   )

The Hunch*

She wore red like a razor—
cut quite a figure

standing there, her
slender danger

dividing day   5
from night, there

from here. Where
I hoped to be is near

her & her
fragrant, flammable hair—   10

words like *always*
entering my mouth

that once only gargled doubt.

You see, I been used
before like a car . . .   15

° *Spiritus Mundi:* Literally, "Spirit of the World" (Latin). Yeats believed all souls to be connected by a "Great Memory."   ° *twenty centuries:* The centuries between the birth of Christ and the twentieth century, in which Yeats was writing.   *Like "The Hunch," the other poems in Kevin Young's collection *Black Maria* (which rhymes with *pariah*) recreate the world of hard-boiled detective movies. The action takes place in "Shadow-town" and conveys the adventures of a "soft-boiled" private eye, A.K.A. Jones, and a "femme fatale" named Delilah Redbone. *Black Maria* is a slang term for a police van (as well as for a hearse).

Between us, this sweating, a grandfather
clock's steady tick, soundtrack
of saxophones sighing.

It's been too long—
a whole week   20

since love burned
me like rye. I had begun

to see the glass
as never empty

& that scared me.   25

She fills me
like the lake

fills a canoe—
no rescue —& to swim

I never learned how.   30

ADAM ZAGAJEWSKI (1945–   )

Poetry Searches for Radiance

Translated by Clare Cavanagh

Poetry searches for radiance,
poetry is the kingly road
that leads us farthest.
We seek radiance in a gray hour,
at noon or in the chimneys of the drawn,   5
even on a bus, in November,
while an old priest nods beside us.

The waiter in a Chinese restaurant bursts into tears
and no one can think why.
Who knows, this may also be a quest,   10
like that moment at the seashore
when a predatory ship appeared on the horizon
and stopped short, held still for a long while.
And also moments of deep joy

and countless moments of anxiety.   15
Let me see, I ask.
Let me persist, I say.

A cold rain falls at night.
In the streets and avenues of my city
quiet darkness is hard at work.   20
Poetry searches for radiance.

CHAPTER 35

BIOGRAPHICAL SKETCHES OF SELECTED POETS

SHERMAN ALEXIE (1966 –   ) a Spokane/Coeur d'Alene Indian, grew up on the Spokane Indian Reservation in Wellpinit, Washington, about fifty miles northwest of Spokane, where approximately 1,100 Spokane tribal members live. Alexie has published short stories, novels, and poetry. He was named one of *Granta's* Best of Young American Novelists, and his first novel, *Reservation Blues* (1995), won the Before Columbus Foundation's American Book Award and the Murray Morgan Prize. His second novel, *Indian Killer* (1996), was named one of *People's* Best of Pages and was a *New York Times* Notable Book. In 1997, he and Chris Eyre collaborated on a film project based on the short story "This Is What It Means to Say Phoenix, Arizona" (1993) (p. 287), and the screenplay eventually became *Smoke Signals*, which was released in 1998. To date, Alexie has written sixteen books, his most recent being *Ten Little Indians* (2003), a collection of short stories, as well as two collections of poetry in 2005—*Il powaw della fine del mondo* and *Dangerous Astronomy*.

MAYA ANGELOU (1928–   ), born Marguerite Johnson in St. Louis, lived with her grandmother in Stamps, Arkansas, where she graduated from Lafayette County Training School. She has worked as a cook, streetcar conductor, screenwriter, singer, dancer, and actress. Professor of American studies at Wake Forest University (Winston-Salem, North Carolina), Angelou was nominated for the National Book Award (for *I Know Why the Caged Bird Sings*) and the Pulitzer Prize (for *Just Give Me a Cool Drink of Water 'Fore I Die,* 1974). She won an Emmy for her role in *Roots* (1977) and a Grammy for an album of her poem "On the Pulse of Morning," which she read at the 1993 inauguration of President Bill Clinton. Angelou's collected poems, *The Complete Collected Poems of Maya Angelou*, was published in 1994, Critic Carol E. Neubauer notes that "through all of her verse, Angelou reaches out to touch the lives of others and to offer them hope and confidence in place of humiliation and despair." Angelou summarizes her work in this way: "I speak to the black experience, but I am always talking about the human condition — about what we can endure, dream, fail at, and still survive."

MARGARET ATWOOD (1939–   ) was born in Ottawa, Canada, and grew up in Toronto. She received her bachelor's degree from the University of Toronto and her master's from Radcliffe College. After her first book of poetry, *Double Persephone* (1962), she published *The Circle Game* (1966), winner of Canada's highest literary honor, the Governor General's Award. She gained even greater prominence with novels — *The Handmaid's Tale* (1985), which was made into a movie, *Cat's Eye* (1988), and *The Robber Bride* (1993)— as well as other volumes of poetry, short stories, critical essays, radio and television scripts, and children's books. Her novel *The Blind Assassin* won the 2000 Booker Prize for fiction. Her most recent book is *Oryx and Crake,* published in 2003. She teaches at the University of British Columbia at Vancouver. Critic Carolyn Allen compares her to feminist writers Marge Piercy, Alice Munro, and Adrienne Rich, noting that "Atwood's increasingly unmistakable voice comes in part from her willingness to create women who attempt transformations and almost — but not quite — become trees, roots, foxes. By failing to change themselves into what they cannot be, they become instead what they most truly are." As Atwood explained in an interview with critic Linda Sandler, "You can't write poetry unless you're willing to immerse yourself in language — not just in words, but in words of a certain potency. It's like learning a foreign language."

W(YSTAN) H(UGH) AUDEN (1907–1973), son of an English physician, earned a scholarship to Oxford University, where he studied T. S. Eliot's poetry. He and his writer friends — Stephen Spender, Cecil Day-Lewis, Christopher Isherwood, and Louis MacNeice (known as the "Auden Generation")— exerted considerable influence on modern literature. Auden left England in 1939 and became a United States citizen in 1946. Among his many works probing the mysteries of religion, psychology, and politics are *The Double Man* (1941); *The Age of Anxiety* (1947), winner of the 1948 Pulitzer Prize; and *The Shield of Achilles* (1955), winner of the 1956 National Book Award. Seamus Heaney, noted critic and Nobel Prize-winning poet, described Auden as "an epoch-making poet on public themes, the register of a new sensibility, a great sonneteer, a writer of perfect light verse, a prospector of literature at its most illiterate roots and a dandy of lexicography at its most extravagant reaches." In a 1971 interview with Daniel Halpern, Auden commented, "Truth in poetry is very important to me. I think you must feel, when you read a poem, that it says something about life which you recognize to be true."

ELIZABETH BISHOP (1911–1979) was born in Worcester, Massachusetts, and raised by her grandparents in Nova Scotia. She was educated at Vassar College, where she earned her BA in 1934; after graduation, she traveled widely, living in New York, Mexico, France, Spain, North Africa, Ireland, and Italy. For four years, she lived in Key West, Florida — an experience that informed some of the poems in her first volume, *North and South* (1946)— and for sixteen years, she lived in Brazil. These varied settings and her experiences there continued to influence her poems, such as those in the 1965 volume *Questions of Travel,* and much of her later work. *Poems: North and South — A Cold Spring* (1955) won the Pulitzer

Prize; *Complete Poems* (1969) won the National Book Award; her last volume, *Geography III* (1976), established her as a major figure in contemporary literature. Her poetry, like that of Marianne Moore, her longtime friend and mentor, is admired for its fastidious attention to the natural world, as well as for its muted irony and humor. Poets Robert Lowell and Randall Jarrell thought her work exquisite; Lowell modeled his "Skunk Hour" after Bishop, to whom the poem is dedicated. Her *Collected Prose,* published in 1984, includes autobiographical sketches, travel accounts, a memoir of Marianne Moore, and short stories. Bishop was awarded the Fellowship of the Academy of American Poets in 1964 and served as a chancellor of the academy from 1966 to 1979. She lived in Cambridge, Massachusetts, during the last years of her life, and she taught at Harvard University.

WILLIAM BLAKE (1757–1827) was born in London, England, and educated entirely at home. As a boy, he read Milton, Shakespeare, and the Bible and developed his knowledge of French, Italian, Latin, Greek, and Hebrew. At fourteen, he was apprenticed to an engraver. His talent for art flourished, and he was eventually made a member of London's Royal Academy. He married Catherine Boucher in 1782, and the two worked together for the rest of their lives developing colored engravings of Blake's poems. His first book, *Poetical Sketches* (1783), was printed by friends; in 1789, he published *Songs of Innocence,* followed in 1794 by *Songs of Experience.* At times deceptively simple, at times radically outspoken, these lyrics express Blake's ardent belief in the freedom of the imagination and his scorn for rationalism and materialism. Also issued during this period were his mystical and prophetic works, *The Book of Thel* (1789) and *The Marriage of Heaven and Hell* (1791). In 1793, the Blakes moved to Lambeth, south of London; here Blake began work on *The Book of Job,* arguably his finest illustrations, completed when he was nearly seventy. Largely dismissed in his time as the products of an eccentric, even a madman, Blake's books attracted no more than a small following of readers. He died a pauper and was buried in an unmarked grave. Still, his influence on poetry and art, and even on contemporary popular culture, has been enormous and profound. An idealist and a visionary, Blake held his convictions to the end, best articulated in *The Marriage of Heaven and Hell:* "If the doors of perception were cleansed every thing would appear to man as it is: infinite."

ANNE BRADSTREET (1612–1672) was born in Northampton, England, the daughter of Thomas Dudley, former steward to the earl of London. At sixteen, she married Simon Bradstreet and two years later sailed for America with her husband and father, both of whom eventually became governors of the Massachusetts Bay colony. She lived in Ipswich, then at Andover, and had eight children. In 1650, her first collection of poems, *The Tenth Muse,* was published in London without her knowledge by her brother-in-law, who thus bestowed on Bradstreet the unexpected honor of being the first American poet to be published in England. Readers who encountered the book were promised on the title page "Several Poems, compiled with great variety of Wit and Learning, full of delight" composed by an anonymous American "Gentlewoman in those parts." The book concerns itself with historical, cosmological, and metaphysical matters; the works are conventional in style, and show the influence of earlier English poets, notably Edmund Spenser, Sir Philip Sidney and Sir Walter Raleigh. Along with poems on the familiar poetic preoccupations of the age — time and mutability — the volume contains elegies on Sidney and Queen Elizabeth. A second edition, with corrections and additions, appeared in Boston six years after the poet's death. In this collection, Bradstreet turns more frequently toward the personal in subject, often addressing domestic topics from a religious point of view. The second edition contains elegies on her children and poems to her beloved husband.

GWENDOLYN BROOKS (1917–2000) former Poet Laureate of Illinois, was, in 1950, the first African-American to win a Pulitzer Prize (for her second book of poems, *Annie Allen*). Born in Topeka, Kansas, Brooks was raised in a section of Chicago called "Bronzeville," which provided the setting for her first published poetry collection, *A Street in Bronzeville* (1945). Other collections include *The Bean Eaters* (1960), *In the Mecca* (1968), and *The World of Gwendolyn Brooks* (1971). Brooks also published a novel, *Maud Martha* (1953), and *Report from Part One: An Autobiography* (1972). In a review of *Annie Allen,* Langston Hughes, prominent poet of the Harlem Renaissance, noted that "the people and the poems in Gwendolyn Brooks's book are alive, reaching and very much of today." Brooks's desire to reach all African-Americans is revealed in a 1974 interview in which she explained that she wanted "to develop a style that will appeal to black people in taverns, black people in gutters, schools, offices, factories, prisons, the consulate; I wish to reach black people in pulpits, black people in mines, on farms, on thrones."

ROBERT BROWNING (1812–1889) was born in Camberwell, a London suburb, into a family of religious dissenters. He received little formal education; much of his learning he gained from his father's library. At an early age, he wrote poems in the manner of the romantic poet Percy Bysshe Shelley, under whose influence he briefly became a vegetarian and touted atheistic principles. Although his poetry attracted little attention until the publication of *Paracelsus* (1835) and *Bells and Pomegranates* (1841–1846), his first volume, *Pauline: A Fragment of a Confession,* published anonymously in 1833, prompted a strong reaction from the philosopher John Stuart Mill: in Browning's poems, Mill noted "a more intense and morbid self-consciousness than I ever knew in any sane human being." Such censure may have been responsible for Browning's subsequent turning in his work to the creation of dramatic characters and his development of the dramatic monologue, a literary form now associated almost exclusively with him. In 1846, he married Elizabeth Barrett, and the couple moved to Florence, where he composed *Men and Women* (1855) and *Dramatis Personae* (1864). After the death of his wife, Browning returned to London, where he wrote his masterpiece, *The Ring and the Book* (1869). He died in 1889 while visiting his son in Venice. His request for burial in Florence being impossible to fulfill, his body was returned to England and buried in Poets' Corner in Westminster Abbey. Browning was one of the most famous poets of the Victorian Age; his work — especially his dramatic monologues — had great influence on early twentieth-century writers, notably Ezra Pound.

GEOFFREY CHAUCER (c. 1340–1400), born in London sometime between 1340 and 1344, was the son of a prosperous wine merchant and his wife. Although little is known of his early education, his later works reflect his knowledge of French, Italian, and Latin. A skilled professional soldier, Chaucer fought in the Hundred Years War and did not begin working on *The Canterbury Tales* until he was in his early forties. The book, which was left unfinished when he died, depicts a journey by some pilgrims going to the shrine of the martyr St. Thomas Becket. On the way, they amuse themselves by telling stories that are interlinked with interludes in which the characters reveal much about themselves. Although Chaucer wrote numerous literary works, he is best remembered for his *Canterbury Tales*. After his death in London on October 25, 1400, he was buried in Westminster Abbey, in the part of the cathedral which later became known as Poets' Corner.

WANDA COLEMAN (1946–   ), a native of Los Angeles, is the author of eight collections of poetry, including *Bathwater Wine* (1998), which won the 1999 Lenore Marshall Poetry Prize, and a novel, *Mambo Hips and Make Believe* (1999). A former columnist for the *Los Angeles Times Magazine*, Coleman has published poetry and prose in a wide variety of literary journals and anthologies. *Mecurochrome: New Poems* (2001) was a finalist for the National Book Award in 2001. Her latest collection, *The Riot Inside Me: More Trials & Tremors,* was published in 2005.

SAMUEL TAYLOR COLERIDGE (1772–1834) was born at Ottery St. Mary, Devon, England, where his father was vicar. He entered Jesus College, Cambridge, in 1791, intending a profession in the Church of England, but abandoned his studies in 1793. Though readmitted to the university in 1794, he never returned to take his degree. His first poems were published that year, but it was only in 1798, with the publication of *Lyrical Ballads,* that his mature writing appeared. This book was a collaborative venture between Coleridge and his friend William Wordsworth. Here and in their later poems, the two not only laid the foundations of English romanticism but also redefined the contours of English poetic form. Coleridge experimented with preexisting forms ranging from the ballad (*Lyrical Ballads* included his masterpiece, *The Rime of the Ancient Mariner*) to the ode. His visionary fragment "Kubla Khan" was written in 1797. Despite his falling-out with Wordsworth after 1810 and the decline of his poetic powers (due in part to a long-term opium addiction), Coleridge continued to write philosophical and social tracts, as well as sermons and literary criticism. His magnum opus, *Biographia Literaria,* was written in this later period. Revolutionary in thought, catholic in work and taste, Coleridge has inspired generations of poets — of whom he offered a definition in *Biographia Literaria:* "The poet, described in *ideal* perfection, brings the whole soul of man into activity, with the subordination of its faculties to each other, according to their relative worth and dignity. He diffuses a tone and spirit of unity, that blends, and (as it were) *fuses,* each into each, by that synthetic and magical power . . . imagination."

BILLY COLLINS (1941–   ) was born in New York City and currently resides in Somers, New York. Since the publication of his first book, *The Apple That Astonished Paris* (1988), he has established himself as a prominent voice in contemporary American poetry. He has received many awards, among them the Bess Hokin Prize, the Frederick Bock Prize, the Oscar Blumenthal Prize, and the Levinson Prize awarded by *Poetry* magazine. His work has appeared in a variety of journals and anthologies, including the Pushcart Prize anthology and *The Best American Poetry* for 1992, 1993, and 1997; his books of poetry include *Nine Horses* (2002), *Sailing Alone around the Room: New and Selected Poems* (2001); *Picnic, Lightning* (1998); *The Art of Drowning* (1995), a finalist for the Lenore Marshall Prize; and *Questions about Angels* (1991), selected for the National Poetry Series and reissued in 1999. The recipient of a Guggenheim Fellowship and a grant from the National Endowment for the Arts, Collins served as Poet Laureate of the United States between 2001 and 2003. His poems, often about ordinary people and situations, have made him one of the country's most popular poets. His Poetry 180 program offers a poem a day for high school students during their approximately 180-day school year. Collins is a professor of English at Lehman College, City University of New York.

E(DWARD) E(STLIN) CUMMINGS (1894–1962), born in Cambridge, Massachusetts, completed his undergraduate and graduate degrees at Harvard. He served as an ambulance driver during World War I and then spent several years studying art in Paris. *Tulips and Chimneys* (1923), his first book of poems, received both praise and criticism for its idiosyncratic capitalization (such as the use of only lowercase letters in his name), diction, punctuation, and typography. The publication of his *Complete Poems: 1904–1962* (1994), a collection of his twelve volumes of verse, affirms his lasting literary reputation. Best known as an experimental poet, the versatile Cummings was also a talented painter, prose writer, translator, and playwright. He won two Guggenheim fellowships (1933, 1951), a special citation from the National Book Awards (1955), and the Bollingen Prize in Poetry (1957). According to critic Malcolm Cowley, Cummings "suffers from comparison with those who built on a larger scale . . . but still he is unsurpassed in his field." Noted poet Randall Jarrell concluded, "No one else . . . has ever made avant-garde, experimental poems so attractive to the general and special reader."

EMILY DICKINSON (1830–1886), born into a prominent Amherst, Massachusetts, family, attended Amherst Academy and Mount Holyoke Female Seminary. She rarely left her hometown—and, except for extended stays in Cambridge in 1864 and 1865, she rarely left her home after that. In her lifetime, Dickinson published anonymously only seven of her poems, and most of these had been edited to make them more conventional. In 1955, Thomas H. Johnson edited the definitive Dickinson canon of 1,775 poems. He attributes her obscurity during the nineteenth century to her experimentation "in meters, rhyme, capitals, grammar, and punctuation." Noted writer Joyce Carol Oates calls her "the most paradoxical of poets" because, despite "the extraordinary intimacy of her poetry," her voice has "a tone of the purest anonymity." Oates considers Dickinson a "poet of the soul" — indeed, "our most endlessly fascinating American poet." Fascinating, indeed, is the way Dickinson saw poetry as a moment of great intensity. As she told her literary adviser Thomas Wentworth Higginson, "If I read a book and it makes my whole body so cold no fire can warm me, I know *that* is poetry. If I feel physically as if the top of my head were taken off, I know *that* is poetry."

JOHN DONNE (1572–1631) was born in London, England. Though educated at Oxford and Cambridge universities, he left both without receiving any degree. During the 1590s, he traveled widely, read voraciously, and was a courtier in Queen Elizabeth's court. In 1601, he married Ann Moore, still a minor, an offense for which he was briefly imprisoned and left unemployed. The next twenty years were difficult for Donne: he supported his steadily growing family with a series of makeshift jobs; when Ann died in 1617, he was left with seven children. In 1621, however, Donne's prospects changed: King James, convinced of Donne's promise as a preacher, made him the dean of St. Paul's Cathedral in London, a position he held until his death in 1631. Donne's poetry, known as "metaphysical," is characterized by passionate thought and intellectual playfulness; it delights in puns, paradox, poses, and conceits. His career is generally seen as divided between the love poetry of his early years and his later poems of religious devotion. In love poems such as "The Good Morrow" and "Song: Go and Catch a Falling Star," Donne interjected life into the tired conventions of 1590s love poetry. Similarly, in his *Holy Sonnets,* he infused English religious verse with sinewy toughness; "Batter My Heart, Three-Personed God" and "Death Be Not Proud" are fine examples. His poetry fell out of favor in the seventeenth and eighteenth centuries but has since been reclaimed as one of the treasures of English Renaissance literature.

T(HOMAS) S(TEARNS) ELIOT (1888–1965), born in St. Louis, received his undergraduate, master's, and doctoral degrees from Harvard and then emigrated to England, where he worked in London as a bank clerk and book editor. In 1927, he became a British citizen and declared himself an "Anglo-Catholic in religion, royalist in politics, and classicist in literature." He won prestigious professorships at Cambridge and Harvard, the Nobel Prize in Literature (1948), the British Order of Merit, the Emerson-Thoreau Medal from the American Academy of Arts and Sciences (1959), and the U.S. Medal of Freedom (1964). His best-known works of poetry include "The Love Song of J. Alfred Prufrock" (1917), *The Waste Land* (1922), *The Four Quartets* (1943), and *Old Possum's Book of Practical Cats* (1939), the basis for the long-running musical *Cats*. His friend Ezra Pound, upon reading the manuscript of *The Waste Land,* suggested revisions but immediately recognized it as a work of genius, saying that Eliot's poem was enough "to make the rest of us shut up shop." To those who called this work social criticism, Eliot modestly replied that it was merely "the relief of a personal and wholly insignificant grouse against life . . . just a piece of rhythmical grumbling."

MARTÍN ESPADA (1957–   ) was born in Brooklyn, New York, and was early immersed in political activism by his father, a leader in the Puerto Rican community. "Long Island was tough when you were the only Puerto Rican in town. I needed a way to respond," Espada has said. "I think writing poetry is a great way to assert your humanity. So I started to do that, and I never looked back." In his poetry, Espada strikes out against oppression, giving voice to the struggles of the poor and the working class; his poems seek to move "beyond victimization; they document not only repression, but resistance; they celebrate as well as denounce." *Imagine the Angels of Bread,* his 1996 collection, won the American Book Award. Other books of poetry include *Rebellion Is the Circle of a Lover's Hand* (1990), *City of Coughing and Dead Radiators* (1993), and *A Mayan Astronomer in Hell's Kitchen: Poems* (2000). He has edited several anthologies, including *El Coro: A Chorus of Latino and Latina Poets* (1997) and *Poetry like Bread: Poets of the Imagination from Curbstone Press* (1994). His collection of essays, *Zapata's Disciple,* appeared in 1998. In 2003, Espada published *Albanza: New and Selected Poems 1982–2002,* for which he received the Patterson Award for Sustained Literary Achievement. The recipient of a Massachusetts Artists' Fellowship, a PEN/Revson Fellowship, a PEN/Voelker Award for Poetry, and the Paterson Poetry Prize, Espada teaches at the University of Massachusetts.

ROBERT FROST (1874–1963) moved to New England from his birthplace of San Francisco and attended Dartmouth College and Harvard without receiving a degree. In 1900, he settled on a New Hampshire dairy farm, writing many of his works there. Twenty years later, he helped to establish the Bread Loaf School of English at Middlebury College in Vermont. Frost enjoyed enormous popularity as a revered poet, receiving honorary degrees from prestigious universities and winning major prizes, including the Pulitzer for *New Hampshire, Collected Poems, A Further Range,* and *Witness Tree.* He served as Poet Laureate of the United States between 1958 and 1959. In 1961, at the inauguration of President John F. Kennedy, he recited from memory his poem "The Gift Outright" because poor eyesight at age eighty-seven prevented him from reading. "Stopping by Woods on a Snowy Evening," observed critic Donald J. Greiner, "has immortality written all over it" and "deserves its place alongside the many novels and stories that ponder the fate of those who dare to plunge beyond the safety of the clearing to the darkness of the woods." Frost himself, in a letter to poet-critic Louis Untermeyer in 1923, called this poem his "best bid for remembrance."

NIKKI GIOVANNI (1943–   ) was born in Knoxville, Tennessee, and raised in the Lincoln Heights neighborhood of Cincinnati, Ohio. In 1960, she entered Fisk University, where she worked with the Writers' Workshop, edited the literary magazine, and became involved in the Student Non-Violent Coordinating Committee (SNCC); after earning her BA, she attended graduate school at the University of Pennsylvania. During the late 1960s, Giovanni became involved in the Black Arts movement; in her first three collections of poems — *Black Feeling, Black Talk* (1968), *Black Judgement* (1968), and *Re: Creation* (1970) — she explores the interpretation of identity and experience through a black consciousness. Her work of the 1970s treats her experience as a single mother; the volumes *Spin a Soft Black Song* (1971), *Ego-Tripping* (1973), and *Vacation Time* (1980) are collections of poems for children.

Giovanni returned to more explicitly political subjects in *Those Who Ride the Night Winds* (1983); more recently, she published *Selected Poems of Nikki Giovanni* (1996), *Love Poems* (1997), *Blues for All the Changes: New Poems* (1999), *Quilting the Black-Eyed Pea: Poems and Not-Quite Poems* (2002), and *The Collected Poetry of Nikki Giovanni: 1968–1998* (2003). Her honors include the NAACP Image Award for Literature (1998) and the Langston Hughes Award for Distinguished Contributions to Arts and Letters (1996). She is now a professor of English and Black Studies at Virginia Tech. About the popular adage, "Write about what you know," Giovanni offers the following response: "I resent people who say writers write from experience. Writers don't write from experience, though many are hesitant to admit that they don't. I want to be clear about this. If you wrote from experience, you'd get maybe one book, maybe three poems. Writers write from empathy."

LOUISE GLÜCK (1943–   ) was born in New York City; she attended Sarah Lawrence College and Columbia University and then taught at the University of North Carolina at Greensboro, the University of Virginia, the University of Iowa, and the University of Cincinnati. Among her many awards and honors are Columbia University's Academy of American Poets Prize (1967), a Rockefeller Foundation grant (1968), a National Endowment for the Arts grant (1969–1970), and a Guggenheim Fellowship (1975–1976). Glück's first collection of poetry, *First Born,* appeared in 1968. It was followed in 1975 by *The House on Marshland,* which brought her national recognition. She won the American Academy Award in 1981 and the National Book Critics Circle Award in 1985 for *The Triumph of Achilles.* Glück also served as Poet Laureate of the United States between 2003 and 2004. Her most recent collections include *Meadowlands* (1996), *Vita Nova* (1999), and the *Seven Ages* (2001). Critic Deno Trakis suggests that although the world of Glück's poems is "bleak"—portraying people "isolated from family, or bitter from rejected love, or disappointed with what life has to offer"—it is "depicted with a lyrical grace, and her poems are attractive if disturbing." Perhaps Glück's outlook on her career is expressed by her persona in "To Autumn": "I am no longer young. What / of it? Summer approaches and the long / decaying days of autumn when I shall begin / the great poems of my middle period."

THOMAS HARDY (1840–1928), born in Dorsetshire, England, became a full-time writer after working as an architect in London. This versatile writer published fourteen novels, eight volumes of poetry, four short story collections, two plays, and a variety of essays, prefaces, and other nonfiction prose. His best-known novels are *Far from the Madding Crowd* (1874), *The Return of the Native* (1878), *The Mayor of Casterbridge* (1886), *Tess of the D'Urbervilles* (1891), and *Jude the Obscure* (1896). Recipient of many honors, Hardy was the last great Victorian poet. The American poet-critic John Crowe Ransom connected Hardy to the next generation of poets "by reason of his naturalism and rebellion against the dogma," and Ezra Pound, W. H. Auden, and D. H. Lawrence — prominent poets of this next generation — acknowledged Hardy's influence on them. Often called a pessimist, Hardy regarded himself as a "meliorist" — someone who believes the world can be improved by human effort. In his preface to *Late Lyrics and Earlier* (1922), Hardy wrote that pain "shall be kept down to a minimum by loving kindness, operating through scientific knowledge, and actuated by the modicum of free will."

ROBERT HAYDEN (1913–1980), born Asa Bundy Sheffey in Detroit, was renamed by his adoptive parents. After his studies at Detroit City College (now Wayne State University) and the University of Michigan, Hayden taught at Fisk University and the University of Michigan. He published four significant volumes of poetry and in 1966 gained international recognition by winning the Grand Prize for Poetry in English at the First World Festival of Negro Arts in Dakar, Senegal, for *A Ballad of Remembrance.* Elected in 1975 to the Academy of American Poets, Hayden became the first African-American appointed Poet Laureate of the United States (1976–78). His *Collected Poems,* reissued in 1995 with an introduction by noted scholar Arnold Rampersad, reaffirms his literary reputation. Critic Wilbur Williams noted that "Hayden's characteristically soft-spoken and fluid voice derives much of its power from the evident contrast between the maelstrom of anguish [from] which it originates and the quiet reflecting pool of talk into which it is inevitably channeled." Hayden stated that he experimented with new forms and techniques "to arrive at something really my own, something patterned, wild, and free."

SEAMUS HEANEY (1939–   ) comes from a Roman Catholic family in the predominantly Protestant town of Mossbawn, County Derry, Northern Ireland. After attending Queen's University, Belfast, and St. Joseph's College of Education, he left Northern Ireland in 1972 and eventually settled in Dublin in the Irish Republic. This influential contemporary Irish poet has received most of the literary prizes awarded in Ireland and England as well as the 1995 Nobel Prize in Literature — the third Irish writer to receive this award, joining W. B. Yeats (1923) and Samuel Beckett (1969). For his translation of *Beowulf,* dedicated to his friend, British poet Ted Hughes, Heaney was awarded the 1999 Whitbread Prize for Poetry. Heaney's other works include *Crediting Poetry: The Nobel Lecture* (1996) and *Open Ground: Selected Poems 1966–1996* (1998), which was named a *New York Times* Notable Book. Heaney's poetry, William Grimes observed, "is rooted in the Irish soil . . . as though Ireland's wet peat were a storehouse of images and memories. At the same time [he] moves easily from the homely images of farm and village to larger issues of history, language, and national identity." Nobel Prize–winning poet Derek Walcott called Heaney "the guardian spirit of Irish poetry." Heaney metaphorically depicts the hard, patient work of poetry in "Digging," the first poem in his first book, *Death of a Naturalist* (1966): "Between my fingers and my thumb / The squat pen rests. / I'll dig with it." His most recent works include a poetry collection, *Electric Light* (2001); essays, *Finders Keepers: Selected Prose 1971–2001* (2002); and a translation, *The Burial at Thebes: A Version of Sophocles' Antigone* (2004).

ROBERT HERRICK (1591–1674) was the seventh child and fourth son born to a London goldsmith, Nicholas, and his wife, Julia Stone Herrick. When Herrick was fourteen months old, his father died. As a young man, Herrick took holy orders and became a vicar in the Catholic Church. His most famous work was *Hesperides; or, the Works Both Human and Divine of Robert Herrick, Esq.* (1648). Influenced by classical Roman poetry, he wrote on pastoral themes, dealing primarily with English country life and village customs.

GERARD MANLEY HOPKINS (1844–1889) was born into a cultivated London family and attended Oxford, where the renowned aesthetic critic Walter Pater and the Anglican High Church movement leader Cardinal John Henry Newman influenced him. As a result, Hopkins converted to Roman Catholicism and became a Jesuit priest. His long poem *The Wreck of the Deutschland* appeared in 1875; his shorter, more accessible nature poems were published in 1918. "The Windhover," his most famous sonnet with a typically religious theme, explores ways to praise, revere, and serve God. Hopkins is best known for his unusual metrical system, which he named "sprung rhythm." Stylistically, his poems boldly experiment with imagery, syntax, and rhythm. Thematically, they connect nature and Christianity with passionate, sometimes anguished, intensity. Critic Jerome Bump has observed that this "idiosyncratic creativity" made Hopkins's style "so radically different from that of his contemporaries" that much of his work was not fully recognized until after his death. Hopkins believed that nature, like the Bible, offers moral instruction: "This world is word, expression, news of God," and "it is a book he has written . . . a poem of beauty. . . ."

JOHN KEATS (1795–1821) was born in London, England, the eldest of four children. After his father's death in 1804, Keats's mother moved the family to Edmonton; she died of tuberculosis in 1810. Keats studied medicine at Guy's Hospital, intending to become a surgeon, but gave up that goal in 1816 for a life of writing. His first poems were composed in 1814; in 1816, *The Examiner* printed his sonnet "On First Looking into Chapman's Homer" and hailed Keats, alongside Percy Bysshe Shelley, as one of the most promising writers of his generation. His *Poems* (1817), however, appeared to little applause. Keats began work on his long poem *Endymion*, published in 1818, but by then his brother Tom had become ill with tuberculosis, and Keats devoted much time to nursing him. The strain, combined with the withering attacks *Endymion* received, almost forced Keats to give up poetry altogether. In 1818, after Tom's death, he moved to Hampstead, where he met and fell in love with Fanny Brawne. He finished *Hyperion,* wrote lyrics such as "La Belle Dame sans Merci," and completed the great odes of 1819, for which he is chiefly remembered. In the winter of 1820, he fell seriously ill with tuberculosis and sailed for Italy. He died in Rome that summer, at age twenty-five. Despite his doubts over the permanence of his achievement — he requested that the inscription on his tombstone be "Here lies one whose name was writ in water" — Keats exerted enormous influence on later poets, notably Alfred, Lord Tennyson and Matthew Arnold; he remains one of the best-loved poets of the English Romantic period. Of poetry's aim, Keats wrote: "Poetry should surprise by a fine excess, and not by singularity. It should strike the reader as a wording of his own highest thoughts, and appear almost as a remembrance."

YUSEF KOMUNYAKAA (1947–   ) was born the oldest of five children in Bogalusa, Louisiana. After high school, he enlisted in the Army. He served as a war correspondent for the *Southern Cross* during the Vietnam War, and he was awarded a Bronze Star. His experiences during the war became the basis for one of his most important collections of poetry, *Dien Cai Dau* (1988). In addition to this collection, Komunyakaa's numerous books of poems include *Copacetic* (1984), *I Apologize for the Eyes in My Head* (1986), *Magic City* (1992), *Thieves of Paradise* (1998), *Talking Dirty to the Gods* (2000), *Taboo* (2004), and two collections of new and collected poems — one of which, *Neon Vernacular* (1993), won the Pulitzer Prize in 1994. His most recent poetry collection, *Pleasure Dome: New and Collected Poems, 1975–1999,* was published in 2001. The recipient of numerous prizes and awards, Komunyakaa has also coedited two anthologies of jazz poetry and worked on various musical and lyrical collaborations with musicians and artists from around the world. Elected a chancellor of the Academy of American Poets in 1999, he is currently a professor in the Council of Humanities and Creative Writing Program at Princeton University.

TED KOOSER (1939–   ) was born in Ames, Iowa, and received his BA from Iowa State and his MA in English from the University of Nebraska–Lincoln. He is the author of ten collections of poetry, including *Delights and Shadows* (2004), *Winter Morning Walks: One Hundred Postcards to Jim Harrison* (2000), *Weather Central* (1994), *One World at a Time* (1985), and *Sure Signs* (1980). His fiction and nonfiction books include *Braided Creek: A Conversation in Poetry* (2003) and *Local Wonders: Seasons in the Bohemian Alps* (2002). In 2004, Kooser was named Poet Laureate of the United States. He is now a visiting professor at the University of Nebraska–Lincoln. His latest works are *Flying at Night: Poems 1965–1985* (Pitt Poetry Series) (2005) and *The Poetry Repair Manual: Practical Advice for Beginning Poets* (2005).

LI-YOUNG LEE (1957–   ) Li-Young Lee was born in Jakarta, Indonesia, of Chinese parents. His father, who was a personal physician to Mao Zedong while in China, relocated his family to Indonesia, where he helped found Gamaliel University. In 1959, the Lee family fled Indonesia to escape anti-Chinese sentiment. After a five-year journey through Hong Kong, Macau, and Japan, they settled in the United States in 1964. Li-Young Lee attended the University of Pittsburgh, the University of Arizona, and the State University of New York at Brockport. His collections of poetry include *Book of My Nights* (2001), *The City in Which I Love You* (1991), and *Rose* (1986), as well as a memoir entitled *The Winged Seed: A Remembrance* (1995), which received an American Book Award from the Before Columbus Foundation. Other honors include a Lannan Literary Award, a Whiting Writer's Award, and a Guggenheim Foundation fellowship.

CLAUDE MCKAY (1890–1948), born in Jamaica, received part of his education from a well-read older brother. Two early volumes of poetry won him an award and stipend from the Jamaican Institute of Arts and Sciences to study at Tuskeegee Institute and at Kansas State College. In 1914, he traveled to New York City, and his works *Harlem Shadows* (1922) and *Home to Harlem* (1927) established him as an important writer of the Harlem Renaissance. His best work is collected in *The Passion of Claude McKay: Selected Poetry and Prose, 1912–1948.* Written in traditional meter and rhyme, his poetry expresses powerful, compressed passion about topics both personal and social. His elegant control disguises his anger, as seen in his descriptions of the New York City that he both loved and hated. According to critic Arthur D. Prayton, "McKay does not seek to hide his bitterness, but having preserved his vision as a poet and his status as a human being, he can transcend bitterness." Something of this transcendence appears in McKay's "If We Must Die": "Like men will face the murderous, cowardly push. / Press to the wall, dying, but fighting back."

EDNA ST. VINCENT MILLAY (1892–1950) was born in Rockland, Maine. Her mother raised her three daughters on her own, and she encouraged her girls to be ambitious and self-sufficient, teaching them an appreciation of music and literature. After attending Vassar College on a scholarship, Millay published several collections of poems and a play in verse. She moved to New York City's Greenwich Village, where she led a notoriously bohemian lifestyle, living for a time in a nine-foot-wide attic and maintaining an "open marriage" with her husband for twenty-six years. Her most famous collection of poetry is *Renascence and Other Poems* (1917).

JOHN MILTON (1608–1674) was born in London's Cheapside district, the son of a businessman. He was educated at St. Paul's, where he showed a great aptitude for languages, mastering both Latin and Greek before turning to Hebrew and modern European tongues. After his graduation from Christ's College, Cambridge, where he earned his BA in 1629 and his MA in 1632, Milton returned to his father's house in Buckinghamshire and continued his education, reading day and night for six years. In 1634, he wrote the masque popularly known as *Comus,* and in 1637, he wrote the great elegy *Lycidas* for a college classmate who had drowned. From 1640 to 1660, Milton was embroiled in the political-religious controversies of the time, publishing tract after tract in what are known as the pamphlet wars. For a time, he was imprisoned at peril of his life, but at the intervention of friends (the poet Andrew Marvell among them), he was released. In 1663, blind and impoverished, Milton began work on his masterpiece, a long poem aimed at "justifying the ways of God to men." *Paradise Lost* was published in 1667 and was at once recognized as a supreme epic achievement. It was followed by *Paradise Regained* in 1671 and *Samson Agonistes,* a tragedy, in 1674. Combining Renaissance learning and Latinate style with a staunchly Reformation temperament, Milton's work continues to inspire and challenge readers three centuries after his death. He wrote, in *The Reason of Church Government,* "By labor and intent study (which I take to be my portion in this life), joined with the strong propensity of nature, I might perhaps leave something so written to after-times, as they should not willingly let it die."

N(AVARRE) SCOTT MOMADAY (1934–   ) was born in Lawton, Oklahoma, and studied at the University of New Mexico and Stanford University, where he received his PhD in 1963. In 1969, he became the first Native American writer to win a Pulitzer Prize, awarded for his first novel, *House Made of Dawn* (1969). His autobiographical work *The Names: A Memoir* (1976) recounts his growing up in New Mexico. His other publications include volumes of poetry —*Angle of Geese and Other Poems* (1974) and *Gourd Dancer* (1976)— and *The Way to Rainy Mountain* (1969), a collection of personal and historical narratives interwoven with tales from Kiowa mythology. He also wrote another novel, *The Ancient Child* (1989), and a collection of poems and narratives that he illustrated, *In the Presence of Sun* (1991). In 1993, he published *Circle of Wonder: A Native American Christmas Story* and *The Native Americans: Indian Country.* A collection of essays, *The Man Made of Words,* was published in 1997. Critic Roger Dickinson-Brown referred to Momaday's work as "a fusion of alien cultures and . . . extraordinary experiments in different literary forms." Momaday, who considers himself primarily a poet, has stated that he returns again and again to his Kiowa culture for inspiration because it has "a certain strength and beauty I find missing in the modern world."

PAT MORA (1942–   ), a leading figure in contemporary Hispanic poetry, was born in El Paso, Texas. She received a BA from Texas Western College in 1963 and an MA from the University of Texas, El Paso, in 1967. In addition to writing poetry, nonfiction, and children's books, Mora has taught at the University of New Mexico, where she held the position of Distinguished Visiting Professor. Her recent books include *My Own True Name: New and Selected Poems for Young Adults, 1984–1999* (2000); *Aunt Carmen's Book of Practical Saints* (1997); and *Agua Santa: Holy Water* (1995). In addition to her books of poetry, Mora is the author of numer-ous children's books, including *A Birthday Basket for Tia* (1992), and a memoir. Her most recent works include *Doña Flor: A Tall Tale About a Giant Woman with a Great Big Heart* (2005) and *The Song of Francis and the Animals* (2005).

SHARON OLDS (1942–   ), born in San Francisco, attended Stanford and Co-lumbia, where she received her PhD in 1972. Her poetry collections include *The Dead and the Living* (1983), winner of both the Lamont Poetry Award and the Na-tional Book Critics Circle Award; *The Gold Cell* (1987); *The Father* (1992); *The Wellspring* (1995); *Blood, Tin, Straw* (1999); and *Unswept Room* (2002). She re-ceived major grants from New York state, the National Endowment for the Arts, and the Guggenheim Foundation. She served as the New York State Poet Laure-ate from 1998 to 2000. More recently, she published the poetry collection *Strike Sparks: Selected Poems* in 2004. Because she so graphically details personal traumas, some critics place her in the confessional tradition of Sylvia Plath. However, Olds's poems have a less tormented tone and are more easily understood. Her style com-bines grotesque humor and straightforward reporting in a manner that *Poetry* magazine critic Lisel Mueller has called "a proud, urgent human voice." This persona is well illus-trated in these lines from Olds's poem "35/10," published a few years after she turned thirty-five: "Brushing out my daughter's dark / silken hair before the mirror / I see the grey gleaming on my head, / . . . it's an old / story — the oldest we have on our planet — / the story of replacement."

MARY OLIVER (1935–   ) was born in Maple Heights, Ohio. A widely renowned nature writer, she is the author of several volumes of poetry, including *Why I Wake Early* (2004); *Owls and Other Fantasies: Poems and Essays* (2003); *Winter Hours: Prose, Prose Poems, and Poems* (1999); *West Wind* (1997); *White Pine* (1994); *New and Selected Poems* (1992), which won the National Book Award; and *American Primitive* (1983), for which she won the Pulitzer Prize in 1983. Her books of prose include *Long Life: Essays and Other Writings* (2004); *Rules for the Dance: A Handbook for Writing and Reading Metrical Verse* (1998); *Blue Pastures* (1995); and *A Poetry Handbook* (1994). Mary Oliver holds the Catharine Osgood Foster Chair for Distinguished Teaching at Bennington College. Her most recent work is *New and Selected Poems: Volume Two* (2005).

JUDITH ORTIZ COFER (1952–   ) was born in Hormigueros, Puerto Rico, and moved north with her family in 1960. The Cofers settled in Paterson, New Jersey; much of her memory of that time ("all in shades of gray") is vividly recorded in her collection of essays and poetry, *Silent Dancing: A Partial Remembrance of a Puerto Rican Childhood* (1991). She is the author of two additional collections of essays, *The Year of Revolution* (1998) and *Woman in Front of the Sun: On Becoming a Writer* (2000); a novel, *The Line of the Sun* (1989); two books of poetry, *Terms of Survival* and *Reaching for the Mainland* (both 1987); *The Latin Deli: Prose and Poetry* (1993); and *The Year of Our Revolution: Selected and New Prose and Poetry* (1998). Her collection *An Island like You: Stories of the Barrio* (1996) won the first Pura Belpre Award and was named a Best Book of the Year 1995–1996 by the American Library Association. Her most recent books are *The Meaning of Consuelo* (2003), *Call Me Maria* (2004), and *A Love Story Beginning in Spanish: Poems* (2005). She is currently professor of English and director of the Creative Writing Program at the University of Georgia. Of her bilingual writing life, Cofer has said, "The 'infinite variety' and power of language interest me. I never cease to experiment with it. As a native Puerto Rican, my first language was Spanish. It was a challenge, not only to learn English, but to master it enough to teach it and — the ultimate goal — to write poetry in it."

LINDA PASTAN (1932–   ), born in The Bronx, New York, received her BA from Radcliffe College, her MLS from Simmons College, and her MA from Brandeis University. Her publications include *A Perfect Circle of Sun* (1971); *On the Way to the Zoo* (1975); *Aspects of Eve* (1977); *The Five Stages of Grief* (1978), winner of the Poetry Society of America award; *PM/AM: New and Selected Poems* (1983), American Book Award nominee; *The Imperfect Paradise* (1988); *Heroes in Disguise* (1991); and *An Early Afterlife* (1995). Her most recent collection is *The Last Uncle* (2002). She has received fellowships from the Bread Loaf Writers' Conference and the National Endowment for the Arts. She was Poet Laureate for Maryland from 1991 through 1994. According to prominent feminist critic Sandra M. Gilbert, Pastan "broods on the rewards as well as the risks of domesticity" because she is "quite self-consciously a *woman* poet" who "austerely ordains the necessity of acquiescence in the ordinary." Pastan has explained how she writes poetry: "By allowing myself to follow a poem wherever it wants to take me, I find that I often stumble upon truths about myself, my world, that I scarcely suspected I knew"; she then compares the writing process to "following the thread through the labyrinth, trying at all costs to avoid the minotaur."

OCTAVIO PAZ (1914–1998) was born in Mexico City to parents of Spanish and Mexican descent. He was educated at the National University of Mexico in law and literature, and under the encouragement of poet Pablo Neruda, he began his poetic career in his teens by founding an avant-garde literary magazine, *Barandal*, and publishing his first book of poems, *Luna silvestre* (1933). In his youth, Paz spent time in the United States and in Spain, where he was influenced by the modernist and surrealist movements. His sequence of prose poems, *Aguila o sol?* (*Eagle or Sun?*) (1951) is a visionary mapping of Mexico in terms of its past, present, and future, and *Piedra de Sol* (*Sun Stone*) (1957) borrows its structure from the Aztec calendar. This long poem, and Paz's sociocultural analysis of Mexico, *El laberinto de la soledad* (*The Labyrinth of Solitude*) (1950), established him as a major literary figure in the 1950s. In 1962, he became Mexico's ambassador to India but resigned six years later in protest when government forces massacred student demonstrators in Mexico City. He was awarded the Nobel Prize in Literature in 1990.

MARGE PIERCY (1936–   ) grew up poor and white in a predominantly black neighborhood in Detroit. She received a bachelor's degree from the University of Michigan in 1957 and a master's degree from Northwestern University in 1958. Her publications include *Woman on the Edge of Time* (1976), *Circles on the Water* (1982), *Braided Lives* (1982), and *The Longings of Women* (1994). In addition to her novels and a collection of essays, Piercy has written numerous collections of poetry, including *What are Big Girls Made Of?* (1997). Her volume of poetry, *The Art of Blessing the Day: Poems with a Jewish Theme* (1999), celebrates the traditions of her religion. Author Erica Jong called the often-controversial Piercy "an immensely gifted poet and novelist whose range and versatility have made it hard for her talents to be adequately appreciated critically." Piercy has said that she wants her writing to be "useful" so "readers will find poems that speak to and for them, will take those poems into their lives and say them to each other and put them up on the bathroom wall and remember bits and pieces of them in stressful or quiet moments." Her most recent work, *Sex Wars: A Novel of the Turbulent Post–Civil War Period*, was published in 2005.

ROBERT PINSKY (1940–   ) was born in the seashore resort of Long Branch, New Jersey. He attended Rutgers College and then Stanford University, where he held a Stegner Fellowship in Creative Writing. Pinsky is the author of six books of poetry: *Sadness and Happiness* (1975); *An Explanation of America* (1980); *History of My Heart* (1984); *The Want Bone* (1990); *The Figured Wheel: New and Collected Poems 1966–1996* (1996), which won the 1997 Lenore Poetry Prize and was a Pulitzer Prize nominee; and *Jersey Rain* (2000). Two of his four books of criticism are *The Sounds of Poetry* (1998), which was a finalist for the National Book Critics Circle Award, and *The Situation of Poetry* (1977). His best-selling translation of *The Inferno of Dante* (1994) was called by critic Stephen Greenblatt "the premier modern text for English-language readers to experience Dante's power." Pinsky's honors include an American Academy of Arts and Letters award, the Oscar Blumenthal Prize, the William Carlos Williams Award, and a Guggenheim Foundation Fellowship. In 1997, he was named the thirty-ninth Poet Laureate of the United States, a position he held for an unprecedented three years. A member of the American Academy of Arts and Sciences and the American Academy of Arts and Letters, he currently teaches in the graduate writing program at Boston University. Stressing the vocal nature of poetry — as apart from its merely *literary* existence — Pinsky has said, "A poem is something that occurs, a poem takes place, in a reader's voice."

SYLVIA PLATH (1932–1963) was born in Boston to Polish-German parents who taught at Boston University. She graduated from Smith College in 1955 and then won a Fulbright Fellowship to Cambridge University (MA, 1957), where she met and married poet Ted Hughes. Having won a *Mademoiselle* magazine prize (1953), an award from *Poetry* magazine (1957), and a Yaddo writers' colony fellowship (1959), she began a promising career. After *A Winter Ship* (1960) came *The Colossus and Other Poems* (1962) and a novel, *The Bell Jar,* (1963). Plath committed suicide at age thirty-one, soon after her seven-year marriage to Hughes ended. Her posthumous works are *Ariel* (1965); *Crossing the Water* (1971); *Winter Trees* (1971); *Letters Home by Sylvia Plath: Correspondence 1950–1963* (1975); *Johnny Panic and the Bible of Dreams and Other Prose Writings* (1977); and her *Collected Poems,* a 1982 Pulitzer Prize winner. In the introduction to *Ariel,* Robert Lowell praised her as "one of those super-real, hypnotic, great classical heroines." In a 1958 journal entry, Plath prophesied: "coming again to make and make in the face of the flux; making of the moment something of permanence. That is the lifework. . . . My life, I feel, will not be lived until there are books and stories which relive it perpetually in time."

EZRA POUND (1885–1972), born in Hailey, Idaho, spent his childhood near Philadelphia. He graduated from Hamilton College in 1905 and received an MA from the University of Pennsylvania in 1906. After his first volume, *A Lume Spento* (1908), he published *Personae and Exultations of Ezra Pound* (1913), *Homage to Sextus Propertius* (1919), and *Hugh Selwyn Mauberley* (1920). In 1917, he began his best-known work — a series of cantos that eventually included *The Pisan Cantos* (1948) and *Thrones: Cantos 96 — 109* (1959). During World War II, Pound fervently supported Mussolini and broadcast Fascist propaganda over Italian radio. After the war, he was arrested for treason against the United States and was incarcerated in a mental hospital in Washington, D.C., from 1946 to 1958. A motivating force behind modern poetry, Pound won the Bollingen–Library of Congress Award in 1948. Critic Robert Hillyer protested bitterly that Pound's Fascist and anti-Semitic poems were "the vehicle of contempt for America" and that the prize-winning *Pisan Cantos* were a "ruthless mockery" of America's war dead. Leader of the Imagist poets, Pound experimented with poetic images to express "an intellectual and emotional complex in an instant of time." He once told an interviewer, "You cannot have literature without curiosity and when a writer's curiosity dries out he is finished."

ADRIENNE RICH (1929–   ), born and raised in Baltimore, began her prolific publishing career during her senior year at Radcliffe when her first book, *A Change of World,* was published by W. H. Auden in the Yale Series of Younger Poets. After graduating in 1951, she studied at Oxford. She has received Guggenheim fellowships, a Poetry Society of America award, a National Institute of Arts and Letters award, a Bollingen Foundation grant, and a National Endowment for the Arts grant. Rich writes about feminist issues in her many poetry collections, including *Twenty-one Love Poems* (1976); *The Dream of a Common Language,*

Poems 1974–1977 (1978); *The Fact of a Doorframe: Poems Selected and New 1950–1984* (1985); *Dark Fields of the Republic: Poems, 1991–1995* (1995); *Time's Power: Poems, 1985–88* (1989); and *Midnight Salvage: Poems (1995–1998).* Her most recent collections are *Fox: Poems 1998–2000,* published in 2001, and *The School Among the Ruins: Poems 2000–2004,* published in 2004. *The Diamond Cutters and Other Poems* (1955) won the Poetry Society of America Award, and *Diving into the Wreck: Poems 1971–1972* (1973) won the 1974 National Book Award. William Heyen noted that Rich's work describes years of conflict as woman, wife, mother, and poet. Rich once commented, "Instead of poems *about* experiences I am getting poems that *are* experiences, that contribute to my knowledge and my emotional life even while they reflect and assimilate it."

EDWIN ARLINGTON ROBINSON (1869–1935), a descendant of the Puritan poet Anne Bradstreet, was born in Head Tide, Maine, where his father had a grain and lumber business. He grew up in Gardiner, Maine (the inspiration for his fictitious Tilbury Town) and then studied for two years at Harvard before his family's financial difficulties halted his education. He went on to publish *The Torrent and the Night Before* (1896), *The Children of the Night* (1897), and *Captain Craig* (1902). In 1916, *The Man against the Sky* confirmed his reputation as a major poet. Pulitzer Prizes were awarded for his *Collected Poems* (1921), *The Man Who Died Twice* (1924), and *Tristram* (1927). Robert Frost, in his introduction to Robinson's posthumous *King Jasper* (1935), characterized Robinson as a poet who "stayed content with the old-fashioned way to be new," unlike contemporary experimentalists who used poetry to express their grievances against society; he praised Robinson's skillful blending of playful humor and profound melancholy. Robinson commented in a 1916 interview with poet Joyce Kilmer that poetry is both "undefinable" and "unmistakable: a language which tells us, through a more or less emotional experience, something that cannot be said."

THEODORE ROETHKE (1908–1963) was born and grew up in Saginaw, Michigan, where his father owned a twenty-five-acre greenhouse complex that inspired much of his symbolism. After completing his education at the University of Michigan and Harvard, he taught English at Lafayette College, Penn State, Bennington College, and the University of Washington, where he became poet-in-residence a year before he died. He won the Pulitzer Prize (1954) and two National Book Awards (1959 and 1965) for *Words for the Wind* (1958) and *The Far Field* (1964), respectively. Poet and critic Stanley Kunitz praised his rare gifts as a writer: "The ferocity of Roethke's imagination makes most contemporary poetry seem pale and tepid in contrast. Even his wit is murderous. . . . What Roethke brings us is news of the root, of the minimal, of the primordial. The sub-human is given tongue; and the tongue proclaims the agony of coming alive, the painful miracle of growth." Roethke once explained that he wrote about "trivial and vulgar" details "as barely and honestly as possible, symbolically, what few nuggets of observation and, let us hope, spiritual wisdom I have managed to seize upon in the course of a conventional albeit sometimes disordered existence."

CHRISTINA ROSSETTI (1830–1894) was born in London, England, the daughter of a Neapolitan political exile and sister of the poet-painter Dante Gabriel Rossetti. She was educated at home by her mother. While still a child, she showed such poetic promise that her grandfather had small collections of her poems published when she was twelve and fifteen. Her first mature volume of verse, *Goblin Market and Other Poems,* was published in 1862; before that, lyrics such as "An End" and "Dream Lane" had been published in magazines under her pseudonym, Ellen Alleyne. *Goblin Market* was followed by *The Prince's Progress and Other Poems* (1866) and *Sing Song: A Nursery Rhyme Book* (1872). By the 1880s, ill health had made her an invalid, but she continued to write poetry. *A Pageant and Other Poems,* published in 1881, contains her sonnet sequence *Monna Innominata.* It was followed by *Time Flies: A Reading Diary* (1885) and *The Face of the Deep: A Devotional Commentary on the Apocalypse* (1892), her last published work. Highly accomplished in its verbal precision and metrical invention, her verse bears the influence of the Pre-Raphaelite movement, which her brother Dante Gabriel Rossetti helped to found. Her brother William edited her complete works (1904) after her death.

SONIA SANCHEZ (1934–   ) moved from her birthplace of Birmingham, Alabama, to New York City, where she later studied political science and poetry at Hunter College (BA, 1955) and New York University. Her publications include *Homecoming* (1969); *It's a New Day: Poems for Young Brothas and Sistuhs* (1971); *A Blues Book for Blue Black Magical Women* (1973); *I'm Black When I'm Singing, I'm Blue When I Ain't* (1982); *homegirls & handgrenades* (1984); *Like the Singing Coming off the Drums: Love Poems* (1998); and *Shake Loose My Skin: New and Selected Poems* (1999). She has received grants from the National Institute of Arts and Letters and the National Endowment for the Arts and won the American Book Award. Critic C. W. E. Bigsby finds her work distinguished by "language which catches the nuance of the spoken word, the rhythms of the street, and of a music which is partly jazz and partly a lyricism which underlies ordinary conversation." A strong black feminist advocate, Sanchez supports change, not through rage, violence, or substance abuse but through political astuteness, moral power, and strong family relationships. Sanchez has declared, "I recognize that my writing must serve a dual purpose. It must be a clarion call to the values of change while it also speaks to the beauty of a nonexploitative age." She was the 2001 recipient of the Robert Frost medal in poetry. In 2004, she celebrated the release of a new CD titled *The Full Moon of Sonia.*

CARL SANDBURG (1878–1967) was born in Galesburg, Illinois, to Swedish immigrant parents. He studied at Lombard College and later wrote for *Poetry* magazine. His volumes of verse, often about industrialized America, include *Chicago Poems* (1915), *Corn Huskers* (1918), *Smoke and Steel* (1920), and *Good Morning, America* (1928); in 1951 he won the Pulitzer Prize for his *Complete Poems.* He also wrote prose works, such as *Abraham Lincoln: The Prairie Years* (1926) and *Abraham Lincoln: The War Years* (1940). On his seventy-fifth birthday, in 1953, Governor Adlai Stevenson proclaimed Carl Sandburg Day in Illinois, and a representative of King Gustav VI of Sweden decorated him with the Commander Order of the Northern Star. According to historian Henry Steele Commager, Sandburg "celebrates what is best in us, and recalls us to our heritage and our humanity." In notes to his *Complete Poems,* Sandburg affirmed his purpose as a poet "of streets and struggles, of dust and combat, of violence wanton or justified, of plain folk living close to a hard earth." On his eighty-fifth birthday, in 1963, when he published his final book, *Honey and Salt,* Sandburg confessed, "Being a poet is a damn dangerous business."

WILLIAM SHAKESPEARE (1564–1616) was born in Stratford-upon-Avon and was probably educated at the King Edward IV Grammar School in Stratford, where he learned Latin and some Greek and read the Roman dramatists. At eighteen, he married Anne Hathaway, a woman seven or eight years his senior, and together they raised a family. Little is known about Shakespeare's activities between 1585 and 1592, but in 1594, Shakespeare joined the Lord Chamberlain's Men, the most popular of the companies acting at the royal court. The acting troupe would eventually build, and, in 1599, open the Globe, a new playhouse that became the most famous theater of its time. Although Shakespeare was regarded as the foremost dramatist of his time, the overarching sentiment of the era was that poetry, not playwriting, would be the means toward enduring fame, and so he focused on the sonnet form. Composed between 1593 and 1601, Shakespeare's sonnets are considered immortal expressions of love and beauty. Shakespeare then turned his attentions to drama, writing more than thirty plays during his lifetime, including histories, comedies, tragedies, and romances. Although he chose the dramatic form for these stories, his plays were often written in verse, especially iambic pentameter, and many scenes contain within them "hidden sonnets" with perfect rhymes. His most famous and celebrated plays include *Romeo and Juliet, Julius Caesar, Hamlet, Othello, King Lear, Macbeth,* and *The Tempest.* Shakespeare retired from the stage in 1612, four years before his death.

TUPAC SHAKUR (1971–1996) was born Lesane Parish Crooks in Brooklyn, New York, but his mother soon changed his name to Tupac Amaru after an Inca Indian revolutionary. His father, a Black Panther, was sentenced to sixty years in prison for his part in a fatal armored car robbery when Shakur was two years old, and the singer was raised by his mother, also a Black Panther. After winning a scholarship to the prestigious Baltimore School of the Arts, he began writing raps and acting. The single "Brenda's Got a Baby" launched his career and landed him a role in the motion picture *Juice* (1992). From there, he appeared in *Poetic Justice* (1993) and went on to release a platinum album, *Me Against the World* (1995). In addition to writing rap lyrics, Shakur wrote poetry that combined elements of the street and hip-hop culture with lyrical forms. Shakur, who was arrested eight times by the time he was twenty, was notorious for promoting the "Thug Life," which glorified living and dying by the gun. On September 7, 1996, he was shot by unknown gunmen in Las Vegas. He died of respiratory failure six days later. His murderers were never apprehended.

PERCY BYSSHE SHELLEY (1792–1822) was born at Field Place, near Horsham, West Sussex, England. He attended Oxford but was expelled after he published his pamphlet *The Necessity of Atheism* (1811). He eloped to Scotland with Harriet Westbrook, a move that, combined with his refusal to retract his pamphlet, caused a permanent break with his family. While in Scotland, Shelley corresponded with the radical thinker William Godwin, published a series of political works, and composed his poem *Queen Mab* (1813). After moving to London, Shelley joined Godwin and fell in love with Godwin's sixteen-year-old daughter, Mary (later Mary Shelley, author of *Frankenstein*). Despite the birth of Shelley's daughter by Harriet, Shelley and Mary Godwin ran off to the Continent in 1814, spending the summer of 1816 at Lake Geneva with the poet and celebrity George Gordon, Lord Byron. Harriet drowned herself that autumn, and Shelley immediately married Mary. In 1818, they left England permanently and settled in Italy, living first in Venice with Byron. Shelley completed his long poem *Prometheus Unbound* in 1819; that year and the next constituted his most productive period. "Ode to the West Wind" and many of his important lyrics belong to this time. He drowned in a tempest at age twenty-nine when his boat went down in the Gulf of Spezia. Grudgingly admired in his own day, his poetry was a major influence on later nineteenth-century poets such as Tennyson and Robert Browning. Mary Shelley collected his *Poetical Works* in 1839.

(AKINWANDE OLUWOLE) WOLE SOYINKA (1934–   ) was born in western Nigeria; his parents were both educators. In *Aké: The Years of Childhood* (1981), he wrote about growing up under colonial rule. Soyinka attended the University College of Ibadan and the University of Leeds. His *Collected Plays* (Vol. 1, 1973; Vol. 2, 1974), along with major works such as *Death and the King's Horseman* (1975) and *The Interpreters* (1965), led to his winning the Nobel Prize in Literature in 1986. The Swedish Academy described him as "a writer who in a wide cultural perspective and with poetic overtures fashions the drama of existence." In addition to his analytical work *Myth, Literature, and the African World* (1976), he has published two volumes based on lectures at the W. E. B. Du Bois Institute at Harvard: *Open Sore of a Continent: A Personal Narrative of the Nigerian Crisis* (1996) and *The Burden of Memory, the Muse of Forgiveness* (1999). A deeply committed political writer and activist, Soyinka endured repeated imprisonment for his outspoken beliefs. Despite this persecution, in 1999 he returned to his homeland after a long absence. Soyinka explained, "I would be frankly ill at ease with myself if I failed to call attention to the public for . . . its . . . abdication of basic rights to official crooks, thugs, touts and other . . . scum of society." His most recent play, *King Baabu,* was published in 2001.

WILLIAM STAFFORD (1914–1993) was born in Hutchinson, Kansas, and received a BA and an MA from the University of Kansas at Lawrence and, in 1954, a PhD from the University of Iowa. During World War II, Stafford, a conscientious objector, worked in civilian public service camps — an experience he recorded in the prose memoir *Down My Heart* (1947). In 1948, Stafford moved to Oregon to teach at Lewis and Clark College. Though he traveled and read his work widely, he continued to teach at Lewis and Clark until 1980. His first major collection of poems, *Traveling Through the Dark* (1962), was published when Stafford was forty-eight and won the National Book Award in 1963. He went on to publish more than sixty-five volumes of poetry and prose. He served as Poet Laureate of the United States from 1970 to 1971.

WALLACE STEVENS (1879–1955) was born in Reading, Pennsylvania, son of a prominent attorney and a schoolteacher. He attended Harvard, where he began writing poetry, and New York Law School. In 1916, he took a job with the Hartford Accident and Indemnity Company, which afforded him and his family a prosperous life, and he continued writing poetry. For his life work, he was awarded the Bollingen Prize in 1949, and in 1955 he won both the Pulitzer Prize and the National Book Award for his *Collected Poems.* As critic Richard Gray noted, Stevens's poems fuse elements of the ancient, the Romantic, and the American poet: "Stevens returned the poet to his ancient role of bard or myth-maker, offering purpose and a sense of meaning to his tribe. And to this he added another more peculiarly Romantic and American dimension, which was that of hero." His poem "Of Modern Poetry" defines "the poem of the act of the mind." In a letter to his wife, Stevens wrote, "The priest in me worshipped one God at one shrine; the poet another God at another shrine. The priest worshipped Mercy and Love; the poet Beauty and Might."

WISLAWA SZYMBORSKA (1923–   ) was born in Bnin (now a part of Kórnik) in western Poland. She studied Polish literature and sociology at Jagiellonian University in Krakow. She has published more than fifteen books of poetry, and her poems have been translated into many languages. Collections of her work available in English include *Miracle Fair: Selected Poems of Wislawa Szymborska* (2001); *View with a Grain of Sand: Selected Poems* (1995); *People on a Bridge* (1990); and *Sounds, Feelings, Thoughts: Seventy Poems* (1981). Wislawa Szymborska won the Nobel Prize in Literature in 1996.

ALFRED, LORD TENNYSON (1809–1892) was born in Somersby, Lincolnshire, England, and was educated at Trinity College, Cambridge, but left in 1831 without taking a degree. Tennyson's early collection *Poems, Chiefly Lyrical* (1830) was not well received. Neither was *Poems* (1832), which included major works such as "The Lady of Shallott" and "The Lotos-Eaters." In the ten years following the publication of *Poems,* Tennyson revised earlier works and continued to write poetry. Finally, in 1842, two volumes of *Poems* were published and well received. Among the new works in these volumes were "Ulysses," "Locksley Hall," and "Morte d'Arthur." Tennyson had begun writing a poem in memory of his best friend, Arthur Hallam in 1834; in 1850, *In Memoriam* was published. Also in 1850, Tennyson succeeded William Wordsworth as Poet Laureate of England. In 1855, he published *Maud and Other Poems,* which included the title work and "The Charge of the Light Brigade." From 1859 to 1885, he issued his series of Arthurian poems, *Idylls of the King.* He continued to write poems and plays until his death in 1892. A meticulous craftsman with an ear for the music of verse and the fluctuations of thought, Tennyson stands with Robert Browning as creator of the Victorian dramatic monologue. His variety of verse forms extended the range of metrical poetry in English. Though his reputation declined somewhat after his death, T. S. Eliot and other poets of the twentieth century acknowledged the influence of his work. Of Tennyson's technical accomplishment in *In Memoriam,* Eliot wrote: "I do not think any poet in English has ever had a finer ear for vowel sound, as well as a subtler feeling for some moods of anguish."

MONA VAN DUYN (1921–2004) was born in Waterloo, Iowa. Van Duyn taught widely in the United States and abroad, most recently at Washington University. She is the author of nine books of poems: *Firefall* (1994); *If It Be Not I: Collected Poems, 1959–1982* (1994); *Near Changes* (1990), for which she won a Pulitzer Prize; *Letters from a Father and Other Poems* (1982); *Merciful Disguises* (1973, reissued 1982); *Bedtime Stories* (1972); *To See, to Take* (1970), recipient of the National Book Award; *A Time of Bees* (1964); and *Valentines to the Wide World* (1959). With her husband, Jarvis Thurston, she founded *Perspective: A Quarterly of Literature* in 1947 and coedited it until 1970. She received numerous prizes and awards, including the Bollingen Prize, the Hart Crane Memorial Award, and the Shelley Memorial Prize, as well as fellowships from the Academy of American Poets, the American Academy of Arts and Sciences, the Guggenheim Foundation, and the National Endowment for the Arts. She served as Poet Laureate of the United States (1992–1993) and was a chancellor of the Academy of American Poets. Of her work, Joseph Parisi has written: "From the publication of Mona Van Duyn's first book, her mastery of the art was immediately apparent, and each of her succeeding volumes has demonstrated the consistency of her strengths — her subtle intelligence and formidable technical skill, her gift for humor and satire, her formal elegance and especially her understanding of the vagaries and vulnerabilities of the human heart."

WALT WHITMAN (1819–1892) was born in Long Island, New York. After only six years of formal education, he left school and eventually became a newspaper reporter and editor. He worked as a part-time carpenter while writing his major work *Leaves of Grass,* which he continued to revise and expand until his death. In 1862, when his brother was wounded in the Civil War, Whitman went to Washington to work as a hospital nurse volunteer, an experience that led to *Drum-Taps* (1865); a later edition of this volume included the poem "When Lilacs Last in the Door-Yard Bloom'd." "Whitman has been an inescapable influence not only for most significant American poets after him," critic Harold Bloom has concluded, "but also for the most gifted writers of narrative fiction." Justifying the validity of the nontraditional forms of poetry he created, Whitman asserted, "The rhyme and conformity of perfect poems show the free growth of metrical laws and bud from them as unerringly and loosely as lilacs or roses on a bush, and take shapes as compact as the shapes of chestnuts and oranges and melons and peas, and shed the perfume impalpable to form."

RICHARD WILBUR (1921–   ), was born in New York City and grew up on a farm in North Caldwell, New Jersey. He graduated from Amherst in 1942, served in the infantry during World War II, and received his MA from Harvard in 1947. He began writing poetry in the army, and he has taught at Harvard, Wellesley, and Wesleyan. He won the Pulitzer Prize, the Edna St. Vincent Millay Memorial Award, and the National Book Award in 1957 for *Things of This World* (1956). Other works include *The Beautiful Changes and Other Poems* (1947); *Ceremony and Other Poems* (1950); *Poems, 1943–1956* (1957); *The Poems of Richard Wilbur* (1963); and *New and Collected Poems* (1989). Named Poet Laureate of the United States in 1987, Wilbur also has written translations, nonfiction, and operetta lyrics. Poet and critic Donald Hall praised Wilbur's "capacity for drawing sympathetically on the world of the past without getting out of touch with the present." Wilbur advocates a "strictness of form" to structure his poetry because the "strength of the genie," he believes, "comes of his being confined in a bottle." Beyond his scholarly life, Wilbur seeks "non-verbal" activities because, as he has explained, it is "good for a writer to move into words out of silence as much as he can." His most recent collection, *Collected Poems: 1943–2004,* was published in 2004.

WILLIAM CARLOS WILLIAMS (1883–1963) was born in Rutherford, New Jersey, to a British father and a mother of French, Dutch, and Spanish ancestry. He read the classics at home, attended private schools in Geneva and Paris, and then attended high school in New York City. Having studied medicine at the University of Pennsylvania (MD, 1906) Williams was a pediatrician for over forty years. He published widely in several genres — poetry, fiction, autobiography, essays, and drama. His many honors include the National Book Award (1950), the Bollingen Prize in Poetry (1952), and a posthumous Pulitzer Prize (1963) for *Pictures from Brueghel and Other Poems.* Perhaps his best-known work is *Paterson* (1946–1958). Williams's poetry, according to poet Randall Jarrell, "is more remarkable for its empathy, sympathy, its muscular and emotional identification with its subjects, than any other modern poetry except Rilke's." Reflecting on the origins of modern poetry and of his own work, Williams speculated that "it was the French painters rather than the writers who influenced us, and their influence was very great; they created an atmosphere of release, color-release, from stereotypical forms, trite subjects."

WILLIAM WORDSWORTH (1770–1850) was born in Cockermouth, Cumberland, England, and educated at Hawkshead in the Lake District and at St. John's College, Cambridge. In 1790, he embarked on a walking tour through France and Switzerland, commemorated in his early collection of poems, *Descriptive Sketches* (published in 1793). While in France, Wordsworth became devoted to the ideals of the French Revolution. On returning to England, he took up residence with his sister, Dorothy, who was to have a profound effect on his early poetry. Settling at Somerset, he developed a friendship with Samuel Taylor Coleridge, and the two began to compose the poems that would appear in *Lyrical Ballads* (1798); the volume's preface, written by Wordsworth, is essentially the manifesto of early English Romantic poetry. In 1802, after a year in Germany with Coleridge and Dorothy, Wordsworth married Mary Hutchinson and began work on his long autobiographical poem *The Prelude,* in which he traces the growth of a poet's mind. The first thirteen books of *The Prelude* were published in 1805; a revised edition appeared posthumously in 1850. In later life, Wordsworth became a kind of institution — he was appointed Poet Laureate of England in 1843 — receiving visits from admirers and political sympathizers at his home, Rydal Mount, in the English Lake District. His poetic powers waned in old age, and his conservatism fell under criticism by the younger generation of English Romantic poets; still, his revolutionary early work, his experiment with new verse forms, and his opening of new territory for poetry remain a deep and enduring legacy.

WILLIAM BUTLER YEATS (1865–1939) came from an upper-middle-class Anglo-Irish family in Dublin. He was educated in London and Dublin, where he attended the Metropolitan School of Art from 1884 to 1886. In 1923, he won the Nobel Prize in Literature in recognition not only of his achievements as a poet but also of his tireless efforts to promote Irish literature. As leader of the Celtic Renaissance in Ireland, Yeats celebrated nationalism in his early poetry, such as *The Wanderings of Oislin* (1889), based on Irish legend. His later poems, often mystical and deeply symbolic, reflect more expansive universal themes. Besides his highly regarded volumes of poetry, such as *The Wild Swans at Coole* (1917), *The*

Tower (1928), and *The Winding Stair and Other Poems* (1929), his legacy includes plays and essays. Renowned poet and critic T. S. Eliot praised Yeats for being among the few poets "whose history was the history of our own time, who are part of the consciousness of our age, which cannot be understood without them." Yeats's *Autobiographies* contains the following comment on the connection between art and artist: "When great artists were at their most creative the result was not simply a work of art, but rather the 're-creation of the man through that art.'"

 ADAM ZAGAJEWSKI (1945–   ) was born in Lwów, Poland, and spent his childhood in Silesia and then in Krakow, where he graduated from Jagiellonian University. Zagajewski first became well known as one of the leading poets of the "Generation of 1968," or the Polish New Wave, and is one of Poland's best known contemporary poets. His books of poetry in English include *Mysticism for Beginners* (1997); *Tremor* (1985); and *Canvas* (1991). He is also the author of a memoir, *Another Beauty* (2000); and of the prose collections, *Two Cities* (1991) and *Solitude and Solidarity* (1986). His poems and essays have been translated into many languages. Since 1988, he has served as Visiting Associate Professor of English in the Creative Writing Program at the University of Houston. He is currently coeditor of *Zeszyty literackie* (Literary Review), which is published in Paris. More recently, he published another poetry collection, *Without End,* as well as a collection of essays, *A Defense of Ardor* in 2004.

4| DRAMA

CHAPTER 36

UNDERSTANDING DRAMA

Dramatic Literature

The distinctive appearance of a script, with its stage directions, character parts, and divisions into acts and scenes, identifies **drama** as a unique form of literature. A play is written to be performed in front of an audience by actors who take on the roles of the characters and who present the story through dialogue and action. (An exception is **closet drama**, which is meant to be read, not performed.) Indeed, the term *theater* comes from the Greek word *theasthai*, which means "to view" or "to see." Thus, drama is different from novels and short stories, which are meant to be read.

Origins of Modern Drama

The Ancient Greek Theater

The dramatic presentations of ancient Greece developed out of religious rites performed to honor gods or to mark the coming of spring. Playwrights such as Aeschylus (525–456 B.C.), Sophocles (496–406 B.C.), and Euripides (480?–406 B.C.) wrote plays to be performed and judged at competitions held during the yearly Dionysian festivals. Works were chosen by a selection board and evaluated by a panel of judges. To compete in the contest, writers had to submit three tragedies, which could be either based on a common theme or unrelated, and one comedy. Unfortunately, relatively few of these ancient Greek plays survive today.

The open-air semicircular ancient Greek theater, built into the side of a hill, looked much like a primitive version of a modern sports stadium. Some Greek theaters, such as the Athenian theater, could seat almost seventeen thousand spectators. Sitting in tiered seats, the audience would look down on the **orchestra**, or "dancing place," occupied by the **chorus**—originally a group of men (led by an individual called the **choragos**) who danced and chanted, then later a group of onlookers who commented on the drama. Raised a few steps above the orchestra was a platform on which the actors performed. Behind this platform was a **skene**, or building, that originally served as a resting place or dressing room. (The modern word *scene* is derived from the Greek *skene*.) Behind the skene was a line of pillars called a **colonnade**, which was covered by a roof. Actors used the skene for

Grand Theater at Ephesus (3rd century B.C.), a Greek settlement in what is now Turkey.

entrances and exits; beginning with the plays of Sophocles, painted backdrops were hung there. These backdrops, however, were most likely more decorative than realistic. Historians believe that realistic props and scenery were probably absent from the ancient Greek theater. Instead, the setting was suggested by the play's dialogue, and the audience had to imagine the specific physical details of a scene.

Two mechanical devices were used. One, a rolling cart or platform, was sometimes employed to introduce action that had occurred offstage. For example, actors frozen in position could be rolled onto the roof of the skene to illustrate an event such as the killing of Oedipus's father, which occurred before the play began. Another mechanical device, a small crane, was used to show gods ascending to or descending from heaven. Such devices enabled playwrights to dramatize the myths that were celebrated at the Dionysian festivals.

The ancient Greek theater was designed to enhance acoustics. The flat stone wall of the skene reflected the sound from the orchestra and the stage, and the curved shape of the amphitheater captured the sound, enabling the audience to hear the lines spoken by the actors. Each actor wore a stylized mask, or **persona**, to convey to the audience the personality traits of the particular character being portrayed — a king, a soldier, a wise old man, a young girl (female roles were played by men). The mouths of these masks were probably constructed so they amplified the voice and projected it into the audience. In addition, the actors wore *kothorni*, high shoes that elevated them above the stage, perhaps also helping to project their voices. Due to the excellent acoustics, audiences who see plays performed in these ancient theaters today can hear clearly without microphones or speaker systems.

Because actors wore masks and because males played the parts of women and gods as well as men, acting methods in the ancient Greek theater were probably not realistic. In their masks, high shoes, and full-length tunics (called *chiton*), actors could not hope to appear natural or to mimic the attitudes of everyday life. Instead, they probably recited their lines while standing in stylized poses, with emotions conveyed more by gesture and tone than by action. Typically, three actors had all the speaking roles. One actor — the **protagonist** — would play the central role and have the largest speaking part. Two other actors would divide the remaining lines between them. Although other characters would come on and off the stage, they would usually not have speaking roles.

Ancient Greek tragedies were typically divided into five parts. The first part was the **prologos**, or prologue, in which an actor gave the background or explanations that the audience needed to follow the rest of the drama. Then came the **párodos**, in which the chorus entered and commented on the events presented in the prologue. Following this were several **episodia**, or episodes, in which characters spoke to one another on the stage and developed the central conflict of the play. Alternating with episodes were **stasimon** (choral odes), in which the chorus commented on the exchanges that had taken place during the preceding episode. Frequently, the choral odes were divided into *strophes*, or stanzas, which were recited or sung as the chorus moved across the orchestra in one direction, and *antistrophes*, which were recited as it moved in the opposite direction. (Interestingly, the chorus stood between the audience and the actors, often functioning as an additional audience, expressing the political, social, and moral views of the community.) The fifth part was the **exodos**, the last scene of the play, during which the conflict was resolved and the actors left the stage.

Using music, dance, and verse — as well as a variety of architectural and technical innovations — the ancient Greek theater was able to convey the traditional themes of tragedy. Thus, the theater powerfully expressed ideas that were central to the religious festivals in which they first appeared: the reverence for the cycles of life and death, the unavoidable dictates of the gods, and the inscrutable workings of fate.

The Elizabethan Theater

The Elizabethan theater, influenced by the classical traditions of Roman and Greek dramatists, traces its roots back to local religious pageants performed at medieval festivals during the twelfth and thirteenth centuries. Town guilds — organizations of craftsmen who worked in the same profession — reenacted Old and New Testament stories: the fall of man, Noah and the flood, David and Goliath, and the crucifixion of Christ, for example. Church fathers encouraged these plays because they brought the Bible to a largely illiterate audience. Sometimes these spectacles, called **mystery plays**, were presented in the market square or on the church steps, and at other times actors appeared on movable stages or wagons called **pageants**, which could be wheeled to a given location. (Some of these wagons were quite elaborate, with trapdoors and pulleys and an upper tier that simulated heaven.) As mystery plays became more popular, they were performed in series over several days, presenting an entire cycle of a holiday — the crucifixion and resurrection of Christ during Easter, for example.

Related to mystery plays are **morality plays**, which developed in the fourteenth and fifteenth centuries. Unlike mystery plays, which depict scenes from the Bible, morality plays allegorize the Christian way of life. Typically, characters representing various virtues and vices struggle or debate over the soul of man. *Everyman* (1500), the best known of these plays, dramatizes the good and bad qualities of Everyman and shows his struggle to determine what is of value to him as he journeys toward death.

By the middle of the sixteenth century, mystery and morality plays had lost ground to a new secular drama. One reason for this decline was that mystery and morality plays were associated with Catholicism and consequently discouraged by the Protestant clergy. In addition, newly discovered plays of ancient Greece and Rome introduced a dramatic tradition that supplanted the traditions of religious drama. English plays that followed the classic model were sensational and bombastic, often dealing with murder, revenge, and blood retribution. Appealing to privileged classes and commoners alike, these plays were extremely popular. (One source estimates that between 20,000 and 25,000 people attended performances each week.)

In spite of the popularity of the theater, actors and playwrights encountered a number of difficulties. First, they faced opposition from city officials who were averse to theatrical presentations because they thought that the crowds attending these performances spread disease. Puritans opposed the theater because they thought plays were immoral and sinful. Finally, some people attached to the royal court opposed the theater because they thought that the playwrights undermined the authority of Queen Elizabeth by spreading politically seditious ideas. As a result, during Elizabeth's reign, performances were placed under the strict control of the **Master of Revels**, a public official who had the power to censor plays (and did so with great regularity) and to grant licenses for performances.

Acting companies that wanted to put on a performance had to obtain a license — possible only with the patronage of a powerful nobleman — and to perform the play in an area designated by the queen. Despite these difficulties, a number of actors and playwrights gained a measure of financial independence by joining together and forming acting companies. These companies of professional actors performed works such as Christopher Marlowe's *Tamburlaine* and Thomas Kyd's *The Spanish Tragedy* in tavern courtyards and then eventually in permanent theaters. According to scholars, the structures of the Elizabethan theater evolved from these tavern courtyards.

William Shakespeare's plays were performed in the Globe Theatre (a corner of which was unearthed in December 1988). Although scholars do not know the exact design of the original Globe, drawings from the period provide a good idea of its physical features. The major difference between the Globe and today's theaters is the multiple stages on which action could be performed. The Globe consisted of a large main **stage** that extended out into the open-air **yard** where the **groundlings**, or common people, stood. Spectators who paid more sat on small stools in two or three levels of galleries that extended in front of and around the stage. (The theater could probably seat almost two thousand people at a performance.) Most of the play's action occurred on the stage, which had no curtain and could be seen from three sides. Beneath the stage was a space called the **hell**, which could be reached when the floorboards were removed. This space enabled actors to "disappear" or descend into a hole or grave when the play called for such action. Above the stage was a roof called the **heavens**, which protected the actors from the weather and contained ropes and pulleys used to lower props or to create special effects.

At the rear of the stage was a narrow **alcove** covered by a curtain that could be open or closed. This curtain, often painted, functioned as a decorative rather than a realistic backdrop. The main function of this alcove was to enable actors to hide or disappear when the script called for them to do so. Some Elizabethan theaters contained a **rear stage** instead of an alcove. Because the rear stage was concealed by a curtain, props could be arranged on it ahead of time. When the action on the rear stage was finished, the curtain would be closed and the action would continue on the front stage.

On either side of the rear stage was a door through which the actors could enter and exit the front stage. Above the rear stage was a curtained stage called the **chamber**, which functioned as a balcony or as any other setting located above the action taking place on the stage below. On either side of the chamber were casement windows, which actors could use when a play called for a conversation with someone leaning out a window or standing on a balcony. Above the chamber was the **music gallery**, a balcony that housed the musicians who provided musical interludes throughout the play (and that doubled as a stage if the play required it). The **huts**, windows located above the music gallery, could be used by characters playing lookouts or sentries. Because of the many acting sites, more than one action could take place simultaneously. For example, lookouts could stand in the towers of Hamlet's castle while Hamlet and Horatio walked the walls below.

During Shakespeare's time, the theater had many limitations that challenged the audience's imagination. Because women did not perform on the stage, young boys — usually between the ages of ten and twelve — played all the women's parts. In addition, there was no artificial lighting, so plays had to be performed in daylight. Rain, wind, or clouds could disrupt a performance or ruin an image — such as "the morn in russet mantle clad" — that the audience was asked to imagine. Finally, because few sets and props were used, the audience often had to visualize the high walls of a castle or the trees of a forest. The plays were performed without intermission, except for musical interludes that occurred at various points. Thus, the experience of seeing one of Shakespeare's plays staged in the Elizabethan theater was different from seeing it staged today in a modern theater.

Today, a reconstruction of the Globe Theatre stands on the south bank of the Thames River in London. In the 1940s, the late American actor Sam Wanamaker visited London and was shocked to find nothing that commemorated the site of the original Globe. He eventually decided to try to raise enough money to

The Globe Playhouse,
1599–1613

A CONJECTURAL

RECONSTRUCTION

KEY

AA Main entrance
B   The Yard
CC Entrances to lowest gallery
D   Entrances to staircase and upper
    galleries
E   Corridor serving the different sections
    of the middle gallery
F   Middle gallery ('Twopenny Rooms')
G   'Gentlemen's Rooms' or 'Lords' Rooms'
H   The stage

J   The hanging being put up round the
    stage
K   The 'Hell' under the stage
L   The stage trap, leading down to the
    Hell
MM Stage doors
N   Curtained 'place behind the stage'
O   Gallery above the stage, used as re-
    quired sometimes by musicians, some-
    times by spectators, and often as part
    of the play
P   Back-stage area (the tiring-house)
Q   Tiring-house door
R   Dressing-rooms
S   Wardrobe and storage
T   The hut housing the machine for
    lowering enthroned gods, etc., to the
    stage
U   The 'Heavens'
W   Hoisting the playhouse flag

The Globe Playhouse, 1599–1613; a conjectural reconstruction. From C. Walter Hodges *The Globe Restored: A Study of the Elizabethan Theatre.* New York: Norton, 1973.

reconstruct the Globe in its original location. The Globe Playhouse Trust was founded in the 1970s, but the actual construction of the new theater did not begin until the 1980s. After a number of setbacks — for example, the Trust ran out of funds after the construction of a large underground "diaphragm" wall needed to keep out the river water — the project was finally completed. The first performance at the reconstructed Globe was given on June 14, 1996, Sam Wanamaker's birthday.

Aerial view of the reconstructed Globe Theatre in London.

The Modern Theater

Unlike the theaters of ancient Greece and Elizabethan England, seventeenth- and eighteenth-century theaters — such as the Palais Royal, where the great French playwright Molière presented many of his plays — were covered by a roof, beautifully decorated, and illuminated by candles so that plays could be performed at night. The theater remained brightly lit even during performances, partly because there was no easy way to extinguish hundreds of candles and partly because people went to the theater as much to see each other as to see the play. A curtain opened and closed between acts. The audience of about five hundred spectators sat in a long room and viewed the play on a **picture-frame stage**. This type of stage contained the action within a **proscenium arch** that surrounded the opening through which the audience viewed the performance. Thus, the action seemed to take place in an adjoining room with one of its walls cut away. Painted scenery (some of it quite elaborate), intricately detailed costumes, and stage makeup were commonplace, and for the first time women performed female roles. In addition, a complicated series of ropes, pulleys, and cranks enabled stagehands to change scenery quickly, and sound-effects machines could give audiences the impression that they were hearing a galloping horse or a raging thunderstorm. Because the theaters were small, audiences were relatively close to the stage, so actors could use subtle movements and facial expressions to enhance their performances.

Many of the first innovations in the theater were quite basic. For example, the first stage lighting was produced by candles lining the front of the stage. This method of lighting was not only ineffective — actors were lit from below and had to step forward to be fully illuminated — but also dangerous. Costumes and even entire theaters could (and did) catch fire. Later, covered lanterns with reflectors provided better lighting. In the nineteenth century, a device that used an oxyhydrogen flame directed on a cylinder of lime created extremely bright illumination that could, with the aid of a lens, be concentrated into a spotlight. (It is from this method of stage lighting that we get the expression *to be in the limelight*.)

Eventually, in the twentieth century, electric lights provided a dependable and safe way of lighting the stage. Electric spotlights, footlights, and ceiling light bars made the actors clearly visible and enabled playwrights to create special effects. In Arthur Miller's *Death of a Salesman* (p. 1581), for example, lighting focuses attention on action in certain areas of the stage while leaving other areas in complete darkness.

Along with electric lighting came other innovations, such as electronic amplification. Microphones made it possible for actors to speak conversationally and to avoid using unnaturally loud "stage diction" to project their voices to the rear of the theater. Microphones placed at various points around the stage enabled actors and actresses to interact naturally and to deliver their lines audibly even without facing the audience. More recently, small wireless microphones eliminated the unwieldy wires and the "dead spaces" left between upright or hanging microphones, allowing characters to move freely around the stage.

The true revolutions in staging came with the advent of **realism** in the middle of the nineteenth century. Until this time, scenery was painted on canvas backdrops that trembled visibly, especially when they were intersected by doors through which actors and actresses entered. With realism came settings that were accurate down to the smallest detail. (Improved lighting, which revealed the inadequacies of painted backdrops, made such realistic stage settings necessary.) Backdrops were replaced by the **box set**, three flat panels arranged to form connected walls, with the fourth wall removed to give the audience the illusion of looking into a room. The room itself was decorated with real furniture, plants, and pictures on the walls; the door of one room might connect to another completely furnished room, or a window might open to a garden filled with realistic foliage. In addition, new methods of changing scenery were employed. Elevator stages, hydraulic lifts, and moving platforms enabled directors to make complicated changes in scenery out of the audience's view.

During the late nineteenth and early twentieth centuries, however, some playwrights reacted against what they saw as the excesses of realism. They introduced **surrealistic** stage settings, in which color and scenery mirrored the uncontrolled images of dreams, and **expressionistic** stage settings, in which costumes and scenery were exaggerated and distorted to reflect the workings of a troubled, even unbalanced mind. In addition, playwrights used lighting to create areas of light, shadow, and color that reinforced the themes of the play or reflected the emotions of the protagonist. Eugene O'Neill's *The Emperor Jones*, for example, used a series of expressionistic scenes to show the mental state of the terrified protagonist.

Sets in contemporary plays run the gamut from realistic to fantastic, from a detailed re-creation of a room in a production of Tennessee Williams's *The Glass Menagerie* (p. 1998) to a dreamlike set for *The Emperor Jones* and Edward Albee's *The Sandbox*. Motorized devices, such as revolving turntables, and *wagons*— scenery mounted on wheels—make possible rapid changes of scenery. The Broadway musical *Les Misérables*, for example, required scores of elaborate sets — Parisian slums, barricades, walled gardens — to be shifted as the audience watched. A gigantic barricade constructed on stage at one point in the play was later rotated to show the carnage that had taken place on both sides of a battle. Light, sound, and smoke were used to heighten the impact of the scene.

Today, as dramatists attempt to break down the barriers that separate audiences from the action they are viewing, plays are not limited to the picture-frame stage; in fact, they are performed on many different kinds of stages. Some plays take place on a **thrust stage**, which has an area that projects out into the audience. Other plays are performed on an **arena stage**, with the audience surrounding the actors. (This kind of performance is often called **theater in the round**.) In

Thrust-Stage Theater. With seats on three sides of the stage area, the thrust stage and its background can assume many forms other than the conventional living-room interior in the illustration. Entrances can be made from the aisles, from the sides, through the stage floor, and from the back.

Arena Theater. The audience surrounds the stage area, which may or may not be raised. Use of scenery is limited — perhaps to a single piece of scenery standing alone in the middle of the stage.

addition, experiments have been done with **environmental staging**, in which the stage surrounds the audience or several stages are situated at various locations throughout the audience. Plays may also be performed outdoors, in settings ranging from parks to city streets.

Some playwrights even try to blur the line that divides the audience from the stage by having actors move through or sit in the audience — or even by eliminating the stage entirely. For example, *Tony 'n Tina's Wedding*, a **participatory drama** created in 1988 by the theater group Artificial Intelligence, takes place not in a theater but at a church where a wedding is performed and then at a catering hall where the wedding reception is held. Throughout the play, the members of the audience function as guests, joining in the wedding celebration and mingling with the actors, who improvise freely. Recent examples of such interactive drama include *Grandma Sylvia's Funeral* and *Off the Wall*, in which audiences "attend" an art auction. Today, no single architectural form defines the theater. The modern stage is a flexible space suited to the many varieties of contemporary theatrical production.

Tragedy and Comedy

Tragedy

In his *Poetics*, Aristotle (384–322 B.C.) sums up ancient Greek thinking about drama when he defines a **tragedy**—a drama treating a serious subject and involving persons of significance. According to Aristotle, when the members of an audience see a tragedy, they should feel both pity (and thus closeness to the protagonist) and fear (and thus revulsion) because they recognize in themselves the potential for similar reactions. The purging of these emotions that audience members experience as they see the dramatic action unfold is called **catharsis**. For catharsis to occur, the protagonist of a tragedy must be worthy of the audience's attention and sympathy. Because of his or her exalted position, the fall of a tragic protagonist is greater than that of an average person; therefore, it arouses more pity and fear in the audience. Often the entire society suffers as a result of the actions of the protagonist. Before the action of Sophocles' *Oedipus the King* (p. 1786), for example, Oedipus has freed Thebes from the deadly grasp of the Sphinx by answering her riddle and, as a result, has been welcomed as king. But because of his sins, Oedipus is an affront to the gods and brings famine and pestilence to the city. When his fall finally comes, it is sudden and absolute.

According to Aristotle, the protagonist of a tragedy is neither all good nor all evil, but a mixture of the two. The protagonist is like the rest of us — only more exalted and possessing some weakness or flaw **(hamartia)**. This tragic flaw — perhaps narrowness of vision or overwhelming pride **(hubris)** — is typically the element that creates the conditions for tragedy. Shakespeare's Romeo and Juliet, for example, are so much in love they think they can ignore the blood feud that rages between their two families. However, their naive efforts to sustain their love despite the feud lead them to their tragic deaths. Similarly, Richard III's blind ambition to gain the throne causes him to murder all those who stand in his way. His unscrupulousness sets into motion the forces that eventually cause his death.

Irony — a discrepancy between what characters say and what the audience believes to be true — is central to tragedy. **Dramatic irony** (also called **tragic irony**) emerges from a situation in which the audience knows more about the dramatic situation than a character does. As a result, the character's words and actions may be consistent with what he or she expects but at odds with what the audience knows will happen. Thus, a character may say or do something that causes the audience to infer a meaning beyond what the character intends or realizes. The dramatic irony is clear, for example, when Oedipus announces that whoever has disobeyed the dictates of the gods will be exiled. The audience knows, although Oedipus does not, that he has just condemned himself. **Cosmic irony**, also called **irony of fate**, occurs when God, fate, or some larger, uncontrollable force seems to be intentionally deceiving characters into believing they can escape their fate. Too late, they realize that trying to avoid their destiny is futile. Years before Oedipus was born, for example, the oracle of Apollo foretold that Oedipus would kill his parents. Naturally, his parents attempted to thwart the prophecy, but ironically, their actions ensured that the prophecy would be fulfilled.

At some point in a tragedy — after the climax — the protagonist recognizes the reasons for his or her downfall. This recognition (and the accompanying acceptance) elevate tragic protagonists to grandeur and give their suffering meaning. Without this recognition, there would be no tragedy, just **pathos** — suffering that exists simply to satisfy the sentimental or morbid sensibilities of the audience. In spite of the death of the protagonist, then, tragedy enables the audience to see the nobility of the character and thus to experience a sense of elation. In Shakespeare's *King Lear*, for example, a king at the height of his powers decides to divide his kingdom among his three daughters. Later, he realizes that without his power, he is just a bothersome old man to his ambitious children. Only after going mad does he understand the vanity of his former existence; he dies a humbled but enlightened man.

According to Aristotle, a tragedy achieves the illusion of reality when it has **unity of action**— that is, when the play contains only those actions that lead to its tragic outcome. Later critics interpreted this constraint to mean that including subplots or mixing tragic and comic elements would destroy this unity. To the concept of unity of action, these later critics added two other requirements: **unity of place** — the requirement that the play have a single setting — and **unity of time**— the requirement that the events depicted by the play take no longer than the actual duration of the play (or, at most, a single day).

The **three unities** have had a long and rather uneven history. In some of his plays — *The Tempest* and *The Comedy of Errors*, for example — Shakespeare observed the unities. Most of the time, however, he had no compunctions about writing plays with subplots and frequent changes of location. He also wrote **tragicomedies**, such as *The Merchant of Venice*, which have a serious theme appropriate for tragedy but end happily, usually because of a sudden turn of events. During the eighteenth century, with its emphasis on classic form, the unities were adhered to quite strictly. In the late eighteenth and early nineteenth centuries, with the onset of romanticism and its emphasis on the natural, interest in the unities of place and time waned. Even though some modern plays (particularly one-act plays) do observe the unities — *Trifles* (p. 1372), for instance, has a single setting and takes place during a period of time that corresponds to the length of the play — few modern dramatists strictly adhere to them.

Ideas about appropriate subjects for tragedy have also changed. For Aristotle, the protagonist of a tragedy had to be exceptional — a king, for example. The protagonists of Greek tragedies were usually historical or mythical figures. Shakespeare often used kings and princes as protagonists — Richard II and Hamlet, for example — but he also used people of lesser rank, as in *Romeo and Juliet* and *A Midsummer Night's Dream* (p. 1828). In our times, interest in the lives of monarchs has been overshadowed by involvement in the lives of ordinary people. Modern tragedies — *Death of a Salesman*, for example — are more likely to focus on a traveling salesman than on a king.

With the rise of the middle class in the nineteenth century, ideas about the nature of tragedy changed. Responding to the age's desire for sentimentality, playwrights produced **melodramas**, sensational plays that appealed mainly to the emotions. Melodramas include many of the elements of tragedy but end happily and often rely on conventional plots and stock characters. Because the protagonists in melodramas — often totally virtuous heroines suffering at the hands of impossibly wicked villains — helplessly endure their tribulations without ever gaining insight or enlightenment, they never achieve tragic status. As a result, they remain cardboard cutouts who exist only to exploit the emotions of the audience. Melodrama survives today in many films and in television soap operas.

Realism, which arose in the late nineteenth century as a response to the artificiality of melodrama, presented serious (and sometimes tragic) themes and believable characters in the context of everyday contemporary life. Writers of realistic drama used their plays to educate their audiences about the problems of the society in which they lived. For this reason, realistic drama focuses on the commonplace and eliminates the unlikely coincidences and excessive sentimentality of melodrama. Dramatists such as Henrik Ibsen scrutinize the lives of ordinary people, not larger-than-life characters. After great suffering, these characters rise above the limitations of their mediocre lives and exhibit courage or emotional strength. The insight they gain often focuses attention on a social problem — the restrictive social conventions that define the behavior of women in nineteenth-century marriages, for example. Realistic drama also features settings and props similar to those used in people's daily lives and includes dialogue that reflects the way people actually speak.

Developing alongside realism was a literary movement called **naturalism**. Like realism, naturalism rejected the unrealistic plots and sentimentality of melodrama, but unlike realism, naturalism sought to explore the depths of the human condition. Influenced by Charles Darwin's ideas about evolution and natural selection and Karl Marx's ideas about economic forces that shape people's lives, naturalism is a pessimistic philosophy that presents a world that is at worst hostile and at best indifferent to human concerns. It portrays human beings as higher-order animals who are driven by basic instincts — especially hunger, fear, greed, and sexuality — and who are subject to economic, social, and biological forces beyond their understanding or control. For these reasons, it is well suited to tragic themes.

The nineteenth-century French writer Émile Zola did much to develop the theory of naturalism, as did the American writers Stephen Crane, Frank Norris, and Theodore Dreiser. Naturalism also finds its way into the work of contemporary dramatists, such as Arthur Miller. Unlike other tragic characters, the protagonists of naturalist works are crushed not by the gods or by fate but by poverty, animal drives, or social class. Willy Loman in *Death of a Salesman,* for example, is subject to the economic forces of a society that does not value its workers and discards those it no longer finds useful.

Comedy

A **comedy** treats themes and characters with humor and typically has a happy ending. Whereas tragedy focuses on the hidden dimensions of the tragic hero's character, comedy focuses on the public persona, the protagonist as a social being. Tragic figures are typically seen in isolation, questioning the meaning of their lives and trying to comprehend their suffering. Hamlet — draped in sable, longing for death, and self-consciously contemplating his duty — epitomizes the isolation of the tragic hero.

Unlike tragic heroes, comic figures are seen in the public arena, where people intentionally assume the masks of pretension and self-importance. The purpose of comedy is to strip away these masks and expose human beings for what they are. Whereas tragedy reveals the nobility of the human condition, comedy reveals its inherent folly, portraying human beings as selfish, hypocritical, vain, weak, irrational, and capable of self-delusion. Thus, the basic function of comedy is critical — to tell people that things are not what they seem and that appearances are not necessarily reality. In the comic world, nothing is solid or predictable, and accidents and coincidences are more important to the plot than reason. Many of Shakespeare's comedies, for example, depend on exchanged or confused identities. The wordplay and verbal nonsense of comedy add to this general confusion.

Comedies typically rely on certain familiar plot devices. Many comedies begin with a startling or unusual situation that attracts the audience's attention. In Shakespeare's *A Midsummer Night's Dream* (p. 1828), for example, Theseus, the duke of Athens, rules that Hermia will either marry the man her father has chosen for her or be put to death. Such an event could lead to tragedy if comedy did not intervene to save the day.

Comedy often depends on obstacles and hindrances to further its plot: the more difficult the problems the lovers face, the more satisfying their eventual triumph will be. For this reason, the plot of a comedy is usually more complex than the plot of a tragedy. Compare the rather straightforward plot of *Hamlet* (p. 1656) — a prince ordered to avenge his murdered father's death is driven mad with indecision and, after finally acting decisively, is killed himself — with the mix-ups, mistaken identities, and general confusion of *A Midsummer Night's Dream*.

Finally, comedies have happy endings. Whereas tragedy ends with death, comedy ends with an affirmation of life. Eventually, the confusion and misunderstandings reach a point where some resolution must be achieved: the difficulties of the lovers are overcome, the villains are banished, and the lovers marry — or at least express their intention to do so. In this way, the lovers establish their connection with the rest of society, and its values are affirmed.

The first comedies, written in Greece in the fifth century B.C., heavily satirized the religious and social issues of the day and were characterized by bawdy humor. In the fourth and third centuries B.C., this **Old Comedy** gave way to **New Comedy**, a comedy of romance with stock characters — lovers and untrustworthy servants, for example — and conventional settings. Lacking the bitter satire and bawdiness of Old Comedy, New Comedy depends on outrageous plots, mistaken identities, young lovers, interfering parents, and conniving servants. Ultimately, the young lovers outwit all those who stand between them and, in so doing, affirm the primacy of youth and love over old age and death.

Old and New Comedy represent two distinct lines of humor that extend to modern times. Old Comedy depends on **satire** — biting humor that diminishes a person, idea, or institution by ridiculing it or holding it up to scorn. Unlike most comedy, which exists simply to make people laugh, satire is social criticism, deriding hypocrisy, pretension, and vanity or condemning vice. At its best, satire appeals to the intellect, has a serious purpose, and arouses thoughtful laughter. New Comedy may also be satiric, but the satire is often tempered by elements of **farce**, comedy in which stereotypical characters engage in boisterous horseplay and slapstick humor, all the while making jokes and sexual innuendoes — as they do in Anton Chekhov's *The Brute* (p. 1293).

English comedy got its start in the sixth century A.D. in the form of farcical episodes that appeared in morality plays. During the Renaissance, comedy developed rapidly, beginning in 1533 with Nicholas Udall's *Ralph Roister Doister* and eventually evolving into Shakespeare's **romantic comedy**— such as *A Midsummer Night's Dream*, in which love is the main subject and idealized heroines and lovers endure great difficulties until the inevitable happy ending is reached.

Also during the Renaissance, particularly in the latter part of the sixteenth century, writers such as Ben Jonson experimented with a different type of comedy — the **comedy of humours**, which focuses on characters whose behavior is controlled by a characteristic trait, or *humour*. During the Renaissance, a person's temperament was thought to be determined by the mix of fluids, or humours, in the body. When one humour dominated, a certain type of disposition resulted. Playwrights capitalized on this belief, writing comedies in which characters are motivated by stereotypical behaviors that result from the imbalance of the humours. In comedies such as Jonson's *Volpone* and *The Alchemist*, characters such as the suspicious husband and the miser can be manipulated by others because of their predictable dispositions.

Closely related to the comedy of humours is the satiric **comedy of manners**, which developed during the sixteenth century and achieved great popularity in the nineteenth century. This form focuses on the manners and customs of society and directs its satire against characters who violate social conventions and rules of behavior. These plays tend to be memorable more for their witty dialogue than for their development of characters or setting. Oliver Goldsmith's *She Stoops to Conquer*, George Bernard Shaw's *Pygmalion*, and even some of the television sitcoms of today are examples of this type of comedy.

In the eighteenth century, a reaction against the perceived immorality of the comedy of manners led to **sentimental comedy**, which eventually achieved great popularity. This kind of comedy relies on sentimental emotion rather than on wit or humor to move an audience. It also dwells on the virtues rather than on the vices of life. The heroes of sentimental comedy are unimpeachably noble, moral, and honorable; the pure, virtuous, middle-class heroines suffer trials and tribulations calculated to move the audience to tears rather than to laughter. Eventually, the distress of the hero and heroine is resolved in a sometimes contrived (but always happy) ending. Sir Richard Steele's *The Conscious Lovers* (1722) is an example of sentimental comedy.

In his 1877 essay *The Idea of Comedy*, novelist and critic George Meredith suggests that comedy that appeals to the intellect should be called **high comedy**. Shakespeare's *As You Like It* and George Bernard Shaw's *Pygmalion* can be characterized as high comedy. When comedy has little or no intellectual appeal, according to Meredith, it is **low comedy**. Low comedy appears in parts of Shakespeare's *The Taming of the Shrew* and as comic relief in *Macbeth*.

The twentieth century developed its own characteristic comic forms, reflecting the uncertainty and pessimism of a period characterized by two world wars, the Holocaust, and nuclear destruction, as well as threats posed by environmental pollution and ethnic and racial conflict — and, in this century, the terrorist attacks of September 11, 2001. Combining laughter and hints of tragedy, these modern tragicomedies feature **antiheroes**, characters who, instead of manifesting dignity and power, are ineffectual or petty. Their plight frequently elicits laughter, not pity and fear, from the audience. **Black** or **dark comedies**, for example, rely for their comedy on the morbid and the absurd. These works are usually so satiric and bitter that they threaten to slip over the edge into tragedy. The screenplay of Joseph Heller's novel *Catch-22*, which ends with a character dropping bombs on his own men, is a classic example of such comedy. **Theater of the absurd**, which includes comedies such as Samuel Beckett's *Waiting for Godot* and Tom Stoppard's *Rosencrantz and Guildenstern Are Dead*, begins with the assumption that the human condition is irrational. Typically, this type of drama does not have a conventional plot; instead, it presents a series of apparently unrelated images and illogical exchanges of dialogue meant to reinforce the idea that human beings live in a remote, confusing, and often incomprehensible universe. Absurdist dramas seem to go in circles, never progressing to a climax or achieving a resolution, thus reinforcing the theme of the endless and meaningless repetition that characterizes modern life.

Defining Drama

Dramatic works differ from other prose works in a number of fairly obvious ways. For one thing, plays look different on the page: generally, they are divided into **acts** and **scenes**; they include **stage directions** that specify characters' entrances and exits and describe what settings look like and how characters look and act; and they consist primarily of **dialogue**, lines spoken by the characters. And, of course, plays are different from other prose works in that they are written not to be read but to be performed in front of an audience.

Unlike novels and short stories, plays do not usually have narrators to tell the audience what a character is thinking or what happened in the past; for the most part, the audience knows only what characters reveal. To compensate for the absence of a narrator, playwrights can use **monologues** (extended speeches by one character), **soliloquies** (monologues in which a character expresses private thoughts while alone on stage), or **asides** (brief comments by a character who reveals thoughts by speaking directly to the audience without being heard by the other characters). In addition to these dramatic techniques, a play can also use costumes, scenery, props, music, lighting, and other techniques to enhance its impact on the audience.

The play that follows, Anton Chekhov's *The Brute* (1888), is typical of modern drama in many respects. A one-act play translated from Russian, it is essentially a struggle of wills between two headstrong characters, a man and a woman, with action escalating through the characters' increasingly heated exchanges of dialogue. Stage directions briefly describe the setting—"*the drawing room of a country house*"—and announce the appearance of various props. They also describe the major characters' appearances as well as their actions, gestures, and emotions. Because the play is a **farce**, it features broad physical comedy, asides, wild dramatic gestures, and elaborate figures of speech, all designed to enhance its comic effect.

ANTON CHEKHOV (1860–1904) is an important nineteenth-century Russian playwright and short story writer. He became a doctor and, as a young adult, supported the rest of his family after his father's bankruptcy. After his early adult years in Moscow, Chekhov spent the rest of his life in the country, moving to Yalta, a resort town in Crimea, for his health (he suffered from tuberculosis). He continued to write plays, mostly for the Moscow Art Theatre, although he could not supervise their production as he would have wished. His plays include *The Seagull* (1896), *Uncle Vanya* (1898), *The Three Sisters* (1901), and *The Cherry Orchard* (1904).

    The Brute, or *The Bear* (1888), is one of a number of one-act farces Chekhov wrote just before his major plays. It is based on a French farce (*Les Jurons de Cadillac* by Pierre Breton) about a man who cannot refrain from swearing. The woman he loves offers to marry him if he can avoid swearing for one hour; he is unable to do it, but he fails so charmingly that she agrees to marry him anyway.

Cultural Context The custom of dueling is a form of conflict resolution that has been popular throughtout history and in many different countries. Generally speaking, as in *The Brute*, duels are fought as a matter of honor—whether in response to an insult, an offense to one's character, or an affront to one's dignity. Once a challenge to a duel has been issued, negotiators (called *seconds*) agree on the time, place, and weaponry involved, as well as the point of surrender—whether it be first blood drawn or death. In a pistol duel, the participants stand back to back, count off a predetermined number of paces, turn, and fire. Today, dueling is illegal in most countries, and killing someone in the course of a duel is considered murder.

The Brute

A JOKE IN ONE ACT (1888)

Translated by Eric Bentley

CHARACTERS

Mrs. Popov, *widow and landowner, small, with dimpled cheeks*

Mr. Grigory S. Smirnov, *gentleman farmer, middle-aged*

Luka, *Mrs. Popov's footman, an old man*

Gardener
Coachman
Hired Men

SCENE

The drawing room of a country house. Mrs. Popov, in deep mourning, is staring hard at a photograph. Luka is with her.

LUKA: It's not right, ma'am, you're killing yourself. The cook has gone off with the maid to pick berries. The cat's having a high old time in the yard catching birds. Every living thing is happy. But you stay moping here in the house like it was a convent, taking no pleasure in nothing. I mean it, ma'am! It must be a full year since you set foot out of doors.

MRS. POPOV: I must never set foot out of doors again, Luka. Never! I have nothing to set foot out of doors *for*. My life is done. *He* is in his grave. I have buried myself alive in this house. We are *both* in our graves.

LUKA: You're off again, ma'am. I just won't listen to you no more. Mr. Popov is dead, but what can we do about that? It's God's doing. God's will be done. You've cried over him, you've done your share of mourning, haven't you? There's a limit to everything. You can't go on weeping and wailing forever. My old lady died, for that matter, and I wept and wailed over her a whole month long. Well, that was it. I couldn't weep and wail all my life. She just wasn't worth it. *(He sighs.)* As for the neighbors, you've forgotten all about them, ma'am. You don't visit them and you don't let them visit you. You and I are like a pair of spiders — excuse the expression, ma'am — here we are in this house like a pair of spiders, we never see the light of day. And it isn't like there was no nice people around either. The whole county's swarming with 'em. There's a regiment quartered at Riblov, and the officers are so good-looking! The girls can't take their eyes off them — There's a ball at the camp every Friday — The military band plays most every day of the week — What do you say, ma'am? You're young, you're pretty, you could enjoy yourself! Ten years from now you may want to strut and show your feathers to the officers, and it'll be too late.

MRS. POPOV: *(firmly)* You must never bring this subject up again, Luka. Since Popov died, life has been an empty dream to me, you know that. *You* may think I am alive. Poor ignorant Luka! You are wrong. I am dead. I'm in my grave. Never more shall I see the light of day, never strip from my body this . . . raiment of death! Are you listening, Luka? Let his ghost learn how I love him! Yes, *I* know, and *you* know, he was often unfair to me, he was cruel to me, and he was unfaithful to me. What of it? *I* shall be faithful to *him*, that's all. I will show him how *I* can love. Hereafter, in a better world than this, he will welcome me back, the same loyal girl I always was —

5 LUKA: Instead of carrying on this way, ma'am, you should go out in the garden and take a bit of a walk, ma'am. Or why not harness Toby and take a drive? Call on a couple of the neighbours, ma'am?

MRS. POPOV: *(breaking down)* Oh, Luka!

LUKA: Yes, ma'am? What have I said, ma'am? Oh, dear!

MRS. POPOV: Toby! You said Toby! He adored that horse. When he drove me out to the Korchagins and the Vlasovs, it was always with Toby! He was a wonderful driver, do you remember, Luka? So graceful! So strong! I can see him now, pulling at those reins with all his might and main! Toby! Luka, tell them to give Toby an extra portion of oats today.

LUKA: Yes, ma'am.

A bell rings.

10 MRS. POPOV: Who is that? Tell them I'm not at home.

LUKA: Very good, ma'am. *(Exit.)*

MRS. POPOV: *(gazing again at the photograph)* You shall see, my Popov, how a wife can love and forgive. Till death do us part. Longer than that. Till death re-unite us forever! (*Suddenly a titter breaks through her tears.*) Aren't you ashamed of yourself, Popov? Here's your little wife, being good, being faithful, so faithful she's locked up here waiting for her own funeral, while you — doesn't it make you ashamed, you naughty boy? You were terrible, you know. You were unfaithful, and you made those awful scenes about it, you stormed out and left me alone for weeks—

Enter Luka.

LUKA: (*upset*) There's someone asking for you, ma'am. Says he must—

MRS. POPOV: I suppose you told him that since my husband's death I see no one?

LUKA: Yes, ma'am. I did, ma'am. But he wouldn't listen, ma'am. He says it's   15
urgent.

MRS. POPOV: (*shrilly*) I see no one!!

LUKA: He won't take no for an answer, ma'am. He just curses and swears and comes in anyway. He's a perfect monster, ma'am. He's in the dining room right now.

MRS. POPOV: In the dining room, is he? I'll give him his come-uppance. Bring him in here this minute.

Exit Luka.

(*Suddenly sad again.*) Why do they do this to me? Why? Insulting my grief, intruding on my solitude? (*She sighs.*) I'm afraid I'll have to enter a convent. I will, I *must* enter a convent!

Enter Mr. Smirnov and Luka.

SMIRNOV: (*to Luka*) Dolt! Idiot! You talk too much! (*Seeing Mrs. Popov. With dignity.*) May I have the honor of introducing myself, madam? Grigory S. Smirnov, landowner and lieutenant of artillery, retired. Forgive me, madam, if I disturb your peace and quiet, but my business is both urgent and weighty.

MRS. POPOV: (*declining to offer him her hand*) What is it you wish, sir?   20

SMIRNOV: At the time of his death, your late husband — with whom I had the honor to be acquainted, ma'am — was in my debt to the tune of twelve hundred rubles. I have two notes to prove it. Tomorrow, ma'am, I must pay the interest on a bank loan. I have therefore no alternative, ma'am, but to ask you to pay me the money today.

MRS. POPOV: Twelve hundred rubles? But what did my husband owe it to you for?

SMIRNOV: He used to buy his oats from me, madam.

MRS. POPOV: (*to Luka, with a sigh*) Remember what I said, Luka: tell them to give Toby an extra portion of oats today!

Exit Luka.

My dear Mr. — what was the name again?

SMIRNOV: Smirnov, ma'am.   25

MRS. POPOV: My dear Mr. Smirnov, if Mr. Popov owed you money, you shall
be paid — to the last ruble, to the last kopeck. But today — you must
excuse me, Mr. — what was it?

SMIRNOV: Smirnov, ma'am.

MRS. POPOV: Today, Mr. Smirnov, I have no ready cash in the house.
(*Smirnov starts to speak.*) Tomorrow, Mr. Smirnov, no, the day after
tomorrow, all will be well. My steward will be back from town. I shall see
that he pays what is owing. Today, no. In any case, today is exactly seven
months from Mr. Popov's death. On such a day you will understand that
I am in no mood to think of money.

SMIRNOV: Madam, if you don't pay up now, you can carry me out feet
foremost. They'll seize my estate.

30 MRS. POPOV: You can have your money. (*He starts to thank her.*) Tomorrow.
(*He again starts to speak.*) That is: the day after tomorrow.

SMIRNOV: I don't need the money the day after tomorrow. I need it today.

MRS. POPOV: I'm sorry, Mr. —

SMIRNOV: (*shouting*) Smirnov!

MRS. POPOV: (*sweetly*) Yes, of course. But you can't have it today.

35 SMIRNOV: But I can't wait for it any longer!

MRS. POPOV: Be sensible, Mr. Smirnov. How can I pay you if I don't have it?

SMIRNOV: You don't have it?

MRS. POPOV: I don't have it.

SMIRNOV: Sure?

40 MRS. POPOV: Positive.

SMIRNOV: Very well. I'll make a note to that effect. (*Shrugging.*) And then
they want me to keep cool. I meet the tax commissioner on the street, and
he says, "Why are you always in such a bad humor, Smirnov?" Bad humor!
How can I help it, in God's name? I need money, I need it desperately. Take
yesterday: I leave home at the crack of dawn, I call on all my debtors. Not a
one of them pays up. Footsore and weary. I creep at midnight into some
little dive, and try to snatch a few winks of sleep on the floor by the vodka
barrel. Then today, I come here, fifty miles from home, saying to myself,
"At last, at last, I can be sure of something," and you're not in the mood!
You give me a mood! Christ, how can I help getting all worked up?

MRS. POPOV: I thought I'd made it clear, Mr. Smirnov, that you'll get your
money the minute my steward is back from town.

SMIRNOV: What the hell do I care about your steward? Pardon the expression,
ma'am. But it was you I came to see.

MRS. POPOV: What language! What a tone to take to a lady! I refuse to hear
another word. (*Quickly, exit.*)

45 SMIRNOV: Not in the mood, huh? "Exactly seven months since Popov's death,"
huh? How about me? (*Shouting after her.*) Is there this interest to pay, or isn't
there? I'm asking you a question: is there this interest to pay, or isn't there?
So your husband died, and you're not in the mood, and your steward's gone
off some place, and so forth and so on, but what can *I* do about all that,
huh? What do *you* think I should do? Take a running jump and shove my

head through the wall? Take off in a balloon? You don't know my *other* debtors. I call on Gruzdeff. Not at home. I look for Yaroshevitch. He's hiding out. I find Kooritsin. He kicks up a row, and I have to throw him through the window. I work my way right down the list. Not a kopeck. Then I come to you, and God damn it to hell, if you'll pardon the expression, you're not in the mood! (*Quietly, as he realizes he's talking to air.*) I've spoiled them all, that's what, I've let them play me for a sucker. Well, I'll show them. I'll show this one. I'll stay right here till she pays up. Ugh! (*He shudders with rage.*) I'm in a rage! I'm in a positively towering rage! Every nerve in my body is trembling at forty to the dozen! I can't breathe, I feel ill, I think I'm going to faint, hey, you there!

Enter Luka.

LUKA: Yes, sir? Is there anything you wish, sir?
SMIRNOV: Water! Water! No, make it vodka.

Exit Luka.

Consider the logic of it. A fellow creature is desperately in need of cash, so desperately in need that he has to seriously contemplate hanging himself, and this woman, this mere chit of a girl, won't pay up, and why not? Because, forsooth, she isn't in the mood! Oh, the logic of women! Come to that, I never have liked them, I could do without the whole sex. Talk to a woman? I'd rather sit on a barrel of dynamite, the very thought gives me gooseflesh. Women! Creatures of poetry and romance! Just to see one in the distance gets me mad. My legs start twitching with rage. I feel like yelling for help.

Enter Luka, handing Smirnov a glass of water.

LUKA: Mrs. Popov is indisposed, sir. She is seeing no one.
SMIRNOV: Get out.

Exit Luka.

Indisposed, is she? Seeing no one, huh? Well, she can see me or not, but I'll be here, I'll be right here till she pays up. If you're sick for a week, I'll be here for a week. If you're sick for a year, I'll be here for a year. You won't get around *me* with your widow's weeds and your schoolgirl dimples. I know all about dimples. (*Shouting through the window.*) Semyon, let the horses out of those shafts, we're not leaving, we're staying, and tell them to give the horses some oats, yes, oats, you fool, what do you think? (*Walking away from the window.*) What a mess, what an unholy mess! I didn't sleep last night, the heat is terrific today, not a damn one of 'em has paid up, and here's this — this skirt in mourning that's not in the mood! My head aches, where's that —(*He drinks from the glass.*) Water, ugh! You there!

Enter Luka.

LUKA: Yes, sir. You wish for something, sir?

50

SMIRNOV: Where's that confounded vodka I asked for?

Exit Luka.

> (*Smirnov sits and looks himself over.*) Oof! A fine figure of a man *I* am!
> Unwashed, uncombed, unshaven, straw on my vest, dust all over me.
> The little woman must've taken me for a highwayman. (*Yawns.*) I suppose
> it wouldn't be considered polite to barge into a drawing room in this state,
> but who cares? I'm not a visitor, I'm a creditor — most unwelcome of guests,
> second only to Death.

Enter Luka.

LUKA: (*handing him the vodka*) If I may say so, sir, you take too many
    liberties, sir.
SMIRNOV: What?!
LUKA: Oh, nothing, sir, nothing.
55 SMIRNOV: Who in hell do you think you're talking to? Shut your mouth!
LUKA: (*aside*) There's an evil spirit abroad. The Devil must have sent him.
    Oh! (*Exit Luka.*)
SMIRNOV: What a rage I'm in! I'll grind the whole world to powder. Oh, I feel
    ill again. You there!

Enter Mrs. Popov.

MRS. POPOV: (*looking at the floor*) In the solitude of my rural retreat,
    Mr. Smirnov, I've long since grown unaccustomed to the sound of the
    human voice. Above all, I cannot bear shouting. I must beg you not to
    break the silence.
SMIRNOV: Very well. Pay me my money and I'll go.
60 MRS. POPOV: I told you before, and I tell you again, Mr. Smirnov. I have no
    cash, you'll have to wait till the day after tomorrow. Can I express myself
    more plainly?
SMIRNOV: And *I* told *you* before, and *I* tell *you* again, that I need the money
    today, that the day after tomorrow is too late, and that if you don't pay, and
    pay now, I'll have to hang myself in the morning!
MRS. POPOV: But I have no cash. This is quite a puzzle.
SMIRNOV: You won't pay, huh?
MRS. POPOV: I *can't* pay, Mr. Smirnov.
65 SMIRNOV: In that case, I'm going to sit here and wait. (*Sits down.*) You'll
    pay up the day after tomorrow? Very good. Till the day after tomorrow,
    here I sit. (*Pause. He jumps up.*) Now look, do I have to pay that interest
    tomorrow, or don't I? Or do you think I'm joking?
MRS. POPOV: I must ask you not to raise your voice, Mr. Smirnov. This is not a
    stable.
SMIRNOV: Who said it was? Do I have to pay the interest tomorrow or not?
MRS. POPOV: Mr. Smirnov, do you know how to behave in the presence
    of a lady?
SMIRNOV: No, madam, I do not know how to behave in the presence of a lady.

MRS. POPOV: Just what I thought. I look at you, and I say: ugh! I hear you talk,   70
and I say to myself: "That man doesn't know how to talk to a lady."

SMIRNOV: You'd like me to come simpering to you in French, I suppose.
"*Enchanté, madame! Merci beaucoup* for not paying zee money, *madame!*
Pardonnez-moi if I 'ave disturbed you, *madame!* How *charmante* you look in
mourning, *madame!*"

MRS. POPOV: Now you're being silly, Mr. Smirnov.

SMIRNOV: (*mimicking*) "Now you're being silly, Mr. Smirnov." "You don't know
how to talk to a lady, Mr. Smirnov." Look here, Mrs. Popov, I've known
more women than you've known pussy cats. I've fought three duels on
their account. I've jilted twelve, and been jilted by nine others. Oh, yes,
Mrs. Popov, I've played the fool in my time, whispered sweet nothings,
bowed and scraped and endeavored to please. Don't tell me I don't know
what it is to love, to pine away with longing, to have the blues, to melt like
butter, to be weak as water. I was full of tender emotion. I was carried away
with passion. I squandered half my fortune on the sex. I chattered about
women's emancipation. But there's an end to everything, dear madam.
Burning eyes, dark eyelashes, ripe, red lips, dimpled cheeks, heaving
bosoms, soft whisperings, the moon above; the lake below — I don't give a
rap for that sort of nonsense any more, Mrs. Popov. I've found out about
women. Present company excepted, they're liars. Their behavior is mere
play acting; their conversation is sheer gossip. Yes, dear lady, women,
young or old, are false, petty, vain, cruel, malicious, unreasonable. As for
intelligence, any sparrow could give them points. Appearances, I admit,
can be deceptive. In appearance, a woman may be all poetry and romance,
goddess and angel, muslin and fluff. To look at her exterior is to be
transported to heaven. But I have looked at her interior, Mrs. Popov, and
what did I find there — in her very soul? A crocodile. (*He has gripped the
back of the chair so firmly that it snaps.*) And, what is more revolting, a
crocodile with an illusion, a crocodile that imagines tender sentiments are
its own special province, a crocodile that thinks itself queen of the realm
of love! Whereas, in sober fact, dear madam, if a woman can love anything
except a lapdog you can hang me by the feet on that nail. For a man, love
is suffering, love is sacrifice. A woman just swishes her train around
and tightens her grip on your nose. Now, you're a woman, aren't you,
Mrs. Popov? You must be an expert on some of this. Tell me, quite frankly,
did you ever know a woman to be — faithful, for instance? Or even sincere?
Only old hags, huh? Though some women are old hags from birth. But as
for the others? You're right: a faithful woman is a freak of nature — like a
cat with horns.

MRS. POPOV: Who *is* faithful, then? Who *have* you cast for the faithful lover?
Not man?

SMIRNOV: Right first time, Mrs. Popov: man.   75

MRS. POPOV: (*going off into a peal of bitter laughter*) Man! Man is faithful! that's
a new one! (*Fiercely.*) What right do you have to say this, Mr. Smirnov?
Men faithful? Let me tell you something. Of all the men I have ever known

my late husband Popov was the best. I loved him, and there are women
who know how to love, Mr. Smirnov. I gave him my youth, my happiness,
my life, my fortune. I worshipped the ground he trod on — and what
happened? The best of men was unfaithful to me, Mr. Smirnov. Not once
in a while. All the time. After he died, I found his desk drawer full of love
letters. While he was alive, he was always going away for the week-end. He
squandered my money. He made love to other women before my very eyes.
But, in spite of all, Mr. Smirnov, *I* was faithful. Unto death. And beyond.
I am *still* faithful, Mr. Smirnov! Buried alive in this house, I shall wear
mourning till the day I, too, am called to my eternal rest.

SMIRNOV: *(laughing scornfully)* Expect me to believe that? As if I couldn't see
through all this hocus-pocus. Buried alive! Till you're called to your eternal
rest! Till when? Till some little poet — or some little subaltern with his
first moustache — comes riding by and asks: "Can that be the house of the
mysterious Tamara who for love of her late husband has buried herself
alive, vowing to see no man?" Ha!

MRS. POPOV: *(flaring up)* How dare you? How dare you insinuate —?

SMIRNOV: You may have buried yourself alive, Mrs. Popov, but you haven't
forgotten to powder your nose.

80 MRS. POPOV: *(incoherent)* How dare you? How —?

SMIRNOV: Who's raising his voice now? Just because I call a spade a spade.
Because I shoot straight from the shoulder. Well, don't shout at me, I'm not
your steward.

MRS. POPOV: I'm not shouting, you're shouting! Oh, leave me alone!

SMIRNOV: Pay me the money, and I will.

MRS. POPOV: You'll get no money out of me!

85 SMIRNOV: Oh, so that's it!

MRS. POPOV: Not a ruble, not a kopeck. Get out! Leave me alone!

SMIRNOV: Not being your husband, I must ask you not to make scenes with
me. *(He sits.)* I don't like scenes.

MRS. POPOV: *(choking with rage)* You're sitting down?

SMIRNOV: Correct, I'm sitting down.

90 MRS. POPOV: I asked you to leave!

SMIRNOV: Then give me the money. *(Aside.)* Oh, what a rage I'm in,
what a rage!

MRS. POPOV: The impudence of the man! I won't talk to you a moment
longer. Get out. *(Pause.)* Are you going?

SMIRNOV: No.

MRS. POPOV: No?!

95 SMIRNOV: No.

MRS. POPOV: On your head be it. Luka!

Enter Luka.

Show the gentleman out, Luka.

LUKA: *(approaching)* I'm afraid, sir, I'll have to ask you, um, to leave, sir,
now, um—

SMIRNOV: *(jumping up)* Shut your mouth, you old idiot! Who do you think you're talking to? I'll make mincemeat of you.

LUKA: *(clutching his heart)* Mercy on us! Holy saints above! *(He falls into an armchair.)* I'm taken sick! I can't breathe!!

MRS. POPOV: Then where's Dasha? Dasha! Dasha! Come here at once! *(She rings.)*   100

LUKA: They gone picking berries, ma'am, I'm alone here —Water, water, I'm taken sick!

MRS. POPOV: *(to Smirnov)* Get out, you!

SMIRNOV: Can't you even be polite with me, Mrs. Popov?

MRS. POPOV: *(clenching her fists and stamping her feet)* With you? You're a wild animal, you were never house-broken!

SMIRNOV: What? What did you say?   105

MRS. POPOV: I said you were a wild animal, you were never house-broken.

SMIRNOV: *(advancing upon her)* And what right do you have to talk to me like that?

MRS. POPOV: Like what?

SMIRNOV: You have insulted me, madam.

MRS. POPOV: What of it? Do you think I'm scared of you?   110

SMIRNOV: So you think you can get away with it because you're a woman. A creature of poetry and romance, huh? Well, it doesn't go down with me. I hereby challenge you to a duel.

LUKA: Mercy on us! Holy saints alive! Water!

SMIRNOV: I propose we shoot it out.

MRS. POPOV: Trying to scare me again? Just because you have big fists and a voice like a bull? You're a brute.

SMIRNOV: No one insults Grigory S. Smirnov with impunity! And I don't care   115 if you *are* a female.

MRS. POPOV: *(trying to outshout him)* Brute, brute, brute!

SMIRNOV: The sexes are equal, are they? Fine: then it's just prejudice to expect men alone to pay for insults. I hereby challenge—

MRS. POPOV: *(screaming)* All right! You want to shoot it out? All right! Let's shoot it out!

SMIRNOV: And let it be here and now!

MRS. POPOV: Here and now! All right! I'll have Popov's pistols here in one   120 minute! *(Walks away, then turns.)* Putting one of Popov's bullets through your silly head will be a pleasure! Au revoir. *(Exit.)*

SMIRNOV: I'll bring her down like a duck, a sitting duck. I'm not one of your little poets, I'm no little subaltern with his first moustache. No, sir, there's no weaker sex where I'm concerned!

LUKA: Sir! Master! *(He goes down on his knees.)* Take pity on a poor old man, and do me a favor: go away. It was bad enough before, you nearly scared me to death. But a duel—!

SMIRNOV: *(ignoring him)* A duel! That's equality of the sexes for you! That's women's emancipation! Just as a matter of principle I'll bring her down like a duck. But what a woman! "Putting one of Popov's bullets through your silly head . . ." Her cheeks were flushed, her eyes were gleaming! And, by God, she's accepted the challenge! I never knew a woman like this before!

LUKA: Sir! Master! Please go away! I'll always pray for you!

125   SMIRNOV: *(again ignoring him)* What a woman! Phew!! *She's no sour puss, she's no cry baby.* She's fire and brimstone. She's a human cannon ball. What a shame I have to kill her!

LUKA: *(weeping)* Please, kind sir, please, go away!

SMIRNOV: *(as before)* I like her, isn't that funny? With those dimples and all? I like her. I'm even prepared to consider letting her off that debt. And where's my rage? It's gone. I never knew a woman like this before.

Enter Mrs. Popov with pistols.

MRS. POPOV: *(boldly)* Pistols, Mr. Smirnov! *(Matter of fact.)* But before we start, you'd better show me how it's done. I'm not too familiar with these things. In fact I never gave a pistol a second look.

LUKA: Lord, have mercy on us, I must go hunt up the gardener and the coachman. Why has this catastrophe fallen upon us, O Lord? *(Exit.)*

130   SMIRNOV: *(examining the pistols)* Well, it's like this. There are several makes: one is the Mortimer, with capsules, especially constructed for dueling. What you have here are Smith and Wesson triple-action revolvers, with extractor, first-rate job, worth ninety rubles at the very least. You hold it this way. *(Aside.)* My God, what eyes she has! They're setting me on fire.

MRS. POPOV: This way?

SMIRNOV: Yes, that's right. You cock the trigger, take aim like this, head up, arm out like this. Then you just press with this finger here, and it's all over. The main thing is, keep cool, take slow aim, and don't let your arm jump.

MRS. POPOV: I see. And if it's inconvenient to do the job here, we can go out in the garden.

SMIRNOV: Very good. Of course, I should warn you: I'll be firing in the air.

135   MRS. POPOV: What? This is the end. Why?

SMIRNOV: Oh, well—because—for private reasons.

MRS. POPOV: Scared, huh? *(She laughs heartily.)* Now don't you try to get out of it, Mr. Smirnov. My blood is up. I won't be happy till I've drilled a hole through that skull of yours. Follow me. What's the matter? Scared?

SMIRNOV: That's right. I'm scared.

MRS. POPOV: Oh, come on, what's the matter with you?

140   SMIRNOV: Well, um, Mrs. Popov, I, um, I like you.

MRS. POPOV: *(laughing bitterly)* Good God! He likes me, does he? The gall of the man. *(Showing him the door.)* You may leave, Mr. Smirnov.

SMIRNOV: *(Quietly puts the gun down, takes his hat, and walks to the door. Then he stops and the pair look at each other without a word. Then, approaching gingerly.)* Listen, Mrs. Popov. Are you still mad at me? I'm in the devil of a temper myself, of course. But then, you see — what I mean is — it's this way — the fact is — *(Roaring.)* Well, is it my fault, damn it, if I like you? *(Clutches the back of a chair. It breaks.)* Christ, what fragile furniture you have here. I like you. Know what I mean? I could fall in love with you.

MRS. POPOV: I hate you. Get out!

SMIRNOV: What a woman! I never saw anything like it. Oh, I'm lost, I'm done for, I'm a mouse in a trap.

MRS. POPOV: Leave this house, or I shoot! 145

SMIRNOV: Shoot away! What bliss to die of a shot that was fired by that little velvet hand! To die gazing into those enchanting eyes. I'm out of my mind. I know: you must decide at once. Think for one second, then decide. Because if I leave now, I'll never be back. Decide! I'm a pretty decent chap. Landed gentleman, I should say. Ten thousand a year. Good stable. Throw a kopeck up in the air, and I'll put a bullet through it. Will you marry me?

MRS. POPOV: *(indignant, brandishing the gun)* We'll shoot it out! Get going! Take your pistol!

SMIRNOV: I'm out of my mind. I don't understand anything any more. *(Shouting.)* You there! That vodka!

MRS. POPOV: No excuses! No delays! We'll shoot it out!

SMIRNOV: I'm out of my mind. I'm falling in love. I *have* fallen in love. 150 *(He takes her hand vigorously; she squeals.)* I love you. *(He goes down on his knees.)* I love you as I've never loved before. I jilted twelve, and was jilted by nine others. But I didn't love a one of them as I love you. I'm full of tender emotion. I'm melting like butter. I'm weak as water. I'm on my knees like a fool, and I offer you my hand. It's a shame, it's a disgrace. I haven't been in love in five years. I took a vow against it. And now, all of a sudden, to be swept off my feet, it's a scandal. I offer you my hand, dear lady. Will you or won't you? You won't? Then don't! *(He rises and walks toward the door.)*

MRS. POPOV: I didn't say anything.

SMIRNOV: *(stopping)* What?

MRS. POPOV: Oh, nothing, you can go. Well, no, just a minute. No, you can go. Go! I detest you! But, just a moment. Oh, if you knew how furious I feel! *(Throws the gun on the table.)* My fingers have gone to sleep holding that horrid thing. *(She is tearing her handkerchief to shreds.)* And what are you standing around for? Get out of here!

SMIRNOV: Goodbye.

MRS. POPOV: Go, go, go! *(Shouting.)* Where are you going? Wait a minute! 155 No, no, it's all right, just go. I'm fighting mad. Don't come near me, don't come near me!

SMIRNOV: *(who is coming near her)* I'm pretty disgusted with myself — falling in love like a kid, going down on my knees like some moongazing whipper-snapper, the very thought gives me gooseflesh. *(Rudely.)* I love you. But it doesn't make sense. Tomorrow, I have to pay that interest, and we've already started mowing. *(He puts his arm about her waist.)* I shall never forgive myself for this.

MRS. POPOV: Take your hands off me, I hate you! Let's shoot it out!

A long kiss. Enter Luka with an axe, the Gardener with a rake, the coachman with a pitchfork, hired men with sticks.

LUKA: (*seeing the kiss*) Mercy on us! Holy saints above!

MRS. POPOV: (*dropping her eyes*) Luka, tell them in the stable that Toby is *not* to have any oats today.

❖ ❖ ❖

A Note on Translations

Many dramatic works that we read or see are translations from another language. For example, Ibsen wrote in Norwegian, Sophocles in Greek, Molière in French, and Chekhov in Russian. Before English-speaking viewers or readers can evaluate the language of a translated play, they must understand that the language they hear or read is the translator's interpretation of what the playwright intended to communicate. Translation is interpretation, not just a search for literal equivalents; as a result, a translation is always different from the original. Moreover, because translators make different choices, two translations of the same work into English can vary considerably.

Compare these two versions of an exchange of dialogue from two translations of the same Chekhov play, called *The Brute* in the translation that begins on page 1293 and *The Bear* in the alternate version.

From *The Brute*

SMIRNOV: You'd like me to come simpering to you in French, I suppose. "*Enchanté, madame! Merci beaucoup* for not paying zee money, *madame! Pardonnez-moi* if I 'ave disturbed you, *madame!* How *charmante* you look in mourning, *madame!*"

MRS. POPOV: Now you're being silly, Mr. Smirnov.

SMIRNOV: (*mimicking*) "Now you're being silly, Mr. Smirnov." "You don't know how to talk to a lady, Mr. Smirnov." Look here, Mrs. Popov. I've known more women than you've known pussy cats. I've fought three duels on their account. I've jilted twelve, and been jilted by nine others. Oh, yes, Mrs. Popov, I've played the fool in my time, whispered sweet nothings, bowed and scraped and endeavored to please. Don't tell me I don't know what it is to love, to pine away with longing, to have the blues, to melt like butter, to be weak as water. I was full of tender emotion. I was carried away with passion. I squandered half my fortune on the sex. I chattered about women's emancipation. But there's an end to everything, dear madam. . . . (1.71–73)

From *The Bear*

SMIRNOV: Ach, it's astonishing! How would you like me to talk to you? In French, perhaps? (*Lisps in anger.*) Madame, *je vous prie.* . . . how happy I am that you're not paying me the money. . . . Ah, pardon, I've made you uneasy! Such lovely weather we're having today! And you look so becoming in your mourning dress. (*Bows and scrapes.*)

MRS. POPOV: That's rude and not very clever!

SMIRNOV: *(teasing)* Rude and not very clever! I don't know how to behave in the company of ladies. Madam, in my time I've seen far more women than you've seen sparrows. Three times I've fought duels over women; I've jilted twelve women, nine have jilted me! Yes! There was a time when I played the fool; I became sentimental over women, used honeyed words, fawned on them, bowed and scraped. . . . I loved, suffered, sighed at the moon; I became limp, melted, shivered . . . I loved passionately, madly, every which way, devil take me, I chattered away like a magpie about the emancipation of women, ran through half my fortune as a result of my tender feelings; but now, if you will excuse me, I'm on to your ways! I've had enough!

Although both translations convey Smirnov's anger and frustration, they use different words (with different connotations), different phrasing — and even different stage directions. In *The Bear,* for instance, only one French phrase is used, whereas *The Brute* uses several and specifies a French accent as well; other differences between the two translations include *The Bear*'s use of "teasing," "sparrows," and "I've had enough!" where *The Brute* uses "mimicking," "pussy cats," and "But there's an end to everything, dear madam." (Elsewhere in the play, *The Bear* uses profanity while *The Brute* uses more polite language.) Many words and idiomatic expressions used in daily speech cannot be translated exactly from one language to another; as a result, the two translators make different choices to try to convey a sense of the original.

Recognizing Kinds of Drama

The dramatic tradition stretches back to antiquity, with some of the earliest known plays dating back to the sixth century B.C. This long lifespan has produced numerous developments in the form and conventions of drama.

Traditionally, plays are divided into **acts**, which are further divided into **scenes**. In between acts, there is sometimes an **intermission**, a pause in the action that can be used to heighten the dramatic tension created at the end of the previous scene (as well as to represent the passage of time between one act and the next). The number of acts in a play can range from one to five, depending on the length and scope of the play itself. Shakespeare's *Hamlet* and *A Midsummer's Night's Dream* both have five acts, but most full-length contemporary plays have just two or three.

Some shorter plays have only one act. In a **one-act play** such as Chekov's *The Brute*, the playwright is faced with the challenge of creating a dramatic work that includes all the elements that are part of longer plays — exposition, conflict, climax, and resolution. Because these plays are shorter, their imagery and dialogue are often more concise. In fact, because there is less time to devote to character development, subtext, or the consequences of events, one-act plays differ from full-length plays in the same way that short stories differ from novels.

An even more recent development in drama is the **ten-minute play** — a play in which all the actors are onstage and all events take place within a ten-minute time period (see Chapter 37). On an even smaller scale, a **monologue**—an extended speech delivered by one character—can stand alone as a complete dramatic work. Some contemporary plays—including Eve Ensler's *The Vagina Monologues* and Claudia Shear's *Blown Sideways through Life*—are composed entirely of a series of interrelated dramatic monologues.

Some contemporary drama is **improvisational**, which means that it is either partially or completely unscripted. This dramatic tradition is a descendant of **commedia dell'arte**, an Italian form of improvisational theater that began in the sixteenth century and was popular until the eighteenth century. Today, many theater actors are trained in "improv" work, which challenges them to sharpen their concentration and trust in their own instincts rather than relying solely on a script. Some improvisational plays rely on audience participation, requiring actors to improvise in response to audience members' spontaneous contributions to the play.

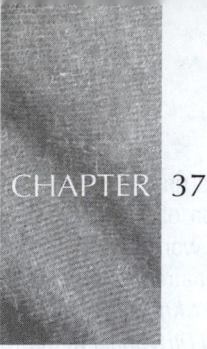

CHAPTER 37

DRAMA SAMPLER:
TEN-MINUTE PLAYS

Many different types and forms of drama have emerged throughout the long history of playwriting. In recent years, theater has become a bit more experimental in nature, as evidenced by the proliferation of improvisational plays as well as one-act and ten-minute plays. While one-act plays have the luxury of a more extended period in which to accomplish exposition, dramatic tension, climax, and denouement, the **ten-minute play** offers a very small window of opportunity in which the playwright can create meaning. In fact, the ten-minute play is, in a sense, the dramatic equivalent of the **haiku** in poetry in that it is intended to be taken in all at once, and thus to have a particularly intense impact on the audience.

Since a page of script roughly translates into a minute of time onstage, a ten-minute play is generally limited to about ten pages in length. Despite its brevity, however, a ten-minute play is more than just a scene: it must begin with **exposition**, introduce a **conflict** (usually relatively early in the play), and provide a **resolution**, just as any other complete dramatic work does. A ten-minute play is also more than just a **monologue**; it always includes at least two characters.

Ten-minute plays are generally staged in groups, allowing the audience to watch several plays in sequence. For this reason, large casts and elaborate staging are rare. The most popular venue for a ten-minute play is a dramatic festival, and numerous competitions offer prizes that include the staging of an author's play. The most prominent contest is sponsored by the Actors Theatre of Louisville, which stages the annual Humana Festival of New American Plays.

The five ten-minute plays in this sampler treat a variety of topics. In Jane Martin's *Beauty*, the two protagonists trade lives, with unexpected consequences; in *Tape*, by José Rivera, the protagonist is forced to confront his entire life and face up to his own truths; in Billy Goda's *No Crime*, a job interview takes an unexpected turn; in *I Dream Before I Take the Stand*, Arlene Hutton's protagonist faces a hostile interrogator; and in *Nine Ten*, by Warren Leight, five strangers are brought together for jury duty. Although each playwright addresses the challenges of the ten-minute play format in a different fashion, each of these plays relies on dialogue, pauses, subtext, and the power of suggestion to create meaning in a short span of time.

JANE MARTIN, a prize-winning playwright, has never made a public appearance or spoken about any of her works. In addition, she has never given an interview, and no picture of her has ever been published. As one critic wryly observed, Martin is "America's best known, unknown playwright." Martin first came to the attention of American theater audiences with her collection of monologues, *Talking With . . . ,* a work that premiered at the 1981 Humana Festival of New American Plays at the Actors Theatre of Louisville, Kentucky. Her other works include *Vital Signs* and *What Mama Don't Know;* her full-length plays include *Cementville;* the Pulitzer Prize–nominated *Keely and Du* (winner of the 1994 American Theatre Critics Association New Play Award); *Criminal Hearts;* and *Middle Aged White Guys.* Martin's name is widely believed to be a pseudonym. Jon Jory, artistic director of the Actors Theatre of Louisville — and director of the premieres of all of Martin's plays — is spokesperson for the playwright and, according to some people, may actually be the playwright behind the pen name. Jory has repeatedly denied this; in a 1994 interview, he said that Martin "feels she could not write plays if people knew who she was, regardless of her identity or gender." In Jory's opinion, "The point in the end is the plays themseleves. . . . But if Jane's anonymity is a P. T. Barnum publicity stunt, it's one of the longest circus acts going."

Beauty (2000)

<u>CHARACTERS</u>
Carla
Bethany

An apartment. Minimalist set. A young woman, Carla, on the phone.

CARLA: In love with me? You're in love with me? Could you describe yourself again? Uh-huh. Uh-huh. And you spoke to me? (*A knock at the door.*) Listen, I always hate to interrupt a marriage proposal, but . . . could you possibly hold that thought? (*Puts phone down and goes to door. Bethany, the same age as Carla and a friend, is there. She carries the sort of Mideastern lamp we know of from Aladdin.*)

BETHANY: Thank God you were home. I mean, you're not going to believe this!

CARLA: Somebody on the phone. (*Goes back to it.*)

BETHANY: I mean, I just had a beach urge, so I told them at work my uncle was dying . . .

5   CARLA: (*motions to Bethany for quiet*) And you were the one in the leather jacket with the tattoo? What was the tattoo? (*Carla again asks Bethany, who is gesturing wildly that she should hang up, to cool it.*) Look, a screaming eagle from shoulder to shoulder, maybe. There were a lot of people in the bar.

BETHANY: (*gesturing and mouthing*) I have to get back to work.

CARLA: (*on phone*) See, the thing is, I'm probably not going to marry someone I can't remember . . . particularly when I don't drink. Sorry. Sorry. Sorry. (*She hangs up.*) Madness.

BETHANY: So I ran out to the beach . . .

CARLA: This was some guy I never met who apparently offered me a beer . . .

BETHANY: . . . low tide and this . . . (*The lamp.*) . . . was just sitting there, lying   10
    there . . .

CARLA: . . . and he tracks me down . . .

BETHANY: . . . on the beach, and I lift this lid thing . . .

CARLA: . . . and seriously proposes marriage.

BETHANY: . . . and a genie comes out.

CARLA: I mean, that's twice in a . . . what?   15

BETHANY: A genie comes out of this thing.

CARLA: A genie?

BETHANY: I'm not kidding, the whole Disney kind of thing, swirling smoke,
    and then this twenty-foot-high, see-through guy in like an Arabian outfit.

CARLA: Very funny.

BETHANY: Yes, funny, but twenty feet high! I look up and down the beach, I'm   20
    alone. I don't have my pepper spray or my hand alarm. You know me, when
    I'm petrified I joke. I say his voice is too high for Robin Williams, and he
    says he's a castrati. Naturally. Who else would I meet?

CARLA: What's a castrati?

BETHANY: You know . . .

The appropriate gesture.

CARLA: Bethany, dear one, I have three modeling calls. I am meeting Ralph
    Lauren!

BETHANY: Okay, good. Ralph Lauren. Look, I am not kidding!

CARLA: You're not kidding what?!   25

BETHANY: There is a genie in this thingamajig.

CARLA: Uh-huh. I'll be back around eight.

BETHANY: And he offered me *wishes!*

CARLA: Is this some elaborate practical joke because it's my birthday?

BETHANY: No, happy birthday, but I'm like crazed because I'm on this deserted   30
    beach with a twenty-foot-high, see-through genie, so like sarcastically . . .
    you know how I need a new car . . . I said fine, gimme 25,000 dollars . . .

CARLA: On the beach with the genie?

BETHANY: Yeah, right, exactly, and it rains down out of the sky.

CARLA: Oh sure.

BETHANY: (*pulling a wad out of her purse*) Count it, those are thousands. I lost
    one in the surf.

*Carla sees the top bill. Looks at Bethany, who nods encouragement. Carla thumbs
through them.*

CARLA: These look real.   35

BETHANY: Yeah.

CARLA: And they rained down out of the sky?

BETHANY: Yeah.

CARLA: You've been really strange lately, are you dealing?

BETHANY: Dealing what, I've even given up chocolate.   40

CARLA: Let me see the genie.

BETHANY: Wait, wait.

CARLA: Bethany, I don't have time to screw around. Let me see the genie or let me go on my appointments.

BETHANY: Wait! So I pick up the money . . . see, there's sand on the money . . . and I'm like nuts so I say, you know, "Okay, look, ummm, big guy, my uncle is in the hospital" . . . because as you know when I said to the people at work my uncle was dying, I was on one level telling the truth although it had nothing to do with the beach, but he was in Intensive Care after the accident, and that's on my mind, so I say, okay, Genie, heal my uncle . . . which is like impossible given he was hit by two trucks, and the genie says, "Yes, Master" . . . like they're supposed to say, and he goes into this like kind of whirlwind, kicking up sand and stuff, and I'm like, "Oh my God!" and the air clears, and he bows, you know, and says, "It is done, Master," and I say, "Okay, whatever-you-are, I'm calling on my cell phone," and I get it out and I get this doctor who is like dumbstruck who says my uncle came to, walked out of Intensive Care and left the hospital! I'm not kidding, Carla.

45 CARLA: On your mother's grave?

BETHANY: On my mother's grave.

They look at each other.

CARLA: Let me see the genie.

BETHANY: No, no, look, that's the whole thing . . . I was just, like, reacting, you know, responding, and that's already two wishes . . . although I'm really pleased about my uncle, the $25,000 thing, I could have asked for $10 million, and there is only one wish left.

CARLA: So ask for $10 million.

50 BETHANY: I don't think so. I don't think so. I mean, I gotta focus in here. Do you have a sparkling water?

CARLA: No. Bethany, I'm missing Ralph Lauren now. Very possibly my one chance to go from catalogue model to the very, very big time, so, if you are joking, stop joking.

BETHANY: Not joking. See, see, the thing is, I know what I want. In my guts. Yes. Underneath my entire bitch of a life is this unspoken, ferocious, all-consuming urge . . .

CARLA: (*trying to get her to move this along*) Ferocious, all-consuming urge . . .

BETHANY: I want to be like you.

55 CARLA: Me?

BETHANY: Yes.

CARLA: Half the time you don't even like me.

BETHANY: Jealous. The ogre of jealousy.

CARLA: You're the one with the $40,000 job straight out of school. You're the one who has published short stories. I'm the one hanging on by her fingernails in modeling. The one who has creeps calling her on the phone. The one who had to have a nose job.

60 BETHANY: I want to be beautiful.

CARLA: You are beautiful.

BETHANY: Carla, I'm not beautiful.

CARLA: You have charm. You have personality. You know perfectly well you're pretty.

BETHANY: "Pretty," see, that's it. Pretty is the minor leagues of beautiful. Pretty is what people discover about you after they know you. Beautiful is what knocks them out across the room. Pretty, you get called a couple of times a year; *beautiful* is twenty-four hours a day.

CARLA: Yeah? So?

65

BETHANY: So?! We're talking *beauty* here. Don't say "So?" Beauty is the real deal. You are the center of any moment of your life. People stare. Men flock. I've seen you get offered discounts on makeup for no reason. Parents treat beautiful children better. Studies show your income goes up. You can have sex anytime you want it. Men have to know me. That takes up to a year. I'm continually horny.

CARLA: Bethany, I don't even like sex. I can't have a conversation without men coming on to me. I have no privacy. I get hassled on the street. They start pressuring me from the beginning. Half the time, it never occurs to them to start with a conversation. Smart guys like you. You've had three long-term relationships, and you're only twenty-three. I haven't had one. The good guys, the smart guys are scared to death of me. I'm surrounded by male bimbos who think a preposition is when you go to school away from home. I have no woman friends except you. I don't even want to talk about this!

BETHANY: I knew you'd say something like this. See, you're "in the club" so you can say this. It's the way beauty functions as an elite. You're trying to keep it all for yourself.

CARLA: I'm trying to tell you it's no picnic.

BETHANY: But it's what everybody wants. It's the nasty secret at large in the world. It's the unspoken tidal desire in every room and on every street. It's the unspoken, the soundless whisper . . . millions upon millions of people longing hopelessly and forever to stop being whatever they are and be beautiful, but the difference between those ardent multitudes and me is that I have a goddamn genie and one more wish!

70

CARLA: Well, it's not what I want. This is me, Carla. I have never read a whole book. Page six, I can't remember page four. The last thing I read was *The Complete Idiot's Guide to WordPerfect*. I leave dinner parties right after the dessert because I'm out of conversation. You know the dumb blond joke about the application where it says, "Sign here," she put Sagittarius? I've done that. Only beautiful guys approach me, and that's because they want to borrow my eye shadow. I barely exist outside a mirror! You don't want to *be me*.

BETHANY: None of you tell the truth. That's why you have no friends. We can all see you're just trying to make us feel better because we aren't in your league. This only proves to me it should be my third wish. Money can only buy things. Beauty makes you the center of the universe.

Bethany picks up the lamp.

CARLA: Don't do it. Bethany, don't wish it! I am telling you you'll regret it.

Bethany lifts the lid. There is a tremendous crash, and the lights go out. Then they flicker and come back up, revealing Bethany and Carla on the floor where they have been thrown by the explosion. We don't realize it at first, but they have exchanged places.

CARLA/BETHANY: Oh God.

75 BETHANY/CARLA: Oh God.

CARLA/BETHANY: Am I bleeding? Am I dying?

BETHANY/CARLA: I'm so dizzy. You're not bleeding.

CARLA/BETHANY: Neither are you.

BETHANY/CARLA: I feel so weird.

80 CARLA/BETHANY: Me too. I feel . . . (*Looking at her hands.*) Oh, my God, I'm wearing your jewelry. I'm wearing your nail polish.

BETHANY/CARLA: I know I'm over here, but I can see myself over there.

CARLA/BETHANY: I'm wearing your dress. I have your legs!!

BETHANY/CARLA: These aren't my shoes. I can't meet Ralph Lauren wearing these shoes!

CARLA/BETHANY: I wanted to be beautiful, but I didn't want to be you.

85 BETHANY/CARLA: Thanks a lot!!

CARLA/BETHANY: I've got to go. I want to pick someone out and get laid.

BETHANY/CARLA: You can't just walk out of here in my body!

CARLA/BETHANY: Wait a minute. Wait a minute. What's eleven eighteenths of 1,726?

BETHANY/CARLA: Why?

90 CARLA/BETHANY: I'm a public accountant. I want to know if you have my brain.

BETHANY/CARLA: One hundred thirty-two and a half.

CARLA/BETHANY: You have my brain.

BETHANY/CARLA: What shade of Rubenstein lipstick does Cindy Crawford wear with teal blue?

CARLA/BETHANY: Raging Storm.

95 BETHANY/CARLA: You have my brain. You poor bastard.

CARLA/BETHANY: I don't care. Don't you see?

BETHANY/CARLA: See what?

CARLA/BETHANY: We both have the one thing, the one and only thing everybody wants.

BETHANY/CARLA: What is that?

100 CARLA/BETHANY: It's better than beauty for me; it's better than brains for you.

BETHANY/CARLA: What? What?!

CARLA/BETHANY: Different problems.

Blackout.

◇   ◇   ◇

JOSÉ RIVERA (1955–   ) was born in San Juan, Puerto Rico and grew up in a household where the only book was a Bible. When he was four years old, his family moved to New York. Early in his life, he saw a staged version of the play *Rumpelstiltskin* and decided to become a playwright. He has written numerous plays and won several awards, including two Obie Awards, a Fulbright Fellowship, and the Whiting Foundation Writing Award. In 2002, Rivera wrote the screenplay for *The Motorcycle Diaries,* a movie based on a motorcycle trip that Cuban revolutionary Che Guevara took as a young man. In 2005, Rivera became the first Puerto Rican to be nominated for an Academy Award for best adapted screenplay.

Tape (1993)

CHARACTERS
Person
Attendant

A small dark room. No windows. One door. A Person is being led in by an Attendant. In the room is a simple wooden table and chair. On the table is a large reel-to-reel tape recorder, a glass of water, and a pitcher of water.

PERSON: Dark in here.
ATTENDANT: I'm sorry.
PERSON: No, I know it's not your fault.
ATTENDANT: I'm afraid of those lights . . .   5
PERSON: I guess, what does it matter now?
ATTENDANT: . . . not very bright.
PERSON: Who cares, really?
ATTENDANT: We don't want to cause you any undue suffering. If it's too dark in here, I'll make sure one of the other attendants replaces the light bulb.

(The Person looks at the Attendant.)

PERSON: Any "undue suffering"?   10
ATTENDANT: That's right. *(The Person looks at the room.)*
PERSON: Is this where I'll be?
ATTENDANT: That's right.
PERSON: Will you be outside?
ATTENDANT: Yes.   15
PERSON: The entire time?
ATTENDANT: The entire time.
PERSON: Is it boring?
ATTENDANT: I'm sorry?
PERSON: Is it boring? You know. Waiting outside all the time.   20
ATTENDANT: *(Soft smile.)* It's my job. It's what I do.
PERSON: Of course. *(Beat.)* Will I get anything to eat or drink?
ATTENDANT: Well, we're not really set up for that. We don't have what you'd call a kitchen. But we can send out for things. Little things. Cold food.

PERSON: I understand.

ATTENDANT: Soft drinks.

25   PERSON: *(Hopefully.)* Beer?

ATTENDANT: I'm afraid not.

PERSON: Not even on special occasions like my birthdays?

ATTENDANT: *(Thinking.)* I guess maybe on your birthday.

PERSON: *(Truly appreciative.)* Great, thanks. *(Beat.)*

30   ATTENDANT: Do you have any more questions before we start? Because if you
     do, that's okay. It's okay to ask as many questions as you want. I'm sure
     you're very curious. I'm sure you'd like to know as much as possible, so you
     can figure out how it all fits together and what it all means. So please ask.
     That's why I'm here. Don't worry about the time. We have a lot of time.
     (Beat.)

PERSON: I don't have any questions.

ATTENDANT: *(Disappointed.)* Are you sure?

PERSON: There's not much I really have to know is there? Really?

ATTENDANT: No, I guess not. I just thought . . .

35   PERSON: It's okay. I appreciate it. I guess I really want to sit.

ATTENDANT: Sit. *(The person sits on the chair and faces the tape recorder.)*

PERSON: Okay, I'm sitting.

ATTENDANT: Is it . . . comfortable?

PERSON: Does it matter? Does it really fucking matter?

40   ATTENDANT: No. I suppose not. *(The Attendant looks sad. The Person looks at
     the Attendant and feels bad.)*

PERSON: Hey I'm sorry. I know it's not your fault. I know you didn't mean it.
     I'm sorry.

ATTENDANT: It's all right.

PERSON: What's your name anyway? Do you have a name?

ATTENDANT: Not really. It's not allowed.

45   PERSON: Really? Not allowed? Who says?

ATTENDANT: The rules say.

PERSON: Have you actually seen these rules? Are they in writing?

ATTENDANT: Oh yes. There's a long and extensive training course.

PERSON: *(Surprised.)* There is?

50   ATTENDANT: Oh yes. It's quite rigorous.

PERSON: Imagine that.

ATTENDANT: You have to be a little bit of everything. Confidant, confessor,
     friend, stern taskmaster. Guide.

PERSON: I guess that would take time.

ATTENDANT: My teachers were all quite strong and capable. They really
     pushed me. I was grateful. I knew I had been chosen for something unique
     and exciting. Something significant. Didn't mind the hard work and sleep-
     less nights.

55   PERSON: *(Surprised.)* Oh? You sleep?

ATTENDANT: *(Smiles.)* When I can. *(Beat.)*

PERSON: Do you dream? *(Beat.)*

ATTENDANT: No. (*Beat.*) That's not allowed. (*Beat.*)

PERSON: I'm sorry.

ATTENDANT: No. It's something you get used to.   60

PERSON: (*Trying to be chummy.*) I know. I went years and years without being able to remember one single dream I had. It really scared the shit out of me when I was ten and . . .

ATTENDANT: I know.

PERSON: I'm sorry.

ATTENDANT: I said I know. I know that story. When you were ten.

PERSON: Oh. Yeah. I guess you would know everything. Every story.   65

ATTENDANT: (*Apologetic.*) It's part of the training.

PERSON: I figured. (*A long uncomfortable silence.*)

ATTENDANT: (*Softly.*) Have you ever operated a reel-to-reel tape recorder before?

PERSON: No I haven't. I mean — no.

ATTENDANT: It's not hard.   70

PERSON: I, uhm, these things were pretty obsolete by the time I was old enough to afford stereo equipment, you know, I got into cassettes, and, later, CDs, but never one of these jobbies.

ATTENDANT: It's not hard. (*Demonstrates.*) On here. Off here. Play. Pause. Rewind.

PERSON: (*Surprised.*) Rewind?

ATTENDANT: In some cases the quality of the recording is so poor . . . you'll want to rewind it until you understand.

PERSON: No fast forward?   75

ATTENDANT: No.

PERSON: It looks like a pretty good one. Sturdy. Very strong.

ATTENDANT: They get a lot of use.

PERSON: I bet. (*Beat.*) Is this the only tape? (*The Attendant laughs out loud— then quickly stops.*)

ATTENDANT: No.   80

PERSON: I didn't think so.

ATTENDANT: There are many more.

PERSON: How many? A lot?

ATTENDANT: There are ten thousand boxes.

PERSON: *Ten* thousand?   85

ATTENDANT: I'm afraid so.

PERSON: Did I really . . .

ATTENDANT: I'm afraid you did.

PERSON: So . . . everyone goes into a room like this?

ATTENDANT: Exactly like this. There's no differentiation. Everyone's equal.   90

PERSON: For once.

ATTENDANT: What isn't equal, of course, is the . . . amount of time you spend here listening.

PERSON: Oh God.

ATTENDANT: (*Part of the training.*) Listening, just to yourself. To your voice.

95   **PERSON:** I know.

ATTENDANT: Listening, word by word, to every lie you ever told while you were alive.

PERSON: Oh God!

ATTENDANT: Every ugly lie to every person, every single time, every betrayal, every lying thought, every time you lied to yourself, deep in your mind, we were listening, we were recording, and it's all in these tapes, ten thousand boxes of them, in your own words, one lie after the next, over and over, until we're finished. So the amount of time varies. The amount of time you spend here all depends on how many lies you told. How many boxes of tape we have to get through together.

PERSON: *(Almost in tears.)* I'm sorry . . .

100   **ATTENDANT:** Too late.

PERSON: I said I'm sorry! I said I'm sorry! I said it a million times! What happened to forgiveness? I don't want to be here! I don't want this! I don't want to listen! I don't want to hear myself! I didn't mean to say the things that I said! I don't want to listen!

ATTENDANT: Yes, well. Neither did we. Neither did we. *(The Attendant looks sadly at the Person. The Attendant turns on the tape recorder. The Attendant hits the Play button, the reels spin slowly, and the tape starts snaking its way through the machine. Silence. The Attendant leaves the room, leaving the Person all alone. The Person nervously pours a glass of water, accidentally spilling water on the floor. From the depths of the machine comes a long-forgotten voice.)*

WOMAN'S VOICE: "Where have you been? Do you know I've been looking all over? Jesus Christ! I went to Manny's! I went to the pharmacy! The school! I even called the police! Look at me, Jesus Christ, I'm shaking! Now look at me — look at me and tell me where the hell you were! Tell me right now!" *(Silence. As the Person waits for the lying response, the lights fade to black.)*

◆ ◆ ◆

BILLY GODA is a screenwriter and playwright who earned an MFA in playwriting at Columbia University, where he also studied screenwriting. While he was at Columbia, his play *Georgia Cowboy* was selected as his graduating class production. Recent screenplays include *The Cretan Bull* and *Two-Arm Bandit*. *No Crime* was originally published in the *Best American Short Play Series 1998–1999*.

No Crime

CHARACTERS

Cal Roberts, a good looking thirty-year-old man
Jim Abner, a big, egotistical fifty-year-old man

Cal is in Jim Abner's office. It is a large office with a great deal of room, light, and a nice view. Jim has his cowboy boots up on his desk.

JIM: A time comes in a man's life when fifteen minutes can change his future, change his life; these could be your fifteen minutes, Cal.

Pause as Jim takes a tin of Skoal chewing tobacco out of his desk, packs it down, and takes a dip. He will spit throughout the scene.

You're one of three finalists for this position. Now it all depends upon your interview. Whichever one of you has the best interview, that's the one I'll hire. (Jim *spits*). Nasty habit. I've already met with the other two, so it's up to you now, Cal. It's up to you. (Jim *spits*.) What do you have to say about that?

CAL: I look forward to the challenge . . .

JIM: Yeah, yeah, yeah, one of the others said that also. Every time we interview I get that answer: "looking forward to something." You must get it out of a book. Were you reading one of those "what to say in an interview" books?

CAL: I wasn't . . .

JIM: I hope not. We need original thinking here. This law firm's been around for fifty-two years, and we've become so damn successful by original thinking; not by memorizing some damn answers in a how to be interviewed book. Are you aware of the success this firm has accomplished?   5

CAL: I am very aware of that . . .

JIM: We've been involved in some of the most important criminal cases in this country, and you know what nearly every one of them have in common? (*Pause.*) I'm asking what do these cases have in common? You said you know about our firm . . .

CAL: That you've improved the situation of the defendant. You've either plea bargained for a much lesser charge or you've had your client acquitted.

JIM: That's good, very good. Dave told you to say that, didn't he? (*Laughing.*) That s.o.b.'s ruining all my fun. That question usually scares the pants off the applicant . . .

CAL: However, in 1988, the state versus Max Mainer, he received a life sentence. In 1994, Tony Giovano received three consecutive life sentences for multiple murders, and I wonder if you shouldn't have gone with the insanity plea . . .   10

JIM: All right, Cal, you've done your homework; I don't need a history lesson. (*Pause.*) There is only one thing that matters when a client walks through that door. Do you know what that is?

CAL: That he can pay the bill for our legal services.

JIM: (*Laughing.*) Well, yes that too. Make that two things that matter. If he can pay our bill and if there is at least a slight chance of our improving his situation. If there is not that possibility we will reject the case no matter how much money they offer. If you lose cases you lose your reputation. We do not take kindly to losing cases here.

CAL: I understand.

JIM: When we went down with the Giovano fiasco, two very prestigious clients walked out the door with his guilty verdict. (Jim *spits*.) How is Dave?   15

CAL: He's fine.

JIM: Dave speaks very highly of you.

CAL: Thank you.

JIM: I said Dave does, not me. I don't know you yet. That's one of the main reasons you're sitting in that chair right now — that crazy bastard's a very good friend of mine. At Harvard Law, he saved my butt more than once forcing me to study something other than women and beer. I never understood why he decided to become a professor, without a doubt he could have been one of the top litigates in the country. We could have been partners. (*Pause.*) I have numerous applications with excellent resumes, but you have an ace in your pocket by the name of Dave Horowitz. That recommendation gives you the rail position. What do you have to say about that?

20 CAL: I think Dave's an excellent judge of character.

JIM: (*Laughing.*) I'm sure you do. He says you'll do whatever it takes to improve your situation — that's the feeling he gets from you. That's an important feeling, very important. What did Dave teach you, Cal? You better not give me a course title.

CAL: How to shoot a gun. How to aim and hit a target.

JIM: Well that's good, but I'm not interviewing you for our rifle team.

CAL: Everyone has a price, that becomes, that is, a weakness, and it's up to me, as a lawyer, as a thinking man, to find out what that is, and then, if need be, to use it. Ready, aim, fire, so to speak.

Long pause.
Jim spits.

25 JIM: A client walks into your office, sits down in your leather arm chair, Cal, lights a cigar, and then tells you the truth of his case, let's say he cracked some lady on the head with a baseball bat splattering her brains all over the sidewalk . . . (Jim *spits.*) . . . and he played Mickey Mantle on her head because he was ordered to by his, let's call it a supervisor, and he did not question his supervisor's authority. What would you do? How would you feel, Cal? This client has confessed his guilt to you. He has confessed to this horrible, this heinous crime of an innocent lady's head being smashed open. What would you do in defending a client that was guilty, and your only hope of winning the case was by twisting the truth?

Long pause.

CAL: I cannot accurately answer that question.

JIM: Why not?

CAL: He is my client?

JIM: That's what I said . . .

30 CAL: He has already agreed to use our firm as his representation?

JIM: Correct . . .

CAL: He is not guilty.

JIM: Cal, he has confessed to you . . .

CAL: He is innocent . . .

35 JIM: He has told you about the murder . . .

CAL: He did not commit . . .

JIM: He bashed a lady's head in with a bat! Splattering her blood . . .

CAL: Blood on the sidewalk from someone else's bat . . .

JIM: Are you stupid, son?! What is wrong with you? I have told you, he has told you . . .

CAL: You say that my client is guilty, well I say that is impossible, Jim. It is impossible to say he is guilty. He is innocent until someone from the DA's office can persuade a jury of twelve to say he is not innocent. He is innocent until a verdict of guilty is returned. This is why I can not accurately answer your question; this is why your question becomes irrelevant. If he is my client then he is innocent, and it was someone else's bat. Who are the witnesses, Jim? Do you have eyewitnesses? Did he confess to the police? I don't think he confessed or he wouldn't be in my office. Only if he confessed to the police would I start with the idea of his guilt as a possibility. A possibility that I would evaluate and attempt to repudiate. Has our hypothetical client confessed to the police?   40

JIM: We'll say he has not.

CAL: Then he is not guilty. Then the only thing which can be proved is that some lady's head has been struck with a blunt object causing her death. What other evidence exists, Jim? Is there any other evidence?

Jim spits.

JIM: Your conscience.

CAL: My conscience is not on trial.

Pause.

JIM: Would you like a dip of tobacco? Green, Skoal, longcut. Dave's the idiot that started me dipping; he thinks he's a Jewish cowboy from New York. I always chew tobacco when I think — that's as long as no women are around.   45

CAL: Yes, thank you.

Jim passes the tin to Cal. Cal packs it down and places a dip in his mouth.

JIM: I spit in this bronze cup. It was a present from my daughter. See that: "World's Greatest Dad."

CAL: That's a nice spit cup, sir.

JIM: I never hired a lawyer that dips tobacco.

CAL: It helps me think.   50

JIM: So your hypothetical client is not guilty?

CAL: No, he isn't.

JIM: I like that answer. I like the logic. The logic of truth not existing until it's been proven again.

CAL: And it can be a very difficult thing to prove.

Pause.
Jim spits and then gives Cal an empty-cup to spit in.

JIM: My instincts seem to be the same as Dave's, and I go with my instincts, Cal. I'm betting you'll be a fine addition to this team.   55

CAL: Thank you. I'll do my best . . .

JIM: Is that another answer out of that damn book?

CAL: No, it's not.

JIM: When you start at this firm, you start on probation, so I can see if you have what it takes to succeed.

60 CAL: That's fine.

JIM: You'll do some leg work for me, gathering some background information. Let's see what questions you come up with, what possibilities you create. (*Jim spits.*) I ask everyone if they'd like a dip of tobacco. No one ever says yes. Most people think it's disgusting.

CAL: Maybe that's why we like it.

JIM: Yes, yes, maybe that is why. I want you to meet someone, Cal. (*Jim buzzes the secretary.*) Send him in.

A man enters the office.

Cal, this will be your first client. His name is John Stutts. He bashed an elderly lady's head in with a baseball bat.

Lights down.

◆ ◆ ◆

ARLENE HUTTON is a MacDowell Colony fellow and a member of the Dramatists' Guild. Her first full-length play, *Last Train to Nibroc* (2000), received a 2000 New York Drama League nomination for Best Play and was produced regionally more than fifty times. *As It Is in Heaven*, her second play, premiered in Edinburgh and received a highly acclaimed four-month run at the Actors' Co-op in Los Angeles. She teaches at Fordham University.

I Dream Before I Take the Stand (1998)

CHARACTERS

She: a petite woman
He: a man, probably a lawyer

Casting Note: *The man is age 25–50, the woman 20–50, both of any race. The woman should be petite in height or very slim if taller, but the specific hair color lines may be changed with the author's permission.*

Set: *A chair.*

Time: *Right now.*

Lights up on a petite woman sitting in a chair. It is possible that the lights begin the play full and soft, narrowing very slowly throughout, so that by the end of the play only a narrow spot is focused on the woman, like an interrogation room. The man, a lawyer, walks around her throughout, at first in the full circle or light, later appearing in and out of the focused light. Perhaps by the end of the play, the light has narrowed on the woman, and the man is barely seen. There are many ways to present this play, but the pauses are a part of the dialogue.

SHE: I was walking through the park.
HE: Why were you in the park?
SHE: I was on my way to work.
HE: Do you have to walk through the park to get to work?
SHE: No.   5
HE: Do you always walk through the park to work?
SHE: No.
HE: Why did you walk through the park that day?
SHE: It was a beautiful day. I like to walk to work through the park when the
     weather's good.

Pause.

HE: Were you in a hurry?   10
SHE: I was on my way to work.
HE: Were you late?
SHE: No, I would have been on time.
HE: Were you strolling or walking fast?
SHE: I always walk fairly quickly.   15
HE: Why? The park is not safe?
SHE: I guess not.
HE: Yet you walk through it to get to work.
SHE: There are lots of people around.
HE: But you walk quickly through the park.   20
SHE: Yes.

Pause.

HE: How do you walk?
SHE: Which way?
HE: Do you swing your arms?
SHE: I don't know.   25
HE: Were you carrying anything?
SHE: Just my purse.
HE: So your arms were free to swing along as you walked.
SHE: Maybe.
HE: Or maybe you walk with them folded.   30
SHE: I don't know what you mean.
HE: Perhaps you fold your arms.

He demonstrates.

SHE: Maybe.
HE: So sometimes you swing your arms and sometimes you fold them.
SHE: I guess.   35

HE: What else would you do with them?
SHE: I guess you're right.

Pause.

HE: So you were walking through the park that day on your way to work.
SHE: Yes. I already said that.

Pause.

40   HE: What were you wearing?
SHE: A skirt and a top.
HE: What color was the skirt?
SHE: It was a print.
HE: What color?
45   SHE: Black and red.
HE: And the top?
SHE: What?
HE: What color was the top?
SHE: Black.
50   HE: Just black?
SHE: It had a little red flower on it.
HE: The fabric?
SHE: No. A decoration.
HE: Where?
55   SHE: In the center of the neckline.
HE: A rose.
SHE: I guess. It was tiny.
HE: It was in the fabric?
SHE: No. It was a small ribbon.
60   HE: Like the little flowers on lingerie.
SHE: Like that.
HE: How sweet. (*A pause*) Were you wearing jewelry?
SHE: No. Just a watch.
HE: An expensive watch?
65   SHE: No.
HE: An expensive *looking* watch?
SHE: No. Just a Timex.
HE: So that you could hurry through the park to be at work on time.
SHE: Of course.
70   HE: No other jewelry?
SHE: No.
HE: Why not?
SHE: I don't wear jewelry in the park.
HE: Why not?
75   SHE: I don't want to attract attention.
HE: You don't want to get mugged.
SHE: Right.

Pause.

HE: Your hair is up today. Were you wearing it that way in the park?

SHE: No. I was wearing it down.

HE: Why?   80

SHE: It probably wasn't quite dry.

HE: You go out with wet hair? Why?

SHE: In nice weather.

HE: Why?

SHE: It feels good.   85

HE: And you color your hair.

SHE: Yes.

HE: And why is that?

SHE: I like it.

HE: Why? What is your natural color?   90

SHE: Like this when I was in college.

HE: But now?

SHE: I don't know.

HE: You don't know what color your hair is?

SHE: It's been a while —   95

HE: What color do you think it is?

SHE: I imagine it's sort of a dirty blonde with a little gray. (Note: *"dirty blonde"*
    can be "mousy brown," depending on the hair color of the actress. "With a little
    gray" can be omitted.)

HE: But you don't really know.

SHE: Not really.

HE: (*optional pause*) Do you think you are more attractive with colored hair?   100

SHE: I don't know.

HE: Then why do you color it?

SHE: I guess so.

HE: What?

SHE: I guess I think I'm —   105

HE: So you color your hair to be more attractive.

SHE: I guess.

HE: But your fingernails are not painted.

SHE: No.

HE: Do you sometimes paint your fingernails?   110

SHE: Sometimes I wear nail polish.

HE: Were your fingernails painted that day?

SHE: I think so.

HE: What nail color did you use?

SHE: A pink polish.   115

HE: Not red.

SHE: No. Just pink.

HE: Why?

SHE: To match my make-up.

120   HE: You were wearing make-up?

SHE: Yes.

HE: Do you always wear make-up to the park?

SHE: No.

HE: Then why were you wearing it that day?

125   SHE: I was on my way to work.

HE: What sort of make-up were you wearing?

SHE: What brand?

HE: Which items of make-up had you put on? Lipstick?

SHE: Yes.

130   HE: What color?

SHE: The actual name?

HE: What color would *you* call the lipstick you wore?

SHE: A sort of peach, maybe, with a darker —

HE: You were wearing two colors on your lips?

135   SHE: Well, yes.

HE: How does one do that?

SHE: It's a lip liner with a brush and then a tube lipstick.

HE: You outline your lips before you put on your lipstick.

SHE: Yes. It's —

140   HE: You add definition to your lips.

SHE: Sort of.

HE: To emphasize them. You emphasize your lips.

SHE: It's just the way you put on make-up.

Possibly a pause.

HE: What other make-up were you wearing?

145   SHE: A little powder.

HE: Why?

SHE: So my nose wouldn't be shiny.

HE: And why would it?

SHE: It was a fairly warm day.

150   HE: You might have perspired a little.

SHE: Maybe.

HE: And was there color on your cheeks?

SHE: Yes. I use a little blush.

HE: Color on the eyes?

155   SHE: Eyeliner. Maybe a little eye shadow.

HE: Mascara.

SHE: No.

HE: Are you sure?

SHE: Yes. I don't use mascara.

160   HE: Why not?

SHE: It bothers my contact lenses.

HE: Were you wearing contact lenses in the park?

SHE: Yes.

HE: You weren't wearing glasses?
SHE: No.   165
HE: But you are wearing glasses now.
SHE: Sometimes I wear contact lenses.
HE: You were wearing contact lenses in the park.
SHE: I already said that.
HE: Your hair was down and you were wearing make-up and contact lenses.   170
SHE: I already said that.
HE: Your hair was down and you were wearing make-up and contact lenses.
SHE: Yes.

A pause.

HE: Were you wearing perfume?
SHE: Cologne.   175
HE: Do you always wear perfume?
SHE: Cologne. I was wearing cologne.
HE: Do you always wear cologne?
SHE: Usually.
HE: In the park?   180
SHE: To work.
HE: And it was a warm day.
SHE: Yes. But what does that —
HE: You were walking through the park on your way to work dressed in your skirt
    and top. Your hair was down and you were wearing make-up and perfume.
SHE: Cologne.   185

A long pause. She has won this round, and he must regroup.

HE: You were walking through the park.
SHE: Yes.
HE: You passed a man sitting on a bench.
SHE: (*after a slight pause*) There were lots of people sitting on benches.
HE: You passed many people.   190
SHE: Yes.
HE: The park was crowded.
SHE: No.
HE: The park was not empty.
SHE: No. But there were a lot of people.   195
HE: Did you see anyone you knew?
SHE: No.
HE: No neighbors or friends or familiar faces?
SHE: No.
HE: You walked past the people sitting on benches.   200
SHE: Yes.
HE: There was a man sitting on a bench by himself.
SHE: I didn't notice he was alone.
HE: He spoke to you.

205   SHE: Yes.

HE: You spoke to him.

SHE: No.

HE: He spoke to you.

SHE: Yes.

210   HE: What did he say?

SHE: He just said hello.

HE: And what did you do?

SHE: I nodded to him and kept on walking.

HE: Did you know him?

215   SHE: No.

HE: Had you ever seen him before?

SHE: No.

HE: He was a stranger.

SHE: Yes.

220   HE: Yet you nodded at him. Did you smile as you nodded?

SHE: Yes.

HE: Why?

SHE: It was a beautiful day. I was just passing by and he said hello.

HE: Do you always acknowledge comments from strangers on the street?

225   SHE: Not always.

HE: Then why did you acknowledge this man?

SHE: It was such a nice day. And I don't like to be rude.

HE: So this stranger said hello and you smiled and nodded.

SHE: That's right.

230   HE: Did you speak to other people sitting on the benches?

SHE: No.

HE: Did you speak to anyone else in the park?

SHE: No.

HE: Why not?

235   SHE: No one else spoke to me.

HE: But when a strange man said hello you smiled and nodded at him.

SHE: Yes. There were lots of people —

HE: Did you stop to smile and nod?

SHE: What?

240   HE: Did you stop still in front of the man to smile at him?

SHE: No. I kept walking.

HE: Why didn't you stop?

SHE: I didn't think about it. It was just a casual hello. I just kept walking. It
    was nothing.

HE: Not really. (*Pause.*) What were you wearing?

245   SHE: What?

HE: What were you wearing?

SHE: I told you.

HE: You have to answer. What were you wearing?

SHE: A skirt and a top.

HE: To go to work? 250
SHE: I had a jacket in the office.
HE: What kind of skirt?
SHE: A printed one.
HE: A red and black print.
SHE: Yes. 255
HE: Was it long or short?
SHE: What?
HE: The skirt. Was it below your knees?
SHE: No.
HE: It came above your knees. 260
SHE: Yes.
HE: It was tight. It clung to your body?
SHE: No. It was gathered. A full skirt.
HE: So it might have moved when you walked.
SHE: I don't know. 265
HE: What was the fabric?
SHE: Chiffon.
HE: Chiffon is a sheer fabric.
SHE: It was lined.
HE: What was the lining? 270
SHE: The lining was chiffon, too.
HE: So you were wearing a see-through mini skirt.
SHE: No.
HE: Describe the blouse.
SHE: What? 275
HE: You were wearing a top.
SHE: Yes. A T-shirt.
HE: A knit top.
SHE: Yes.
HE: Did it have sleeves? 280
SHE: No. It was sleeveless.
HE: A tank top. It was tight.
SHE: No.
HE: It fitted closely on your body. What color was it?
SHE: I already told you. 285
HE: What color was it?
SHE: (*an outburst*) Black.
HE: With a little red flower. (*Possibly a pause.*) Were you wearing underwear?
SHE: (*surprised at this question*) Yes.
HE: Were you wearing a slip? 290
SHE: No.
HE: Why not?
SHE: It was warm out. And the skirt was lined.
HE: Were you wearing panty hose?
SHE: No. 295

HE: Your legs were bare.

SHE: Yes.

HE: No socks?

SHE: I told you. I was wearing sandals.

300 **HE:** For the office?

SHE: I keep stockings and pumps in my desk.

HE: Along with a jacket.

SHE: Yes.

HE: You walk through the park half naked and cover up for the office.

305 **SHE:** (*After a pause*) It's air-conditioned.

HE: What?

SHE: The office. It's air-conditioned. It gets cold.

HE: But the park was hot.

SHE: Yes.

310 **HE:** So you don't wear much clothing. Were your legs shaved?

SHE: Yes.

HE: Why do you shave your legs?

SHE: I just do.

HE: It looks better.

315 **SHE:** Yes.

HE: So you weren't wearing pantyhose.

SHE: I already said that.

HE: No stockings at all.

SHE: I was wearing sandals.

320 **HE:** Were you wearing a bra?

SHE: What?

HE: Were you wearing a bra?

SHE: Yes.

HE: What size?

325 **SHE:** Thirty-four.

HE: Thirty-four what?

SHE: Just thirty-four.

HE: What cup size are you?

SHE: Um, uh, B or C.

330 **HE:** You don't know?

SHE: It depends on the bra. What brand.

HE: What was the cup size of the bra you had on the day?

SHE: It didn't have a cup size. It was just a 34.

HE: Why didn't it have a cup size? Don't most bras have a cup size?

335 **SHE:** It wasn't sized that way. It didn't have an underwire.

HE: So it was an elastic sort of bra.

SHE: I don't know. Maybe.

A *slight pause.*

HE: How tall are you?

SHE: Five foot three.

HE: You are considered a petite woman, then.   340
SHE: I guess so.
HE: But thirty-four B or C is a fairly large bra size for a small woman.
SHE: It's average.
HE: Not for a petite woman. You wouldn't say your breasts were small.
SHE: My . . .   345
HE: Your breasts. They are not small breasts.
SHE: I don't know.
HE: You don't know you have large breasts?
SHE: They're average.
HE: Do you always wear a bra?   350
SHE: When?
HE: When you walk through the park, do you always wear a bra?
SHE: Yes.
HE: Why?
SHE: I feel more comfortable.   355
HE: Because you have large breasts.
SHE: (*No answer*).
HE: You would not say that you have small breasts.
SHE: No . . .
HE: You have a large bust. But you were wearing a tank top.   360
SHE: It was hot.
HE: You were wearing a tight T-shirt. How wide were the straps on your tank
    top?
SHE: I don't know.
HE: Wide enough to cover the bra straps?
SHE: Well, yes.   365
HE: You were carrying a purse.
SHE: Yes.
HE: What kind?
SHE: A small leather one.
HE: You were carrying it in your hand.   370
SHE: No.
HE: It had a strap.
SHE: Yes.
HE: How were you carrying your purse?
SHE: On my shoulder. The strap was on my shoulder.   375
HE: Could it cause your tank top strap to shift?
SHE: What?
HE: The strap on your tank top. Could your purse strap have caused it to shift?
SHE: I guess.
HE: Revealing your bra strap.   380
SHE: Maybe.
HE: So your bra straps could have been showing as you walked through the
    park.
SHE: I don't know.

Pause.

HE: What color was your underwear?

385　SHE: What does it matter?

HE: What color was your underwear?

SHE: (*overlapping*) Black.

HE: The bra or the panties?

SHE: Both.

390　HE: They matched?

SHE: Yes.

HE: Did they have lace?

SHE: Yes.

HE: You were wearing a black lacy bra and panties?

395　SHE: That's right.

HE: Why not white or beige?

SHE: To match the tank top and skirt.

HE: Why? Did you expect anyone to see your underwear that day?

SHE: What?

400　HE: (*doesn't answer*).

SHE: No.

HE: Did you have a date with a boyfriend later?

SHE: No.

HE: Then why did it have to match?

405　SHE: What?

HE: The underwear. The bra and panties.

SHE: In case it . . . in case the tank strap . . .

HE: So you expected the bra strap to be seen.

SHE: Not necessarily.

410　HE: But you thought it might.

SHE: I didn't really think about it. It's just what I put on that morning.

HE: Black lacy underwear is considered sexy.

SHE: I guess.

HE: It is sexier than white or beige.

415　SHE: I guess so.

HE: Black is considered a sexy color. So is red.

SHE: I don't know.

HE: Your skirt was black and red. Your top was black with a little red ribbon
flower on it. Your bra and panties were black.

SHE: That's right.

420　HE: So why were you wearing sexy underwear if no one was to see it?

SHE: I just like it.

HE: Why?

SHE: It makes me feel . . .

HE: Sexier.

425　SHE: Prettier.

HE: More sensual.

SHE: More feminine.

HE: You walked through the park wearing sexy underwear and revealing clothes and you smiled and nodded at a man you did not know.

SHE: No.

HE: No?   430

SHE: Not like that.

HE: You walked through the park.

SHE: Yes.

HE: You were wearing black lacy underwear.

SHE: Yes.   435

HE: You were wearing a tight tank top and a see-through skirt.

SHE: I . . .

HE: You nodded at a strange man.

SHE: Okay.

HE: You smiled at him.   440

SHE: Okay.

HE: Your bra strap had slipped, and you felt sexy.

SHE: No.

HE: It was a hot day.

SHE: Yes.   445

HE: Your legs were bare. Your thighs were warm.

SHE: No.

HE: The weather was warm.

SHE: Yes.

HE: You were walking quickly.   450

SHE: Yes.

HE: You worked up a sweat.

SHE: I don't know.

HE: It is likely you were perspiring.

SHE: I guess.   455

HE: Your clothes were clinging to you.

SHE: No.

HE: You were moist with sweat and the chiffon lining of your skirt was cling-ing to your legs as you walked. Your knit top was damp and clung closely to your body.

SHE: That's not right.

HE: It was a hot day. You were walking quickly. You were perspiring.   460

SHE: (*no answer*).

HE: Your clothes were warm and sticky. The shape of your body was revealed. Have your breasts been artificially enlarged?

SHE: No.

HE: Or reduced?

SHE: No.   465

HE: They have not been altered in any way.

SHE: No.

HE: So your breasts are not, shall we say, unnaturally firm.

SHE: I guess not.

470   HE: And your bra had no underwire.

       SHE: We've been through that.

       HE: So your breasts had little support.

       SHE: I was wearing a bra.

       HE: You were walking quickly.

475   SHE: Yes.

       HE: Your breasts were bouncing.

       SHE: I don't know.

       HE: Your strap might have slipped. Your breasts had no support.

       SHE: I was wearing a bra.

480   HE: You were swinging your arms.

       SHE: You said that.

       HE: You were either swinging your arms or your arms were folded holding up your breasts.

       SHE: I don't know.

       HE: Tank tops are low cut.

485   SHE: It wasn't really —

       HE: You folded your arms under your breasts to show your cleavage.

       SHE: No.

       HE: Might you have folded your arms?

       SHE: Not to —

490   HE: Is it possible you folded your arms?

       SHE: Maybe.

       HE: Or you were swinging your arms?

       SHE: No.

       HE: You were walking quickly.

495   SHE: Yes. To —

       HE: Then you were swinging your arms.

       SHE: I don't know.

       HE: You were swaying your hips.

       SHE: No.

500   HE: You were swinging your arms and your breasts were bouncing.

       SHE: No.

       HE: Your large breasts were bouncing and your strap was showing.

       SHE: No.

       HE: If you were walking at a fast pace your breasts would bounce and your hips away.

505   SHE: I didn't think about it.

       HE: That's right (*Pause.*) What size panties?

       SHE: What?

       HE: What size were your panties?

       SHE: Medium, I guess.

510   HE: You don't know?

       SHE: I don't remember.

       HE: What size panties do you usually buy?

       SHE: Medium or small. It depends.

HE: On what?

SHE: On what's on sale, the style, I don't know. 515

HE: What style?

SHE: I don't know what you mean.

HE: What style were those panties? Bikini panties?

SHE: That's right.

HE: Why? 520

SHE: Why what?

HE: Why were you wearing bikini panties?

SHE: They matched the bra.

HE: Wouldn't a looser fitting panty be more comfortable?

SHE: Not really. 525

HE: Bikini panties allow your thighs to touch each other.

SHE: Stop it.

HE: It was a very hot day. You walked quickly through the park wearing sexy clothes with your breasts bouncing and your thighs damp and you smiled and nodded at a stranger.

SHE: That's not it.

HE: You were walking through the park. 530

SHE: Yes.

HE: It was a hot day.

SHE: Yes.

HE: You smiled at a stranger. And he followed you.

SHE: I didn't know. 535

HE: What?

SHE: I didn't know that he had followed me.

HE: When did you notice that he followed you?

SHE: When he grabbed me.

HE: Not before? 540

SHE: He grabbed me from behind. I didn't see him.

HE: You didn't turn when you heard someone behind you?

SHE: There was loud music. I didn't hear anything.

HE: The music was so loud you didn't hear someone behind you?

SHE: There was a machine . . . 545

HE: A lawnmower?

SHE: Louder. An edger. There was loud music and loud noise. I didn't hear him.

HE: You went into the park.

SHE: To walk to work.

HE: You were wearing suggestive clothing. 550

SHE: No.

HE: You signaled to a man.

SHE: No.

HE: You enticed him.

SHE: No. 555

HE: You led him on.

SHE: No.

HE: You acknowledged him.

SHE: (*no answer*).

560 HE: You smiled at him.

SHE: Yes.

The lights are beginning to dim, leaving an ever-brightening single spot focused in the woman's eyes, like an interrogation room. Perhaps the man fades into the background during the rest of the play. Or maybe not.

HE: (*he verbally rapes her*) You left your glasses off. Your dyed hair was bobbing in the breeze. You had painted nails and wore rouge. Your body was scented. You were wearing a revealing outfit, you were feeling sexy in your dainty black lacy undies and your tight shirt and your sheer skirt, and you were shaking your breasts and rolling your hips at this man.

SHE: (*quite possibly a scream*) No!

A very long pause.

HE: Start at the beginning.

565 SHE: What?

HE: Start at the beginning.

SHE: I was walking through the park.

HE: And?

SHE: It was a nice day. (*Pause.*) It was a nice day.

(*Blackout.*)

◆ ◆ ◆

WARREN LEIGHT (1957–   ), a widely acclaimed writer and director, is a writer/producer for the television series *Law and Order: Criminal Intent.* His play *Side Man* (1998) was nominated for a Pulitzer Prize and won Broadway's 1999 Tony Award for Best Play. His other plays include *Glimmer, Glimmer and Shine* (2001); *No Foreigners Beyond This Point;* and *James and Annie.* His screen credits include *Dear God* (1996) and *The Night We Never Met* (1993).

Nine Ten (2001)

CHARACTERS
Leslie
John
Kearrie
Nick
Lyris

Jury Duty Grand Hall. Morning.

John, a slightly awkward bond trader, sits on a bench. Very neat, buttoned down. He reads a perfectly folded Wall Street Journal. *Lyris Touzet, a dancer, enters, almost spills her coffee on him.*

LYRIS: Is this Part B?

JOHN: What?

LYRIS: Part B, or not part B?

JOHN: Ah . . . that is the question.

LYRIS: Are you making fun of me?   5

JOHN: No no. Um, let me look at your . . . (*She hands him a slip of paper, he reads it.*) Where you are is where you're supposed to be.

She sits next to him. He needs a little more personal space than she does.

LYRIS: Why do they call us at eight thirty? It's like, nine already, and they haven't said anything.

JOHN: They build in a grace period.

LYRIS: They what?

JOHN: They say eight thirty so that most people get here by nine. And around   10
nine ten they start calling names.

LYRIS: You knew this, and you came at eight-thirty?

JOHN: Eight actually.

LYRIS: Eight A.M.? You must hate your wife.

JOHN: I don't see her much. We both have to be at work at six.

LYRIS: You punch in at six?   15

JOHN: Well, I don't . . . punch in exactly. But, the desk opens at six so . . . .

LYRIS: Your desk opens?

JOHN: Sorry. Trading desk. Bonds. Euros, mostly. From my desk, I'm up so high, on a clear day, you can see Europe.

At a bench opposite, Nick Theron *works the* Times *crossword puzzle as* Leslie Rudin *arrives, pissed off and hyper.*

LESLIE: Part B?   20

NICK: Must be.

LYRIS: Have they called any —

NICK: Does it look like it? (*She looks to the court officer's desk, downstage left.*) Every once in a while this guy comes out and says we should wait. Which is . . . helpful.

LESLIE: I tried to get out of it on the phone and they said it was my third postponement and I had to come down here in person on the day of and that I wasn't going to get out anyway. And I finally get here — do they just change the names of the subway lines for spite lately?— and there's a line a mile long to get through security and they go through my purse like I'm a serial killer and it turns out if I want to smoke I'm going to have to go down and outside, and then wait on line again for them to check my bag. This just sucks.

NICK: I'm going to tell the judge that I'm a felon. He won't even question it.   25
And he'll tell me felons can't serve. I'll act offended at this. And then he'll just let me go back to my life.

LESLIE: (*impressed*) That's good.

NICK: Racial profiling. A two-way street.

Over to John *and* Lyris.

LYRIS: My brother's in the same building. Security guard. You probably don't know him.

Kearrie, *a tough businesswoman, enters, rushed.*

KEARRIE: Part B?

30 **LYRIS AND JOHN:** Or not part B?

KEARRIE: It's too early for cute. (*They look at her, she means it.*) Have they started to give out postponements yet?

LYRIS: No one gets postponement.

KEARRIE: I'm on a flight tomorrow. (*Pulls something out of her bag.*) I've got a ticket.

John *takes another look at her.*

JOHN: Kearrie?

35 **KEARRIE:** What?

JOHN: It's me, John. . . .

KEARRIE: Right. John. That narrows it down.

JOHN: John McCormack. From Wharton.

Kearrie *still doesn't place him.*

LYRIS: (*to John*) You sure leave an impression.

40 **JOHN:** Story of my life. (*To Kearrie.*) Case study. Euro-economic unity.

KEARRIE: You got an A, I got a B plus. Even though we worked together.

JOHN: (*to Lyris*) You know about Irish Alzheimer's . . . you forget everything except your grudges.

KEARRIE: You went to Gold and Strauss when we graduated, right?

JOHN: Still there.

45 **KEARRIE:** (*grades him a loser*) You're kidding. You are not still at—

JOHN: Just the last ten years. Kearrie this is—

LYRIS: Lyris Touzet. Spiritual dancer. And healer.

JOHN: Lyris this is Kearrie Whitman. We went to Wharton together. Class of 91.

LYRIS: I must have missed you two by like . . . one year.

Leslie *and* Nick. *He has no hope of attending to his crossword puzzle.* Leslie *must talk or die.*

50 **LESLIE:** I'm out in the Hamptons. One week after Labor Day. Paradise found. The assholes are gone. The beaches are empty. The water is warm.

NICK: Sharks are hungry.

LESLIE: No sharks in the Hamptons. Professional courtesy.

NICK: Touché.

LESLIE: I think I'll stay another day. Then I remember . . . fuck me —eight thirty summons. Drive in at midnight. Get stuck in traffic. The L.I.E. has got to be the only road in the world that has traffic jams at two A.M. By the time I get to my garage it's locked for the night. You ever try to find a space on the right side of the street at two A.M.?

Back to John *and* Lyris *chatting.* Kearrie *plays with her Palm Pilot.*

JOHN: It's funny, I always wanted to be a spiritual dancer. 55
LYRIS: You're making fun of me.
JOHN: I'm not. . . . swear to god. But what is a—
LYRIS: I heal people, through movement. Rhythm. Every person has their own . . . pulse. Below the surface, that—
KEARRIE: Fuck me!
LYRIS: I help them to get in touch with their inner— 60
KEARRIE: (*Turns to them.*) Fuck me fuck me fuck . . .
JOHN: What's hers?

Kearrie *now rants in their direction, about her Palm Pilot.*

KEARRIE: Money on the table. I've got a watch list. It's programmed to signal me when there's a discrepancy between euro prices and ADRs. The spread is sitting there. Sitting there. It's blinking—buy me. Buy me. I try to buy and my damn signal fades. What's the point of fucking having a watch list if you can't follow up on it. This whole building should be wired. This city is . . . in the stone ages.
LYRIS: (*to* John) Some people are harder cases than others.

Over to Nick *and* Leslie.

NICK: My neighborhood, downtown, they're *always* filming. Some sequel to a 65 sequel to a disaster flick. *Mortal Danger Times Four.* Whatever. Which means like—
LESLIE: They take every parking place. Big lights up—
NICK: — all night long.
LESLIE: Idiots in walkie-talkies saying don't walk there. On your own street. Call the cops to complain, they don't care. No one in this city cares. The film crew can be, like, setting off concussion bombs, and nobody does anything.

Back to John *and* Lyris.

JOHN: (*to* Lyris) I can't.
LYRIS: Everybody can move. Even you . . . Stand up. 70

He doesn't.

LYRIS: (*loud*) STAND UP!

Nick *and* Leslie *hear this. Look over to* John *and* Lyris. John *doesn't want to attract attention, so he stands.* John *and* Lyris *now overlap with* Nick *and* Leslie. Kearrie *is in her own world.*)

LYRIS: (*to* John) Just start to, sway a little . . . from your hips.
LESLIE: (*to* Nick) That is sick the way he's flirting with her.

John *sits back down.*

JOHN: I can't.

75 **LYRIS:** Yes you can.

NICK: (*to* Leslie) How do you know it's his fault?

LESLIE: (*to* Nick) It's always the guy's fault. I date cops. Believe me. I know.

JOHN: (*to* Lyris) I don't like to. Move. I like things as they are. I've had the same job for ten years.

KEARRIE: (*on her cell phone, to her office*) Here? It's a fucking hellhole. What do you think? Ah-huh. Ah-huh. Ah-huh. Look — keep that on hold.

80 **JOHN:** (*to* Lyris, *oblivious to* Kearrie) Same office, same view. Married my junior high school sweetheart. We take the same train to work. We have the same lunch. Tuna. On rye. No mayo.

LYRIS: No mayo?

JOHN: It's not so bad, once you get used to it.

KEARRIE: (*into phone*) Yeah as soon as they call roll, I show my plane ticket . . . and I'm out of here.

Now, from downstage left, a court officer enters.

COURT OFFICER: Hello folks. Welcome to New York County Jury Duty. Before you all come up to me . . .

85 **KEARRIE:** Excuse me, I have a flight to —

NICK: I have a record —

COURT OFFICER: (He *drowns her out.*) — with your reasons for why you shouldn't be here, let me tell you: I've heard them all. On the bright side, most of you will get to go back to your life in two or three days.

LESLIE, NICK, KEARRIE, JOHN, *and* LYRIS *all groan. Two days is eternity.*

COURT OFFICER: And we are as happy to have you, as you are happy to be here. First things first. Check your summons, and be sure you're in the right place. This is Civil Court. Part B. 60 Centre Street. Today is Monday, September 10th . . . Two thousand and one.

Blackout.

❖ ❖ ❖

Reading and Reacting

1. Do you think any of the characters in the five plays in this chapter are fully developed individuals, or do you see most (or all) of them as stereotypes? Given the limits of its form, can a ten-minute play ever really develop a character?

2. With the exception of *Nine Ten*, all the plays in this chapter have only two characters. Should any additional parts have been written for the four two-character plays? Are all the characters in *Nine Ten* necessary?

3. The play *Tape* was written for two actors of either gender. Could the roles in the other plays in this chapter also be portrayed by actors of either gender? By actors of any age? Of any race?

4. Identify the central conflict in each play. What do you see as the **climax**, or highest point of tension, in each? Where does the climax generally occur in these plays?

5. Each play in this chapter has a single setting, and each of these settings is described very minimally. Do any settings seem to require more detailed descriptions? If you were going to expand each play, would you show any additional settings?

6. Considering the subject matter of each of the five plays in this chapter, what kinds of topics seem to be most appropriate for ten-minute plays? Why do you think this is so? What kinds of topics, if any, would *not* be suitable for ten-minute plays?

WRITING SUGGESTIONS

1. Assume you are a director writing notes for an actor who is to play a role in one of this chapter's plays. Write a character sketch in which you outline the character's background and explain his or her emotions, actions, conflicts, and motivation.

2. Choose a scene from one of the longer plays in this text that has a definite beginning, middle, and end. Rewrite this scene as a self-contained ten-minute play. (If you like, you can update the scene to the present time, change the characters' names or genders, and make other changes you see as necessary.)

3. Write an original ten-minute play for two characters.

CHAPTER 38

READING AND WRITING ABOUT DRAMA

Reading Drama

When you read a play, you will notice features it shares with works of fiction — for instance, the use of language and symbols, the interaction among characters, and the development of a theme or themes. In addition, you will notice features that distinguish it from fiction — for example, the presence of stage directions and the division of the play into acts and scenes.

The following guidelines, designed to help you explore works of dramatic literature, focus on issues that are examined in depth in chapters to come:

- *Trace the play's **plot**.* What conflicts are present? Where does the rising action reach a climax? Where does the falling action begin? What techniques move the action along? (See Chapter 39.)
- *Analyze the play's **characters**.* Who are the central characters? What are their most distinctive traits? How do you learn about their personalities, backgrounds, appearances, and strengths and weaknesses? (See Chapter 40.)
- *Consider how the characters interact with one another.* Do the characters change and grow in response to the play's events, or do they remain essentially unchanged? (See Chapter 40.)
- *Examine the play's **language**.* How does **dialogue** reveal characters' emotions, conflicts, opinions, and motivation? (See Chapter 40.)
- *Look for **soliloquies** or **asides**.* What do they contribute to your knowledge of the play's characters and events? (See Chapter 40.)
- *Read the play's **stage directions**.* What do you learn from the descriptions of the characters, including their dress, gestures, and facial expressions? (See Chapter 40.) What information do you gain from studying the playwright's descriptions of the play's setting? Do the stage directions include information about lighting, props, music, or sound effects? (See Chapter 41.)
- *Consider the play's **staging**.* Where and when does the action take place? What techniques are used to convey a sense of time and place to the audience? (See Chapter 41.)

- *Try to identify the play's **themes**.* What main idea does the play communicate? What additional themes are explored? (See Chapter 42.)
- *Identify any symbols in the play.* How do these symbols help you to understand the play's themes? (See Chapter 42.)

Active Reading

As you read a play about which you plan to write, you follow the same process that guides you when you read any work of literature. You read actively, marking the text as you proceed. Then, you go on to select a topic and develop ideas about it, decide on a thesis, prepare an outline, and write and revise several drafts.

Kimberly Allison, a student in an Introduction to Literature course, was given the following assignment.

> Without consulting any outside sources, write a three- to five-page essay about any play in our literature anthology. You may focus on action, character, staging, or theme, or you may consider more than one of these elements.

Previewing

Kim decided to write her paper on Susan Glaspell's play *Trifles*, which begins on page 1372. She began by previewing *Trifles*, noting its brief length, its one-act structure, its list of characters, and its setting in John Wright's farmhouse. Kim noticed immediately that John Wright does not appear in the play, and his absence aroused her curiosity.

Highlighting and Annotating

As Kim read *Trifles*, she highlighted the dialogue and stage directions she thought she might later want to examine more closely, noted possible links among ideas, identified patterns of action and language, and jotted down her own observations and questions. She found herself especially interested in the female and male characters' different reactions to the objects discovered in the house and in the interaction between women and men.

The following highlighted and annotated passage illustrates some of her responses to the play.

The men laugh; the women looked abashed.

> *Why do the men and women react so differently?*

COUNTY ATTORNEY: (*rubbing his hands over the stove*) Frank's fire didn't do much up there, did it? Well, let's go out to the barn and get that cleared up.

The men go outside.

MRS. HALE: (*resentfully*) I don't know as there's anything

so strange, our takin' up our time with little things

while we're waiting for them to get the evidence

(*She sits down at the big table smoothing out a block with*

decision.) I don't see as it's anything to laugh about.

MRS. PETERS: (*apologetically*) Of course they've got

awful important things on their minds.

Pulls up a chair and joins Mrs. Hale at the table.

[Handwritten annotations: "Why do the men go and the women stay?"; "little things"; "Like what? Why does she make excuses for the men?"]

Kim's highlighting and annotations — most of which, like those above, focused on the play's characters — suggested some interesting possibilities for her essay.

Writing about Drama

Planning an Essay

Even after Kim decided to write about the play's characters, she knew she had to narrow her focus. Her notes suggested that gender roles in general, and the role of the women in particular, would make an interesting topic, so she decided to explore this idea further.

Choosing a Topic

To help her decide on a direction for her paper, Kim wrote the following entry in her journal.

What is the role of the women in this play? Although the two women have gone with their husbands to pick up some items for Mrs. Wright, they seem to be primarily interested in why Mrs. Wright would leave her house in such disarray. They find several objects that suggest that Mrs. Wright was lonely and that she was dominated by her husband. But these women are left on their own and seem to band together. Their guilt about not visiting Mrs. Wright also seems to connect them with the murder suspect. The women find the details, or "trifles," of Mrs. Wright's life interesting and learn from them the facts surrounding the murder; the men wander aimlessly around the house and yard. The real clue to the

murder appears to be Mrs. Wright's messy house, but the men
do not seem to understand the implications of the disorder.
The women have an understanding that comes from their own
experiences as women, which the men are unable to tap into.

At this point, Kim concluded that the role of the women in *Trifles* would be the
best focus for her paper. As she went on to gather ideas to write about, she also
planned to examine the ways in which the women interacted with the men.

Finding Something to Say: Brainstorming

Kim's next step was to develop the specific ideas to discuss in her paper. She reread
the play and her annotations, keeping her topic (the role of women) in mind as
she brainstormed.

Sheriff Peters says there is nothing in the kitchen but
"kitchen stuff"; he thinks Mrs. Wright is a typical woman,
worried about her preserves while imprisoned for murder.

Mrs. Hale feels animosity toward the men for laughing
about the women's interest in the quilt; she regrets not
visiting Mrs. Wright; she feels sorry for Mrs. Wright
because she had no children.

Mr. Henderson eventually sides with the other two men,
claiming that women's worries are trifles.

Mr. Hale mentions Mr. Wright's stinginess; he seems to
know Mr. Wright best.

Men think women are shallow and worry only about
trifles.

Women empathize with Mrs. Wright because they understand
how she was treated.

Mrs. Peters (wife of Sheriff) empathizes with
Mrs. Wright's loss of bird; notes that keeping house was
Mrs. Wright's duty.

Mrs. Wright seems trapped in the house; loses control
after her bird is killed.

John Wright strips wife of her identity; controls her
every move; stops her from singing, which she enjoys; kills
canary.

When she reread her notes, the first thing Kim noticed was that the women and
men have two entirely different attitudes about women's lives and concerns: the
men think their own work is much more important than that of the women,
which they see as trivial; the women realize they are not much different from
Mrs. Wright. Now Kim saw that in order to discuss the role of women in the play,
she first had to define that role in relation to the role of the men.

Seeing Connections: Listing

At this point, Kim decided that listing ideas under the heads *Men* and *Women* could help her clarify the differences between men's and women's roles.

Men	Women
Work outside the home	Make preserves
Make decisions about financial expenditures	Clean house
	Make quilts
Think women should do just housework	Raise children
	Go to ladies' clubs for socializing
Create and enforce law	Follow laws that men create
Dictate wives' actions	Subordinate their desires, to their husbands
Have separate identities and power	Act defiantly to break boundaries set by social role
Act in ways that are accepted by society	

Listing enabled Kim to confirm her idea that the men's and the women's roles are defined very differently in *Trifles*. In fact, both men and women seem to agree that they have different responsibilities, and both seem to understand and accept the fact that power is unevenly distributed.

Deciding on a Thesis

Kim's listing clarified her understanding of the limited role women have in the society portrayed in *Trifles*. This, in turn, enabled her to develop the following **thesis statement**.

```
The central focus of Trifles is not on finding out who killed
Mr. Wright, but on defining the limited, even subservient,
role of women like Mrs. Wright.
```

Preparing an Outline

Guided by her thesis statement and the information she had collected in her notes, Kim made a scratch outline, arranging her supporting details in a logical order under appropriate headings:

<u>Mrs. Hale and Mrs. Peters had limited roles</u>
   —Subservient to husbands
   —Restricted to performing domestic chores
   —Confined to kitchen
   —Identified with Minnie Wright's loneliness
<u>Minnie Wright had limited role</u>
   —Did what husband told her to do
   —Had no link with outside world
   —Couldn't sing
   —Had no friends
   —Had no identity

Drafting an Essay

Following her tentative thesis and her scratch outline, Kim wrote the following first draft of her essay. Before she began, she reviewed her notes and her highlighting of the play to look for details that would illustrate and support her generalizations about it.

first draft

The Women's Role in Trifles

Susan Glaspell's Trifles seems to focus on the murder of John Wright. Mr. Wright had little concern for his wife's opinions. Mr. Hale suggested that Minnie Wright was powerless against her husband, and Sheriff Henry Peters questioned whether Minnie was allowed to quilt her log cabin pattern. Perhaps, because Mr. Wright did not spend his money freely, he would have made Minnie knot the quilt because it cost less. Minnie was controlled by her husband. He forced her to perform repetitive domestic chores. The central focus of Trifles is not on finding out who killed Mr. Wright but on defining the limited, even subservient role of women like Mrs. Wright.

Mrs. Peters and Mrs. Hale were similar to Minnie. Mrs. Peters and Mrs. Hale also performed domestic chores and had to do what their husbands wanted them to do, and they too were confined to Mrs. Wright's kitchen. The kitchen was the focal point of the play. Mrs. Peters and Mrs. Hale remained confined to the kitchen while their husbands exercised their freedom to enter and exit the house at will. This mirrored Minnie's life because she stayed home while her husband went to work and into town. The two women discussed Minnie's isolation. Beginning to identify with Minnie's loneliness, Mrs. Peters and Mrs. Hale recognized that while they were busy in their own homes, they had, in fact, participated in isolating and confining Minnie.

Eventually, the women found that the kitchen held the clues to Mrs. Wright's loneliness and to the details of the murder. The two women discovered that Minnie's only connection to the outside world was her bird. Minnie too was a caged bird because she was kept from singing and communicating with others by her husband. And piecing together the evidence, the women came to believe that John Wright had broken the bird's neck.

At the same time, Mrs. Peters and Mrs. Hale discovered the connection between the dead canary and Minnie's situation, and they began to recognize that they had to band together in order to exert their strength against the men. They realized that Minnie's independence and identity were crushed by her husband and that their own husbands believed women's lives were trivial and unimportant. The revelation that Mrs. Peters and Mrs. Hale experienced encouraged them to commit an act as rebellious as the one that got Minnie in trouble: they concealed their discovery from their husbands and from the law.

Because Mrs. Hale and Mrs. Peters empathized with Minnie's situation, they suppressed the evidence they found and endured the men's insults. And in this way, the women attempted to break through the boundaries of their social roles, just as Minnie had done before them.

First Draft: Commentary

When Kim reread her first draft, she realized that she had gone beyond the scope of her tentative thesis statement and scratch outline. She had considered not just the women's subservient role but also the actions they take to break free of this role. She decided to revise her thesis statement to reflect this new emphasis — and then to expand her paper to develop this aspect of her thesis more fully.

Kim's peer review group made the general suggestion that she develop her paper further. In addition, they thought that her paper's sentences seemed choppy — many needed to be linked with transitional words and phrases — and that her introduction was unfocused.

When Kim met with her instructor to discuss her revision plans, he encouraged her to expand her paper's focus and to use quotations and specific examples to support her ideas. He also reminded her to use the present tense in her paper — not "Mrs. Peters and Mrs. Hale *were* similar to Minnie" but "Mrs. Peters and Mrs. Hale *are* similar to Minnie." (Only events that occurred *before* the time in which the play takes place — for example, the murder itself or Minnie's girlhood experiences — should be described in past tense.)

After meeting with her instructor, Kim made a new scratch outline to guide her as she continued to revise.

<u>Subservient role of women</u>
  —Minnie's husband didn't respect her opinion
  —Her husband didn't let her sing
  —Minnie could perform only domestic chores
<u>Confinement of women in home</u>
  —Mrs. Hale and Mrs. Peters are confined to kitchen
  —Minnie was lonely at home because she had no children
  —Minnie didn't belong to Ladies Aid
  —Minnie was a caged bird
<u>Women's defiance</u>
  —Mrs. Hale and Mrs. Peters solve "mystery"
  —They realize they must band together
  —They take action
  —They defy men's law

Revising and Editing an Essay

Before she wrote her next draft, Kim reviewed the suggestions she had recorded in meetings with classmates and with her instructor. Then, she incorporated this material, along with her own new ideas, into her second draft, which follows.

second draft

Confinement and Rebellion in <u>Trifles</u>

Susan Glaspell's play <u>Trifles</u> involves the solving of a murder. Two women, Mrs. Peters and Mrs. Hale, discover that Mrs. Wright, who remains in jail throughout the play, has indeed murdered her husband. Interestingly, the women make this discovery through the examination of evidence in Mrs. Wright's kitchen, which their husbands, Sheriff Henry Peters and farmer Lewis Hale, along with the county attorney, Mr. Henderson, dismiss as women's "trifles." The focus of <u>Trifles</u>, however, is not on the murder of John Wright but on the subservient role of women, the confinement of the wife in the home, and the desperate measures women must take to achieve autonomy.

The role of Minnie Wright becomes evident in the first few minutes of the play, when Mr. Hale declares, "I didn't know as what his wife wanted made much difference to John—" (1373). Minnie's powerlessness is further revealed when the women discuss how Mr. Wright forced her to give up the thing she loved—singing. Both of these observations suggest that Minnie's every action was controlled and stifled by her husband. She was not allowed to make decisions or be an individual; instead, she was expected only to perform domestic chores.

Doing domestic chores was the only part of life that Minnie was allowed to exert some power over, a condition that is shared by Mrs. Peters and Mrs. Hale, whom we assume work only in the home and whose behavior as wives is determined by their husbands.

The men are free to walk throughout the house and outside of it while the women are, not surprisingly, confined to the kitchen, just as Mrs. Wright had been confined to the house. Early in the play, Mrs. Hale refers to Minnie's isolation, saying she "kept so much to herself. She didn't even belong to the Ladies Aid" (1377). Mrs. Hale goes on to mention Mrs. Wright's lack of nice clothing, which further suggests her confinement in the home: if she never left her home, she wouldn't need to look nice, and why would she want to leave home if she had no nice clothes? Minnie's isolation is further revealed when Mrs. Hale mentions her lack of children: "Not having children makes less work—but it makes a quiet house, and Wright out to work all day, and no company when he did come in" (1380). Minnie's only connection to the outside world was her bird, which becomes the symbol of her confinement because she herself was a caged bird. In a sense, Mr. Wright strangled her, as he did the bird, by preventing her from talking to other people in the community. Unlike the men, Mrs. Peters and Mrs. Hale realize the connection between the dead canary and Minnie's situation as "<u>Their eyes meet</u>" and they share "<u>A look of growing comprehension, of horror</u>" (1380).

The comprehension that Mrs. Peters and Mrs. Hale experience urges them to rebel by concealing their discovery from their husbands and from the law. Mrs. Peters does concede that "the law is the law"

(1378), but she also seems to believe that because Mr. Wright treated his wife badly, treating her as a domestic slave and isolating her from the world, Minnie was justified in killing him. And Mrs. Peters knows that even if Minnie had been able to communicate the abuse she suffered, the law would not take the abuse into account because the men on the jury would not be sympathetic to a woman's complaints about how her husband treated her.

The dialogue in <u>Trifles</u> reveals a huge difference in how women and men view their experiences. From the opening of the play, the gulf between the men and women emerges, and as the play progresses, the polarization of the male and female characters becomes clearer. Once the men leave the kitchen to find what they consider to be significant criminal evidence, the men and women are divided physically as well as emotionally. The men create their own community, as do the women. With the women alone in the kitchen, the focus of the dialogue is on the female experience. The women discuss the preserves, the quilt, and the disarray in the kitchen, emphasizing that Mrs. Wright would not have left her home in disorder unless she had been distracted by some more pressing situation.

Minnie Wright seems to have accepted her servitude voluntarily, making work in the home her main interest. But the men trivialize Mrs. Wright's and other women's significance when they criticize her role as a homemaker. The county attorney condemns her, sarcastically observing, "I shouldn't say she had the homemaking instinct" (1376). Minnie attempted to

keep her home clean and do her chores, but the cold
exploded her preserves, and her husband dirtied the
towels. What caused Minnie to neglect her chores is
something of great importance: her longing for
independence and freedom from the servitude she once
accepted voluntarily.

What makes this play most interesting is that
Mrs. Hale and Mrs. Peters come to realize that they
too have volunteered to be subservient to their
husbands. They understand that their husbands will
trivialize their discovery about the murder, as the
men earlier trivialized their discussions of Minnie's
daily tasks. Therefore, the women band together and
conceal the information, breaking through their
subservient roles as wives. And, in the end, they find
their own independence and significance in society.

Second Draft: Commentary

When she read her second draft, Kim had mixed feelings about it. She thought it was an improvement over her first draft, primarily because she had expanded the focus of her discussion and added specific details and quotations to support her points. She also believed her essay was now clearer, with a more specific thesis statement and smoother transitions.

Still, Kim thought that the logic of her discussion was somewhat difficult to follow, and she thought clearer topic sentences might correct this problem by guiding readers more smoothly through her essay. She also thought her organization, which did not follow her revised scratch outline, was somewhat confusing. (For example, she discussed the women's subservient role in two different parts of her essay — paragraphs 2 and 7.) In addition, Kim thought her third paragraph could be developed further, and she still believed her essay needed additional supporting details and quotations throughout. After rereading her notes, she wrote her final draft, which appears on the following pages.

Allison 1

Kimberly Allison

English 1013

Professor Johnson

3 Mar. 2006

Desperate Measures: Acts of Defiance in <u>Trifles</u>

Susan Glaspell wrote her best-known play,
<u>Trifles</u>, in 1916, at a time when married women were
beginning to challenge their socially defined roles,
realizing that their identities as wives kept them in
a subordinate position in society. Because women were
demanding more autonomy, traditional institutions
such as marriage, which confined women to the home
and made them mere extensions of their husbands, were
beginning to be reexamined.

Evidently touched by these concerns, Glaspell
chose as her play's protagonist a married woman,
Minnie Wright, who challenged society's expectations
in a very extreme way: by murdering her husband.
Minnie's defiant act has occurred before the action
begins; during the play, two women, Mrs. Peters and
Mrs. Hale, who accompany their husbands on an
investigation of the murder scene, piece together the
details of the situation surrounding the murder. As
the events unfold, however, it becomes clear that the
focus of <u>Trifles</u> is not on who killed John Wright but
on the themes of the subordinate role of women, the
confinement of the wife in the home, and the
experiences all women share. With these themes,
Glaspell shows her audience the desperate measures
women had to take to achieve autonomy.

[margin annotations:]

Opening sentence identifies author and work.

Introduction places play in historical context.

Thesis statement

Allison 2

The subordinate role of women, particularly
Minnie's role in her marriage, becomes evident in the
first few minutes of the play, when Mr. Hale observes
that the victim, John Wright, had little concern for
his wife's opinions: "I didn't know as what his wife
wanted made much difference to John——" (1373). Here
Mr. Hale suggests that Mrs. Wright was powerless
against the wishes of her husband. Indeed, as these
characters imply, Mrs. Wright's every act and thought
were controlled by her husband, who tried to break
her spirit by forcing her to stay alone in the house,
performing repetitive domestic chores. Mrs. Wright's
only source of power in the household was her kitchen
work, a situation that Mrs. Peters and Mrs. Hale
understand because their own behavior is also
determined by their husbands. Therefore, when Sheriff
Peters makes fun of Minnie's concern about her
preserves, saying, "Well, can you beat the women!
Held for murder and worryin' about her preserves"
(1375), he is, in a sense, criticizing all three of
the women for worrying about domestic matters rather
than about the murder that has been committed.
Indeed, the sheriff's comment suggests that he
assumes women's lives are trivial, an attitude that
influences the thoughts and speech of all three men.

Mrs. Peters and Mrs. Hale are similar to Minnie
Wright in another way as well: throughout the play,
they are confined to the kitchen of the Wrights'
house. As a result, the kitchen becomes the focal
point of the play—and, ironically, the women find

> Topic sentence identifies first point, paper will discuss: women's subordinate role.

> Topic sentence introduces second point paper will discuss: women's confinement in the home.

Allison 3

that the kitchen holds the clues to Mrs. Wright's
loneliness and to the details of the murder. Mrs.
Peters and Mrs. Hale remain confined to the kitchen
while their husbands enter and exit the house at
will. This situation mirrors Minnie Wright's daily
life, as she remained in the home while her husband
went to work and into town. As they move about the
kitchen, the two women discuss Minnie Wright's
isolation: "Not having children makes less work—but
it makes a quiet house, and Wright out to work all
day, and no company when he did come in" (1380).
Beginning to identify with Mrs. Wright's loneliness,
Mrs. Peters and Mrs. Hale recognize that, busy in
their own homes, they have participated in isolating
and confining Minnie Wright. Mrs. Hale declares, "Oh,
I <u>wish</u> I'd come over here once in a while! That was a
crime! That was a crime! Who's going to punish that?
. . . I might have known she needed help" (1382)!

Transitional
paragraph
discusses
women's
observations
and conclusions.

Soon the two women discover that Mrs. Wright's
only connection to the outside world was her bird,
the symbol of her confinement; she herself was a caged
bird who was kept from singing and communicating with
others because of her husband. And piecing together
the evidence—the disorderly kitchen, the misstitched
quilt pieces, and the dead canary—the women come to
believe that John Wright broke the bird's neck, just
as he had broken his wife's spirit. At this point,
Mrs. Peters and Mrs. Hale understand the connection
between the dead canary and Minnie Wright's
motivation. The stage directions describe the moment
when the women become aware of the truth behind the

Allison 4

murder: "<u>Their eyes meet</u>," and the women share "<u>A look of growing comprehension, of horror</u>" (1380).

Through their observations and discussions in Mrs. Wright's kitchen, Mrs. Hale and Mrs. Peters come to understand the commonality of women's experiences. Mrs. Hale speaks for both of them when she says, "I know how things can be—for women. . . . We all go through the same things—it's all just a different kind of the same thing" (1382). And once the two women realize the experiences they share, they begin to recognize that they must join together in order to challenge their male-oriented society; although their experiences may seem trivial to the men, the "trifles" of their lives are significant to them. They realize that Minnie's independence and identity were crushed by her husband and that their own husbands also believe that women's lives are trivial and unimportant. This realization leads them to commit an act as defiant as the one that got Minnie into trouble: they conceal their discovery from their husbands and from the law.

Significantly, Mrs. Peters does acknowledge that "the law is the law" (1378), yet she still seems to believe that because Mr. Wright treated his wife badly, she is justified in killing him. They also realize, however, that for men the law is black and white and that an all-male jury will not take into account the extenuating circumstances that prompted Minnie Wright to kill her husband. And even if Mrs. Wright were allowed to communicate to the all-male court the psychological abuse she has suffered, the

> Topic sentence introduces third point paper will discuss: experiences women share.

Allison 5

law would undoubtedly view her experience as trivial because a woman who complained about how her husband treated her would be seen as ungrateful.

Nevertheless, because Mrs. Hale and Mrs. Peters empathize with Mrs. Wright's situation, they suppress the evidence they find, enduring their husbands' condescension rather than standing up to them. And through this desperate action, the women break through the boundaries of their social role, just as Minnie Wright has done. Although Mrs. Wright is imprisoned for her crime, she has freed herself; and although Mrs. Peters and Mrs. Hale conceal their knowledge, fearing the men will laugh at them, these women are really challenging society and, in this way, freeing themselves as well.

In <u>Trifles</u>, Susan Glaspell addresses many of the problems shared by early-twentieth-century women, including their subordinate status and their confinement in the home. In order to emphasize the pervasiveness of these problems and the desperate measures women had to take to break out of restrictive social roles, Glaspell does more than focus on the plight of a woman who has ended her isolation and loneliness by committing a heinous crime against society. By presenting characters who demonstrate the vast differences between male and female experience, she illustrates how men define the roles of women and how women must challenge these roles in search of their own significance in society and their eventual independence.

Conclusion places play in historical context.

Final Draft: Commentary

Kim made many changes in her final draft. Although her focus is much the same as it was in her previous draft, she expanded her paper considerably. Most important, she added a discussion of the commonality of women's experience in paragraph 6 and elsewhere, and this material helps to explain what motivates Mrs. Hale and Mrs. Peters to conceal evidence from their husbands.

As she expanded her essay, Kim added explanations, details, and quotations, taking care to provide accurate page numbers in parentheses after each quotation. (Because students were required to use a play from this anthology, and no outside sources, Kim's instructor did not require a works-cited page.) She also worked hard to make her topic sentences clearer, and she used information from her class notes to help her write a new introduction and conclusion that discussed the status of women at the time in which *Trifles* was written. Finally, she added a new title and revised her thesis statement to emphasize the focus of her essay on the "desperate measures" all three women are driven to in response to their social situation.

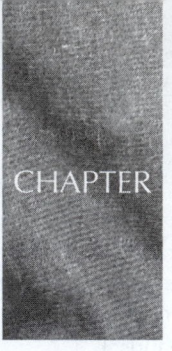
PLOT

> Great character creation is a fine thing in a drama, but the sum of all its characters is the story that they enact. Aristotle puts the plot at the head of the dramatic elements; of all these he thinks plot the most difficult and the most expressive. And he is right.
>
> —Stark Young, *The Theatre*

Plot denotes the way events are arranged in a work of literature. Although the conventions of drama require that the plot of a play be presented somewhat differently from the plot of a short story, the same components of plot are present in both. Plot in a dramatic work, like plot in a short story, consists of conflicts that are revealed, intensified, and resolved through the characters' actions. (See Chapter 12 for a discussion of conflict.)

Plot Structure

In 1863, the German critic Gustav Freytag devised a pyramid to represent a prototype for the plot of a dramatic work. According to Freytag, a play typically begins with **exposition**, which presents characters and setting and introduces the basic situation in which the characters are involved. Then, during the **rising action**, complications develop, conflicts emerge, suspense builds, and crises occur. The rising action culminates in a **climax**, a point at which the plot's tension peaks. Finally, during the **falling action**, the intensity subsides, eventually winding down to a **resolution**, or **denouement**, in which all loose ends are tied up.

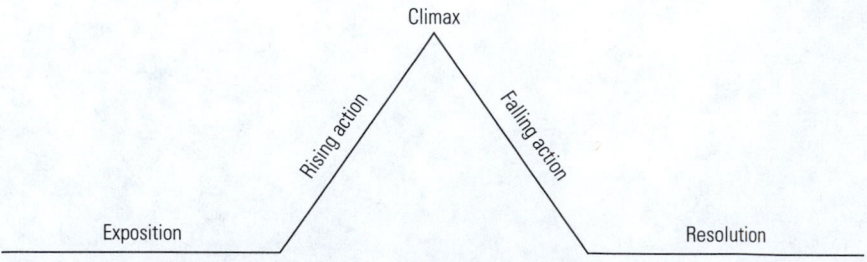

The familiar plot of a detective story follows Freytag's concept of plot: the exposition section includes the introduction of the detective and the explanation of the crime; the rising action develops as the investigation of the crime proceeds, with suspense increasing as the solution approaches; the high point of the action, the climax, comes with the revelation of the crime's solution; and the falling action presents the detective's explanation of the solution. The story concludes with a resolution that typically includes the capture of the criminal and the restoration of order.

The action of Susan Glaspell's one-act play *Trifles* (p. 1372), which in many ways resembles a detective story, can be diagrammed as follows:

Women find canary; motive for crime revealed

Mrs. Hale and Mrs. Peters investigate

Mrs. Hale and Mrs. Peters reconstruct events

Characters and setting introduced; crime identified; background provided by Mr. Hale

Women conceal evidence; characters leave Wright house

Of course, the plot of a complex dramatic work rarely conforms to the neat pattern represented by Freytag's pyramid. For example, a play can lack exposition entirely: because long stretches of exposition can be dull, a playwright may decide to arouse audience interest by moving directly into conflict, as Sophocles does in *Oedipus the King* (p. 1786) and as Milcha Sanchez-Scott does in *The Cuban Swimmer* (p. 1772). Similarly, because audiences tend to lose interest after the play's climax is reached, a playwright may choose to dispense with extended falling action. Thus, after Hamlet's death, the play ends quite abruptly, with no real resolution.

Plot and Subplot

While the main plot is developing, a parallel plot, called a **subplot**, may be developing alongside it. This structural device is common in the works of Shakespeare and in many other plays as well. The subplot's function may not immediately be clear, so at first it may seem to draw attention away from the main plot. Ultimately, however, the subplot reinforces elements of the primary plot. In Henrik Ibsen's *A Doll House* (p. 1454), for example, the threat of Dr. Rank's impending death parallels the threat of Nora's approaching exposure; for both of them, time is running out.

In Shakespeare's *King Lear*, a more elaborate subplot involves the earl of Gloucester, who, like Lear, misjudges his children, favoring a deceitful son who does not deserve his support and overlooking a more deserving one. Both families suffer greatly as a result of the fathers' misplaced loyalties. Thus, the parallel plot places additional emphasis on Lear's poor judgment and magnifies the consequences of his misguided acts: both fathers, and all but one of the five children, are dead by the play's end. A subplot can also set up a contrast — as it does in *Hamlet* (p. 1656), where Fortinbras acts decisively to avenge his father, an action that underscores Hamlet's hesitation and procrastination when faced with a similar challenge.

Plot Development

In a dramatic work, plot unfolds through **action**: what characters say and do. Generally, a play does not include a narrator. Instead, dialogue, stage directions, and various staging techniques work together to move the play's action along.

Exchanges of **dialogue** reveal what is happening — and, sometimes, indicate what happened in the past or suggest what will happen in the future. Characters can recount past events to other characters, announce an intention to take some action in the future, or summarize events that are occurring offstage. In such cases, dialogue takes the place of formal narrative.

On the printed page, **stage directions** efficiently move readers from one location and time period to another by specifying entrances and exits and identifying the play's structural divisions — acts and scenes — and their accompanying changes of setting.

Staging techniques can also advance a play's action. For example, a change in **lighting** can shift the focus to another part of the stage — and thus to another place and time. An adjustment of **scenery** or **props** — for instance, a breakfast table, complete with morning paper, replacing a bedtime setting — can indicate that the action has moved forward in time, as can a change of costumes. **Music** can also move a play's action along, predicting excitement or doom or a romantic interlude — or a particular character's entrance.

In Tennessee Williams's *The Glass Menagerie* (p. 1998), unusual staging devices — such as words projected on a screen that preview words to be spoken by a character and visual images on screen that predict scenes to follow — were designed to help keep the action moving. For example, a screen image of blue roses leads into a scene in which Laura tells her mother how Jim gave her the nickname "Blue Roses." Other staging techniques are also used to advance the plot. For example, toward the end of scene 5, stage directions announce, *"The Dance-Hall Music Changes To A Tango That Has A Minor and Somewhat Ominous Tone"*; a "music legend" repeated throughout the play serves as a signature in scenes focusing on Laura.

Occasionally, a play does have a formal narrator. In Thornton Wilder's play *Our Town* (1938), a character known as the Stage Manager functions as a narrator, not only describing the play's setting and introducing the characters to the audience but also soliciting questions from characters scattered around the audience, prompting characters, and interrupting dialogue. In *The Glass Menagerie*, the protagonist, Tom Wingfield, also serves as a narrator, summarizing what has happened and moving readers on to the next scene: "After the fiasco at Rubicam's Business College, the idea of getting a gentleman caller for Laura began to play a more important part in Mother's calculations" (scene 3).

Flashbacks

Many plays — such as *The Glass Menagerie* and Arthur Miller's *Death of a Salesman* (p. 1581) — include **flashbacks**, which depict events that occurred before the play's main action. Dialogue can also summarize events that occurred earlier, thereby overcoming the limitations set by the chronological action on stage. Thus, Mr. Hale in *Trifles* tells the other characters how he discovered John Wright's murder, and Nora in *A Doll House* confides her secret past to her friend Kristine. As characters on stage are brought up to date, the audience is also given necessary information — facts that are essential to an understanding of the characters' motivation. (In less realistic dramas, characters can interrupt the action to deliver long monologues or soliloquies that fill in background details — or even address the audience directly, as Tom does in *The Glass Menagerie*.)

Foreshadowing

In addition to revealing past events, dialogue can **foreshadow**, or look ahead to, future action. In many cases, seemingly unimportant comments have significance that becomes clear as the play develops. For example, in act 3 of *A Doll House*, Torvald Helmer says to Kristine, "An exit should always be effective, Mrs. Linde, but that's what I can't get Nora to grasp." At the end of the play, Nora's exit is not only effective but also memorable.

Elements of staging can also suggest events to come. In *The Glass Menagerie*, the ever-present photograph of the absent father — who, Tom tells the audience in scene 1, may be seen as a symbol of "the long delayed but always expected something that we live for" — foreshadows Tom's escape. Various bits of **stage business** — gestures or movements designed to attract the audience's attention — may also foreshadow future events. In *A Doll House*, Nora's sneaking forbidden macaroons seems at first to suggest her fear of her husband, but her actions actually foreshadow her eventual defiance of his authority.

✔ **CHECKLIST** **Writing about Plot**

☐ What happens in the play?

☐ What is the play's central conflict? How is it resolved? What other conflicts are present?

☐ What section of the play constitutes its rising action?

---

continued on next page

- Where does the play's climax occur?

- What crises can you identify?

- How is suspense created?

- What section of the play constitutes its falling action?

- Does the play contain a subplot? What is its purpose? How is it related to the main plot?

- How do characters' actions advance the play's plot?

- How does dialogue advance the play's plot?

- How do stage directions advance the play's plot?

- How do staging techniques advance the play's plot?

- Does the play include a narrator?

- Does the play include flashbacks? Foreshadowing? Does the play's dialogue contain summaries of past events or references to events in the future? How does the use of flashbacks or foreshadowing advance the play's plot?

EMILY RODERER received her MFA in creative writing from Virginia Commonwealth University. As a third-year MFA student, she submitted the script for *Scheherazade* to the National Ten-Minute Play Contest, and the play was one of six winners selected from more than two thousand scripts. *Scheherazade* was performed at the Actors Theatre of Louisville in Kentucky. Roderer currently teaches English at VCU.

Cultural Context *The Thousand and One Nights* (also known as the *Arabian Nights Entertainments*) is a collection of medieval Middle Eastern stories presented in the style of a frame tale: an overarching story line frames the delivery of numerous folktales and stories within the larger story. In the story of Scheherazade, a king is betrayed by his wife and orders her to be executed. Distrustful of women, he decides that he will marry a different woman every few days, spend the wedding night with her, and have her executed at dawn. This pattern continues until he marries Scheherazade, who, after their wedding night and the nights that follow, tells the king stories that end at dawn in cliff-hangers. The king repeatedly postpones her execution in order to hear the conclusion of each story, and by the end of a thousand and one nights, she has given birth to three sons and proved herself faithful to him. The tales themselves vary widely and include historical tales, love stories, tragedies, comedies, poems, and Muslim religious legends.

Scheherazade (1998)

CHARACTERS
Girl, *young, perhaps sixteen years old*
Man, *older*

SETTING

The early part of the twentieth century. The deck of a ship bound for North America from the Continent.

The deck of a ship. Sounds of crowd, waves, and ship fade in the background. A girl, sixteen, sits in a deck chair near a man. The man is writing in a ledger.

GIRL: Are you a writer?

MAN: No.

GIRL: What are you doing?

MAN: Excuse me. Should you be talking to strangers?

GIRL: Strangers? We've been trapped on board with these people for almost   5
two weeks. Don't you feel like you've known each and every one of them
your whole life?

MAN: No.

GIRL: I do. And the rain! I've been trapped in a cabin with my aunt and my
cousin for three days. I could jump overboard.

MAN: *(continues writing)* How dramatic.

GIRL: How do you keep from being bored?

MAN: *(still writing)* I work.   10

GIRL: *(doesn't take the hint)* What do you do?

MAN: I'm a banker.

GIRL: You loan people money?

MAN: Where is your aunt?

GIRL: I don't know, and I don't care. *(The man is writing again.)* I hate work.   15

MAN: You have to earn your keep?

GIRL: I won't have to. I'm going to marry a rich man who will take care of me.

MAN: And if you don't?

GIRL: I'll be a writer. I'm very good at stories. I've imagined a story for nearly
every person on deck. Would you like to hear one?

MAN: Do I have a choice?   20

GIRL: See the woman over there with the funny hat and the shoes that don't fit?

MAN: Yes.

GIRL: The man to her left with the spectacle is a rich suitor. She's been tempting him the whole trip. He wants her to marry him, but she doesn't love
him. She's in love with the bald man with his back to us. I've seen her pass
notes to him every day. They've been lovers for years. It's so obvious, you'd
think the man with the spectacle would realize, but he's a fool, so he doesn't.
She marries one of these rich old fools once every . . . five years. Slowly, she
poisons them with arsenic. When the old man croaks she sends for her bald

lover and meets him on a boat, like this one, bound for Asia or Europe or maybe South America. They travel for a while together. Reaping the benefits of their merciless endeavor. Then, en route back to the United States, they find another of these bumbling idiots, like the man with the spectacle, and the wicked cycle starts all over again.

25 MAN: And your reasoning?

GIRL: The man with the spectacle is obviously a fool. Have you spoken to him? The woman is obviously a temptress, that's why she wears those ridiculous hats and shoes that don't fit. And the bald man is obviously her lover because he's constantly at her disposal, and she passes him notes night and day.

MAN: The bald man is a steward on this ship. He takes dinner orders. The woman is a wealthy heiress prone to wearing eccentric clothing, and the fool is a fool trying to convince her to invest in his business.

GIRL: How do you know all that?

MAN: I've had dinner with them three times.

GIRL: But isn't my story more interesting?

30 MAN: Yes, but only because they are so boring. And your story isn't remotely believable.

GIRL: Why not?

MAN: Because that woman isn't remotely enticing, and she'd have to be to lure money away from rich old fools.

GIRL: Enticing? Is that what you have to be?

MAN: Yes.

35 GIRL: And if you're not?

MAN: Well, some people have to work to earn their keep.

GIRL: Some people have to tutor their cousin in art and history and read to their aunt and get her shawl whenever she asks, and if you do something she doesn't like you apologize, and when she threatens to leave you at home on her next trip, you cry and plead, because you know being left at home is worse than being with her.

MAN: Not such a bad job, is it?

GIRL: It might be, if that's all you could do.

40 MAN: I have to go to work every day and count money and sign loans or not sign loans and refuse people money that they may have needed but you couldn't in good conscience let them have. And maybe they needed it because a baby was on the way or their mother was ill or they couldn't find work. Those are not easy decisions.

GIRL: You do all that?

MAN: Sometimes.

GIRL: I would like to do that. I would give them the money, if they needed it.

MAN: That's why little girls don't work in banks.

45 GIRL: Little girl. (*She laughs.*) That's why they study art and visit Europe with their aunts and wear gloves to parties.

MAN: Yes. (*She is silent. He is content for a moment and returns to work.*) Sometimes, I give them the money.

GIRL: I knew you did.

MAN: I make them pay it back.

GIRL: Of course, so, you can loan it to other people.

MAN: Yes, sometimes.   50

GIRL: I thought you had a kind face, an imaginative face. That's why I thought you were a writer. You looked as though you understood people.

MAN: Humph.

GIRL: Don't you ever imagine stories?

MAN: (laughs) My job in the bank is so much more interesting.

GIRL: Tell me a story.   55

MAN: I don't tell stories.

GIRL: Everyone tells stories.

MAN: Not me.

GIRL: Not ever?

MAN: No.   60

GIRL: Never to your son or daughter?

MAN: I don't have any children.

GIRL: Never to a niece or nephew?

MAN: I don't have any family.

GIRL: Never to a lover?   65

MAN: You're too young to be talking about lovers.

GIRL: No, I'm not. I have to know all about them to be a writer.

MAN: Well, then you're too young to be talking about them to me.

GIRL: Then, say something, anything.

MAN: (He starts softly, as if he is telling a secret.) The man and woman behind   70
us. The two sketching. Don't look.

GIRL: Yes.

MAN: They're both world famous artists. They're married, but they're traveling together as brother and sister.

GIRL: Why?

MAN: Because they don't like to have attention drawn to themselves. They pick their subjects from ordinary people. If people knew they were famous artists, they would behave differently in front of them and none of their art would be real.

GIRL: How do you know?   75

MAN: I had dinner with them last night.

GIRL: And they told you all this?

MAN: I have an honest face. They thought they could trust me, and I believe they've already finished sketching me.

GIRL: Are you going to be in a painting?

MAN: Probably not. I was a useful exercise in the human form, but you never   80
know. They could choose anyone as the subject for their next masterpiece.

GIRL: Anyone?

MAN: Anyone.

GIRL: (She becomes self-conscious.) How will you know, if they've used you in a painting?

MAN: You wouldn't, unless you asked.

85 GIRL: I'm not going to ask.

MAN: Why not? What's the harm?

GIRL: I'm not going to ask because you're not telling the truth.

MAN: I wouldn't lie.

GIRL: But you would tell a story.

90 MAN: I don't tell stories.

GIRL: You'd never tell me to go over and ask them if I was to be in their next painting, if they were really artists.

MAN: *(laughs)* Then, you learned something about telling a story.

GIRL: I knew it was a story!

MAN: But you believed me until the end.

95 GIRL: I didn't.

MAN: The trick is not to make the story too outrageous or ridiculous.

GIRL: How do you know about stories, if you don't tell them?

MAN: I used to tell stories.

GIRL: When?

100 MAN: That was a very long time ago.

GIRL: Who did you tell stories to?

MAN: A woman I used to know.

GIRL: Your wife?

MAN: No.

105 GIRL: Your lover?

MAN: How old are you?

GIRL: Why?

MAN: You shouldn't be discussing people's lovers. Why don't you have another try?

GIRL: Was she your mistress?

110 MAN: I meant why don't you tell another story?

GIRL: I know what you meant. What kind?

MAN: Tell me one that I'll believe.

GIRL: That's an awful lot of pressure.

MAN: I have faith in you.

115 GIRL: Who would you like me to tell a story about?

MAN: Anyone?

GIRL: Anyone on deck.

MAN: You.

GIRL: Me? *(Pause.)* I'm sixteen. I'm traveling with my aunt and my cousin, Amy. We've been abroad for the summer. My aunt took us to Europe for a bit of "culture." In my aunt's view, the trip was a miserable failure. She hired a third-rate governess to tutor us in French and take us to museums. The governess ran off with our cook.

120 MAN: Was he handsome?

GIRL: No, he was hideous. It wasn't romantic. She was a shrew. He had a bit of money saved. I heard them discussing it in the garden one night. That's the only reason she went off with him.

MAN: Not in the least bit exciting.

GIRL: It was sad. She didn't love him. When she left she pulled me aside and said, "Learn how to fend for yourself. Work if you have to, but it's easier if you find someone to do it for you."

MAN: Not very romantic.

GIRL: No, I'd never marry for money. 125

MAN: Humph.

GIRL: My aunt was forced to be chaperon. She has gout and couldn't keep up with us. Amy and I smoked our first cigarette in the gardens at Versailles. Does that shock you?

MAN: No.

GIRL: The gardens are lovely. My aunt's gout got the worst of her, and we had to stay penned in the hotel room. She tried to occupy us. Amy is eighteen, and my Aunt had wealthy suitors visit almost every day. One was an Italian nobleman. He fell in love with me. He visited every day and passed me notes. The trip ended abruptly when my aunt discovered us. She was very angry.

MAN: Because you're too young. 130

GIRL: No, she doesn't care about me. I have no money. She doesn't want me to marry well. She doesn't want me to marry at all. She wants me to take care of her in her old age.

MAN: You've read too many romantic novels.

GIRL: It's all true.

MAN: I believed the first part. The second part is stolen.

GIRL: He's followed me on board. He's so in love with me, he's following me 135
back to America. He wants to elope. He's been watching us this whole time. See him. The handsome, dark man, with the wide brim hat. He thinks he's inconspicuous. Don't stare. I only decided to speak with you, because I saw him coming over, and I thought he might try to kiss me. We'd be discovered.

MAN: Now, you're being outrageous.

GIRL: It's a good story.

MAN: Oh yes. Very good for you.

GIRL: You halfway believed me.

MAN: Until it became ridiculous. 140

GIRL: It was more exciting than your story.

MAN: Yes, but you believed me.

GIRL: Only for a moment.

MAN: Your story would have been more believable, if the nobleman hadn't been rich.

GIRL: No? 145

MAN: Or maybe not a nobleman at all.

GIRL: No?

MAN: No, a commoner and your wealthy aunt threatened to cut you off if you married him.

GIRL: That's not a very happy story.

150 MAN: No, but maybe closer to the truth.

GIRL: But what if her money was really mine, at least some of it. And what if, I just couldn't get to it.

MAN: You'd still be in a pinch.

GIRL: But what if there was someone who could help me?

MAN: You have a fine imagination.

155 GIRL: And what if that person was the banker who controlled that money and all he had to do was help me just a little.

MAN: If only things were so simple.

GIRL: Did you tell the woman stories?

MAN: Oh yes.

GIRL: Were they believable?

160 MAN: They were hopeful.

GIRL: What happened to her?

MAN: Let's just say, she had an aunt who didn't approve.

GIRL: What if someone could have helped her?

MAN: I would have been very happy.

165 GIRL: And you would have paid every penny back?

MAN: Yes.

GIRL: I believe you.

Reading and Reacting

1. Scheherazade, a character from *The Thousand and One Nights*, tells mesmerizing stories to postpone her execution. In what sense is the girl in this play like Scheherazade?

2. The exposition provided in the play's stage directions is quite minimal. How do you picture the two characters and the setting?

3. What specific information does the audience learn about the two characters? How certain are you that all this information is true?

4. This play has a single setting and virtually no action. What moves the plot along? Is this enough?

5. How does the man feel about his work? What does he mean when he says, "Some people have to work to earn their keep"? How does this statement foreshadow the play's ending?

6. At the beginning of the play, the girl tells the man a story about some of the other passengers; later on, he tells her one. What do these two stories have in common? How are they different?

7. Which parts of the stories that the characters tell do you see as believable? Which parts do you see as "ridiculous" — or even "outrageous"? Why?

8. Do you believe the story that the girl tells about herself? Which elements seem plausible? Which, if any, do not?

9. Do you see the plot of *Scheherazade* as realistic? Are any elements improbable? Explain.

10. At the end of the play, exactly what has happened? Do you think the characters have made an alliance of any sort? Do you think their story will continue?

11. **JOURNAL ENTRY** Twice, the man tells the girl, "I don't tell stories," and, in fact, he never tells a story about his own life. Invent a suitable story, one that seems realistic and not "outrageous."

12. **CRITICAL PERSPECTIVE** In their introduction to *30 Ten-Minute Plays for 2 Actors*, editors Michael Bigelow Dixon, Amy Wegener, and Karen C. Petruska try to account for the ten-minute play's popularity. They note that "its brevity relates directly to the restlessness of the American character. Americans aren't about lingering or loitering . . . and neither are these plays." They continue as follows:

> Things *happen* in these plays! Because they move so quickly, the plays are just long enough to satisfy the American need to get to the root of problems and short enough to allow us to move along once the dramatic problem's been dealt with.

Do you think these comments apply to *Scheherazade?* For example, what "things happen" in the play? Does it indeed move quickly? Is it just the right length, or should it have been longer — or shorter?

Related Works: "Hills Like White Elephants" (p. 148), "Sleepy Time Gal" (p. 154), "Gryphon" (p. 248), "Gretel in Darkness" (p. 852), "Cinderella," (p. 882), *No Crime* (p. 1316)

SUSAN GLASPELL (1882–1948) was born in Davenport, Iowa, and graduated from Drake University in 1899. First a reporter and then a freelance writer, she lived in Chicago (where she was part of the Chicago Renaissance that included poet Carl Sandburg and novelist Theodore Dreiser) and later in Greenwich Village. Her works include two plays in addition to *Trifles, The Verge* (1921) and *Alison's House* (1930), and several novels, including *Fidelity* (1915) and *The Morning Is Near Us* (1939). With her husband, George Cram Cook, she founded the Provincetown Players, which became the staging ground for innovative plays by Eugene O'Neill, among others.

Glaspell herself wrote plays for the Provincetown Players, beginning with *Trifles,* which she created for the 1916 season although she had never previously written a drama. The play opened on August 8, 1916, with Glaspell and her husband in the cast. Glaspell said she wrote *Trifles* in one afternoon, sitting in the empty theater and looking at the bare stage: "After a time, the stage became a kitchen — a kitchen there all by itself." She remembered a murder trial she had covered in Iowa in her days as a reporter, and the story began to play itself out on the stage as she gazed. Throughout her revisions, she said, she returned to look at the stage to see whether the events she was recording came to life on it. Although Glaspell later rewrote *Trifles* as a short story called "A Jury of Her Peers," the play remains her most successful and memorable work.

> **Cultural Context** One of the main themes of this play is the contrast between the sexes in terms of their roles, rights, and responsibilities. In 1916, when *Trifles* was first produced, women were not allowed to serve on juries in most states. This circumstance was in accordance with other rights denied to women, including the right to vote, which was not ratified in all states until 1920. Unable to participate in the most basic civic functions, women largely discussed politics only among themselves and were relegated to positions of lesser status. However, their influence could still be deeply felt, as it is in this play.

Trifles (1916)

CHARACTERS

George Henderson, *county attorney*	**Mrs. Peters**
Henry Peters, *sheriff*	**Mrs. Hale**
Lewis Hale, *a neighboring farmer*	

SCENE

The kitchen in the now abandoned farmhouse of John Wright, a gloomy kitchen, and left without having been put in order — unwashed pans under the sink, a loaf of bread outside the breadbox, a dish towel on the table — other signs of incompleted work. At the rear the outer door opens and the Sheriff comes in followed by the County Attorney and Hale. The Sheriff and Hale are men in middle life, the County Attorney is a young man; all are much bundled up and go at once to the stove. They are followed by two women — the Sheriff's wife first; she is a slight wiry woman, a thin nervous face. Mrs. Hale is larger and would ordinarily be called more comfortable looking, but she is disturbed now and looks fearfully about as she enters. The women have come in slowly, and stand close together near the door.

COUNTY ATTORNEY: *(rubbing his hands)* This feels good. Come up to the fire, ladies.

MRS. PETERS: *(after taking a step forward)* I'm not — cold.

SHERIFF: *(unbuttoning his overcoat and stepping away from the stove as if to mark the beginning of official business)* Now, Mr. Hale, before we move things about, you explain to Mr. Henderson just what you saw when you came here yesterday morning.

COUNTY ATTORNEY: By the way, has anything been moved? Are things just as you left them yesterday?

5 SHERIFF: *(looking about)* It's just the same. When it dropped below zero last night I thought I'd better send Frank out this morning to make a fire for us — no use getting pneumonia with a big case on, but I told him not to touch anything except the stove — and you know Frank.

COUNTY ATTORNEY: Somebody should have been left here yesterday.

SHERIFF: Oh — yesterday. When I had to send Frank to Morris Center for that man who went crazy — I want you to know I had my hands full yesterday. I

knew you could get back from Omaha by today and as long as I went over
everything here myself —

COUNTY ATTORNEY: Well, Mr. Hale, tell just what happened when you came
here yesterday morning.

HALE: Harry and I had started to town with a load of potatoes. We came along
the road from my place and as I got here I said, "I'm going to see if I can't
get John Wright to go in with me on a party telephone." I spoke to Wright
about it once before and he put me off, saying folks talked too much
anyway, and all he asked was peace and quiet — I guess you know about
how much he talked himself; but I thought maybe if I went to the house
and talked about it before his wife, though I said to Harry that I didn't
know as what his wife wanted made much difference to John —

COUNTY ATTORNEY: Let's talk about that later, Mr. Hale. I do want to talk   10
about that, but tell now just what happened when you got to the house.

HALE: I didn't hear or see anything; I knocked at the door, and still it was all
quiet inside. I knew they must be up, it was past eight o'clock. So I knocked
again, and I thought I heard somebody say, "Come in." I wasn't sure, I'm not
sure yet, but I opened the door — this door (*indicating the door by which the
two women are still standing*) and there in that rocker —(*pointing to it*) sat
Mrs. Wright.

They all look at the rocker.

COUNTY ATTORNEY: What — was she doing?

HALE: She was rockin' back and forth. She had her apron in her hand and was
kind of — pleating it.

COUNTY ATTORNEY: And how did she —look?

HALE: Well, she looked queer.   15

COUNTY ATTORNEY: How do you mean — queer?

HALE: Well, as if she didn't know what she was going to do next. And kind of
done up.

COUNTY ATTORNEY: How did she seem to feel about your coming?

HALE: Why, I don't think she minded — one way or other. She didn't pay
much attention. I said, "How do, Mrs. Wright, it's cold, ain't it?" And she
said, "Is it?"— and went on kind of pleating at her apron. Well, I was surprised; she didn't ask me to come up to the stove, or to set down, but just
sat there, not even looking at me, so I said, "I want to see John." And then
she —laughed. I guess you would call it a laugh. I thought of Harry and the
team outside, so I said a little sharp: "Can't I see John?" "No," she says, kind
o' dull like. "Ain't he home?" says I. "Yes," says she, "he's home." "Then why
can't I see him?" I asked her, out of patience. "'Cause he's dead," says she.
"*Dead?*" says I. She just nodded her head, not getting a bit excited, but
rockin' back and forth. "Why — where is he?" says I, not knowing what to
say. She just pointed upstairs — like that. (*Himself pointing to the room
above.*) I got up, with the idea of going up there. I walked from there to
here — then I says, "Why, what did he die of?" "He died of a rope round his
neck," says she, and just went on pleatin' at her apron. Well, I went out and

called Harry. I thought I might — need help. We went upstairs and there
he was lyin'—

20   COUNTY ATTORNEY: I think I'd rather have you go into that upstairs, where
you can point it all out. Just go on now with the rest of the story.

HALE: Well, my first thought was to get that rope off. It looked . . . (*stops, his
face twitches*) . . . but Harry, he went up to him, and he said, "No, he's dead
all right, and we'd better not touch anything." So we went back down stairs.
She was still sitting that same way. "Has anybody been notified?" I asked.
"No," says she, unconcerned. "Who did this, Mrs. Wright?" said Harry. He
said it businesslike — and she stopped pleatin' of her apron. "I don't know,"
she says. "You don't *know?*" says Harry. "No," says she. "Weren't you sleepin'
in the bed with him?" says Harry. "Yes," says she, "but I was on the inside."
"Somebody slipped a rope round his neck and strangled him and you didn't
wake up?" says Harry. "I didn't wake up," she said after him. We must 'a
looked as if we didn't see how that could be, for after a minute she said, "I
sleep sound." Harry was going to ask her more questions but I said maybe we
ought to let her tell her story first to the coroner, or the sheriff, so Harry
went fast as he could to Rivers' place, where there's a telephone.

COUNTY ATTORNEY: And what did Mrs. Wright do when she knew that you
had gone for the coroner?

HALE: She moved from that chair to this one over here (*pointing to a small
chair in the corner*) and just sat there with her hands held together and
looking down. I got a feeling that I ought to make some conversation, so
I said I had come in to see if John wanted to put in a telephone, and at that
she started to laugh, and then she stopped and looked at me — scared.
(*The County Attorney, who has had his notebook out, makes a note.*) I dunno,

In this scene from the Provincetown Players' 1917 production of Susan Glaspell's *Trifles,* the
three men discuss the crime while Mrs. Peters and Mrs. Hale look on.

maybe it wasn't scared. I wouldn't like to say it was. Soon Harry got back, and then Dr. Lloyd came, and you, Mr. Peters, and so I guess that's all I know that you don't.

COUNTY ATTORNEY: *(looking around)* I guess we'll go upstairs first — and then out to the barn and around there. *(To the Sheriff.)* You're convinced that there was nothing important here — nothing that would point to any motive.

SHERIFF: Nothing here but kitchen things. 25

The County Attorney, after again looking around the kitchen, opens the door of a cupboard closet. He gets up on a chair and looks on a shelf. Pulls his hand away, sticky.

COUNTY ATTORNEY: Here's a nice mess.

The women draw nearer.

MRS. PETERS: *(to the other woman)* Oh, her fruit; it did freeze. *(To the County Attorney.)* She worried about that when it turned so cold. She said the fire'd go out and her jars would break.

SHERIFF: Well, can you beat the women! Held for murder and worryin' about her preserves.

COUNTY ATTORNEY: I guess before we're through she may have something more serious than preserves to worry about.

HALE: Well, women are used to worrying over trifles. 30

The two women move a little closer together.

COUNTY ATTORNEY: *(with the gallantry of a young politician)* And yet, for all their worries, what would we do without the ladies? *(The women do not unbend. He goes to the sink, takes a dipperful of water from the pail and pouring it into a basin, washes his hands. Starts to wipe them on the roller towel, turns it for a cleaner place.)* Dirty towels! *(Kicks his foot against the pans under the sink.)* Not much of a housekeeper, would you say, ladies?

MRS. HALE: *(stiffly)* There's a great deal of work to be done on a farm.

COUNTY ATTORNEY: To be sure. And yet *(with a little bow to her)* I know there are some Dickson county farmhouses which do not have such roller towels.

He gives it a pull to expose its full length again.

MRS. HALE: Those towels get dirty awful quick. Men's hands aren't always as clean as they might be.

COUNTY ATTORNEY: Ah, loyal to your sex, I see. But you and Mrs. Wright 35 were neighbors. I suppose you were friends, too.

MRS. HALE: *(shaking her head)* I've not seen much of her of late years. I've not been in this house — it's more than a year.

COUNTY ATTORNEY: And why was that? You didn't like her?

MRS. HALE: I liked her all well enough. Farmers' wives have their hands full, Mr. Henderson. And then —

COUNTY ATTORNEY: Yes —?

40   MRS. HALE: *(looking about)* It never seemed a very cheerful place.

COUNTY ATTORNEY: No — it's not cheerful. I shouldn't say she had the homemaking instinct.

MRS. HALE: Well, I don't know as Wright had, either.

COUNTY ATTORNEY: You mean that they didn't get on very well?

MRS. HALE: No, I don't mean anything. But I don't think a place'd be any cheerfuller for John Wright's being in it.

45   COUNTY ATTORNEY: I'd like to talk more of that a little later. I want to get the lay of things upstairs now.

He goes to the left, where three steps lead to a stair door.

SHERIFF: I suppose anything Mrs. Peters does'll be all right. She was to take in some clothes for her, you know, and a few little things. We left in such a hurry yesterday.

COUNTY ATTORNEY: Yes, but I would like to see what you take, Mrs. Peters, and keep an eye out for anything that might be of use to us.

MRS. PETERS: Yes, Mr. Henderson.

The women listen to the men's steps on the stairs, then look about the kitchen.

MRS. HALE: I'd hate to have men coming into my kitchen, snooping around and criticizing.

She arranges the pans under sink which the County Attorney had shoved out of place.

50   MRS. PETERS: Of course it's no more than their duty.

MRS. HALE: Duty's all right, but I guess that deputy sheriff that came out to make the fire might have got a little of this on. *(Gives the roller towel a pull.)* Wish I'd thought of that sooner. Seems mean to talk about her for not having things slicked up when she had to come away in such a hurry.

MRS. PETERS: *(who has gone to a small table in the left rear corner of the room, and lifted one end of a towel that covers a pan)* She had bread set.

Stands still.

MRS. HALE: *(eyes fixed on a loaf of bread beside the breadbox, which is on a low shelf at the other side of the room. Moves slowly toward it.)* She was going to put this in there. *(Picks up loaf, then abruptly drops it. In a manner of returning to familiar things.)* It's a shame about her fruit. I wonder if it's all gone. *(Gets up on the chair and looks.)* I think there's some here that's all right, Mrs. Peters. Yes — here; *(holding it toward the window)* this is cherries, too. *(Looking again.)* I declare I believe that's the only one. *(Gets down, bottle in her hand. Goes to the sink and wipes it off on the outside.)* She'll feel awful bad after all her hard work in the hot weather. I remember the afternoon I put up my cherries last summer.

She puts the bottle on the big kitchen table, center of the room. With a sigh, is about to sit down in the rocking-chair. Before she is seated realizes what chair it is; with a slow look at it, steps back. The chair which she has touched rocks back and forth.

MRS. PETERS: Well, I must get those things from the front room closet. (*She goes to the door at the right, but after looking into the other room, steps back.*) You coming with me, Mrs. Hale? You could help me carry them.

They go in the other room; reappear, Mrs. Peters carrying a dress and skirt, Mrs. Hale following with a pair of shoes.

MRS. PETERS: My, it's cold in there.   55

She puts the clothes on the big table, and hurries to the stove.

MRS. HALE: (*examining her skirt*) Wright was close. I think maybe that's why she kept so much to herself. She didn't even belong to the Ladies Aid. I suppose she felt she couldn't do her part, and then you don't enjoy things when you feel shabby. She used to wear pretty clothes and be lively, when she was Minnie Foster, one of the town girls singing in the choir. But that — oh, that was thirty years ago. This all you was to take in?

MRS. PETERS: She said she wanted an apron. Funny thing to want, for there isn't much to get you dirty in jail, goodness knows. But I suppose just to make her feel more natural. She said they was in the top drawer in this cupboard. Yes, here. And then her little shawl that always hung behind the door. (*Opens stair door and looks.*) Yes, here it is.

Quickly shuts door leading upstairs.

MRS. HALE: (*abruptly moving toward her*) Mrs. Peters?
MRS. PETERS: Yes, Mrs. Hale?
MRS. HALE: Do you think she did it?   60
MRS. PETERS: (*in a frightened voice*) Oh, I don't know.
MRS. HALE: Well, I don't think she did. Asking for an apron and her little shawl. Worrying about her fruit.
MRS. PETERS: (*starts to speak, glances up, where footsteps are heard in the room above. In a low voice.*) Mr. Peters says it looks bad for her. Mr. Henderson is awful sarcastic in a speech and he'll make fun of her sayin' she didn't wake up.
MRS. HALE: Well, I guess John Wright didn't wake when they was slipping that rope under his neck.
MRS. PETERS: No, it's strange. It must have been done awful crafty and still.   65
They say it was such a — funny way to kill a man, rigging it all up like that.
MRS. HALE: That's just what Mr. Hale said. There was a gun in the house. He says that's what he can't understand.
MRS. PETERS: Mr. Henderson said coming out that what was needed for the case was a motive; something to show anger, or — sudden feeling.
MRS. HALE: (*who is standing by the table*) Well, I don't see any signs of anger around here. (*She puts her hand on the dish towel which lies on the table, stands looking down at table, one half of which is clean, the other half messy.*) It's wiped to here. (*Makes a move as if to finish work, then turns and looks at loaf of bread outside the breadbox. Drops towel. In that voice of coming back to familiar things.*) Wonder how they are finding things upstairs. I hope she

had it a little more red-up° up there. You know, it seems kind of *sneaking*.
Locking her up in town and then coming out here and trying to get her
own house to turn against her!

MRS. PETERS: But Mrs. Hale, the law is the law.

70 **MRS. HALE:** I s'pose 'tis. (*Unbuttoning her coat.*) Better loosen up your things,
Mrs. Peters. You won't feel them when you go out.

*Mrs. Peters takes off her fur tippet, goes to hang it on hook at back of room, stands
looking at the under part of the small corner table.*

MRS. PETERS: She was piecing a quilt.

She brings the large sewing basket and they look at the bright pieces.

MRS. HALE: It's log cabin pattern. Pretty, isn't it? I wonder if she was goin' to
quilt it or just knot it?

*Footsteps have been heard coming down the stairs. The Sheriff enters followed by Hale
and the County Attorney.*

SHERIFF: They wonder if she was going to quilt it or just knot it!

The men laugh; the women look abashed.

COUNTY ATTORNEY: (*rubbing his hands over the stove*) Frank's fire didn't do
much up there, did it? Well, let's go out to the barn and get that cleared up.

The men go outside.

75 **MRS. HALE:** (*resentfully*) I don't know as there's anything so strange, our takin'
up our time with little things while we're waiting for them to get the
evidence. (*She sits down at the big table smoothing out a block with decision.*)
I don't see as it's anything to laugh about.

MRS. PETERS: (*apologetically*) Of course they've got awful important things on
their minds.

Pulls up a chair and joins Mrs. Hale at the table.

MRS. HALE: (*examining another block*) Mrs. Peters, look at this one. Here, this
is the one she was working on, and look at the sewing! All the rest of it has
been so nice and even. And look at this! It's all over the place! Why, it
looks as if she didn't know what she was about!

*After she has said this they look at each other, then start to glance back at the door.
After an instant Mrs. Hale has pulled at a knot and ripped the sewing.*

MRS. PETERS: Oh, what are you doing, Mrs. Hale?

MRS. HALE: (*mildly*) Just pulling out a stitch or two that's not sewed very
good. (*Threading a needle.*) Bad sewing always made me fidgety.

80 **MRS. PETERS:** (*nervously*) I don't think we ought to touch things.

---

red-up: Spruced-up (slang).

MRS. HALE: I'll just finish up this end. (*Suddenly stopping and leaning forward.*) Mrs. Peters?

MRS. PETERS: Yes, Mrs. Hale?

MRS. HALE: What do you suppose she was so nervous about?

MRS. PETERS: Oh — I don't know. I don't know as she was nervous. I sometimes sew awful queer when I'm just tired. (*Mrs. Hale starts to say something, looks at Mrs. Peters, then goes on sewing.*) Well, I must get these things wrapped up. They may be through sooner than we think. (*Putting apron and other things together.*) I wonder where I can find a piece of paper, and string.

MRS. HALE: In that cupboard, maybe. 85

MRS. PETERS: (*looking in cupboard*) Why, here's a birdcage. (*Holds it up.*) Did she have a bird, Mrs. Hale?

MRS. HALE: Why, I don't know whether she did or not — I've not been here for so long. There was a man around last year selling canaries cheap, but I don't know as she took one; maybe she did. She used to sing real pretty herself.

MRS. PETERS: (*glancing around*) Seems funny to think of a bird here. But she must have had one, or why would she have a cage? I wonder what happened to it.

MRS. HALE: I s'pose maybe the cat got it.

MRS. PETERS: No, she didn't have a cat. She's got that feeling some people 90 have about cats — being afraid of them. My cat got in her room and she was real upset and asked me to take it out.

MRS. HALE: My sister Bessie was like that. Queer, ain't it?

MRS. PETERS: (*examining the cage*) Why, look at this door. It's broke. One hinge is pulled apart.

MRS. HALE: (*looking too*) Looks as if someone must have been rough with it.

MRS. PETERS: Why, yes.

She brings the cage forward and puts it on the table.

MRS. HALE: I wish if they're going to find any evidence they'd be about it. I 95 don't like this place.

MRS. PETERS: But I'm awful glad you came with me, Mrs. Hale. It would be lonesome for me sitting here alone.

MRS. HALE: It would, wouldn't it? (*Dropping her sewing.*) But I tell you what I do wish, Mrs. Peters. I wish I had come over sometimes when *she* was here. I —(*looking around the room*)— wish I had.

MRS. PETERS: But of course you were awful busy, Mrs. Hale — your house and your children.

MRS. HALE: I could've come. I stayed away because it weren't cheerful — and that's why I ought to have come. I — I've never liked this place. Maybe because it's down in a hollow and you don't see the road. I dunno what it is but it's a lonesome place and always was. I wish I had come over to see Minnie Foster sometimes. I can see now —

Shakes her head.

100   MRS. PETERS: Well, you mustn't reproach yourself, Mrs. Hale. Somehow we just don't see how it is with other folks until — something comes up.

MRS. HALE: Not having children makes less work — but it makes a quiet house, and Wright out to work all day, and no company when he did come in. Did you know John Wright, Mrs. Peters?

MRS. PETERS: Not to know him; I've seen him in town. They say he was a good man.

MRS. HALE: Yes — good; he didn't drink, and kept his word as well as most, I guess, and paid his debts. But he was a hard man, Mrs. Peters. Just to pass the time of day with him — (*Shivers.*) Like a raw wind that gets to the bone. (*Pauses, her eye falling on the cage.*) I should think she would 'a wanted a bird. But what do you suppose went with it?

MRS. PETERS: I don't know, unless it got sick and died.

She reaches over and swings the broken door, swings it again. Both women watch it.

105   MRS. HALE: You weren't raised round here, were you? (*Mrs. Peters shakes her head.*) You didn't know — her?

MRS. PETERS: Not till they brought her yesterday.

MRS. HALE: She — come to think of it, she was kind of like a bird herself — real sweet and pretty, but kind of timid and — fluttery. How — she — did — change. (*Silence; then as if struck by a happy thought and relieved to get back to everyday things.*) Tell you what, Mrs. Peters, why don't you take the quilt in with you? It might take up her mind.

MRS. PETERS: Why, I think that's a real nice idea, Mrs. Hale. There couldn't possibly be any objection to it, could there? Now, just what would I take? I wonder if her patches are in here — and her things.

They look in the sewing basket.

MRS. HALE: Here's some red. I expect this has got sewing things in it. (*Brings out a fancy box.*) What a pretty box. Looks like something somebody would give you. Maybe her scissors are in here. (*Opens box. Suddenly puts her hand to her nose.*) Why — (*Mrs. Peters bends nearer, then turns her face away.*) There's something wrapped up in this piece of silk.

110   MRS. PETERS: Why, this isn't her scissors.

MRS. HALE: (*lifting the silk*) Oh, Mrs. Peters — it's —

Mrs. Peters bends closer.

MRS. PETERS: It's the bird.

MRS. HALE: (*jumping up*) But, Mrs. Peters — look at it! Its neck! Look at its neck! It's all — other side *to*.

MRS. PETERS: Somebody — wrung — its — neck.

Their eyes meet. A look of growing comprehension, of horror. Steps are heard outside. Mrs. Hale slips box under quilt pieces, and sinks into her chair. Enter Sheriff and County Attorney. Mrs. Peters rises.

COUNTY ATTORNEY: *(as one turning from serious things to little pleasantries)*   115
    Well, ladies, have you decided whether she was going to quilt it or knot it?
MRS. PETERS: We think she was going to — knot it.
COUNTY ATTORNEY: Well, that's interesting, I'm sure. *(Seeing the birdcage.)*
    Has the bird flown?
MRS. HALE: *(putting more quilt pieces over the box)* We think the — cat got it.
COUNTY ATTORNEY: *(preoccupied)* Is there a cat?

Mrs. Hale glances in a quick covert way at Mrs. Peters.

MRS. PETERS: Well, not *now*. They're superstitious, you know. They leave.   120
COUNTY ATTORNEY: *(to Sheriff Peters, continuing an interrupted conversation)*
    No sign at all of anyone having come from the outside. Their own rope.
    Now let's go up again and go over it piece by piece. *(They start upstairs.)*
    It would have to have been someone who knew just the —

Mrs. Peters sits down. The two women sit there not looking at one another, but as if peering into something and at the same time holding back. When they talk now it is in the manner of feeling their way over strange ground, as if afraid of what they are saying, but as if they can not help saying it.

MRS. HALE: She liked the bird. She was going to bury it in that pretty box.
MRS. PETERS: *(in a whisper)* When I was a girl — my kitten — there was a boy
    took a hatchet, and before my eyes — and before I could get there —*(Covers*
    her face an instant.) If they hadn't held me back I would have —*(catches*
    herself, looks upstairs where steps are heard, falters weakly)—hurt him.
MRS. HALE: *(with a slow look around her)* I wonder how it would seem never to
    have had any children around. *(Pause.)* No, Wright wouldn't like the
    bird — a thing that sang. She used to sing. He killed that, too.
MRS. PETERS: *(moving uneasily)* We don't know who killed the bird.   125
MRS. HALE: I knew John Wright.
MRS. PETERS: It was an awful thing was done in this house that night,
    Mrs. Hale. Killing a man while he slept, slipping a rope around his neck
    that choked the life out of him.
MRS. HALE: His neck. Choked the life out of him.

Her hand goes out and rests on the birdcage.

MRS. PETERS: *(with rising voice)* We don't know who killed him. We don't
    know.
MRS. HALE: *(her own feeling not interrupted)* If there'd been years and years of   130
    nothing, then a bird to sing to you, it would be awful — still, after the bird
    was still.
MRS. PETERS: *(something within her speaking)* I know what stillness is. When
    we homesteaded in Dakota, and my first baby died — after he was two years
    old, and me with no other then—
MRS. HALE: *(moving)* How soon do you suppose they'll be through, looking for
    the evidence?

MRS. PETERS: I know what stillness is. (*Pulling herself back.*) The law has got
to punish crime, Mrs. Hale.

MRS. HALE: (*not as if answering that*) I wish you'd seen Minnie Foster when
she wore a white dress with blue ribbons and stood up there in the choir
and sang. (*A look around the room.*) Oh, I *wish* I'd come over here once in a
while! That was a crime! That was a crime! Who's going to punish that?

135 MRS. PETERS: (*looking upstairs*) We mustn't — take on.

MRS. HALE: I might have known she needed help! I know how things can
be — for women. I tell you, it's queer, Mrs. Peters. We live close together
and we live far apart. We all go through the same things — it's all just a
different kind of the same thing. (*Brushes her eyes; noticing the bottle of fruit,
reaches out for it.*) If I was you I wouldn't tell her her fruit was gone. Tell her
it *ain't*. Tell her it's all right. Take this in to prove it to her. She — she may
never know whether it was broke or not.

MRS. PETERS: (*takes the bottle, looks about for something to wrap it in; takes
petticoat from the clothes brought from the other room, very nervously begins
winding this around the bottle. In a false voice*) My, it's a good thing the men
couldn't hear us. Wouldn't they just laugh! Getting all stirred up over a
little thing like a — dead canary. As if that could have anything to do
with — with — wouldn't they *laugh!*

The men are heard coming down stairs.

MRS. HALE: (*under her breath*) Maybe they would — maybe they wouldn't.

COUNTY ATTORNEY: No, Peters, it's all perfectly clear except a reason for
doing it. But you know juries when it comes to women. If there was some
definite thing. Something to show — something to make a story about — a
thing that would connect up with this strange way of doing it—

The women's eyes meet for an instant. Enter Hale from outer door.

140 HALE: Well, I've got the team around. Pretty cold out there.

COUNTY ATTORNEY: I'm going to stay here a while by myself. (*To the Sheriff.*)
You can send Frank out for me, can't you? I want to go over everything. I'm
not satisfied that we can't do better.

SHERIFF: Do you want to see what Mrs. Peters is going to take in?

The County Attorney goes to the table, picks up the apron, laughs.

COUNTY ATTORNEY: Oh, I guess they're not very dangerous things the ladies
have picked out. (*Moves a few things about, disturbing the quilt pieces which
cover the box. Steps back.*) No, Mrs. Peters doesn't need supervising. For
that matter, a sheriff's wife is married to the law. Ever think of it that way,
Mrs. Peters?

MRS. PETERS: Not — just that way.

145 SHERIFF: (*chuckling*) Married to the law. (*Moves toward the other room.*) I just
want you to come in here a minute, George. We ought to take a look at
these windows.

COUNTY ATTORNEY: *(scoffingly)* Oh, windows!

SHERIFF: We'll be right out, Mr. Hale.

Hale goes outside. The Sheriff follows the County Attorney into the other room. Then Mrs. Hale rises, hands tight together, looking intensely at Mrs. Peters, whose eyes make a slow turn, finally meeting Mrs. Hale's. A moment Mrs. Hale holds her, then her own eyes point the way to where the box is concealed. Suddenly Mrs. Peters throws back quilt pieces and tries to put the box in the bag she is wearing. It is too big. She opens box, starts to take bird out, cannot touch it, goes to pieces, stands there helpless. Sound of a knob turning in the other room. Mrs. Hale snatches the box and puts it in the pocket of her big coat. Enter County Attorney and Sheriff.

COUNTY ATTORNEY: *(facetiously)* Well, Henry, at least we found out that she was not going to quilt it. She was going to — what is it you call it, ladies?

MRS. HALE: *(her hand against her pocket)* We call it — knot it, Mr. Henderson.

Reading and Reacting

1. What key events have occurred before the start of the play? Why do you suppose these events are not presented in the play itself?
2. What are the "trifles" to which the title refers? How do these "trifles" advance the play's plot?
3. Glaspell's short story version of *Trifles* is called "A Jury of Her Peers." Who are Mrs. Wright's peers? What do you suppose the verdict would be if she were tried for her crime in 1916, when only men were permitted to serve on juries? If the trial were held today, do you think a jury might reach a different verdict?
4. *Trifles* is a one-act play, and all its action occurs in the Wrights' kitchen. Does this confined setting restrict the flow of the plot? Are there any advantages to this setting? Explain.
5. All background information about Mrs. Wright is provided by Mrs. Hale. Do you consider her to be a reliable source of information? Why or why not?
6. Mr. Hale's summary of his conversation with Mrs. Wright is the reader's only chance to hear her version of events. How might the play be different if Mrs. Wright appeared as a character?
7. *Trifles* is a relatively slow-moving, "talky" play, with very little physical action. Is this a weakness of the play, or is the slow development consistent with the effect Glaspell is trying to achieve? Explain.
8. How does each of the following events advance the play's action: the men's departure from the kitchen, the discovery of the quilt pieces, the discovery of the dead bird?
9. How do the county attorney's sarcastic comments and his patronizing attitude toward Mrs. Hale and Mrs. Peters advance the play's action?
10. How do Mrs. Peters's memories of her own life advance the action?
11. What assumptions about women do the male characters make? In what ways do the female characters support or challenge these assumptions?

12. In what sense is the process of making a quilt an appropriate metaphor for the plot of *Trifles*?

13. **JOURNAL ENTRY** Do you think Mrs. Hale and Mrs. Peters do the right thing by concealing evidence?

14. **CRITICAL PERSPECTIVE** In *American Drama from the Colonial Period through World War I*, Gary A. Richardson says that in *Trifles*, Glaspell developed a new structure for her action:

> While action in the traditional sense is minimal, Glaspell is nevertheless able to rivet attention on the two women, wed the audience to their perspective, and make a compelling case for the fairness of their actions. Existing on the margins of their society, Mrs. Peters and Mrs. Hale become emotional surrogates for the jailed Minnie Wright, effectively exonerating her action as "justifiable homicide."
> *Trifles* is carefully crafted to match Glaspell's subject matter — the action meanders, without a clearly delineated beginning, middle, or end . . . .

Exactly how does Glaspell "rivet attention on" Mrs. Hale and Mrs. Peters? Do you agree that the play's action "meanders, without a clearly delineated beginning, middle, and end"? If so, do you too see this "meandering" as appropriate for Glaspell's subject matter?

Related Works: "I Stand Here Ironing" (p. 309), "The Cask of Amontillado" (p. 350), "Everyday Use" (p. 469), "The Disappearance" (p. 371), "The Yellow Wallpaper" (p. 421), "Eveline" (p. 722), "Harlem" (p. 940), "After great pain, a formal feeling comes —" (p. 1159), *A Doll House* (p. 1454)

LORRAINE HANSBERRY (1930–1965) was born in Chicago and was raised by politically active parents who surrounded themselves with some of the most influential and important African-American intellectuals of the time. Her inspiration for *A Raisin in the Sun* came from her own experiences: her father moved their family into the white, middle-class suburb of Woodlawn at a time when Chicago was still legally segregated. Her family frequently faced the threats of racist mobs, but as a result of her father's lawsuit against the city's housing practices, the Illinois Supreme Court declared the housing segregation laws unconstitutional. *A Raisin in the Sun*, the first play written by an African-American woman to be produced on Broadway, received the best play award from the New York Drama Critics' Circle. In 1961, a film version of the play, starring Sidney Poitier, Claudia McNeil, and Ruby Dee received a special award at the Cannes Film Festival. Lorraine Hansberry died of cancer at the age of 34.

Cultural Context The action of this play is probably set around 1957, during a time of segregation and overt racism. Some particularly harmful manifestations of this racism were seen in the housing market, where unlawful practices kept African-Americans from buying homes. One such practice was *blockbusting*, where realtors persuaded white homeowners to sell their homes by warning them that the presence of African-Americans in their neighborhoods would increase the crime rate and decrease their property value. Another practice, known as *steering* directed minorities to or away from particular neighborhoods. Finally, *redlining* was the practice of denying mortgage loans or home insurance to minorities buying in certain neighborhoods (regardless of their financial qualifications). These practices were in effect at the time this play was written and were not outlawed until the Fair Housing Amendments Act of 1988.

A Raisin in the Sun (1959)

CHARACTERS (in order of appearance)

Ruth Younger	**George Murchison**
Travis Younger	**Mrs. Johnson**
Walter Lee Younger, brother	**Karl Lindner**
Beneatha Younger	**Bobo**
Lena Younger, Mama	**Moving men**
Joseph Asagas	

The action of the play is set in Chicago's Southside, sometime between World War II and the present.

ACT 1
SCENE 1 (FRIDAY MORNING.)

The Younger living room would be a comfortable and well-ordered room if it were not for a number of indestructible contradictions to this state of being. Its furnishings are typical and undistinguished and their primary feature now is that they have clearly had to accommodate the living of too many people for too many years — and they are tired. Still, we can see that at some time, a time probably no longer remembered by the family (except perhaps for Mama), the furnishings of this room were actually selected with care and love and even hope-and brought to this apartment and arranged with taste and pride.

That was a long time ago. Now the once loved pattern of the couch upholstery has to fight to show itself from under acres of crocheted doilies and couch covers which have themselves finally come to be more important than the upholstery. And here a table or a chair has been moved to disguise the worn places in the carpet, but the carpet has fought back by showing its weariness, with depressing uniformity, elsewhere on its surface.

Weariness has, in fact, won in this room. Everything has been polished, washed, sat on, used, scrubbed too often. All pretenses but living itself have long since vanished from the very atmosphere of this room.

Moreover, a section of this room, for it is not really a room unto itself, though the landlord's lease would make it seem so, slopes backward to provide a small kitchen area, where the family prepares the meals that are eaten in the living room proper, which must also serve as dining room. The single window that has been provided for these "two" rooms is located in this kitchen area. The sole natural light the family may enjoy in the course of a day is only that which fights its way through this little window.

At left, a door leads to a bedroom which is shared by Mama and her daughter, Beneatha. At right, opposite, is a second room (which in the beginning of the life of this apartment was probably a breakfast room) which serves as a bedroom for Walter and his wife, Ruth.

Time: Sometime between World War II and the present.
Place: Chicago's Southside.

At Rise: It is morning dark in the living room. Travis is asleep on the make-down bed at center. An alarm clock sounds from within the bedroom at right, and presently Ruth enters from that room and closes the door behind her. She crosses sleepily toward the window. As she passes her sleeping son she reaches down and shakes him a little. At the window she raises the shade and a dusky Southside morning light comes in feebly. She fills a pot with water and puts it on to boil. She calls to the boy, between yawns, in a slightly muffled voice.

Ruth is about thirty. We can see that she was a pretty girl, even exceptionally so, but now it is apparent that life has been little that she expected, and disappointment has already begun to hand in her face. In a few years, before thirty-five even, she will be known among her people as a "settled woman."

She crosses to her son and gives him a good, final, rousing shake.

RUTH: Come on now, boy, it's seven thirty! (*Her son sits up at last, in a stupor of sleepiness.*) I say hurry up, Travis! You ain't the only person in the world got to use a bathroom! (*The child, a sturdy, handsome little boy of ten or eleven, drags himself out of the bed and almost blindly takes his towels and "today's clothes" from drawers and a closet and goes out to the bathroom, which is in an outside hall and which is shared by another family or families on the same floor. Ruth crosses to the bedroom door at right and opens it and calls in to her husband.*) Walter Lee! . . . It's after seven thirty! Lemme see you do some waking up in there now! (*She waits.*) You better get up from there, man! It's after seven thirty I tell you. (*She waits again.*) All right, you just go ahead and lay there and next thing you know Travis be finished and Mr. Johnson'll be in there and you'll be fussing and cussing round here like a madman! And be late too! (*She waits, at the end of patience.*) Walter Lee — it's time for you to GET UP!

She waits another second and then starts to go into the bedroom, but is apparently satisfied that her husband has begun to get up. She stops, pulls the door to, and returns to the kitchen area. She wipes her face with a moist cloth and runs her fingers through her sleep-disheveled hair in a vain effort and ties an apron around her housecoat. The bedroom door at right opens and her husband stands in the doorway in his pajamas, which are rumpled and mismated. He is a lean, intense young man in his middle thirties, inclined to quick nervous movements and erratic speech habits — and always in his voice there is a quality of indictment.

WALTER: Is he out yet?

RUTH: What you mean *out*? He ain't hardly got in there good yet.

WALTER: (*wandering in, still more oriented to sleep than to a new day*) Well, what was you doing all that yelling for if I can't even get in there yet? (*Stopping and thinking.*) Check coming today?

5 **RUTH:** They said Saturday and this is just Friday and I hopes to God you ain't going to get up here first thing this morning and start talking to me 'bout no money — 'cause I 'bout don't want to hear it.

WALTER: Something the matter with you this morning?

RUTH: No — I'm just sleepy as the devil. What kind of eggs you want?

WALTER: Not scrambled. (*Ruth starts to scramble eggs.*) Paper come? (*Ruth points impatiently to the rolled up Tribune on the table, and he gets it and spreads it out and vaguely reads the front page.*) Set off another bomb yesterday.

RUTH: (*maximum indifference*) Did they?

WALTER: (*looking up*) What's the matter with you?   10

RUTH: Ain't nothing the matter with me. And don't keep asking me that this morning.

WALTER: Ain't nobody bothering you. (*Reading the news of the day absently again.*) Say Colonel McCormick is sick.

RUTH: (*affecting tea-party interest*) Is he now? Poor thing.

WALTER: (*sighing and looking at his watch*) Oh, me (*He waits.*) Now what is that boy doing in that bathroom all this time? He just going to have to start getting up earlier. I can't be being late to work on account of him fooling around in there.

RUTH: (*turning on him*) Oh, no he ain't going to be getting up no earlier   15
no such thing! It ain't his fault that he can't get to bed no earlier nights 'cause he got a bunch of crazy good-for-nothing clowns sitting up running their mouths in what is supposed to be his bedroom after ten o'clock at night.

WALTER: That's what you mad about, ain't it? The things I want to talk about with my friends just couldn't be important in your mind, could they?

He rises and finds a cigarette in her handbag on the table and crosses to the little window and looks out, smoking and deeply enjoying this first one.

RUTH: (*almost matter of factly, a complaint too automatic to deserve emphasis*) Why you always got to smoke before you eat in the morning?

WALTER: (*at the window*) Just look at 'em down there . . . Running and racing to work . . . (*He turns and faces his wife and watches her a moment at the stove, and then, suddenly*) You look young this morning, baby.

RUTH: (*indifferently*) Yeah?

WALTER: Just for a second — stirring them eggs. Just for a second it was — you   20
looked real young again. (*He reaches for her, she crosses away. Then, drily.*) It's gone now — you look like yourself again!

RUTH: Man, if you don't shut up and leave me alone.

WALTER: (*looking out to the street again*) First thing a man ought to learn in life is not to make love to no colored woman first thing in the morning. You all some eeeevil people at eight o'clock in the morning.

Travis appears in the hall doorway, almost fully dressed and quite wide awake news, his towels and pajamas across his shoulders. He opens the door and signals for his father to make the bathroom in a hurry.

TRAVIS: (*watching the bathroom*) Daddy, come on!

Walter gets his bathroom utensils and flies out to the bathroom.

RUTH: Sit down and have your breakfast, Travis.

25 **TRAVIS:** Mama, this is Friday. (*Gleefully.*) Check coming tomorrow, huh?

RUTH: You get your mind off money and eat your breakfast.

TRAVIS: (*eating*) This is the morning we supposed to bring the fifty cents to school.

RUTH: Well, I ain't got no fifty cents this morning.

TRAVIS: Teacher say we have to.

30 **RUTH:** I don't care what teacher say. I ain't got it. Eat your breakfast, Travis.

TRAVIS: I *am* eating.

RUTH: Hush up now and just eat!

The boy gives her an exasperated look for her lack of understanding, and eats grudgingly.

TRAVIS: You think Grandmama would have it?

RUTH: No! And I want you to stop asking your grandmother for money, you hear me?

35 **TRAVIS:** (*outraged*) Gaaaleee! I don't ask her, she just gimme it sometimes!

RUTH: Travis Willard Younger — I got too much on me this morning to be —

TRAVIS: Maybe Daddy —

RUTH: *Travis!*

The boy hushes abruptly. They are both quiet and tense for several seconds.

TRAVIS: (*presently*) Could I maybe go carry some groceries in front of the supermarket for a little while after school then?

40 **RUTH:** Just hush, I said (*Travis jabs his spoon into his cereal bowl viciously, and rests his head in anger upon his fists.*) If you through eating, you can get over there and make up your bed.

The boy obeys stiffly and crosses the room, almost mechanically, to the bed and more or less folds the bedding into a heap, then angrily gets his books and cap.

TRAVIS: (*sulking and standing apart from her unnaturally*) I'm gone.

RUTH: (*looking up from the stove to inspect him automatically*) Come here. (*He crosses to her and she studies his head.*) If you don't take this comb and fix this here head, you better! (*Travis puts down his books with a great sign of oppression, and crosses to the mirror. His mother mutters under her breath about his "slubbornness."*) 'Bout to march out of here with that head looking just like chickens slept in it! I just don't know where you get your slubborn way . . . And get your jacket, too. Looks chilly out this morning.

TRAVIS: (*with conspicuously brushed hair and jacket*) I'm gone.

RUTH: Get carfare and milk money — (*Waving one finger.*) — and not a single penny for no caps, you hear me?

45 **TRAVIS:** (*with sullen politeness*) Yes'm.

He turns in outrage to leave. His mother watches after him as in his frustration he approaches the door almost comically. When she speaks to him, her voice has become a very gentle tease.

RUTH: *(mocking; as she thinks he would say it)* Oh, Mama makes me so mad sometimes, I don't know what to do! *(She waits and continues to his back as he stands stock-still in front of the door.)* I wouldn't kiss that woman good-bye for nothing in this world this morning! *(The boy finally turns around and rolls his eyes at her, knowing the mood has changed and he is vindicated, he does not, however, move toward her yet.)* Not for nothing in this world! *(She finally laughs aloud at him and holds out her arms to him and we see that it is a way between them, very old and practiced. He crosses to her and allows her to embrace him warmly but keeps his face fixed with masculine rigidity. She holds him back from her presently and looks at him and runs her fingers over the features of his face. With utter gentleness—.)* Now—whose little old angry man are you?

TRAVIS: *(the masculinity and gruffness start to fade at last)* Aw gaalee—Mama...

RUTH: *(mimicking)* Aw—gaaaaalleeeee, Mama! *(She pushes him, with rough playfulness and finality, toward the door.)* Get on out of here or you going to be late.

TRAVIS: *(in the face of love, new aggressiveness)* Mama, could I *please* go carry groceries?

RUTH: Honey, it's starting to get so cold evenings.   50

WALTER: *(coming in from the bathroom and drawing a make-believe gun from a make-believe holster and shooting at his son)* What is it he wants to do?

RUTH: Go carry groceries after school at the supermarket.

WALTER: Well, let him go...

TRAVIS: *(quickly, to the ally)* I have to—she won't gimme the fifty cents...

WALTER: *(to his wife only)* Why not?   55

RUTH: *(simply, and with flavor)* 'Cause we don't have it.

WALTER: *(to Ruth only)* What you tell the boy things like that for? *(Reaching down into his pants with a rather important gesture.)* Here, son—

He hands the boy the coin, but his eyes are directed to his wife's. Travis takes the money happily.

TRAVIS: Thanks, Daddy.

He starts out. Ruth watches both of them with murder in her eyes. Walter stands and stares back at her with defiance, and suddenly reaches into his pocket again on an afterthought.

WALTER: *(without even looking at his son, still staring hard at his wife)* In fact, here's another fifty cents... Buy yourself some fruit today—or take a taxi-cab to school or something!

TRAVIS: Whoopee—   60

He leaps up and clasps his father around the middle with his legs, and they face each other in mutual appreciation; slowly Walter Lee peeks around the boy to catch the violent rays from his wife's eyes and draws his head back as if shot.

WALTER: You better get down now—and get to school, man.

TRAVIS: *(at the door)* O.K. Good-bye.

He exits.

WALTER: *(after him, pointing with pride)* That's my boy. *(She looks at him in disgust and turns back to her work.)* You know what I was thinking 'bout in the bathroom this morning?

RUTH: No.

65 WALTER: How come you always try to be so pleasant!

RUTH: What is there to be pleasant 'bout!

WALTER: You want to know what I was thinking 'bout in the bathroom or not!

RUTH: I know what you thinking 'bout.

WALTER: *(ignoring her)* 'Bout what me and Willy Harris was talking about last night.

70 RUTH: *(immediately — a refrain)* Willy Harris is a good-for-nothing loudmouth.

WALTER: Anybody who talks to me has got to be a good-for-nothing loudmouth, ain't he? And what you know about who is just a good-for-nothing loudmouth? Charlie Atkins was just a "good-for-nothing loudmouth" too, wasn't he! When he wanted me to go in the dry-cleaning business with him. And now — he's grossing a hundred thousand a year. A hundred thousand dollars a year! You still call *him* a loudmouth!

RUTH: *(bitterly)* Oh, Walter Lee . . .

She folds her head on her arms over the table.

WALTER: *(rising and coming to her and standing over her)* You tired, ain't you? Tired of everything. Me, the boy, the way we live — this beat-up hole — everything. Ain't you? *(She doesn't look up, doesn't answer)* So tired — moaning and groaning all the time, but you wouldn't do nothing to help, would you? You couldn't be on my side that long for nothing, could you?

RUTH: Walter, please leave me alone.

75 WALTER: A man needs for a woman to back him up . . .

RUTH: Walter —

WALTER: Mama would listen to you. You know she listen to you more than she do me and Bennie. She think more of you. All you have to do is just sit down with her when you drinking your coffee one morning and talking 'bout things like you do and —*(He sits down beside her and demonstrates graphically what he thinks her methods and tone should be.)*— you just sip your coffee, see, and say easy like that you been thinking 'bout that deal Walter Lee is so interested in, 'bout the store and all, and sip some more coffee, like what you saying ain't really that important to you-And the next thing you know, she be listening good and asking you questions and when I come home — I can tell her the details. This ain't no fly-by-night proposition, baby. I mean we figured it out, me and Willy and Bobo.

RUTH: *(with a frown)* Bobo?

WALTER: Yeah. You see, this little liquor store we got in mind cost seventy-five thousand and we figured the initial investment on the place be 'bout thirty thousand, see. That be ten thousand each. Course, there's a couple of hundred you got to pay so's you don't spend your life just waiting for them clowns to let your license get approved —

80 RUTH: You mean graft?

Walter: *(frowning impatiently)* Don't call it that. See there, that just goes to show you what women understand about the world. Baby, don't *nothing* happen for you in the world 'less you pay *somebody* off!

Ruth: Walter, leave me alone! *(She raises her head and stares at him vigorously—then says, more quietly.)* Eat your eggs, they gonna be cold.

Walter: *(straightening up from her and looking off)* That's it. There you are. Man say to his woman: I got me a dream. His woman say: Eat your eggs. *(Sadly, but gaining in power.)* Man say: I got to take hold of this here world, baby I And a woman will say: Eat your eggs and go to work. *(Passionately now.)* Man say: I got to change my life, I'm choking to death, baby! And his woman say—*(In utter anguish as he brings his fists down on his thighs.)*—Your eggs is getting cold!

Ruth: *(softly)* Walter, that ain't none of our money.

Walter: *(not listening at all or even looking at her)* This morning, I was lookin' in   85
the mirror and thinking about it . . . I'm thirty-five years old; I been married eleven years and I got a boy who sleeps in the living room —*(Very, very quietly.)*— and all I got to give him is stories about how rich white people live . . .

Ruth: Eat your eggs, Walter.

Walter: *(slams the table and jumps up)*— DAMN MY EGGS — DAMN ALL THE EGGS THAT EVER WAS!

Ruth: Then go to work.

Walter: *(looking up at her)* See — I'm trying to talk to you 'bout myself — *(Shaking his head with the repetition.)*— and all you can say is eat them eggs and go to work.

Ruth: *(wearily)* Honey, you never say nothing new. I listen to you every day,   90
every night and every morning, and you never say nothing new. *(Shrugging)* So you would rather *be* Mr. Arnold than be his chauffeur. So — I would *rather* be living in Buckingham Palace.

Walter: That is just what is wrong with the colored woman in this world . . . Don't understand about building their men up and making 'em feel like they somebody. Like they can do something.

Ruth: *(drily, but to hurt)* There *are* colored men who do things.

Walter: No thanks to the colored woman.

Ruth: Well, being a colored woman, I guess I can't help myself none.

She rises and gets the ironing board and sets it up and attacks a huge pile of rough-dried clothes, sprinkling them in preparation for the ironing and then rolling them into tight fat balls.

Walter: *(mumbling)* We one group of men tied to a race of women with small   95
minds!

His sister Beneatha enters. She is about twenty, as slim and intense as her brother. She is not as pretty as her sister-in-law, but her lean, almost intellectual face has a handsomeness of its own. She wears a bright-red flannel nightie, and her thick hair stands wildly about her head. Her speech is a mixture of many things; it is different from the rest of the family's insofar as education has permeated her sense of

English — and perhaps the Midwest rather than the South has finally — at last — won out in her inflection; but not altogether, because over all of it is a soft slurring and transformed use of vowels which is the decided influence of the Southside. She passes through the room without looking at either Ruth or Walter and goes to the outside door and looks, a little blindly, out to the bathroom. She sees that it has been lost to the Johnsons. She closes the door with a sleepy vengeance and crosses to the table and sits down a little defeated.

BENEATHA: I am going to start timing those people.

WALTER: You should get up earlier.

BENEATHA: *(her face in her hands. She is still fighting the urge to go back to bed)* Really — would you suggest dawn? Where's the paper?

WALTER: *(pushing the paper across the table to her as he studies her almost clinically, as though he has never seen her before)* You a horrible-looking chick at this hour.

100 BENEATHA: *(drily)* Good morning, everybody.

WALTER: *(senselessly)* How is school coming?

BENEATHA: *(in the same spirit)* Lovely. Lovely. And you know, biology is the greatest. *(Looking up at him.)* I dissected something that looked just like you yesterday.

WALTER: I just wondered if you've made up your mind and everything.

BENEATHA: *(gaining in sharpness and impatience)* And what did I answer yesterday morning — and the day before that?

105 RUTH: *(from the ironing board, like someone disinterested and old)* Don't be so nasty, Bennie.

BENEATHA: *(still to her brother)* And the day before that and the day before that!

WALTER: *(defensively)* I'm interested in you. Something wrong with that? Ain't many girls who decide —

WALTER AND BENEATHA *(in unison):* "to be a doctor."

Silence.

WALTER: Have we figured out yet just exactly how much medical school is going to cost?

110 RUTH: Walter Lee, why don't you leave that girl alone and get out of here to work?

BENEATHA: *(exits to the bathroom and bangs on the door)* Come on out of there, please!

She comes back into the room.

WALTER: *(looking at his sister intently)* You know the check is coming tomorrow.

BENEATHA: *(turning on him with a sharpness all her own)* That money belongs to Mama, Walter, and it's for her to decide how she wants to use it. I don't care if she wants to buy a house or a rocket ship or just nail it up somewhere and look at it. It's hers. Not ours — *hers.*

WALTER: *(bitterly)* Now ain't that fine! You just got your mother's interest at heart, ain't you, girl? You such a nice girl — but if Mama got that money she can always take a few thousand and help you through school too — can't she?

BENEATHA: I have never asked anyone around here to do anything for me!   115

WALTER: No! And the line between asking and just accepting when the time comes is big and wide — ain't it!

BENEATHA: (with fury) What do you want from me, Brother — that I quit school or just drop dead, which!

WALTER: I don't want nothing but for you to stop acting holy 'round here. Me and Ruth done made some sacrifices for you — why can't you do something for the family?

RUTH: Walter, don't be dragging me in it.

WALTER: You are in it — Don't you get up and go work in somebody's kitchen   120 for the last three years to help put clothes on her back?

RUTH: Oh, Walter — that's not fair . . .

WALTER: It ain't that nobody expects you to get on your knees and say thank you, Brother; thank you, Ruth; thank you, Mama — and thank you, Travis, for wearing the same pair of shoes for two semesters —

BENEATHA: (dropping to her knees) Well — I do — all right? — thank everybody! And forgive me for ever wanting to be anything at all (Pursuing him on her knees across the floor.) FORGIVE ME, FORGIVE ME, FORGIVE ME!

RUTH: Please stop it! Your mama'll hear you.

WALTER: Who the hell told you you had to be a doctor? If you so crazy 'bout   125 messing 'round with sick people — then go be a nurse like other women — or just get married and be quiet . . .

BENEATHA: Well — you finally got it said . . . It took you three years but you finally got it said. Walter, give up; leave me alone — it's Mama's money.

WALTER: *He was my father, too!*

BENEATHA: So what? He was mine, too — and Travis' grandfather — but the insurance money belongs to Mama. Picking on me is not going to make her give it to you to invest in any liquor stores — (Under breath, dropping into a chair.) — and I for one say, God bless Mama for that!

WALTER: (to Ruth) See — did you hear? Did you hear!

RUTH: Honey, please go to work.   130

WALTER: Nobody in this house is ever going to understand me.

BENEATHA: Because you're a nut.

WALTER: Who's a nut?

BENEATHA: You — you are a nut. Thee is mad, boy.

WALTER: (looking at his wife and his sister from the door, very sadly) The world's   135 most backward race of people, and that's a fact.

BENEATHA: (turning slowly in her chair) And then there are all those prophets who would lead us out of the wilderness — (Walter slams out of the house) — into the swamps!

RUTH: Bennie, why you always gotta be pickin' on your brother? Can't you be a little sweeter sometimes? (Door opens. Walter walks in. He fumbles with his cap, starts to speak, clear throat, looks everywhere but at Ruth. Finally:)

WALTER: (to Ruth) I need some money for carfare.

RUTH: (*looks at him, then warms; teasing, but tenderly*) Fifty cents? (*She goes to her bag and gets money.*) Here—take a taxi!

Walter exits. Mama enters. She is a woman in her early sixties, full-bodied and strong. She is one of those women of a certain grace and beauty who wear it so unobtrusively that it takes a while to notice. Her dark-brown face is surrounded by the total whiteness of her hair, and, being a woman who has adjusted to many things in life and overcome many more, her face is full of strength. She has, we can see, wit and faith of a kind that keep her eyes lit and full of interest and expectancy. She is, in a word, a beautiful woman. Her bearing is perhaps most like the noble bearing of the women of the Hereros of Southwest Africa—rather as if she imagines that as she walks she still bears a basket or a vessel upon her head. Her speech, on the other hand, is as careless as her carriage is precise—she is inclined to slur everything—but her voice is perhaps not so much quiet as simply soft.

140 **MAMA:** Who that 'round here slamming doors at this hour?

She crosses through the room, goes to the window, opens it, and brings in a feeble little plant growing doggedly in a small pot on the window sill. She feels the dirt and puts it back out.

RUTH: That was Walter Lee. He and Bennie was at it again.

MAMA: My children and they tempers. Lord, if this little old plant don't get more sun than it's been getting it ain't never going to see spring again. (*She turns from the window.*) What's the matter with you this morning, Ruth? You looks right peaked. You aiming to iron all them things? Leave some for me. I'll get to 'em this afternoon. Bennie honey, it's too drafty for you to be sitting 'round half dressed. Where's you robe?

BENEATHA: In the cleaners.

MAMA: Well, go get mine and put it on.

145 **BENEATHA:** I'm not cold, Mama, honest.

MAMA: I know—but you so thin

BENEATHA: (*irritably*) Mama, I'm not cold.

MAMA: (*seeing the make down bed as Travis has left it*) Lord have mercy, look at that poor bed. Bless his heart—he tries, don't he?

She moves to the bed Travis has sloppily made up.

RUTH:. No—he don't half try at all 'cause he knows you going to come along behind him and fix everything. That's just how come he don't know how to do nothing right now—you done spoiled that boy so.

150 **MAMA:** (*folding bedding*) Well—he's a little boy. Ain't supposed to know 'bout housekeeping. My baby, that's what he is. What you fix for his breakfast this morning?

RUTH: (*angrily*) I feed my son, Lena!

MAMA: I ain't meddling—(*Under breath; busy-bodyish.*) I just noticed all last week he had cold cereal, and when it starts getting this chilly in the fall a child ought to have some hot grits of something when he goes out in the cold—

RUTH: *(furious)* I gave him hot oats—is that all right!

MAMA: I ain't meddling. *(Pause.)* Put a lot of nice butter on it? *(Ruth shoots her an angry look and does not reply.)* He likes lots of butter.

RUTH: *(exasperated)* Lena—   155

MAMA: *(to Beneatha. Mama is inclined to wander conversationally sometimes)* What was you and your brother fussing 'bout this morning?

BENEATHA: It's not important, Mama.

She gets up and goes to look out at the bathroom, which is apparently free, and she picks up her towels and rushes out.

MAMA: What was they fighting about?

RUTH: Now you know as well as I do.

MAMA: *(shaking her head)* Brother still worrying hisself sick about that money?   160

RUTH: You know he is.

MAMA: You had breakfast?

RUTH: Some coffee.

MAMA: Girl, you better start eating and looking after yourself better. You almost thin as Travis.

RUTH: Lena—   165

MAMA: Un-hunh?

RUTH: What are you going to do with it?

MAMA: Now don't you start, child. It's too early in the morning to be talking about money. It ain't Christian.

RUTH: It's just that he got his heart set on that store—

MAMA: You mean that liquor store that Willy Harris want him to invest in?   170

RUTH: Yes—

MAMA: We ain't no business people, Ruth. We just plain working folks.

RUTH: Ain't nobody business people till they go into business. Walter Lee say colored people ain't never going to start getting ahead till they start gambling on some different kinds of things in the world—investments and things.

MAMA: What done got into you, girl? Walter Lee done finally sold you on investing.

RUTH: No. Mama, something is happening between Walter and me. I don't   175
know what it is—but he needs something—something I can't give him any more. He needs this chance, Lena.

MAMA: *(frowning deeply)* But liquor, honey—

RUTH: Well—like Walter say—I spec people going to always be drinking themselves some liquor.

MAMA: Well—whether they drinks it or not ain't none of my business. But whether I go into business selling it to 'em *is*, and I don't want that on my ledger this late in life. *(Stopping suddenly and studying her daughter (in law.)* Ruth Younger, what's the matter with you today? You look like you could fall over right there.

RUTH: I'm tired.

MAMA: Then you better stay home from work today.   180

RUTH: I can't stay home. She'd be calling up the agency and screaming at them, "My girl didn't come in today— send me somebody! My girl didn't come in!" Oh, she just have a fit. . .

MAMA: Well, let her have it. I'll just call her up and say you got the flu—

RUTH: *(laughing)* Why the flu?

MAMA: 'Cause it sounds respectable to 'em. Something white people get, too. They know 'bout the flu. Otherwise they think you been cut up or something when you tell 'em you sick.

185   **RUTH:** I got to go in. We need the money.

MAMA: Somebody would of thought my children done all but starved to death the way they talk about money here late. Child, we got a great big old check coming tomorrow.

RUTH: *(sincerely, but also self-righteously)* Now that's your money. It ain't got nothing to do with me. We all feel like that—Walter and Bennie and me—even Travis.

MAMA: *(thoughtfully, and suddenly very far away)* Ten thousand dollars—

RUTH: Sure is wonderful.

190   **MAMA:** Ten thousand dollars.

RUTH: You know what you should do, Miss Lena? You should take yourself a trip somewhere. To Europe or South America or someplace—

MAMA: *(throwing up her hands at the thought)* Oh, child!

RUTH: I'm serious. Just pack up and leave! Go on away and enjoy yourself some. Forget about the family and have yourself a ball for once in your life—

MAMA: *(drily)* You some like I'm just about ready to die. Who'd go with me? What I look like wandering 'round Europe by myself?

195   **RUTH:** Shoot— these here rich white women do it all the time. They don't think nothing of packing up they suitcases and piling on one of them big steamships and— swoosh!— they gone, child.

MAMA: Something always told me I wasn't no rich white woman.

RUTH: Well— what are you going to do with it then?

MAMA: I ain't rightly decided. *(Thinking. She speaks now with emphasis.)* Some of it got to be put away for Beneatha and her schoolin'— and ain't nothing going to touch that part of it. Nothing *(She waits several seconds, trying to make up her mind about something, and looks at Ruth a little tentatively before going on.)* Been thinking that we maybe could meet the notes on a little old two-story somewhere, with a yard where Travis could play in the summertime, if we use part of the insurance for a down payment and everybody kind of pitch in. I could maybe take on a little day work again, few days a week—

RUTH: *(studying her mother-in-law furtively and concentrating on her ironing, anxious to encourage without seeming to)* Well, Lord knows, we've put enough rent into this here rat trap to pay for four houses by now.

200   **MAMA:** *(looking up at the words "rat trap" and then looking around and leaning back and sighing—in a suddenly reflective mood—)* "Rat trap"— yes, that's all it is. *(Smiling.)* I remember just as well the day me and Big Walter moved in here. Hadn't been married but two weeks and wasn't planning on living

here no more than a year. (*She shakes her head at the dissolved dream.*) We was going to set away, little by little, don't you know, and buy a little place out in Morgan Park. We had even picked out the house. (*Chuckling a little.*) Looks right dumpy today. But Lord, child, you should know all the dreams I had 'bout buying that house and fixing it up and making me a little garden in the back—(*She waits and stops smiling.*) And didn't none of it happen.

Dropping her hands in a futile gesture.

RUTH: (*keep her head down, ironing*) Yes, life can be a barrel of disappointments, sometimes.

MAMA: Honey, Big Walter would come in here some nights back then and slump down on that couch there and just look at the rug, and look at me and look at the rug and then back at me — and I'd know he was down then . . . really down. (*After a second very long and thoughtful pause; she is seeing back to times that only she can see.*) And then, Lord, when I lost that baby—little Claude—I almost thought I was going to lose Big Walter too. Oh, that man grieved hisself! He was one man to love his children.

RUTH: Ain't nothin' can tear at you lik losin' your baby.

MAMA: I guess that's how come that man finally worked hisself to death like he done. Like he was fighting his own war with this here world that took his baby from him.

RUTH: He sure was a fine man, all right. I always liked Mr. Younger.   205

MAMA: Crazy 'bout his children! God knows there was plenty wrong with Walter Younger—hard-headed, mean, kind of wild with women—plenty wrong with him. But he sure loved his children. Always wanted them to have something—be something. That's where Brother gets all these notions, I reckon. Big Walter used to say, he'd get right wet in the eyes sometimes, lean his head back with the water standing in his eyes and say, "Seem like God didn't see fit to give the black man nothing but dreams—but He did give us children to make them dreams seem worthwhile." (*She smiles.*) He could talk like that, don't you know.

RUTH: Yes, he sure could. He was a good man, Mr. Younger.

MAMA: Yes, a fine man—just couldn't never catch up with his dreams, that's all.

Beneatha comes in, brushing her hair and looking up to the ceiling, where the sound of a vacuum cleaner has started up.

BENEATHA: What could be so dirty on that woman's rugs that she has to vacuum them every single day?

RUTH: I wish certain young women 'round here who I could name would take   210
inspiration about certain rugs in a certain apartment I could also mention.

BENEATHA: (*shrugging*) How much cleaning can a house need, for Christ's sakes.

MAMA: (*not liking the Lord's name used thus*) Bennie!

RUTH: Just listen to her —just listen!

BENEATHA: Oh, God!

MAMA: If you use the Lord's name just one more time—   215

BENEATHA: (*a bit of a whine*) Oh, Mama—

RUTH: Fresh—just fresh as salt, this girl!

BENEATHA: *(drily)* Well—if the salt loses its savor—

MAMA: Now that will do. I just ain't going to have you 'round here reciting the scriptures in vain—you hear me?

220 BENEATHA: How did I manage to get on everybody's wrong side by just walking into a room?

RUTH: If you weren't so fresh—

BENEATHA: Ruth, I'm twenty years old.

MAMA: What time you be home from school today?

BENEATHA: Kind of late. *(With enthusiasm.)* Madeline is going to start my guitar lessons today.

Mama and Ruth look up with the same expression.

225 MAMA: Your *what* kind of lessons?

BENEATHA: Guitar.

RUTH: Oh, Father!

MAMA: How come you done taken it in your mind to learn to play the guitar?

BENEATHA: I just want to, that's all.

230 MAMA: *(smiling)* Lord, child, don't you know what to do with yourself? How long it going to be before you get tired of this now—like you got tired of that little play-acting group you joined last year? *(Looking at Ruth.)* And what was it the year before that?

RUTH: The horseback-riding club for which she bought that fifty-five-dollar riding habit that's been hanging in the closer ever since!

MAMA: *(to Beneatha)* Why you got to flit so from one thing to another, baby?

BENEATHA: *(sharply)* I just want to learn to play the guitar. Is there anything wrong with that?

MAMA: Ain't nobody trying to stop you. I just wonders sometimes why you has to flit so from one thing to another all the time. You ain't never done nothing with all that camera equipment you brought home—

235 BENEATHA: I don't flit! I—I experiment with different forms of expression—

RUTH: Like riding a horse?

BENEATHA: —People have to express themselves one way or another.

MAMA: What is it you want to express?

BENEATHA: *(angrily)* Me! *(Mama and Ruth look at each other and burst into raucous laughter.)* Don't worry—I don't expect you to understand.

240 MAMA: *(to change the subject)* Who you going out with tomorrow night?

BENEATHA: *(with displeasure)* George Murchison again.

MAMA: *(pleased)* Oh you getting a little sweet on him?

RUTH: You ask me, this child ain't sweet on nobody but herself—*(under breath.)* Express herself!

They laugh.

BENEATHA: Oh I like George all right, Mama. I mean I like him enough to go out with him and stuff, but—

245 RUTH: *(for devilment)* What does *and stuff* mean?

BENEATHA: Mind your own business.

MAMA: Stop picking at her now, Ruth. (*She chuckles — then a suspicious sudden look at her daughter as she turns in her chair for emphasis.*) What DOES it mean?

BENEATHA: (*wearily*) Oh, I just mean I couldn't ever really be serious about George. He's — he's so shallow.

RUTH: Shallow — what do you mean he's shallow? He's *rich!*

MAMA: Hush, Ruth.   250

BENEATHA: I know he's rich. He knows he's rich, too.

RUTH: Well — what other qualities a man got to have to satisfy you, little girl?

BENEATHA: You wouldn't even begin to understand. Anybody who married Walter could not possibly understand.

Mama (outraged) What kind of way is that to talk about your brother?

BENEATHA: Brother is a flip — let's face it.   255

MAMA: (*to Ruth, helplessly*) What's a flip?

RUTH: (*glad to add kindling*) She's saying he's crazy.

BENEATHA: Not crazy. Brother isn't really crazy yet — he — he's an elaborate neurotic.

MAMA: Hush your mouth!

BENEATHA: As for George. Well. George looks good — he's got a beautiful   260
car and he takes me to nice places and, as my sister-in-law says, he is probably the richest boy I will ever get to know and I even like him some-times — but if the Youngers are sitting around waiting to see if their little Bennie is going to tie up the family with the Murchisons, they are wast-ing their time.

RUTH: You mean you wouldn't marry George Murchison if he asked you some-day? That pretty, rich thing? Honey, I knew you was odd —

BENEATHA: No I would not marry him if all I felt for him was what I feel now. Besides, George's family wouldn't really like it.

MAMA: Why not?

BENEATHA: Oh, Mama — The Murchisons are honest-to-God-real-*live*-rich colored people, and the only people in the world who are more snobbish than rich white people are rich colored people. I thought everybody knew that. I've met Mrs. Murchison. She's a scene!

MAMA: You must not dislike people 'cause they well off, honey.   265

BENEATHA: Why not? It makes just as much sense as disliking people 'cause they are poor, and lots of people do that.

RUTH: (*a wisdom-of-the-ages manner. To Mama*) Well, she'll get over some of this —

BENEATHA: Get over it? What are you talking about, Ruth? Listen, I'm going to be a doctor. I'm not worried about who I'm going to marry yet — if I ever get married.

MAMA AND RUTH: *If!*

MAMA: Now, Bennie —   270

BENEATHA: Oh, I probably will . . . but first I'm going to be a doctor, and George, for one, still thinks that's pretty funny. I couldn't be bothered with

that. I am going to be a doctor and everybody around here better understand that!

MAMA: *(kindly)* 'Course you going to be a doctor, honey, God willing.

BENEATHA: *(drily)* God hasn't got a thing to do with it.

MAMA: Beneatha — that just wasn't necessary.

275   BENEATHA: Well — neither is God. I get sick of hearing about God.

MAMA: Beneatha!

BENEATHA: I mean it! I'm just tired of hearing about God all the time. What
has He got to do with anything? Does He pay tuition?

MAMA: You 'bout to get your fresh little jaw slapped!

RUTH: That's just what she needs, all right!

280   BENEATHA: Why? Why can't I say what I want to around here, like everybody
else?

MAMA: It don't sound nice for a young girl to say things like that — you wasn't
brought up that way. Me and your father went to trouble of get you and
Brother to church every Sunday.

BENEATHA: Mama, you don't understand. It's all a matter of ideas, and God is
just one idea I don't accept. It's not important. I am not going out and being immoral or commit crimes because I don't believe in God. I don't even
think about it. It's just that I get tired of Him getting credit for all the
things the human race achieves through its own stubborn effort. There simply is no blasted God — there is only man and it is *He* who makes miracles!

*Mama absorbs this speech, studies her daughter, and rises slowly and crosses to Beneatha
and slaps her powerfully across the face. After, there is only silence and the daughter drops
her eyes from her mother's face, and Mama is very tall before her.*

MAMA: Now — you say after me, in my mother's house there is still God. *(There
is a long pause and Beneatha stares at the floor wordlessly. Mama repeats the
phrase with precision and cool emotion.)* In my mother's house there is still God.

BENEATHA: In my mother's house there is still God.
A long pause,

285   MAMA: *(walking away from Beneatha, too disturbed for triumphant posture. Stopping and turning back to her daughter)* There are some ideas we ain't going to
have in this house. Not long as I am at the head of this family.

BENEATHA: Yes, ma'am.

Mama walks out of the room.

RUTH: *(almost gently, with profound understanding)* You think you a woman.
Bennie — but you still a little girl. What you did was childish — so you got
treated like a child.

BENEATHA: I see. *(Quietly.)* I also see that everybody thinks it's all right for
Mama to be a tyrant. But all the tyranny in the world will never put a God
in the heavens!

She picks up her books and goes out. Pause.

RUTH: *(goes to Mama's door)* She said she was sorry.

290   MAMA: *(coming out, going to her plant)* They frightens me, Ruth. My children.

RUTH: You got good children, Lena. They just a little off sometimes—but they're good.

MAMA: No—there's something come down between me and them that don't let us understand each other and I don't know what it is. One done almost lost his mind thinking 'bout money all the time and the other done commence to talk about things I can't seem to understand in no form or fashion. What is it that's changing, Ruth.

RUTH: *(soothingly, older than her years)* Now . . . you taking it all too seriously. You just got strong-willed children and it takes a strong woman like you to keep 'em in hand.

MAMA: *(looking at her plant and sprinkling a little water on it)* They spirited all right, my children. Got to admit they got spirit—Bennie and Walter Like this little old plant that ain't never had enough sunshine or nothing—and look at it. . .

She has her back to Ruth, who has had to stop ironing and lean against something and put the back of her hand to her forehead.

RUTH: *(trying to keep Mama from noticing)* You . . . sure . . . loves that little old thing, don't you?

295

MAMA: Well, I always wanted me a garden like I used to see sometimes at the back of the houses down home. This plant is close as I ever got to having one. *(She looks out of the window as she replaces the plant.)* Lord, ain't nothing as dreary as the view from this window on a dreary day, is there? Why ain't you singing this morning, Ruth? Sing that "No Ways Tired." That song always lifts me up so—*(She turns at last to see that Ruth has slipped quietly to the floor, in a state of semiconsciousness.)* Ruth! Ruth honey—what's the matter with you . . . Ruth!

Curtain.

SCENE 2 *(The following morning.)*

It is the following morning; a Saturday morning, and house cleaning is in progress at the Youngers'. Furniture has been shoved hither and yon and Mama is giving the kitchen area walls a washing down. Beneatha, in dungarees, with a handkerchief tied around her face, is spraying insecticide into the cracks in the walls. As they work, the radio is on and a Southside disk jockey program is inappropriately filling the house with a rather exotic saxophone blues. Travis, the sole idle one, is leaning on his arms, looking out of the window.

TRAVIS: Grandmama, that stuff Bennie is using smells awful. Can I go downstairs, please?

MAMA: Did you get all them chores done already? I ain't seen you doing much.

TRAVIS: Yes'm—finished early. Where did Mama go this morning?

MAMA: *(looking at Beneatha)* She had to go on a little errand.

The phone rings. Beneatha runs to answer it and reaches it before Walter, who has entered from bedroom.

5

TRAVIS: Where?

MAMA: To tend to her business.

BENEATHA: Haylo . . . (*Disappointed.*) Yes, he is. (*She tosses the phone to Walter, who barely catches it.*) It's Willie Harris again.

WALTER: (*as privately as possible under Mama's gaze*) Hello, Willie. Did you get the papers from the lawyer? . . . No, not yet. I told you the mailman doesn't get here till ten-thirty . . . No, I'll come there . . . Yeah! Right away. (*He hangs up and goes for his coat.*)

BENEATHA: Brother, where did Ruth go?

10 WALTER: (*as he exits*) How should I know!

TRAVIS: Aw come on, Grandma. Can I go outside?

MAMA: Oh, I guess so. You stay right in front of the house, though, and keep a good lookout for the postman.

TRAVIS: Yes'm. (*He darts into bedroom for stickball and bat, reenters, and sees Beneatha on her knees spraying under sofa with behind upraised. He edges closer to the target, takes aim, and lets her have it. She screams.*) Leave them poor little cockroaches alone, they ain't bothering you none! (*He runs as she swings the spraygun at him viciously and playfully.*) Grandma! Grandma!

MAMA: Look out there, girl, before you be spilling some of that stuff on that child!

15 TRAVIS: (*safely behind the bastion of Mama*) That's right—look out, now! (*He exits.*)

BENEATHA: (*drily*) I can't imagine that it would hurt him—it has never hurt the roaches.

MAMA: Well, little boys' hides ain't as tough as Southside roaches. You better get over there behind the bureau. I seen one marching out of there like Napoleon yesterday.

BENEATHA: There's really only one way to get rid of them, Mama—

MAMA: How?

20 BENEATHA: Set fire to this building! Mama, where did Ruth go?

MAMA: (*Looking at her with meaning*) To the doctor, I think.

BENEATHA: The doctor? What's the matter? (*They exchange glances.*) You don't think—

MAMA: (*with her sense drama*) Now I ain't saying what I think. But I ain't never been wrong 'bout a woman neither.

The phone rings.

BENEATHA: (*at the phone*) Hay-lo . . . (*Pause, and a moment of recognition.*) Well—when did you get back! . . . And how was it? . . . Of course I've missed you—in my way . . . This morning? No . . . house cleaning and all that and Mama hates it if I let people come over when the house is like this . . . You *have?* Well, that's different . . . What is it— Oh, what the hell, come on over . . . Right, see you then. *Arrivederci.*

She hangs up.

25 MAMA: (*who has listened vigorously, as is her habit*) Who is that you inviting over here with this house looking like this? You ain't got the pride you was born with!

BENEATHA: Asagai doesn't care how houses look, Mama—he's an intellectual.

MAMA: *Who?*

BENEATHA: Asagai—Joseph Asagai. He's an African boy I met on campus. He's been studying in Canada all summer.

MAMA: What's his name?

BENEATHA: Asagai, Joseph. Ah-sah-guy . . . He's from Nigeria.   30

MAMA: Oh, that's the little country that was founded by slaves way back . . .

BENEATHA: No, Mama—that's Liberia.

MAMA: I don't think I never met no African before.

BENEATHA: Well, do me a favor and don't ask him a whole lot of ignorant questions about Africans. I mean, do they wear clothes and all that—

MAMA: Well, now, I guess if you think we so ignorant 'round here maybe you   35
shouldn't bring your friends here—

BENEATHA: It's just that people ask such crazy things. All anyone seems to know about when it comes to Africa is Tarzan—

MAMA: *(indignantly)* Why should I know anything about Africa?

BENEATHA: Why do you give money at church for the missionary work?

MAMA: Well, that's to help save people.

BENEATHA: You mean save them from *heathenism*—   40

MAMA: *(innocently)* Yes.

BENEATHA: I'm afraid they need more salvation from the British and the French.

Ruth comes in forlornly and pulls off her coat with dejection. They both turn to look at her.

RUTH: *(dispiritedly)* Well, I guess from all the happy faces—everybody knows.

BENEATHA: You pregnant?

MAMA: Lord have mercy, I sure hope it's a little old girl. Travis ought to have a   45
sister.

Beneatha and Ruth give her a hopeless look for his grandmotherly enthusiasm.

BENEATHA: How far along are you?

RUTH: Two months.

BENEATHA: Did you mean to? I mean did you plan it or was it an accident?

MAMA: What do you know about planning or not planning?

BENEATHA: Oh, Mama.   50

RUTH: *(wearily)* She's twenty years old, Lena.

BENEATHA: Did you plan it, Ruth?

RUTH: Mind your own business.

BENEATHA: It is my business—where is he going to live, on the *roof?* (*There is silence following the remark as the three women react to the sense of it.*) Gee—I didn't mean that, Ruth, honest. Gee, I don't feel like that at all. I—I think it is wonderful.

RUTH: *(dully)* Wonderful.   55

BENEATHA: Yes—really.

MAMA: *(looking at Ruth, worried)* Doctor say everything going to be all right?

RUTH: *(far away)* Yes—she says everything is going to be fine . . .

MAMA: *(immediately suspicious)* "She"—What doctor you went to?

Ruth folds over, near hysteria.

60 MAMA: *(worriedly hovering over Ruth)* Ruth honey — what's the matter with you — you sick?

Ruth has her fists clenched on her thighs and is fighting hard to suppress a scream that seems to be rising in her.

BENEATHA: What's the matter with her, Mama?

MAMA: *(working her fingers in Ruth's shoulders to relax her)* She be all right. Women gets right depressed sometimes when they get her way. *(Speaking softly, expertly, rapidly.)* Now you just relax. That's right . . . just lean back, don't think 'bout nothing at all . . . nothing at all —

RUTH: I'm all right . . .

The glassy eyed look melts and then she collapses into a fit of heavy sobbing. The belt rings.

BENEATHA: Oh, my God — that must be Asagai.

65 MAMA: *(to Ruth)* Come on now, honey. You need to lie down and rest awhile . . . then have some nice hot food.

They exit, Ruth's weight on her mother-in-law. Beneatha, herself profoundly disturbed, opens the door to admit a rather dramatic-looking young man with a large package.

ASAGAI: Hello, Alaiyo —

BENEATHA: *(holding the door open and regarding him with pleasure)* Hello . . . *(Long pause.)* Well — come in. And please excuse everything. My mother was very upset about my letting anyone come here with the place like this.

ASAGAI: *(coming into the room)* You look disturbed too . . . Is something wrong?

BENEATHA: *(still at the door, absently)* Yes . . . we've all got acute ghetto-itsu. *(She smiles and comes toward him, finding a cigarette and sitting.)* So — sit down! No! Wait! *(She whips the spraygun off sofa where she had left it and puts the cushions back. At last perches on arm of sofa. He sits.)* So, how was Canada?

70 ASAGAI: *(a sophisticate)* Canadian.

BENEATHA: *(looking at him)* Asagai, I'm very glad you are back.

ASAGAI: *(looking back at her in turn)* Are you really?

BENEATHA: Yes — very.

ASAGAI: Why? — you were quite glad when I went away. What happened?

75 BENEATHA: You went away.

ASAGAI: Ahhhhhhhh.

BENEATHA: Before — you wanted to be so serious before there was time.

ASAGAI: How much time must there be before one knows what one feels?

BENEATHA: *(stalling this particular conversation. Her hands pressed together, in a deliberately childish gesture)* What did you bring me?

80 ASAGAI: *(handing her the package)* Open it and see.

BENEATHA: *(eagerly opening the package and drawing out some records and the colorful robes of a Nigerian woman)* Oh Asagai! . . . You got them for me! . . . How beautiful . . . and the records tool *(She lifts out the robes and runs to the mirror with them and holds the drapery up in front of herself.)*

ASAGAI: *(coming to her at the mirror)* I shall have to teach you how to drape it properly. *(He flings the material about her for the moment and stands back to look at her.)* Ah-Oh-pay-gay-day, oh-gbab-mu-shay. *(A Yoruba exclamation for admiration.)* You wear it well . . . very well . . . mutilated hair and all.

BENEATHA: *(turning suddenly)* My hair — what's wrong with my hair?

Asagai *(shrugging)* Were you born with it like that?

BENEATHA: *(reaching up to touch it)* No . . . of course not.

She looks back to the mirror, disturbed.

ASAGAI: *(smiling)* How then?   85
BENEATHA: You know perfectly well how . . . as crinkly as yours . . . that's how.
ASAGAI: And it is ugly to you that way?
BENEATHA: *(quickly)* Oh, no — not ugly . . . *(More slowly, apologetically.)* But it's so hard to manage when it's, well — raw.
ASAGAI: And so to accommodate that — you mutilate it every week?
BENEATHA: It's not mutilation!   90
ASAGAI: *(laughing aloud at her seriousness)* Oh . . . please! I am only teasing you because you are so very serious about these things. *(He stands back from her and folds his arms across his chest as he watches her pulling at her hair and frowning in the mirror.)* Do you remember the first time you met me at school?

(He laughs.) You came up to me and you said — and I thought you were the most serious little thing I had ever seen — you said: *(He imitates her.)* "Mr. Asagai — I want very much to talk with you. About Africa. You see, Mr. Asagai, I am looking for my *identity!*"

He laughs.

BENEATHA: *(turning to him, not laughing)* Yes —

Her face is quizzical, profoundly disturbed.

ASAGAI: *(still teasing and reaching out and taking her face in his hands and turning her profile to him)* Well . . . it is true that this is not so much a profile of a Hollywood queen as perhaps a queen of the Nile — *(A mock dismissal of the importance of the question.)* But what does it matter. Assimilationism is so popular in your country.

BENEATHA: *(wheeling, passionately, sharply)* I am not an assimilationist!   95
ASAGAI: *(the protest hangs in the room for a moment and Asagai studies her, his laughter fading)* Such a serious one. *(There is a pause.)* So — you like the robes? You must take excellent care of them — they are from my sister's personal wardrobe.
BENEATHA: *(with incredulity)* You — you sent all the way home — for me?
ASAGAI: *(with charm)* For you — I would do much more . . . Well, that is what I came for. I must go.
BENEATHA: Will you call me Monday?
ASAGAI: Yes . . . We have a great deal to talk about. I mean about identity and   100
time and all that.
BENEATHA: Time?

ASAGAI: Yes. About how much time one needs to know what one feels.

BENEATHA: You see! You never understood that there is more than one kind of feeling which can exist between a man and a woman — or, at least, there should be.

ASAGAI: *(shaking his head negatively but gently)* No. Between a man and a woman there need be only one kind of feeling. I have that for you . . . Now even . . . right this moment . . .

105 BENEATHA: I know — and by itself — it won't do. I can find that anywhere.

ASAGAI: For a woman it should be enough.

BENEATHA: I know — because that's what it says in all the novels that men write. But it isn't. Go ahead and laugh — but I'm not interested in being someone's little episode in America or — *(With feminine vengeance.)* — one of them! *(Asagai has burst into laughter again.)* That's funny as hell, huh!

ASAGAI: It's just that every American girl I have known has said that to me. White — black — in this you are all the same. And the same speech, too!

BENEATHA: *(angrily)* Yuk, yuk, yuk!

110 ASAGAI: It's how you can be sure that the world's most liberated women are not liberated at all. You all talk about it too much!

Mama enters and is immediately all social charm because of the presence of a guest.

BENEATHA: Oh — Mama — this is Mr. Asagai.

MAMA: How do you do?

ASAGAI: *(total politeness to an elder)* How do you do, Mrs. Younger. Please forgive me for coming at such an outrageous hour on a Saturday.

MAMA: Well, you are quite welcome. I just hope you understand that our house don't always look like this. *(Chatterish.)* You must come again. I would love to hear all about — *(Not sure of the name.)* — your country. I think it's so sad the way our American Negroes don't know nothing about Africa 'cept. Tarzan and all that. And all that money they pour into these churches when they ought to be helping you people over there drive out them French and Englishmen done taken away your land.

The mother flashes a slightly superior look at her daughter upon completion of the recitation.

115 ASAGAI: *(taken aback by this sudden and acutely unrelated expression of sympathy)* Yes . . . yes . . .

MAMA: *(smiling at him suddenly and relaxing and looking him over)* How many miles is it from here to where you come from?

ASAGAI: Many thousands.

MAMA: *(looking at him as she would Walter)* I bet you don't half look after yourself, being away from your mama either. I spec you better come 'round here from time to time to get yourself some decent homecooked meals . . .

ASAGAI: *(moved)* Thank you. Thank you very much. *(They are all quiet, then-)* Well . . . I must go. I will call you Monday, Alaiyo.

120 MAMA: What's that he call you?

ASAGAI: Oh — "Alaiyo." I hope you don't mind. It is what you would call a nickname, I think. It is a Yotuba word. I am a Yoruba.

MAMA: *(looking at Beneatha)* I—I thought he was from—*(Uncertain.)*

ASAGAI: *(understanding)* Nigeria is my country. Yoruba is my tribal origin-

BENEATHA: You didn't tell us what Alaiyo means . . . for all I know, you might be calling me Little Idiot or something . . .

ASAGAI: Well . . . let me see . . . I do not know how just to explain it . . . The   125
sense of a thing can be so different when it changes languages.

BENEATHA: You're evading.

ASAGAI: No—really it is difficult . . . *(Thinking.)* It means . . . it means One for Whom Bread—Food—Is Not Enough. *(He looks at her.)* Is that all right?

BENEATHA: *(understanding, softly)* Thank you.

MAMA: *(looking from one to the other and not understanding any of it)* Well . . . that's nice . . . You must come see us again—Mr.—

ASAGAI: Ah-sah-guy . . .   130

MAMA: Yes . . . Do come again.

ASAGAI: Good-bye.

He exits.

MAMA: *(after him)* Lord, that's a pretty thing just went out here! *(Insinuatingly, to her daughter.)* Yes, I guess I see why we done commence to get so interested in Africa 'round here. Missionaries may aunt Jenny!

She exits.

BENEATHA: Oh, Mama! . . .

She picks up the Nigerian dress and holds it up to her in front of the mirror again. She sets the headdress on haphazardly and then notices her hair again and clutches at it and then replaces the headdress and frowns at herself. Then she starts to wriggle in front of the mirror as she thinks a Nigerian woman might. Travis enters and stands regarding her.

TRAVIS: What's the matter, girl, you cracking up?   135

BENEATHA: Shut up.

She pulls the headdress off and looks at herself in the mirror and clutches at her hair again and squinches her eyes as if trying to imagine something. Then, suddenly, she gets her raincoat and kerchief and hurriedly prepares for going out.

MAMA: *(coming back into the room)* She's resting now. Travis, baby, run next door and ask Miss Johnson to please let me have a little kitchen cleanser. This here can is empty as Jacob's kettle.

TRAVIS: I just came in.

MAMA: Do as you told. *(He exits and she looks at her daughter.)* Where you going?

BENEATHA: *(halting at the door)* To become a queen of the Nile!   140

She exits in a breathless blaze of glory. Ruth appears in the bedroom doorway.

MAMA: Who told you to get up?

RUTH: Ain't nothing wrong with me to be lying in no bed for. Where did Bennie go?

MAMA: *(drumming her fingers)* Fat as I could make out— to Egypt. *(Ruth just looks at her.)* What time is it getting to?

RUTH: Ten twenty. And the mailman going to ring that bell this morning just like he done ever morning for the last umpteen years.

Travis comes in with the cleanser can.

145 TRAVIS: She say to tell you that she don't have much.

MAMA: *(angrily)* Lord, some people I could name sure is tight-fisted! *(Directing her grandson.)* Mark two cans of cleanser on the list there. If she that hard up for kitchen cleanser, I sure don't want to forget to get her none!

RUTH: Lena—maybe the woman is just short on cleanser—

MAMA: *(not listening)*— Much baking powder as she done borrowed from me all these years, she could of done gone into the baking business!

The bell sounds suddenly and sharply and all three are stunned—serious and silent— midspeech. In spite of all the other conversations and distractions of the morning, this is what they have been waiting for, even Travis, who looks helplessly from his mother to his grandmother. Ruth is the first to come to life again.

RUTH: *(to Travis)* Get down them steps, boy!

Travis snaps to life and flies out to get the mail.

150 MAMA: *(her eyes wide, her hand to her breast)* You mean it done really come?

RUTH: *(excited)* Oh, Miss Lena!

MAMA: *(collecting herself)* Well . . . I don't know what we all so excited about round here for. We known it was coming for months.

RUTH: That's a whole lot different from having it come and being able to hold it in your hands . . . a piece of paper worth ten thousand dollars . . . *(Travis bursts back into the room. He holds the envelope high above his head, like a little dancer, his face is radiant and he is breathless. He moves to his grandmother with sudden slow ceremony and puts the envelope into her hands. She accepts it, and then merely holds it and looks at it.)* Come on! Open it . . . Lord have mercy, I wish Walter Lee was here!

TRAVIS: Open it, Grandmama!

155 MAMA: *(staring at it)* Now you all be quiet. It's just a check.

RUTH: Open it. . .

MAMA: *(still staring at it)* Now don't act silly . . . We ain't never been no people to act silly 'bout no money—

RUTH: *(swiftly)* We ain't never had none before— OPEN IT!

Mama finally makes a good strong tear and pulls out the thin blue slice of paper and inspects it closely. The boy and his mother study it raptly over Mama's shoulders.

MAMA: Travis! *(She is counting off with doubt.)* Is that the right number of zeros?

160 TRAVIS: Yes'm . . . ten thousand dollars. Gaalee, grandmama, you rich.

MAMA: *(She holds the check away from her, still looking at it. Slowly her face sobers into a mask of unhappiness)* Ten thousand dollars. *(She hands it to Ruth.)* Put it away somewhere, Ruth. *(She does not look at Ruth; her eyes seem to be seeing something somewhere very far off.*) Ten thousand dollars they give you, Ten thousand dollars.

TRAVIS: (*to his mother, sincerely*) What's the matter with Grandmama — don't she want to be rich?

RUTH: (*distractedly*) You go on out and play now, baby. (*Travis exits. Mama starts wiping dishes absently, humming intently to herself. Ruth turns to her; with kind exasperation.*) You've gone and got yourself upset.

MAMA: (*not looking at her*) I spec if it wasn't for you all . . . I would just put that money away or give it to the church or something.

RUTH: Now what kind of talk is that, Mr. Younger would just be plain mad if   165
he could hear you talking foolish like that.

MAMA: (*stopping and staring off*) Yes . . . he sure would. (*Sighing.*) We got enough to do with that money, all right. (*She halts then, and turns and looks at her daughter-in-law hard; Ruth avoids her eyes and Mama wipes her hands with finality and starts to speak firmly to Ruth.*) Where did you go today, girl?

RUTH: To the doctor.

MAMA: (*impatiently*) Now, Ruth . . . you know better than that. Old Doctor Jones is strange enough in his way but there ain't nothing 'bout him make somebody slip and call him "she" — like you done this morning.

RUTH: Well, that's what happened — my tongue slipped.

MAMA: You went to see that woman, didn't you?   170

RUTH: (*defensively, giving herself away*) What woman you talking about?

MAMA: (*angrily*): That woman who —

Walter enters in great excitement.

WALTER: Did it come?

MAMA: (*quietly*) Can't you give people a Christian greeting before you start asking about money?

WALTER: (*to Ruth*) Did it come? (*Ruth unfolds the check and lays it quietly before*   175
him, watching him intently with thoughts of her own. Walter sits down and grasps it close and counts off the zeros.) Ten thousand dollars — (*He turns suddenly, frantically to his mother and draws some papers out of his breast pocket.*)
Mama — look. Old Willy Harris put everything on paper —

MAMA: Son — I think you ought to talk to your wife . . . I'll go on out and leave you alone if you want —

WALTER: I can talk to her later — Mama, look —

MAMA: Son —

WALTER: WILL SOMEBODY PLEASE LISTEN TO ME TODAY!

MAMA: (*quietly*) I don't 'low no yellin' in this house, Walter Lee, and you know   180
it — (*Walter stares at them in frustration and starts to speak several times.*) And there ain't going to be no investing in no liquor stores.

WALTER: But, Mama, you ain't even looked at it.

MAMA: I don't aim to have to speak on that again.

A long pause.

WALTER: You ain't looked at it and you don't aim to have to speak on that again? You ain't even looked at it and *you* have decided — (*Crumpling his papers.*) Well, *you* tell that to my boy tonight when you put him to sleep on the living-room couch . . . (*Turning to Mama and speaking directly on her.*) Yeah — and tell it to my wife, Mama, tomorrow when she has to go out of here to look after somebody else's kids. And tell it to *me*, Mama, every time we need a new pair of curtains and I have to watch *you* go out and work in somebody's kitchen. Yeah, you tell me then!

Walter starts out.

RUTH: Where you going?
185 WALTER: I'm going out!
RUTH: Where?
WALTER: Just out of this house somewhere —
RUTH: (*getting her coat*) I'll come too.
WALTER: I don't want you to come!
190 RUTH: I got something to talk to you about, Walter.
WALTER: That's too bad.
MAMA: (*still quietly*) Walter Lee — (*She waits and he finally turns and looks at her.*) Sit down.
WALTER: I'm a grown man, Mama.
MAMA: Ain't nobody said you wasn't grown. But you still in my house and my presence. And as long as you are — you'll talk to your wife civil. Now sit down.
195 RUTH: (*suddenly*) Oh, let him go on out and drink himself to death! He makes me sick to my stomach! (*She flings her coat against him and exits to bedroom.*)
WALTER: (*violently flinging the coat after her*) And you turn mine too, baby! (*The door slams behind her.*) That was my biggest mistake —
MAMA: (*still quietly*) Walter, what is the matter with you?
WALTER: Matter with me? Ain't nothing the matter with *me*!
MAMA: Yes there is. Something eating you up like a crazy man. Something more than me not giving you this money. The past few years I been watching it happen to you. You get all nervous acting and kind of wild in the eyes — (*Walter jumps up impatiently at her words.*) I said sit there now, I'm talking to you!
200 WALTER: Mama — I don't need no nagging at me today.
MAMA: Seem like you getting to a place where you always tied up in some kind of knot about something. But if anybody ask you 'bout it you just yell at 'em and bust out the house and go out and drink somewheres. Walter Lee, people can't live with that. Ruth's a good, patient girl in her way — but you getting to be too much. Boy, don't make the mistake of driving that girl away from you.
WALTER: Why — what she do for me?
MAMA: She loves you.
WALTER: Mama — I'm going out I want to go off somewhere and be by myself for a while.

MAMA: I'm sorry 'bout your liquor store, son. It just wasn't the thing for us to   205
do. That's what I want to tell you about —

WALTER: I got to go out, Mama —

He rises.

MAMA: It's dangerous, son.

WALTER: What's dangerous?

MAMA: When a man goes outside his home to look for peace.

WALTER: *(beseechingly)* Then why can't there never be no peace in this house   210
then?

MAMA: You done found it in some other house?

WALTER: No — there ain't no woman! Why do women always think there's a
woman somewhere when a man gets restless *(Picks up the check.)* Do you
know what this money means to me? Do you know what this money can do
for us? *(Puts it back.)* Mama — Mama — I want so many things . . .

MAMA: Yes, son—

WALTER: I want so many things that they are driving me kind of crazy . . .
Mama — look at me.

MAMA: I'm looking at you. You a good-looking boy. You got a job, a nice wife,   215
a fine boy, and —

WALTER: A job. *(Looks at her.)* Mama, a job? I open and close car doors all day
long. I drive a man around in his limousine and I say, "Yes, sir; no, sir; very
good, sir; shall I take the Drive, sir?" Mama, that ain't no kind of job . . .
that ain't nothing at all. *(Very quietly.)* Mama, I don't know if I can make
you understand.

MAMA: Understand what, baby?

WALTER: *(quietly)* Sometimes it's like I can see the future stretched out in
front of me — just plain as day. The future Mama. Hanging over there at
the edge of my days. Just waiting for me — a big, looming blank space —
full of *nothing*. Just waiting for *me*. But it don't have to be. *(Pause. Kneeling
beside her chair.)* Mama — sometimes when I'm downtown and I pass them
cool, quiet looking restaurants where them white boys are sitting back and
talking 'bout things . . . sitting there turning deals worth millions of dollars
. . . sometimes I see guys don't look much older than me —

MAMA: Son — how come you talk so much 'bout money?   220

WALTER: *(with immense passion)* Because it is life, Mama!

MAMA: *(quietly)* Oh —*(Very quietly.)* So now it's life. Money is life. Once
upon a time freedom used to be life — now it's money. I guess the world really do change . . .

WALTER: No — it was always money, Mama. We just didn't know about it.

MAMA: No . . . something has changed. *(She looks at him.)* You something
new, boy. In my time we was worried about not being lynched and getting
to the North if we could and how to stay alive and still have a pinch of
dignity too . . . Now here come you and Beneatha — talking 'bout things
we ain't never even thought about hardly, me and your daddy. You ain't satisfied or proud of nothing we done. I mean that you had a home; that we

kept you out of trouble till you was grown; that you don't have to ride to work on the back of nobody's streetcar — You my children — but how different we done become.

WALTER: *(a long beat. He pats her hand and gets up)* You just don't understand, Mama, you just don't understand.

225 MAMA: Son — do you know your wife is expecting another baby? *(Walter stands, stunned, and absorbs what his mother has said.)* That's what she wanted to talk to you about. *(Walter sinks down into a chair.)* This ain't for me to be telling — but you ought to know. *(She waits.)* I think Ruth is thinking 'bout getting rid of that child.

WALTER: *(slowly understanding)* —No — no — Ruth wouldn't do that.

MAMA: When the world gets ugly enough — a woman will do anything for her family. *The part that's already living.*

WALTER: You don't know Ruth, Mama, if you think she would do that.

Ruth opens the bedroom door and stands there a little limp.

RUTH: *(beaten)* Yes I would too, Walter. *(Pause.)* I gave her a five-dollar down payment.

There is total silence as the man stares at his wife and the mother stares at her son.

230 MAMA: *(presently)* Well —*(Tightly.)* Well — son, I'm waiting to hear you say something . . . *(She waits.)* I'm waiting to hear how you be your father's son. Be the man he was . . . *(Pause. The silence shouts.)* Your wife say she going to destroy your child. And I'm waiting to hear you talk like him and say we a people who give children life, not who destroys them —*(She rises.)* I'm waiting to see you stand up and look like your daddy and say we done give up one baby to poverty and that we ain't going to give up nary another one . . . I'm waiting.

WALTER: Ruth —*(He can say nothing.)*

MAMA: If you a son of mine, tell her! *(Walter picks up his keys and his coat and walks out. She continues, bitterly.)* You . . . you are a disgrace to your father's memory. Somebody get me my hat!

Curtain.

ACT 2
SCENE 1

TIME: *Later the same day.*

At rise. Ruth is ironing again. She has the radio going. Presently Beneatha's bedroom door opens and Ruth's mouth falls and she puts down the iron in fascination.

RUTH: What have we got on tonight!

BENEATHA: *(emerging grandly from the doorway so that we can see her thoroughly robed in the costume Asagai brought)* You are looking at what a well-dressed Nigerian woman wears —*(She parades for Ruth, her hair completely hidden by the headdress; she is coquettishly fanning herself with an ornate oriental fan, mistakenly more like Butterfly than any Nigerian that ever was.)* Isn't it beautiful? *(She promenades to the radio and, with an arrogant flourish, turns off the good*

loud blues that is playing.) Enough of this assimilationist junk! (*Ruth follows her with her eyes as she goes to the phonograph and puts on a record and turns and waits ceremoniously for the music to come up. Then, with a shout —*)
OCOMOGOSIAY!

Ruth jumps. The music comes up, a lovely Nigerian melody. Beneatha listens, enraptured, her eyes far way — "back to the past." She begins to dance. Ruth is dumfounded.

RUTH: What kind of dance is that?
BENEATHA: A folk dance.
RUTH: What kind of folks do that, honey?
BENEATHA: It's from Nigeria. It's a dance of welcome.
RUTH: Who you welcoming?
BENEATHA: The men back to the village.
RUTH: Where they been?
BENEATHA: How should I know — out hunting or something. Anyway, they are coming back now . . .
RUTH: Well, that's good.
BENEATHA: (*with the record*)

> Alundi, alundi
> Alundi alunya
> Jop pu a jeepua
> Ang gu soooooooooo
> Ai yai yae . . .
> Ayehaye — alundi . . .

Walter comes in during this performance, he has obviously been drinking. He leans against the door heavily and watches his sister, at first with distaste. Then his eyes look off — "back to the past" — as he lifts both his fists to the roof, screaming.

WALTER: YEAH . . . AND ETHIOPIA, STRETCH FORTH HER HANDS AGAIN! . . .
RUTH: (*drily, looking at him*) Yes — and Africa sure is claiming her own tonight. (*She gives them both up and starts ironing again.*)
WALTER: (*all in a drunken, dramatic shout*) Shut up! . . . I'm diggin them drums . . . them drums move me! . . . (*He makes his weaving way to his wife's face and leans in close to her.*) In my *heart of hearts* —(*He thumps his chest.*)— I am much warrior!
RUTH: (*without even looking up*) In your heart of hearts you are much drunkard.
WALTER: (*coming away from her and starting to wander around the room, shouting*) Me and Jomo . . . (*Intently, in his sister's face. She has stopped dancing to watch him in this unknown mood.*) That's my man, Kenyatta. (*Shouting and thumping his chest.*) FLAMING SPEAR! HOT DAMN! (*He is suddenly in possession of an imaginary spear and actively spearing enemies all over the room.*) OCOMOGOSIAY . . .
BENEATHA: (*to encourage Walter, thoroughly caught up with this side of him*) OCOMOGOSIAY, FLAMING SPEAR!
WALTER: THE LION IS WAKING . . . OWIMOWEH!

He pulls his shirt open and leaps up on the table and gestures with his spear.

20 BENEATHA: OWIMOWEH!

WALTER: (*on the table, very far gone, his eyes pure glass sheets. He sees what we cannot, that he is a leader of his people, a great chief, a descendant of Chaka, and that the hour to march has come*) Listen, my black brothers —

BENEATHA: OCOMOGOSIAY!

WALTER: Do you hear the waters rushing against the shores of the coast-lands —

BENEATHA: OCOMOGOSIAY!

25 WALTER: Do you hear the screeching of the cocks in yonder hills beyond where the chiefs meet in council for the coming of the mighty war —

BENEATHA: OCOMOGOSIAY!

And now the lighting shifts subtly to suggest the world of Walter's imagination, and the mood shifts from pure comedy. It is the inner Walter speaking: the Southside chauffeur has assumed an unexpected majesty.

WALTER: —Do you hear the beating of the wings of the birds flying low over the mountains and the low places of our land —

BENEATHA: OCOMOGOSIAY!

WALTER: —Do you hear the singing of the women, singing the war songs of our fathers to the babies in the great houses? Singing the sweet war songs! (*The doorbell rings.*) OH, DO YOU HEAR, MY *BLACK BROTHERS!*

30 BENEATHA: (*completely gone*) We hear you, Flaming spear —

Ruth shuts off the phonograph and opens the door. George Murchison enters.

WALTER: Telling us to prepare for the GREATNESS OF THE TIME! (*Lights back to normal. He turns and sees George.*) Black Brother!

He extends his hand for the fraternal clasp.

GEORGE: Black Brother, hell!

RUTH: (*having had enough, and embarrassed for the family*) Beneatha, you got company — what's the matter with you? Walter Lee Younger, get down off that table and stop acting like a fool . . .

Walter comes down off the table suddenly and makes a quick exit to the bathroom.

RUTH: He's had a little to drink . . . I don't know what her excuse is.

35 GEORGE: (*to Beneatha*) Look honey, we're going to the theater — we're not going to be *in* it . . . so go change, huh?

Beneatha looks at him and slowly, ceremoniously, lifts her hands and pulls off the head-dress. Her hair is close-cropped and unstraightened. George freezes mid-sentence and Ruth's eyes all but fall out of her head.

GEORGE: What in the name of —

RUTH: (*touching Beneatha's hair*) Girl, you done lost your natural mind? Look at your head!

GEORGE: What have you done to your head — I mean your hair!

BENEATHA: Nothing — except cut it off.

RUTH: Now that's the truth — it's what ain't been done to it! You expect this   40
boy to go out with you with your head all nappy like that?

BENEATHA: *(looking at George)* That's up to George. If he's ashamed of his
heritage —

GEORGE: Oh, don't be so proud of yourself, Bennie — just because you look
eccentric.

BENEATHA: How can something that's natural be eccentric?

GEORGE: That's what being eccentric means — being natural. Get dressed.

BENEATHA: I don't like that, George.   45

RUTH: Why must you and your brother make an argument out of everything
people say?

BENEATHA: Because I hate assimilationist Negroes!

RUTH: Will somebody please tell me what assimila-whoever means!

GEORGE: Oh, it's just a college girl's way of calling people Uncle Toms — but
that isn't what it means at all.

RUTH: Well, what does it means?   50

BENEATHA: *(cutting George off and staring at him as she replies to Ruth)* It means
someone who is willing to give up his own culture and submerge himself
completely in the dominant, and in this case *oppressive* culture!

GEORGE: Oh, dear, dear, dear! Here we go! A lecture on the African past! On
our Great West African Heritage! In one second we will hear all about the
great Ashanti empires, the great Songhay civilizations; and the great sculpture
of Benin — and then some poetry in the Bantu — and the whole monologue
will end with the word *heritage*! *(Nastily.)* Let's face it, baby, your heritage is
nothing but a bunch of raggedy-assed spirituals and some grass huts!

BENEATHA: GRASS HUTS! *(Ruth crosses to her and forcibly pushes her toward
the bedroom.)* See there . . . you are standing there in your splendid ignorance talking about people who were the first to smelt iron on the face of
the earth! *(Ruth is pushing her through the door.)* The Ashanti were performing surgical operations when the English —*(Ruth pulls the door to, with Beneatha on the other side, and smiles graciously at George. Beneatha opens the door
and shouts the end of the sentence defiantly at George.)*— were still tatooing
themselves with blue dragons! *(She goes back inside.)*

RUTH: Have a seat, George. *(They both sit. Ruth folds her hands rather primly on
her lap, determined to demonstrate the civilization of the family.)* Warm, ain't it?
I mean for September. *(Pause.)* Just like they always say about Chicago
weather. If it's too hot or cold for you, just wait a minute and it'll change.
(She smiles happily at this cliché of cliché.) Everybody say it's got to do with
them bombs and things they keep setting off. *(Pause.)* Would you like a
nice cold beer?

GEORGE: No, thank you. I don't care for beer. *(He looks at his watch.)* I hope   55
she hurries up.

RUTH: What time is the show?

GEORGE: It's an eight-thirty curtain. That's just Chicago, though. In New York
standard curtain time is eight forty.

He is rather proud of this knowledge.

RUTH: (*properly appreciating it*) You get to New York a lot?
GEORGE: (*offhand*) Few times a year.
60 **RUTH:** Oh — that's nice. I've never been to New York.

Walter enters. We feel he has relieved himself, but the edge of unreality is still with him.

WALTER: New York ain't got nothing Chicago ain't. Just a bunch of hustling people all squeezed up together — being "Eastern."

He turns his face into a screw of displeasure.

GEORGE: Oh — you've been?
WALTER: Plenty of times.
RUTH: (*Shocked at the lie*) Walter Lee Younger!
65 **WALTER:** (*staring her down*) Plenty! (*Pause.*) What we got to drink in this house? Why don't you offer this man some refreshment. (*To George.*) They don't know how to entertain people in this house, man.
GEORGE: Thank you — I don't really care for anything.
WALTER: (*feeling his head, sobriety coming*) Where's Mama?
RUTH: She ain't come back yet.
WALTER: (*looking Murchison over from head to toe, scrutinizing his carefully casual tweed sports jacket over cashmere V-neck sweater over soft eyelet shirt and tie, and soft slacks, finished off with white buckskin shoes*) Why all you college boys wear them faggoty-looking white shoes?
70 **RUTH:** Walter Lee!

George Murchison ignores the remark.

WALTER: (*to Ruth*) Well, they look crazy as hell — white shoes, cold as it is.
RUTH: (*crushed*) You have to excuse him —
75 **WALTER:** No he don't! Excuse me for what? What you always excusing me for! I'll excuse myself when I needs to be excused! (*A pause.*) They look as funny as them black knee socks Beneatha wears out of here all the time.
RUTH: It's the college *style*, Walter.
WALTER: Style, hell. She looks like she got burnt legs or something!
RUTH: Oh, Walter —
WALTER: (*an irritable mimic*) Oh, Walter! Oh, Walter! (*To Murchison.*) How's your old man making out? I understand you all going to buy that big hotel on the Drive? (*He finds a beer in the refrigerator, wanders over to Murchison, sipping and wiping his lips with the back of his hand, and straddling a chair backwards to talk to the other man.*) Shrewed move. Your old man is all right, man. (*Tapping his head and half winking for emphasis.*) I mean he knows how to operate. I mean he thinks *big*, you know what I mean, I mean for a *home*, you know? But I think he's kind of running out of ideas now. I'd like to talk to him, Listen, man, I got some plans that could turn this city upside down. I mean think like he does. *Big*. Invest big, gamble big, hell, lose *big* if you have to, you know what I mean. It's hard to find a man on this whole Southside who understands my kinds of thinking — you dig? (*He scrutinizes*

Murchison again, drinks his beer, squints his eyes and leans in close, confidential, man to man.) Me and you ought to sit down and talk sometimes, man. Man, I got me some ideas . . .

MURCHISON: *(with boredom)* Yeah — sometimes we'll have to do that, Walter. 80

WALTER: *(understanding the indifference, and offended)* Yeah — well, when you get the time, man. I know you a busy little boy.

RUTH: *Walter, please*

WALTER: *(bitterly, hurt)* I know ain't nothing in this world as buys as you col-ored college boys with your fraternity pins and white shoes . . .

RUTH: *(covering her face with humiliation)* Oh, Walter Lee —

WALTER: I see you all all the time — with the books tucked under your 85 arms — going to your *(British A — a mimic.)* "clahsses." And for what! What the hell you learning over there? Filling up your heads —*(Counting off on his fingers.)* — with the sociology and the psychology — but they teaching you how to be a man? How to take over and run the world? They teaching you how to run a rubber plantation or a steel mill? Naw —just to talk proper and read books and wear them faggoty-looking white shoes . . .

GEORGE: *(looking at him with distaste, a little above it all)* You're all wacked up with bitterness, man.

WALTER: *(intently, almost quietly, between the teeth, glaring at the boy)* And you — ain't you bitter, man! Ain't you just about had it yet? Don't you see no stars gleaming that you can't reach out and grab? You happy?—You con-tented son-of-a-bitch — you happy? You got it made? Bitter? Man, I'm a volcano. Bitter? Here I am a giant — surrounded by ants! Ants who can't even understand what it is the giant is talking about.

RUTH: *(passionately and suddenly)* Oh, Walter — ain't you with nobody!

WALTER: *(violently)* No! 'Cause ain't nobody with me! Not even my own mother!

RUTH: Walter, that's a terrible thing to say! 90

Beneatha enters, dressed for the evening in a cocktail dress and earrings, hair natural.

GEORGE: Well —hey —*(Crosses to Beneatha; thoughtful, with emphasis, since this is a reversal.)* You look great!

WALTER: *(seeing his sister's hair for the first time)* What's the matter with your head?

BENEATHA: *(tired of the jokes now)* I cut it off, Brother.

WALTER: *(coming close to inspect it and walking around her)* Well, I'll be damned. So that's what they mean by the African bush.

BENEATHA: Ha ha. Let's go, George. 95

GEORGE: *(looking at her)* You know something? I like it. It's sharp. I mean it re-ally is. *(Helps her into her wrap.)*

RUTH: Yes — I think so, too. *(She goes to the mirror and starts to clutch at her hair.)*

WALTER: Oh no! You leave yours alone, baby. You might turn out to have a pin-shaped head or something!

BENEATHA: See you all later.

RUTH: Have a nice time. 100

GEORGE: Thanks. Good night. *(Half out the door, he reopens it. To Walter.)* Good night, Prometheus!

Beneatha and George exit.

WALTER: (*to Ruth*) Who is Prometheus?

RUTH: I don't know. Don't worry about it.

WALTER: (*in fury, pointing after George*) See there — they get to a point where they can't insult you man to man — they got to go talk about something ain't nobody never heard of!

105 **RUTH:** How do you know it was an insult? (*To humor him.*) Maybe Prometheus is a nice fellow.

WALTER: Prometheus! I bet there ain't even no such thing! I bet that simple-minded clown —

RUTH: Walter —

She stops what she is doing and looks at him.

WALTER: (*yelling*) Don't start!

RUTH: Start what?

110 **WALTER:** Your nagging! Where was I? Who was I with? How much money did I spend?

RUTH: (*plaintively*) Walter Lee — why don't we just try to talk about it. . .

WALTER: (*not listening*) I been out talking with people who understand me. People who care about the things I got on my mind.

RUTH: (*wearily*) I guess that means people like Willy Harris.

WALTER: Yes, people like Willy Harris.

115 **RUTH:** (*with a sudden flash of impatience*) Why don't you all just hurry up and go into the banking business and stop talking about it!

WALTER: Why? You want to know why? Cause we all tied up in a race of people that don't know how to do nothing but moan, pray and have babies!

The line is too bitter even for him and he looks at her and sits down.

RUTH: Oh, Walter. . . (*Softly.*) Honey, why can't you stop fighting me?

WALTER: (*without thinking*) Who's fighting you? Who even cares about you?

This line begins the retardation of his mood.

RUTH: Well —(*She waits a long time, and then with resignation starts to put away her things.*) I guess I might as well go on to bed . . . (*More or less to herself.*) I don't know where we lost it . . . but we have . . . (*Then, to him.*) I — I'm sorry about this new baby, Walter. I guess maybe I better go on and do what I started . . . I guess I just didn't realize how bad things was with us . . . I guess I just didn't really realize —(*She starts out to the bedroom and stops.*) You want some hot milk?

120 **WALTER:** Hot milk?

RUTH: Yes —hot milk.

WALTER: Why hot milk?

RUTH: 'Cause after all that liquor you come home with you ought to have something hot in your stomach.

WALTER: I don't want hot milk.

125 **RUTH:** You want some coffee then?

Walter: No, I don't want no coffee. I don't want nothing hot to drink. *(Almost plaintively.)* Why you always trying to give me something to eat?

Ruth: *(standing and looking at him helplessly)* What *else* can I give you, Walter Lee Younger?

She stands and looks at him and presently turns to go out again. He lifts his head and watches her going away from him in a new mood which began to emerge when he asked her "Who cares about you?"

Walter: It's been rough, ain't it, baby? *(She hears and stops but does not turn around and he continues to her back.)* I guess between two people there ain't never as much understood as folks generally thinks there is. I mean like between me and you — *(She turns to face him.)* How we gets to the place where we scared to talk softness to each other. *(He waits, thinking hard himself.)* Why you think it got to be like that? *(He is thoughtful, almost as a child would be.)* Ruth, what is it gets into people ought to be close?

Ruth: I don't know, honey, I think about it a lot.

Walter: On account of you and me, you mean? The way things are with us. The way something done come down between us.

Ruth: There ain't so much between us, Walter . . . Not when you come to me and try to talk to me. Try to be with me . . . a little even.

Walter: *(total honesty)* Sometimes . . . sometimes . . . I don't even know how to try.

Ruth: Walter —

Walter: Yes?

Ruth: *(coming to him, gently and with misgiving, but coming to him)* Honey . . . life don't have to be like this. I mean sometimes people can do things so that things are better . . . You remember how we used to talk when Travis was born . . . about the way we were going to live . . . the kind of house. . . *(She is stroking his head.)* Well, it's all starting to slip away from us. . .

He turns her to him and they look at each other and kiss, tenderly and hungrily. The door opens and Mama enters—Walter breaks away and jumps up. A beat.

Walter: Mama, where have you been?

Mama: My — them steps is longer than they used to be. Whew! *(She sits down and ignores him.)* How you feeling this evening, Ruth?

Ruth shrugs, disturbed at having been interrupted and watching her husband knowingly.

Walter: Mama, where have you been all day?

Mama: *(still ignoring him and leaning on the table and changing to more comfortable shoes)* Where's Travis?

Ruth: I let him go out earlier and he ain't come back yet. Boy, is he going to get it!

Walter: Mama!

Mama: *(as if she has heard him for the first time)* Yes, son?

Walter: Where did you go this afternoon?

Mama: I went downtown to tend to some business that I had to tend to.

145 **WALTER:** What kind of business?

MAMA: You know better than to question me like a child, Brother.

WALTER: *(rising and bending over the table)* Where were you, Mama? *(Bringing his fists down and shouting.)* Mama, you didn't go do something with that insurance money, something crazy?

The front door opens slowly, interrupting him, and Travis peeks his head in, less than hopefully.

TRAVIS: *(to his mother)* Mama, I —

RUTH: "Mama I" nothing! You're going to get it, boy! Get on in that bedroom and get yourself ready!

150 **TRAVIS:** But I —

MAMA: Why don't you all never let the child explain hisself.

RUTH: Keep out of it now, Lena.

Mama clamps her lips together, and Ruth advances toward her son menacingly.

RUTH: A thousand times I have told you not to go off like that —

MAMA: *(holding out her arms to her grandson)* Well — at least let me tell him something. I want him to be the first one to hear . . . Come here, Travis. *(The boy obeys, gladly.)* Travis — *(She takes him by the shoulder and looks into his face.)* — you know that money we got in the mail this morning?

155 **TRAVIS:** Yes'm —

MAMA: Well — what you think your grandmama gone and done with that money?

TRAVIS: I don't know, Grandmama.

MAMA: *(putting her finger on his nose for emphasis)* She went out and she bought you a house! *(The explosion comes from Walter at the end of the revelation and he jumps up and turns away from all of them in a fury. Mama continues, to Travis.)* You glad about the house? It's going to be yours when you get to be a man.

TRAVIS: Yeah — I always wanted to live in a house.

160 **MAMA:** All right, gimme some sugar then — *(Travis puts his arms around her neck as she watches her son over the boy's shoulder. Then, to Travis, after the embrace.)* Now when you say your prayers tonight, you thank God and your grandfather — 'cause it was him who give you the house — in his way.

RUTH: *(taking the boy from Mama and pushing him toward the bedroom)* Now you get out of here and get ready for your beating.

TRAVIS: Aw, Mama —

RUTH: Get on in there — *(Closing the door behind him and turning radiantly to her mother-in-law.)* So you went and did it!

MAMA: *(quietly, looking at her son with pain)* Yes, I did.

165 **RUTH:** *(raising both arms classically)* PRAISE GOD! *(Looks at Walter a moment, who says nothing. She crosses rapidly to her husband.)* Please, honey — let me be glad . . . you be glad too. *(She has laid her hands on his shoulders, but he shakes himself free of her roughly, without turning to face her.)* Oh, Walter . . . a home . . . a home. *(She comes back to Mama.)* Well — where is it? How big is it? How much it going to cost?

MAMA: Well —

RUTH: When we moving?

MAMA: (*smiling at her*) First of the month.

RUTH: (*throwing back her head with jubilance*) Praise God!

MAMA: (*tentatively, still looking at her son's back turned against her and Ruth*)   170
It's — it's a nice house too . . . (*She cannot help speaking directly to him. An imploring quality in her voice, her manner, makes her almost like a girl now.*) Three bedrooms — nice big one for you and Ruth . . . Me and Beneatha still have to share our room, but Travis have one of his own — and (*With difficulty.*) I figure if the — new baby — is a boy, we could get one of them double-decker outfits . . . And there's a yard with a little patch of dirt where I could maybe get to grow me a few flowers . . . And a nice big basement . . .

RUTH: Walter honey, be glad —

MAMA: (*still to his back, fingering things on the table*) 'Course I don't want to make it sound fancier than it is . . . It's just a plain little old house — but it's made good and solid — and it will be *ours*. Walter Lee — it makes a difference in a man when he can walk on floors that belong to *him* . . .

RUTH: Where is it?

MAMA: (*frightened at this telling*) Well — well — it's out there in Clybourne Park —

Ruth's radiance fades abruptly, and Walter finally turns slowly to face his mother with incredulity and hostility.

RUTH: Where?   175

MAMA: (*matter of factly*) Four o six Clybourne Street, Clybourne Park.

RUTH: Clybourne Park? Mama, there ain't no colored people living in Clybourne Park.

MAMA: (*almost idiotically*) Well, I guess there's going to be some now.

WALTER: (*bitterly*) So that's the peace and comfort you went out and bought for us today!

MAMA: (*raising her eyes to meet his finally*) Son — I just tried to find the nicest   180
place for the least amount of money for my family.

RUTH: (*trying to recover from the shock*) Well — well —'course I ain't one never been 'fraid of no crackers, mind you — but — well, wasn't there no other houses nowhere?

MAMA: Them houses they put up for colored in them areas way out all seem to cost twice as much as other houses. I did the best I could.

RUTH: (*struck senseless with the news, in its various degrees of goodness and trouble, she sits a moment, her fists propping her chin in thought, and then she starts to rise, bringing her fists down with vigor, the radiance spreading from cheek to cheek again*) Well — well — All I can say is — if this is my time in life — MY TIME — to say good-bye — (*And she builds with momentum as she starts to circle the room with an exuberant, almost tearfully happy release.*) — to these God-damned cracking walls! — (*She pounds the walls.*) — and these marching roaches! — (*She wipes at an imaginary army of marching reaches.*) —

and this cramped little closet which ain't now or never was no kitchen!. . . then I say it loud and good, HALLELUJAH! AND GOOD-BYE MISERY . . . I DON'T NEVER WANT TO SEE YOUR UGLY FACE AGAIN! (*She laughs joyously, having practically destroyed the apartment, and flings her arms up and lets them come down happily, slowly, reflectively, over her abdomen, aware for the first time perhaps that the life therein pulses with happiness and not despair.*) Lena?

MAMA: (*moved, watching her happiness*) Yes, honey?

185   **RUTH:** (*looking off*) Is there — is there a whole lot of sunlight?

MAMA: (*understanding*) Yes, child, there's a whole lot of sunlight.

Long pause.

RUTH: (*collecting herself and going to the door of the room Travis is in*) Well — I guess I better see 'bout Travis. (*To Mama.*) Lord, I sure don't feel like whipping nobody today!

She exits.

MAMA: (*the mother and son are left alone now and the mother waits a long time, considering deeply, before she speaks*) Son — you — you understand what I done, don't you? (*Walter is silent and sullen.*) I — I just seen my family falling apart today . . . just falling to pieces in front of my eyes . . . We couldn't of gone on like we was today. We was going backwards 'stead of forwards — talking 'bout killing babies and wishing each other was dead . . . When it gets like that in life — you just got to do something different, push on out and do something bigger . . . (*She waits.*) I wish you say something, son . . . I wish you'd say how deep inside you you think I done the right thing —

WALTER: (*crossing slowly to his bedroom door and finally turning there and speaking measuredly*) What you need me to say you done right for? *You* the head of this family. You run our lives like you want to. It was your money and you did what you wanted with it. So what you need for me to say it was all right for? (*Bitterly, to hurt her as deeply as he knows is possible.*) So you butchered up a dream of mine — you — who always talking 'bout your children's dreams . . .

190   **MAMA:** Walter Lee —

He just closes the door behind him. Mama sits alone, thinking heavily.

Curtain.

SCENE 2

TIME: *Friday night, a few weeks later.*

At rise: Packing crates mark the intention of the family to move. Beneatha and George come in, presumably from an evening out again.

GEORGE: O.K. . . . O.K., whatever you say . . . (*They both sit on the couch. He tries to kiss her. She moves away.*) Look, we've had a nice evening, let's not spoil it, huh? . . .

He again turns her head and tries to nuzzle in and she turns away from him, not with distaste but with momentary lack of interest; in a mood to pursue what they were talking about.

BENEATHA:　I'm *trying* to talk to you.

GEORGE:　We always talk.

BENEATHA:　Yes — and I love to talk.

GEORGE:　*(exasperated 'rising)* I know it and I don't mind it sometimes . . . I 　　　5
want you to cut it out, see — The moody stuff, I mean. I don't like it. You're
a nice-looking girl . . . all over. That's all you need, honey, forget the atmosphere. Guys aren't going to go for the atmosphere — they're going to go for
what they see. Be glad for that. Drop the Garbo routine. It doesn't go with
you. As for myself, I want a nice —(*Groping.*)— simple (*Thoughtfully.*)—
sophisticated girl . . . not a poet — O.K.?

He starts to kiss her, she rebuffs him again and he jumps up.

BENEATHA:　Why are you angry, George?

GEORGE:　Because this is stupid! I don't go out with you to discuss the nature of
"quiet desperation" or to hear all about your thoughts — because the world
will go on thinking what it thinks regardless —

BENEATHA:　Then why read books? Why go to school?

GEORGE:　*(with artificial patience, counting on his fingers)* It's simple. You read
books — to learn facts — to get grades — to pass the course — to get a degree. That's all — it has nothing to do with thoughts.

A long pause.

BENEATHA:　I see. (*He starts' to sit.*) Good night, George.　　　10

George looks at her a little oddly, and starts to exit. He meets Mama coming in.

GEORGE:　Oh — hello, Mrs. Younger.

MAMA:　Hello George how you feeling?

GEORGE:　Fine — fine, how are you?

MAMA:　Oh, a little tired. You know them steps can get you after a day's work.
You all have a nice time tonight?

GEORGE:　Yes — a fine time. A fine time.　　　15

MAMA:　Well, good night.

GEORGE:　Good night. (*He exits. Mama closes the door behind her.*) Hello, honey.
What you sitting like that for?

BENEATHA:　I'm just sitting.

MAMA:　Didn't you have a nice time?

BENEATHA:　No.　　　20

MAMA:　No? What's the matter?

BENEATHA:　Mama, George is a fool — honest. (*She rises.*)

MAMA:　*(hustling around unloading the packages she has entered with. She stops.*) Is
he, baby?

BENEATHA:　Yes.

Beneatha makes up Travis's bed as she talks.

MAMA:　You sure?　　　25

BENEATHA: Yes.

MAMA: Well — I guess you better not waste your time with no fools.

Beneatha looks up at her mother, watching her put groceries in the refrigerator. Finally she gathers up her things and starts into the bedroom. At the door she stops and looks back at her mother.

BENEATHA: Mama —

MAMA: Yes, baby —

30 **BENEATHA:** Thank you.

MAMA: For what?

BENEATHA: For understanding me this time.

She exits quickly and the mother stands, smiling a little, looking at the place where Beneatha just stood, Ruth enters.

RUTH: Now don't you fool with any of this stuff, Lena —

MAMA: Oh, I just thought I'd sort a few things out. Is Brother here?

35 **RUTH:** Yes.

MAMA: *(with concern)* Is he —

RUTH: *(reading her eyes)* Yes.

Mama is silent and someone knocks on the door. Mama and Ruth exchange weary and knowing glances and Ruth opens it to admit the neighbor, Mrs. Johnson who is a rather squeaky wide-eyed lady of no particular age, with a newspaper under her arm.

MAMA: *(changing her expression to acute delight and a ringing cheerful greeting)* Oh — hello there, Johnson.

JOHNSON: *(this is a woman who decided long ago to be enthusiastic about EVERY-THING in life and she is inclined to wave her wrist vigorously at the height of her exclamatory comments)* Hello there, yourself! H'you this evening, Ruth?

40 **RUTH:** *(not much of a deceptive type)* Fine, Mis' Johnson, h'you?

JOHNSON: Fine. *(Reaching out quickly, playfully, and patting Ruth's stomach.)* Ain't you starting to poke out none yet! *(She mugs with delight at the over familiar remark and her eyes dart around looking at the crates and packing preparation; Mama's face is a cold sheet of endurance.)* Oh, ain't we getting ready round here, though! Yessir! Lookathere! I'm telling you the Youngers is really getting ready to "move on up a little higher!" — Bless God!

MAMA: *(a little drily, doubting the total sincerity of the Blesser)* Bless God.

JOHNSON: He's good, ain't He?

MAMA: Oh yes, He's good.

45 **JOHNSON:** I mean sometimes He works in mysterious ways . . . but He works, don't He!

MAMA: *(the same)* Yes, he does.

JOHNSON: I'm just soooooo happy for y'all. And this here child — *(About Ruth.)* looks like she could just pop open with happiness, don't she. Where's all the rest of the family?

MAMA: Bennie's gone to bed —

JOHNSON: Ain't no . . . (*The implication is pregnancy.*) sickness done hit you — I hope . . . ?

MAMA: No — she just tired. She was out this evening.   50

JOHNSON: (*all is a coo, an emphatic coo*) Aw — ain't that lovely. She still going out with the little Murchison boy?

MAMA: (*drily*) Ummmm huh.

JOHNSON: That's lovely. You sure got lovely children, Younger. Me and Isaiah talks all the time 'bout what fine children you was blessed with. We sure do.

MAMA: Ruth, give Mis' Johnson a piece of sweet potato pie and some milk.

JOHNSON: Oh honey, I can't stay hardly a minute — I just dropped in to see if   55 there was anything I could do. (*Accepting the food easily.*) I guess y'all seen the news what's all over the colored paper this week . . .

MAMA: No — didn't get mine yet this week.

JOHNSON: (*lifting her head and blinking with the spirit of catastrophe*) You mean you ain't read 'bout them colored people that was bombed out their place out there?

Ruth straightens with concern and takes the paper and reads it. Johnson notices her and feeds commentary.

JOHNSON: Ain't it something how bad these here white folks is getting here in Chicago! Lord, getting so you think you right down in Mississippi! (*With a tremendous and rather insincere sense of melodrama.*) 'Course I thinks it's wonderful how our folk keeps on pushing out. You hear some of these Negroes round here talking 'bout how they don't go where they ain't wanted and all that — but not me, honey! (*This is a lie.*) Wilhemenia Othella Johnson goes anywhere, any time she feels like it! (*With head movement for emphasis.*) Yes I do! Why if we left it up to these here crackers, the poor niggers wouldn't have nothing — (*She clasps her hand over her mouth.*) Oh, I always forgets you don't 'low that word in your house.

MAMA: (*quietly, looking at her*) No — I don't 'low it.

JOHNSON: (*vigorously again*) Me neither! I was just telling Isaiah yesterday   60 when he come using it in front of me — I said, "Isaiah, it's just like Mis' Younger says all the time —"

MAMA: Don't you want some more pie?

JOHNSON: No — no thank you; this was lovely. I got to get on over home and have my midnight coffee, I hear some people say it don't let them sleep but I finds I can't close my eyes right lessen I done had that laaaast cup of coffee . . . (*She waits. A beat. Undaunted.*) My Goodnight coffee, I calls it!

MAMA: (*with much eye-rolling and communication between herself and Ruth*) Ruth, why don't you give Mis' Johnson some coffee.

Ruth gives Mama an unpleasant look for her kindness.

JOHNSON: (*accepting the coffee*) Where's Brother tonight?

MAMA: He's lying down.   65

JOHNSON: MMmmmmm, he sure gets his beauty rest, don't he? Good-looking man. Sure is a good-looking man! (*Reaching out to pat Ruth's stomach again.*)

I guess that's how come we keep on having babies around here. (*She winks at Mama.*) One thing 'bout Brother, he always know how to have a *good* time. And soooooo ambitious! I bet it was his idea y'all moving out to Clybourne Park. Lord — I bet this time next month y'all's names will have been in the papers plenty —(*Holding up her hands to mark off each word of the headline she can see in front of her.*) "NEGROES INVADE CLYBOURNE PARK—BOMBED!"

MAMA: (*she and Ruth look at the woman in amazement*) We ain't exactly moving out there to get bombed.

JOHNSON: Oh honey — you know I'm praying to God every day that don't nothing like that happen! But you have to think of life like it is — and these here Chicago peckerwoods is some baaaad peckerwoods.

MAMA: (*wearily*) We done thought about all that Mis' Johnson.

Beneatha comes out of the bedroom in her robe and passes through to the bathroom. Mrs. Johnson turns.

70   JOHNSON: Hello there, Bennie!

BENEATHA: (*crisply*) Hello, Mrs. Johnson.

JOHNSON: How is school?

BENEATHA: (*crisply*) Fine, thank you. (*She goes out.*)

JOHNSON: (*insulted*) Getting so she don't have much to say to nobody.

75   MAMA: The child was on her way to the bathroom.

JOHNSON: I know — but sometimes she act like ain't got time to pass the time of day with nobody ain't been to college. Oh — I ain't criticizing her none. It's just — you know how some of our young people gets when they get a little education. (*Mama and Ruth say nothing, just look at her.*) Yes — well. Well, I guess I better get on home. (*Unmoving.*) 'Course I can understand how she must be proud and everything — being the only one in the family to make something of herself. I know just being a chauffeur ain't never satisfied Brother none. He shouldn't feel like that, though. Ain't nothing wrong with being a chauffeur.

MAMA: There's plenty wrong with it.

JOHNSON: What?

MAMA: Plenty. My husband always said being any kind of a servant wasn't a fit thing for a man to have to be. He always said a man's hands was made to make things, or to turn the earth with — not to drive nobody's car for 'em — or —(*She looks at her own hands.*) carry they slop jars. And my boy is just like him — he wasn't meant to wait on nobody.

80   JOHNSON: (*rising, somewhat offended*) Mmmmmmmmmm. The Youngers is too much for me! (*She looks around.*) You sure one proud acting bunch of colored folks. Well — I always thinks like Booker T. Washington said that time —"Education has spoiled many a good plow hand"—

MAMA: Is that what old Booker T. said?

JOHNSON: He sure did.

MAMA: Well, it sounds just like him. The fool.

JOHNSON: (*indignantly*) Well — he was one of our great men.

MAMA: Who said so? 85

JOHNSON: (*nonplussed*) You know, me and you ain't never agreed about some things, Lena *Younger*. I guess I better be going —

RUTH: (quickly) Good night.

JOHNSON: Good night. Oh —(*Thrusting it at her.*) You can keep the paper! (*With a trill.*) 'Night.

MAMA: Good night, Mis' Johnson.

Mrs. Johnson exits.

RUTH: If ignorance was gold. 90

MAMA: Shush. Don't talk about folks behind their backs.

RUTH: You do.

MAMA: I'm old and corrupted. (*Beneatha enters.*) You was rude to Mis' Johnson, Beneatha, and I don't like it at all.

BENEATHA: (*at her door*) Mama, if there are two things we, as a people, have got to overcome, one is the Klu Klux Klan — and the other is Mrs. Johnson. (*She exits.*)

MAMA: Smart aleck. 95

The phone rings.

RUTH: I'll get it.

MAMA: Lord, ain't this a popular place tonight.

RUTH: (*at the phone*) Hello — Just a minute. (*Goes to door.*) Walter, it's Mrs. Arnold. (*Waits. Goes back to the phone. Tense.*) Hello. Yes, this is his wife speaking. He's lying down now. Yes . . . well, he'll be in tomorrow. He's been very sick. Yes — I know we should have called, but we were so sure he'd be able to come in today. Yes — yes, I'm very sorry. Yes . . . Thank you very much. (*She hangs up. Walter is standing in the doorway of the bedroom behind her.*) That was Mrs. Arnold.

WALTER: (*indifferently*) Was it?

RUTH: She said if you don't come in tomorrow that they are getting a new 100 man . . .

WALTER: Ain't that sad — ain't that crying sad.

RUTH: She said Mr. Arnold has had to take a cab for three days . . . Walter, you ain't been to work for three days! (*This is a revelation to her.*) Where you been, Walter Lee Younger? (*Walter looks at her and starts to laugh.*) You're going to lose your job.

WALTER: That's right . . . (*He turns on the radio.*)

RUTH: Oh, Walter, and with your mother working like a dog every day —

A steamy, deep blues pours into the room.

WALTER: That's sad too — Everything is sad. 105

MAMA: What you been doing for these three days, son?

WALTER: Mama — you don't know all the things a man what got leisure can find to do in this city . . . What's this — Friday night? Well — Wednesday I borrowed Willey Harris' car and I went for a drive . . . just me and myself and I drove and drove . . . Way out . . . way past South Chicago, and I parked the car and I sat and looked at the steel mills all day long. I just sat in the car and looked at them big black chimneys for hours. Then I drove back and I went to the Green Hat. (*Pause.*) And Thursday — Thursday I borrowed the car again and I got in it and I pointed it the other way and I drove the other way — for hours — way, way up to Wisconsin, and I looked at the farms. I just drove and looked at the farms. Then I drove back and I went to the Green Hat. (*Pause.*) And today — today I didn't get the car. Today I just walked. All over the Southside. And I looked at the Negroes and they looked at me and finally I just sat down on the curb at Thirty-ninth and South Parkway and I just sat there and watched the Negroes go by. And then I went to the Green Hat. You all sad? You all depressed? And you know where I am going right now —

Ruth goes out quietly.

MAMA: Oh, Big Walter, is this the harvest of our days?

WALTER: You know what I like about the Green Hat? I like this little cat they got there who blows a sax . . . He blows. He talks to me. He ain't but 'bout five feet tall and he's got a conked head and his eyes is always closed and he's all music —

110 **MAMA:** (*rising and getting some papers out of her handbag*) Walter —

WALTER: And there's this other guy who plays the piano . . . and they got a sound. I mean they can work on some music . . . They got the best little combo in the world in the Green Hat . . . You can just sit there and drink and listen to them three men play and you realize that don't nothing matter worth a damn, but just being there —

MAMA: I've helped do it to you, haven't I, son? Walter I been wrong.

WALTER: Naw — you ain't never been wrong about nothing, Mama.

MAMA: Listen to me, now. I say I been wrong son. That I been doing to you what the rest of the world been doing to you. (*She turns off the radio.*) Walter —(*She stops and he looks up slowly at her and she meets his eyes pleadingly.*) What you ain't never understood is that I ain't got nothing, don't own nothing, ain't never really wanted nothing that wasn't for you. There ain't nothing as precious to me . . . There ain't nothing worth holding on to, money, dreams, nothing else — if it means — if it means it's going to destroy my boy. (*She takes an envelope out of her handbag and puts it in front of him and he watches her without speaking or moving.*) I paid the man thirty-five hundred dollars down on the house. That leaves sixty-five hundred dollars. Monday morning I want you to take this money and take three thousand dollars and put it in a savings account for Beneatha's medical schooling. The rest you put in a checking account — with your name on it. And from now on any penny that come out of it or that go in it is for you to look after. For you to decide. (*She drops her hands a little helplessly.*) It ain't much, but it's all I got in the world and I'm putting it in your hands. I'm telling you to be the head of this family from now on like you supposed to be.

115 **WALTER:** (*stares at the money*) You trust me like that Mama?

MAMA: I ain't never stop trusting you. Like I ain't never stop loving you.

She goes out, and Walter sits looking at the money on the table. Finally, in a decisive gesture, he gets up, and, in mingled joy and desperation, picks up the money. At the same moment, Travis enters for bed.

TRAVIS: *(sweetly, more sweetly than we have ever known him)* What's the matter, Daddy? You drunk?

WALTER: *(sweetly, more sweetly than we have ever known him)* No, Daddy ain't drunk. Daddy ain't going to never be drunk again . . .

TRAVIS: Well, good night, Daddy.

The father has come from behind the couch and leans over, embracing his son.

WALTER: Son, I feel like talking to you tonight.   120

TRAVIS: About what?

WALTER: Oh, about a lot of things. About you and what kind of man you going to be when you grow up . . . Son — son, what do you want to be when you grow up?

TRAVIS: A bus driver.

WALTER: *(laughing a little)*: A what? Man, that ain't nothing to want to be!

TRAVIS: Why not?   125

WALTER: 'Cause, man — it ain't big enough — you know what I mean.

TRAVIS: I don't know then. I can't make up my mind. Sometimes Mama asks me that too. And sometimes when I tell her I just want to be like you — she says she don't want me to be like that and sometimes she says she does. . . .

WALTER: *(gathering him up in his arms)* You know what, Travis? In seven years you going to be seventeen years old. And things is going to be very different with us in seven years, Travis. . . . One day when you are seventeen I'll come home — home from my office downtown somewhere —

TRAVIS: You don't work in no office, Daddy.

WALTER: No — but after tonight. After what your daddy gonna do tonight,   130 there's going to be offices — a whole lot of offices. . . .

TRAVIS: What you gonna do tonight, Daddy?

WALTER: You wouldn't understand yet, son, but your daddy's gonna make a transaction . . . a business transaction that's going to change our lives. . . . That's how come one day when you 'bout seventeen years old I'll come home and I'll be pretty tired, you know what I mean, after a day of conference and secretaries getting things wrong the way they do . . . just a plain black Chrysler, I think, with white walls — no — black tires. More elegant. Rich people don't have to be flashy . . . though I'll have to get something a little sportier for Ruth — maybe a Cadillac convertible to do her shopping in. . . . And I'll come up the steps to the house and the gardener will be clipping away at the hedges and he'll say, "Good evening, Mr. Younger." And I'll say, "Hello, Jefferson, how are you this evening?" And I'll go inside and Ruth will come downstairs and meet me at the door and we'll kiss each other and she'll take my arm and we'll go up to your room to see you sitting on the floor with the catalogues of all the great schools in American around you. . . . All the great schools in the world! And — and I'll say, all right son — it's your seventeenth birthday, what is it you've decided? . . . Just tell me where you want to go to school and you'll go. Just tell me, what it is you want to be — and you'll *be* it. . . . Whatever you want to be — Yessir! (*He holds his arms open for Travis.*) You just name it, son . . . (*Travis leaps into them.*) and I hand you the world!

Walter's voice has risen in pitch and hysterical promise and on the last line he lifts Travis high.

Blackout.

SCENE 3

TIME: *Saturday, moving day, one week later.*

Before the curtain rises, Ruth's voice, a strident, dramatic church alto, cuts through the silence.

It is, in the darkness, a triumphant surge, a penetrating statement of expectation: "Oh, Lord, I don't feel no ways tired! Children, oh, glory hallelujah!"

As the curtain rises we see that Ruth is alone in the living room, finishing up the family's packing. It is moving day. She is nailing crates and trying cartons. Beneatha enters, carrying a guitar case, and watches her exuberant sister-in-law.

RUTH: Hey!

BENEATHA: (*putting away the case*) Hi.

RUTH: (*pointing at a package*) Honey — look in that package there and see what I found on sale this morning at the South Center. (*Ruth gets up and moves to the package and draws out some curtains.*) Lookahere — hand-turned hems!

BENEATHA: How do you know the window size out there?

5   RUTH: (*who hadn't thought of that*) Oh — Well, they bound to fit something in the whole house. Anyhow, they was too good a bargain to pass up. (*Ruth slaps her head, suddenly remembering something.*) Oh, Bennie — I meant to put a special note on that carton over there. That's your mama's good china and she wants 'em to be very careful with it.

BENEATHA: I'll do it.

Beneatha finds a piece of paper and starts to draw large letters on it.

RUTH: You know what I'm going to do soon as I get in that new house?

BENEATHA: What?

RUTH: Honey — I'm going to run me a tub of water up to here . . . (*With her fingers practically up to her nostrils.*) And I'm going to get in it — and I am going to sit . . . and sit . . . and sit in that hot water and the first person who knocks to tell *me* to hurry up and come out —

10   BENEATHA: Gets shot at sunrise.

RUTH: (*laughing happily*) You said it, sister! (*Noticing how large Beneatha is absent-mindedly making the note*): Honey, they ain't going to read that from no air-plane.

BENEATHA: (*laughing herself*) I guess I always think things have more emphasis if they are big, somehow.

RUTH: (*looking up at her and smiling*). You and your brother seem to have that as a philosophy of life. Lord, that man — done changed so 'round here. You know — you know what we did last might? Me and Walter Lee?

BENEATHA: What?

RUTH: (*smiling to herself*) We went to the movies. (*Looking at Beneatha to see if she understands.*) We went to the movies. You know the last time me and Walter went to the movies together?

BENEATHA: No.

RUTH: Me neither. That's how long it been. (*Smiling again.*) But we went last night. The picture wasn't much good, but that didn't seem to matter. We went — and we held hands.

BENEATHA: Oh, Lord!

RUTH: We held hands — and you know what?

BENEATHA: What?

RUTH: When we come out of the show it was late and dark and all the stores and things was closed up . . . and it was kind of chilly and there wasn't many people on the streets . . . and we was still holding hands, me and Walter.

BENEATHA: You're killing me.

Walter enters with a large package. His happiness is deep in him; he cannot keep still with his newfound exuberance. He is singing and wiggling and snapping his fingers. He puts his package in a corner and puts a phonograph record, which he has brought in with him, on the record player. As the music, soulful and sensuous, comes up he dances over to Ruth and tries to get her to dance with him. She gives in at last to his raunchiness and in a fit of giggling allows herself to be drawn into his mood. They dip and she melts into his arms in a classic, body melting "slow drag."

BENEATHA: (*regarding them a long time as they dance, then drawing in her breath for a deeply exaggerated comment which she does not particularly mean*) Talk about — olddddddddddd-fashion edddddddd — Negroes!

WALTER: (*stopping momentarily*) What kind of Negroes?

He says this in fun, He is not angry with her today, nor with anyone. He starts to dance with his wife again.

BENEATHA: Old-fashioned.

WALTER: (*as he dances with Ruth*) You know, when these *New Negroes* have their convention —(*Pointing at his sister.*)— that is going to be the chairman of the Committee on Unending Agitation. (*He goes on dancing, then stops.*) Race, race, race! . . . Girl, I do believe you are the first person in the history of the entire human race to successfully brainwash yourself. (*Beneatha breaks up and he goes on dancing. He stops again, enjoying his tease.*) Damn, even then N double A C P takes a holiday sometimes! (*Beneatha and Ruth laugh. He dances with Ruth some more and starts to laugh and stops and pantomimes someone over an operating table.*) I can just see that chick someday looking down at some poor cat on an operating table and before she starts to slice him, she says . . . (*Pulling his sleeves back maliciously.*) "By the way, what are your views on civil rights down there? . . ."

He laughs at her again and starts to dance happily. The bell sounds.

BENEATHA: Sticks and stones may break my bones but . . . words will never
hurt me!

*Beneatha goes to the door and opens it as Walter and Ruth go on with the clowning.
Beneatha is somewhat surprised to see a quiet looking middle-aged white man in a business suit holding his hat and a briefcase in his hand and consulting a small piece of paper.*

MAN: Uh — how do you do, miss. I am looking for a Mrs. — (*He looks at the slip
of paper.*) Mrs. Lena Younger? (*He stops short, struck dumb at the sight of the
oblivious Walter and Ruth.*)

BENEATHA: (*smoothing her hair with slight embarrassment*) Oh — yes, that's my
mother. Excuse me. (*She closes the door and turns to quiet the other two.*)
Ruth! Brother! (*Enunciating precisely but soundlessly: "There's a white man at
the door!" They stop dancing, Ruth cuts off the phonograph, Beneatha opens the
door. The man casts a curious quick glance at all of them.*) Uh — come in
please.

30 MAN: (*coming in*) Thank you.

BENEATHA: My mother isn't here just now. Is it business?

MAN: Yes . . . well, of a sort.

WALTER: (*freely, the Man of the House*) Have a seat. I'm Mrs. Younger's son. I
look after most of her business matters.

Ruth and Beneatha exchange amused glances.

MAN: (*regarding Walter, and sitting*) Well my name is Karl Lindner . . .

35 WALTER: (*stretching out his hand*) Walter Younger. This is my wife — (*Ruth nods
politely.*) — and my sister.

LINDNER: How do you do.

WALTER: (*amiably, as he sits himself easily on a chair, leaning forward on his knees
with interest and looking expectantly into the newcomer's face*) What can we do
for you, Mr. Lindner!

LINDNER: (*some minor shuffling of the hat and briefcase on his knees*) Well — I am
a representative of the Clybourne Park Improvement Association —

WALTER: (*pointing*) Why don't you sit your things on the floor?

40 LINDNER: Oh — yes. Thank you. (*He slides the briefcase and hat under the
chair.*) And as I was saying — I am from the Clybourne Park Improvement
Association and we have had it brought to our attention at the last meeting
that you people — or at least your mother — has bought a piece of residential property at — (*He digs for the slip of paper again.*) — four o six Clybourne
Street . . .

WALTER: That's right. Care for something to drink? Ruth, get Mr. Lindner a beer.

LINDNER: (*upset for some reason*) Oh — no, really. I mean thank you very
much, but no thank you.

RUTH: (*innocently*) Some coffee?

LINDNER: Thank you, nothing at all.

Beneatha a watching the man carefully.

LINDNER: Well, I don't know how much you folks know about our organiza-   45
tion. (*He is a gentle man; thoughtful and somewhat labored in his manner.*) It is
one of these community organizations set up to look after — oh, you know,
things like block upkeep and special projects and we also have what we call
our New Neighbors Orientation Committee . . .

BENEATHA: (*drily*) Yes — and what do they do?

LINDNER: (*turning a little to her and then returning the main force to Walter*)
Well — it's what you might call a sort of welcoming committee, I guess. I
mean they, we — I'm the chairman of the committee — go around and see
the new people who move into the neighborhood and sort of give them the
lowdown on the way we do things out in Glybourne Park.

BENEATHA: (*with appreciation of the two meanings, which escape Ruth and Walter*)
Un-huh.

LINDNER: And we also have the category of what the association calls —(*He
looks elsewhere.*) — uh — special community problems . . .

BENEATHA: Yes — and what are some of those?   50

WALTER: Girl, let the man talk.

LINDNER: (*with understated relief*) Thank you. I would sort of like to explain
this thing in my own way. I mean I want to explain to you in a certain way.

WALTER: Go ahead.

LINDNER: Yes. Well. I'm going to try to get right to the point. I'm sure we'll all
appreciate that in the long run.

BENEATHA: Yes.   55

WALTER: Be still now!

LINDNER: Well —

RUTH: (*still innocently*) Would you like another chair — you don't look comfortable.

LINDNER: (*more frustrated than annoyed*) No, thank you very much. Please.
Well — to get right to the point, I —(*A great breath, and he is off at last.*) I
am sure you people must be aware of some of the incidents which have happened in various parts of the city when colored people have moved into
certain areas —(*Beneatha exhales heavily and starts tossing a piece of fruit up
and down in the air.*) Well —because we have what I think is going to be a
unique type of organization in American community life — not only do we
deplore that kind of thing —but we are trying to do something about it.
(*Beneatha stops tossing and turns with a new and quizzical interest to the man.*)
We feel —(*gaining confidence in his mission because of the interest in the faces
of the people he is talking to.*) — we feel that most of the trouble in this world,
when you come right down to it —(*He hits his knee for emphasis.*) —most of
the trouble exists because people just don't sit down and talk to each other.

RUTH: (*nodding as she might in church, pleased with the remark*) You can say that   60
again, mister.

LINDNER: (*more encouraged by such affirmation*) That we don't try hard enough
in this world to understand the other fellow's problem. The other guy's
point of view.

RUTH: Now that's right.

Beneatha and Walter merely watch and listen with genuine interest.

LINDNER: Yes — that's the way we feel out in Clybourne Park. And that's why
I was elected to come here this afternoon and talk to you people. Friendly
like, you know, the way people should talk to each other and see if we
couldn't find some way to work this thing out. As I say, the whole business
is a matter of *caring* about the other fellow. Anybody can see that you are a
nice family of folks, hard working and honest I'm sure. (*Beneatha frowns
slightly, quizzically, her head tilted regarding him.*) Today everybody knows
what it means to be on the outside of *something*. And of course, there is
always somebody who is out to take advantage of people who don't always
understand.

WALTER: What do you mean?

65 LINDNER: Well — you see our community is made up of people who've worked
hard as the dickens for years to build up that little community. They're not
rich and fancy people; just hard-working, honest people who don't really
have much but those little homes and a dream of the kind of community
they want to raise their children in. Now, I don't say we are perfect and
there is a lot wrong in some of the things they want. But you've got to admit that a man, right or wrong, has the right to want to have the neighborhood he lives in a certain kind of way. And at the moment the overwhelming majority of our people out there feel that people get along better, take
more of a common interest in the life of the community, when they share a
common background. I want you to believe me when I tell you that race
prejudice simply doesn't enter into it. It is a matter of the people of
Clybourne Park believing, rightly or wrongly, as I say, that for the happiness
of all concerned that our Negro families are happier when they live in their
own communities.

BENEATHA: (*with a grand and bitter gesture*) This, friends, is the Welcoming
Committee!

WALTER: (*dumfounded, looking at Lindner*) Is this what you came marching all
the way over here to tell us?

LINDNER: Well, now we've been having a fine conversation. I hope you'll hear
me all the way through.

WALTER: (*tightly*) Go ahead, man.

70 LINDNER: You see — in the face of all the things I have said, we are prepared
to make your family a very generous offer . . .

BENEATHA: Thirty pieces and not a coin less!

WALTER: Yeah?

LINDNER: (*putting on his glasses drawing a form out of the briefcase*) Our association is prepared, through the collective effort of our people, to buy the
house from you at a financial gain to your family.

RUTH: Lord have mercy, ain't this the living gall!

75 WALTER: All right, you through?

LINDNER: Well, I want to give you the exact terms of the financial
arrangement —

WALTER: We don't want to hear no exact terms of no arrangements. I want to know if you got any more to tell us 'bout getting together?

LINDNER: *(taking off his glasses)* Well — I don't suppose that you feel . . .

WALTER: Never mind how I feel — you got any more or say 'bout how people ought to sit down and talk to each other? . . . Get out of my house, man.

He turns his back and walks to the door.

LINDNER: *(looking around at the hostile faces and reaching and assembling his hat and*   80
briefcase) Well — I don't understand why you people are reacting this way. What do you think you are going to gain by moving into a neighborhood where you just aren't wanted and where some elements — well — people can get awful worked up when they feel that their whole way of life and every-thing they've ever worked for is threatened.

WALTER: Get out.

LINDNER: *(at the door, holding a small card)* Well — I'm sorry it went like this.

WALTER: Get out.

LINDNER: *(almost sadly regarding Walter)* You just can't force people to change their hearts, son.

He turns and puts his card on a table and exits. Walter pushes the door to with stinging hatred, and stands looking at it. Ruth just sits and Beneatha just stands. They say noth-ing. Mama and Travis enter.

MAMA: Well — this all the packing got done since I left out of here this morn-   85
ing. I testify before God that my children got all the energy of the *dead!* What time the moving men due?

BENEATHA: Four o'clock. You had a caller, Mama.

She is smiling teasingly.

MAMA: Sure enough — who?

BENEATHA: *(her arms folded saucily)* The Welcoming Committee.

Walter and Ruth giggle.

MAMA: *(innocently)* Who?

BENEATHA: The Welcoming Committee. They said they're sure going to be   90
glad to see you when you get there.

WALTER: *(devilishly)* Yeah, they said they can't hardly wait to see your face.

Laughter

MAMA: *(sensing their facetiousness)* What's the matter with you all?

WALTER: Ain't nothing the matter with us. We just telling you 'bout the gentleman who came to see you this afternoon. From the Clybourne Park Improvement Association.

MAMA: What he want?

RUTH: *(in the same mood as Beneatha and Walter)* To welcome you, honey.   95

WALTER: He said they can't hardly wait. He said the one thing they don't have, that they just *dying* to have out there is a fine family of fine colored people! *(To Ruth and Beneatha.)* Ain't that right!

RUTH: (*mockingly*) Yeah! He left his card —

BENEATHA: (*handing card to Mama*) In case.

Mama reads and throws it on the floor — understanding and looking off as she draws her chair up to the table on which she has put her plant and some sticks and some card.

MAMA: Father, give us strength. (*Knowingly — and without fun.*) Did he threaten us?

100 BENEATHA: Oh — Mama — they don't do it like that any more. He talked Brotherhood. He said everybody ought to learn how to sit down and hate each other with good Christian fellowship.

She and Walter shake hands to ridicule the remark.

MAMA: (*sadly*) Lord, protect us . . .

RUTH: You should hear the money those folks raised to buy the house from us. All we paid and then some.

BENEATHA: What they think we going to do — eat 'em?

RUTH: No, honey, marry 'em.

105 MAMA: (*shaking her head*) Lord, Lord, Lord . . .

RUTH: Well — that's the way the crackers crumble. (*A beat.*) Joke.

BENEATHA: (*laughingly noticing what her mother is doing*) Mama, what are you doing?

MAMA: Fixing my plant so it won't get hurt none on the way . . .

BENEATHA: Mama, you going to take *that* to the new house?

110 MAMA: Un-huh —

BENEATHA: That raggedy-looking old thing?

MAMA: (*stopping and looking at her*) It expresses ME!

RUTH: (*with delight, to Beneatha*) So there, Miss Thing!

Walter comes to Mama suddenly and bends down behind her and squeezes her in his arms with all his strength. She is overwhelmed by the suddenness of it and, though delighted, her manner is like that of Ruth and Travis.

MAMA: Look out now, boy! You make me mess up my thing here!

115 WALTER: (*his face lit, he slips down on his knees beside her, his arms still about her*) Mama . . . you know what it means to climb up in the chariot?

MAMA: (*gruffly, very happy*) Get on away from me now . . .

RUTH: (*near the gift-wrapped package, trying to catch Walter's eye*) Psst —

WALTER: What the old song say, Mama . . .

RUTH: Walter — Now?

She is pointing at the package.

120 WALTER: (*speaking the lines, sweetly, playfully, in his mother's face*)

I got wings . . . you got wings . . .
All God's children got wings . . .

MAMA: Boy — get out of my face and do some work . . .

WALTER:
> When I get to heaven gonna put on my wings,
> Gonna fly all over God's heaven . . .

BENEATHA: (*teasingly, from across the room*) Everybody talking 'bout heaven ain't going there!

WALTER: (*to Ruth, who is carrying the box across to them*) I don't know, you think we ought to give her that . . . Seems to me she ain't been very appreciative around here.

MAMA: (*eying the box, which is obviously a gift*) What is that? 125

WALTER: (*taking it from Ruth and putting it on the table in front of Mama*) Well — what you all think? Should we give it to her?

RUTH: Oh — she was pretty good today.

MAMA: I'll good you —

She turns her eyes to the box again.

BENEATHA: Open it, Mama.

She stands up, looks at it, turns and looks at all of them, and then presses her hands together does not open the package.

WALTER: (*sweetly*) Open it, Mama. It's for you. (*Mama looks in his eyes. It is the* 130
first present in her life without its being Christmas. Slowly she opens her package and lifts out, one by one, a brand-new sparkling set of gardening tools. Walter continues, prodding.) Ruth made up the note — read it . . .

MAMA: (*picking up the card and adjusting her glasses*) "To our own Mrs. Miniver — Love from Brother, Ruth, and Beneatha." Ain't that lovely . . .

TRAVIS: (*tugging at his father's sleeve*) Daddy, can I give her mine now?

WALTER: All right, son. (*Travis flies to get his gift.*)

MAMA: Now I don't have to use my knives and forks no more . . .

WALTER: Travis didn't want to go in with the rest of us, Mama. He got his 135
own. (*Somewhat amused.*) We don't know what it is . . .

TRAVIS: (*racing back in the room with a large hatbox and putting it in front of his grandmother*) Here!

MAMA: Lord have mercy, baby. You done gone and bought your grandmother a hat?

TRAVIS: (*very proud*) Open it!

She does and lifts out an elaborate, but very elaborate, wide gardening hat, and all the adults break up at the sight of it.

RUTH: Travis, honey, what is that?

TRAVIS: (*who thinks it is beautiful and appropriate*) It's a gardening hat! Like the 140
ladies always have on in the magazines when they work in their gardens.

BENEATHA: (*giggling fiercely*) Travis — we were trying to make Mama Mrs. Miniver — not Scarlett O'Hara!

MAMA: (*indignantly*) What's the matter with you all! This here is a beautiful hat! (*Absurdly.*) I always wanted me one just like it!

She pops it on her head to prove it to her grandson, and the hat is ludicrous and considerably oversized.

RUTH: Hot dog! Go, Mama!

WALTER: *(doubled over with laughter)* I'm sorry, Mama — but you look like you ready to go out and chop you some cotton sure enough!

They all laugh except Mama, out of deference to Travis's feelings.

145   MAMA: *(gathering the boy up to her)* Bless your heart — this is the prettiest hat I ever owned — *(Walter, Ruth, and Beneatha chime in — noisily, festively, and insincerely congratulating Travis on his gift.)* What are we all standing around here for? We ain't finished packin' yet. Bennie, you ain't packed one book.

The bell rings.

BENEATHA: That couldn't be the movers . . . it's not hardly two good yet —

Beneatha goes into her room. Mama starts for door.

WALTER: *(turning, stiffening)* Wait — wait — I'll get it.

He stands and looks at the door.

MAMA: You expecting company, son?

WALTER: *(just looking at the door)* Yeah — yeah . . .

Mama looks at Ruth, and they exchange innocent and unfrightened glances.

150   MAMA: *(not understanding)* Well, let them in, son.

BENEATHA: *(from her room)* We need some more string.

MAMA: Travis — you run to the hardware and get me some string cord.

Mama goes out and Walter turns and looks at Ruth. Travis goes to a dish for money.

RUTH: Why don't you answer the door, man?

WALTER: *(suddenly bounding across the floor to embrace her)* 'Cause sometimes it hard to let the future begin! *(Stooping down in her face.)*

I got wings! You got wings!

All God's children got wings!

He crosses to the door and throws it open. Standing there is a very slight little man in a not-too-prosperous business suit and with haunted frightened eyes and a hat pulled down tightly, brim up, around his forehead. Travis passes between the men and exits. Walter leans deep in the man's face, still in his jubilance.

When I get to heaven gonna put on my wings,

Gonna fly all over God's heaven . . .

The little man just stares at him.

Heaven —

Suddenly he stops and looks past the little man into the empty hallways.

Where's Willy, man?

BOBO: He ain't with me.   155

WALTER: (*not disturbed*) Oh — come on in. You know my wife.

BOBO: (*dumbly, taking off his hat*) Yes — h'you, Miss Ruth.

RUTH: (*quietly, a mood apart form her husband, already seeing Bobo*) Hello, Bobo.

WALTER: You right on time today . . . Right on time. That's the way! (*He slaps Bobo on his back.*) Sit down . . . lemme hear.

Ruth stands stiffly and quietly in back of them, as though somehow she senses death, her eyes fixed on her husband.

BOBO: (*his frightened eyes on the floor, his hat in his hands*) Could I please get a   160
drink of water, before I tell you about it, Walter Lee?

Walter does not take his eyes off the man. Ruth goes blindly to the tap and gets a glass of water and brings it to Bobo.

WALTER: There ain't nothing wrong, is there?

BOBO: Lemme tell you —

WALTER: Man — didn't nothing go wrong?

BOBO: Lemme tell you — Walter Lee. (*Looking at Ruth and talking to her more than to Walter.*) You know how it was. I got to tell you how it was. I mean first I got to tell you how it was all the way . . . I mean about the money I put in, Walter Lee . . .

WALTER: (*with taut agitation now*) What about the money you put in?   165

BOBO: Well — it wasn't much as we told you — me and Willy — (*He stops.*) I'm sorry, Walter. I got a bad feeling about it. I got a real bad feeling about it . . .

WALTER: Man, what you telling me about all this for? . . . Tell me what happened in Springfield . . .

BOBO: Springfield.

RUTH: (*like a dead woman*) What was supposed to happen in Springfield?

BOBO: (*to her*) This deal that me and Walter went into with Willy — Me and   170
Willy was going to go down to Springfield and spread some money 'round so's we wouldn't have to wait so long for the liquor license . . . That's what we were going to do. Everybody said that was the way you had to do, you understand, Miss Ruth?

WALTER: Man — what happened down there?

BOBO: (*a pitiful man, near tears*) I'm trying to tell you, Walter.

WALTER: (*screaming at him suddenly*) THEN TELL ME, GODDAMMIT . . . WHAT'S THE MATTER WITH YOU?

BOBO: Man . . . I didn't go to no Springfield, yesterday.

WALTER: (*halted, life hanging in the moment*) Why not?   175

BOBO: (*the long way, the hard way to tell*) 'Cause I didn't have no reasons to . . .

WALTER: Man, what are you talking about!

BOBO: I'm talking about the fact that when I got to the train station yesterday morning — eight o'clock like we planned . . . Man — *Willy didn't never show up.*

WALTER: Why . . . where was he . . . where is he?

180 **BOBO:** That's what I'm trying to tell you . . . I don't know . . . I waited six hours . . . I called his house . . . and I waited . . . six hours . . . I waited in that train station six hours . . . (*Breaking into tears.*) That was all the extra money I had in the world . . . (*Looking up at Walter with the tears running down his face.*) Man, Willy is gone.

WALTER: Gone, what you mean Willy is gone? Gone where? You mean he went by himself. You mean he went off to Springfield by himself — to take care of getting the license —(*Turns and looks anxiously at Ruth.*) You mean maybe he didn't want too many people in on the business down there? (*Looks to Ruth again, as before.*) You know Willy got his own ways. (*Looks back to Bobo.*) Maybe you was late yesterday and he just went on down there without you. Maybe — maybe — he's been callin' you at home tryin' to tell you what happened or something. Maybe — maybe — he just got sick. He's somewhere — he's got to be somewhere. We just got to find him — me and you got to find him. (*Grabs Bobo senselessly by the cellar and starts to shake him.*) We got to!

BOBO: (*in sudden angry, frightened agony*) Wha's the matter with you, Walter! When a cat take off with your money be don't leave you no road maps!

WALTER: (*turning madly, as though he is looking for Willy in the very room*) Willy! . . . Willy . . . don't do it . . . Please don't do it . . . Man, not with that money . . . Man, please, not with that money . . . Oh, God . . . Don't let it be true . . . (*He is wandering around, crying out for Willy and looking for him or perhaps for help from God.*) Man . . . I trusted you . . . Man, I put my life in your hands . . . (*He starts to crumple down on the floor as Ruth just covers her face in horror. Mama opens the door and comes into the room, with Beneatha behind her.*) Man . . . (*He starts to pound the floor with his fists, sobbing wildly.*)

THAT MONEY IS MADE OUT OF MY FATHER'S FLASH —

BOBO: (*standing over him helplessly*) I'm sorry, Walter . . . (*only Walter's sobs reply. Bobo puts on his hat.*) I had my life staked on this deal, too . . .

He exits.

185 **MAMA:** (*to Walter*) Son —(*She goes to him, bends down to him, talks to his bent head.*) Son . . . Is it gone? Son, I gave you sixty-five hundred dollars. Is it gone? All of it? Beneatha's money too?

WALTER: (*lifting his head slowly*) Mama . . . I never . . . went to the bank at all . . .

MAMA: (*not wanting to believe him*) You mean . . . your sister's school money . . . you used that too . . . Walter? . . .

WALTER: Yessss! All of it . . . It's all gone . . .

There is total silence. Ruth stands with her face covered with her hands; Beneatha leans forlornly against a wall, fingering a piece of red ribbon from the mother's gift. Mama stops and looks at her son without recognition and then, quite without thinking about it, starts to beat him senselessly in the face. Beneatha goes to them and stops it.

BENEATHA: Mama!

Mama stops and looks at both of her children and rises slowly and wanders vaguely, aimlessly away from them.

MAMA: I seen . . . him . . . night after night . . . come in . . . and look at that   190
rug . . . and then look at me . . . the red showing in his eyes . . . the veins
moving in his head . . . I seen him grow thin and old before he was forty . . .
working and working and working like somebody's old horse . . . killing
himself . . . and you — you give it all away in a day — *(She raises her arms to
strike him again.)*

BENEATHA: Mama —

MAMA: Oh, God . . . *(She looks up to Him.)* Look down here — and show me
the strength.

BENEATHA: Mama —

MAMA: *(folding over)* Strength . . .

BENEATHA: *(plaintively)* Mama . . .   195

MAMA: Strength!

Curtain.

ACT 3

TIME: *An hour later.*

*At curtain, there is a sullen light of gloom in the living room, gray light not unlike that
which began the first scene of Act 1. At left we can see Walter within his room, alone
with himself. He is stretched out on the bed, his shirt out and open, his arms under his
head. He does not smoke, he does not cry out, he merely lies there, looking up at the ceiling, much as if he were alone in the world.*

*In the living room Beneatha sits at the table, still surrounded by the now almost ominous packing crates. She sits looking off. We feel that this is a mood struck perhaps an
hour before, and it lingers now, full of the empty sound of profound disappointment. We
see on a line from her brother's bedroom the sameness of their attitudes. Presently the bell
rings and Beneatha rises without ambition or interest in answering. It is Asagai, smiling
broadly, striding into the room with energy and happy expectation and conversations.*

ASAGAI: I came over . . . I had some free time. I thought I might help with the
packing. Ah, I like the look of packing crates! A household in preparation
for a journey! It depresses some people . . . but for me . . . it is another feeling. Something full of the flow of life, do you understand? Movement,
progress . . . It makes me think of Africa.

BENEATHA: Africa!

ASAGAI: What kind of a mood is this? Have I told you how deeply you move
me?

BENEATHA: He gave away the money, Asagai . . .

ASAGAI: Who gave away what money?   5

BENEATHA: The insurance money. My brother gave it away.

ASAGAI: Gave it away?

BENEATHA: He made an investment! With a man even Travis wouldn't have
trusted with his most worn out marbles.

ASAGAI: And it's gone?

10 BENEATHA: Gone!

ASAGAI: I'm very sorry . . . And you, now?

BENEATHA: Me? . . . Me? . . . Me, I'm nothing . . . Me. When I was very small
. . . we used to take our sleds out in the wintertime and the only hills we
had were the ice-covered stone steps of some houses down the street. And
we used to fill them in with snow and make them smooth and slide down
them all day . . . and it was very dangerous, you know . . . far too steep . . .
and sure enough one day a kid named Rufus came down too fast and hit the
sidewalk and we saw his face just split open right there in front of us . . .
And I remember standing there looking at his bloody open face thinking
that was the end of Rufus. But the ambulance came and they took him to
the hospital and they fixed the broken bones and they sewed it all up . . .
and the next time I saw Rufus he just had a little line down the middle of
his face . . . I never got over that . . .

ASAGAI: What?

BENEATHA: That that was what one person could do for another, fix him
up — sew up the problem, make him all right again. That was the most
marvelous thing in the world . . . I wanted to do that, I always thought it
was the one concrete thing in the world that a human being could do. Fix
up the sick, you know — and make them whole again. This was truly being
God . . .

15 ASAGAI: You wanted to be God?

BENEATHA: No — I wanted to cure. It used to be so important to me. I wanted
to cure. It used to matter. I used to care. I mean about people and how their
bodies hurt . . .

ASAGAI: And you've stopped caring?

BENEATHA: Yes — I think so.

ASAGAI: Why?

20 BENEATHA: *(bitterly)* Because it doesn't seem deep enough, close enough to
what ails mankind! It was a child's way of seeing things — or an idealist's.

ASAGAI: Children see things very well sometimes — and idealists even better.

BENEATHA: I know that's what you think. Because you are still where I left off.
You with all your talk and dreams about Africa! You still think you can
patch up the world. Cure the Great Sore of Colonialism — *(Loftily, mocking
it.)* with the Penicillin of Independent —!

ASAGAI: Yes!

BENEATHA: Independence *and then what?* What about all the crooks and
thieves and just plain idiots who will come into power and steal and plun-
der the same as before — only now they will be black and do it in the name
of the new Independence — WHAT ABOUT THEM?!

25 ASAGAI: That will be the problem for another time. First we must get there.

BENEATHA: And where does it end?

ASAGAI: End? Who even spoke of an end? To life? To living?

BENEATHA: An end to misery! To stupidity! Don't you see there isn't any real
progress, Asagai, there is only one large circle that we march in, around and

around, each of us with our own little picture in front of us — our own little mirage that we think is the future.

ASAGAI: That is the mistake.

BENEATHA: What?   30

ASAGAI: What you just said — about the circle. It isn't a circle — it is simply a long line — as in geometry, you know, one that reaches into infinity. And because we cannot see the end — we also cannot see how it changes. And it is very odd but those who see the changes — who dream, who will not give up — are called idealists . . . and those who see only the circle — we call *them* the "realists"!

BENEATHA: Asagai, while I was sleeping in that bed in there, people went out and took the future right out of my hands! And nobody asked me, nobody consulted me — they just went out and changed my life!

ASAGAI: Was it your money?

BENEATHA: What?

ASAGAI: Was it your money he gave away?   35

BENEATHA: It belonged to all of us.

ASAGAI: But did you earn it? Would you have had it at all if your father had not died?

BENEATHA: No.

ASAGAI: Then isn't there something wrong in a house — in a world — where all dreams, good or bad, must depend on the death of a man? I never thought to see *you* like this, Alaiyo. You! Your brother made a mistake and you are grateful to him so that now you can give up the ailing human race on account of it! You talk about what good is struggle, what good is anything! Where are we all going and why are we bothering!

BENEATHA: AND YOU CANNOT ANSWER IT!   40

ASAGAI: *(shouting over her)* I LIVE THE ANSWER! *(Pause.)* In my village at home it is the exceptional man who can even read a newspaper . . . or who ever sees a book at all. I will go home and much of what I will have to say will seem strange to the people of my village. But I will teach and work and things will happen, slowly and swiftly. At times it will seem that nothing changes at all . . . and then again the sudden dramatic events which make history leap into the future. And then quiet again. Retrogression even. Guns, murder, revolution. And I even will have moments when I wonder if the quiet was not better than all that death and hatred. But I will look about my village at the illiteracy and disease and ignorance and I will not wonder long. And perhaps . . . perhaps I will be a great man . . . I mean perhaps I will hold on to the substance of truth and find my way always with the right course . . . and perhaps for it I will be butchered in my bed some night by the servants of empire . . .

BENEATHA: *The martyr!*

ASAGAI: *(he smiles)* . . . or perhaps I shall live to be a very old man, respected and esteemed in my new nation . . . And perhaps I shall hold office and this is what I'm trying to tell you, Alaiyo: perhaps the things I believe now for my country will be wrong and outmoded, and I will not understand and do terrible things to have things my way or merely to keep my power. Don't you see that there will be young men and women — not British soldiers then, but my own black countrymen — to step out of the shadows some evening and slit my then useless throat? Don't you see they have always been there . . . that they always will be. And that such a thing as my own death will be an advance? They who might kill me even . . . actually replenish all that I was.

BENEATHA: Oh, Asagai, I know all that.

45 **ASAGAI:** Good! Then stop moaning and groaning and tell me what you plan to do.

BENEATHA: Do?

ASAGAI: I have a bit of a suggestion.

BENEATHA: What?

ASAGAI: (*rather quietly for him*) That when it is all over — that you come home with me —

50 **BENEATHA:** (*staring at him and crossing away with exasperation*) Oh — Asagai — at this moment you decide to be romantic!

ASAGAI: (*quickly understanding the misunderstanding*) My dear, young creature of the New World — I do not mean across the city — I mean across the ocean: home — to Africa.

BENEATHA: (*slowly understanding and turning to him with murmured amazement*) To Africa?

ASAGAI: Yes! . . . (*smiling and lifting his arms playfully.*) Three hundred years later the African Prince rose up out of the seas and swept the maiden back across the middle passage over which her ancestors had come —

BENEATHA: (*unable to play*) To — to Nigeria?

55 **ASAGAI:** Nigeria, Home. (*Coming to her with genuine romantic flippancy.*) I will show you our mountains and our stars, and give you cool drinks from gourds and teach you the old songs and the ways of our people — and, in time, we will pretend that —(*Very softly*)— you have only been away for a day. Say that you'll come —(*He swings her around and takes her full in his arms in a kiss which proceeds to passion.*)

BENEATHA: (*pulling away suddenly*) You're getting me all mixed up —

ASAGAI: Why?

BENEATHA: Too many things — too many things have happened today. I must sit down and think. I don't know what I feel about anything right this minute.

She promptly sits down and props her chin on her fist.

ASAGAI: (*charmed*) All right, I shall leave you. No — don't get up. (*Touching her, gently, sweetly*) Just sit awhile and think . . . Never be afraid to sit awhile and think. (*He goes to door and looks at her.*) How often I have looked at you and said, "Ah — so this is what the New World hath finally wrought . . ."

He exits. Beneatha sits on alone. Presently Walter enters from his room and starts to rummage through things, feverishly looking for something. She looks up and turns in her seat.

BENEATHA: (*hissingly*) Yes — just look at what the New World hath wrought!   60
. . . Just look! (*She gestures with bitter disgust.*) There he is! *Monsieur le petit bourgeois noir*° — himself! There he is — Symbol of a Rising Class! Entrepreneur! Titan of the system! (*Walter ignores her completely and continues frantically and destructively looking for something and hurling things to floor and tearing things out of their place in his search. Beneatha ignores the eccentricity of his actions and goes on with the monologue of insult.*) Did you dream of yachts on Lake Michigan, Brother? Did you see yourself on that Great Day sitting down at the Conference Table, surrounded by all the mighty bald-headed-men in America? All halted, waiting, breathless, waiting for your pronouncements on industry? Waiting for you — Chairman of the Board! (*Walter finds what he is looking for — a small piece of white paper — and pushes it in his pocket and puts on his coat and rushes out without ever having looked at her. She shouts after him.*) I look at you and I see the final triumph of stupidity in the world!

The door slams and she returns to just sitting again. Ruth comes quickly out of Mama's room.

RUTH: Who was that?
BENEATHA: Your husband.
RUTH: Where did he go?
BENEATHA: Who knows — maybe he has an appointment at U.S. Steel.
RUTH: (*anxiously, with frightened eyes*) You didn't say nothing bad to him, did you?
BENEATHA: Bad? Say anything bad to him? No — I told him he was a sweet boy   65
and full of dreams and everything is strictly peachy keen, as the ofay kids say!

Mama enters from her bedroom. She is lost, vague, trying to catch hold, to make some sense of her former command of the world, but it still eludes her. A sense of waste overwhelms her gait; a measure of apology rides on her shoulders. She goes to her plant, which has remained on the table, looks at it, picks it up and takes it to the window sill and sits it outside, and she stands and looks at it a long moment. Then she closes the window, straightens her body with effort and turns around to her children.

MAMA: Well — ain't it a mess in here, though? (*A false cheerfulness, a beginning of something.*) I guess we all better stop moping around and get some work done. All this unpacking and everything we got to do. (*Ruth raises her head slowly in response to the sense of the line; and Beneatha in similar manner turns very slowly to look at her mother.*) One of you all better call the moving people and tell 'em not to come.
RUTH: Tell 'em not to come?
MAMA: Of course, baby. Ain't no need in 'em coming all the way here and having to go back. They charges for that too. (*She sits down, fingers to her brow, thinking.*) Lord, ever since I was a little girl, I always remembers people saying, "Lena — Lena Eggleston, you aims too high all the time. You needs to slow down and see life a little more like it is. Just slow down some." That's what they always used to say down home — "Lord, that Lena Eggleston is a high-minded thing. She'll get her due one day!"

°*Monsieur le petit bourgeois noir.* French for *Mr. Black Bourgoisie.*

70 **RUTH:** No, Lena . . .
MAMA: Me and Big Walter just didn't never learn right.
RUTH: Lena, no! We gotta go. Bennie — tell her . . .

She rises and crosses to Beneatha with her arms outstretched. Beneatha doesn't respond.

Tell her we can still move . . . the notes ain't but a hundred and twenty-five a
month. We got four grown people in this house — we can work . . .
MAMA: (*to herself*) Just aimed too high all the time —
RUTH: (*turning and going to Mama fast — the words pouring out with urgency and
desperation*) Lena — I'll work . . . I'll work twenty hours a day in all the
kitchens in Chicago . . . I'll strap my baby on my back if I have to and scrub
all the floors in America and wash all the sheets in America if I have to —
but we got to MOVE! We got to get OUT OF HERE!!

Mama reaches out absently and pats Ruth's hand.

75 **MAMA:** No — I sees things differently now. Been thinking 'bout some of the
things we could do to fix this place up some. I seen a second-hand bureau
over on Maxwell Street just the other day that could fit right there. (*She
points to where the new furniture might go. Ruth wanders away from her.*)
Would need some new handles on it and then a little varnish and it look
like something brand-new. And — we can put up them new curtains in the
kitchen . . . Why this place be looking fine. Cheer us all up so that we forget trouble ever come . . . (*To Ruth.*) And you could get some nice screens
to put up in your room round the baby's bassinet . . . (*She looks at both of
them pleadingly.*) Sometimes you just got to know when to give up some
things . . . and hold on to what you got. . .

*Walter enters from the outside, looking spent and leaning against the door, his coat hang-
ing from him.*

MAMA: Where you been, son?
WALTER: (*breathing hard*) Made a call.
MAMA: To The Man. (*He heads for his room.*)
80 **MAMA:** What man, baby?
WALTER: (*stops in the door*) The Man, Mama. Don't you know who The Man is?
RUTH: Walter Lee?
WALTER: *The Man.* Like the guys in the streets say — The Man. Captain
Boss — Mistuh Charley . . . Old Cap'n Please Mr. Bossman . . .
BENEATHA: (*suddenly*) Lindner!
85 **WALTER:** That's right! That's good. I told him to come right over.
BENEATHA: (*fiercely, understanding*) For what? What do you want to see him
for!
WALTER: (*looking at his sister*) We going to do business with him.
MAMA: What you talking 'bout, son?
WALTER: Talking 'bout life, Mama. You all always telling me to see life like it
is. Well — I laid in there on my back today . . . and I figured it out. Life just
like it is. Who gets and who don't get. (*He sits down with his coat on and*

laughs.) Mama, you know it's all divided up. Life is. Sure enough, Between the takers and the "tooken." (*He laughs.*) I've figured it our finally. (*He looks around at them.*) Yeah. Some of us always getting "tooken." (*He laughs.*) People like Willy Harris, they don't never get "tooken." And you know why the rest of us do? 'Cause we all mixed up. Mixed up bad. We get to looking 'round for the right and the wrong, and we worry about it and cry about it and stay up nights trying to figure our 'bout the wrong and the right of things all the time . . . And all the time, man, them takers is out there operating, just taking and taking. Willy Harris? Shoot —Willy Harris don't even count. He don't even count in the big scheme of things. But I'll say one thing for old Willy Harris . . . he's taught me something. He's taught me to keep my eye on what counts in this world. Yeah —(*Shouting out a little.*) Thanks, Willy!

RUTH: What did you call that man for, Walter Lee?   90

WALTER: Called him to tell him to come on over to the show: Gonna put on a show for the man. Just what he wants to see. You see, Mama, the man came here today and he told us that them people out there where you want us to move — well they do upset they willing to pay us *not* to move! (*He laughs again.*) And — and oh, Mama — you would have been proud of the way me and Ruth and Bennie acted. We told him to get out . . . Lord have mercy! We told the man to get out! Oh, we was some proud folks this afternoon, yeah. (*He lights a cigarette.*) We were still full of that old-time stuff . . .

RUTH: (*coming toward him slowly*) You talking 'bout taking them people's money to keep us from moving in that house?

WALTER: I ain't just talking 'bout it, baby — I'm telling you that's what's going to happen!

BENEATHA: Oh, God! Where is the bottom! Where is the real honest-to-God bottom so he can't go any farther!

WALTER: See — that's the old stuff. You and that boy that was here today.   95 You all want everybody to carry a flag and a spear and sing some marching songs, huh? You wanna spend your life looking into things and trying to find the right and the wrong part, huh? Yeah. You know what's going to happen to that boy someday —he'll find himself sitting in a dungeon, locked in forever — and the takers will have the key! Forget it, baby! There ain't no causes — there ain't nothing but taking in this world, and he who takes most is smartest — and it don't make a damn bit of difference *how.*

MAMA: You making something inside me cry, son. Some awful pain inside me.

WALTER: Don't cry, Mama. Understand. That white man is going to walk in that door able to write checks for more money than we ever had. It's important to him and I'm going to help him . . . I'm going to put on the show, Mama.

MAMA: Son — I come from five generations of people who was slaves and sharecroppers — but ain't nobody in my family never let nobody pay 'em no money that was a way of telling us we wasn't fit to walk the earth. We ain't never been that poor. (*Raising her eyes and looking at him.*) We ain't never been that — dead inside.

BENEATHA: Well—we are dead now. All the talk about dreams and sunlight that goes on in this house. It's all dead now.

100 WALTER: What's the matter with you all! I didn't make this world! It was give to me this way! Hell, yes, I want me some yachts someday! Yes, I want to hang some real pearls round my wife's neck. Ain't she supposed to wear no pearls? Somebody tell me — tell me, who decides which women is suppose to wear pearls in this world. I tell you I am a *man*— and I think my wife should wear some pearls in this world!

This last line hangs a good while and Walter begins to move about the room. The word "Man" has penetrated his consciousness; he mumbles it to himself repeatedly between strange agitated pauses as he moves about.

MAMA: Baby, how you going to feel on the inside?

WALTER: Fine! . . . Going to feel fine . . . a man . . .

MAMA: You won't have nothing left then, Walter Lee.

WALTER: (*coming to her*) I'm going to feel fine, Mama. I'm going to look that son-of-a-bitch in the eyes and say —(*He falters.*)— and say, "All right, Mr. Lindner —(*He falters eve more.*)— that's *your* neighborhood out there! You got the right to keep it like you want! You got the right to have it like you want! Just write the check and — the house is yours." And — and I am going to say —(*His voice almost breaks.*) And you — you people just put the money in my hand and you won't have to live next to this bunch of stinking niggers! . . ." (*He straightens up and moves away from his mother, walking, around the room.*) And maybe — maybe I'll just get down on my black knees . . . (*He does so, Ruth and Bennie and Mama watch him in frozen horror.*) "Captain, Mistuh, Bossman —(*Groveling and grinning and wringing his hands in profoundly anguished imitation of the slow-witted movie stereotype.*) A hee-hee-hee! Oh, Yassuhboss! Yassssssuh! Great white —(*Voice breaking, he forces himself to go on.*)— Father, just gi' ussen de money, fo' God's sake, and we's — we's ain't gwine come out deh and dirty up yo' white folks neighborhood . . ." (*He breaks down completely.*) And I'll feel fine! Fine! FINE! (*He gets up and goes into the bedroom.*)

105 BENEATHA: That is not a man. That is nothing but a roothless rat.

MAMA: Yes — death done come in this here house. (*She is nodding, slowly, reflectively.*) Done come walking in my house on the lips of my children. You what supposed to be my beginning again. You — what supposed to be my harvest. (*To Beneatha.*) You — you mourning your brother?

BENEATHA: He's no brother of mine.

MAMA: What you say?

BENEATHA: I said that that individual in that room is no brother of mine.

110 MAMA: That's what I thought you said. You feeling like you better than he is today? (*Beneatha does not answer.*) Yes? What you tell him a minute ago? That he wasn't a man? Yes? You give him up for me? You done wrote his epitaph too —like the rest of the world? Well, who give you the privilege?

BENEATHA: Be on my side for once! You saw what he just did, Mama! You saw him — down on his knees. Wasn't it you who taught me to despise any man who would do that? Do what he's going to do?

MAMA: Yes — I taught you that Me and your daddy. But I thought I taught you something else too . . . I thought I taught you to love him.

BENEATHA: Love him? There is nothing left to love.

MAMA: There is *always* something left to love. And if you ain't learned that, you ain't learned nothing. *(Looking at her.)* Have you cried for that boy today? I don't mean for yourself and for the family 'cause we lost the money. I mean for him: what he been through and what it done to him. Child, when do you think is the time to love somebody the most? When they done good and made things easy for everybody? Well then you ain't through learning — because that ain't the time at all. It's when he's at his lowest and can't believe in hisself 'cause the world done whipped him so! When you starts measuring somebody, measure him right, child, measure him right. Make sure you done taken into account what hills and valleys he come through before he got to wherever he is.

Travis bursts into the room at the end of the speech, leaving the door open.

TRAVIS: Grandmama — the moving men are downstairs! The truck just pulled   115
up.

MAMA: *(turning and looking at him)* Are they, baby? They downstairs?

She sighs and sits. Lindner appears in the doorway. He peers in and knocks lightly, to gain attention, and comes in. All turn to look at him.

LINDNER: *(hat and briefcase in hand)* Uh — hello . . .

Ruth crosses mechanically to the bedroom door and opens it and lets it swing open freely and slowly as the lights come up on Walter within, still in his coat, sitting at the far corner of the room. He looks up and out through the room to Lindner.

RUTH: He's here.

A long minute passes and Walter slowly gets up.

LINDNER: *(coming to the table with efficiency, putting his briefcase on the table and starting to unfold papers and unscrew fountain pens).* Well, I certainly was glad to hear from you people. *(Walter has begun the trek out of the room, slowly and awkwardly, rather like a small boy, passing the back of his sleeve across his mouth from time to time.)* Life can really be so much simpler than people let it be most of the time. Well — with whom do I negotiate? You, Mrs. Younger, or your son here? *(Mama sits with her hands folded on her lap and her eyes closed as Walter advances. Travis goes closer to Lindner and looks at the papers curiously.)* Just some official papers, sonny.

RUTH: Travis, you go downstairs —   120

MAMA: *(opening her eyes and looking into Walter's)* No. Travis, you stay right here. And you make him understand what you doing, Walter Lee. You teach him good. Like Willy Harris taught you. You show where our five generations done come to. *(Walter looks from her to the boy, who grins at him innocently.)* Go ahead, son — *(She folds her hands and closes her eyes.)* Go ahead.

WALTER: *(at last crosses to Lindner, who is reviewing the contract)* Well, Mr. Lindner. *(Beneatha turns away.)* We called you — *(There is a profound, simple groping* quality in his speech.) — because, well me and my family (*He looks around and shifts from one foot to the other.*) Well — we are very plain people . . .

LINDNER: Yes —

WALTER: I mean — I have worked as a chauffeur most of my life — and my wife here, she does domestic work in people's kitchens. So does my mother. I mean — we are plain people . . .

125   LINDNER: Yes, Mr. Younger —

WALTER: (*really like a small boy, looking down at his shoes and then up at the man*) And — uh — well, my father, well, he was a laborer most of his life . . .

LINDNER: (*absolutely confused*) Uh, yes — yes, I understand. (*He turns back to the contract.*)

WALTER: (*a beat; staring at him*) And my father — (*With sudden intensity.*) My father almost *beat a man to death* once because this man called him a bad name or something, you know what I mean?

LINDNER: (*looking up, frozen*) No, no, I'm afraid I don't —

130   WALTER: (*a heat, The tension hangs; then Walter steps back from it*) Yeah. Well — what I mean is that we come from people who had a lot of *pride,* I mean — we are very proud people. And that's my sister over there and she's going to be a doctor — and we are very proud —

LINDNER: Well — I am sure that is very nice, but —

WALTER: What I am telling you is that we called you over here to tell you that we are very proud and that this — (*Signaling to Travis.*) Travis, come here. (*Travis crosses and Walter draws him before him facing the man.*) This is my son, and he makes the sixth generation our family in this country. And we have all thought about your offer —

LINDNER: Well, good . . . good —

WALTER: And we have decided to move into our house because my father — my father — he earned it for us brick by brick. (*Mama has her eyes closed and is rocking back and forth as though she were in church, with her head nodding the Amen yes.*) We don't want to make no trouble for nobody or fight no causes, and we will try to be good neighbors. And that's *all* we got to say about that. (*He looks the man absolutely in the eyes.*) We don't want your money. (*He turns and walks away.*)

135   LINDNER: (*looking around at all of them*) I take it then — that you have decided to occupy.

BENEATHA: That's what the man said.

LINDNER: (*to Mama in her reverie*) Then I would like to appeal to you, Mrs. Younger. You are older and wiser and understand things better I am sure . . .

MAMA: I am afraid you don't understand. My son said we was going to move and there ain't nothing left for me to say. (*Briskly.*) You know how these young folks is nowadays, mister. Can't do a thing with 'em! (*As he opens his mouth, she rises.*) Good-bye.

LINDNER: (*folding up his materials*) Well — if you are that final about it . . . there is nothing left for me to say. (*He finishes, almost ignored by the family, who are concentrating on Walter Lee. At the door Lindner halts and looks around.*) I sure hope you people know what you're getting into.

He shakes his head and exits.

RUTH: *(looking around and coming to life)* Well, for God's sake — if the moving   140
men are here — LET'S GET THE HELL OUT OF HERE!

MAMA: *(into action)* Ain't it the truth! Look at all this here mess. Ruth, put
Travis' good jacket on him . . . Walter Lee, fix your tie and tuck your shirt
in, you look like somebody's hoodlum! Lord have mercy, where is my plant?
*(She flies to get it amid the general bustling of the family, who are deliberately try-
ing to ignore the nobility of the past moment.)* You all start on down . . . Travis
child, don't go empty-handed . . . Ruth, where did I put that box with my
skillets in it? I want to be in charge of it myself . . . I'm going to make us the
biggest dinner we ever ate tonight . . . Beneatha, what's the matter with
them stockings? Pull them things up girl . . .

*The family starts to file out as two moving men appear and begin to carry out the heavier
pieces of furniture, bumping into the family as they move about.*

BENEATHA: Mama, Asagai asked me to marry him today and go to Africa —

MAMA: *(in the middle of her getting-ready activity)* He did? You ain't old enough
to marry nobody — *(Seeing the moving men lifting one of her chairs precariously.)*
Darling, that ain't no bale of cotton, please handle it so we can sit in it
again! I had that chair twenty-five years . . .

The movers sigh with exasperation and go on with their work.

BENEATHA: *(girlishly and unreasonably trying to pursue the conversation)* To go to
Africa, Mama — be a doctor in Africa . . .

MAMA: *(distracted)* Yes, baby —

WALTER: Africa! What he want you to go to Africa for?

BENEATHA: To practice there . . .   145

WALTER: Girl, if you don't get all them silly ideas our your head! You better
marry yourself a man with some loot . . .

BENEATHA: *(angrily, precisely as in the first scene of the play)* What have you got
to do with who I marry!

WALTER: Plenty. Now I think George Murchison —

BENEATHA: George Murchison! I wouldn't marry him if he was Adam and I was
Eve!

*Walter and Beneatha go out yelling at each other vigorously and the anger is loud and real
till their voices diminish. Ruth stands at the door and turns to Mama and smiles knowingly.*

MAMA: *(fixing her hat at last)* Yeah — they something all right, my children . . .   150

RUTH: Yeah — they're something. Let's go, Lena.

MAMA: *(stalling, starting to look around at the house)* Yes — I'm coming. Ruth —

RUTH: Yes?

MAMA: *(quietly, woman to woman)* He finally come into his manhood today,
didn't he? Kind of like a rainbow after the rain . . .

RUTH: *(biting her lip lest her own pride explode in front of Mama)* Yes, Lena.   155

Walter's voice calls for them raucously.

WALTER: *(off stage)* Y'all come on! These people charges by the hour, you know!
MAMA: *(waving Ruth out vaguely)* All right, honey — go on down. I be down
   directly.

*Ruth hestitates, then exits. Mama stands, at last alone in the living room, her plant on
the table before her as the lights starts to come down. She looks around at all the walls
and ceilings and suddenly, despite herself, while the children call below, a great heaving
thing rises in her and she puts her fist to her mouth to stifle it, takes a final desperate look,
pulls her coat about her, pats her hat, and goes out. The lights dim down. The door opens
and she comes back in, grabs her plant, and goes out for the last time.*

Curtain.

Reading and Reacting

1. The title of this play is an allusion to Langston Hughes's poem "Harlem" (p.
   940). How does this title help to explain what motivates the main characters at various points in the play?
2. What conflicts are developed in *A Raisin in the Sun*? How is each of these
   conflicts central to the plot?
3. What ideas does Walter have about education, success, and raising children?
   How are his ideas different from Ruth's?
4. Does Walter love Ruth? Why do you think he treats her the way he does?
   Do you see him as a sympathetic character?
5. Why does Walter refuse to sign the paper Mr. Lindner brings? What do
   you think Mama means when she says to Ruth at the end of the play, "He
   [Walter] finally come into his manhood today, didn't he? Kind of like a rainbow after the rain."
6. What does the subplot about Beneatha's choice between George and Asagai
   contribute to the plot?
7. When the play was first staged in 1959, several cuts were made to shorten
   it. For instance, the scene in which Beneatha unveils her natural hair was
   eliminated. The scene in which Travis recounts the killing of the rat and
   the scene describing Mrs. Johnson's visit were also cut. What does each of
   these scenes contribute to the play? Are they essential to the plot?
8. Walter's bedtime scene with Travis (act 2, scene 2) was cut from the 1959
   performance, but Hansberry thought it should be restored. Do you agree?
   Why or why not?
9. In her stage directions, Hansberry describes her characters' speech very
   carefully. For example, Beneatha's speech is "*a mixture of many things; it is
   different from the family's insofar as education has permeated her sense of English*" (act 1, scene 1). Study the speech of each of the play's characters,
   and consider what their language reveals about them. How do the differences in the various characters' use of language help to convey a central
   theme of the play?

10. Do you see this play as relevant only to the struggles of an urban black family in the period after World War II, or do you see its themes as universal? Do you think it is dated? Explain.

11. JOURNAL ENTRY Some critics contend than Hansberry attempts to force a happy ending by transforming her characters into an acceptable middle-class family. Hansberry herself, however, denied the play's ending was optimistic. Do you think the play has a happy ending? Do you think it should?

12. CRITICAL PERSPECTIVE In his 1967 study *The Crisis of the Negro Intellectual*, African-American social and cultural critic Harold Cruse criticized Hansberry's play, calling it "psychologically uncomplicated" and "bourgeois" because it sees integration as a positive good. Cruse also discussed the critical reaction to the play:

> When *Raisin* burst on the scene with a Negro star, a Negro director plus a young Negro woman playwright, everybody on Broadway was startled and very apprehensive about what this play might say. What obviously elated the drama critics was the very relieving discovery that what the publicity buildup actually heralded was not the arrival of belligerent forces from across the color line to settle some long-standing racial accounts on stage, but a good old-fashioned, home-spun saga of some good working-class folk in pursuit of the American Dream. And what could possibly be thematically objectionable about that? Only because it was about Negroes was this play acceptable. . . . If this play — which is so "American" that many whites did not consider it a "Negro play"— had ever been staged by white actors it would be judged second-rate.

Do you see this play as simply "a good old-fashioned" saga of working-class people in search of the American Dream, or do you see it as a uniquely African-American work? Do you agree that the race of the characters is all that distinguishes the play and keeps it from being "second-rate"?

Related Works: "The Water Faucet Vision" (p. 240), "I Stand Here Ironing" (p. 309), "Everyday Use" (p. 469), "Sonny's Blues" (p. 620), "Harlem" (p. 940), *Death of a Salesman* (p. 1581), *Fences* (p. 1939)

HENRIK IBSEN (1828–1906), Norway's foremost dramatist, was born into a prosperous family; however, his father, lost his fortune when Ibsen was six. When Ibsen was fifteen, he was apprenticed to an apothecary away from home and was permanently estranged from his family. During his apprenticeship, he studied to enter the university and wrote plays. Although he did not pass the university entrance exam, his second play, *The Warrior's Barrow* (1850), was produced by the Christiania Theatre in 1850. He began a life in the theater, writing plays and serving as artistic director of a theatrical company. Disillusioned by the public's lack of interest in theater, he left Norway, living with his wife and son in Italy and Germany between 1864 and 1891. By the time he returned to Norway, he was famous and revered. Ibsen's most notable plays include *Brand* (1865), *Peer Gynt* (1867), *A Doll House* (1879), *Ghosts* (1881), *An Enemy of the People* (1882), *The Wild Duck* (1884), *Hedda Gabler* (1890), and *When We Dead Awaken* (1899).

A Doll House marks the beginning of Ibsen's successful realist period, during which he explored the ordinary lives of small-town people — in this case, writing what he called "a modern tragedy." Ibsen based the play on a true story, which closely paralleled the main events of the play: a wife borrows money to finance a trip for an ailing husband, repayment is demanded, she forges a check and is discovered. (In the real-life story, however, the husband demanded a divorce, and the wife had a nervous breakdown and was committed to a mental institution.) The issue in *A Doll House,* he said, is that there are "two kinds of moral law, . . . one in man and a completely different one in woman. They do not understand each other . . . ." Nora and Helmer's marriage is destroyed because they cannot comprehend or accept their differences. The play begins conventionally but does not fulfill the audience's expectations for a tidy resolution; as a result, it was not successful when first performed. Nevertheless, the publication of *A Doll House* made Ibsen internationally famous.

Cultural Context: During the nineteenth century, the law treated women only a little better than it did children. They could not vote, and they were not considered able to handle their own financial affairs. A woman could not borrow money in her own name, and when she married, her finances were placed under the control of her husband. Moreover, working outside the home was out of the question for a middle-class woman. So, if a woman were to leave her husband, she was not likely to have any way of supporting herself, and she would lose the custody of her children. At the time when *A Doll House* was first performed, most viewers were offended by the way Nora spoke to her husband, and Ibsen was considered an anarchist for suggesting that a woman could leave her family in search of herself. However, Ibsen argued that he was merely asking people to look at, and think about, the social structure they supported.

A Doll House   (1879)

Translated by Rolf Fjelde

CHARACTERS

Torvald Helmer, *a lawyer*	**Nils Krogstad,** *a bank clerk*
Nora, *his wife*	**The Helmers' three small**
Dr. Rank	**children**
Mrs. Linde	**Anne-Marie,** *their nurse*
A Delivery Boy	**Helene,** *a maid*

The action takes place in Helmer's residence.

ACT 1

A comfortable room, tastefully but not expensively furnished. A door to the right in the back wall leads to the entryway; another to the left leads to Helmer's study. Between these doors, a piano. Midway in the left-hand wall a door, and further back a window. Near the window a round table with an armchair and a small sofa. In the right-hand wall, toward the rear, a door, and nearer the foreground a porcelain stove with two armchairs and a rocking chair beside it. Between the stove and the side door, a small table. Engravings on the walls. An étagère with china figures and other small art objects; a small bookcase with richly bound books; the floor carpeted; a fire burning in the stove. It is a winter day.

A bell rings in the entryway; shortly after we hear the door being unlocked. Nora comes into the room, humming happily to herself; she is wearing street clothes and carries an armload of packages, which she puts down on the table to the right. She has left the hall door open; and through it a Delivery Boy is seen, holding a Christmas tree and a basket, which he gives to the Maid who let them in.

NORA: Hide the tree well, Helene. The children mustn't get a glimpse of it till this evening, after it's trimmed. *(To the Delivery Boy, taking out her purse.)* How much?

DELIVERY BOY: Fifty, ma'am.

NORA: There's a crown. No, keep the change. *(The Boy thanks her and leaves. Nora shuts the door. She laughs softly to herself while taking off her street things. Drawing a bag of macaroons from her pocket, she eats a couple, then steals over and listens at her husband's study door.)* Yes, he's home. *(Hums again as she moves to the table right.)*

HELMER: *(from the study)* Is that my little lark twittering out there?

NORA: *(busy opening some packages)* Yes, it is.   5

HELMER: Is that my squirrel rummaging around?

NORA: Yes!

HELMER: When did my squirrel get in?

NORA: Just now. *(Putting the macaroon bag in her pocket and wiping her mouth.)* Do come in, Torvald, and see what I've bought.

HELMER: Can't be disturbed. *(After a moment he opens the door and peers in, pen*   10
in hand.) Bought, you say? All that there? Has the little spendthrift been out throwing money around again?

NORA: Oh, but Torvald, this year we really should let ourselves go a bit. It's the first Christmas we haven't had to economize.

HELMER: But you know we can't go squandering.

NORA: Oh yes, Torvald, we can squander a little now. Can't we? Just a tiny, wee bit. Now that you've got a big salary and are going to make piles and piles of money.

HELMER: Yes — starting New Year's. But then it's a full three months till the raise comes through.

NORA: Pooh! We can borrow that long.   15

HELMER: Nora! *(Goes over and playfully takes her by the ear.)* Are your scatterbrains off again? What if today I borrowed a thousand crowns, and you squandered them over Christmas week, and then on New Year's Eve a roof tile fell on my head, and I lay there —

NORA: *(putting her hand on his mouth)* Oh! Don't say such things!

HELMER: Yes, but what if it happened — then what?

NORA: If anything so awful happened, then it just wouldn't matter if I had debts or not.

HELMER: Well, but the people I'd borrowed from?   20

NORA: Them? Who cares about them! They're strangers.

HELMER: Nora, Nora, how like a woman! No, but seriously, Nora, you know
what I think about that. No debts! Never borrow! Something of freedom's
lost — and something of beauty, too — from a home that's founded on
borrowing and debt. We've made a brave stand up to now, the two of us;
and we'll go right on like that the little while we have to.

NORA: *(going toward the stove)* Yes, whatever you say, Torvald.

HELMER: *(following her)* Now, now, the little lark's wings mustn't droop.
Come on, don't be a sulky squirrel. *(Taking out his wallet.)* Nora, guess what
I have here.

25   NORA: *(turning quickly)* Money!

HELMER: There, see. *(Hands her some notes.)* Good grief, I know how costs go
up in a house at Christmastime.

NORA: Ten — twenty — thirty — forty. Oh, thank you, Torvald; I can manage
no end on this.

HELMER: You really will have to.

NORA: Oh yes, I promise I will! But come here so I can show you everything I
bought. And so cheap! Look, new clothes for Ivar here — and a sword.
Here a horse and a trumpet for Bob. And a doll and a doll's bed here for
Emmy; they're nothing much, but she'll tear them to bits in no time
anyway. And here I have dress material and handkerchiefs for the maids.
Old Anne-Marie really deserves something more.

30   HELMER: And what's in that package there?

NORA: *(with a cry)* Torvald, no! You can't see that till tonight!

HELMER: I see. But tell me now, you little prodigal, what have you thought of
for yourself?

NORA: For myself? Oh, I don't want anything at all.

HELMER: Of course you do. Tell me just what — within reason — you'd most
like to have.

35   NORA: I honestly don't know. Oh, listen, Torvald —

HELMER: Well?

NORA: *(fumbling at his coat buttons, without looking at him)* If you want to give
me something, then maybe you could — you could —

HELMER: Come on, out with it.

NORA: *(hurriedly)* You could give me money, Torvald. No more than you think
you can spare; then one of these days I'll buy something with it.

40   HELMER: But Nora —

NORA: Oh, please, Torvald darling, do that! I beg you, please. Then I could
hang the bills in pretty gilt paper on the Christmas tree. Wouldn't that
be fun?

HELMER: What are those little birds called that always fly through their
fortunes?

NORA: Oh yes, spendthrifts; I know all that. But let's do as I say, Torvald;
then I'll have time to decide what I really need most. That's very sensible,
isn't it?

HELMER: *(smiling)* Yes, very — that is, if you actually hung onto the money I
give you, and you actually used it to buy yourself something. But it goes for

the house and for all sorts of foolish things, and then I only have to lay out some more.

NORA: Oh, but Torvald —   45

HELMER: Don't deny it, my dear little Nora. (*Putting his arm around her waist.*) Spendthrifts are sweet, but they use up a frightful amount of money. It's incredible what it costs a man to feed such birds.

NORA: Oh, how can you say that! Really, I save everything I can.

HELMER: (*laughing*) Yes, that's the truth. Everything you can. But that's nothing at all.

NORA: (*humming, with a smile of quiet satisfaction*) Hm, if you only knew what expenses we larks and squirrels have, Torvald.

HELMER: You're an odd little one. Exactly the way your father was. You're   50 never at a loss for scaring up money; but the moment you have it, it runs right out through your fingers; you never know what you've done with it. Well, one takes you as you are. It's deep in your blood. Yes, these things are hereditary, Nora.

NORA: Ah, I could wish I'd inherited many of Papa's qualities.

HELMER: And I couldn't wish you anything but just what you are, my sweet little lark. But wait; it seems to me you have a very — what should I call it? — a very suspicious look today —

NORA: I do?

HELMER: You certainly do. Look me straight in the eye.

NORA: (*looking at him*) Well?   55

HELMER: (*shaking an admonitory finger*) Surely my sweet tooth hasn't been running riot in town today, has she?

NORA: No. Why do you imagine that?

HELMER: My sweet tooth really didn't make a little detour through the confectioner's?

NORA: No, I assure you, Torvald —

HELMER: Hasn't nibbled some pastry?   60

NORA: No, not at all.

HELMER: Nor even munched a macaroon or two?

NORA: No, Torvald, I assure you, really —

HELMER: There, there now. Of course I'm only joking.

NORA: (*going to the table, right*) You know I could never think of going   65 against you.

HELMER: No, I understand that; and you *have* given me your word. (*Going over to her.*) Well, you keep your little Christmas secrets to yourself, Nora darling. I expect they'll come to light this evening, when the tree is lit.

NORA: Did you remember to ask Dr. Rank?

HELMER: No. But there's no need for that; it's assumed he'll be dining with us. All the same, I'll ask him when he stops by here this morning. I've ordered some fine wine. Nora, you can't imagine how I'm looking forward to this evening.

NORA: So am I. And what fun for the children, Torvald!

HELMER: Ah, it's so gratifying to know that one's gotten a safe, secure job, and   70 with a comfortable salary. It's a great satisfaction, isn't it?

NORA: Oh, it's wonderful!

HELMER: Remember last Christmas? Three whole weeks before, you shut yourself in every evening till long after midnight, making flowers for the Christmas tree, and all the other decorations to surprise us. Ugh, that was the dullest time I've ever lived through.

NORA: It wasn't at all dull for me.

HELMER: (*smiling*) But the outcome *was* pretty sorry, Nora.

75   NORA: Oh, don't tease me with that again. How could I help it that the cat came in and tore everything to shreds.

HELMER: No, poor thing, you certainly couldn't. You wanted so much to please us all, and that's what counts. But it's just as well that the hard times are past.

NORA: Yes, it's really wonderful.

HELMER: Now I don't have to sit here alone, boring myself, and you don't have to tire your precious eyes and your fair little delicate hands —

NORA: (*clapping her hands*) No, is it really true, Torvald, I don't have to? Oh, how wonderfully lovely to hear! (*Taking his arm.*) Now I'll tell you just how I've thought we should plan things. Right after Christmas — (*The doorbell rings.*) Oh, the bell. (*Straightening the room up a bit.*) Somebody would have to come. What a bore!

80   HELMER: I'm not at home to visitors, don't forget.

MAID: (*from the hall doorway*) Ma'am, a lady to see you —

NORA: All right, let her come in.

MAID: (*to Helmer*) And the doctor's just come too.

HELMER: Did he go right to my study?

85   MAID: Yes, he did.

Helmer goes into his room. The Maid shows in Mrs. Linde, dressed in traveling clothes, and shuts the door after her.

MRS. LINDE: (*in a dispirited and somewhat hesitant voice*) Hello, Nora.

NORA: (*uncertain*) Hello —

MRS. LINDE: You don't recognize me.

NORA: No, I don't know — but wait, I think — (*Exclaiming.*) What! Kristine! Is it really you?

90   MRS. LINDE: Yes, it's me.

NORA: *Kristine!* To think I didn't recognize you. But then, how could I? (*More quietly.*) How you've changed, Kristine!

MRS. LINDE: Yes, no doubt I have. In nine — ten long years.

NORA: Is it so long since we met! Yes, it's all of that. Oh, these last eight years have been a happy time, believe me. And so now you've come in to town, too. Made the long trip in the winter. That took courage.

MRS. LINDE: I just got here by ship this morning.

95   NORA: To enjoy yourself over Christmas, of course. Oh, how lovely! Yes, enjoy ourselves, we'll do that. But take your coat off. You're not still cold? (*Helping her.*) There now, let's get cozy here by the stove. No, the easy chair there!

I'll take the rocker here. (*Seizing her hands.*) Yes, now you have your old look again; it was only in that first moment. You're a bit more pale, Kristine — and maybe a bit thinner.

MRS. LINDE: And much, much older, Nora.

NORA: Yes, perhaps a bit older; a tiny, tiny bit; not much at all. (*Stopping short; suddenly serious.*) Oh, but thoughtless me, to sit here, chattering away. Sweet, good Kristine, can you forgive me?

MRS. LINDE: What do you mean, Nora?

NORA: (*softly*) Poor Kristine, you've become a widow.

MRS. LINDE: Yes, three years ago.   100

NORA: Oh, I knew it, of course; I read it in the papers. Oh, Kristine, you must believe me; I often thought of writing you then, but I kept postponing it, and something always interfered.

MRS. LINDE: Nora dear, I understand completely.

NORA: No, it was awful of me, Kristine. You poor thing, how much you must have gone through. And he left you nothing?

MRS. LINDE: No.

NORA: And no children?

MRS. LINDE: No.   105

NORA: Nothing at all, then?

MRS. LINDE: Not even a sense of loss to feed on.

NORA: (*looking incredulously at her*) But Kristine, how could that be?

MRS. LINDE: (*smiling wearily and smoothing her hair*) Oh, sometimes it   110
happens, Nora.

NORA: So completely alone. How terribly hard that must be for you. I have three lovely children. You can't see them now; they're out with the maid. But now you must tell me everything —

MRS. LINDE: No, no, no, tell me about yourself.

NORA: No, you begin. Today I don't want to be selfish. I want to think only of you today. But there *is* something I must tell you. Did you hear of the wonderful luck we had recently?

MRS. LINDE: No, what's that?

NORA: My husband's been made manager in the bank, just think!   115

MRS. LINDE: Your husband? How marvelous!

NORA: Isn't it? Being a lawyer is such an uncertain living, you know, especially if one won't touch any cases that aren't clean and decent. And of course Torvald would never do that, and I'm with him completely there. Oh, we're simply delighted, believe me! He'll join the bank right after New Year's and start getting a huge salary and lots of commissions. From now on we can live quite differently — just as we want. Oh, Kristine, I feel so light and happy! Won't it be lovely to have stacks of money and not a care in the world?

MRS. LINDE: Well, anyway, it would be lovely to have enough for necessities.

NORA: No, not just for necessities, but stacks and stacks of money!

120   MRS. LINDE: (*smiling*) Nora, Nora, aren't you sensible yet? Back in school you
were such a free spender.

NORA: (*with a quiet laugh*) Yes, that's what Torvald still says. (*Shaking her
finger.*) But "Nora, Nora" isn't as silly as you all think. Really, we've been in
no position for me to go squandering. We've had to work, both of us.

MRS. LINDE: You too?

NORA: Yes, at odd jobs — needlework, crocheting, embroidery, and such —
(*casually*) and other things too. You remember that Torvald left the
department when we were married? There was no chance of promotion in
his office, and of course he needed to earn more money. But that first year
he drove himself terribly. He took on all kinds of extra work that kept him
going morning and night. It wore him down, and then he fell deathly ill.
The doctors said it was essential for him to travel south.

MRS. LINDE: Yes, didn't you spend a whole year in Italy?

125   NORA: That's right. It wasn't easy to get away, you know. Ivar had just been
born. But of course we had to go. Oh, that was a beautiful trip, and it saved
Torvald's life. But it cost a frightful sum, Kristine.

MRS. LINDE: I can well imagine.

NORA: Four thousand, eight hundred crowns it cost. That's really a lot of
money.

MRS. LINDE: But it's lucky you had it when you needed it.

NORA: Well, as it was, we got it from Papa.

130   MRS. LINDE: I see. It was just about the time your father died.

NORA: Yes, just about then. And, you know, I couldn't make that trip
out to nurse him. I had to stay here, expecting Ivar any moment, and with
my poor sick Torvald to care for. Dearest Papa, I never saw him again,
Kristine. Oh, that was the worst time I've known in all my
marriage.

MRS. LINDE: I know how you loved him. And then you went off to Italy?

NORA: Yes. We had the means now, and the doctors urged us. So we left
a month after.

MRS. LINDE: And your husband came back completely cured?

135   NORA: Sound as a drum!

MRS. LINDE: But — the doctor?

NORA: Who?

MRS. LINDE: I thought the maid said he was a doctor, the man who came
in with me.

NORA: Yes, that was Dr. Rank — but he's not making a sick call. He's our
closest friend, and he stops by at least once a day. No, Torvald hasn't had
a sick moment since, and the children are fit and strong, and I am, too.
(*Jumping up and clapping her hands.*) Oh, dear God, Kristine, what a
lovely thing to live and be happy! But how disgusting of me — I'm
talking of nothing but my own affairs. (*Sits on a stool close by Kristine,
arms resting across her knees.*) Oh, don't be angry with me! Tell me, is it
really true that you weren't in love with your husband? Why did you
marry him, then?

MRS. LINDE: My mother was still alive, but bedridden and helpless — and   140
I had my two younger brothers to look after. In all conscience, I didn't
think I could turn him down.

NORA: No, you were right there. But was he rich at the time?

MRS. LINDE: He was very well off, I'd say. But the business was shaky, Nora.
When he died, it all fell apart, and nothing was left.

NORA: And then —?

MRS. LINDE: Yes, so I had to scrape up a living with a little shop and a little
teaching and whatever else I could find. The last three years have been like
one endless workday without a rest for me. Now it's over, Nora. My poor
mother doesn't need me, for she's passed on. Nor the boys, either; they're
working now and can take care of themselves.

NORA: How free you must feel —   145

MRS. LINDE: No — only unspeakably empty. Nothing to live for now.
(*Standing up anxiously.*) That's why I couldn't take it any longer out in that
desolate hole. Maybe here it'll be easier to find something to do and keep
my mind occupied. If I could only be lucky enough to get a steady job,
some office work —

NORA: Oh, but Kristine, that's so dreadfully tiring, and you already look so
tired. It would be much better for you if you could go off to a bathing resort.

MRS. LINDE: (*going toward the window*) I have no father to give me travel
money, Nora.

NORA: (*rising*) Oh, don't be angry with me.

MRS. LINDE: (*going to her*) Nora dear, don't you be angry with me. The worst   150
of my kind of situation is all the bitterness that's stored away. No one to
work for, and yet you're always having to snap up your opportunities. You
have to live; and so you grow selfish. When you told me the happy change
in your lot, do you know I was delighted less for your sakes than for mine?

NORA: How so? Oh, I see. You think Torvald could do something for you.

MRS. LINDE: Yes, that's what I thought.

NORA: And he will, Kristine! Just leave it to me; I'll bring it up so
delicately — find something attractive to humor him with. Oh, I'm so
eager to help you.

MRS. LINDE: How very kind of you, Nora, to be so concerned over
me — doubly kind, considering you really know so little of life's burdens
yourself.

NORA: I —? I know so little —?   155

MRS. LINDE: (*smiling*) Well my heavens — a little needlework and
such — Nora, you're just a child.

NORA: (*tossing her head and pacing the floor*) You don't have to act so superior.

MRS. LINDE: Oh?

NORA: You're just like the others. You all think I'm incapable of anything
serious —

MRS. LINDE: Come now —   160

NORA: That I've never had to face the raw world.

MRS. LINDE: Nora dear, you've just been telling me all your troubles.

NORA: Hm! Trivial! (*Quietly.*) I haven't told you the big thing.

MRS. LINDE: Big thing? What do you mean?

165 NORA: You look down on me so, Kristine, but you shouldn't. You're proud that you worked so long and hard for your mother.

MRS. LINDE: I don't look down on a soul. But it *is* true: I'm proud — and happy, too — to think it was given to me to make my mother's last days almost free of care.

NORA: And you're also proud thinking of what you've done for your brothers.

MRS. LINDE: I feel I've a right to be.

NORA: I agree. But listen to this, Kristine — I've also got something to be proud and happy for.

170 MRS. LINDE: I don't doubt it. But whatever do you mean?

NORA: Not so loud. What if Torvald heard! He mustn't, not for anything in the world. Nobody must know, Kristine. No one but you.

MRS. LINDE: But what is it, then?

NORA: Come here. (*Drawing her down beside her on the sofa.*) It's true — I've also got something to be proud and happy for. I'm the one who saved Torvald's life.

MRS. LINDE: Saved —? Saved how?

175 NORA: I told you about the trip to Italy. Torvald never would have lived if he hadn't gone south —

MRS. LINDE: Of course; your father gave you the means —

NORA: (*smiling*) That's what Torvald and all the rest think, but —

MRS. LINDE: But —?

NORA: Papa didn't give us a pin. I was the one who raised the money.

180 MRS. LINDE: You? That whole amount?

NORA: Four thousand, eight hundred crowns. What do you say to that?

MRS. LINDE: But Nora, how was it possible? Did you win the lottery?

NORA: (*disdainfully*) The lottery? Pooh! No art to that.

MRS. LINDE: But where did you get it from then?

185 NORA: (*humming, with a mysterious smile*) Hmm, tra-la-la-la.

MRS. LINDE: Because you couldn't have borrowed it.

NORA: No? Why not?

MRS. LINDE: A wife can't borrow without her husband's consent.

NORA: (*tossing her head*) Oh, but a wife with a little business sense, a wife who knows how to manage —

190 MRS. LINDE: Nora, I simply don't understand —

NORA: You don't have to. Whoever said I *borrowed* the money? I could have gotten it other ways. (*Throwing herself back on the sofa.*) I could have gotten it from some admirer or other. After all, a girl with my ravishing appeal —

MRS. LINDE: You lunatic.

NORA: I'll bet you're eaten up with curiosity, Kristine.

MRS. LINDE: Now listen here, Nora — you haven't done something indiscreet?

NORA: (*sitting up again*) Is it indiscreet to save your husband's life?   195

MRS. LINDE: I think it's indiscreet that without his knowledge you —

NORA: But that's the point: he mustn't know! My Lord, can't you understand? He mustn't ever know the close call he had. It was to *me* the doctors came to say his life was in danger — that nothing could save him but a stay in the south. Didn't I try strategy then! I began talking about how lovely it would be for me to travel abroad like other young wives; I begged and I cried; I told him please to remember my condition, to be kind and indulge me; and then I dropped a hint that he could easily take out a loan. But at that, Kristine, he nearly exploded. He said I was frivolous, and it was his duty as man of the house not to indulge me in whims and fancies — as I think he called them. Aha, I thought, now you'll just have to be saved — and that's when I saw my chance.

MRS. LINDE: And your father never told Torvald the money wasn't from him?

NORA: No, never. Papa died right about then. I'd considered bringing him into my secret and begging him never to tell. But he was too sick at the time — and then, sadly, it didn't matter.

MRS. LINDE: And you've never confided in your husband since?   200

NORA: For heaven's sake, no! Are you serious? He's so strict on that subject. Besides — Torvald, with all his masculine pride — how painfully humiliating for him if he ever found out he was in debt to me. That would just ruin our relationship. Our beautiful, happy home would never be the same.

MRS. LINDE: Won't you ever tell him?

NORA: (*thoughtfully, half smiling*) Yes — maybe sometime, years from now, when I'm no longer so attractive. Don't laugh! I only mean when Torvald loves me less than now, when he stops enjoying my dancing and dressing up and reciting for him. Then it might be wise to have something in reserve — (*Breaking off.*) How ridiculous! That'll never happen — Well, Kristine, what do you think of my big secret? I'm capable of something too, hm? You can imagine, of course, how this thing hangs over me. It really hasn't been easy meeting the payments on time. In the business world there's what they call quarterly interest and what they call amortization, and these are always so terribly hard to manage. I've had to skimp a little here and there, wherever I could, you know. I could hardly spare anything from my house allowance, because Torvald has to live well. I couldn't let the children go poorly dressed; whatever I got for them, I felt I had to use up completely — the darlings!

MRS. LINDE: Poor Nora, so it had to come out of your own budget, then?

NORA: Yes, of course. But I was the one most responsible, too. Every time   205
Torvald gave me money for new clothes and such, I never used more than half; always bought the simplest, cheapest outfits. It was a godsend that everything looks so well on me that Torvald never noticed. But it did weigh me down at times, Kristine. It *is* such a joy to wear fine things. You understand.

MRS. LINDE: Oh, of course.

NORA: And then I found other ways of making money. Last winter I was lucky enough to get a lot of copying to do. I locked myself in and sat writing every evening till late in the night. Ah, I was tired so often, dead tired. But still it was wonderful fun, sitting and working like that, earning money. It was almost like being a man.

MRS. LINDE: But how much have you paid off this way so far?

NORA: That's hard to say, exactly. These accounts, you know, aren't easy to figure. I only know that I've paid out all I could scrape together. Time and again I haven't known where to turn. (*Smiling.*) Then I'd sit here dreaming of a rich old gentleman who had fallen in love with me —

210 MRS. LINDE: What! Who is he?

NORA: Oh, really! And that he'd died, and when his will was opened, there in big letters it said, "All my fortune shall be paid over in cash, immediately, to that enchanting Mrs. Nora Helmer."

MRS. LINDE: But Nora dear — who *was* this gentleman?

NORA: Good grief, can't you understand? The old man never existed; that was only something I'd dream up time and again whenever I was at my wits' end for money. But it makes no difference now; the old fossil can go where he pleases for all I care; I don't need him or his will — because now I'm free. (*Jumping up.*) Oh, how lovely to think of that, Kristine! Carefree! To know you're carefree, utterly carefree; to be able to romp and play with the children, and to keep up a beautiful, charming home — everything just the way Torvald likes it! And think, spring is coming, with big blue skies. Maybe we can travel a little then. Maybe I'll see the ocean again. Oh yes, it *is* so marvelous to live and be happy!

The front doorbell rings.

MRS. LINDE: (*rising*) There's the bell. It's probably best that I go.

215 NORA: No, stay. No one's expected. It must be for Torvald.

MAID: (*from the hall doorway*) Excuse me, ma'am — there's a gentleman here to see Mr. Helmer, but I didn't know — since the doctor's with him —

NORA: Who is the gentleman?

KROGSTAD: (*from the doorway*) It's me, Mrs. Helmer.

Mrs. Linde starts and turns away toward the window.

NORA: (*stepping toward him, tense, her voice a whisper*) You? What is it? Why do you want to speak to my husband?

220 KROGSTAD: Bank business — after a fashion. I have a small job in the investment bank, and I hear now your husband is going to be our chief —

NORA: In other words, it's —

KROGSTAD: Just dry business, Mrs. Helmer. Nothing but that.

NORA: Yes, then please be good enough to step into the study. (*She nods indifferently as she sees him out by the hall door, then returns and begins stirring up the stove.*)

MRS. LINDE: Nora — who was that man?

225 NORA: That was a Mr. Krogstad — a lawyer.

MRS. LINDE: Then it really was him.

NORA: Do you know that person?

MRS. LINDE: I did once — many years ago. For a time he was a law clerk in our town.

NORA: Yes, he's been that.

MRS. LINDE: How he's changed.   230

NORA: I understand he had a very unhappy marriage.

MRS. LINDE: He's a widower now.

NORA: With a number of children. There now, it's burning. (*She closes the stove door and moves the rocker a bit to one side.*)

MRS. LINDE: They say he has a hand in all kinds of business.

NORA: Oh? That may be true: I wouldn't know. But let's not think about   235
business. It's so dull.

Dr. Rank enters from Helmer's study.

RANK: (*still in the doorway*) No, no, really — I don't want to intrude, I'd just as soon talk a little while with your wife. (*Shuts the door, then notices Mrs. Linde.*) Oh, beg pardon. I'm intruding here too.

NORA: No, not at all. (*Introducing him.*) Dr. Rank, Mrs. Linde.

RANK: Well now, that's a name much heard in this house. I believe I passed the lady on the stairs as I came.

MRS. LINDE: Yes, I take the stairs very slowly. They're rather hard on me.

RANK: Uh-hm, some touch of internal weakness?   240

MRS. LINDE: More overexertion, I'd say.

RANK: Nothing else? Then you're probably here in town to rest up in a round of parties?

MRS. LINDE: I'm here to look for work.

RANK: Is that the best cure for overexertion?

MRS. LINDE: One has to live, Doctor.   245

RANK: Yes, there's a common prejudice to that effect.

NORA: Oh, come on, Dr. Rank — you really do want to live yourself.

RANK: Yes, I really do. Wretched as I am, I'll gladly prolong my torment indefinitely. All my patients feel like that. And it's quite the same, too, with the morally sick. Right at this moment there's one of those moral invalids in there with Helmer —

MRS. LINDE: (*softly*) Ah!

NORA: Who do you mean?   250

RANK: Oh, it's a lawyer, Krogstad, a type you wouldn't know. His character is rotten to the root — but even he began chattering all-importantly about how he had to *live*.

NORA: Oh? What did he want to talk to Torvald about?

RANK: I really don't know. I only heard something about the bank.

NORA: I didn't know that Krog — that this man Krogstad had anything to do with the bank.

RANK: Yes, he's gotten some kind of berth down there. (*To Mrs. Linde.*)   255
I don't know if you also have, in your neck of the woods, a type of person

who scuttles about breathlessly, sniffing out hints of moral corruption, and then maneuvers his victim into some sort of key position where he can keep an eye on him. It's the healthy these days that are out in the cold.

MRS. LINDE: All the same, it's the sick who most need to be taken in.

RANK: (*with a shrug*) Yes, there we have it. That's the concept that's turning society into a sanatorium.

Nora, lost in her thoughts, breaks out into quiet laughter and claps her hands.

RANK: Why do you laugh at that? Do you have any real idea of what society is?

NORA: What do I care about dreary old society? I was laughing at something quite different — something terribly funny. Tell me, Doctor — is everyone who works in the bank dependent now on Torvald?

260 **RANK:** Is that what you find so terribly funny?

NORA: (*smiling and humming*) Never mind, never mind! (*Pacing the floor.*) Yes, that's really immensely amusing: that we — that Torvald has so much power now over all those people. (*Taking the bag out of her pocket.*) Dr. Rank, a little macaroon on that?

RANK: See here, macaroons! I thought they were contraband here.

NORA: Yes, but these are some that Kristine gave me.

MRS. LINDE: What? I —?

265 **NORA:** Now, now, don't be afraid. You couldn't possibly know that Torvald had forbidden them. You see, he's worried they'll ruin my teeth. But hmp! Just this once! Isn't that so, Dr. Rank? Help yourself! (*Puts a macaroon in his mouth.*) And you too, Kristine. And I'll also have one, only a little one — or two, at the most. (*Walking about again.*) Now I'm really tremendously happy. Now there's just one last thing in the world that I have an enormous desire to do.

RANK: Well! And what's that?

NORA: It's something I have such a consuming desire to say so Torvald could hear.

RANK: And why can't you say it?

270 **NORA:** I don't dare. It's quite shocking.

MRS. LINDE: Shocking?

RANK: Well, then it isn't advisable. But in front of us you certainly can. What do you have such a desire to say so Torvald could hear?

NORA: I have such a huge desire to say — to hell and be damned!

RANK: Are you crazy?

MRS. LINDE: My goodness, Nora!

275 **RANK:** Go on, say it. Here he is.

NORA: (*hiding the macaroon bag*) Shh, shh, shh!

Helmer comes in from his study, hat in hand, overcoat over his arm.

NORA: (*going toward him*) Well, Torvald dear, are you through with him?

HELMER: Yes, he just left.

NORA: Let me introduce you — this is Kristine, who's arrived here in town.

HELMER: Kristine —? I'm sorry, but I don't know — 280

NORA: Mrs. Linde, Torvald dear. Mrs. Kristine Linde.

HELMER: Of course. A childhood friend of my wife's, no doubt?

MRS. LINDE: Yes, we knew each other in those days.

NORA: And just think, she made the long trip down here in order to talk
with you.

HELMER: What's this? 285

MRS. LINDE: Well, not exactly —

NORA: You see, Kristine is remarkably clever in office work, and so she's
terribly eager to come under a capable man's supervision and add more to
what she already knows —

HELMER: Very wise, Mrs. Linde.

NORA: And then when she heard that you'd become a bank manager — the
story was wired out to the papers — then she came in as fast as she could
and — Really, Torvald, for my sake you can do a little something for
Kristine, can't you?

HELMER: Yes, it's not at all impossible. Mrs. Linde, I suppose you're a widow? 290

MRS. LINDE: Yes.

HELMER: Any experience in office work?

MRS. LINDE: Yes, a good deal.

HELMER: Well, it's quite likely that I can make an opening for you —

NORA: (clapping her hands) You see, you see! 295

HELMER: You've come at a lucky moment, Mrs. Linde.

MRS. LINDE: Oh, how can I thank you?

HELMER: Not necessary. (Putting his overcoat on.) But today you'll have to
excuse me —

RANK: Wait, I'll go with you. (He fetches his coat from the hall and warms
it at the stove.)

NORA: Don't stay out long, dear. 300

HELMER: An hour; no more.

NORA: Are you going too, Kristine?

MRS. LINDE: (putting on her winter garments) Yes, I have to see about a room now.

HELMER: Then perhaps we can all walk together.

NORA: (helping her) What a shame we're so cramped here, but it's quite 305
impossible for us to —

MRS. LINDE: Oh, don't even think of it! Good-bye, Nora dear, and thanks for
everything.

NORA: Good-bye for now. Of course you'll be back this evening. And you too,
Dr. Rank. What? If you're well enough? Oh, you've got to be! Wrap up
tight now.

*In a ripple of small talk the company moves out into the hall; children's voices are heard
outside on the steps.*

NORA: There they are! There they are! (*She runs to open the door. The children come in with their nurse, Anne-Marie.*) Come in, come in! (*Bends down and kisses them.*) Oh, you darlings —! Look at them, Kristine. Aren't they lovely!

RANK: No loitering in the draft here.

310 HELMER: Come, Mrs. Linde — this place is unbearable now for anyone but mothers.

Dr. Rank, Helmer, and Mrs. Linde go down the stairs. Anne-Marie goes into the living room with the children. Nora follows, after closing the hall door.

NORA: How fresh and strong you look. Oh, such red cheeks you have! Like apples and roses. (*The children interrupt her throughout the following.*) And it was so much fun? That's wonderful. Really? You pulled both Emmy and Bob on the sled? Imagine, all together! Yes, you're a clever boy, Ivar. Oh, let me hold her a bit, Anne-Marie. My sweet little doll baby! (*Takes the smallest from the nurse and dances with her.*) Yes, yes, Mama will dance with Bob as well. What? Did you throw snowballs? Oh, if I'd only been there! No, don't bother, Anne-Marie — I'll undress them myself. Oh yes, let me. It's such fun. Go in and rest; you look half frozen. There's hot coffee waiting for you on the stove. (*The nurse goes into the room to the left. Nora takes the children's winter things off, throwing them about, while the children talk to her all at once.*) Is that so? A big dog chased you? But it didn't bite? No, dogs never bite little, lovely doll babies. Don't peek in the packages, Ivar! What is it? Yes, wouldn't you like to know. No, no, it's an ugly something. Well? Shall we play? What shall we play? Hide-and-seek? Yes, let's play hide-and-seek. Bob must hide first. I must? Yes, let me hide first. (*Laughing and shouting, she and the children play in and out of the living room and the adjoining room to the right. At last Nora hides under the table. The children come storming in, search, but cannot find her, then hear her muffled laughter, dash over to the table, lift the cloth up and find her. Wild shouting. She creeps forward as if to scare them. More shouts. Meanwhile, a knock at the hall door; no one has noticed it. Now the door half opens, and Krogstad appears. He waits a moment; the game goes on.*)

KROGSTAD: Beg pardon, Mrs. Helmer —

NORA: (*with a strangled cry, turning and scrambling to her knees*) Oh! What do you want?

KROGSTAD: Excuse me. The outer door was ajar; it must be someone forgot to shut it —

315 NORA: (*rising*) My husband isn't home, Mr. Krogstad.

KROGSTAD: I know that.

NORA: Yes — then what do you want here?

KROGSTAD: A word with you.

NORA: With —? (*To the children, quietly.*) Go in to Anne-Marie. What? No, the strange man won't hurt Mama. When he's gone, we'll play some more. (*She leads the children into the room to the left and shuts the door after them. Then, tense and nervous.*) You want to speak to me?

KROGSTAD: Yes, I want to.   320

NORA: Today? But it's not yet the first of the month —

KROGSTAD: No, it's Christmas Eve. It's going to be up to you how merry a Christmas you have.

NORA: What is it you want? Today I absolutely can't —

KROGSTAD: We won't talk about that till later. This is something else. You do have a moment to spare, I suppose?

NORA: Oh yes, of course — I do, except —   325

KROGSTAD: Good. I was sitting over at Olsen's Restaurant when I saw your husband go down the street —

NORA: Yes?

KROGSTAD: With a lady.

NORA: Yes. So?

KROGSTAD: If you'll pardon my asking: wasn't that lady a Mrs. Linde?   330

NORA: Yes.

KROGSTAD: Just now come into town?

NORA: Yes, today.

KROGSTAD: She's a good friend of yours?

NORA: Yes, she is. But I don't see —   335

KROGSTAD: I also knew her once.

NORA: I'm aware of that.

KROGSTAD: Oh? You know all about it. I thought so. Well, then let me ask you short and sweet: is Mrs. Linde getting a job in the bank?

NORA: What makes you think you can cross-examine me, Mr. Krogstad — you, one of my husband's employees? But since you ask, you might as well know — yes, Mrs. Linde's going to be taken on at the bank. And I'm the one who spoke for her, Mr. Krogstad. Now you know.

KROGSTAD: So I guessed right.   340

NORA: (pacing up and down) Oh, one does have a tiny bit of influence, I should hope. Just because I am a woman, don't think it means that —When one has a subordinate position, Mr. Krogstad, one really ought to be careful about pushing somebody who — hm —

KROGSTAD: Who has influence?

NORA: That's right.

KROGSTAD: (in a different tone) Mrs. Helmer, would you be good enough to use your influence on my behalf?

NORA: What? What do you mean?   345

KROGSTAD: Would you please make sure that I keep my subordinate position in the bank?

NORA: What does that mean? Who's thinking of taking away your position?

KROGSTAD: Oh, don't play the innocent with me. I'm quite aware that your friend would hardly relish the chance of running into me again; and I'm also aware now whom I can thank for being turned out.

NORA: But I promise you —

KROGSTAD: Yes, yes, yes, to the point: there's still time, and I'm advising you   350
to use your influence to prevent it.

NORA: But Mr. Krogstad, I have absolutely no influence.

KROGSTAD: You haven't? I thought you were just saying —

NORA: You shouldn't take me so literally. I! How can you believe that I have any such influence over my husband?

KROGSTAD: Oh, I've known your husband from our student days. I don't think the great bank manager's more steadfast than any other married man.

355 **NORA:** You speak insolently about my husband, and I'll show you the door.

KROGSTAD: The lady has spirit.

NORA: I'm not afraid of you any longer. After New Year's, I'll soon be done with the whole business.

KROGSTAD: *(restraining himself)* Now listen to me, Mrs. Helmer. If necessary, I'll fight for my little job in the bank as if it were life itself.

NORA: Yes, so it seems.

360 **KROGSTAD:** It's not just a matter of income; that's the least of it. It's something else — All right, out with it! Look, this is the thing. You know, just like all the others, of course, that once, a good many years ago, I did something rather rash.

NORA: I've heard rumors to that effect.

KROGSTAD: The case never got into court; but all the same, every door was closed in my face from then on. So I took up those various activities you know about. I had to grab hold somewhere; and I dare say I haven't been among the worst. But now I want to drop all that. My boys are growing up. For their sakes, I'll have to win back as much respect as possible here in town. That job in the bank was like the first rung in my ladder. And now your husband wants to kick me right back down in the mud again.

NORA: But for heaven's sake, Mr. Krogstad, it's simply not in my power to help you.

KROGSTAD: That's because you haven't the will to — but I have the means to make you.

365 **NORA:** You certainly won't tell my husband that I owe you money?

KROGSTAD: Hm — what if I told him that?

NORA: That would be shameful of you. *(Nearly in tears.)* This secret — my joy and my pride — that he should learn it in such a crude and disgusting way — learn it from you. You'd expose me to the most horrible unpleasantness —

KROGSTAD: Only unpleasantness?

NORA: *(vehemently)* But go on and try. It'll turn out the worse for you, because then my husband will really see what a crook you are, and then you'll *never* be able to hold your job.

370 **KROGSTAD:** I asked if it was just domestic unpleasantness you were afraid of.

NORA: If my husband finds out, then of course he'll pay what I owe at once, and then we'd be through with you for good.

KROGSTAD: *(a step closer)* Listen, Mrs. Helmer — you've either got a very bad memory, or else no head at all for business. I'd better put you a little more in touch with the facts.

NORA: What do you mean?

KROGSTAD: When your husband was sick, you came to me for a loan of four thousand, eight hundred crowns.

NORA: Where else could I go? 375

KROGSTAD: I promised to get you that sum —

NORA: And you got it.

KROGSTAD: I promised to get you that sum, on certain conditions. You were so involved in your husband's illness, and so eager to finance your trip, that I guess you didn't think out all the details. It might just be a good idea to remind you. I promised you the money on the strength of a note I drew up.

NORA: Yes, and that I signed.

KROGSTAD: Right. But at the bottom I added some lines for your father to 380 guarantee the loan. He was supposed to sign down there.

NORA: Supposed to? He did sign.

KROGSTAD: I left the date blank. In other words, your father would have dated his signature himself. Do you remember that?

NORA: Yes, I think —

KROGSTAD: Then I gave you the note for you to mail to your father. Isn't that so?

NORA: Yes. 385

KROGSTAD: And naturally you sent it at once — because only some five, six days later you brought me the note, properly signed. And with that, the money was yours.

NORA: Well, then; I've made my payments regularly, haven't I?

KROGSTAD: More or less. But — getting back to the point — those were hard times for you then, Mrs. Helmer.

NORA: Yes, they were.

KROGSTAD: Your father was very ill, I believe. 390

NORA: He was near the end.

KROGSTAD: He died soon after?

NORA: Yes.

KROGSTAD: Tell me, Mrs. Helmer, do you happen to recall the date of your father's death? The day of the month, I mean.

NORA: Papa died the twenty-ninth of September. 395

KROGSTAD: That's quite correct; I've already looked into that. And now we come to a curious thing — (*taking out a paper*) which I simply cannot comprehend.

NORA: Curious thing? I don't know —

KROGSTAD: This is the curious thing: that your father co-signed the note for your loan three days after his death.

NORA: How —? I don't understand.

KROGSTAD: Your father died the twenty-ninth of September. But look. 400 Here your father dated his signature October second. Isn't that curious, Mrs. Helmer? (*Nora is silent.*) Can you explain it to me? (*Nora remains silent.*) It's also remarkable that the words "October second" and the year aren't written in your father's hand, but rather in one that I think I know. Well, it's easy to understand. Your father forgot perhaps to date his signature, and then someone or other added it, a bit sloppily, before anyone knew of his death. There's nothing wrong in that. It all comes down to the signature. And there's no question about *that*, Mrs. Helmer. It really *was* your father who signed his own name here, wasn't it?

NORA: (*after a short silence, throwing her head back and looking squarely at him*) No, it wasn't. *I* signed Papa's name.

KROGSTAD: Wait, now — are you fully aware that this is a dangerous confession?

NORA: Why? You'll soon get your money.

KROGSTAD: Let me ask you a question — why didn't you send the paper to your father?

405 NORA: That was impossible. Papa was so sick. If I'd asked him for his signature, I also would have had to tell him what the money was for. But I couldn't tell him, sick as he was, that my husband's life was in danger. That was just impossible.

KROGSTAD: Then it would have been better if you'd given up the trip abroad.

NORA: I couldn't possibly. The trip was to save my husband's life. I couldn't give that up.

KROGSTAD: But didn't you ever consider that this was a fraud against me?

NORA: I couldn't let myself be bothered by that. You weren't any concern of mine. I couldn't stand you, with all those cold complications you made, even though you knew how badly off my husband was.

410 KROGSTAD: Mrs. Helmer, obviously you haven't the vaguest idea of what you've involved yourself in. But I can tell you this: it was nothing more and nothing worse than I once did — and it wrecked my whole reputation.

NORA: You? Do you expect me to believe that you ever acted bravely to save your wife's life?

KROGSTAD: Laws don't inquire into motives.

NORA: Then they must be very poor laws.

KROGSTAD: Poor or not — if I introduce this paper in court, you'll be judged according to law.

415 NORA: This I refuse to believe. A daughter hasn't a right to protect her dying father from anxiety and care? A wife hasn't a right to save her husband's life? I don't know much about laws, but I'm sure that somewhere in the books these things are allowed. And you don't know anything about it — you who practice the law? You must be an awful lawyer, Mr. Krogstad.

KROGSTAD: Could be. But business — the kind of business we two mixed up in — don't you think I know about that? All right. Do what you want now. But I'm telling you *this*: if I get shoved down a second time, you're going to keep me company. (*He bows and goes out through the hall.*)

NORA: *(pensive for a moment, then tossing her head)* Oh, really! Trying to frighten me! I'm not so silly as all that. *(Begins gathering up the children's clothes, but soon stops.)* But —? No, but that's impossible! I did it out of love.

THE CHILDREN: *(in the doorway, left)* Mama, that strange man's gone out the door.

NORA: Yes, yes, I know it. But don't tell anyone about the strange man. Do you hear? Not even Papa!

THE CHILDREN: No, Mama. But now will you play again? 420

NORA: No, not now.

THE CHILDREN: Oh, but Mama, you promised.

NORA: Yes, but I can't now. Go inside; I have too much to do. Go in, go in, my sweet darlings. *(She herds them gently back in the room and shuts the door after them. Settling on the sofa, she takes up a piece of embroidery and makes some stitches, but soon stops abruptly.)* No! *(Throws the work aside, rises, goes to the hall door and calls out.)* Helene! Let me have the tree in here. *(Goes to the table, left, opens the table drawer, and stops again.)* No, but that's utterly impossible!

MAID: *(with the Christmas tree)* Where should I put it, ma'am?

NORA: There. The middle of the floor. 425

MAID: Should I bring anything else?

NORA: No, thanks. I have what I need.

The Maid, who has set the tree down, goes out.

NORA: *(absorbed in trimming the tree)* Candles here — and flowers here. That terrible creature! Talk, talk, talk! There's nothing to it at all. The tree's going to be lovely. I'll do anything to please you, Torvald. I'll sing for you, dance for you —

Helmer comes in from the hall, with a sheaf of papers under his arm.

NORA: Oh! You're back so soon?

HELMER: Yes. Has anyone been here? 430

NORA: Here? No.

ER: That's odd. I saw Krogstad leaving the front door.

NORA: So? Oh yes, that's true. Krogstad was here a moment.

HELMER: Nora, I can see by your face that he's been here, begging you to put in a good word for him.

NORA: Yes. 435

HELMER: And it was supposed to seem like your own idea? You were to hide it from me that he'd been here. He asked you that, too, didn't he?

NORA: Yes, Torvald, but —

HELMER: Nora, Nora, and you could fall for that? Talk with that sort of person and promise him anything? And then in the bargain, tell me an untruth.

NORA: An untruth —?

HELMER: Didn't you say that no one had been here? *(Wagging his finger.)* My 440 little songbird must never do that again. A songbird needs a clean beak to

warble with. No false notes. (*Putting his arm about her waist.*) That's the way
it should be, isn't it? Yes, I'm sure of it. (*Releasing her.*) And so, enough of
that. (*Sitting by the stove.*) Ah, how snug and cozy it is here. (*Leafing among
his papers.*)

NORA: (*busy with the tree, after a short pause*) Torvald!

HELMER: Yes.

NORA: I'm so much looking forward to the Stenborgs' costume party, day after
tomorrow.

HELMER: And I can't wait to see what you'll surprise me with.

445   NORA: Oh, that stupid business!

HELMER: What?

NORA: I can't find anything that's right. Everything seems so ridiculous,
so inane.

HELMER: So my little Nora's come to *that* recognition?

NORA: (*going behind his chair, her arms resting on its back*) Are you very busy,
Torvald?

450   HELMER: Oh —

NORA: What papers are those?

HELMER: Bank matters.

NORA: Already?

HELMER: I've gotten full authority from the retiring management to make all
necessary changes in personnel and procedure. I'll need Christmas week for
that. I want to have everything in order by New Year's.

455   NORA: So that was the reason this poor Krogstad —

HELMER: Hm.

NORA: (*still leaning on the chair and slowly stroking the nape of his neck*) If you
weren't so very busy, I would have asked you an enormous favor, Torvald.

HELMER: Let's hear. What is it?

NORA: You know, there isn't anyone who has your good taste — and I want so
much to look well at the costume party. Torvald, couldn't you take over and
decide what I should be and plan my costume?

460   HELMER: Ah, is my stubborn little creature calling for a lifeguard?

NORA: Yes, Torvald, I can't get anywhere without your help.

HELMER: All right — I'll think it over. We'll hit on something.

NORA: Oh, how sweet of you. (*Goes to the tree again. Pause.*) Aren't the red
flowers pretty —? But tell me, was it really such a crime that this Krogstad
committed?

HELMER: Forgery. Do you have any idea what that means?

465   NORA: Couldn't he have done it out of need?

HELMER: Yes, or thoughtlessness, like so many others. I'm not so heartless that
I'd condemn a man categorically for just one mistake.

NORA: No, of course not, Torvald!

HELMER: Plenty of men have redeemed themselves by openly confessing their
crimes and taking their punishment.

NORA: Punishment —?

HELMER: But now Krogstad didn't go that way. He got himself out by sharp practices, and that's the real cause of his moral breakdown. 470

NORA: Do you really think that would —?

HELMER: Just imagine how a man with that sort of guilt in him has to lie and cheat and deceive on all sides, has to wear a mask even with the nearest and dearest he has, even with his own wife and children. And with the children, Nora — that's where it's most horrible.

NORA: Why?

HELMER: Because that kind of atmosphere of lies infects the whole life of a home. Every breath the children take in is filled with the germs of something degenerate.

NORA: (*coming closer behind him*) Are you sure of that? 475

HELMER: Oh, I've seen it often enough as a lawyer. Almost everyone who goes bad early in life has a mother who's a chronic liar.

NORA: Why just — the mother?

HELMER: It's usually the mother's influence that's dominant, but the father's works in the same way, of course. Every lawyer is quite familiar with it. And still this Krogstad's been going home year in, year out, poisoning his own children with lies and pretense; that's why I call him morally lost. (*Reaching his hands out toward her.*) So my sweet little Nora must promise me never to plead his cause. Your hand on it. Come, come, what's this? Give me your hand. There, now. All settled. I can tell you it'd be impossible for me to work alongside of him. I literally feel physically revolted when I'm anywhere near such a person.

NORA: (*withdraws her hand and goes to the other side of the Christmas tree*) How hot it is here! And I've got so much to do.

HELMER: (*getting up and gathering his papers*) Yes, and I have to think about 480 getting some of these read through before dinner. I'll think about your costume, too. And something to hang on the tree in gilt paper, I may even see about that. (*Putting his hand on her head.*) Oh you, my darling little songbird. (*He goes into his study and closes the door after him.*)

NORA: (*softly, after a silence*) Oh, really! It isn't so. It's impossible. It must be impossible.

ANNE-MARIE: (*in the doorway, left*) The children are begging so hard to come in to Mama.

NORA: No, no, no, don't let them in to me! You stay with them, Anne-Marie.

ANNE-MARIE: Of course, ma'am. (*Closes the door.*)

NORA: (*pale with terror*) Hurt my children —! Poison my home? (*A moment's* 485 *pause; then she tosses her head.*) That's not true. Never. Never in all the world.

ACT 2

Same room. Beside the piano the Christmas tree now stands stripped of ornaments, burned-down candle stubs on its ragged branches. Nora's street clothes lie on the sofa. Nora, alone in the room, moves restlessly about; at last she stops at the sofa and picks up her coat.

NORA: (*dropping the coat again*) Someone's coming! (*Goes toward the door, listens.*) No — there's no one. Of course — nobody's coming today, Christmas Day — or tomorrow, either. But maybe —(*Opens the door and looks out.*) No, nothing in the mailbox. Quite empty. (*Coming forward.*) What nonsense! He won't do anything serious. Nothing terrible could happen. It's impossible. Why, I have three small children.

Anne-Marie, with a large carton, comes in from the room to the left.

ANNE-MARIE: Well, at last I found the box with the masquerade clothes.
NORA: Thanks. Put it on the table.
ANNE-MARIE: (*does so*) But they're all pretty much of a mess.
5   NORA: Ahh! I'd love to rip them in a million pieces!
ANNE-MARIE: Oh, mercy, they can be fixed right up. Just a little patience.
NORA: Yes, I'll go get Mrs. Linde to help me.
ANNE-MARIE: Out again now? In this nasty weather? Miss Nora will catch cold — get sick.
NORA: Oh, worse things could happen — How are the children?
10   ANNE-MARIE: The poor mites are playing with their Christmas presents, but —
NORA: Do they ask for me much?
ANNE-MARIE: They're so used to having Mama around, you know.
NORA: Yes. But Anne-Marie, I *can't* be together with them as much as I was.
ANNE-MARIE: Well, small children get used to anything.
15   NORA: You think so? Do you think they'd forget their mother if she was gone for good?
ANNE-MARIE: Oh, mercy — gone for good!
NORA: Wait, tell me, Anne-Marie — I've wondered so often — how could you ever have the heart to give your child over to strangers?
20   ANNE-MARIE: But I had to, you know, to become little Nora's nurse.
NORA: Yes, but how could you *do* it?
ANNE-MARIE: When I could get such a good place? A girl who's poor and who's gotten in trouble is glad enough for that. Because that slippery fish, he didn't do a thing for me, you know.
NORA: But your daughter's surely forgotten you.
ANNE-MARIE: Oh, she certainly has not. She's written to me, both when she was confirmed and when she was married.
NORA: (*clasping her about the neck*) You old Anne-Marie, you were a good mother for me when I was little.
ANNE-MARIE: Poor little Nora, with no other mother but me.
25   NORA: And if the babies didn't have one, then I know that you'd —What silly talk! (*Opening the carton.*) Go in to them. Now I'll have to — Tomorrow you can see how lovely I'll look.
ANNE-MARIE: Oh, there won't be anyone at the party as lovely as Miss Nora. (*She goes off into the room, left.*)
NORA: (*begins unpacking the box, but soon throws it aside*) Oh, if I dared to go out. If only nobody would come. If only nothing would happen here while

I'm out. What craziness — nobody's coming. Just don't think. This muff — needs a brushing. Beautiful gloves, beautiful gloves. Let it go. Let it go! One, two, three, four, five, six — *(With a cry.)* Oh, there they are! *(Poises to move toward the door, but remains irresolutely standing. Mrs. Linde enters from the hall, where she has removed her street clothes.)*

NORA: Oh, it's you, Kristine. There's no one else out there? How good that you've come.

MRS. LINDE: I hear you were up asking for me.

NORA: Yes, I just stopped by. There's something you really can help me with. Let's get settled on the sofa. Look, there's going to be a costume party tomorrow evening at the Stenborgs' right above us, and now Torvald wants me to go as a Neapolitan peasant girl and dance the tarantella that I learned in Capri.

MRS. LINDE: Really, are you giving a whole performance?

NORA: Torvald says yes, I should. See, here's the dress. Torvald had it made for me down there; but now it's all so tattered that I just don't know —

MRS. LINDE: Oh, we'll fix that up in no time. It's nothing more than the trimmings — they're a bit loose here and there. Needle and thread? Good, now we have what we need.

NORA: Oh, how sweet of you!

MRS. LINDE: *(sewing)* So you'll be in disguise tomorrow, Nora. You know what? I'll stop by then for a moment and have a look at you all dressed up. But listen, I've absolutely forgotten to thank you for that pleasant evening yesterday.

NORA: *(getting up and walking about)* I don't think it was as pleasant as usual yesterday. You should have come to town a bit sooner, Kristine — Yes, Torvald really knows how to give a home elegance and charm.

MRS. LINDE: And you do, too, if you ask me. You're not your father's daughter for nothing. But tell me, is Dr. Rank always so down in the mouth as yesterday?

NORA: No, that was quite an exception. But he goes around critically ill all the time — tuberculosis of the spine, poor man. You know, his father was a disgusting thing who kept mistresses and so on — and that's why the son's been sickly from birth.

MRS. LINDE: *(lets her sewing fall to her lap)* But my dearest Nora, how do you know about such things?

NORA: *(walking more jauntily)* Hmp! When you've had three children, then you've had a few visits from — from women who know something of medicine, and they tell you this and that.

MRS. LINDE: *(resumes sewing; a short pause)* Does Dr. Rank come here every day?

NORA: Every blessed day. He's Torvald's best friend from childhood, and *my* good friend, too. Dr. Rank almost belongs to this house.

MRS. LINDE: But tell me — is he quite sincere? I mean, doesn't he rather enjoy flattering people?

NORA: Just the opposite. Why do you think that?

45 MRS. LINDE: When you introduced us yesterday, he was proclaiming that
he'd often heard my name in this house; but later I noticed that your
husband hadn't the slightest idea who I really was. So how could Dr.
Rank —?

NORA: But it's all true, Kristine. You see, Torvald loves me beyond words, and,
as he puts it, he'd like to keep me all to himself. For a long time he'd almost
be jealous if I even mentioned any of my old friends back home. So of
course I dropped that. But with Dr. Rank I talk a lot about such things,
because he likes hearing about them.

MRS. LINDE: Now listen, Nora; in many ways you're still like a child. I'm
a good deal older than you, with a little more experience. I'll tell you
something: you ought to put an end to all this with Dr. Rank.

NORA: What should I put an end to?

MRS. LINDE: Both parts of it, I think. Yesterday you said something about
a rich admirer who'd provide you with money —

50 NORA: Yes, one who doesn't exist — worse luck. So?

MRS. LINDE: Is Dr. Rank well off?

NORA: Yes, he is.

MRS. LINDE: With no dependents?

NORA: No, no one. But —

55 MRS. LINDE: And he's over here every day?

NORA: Yes, I told you that.

MRS. LINDE: How can a man of such refinement be so grasping?

NORA: I don't follow you at all.

MRS. LINDE: Now don't try to hide it, Nora. You think I can't guess who
loaned you the forty-eight hundred crowns?

60 NORA: Are you out of your mind? How could you think such a thing! A friend
of ours, who comes here every single day. What an intolerable situation
that would have been!

MRS. LINDE: Then it really wasn't him.

NORA: No, absolutely not. It never even crossed my mind for a moment —
And he had nothing to lend in those days; his inheritance came later.

MRS. LINDE: Well, I think that was a stroke of luck for you, Nora dear.

NORA: No, it never would have occurred to me to ask Dr. Rank — Still, I'm
quite sure that if I had asked him —

65 MRS. LINDE: Which you won't, of course.

NORA: No, of course not. I can't see that I'd ever need to. But I'm quite
positive that if I talked to Dr. Rank —

MRS. LINDE: Behind your husband's back?

NORA: I've got to clear up this other thing; *that's* also behind his back. I've *got*
to clear it all up.

MRS. LINDE: Yes, I was saying that yesterday, but —

70 NORA: (*pacing up and down*) A man handles these problems so much better
than a woman —

MRS. LINDE: One's husband does, yes.

NORA: Nonsense. (*Stopping.*) When you pay everything you owe, then you get
your note back, right?

MRS. LINDE: Yes, naturally.

NORA: And can rip it into a million pieces and burn it up — that filthy scrap of paper!

MRS. LINDE: *(looking hard at her, laying her sewing aside, and rising slowly)* Nora, you're hiding something from me.   75

NORA: You can see it in my face?

MRS. LINDE: Something's happened to you since yesterday morning. Nora, what is it?

NORA: *(hurrying toward her)* Kristine! *(Listening.)* Shh! Torvald's home. Look, go in with the children a while. Torvald can't bear all this snipping and stitching. Let Anne-Marie help you.

MRS. LINDE: *(gathering up some of the things)* All right, but I'm not leaving here until we've talked this out. *(She disappears into the room, left, as Torvald enters from the hall.)*

NORA: Oh, how I've been waiting for you, Torvald dear.   80

HELMER: Was that the dressmaker?

NORA: No, that was Kristine. She's helping me fix up my costume. You know, it's going to be quite attractive.

HELMER: Yes, wasn't that a bright idea I had?

NORA: Brilliant! But then wasn't I good as well to give in to you?

HELMER: Good — because you give in to your husband's judgment? All right,   85
you little goose, I know you didn't mean it like that. But I won't disturb you. You'll want to have a fitting, I suppose.

NORA: And you'll be working?

HELMER: Yes. *(Indicating a bundle of papers.)* See. I've been down to the bank. *(Starts toward his study.)*

NORA: Torvald.

HELMER: *(stops)* Yes.

NORA: If your little squirrel begged you, with all her heart and soul, for   90
something —?

HELMER: What's that?

NORA: Then would you do it?

HELMER: First, naturally, I'd have to know what it was.

NORA: Your squirrel would scamper about and do tricks, if you'd only be sweet and give in.

HELMER: Out with it.   95

NORA: Your lark would be singing high and low in every room—

HELMER: Come on, she does that anyway.

NORA: I'd be a wood nymph and dance for you in the moonlight.

HELMER: Nora — don't tell me it's that same business from this morning?

NORA: *(coming closer)* Yes, Torvald, I beg you, please!   100

HELMER: And you actually have the nerve to drag that up again?

NORA: Yes, yes, you've got to give in to me; you *have* to let Krogstad keep his job in the bank.

HELMER: My dear Nora, I've slated his job for Mrs. Linde.

NORA: That's awfully kind of you. But you could just fire another clerk instead of Krogstad.

105 HELMER: This is the most incredible stubbornness! Because you go and give an
        impulsive promise to speak up for him, I'm expected to—
    NORA: That's not the reason, Torvald. It's for your own sake. That man does
        writing for the worst papers; you said it yourself. He could do you any
        amount of harm. I'm scared to death of him—
    HELMER: Ah, I understand. It's the old memories haunting you.
    NORA: What do you mean by that?
    HELMER: Of course, you're thinking about your father.
110 NORA: Yes, all right. Just remember how those nasty gossips wrote in the
        papers about Papa and slandered him so cruelly. I think they'd have had
        him dismissed if the department hadn't sent you up to investigate, and
        if you hadn't been so kind and open-minded toward him.
    HELMER: My dear Nora, there's a notable difference between your father and
        me. Your father's official career was hardly above reproach. But mine is; and
        I hope it'll stay that way as long as I hold my position.
    NORA: Oh, who can ever tell what vicious minds can invent? We could be so
        snug and happy now in our quiet, carefree home — you and I and the
        children, Torvald! That's why I'm pleading with you so—
    HELMER: And just by pleading for him you make it impossible for me to
        keep him on. It's already known at the bank that I'm firing Krogstad. What
        if it's rumored around now that the new bank manager was vetoed by his
        wife—
    NORA: Yes, what then —?
115 HELMER: Oh yes — as long as our little bundle of stubbornness gets her
        way —! I should go and make myself ridiculous in front of the whole
        office — give people the idea I can be swayed by all kinds of outside
        pressure. Oh, you can bet I'd feel the effects of that soon enough!
        Besides — there's something that rules Krogstad right out at the bank
        as long as I'm the manager.
    NORA: What's that?
    HELMER: His moral failings I could maybe overlook if I had to—
    NORA: Yes, Torvald, why not?
    HELMER: And I hear he's quite efficient on the job. But he was a crony of mine
        back in my teens — one of those rash friendships that crop up again and
        again to embarrass you later in life. Well, I might as well say it straight out:
        we're on a first-name basis. And that tactless fool makes no effort at all to
        hide it in front of others. Quite the contrary — he thinks that entitles him
        to take a familiar air around me, and so every other second he comes
        booming out with his "Yes, Torvald!" and "Sure thing, Torvald!" I tell you,
        it's been excruciating for me. He's out to make my place in the bank
        unbearable.
120 NORA: Torvald, you can't be serious about all this.
    HELMER: Oh no? Why not?
    NORA: Because these are such petty considerations.
    HELMER: What are you saying? Petty? You think I'm petty!
    NORA: No, just the opposite, Torvald dear. That's exactly why—

HELMER: Never mind. You call my motives petty; then I might as well be just   125
that. Petty! All right! We'll put a stop to this for good. (*Goes to the hall door
and calls.*) Helene!

NORA: What do you want?

HELMER: (*searching among his papers*) A decision. (*The Maid comes in.*) Look here;
take this letter; go out with it at once. Get hold of a messenger and have him
deliver it. Quick now. It's already addressed. Wait, here's some money.

MAID: Yes, sir. (*She leaves with the letter.*)

HELMER: (*straightening his papers*) There, now, little Miss Willful.

NORA: (*breathlessly*) Torvald, what was that letter?   130

HELMER: Krogstad's notice.

NORA: Call it back, Torvald! There's still time. Oh, Torvald, call it back! Do
it for my sake — for your sake, for the children's sake! Do you hear, Torvald;
do it! You don't know how this can harm us.

HELMER: Too late.

NORA: Yes, too late.

HELMER: Nora dear, I can forgive you this panic, even though basically you're   135
insulting me. Yes, you are! Or isn't it an insult to think that *I* should be
afraid of a courtroom hack's revenge? But I forgive you anyway, because this
shows so beautifully how much you love me. (*Takes her in his arms.*) This is
the way it should be, my darling Nora. Whatever comes, you'll see: when it
really counts, I have strength and courage enough as a man to take on the
whole weight myself.

NORA: (*terrified*) What do you mean by that?

HELMER: The whole weight, I said.

NORA: (*resolutely*) No, never in all the world.

HELMER: Good. So we'll share it, Nora, as man and wife. That's as it should
be. (*Fondling her.*) Are you happy now? There, there, there — not these
frightened dove's eyes. It's nothing at all but empty fantasies — Now you
should run through your tarantella and practice your tambourine. I'll go to
the inner office and shut both doors, so I won't hear a thing; you can make
all the noise you like. (*Turning in the doorway.*) And when Rank comes, just
tell him where he can find me. (*He nods to her and goes with his papers into
the study, closing the door.*)

NORA: (*standing as though rooted, dazed with fright, in a whisper*) He really could   140
do it. He will do it. He'll do it in spite of everything. No, not that, never,
never! Anything but that! Escape! A way out — (*The doorbell rings.*)
Dr. Rank! Anything but that! *Anything*, whatever it is! (*Her hands pass
over her face, smoothing it; she pulls herself together, goes over and opens the
hall door. Dr. Rank stands outside, hanging his fur coat up. During the following
scene, it begins getting dark.*)

NORA: Hello, Dr. Rank. I recognized your ring. But you mustn't go in to
Torvald yet; I believe he's working.

RANK: And you?

NORA: For you, I always have an hour to spare — you know that. (*He has
entered, and she shuts the door after him.*)

RANK: Many thanks. I'll make use of these hours while I can.

145   NORA: What do you mean by that? While you can?

RANK: Does that disturb you?

NORA: Well, it's such an odd phrase. Is anything going to happen?

RANK: What's going to happen is what I've been expecting so long — but I honestly didn't think it would come so soon.

NORA: *(gripping his arm)* What is it you've found out? Dr. Rank, you have to tell me!

150   RANK: *(sitting by the stove)* It's all over with me. There's nothing to be done about it.

NORA: *(breathing easier)* Is it you — then —?

RANK: Who else? There's no point in lying to one's self. I'm the most miserable of all my patients, Mrs. Helmer. These past few days I've been auditing my internal accounts. Bankrupt! Within a month I'll probably be laid out and rotting in the churchyard.

NORA: Oh, what a horrible thing to say.

RANK: The thing itself is horrible. But the worst of it is all the other horror before it's over. There's only one final examination left; when I'm finished with that, I'll know about when my disintegration will begin. There's something I want to say. Helmer with his sensitivity has such a sharp distaste for anything ugly. I don't want him near my sickroom.

155   NORA: Oh, but Dr. Rank—

RANK: I won't have him in there. Under no condition. I'll lock my door to him — As soon as I'm completely sure of the worst, I'll send you my calling card marked with a black cross, and you'll know then the wreck has started to come apart.

NORA: No, today you're completely unreasonable. And I wanted you so much to be in a really good humor.

RANK: With death up my sleeve? And then to suffer this way for somebody else's sins. Is there any justice in that? And in every single family, in some way or another, this inevitable retribution of nature goes on —

NORA: *(her hands pressed over her ears)* Oh, stuff! Cheer up! Please — be gay!

160   RANK: Yes, I'd just as soon laugh at it all. My poor, innocent spine, serving time for my father's gay army days.

NORA: *(by the table, left)* He was so infatuated with asparagus tips and *pâté de foie gras*, wasn't that it?

RANK: Yes — and with truffles.

NORA: Truffles, yes. And then with oysters, I suppose?

RANK: Yes, tons of oysters, naturally.

165   NORA: And then the port and champagne to go with it. It's so sad that all these delectable things have to strike at our bones.

RANK: Especially when they strike at the unhappy bones that never shared in the fun.

NORA: Ah, that's the saddest of all.

RANK: *(looks searchingly at her)* Hm.

NORA: *(after a moment)* Why did you smile?

RANK: No, it was you who laughed. 170

NORA: No, it was you who smiled, Dr. Rank!

RANK: (getting up) You're even a bigger tease than I'd thought.

NORA: I'm full of wild ideas today.

RANK: That's obvious.

NORA: (putting both hands on his shoulders) Dear, dear Dr. Rank, you'll never 175
die for Torvald and me.

RANK: Oh, that loss you'll easily get over. Those who go away are soon
forgotten.

NORA: (looks fearfully at him) You believe that?

RANK: One makes new connections, and then —

NORA: Who makes new connections?

RANK: Both you and Torvald will when I'm gone. I'd say you're well under 180
way already. What was that Mrs. Linde doing here last evening?

NORA: Oh, come — you can't be jealous of poor Kristine?

RANK: Oh yes, I am. She'll be my successor here in the house. When I'm
down under, that woman will probably —

NORA: Shh! Not so loud. She's right in there.

RANK: Today as well. So you see.

NORA: Only to sew on my dress. Good gracious, how unreasonable you are. 185
(Sitting on the sofa.) Be nice now, Dr. Rank. Tomorrow you'll see how
beautifully I'll dance; and you can imagine then that I'm dancing only
for you — yes, and of course for Torvald, too — that's understood. (Takes
various items out of the carton.) Dr. Rank, sit over here and I'll show you
something.

RANK: (sitting) What's that?

NORA: Look here. Look.

RANK: Silk stockings.

NORA: Flesh-colored. Aren't they lovely? Now it's so dark here, but tomorrow —
No, no, no, just look at the feet. Oh well, you might as well look at the rest.

RANK: Hm — 190

NORA: Why do you look so critical? Don't you believe they'll fit?

RANK: I've never had any chance to form an opinion on that.

NORA: (glancing at him a moment) Shame on you. (Hits him lightly on the ear
with the stockings.) That's for you. (Puts them away again.)

RANK: And what other splendors am I going to see now?

NORA: Not the least bit more, because you've been naughty. (She hums a little
and rummages among her things.) 195

RANK: (after a short silence) When I sit here together with you like this,
completely easy and open, then I don't know — I simply can't
imagine — whatever would have become of me if I'd never come into this
house.

NORA: (smiling) Yes, I really think you feel completely at ease with us.

RANK: (more quietly, staring straight ahead) And then to have to go away
from it all —

NORA: Nonsense, you're not going away.

200 RANK: *(his voice unchanged)* — and not even be able to leave some poor show
        of gratitude behind, scarcely a fleeting regret — no more than a vacant
        place that anyone can fill.

NORA: And if I asked you now for —? No —

RANK: For what?

NORA: For a great proof of your friendship —

RANK: Yes, yes?

205 NORA: No, I mean — for an exceptionally big favor —

RANK: Would you really, for once, make me so happy?

NORA: Oh, you haven't the vaguest idea what it is.

RANK: All right, then tell me.

NORA: No, but I can't, Dr. Rank — it's all out of reason. It's advice and help,
        too — and a favor —

210 RANK: So much the better. I can't fathom what you're hinting at. Just speak
        out. Don't you trust me?

NORA: Of course. More than anyone else. You're my best and truest friend,
        I'm sure. That's why I want to talk to you. All right, then, Dr. Rank:
        there's something you can help me prevent. You know how deeply, how
        inexpressibly dearly Torvald loves me; he'd never hesitate a second to
        give up his life for me.

RANK: *(leaning close to her)* Nora — do you think he's the only one —

NORA: *(with a slight start)* Who —?

RANK: Who'd gladly give up his life for you.

215 NORA: *(heavily)* I see.

RANK: I swore to myself you should know this before I'm gone. I'll never find
        a better chance. Yes, Nora, now you know. And also you know now that
        you can trust me beyond anyone else.

NORA: *(rising, natural and calm)* Let me by.

RANK: *(making room for her, but still sitting)* Nora —

NORA: *(in the hall doorway)* Helene, bring the lamp in. *(Goes over to the stove.)*
        Ah, dear Dr. Rank, that was really mean of you.

220 RANK: *(getting up)* That I've loved you just as deeply as somebody else? Was
        that mean?

NORA: No, but that you came out and told me. That was quite
        unnecessary —

RANK: What do you mean? Have you known —?

The Maid comes in with the lamp, sets it on the table, and goes out again.

RANK: Nora — Mrs. Helmer — I'm asking you: have you known about it?

NORA: Oh, how can I tell what I know or don't know? Really, I don't know
        what to say —Why did you have to be so clumsy, Dr. Rank! Everything
        was so good.

225 RANK: Well, in any case, you now have the knowledge that my body and soul
        are at your command. So won't you speak out?

NORA: *(looking at him)* After that?

RANK: Please, just let me know what it is.

NORA: You can't know anything now.

RANK: I have to. You mustn't punish me like this. Give me the chance to do whatever is humanly possible for you.

NORA: Now there's nothing you can do for me. Besides, actually, I don't 230 need any help. You'll see — it's only my fantasies. That's what it is. Of course! (*Sits in the rocker, looks at him, and smiles.*) What a nice one you are, Dr. Rank. Aren't you a little bit ashamed, now that the lamp is here?

RANK: No, not exactly. But perhaps I'd better go — for good?

NORA: No, you certainly can't do that. You must come here just as you always have. You know Torvald can't do without you.

RANK: Yes, but *you?*

NORA: You know how much I enjoy it when you're here.

RANK: That's precisely what threw me off. You're a mystery to me. So many 235 times I've felt you'd almost rather be with me than with Helmer.

NORA: Yes — you see, there are some people that one loves most and other people that one would almost prefer being with.

RANK: Yes, there's something to that.

NORA: When I was back home, of course I loved Papa most. But I always thought it was so much fun when I could sneak down to the maids' quarters, because they never tried to improve me, and it was always so amusing, the way they talked to each other.

RANK: Aha, so it's *their* place that I've filled.

NORA: (*jumping up and going to him*) Oh, dear, sweet Dr. Rank, that's not what 240 I mean at all. But you can understand that with Torvald it's just the same as with Papa—

The Maid enters from the hall.

MAID: Ma'am — please! (*She whispers to Nora and hands her a calling card.*)

NORA: (*glancing at the card*) Ah! (*Slips it into her pocket.*)

RANK: Anything wrong?

NORA: No, no, not at all. It's only some — it's my new dress—

RANK: Really? But — there's your dress. 245

NORA: Oh, that. But this is another one — I ordered it — Torvald mustn't know—

RANK: Ah, now we have the big secret.

NORA: That's right. Just go in with him — he's back in the inner study. Keep him there as long as—

RANK: Don't worry. He won't get away. (*Goes into the study.*)

NORA: (*to the Maid*) And he's standing waiting in the kitchen? 250

MAID: Yes, he came up by the back stairs.

NORA: But didn't you tell him somebody was here?

MAID: Yes, but that didn't do any good.

NORA: He won't leave?

MAID: No, he won't go till he's talked with you, ma'am. 255

NORA: Let him come in, then — but quietly. Helene, don't breathe a word about this. It's a surprise for my husband.

MAID: Yes, yes, I understand —(*Goes out.*)

NORA: This horror — it's going to happen. No, no, no, it can't happen, it mustn't. (*She goes and bolts Helmer's door. The Maid opens the hall door for Krogstad and shuts it behind him. He is dressed for travel in a fur coat, boots, and a fur cap.*)

NORA: (*going toward him*) Talk softly. My husband's home.

260   **KROGSTAD:** Well, good for him.

NORA: What do you want?

KROGSTAD: Some information.

NORA: Hurry up, then. What is it?

KROGSTAD: You know, of course, that I got my notice.

265   **NORA:** I couldn't prevent it, Mr. Krogstad. I fought for you to the bitter end, but nothing worked.

KROGSTAD: Does your husband's love for you run so thin? He knows everything I can expose you to, and all the same he dares to—

NORA: How can you imagine he knows anything about this?

KROGSTAD: Ah, no — I can't imagine it either, now. It's not at all like my fine Torvald Helmer to have so much guts—

NORA: Mr. Krogstad, I demand respect for my husband!

270   **KROGSTAD:** Why, of course — all due respect. But since the lady's keeping it so carefully hidden, may I presume to ask if you're also a bit better informed than yesterday about what you've actually done?

NORA: More than you ever could teach me.

KROGSTAD: Yes, I *am* such an awful lawyer.

NORA: What is it you want from me?

KROGSTAD: Just a glimpse of how you are, Mrs. Helmer. I've been thinking about you all day long. A cashier, a night-court scribbler, a — well, a type like me also has a little of what they call a heart, you know.

275   **NORA:** Then show it. Think of my children.

KROGSTAD: Did you or your husband ever think of mine? But never mind. I simply wanted to tell you that you don't need to take this thing too seriously. For the present, I'm not proceeding with any action.

NORA: Oh no, really! Well — I knew that.

KROGSTAD: Everything can be settled in a friendly spirit. It doesn't have to get around town at all; it can stay just among us three.

NORA: My husband must never know anything of this.

280   **KROGSTAD:** How can you manage that? Perhaps you can pay me the balance?

NORA: No, not right now.

KROGSTAD: Or you know some way of raising the money in a day or two?

NORA: No way that I'm willing to use.

KROGSTAD: Well, it wouldn't have done you any good, anyway. If you stood in front of me with a fistful of bills, you still couldn't buy your signature back.

285   **NORA:** Then tell me what you're going to do with it.

KROGSTAD: I'll just hold onto it — keep it on file. There's no outsider who'll even get wind of it. So if you've been thinking of taking some desperate step—

NORA: I have.

KROGSTAD: Been thinking of running away from home—

NORA: I have!

KROGSTAD: Or even of something worse—   290

NORA: How could you guess that?

KROGSTAD: You can drop those thoughts.

NORA: How could you guess I was thinking of *that*?

KROGSTAD: Most of us think about *that* at first. I thought about it too, but I
    discovered I hadn't the courage—

NORA: *(lifelessly)* I don't either.   295

KROGSTAD: *(relieved)* That's true, you haven't the courage? You too?

NORA: I don't have it — I don't have it.

KROGSTAD: It would be terribly stupid, anyway. After that first storm at
    home blows out, why, then — I have here in my pocket a letter for your
    husband—

NORA: Telling everything?

KROGSTAD: As charitably as possible.   300

NORA: *(quickly)* He mustn't ever get that letter. Tear it up. I'll find some way
    to get money.

KROGSTAD: Beg pardon, Mrs. Helmer, but I think I just told you—

NORA: Oh, I don't mean the money I owe you. Let me know how much you
    want from my husband, and I'll manage it.

KROGSTAD: I don't want any money from your husband.

NORA: What do you want, then?   305

KROGSTAD: I'll tell you what. I want to recoup, Mrs. Helmer; I want to get
    on in the world — and there's where your husband can help me. For a year
    and a half I've kept myself clean of anything disreputable — all that time
    struggling with the worst conditions; but I was satisfied, working my way up
    step by step. Now I've been written right off, and I'm just not in the mood
    to come crawling back. I tell you, I want to move on. I want to get back in
    the bank — in a better position. Your husband can set up a job for me—

NORA: He'll never do that!

KROGSTAD: He'll do it. I know him. He won't dare breathe a word of protest.
    And once I'm in there together with him, you just wait and see! Inside of
    a year, I'll be the manager's right-hand man. It'll be Nils Krogstad, not
    Torvald Helmer, who runs the bank.

NORA: You'll never see the day!

KROGSTAD: Maybe you think you can—   310

NORA: I have the courage now —for *that*.

KROGSTAD: Oh, you don't scare me. A smart, spoiled lady like you—

NORA: You'll see; you'll see!

KROGSTAD: Under the ice, maybe? Down in the freezing, coal-black water?
    There, till you float up in the spring, ugly, unrecognizable, with your hair
    falling out —

NORA: You don't frighten me.   315

KROGSTAD: Nor do you frighten me. One doesn't do these things, Mrs. Helmer.
    Besides, what good would it be? I'd still have him safe in my pocket.

NORA: Afterwards? When I'm no longer — ?

KROGSTAD: Are you forgetting that *I'll* be in control then over your final reputation? (*Nora stands speechless, staring at him.*) Good; now I've warned you.
Don't do anything stupid. When Helmer's read my letter, I'll be waiting for
his reply. And bear in mind that it's your husband himself who's forced me
back to my old ways. I'll never forgive him for that. Good-bye, Mrs. Helmer.
(*He goes out through the hall.*)

NORA: (*goes to the hall door, opens it a crack, and listens*) He's gone. Didn't leave
the letter. Oh no, no, that's impossible too! (*Opening the door more and
more.*) What's that? He's standing outside — not going downstairs. He's
thinking it over? Maybe he'll — ? (*A letter falls in the mailbox; then Krogstad's
footsteps are heard, dying away down a flight of stairs. Nora gives a muffled cry
and runs over toward the sofa table. A short pause.*) In the mailbox. (*Slips warily
over to the hall door.*) It's lying there. Torvald, Torvald — now we're lost!

320 MRS. LINDE: (*entering with the costume from the room, left*) There now, I can't
see anything else to mend. Perhaps you'd like to try —

NORA: (*in a hoarse whisper*) Kristine, come here.

MRS. LINDE: (*tossing the dress on the sofa*) What's wrong? You look upset.

NORA: Come here. See that letter? *There!* Look — through the glass in the
mailbox.

MRS. LINDE: Yes, yes, I see it.

325 NORA: That letter's from Krogstad —

MRS. LINDE: Nora — it's Krogstad who loaned you the money!

NORA: Yes, and now Torvald will find out everything.

MRS. LINDE: Believe me, Nora, it's best for both of you.

NORA: There's more you don't know. I forged a name.

330 MRS. LINDE: But for heaven's sake — ?

NORA: I only want to tell you that, Kristine, so that you can be my witness.

MRS. LINDE: Witness? Why should I — ?

NORA: If I should go out of my mind — it could easily happen —

MRS. LINDE: Nora!

335 NORA: Or anything else occurred — so I couldn't be present here —

MRS. LINDE: Nora, Nora, you aren't yourself at all!

NORA: And someone should try to take on the whole weight, all of the guilt,
you follow me —

MRS. LINDE: Yes, of course, but why do you think — ?

NORA: Then you're the witness that it isn't true, Kristine. I'm very much
myself; my mind right now is perfectly clear; and I'm telling you: nobody
else has known about this; I alone did everything. Remember that.

340 MRS. LINDE: I will. But I don't understand all this.

NORA: Oh, how could you ever understand it? It's the miracle now that's going
to take place.

MRS. LINDE: The miracle?

NORA: Yes, the miracle. But it's so awful, Kristine. It mustn't take place, not
for anything in the world.

MRS. LINDE: I'm going right over and talk with Krogstad.

345 NORA: Don't go near him; he'll do you some terrible harm!

MRS. LINDE: There was a time once when he'd gladly have done anything for me.

NORA: He?

MRS. LINDE: Where does he live?

NORA: Oh, how do I know? Yes. (*Searches in her pocket.*) Here's his card. But the letter, the letter —!

HELMER: (*from the study, knocking on the door*) Nora!   350

NORA: (*with a cry of fear*) Oh! What is it? What do you want?

HELMER: Now, now, don't be so frightened. We're not coming in. You locked the door — are you trying on the dress?

NORA: Yes, I'm trying it. I'll look just beautiful, Torvald.

MRS. LINDE: (*who has read the card*) He's living right around the corner.

NORA: Yes, but what's the use? We're lost. The letter's in the box.   355

MRS. LINDE: And your husband has the key?

NORA: Yes, always.

MRS. LINDE: Krogstad can ask for his letter back unread; he can find some excuse —

NORA: But it's just this time that Torvald usually —

MRS. LINDE: Stall him. Keep him in there. I'll be back as quick as I can.   360
(*She hurries out through the hall entrance.*)

NORA: (*goes to Helmer's door, opens it, and peers in*) Torvald!

HELMER: (*from the inner study*) Well — does one dare set foot in one's own living room at last? Come on, Rank, now we'll get a look —(*In the doorway.*) But what's this?

NORA: What, Torvald dear?

HELMER: Rank had me expecting some grand masquerade.

RANK: (*in the doorway*) That was my impression, but I must have been wrong.   365

NORA: No one can admire me in my splendor — not till tomorrow.

HELMER: But Nora dear, you look so exhausted. Have you practiced too hard?

NORA: No, I haven't practiced at all yet.

HELMER: You know, it's necessary —

NORA: Oh, it's absolutely necessary, Torvald. But I can't get anywhere without   370
your help. I've forgotten the whole thing completely.

HELMER: Ah, we'll soon take care of that.

NORA: Yes, take care of me, Torvald, please! Promise me that? Oh, I'm so nervous. That big party —You must give up everything this evening for me. No business — don't even touch your pen. Yes? Dear Torvald, promise?

HELMER: It's a promise. Tonight I'm totally at your service — you little helpless thing. Hm —but first there's one thing I want to —(*Goes toward the hall door.*)

NORA: What are you looking for?

HELMER: Just to see if there's any mail.   375

NORA: No, no, don't do that, Torvald!

HELMER: Now what?

NORA: Torvald, please. There isn't any.

HELMER: Let me look, though. (*Starts out. Nora, at the piano, strikes the first notes of the tarantella. Helmer, at the door, stops.*) Aha!

380 NORA: I can't dance tomorrow if I don't practice with you.

HELMER: *(going over to her)* Nora dear, are you really so frightened?

NORA: Yes, so terribly frightened. Let me practice right now; there's still time before dinner. Oh, sit down and play for me, Torvald. Direct me. Teach me, the way you always have.

HELMER: Gladly, if it's what you want. *(Sits at the piano.)*

NORA: *(snatches the tambourine up from the box, then a long, varicolored shawl, which she throws around herself, whereupon she springs forward and cries out)* Play for me now! Now I'll dance!

Helmer plays and Nora dances. Rank stands behind Helmer at the piano and looks on.

385 HELMER: *(as he plays)* Slower. Slow down.

NORA: Can't change it.

HELMER: Not so violent, Nora!

NORA: Has to be just like this.

HELMER: *(stopping)* No, no, that won't do at all.

390 NORA: *(laughing and swinging her tambourine)* Isn't that what I told you?

RANK: Let me play for her.

HELMER: *(getting up)* Yes, go on. I can teach her more easily then.

Rank sits at the piano and plays; Nora dances more and more wildly. Helmer has stationed himself by the stove and repeatedly gives her directions; she seems not to hear them; her hair loosens and falls over her shoulders; she does not notice, but goes on dancing. Mrs. Linde enters.

MRS. LINDE: *(standing dumbfounded at the door)* Ah —!

NORA: *(still dancing)* See what fun, Kristine!

395 HELMER: But Nora darling, you dance as if your life were at stake.

NORA: And it is.

HELMER: Rank, stop! This is pure madness. Stop it, I say!

Rank breaks off playing, and Nora halts abruptly.

HELMER: *(going over to her)* I never would have believed it. You've forgotten everything I taught you.

NORA: *(throwing away the tambourine)* You see for yourself.

400 HELMER: Well, there's certainly room for instruction here.

NORA: Yes, you see how important it is. You've got to teach me to the very last minute. Promise me that, Torvald?

HELMER: You can bet on it.

NORA: You mustn't, either today or tomorrow, think about anything else but me; you mustn't open any letters — or the mailbox—

HELMER: Ah, it's still the fear of that man—

405 NORA: Oh yes, yes, that too.

HELMER: Nora, it's written all over you — there's already a letter from him out there.

NORA: I don't know. I guess so. But you mustn't read such things now; there mustn't be anything ugly between us before it's all over.

RANK: *(quietly to Helmer)* You shouldn't deny her.

HELMER: *(putting his arm around her)* The child can have her way. But tomorrow night, after you've danced —

NORA: Then you'll be free.   410

MAID: *(in the doorway, right)* Ma'am, dinner is served.

NORA: We'll be wanting champagne, Helene.

MAID: Very good, ma'am. *(Goes out.)*

HELMER: So — a regular banquet, hm?

NORA: Yes, a banquet — champagne till daybreak! *(Calling out.)* And some   415
macaroons, Helene. Heaps of them — just this once.

HELMER: *(taking her hands)* Now, now, now — no hysterics. Be my own little
lark again.

NORA: Oh, I will soon enough. But go on in — and you, Dr. Rank. Kristine,
help me put up my hair.

RANK: *(whispering, as they go)* There's nothing wrong — really wrong, is there?

HELMER: Oh, of course not. It's nothing more than this childish anxiety I was
telling you about. *(They go out, right.)*

NORA: Well?   420

MRS. LINDE: Left town.

NORA: I could see by your face.

MRS. LINDE: He'll be home tomorrow evening. I wrote him a note.

NORA: You shouldn't have. Don't try to stop anything now. After all, it's a
wonderful joy, this waiting here for the miracle.

MRS. LINDE: What is it you're waiting for?   425

NORA: Oh, you can't understand that. Go in to them: I'll be along in
a moment.

*Mrs. Linde goes into the dining room. Nora stands a short while as if composing herself;
then she looks at her watch.*

NORA: Five. Seven hours to midnight. Twenty-four hours to the midnight
after, and then the tarantella's done. Seven and twenty-four? Thirty-one
hours to live.

HELMER: *(in the doorway, right)* What's become of the little lark?

NORA: *(going toward him with open arms)* Here's your lark!

ACT 3

*Same scene. The table, with chairs around it, has been moved to the center of the room.
A lamp on the table is lit. The hall door stands open. Dance music drifts down from the
floor above. Mrs. Linde sits at the table, absently paging through a book, trying to read,
but apparently unable to focus her thoughts. Once or twice she pauses, tensely listening
for a sound at the outer entrance.*

MRS. LINDE: *(glancing at her watch)* Not yet — and there's hardly any time left.
If only he's not —*(Listening again.)* Ah, there he is. *(She goes out in the hall
and cautiously opens the outer door. Quiet footsteps are heard on the stairs. She
whispers:)* Come in. Nobody's here.

KROGSTAD: *(in the doorway)* I found a note from you at home. What's back of
all this?

MRS. LINDE: I just *had* to talk to you.

KROGSTAD: Oh? And it just *had* to be here in this house?

5   MRS. LINDE: At my place it was impossible; my room hasn't a private
entrance. Come in; we're all alone. The maid's asleep, and the Helmers
are at the dance upstairs.

KROGSTAD: *(entering the room)* Well, well, the Helmers are dancing tonight?
Really?

MRS. LINDE: Yes, why not?

KROGSTAD: How true — why not?

MRS. LINDE: All right, Krogstad, let's talk.

10   KROGSTAD: Do we two have anything more to talk about?

MRS. LINDE: We have a great deal to talk about.

KROGSTAD: I wouldn't have thought so.

MRS. LINDE: No, because you've never understood me, really.

KROGSTAD: Was there anything more to understand — except what's all too
common in life? A calculating woman throws over a man the moment
a better catch comes by.

15   MRS. LINDE: You think I'm so thoroughly calculating? You think I broke it off
lightly?

KROGSTAD: Didn't you?

MRS. LINDE: Nils — is that what you really thought?

KROGSTAD: If you cared, then why did you write me the way you did?

MRS. LINDE: What else could I do? If I had to break off with you, then it was
my job as well to root out everything you felt for me.

20   KROGSTAD: *(wringing his hands)* So that was it. And this — all this, simply
for money!

MRS. LINDE: Don't forget I had a helpless mother and two small brothers. We
couldn't wait for you, Nils; you had such a long road ahead of you then.

KROGSTAD: That may be; but you still hadn't the right to abandon me for
somebody else's sake.

MRS. LINDE: Yes — I don't know. So many, many times I've asked myself if
I did have that right.

KROGSTAD: *(more softly)* When I lost you, it was as if all the solid ground
dissolved from under my feet. Look at me; I'm a half-drowned man now,
hanging onto a wreck.

25   MRS. LINDE: Help may be near.

KROGSTAD: It was near — but then you came and blocked it off.

MRS. LINDE: Without my knowing it, Nils. Today for the first time I learned
that it's you I'm replacing at the bank.

KROGSTAD: All right — I believe you. But now that you know, will you step
aside?

MRS. LINDE: No, because that wouldn't benefit you in the slightest.

30   KROGSTAD: Not "benefit" me, hm! I'd step aside anyway.

MRS. LINDE: I've learned to be realistic. Life and hard, bitter necessity have
taught me that.

KROGSTAD: And life's taught me never to trust fine phrases.

MRS. LINDE: Then life's taught you a very sound thing. But you do have to trust in actions, don't you?

KROGSTAD: What does that mean?

MRS. LINDE: You said you were hanging on like a half-drowned man to a wreck.   35

KROGSTAD: I've good reason to say that.

MRS. LINDE: I'm also like a half-drowned woman on a wreck. No one to suffer with; no one to care for.

KROGSTAD: You made your choice.

MRS. LINDE: There wasn't any choice then.

KROGSTAD: So — what of it?   40

MRS. LINDE: Nils, if only we two shipwrecked people could reach across to each other.

KROGSTAD: What are you saying?

MRS. LINDE: Two on one wreck are at least better off than each on his own.

KROGSTAD: Kristine!

MRS. LINDE: Why do you think I came into town?   45

KROGSTAD: Did you really have some thought of me?

MRS. LINDE: I have to work to go on living. All my born days, as long as I can remember, I've worked, and it's been my best and my only joy. But now I'm completely alone in the world; it frightens me to be so empty and lost. To work for yourself — there's no joy in that. Nils, give me something— someone to work for.

KROGSTAD: I don't believe all this. It's just some hysterical feminine urge to go out and make a noble sacrifice.

MRS. LINDE: Have you ever found me to be hysterical?

KROGSTAD: Can you honestly mean this? Tell me — do you know everything   50 about my past?

MRS. LINDE: Yes.

KROGSTAD: And you know what they think I'm worth around here.

MRS. LINDE: From what you were saying before, it would seem that with me you could have been another person.

KROGSTAD: I'm positive of that.

MRS. LINDE: Couldn't it happen still?   55

KROGSTAD: Kristine — you're saying this in all seriousness? Yes, you are! I can see it in you. And do you really have the courage, then —?

MRS. LINDE: I need to have someone to care for; and your children need a mother. We both need each other. Nils, I have faith that you're good at heart — I'll risk everything together with you.

KROGSTAD: (gripping her hands) Kristine, thank you, thank you — Now I know I can win back a place in their eyes. Yes — but I forgot—

MRS. LINDE: (listening) Shh! The tarantella. Go now! Go on!

KROGSTAD: Why? What is it?   60

MRS. LINDE: Hear the dance up there? When that's over, they'll be coming down.

KROGSTAD: Oh, then I'll go. But — it's all pointless. Of course, you don't know the move I made against the Helmers.

MRS. LINDE: Yes, Nils, I know.

KROGSTAD: And all the same, you have the courage to —?

65 MRS. LINDE: I know how far despair can drive a man like you.

KROGSTAD: Oh, if I only could take it all back.

MRS. LINDE: You easily could — your letter's still lying in the mailbox.

KROGSTAD: Are you sure of that?

MRS. LINDE: Positive. But—

70 KROGSTAD: *(looks at her searchingly)* Is that the meaning of it, then? You'll save your friend at any price. Tell me straight out. Is that it?

MRS. LINDE: Nils — anyone who's sold herself for somebody else once isn't going to do it again.

KROGSTAD: I'll demand my letter back.

MRS. LINDE: No, no.

KROGSTAD: Yes, of course. I'll stay here till Helmer comes down; I'll tell him to give me my letter again — that it only involves my dismissal — that he shouldn't read it—

75 MRS. LINDE: No, Nils, don't call the letter back.

KROGSTAD: But wasn't that exactly why you wrote me to come here?

MRS. LINDE: Yes, in that first panic. But it's been a whole day and night since then, and in that time I've seen such incredible things in this house. Helmer's got to learn everything; this dreadful secret has to be aired; those two have to come to a full understanding; all these lies and evasions can't go on.

KROGSTAD: Well, then, if you want to chance it. But at least there's one thing I can do, and do right away—

MRS. LINDE: *(listening)* Go now, go, quick! The dance is over. We're not safe another second.

80 KROGSTAD: I'll wait for you downstairs.

MRS. LINDE: Yes, please do; take me home.

KROGSTAD: I can't believe it; I've never been so happy. *(He leaves by way of the outer door; the door between the room and the hall stays open.)*

MRS. LINDE: *(straightening up a bit and getting together her street clothes)* How different now! How different! Someone to work for, to live for — a home to build. Well, it is worth the try! Oh, if they'd only come! *(Listening.)* Ah, there they are. Bundle up. *(She picks up her hat and coat. Nora's and Helmer's voices can be heard outside; a key turns in the lock, and Helmer brings Nora into the hall almost by force. She is wearing the Italian costume with a large black shawl about her; he has on evening dress, with a black domino open over it.)*

NORA: *(struggling in the doorway)* No, no, no, not inside! I'm going up again. I don't want to leave so soon.

85 HELMER: But Nora dear—

NORA: Oh, I beg you, please, Torvald. From the bottom of my heart, *please*— only an hour more!

HELMER: Not a single minute, Nora darling. You know our agreement. Come on, in we go; you'll catch cold out here. *(In spite of her resistance, he gently draws her into the room.)*

MRS. LINDE: Good evening.

NORA: Kristine!

HELMER: Why, Mrs. Linde — are you here so late? 90

MRS. LINDE: Yes, I'm sorry, but I did want to see Nora in costume.

NORA: Have you been sitting here, waiting for me?

MRS. LINDE: Yes. I didn't come early enough; you were all upstairs; and then I thought I really couldn't leave without seeing you.

HELMER: (removing Nora's shawl) Yes, take a good look. She's worth looking at, I can tell you that, Mrs. Linde. Isn't she lovely?

MRS. LINDE: Yes, I should say — 95

HELMER: A dream of loveliness, isn't she? That's what everyone thought at the party, too. But she's horribly stubborn — this sweet little thing. What's to be done with her? Can you imagine, I almost had to use force to pry her away.

NORA: Oh, Torvald, you're going to regret you didn't indulge me, even for just a half hour more.

HELMER: There, you see. She danced her tarantella and got a tumultuous hand — which was well earned, although the performance may have been a bit too naturalistic — I mean it rather overstepped the proprieties of art. But never mind — what's important is, she made a success, an overwhelming success. You think I could let her stay on after that and spoil the effect? Oh no; I took my lovely little Capri girl — my capricious little Capri girl, I should say — took her under my arm; one quick tour of the ballroom, a curtsy to every side, and then — as they say in novels — the beautiful vision disappeared. An exit should always be effective, Mrs. Linde, but that's what I can't get Nora to grasp. Phew, it's hot in here. (Flings the domino on a chair and opens the door to his room.) Why's it dark in here? Oh yes, of course. Excuse me. (He goes in and lights a couple of candles.)

NORA: (in a sharp, breathless whisper) So?

MRS. LINDE: (quietly) I talked with him. 100

NORA: And —?

MRS. LINDE: Nora — you must tell your husband everything.

NORA: (dully) I knew it.

MRS. LINDE: You've got nothing to fear from Krogstad, but you have to speak out.

NORA: I won't tell. 105

MRS. LINDE: Then the letter will.

NORA: Thanks, Kristine. I know now what's to be done. Shh!

HELMER: (reentering) Well, then, Mrs. Linde — have you admired her?

MRS. LINDE: Yes, and now I'll say good night.

HELMER: Oh, come, so soon? Is this yours, this knitting? 110

MRS. LINDE: Yes, thanks. I nearly forgot it.

HELMER: Do you knit, then?

MRS. LINDE: Oh yes.

HELMER: You know what? You should embroider instead.

MRS. LINDE: Really? Why? 115

HELMER: Yes, because it's a lot prettier. See here, one holds the embroidery so, in the left hand, and then one guides the needle with the right — so — in an easy, sweeping curve — right?

MRS. LINDE: Yes, I guess that's —

HELMER: But, on the other hand, knitting — it can never be anything but ugly. Look, see here, the arms tucked in, the knitting needles going up and down — there's something Chinese about it. Ah, that was really a glorious champagne they served.

MRS. LINDE: Yes, good night, Nora, and don't be stubborn any more.

120   HELMER: Well put, Mrs. Linde!

MRS. LINDE: Good night, Mr. Helmer.

HELMER: *(accompanying her to the door)* Good night, good night. I hope you get home all right. I'd be very happy to — but you don't have far to go. Good night, good night. *(She leaves. He shuts the door after her and returns.)* There, now, at last we got her out the door. She's a deadly bore, that creature.

NORA: Aren't you pretty tired, Torvald?

HELMER: No, not a bit.

125   NORA: You're not sleepy?

HELMER: Not at all. On the contrary, I'm feeling quite exhilarated. But you? Yes, you really look tired and sleepy.

NORA: Yes, I'm very tired. Soon now I'll sleep.

HELMER: See! You see! I was right all along that we shouldn't stay longer.

NORA: Whatever you do is always right.

130   HELMER: *(kissing her brow)* Now my little lark talks sense. Say, did you notice what a time Rank was having tonight?

NORA: Oh, was he? I didn't get to speak with him.

HELMER: I scarcely did either, but it's a long time since I've seen him in such high spirits. *(Gazes at her a moment, then comes nearer her.)* Hm — it's marvelous, though, to be back home again — to be completely alone with you. Oh, you bewitchingly lovely young woman!

NORA: Torvald, don't look at me like that!

HELMER: Can't I look at my richest treasure? At all that beauty that's mine, mine alone — completely and utterly.

135   NORA: *(moving around to the other side of the table)* You mustn't talk to me that way tonight.

HELMER: *(following her)* The tarantella is still in your blood, I can see — and it makes you even more enticing. Listen. The guests are beginning to go. *(Dropping his voice.)* Nora — it'll soon be quiet through this whole house.

NORA: Yes, I hope so.

HELMER: You do, don't you, my love? Do you realize — when I'm out at a party like this with you — do you know why I talk to you so little, and keep such a distance away; just send you a stolen look now and then — you know why I do it? It's because I'm imagining then that you're my secret darling, my secret young bride-to-be, and that no one suspects there's anything between us.

NORA: Yes, yes; oh, yes, I know you're always thinking of me.

140   HELMER: And then when we leave and I place the shawl over those fine young rounded shoulders — over that wonderful curving neck — then I pretend that you're my young bride, that we're just coming from the wedding, that for the first time I'm bringing you into my house — that for the first time I'm alone with you — completely alone with you, your trembling young

beauty! All this evening I've longed for nothing but you. When I saw you turn and sway in the tarantella — my blood was pounding till I couldn't stand it — that's why I brought you down here so early —

Nora: Go away, Torvald! Leave me alone. I don't want all this.

Helmer: What do you mean? Nora, you're teasing me. You will, won't you? Aren't I your husband — ?

A knock at the outside door.

Nora: *(startled)* What's that?

Helmer: *(going toward the hall)* Who is it?

Rank: *(outside)* It's me. May I come in a moment?   145

Helmer: *(with quiet irritation)* Oh, what does he want now? *(Aloud.)* Hold on. *(Goes and opens the door.)* Oh, how nice that you didn't just pass us by!

Rank: I thought I heard your voice, and then I wanted so badly to have a look in. *(Lightly glancing about.)* Ah, me, these old familiar haunts. You have it snug and cozy in here, you two.

Helmer: You seemed to be having it pretty cozy upstairs, too.

Rank: Absolutely. Why shouldn't I? Why not take in everything in life? As much as you can, anyway, and as long as you can. The wine was superb —

Helmer: The champagne especially.   150

Rank: You noticed that too? It's amazing how much I could guzzle down.

Nora: Torvald also drank a lot of champagne this evening.

Rank: Oh?

Nora: Yes, and that always makes him so entertaining.

Rank: Well, why shouldn't one have a pleasant evening after a well spent day?   155

Helmer: Well spent? I'm afraid I can't claim that.

Rank: *(slapping him on the back)* But I can, you see!

Nora: Dr. Rank, you must have done some scientific research today.

Rank: Quite so.

Helmer: Come now — little Nora talking about scientific research!   160

Nora: And can I congratulate you on the results?

Rank: Indeed you may.

Nora: Then they were good?

Rank: The best possible for both doctor and patient — certainty.

Nora: *(quickly and searchingly)* Certainty?   165

Rank: Complete certainty. So don't I owe myself a gay evening afterwards?

Nora: Yes, you're right, Dr. Rank.

Helmer: I'm with you — just so long as you don't have to suffer for it in the morning.

Rank: Well, one never gets something for nothing in life.

Nora: Dr. Rank — are you very fond of masquerade parties?   170

Rank: Yes, if there's a good array of odd disguises —

Nora: Tell me, what should we two go as at the next masquerade?

Helmer: You little featherhead — already thinking of the next!

Rank: We two? I'll tell you what: you must go as Charmed Life —

In this scene Doctor Rank, Helmer, and Nora have just returned from the party; Nora is wearing her tarantella costume.

175 HELMER: Yes, but find a costume for *that!*

RANK: Your wife can appear just as she looks every day.

HELMER: That was nicely put. But don't you know what you're going to be?

RANK: Yes, Helmer, I've made up my mind.

HELMER: Well?

180 RANK: At the next masquerade I'm going to be invisible.

HELMER: That's a funny idea.

RANK: They say there's a hat — black, huge — have you never heard of the hat that makes you invisible? You put it on, and then no one on earth can see you.

HELMER: (*suppressing a smile*) Ah, of course.

RANK: But I'm quite forgetting what I came for. Helmer, give me a cigar, one of the dark Havanas.

185 HELMER: With the greatest of pleasure. (*Holds out his case.*)

RANK: Thanks. (*Takes one and cuts off the tip.*)

NORA: (*striking a match*) Let me give you a light.

RANK: Thank you. (*She holds the match for him; he lights the cigar.*) And now good-bye.

HELMER: Good-bye, good-bye, old friend.

190 NORA: Sleep well, Doctor.

RANK: Thanks for that wish.

NORA: Wish me the same.

RANK: You? All right, if you like — Sleep well. And thanks for the light. (*He nods to them both and leaves.*)

HELMER: (*his voice subdued*) He's been drinking heavily.

NORA: *(absently)* Could be. *(Helmer takes his keys from his pocket and goes out in*   195
the hall.) Torvald — what are you after?

HELMER: Got to empty the mailbox; it's nearly full. There won't be room for
the morning papers.

NORA: Are you working tonight?

HELMER: You know I'm not. Why — what's this? Someone's been at the
lock.

NORA: At the lock —?

HELMER: Yes, I'm positive. What do you suppose —? I can't imagine one of the   200
maids —? Here's a broken hairpin. Nora, it's yours —

NORA: *(quickly)* Then it must be the children —

HELMER: You'd better break them of that. Hm, hm — well, opened it after all.
(Takes the contents out and calls into the kitchen.) Helene! Helene, would you
put out the lamp in the hall. *(He returns to the room, shutting the hall door,
then displays the handful of mail.)* Look how it's piled up. *(Sorting through
them.)* Now what's this?

NORA: *(at the window)* The letter! Oh, Torvald, no!

HELMER: Two calling cards — from Rank.

NORA: From Dr. Rank?   205

HELMER: *(examining them)* "Dr. Rank, Consulting Physician." They were on
top. He must have dropped them in as he left.

NORA: Is there anything on them?

HELMER: There's a black cross over the name. See? That's a gruesome notion.
He could almost be announcing his own death.

NORA: That's just what he's doing.

HELMER: What! You've heard something? Something he's told you?   210

NORA: Yes. That when those cards came, he'd be taking his leave of us. He'll
shut himself in now and die.

HELMER: Ah, my poor friend! Of course I knew he wouldn't be here much
longer. But so soon — And then to hide himself away like a wounded animal.

NORA: If it has to happen, then it's best it happens in silence — don't you
think so, Torvald?

HELMER: *(pacing up and down)* He'd grown right into our lives. I simply
can't imagine him gone. He with his suffering and loneliness — like
a dark cloud setting off our sunlit happiness. Well, maybe it's best this way.
For him, at least. *(Standing still.)* And maybe for us too, Nora. Now we're
thrown back on each other, completely. *(Embracing her.)* Oh you, my darling wife, how can I hold you close enough? You know what, Nora — time
and again I've wished you were in some terrible danger, just so I could stake
my life and soul and everything, for your sake.

NORA: *(tearing herself away, her voice firm and decisive)* Now you must read your   215
mail, Torvald.

HELMER: No, no, not tonight. I want to stay with you, dearest.

NORA: With a dying friend on your mind?

HELMER: You're right. We've both had a shock. There's ugliness between
us — these thoughts of death and corruption. We'll have to get free of
them first. Until then — we'll stay apart.

NORA: *(clinging about his neck)* Torvald — good night! Good night!

220 HELMER: *(kissing her on the cheek)* Good night, little songbird. Sleep well, Nora. I'll be reading my mail now. *(He takes the letters into his room and shuts the door after him.)*

NORA: *(with bewildered glances, groping about, seizing Helmer's domino, throwing it around her, and speaking in short, hoarse, broken whispers)* Never see him again. Never, never. *(Putting her shawl over her head.)* Never see the children either — them, too. Never, never. Oh, the freezing black water! The depths — down — Oh, I wish it were over — He has it now; he's reading it — now. Oh no, no, not yet. Torvald, good-bye, you and the children —*(She starts for the hall; as she does, Helmer throws open his door and stands with an open letter in his hand.)*

HELMER: Nora!

NORA: *(screams)* Oh —!

HELMER: What is this? You know what's in this letter?

225 NORA: Yes, I know. Let me go! Let me out!

HELMER: *(holding her back)* Where are you going?

NORA: *(struggling to break loose)* You can't save me, Torvald!

HELMER: *(slumping back)* True! Then it's true what he writes? How horrible! No, no, it's impossible — it can't be true.

NORA: It *is* true. I've loved you more than all this world.

230 HELMER: Ah, none of your slippery tricks.

NORA: *(taking one step toward him)* Torvald —!

HELMER: What *is* this you've blundered into!

NORA: Just let me loose. You're not going to suffer for my sake. You're not going to take on my guilt.

HELMER: No more playacting. *(Locks the hall door.)* You stay right here and give me a reckoning. You understand what you've done? Answer! You understand?

235 NORA: *(looking squarely at him, her face hardening)* Yes. I'm beginning to understand everything now.

HELMER: *(striding about)* Oh, what an awful awakening! In all these eight years — she who was my pride and joy — a hypocrite, a liar — worse, worse — a criminal! How infinitely disgusting it all is! The shame! *(Nora says nothing and goes on looking straight at him. He stops in front of her.)* I should have suspected something of the kind. I should have known. All your father's flimsy values — Be still! All your father's flimsy values have come out in you. No religion, no morals, no sense of duty — Oh, how I'm punished for letting him off! I did it for your sake, and you repay me like this.

NORA: Yes, like this.

HELMER: Now you've wrecked all my happiness — ruined my whole future. Oh, it's awful to think of. I'm in a cheap little grafter's hands; he can do anything he wants with me, ask for anything, play with me like a puppet — and I can't breathe a word. I'll be swept down miserably into the depths on account of a featherbrained woman.

NORA: When I'm gone from this world, you'll be free.

HELMER: Oh, quit posing. Your father had a mess of those speeches too. What   240
good would that ever do me if you were gone from this world, as you say?
Not the slightest. He can still make the whole thing known; and if he does,
I could be falsely suspected as your accomplice. They might even think that
I was behind it — that I put you up to it. And all that I can thank you
for — you that I've coddled the whole of our marriage. Can you see now
what you've done to me?

NORA: *(icily calm)* Yes.

HELMER: It's so incredible, I just can't grasp it. But we'll have to patch up whatever we can. Take off the shawl. I said, take if off! I've got to appease him
somehow or other. The thing has to be hushed up at any cost. And as for you
and me, it's got to seem like everything between us is just as it was — to the
outside world, that is. You'll go right on living in this house, of course. But you
can't be allowed to bring up the children; I don't dare trust you with them —
Oh, to have to say this to someone I've loved so much! Well, that's done with.
From now on happiness doesn't matter; all that matters is saving the bits and
pieces, the appearance —*(The doorbell rings. Helmer starts.)* What's that? And
so late. Maybe the worst —? You think he'd —? Hide, Nora! Say you're sick.
(Nora remains standing motionless. Helmer goes and opens the door.)

MAID: *(half dressed, in the hall)* A letter for Mrs. Helmer.

HELMER: I'll take it. *(Snatches the letter and shuts the door.)* Yes, it's from him.
You don't get it; I'm reading it myself.

NORA: Then read it.   245

HELMER: *(by the lamp)* I hardly dare. We may be ruined, you and I. But — I've
got to know. *(Rips open the letter, skims through a few lines, glances at an enclosure, then cries out joyfully.)* Nora! *(Nora looks inquiringly at him.)* Nora!
Wait —better check it again —Yes, yes, it's true. I'm saved. Nora, I'm saved!

NORA: And I?

HELMER: You too, of course. We're both saved, both of us. Look. He's sent back
your note. He says he's sorry and ashamed — that a happy development in
his life — oh, who cares what he says! Nora, we're saved! No one can hurt
you. Oh, Nora, Nora —but first, this ugliness all has to go. Let me see —
(Takes a look at the note.) No, I don't want to see it; I want the whole thing
to fade like a dream. *(Tears the note and both letters to pieces, throws them into
the stove and watches them burn.)* There — now there's nothing left — He
wrote that since Christmas Eve you — Oh, they must have been three terrible days for you, Nora.

NORA: I fought a hard fight.

HELMER: And suffered pain and saw no escape but — No, we're not going to   250
dwell on anything unpleasant. We'll just be grateful and keep on repeating:
it's over now, it's over! You hear me, Nora? You don't seem to realize — it's
over. What's it mean — that frozen look? Oh, poor little Nora, I
understand. You can't believe I've forgiven you. But I have, Nora; I swear
I have. I know that what you did, you did out of love for me.

NORA: That's true.

HELMER: You loved me the way a wife ought to love her husband. It's simply
the means that you couldn't judge. But you think I love you any the less for

not knowing how to handle your affairs? No, no — just lean on me; I'll guide you and teach you. I wouldn't be a man if this feminine helplessness didn't make you twice as attractive to me. You mustn't mind those sharp words I said — that was all in the first confusion of thinking my world had collapsed. I've forgiven you, Nora; I swear I've forgiven you.

NORA: My thanks for your forgiveness. (*She goes out through the door, right.*)

HELMER: No, wait — (*Peers in.*) What are you doing in there?

255   NORA: (*inside*) Getting out of my costume.

HELMER: (*by the open door*) Yes, do that. Try to calm yourself and collect your thoughts again, my frightened little songbird. You can rest easy now; I've got wide wings to shelter you with. (*Walking about close by the door.*) How snug and nice our home is, Nora. You're safe here; I'll keep you like a hunted dove I've rescued out of a hawk's claws. I'll bring peace to your poor, shuddering heart. Gradually it'll happen, Nora; you'll see. Tomorrow all this will look different to you; then everything will be as it was. I won't have to go on repeating I forgive you; you'll feel it for yourself. How can you imagine I'd ever conceivably want to disown you — or even blame you in any way? Ah, you don't know a man's heart, Nora. For a man there's something indescribably sweet and satisfying in knowing he's forgiven his wife — and forgiven her out of a full and open heart. It's as if she belongs to him in two ways now: in a sense he's given her fresh into the world again, and she's become his wife and his child as well. From now on that's what you'll be to me — you little, bewildered, helpless thing. Don't be afraid of anything, Nora; just open your heart to me, and I'll be conscience and will to you both — (*Nora enters in her regular clothes.*) What's this? Not in bed? You've changed your dress?

NORA: Yes, Torvald, I've changed my dress.

HELMER: But why now, so late?

NORA: Tonight I'm not sleeping.

260   HELMER: But Nora dear—

NORA: (*looking at her watch*) It's still not so very late. Sit down, Torvald; we have a lot to talk over. (*She sits at one side of the table.*)

HELMER: Nora — what is this? That hard expression—

NORA: Sit down. This'll take some time. I have a lot to say.

HELMER: (*sitting at the table directly opposite her*) You worry me, Nora. And I don't understand you.

265   NORA: No, that's exactly it. You don't understand me. And I've never understood you either — until tonight. No, don't interrupt. You can just listen to what I say. We're closing out accounts, Torvald.

HELMER: How do you mean that?

NORA: (*after a short pause*) Doesn't anything strike you about our sitting here like this?

HELMER: What's that?

NORA: We've been married now eight years. Doesn't it occur to you that this is the first time we two, you and I, man and wife, have ever talked seriously together?

270   HELMER: What do you mean — seriously?

NORA: In eight whole years — longer even — right from our first acquaintance, we've never exchanged a serious word on any serious thing.

HELMER: You mean I should constantly go and involve you in problems you couldn't possibly help me with?

NORA: I'm not talking of problems. I'm saying that we've never sat down seriously together and tried to get to the bottom of anything.

HELMER: But dearest, what good would that ever do you?

NORA: That's the point right there: you've never understood me. I've been wronged greatly, Torvald — first by Papa, and then by you.   275

HELMER: What! By us — the two people who've loved you more than anyone else?

NORA: *(shaking her head)* You never loved me. You've thought it fun to be in love with me, that's all.

HELMER: Nora, what a thing to say!

NORA: Yes, it's true now, Torvald. When I lived at home with Papa, he told me all his opinions, so I had the same ones too; or if they were different I hid them, since he wouldn't have cared for that. He used to call me his doll-child, and he played with me the way I played with my dolls. Then I came into your house —

HELMER: How can you speak of our marriage like that?   280

NORA: *(unperturbed)* I mean, then I went from Papa's hands into yours. You arranged everything to your own taste, and so I got the same taste as you — or I pretended to; I can't remember. I guess a little of both, first one, then the other. Now when I look back, it seems as if I'd lived here like a beggar — just from hand to mouth. I've lived by doing tricks for you, Torvald. But that's the way you wanted it. It's a great sin what you and Papa did to me. You're to blame that nothing's become of me.

HELMER: Nora, how unfair and ungrateful you are! Haven't you been happy here?

NORA: No, never. I thought so — but I never have.

HELMER: Not — not happy!

NORA: No, only lighthearted. And you've always been so kind to me. But our   285
home's been nothing but a playpen. I've been your doll-wife here, just as at home I was Papa's doll-child. And in turn the children have been my dolls. I thought it was fun when you played with me, just as they thought it fun when I played with them. That's been our marriage, Torvald.

HELMER: There's some truth in what you're saying — under all the raving exaggeration. But it'll all be different after this. Playtime's over; now for the schooling.

NORA: Whose schooling — mine or the children's?

HELMER: Both yours and the children's, dearest.

NORA: Oh, Torvald, you're not the man to teach me to be a good wife to you.

HELMER: And you can say that?   290

NORA: And I — how am I equipped to bring up children?

HELMER: Nora!

NORA: Didn't you say a moment ago that that was no job to trust me with?

HELMER: In a flare of temper! Why fasten on that?

295 NORA: Yes, but you were so very right. I'm not up to the job. There's another job I have to do first. I have to try to educate myself. You can't help me with that. I've got to do it alone. And that's why I'm leaving you now.

HELMER: *(jumping up)* What's that?

NORA: I have to stand completely alone, if I'm ever going to discover myself and the world out there. So I can't go on living with you.

HELMER: Nora, Nora!

NORA: I want to leave right away. Kristine should put me up for the night —

300 HELMER: You're insane! You've no right! I forbid you!

NORA: From here on, there's no use forbidding me anything. I'll take with me whatever is mine. I don't want a thing from you, either now or later.

HELMER: What kind of madness is this!

NORA: Tomorrow I'm going home — I mean, home where I came from. It'll be easier up there to find something to do.

HELMER: Oh, you blind, incompetent child!

305 NORA: I must learn to be competent, Torvald.

HELMER: Abandon your home, your husband, your children! And you're not even thinking what people will say.

NORA: I can't be concerned about that. I only know how essential this is.

HELMER: Oh, it's outrageous. So you'll run out like this on your most sacred vows.

NORA: What do you think are my most sacred vows?

310 HELMER: And I have to tell you that! Aren't they your duties to your husband and children?

NORA: I have other duties equally sacred.

HELMER: That isn't true. What duties are they?

NORA: Duties to myself.

HELMER: Before all else, you're a wife and a mother.

315 NORA: I don't believe in that any more. I believe that, before all else, I'm a human being, no less than you — or anyway, I ought to try to become one. I know the majority thinks you're right, Torvald, and plenty of books agree with you, too. But I can't go on believing what the majority says, or what's written in books. I have to think over these things myself and try to understand them.

HELMER: Why can't you understand your place in your own home? On a point like that, isn't there one everlasting guide you can turn to? Where's your religion?

NORA: Oh, Torvald, I'm really not sure what religion is.

HELMER: What —?

NORA: I only know what the minister said when I was confirmed. He told me religion was this thing and that. When I get clear and away by myself, I'll go into that problem too. I'll see if what the minister said was right, or, in any case, if it's right for me.

320 HELMER: A young woman your age shouldn't talk like that. If religion can't move you, I can try to rouse your conscience. You do have some moral feeling? Or, tell me — has that gone too?

NORA: It's not easy to answer that, Torvald. I simply don't know. I'm all confused about these things. I just know I see them so differently from you.

I find out, for one thing, that the law's not at all what I'd thought — but I can't get it through my head that the law is fair. A woman hasn't a right to protect her dying father or save her husband's life! I can't believe that.

HELMER: You talk like a child. You don't know anything of the world you live in.

NORA: No, I don't. But now I'll begin to learn for myself. I'll try to discover who's right, the world or I.

HELMER: Nora, you're sick; you've got a fever. I almost think you're out of your head.

NORA: I've never felt more clearheaded and sure in my life. 325

HELMER: And — clearheaded and sure — you're leaving your husband and children?

NORA: Yes.

HELMER: Then there's only one possible reason.

NORA: What?

HELMER: You no longer love me. 330

NORA: No. That's exactly it.

HELMER: Nora! You can't be serious!

NORA: Oh, this is so hard, Torvald — you've been so kind to me always. But I can't help it. I don't love you any more.

HELMER: *(struggling for composure)* Are you also clearheaded and sure about that?

NORA: Yes, completely. That's why I can't go on staying here. 335

HELMER: Can you tell me what I did to lose your love?

NORA: Yes, I can tell you. It was this evening when the miraculous thing didn't come — then I knew you weren't the man I'd imagined.

HELMER: Be more explicit; I don't follow you.

NORA: I've waited now so patiently eight long years — for, my Lord, I know miracles don't come every day. Then this crisis broke over me, and such a certainty filled me: *now* the miraculous event would occur. While Krogstad's letter was lying out there, I never for an instant dreamed that you could give in to his terms. I was so utterly sure you'd say to him: go on, tell your tale to the whole wide world. And when he'd done that —

HELMER: Yes, what then? When I'd delivered my own wife into shame and 340 disgrace — !

NORA: When he'd done that, I was so utterly sure that you'd step forward, take the blame on yourself and say: I am the guilty one.

HELMER: Nora — !

NORA: You're thinking I'd never accept such a sacrifice from you? No, of course not. But what good would my protests be against you? That was the miracle I was waiting for, in terror and hope. And to stave that off, I would have taken my life.

HELMER: I'd gladly work for you day and night, Nora — and take on pain and deprivation. But there's no one who gives up honor for love.

NORA: Millions of women have done just that. 345

HELMER: Oh, you think and talk like a silly child.

NORA: Perhaps. But you neither think nor talk like the man I could join my-self to. When your big fright was over — and it wasn't from any threat against me, only for what might damage you — when all the danger was past, for you it was just as if nothing had happened. I was exactly the same, your little lark, your doll, that you'd have to handle with double care now that I'd turned out so brittle and frail. *(Gets up.)* Torvald — in that instant it dawned on me that for eight years I've been living here with a stranger, and that I'd even conceived three children — oh, I can't stand the thought of it! I could tear myself to bits.

HELMER: *(heavily)* I see. There's a gulf that's opened between us — that's clear. Oh, but Nora, can't we bridge it somehow?

NORA: The way I am now, I'm no wife for you.

350 HELMER: I have the strength to make myself over.

NORA: Maybe — if your doll gets taken away.

HELMER: But to part! To part from you! No, Nora, no — I can't imagine it.

NORA: *(going out, right)* All the more reason why it has to be. *(She reenters with her coat and a small overnight bag, which she puts on a chair by the table.)*

HELMER: Nora, Nora, not now! Wait till tomorrow.

355 NORA: I can't spend the night in a strange man's room.

HELMER: But couldn't we live here like brother and sister —

NORA: You know very well how long that would last. *(Throws her shawl about her.)* Good-bye, Torvald. I won't look in on the children. I know they're in better hands than mine. The way I am now, I'm no use to them.

HELMER: But someday, Nora — someday —?

NORA: How can I tell? I haven't the least idea what'll become of me.

360 HELMER: But you're my wife, now and wherever you go.

NORA: Listen, Torvald — I've heard that when a wife deserts her husband's house just as I'm doing, then the law frees him from all responsibility. In any case, I'm freeing you from being responsible. Don't feel yourself bound, any more than I will. There has to be absolute freedom for us both. Here, take your ring back. Give me mine.

HELMER: That too?

NORA: That too.

HELMER: There it is.

365 NORA: Good. Well, now it's all over. I'm putting the keys here. The maids know all about keeping up the house — better than I do. Tomorrow, after I've left town, Kristine will stop by to pack up everything that's mine from home. I'd like those things shipped up to me.

HELMER: Over! All over! Nora, won't you ever think about me?

NORA: I'm sure I'll think of you often, and about the children and the house here.

HELMER: May I write you?

NORA: No — never. You're not to do that.

370 HELMER: Oh, but let me send you —

NORA: Nothing. Nothing.

HELMER: Or help you if you need it.

NORA: No. I accept nothing from strangers.

HELMER: Nora — can I never be more than a stranger to you?

375 NORA: *(picking up the overnight bag)* Ah, Torvald — it would take the greatest miracle of all —

HELMER: Tell me the greatest miracle!

NORA: You and I both would have to transform ourselves to the point
that — Oh, Torvald, I've stopped believing in miracles.

HELMER: But I'll believe. Tell me! Transform ourselves to the point that —?

NORA: That our living together could be a true marriage. (*She goes out down
the hall.*)

HELMER: (*sinks down on a chair by the door, face buried in his hands*) Nora! Nora!   380
(*Looking about and rising.*) Empty. She's gone. (*A sudden hope leaps in him.*)
The greatest miracle —?

From below, the sound of a door slamming shut.

Reading and Reacting

1. What is your attitude toward Nora at the beginning of the play? How does
your attitude toward her change as the play progresses? What actions and
lines of dialogue change your assessment of her?

2. List the key events that have occurred before the start of the play. How do
we learn of each event?

4. Explain the role of each of the following in advancing the play's action:
the Christmas tree, the locked mailbox, the telegram Dr. Rank receives,
Dr. Rank's calling cards.

5. In act 2, Torvald says, "Whatever comes, you'll see: when it really counts,
I have strength and courage enough as a man to take on the whole weight
myself." How does this statement influence Nora's subsequent actions?

6. How do the upcoming costume party and Nora's dance influence the
development of the play's plot?

7. Explain how each of the following foreshadows events that will occur later
in the play: Torvald's comments about Krogstad's children (act 1); Torvald's
attitude toward Nora's father (act 2); Krogstad's suggestions about suicide
(act 2).

8. In addition to the play's main plot — which concerns the blackmail of Nora
by Krogstad and her attempts to keep her crime secret from Torvald — the
play contains several subplots. Some of them began to develop before the
start of the play, and some unfold alongside the main plot. Identify these
subplots. How do they advance the themes of survival, debt, sacrifice, and
duty that run through the play?

9. Is Kristine Linde as much of a "modern woman" as Nora? Is she actually *more*
of a modern woman? Explain.

10. Is Mrs. Linde essential to the play? How might the play be different
without her?

11. Do you think *A Doll House* is primarily about the struggle between the needs
of the individual and the needs of society, or about the conflict between
women's roles in the family and in the larger society? Explain.

12. JOURNAL ENTRY Nora makes a drastic decision at the end of the play. Do
you think she overreacts? What other options does she have? What other
options might she have today?

13. CRITICAL PERSPECTIVE Since its earliest performances, there has been much
comment on the conclusion of *A Doll House*. Many viewers have found the

play's ending unrealistically harsh. In fact, a famous German actress refused to play the scene as written because she insisted she would never leave her children. (Ibsen reluctantly rewrote the ending for her; in this version, Helmer forces Nora to the doorway of the children's bedroom, and she sinks to the floor as the curtain falls.) Moreover, many critics have found it hard to accept Nora's sudden transformation from, in the words of Elizabeth Hardwick in her essay "Ibsen's Women," "the girlish, charming wife to the radical, courageous heroine setting out alone."

What is your response to the play's ending? Do you think it makes sense in light of what we have learned about Nora and her marriage? Or do you agree with Hardwick that Nora's abandonment of her children is not only implausible but also a "rather casual" gesture that "drops a stain on our admiration of Nora"?

Related Works: "The Story of an Hour" (p. 197), "The Yellow Wallpaper" (p. 421), "The Rocking-Horse Winner" (p. 525), "The Chrysanthemums" (p. 783), "Marks" (p. 1211), "Barbie Doll" (p. 1211), *The Stronger* (p. 1520)

WRITING SUGGESTIONS: Plot

1. Central to the plots of both *Trifles* and *A Doll House* is a woman who commits a crime. Compare and contrast the desperate situations that motivate the two women. Then, consider the parallels and contrasts between the reactions of other characters in the two plays to each woman's crime. If you like, you may also discuss the crime committed by Emily Grierson in "A Rose for Emily" (p. 216).

2. Write an essay in which you compare the influence of Nora's father on the plot of *A Doll House* with the influence of Catherine's father on the plot of *Proof* (p. 1526).

3. Write a monologue for Mama in *A Raisin in the Sun* (or Nora in *A Doll House*), including everything you think she would like to tell her children. Or, write a monologue for Mrs. Wright in *Trifles* in which she describes her marriage and explains the motivation for her crime.

4. Although Beneatha in *A Raisin in the Sun* wants to be a doctor, she is constantly encouraged by Mama and Walter, as well as by George and Asagai, to marry and settle down. Write an essay in which you examine how Beneatha's struggle to achieve her full potential is similar to and different from that of a more contemporary female character, such as Dee in "Everyday Use" (p. 469). Or, compare Beneatha's dilemma to the one faced by the protagonists of such works as *A Doll House*, "A&P" (p. 230), and "Eveline" (p. 722), who struggle between conforming to the expectations of their families (or society) and doing what is best for themselves.

5. In its focus on its characters' need to embellish facts, *Scheherazade* (p. 1365) reveals the fine line between lies and truth. Consider the advantages and disadvantages of this kind of creative storytelling in another work — for example, *A Doll House* or "Gryphon" (p. 248).

CHAPTER 40

CHARACTER

A sensible playwright would write a play with three or four people.
Three is best. A man and his dog is even better.

—Tom Stoppard

In Tennessee Williams's 1945 play *The Glass Menagerie* (p. 1998), the protagonist, Tom Wingfield, functions as the play's narrator. Stepping out of his role as a character and speaking directly to the audience, he directs the play's action, music, lighting, and other elements. In addition, he summarizes characters' actions, explains what motivates them, and discusses the significance of their behavior in the context of the play — commenting on his own character's actions as well. As narrator, Tom also presents useful background information about the characters. For instance, when he introduces his coworker, Jim, he prepares the audience for Jim's entrance and helps them to understand his subsequent actions:

> In high school Jim was a hero. He had tremendous Irish good nature and vitality with the scrubbed and polished look of white chinaware. He seemed to move in a continual spotlight. . . . But Jim apparently ran into more interference after his graduation. . . . His speed had definitely slowed. Six years after he left high school he was holding a job that wasn't much better than mine. (scene 6)

Most plays, however, do not include narrators who present background. Instead, the audience learns about characters from their own words and from comments by others about them, as well as from the characters' actions and from the playwright's stage directions. Also, at a performance, the audience gains insight into characters from the way actors interpret them.

Characters in plays, like characters in novels and short stories, may be **round** or **flat, static,** or **dynamic.** Generally speaking, major characters are likely to be round, whereas minor characters are likely to be flat. Through the language and the actions of the characters, audiences learn whether the characters are multidimensional, skimpily developed, or perhaps merely **foils,** players whose main purpose is to shed light on more important characters. Audiences also learn about the emotions, attitudes, and values that help to shape the characters — their hopes and fears, their strengths and weaknesses. In addition, by comparing characters' early words and actions with later ones, audiences learn from the play whether or not characters grow and change emotionally.

Characters' Words

Characters' words reveal the most about their attitudes, feelings, beliefs, and values. Sometimes information is communicated (to other characters as well as to the audience) in a **monologue**— an extended speech by one character. This device is used throughout August Strindberg's *The Stronger* (p. 1520). A **soliloquy**— a monologue revealing a character's thoughts and feelings, directed at the audience and presumed not to be heard by other characters — can also convey information about a character. For example, Hamlet's well-known soliloquy that begins "To be or not to be" eloquently communicates his distraught mental state —his resentment of his mother and uncle, his confusion about what course of action to take, and his suicidal thoughts. Finally, **dialogue**— an exchange of words between two characters — can reveal misunderstanding or conflict between them, or it can show their agreement, mutual support, or similar beliefs.

In Henrik Ibsen's *A Doll House* (p. 1454), dialogue reveals a good deal about the characters. Nora Helmer, the spoiled young wife, has broken the law and kept her crime secret from her husband. Through her words, we learn about her motivation, her values, her emotions, and her reactions to other characters and to her potentially dangerous situation. We learn, for instance, that she is flirtatious —"If your little squirrel begged you, with all her heart and soul . . ."— and that she is childishly unrealistic about the consequences of her actions. When her husband, Torvald, asks what she would do if he was seriously injured, leaving her in debt, she says, "If anything so awful happened, then it just wouldn't matter if I had debts or not." When Torvald presses, "Well, but the people I'd borrowed from?" she dismisses them: "Them? Who cares about them! They're strangers." As the play progresses, Nora's lack of understanding of the power of the law becomes more and more significant as she struggles with her moral and ethical dilemma.

The inability of both Nora and Torvald to confront ugly truths is also revealed through their words. When, in act 1, Nora tells Krogstad, her blackmailer, that his revealing her secret could expose her to "the most horrible unpleasantness," he responds, "Only unpleasantness?" Yet later on, in act 3, Torvald echoes her language, fastidiously dismissing the horror with, "No, we're not going to dwell on anything unpleasant."

The ease with which Torvald is able to dismiss his dying friend Dr. Rank in act 3 ("He with his suffering and loneliness — like a dark cloud setting off our sunlit happiness. Well, maybe it's best this way.") foreshadows the lack of support he will give Nora immediately thereafter. Especially revealing is his use of *I* and *my* and *me*, which convey his self-centeredness:

> Now you've wrecked all my happiness — ruined my whole future. Oh, it's awful to think of. I'm in a cheap little grafter's hands; he can do anything he wants with me, ask for anything, play with me like a puppet — and I can't breathe a word. I'll be swept down miserably into the depths on account of a featherbrained woman.

Just as Torvald's words reveal that he has not been changed by the play's events, Nora's words show that she has changed significantly. Her dialogue near the end of act 3 shows that she has become a responsible, determined woman — one who understands her situation and her options and is no longer blithely oblivious to her duties. When she says, "I've never felt more clearheaded and sure in my life," she is calm and decisive. When she says, "Our home's been nothing but a playpen. I've been your doll-wife here, just as at home I was Papa's doll-child," she reveals a new self-awareness. And, when she confronts her husband, she displays — perhaps for the first time in their relationship — complete honesty.

Sometimes what other characters say to (or about) a character can reveal more to an audience than the character's own words. For instance, in *A Doll House*, when the dying Dr. Rank says, apparently without malice, "[Torvald] Helmer with his sensitivity has such a sharp distaste for anything ugly," the audience not only thinks ill of the man who is too "sensitive" to visit his sick friend but also questions his ability to withstand situations that may be emotionally or morally "ugly" as well.

When a character is offstage for much (or even all) of the action, the audience must rely on other characters' assessments of the absent character. In Susan Glaspell's *Trifles* (p. 1372), the play's focus is on an absent character, Minnie Wright, who is described solely through other characters' remarks. The evidence suggests that Mrs. Wright killed her husband, and only Mrs. Hale's and Mrs. Peters's comments about Mrs. Wright's dreary life can delineate her character and suggest a likely motive for the murder. Although Mrs. Wright never appears on stage, we learn essential information from the other women about her: that as a young girl she liked to sing and that more recently she was so distraught about the lack of beauty in her life that even her sewing revealed her distress. Similarly, the father in *The Glass Menagerie* never appears (and therefore never speaks), but the play's other characters describe him as "A telephone man who — fell in love with long-distance!" — the absent husband and father who symbolizes abandonment and instability to Laura and Amanda and the possibility of freedom and escape to Tom.

Whether a character's words are in the form of a monologue, a soliloquy, or dialogue, and whether they reveal information about the character who is speaking or about someone else, such words are always revealing. Explicitly or implicitly, they convey a character's nature, attitudes, and relationships with other characters.

The language characters use can vary widely. A character may, for instance, use learned words, foreign words, elaborate figures of speech, irony or sarcasm, regionalisms, slang, jargon, clichés, or profanity. Words can also be used to indicate tone — for example, to express irony. Any of these uses of language may communicate vital information to the audience about a character's background, attitudes, and motivation. And, of course, a character's language may change as a play progresses, and this change too may be revealing.

Formal and Informal Language

One character in a dramatic work may speak very formally, using absolutely correct grammar, a learned vocabulary, and long, complex sentences; another may speak in an informal style, using conversational speech, colloquialisms, and slang.

At times, two characters with different levels of language may be set in opposition for dramatic effect, as they are in Irish playwright George Bernard Shaw's classic play *Pygmalion* (1912), which updates the ancient Greek myth of a sculptor who creates (and falls in love with) a statue of a woman. In Shaw's version, a linguistics professor sets out to teach "proper" speech and manners to a lowly flower seller. Throughout the play, the contrasting language of Henry Higgins, the professor, and Eliza Doolittle, the flower seller, indicates their differing social standing. The following exchange illustrates this contrast:

LIZA: I ain't got no mother. Her that turned me out was my sixth stepmother.
　　　But I done without them. And I'm a good girl, I am.
HIGGINS: Very well, then, what on earth is all this fuss about?

A character's accent or dialect may also be significant. In **comedies of manners,** for instance, rustic or provincial characters, identified by their speech, are often objects of humor. In *Pygmalion*, Eliza Doolittle uses cockney dialect, the dialect spoken in the East End of London. At first, her colorful, distinctive language (complete with expressions like *Nah-ow, garn,* and *ah-ah-ah-ow-ow-ow-oo*) and her nonstandard grammatical constructions make her an object of ridicule; later, the transformation of her speech reveals the dramatic changes in her character.

Plain and Elaborate Language

A character's speech may be simple and straightforward or complex and convoluted; it may be plain and unadorned or embellished with elaborate **figures of speech.** The relative complexity or lack of complexity of a character's speech may have different effects on the audience. For example, a character whose language is simple and unsophisticated may seem to be unintelligent, unenlightened, gullible, or naive — especially if he or she also uses slang, dialect, or colloquial expressions. Conversely, a character's plain, down-to-earth language may convey common sense or intelligence. Plain language may also be quite emotionally powerful. Thus, Willy Loman's speech in act 2 of *Death of a Salesman* (p. 1581), about an eighty-four-year-old salesman named Dave Singleman, moves the audience with its sincerity and directness:

> Do you know? When he died — and by the way he died the death of a
> salesman, in his green velvet slippers in the smoker of the New York,
> New Haven and Hartford, going into Boston — when he died, hundreds
> of salesmen and buyers were at his funeral. Things were sad on a lotta trains
> for months after that.

Like plain speech, elaborate language may have different effects in different contexts. Sometimes, use of figures of speech can make a character seem to have depth and insight and analytical skills absent in other characters. In the following excerpt from a soliloquy in act 1 scene 2 of *Hamlet*, for example, complex language reveals the depth of Hamlet's anguished self-analysis:

HAMLET: O, that this too too solid flesh would melt,
    Thaw, and resolve itself into a dew!
    Or that the Everlasting had not fix'd
    His canon 'gainst self-slaughter! O God! O God!
    How weary, stale, flat, and unprofitable
    Seem to me all the uses of this world!
    Fie on't, O fie, 'tis an unweeded garden,
    That grows to seed. . . .

In these lines, Hamlet compares the world to a garden gone to seed. His use of imagery and figures of speech vividly communicates his feelings about the world and his internal struggle against the temptation to commit suicide.

Sometimes, however, elaborate language may make a character seem aloof, pompous, or even untrustworthy. In the following passages from Shakespeare's *King Lear*, Goneril and Regan, the deceitful daughters, use complicated verbal constructions to conceal their true feelings from their father, King Lear. Cordelia — the loyal, loving daughter — uses simple, straightforward language that suggests her sincerity and lack of artifice. Compare the three speeches:

GONERIL: Sir, I love you more than words can wield the matter;
    Dearer than eyesight, space, and liberty;
    Beyond what can be valued, rich or rare;
    No less than life, with grace, health, beauty, honour;
    As much as child e'er lov'd, or father found;
    A love that makes breath poor, and speech unable.
    Beyond all manner of so much I love you. . . .
REGAN: Sir, I am made
    Of the selfsame metal that my sister is,
    And prize me at her worth. In my true heart
    I find she names my very deed of love;
    Only she comes too short, that I profess
    Myself an enemy to all other joys
    Which the most precious square of sense possesses,
    And find I am alone felicitate
    In your dear Highness' love. . . .
CORDELIA: Unhappy that I am, I cannot heave
    My heart into my mouth. I love your Majesty
    According to my bond; no more no less. . . .

Cordelia's unwillingness, even when she is prodded by Lear, to exaggerate her feelings or misrepresent her love through inflated language shows the audience her honesty and nobility. The contrast between her language and that of her sisters makes their very different motives clear to the audience.

Tone

Tone reveals a character's mood or attitude. Tone can be flat or emotional, bitter or accepting, affectionate or aloof, anxious or calm. Contrasts in tone can indicate differences in outlook or emotional state between two characters; changes in tone from one point in a play to another can suggest corresponding changes within a character. At the end of *A Doll House*, for instance, Nora is resigned to what she must do, and her language is appropriately controlled. Her husband, however, is desperate to change her mind, and his language reflects this desperation. The following exchanges from act 3 of the play illustrate their contrasting emotional states:

HELMER: But to part! To part from you! No, Nora, no — I can't imagine it.
NORA: *(going out, right)* All the more reason why it has to be.
HELMER: Over! All over! Nora, won't you ever think about me?
NORA: I'm sure I'll think of you often, and about the children and the
     house here.

In earlier scenes between the two characters, Nora is emotional — at times, hysterical — and her husband is considerably more controlled. As the above exchange indicates, both Nora and Torvald Helmer change drastically during the course of the play.

Irony

Irony, a contradiction or discrepancy between two different levels of meaning, can reveal a great deal about character. **Verbal irony** — a contradiction between what a character says and what he or she means — is very important in drama, where the verbal interplay between characters may carry the weight of the play. For example, when Nora and Dr. Rank discuss the latest news about his health in *A Doll House*, there is deep irony in his use of the phrase "complete certainty." Although the phrase usually suggests reassuring news, here it is meant to suggest death, and both Nora and Dr. Rank understand this.

    Dramatic irony depends on the audience's knowing something that a character has not yet realized, or on one character's knowing something that other characters do not know. In some cases, dramatic irony is created by an audience's awareness of historical background or events of which characters are unaware. Familiar with the story of Oedipus, for instance, the audience knows that the man who has caused all the problems in Thebes — the man Oedipus vows to find and take revenge on — is Oedipus himself. In other cases, dramatic irony emerges when the audience learns something — something the characters do not yet know or comprehend — from a play's unfolding action. The central irony in *A Doll House*, for example, is that the family's "happy home" rests on a foundation of secrets, lies, and deception. Torvald does not know about the secrets, and Nora does not understand how they have poisoned her marriage. The audience, however, quickly becomes aware of the atmosphere of deceit — and aware of how it threatens the family's happiness.

Dramatic irony may also be conveyed through dialogue. Typically, dramatic irony is revealed when a character says something that gives the audience information that other characters, offstage at the time, do not know. In *A Doll House*, the audience knows — because Nora has explained her situation to Kristine — that Nora spent the previous Christmas season hard at work, earning money to pay her secret debt. Torvald, however, remains unaware of her activities and believes her story that she was using the time to make holiday decorations, which the cat destroyed. This belief is consistent with his impression of Nora as an irresponsible child, yet the audience has quite a different impression of her. This discrepancy, one of many contradictions between the audience's view of Nora and Torvald's view of her, helps to create dramatic tension in the play.

Finally, **asides** (comments to the audience that other characters do not hear) can create dramatic irony by undercutting dialogue, providing ironic contrast between what the characters on stage know and what the audience knows. In Anton Chekhov's *The Brute* (p. 1293), for example, the audience knows that Mr. Smirnov is succumbing to Mrs. Popov's charms because he says, in an aside, "My God, what eyes she has! They're setting me on fire." Mrs. Popov, however, is not yet aware of his infatuation. The discrepancy between the audience's awareness and the character's adds to the play's humor.

Characters' Actions

Through their actions, characters convey their values and attitudes to the audience. Actions also reveal aspects of a character's personality. When Laura Wingfield, a character in *The Glass Menagerie*, hides rather than face the "gentleman caller," audiences see how shy she is; when Nora in *A Doll House* plays hide-and-seek with her children, eats forbidden macaroons, and takes childish joy in Christmas, her immaturity is apparent.

Audiences also learn about characters from what they do *not* do. Thus, Nora's failure to remain in touch with her friend Kristine, who has had a hard life, reveals her selfishness, and the failure of Mrs. Peters and Mrs. Hale in *Trifles* to give their evidence to the sheriff indicates their support for Mrs. Wright and their understanding of what motivated her to take such drastic action.

Audiences also learn a good deal about characters by observing how they interact with other characters. In William Shakespeare's *Othello*, Iago is the embodiment of evil, and as the play's action unfolds, we discover his true nature. He reveals the secret marriage of Othello and Desdemona to her father; he schemes to arouse Othello's jealousy, making him believe Desdemona has been unfaithful with his lieutenant, Cassio; he persuades Cassio to ask Desdemona to plead his case with Othello, knowing this act will further arouse Othello's suspicions; he encourages Othello to be suspicious of Desdemona's defense of Cassio; he plants Desdemona's handkerchief in Cassio's room; and, finally, he persuades Othello to kill Desdemona and then kills his own wife, Emilia, to prevent her from exposing his role in the intrigue. As the play progresses, then, Iago's dealings with others consistently reveal him to be evil and corrupt.

Stage Directions

When we read a play, we also read the playwright's italicized **stage directions,** the notes that concern **staging**— the scenery, props, lighting, music, sound effects, costumes, and other elements that contribute to the way the play looks and sounds to an audience (see Chapter 41). In addition to commenting on staging, stage directions may supply physical details about the characters, suggesting their age, appearance, movements, gestures, and facial expressions. These details may in turn convey additional information about characters: appearance may reveal social position or economic status, expressions may reveal attitudes, and so on. Stage directions may also indicate the manner in which a line of dialogue is to be delivered —*haltingly, confidently, hesitantly,* or *loudly,* for instance. The way a line is spoken may reveal a character to be excited, upset, angry, shy, or disappointed. Finally, stage directions may indicate *changes* in characters —for instance, a character whose speech is described as timid in early scenes may deliver lines emphatically and forcefully later on in the play.

Some stage directions provide a good deal of detail about character; others do little more than list characters' names. Arthur Miller is one playwright who often provides detailed information about character through stage directions. In *Death of a Salesman*, for instance, Miller's stage directions at the beginning of act 1 characterize Willy Loman immediately and specifically:

> He is past sixty years of age, dressed quietly. Even as he crosses the stage to the doorway of the house, his exhaustion is apparent. He unlocks the door, comes into the kitchen, and thankfully lets his burden down, feeling the soreness of his palms. A word-sigh escapes his lips. . .

Subsequent stage directions indicate how lines are to be spoken. For example, in the play's opening lines, Willy's wife Linda calls out to him *"with some trepidation"*; Linda speaks *"very carefully, delicately,"* and Willy speaks *"with casual irritation."* These instructions to readers (and actors) are meant to suggest the strained relationship between the two characters.

George Bernard Shaw is notorious for the full character description in his stage directions. In these directions — seen by readers of the play but not heard by audiences —he communicates complex information about characters' attitudes and values, motivation and reactions, and relationships with other characters. In doing so, Shaw functions as a narrator, explicitly communicating his own attitudes toward various characters. (Unlike the voice of Tom Wingfield in *The Glass Menagerie*, however, the voice in Shaw's stage directions is not also the voice of a character in the play; it is the voice of the playwright.) Shaw's stage directions for *Pygmalion* initially describe Eliza Doolittle as follows:

> She is not at all an attractive person. She is perhaps eighteen, perhaps twenty, hardly older. She wears a little sailor hat of black straw that has long been exposed to the dust and soot of London and has seldom if ever been brushed. Her hair needs washing rather badly; its mousy color can hardly be natural. She wears a shoddy black coat

that reaches nearly to her knees and is shaped to her waist. She has a brown skirt with a coarse apron. Her boots are much the worse for wear. She is no doubt as clean as she can afford to be; but compared to the ladies she is very dirty. Her features are no worse than theirs; but their condition leaves something to be desired; and she needs the services of a dentist.

Rather than providing an objective summary of the character's most notable physical attributes, Shaw injects subjective comments (*"seldom if ever brushed"*; *"color can hardly be natural"*; *"no doubt as clean as she can afford to be"*) that reveal his attitude toward Eliza. This initially supercilious attitude, which he has in common with Professor Higgins, is tempered considerably by the end of the play, helping to make Eliza's transformation more obvious to readers than it would be if measured by her words and actions alone. By act 5, the tone of the stage directions characterizing Eliza has changed to admiration: *"Eliza enters, sunny, self-possessed, and giving a staggeringly convincing exhibition of ease of manner."*

Stage directions in *Hamlet* are not nearly as comprehensive. Characters are introduced with only the barest identifying tags: "Claudius, *King of Denmark*"; "Hamlet, *Son to the former, and nephew to the present King*"; "Gertrude, *Queen of Denmark, mother to Hamlet*." Most stage directions do little more than chronicle the various characters' entrances and exits or specify particular physical actions: "*Enter Ghost*"; "*Spreads his arms*"; "*Ghost beckons Hamlet*"; "*He kneels*"; "*Sheathes his sword*"; "*Leaps in the grave.*" Occasionally, stage directions specify a prop ("*Puts down the skull*"); a sound effect ("*A noise within*"); or a costume ("*Enter the ghost in his night-gown*"). Such brevity is typical of Shakespeare's plays, in which characters are delineated almost solely by their words — and, not incidentally, by the way actors have interpreted the characters over the years. In fact, because Shakespeare's stage directions only suggest characters' gestures, physical reactions, movements, and facial expressions, actors have been left quite free to experiment, reading various interpretations into Shakespeare's characters.

Actors' Interpretations

When we watch a play, we gain insight into a character not merely through what the character says and does or how other characters react, but also through the way an actor interprets the role. If a playwright does not specify a character's mannerisms, gestures, or movements, or does not indicate how a line is to be delivered (and sometimes even if he or she does), an actor is free to interpret the role as he or she believes it should be played. Even when a playwright *does* specify such actions, the actor has a good deal of freedom to decide which gestures or expressions will convey a particular emotion.

In "Some Thoughts on Playwriting," American dramatist Thornton Wilder argues that "the theatre is an art which reposes upon the work of many collaborators" rather than on "one governing selecting will." Citing examples from Shakespeare and Ibsen, Wilder illustrates the great degree of "intervention" that may occur in dramatic productions. For instance, Wilder observes, Shakespeare's Shylock has been portrayed by two different actors as "noble, wronged and indignant" and as "a vengeful and hysterical buffoon"— and both performances were considered legitimate interpretations. As noted earlier, the absence of detailed stage directions in Shakespeare's plays makes possible (and perhaps even encourages) such widely diverging interpretations. However, as Wilder points out, even when playing roles created by a dramatist such as Ibsen, whose stage directions are typically quite specific, actors and directors have a good deal of leeway. Thus, actress Janet McTeer, who played the part of Ibsen's Nora in the 1997 London production of *A Doll House,* saw Nora and Torvald, despite their many problems, as "the perfect couple," deeply in love and involved in a passionate marriage. "You have to make that marriage sexually credible," McTeer told the *New York Times,* "to imagine they have a wonderful time in bed, so there becomes something to lose. If you play them as already past it or no longer attracted to each other, then there is no play." This interpretation is not inconsistent with the play, but it does go beyond what Ibsen actually wrote.

Similarly, the role of Catherine in David Auburn's *Proof* (p. 1526) has been played by several actresses — among them Mary-Louise Parker, Jennifer Jason Leigh, Anne Heche, Gwyneth Paltrow, and Lea Salonga — and each actress has interpreted this complex character in a different way. As *New York Times* theater critic John Rockwell observes, "Catherine can be loopy-ethereal-sexy (Ms. Parker), earthy and even a little bitter (Ms. Leigh), or adorable-needy-fragile (Ms. Heche), and Mr. Auburn's structure and characters and ideas still work."

Irish playwright Samuel Beckett devotes a good deal of attention to indicating actors' movements and gestures and their physical reactions to one another. In his 1952 play *Waiting for Godot,* for example, Beckett's stage directions seem to choreograph every gesture, every emotion, every intention:

- *(he looks at them ostentatiously in turn to make it clear they are both meant)*
- *Vladimir seizes Lucky's hat. Silence of Lucky. He falls. Silence. Panting of the victors.*
- *Estragon hands him the boot. Vladimir inspects it, throws it down angrily.*
- *Estragon pulls, stumbles, falls. Long silence.*
- *He goes feverishly to and fro, halts finally at extreme left, broods.*

Beckett provides full and obviously carefully thought-out stage directions and, in so doing, attempts to retain a good deal of control over his characters. Still, in a 1988 production of *Godot,* director Mike Nichols and comic actors Robin Williams and Steve Martin felt free to improvise, adding gestures and movements not specified or even hinted at — and most critics believed that this production remained true to the tragicomic spirit of Beckett's existentialist play. In a sense, then, the playwright's words on the page are just the beginning of the characters' lives on the stage.

✔CHECKLIST   **Writing about Character**

☐ Does any character serve as a narrator? If so, what information does this narrator supply about the other characters? How reliable is the narrator?

☐ Are the major characters fully developed?

☐ What do the minor characters contribute to the play?

☐ Do the major characters change and grow during the course of the play, or do they remain essentially unchanged?

☐ Does the play include monologue or soliloquies? What do these extended speeches reveal about the characters?

☐ What is revealed about the characters through dialogue?

☐ Do characters use foreign words, regionalisms, slang, jargon, clichés, or profanity? What does such use of language reveal about characters? About the play's theme?

☐ Is the characters' language formal or informal?

☐ Do characters speak in dialect? Do they have accents?

☐ Is the characters' language plain or elaborate?

☐ Do different characters have different styles or levels of language? What is the significance of these differences?

☐ In what way does language reveal characters' emotional states?

☐ Does the tone of any character's language change significantly as the play progresses? What does this change reveal?

☐ Does the play include verbal irony? Dramatic irony? How is irony conveyed? What purpose does irony achieve?

☐ What is revealed about the characters through what others say about them?

☐ What is revealed about characters through their actions?

☐ What is revealed about characters through the playwright's stage directions?

☐ How might different actors' interpretations change an audience's understanding of the characters?

AUGUST STRINDBERG (1849–1912) was born in Stockholm, Sweden, the child of a shipping merchant and his former maid. He studied at Uppsala University but left the university without a degree. By 1872, he had moved into the artistic circles in Stockholm and had begun work as a journalist.

In 1874, Strindberg was appointed assistant librarian at the Royal Library in Stockholm. Beginning the first of several stormy marriages, he struggled over the next few years; in 1879, he declared bankruptcy. During the same period, he wrote the novel that marked his breakthrough as a writer, *The Red Room* (1879). In 1881, he left the Royal Library to devote himself to writing, and in 1883, he left Sweden to join an artists' colony near Paris. His restlessness continued, however, and he soon moved to Switzerland, later living in Denmark, Germany, and Austria before returning at last to Stockholm.

Strindberg was a prolific artist, and his work includes novels, plays, poetry, and paintings. He is considered one of the most influential dramatists in literature.

The Stronger has been called a monodrama, a dramatic monologue, and a battle of brains in one scene. *The Stronger* was the kind of experimental work being encouraged in the late nineteenth century at the Théâtre Libre in Paris, for which Strindberg wrote several plays while hoping to form his own experimental theater in Stockholm. Though written in 1889, *The Stronger* did not premiere on stage until 1907.

Cultural Context The explicit nature of Strindberg's subject matter (*The Stronger*, for example, is about a meeting between an actress and her husband's mistress) shocked and sometimes scandalized his nineteenth-century contemporaries. As a result, Strindberg often had difficulty getting his plays performed in commercial theaters, and for ths reason, he and other playwrights became involved with the Independent Theater movement. By producing plays outside the control of official censors, they were able to attract an audience for their work, and their subject matter reflected their rebellion against the mores and standards of their societies.

The Stronger (1889)

Translated by Elizabeth Sprigge

CHARACTERS

Mrs. X., *actress, married*
Miss Y., *actress, unmarried*
A Waitress
SCENE

A corner of a ladies' café [in Stockholm in the eighteen eighties].° Two small wrought-iron tables, a red plush settee and a few chairs.

Miss Y. is sitting with a half-empty bottle of beer on the table before her, reading an illustrated weekly which from time to time she exchanges for another.

Mrs. X. enters, wearing a winter hat and coat and carrying a decorative Japanese basket.

°[*In Stockholm in the eighteen eighties*] Brackets indicate translator's addition to scene.

MRS. X: Why, Millie, my dear, how are you? Sitting here all alone on Christmas Eve like some poor bachelor.

Miss Y. looks up from her magazine, nods, and continues to read.

MRS. X: You know it makes me feel really sad to see you. Alone. Alone in a café and on Christmas Eve of all times. It makes me feel as sad as when once in Paris I saw a wedding party at a restaurant. The bride was reading a comic paper and the bridegroom playing billiards with the witnesses. Ah me, I said to myself, with such a beginning how will it go, and how will it end? He was playing billiards on his wedding day! And she, you were going to say, was reading a comic paper on hers. But that's not quite the same.

A waitress brings a cup of chocolate to Mrs. X. and goes out.

MRS. X: Do you know, Amelia, I really believe now you would have done better to stick to him. Don't forget I was the first who told you to forgive him. Do you remember? Then you would be married now and have a home. Think how happy you were that Christmas when you stayed with your finance's people in the country. How warmly you spoke of domestic happiness! You really quite longed to be out of the theatre. Yes, Amelia dear, home is best — next best to the stage, and as for children — but you couldn't know anything about that.

Miss Y.'s expression is disdainful. Mrs. X. sips a few spoonfuls of chocolate, then opens her basket and displays some Christmas presents.

MRS. X: Now you must see what I have bought for my little chicks. *(Takes out a doll.)* Look at this. That's for Lisa. Do you see how she can roll her eyes and turn her head. Isn't she lovely? And here's a toy pistol for Maja.° *(She loads the pistol and shoots it at Miss Y. who appears frightened.)*

MRS. X: Were you scared? Did you think I was going to shoot you? Really, I didn't think you'd believe that of me. Now if *you* were to shoot *me* it wouldn't be so surprising, for after all I did get in your way, and I know you never forget it — although I was entirely innocent. You still think I intrigued to get you out of the Grand Theatre, but I didn't. I didn't, however much you think I did. Well, it's no good talking, you will believe it was me . . . *(Takes out a pair of embroidered slippers.)* And these are for my old man, with tulips on them that I embroidered myself. As a matter of fact I hate tulips, but he has to have tulips on everything.

5

Miss Y. looks up, irony and curiosity in her face.

MRS. X: *(putting one hand in each slipper)* Look what small feet Bob has, hasn't he? And you ought to see the charming way he walks — you've never seen him in slippers, have you?

Miss Y. laughs.

°*Maja:* Pronounced "Maya."

MRS. X: Look, I'll show you. (*She makes the slippers walk across the table, and Miss Y. laughs again.*)

MRS. X: But when he gets angry, look, he stamps his foot like this. "Those damn girls who can never learn how to make coffee! Blast! That silly idiot hasn't trimmed the lamp properly!" Then there's a draught under the door and his feet get cold. "Hell, it's freezing, and the damn fools can't even keep the stove going!" (*She rubs the sole of one slipper against the instep of the other. Miss Y roars with laughter.*)

MRS. X: And then he comes home and has to hunt for his slippers, which Mary has pushed under the bureau . . . Well, perhaps it's not right to make fun of one's husband like this. He's sweet anyhow, and a good, dear husband. You ought to have had a husband like him, Amelia. What are you laughing at? What is it? Eh? And, you see, I know he is faithful to me. Yes, I know it. He told me himself — what *are* you giggling at?— that while I was on tour in Norway that horrible Frederica came and tried to seduce him. Can you imagine anything more abominable? (*Pause.*) I'd have scratched her eyes out if she had come around while I was at home. (*Pause.*) I'm glad Bob told me about it himself, so I didn't just hear it from gossip. (*Pause.*) And, as a matter of fact, Frederica wasn't the only one. I can't think why, but all the women in the Company° seem to be crazy about my husband. They must think his position gives him some say in who is engaged at the Theatre. Perhaps you have run after him yourself? I don't trust you very far, but I know he has never been attracted by you, and you always seemed to have some sort of grudge against him, or so I felt. (*Pause. They look at one another guardedly.*)

10   MRS. X: Do come and spend Christmas Eve with us tonight, Amelia — just to show that you're not offended with us, or anyhow not with me. I don't know why, but it seems specially unpleasant not to be friends with you. Perhaps it's because I did get in your way that time . . . (*slowly*) or — I don't know — really, I don't know at all why it is.

Pause. Miss Y. gazes curiously at Mrs. X.

MRS. X: (*thoughtfully*) It was so strange when we were getting to know one another. Do you know, when we first met, I was frightened of you, so frightened I didn't dare let you out of my sight. I arranged all my goings and comings to be near you. I dared not be your enemy, so I became your friend. But when you came to our home, I always had an uneasy feeling, because I saw my husband didn't like you, and that irritated me — like when a dress doesn't fit. I did all I could to make him be nice to you, but it was no good — until you went and got engaged. Then you became such tremendous friends that at first it looked as if you only dared show your real feelings then — when you were safe. And then, let me see, how was it after that? I wasn't jealous — that's queer. And I remember at the christening,

---

° *in the Company:* Translator's addition.

when you were the godmother, I told him to kiss you. He did, and you were so upset . . . As a matter of fact I didn't notice that then . . . I didn't think about it afterwards either . . . I've never thought about it — until *now!* (*Rises abruptly.*) Why don't you say something? You haven't said a word all this time. You've just let me go on talking. You have sat there with your eyes drawing all these thoughts out of me — they were there in me like silk in a cocoon — thoughts. . . Mistaken thoughts? Let me think. Why did you break off your engagement? Why did you never come to our house after that? Why don't you want to come to us tonight?

Miss Y. makes a motion, as if about to speak.

Mrs. X: No. You don't need to say anything, for now I see it all. That was why — and why — and why. Yes. Yes, that's why it was. Yes, yes, all the pieces fit together now. That's it. I won't sit at the same table as you. (*Moves her things to the other table.*) That's why I have to embroider tulips, which I loathe, on his slippers — because you liked tulips. (*Throws the slippers on the floor.*) That's why we have to spend the summer on the lake — because you couldn't bear the seaside. That's why my son had to be called Eskil — because it was your father's name. That's why I had to wear your colours, read your books, eat the dishes you liked, drink your drinks — your choco-late, for instance. That's why — oh my God, it's terrible to think of, terri-ble! Everything, everything came to me from you — even your passions. Your soul bored into mine like a worm into an apple, and ate and ate and burrowed and burrowed, till nothing was left but the skin and a little black mould. I wanted to fly from you, but I couldn't. You were there like a snake, your black eyes fascinating me. When I spread my wings, they only dragged me down. I lay in the water with my feet tied together, and the harder I worked my arms, the deeper I sank — down, down, till I reached the bot-tom, where you lay in waiting like a giant crab to catch me in your claws — and now here I am. Oh how I hate you! I hate you, I hate you! And you just go on sitting there, silent, calm, indifferent, not caring whether the moon is new or full, if it's Christmas or New Year, if other people are happy or unhappy. You don't know how to hate or to love. You just sit there without moving — like a cat° at a mouse-hole. You can't drag your prey out, you can't chase it, but you can out-stay it. Here you sit in your corner — you know they call it the rat-trap after you — reading the papers to see if anyone's ruined or wretched or been thrown out of the Company. Here you sit sizing up your victims and weighing your chances — like a pilot his shipwrecks for the salvage. (*Pause.*) Poor Amelia! Do you know, I couldn't be more sorry for you. I know you are miserable, miserable like some wounded creature, and vicious because you are wounded. I can't be angry with you. I should like to be, but after all you are the small one — and as for your affair with Bob, that doesn't worry me in the least. Why should it matter to me?

°*cat:* In Swedish, "stork."

And if you, or somebody else taught me to drink chocolate, what's the difference? (*Drinks a spoonful. Smugly.*) Chocolate is very wholesome anyhow. And if I learnt from you how to dress, *tant mieux!* — that only gave me a stronger hold over my husband, and you have lost what I gained. Yes, to judge from various signs, I think you have now lost him. Of course, you meant me to walk out, as you once did, and which you're now regretting. But I won't do that, you may be sure. One shouldn't be narrow-minded, you know. And why should nobody else want what I have? (*Pause.*) Perhaps, my dear, taking everything into consideration, at this moment it is I who am the stronger. You never got anything from me, you just gave away — from yourself. And now, like the thief in the night, when you woke up I had what you had lost. Why was it then that everything you touched became worthless and sterile? You couldn't keep a man's love — for all your tulips and your passions — but I could. You couldn't learn the art of living from your books — but I learnt it. You bore no little Eskil, although that was your father's name. (*Pause.*) And why is it you are silent — everywhere, always silent? Yes, I used to think this was strength, but perhaps it was because you hadn't anything to say, because you couldn't think of anything. (*Rises and picks up the slippers.*) Now I am going home, taking the tulips with me — *your* tulips. You couldn't learn from others, you couldn't bend, and so you broke like a dry stick. I did not. Thank you, Amelia, for all your good lessons. Thank you for teaching my husband how to love. Now I am going home — to love him.

Exit.

Reading and Reacting

1. Summarize the plot of *The Stronger*. What actually happens during the play? What events have occurred before the play begins?
2. Explain the nature of the conflict between Mrs. X and Miss Y. Is this conflict entirely personal, or is it professional as well?
3. Why do you suppose Strindberg structures this play as a monologue? Would exchanges of dialogue strengthen the play? What do you suppose Miss Y would like to tell Mrs. X?
4. Is Miss Y a flat character? Is she a foil for Mrs. X? Explain.
5. Both Miss Y and Mrs. X are actresses. What significance, if any, do you see in this fact?
6. What does the audience learn about Bob, Mrs. X's husband, during the course of the play? What more can we infer about him?
7. As she continues to speak, Mrs. X's similes—for example, "Your soul bored into mine like a worm into an apple"—grow increasingly vivid. Identify as many similes as you can. What does this language reveal about Mrs. X's character? How does it move the play's action along?
8. As the play progresses, Mrs. X gains knowledge and self-awareness. What does she learn?
9. List all the play's props—for example, the toy gun and the slippers. What function does each of these props serve? Are they all necessary?

10. **JOURNAL ENTRY** Which of the two women do you see as "the stronger" in this play? Explain your position.

11. **CRITICAL PERSPECTIVE** In her notes on the play, director Tracy Campbell makes the following observations about the play's two characters:

> To be stronger, two things have to be compared with one overcoming the other. The two are both women, both have hopes and dreams, both have very real fears. But that's where the comparisons end. Mrs. X and Miss Y are not the same kind of woman; they have similar hopes and dreams but they are motivated differently; their fears of loneliness may be the same, but how the two women face this fear is very different.

How are these two women similar? How are they different? What do you think each woman fears, and how does each one face her fears?

Related Works: "Hills Like White Elephants" (p. 148), "The Storm" (p. 281), "Big Black Good Man" (p. 339), "The Faithful Wife" (p. 909), "General Review of the Sex Situation" (p. 1075), *Small World* (p. 1763)

DAVID AUBURN (1969–   ) was born in Chicago and grew up in Columbus, Ohio, and in Arkansas before returning to Chicago for college. Having spent time in Los Angeles on a screenwriting fellowship, Auburn moved to New York to become a playwright. He enrolled in the playwriting program at Juilliard and had his first full-length play, *Skyscraper* (1998), produced off-Broadway in 1997. The production attracted the attention of the Manhattan Theatre Club, which told Auburn, "Keep us in mind for your next play and send it to us." He did, and that play was *Proof* (2000), his first Broadway production. *Proof* was awarded the 2001 Pulitzer Prize for drama and the 2001 Tony Award; Auburn also received a Dramatists Guild's Hull-Warriner Award. His other plays include *Fifth Planet* (1998), *Miss You* (1998), and *The Next Life*. His short play *What Do You Believe about the Future?* (1996) appeared in *Harper's* magazine and was adapted for the screen. Winner of the Joseph Kesselring Prize for drama, Auburn has received the Helen Merrill Playwriting Award and a Guggenheim Foundation Fellowship.

Cultural Context The number of women in mathematics—traditionally a male-dominated field—has grown slowly but steadily in the last thirty years. According to a study published in the 1990s, women accounted for nearly half the approximately 7,500 bachelor's degrees in math awarded by colleges and universities in the United States during the 1980s. The percentage of American women earning PhDs in math has also risen, climbing above twenty percent. Despite these gains, discrimination against the notion of women excelling in math and science still exists. In January 2005, Dr. Lawrence Summers, the President of Harvard University, hypothesized that innate genetic differences between men and women might be one reason why "fewer women succeed in math and science careers." These comments—from the leader of a prestigious university—sparked international controversy.

Proof (2001)

SETTING

THE BACK PORCH OF A HOUSE IN CHICAGO

CHARACTERS

Robert, *fifties*   **Hal,** *twenty-eight*
Catherine, *twenty-five*   **Claire,** *twenty-nine*

ACT 1

SCENE 1

*Night. Catherine sits in a chair. She is exhausted, haphazardly dressed. Eyes closed.
Robert is standing behind her. He is Catherine's father. Rumpled academic look.
Catherine does not know he is there. After a moment:*

ROBERT: Can't sleep?

CATHERINE: Jesus, you scared me.

ROBERT: Sorry.

CATHERINE: What are you doing here?

5   ROBERT: I thought I'd check up on you. Why aren't you in bed?

CATHERINE: Your student is still here. He's up in your study.

ROBERT: He can let himself out.

CATHERINE: I might as well wait up till he's done.

ROBERT: He's not my student anymore. He's teaching now. Bright kid.

Beat.

10   CATHERINE: What time is it?

ROBERT: It's almost one.

CATHERINE: Huh.

ROBERT: After midnight . . .

CATHERINE: So?

15   ROBERT: So: (*He indicates something on the table behind him: a bottle of
champagne.*) Happy birthday.

CATHERINE: Dad.

ROBERT: Do I ever forget?

CATHERINE: Thank you.

ROBERT: Twenty-five. I can't believe it.

20   CATHERINE: Neither can I. Should we have it now?

ROBERT: It's up to you.

CATHERINE: Yes.

ROBERT: You want me to open it?

CATHERINE: Let me. Last time you opened a bottle of champagne out here you
broke a window.

25   ROBERT: That was a long time ago. I resent your bringing it up.

CATHERINE: You're lucky you didn't lose an eye.

Pop. The bottle foams.

ROBERT: Twenty-five!
CATHERINE: I feel old.
ROBERT: You're a kid.
CATHERINE: Glasses?   30
ROBERT: Goddamn it, I forgot the glasses. Do you want me to—
CATHERINE: Nah.

Catherine drinks from the bottle. A long pull. Robert watches her.

ROBERT: I hope you like it. I wasn't sure what to get you.
CATHERINE: This is the worst champagne I have ever tasted.
ROBERT: I am proud to say I don't know anything about wines. I hate those   35
    kind of people who are always talking about "vintages."
CATHERINE: It's not even champagne.
ROBERT: The bottle was the right shape.
CATHERINE: "Great Lakes Vineyards." I didn't know they made wine in
    Wisconsin.
ROBERT: A girl who's drinking from the bottle shouldn't complain. Don't
    guzzle it. It's an elegant beverage. Sip.
CATHERINE: *(offering the bottle)* Do you—   40
ROBERT: No, go ahead.
CATHERINE: You sure?
ROBERT: Yeah. It's your birthday.
CATHERINE: Happy birthday to me.
ROBERT: What are you going to do on your birthday?   45
CATHERINE: Drink this. Have some.
ROBERT: No. I hope you're not spending your birthday alone.
CATHERINE: I'm not alone.
ROBERT: I don't count.
CATHERINE: Why not?   50
ROBERT: I'm your old man. Go out with some friends.
CATHERINE: Right.
ROBERT: Your friends aren't taking you out?
CATHERINE: No.
ROBERT: Why not?   55
CATHERINE: Because in order for your friends to take you out you generally
    have to have friends.
ROBERT: *(dismissive)* Oh—
CATHERINE: It's funny how that works.
ROBERT: You have friends. What about that cute blonde, what was her name?
CATHERINE: What?   60
ROBERT: She lives over on Ellis Avenue — you used to spend every minute
    together.
CATHERINE: Cindy Jacobsen?
ROBERT: Cindy Jacobsen!

Larry Bryggman as Robert and Mary-Louise Parker as Catherine in the Broadway production of *Proof*.

CATHERINE: That was in *third grade*, Dad. Her family moved to Florida in 1983.
65 ROBERT: What about Claire?
CATHERINE: She's not my friend, she's my sister. And she's in New York. And I don't like her.
ROBERT: I thought she was coming in.
CATHERINE: Not till tomorrow.

Beat.

ROBERT: My advice, if you find yourself awake late at night, is to sit down and do some mathematics.
70 CATHERINE: Oh please.
ROBERT: We could do some together.
CATHERINE: No.
ROBERT: Why not?
CATHERINE: I can't think of anything worse. You sure you don't want any?
75 ROBERT: Yeah, thanks. You used to love it.
CATHERINE: Not anymore.
ROBERT: You knew what a prime number was before you could read.
CATHERINE: Well now I've forgotten.

ROBERT: *(Hard)* Don't waste your talent, Catherine.

Beat.

CATHERINE: I knew you'd say something like that.   80

ROBERT: I realize you've had a difficult time.

CATHERINE: Thanks.

ROBERT: That's not an excuse. Don't be lazy.

CATHERINE: I haven't been lazy, I've been taking care of you.

ROBERT: Kid, I've seen you. You sleep till noon, you eat junk, you don't work,   85
the dishes pile up in the sink. If you go out it's to buy magazines. You come
back with a stack of magazines this high — I don't know how you read that
crap. And those are the good days. Some days you don't get up, you don't
get out of bed.

CATHERINE: Those are the good days.

ROBERT: Bullshit. Those days are lost. You threw them away. And you'll never
know what else you threw away with them — the work you lost, the ideas
you didn't have, discoveries you never made because you were moping in
your bed at four in the afternoon. *(Beat.)* You know I'm right. *(Beat.)*

CATHERINE: I've lost a few days.

ROBERT: How many?

CATHERINE: Oh, I don't know.   90

ROBERT: I bet you do.

CATHERINE: What?

ROBERT: I bet you count.

CATHERINE: Knock it off.

ROBERT: Well do you know or don't you?   95

CATHERINE: I don't.

ROBERT: Of course you do. How many days have you lost?

CATHERINE: A month. Around a month.

ROBERT: Exactly.

CATHERINE: Goddamn it, I don't —   100

ROBERT: *How many?*

CATHERINE: Thirty-three days.

ROBERT: Exactly?

CATHERINE: I don't know.

ROBERT: Be precise, for Chrissake.   105

CATHERINE: I slept till noon today.

ROBERT: Call it thirty-three and a quarter days.

CATHERINE: Yes, all right.

ROBERT: You're kidding!

CATHERINE: No.   110

ROBERT: Amazing number!

CATHERINE: It's a depressing fucking number.

ROBERT: Catherine, if every day you say you've lost were a year, it would be a
very interesting fucking number.

CATHERINE: Thirty-three and a quarter years is not interesting.

115   ROBERT: Stop it. You know exactly what I mean.
       CATHERINE: *(conceding)* 1729 weeks.
       ROBERT: 1729. Great number. The smallest number expressible —
       CATHERINE: — expressible as the sum of two cubes in two different ways.
       ROBERT: 12 cubed plus 1 cubed equals 1729.
120   CATHERINE: And 10 cubed plus 9 cubed. Yes, we've got it, thank you.
       ROBERT: You see? Even your depression is mathematical. Stop moping and get
           to work. The kind of potential you have —
       CATHERINE: I haven't done anything good.
       ROBERT: You're young. You've got time.
       CATHERINE: I do?
125   ROBERT: *Yes.*
       CATHERINE: By the time you were my age you were famous.
       ROBERT: By the time I was your age I'd already done my best work.

       Beat.

       CATHERINE: What about after?
       ROBERT: After what?
130   CATHERINE: After you got sick.
       ROBERT: What about it?
       CATHERINE: You couldn't work then.
       ROBERT: No, if anything I was sharper.
       CATHERINE: *(She can't help it: she laughs.)* Dad.
135   ROBERT: I was. Hey, it's true. The clarity — that was the amazing thing.
           No doubts.
       CATHERINE: You were happy?
       ROBERT: Yeah, I was busy.
       CATHERINE: Not the same thing.
       ROBERT: I don't see the difference. I knew what I wanted to do and I did it.

           If I wanted to work a problem all day long, I did it.
           If I wanted to look for information — secrets, complex and tantalizing
       messages — I could find them all around me. In the air. In a pile of fallen
       leaves some neighbor raked together. In box scores in the paper, written in
       the steam coming up off a cup of coffee. The whole world was talking to me.
           If I just wanted to close my eyes, sit quietly on the porch and listen for
       the messages, I did that.
           It was wonderful.

       Beat.

       CATHERINE: How old were you? When it started.
140   ROBERT: Mid-twenties. Twenty-three, four. *(Beat.)* Is that what you're worried
           about?
       CATHERINE: I've thought about it.
       ROBERT: Just getting a year older means nothing, Catherine.
       CATHERINE: It's not just getting older.

ROBERT: It's me.   145

Beat.

CATHERINE: I've thought about it.

ROBERT: Really?

CATHERINE: How could I not?

ROBERT: Well if that's why you're worried you're not keeping up with the medical literature. There are all kinds of factors. It's not simply something you inherit. Just because I went bughouse doesn't mean you will.

CATHERINE: Dad . . .   150

ROBERT: Listen to me. Life changes fast in your early twenties and it shakes you up. You're feeling down. It's been a bad week. You've had a lousy couple years, no one knows that better than me. But you're gonna be okay.

CATHERINE: Yeah?

ROBERT: Yes. I promise you. Push yourself. Don't read so many magazines. Sit down and get the machinery going and I swear to God you'll feel fine. The simple fact that we can talk about this together is a good sign.

CATHERINE: A good sign?

ROBERT: Yes!   155

CATHERINE: How could it be a good sign?

ROBERT: Because! Crazy people don't sit around wondering if they're nuts.

CATHERINE: They don't?

ROBERT: Of course not. They've got better things to do. Take it from me. A very good sign that you're crazy is an inability to ask the question "Am I crazy?"

CATHERINE: Even if the answer is yes?   160

ROBERT: Crazy people don't ask. You see?

CATHERINE: Yes.

ROBERT: So if you're asking . . .

CATHERINE: I'm not.

ROBERT: But if you were, it would be a very good sign.   165

CATHERINE: A good sign . . .

ROBERT: A good sign that you're fine.

CATHERINE: Right.

ROBERT: You see? You've just gotta think these things through. Now come on, what do you say? Let's call it a night; you go up, get some sleep, and then in the morning you can—

CATHERINE: Wait. No.   170

ROBERT: What's the matter?

CATHERINE: It doesn't work.

ROBERT: Why not?

CATHERINE: It doesn't make sense.

ROBERT: Sure it does.   175

CATHERINE: No.

ROBERT: Where's the problem?

CATHERINE: The problem is you are crazy!

ROBERT: What difference does that make?

180   CATHERINE: You admitted — You just told me that you are.
        ROBERT: So?
        CATHERINE: You said a crazy person would never admit that.
        ROBERT: Yeah, but it's . . . Oh. I see.
        CATHERINE: So?
185   ROBERT: It's a point.
        CATHERINE: So how can you admit it?
        ROBERT: Well. Because I'm also dead. *(Beat.)* Aren't I?
        CATHERINE: You died a week ago.
        ROBERT: Heart failure. Quick. The funeral's tomorrow.
190   CATHERINE: That's why Claire's flying in from New York.
        ROBERT: Yes.
        CATHERINE: You're sitting here. You're giving me advice. You brought me
           champagne.
        ROBERT: Yes.

Beat.

        CATHERINE: Which means . . .
195   ROBERT: For you?
        CATHERINE: Yes.
        ROBERT: For you, Catherine, my daughter, who I love very much . . .
           It could be a bad sign.

*They sit together for a moment. Noise off. Hal enters, semi-hip clothes. He carries a
backpack and a jacket, folded. He lets the door go and it bangs shut. Catherine sits up
with a jolt.*

        CATHERINE: What?
        HAL: Oh God, sorry — did I wake you?
200   CATHERINE: What?
        HAL: Were you asleep?

Beat. Robert is gone.

        CATHERINE: You scared me, for Chrissake. What are you doing?
        HAL: I'm sorry. I didn't realize it had gotten so late. I'm done for the night.
        CATHERINE: Good.
205   HAL: Drinking alone?

Catherine realizes she is holding the champagne bottle. She puts it down quickly.

        CATHERINE: Yes.
        HAL: Champagne, huh?
        CATHERINE: Yes.
        HAL: Celebrating?
210   CATHERINE: No. I just like champagne.
        HAL: It's festive.
        CATHERINE: What?
        HAL: Festive. *(He makes an awkward "party" gesture.)*

CATHERINE: Do you want some?

HAL: Sure.   215

CATHERINE: (*gives him the bottle*) I'm done. You can take the rest with you.

HAL: Oh. No thanks.

CATHERINE: Take it, I'm done.

HAL: No, I shouldn't. I'm driving. (*Beat.*) Well I can let myself out.

CATHERINE: Good.   220

HAL: When should I come back?

CATHERINE: Come back?

HAL: Yeah. I'm nowhere near finished. Maybe tomorrow?

CATHERINE: We have a funeral tomorrow.

HAL: God, you're right, I'm sorry. I was going to attend, if that's all right.   225

CATHERINE: Yes.

HAL: What about Sunday? Will you be around?

CATHERINE: You've had three days.

HAL: I'd love to get in some more time up there.

CATHERINE: How much longer do you need?   230

HAL: Another week. At least.

CATHERINE: Are you joking?

HAL: No. Do you know how much stuff there is?

CATHERINE: A week?

HAL: I know you don't need anybody in your hair right now. Look, I spent the   235
last couple days getting everything sorted out. It's mostly notebooks. He
dated them all; now that I've got them in order I don't have to work here.
I could take some stuff home, read it, bring it back.

CATHERINE: No.

HAL: I'll be careful.

CATHERINE: My father wouldn't want anything moved and I don't want
anything to leave this house.

HAL: Then I should work here. I'll stay out of the way.

CATHERINE: You're wasting your time.   240

HAL: Someone needs to go through your dad's papers.

CATHERINE: There's nothing up there. It's garbage.

HAL: There are a hundred and three notebooks.

CATHERINE: I've looked at those. It's gibberish.

HAL: Someone should read them.   245

CATHERINE: He was crazy.

HAL: Yes, but he wrote them.

CATHERINE: He was a graphomaniac, Harold. Do you know what that is?

HAL: I know. He wrote compulsively. Call me Hal.

CATHERINE: There's no connection between the ideas. There's no ideas. It's like   250
a monkey at a typewriter. A hundred and three notebooks full of bullshit.

HAL: Let's make sure they're bullshit.

CATHERINE: I'm sure.

HAL: I'm prepared to look at every page. Are you?

CATHERINE: No. *I'm* not crazy.

Beat.

255 HAL: Well, I'm gonna be late . . . Some friends of mine are in this band.
They're playing at a bar up on Diversey. Way down the bill, they're probably
going on around two, two-thirty. I said I'd be there.

CATHERINE: Great.

HAL: They're all in the math department. They're really good.
They have this great song — you'd like it — called "i" — lower-case I. They
just stand there and don't play anything for three minutes.

CATHERINE: "Imaginary Number."

HAL: It's a math joke. You see why they're way down the bill.

260 CATHERINE: Long drive to see some nerds in a band.

HAL: God I hate when people say that. It is not that long a drive.

CATHERINE: So they are nerds.

HAL: Oh they're raging geeks. But they're geeks who, you know, can dress
themselves . . . hold down a job at a major university . . . Some of them have
switched from glasses to contacts. They play sports, they play in a band, they
get laid surprisingly often, so in that sense they sort of make you question
the whole set of terms: geek, nerd, wonk, dweeb, dilbert, paste-eater.

CATHERINE: You're in this band, aren't you?

265 HAL: Okay, yes. I play drums. You want to come? I never sing, I swear to God.

CATHERINE: No thanks.

HAL: All right. Look, Catherine, Monday: what do you say?

CATHERINE: Don't you have a job?

HAL: Yeah, I have a full teaching load this quarter plus my own work.

270 CATHERINE: Plus band practice.

HAL: I don't have time to do this but I'm going to. If you'll let me. *(Beat.)*
I loved your dad. I don't believe a mind like his can just shut down.
He had lucid moments. He had a lucid year, a whole year four years ago.

CATHERINE: It wasn't a year. It was more like nine months.

HAL: A school year. He was advising students . . . I was stalled on my Ph.D.
I was this close to quitting. I met with your dad and he put me on the right
track with my research. I owe him.

CATHERINE: Sorry.

275 HAL: Look. Let me — You're twenty-five, right?

CATHERINE: How old are you?

HAL: It doesn't matter. Listen.

CATHERINE: Fuck you, how old are you?

HAL: I'm twenty-eight, all right? When your dad was younger than both of us,
he made major contributions to three fields: game theory, algebraic geometry,
and nonlinear operator theory. Most of us never get our heads around one.
He basically invented the mathematical techniques for studying rational
behavior, and he gave the astrophysicists plenty to work over too. Okay?

280 CATHERINE: Don't lecture me.

HAL: I'm not. I'm telling you, if I came up with one-tenth of the shit your dad produced, I could write my own ticket to any math department in the country.

Beat.

CATHERINE: Give me your backpack.

HAL: What?

CATHERINE: Give me your backpack.

HAL: Why? 285

CATHERINE: I want to look inside it.

HAL: What?

CATHERINE: Open it and give it to me.

HAL: Oh come on.

CATHERINE: You're not taking anything out of this house. 290

HAL: I wouldn't do that.

CATHERINE: You're hoping to find something upstairs that you can publish.

HAL: Sure.

CATHERINE: Then you can write your own ticket.

HAL: What? No! It would be under your dad's name. It would be for your dad. 295

CATHERINE: I don't believe you. You have a notebook in that backpack.

HAL: What are you talking about?

CATHERINE: Give it to me.

HAL: You're being a little bit paranoid.

CATHERINE: *Paranoid?* 300

HAL: Maybe a little.

CATHERINE: Fuck you, *Hal. I know* you have one of my notebooks.

HAL: I think you should calm down and think about what you're saying.

CATHERINE: I'm saying you're lying to me and stealing my family's property.

HAL: And I think that sounds paranoid. 305

CATHERINE: Just because I'm paranoid doesn't mean there isn't something in that backpack.

HAL: *You just said yourself there's nothing up there.* Didn't you?

CATHERINE: I—

HAL: Didn't you say that?

CATHERINE: Yes. 310

HAL: So what would I take? Right?

Beat.

CATHERINE: You're right.

HAL: Thank you.

CATHERINE: So you don't need to come back.

HAL: (*Sighs.*) Please. Someone should know for sure whether— 315

CATHERINE: *I lived with him.* I spent my life with him. I fed him. Talked to him. Tried to listen when he talked. Talked to people who weren't there . . . Watched him shuffling around like a ghost. A very smelly ghost. He was filthy. I had to make sure he bathed. My own father.

HAL: I'm sorry. I shouldn't have . . .

CATHERINE: After my mother died it was just me here. I tried to keep him happy no matter what idiotic project he was doing. He used to read all day. He kept demanding more and more books. I took them out of the library by the carload. We had hundreds upstairs. Then I realized he wasn't reading: he believed aliens were sending him messages through the Dewey decimal numbers on the library books. He was trying to work out the code.

HAL: What kind of messages?

320 CATHERINE: Beautiful mathematics. The most elegant proofs, perfect proofs, proofs like music.

HAL: Sounds good.

CATHERINE: Plus fashion tips, knock-knock jokes — I mean it was *nuts*, okay?

HAL: He was ill. It was a tragedy.

CATHERINE: Later the writing phase: scribbling nineteen, twenty hours a day . . . I ordered him a case of notebooks and he used every one.

I dropped out of school . . .

I'm glad he's dead.

325 HAL: I understand why you'd feel that way.

CATHERINE: Fuck you.

HAL: You're right. I can't imagine dealing with that. It must have been awful. I know you—

CATHERINE: You don't know me. I want to be alone. I don't want him around.

HAL: *(confused)* Him? I don't—

330 CATHERINE: You. I don't want you here.

HAL: Why?

CATHERINE: He's dead.

HAL: But I'm not—

CATHERINE: *He's* dead; I don't need any *protégés* around.

335 HAL: There will be others.

CATHERINE: What?

HAL: You think I'm the only one? People are already working over his stuff. Someone's gonna read those notebooks.

CATHERINE: I'll do it.

HAL: No, you—

340 CATHERINE: He's my father, I'll do it.

HAL: You can't.

CATHERINE: Why not?

HAL: You don't have the math. It's all just squiggles on a page. You wouldn't know the good stuff from the junk.

CATHERINE: It's all junk.

345 HAL: If it's not we can't afford to miss any through carelessness.

CATHERINE: I know mathematics.

HAL: If there was anything up there it would be pretty high-order. It would take a professional to recognize it.

CATHERINE: I think I could recognize it.

HAL: *(Patient)* Cathy . . .

CATHERINE: *What?*   350

HAL: I know your dad taught you some basic stuff, but come on.

CATHERINE: You don't think I could do it.

HAL: I'm sorry: I know that you couldn't. *(Beat. Catherine snatches his back-pack.)* Hey! Oh come on. Give me a break. *(Catherine opens the backpack and rifles through it.)* This isn't an airport.

Catherine removes items one by one. A water bottle. Some workout clothes. An orange. Drumsticks. Nothing else. She puts everything back in and gives it back. Beat.

CATHERINE: You can come tomorrow.

Beat. They are both embarrassed.

HAL: The university health service is uh very good.   355
    My mom died a couple years ago and I was pretty broken up. Also my work wasn't going that well . . . I went over and talked to this doctor. I saw her for a couple months and it really helped.

CATHERINE: I'm fine.

Beat.

HAL: Also exercise is great. I run along the lake a couple of mornings a week. It's not too cold yet. If you wanted to come sometime I could pick you up. We wouldn't have to talk . . .

CATHERINE: No thanks.

HAL: All right. I'm gonna be late for the show. I better go.

CATHERINE: Okay.   360

Beat.

HAL: It's seriously like twenty minutes up to the club. We go on, we play, we're terrible but we buy everyone drinks afterward to make up for it. You're home by four, four-thirty, tops . . .

CATHERINE: Good night.

HAL: Good night. *(He starts to exit. He has forgotten his jacket.)*

CATHERINE: Wait, your coat.

HAL: No, you don't have to —   365

Catherine picks up his jacket. As she does, a composition book that was folded up in the coat falls to the floor. Beat. She picks it up, trembling with rage.

CATHERINE: I'm *paranoid?*

HAL: Wait.

CATHERINE: You think I should go *jogging?*

HAL: Just hold on.

CATHERINE: Get out!   370

HAL: Can I please just —

CATHERINE: Get the fuck out of my house.

HAL: Listen to me for a *minute.*

CATHERINE: *(Waving the book)* You stole this!

375 HAL: Let me *explain!*

CATHERINE: You stole it from *me*, you stole it from my *father*—

Hal snatches the book.

HAL: I want to show you something. Will you calm down?

CATHERINE: Give it back.

HAL: Just wait a minute.

380 CATHERINE: I'm calling the police. *(She picks up the phone and dials.)*

HAL: Don't. Look, I borrowed the book, all right? I'm sorry, I just picked it up before I came downstairs and thought I'd—

CATHERINE: *(On phone)* Hello?

HAL: I did it for a reason.

CATHERINE: Hello, police? I—Yes, I'd like to report a robbery in progress.

385 HAL: I noticed something—something your father wrote. All right? Not math, something he *wrote*. Here, let me show you.

CATHERINE: A *robbery*.

HAL: Will you put the fucking phone down and listen to me?

CATHERINE: *(On phone)* Yes, I'm at 5724 South—

HAL: It's about you. See? *You*. It was written about you. Here's your name: Cathy. See?

390 CATHERINE: South . . .

Catherine pauses. She seems to be listening. Hal reads.

HAL: "A good day. Some very good news from Catherine." I didn't know what that referred to, but I thought you might . . .

CATHERINE: When did he write this?

HAL: I think four years ago. The handwriting is steady. It must have been during his remission. There's more. *(A moment. Catherine hangs up the phone.)* "Machinery not working yet but I am patient." "The machinery" is what he called his mind, his ability to do mathematics.

CATHERINE: I know.

395 HAL: *(reads)* "I know I'll get there. I am an auto mechanic who after years of greasy work on a hopeless wreck turns the ignition and hears a faint cough. I am not driving yet, but there's cause for optimism. Talking with students helps. So does being outside, eating meals in restaurants, riding buses, all the activities of 'normal' life.

"Most of all Cathy. The years she has lost caring for me. I almost wrote 'wasted.' Yet her refusal to let me be institutionalized—her keeping me at home, caring for me herself, has certainly saved my life. Made writing this possible. Made it possible to imagine doing math again. Where does her strength come from? I can never repay her.

"Today is her birthday: she is twenty-one. I'm taking her to dinner." Dated September 4. That's tomorrow.

CATHERINE: It's today.

HAL: You're right. (*He gives her the book.*) I thought you might want to see it. I shouldn't have tried to sneak it out. Tomorrow I was going to — it sounds stupid now. I was going to wrap it. Happy birthday.

Hal exits. Catherine is alone. She puts her head in her hands. She weeps. Eventually she stops, wipes her eyes. From off: a police siren, drawing closer.

CATHERINE: Shit.

Fade

SCENE 2

The next morning. Claire, stylish, attractive, drinks coffee from a mug. She has brought bagels and fruit on a tray out to the porch. She arranges them on two plates. She notices the champagne bottle lying on the floor. She picks it up and sets it on a table. Catherine enters. Her hair is wet from a shower.

CLAIRE: Better. Much.
CATHERINE: Thanks.
CLAIRE: Feel better?
CATHERINE: Yeah.
CLAIRE: You look a million times better. Have some coffee.   5
CATHERINE: Okay.
CLAIRE: How do you take it?
CATHERINE: Black.
CLAIRE: Have a little milk. (*She pours.*) Want a banana? It's a good thing
    I brought food: there was nothing in the house.
CATHERINE: I've been meaning to go shopping.   10
CLAIRE: Have a bagel.
CATHERINE: No. I hate breakfast. (*Beat.*)
CLAIRE: You didn't put on the dress.
CATHERINE: Didn't really feel like it.
CLAIRE: Don't you want to try it on? See if it fits?   15
CATHERINE: I'll put it on later.

Beat.

CLAIRE: If you want to dry your hair I have a hair dryer.
CATHERINE: Nah.
CLAIRE: Did you use that conditioner I brought you?
CATHERINE: No, shit, I forgot.   20
CLAIRE: It's my favorite. You'll love it, Katie. I want you to try it.
CATHERINE: I'll use it next time.
CLAIRE: You'll like it. It has jojoba.
CATHERINE: What is "jojoba"?
CLAIRE: It's something they put in for healthy hair.   25
CATHERINE: Hair is dead.
CLAIRE: What?

CATHERINE: It's dead tissue. You can't make it "healthy."

CLAIRE: Whatever, it's something that's good for your hair.

30 CATHERINE: What, a chemical?

CLAIRE: No, it's organic.

CATHERINE: Well it can be organic and still be a chemical.

CLAIRE: I don't know what it is.

CATHERINE: Haven't you ever heard of organic chemistry?

35 CLAIRE: It makes my hair feel, look, and smell good. That's the extent of my
     information about it. You might like it if you decide to use it.

CATHERINE: Thanks, I'll try it.

CLAIRE: Good. (*Beat.*) If the dress doesn't fit we can go downtown and
     exchange it.

CATHERINE: Okay.

CLAIRE: I'll take you to lunch.

40 CATHERINE: Great.

CLAIRE: Maybe Sunday before I go back. Do you need anything?

CATHERINE: Like clothes?

CLAIRE: Or anything. While I'm here.

CATHERINE: Nah, I'm cool.

Beat.

45 CLAIRE: I thought we'd have some people over tonight. If you're
     feeling okay.

CATHERINE: I'm feeling okay, Claire, stop saying that.

CLAIRE: You don't have any plans?

CATHERINE: No.

CLAIRE: I ordered some food. Wine, beer.

50 CATHERINE: We are burying Dad this afternoon.

CLAIRE: I think it will be all right. Anyone who's been to the funeral and
     wants to come over for something to eat can. And it's the only time I can
     see any old Chicago friends. It'll be nice. It's a funeral but we don't have to
     be completely grim about it. *If* it's okay with you.

CATHERINE: Yes, sure.

CLAIRE: It's been a stressful time. It would be good to relax in a low-key way.
     Mitch says Hi.

CATHERINE: Hi Mitch.

55 CLAIRE: He's really sorry he couldn't come.

CATHERINE: Yeah, he's gonna miss all the fun.

CLAIRE: He wanted to see you. He sends his love. I told him you'd see him
     soon enough. (*Beat.*) We're getting married.

CATHERINE: No shit.

CLAIRE: Yes! We just decided.

60 CATHERINE: Yikes.

CLAIRE: Yes!

CATHERINE: When?

CLAIRE: January.

CATHERINE: Huh.

CLAIRE: We're not going to do a huge thing. His folks are gone too. Just City   65
Hall, then a big dinner at our favorite restaurant for all our friends. And
you, of course. I hope you'll be in the wedding.

CATHERINE: Yeah. Of course. Congratulations, Claire, I'm really happy for you.

CLAIRE: Thanks. Me too. We just decided it was time. His job is great. I just
got promoted . . .

CATHERINE: Huh.

CLAIRE: You will come?

CATHERINE: Yes, sure. January? I mean, I don't have to check my calendar or   70
anything. Sure.

CLAIRE: That makes me very happy. *(Beat. From here on Claire treads gingerly.)*

CLAIRE: How are you?

CATHERINE: Okay.

CLAIRE: How are you feeling about everything?

CATHERINE: About "everything"?   75

CLAIRE: About Dad.

CATHERINE: What about him?

CLAIRE: How are you feeling about his death? Are you all right?

CATHERINE: Yes, I am.

CLAIRE: Honestly?   80

CATHERINE: Yes.

CLAIRE: I think in some ways it was the "right time." If there is ever a right time.
Do you know what you want to do now?

CATHERINE: No.

CLAIRE: Do you want to stay here?

CATHERINE: I don't know.   85

CLAIRE: Do you want to go back to school?

CATHERINE: I haven't thought about it.

CLAIRE: Well there's a lot to think about.
How do you feel?

CATHERINE: Physically? Great. Except my hair seems kind of unhealthy,
I wish there were something I could do about that.

CLAIRE: Come on, Catherine.   90

CATHERINE: What is the point of all these questions?

Beat.

CLAIRE: Katie, some policemen came by while you were in the shower.

CATHERINE: Yeah?

CLAIRE: They said they were "checking up" on things here. Seeing how
everything was this morning.

CATHERINE: *(neutral)* That was nice.   95

CLAIRE: They told me they responded to a call last night and came to the house.

CATHERINE: Yeah?

CLAIRE: Did you call the police last night?

CATHERINE: Yeah.

100   CLAIRE: Why?
CATHERINE: I thought the house was being robbed.
CLAIRE: But it wasn't.
CATHERINE: No. I changed my mind.

Beat.

CLAIRE: First you call 911 with an emergency and then you hang up on them—
105   CATHERINE: I didn't really want them to come.
CLAIRE: So why did you call?
CATHERINE: I was trying to get this guy out of the house.
CLAIRE: Who?
CATHERINE: One of Dad's students.
110   CLAIRE: Dad hasn't had any students for years.
CATHERINE: No, he *was* Dad's student. Now he's—he's a mathematician.
CLAIRE: Why was he in the house in the first place?
CATHERINE: Well he's been coming here to look at Dad's notebooks.
CLAIRE: In the middle of the night?
115   CATHERINE: It was late. I was waiting for him to finish, and last night I
          thought he might have been stealing them.
CLAIRE: Stealing the notebooks.
CATHERINE: *Yes.* So I told him to go.
CLAIRE: Was he stealing them?
CATHERINE: Yes. That's why I called the police—
120   CLAIRE: What is this man's name?
CATHERINE: Hal. Harold. Harold Dobbs.
CLAIRE: The police said you were the only one here.
CATHERINE: He left before they got here.
CLAIRE: With the notebooks?
125   CATHERINE: No, Claire, don't be stupid, there are over a hundred notebooks.
          He was only stealing *one,* but he was stealing it so he could give it *back* to
          me, so I let him go so he could play with his band on the north side.
CLAIRE: His band?
CATHERINE: He was late. He wanted me to come with him but I was like,
          Yeah, right.

Beat.

CLAIRE: *(gently)* Is "Harold Dobbs" your boyfriend?
CATHERINE: No!
130   CLAIRE: Are you sleeping with him?
CATHERINE: What? Euughh! No! He's a math geek!
CLAIRE: And he's in a band? A rock band?
CATHERINE: No, a marching band. He plays trombone. Yes, a rock band!
CLAIRE: What is the name of his band?
135   CATHERINE: How should I know?
CLAIRE: "Harold Dobbs" didn't tell you the name of his rock band?

CATHERINE: No. I don't know. Look in the paper. They were playing last night. They do a song called "Imaginary Number" that doesn't exist.

Beat.

CLAIRE: I'm sorry, I'm just trying to understand: is "Harold Dobbs"—
CATHERINE: Stop saying "Harold Dobbs."
CLAIRE: Is this . . . person . . .   140
CATHERINE: *Harold Dobbs exists.*
CLAIRE: I'm sure he does.
CATHERINE: He's a mathematician at the University of Chicago. Call the fucking math department.
CLAIRE: Don't get upset. I'm just trying to understand! I mean if you found out some creepy grad student was trying to take some of Dad's papers and you called the police, I'd understand, and if you were out here partying, drinking with your boyfriend, I'd understand. But the two stories don't go together.
CATHERINE: Because you made up the "boyfriend" story. I was here *alone.*   145
CLAIRE: Harold Dobbs wasn't here?
CATHERINE: No, he — *Yes,* he was here, but we weren't partying!
CLAIRE: You weren't drinking with him?
CATHERINE: No!
CLAIRE: *(She holds up the champagne bottle.)* This was sitting right here.   150
Who were you drinking champagne with?

Catherine hesitates.

CATHERINE: With no one.
CLAIRE: Are you sure?
CATHERINE: Yes.

Beat.

CLAIRE: The police said you were abusive. *(Catherine doesn't say anything.)*
They said you're lucky they didn't haul you in.
CATHERINE: These guys were assholes, Claire. They wouldn't go away. They   155
wanted me to fill out a report . . .
CLAIRE: Were you abusive?
CATHERINE: This one cop kept spitting on me when he talked. It was disgusting.
CLAIRE: Did you use the word "dickhead"?
CATHERINE: Oh I don't remember.
CLAIRE: Did you tell one cop . . . to go fuck the other cop's mother?   160
CATHERINE: *No.*
CLAIRE: That's what they said.
CATHERINE: Not with that phrasing.
CLAIRE: Did you strike one of them?
CATHERINE: They were trying to come in the house!   165

CLAIRE: Oh my God.

CATHERINE: I might have *pushed* him a little.

CLAIRE: They said you were either drunk or disturbed.

CATHERINE: They wanted to come in here and *search my house—*

170 CLAIRE: *You* called *them.*

CATHERINE: Yes but I didn't actually *want* them to come. But they did come and then they started acting like they owned the place, pushing me around, calling me "girly," smirking at me, laughing: they were assholes.

CLAIRE: These guys seemed perfectly nice. They were off-duty and they took the trouble to come back here at the end of their shift to check up on you. They were very polite.

CATHERINE: Well people are nicer to you.

Beat.

CLAIRE: Katie. Would you like to come to New York?

175 CATHERINE: Yes, I told you, I'll come in January.

CLAIRE: You could come sooner. We'd love to have you. You could stay with us. It'd be fun.

CATHERINE: I don't want to.

CLAIRE: Mitch has become an *excellent* cook. It's like his hobby now. He buys all these gadgets. Garlic press, olive oil sprayer . . . Every night there's something new. Delicious, wonderful meals. The other day he made vegetarian chili!

CATHERINE: What the fuck are you talking about?

180 CLAIRE: Stay with us for a while. We would have so much fun.

CATHERINE: Thanks, I'm okay here.

CLAIRE: Chicago is dead. New York is so much more fun, you can't believe it.

CATHERINE: The "fun" thing is really not where my focus is at the moment.

CLAIRE: I think New York would be a really fun and . . . safe . . . place for you to—

185 CATHERINE: I don't need a safe place and I don't want to have any fun! I'm perfectly fine here.

CLAIRE: You look tired. I think you could use some downtime.

CATHERINE: Downtime?

CLAIRE: Katie, please. You've had a very hard time.

CATHERINE: I'm *perfectly okay.*

190 CLAIRE: I think you're upset and exhausted.

CATHERINE: I was *fine* till you got here.

CLAIRE: Yes, but you —

HAL: *(from off)* Catherine?

CLAIRE: Who is that?

Beat. Hal enters.

195 HAL: Hey, I—

Catherine stands and points triumphantly at him.

CATHERINE: *Harold Dobbs!*

HAL: (*confused*) Hi.

CATHERINE: *Okay?* I really don't need this, Claire. I'm fine, you know, I'm totally fine, and then you swoop in here with these questions, and "Are you okay?" and your soothing tone of voice and "Oh, the poor policemen"— I think the police can handle themselves!— and bagels and bananas and jojoba and "Come to New York" and vegetarian *chili*. I mean it really pisses me off so just *save* it.

Beat.

CLAIRE: (*Smoothly, to Hal*) I'm Claire. Catherine's sister.

HAL: Oh, hi. Hal. Nice to meet you. (*Uncomfortable beat.*) I . . . hope it's not   200
too early. I was just going to try to get some work done before the uh — if uh if . . .

CLAIRE: Yes!

CATHERINE: Sure, okay.

Hal exits. A moment.

CLAIRE: That's Harold Dobbs?

CATHERINE: Yes.

CLAIRE: He's cute.   205

CATHERINE: (*disgusted*) Eugh.

CLAIRE: He's a mathematician?

CATHERINE: I think you owe me an apology, Claire.

CLAIRE: We need to make some decisions. But I shouldn't have tried to start first thing in the morning. I don't want an argument. (*Beat.*) Maybe Hal would like a bagel?

Beat. Catherine doesn't take the hint. She exits.

Fade

SCENE 3

Night. Inside the house a party is in progress. Loud music from a not-very-good but enthusiastic band. Catherine is alone on the porch. She wears a flattering black dress. Inside, the band finishes a number. Cheers, applause. After a moment Hal comes out. He wears a dark suit. He has taken off his tie. He is sweaty and revved up from playing. He holds two bottles of beer. Catherine regards him. A beat.

CATHERINE: I feel that for a funeral reception this might have gotten a bit out of control.

HAL: Aw come on. It's great. Come on in.

CATHERINE: I'm okay.

HAL: We're done playing, I promise.

CATHERINE: No thanks.   5

HAL: Do you want a beer?

CATHERINE: I'm okay.

HAL: I brought you one.

Beat. Catherine hesitates.

CATHERINE: Okay. *(She takes it, sips.)* How many people are in there?
10 HAL: It's down to about forty.
CATHERINE: Forty?
HAL: Just the hardcore partyers.
CATHERINE: My sister's friends.
HAL: No, mathematicians. Your sister's friends left hours ago. The guys were
     really pleased to be asked to participate. They worshipped your dad.
15 CATHERINE: It was Claire's idea.
HAL: It was good.
CATHERINE: *(concedes)* The performance of "Imaginary Number" was . . . sort
     of . . . moving.
HAL: Good funeral. I mean not "good," but—
CATHERINE: No. Yeah.
20 HAL: Can you believe how many people came?
CATHERINE: I was surprised.
HAL: I think he would have liked it. *(Catherine looks at him.)* Sorry, it's not my
     place to—
CATHERINE: No, you're right. Everything was better than I thought.

Beat.

HAL: You look great.
25 CATHERINE: *(indicates the dress)* Claire gave it to me.
HAL: I like it.
CATHERINE: It doesn't really fit.
HAL: No, Catherine, it's good.

A moment. Noise from inside.

CATHERINE: When do you think they'll leave?
30 HAL: No way to know. Mathematicians are insane. I went to this conference
     in Toronto last fall. I'm young, right? I'm in shape, I thought I could
     hang with the big boys. Wrong. I've never been so exhausted in my life.
     Forty-eight straight hours of partying, drinking, drugs, papers, lectures . . .
CATHERINE: Drugs?
HAL: Yeah. Amphetamines mostly. I mean, I don't. Some of the older guys are
     really hooked.
CATHERINE: Really?
HAL: Yeah, they think they need it.
35 CATHERINE: Why?
HAL: They think math's a young man's game. Speed keeps them racing,
     makes them feel sharp. There's this fear that your creativity peaks around
     twenty-three and it's all downhill from there. Once you hit fifty it's over,
     you might as well teach high school.
CATHERINE: That's what my father thought.

HAL: I dunno. Some people stay prolific.

CATHERINE: Not many.

HAL: No, you're right. Really original work — it's all young guys.   40

CATHERINE: Young guys.

HAL: Young people.

CATHERINE: But it is men, mostly.

HAL: There are some women.

CATHERINE: Who?   45

HAL: There's a woman at Stanford, I can't remember her name.

CATHERINE: Sophie Germain.

HAL: Yeah? I've probably seen her at meetings, I just don't think I've met her.

CATHERINE: She was born in Paris in 1776.

Beat.

HAL: So I've definitely never met her.   50

CATHERINE: She was trapped in her house.

The French Revolution was going on, the Terror. She had to stay inside for safety and she passed the time reading in her father's study. The Greeks . . . Later she tried to get a real education but the schools didn't allow women. So she wrote letters. She wrote to Gauss. She used a man's name. Uh — Antoine-August Le Blanc. She sent him some proofs involving a certain kind of prime number, important work. He was delighted to correspond with such a brilliant young man. Dad gave me a book about her.

HAL: I'm stupid. Sophie Germain, of course.

CATHERINE: You know her?

HAL: Germain Primes.

CATHERINE: Right.   55

HAL: They're famous. Double them and add one, and you get another prime.

Like two. Two is prime, doubled plus one is five: also prime.

CATHERINE: Right. Or $92{,}305 \times 2^{16{,}998} + 1$.

HAL: *(startled)* Right.

CATHERINE: That's the biggest one. The biggest one known . . .

Beat.

HAL: Did he ever find out who she was? Gauss.   60

CATHERINE: Yeah. Later a mutual friend told him the brilliant young man was a woman.

He wrote to her: "A taste for the mysteries of numbers is excessively rare, but when a person of the sex which, according to our customs and prejudices, must encounter infinitely more difficulties than men to familiarize herself with these thorny researches, succeeds nevertheless in penetrating the most obscure parts of them, then without a doubt she must have the noblest courage, quite extraordinary talents, and superior genius."

(Now self-conscious.) I memorized it . . .

Hal stares at her. He suddenly kisses her, then stops, embarrassed. He moves away.

HAL: Sorry. I'm a little drunk.

CATHERINE: It's okay. (*Uncomfortable beat.*) I'm sorry about yesterday. I wasn't helpful. About the work you're doing. Take as long as you need upstairs.

65   HAL: You were fine. I was pushy.

CATHERINE: I was awful.

HAL: No. My timing was terrible. Anyway, you're probably right.

CATHERINE: What?

HAL: About it being junk.

70   CATHERINE: (*nods*) Yes.

HAL: I read through a lot of stuff today, just skimming. Except for the book I stole—

CATHERINE: Oh God, I'm sorry about that.

HAL: No, you were right.

CATHERINE: I shouldn't have called the police.

75   HAL: It was my fault.

CATHERINE: No.

HAL: The point is, that book—I'm starting to think it's the only lucid one, really. And there's no math in it.

CATHERINE: No.

HAL: I mean, I'll keep reading, but if I don't find anything in a couple of days . . .

CATHERINE: Back to the drums.

HAL: Yeah.

80   CATHERINE: And your own research.

HAL: Such as it is.

CATHERINE: What's wrong with it?

HAL: It's not exactly setting the world on fire.

CATHERINE: Oh come on.

85   HAL: It sucks, basically.

CATHERINE: Harold.

HAL: My papers get turned down. For the right reasons—my stuff is trivial. The big ideas aren't there.

CATHERINE: It's not about big ideas. It's work. You've got to chip away at a problem.

HAL: That's not what your dad did.

90   CATHERINE: I think it was, in a way. He'd attack a question from the side, from some weird angle, sneak up on it, grind away at it. He was slogging. He was just so much faster than anyone else that from the outside it looked magical.

HAL: I don't know.

CATHERINE: I'm just guessing.

HAL: Plus the work was beautiful. You can read it for pleasure. It's streamlined: no wasted moves, like a ninety-five-mile-an-hour fastball. It's just . . . elegant.

CATHERINE: Yeah.

HAL: And that's what you can never duplicate. At least I can't. It's okay.   95
At a certain point you realize it's not going to happen, you readjust your
expectations. I enjoy teaching.

CATHERINE: You might come up with something.

HAL: I'm twenty-eight, remember? On the downhill slope.

CATHERINE: Have you tried speed? I've heard it helps.

HAL: *(laughs)* Yeah.

Beat.

CATHERINE: So, Hal.   100

HAL: Yeah?

CATHERINE: What do you do for sex?

HAL: What?

CATHERINE: At your conferences.

HAL: Uh, I uh —   105

CATHERINE: Isn't that why people hold conferences? Travel. Room service.
Tax-deductible sex in big hotel beds.

HAL: *(laughs, nervous)* Maybe. I don't know.

CATHERINE: So what do you do? All you guys.

Beat. Is she flirting with him? Hal is not sure.

HAL: Well we are scientists.

CATHERINE: So?   110

HAL: So there's a lot of experimentation.

CATHERINE: *(laughs)* I see.

*Beat. Catherine goes to him. She kisses him. A longer kiss. It ends. Hal is surprised and
pleased.*

HAL: Huh.

CATHERINE: That was nice.

HAL: Really?   115

CATHERINE: Yes.

HAL: Again?

CATHERINE: Yes.

Kiss.

HAL: I always liked you.

CATHERINE: You did?   120

HAL: Even before I knew you. I'd catch glimpses of you when you visited your
dad's office at school. I wanted to talk to you, but I thought, No, you do not
flirt with your doctoral adviser's daughter.

CATHERINE: Especially when your adviser's crazy.

HAL: Especially then.

Kiss.

CATHERINE: You came here once. Four years ago. Remember?

125 **HAL:** Sure. I can't believe you do. I was dropping off a draft of my thesis for
your dad. Jesus I was nervous.
CATHERINE: You looked nervous.
HAL: I can't believe you remember that.
CATHERINE: I remember you. *(Kiss.)* I thought you seemed . . . not boring.

They continue to kiss.

Fade

SCENE 4

*The next morning. Catherine alone on the porch, in a robe. Hal enters, half-dressed.
He walks up behind her quietly. She hears him and turns.*

HAL: How long have you been up?
CATHERINE: A while.
HAL: Did I oversleep?
CATHERINE: No.

Beat. Morning-after awkwardness.

5 **HAL:** Is your sister up?
CATHERINE: No. She's flying home in a couple hours. I should probably
wake her.
HAL: Let her sleep. She was doing some pretty serious drinking with the
theoretical physicists last night.
CATHERINE: I'll make her some coffee when she gets up.

Beat.

HAL: Sunday mornings I usually go out. Get the paper, have some breakfast.
10 **CATHERINE:** Okay.

Beat.

HAL: Do you want to come?
CATHERINE: Oh. No. I ought to stick around until Claire leaves.
HAL: All right. Do you mind if I stay?
CATHERINE: No. You can work if you want.
15 **HAL:** *(Taken aback)* Okay.
CATHERINE: Okay.
HAL: Should I?
CATHERINE: If you want to.
HAL: Do you want me to go?
20 **CATHERINE:** Do you want to go?
HAL: I want to stay here with you.
CATHERINE: Oh . . .
HAL: I want to spend the day with you if possible. I'd like to spend as much
time with you as I can unless of course I'm coming on *way* too strong right
now and scaring you in which case I'll begin backpedaling immediately . . .

(*Catherine laughs. Her relief is evident; so is his. They kiss.*) How embarrassing is it if I say last night was wonderful?

CATHERINE: It's only embarrassing if I don't agree.

HAL: Uh, so . . .   25

CATHERINE: Don't be embarrassed. (*They kiss. After a moment she breaks off. She hesitates, making a decision. Then she takes a chain from around her neck. There is a key on the chain. She tosses it to Hal.*) Here.

HAL: What's this?

CATHERINE: It's a key.

HAL: Ah.

CATHERINE: Try it.   30

HAL: Where?

CATHERINE: Bottom drawer of the desk in my dad's office.

HAL: What's in there?

CATHERINE: There's one way to find out, Professor.

HAL: Now? (*Catherine shrugs. He laughs, unsure if this is a joke or not.*) Okay.   35

Hal kisses her quickly, then goes inside. Catherine smiles to herself. She is happy, on the edge of being giddy. Claire enters, hungover. She sits down, squinting.

CATHERINE: Good morning.

CLAIRE: Please don't yell please!

CATHERINE: Are you all right?

CLAIRE: No. (*Beat. She clutches her head.*) Those fucking physicists.

CATHERINE: What happened?   40

CLAIRE: Thanks a *lot* for leaving me all alone with them.

CATHERINE: Where were your friends?

CLAIRE: My stupid friends left — it was only eleven o'clock! — they all had to get home and pay their babysitters or bake bread or something. I'm left alone with these lunatics . . .

CATHERINE: Why did you drink so much?

CLAIRE: I thought I could keep up with them. I thought they'd stop. They   45
didn't. Oh God. "Have another tequila . . ."

CATHERINE: Do you want some coffee?

CLAIRE: In a minute. (*Beat.*) That *band.*

CATHERINE: Yeah.

CLAIRE: They were terrible.

CATHERINE: They were okay. They had fun. I think.   50

CLAIRE: Well as long as everyone had fun. (*Beat.*) Your dress turned out all right.

CATHERINE: I love it.

CLAIRE: You do.

CATHERINE: Yeah, it's wonderful.

CLAIRE: I was surprised you even wore it.   55

CATHERINE: I love it, Claire. Thanks.

CLAIRE: (*surprised*) You're welcome. You're in a good mood.

CATHERINE: Should I not be?

CLAIRE: Are you kidding? No. I'm thrilled. *(Beat.)* I'm leaving in a few hours.

60 CATHERINE: I know.

CLAIRE: The house is a wreck. Don't clean it up yourself. I'll hire someone to come in.

CATHERINE: Thanks. You want your coffee?

CLAIRE: No, thanks.

CATHERINE: *(starting in)* It's no trouble.

65 CLAIRE: Hold on a sec, Katie. I just . . . *(She takes a breath.)* I'm leaving soon. I—

CATHERINE: You said. I know.

CLAIRE: I'd still like you to come to New York.

CATHERINE: Yes: January.

CLAIRE: I'd like you to move to New York.

70 CATHERINE: Move?

CLAIRE: Would you think about it? For me? You could stay with me and Mitch at first. There's plenty of room. Then you could get your own place. I've already scouted some apartments for you, really cute places.

CATHERINE: What would I do in New York?

CLAIRE: What are you doing here?

CATHERINE: I live here.

75 CLAIRE: You could do whatever you want. You could work, you could go to school.

CATHERINE: I don't know, Claire. This is pretty major.

CLAIRE: I realize that.

CATHERINE: I know you mean well. I'm just not sure what I want to do. I mean to be honest you were right yesterday. I do feel a little confused. I'm tired. It's been a pretty weird couple of years. I think I'd like to take some time to figure things out.

CLAIRE: You could do that in New York.

80 CATHERINE: And I could do it here.

CLAIRE: But it would be much easier for me to get you set up in an apartment in New York, and—

CATHERINE: I don't need an apartment, I'll stay in the house.

CLAIRE: We're selling the house.

Beat.

CATHERINE: What?

85 CLAIRE: We — I'm selling it.

CATHERINE: *When?*

CLAIRE: I'm hoping to do the paperwork this week. I know it seems sudden.

CATHERINE: No one was here looking at the place, who are you selling it to?

CLAIRE: The university. They've wanted the block for years.

90 CATHERINE: *I live here.*

CLAIRE: Honey, now that Dad's gone it doesn't make sense. It's in bad shape. It costs a fortune to heat. It's time to let it go. Mitch agrees, it's a very smart move. We're lucky, we have a great offer—

CATHERINE: Where am I supposed to live?

CLAIRE: Come to New York.

CATHERINE: I can't believe this.

CLAIRE: It'll be so good. You deserve a change. This would be a whole new   95
adventure for you.

CATHERINE: Why are you doing this?

CLAIRE: I want to help.

CATHERINE: By kicking me out of my *house?*

CLAIRE: It was my house too.

CATHERINE: You haven't lived here for years.   100

CLAIRE: I know that. You were on your own. I really regret that, Katie.

CATHERINE: Don't.

CLAIRE: I know I let you down. I feel awful about it. Now I'm trying to help.

CATHERINE: You want to help *now?*

CLAIRE: Yes.   105

CATHERINE: Dad is dead.

CLAIRE: I know.

CATHERINE: He's dead. Now that he's dead you fly in for the weekend and
decide you want to help? *You're late.* Where have you been?

CLAIRE: I —

CATHERINE: Where were you five years ago? You weren't helping then.   110

CLAIRE: I was working.

CATHERINE: I was *here*. I lived with him *alone*.

CLAIRE: I was working fourteen-hour days. I paid every bill here. I paid off the
mortgage on this three-bedroom house while I was living in a studio in
Brooklyn.

CATHERINE: You had your life. You got to finish school.

CLAIRE: You could have stayed in school!   115

CATHERINE: How?

CLAIRE: I would have done anything — I told you that. I told you a million
times to do anything you wanted.

CATHERINE: What about Dad? Someone had to take care of him.

CLAIRE: He was ill. He should have been in a full-time professional-care
situation.

CATHERINE: He didn't belong in the nuthouse.   120

CLAIRE: He might have been better off.

CATHERINE: How can you say that?

CLAIRE: This is where I'm meant to feel guilty, right?

CATHERINE: Sure, go for it.

CLAIRE: I'm heartless. My own father.   125

CATHERINE: He needed to be here. In his own house, near the university, near
his students, near everything that made him happy.

CLAIRE: Maybe. Or maybe some real professional care would have done
him more good than rattling around in a filthy house with *you* looking
after him.
I'm sorry, Catherine, it's not your fault. It's my fault for letting you do it.

CATHERINE: I was right to keep him here.

CLAIRE: No.

130 CATHERINE: What about his remission? Four years ago. He was healthy for
almost a year.

CLAIRE: And then he went right downhill again.

CATHERINE: He might have been worse in a hospital.

CLAIRE: And he *might* have been *better*. Did he ever do any work again?

CATHERINE: No.

135 CLAIRE: *No. (Beat.)* And you might have been better.

CATHERINE: *(keeping her voice under control)* Better than what?

CLAIRE: Living here with him didn't do you any good. You said that yourself.
You had so much talent . . .

CATHERINE: You think I'm like Dad.

CLAIRE: I think you have some of his talent and some of his tendency
toward . . . instability.

Beat.

140 CATHERINE: Claire, in addition to the "cute apartments" that you've
"scouted" for me in New York, would you by any chance also have
devoted some of your considerable energies toward scouting out another
type of —

CLAIRE: *No.*

CATHERINE: —living facility for your bughouse little sister?

CLAIRE: *No!* Absolutely not. That is not what this is about.

CATHERINE: Don't lie to me, Claire. I'm smarter than you.

Beat.

145 CLAIRE: The resources . . . I've investigated —

CATHERINE: Oh my *God.*

CLAIRE: —if you *wanted* to, all I'm saying is, the doctors in New York and the
people are the *best*, and they —

CATHERINE: *Fuck you.*

CLAIRE: It would be entirely up to you. You wouldn't *live* anywhere, you can —

150 CATHERINE: I hate you.

CLAIRE: Don't yell, please. Calm down.

CATHERINE: *I hate you.* I —

Hal enters, holding a notebook. Claire and Catherine stop suddenly. Beat.

CLAIRE: What are you doing here? . . .

Claire stares at Catherine

HAL: How long have you known about this?

155 CATHERINE: A while.

HAL: Why didn't you tell me about it?

CATHERINE: I wasn't sure I wanted to.

Beat.

HAL: Thank you.

CATHERINE: You're welcome.

CLAIRE: What's going on? 160

HAL: God, Catherine, thank you.

CATHERINE: I thought you'd like to see it.

CLAIRE: What is it?

HAL: It's incredible.

CLAIRE: What *is* it? 165

HAL: Oh, uh, it's a result. A proof. I mean it looks like a proof. I mean it is a proof, a very long proof, I haven't read it all of course, or checked it, I don't even know if I *could* check it, but if it *is* a proof of what I think it's a proof of, it's . . . a very . . . *important* . . . proof.

CLAIRE: What does it prove?

HAL: It looks like it proves a theorem . . . a mathematical theorem about prime numbers, something mathematicians have been trying to prove since . . . since there were mathematicians, basically. Most people thought it couldn't be done.

CLAIRE: Where did you find it?

HAL: In your father's desk. Cathy told me about it. 170

CLAIRE: You know what this is?

CATHERINE: Sure.

CLAIRE: Is it good?

CATHERINE: Yes.

HAL: It's historic. If it checks out. 175

CLAIRE: What does it say?

HAL: I don't know yet. I've just read the first few pages.

CLAIRE: But what does it mean?

HAL: It means that during a time when everyone thought your dad was crazy . . . or barely functioning . . . he was doing some of the most important mathematics in the world. If it checks out, it means you publish instantly. It means newspapers all over the world are going to want to talk to the person who found this notebook.

CLAIRE: Cathy. 180

HAL: Cathy.

CATHERINE: I didn't find it.

HAL: Yes you did.

CATHERINE: No.

CLAIRE: Well did you find it or did Hal find it? 185

HAL: I didn't find it.

CATHERINE: I didn't find it.

I wrote it.

Curtain

ACT 2

SCENE 1

Robert is alone on the porch. He sits quietly, enjoying a drink, the quiet, the September afternoon. A notebook nearby, unopened. He closes his eyes, apparently dozing. It is four years earlier than the events in Act One. Catherine enters quietly. She stands behind her father for a moment.

ROBERT: Hello.

CATHERINE: How did you know I was here?

ROBERT: I heard you.

CATHERINE: I thought you were asleep.

5 ROBERT: On an afternoon like this? No.

CATHERINE: Do you need anything?

ROBERT: No.

CATHERINE: I'm going to the store.

ROBERT: What's for dinner?

10 CATHERINE: What do you want?

ROBERT: Not spaghetti.

CATHERINE: All right.

ROBERT: Disgusting stuff.

CATHERINE: That's what I was going to make.

15 ROBERT: I had a feeling. Good thing I spoke up. You make it too much.

CATHERINE: What do you want?

ROBERT: What do you have a taste for?

CATHERINE: Nothing.

ROBERT: Nothing at all?

20 CATHERINE: I don't care. I thought pasta would be easy.

ROBERT: Pasta, oh God, don't even say the word "pasta." It sounds so hopeless, like surrender: "Pasta would be easy." Yes, yes, it would. Pasta. It doesn't *mean* anything. It's just a euphemism people invented when they got sick of eating spaghetti.

CATHERINE: Dad, what do you want to eat?

ROBERT: I don't know.

CATHERINE: Well I don't know what to get.

25 ROBERT: I'll shop.

CATHERINE: No.

ROBERT: I'll do it.

CATHERINE: No, Dad, rest.

ROBERT: I wanted to take a walk anyway.

30 CATHERINE: Are you sure?

ROBERT: Yes. What about a walk to the lake? You and me.

CATHERINE: All right.

ROBERT: I would love to go to the lake. Then on the way home we'll stop at the store, see what jumps out at us.

CATHERINE: It's warm. It would be nice, if you're up for it.

ROBERT: You're damn right I'm up for it. We'll work up an appetite. Give me   35
ten seconds, let me put this stuff away and we're out the door.

CATHERINE: I'm going to school.

Beat.

ROBERT: When?

CATHERINE: I'm gonna start at Northwestern at the end of the month.

ROBERT: Northwestern?

CATHERINE: They were great about my credits. They're taking me in as a   40
sophomore. I wasn't sure when to talk to you about it.

ROBERT: Northwestern?

CATHERINE: Yes.

ROBERT: What's wrong with Chicago?

CATHERINE: You still teach there. I'm sorry, it's too weird, taking classes in
your department.

ROBERT: It's a long drive.   45

CATHERINE: Not that long, half an hour.

ROBERT: Still, twice a day . . .

CATHERINE: Dad, I'd live there.

Beat.

ROBERT: You'd actually want to live in Evanston?

CATHERINE: Yes. I'll still be close. I can come home whenever you want.   50
You've been well — really well — for almost seven months.
I don't think you need me here every minute of the day.

Beat.

ROBERT: This is all a done deal? You're in.

CATHERINE: Yes.

ROBERT: You're sure.

CATHERINE: Yes.

ROBERT: Who pays for it?   55

CATHERINE: They're giving me a free ride, Dad. They've been great.

ROBERT: On tuition, sure. What about food, books, clothes, gas, meals out —
do you plan to have a social life?

CATHERINE: I don't know.

ROBERT: You gotta pay your own way on dates, at least the early dates, say the
first three, otherwise they expect something.

CATHERINE: The money will be fine. Claire's gonna help out.   60

ROBERT: When did you talk to Claire?

CATHERINE: I don't know, a couple weeks ago.

ROBERT: You talk to her before you talk to me?

CATHERINE: There were a lot of details to work out. She was great, she offered
to take care of all the expenses.

ROBERT: This is a big step. A different *city*—   65

CATHERINE: It's not even a long-distance phone call.

ROBERT: It's a huge place. They're serious up there. I mean serious. Yeah the
football's a disaster but the math guys don't kid around. You haven't been in
school. You sure you're ready? You can get buried up there.

CATHERINE: I'll be all right.

ROBERT: You're way behind.

70 CATHERINE: I know.

ROBERT: A year, at least.

CATHERINE: Thank you, *I know*. Look, I don't know if this is a good idea.
I don't know if I can handle the work. I don't know if I can handle *any* of it.

ROBERT: For Chrissake, Catherine, you should have talked to me.

CATHERINE: Dad. Listen. If you ever . . . if for any reason it ever turned out
that you needed me here full-time again—

75 ROBERT: *I won't*. That's not—

CATHERINE: I can always take a semester off, or—

ROBERT: No. Stop it. I just — the end of the *month?* Why didn't you say
something before?

CATHERINE: Dad, come on. It took a while to set this up, and until recently,
until very recently, you weren't—

ROBERT: You just said yourself I've been fine.

80 CATHERINE: Yes, but I didn't know —*I hoped*, but I didn't *know*, no one knew
if this would last. I told myself to wait until I was sure about you. That you
were feeling okay again. Consistently okay.

ROBERT: So I'm to take this conversation as a vote of confidence? I'm
honored.

CATHERINE: Take it however you want. I believed you'd get better.

ROBERT: Well thank you very much.

CATHERINE: Don't thank me. I had to. I was living with you.

85 ROBERT: All right, that's enough, Catherine. Let's stay on the subject.

CATHERINE: This is the subject! There were *library books* upstairs stacked up
to the ceiling, do you remember that? You were trying to decode *messages*—

ROBERT: The fucking books are gone, I took them back myself. Why do you
bring that garbage up?

*Knocking offstage. Beat. Catherine goes inside to answer the door. She returns with
Hal. He carries a manila envelope. He is nervous.*

ROBERT: Mr. Dobbs.

HAL: Hi. I hope it's not a bad time.

90 ROBERT: Yes it is, actually, you couldn't have picked worse.

HAL: Oh, I uh—

ROBERT: You interrupted an argument.

HAL: I'm sorry. I can come back.

ROBERT: It's all right. We needed a break.

95 HAL: Are you sure?

ROBERT: Yes. The argument was about dinner. We don't know what to eat.
What's your suggestion?

A beat while Hal is on the spot.

HAL: Uh, there's a great pasta place not too far from here.
ROBERT: *No!*
CATHERINE: *(with Robert):* That is a *brilliant* idea.
ROBERT: Oh dear Jesus God, no.   100
CATHERINE: *(with Robert):* What's it called? Give me the address.
ROBERT: No! Sorry. Wrong answer, but thank you for trying.

Hal stands there, looking at both of them.

HAL: I can come back.
ROBERT: Stay. *(To Catherine.)* Where are you going?
CATHERINE: Inside.   105
ROBERT: What about dinner?
CATHERINE: What about him?
ROBERT: What are you doing here, Dobbs?
HAL: My timing sucks. I am really sorry.
ROBERT: Don't be silly.   110
HAL: I'll come to your office.
ROBERT: Stop. Sit down. Glad you're here. Don't let the dinner thing throw
    you, you'll bounce back. *(To Catherine.)* This should be easier. Let's back off
    the problem, let it breathe, come at it again when it's not looking.
CATHERINE: Fine. *(Exiting.)* Excuse me.
ROBERT: Sorry, I'm rude. Hal, this is my daughter Catherine. *(To Catherine.)*
    Don't go, have a drink with us. Catherine, Harold Dobbs.
CATHERINE: Hi.   115
HAL: Hi.
ROBERT: Hal is a grad student. He's doing his Ph.D., very promising stuff.
    Unfortunately for him, his work coincided with my return to the
    department and he got stuck with me.
HAL: No, no, it's been — I've been very lucky.
CATHERINE: How long have you been at U. of C.?
HAL: Well I've been working on my thesis for—   120
ROBERT: Hal's in our "Infinite" program. As he approaches completion of his
    dissertation, time approaches infinity. Would you like a drink, Hal?
HAL: Yes I would. And uh, with all due respect . . .

Hall hands Robert the envelope.

ROBERT: Really? *(He opens it and looks inside.)* You must have had an interest-
    ing few months.
HAL: *(cheerfully)* Worst summer of my life.
ROBERT: Congratulations.   125
HAL: It's just a draft. Based on everything we talked about last spring. *(Robert*
    pours a drink. Hal babbles.) I wasn't sure if I should wait till the quarter
    started, or if I should give it to you *now*, or hold off, do another draft, but
    I figured fuck it, I, I mean I just . . . let's just get it *over* with, so I thought I'd
    just come over and see if you were home, and—

ROBERT: Drink this.

HAL: Thanks. (*He drinks.*) I decided, I don't know, if it feels done, maybe
　　　it is.

ROBERT: Wrong. If it feels done, there are major errors.

130　HAL: Uh, I—

ROBERT: That's okay, that's good, we'll find them and fix them. Don't worry.
　　　You're on your way to a solid career, you'll be teaching younger, more
　　　irritating versions of yourself in no time.

HAL: Thank you.

ROBERT: Catherine's in the math department at Northwestern, Hal.

Catherine looks up, startled.

HAL: Oh, who are you working with?

135　CATHERINE: I'm just starting this fall. Undergrad.

ROBERT: She's starting in . . . three weeks?

CATHERINE: A little more.

Beat.

ROBERT: They have some good people at Northwestern. O'Donohue.
　　　Kaminsky.

CATHERINE: Yes.

140　ROBERT: They will work your ass off.

CATHERINE: I know.

ROBERT: You'll have to run pretty hard to catch up.

CATHERINE: I think I can do it.

ROBERT: Of course you can. (*Beat.*)

145　HAL: You must be excited.

CATHERINE: I am.

HAL: First year of school can be great.

CATHERINE: Yeah?

HAL: Sure, all the new people, new places, getting out of the house.

150　CATHERINE: (*Embarrassed*) Yes.

HAL: (*Embarrassed*) Or, no I—

ROBERT: Absolutely, getting the hell out of here, thank God, it's about time.
　　　I'll be glad to see the back of her.

CATHERINE: You will?

ROBERT: Of course. Maybe I want to have the place to myself for a while,
　　　did that ever occur to you? (*To Hal.*) It's awful the way children
　　　sentimentalize their parents. (*To Catherine.*) We could use some quiet
　　　around here.

155　CATHERINE: Oh don't worry, I'll come back. I'll be here every Sunday cooking
　　　up big vats of pasta to last you through the week.

ROBERT: And I'll drive up, strut around Evanston, embarrass you in front of
　　　your classmates.

CATHERINE: Good. So we'll be in touch.

ROBERT: Sure. And if you get stuck with a problem, give me a call.

CATHERINE: Okay. Same to you.

ROBERT: Fine. Make sure to get me your number. (*To Hal.*) I'm actually   160
looking forward to getting some work done.

HAL: Oh, what are you working on?

ROBERT: Nothing. (*Beat.*) Nothing at the moment.

Which I'm glad of, really. This is the time of year when you don't want
to be tied down to anything. You want to be outside. I love Chicago in
September. Perfect skies. Sailboats on the water. Cubs losing. Warm, the
sun still hot . . . with the occasional blast of Arctic wind to keep you on
your toes, remind you of winter. Students coming back, bookstores full,
everybody busy.

I was in a bookstore yesterday. Completely full, students buying books . . .
browsing . . . Students do a hell of a lot of browsing, don't they? Just
browsing. You see them shuffling around with their backpacks, goofing off,
taking up space. You'd call it loitering except every once in a while they
pick up a book and flip the pages: "browsing." I admire it. It's an honest
way to kill an afternoon. In the back of a used bookstore, or going through
a crate of somebody's old record albums — not looking for anything,
just looking, what the hell, touching the old book jackets, seeing what
somebody threw out, seeing what they underlined . . . Maybe you find
something great, like an old thriller with a painted cover from the forties,
or a textbook one of your professors used when *he* was a student — his
name is written in it very carefully . . . Yeah, I like it. I like watching the
students. Wondering what they're gonna buy, what they're gonna read.
What kind of ideas they'll come up with when they settle down and get
to work . . .

I'm not doing much right now. It does get harder. It's a stereotype that
happens to be true, unfortunately for me — unfortunately for you, for all
of us.

CATHERINE: Maybe you'll get lucky.

ROBERT: Maybe I will. Maybe you'll pick up where I left off.

CATHERINE: Don't hold your breath.   165

ROBERT: Don't underestimate yourself.

CATHERINE: Anyway.

Beat.

ROBERT: Another drink? Cathy? Hal?

CATHERINE: No thanks.

HAL: Thanks, I really should get going.   170

ROBERT: Are you sure?

HAL: Yes.

ROBERT: I'll call you when I've looked at this. Don't think about it till then.
Enjoy yourself, see some movies.

HAL: Okay.

ROBERT: You can come by my office in a week. Call it—   175

HAL: The eleventh?

ROBERT: Yes, we'll . . . (*Beat. He turns to Catherine. Grave*) I am sorry. I used to
have a pretty good memory for numbers. Happy birthday.

CATHERINE: Thank you.

ROBERT: I am so sorry. I'm embarrassed.

180   CATHERINE: Dad, don't be stupid.

ROBERT: I didn't get you anything.

CATHERINE: Don't worry about it.

ROBERT: I'm taking you out.

CATHERINE: You don't have to.

185   ROBERT: We are going out. I didn't want to shop and cook. Let's go to dinner.
Let's get the hell out of this neighborhood. What do you want to eat? Let's
go to the North Side. Or Chinatown. Or Greektown. I don't know what's
good anymore.

CATHERINE: Whatever you want.

ROBERT: Whatever *you* want goddamnit, Catherine, it's your birthday.

Beat.

CATHERINE: Steak.

ROBERT: Steak. Yes.

190   CATHERINE: No, first beer, really cold beer. Really cheap beer.

ROBERT: Done.

CATHERINE: That Chicago beer that's watery with no flavor and you can just
drink *gallons* of it.

ROBERT: They just pump the water out of Lake Michigan and bottle it.

CATHERINE: It's so awful.

195   ROBERT: I have a taste for it myself.

CATHERINE: Then the steak, grilled really black, and potatoes and creamed
spinach.

ROBERT: I remember a place. If it's still there I think it will do the trick.

CATHERINE: And dessert.

ROBERT: That goes without saying. It's your birthday, hooray. And there's the
solution to our dinner problem. Thank you for reminding me,
Harold Dobbs.

200   CATHERINE: (*To Hal.*) We're being rude. Do you want to come?

HAL: Oh, no, I shouldn't.

ROBERT: Why not? Please, come.

CATHERINE: Come on.

A tiny moment between Hal and Catherine. Hal wavers, then

HAL: No, I can't, I have plans. Thank you, though. Happy birthday.

205   CATHERINE: Thanks. Well. I'll let you out.

ROBERT: I'll see you on the eleventh, Hal.

HAL: Great.

CATHERINE: I'm gonna change my clothes, Dad. I'll be ready in a sec.

*Hal and Catherine exit. A moment. It's darker. Robert looks out at the evening.
Eventually he picks up the notebook and a pen. He sits down. He opens to a blank page.
He writes.*

ROBERT: "September fourth. A good day . . ." (*He continues to write.*)

Fade

SCENE 2

Morning. An instant after the end of Act One: Catherine, Claire, and Hal.

HAL: You wrote this?

CATHERINE: Yes.

CLAIRE: You mean Dad dictated it to you?

CATHERINE: No, its my proof. It's mine, I wrote it.

CLAIRE: When?   5

CATHERINE: I started after I quit school. I finished a few months before Dad died.

CLAIRE: Did he see it?

CATHERINE: No. He didn't know I was working on it. It wouldn't have mattered to him anyway, he was too sick.

HAL: I don't understand — you did this by yourself?

CATHERINE: Yes.   10

CLAIRE: It's in Dad's notebook.

CATHERINE: I used one of his blank books. There were a bunch of them upstairs.

Beat.

CLAIRE: (*To Hal.*) Tell me exactly where you found this.

HAL: In his study.

CATHERINE: In his desk. I gave him the —   15

CLAIRE: (*To Catherine.*) Hold on. (*To Hal.*) Where did you find it?

HAL: In the bottom drawer of the desk in the study, a locked drawer: Catherine gave me the key.

CLAIRE: Why was the drawer locked?

CATHERINE: It's mine, it's the drawer I keep my private things in. I've used it for years.

CLAIRE: (*To Hal.*) Was there anything else in the drawer?   20

HAL: No.

CATHERINE: No, that's the only —

CLAIRE: Can I see it? (*Hal gives Claire the book. She pages through it. Beat.*) I'm sorry, I just . . . (*To Catherine.*) The book was in the . . . You told him where to find it . . . You gave him the key . . . You wrote this incredible thing and you didn't *tell* anyone?

CATHERINE: I'm telling you both now. After I dropped out of school I had nothing to do. I was depressed, really depressed, but at a certain point I decided, Fuck it, I don't need them. It's just math, I can do it on my own. So I kept working here. I worked at night, after Dad had gone to sleep. It was hard but I did it.

Beat.

CLAIRE: Catherine, I'm sorry but I just find this very hard to believe.   25

CATHERINE: Claire. I wrote. The proof.

CLAIRE: I'm sorry, I —
CATHERINE: Claire . . .
CLAIRE: This is Dad's handwriting.
30   CATHERINE: It's not.
CLAIRE: It looks exactly like it.
CATHERINE: It's my writing.
CLAIRE: I'm sorry—
CATHERINE: Ask Hal, he's been looking at Dad's writing for weeks.

Claire gives Hal the book. He looks at it. Beat.

35   HAL: I don't know.
CATHERINE: Hal, come on.
CLAIRE: What does it look like?
HAL: It looks . . . I don't know what Catherine's handwriting looks like.
CATHERINE: It *looks* like *that.*
40   HAL: Okay. It . . . Okay. (*Beat. He hands the book back.*)
CLAIRE: I think — you know what? I think it's early, and people are tired and
   not in the best state to make decisions about emotional things, so maybe
   we should all just take a breath . . .
CATHERINE: You don't believe me?
CLAIRE: I don't know. I really don't know anything about this.
CATHERINE: Never mind. I don't know why I expected you to believe me
   about *anything.*
45   CLAIRE: Could you *tell* us the proof? That would show it was yours.
CATHERINE: You wouldn't understand it.
CLAIRE: Tell it to Hal.
CATHERINE: (*taking the book*) We could talk through it together. It might take
   a while.
CLAIRE: (*taking the book*) You can't use the book.
50   CATHERINE: For God's sake, it's forty pages long. I didn't *memorize* it. It's not a
   muffin recipe.
      This is stupid. It's my book, my writing, my key, my drawer, my proof.
   Hal, tell her!
HAL: Tell her what?
CATHERINE: Whose book is that?
HAL: I don't know.
CATHERINE: What is the matter with you? You've been looking at his other
   stuff, you know there's nothing even remotely like this!
55   HAL: Look, Catherine —
CATHERINE: We'll go through the proof together. We'll sit down — if Claire
   will *please* let me have my book back—
CLAIRE: (*giving her the book*) All right, talk him through it.
HAL: That might take days and it still wouldn't show that she wrote it.
CATHERINE: Why not?
60   HAL: Your dad might have written it and explained it to you later. I'm not
   saying he did, I'm just saying there's no proof that you wrote this.

CATHERINE: Of course there isn't, but come on! He didn't do this, he couldn't have. He didn't do any mathematics at all for years. Even in the good year he couldn't work: you *know* that. You're supposed to be a scientist.

Beat.

HAL: You're right. Okay. Here's my suggestion. I know three or four guys at the department, very sharp, disinterested people who knew your father, knew his work. Let me take this to them.

CATHERINE: What?

HAL: I'll tell them we've found something, something potentially major, we're not sure about the authorship; I'll sit down with them. We'll go through the thing carefully—

CLAIRE: Good.   65

HAL: —and figure out exactly what we've got. It would only take a couple of days, probably, and then we'd have a lot more information.

CLAIRE: I think that's an excellent suggestion.

CATHERINE: You can't.

CLAIRE: Catherine.

CATHERINE: No! You can't take it.   70

HAL: I'm not "taking" it.

CATHERINE: This is what you wanted.

HAL: Oh come on, Jesus.

CATHERINE: You don't waste any time, do you? No hesitation.
  You can't wait to show them your brilliant discovery.

HAL: I'm trying to determine what this is.   75

CATHERINE: I'm telling you what it is.

HAL: You don't know!

CATHERINE: *I wrote it.*

HAL: *It's your father's handwriting. (Beat. Pained.)* At least it looks an awful lot like the writing in the other books. Maybe your writing looks exactly like his, I don't know.

CATHERINE: *(softly)* It does look like his.
  I didn't show this to anyone else. I could have. I wanted you to be the first to see it. I didn't know I wanted that until last night. It's *me*. I trusted you.   80

HAL: I know.

CATHERINE: Was I wrong?

HAL: No. I—

CATHERINE: I should have known she wouldn't believe me but why don't you?

HAL: This is one of his notebooks. The exact same kind he used.   85

CATHERINE: I told you. I just used one of his blank books. There were extras.

HAL: There aren't any extra books in the study.

CATHERINE: There were when I started writing the proof. I bought them for him. He must have used the rest up later.

HAL: And the writing.

CATHERINE: You want to test the handwriting?   90

HAL: No. It doesn't matter. He could have dictated it to you for Chrissake. It still doesn't make sense.

CATHERINE: Why not?

HAL: I'm a mathematician.

CATHERINE: Yes.

95 **HAL:** I know how hard it would be to come up with something like this. I mean it's impossible. You'd have to be . . . you'd have to be your dad, basically. Your dad at the peak of his powers.

CATHERINE: I'm a mathematician too.

HAL: Not like your dad.

CATHERINE: Oh, he's the only one who could have done this?

HAL: The only one I know.

100 **CATHERINE:** Are you sure?

HAL: Your father was the most—

CATHERINE: Just because you and the rest of the geeks worshipped him doesn't mean he wrote this proof, Hal!

HAL: He was the *best*. My generation hasn't produced anything like him. He revolutionized the field twice before he was twenty-two. I'm sorry, Catherine, but you took some classes at Northwestern for a few months.

CATHERINE: My education wasn't at Northwestern. It was living in this house for twenty-five years.

105 **HAL:** Even so, it doesn't matter. This is too advanced. I don't even understand most of it.

CATHERINE: You think it's too advanced.

HAL: Yes.

CATHERINE: It's too advanced for *you*.

HAL: You could not have done this work.

110 **CATHERINE:** But what if I did?

HAL: Well what if?

CATHERINE: It would be a real disaster for you, wouldn't it? And for the other geeks who *barely* finished their Ph.D.'s, who are marking time doing *lame* research, bragging about the conferences they go to —*wow*— playing in an *awful* band, and whining that they're intellectually past it at twenty-eight, *because they are*.

Beat. Hal hesitates, then abruptly exits. Beat. Catherine is furious and so upset she looks dazed.

CLAIRE: Katie. Let's go inside. Katie?

Catherine opens the book, tries to rip out the pages, destroy it. Claire goes to take it from her. They struggle. Catherine gets the book away. They stand apart, breathing hard. After a moment, Catherine throws the book to the floor. She exits.

Fade

SCENE 3

The next day. The porch is empty. Knocking off. No one appears. After a moment Hal comes around the side of the porch and knocks on the back door.

HAL: Catherine?

Claire enters.

HAL: I thought you were leaving.
CLAIRE: I had to delay my flight.

Beat.

HAL: Is Catherine here?
CLAIRE: I don't think this is a good time, Hal.   5
HAL: Could I see her?
CLAIRE: Not now.
HAL: What's the matter?
CLAIRE: She's sleeping.
HAL: Can I wait here until she gets up?   10
CLAIRE: She's been sleeping since yesterday. She won't get up. She won't eat,
   won't talk to me. I couldn't go home. I'm going to wait until she seems okay
   to travel.
HAL: Jesus, I'm sorry.
CLAIRE: Yes.
HAL: I'd like to talk to her.
CLAIRE: I don't think that's a good idea.   15
HAL: Has she said anything?
CLAIRE: About you? No.
HAL: Yesterday . . . I know I didn't do what she wanted.
CLAIRE: Neither of us did.
HAL: I didn't know what to say. I feel awful.   20
CLAIRE: Why did you sleep with her?

Beat.

HAL: I'm sorry, that's none of your business.
CLAIRE: Bullshit. I have to take care of her. It's a little bit harder with you
   jerking her around.
HAL: I wasn't jerking her around. It just happened.
CLAIRE: Your timing was not great.   25
HAL: It wasn't *my* timing, it was *both* of our—
CLAIRE: Why'd you do it? You know what she's like. She's fragile and you took
   advantage of her.
HAL: No. It's what we both wanted. I didn't mean to hurt her.
CLAIRE: You did.
HAL: I'd like to talk to Catherine, please.   30
CLAIRE: You can't.
HAL: Are you taking her away?
CLAIRE: Yes.
HAL: To New York.
CLAIRE: Yes.   35
HAL: Just going to drag her to New York.

CLAIRE: If I have to.

HAL: Don't you think she should have some say in whether or not she goes?

CLAIRE: If she's not going to speak, what else can I do?

40 HAL: Let me try. Let me talk to her.

CLAIRE: Hal, give up. This has nothing to do with you.

HAL: I know her. She's tougher than you think, Claire.

CLAIRE: What?

HAL: She can handle herself. She can handle talking to me — maybe it would help. Maybe she'd like it.

45 CLAIRE: Maybe she'd *like* it? Are you out of your *mind?* You're the reason she's up there right now! You have *no idea* what she needs. You don't know her! She's my sister. Jesus, you fucking mathematicians: you *don't think.* You don't know what you're doing. You stagger around creating these catastrophes and it's people like me who end up flying in to clean them up. *(Beat.)* She needs to get out of Chicago, out of this house. I'll give you my number in New York. You can call her once she's settled there. That's it, that's the deal.

HAL: Okay. *(Beat. He doesn't move.)*

CLAIRE: I don't mean to be rude but I have a lot to do.

HAL: There's one more thing. You're not going to like it.

CLAIRE: Sure, take the notebook.

50 HAL: *(startled)* I —

CLAIRE: Hold on a sec, I'll get it for you. *(She goes inside and returns with the notebook. She gives it to Hal.)*

HAL: I thought this would be harder.

CLAIRE: Don't worry, I understand. It's very sweet you want to see Catherine but of course you'd like to see the notebook too.

HAL: *(Huffy)* It's — No, it's my responsibility — as a professional I can't turn my back on the necessity of the —

55 CLAIRE: Relax. I don't care. Take it. What would I do with it?

HAL: You sure?

CLAIRE: Yes, of course.

HAL: You trust me with this?

CLAIRE: Yes.

60 HAL: You just said I don't know what I'm doing.

CLAIRE: I think you're a little bit of an idiot but you're not dishonest. Someone needs to figure out what's in there. I can't do it. It should be done here, at Chicago: my father would like that. When you decide what we've got let me know what the family should do.

HAL: Thanks.

CLAIRE: Don't thank me, it's by far the most convenient option available. I put my card in there, call me whenever you want.

HAL: Okay.

Hal starts to exit. Claire hesitates, then

65 CLAIRE: Hal.

HAL: Yeah?

CLAIRE: Can you tell me about it? The proof. I'm just curious.
HAL: It would take some time. How much math have you got?

Beat.

CLAIRE: I'm a currency analyst. It helps to be very quick with numbers. I am.
I probably inherited about one one-thousandth of my father's ability. It's enough.
Catherine got more. I'm not sure how much.

Fade

SCENE 4

Winter. About three and a half years earlier. Robert is on the porch. He wears a T-shirt. He writes in a notebook. After a moment we hear Catherine's voice from offstage.

CATHERINE: Dad? (*She enters wearing a parka. She sees her father and stops.*)
What are you doing out here?
ROBERT: Working.
CATHERINE: It's December. It's thirty degrees.
ROBERT: I know.

Catherine stares at him, baffled.

CATHERINE: Don't you need a coat?   5
ROBERT: Don't you think I can make that assessment for myself?

Beat.

CATHERINE: Aren't you cold?
ROBERT: Of course I am! I'm freezing my ass off!
CATHERINE: So what are you *doing* out here?
ROBERT: Thinking! Writing!   10
CATHERINE: You're gonna freeze.
ROBERT: It's too hot in the house. The radiators dry out the air. Also the clanking — I can't concentrate. If the house weren't so old, we'd have central air heating, but we don't, so I have to come out here to get any work done.
CATHERINE: I'll turn off the radiators. They won't make any noise. Come inside, it isn't safe.
ROBERT: I'm okay.
CATHERINE: I've been calling. Didn't you hear the phone?   15
ROBERT: It's a distraction.
CATHERINE: I didn't know what was going on. I had to drive all the way down here.
ROBERT: I can see that.
CATHERINE: I had to skip class. (*She brings Robert a coat and he puts it on.*)
Why don't you answer the phone?
ROBERT: Well I'm sorry, Catherine, but it's a question of priorities, and work   20
takes priority, you know that.

CATHERINE: You're working?

ROBERT: Goddamnit, I am working! I say "I"—The machinery. The machinery is working. Catherine, it's on full-blast. All the cylinders are firing, I'm
on fire. That's why I came out here, to cool off. I haven't felt like this for
years.

CATHERINE: You're kidding.

ROBERT: No!

25   CATHERINE: I don't believe it.

ROBERT: I don't believe it either! But it's true. It started about a week ago. I
woke up, came downstairs, made a cup of coffee, and before I could pour in
the milk it was like someone turned the *light* on in my head.

CATHERINE: Really?

ROBERT: Not the light, the whole *power grid. I lit up,* and it's like no time has
passed since I was twenty-one.

CATHERINE: You're kidding!

30   ROBERT: No! I'm back! I'm back in touch with the source — the font, the —
whatever the source of my creativity was all those years ago. I'm in contact
with it again. I'm *sitting* on it. It's a geyser and I'm shooting right up into
the air on top of it.

CATHERINE: My God.

ROBERT: I'm not talking about divine inspiration. It's not funneling down into
my head and onto the page. It'll take *work* to shape these things; I'm not
saying it won't be a tremendous amount of work. It *will* be a tremendous
amount of work. It's not going to be easy. But the raw material is there. It's
like I've been driving in traffic and now the lanes are opening up before me
and I can *accelerate.* I see whole landscapes — places for the work to go,
new techniques, revolutionary possibilities. I'm going to get whole branches
of the profession talking to each other. I — I'm sorry, I'm being rude. How's
school?

CATHERINE: *(taken aback)* Fine.

ROBERT: You're working hard?

35   CATHERINE: Sure.

ROBERT: Faculty treating you all right?

CATHERINE: Yes. Dad—

ROBERT: Made any friends?

CATHERINE: Of course. I—

40   ROBERT: Dating?

CATHERINE: Dad, hold on.

ROBERT: No details necessary if you don't want to provide them. I'm just
interested.

CATHERINE: School's great. I want to talk about what you're doing.

ROBERT: Great, let's talk.

45   CATHERINE: This work.

ROBERT: Yes.

CATHERINE: *(indicating the notebooks)* Is it here?

ROBERT: Part of it, yes.

CATHERINE: Can I see it?

ROBERT: It's all at a very early stage.   50

CATHERINE: I don't mind.

ROBERT: Nothing's actually complete, to be honest. It's all in progress. I think
we're talking years.

CATHERINE: That's okay. I don't care. Just let me see anything.

ROBERT: You really want to?

CATHERINE: Yes.   55

ROBERT: You're genuinely interested.

CATHERINE: Dad, of course!

ROBERT: Of course. It's your field.

CATHERINE: Yes.

ROBERT: You know how happy that makes me.   60

Beat.

CATHERINE: Yes.

ROBERT: I think there's enough here to keep me working the rest of
my life.

Not just me.

I was starting to imagine I was finished, Catherine. Really finished. Don't
get me wrong, I was grateful I could go to my office, have a life, but secretly
I was terrified I'd never work again. Did you know that?

CATHERINE: I wondered.

ROBERT: I was absolutely fucking terrified.

Then I remembered something and a part of the terror went away.
I remembered you.

Your creative years were just beginning. You'd get your degree, do your
own work. You were just getting started. If you hadn't gone into math,
that would have been all right. Claire's done well for herself. I'm satisfied
with her.

I'm proud of you.

I don't mean to embarrass you. It's part of the reason we have children.
We hope they'll survive us, accomplish what we can't.

Now that I'm back in the game I admit I've got another idea, a
better one.

CATHERINE: What?   65

ROBERT: I know you've got your own work. I don't want you to neglect that.
You can't neglect it. But I could probably use some help. Work with me. If
you want to, if you can work it out with your class schedule and everything
else, I could help you with that, make some calls, talk to your teachers . . .

I'm getting ahead of myself.

Well, Jesus, look, enough bullshit. You asked to see something. Let's start
with this. I've roughed something out. General outline for a proof. Major
result. Important. It's not finished but you can see where it's going. Let's see.
(He selects a notebook.) Here. *(He gives it to Catherine. She opens it and
reads.)* It's very rough.

After a long moment Catherine closes the notebook. A beat. She sits down next to Robert.

CATHERINE: Dad. Let's go inside.

ROBERT: The gaps might make it hard to follow. We can talk it through.

CATHERINE: You're cold. Let's go in.

70 **ROBERT:** Maybe we could work on this together. This might be a great place to start. What about it? What do you think? Let's talk it through.

CATHERINE: Not now. I'm cold too. It's really freezing out here. Let's go inside.

ROBERT: I'm telling you it's stifling in there, goddamn it. The radiators. Look, read out the first couple of lines. That's how we start: you read, and we go line by line, out loud, through the argument. See if there's a better way, a shorter way. Let's collaborate.

CATHERINE: No. Come on.

ROBERT: I've been waiting years for this. This is something I want to do. Come on, let's do some work together.

75 **CATHERINE:** We can't do it out here. It's freezing cold. I'm taking you in.

ROBERT: Not until we *talk about the proof.*

CATHERINE: No.

ROBERT: *Goddamnit, Catherine, open the goddamn book and read me the lines.*

Beat. Catherine, opens the book. She reads slowly, without inflection.

CATHERINE: "Let X equal the quantity of all quantities of X. Let X equal the cold. It is cold in December. The months of cold equal November through February. There are four months of cold and four of heat, leaving four months of indeterminate temperature. In February it snows. In March the lake is a lake of ice. In September the students come back and the bookstores are full. Let X equal the month of full bookstores. The number of books approaches infinity as the number of months of cold approaches four. I will never be as cold now as I will in the future. The future of cold is infinite. The future of heat is the future of cold. The bookstores are infinite and so are never full except in September . . ." (*She stops reading and slowly closes the book. Robert is shivering uncontrollably. She puts her arms around him and helps him to his feet.*) It's all right. We'll go inside.

80 **ROBERT:** I'm cold.

CATHERINE: We'll warm you up.

ROBERT: Don't leave. Please.

CATHERINE: I won't. Let's go inside.

Fade

SCENE 5

The present. A week after the events in Scene 3. Claire on the porch. Coffee in takeout cups. Claire takes a plane ticket out of her purse, checks the itinerary. A moment. Catherine enters with bags for travel. Claire gives her a cup of coffee. Catherine drinks in silence. Beat.

CATHERINE: Good coffee.

CLAIRE: It's all right, isn't it? (*Beat.*) We have a place where we buy all our coffee. They roast it themselves, they have an old roaster down in the basement. You can smell it on the street. Some mornings you can smell it from
our place, four stories up. It's wonderful. "Manhattan's Best": some magazine
wrote it up. Who knows. But it is very good.

CATHERINE: Sounds good.

CLAIRE: You'll like it.

CATHERINE: Good.   5

Beat.

CLAIRE: You look nice.

CATHERINE: Thanks, so do you.

Beat.

CLAIRE: It's bright.

CATHERINE: Yes.

CLAIRE: It's one of the things I do miss. All the space, the light. You could sit   10
out here all morning.

CATHERINE: It's not that warm.

CLAIRE: Are you cold?

CATHERINE: Not really. I just —

CLAIRE: It has gotten chilly. I'm sorry. Do you want to go in?

CATHERINE: I'm okay.   15

CLAIRE: I just thought it might be nice to have a quick cup of coffee out here.

CATHERINE: No, it is.

CLAIRE: Plus the kitchen's all put away. If you're cold —

CATHERINE: I'm not. Not really.

CLAIRE: Want your jacket?   20

CATHERINE: Yeah, okay. (*Claire gives it to her. She puts it on.*) Thanks.

CLAIRE: It's that time of year.

CATHERINE: Yes. You can feel it coming. (*Beat. She stares out at the yard.*)

CLAIRE: Honey, there's no hurry.

CATHERINE: I know.   25

CLAIRE: If you want to hang out, be alone for a while —

CATHERINE: No. It's no big deal.

CLAIRE: We don't have to leave for twenty minutes or so.

CATHERINE: I know. Thanks, Claire.

CLAIRE: You're all packed.   30

CATHERINE: Yes.

CLAIRE: If you missed anything it doesn't really matter. The movers will send
us everything next month. (*Catherine doesn't move. Beat.*) I know this is
hard.

CATHERINE: It's fine.

CLAIRE: This is the right decision.

CATHERINE: I know . . .   35

CLAIRE: I want to do everything I can to make this a smooth transition for
you. So does Mitch.
CATHERINE: Good.
CLAIRE: The actual departure is the hardest part. Once we get there we can
relax. Enjoy ourselves.
CATHERINE: I know.

Beat.

40   CLAIRE: You'll love New York.
CATHERINE: I can't wait.
CLAIRE: You'll love it. It's the most exciting city.
CATHERINE: I know.
CLAIRE: It's not like Chicago, it's really alive.
45   CATHERINE: I've read about that.
CLAIRE: I think you'll truly feel at home there.
CATHERINE: You know what I'm looking forward to?
CLAIRE: What?
CATHERINE: Seeing Broadway musicals.

Beat.

50   CLAIRE: Mitch can get us tickets to whatever you'd like.
CATHERINE: And Rockefeller Center in winter — all the skaters!
CLAIRE: Well, you —
CATHERINE: Also, the many fine museums!

Beat.

CLAIRE: I know how hard this is for you.
55   CATHERINE: Listening to you say how hard it is for me is what's hard for me.
CLAIRE: Once you're there you'll see all the possibilities that are available.
CATHERINE: Restraints, lithium, electroshock.
CLAIRE: *Schools.* In the New York area alone there's NYU, Columbia—
CATHERINE: Bright college days! Football games, road trips, necking on the
"quad."
60   CLAIRE: Or if that's not what you want we can help you find a job. Mitch has
terrific contacts all over town.
CATHERINE: Does he know anyone in the phone-sex industry?
CLAIRE: I want to make this as easy a transition as I can.
CATHERINE: It's going to be *easy*, Claire, it's gonna be so fucking easy you
won't believe it.
CLAIRE: Thank you.
65   CATHERINE: I'm going to sit quietly on the plane to New York. And live quietly
in a cute apartment. And answer Dr. Von Heimlich's questions very politely.
CLAIRE: You can see any doctor you like, or you can see no doctor.
CATHERINE: I would like to see a doctor called Dr. Von Heimlich: please find
one. And I would like him to wear a monocle. And I'd like him to have a
very soft, very well-upholstered couch, so that I'll be perfectly comfortable
while I'm blaming everything on you.

Beat.

CLAIRE: Don't come.
CATHERINE: No, I'm coming.
CLAIRE: Stay here, see how you do.   70
CATHERINE: I could.
CLAIRE: You can't take care of yourself for *five days*.
CATHERINE: Bullshit!
CLAIRE: You *slept all week*. I had to cancel my flight. I missed a week of
    work — I was this close to taking you to the hospital! I couldn't believe it
    when you finally dragged yourself up.
CATHERINE: I was tired!   75
CLAIRE: You were completely out of it, Catherine, you weren't speaking!
CATHERINE: I didn't want to talk to you.

Beat.

CLAIRE: Stay here if you hate me so much.
CATHERINE: And do what?
CLAIRE: You're the genius, figure it out.   80

*Claire is upset, near tears. She digs in her bag, pulls out a plane ticket, throws it on the
table. She exits. Catherine is alone. She can't quite bring herself to leave the porch. A
moment. Hal enters — not through the house, from the side. He is badly dressed and
looks very tired. He is breathless from running.*

HAL: You're still here. (*Catherine is surprised. She doesn't speak.*) I saw Claire
    leaving out front. I wasn't sure if you —(*He holds up the notebook.*) This
    fucking thing . . . checks out.
        I have been over it, *twice*, with two different sets of guys, old geeks *and*
    young geeks. It is *weird*. I don't know where the techniques came from.
    Some of the moves are very hard to follow. But we can't find anything
    wrong with it! There might be something wrong with it but we can't find it.
    I have not slept. (*He catches his breath.*) It works. I thought you might want
    to know.
CATHERINE: I already knew.

Beat.

HAL: I had to swear these guys to secrecy. They were jumping out of their
    skins. See, one e-mail and it's all over. I threatened them. I think we're safe,
    they're physical cowards. (*Beat.*) I had to see you.
CATHERINE: I'm leaving.
HAL: I know. Just wait for a minute, please?   85
CATHERINE: What do you want? You have the book. She told me you came
    by for it and she gave it to you. You can do whatever you want with it.
    Publish it.
HAL: Catherine.
CATHERINE: Get Claire's permission and publish it. She doesn't care. She
    doesn't know anything about it anyway.

Hal: I don't want Claire's permission.

90   Catherine: You want mine? Publish. Go for it. Have a press conference. Tell the world what my father discovered.

Hal: I don't want to.

Catherine: Or fuck my father, pass it off as your own work. Who cares? Write your own ticket to any math department in the country.

Hal: I don't think your father wrote it.

Beat.

Catherine: You thought so last week.

95   Hal: That was last week. I spent this week reading the proof. I think I understand it, more or less. It uses a lot of newer mathematical techniques, things that were developed in the last decade. Elliptic curves. Modular forms. I think I learned more mathematics this week than I did in four years of grad school.

Catherine: So?

Hal: So the proof is very . . . hip.

Catherine: Get some sleep, Hal.

Hal: What was your father doing the last ten years? He wasn't well, was he?

100 Catherine: Are you done?

Hal: I don't think he would have been able to master those new techniques.

Catherine: But he was a genius.

Hal: But he was nuts.

Catherine: So he read about them later.

105 Hal: Maybe. The books he would have needed are upstairs.

Beat.

Your dad dated everything. Even his most incoherent entries he dated. There are no dates in this.

Catherine: The handwriting —

Hal: —looks like your dad's. Parents and children sometimes have similar handwriting, especially if they've spent a lot of time together.

Beat.

Catherine: Interesting theory.

Hal: I like it.

110 Catherine: I like it too. It's what I told you last week.

Hal: I know.

Catherine: You blew it.

Hal: I—

Catherine: It's too bad, the rest of it was really good. All of it: "I loved your dad." "I always liked you." "I'd like to spend every minute with you . . ." It's killer stuff. You got laid *and* you got the notebook! You're a genius!

115 Hal: You're giving me way too much credit. (*Beat.*) I don't expect you to be happy with me. I just wanted . . . I don't know. I was hoping to discuss some of this with you before you left. Purely professional. I don't expect anything else.

CATHERINE: Forget it.

HAL: I mean we have questions. Working on this must have been amazing. I'd love just to hear you talk about some of it.

CATHERINE: No.

HAL: You'll have to deal with it eventually, you know. You can't ignore it, you'll have to get it published. You'll have to talk to someone.

Take it, at least. Then I'll go. Here.

CATHERINE: I don't want it. 120

HAL: Come on, Catherine. I'm trying to correct things.

CATHERINE: You *can't*. Do you hear me?

You think you've figured something out? You run over here so pleased with yourself because you changed your mind. Now you're certain. You're so . . . *sloppy*. You don't know anything. The book, the math, the dates, the writing, all that stuff you decided with your buddies, it's just evidence. It doesn't finish the job. It doesn't prove anything.

HAL: Okay, what would?

CATHERINE: *Nothing*.

You should have trusted me.

Beat.

HAL: I know (*Beat. Catherine gathers her things.*) So Claire sold the house? 125

CATHERINE: Yes.

HAL: Stay in Chicago. You're an adult.

CATHERINE: She wants me in New York. She wants to look after me.

HAL: Do you need looking after?

CATHERINE: She thinks I do. 130

HAL: You looked after your dad for five years.

CATHERINE: So maybe it's my turn.

I kick and scream, but I don't know. Being taken care of, it doesn't sound so bad. I'm tired.

And the house is a wreck, let's face it. It was my dad's house . . .

Beat.

HAL: Nice house.

CATHERINE: It's old.

HAL: I guess. 135

CATHERINE: It's drafty as hell. The winters are rough.

HAL: That's just Chicago.

CATHERINE: Either it's freezing inside, or the steam's on full-blast and you're stifling.

HAL: I don't mind cold weather. Keeps you alert.

CATHERINE: Wait a few years. 140

HAL: I've lived here all my life.

CATHERINE: Yeah?

HAL: Sure. Just like you.

CATHERINE: Still. I don't think I should spend another winter here.

Beat.

145 HAL: There is nothing wrong with you.
CATHERINE: I think I'm like my dad.
HAL: I think you are too.
CATHERINE: I'm . . . *afraid* I'm like my dad.
HAL: You're not him.
150 CATHERINE: Maybe I will be.
HAL: Maybe. Maybe you'll be better.

Pause. Hal hands her the book. This time Catherine takes it. She sits. She looks down at the book, runs her fingers over the cover.

CATHERINE: It didn't feel "amazing" or — what word did you use?
HAL: Yeah, amazing.
CATHERINE: Yeah. It was just connecting the dots.
    Some nights I could connect three or four. Some nights they'd be really far apart, I'd have no idea how to get to the next one, if there was a next one.
155 HAL: He really never knew?
CATHERINE: No. I worked after midnight. He was usually in bed.
HAL: Every night?
CATHERINE: No. When I got stuck I watched TV. Sometimes if he couldn't sleep he'd come downstairs, sit with me. We'd talk. Not about math, he couldn't. About the movie we were watching. I'd explain the stories.
    Or about fixing the heat. Decide we didn't want to. We liked the radiators even though they clanked in the middle of the night, made the air dry.
    Or we'd plan breakfast, talk about what we were gonna eat together in the morning.
    Those nights were usually pretty good.
    I know . . . it works . . . But all I can see are the compromises, the approximations, places where it's stitched together. It's lumpy. Dad's stuff was way more elegant. When he was young.

Beat.

HAL: Talk me through it? Whatever's bothering you. Maybe you'll improve it.
160 CATHERINE: I don't know . . .
HAL: Pick anything. Give it a shot? Maybe you'll discover something elegant.

A moment, Hal sits next to Catherine. Eventually she opens the book, turns the pages slowly, finding a section. She looks at him.

CATHERINE: Here.

She begins to speak.

Curtain

Reading and Reacting

1. How are Catherine and her father alike? Why are their similarities important?

2. What role does the academic discipline of mathematics play in *Proof*? How would the play be different if Catherine and Robert shared another academic or professional interest instead of mathematics?

3. What does the following exchange from act 1, scene 1, reveal about Catherine and Robert?

> CATHERINE: By the time you were my age you were famous.
> ROBERT: By the time I was your age I'd already done my best work.

4. Robert had a mental breakdown when he was in his mid-twenties; now, Catherine is afraid the same thing is happening to her. Do you think her fears are justified? Why or why not?

5. What has Catherine given up for her father? Does she think her sacrifice has been worth it? Do you?

6. How do you interpret the play's title? Consider all its possible meanings.

7. Why do you think Hal doubts that Catherine could have written the proof? Could it be because he worships Robert? Because Catherine is so young? Because she has no reputation as a mathematician? Because she does not have a PhD? Because she is female? Because she has a family history of mental illness? Which of these explanations seems most likely? Which seems least likely? Why?

8. Is Claire essential to the play? Do you see her as a fully developed character or merely as a foil for Catherine?

9. Act 1 ends with Catherine announcing, "I wrote it." What stage directions would you write for this dramatic moment if you wanted to indicate Catherine's gestures, expression, and tone — and Hal's and Claire's reactions?

10. Which stereotypes about mathematicians does this play promote? Which does it challenge? For example, are Hal and his friends "typical" mathematicians? Is Robert? Is Catherine?

11. In act 1, scene 3, Hal explains why some mathematicians take amphetamines:

> They think math's a young man's game. Speed keeps them racing, makes them feel sharp. There's this fear that your creativity peaks around twenty-three and it's all downhill from there. Once you hit fifty it's over, you might as well teach high school.

In what way does this speech provide insight into the motivation of the three mathematicians in this play (Robert, Hal, and Catherine)?

12. What purpose does Catherine's story about Sophie Germain (act 1, scene 3) serve in the play?

13. In defiance of Catherine's wishes, Claire decides to sell the family home and gives the notebook to Hal. Do you think that either (or both) of these actions is justified?

14. Robert is dead when the play begins, yet he functions as a character who interacts with his daughter. Would the play have worked without him? Would it have been stronger? What, if anything, does his presence add?

15. What do you see as the central theme of this play? For example, is its focus on mathematics? Genius? Heredity? Family relationships? Professional rivalry? Feminism? Mental illness? Explain your choice.

16. Would you say *Proof* has a happy ending? Explain.

17. JOURNAL ENTRY Do you believe Catherine really wrote the proof? Why or why not?

18. CRITICAL PERSPECTIVE In his review of *Proof* for the *New York Times*, critic Bruce Weber discusses the play's characterizations of mathematicians:

> Without any baffling erudition—if you know what a prime number is, there won't be a single line of dialogue you find perplexing—the play presents mathematicians as both blessed and bedeviled by the gift for abstraction that ties them achingly to one another and separates them, also achingly, from concrete-minded folks like you and me. And perhaps most satisfying of all, it does so without a moment of meanness.

How are the play's characters "blessed" by mathematics? How are they "bedeviled" by it? How does mathematics unite them? How does it separate them from ordinary people?

Related Works: "Gryphon" (p. 248), "Doe Season" (p. 512), "Mathemaku # 10" (p. 827) "ABC" (p. 900), "My Son, My Executioner" (p. 961), "Do not go gentle into that good night" (p. 1065), *Trifles* (p. 1372)

ARTHUR MILLER (1915–2005) was born in New York City and graduated in 1938 from the University of Michigan, where he began to write plays. His first big success, which won the New York Drama Critics Circle Award, was *All My Sons* (1947), about a man who has knowingly manufactured faulty airplane parts during World War II. Other significant plays are *The Crucible* (1953), based on the Salem witch trials of 1692, which Miller saw as parallel to contemporary investigations by the House Un-American Activities Committee; *A View from the Bridge* (1955); and *After the Fall* (1955). He was married for a time to actress Marilyn Monroe and wrote the screenplay for her movie *The Misfits* (1961). His play *The Last Yankee* opened off-Broadway in 1993, *Broken Glass* was both published and performed in 1994, and *Mr. Peter's Connection* was published in 1998. In 2001, Miller was awarded an NEH fellowship and the John H. Finney Award for Exemplary Service to New York City.

Death of a Salesman is Miller's most significant work, a play that quickly became an American classic. Miller said he was very much influenced by the structure of Greek tragedy, and in his play he shows that a tragedy can also be the story of an ordinary person told in realistic terms. The play is frequently produced, and each production interprets it a bit differently. When Miller directed *Death of a Salesman* in China in 1983, audiences perceived it as primarily the story of the mother. In the 1983 Broadway production, Miller himself realized "at a certain point that it was far more the story of Biff, the son, than it was of Willy Loman, the salesman of the title."

> **Cultural Context** At the time *Death of a Salesman* was written in 1949, the United States was experiencing the largest economic expansion in its history. After World War II, soldiers returned home, women left the factory jobs they had held while men were at war, and consumer goods were developed and manufactured at exponential rates. As companies expanded and were consolidated, large, impersonal corporations began to replace the mom-and-pop businesses that had dominated the American scene. The foot soldiers of these corporations were the traveling salesmen who moved from town to town and covered large territories in a relentless effort to generate clients and sales. During the same period, the American suburbs began to appear, with a mass movement of population from older urban neighborhoods to massive housing developments such as those constructed in Levittown, Long Island, in 1946. It is against this background that the events of the play unfold.

Death of a Salesman (1949)
CERTAIN PRIVATE CONVERSATIONS IN TWO ACTS
AND A REQUIEM

CHARACTERS

Willy Loman	**The Woman**
Linda, *his wife*	**Howard Wagner**
Biff ⎫	**Jenny**
Happy ⎭ *his sons*	**Stanley**
Uncle Ben	**Miss Forsythe**
Charley	**Letta**
Bernard	

The action takes place in Willy Loman's house and yard and in various places he visits in the New York and Boston of today.

Throughout the play, in the stage directions, left and right mean stage left and stage right.

ACT 1

A melody is heard, played upon a flute. It is small and fine, telling of grass and trees and the horizon. The curtain rises.

Before us is the Salesman's house. We are aware of towering, angular shapes behind it, surrounding it on all sides. Only the blue light of the sky falls upon the house and forestage; the surrounding area shows an angry glow of orange. As more light appears, we see a solid vault of apartment houses around the small, fragile-seeming home. An air of the dream clings to the place, a dream rising out of reality. The kitchen at center seems actual enough, for there is a kitchen table with three chairs, and a refrigerator. But no other fixtures are seen. At the back of the kitchen there is a draped entrance, which leads to the living room. To the right of the kitchen, on a level raised two feet, is a bedroom furnished only with a brass bedstead and a straight chair. On a shelf over the bed a silver athletic trophy stands. A window opens onto the apartment house at the side.

Behind the kitchen, on a level raised six and a half feet, is the boys' bedroom, at present barely visible. Two beds are dimly seen, and at the back of the room a dormer window. (This bedroom is above the unseen living room.) At the left a stairway curves up to it from the kitchen.

The entire setting is wholly or, in some places, partially transparent. The roofline of the house is one-dimensional; under and over it we see the apartment buildings. Before the house lies an apron, curving beyond the forestage into the orchestra. This forward area serves as the back yard as well as the locale of all Willy's imaginings and of his city scenes. Whenever the action is in the present the actors observe the imaginary wall-lines, entering the house only through the door at the left. But in the scenes of the past these boundaries are broken, and characters enter or leave a room by stepping "through" a wall onto the forestage.

From the right, Willy Loman, the Salesman, enters, carrying two large sample cases. The flute plays on. He hears but is not aware of it. He is past sixty years of age, dressed quietly. Even as he crosses the stage to the doorway of the house, his exhaustion is apparent. He unlocks the door, comes into the kitchen, and thankfully lets his burden down, feeling the soreness of his palms. A word-sigh escapes his lips — it might be "Oh, boy, oh, boy." He closes the door, then carries his cases out into the living room, through the draped kitchen doorway.

Linda, his wife, has stirred in her bed at the right. She gets out and puts on a robe, listening. Most often jovial, she has developed an iron repression of her exceptions to Willy's behavior — she more than loves him, she admires him, as though his mercurial nature, his temper, his massive dreams and little cruelties, served her only as sharp reminders of the turbulent longings within him, longings which she shares but lacks the temperament to utter and follow to their end.

LINDA: *(hearing Willy outside the bedroom, calls with some trepidation)* Willy!

WILLY: It's all right. I came back.

LINDA: Why? What happened? *(Slight pause.)* Did something happen, Willy?

WILLY: No, nothing happened.

5 **LINDA:** You didn't smash the car, did you?

WILLY: *(with casual irritation)* I said nothing happened. Didn't you hear me?

LINDA: Don't you feel well?

WILLY: I am tired to the death. *(The flute has faded away. He sits on the bed beside her, a little numb.)* I couldn't make it. I just couldn't make it, Linda.

LINDA: *(very carefully, delicately)* Where were you all day? You look terrible.

10 **WILLY:** I got as far as a little above Yonkers. I stopped for a cup of coffee. Maybe it was the coffee.

LINDA: What?

WILLY: *(after a pause)* I suddenly couldn't drive any more. The car kept going onto the shoulder, y'know?

LINDA: *(helpfully)* Oh. Maybe it was the steering again. I don't think Angelo knows the Studebaker.

WILLY: No, it's me, it's me. Suddenly I realize I'm goin' sixty miles an hour and I don't remember the last five minutes. I'm — I can't seem to — keep my mind to it.

15 **LINDA:** Maybe it's your glasses. You never went for your new glasses.

WILLY: No, I see everything. I came back ten miles an hour. It took me nearly four hours from Yonkers.

LINDA: *(resigned)* Well, you'll just have to take a rest, Willy, you can't continue this way.

WILLY: I just got back from Florida.

LINDA: But you didn't rest your mind. Your mind is overactive, and the mind is what counts, dear.

WILLY: I'll start out in the morning. Maybe I'll feel better in the morning. *(She* 20 *is taking off his shoes.)* These goddam arch supports are killing me.

LINDA: Take an aspirin. Should I get you an aspirin? It'll soothe you.

WILLY: *(with wonder)* I was driving along, you understand? And I was fine. I was even observing the scenery. You can imagine, me looking at scenery, on the road every week of my life. But it's so beautiful up there, Linda, the trees are so thick, and the sun is warm. I opened the windshield and just let the warm air bathe over me. And then all of a sudden I'm goin' off the road! I'm tellin' ya, I absolutely forgot I was driving. If I'd've gone the other way over the white line I might've killed somebody. So I went on again — and five minutes later I'm dreamin' again, and I nearly — *(He presses two fingers against his eyes.)* I have such thoughts, I have such strange thoughts.

LINDA: Willy, dear. Talk to them again. There's no reason why you can't work in New York.

WILLY: They don't need me in New York. I'm the New England man. I'm vital in New England.

LINDA: But you're sixty years old. They can't expect you to keep traveling   25 every week.

WILLY: I'll have to send a wire to Portland. I'm supposed to see Brown and Morrison tomorrow morning at ten o'clock to show the line. Goddammit, I could sell them! *(He starts putting on his jacket.)*

LINDA: *(taking the jacket from him)* Why don't you go down to the place tomorrow and tell Howard you've simply got to work in New York? You're too accommodating, dear.

WILLY: If old man Wagner was alive I'd a been in charge of New York now! That man was a prince, he was a masterful man. But that boy of his, that Howard, he don't appreciate. When I went north the first time, the Wagner Company didn't know where New England was!

LINDA: Why don't you tell those things to Howard, dear?

WILLY: *(encouraged)* I will, I definitely will. Is there any cheese?   30

LINDA: I'll make you a sandwich.

WILLY: No, go to sleep. I'll take some milk. I'll be up right away. The boys in?

LINDA: They're sleeping. Happy took Biff on a date tonight.

WILLY: *(interested)* That so?

LINDA: It was so nice to see them shaving together, one behind the other, in   35 the bathroom. And going out together. You notice? The whole house smells of shaving lotion.

WILLY: Figure it out. Work a lifetime to pay off a house. You finally own it, and there's nobody to live in it.

LINDA: Well, dear, life is a casting off. It's always that way.

WILLY: No, no, some people — some people accomplish something. Did Biff say anything after I went this morning?

LINDA: You shouldn't have criticized him, Willy, especially after he just got off the train. You mustn't lose your temper with him.

40 WILLY: When the hell did I lose my temper? I simply asked him if he was making any money. Is that a criticism?

LINDA: But, dear, how could he make any money?

WILLY: (*worried and angered*) There's such an undercurrent in him. He became a moody man. Did he apologize when I left this morning?

LINDA: He was crestfallen, Willy. You know how he admires you. I think if he finds himself, then you'll both be happier and not fight any more.

WILLY: How can he find himself on a farm? Is that a life? A farmhand? In the beginning, when he was young, I thought, well, a young man, it's good for him to tramp around, take a lot of different jobs. But it's more than ten years now and he has yet to make thirty-five dollars a week!

45 LINDA: He's finding himself, Willy.

WILLY: Not finding yourself at the age of thirty-four is a disgrace!

LINDA: Shh!

WILLY: The trouble is he's lazy, goddammit!

LINDA: Willy, please!

50 WILLY: Biff is a lazy bum!

LINDA: They're sleeping. Get something to eat. Go on down.

WILLY: Why did he come home? I would like to know what brought him home.

LINDA: I don't know. I think he's still lost, Willy. I think he's very lost.

WILLY: Biff Loman is lost. In the greatest country in the world a young man with such — personal attractiveness, gets lost. And such a hard worker. There's one thing about Biff — he's not lazy.

55 LINDA: Never.

WILLY: (*with pity and resolve*) I'll see him in the morning; I'll have a nice talk with him. I'll get him a job selling. He could be big in no time. My God! Remember how they used to follow him around in high school? When he smiled at one of them their faces lit up. When he walked down the street . . . (*He loses himself in reminiscences.*)

LINDA: (*trying to bring him out of it*) Willy, dear, I got a new kind of American-type cheese today. It's whipped.

WILLY: Why do you get American when I like Swiss?

LINDA: I just thought you'd like a change —

60 WILLY: I don't want a change! I want Swiss cheese. Why am I always being contradicted?

LINDA: (*with a covering laugh*) I thought it would be a surprise.

WILLY: Why don't you open a window in here, for God's sake?

LINDA: (*with infinite patience*) They're all open, dear.

WILLY: The way they boxed us in here. Bricks and windows, windows and bricks.

65 LINDA: We should've bought the land next door.

WILLY: The street is lined with cars. There's not a breath of fresh air in the neighborhood. The grass don't grow any more, you can't raise a carrot in the back yard. They should've had a law against apartment houses. Remember those two beautiful elm trees out there? When I and Biff hung the swing between them?

LINDA: Yeah, like being a million miles from the city.

WILLY: They should've arrested the builder for cutting those down. They massacred the neighborhood. (*Lost.*) More and more I think of those days, Linda. This time of year it was lilac and wisteria. And then the peonies would come out, and the daffodils. What fragrance in this room!

LINDA: Well, after all, people had to move somewhere.

WILLY: No, there's more people now. 70

LINDA: I don't think there's more people. I think —

WILLY: There's more people! That's what's ruining this country! Population is getting out of control. The competition is maddening! Smell the stink from that apartment house! And another on the other side . . . How can they whip cheese?

On Willy's last line, Biff and Happy raise themselves up in their beds, listening.

LINDA: Go down, try it. And be quiet.

WILLY: (*turning to Linda, guiltily*) You're not worried about me, are you, sweetheart?

BIFF: What's the matter? 75

HAPPY: Listen!

LINDA: You've got too much on the ball to worry about.

WILLY: You're my foundation and my support, Linda.

LINDA: Just try to relax, dear. You make mountains out of molehills.

WILLY: I won't fight with him any more. If he wants to go back to Texas, let 80
him go.

LINDA: He'll find his way.

WILLY: Sure. Certain men just don't get started till later in life. Like Thomas Edison, I think. Or B. F. Goodrich. One of them was deaf. (*He starts for the bedroom doorway.*) I'll put my money on Biff.

LINDA: And Willy — if it's warm Sunday we'll drive in the country. And we'll open the windshield, and take lunch.

WILLY: No, the windshields don't open on the new cars.

LINDA: But you opened it today. 85

WILLY: Me? I didn't. (*He stops.*) Now isn't that peculiar! Isn't that remarkable —
(*He breaks off in amazement and fright as the flute is heard distantly.*)

LINDA: What, darling?

WILLY: That is the most remarkable thing.

LINDA: What, dear?

WILLY: I was thinking of the Chevvy. (*Slight pause.*) Nineteen twenty-eight . . . 90
when I had that red Chevvy — (*Breaks off.*) That funny? I coulda sworn
I was driving that Chevvy today.

LINDA: Well, that's nothing. Something must've reminded you.

WILLY: Remarkable. Ts. Remember those days? The way Biff used to simonize
that car? The dealer refused to believe there was eighty thousand miles on

it. (*He shakes his head.*) Heh! (*To Linda.*) Close your eyes, I'll be right up. (*He walks out of the bedroom.*)

HAPPY: (*to Biff*) Jesus, maybe he smashed up the car again!

LINDA: (*calling after Willy*) Be careful on the stairs, dear! The cheese is on the middle shelf! (*She turns, goes over to the bed, takes his jacket, and goes out of the bedroom.*)

Light has risen on the boys' room. Unseen, Willy is heard talking to himself, "Eighty thousand miles," and a little laugh. Biff gets out of bed, comes downstage a bit, and stands attentively. Biff is two years older than his brother Happy, well built, but in these days bears a worn air and seems less self-assured. He has succeeded less, and his dreams are stronger and less acceptable than Happy's. Happy is tall, powerfully made. Sexuality is like a visible color on him, or a scent that many women have discovered. He, like his brother, is lost, but in a different way, for he has never allowed himself to turn his face toward defeat and is thus more confused and hard-skinned, although seemingly more content.

95 **HAPPY:** (*getting out of bed*) He's going to get his license taken away if he keeps that up. I'm getting nervous about him, y'know, Biff?

BIFF: His eyes are going.

HAPPY: No, I've driven with him. He sees all right. He just doesn't keep his mind on it. I drove into the city with him last week. He stops at a green light and then it turns red and he goes. (*He laughs.*)

BIFF: Maybe he's color-blind.

Jo Mielziner's celebrated set for the premiere production of Arthur Miller's *Death of a Salesman,* starring Lee J. Cobb, showing the cut-away house and the downstage playing area.

HAPPY: Pop? Why he's got the finest eye for color in the business. You know that.

BIFF: *(sitting down on his bed)* I'm going to sleep. 100

HAPPY: You're not still sour on Dad, are you, Biff?

BIFF: He's all right, I guess.

WILLY: *(underneath them, in the living room)* Yes, sir, eighty thousand miles — eighty-two thousand!

BIFF: You smoking?

HAPPY: *(holding out a pack of cigarettes)* Want one? 105

BIFF: *(taking a cigarette)* I can never sleep when I smell it.

WILLY: What a simonizing job, heh!

HAPPY: *(with deep sentiment)* Funny, Biff, y'know? Us sleeping in here again? The old beds. *(He pats his bed affectionately.)* All the talk that went across those two beds, huh? Our whole lives.

BIFF: Yeah. Lotta dreams and plans.

HAPPY: *(with a deep and masculine laugh)* About five hundred women would 110 like to know what was said in this room.

They share a soft laugh.

BIFF: Remember that big Betsy something — what the hell was her name — over on Bushwick Avenue?

HAPPY: *(combing his hair)* With the collie dog!

BIFF: That's the one. I got you in there, remember?

HAPPY: Yeah, that was my first time — I think. Boy, there was a pig! *(They laugh, almost crudely.)* You taught me everything I know about women. Don't forget that.

BIFF: I bet you forgot how bashful you used to be. Especially with girls. 115

HAPPY: Oh, I still am, Biff.

BIFF: Oh, go on.

HAPPY: I just control it, that's all. I think I got less bashful and you got more so. What happened, Biff? Where's the old humor, the old confidence? *(He shakes Biff's knee. Biff gets up and moves restlessly about the room.)* What's the matter?

BIFF: Why does Dad mock me all the time?

HAPPY: He's not mocking you, he — 120

BIFF: Everything I say there's a twist of mockery on his face. I can't get near him.

HAPPY: He just wants you to make good, that's all. I wanted to talk to you about Dad for a long time, Biff. Something's — happening to him. He — talks to himself.

BIFF: I noticed that this morning. But he always mumbled.

HAPPY: But not so noticeable. It got so embarrassing I sent him to Florida. And you know something? Most of the time he's talking to you.

BIFF: What's he say about me? 125

HAPPY: I can't make it out.

BIFF: What's he say about me?

HAPPY: I think the fact that you're not settled, that you're still kind of up in the air . . .

BIFF: There's one or two other things depressing him, Happy.

130 **HAPPY:** What do you mean?

BIFF: Never mind. Just don't lay it all to me.

HAPPY: But I think if you just got started — I mean — is there any future for you out there?

BIFF: I tell ya, Hap, I don't know what the future is. I don't know — what I'm supposed to want.

HAPPY: What do you mean?

135 **BIFF:** Well, I spent six or seven years after high school trying to work myself up. Shipping clerk, salesman, business of one kind or another. And it's a measly manner of existence. To get on that subway on the hot mornings in summer. To devote your whole life to keeping stock, or making phone calls, or selling or buying. To suffer fifty weeks of the year for the sake of a two-week vacation, when all you really desire is to be outdoors, with your shirt off. And always to have to get ahead of the next fella. And still — that's how you build a future.

HAPPY: Well, you really enjoy it on a farm? Are you content out there?

BIFF: *(with rising agitation)* Hap, I've had twenty or thirty different kinds of jobs since I left home before the war, and it always turns out the same. I just realized it lately. In Nebraska when I herded cattle, and the Dakotas, and Arizona, and now in Texas. It's why I came home now, I guess, because I realized it. This farm I work on, it's spring there now, see? And they've got about fifteen new colts. There's nothing more inspiring or — beautiful than the sight of a mare and a new colt. And it's cool there now, see? Texas is cool now, and it's spring. And whenever spring comes to where I am, I suddenly get the feeling, my God, I'm not gettin' anywhere! What the hell am I doing, playing around with horses, twenty-eight dollars a week! I'm thirty-four years old, I oughta be makin' my future. That's when I come running home. And now, I get here, and I don't know what to do with myself. *(After a pause.)* I've always made a point of not wasting my life, and every time I come back here I know that all I've done is to waste my life.

HAPPY: You're a poet, you know that, Biff? You're a — you're an idealist!

BIFF: No, I'm mixed up very bad. Maybe I oughta get married. Maybe I oughta get stuck into something. Maybe that's my trouble. I'm like a boy. I'm not married, I'm not in business, I just — I'm like a boy. Are you content, Hap? You're a success, aren't you? Are you content?

140 **HAPPY:** Hell, no!

BIFF: Why? You're making money, aren't you?

HAPPY: *(moving about with energy, expressiveness)* All I can do now is wait for the merchandise manager to die. And suppose I get to be merchandise manager? He's a good friend of mine, and he just built a terrific estate on Long Island. And he lived there about two months and sold it, and now he's building another one. He can't enjoy it once it's finished. And I know that's just what I would do. I don't know what the hell I'm workin' for. Sometimes I sit in my apartment — all alone. And I think of the rent I'm paying. And it's crazy. But then, it's what I always wanted. My own apartment, a car, and plenty of women. And still, goddammit, I'm lonely.

BIFF: *(with enthusiasm)* Listen, why don't you come out West with me?

HAPPY: You and I, heh?

BIFF: Sure, maybe we could buy a ranch. Raise cattle, use our muscles. Men   145
built like we are should be working out in the open.

HAPPY: *(avidly)* The Loman Brothers, heh?

BIFF: *(with vast affection)* Sure, we'd be known all over the counties!

HAPPY: *(enthralled)* That's what I dream about, Biff. Sometimes I want to just
rip my clothes off in the middle of the store and outbox that goddam merchandise manager. I mean I can outbox, outrun, and outlift anybody in that
store, and I have to take orders from those common, petty sons-of-bitches
till I can't stand it any more.

BIFF: I'm telln' you, kid, if you were with me I'd be happy out there.

HAPPY: *(enthused)* See, Biff, everybody around me is so false that I'm   150
constantly lowering my ideals . . .

BIFF: Baby, together we'd stand up for one another, we'd have someone to trust.

HAPPY: If I were around you —

BIFF: Hap, the trouble is we weren't brought up to grub for money. I don't know
how to do it.

HAPPY: Neither can I!

BIFF: Then let's go!   155

HAPPY: The only thing is — what can you make out there?

BIFF: But look at your friend. Builds an estate and then hasn't the peace of
mind to live in it.

HAPPY: Yeah, but when he walks into the store the waves part in front of him.
That's fifty-two thousand dollars a year coming through the revolving door,
and I got more in my pinky finger than he's got in his head.

BIFF: Yeah, but you just said —

HAPPY: I gotta show some of those pompous, self-important executives over   160
there that Hap Loman can make the grade. I want to walk into the store
the way he walks in. Then I'll go with you, Biff. We'll be together yet, I
swear. But take those two we had tonight. Now weren't they gorgeous
creatures?

BIFF: Yeah, yeah, most gorgeous I've had in years.

HAPPY: I get that any time I want, Biff. Whenever I feel disgusted. The only
trouble is, it gets like bowling or something. I just keep knockin' them over
and it doesn't mean anything. You still run around a lot?

BIFF: Naa. I'd like to find a girl — steady, somebody with substance.

HAPPY: That's what I long for.

BIFF: Go on! You'd never come home.   165

HAPPY: I would! Somebody with character, with resistance! Like Mom,
y'know? You're gonna call me a bastard when I tell you this. That girl
Charlotte I was with tonight is engaged to be married in five weeks.
(He tries on his new hat.)

BIFF: No kiddin'!

HAPPY: Sure, the guy's in line for the vice-presidency of the store. I don't know
what gets into me, maybe I just have an overdeveloped sense of competition or something, but I went and ruined her, and furthermore I can't get

rid of her. And he's the third executive I've done that to. Isn't that a crummy characteristic? And to top it all, I go to their weddings! (*Indignantly, but laughing.*) Like I'm not supposed to take bribes. Manufacturers offer me a hundred-dollar bill now and then to throw an order their way. You know how honest I am, but it's like this girl, see. I hate myself for it. Because I don't want the girl, and, still, I take it and — I love it!

Biff: Let's go to sleep.

170 **Happy:** I guess we didn't settle anything, heh?

Biff: I just got one idea that I think I'm going to try.

Happy: What's that?

Biff: Remember Bill Oliver?

Happy: Sure, Oliver is very big now. You want to work for him again?

175 **Biff:** No, but when I quit he said something to me. He put his arm on my shoulder, and he said, "Biff, if you ever need anything, come to me."

Happy: I remember that. That sounds good.

Biff: I think I'll go to see him. If I could get ten thousand or even seven or eight thousand dollars I could buy a beautiful ranch.

Happy: I bet he'd back you. 'Cause he thought highly of you, Biff, I mean, they all do. You're well liked, Biff. That's why I say to come back here, and we both have the apartment. And I'm tellin' you, Biff, any babe you want . . .

Biff: No, with a ranch I could do the work I like and still be something. I just wonder though. I wonder if Oliver still thinks I stole that carton of basketballs.

180 **Happy:** Oh, he probably forgot that long ago. It's almost ten years. You're too sensitive. Anyway, he didn't really fire you.

Biff: Well, I think he was going to. I think that's why I quit. I was never sure whether he knew or not. I know he thought the world of me, though. I was the only one he'd let lock up the place.

Willy: (*below*) You gonna wash the engine, Biff?

Happy: Shh!

Biff looks at Happy, who is gazing down, listening. Willy is mumbling in the parlor.

Happy: You hear that?

They listen. Willy laughs warmly.

185 **Biff:** (*growing angry*) Doesn't he know Mom can hear that?

Willy: Don't get your sweater dirty, Biff!

A look of pain crosses Biff's face.

Happy: Isn't that terrible? Don't leave again, will you? You'll find a job here. You gotta stick around. I don't know what to do about him, it's getting embarrassing.

Willy: What a simonizing job!

Biff: Mom's hearing that!

190 **Willy:** No kiddin', Biff, you got a date? Wonderful!

Happy: Go on to sleep. But talk to him in the morning, will you?

BIFF: (*reluctantly getting into bed*) With her in the house. Brother!

HAPPY: (*getting into bed*) I wish you'd have a good talk with him.

The light on their room begins to fade.

BIFF: (*to himself in bed*) That selfish, stupid . . .

HAPPY: Sh . . . Sleep, Biff.

195

Their light is out. Well before they have finished speaking, Willy's form is dimly seen below in the darkened kitchen. He opens the refrigerator, searches in there, and takes out a bottle of milk. The apartment houses are fading out, and the entire house and surroundings become covered with leaves. Music insinuates itself as the leaves appear.

WILLY: Just wanna be careful with those girls, Biff, that's all. Don't make any promises. No promises of any kind. Because a girl, y'know, they always believe what you tell'em, and you're very young, Biff, you're too young to be talking seriously to girls.

Light rises on the kitchen. Willy, talking, shuts the refrigerator door and comes downstage to the kitchen table. He pours milk into a glass. He is totally immersed in himself, smiling faintly.

WILLY: Too young entirely, Biff. You want to watch your schooling first. Then when you're all set, there'll be plenty of girls for a boy like you. (*He smiles broadly at a kitchen chair.*) That so? The girls pay for you? (*He laughs.*) Boy, you must really be makin' a hit.

Willy is gradually addressing — physically — a point offstage, speaking through the wall of the kitchen, and his voice has been rising in volume to that of a normal conversation.

WILLY: I been wondering why you polish the car so careful. Ha! Don't leave the hubcaps, boys. Get the chamois to the hubcaps. Happy, use newspaper on the windows, it's the easiest thing. Show him how to do it, Biff! You see, Happy? Pad it up, use it like a pad. That's it, that's it, good work. You're doin' all right, Hap. (*He pauses, then nods in approbation for a few seconds, then looks upward.*) Biff, first thing we gotta do when we get time is clip that big branch over the house. Afraid it's gonna fall in a storm and hit the roof. Tell you what. We get a rope and sling her around, and then we climb up there with a couple of saws and take her down. Soon as you finish the car, boys, I wanna see ya. I got a surprise for you, boys.

BIFF: (*offstage*) Whatta ya got, Dad?

WILLY: No, you finish first. Never leave a job till you're finished — remember that. (*Looking toward the "big trees."*) Biff, up in Albany I saw a beautiful hammock. I think I'll buy it next trip, and we'll hang it right between those two elms. Wouldn't that be something? Just swingin' there under those branches. Boy, that would be . . .

200

Young Biff and Young Happy appear from the direction Willy was addressing. Happy carries rags and a pail of water. Biff, wearing a sweater with a block "S," carries a football.

BIFF: (*pointing in the direction of the car offstage*) How's that, Pop, professional?

WILLY: Terrific. Terrific job, boys. Good work, Biff.

HAPPY: Where's the surprise, Pop?

WILLY: In the back seat of the car.

205 HAPPY: Boy! (*He runs off.*)

BIFF: What is it, Dad? Tell me, what'd you buy?

WILLY: (*laughing, cuffs him*) Never mind, something I want you to have.

BIFF: (*turns and starts off*) What is it, Hap?

HAPPY: (*offstage*) It's a punching bag!

210 BIFF: Oh, Pop!

WILLY: It's got Gene Tunney's° signature on it!

Happy runs onstage with a punching bag.

BIFF: Gee, how'd you know we wanted a punching bag?

WILLY: Well, it's the finest thing for the timing.

HAPPY: (*lies down on his back and pedals with his feet*) I'm losing weight, you
notice, Pop?

215 WILLY: (*to Happy*) Jumping rope is good too.

BIFF: Did you see the new football I got?

WILLY: (*examining the ball*) Where'd you get a new ball?

BIFF: The coach told me to practice my passing.

WILLY: That so? And he gave you the ball, heh?

220 BIFF: Well, I borrowed it from the locker room. (*He laughs confidentially.*)

WILLY: (*laughing with him at the theft*) I want you to return that.

HAPPY: I told you he wouldn't like it!

BIFF: (*angrily*) Well, I'm bringing it back!

WILLY: (*stopping the incipient argument, to Happy*) Sure, he's gotta practice with
a regulation ball, doesn't he? (*To Biff.*) Coach'll probably congratulate you
on your initiative!

225 BIFF: Oh, he keeps congratulating my initiative all the time, Pop.

WILLY: That's because he likes you. If somebody else took that ball there'd be
an uproar. So what's the report, boys, what's the report?

BIFF: Where'd you go this time, Dad? Gee we were lonesome for you.

WILLY: (*pleased, puts an arm around each boy and they come down to the apron*)
Lonesome, heh?

BIFF: Missed you every minute.

230 WILLY: Don't say? Tell you a secret, boys. Don't breathe it to a soul. Someday
I'll have my own business, and I'll never have to leave home any more.

HAPPY: Like Uncle Charley, heh?

WILLY: Bigger than Uncle Charley! Because Charley is not —liked. He's liked,
but he's not — well liked.

BIFF: Where'd you go this time, Dad?

WILLY: Well, I got on the road, and I went north to Providence. Met the Mayor.

°*Gene Tunney's:* James Joseph ("Gene") Tunney (1897–1978)—American boxer, world heavyweight champion
from his defeat of Jack Dempsey in 1926 until his retirement in 1928.

BIFF: The Mayor of Providence! 235

WILLY: He was sitting in the hotel lobby.

BIFF: What'd he say?

WILLY: He said, "Morning!" And I said, "You've got a fine city here, Mayor." And then he had coffee with me. And then I went to Waterbury. Waterbury is a fine city. Big clock city, the famous Waterbury clock. Sold a nice bill there. And then Boston — Boston is the cradle of the Revolution. A fine city. And a couple of other towns in Mass., and on to Portland and Bangor and straight home!

BIFF: Gee, I'd love to go with you sometime, Dad.

WILLY: Soon as summer comes. 240

HAPPY: Promise?

WILLY: You and Hap and I, and I'll show you all the towns. America is full of beautiful towns and fine, upstanding people. And they know me, boys, they know me up and down New England. The finest people. And when I bring you fellas up, there'll be open sesame for all of us, 'cause one thing, boys: I have friends. I can park my car in any street in New England, and the cops protect it like their own. This summer, heh?

BIFF AND HAPPY: (*together*) Yeah! You bet!

WILLY: We'll take our bathing suits.

HAPPY: We'll carry your bags, Pop! 245

WILLY: Oh, won't that be something! Me comin' into the Boston store with you boys carryin' my bags. What a sensation!

Biff is prancing around, practicing passing the ball.

WILLY: You nervous, Biff, about the game?

BIFF: Not if you're gonna be there.

WILLY: What do they say about you in school, now that they made you captain?

HAPPY: There's a crowd of girls behind him everytime the classes change. 250

BIFF: (*taking Willy's hand*) This Saturday, Pop, this Saturday — just for you, I'm going to break through for a touchdown.

HAPPY: You're supposed to pass.

BIFF: I'm takin' one play for Pop. You watch me, Pop, and when I take off my helmet, that means I'm breakin' out. Then you watch me crash through that line!

WILLY: (*kisses Biff*) Oh, wait'll I tell this in Boston!

Bernard enters in knickers. He is younger than Biff, earnest and loyal, a worried boy.

BERNARD: Biff, where are you? You're supposed to study with me today. 255

WILLY: Hey, looka Bernard. What're you lookin' so anemic about, Bernard?

BERNARD: He's gotta study, Uncle Willy. He's got Regents next week.

HAPPY: (*tauntingly, spinning Bernard around*) Let's box, Bernard!

BERNARD: Biff! (*He gets away from Happy.*) Listen, Biff, I heard Mr. Birnbaum say that if you don't start studyin' math he's gonna flunk you, and you won't graduate. I heard him!

WILLY: You better study with him, Biff. Go ahead now. 260

BERNARD: I heard him!

BIFF: Oh, Pop, you didn't see my sneakers! (*He holds up a foot for Willy to look at.*)

WILLY: Hey, that's a beautiful job of printing!

BERNARD: (*wiping his glasses*) Just because he printed University of Virginia on his sneakers doesn't mean they've got to graduate him, Uncle Willy!

265 **WILLY:** (*angrily*) What're you talking about? With scholarships to three universities they're gonna flunk him?

BERNARD: But I heard Mr. Birnbaum say —

WILLY: Don't be a pest, Bernard! (*To his boys.*) What an anemic!

BERNARD: Okay, I'm waiting for you in my house, Biff.

Bernard goes off. The Lomans laugh.

WILLY: Bernard is not well liked, is he?

270 **BIFF:** He's liked, but he's not well liked.

HAPPY: That's right, Pop.

WILLY: That's just what I mean. Bernard can get the best marks in school, y'understand, but when he gets out in the business world, y'understand, you are going to be five times ahead of him. That's why I thank Almighty God you're both built like Adonises. Because the man who makes an appearance in the business world, the man who creates personal interest, is the man who gets ahead. Be liked and you will never want. You take me, for instance. I never have to wait in line to see a buyer. "Willy Loman is here!" That's all they have to know, and I go right through.

BIFF: Did you knock them dead, Pop?

WILLY: Knocked 'em cold in Providence, slaughtered 'em in Boston.

275 **HAPPY:** (*on his back, pedaling again*) I'm losing weight, you notice, Pop?

Linda enters, as of old, a ribbon in her hair, carrying a basket of washing.

LINDA: (*with youthful energy*) Hello, dear!

WILLY: Sweetheart!

LINDA: How'd the Chevvy run?

WILLY: Chevrolet, Linda, is the greatest car ever built. (*To the boys.*) Since when do you let your mother carry wash up the stairs?

280 **BIFF:** Grab hold there, boy!

HAPPY: Where to, Mom?

LINDA: Hang them up on the line. And you better go down to your friends, Biff. The cellar is full of boys. They don't know what to do with themselves.

BIFF: Ah, when Pop comes home they can wait!

WILLY: (*laughs appreciatively*) You better go down and tell them what to do, Biff.

285 **BIFF:** I think I'll have them sweep out the furnace room.

WILLY: Good work, Biff.

BIFF: (*goes through wall-line of kitchen to doorway at back and calls down*) Fellas! Everybody sweep out the furnace room! I'll be right down!

VOICES: All right! Okay, Biff.

BIFF: George and Sam and Frank, come out back! We're hangin' up the wash! Come on, Hap, on the double! (*He and Happy carry out the basket.*)

LINDA: The way they obey him!   290

WILLY: Well, that's training, the training. I'm tellin' you, I was sellin' thousands and thousands, but I had to come home.

LINDA: Oh, the whole block'll be at that game. Did you sell anything?

WILLY: I did five hundred gross in Providence and seven hundred gross in Boston.

LINDA: No! Wait a minute, I've got a pencil. (*She pulls pencil and paper out of her apron pocket.*) That makes your commission . . . Two hundred — my God! Two hundred and twelve dollars!

WILLY: Well, I didn't figure it yet, but . . .   295

LINDA: How much did you do?

WILLY: Well, I — I did — about a hundred and eighty gross in Providence. Well, no — it came to — roughly two hundred gross on the whole trip.

LINDA: (*without hesitation*) Two hundred gross. That's . . . (*She figures.*)

WILLY: The trouble was that three of the stores were half closed for inventory in Boston. Otherwise I woulda broke records.

LINDA: Well, it makes seventy dollars and some pennies. That's very good.   300

WILLY: What do we owe?

LINDA: Well, on the first there's sixteen dollars on the refrigerator —

WILLY: Why sixteen?

LINDA: Well, the fan belt broke, so it was a dollar eighty.

WILLY: But it's brand new.   305

LINDA: Well, the man said that's the way it is. Till they work themselves in, y'know.

They move through the wall-line into the kitchen.

WILLY: I hope we didn't get stuck on that machine.

LINDA: They got the biggest ads of any of them!

WILLY: I know, it's a fine machine. What else?

LINDA: Well, there's nine-sixty for the washing machine. And for the vacuum   310
cleaner there's three and a half due on the fifteenth. Then the roof, you got twenty-one dollars remaining.

WILLY: It don't leak, does it?

LINDA: No, they did a wonderful job. Then you owe Frank for the carburetor.

WILLY: I'm not going to pay that man! That goddam Chevrolet, they ought to prohibit the manufacture of that car!

LINDA: Well, you owe him three and a half. And odds and ends, comes to around a hundred and twenty dollars by the fifteenth.

WILLY: A hundred and twenty dollars! My God, if business don't pick up I   315
don't know what I'm gonna do!

LINDA: Well, next week you'll do better.

WILLY: Oh, I'll knock them dead next week. I'll go to Hartford. I'm very well liked in Hartford. You know, the trouble is, Linda, people don't seem to take to me.

They move onto the forestage.

LINDA: Oh, don't be foolish.

WILLY: I know it when I walk in. They seem to laugh at me.

320 **LINDA:** Why? Why would they laugh at you? Don't talk that way, Willy.

Willy moves to the edge of the stage. Linda goes into the kitchen and starts to darn stockings.

WILLY: I don't know the reason for it, but they just pass me by. I'm not noticed.

LINDA: But you're doing wonderful, dear. You're making seventy to a hundred dollars a week.

WILLY: But I gotta be at it ten, twelve hours a day. Other men — I don't know — they do it easier. I don't know why — I can't stop myself — I talk too much. A man oughta come in with a few words. One thing about Charley. He's a man of few words, and they respect him.

LINDA: You don't talk too much, you're just lively.

325 **WILLY:** (*smiling*) Well, I figure, what the hell, life is short, a couple of jokes. (*To himself.*) I joke too much! (*The smile goes.*)

LINDA: Why? You're —

WILLY: I'm fat. I'm very —foolish to look at, Linda. I didn't tell you, but Christmas time I happened to be calling on F. H. Stewarts, and a salesman I know, as I was going in to see the buyer, I heard him say something about — walrus. And I — I cracked him right across the face. I won't take that. I simply will not take that. But they do laugh at me. I know that.

LINDA: Darling . . .

WILLY: I gotta overcome it. I know I gotta overcome it. I'm not dressing to advantage, maybe.

330 **LINDA:** Willy, darling, you're the handsomest man in the world —

WILLY: Oh, no, Linda.

LINDA: To me you are. (*Slight pause.*) The handsomest.

From the darkness is heard the laughter of a woman. Willy doesn't turn to it, but it continues through Linda's lines.

LINDA: And the boys, Willy. Few men are idolized by their children the way you are.

Music is heard as behind a scrim, to the left of the house, The Woman, dimly seen, is dressing.

WILLY: (*with great feeling*) You're the best there is, Linda, you're a pal, you know that? On the road — on the road I want to grab you sometimes and just kiss the life outa you.

The laughter is loud now, and he moves into a brightening area at the left, where The Woman has come from behind the scrim and is standing, putting on her hat, looking into a "mirror" and laughing.

335 **WILLY:** 'Cause I get so lonely — especially when business is bad and there's nobody to talk to. I get the feeling that I'll never sell anything again, that I won't make a living for you, or a business, a business for the boys. (*He talks through The Woman's subsiding laughter; The Woman primps at the "mirror."*) There's so much I want to make for —

THE WOMAN: Me? You didn't make me, Willy. I picked you.

WILLY: *(pleased)* You picked me?

THE WOMAN: *(who is quite proper-looking, Willy's age)* I did. I've been sitting at that desk watching all the salesmen go by, day in, day out. But you've got such a sense of humor, and we do have such a good time together, don't we?

WILLY: Sure, sure. *(He takes her in his arms.)* Why do you have to go now?

THE WOMAN: It's two o'clock . . .   340

WILLY: No, come on in! *(He pulls her.)*

THE WOMAN: . . . my sisters'll be scandalized. When'll you be back?

WILLY: Oh, two weeks about. Will you come up again?

THE WOMAN: Sure thing. You do make me laugh. It's good for me. *(She squeezes his arm, kisses him.)* And I think you're a wonderful man.

WILLY: You picked me, heh?   345

THE WOMAN: Sure. Because you're so sweet. And such a kidder.

WILLY: Well, I'll see you next time I'm in Boston.

THE WOMAN: I'll put you right through to the buyers.

WILLY: *(slapping her bottom)* Right. Well, bottoms up!

THE WOMAN: *(slaps him gently and laughs)* You just kill me, Willy. *(He suddenly*   350
    grabs her and kisses her roughly.) You kill me. And thanks for the stockings.
    I love a lot of stockings. Well, good night.

WILLY: Good night. And keep your pores open!

THE WOMAN: Oh, Willy!

*The Woman bursts out laughing, and Linda's laughter blends in. The Woman disappears
into the dark. Now the area at the kitchen table brightens. Linda is sitting where she was
at the kitchen table, but now is mending a pair of silk stockings.*

LINDA: You are, Willy. The handsomest man. You've got no reason to feel
    that —

WILLY: *(coming out of The Woman's dimming area and going over to Linda)* I'll
    make it all up to you, Linda, I'll —

LINDA: There's nothing to make up, dear. You're doing fine, better than —   355

WILLY: *(noticing her mending)* What's that?

LINDA: Just mending my stockings. They're so expensive —

WILLY: *(angrily, taking them from her)* I won't have you mending stockings in
    this house! Now throw them out!

Linda puts the stockings in her pocket.

BERNARD: *(entering on the run)* Where is he? If he doesn't study!

WILLY: *(moving to the forestage, with great agitation)* You'll give him the   360
    answers!

BERNARD: I do, but I can't on a Regents! That's a state exam! They're liable to
    arrest me!

WILLY: Where is he? I'll whip him, I'll whip him!

LINDA: And he'd better give back that football, Willy, it's not nice.

WILLY: Biff! Where is he? Why is he taking everything?

LINDA: He's too tough with the girls, Willy. All the mothers are afraid of him!   365

WILLY: I'll whip him!

BERNARD: He's driving the car without a license!

The Woman's laugh is heard.

WILLY: Shut up!

LINDA: All the mothers—

370 WILLY: Shut up!

BERNARD: *(backing quietly away and out)* Mr. Birnbaum says he's stuck up.

WILLY: Get outa here!

BERNARD: If he doesn't buckle down he'll flunk math! *(He goes off.)*

LINDA: He's right, Willy, you've gotta—

375 WILLY: *(exploding at her)* There's nothing the matter with him! You want him
     to be a worm like Bernard? He's got spirit, personality . . .

*As he speaks, Linda, almost in tears, exits into the living room. Willy is alone in the
kitchen, wilting and staring. The leaves are gone. It is night again, and the apartment
houses look down from behind.*

WILLY: Loaded with it. Loaded! What is he stealing? He's giving it back, isn't
     he? Why is he stealing? What did I tell him? I never in my life told him
     anything but decent things.

*Happy in pajamas has come down the stairs; Willy suddenly becomes aware of Happy's
presence.*

HAPPY: Let's go now, come on.

WILLY: *(sitting down at the kitchen table)* Huh! Why did she have to wax the
     floors herself? Everytime she waxes the floors she keels over. She knows that!

HAPPY: Shh! Take it easy. What brought you back tonight?

380 WILLY: I got an awful scare. Nearly hit a kid in Yonkers. God! Why didn't I go
     to Alaska with my brother Ben that time! Ben! That man was a genius,
     that man was success incarnate! What a mistake! He begged me to go.

HAPPY: Well, there's no use in —

WILLY: You guys! There was a man started with the clothes on his back and
     ended up with diamond mines!

HAPPY: Boy, someday I'd like to know how he did it.

WILLY: What's the mystery? The man knew what he wanted and went out and
     got it! Walked into a jungle, and comes out, the age of twenty-one, and he's
     rich! The world is an oyster, but you don't crack it open on a mattress!

385 HAPPY: Pop, I told you I'm gonna retire you for life.

WILLY: You'll retire me for life on seventy goddam dollars a week? And your
     women and your car and your apartment, and you'll retire me for life!
     Christ's sake, I couldn't get past Yonkers today! Where are you guys, where
     are you? The woods are burning! I can't drive a car!

*Charley has appeared in the doorway. He is a large man, slow of speech, laconic, im-
movable. In all he says, despite what he says, there is pity, and now, trepidation. He has
a robe over his pajamas, slippers on his feet. He enters the kitchen.*

CHARLEY: Everything all right?

HAPPY: Yeah, Charley, everything's . . .

WILLY: What's the matter?

CHARLEY: I heard some noise. I thought something happened. Can't we do   390
something about the walls? You sneeze in here, and in my house hats blow off.

HAPPY: Let's go to bed, Dad. Come on.

Charley signals to Happy to go.

WILLY: You go ahead, I'm not tired at the moment.

HAPPY: (*to Willy*) Take it easy, huh? (*He exits.*)

WILLY: What're you doin' up?

CHARLEY: (*sitting down at the kitchen table opposite Willy*) Couldn't sleep good.   395
I had a heartburn.

WILLY: Well, you don't know how to eat.

CHARLEY: I eat with my mouth.

WILLY: No, you're ignorant. You gotta know about vitamins and things like that.

CHARLEY: Come on, let's shoot. Tire you out a little.

WILLY: (*hesitantly*) All right. You got cards?   400

CHARLEY: (*taking a deck from his pocket*) Yeah, I got them. Someplace. What is
it with those vitamins?

WILLY: (*dealing*) They build up your bones. Chemistry.

CHARLEY: Yeah, but there's no bones in a heartburn.

WILLY: What are you talkin' about? Do you know the first thing about it?

CHARLEY: Don't get insulted.   405

WILLY: Don't talk about something you don't know anything about.

They are playing. Pause.

CHARLEY: What're you doin' home?

WILLY: A little trouble with the car.

CHARLEY: Oh. (*Pause.*) I'd like to take a trip to California.

WILLY: Don't say.   410

CHARLEY: You want a job?

WILLY: I got a job, I told you that. (*After a slight pause.*) What the hell are you
offering me a job for?

CHARLEY: Don't get insulted.

WILLY: Don't insult me.

CHARLEY: I don't see no sense in it. You don't have to go on this way.   415

WILLY: I got a good job. (*Slight pause.*) What do you keep comin' in here for?

CHARLEY: You want me to go?

WILLY: (*after a pause, withering*) I can't understand it. He's going back to Texas
again. What the hell is that?

CHARLEY: Let him go.

WILLY: I got nothin' to give him, Charley, I'm clean, I'm clean.   420

CHARLEY: He won't starve. None a them starve. Forget about him.

WILLY: Then what have I got to remember?

CHARLEY: You take it too hard. To hell with it. When a deposit bottle is
broken you don't get your nickel back.

WILLY: That's easy enough for you to say.

425   CHARLEY: That ain't easy for me to say.

WILLY: Did you see the ceiling I put up in the living room?

CHARLEY: Yeah, that's a piece of work. To put up a ceiling is a mystery to me. How do you do it?

WILLY: What's the difference?

CHARLEY: Well, talk about it.

430   WILLY: You gonna put up a ceiling?

CHARLEY: How could I put up a ceiling?

WILLY: Then what the hell are you bothering me for?

CHARLEY: You're insulted again.

WILLY: A man who can't handle tools is not a man. You're disgusting.

435   CHARLEY: Don't call me disgusting, Willy.

Uncle Ben, carrying a valise and an umbrella, enters the forestage from around the right corner of the house. He is a stolid man, in his sixties, with a mustache and an authoritative air. He is utterly certain of his destiny, and there is an aura of far places about him. He enters exactly as Willy speaks.

WILLY: I'm getting awfully tired, Ben.

Ben's music is heard. Ben looks around at everything.

CHARLEY: Good, keep playing; you'll sleep better. Did you call me Ben?

Ben looks at his watch.

WILLY: That's funny. For a second there you reminded me of my brother Ben.

BEN: I have only a few minutes. (*He strolls, inspecting the place. Willy and Charley continue playing.*)

440   CHARLEY: You never heard from him again, heh? Since that time?

WILLY: Didn't Linda tell you? Couple of weeks ago we got a letter from his wife in Africa. He died.

CHARLEY: That so.

BEN: (*chuckling*) So this is Brooklyn, eh?

CHARLEY: Maybe you're in for some of his money.

445   WILLY: Naa, he had seven sons. There's just one opportunity I had with that man . . .

BEN: I must make a train, William. There are several properties I'm looking at in Alaska.

WILLY: Sure, sure! If I'd gone with him to Alaska that time, everything would've been totally different.

CHARLEY: Go on, you'd froze to death up there.

WILLY: What're you talking about?

450   BEN: Opportunity is tremendous in Alaska, William. Surprised you're not up there.

WILLY: Sure, tremendous.

CHARLEY: Heh?

WILLY: There was the only man I ever met who knew the answers.

CHARLEY: Who?

BEN: How are you all? 455

WILLY: *(taking a pot, smiling)* Fine, fine.

CHARLEY: Pretty sharp tonight.

BEN: Is Mother living with you?

WILLY: No, she died a long time ago.

CHARLEY: Who? 460

BEN: That's too bad. Fine specimen of a lady, Mother.

WILLY: *(to Charley)* Heh?

BEN: I'd hoped to see the old girl.

CHARLEY: Who died?

BEN: Heard anything from Father, have you? 465

WILLY: *(unnerved)* What do you mean, who died?

CHARLEY: *(taking a pot)* What're you talkin' about?

BEN: *(looking at his watch)* William, it's half-past eight!

WILLY: *(as though to dispel his confusion he angrily stops Charley's hand)* That's my
build!

CHARLEY: I put the ace — 470

WILLY: If you don't know how to play the game I'm not gonna throw my
money away on you!

CHARLEY: *(rising)* It was my ace, for God's sake!

WILLY: I'm through, I'm through!

BEN: When did Mother die?

WILLY: Long ago. Since the beginning you never knew how to play cards. 475

CHARLEY: *(picks up the cards and goes to the door)* All right! Next time I'll bring
a deck with five aces.

WILLY: I don't play that kind of game!

CHARLEY: *(turning to him)* You should be ashamed of yourself!

WILLY: Yeah?

CHARLEY: Yeah! *(He goes out.)* 480

WILLY: *(slamming the door after him)* Ignoramus!

BEN: *(as Willy comes toward him through the wall-line of the kitchen)* So you're
William.

WILLY: *(shaking Ben's hand)* Ben! I've been waiting for you so long! What's the
answer? How did you do it?

BEN: Oh, there's a story in that.

Linda enters the forestage, as of old, carrying the wash basket.

LINDA: Is this Ben? 485

BEN: *(gallantly)* How do you do, my dear.

LINDA: Where've you been all these years? Willy's always wondered why you —

WILLY: *(pulling Ben away from her impatiently)* Where is Dad? Didn't you follow
him? How did you get started?

BEN: Well, I don't know how much you remember.

WILLY: Well, I was just a baby, of course, only three or four years old — 490

BEN: Three years and eleven months.

WILLY: What a memory, Ben!

BEN: I have many enterprises, William, and I have never kept books.

WILLY: I remember I was sitting under the wagon in — was it Nebraska?

495 BEN: It was South Dakota, and I gave you a bunch of wild flowers.

WILLY: I remember you walking away down some open road.

BEN: *(laughing)* I was going to find Father in Alaska.

WILLY: Where is he?

BEN: At that age I had a very faulty view of geography, William. I discovered after a few days that I was heading due south, so instead of Alaska, I ended up in Africa.

500 LINDA: Africa!

WILLY: The Gold Coast!

BEN: Principally, diamond mines.

LINDA: Diamond mines!

BEN: Yes, my dear. But I've only a few minutes—

505 WILLY: No! Boys! Boys! *(Young Biff and Happy appear.)* Listen to this. This is your Uncle Ben, a great man! Tell my boys, Ben!

BEN: Why, boys, when I was seventeen I walked into the jungle, and when I was twenty-one I walked out. *(He laughs.)* And by God I was rich.

WILLY: *(to the boys)* You see what I been talking about? The greatest things can happen!

BEN: *(glancing at his watch)* I have an appointment in Ketchikan Tuesday week.

WILLY: No, Ben! Please tell about Dad. I want my boys to hear. I want them to know the kind of stock they spring from. All I remember is a man with a big beard, and I was in Mamma's lap, sitting around a fire, and some kind of high music.

510 BEN: His flute. He played the flute.

WILLY: Sure, the flute, that's right!

New music is heard, a high, rollicking tune.

BEN: Father was a very great and a very wild-hearted man. We would start in Boston, and he'd toss the whole family into the wagon, and then he'd drive the team right across the country; through Ohio, and Indiana, Michigan, Illinois, and all the Western states. And we'd stop in the towns and sell the flutes that he'd made on the way. Great inventor, Father. With one gadget he made more in a week than a man like you could make in a lifetime.

WILLY: That's just the way I'm bringing them up, Ben — rugged, well liked, all-around.

BEN: Yeah? *(To Biff.)* Hit that, boy — hard as you can. *(He pounds his stomach.)*

515 BIFF: Oh, no, sir!

BEN: *(taking boxing stance)* Come on, get to me! *(He laughs.)*

WILLY: Go to it, Biff! Go ahead, show him!

BIFF: Okay! *(He cocks his fist and starts in.)*

LINDA: *(to Willy)* Why must he fight, dear?

520 BEN: *(sparring with Biff)* Good boy! Good boy!

WILLY: How's that, Ben, heh?

HAPPY: Give him the left, Biff!

LINDA: Why are you fighting?

BEN: Good boy! (*Suddenly comes in, trips Biff, and stands over him, the point of his umbrella poised over Biff's eye.*)

LINDA: Look out, Biff!   525

BIFF: Gee!

BEN: (*patting Biff's knee*) Never fight fair with a stranger, boy. You'll never get out of the jungle that way. (*Taking Linda's hand and bowing.*) It was an honor and a pleasure to meet you, Linda.

LINDA: (*withdrawing her hand coldly, frightened*) Have a nice — trip.

BEN: (*to Willy*) And good luck with your — what do you do?

WILLY: Selling.   530

BEN: Yes. Well . . . (*He raises his hand in farewell to all.*)

WILLY: No, Ben, I don't want you to think . . . (*He takes Ben's arm to show him.*) It's Brooklyn, I know, but we hunt too.

BEN: Really, now.

WILLY: Oh, sure, there's snakes and rabbits and — that's why I moved out here. Why, Biff can fell any one of these trees in no time! Boys! Go right over to where they're building the apartment house and get some sand. We're gonna rebuild the entire front stoop right now! Watch this, Ben!

BIFF: Yes, sir! On the double, Hap!   535

HAPPY: (*as he and Biff run off*) I lost weight, Pop, you notice?

Charley enters in knickers, even before the boys are gone.

CHARLEY: Listen, if they steal any more from that building the watchman'll put the cops on them!

LINDA: (*to Willy*) Don't let Biff . . .

Ben laughs lustily.

WILLY: You shoulda seen the lumber they brought home last week. At least a dozen six-by-tens worth all kinds of money.

CHARLEY: Listen, if that watchman—   540

WILLY: I gave them hell, understand. But I got a couple of fearless characters there.

CHARLEY: Willy, the jails are full of fearless characters.

BEN: (*clapping Willy on the back, with a laugh at Charley*) And the stock exchange, friend!

WILLY: (*joining in Ben's laughter*) Where are the rest of your pants?

CHARLEY: My wife bought them.   545

WILLY: Now all you need is a golf club and you can go upstairs and go to sleep. (*To Ben.*) Great athlete! Between him and his son Bernard they can't hammer a nail!

BERNARD: (*rushing in*) The watchman's chasing Biff!

WILLY: *(angrily)* Shut up! He's not stealing anything!

LINDA: *(alarmed, hurrying off left)* Where is he? Biff, dear! *(She exits.)*

550 WILLY: *(moving toward the left, away from Ben)* There's nothing wrong. What's the matter with you?

BEN: Nervy boy. Good!

WILLY: *(laughing)* Oh, nerves of iron, that Biff!

CHARLEY: Don't know what it is. My New England man comes back and he's bleedin', they murdered him up there.

WILLY: It's contacts, Charley, I got important contacts!

555 CHARLEY: *(sarcastically)* Glad to hear it, Willy. Come in later, we'll shoot a little casino. I'll take some of your Portland money. *(He laughs at Willy and exits.)*

WILLY: *(turning to Ben)* Business is bad, it's murderous. But not for me, of course.

BEN: I'll stop by on my way back to Africa.

WILLY: *(longingly)* Can't you stay a few days? You're just what I need, Ben, because I — I have a fine position here, but I — well, Dad left when I was such a baby and I never had a chance to talk to him and I still feel — kind of temporary about myself.

BEN: I'll be late for my train.

They are at opposite ends of the stage.

560 WILLY: Ben, my boys — can't we talk? They'd go into the jaws of hell for me, see, but I —

BEN: William, you're being first-rate with your boys. Outstanding, manly chaps!

WILLY: *(hanging on to his words)* Oh, Ben, that's good to hear! Because sometimes I'm afraid that I'm not teaching them the right kind of — Ben, how should I teach them?

BEN: *(giving great weight to each word, and with a certain vicious audacity)* William, when I walked into the jungle, I was seventeen. When I walked out I was twenty-one. And, by God, I was rich! *(He goes off into darkness around the right corner of the house.)*

WILLY: . . . was rich! That's just the spirit I want to imbue them with! To walk into a jungle! I was right! I was right! I was right!

Ben is gone, but Willy is still speaking to him as Linda, in nightgown and robe, enters the kitchen, glances around for Willy, then goes to the door of the house, looks out and sees him. Comes down to his left. He looks at her.

565 LINDA: Willy, dear? Willy?

WILLY: I was right!

LINDA: Did you have some cheese? *(He can't answer.)* It's very late, darling. Come to bed, heh?

WILLY: *(looking straight up)* Gotta break your neck to see a star in this yard.

LINDA: You coming in?

570 WILLY: What ever happened to that diamond watch fob? Remember? When Ben came from Africa that time? Didn't he give me a watch fob with a diamond in it?

LINDA: You pawned it, dear. Twelve, thirteen years ago. For Biff's radio
   correspondence course.

WILLY: Gee, that was a beautiful thing. I'll take a walk.

LINDA: But you're in your slippers.

WILLY: (*starting to go around the house at the left*) I was right! I was! (*Half to
   Linda, as he goes, shaking his head.*) What a man! There was a man worth
   talking to. I was right!

LINDA: (*calling after Willy*) But in your slippers, Willy!   575

*Willy is almost gone when Biff, in his pajamas, comes down the stairs and enters the
kitchen.*

BIFF: What is he doing out there?

LINDA: Sh!

BIFF: God Almighty, Mom, how long has he been doing this?

LINDA: Don't, he'll hear you.

BIFF: What the hell is the matter with him?   580

LINDA: It'll pass by morning.

BIFF: Shouldn't we do anything?

LINDA: Oh, my dear, you should do a lot of things, but there's nothing to do,
   so go to sleep.

Happy comes down the stairs and sits on the steps.

HAPPY: I never heard him so loud, Mom.

LINDA: Well, come around more often; you'll hear him. (*She sits down at the*   585
   table and mends the lining of Willy's jacket.)

BIFF: Why didn't you ever write me about this, Mom?

LINDA: How would I write to you? For over three months you had no address.

BIFF: I was on the move. But you know I thought of you all the time. You
   know that, don't you, pal?

LINDA: I know, dear, I know. But he likes to have a letter. Just to know that
   there's still a possibility for better things.

BIFF: He's not like this all the time, is he?   590

LINDA: It's when you come home he's always the worst.

BIFF: When I come home?

LINDA: When you write you're coming, he's all smiles, and talks about the
   future, and —he's just wonderful. And then the closer you seem to come,
   the more shaky he gets, and then, by the time you get here, he's arguing,
   and he seems angry at you. I think it's just that maybe he can't bring
   himself to — to open up to you. Why are you so hateful to each other?
   Why is that?

BIFF: (*evasively*) I'm not hateful, Mom.

LINDA: But you no sooner come in the door than you're fighting!   595

BIFF: I don't know why. I mean to change. I'm tryin', Mom, you understand?

LINDA: Are you home to stay now?

BIFF: I don't know. I want to look around, see what's doin'.

LINDA: Biff, you can't look around all your life, can you?

600 BIFF: I just can't take hold, Mom. I can't take hold of some kind of a life.

LINDA: Biff, a man is not a bird, to come and go with the springtime.

BIFF: Your hair . . . (*He touches her hair.*) Your hair got so gray.

LINDA: Oh, it's been gray since you were in high school. I just stopped dyeing it, that's all.

BIFF: Dye it again, will ya? I don't want my pal looking old. (*He smiles.*)

605 LINDA: You're such a boy! You think you can go away for a year and . . . You've got to get it into your head now that one day you'll knock on this door and there'll be strange people here—

BIFF: What are you talking about? You're not even sixty, Mom.

LINDA: But what about your father?

BIFF: (*lamely*) Well, I meant him too.

HAPPY: He admires Pop.

610 LINDA: Biff, dear, if you don't have any feeling for him, then you can't have any feeling for me.

BIFF: Sure I can, Mom.

LINDA: No. You can't just come to see me, because I love him. (*With a threat, but only a threat, of tears.*) He's the dearest man in the world to me, and I won't have anyone making him feel unwanted and low and blue. You've got to make up your mind now, darling, there's no leeway any more. Either he's your father and you pay him that respect, or else you're not to come here. I know he's not easy to get along with — nobody knows that better than me —but . . .

WILLY: (*from the left, with a laugh*) Hey, hey, Biffo!

BIFF: (*starting to go out after Willy*) What the hell is the matter with him? (*Happy stops him.*)

615 LINDA: Don't — don't go near him!

BIFF: Stop making excuses for him! He always, always wiped the floor with you. Never had an ounce of respect for you.

HAPPY: He's always had respect for—

BIFF: What the hell do you know about it?

HAPPY: (*surlily*) Just don't call him crazy!

620 BIFF: He's got no character — Charley wouldn't do this. Not in his own house — spewing out that vomit from his mind.

HAPPY: Charley never had to cope with what he's got to.

BIFF: People are worse off than Willy Loman. Believe me, I've seen them!

LINDA: Then make Charley your father, Biff. You can't do that, can you? I don't say he's a great man. Willy Loman never made a lot of money. His name was never in the paper. He's not the finest character that ever lived. But he's a human being, and a terrible thing is happening to him. So attention must be paid. He's not to be allowed to fall into his grave like an old dog. Attention, attention must be finally paid to such a person. You called him crazy—

BIFF: I didn't mean—

625 LINDA: No, a lot of people think he's lost his —balance. But you don't have to be very smart to know what his trouble is. The man is exhausted.

HAPPY: Sure!

LINDA: A small man can be just as exhausted as a great man. He works for a company thirty-six years this March, opens up unheard-of territories to their trademark, and now in his old age they take his salary away.

HAPPY: (*indignantly*) I didn't know that, Mom.

LINDA: You never asked, my dear! Now that you get your spending money someplace else you don't trouble your mind with him.

HAPPY: But I gave you money last—   630

LINDA: Christmas time, fifty dollars! To fix the hot water it cost ninety-seven fifty! For five weeks he's been on straight commission, like a beginner, an unknown!

BIFF: Those ungrateful bastards!

LINDA: Are they any worse than his sons? When he brought them business, when he was young, they were glad to see him. But now his old friends, the old buyers that loved him so and always found some order to hand him in a pinch — they're all dead, retired. He used to be able to make six, seven calls a day in Boston. Now he takes his valises out of the car and puts them back and takes them out again and he's exhausted. Instead of walking he talks now. He drives seven hundred miles, and when he gets there no one knows him any more, no one welcomes him. And what goes through a man's mind, driving seven hundred miles home without having earned a cent? Why shouldn't he talk to himself? Why? When he has to go to Charley and borrow fifty dollars a week and pretend to me that it's his pay? How long can that go on? How long? You see what I'm sitting here and waiting for? And you tell me he has no character? The man who never worked a day but for your benefit? When does he get the medal for that? Is this his reward — to turn around at the age of sixty-three and find his sons, who he loved better than his life, one a philandering bum—

HAPPY: Mom!

LINDA: That's all you are, my baby! (*To Biff.*) And you! What happened to the   635
love you had for him? You were such pals! How you used to talk to him on the phone every night! How lonely he was till he could come home to you!

BIFF: All right, Mom. I'll live here in my room, and I'll get a job. I'll keep away from him, that's all.

LINDA: No, Biff. You can't stay here and fight all the time.

BIFF: He threw me out of this house, remember that.

LINDA: Why did he do that? I never knew why.

BIFF: Because I know he's a fake and he doesn't like anybody around who   640
knows!

LINDA: Why a fake? In what way? What do you mean?

BIFF: Just don't lay it all at my feet. It's between me and him — that's all I have to say. I'll chip in from now on. He'll settle for half my pay check. He'll be all right. I'm going to bed. (*He starts for the stairs.*)

LINDA: He won't be all right.

BIFF: (*turning on the stairs, furiously*) I hate this city and I'll stay here. Now what do you want?

LINDA: He's dying, Biff.   645

Happy turns quickly to her, shocked.

BIFF: *(after a pause)* Why is he dying?

LINDA: He's been trying to kill himself.

BIFF: *(with great horror)* How?

LINDA: I live from day to day.

650 BIFF: What're you talking about?

LINDA: Remember I wrote you that he smashed up the car again? In February?

BIFF: Well?

LINDA: The insurance inspector came. He said that they have evidence. That all these accidents in the last year — weren't — weren't — accidents.

HAPPY: How can they tell that? That's a lie.

655 LINDA: It seems there's a woman . . . *(She takes a breath as —)*

BIFF: *(sharply but contained)* What woman?

LINDA: *(simultaneously)* . . . and this woman . . .

LINDA: What?

BIFF: Nothing. Go ahead.

660 LINDA: What did you say?

BIFF: Nothing. I just said what woman?

HAPPY: What about her?

LINDA: Well, it seems she was walking down the road and saw his car. She says that he wasn't driving fast at all, and that he didn't skid. She says he came to that little bridge, and then deliberately smashed into the railing, and it was only the shallowness of the water that saved him.

BIFF: Oh, no, he probably just fell asleep again.

665 LINDA: I don't think he fell asleep.

BIFF: Why not?

LINDA: Last month . . . *(With great difficulty.)* Oh, boys, it's so hard to say a thing like this! He's just a big stupid man to you, but I tell you there's more good in him than in many other people. *(She chokes, wipes her eyes.)* I was looking for a fuse. The lights blew out, and I went down the cellar. And behind the fuse box — it happened to fall out — was a length of rubber pipe — just short.

HAPPY: No kidding?

LINDA: There's a little attachment on the end of it. I knew right away. And sure enough, on the bottom of the water heater there's a new little nipple on the gas pipe.

670 HAPPY: *(angrily)* That — jerk.

BIFF: Did you have it taken off?

LINDA: I'm — I'm ashamed to. How can I mention it to him? Every day I go down and take away that little rubber pipe. But, when he comes home, I put it back where it was. How can I insult him that way? I don't know what to do. I live from day to day, boys. I tell you, I know every thought in his mind. It sounds so old-fashioned and silly, but I tell you he put his whole life into you and you've turned your backs on him. *(She is bent over in the chair, weeping, her face in her hands.)* Biff, I swear to God! Biff, his life is in your hands!

HAPPY: *(to Biff)* How do you like that damned fool!

BIFF: *(kissing her)* All right, pal, all right. It's all settled now. I've been remiss. I know that, Mom, but now I'll stay, and I swear to you, I'll apply myself. *(Kneeling in front of her, in a fever of self-reproach.)* It's just — you see, Mom, I don't fit in business. Not that I won't try. I'll try, and I'll make good.

HAPPY: Sure you will. The trouble with you in business was you never tried to please people.　675

BIFF: I know, I—

HAPPY: Like when you worked for Harrison's. Bob Harrison said you were tops, and then you go and do some damn fool thing like whistling whole songs in the elevator like a comedian.

BIFF: *(against Happy)* So what? I like to whistle sometimes.

HAPPY: You don't raise a guy to a responsible job who whistles in the elevator!

LINDA: Well, don't argue about it now.　680

HAPPY: Like when you'd go off and swim in the middle of the day instead of taking the line around.

BIFF: *(his resentment rising)* Well, don't you run off? You take off sometimes, don't you? On a nice summer day?

HAPPY: Yeah, but I cover myself!

LINDA: Boys!

HAPPY: If I'm going to take a fade the boss can call any number where I'm　685 supposed to be and they'll swear to him that I just left. I'll tell you something that I hate to say, Biff, but in the business world some of them think you're crazy.

BIFF: *(angered)* Screw the business world!

HAPPY: All right, screw it! Great, but cover yourself!

LINDA: Hap, Hap!

BIFF: I don't care what they think! They've laughed at Dad for years, and you know why? Because we don't belong in this nut-house of a city! We should be mixing cement on some open plain, or — or carpenters. A carpenter is allowed to whistle!

Willy walks in from the entrance of the house, at left.

WILLY: Even your grandfather was better than a carpenter. *(Pause. They　690 watch him.)* You never grew up. Bernard does not whistle in the elevator, I assure you.

BIFF: *(as though to laugh Willy out of it)* Yeah, but you do, Pop.

WILLY: I never in my life whistled in an elevator! And who in the business world thinks I'm crazy?

BIFF: I didn't mean it like that, Pop. Now don't make a whole thing out of it, will ya?

WILLY: Go back to the West! Be a carpenter, a cowboy, enjoy yourself!

LINDA: Willy, he was just saying —　695

WILLY: I heard what he said!

HAPPY: *(trying to quiet Willy)* Hey, Pop, come on now . . .

WILLY: *(continuing over Happy's line)* They laugh at me, heh? Go to Filene's, go to the Hub, go to Slattery's, Boston. Call out the name Willy Loman and see what happens! Big shot!

BIFF: All right, Pop.

700 WILLY: Big!

BIFF: All right!

WILLY: Why do you always insult me?

BIFF: I didn't say a word. *(To Linda.)* Did I say a word?

LINDA: He didn't say anything, Willy.

705 WILLY: *(going to the doorway of the living room)* All right, good night, good night.

LINDA: Willy, dear, he just decided . . .

WILLY: *(to Biff)* If you get tired hanging around tomorrow, paint the ceiling I put up in the living room.

BIFF: I'm leaving early tomorrow.

HAPPY: He's going to see Bill Oliver, Pop.

710 WILLY: *(interestedly)* Oliver? For what?

BIFF: *(with reserve, but trying, trying)* He always said he'd stake me. I'd like to go into business, so maybe I can take him up on it.

LINDA: Isn't that wonderful?

WILLY: Don't interrupt. What's wonderful about it? There's fifty men in the City of New York who'd stake him. *(To Biff.)* Sporting goods?

BIFF: I guess so. I know something about it and—

715 WILLY: He knows something about it! You know sporting goods better than Spalding, for God's sake! How much is he giving you?

BIFF: I don't know, I didn't even see him yet, but—

WILLY: Then what're you talkin' about?

BIFF: *(getting angry)* Well, all I said was I'm gonna see him, that's all!

WILLY: *(turning away)* Ah, you're counting your chickens again.

720 BIFF: *(starting left for the stairs)* Oh, Jesus, I'm going to sleep!

WILLY: *(calling after him)* Don't curse in this house!

BIFF: *(turning)* Since when did you get so clean!

HAPPY: *(trying to stop them)* Wait a . . .

WILLY: Don't use that language to me! I won't have it!

725 HAPPY: *(grabbing Biff, shouts)* Wait a minute! I got an idea. I got a feasible idea. Come here, Biff, let's talk this over now, let's talk some sense here. When I was down in Florida last time, I thought of a great idea to sell sporting goods. It just came back to me. You and I, Biff — we have a line, the Loman Line. We train a couple of weeks, and put on a couple of exhibitions, see?

WILLY: That's an idea!

HAPPY: Wait! We form two basketball teams, see? Two water-polo teams. We play each other. It's a million dollars' worth of publicity. Two brothers, see? The Loman Brothers. Displays in the Royal Palms — all the hotels. And banners over the ring and the basketball court: "Loman Brothers." Baby, we could sell sporting goods!

WILLY: That is a one-million-dollar idea.

LINDA: Marvelous!

BIFF: I'm in great shape as far as that's concerned.   730

HAPPY: And the beauty of it is, Biff, it wouldn't be like a business. We'd be out playin' ball again . . .

BIFF: (*enthused*) Yeah, that's . . .

WILLY: Million-dollar . . .

HAPPY: And you wouldn't get fed up with it, Biff. It'd be the family again. There'd be the old honor, and comradeship, and if you wanted to go off for a swim or somethin'—well, you'd do it! Without some smart cooky gettin' up ahead of you!

WILLY: Lick the world! You guys together could absolutely lick the civilized   735
world.

BIFF: I'll see Oliver tomorrow. Hap, if we could work that out . . .

LINDA: Maybe things are beginning to—

WILLY: (*wildly enthused, to Linda*) Stop interrupting! (*To Biff.*) But don't wear sport jacket and slacks when you see Oliver.

BIFF: No, I'll—

WILLY: A business suit, and talk as little as possible, and don't crack any jokes.   740

BIFF: He did like me. Always liked me.

LINDA: He loved you!

WILLY: (*to Linda*) Will you stop! (*To Biff.*) Walk in very serious. You are not applying for a boy's job. Money is to pass. Be quiet, fine, and serious. Everybody likes a kidder, but nobody lends him money.

HAPPY: I'll try to get some myself, Biff. I'm sure I can.

WILLY: I can see great things for you, kids, I think your troubles are over. But   745
remember, start big and you'll end big. Ask for fifteen. How much you gonna ask for?

BIFF: Gee, I don't know —

WILLY: And don't say "Gee." "Gee" is a boy's word. A man walking in for fifteen thousand dollars does not say "Gee!"

BIFF: Ten, I think, would be top though.

WILLY: Don't be so modest. You always started too low. Walk in with a big laugh. Don't look worried. Start off with a couple of your good stories to lighten things up. It's not what you say, it's how you say it —because personality always wins the day.

LINDA: Oliver always thought the highest of him —   750

WILLY: Will you let me talk?

BIFF: Don't yell at her, Pop, will ya?

WILLY: (*angrily*) I was talking, wasn't I!

BIFF: I don't like you yelling at her all the time, and I'm tellin' you, that's all.

WILLY: What're you, takin' over this house?   755

LINDA: Willy —

WILLY: (*turning on her*) Don't take his side all the time, goddammit!

BIFF: (*furiously*) Stop yelling at her!

WILLY: (*suddenly pulling on his cheek, beaten down, guilt ridden*) Give my best to Bill Oliver —he may remember me. (*He exits through the living room doorway.*)

760 LINDA: *(her voice subdued)* What'd you have to start that for? *(Biff turns away.)* You see how sweet he was as soon as you talked hopefully? *(She goes over to Biff.)* Come up and say good night to him. Don't let him go to bed that way.

HAPPY: Come on, Biff, let's buck him up.

LINDA: Please, dear. Just say good night. It takes so little to make him happy. Come. *(She goes through the living room doorway, calling upstairs from within the living room.)* Your pajamas are hanging in the bathroom. Willy!

HAPPY: *(looking toward where Linda went out)* What a woman! They broke the mold when they made her. You know that, Biff?

BIFF: He's off salary. My God, working on commission!

765 HAPPY: Well, let's face it: he's no hot-shot selling man. Except that sometimes, you have to admit, he's a sweet personality.

BIFF: *(deciding)* Lend me ten bucks, will ya? I want to buy some new ties.

HAPPY: I'll take you to a place I know. Beautiful stuff. Wear one of my striped shirts tomorrow.

BIFF: She got gray. Mom got awful old. Gee, I'm gonna go in to Oliver tomorrow and knock him for a —

HAPPY: Come on up. Tell that to Dad. Let's give him a whirl. Come on.

770 BIFF: *(steamed up)* You know, with ten thousand bucks, boy!

HAPPY: *(as they go into the living room)* That's the talk, Biff, that's the first time I've heard the old confidence out of you! *(From within the living room, fading off.)* You're gonna live with me, kid, and any babe you want you just say the word . . . *(The last lines are hardly heard. They are mounting the stairs to their parents' bedroom.)*

LINDA: *(entering her bedroom and addressing Willy, who is in the bathroom. She is straightening the bed for him)* Can you do anything about the shower? It drips.

WILLY: *(from the bathroom)* All of a sudden everything falls to pieces! Goddam plumbing, oughta be sued, those people. I hardly finished putting it in and the thing . . . *(His words rumble off.)*

LINDA: I'm just wondering if Oliver will remember him. You think he might?

775 WILLY: *(coming out of the bathroom in his pajamas)* Remember him? What's the matter with you, you crazy? If he'd've stayed with Oliver he'd be on top by now! Wait'll Oliver gets a look at him. You don't know the average caliber any more. The average young man today —*(he is getting into bed)*— is got a caliber of zero. Greatest thing in the world for him was to bum around.

Biff and Happy enter the bedroom. Slight pause.

WILLY: *(stops short, looking at Biff)* Glad to hear it, boy.

HAPPY: He wanted to say good night to you, sport.

WILLY: *(to Biff)* Yeah. Knock him dead, boy. What'd you want to tell me?

BIFF: Just take it easy, Pop. Good night. *(He turns to go.)*

780 WILLY: *(unable to resist)* And if anything falls off the desk while you're talking to him — like a package or something — don't you pick it up. They have office boys for that.

LINDA: I'll make a big breakfast —

WILLY: Will you let me finish? (*To Biff.*) Tell him you were in the business in
the West. Not farm work.

BIFF: All right, Dad.

LINDA: I think everything —

WILLY: (*going right through her speech*) And don't undersell yourself. No less   785
than fifteen thousand dollars.

BIFF: (*unable to bear him*) Okay. Good night, Mom. (*He starts moving.*)

WILLY: Because you got a greatness in you, Biff, remember that. You got all
kinds a greatness . . . (*He lies back, exhausted. Biff walks out.*)

LINDA: (*calling after Biff*) Sleep well, darling!

HAPPY: I'm gonna get married, Mom. I wanted to tell you.

LINDA: Go to sleep, dear.   790

HAPPY: (*going*) I just wanted to tell you.

WILLY: Keep up the good work. (*Happy exits.*) God . . . remember that Ebbets
Field game? The championship of the city?

LINDA: Just rest. Should I sing to you?

WILLY: Yeah. Sing to me. (*Linda hums a soft lullaby.*) When that team came
out — he was the tallest, remember?

LINDA: Oh, yes. And in gold.   795

*Biff enters the darkened kitchen, takes a cigarette, and leaves the house. He comes
downstage into a golden pool of light. He smokes, staring at the night.*

WILLY: Like a young god. Hercules — something like that. And the sun, the sun
all around him. Remember how he waved to me? Right up from the field,
with the representatives of three colleges standing by? And the buyers I
brought, and the cheers when he came out — Loman, Loman, Loman! God
Almighty, he'll be great yet. A star like that, magnificent, can never really
fade away!

*The light on Willy is fading. The gas heater begins to glow through the kitchen wall, near
the stairs, a blue flame beneath red coils.*

LINDA: (*timidly*) Willy, dear, what has he got against you?

WILLY: I'm so tired. Don't talk any more.

Biff slowly returns to the kitchen. He stops, stares toward the heater.

LINDA: Will you ask Howard to let you work in New York?

WILLY: First thing in the morning. Everything'll be all right.   800

*Biff reaches behind the heater and draws out a length of rubber tubing. He is horrified
and turns his head toward Willy's room, still dimly lit, from which the strains of Linda's
desperate but monotonous humming rise.*

WILLY: (*staring through the window into the moonlight*) Gee, look at the moon
moving between the buildings!

Biff wraps the tubing around his hand and quickly goes up the stairs. Curtain.

ACT 2

Music is heard, gay and bright. The curtain rises as the music fades away. Willy, in shirt sleeves, is sitting at the kitchen table, sipping coffee, his hat in his lap. Linda is filling his cup when she can.

WILLY: Wonderful coffee. Meal in itself.

LINDA: Can I make you some eggs?

WILLY: No. Take a breath.

LINDA: You look so rested, dear.

5   **WILLY:** I slept like a dead one. First time in months. Imagine, sleeping till ten on a Tuesday morning. Boys left nice and early, heh?

LINDA: They were out of here by eight o'clock.

WILLY: Good work!

LINDA: It was so thrilling to see them leaving together. I can't get over the shaving lotion in this house.

WILLY: *(smiling)* Mmm —

10   **LINDA:** Biff was very changed this morning. His whole attitude seemed to be hopeful. He couldn't wait to get downtown to see Oliver.

WILLY: He's heading for a change. There's no question, there simply are certain men that take longer to get — solidified. How did he dress?

LINDA: His blue suit. He's so handsome in that suit. He could be a — anything in that suit!

Willy gets up from the table. Linda holds his jacket for him.

WILLY: There's no question, no question at all. Gee, on the way home tonight I'd like to buy some seeds.

LINDA: *(laughing)* That'd be wonderful. But not enough sun gets back there. Nothing'll grow any more.

15   **WILLY:** You wait, kid, before it's all over we're gonna get a little place out in the country, and I'll raise some vegetables, a couple of chickens . . .

LINDA: You'll do it yet, dear.

Willy walks out of his jacket. Linda follows him.

WILLY: And they'll get married, and come for a weekend. I'd build a little guest house. 'Cause I got so many fine tools, all I'd need would be a little lumber and some peace of mind.

LINDA: *(joyfully)* I sewed the lining . . .

WILLY: I could build two guest houses, so they'd both come. Did he decide how much he's going to ask Oliver for?

20   **LINDA:** *(getting him into the jacket)* He didn't mention it, but I imagine ten or fifteen thousand. You going to talk to Howard today?

WILLY: Yeah. I'll put it to him straight and simple. He'll just have to take me off the road.

LINDA: And Willy, don't forget to ask for a little advance, because we've got the insurance premium. It's the grace period now.

WILLY: That's a hundred . . .?

LINDA: A hundred and eight, sixty-eight. Because we're a little short again.

WILLY: Why are we short?   25

LINDA: Well, you had the motor job on the car . . .

WILLY: That goddam Studebaker!

LINDA: And you got one more payment on the refrigerator . . .

WILLY: But it just broke again!

LINDA: Well, it's old, dear.   30

WILLY: I told you we should've bought a well-advertised machine. Charley bought a General Electric and it's twenty years old and it's still good, that son-of-a-bitch.

LINDA: But, Willy—

WILLY: Whoever heard of a Hastings refrigerator? Once in my life I would like to own something outright before it's broken! I'm always in a race with the junkyard! I just finished paying for the car and it's on its last legs. The refrigerator consumes belts like a goddam maniac. They time those things. They time them so when you finally paid for them, they're used up.

LINDA: (buttoning up his jacket as he unbuttons it) All told, about two hundred dollars would carry us, dear. But that includes the last payment on the mortgage. After this payment, Willy, the house belongs to us.

WILLY: It's twenty-five years!   35

LINDA: Biff was nine years old when we bought it.

WILLY: Well, that's a great thing. To weather a twenty-five year mortgage is—

LINDA: It's an accomplishment.

WILLY: All the cement, the lumber, the reconstruction I put in this house! There ain't a crack to be found in it any more.

LINDA: Well, it served its purpose.   40

WILLY: What purpose? Some stranger'll come along, move in, and that's that. If only Biff would take this house, and raise a family . . . (He starts to go.) Good-by, I'm late.

LINDA: (suddenly remembering) Oh, I forgot! You're supposed to meet them for dinner.

WILLY: Me?

LINDA: At Frank's Chop House on Forty-eighth near Sixth Avenue.

WILLY: Is that so! How about you?   45

LINDA: No, just the three of you. They're gonna blow you to a big meal!

WILLY: Don't say! Who thought of that?

LINDA: Biff came to me this morning, Willy, and he said, "Tell Dad, we want to blow him to a big meal." Be there six o'clock. You and your two boys are going to have dinner.

WILLY: Gee whiz! That's really somethin'. I'm gonna knock Howard for a loop, kid. I'll get an advance, and I'll come home with a New York job. Goddammit, now I'm gonna do it!

LINDA: Oh, that's the spirit, Willy!   50

WILLY: I will never get behind a wheel the rest of my life!

LINDA: It's changing, Willy, I can feel it changing!

WILLY: Beyond a question. G'by, I'm late. (*He starts to go again.*)

LINDA: (*calling after him as she runs to the kitchen table for a handkerchief*) You got your glasses?

55 **WILLY:** (*feels for them, then comes back in*) Yeah, yeah, got my glasses.

LINDA: (*giving him the handkerchief*) And a handkerchief.

WILLY: Yeah, handkerchief.

LINDA: And your saccharine?

WILLY: Yeah, my saccharine.

60 **LINDA:** Be careful on the subway stairs.

She kisses him, and a silk stocking is seen hanging from her hand. Willy notices it.

WILLY: Will you stop mending stockings? At least while I'm in the house. It gets me nervous. I can't tell you. Please.

Linda hides the stocking in her hand as she follows Willy across the forestage in front of the house.

LINDA: Remember, Frank's Chop House.

WILLY: (*passing the apron*) Maybe beets would grow out there.

LINDA: (*laughing*) But you tried so many times.

65 **WILLY:** Yeah. Well, don't work hard today. (*He disappears around the right corner of the house.*)

LINDA: Be careful!

As Willy vanishes, Linda waves to him. Suddenly the phone rings. She runs across the stage and into the kitchen and lifts it.

LINDA: Hello? Oh, Biff! I'm so glad you called, I just . . . Yes, sure, I just told him. Yes, he'll be there for dinner at six o'clock, I didn't forget. Listen, I was just dying to tell you. You know that little rubber pipe I told you about? That he connected to the gas heater? I finally decided to go down the cellar this morning and take it away and destroy it. But it's gone! Imagine? He took it away himself, it isn't there! (*She listens.*) When? Oh, then you took it. Oh — nothing, it's just that I'd hoped he'd taken it away himself. Oh, I'm not worried, darling, because this morning he left in such high spirits, it was like the old days! I'm not afraid any more. Did Mr. Oliver see you? . . . Well, you wait there then. And make a nice impression on him, darling. Just don't perspire too much before you see him. And have a nice time with Dad. He may have big news too! . . . That's right, a New York job. And be sweet to him tonight, dear. Be loving to him. Because he's only a little boat looking for a harbor. (*She is trembling with sorrow and joy.*) Oh, that's wonderful, Biff, you'll save his life. Thanks, darling. Just put your arm around him when he comes into the restaurant. Give him a smile. That's the boy . . . Good-by, dear. . . . You got your comb? . . . That's fine. Good-by, Biff dear.

In the middle of her speech, Howard Wagner, thirty-six, wheels in a small typewriter table on which is a wire-recording machine and proceeds to plug it in. This is on the left

forestage. Light slowly fades on Linda as it rises on Howard. Howard is intent on thread-
ing the machine and only glances over his shoulder as Willy appears.

WILLY: Pst! Pst!

HOWARD: Hello, Willy, come in.

WILLY: Like to have a little talk with you, Howard.   70

HOWARD: Sorry to keep you waiting. I'll be with you in a minute.

WILLY: What's that, Howard?

HOWARD: Didn't you ever see one of these? Wire recorder.

WILLY: Oh. Can we talk a minute?

HOWARD: Records things. Just got delivery yesterday. Been driving me crazy,   75
the most terrific machine I ever saw in my life. I was up all night with it.

WILLY: What do you do with it?

HOWARD: I bought it for dictation, but you can do anything with it. Listen to
this. I had it home last night. Listen to what I picked up. The first one is
my daughter. Get this. (*He flicks the switch and "Roll out the Barrel" is heard
being whistled.*) Listen to that kid whistle.

WILLY: That is lifelike, isn't it?

HOWARD: Seven years old. Get that tone.

WILLY: Ts, ts. Like to ask a little favor if you . . .   80

The whistling breaks off, and the voice of Howard's Daughter is heard.

HIS DAUGHTER: "Now you, Daddy."

HOWARD: She's crazy for me! (*Again the same song is whistled.*) That's me! Ha!
(*He winks.*)

WILLY: You're very good!

The whistling breaks off again. The machine runs silent for a moment.

HOWARD: Sh! Get this now, this is my son.

HIS SON: "The capital of Alabama is Montgomery; the capital of Arizona is   85
Phoenix; the capital of Arkansas is Little Rock; the capital of California is
Sacramento . . ." (*And on, and on.*)

HOWARD: (*holding up five fingers*) Five years old, Willy!

WILLY: He'll make an announcer some day!

HIS SON: (*continuing*) "The capital . . ."

HOWARD: Get that — alphabetical order! (*The machine breaks off suddenly.*)
Wait a minute. The maid kicked the plug out.

WILLY: It certainly is a—   90

HOWARD: Sh, for God's sake!

HIS SON: "It's nine o'clock, Bulova watch time. So I have to go to sleep."

WILLY: That really is—

HOWARD: Wait a minute! The next is my wife.

They wait.

HOWARD'S VOICE: "Go on, say something." (*Pause.*) "Well, you gonna talk?"   95

HIS WIFE: "I can't think of anything."

HOWARD'S VOICE: "Well, talk — it's turning."

HIS WIFE: (*shyly, beaten*) "Hello." (*Silence.*) "Oh, Howard, I can't talk into this . . ."

HOWARD: (*snapping the machine off*) That was my wife.

100   WILLY: That is a wonderful machine. Can we —

HOWARD: I tell you, Willy, I'm gonna take my camera, and my bandsaw, and all my hobbies, and out they go. This is the most fascinating relaxation I ever found.

WILLY: I think I'll get one myself.

HOWARD: Sure, they're only a hundred and a half. You can't do without it. Supposing you wanna hear Jack Benny, see? But you can't be at home at that hour. So you tell the maid to turn the radio on when Jack Benny comes on, and this automatically goes on with the radio . . .

WILLY: And when you come home you . . .

105   HOWARD: You can come home twelve o'clock, one o'clock, any time you like, and you get yourself a Coke and sit yourself down, throw the switch, and there's Jack Benny's program in the middle of the night!

WILLY: I'm definitely going to get one. Because lots of time I'm on the road, and I think to myself, what I must be missing on the radio!

HOWARD: Don't you have a radio in the car?

WILLY: Well, yeah, but who ever thinks of turning it on?

HOWARD: Say, aren't you supposed to be in Boston?

110   WILLY: That's what I want to talk to you about, Howard. You got a minute?

He draws a chair in from the wing.

HOWARD: What happened? What're you doing here?

WILLY: Well . . .

HOWARD: You didn't crack up again, did you?

WILLY: Oh, no. No . . .

115   HOWARD: Geez, you had me worried there for a minute. What's the trouble?

WILLY: Well, to tell you the truth, Howard, I've come to the decision that I'd rather not travel any more.

HOWARD: Not travel! Well, what'll you do?

WILLY: Remember, Christmas time, when you had the party here? You said you'd try to think of some spot for me here in town.

HOWARD: With us?

120   WILLY: Well, sure.

HOWARD: Oh, yeah, yeah. I remember. Well, I couldn't think of anything for you, Willy.

WILLY: I tell ya, Howard. The kids are all grown up, y'know. I don't need much any more. If I could take home — well, sixty-five dollars a week, I could swing it.

HOWARD: Yeah, but Willy, see I —

WILLY: I tell ya why, Howard. Speaking frankly and between the two of us, y'know — I'm just a little tired.

HOWARD: Oh, I could understand that, Willy. But you're a road man, Willy,   125
and we do a road business. We've only got a half-dozen salesmen on the
floor here.

WILLY: God knows, Howard, I never asked a favor of any man. But I was with
the firm when your father used to carry you in here in his arms.

HOWARD: I know that, Willy, but—

WILLY: Your father came to me the day you were born and asked me what I
thought of the name of Howard, may he rest in peace.

HOWARD: I appreciate that, Willy, but there just is no spot here for you. If I
had a spot I'd slam you right in, but I just don't have a single, solitary spot.

He looks for his lighter. Willy has picked it up and gives it to him. Pause.

WILLY: *(with increasing anger)* Howard, all I need to set my table is fifty dollars   130
a week.

HOWARD: But where am I going to put you, kid?

WILLY: Look, it isn't a question of whether I can sell merchandise, is it?

HOWARD: No, but it's a business, kid, and everybody's gotta pull his own
weight.

WILLY: *(desperately)* Just let me tell you a story, Howard —

HOWARD: 'Cause you gotta admit, business is business.   135

WILLY: *(angrily)* Business is definitely business, but just listen for a minute. You
don't understand this. When I was a boy — eighteen, nineteen — I was
already on the road. And there was a question in my mind as to whether
selling had a future for me. Because in those days I had a yearning to go to
Alaska. See, there were three gold strikes in one month in Alaska, and I
felt like going out. Just for the ride, you might say.

HOWARD: *(barely interested)* Don't say.

WILLY: Oh, yeah, my father lived many years in Alaska. He was an adventurous
man. We've got quite a little streak of self-reliance in our family. I thought I'd
go out with my older brother and try to locate him, and maybe settle in the
North with the old man. And I was almost decided to go, when I met a salesman in the Parker House. His name was Dave Singleman. And he was eighty-
four years old, and he'd drummed merchandise in thirty-one states. And old
Dave, he'd go up to his room, y'understand, put on his green velvet slippers —
I'll never forget — and pick up his phone and call the buyers, and without
ever leaving his room, at the age of eighty-four, he made his living. And
when I saw that, I realized that selling was the greatest career a man could
want. 'Cause what could be more satisfying than to be able to go, at the age
of eighty-four, into twenty or thirty different cities, and pick up a phone, and
be remembered and loved and helped by so many different people? Do you
know? when he died — and by the way he died the death of a salesman, in his
green velvet slippers in the smoker of the New York, New Haven and Hartford, going into Boston — when he died, hundreds of salesmen and buyers
were at his funeral. Things were sad on a lotta trains for months after that.
(He stands up. Howard has not looked at him.) In those days there was personality in it, Howard. There was respect, and comradeship, and gratitude in it.

Today, it's all cut and dried, and there's no chance for bringing friendship to bear — or personality. You see what I mean? They don't know me any more.

HOWARD: *(moving away, to the right)* That's just the thing, Willy.

140 WILLY: If I had forty dollars a week — that's all I'd need. Forty dollars, Howard.

HOWARD: Kid, I can't take blood from a stone, I—

WILLY: *(desperation is on him now)* Howard, the year Al Smith was nominated, your father came to me and—

HOWARD: *(starting to go off)* I've got to see some people, kid.

WILLY: *(stopping him)* I'm talking about your father! There were promises made across this desk! You mustn't tell me you've got people to see — I put thirty-four years into this firm, Howard, and now I can't pay my insurance! You can't eat the orange and throw the peel away — a man is not a piece of fruit! *(After a pause.)* Now pay attention. Your father — in 1928 I had a big year. I averaged a hundred and seventy dollars a week in commissions.

145 HOWARD: *(impatiently)* Now, Willy, you never averaged—

WILLY: *(banging his hand on the desk)* I averaged a hundred and seventy dollars a week in the year of 1928! And your father came to me — or rather, I was in the office here — it was right over this desk — and he put his hand on my shoulder—

HOWARD: *(getting up)* You'll have to excuse me, Willy, I gotta see some people. Pull yourself together. *(Going out.)* I'll be back in a little while.

On Howard's exit, the light on his chair grows very bright and strange.

WILLY: Pull myself together! What the hell did I say to him? My God, I was yelling at him! How could I! *(Willy breaks off, staring at the light, which occupies the chair, animating it. He approaches this chair, standing across the desk from it.)* Frank, Frank, don't you remember what you told me that time? How you put your hand on my shoulder, and Frank . . . *(He leans on the desk and as he speaks the dead man's name he accidentally switches on the recorder, and instantly —)*

HOWARD'S SON: "... of New York is Albany. The capital of Ohio is Cincinnati, the capital of Rhode Island is . . ." *(The recitation continues.)*

150 WILLY: *(leaping away with fright, shouting)* Ha! Howard! Howard! Howard!

HOWARD: *(rushing in)* What happened?

WILLY: *(pointing at the machine, which continues nasally, childishly, with the capital cities)* Shut it off! Shut it off!

HOWARD: *(pulling the plug out)* Look, Willy . . .

WILLY: *(pressing his hands to his eyes)* I gotta get myself some coffee. I'll get some coffee . . .

Willy starts to walk out. Howard stops him.

155 HOWARD: *(rolling up the cord)* Willy, look . . .

WILLY: I'll go to Boston.

HOWARD: Willy, you can't go to Boston for us.

WILLY: Why can't I go?

HOWARD: I don't want you to represent us. I've been meaning to tell you for a long time now.

WILLY: Howard, are you firing me?   160

HOWARD: I think you need a good long rest, Willy.

WILLY: Howard—

HOWARD: And when you feel better, come back, and we'll see if we can work something out.

WILLY: But I gotta earn money, Howard. I'm in no position—

HOWARD: Where are your sons? Why don't your sons give you a hand?   165

WILLY: They're working on a very big deal.

HOWARD: This is no time for false pride, Willy. You go to your sons and tell them that you're tired. You've got two great boys, haven't you?

WILLY: Oh, no question, no question, but in the meantime . . .

HOWARD: Then that's that, heh?

WILLY: All right, I'll go to Boston tomorrow.   170

HOWARD: No, no.

WILLY: I can't throw myself on my sons. I'm not a cripple!

HOWARD: Look, kid, I'm busy this morning.

WILLY: (*grasping Howard's arm*) Howard, you've got to let me go to Boston!

HOWARD: (*hard, keeping himself under control*) I've got a line of people to see   175
this morning. Sit down, take five minutes, and pull yourself together, and
then go home, will ya? I need the office, Willy. (*He starts to go, turns,
remembering the recorder, starts to push off the table holding the recorder.*) Oh,
yeah. Whenever you can this week, stop by and drop off the samples. You'll
feel better, Willy, and then come back and we'll talk. Pull yourself together,
kid, there's people outside.

*Howard exits, pushing the table off left. Willy stares into space, exhausted. Now the mu-
sic is heard — Ben's music — first distantly, then closer, closer. As Willy speaks, Ben
enters from the right. He carries valise and umbrella.*

WILLY: Oh, Ben, how did you do it? What is the answer? Did you wind up the
Alaska deal already?

BEN: Doesn't take much time if you know what you're doing. Just a short
business trip. Boarding ship in an hour. Wanted to say good-by.

WILLY: Ben, I've got to talk to you.

BEN: (*glancing at his watch*) Haven't the time, William.

WILLY: (*crossing the apron to Ben*) Ben, nothing's working out. I don't know   180
what to do.

BEN: Now, look here, William. I've bought timberland in Alaska and I need a
man to look after things for me.

WILLY: God, timberland! Me and my boys in those grand outdoors!

BEN: You've a new continent at your doorstep, William. Get out of these
cities, they're full of talk and time payments and courts of law. Screw on
your fists and you can fight for a fortune up there.

WILLY: Yes, yes! Linda! Linda!

Linda enters as of old, with the wash.

185 LINDA: Oh, you're back?

BEN: I haven't much time.

WILLY: No, wait! Linda, he's got a proposition for me in Alaska.

LINDA: But you've got — *(To Ben.)* He's got a beautiful job here.

WILLY: But in Alaska, kid, I could—

190 LINDA: You're doing well enough, Willy!

BEN: *(to Linda)* Enough for what, my dear?

LINDA: *(frightened of Ben and angry at him)* Don't say those things to him! Enough to be happy right here, right now. *(To Willy, while Ben laughs.)* Why must everybody conquer the world? You're well liked, and the boys love you, and someday — *(to Ben)* — why, old man Wagner told him just the other day that if he keeps it up he'll be a member of the firm, didn't he, Willy?

WILLY: Sure, sure. I am building something with this firm, Ben, and if a man is building something he must be on the right track, mustn't he?

BEN: What are you building? Lay your hand on it. Where is it?

195 WILLY: *(hesitantly)* That's true, Linda, there's nothing.

LINDA: Why? *(To Ben.)* There's a man eighty-four years old—

WILLY: That's right, Ben, that's right. When I look at that man I say, what is there to worry about?

BEN: Bah!

WILLY: It's true, Ben. All he has to do is go into any city, pick up the phone, and he's making his living and you know why?

200 BEN: *(picking up his valise)* I've got to go.

WILLY: *(holding Ben back)* Look at this boy!

Biff, in his high school sweater, enters carrying suitcase. Happy carries Biff's shoulder guards, gold helmet, and football pants.

WILLY: Without a penny to his name, three great universities are begging for him, and from there the sky's the limit, because it's not what you do, Ben. It's who you know and the smile on your face! It's contacts, Ben, contacts! The whole wealth of Alaska passes over the lunch table at the Commodore Hotel, and that's the wonder, the wonder of this country, that a man can end with diamonds here on the basis of being liked! *(He turns to Biff.)* And that's why when you get out on that field today it's important. Because thousands of people will be rooting for you and loving you. *(To Ben, who has again begun to leave.)* And Ben! when he walks into a business office his name will sound out like a bell and all the doors will open to him! I've seen it, Ben, I've seen it a thousand times! You can't feel it with your hand like timber, but it's there!

BEN: Good-by, William.

WILLY: Ben, am I right? Don't you think I'm right? I value your advice.

205 BEN: There's a new continent at your doorstep, William. You could walk out rich. Rich. *(He is gone.)*

WILLY: We'll do it here, Ben! You hear me? We're gonna do it here!

Young Bernard rushes in. The gay music of the boys is heard.

BERNARD: Oh, gee, I was afraid you left already!

WILLY: Why? What time is it?

BERNARD: It's half-past one!

WILLY: Well, come on, everybody! Ebbets Field° next stop! Where's the pennants?   210
  (*He rushes through the wall-line of the kitchen and out into the living room.*)

LINDA: (*to Biff*) Did you pack fresh underwear?

BIFF: (*who has been limbering up*) I want to go!

BERNARD: Biff, I'm carrying your helmet, ain't I?

HAPPY: No, I'm carrying the helmet.

BERNARD: Oh, Biff, you promised me.   215

HAPPY: I'm carrying the helmet.

BERNARD: How am I going to get in the locker room?

LINDA: Let him carry the shoulder guards. (*She puts her coat and hat on in the
  kitchen.*)

BERNARD: Can I, Biff? 'Cause I told everybody I'm going to be in the locker
  room.

HAPPY: In Ebbets Field it's the clubhouse.   220

BERNARD: I meant the clubhouse. Biff!

HAPPY: Biff!

BIFF: (*grandly, after a slight pause*) Let him carry the shoulder guards.

HAPPY: (*as he gives Bernard the shoulder guards*) Stay close to us now.

Willy rushes in with the pennants.

WILLY: (*handing them out*) Everybody wave when Biff comes out on the field.   225
  (*Happy and Bernard run off.*) You set now, boy?

The music has died away.

BIFF: Ready to go, Pop. Every muscle is ready.

WILLY: (*at the edge of the apron*) You realize what this means?

BIFF: That's right, Pop.

WILLY: (*feeling Biff's muscles*) You're comin' home this afternoon captain of the
  All-Scholastic Championship Team of the City of New York.

BIFF: I got it, Pop. And remember, pal, when I take off my helmet, that   230
  touchdown is for you.

WILLY: Let's go! (*He is starting out, with his arm around Biff, when Charley
  enters, as of old, in knickers.*) I got no room for you, Charley.

CHARLEY: Room? For what?

WILLY: In the car.

CHARLEY: You goin' for a ride? I wanted to shoot some casino.

WILLY: (*furiously*) Casino! (*Incredulously.*) Don't you realize what today is?   235

°*Ebbets Field:* The home park of the Brooklyn Dodgers.

LINDA: Oh, he knows, Willy. He's just kidding you.

WILLY: That's nothing to kid about!

CHARLEY: No, Linda, what's goin' on?

LINDA: He's playing in Ebbets Field.

240   CHARLEY: Baseball in this weather?

WILLY: Don't talk to him. Come on, come on! (*He is pushing them out.*)

CHARLEY: Wait a minute, didn't you hear the news?

WILLY: What?

CHARLEY: Don't you listen to the radio? Ebbets Field just blew up.

245   WILLY: You go to hell! (*Charley laughs. Pushing them out.*) Come on, come on!
We're late.

CHARLEY: (*as they go*) Knock a homer, Biff, knock a homer!

WILLY: (*the last to leave, turning to Charley*) I don't think that was funny,
Charley. This is the greatest day of his life.

CHARLEY: Willy, when are you going to grow up?

WILLY: Yeah, heh? When this game is over, Charley, you'll be laughing out of
the other side of your face. They'll be calling him another Red Grange.°
Twenty-five thousand a year.

250   CHARLEY: (*kidding*) Is that so?

WILLY: Yeah, that's so.

CHARLEY: Well, then, I'm sorry, Willy. But tell me something.

WILLY: What?

CHARLEY: Who is Red Grange?

255   WILLY: Put up your hands. Goddam you, put up your hands!

*Charley, chuckling, shakes his head and walks away, around the left corner of the stage.
Willy follows him. The music rises to a mocking frenzy.*

WILLY: Who the hell do you think you are, better than everybody else? You
don't know everything, you big, ignorant, stupid . . . Put up your hands!

*Light rises, on the right side of the forestage, on a small table in the reception room
of Charley's office. Traffic sounds are heard. Bernard, now mature, sits whistling to
himself. A pair of tennis rackets and an overnight bag are on the floor beside him.*

WILLY: (*offstage*) What are you walking away for? Don't walk away! If you're
going to say something say it to my face! I know you laugh at me behind my
back. You'll laugh out of the other side of your goddam face after this game.
Touchdown! Touchdown! Eighty thousand people! Touchdown! Right
between the goal posts.

*Bernard is a quiet, earnest, but self-assured young man. Willy's voice is coming from
right upstage now. Bernard lowers his feet off the table and listens. Jenny, his father's
secretary, enters.*

° *Red Grange:* Harold Edward ("Red") Grange (1903–1991)—American football player. A running back for the
New York Yankees football team and the Chicago Bears, Grange was elected to the Football Hall of Fame in 1963.

JENNY: (*distressed*) Say, Bernard, will you go out in the hall?

BERNARD: What is that noise? Who is it?

JENNY: Mr. Loman. He just got off the elevator.   260

BERNARD: (*getting up*) Who's he arguing with?

JENNY: Nobody. There's nobody with him. I can't deal with him any more, and your father gets all upset everytime he comes. I've got a lot of typing to do, and your father's waiting to sign it. Will you see him?

WILLY: (*entering*) Touchdown! Touch — (*He sees Jenny.*) Jenny, Jenny, good to see you. How're ya? Workin'? Or still honest?

JENNY: Fine. How've you been feeling?

WILLY: Not much any more, Jenny. Ha, ha! (*He is surprised to see the rackets.*)   265

BERNARD: Hello, Uncle Willy.

WILLY: (*almost shocked*) Bernard! Well, look who's here! (*He comes quickly, guiltily, to Bernard and warmly shakes his hand.*)

BERNARD: How are you? Good to see you.

WILLY: What are you doing here?

BERNARD: Oh, just stopped by to see Pop. Get off my feet till my train leaves.   270
I'm going to Washington in a few minutes.

WILLY: Is he in?

BERNARD: Yes, he's in his office with the accountant. Sit down.

WILLY: (*sitting down*) What're you going to do in Washington?

BERNARD: Oh, just a case I've got there, Willy.

WILLY: That so? (*indicating the rackets*) You going to play tennis there?   275

BERNARD: I'm staying with a friend who's got a court.

WILLY: Don't say. His own tennis court. Must be fine people, I bet.

BERNARD: They are, very nice. Dad tells me Biff's in town.

WILLY: (*with a big smile*) Yeah, Biff's in. Working on a very big deal, Bernard.

BERNARD: What's Biff doing?   280

WILLY: Well, he's been doing very big things in the West. But he decided to establish himself here. Very big. We're having dinner. Did I hear your wife had a boy?

BERNARD: That's right. Our second.

WILLY: Two boys! What do you know!

BERNARD: What kind of a deal has Biff got?

WILLY: Well, Bill Oliver — very big sporting-goods man — he wants Biff very   285
badly. Called him in from the West. Long distance, carte blanche, special deliveries. Your friends have their own private tennis court?

BERNARD: You still with the old firm, Willy?

WILLY: (*after a pause*) I'm — I'm overjoyed to see how you made the grade, Bernard, overjoyed. It's an encouraging thing to see a young man really — really — Looks very good for Biff — very — (*He breaks off, then.*) Bernard — (*He is so full of emotion, he breaks off again.*)

BERNARD: What is it, Willy?

WILLY: (*small and alone*) What — what's the secret?

BERNARD: What secret?   290

WILLY: How — how did you? Why didn't he ever catch on?

BERNARD: I wouldn't know that, Willy.

WILLY: *(confidentially, desperately)* You were his friend, his boyhood friend. There's something I don't understand about it. His life ended after that Ebbets Field game. From the age of seventeen nothing good ever happened to him.

BERNARD: He never trained himself for anything.

295 WILLY: But he did, he did. After high school he took so many correspondence courses. Radio mechanics; television; God knows what, and never made the slightest mark.

BERNARD: *(taking off his glasses)* Willy, do you want to talk candidly?

WILLY: *(rising, faces Bernard)* I regard you as a very brilliant man, Bernard. I value your advice.

BERNARD: Oh, the hell with the advice, Willy. I couldn't advise you. There's just one thing I've always wanted to ask you. When he was supposed to graduate, and the math teacher flunked him —

WILLY: Oh, that son-of-a-bitch ruined his life.

300 BERNARD: Yeah, but, Willy, all he had to do was go to summer school and make up that subject.

WILLY: That's right, that's right.

BERNARD: Did you tell him not to go to summer school?

WILLY: Me? I begged him to go. I ordered him to go!

BERNARD: Then why wouldn't he go?

305 WILLY: Why? Why! Bernard, that question has been trailing me like a ghost for the last fifteen years. He flunked the subject, and laid down and died like a hammer hit him!

BERNARD: Take it easy, kid.

WILLY: Let me talk to you — I got nobody to talk to. Bernard, Bernard, was it my fault? Y'see? It keeps going around in my mind, maybe I did something to him. I got nothing to give him.

BERNARD: Don't take it so hard.

WILLY: Why did he lay down? What is the story there? You were his friend!

310 BERNARD: Willy, I remember, it was June, and our grades came out. And he'd flunked math.

WILLY: That son-of-a-bitch!

BERNARD: No, it wasn't right then. Biff just got very angry, I remember, and he was ready to enroll in summer school.

WILLY: *(surprised)* He was?

BERNARD: He wasn't beaten by it at all. But then, Willy, he disappeared from the block for almost a month. And I got the idea that he'd gone up to New England to see you. Did he have a talk with you then?

Willy stares in silence.

315 BERNARD: Willy?

WILLY: *(with a strong edge of resentment in his voice)* Yeah, he came to Boston. What about it?

BERNARD: Well, just that when he came back — I'll never forget this, it always
  mystifies me. Because I'd thought so well of Biff, even though he'd always
  taken advantage of me. I loved him, Willy, y'know? And he came back after
  that month and took his sneakers — remember those sneakers with "University of Virginia" printed on them? He was so proud of those, wore them
  every day. And he took them down in the cellar, and burned them up in
  the furnace. We had a fist fight. It lasted at least half an hour. Just the two
  of us, punching each other down the cellar, and crying right through it. I've
  often thought of how strange it was that I knew he'd given up his life.
  What happened in Boston, Willy?

Willy looks at him as at an intruder.

BERNARD: I just bring it up because you asked me.
WILLY: *(angrily)* Nothing. What do you mean, "What happened?" What's that
  got to do with anything?
BERNARD: Well, don't get sore.   320
WILLY: What are you trying to do, blame it on me? If a boy lays down is that
  my fault?
BERNARD: Now, Willy, don't get —
WILLY: Well, don't — don't talk to me that way! What does that mean, "What
  happened?"

Charley enters. He is in his vest, and he carries a bottle of bourbon.

CHARLEY: Hey, you're going to miss that train. *(He waves the bottle.)*
BERNARD: Yeah, I'm going. *(He takes the bottle.)* Thanks, Pop. *(He picks up his* 325
  rackets and bag.) Good-by, Willy, and don't worry about it. You know, "If at
  first you don't succeed . . ."
WILLY: Yes, I believe in that.
BERNARD: But sometimes, Willy, it's better for a man just to walk away.
WILLY: Walk away?
BERNARD: That's right.
WILLY: But if you can't walk away?   330
BERNARD: *(after a slight pause)* I guess that's when it's tough. *(Extending his*
  hand.) Good-by, Willy.
WILLY: *(shaking Bernard's hand)* Good-by, boy.
CHARLEY: *(an arm on Bernard's shoulder)* How do you like this kid? Gonna
  argue a case in front of the Supreme Court.
BERNARD: *(protesting)* Pop!
WILLY: *(genuinely shocked, pained, and happy)* No! The Supreme Court!   335
BERNARD: I gotta run, 'By, Dad!
CHARLEY: Knock 'em dead, Bernard!

Bernard goes off.

WILLY: *(as Charley takes out his wallet)* The Supreme Court! And he didn't
  even mention it!
CHARLEY: *(counting out money on the desk)* He don't have to — he's gonna do it.

340   **WILLY:** And you never told him what to do, did you? You never took any
interest in him.

CHARLEY: My salvation is that I never took any interest in anything. There's
some money — fifty dollars. I got an accountant inside.

WILLY: Charley, look . . . (*With difficulty.*) I got my insurance to pay. If you can
manage it — I need a hundred and ten dollars.

Charley doesn't reply for a moment; merely stops moving.

WILLY: I'd draw it from my bank but Linda would know, and I . . .

CHARLEY: Sit down, Willy.

345   **WILLY:** (*moving toward the chair*) I'm keeping an account of everything,
remember. I'll pay every penny back. (*He sits.*)

CHARLEY: Now listen to me, Willy.

WILLY: I want you to know I appreciate . . .

CHARLEY: (*sitting down on the table*) Willy, what're you doin'? What the hell is
goin' on in your head?

WILLY: Why? I'm simply . . .

350   **CHARLEY:** I offered you a job. You can make fifty dollars a week. And I won't
send you on the road.

WILLY: I've got a job.

CHARLEY: Without pay? What kind of a job is a job without pay? (*He rises.*)
Now, look, kid, enough is enough. I'm no genius but I know when I'm
being insulted.

WILLY: Insulted!

CHARLEY: Why don't you want to work for me?

355   **WILLY:** What's the matter with you? I've got a job.

CHARLEY: Then what're you walkin' in here every week for?

WILLY: (*getting up*) Well, if you don't want me to walk in here —

CHARLEY: I am offering you a job.

WILLY: I don't want your goddam job!

360   **CHARLEY:** When the hell are you going to grow up?

WILLY: (*furiously*) You big ignoramus, if you say that to me again I'll rap you
one! I don't care how big you are! (*He's ready to fight.*)

Pause.

CHARLEY: (*kindly, going to him*) How much do you need, Willy?

WILLY: Charley, I'm strapped. I'm strapped. I don't know what to do. I was just
fired.

CHARLEY: Howard fired you?

365   **WILLY:** That snotnose. Imagine that? I named him. I named him Howard.

CHARLEY: Willy, when're you gonna realize that them things don't mean anything? You named him Howard, but you can't sell that. The only thing you
got in this world is what you can sell. And the funny thing is that you're a
salesman, and you don't know that.

WILLY: I've always tried to think otherwise, I guess. I always felt that if a man
was impressive, and well liked, that nothing —

CHARLEY: Why must everybody like you? Who liked J. P. Morgan?° Was he
impressive? In a Turkish bath he'd look like a butcher. But with his pockets
on he was very well liked. Now listen, Willy, I know you don't like me, and
nobody can say I'm in love with you, but I'll give you a job because — just
for the hell of it, put it that way. Now what do you say?

WILLY: I — I just can't work for you, Charley.

CHARLEY: What're you, jealous of me?   370

WILLY: I can't work for you, that's all, don't ask me why.

CHARLEY: (angered, takes out more bills) You been jealous of me all your life,
you damned fool! Here, pay your insurance. (He puts the money in Willy's
hand.)

WILLY: I'm keeping strict accounts.

CHARLEY: I've got some work to do. Take care of yourself. And pay your
insurance.

WILLY: (moving to the right) Funny, y'know? After all the highways, and the   375
trains, and the appointments, and the years, you end up worth more dead
than alive.

CHARLEY: Willy, nobody's worth nothin' dead. (After a slight pause.) Did you
hear what I said?

Willy stands still, dreaming.

CHARLEY: Willy!

WILLY: Apologize to Bernard for me when you see him. I didn't mean to argue
with him. He's a fine boy. They're all fine boys, and they'll end up big — all
of them. Someday they'll all play tennis together. Wish me luck, Charley.
He saw Bill Oliver today.

CHARLEY: Good luck.

WILLY: (on the verge of tears) Charley, you're the only friend I got. Isn't that a   380
remarkable thing? (He goes out.)

CHARLEY: Jesus!

*Charley stares after him a moment and follows. All light blacks out. Suddenly raucous
music is heard, and a red glow rises behind the screen at right. Stanley, a young waiter,
appears, carrying a table, followed by Happy, who is carrying two chairs.*

STANLEY: (putting the table down) That's all right, Mr. Loman, I can handle it
myself. (He turns and takes the chairs from Happy and places them at the table.)

HAPPY: (glancing around) Oh, this is better.

STANLEY: Sure, in the front there you're in the middle of all kinds a noise.
Whenever you got a party, Mr. Loman, you just tell me and I'll put you back
here. Y'know, there's a lotta people they don't like it private, because when
they go out they like to see a lotta action around them because they're sick
and tired to stay in the house by theirself. But I know you, you ain't from
Hackensack. You know what I mean?

° *J. P. Morgan:* John Pierpont Morgan (1837–1913) — American financier.

385 HAPPY: (*sitting down*) So, how's it coming, Stanley?

STANLEY: Ah, it's a dog's life. I only wish during the war they'd a took me in the Army. I coulda been dead by now.

HAPPY: My brother's back, Stanley.

STANLEY: Oh, he come back, heh? From the Far West.

HAPPY: Yeah, big cattle man, my brother, so treat him right. And my father's coming too.

390 STANLEY: Oh, your father too!

HAPPY: You got a couple of nice lobsters?

STANLEY: Hundred per cent, big.

HAPPY: I want them with the claws.

STANLEY: Don't worry, I don't give you no mice. (*Happy laughs.*) How about some wine? It'll put a head on the meal.

395 HAPPY: No. You remember, Stanley, that recipe I brought you from overseas? With the champagne in it?

STANLEY: Oh, yeah, sure. I still got it tacked up yet in the kitchen. But that'll have to cost a buck apiece anyways.

HAPPY: That's all right.

STANLEY: What'd you, hit a number or somethin'?

HAPPY: No, it's a little celebration. My brother is — I think he pulled off a big deal today. I think we're going into business together.

400 STANLEY: Great! That's the best for you. Because a family business, you know what I mean?— that's the best.

HAPPY: That's what I think.

STANLEY: 'Cause what's the difference? Somebody steals? It's in the family. Know what I mean? (*Sotto voce.*) Like this bartender here. The boss is goin' crazy what kinda leak he's got in the cash register. You put it in but it don't come out.

HAPPY: (*raising his head*) Sh!

STANLEY: What?

405 HAPPY: You notice I wasn't lookin' right or left, was I?

STANLEY: No.

HAPPY: And my eyes are closed.

STANLEY: So what's the—

HAPPY: Strudel's comin'.

410 STANLEY: (*catching on, looks around*) Ah, no, there's no—

He breaks off as a furred, lavishly dressed Girl enters and sits at the next table. Both follow her with their eyes.

STANLEY: Geez, how'd ya know?

HAPPY: I got radar or something. (*Staring directly at her profile.*) Oooooooo . . . Stanley.

STANLEY: I think that's for you, Mr. Loman.

HAPPY: Look at that mouth. Oh, God. And the binoculars.

415 STANLEY: Geez, you got a life, Mr. Loman.

HAPPY: Wait on her.

STANLEY: *(going to The Girl's table)* Would you like a menu, ma'am?

GIRL: I'm expecting someone, but I'd like a—

HAPPY: Why don't you bring her—excuse me, miss, do you mind? I sell champagne, and I'd like you to try my brand. Bring her a champagne, Stanley.

GIRL: That's awfully nice of you.   420

HAPPY: Don't mention it. It's all company money. *(He laughs.)*

GIRL: That's a charming product to be selling, isn't it?

HAPPY: Oh, gets to be like everything else. Selling is selling, y'know.

GIRL: I suppose.

HAPPY: You don't happen to sell, do you?   425

GIRL: No, I don't sell.

HAPPY: Would you object to a compliment from a stranger? You ought to be on a magazine cover.

GIRL: *(looking at him a little archly)* I have been.

Stanley comes in with a glass of champagne.

HAPPY: What'd I say before, Stanley? You see? She's a cover girl.

STANLEY: Oh, I could see, I could see.   430

HAPPY: *(to The Girl)* What magazine?

GIRL: Oh, a lot of them. *(She takes the drink.)* Thank you.

HAPPY: You know what they say in France, don't you? "Champagne is the drink of the complexion"—Hya, Biff!

Biff has entered and sits with Happy.

BIFF: Hello, kid. Sorry I'm late.

HAPPY: I just got here. Uh, Miss—?   435

GIRL: Forsythe.

HAPPY: Miss Forsythe, this is my brother.

BIFF: Is Dad here?

HAPPY: His name is Biff. You might've heard of him. Great football player.

GIRL: Really? What team?   440

HAPPY: Are you familiar with football?

GIRL: No, I'm afraid I'm not.

HAPPY: Biff is quarterback with the New York Giants.

GIRL: Well, that is nice, isn't it? *(She drinks.)*

HAPPY: Good health.   445

GIRL: I'm happy to meet you.

HAPPY: That's my name. Hap. It's really Harold, but at West Point they called me Happy.

GIRL: *(now really impressed)* Oh, I see. How do you do? *(She turns her profile.)*

BIFF: Isn't Dad coming?

HAPPY: You want her?   450

BIFF: Oh, I could never make that.

HAPPY: I remember the time that idea would never come into your head. Where's the old confidence, Biff?

BIFF: I just saw Oliver—

HAPPY: Wait a minute. I've got to see that old confidence again. Do you want her? She's on call.

455   BIFF: Oh, no. (*He turns to look at The Girl.*)

HAPPY: I'm telling you. Watch this. (*Turning to The Girl.*) Honey? (*She turns to him.*) Are you busy?

GIRL: Well, I am . . . but I could make a phone call.

HAPPY: Do that, will you, honey? And see if you can get a friend. We'll be here for a while. Biff is one of the greatest football players in the country.

GIRL: (*standing up*) Well, I'm certainly happy to meet you.

460   HAPPY: Come back soon.

GIRL: I'll try.

HAPPY: Don't try, honey, try hard.

The Girl exits. Stanley follows, shaking his head in bewildered admiration.

HAPPY: Isn't that a shame now? A beautiful girl like that? That's why I can't get married. There's not a good woman in a thousand. New York is loaded with them, kid!

BIFF: Hap, look —

465   HAPPY: I told you she was on call!

BIFF: (*strangely unnerved*) Cut it out, will ya? I want to say something to you.

HAPPY: Did you see Oliver?

BIFF: I saw him all right. Now look, I want to tell Dad a couple of things and I want you to help me.

HAPPY: What? Is he going to back you?

470   BIFF: Are you crazy? You're out of your goddam head, you know that?

HAPPY: Why? What happened?

BIFF: (*breathlessly*) I did a terrible thing today, Hap. It's been the strangest day I ever went through. I'm all numb, I swear.

HAPPY: You mean he wouldn't see you?

BIFF: Well, I waited six hours for him, see? All day. Kept sending my name in. Even tried to date his secretary so she'd get me to him, but no soap.

475   HAPPY: Because you're not showin' the old confidence, Biff. He remembered you, didn't he?

BIFF: (*stopping Happy with a gesture*) Finally, about five o'clock, he comes out. Didn't remember who I was or anything. I felt like such an idiot, Hap.

HAPPY: Did you tell him my Florida idea?

BIFF: He walked away. I saw him for one minute. I got so mad I could've torn the walls down! How the hell did I ever get the idea I was a salesman there? I even believed myself that I'd been a salesman for him! And then he gave me one look and — I realized what a ridiculous lie my whole life has been! We've been talking in a dream for fifteen years. I was a shipping clerk.

HAPPY: What'd you do?

480   BIFF: (*with great tension and wonder*) Well, he left, see. And the secretary went out. I was all alone in the waiting-room. I don't know what came over me,

Hap. The next thing I know I'm in his office — paneled walls, everything. I can't explain it. I — Hap, I took his fountain pen.

HAPPY: Geez, did he catch you?

BIFF: I ran out. I ran down all eleven flights. I ran and ran and ran.

HAPPY: That was an awful dumb — what'd you do that for?

BIFF: *(agonized)* I don't know, I just — wanted to take something, I don't know. You gotta help me, Hap. I'm gonna tell Pop.

HAPPY: You crazy? What for?   485

BIFF: Hap, he's got to understand that I'm not the man somebody lends that kind of money to. He thinks I've been spiting him all these years and it's eating him up.

HAPPY: That's just it. You tell him something nice.

BIFF: I can't.

HAPPY: Say you got a lunch date with Oliver tomorrow.

BIFF: So what do I do tomorrow?   490

HAPPY: You leave the house tomorrow and come back at night and say Oliver is thinking it over. And he thinks it over for a couple of weeks, and gradually it fades away and nobody's the worse.

BIFF: But it'll go on forever!

HAPPY: Dad is never so happy as when he's looking forward to something!

Willy enters.

HAPPY: Hello, scout!

WILLY: Gee, I haven't been here in years!   495

Stanley has followed Willy in and sets a chair for him. Stanley starts off but Happy stops him.

HAPPY: Stanley!

Stanley stands by, waiting for an order.

BIFF: *(going to Willy with guilt, as to an invalid)* Sit down, Pop. You want a drink?

WILLY: Sure, I don't mind.

BIFF: Let's get a load on.

WILLY: You look worried.   500

BIFF: N-no. *(To Stanley.)* Scotch all around. Make it doubles.

STANLEY: Doubles, right. *(He goes.)*

WILLY: You had a couple already, didn't you?

BIFF: Just a couple, yeah.

WILLY: Well, what happened, boy? *(Nodding affirmatively, with a smile.)*   505
Everything go all right?

BIFF: *(takes a breath, then reaches out and grasps Willy's hand)* Pal . . . *(He is smiling bravely, and Willy is smiling too.)* I had an experience today.

HAPPY: Terrific, Pop.

WILLY: That so? What happened?

BIFF: (*high, slightly alcoholic, above the earth*) I'm going to tell you everything from first to last. It's been a strange day. (*Silence. He looks around, composes himself as best he can, but his breath keeps breaking the rhythm of his voice.*) I had to wait quite a while for him, and—

510   **WILLY:** Oliver?

BIFF: Yeah, Oliver. All day, as a matter of cold fact. And a lot of — instances — facts, Pop, facts about my life came back to me. Who was it, Pop? Who ever said I was a salesman with Oliver?

WILLY: Well, you were.

BIFF: No, Dad, I was a shipping clerk.

WILLY: But you were practically—

515   **BIFF:** (*with determination*) Dad, I don't know who said it first, but I was never a salesman for Bill Oliver.

WILLY: What're you talking about?

BIFF: Let's hold on to the facts tonight, Pop. We're not going to get anywhere bullin' around. I was a shipping clerk.

WILLY: (*angrily*) All right, now listen to me—

BIFF: Why don't you let me finish?

520   **WILLY:** I'm not interested in stories about the past or any crap of that kind because the woods are burning, boys, you understand? There's a big blaze going on all around. I was fired today.

BIFF: (*shocked*) How could you be?

WILLY: I was fired, and I'm looking for a little good news to tell your mother, because the woman has waited and the woman has suffered. The gist of it is that I haven't got a story left in my head, Biff. So don't give me a lecture about facts and aspects. I am not interested. Now what've you got to say to me?

Stanley enters with three drinks. They wait until he leaves.

WILLY: Did you see Oliver?

BIFF: Jesus, Dad!

525   **WILLY:** You mean you didn't go up there?

HAPPY: Sure he went up there.

BIFF: I did. I — saw him. How could they fire you?

WILLY: (*on the edge of his chair*) What kind of a welcome did he give you?

BIFF: He won't even let you work on commission?

530   **WILLY:** I'm out! (*Driving.*) So tell me, he gave you a warm welcome?

HAPPY: Sure, Pop, sure!

BIFF: (*driven*) Well, it was kind of —

WILLY: I was wondering if he'd remember you. (*To Happy.*) Imagine, man doesn't see him for ten, twelve years and gives him that kind of a welcome!

HAPPY: Damn right!

535   **BIFF:** (*trying to return to the offensive*) Pop, look —

WILLY: You know why he remembered you, don't you? Because you impressed him in those days.

BIFF: Let's talk quietly and get this down to the facts, huh?

WILLY: *(as though Biff had been interrupting)* Well, what happened? It's great news, Biff. Did he take you into his office or'd you talk in the waiting-room?

BIFF: Well, he came in, see, and—

WILLY: *(with a big smile)* What'd he say? Betcha he threw his arm around you.   540

BIFF: Well, he kinda—

WILLY: He's a fine man. *(To Happy.)* Very hard man to see, y'know.

HAPPY: *(agreeing)* Oh, I know.

WILLY: *(to Biff)* Is that where you had the drinks?

BIFF: Yeah, he gave me a couple of — no, no!   545

HAPPY: *(cutting in)* He told him my Florida idea.

WILLY: Don't interrupt. *(To Biff.)* How'd he react to the Florida idea?

BIFF: Dad, will you give me a minute to explain?

WILLY: I've been waiting for you to explain since I sat down here! What happened? He took you into his office and what?

BIFF: Well — I talked. And — and he listened, see.   550

WILLY: Famous for the way he listens, y'know. What was his answer?

BIFF: His answer was — *(He breaks off, suddenly angry.)* Dad, you're not letting me tell you what I want to tell you!

WILLY: *(accusing, angered)* You didn't see him, did you?

BIFF: I did see him!

WILLY: What'd you insult him or something? You insulted him, didn't you?   555

BIFF: Listen, will you let me out of it, will you just let me out of it!

HAPPY: What the hell!

WILLY: Tell me what happened!

BIFF: *(to Happy)* I can't talk to him!

A single trumpet note jars the ear. The light of green leaves stains the house, which holds the air of night and a dream. Young Bernard enters and knocks on the door of the house.

YOUNG BERNARD: *(frantically)* Mrs. Loman, Mrs. Loman!   560

HAPPY: Tell him what happened!

BIFF: *(to Happy)* Shut up and leave me alone!

WILLY: No, no! You had to go and flunk math!

BIFF: What math? What're you talking about?

YOUNG BERNARD: Mrs. Loman, Mrs. Loman!   565

Linda appears in the house, as of old.

WILLY: *(wildly)* Math, math, math!

BIFF: Take it easy, Pop!

YOUNG BERNARD: Mrs. Loman!

WILLY: *(furiously)* If you hadn't flunked you'd've been set by now!

BIFF: Now, look, I'm gonna tell you what happened, and you're going to listen   570 to me.

YOUNG BERNARD: Mrs. Loman!

BIFF: I waited six hours—

HAPPY: What the hell are you saying?

BIFF: I kept sending in my name but he wouldn't see me. So finally he . . .
   (*He continues unheard as light fades low on the restaurant.*)

575 **YOUNG BERNARD:** Biff flunked math!

LINDA: No!

YOUNG BERNARD: Birnbaum flunked him! They won't graduate him!

LINDA: But they have to. He's gotta go to the university. Where is he? Biff! Biff!

YOUNG BERNARD: No, he left. He went to Grand Central.

580 **LINDA:** Grand — You mean he went to Boston!

YOUNG BERNARD: Is Uncle Willy in Boston?

LINDA: Oh, maybe Willy can talk to the teacher. Oh, the poor, poor boy!

Light on house area snaps out.

BIFF: (*at the table, now audible, holding up a gold fountain pen*) . . . so I'm washed
   up with Oliver, you understand? Are you listening to me?

WILLY: (*at a loss*) Yeah, sure. If you hadn't flunked —

585 **BIFF:** Flunked what? What're you talking about?

WILLY: Don't blame everything on me! I didn't flunk math — you did! What pen?

HAPPY: That was awful dumb, Biff, a pen like that is worth —

WILLY: (*seeing the pen for the first time*) You took Oliver's pen?

BIFF: (*weakening*) Dad, I just explained it to you.

590 **WILLY:** You stole Bill Oliver's fountain pen!

BIFF: I didn't exactly steal it! That's just what I've been explaining to you!

HAPPY: He had it in his hand and just then Oliver walked in, so he got
   nervous and stuck it in his pocket!

WILLY: My God, Biff!

BIFF: I never intended to do it, Dad!

595 **OPERATOR'S VOICE:** Standish Arms, good evening!

WILLY: (*shouting*) I'm not in my room!

BIFF: (*frightened*) Dad, what's the matter? (*He and Happy stand up.*)

OPERATOR: Ringing Mr. Loman for you!

WILLY: I'm not there, stop it!

600 **BIFF:** (*horrified, gets down on one knee before Willy*) Dad, I'll make good, I'll
   make good. (*Willy tries to get to his feet. Biff holds him down.*) Sit down now.

WILLY: No, you're no good, you're no good for anything.

BIFF: I am, Dad, I'll find something else, you understand? Now don't worry
   about anything. (*He holds up Willy's face.*) Talk to me, Dad.

OPERATOR: Mr. Loman does not answer. Shall I page him?

WILLY: (*attempting to stand, as though to rush and silence the Operator*) No, no, no!

605 **HAPPY:** He'll strike something, Pop.

WILLY: No, no . . .

BIFF: (*desperately, standing over Willy*) Pop, listen! Listen to me! I'm telling
   you something good. Oliver talked to his partner about the Florida idea.
   You listening? He — he talked to his partner, and he came to me . . .
   I'm going to be all right, you hear? Dad, listen to me, he said it was just a
   question of the amount!

WILLY: Then you . . . got it?

HAPPY: He's gonna be terrific, Pop!

WILLY: (*trying to stand*) Then you got it, haven't you? You got it! You got it!   610

BIFF: (*agonized, holds Willy down*) No, no. Look, Pop. I'm supposed to have lunch with them tomorrow. I'm just telling you this so you'll know that I can still make an impression, Pop. And I'll make good somewhere, but I can't go tomorrow, see?

WILLY: Why not? You simply —

BIFF: But the pen, Pop!

WILLY: You give it to him and tell him it was an oversight!

HAPPY: Sure, have lunch tomorrow!   615

BIFF: I can't say that —

WILLY: You were doing a crossword puzzle and accidentally used his pen!

BIFF: Listen, kid, I took those balls years ago, now I walk in with his fountain pen? That clinches it, don't you see? I can't face him like that! I'll try elsewhere.

PAGE'S VOICE: Paging Mr. Loman!

WILLY: Don't you want to be anything?   620

BIFF: Pop, how can I go back?

WILLY: You don't want to be anything, is that what's behind it?

BIFF: (*now angry at Willy for not crediting his sympathy*) Don't take it that way! You think it was easy walking into that office after what I'd done to him? A team of horses couldn't have dragged me back to Bill Oliver!

WILLY: Then why'd you go?

BIFF: Why did I go? Why did I go? Look at you! Look at what's become of you!   625

Off left, The Woman laughs.

WILLY: Biff, you're going to go to that lunch tomorrow, or —

BIFF: I can't go. I've got no appointment!

HAPPY: Biff, for . . .!

WILLY: Are you spiting me?

BIFF: Don't take it that way! Goddammit!   630

WILLY: (*strikes Biff and falters away from the table*) You rotten little louse! Are you spiting me?

THE WOMAN: Someone's at the door, Willy!

BIFF: I'm no good, can't you see what I am?

HAPPY: (*separating them*) Hey, you're in a restaurant! Now cut it out, both of you! (*The Girls enter.*) Hello, girls, sit down.

The Woman laughs, off left.

MISS FORSYTHE: I guess we might as well. This is Letta.   635

THE WOMAN: Willy, are you going to wake up?

BIFF: (*ignoring Willy*) How're ya, miss, sit down. What do you drink?

MISS FORSYTHE: Letta might not be able to stay long.

LETTA: I gotta get up very early tomorrow. I got jury duty. I'm so excited! Were you fellows ever on a jury?

640   **BIFF:** No, but I been in front of them! (*The Girls laugh.*) This is my father.

  LETTA: Isn't he cute? Sit down with us, Pop.

  HAPPY: Sit him down, Biff!

  BIFF: (*going to him*) Come on, slugger, drink us under the table. To hell with it! Come on, sit down, pal.

On Biff's last insistence, Willy is about to sit.

THE WOMAN: (*now urgently*) Willy, are you going to answer the door!

The Woman's call pulls Willy back. He starts right, befuddled.

645   **BIFF:** Hey, where are you going?

  WILLY: Open the door.

  BIFF: The door?

  WILLY: The washroom . . . the door . . . where's the door?

  BIFF: (*leading Willy to the left*) Just go straight down.

Willy moves left.

650   **THE WOMAN:** Willy, Willy, are you going to get up, get up, get up, get up?

Willy exits left.

  LETTA: I think it's sweet you bring your daddy along.

  MISS FORSYTHE: Oh, he isn't really your father!

  BIFF: (*at left, turning to her resentfully*) Miss Forsythe, you've just seen a prince walk by. A fine, troubled prince. A hard-working, unappreciated prince. A pal, you understand? A good companion. Always for his boys.

  LETTA: That's so sweet.

655   **HAPPY:** Well, girls, what's the program? We're wasting time. Come on, Biff. Gather round. Where would you like to go?

  BIFF: Why don't you do something for him?

  HAPPY: Me!

  BIFF: Don't you give a damn for him, Hap?

  HAPPY: What're you talking about? I'm the one who—

660   **BIFF:** I sense it, you don't give a good goddam about him. (*He takes the rolled-up hose from his pocket and puts it on the table in front of Happy.*) Look what I found in the cellar, for Christ's sake. How can you bear to let it go on?

  HAPPY: Me? Who goes away? Who runs off and—

  BIFF: Yeah, but he doesn't mean anything to you. You could help him — I can't! Don't you understand what I'm talking about? He's going to kill himself, don't you know that?

  HAPPY: Don't I know it! Me!

  BIFF: Hap, help him! Jesus . . . help him . . . Help me, help me, I can't bear to look at his face! (*Ready to weep, he hurries out, up right.*)

665   **HAPPY:** (*starting after him*) Where are you going?

  MISS FORSYTHE: What's he so mad about?

  HAPPY: Come on, girls, we'll catch up with him.

  MISS FORSYTHE: (*as Happy pushes her out*) Say, I don't like that temper of his!

HAPPY: He's just a little overstrung, he'll be all right!

WILLY: (*off left, as The Woman laughs*) Don't answer! Don't answer! 670

LETTA: Don't you want to tell your father —

HAPPY: No, that's not my father. He's just a guy. Come on, we'll catch Biff, and, honey, we're going to paint this town! Stanley, where's the check! Hey, Stanley!

They exit. Stanley looks toward left.

STANLEY: (*calling to Happy indignantly*) Mr. Loman! Mr. Loman!

Stanley picks up a chair and follows them off. Knocking is heard off left. The Woman enters, laughing. Willy follows her. She is in a black slip; he is buttoning his shirt. Raw, sensuous music accompanies their speech.

WILLY: Will you stop laughing? Will you stop?

THE WOMAN: Aren't you going to answer the door? He'll wake the whole 675
hotel.

WILLY: I'm not expecting anybody.

THE WOMAN: Whyn't you have another drink, honey, and stop being so damn self-centered?

WILLY: I'm so lonely.

THE WOMAN: You know you ruined me, Willy? From now on, whenever you come to the office, I'll see that you go right through to the buyers. No waiting at my desk any more, Willy. You ruined me.

WILLY: That's nice of you to say that. 680

THE WOMAN: Gee, you are self-centered! Why so sad? You are the saddest self-centeredest soul I ever did see-saw. (*She laughs. He kisses her.*) Come on inside, drummer boy. It's silly to be dressing in the middle of the night. (*As knocking is heard.*) Aren't you going to answer the door?

WILLY: They're knocking on the wrong door.

THE WOMAN: But I felt the knocking. And he heard us talking in here. Maybe the hotel's on fire!

WILLY: (*his terror rising*) It's a mistake.

THE WOMAN: Then tell him to go away! 685

WILLY: There's nobody there.

THE WOMAN: It's getting on my nerves, Willy. There's somebody standing out there and it's getting on my nerves!

WILLY: (*pushing her away from him*) All right, stay in the bathroom here, and don't come out. I think there's a law in Massachusetts about it, so don't come out. It may be that new room clerk. He looked very mean. So don't come out. It's a mistake, there's no fire.

The knocking is heard again. He takes a few steps away from her, and she vanishes into the wing. The light follows him, and now he is facing Young Biff, who carries a suitcase. Biff steps toward him. The music is gone.

BIFF: Why didn't you answer?

WILLY: Biff! What are you doing in Boston? 690

BIFF: Why didn't you answer? I've been knocking for five minutes, I called you on the phone—

WILLY: I just heard you. I was in the bathroom and had the door shut. Did anything happen home?

BIFF: Dad—I let you down.

WILLY: What do you mean?

695 **BIFF:** Dad . . .

WILLY: Biffo, what's this about? (*Putting his arm around Biff.*) Come on, let's go downstairs and get you a malted.

BIFF: Dad, I flunked math.

WILLY: Not for the term?

BIFF: The term. I haven't got enough credits to graduate.

700 **WILLY:** You mean to say Bernard wouldn't give you the answers?

BIFF: He did, he tried, but I only got a sixty-one.

WILLY: And they wouldn't give you four points?

BIFF: Birnbaum refused absolutely. I begged him, Pop, but he won't give me those points. You gotta talk to him before they close the school. Because if he saw the kind of man you are, and you just talked to him in your way, I'm sure he'd come through for me. The class came right before practice, see, and I didn't go enough. Would you talk to him? He'd like you, Pop. You know the way you could talk.

WILLY: You're on. We'll drive right back.

705 **BIFF:** Oh, Dad, good work! I'm sure he'll change it for you!

WILLY: Go downstairs and tell the clerk I'm checkin' out. Go right down.

BIFF: Yes, Sir! See, the reason he hates me, Pop—one day he was late for class so I got up at the blackboard and imitated him. I crossed my eyes and talked with a lithp.

WILLY: (*laughing*) You did? The kids like it?

BIFF: They nearly died laughing!

710 **WILLY:** Yeah? What'd you do?

BIFF: The thquare root of thixthy twee is . . . (*Willy bursts out laughing; Biff joins him.*) And in the middle of it he walked in!

Willy laughs and The Woman joins in offstage.

WILLY: (*without hesitating*) Hurry downstairs and—

BIFF: Somebody in there?

WILLY: No, that was next door.

The Woman laughs offstage.

715 **BIFF:** Somebody got in your bathroom!

WILLY: No, it's the next room, there's a party—

THE WOMAN: (*enters, laughing. She lisps this*) Can I come in? There's something in the bathtub, Willy, and it's moving!

Willy looks at Biff, who is staring open-mouthed and horrified at The Woman.

WILLY: Ah — you better go back to your room. They must be finished painting by now. They're painting her room so I let her take a shower here. Go back, go back . . . (*He pushes her.*)

THE WOMAN: (*resisting*) But I've got to get dressed, Willy, I can't—

WILLY: Get out of here! Go back, go back . . . (*Suddenly striving for the ordinary.*) This is Miss Francis, Biff, she's a buyer. They're painting her room. Go back, Miss Francis, go back . . .   720

THE WOMAN: But my clothes, I can't go out naked in the hall!

WILLY: (*pushing her offstage*) Get outa here! Go back, go back!

Biff slowly sits down on his suitcase as the argument continues offstage.

THE WOMAN: Where's my stockings? You promised me stockings, Willy!

WILLY: I have no stockings here!

THE WOMAN: You had two boxes of size nine sheers for me, and I want them!   725

WILLY: Here, for God's sake, will you get outa here!

THE WOMAN: (*enters holding a box of stockings*) I just hope there's nobody in the hall. That's all I hope. (*To Biff.*) Are you football or baseball?

BIFF: Football.

THE WOMAN: (*angry, humiliated*) That's me too. G'night. (*She snatches her clothes from Willy, and walks out.*)

WILLY: (*after a pause*) Well, better get going. I want to get to the school first thing in the morning. Get my suits out of the closet. I'll get my valise. (*Biff doesn't move.*) What's the matter? (*Biff remains motionless, tears falling.*) She's a buyer. Buys for J. H. Simmons. She lives down the hall — they're painting. You don't imagine —(*He breaks off. After a pause.*) Now listen, pal, she's just a buyer. She sees merchandise in her room and they have to keep it looking just so . . . (*Pause. Assuming command.*) All right, get my suits. (*Biff doesn't move.*) Now stop crying and do as I say. I gave you an order. Biff, I gave you an order! Is that what you do when I give you an order? How dare you cry! (*Putting his arm around Biff.*) Now look, Biff, when you grow up you'll understand about these things. You mustn't — you mustn't overemphasize a thing like this. I'll see Birnbaum first thing in the morning.   730

BIFF: Never mind.

WILLY: (*getting down beside Biff*) Never mind! He's going to give you those points. I'll see to it.

BIFF: He wouldn't listen to you.

WILLY: He certainly will listen to me. You need those points for the U. of Virginia.

BIFF: I'm not going there.   735

WILLY: Heh? If I can't get him to change that mark you'll make it up in summer school. You've got all summer to—

BIFF: (*his weeping breaking from him*) Dad . . .

WILLY: (*infected by it*) Oh, my boy . . .

BIFF: Dad . . .

740 **WILLY:** She's nothing to me, Biff. I was lonely, I was terribly lonely.

BIFF: You — you gave her Mama's stockings! (*His tears break through and he rises to go.*)

WILLY: (*grabbing for Biff*) I gave you an order!

BIFF: Don't touch me, you — liar!

WILLY: Apologize for that!

745 **BIFF:** You fake! You phony little fake! You fake! (*Overcome, he turns quickly and weeping fully goes out with his suitcase. Willy is left on the floor on his knees.*)

WILLY: I gave you an order! Biff, come back here or I'll beat you! Come back here! I'll whip you!

Stanley comes quickly in from the right and stands in front of Willy.

WILLY: (*shouts at Stanley*) I gave you an order . . .

STANLEY: Hey, let's pick it up, pick it up, Mr. Loman. (*He helps Willy to his feet.*) Your boys left with the chippies. They said they'll see you home.

A second waiter watches some distance away.

WILLY: But we were supposed to have dinner together.

Music is heard, Willy's theme.

750 **STANLEY:** Can you make it?

WILLY: I'll — sure, I can make it. (*Suddenly concerned about his clothes.*) Do I — I look all right?

STANLEY: Sure, you look all right. (*He flicks a speck off Willy's lapel.*)

WILLY: Here — here's a dollar.

STANLEY: Oh, your son paid me. It's all right.

755 **WILLY:** (*putting it in Stanley's hand*) No, take it. You're a good boy.

STANLEY: Oh, no, you don't have to . . .

WILLY: Here — here's some more, I don't need it any more. (*After a slight pause.*) Tell me — is there a seed store in the neighborhood?

STANLEY: Seeds? You mean like to plant?

As Willy turns, Stanley slips the money back into his jacket pocket.

WILLY: Yes. Carrots, peas . . .

760 **STANLEY:** Well, there's hardware stores on Sixth Avenue, but it may be too late now.

WILLY: (*anxiously*) Oh, I'd better hurry. I've got to get some seeds. (*He starts off to the right.*) I've got to get some seeds, right away. Nothing's planted. I don't have a thing in the ground.

Willy hurries out as the light goes down. Stanley moves over to the right after him, watches him off. The other waiter has been staring at Willy.

STANLEY: (*to the waiter*) Well, whatta you looking at?

The waiter picks up the chairs and moves off right. Stanley takes the table and follows him. The light fades on this area. There is a long pause, the sound of the flute coming over. The light gradually rises on the kitchen, which is empty. Happy appears at the door of the house, followed by Biff. Happy is carrying a large bunch of long-stemmed roses. He enters the kitchen, looks around for Linda. Not seeing her, he turns to Biff, who is just outside the house door, and makes a gesture with his hands, indicating "Not here, I guess." He looks into the living room and freezes. Inside, Linda, unseen, is seated, Willy's coat on her lap. She rises ominously and quietly and moves toward Happy, who backs up into the kitchen, afraid.

HAPPY: Hey, what're you doing up? *(Linda says nothing but moves toward him implacably.)* Where's Pop? *(He keeps backing to the right, and now Linda is in full view in the doorway to the living room.)* Is he sleeping?

LINDA: Where were you?

HAPPY: *(trying to laugh it off)* We met two girls, Mom, very fine types. Here, we   765
brought you some flowers. *(Offering them to her.)* Put them in your room, Ma.

She knocks them to the floor at Biff's feet. He has now come inside and closed the door behind him. She stares at Biff, silent.

HAPPY: Now what'd you do that for? Mom, I want you to have some flowers —

LINDA: *(cutting Happy off, violently to Biff)* Don't you care whether he lives
or dies?

HAPPY: *(going to the stairs)* Come upstairs, Biff.

BIFF: *(with a flare of disgust, to Happy)* Go away from me! *(To Linda.)* What do
you mean, lives or dies? Nobody's dying around here, pal.

LINDA: Get out of my sight! Get out of here!   770

BIFF: I wanna see the boss.

LINDA: You're not going near him!

BIFF: Where is he? *(He moves into the living room and Linda follows.)*

LINDA: *(shouting after Biff)* You invite him for dinner. He looks forward to it all
day —*(Biff appears in his parents' bedroom, looks around, and exits)*— and
then you desert him there. There's no stranger you'd do that to!

HAPPY: Why? He had a swell time with us. Listen, when I —*(Linda comes back*   775
into the kitchen)— desert him I hope I don't outlive the day!

LINDA: Get out of here!

HAPPY: Now look, Mom . . .

LINDA: Did you have to go to women tonight? You and your lousy rotten whores!

Biff re-enters the kitchen.

HAPPY: Mom, all we did was follow Biff around trying to cheer him up!
(To Biff.) Boy, what a night you gave me!

LINDA: Get out of here, both of you, and don't come back! I don't want you   780
tormenting him any more. Go on now, get your things together! *(To Biff.)*
You can sleep in his apartment. *(She starts to pick up the flowers and stops
herself.)* Pick up this stuff, I'm not your maid any more. Pick it up, you
bum, you!

Happy turns his back to her in refusal. Biff slowly moves over and gets down on his knees, picking up the flowers.

LINDA: You're a pair of animals! Not one, not another living soul would have had the cruelty to walk out on that man in a restaurant!

BIFF: *(not looking at her)* Is that what he said?

LINDA: He didn't have to say anything. He was so humiliated he nearly limped when he came in.

HAPPY: But, Mom he had a great time with us —

785   BIFF: *(cutting him off violently)* Shut up!

Without another word, Happy goes upstairs.

LINDA: You! You didn't even go in to see if he was all right!

BIFF: *(still on the floor in front of Linda, the flowers in his hand; with self-loathing)* No. Didn't. Didn't do a damned thing. How do you like that, heh? Left him babbling in a toilet.

LINDA: You louse. You . . .

BIFF: Now you hit it on the nose! *(He gets up, throws the flowers in the wastebasket.)* The scum of the earth, and you're looking at him!

790   LINDA: Get out of here!

BIFF: I gotta talk to the boss, Mom. Where is he?

LINDA: You're not going near him. Get out of this house!

BIFF: *(with absolute assurance, determination)* No. We're gonna have an abrupt conversation, him and me.

LINDA: You're not talking to him!

Hammering is heard from outside the house, off right. Biff turns toward the noise.

795   LINDA: *(suddenly pleading)* Will you please leave him alone?

BIFF: What's he doing out there?

LINDA: He's planting the garden!

BIFF: *(quietly)* Now? Oh, my God!

Biff moves outside, Linda following. The light dies down on them and comes up on the center of the apron as Willy walks into it. He is carrying a flashlight, a hoe and a handful of seed packets. He raps the top of the hoe sharply to fix it firmly, and then moves to the left, measuring off the distance with his foot. He holds the flashlight to look at the seed packets, reading off the instructions. He is in the blue of night.

WILLY: Carrots . . . quarter-inch apart. Rows . . . one-foot rows. *(He measures it off.)* One foot. *(He puts down a package and measures off.)* Beets. *(He puts down another package and measures again.)* Lettuce. *(He reads the package, puts it down.)* One foot — *(He breaks off as Ben appears at the right and moves slowly down to him.)* What a proposition, ts, ts. Terrific, terrific. 'Cause she's suffered, Ben, the woman has suffered. You understand me? A man can't go out the way he came in, Ben, a man has got to add up to something. You can't, you can't — *(Ben moves toward him as though to interrupt.)* You gotta consider, now. Don't answer so quick. Remember, it's a guaranteed twenty-thousand-dollar proposition. Now look, Ben, I want you to go through the ins and outs of this thing with me. I've got nobody to talk to, Ben, and the woman has suffered, you hear me?

BEN: *(standing still, considering)* What's the proposition?   800
WILLY: It's twenty thousand dollars on the barrelhead. Guaranteed, gilt-edged, you understand?
BEN: You don't want to make a fool of yourself. They might not honor the policy.
WILLY: How can they dare refuse? Didn't I work like a coolie to meet every premium on the nose? And now they don't pay off? Impossible!
BEN: It's called a cowardly thing, William.
WILLY: Why? Does it take more guts to stand here the rest of my life ringing   805
up a zero?
BEN: *(yielding)* That's a point, William. *(He moves, thinking, turns.)* And twenty thousand — that *is* something one can feel with the hand, it is there.
WILLY: *(now assured, with rising power)* Oh, Ben, that's the whole beauty of it! I see it like a diamond, shining in the dark, hard and rough, that I can pick up and touch in my hand. Not like — like an appointment! This would not be another damned-fool appointment, Ben, and it changes all the aspects. Because he thinks I'm nothing, see, and so he spites me. But the funeral — *(Straightening up.)* Ben, that funeral will be massive! They'll come from Maine, Massachusetts, Vermont, New Hampshire! All the old-timers with the strange license plates — that boy will be thunder-struck, Ben, because he never realized — I am known! Rhode Island, New York, New Jersey — I am known, Ben, and he'll see it with his eyes once and for all. He'll see what I am, Ben! He's in for a shock, that boy!
BEN: *(coming down to the edge of the garden)* He'll call you a coward.
WILLY: *(suddenly fearful)* No, that would be terrible.
BEN: Yes. And a damned fool.   810
WILLY: No, no, he mustn't, I won't have that! *(He is broken and desperate.)*
BEN: He'll hate you, William.

The gay music of the boys is heard.

WILLY: Oh, Ben, how do we get back to all the great times? Used to be so full of light, and comradeship, the sleigh-riding in winter, and the ruddiness on his cheeks. And always some kind of good news coming up, always something nice coming up ahead. And never even let me carry the valises in the house, and simonizing, simonizing that little red car! Why, why can't I give him something and not have him hate me?
BEN: Let me think about it. *(He glances at his watch.)* I still have a little time. Remarkable proposition, but you've got to be sure you're not making a fool of yourself.

Ben drifts off upstage and goes out of sight. Biff comes down from the left.

WILLY: *(suddenly conscious of Biff, turns and looks up at him, then begins*   815
picking up the packages of seeds in confusion) Where the hell is that seed?
(Indignantly.) You can't see nothing out here! They boxed in the whole goddam neighborhood!
BIFF: There are people all around here. Don't you realize that?

WILLY: I'm busy. Don't bother me.

BIFF: (*taking the hoe from Willy*) I'm saying good-by to you, Pop. (*Willy looks at him, silent, unable to move.*) I'm not coming back any more.

WILLY: You're not going to see Oliver tomorrow?

820 BIFF: I've got no appointment, Dad.

WILLY: He put his arm around you, and you've got no appointment?

BIFF: Pop, get this now, will you? Everytime I've left it's been a fight that sent me out of here. Today I realized something about myself and I tried to explain it to you and I — I think I'm just not smart enough to make any sense out of it for you. To hell with whose fault it is or anything like that. (*He takes Willy's arm.*) Let's just wrap it up, heh? Come on in, we'll tell Mom. (*He gently tries to pull Willy to the left.*)

WILLY: (*frozen, immobile, with guilt in his voice*) No, I don't want to see her.

BIFF: Come on! (*He pulls again, and Willy tries to pull away.*)

825 WILLY: (*highly nervous*) No, no, I don't want to see her.

BIFF: (*tries to look into Willy's face, as if to find the answer there*) Why don't you want to see her?

WILLY: (*more harshly now*) Don't bother me, will you?

BIFF: What do you mean, you don't want to see her? You don't want them calling you yellow, do you? This isn't your fault; it's me, I'm a bum. Now come inside! (*Willy strains to get away.*) Did you hear what I said to you?

Willy pulls away and quickly goes by himself into the house. Biff follows.

LINDA: (*to Willy*) Did you plant, dear?

830 BIFF: (*at the door, to Linda*) All right, we had it out. I'm going and I'm not writing any more.

LINDA: (*going to Willy in the kitchen*) I think that's the best way, dear. 'Cause there's no use drawing it out, you'll just never get along.

Willy doesn't respond.

BIFF: People ask where I am and what I'm doing, you don't know, and you don't care. That way it'll be off your mind and you can start brightening up again. All right? That clears it, doesn't it? (*Willy is silent, and Biff goes to him.*) You gonna wish me luck, scout? (*He extends his hand.*) What do you say?

LINDA: Shake his hand, Willy.

WILLY: (*turning to her, seething with hurt*) There's no necessity to mention the pen at all, y'know.

835 BIFF: (*gently*) I've got no appointment, Dad.

WILLY: (*erupting fiercely*) He put his arm around . . .?

BIFF: Dad, you're never going to see what I am, so what's the use of arguing? If I strike oil I'll send you a check. Meantime forget I'm alive.

WILLY: (*to Linda*) Spite, see?

BIFF: Shake hands, Dad.

840 WILLY: Not my hand.

BIFF: I was hoping not to go this way.

WILLY: Well, this is the way you're going. Good-by.

Biff looks at him a moment, then turns sharply and goes to the stairs.

WILLY: *(stops him with)* May you rot in hell if you leave this house!

BIFF: *(turning)* Exactly what is it that you want from me?

WILLY: I want you to know, on the train, in the mountains, in the valleys,   845
wherever you go, that you cut down your life for spite!

BIFF: No, no.

WILLY: Spite, spite, is the word of your undoing! And when you're down and
out, remember what did it. When you're rotting somewhere beside the
railroad tracks, remember, and don't you dare blame it on me!

BIFF: I'm not blaming it on you!

WILLY: I won't take the rap for this, you hear?

Happy comes down the stairs and stands on the bottom step, watching.

BIFF: That's just what I'm telling you!   850

WILLY: *(sinking into a chair at the table, with full accusation)* You're trying to put
a knife in me — don't think I don't know what you're doing!

BIFF: All right, phony! Then let's lay it on the line. (*He whips the rubber tube
out of his pocket and puts it on the table.*)

HAPPY: You crazy —

LINDA: Biff! *(She moves to grab the hose, but Biff holds it down with his hand.)*

BIFF: Leave it there! Don't move it!   855

WILLY: *(not looking at it)* What is that?

BIFF: You know goddam well what that is.

WILLY: *(caged, wanting to escape)* I never saw that.

BIFF: You saw it. The mice didn't bring it into the cellar! What is this supposed
to do, make a hero out of you? This supposed to make me sorry for you?

WILLY: Never heard of it.   860

BIFF: There'll be no pity for you, you hear it? No pity!

WILLY: *(to Linda)* You hear the spite!

BIFF: No, you're going to hear the truth — what you are and what I am!

LINDA: Stop it!

WILLY: Spite!   865

HAPPY: *(coming down toward Biff)* You cut it now!

BIFF: *(to Happy)* The man don't know who we are! The man is gonna know!
(*To Willy.*) We never told the truth for ten minutes in this house!

HAPPY: We always told the truth!

BIFF: *(turning on him)* You big blow, are you the assistant buyer? You're one of
the two assistants to the assistant, aren't you?

HAPPY: Well, I'm practically —   870

BIFF: You're practically full of it! We all are! And I'm through with it.
(*To Willy.*) Now hear this, Willy, this is me.

WILLY: I know you!

BIFF: You know why I had no address for three months? I stole a suit in Kansas
City and I was in jail. (*To Linda, who is sobbing.*) Stop crying. I'm through
with it.

Linda turns away from them, her hands covering her face.

WILLY: I suppose that's my fault!

875 **BIFF:** I stole myself out of every good job since high school!

WILLY: And whose fault is that?

BIFF: And I never got anywhere because you blew me so full of hot air I could never stand taking orders from anybody! That's whose fault it is!

WILLY: I hear that!

LINDA: Don't, Biff!

880 **BIFF:** It's goddam time you heard that! I had to be boss big shot in two weeks, and I'm through with it!

WILLY: Then hang yourself! For spite, hang yourself!

BIFF: No! Nobody's hanging himself, Willy! I ran down eleven flights with a pen in my hand today. And suddenly I stopped, you hear me? And in the middle of that office building, do you hear this? I stopped in the middle of that building and I saw — the sky. I saw the things that I love in this world. The work and the food and time to sit and smoke. And I looked at the pen and said to myself, what the hell am I grabbing this for? Why am I trying to become what I don't want to be? What am I doing in an office, making a contemptuous, begging fool of myself, when all I want is out there, waiting for me the minute I say I know who I am! Why can't I say that, Willy? (*He tries to make Willy face him, but Willy pulls away and moves to the left.*)

WILLY: (*with hatred, threateningly*) The door of your life is wide open!

BIFF: Pop! I'm a dime a dozen, and so are you!

885 **WILLY:** (*turning on him now in an uncontrolled outburst*) I am not a dime a dozen! I am Willy Loman, and you are Biff Loman!

Biff starts for Willy, but is blocked by Happy. In his fury, Biff seems on the verge of attacking his father.

BIFF: I am not a leader of men, Willy, and neither are you. You were never anything but a hard-working drummer who landed in the ash can like all the rest of them! I'm one dollar an hour, Willy! I tried seven states and couldn't raise it. A buck an hour! Do you gather my meaning? I'm not bringing home any prizes any more, and you're going to stop waiting for me to bring them home!

WILLY: (*directly to Biff*) You vengeful, spiteful mutt!

Biff breaks from Happy. Willy, in fright, starts up the stairs. Biff grabs him.

BIFF: (*at the peak of his fury*) Pop, I'm nothing! I'm nothing, Pop. Can't you understand that? There's no spite in it any more. I'm just what I am, that's all.

Biff's fury has spent itself, and he breaks down, sobbing, holding on to Willy, who dumbly fumbles for Biff's face.

WILLY: (*astonished*) What're you doing? What're you doing? (*To Linda.*) Why is he crying?

BIFF: (*crying, broken*) Will you let me go, for Christ's sake? Will you take that   890
  phony dream and burn it before something happens? (*Struggling to contain
  himself, he pulls away and moves to the stairs.*) I'll go in the morning. Put
  him — put him to bed. (*Exhausted, Biff moves up the stairs to his room.*)

WILLY: (*after a long pause, astonished, elevated*) Isn't that remarkable? Biff — he
  likes me!

LINDA: He loves you, Willy!

HAPPY: (*deeply moved*) Always did, Pop.

WILLY: Oh, Biff! (*Staring wildly.*) He cried! Cried to me! (*He is choking with his
  love, and now cries out his promise.*) That boy — that boy is going to be
  magnificent!

Ben appears in the light just outside the kitchen.

BEN: Yes, outstanding, with twenty thousand behind him.   895

LINDA: (*sensing the racing of his mind, fearfully, carefully*) Now come to bed,
  Willy. It's all settled now.

WILLY: (*finding it difficult not to rush out of the house*) Yes, we'll sleep. Come on.
  Go to sleep, Hap.

BEN: And it does take a great kind of man to crack the jungle.

In accents of dread, Ben's idyllic music starts up.

HAPPY: (*his arm around Linda*) I'm getting married, Pop, don't forget it. I'm
  changing everything. I'm gonna run that department before the year is up.
  You'll see, Mom. (*He kisses her.*)

BEN: The jungle is dark but full of diamonds, Willy.   900

Willy turns, moves, listening to Ben.

LINDA: Be good. You're both good boys, just act that way, that's all.

HAPPY: 'Night, Pop. (*He goes upstairs.*)

LINDA: (*to Willy*) Come, dear.

BEN: (*with greater force*) One must go in to fetch a diamond out.

WILLY: (*to Linda, as he moves slowly along the edge of the kitchen, toward the door*)   905
  I just want to get settled down, Linda. Let me sit alone for a little.

LINDA: (*almost uttering her fear*) I want you upstairs.

WILLY: (*taking her in his arms*) In a few minutes, Linda. I couldn't sleep right
  now. Go on, you look awful tired. (*He kisses her.*)

BEN: Not like an appointment at all. A diamond is rough and hard to the touch.

WILLY: Go on now. I'll be right up.

LINDA: I think this is the only way, Willy.   910

WILLY: Sure, it's the best thing.

BEN: Best thing!

WILLY: The only way. Everything is gonna be — go on, kid, get to bed. You
  look so tired.

LINDA: Come right up.

WILLY: Two minutes.   915

Linda goes into the living room, then reappears in her bedroom. Willy moves just outside the kitchen door.

WILLY: Loves me. *(Wonderingly.)* Always loved me. Isn't that a remarkable thing? Ben, he'll worship me for it!

BEN: *(with promise)* It's dark there, but full of diamonds.

WILLY: Can you imagine that magnificence with twenty thousand dollars in his pocket?

LINDA: *(calling from her room)* Willy! Come up!

920 **WILLY:** *(calling from the kitchen)* Yes! Yes! Coming! It's very smart, you realize that, don't you, sweetheart? Even Ben sees it. I gotta go, baby. 'By! By! *(Going over to Ben, almost dancing.)* Imagine? When the mail comes he'll be ahead of Bernard again!

BEN: A perfect proposition all around.

WILLY: Did you see how he cried to me? Oh, if I could kiss him, Ben!

BEN: Time, William, time!

WILLY: Oh, Ben, I always knew one way or another we were gonna make it, Biff and I!

925 **BEN:** *(looking at his watch)* The boat. We'll be late. *(He moves slowly off into the darkness.)*

WILLY: *(elegiacally, turning to the house)* Now when you kick off, boy, I want a seventy-yard boot, and get right down the field under the ball, and when you hit, hit low and hit hard, because it's important, boy. *(He swings around and faces the audience.)* There's all kinds of important people in the stands, and the first thing you know . . . *(Suddenly realizing he is alone.)* Ben! Ben, where do I . . . ? *(He makes a sudden movement of search.)* Ben, how do I . . . ?

LINDA: *(calling)* Willy, you coming up?

WILLY: *(uttering a gasp of fear, whirling about as if to quiet her)* Sh! *(He turns around as if to find his way; sounds, faces, voices, seem to be swarming in upon him and he flicks at them, crying.)* Sh! Sh! *(Suddenly music, faint and high, stops him. It rises in intensity, almost to an unbearable scream. He goes up and down on his toes, and rushes off around the house.)* Shhh!

LINDA: Willy?

There is no answer. Linda waits. Biff gets up off his bed. He is still in his clothes. Happy sits up. Biff stands listening.

930 **LINDA:** *(with real fear)* Willy, answer me! Willy!

There is the sound of a car starting and moving away at full speed.

LINDA: No!

BIFF: *(rushing down the stairs)* Pop!

As the car speeds off, the music crashes down in a frenzy of sound, which becomes the soft pulsation of a single cello string. Biff slowly returns to his bedroom. He and Happy gravely don their jackets. Linda slowly walks out of her room. The music has developed into a dead march. The leaves of day are appearing over everything. Charley and Bernard, somberly dressed, appear and knock on the kitchen door. Biff and Happy slowly descend the stairs to the kitchen as Charley and Bernard enter. All stop a moment when Linda, in clothes of mourning, bearing a little bunch of roses, comes through the draped doorway into the kitchen. She goes to Charley and takes his arm. Now all move toward the audience, through the wall-line of the kitchen. At the limit of the apron, Linda lays down the flowers, kneels, and sits back on her heels. All stare down at the grave.

REQUIEM

CHARLEY: It's getting dark, Linda.

Linda doesn't react. She stares at the grave.

BIFF: How about it, Mom? Better get some rest, heh? They'll be closing the gate soon.

Linda makes no move. Pause.

HAPPY: (*deeply angered*) He had no right to do that! There was no necessity for it. We would've helped him.

CHARLEY: (*grunting*) Hmmm.

BIFF: Come along, Mom. 5

LINDA: Why didn't anybody come?

CHARLEY: It was a very nice funeral.

LINDA: But where are all the people he knew? Maybe they blame him.

CHARLEY: Naa. It's a rough world, Linda. They wouldn't blame him.

LINDA: I can't understand it. At this time especially. First time in thirty-five 10 years we were just about free and clear. He only needed a little salary. He was even finished with the dentist.

CHARLEY: No man only needs a little salary.

LINDA: I can't understand it.

BIFF: There were a lot of nice days. When he'd come home from a trip; or on Sundays, making the stoop; finishing the cellar; putting on the new porch; when he built the extra bathroom; and put up the garage. You know something, Charley, there's more of him in that front stoop than in all the sales he ever made.

CHARLEY: Yeah. He was a happy man with a batch of cement.

LINDA: He was so wonderful with his hands. 15

BIFF: He had the wrong dreams. All, all, wrong.

HAPPY: (*almost ready to fight Biff*) Don't say that!

BIFF: He never knew who he was.

CHARLEY: (*stopping Happy's movement and reply. To Biff.*) Nobody dast blame this man. You don't understand: Willy was a salesman. And for a salesman, there is no rock bottom to the life. He don't put a bolt to a nut, he don't tell you the law or give you medicine. He's a man out there in the blue, riding on a smile and a shoeshine. And when they start not smiling back — that's an earthquake. And then you get yourself a couple of spots on your hat, and you're finished. Nobody dast blame this man. A salesman is got to dream, boy. It comes with the territory.

20 **BIFF:** Charley, the man didn't know who he was.

HAPPY: (*infuriated*) Don't say that!

BIFF: Why don't you come with me, Happy?

HAPPY: I'm not licked that easily. I'm staying right in this city, and I'm gonna beat this racket! (*He looks at Biff, his chin set.*) The Loman Brothers!

BIFF: I know who I am, kid.

25 **HAPPY:** All right, boy. I'm gonna show you and everybody else that Willy Loman did not die in vain. He had a good dream. It's the only dream you can have — to come out number-one man. He fought it out here, and this is where I'm gonna win it for him.

BIFF: (*with a hopeless glance at Happy, bends toward his mother*) Let's go, Mom.

LINDA: I'll be with you in a minute. Go on, Charley. (*He hesitates.*) I want to, just for a minute. I never had a chance to say good-by.

Charley moves away, followed by Happy. Biff remains a slight distance up and left of Linda. She sits there, summoning herself. The flute begins, not far away, playing behind her speech.

LINDA: Forgive me, dear. I can't cry. I don't know what it is, but I can't cry. I don't understand it. Why did you ever do that? Help me, Willy, I can't cry. It seems to me that you're just on another trip. I keep expecting you. Willy, dear, I can't cry. Why did you do it? I search and search and I search, and I can't understand it, Willy. I made the last payment on the house today. Today, dear. And there'll be nobody home. (*A sob rises in her throat.*) We're free and clear. (*Sobbing more fully, released.*) We're free. (*Biff comes slowly toward her.*) We're free . . . We're free . . .

Biff lifts her to her feet and moves out up right with her in his arms. Linda sobs quietly. Bernard and Charley come together and follow them, followed by Happy. Only the music of the flute is left on the darkening stage as over the house the hard towers of the apartment buildings rise into sharp focus, and—

The Curtain Falls

Reading and Reacting

1. With which character in the play do you most identify? Why?
2. Is Willy a likeable character? What words and actions — both Willy's and those of other characters — help you form your conclusion?
3. How does the existence of The Woman affect your overall impression of Willy? What does she reveal about his character?
4. What does Willy's attitude toward his sons indicate about his character? How is this attitude revealed?
5. Does this play have a hero? A villain? Explain.

6. In the absence of a narrator, what devices does Miller use to provide exposition — basic information about character and setting?

7. The conversation between Biff and Happy in act 1 reveals many of their differences. List some of the differences between these two characters.

8. In numerous remarks, Willy expresses his philosophy of business. Summarize some of his key ideas about the business world. How realistic do you think these ideas are? How do these ideas help to delineate his character?

9. In act 1, Linda tells Willy, "Few men are idolized by their children the way you are." Is she sincere, is she being ironic, or is she just trying to make Willy feel better?

10. How do the frequent flashbacks help to explain what motivates Willy? How else could this background information have been presented in the play? Are there advantages to using flashbacks instead of the alternative you suggest?

11. Is Linda simply a stereotype of the long-suffering wife, or is she an individualized, multidimensional character? Explain.

12. Willy Loman lives in Brooklyn, New York; his "territory" is New England. What is the significance to him of the "faraway places"— Africa, Alaska, California, Texas, and the like — mentioned in the play?

13. What purpose does Bernard serve in the play?

14. The play concludes with a requiem. What is a requiem? What information about each of the major characters is supplied in this brief section? Is this information essential to your understanding or appreciation of the play, or would the play have been equally effective without the requiem? Explain.

15. **JOURNAL ENTRY** Do you believe Willy Loman is an innocent victim of the society in which he lives, or do you believe there are flaws in his character that make him at least partially responsible for his own misfortune? Explain.

16. **CRITICAL PERSPECTIVE** Writing just after Miller's death in 2005, playwright David Mamet notes that at the end of *Death of a Salesman*, Miller has offered no solution to Willy's problems but instead "has reconciled us to the notion that there is no solution — that it is the human lot to try and fail, and that no one is immune from self-deception." Mamet goes on to explain the value of Miller's plays by comparing "bad drama" and "good drama":

> Bad drama reinforces our prejudices. It informs us of what we knew when we came into the theater . . . .
>
> The good drama survives because it appeals not to the fashion of the moment, but to the problems both universal and eternal, as they are insoluble.
>
> To find beauty in the sad, hope in the midst of loss, and dignity in failure is great poetic art.

According to Mamet's criteria, do you agree that *Death of a Salesman* qualifies as "good drama"? Do you think it is great drama?

Related Works: "A Primer for the Punctuation of Heart Disease" (p. 156), "Do not go gentle into that good night" (p. 1065), "Those Winter Sundays" (p. 1059), "The Love Song of J. Alfred Prufrock" (p. 1172), *Oedipus the King* (p. 1786), *Fences* (p. 1939)

WILLIAM SHAKESPEARE (1564–1616) is recognized as the greatest of English writers, but many details about his life are based on conjecture or tradition. The earliest dependable information concerning Shakespeare is found in the parish registers of Stratford-upon-Avon's Holy Trinity Church, where his baptism was recorded on April 26, 1564. Although his date of birth cannot be determined with certainty, tradition has assigned it to April 23, 1564. Little is known about his early life, but reliable information about significant events is available in church documents. For example, he married Ann Hathaway in 1582 and had three children — Susanna in 1583 and the twins Judith and Hamnet in 1585.

Soon after the birth of his children, Shakespeare left Stratford for London. Upon his arrival in the capital, he set out to establish himself in London's literary world. His first step toward achieving this goal occurred in 1592, when he published his narrative poem *Venus and Adonis;* the following year, he published a second poem, *The Rape of Lucrece.*

By 1594, Shakespeare had become quite involved with the London stage. For approximately twenty years, Shakespeare enjoyed a successful professional career in London — as actor, playwright, shareholder in the Lord Chamberlain's Men (an acting company), part owner of the Globe Theatre (from 1599), and author of at least thirty-six plays. The income derived from these activities brought him significant wealth and enabled him, sometime between 1610 and 1613, to retire from the theater and to return to Stratford-upon-Avon, where he owned considerable property. On April 23, 1616, Shakespeare died at age fifty-two in Stratford and was buried two days later in Holy Trinity Church.

It is difficult to date many of Shakespeare's plays exactly because they must be dated by records of their first performance (often hard to come by) and by topical references in the text. Shakespeare's company probably first staged *Hamlet* at the Globe Theatre in 1600 or 1601, but some scholars believe the play was composed as early as 1598.

An audience at the reconstructed Globe Theatre in London.

Hamlet has been called Shakespeare's most complex and most confusing play, yet it is also the play most frequently performed, read, and written about. Shakespeare's audience would have recognized *Hamlet* as a **revenge tragedy**—a play in which the hero discovers that a close relative has been murdered, experiences considerable trouble in identifying the murderer, and, after overcoming numerous obstacles, avenges the death by killing the murderer. Frequently, revenge tragedies featured murders, physical mutilations, and ghosts, all enacted with grand style and bold rhetoric. These plays were extremely popular productions that were the action movies of their day.

Hamlet, however, is different from the typical revenge tragedy. Because the Ghost gives him the necessary information, Hamlet has no need to search for the cause of his father's death or find the murderer. In fact, the only impediments to Hamlet's revenge are the impediments he himself creates. And, by the time the delay ends and Hamlet avenges his father's death, the loss is immense: his mother, the woman he loves, her father and brother, and Hamlet himself are all dead. Although the argument that there would be no play if Hamlet had immediately avenged his father may be valid, it fails to satisfy those who ponder the tragic cost of Hamlet's inaction.

Cultural Context The appearance of a ghost was a longstanding tradition in Renaissance drama. The ghost appeared in Elizabethan revenge tragedies as a plot device to help further the action and prompt a reaction from the hero. For a Renaissance audience, the dramatic representation of a ghost from purgatory would evoke a rich context of legends and lore derived from paintings, illuminated manuscript, prints, and narratives. Moreover, stories involving ghosts were a frequent element of medieval sermons. However, Shakespeare's ghost transcends the traditions of the revenge tragedy. His use of the ghost not only as a plot device but also as a character who may or may not be telling the truth adds depth and complexity to the play.

Hamlet
Prince of Denmark* (c. 1600)

CHARACTERS

Claudius, *King of Denmark*	**Reynaldo,** *servant to Polonius*
Hamlet, *son to the former and nephew*	**Players**
to the present King	**Two Clowns,** *grave-diggers*
Polonius, *Lord Chamberlain*	**Fortinbras,** *Prince of Norway*
Horatio, *friend to Hamlet*	**A Captain**
Laertes, *son to Polonius*	**English Ambassadors**
Courtiers { **Voltimand**	**Ghost of Hamlet's Father**
Cornelius	**Gertrude,** *Queen of Denmark and mother*
Rosencrantz	*of Hamlet*
Guildenstern	**Ophelia,** *daughter to Polonius*
Osric	**Lords, Ladies, Officers,**
A Gentleman	**Soldiers, Sailors**
A Priest	**Messengers, and other**
Francisco, *a soldier*	**Attendants**
Officers { **Marcellus**	
Bernardo	

ACT 1
SCENE 1

Elsinore. A platform before the castle.

Francisco at his post. Enter to him Bernardo.

BERNARDO: Who's there?

FRANCISCO: Nay, answer me: stand, and unfold yourself.

BERNARDO: Long live the king!

FRANCISCO: Bernardo?

5 BERNARDO: He.

FRANCISCO: You come most carefully upon your hour.

BERNARDO: 'Tis now struck twelve; get thee to bed, Francisco.

FRANCISCO: For this relief much thanks: 'tis bitter cold,
  And I am sick at heart.

10 BERNARDO: Have you had quiet guard?

FRANCISCO: Not a mouse stirring.

BERNARDO: Well, good-night.
  If you do meet Horatio and Marcellus,
  The rivals of my watch, bid them make haste.

15 FRANCISCO: I think I hear them. — Stand, ho! Who is there?

---

* Note that individual lines are numbered in the following play. When a line is shared by one or more characters, it is counted as one line.

Enter Horatio and Marcellus.

HORATIO: Friends to this ground.
MARCELLUS: And liegemen to the Dane.
FRANCISCO: Give you good-night.
MARCELLUS: O, farewell, honest soldier:
    Who hath reliev'd you?   20
FRANCISCO: Bernardo has my place.
Give you good-night.

Exit.

MARCELLUS: Holla! Bernardo!
BERNARDO: Say.
    What, is Horatio there?   25
HORATIO: A piece of him.
BERNARDO: Welcome, Horatio:— welcome, good Marcellus.
MARCELLUS: What, has this thing appear'd again to-night?
BERNARDO: I have seen nothing.
MARCELLUS: Horatio says 'tis but our fantasy,   30
    And will not let belief take hold of him
    Touching this dreaded sight, twice seen of us:
    Therefore I have entreated him along
    With us to watch the minutes of this night;
    That, if again this apparition come   35
    He may approve our eyes and speak to it.
HORATIO: Tush, tush, 'twill not appear.
BERNARDO: Sit down awhile,
    And let us once again assail your ears,
    That are so fortified against our story,   40
    What we two nights have seen.
HORATIO: Well, sit we down,
    And let us hear Bernardo speak of this.
BERNARDO: Last night of all,
    When yon same star that's westward from the pole   45
    Had made his course to illume that part of heaven
    Where now it burns, Marcellus and myself,
    The bell then beating one,—
MARCELLUS: Peace, break thee off; look where it comes again!

Enter Ghost, armed.

BERNARDO: In the same figure, like the king that's dead.   50
MARCELLUS: Thou art a scholar; speak to it, Horatio.
BERNARDO: Looks it not like the king? mark it, Horatio.
HORATIO: Most like:— it harrows me with fear and wonder.
BERNARDO: It would be spoke to.
MARCELLUS: Question it, Horatio.   55

HORATIO: What art thou, that usurp'st this time of night,
 Together with that fair and warlike form
 In which the majesty of buried Denmark
 Did sometimes march? by heaven I charge thee, speak!
60 MARCELLUS: It is offended.
BERNARDO: See, it stalks away!
HORATIO: Stay! speak, speak! I charge thee, speak!

Exit Ghost.

MARCELLUS: 'Tis gone, and will not answer.
BERNARDO: How now, Horatio! you tremble and look pale:
65 Is not this something more than fantasy?
 What think you on't?
HORATIO: Before my God, I might not this believe
 Without the sensible and true avouch
 Of mine own eyes.
70 MARCELLUS: Is it not like the king?
HORATIO: As thou art to thyself:
 Such was the very armor he had on
 When he the ambitious Norway combated;
 So frown'd he once when, in an angry parle,°
75 He smote the sledded Polacks on the ice.
 'Tis strange.
MARCELLUS: Thus twice before, and just at this dead hour,
 With martial stalk hath he gone by our watch.
HORATIO: In what particular thought to work I know not;
80 But, in the gross and scope of my opinion,
 This bodes some strange eruption to our state.
MARCELLUS: Good now, sit down, and tell me, he that knows,
 Why this same strict and most observant watch
 So nightly toils the subject of the land;
85 And why such daily cast of brazen cannon,
 And foreign mart for implements of war;
 Why such impress of shipwrights, whose sore task
 Does not divide the Sunday from the week;
 What might be toward, that this sweaty haste
90 Doth make the night joint-laborer with the day:
 Who is't that can inform me?
HORATIO: That can I;
 At least, the whisper goes so. Our last king,
 Whose image even but now appear'd to us,
95 Was, as you know, by Fortinbras of Norway,
 Thereto prick'd on by a most emulate pride,

° *parle:* Parley, or conference.

Dar'd to the combat; in which our valiant Hamlet,—
For so this side of our known world esteem'd him,—
Did slay this Fortinbras; who, by a seal'd compact,
Well ratified by law and heraldry, 　　　　　　　　　　100
Did forfeit, with his life, all those his lands.
Which he stood seiz'd of,° to the conqueror:
Against the which, a moiety competent°
Was gagéd° by our king; which had return'd
To the inheritance of Fortinbras, 　　　　　　　　　　105
Had he been vanquisher; as by the same cov'nant,
And carriage of the article design'd,
His fell to Hamlet. Now, sir, young Fortinbras,
Of unimproved mettle hot and full,
Hath in the skirts of Norway, here and there, 　　　　110
Shark'd up a list of landless resolutes,
For food and diet, to some enterprise
That hath a stomach in't: which is no other,—
As it doth well appear unto our state,—
But to recover of us by strong hand, 　　　　　　　　115
And terms compulsatory, those foresaid lands
So by his father lost: and this, I take it,
Is the main motive of our preparations,
The source of this our watch, and the chief head
Of this post-haste and romage° in the land. 　　　　120

BERNARDO: I think it be no other, but e'en so:
　　Well may it sort that this portentous figure
　　Comes armed through our watch; so like the king
　　That was and is the question of these wars.

HORATIO: A mote it is to trouble the mind's eye. 　　125
　　In the most high and palmy state of Rome,
　　A little ere the mightiest Julius fell,
　　The graves stood tenantless, and the sheeted dead
　　Did squeak and gibber in the Roman streets:
　　As, stars with trains of fire and dews of blood, 　　130
　　Disasters in the sun; and the moist star,
　　Upon whose influence Neptune's empire stands,
　　Was sick almost to doomsday with eclipse:
　　And even the like precurse of fierce events,—
　　As harbingers preceding still the fates, 　　　　　135
　　And prologue to the omen coming on,—
　　Have heaven and earth together demonstrated

° *seiz'd of:* Possessed.　　° *moiety competent:* A sufficient portion of his lands.　　° *gagéd:* Engaged or pledged.
° *post-haste and romage:* General activity.

Unto our climature and countrymen.—
But, soft, behold! lo, where it comes again!

Re-enter Ghost.

140   I'll cross it, though it blast me.— Stay, illusion!
If thou hast any sound or use of voice,
Speak to me:
If there be any good thing to be done,
That may to thee do ease, and grace to me,
145   Speak to me:
If thou art privy to thy country's fate,
Which, happily,° foreknowing may avoid,
O, speak!
Or if thou has uphoarded in thy life
150   Extorted treasure in the womb of earth,
For which, they say, you spirits oft walk in death,

Cock crows.

Speak of it:— stay, and speak!— Stop it, Marcellus.
MARCELLUS: Shall I strike at it with my partisan?°
HORATIO: Do, if it will not stand.
155   BERNARDO: 'Tis here!
HORATIO: 'Tis here!
MARCELLUS: 'Tis gone!

Exit Ghost.

We do it wrong, being so majestical,
To offer it the show of violence;
160   For it is, as the air, invulnerable,
And our vain blows malicious mockery.
BERNARDO: It was about to speak when the cock crew.
HORATIO: And then it started like a guilty thing
Upon a fearful summons. I have heard,
165   The cock, that is the trumpet to the morn,
Doth with his lofty and shrill-sounding throat
Awake the god of day; and at his warning,
Whether in sea or fire, in earth or air,
The extravagant and erring spirit hies
170   To his confine: and of the truth herein
This present object made probation.°
MARCELLUS: It faded on the crowing of the cock.
Some say that ever 'gainst that season comes
Wherein our Saviour's birth is celebrated,

° *happily:* Haply, or perhaps.   ° *partisan:* Pike.   ° *probation:* Proof.

The bird of dawning singeth all night long: 175
And then, they say, no spirit can walk abroad;
The nights are wholesome; then no planets strike,
No fairy takes, nor witch hath power to charm;
So hallow'd and so gracious is the time.

HORATIO: So have I heard, and do in part believe. 180
But, look, the morn, in russet mantle clad,
Walks o'er the dew of yon high eastern hill:
Break we our watch up: and, by my advice,
Let us impart what we have seen to-night
Unto young Hamlet; for, upon my life, 185
This spirit, dumb to us, will speak to him:
Do you consent we shall acquaint him with it,
As needful in our loves, fitting our duty?

MARCELLUS: Let's do't, I pray; and I this morning know
Where we shall find him most conveniently. 190

Exeunt.

SCENE 2

Elsinore. A room of state in the castle.

Enter the King, Queen, Hamlet, Polonius, Laertes, Voltimand, Cornelius, Lords, and Attendants.

KING: Though yet of Hamlet our dear brother's death
The memory be green; and that it us befitted
To bear our hearts in grief, and our whole kingdom
To be contracted in one brow of woe;
Yet so far hath discretion fought with nature 5
That we with wisest sorrow think on him,
Together with remembrance of ourselves.
Therefore our sometime sister, now our queen,
The imperial jointress of this warlike state,
Have we, as 'twere with defeated joy,— 10
With one auspicious and one dropping eye,
With mirth and funeral, and with dirge in marriage,
In equal scale weighing delight and dole,—
Taken to wife: nor have we herein barr'd
Your better wisdoms, which have freely gone 15
With this affair along:—for all, our thanks.
Now follows that you know, young Fortinbras,
Holding a weak supposal of our worth,
Or thinking by our late dear brother's death
Our state to be disjoint and out of frame, 20
Colleagued with the dream of his advantage,
He hath not fail'd to pester us with message,

Importing the surrender of those lands
Lost by his father, with all bonds of law,
25   To our most valiant brother. So much for him. —
Now for ourself, and for this time of meeting:
Thus much the business is: — we have here writ
To Norway, uncle of young Fortinbras, —
Who, impotent and bed-rid, scarcely hears
30   Of this his nephew's purpose, — to suppress
His further gait herein; in that the levies,
The lists, and full proportions, are all made
Out of his subject: — and we here despatch
You, good Cornelius, and you, Voltimand,
35   For bearers of this greeting to old Norway;
Giving to you no further personal power
To business with the king more than the scope
Of these dilated articles allow.
Farewell; and let your haste commend your duty.

40   **CORNELIUS** and **VOLTIMAND**: In that and all things will we show
our duty.

KING: We doubt it nothing: heartily farewell.

Exeunt Voltimand and Cornelius.

And now, Laertes, what's the news with you?
You told us of some suit; what is't, Laertes?
You cannot speak of reason to the Dane,
45   And lose your voice: what wouldst thou beg, Laertes,
That shall not be my offer, nor thy asking?
The head is not more native to the heart,
The hand more instrumental to the mouth,
Than is the throne of Denmark to thy father.
50   What wouldst thou have, Laertes?

LAERTES: Dread my lord,
Your leave and favor to return to France;
From whence though willingly I came to Denmark,
To show my duty in your coronation;
55   Yet now, I must confess, that duty done,
My thoughts and wishes bend again toward France.
And bow them to your gracious leave and pardon.

KING: Have you your father's leave? What says Polonius?

POLONIUS: He hath, my lord, wrung from me my slow leave
60   By laborsome petition; and at last
Upon his will I seal'd my hard consent:
I do beseech you, give him leave to go.

KING: Take thy fair hour, Laertes; time be thine,
And thy best graces spend it at thy will! —
65   But now, my cousin Hamlet, and my son, —

HAMLET: [*Aside*] A little more than kin, and less than kind.

KING: How is it that the clouds still hang on you?

HAMLET: Not so, my lord; I am too much i' the sun.

QUEEN: Good Hamlet, cast thy nighted color off,
 And let thine eye look like a friend on Denmark.   70
 Do not for ever with thy vailed° lids
 Seek for thy noble father in the dust:
 Thou know'st 'tis common,— all that live must die,
 Passing through nature to eternity.

HAMLET: Ay, madam, it is common.   75

QUEEN: If it be,
 Why seems it so particular with thee?

HAMLET: Seems, madam! nay, it is; I know not seems.
 'Tis not alone my inky cloak, good mother,
 Nor customary suits of solemn black,   80
 Nor windy suspiration of forc'd breath,
 No, nor the fruitful river in the eye,
 Nor the dejected 'havior of the visage,
 Together with all forms, moods, shows of grief,
 That can denote me truly: these, indeed, seem;   85
 For they are actions that a man might play:
 But I have that within which passeth show;
 These but the trappings and the suits of woe.

KING: 'Tis sweet and cómmendable in your nature, Hamlet,
 To give these mourning duties to your father: 90
 But, you must know, your father lost a father;
 That father lost, lost his; and the survivor bound,
 In filial obligation, for some term
 To do obsequious sorrow: but to persever
 In obstinate condolement is a course   95
 Of impious stubbornness; 'tis unmanly grief:
 It shows a will most incorrect to heaven;
 A heart unfortified, a mind impatient;
 An understanding simple and unschool'd:
 For what we know must be, and is as common   100
 As any the most vulgar thing to sense,°
 Why should we, in our peevish opposition,
 Take it to heart? Fie! 'tis a fault to heaven,
 A fault against the dead, a fault to nature,
 To reason most absurd; whose common theme   105
 Is death of fathers, and who still° hath cried,
 From the first corse till he that died to-day,
 This must be so. We pray you, throw to earth

° *vailed:* Downcast. ° *any . . . sense:* Anything that is very commonly seen or heard. ° *still:* Ever, or always.

This unprevailing woe; and think of us
110 As of a father: for let the world take note
You are the most immediate to our throne;
And with no less nobility of love
Than that which dearest father bears his son
Do I impart toward you. For your intent
115 In going back to school in Wittenberg,
It is most retrograde to our desire:
And we beseech you bend you to remain
Here, in the cheer and comfort of our eye,
Our chiefest courtier, cousin, and our son.
120 QUEEN: Let not thy mother lose her prayers, Hamlet:
I pray thee, stay with us; go not to Wittenberg.
HAMLET: I shall in all my best obey you, madam.
KING: Why, 'tis a loving and a fair reply:
Be as ourself in Denmark. — Madam, come;
125 This gentle and unforc'd accord of Hamlet
Sits smiling to my heart: in grace whereof,
No jocund health that Denmark drinks to-day
But the great cannon to the clouds shall tell;
And the king's rouse° the heavens shall bruit° again,
130 Re-speaking earthly thunder. Come away.

Exeunt all but Hamlet.

HAMLET: O, that this too too solid flesh would melt,
Thaw, and resolve itself into a dew!
Or that the Everlasting had not fix'd
His canon 'gainst self-slaughter! O God! O God!
135 How weary, stale, flat, and unprofitable
Seem to me all the uses of this world!
Fie on't! O fie! 'tis an unweeded garden,
That grows to seed; things rank and gross in nature
Possess it merely. That it should come to this!
140 But two months dead! — nay, not so much, not two:
So excellent a king; that was, to this,
Hyperion° to a satyr: so loving to my mother,
That he might not beteem the winds of heaven
Visit her face too roughly. Heaven and earth!
145 Must I remember? why, she would hang on him
As if increase of appetite had grown
By what it fed on: and yet, within a month, —
Let me not think on't, — Frailty, thy name is woman! —
A little month; or ere those shoes were old

° *rouse:* Drink.　° *bruit:* Echo.　° *Hyperion:* The Greek sun-god, the brightest and most beautiful of the gods.

With which she follow'd my poor father's body　　　　　　　150
Like Niobe, all tears;—why she, even she,—
O God! a beast, that wants discourse of reason,
Would have mourn'd longer,—married with mine uncle,
My father's brother; but no more like my father
Than I to Hercules: within a month;　　　　　　　　　　155
Ere yet the salt of most unrighteous tears
Had left the flushing in her galled eyes,
She married:— O, most wicked speed, to post
With such dexterity to incestuous sheets!
It is not, nor it cannot come to good;　　　　　　　　　160
But break, my heart,—for I must hold my tongue!

Enter Horatio, Marcellus, and Bernardo.

HORATIO:　Hail to your lordship!
HAMLET:　　　　　　　　　　I am glad to see you well:
　　Horatio,— or I do forget myself.
HORATIO:　The same, my lord, and your poor servant ever.　　165
HAMLET:　Sir, my good friend; I'll change that name with you:
　　And what make you from Wittenberg, Horatio?—Marcellus?
MARCELLUS:　My good lord,—
HAMLET:　I am very glad to see you.— Good even, sir.—
　　But what, in faith, make you from Wittenberg?　　　　　170
HORATIO:　A truant disposition, good my lord.
HAMLET:　I would not hear your enemy say so;
　　Nor shall you do mine ear that violence,
　　To make it truster of your own report
　　Against yourself: I know you are no truant.　　　　　　175
　　But what is your affair in Elsinore?
　　We'll teach you to drink deep ere you depart.
HORATIO:　My lord, I came to see your father's funeral.
HAMLET:　I pray thee, do not mock me, fellow-student;
　　I think it was to see my mother's wedding.　　　　　　180
HORATIO:　Indeed, my lord, it follow'd hard upon.
HAMLET:　Thrift, thrift, Horatio! the funeral-bak'd meats
　　Did coldly furnish forth the marriage tables.
　　Would I had met my dearest foe° in heaven
　　Ere I had ever seen that day, Horatio!—　　　　　　　185
　　My father,—methinks I see my father.
HORATIO:　Where, my lord?
HAMLET:　　　　　　　　　In my mind's eye, Horatio.
HORATIO:　I saw him once; he was a goodly° king.
HAMLET:　He was a man, take him for all in all,　　　　　190
　　I shall not look upon his like again.

° *dearest foe:* Worst enemy.　　° *goodly:* Handsome.

HORATIO: My lord, I think I saw him yester-night.

HAMLET: Saw who?

HORATIO: My lord, the king your father.

195 HAMLET: The king my father!

HORATIO: Season your admiration° for awhile
       With an attent ear, till I may deliver,
       Upon the witness of these gentlemen,
       This marvel to you.

200 HAMLET: For God's love, let me hear.

HORATIO: Two nights together had these gentlemen,
       Marcellus and Bernardo, in their watch,
       In the dead vast and middle of the night,
       Been thus encounter'd. A figure like your father,
205   Arm'd at all points exactly, cap-a-pe,°
       Appears before them, and with solemn march
       Goes slow and stately by them: thrice he walk'd
       By their oppress'd° and fear-surprised eyes,
       Within his truncheon's length; whilst they, distill'd
210   Almost to jelly with the act of fear,
       Stand dumb, and speak not to him. This to me
       In dreadful secrecy impart they did;
       And I with them the third night kept the watch:
       Where, as they had deliver'd, both in time,
215   Form of the thing, each word made true and good,
       The apparition comes: I knew your father;
       These hands are not more like.

HAMLET: But where was this?

MARCELLUS: My lord, upon the platform where we watch'd.

220 HAMLET: Did you not speak to it?

HORATIO: My lord, I did;
       But answer made it none: yet once methought
       It lifted up its head, and did address
       Itself to motion, like as it would speak:
225   But even then the morning cock crew loud,
       And at the sound it shrunk in haste away,
       And vanish'd from our sight.

HAMLET: 'Tis very strange.

HORATIO: As I do live, my honor'd lord, 'tis true;
230   And we did think it writ down in our duty
       To let you know of it.

HAMLET: Indeed, indeed, sirs, but this troubles me.
       Hold you the watch to-night?

MARCELLUS and BERNARDO: We do, my lord.

° *admiration:* Astonishment.   ° *cap-a-pe:* From head to toe.   ° *oppress'd:* Overwhelmed.

HAMLET: Arm'd, say you?   235
MARCELLUS and BERNARDO: Arm'd, my lord.
HAMLET: From top to toe?
MARCELLUS and BERNARDO: My lord, from head to foot.
HAMLET: Then saw you not his face?
HORATIO: O yes, my lord; he wore his beaver up.   240
HAMLET: What, look'd he frowningly?
HORATIO: A countenance more in sorrow than in anger.
HAMLET: Pale or red?
HORATIO: Nay, very pale.
HAMLET: And fix'd his eyes upon you?   245
HORATIO: Most constantly.
HAMLET: I would I had been there.
HORATIO: It would have much amaz'd you.
HAMLET: Very like, very like. Stay'd it long?
HORATIO: While one with moderate haste might tell° a hundred.   250
MARCELLUS and BERNARDO: Longer, longer.
HORATIO: Not when I saw't.
HAMLET: His beard was grizzled,— no?
HORATIO: It was, as I have seen it in his life,
   A sable silver'd.   255
HAMLET: I will watch to-night;
   Perchance 'twill walk again.
HORATIO: I warrant it will.
HAMLET: If it assume my noble father's person
   I'll speak to it, though hell itself should gape   260
   And bid me hold my peace. I pray you all,
   If you have hitherto conceal'd this sight,
   Let it be tenable in your silence still;
   And whatsoever else shall hap to-night,
   Give it an understanding, but no tongue: 265
   I will requite your loves. So, fare ye well:
   Upon the platform, 'twixt eleven and twelve,
   I'll visit you.
ALL: Our duty to your honor.
HAMLET: Your loves, as mine to you: farewell.   270

Exeunt Horatio, Marcellus, and Bernardo.

   My father's spirit in arms; all is not well;
   I doubt some foul play: would the night were come!
   Till then sit still, my soul: foul deeds will rise,
   Though all the earth o'erwhelm them, to men's eyes.

Exit.

° *tell:* Count

SCENE 3

A room in Polonius' house.

Enter Laertes and Ophelia.

LAERTES: My necessaries are embark'd: farewell:
    And, sister, as the winds give benefit,
    And convoy° is assistant, do not sleep,
    But let me hear from you.

5 OPHELIA: Do you doubt that?
LAERTES: For Hamlet, and the trifling of his favor,
    Hold it a fashion and a toy in blood:
    A violet in the youth of primy nature,
    Forward, not permanent, sweet, not lasting,
10   The perfume and suppliance of a minute;
    No more.
OPHELIA: No more but so?
LAERTES: Think it no more:
    For nature, crescent,° does not grow alone
15   In thews and bulk; but as this temple° waxes,
    The inward service of the mind and soul
    Grows wide withal. Perhaps he loves you now;
    And now no soil nor cautel° doth besmirch
    The virtue of his will: but you must fear,
20   His greatness weigh'd, his will is not his own;
    For he himself is subject to his birth:
    He may not, as unvalu'd persons do,
    Carve for himself; for on his choice depends
    The safety and the health of the whole state;
25   And therefore must his choice be circumscrib'd
    Unto the voice and yielding of that body
    Whereof he is the head. Then if he says he loves you,
    It fits your wisdom so far to believe it
    As he in his particular act and place
30   May give his saying deed; which is no further
    Than the main° voice of Denmark goes withal.
    Then weigh what loss your honor may sustain
    If with too credent ear you list his songs,
    Or lose your heart, or your chaste treasure open
35   To his unmaster'd importunity.
    Fear it, Ophelia, fear it, my dear sister;
    And keep within the rear of your affection,
    Out of the shot and danger of desire.

° *convoy:* Means of conveyance.   ° *crescent:* Growing.   ° *temple:* Body.   ° *cautel:* Deceit.   ° *main:* Strong, or mighty.

The chariest maid is prodigal enough
If she unmask her beauty to the moon: 40
Virtue itself scrapes not calumnious strokes:
The canker galls the infants of the spring
Too oft before their buttons be disclos'd;
And in the morn and liquid dew of youth
Contagious blastments are most imminent.   45
Be wary, then; best safety lies in fear:
Youth to itself rebels, though none else near.
OPHELIA: I shall the effect of this good lesson keep
As watchman to my heart. But, good my brother,
Do not, as some ungracious pastors do,   50
Show me the steep and thorny way to heaven;
Whilst like a puff'd and reckless libertine,
Himself the primrose path of dalliance treads,
And recks not his own rede.°
LAERTES: O, fear me not.   55
I stay too long:—but here my father comes.

Enter Polonius.

A double blessing is a double grace;
Occasion smiles upon a second leave.

POLONIUS: Yet here, Laertes! aboard, aboard, for shame!
The wind sits in the shoulder of your sail,   60
And you are stay'd for. There,—my blessing with you!

Laying his hand on Laertes' head.

And these few precepts in thy memory
See thou character.° Give thy thoughts no tongue,
Nor any unproportion'd thought his act.
Be thou familiar, but by no means vulgar.   65
The friends thou hast, and their adoption tried,
Grapple them to thy soul with hoops of steel;
But do not dull thy palm with entertainment
Of each new-hatch'd, unfledg'd comrade. Beware
Of entrance to a quarrel; but, being in,   70
Bear't that the opposéd may beware of thee.
Give every man thine ear, but few thy voice:
Take each man's censure,° but reserve thy judgment.
Costly thy habit as thy purse can buy,
But not express'd in fancy; rich, not gaudy: 75
For the apparel oft proclaims the man;
And they in France of the best rank and station

° *rede:* Counsel.   ° *in . . . character:* Engrave in your mind.   ° *censure:* Opinion.

Are most select and generous chief in that.
Neither a borrower nor a lender be:
80 For a loan oft loses both itself and friend;
And borrowing dulls the edge of husbandry.
This above all, — to thine own self be true;
And it must follow, as the night the day,
Thou canst not then be false to any man.
85 Farewell: my blessing season this in thee!

LAERTES: Most humbly do I take my leave, my lord.

POLONIUS: The time invites you; go, your servants tend.°

LAERTES: Farewell, Ophelia; and remember well
What I have said to you.

90 OPHELIA: 'Tis in my memory lock'd,
And you yourself shall keep the key of it.

LAERTES: Farewell. [*Exit.*]

POLONIUS: What is't, Ophelia, he hath said to you?

OPHELIA: So please you, something touching the Lord Hamlet.

95 POLONIUS: Marry, well bethought:
'Tis told me he hath very oft of late
Given private time to you; and you yourself
Have of your audience been most free and bounteous:
If it be so, — as so 'tis put on me,
100 And that in way of caution, — I must tell you,
You do not understand yourself so clearly
As it behoves my daughter and your honor.
What is between you? give me up the truth.

OPHELIA: He hath, my lord, of late made many tenders
105 Of his affection to me.

POLONIUS: Affection! pooh! you speak like a green girl,
Unsifted in such perilous circumstance.
Do you believe his tenders,° as you call them?

OPHELIA: I do not know, my lord, what I should think.

110 POLONIUS: Marry, I'll teach you: think yourself a baby;
That you have ta'en these tenders for true pay,
Which are not sterling. Tender yourself more dearly;
Or, — not to crack the wind of the poor phrase,
Wronging it thus, — you'll tender me a fool.

115 OPHELIA: My lord, he hath impórtun'd me with love
In honorable fashion.

POLONIUS: Ay, fashion you may call it; go to, go to.

OPHELIA: And hath given countenance to his speech, my lord,
With almost all the holy vows of heaven.

120 POLONIUS: Ay, springes to catch woodcocks. I do know,
When the blood burns, how prodigal the soul

° *tend:* Wait.   ° *tenders:* Offers.

Lends the tongue vows: these blazes, daughter,
Giving more light than heat,—extinct in both,
Even in their promise, as it is a-making,—
You must not take for fire. From this time   125
Be somewhat scanter of your maiden presence;
Set your entreatments at a higher rate
Than a command to parley. For Lord Hamlet,
Believe so much in him, that he is young;
And with a larger tether may he walk   130
Than may be given you: in few, Ophelia,
Do not believe his vows; for they are brokers,°—
Not of that die which their investments show,
But mere implorators of unholy suits,
Breathing like sanctified and pious bawds,   135
The better to beguile. This is for all,—
I would not, in plain terms, from this time forth,
Have you so slander any moment leisure
As to give words or talk with the Lord Hamlet.
Look to't, I charge you; come your ways.   140

OPHELIA: I shall obey, my lord.

Exeunt.

SCENE 4

The platform.

Enter Hamlet, Horatio, and Marcellus.

HAMLET: The air bites shrewdly; it is very cold.
HORATIO: It is a nipping and an eager air.
HAMLET: What hour now?
HORATIO: I think it lacks of twelve.
MARCELLUS: No, it is struck.   5
HORATIO: Indeed? I heard it not: then it draws near the season
        Wherein the spirit held his wont to walk.

A flourish of trumpets, and ordnance shot off within.

        What does this mean, my lord?
HAMLET: The king doth wake to-night, and takes his rouse,
        Keeps wassail, and the swaggering upspring° reels;   10
        And, as he drains his draughts of Rhenish down,
        The kettle-drum and trumpet thus bray out
        The triumph of his pledge.°
HORATIO: Is it a custom?

° *brokers:* Procurers.   ° *upspring:* A dance.   ° *triumph . . . pledge:* The glory of his toasts.

15 **HAMLET:** Ay, marry, is't:
        But to my mind, — though I am native here,
        And to the manner born, — it is a custom
        More honor'd in the breach than the observance.
        This heavy-headed revel east and west
20   Makes us traduc'd and tax'd of other nations:
        They clepe us drunkards, and with swinish phrase
        Soil our addition;° and, indeed, it takes
        From our achievements, though perform'd at height,
        The pith and marrow of our attribute.
25   So oft it chances in particular men
        That, for some vicious mole of nature in them,
        As in their birth, — wherein they are not guilty,
        Since nature cannot choose his origin, —
        By the o'ergrowth of some complexion,
30   Oft breaking down the pales and forts of reason;
        Or by some habit, that too much o'erleavens
        The form of plausive° manners; — that these men, —
        Carrying, I say, the stamp of one defect,
        Being nature's livery or fortune's star, —
35   Their virtues else, — be they as pure as grace,
        As infinite as man may undergo, —
        Shall in the general censure take corruption
        From that particular fault: the dram of evil
        Doth all the noble substance of a doubt
40   To his own scandal.
  HORATIO: Look, my lord, it comes!

Enter Ghost.

  HAMLET: Angels and ministers of grace defend us! —
        Be thou a spirit of health or goblin damn'd,
        Bring with thee airs from heaven or blasts from hell,
45   Be thy intents wicked or charitable,
        Thou com'st in such a questionable shape
        That I will speak to thee: I'll call thee Hamlet,
        King, father, royal Dane: O, answer me!
        Let me not burst in ignorance; but tell
50   Why thy canóniz'd bones, hearsèd in death,
        Have burst their cerements;° why the sepulchre,
        Wherein we saw thee quietly in-urn'd,
        Hath op'd his ponderous and marble jaws
        To cast thee up again! What may this mean,
55   That thou, dead corpse, again in còmplete steel,
        Revisit'st thus the glimpses of the moon,

° *addition:* Reputation.   ° *plausive:* Pleasing.   ° *cerements:* Burial garments

Making night hideous and we° fools of nature
So horridly to shake our disposition
With thoughts beyond the reaches of our souls?
Say, why is this? wherefore? what should we do?   60

Ghost beckons Hamlet.

HORATIO: It beckons you to go away with it,
    As if it some impartment did desire
    To you alone.
MARCELLUS: Look, with what courteous action
    It waves you to a more removed ground: 65
    But do not go with it.
HORATIO: No, by no means.
HAMLET: It will not speak; then will I follow it.
HORATIO: Do not, my lord.
HAMLET: Why, what should be the fear?   70
    I do not set my life at a pin's fee;
    And for my soul, what can it do to that,
    Being a thing immortal as itself?
    It waves me forth again; — I'll follow it.
HORATIO: What if it tempt you toward the flood, my lord.   75
    Or to the dreadful summit of the cliff
    That beetles o'er his base into the sea,
    And there assume some other horrible form,
    Which might deprive your sovereignty of reason,
    And draw you into madness? think of it: 80
    The very place puts toys of desperation,
    Without more motive, into every brain
    That looks so many fathoms to the sea
    And hears it roar beneath.
HAMLET: It waves me still.—   85
    Go on; I'll follow thee.
MARCELLUS: You shall not go, my lord.
HAMLET: Hold off your hands.
HORATIO: Be rul'd; you shall not go.
HAMLET: My fate cries out,   90
    And makes each petty artery in this body
    As hardy as the Némean lion's° nerve.—

Ghost beckons.

    Still am I call'd; — unhand me, gentlemen; —[*Breaking from them*]
    By heaven, I'll make a ghost of him that lets° me.
    I say, away! — Go on; I'll follow thee.   95

° *we:* Us.   ° *Némean lion's:* The fierce lion that Hercules was called upon to slay as one of his "twelve labors."
° *lets:* Hinders.

Exeunt Ghost and Hamlet.

HORATIO: He waxes desperate with imagination.
MARCELLUS: Let's follow; 'tis not fit thus to obey him.
HORATIO: Have after.— To what issue will this come?
MARCELLUS: Something is rotten in the state of Denmark.
100   **HORATIO:** Heaven will direct it.
MARCELLUS: Nay, let's follow him.

Exeunt.

SCENE 5

A more remote part of the platform.

Enter Ghost and Hamlet.

HAMLET: Where wilt thou lead me? speak, I'll go no further.
GHOST: Mark me.
HAMLET: I will.
GHOST: My hour is almost come,
5   When I to sulphurous and tormenting flames
         Must render up myself.
HAMLET: Alas, poor ghost!
GHOST: Pity me not, but lend thy serious hearing
         To what I shall unfold.
10   **HAMLET:**   Speak; I am bound to hear.
GHOST: So art thou to revenge, when thou shalt hear.
HAMLET: What?
GHOST: I am thy father's spirit;
         Doom'd for a certain term to walk the night,
15   And, for the day, confin'd to waste in fires
         Till the foul crimes° done in my days of nature
         Are burnt and purg'd away. But that I am forbid
         To tell the secrets of my prison-house,
         I could a tale unfold whose lightest word
20   Would harrow up thy soul; freeze thy young blood;
         Make thy two eyes, like stars, start from their spheres;
         Thy knotted and combined locks to part,
         And each particular hair to stand on end,
         Like quills upon the fretful porcupine:
25   But this eternal blazon° must not be
         To ears of flesh and blood.— List, list, O, list!—
         If thou didst ever thy dear father love,—
HAMLET: O God!

° *foul crimes:* Sins or faults.   ° *eternal blazon:* Disclosure of information concerning the other world.

GHOST: Revenge his foul and most unnatural murder.
HAMLET: Murder!   30
GHOST: Murder — most foul, as in the best it is;
    But this most foul, strange, and unnatural.
HAMLET: Haste me to know't, that I, with wings as swift
    As meditation or the thoughts of love,
    May sweep to my revenge.   35
GHOST: I find thee apt;
    And duller shouldst thou be than the fat weed
    That rots itself in ease on Lethe° wharf,
    Wouldst thou not stir in this. Now, Hamlet,
    'Tis given out that, sleeping in mine orchard,   40
    A serpent stung me; so the whole ear of Denmark
    Is by a forged process of my death
    Rankly abus'd: but know, thou noble youth,
    The serpent that did sting thy father's life
    Now wears his crown.   45
HAMLET: O my prophetic soul! mine uncle!
GHOST: Ay, that incestuous, that adulterate beast,
    With witchcraft of his wit, with traitorous gifts,—
    O wicked wit and gifts that have the power
    So to seduce! — won to his shameful lust   50
    The will of my most seeming virtuous queen:
    O Hamlet, what a falling-off was there!
    From me, whose love was of that dignity
    That it went hand in hand even with the vow
    I made to her in marriage: and to decline   55
    Upon a wretch whose natural gifts were poor
    To those of mine!
    But virtue, as it never will be mov'd,
    Though lewdness court it in a shape of heaven;
    So lust, though to a radiant angel link'd,   60
    Will sate itself in a celestial bed
    And prey on garbage.
    But, soft! methinks I scent the morning air;
    Brief let me be. — Sleeping within mine orchard,
    My custom always in the afternoon,   65
    Upon my sécure hour thy uncle stole,
    With juice of cursed hebenon° in a vial,
    And in the porches of mine ears did pour
    The leperous distilment; whose effect
    Holds such an enmity with blood of man   70
    That, swift as quicksilver, it courses through

° *Lethe:* The river of forgetfulness of the past, out of which the dead drink.   ° *hebenon:* Ebony.

The natural gates and alleys of the body;
And with a sudden vigor it doth posset°
And curd, like eager° droppings into milk,
75   The thin and wholesome blood: so did it mine;
And a most instant tetter bark'd about,
Most lazar-like,° with vile and loathsome crust,
All my smooth body.
Thus was I, sleeping, by a brother's hand,
80   Of life, of crown, of queen, at once despatch'd:
Cut off even in the blossoms of my sin,
Unhousel'd, unanointed, unanel'd;
No reckoning made, but sent to my account
With all my imperfections on my head:
85   O, horrible! O, horrible! most horrible!
If thou hast nature in thee, bear it not;
Let not the royal bed of Denmark be
A couch for luxury° and damned incest.
But, howsoever thou pursu'st this act,
90   Taint not thy mind, nor let thy soul contrive
Against thy mother aught: leave her to heaven,
And to those thorns that in her bosom lodge,
To prick and sting her. Fare thee well at once!
The glowworm shows the matin to be near,
95   And 'gins to pale his uneffectual fire:
Adieu, adieu! Hamlet, remember me. [*Exit.*]
Hamlet: O all you host of heaven! O earth! what else?
And shall I couple hell?— O, fie!— Hold, my heart;
And you, my sinews, grow not instant old,
100   But bear me stiffly up.— Remember thee!
Ay, thou poor ghost, while memory holds a seat
In this distracted globe. Remember thee!
Yea, from the table of my memory
I'll wipe away all trivial fond° recórds,
105   All saws of books, all forms, all pressures past,
That youth and observation copied there;
And thy commandment all alone shall live
Within the book and volume of my brain,
Unmix'd with baser matter: yes, by heaven.—
110   O most pernicious woman!
O villain, villain, smiling, damned villain!
My tables,—meet it is I set it down,

° *posset:* Coagulate.   ° *eager:* Acid.   ° *lazar-like:* Like a leper, whose skin is rough.   ° *luxury:* Lechery.
° *fond:* Foolish.

That one may smile, and smile, and be a villain;
At least, I am sure, it may be so in Denmark:

Writing.

So, uncle, there you are. Now to my word;   115
It is, *Adieu, adieu! remember me:*
I have sworn't.
Horatio: [*Within*] My lord, my lord,—
Marcellus: [*Within*]   Lord Hamlet,—
Horatio: [*Within*]   Heaven secure him!   120
Marcellus: [*Within*] So be it!
Horatio: [*Within*] Illo, ho, ho, my lord!
Hamlet: Hillo, ho, ho, boy! come, bird, come.°

Enter Horatio and Marcellus.

Marcellus: How is't, my noble lord?
Horatio: What news, my lord?   125
Hamlet: O, wonderful!
Horatio: Good my lord, tell it.
Hamlet: No; you'll reveal it.
Horatio: Not I, my lord, by heaven.
Marcellus: Nor I, my lord.   130
Hamlet: How say you, then; would heart of man once think it?—
But you'll be secret?
Horatio and **Marcellus:** Ay, by heaven, my lord.
Hamlet: There's ne'er a villain dwelling in all Denmark
But he's an arrant knave.   135
Horatio: There needs no ghost, my lord, come from the grave
To tell us this.
Hamlet: Why, right; you are i' the right;
And so, without more circumstance at all,
I hold it fit that we shake hands and part: 140
You, as your business and desire shall point you,—
For every man has business and desire,
Such as it is;— and for mine own poor part,
Look you, I'll go pray.
Horatio: These are but wild and whirling words, my lord.   145
Hamlet: I'm sorry they offend you, heartily;
Yes, faith, heartily.
Horatio: There's no offence, my lord.
Hamlet: Yes, by Saint Patrick, but there is, Horatio,
And much offence too. Touching this vision here,—   150
It is an honest ghost, that let me tell you:

° *Hillo . . . come:* Hamlet uses the word "bird" because this is a falconer's call.

For you desire to know what is between us,
O'ermaster't as you may. And now, good friends,
As you are friends, scholars, and soldiers,
155   Give me one poor request.
HORATIO: What is't, my lord? we will.
HAMLET: Never make known what you have seen to-night.
HORATIO and MARCELLUS: My lord, we will not.
HAMLET: Nay, but swear't.
160   HORATIO: In faith,
My lord, not I.
MARCELLUS: Nor I, my lord, in faith.
HAMLET: Upon my sword.
MARCELLUS: We have sworn, my lord, already.
165   HAMLET: Indeed, upon my sword, indeed.
GHOST: [*Beneath*] Swear.
HAMLET: Ha, ha, boy! say'st thou so? art thou there, truepenny?—
Come on,— you hear this fellow in the cellarage,—
Consent to swear.
170   HORATIO: Propose the oath, my lord.
HAMLET: Never to speak of this that you have seen,
Swear by my sword.
GHOST: [*Beneath*] Swear.
HAMLET: *Hic et ubique?*° then we'll shift our ground.—
175   Come hither, gentlemen,
And lay your hands again upon my sword:
Never to speak of this that you have heard,
Swear by my sword.
GHOST: [*Beneath*] Swear.
180   HAMLET: Well said! old mole! canst work i' the earth so fast?
A worthy pioneer!°— Once more remove, good friends.
HORATIO: O day and night, but this is wondrous strange!
HAMLET: And therefore as a stranger give it welcome.
There are more things in heaven and earth, Horatio,
185   Than are dreamt of in your philosophy.
But come;—
Here, as before, never, so help you mercy,
How strange or odd soe'er I bear myself,—
As I, perchance, hereafter shall think meet
190   To put an antic disposition on,—
That you, at such times seeing me, never shall,
With arms encumber'd° thus, or this headshake,
Or by pronouncing of some doubtful phrase,

° *Hic et ubique:* "Here and everywhere" (Latin).   ° *pioneer:* A soldier who digs trenches and undermines fortresses.   ° *encumber'd:* Folded.

As, *Well, well, we know;*— or, *We could, an if we would;*—
Or, *If we list to speak;*— or, *There be, an if they might;*— 195
Or such ambiguous giving out, to note
That you know aught of me:— this not to do,
So grace and mercy at your most need help you,
Swear.

GHOST: [*Beneath*] Swear. 200

HAMLET: Rest, rest, perturbed spirit!— So, gentlemen,
With all my love I do commend to you:
And what so poor a man as Hamlet is
May do, to express his love and friending to you,
God willing, shall not lack. Let us go in together; 205
And still your fingers on your lips, I pray.
The time is out of joint:— O cursed spite,
That ever I was born to set it right!—
Nay, come, let's go together.

Exeunt.

ACT 2
SCENE 1

A room in Polonius' house.

Enter Polonius and Reynaldo.

POLONIUS: Give him this money and these notes, Reynaldo.

REYNALDO: I will, my lord.

POLONIUS: You shall do marvelous wisely, good Reynaldo,
Before you visit him, to make inquiry
On his behavior. 5

REYNALDO: My lord, I did intend it.

POLONIUS: Marry, well said; very well said. Look you, sir,
Inquire me first what Danskers° are in Paris;
And how, and who, what means, and where they keep,
What company, at what expense; and finding, 10
By this encompassment and drift of question,
That they do know my son, come you more nearer
Than your particular demands will touch it:
Take you, as 'twere, some distant knowledge of him;
As thus, *I know his father and his friends,* 15
And in part him;— do you mark this, Reynaldo?

REYNALDO: Ay, very well, my lord.

POLONIUS: *And in part him;*— but, you may say, *not well:*
But if't be he I mean, he's very wild;

° *Danskers:* Danes.

20 *Addicted so and so*; and there put on him
What forgeries you please; marry, none so rank
As may dishonor him; take heed of that;
But, sir, such wanton, wild, and usual slips
As are companions noted and most known
25 To youth and liberty.

REYNALDO: As gaming, my lord.

POLONIUS: Ay, or drinking, fencing, swearing, quarreling,
Drabbing:°— you may go so far.

REYNALDO: My lord, that would dishonor him.

30 POLONIUS: Faith, no; as you may season it in the charge.
You must not put another scandal on him,
That he is open to incontinency;
That's not my meaning: but breathe his faults so quaintly
That they may seem the taints of liberty;
35 The flash and outbreak of a fiery mind;
A savageness in unreclaimed blood,
Of general assault.

REYNALDO: But, my good lord,—

POLONIUS: Wherefore should you do this?

40 REYNALDO: Ay, my lord,
I would know that.

POLONIUS: Marry, sir, here's my drift;
And I believe it is a fetch of warrant:°
You laying these slight sullies on my son.
45 As 'twere a thing a little soil'd i' the working,
Mark you,
Your party in converse, him you would sound,
Having ever seen in the prenominate crimes
The youth you breathe of guilty, be assur'd
50 He closes with you in this consequence;
Good sir, or so; or *friend*, or *gentleman*,—
According to the phrase or the addition°
Of man and country.

REYNALDO: Very good, my lord.

55 POLONIUS: And then, sir, does he this,—he does,—
What was I about to say?— By the mass, I was
About to say something:— where did I leave?

REYNALDO: At *closes in the consequence,*
At *friend or so,* and *gentleman.*

60 POLONIUS: At — closes in the consequence,— ay, marry;
He closes with you thus:—*I know the gentleman;
I saw him yesterday, or t'other day,*

° *Drabbing:* Going about with loose women.   ° *fetch of warrant:* A good device.   ° *addition:* Form of address.

Or then, or then; with such, or such; and, as you say,
There was he gaming; there o'ertook in's rouse;
There falling out at tennis: or perchance,   65
I saw him enter such a house of sale,—
Videlicet,° a brothel,— or so forth.—
See you now;
Your bait of falsehood takes this carp of truth:
And thus do we of wisdom and of reach,   70
With windlasses, and with assays of bias,
By indirections find directions out:
So, by my former lecture and advice,
Shall you my son. You have me, have you not?

REYNALDO: My lord, I have.   75
POLONIUS: God b' wi' you; fare you well.
REYNALDO: Good my lord!
POLONIUS: Observe his inclination in yourself.
REYNALDO: I shall, my lord.
POLONIUS: And let him ply his music.   80
REYNALDO: Well, my lord.
POLONIUS: Farewell!

Exit Reynaldo.

Enter Ophelia.

How now, Ophelia! what's the matter?
OPHELIA: Alas, my lord, I have been so affrighted.
POLONIUS: With what, i' the name of God?   85
OPHELIA: My lord, as I was sewing in my chamber,
Lord Hamlet,— with his doublet all unbrac'd;
No hat upon his head; his stockings foul'd,
Ungarter'd, and down-gyved° to his ankle;
Pale as his shirt; his knees knocking each other;   90
And with a look so piteous in purport
As if he had been loosed out of hell
To speak of horrors,— he comes before me.
POLONIUS: Mad for thy love?
OPHELIA: My lord, I do not know;   95
But truly I do fear it.
POLONIUS: What said he?
OPHELIA: He took me by the wrist, and held me hard;
Then goes he to the length of all his arm;
And with his other hand thus o'er his brow,   100
He falls to such perusal of my face
As he would draw it. Long stay'd he so;

° *Videlicet:* That is; namely (Latin).   ° *down-gyved:* Dangling like chains.

At last,— a little shaking of mine arm,
And thrice his head thus waving up and down,—
105   He rais'd a sigh so piteous and profound
That it did seem to shatter all his bulk
And end his being; that done, he lets me go:
And, with his head over his shoulder turn'd,
He seem'd to find his way without his eyes;
110   For out o' doors he went without their help,
And to the last bended their light on me.

POLONIUS: Come, go with me: I will go seek the king.
This is the very ecstasy° of love;
Whose violent property fordoes itself,°
115   And leads the will to desperate undertakings,
As oft as any passion under heaven
That does afflict our nature. I am sorry,—
What, have you given him any hard words of late?

OPHELIA: No, my good lord; but, as you did command,
120   I did repel his letters, and denied
His access to me.

POLONIUS: That hath made him mad.
I am sorry that with better heed and judgment
I had not quoted him: I fear'd he did but trifle,
125   And meant to wreck thee; but, beshrew my jealousy!
It seems it is as proper to our age
To cast beyond ourselves in our opinions
As it is common for the younger sort
To lack discretion. Come, go we to the king:
130   This must be known; which, being kept close, might move
More grief to hide than hate to utter love.

Exeunt.

SCENE 2

A room in the castle.

Enter King, Queen, Rosencrantz, Guildenstern, and Attendants.

KING: Welcome, dear Rosencrantz and Guildenstern!
Moreover that we much did long to see you,
The need we have to use you did provoke
Our hasty sending. Something have you heard
5   Of Hamlet's transformation; so I call it,
Since nor the exterior nor the inward man
Resembles that it was. What it should be,

° *ecstasy:* Madness.   ° *fordoes itself:* Destroys itself.

More than his father's death, that thus hath put him
So much from the understanding of himself,
I cannot dream of: I entreat you both,   10
That being of so young days brought up with him,
And since so neighbor'd to his youth and humor,
That you vouchsafe your rest here in our court
Some little time: so by your companies
To draw him on to pleasures, and to gather,   15
So much as from occasion you may glean,
Whether aught, to us unknown, afflicts him thus,
That, open'd, lies within our remedy.

QUEEN: Good gentlemen, he hath much talk'd of you;
And sure I am two men there are not living   20
To whom he more adheres. If it will please you
To show us so much gentry and good-will
As to expend your time with us awhile,
For the supply and profit of our hope,
Your visitation shall receive such thanks   25
As fits a king's remembrance.

ROSENCRANTZ: Both your majesties
Might, by the sovereign power you have of us,
Put your dread pleasures more into command
Than to entreaty.   30

GUILDENSTERN: We both obey,
And here give up ourselves, in the full bent,
To lay our service freely at your feet,
To be commanded.

KING: Thanks, Rosencrantz and gentle Guildenstern.   35

QUEEN: Thanks, Guildenstern and gentle Rosencrantz:
And I beseech you instantly to visit
My too-much-changed son.— Go, some of you,
And bring these gentlemen where Hamlet is.

GUILDENSTERN: Heavens make our presence and our practices   40
Pleasant and helpful to him!

QUEEN: Ay, amen!

Exeunt Rosencrantz, Guildenstern, and some Attendants.

Enter Polonius.

POLONIUS: The ambassadors from Norway, my good lord,
Are joyfully return'd.

KING: Thou still has been the father of good news.   45

POLONIUS: Have I, my lord? Assure you, my good liege,
I hold my duty, as I hold my soul,
Both to my God and to my gracious king:
And I do think,— or else this brain of mine

50   Hunts not the trail of policy° so sure
        As it hath us'd to do,—that I have found
        The very cause of Hamlet's lunacy.
KING: O, speak of that; that do I long to hear.
POLONIUS: Give first admittance to the ambassadors;
55   My news shall be the fruit to that great feast.
KING: Thyself do grace to them, and bring them in.

Exit Polonius.

        He tells me, my sweet queen, that he hath found
        The head and source of all your son's distemper.
QUEEN: I doubt it is no other but the main,—
60   His father's death and our o'erhasty marriage.
KING: Well, we shall sift him.

Re-enter Polonius, with Voltimand and Cornelius.

                        Welcome, my good friends!
        Say, Voltimand, what from our brother Norway?
VOLTIMAND: Most fair return of greetings and desires.
65   Upon our first, he sent out to suppress
        His nephew's levies; which to him appear'd
        To be a preparation 'gainst the Polack;
        But, better look'd into, he truly found
        It was against your highness: whereat griev'd,—
70   That so his sickness, age, and impotence
        Was falsely borne in hand,—sends out arrests
        On Fortinbras; which he, in brief, obeys;
        Receives rebuke from Norway; and, in fine,
        Makes vows before his uncle never more
75   To give the assay of arms against your majesty.
        Whereon old Norway, overcome with joy,
        Gives him three thousand crowns in annual fee;
        And his commission to employ those soldiers,
        So levied as before, against the Polack:
80   With an entreaty, herein further shown, [*gives a paper*]
        That it might please you to give quiet pass
        Through your dominions for this enterprise,
        On such regards of safety and allowance
        As therein are set down.

85 **KING:**   It likes us well;
        And at our more consider'd time we'll read,
        Answer, and think upon this business.
        Meantime we thank you for your well-took labor:

° *trail of policy:* Statecraft.

Go to your rest; at night we'll feast together:
Most welcome home!   90

Exeunt Voltimand and Cornelius.

POLONIUS: This business is well ended.—
My liege, and madam,— to expostulate
What majesty should be, what duty is,
Why day is day, night night, and time is time,
Were nothing but to waste night, day, and time.   95
Therefore, since brevity is the soul of wit,
And tediousness the limbs and outward flourishes,
I will be brief:— your noble son is mad:
Mad call I it; for to define true madness,
What is't but to be nothing else but mad?   100
But let that go.
QUEEN: More matter with less art.
POLONIUS: Madam, I swear I use no art at all.
That he is mad, 'tis true 'tis pity;
And pity 'tis 'tis true: a foolish figure;   105
But farewell it, for I will use no art.
Mad let us grant him, then: and now remains
That we find out the cause of this effect;
Or rather say, the cause of this defect,
For this effect defective comes by cause: 110
Thus it remains, and the remainder thus.
Perpend.
I have a daughter,—have whilst she is mine,—
Who, in her duty and obedience, mark,
Hath given me this: now gather, and surmise   115

Reads

> To the celestial, and my soul's idol, the most beautified Ophelia,—

That's an ill phrase, a vile phrase,—*beautified* is a vile phrase: but you shall
hear. Thus:

Reads

> In her excellent white bosom, these, &c.

QUEEN: Came this from Hamlet to her?   120
POLONIUS: Good madam, stay a while; I will be faithful.

Reads

> Doubt thou the stars are fire;
>   Doubt that the sun doth move;
> Doubt truth to be a liar;
>   But never doubt I love.   125

O dear Ophelia, I am ill at these numbers, I have not art to reckon my groans: but
that I love thee best, O most best, believe it. Adieu.
Thine evermore, most dear lady, whilst this machine is to him,

Hamlet

This, in obedience, hath my daughter show'd me:

130   And more above, hath his solicitings,
As they fell out by time, by means, and place,
All given to mine ear.

KING: But how hath she
Receiv'd his love?

135 POLONIUS: What do you think of me?

KING: As of a man faithful and honorable.

POLONIUS: I would fain prove so. But what might you think,
When I had seen this hot love on the wing,—
As I perceiv'd it, I must tell you that,

140   Before my daughter told me,— what might you,
Or my dear majesty your queen here, think,
If I had play'd the desk or table-book;°
Or given my heart a winking, mute and dumb;
Or look'd upon this love with idle sight;—

145   What might you think? No, I went round to work,
And my young mistress thus I did bespeak:
Lord Hamlet is a prince out of thy sphere;
This must not be: and then I precepts gave her,
That she should lock herself from his resort,

150   Admit no messengers, receive no tokens.
Which done, she took the fruits of my advice;
And he, repulsed,— a short tale to make,—
Fell into a sadness; then into a fast;
Thence to a watch; thence into a weakness;

155   Thence to a lightness; and, by this declension,
Into the madness wherein now he raves
And all we wail for.

KING: Do you think 'tis this?

QUEEN: It may be, very likely.

160 POLONIUS: Hath there been such a time,— I'd fain know that,—
That I have positively said, *'Tis so,*
When it prov'd otherwise?

KING: Not that I know.

POLONIUS: Take this from this, if this be otherwise: [*Pointing to his head and*
shoulder]

165   If circumstances lead me, I will find
Where truth is hid, though it were hid indeed
Within the center.

° *table-book:* Memorandum pad.

KING: How may we try it further?

POLONIUS: You know, sometimes he walks four hours together

   Here in the lobby.   170

QUEEN: So he does, indeed.

POLONIUS: At such a time I'll loose my daughter to him:

   Be you and I behind an arras° then;

   Mark the encounter: if he love her not,

   And be not from his reason fall'n thereon,   175

   Let me be no assistant for a state,

   But keep a farm and carters.

KING: We will try it.

QUEEN: But look, where sadly the poor wretch comes reading.

POLONIUS: Away, I do beseech you, both away: 180

   I'll board° him presently:— O, give me leave.

Exeunt King, Queen, and Attendants.

Enter Hamlet, reading.

   How does my good Lord Hamlet?

HAMLET: Well, God-a-mercy.

POLONIUS: Do you know me, my lord?

HAMLET: Excellent, excellent well; you're a fishmonger.   185

POLONIUS: Not I, my lord.

HAMLET: Then I would you were so honest a man.

POLONIUS: Honest, my lord!

HAMLET: Ay, sir; to be honest, as this world goes, is to be one man picked out

   of ten thousand.   190

POLONIUS: That's very true, my lord.

HAMLET: For if the sun breed maggots in a dead dog, being a god kissing

   carrion,— Have you a daughter?

POLONIUS: I have, my lord.

HAMLET: Let her not walk i' the sun: conception is a blessing; but not as your   195

   daughter may conceive:—friend, look to't.

POLONIUS: How say you by that?—[*Aside*] Still harping on my daughter:—

   yet he knew me not at first; he said I was a fishmonger: he is far gone, far

   gone: and truly in my youth I suffered much extremity for love; very near

   this. I'll speak to him again.—What do you read, my lord?   200

HAMLET: Words, words, words.

POLONIUS: What is the matter, my lord?

HAMLET: Between who?

POLONIUS: I mean, the matter that you read, my lord.

HAMLET: Slanders, sir: for the satirical slave says here that old men have gray   205

   beards; that their faces are wrinkled; their eyes purging thick amber and

   plum-tree gum; and that they have a plentiful lack of wit, together with

---

° *arras:* Tapestry, hung some distance away from a wall.   ° *board:* Address.

most weak hams: all which, sir, though I most powerfully and potently
believe, yet I hold it not honesty to have it thus set down; for you yourself,
210   sir, should be old as I am, if, like a crab, you could go backward.

Polonius: [*Aside*] Though this be madness, yet there is method in't.—ill you
walk out of the air, my lord?

Hamlet: Into my grave?

Polonius: Indeed, that is out o' the air.—[*Aside*] How pregnant° sometimes
215   his replies are! a happiness that often madness hits on, which reason and
sanity could not so prosperously be delivered of. I will leave him, and suddenly contrive the means of meeting between him and my daughter.—
More honorable lord, I will most humbly take my leave of you.

Hamlet: You cannot, sir, take from me anything that I will more willingly
220   part withal,—except my life, except my life, except my life.

Polonius: Fare you well, my lord.

Hamlet: These tedious old fools!

Enter Rosencrantz and Guildenstern.

Polonius: You go to seek the Lord Hamlet; there he is.

Rosencrantz: [*To Polonius*] God save you, sir!

Exit Polonius.

225   **Guildenstern:** Mine honored lord!

Rosencrantz: My most dear lord!

Hamlet: My excellent good friends! How dost thou, Guildenstern? Ah,
Rosencrantz? Good lads, how do ye both?

Rosencrantz: As the indifferent children of the earth.

230   **Guildenstern:** Happy in that we are not overhappy; on fortune's cap we are
not the very button.

Hamlet: Nor the soles of her shoe?

Rosencrantz: Neither, my lord.

Hamlet: Then you live about her waist, or in the middle of her favors?

235   **Guildenstern:** Faith, her privates we.

Hamlet: In the secret parts of fortune? O, most true; she is a strumpet.
What's the news?

Rosencrantz: None, my lord, but that the world's grown honest.

Hamlet: Then is doomsday near: but your news is not true. Let me question
240   more in particular: what have you, my good friends, deserved at the hands
of fortune, that she sends you to prison hither?

Guildenstern: Prison, my lord!

Hamlet: Denmark's a prison.

Rosencrantz: Then is the world one.

245   **Hamlet:** A goodly one; in which there are many confines, wards, and dun-
geons, Denmark being one o' the worst.

° *pregnant:* Ready, and clever.

ROSENCRANTZ: We think not so, my lord.

HAMLET: Why, then, 'tis none to you; for there is nothing either good or bad, but thinking makes it so: to me it is a prison.

ROSENCRANTZ: Why, then, your ambition makes it one; 'tis too narrow for your mind.   250

HAMLET: O God, I could be bounded in a nutshell, and count myself a king of infinite space, were it not that I have bad dreams.

GUILDENSTERN: Which dreams, indeed, are ambition; for the very substance of the ambitious is merely the shadow of a dream.   255

HAMLET: A dream itself is but a shadow.

ROSENCRANTZ: Truly, and I hold ambition of so airy and light a quality that it is but a shadow's shadow.

HAMLET: Then are our beggars bodies, and our monarchs and outstretched heroes the beggars' shadows. Shall we to the court? for, by my fay, I cannot reason.   260

ROSENCRANTZ and GUILDENSTERN: We'll wait upon you.

HAMLET: No such matter: I will not sort you with the rest of my servants, for, to speak to you like an honest man, I am most dreadfully attended. But, in the beaten way of friendship, what make you at Elsinore?   265

ROSENCRANTZ: To visit you, my lord; no other occasion.

HAMLET: Beggar that I am, I am even poor in thanks; but I thank you: and sure, dear friends, my thanks are too dear a halfpenny. Were you not sent for? Is it your own inclining? Is it a free visitation? Come, deal justly with me: come, come; nay, speak.   270

GUILDENSTERN: What should we say, my lord?

HAMLET: Why, anything — but to the purpose. You were sent for; and there is a kind of confession in your looks, which your modesties have not craft enough to color: I know the good king and queen have sent for you.

ROSENCRANTZ: To what end, my lord?   275

HAMLET: That you must teach me. But let me conjure you, by the rights of our fellowship, by the consonancy of our youth, by the obligation of our ever-preserved love, and by what more dear a better proposer could charge you withal, be even and direct with me, whether you were sent for or no?

ROSENCRANTZ: What say you? [*To Guildenstern*]   280

HAMLET: [*Aside*] Nay, then, I have an eye of you. — If you love me, hold not off.

GUILDENSTERN: My lord, we were sent for.

HAMLET: I will tell you why; so shall my anticipation prevent your discovery, and your secrecy to the king and queen moult no feather. I have of late, — but wherefore I know not, — lost all my mirth, forgone all custom of exercises; and, indeed, it goes so heavily with my disposition that this goodly frame, the earth, seems to me a sterile promontory; this most excellent canopy, the air, look you, this brave o'erhanging firmament, this majestical roof fretted° with golden fire, — why, it appears no other thing to me than   285

      290

° *roof fretted:* A roof with fretwork.

a foul and pestilent congregation of vapors. What a piece of work is man! How noble in reason! how infinite in faculties! in form and moving, how express and admirable! in action, how like an angel! in apprehension, how like a god! the beauty of the world! the paragon of animals! And yet, to me, what is this quintessence of dust? man delights not me; no, nor woman neither, though by your smiling you seem to say so.

ROSENCRANTZ: My lord, there was no such stuff in my thoughts.

HAMLET: Why did you laugh, then, when I said, *Man delights not me?*

ROSENCRANTZ: To think, my lord, if you delight not in man, what lenten en- tertainment° the players shall receive from you: we coted° them on the way; and hither are they coming, to offer you service.

HAMLET: He that plays the king shall be welcome,—his majesty shall have tribute of me; the adventurous knight shall use his foil and target; the lover shall not sigh gratis; the humorous° man shall end his part in peace; the clown shall make those laugh whose lungs are tickled o' the sere;° and the lady shall say her mind freely, or the blank verse shall halt° for't.—What players are they?

ROSENCRANTZ: Even those you were wont to take delight in,— the tragedi- ans of the city.

HAMLET: How chances it they travel? their residence, both in reputation and profit, was better both ways.

ROSENCRANTZ: I think their inhibition° comes by the means of the late innovation.

HAMLET: Do they hold the same estimation they did when I was in the city? Are they so followed?

ROSENCRANTZ: No, indeed, they are not.

HAMLET: How comes it? do they grow rusty?

ROSENCRANTZ: Nay, their endeavor keeps in the wonted pace; but there is, sir, an aery° of children, little eyases,° that cry out on the top of question, and are most tyrannically clapped for't: these are now the fashion; and so berattle the common stages,— so they call them,— that many wearing rapiers are afraid of goose-quills, and dare scarce come thither.

HAMLET: What, are they children? who maintains 'em? how are they escoted?° Will they pursue the quality° no longer than they can sing? will they not say afterwards, if they should grow themselves to common players,— as it is most like, if their means are no better,— their writers do them wrong, to make them exclaim against their own succession?

ROSENCRANTZ: Faith, there has been much to do on both sides; and the na- tion holds it no sin to tarre° them to controversy: there was for awhile no money bid for argument, unless the poet and the player went to cuffs in the question.

° *lenten entertainment:* Poor reception.   ° *coted:* Passed.   ° *humorous:* Eccentric.   ° *whose lungs* . . . *sere:* Whose lungs, for laughter, are easily tickled.   ° *halt:* Limp.   ° *inhibition:* Difficulty, preventing them from remaining in the capital.   ° *aery:* Brood of birds of prey.   ° *little eyases:* Young hawks; a reference to the boys' companies that became popular rivals of Shakespeare's company of players.   ° *escoted:* Financially supported.   ° *quality:* Profession.   ° *to tarre:* To egg them on.

HAMLET: Is't possible?

GUILDENSTERN: O, there has been much throwing about of brains.

HAMLET: Do the boys carry it away?

ROSENCRANTZ: Ay, that they do, my lord; Hercules and his load° too.   335

HAMLET: It is not strange; for mine uncle is king of Denmark, and those that
would make mouths at him while my father lived, give twenty, forty, fifty,
an hundred ducats a-piece for his picture in little. 'Sblood, there is something in this more than natural, if philosophy could find it out.

Flourish of trumpets within.

GUILDENSTERN: There are the players.   340

HAMLET: Gentlemen, you are welcome to Elsinore. Your hands, come: the ap-
purtenance of welcome is fashion and ceremony: let me comply with you in
this garb; lest my extent° to the players, which, I tell you, must show fairly
outward, should more appear like entertainment° than yours. You are welcome: but my uncle-father and aunt-mother are deceived.   345

GUILDENSTERN: In what, my dear lord?

HAMLET: I am but mad north-north-west: when the wind is southerly I know a
hawk from a handsaw.

Enter Polonius.

POLONIUS: Well be with you, gentlemen!

HAMLET: Hark you, Guildenstern;— and you too;— at each ear a hearer: that   350
great baby you see there is not yet out of his swathing-clouts.

ROSENCRANTZ: Happily he's the second time come to them; for they say an
old man is twice a child.

HAMLET: I will prophesy he comes to tell me of the players; mark it. You say
right, sir: o' Monday morning; 'twas so indeed.   355

POLONIUS: My lord, I have news to tell you.

HAMLET: My lord, I have news to tell you. When Roscius was an actor
in Rome,—

POLONIUS: The actors are come hither, my lord.

HAMLET: Buzz, buzz!   360

POLONIUS: Upon mine honor,—

HAMLET: Then came each actor on his ass,—

POLONIUS: The best actors in the world, either for tragedy, comedy, history,
pastoral, pastoral-comical, historical-pastoral, tragical-historical, tragical-
comical-historical-pastoral, scene individable,° or poem unlimited:°   365
Seneca cannot be too heavy nor Plautus too light. For the law of writ and
the liberty,° these are the only men.

°*his load:* The globe, or the world.   °*extent:* Show of friendliness.   °*entertainment:* Welcome.
°*scene individable:* A play that observes the unities of time and place.   °*poem unlimited:* A typical multiscene
Elizabethan drama, not restricted by the unities; examples are *Hamlet, Macbeth, King Lear,* and nearly any other
play by Shakespeare.   °*For the law . . . liberty:* For the laws of the unities and for playwriting that is not so
restricted.

HAMLET: O Jephthah, judge of Israel, what a treasure hadst thou!
POLONIUS: What a treasure had he, my lord?
370 HAMLET: Why—

> One fair daughter, and no more,
> The which he loved passing well.

POLONIUS: [*Aside*] Still on my daughter.
HAMLET: Am I not i' the right, old Jephthah?
375 POLONIUS: If you call me Jephthah, my lord, I have a daughter that I love
   passing well.
HAMLET: Nay, that follows not.
POLONIUS: What follows, then, my lord?
HAMLET: Why—

380
> As by lot, God wot,
> and then, you know,
> It came to pass, as most like it was,

the first row of the pious chanson will show you more; for look where my
abridgement comes.

Enter four or five Players.

385 You are welcome, masters; welcome, all:—I am glad to see thee well:—
welcome, good friends.— O, my old friend! Thy face is valanced since I saw
thee last; comest thou to beard me in Denmark?—What, my young lady and
mistress! By'r lady, your ladyship is nearer heaven than when I saw you last,
by the altitude of a chopine.° Pray God, your voice, like a piece of uncurrent
390 gold, be not cracked within the ring.—Masters, you are all welcome. We'll
e'en to't like French falconers, fly at anything we see: we'll have a speech
straight: come, give us a taste of your quality; come, a passionate speech.
1ST PLAYER: What speech, my lord?
HAMLET: I heard thee speak me a speech once,—but it was never acted; or, if
395 it was, not above once; for the play, I remember, pleased not the million;
'twas caviare to the general: but it was,— as I received it, and others whose
judgments in such matters cried in the top of mine,— an excellent play, well
digested in the scenes, set down with as much modesty as cunning. I remember, one said there were no sallets in the lines to make the matter savory, nor
400 no matter in the phrase that might indite the author of affectation; but
called it an honest method, as wholesome as sweet, and by very much more
handsome than fine. One speech in it I chiefly loved: 'twas Aeneas' tale to
Dido; and thereabout of it especially where he speaks of Priam's slaughter: if
it live in your memory, begin at this line;—let me see, let me see:—

405
> The rugged Pyrrhus, like the Hyrcanian beast,°

° *chopine:* A wooden stilt more than a foot high used under a woman's shoe; a Venetian fashion introduced into
England.   ° *The rugged . . .:* This speech is an example of the declamatory style of drama, which Shakespeare
surely must have considered outmoded.

—it is not so:—it begins with Pyrrhus:—

> The rugged Pyrrhus,—he whose sable arms,
> Black as his purpose, did the night resemble
> When he lay couched in the ominous horse,—
> Hath now this dread and black complexion smear'd
> With heraldry more dismal; head to foot
> Now is he total gules; horridly trick'd
> With blood of fathers, mothers, daughters, sons,
> Bak'd and impasted with the parching streets,
> That lend a tyrannous and damned light
> To their vile murders: roasted in wrath and fire,
> And thus o'er-sized with coagulate gore,
> With eyes like carbuncles, the hellish Pyrrhus
> Old grandsire Priam seeks.—

So proceed you.

POLONIUS: 'Fore God, my lord, well spoken, with good accent and
good discretion.

1ST PLAYER: Anon he finds him
Striking too short at Greeks; his antique sword,
Rebellious to his arm, lies where it falls,
Repugnant to command: unequal match'd,
Pyrrhus at Priam drives; in rage strikes wide;
But with the whiff and wind of his fell sword
The unnerved father falls. Then senseless Ilium,
Seeming to feel this blow, with flaming top
Stoops to his base; and with a hideous crash
Takes prisoner Pyrrhus' ear: for, lo! his sword,
Which was declining on the milky head
Of reverend Priam, seem'd i' the air to stick:
So, as a painted tyrant, Pyrrhus stood;
And, like a neutral to his will and matter,
Did nothing.
But as we often see, against some storm,
A silence in the heavens, the rack stand still,
The blood winds speechless, and the orb below
As hush as death, anon the dreadful thunder
Doth rend the region; so, after Pyrrhus' pause,
A roused vengeance sets him new a-work;
And never did the Cyclops' hammers fall
On Mars his armor, forg'd for proof eterne,
With less remorse than Pyrrhus' bleeding sword
Now falls on Priam.—
Out, out, thou strumpet, Fortune! All you gods,
In general synod, take away her power;
Break all the spokes and fellies from her wheel,
And bowl the round knave down the hill of heaven,
As low as to the fiends!

410

415

420

425

430

435

440

445

450

POLONIUS: This is too long.

HAMLET: It shall to the barber's, with your beard. — Pr'ythee, say on. — He's

455   for a jig, or a tale of bawdry, or he sleeps: — say on; come to Hecuba.

1ST PLAYER: But who, O, who had seen the mobled queen,—

HAMLET: *The mobled queen?*

POLONIUS: That's good; *mobled queen* is good.

1ST PLAYER: Run barefoot up and down, threatening the flames

460   With bissom rheum; a clout upon that head

Where late the diadem stood; and, for a robe,

About her lank and all o'er-teemed loins,

A blanket, in the alarm of fear caught up;—

Who this had seen, with tongue in venom steep'd,

465   'Gainst Fortune's state would treason have pronounc'd:

But if the gods themselves did see her then,

When she saw Pyrrhus make malicious sport

In mincing with his sword her husband's limbs,

The instant burst of clamor that she made,—

470   Unless things mortal move them not at all,—

Would have made milch the burning eyes of heaven,

And passion in the gods.

POLONIUS: Look, whether he has not turn'd his color, and has tears in's

eyes. — Pray you, no more.

475 HAMLET: 'Tis well; I'll have thee speak out the rest soon. — Good my lord,

will you see the players well bestowed? Do you hear, let them be well

used; for they are the abstracts and brief chronicles of the time; after

your death you were better have a bad epitaph than their ill report while

you live.

480 POLONIUS: My lord, I will use them according to their desert.

HAMLET: God's bodikin, man, better: use every man after his desert, and who

should scape whipping? Use them after your own honor and dignity: the

less they deserve the more merit is in your bounty. Take them in.

POLONIUS: Come, sirs.

485 HAMLET: Follow him, friends: we'll hear a play to-morrow.

Exit Polonius with all the Players but the First.

Dost thou hear me, old friend; can you play the Murder of Gonzago?

1ST PLAYER: Ay, my lord.

HAMLET: We'll ha't to-morrow night. You could, for a need, study a speech

of some dozen or sixteen lines which I would set down and insert in't?

490   could you not?

1ST PLAYER: Ay, my lord.

HAMLET: Very well. — Follow that lord; and look you mock him not.

Exit First Player.

—My good friends, [*to Rosencrantz and Guildenstern*] I'll leave you till night:

you are welcome to Elsinore.

ROSENCRANTZ: Good my lord! 495

Exeunt Rosencrantz and Guildenstern.

HAMLET: Ay, so God b' wi' ye! — Now I am alone.
O, what a rogue° and peasant slave am I!
Is it not monstrous that this player here,
But in a fiction, in a dream of passion,
Could force his soul so to his own conceit° 500
That from her working all his visage wan'd;
Tears in his eyes, distraction in's aspéct,
A broken voice, and his whole function suiting
With forms to his conceit? And all for nothing!
For Hecuba? 505
What's Hecuba to him or he to Hecuba,
That he should weep for her? What would he do,
Had he the motive and the cue for passion
That I have? He would drown the stage with tears,
And cleave the general ear with horrid speech; 510
Make mad the guilty, and appal the free;
Confound the ignorant, and amaze, indeed,
The very faculties of eyes and ears.
Yet I,
A dull and muddy-mettled rascal, peak, 515
Like John-a-dreams, unpregnant of my cause,
And can say nothing; no, not for a king
Upon whose property and most dear life
A damn'd defeat was made. Am I a coward?
Who calls me villain? breaks my pate across? 520
Plucks off my beard and blows it in my face?
Tweaks me by the nose? gives me the lie i' the throat,
As deep as to the lungs? who does me this, ha?
'Swounds, I should take it: for it cannot be
But I am pigeon-liver'd, and lack gall 525
To make oppression bitter; or ere this
I should have fatted all the region kites
With this slave's offal: — bloody, bawdy villain!
Remorseless, treacherous, lecherous, kindless villain!
O, vengeance! 530
Why, what an ass am I! This is most brave,
That I, the son of a dear father murder'd,
Prompted to my revenge by heaven and hell,
Must, like a whore, unpack my heart with words,
And fall a-cursing like a very drab, 535

° *rogue:* Wretched creature.   ° *conceit:* Conception.

A scullion!
Fie upon't! foh!— About, my brain! I have heard
That guilty creatures, sitting at a play,
Have by the very cunning of the scene
540   Been struck so to the soul that presently
They have proclaim'd their malefactions;
For murder, though it have no tongue, will speak
With most miraculous organ. I'll have these players
Play something like the murder of my father
545   Before mine uncle: I'll observe his looks;
I'll tent° him to the quick: if he but blench,
I know my course. The spirit that I have seen
May be the devil: and the devil hath power
To assume a pleasing shape; yea, and perhaps
550   Out of my weakness and my melancholy,—
As he is very potent with such spirits,—
Abuses me to damn me: I'll have grounds
More relative than this:— the play's the thing
Wherein I'll catch the conscience of the king. [*Exit.*]

ACT 3
SCENE 1

A room in the castle.

Enter King, Queen, Polonius, Ophelia, Rosencrantz, and Guildenstern.

KING: And can you, by no drift of circumstance,
        Get from him why he puts on this confusion,
        Grating so harshly all his days of quiet
        With turbulent and dangerous lunacy?
5   ROSENCRANTZ: He does confess he feels himself distracted;
        But from what cause he will by no means speak.
    GUILDENSTERN: Nor do we find him forward to be sounded;
        But, with a crafty madness, keeps aloof
        When we would bring him on to some confession
10   Of his true state.
    QUEEN: Did he receive you well?
    ROSENCRANTZ: Most like a gentleman.

    GUILDENSTERN: But with much forcing of his disposition.

    ROSENCRANTZ: Niggard of question; but, of our demands,
15   Most free in his reply.

° *tent:* Probe.

QUEEN: Did you assay him
    To any pastime?

ROSENCRANTZ: Madam, it so fell out that certain players
    We o'er-raught on the way: of these we told him;
    And there did seem in him a kind of joy   20
    To hear of it: they are about the court;
    And, as I think, they have already order
    This night to play before him.

POLONIUS: 'Tis most true:
    And he beseech'd me to entreat your majesties   25
    To hear and see the matter.

KING: With all my heart; and it doth much content me
    To hear him so inclin'd.
    Good gentlemen, give him a further edge,
    And drive his purpose on to these delights.   30
ROSENCRANTZ: We shall, my lord.

Exeunt Rosencrantz and Guildenstern.

KING: Sweet Gertrude, leave us too;
    For we have closely sent for Hamlet hither
    That he, as 'twere by accident, may here
    Affront Ophelia: 35
    Her father and myself,—lawful espials,°—
    Will so bestow ourselves that, seeing, unseen,
    We may of their encounter frankly judge;
    And gather by him, as he is behav'd,
    If't be the affliction of his love or no   40
    That thus he suffers for.
QUEEN: I shall obey you:—
    And for your part, Ophelia, I do wish
    That your good beauties be the happy cause
    Of Hamlet's wildness: so shall I hope your virtues   45
    Will bring him to his wonted way again,
    To both your honors.
OPHELIA: Madam, I wish it may.

Exit Queen.

POLONIUS: Ophelia, walk you here.— Gracious, so please you,
    We will bestow ourselves.—[*To Ophelia*] Read on this book;   50
    That show of such an exercise may color
    Your loneliness.—We are oft to blame in this,—
    'Tis too much prov'd,— that with devotion's visage

° *espials:* Spies.

And pious action we do sugar o'er
55   The devil himself.

KING: [*Aside*]   O, 'tis too true!
How smart a lash that speech doth give my conscience!
The harlot's cheek, beautied with plastering art,
Is not more ugly to the thing that helps it
60   Than is my deed to my most painted word:
O heavy burden!

POLONIUS: I hear him coming: let's withdraw, my lord.

Exeunt King and Polonius.

Enter Hamlet.

HAMLET: To be, or not to be,—that is the question:
Whether 'tis nobler in the mind to suffer
65   The slings and arrows of outrageous fortune,
Or to take arms against a sea of troubles,
And by opposing end them?—To die,—to sleep,—
No more; and by a sleep to say we end
The heart-ache and the thousand natural shocks
70   That flesh is heir to,—'tis a consummation
Devoutly to be wish'd. To die,—to sleep;—
To sleep! perchance to dream:—ay, there's the rub;
For in that sleep of death what dreams may come,
When we have shuffled off this mortal coil,
75   Must give us pause: there's the respect
That makes a calamity of so long life;
For who would bear the whips and scorns of time,
The oppressor's wrong, the proud man's contumely,
The pangs of déspis'd love, the law's delay,
80   The insolence of office, and the spurns
That patient merit of the unworthy takes,
When he himself might his quietus make
With a bare bodkin?° who would fardels° bear,
To grunt° and sweat under a weary life,
85   But that the dread of something after death,—
The undiscover'd country, from whose bourn°
No traveler returns,—puzzles the will,
And makes us rather bear those ills we have
Than to fly to others that we know not of?
90   Thus conscience does make cowards of us all;
And thus the native hue of resolution
Is sicklied o'er with the pale cast of thought;
And enterprises of great pith and moment,

° *bodkin:* Stiletto.   ° *fardels:* Burdens.   ° *grunt:* Groan.   ° *bourn:* Boundary.

With this regard, their currents turn awry,
And lose the name of action. — Soft you now!   95
The fair Ophelia. — Nymph, in thy orisons°
Be all my sins remember'd.

OPHELIA: Good my lord,
How does your honor for this many a day?

HAMLET: I humbly thank you; well, well, well.   100

OPHELIA: My lord, I have remembrances of yours,
That I have longed long to re-deliver;
I pray you, now receive them.

HAMLET: No, not I;
I never gave you aught.   105

OPHELIA: My honor'd lord, you know right well you did;
And with them, words of so sweet breath compos'd
As made the things more rich: their perfume lost,
Take these again; for to the noble mind
Rich gifts wax poor when givers prove unkind.   110
There, my lord.

HAMLET: Ha, ha! are you honest?

OPHELIA: My lord?

HAMLET: Are you fair?

OPHELIA: What means your lordship?   115

HAMLET: That if you be honest and fair, your honesty should admit no
discourse to your beauty.

OPHELIA: Could beauty, my lord, have better commerce than with honesty?

HAMLET: Ay, truly; for the power of beauty will sooner transform honesty from
what it is to a bawd than the force of honesty can translate beauty into his   120
likeness: this was sometime a paradox, but now the time gives it proof. I did
love you once.

OPHELIA: Indeed, my lord, you made me believe so.

HAMLET: You should not have believed me; for virtue cannot so inoculate our
old stock but we shall relish of it: I loved you not.   125

OPHELIA: I was the more deceived.

HAMLET: Get thee to a nunnery: why wouldst thou be a breeder of sinners? I am
myself indifferent° honest; but yet I could accuse me of such things that it
were better my mother had not borne me: I am very proud, revengeful, ambitious; with more offences at my beck than I have thoughts to put them in,   130
imagination to give them shape, or time to act them in. What should such
fellows as I do crawling between heaven and earth? We are arrant knaves,
all; believe none of us. Go thy ways to a nunnery. Where's your father?

OPHELIA: At home, my lord.

HAMLET: Let the doors be shut upon him, that he may play the fool nowhere   135
but in's own house. Farewell.

° *orisons:* Prayers.   ° *indifferent:* Tolerably.

OPHELIA: O, help him, you sweet heavens!

HAMLET: If thou dost marry, I'll give thee this plague for thy dowry,—be thou
as chaste as ice, as pure as snow, thou shalt not escape calumny. Get thee to
140   a nunnery, go: farewell. Or, if thou wilt needs marry, marry a fool; for wise
men know well enough what monsters you make of them. To a nunnery, go;
and quickly too. Farewell.

OPHELIA: O heavenly powers, restore him!

HAMLET: I have heard of your paintings too, well enough; God has given you
145   one face and you make yourselves another: you jig, you amble, and you lisp,
and nickname God's creatures, and make your wantonness your ignorance.
Go to, I'll no more on't; it hath made me mad. I say, we will have no more
marriages: those that are married already, all but one, shall live; the rest
shall keep as they are. To a nunnery, go. [*Exit.*]

150 OPHELIA: O, what a noble mind is here o'erthrown!
The courtier's, soldier's, scholar's eye, tongue, sword:
The expectancy and rose of the fair state,
The glass of fashion and the mould of form,
The observ'd of all observers,— quite, quite down!
155   And I, of ladies most deject and wretched
That suck'd the honey of his music vows,
Now see that noble and most sovereign reason,
Like sweet bells jangled, out of tune and harsh;
That unmatch'd form and feature of blown° youth
160   Blasted with ecstasy: O, woe is me,
To have seen what I have seen, see what I see!

Re-enter King and Polonius.

KING: Love! his affections do not that way tend;
Nor what he spake, though it lack'd form a little,
Was not like madness. There's something in his soul
165   O'er which his melancholy sits on brood;
And I do doubt° the hatch and the disclose
Will be some danger: which for to prevent,
I have in quick determination
Thus set it down:—he shall with speed to England
170   For the demand of our neglected tribute:
Haply, the seas and countries different,
With variable objects, shall expel
This something-settled matter in his heart;
Whereon his brains still beating puts him thus
175   From fashion of himself. What think you on't?

POLONIUS: It shall do well: but yet do I believe
The origin and commencement of his grief

° *blown:* Full-blown.   ° *doubt:* Fear.

Sprung from neglected love.— How now, Ophelia!
You need not tell us what Lord Hamlet said;
We heard it all.— My lord, do as you please;   180
But if you hold it fit, after the play,
Let his queen mother all alone entreat him
To show his grief: let her be round with him;
And I'll be plac'd, so please you, in the ear
Of all their conference. If she finds him not,°   185
To England send him; or confine him where
Your wisdom best shall think.

KING: It shall be so:
Madness in great ones must not unwatch'd go.

Exeunt.

SCENE 2

A hall in the castle.

Enter Hamlet and certain Players.

HAMLET: Speak the speech, I pray you, as I pronounced it to you, trippingly on
the tongue: but if you mouth it, as many of your players do, I had as lief the
town-crier spoke my lines. Nor do not saw the air too much with your
hand, thus; but use all gently: for in the very torrent, tempest, and, as I may
say, the whirlwind of passion, you must acquire and beget a temperance that   5
may give it smoothness. O, it offends me to the soul, to hear a robustious
periwigpated fellow tear a passion to tatters, to very rags, to split the ears of
the groundlings, who, for the most part, are capable of nothing but inexplicable dumb shows and noise: I could have such a fellow whipped for
o'erdoing Termagant;° it out-herods Herod:° pray you, avoid it.   10
1ST PLAYER: I warrant your honor.
HAMLET: Be not too tame neither, but let your own discretion be your tutor;
suit the action to the word, the word to the action; with this special observance, that you o'erstep not the modesty of nature: for anything so overdone is from the purpose of playing, whose end, both at the first and now,   15
was and is, to hold, as 'twere, the mirror up to nature; to show virtue her
own feature, scorn her own image, and the very age and body of the time
his form and pressure. Now, this overdone or come tardy off, though it
make the unskilful laugh, cannot but make the judicious grieve; the censure
of the which one must, in your allowance, o'erweigh a whole theater of   20
others. O, there be players that I have seen play,— and heard others praise,
and that highly,— not to speak it profanely, that, neither having the accent
of Christians, nor the gait of Christian, pagan, nor man, have so strutted

---

° *finds him not:* Does not find him out.   ° *Termagant:* A violent pagan deity, supposedly Mohammedan.
° *out-herods Herod:* Outrants the ranting Herod, who figures in medieval drama.

and bellowed that I have thought some of nature's journeymen had made
25   men, and not made them well, they imitated humanity so abominably.

1ST PLAYER: I hope we have reformed that indifferently with us, sir.

HAMLET: O, reform it altogether. And let those that play your clowns speak
no more than is set down for them: for there be of them that will themselves laugh, to set on some quantity of barren spectators to laugh too;
30   though, in the meantime, some necessary question of the play be then to be
considered: that's villainous, and shows a most pitiful ambition in the fool
that uses it. Go, make you ready.

Exeunt Players.

Enter Polonius, Rosencrantz, and Guildenstern.

How now, my lord! will the king hear this piece of work?

POLONIUS: And the queen, too, and that presently.

35   HAMLET: Bid the players make haste.

Exit Polonius.

Will you two help to hasten them?

ROSENCRANTZ and GUILDENSTERN: We will, my lord. [*Exeunt.*]

HAMLET: What, ho, Horatio!

Enter Horatio.

HORATIO: Here, sweet lord, at your service.

40   HAMLET: Horatio, thou art e'en as just a man
As e'er my conversation cop'd withal.

HORATIO: O, my dear lord,—

HAMLET: Nay, do not think I flatter;
For what advancement may I hope from thee,
45   That no revénue hast, but thy good spirits,
To feed and clothe thee? Why should the poor be flatter'd?
No, let the candied tongue lick ábsurd pomp;
And crook the pregnant hinges of the knee
Where thrift may follow fawning. Dost thou hear?
50   Since my dear soul was mistress of her choice,
And could of men distinguish, her election
Hath seal'd thee for herself: for thou hast been
As one, in suffering all, that suffers nothing;
A man that Fortune's buffets and rewards
55   Hast ta'en with equal thanks: and bless'd are those
Whose blood and judgment are so well commingled
That they are not a pipe for Fortune's finger
To sound what stop she please. Give me that man
That is not passion's slave, and I will wear him
60   In my heart's core, ay, in my heart of heart,
As I do thee.— Something too much of this.—

There is a play to-night before the king;
One scene of it comes near the circumstance
Which I have told thee of my father's death:
I pr'ythee, when thou see'st that act a-foot,   65
Even with the very comment of thy soul
Observe mine uncle: if this his occulted guilt
Do not itself unkennel in one speech,
It is a damned ghost that we have seen;
And my imaginations are as foul   70
As Vulcan's stithy.° Give him heedful note:
For I mine eyes will rivet to his face;
And, after, we will both our judgments join
In censure of his seeming.

HORATIO: Well, my lord: 75
If he steal aught the whilst this play is playing,
And scape detecting, I will pay the theft.

HAMLET: They are coming to the play; I must be idle:°
Get you a place.

Danish march. A flourish. Enter King, Queen, Polonius, Ophelia, Rosencrantz, Guild-
enstern, and others.

KING: How fares our cousin Hamlet?   80

HAMLET: Excellent, i'faith; of the chameleon's dish: I eat the air,°
promise-crammed: you cannot feed capons so.

KING: I have nothing with this answer, Hamlet; these words are not mine.

HAMLET: No, nor mine now. [*To Polonius*] My lord, you played once i' the
university, you say?   85

POLONIUS: That did I, my lord, and was accounted a good actor.

HAMLET: And what did you enact?

POLONIUS: I did enact Julius Caesar: I was killed i' the Capitol; Brutus
killed me.

HAMLET: It was a brute part of him to kill so capital a calf there.— Be the   90
players ready.

ROSENCRANTZ: Ay, my lord; they stay upon your patience.

QUEEN: Come hither, my good Hamlet, sit by me.

HAMLET: No, good mother, here's metal more attractive.

POLONIUS: O, ho! do you mark that? [*To the King*]   95

HAMLET: Lady, shall I lie in your lap? [*Lying down at Ophelia's feet*]

OPHELIA: No, my lord.

HAMLET: I mean, my head upon your lap?

OPHELIA: Ay, my lord.

HAMLET: Do you think I meant country matters?   100

OPHELIA: I think nothing, my lord.

° *stithy:* Smithy.   ° *idle:* Foolish.   ° *of the chameleon's . . . the air:* Chameleons were believed to live on air.

HAMLET: That's a fair thought to lie between maids' legs.

OPHELIA: What is, my lord?

HAMLET: Nothing.

105 OPHELIA: You are merry, my lord.

HAMLET: Who, I?

OPHELIA: Ay, my lord.

HAMLET: O, your only jig-maker. What should a man do but be merry? for, look
you, how cheerfully my mother looks, and my father died within's two hours.

110 OPHELIA: Nay, 'tis twice two months, my lord.

HAMLET: So long? Nay, then, let the devil wear black, for I'll have a suit of
sables. O heavens! die two months ago, and not forgotten yet? Then there's
hope a great man's memory may outlive his life half a year: but, by'r lady, he
must build churches, then; or else shall he suffer not thinking on, with the
115 hobby-horse, whose epitaph is, *For, O, for, O, the hobby-horse is forgot.*

Trumpets sound. The dumb show enters.

*Enter a King and a Queen, very lovingly; the Queen embracing him and he her. She
kneels, and makes show of protestation unto him. He takes her up, and declines his head
upon her neck: lays him down upon a bank of flowers: she, seeing him asleep, leaves
him. Anon comes in a fellow, takes off his crown, kisses it, and pours poison in the
King's ears, and exit. The Queen returns; finds the King dead, and makes passionate action. The Poisoner, with some two or three Mutes, comes in again, seeming to lament
with her. The dead body is carried away. The Poisoner woos the Queen with gifts: she
seems loth and unwilling awhile, but in the end accepts his love.*

Exeunt.

OPHELIA: What means this, my lord?

HAMLET: Marry, this is miching mallecho;° it means mischief.

OPHELIA: Belike this show imports the argument of the play.

Enter Prologue.

HAMLET: We shall know by this fellow: the players cannot keep counsel;
120 they'll tell all.

OPHELIA: Will he tell us what this show meant?

HAMLET: Ay, or any show that you'll show him: be not you ashamed to show,
he'll not shame to tell you what it means.

OPHELIA: You are naught, you are naught: I'll mark the play.

125 PROLOGUE:

> *For us, and for our tragedy,*
> *Here stooping to your clemency,*
> *We beg your hearing patiently.*

HAMLET: Is this a prologue, or the posy° of a ring?

° *miching mallecho:* A sneaking misdeed.   ° *posy:* Motto or inscription.

OPHELIA: 'Tis brief, my lord.   130

HAMLET: As woman's love.

Enter a King and a Queen.

PROLOGUE KING: Full thirty times hath Phoebus' cart gone round
  Neptune's salt wash and Tellus' orbed ground,°
  And thirty dozen moons with borrow'd sheen
  About the world have times twelve thirties been,   135
  Since love our hearts, and Hymen did our hands
  Unite commutual in most sacred bands.
PROLOGUE QUEEN: So many journeys may the sun and moon
  Make us again count o'er ere love be done!
  But, woe is me, you are so sick of late,   140
  So far from cheer and from your former state
  That I distrust you.° Yet, though I distrust,
  Discomfort you, my lord, it nothing must:
  For women's fear and love holds quantity,°
  In neither aught, or in extremity.   145
  Now, what my love is, proof hath made you know;
  And as my love is siz'd, my fear is so:
  Where love is great, the littlest doubts are fear;
  Where little fears grow great, great love grows there.
PROLOGUE KING: Faith, I must leave thee, love, and shortly too;   150
  My operant powers their functions leave° to do:
  And thou shalt live in this fair world behind,
  Honor'd, belov'd; and haply one as kind
  For husband shalt thou,—
PROLOGUE QUEEN: O, confound the rest!   155
  Such love must needs be treason in my breast:
  In second husband let me be accurst!
  None wed the second but who kill'd the first.
HAMLET: [*Aside*] Wormwood, wormwood.
PROLOGUE QUEEN: The instances that second marriage move   160
  Are base respects of thrift, but none of love:
  A second time I kill my husband, dead,
  When second husband kisses me in bed.
PROLOGUE KING: I do believe you think what now you speak;
  But what we do determine oft we break.   165
  Purpose is but the slave to memory;
  Of violent birth, but poor validity:
  Which now, like fruit unripe, sticks on the tree;
  But fall unshaken when they mellow be.

° *orbed ground:* The globe.   ° *distrust you:* Worry about you.   ° *holds quantity:* Correspond in degree.
° *leave:* Cease.

170   Most necessary 'tis that we forget
         To pay ourselves what to ourselves is debt:
         What to ourselves in passion we propose,
         The passion ending, doth the purpose lose.
         The violence of either grief or joy
175   Their own enactures with themselves destroy:
         Where joy most revels grief doth most lament;
         Grief joys, joy grieves, on slender accident.
         This world is not for aye; nor 'tis not strange
         That even our loves should with our fortunes change;
180   For 'tis a question left us yet to prove
         Whether love lead fortune or else fortune love.
         The great man down, you mark his favorite flies;
         The poor advanc'd makes friends of enemies.
         And hitherto doth love on fortune tend:
185   For who not needs shall never lack a friend;
         And who in want a hollow friend doth try,
         Directly seasons him his enemy.
         But, orderly to end where I begun,—
         Our wills and fates do so contrary run
190   That our devices still are overthrown;
         Our thoughts are ours, their ends none of our own:
         So think thou wilt no second husband wed;
         But die thy thoughts when thy first lord is dead.
PROLOGUE QUEEN: Nor earth to me give food, nor heaven light!
195   Sport and repose lock from me day and night!
         To desperation turn my trust and hope!
         An anchor's° cheer in prison be my scope!
         Each opposite, that blanks the face of joy,
         Meet what I would have well, and it destroy!
200   Both here and hence, pursue me lasting strife,
         If, once a widow, ever I be wife!
HAMLET: If she should break it now! [*To Ophelia*]
PROLOGUE KING: 'Tis deeply sworn. Sweet, leave me here awhile;
         My spirits grow dull, and fain I would beguile
205   The tedious day with sleep. [*Sleeps*]
PROLOGUE QUEEN: Sleep rock thy brain,
         And never come mischance between us twain! [*Exit.*]
HAMLET: Madam, how like you this play?
QUEEN: The lady doth protest too much, methinks.
210 **HAMLET:** O, but she'll keep her word.
KING: Have you heard the argument? Is there no offence in't?
HAMLET: No, no, they do but jest, poison in jest; no offence i' the world.

° *anchor's:* Anchorite's, or hermit's.

KING: What do you call the play?

HAMLET: The Mouse-trap. Marry, how? Tropically.° This play is the image of a murder done in Vienna: Gonzago is the duke's name: his wife, Baptista: you shall see anon; 'tis a knavish piece of work: but what o' that? your majesty, and we that have free souls, it touches us not: let the galled jade wince, our withers are unwrung. 215

Enter Lucianus.

This is one Lucianus, nephew to the king.

OPHELIA: You are a good chorus, my lord. 220

HAMLET: I could interpret between you and your love, if I could see the puppets dallying.

OPHELIA: You are keen, my lord, you are keen.

HAMLET: It would cost you a groaning to take off my edge.

OPHELIA: Still better, and worse. 225

HAMLET: So you must take your husbands.— Begin, murderer; pox, leave thy damnable faces and begin. Come:— *The croaking raven doth bellow for revenge.*

LUCIANUS: Thoughts black, hands apt, drugs fit, and time agreeing;
Confederate season, else no creature seeing; 230
Thou mixture rank, of midnight weeds collected,
With Hecate's ban° thrice blasted, thrice infected,
Thy natural magic and dire property
On wholesome life usurp immediately.

Pours the poison into the sleeper's ears.

HAMLET: He poisons him i' the garden for's estate. His name's Gonzago: the 235
story is extant, and writ in choice Italian: you shall see anon how the murderer gets the love of Gonzago's wife.

OPHELIA: The king rises.

HAMLET: What, frighted with false fire!

QUEEN: How fares my lord? 240

POLONIUS: Give o'er the play.

KING: Give me some light:— away!

ALL: Lights, lights, lights!

Exeunt all but Hamlet and Horatio.

HAMLET:

Why, let the stricken deer go weep, 245
The hart ungalled play;
For some must watch, while some must sleep:
So runs the world away.—

° *Tropically:* Figuratively, or metaphorically; by means of a "trope."   ° *Hecate's ban:* The spell of the goddess of witchcraft.

Would not this, sir, and a forest of feathers, if the rest of my fortunes turn
250   Turk with me, with two Provencial roses on my razed shoes, get me a
fellowship in a cry° of players, sir?

HORATIO: Half a share.

HAMLET: A whole one, I.

> For thou dost know, O Damon dear,
255   >   This realm dismantled was
> Of Jove himself; and now reigns here
>   A very, very — pajock.°

HORATIO: You might have rhymed.

HAMLET: O good Horatio, I'll take the ghost's word for a thousand pound.
260   Didst perceive?

HORATIO: Very well, my lord.

HAMLET: Upon the talk of the poisoning,—

HORATIO: I did very well note him.

HAMLET: Ah, ha!— Come, some music! come, the recorders!—

265   > For if the king like not the comedy,
> Why, then, belike,—he likes it not, perdy.

Come, some music!

Re-enter Rosencrantz and Guildenstern.

GUILDENSTERN: Good my lord, vouchsafe me a word with you.

HAMLET: Sir, a whole history.

270   GUILDENSTERN: The king, sir,—

HAMLET: Ay, sir, what of him?

GUILDENSTERN: Is, in his retirement, marvelous distempered.

HAMLET: With drink, sir?

GUILDENSTERN: No, my lord, rather with choler.

275   HAMLET: Your wisdom should show itself more richer to signify this to his
doctor; for, for me to put him to his purgation would perhaps plunge him
into far more choler.

GUILDENSTERN: Good my lord, put your discourse into some frame, and start
not so wildly from my affair.

280   HAMLET: I am tame, sir:— pronounce.

GUILDENSTERN: The queen, your mother, in most great affliction of spirit,
hath sent me to you.

HAMLET: You are welcome.

GUILDENSTERN: Nay, good my lord, this courtesy is not of the right breed. If it
285   shall please you to make me a wholesome answer, I will do you mother's
commandment: if not, your pardon and my return shall be the end of my
business.

HAMLET: Sir, I cannot.

° *cry:* Company.   ° *pajock:* Peacock.

GUILDENSTERN: What, my lord?

HAMLET: Make you a wholesome answer; my wit's diseas'd: but, sir, such an-   290
swer as I can make, you shall command; or, rather, as you say, my mother:
therefore no more, but to the matter: my mother, you say,—

ROSENCRANTZ: Then thus she says: your behavior hath struck her into amazement and admiration.

HAMLET: O wonderful son, that can so astonish a mother!—But is there no   295
sequel at the heels of this mother's admiration?

ROSENCRANTZ: She desires to speak with you in her closet° ere you go to bed.

HAMLET: We shall obey, were she ten times our mother. Have you any further
trade with us?

ROSENCRANTZ: My lord, you once did love me.   300

HAMLET: So I do still, by these pickers and stealers.°

ROSENCRANTZ: Good, my lord, what is your cause of distemper? you do,
surely, bar the door upon your own liberty if you deny your griefs to
your friend.

HAMLET: Sir, I lack advancement.   305

ROSENCRANTZ: How can that be, when you have the voice of the king
himself for your succession in Denmark?

HAMLET: Ay, but *While the grass grows,*—the proverb is something musty.

Re-enter the Players, with recorders.

O, the recorders:—let me see one.—To withdraw with you:—why do you
go about to recover the wind of me, as if you would drive me into a toil?   310

GUILDENSTERN: O, my lord, if my duty be too bold, my love is too
unmannerly.

HAMLET: I do not well understand that. Will you play upon this pipe?

GUILDENSTERN: My lord, I cannot.

HAMLET: I pray you.   315

GUILDENSTERN: Believe me, I cannot.

HAMLET: I do beseech you.

GUILDENSTERN: I know no touch of it, my lord.

HAMLET: 'Tis as easy as lying: govern these ventages° with your finger and
thumb, give it breath with your mouth, and it will discourse most eloquent   320
music. Look you, these are the stops.

GUILDENSTERN: But these cannot I command to any utterance of harmony; I
have not the skill.

HAMLET: Why, look you now, how unworthy a thing you make of me! You
would play upon me; you would seem to know my stops; you would pluck   325
out the heart of my mystery; you would sound me from my lowest note to
the top of my compass: and there is much music, excellent voice, in this
little organ; yet cannot you make it speak. 'Sblood, do you think that I am
easier to be played on than a pipe? Call me what instrument you will,
though you can fret me you cannot play upon me.   330

° *closet:* Boudoir.   ° *pickers and stealers:* Fingers.   ° *ventages:* Holes.

Enter Polonius.

God bless you, sir!

POLONIUS: My lord, the queen would speak with you, and presently.

HAMLET: Do you see yonder cloud that's almost in shape of a camel?

POLONIUS: By the mass, and 'tis like a camel indeed.

335 HAMLET: Methinks it is like a weasel.

POLONIUS: It is backed like a weasel.

HAMLET: Or like a whale?

POLONIUS: Very like a whale.

HAMLET: Then will I come to my mother by and by.—They fool me to the

340   top of my bent.—I will come by and by.

POLONIUS: I will say so.

HAMLET: By and by is easily said.

Exit Polonius.

Leave me, friends.

Exeunt Rosencrantz, Guildenstern, Horatio, and Players.

'Tis now the very witching time of night,

345   When churchyards yawn, and hell itself breathes out

Contagion to this world: now could I drink hot blood,

And do such bitter business as the day

Would quake to look on. Soft! now to my mother.—

O heart, lose not thy nature; let not ever

350   The soul of Nero° enter this firm bosom:

Let me be cruel, not unnatural:

I will speak daggers to her, but use none;

My tongue and soul in this be hypocrites,—

How in my words soever she be shent,

355   To give them seals never, my soul, consent! [*Exit.*]

SCENE 3

A room in the castle.

Enter King, Rosencrantz, and Guildenstern.

KING: I like him not; nor stands it safe with us

To let his madness range. Therefore prepare you;

I your commission with forthwith despatch,

And he to England shall along with you:

5   The terms of our estate may not endure

Hazard so dangerous as doth hourly grow

Out of his lunacies.

° *Nero:* The Roman emperor Nero killed his mother, a crime of which Hamlet does not want to be guilty.

GUILDENSTERN: We will ourselves provide:
   Most holy and religious fear it is
   To keep those many many bodies safe   10
   That live and feed upon your majesty.
ROSENCRANTZ: The single and peculiar life is bound,
   With all the strength and armor of the mind,
   To keep itself from 'noyance; but much more
   That spirit upon whose weal depend and rest   15
   The lives of many. The cease of majesty
   Dies not alone; but like a gulf doth draw
   What's near it with it: it is a massy wheel,
   Fix'd on the summit of the highest mount,
   To whose huge spokes ten thousand lesser things   20
   Are mortis'd and adjoin'd; which, when it falls,
   Each small annexment, petty consequence,
   Attends the boisterous ruin. Never alone
   Did the king sigh, but with a general groan.
KING: Arm you, I pray you, to this speedy voyage;   25
   For we will fetters put upon this fear,
   Which now goes too free-footed.
ROSENCRANTZ and GUILDENSTERN: We will haste us.

Exeunt Rosencrantz and Guildenstern.

Enter Polonius.

POLONIUS: My lord, he's going to his mother's closet:
   Behind the arras I'll convey myself   30
   To hear the process; I'll warrant she'll tax him home:°
   And, as you said, and wisely was it said,
   'Tis meet that some more audience than a mother,
   Since nature makes them partial, should o'erhear
   The speech, of vantage. Fare you well, my liege: 35
   I'll call upon you ere you go to bed,
   And tell you what I know.

KING: Thanks, dear my lord.

Exit Polonius.

   O, my offence is rank, it smells to heaven;
   It hath the primal eldest curse upon't,—   40
   A brother's murder!— Pray can I not,
   Though inclination be as sharp as will:
   My stronger guilt defeats my strong intent;
   And, like a man to double business bound,

° *tax him home:* Reprove him properly.

45   I stand in pause where I shall first begin,
    And both neglect. What if this cursed hand
    Were thicker than itself with brother's blood,—
    Is there not rain enough in the sweet heavens
    To wash it white as snow? Whereto serves mercy
50   But to confront the visage of offence?
    And what's in prayer but this twofold force,—
    To be forestalled ere we come to fall,
    Or pardon'd being down? Then I'll look up;
    My fault is past. But, O, what form of prayer
55   Can serve my turn? Forgive me my foul murder?—
    That cannot be; since I am still possess'd
    Of those effects for which I did the murder,—
    My crown, mine own ambition, and my queen.
    May one be pardon'd and retain the offence?°
60   In the corrupted currents of this world
    Offence's gilded hand may shove by justice;
    And oft 'tis seen the wicked prize itself
    Buys out the law: but 'tis not so above;
    There is no shuffling,— there the action lies
65   In his true nature; and we ourselves compell'd,
    Even to the teeth and forehead of our faults,
    To give in evidence. What then? what rests?°
    Try what repentance can: what can it not?
    Yet what can it when one can not repent?
70   O wretched state! O bosom black as death!
    O limed° soul, that, struggling to be free,
    Art more engag'd! Help, angels! make assay:
    Bow, stubborn knees; and, heart, with strings of steel,
    Be soft as sinews of the new-born babe!
75   All may be well. [*Retires and kneels*]

Enter Hamlet.

HAMLET: Now might I do it pat, now he is praying;
    And now I'll do't — and so he goes to heaven;
    And so am I reveng'd:— that would be scann'd:
    A villain kills my father; and for that,
80   I, his sole son, do this same villain send
    To heaven.
    O, this is hire and salary, not revenge.
    He took my father grossly, full of bread;
    With all his crimes broad blown, as flush as May;
85   And how his audit stands who knows save heaven?

° *retain the offence:* Retain the gains won by the offense.   ° *rests:* Remains.   ° *limed:* Snared.

But in our circumstance and course of thought
'Tis heavy with him: and am I, then, reveng'd,
To take him in the purging of his soul,
When he is fit and season'd for his passage?
No.   90
Up, sword; and know thou a more horrid hent:°
When he is drunk, asleep, or in his rage;
Or in the incestuous pleasure of his bed;
At gaming, swearing; or about some act
That has no relish of salvation in't;—   95
Then trip him, that his heels may kick at heaven;
And that his soul may be as damn'd and black
As hell, whereto it goes. My mother stays:
This physic but prolongs thy sickly days. [*Exit.*]

The King rises and advances.

KING: My words fly up, my thoughts remain below: 100
    Words without thoughts never to heaven go. [*Exit.*]

                        SCENE 4

Another room in the castle.

Enter Queen and Polonius.

POLONIUS: He will come straight. Look you lay home to him:
    Tell him his pranks have been too broad to bear with,
    And that your grace hath screen'd and stood between
    Much heat and him. I'll silence me e'en here.
    Pray you, be round with him.   5
HAMLET: [*Within*] Mother, mother, mother!
QUEEN: I'll warrant you:
    Fear me not:— withdraw, I hear him coming.

Polonius goes behind the arras.

Enter Hamlet.

HAMLET: Now, mother, what's the matter?
QUEEN: Hamlet, thou hast thy father much offended.   10
HAMLET: Mother, you have my father much offended.
QUEEN: Come, come, you answer with an idle tongue.
HAMLET: Go, go, you question with a wicked tongue.
QUEEN: Why, how now, Hamlet!
HAMLET: What's the matter now?   15
QUEEN: Have you forgot me?

° *hent:* Opportunity.

HAMLET: No, by the rood, not so:
    You are the queen, your husband's brother's wife;
    And,— would it were not so!— you are my mother.
20 QUEEN: Nay, then, I'll set those to you that can speak.
HAMLET: Come, come, and sit you down; you shall not budge;
    You go not till I set you up a glass
    Where you may see the inmost part of you.
QUEEN: What wilt thou do? thou wilt not murder me?—
25   Help, help, ho!
POLONIUS: [*Behind*] What, ho! help, help, help!
HAMLET: How now! a rat?
    [*Draws.*]
    Dead, for a ducat, dead! [*Makes a pass through the arras*]
30 POLONIUS: [*Behind*] O, I am slain! [*Falls and dies.*]
QUEEN: O me, what hast thou done?
HAMLET: Nay, I know not:
    Is it the king? [*Draws forth Polonius*]
QUEEN: O, what a rash and bloody deed is this!
35 HAMLET: A bloody deed!— almost as bad, good mother,
    As kill a king and marry with his brother.
QUEEN: As kill a king!
HAMLET: Ay, lady, 'twas my word.—
    Thou wretched, rash, intruding fool, farewell! [*To Polonius*]
40   I took thee for thy better: take thy fortune;
    Thou find'st to be too busy is some danger.—
    Leave wringing of your hands: peace; sit you down,
    And let me wring your heart: for so I shall,
    If it be made of penetrable stuff;
45   If damned custom have not braz'd it so
    That it is proof and bulwark against sense.
QUEEN: What have I done, that thou dar'st wag thy tongue
    In noise so rude against me?
HAMLET: Such an act
50   That blurs the grace and blush of modesty;
    Calls virtue hypocrite; takes off the rose
    From the fair forehead of an innocent love,
    And sets a blister there; makes marriage-vows
    As false as dicers' oaths: O, such a deed
55   As from the body of contraction plucks
    The very soul, and sweet religion makes
    A rhapsody of words: heaven's face doth glow;
    Yea, this solidity and compound mass,
    With tristful° visage, as against the doom,
60   Is thought-sick at the act.

° *tristful:* Gloomy.

QUEEN: Ah me, what act,
    That roars so loud, and thunders in the index?
HAMLET: Look here upon this picture and on this,—
    The counterfeit presentment of two brothers.
    See what grace was seated on this brow;   65
    Hyperion's curls; the front of Jove himself;
    An eye like Mars, to threaten and command;
    A station like the herald Mercury
    New-lighted on a heaven-kissing hill;
    A combination and a form, indeed,   70
    Where every god did seem to set his seal,
    To give the world assurance of a man:
    This was your husband.— Look you now, what follows:
    Here is your husband, like a mildew'd ear
    Blasting his wholesome brother. Have you eyes?   75
    Could you on this fair mountain leave to feed,
    And batten on this moor? Ha! have you eyes?
    You cannot call it love; for at your age
    The hey-day in the blood is tame, it's humble,
    And waits upon the judgment: and what judgment   80
    Would step from this to this? Sense, sure, you have,
    Else could you not have motion: but sure that sense
    Is apoplex'd: for madness would not err;
    Nor sense to ecstasy was ne'er so thrill'd
    But it reserv'd some quantity of choice   85
    To serve in such a difference. What devil was't
    That thus hath cozen'd you at hoodman-blind?°
    Eyes without feeling, feeling without sight,
    Ears without hand or eyes, smelling sans all,
    Or but a sickly part of one true sense   90
    Could not so mope.
    O shame! where is thy blush! Rebellious hell,
    If thou canst mutine in a matron's bones,
    To flaming youth let virtue be as wax,
    And melt in her own fire: proclaim no shame   95
    When the compulsive ardor gives the charge,
    Since frost itself as actively doth burn,
    And reason panders° will.
QUEEN: O Hamlet, speak no more:
    Thou turn'st mine eyes into my very soul;   100
    And there I see such black and grained spots
    As will not leave their tinct.°

° *cozen'd . . . hoodman-blind:* Tricked you at blindman's buff.   ° *panders:* Becomes subservient to.
° *As will not . . . tinct:* As will not yield up their color.

HAMLET: Nay, but to live
         In the rank sweat of an enseamed bed,
105   Stew'd in corruption, honeying and making love
         Over the nasty sty,—
     QUEEN: O, speak to me no more;
         These words like daggers enter in mine ears;
         No more, sweet Hamlet.
110 HAMLET: A murderer and a villain;
         A slave that is not twentieth part the tithe
         Of your precedent lord; a vice of kings;°
         A cutpurse of the empire and the rule,
         That from a shelf the precious diadem stole,
115   And put it in his pocket!
     QUEEN: No more.
     HAMLET: A king of shreds and patches,—

Enter Ghost.

         Save me, and hover o'er me with your wings,
         You heavenly guards!—What would your gracious figure?
120 QUEEN: Alas, he's mad!
     HAMLET: Do you not come your tardy son to chide,
         That, laps'd in time and passion, lets go by
         The important acting of your dread command?
         O, say!
125 GHOST: Do not forget: this visitation
         Is but to whet thy almost blunted purpose.
         But, look, amazement on thy mother sits:
         O, step between her and her fighting soul,—
         Conceit in weakest bodies strongest works,—
130   Speak to her, Hamlet.
     HAMLET: How is it with you, lady?
     QUEEN: Alas, how is't with you,
         That you do bend your eye on vacancy,
         And with the incorporal air do hold discourse?
135   Forth at your eyes your spirits wildly peep;
         And, as the sleeping soldiers in the alarm,
         Your bedded hair, like life in excrements,°
         Starts up and stands on end. O gentle son,
         Upon the heat and flame of thy distemper
140   Sprinkle cool patience. Whereon do you look?
     HAMLET: On him, on him! Look you, how pale he glares!
         His form and cause conjoin'd, preaching to stones,

°*a vice of kings:* A buffoon among kings; the character "Vice" in morality plays.   °*in excrements:* In out-
growths or extremities.

Would make them capable.— Do not look upon me;
Lest with this piteous action you convert
My stern effects: then what I have to do   145
Will want true color; tears perchance for blood.
QUEEN: To whom do you speak this?
HAMLET: Do you see nothing there?
QUEEN: Nothing at all; yet all that is I see.
HAMLET: Nor did you nothing hear?   150
QUEEN: No, nothing but ourselves.
HAMLET: Why, look you there! look, how it steals away!
    My father, in his habit as he liv'd!
    Look, where he goes, even now, out at the portal!

Exit Ghost.

QUEEN: This is the very coinage of your brain: 155
    This bodiless creation ecstasy
    Is very cunning in.
HAMLET: Ecstasy!
    My pulse, as yours, doth temperately keep time.
    And makes as healthful music: it is not madness   160
    That I have utter'd: bring me to the test,
    And I the matter will re-word; which madness
    Would gambol from. Mother, for love of grace,
    Lay not that flattering unction to your soul,
    That not your trespass, but my madness speaks: 165
    It will but skin and film the ulcerous place,
    Whilst rank corruption, mining all within,
    Infects unseen. Confess yourself to Heaven;
    Repent what's past; avoid what is to come;
    And do not spread the compost on the weeds,   170
    To make them ranker. Forgive me this my virtue;
    For in the fatness° of these pursy times
    Virtue itself of vice must pardon beg,
    Yea, curb and woo for leave to do him good.
QUEEN: O Hamlet, thou hast cleft my heart in twain.   175
HAMLET: O, throw away the worser part of it,
    And live the purer with the other half.
    Good-night: but go not to mine uncle's bed;
    Assume a virtue, if you have it not.
    That monster custom, who all sense doth eat,   180
    Of habits devil, is angel yet in this,—
    That to the use of actions fair and good
    He likewise gives a frock or livery

° *fatness.* Corruption.

That aptly is put on. Refrain to-night;
185   And that shall lend a kind of easiness
To the next abstinence: the next more easy;
For use almost can change the stamp of nature,
And either curb the devil, or throw him out
With wondrous potency. Once more, good-night:
190   And when you are desirous to be bless'd,
I'll blessing beg of you.— For this same lord [*pointing to Polonius*]
I do repent: but Heaven hath pleas'd it so,
To punish me with this, and this with me,
That I must be their° scourge and minister.
195   I will bestow him, and will answer well
The death I gave him. So, again, good-night.—
I must be cruel only to be kind:
Thus bad begins and worse remains behind.—
One word more, good lady.
200   QUEEN: What shall I do?
HAMLET: Not this, by no means, that I bid you do:
Let the bloat king tempt you again to bed;
Pinch wanton on your cheek; call you his mouse;
And let him, for a pair of reechy kisses,
205   Or paddling in your neck with his damn'd fingers,
Make you to ravel all this matter out,
That I essentially am not in madness,
But mad in craft. 'Twere good you let him know;
For who that's but a queen, fair, sober, wise,
210   Would from a paddock,° from a bat, a gib,°
Such dear concernings hide? who would do so?
No, in despite of sense and secrecy,
Unpeg the basket on the house's top,
Let the birds fly, and, like the famous ape,
215   To try conclusions, in the basket creep,
And break your own neck down.
QUEEN: Be thou assur'd, if words be made of breath
And breath of life, I have not life to breathe
What thou hast said to me.
220   HAMLET: I must to England; you know that?
QUEEN: Alack,
I had forgot: 'tis so concluded on.
HAMLET: There's letters seal'd: and my two school-fellows,—
Whom I will trust as I will adders fang'd,
225   They bear the mandate; they must sweep my way,
And marshal me to knavery. Let it work;

° *their:* Heaven's, or the heavens'.   ° *paddock:* Toad.   ° *gib:* Tomcat.

For 'tis the sport to have the éngineer
Hoist with his own petard: and't shall go hard
But I will delve one yard below their mines,
And blow them at the moon: O, 'tis most sweet,   230
When in one line two crafts directly meet. —
This man shall set me packing:
I'll lug the guts into the neighbor room. —
Mother, good-night. — Indeed, this counsellor
Is now most still, most secret, and most grave,   235
Who was in life a foolish prating knave.
Come, sir, to draw toward an end with you: —
Good-night, mother.

Exeunt severally; Hamlet dragging out Polonius.

ACT 4
SCENE 1

A room in the castle.

Enter King, Queen, Rosencrantz, and Guildenstern.

KING: There's matter in these sighs, these prófound heaves:
    You must translate: 'tis fit we understand them.
    Where is your son?
QUEEN: Bestow this place on us a little while. [*To Rosencrantz and*
    Guildenstern, who go out]   5
    Ah, my good lord, what have I seen to-night!
KING: What, Gertrude? How does Hamlet?
QUEEN: Mad as the sea and wind, when both contend
    Which is the mightier: in his lawless fit,
    Behind the arras hearing something stir,   10
    He whips his rapier out, and cries, *A rat, a rat!*
    And, in this brainish apprehension,° kills
    The unseen good old man.
KING: O heavy deed!
    It had been so with us had we been there: 15
    His liberty is full of threats to all;
    To you yourself, to us, to every one.
    Alas, how shall this bloody deed be answer'd?
    It will be laid to us, whose providence
    Should have kept short, restrain'd, and out of haunt   20
    This mad young man: but so much was our love,
    We would not understand what was most fit;
    But, like the owner of a foul disease,

° *brainish apprehension:* Mad notion.

To keep it from divulging, let it feed
25   Even on the pith of life. Where is he gone?
QUEEN: To draw apart the body he hath kill'd:
O'er whom his very madness, like some ore
Among a mineral of metals base,
Shows itself pure; he weeps for what is done.
30 KING: O Gertrude, come away!
The sun no sooner shall the mountains touch
But we will ship him hence: and this vile deed
We must, with all our majesty and skill,
Both countenance and excuse.— Ho, Guildenstern!

Enter Rosencrantz and Guildenstern.

35   Friends both, go join you with some further aid:
Hamlet in madness hath Polonius slain,
And from his mother's closet hath he dragg'd him:
Go seek him out; speak fair, and bring the body
Into the chapel. I pray you, haste in this.

Exeunt Rosencrantz and Guildenstern.

40   Come, Gertrude, we'll call up our wisest friends;
And let them know both what we mean to do
And what's untimely done: so haply slander,—
Whose whisper o'er the world's diameter,
As level as the cannon to his blank,
45   Transports his poison'd shot,— may amiss our name,
And hit the woundless air.— O, come away!
My soul is full of discord and dismay.

Exeunt.

SCENE 2

Another room in the castle.

Enter Hamlet.

HAMLET: Safely stowed.
ROSENCRANTZ and GUILDENSTERN: [*Within*] Hamlet! Lord Hamlet!
HAMLET: What noise? who calls on Hamlet?
O, here they come.

Enter Rosencrantz and Guildenstern.

5 ROSENCRANTZ: What have you done, my lord, with the dead body?
HAMLET: Compounded it with dust, whereto 'tis kin.
ROSENCRANTZ: Tell us where 'tis, that we may take it thence,
And bear it to the chapel.

HAMLET: Do not believe it.

ROSENCRANTZ: Believe what? 10

HAMLET: That I can keep your counsel, and not mine own. Besides, to be demanded of a sponge!— what replication should be made by the son of a king?

ROSENCRANTZ: Take you me for a sponge, my lord?

HAMLET: Ay, sir; that soaks up the king's countenance, his rewards, his 15 authorities. But such officers do the king best service in the end: he keeps them, like an ape, in the corner of his jaw; first mouthed, to be last swallowed: when he needs what you have gleaned, it is but squeezing you, and, sponge, you shall be dry again.

ROSENCRANTZ: I understand you not, my lord. 20

HAMLET: I am glad of it: a knavish speech sleeps in a foolish ear.

ROSENCRANTZ: My lord, you must tell us where the body is, and go with us to the king.

HAMLET: The body is with the king, but the king is not with the body. The king is a thing,— 25

GUILDENSTERN: A thing, my lord!

HAMLET: Of nothing: bring me to him.
　　　　Hide fox, and all after.

Exeunt.

SCENE 3

Another room in the castle.

Enter King, attended.

KING: I have sent to seek him, and to find the body.
　　　　How dangerous is it that this man goes loose!
　　　　Yet must not we put the strong law on him:
　　　　He's lov'd of the distracted multitude,
　　　　Who like not in their judgment, but their eyes; 5
　　　　And where 'tis so, the offender's scourge is weigh'd,
　　　　But never the offence. To bear all smooth and even,
　　　　This sudden sending him away must seem
　　　　Deliberate pause: diseases desperate grown
　　　　By desperate appliance are reliev'd, 10
　　　　Or not at all.

Enter Rosencrantz.

　　　　　　　　How now! what hath befallen!

ROSENCRANTZ: Where the dead body is bestow'd, my lord,
　　　　We cannot get from him.

KING:　　　　　　　But where is he? 15

ROSENCRANTZ: Without, my lord; guarded, to know your pleasure.

KING: Bring him before us.

ROSENCRANTZ: Ho, Guildenstern! bring in my lord.

Enter Hamlet and Guildenstern.

KING: Now, Hamlet, where's Polonius?

20   HAMLET: At supper.

KING: At supper! where?

HAMLET: Not where he eats, but where he is eaten: a certain convocation of
politic worms are e'en at him. Your worm is your only emperor for diet: we
fat all creatures else to fat us, and we fat ourselves for maggots: your fat king
25   and your lean beggar is but variable service,—two dishes, but to one table:
that's the end.

KING: Alas, alas!

HAMLET: A man may fish with the worm that hath eat of a king, and eat of
the fish that hath fed of that worm.

30   KING: What does thou mean by this?

HAMLET: Nothing but to show you how a king may go a progress through the
guts of a beggar.

KING: Where is Polonius?

HAMLET: In heaven; send thither to see: if your messenger find him not there,
35   seek him i' the other place yourself. But, indeed, if you find him not within
this month, you shall nose him as you go up the stairs into the lobby.

KING: Go seek him there. [*To some Attendants*]

HAMLET: He will stay till ye come.

Exeunt Attendants.

KING: Hamlet, this deed, for thine especial safety,—
40   Which we do tender, as we dearly grieve
For that which thou hast done,—must send thee hence
With fiery quickness: therefore prepare thyself;
The bark is ready, and the wind at help,
The associates tend, and everything is bent
45   For England.

HAMLET: For England!

KING: Ay, Hamlet.

HAMLET: Good.

KING: So is it, if thou knew'st our purposes.

50   HAMLET: I see a cherub that sees them.—But, come; for England!—
Farewell, dear mother.

KING: Thy loving father, Hamlet.

HAMLET: My mother: father and mother is man and wife; man and wife is one
flesh; and so, my mother.—Come, for England! [*Exit.*]

55   KING: Follow him at foot; tempt him with speed aboard;
Delay it not; I'll have him hence to-night:
Away! for everything is seal'd and done
That else leans on the affair, pray you, make haste.

Exeunt Rosencrantz and Guildenstern.

And, England, if my love thou hold'st at aught,—
As my great power thereof may give thee sense,   60
Since yet thy cicatrice looks raw and red
After the Danish sword, and thy free awe
Pays homage to us,— thou mayst not coldly set
Our sovereign process; which imports at full,
By letters conjuring to that effect,   65
The present death of Hamlet. Do it, England;
For like the hectic in my blood he rages,
And thou must cure me: till I know 'tis done,
Howe'er my haps, my joys will ne'er begin. [*Exit.*]

SCENE 4

A plain in Denmark.

Enter Fortinbras, and Forces marching.

FORTINBRAS: Go, from me greet the Danish king:
    Tell him that, by his license, Fortinbras
    Craves the conveyance of a promis'd march
    Over his kingdom. You know the rendezvous,
    If that his majesty would aught with us,   5
    We shall express our duty in his eye,
    And let him know so.
CAPTAIN: I will do't, my lord.
FORTINBRAS: Go softly on.

Exeunt Fortinbras and Forces.

Enter Hamlet, Rosencrantz, Guildenstern, &c.

HAMLET: Good sir, whose powers are these?   10
CAPTAIN: They are of Norway, sir.
HAMLET: How purpos'd, sir, I pray you?
CAPTAIN: Against some part of Poland.
HAMLET: Who commands them, sir?
CAPTAIN: The nephew to old Norway, Fortinbras.   15
HAMLET: Goes it against the main of Poland, sir,
    Or for some frontier?
CAPTAIN: Truly to speak, and with no addition,
    We go to gain a little patch of ground
    That hath in it no profit but the name.   20
    To pay five ducats, five, I would not farm it;
    Nor will it yield to Norway or the Pole
    A ranker° rate should it be sold in fee.

° *ranker:* Dearer.

HAMLET: Why, then the Polack never will defend it.

25 CAPTAIN: Yes, it is already garrison'd.

HAMLET: Two thousand souls and twenty thousand ducats
    Will not debate the question of this straw:
    This is the imposthume° of much wealth and peace,
    That inward breaks, and shows no cause without
30   Why the man dies.—I humbly thank you, sir.

CAPTAIN: God b' wi' you, sir. [*Exit.*]

ROSENCRANTZ: Will't please you go, my lord?

HAMLET: I'll be with you straight. Go a little before.

Exeunt all but Hamlet.

    How all occasions do inform against me,
35   And spur my dull revenge! What is a man,
    If his chief good and market of his time
    Be but to sleep and feed? a beast, no more.
    Sure he that made us with such large discourse,°
    Looking before and after, gave us not
40   That capability and godlike reason
    To fust° in us unus'd. Now, whether it be
    Bestial oblivion or some craven scruple
    Of thinking too precisely on the event,—
    A thought which, quarter'd, hath but one part wisdom
45   And ever three parts coward,—I do not know
    Why yet I live to say, *This thing's to do;*
    Sith° I have cause, and will, and strength, and means
    To do't. Examples, gross as earth, exhort me:
    Witness this army, of such mass and charge,
50   Led by a delicate and tender prince;
    Whose spirit, with divine ambition puff'd,
    Makes mouths at the invisible event;
    Exposing what is mortal and unsure
    To all that fortune, death, and danger dare,
55   Even for an egg-shell. Rightly to be great
    Is not to stir without great argument,
    But greatly to find quarrel in a straw
    When honor's at the stake. How stand I, then,
    That have a father kill'd, a mother stain'd,
60   Excitements of my reason and my blood,
    And let all sleep? while, to my shame, I see
    The imminent death of twenty thousand men,
    That, for a fantasy and trick of fame,
    Go to their graves like beds; fight for a plot

° *imposthume:* Ulcer.   ° *discourse:* Reasoning faculty.   ° *fust:* Grow musty.   ° *Sith:* Since.

Whereon the numbers cannot try the cause, 65
Which is not tomb enough and continent°
To hide the slain?— O, from this time forth,
My thoughts be bloody, or be nothing worth! [*Exit.*]

SCENE 5

Elsinore. A room in the castle.

Enter Queen and Horatio.

QUEEN: I will not speak with her.
HORATIO: She is importunate; indeed, distract:
    Her mood will needs be pitied.
QUEEN: What would she have?
HORATIO: She speaks much of her father; says she hears 5
    There's tricks i' the world; and hems, and beats her heart;
    Spurns enviously at straws; speaks things in doubt,
    That carry but half sense: her speech is nothing,
    Yet the unshapéd use of it doth move
    The hearers to collection; they aim at it, 10
    And botch the words up fit to their own thoughts;
    Which, as her winks, and nods, and gestures yield them,
    Indeed would make one think there might be thought,
    Though nothing sure, yet much unhappily.
    'Twere good she were spoken with; for she may strew 15
    Dangerous conjectures in ill-breeding minds.
QUEEN: Let her come in.

Exit Horatio.

    To my sick soul, as sin's true nature is,
    Each toy seems prologue to some great amiss:
    So full of artless jealousy is guilt, 20
    It spills itself in fearing to be spilt.

Re-enter Horatio and Ophelia.

OPHELIA: Where is the beauteous majesty of Denmark?
QUEEN: How now, Ophelia!
OPHELIA: [*Sings*]

      How should I your true love know 25
        From another one?
      By his cockle hat and staff,
        And his sandal shoon.

° *continent:* Container.

QUEEN: Alas, sweet lady, what imports this song?
30 OPHELIA: Say you? nay, pray you, mark.

Sings

> He is dead and gone, lady,
>   He is dead and gone;
> At his head a grass green turf,
>   At his heels a stone.

35 QUEEN: Nay, but, Ophelia,—
OPHELIA: Pray you, mark.

Sings

> White his shroud as the mountain snow,

Enter King.

QUEEN: Alas, look here, my lord.
OPHELIA: [*Sings*]
40
> Larded with sweet flowers;
> Which bewept to the grave did go
> With true-love showers.

KING: How do you, pretty lady?
OPHELIA: Well, God 'ild you!° They say the owl was a baker's daughter.
45   Lord, we know what we are, but know not what we may be.
      God be at your table!
KING: Conceit upon her father.

OPHELIA: Pray you, let's have no words of this; but when they ask you what it
    means, say you this:

Sings.

50
> To-morrow is Saint Valentine's day
>   All in the morning betime,
> And I a maid at your window,
>   To be your Valentine.
> Then up he rose, and donn'd his clothes,
55
>   And dupp'd the chamber-door;
> Let in the maid, that out a maid
>   Never departed more.

KING: Pretty Ophelia!
OPHELIA: Indeed, la, without an oath, I'll make an end on't;

Sings

60
> By Gis° and by Saint Charity,
>   Alack, and fie for shame!

° *ild you:* Yield you — i.e., reward you.   ° *Gis:* A contraction for "by Jesus."

Young men will do't, if they come to't;
   By cock, they are to blame.
Quoth she, before you tumbled me,
   You promis'd me to wed.   65
So would I ha' done, by yonder sun,
   An thou hadst not come to my bed.

KING: How long hath she been thus?

OPHELIA: I hope all will be well. We must be patient: but I cannot choose but
weep, to think they should lay him i' the cold ground. My brother shall   70
know of it: and so I thank you; for your good counsel.— Come, my
coach!— Good-night, ladies; good-night, sweet ladies; good-night, good-
night. [*Exit.*]

KING: Follow her close; give her good watch, I pray you.

Exit Horatio.

O, this is the poison of deep grief; it springs   75
All from her father's death. O Gertrude, Gertrude,
When sorrows come, they come not single spies,
But in battalions! First, her father slain:
Next, your son gone; and he most violent author
Of his own just remove: the people muddied,   80
Thick and unwholesome in their thoughts and whispers
For good Polonius' death; and we have done but greenly
In hugger-mugger° to inter him: poor Ophelia
Divided from herself and her fair judgment,
Without the which we are pictures, or mere beasts: 85
Last, and as much containing as all these,
Her brother is in secret come from France;
Feeds on his wonder, keeps himself in clouds,
And wants not buzzers to infect his ear
With pestilent speeches of his father's death;   90
Wherein necessity, of matter beggar'd,
Will nothing stick our person to arraign
In ear and ear. O my dear Gertrude, this,
Like to a murdering piece,° in many places
Gives me superfluous death.   95

A noise within.

QUEEN: Alack, what noise is this?

KING: Where are my Switzers?° let them guard the door.

Enter a Gentleman.

What is the matter?

° *In hugger-mugger:* In great secrecy and haste.   ° *murdering piece:* A cannon.   ° *Switzers:* Bodyguard of
Swiss mercenaries.

GENTLEMAN: Save yourself, my lord:
100   The ocean, overpeering of his list,
         Eats not the flats with more impetuous haste
         Than young Laertes, in a riotous head,
         O'erbears your officers. The rabble call him lord;
         And, as the world were now but to begin,
105   Antiquity forgot, custom not known,
         The ratifiers and props of every word,
         They cry, *Choose we, Laertes shall be king!*
         Caps, hands, and tongues applaud it to the clouds,
         Laertes shall be king, Laertes king!
110 QUEEN: How cheerfully on the false trail they cry!
         O, this is counter, you false Danish dogs!
     KING: The doors are broke.

Noise within.

Enter Laertes armed; Danes following.

     LAERTES: Where is this king?— Sirs, stand you all without.
     DANES: No, let's come in.
115 LAERTES: I pray you, give me leave.
     DANES: We will, we will. [*They retire without the door.*]
     LAERTES: I thank you:— keep the door.— O thou vile king,
         Give me my father!
     QUEEN: Calmly, good Laertes.
120 LAERTES: That drop of blood that's calm proclaims me bastard;
         Cries cuckold to my father; brands the harlot
         Even here, between the chaste unsmirched brow
         Of my true mother.
     KING: What is the cause, Laertes,
125   That thy rebellion looks so giant-like?—
         Let him go, Gertrude; do not fear our person:
         There's such divinity doth hedge a king,
         That treason can but peep to what it would,
         Acts little of his will.— Tell me, Laertes,
130   Why thou art thus incens'd.— Let him go, Gertrude:—
         Speak, man.
     LAERTES: Where is my father?
     KING: Dead.
     QUEEN: But not by him.
135 KING: Let him demand his fill.
     LAERTES: How came he dead? I'll not be juggled with:
         To hell, allegiance! vows, to the blackest devil!
         Conscience and grace, to the profoundest pit!
         I dare damnation:— to this point I stand,—
140   That both the worlds I give to negligence,

Let come what comes; only I'll be reveng'd
Most thoroughly for my father.
KING: Who shall stay you?
LAERTES: My will, not all the world:
   And for my means, I'll husband them so well,   145
   They shall go far with little.
KING: Good Laertes,
   If you desire to know the certainty
   Of your dear father's death, is't writ in your revenge
   That, sweepstake, you will draw both friend and foe,   150
   Winner or loser?
LAERTES: None but his enemies.
KING: Will you know them, then?
LAERTES: To his good friends thus wide I'll ope my arms;
   And, like the kind life-rendering pelican,°   155
   Repast them with my blood.
KING: Why, now you speak
   Like a good child and a true gentleman.
   That I am guiltless of your father's death,
   And am most sensible in grief for it,   160
   It shall as level to your judgment pierce
   As day does to your eye.
DANES: [*Within*]   Let her come in.
LAERTES: How now! what noise is that?

Re-enter Ophelia, fantastically dressed with straws and flowers.

   O heat, dry up my brains! tears seven times salt   165
   Burn out the sense and virtue of mine eyes!—
   By heaven, thy madness shall be paid by weight
   Till our scale turn the beam. O rose of May!
   Dear maid, kind sister, sweet Ophelia!—
   O heavens! is't possible a young maid's wits   170
   Should be as mortal as an old man's life!
   Nature is fine in love; and where 'tis fine
   It sends some precious instance of itself
   After the thing it loves.
OPHELIA: [*Sings*]   175

      They bore him barefac'd on the bier;
         Hey no nonny, nonny, hey nonny;
      And on his grave rain'd many a tear,—
         Fare you well, my dove!

LAERTES: Hadst thou thy wits, and didst persuade revenge,   180
   It could not move thus.

° *life-rendering pelican:* The mother pelican was believed to draw blood from herself to feed her young.

OPHELIA: You must sing, *Down-a-down, and you call him a-down-a.* O, how the wheel becomes it! It is the false steward, that stole his master's daughter.

LAERTES: This nothing's more than matter.

185 OPHELIA: There's rosemary, that's for remembrance; pray, love, remember: and there is pansies that's for thoughts.

LAERTES: A document in madness,— thoughts and remembrance fitted.

OPHELIA: There's fennel for you, and columbines:— there's rue for you; and here's some for me:— we may call it herb-grace o' Sundays:—

190 O, you must wear your rue with a difference.— There's a daisy:— I would give you some violets, but they withered all when my father died:— they say, he made a good end,—

Sings

> For bonny sweet Robin is all my joy,—

LAERTES: Thoughts and affliction, passion, hell itself,
195 She turns to favor and to prettiness.

OPHELIA: [*Sings*]

> And will he not come again?
> And will he not come again?
>   No, no, he is dead,
200 >   Go to thy death-bed,
> He never will come again.
> His beard was as white as snow
> All flaxen was his poll:
>   He is gone, he is gone,
205 >   And we cast away moan:
> God ha' mercy on his soul!

And of all Christian souls, I pray God.— God b' wi' ye. [*Exit.*]

LAERTES: Do you see this, O God?

KING: Laertes, I must commune with your grief,
210 Or you deny me right. Go but apart,
Make choice of whom your wisest friends you will,
And they shall hear and judge 'twixt you and me:
If by direct or by collateral hand
They find us touch'd, we will our kingdom give,
215 Our crown, our life, and all that we call ours,
To you in satisfaction; but if not,
Be you content to lend your patience to us,
And we shall jointly labor with your soul
To give it due content.

220 LAERTES: Let this be so;
His means of death, his obscure burial,—
No trophy, sword, nor hatchment° o'er his bones

° *hatchment:* A tablet with coat of arms.

No noble rite nor formal ostentation,—
Cry to be heard, as 'twere from heaven to earth,
That I must call't in question.   225
KING: So you shall;
And where the offence is, let the great axe fall.
I pray you, go with me.

Exeunt.

SCENE 6

Another room in the castle.

Enter Horatio and a Servant.

HORATIO: What are they that would speak with me?
SERVANT: Sailors, sir: they say they have letters for you.
HORATIO: Let them come in.—

Exit Servant.

I do not know from what part of the world
I should be greeted, if not from Lord Hamlet.   5

Enter Sailors.

1ST SAILOR: God bless you, sir.
HORATIO: Let him bless thee too.
1ST SAILOR: He shall, sir, an't please him. There's a letter for you, sir; it comes
from the ambassador that was bound for England; if your name be Horatio,
as I am let to know it is.   10
HORATIO: [*Reads*] *Horatio, when thou shalt have overlooked this, give these*
fellows some means to the king: they have letters for him. Ere we were two
days old at sea, a pirate of very warlike appointment gave us chase. Finding
ourselves too slow of sail, we put on a compelled valor; and in the
grapple I boarded them; on the instant they got clear of our ship; so I alone   15
became their prisoner. They have dealt with me like thieves of mercy: but
they knew what they did; I am to do a good turn for them. Let the king
have the letters I have sent; and repair thou to me with as much haste as thou
wouldst fly death. I have words to speak in thine ear will make thee dumb;
yet are they much too light for the bore of the matter. These good fellows   20
will bring thee where I am. Rosencrantz and Guildenstern hold their course
for England: of them I have much to tell thee. Farewell. He that thou knowest
thine.

Hamlet

Come, I will give you way for these your letters;   25
And do't the speedier, that you may direct me
To him from whom you brought them.

Exeunt.

SCENE 7

Another room in the castle.

Enter King and Laertes.

KING: Now must your conscience my acquittance seal,
And you must put me in your heart for friend,
Sith you have heard, and with a knowing ear,
That he which hath your noble father slain
5   Pursu'd my life.

LAERTES: It well appears:—but tell me
Why you proceeded not against these feats,
So crimeful and so capital in nature.
As by your safety, wisdom, all things else,
10   You mainly were stirr'd up.

KING: O, for two special reasons;
Which may to you, perhaps, seem much unsinew'd,
But yet to me they are strong. The queen his mother
Lives almost by his looks; and for myself,—
15   My virtue or my plague, be it either which,—
She's so conjunctive to my life and soul,
That, as the star moves not but in his sphere,
I could not but by her. The other motive,
Why to a public count I might not go,
20   Is the great love the general gender bear him;
Who, dipping all his faults in their affection,
Would, like the spring that turneth wood to stone,
Convert his gyves to graces; so that my arrows,
Too slightly timber'd for so loud a wind,
25   Would have reverted to my bow again,
And not where I had aim'd them.

LAERTES: And so have I a noble father lost;
A sister driven into desperate terms,—
Whose worth, if praises may go back again,
30   Stood challenger on mount of all the age
For her perfections:—but my revenge will come.

KING: Break not your sleeps for that: you must not think
That we are made of stuff so flat and dull
That we can let our beard be shook with danger,
35   And think it pastime. You shortly shall hear more:
I lov'd your father, and we love ourself;
And that, I hope, will teach you to imagine,—

Enter a Messenger.

How now! what news?

MESSENGER: Letters, my lord, from Hamlet:
40   This to your majesty; this to the queen.

KING: From Hamlet! Who brought them?
MESSENGER: Sailors, my lord, they say; I saw them not:
    They were given me by Claudio,—he receiv'd them
    Of him that brought them.
KING: Laertes, you shall hear them.—Leave us.   45

Exit Messenger.

    [Reads] High and mighty,—You shall know I am set naked on your kingdom.
    To-morrow shall I beg leave to see your kingly eyes: when I shall, first asking
    your pardon thereunto, recount the occasions of my sudden and more strange
    return.   *Hamlet*

    What should this mean? Are all the rest come back?   50
    Or is it some abuse,° and no such thing?
LAERTES: Know you the hand?
KING: 'Tis Hamlet's character:°—*Naked,*—
    And in a postscript here, he says, *alone.*
    Can you advise me?   55
LAERTES: I am lost in it, my lord. But let him come;
    It warms the very sickness in my heart,
    That I shall live, and tell him to his teeth,
    Thus diddest thou.
KING: If it be so, Laertes,—   60
    As how should it be so? how otherwise?—
    Will you be rul'd by me?
LAERTES: Ay, my lord:
    So you will not o'errule me to a peace.
KING: To thine own peace. If he be now return'd,—   65
    As checking at his voyage, and that he means
    No more to undertake it,—I will work him
    To an exploit, now ripe in my device,
    Under the which he shall not choose but fall:
    And for his death no wind of blame shall breathe;   70
    But even his mother shall uncharge the practice
    And call it accident.
LAERTES: My lord, I will be rul'd;
    The rather if you could devise it so
    That I might be the organ.   75
KING: It falls right.
    You have been talk'd of since your travel much,
    And that in Hamlet's hearing, for a quality
    Wherein they say you shine: your sum of parts
    Did not together pluck such envy from him   80

° *abuse:* Ruse.   ° *character:* Handwriting.

As did that one; and that, in my regard,
Of the unworthiest siege.

LAERTES: What part is that, my lord?

KING: A very riband in the cap of youth,
85   Yet needful too; for youth no less becomes
The light and careless livery that it wears
Than settled age his sables and his weeds,
Importing health and graveness.—Two months since,
Here was a gentleman of Normandy,—
90   I've seen myself, and serv'd against, the French,
And they can well on horseback: but this gallant
Had witchcraft in't; he grew unto his seat;
And to such wondrous doing brought his horse,
As he had been incorps'd and demi-natur'd°
95   With the brave beast: so far he topp'd my thought,
That I, in forgery of shapes and tricks,°
Come short of what he did.

LAERTES: A Norman was't?

KING: A Norman.

100 LAERTES: Upon my life, Lamond.

KING: The very same.

LAERTES: I know him well: he is the brooch, indeed,
And gem of all the nation.

KING: He made confession of you;
105   And gave you such a masterly report
For art and exercise in your defence,
And for your rapier most especially,
That he cried out, 'twould be a sight indeed
If one could match you: the scrimers° of their nation,
110   He swore, had neither motion, guard, nor eye,
If you oppos'd them. Sir, this report of his
Did Hamlet so envenom with his envy,
That he could nothing do but wish and beg
Your sudden coming o'er, to play with him.
115   Now, out of this,—

LAERTES: What out of this, my lord?

KING: Laertes, was your father dear to you?
Or are you like the painting of a sorrow,
A face without a heart?

120 LAERTES: Why ask you this?

KING: Not that I think you did not love your father;
But that I know love is begun by time;

° *As . . . demi-natur'd:* Made as one body and formed into half man, half horse — or centaur.   ° *in forgery . . .*
tricks: In imagining tricks of horsemanship.   ° *scrimers:* Fencers.

And that I see, in passages of proof,°
Time qualifies the spark and fire of it.
There lives within the very flame of love   125
A kind of wick or snuff that will abate it;
And nothing is at a like goodness still;
For goodness, growing to a pleurisy,°
Dies in his own too much: that we would do
We should do when we would; for this *would* changes,   130
And hath abatements and delays as many
As there are tongues, or hands, or accidents;
And then this *should* is like a spendthrift sigh
That hurts by easing. But to the quick o' the ulcer:
Hamlet comes back: what would you undertake   135
To show yourself your father's son in deed
More than in words?
LAERTES: To cut his throat i' the church.
KING: No place, indeed, should murder sanctuarize;
Revenge should have no bounds. But, good Laertes,   140
Will you do this, keep close within your chamber.
Hamlet return'd shall know you are come home:
We'll put on those shall praise your excellence,
And set a double varnish on the fame
The Frenchman gave you; bring you, in fine, together,   145
And wager on yours heads: he, being remiss,°
Most generous, and free from all contriving,
Will not peruse the foils; so that, with ease,
Or with a little shuffling, you may choose
A sword unbated, and, in a pass of practice,   150
Requite him for your father.
LAERTES: I will do't it:
And, for that purpose, I'll anoint my sword.
I bought an unction of a mountebank,
So mortal that but dip a knife in it,   155
Where it draws blood no cataplasm so rare,°
Collected from all simples that have virtue
Under the moon, can save the thing from death
That is but scratch'd withal: I'll touch my point
With this contagion, that, if I gall him slightly,   160
It may be death.

KING: Let's further think of this;
Weigh what convenience both of time and means
May fit us to our shape: if this should fail,

° *passages of proof:* The evidence of experience.   ° *pleurisy:* Plethora, an excess of blood.   ° *remiss:* Unguarded and free from suspicion.   ° *no cataplasm so rare:* No poultice, however remarkably efficacious.

165   And that our drift look through our bad performance,
         'Twere better not assay'd: therefore this project
         Should have a back or second, that might hold
         If this should blast in proof. Soft! let me see:—
         We'll make a solemn wager on your cunnings,—
170   I ha't:
         When in your motion you are hot and dry,—
         As make your bouts more violent to that end,—
         And that he calls for drink, I'll have prepar'd him
         A chalice for the nonce;° whereon but sipping,
175   If he by chance escape your venom'd stuck
         Our purpose may hold there.

Enter Queen.

                              How now, sweet queen!
QUEEN: One woe doth tread upon another's heel,
        So fast they follow:— your sister's drown'd, Laertes.
180 LAERTES: Drown'd! O, where?
     QUEEN: There is a willow grows aslant a brook,
        That shows his hoar leaves in the glassy stream;
        There with fantastic garlands did she come
        Of crowflowers, nettles, daisies, and long purples,
185   That liberal shepherds give a grosser name,
        But our cold maids do dead men's fingers call them.
        There, on the pendant boughs her coronet weeds
        Clambering to hang, an envious° sliver broke;
        When down her weedy trophies and herself
190   Fell in the weeping brook. Her clothes spread wide;
        And, mermaid-like, awhile they bore her up:
        Which time she chanted snatches of old tunes;
        As one incapable of her own distress,
        Or like a creature native and indu'd
195   Unto that element: but long it could not be
        Till that her garments, heavy with their drink,
        Pull'd the poor wretch from her melodious lay
        To muddy death.
     LAERTES: Alas, then, she is drown'd?
200 QUEEN: Drown'd, drown'd.
     LAERTES: Too much of water hast thou, poor Ophelia,
        And therefore I forbid my tears: but yet
        It is our trick; nature her custom holds,
        Let shame say what it will: when these are gone,
205   The woman will be out.°— Adieu, my lord:

° *nonce:* Purpose.   ° *envious:* Malicious.   ° *The women . . . out:* I.e., "I shall be ruthless."

I have a speech of fire, that fain would blaze,
But that this folly douts it.° [*Exit.*]
KING: Let's follow, Gertrude;
    How much I had to do to calm his rage!
    Now fear I this will give it start again;   210
    Therefore let's follow.

Exeunt.

ACT 5

SCENE 1

A churchyard.

Enter two Clowns° with spades, &c.

1ST CLOWN: Is she to be buried in Christian burial that wilfully seeks her
    own salvation?
2ND CLOWN: I tell thee she is; and therefore make her grave straight: the
    crowner° hath sat on her, and finds it Christian burial.
1ST CLOWN: How can that be, unless she drowned herself in her own defence? 5
2ND CLOWN: Why, 'tis found so.
1ST CLOWN: It must be *se offendendo,*° it cannot be else. For here lies the
    point: if I drown myself wittingly, it argues an act: and an act hath three
    branches; it is to act, to do, and to perform: argal,° she drowned herself
    wittingly.   10
2ND CLOWN: Nay, but hear you, goodman delver,—
1ST CLOWN: Give me leave. Here lies the water; good: here stands the man;
    good: if the man go to this water and drown himself, it is, will he, nill he,
    he goes,—mark you that: but if the water come to him and drown him, he
    drowns not himself: argal, he that is not guilty of his own death shortens 15
    not his own life.
2ND CLOWN: But is this law?
1ST CLOWN: Ay, marry, is't; crowner's quest law.
2ND CLOWN: Will you ha' the truth on't? If this had not been a gentlewoman
    she should have been buried out of Christian burial.   20
1ST CLOWN: Why, there thou say'st: and the more pity that great folks should
    have countenance in this world to drown or hang themselves more than
    their even-Christian.°— Come, my spade. There is no ancient gentlemen
    but gardeners, ditchers, and grave-makers; they hold up Adam's profession.
2ND CLOWN: Was he a gentleman?   25
1ST CLOWN: He was the first that ever bore arms.
2ND CLOWN: Why, he had none.

° *douts it:* Drowns it.   ° *Clowns:* Rustic fellows.   ° *crowner:* Coroner.   ° *se offendendo:* In self-offense;
he means *se defendendo,* in self-defense.   ° *argal:* He means *ergo,* therefore.   ° *even-Christian:* Fellow
Christian.

1st Clown: What, art a heathen? How dost thou understand the Scripture? The Scripture says, Adam digged: could he dig without arms? I'll put an-
30 other question to thee: if thou answerest me not to the purpose, confess thyself,°—

2nd Clown: Go to.

1st Clown: What is he that builds stronger than either the mason, the shipwright, or the carpenter?

35 2nd Clown: The gallows-maker; for that frame outlives a thousand tenants.

1st Clown: I like thy wit well, in good faith: the gallows does well; but how does it well? it does well to those that do ill: now thou dost ill to say the gallows is built stronger than the church: argal, the gallows may do well to thee. To't again, come.

40 2nd Clown: Who builds stronger than a mason, a shipwright, or a carpenter?

1st Clown: Ay, tell me that, and unyoke.

2nd Clown: Marry, now I can tell.

1st Clown: To't.

2nd Clown: Mass, I cannot tell.

Enter Hamlet and Horatio, at a distance.

45 1st Clown: Cudgel thy brains no more about it, for your dull ass will not mend his pace with beating; and when you are asked this question next, say a grave-maker; the houses that he makes last till doomsday. Go, get thee to Yaughan: fetch me a stoup of liquor.

Exit Second Clown.

Digs and sings.

> In youth, when I did love, did love,
50 >   Methought it was very sweet,
> To contract, O, the time, for, ah, my behove,°
>   O, methought there was nothing meet.

Hamlet: Has this fellow no feeling of his business, that he sings at grave-making?

55 Horatio: Custom hath made it in him a property of easiness.

Hamlet: 'Tis e'en so: the hand of little employment hath the daintier sense.

1st Clown: [*Sings*]

> But age, with his stealing steps,
>   Hath claw'd me in his clutch,
60 > And hath shipp'd me intil the land,
>   As if I had never been such.

Throws up a skull.

° *confess thyself:* "Confess thyself an ass," perhaps.   ° *behove:* Behoof, or advantage.

HAMLET: That skull had a tongue in it, and could sing once: how the knave
    joels° it to the ground, as if it were Cain's jawbone, that did the first
    murder! This might be the pate of a politician, which this ass now
    o'erreaches; one that would circumvent God, might it not?   65
HORATIO: It might, my lord.
HAMLET: Or of a courtier; which could say, *Good-morrow, sweet lord! How dost
    thou, good lord?* This might be my lord such-a-one, that praised my lord
    such-a-one's horse, when he meant to beg it,—might it not?
HORATIO: Ay, my lord.   70
HAMLET: Why, e'en so: and now my Lady Worm's; chapless,° and knocked
    about the mazard° with a sexton's spade: here's fine revolution, an we had
    the trick to see't. Did these bones cost no more the breeding but to play at
    loggats° with 'em? Mine ache to think on't.
1ST CLOWN: [*Sings*]   75

> A pick-axe and a spade, a spade,
>   For and a shrouding sheet:
> O, a pit of clay for to be made
>   For such a guest is meet.

Throws up another.

HAMLET: There's another: why may not that be the skull of a lawyer? Where   80
    be his quiddits° now, his quillets,° his cases, his tenures, and his tricks? why
    does he suffer this rude knave now to knock him about the sconce with a
    dirty shovel, and will not tell him of his action of battery? Hum! This fellow
    might be in's time a great buyer of land, with his statutes, his recognizances,
    his fines, his double vouchers, his recoveries: is this the fine of his fines, and   85
    the recovery of his recoveries, to have his fine pate full of fine dirt? will his
    vouchers vouch him no more of his purchases, and double ones too, than
    the length and breadth of a pair of indentures? The very conveyances of his
    lands will hardly lie in this box; and must the inheritor himself have no
    more, ha?   90
HORATIO: Not a jot more, my lord.
HAMLET: Is not parchment made of sheep-skins?
HORATIO: Ay, my lord, and of calf-skins too.
HAMLET: They are sheep and calves which seek out assurance in that. I will
    speak to this fellow.—Whose grave's this, sir?   95
1ST CLOWN: Mine, sir.—[*Sings*]

> O, a pit of clay for to be made
>   For such a guest is meet.

° *joels:* Throws.   ° *chapless:* Without a lower jaw.   ° *mazard:* Head.   ° *loggats:* A game in which small
pieces of wood are hurled at a stake.   ° *quiddits:* Quiddities, "whatnesses"—that is, hair-splittings.
° *quillets:* Quibbling distinctions.

HAMLET: I think it be thine indeed; for thou liest in't.

100   1ST CLOWN: You lie out on't, sir, and therefore it is not yours: for my part, I do
not lie in't, and yet it is mine.

HAMLET: Thou dost lie in't, to be in't, and say it is thine: 'tis for the dead, not
for the quick; therefore thou liest.

1ST CLOWN: 'Tis a quick lie, sir: 'twill away again from me to you.

105   HAMLET: What man dost thou dig it for?

1ST CLOWN: For no man, sir.

HAMLET: What woman, then?

1ST CLOWN: For none, neither.

HAMLET: Who is to be buried in't?

110   1ST CLOWN: One that was a woman, sir; but, rest her soul, she's dead.

HAMLET: How absolute the knave is! we must speak by the card, or equivoca-
tion will undo us. By the Lord, Horatio, these three years I have taken note
of it; the age is grown so picked° that the toe of the peasant comes so near
the heel of the courtier, he galls his kibe.°—How long hast thou been a
115   grave-maker?

1ST CLOWN: Of all the days i' the year, I came to't that day that our last King
Hamlet o'ercame Fortinbras.

HAMLET: How long is that since?

1ST CLOWN: Cannot you tell that? every fool can tell that: it was the very day
120   that young Hamlet was born,—he that is mad, and sent into England.

HAMLET: Ay, marry, why was he sent into England?

1ST CLOWN: Why, because he was mad: he shall recover his wits there; or, if
he do not, it's no great matter there.

HAMLET: Why?

125   1ST CLOWN: 'Twill not be seen in him there; there the men are as mad as he.

HAMLET: How came he mad?

1ST CLOWN: Very strangely, they say.

HAMLET: How strangely?

1ST CLOWN: Faith, e'en with losing his wits.

130   HAMLET: Upon what ground?

1ST CLOWN: Why, here in Denmark: I have been sexton here, man and boy,
thirty years.

HAMLET: How long will a man lie i' the earth ere he rot?

1ST CLOWN: Faith, if he be not rotten before he die,—as we have many
135   pocky corses now-a-days, that will scarce hold the laying in,—he will last
you some eight year or nine year: a tanner will last you nine year.

HAMLET: Why he more than another?

1ST CLOWN: Why, sir, his hide is so tanned with his trade that he will keep
out water a great while; and your water is a sore decayer of your whoreson
140   dead body. Here's a skull now; this skull has lain in the earth three-and-
twenty years.

° *picked:* Refined or educated.   ° *galls his kibe:* Rubs and irritates the chilblain sore on the courtier's heel.

Richard Burton (left), Laurence Olivier (middle), and Mel Gibson (right) have all played the role of Hamlet.

HAMLET: Whose was it?

1ST CLOWN: A whoreson mad fellow's it was: whose do you think it was?

HAMLET: Nay, I know not.

1ST CLOWN: A pestilence on him for a mad rogue! 'a poured a flagon of   145
Rhenish on my head once. This same skull, sir, was Yorick's skull, the
king's jester.

HAMLET: This?

1ST CLOWN: E'en that.

HAMLET: Let me see. [*Takes the skull*] — Alas, poor Yorick! — I knew him,   150
Horatio; a fellow of infinite jest, of most excellent fancy: he hath borne me
on his back a thousand times; and now, how abhorred in my imagination it
is! my gorge rises at it. Here hung those lips that I have kissed I know not
how oft. Where be your gibes now? your gambols? your songs? your flashes
of merriment, that were wont to set the table on a roar? Not one now, to   155
mock your own grinning? quite chap-fallen? Now get you to my lady's
chamber, and tell her, let her paint an inch thick, to this favor° she must
come; make her laugh at that. — Pr'ythee, Horatio, tell me one thing.

HORATIO: What's that, my lord?

HAMLET: Dost thou think Alexander looked o' this fashion i' the earth?   160

HORATIO: E'en so.

HAMLET: And smelt so? pah! [*Throws down the skull*]

HORATIO: E'en so, my lord.

HAMLET: To what base uses we may return, Horatio! Why may not imagination trace the noble dust of Alexander till he find it stopping a bung-hole?   165

° *favor:* Face.

HORATIO: 'Twere to consider too curiously to consider so.

HAMLET: No, faith, not a jot; but to follow him thither with modesty enough, and likelihood to lead it: as thus; Alexander died, Alexander was buried, Alexander returneth into dust; the dust is earth; of earth we make loam;

170 and why of that loam whereto he was converted might they not stop a beer-barrel?

> Imperious Caesar, dead and turn'd to clay,
>   Might stop a hole to keep the wind away:
> O, that that earth which kept the world in awe
175 Should patch a wall to expel the winter's flaw!—

But soft! but soft! aside.— Here comes the king.

Enter Priests, &c., in procession; the corpse of Ophelia, Laertes and Mourners following; King, Queen, their Trains, &c.

The queen, the courtiers: who is that they follow?
And with such maimed rites? This doth betoken
The corse they follow did with desperate hand
180 Fordo its own life: 'twas of some estate.
Couch we awhile and mark. [*Retiring with Horatio*]

LAERTES: What ceremony else?

HAMLET: That is Laertes,
A very noble youth: mark.

185 LAERTES: What ceremony else?

1ST PRIEST: Her obsequies have been as far enlarg'd
As we have warrantise: her death was doubtful,
And, but that great command o'ersways the order,
She should in ground unsanctified have lodg'd
190 Till the last trumpet; for charitable prayers,
Shards, flints, and pebbles, should be thrown on her,
Yet here she is allowed her virgin rites,
Her maiden strewments, and the bringing home
Of bell and burial.

195 LAERTES: Must there no more be done?

1ST PRIEST: No more be done:
We should profane the service of the dead
To sing a *requiem,* and such rest to her
As to peace-parted souls.

200 LAERTES: Lay her i' the earth;—
And from her fair and unpolluted flesh
May violets spring!— I tell thee, churlish priest,
A ministering angel shall my sister be
When thou liest howling.

205 HAMLET: What, the fair Ophelia!

QUEEN: Sweets to the sweet: farewell! [*Scattering flowers*]
I hop'd thou shouldst have been my Hamlet's wife;

I thought thy bride-bed to have deck'd, sweet maid,
And not have strew'd thy grave.

LAERTES: O, treble woe   210
Fall ten times treble on that cursed head
Whose wicked deed thy most ingenious sense
Depriv'd thee of!— Hold off the earth awhile,
Till I have caught her once more in mine arms:

Leaps into the grave.

Now pile your dust upon the quick and dead,   215
Till of this flat a mountain you have made,
To o'er-top old Pelion° or the skyish head
Of blue Olympus.

HAMLET: [*Advancing*] What is he whose grief
Bears such an emphasis? whose phrase of sorrow   220
Conjures the wandering stars, and makes them stand
Like wonder-wounded hearers? this is I, Hamlet the
Dane. [*Leaps into the grave*]

LAERTES: The devil take thy soul! [*Grappling with him*]

HAMLET: Thou pray'st not well.   225
I pr'ythee, take thy fingers from my throat;
For, though I am not splenitive and rash,
Yet have I in me something dangerous,
Which let thy wiseness fear: away thy hand.

KING: Pluck them asunder.   230

QUEEN: Hamlet! Hamlet!

ALL: Gentlemen,—

HORATIO: Good my lord, be quiet.

The Attendants part them, and they come out of the grave.

HAMLET: Why, I will fight with him upon this theme
Until my eyelids will no longer wag.   235

QUEEN: O my son, what theme?

HAMLET: I lov'd Ophelia; forty thousand brothers
Could not, with all their quantity of love,
Make up my sum.— What wilt thou do for her?

KING: O, he is mad, Laertes.   240

QUEEN: For love of God, forbear him.

HAMLET: 'Swounds, show me what thou'lt do:
Woul't weep? woul't fight? woul't fast? woul't tear thyself?
Woul't drink up eisel?° eat a crocodile?
I'll do't.— Dost thou come here to whine?   245
To outface me with leaping in her grave?

° *Pelion:* A mountain in Greece.   ° *eisel:* Vinegar.

Be buried quick° with her, and so will I:
And, if thou prate of mountains, let them throw
Millions of acres on us, till our ground,
250   Singeing his pate against the burning zone,°
Make Ossa° like a wart! Nay, an thou'lt mouth,
I'll rant as well as thou.

QUEEN: This is mere madness:
And thus awhile the fit will work on him;
255   Anon, as patient as the female dove,
When that her golden couplets are disclos'd,°
His silence will sit drooping.

HAMLET: Hear you, sir;
What is the reason that you use me thus?
260   I lov'd you ever: but it is no matter;
Let Hercules himself do what he may,
The cat will mew, and dog will have his day. [*Exit.*]

KING: I pray thee, good Horatio, wait upon him.—

Exit Horatio.

[*To Laertes*] Strengthen your patience in our last night's speech;
265   We'll put the matter to the present push.—
Good Gertrude, set some watch over your son.—
This grave shall have a living monument:
An hour of quiet shortly shall we see;
Till then, in patience our proceeding be.

Exeunt.

SCENE 2

A hall in the castle.

Enter Hamlet and Horatio.

HAMLET: So much for this, sir: now let me see the other;
You do remember all the circumstance?
HORATIO: Remember it, my lord!
HAMLET: Sir, in my heart there was a kind of fighting
5   That would not let me sleep: methought I lay
Worse than the mutines in the bilboes.° Rashly,
And prais'd be rashness for it,—let us know,
Our indiscretion sometimes serves us well,
When our deep plots do fail: and that should teach us

° *quick:* Alive.   ° *burning zone:* The fiery zone of the celestial sphere.   ° *Ossa:* A high mountain in Greece.
° *When . . . are disclos'd:* When the golden twins are hatched.   ° *mutines . . . bilboes:* Mutineers in the iron
stocks on board ship.

> There's a divinity that shapes our ends, 10
> Rough-hew them how we will.

HORATIO: This is most certain.

HAMLET: Up from my cabin,
> My sea-gown scarf'd about me, in the dark
> Grop'd I to find out them: had my desire; 15
> Finger'd their packet; and, in fine, withdrew
> To mine own room again: making so bold,
> My fears forgetting manners, to unseal
> Their grand commission; where I found, Horatio,
> O royal knavery! an exact command,— 20
> Larded with many several sorts of reasons,
> Importing Denmark's health and England's too,
> With, ho! such bugs° and goblins in my life,—
> That, on the supervise, no leisure bated,
> No, not to stay the grinding of the axe, 25
> My head should be struck off.

HORATIO: Is't possible?

HAMLET: Here's the commission: read it at more leisure.
> But wilt thou hear me how I did proceed?

HORATIO: I beseech you. 30

HAMLET: Being thus benetted round with villainies,—
> Ere I could make a prologue to my brains,
> They had begun the play,— I sat me down;
> Devis'd a new commission; wrote it fair:
> I once did hold it, as our statists do, 35
> A baseness to write fair, and labor'd much
> How to forget that learning; but, sir, now
> It did me yeoman's service. Wilt thou know
> The effect of what I wrote?

HORATIO: Ay, good my lord. 40

HAMLET: An earnest conjuration from the king,—
> As England was his faithful tributary;
> As love between them like the palm might flourish;
> As peace should still her wheaten garland wear
> And stand a comma° 'tween their amities; 45
> And many such like as's of great charge,—
> That, on the view and know of these contents,
> Without debatement further, more or less,
> He should the bearers put to sudden death,
> Not shriving-time allow'd. 50

HORATIO: How was this seal'd?

° *bugs:* Bugbears.   ° *comma:* Link.

HAMLET: Why, even in that was heaven ordinant.
    I had my father's signet in my purse,
    Which was the model of that Danish seal:
55   Folded the writ up in form of the other;
    Subscrib'd it; gav't the impression; plac'd it safely,
    The changeling never known. Now, the next day
    Was our sea-fight; and what to this was sequent
    Thou know'st already.
60 HORATIO: So Guildenstern and Rosencrantz go to't.
  HAMLET: Why, man, they did make love to this employment;
    They are not near my conscience; their defeat
    Does by their own insinuation° grow:
    'Tis dangerous when the baser nature° comes
65   Between the pass and fell° incensed points
    Of mighty opposites.
  HORATIO: Why, what a king is this!
  HAMLET: Does it not, think'st thee, stand me now upon,°
    He that hath kill'd my king and whor'd my mother;
70   Popp'd in between the election and my hopes;
    Thrown out his angle for my proper life,
    And with such cozenage,°—is't not perfect conscience
    To quit him with this arm? and is't not to be damn'd,
    To let this canker of our nature come
75   In further evil?
  HORATIO: It must be shortly known to him from England
    What is the issue of the business there.
  HAMLET: It will be short: the interim is mine;
    And a man's life's no more than to say One.
80   But I am very sorry, good Horatio,
    That to Laertes I forgot myself;
    For by the image of my cause I see
    The portraiture of his: I'll court his favors:
    But, sure, the bravery° of his grief did put me
85   Into a towering passion.
  HORATIO: Peace; who comes here?

Enter Osric.

OSRIC: Your lordship is right welcome back to Denmark.
  HAMLET: I humbly thank you, sir.—Dost know this water-fly?
  HORATIO: No, my good lord.
90 HAMLET: Thy state is the more gracious; for 'tis a vice to know him. He hath
    much land, and fertile: let a beast be lord of beasts, and his crib shall stand

---

° *insinuation:* By their own "sticking their noses" into the business.   ° *baser nature:* Men of lower rank.   ° *fell:*
Fierce.   ° *Does . . . upon:* I.e., "Don't you think it is my duty?"   ° *cozenage:* Deceit.   ° *bravery:* Ostentation.

at the king's mess: 'tis a chough;° but, as I say, spacious in the possession
of dirt.

OSRIC: Sweet lord, if your lordship were at leisure, I should impart a thing to
you from his majesty.   95

HAMLET: I will receive it with all diligence of spirit. Put your bonnet to his
right use; 'tis for the head.

OSRIC: I thank your lordship, 'tis very hot.

HAMLET: No, believe me, 'tis very cold; the wind is northerly.

OSRIC: It is indifferent cold, my lord, indeed.   100

HAMLET: Methinks it is very sultry and hot for my complexion.

OSRIC: Exceedingly, my lord; it is very sultry, — as't were, — I cannot tell
how. — But, my lord, his majesty bade me signify to you that he has laid
a great wager on your head. Sir, this is the matter, —

HAMLET: I beseech you, remember, —   105

Hamlet moves him to put on his hat.

OSRIC: Nay, in good faith; for mine ease, in good faith. Sir, here is newly come
to court Laertes; believe me, an absolute gentleman, full of most excellent
differences, of very soft society and great showing: indeed, to speak feelingly
of him, he is the card or calendar of gentry, for you shall find in him the
continent of what part a gentleman would see.   110

HAMLET: Sir, his definement suffers no perdition in you; — though, I know, to
divide him inventorially would dizzy the arithmetic of memory, and yet but
yaw neither, in respect of his quick sail. But, in the verity of extolment,
I take him to be a soul of great article; and his infusion of such dearth° and
rareness as, to make true diction of him, his semblable is his mirror; and   115
who else would trace him, his umbrage,° nothing more.

OSRIC: Your lordship speaks most infallibly of him.

HAMLET: The concernancy, sir? why do we wrap the gentleman in our more
rawer breath?

OSRIC: Sir?   120

HORATIO: Is't not possible to understand in another tongue? You will do't
sir, really.

HAMLET: What imports the nomination° of this gentleman?

OSRIC: Of Laertes?

HORATIO: His purse is empty already; all's golden words are spent.   125

HAMLET: Of him, sir.

OSRIC: I know, you are not ignorant, —

HAMLET: I would you did, sir; yet, in faith, if you did, it would not much
approve me.° — Well, sir.

° *his crib . . . chough:* He shall have his trough at the king's table: he is a chattering fool.   ° *dearth:* Rareness,
or excellence.   ° *umbrage:* Shadow.   ° *nomination:* Naming.   ° *if you . . . approve me:* If you, who are a
fool, thought me not ignorant, that would not be particularly to my credit.

130 OSRIC: You are not ignorant of what excellence Laertes is,—

HAMLET: I dare not confess that, lest I should compare with him in excellence; but to know a man well were to know himself.

OSRIC: I mean, sir, for his weapon; but in the imputation laid on him by them, in his meed he's unfellowed.°

135 HAMLET: What's his weapon?

OSRIC: Rapier and dagger.

HAMLET: That's two of his weapons: but, well.

OSRIC: The king, sir, hath wagered with him six Barbary horses: against the which he has imponed,° as I take it, six French rapiers and poniards, with 140 their assigns, as girdle, hangers, and so: three of the carriages, in faith, are very dear to fancy, very responsive to the hilts, most delicate carriages, and of very liberal conceit.

HAMLET: What call you the carriages?

HORATIO: I knew you must be edified by the margent° ere you had done.

145 OSRIC: The carriages, sir, are the hangers.

HAMLET: The phrase would be more german to the matter if we could carry cannon by our sides: I would it might be hangers till then. But, on: six Barbary horses against six French swords, their assigns, and three liberal conceited carriages; that's the French bet against the Danish: why is this 150 imponed, as you call it?

OSRIC: The king, sir, hath laid, that in a dozen passes between you and him he shall not exceed you three hits: he hath laid on twelve for nine; and it would come to immediate trial if your lordship would vouchsafe the answer.

HAMLET: How if I answer no?

155 OSRIC: I mean, my lord, the opposition of your person in trial.°

HAMLET: Sir, I will walk here in the hall: if it please his majesty, it is the breathing time of day with me: let the foils be brought, the gentleman willing, and the king hold his purpose, I will win for him if I can; if not, I will gain nothing but my shame and the odd hits.

160 OSRIC: Shall I re-deliver you° e'en so?

HAMLET: To this effect, sir; after what flourish your nature will.

OSRIC: I commend my duty to your lordship.

HAMLET: Yours, yours.

Exit Osric.

He does well to commend it himself; there are no tongues else for's turn.

165 HORATIO: This lapwing runs away with the shell on his head.°

HAMLET: He did comply with his dug before he sucked it.° Thus has he,— and many more of the same bevy, that I know the drossy age dotes on,—

° *in . . . unfellowed:* In his worth he has no equal. ° *imponed:* Staked. ° *edified . . . margent:* Informed by a note in the margin of your instructions. ° *the opposition . . . trial:* The presence of your person as Laertes' opponent in the fencing contest. ° *re-deliver you:* Carry back your answer. ° *This lapwing . . . head:* This precocious fellow is like a lapwing that starts running when it is barely out of the shell. ° *He . . . sucked it:* He paid compliments to his mother's breast before he sucked it.

only got the tune of the time, and outward habit of encounter; a kind of
yesty collection,° which carries them through and through the most
fanned and winnowed opinions; and do but blow them to their trial,   170
the bubbles are out.

Enter a Lord.

LORD: My lord, his majesty commended him to you by young Osric, who
    brings back to him that you attend him in the hall: he sends to know if
    your pleasure hold to play with Laertes, or that you will take longer time.

HAMLET: I am constant to my purposes; they follow the king's pleasure: if his   175
    fitness speaks, mine is ready; now or whensoever, provided I be so able
    as now.

LORD: The king and queen and all are coming down.

HAMLET: In happy time.

LORD: The queen desires you to use some gentle entertainment to Laertes   180
    before you fall to play.

HAMLET: She well instructs me.

Exit Lord.

HORATIO: You will lose this wager, my lord.

HAMLET: I do not think so; since he went into France I have been in
    continual practice: I shall win at the odds. But thou wouldst not think   185
    how ill all's here about my heart: but it is no matter.

HORATIO: Nay, good my lord,—

HAMLET: It is but foolery; but it is such a kind of gain-giving° as would
    perhaps trouble a woman.

HORATIO: If your mind dislike anything, obey it: I will forestall their repair   190
    hither, and say you are not fit.

HAMLET: Not a whit, we defy augury: there's a special providence in the fall of
    a sparrow. If it be now, 'tis not to come; if it be not to come, it will be now;
    if it be not now, yet it will come: the readiness is all. Since no man has
    aught of what he leaves, what is't to leave betimes?°   195

Enter King, Queen, Laertes, Lords, Osric, and Attendants with foils, &c.

KING: Come, Hamlet, come, and take this hand from me.

The King puts Laertes' hand into Hamlet's.

HAMLET: Give me your pardon, sir: I have done you wrong:
    But pardon't, as you are a gentleman.
    This presence knows, and you must needs have heard,
    How I am punish'd with sore distraction.   200
    What I have done,

° *yesty collection:* Yeasty or frothy affair.   ° *gain-giving:* Misgiving.   ° *what . . . betimes?:* What does an
early death matter?

That might your nature, honor, and exception
Roughly awake, I here proclaim was madness.
Was't Hamlet wrong'd Laertes? Never Hamlet:
205   If Hamlet from himself be ta'en away,
And when he's not himself does wrong Laertes,
Then Hamlet does it not, Hamlet denies it.
Who does it, then? His madness: if't be so,
Hamlet is of the faction that is wrong'd;
210   His madness is poor Hamlet's enemy.
Sir, in this audience,
Let my disclaiming from a purpos'd evil
Free me so far in your most generous thoughts
That I have shot mine arrow o'er the house
215   And hurt my brother.

LAERTES: I am satisfied in nature,
Whose motive, in this case, should stir me most
To my revenge: but in my terms of honor
I stand aloof; and will no reconcilement
220   Till by some elder masters of known honor
I have a voice and precedent of peace
To keep my name ungor'd. But till that time
I do receive your offer'd love like love,
And will not wrong it.

225 **HAMLET:**   I embrace it freely;
And will this brother's wager frankly play.°—
Give us the foils; come on.

LAERTES: Come, one for me.

HAMLET: I'll be your foil, Laertes; in mine ignorance
230   Your skill shall, like a star in the darkest night,
Stick fiery off indeed.

LAERTES: You mock me, sir.

HAMLET: No, by this hand.

KING: Give them the foils, young Osric.
235   Cousin Hamlet,
You know the wager?

HAMLET: Very well, my lord;
Your grace hath laid the odds o' the weaker side.

KING: I do not fear it; I have seen you both;
240   But since he's better'd, we have therefore odds.

LAERTES: This is too heavy, let me see another.

HAMLET: This likes me well. These foils have all a length?

They prepare to play.

° *frankly play:* Fence with a heart free from resentment.

OSRIC: Ay, my good lord.
KING: Set me the stoups of wine upon that table,—
   If Hamlet give the first or second hit,   245
   Or quit in answer of the third exchange,
   Let all the battlements their ordnance fire;
   The king shall drink to Hamlet's better breath;
   And in the cup an union° shall he throw,
   Richer than that which four successive kings   250
   In Denmark's crown have worn. Give me the cups;
   And let the kettle° to the trumpet speak,
   The trumpet to the cannoneer without,
   The cannons to the heavens, the heavens to earth,
   Now the king drinks to Hamlet. — Come, begin;—   255
   And you, the judges, bear a wary eye.
HAMLET: Come on, sir.
LAERTES: Come, my lord.

They play.

HAMLET: One.
LAERTES: No.   260
HAMLET: Judgment.
OSRIC: A hit, a very palpable hit.
LAERTES: Well;— again.
KING: Stay, give me a drink. — Hamlet, this pearl is thine;

   Here's to thy health.—   265

Trumpets sound, and cannon shot off within.

   Give him the cup.

HAMLET: I'll play this bout first; set it by awhile.—
   Come. — Another hit; what say you?

They play.

LAERTES: A touch, a touch, I do confess.
KING: Our son shall win.   270
QUEEN: He's fat, and scant of breath. —
   Here, Hamlet, take my napkin, rub thy brows:
   The queen carouses to thy fortune, Hamlet.
HAMLET: Good madam!
KING: Gertrude, do not drink.   275
QUEEN: I will, my lord; I pray you, pardon me.
KING: [*Aside*] It is the poison'd cup; it is too late.
HAMLET: I dare not drink yet, madam; by and by.

°*an union:* A pearl.   °*kettle:* Kettledrum.

QUEEN: Come, let me wipe thy face.

280   LAERTES: My lord, I'll hit him now.

KING: I do not think't.

LAERTES: [*Aside*] And yet 'tis almost 'gainst my conscience.

HAMLET: Come, for the third, Laertes: you but dally;
        I pray you, pass with your best violence:

285   I am afeard you make a wanton of me.

LAERTES: Say you so? come on.

They play.

OSRIC: Nothing, neither way.

LAERTES: Have at you now!

Laertes wounds Hamlet; then, in scuffling, they change rapiers, and Hamlet wounds Laertes.

KING: Part them; they are incens'd.

290   HAMLET: Nay, come, again.

The Queen falls.

OSRIC: Look to the queen there, ho!

HORATIO: They bleed on both sides. — How is it, my lord?

OSRIC: How is't, Laertes?

LAERTES: Why, as a woodcock to my own springe, Osric;

295   I am justly kill'd with mine own treachery.

HAMLET: How does the queen?

KING: She swoons to see them bleed.

QUEEN: No, no, the drink, the drink, — O my dear Hamlet, —
        The drink, the drink! — I am poison'd. [*Dies.*]

300   HAMLET: O villainy! — Ho! let the door be lock'd:
        Treachery! seek it out.

Laertes falls.

LAERTES: It is here, Hamlet: Hamlet, thou art slain;
        No medicine in the world can do thee good;
        In thee there is not half an hour of life;

305   The treacherous instrument is in thy hand,
        Unbated and envenom'd: the foul practice
        Hath turn'd itself on me; lo, here I lie,
        Never to rise again: thy mother's poison'd:
        I can no more: — the king, the king's to blame.

310   HAMLET: The point envenom'd too! —
        Then venom to thy work. [*Stabs the King.*]

OSRIC and LORDS: Treason! treason!

KING: O, yet defend me, friends; I am but hurt.

HAMLET: Here, thou incestuous, murderous, damned Dane,
    Drink off this potion.—Is thy union here? 315
    Follow my mother.

King dies.

LAERTES: He is justly serv'd;
    It is a poison temper'd by himself.—
    Exchange forgiveness with me, noble Hamlet:
    Mine and my father's death come not upon thee, 320
    Nor thine on me! [*Dies.*]

HAMLET: Heaven make thee free of it! I follow thee.—
    I am dead, Horatio.—Wretched queen, adieu!—
    You that look pale and tremble at this chance,
    That art but mutes or audience to this act, 325
    Had I but time,—as this fell sergeant, death,
    Is strict in his arrest,—O, I could tell you,—
    But let it be.—Horatio, I am dead;
    Thou liv'st; report me and my cause aright
    To the unsatisfied.° 330

HORATIO: Never believe it:
    I am more an antique Roman than a Dane,—
    Here's yet some liquor left.

HAMLET: As thou'rt a man,
    Give me the cup; let go; by heaven, I'll have't.— 335
    O good Horatio, what a wounded name,
    Things standing thus unknown, shall live behind me!
    If thou didst ever hold me in thy heart,
    Absent thee from felicity awhile,
    And in this harsh world draw thy breath in pain, 340
    To tell my story.—

March afar off, and shot within.

                  What warlike noise is this?

OSRIC: Young Fortinbras, with conquest come from Poland,
    To the ambassadors of England gives
    This warlike volley. 345

HAMLET: O, I die, Horatio;
    The potent poison quite o'er-crows my spirit:
    I cannot live to hear the news from England;
    But I do prophesy the election lights
    On Fortinbras: he has my dying voice; 350

° *the unsatisfied:* The uninformed.

So tell him, with the occurrents, more and less,
Which have solicited. °— The rest is silence. [*Dies.*]

HORATIO: Now cracks a noble heart.— Good-night, sweet prince,
And flights of angels sing thee to thy rest!

355   Why does the drum come hither?

March within. Enter Fortinbras, the English Ambassadors, and others.

FORTINBRAS: Where is this sight?

HORATIO: What is it you would see?
If aught of woe or wonder, cease your search.

FORTINBRAS: This quarry cries on havoc.°— O proud death,

360   What feast is toward in thine eternal cell,
That thou so many princes at a shot
So bloodily hast struck?

1ST AMBASSADOR: The sight is dismal;
And our affairs from England come too late:

365   The ears are senseless that should give us hearing,
To tell him his commandment is fulfill'd,
That Rosencrantz and Guildenstern are dead:
Where should we have our thanks?

HORATIO: Not from his mouth,

370   Had it the ability of life to thank you:
He never gave commandment for their death.
But since, so jump° upon this bloody question,
You from the Polack wars, and you from England,
Are here arriv'd, give order that these bodies

375   High on a stage be placed to the view;
And let me speak to the yet unknowing world
How these things came about: so shall you hear
Of carnal, bloody, and unnatural acts;
Of accidental judgments, casual slaughters;

380   Of deaths put on by cunning and forc'd cause;
And, in this upshot, purposes mistook
Fall'n on the inventors' heads: all this can I
Truly deliver.

FORTINBRAS: Let us haste to hear it,

385   And call the noblest to the audience.
For me, with sorrow I embrace my fortune:
I have some rights of memory in this kingdom,°
Which now to claim my vantage doth invite me.

HORATIO: Of that I shall have also cause to speak,

390   And from his mouth whose voice will draw on more:

° *So tell him . . . solicited:* So tell him, together with the events, more or less, that have brought on this tragic affair.
° *This quarry . . . havoc:* This collection of dead bodies cries out havoc.   ° *so jump:* So opportunely.   ° *I have
. . . kingdom:* I have some unforgotten rights to this kingdom.

But let this same be presently perform'd,
Even while men's minds are wild: lest more mischance
On plots and errors happen.
FORTINBRAS: Let four captains
Bear Hamlet like a soldier to the stage;   395
For he was likely, had he been put on,°
To have prov'd most royally: and, for his passage,
The soldier's music and the rites of war
Speak loudly for him.—
Take up the bodies.— Such a sight as this   400
Becomes the field, but here shows much amiss.
Go, bid the soldiers shoot.

A dead march.

Exeunt, bearing off the dead bodies: after which a peal of ordnance is shot off.

Reading and Reacting

1. What are Hamlet's most notable character traits? Do you see these traits as generally positive or negative?

2. Review each of Hamlet's soliloquies. Judging from his own words, do you believe his assessments of his own problems are accurate? Are his assessments of other characters' behavior accurate? Point to examples from the soliloquies that reveal Hamlet's insight or lack of insight.

3. Is Hamlet a sympathetic character? Where (if anywhere) do you find yourself growing impatient with him or disagreeing with him?

4. What is the emotional impact on the audience of having Hamlet behave so cruelly toward Ophelia after his "To be or not to be" soliloquy (act 3, scene 1)?

5. What do other characters' comments reveal about Hamlet's character *before* the key events in the play begin to unfold? For example, in what way has Hamlet changed since he returned to the castle and found out about his father's death?

6. Claudius is presented as the play's villain. Is he all bad, or does he have any redeeming qualities?

7. List those in the play whom you believe to be flat characters. Why do you characterize each individual in this way? What does each of these flat characters contribute to the play?

8. Is Fortinbras simply Hamlet's foil, or does he have another essential role? Explain.

9. Each of the play's major characters has one or more character flaws that influence plot development. What specific weaknesses do you see in Claudius, Gertrude, Polonius, Laertes, Ophelia, and Hamlet himself? Through what

° *put on:* Tested by succession to the throne.

words or actions is each weakness revealed? How does each weakness contribute to the play's plot?

10. Why doesn't Hamlet kill Claudius as soon as the Ghost tells him what Claudius did? Why doesn't he kill him when he has the chance in act 3? What words and actions reveal Hamlet's motivation for hesitating? What are the implications of his failure to act?

11. Why does Hamlet pretend to be insane? Why does he arrange for the "play within a play" to be performed? Why does he agree to the duel with Laertes? In each case, what words or actions reveal his motivation to the audience?

12. Is the Ghost an essential character, or could the information he reveals and the reactions he arouses come from another source? Explain. (Keep in mind that the ghost is a stock character in Elizabethan revenge tragedies.)

13. Describe Hamlet's relationship with his mother. Do you consider this a typical mother/son relationship? Why or why not?

14. In the graveyard scene (act 5, scene 1), the gravediggers make many ironic comments. In what way do these comments shed light on the events taking place in the play?

15. **JOURNAL ENTRY** Both Gertrude and Ophelia are usually seen as weak women, firmly under the influence of the men in their lives. Do you think this characterization of them as passive and dependent is accurate? Why or why not?

16. **CRITICAL PERSPECTIVE** In *The Meaning of Shakespeare*, (1951), Harold Goddard reads *Hamlet* as, in part, a play about war, with a grimly ironic conclusion in that "all the Elder Hamlet's conquests have been for nothing — for less than nothing. Fortinbras, his former enemy, is to inherit the kingdom! Such is the end to which the Ghost's thirst for vengeance has led." Goddard goes on to describe the play's ending:

> The dead Hamlet is borne out "like a soldier" and the last rites over his body are to be the rites of war. The final word of the text is "shoot." The last sounds we hear are a dead march and the reverberations of ordnance being shot off. The end crowns the whole. The sarcasm of fate could go no further. Hamlet, who aspired to nobler things, is treated at death as if he were the mere image of his father: a warrior. Shakespeare knew what he was about in making the conclusion of his play martial. Its theme has been war as well as revenge. It is the story of the Minotaur over again, of that monster who from the beginning of human strife has exacted his annual tribute of youth. No sacrifice ever offered to it was more precious than Hamlet. But he was not the last.

> If ever a play seems expressly written for the twentieth century, it is *Hamlet*. It should be unnecessary to underscore its pertinence to an age in which, twice within three decades, the older generation has called on the younger generation to settle a quarrel with the making of which it had nothing to do. So taken, *Hamlet* is an allegory of our time. Imagination or violence, Shakespeare seems to say, there is no other alternative.

Can you find other evidence in the play to support the idea that war (and, more specifically, the futility of war) is one of its major themes? Do you agree that the play is, in this respect, "an allegory of our time"?

Related Works: "The Cask of Amontillado" (p. 350), "Young Goodman Brown" (p. 489), "Hamlet" (p. 1656), *Oedipus the King* (p. 1786)

WRITING SUGGESTIONS: Character

1. In *Death of a Salesman*, each character pursues his or her version of the American Dream. Choose two characters, define their concept of the American dream, and explain how each tries to make the dream a reality. In each case, consider the obstacles the character encounters, and try to account for the character's success or lack of success. If you like, you may also consider other works in which the American Dream is central — for example, "The Third and Final Continent" (p. 261), "Two Kinds" (p. 791), "Immigrants" (p. 1025), *The Cuban Swimmer* (p. 1772), or *Fences* (p. 1939).

2. Many of the female characters in this chapter's plays — for example, Mrs. X (*The Stronger*), Catherine (*Proof*), Linda (*Death of a Salesman*), and Ophelia (*Hamlet*) — are, in one way or another, in conflict with men. Focusing on female characters in two different plays, define each conflict, and consider whether it is resolved in the play. (If you like, you may also discuss a female character in a play in another chapter.)

3. Minor characters are often flat characters; in many cases, their sole function is to advance the plot or to highlight a particular trait in a major character. Sometimes, however, minor characters may be of more than minor importance. Choose one minor character from *Death of a Salesman* or *Hamlet* (or from a play in another chapter), and write a paper in which you discuss what this character contributes and how the play would be different without him or her.

4. Watch a film version of one of the four plays in this chapter, and write an essay in which you evaluate the actor's interpretation of the central character.

5. Three of this chapter's four plays explore complex relationships between parents and children. Write an essay in which you compare and contrast two of these three relationships: Catherine's relationship with her father, Willy Loman's relationships with his sons, or Hamlet's relationship with his mother.

6. In several other plays in this anthology, as in *Proof*, the past is an important influence on characters' lives in the present. Write an essay in which you discuss the importance of the past on the present in *Proof* and one or two other plays — for example, *The Glass Menagerie* or *A Doll House*.

CHAPTER 41

STAGING

> In reading a play rather than witnessing it on stage, we . . . have to imagine what it might look like in performance, projecting in our mind's eye an image of the setting and the props, as well as the movements, gestures, facial expressions, and vocal intonations of the characters.
>
> —Carl H. Klaus, Miriam Gilbert, and Braford S. Field, Jr., *Stages of Drama*

Staging refers to the physical elements of a play's production that determine how the play looks and sounds to an audience. It encompasses the **stage settings**, or **sets**—furnishings, scenery, props, and lighting — as well as the costumes, sound effects, and music that bring the play to life on the stage. In short, staging is everything that goes into making a written script a play.

Contemporary staging in the West has traditionally concentrated on re-creating the outside world. This concept of staging, which has dominated Western theatrical productions for centuries, would seem alien in many non-Western theaters. Japanese **Kabuki dramas** and **No plays**, for example, depend on staging conventions that make no attempt to mirror reality. Scenery and costumes are largely symbolic, and often actors wear highly stylized makeup or masks. Although some European and American playwrights have been strongly influenced by non-Western staging, the majority of plays being produced in the West still try to create the illusion of reality.

Stage Directions

Usually a playwright presents instructions for the staging of a play in **stage directions**—notes that comment on the scenery, the movements of the performers, the lighting, and the placement of props. (In the absence of detailed stage directions, dialogue can provide information about staging.) Sometimes these stage directions are quite simple, leaving much to the imagination of the director. Consider how little specific information about the setting of the play is provided in these stage directions from act 1 of Samuel Beckett's 1952 absurdist play *Waiting for Godot*:

A country road. A tree. Evening.

Often, however, playwrights furnish much more detailed information about staging. Consider these stage directions from act 1 of Anton Chekhov's *The Cherry Orchard:*

A room, which has always been called the nursery. One of the doors leads into Anya's room. Dawn, sun rises during the scene. May, the cherry trees in flower, but it is cold in the garden with the frost of the early morning. Windows closed.

Enter Dunyasha with a candle and Lopahin with a book in his hand.

These comments indicate that the first act takes place in a room with more than one door and that several windows reveal cherry trees in bloom. They also specify that the lighting should simulate the sun rising at dawn and that certain characters should enter carrying particular props. Still, Chekhov leaves it up to those staging the play to decide on the costumes for the characters and on the furniture to be placed around the room.

Some stage directions are even more specific. Irish playwright George Bernard Shaw's long, complex stage directions are legendary in the theater. Note the degree of detail he provides in these stage directions from his 1906 comedy *The Doctor's Dilemma:*

The consulting-room has two windows looking on Queen Anne Street. Between the two is a marble-topped console, with haunched gilt legs ending in sphinx claws. The huge pier-glass [a long narrow mirror that fits between two windows] which surmounts it is mostly disabled from reflection by elaborate painting on its surface of palms, ferns, lilies, tulips, and sunflowers. The adjoining wall contains the fireplace, with two arm-chairs before it. As we happen to face the corner we see nothing of the other two walls. On the right of the fireplace, or rather on the right of any person facing the fireplace, is the door. On the left is the writing-table at which Redpenny [a medical student] sits. It is an untidy table with a microscope, several test tubes, and a spirit lamp [an alcohol burner] standing up through its litter of papers. There is a couch in the middle of the room, at right angles to the console, and parallel to the fireplace. A chair stands between the couch and the window. Another in the corner. Another at the other end of the windowed wall. . . . The wallpaper and carpets are mostly green. . . . The house, in fact, was so well furnished in the middle of the XIXth century that it stands unaltered to this day and is still quite presentable.

Not only does Shaw indicate what furniture is to be placed on stage, but he also includes a good deal of physical description — specifying, for example, "gilt legs ending in sphinx claws" and "test tubes and a spirit lamp" that clutter the writing table. In addition, he defines furniture placement and specifies color.

Regardless of how detailed the stage directions are, they do not eliminate the need for creative interpretations on the part of the producer, director, set designers, and actors (See "Actors' Interpretations," p. 1517). Stage directions — and, for that matter, the entire script — are the foundation on which to construct the play that the audience finally sees. Many directors see stage directions as suggestions, not requirements, and some consider them more confusing than helpful. Therefore, some directors may choose to interpret a play's stage directions quite loosely — or even to ignore them entirely.

The Uses of Staging

Various elements of staging communicate important information about characters and their motivation as well as about the play's theme.

Costumes

Costumes establish the historical period in which a play is set and provide insight into the characters who wear them. When Hamlet first appears on stage, he is profoundly disillusioned and quite melancholy. This fact was immediately apparent to Shakespeare's audience because Hamlet is dressed in sable, which to the Elizabethans signified a melancholy nature. In Tennessee Williams's *The Glass Menagerie* (p. 1998), Laura's dress of soft violet material and her hair ribbon reflect her delicate, childlike innocence. In contrast, her mother's "*imitation velvety-looking cloth [coat] with imitation fur collar*" and her "*enormous black patent-leather pocketbook*" reveal her somewhat pathetic attempt to achieve respectability. Later in the play, awaiting the "gentleman caller," Laura's mother wears a dress that is both outdated and inappropriately youthful, suggesting both her need to relive her own past and her increasingly desperate desire to marry off her daughter.

Props and Furnishings

Props (short for *properties*) can also help audiences to interpret a play's characters and themes. For example, the handkerchief in Shakespeare's *Othello* gains significance as the play progresses: it begins as an innocent object and ends as the piece of evidence that convinces Othello his wife is committing adultery. Sometimes props can have symbolic significance. During the Renaissance, flowers had symbolic meaning. In act 4 of *Hamlet*, Ophelia, who is mad, gives flowers to various characters. In a note to the play, the critic Thomas Parrott points out the symbolic significance of her gifts: to Claudius, the murderer of Hamlet's father, she gives fennel and columbines, which signify flattery and ingratitude; to the Queen, she gives rue and daisies, which symbolize sadness and unfaithfulness. Although modern audiences would not understand the significance of these flowers, many people in Shakespeare's Elizabethan audience would have been aware of their meaning.

The **furnishings** in a room can also reveal a lot about a play's characters and themes. Willy Loman's house in Arthur Miller's *Death of a Salesman* (p. 1581) is sparsely furnished, revealing the declining financial status of the family. The kitchen contains a table and three chairs and the bedroom only a brass bed and a straight chair. Over the bed on a shelf is Biff's silver athletic trophy, a constant reminder of his loss of status. Like Willy Loman's house, the Wingfield apartment in *The Glass Menagerie* reflects its inhabitants' modest economic circumstances. For example, the living room, which contains a sofa that opens into a bed, also serves as a bedroom for Laura. In addition, one piece of furniture highlights a central theme of the play: an old-fashioned cabinet in the living room displays a collection of transparent glass animals that, like Laura, are too fragile to be removed from their surroundings.

Scenery and Lighting

Playwrights often use **scenery and lighting** to create imaginative stage settings. In *Death of a Salesman*, the house is surrounded by *"towering angular shapes"* of apartment houses that emphasize the *"small, fragile-seeming home."* Arthur Miller calls for a set that is *"wholly, or in some places, transparent."* Whenever the action is in the present, the actors observe the imaginary boundaries that separate rooms or mark the exterior walls of the house. But when the characters reenact past events, they walk over the boundaries and come to the front of the stage. By lighting up and darkening different parts of the stage, Miller shifts from the present to the past and back again.

The set of *The Glass Menagerie* is also innovative, combining imaginative backdrops with subtle lighting. As the curtain rises, the audience sees the dark rear wall of the Wingfield tenement, which is flanked on both sides by alleys lined with clotheslines, garbage cans, and fire escapes. After Tom delivers his opening narrative, the rear wall becomes transparent, revealing the interior of the Wingfield apartment. To create this effect, Williams used a **scrim**, a curtain that when illuminated from the front appears solid but when illuminated from the back becomes transparent. For Williams, such "atmospheric touches" represented a new direction in theater that contrasted with the theater of "realistic conventions."

Contemporary playwrights often use sets that combine realistic and nonrealistic elements. In his 1988 Tony Award-winning play *M. Butterfly*, for example, David Henry Hwang employs not only scrims but also a large red lacquered ramp that runs from the bottom to the top of the stage. The action takes place beneath, on, and above the ramp, creating an effect not unlike that created by Shakespeare's multiple stages. At several points in the play, a character who acts as the narrator sits beneath the ramp, addressing the audience, while at the same time a character on top of the ramp acts out the narrator's words.

Music and Sound Effects

Staging involves more than visual elements such as costumes and scenery; it also involves **music and sound effects**. The stage directions for *Death of a Salesman*, for example, begin, *"A melody is heard, played upon a flute."* Although not specifically identified, the music is described as *"small and fine, telling of grass and trees and the horizon."* Interestingly, this music stands in stark contrast to the claustrophobic urban setting of the play. Music also plays a major role in *The Glass Menagerie*, where a single recurring tune, like circus music, weaves in and out of the play. This musical motif gives emotional impact to certain lines and suggests the fantasy world into which Laura has retreated.

Sound effects play an important part in Henrik Ibsen's *A Doll House* (p. 1454). At the very end of the play, after his wife has left him, Torvald Helmer sits alone on the stage. In the following stage directions, the final sound effect cuts short Helmer's attempt at self-deluding optimism:

HELMER: (*sinks down on a chair by the door, face buried in his hands*) Nora! Nora! (*Looking about and rising.*) Empty. She's gone. (*A sudden hope leaps in him.*) The greatest miracle —?

From below, the sound of a door slamming shut.

When you read a play, it may be difficult to appreciate the effect that staging can have on a performance. As you read, pay particular attention to the stage directions, and use your imagination to visualize the scenes the playwright describes. In addition, try to imagine the play's sights and sounds, and consider the options for staging that are suggested as characters speak to one another. Although even such careful reading cannot substitute for actually seeing a play performed, it can help you imagine the play as it might appear on the stage.

A Final Note

Because of a play's limited performance time, and because of space and financial limitations, not every action or event can be represented on stage. Frequently, incidents that would involve many actors or require elaborate scenery are only suggested. For example, a violent political riot may be suggested by a single scuffle, a full-scale wedding by the kiss between bride and groom, a gala evening at the opera by a well-dressed group in box seats, and a trip to an exotic locale by a departure scene. Other events are suggested by sounds offstage — for example, the roar of a crowd may suggest an athletic event.

✔ CHECKLIST   Writing about Staging

☐ What information about staging is specified in the stage directions of the play?

☐ What information about staging is suggested by the play's dialogue?

☐ What information about staging is left to the imagination?

☐ How might different decisions about staging change the play?

☐ Do the stage directions provide information about how characters are supposed to look or behave?

☐ What costumes are specified? In what ways do costumes provide insight into the characters who wear them?

☐ What props play an important part in the play? Do these props have symbolic meaning?

- Is the scenery special or unusual in any way?

- What kind of lighting is specified by the stage directions? In what way does this lighting affect your reaction to the play?

- How are music and sound effects used in the play? Are musical themes associated with any characters? Do music or sound effects heighten the emotional impact of certain lines?

- What events occur offstage? Why? How are they suggested?

- How does staging help to communicate the play's themes?

TRACEY SCOTT WILSON was born and raised in Newark, New Jersey. She received a BA from Rutgers University and an MA from Temple University. Wilson won the 2002 Helen Merrill Award for Emerging Artists, and her play *The Story* was a finalist for the Susan Smith Blackburn Prize. In 2004, she won the Kesselring Prize for Exceptional Promise and the Whiting Award.

Cultural Context As *Small World* suggests, dating today has become much more complicated, and perhaps more impersonal, than it was in the past. The Internet has made online dating a popular enterprise, with chat rooms, personals, and dating services targeting specific groups with shared interests. Often, clients can communicate and even fall in love without ever seeing each other face to face. Moreover, because of the fast pace of modern society, many singles opt to engage in less traditional forms of dating, including "speed dating," in which individuals spend five minutes with each other before rotating to the next table and the next prospective partner. Clearly, the complexities of the modern world have changed dating significantly.

Small World (2001)

CHARACTERS
Man 1
Man 2
Man 3
Woman 1
Woman 2
Woman 3

Lights up on 3 couples meeting at separate benches. They have never met before. It is a first date for all. Until specified, Man 1 only speaks to Woman 1, Man 2 only speaks to Woman 2, and Man 3 only speaks to Woman 3. When it reads, Man 1, 2, and so on, the characters are speaking simultaneously. Also (. . .) indicates that the characters are finishing the previous sentence.

MAN 1: Stacy?

WOMAN 1: Bob?

MAN 2: Lucy?

WOMAN 2: Bill?

5 MAN 3: Alice?

WOMAN 3: Tim?

ALL: Hi!

MAN 1: I've never been on one of these blind . . .

MAN 2: . . . computer . . .

10 MAN 3: . . . newspaper ad . . .

MAN 1, 2, 3: dates before.

WOMAN 1, 2, 3: Neither have I.

They sit.

MAN 1, 2: It's beautiful here in the park.

MAN 3: Maybe we should have gone to the park.

15 WOMAN 1, 2: Yes.

WOMAN 3: No.

MAN 3: Oh.

WOMAN 3: I have allergies. (*Pause.*) But still you . . .

WOMAN 1, 2, 3: . . . couldn't ask for a more . . .

20 WOMAN 1: Beautiful . . .

WOMAN 2: Wonderful . . .

WOMAN 3: Pretty . . .

WOMAN 1, 2, 3: day today.

MAN 1, 2: Would you like to go for a walk around the . . .

25 MAN 1: Lake.

MAN 2: Flower garden.

MAN 3: Wanna go to a movie?

WOMAN 1: Maybe in a minute.

WOMAN 2: I'd like to sit here for a few minutes.

30 WOMAN 3: Can we talk first?

MAN 1, 2, 3: OK.

ALL: So . . .

WOMAN 1, 2: I understand you work in . . .

WOMAN 1: . . . the health care . . .

35 WOMAN 2: . . . the music . . .

WOMAN 1, 2: industry.

WOMAN 3: I am so lonely.

MAN 1: Yes, I am a home health aid for the elderly.

MAN 2: Yes, I'm writing a book on jazz.

40 MAN 3: I . . . uh . . .

WOMAN 1, 2: That's . . .

WOMAN 1: Wonderful.

WOMAN 2: Exciting.

WOMAN 3: Please help me.

MAN 1, 2: So . . . 45

MAN 3: Uh . . .

MAN 1, 2: What do you do?

MAN 3: How can I help you?

WOMAN 1: Oh, I'm just an office manager for a small office.

WOMAN 2: I'm a computer consultant. 50

WOMAN 3: Just be real with me.

WOMAN 1, 2: But I really want to . . .

WOMAN 3: Be really, really, really, really, really real with me.

WOMAN 1: . . . work in TV.

WOMAN 2: . . . own a farm someday. 55

WOMAN 3: Unorchestrate your emotions to my song.

MAN 1: Interesting.

MAN 2: Great.

MAN 3: Wait a minute.

MAN 1: I have a friend . . . 60

MAN 2: I know someone . . .

MAN 3: Have you read that book . . . ?

MAN 1: Works in TV.

MAN 2: Who owns a farm.

MAN 3: (*Recalling title of book.*) Think It . . . 65

WOMAN 3: Say It . . .

MAN 3: Speak It . . .

MAN 3, WOMAN 3: Now! *The Interactive Guide to Kicking Your Inner Child's Ass.*

MAN 1: She says TV is . . .

MAN 2: He says farming is . . . 70

MAN 3: I love that book.

MAN 1, 2: a lot of work.

MAN 3: It changed my life.

MAN 1, 2: . . . but rewarding.

WOMAN 1: Yeah. 75

WOMAN 2: Yup.

WOMAN 3: It changed my life too. (*Pause.*) Before I read that book I was so polite all the time. I was into . . .

WOMAN 3, MAN 3: Pseudo-Ultra-Judo-Fake Bonding.

WOMAN 3: Like it says in the book! I would have met you here today and just had a . . .

WOMAN 1, 2: So . . . 80

WOMAN 3: shallow conversation . . .

WOMAN 1, 2: It must be really rewarding to . . .

WOMAN 3: . . . about nothing.

WOMAN 1: . . . help the elderly . . .

WOMAN 2: . . . write about jazz. 85

WOMAN 3: But because of that book I feel strong enough to say to you: HELP ME!

Man 1, 2: It's so rewarding.

Man 1: I couldn't even begin to tell you.

Man 2: Jazz is my life.

90 **Man 3:** I will help you. What's wrong?

Woman 3: You see I'm not really over my . . .

Lights up on Man 1.

Woman 3: . . . last boyfriend.

Man 1: (*to* Woman 1) Some people get depressed when they look at the elderly.

Woman 3: He told me he was a home health aide for the elderly.

95 **Man 1:** (*to* Woman 1) But I don't. I feel hopeful . . .

Woman 3: But he only had one patient.

Man 1: . . . to have lived so long and experienced so much.

Woman 3: . . . his mother.

Man 1: (*to* Woman 1) It's a beautiful thing.

100 **Woman 1:** (*to* Man 1) Wow . . .

Man 3: Ewwwww.

Woman 3: Every time I would go over to his house, he would excuse himself every few minutes and go into another room. I just thought he had a bladder problem, but them one day I heard someone talking. I asked him (*to* Man 1.) who was that? . . .

Man 1: (*to* Woman 3) No one. You're hearing things. I live alone.

Woman 3: (*to* Man 3) But one day, I tiptoed behind him and peeked in the room. There was an old woman in a chair. He was calling her . . .

105 **Man 1:** Momma.

Woman 3: (*to* Man 3) I was very understanding. (*to* Man 1.) Oh, honey. Is this your mother? You take care of her too? That's nothing to be ashamed of. It's sweet. Your mother and all those others too. (*to* Man 3.) Then this woman, who is like so wrinkled a prune would stare in awe, says . . .

Woman 2: (*as mother*) Who are you! Who are you! I'm his one and only patient! His one and only! Get out! I'm the only one who gets her feet shaved around here. You're stepping on my toenail clippings! GET OUT! GET OUT!

Woman 3: Two days later he was like:

Man 1: (*to* Woman 3) I tried to be a home health worker, but Momma takes up all of my time. I love Momma, I love Momma, I love Momma. I do. Before that she and Grandma took up all of my time. I love Grandma, I love Grandma, I love Grandma. I do. But Grandma is dead now, and soon . . . Momma will be dead too. Then you can move into my house, and we'll have kids. Two boys and two girls. We'll teach them to be good little home health workers, too, cause, like Momma says, by the time we grow old our Social Security check won't buy us a cup of milk.

110 **Woman 1:** (*to* Man 1) You are so noble.

Man 3: Ew.

Woman 3: But still I think of him.

MAN 3: I know what you mean. I'm still hung up on my girl-friend too.

Lights up on Woman 2.

MAN 3: She said she wanted to be a farmer.
WOMAN 2: (*to* Man 2) I know it's a lot of work, but to be out in the fresh   115
country air . . .
MAN 3: . . . a chicken farmer.
WOMAN 2: (*to* Man 2) Communing with nature every day. Feeding the land.
Feeding the chickens.
MAN 3: But that is not all she wanted to do with those chickens.

Man 3 *squirms in his chair.*

WOMAN 2: (*to* Man 3) What's wrong with you?
MAN 3: I've got hay in my butt. God, that is the last time we go to a farm.   120
WOMAN 2: What? No!
MAN 3: Yes, it is.
WOMAN 2: But farming is my life.
MAN 3: But you don't own a farm, I don't understand why we have to sneak in
other people's barns to make love all the time. At first, it was exciting, but
now it's just weird.
WOMAN 2: You're so conventional.   125
MAN 3: I am not . . . I . . .

There is the sound of a chicken.

MAN 3: What was that?

Sound of a chicken.

WOMAN 2: Nothing.
MAN 3: Yes, it was.

Sound of a chicken.

MAN 3: It sounded like . . . (*to* Woman 3.) I opened the door and there were   130
all these chickens. Chickens everywhere.
MAN 3: (*to* Woman 2) What the . . .
WOMAN 2: Don't touch them. I love them. See how soft and gentle.
MAN 3: You can't . . . We can't keep chickens in the apartment.
WOMAN 2: Quiet. Don't yell in front of them. (*Pause.*) See, they are sweet and
gentle. Like kittens with feathers. But sexy. Very sexy. That clucking drives
me wild. Please just touch the chickens, baby! Touch the chickens!
MAN 2: (*to* Woman 2) I love nature too.   135
WOMAN 3: (*to* Man 3) Yuuccch.
MAN 3: What is wrong with us?
WOMAN 3: For me it has been a pattern. A pattern of unhealthy relationships.
The other guy I dated.

Light up on Man 2.

Woman 3: A die-hard jazz lover.

140 **Man 2:** (*to* Woman 2) Jazz is truly the only great American art form.

Woman 3: So I thought.

Man 2: In its rhythms we hear America. In its tunes we see ourselves.

Woman 3: I studied everything I could about jazz just so I could get close to him. I bought thousands of recordings. One day I bought him this rare Miles Davis recording. It took me six months to find it. I was going to surprise him and slip it in his record collection. I must have hit some secret door because . . . (*to* Man 2.) Honey . . .

Man 2: Yeah, baby.

145 **Woman 3:** Uh . . . I wanted to give you this. (*Hands him CD.*)

Man 2: Oh wow. Miles Davis session number 73. Oh wow baby, thank you, thank you.

Woman 3: Uh-huh. Um . . . I was going to put it in with your other records . . . and surprise you.

Man 2: Uh-huh. This is perfect.

Woman 3: And I found this.

Woman 3 *shows him CD.*

150 **Man 2:** Oh . . . Uh . . . Yeah, you know. I was holding that for my . . . mother. My mother . . .

Woman 3: (*to* Man 3) A Yanni CD.

Woman 3: (*to* Man 2) No, you weren't.

She dumps a whole batch of CDs at his feet.

Woman 3: Yanni, John Tesh, Enya, Celine Dion, Phil Collins . . . What is this about? I thought you were cool.

Man 2: Hey! Be careful. You're going to scratch them. (*Pause.*) One night I couldn't sleep, all right. So, I turned on the radio. They were playing "Desert Siren' by Yanni. (*He hums tune.*) It was so relaxing. (*He hums tune.*) So calming. (*He hums tune.*) Yanni is beautiful. (*He hums tune.*) Someday he'll be appreciated. (*He hums tune.*) Someday . . . (*He hums*) Someday.

155 **Woman 2:** (*to* Man 2) I want you to teach me everything you know about music.

Man 3: (*shudders*) John Tesh. Ewww.

Woman 3: So, you see. It must be me.

Man 3: No, no, no. Don't assume that. I dated this woman.

Woman 1: (*to* Man 1) I know TV is supposed to be this vast wasteland.

160 **Man 3:** Who wanted to work in TV.

Woman 1: (*to* Man 1) But I think it is a powerful and effective medium . . .

Man 3: So, she watched a lot of TV.

Woman 1: (*to* Man 1) . . . to communicate and express ideas.

Man 3: But then I noticed she began to watch only one program.

Theme from The Jeffersons plays.

165 **Man 3:** (*to* Woman 1) Honey, do we have to watch . . .

Woman 1: Shhhhh.

Man 3: But you've seen this episode a hundred times already.

WOMAN 1: Shhhhh.

MAN 3: All day and night. *The Jeffersons*. She would tape the show and watch it in fast forward and reverse.

WOMAN 1: (*pointing to TV*) See! Right there! Right there!   170

MAN 3: What?

WOMAN 1: Lionel just said . . . Pop Taht Tuoba Erus Ton Mi.

MAN 3: What?

WOMAN 1: He said: Pop Taht Tuoba Erus Ton Mi.

MAN 3: What? What are you saying?   175

WOMAN 1: Oh, I have a little language for Lionel. You see, I believe he's giving me a message, so I speak his lines backwards so I can understand.

MAN 3: Giving you a message?

WOMAN 1: Yes. Us. Us a message. To the world.

MAN 3: Uh . . .

WOMAN 1: Did you know Lionel created the show *Good Times* . . .   180

MAN 3: Uh . . . Honey . . .

WOMAN 1: And the man that replaced him on the show was his brother. His very own brother.

MAN 3: Honey, I . . .

WOMAN 1: But he's gone now. No word of him since 1979. I can't find him. But I will. I know I will. Pop Taht Tuobs Erus Ton Mi Pop. Taht Tuoba Erus Ton Mi Pop. Taht Tuoba Erus Ton Mi.

MAN 1: (*to* Woman 1) I've never thought of TV that way before.   185

WOMAN 3: (*to* Man 3) I'll never watch. *The Jeffersons* again. (*Pause.*) In honor of you.

MAN 3: Listen, I have to tell you . . .

MAN 1, 2, 3: I really like you.

MAN 1: You're wonderful . . .

MAN 2: . . . Terrific . . .   190

MAN 3: You've touched my inner song and let me tell you baby, it ain't playing Yanni.

Girls smile and laugh in unison.

WOMAN 1, 2, 3: Well . . .

WOMAN 1: I think you're great . . .

WOMAN 2: Fantastic. . .

WOMAN 3: You've touched my inner song . . .   195

WOMAN 1, 2, 3: . . . too.

MAN 1, 2, 3: I would love to . . .

MAN 1: Get to know you.

MAN 2: Spend some more time with you.

MAN 3: Coordinate your soul with mine.   200

WOMAN 1, 2, 3: (*they all sigh*) Great!

MAN 1, 2: But first I have to . . .

MAN 1: Stop at home for a minute.

MAN 2: Stop by the record store.

MAN 3: My afternoon is completely free.   205

WOMAN 1: Oh, I suppose you have to check on your patients?
WOMAN 2: Are you buying the latest jazz CD?
MAN 1, 2: Uh . . . Yeah . . . Yeah . . .
WOMAN 1, 2: Oh, that works out because I have to . . .
210 WOMAN 1: Set my VCR to record a program.
WOMAN 2: Stop by this new chicken farm.
WOMAN 3: My afternoon is free too.
WOMAN 1, 2, MAN 1, 2: So, I'll meet you later then.
ALL: Great!
215 WOMAN 1, 2, 3: But I tell you, I just can't believe someone like you . . .
WOMAN 1: . . . isn't taken . . .
WOMAN 2: . . . hasn't been snatched up yet . . .
WOMAN 3: . . . is free . . .
MAN 1, 2, 3: Well, I can't believe you are . . .
220 MAN 1: . . . available . . .
MAN 2: . . . not married . . .
MAN 3: . . . unattached.
ALL: There are just so many crazy people out there.

They all laugh.

WOMAN 1: I'm telling you . . .
225 MAN 1: You got that right.
WOMAN 2: Tell me about it . . .
MAN 2: I could tell you stories.
WOMAN 3: Hell, between the two of us . . .
MAN 3: I guess we dated every crazy person out there.
230 WOMAN 1, 2: My last boyfriend . . .
MAN 1, 2: . . . girlfriend . . .

Lights up on Man 3 *and* Woman 3.

MAN 1, 2, WOMAN 1, 2: . . . was a pathological liar!

They gasp in disbelief.

WOMAN 1: Really?
MAN 1: No kidding.
235 WOMAN 2: What are the chances of that?
MAN 2: It really is a small world. (*Pause.*) A small world.

Reading and Reacting

1. What information do the stage directions for *Small World* provide? Should Wilson have provided more information? For example, should she have specified the characters's ages or described their appearance and dress?
2. If you were designing a set for *Small World*, what would it look like? What props would you use? Where would you place the characters?
3. How does Wilson use lighting? Sound effects? What do these elements contribute to the play?

4. The opening exchange of dialogue tells us that Wilson's characters are named Stacy, Bob, Lucy, Bill, Alice, and Tim. Why do you suppose she selected these names? Why doesn't she refer to them by name?

5. Why does Wilson have the characters speak simultaneously? What impression do you think she is trying to convey? Is she successful?

6. Are all the characters equally important? Or, is one character (or one couple) more important than the others? How can you tell?

7. As the play progresses, various interconnections between characters become apparent. Identify some of these interconnections. Why are they important?

8. Do you see the play's last line — "It's really a small world. (*Pause.*) A small world" — as ironic? Why or why not?

9. At the end of the play, Man 1 and 2 and Woman 1 and 2 each say that their last relationship was with "a pathological liar." Are any of the characters in the play lying to themselves, or to others? How do you know?

10. What comment do you think *Small World* is making about dating? About relationships? About people in general?

11. **JOURNAL ENTRY** How accurate is the dating scenario Wilson presents? In terms of your own experience, is it at all familiar?

12. **CRITICAL PERSPECTIVE** In a 2005 interview about her play *The Story*, Wilson said, "I guess I am a political playwright because I like to write about social issues, but I try to avoid being didactic at all cost. That is deadly."

What social issue is Wilson writing about in *Small World*? Do you think *Small World* in any sense is a political play? Explain.

Related Works: "The Story of an Hour" (p. 197), "Shiloh" (p. 316), "Nice Car, Camille" (p. 862), "Cinderella" (p. 882), "Oh, my love is like a red, red rose" (p. 944), "Fox Trot Fridays" (p. 1170), "Barbie Doll" (p. 1211), *Beauty* (p. 1308), *The Stronger* (p. 1520)

MILCHA SANCHEZ-SCOTT (1955–) is a Los Angeles–based writer of plays that include *Dog Lady* and *The Cuban Swimmer,* both one-act plays (1984); *Roosters,* published in *On New Ground: Contemporary Hispanic American Plays* (1987); and *Stone Wedding,* produced at the Los Angeles Theater Center (1988). Also produced by the Los Angeles Theater Center was her play *Carmen,* adapted from Georges Bizet's opera of the same title.

Born in Bali, Sanchez-Scott is the daughter of an Indonesian mother and a Colombian-Mexican father. Her early childhood was spent in Mexico, South America, and Britain; her family moved to San Diego when she was fourteen.

Writing in *Time* magazine, William A. Henry observes that the visionary or hallucinatory elements in Sanchez-Scott's plays derive from the Latin American "magic realism" tradition of Jorge Luis Borges and Gabriel García Márquez. For example, Henry notes that in *Roosters,* what seems "a straightforward depiction of the life of farmlands gives way to mysterious visitations, symbolic cockfights enacted by dancers, virginal girls wearing wings, archetypal confrontations between father and son."

In 1984, the New York production of *The Cuban Swimmer* was noteworthy for an ingeniously designed set that realistically re-created on stage Pacific Ocean waves, a helicopter, and a boat. According to the *New York Times,* "The audience [could] almost feel the resisting tides and the California oil slick . . . represented by a watery-blue floor and curtain." Jeannette Mirabel, as the Cuban swimmer, made an "auspicious" debut in the play, according to the *Times:* "In a tour de force of balletic movements, she [kept] her arms fluttering in the imaginary waters throughout the play."

Cultural Context In 1980, in the wake of numerous incidences of dissent and rebellion, Fidel Castro deported a large number of Cubans and allowed many others to leave. In the resulting exodus, which became known as the Mariel boatlift, more than 120,000 undocumented Cubans arrived in Florida, placing tremendous strain on United States facilities. In 1984, an agreement was made between the two countries that limited the number of Cuban immigrants to 20,000 per year. Over time, the United States relaxed this quota, but the resulting abundance of refugees prompted the US government to reinstate it in the mid-1990s. In 1996, the Cuban Adjustment Act was passed, stating that Cubans who reached dry land would be allowed to become permanent residents of the United States, but those who were intercepted while still at sea would be returned to Cuba. In 1999, the plight of Cuban refugees was reflected in the story of Elian Gonzalez, a six-year-old boy who was found clinging to an inner tube but was later returned to Cuba in accordance with the 1996 act.

The Cuban Swimmer (1984)

CHARACTERS

Margarita Suárez, *the swimmer*   **Abuela,** *her grandmother*
Eduardo Suárez, *her father, the coach*   **Voice of Mel Munson**
Simón Suárez, *her brother*   **Voice of Mary Beth White**
Aída Suárez, *her mother*   **Voice of Radio Operator**

SETTING

The Pacific Ocean between San Pedro and Catalina Island.

TIME

Summer.

Live conga drums can be used to punctuate the action of the play.

SCENE 1

Pacific Ocean. Midday. On the horizon, in perspective, a small boat enters upstage left, crosses to upstage right, and exits. Pause. Lower on the horizon, the same boat, in larger perspective, enters upstage right, crosses and exits upstage left. Blackout.

SCENE 2

Pacific Ocean. Midday. The swimmer, Margarita Suárez, is swimming. On the boat following behind her are her father, Eduardo Suárez, holding a megaphone, and Simón, her brother, sitting on top of the cabin with his shirt off, punk sunglasses on, binoculars hanging on his chest.

EDUARDO: *(leaning forward, shouting in time to Margarita's swimming)* Uno, dos, uno, dos. Y uno, dos . . . keep your shoulders parallel to the water.

SIMÓN: I'm gonna take these glasses off and look straight into the sun.

EDUARDO: *(through megaphone)* Muy bien, muy bien . . . but punch those arms in, baby.

SIMÓN: *(looking directly at the sun through binoculars)* Come on, come on, zap me. Show me something. *(He looks behind at the shoreline and ahead at the sea.)* Stop! Stop, Papi! Stop!

Aída Suárez and Abuela, the swimmer's mother and grandmother, enter running from the back of the boat.

AÍDA and **ABUELA:** Qué? Qué es?   5

AÍDA: Es un shark?

EDUARDO: Eh?

ABUELA: Que es un shark dicen?

Eduardo blows whistle. Margarita looks up at the boat.

SIMÓN: No, Papi, no shark, no shark. We've reached the halfway mark.

ABUELA: *(looking into the water)* A dónde está?   10

AÍDA: It's not in the water.

ABUELA: Oh, no? Oh, no?

AÍDA: No! A poco do you think they're gonna have signs in the water to say you are halfway to Santa Catalina? No. It's done very scientific. A ver, hijo, explain it to your grandma.

SIMÓN: Well, you see, Abuela — *(He points behind.)* There's San Pedro. *(He points ahead.)* And there's Santa Catalina. Looks halfway to me.

Abuela shakes her head and is looking back and forth, trying to make the decision, when suddenly the sound of a helicopter is heard.

ABUELA: *(looking up)* Virgencita de la Caridad del Cobre. Qué es eso?   15

Sound of helicopter gets closer. Margarita looks up.

MARGARITA: Papi, Papi!

A small commotion on the boat, with Everybody pointing at the helicopter above. Shadows of the helicopter fall on the boat. Simón looks up at it through binoculars.

Papi — qué es? What is it?

EDUARDO: *(through megaphone)* Uh . . . uh . . . uh, un momentico . . . mi hija. . . . Your papi's got everything under control, understand? Uh . . . you just keep stroking. And stay . . . uh . . . close to the boat.

SIMÓN: Wow, *Papi!* We're on TV, man! Holy Christ, we're all over the fucking U.S.A.! It's Mel Munson and Mary Beth White!

AÍDA: *Por Dios!* Simón, don't swear. And put on your shirt.

Aída fluffs her hair, puts on her sunglasses and waves to the helicopter. Simón leans over the side of the boat and yells to Margarita.

20 SIMÓN: Yo, Margo! You're on TV, man.

EDUARDO: Leave your sister alone. Turn on the radio.

MARGARITA: *Papi! Qué está pasando?*

ABUELA: *Que es la televisión dicen?* (*She shakes her head.*) *Porque como yo no puedo ver nada sin mis espejuelos.*

Abuela rummages through the boat, looking for her glasses. Voices of Mel Munson and Mary Beth White are heard over the boat's radio.

MEL'S VOICE: As we take a closer look at the gallant crew of *La Havana* . . . and there . . . yes, there she is . . . the little Cuban swimmer from Long Beach, California, nineteen-year-old Margarita Suárez. The unknown swimmer is our Cinderella entry . . . a bundle of tenacity, battling her way through the choppy, murky waters of the cold Pacific to reach the Island of Romance . . . Santa Catalina . . . where should she be the first to arrive, two thousand dollars and a gold cup will be waiting for her.

25 AÍDA: Doesn't even cover our expenses.

ABUELA: *Qué dice?*

EDUARDO: Shhhh!

MARY BETH'S VOICE: This is really a family effort, Mel, and—

MEL'S VOICE: Indeed it is. Her trainer, her coach, her mentor, is her father, Eduardo Suárez. Not a swimmer himself, it says here, Mr. Suárez is head usher of the Holy Name Society and the owner-operator of Suárez Treasures of the Sea and Salvage Yard. I guess it's one of those places—

30 MARY BETH'S VOICE: If I might interject a fact here, Mel, assisting in this swim is Mrs. Suárez, who is a former Miss Cuba.

MEL'S VOICE: And a beautiful woman in her own right. Let's try and get a closer look.

Helicopter sound gets louder. Margarita, frightened, looks up again.

MARGARITA: *Papi!*

EDUARDO: (*through megaphone*) *Mi hija,* don't get nervous . . . it's the press. I'm handling it.

AÍDA: I see how you're handling it.

35 EDUARDO: (*through megaphone*) Do you hear? Everything is under control. Get back into your rhythm. Keep your elbows high and kick and kick and kick and kick . . .

ABUELA: (*finds her glasses and puts them on*) *Ay sí, es la televisión* . . . (*She points to helicopter.*) *Qué lindo mira* . . . (*She fluffs her hair, gives a big wave.*) *Aló América! Viva mi Margarita, viva todo los Cubanos en los Estados Unidos!*

Aída: *Ay por Dios*, Cecilia, the man didn't come all this way in his helicopter
to look at you jumping up and down, making a fool of yourself.

Abuela: I don't care. I'm proud.

Aída: He can't understand you anyway.

Abuela: *Viva . . . (She stops.) Simón, comó se dice viva?*   40

Simón: Hurray.

Abuela: Hurray for *mi Margarita y* for all the Cubans living *en* the United
States, *y un abrazo . . . Simón, abrazo . . .*

Simón: A big hug.

Abuela: *Sí,* a big hug to all my friends in Miami, Long Beach, Union City,
except for my son Carlos, who lives in New York in sin! He lives . . .
(she crosses herself) in Brooklyn with a Puerto Rican woman in sin! *No
decente . . .*

Simón: Decent.   45

Abuela: Carlos, *no decente.* This family, *decente.*

Aída: Cecilia, *por Dios.*

Mel's Voice: Look at that enthusiasm. The whole family has turned out
to cheer little Margarita on to victory! I hope they won't be too
disappointed.

Mary Beth's Voice: She seems to be making good time, Mel.

Mel's Voice: Yes, it takes all kinds to make a race. And it's a testimonial   50
to the all-encompassing fairness . . . the greatness of this, the Wrigley
Invitational Women's Swim to Catalina, where among all the professionals
there is still room for the amateurs . . . like these, the simple people we see
below us on the ragtag *La Havana*, taking their long-shot chance to victory.
Vaya con Dios!

*Helicopter sound fading as family, including Margarita, watch silently. Static as Simón
turns radio off. Eduardo walks to bow of boat, looks out on the horizon.*

Eduardo: *(to himself)* Amateurs.

Aída: Eduardo, that person insulted us. Did you hear, Eduardo? That he called
us a simple people in a ragtag boat? Did you hear . . . ?

Abuela: *(clenching her fist at departing helicopter) Mal-Rayo los parta!*

Simón: *(same gesture)* Asshole!

Aída follows Eduardo as he goes to side of boat and stares at Margarita.

Aída: This person comes in his helicopter to insult your wife, your family, your   55
daughter . . .

Margarita: *(pops her head out of the water)* Papi?

Aída: Do you hear me, Eduardo? I am not simple.

Abuela: *Sí.*

Aída: I am complicated.

Abuela: *Sí, demasiada complicada.*   60

Aída: Me and my family are not so simple.

Simón: Mom, the guy's an asshole.

Abuela: *(shaking her fist at helicopter)* Asshole!

Aída: If my daughter was simple, she would not be in that water swimming.

65 **MARGARITA:** Simple? *Papi* . . . ?

AÍDA: *Ahora,* Eduardo, this is what I want you to do. When we get to Santa
     Catalina, I want you to call the TV station and demand an apology.

EDUARDO: *Cállete mujer! Aquí mando yo.* I will decide what is to be done.

MARGARITA: *Papi,* tell me what's going on.

EDUARDO: Do you understand what I am saying to you, Aída?

70 **SIMÓN:** *(leaning over side of boat, to Margarita)* Yo Margo! You know that Mel
     Munson guy on TV? He called you a simple amateur and said you didn't
     have a chance.

ABUELA: *(leaning directly behind Simón.) Mi hija, insultó a la familia.
     Desgraciado!*

AÍDA: *(leaning in behind Abuela)* He called us peasants! And your father is not
     doing anything about it. He just knows how to yell at me.

EDUARDO: *(through megaphone)* Shut up! All of you! Do you want to break her
     concentration? Is that what you are after? Eh?

Abuela, Aída, and Simón shrink back. Eduardo paces before them.

> Swimming is rhythm and concentration. You win a race *aquí. (Pointing to
> his head.)* Now . . . *(to Simón)* you, take care of the boat, Aída y Mama . . .
> do something. Anything. Something practical.

Abuela and Aída get on knees and pray in Spanish.

> Hija, give it everything, eh? . . . *por la familia. Uno . . . dos.* . . . You
> must win.

*Simón goes into cabin. The prayers continue as lights change to indicate bright sunlight,
later in the afternoon.*

SCENE 3

*Tableau for a couple of beats. Eduardo on bow with timer in one hand as he counts
strokes per minute. Simón is in the cabin steering, wearing his sunglasses, baseball cap
on backward. Abuela and Aída are at the side of the boat, heads down, hands folded,
still muttering prayers in Spanish.*

AÍDA and **ABUELA:** *(crossing themselves) En el nombre del Padre, del Hijo y del
     Espíritu Santo amén.*

EDUARDO: *(through megaphone)* You're stroking seventy-two!

SIMÓN: *(singing)* Mama's stroking, Mama's stroking seventy-two. . . .

EDUARDO: *(through megaphone)* You comfortable with it?

5 **SIMÓN:** *(singing)* Seventy-two, seventy-two, seventy-two for you.

AÍDA: *(looking at the heavens)* Ay, Eduardo, *ven acá,* we should be grateful that
     Nuestro Señor gave us such a beautiful day.

ABUELA: *(crosses herself) Si, gracias a Dios.*

EDUARDO: She's stroking seventy-two, with no problem. *(He throws a kiss to
     the sky.)* It's a beautiful day to win.

AÍDA: *Qué hermoso!* So clear and bright. Not a cloud in the sky. *Mira! Mira!*
     Even rainbows on the water . . . a sign from God.

SIMÓN: (*singing*) Rainbows on the water . . . you in my arms . . .   10

ABUELA and EDUARDO: (*Looking the wrong way.*) Dónde?

AÍDA: (*pointing toward Margarita*) There, dancing in front of Margarita, leading her on . . .

EDUARDO: Rainbows on . . . Ay coño! It's an oil slick! You . . . you . . . (*To Simón.*) Stop the boat. (*Runs to bow, yelling.*) Margarita! Margarita!

On the next stroke, Margarita comes up all covered in black oil.

MARGARITA: Papi! Papi . . . !

Everybody goes to the side and stares at Margarita, who stares back. Eduardo freezes.

AÍDA: Apúrate, Eduardo, move . . . what's wrong with you . . . no me oíste, get   15
my daughter out of the water.

EDUARDO: (*softly*) We can't touch her. If we touch her, she's disqualified.

AÍDA: But I'm her mother.

EDUARDO: Not even by her own mother. Especially by her own mother. . . . You always want the rules to be different for you, you always want to be the exception. (*To Simón.*) And you . . . you didn't see it, eh? You were playing again?

SIMÓN: Papi, I was watching . . .

AÍDA: (*interrupting*) Pues, do something Eduardo. You are the big coach,   20
the monitor.

SIMÓN: Mentor! Mentor!

EDUARDO: How can a person think around you? (*He walks off to bow, puts head in hands.*)

ABUELA: (*looking over side*) Mira como todos los little birds are dead. (*She crosses herself.*)

AÍDA: Their little wings are glued to their sides.

SIMÓN: Christ, this is like the La Brea tar pits.   25

AÍDA: They can't move their little wings.

ABUELA: Esa niña tiene que moverse.

SIMÓN: Yeah, Margo, you gotta move, man.

Abuela and Simón gesture for Margarita to move. Aída gestures for her to swim.

ABUELA: Anda niña, muévete.

AÍDA: Swim, hija, swim or the aceite will stick to your wings.   30

MARGARITA: Papi?

ABUELA: (*taking megaphone*) Your papi say "move it!"

Margarita with difficulty starts moving.

ABUELA, AÍDA AND SIMÓN: (*laboriously counting*) Uno, dos . . . uno, dos . . . anda . . . uno, dos.

EDUARDO: (*running to take megaphone from Abuela*) Uno, dos . . .

Simón races into cabin and starts the engine. Abuela, Aída and Eduardo count together.

SIMÓN: (*looking ahead*) Papi, it's over there!   35

EDUARDO: Eh?

SIMÓN: *(pointing ahead and to the right)* It's getting clearer over there.
EDUARDO: *(through megaphone)* Now pay attention to me. Go to the right.

Simón, Abuela, Aída and Eduardo all lean over side. They point ahead and to the right, except Abuela, who points to the left.

FAMILY: *(shouting together)* Para yá! Para yá!

Lights go down on boat. A special light on Margarita, swimming through the oil, and on Abuela, watching her.

40   ABUELA: *Sangre de mi sangre,* you will be another to save us. En Bolondron, where your great-grandmother Luz Suárez was born, they say one day it rained blood. All the people, they run into their houses. They cry, they pray, *pero* your great-grandmother Luz she had *cojones* like a man. She run outside. She look straight at the sky. She shake her fist. And she say to the evil one, "Mira . . . *(beating her chest) coño, Diablo, aquí estoy si me quieres.*" And she open her mouth, and she drunk the blood.

Blackout
SCENE 4

Lights up on boat. Aída and Eduardo are on deck watching Margarita swim. We hear the gentle, rhythmic lap, lap, lap of the water, then the sound of inhaling and exhaling as Margarita's breathing becomes louder. Then Margarita's heartbeat is heard, with the lapping of the water and the breathing under it. These sounds continue beneath the dialogue to the end of the scene.

AÍDA: *Dios mío.* Look how she moves through the water. . . .
EDUARDO: You see, it's very simple. It is a matter of concentration.
AÍDA: The first time I put her in water she came to life, she grew before my eyes. She moved, she smiled, she loved it more than me. She didn't want my breast any longer. She wanted the water.
EDUARDO: And of course, the rhythm. The rhythm takes away the pain and helps the concentration.

Pause. Aída and Eduardo watch Margarita.

5   AÍDA: Is that my child or a seal. . . .
EDUARDO: Ah, a seal, the reason for that is that she's keeping her arms very close to her body. She cups her hands, and then she reaches and digs, reaches and digs.
AÍDA: To think that a daughter of mine . . .
EDUARDO: It's the training, the hours in the water. I used to tie weights around her little wrists and ankles.
AÍDA: A spirit, an ocean spirit, must have entered my body when I was carrying her.
10   EDUARDO: *(to Margarita)* Your stroke is slowing down.

Pause. We hear Margarita's heartbeat with the breathing under, faster now.

AÍDA: Eduardo, that night, the night on the boat . . .

EDUARDO: Ah, the night on the boat again . . . the moon was . . .

AÍDA: The moon was full. We were coming to America. . . . *Qué romantico.*

Heartbeat and breathing continue.

EDUARDO: We were cold, afraid, with no money, and on top of everything, you were hysterical, yelling at me, tearing at me with your nails. *(Opens his shirt, points to the base of his neck.)* Look, I still bear the scars . . . telling me that I didn't know what I was doing . . . saying that we were going to die. . . .

AÍDA: You took me, you stole me from my home . . . you didn't give me a chance to prepare. You just said we have to go now, now! Now, you said. You didn't let me take anything. I left everything behind. . . . I left everything behind.   15

EDUARDO: Saying that I wasn't good enough, that your father didn't raise you so that I could drown you in the sea.

AÍDA: You didn't let me say even a good-bye. You took me, you stole me, you tore me from my home.

EDUARDO: I took you so we could be married.

AÍDA: That was in Miami. But that night on the boat, Eduardo. . . . We were not married, that night on the boat.

EDUARDO: *No pasó nada!* Once and for all get it out of your head, it was cold, you hated me, and we were afraid. . . .   20

AÍDA: *Mentiroso!*

EDUARDO: A man can't do it when he is afraid.

AÍDA: Liar! You did it very well.

EDUARDO: I did?

AÍDA: *Sí.* Gentle. You were so gentle and then strong . . . my passion for you so deep. Standing next to you . . . I would ache . . . looking at your hands I would forget to breathe, you were irresistible.   25

EDUARDO: I was?

AÍDA: You took me into your arms, you touched my face with your fingertips . . . you kissed my eyes . . . *la esquina de la boca y* . . .

EDUARDO: *Sí, sí,* and then . . .

AÍDA: I look at your face on top of mine, and I see the lights of Havana in your eyes. That's when you seduced me.

EDUARDO: Shhh, they're gonna hear you.   30

Lights go down. Special on Aída.

AÍDA: That was the night. A woman doesn't forget those things . . . and later that night was the dream . . . the dream of a big country with fields of fertile land and big, giant things growing. And there by a green, slimy pond I found a giant pea pod and when I opened it, it was full of little, tiny baby frogs.

Aída crosses herself as she watches Margarita. We hear louder breathing and heartbeat.

MARGARITA: Santa Teresa. Little Flower of God, pray for me. San Martín de Porres, pray for me. Santa Rosa de Lima, *Virgencita de la Caridad del Cobre*, pray for me. . . . Mother pray for me.

SCENE 5

Loud howling of wind is heard, as lights change to indicate unstable weather, fog and mist. Family on deck, braced and huddled against the wind. Simón is at the helm.

AÍDA: Ay *Dios mío, qué viento.*

EDUARDO: *(through megaphone)* Don't drift out . . . that wind is pushing you out. *(To Simón.)* You! Slow down. Can't you see your sister is drifting out?

SIMÓN: It's the wind, *Papi.*

AÍDA: Baby, don't go so far. . . .

5   ABUELA: *(to heaven)* Ay *Gran Poder de Dios, quita este maldito viento.*

SIMÓN: Margo! Margo! Stay close to the boat.

EDUARDO: Dig in. Dig in hard. . . . Reach down from your guts and dig in.

ABUELA: *(to heaven)* Ay *Virgen de la Caridad del Cobre, por lo más tú quieres a pararla.*

AÍDA: *(putting her hand out, reaching for Margarita)* Baby, don't go far.

Abuela crosses herself. Action freezes. Lights get dimmer, special on Margarita. She keeps swimming, stops, starts again, stops, then, finally exhausted, stops altogether. The boat stops moving.

10   EDUARDO: What's going on here? Why are we stopping?

SIMÓN: *Papi,* she's not moving! Yo Margo!

The family all run to the side.

EDUARDO: *Hija!* . . . *Hijita!* You're tired, eh?

AÍDA: *Por supuesto* she's tired. I like to see you get in the water, waving your arms and legs from San Pedro to Santa Catalina. A person isn't a machine, a person has to rest.

SIMÓN: Yo, Mama! Cool out, it ain't fucking brain surgery.

15   EDUARDO: *(to Simón)* Shut up, you. *(Louder to Margarita.)* I guess your mother's right for once, huh? . . . I guess you had to stop, eh? . . . Give your brother, the idiot . . . a chance to catch up with you.

SIMÓN: *(clowning like Mortimer Snerd)* Dum dee dum dee dum ooops, ah shucks . . .

EDUARDO: I don't think he's Cuban.

SIMÓN: *(like Ricky Ricardo)* Oye, Lucy! I'm home! Ba ba lu!

EDUARDO: *(joins in clowning, grabbing Simón in a headlock)* What am I gonna do with this idiot, eh? I don't understand this idiot. He's not like us, Margarita. *(Laughing.)* You think if we put him into your bathing suit with a cap on his head . . . *(He laughs hysterically.)* You think anyone would know . . . huh? Do you think anyone would know? *(Laughs.)*

20   SIMÓN: *(vamping)* Ay, *mi amor.* Anybody looking for tits would know.

Eduardo slaps Simón across the face, knocking him down. Aída runs to Simón's aid. Abuela holds Eduardo back.

MARGARITA: *Mía culpa! Mía culpa!*

ABUELA: *Qué dices hija?*

MARGARITA: *Papi,* it's my fault, it's all my fault. . . . I'm so cold, I can't move. . . . I put my face in the water . . . and I hear them whispering . . . laughing at me. . . .

AÍDA: Who is laughing at you?

MARGARITA: The fish are all biting me . . . they hate me . . . they whisper   25
about me. She can't swim, they say. She can't glide. She has no grace. . . . Yellowtails, bonita, tuna, man-o'-war, snub-nose sharks, *los baracudas* . . . they all hate me . . . only the dolphins care . . . and sometimes I hear the whales crying . . . she is lost, she is dead. I'm so numb, I can't feel. *Papi! Papi!* Am I dead?

EDUARDO: *Vamos,* baby, punch those arms in. Come on . . . do you hear me?

MARGARITA: *Papi* . . . *Papi* . . . forgive me. . . .

All is silent on the boat. Eduardo drops his megaphone, his head bent down in dejection. Abuela, Aída, Simón, all leaning over the side of the boat. Simón slowly walks away.

AÍDA: *Mi hija, qué tienes?*

SIMÓN: Oh, Christ, don't make her say it. Please don't make her say it.

ABUELA: Say what? *Qué cosa?*   30

SIMÓN: She wants to quit, can't you see she's had enough?

ABUELA: *Mira, para eso. Esta niña* is turning blue.

AÍDA: *Oyeme, mi hija.* Do you want to come out of the water?

MARGARITA: *Papi?*

SIMÓN: *(to Eduardo)* She won't come out until *you* tell her.   35

AÍDA: Eduardo . . . answer your daughter.

EDUARDO: *Le dije* to concentrate . . . concentrate on your rhythm. Then the rhythm would carry her . . . ay, it's a beautiful thing, Aída. It's like yoga, like meditation, the mind over matter . . . the mind controlling the body . . . that's how the great things in the world have been done. I wish you . . . I wish my wife could understand.

MARGARITA: *Papi?*

SIMÓN: *(to Margarita)* Forget him.

AÍDA: *(imploring)* Eduardo, *por favor.*   40

EDUARDO: *(walking in circles)* Why didn't you let her concentrate? Don't you understand, the concentration, the rhythm is everything. But no, you wouldn't listen. *(Screaming to the ocean.)* Goddamn Cubans, why, God, why do you make us go everywhere with our families? *(He goes to back of boat.)*

AÍDA: *(opening her arms) Mi hija, ven,* come to *Mami. (Rocking.)* Your *mami* knows.

Abuela has taken the training bottle, puts it in a net. She and Simón lower it to Margarita.

SIMÓN: Take this. Drink it. *(As Margarita drinks, Abuela crosses herself.)*
ABUELA: *Sangre de mi sangre.*

Music comes up softly. Margarita drinks, gives the bottle back, stretches out her arms, as if on a cross. Floats on her back. She begins a graceful backstroke. Lights fade on boat as special lights come up on Margarita. She stops. Slowly turns over and starts to swim, gradually picking up speed. Suddenly as if in pain she stops, tries again, then stops in pain again. She becomes disoriented and falls to the bottom of the sea. Special on Margarita at the bottom of the sea.

45   **MARGARITA:** *Ya no puedo . . .* I can't. . . . A person isn't a machine . . . *es mi culpa . . .* Father forgive me . . . *Papi! Papi!* One, two. *Uno, dos. (Pause.) Papi! A dónde estás? (Pause.)* One, two, one, two. *Papi! Ay, Papi!* Where are you . . . ? Don't leave me. . . . Why don't you answer me? *(Pause. She starts to swim, slowly.) Uno, dos, uno, dos.* Dig in, dig in. *(Stops swimming.) Por favor, Papi! (Starts to swim again.)* One, two, one, two. Kick from your hip, kick from your hip. *(Stops swimming. Starts to cry.)* Oh God, please. . . . *(Pause.)* Hail Mary, full of grace . . . dig in, dig in . . . the Lord is with thee. . . . *(She swims to the rhythm of her Hail Mary.)* Hail Mary, full of grace . . . dig in, dig in . . . the Lord is with thee . . . dig in, dig in. . . . Blessed art thou among women. . . . *Mami,* it hurts. You let go of my hand. I'm lost. . . . And blessed is the fruit of thy womb, now and at the hour of our death. Amen. I don't want to die, I don't want to die.

Margarita is still swimming. Blackout. She is gone.

SCENE 6

Lights up on boat, we hear radio static. There is a heavy mist. On deck we see only black outline of Abuela with shawl over her head. We hear the voices of Eduardo, Aída, and Radio Operator.

EDUARDO'S VOICE: *La Havana!* Coming from San Pedro. Over.
RADIO OPERATOR'S VOICE: Right, DT6-6, you say you've lost a swimmer.
AÍDA'S VOICE: Our child, our only daughter . . . listen to me. Her name is Margarita Inez Suárez, she is wearing a black one-piece bathing suit cut high in the legs with a white racing stripe down the sides, a white bathing cap with goggles and her whole body covered with a . . . with a . . .
EDUARDO'S VOICE: With lanolin and paraffin.
5   **AÍDA'S VOICE:** *Sí . . . con lanolin and paraffin.*

More radio static. Special on Simón, on the edge of the boat.

SIMÓN: Margo! Yo Margo! *(Pause.)* Man don't do this. *(Pause.)* Come on. . . . Come on. . . . *(Pause.)* God, why does everything have to be so hard? *(Pause.)* Stupid. You know you're not supposed to die for this. Stupid. It's his dream and he can't even swim. *(Pause.)* Punch those arms in. Come home. Come home. I'm your little brother. Don't forget what Mama said. You're not supposed to leave me behind. *Vamos,* Margarita, take your little brother, hold his hand tight when you cross the street. He's so little. (*Pause.*) Oh, Christ, give us a sign. . . . I know! I know! Margo, I'll send you a message . . . like mental telepathy. I'll hold my breath, close my eyes, and I'll bring you home. (*He takes a deep breath; a few beats.*) This time I'll beep . . . I'll send out sonar signals like a dolphin. (*He imitates dolphin sounds.*)

The sound of real dolphins takes over from Simón, then fades into sound of Abuela saying the Hail Mary in Spanish, as full lights come up slowly.

SCENE 7

Eduardo coming out of cabin, sobbing, Aída holding him. Simón anxiously scanning the horizon. Abuela looking calmly ahead.

EDUARDO: *Es mi culpa, sí, es mi culpa.* (*He hits his chest.*)

AÍDA: *Ya, ya viejo* . . . it was my sin . . . I left my home.

EDUARDO: Forgive me, forgive me. I've lost our daughter, our sister, our granddaughter, *mi carne, mi sangre, mis ilusiones.* (*To heaven.*) *Dios mío,* take me . . . take me, I say . . . Goddammit, take me!

SIMÓN: I'm going in.

AÍDA AND EDUARDO: No!   5

EDUARDO: (*grabbing and holding Simón, speaking to heaven*) God, take me, not my children. They are my dreams, my illusions . . . and not this one, this one is my mystery . . . he has my secret dreams. In him are the parts of me I cannot see.

Eduardo embraces Simón. Radio static becomes louder.

AÍDA: I . . . I think I see her.

SIMÓN: No, it's just a seal.

ABUELA: (*looking out with binoculars*) *Mi nietacita, dónde estás?* (*She feels her heart.*) I don't feel the knife in my heart . . . my little fish is not lost.

Radio crackles with static. As lights dim on boat, Voices of Mel and Mary Beth are heard over the radio.

MEL'S VOICE: Tragedy has marred the face of the Wrigley Invitational   10
Women's Race to Catalina. The Cuban swimmer, little Margarita Suárez, has reportedly been lost at sea. Coast Guard and divers are looking for her as we speak. Yet in spite of this tragedy the race must go on because . . .

MARY BETH'S VOICE: (*interrupting loudly*) Mel!

MEL'S VOICE: (*startled*) What!

MARY BETH'S VOICE: Ah . . . excuse me, Mel . . . we have a winner. We've just received word from Catalina that one of the swimmers is just fifty yards from the breakers . . . it's, oh, it's . . . Margarita Suárez!

Special on family in cabin listening to radio.

MEL'S VOICE: What? I thought she died!

Special on Margarita, taking off bathing cap, trophy in hand, walking on the water.

15 MARY BETH'S VOICE: Ahh . . . unless . . . unless this is a tragic . . . No . . .
there she is, Mel. Margarita Suárez! The only one in the race wearing
a black bathing suit cut high in the legs with a racing stripe down
the side.

Family cheering, embracing.

SIMÓN: (*screaming*) Way to go, Margo!

MEL'S VOICE: This is indeed a miracle! It's a resurrection! Margarita Suárez,
with a flotilla of boats to meet her, is now walking on the waters, through
the breakers . . . onto the beach, with crowds of people cheering her on.
What a jubilation! This is a miracle!

Sound of crowds cheering. Lights and cheering sounds fade.

Blackout

Reading and Reacting

1. *The Cuban Swimmer* is a short play with a single setting. In what other locations could Sanchez-Scott have set the play's action? What might she
have gained or lost by adding these settings?

2. What lighting and sound effects does the play call for? In what way do these
effects advance the action of the play? In what way — if any — do they help
to communicate the play's theme?

3. Although most of the play is in English, the characters frequently speak
Spanish. What are the advantages and disadvantages of this use of Spanish?
How does the mixing of English and Spanish reflect one of the play's
themes?

4. What function do the voices of Mel and Mary Beth serve in the play?

5. What conflicts develop among the family members as the play proceeds?
How might these conflicts represent the problems of other immigrant
groups?

6. In what sense is Mel's final comment "This is a miracle!" true? In what sense
is it ironic?

7. Do you think this play comments on the position of women in American
culture? In Cuban-American culture? Explain.

8. Could this play be seen as an allegory? What is the value of seeing it in
this way?

9. During much of the play, Margarita is swimming in full view of the audience. Suggest three ways in which a director could convey this effect on
stage. Which way would you choose if you were directing the play?

10. As the headnote to the play explains, the 1984 New York production of
The Cuban Swimmer had an extremely realistic set. Could the play be
staged unrealistically, with the characters on a raised platform instead of

a boat? How do you think this kind of set would change the audience's reaction?

11. **JOURNAL ENTRY** Are you able to empathize with Margarita's struggle? What elements of the play make it easy, (or difficult) for you to do so?

12. **CRITICAL PERSPECTIVE** In a 1998 article in the *New York Times*, theater critic Brooks Atkinson said, "Nothing is better for good actors than a stage with no scenery."

How do you interpret Atkinson's comment? Do you think this remark could be applied to the staging of *The Cuban Swimmer*?

Related Works: "The Secret Lion" (p. 170), "The Water Faucet Vision" (p. 240), "Two Kinds" (p. 791), "How to Write the Great American Indian Novel" (p. 887), "Baca Grande" (p. 905), "Harlem" (p. 940), "La Florida" (p. 1232)

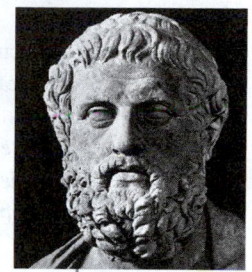

SOPHOCLES (496–406 B.C.), along with Aeschylus and Euripides, is one of the three great Greek tragic dramatists. He lived during the flowering and subsequent decline of fifth-century B.C. Athens — the high point of Greek civilization. Born as Greece struggled against the Persian Empire and moved to adopt democracy, he lived as an adult under Pericles during the golden age of Athens and died as it became clear that Athens would lose the Peloponnesian War. Sophocles was an active participant in the public life of Athens, serving as a collector of tribute from Athenian subjects and later as a general. He wrote at least 120 plays, but only seven have survived, including three plays about Oedipus: *Oedipus the King* (c. 430 B.C.), *Oedipus at Colonus* (411? B.C.), and *Antigone* (441 B.C.).

Oedipus the King, or *Oedipus Rex* (sometimes called *Oedipus the Tyrant*), was performed shortly after a great plague in Athens (probably in 429 or 425 B.C.) and as Athens was falling into decline. The play opens with an account of a plague in Thebes, Oedipus's kingdom. Over the years, *Oedipus the King* has attracted impressive critical attention, from Aristotle's use of it as a model for his definition of tragedy to Freud's use of its power as evidence of the validity of the "Oedipus complex."

Cultural Context During the period in which *Oedipus* was written, the Greeks were especially interested in the relationship between greatness and *hubris,* the excessive pride and ambition that leads to the downfall of a hero in classical tragedy. They were fascinated by the idea that hubris can bring destruction: that the same traits that can elevate a person to greatness can also cause his or her ruin. This theme recurs throughout classical literature and was especially relevant between 431 and 404 B.C., when the second Peloponnesian War (which Athens lost) was raging between Athens and Sparta. After a Spartan army invaded Attica in 431 B.C., the Athenians retreated behind the walls of their city while the Athenian fleet began raids. Between 430 and 428 B.C., a plague (which the Athenians believed was inflicted upon them by the gods) wiped out at least a quarter of the Athenian population. It is during this tumultuous time that Sophocles wrote of Oedipus and his troubles.

Oedipus the King* (c. 430 b.c.)

Translated by Thomas Gould

CHARACTERS

Oedipus,° the King of Thebes   **Tiresias,** a blind seer or prophet
Priest of Zeus, leader of the suppliants   **Jocasta,** the queen of Thebes
Creon, Oedipus's brother-in-law   **Messenger,** from Corinth, once a shepherd
Chorus, a group of Theban elders   **Herdsman,** once a servant of Laius
Choragos, spokesman of the Chorus   **Second Messenger,** a servant of Oedipus

MUTES

Suppliants, Thebans seeking Oedipus's help
Attendants, for the Royal Family
Servants, to lead Tiresias and Oedipus
Antigone, daughter of Oedipus and Jocasta
Ismene, daughter of Oedipus and Jocasta

The action takes place during the day in front of the royal palace in Thebes. There are two altars (left and right) on the proscenium and several steps leading down to the orchestra. As the play opens, Thebans of various ages who have come to beg Oedipus for help are sitting on these steps and in part of the orchestra. These suppliants are holding branches of laurel or olive which have strips of wool° wrapped around them. Oedipus enters from the palace (the central door of the skene).

PROLOGUE°

OEDIPUS: My children, ancient Cadmus'° newest care,
    why have you hurried to those seats, your boughs
    wound with the emblems of the suppliant?
    The city is weighed down with fragrant smoke,
5   with hymns to the Healer° and the cries of mourners.
    I thought it wrong, my sons, to hear your words
    through emissaries, and have come out myself,
    I, Oedipus, a name that all men know.

Oedipus addresses the Priest.

    Old man — for it is fitting that you speak
10   for all — what is your mood as you entreat me,
    fear or trust? You may be confident

---

*Note that individual lines are numbered in the following play. When a line is shared by two or more characters, it is counted as one line.   °*Oedipus:* The name, meaning "swollen foot," refers to the mutilation of Oedipus's feet by his father, Laius, before the infant was sent to Mount Cithaeron to be put to death by exposure. °*wool:* Branches wrapped with wool are traditional symbols of prayer or supplication.   °*Prologue:* The portion of the play containing the exposition, or explanation, of what has gone before and what is now happening.   °*Cadmus:* Oedipus's great-great-grandfather (although Oedipus does not know this) and the founder of Thebes.   °*Healer:* Apollo, god of prophecy, light, healing, justice, purification, and destruction.

that I'll do anything. How hard of heart
   if an appeal like this did not rouse my pity!
PRIEST: You, Oedipus, who hold the power here,
   you see our several ages, we who sit   15
   before your altars — some not strong enough
   to take long flight, some heavy in old age,
   the priests, as I of Zeus,° and from our youths
   a chosen band. The rest sit with their windings
   in the markets, at the twin shrines of Pallas,°   20
   and the prophetic embers of Ismēnos.°
   Our city, as you see yourself, is tossed
   too much, and can no longer lift its head
   above the troughs of billows red with death.
   It dies in the fruitful flowers of the soil,   25
   it dies in its pastured herds, and in its women's
   barren pangs. And the fire-bearing god°
   has swooped upon the city, hateful plague,
   and he has left the house of Cadmus empty.
   Black Hades° is made rich with moans and weeping.   30
   Not judging you an equal of the gods,
   do I and the children sit here at your hearth,
   but as the first of men, in troubled times
   and in encounters with divinities.
   You came to Cadmus' city and unbound   35
   the tax we had to pay to the harsh singer,°
   did it without a helpful word from us,
   with no instruction; with a god's assistance
   you raised up our life, so we believe.
   Again now Oedipus, our greatest power,   40
   we plead with you, as suppliants, all of us,
   to find us strength, whether from a god's response,
   or learned in some way from another man.

°*Zeus:* Father and king of the gods.   °*Pallas:* Athena, goddess of wisdom, arts, crafts, and war.
°*Ismēnos:* A reference to the temple of Apollo near the river Ismēnos in Thebes. Prophecies were made here by "reading" the ashes of the altar fires.   °*fire-bearing god:* Contagious fever viewed as a god.   °*Black Hades:* Refers both to the underworld where the spirits of the dead go and to the god of the underworld.
°*harsh singer:* The Sphinx, a monster with a woman's head, a lion's body, and wings. The "tax" from which Oedipus freed Thebes was the destruction of all the young men who failed to solve the Sphinx's riddle and were subsequently devoured. The Sphinx always asked the same riddle: "What goes on four legs in the morning, two legs at noon, and three legs in the evening, and yet is weakest when supported by the largest number of feet?" Oedipus discovered the correct answer — man, who crawls in infancy, walks in his prime, and uses a stick in old age — and thus ended the Sphinx's reign of terror. The Sphinx destroyed herself when Oedipus answered the riddle. Oedipus's reward for freeing Thebes of the Sphinx was the throne and the hand of the recently widowed Jocasta.

I know that the experienced among men
45   give counsels that will prosper best of all.
Noblest of men, lift up our land again!
Think also of yourself; since now the land
calls you its Savior for your zeal of old,
oh let us never look back at your rule
50   as men helped up only to fall again!
Do not stumble! Put our land on firm feet!
The bird of omen was auspicious then,
when you brought that luck; be that same man again!
The power is yours; if you will rule our country,
55   rule over men, not in an empty land.
A towered city or a ship is nothing
if desolate and no man lives within.

OEDIPUS: Pitiable children, oh I know, I know
the yearnings that have brought you. Yes, I know
60   that you are sick. And yet, though you are sick,
there is not one of you so sick as I.
For your affliction comes to each alone,
for him and no one else, but my soul mourns
for me and for you, too, and for the city.
65   You do not waken me as from a sleep,
for I have wept, bitterly and long,
tried many paths in the wanderings of thought,
and the single cure I found by careful search
I've acted on: I sent Menoeceus' son,
70   Creon, brother of my wife, to the Pythian
halls of Phoebus,° so that I might learn
what I must do or say to save this city.
Already, when I think what day this is,
I wonder anxiously what he is doing.
75   Too long, more than is right, he's been away.
But when he comes, then I shall be a traitor
if I do not do all that the god reveals.

PRIEST: Welcome words! But look, those men have signaled
that it is Creon who is now approaching!
80 OEDIPUS: Lord Apollo! May he bring Savior Luck,
a Luck as brilliant as his eyes are now!

PRIEST: His news is happy, it appears. He comes,
forehead crowned with thickly berried laurel.°

OEDIPUS: We'll know, for he is near enough to hear us.

Enter Creon along one of the parados.

°*Pythian halls . . . Phoebus:* The temple of Phoebus, Apollo's oracle or prophet at Delphi.   °*laurel:* Creon is wearing a garland of laurel leaves, sacred to Apollo.

Lord, brother in marriage, son of Menoeceus!   85
  What is the god's pronouncement that you bring?
CREON: It's good. For even troubles, if they chance
  to turn out well, I always count as lucky.
OEDIPUS: But what was the response? You seem to say
  I'm not to fear — but not to take heart either.   90
CREON: If you will hear me with these men present,
  I'm ready to report — or go inside.

Creon moves up the steps toward the palace.

OEDIPUS: Speak out to all! The grief that burdens me
  concerns these men more than it does my life.
CREON: Then I shall tell you what I heard from the god.   95
  The task Lord Phoebus sets for us is clear:
  drive out pollution sheltered in our land,
  and do not shelter what is incurable.
OEDIPUS: What is our trouble? How shall we cleanse ourselves?
CREON: We must banish or murder to free ourselves   100
  from a murder that blows storms through the city.
OEDIPUS: What man's bad luck does he accuse in this?
CREON: My Lord, a king named Laius ruled our land
  before you came to steer the city straight.
OEDIPUS: I know. So I was told — I never saw him.   105
CREON: Since he was murdered, you must raise your hand
  against the men who killed him with their hands.
OEDIPUS: Where are they now? And how can we ever find
  the track of ancient guilt now hard to read?
CREON: In our own land, he said. What we pursue,   110
  that can be caught; but not what we neglect.
OEDIPUS: Was Laius home, or in the countryside —
  or was he murdered in some foreign land?
CREON: He left to see a sacred rite, he said;
  He left, but never came home from his journey.   115
OEDIPUS: Did none of his party see it and report —
  someone we might profitably question?
CREON: They were all killed but one, who fled in fear,
  and he could tell us only one clear fact.
OEDIPUS: What fact? One thing could lead us on to more   120
  if we could get a small start on our hope.
CREON: He said that bandits chanced on them and killed him —
  with the force of many hands, not one alone.
OEDIPUS: How could a bandit dare so great an act —
  unless this was a plot paid off from here!   125
CREON: We thought of that, but when Laius was killed,
  we had no one to help us in our troubles.
OEDIPUS: It was your very kingship that was killed!

What kind of trouble blocked you from a search?

130   **CREON:** The subtle-singing Sphinx asked us to turn
    from the obscure to what lay at our feet.

  OEDIPUS: Then I shall begin again and make it plain.
    It was quite worthy of Phoebus, and worthy of you,
    to turn our thoughts back to the murdered man,

135   and right that you should see me join the battle
    for justice to our land and to the god.
    Not on behalf of any distant kinships,
    it's for myself I will dispel this stain.
    Whoever murdered him may also wish

140   to punish me — and with the selfsame hand.
    In helping him I also serve myself.
    Now quickly, children: up from the altar steps,
    and raise the branches of the suppliant!
    Let someone go and summon Cadmus' people:
    say I'll do anything.

Exit an Attendant along one of the parados.

145   Our luck will prosper
    if the god is with us, or we have already fallen.

  PRIEST: Rise, my children; that for which we came,
    he has himself proclaimed he will accomplish.
    May Phoebus, who announced this, also come

150   as Savior and reliever from the plague.

*Exit Oedipus and Creon into the palace. The Priest and the Suppliants exit left and right
along the parados. After a brief pause, the Chorus (including the Choragos) enters the
orchestra from the parados.*

PARADOS°

STROPHE 1°

  CHORUS: Voice from Zeus,° sweetly spoken, what are you
    that have arrived from golden
    Pytho° to our shining
    Thebes? I am on the rack, terror

155   shakes my soul.
    Delian Healer,° summoned by "iē!"
    I await in holy dread what obligation, something new

° *Parados:* A song sung by the Chorus on first entering.   ° *Strophe:* Probably refers to the direction in which the
Chorus danced while reciting specific stanzas. *Strophe* may have indicated dance steps to stage left, *antistrophe*
to stage right.   ° *Voice from Zeus:* A reference to Apollo's prophecy. Zeus taught Apollo how to prophesy
° *Pytho:* Delphi.   ° *Delian Healer:* Apollo.

or something back once more with the revolving years,
  you'll bring about for me.
Oh tell me, child of golden Hope,
  deathless Response!   160

ANTISTROPHE 1

I appeal to you first, daughter of Zeus,
  deathless Athena,
  and to your sister who protects this land,
Artemis,° whose famous throne is the whole circle   165
  of the marketplace,
and Phoebus, who shoots from afar: iō!
Three-fold defenders against death, appear!
If ever in the past, to stop blind ruin
  sent against the city,   170
you banished utterly the fires of suffering,
  come now again!

STROPHE 2

Ah! Ah! Unnumbered are the miseries
I bear. The plague claims all
our comrades. Nor has thought found yet a spear   175
by which a man shall be protected. What our glorious
earth gives birth to does not grow. Without a birth
from cries of labor
  do the women rise.
One person after another   180
  you may see, like flying birds,
faster than indomitable fire, sped
to the shore of the god that is the sunset.°

ANTISTROPHE 2

And with their deaths unnumbered dies the city.
Her children lie unpitied on the ground,   185
spreading death, unmourned.
Meanwhile young wives, and gray-haired mothers with them,
on the shores of the altars, from this side and that,
suppliants from mournful trouble,
  cry out their grief.   190
A hymn to the Healer shines,
  the flute a mourner's voice.
Against which, golden goddess, daughter of Zeus,
  send lovely Strength.

° *Artemis:* Goddess of virginity, childbirth, and hunting.   ° *god . . . sunset:* Hades, god of the underworld.

STROPHE 3

195   Causing raging Ares°— who,
        armed now with no shield of bronze,
     burns me, coming on amid loud cries—
     to turn his back and run from my land,
     with a fair wind behind, to the great
200   hall of Amphitritē,°
     or to the anchorage that welcomes no one,
     Thrace's troubled sea!
     If night lets something get away at last,
205   it comes by day.
     Fire-bearing god . . .
        you who dispense the might of lightning,
     Zeus! Father! Destroy him with your thunderbolt!

Enter Oedipus from the palace.

ANTISTROPHE 3

     Lycēan Lord!° From your looped
        bowstring, twisted gold,
210   I wish indomitable missiles might be scattered
     and stand forward, our protectors; also fire-bearing
     radiance of Artemis, with which
        she darts across the Lycian mountains.
     I call the god whose head is bound in gold,
215   with whom this country shares its name,
     Bacchus,° wine-flushed, summoned by "euoi!,"
        Maenads' comrade,
     to approach ablaze
        with gleaming . . .
220   pine, opposed to that god-hated god.

EPISODE 1°

OEDIPUS: I hear your prayer. Submit to what I say
     and to the labors that the plague demands
     and you'll get help and a relief from evils.
225   I'll make the proclamation, though a stranger
     to the report and to the deed. Alone,
     had I no key, I would soon lose the track.
     Since it was only later that I joined you,

°*Ares:* God of war and destruction.   °*Amphitritē:* The Atlantic Ocean.   °*Lycēan Lord:* Apollo.
°*Bacchus:* Dionysus, god of fertility and wine.   °*Episode:* The portion of ancient Greek plays that appears between choric songs.

to all the sons of Cadmus I say this:
whoever has clear knowledge of the man
who murdered Laius, son of Labdacus,   230
I command him to reveal it all to me —
nor fear if, to remove the charge, he must
accuse himself: his fate will not be cruel —
he will depart unstumbling into exile.
But if you know another, or a stranger,   235
to be the one whose hand is guilty, speak:
I shall reward you and remember you.
But if you keep your peace because of fear,
and shield yourself or kin from my command,
hear you what I shall do in that event: 240
I charge all in this land where I have throne
and power, shut out that man — no matter who—
both from your shelter and all spoken words,
nor in your prayers or sacrifices make
him partner, nor allot him lustral° water.   245
All men shall drive him from their homes: for he
is the pollution that the god-sent Pythian
response has only now revealed to me.
In this way I ally myself in war
with the divinity and the deceased.°   250
And this curse, too, against the one who did it,
whether alone in secrecy, or with others:
may he wear out his life unblest and evil!
I pray this, too: if he is at my hearth
and in my home, and I have knowledge of him,   255
may the curse pronounced on others come to me.
All this I lay to you to execute,
for my sake, for the god's, and for this land
now ruined, barren, abandoned by the gods.
Even if no god had driven you to it,   260
you ought not to have left this stain uncleansed,
the murdered man a nobleman, a king!
You should have looked! But now, since, as it happens,
It's I who have the power that he had once,
and have his bed, and a wife who shares our seed,   265
and common bond had we had common children
(had not his hope of offspring had bad luck—
but as it happened, luck lunged at his head);
because of this, as if for my own father,

° *lustral:* Purifying.   ° *the deceased:* Laius.

270   I'll fight for him, I'll leave no means untried,
     to catch the one who did it with his hand,
     for the son of Labdacus, of Polydōrus,
     of Cadmus before him, and of Agēnor.°
     This prayer against all those who disobey:
275   the gods send out no harvest from their soil,
     nor children from their wives. Oh, let them die
     victims of this plague, or of something worse.
     Yet for the rest of us, people of Cadmus,
     we the obedient, may Justice, our ally,
280   and all the gods, be always on our side!

CHORAGOS:° I speak because I feel the grip of your curse:
     the killer is not I. Nor can I point
     to him. The one who set us to this search,
     Phoebus, should also name the guilty man.

285 **OEDIPUS:** Quite right, but to compel unwilling gods—
     no man has ever had that kind of power.

CHORAGOS: May I suggest to you a second way?

OEDIPUS: A second or a third — pass over nothing!

CHORAGOS: I know of no one who sees more of what
290   Lord Phoebus sees than Lord Tiresias.
     My Lord, one might learn brilliantly from him.

OEDIPUS: Nor is this something I have been slow to do.
     At Creon's word I sent an escort — twice now!
295   I am astonished that he has not come.

CHORAGOS: The old account is useless. It told us nothing.

OEDIPUS: But tell it to me. I'll scrutinize all stories.

CHORAGOS: He is said to have been killed by travelers.

OEDIPUS: I have heard, but the one who did it no one sees.

300 **CHORAGOS:** If there is any fear in him at all,
     he won't stay here once he has heard that curse.

OEDIPUS: He won't fear words: he had no fear when he did it.

Enter Tiresias from the right, led by a Servant and two of Oedipus's Attendants.

CHORAGOS: Look there! There is the man who will convict him!
     It's the god's prophet they are leading here,
305   one gifted with the truth as no one else.

OEDIPUS: Tiresias, master of all omens—
     public and secret, in the sky and on the earth—
     your mind, if not your eyes, sees how the city
     lives with a plague, against which Thebes can find
310   no Saviour or protector, Lord, but you.
     For Phoebus, as the attendants surely told you,

° *son . . . Agēnor:* Refers to Laius by citing his genealogy.   ° *Choragos:* Leader of the Chorus and principal commentator on the play's action.

returned this answer to us: liberation
from the disease would never come unless
we learned without a doubt who murdered Laius—
put them to death, or sent them into exile.
Do not begrudge us what you may learn from birds   315
or any other prophet's path you know!
Care for yourself, the city, care for me,
care for the whole pollution of the dead!
We're in your hands. To do all that he can
to help another is man's noblest labor.   320

TIRESIAS: How terrible to understand and get
no profit from the knowledge! I knew this,
but I forgot, or I had never come.

OEDIPUS: What's this? You've come with very little zeal.

TIRESIAS: Let me go home! If you will listen to me,   325
You will endure your troubles better — and I mine.

OEDIPUS: A strange request, not very kind to the land
that cared for you — to hold back this oracle!

TIRESIAS: I see your understanding comes to you
inopportunely. So that won't happen to me . . .   330

OEDIPUS: Oh, by the gods, if you understand about this,
don't turn away! We're on our knees to you.

TIRESIAS: None of you understands! I'll never bring
my grief to light — I will not speak of yours.

OEDIPUS: You know and won't declare it! Is your purpose   335
to betray us and to destroy this land!

TIRESIAS: I will grieve neither of us. Stop this futile
cross-examination. I'll tell you nothing!

OEDIPUS: Nothing? You vile traitor! You could provoke
a stone to anger! You still refuse to tell?   340
Can nothing soften you, nothing convince you?

TIRESIAS: You blamed anger in me — you haven't seen.
The kind that lives with you, so you blame me.

OEDIPUS: Who wouldn't fill with anger, listening
to words like yours which now disgrace this city?   345

TIRESIAS: It will come, even if my silence hides it.

OEDIPUS: If it will come, then why won't you declare it?

TIRESIAS: I'd rather say no more. Now if you wish,
respond to that with all your fiercest anger!

OEDIPUS: Now I am angry enough to come right out   350
with this conjecture: you, I think, helped plot
the deed; you did it — even if your hand,
cannot have struck the blow. If you could see,
I should have said the deed was yours alone.

TIRESIAS: Is that right! Then I charge you to abide   355
by the decree you have announced: from this day

            say no word to either these or me,
            for you are the vile polluter of this land!

       OEDIPUS: Aren't you appalled to let a charge like that
360   come bounding forth? How will you get away?

       TIRESIAS: You cannot catch me. I have the strength of truth.

       OEDIPUS: Who taught you this? Not your prophetic craft!

       TIRESIAS: You did. You made me say it. I didn't want to.

       OEDIPUS: Say what? Repeat it so I'll understand.

365   TIRESIAS: I made no sense? Or are you trying me?

       OEDIPUS: No sense I understood. Say it again!

       TIRESIAS: I say you are the murderer you seek.

       OEDIPUS: Again that horror! You'll wish you hadn't said that.

       TIRESIAS: Shall I say more, and raise your anger higher?

370   OEDIPUS: Anything you like! Your words are powerless.

       TIRESIAS: You live, unknowing, with those nearest to you
            in the greatest shame. You do not see the evil.

       OEDIPUS: You won't go on like that and never pay!

       TIRESIAS: I can if there is any strength in truth.

375   OEDIPUS: In truth, but not in you! You have no strength,
            blind in your ears, your reason, and your eyes.

       TIRESIAS: Unhappy man! Those jeers you hurl at me
            before long all these men will hurl at you.

       OEDIPUS: You are the child of endless night; it's not
380   for me or anyone who sees to hurt you.

       TIRESIAS: It's not my fate to be struck down by you.
            Apollo is enough. That's his concern.

       OEDIPUS: Are these inventions Creon's or your own?

       TIRESIAS: No, your affliction is yourself, not Creon.

385   OEDIPUS: Oh success! — in wealth, kingship, artistry,
            in any life that wins much admiration —
            the envious ill will stored up for you!
            to get at my command, a gift I did not
            seek, which the city put into my hands,
390   my loyal Creon, colleague from the start,
            longs to sneak up in secret and dethrone me.
            So he's suborned this fortuneteller — schemer!
            deceitful beggar-priest! — who has good eyes
            for gains alone, though in his craft he's blind.
395   Where were your prophet's powers ever proved?
            Why, when the dog who chanted verse° was here,
            did you not speak and liberate this city?
            Her riddle wasn't for a man chancing by
            to interpret; prophetic art was needed,

°*dog . . . verse:* The Sphinx.

but you had none, it seems—learned from birds   400
or from a god. I came along, yes I,
Oedipus the ignorant, and stopped her—
by using thought, not augury from birds.
And it is I whom you now wish to banish,
so you'll be close to the Creontian throne.   405
You—and the plot's concocter—will drive out
pollution to your grief: you look quite old
or you would be the victim of that plot!

CHORAGOS: It seems to us that this man's words were said
in anger, Oedipus, and yours as well.   410
Insight, not angry words, is what we need,
the best solution to the god's response.

TIRESIAS: You are the king, and yet I am your equal
in my right to speak. In that I too am Lord.
for I belong to Loxias,° not you.   415
I am not Creon's man. He's nothing to me.
Hear this, since you have thrown my blindness at me:
Your eyes can't see the evil to which you've come,
nor where you live, nor who is in your house.
Do you know your parents? Not knowing, you are   420
their enemy, in the underworld and here.
A mother's and a father's double-lashing
terrible-footed curse will soon drive you out.
Now you can see, then you will stare into darkness.
What place will not be harbor to your cry,   425
or what Cithaeron° not reverberate
when you have heard the bride-song in your palace
to which you sailed? Fair wind to evil harbor!
Nor do you see how many other woes
will level you to yourself and to your children.   430
So, at my message, and at Creon, too,
splatter muck! There will never be a man
ground into wretchedness as you will be.

OEDIPUS: Am I to listen to such things from him!
May you be damned! Get out of here at once!   435
Go! Leave my palace! Turn around and go!

Tiresias begins to move away from Oedipus.

TIRESIAS: I wouldn't have come had you not sent for me.
OEDIPUS: I did not know you'd talk stupidity,
or I wouldn't have rushed to bring you to my house.
TIRESIAS: Stupid I seem to you, yet to your parents   440

°*Loxias:* Apollo.   °*Cithaeron:* The mountain on which Oedipus was to be exposed as an infant.

who gave you natural birth I seemed quite shrewd.

OEDIPUS: Who? Wait! Who is the one who gave me birth?

TIRESIAS: This day will give you birth,° and ruin too.

OEDIPUS: What murky, riddling things you always say!

445   **TIRESIAS:** Don't you surpass us all at finding out?

OEDIPUS: You sneer at what you'll find has brought me greatness.

TIRESIAS: And that's the very luck that ruined you.

OEDIPUS: I wouldn't care, just so I saved the city.

TIRESIAS: In that case I shall go. Boy, lead the way!

450   **OEDIPUS:** Yes, let him lead you off. Here, underfoot,
you irk me. Gone, you'll cause no further pain.

TIRESIAS: I'll go when I have said what I was sent for.
Your face won't scare me. You can't ruin me.
I say to you, the man whom you have looked for

455   as you pronounced your curses, your decrees
on the bloody death of Laius — he is here!
A seeming stranger, he shall be shown to be
a Theban born, though he'll take no delight
in that solution. Blind, who once could see,

460   a beggar who was rich, through foreign lands
he'll go and point before him with a stick.
To his beloved children, he'll be shown
a father who is also brother; to the one
who bore him, son and husband; to his father,

465   his seed-fellow and killer. Go in
and think this out; and if you find I've lied,
say then I have no prophet's understanding!

Exit Tiresias, led by a Servant. Oedipus exits into the palace with his Attendants.

<u>STASIMON 1°</u>
STROPHE 1

CHORUS: Who is the man of whom the inspired
rock of Delphi° said

470   he has committed the unspeakable
with blood-stained hands?
Time for him to ply a foot
mightier than those of the horses
of the storm in his escape;

475   upon him mounts and plunges the weaponed
son of Zeus,° with fire and thunderbolts,

° *This day . . . birth:* On this day, you will learn who your parents are.   ° *Stasimon:* Greek choral ode between episodes.   ° *rock of Delphi:* Apollo's oracle at Delphi.   ° *son of Zeus:* Apollo.

and in his train the dreaded goddesses
of Death, who never miss.

ANTISTROPHE 1

The message has just blazed,
    gleaming from the snows 480
of Mount Parnassus: we must track
    everywhere the unseen man.
He wanders, hidden by wild
forests, up through caves
    and rocks, like a bull, 485
anxious, with an anxious foot, forlorn.
He puts away from him the mantic° words come from earth's
navel,° at its center, yet these live
forever and still hover round him.

STROPHE 2

Terribly he troubles me, 490
    the skilled interpreter of birds!°
I can't assent, nor speak against him.
    Both paths are closed to me.
I hover on the wings of doubt,
    not seeing what is here nor what's to come. 495
What quarrel started in the house of Labdacus°
or in the house of Polybus,°
    either ever in the past
    or now, I never
heard, so that . . . with this fact for my touchstone 500
I could attack the public
    fame of Oedipus, by the side of the Labdaceans
an ally, against the dark assassination.

ANTISTROPHE 2

No, Zeus and Apollo
    understand and know things
mortal; but that another man
    can do more as a prophet than I can— 505
for that there is no certain test,
    though, skill to skill,

°*mantic:* prophetic.   °*earth's navel:* Delphi.   °*interpreter of birds:* Tiresias. The Chorus is troubled by his accusations.   °*house of Labdacus:* The line of Laius.   °*Polybus:* Oedipus's foster father.

510   one man might overtake another.
     No, never, not until
         I see the charges proved,
     when someone blames him shall I nod assent.
     For once, as we all saw, the winged maiden° came
515   against him: he was seen then to be skilled,
         proved, by that touchstone, dear to the people. So,
     never will my mind convict him of the evil.

<u>EPISODE 2</u>

Enter Creon from the right door of the skene and speaks to the Chorus.

CREON: Citizens, I hear that a fearful charge
     is made against me by King Oedipus!
520   I had to come. If, in this crisis,
     he thinks that he has suffered injury
     from anything that I have said or done,
     I have no appetite for a long life —
     bearing a blame like that! It's no slight blow
525   the punishment I'd take from what he said:
     it's the ultimate hurt to be called traitor
     by the city, by you, by my own people!
CHORAGOS: The thing that forced that accusation out
     could have been anger, not the power of thought.
530 **CREON:** But who persuaded him that thoughts of mine
     had led the prophet into telling lies?
CHORAGOS: I do not know the thought behind his words.
CREON: But did he look straight at you? Was his mind right
     when he said that I was guilty of this charge?
535 **CHORAGOS:** I have no eyes to see what rulers do.
     But here he comes himself out of the house.

Enter Oedipus from the palace.

OEDIPUS: What? You here? And can you really have
     the face and daring to approach my house
     when you're exposed as its master's murderer
540   and caught, too, as the robber of my kingship?
     Did you see cowardice in me, by the gods,
     or foolishness, when you began this plot?
     Did you suppose that I would not detect
     your stealthy moves, or that I'd not fight back?
545   It's your attempt that's folly, isn't it —
     tracking without followers or connections,
     kingship which is caught with wealth and numbers?

° *winged maiden:* The Sphinx.

CREON: Now wait! Give me as long to answer back!
　　Judge me for yourself when you have heard me!
OEDIPUS: You're eloquent, but I'd be slow to learn　　　　　　550
　　from you, now that I've seen your malice toward me.
CREON: That I deny. Hear what I have to say.
OEDIPUS: Don't you deny it! You are the traitor here!
CREON: If you consider mindless willfulness
　　a prized possession, you are not thinking sense.　　　　　555
OEDIPUS: If you think you can wrong a relative
　　and get off free, you are not thinking sense.
CREON: Perfectly just, I won't say no. And yet
　　what is this injury you say I did you?
OEDIPUS: Did you persuade me, yes or no, to send　　　　　560
　　someone to bring that solemn prophet here?
CREON: And I still hold to the advice I gave.
OEDIPUS: How many years ago did your King Laius . . .
CREON: Laius! Do what? Now I don't understand.
OEDIPUS: Vanish — victim of a murderous violence?　　　　　565
CREON: That is a long count back into the past.
OEDIPUS: Well, was this seer then practicing his art?
CREON: Yes, skilled and honored just as he is today.
OEDIPUS: Did he, back then, ever refer to me?
CREON: He did not do so in my presence ever.　　　　　　570
OEDIPUS: You did inquire into the murder then.
CREON: We had to, surely, though we discovered nothing.
OEDIPUS: But the "skilled" one did not say this then? Why not?
CREON: I never talk when I am ignorant.
OEDIPUS: But you're not ignorant of your own part.　　　　　575
CREON: What do you mean? I'll tell you if I know.
OEDIPUS: Just this: if he had not conferred with you
　　he'd not have told about my murdering Laius.
CREON: If he said that, you are the one who knows.
　　But now it's fair that you should answer me.　　　　　　580
OEDIPUS: Ask on! You won't convict me as the killer.
CREON: Well then, answer. My sister is your wife?
OEDIPUS: Now there's a statement that I can't deny.
CREON: You two have equal power in this country?
OEDIPUS: She gets from me whatever she desires.　　　　　　585
CREON: And I'm a third? The three of us are equals?
OEDIPUS: That's where you're treacherous to your kinsman!
CREON: But think about this rationally, as I do.
　　First look at this: do you think anyone
　　prefers the anxieties of being king　　　　　　　　　　590
　　to untroubled sleep — if he has equal power?
　　I'm not the kind of man who falls in love
　　with kingship. I am content with a king's power.

And so would any man who's wise and prudent.
595 I get all things from you, with no distress;
as king I would have onerous duties, too.
How could the kingship bring me more delight
than this untroubled power and influence?
I'm not misguided yet to such a point
600 that profitable honors aren't enough.
As it is, all wish me well and all salute;
those begging you for something have me summoned,
for their success depends on that alone.
Why should I lose all this to become king?
605 A prudent mind is never traitorous.
Treason's a thought I'm not enamored of;
nor could I join a man who acted so.
In proof of this, first go yourself to Pytho
and ask if I brought back the true response.
610 Then, if you find I plotted with that portent
reader,° don't have me put to death by your vote
only — I'll vote myself for my conviction.
Don't let an unsupported thought convict me!
It's not right mindlessly to take the bad
615 for good or to suppose the good are traitors.
Rejecting a relation who is loyal
is like rejecting life, our greatest love.
In time you'll know securely without stumbling,
for time alone can prove a just man just,
620 though you can know a bad man in a day.

CHORAGOS: Well said, to one who's anxious not to fall.
Swift thinkers, Lord, are never safe from stumbling.

OEDIPUS: But when a swift and secret plotter moves
against me, I must make swift counterplot.
625 If I lie quiet and await his move,
he'll have achieved his aims and I'll have missed.

CREON: You surely cannot mean you want me exiled!

OEDIPUS: Not exiled, no. Your death is what I want!

630 CREON: If you would first define what envy is . . .

OEDIPUS: Are you still stubborn? Still disobedient?

CREON: I see you cannot think!

OEDIPUS: For me I can.

CREON: You should for me as well!

OEDIPUS: But you're a traitor!

CREON: What if you're wrong?

OEDIPUS: Authority must be maintained.

°*portent reader:* Apollo's oracle or prophet.

CREON: Not if the ruler's evil.

OEDIPUS: Hear that, Thebes!   635

CREON: It is my city too, not yours alone!

CHORAGOS: Please don't, my Lords! Ah, just in time, I see
    Jocasta there, coming from the palace.
    With her help you must settle your quarrel.

Enter Jocasta from the palace.

JOCASTA: Wretched men! What has provoked this ill-
    advised dispute? Have you no sense of shame,   640
    with Thebes so sick, to stir up private troubles?
    Now go inside! And Creon, you go home!
    Don't make a general anguish out of nothing!

CREON: My sister, Oedipus your husband here
    sees fit to do one of two hideous things: 645
    to have me banished from the land — or killed!

OEDIPUS: That's right: I caught him, Lady, plotting harm
    against my person — with a malignant science.

CREON: May my life fail, may I die cursed, if I
    did any of the things you said I did!   650

JOCASTA: Believe his words, for the god's sake, Oedipus,
    in deference above all to his oath
    to the gods. Also for me, and for these men!

KOMMOS°

STROPHE 1

CHORUS: Consent, with will and mind,
    my king, I beg of you!   655

OEDIPUS: What do you wish me to surrender?

CHORUS: Show deference to him who was not feeble in time past
    and is now great in the power of his oath!

OEDIPUS: Do you know what you're asking?

CHORUS: Yes.

OEDIPUS: Tell me then.

CHORUS: Never to cast into dishonored guilt, with an unproved   660
    assumption, a kinsman who has bound himself by curse.

OEDIPUS: Now you must understand, when you ask this,
    you ask my death or banishment from the land.

STROPHE 2

CHORUS: No, by the god who is the foremost of all gods,
    the Sun! No! Godless,   665
        friendless, whatever death is worst of all,
    let that be my destruction, if this
        thought ever moved me!
    But my ill-fated soul

° *Kommos:* A dirge or lament sung by the Chorus and one or more of the chief characters.

670 this dying land
 wears out — the more if to these older troubles
 she adds new troubles from the two of you!

OEDIPUS: Then let him go, though it must mean my death,
 or else disgrace and exile from the land.

675 My pity is moved by your words, not by his —
 he'll only have my hate, wherever he goes.

CREON: You're sullen as you yield; you'll be depressed
 when you've passed through this anger. Natures like yours
 are hardest on themselves. That's as it should be.

680 OEDIPUS: Then won't you go and let me be?

CREON: I'll go.
 Though you're unreasonable, they know I'm righteous.

Exit Creon.

ANTISTROPHE 1

CHORUS: Why are you waiting, Lady?
 Conduct him back into the palace!

JOCASTA: I will, when I have heard what chanced.

685 CHORUS: Conjectures — words alone, and nothing based on thought.
 But even an injustice can devour a man.

JOCASTA: Did the words come from both sides?

CHORUS: Yes.

JOCASTA: What was said?

CHORUS: To me it seems enough! enough! the land already troubled,
 that this should rest where it has stopped.

690 OEDIPUS: See what you've come to in your honest thought,
 in seeking to relax and blunt my heart?

ANTISTROPHE 2

CHORUS: I have not said this only once, my Lord.
 That I had lost my sanity,
  without a path in thinking —
695 be sure this would be clear
  if I put you away
 who, when my cherished land
  wandered crazed
 with suffering, brought her back on course.
700 Now, too, be a lucky helmsman!

JOCASTA: Please, for the god's sake, Lord, explain to me
 the reason why you have conceived this wrath?

OEDIPUS: I honor you, not them,° and I'll explain
 to you how Creon has conspired against me.

705 JOCASTA: All right, if that will explain how the quarrel started.

° *them:* The Chorus.

OEDIPUS: He says I am the murderer of Laius!

JOCASTA: Did he claim knowledge or that someone told him?

OEDIPUS: Here's what he did: he sent that vicious seer
    so he could keep his own mouth innocent.

JOCASTA: Ah then, absolve yourself of what he charges!   710
    Listen to this and you'll agree, no mortal
    is ever given skill in prophecy.
    I'll prove this quickly with one incident.
    It was foretold to Laius — I shall not say
    by Phoebus himself, but by his ministers—   715
    that when his fate arrived he would be killed
    by a son who would be born to him and me.
    And yet, so it is told, foreign robbers
    murdered him, at a place where three roads meet.
    As for the child I bore him, not three days passed   720
    before he yoked the ball-joints of its feet,°
    then cast it, by others' hands, on a trackless mountain.
    That time Apollo did not make our child
    a patricide, or bring about what Laius
    feared, that he be killed by his own son.   725
    That's how prophetic words determined things!
    Forget them. The things a god must track
    he will himself painlessly reveal.

OEDIPUS: Just now, as I was listening to you, Lady,
    what a profound distraction seized my mind!   730

JOCASTA: What made you turn around so anxiously?

OEDIPUS: I thought you said that Laius was attacked
    and butchered at a place where three roads meet.

JOCASTA: That is the story, and it is told so still.

OEDIPUS: Where is the place where this was done to him?   735

JOCASTA: The land's called Phocis, where a two-forked road
    comes in from Delphi and from Daulia.

OEDIPUS: And how much time has passed since these events?

JOCASTA: Just prior to your presentation here
    as king this news was published to the city.   740

OEDIPUS: Oh, Zeus, what have you willed to do to me?

JOCASTA: Oedipus, what makes your heart so heavy?

OEDIPUS: No, tell me first of Laius' appearance,
    what peak of youthful vigor he had reached.

JOCASTA: A tall man, showing his first growth of white.   745
    He had a figure not unlike your own.

OEDIPUS: Alas! It seems that in my ignorance
    I laid those fearful curses on myself.

° *ball-joints of its feet:* The ankles.

JOCASTA: What is it, Lord? I flinch to see your face.

750 OEDIPUS: I'm dreadfully afraid the prophet sees.
But I'll know better with one more detail.

JOCASTA: I'm frightened too. But ask: I'll answer you.

OEDIPUS: Was his retinue small, or did he travel
with a great troop, as would befit a prince?

755 JOCASTA: There were just five in all, one a herald.
There was a carriage, too, bearing Laius.

OEDIPUS: Alas! Now I see it! But who was it,
Lady, who told you what you know about this?

JOCASTA: A servant who alone was saved unharmed.

760 OEDIPUS: By chance, could he be now in the palace?

JOCASTA: No, he is not. When he returned and saw
you had the power of the murdered Laius,
he touched my hand and begged me formally
to send him to the fields and to the pastures,

765 so he'd be out of sight, far from the city.
I did. Although a slave, he well deserved
to win this favor, and indeed far more.

OEDIPUS: Let's have him called back in immediately.

JOCASTA: That can be done, but why do you desire it?

770 OEDIPUS: I fear, Lady, I have already said
too much. That's why I wish to see him now.

JOCASTA: Then he shall come; but it is right somehow
that I, too, Lord, should know what troubles you.

OEDIPUS: I've gone so deep into the things I feared

775 I'll tell you everything. Who has a right
greater than yours, while I cross through this chance?
Polybus of Corinth was my father,
my mother was the Dorian Meropē.
I was first citizen, until this chance

780 attacked me — striking enough, to be sure,
but not worth all the gravity I gave it.
This: at a feast a man who'd drunk too much
denied, at the wine, I was my father's son.
I was depressed and all that day I barely

785 held it in. Next day I put the question
to my mother and father. They were enraged
at the man who'd let this fiction fly at me.
I was much cheered by them. And yet it kept
grinding into me. His words kept coming back.

790 Without my mother's or my father's knowledge
I went to Pytho. But Phoebus sent me away
dishonoring my demand. Instead, other
wretched horrors he flashed forth in speech.
He said that I would be my mother's lover,

795 show offspring to mankind they could not look at,

and be his murderer whose seed I am.°
When I heard this, and ever since, I gauged
the way to Corinth by the stars alone,
running to a place where I would never see
the disgrace in the oracle's words come true.   800
But I soon came to the exact location
where, as you tell of it, the king was killed.
Lady, here is the truth. As I went on,
when I was just approaching those three roads,
a herald and a man like him you spoke of   805
came on, riding a carriage drawn by colts.
Both the man out front and the old man himself°
tried violently to force me off the road.
The driver, when he tried to push me off,
I struck in anger. The old man saw this, watched   810
me approach, then leaned out and lunged down
with twin prongs° at the middle of my head!
He got more than he gave. Abruptly — struck
once by the staff in this my hand — he tumbled
out, head first, from the middle of the carriage.   815
And then I killed them all. But if there is
a kinship between Laius and this stranger,
who is more wretched than the man you see?
Who was there born more hated by the gods?
For neither citizen nor foreigner   820
may take me in his home or speak to me.
No, they must drive me off. And it is I
who have pronounced these curses on myself!
I stain the dead man's bed with these my hands,
by which he died. Is not my nature vile?   825
Unclean?—if I am banished and even
in exile I may not see my own parents,
or set foot in my homeland, or else be yoked
in marriage to my mother, and kill my father,
Polybus, who raised me and gave me birth?   830
If someone judged a cruel divinity
did this to me, would he not speak the truth?
You pure and awful gods, may I not ever
see that day, may I be swept away
from men before I see so great and so   835
calamitous a stain fixed on my person!

CHORAGOS: These things seem fearful to us, Lord, and yet,
    until you hear it from the witness, keep hope!

°*be . . . am:* I would murder my father.   °*old man himself:* Laius.   °*lunged . . . prongs:* Laius strikes Oedipus with a two-pronged horse goad, or whip.

OEDIPUS: That is the single hope that's left to me,
840   to wait for him, that herdsman — until he comes.

JOCASTA: When he appears, what are you eager for?

OEDIPUS: Just this: if his account agrees with yours
           then I shall have escaped this misery.

JOCASTA: But what was it that struck you in my story?

845 **OEDIPUS:** You said he spoke of robbers as the ones
           who killed him. Now: if he continues still
           to speak of many, then I could not have killed him.
           One man and many men just do not jibe.
           But if he says one belted man, the doubt
850   is gone. The balance tips toward me. I did it.

JOCASTA: No! He told it as I told you. Be certain.
           He can't reject that and reverse himself.
           The city heard these things, not I alone.
           But even if he swerves from what he said,
855   he'll never show that Laius' murder, Lord,
           occurred just as predicted. For Loxias
           expressly said my son was doomed to kill him.
           The boy — poor boy — he never had a chance
           to cut him down, for he was cut down first.
860   Never again, just for some oracle
           will I shoot frightened glances right and left.

OEDIPUS: That's full of sense. Nonetheless, send a man
           to bring that farm hand here. Will you do it?

JOCASTA: I'll send one right away. But let's go in.
865   Would I do anything against your wishes?

Exit Oedipus and Jocasta through the central door into the palace.

STASIMON 2

STROPHE 1

CHORUS: May there accompany me
           the fate to keep a reverential purity in what I say,
           in all I do, for which the laws have been set forth
           and walk on high, born to traverse the brightest,
870   highest upper air; Olympus° only
           is their father, nor was it
           mortal nature
           that fathered them, and never will
           oblivion lull them into sleep;
875   the god in them is great and never ages.

ANTISTROPHE 1

The will to violate, seed of the tyrant,
if it has drunk mindlessly of wealth and power,

° *Olympus:* Mount Olympus, home of the gods, and treated as a god itself.

without a sense of time or true advantage,
mounts to a peak, then
plunges to an abrupt . . . destiny,   880
where the useful foot
is of no use. But the kind
of struggling that is good for the city
I ask the god never to abolish.
The god is my protector: never will I give that up.   885

STROPHE 2

But if a man proceeds disdainfully
        in deeds of hand or word
and has no fear of Justice
        or reverence for shrines of the divinities
(may a bad fate catch him   890
        for his luckless wantonness!),
if he'll not gain what he gains with justice
and deny himself what is unholy,
or if he clings, in foolishness, to the untouchable
(what man, finally, in such an action, will have strength   895
enough to fend off passion's arrows from his soul?),
if, I say, this kind of
        deed is held in honor—
why should I join the sacred dance?

ANTISTROPHE 2

No longer shall I visit and revere   900
        Earth's navel,° the untouchable,
nor visit Abae's° temple,
        or Olympia,°
if the prophecies are not matched by events
        for all the world to point to.   905
No, you who hold the power, if you are rightly called
Zeus the king of all, let this matter not escape you
and your ever-deathless rule,
for the prophecies to Laius fade . . .
and men already disregard them;   910
nor is Apollo anywhere
        glorified with honors.
Religion slips away.

EPISODE 3

*Enter Jocasta from the palace carrying a branch wound with wool and a jar of incense.
She is attended by two women.*

°*Earth's navel:* Delphi.   °*Abae's:* Abae was a town in Phocis where there was another oracle of Apollo.
°*Olympia:* Site of the oracle of Zeus.

JOCASTA: Lords of the realm, the thought has come to me
915   to visit shrines of the divinities
           with suppliant's branch in hand and fragrant smoke.
           For Oedipus excites his soul too much
           with alarms of all kinds. He will not judge
           the present by the past, like a man of sense.
920   He's at the mercy of all terror-mongers.

Jocasta approaches the altar on the right and kneels.

           Since I can do no good by counseling,
           Apollo the Lycēan! — you are the closest —
           I come a suppliant, with these my vows,
           for a cleansing that will not pollute him.
925   For when we see him shaken we are all
           afraid, like people looking at their helmsman.

*Enter a Messenger along one of the parados. He sees Jocasta at the altar and then
addresses the Chorus.*

MESSENGER: I would be pleased if you would help me, stranger.
           Where is the palace of King Oedipus?
           Or tell me where he is himself, if you know.
930 CHORUS: This is his house, stranger. He is within.
           This is his wife and mother of his children.
MESSENGER: May she and her family find prosperity,
           if, as you say, her marriage is fulfilled.
JOCASTA: You also, stranger, for you deserve as much
935   for your gracious words. But tell me why you've come.
           What do you wish? Or what have you to tell us?
MESSENGER: Good news, my Lady, both for your house and husband.
JOCASTA: What is your news? And who has sent you to us?
MESSENGER: I come from Corinth. When you have heard my news
940   you will rejoice, I'm sure — and grieve perhaps.
JOCASTA: What is it? How can it have this double power?
MESSENGER: They will establish him their king, so say
           the people of the land of Isthmia.°
JOCASTA: But is old Polybus not still in power?
945 MESSENGER: He's not, for death has clasped him in the tomb.
JOCASTA: What's this? Has Oedipus' father died?
MESSENGER: If I have lied then I deserve to die.
JOCASTA: Attendant! Go quickly to your master,
           and tell him this.

Exit an Attendant into the palace.

°*land of Isthmia:* Corinth, Greek city-state situated on an isthmus.

Oracles of the gods!
Where are you now? The man whom Oedipus   950
fled long ago, for fear that he should kill him —
he's been destroyed by chance and not by him!

Enter Oedipus from the palace.

OEDIPUS: Darling Jocasta, my beloved wife,
  Why have you called me from the palace?
JOCASTA: First hear what this man has to say. Then see   955
  what the god's grave oracle has come to now!
OEDIPUS: Where is he from? What is this news he brings me?
JOCASTA: From Corinth. He brings news about your father:
  that Polybus is no more! that he is dead!
OEDIPUS: What's this, old man? I want to hear you say it.   960
MESSENGER: If this is what must first be clarified,
  please be assured that he is dead and gone.
OEDIPUS: By treachery or by the touch of sickness?
MESSENGER: Light pressures tip agéd frames into their sleep.
OEDIPUS: You mean the poor man died of some disease.   665
MESSENGER: And of the length of years that he had tallied.
OEDIPUS: Aha! Then why should we look to Pytho's vapors,°
  or to the birds that scream above our heads?°
  If we could really take those things for guides,
  I would have killed my father. But he's dead!   970
  He is beneath the earth, and here am I,
  who never touched a spear. Unless he died
  of longing for me and I "killed" him that way!
  No, in this case, Polybus, by dying, took
  the worthless oracle to Hades with him.   975
JOCASTA: And wasn't I telling you that just now?
OEDIPUS: You were indeed. I was misled by fear.
JOCASTA: You should not care about this anymore.
OEDIPUS: I must care. I must stay clear of my mother's bed.
JOCASTA: What's there for man to fear? The realm of chance   980
  prevails. True foresight isn't possible.
  His life is best who lives without a plan.
  This marriage with your mother — don't fear it.
  How many times have men in dreams, too, slept
  with their own mothers! Those who believe such things   985
  mean nothing endure their lives most easily.
OEDIPUS: A fine, bold speech, and you are right, perhaps,
  except that my mother is still living,
  so I must fear her, however well you argue.

°*Pytho's vapors:* Prophecies of the oracle at Delphi.   °*birds . . . heads:* Prophecies derived from interpreting
the flights of birds.

990 JOCASTA: And yet your father's tomb is a great eye.

OEDIPUS: Illuminating, yes. But I still fear the living.

MESSENGER: Who is the woman who inspires this fear?

OEDIPUS: Meropē, Polybus' wife, old man.

MESSENGER: And what is there about her that alarms you?

995 OEDIPUS: An oracle, god-sent and fearful, stranger.

MESSENGER: Is it permitted that another know?

OEDIPUS: It is. Loxias once said to me

    I must have intercourse with my own mother

    and take my father's blood with these my hands.

1000 So I have long lived far away from Corinth.

    This has indeed brought much good luck, and yet,

    to see one's parents' eyes is happiest.

MESSENGER: Was it for this that you have lived in exile?

OEDIPUS: So I'd not be my father's killer, sir.

1005 MESSENGER: Had I not better free you from this fear,

    my Lord? That's why I came — to do you service.

OEDIPUS: Indeed, what a reward you'd get for that!

MESSENGER: Indeed, this is the main point of my trip,

    to be rewarded when you get back home.

1010 OEDIPUS: I'll never rejoin the givers of my seed!°

MESSENGER: My son, clearly you don't know what you're doing.

OEDIPUS: But how is that, old man? For the gods' sake, tell me!

MESSENGER: If it's because of them you won't go home.

OEDIPUS: I fear that Phoebus will have told the truth.

1015 MESSENGER: Pollution from the ones who gave you seed?

OEDIPUS: That is the thing, old man, I always fear.

MESSENGER: Your fear is groundless. Understand that.

OEDIPUS: Groundless? Not if I was born their son.

MESSENGER: But Polybus is not related to you.

1020 OEDIPUS: Do you mean Polybus was not my father?

MESSENGER: No more than I. We're both the same to you.

OEDIPUS: Same? One who begot me and one who didn't?

MESSENGER: He didn't beget you any more than I did.

OEDIPUS: But then, why did he say I was his son?

1025 MESSENGER: He got you as a gift from my own hands.

OEDIPUS: He loved me so, though from another's hands?

MESSENGER: His former childlessness persuaded him.

OEDIPUS: But had you bought me, or begotten me?

MESSENGER: Found you. In the forest hallows of Cithaeron.

1030 OEDIPUS: What were you doing traveling in that region?

MESSENGER: I was in charge of flocks which grazed those mountains.

OEDIPUS: A wanderer who worked the flocks for hire?

°*givers of my seed:* Meaning, i.e., my parents." Oedipus still thinks Meropē and Polybus are his parents.

Messenger: Ah, but that day I was your savior, son.

Oedipus: From what? What was my trouble when you took me?

Messenger: The ball-joints of your feet might testify. 1035

Oedipus: What's that? What makes you name that ancient trouble?

Messenger: Your feet were pierced and I am your rescuer.

Oedipus: A fearful rebuke those tokens left for me!

Messenger: That was the chance that names you who you are.

Oedipus: By the gods, did my mother or my father do this? 1040

Messenger: That I don't know. He might who gave you to me.

Oedipus: From someone else? You didn't chance on me?

Messenger: Another shepherd handed you to me.

Oedipus: Who was he? Do you know? Will you explain!

Messenger: They called him one of the men of — was it Laius? 1045

Oedipus: The one who once was king here long ago?

Messenger: That is the one! The man was shepherd to him.

Oedipus: And is he still alive so I can see him?

Messenger: But you who live here ought to know that best.

Oedipus: Does any one of you now present know 1050
about the shepherd whom this man has named?
Have you seen him in town or in the fields? Speak out!
The time has come for the discovery!

Laurence Olivier as Oedipus, framed by a masked member of the Chorus and Jocasta. In this scene from the landmark 1945 production of *Oedipus the King,* the doomed King seems to finally recognize the "truth" that he has been seeking.

CHORAGOS: The man he speaks of, I believe, is the same
1055   as the field hand you have already asked to see.
            But it's Jocasta who would know this best.
OEDIPUS: Lady, do you remember the man we just
            now sent for — is that the man he speaks of?
JOCASTA: What? The man he spoke of? Pay no attention!
1060   His words are not worth thinking about. It's nothing.
OEDIPUS: With clues like this within my grasp, give up?
            Fail to solve the mystery of my birth?
JOCASTA: For the love of the gods, and if you love your life,
            give up this search! My sickness is enough.
1065 OEDIPUS: Come! Though my mothers for three generations
            were in slavery, you'd not be lowborn!
JOCASTA: No, listen to me! Please! Don't do this thing!
OEDIPUS: I will not listen; I will search out the truth.
JOCASTA: My thinking is for you — it would be best.
1070 OEDIPUS: This "best" of yours is starting to annoy me.
JOCASTA: Doomed man! Never find out who you are!
OEDIPUS: Will someone go and bring that shepherd here?
            Leave her to glory in her wealthy birth!
JOCASTA: Man of misery! No other name
1075   shall I address you by, ever again.

Exit Jocasta into the palace after a long pause.

CHORAGOS: Why has your lady left, Oedipus,
            hurled by a savage grief? I am afraid
            disaster will come bursting from this silence.
OEDIPUS: Let it burst forth! However low this seed
1080   of mine may be, yet I desire to see it.
            She, perhaps — she has a woman's pride —
            is mortified by my base origins.
            But I who count myself the child of Chance,
            the giver of good, shall never know dishonor.
1085   She is my mother,° and the months my brothers
            who first marked out my lowness, then my greatness.
            I shall not prove untrue to such a nature
            by giving up the search for my own birth.

STASIMON 3
STROPHE

CHORUS: If I have mantic power°
1090   and excellence in thought,
            by Olympus,

° *She . . . mother:* Chance is my mother.   ° *If . . . mantic power:* If I am a prophet

you shall not, Cithaeron, at tomorrow's
full moon,
fail to hear us celebrate you as the countryman
of Oedipus, his nurse and mother,   1095
or fail to be the subject of our dance,
    since you have given pleasure
to our king.
Phoebus, whom we summon by "iē!,"
may this be pleasing to you!   1100

ANTISTROPHE

Who was your mother, son?
which of the long-lived nymphs
after lying with Pan,°
    the mountain roaming . . . Or was it a bride
of Loxias?°   1105
For dear to him are all the upland pastures.
Or was it Mount Cyllēnē's lord,°
or the Bacchic god,°
    dweller of the mountain peaks,
who received you as a joyous find   1110
from one of the nymphs of Helicon,
the favorite sharers of his sport?

EPISODE 4

OEDIPUS: If someone like myself, who never met him,
  may calculate — elders, I think I see
  the very herdsman we've been waiting for.   1115
  His many years would fit that man's age,
  and those who bring him on, if I am right,
  are my own men. And yet, in real knowledge,
  you can outstrip me, surely: you've seen him.

*Enter the old Herdsman escorted by two of Oedipus's Attendants. At first, the Herdsman
will not look at Oedipus.*

CHORAGOS: I know him, yes, a man of the house of Laius,   1120
  a trusty herdsman if he ever had one.
OEDIPUS: I ask you first, the stranger come from Corinth:
  is this the man you spoke of?
MESSENGER: That's he you see.
OEDIPUS: Then you, old man. First look at me! Now answer:
  did you belong to Laius' household once?   1125
HERDSMAN: I did. Not a purchased slave but raised in the palace.

°*Pan:* God of shepherds and woodlands, half man and half goat.   °*Loxias:* Apollo.   °*Mount Cyllēnē's lord:*
Hermes, messenger of the gods.   °*Bacchic god:* Dionysus.

OEDIPUS: How have you spent your life? What is your work?

HERDSMAN: Most of my life now I have tended sheep.

OEDIPUS: Where is the usual place you stay with them?

1130 HERDSMAN: On Mount Cithaeron. Or in that district.

OEDIPUS: Do you recall observing this man there?

HERDSMAN: Doing what? Which is the man you mean?

OEDIPUS: This man right here. Have you had dealings with him?

HERDSMAN: I can't say right away. I don't remember.

1135 MESSENGER: No wonder, master. I'll bring clear memory
           to his ignorance. I'm absolutely sure
           he can recall it, the district was Cithaeron,
           he with a double flock, and I, with one,
           lived close to him, for three entire seasons,
1140   six months along, from spring right to Arcturus.°
           Then for the winter I'd drive mine to my fold,
           and he'd drive his to Laius' pen again.
           Did any of the things I say take place?

HERDSMAN: You speak the truth, though it's from long ago.

1145 MESSENGER: Do you remember giving me, back then,
           a boy I was to care for as my own?

HERDSMAN: What are you saying? Why do you ask me that?

MESSENGER: There, sir, is the man who was that boy!

1150 HERDSMAN: Damn you! Shut your mouth! Keep your silence!

OEDIPUS: Stop! Don't you rebuke his words.
           Your words ask for rebuke far more than his.

HERDSMAN: But what have I done wrong, most royal master?

OEDIPUS: Not telling of the boy of whom he asked.

HERDSMAN: He's ignorant and blundering toward ruin.

1155 OEDIPUS: Tell it willingly — or under torture.

HERDSMAN: Oh god! Don't — I am old — don't torture me!

OEDIPUS: Here! Someone put his hands behind his back!

HERDSMAN: But why? What else would you find out, poor man?

OEDIPUS: Did you give him the child he asks about?

1160 HERDSMAN: I did. I wish that I had died that day!

OEDIPUS: You'll come to that if you don't speak the truth.

HERDSMAN: It's if I speak that I shall be destroyed.

OEDIPUS: I think this fellow struggles for delay.

HERDSMAN: No, no! I said already that I gave him.

1165 OEDIPUS: From your own home, or got from someone else?

HERDSMAN: Not from my own. I got him from another.

OEDIPUS: Which of these citizens? What sort of house?

HERDSMAN: Don't — by the gods! — don't, master, ask me more!

OEDIPUS: It means your death if I must ask again.

1170 HERDSMAN: One of the children of the house of Laius.

°*Arcturus:* A star that is first seen in September in the sky over Greece.

OEDIPUS: A slave — or born into the family?

HERDSMAN: I have come to the dreaded thing, and I shall say it.

OEDIPUS: And I to hearing it, but hear I must.

HERDSMAN: He was reported to have been — his son.
　　　Your lady in the house could tell you best.　　　　1175

OEDIPUS: Because she gave him to you?

HERDSMAN:　　　　　　　　Yes, my lord.

OEDIPUS: What was her purpose?

HERDSMAN:　　　　　　　I was to kill the boy.

OEDIPUS: The child she bore?

HERDSMAN:　　　　　　She dreaded prophecies.

OEDIPUS: What were they?

HERDSMAN:　　　　　　　The word was that he'd kill his parents.

OEDIPUS: Then why did you give him up to this old man?　　　1180

HERDSMAN: In pity, master — so he would take him home,
　　　to another land. But what he did was save him
　　　for this supreme disaster. If you are the one
　　　he speaks of — know your evil birth and fate!

OEDIPUS: Ah! All of it was destined to be true!　　　　1185
　　　Oh light, now may I look my last upon you,
　　　shown monstrous in my birth, in marriage monstrous,
　　　a murderer monstrous in those I killed.

Exit Oedipus, running into the palace.

<u>STASIMON 4</u>

STROPHE 1

CHORUS: Oh generations of mortal men,
　　　while you are living, I will　　　　　　1190
　　　　　appraise your lives at zero!
　　　What man
　　　comes closer to seizing lasting blessedness
　　　than merely to seize its semblance,
　　　and after living in this semblance, to plunge?　　　1195
　　　With your example before us,
　　　with your destiny, yours,
　　　　　suffering Oedipus, no mortal
　　　can I judge fortunate.

ANTISTROPHE 1　　　　　　　　1200

For he,° outranging everybody,
　　　shot his arrow° and became the lord
　　　　　of wide prosperity and blessedness,

° *he:* Oedipus.　　　° *shot his arrow:* Took his chances; made a guess at the Sphinx's riddle.

oh Zeus, after destroying
the virgin with the crooked talons,°
1205   singer of oracles; and against death,
in my land, he arose a tower of defense.
From which time you were called my king
and granted privileges supreme — in mighty
Thebes the ruling lord.

STROPHE 2

1210   But now — whose story is more sorrowful than yours?
Who is more intimate with fierce calamities,
with labors, now that your life is altered?
Alas, my Oedipus, whom all men know:
one great harbor°—
1215   one alone sufficed for you,
as son and father,
when you tumbled,° plowman° of the woman's chamber.
How, how could your paternal
1220   furrows, wretched man,
endure you silently so long.

ANTISTROPHE 2

Time, all-seeing, surprised you living an unwilled life
and sits from of old in judgment on the marriage, not a marriage,
where the begetter is the begot as well.
Ah, son of Laius . . . ,
1225   would that — oh, would that
I had never seen you!
I wail, my scream climbing beyond itself
from my whole power of voice. To say it straight:
from you I got new breath —
1230   but I also lulled my eye to sleep.°

EXODOS°

Enter the Second Messenger from the palace.

SECOND MESSENGER: You who are first among the citizens,
what deeds you are about to hear and see!
What grief you'll carry, if, true to your birth,
you still respect the house of Labdacus!
1235   Neither the Ister nor the Phasis river
could purify this house, such suffering

°*virgin . . . talons:* The Sphinx.   °*one great harbor:* Metaphorical allusion to Jocasta's body.   °*tumbled:*
Were born and had sex.   °*plowman:* Plowing is used here as a sexual metaphor.   °*I . . . sleep:* I failed
to see the corruption you brought.   °*Exodos:* The final scene, containing the play's resolution.

does it conceal, or soon must bring to light —
willed this time, not unwilled. Griefs hurt worst
which we perceive to be self-chosen ones.

CHORAGOS: They were sufficient, the things we knew before, 1240
  to make us grieve. What can you add to those?

SECOND MESSENGER: The thing that's quickest said and quickest heard:
  our own, our royal one, Jocasta's dead.

CHORAGOS: Unhappy queen! What was responsible?

SECOND MESSENGER: Herself. The bitterest of these events 1245
  is not for you, you were not there to see,
  but yet, exactly as I can recall it,
  you'll hear what happened to that wretched lady.
  She came in anger through the outer hall,
  and then she ran straight to her marriage bed, 1250
  tearing her hair with the fingers of both hands.
  Then, slamming shut the doors when she was in,
  she called to Laius, dead so many years,
  remembering the ancient seed which caused
  his death, leaving the mother to the son 1255
  to breed again an ill-born progeny.
  She mourned the bed where she, alas, bred double —
  husband by husband, children by her child.
  From this point on I don't know how she died,
  for Oedipus then burst in with a cry, 1260
  and did not let us watch her final evil.
  Our eyes were fixed on him. Wildly he ran
  to each of us, asking for his spear
  and for his wife — no wife: where he might find
  the double mother-field, his and his children's. 1265
  He raved, and some divinity then showed him —
  for none of us did so who stood close by.
  With a dreadful shout — as if some guide were leading —
  he lunged through the double doors; he bent the hollow
  bolts from the sockets, burst into the room, 1270
  and there we saw her, hanging from above,
  entangled in some twisted hanging strands.
  He saw, was stricken, and with a wild roar
  ripped down the dangling noose. When she, poor woman,
  lay on the ground, there came a fearful sight: 1275
  he snatched the pins of worked gold from her dress,
  with which her clothes were fastened: these he raised
  and struck into the ball-joints of his eyes.°
  He shouted that they would no longer see
  the evils he had suffered or had done, 1280

° *ball-joints of his eyes:* His eyeballs. Oedipus blinds himself in both eyes at the same time.

> see in the dark those he should not have seen,
> and know no more those he once sought to know.
> While chanting this, not once but many times
> he raised his hand and struck into his eyes.

1285
> Blood from his wounded eyes poured down his chin,
> not freed in moistening drops, but all at once
> a stormy rain of black blood burst like hail.
> These evils, coupling them, making them one,

1290
> have broken loose upon both man and wife.
> The old prosperity that they had once
> was true prosperity, and yet today,
> mourning, ruin, death, disgrace, and every
> evil you could name — not one is absent.

CHORAGOS: Has he allowed himself some peace from all this grief?

1295 **SECOND MESSENGER:** He shouts that someone slide the bolts and show
> to all the Cadmeians the patricide,
> his mother's — I can't say it, it's unholy —
> so he can cast himself out of the land,
> not stay and curse his house by his own curse.

1300
> He lacks the strength, though, and he needs a guide,
> for his is a sickness that's too great to bear.
> Now you yourself will see: the bolts of the doors
> are opening. You are about to see
> a vision even one who hates must pity.

Enter the blinded Oedipus from the palace, led in by a household Servant.

1305 **CHORAGOS:** Terrifying suffering for men to see,
> more terrifying than any I've ever
> come upon. Oh man of pain
> what madness reached you? Which god from far off,
> surpassing in range his longest spring,

1310
> struck hard against your god-abandoned fate?
> Oh man of pain,
> I cannot look upon you — though there's so much
> I would ask you, so much to hear,
> so much that holds my eyes —

1315
> such is the shudder you produce in me.

OEDIPUS: Ah! Ah! I am a man of misery.
> Where am I carried? Pity me! Where
> is my voice scattered abroad on wings?
> Divinity, where has your lunge transported me?

1320 **CHORAGOS:** To something horrible, not to be heard or seen.

KOMMOS
STROPHE 1

OEDIPUS: Oh, my cloud
> of darkness, abominable, unspeakable as it attacks me,

not to be turned away, brought by an evil wind!
Alas!
Again alas! Both enter me at once: 1325
the sting of the prongs,° the memory of evils!
CHORUS: I do not marvel that in these afflictions
you carry double griefs and double evils.

ANTISTROPHE 1

OEDIPUS: Ah, friend,
so you at least are there, resolute servant! 1330
Still with a heart to care for me, the blind man.
Oh! Oh!
I know that you are there. I recognize
even inside my darkness, that voice of yours.
CHORUS: Doer of horror, how did you bear to quench 1335
your vision? What divinity raised your hand?

STROPHE 2

OEDIPUS: It was Apollo there, Apollo, friends,
who brought my sorrows, vile sorrows to their perfection,
these evils that were done to me.
But the one who struck them with his hand, 1340
that one was none but I, in wretchedness.
For why was I to see
when nothing I could see would bring me joy?
CHORUS: Yes, that is how it was.
OEDIPUS: What could I see, indeed, 1345
or what enjoy — what greeting
is there I could hear with pleasure, friends?
Conduct me out of the land
as quickly as you can!
Conduct me out, my friends, 1350
the man utterly ruined,
supremely cursed,
the man who is by gods
the most detested of all men!
CHORUS: Wretched in disaster and in knowledge: 1355
oh, I could wish you'd never come to know!

ANTISTROPHE 2

OEDIPUS: May he be destroyed, whoever freed the savage shackles
from my feet when I'd been sent to the wild pasture,
whoever rescued me from murder
and became my savior — 1360

°*prongs:* Refers both to the whip that Laius used and to the two gold pins that Oedipus used to blind himself.

a bitter gift:
if I had died then,
I'd not have been such grief to self and kin.

CHORUS: I also would have had it so.

1365 OEDIPUS: I'd not have returned to be my father's
murderer; I'd not be called by men
my mother's bridegroom.
Now I'm without a god,
child of a polluted parent,
1370 fellow progenitor with him
who gave me birth in misery.
If there's an evil that
surpasses evils, that
has fallen to the lot of Oedipus.

1375 CHORAGOS: How can I say that you have counseled well?
Better not to be than live a blind man.

OEDIPUS: That this was not the best thing I could do —
don't tell me that, or advise me any more!
Should I descend to Hades and endure
1380 to see my father with these eyes? Or see
my poor unhappy mother? For I have done,
to both of these, things too great for hanging.
Or is the sight of children to be yearned for,
to see new shoots that sprouted as these did?
1385 Never, never with these eyes of mine!
Nor city, nor tower, nor holy images
of the divinities! For I, all-wretched,
most nobly raised — as no one else in Thebes —
deprived myself of these when I ordained
1390 that all expel the impious one — god-shown
to be polluted, and the dead king's son!°
Once I exposed this great stain upon me,
could I have looked on these with steady eyes?
No! No! And if there were a way to block
1395 the source of hearing in my ears, I'd gladly
have locked up my pitiable body,
so I'd be blind and deaf. Evils shut out —
that way my mind could live in sweetness.
Alas, Cithaeron, why did you receive me?
1400 Or when you had me, not killed me instantly?
I'd not have had to show my birth to mankind.
Polybus, Corinth, halls — ancestral,
they told me — how beautiful was your ward,
a scar that held back festering disease!

°*1 . . . son:* Oedipus refers to his own curse against the murderer as well as his sins of patricide and incest.

Evil my nature, evil my origin.   1405
You, three roads, and you, secret ravine,
you oak grove, narrow place of those three paths
that drank my blood° from these hands, from him
who fathered me, do you remember still
the things I did to you? When I'd come here,   1410
what I then did once more? Oh marriages! Marriages!
You gave us life and when you'd planted us
you sent the same seed up, and then revealed
fathers, brothers, sons, and kinsman's blood,
and brides, and wives, and mothers, all the most   1415
atrocious things that happen to mankind!
One should not name what never should have been.
Somewhere out there, then, quickly, by the gods,
cover me up, or murder me, or throw me
to the ocean where you will never see me more!   1420

Oedipus moves toward the Chorus and they back away from him.

Come! Don't shrink to touch this wretched man!
Believe me, do not be frightened! I alone
of all mankind can carry these afflictions.

Enter Creon from the palace with Attendants.

CHORAGOS: Tell Creon what you wish for. Just when we need him
he's here. He can act, he can advise you.   1425
He's now the land's sole guardian in your place.
OEDIPUS: Ah! Are there words that I can speak to him?
What ground for trust can I present? It's proved
that I was false to him in everything.
CREON: I have not come to mock you, Oedipus,   1430
nor to reproach you for your former falseness.
You men, if you have no respect for sons
of mortals, let your awe for the all-feeding
flames of lordy Hēlius° prevent
your showing unconcealed so great a stain,   1435
abhorred by earth and sacred rain and light.
Escort him quickly back into the house!
If blood kin only see and hear their own
afflictions, we'll have no impious defilement.
OEDIPUS: By the gods, you've freed me from one terrible fear,   1440
so nobly meeting my unworthiness:
grant me something — not for me; for you!
CREON: What do you want that you should beg me so?
OEDIPUS: To drive me from the land at once, to a place

°*my blood:* I.e., "the blood of my father, Laius."   °*Hēlius:* The sun.

1445   where there will be no man to speak to me!
       CREON: I would have done just that — had I not wished
           to ask first of the god what I should do.
       OEDIPUS: His answer was revealed in full — that I,
           the patricide, unholy, be destroyed.
1450   CREON: He said that, but our need is so extreme,
           it's best to have sure knowledge what must be done.
       OEDIPUS: You'll ask about a wretched man like me?
       CREON: Is it not time you put your trust in the god?
       OEDIPUS: But I bid you as well, and shall entreat you.
1455   Give her who is within what burial
           you will — you'll give your own her proper rites;
           but me — do not condemn my fathers' land
           to have me dwelling here while I'm alive,
           but let me live on mountains — on Cithaeron
1460   famed as mine, for my mother and my father,
           while they yet lived, made it my destined tomb,
           and I'll be killed by those who wished my ruin!
           And yet I know: no sickness will destroy me,
           nothing will: I'd never have been saved
1465   when left to die unless for some dread evil.
           Then let my fate continue where it will!
           As for my children, Creon, take no pains
           for my sons — they're men and they will never lack
           the means to live, wherever they may be —
1470   but my two wretched, pitiable girls,
           who never ate but at my table, never
           were without me — everything that I
           would touch, they'd always have a share of it —
           please care for them! Above all, let me touch
1475   them with my hands and weep aloud my woes!
           Please, my Lord!
           Please, noble heart! Touching with my hands,
           I'd think I held them as when I could see.

Enter Antigone and Ismene from the palace with Attendants.

       What's this?
1480   Oh gods! Do I hear, somewhere, my two dear ones
           sobbing? Has Creon really pitied me
           and sent to me my dearest ones, my children?
           Is that it?
       CREON: Yes, I prepared this for you, for I knew
1485   you'd feel this joy, as you have always done.
       OEDIPUS: Good fortune, then, and, for your care, be guarded
           far better by divinity than I was!
           Where are you, children? Come to me! Come here

to these my hands, hands of your brother, hands
of him who gave you seed, hands that made   1490
these once bright eyes to see now in this fashion.

Oedipus embraces his daughters.

He, children, seeing nothing, knowing nothing,
he fathered you where his own seed was plowed.
I weep for you as well, though I can't see you,
imagining your bitter life to come,   1495
the life you will be forced by men to live.
What gatherings of townsmen will you join,
what festivals, without returning home
in tears instead of watching holy rites?
And when you've reached the time for marrying,   1500
where, children, is the man who'll run the risk
of taking on himself the infamy
that will wound you as it did my parents?
What evil is not here? Your father killed
his father, plowed the one who gave him birth,   1505
and from the place where he was sown, from there
he got you, from the place he too was born.
These are the wounds: then who will marry you?
No man, my children. No, it's clear that you
must wither in dry barrenness, unmarried.   1510

Oedipus addresses Creon.

Son of Menoeceus! You are the only father
left to them — we two who gave them seed
are both destroyed: watch that they don't become
poor, wanderers, unmarried — they are your kin.
Let not my ruin be their ruin, too!   1515
No, pity them! You see how young they are,
bereft of everyone, except for you.
Consent, kind heart, and touch me with your hand!

Creon grasps Oedipus's right hand.

You, children, if you had reached an age of sense,
I would have counseled much. Now, pray you may live   1520
always where it's allowed, finding a life
better than his was, who gave you seed.
CREON: Stop this now. Quiet your weeping. Move away, into the house.
OEDIPUS: Bitter words, but I obey them.
CREON: There's an end to all things.
OEDIPUS: I have first this request.
CREON: Tell me. I shall judge when I will hear it.   1525
OEDIPUS: Banish me from my homeland.

CREON: You must ask that of the god.
OEDIPUS: But I am the gods' most hated man!
CREON: Then you will soon get what you want.
OEDIPUS: Do you consent?
CREON: I never promise when, as now, I'm ignorant.
OEDIPUS: Then lead me in.
CREON: Come. But let your hold fall from your children.
OEDIPUS: Do not take them from me, ever!
1530   CREON: Do not wish to keep all of the power.
       You had power, but that power did not follow you through life.

*Oedipus's daughters are taken from him and led into the palace by Attendants. Oedipus
is led into the palace by a Servant. Creon and the other Attendants follow. Only the
Chorus remains.*

CHORUS: People of Thebes, my country, see: here is that Oedipus —
       he who "knew" the famous riddle, and attained the highest power,
       whom all citizens admired, even envying his luck!
1535   See the billows of wild troubles which he has entered now!
       Here is the truth of each man's life: we must wait, and see his end,
       scrutinize his dying day, and refuse to call him happy
       till he has crossed the border of his life without pain.

Exit the Chorus along each of the parados.

Reading and Reacting

1. The ancient Greeks used no scenery in their theatrical productions. In the absence of scenery, how is the setting established at the beginning of *Oedipus the King*?

2. In order not to detract from the language of *Oedipus the King*, some contemporary productions use very simple costumes. Do you agree with this decision? If so, why? If not, what kind of costumes would you use?

3. In some recent productions of *Oedipus the King*, actors wear copies of ancient Greek masks. What are the advantages and disadvantages of using such masks in a contemporary production of the play?

4. In the ancient Greek theater, the *strophe* and *antistrophe* were sung or chanted by the chorus as it danced back and forth across the stage. If you were staging the play today, would you retain the chorus or do away with it entirely? What would be gained or lost with each alternative?

5. Why does Sophocles have Oedipus blind himself offstage? What would be the effect of having Oedipus perform this act in full view of the audience?

6. In what ways does Sophocles observe the unities of time, place, and action described on page 1288? How does Sophocles manage to present information about what happened years before the action of the play while still maintaining the three unities?

7. The ancient Greek audience that viewed *Oedipus the King* was familiar with the plot of the play. Given this situation, how does Sophocles create

suspense? What are the advantages and disadvantages of using a story that the audience already knows?

8. By the end of the play, what has Oedipus learned about himself? About the gods? About the quest for truth? Is he a tragic or a pathetic figure? (See pages 1286–1287 for a discussion of **tragedy** and **pathos**.)

9. Today, many directors employ **color-blind casting**—that is, they cast an actor in a role without regard to his or her race. Do you think this practice could be used in casting *Oedipus the King*? How, for example, would you react to an African-American Oedipus or to an Asian Creon?

10. JOURNAL ENTRY Do you think Oedipus deserves his fate? Why or why not?

11. CRITICAL PERSPECTIVE In "On Misunderstanding the *Oedipus Rex*," F. R. Dodds argues that Sophocles did not intend that Oedipus's tragedy be seen as rising from a "grave moral flaw." Neither, says Dodds, was Oedipus a "mere puppet" of the gods. Rather, "what fascinates us is the spectacle of a man freely choosing, from the highest motives, a series of actions which lead to his own ruin":

> Oedipus is great, not in virtue of a great worldly position—for his worldly position is an illusion which will vanish like a dream—but in virtue of his inner strength: strength to pursue the truth at whatever personal cost, and strength to accept and endure it when found. . . . Oedipus is great because he accepts the responsibility for all his acts, including those which are objectively most horrible, though subjectively innocent.

Do you agree with Dodds's arguments? Do you see Oedipus as someone who has inner strength or as a morally flawed victim of the gods?

Related Works: "Barn Burning" (p. 356), "Young Goodman Brown" (p. 489), "The Open Boat" (p. 685), "'Out, Out —'" (p. 959), "Leda and the Swan" (p. 1049), "Ulysses" (p. 1233), *Antigone* (p. 1899), *Hamlet* (p. 1656)

WILLIAM SHAKESPEARE (1564–1616) was the best-known dramatist of his era (see biography on p. 1269). *A Midsummer Night's Dream* was first performed in celebration of an aristocratic marriage, in either January 1595 or February 1596; its three levels of love stories, all worked out by the end, make it a suitable wedding entertainment. Uncharacteristically for Shakespeare, there is no central earlier source for the story, though parts of it probably come from Chaucer, Ovid, and English folk legends. The play has always been popular with audiences and has frequently been adapted into other forms, such as ballet and opera. In Seattle in 1979, for example, a musical adaptation used popular songs from the 1950s: Puck sang, "Why Do Fools Fall in Love?" and Oberon entered on a motorcycle and sang "Love Potion Number Nine."

Cultural Context The conditions and restrictions of Elizabethan theater undoubtedly shaped the kinds of plays and characters Shakespeare created. For example, during this period, no women were permitted to perform on the English stage, so all of the female roles in his plays were written for, and performed by, boy actors whose voices had not yet changed. Ironically, some of literature's most beloved female characters, including Ophelia, Desdemona, and Juliet, were originally performed by males. Moreover, many of Shakespeare's plays feature female characters who cross-dress, or pose as males to accomplish certain tasks, further compounding the gender confusion. Actresses were not allowed to play female roles onstage until 1660 when the theaters reopened after being closed during the Puritan Revolution of 1642.

A Midsummer Night's Dream* (c. 1595)

CHARACTERS

Theseus, Duke of Athens
Egeus, father of Hermia
Lysander, beloved of Hermia
Demetrius, in love with Hermia, favoured
by Egeus
Philostrate, Master of the Revels to Theseus
Peter Quince, a carpenter (Prologue)
Nick Bottom, a weaver (Pyramus)
Francis Flute, a bellows-mender (Thisby)
Tom Snout, a tinker (Wall)
Snug, a joiner (Lion)
Robin Starveling, a tailor (Moonshine)
Hippolyta, Queen of the Amazons, betrothed
to Theseus

Hermia, daughter of Egeus, in love with
Lysander
Helena, in love with Demetrius
Oberon, King of the Fairies
Titania, Queen of the Fairies
Puck, or Robin Goodfellow
Peaseblossom
Cobweb   Fairies
Moth
Mustardseed
Other Fairies attending Oberon and
Titania. Attendants on Theseus and
Hippolyta.

ACT 1
SCENE 1

Athens. The palace of Theseus.

Enter Theseus, Hippolyta, Philostrate, and Attendants.

THESEUS: Now, fair Hippolyta,° our nuptial hour
    Draws on apace;° four happy days bring in
    Another moon. But oh, methinks, how slow
    This old moon wanes! She lingers° my desires,
5   Like to a stepdame, or a dowager,
    Long withering out° a young man's revenue.°
HIPPOLYTA: Four days will quickly steep themselves in° night,
    Four nights will quickly dream away the time,
    And then the moon, like to a silver bow
10   New-bent in heaven, shall behold the night
    Of our solemnities.
THESEUS: Go, Philostrate,
    Stir up the Athenian youth to merriments,

---

*Note that individual lines are numbered in the following play. When a line is shared by two or more characters, it is counted as one line.   °*Hippolyta:* Queen of the Amazons, a legendary race of female warriors who lived in southern Russia; Theseus had defeated them in battle.   °*apace:* Quickly.   °*lingers:* Delays. °*withering out:* Making to dwindle.   °*Like . . . revenue:* Like a stepmother or a widowed mother (*dowager*) who has to be provided with an annuity.   °*steep . . . in:* Turn into.

Awake the pert° and nimble spirit of mirth.
Turn melancholy forth to funerals.
The pale companion° is not for our pomp.   15

Exit Philostrate.

Hippolyta, I wooed thee with my sword,
And won thy love, doing thee injuries;
But I will wed thee in another key,
With pomp, with triumph, and with reveling.

Enter Egeus, Hermia, Lysander, and Demetrius.

EGEUS: Happy be Theseus, our renownèd Duke!   20
THESEUS: Thanks, good Egëus. What's the news with thee?
EGEUS: Full of vexation come I, with complaint
    Against my child, my daughter Hermia.
    Stand forth, Demetrius. My noble lord,
    This man hath my consent to marry her.   25
    Stand forth, Lysander. And, my gracious Duke,
    This man hath bewitched the bosom of my child.
    Thou, thou, Lysander, thou hast given her rhymes,
    And interchanged love tokens with my child.
    Thou hast by moonlight at her window sung,   30
    With feigning° voice, verses of feigning love;
    And stolen the impression of her fantasy°
    With bracelets of they hair, rings, gawds,° conceits,°
    Knacks,° trifles, nosegays,° sweetmeats, messengers
    Of strong prevailment in unhardened youth.   35
    With cunning hast thou filched my daughter's heart,
    Turned her obedience, which is due to me,
    To stubborn harsheness. And, my gracious Duke,
    Be it so° she will not here before your Grace
    Consent to marry with Demetrius,   40
    I beg the ancient privilege of Athens,
    As she is mine, I may dispose of her —
    Which shall be either to this gentleman
    Or to her death, according to our law
    Immediately° provided in that case.   45
THESEUS: What say you, Hermia? Be advised,° fair maid,
    To you your father should be as a god,
    One that composed° your beauties — yea, and one

°*pert:* Lively.   °*pale companion:* Melancholy fellow.   °*feigning:* Deceptive.   °*stolen...fantasy:* Made a false impression on her imagination.   °*gawds:* Trifles.   °*conceits:* Pretty compliments.   °*Knacks:* Knickknacks.   °*nosegays:* Bunches of flowers.   °*Be it so:* If.   °*Immediately:* Expressly.   °*Be advised:* Consider.   °*composed:* Formed.

To whom you are but as a form° in wax
50   By him imprinted and within his power
To leave the figure or disfigure it.
Demetrius is a worthy gentleman.

Hermia: So is Lysander.

Theseus: In himself he is;
But in this kind,° wanting° your father's voice,
55   The other must be held the worthier.

Hermia: I would my father looked but with my eyes.

Theseus: Rather your eyes must with his judgment look.

Hermia: I do entreat your Grace to pardon me.
I know not by what power I am made bold,
60   Nor how it may concern my modesty,°
In such a presence here to plead my thoughts;
But I beseech your Grace that I may know
The worst that may befall me in this case
If I refuse to wed Demetrius.

65 **Theseus:** Either to die the death,° or to abjure
Forever the society of men.
Therefore, fair Hermia, question your desires.
Know of° your youth, examine well your blood,
Whether, if you yield not to your father's choice,
70   You can endure the livery of a nun —
For aye° to be in shady cloister mewed,°
To live a barren sister all your life,
Chanting faint hymns to the old fruitless moon.°
Thrice blessèd they that master so their blood,
75   To undergo such maiden pilgrimage;
But earthlier happy° is the rose distilled,°
Than that which, withering on the virgin thorn,
Grows, lives, and dies in single blessedness.

Hermia: So will I grow, so live, so die, my lord,
80   Ere I will yield my virgin patent° up
Unto his lordship, whose unwishèd yoke
My soul consents not to give sovereignty.

Theseus: Take time to pause; and by the next new moon —
The sealing day betwixt my love and me,
85   For everlasting bond of fellowship° —
Upon that day either prepare to die

°*a form:* A shape.   °*in . . . kind:* In this case (i.e., the marriage).   °*wanting:* Being without.   °*how . . . modesty:* Whether it may make me appear immodest.   °*die the death:* Be put to death by the law.   °*Know of:* Remember.   °*For aye:* Forever.   °*mewed:* Caged.   °*to . . . moon:* To Diana, goddess of chastity and the single life.   °*earthlier happy:* Happier on earth.   °*rose distilled:* A rose plucked and its fragrance concentrated into perfume (as opposed to the rose that stays unplucked).   °*virgin patent:* Privilege of my virginity.   °*sealing day . . . fellowship:* The day when we marry.

For disobedience to your father's will,
Or else to wed Demetrius, as he would,
Or on Diana's altar to protest°
For aye austerity and single life.   90

DEMETRIUS: Relent, sweet Hermia. And, Lysander, yield
Thy crazèd title° to my certain right.

LYSANDER: You have her father's love, Demetrius,
Let me have Hermia's. Do you marry him.

EGEUS: Scornful Lysander! True, he hath my love,   95
And what is mine my love shall render° him.
And she is mine, and all my right of her
I do estate° unto Demetrius.

LYSANDER: I am, my lord, as well derived as he,
As well possessed;° my love is more than his;   100
My fortunes every way as fairly ranked,
If not with vantage,° as Demetrius'.
And, which is more than all these boasts can be,
I am beloved of beauteous Hermia.
Why should not I then prosecute my right?   105
Demetrius, I'll avouch it to his head,°
Made love to Nedar's daughter, Helena,
And won her soul, and she, sweet lady, dotes,
Devoutly dotes, dotes in idolatry,
Upon this spotted° and inconstant man.   110

THESEUS: I must confess that I have heard so much,
And with Demetrius thought to have spoke thereof;
But, being overfull of self-affairs,
My mind did lose it. But, Demetrius, come,
And come, Egëus. You shall go with me.   115
I have some private schooling° for you both.
For you, fair Hermia, look you arm yourself
To fit your fancies° to your father's will,
Or else the law of Athens yields you up —
Which by no means we may extenuate —   120
To death, or to a vow of single life.
Come, my Hippolyta. What cheer, my love?
Demetrius and Egëus, go along.
I must employ you in some business.
Against° our nuptial, and confer with you   125
Of something nearly° that concerns yourselves.

°*protest:* Vow.   °*crazèd title:* Flawed claim.   °*render:* Give up to.   °*estate:* Transfer.   °*derived . . .
possessed:* Of as good birth and wealth.   °*vantage:* Advantage, superiority.   °*avouch . . . head:* Declare it
to his face.   °*spotted:* Stained.   °*schooling:* Advice.   °*fit your fancies:* Suit your ideas of love.
Against: In anticipation of.   °*nearly:* Closely.

EGEUS: With duty and desire we follow you.

Exeunt all but Lysander and Hermia.

LYSANDER: How now, my love! Why is your cheek so pale?
How chance the roses there do fade so fast?

130 HERMIA: Belike for want of rain, which I could well
Beteem° them from the tempest of my eyes.

LYSANDER: Aye me! for aught that I could ever read,
Could ever hear by tale or history,
The course of true love never did run smooth,

135 But either it was different in blood —

HERMIA: Oh, cross!° Too high to be enthralled° to low.°

LYSANDER: Or else misgraffèd° in respect of years —

HERMIA: Oh, spite! Too old to be engaged to young.

LYSANDER: Or else it stood upon the choice of friends —

140 HERMIA: Oh, Hell! To choose love by another's eyes.

LYSANDER: Or, if there were a sympathy in choice,
War, death, or sickness did lay siege to it,
Making it momentany° as a sound,
Swift as a shadow, short as any dream;

145 Brief as the lightning is the collied° night,
That, in a spleen,° unfolds both heaven and earth,
And ere a man hath power to say "Behold!"
The jaws of darkness do devour it up.
So quick bright things come to confusion.°

150 HERMIA: If then true lovers have been ever crossed,°
It stands as an edíct in destiny.°
Then let us teach our trial patience,
Because it is a customary cross,
As due to love as thoughts and dreams and sighs,

155 Wishes and tears, poor fancy's° followers.

LYSANDER: A good persuasion. Therefore hear me, Hermia.
I have a widow aunt, a dowager
Of great revénue, and she hath no child.
From Athens is her house remote seven leagues;°

160 And she respects° me as her only son.
There, gentle Hermia, may I marry thee,
And to that place the sharp Athenian law
Cannot pursue us. If thou lovest me, then,
Steal forth thy father's house tomorrow night,

165 And in the wood, a league without the town,

°*Beteem:* Bring forth.   °*cross:* Perversity.   °*enthralled:* Made servant to.   °*low:* One of low birth.
°*misgraffèd:* Ill grafted.   °*momentany:* Momentary.   °*collied:* Coal-black.   °*spleen:* Flash of wrath.
°*confusion:* Here pronounced with four syllables.   °*crossed:* Thwarted.   °*edíct in destiny:* Decree of fate.
°*fancy's:* Love's.   °*seven leagues:* twenty-one miles.   °*respects:* Regards.

Where I did meet thee once with Helena
To do observance to a morn of May,°
There will I stay for thee.

Hermia: My good Lysander!
I swear to thee, by Cupid's strongest bow,
By his best arrow with the golden head,°   170
By the simplicity of Venus' doves,°
By that which knitteth souls and prospers loves,
And by that fire which burned the Carthage Queen°
When the false Troyan under sail was seen —
By all the vows that ever men have broke,   175
In number more than ever women spoke,
In that same place thou hast appointed me,
Tomorrow truly will I meet with thee.

Lysander: Keep promise, love. Look, here comes Helena.

Enter Helena.

Hermia: Godspeed, fair Helena! Whither away?   180
Helena: Call you me fair? That fair again unsay.
Demetrius loves your fair. O happy fair!
Your eyes are lodestars,° and your tongue's sweet air
More tunable than lark to shepherd's ear
When wheat is green, when hawthorn buds appear.   185
Sickness is catching. Oh, were favor° so,
Yours would I catch, fair Hermia, ere I go.
My ear should catch your voice, my eye your eye,
My tongue should catch your tongue's sweet melody.
Were the world mine, Demetrius being bated,°   190
The rest I'd give to be to you translated.°
Oh, teach me how you look, and with what art
You sway the motion° of Demetrius' heart!

Hermia: I frown upon him, yet he loves me still.
Helena: Oh, that your frowns would teach my smiles such skill! 195
Hermia: I give him curses, yet he gives me love.
Helena: Oh, that my prayers could such affection move!
Hermia: The more I hate, the more he follows me.
Helena: The more I love, the more he hateth me.
Hermia: His folly, Helena, is no fault of mine.   200
Helena: None but your beauty. Would that fault were mine!

°*do . . . May:* Observe May Day.   °*golden head:* Cupid has two kinds of arrows, the leaden cause dislike, the golden love.   °*Venus' doves:* Doves were sacred to Venus, goddess of love.   °*Carthage Queen:* Dido, queen of Carthage, fell in love with Aeneas when he visited her after his escape from Troy. Aeneas deserted her, whereupon she mounted a funeral pyre and killed herself in the flames.   °*odestars:* Guiding stars.   °*favor:* Has a double meaning, "beauty" and "affection."   °*bated:* Excepted.   °*translated:* Transformed. °*motion:* Inclination.

HERMIA: Take comfort. He no more shall see my face.
Lysander and myself will fly this place.
Before the time I did Lysander see,
205   Seemed Athens as a paradise to me.
Oh then, what graces in my love do dwell,
That he hath turned a Heven unto a Hell!

LYSANDER: Helen, to you our minds we will unfold.
Tomorrow night, when Phoebe° doth behold
210   Her silver visage in the watery glass,°
Decking with liquid pearl the bladed grass,
A time that lovers' flights doth still° conceal,
Through Athens' gates have we devised to steal.

HERMIA: And in the wood, where often you and I
215   Upon faint primrose beds were wont to lie,
Emptying our bosoms of their counsel sweet,
There my Lysander and myself shall meet,
And thence from Athens turn away our eyes,
To seek new friends and stranger companies.
220   Farewell, sweet playfellow. Pray thou for us,
And good luck grant thee thy Demetrius!
Keep word, Lysander. We must starve our sight
From lovers' food till morrow deep midnight.

LYSANDER: I will, my Hermia. (*Exit Hermia.*) Helena, adieu.
225   As you on him, Demetrius dote on you! (*Exit.*)

HELENA: How happy some o'er other some° can be!
Through Athens I am thought as fair as she.
But what of that? Demetrius thinks not so,
He will not know what all but he do know.
230   And as he errs, doting on Hermia's eyes,
So I, admiring of his qualities.
Things base and vile, holding no quantity,°
Love can transpose to form and dignity.
Love looks not with the eyes, but with the mind;
235   And therefore is winged Cupid painted blind.
Nor hath Love's mind of any judgment taste;°
Wings, and no eyes, figure unheedy haste.
And therefore is Love said to be a child,
Because in choice he is so oft beguiled.
240   As waggish° boys in game themselves forswear,
So the boy Love is perjured everywhere:
For ere Demetrius looked on Hermia's eyne,°

°*Phoebe:* Diana, the moon.   °*in the watery glass:* Reflected in the water.   °*still:* Always.   °*o'er . . . some:* Compared with some others.   °*quantity:* Proportion.   °*Nor . . . taste:* Love has no judgment.   °*waggish:* Frolicsome.   °*eyne:* Eyes.

He hailed down oaths that he was only mine;
And when this hail some heat from Hermia felt,
So he dissolved, and showers of oaths did melt.   245
I will go tell him of fair Hermia's flight.
Then to the wood will he tomorrow night
Pursue her; and for this intelligence°
If I have thanks, it is a dear expense.°
But herein mean I to enrich° my pain,   250
To have his sight thither and back again. (*Exit.*)

SCENE 2

The same. Quince's house.

Enter Quince, Snug, Bottom, Flute, Snout, and Starveling.

QUINCE: Is all our company here?
BOTTOM: You were best to call them generally,° man by man, according to
  the scrip.°
QUINCE: Here is the scroll of every man's name which is thought fit,
  through all Athens, to play in our interlude° before the Duke and the   5
  Duchess on his wedding day at night.
BOTTOM: First, good Peter Quince, say what the play treats on. Then read
  the names of the actors, and so grow to a point.°
QUINCE: Marry,° our play is, *The most lamentable comedy, and most cruel
  death of Pyramus and Thisby.*   10
BOTTOM: A very good piece of work, I assure you, and a merry. Now, good
  Peter Quince, call forth your actors by the scroll. Masters, spread
  yourselves.
QUINCE: Answer as I call you. Nick Bottom, the weaver.
BOTTOM: Ready. Name what part I am for, and proceed.   15
QUINCE: You, Nick Bottom, are set down for Pyramus.
BOTTOM: What is Pyramus? A lover, or a tyrant?
QUINCE: A lover, that kills himself most gallant for love.
BOTTOM: That will ask some tears in the true performing of it. If I do it,
  let the audience look to their eyes, I will move storms, I will condole°   20
  in some measure. To the rest. Yet my chief humor° is for a tyrant.
  I could play Ercles° rarely, or a part to tear a cat° in, to make all split.

"The raging rocks
And shivering shocks
Shall break the locks   25
Of prison gates.

°*intelligence:* Information.   °*dear expense:* Something that costs one dearly.   °*enrich:* Make rich —
by the pleasure of seeing him.   °*generally:* Bottom loves a long word but usually gets it wrong. Here he
means "severally," i.e., separately.   °*scrip:* List.   °*interlude:* Play.   °*grow . . . point:* Come to a conclusion.   *Marry:* Mary; by the Virgin.   °*condole:* Sympathize; Bottom means "lament."   °*humor:* Whim.
°*Ercles:* Hercules, a roaring figure in the old drama.   °*tear a cat:* Proverbial expression for ham acting.

> And Phibbus' car°
> Shall shine from far,
> And make and mar
30   The foolish Fates."

This was lofty! Now name the rest of the players. This is Ercles' vein,
a tyrant's vein. A lover is more condoling.

QUINCE: Francis Flute, the bellows-mender.

FLUTE: Here, Peter Quince.

35 QUINCE: Flute, you must take Thisby on you.

FLUTE: What is Thisby? A wandering knight?

QUINCE: It is the lady that Pyramus must love.

FLUTE: Nay, faith, let not me play a woman. I have a beard coming.

QUINCE: That's all one. You shall play it in a mask, and you may speak as
40   small° as you will.

BOTTOM: An° I may hide my face, let me play Thisby too. I'll speak in a
monstrous little voice, "Thisne, Thisne." "Ah Pyramus, my lover dear!
Thy Thisby dear, and lady dear!"

QUINCE: No, no. You must play Pyramus, and Flute, you Thisby.

45 BOTTOM: Well, proceed.

QUINCE: Robin Starveling, the tailor.

STARVELING: Here, Peter Quince.

QUINCE: Robin Starveling, you must play Thisby's mother. Tom Snout,
the tinker.

50 SNOUT: Here, Peter Quince.

QUINCE: You, Pyramus' father. Myself, Thisby's father. Snug, the joiner,
you, the lion's part. And, I hope, here is a play fitted.

SNUG: Have you the lion's part written? Pray you, if it be, give it me, for I
am slow of study.

55 QUINCE: You may do it extempore, for it is nothing but roaring.

BOTTOM: Let me play the lion too. I will roar that I will do any man's
heart good to hear me; I will roar that I will make the Duke say, "Let
him roar again, let him roar again."

QUINCE: An you should do it too terribly, you would fright the Duchess and
60   the ladies, that they would shriek; and that were enough to hang us all.

ALL: That would hang us, every mother's son.

BOTTOM: I grant you, friends, if you should fright the ladies out of their
wits, they would have no more discretion but to hang us. But I will
aggravate° my voice so that I will roar you as gently as any sucking
65   dove, I will roar you an 'twere any nightingale.

QUINCE: You can play no part but Pyramus; for Pyramus is a sweet-faced
man, a proper° man as one shall see in a summer's day, a most
lovely, gentlemanlike man. Therefore you must needs play Pyramus.

°*Phibbus' car:* Phoebus's Chariot.   °*small:* Shrilly.   °*An:* If.   °*aggravate:* Bottom means "moderate."
°*proper:* Handsome.

BOTTOM: Well, I will undertake it. What beard were I best to play it in?

QUINCE: Why, what you will. 70

BOTTOM: I will discharge it in either your straw-color beard, your orange-tawny beard, your purple-in-grain° beard, or your French-crown-color beard, your perfect yellow.

QUINCE: Some of your French crowns have no hair at all,° and then you will play barefaced. But, masters, here are your parts. And I am to entreat you, 75 request you, and desire you, to con° them by tomorrow night; and meet me in the palace wood, a mile without the town, by moonlight. There will we rehearse, for if we meet in the city, we shall be dogged with company, and our devices known. In the meantime I will draw a bill of properties such as our play wants. I pray you, fail me not. 80

BOTTOM: We will meet, and there we may rehearse most obscenely° and courageously. Take pains, be perfect. Adieu.

QUINCE: At the Duke's Oak we meet.

BOTTOM: Enough. Hold or cut bowstrings.°

Exeunt.

ACT 2
SCENE 1

A wood near Athens.

Enter, from opposite sides, a Fairy, and Puck.

PUCK: How now, spirit! Whither wander you?

FAIRY:

> Over hill, over dale,
>> Thorough° bush, thorough brier,
> Over park, over pale,°
>> Thorough flood, thorough fire,
> I do wander everywhere, 5
> Swifter than the moon's sphere.
> And I serve the Fairy Queen,
> To dew her orbs° upon the green.
> The cowslips° tall her pensioners° be. 10
> In their gold coats spots you see;
> Those be rubies, fairy favors,
> In those freckles live their savors.

I must go seek some dewdrops here,
And hang a pearl in every cowslip's ear. 15

°*purple-in-grain:* Dyed purple. °*French . . . all:* Loss of hair was one of the results of venereal or "French" disease. °*con:* Learn by heart. °*obscenely:* Bottom means "obscurely." °*Hold . . . bowstrings:* A proverbial phrase meaning "Come what may." °*Thorough:* Through. °*pale:* Fence. °*orbs:* Fairy rings; circles of dark grass common in English meadows. °*cowslips:* A wild plant that grows in meadows, with clusters of small yellow-orange flowers on a stem eight to nine inches tall. °*pensioners:* The queen's personal bodyguard, all young men of fine physique and good family.

Farewell, thou lob° of spirits, I'll be gone.
Our Queen and all her elves come here anon.
PUCK: The King doth keep his revels here tonight.
Take heed the Queen come not within his sight;
20   For Oberon is passing° fell° and wrath,
Because that she as her attendant hath
A lovely boy, stolen from an Indian king.
She never had so sweet a changeling,°
And jealous Oberon would have the child
25   Knight of his train,° to trace° the forests wild;
But she perforce withholds the lovèd boy,
Crowns him with flowers, and makes him all her joy.
And now they never meet in grove or green,
By fountain clear or spangled starlight sheen,
30   But they do square,° that all their elves for fear
Creep into acorn cups and hide them there.
FAIRY: Either I mistake your shape and making quite,
Or else you are that shrewd and knavish sprite
Called Robin Goodfellow.° Are not you he
35   That frights the maidens of the villagery;
Skim milk, and somtimes labor in the quern,°
And bootless° make the breathless housewife churn;
And sometimes make the drink to bear no barm;°
Mislead night wanderers, laughing at their harm?
40   Those that Hobgoblin call you, and sweet Puck,
You do their work, and they shall have good luck.
Are not you he?
PUCK: Thou speak'st aright.
I am that merry wanderer of the night.
I jest to Oberon, and make him smile,
45   When I a fat and bean-fed horse beguile,
Neighing in likeness of a filly foal.
And sometime lurk I in a gossip's° bowl,
In very likeness of a roasted crab;°
And when she drinks, against her lips I bob
50   And on her withered dewlap° pour the ale.
The wisest aunt, telling the saddest tale,
Sometime for three-foot stool mistaketh me;
Then slip I from her bum, down topples she,

°*lob:* Lubber, lout.   °*passing:* Exceedingly.   °*fell:* Fierce.   °*changeling:* Child exchanged by fairies. It was a country superstition that the fairies sometimes stole a beautiful child and left an ugly one in its place; here the changeling is the stolen child.   °*train:* Following.   °*trace:* Follow the tracks in.   °*square:* Quarrel. *Robin Goodfellow:* the common name for Puck, the mischief-maker.   °*quern:* Handmill for grinding wheat. °*bootless:* Vainly.   °*barm:* Yeast.   °*gossip's:* Goodwife's (by nature given to gossiping).   °*crab:* Crab apple. Roasted apples were sometimes floated in drinks to give flavor.   °*dewlap:* Loose skin under the chin.

And "tailor"° cries, and falls into a cough,
And then the whole quire° hold their hips and laugh, 55
And waxen in their mirth, and neeze,° and swear
A merrier hour was never wasted there.
But, room, fairy! Here comes Oberon.

FAIRY: And here my mistress. Would that he were gone!

Enter, from one side, Oberon, with his train; from the other, Titania, with hers.

OBERON: Ill met by moonlight,° proud Titania. 60

TITANIA: What, jealous Oberon! Fairies, skip hence.
I have forsworn° his bed and company.

OBERON: Tarry, rash wanton. Am not I thy lord?

TITANIA: Then I must be thy lady. But I know
When thou hast stolen away from fairyland, 65
And in the shape of Corin sat all day,
Playing on pipes of corn,° and versing love
To amorous Phillida.° Why art thou here,
Come from the farthest steppe of India
But that, forsooth, the bouncing Amazon, 70
Your buskined° mistress and your warrior love,
To Theseus must be wedded, and you come
To give their bed joy and prosperity?

OBERON: How canst thou thus for shame, Titania,
Glance at my credit° with Hippolyta, 75
Knowing I know thy love to Theseus?
Didst thou not lead him through the glimmering night
From Perigenia, whom he ravishèd?
And make him with fair Aegle break his faith,
With Ariadne and Antiopa?° 80

TITANIA: These are the forgeries° of jealousy.
And never, since the middle summer's spring,
Met we on hill, in dale, forest, or mead,
By pavèd fountain or by rushy brook,
Or in the beachèd margent° of the sea, 85
To dance our ringlets° to the whistling wind,
But with thy brawls thou hast disturbed our sport.
Therefore° the winds, piping to us in vain,
As in revenge, have sucked up from the sea

°*"tailor"*: Nobody has as yet explained convincingly why she cries "tailor."   °*quire:* Company.   °*neeze:* Sneeze.   °*moonlight:* The constant suggestion of moonlight throughout acts 2, 3, and 4 is worth noting. °*forsworn:* Sworn to avoid.   °*pipes of corn:* Oaten straws, a favorite musical instrument of shepherds. °*shape . . . Phillida:* Like an idle shepherd making love to a shepherdess. Corin and Phillida are typical names in pastoral verse.   °*buskined:* Wearing hunting boots.   °*credit:* Reputation.   °*Perigenia . . . Antiopa:* These details of Theseus's love life Shakespeare found in Plutarch.   °*forgeries:* False inventions.   °*margent:* Margin.   °*ringlets:* Round dances.   °*Therefore . . . which:* Passage perhaps inspired by the extreme weather of the summer of 1594.

90   Contagious fogs, which, falling in the land,
   Have every pelting° river made so proud
   That they have overborne their continents.°
   The ox hath therefore stretched his yoke in vain,
   The plowman lost his sweat, and the green corn°
95   Hath rotted ere his youth attained a beard.
   The fold° stands empty in the drownèd field,
   And crows are fatted with the murrion° flock.
   The nine men's morris° is filled up with mud;
   And the quaint° mazes° in the wanton° green,
100   For lack of tread, are undistinguishable.
   The human mortals want° their winter here.
   No night is now with hymn or carol blest.
   Therefore the moon, the governess of floods,
   Pale in her anger, washes all the air,
105   That rhéumatic diseases do abound.
   And thorough this distemperature° we see
   The seasons alter. Hoary-headed frosts
   Fall in the fresh lap of the crimson rose,
   And on old Hiems° thin and icy crown
110   An odorous chaplet of sweet summer buds
   Is, as in mockery, set. The spring, the summer,
   The childing° autumn, angry winter, change
   Their wonted liveries, and the mazed° world,
   By their increase, now knows not which is which.
115   And this same progeny of evils comes
   From our debate, from our dissension.
   We are their parents and original.

OBERON: Do you amend it, then. It lies in you.
   Why should Titania cross her Oberon?
120   I do but beg a little changeling boy,
   To be my henchman.°

TITANIA: Set your heart at rest.
   The fairyland buys not the child of me.
   His mother was a votaress° of my order.
   And in the spicèd Indian air, by night,
125   Full often hath she gossiped by my side;
   And sat with me on Neptune's yellow sands,

°*pelting:* Paltry.   °*continents:* Banks.   °*corn:* Wheat, oats, barley, rye, but *not* maize.   °*fold:* Sheep-pen.   °*murrion:* Plague-stricken.   °*nine . . . morris:* Popular Elizabethan game.   °*quaint:* Curious.
°*mazes:* Elaborate and intricate paths leading (or misleading) to a center. Those who know the secret can find their way; those who do not are baffled at every turn. To preserve the pattern in a village green, the paths must be re-trod every year. At Hampton Court, there is an ancient maze with high yew hedges in which it is easy to be lost for hours.
°*wanton:* Luxuriant.   °*want:* Lack, i.e., are without the usual winter feasting.   °*distemperature:* Disorder in nature.   °*Hiems:* Winter.   °*childing:* Pregnant, fertile.   °*mazed:* Bewildered.   °*henchman:* Servant.   °*votaress:* Devoted follower.

Marking the embarkèd traders° on the flood,
When we have laughed to see the sails conceive
And grow big-bellied with the wanton wind,
Which she, with pretty and with swimming gait   130
Following — her womb then rich with my young squire—
Would imitate, and sail upon the land,
To fetch me trifles, and return again
As from a voyage, rich with merchandise.
But she, being mortal, of that boy did die,   135
And for her sake do I rear up her boy,
And for her sake I will not part with him.

OBERON: How long within this wood intend you stay?

TITANIA: Perchance till after Theseus' wedding day.   140
If you will patiently dance in our round,
And see our moonlight revels, go with us;
If not, shun me, and I will spare° your haunts.

OBERON: Give me that boy, and I will go with thee.

TITANIA: Not for thy fairy kingdom. Fairies, away!
We shall chide downright, if I longer stay.   145

Exit Titania with her train.

OBERON: Well, go thy way. Thou shalt not from this grove
Till I torment thee for this injury.
My gentle Puck, come hither. Thou rememberest
Since once I sat upon a promontory
And heard a mermaid,° on a dolphin's back,   150
Uttering such dulcet and harmonious breath
That the rude sea grew civil at her song,
And certain stars shot madly from their spheres°
To hear the sea maid's music.

PUCK: I remember.

OBERON: That very time I saw, but thou couldst not,   155
Flying between the cold moon and the earth,
Cupid all armed. A certain aim he took
At a fair° vestal° thronèd by the west,
And loosed his love shaft smartly from his bow,
As it should pierce a hundred thousand hearts.   160
But I might see young Cupid's fiery shaft
Quenched in the chaste beams of the watery moon,
And the imperial votaress° passed on,
In maiden meditation, fancy-free.°

°*embarkèd traders:* Merchant ships.   °*spare:* Avoid.   °*heard a mermaid:* Probably an allusion to one of the elaborate entertainments prepared for Queen Elizabeth.   °*spheres:* Courses.   °*fair . . . fancy-free:* A tactful and complimentary allusion to Queen Elizabeth, the so-called Virgin Queen, whose bosom was impenetrable to Cupid's arrows.   °*vestal:* A woman vowed to virginity.   °*votaress:* One who has made a vow.   °*fancy-free:* Not caught by love.

165   Yet marked I where the bolt° of Cupid fell.
It fell upon a little western flower,
Before milk-white, now purple with love's wound,
And maidens call it love-in-idleness.°
Fetch me that flower, the herb I showed thee once.
170   The juice of it on sleeping eyelids laid
Will make or man or woman madly dote
Upon the next live creature that it sees.
Fetch me this herb, and be thou here again
Ere the leviathan° can swim a league.

175   PUCK: I'll put a girdle round about the earth°
In forty minutes. (*Exit.*)

OBERON: Having once this juice,
I'll watch Titania when she is asleep
And drop the liquor of it in her eyes.
The next thing then she waking looks upon,
180   Be it on lion, bear, or wolf, or bull,
On meddling monkey or on busy ape,
She shall pursue it with the soul of love.
And ere I take this charm from off her sight,
As I can take it with another herb,
185   I'll make her render up her page to me.
But who comes here? I am invisible,°
And I will overhear their conference.

Enter Demetrius, Helena following him.

DEMETRIUS: I love thee not, therefore pursue me not.
Where is Lysander and fair Hermia?
190   The one I'll slay, the other slayeth me.
Thou told'st me they were stolen unto this wood,
And here am I, and wode° within this wood,
Because I cannot meet my Hermia.
Hence, get thee gone, and follow me no more.

195   HELENA: You draw me, you hardhearted adamant.°
But yet you draw not iron, for my heart
Is true as steel. Leave you° your power to draw,
And I shall have no power to follow you.

DEMETRIUS: Do I entice you? Do I speak you fair?
200   Or, rather, do I not in plainest truth
Tell you I do not nor I cannot love you?

HELENA: And even for that do I love you the more.
I am your spaniel, and, Demetrius,

°*bolt:* Arrow.   °*love-in-idleness:* Wild pansy.   °*leviathan:* Whale.   °*I'll . . . earth:* I'll fly round the earth.
°*I am invisible:* Presumably Oberon here puts on a cloak to symbolize invisibility.   °*wode:* Mad.
°*adamant:* Lodestone, a very hard magnetic stone.   °*Leave you:* If you will leave off.

The more you beat me, I will fawn on you.
Use me but as your spaniel, spurn me, strike me,   205
Neglect me, lose me — only give me leave,
Unworthy as I am, to follow you.
What worser place can I beg in your love—
And yet a place of high respect with me—
Than to be usèd as you use your dog?   210

DEMETRIUS: Tempt not too much the hatred of my spirit,
For I am sick when I do look on thee.

HELENA: And I am sick when I look not on you.

DEMETRIUS: You do impeach° your modesty too much,
To leave the city, and commit yourself   215
Into the hands of one that loves you not;
To trust the opportunity of night
And the ill counsel of a desert place
With the rich worth of your virginity.

HELENA: Your virtue is my privilege. For that   220
It is not night when I do see your face,
Therefore I think I am not in the night.
Nor doth this wood lack worlds of company,
For you in my respect° are all the world.
Then how can it be said I am alone   225
When all the world is here to look on me?

DEMETRIUS: I'll run from thee and hide me in the brakes,°
And leave thee to the mercy of wild beasts.

HELENA: The wildest hath not such a heart as you.
Run when you will, the story shall be changed.   230
Apollo flies, and Daphne holds the chase;°
The dove pursues the griffin;° the mild hind
Makes speed to catch the tiger — bootless° speed
When cowardice pursues, and valor flies.

DEMETRIUS: I will not stay thy questions, let me go.   235
Or, if thou follows me, do not believe
But I shall do thee mischief in the wood.

HELENA: Aye, in the temple, in the town, the field,
You do me mischief. Fie, Demetrius!
Your wrongs do set a scandal on my sex.   240
We cannot fight for love, as men may do;
We should be wooed, and were not made to woo.

Exit Demetrius.

I'll follow thee, and make a Heaven of Hell,
To die upon the hand I love so well. (*Exit.*)

°*impeach:* Discredit.   °*respect:* Estimation.   °*brakes:* Bushes.   °*Apollo . . . chase:* The natural order is reversed; the meek pursues the strong. According to legend, Apollo pursued Daphne, who was turned into a laurel bush.   °*griffin:* A fabulous beast, eagle in front and lion behind.   °*bootless:* Vain.

245 **OBERON:** Fare thee well, nymph. Ere he do leave this grove,
Thou shalt fly him, and he shall seek thy love.

Re-enter Puck.

Hast thou the flower there? Welcome, wanderer.
PUCK: Aye, there it is.
OBERSON: I pray thee, give it me.
I know a bank where the wild thyme blows,
250 Where oxlips° and the nodding violet grows;
Quite overcanopied with luscious woodbine,°
With sweet musk roses, and with eglantine.°
There sleeps Titania sometime of the night,
Lulled in these flowers with dances and delight.
255 And there the snake throws her enameled° skin,
Weed° wide enough to wrap a fairy in.
And with the juice of this I'll streak her eyes,
And make her full of hateful fantasies.
Take thou some of it, and seek through this grove.
260 A sweet Athenian lady is in love
With a disdainful youth. Anoint his eyes;
But do it when the next thing he espies
May be the lady. Thou shalt know the man
By the Athenian garments he hath on.
265 Effect it with some care, that he may prove
More fond° on her than she upon her love.
And look thou meet me ere the first cock crow.
PUCK: Fear not, my lord, your servant shall do so.

Exeunt.

SCENE 2

Another part of the wood.

Enter Titania, with her train.

TITANIA: Come, now a roundel° and a fairy song,
Then, for the third part of a minute, hence —
Some to kill cankers° in the musk-rose buds,
Some war with reremice° for their leathern wings,
5 To make my small elves coats, and some keep back
The clamorous owl that nightly hoots and wonders
At our quaint spirits. Sing me now asleep,
Then to your offices, and let me rest.

The fairies sing.

°*oxlips:* Cross between primroses and cowslips. °*woodbine:* Honeysuckle. °*eglantine:* Sweetbrier.
°*enameled:* Shiny. °*Weed:* Garment. °*fond:* Foolishly doting. °*roundel:* Round dance. °*cankers:*
Cankerworms. °*reremice:* Bats.

1ST FAIRY:

> You spotted snakes with double tongue,
>> Thorny hedgehogs, be not seen.
> Newts and blindworms,° do no wrong,   10
>> Come not near our fairy Queen.

CHORUS:

> Philomel,° with melody
> Sing in our sweet lullaby;
> Lulla, lulla, lullaby, lulla, lulla, lullaby.   15
>> Never harm,
>> Nor spell, nor charm,
> Come our lovely lady nigh.
> So, good night, with lullaby.

1ST FAIRY:

> Weaving spiders, come not here.   20
>> Hence, you long-legged spinners, hence!
>>> Beetles black, approach not near.
>>> Worm nor snail, do no offense.

CHORUS:

> Philomel, with melody
> Sing in our sweet lullaby;   25
> Lulla, lulla, lullaby, lulla, lulla, lullaby.
>> Never harm,
>> Nor spell, nor charm,
> Come our lovely lady nigh.
> So, good night, with lullaby.   30

2ND FAIRY: Hence, away! Now all is well.
One aloof stand sentinel.

Exeunt Fairies. Titania sleeps.

Enter Oberon, and squeezes the flower on Titania's eyelids.

OBERON: What thou seest when thou dost wake,
Do it for thy truelove take,
Love and languish for his sake.   35
Be it ounce,° or cat, or bear,
Pard,° or boar with bristled hair,
In thy eye that shall appear
When thou wakest, it is thy dear.
Wake when some vile thing is near. *(Exit.)*   40

Enter Lysander and Hermia.

LYSANDER: Fair love, you faint with wandering in the wood,
And to speak troth, I have forgot our way.

°*blindworms:* Slow worms, small harmless snakelike creatures (actually legless lizards), common in the English countryside.   °*Philomel:* The nightingale.   °*ounce:* Lynx.   °*Pard:* Leopard.

We'll rest us, Hermia, if you think it good,
And tarry for the comfort of the day.

45 **HERMIA:** Be it so, Lysander. Find you out a bed,
For I upon this bank will rest my head.

LYSANDER: One turf shall serve as pillow for us both—
One heart, one bed, two bosoms, and one troth.°

HERMIA: Nay, good Lysander, for my sake, my dear,
50   Lie further off yet, do not lie so near.

LYSANDER: Oh, take the sense, sweet, of my innocence!
Love takes the meaning in love's conference.
I mean that my heart unto yours is knit
So that but one heart we can make of it.
55   Two bosoms interchainèd with an oath,
So then two bosoms and a single troth.
Then by your side no bedroom me deny
For lying so, Hermia, I do not lie.

HERMIA: Lyander riddles very prettily.
60   Now much beshrew° my manners and my pride,
If Hermia meant to say Lysander lied.
But, gentle friend, for love and courtesy
Lie further off; in human modesty,
Such separation as may well be said
65   Becomes a virtuous bachelor and a maid,
So far be distant. And good night, sweet friend.
Thy love ne'er alter till thy sweet life end!

LYSANDER: Amen, amen, to that fair prayer say I,
And then end life when I end loyalty!
70   Here is my bed. Sleep give thee all his rest!

HERMIA: With half that wish the wisher's eye be pressed! *(They sleep.)*

Enter Puck.

PUCK: Through the forest have I gone,
But Athenian found I none
On whose eyes I might approve°
75   This flower's force in stirring love.
Night and silence.—Who is here?
Weeds of Athens he doth wear.
This is he, my master said,
Despisèd the Athenian maid,
80   And here the maiden, sleeping sound
On the dank and dirty ground.
Pretty soul! She durst not lie
Near this lacklove, this kill-courtesy.
Churl,° upon thy eyes I throw

° *troth:* Truth.   ° *beshrew:* Plague on.   ° *approve:* Test.   ° *Churl:* Boor.

All the power this charm doth owe.   85
When thou wakest, let love forbid
Sleep his seat on thy eyelid.
So awake when I am gone,
For I must now to Oberon. *(Exit.)*

Enter Demetrius and Helena, running.

Helena: Stay, though thou kill me, sweet Demetrius.   90
Demetrius: I charge thee, hence, and do not haunt me thus.
Helena: Oh, wilt thou darkling° leave me? Do not so.
Demetrius: Stay, on thy peril.° I alone will go. *(Exit.)*
Helena: Oh, I am out of breath in this fond° chase!
  The more my prayer, the lesser is my grace.   95
  Happy is Hermia, whereso'er she lies,
  For she hath blessèd and attractive eyes.
  How came her eyes so bright? Not with salt tears;
  If so, my eyes are oftener washed than hers.
  No, no, I am as ugly as a bear,   100
  For beasts that meet me run away for fear.
  Therefore no marvel though Demetrius
  Do, as a monster, fly my presence thus.
  What wicked and dissembling° glass of mine
  Made me compare with Hermia's sphery° eyne?   105
  But who is here? Lysander! On the ground!
  Dead? Or asleep? I see no blood, no wound.
  Lysander, if you live, good sir, awake.
Lysander: *(Awaking)* And run through fire I will for thy sweet sake.
  Transparent° Helena! Nature shows art,   110
  That through thy bosom makes me see thy heart.
  Where is Demetrius? Oh, how fit a word
  Is that vile name to perish on my sword!
Helena: Do not say so, Lysander, say not so.
  What though he love your Hermia? Lord, what though?   115
  Yet Hermia still loves you. Then be content.
Lysander: Content with Hermia! No, I do repent
  The tedious minutes I with her have spent.
  Not Hermia but Helena I love.
  Who will not change a raven for a dove?   120
  The will of man is by his reason swayed,
  And reason says you are the worthier maid.
  Things growing are not ripe until their season.
  So I, being young, till now ripe not to reason;

°*darkling:* In the dark.   °*on thy peril:* Or harm will come to you.   °*fond:* Foolish.   °*dissembling:* Deceiving.   °*sphery:* Starlike.   °*Transparent:* Clearly understandable because her emotions are so obvious.

125 And touching now the point° of human skill,
Reason becomes the marshal° to my will,°
And leads me to your eyes, where I o'erlook
Love's stories, written in love's richest book.

HELENA: Wherefore was I to this keen mockery born?
130 When at your hands did I deserve this scorn?
Is't not enough, is't not enough, young man,
That I did never, no, nor never can,
Deserve a sweet look from Demetrius' eye,
But you must flout my insufficiency?
135 Good troth, you do me wrong, good sooth,° you do,
In such disdainful manner me to woo.
But fare you well. Perforce I must confess
I thought you lord of more true gentleness.
Oh, that a lady, of one man refused,
140 Should of another therefore be abused! (*Exit.*)

LYSANDER: She sees not Hermia. Hermia, sleep thou there.
And never mayst thou come Lysander near!
For as a surfeit of the sweetest things
The deepest loathing to the stomach brings,
145 Or as the heresies that men do leave
Are hated most of those they did deceive,
So thou, my surfeit and my heresy,
Of all be hated, but the most of me!
And, all my powers, address your love and might
150 To honor Helen and to be her knight! (*Exit.*)

HERMIA: (*Awaking*) Help me, Lysander, help me! Do thy best
To pluck this crawling serpent from my breast!
Aye me, for pity! What a dream was here!
Lysander, look how I do quake with fear.
155 Methought a serpent eat my heart away,
And you sat smiling at his cruel prey.
Lysander! What, removed? Lysander! Lord!
What, out of hearing? Gone? No sound, no word?
Alack, where are you? Speak, an if you hear,
160 Speak, of all loves! I swoon almost with fear.
No? Then I well perceive you are not nigh.
Either death or you I'll find immediately. (*Exit.*)

ACT 3
SCENE 1

The wood. Titania lying asleep.

Enter Quince, Snug, Bottom, Flute, Snout, and Starveling.

°*point*: High spot.   °*marshal*: Director.   °*will*: Passion.   °*sooth*: Truth.

BOTTOM: Are we all met?

QUINCE: Pat, pat, and here's a marvelous convenient place for our
rehearsal. This green plot shall be our stage, this hawthorn brake°
our tiring-house;° and we will do it in action as we will do it before
the Duke.   5

BOTTOM: Peter Quince—

QUINCE: What sayest thou, bully Bottom?

BOTTOM: There are things in this comedy of Pyramus and Thisby that
will never please. First, Pyramus must draw a sword to kill himself,
which the ladies cannot abide. How answer you that?   10

SNOUT: By'r lakin,° a parlous fear.

STARVELING: I believe we must leave the killing out, when all is done.

BOTTOM: Not a whit. I have a device to make all well. Write me a
prologue, and let the prologue seem to say we will do no harm with
our swords, and that I Pyramus is not killed indeed. And, for the more   15
better assurance, tell them that Pyramus am not Pyramus, but
Bottom the weaver. This will put them out of fear.

QUINCE: Well, we will have such a prologue, and it shall be written in
eight and six.°

BOTTOM: No, make it two more. Let it be written in eight and eight.   20

SNOUT: Will not the ladies be afeard of the lion?

STARVELING: I fear it, I promise you.

BOTTOM: Masters, you ought to consider with yourselves. To bring in —
God shield us! — a lion among ladies° is a most dreadful thing; for
there is not a more fearful wildfowl than your lion living, and we   25
ought to look to 't.

SNOUT: Therefore another prologue must tell he is not a lion.

BOTTOM: Nay, you must name his name, and half his face must be seen
through the lion's neck. And he himself must speak through, saying
thus, or to the same defect°—"Ladies"—or "Fair ladies—I would wish   30
you"—or "I would request you"—or "I would entreat you—not to
fear, not to tremble. My life for yours. If you think I come hither as a
lion, it were pity of my life. No, I am no such thing, I am a man as
other men are." And there indeed let him name his name, and tell
them plainly he is Snug the joiner.   35

QUINCE: Well, it shall be so. But there is two hard things: that is, to bring the
moonlight into a chamber, for you know Pyramus and Thisby meet by
moonlight.

SNOUT: Doth the moon shine that night we play our play?

BOTTOM: A calendar, a calendar! Look in the almanac. Find out   40
moonshine, find out moonshine.

°*brake:* Thicket.   °*tiring-house:* Dressing room.   °*By'r lakin:* By our little lady, i.e., the Virgin Mary.
°*eight and six:* The common ballad meter of alternating lines of six and eight syllables.   °*lion . . . ladies:*
Allusion to a pamphlet describing the baptismal ceremony for the infant son of King James VI of Scotland.
°*defect:* Bottom means "effect."

QUINCE: Yes, it doth shine that night.

BOTTOM: Why, then may you leave a casement° of the great-chamber°
window, where we play, open, and the moon may shine in at

45   the casement.

QUINCE: Aye, or else one must come in with a bush of thorns and a
lantern,° and say he comes to disfigure,° or to present, the person of
moonshine. Then, there is another thing. We must have a wall in the
great chamber, for Pyramus and Thisby, says the story, did talk

50   through the chink of a wall.

SNOUT: You can never bring in a wall. What say you, Bottom?

BOTTOM: Some man or other must present wall. And let him have some
plaster, or some loam,° or some roughcast° about him, to signify
wall. And let him hold his fingers thus, and through that cranny

55   shall Pyramus and Thisby whisper.

QUINCE: If that may be, then all is well. Come, sit down, every mother's
son, and rehearse your parts. Pyramus, you begin. When you have
spoken your speech, enter into that brake. And so every one
according to his cue.

Enter Puck behind.

60   **PUCK:** What hempen homespuns° have we swaggering here,
So near the cradle of the Fairy Queen?
What, a play toward!° I'll be an auditor —
An actor too perhaps, if I see cause.

QUINCE: Speak, Pyramus. Thisby, stand forth.

65   **BOTTOM:** "Thisby, the flowers of odious savors sweet —"

QUINCE: Odors, odors.

BOTTOM: "— odors savors sweet.
So hath thy breath, my dearest Thisby dear.
But hark, a voice! Stay thou but here awhile,

70   And by and by I will to thee appear." (*Exit.*)

PUCK: A stranger Pyramus than e'er played here. (*Exit.*)

FLUTE: Must I speak now?

QUINCE: Aye, marry must you, for you must understand he goes but to see
a noise that he heard, and is to come again.

75   **FLUTE:** "Most radiant Pyramus, most lily-white of hue,
Of color like the red rose on triumphant brier,
Most briskly juvenal,° and eke°most lovely Jew,
As true as truest horse, that yet would never tire,
I'll meet thee, Pyramus, at Ninny's tomb."

°*casement:* Window opening on a hinge.   °*great-chamber:* Hall of a great house.   °*bush . . . lantern:* Supposedly carried by the man in the moon.   °*disfigure:* Quince means "prefigure."   °*loam:* Preparation of
clay used for covering walls.   °*roughcast:* Rough plaster.   °*hempen homespuns:* Coarse clothing spun at
home, i.e., country clowns.   °*toward:* In hand.   °*juvenal:* Youth.   °*eke:* Also.

QUINCE: "Ninus' tomb," man. Why, you must not speak that yet. That　　80
　　you answer to Pyramus. You speak all your part at once, cues and all.
　　Pyramus enter. Your cue is past. It is "never tire."
FLUTE: Oh —"As true as truest horse, that yet would never tire."

Re-enter Puck, and Bottom with an ass's head.

BOTTOM: "If I were fair, Thisby, I were only thine."
QUINCE: Oh, monstrous! Oh, strange! We are haunted. Pray, masters! Fly,　　85
　　masters! Help!

Exeunt Quince, Snug, Flute, Snout, and Starveling.

PUCK: I'll follow you, I'll lead you about a round,°
　　Through bog, through bush, through brake, through brier.
　　Sometime a horse I'll be, sometime a hound,
　　　　A hog, a headless bear, sometime a fire,　　90
　　And neigh, and bark, and grunt, and roar, and burn,
　　　　Like horse, hound, hog, bear, fire, at every turn. (*Exit.*)
BOTTOM: Why do they run away? This is a knavery of them to make me
　　afeard.

Re-enter Snout.

SNOUT: O Bottom, thou art changed! What do I see on thee?　　95
BOTTOM: What do you see? You see an asshead of your own, do you?

Exit Snout.

Re-enter Quince.

QUINCE: Bless thee, Bottom! Bless thee! Thou art translated.° (*Exit.*)
BOTTOM: I see their knavery. This is to make an ass of me, to fright me, if
　　they could. But I will not stir from this place, do what they can. I will
　　walk up and down here, and I will sing, that they shall hear I am not afraid.　　100

Sings.

　　　　"The ousel° cock so black of hue,
　　　　With orange-tawny bill,
　　　　The throstle° with his note so true,
　　　　The wren° with little quill;"°　　105

TITANIA: (*Awaking*) What angel wakes me from my flower bed?
BOTTOM: (*Sings.*)

　　　　"The finch, the sparrow, and the lark,
　　　　The plainsong° cuckoo gray,
　　　　Whose note full many a man doth mark,
　　　　And dares not answer nay—"　　110

°*about a round:* Roundabout.　　°*translated:* Transformed.　　°*ousel:* Blackbird.　　°*throstle:* Thrush.
wren: The smallest of English birds.　　°*quill:* Feather.　　°*plainsong:* Singing a simple melody.

for indeed who would set his wit to° so foolish a bird? Who would
give a bird the lie, though he cry "cuckoo" never so?

Titania: I pray thee, gentle mortal, sing again.
Mine ear is much enamored of thy note,
115   So is mine eye enthrallèd° to thy shape.
And thy fair virtue's force perforce doth move me
On the first view to say, to swear, I love thee.

Bottom: Methinks, mistress, you should have little reason for that. And
yet, to say the truth, reason and love keep little company together
120   nowadays; the more the pity, that some honest neighbors will not
make them friends. Nay, I can gleek° upon occasion.

Titania: Thou art as wise as thou art beautiful.

Bottom: Not so, neither. But if I had wit enough to get out of this wood,
I have enough to serve mine own turn.

125   **Titania:** Out of this wood do not desire to go.
Thou shalt remain here, whether thou wilt or no.
I am a spirit of no common rate.
The summer still° doth tend° upon my state;
And I do love thee. Therefore go with me.
130   I'll give thee fairies to attend on thee,
And they shall fetch thee jewels from the deep,
And sing while thou on pressèd flowers dost sleep.
And I will purge thy mortal grossness so
That thou shalt like an airy spirit go.
135   Peaseblossom! Cobweb! Moth! And Mustardseed!

Enter Peaseblossom, Cobweb, Moth, and Mustardseed.

1st Fairy: Ready.
2nd Fairy: And I.
3rd Fairy: And I.
4th Fairy: And I.
140   **All:**   Where shall we go?
Titania: Be kind and courteous to this gentleman.
Hop in his walks, and gambol° in his eyes.
Feed him with apricocks° and dewberries,°
With purple grapes, green figs, and mulberries.
145   The honey bags steal from the humblebees,
And for night tapers crop their waxen thighs,
And light them at the fiery glowworm's eyes,
To have my love to bed and to arise.
And pluck the wings from painted butterflies,
150   To fan the moonbeams from his sleeping eyes.
Nod to him, elves, and do him courtesies.

°*set . . . to:* Try to answer.   °*enthrallèd:* Enslaved.   °*gleek:* Wisecrack.   °*still:* Always.   °*tend:* Attend.   °*gambol:* Caper.   °*apricocks:* Apricots.   °*dewberries:* Blackberries.

1ST FAIRY: Hail, mortal!
2ND FAIRY: Hail!
3RD FAIRY: Hail!
4TH FAIRY: Hail!   155
BOTTOM: I cry your Worship's mercy,° heartily. I beseech your Worship's name.
COBWEB: Cobweb.
BOTTOM: I shall desire you of more acquaintance, good Master Cobweb. If
  I cut my finger, I shall make bold with you.° You name, honest gentleman?
PEASEBLOSSOM: Peaseblossom.°   160
BOTTOM: I pray you, commend me to Mistress Squash,° your mother, and
  to Master Peascod,° your father. Good Master Peaseblossom, I shall
  desire you of more acquaintance too. Your name, I beseech you, sir?
MUSTARDSEED: Mustardseed.
BOTTOM: Good Master Mustardseed, I know your patience well. That   165
  same cowardly, giantlike ox beef hath devoured many a gentleman of
  your house. I promise you your kindred hath made my eyes water ere now.
  I desire your more acquaintance, good Master Mustardseed.
TITANIA: Come, wait upon him; lead him to my bower.
  The moon methinks looks with a watery eye,   170
  And when she weeps, weeps every little flower,
  Lamenting some enforcèd chastity.
  Tie up my love's tongue, bring him silently.

Exeunt.

SCENE 2

Another part of the wood.

Enter Oberon.

OBERON: I wonder if Titania be awaked,
  Then, what it was that next came in her eye,
  Which she must dote on in extremity.

Enter Puck.

  How now, mad spirit!
                          Here comes my messenger.
  What night rule° now about this haunted grove?   5
PUCK: My mistress with a monster is in love.
  Near to her close and consecrated bower,
  While she was in her dull and sleeping hour,
  A crew of patches,° rude mechanicals,°
  That work for bread upon Athenian stalls,°   10

°*I . . . mercy:* I beg your pardon.   °*Cobweb . . . you:* An ancient means of first aid for a cut finger.   °*Pease-*
blossom: The blossom of a garden pea.   °*Squash:* The unripe peapod.   °*Peascod:* The full pod.
°*night rule:* Mischief.   °*patches:* Clowns.   °*mechanicals:* Workingmen.   °*stalls:* Shops.

Were met together to rehearse a play,
Intended for great Theseus' nuptial day.
The shallowest thickskin of that barren° sort,
Who Pyramus presented,° in their sport

15   Forsook his scene, and entered in a brake,
When I did him at this advantage take,
An ass's nole° I fixèd on his head.
Anon his Thisbe must be answerèd,
And forth my mimic° comes. When they him spy,

20   As wild geese that the creeping fowler eye,
Or russet-pated choughs,° many in sort,
Rising and cawing at the gun's report,
Sever themselves and madly sweep the sky,
So at his sight away his fellows fly.

25   And, at our stamp, here o'er and o'er one falls,
He murder cries, and help from Athens calls.
Their sense thus weak, lost with their fears thus strong,
Made senseless things begin to do them wrong;
For briers and thorns at their apparel snatch,

30   Some sleeves, some hats, from yielders all things catch.
I led them on in this distracted fear,
And left sweet Pyramus translated there,
When in that moment, so it came to pass,
Titania waked, and straightway loved an ass.

35   **OBERON:** This falls out better than I could devise.
But hast thou yet latched° the Athenian's eyes
With the love juice, as I did bid thee do?

PUCK: I took him sleeping — that is finished too —
And the Athenian woman by his side,

40   That, when he waked, of force she must be eyed.

Enter Hermia and Demetrius.

OBERON: Stand close. This is the same Athenian.
PUCK: This is the woman, but not this the man.
DEMETRIUS: Oh, why rebuke you him that loves you so?
Lay breath so bitter on your bitter foe.

45   **HERMIA:** Now I but chide, but I should use thee worse,
For thou, I fear, hast given me cause to curse.
If thou hast slain Lysander in his sleep,
Being o'er shoes in blood, plunge in the deep,
And kill me too.

50   The sun was not so true unto the day
As he to me. Would he have stolen away

°*barren:* Empty-headed.   °*presented:* Represented.   °*nole:* noddle, head.   °*mimic:* Actor.   °*russet-pated choughs:* Gray-headed jackdaws.   °*latched:* Caught, i.e., charmed.

From sleeping Hermia? I'll believe as soon
This whole earth may be bored, and that the moon
May through the center° creep, and so displease
Her brother's noontide with the Antipodes.°   55
It cannot be but thou hast murdered him.
So should a murderer look, so dead,° so grim.

DEMETRIUS: So should the murdered look, and so should I,
    Pierced through the heart with your stern cruelty.
    Yet you, the murderer, look as bright, as clear,   60
    As yonder Venus° in her glimmering sphere.

HERMIA: What's this to my Lysander? Where is he?
    Ah, good Demetrius, wilt thou give him me?

DEMETRIUS: I had rather give his carcass to my hounds.

HERMIA: Out, dog! Out, cur! Thou drivest me past the bounds   65
    Of maiden's patience. Hast thou slain him, then?
    Henceforth be never numbered among men!
    Oh, once tell true, tell true, even for my sake!
    Durst thou have looked upon him being awake.
    And hast thou killed him sleeping? Oh, brave touch.°   70
    Could not a worm, an adder, do so much?
    An adder did it, for with doubler tongue
    Than thine, thou serpent, never adder stung.

DEMETRIUS: You spend your passion on a misprised° mood.
    I am not guilty of Lysander's blood,   75
    Nor is he dead, for aught that I can tell.

HERMIA: I pray thee, tell me then that he is well.

DEMETRIUS: An if I could, what should I get therefore?

HERMIA: A privilege never to see me more.
    And from thy hated presence part I so.   80
    See me no more, whether he be dead or so. (*Exit.*)

DEMETRIUS: There is no following her in this fierce vein.
    Here therefore for a while I will remain.
    So sorrow's heaviness doth heavier grow
    For debt that bankrupt sleep doth sorrow owe,°   85
    Which now in some slight measure it will pay
    If for his tender° here I make some stay. (*Lies down and sleeps*)

OBERON: What hast thou done? Thou hast mistaken quite,
    And laid the love juice on some truelove's sight,
    Of thy misprision° must perforce ensue   90
    Some true love turned, and not a false turned true.

°*center:* The center of the earth.   °*so . . . Antipodes:* The moon will pass through the earth and appear at the other side, to the annoyance of the sun, who is shining there.   °*dead:* Deadly.   °*Venus:* The planet. °*touch:* Feat.   °*misprised:* Mistaken.   °*So . . . owe:* A man in sorrow cannot sleep; sleep's debt to sorrow thus becomes heavier.   °*tender:* Offer, i.e., sleep.   °*misprision:* Mistake.

PUCK: Then fate o'errules, that, one man holding troth,
    A million fail, confounding oath on oath.°
OBERON: About the wood go swifter than the wind,
95   And Helena of Athens look thou find.
    All fancy-sick° she is and pale of cheer,°
    With sighs of love that costs the fresh blood° dear.
    By some illusion° see thou bring her here.
    I'll charm his eyes against° she do appear.
100 PUCK: I go, I go, look how I go,
    Swifter than arrow from the Tartar's° bow. (*Exit.*)
OBERON: Flower of this purple dye,
    Hit with Cupid's archery,
    Sink in apple of his eye.
105   When his love he doth espy,
    Let her shine as gloriously
    As the Venus of the sky.
    When thou wakest, if she be by,
    Beg of her for remedy.

Re-enter Puck.

110 PUCK: Captain of our fairy band,
    Helena is here at hand,
    And the youth, mistook by me,
    Pleading for a lover's fee.
    Shall we their fond pageant see?
115   Lord, what fools these mortals be!
OBERON: Stand aside. The noise they make
    Will cause Demetrius to awake.
PUCK: Then will two at once woo one,
    That must needs be sport alone.
120   And those things do best please me
    That befall preposterously.

Enter Lysander and Helena.

LYSANDER: Why should you think that I should woo in scorn?
    Scorn and derision never come in tears.
    Look, when I vow, I weep, and vows so born
125   In their nativity all truth appears.
    How can these things in me seem scorn to you,
    Bearing the badge of faith to prove them true?
HELENA: You do advance your cunning more and more.

°*Then . . . oath:* Then fate overrules my efforts; for every man true in love, a million are false, breaking oath after oath. °*fancy-sick:* Lovesick. °*cheer:* Face. °*sighs . . . blood:* It was believed that sighs consumed the heart's blood. °*illusion:* Deception. °*against:* By the time that. °*Tartar's:* The Tartars, who lived in Siberia, were famous bowmen.

When truth kills truth, oh, devilish-holy fray!
These vows are Hermia's. Will you give her o'er?   130
Weigh oath with oath, and you will nothing weigh.
Your vows to her and me, put in two scales,
Will even weigh — and both as light as tales.
LYSANDER: I had no judgment when to her I swore.
HELENA: Nor none, in my mind, now you give her o'er.   135
LYSANDER: Demetrius loves her, and he loves not you.
DEMETRIUS: (*Awaking*) O Helen, goddess, nymph, perfect, divine!
To what, my love, shall I compare thine eyne?
Crystal is muddy. Oh, how ripe in show
Thy lips, those kissing cherries, tempting grow!   140
That pure congealèd white, high Taurus'° snow,
Fanned with the eastern wind, turns to a crow
When thou hold'st up thy hand. Oh, let me kiss
This princess of pure white, this seal° of bliss!
HELENA: Oh, spite! Oh, Hell! I see you all are bent   145
To set against me for your merriment.
If you were civil and knew courtesy,
You would not do me thus much injury.
Can you not hate me, as I know you do,
But you must join in souls to mock me too?   150
If you were men, as men you are in show,
You would not use a gentle lady so —
To vow, and swear, and superpraise my parts,
When I am sure you hate me with your hearts.
You both are rivals, and love Hermia,   155
And now both rivals, to mock Helena.
A trim° exploit, a manly enterprise,
To conjure tears up in a poor maid's eyes
With your derision! None of noble sort
Would so offend a virgin, and extort   160
A poor soul's patience, all to make you sport.
LYSANDER: You are unkind, Demetrius. Be not so;
For you love Hermia — this you know I know.
And here, with all goodwill, with all my heart,
In Hermia's love I yield you up my part.   165
And yours of Helena to me bequeath,
Whom I do love, and will do till my death.
HELENA: Never did mockers waste more idle breath.
DEMETRIUS: Lysander, keep thy Hermia. I will none.
If e'er I loved her, all that love is gone.   170

°*Taurus'*: The Taurus mountains are in Asia Minor.   °*seal*: Guarantee.   °*trim*: Fine.

My heart to her but as guest-wise sojourned,°
And now to Helen is it home returned,
There to remain.

LYSANDER: Helen, it is not so.

DEMETRIUS: Disparage not the faith thou dost not know,

175   Lest, to thy peril, thou aby° it dear.
Look where thy love comes — yonder is thy dear.

Re-enter Hermia.

HERMIA: Dark night, that from the eye his function takes,
The ear more quick of apprehension makes.
Wherein it doth impair the seeing sense,

180   It pays the hearing double recompense.
Thou art not by mine eye, Lysander, found;
Mine ear, I thank it, brought me to thy sound.
But why unkindly didst thou leave me so?

LYSANDER: Why should he stay whom love doth press to go?

185   **HERMIA:** What love could press Lysander from my side?

LYSANDER: Lysander's love, that would not let him bide
Fair Helena, who more engilds the night
Than all yon fiery oes° and eyes of light.
Why seek'st thou me? Could not this make thee know,

190   The hate I bare thee made me leave thee so?

HERMIA: You speak not as you think. It cannot be.

HELENA: Lo, she is one of this confederacy!
Now I perceive they have conjoined all three
To fashion this false sport, in spite of me.°

195   Injurious Hermia! Most ungrateful maid!
Have you conspired, have you with these contrived°
To bait° me with this foul derision?
Is all the counsel that we two have shared,
The sister's vows, the hours that we have spent,

200   When we have chid the hasty-footed time
For parting us — Oh, is it all forgot?
All school days' friendship, childhood innocence?
We, Hermia, like two artificial° gods,
Have with our needles created both one flower,

205   Both on one sampler,° sitting on one cushion,
Both warbling of one song, both in one key —
As if our hands, our sides, voices, and minds
Had been incorporate.° So we grew together,

°*guest-wise sojourned:* Made a short stay.   °*aby:* Abide, pay for.   °*oes:* Circles, i.e., stars, with a pun on
"o" and "i."   °*in . . . me:* To spite me.   °*contrived:* Devised, plotted.   °*bait:* Taunt.   °*artificial:* Creative.   °*sampler:* Piece of embroidery.   °*incorporate:* In one body.

Like to a double cherry, seeming parted
But yet a union in partition — 210
Two lovely berries molded on one stem.
So, with two seeming bodies, but one heart,
Two of the first, like coats in heraldry,
Due but to one, and crownèd with one crest.°
And will you rent our ancient love asunder, 215
To join with men in scorning your poor friend?
It is not friendly, 'tis not maidenly.
Our sex, as well as I, may chide you for it,
Though I alone do feel the injury.

Hermia: I am amazèd at your passionate words. 220
I scorn you not. It seems that you scorn me.

Helena: Have you not set Lysander, as in scorn,
To follow me and praise my eyes and face?
And made your other love, Demetrius,
Who even but now did spurn me with his foot, 225
To call me goddess, nymph, divine and rare,
Precious, celestial! Wherefore speaks he this
To her he hates? And wherefore doth Lysander
Deny your love, so rich within his soul,
And tender me, forsooth, affection, 230
But by your setting on, by your consent?
What though I be not so in grace as you,
So hung upon with love, so fortunate,
But miserable most, to love unloved?
This you should pity rather than despise. 235

Hermia: I understand not what you mean by this.

Helena: Aye, do, persever,° counterfeit sad looks,
Make mouths upon me when I turn my back,
Wink each at other, hold the sweet jest up.
This sport, well carried, shall be chronicled.° 240
If you have any pity, grace, or manners,
You would not make me such an argument.°
But fare ye well. 'Tis partly my own fault,
Which death or absence soon shall remedy.

Lysander: Stay, gentle Helena, hear my excuse. 245
My love, my life, my soul, fair Helena!

Helena: Oh, excellent!

Hermia: Sweet, do not scorn her so.

Demetrius: If she cannot entreat, I can compel.

Lysander: Thou canst compel no more than she entreat.

°*Two . . . crest:* Two bodies with a single heart — an elaborate mataphor from heraldry. After marriage, the coats of arms of husband and wife are united in one coat under one crest.   °*persever:* Keep it up.   °*chronicled:* Recorded in the history book.   °*argument:* Subject for a story.

250 Thy threats have no more strength than her weak prayers.
     Helen, I love thee, by my life, I do.
     I swear by that which I will lose for thee,
     To prove him false that says I love thee not.
DEMETRIUS: I say I love thee more than he can do.
255 LYSANDER: If thou say so, withdraw, and prove it too.
DEMETRIUS: Quick, come!
HERMIA: Lysander, whereto tends all this?
LYSANDER: Away, you Ethiope!°
DEMETRIUS: No, no, he'll—
     Seem to break loose,° take on as you would follow,
     But yet come not. You are a tame man, go!
260 LYSANDER: Hang off, thou cat, thou bur! Vile thing, let loose,
     Or I will shake thee from me like a serpent!
HERMIA: Why are you grown so rude? What change is this?
     Sweet love—
LYSANDER: Thy love! Out, tawny° Tartar, out!
     Out, loathèd medicine! Hated potion, hence!
HERMIA: Do you not jest?
265 HELENA: Yes, sooth, and so do you.
LYSANDER: Demetrius, I will keep my word with thee.
DEMETRIUS: I would I had your bond,° for I perceive
     A weak bond° holds you. I'll not trust your word.
LYSANDER: What, should I hurt her, strike her, kill her dead?
270 Although I hate her, I'll not harm her so.
HERMIA: What, can you do me greater harm than hate?
     Hate me! Wherefore? Oh, me! What news, my love!
     Am not I Hermia? Are not you Lysander?
     I am as fair now as I was erewhile.°
275 Since night you loved me, yet since night you left me.
     Why, then you left me — Oh, the gods forbid—
     In earnest, shall I say?
LYSANDER: Aye, by my life,
     And never did desire to see thee more.
     Therefore be out of hope, of question, of doubt;
280 Be certain, nothing truer. 'Tis no jest
     That I do hate thee, and love Helena.
HERMIA: Oh, me! You juggler! You canker blossom!°
     You thief of love! What, have you come by night

°*Ethiope:* Ethiopian. From the number of references to the dark complexion of different women in Shakespeare's plays, it is evident that one of the boy actors was dark-skinned.   °*No . . . loose:* There is a difficulty of reading here. Hermia is clutching Lysander; Demetrius taunts him, saying that he pretends to want a fight but is in reality willing enough to be held back by a woman.   °*tawny:* dark-skinned.   °*bond:* Written agreement. °*weak bond:* i.e., Hermia.   °*erewhile:* A short while ago.   °*canker blossom:* Worm in the bud.

And stolen my love's heart from him?

HELENA: Fine, i'faith!
Have you no modesty, no maiden shame,   285
No touch of bashfulness? What, will you tear
Impatient answers from my gentle tongue?
Fie, fie! You counterfeit, you puppet,° you!

HERMIA: Puppet? Why so? Aye, that way goes the game.
Now I perceive that she hath made compare   290
Between our statures, she hath urged her height.
And with her personage, her tall personage,
Her height, forsooth, she hath prevailed with him.
And are you grown so high in his esteem
Because I am so dwarfish and so low?   295
How low am I, thou painted maypole?° Speak—
How long am I? I am not yet so low
But that my nails can reach unto thine eyes.

HELENA: I pray you, though you mock me, gentlemen,
Let her not hurt me. I was never curst,°   300
I have no gift at all in shrewishness.
I am a right maid° for my cowardice.
Let her not strike me. You perhaps may think,
Because she is something lower than myself,
That I can match her.

HERMIA: Lower! Hark again.   305

HELENA: Good Hermia, do not be so bitter with me.
I evermore did love you, Hermia,
Did ever keep your counsels, never wronged you,
Save that, in love unto Demetrius,
I told him of your stealth unto this wood.   310
He followed you, for love I followed him;
But he hath chid° me hence, and threatened me
To strike me, spurn me, nay, to kill me too.
And now, so you will let me quiet go,
To Athens will I bear my folly back,   315
And follow you no further. Let me go.
You see how simple and how fond I am.

HERMIA: Why, get you gone. Who is't that hinders you?

HELENA: A foolish heart, that I leave here behind.

HERMIA: What, with Lysander?

HELENA: With Demetrius.   320

LYSANDER: Be not afraid. She shall not harm thee, Helena.

DEMETRIUS: No, sir, she shall not, though you take her part.

°*puppet:* Doll.   °*maypole:* Unlike Hermia, Helena is tall and thin.   °*curst:* Bad-tempered.   °*right maid:*
Truly feminine.   °*chid:* Scolded.

HELENA: Oh, when she's angry, she is keen and shrewd!°
She was a vixen when she went to school,
325   And though she be but little, she is fierce.
HERMIA: Little again! Nothing but low and little!
Why will you suffer her to flout me thus?
Let me come to her.
LYSANDER: Get you gone, you dwarf,
You minimus,° of hindering knotgrass° made,
You bead, you acorn.
330 **DEMETRIUS:**   You are too officious
In her behalf that scorns your services.
Let her alone. Speak not of Helena,
Take not her part; for it thou dost intend
Never so little show of love to her,
Thou shalt aby it.
335 **LYSANDER:**   Now she holds me not.
Now follow, if thou darest, to try whose right,
Of thine or mine, is most in Helena.
DEMETRIUS: Follow! Nay, I'll go with thee, cheek by jole.°

Exeunt Lysander and Demetrius.

HERMIA: You, mistress, all this coil° is 'long of you.
Nay, go not back.
340 **HELENA:**   I will not trust you, I,
Nor longer stay in your curst company.
Your hands than mine are quicker for a fray,
My legs are longer though, to run away. (*Exit.*)
HERMIA: I am amazed, and know not what to say. (*Exit.*)
345 **OBERON:** This is thy negligence. Still thou mistakest,
Or else committ'st thy knaveries willfully.
PUCK: Believe me, King of Shadows, I mistook.
Did not you tell me I should know the man
By the Athenian garments he had on?
350   And so far blameless proves my enterprise
That I have 'nointed an Athenian's eyes.
And so far am I glad it so did sort,
As this their jangling° I esteem a sport.
OBERON: Thou see'st these lovers seek a place to fight.
355   Hie° therefore, Robin, overcast the night.
The starry welkin° cover thou anon°
With drooping fog, as black as Acheron,°

°*shrewd:* A shrew.   °*minimus:* Littlest thing.   °*hindering knotgrass:* A clinging weed believed to stunt
growth.   °*cheek by jole:* Cheek by jowl; that is, closely.   °*coil:* Tumult.   °*jangling:* Wrangling.   °*Hie:*
Hasten.   °*welkin:* Sky.   °*anon:* At once.   °*Acheron:* River in the underworld.

And lead these testy rivals to astray
As one come not within another's way.
Like to Lysander sometime frame thy tongue,　　360
Then stir Demetrius up with bitter wrong.
And sometime rail thou like Demetrius,
And from each other look thou lead them thus
Till o'er their brows death-counterfeiting sleep
With leaden° legs and batty wings doth creep.　　365
Then crush this herb into Lysander's eye,
Whose liquor hath this virtuous property,
To take from thence all error with his might,
And make his eyeballs roll with wonted sight.
When they next wake, all this derision°　　370
Shall seem a dream and fruitless vision,
And back to Athens shall the lovers wend,
With league whose date till death shall never end.°
Whiles I in this affair do thee employ,
I'll to my Queen and beg her Indian boy.　　375
And then I will her charmèd eye release
From monster's view, and all things shall be peace.

PUCK: My fairy lord, this must be done with haste,
For night's swift dragons° cut the clouds full fast,
And yonder shines Aurora's° harbinger,°　　380
At whose approach, ghosts, wandering here and there,
Troop home to churchyards. Damnèd spirits all,
That in crossways° and floods have burial,
Already to their wormy beds are gone.
For fear lest day should look their shames upon,　　385
They willfully themselves exíle from light,
And must for aye° consort with black-browed night.

OBERON: But we are spirits of another sort.°
I with the morning's love have oft made sport,
And, like a forester, the groves may tread　　390
Even till the eastern gate, all fiery-red,
Opening on Neptune with fair blessèd beams,
Turns into yellow gold his salt green streams.
But, notwithstanding, haste. Make no delay.
We may effect this business yet ere day. (*Exit.*)　　395

PUCK: Up and down, up and down,
I will lead them up and down.

°*leaden:* Heavy.　　°*derision:* Mockery.　　°*With . . . end:* United everlastingly.　　°*night's . . . dragons:*
Dragons that draw the chariot of Night.　　°*Aurora's:* The dawn's.　　°*harbinger:* Forerunner.　　°*cross-*
ways: Crossroads, where suicides were buried.　　°*for aye:* Forever.　　°*another sort:* Not damned or infernal
and thus able to endure daylight.

I am feared in field and town.
Goblin, lead them up and down.
400   Here comes one.

Re-enter Lysander.

LYSANDER: Where art thou, proud Demetrius? Speak thou now.
PUCK: Here, villain, drawn° and ready. Where art thou?
LYSANDER: I will be with thee straight.
PUCK: Follow me, then,
        To plainer° ground.

Exit Lysander, as following the voice.

Re-enter Demetrius.

405   DEMETRIUS: Lysander! Speak again.
        Thou runaway, thou coward, art thou fled?
        Speak! In some bush? Where does thou hide thy head?
    PUCK: Thou coward, art thou bragging to the stars,
        Telling the bushes that thou look'st for wars,
        And wilt not come? Come, recreant.° Come, thou child,
410   I'll whip thee with a rod. He is defiled
        That draws a sword on thee.
    DEMETRIUS: Yea, art thou there?
    PUCK: Follow my voice. We'll try no manhood here.°

Exeunt.

Re-enter Lysander.

415   LYSANDER: He goes before me and still dares me on.
        When I come where he calls, then he is gone.
        The villain is much lighter-heeled than I,
        I followed fast, but faster he did fly,
        That fallen am I in dark uneven way,
        And here will rest me. (*Lies down.*) Come, thou gentle day!
420   For if but once thou show me thy gray light,
        I'll find Demetrius, and revenge this spite. (*Sleeps.*)

Re-enter Puck and Demetrius.

    PUCK: Ho, ho, ho! Coward, why comest thou not?
    DEMETRIUS: Abide° me, if thou darest, for well I wot°
        Thou runn'st before me, shifting every place,
        And darest not stand, nor look me in the face.
425   Where art thou now?

°*drawn:* With sword drawn.   °*plainer:* Flatter.   °*recreant:* Traitor.   °*We'll . . . here:* We will not make
trial of your courage here.   °*Abide:* Wait for.   °*wot:* Know.

PUCK: Come hither. I am here.
DEMETRIUS: Nay, then, thou mock'st me. Thou shalt buy this dear
    If ever I thy face by daylight see.
    Now, go thy way. Faintness constaineth me   430
    To measure out my length on this cold bed.
    By day's approach look to be visited. (*Lies down and sleeps*)

Re-enter Helena.

HELENA: O weary night, O long and tedious night,
      Abate° thy hours! Shine comforts from the east,
    That I may back to Athens by daylight,   435
      From these that my poor company detest.
    And sleep, that sometimes shuts up sorrow's eye,
    Steal me awhile from mine own company. (Lies down and sleeps)
PUCK: Yet but three? Come one more,
      Two of both kinds makes up four.   440
    Here she comes, curst and sad.
      Cupid is a knavish lad,
    Thus to make poor females mad.

Re-enter Hermia.

HERMIA: Never so weary, never so in woe,
      Bedabbled with the dew, and torn with briers,   445
    I can no further crawl, no further go,
      My legs can keep no pace with my desires.
    Here will I rest me till the break of day.
      Heavens shield Lysnder, if they mean a fray! (Lies down and sleeps)
PUCK: On the ground   450
    Sleep sound.
    I'll apply
    To your eye,
    Gentle lover, remedy.

Squeezing the juice on Lysander's eye.

    When thou wakest,   455
    Thou takest
    True delight
    In the sight
    Of thy former lady's eye.
    And the country proverb known,   460
    That every man should take his own,
    In your waking shall be shown.
    Jack shall have Jill,
    Nought shall go ill,
The man shall have his mare again, and all shall be well. (*Exit.*)   465

°*Abate:* Shorten.

A still from Michael Hoffman's 1999 film adaptation of Shakespeare's *A Midsummer Night's Dream* with Kevin Kline as Bottom and Michelle Pfeiffer as Titania.

ACT 4
SCENE 1

The same. Lysander, Demetrius, Helena, and Hermia, lying asleep.

Enter Titania and Bottom; Peaseblossom, Cobweb, Moth, Mustardseed, and other Fairies attending; Oberon behind unseen.

TITANIA: Come, sit thee down upon this flowery bed,
While I thy amiable cheeks do coy,°
And stick musk roses in thy sleek smooth head,
And kiss thy fair large ears, my gentle joy.

5 **BOTTOM:** Where's Peaseblossom?

PEASEBLOSSOM: Ready.

BOTTOM: Scratch my head, Peaseblossom. Where's Mounsieur Cobweb?

COBWEB: Ready.

BOTTOM: Mounsieur Cobweb, good mounsieur, get you your weapons in
10 your hand, and kill me a red-hipped humblebee on the top of a thistle,
and, good mounsieur, bring me the honey bag. Do not fret yourself
too much in the action, mounsieur, and, good mounsieur, have a
care the honey bag break not. I would be loath to have you
overflown with a honey bag, signior. Where's Mounsieur
15 Mustardseed?

MUSTARDSEED: Ready.

BOTTOM: Give me your neaf,° Mounsieur Mustardseed. Pray you, leave your
courtesy,° good mounsieur.

°*coy:* Caress.   °*neaf:* Fist.   °*leave . . . courtesy:* There's no need to bow.

Bottom being pampered by fairy attendants in the Hartford Stage Production of *A Midsummer Night's Dream.*

MUSTARDSEED: What's your will?

BOTTOM: Nothing, good mounsieur, but to help Cavalery° Cobweb to   20
scratch. I must to the barber's, mounsieur, for methinks I am marvelous
hairy about the face, and I am such a tender ass, if my hair do but tickle me,
I must scratch.

TITANIA: What, wilt thou hear some music, my sweet love?

BOTTOM: I have a reasonable good ear in music.   25
Let's have the tongs and the bones.

TITANIA: Or say, sweet love, what thou desirest to eat.

BOTTOM: Truly, a peck of provender. I could munch your good dry oats.
Methinks I have a great desire to a bottle° of hay. Good hay, sweet hay,
hath no fellow.°   30

TITANIA: I have a venturous fairy that shall seek the squirrel's hoard, and
fetch thee new nuts.

BOTTOM: I had rather have a handful or two of dried peas. But I pray
you let none of your people stir me. I have an exposition° of sleep come
upon me.   35

°*Cavalery:* Cavaleiro, a gallant soldier.   °*bottle:* Bundle.   °*fellow:* Equal.   °*exposition:* Bottom means
"disposition."

TITANIA: Sleep thou, and I will wind thee in my arms. Fairies, be gone, and be all ways away.

Exeunt Fairies.

So doth the woodbine the sweet honeysuckle
Gently entwist, the female ivy so
40 Enrings the barky fingers of the elm.
Oh, how I love thee! How I dote on thee!

They sleep.

Enter Puck.

OBERON: *(Advancing)* Welcome, good Robin. See'st thou this sweet sight?
Her dotage now I do begin to pity.
For, meeting her of late behind the wood,
45 Seeking sweet favors for this hateful fool,
I did upbraid her, and fall out with her;
For she his hairy temples then had rounded
With coronet of fresh and fragrant flowers,
And that same dew, which sometime on the buds
50 Was wont to swell, like round and orient pearls,
Stood now within the pretty flowerets' eyes
Like tears that did their own disgrace bewail.
When I had at my pleasure taunted her,
And she in mild terms begged my patience,
55 I then did ask of her her changeling child,
Which straight she gave me, and her fairy sent
To bear him to my bower in fairyland.
And now I have the boy, I will undo
This hateful imperfection of her eyes.
60 And, gentle Puck, take this transformèd scalp
From off the head of this Athenian swain,
That, he awaking when the other do,
May all to Athens back again repair,°
And think no more of this night's accidents
65 But as the fierce vexation of a dream.
But first I will release the Fairy Queen.
      Be as thou wast wont to be,
      See as thou wast wont to see.
      Dian's° bud o'er Cupid's flower
70   Hath such force and blessèd power.
Now, my Titania, wake you, my sweet Queen.
TITANIA: My Oberon! What visions have I seen!
Methought I was enamored of an ass.

°*repair:* Return.   °*Dian:* Diana (see 1.1.73).

Oberon: There lies your love.
Titania: How came these things to pass?
 Oh, how mine eyes do loathe his visage now!   75
Oberon: Silence awhile. Robin, take off this head.
 Titania, music call, and strike more dead
 Than common sleep of all these five° the sense.°
Titania: Music, ho! Music, such as charmeth sleep!

Music, still.

Puck: Now, when thou wakest, with thine own fool's eyes peep.   80
Oberon: Sound, music! Come, my Queen, take hands with me,
 And rock the ground whereon these sleepers be.
 Now thou and I are new in amity,
 And will tomorrow midnight solemnly
 Dance in Duke Theseus' house triumphantly,   85
 And bless it to all fair prosperity.
 There shall the pairs of faithful lovers be
 Wedded, with Theseus, all in jollity.
Puck: Fairy King, attend, and mark.
 I do hear the morning lark.   90
Oberon: Then, my Queen, in silence sad,°
 Trip we after night's shade.
 We the globe can compass soon,
 Swifter than the wandering moon.
Titania: Come, my lord, and in our flight,   95
 Tell me how it came this night
 That I sleeping here was found
 With these mortals on the ground.

Exeunt.

Horns winded° within. Enter Theseus, Hippolyta, Egeus, and train.

Theseus: Go, one of you, find out the forester,
 For now our observation° is performed.   100
 And since we have the vaward° of the day,
 My love shall hear the music of my hounds.
 Uncouple in the western valley, let them go.
 Dispatch, I say, and find the forester.

Exit an Attendant.

 We will, fair Queen, up to the mountain's top,   105
 And mark the musical confusion

°*these five:* Bottom, Demetrius, Lysander, Hermia, and Helena.   °*strike . . . sense:* Make them more dead
asleep than normal.   °*sad:* Serious.   °*winded:* Sounded.   °*observation:* The rites of May (see
1.1.167).   °*vaward:* Forepart.

Of hounds and echo in conjunction.

HIPPOLYTA: I was with Hercules and Cadmus once
When in a wood of Crete they bayed° the bear

110   With hounds of Sparta. Never did I hear
Such gallant chiding;° for, besides the groves,
The skies, the fountains, every region near
Seemed all one mutual cry. I never heard
So musical a discord, such sweet thunder.

115   **THESEUS:** My hounds are bred out of the Spartan kind,
So flewed,° so sanded;° and their heads are hung
With ears that sweep away the morning dew;
Crook-kneed, and dewlapped° like Thessalian bulls;
Slow in pursuit, but matched in mouth like bells,°

120   Each under each.° A cry° more tunable
Was never holloed to, nor cheered with horn,
In Crete, in Sparta, nor in Thessaly.
Judge when you hear. But, soft! What nymphs are these?

EGEUS: My lord, this is my daughter here asleep.

125   And this, Lysander. This Demetrius is,
This Helena, old Nedar's Helena.
I wonder of their being here together.

THESEUS: No doubt they rose up early to observe
The rite of May, and, hearing our intent,

130   Came here in grace of° our solemnity.°
But speak, Egëus, is not this the day
That Hermia should give answer of her choice?

EGEUS: It is, my lord.

THESEUS: Go, bid the huntsmen wake them with their horns.

*Horns and shout within.° Lysander, Demetrius, Helena, and Hermia, wake and
start up.*

135   Good morrow, friends. Saint Valentine° is past.
Begin these wood birds but to couple now?

LYSANDER: Pardon, my lord.

THESEUS: I pray you all, stand up.
I know you two are rival enemies.
How comes this gentle concord in the world,

140   That hatred is so far from jealousy,
To sleep by hate, and fear no enmity?

°*bayed:* Brought to bay.   °*chiding:* Barking.   °*flewed:* With hanging cheeks.   °*sanded:* Sandy colored.
°*dewlapped:* The dewlap is a flap of loose skin hanging down from the throats of cattle and certain kinds of
dog.   °*matched . . . bells:* In a perfect pack of hounds, each hound uttered a different note, the total effect being harmony.   °*Each . . . each:* One a note lower than the other.   °*cry:* Pack of hounds.   °*in grace of:*
In compliment to.   °*solemnity:* Celebration.   °*within:* Offstage.   °*Saint Valentine:* The day on which
birds were supposed to mate.

LYSANDER: My lord, I shall reply amazedly,
Half sleep, half waking. But as yet, I swear,
I cannot truly say how I came here,
But, as I think — for truly would I speak,
And now I do bethink me, so it is — 145
I came with Hermia hither. Our intent
Was to be gone from Athens, where we might,
Without the peril° of the Athenian law —
EGEUS: Enough, enough, my lord, you have enough. 150
I beg the law, the law, upon his head.
They would have stolen away. They would, Demetrius,
Thereby to have defeated you and me,
You of your wife and me of my consent —
Of my consent that she should be your wife. 155
DEMETRIUS: My lord, fair Helen told me of their stealth,
Of this their purpose hither to this wood.
And I in fury hither followed them,
Fair Helena in fancy° following me.
But, my good lord, I wot not by what power — 160
But by some power it is — my love to Hermia,
Melted as the snow, seems to me now
As the remembrance of an idle gaud°
Which in my childhood I did dote upon.
And all the faith, the virtue of my heart, 165
The object and the pleasure of mine eye,
Is only Helena. To her, my lord,
Was I betrothed ere I saw Hermia.
But, like in sickness, did I loathe this food,
But, as in health, come to my natural taste, 170
Now I do wish it, love it, long for it,
And will forevermore be true to it.
THESEUS: Fair lovers, you are fortunately met.
Of this discourse we more will hear anon.
Egëus, I will overbear your will, 175
For in the temple, by and by, with us
These couples shall eternally be knit.
And, for° the morning now is something worn,
Our purposed hunting shall be set aside.
Away with us to Athens! Three and three,° 180
We'll hold a feast in great solemnity.
Come, Hippolyta.

Exeunt Theseus, Hippolyta, Egeus, and train.

°*Without the peril:* Beyond danger.   °*fancy:* Love.   °*gaud:* Trifle.   °*for:* Since.   °*Three and three:*
A triple wedding.

DEMETRIUS: These things seem small and undistinguishable,
Like far-off mountains turnèd into clouds.

185 **HERMIA:** Methinks I see these things with parted eye,
When everything seems double.

HELENA: So methinks.
And I have found Demetrius like a jewel,
Mine own, and not mine own.

DEMETRIUS: Are you sure
That we are awake? It seems to me

190 That yet we sleep, we dream. Do not you think
The Duke was here, and bid us follow him?

HERMIA: Yea, and my father.

HELENA: And Hippolyta.

LYSANDER: And he did bid us follow to the temple.

DEMETRIUS: Why, then, we are awake. Let's follow him,

195 And by the way let us recount our dreams.

Exeunt.

BOTTOM: *(Awaking)* When my cue comes, call me, and I will answer.
My next is "Most fair Pyramus." Heigh-ho! Peter Quince! Flute, the
bellows-mender! Snout, the tinker! Starveling! God's my life, stolen hence,
and left me asleep! I have had a most rare vision. I have had a dream past

200 the wit of man to say what dream it was. Man is but an ass if he go about
to expound this dream. Methought I was — there is no man can tell what.
Methought I was — and methought I had — but man is but a patched° fool
if he will offer to say what methought I had. The eye of man hath not
heard, the ear of man hath not seen, man's hand is not able to taste, his

205 tongue to conceive, nor his heart to report, what my dream was. I will get
Peter Quince to write a ballad of this dream. It shall be called Bottom's
Dream, because it hath no bottom, and I will sing it in the latter end of a
play, before the Duke. Peradventure,° to make it the more gracious, I shall
sing it at her death.° *(Exit.)*

SCENE 2

Athens. Quince's house.

Enter Quince, Flute, Snout, and Starveling.

QUINCE: Have you sent to Bottom's house? Is he come home yet?

STARVELING: He cannot be heard of. Out of doubt he is transported.°

FLUTE: If he come not, then the play is marred. It goes not forward,
doth it?

°*patched:* Wearing a particolored coat, the regular costume worn by a professional fool.   °*Peradventure:* Perchance.   °*at her death:* Thisby's death at the end of the play.   *transported:* Carried off.

QUINCE: It is not possible. You have not a man in all Athens able to discharge 5
    Pyramus but he.

FLUTE: No, he hath simply the best wit of any handicraft man in Athens.

QUINCE: Yea, and the best person too, and he is a very paramour for a sweet
    voice.

FLUTE: You must say "paragon." A paramour is, God bless us, a thing of 10
    naught.°

Enter Snug.

SNUG: Masters, the Duke is coming from the temple, and there is two or three
    lords and ladies more married. If our sport had gone forward, we had all
    been made men.

FLUTE: Oh, sweet bully Bottom! Thus hath he lost sixpence a day during 15
    his life;° he could not have scaped sixpence a day. An the Duke had
    not given him sixpence a day for playing Pyramus, I'll be hanged.
    He would have deserved it. Sixpence a day in Pyramus, or nothing.

Enter Bottom.

BOTTOM: Where are these lads? Where are these hearts?

QUINCE: Bottom! Oh, most courageous day! Oh, most happy hour! 20

BOTTOM: Masters, I am to discourse wonders. But ask me not what, for if I tell
    you I am no true Athenian. I will tell you everything, right as it fell out.

QUINCE: Let us hear, sweet Bottom.

BOTTOM: Not a word of me. All that I will tell you is that the Duke hath
    dined. Get your apparel together, good strings° to your beards, new ribbons 25
    to your pumps.° Meet presently° at the palace. Every man look o'er his
    part, for the short and the long is, our play is preferred.° In any case, let
    Thisby have clean linen, and let not him that plays the lion pare his nails,
    for they shall hang out for the lion's claws. And, most dear actors, eat no
    onions nor garlic, for we are to utter sweet breath, and I do not doubt but to 30
    hear them say it is a sweet comedy. No more words. Away! Go, away!

Exeunt.

ACT 5
SCENE 1

Athens. The palace of Theseus.

Enter Theseus, Hippolyta, Philostrate, Lords, and Attendants.

HIPPOLYTA: 'Tis strange, my Theseus, that these lovers speak of.

THESEUS: More strange than true. I never may believe
    These antique fables, nor these fairy toys.°

°*naught:* Wickedness.   °*sixpence . . . life:* A royal pension of sixpence a day for life.   °*strings:* For tying
on the beards.   °*pumps:* Shoes.   °*presently:* Immediately.   °*preferred:* Accepted.   °*fairy toys:*
Trifling tales about fairies.

Lovers and madmen have such seething brains,
5   Such shaping fantasies,° that apprehend
More than cool reason ever comprehends.
The lunatic, the lover, and the poet
Are of imagination all compact.°
One sees more devils than vast Hell can hold,
10   That is the madman. The lover, all as frantic,
Sees Helen's beauty in a brow of Egypt.°
The poet's eye, in a fine frenzy rolling,
Doth glance from heaven to earth, from earth to heaven,
And as imagination bodies forth
15   The forms of things unknown, the poet's pen
Turns them to shapes, and gives to airy nothing
A local habitation and a name.
Such tricks hath strong imagination
That if it would but apprehend some joy,
20   It comprehends some bringer of that joy;
Or in the night, imagining some fear,
How easy is a bush supposed a bear!

HIPPOLYTA: But all the story of the night told over,
And all their minds transfigured° so together,
25   More witnesseth than fancy's images,
And grows to something of great constancy,°
But, howsoever, strange and admirable.°

THESEUS: Here come the lovers, full of joy and mirth.

Enter Lysander, Demetrius, Hermia, and Helena.

Joy, gentle friends! Joy and fresh days of love
Accompany your hearts!
30   **LYSANDER:**   More than to us
Wait in your royal walks, your board, your bed!
THESEUS: Come now, what masques,° what dances shall we have
To wear away this long age of three hours
Between our after-supper and bedtime?
35   Where is our usual manager of mirth?
What revels are in hand? Is there no play
To ease the anguish of a torturing hour?
Call Philostrate.

PHILOSTRATE: Here, mighty Theseus.

THESEUS: Say, what abridgment° have you for this evening?

°*fantasies:* Fancies.   °*Are . . . compact:* Wholly composed of imagination — which in Shakespeare's time
meant the "power of seeing things."   °*Sees . . . Egypt:* To the lover, a gypsy is as beautiful as Helen of Troy.
Gypsies were thought to be Egyptians.   °*transfigured:* Excited.   °*constancy:* Consistency; the fact that
they are all excited shows that something strange has happened to them.   °*admirable:* Marvelous.
°*masques:* Courtly entertainments.   °*abridgment:* Pastime, entertainment.

What masque? What music? How shall we beguile   40
    The lazy time, if not with some delight?
PHILOSTRATE: There is a brief° how many sports are ripe.°
    Make choice of which your Highness will see first. (*Giving a paper*)
THESEUS: (*Reads.*) "The battle with the Centaurs,° to be sung
    By an Athenian eunuch to the harp."   45
We'll none of that. That have I told my love,
In glory of my kinsman Hercules.
    "The riot of the tipsy Bacchanals,
    Tearing the Thracian singer in their rage."°
That is an old device, and it was played   50
When I from Thebes came last a conqueror.
    "The thrice three Muses mourning for the death
    Of Learning,° late deceased in beggary."
That is some satire, keen and critical,
Not sorting with a nuptial ceremony.   55
    "A tedious brief scene of young Pyramus
    And his love Thisbe, very tragical mirth."
Merry and tragical! Tedious and brief!
That is, hot ice and wondrous strange snow.
How shall we find the concord of this discord?   60
PHILOSTRATE: A play there is, my lord, some ten words long,
    Which is as brief as I have known a play.
    But by ten words, my lord, it is too long,
    Which makes it tedious; for in all the play
    There is not one word apt, one player fitted.   65
    And tragical, my noble lord, it is,
    For Pyramus therein doth kill himself.
    Which, when I saw rehearsed, I must confess
    Made mine eyes water, but more merry tears
    The passion of loud laughter never shed.   70
THESEUS: What are they that do play it?
PHILOSTRATE: Hardhanded men that work in Athens here,
    Which never labored in their minds till now,
    And now have toiled their unbreathed° memories
    With this same play, against° your nuptial.   75
THESEUS: And we will hear it.
PHILOSTRATE: No, my noble lord,
    It is not for you. I have heard it over,
    And it is nothing, nothing in the world—

°*brief:* List.   °*ripe:* Ready.   °*Centaurs:* Creatures half man, half horse.   °*The riot . . . rage":* The story of how Orpheus the singer was torn in pieces by frenzied women worshipers of Bacchus.   °*"death . . . Learning:* Depending on when this portion of the play was last revised, the words most likely refer to the death of either the English poet and dramatist Robert Greene (1592) or the English poet Edmund Spenser (1599).   °*unbreathed:* Unpracticed.   °*against:* In anticipation of.

Unless you can find sport in their intents,°
80   Extremely stretched° and conned with cruel pain,°
To do you service.
THESEUS: I will hear that play,
For never anything can be amiss,
When simpleness and duty tender it.
Go, bring them in, and take your places, ladies.

Exit Philostrate.

85   HIPPOLYTA: I love not to see wretchedness o'ercharged,°
And duty in his service perishing.°
THESEUS: Why, gentle sweet, you shall see no such thing.
HIPPOLYTA: He says they can do nothing in this kind.°
THESEUS: The kinder we, to give them thanks for nothing.
90   Our sport shall be to take what they mistake.
And what poor duty cannot do, noble respect
Takes it in might, not merit.°
Where I have come, great clerks° have purposed
To greet me with premeditated welcomes,
95   Where I have seen them shiver and look pale,
Make periods in the midst of sentences,
Throttle their practiced accent in their fears,
And, in conclusion, dumbly have broke off,
Nor paying me a welcome. Trust me, sweet,
100   Out of this silence yet I picked a welcome,
And in the modesty of fearful° duty
I read as much as from the rattling tongue
Of saucy and audacious eloquence.
Love, therefore, and tongue-tied simplicity
105   In least speak most, to my capacity.°

Re-enter Philostrate.

PHILOSTRATE: So please your Grace, the Prologue is addressed.°
THESEUS: Let him approach.

Flourish of trumpets. Enter Quince for the Prologue.

PROLOGUE: If° we offend, it is with our goodwill.
That you should think, we come not to offend,
110   But with goodwill. To show our simple skill,

°*intents:* Intentions.   °*Extremely stretched:* Overreaching themselves.   °*pain:* Labor.   °*wretchedness o'ercharged:* Poor men trying to do too much.   °*duty . . . perishing:* A subject ruining himself through excess of zeal.   °*this kind:* I.e., acting.   °*noble . . . merit:* A noble mind accepts the good intention for the bad performance.   °*great clerks:* Learned scholars.   °*fearful:* Full of fear.   °*capacity:* Understanding.   °*addressed:* Ready.   °*If . . . know:* Quince, by mistaking his punctuation, makes woeful sense of his words.

> That is the true beginning of our end.
> Consider, then, we come but in despite.°
>   We do not come, as minding to content you,   115
> Our true intent is. All for your delight,
>   We are not here. That you should here repent you,
> The actors are at hand, and, by their show,
> You shall know all, that you are like to know.

THESEUS: This fellow doth not stand upon points.°

LYSANDER: He hath rid his prologue like a rough colt, he knows not
the stop. A good moral, my lord. It is not enough to speak, but to   120
speak true.

HIPPOLYTA: Indeed he hath played on his prologue like a child on a
recorder°— a sound, but not in government.°

THESEUS: His speech was like a tangled chain — nothing impaired, but all
disordered. Who is next?   125

Enter Pyramus and Thisbe. Wall, Moonshine, and Lion.

PROLOGUE: Gentles, perchance you wonder at this show,
>   But wonder on, till truth make all things plain.
> This man is Pyramus, if you would know.
>   This beauteous lady Thisby is certáin.
> This man, with lime and roughcast, doth present   130
>   Wall, that vile Wall which did these lovers sunder,
> And through Wall's chink, poor souls, they are content
>   To whisper. At the which let no man wonder.
> This man, with lanthorn,° dog, and bush of thorn,
>   Presenteth Moonshine; for, if you will know,   135
> By moonshine did these lovers think no scorn
>   To meet at Ninus' tomb, there, there to woo.
> This grisly beast, which Lion hight° by name,
> The trusty Thisby, coming first by night,
> Did scare away, or rather did affright.   140
> And, as she fled, her mantle she did fall,°
>   Which Lion vile with bloody mouth did stain.
> Anon comes Pyramus, sweet youth and tall,
>   And finds his trusty Thisby's mantle slain.
> Whereat, with blade, with bloody blameful blade,   145
>   He bravely broached his boiling bloody breast.
> And Thisby, tarrying in mulberry shade,
>   His dagger drew, and died. For all the rest,
> Let Lion, Moonshine, Wall, and lovers twain
> At large discourse, while here they do remain.   150

°*despite:* Ill will.   °*stand upon points:* Observe his punctuation marks.   °*recorder:* A flutelike musical instrument.   °*government:* Control.   °*lanthorn:* Lantern with sides made of horn.   °*hight:* Called.
°*did fall:* Let fall.

Exeunt Prologue, Pyramus, Thisbe, Lion, and Moonshine.

THESEUS: I wonder if the lion be to speak.

DEMETRIUS: No wonder, my lord. One lion may when many asses do.

WALL: In this same interlude it doth befall

That I, one Snout by name, present a wall,

155 And such a wall, as I would have you think,

That had in it a crannied° hole or chink,

Through which the lovers, Pyramus and Thisby,

Did whisper often very secretly.

This loam, this roughcast, and this stone doth show

160 That I am that same wall. The truth is so.

And this the cranny is, right and siníster,°

Through which the fearful lovers are to whisper.

THESEUS: Would you desire lime and hair to speak better?

DEMETRIUS: It is the wittiest partition that ever I heard discourse,

165 my lord.

THESEUS: Pyramus draws near the wall. Silence!

Re-enter Pyramus.

PYRAMUS: O grim-looked night! O night with hue so black!

O night, which ever art when day is not!

O night, O night! alack, alack, alack,

170 I fear my Thisby's promise is forgot!

And thou, O wall, O sweet, O lovely wall,

That stand'st between her father's ground and mine!

Thou wall, O wall, O sweet and lovely wall,

Show me thy chink, to blink through with mine eyne!

Wall holds up his fingers.

175 Thanks, courteous wall. Jove shield thee well for this!

But what see I? No Thisby do I see.

O wicked wall, through whom I see no bliss!

Cursed be thy stones for thus deceiving me!

THESEUS: The wall, methinks, being sensible,° should curse again.

180 **PYRAMUS:** No, in truth, sir, he should not. "Deceiving me" is Thisby's cue.

She is to enter now, and I am to spy her through the wall. You shall see, it

will fall pat as I told you. Yonder she comes.

Re-enter Thisbe.

THISBE: O wall, full often hast thou heard my moans,

For parting my fair Pyramus and me!

185 My cherry lips have often kissed thy stones,

Thy stones with lime and hair knit up in thee.

°*crannied:* Cracked.   °*siníster:* Left-handed.   °*being sensible:* Having feeling.

PYRAMUS: I see a voice. Now will I to the chink,
    To spy an I can hear my Thisby's face.
    Thisby!
THISBE: My love thou art, my love I think. 190
PYRAMUS: Think what thou wilt, I am thy lover's grace;
    And, like Limander,° am I trusty still.
THISBE: And I like Helen,° till the Fates me kill.
PYRAMUS: Not Shafalus to Procrus° was so true.
THISBE: As Shafalus to Procrus, I to you. 195
PYRAMUS: Oh, kiss me through the hole of this vile wall!
THISBE: I kiss the wall's hole, not your lips at all.
PYRAMUS: Wilt thou at Ninny's tomb meet me straight way?
THISBE: 'Tide life, 'tide death, I come without delay.

Exeunt Pyramus and Thisbe.

WALL: Thus have I, wall, my part dischargèd so; 200
    And, being done, thus wall away doth go. *(Exit.)*
THESEUS: Now is the mural° down between the two neighbors.
DEMETRIUS: No remedy, my lord, when walls are so willful to hear without
    warning.
HIPPOLYTA: This is the silliest stuff that ever I heard. 205
THESEUS: The best in this kind are but shadows,° and the worst are no worse
    if imagination amend them.
HIPPOLYTA: It must be your imagination, then, and not theirs.
THESEUS: If we imagine no worse of them than they of themselves, they
    may pass for excellent men. Here come two noble beasts in, a man and 210
    a lion.

Re-enter Lion and Moonshine.

LION: You, ladies, you, whose gentle hearts do fear
    The smallest monstrous mouse that creeps on floor,
May now perchance both quake and tremble here,
    When lion rough in wildest rage doth roar. 215
Then know that I, one Snug the joiner, am
A lion fell,° nor else no lion's dam;
For, if I should as lion come in strife
Into this place, 'twere pity on my life.°
THESEUS: A very gentle beast, and of a good conscience. 220
DEMETRIUS: The very best at a beast, my lord, that e'er I saw.
LYSANDER: This lion is a very fox for his valor.
THESEUS: True, and a goose for his discretion.

°*Limander:* For "Leander."   °*Helen:* For "Hero," Leander's love.   °*Shafalus to Procrus:* For "Cephalus to
Procris."   °*mural:* Wall.   °*shadows:* Things of no substance.   °*fell:* Fierce.

225 DEMETRIUS: Not so, my lord, for his valor cannot carry his discretion, and the
fox carries the goose.

THESEUS: His discretion, I am sure, cannot carry his valor, for the goose
carries not the fox. It is well. Leave it to his discretion, and let us listen
to the moon.

MOONSHINE: This lanthorn doth the hornèd moon present—

230 DEMETRIUS: He should have worn the horns on his head.

THESEUS: He is no crescent, and his horns are invisible within the
circumference.

MOONSHINE: This lanthorn doth the hornèd moon present,
Myself the man i' the moon do seem to be.

235 THESEUS: This is the greatest error of all the rest. The man should be put into
the lantern. How is it else the man i' the moon?

DEMETRIUS: He dares not come there for the candle, for you see it is already
in snuff.°

HIPPOLYTA: I am aweary of this moon. Would he would change!

240 THESEUS: It appears, by his small light of discretion, that he is in the wane.
But yet, in courtesy, in all reason, we must stay the time.°

LYSANDER: Proceed, Moon.

MOONSHINE: All that I have to say is, to tell you that the lanthorn is the
moon; I, the man i' the moon; this thornbush, my thornbush; and

245 this dog, my dog.

DEMETRIUS: Why, all these should be in the lantern, for all these are in the
moon. But, silence! Here comes Thisbe.

Re-enter Thisbe.

THISBE: This is old Ninny's tomb. Where is my love?

LION: *(Roaring)* Oh—

Thisbe runs off.

250 DEMETRIUS: Well roared, Lion.

THESEUS: Well run, Thisbe.

HIPPOLYTA: Well shone, Moon. Truly, the moon shines with a good grace.

The Lion shakes Thisbe's mantle, and exit.

THESEUS: Well moused,° Lion.

LYSANDER: And so the lion vanished.

255 DEMETRIUS: And then came Pyramus.

Re-enter Pyramus.

PYRAMUS: Sweet Moon, I thank thee for thy sunny beams,
I thank thee, Moon, for shining now so bright.

°*in snuff:* Smoking. Before self-consuming wicks were invented for candles, wicks had to be snuffed (cut) constantly or they would smoke foully. °*stay the time:* See it out. °*moused:* Torn apart as a cat tears a
mouse.

  For, by thy gracious, golden, glittering gleams,
   I trust to take of truest Thisby sight.
    But stay, oh, spite!   260
    But mark, poor knight,
 What dreadful dole° is here!
    Eyes, do you see?
    How can it be?
  Oh, dainty duck! Oh, dear!   265
   Thy mantle good,
   What, stained with blood!
  Approach, ye Furies fell!
   O Fates, come, come,
   Cut thread and thrum,°   270
 Quail,° crush, conclude, and quell!°

THESEUS: This passion, and the death of a dear friend, would go near to make
 a man look sad.

HIPPOLYTA: Beshrew my heart, but I pity the man.

PYRAMUS: O wherefore, Nature, didst thou lions frame?   275
  Since lion vile hath here deflowered my dear,
 Which is — no, no — which was the fairest dame
  That lived, that loved, that liked, that looked with cheer.
   Come, tears, confound.
   Out, sword, and wound   280
  The pap of Pyramus.
   Aye, that let pap,
   Where heart doth hop.

Stabs himself.

  Thus die I, thus, thus, thus.
   Now am I dead,   285
   Now am I fled,
  My soul is in the sky.
   Tongue, lose thy light,
   Moon, take thy flight,

Exit Moonshine.

  Now die, die, die, die, die. *(Dies.)*   290

DEMETRIUS: No die, but an ace,° for him,° for he is but one.

LYSANDER: Less than an ace, man, for he is dead, he is nothing.

THESEUS: With the help of a surgeon he might yet recover, and prove
 an ass.

°*dole:* Dolor, grief.   °*thrum:* The end of the thread in a piece of weaving. So *cut thread and thrum* means "destroy everything."   °*Quail:* Overwhelm.   °*quell:* Slay.   °*ace:* Throw of one.   °*No . . . him:* Demetrius makes a poor pun on *die* (perish) and *die* (singular of *dice*).

295 **HIPPOLYTA:** How chance Moonshine is gone before Thisbe comes back and finds her lover?

THESEUS: She will find him by starlight. Here she comes, and her passion ends the play.

Re-enter Thisbe.

HIPPOLYTA: Methinks she should not use a long one for such a Pyramus. I
300 hope she will be brief.

DEMETRIUS: A mote° will turn the balance, which Pyramus, which Thisbe, is the better — he for a man, God warrant us, she for a woman, God bless us.

LYSANDER: She hath spied him already with those sweet eyes.

305 **DEMETRIUS:** And thus she means, videlicet:°

THISBE:

> Asleep, my love?
> What, dead, my dove?
> O Pyramus, arise!
> Speak, speak. Quite dumb?
310 > Dead, dead? A tomb
> Must cover thy sweet eyes.
> These lily lips,
> This cherry nose,
> These yellow cowslip cheeks,
315 > Are gone, are gone.
> Lovers, make moan.
> His eyes were green as leeks.
> O Sisters Three,°
> Come, come to me,
320 > With hands as pale as milk,
> Lay them in gore,
> Since you have shore
> With shears his thread of silk.
> Tongue, not a word.
325 > Come, trusty sword,
> Come, blade, my breast imbrue.°

Stabs herself.

> And, farewell, friends.
> Thus Thisby ends.
> Adieu, adieu, adieu. (Dies)

330 **THESEUS:** Moonshine and Lion are left to bury the dead.

DEMETRIUS: Aye, and Wall too.

°*mote:* Speck of dust.   °*videlicet:* Namely, "viz."   °*Sisters Three:* The three Fates who sit spinning human destiny.   °*imbrue:* Make bloody.

BOTTOM: *(Starting up)* No, I assure you the wall is down that parted their fathers. Will it please you to see the epilogue, or to hear a Bergomask° dance
between two of our company?

THESEUS: No epilogue, I pray you, for your play needs no excuse. Never 335
excuse, for when the players are all dead, there need none to be blamed.
Marry, if he that writ it had played Pyramus and hanged himself in
Thisbe's garter, it would have been a fine tragedy. And so it is, truly,
and very notably discharged. But, come, your Bergomask. Let your
epilogue alone. 340

A dance.

The iron tongue of midnight hath told twelve.
Lovers, to bed, 'tis almost fairy time.
I fear we shall outsleep the coming morn
As much as we this night have overwatched.
This palpable-gross° play hath well beguiled 345
The heavy gait of night. Sweet friends, to bed.
A fortnight hold we this solemnity,
In nightly revels and new jollity.

Exeunt.

Enter Puck.

PUCK: Now the hungry lion roars,
 And the wolf behowls the moon, 350
Whilst the heavy plowman snores,
 All with weary task fordone.°
Now the wasted brands° do glow,
 Whilst the screech owl, screeching loud,
Puts the wretch that lies in woe 355
 In remembrance of a shroud.
Now it is the time of night
 That the graves, all gaping wide,
Every one lets forth his sprite,
 In the churchway paths to glide. 360
And we fairies, that do run
 By the triple Hecate's° team,
From the presence of the sun,
 Following darkness like a dream,
Now are frolic. Not a mouse 365
Shall disturb this hallowed house.

°*Bergomask:* A rough country-dance named after the province of Bergamo in Italy, whose people were noted for
their rustic manners.   °*palpable-gross:* Crudely gross.   °*fordone:* Overcome.   °*brands:* Firebrands.
°*triple Hecate's:* The goddess Diana is sometimes referred to as three-formed, because she was worshiped as
Luna (or Cynthia), the moon, in heaven; Diana on earth; and Proserpine (or *Hecate*) in Hades.

I am sent with broom before,
To sweep the dust behind the door.

Enter Oberon and Titania with their train.

OBERON: Through the house give glimmering light,
370   By the dead and drowsy fire.
    Every elf and fairy sprite
      Hop as light as bird from brier,
    And this ditty, after me,
    Sing, and dance it trippingly.
375 **TITANIA:** First, rehearse your song by rote,
    To each word a warbling note.
    Hand in hand, with fairy grace,
    Will we sing, and bless this place.

Song and dance.

380 **OBERON:** Now, until the break of day,
    Through this house each fairy stray.
    To the best bridebed will we,
    Which by us shall blessèd be,
    And the issue there create
    Ever shall be fortunate.
385   So shall all the couples three
    Ever true in loving be,
    And the blots of Nature's hand
    Shall not in their issue stand —
    Never mole, harelip, nor scar,
390   Nor mark prodigious,° such as are
    Despisèd in nativity,
    Shall upon their children be.
    With this field dew consecrate,
    Every fairy take his gait,
395   And each several° chamber bless,
    Through this palace, with sweet peace,
    And the owner of it blest,
    Ever shall in safety rest.
    Trip away, make no stay,
400   Meet me all by break of day.

Exeunt Oberon, Titania, and train.

PUCK: If we shadows have offended,
    Think but this, and all is mended,
    That you have but slumbered here

°*prodigious:* Unnatural.   °*several:* Separate.

While these visions did appear,
And this weak and idle theme,
No more yielding but a dream,
Gentles, do not reprehend.
If you pardon, we will mend.
And, as I am an honest Puck,
If we have unearnèd luck
Now to scape the serpent's tongue,°
We will make amends ere long,
Else the Puck a liar call.
So, good night unto you all.
Give me your hands,° if we be friends,
And Robin shall restore amends. (*Exit.*)

405

410

415

Reading and Reacting

1. In what two locations is *A Midsummer Night's Dream* set? How do these two settings help to define the action of the play?

2. This play contains very few stage directions. In the absence of stage directions, how does Shakespeare establish the settings? How does he indicate the actions of the various characters?

3. What costumes might highlight the most distinctive character traits of the following characters: Theseus, Hermia, Bottom, Hippolyta, Oberon, and Puck?

4. Musical interludes occur throughout *A Midsummer Night's Dream* (see act 2, scene 3, for example). How does music help to establish the mood of the play? In what way does it underscore the play's themes?

5. What is the significance of Oberon's flower? What kind of prop would you design to represent it?

6. Would you use a realistic ass's head on Bottom, or would some other alternative be more effective? Explain your answer.

7. Today, the role of Puck is frequently played by a female. How might you explain this casting decision? How would you cast Puck?

8. Theseus's final speech is interrupted by a dance of clowns. What do you think the purpose of this dance is? If you were directing the play, would you include this interlude?

9. How would you use lighting to establish the mood of act 3?

10. **JOURNAL ENTRY** A critic has observed that *A Midsummer Night's Dream* "does not read as well as it plays." What do you think he means? What, if anything, do you think one loses by reading this play instead of seeing it?

11. **CRITICAL PERSPECTIVE** In his commentary on *A Midsummer Night's Dream*, Charles Boyce says, "Scholars generally agree that *A Midsummer Night's Dream* was written to be performed at an aristocratic wedding. Everything in the play is related to the theme of marriage."

°*serpent's tongue:* Hissing.   °*Give . . . hands:* Clap.

What elements of the play do you think are "related to the theme of marriage"? What "message" does Shakespeare's play have for those who are about to be married?

Related Works: "Araby" (p. 395), "Cathedral" (p. 476), "Young Goodman Brown" (p. 489), "The Passionate Shepherd to His Love" (p. 1202), "La Belle Dame sans Merci" (p. 1191), "Not Marble, nor the Gilded Monuments (p. 1223), *The Brute* (p. 1293).

WRITING SUGGESTIONS: Staging

1. Discuss the problems that the original staging of *Oedipus the King* or *A Midsummer Night's Dream* poses for contemporary audiences, and offer some possible solutions.
2. More than one critic has observed that the simplicity of Shakespeare's theater was one of its main strengths. If a character wanted to make himself invisible, all he had to do was declare himself so. If a scene called for a particular setting — a palace or forest, for example — the setting could be established with dialogue. Find two or three examples of this technique, and write an essay in which you discuss whether or not suggestions are more effective in the staging of *A Midsummer Night's Dream* than special effects or realistic settings would be.
3. Discuss and analyze the staging techniques used in a play that is not in this chapter — for example, *Trifles* (p. 1372) or *Tape* (p. 1313).
4. Choose a short story that appears in this anthology, and explain how you would stage it if it were a play. What furnishings, props, costumes, lighting, and sound effects would you choose? What events would occur offstage? Possible subjects for this paper might include "A&P" (p. 230), "The Story of an Hour" (p. 197), or "The Storm" (p. 281).
5. *Small World* and *The Cuban Swimmer* present different problems in staging. Write an essay in which you outline plans for staging *Small World* with a generous budget and *The Cuban Swimmer* with a very limited budget.

CHAPTER 42

THEME

> I can't even count how many times I've heard the line, "Where did the idea for this play come from?" . . . Ideas emerge from plays — not the other way around. . . . I think explanation destroys [a play] and makes it less than it is.
>
> — **Sam Shepard,** Fool for Love *and Other Plays*

Like a short story or a novel, a play is open to interpretation. Readers' reactions are influenced by the language of the text, and audiences' reactions are influenced by the performance on stage. Just as in fiction, every element of a play —its title, its conflicts, its dialogue, its characters, and its staging, for instance —can shed light on its themes.

Titles

The **title** of a play can provide insight into its themes. The ironic title of Susan Glaspell's *Trifles* (p. 1372), for example, suggests that women's concerns with "trifles" may get to the heart of the matter more effectively than the preoccupations of self-important men do. Lorraine Hansberry's *A Raisin in the Sun* is another title that offers clues to the theme of a play. An allusion to Langston Hughes's poem "Harlem" (p. 940), which asks, "what happens to a dream deferred? / Does it dry up / like a raisin in the sun?" the title suggests what happens to an African-American family whose dreams are constantly crushed. Likewise, the title *Fences* (p. 1939) offers clues to a major theme of August Wilson's play, suggesting that the main character in the play is kept from his goals by barriers that are constructed by himself as well as by society. Finally, the title of Anton Chekhov's *The Brute* (p. 1293) effectively calls attention to the play's ideas about male-female relationships. The title may refer to Smirnov, who says that he has never liked women — whom he characterizes as "creatures of poetry and romance." Or, it may refer to Mrs. Popov's late husband, to whose memory she has dedicated her life despite the fact that he was repeatedly unfaithful. Either alternative reinforces the play's tongue-in-cheek characterization of men as "brutes."

Conflicts

The unfolding plot of a play — especially the **conflicts** that develop — can also reveal the play's themes. In Henrik Ibsen's *A Doll House* (p. 1454), for example, at least three major conflicts are present: one between Nora and her husband Torvald, one between Nora and Krogstad (an old acquaintance), and one between Nora and society. Each of these conflicts sheds light on the themes of the play.

Through Nora's conflict with Torvald, Ibsen examines the constraints placed on women and men by marriage in the nineteenth century. Both Nora and Torvald are imprisoned within their respective roles: Nora must be passive and childlike, and Torvald must be proper and always in control. Nora, therefore, expects her husband to be noble and generous and, in a crisis, to sacrifice himself for her. When he fails to live up to her expectations, she is profoundly disillusioned.

Nora's conflict with Krogstad underscores Ibsen's criticisms of the class system in nineteenth-century Norway. At the beginning of the play, Nora finds it "immensely amusing: that we — that Torvald has so much power over . . . people." Krogstad, a bank clerk who is in the employ of Torvald, visits Nora in act 1 to enlist her aid in saving his job. It is clear that she sees him as her social inferior. When Krogstad questions her about a woman with whom he has seen her, she replies, "What makes you think you can cross-examine me, Mr. Krogstad — you, one of my husband's employees?" Nora does not realize that she and Krogstad are, ironically, very much alike: both occupy subordinate positions and therefore have no power to determine their own destinies.

Finally, through Nora's conflict with society, Ibsen examines an important theme of his play: the destructive nature of the forces that subjugate women. Nineteenth-century society was male dominated. A married woman could not borrow money without her husband's signature, own real estate in her own name, or enter into contracts. In addition, all her assets — including inheritances and trust funds — automatically became the property of her husband at the time of marriage. As a result of her sheltered life, Nora at the beginning of the play is completely unaware of the consequences of her actions. Most readers share Dr. Rank's confusion when he asks Nora, "Why do you laugh at that? Do you have any idea of what society is?" It is Nora's disillusionment at finding out that Torvald and the rest of society are not what she has been led to believe they are that ultimately causes her to rebel. By walking out the door at the end of the play, Nora rejects not only her husband and her children (to whom she has no legal right once she leaves), but also society and its laws.

Those three conflicts underscore many of the themes that dominate *A Doll House*. First, the conflicts show that marriage in the nineteenth century imprisons both men and women in narrow, constricting roles. They also show that middle-class Norwegian society is narrow, smug, and judgmental. (Krogstad is looked down upon for a crime years after he committed it, and Nora is looked down upon because she borrows money to save her husband's life.) Finally, the conflicts show that society does not offer individuals — especially women — the freedom to lead happy and fulfilling lives. Only when the social and economic conditions that govern society change, Ibsen suggests, can women and men live together in mutual esteem.

Dialogue

Dialogue can also give insight into a play's themes. Sometimes a character suggests — or even explicitly states — a theme. In act 3 of *A Doll House,* for example, Nora's friend, Mrs. Linde, comes as close as any character to expressing the central concern of the play when she says, "Helmer's got to learn everything; this dreadful secret has to be aired; those two have to come to a full understanding; all these lies can't go on." As the play goes on to demonstrate, the lies that exist both in marriage and in society are obstacles to love and happiness.

One of the main themes of Arthur Miller's *Death of a Salesman* (p. 1581) — the questionable validity of the American Dream, given the nation's social, political, and economic realities — is suggested by the play's dialogue. As his son Biff points out, Willy Loman's stubborn belief in upward mobility and material success is based more on fantasy than on fact:

WILLY: *(with hatred, threatening)* The door of your life is wide open!

BIFF: Pop! I am a dime a dozen, and so are you!

WILLY: *(turning on him now in an uncontrolled outburst)* I am not a dime a dozen! I am Willy Loman, and you are Biff Loman!

> *Biff starts for Willy, but is blocked by Happy. In his fury, Biff seems on the verge of attacking his father.*

BIFF: I am not a leader of men, Willy, and neither are you. You were never anything but a hard-working drummer who landed in the ash can like all the rest of them! I'm one dollar an hour, Willy! I tried seven states and couldn't raise it. A buck an hour! Do you gather my meaning? I'm not bringing home any prizes any more, and you're going to stop waiting for me to bring them home!

Though not explicitly stating the theme of the play, this exchange strongly suggests that Biff rejects the desperate optimism to which Willy clings.

Characters

Because a dramatic work focuses on a central character, or **protagonist**, the development of this character can shed light on a play's themes. Willy Loman in *Death of a Salesman* is developed in great detail. At the beginning of the play, he feels trapped, exhausted, and estranged from his surroundings. As Willy gradually sinks from depression into despair, the action of the play shifts from the present to the past, showing the events that shaped his life. His attitudes, beliefs, dreams, and dashed hopes reveal him to be an embodiment of the major theme of the play — that an unquestioning belief in the American dream of success and upward mobility is unrealistic and possibly destructive.

Nora in *A Doll House* changes a great deal during the course of the play. At the beginning, she is more her husband's possession than an adult capable of shaping her own destiny. Nora's status becomes apparent in the first act when Torvald gently scolds his "little spendthrift" and refers to her as his "little lark" and his "squirrel." She is reduced to childish deceptions, such as hiding her macaroons when her husband enters the room. After Krogstad accuses her of committing forgery and threatens to expose her, she expects her husband to rise to the occasion and take the blame for her. When Torvald instead accuses her of being a hypocrite, a liar, and a criminal, Nora's neat little world comes crashing down. As a result of this experience, Nora changes; no longer is she the submissive and obedient wife. Instead, she becomes assertive — even rebellious — ultimately telling Torvald that their marriage is a sham and that she can no longer stay with him. This abrupt shift in Nora's personality gives the audience a clear understanding of the major themes of the play.

Unlike Willy and Nora, Laura in Tennessee Williams's *The Glass Menagerie* (p. 1998) is a character who changes very little during the course of the play. Laura suffers from such pathological shyness that she is unable to attend typing class, let alone talk to a potential suitor. Although the "gentleman caller" draws Laura out of her shell for a short time, she soon withdraws again. Laura's inability to change reinforces the play's theme that contemporary society, with its emphasis on progress, has no place for people like Laura who live in private worlds "of glass animals and old, worn-out phonograph records."

Staging

Various physical elements, such as props and furnishings, may also convey the themes of a play. In *Death of a Salesman*, Biff's trophy, which is constantly in the audience's view, ironically underscores the futility of Willy's efforts to achieve success. Similarly, the miniature animals in *The Glass Menagerie* reflect the fragility of Laura's character and the futility of her efforts to fit into the modern world. And, in *Trifles*, the depressing farm house, the broken birdcage, and the dead canary suggest Mrs. Wright's misery and the reason she murdered her husband.

Special lighting effects and music can also suggest a play's themes. Throughout *The Glass Menagerie*, for example, words and pictures are projected onto a section of the set between the front room and dining room walls. In scene 1, as Tom's mother, Amanda, tells him about her experiences with her "gentlemen callers," an image of her as a girl greeting callers appears on the screen. As Amanda continues, the words *"Où sont Les Neiges"* — "Where are the snows [of yesteryear]?" — appear on the screen. Later in the play, when Laura and her mother discuss a boy Laura knew, his picture is projected on the screen, showing him as a high school hero carrying a silver cup. In addition to the slides, Williams uses music — a recurring tune, dance music, and "Ave Maria"— to increase the emotional impact of certain scenes. He also uses shafts of light focused on selected areas or characters to create a dreamlike atmosphere for the play. Collectively, the slides, music, and lighting reinforce the theme that those who retreat into the past inevitably become estranged from the present.

A Final Note

As you read, your values and beliefs influence your interpretation of a play's themes. For instance, your interest in the changing status of women could lead you to focus on the submissive, almost passive, role of Willy's wife, Linda, in *Death of a Salesman*. As a result, you could conclude that the play shows how, in the post–World War II United States, women like Linda often sacrificed their own happiness for their husbands. Remember, however, that the play itself, not just your own feelings or assumptions about it, must support your interpretation.

✔ **CHECKLIST   Writing about Theme**

- What is the central theme of the play?

- What other themes can you identify?

- Does the title of the play suggest a theme?

- What conflicts exist in the play? In what way do they shed light on the themes of the play?

- Do any characters' statements express or imply a theme of the play?

- Do any characters change during the play? How do these changes suggest the play's themes?

- Do certain characters resist change? How does their failure to change suggest a theme of the play?

- Do scenery and props help to communicate the play's themes?

- Does music reinforce certain ideas in the play?

- Does lighting underscore the themes of the play?

DAVID HENRY HWANG (1957–   ) was born in Los Angeles. The son of immigrants, Hwang wrote his first play before he graduated from Stanford. *FOB* (Fresh Off the Boat), which was first performed in 1979, won the 1981 Obie as Best New Play of the Season. Hwang attended the Yale School of Drama from 1980 to 1981, and his next two plays, *The Dance and the Railroad* (1981) and *Family Devotions* (1981), were both based on the problems of immigrants trying at the same time to assimilate and to avoid assimilation into a new culture. In 1988, his Broadway hit, *M. Butterfly*, won the Tony Award for best play and established him as a major modern American playwright.

Cultural Context With the advent of the Gold Rush and the burgeoning development of the railroad in the early nineteenth century, a large number of Chinese immigrants arrived to work in the United States. Many of these immigrants viewed their residency as temporary and did not wish to assimilate into American culture. Others wanted to stay but longed for a neighborhood of their own, and as a result, Chinatowns were born, with the largest in San Francisco and New York. Chinatowns, such as the one referred to in this play, are distinguished by bilingual signs, and numerous restaurants, stores, and businesses that serve the Asian population.

Trying to Find Chinatown (1996)

CHARACTERS
Benjamin
Ronnie

SETTING
A street corner on the Lower East Side, New York City. The present.

NOTE ON MUSIC
Obviously, it would be foolish to require that the actor portraying Ronnie perform the specified violin music live. The score of this play can be played on tape over the house speakers, and the actor can feign playing the violin using a bow treated with soap. However, to effect a convincing illusion, it is desirable that the actor possess some familiarity with the violin, or at least another stringed instrument.

Darkness. Over the house speakers, fade in Hendrix-like virtuoso rock 'n' roll riffs—heavy feedback, distortion, phase shifting, wah-wah—amplified over a tiny Fender pugnose.

Lights fade up to reveal that the music's being played over a solid-body electric violin by Ronnie, a Chinese American male in his mid-twenties, dressed in retro sixties clothing, with a few requisite nineties body mutilations. He's playing on a sidewalk for money, his violin case open before him, change and a few stray bills having been left by previous passers-by.

Enter Benjamin, early twenties, blond, blue-eyed, looking like a midwestern tourist in the big city. He holds a scrap of paper in his hands, scanning street signs for an address. He pauses before Ronnie, listens for a while. With a truly bravura run, Ronnie concludes the number, falls in his knees, gasping. Benjamin applauds.

BENJAMIN: Good. That was really great. (*Pause.*) I didn't . . . I mean, a fiddle . . . I mean, I'd heard them at square dances, on country stations and all, but I never . . . wow, this must really be New York City!

He applauds, starts to walk on. Still on his knees Ronnie clears his throat loudly.

BENJAMIN: Oh, I . . . you're not just doing this for your health, right?
He reaches in his packet, pulls out a couple of coins. Ronnie clears his throat again.

BENJAMIN: Look, I'm not a millionaire, I'm just . . .

Benjamin pulls out his wallet, removes a dollar bill. Ronnie nods his head, gestures toward the violin case, as he sits on the sidewalk, takes out a pack of cigarettes, lights one.

RONNIE: And don't call it a "fiddle," OK?
BENJAMIN: Oh, well. I didn't mean to —
RONNIE: You sound like a wuss. A hick. A dipshit.   5
BENJAMIN: It just slipped out. I didn't really —
RONNIE: If this was a fiddle, I'd be sitting here with a cob pipe, stomping my cowboy boots and kicking up hay. Then I'd go home and fuck my cousin.
BENJAMIN: Oh! Well, I don't really think —
RONNIE: Do you see a cob pipe? Am I fucking my cousin?
BENJAMIN: Well, no, not at the moment, but —   10
RONNIE: All right. Then this is a violin, you hand over the money, and I ignore the insult, herein endeth the lesson. (*Pause.*)
BENJAMIN: Listen, a dollar's more than I've ever given to a . . . to someone asking for money.
RONNIE: Yeah, well, this is New York. Welcome to the cost of living.
BENJAMIN: What I mean is, maybe in exchange, you could help me —?
RONNIE: Jesus Christ! Do you see a sign around my neck reading "Big Apple   15
Fucking Tourist Bureau?"
BENJAMIN: I'm just looking for an address, I don't think it's far from here, maybe you could . . . ?

Ronnie snatches the scrap of paper from Benjamin.

RONNIE: You're lucky I'm such a goddamn softie. (*He looks at the paper.*) Oh, fuck you. Just suck my dick, you and the cousin you rode in on.
BENJAMIN: I don't get it! What are you —?
RONNIE: Eat me. You know exactly what I —
BENJAMIN: I'm just asking for a little —   20
RONNIE: 13 Doyers St.? Like you don't know where that is?
BENJAMIN: Of course I don't know! That's why I'm asking —
RONNIE: C'mon, you trailer-park refugee. You don't know that's Chinatown?
BENJAMIN: Sure I know that's Chinatown.
RONNIE: I know you know that's Chinatown.   25
BENJAMIN: So? That doesn't mean I know where Chinatown —
RONNIE: So why is it that you picked me, of all the street musicians in the city — to point you in the direction of Chinatown? Lemme guess — is it the

earring? No, I don't think so. The Hendrix riffs? Guess again, you fucking
moron.

BENJAMIN: Now, wait a minute. I see what you're —

RONNIE: What are you gonna ask me next? Where you can find the best dim
sum in the city? Whether I can direct you to a genuine opium den? Or do I
know how you can meet Miss Saigon for a night of nookie-nookie followed
by a good old-fashioned ritual suicide? (*He picks up his violin.*) Now, get your
white ass off my sidewalk. One dollar doesn't even begin to make up for all
this aggravation. Why don't you go back home and race bullfrogs, or whatever it is you do for —?

30   **BENJAMIN:** Brother, I can absolutely relate to your anger. Righteous rage, I
suppose would be a more appropriate term. To be marginalized, as we are,
by a white racist patriarchy, to the point where the accomplishments of our
people are obliterated from the history books, this is cultural genocide of
the first order, leading to the fact that you must do battle with all Euro-
America's emasculating and brutal stereotypes of Asians — the opium den,
the sexual objectification of the Asian female, the exoticized image of a
tourist's Chinatown which ignores the exploitation of workers, the failure
to unionize, the high rate of mental illness and tuberculosis — against
these, each day, you rage, no, not as a victim, but as a survivor, yes, brother,
a glorious warrior survivor!

Silence.

RONNIE: Say what?

BENJAMIN: So, I hope you can see that my request is not —

RONNIE: Wait, wait.

BENJAMIN: —motivated by sorts of racist assumptions —

35   **RONNIE:** But, but where . . . how did you learn all that?

BENJAMIN: All what?

RONNIE: All that — you know — oppression stuff — tuberculosis . . .

BENJAMIN: It's statistically irrefutable. TB occurs in the community at a rate —

RONNIE: Where did *you* learn it?

40   **BENJAMIN:** Well . . . I took Asian-American studies. In college.

RONNIE: Where did you go to college?

BENJAMIN: University of Wisconsin. Madison.

RONNIE: Madison, Wisconsin?

BENJAMIN: That's not where the bridges are, by the way.

45   **RONNIE:** Huh? Oh, right . . .

BENJAMIN: You wouldn't believe the number of people who—

RONNIE: They have Asian-American studies in Madison, Wisconsin? Since
when?

BENJAMIN: Since the last Third World Unity sit-in and hunger strike. (*Pause.*)
Why do you look so surprised? We're down.

RONNIE: I dunno. It just never occurred to me, the idea of Asian students in
the Midwest going on a hunger strike.

BENJAMIN: Well, a lot of them had midterms that week, so they fasted in 50
shifts. (*Pause.*) The administration never figured it out. The Asian students
put that "they all look alike" stereotype to good use.

RONNIE: OK, so they got Asian-American studies. That still doesn't explain—

BENJAMIN: What?

RONNIE: What *you* were doing taking it?

BENJAMIN: Just like everyone else. I wanted to explore my roots. After a lifetime of assimilation, I wanted to find out who I really am. (*Pause.*)

RONNIE: And did you? 55

BENJAMIN: Sure. I learned to take pride in my ancestors who built the railroads, my Popo who would make me a hot bowl of jok with thousand-day-
old eggs when the white kids chased me home yelling. "Gook! Chink!
Slant-eyes!"

RONNIE: OK, OK, that's enough!

BENJAMIN: Painful to listen to, isn't it?

RONNIE: I don't know what kind of bullshit ethnic studies program they're
running over in Wisconsin, but did they teach you that in order to find
your Asian "roots," it's a good idea first to be Asian? (*Pause.*)

BENJAMIN: Are you speaking metaphorically? 60

RONNIE: No! Literally! Look at your skin!

Ronnie grabs Benjamin's hands, holds them up before his face.

BENJAMIN: You know, it's very stereotypical to think that all Asian skin tones
conform to a single hue.

RONNIE: You're white! Is this some kind of redneck joke or something? Am I
the first person in the world to tell you this?

BENJAMIN: Oh! Oh! Oh!

RONNIE: I know real Asians are scarce in the Midwest, but . . . Jesus! 65

BENJAMIN: No, of course, I . . . I see where your misunderstanding arises.

RONNIE: Yeah. It's called "You white."

BENJAMIN: It's just that—in my hometown of Tribune, Kansas, and then at
school—see, everyone knows me—so this sort of thing never comes up.
(*He offers his hand.*) Benjamin Wong. I forget that a society wedded to
racial constructs constantly forces me to explain my very existence.

RONNIE: Ronnie Chang. Otherwise known as "The Bowman."

BENJAMIN: You see, I was adopted by Chinese-American parents at birth. So 70
clearly, I'm an Asian American—

RONNIE: Even though they could put a picture of you in the dictionary next to
the definition of "WASP."

BENJAMIN: Well, you can't judge my race by my genetic heritage.

RONNIE: If genes don't determine race, what does?

BENJAMIN: Maybe you'd prefer that I continue in denial, masquerading as a
white man?

RONNIE: Listen, you can't just wake up and say, "Gee, I *feel* Black today." 75

BENJAMIN: Brother, I'm just trying to find what you've already got.

RONNIE: What do I got?

BENJAMIN: A home. With your people. Picketing with the laundry workers. Taking refuge from the daily slights against your masculinity in the noble image of Gwan Gung.

RONNIE: Gwan *who*?

80 BENJAMIN: C'mon—the Chinese God of warriors and—what do you take me for? There're altars to him up all over the community.

RONNIE: I dunno what community you're talking about, but it's sure as hell not mine. (*Pause.*)

BENJAMIN: What do you mean?

RONNIE: I mean, if you wanna call Chinatown *your* community, OK, knock yourself out, learn to use chopsticks. Go ahead, try and find your roots in some dim sum parlor with headless ducks hanging in the window. Those places don't tell you a thing about who *I* am.

BENJAMIN: Oh, I get it.

85 RONNIE: You get what?

BENJAMIN: You're one of those self-hating, *assimilated* Chinese Americans, aren't you?

RONNIE: Oh, Jesus.

BENJAMIN: You probably call yourself, "Oriental," right? Look, maybe I can help you. I have some books I can—

RONNIE: Hey, I read all those Asian identity books when you were still slathering on industrial-strength sunblock. (*Pause.*) Sure, I'm Chinese. But folks like you act like that means something. Like all of a sudden, you know who I am. You think identity's that simple? That you can wrap it all up in a neat package and say, "I have ethnicity, therefore I am?" All you fucking ethnic fundamentalists. Always looking for easy answers. You say you're looking for identity, but you can't begin to face the real mysteries of the search. So instead you go skin-deep, and call it a day.

Pause. Ronnie turns away from Benjamin, starts to play his violin—slow and bluesy.

90 BENJAMIN: So what are you? "Just a human being?" That's like saying you *have* no identity. If you asked me to describe my dog. I'd say more than "He's just a dog."

RONNIE: What—you think if I deny the importance of my race, I'm nobody? There're worlds out there, worlds you haven't even begun to understand. Open your eyes. Hear with your ears.

He holds his violin at chest level, does not attempt to play during the following monologue. As he speaks, a montage of rock and jazz tracks fades in and out over the house speakers, bringing to life the styles of music he describes.

I concede—it was called a fiddle long ago—but that was even before the birth of jazz. When the hollering in the fields, the rank injustice of human bondage, the struggle of God's children against the plagues of the devil's white man, when all these boiled up into that bittersweet brew, called by later generations, the blues. That's when fiddlers like Son Sims held their chin rests at their chests and sawed away like the hillbillies still do today. And with the coming of ragtime appeared the pioneer Stuff Smith, who sang as he stroked the catgut, with his raspy Louis Armstrong voice—gruff and sweet like the timbre of horsehair riding south below the fingerboard, and who finally sailed for Europe to find ears that would hear. Europe — where Stephane Grapelli initialed a magical French violin, to be passed from generation to generation —first he, to Jean-Luc Ponty, then Ponty to Didier Lockwood. Listening to Grapelli play "A Nightingale Sang in Berkeley Square" is to understand not only the song of birds, but also how they learn to fly, fall in love on the wing, and finally falter one day, to wait for darkness beneath a London street lamp. And Ponty, he showed us how the modern violin man can accompany the shadow of his own lead lines, which cascade, one over another, into some netherworld beyond the range of human hearing. Joe Venuti, Noel Pointer, Svend Asmussen. Even the Kronos Quartet with their arrangement of "Purple Haze." Now, tell me, could any legacy be more rich, more crowded with mythology and heroes to inspire pride? What can I say if the banging of a gong or the clinking of a pickax on the Transcontinental Railroad fails to move me even as much as one note, played through the violin MIDI controller of Michal Urbaniak?

Ronnie puts his violin to his chin, begins to play a jazz composition of his own invention.

Does it have to sound like Chinese opera before people like you decide that I know who I am? (*Benjamin stands for a long moment, listening to Ronnie play. Then, he drops his dollar into the case, turns, and exits. Ronnie continues to play a long moment. Then Benjamin enters, illuminated in his own special. He sits on the floor of the stage, his feet dangling off the lip. As he speaks, Ronnie continues playing his tune, which becomes underscoring for Benjamin's monologue. As the music continues, does it slowly begin to reflect the influence of Chinese music?*)

BENJAMIN: When I finally found Doyers St., I scanned the buildings for Number 13. Walking down an alley where the scent of freshly steamed char siu bao lingered in the air, I felt immediately that I had entered a world where all things were finally familiar. (*Pause.*) An old woman bumped me with her shopping bag — screaming to her friend in Cantonese, though they walked no more than a few inches apart. Another man — shouting to a vendor in Sze-Yup. A youth, in a white undershirt, perhaps a recent newcomer, bargaining with a grocer in Hokkien. I walked through this ocean of dialects, breathing in the richness with deep gulps, exhilarated by the energy this symphony brought to my step. And when I finally saw the number 13, I nearly wept at my good fortune. An old tenement, paint peeling, inside walls no doubt thick with a century of grease and broken dreams — and yet, to me, a temple — the house where my father was born. I suddenly saw it all: Gung Gung, coming home from his 16-hour days pressing shirts he could never afford to own, bringing with him candies for my father, each sweet wrapped in the hope of a better life. When my father left the ghetto, he swore he would never return. But he had, this day, in the thoughts and memories of his son, just six months after his death. And as I sat on the stoop, I pulled a hua-moi from my pocket, sucked on it, and felt his spirit returning. To the place where his ghost, and the dutiful hearts of all his descendants, would always call home. (*He listens for a long moment.*) And I felt an ache in my heart for all those lost souls, denied this most important of revelations: to know who they truly are. (*Benjamin sits on the stage, sucking his salted plum and listening to the sounds around him. Ronnie continues to play. The two remain oblivious of one another. Lights fade slowly to black.*)

Reading and Reacting

1. What were your first impressions of Benjamin? Of Ronnie? How did your impressions of these two characters change as the play progressed?
2. Why does Ronnie become angry when Benjamin calls his violin a fiddle? Why does he become even angrier when Benjamin asks for directions to Chinatown?
3. What does Benjamin hope to find in Chinatown? Do you think he is successful?
4. During the first half of the play, Benjamin dominates the action. At what point does this situation change? What do you think causes this change?
5. What is the main theme of this play? What other themes are developed?
6. What is the significance of the play's title? In what way does it express the play's main theme? For example, is Benjamin really trying to find Chinatown, or is he looking for something else?
7. What is the central conflict of the play? Is it ever resolved? Explain.
8. Both Ronnie and Benjamin deliver long monologues. What do these characters reveal about themselves in their monologues?
9. How does Hwang use music in the play? How does music help him to convey his ideas?
10. What can you tell about the social class of the two characters? For example, which character do you think has a better education? Which one seems to come from a more privileged background? Is this difference in social class essential to the play?
11. **JOURNAL ENTRY** Is Ronnie correct when he says that Benjamin is white? Is it possible for Benjamin to be both white and Chinese? Explain.
12. **CRITICAL PERSPECTIVE** In an introduction to a collection of Hwang's plays, novelist Maxine Hong Kingston discusses his contributions to Chinese-American theater:

> Chinese American actors are given too few dignified parts to play. If no playwrights like David Hwang came along, a generation of actors who speak our accents would be lost. A novelist can only invent an approximate orthography. For voices, the play's the thing. Chinese American theater, which started out with a bang — firecrackers, drums — keeps dying out. David Henry Hwang gives it life once again.

Do you think that these comments apply to *Trying to Find Chinatown*? For example, does the play convey the authentic voices and accents of its characters? Do you agree that this kind of authenticity is not possible in a novel or short story?

Related Works: "The Water Faucet Vision" (p. 240), "The Disappearance" (p. 371), "Suicide Note" (p. 860), "The Old Poets of China" (p. 875), "How to Write the Great American Indian Novel" (p. 887), "Harlem" (p. 940), "Little Father" (p. 1200), *The Cuban Swimmer* (p. 1772), *A Raisin in the Sun* (p. 1385)

SOPHOCLES (496 – 406 B.C.) (picture and biography on p. 1785) was one of nine generals elected for a military campaign against Samos, a Greek island that was in revolt against Athens. Sophocles' election was due at least in part to the popularity of his play *Antigone*. (Greek plays often centered on problems of the city-state, and the theater was in many ways the center of the state's religious and political life.)

Even though it was written long before *Oedipus the King*, *Antigone* traces the events that befall Oedipus's younger daughter after his banishment from Thebes. Caught between the laws of the gods and the edict of her uncle the king, Antigone follows her conscience despite the fatal consequences to herself. In the 1960s, the story of Antigone was especially meaningful to those Americans who engaged in civil disobedience in struggles for civil rights and against the war in Vietnam.

Cultural Context: The central struggle in this play revolves around Antigone's desire to bury her brother in an honorable way. The ancient Greeks believed that at the moment of death, the spirit of the dead person left the body as a little puff of wind. The body was then prepared for burial according to time-honored rituals, which were primarily performed by female relatives. The burial rituals consisted of three parts: the *prothesis*, or laying out of the body; the *ekphora*, or funeral procession; and the interment of the body or cremated remains of the deceased. Coins were placed over the eyelids of the deceased as payment for the ferryman who would usher the body across the River Styx and into the underworld. Very few other objects were placed in the grave, but elaborate monuments and statues were often erected to ensure that the dead would be remembered.

Antigone* (441 B.C.)

Translated by Dudley Fitts and Robert Fitzgerald

CHARACTERS

Antigone	**Teiresias**
Ismene	**A Sentry**
Eurydice	**A Messenger**
Creon	**Chorus**
Haimon	

SCENE

Before the palace of Creon, King of Thebes. A central double door, and two lateral doors. A platform extends the length of the facade, and from this platform three steps lead down into the "orchestra," or chorus-ground.

TIME

Dawn of the day after the repulse of the Argive army from the assault on Thebes.

---

*Note that individual lines are numbered in the following play. When a line is shared by two or more characters, it is counted as one line.

<u>PROLOGUE</u>°

Antigone and Ismene enter from the central door of the palace.

ANTIGONE: Ismene, dear sister,
    You would think that we had already suffered enough
    For the curse on Oedipus.°
    I cannot imagine any grief
5   That you and I have not gone through. And now—
    Have they told you of the new decree of our King Creon?

ISMENE: I have heard nothing: I know
    That two sisters lost two brothers, a double death
    In a single hour; and I know that the Argive army
10   Fled in the night; but beyond this, nothing.

ANTIGONE: I thought so. And that is why I wanted you
    To come out here with me. There is something we must do.

ISMENE: Why do you speak so strangely?

ANTIGONE: Listen, Ismene:
15   Creon buried our brother Eteocles
    With military honors, gave him a soldier's funeral,
    And it was right that he should; but Polyneices,
    Who fought as bravely and died as miserably,—
    They say that Creon has sworn
20   No one shall bury him, no one mourn for him,
    But his body must lie in the fields, a sweet treasure
    For carrion birds to find as they search for food.
    That is what they say, and our good Creon is coming here
    To announce it publicly; and the penalty—
    Stoning to death in the public square!
25   There it is,
    And now you can prove what you are:
    A true sister, or a traitor to your family.

ISMENE: Antigone, you are mad! What could I possibly do?

ANTIGONE: You must decide whether you will help me or not.

30 ISMENE: I do not understand you. Help you in what?

ANTIGONE: Ismene, I am going to bury him. Will you come?

°*Prologue:* The portion of the play containing the exposition, or explanation, of what has gone before and what is now happening.   °*the curse on Oedipus:* As Sophocles tells in *Oedipus the King,* the king of Thebes discovered that he had lived his life under a curse. Unknowingly, he had slain his father and married his mother. On realizing this terrible truth, Oedipus put out his own eyes and departed into exile. Now, years later, as *Antigone* opens, Antigone and Ismene, daughters of Oedipus, are recalling how their two brothers died. After the abdication of their father, the brothers ruled Thebes together, but they fell to quarreling. When Eteocles expelled Polyneices, the latter returned with an army and attacked the city. The two brothers killed each other in combat, leaving the throne to Creon. The new king of Thebes buried Eteocles with full honors but, calling Polyneices a traitor, decreed that Polyneices' body be left to the crows. This was an especially terrible decree, for a rotting corpse might offend Zeus, bring down plague, blight, and barrenness upon Thebes, and prevent the soul of a dead hero from entering the Elysian Fields, abode of those favored by the gods.

ISMENE: Bury him! You have just said the new law forbids it.

ANTIGONE: He is my brother. And he is your brother, too.

ISMENE: But think of the danger! Think what Creon will do!

ANTIGONE: Creon is not strong enough to stand in my way.   35

ISMENE: Ah sister!
    Oedipus died, everyone hating him
    For what his own search brought to light, his eyes
    Ripped out by his own hand; and Jocasta died,
    His mother and wife at once: she twisted the cords   40
    That strangled her life; and our two brothers died,
    Each killed by the other's sword. And we are left:
    But oh, Antigone,
    Think how much more terrible than these
    Our own death would be if we should go against Creon   45
    And do what he has forbidden! We are only women,
    We cannot fight with men, Antigone!
    The law is strong, we must give in to the law
    In this thing, and in worse. I beg the Dead
    To forgive me, but I am helpless: I must yield   50
    To those in authority. And I think it is dangerous business
    To be always meddling.

ANTIGONE: If that is what you think,
    I should not want you, even if you asked to come.
    You have made your choice, you can be what you want to be.
    But I will bury him; and if I must die,   55
    I say that this crime is holy: I shall lie down
    With him in death, and I shall be as dear
    To him as he to me.
          It is the dead,
    Not the living, who make the longest demands:
    We die for ever . . .
          You may do as you like,   60
    Since apparently the laws of the gods mean nothing to you.

ISMENE: They mean a great deal to me; but I have no strength
    To break laws that were made for the public good.

ANTIGONE: That must be your excuse, I suppose. But as for me,
    I will bury the brother I love.

ISMENE: Antigone,   65
    I am so afraid for you!

ANTIGONE: You need not be:
    You have yourself to consider, after all.

ISMENE: But no one must hear of this, you must tell no one!
    I will keep it a secret, I promise!

ANTIGONE: O tell it! Tell everyone!
    Think how they'll hate you when it all comes out   70
    If they learn that you knew about it all the time!

ISMENE: So fiery! You should be cold with fear.

ANTIGONE: Perhaps. But I am doing only what I must.

ISMENE: But can you do it? I say that you cannot.

75 ANTIGONE: Very well: when my strength gives out,
      I shall do no more.

ISMENE: Impossible things should not be tried at all.

ANTIGONE: Go away, Ismene:
      I shall be hating you soon, and the dead will too,

80   For your words are hateful. Leave me my foolish plan:
      I am not afraid of the danger; if it means death,
      It will not be the worst of deaths — death without honor.

ISMENE: Go then, if you feel that you must.
      You are unwise,

85   But a loyal friend indeed to those who love you.

Exit into the palace. Antigone goes off, left. Enter the Chorus.

PARADOS°
STROPHE 1

CHORUS: Now the long blade of the sun, lying
      Level east to west, touches with glory
      Thebes of the Seven Gates. Open, unlidded
      Eye of golden day! O marching light

90   Across the eddy and rush of Dirce's stream,°
      Striking the white shields of the enemy
      Thrown headlong backward from the blaze of morning!

CHORAGOS:° Polyneices their commander
      Roused them with windy phrases,

95   He the wild eagle screaming
      Insults above our land,
      His wings their shields of snow,
      His crest their marshalled helms.

ANTISTROPHE 1

CHORUS: Against our seven gates in a yawning ring

100   The famished spears came onward in the night;
      But before his jaws were sated with our blood,
      Or pinefire took the garland of our towers,

°*Parados:* A song sung by the Chorus on the entering. Its *strophe* (according to scholarly theory) was sung while
the Chorus danced from stage right to stage left; its *antistrophe,* while the Chorus danced back again. Another
parados follows the prologue of *Oedipus the King.*   °*Dirce's stream:* A river near Thebes.   °*Choragos:*
Leader of the Chorus and principal commentator on the play's action.

He was thrown back; and as he turned, great Thebes—
No tender victim for his noisy power—
Rose like a dragon behind him, shouting war.   105
CHORAGOS: For God hates utterly
The bray of bragging tongues;
And when he beheld their smiling,
Their swagger of golden helms,
The frown of his thunder blasted   110
Their first man from our walls.

STROPHE 2

CHORUS: We heard his shout of triumph high in the air
Turn to a scream; far out in a flaming arc
He fell with his windy torch, and the earth struck him.
And others storming in fury no less than his   115
Found shock of death in the dusty joy of battle.
CHORAGOS: Seven captains at seven gates
Yielded their clanging arms to the god
That bends the battle-line and breaks it.
These two only, brothers in blood,   120
Face to face in matchless rage,
Mirroring each the other's death,
Clashed in long combat.

ANTISTROPHE 2

CHORUS: But now in the beautiful morning of victory
Let Thebes of the many chariots sing for joy!   125
With hearts for dancing we'll take leave of war:
Our temples shall be sweet with hymns of praise,
And the long nights shall echo with our chorus.

SCENE 1

CHORAGOS: But now at last our new King is coming:
Creon of Thebes, Menoeceus' son.   130
In this auspicious dawn of his reign
What are the new complexities
That shifting Fate has woven for him?
What is his counsel? Why has he summoned
The old men to hear him?   135

Enter Creon from the palace, center. He addresses the Chorus from the top step.

CREON: Gentlemen: I have the honor to inform you that our Ship of
State, which recent storms have threatened to destroy, has come
safely to harbor at last, guided by the merciful wisdom of Heaven.
I have summoned you here this morning because I know that I can

140   depend upon you: your devotion to King Laius was absolute; you
never hesitated in your duty to our late ruler Oedipus; and when
Oedipus died, your loyalty was transferred to his children.
Unfortunately, as you know, his two sons, the princes Eteocles and
Polyneices, have killed each other in battle; and I, as the next in
145   blood, have succeeded to the full power of the throne.

I am aware, of course, that no Ruler can expect complete loyalty
from his subjects until he has been tested in office. Nevertheless, I
say to you at the very outset that I have nothing but contempt for the
kind of Governor who is afraid, for whatever reason, to follow the
150   course that he knows is best for the State; and as for the man who
sets private friendship above the public welfare, — I have no use for
him, either. I call God to witness that I saw my country headed for
ruin, I should not be afraid to speak out plainly; and I need hardly
remind you that I would never have any dealings with an enemy of
155   the people. No one values friendship more highly than I; but we must
remember that friends made at the risk of wrecking our Ship are not
real friends at all.

These are my principles, at any rate, and that is why I have made
the following decision concerning the sons of Oedipus: Eteocles, who
160   died as a man should die, fighting for his country, is to be buried
with full military honors, with all the ceremony that is usual when
the greatest heroes die; but his brother Polyneices, who broke his
exile to come back with fire and sword against his native city and the
shrines of his fathers' gods, whose one idea was to spill the blood of
165   his blood and sell his own people into slavery — Polyneices, I say, is to
have no burial: no man is to touch him or say the least prayer for
him; he shall lie on the plain, unburied; and the birds and the
scavenging dogs can do with him whatever they like.

This is my command, and you can see the wisdom behind it.
170   As long as I am King, no traitor is going to be honored with the
loyal man. But whoever shows by word and deed that he is on the
side of the State, — he shall have my respect while he is living and
my reverence when he is dead.

CHORAGOS: If that is your will, Creon son of Menoeceus,
175   You have the right to enforce it: we are yours.

CREON: That is my will. Take care that you do your part.

CHORAGOS: We are old men: let the younger ones carry it out.

CREON: I do not mean that: the sentries have been appointed.

CHORAGOS: Then what is it that you would have us do?

180   CREON: You will give no support to whoever breaks this law.

CHORAGOS: Only a crazy man is in love with death!

CREON: And death it is; yet money talks, and the wisest
Have sometimes been known to count a few coins too many.

Enter Sentry from left.

SENTRY: I'll not say that I'm out of breath from running, King, because   185
every time I stopped to think about what I have to tell you, I felt like
going back. And all the time a voice kept saying, "You fool, don't you
know you're walking straight into trouble?"; and then another voice:
"Yes, but if you let somebody else get the news to Creon first, it will
be even worse than that for you!" But good sense won out, at least I   190
hope it was good sense, and here I am with a story that makes no
sense at all; but I'll tell it anyhow, because, as they say, what's going
to happen's going to happen and—

CREON: Come to the point. What have you to say?

SENTRY: I did not do it. I did not see who did it. You must not punish
me for what someone else has done.   195

CREON: A comprehensive defense! More effective, perhaps,
If I knew its purpose. Come: what is it?

SENTRY: A dreadful thing . . . I don't know how to put it—

CREON: Out with it!

SENTRY: Well, then;
The dead man—
                    Polyneices—

Pause. The Sentry is overcome, fumbles for words. Creon waits impassively.

                    out there—
                                        someone,—   200
New dust on the slimy flesh!

Pause. No sign from Creon.

Someone has given it burial that way, and
Gone . . .

Long pause. Creon finally speaks with deadly control.

CREON: And the man who dared do this?

SENTRY: I swear I
Do not know! You must believe me!
                                        Listen: 205
The ground was dry, not a sign of digging, no,
Not a wheeltrack in the dust, no trace of anyone.
It was when they relieved us this morning: and one of them,
The corporal, pointed to it.
                    There it was,
The strangest—
                    Look: 210
The body, just mounded over with light dust: you see?
Not buried really, but as if they'd covered it
Just enough for the ghost's peace. And no sign
Of dogs or any wild animal that had been there.

215   And then what a scene there was! Every man of us
        Accusing the other: we all proved the other man did it,
        We all had proof that we could not have done it.
        We were ready to take hot iron in our hands,
        Walk through fire, swear by all the gods,
220   *It was not I!*
        I do not know who it was, but it was not I!

Creon's rage has been mounting steadily, but the Sentry is too intent upon his story to notice it.

        And then, when this came to nothing, someone said
        A thing that silenced us and made us stare
        Down at the ground: you had to be told the news,
225   And one of us had to do it! We threw the dice,
        And the bad luck fell to me. So here I am,
        No happier to be here than you are to have me:
        Nobody likes the man who brings bad news.

CHORAGOS: I have been wondering, King: can it be that the gods have
230   done this?

CREON: (*Furiously*) Stop!
        Must you doddering wrecks
        Go out of your heads entirely? "The gods"!
        Intolerable!
235   The gods favor this corpse? Why? How had he served them?
        Tried to loot their temples, burn their images,
        Yes, and the whole State, and its laws with it!
        Is it your senile opinion that the gods love to honor bad men?
        A pious thought! —
                                    No, from the very beginning
240   There have been those who have whispered together,
        Stiff-necked anarchists, putting their heads together,
        Scheming against me in alleys. These are the men,
        And they have bribed my own guard to do this thing.
        (*Sententiously*) Money!
245   There's nothing in the world so demoralizing as money.
        Down go your cities,
        Homes gone, men gone, honest hearts corrupted,
        Crookedness of all kinds, and all for money!
        (*To Sentry*)   But you—
        I swear by God and by the throne of God,
250   The man who has done this thing shall pay for it!
        Find that man, bring him here to me, or your death
        Will be the least of your problems: I'll string you up
        Alive, and there will be certain ways to make you
        Discover your employer before you die;
255   And the process may teach you a lesson you seem to have missed:

The dearest profit is sometimes all too dear:
That depends on the source. Do you understand me?
A fortune won is often misfortune.

SENTRY: King, may I speak?

CREON: Your very voice distresses me.

SENTRY: Are you sure that it is my voice, and not your conscience?   260

CREON: By God, he wants to analyze me now!

SENTRY: It is not what I say, but what has been done, that hurts you.

CREON: You talk too much.

SENTRY: Maybe; but I've done nothing.

CREON: Sold your soul for some silver: that's all you've done.

SENTRY: How dreadful it is when the right judge judges wrong!   265

CREON: Your figures of speech
     May entertain you now; but unless you bring me the man,
     You will get little profit from them in the end.

Exit Creon into the palace.

SENTRY: "Bring me the man"—!
     I'd like nothing better than bringing him the man!   270
     But bring him or not, you have seen the last of me here.
     At any rate, I am safe!

Exit Sentry.

ODE 1°
STROPHE 1

CHORUS: Numberless are the world's wonders, but none
     More wonderful than man; the stormgray sea
     Yields to his prows, the huge crests bear him high;   275
     Earth, holy and inexhaustible, is graven
     With shining furrows where his plows have gone
     Year after year, the timeless labor of stallions.

ANTISTROPHE 1

The lightboned birds and beasts that cling to cover,
The lithe fish lighting their reaches of dim water,   280
All are taken, tamed in the net of his mind;
The lion on the hill, the wild horse windy-maned,
Resign to him; and his blunt yoke has broken
The sultry shoulders of the mountain bull.

STROPHE 2

Words also, and thought as rapid as air,   285
He fashions to his good use; statecraft is his,

°*Ode 1:* The first song sung by the Chorus, who at the same time danced. Here again, as in the parados, *strophe* and *antistrophe* probably divide the song into two movements of the dance: right to left, then left to right.

And his the skill that deflects the arrows of snow,
The spears of winter rain: from every wind
He has made himself secure — from all but one:
290   In the late wind of death he cannot stand.

ANTISTROPHE 2

O clear intelligence, force beyond all measure!
O fate of man, working both good and evil!
When the laws are kept, how proudly his city stands!
When the laws are broken, what of his city then?
295   Never may the anárchic man find rest at my hearth,
Never be it said that my thoughts are his thoughts.

SCENE 2

Reenter Sentry leading Antigone.

CHORAGOS: What does this mean? Surely this captive woman
Is the Princess, Antigone. Why should she be taken?
SENTRY: Here is the one who did it! We caught her
300   In the very act of burying him.—Where is Creon?
CHORAGOS: Just coming from the house.

Enter Creon, center.

CREON: What has happened?
Why have you come back so soon?
SENTRY: *(Expansively)*   O King,
A man should never be too sure of anything:
I would have sworn
305   That you'd not see me here again: your anger
Frightened me so, and the things you threatened me with;
But how could I tell then
That I'd be able to solve the case so soon?
No dice-throwing this time: I was only too glad to come!
310   Here is this woman. She is the guilty one:
We found her trying to bury him.
Take her, then; question her; judge her as you will.
I am through with the whole thing now, and glad of it.
CREON: But this is Antigone! Why have you brought her here?
SENTRY: She was burying him, I tell you!
315   CREON: *(Severely)*   Is this the truth?
SENTRY: I saw her with my own eyes. Can I say more?
CREON: The details: come, tell me quickly!
SENTRY: It was like this:
After those terrible threats of yours, King,
We went back and brushed the dust away from the body.
320   The flesh was soft by now, and stinking,

So we sat on a hill to windward and kept guard.
No napping this time! We kept each other awake.
But nothing happened until the white round sun
Whirled in the center of the round sky over us:
Then, suddenly,   325
A storm of dust roared up from the earth, and the sky
Went out, the plain vanished with all its tress
In the stinging dark. We closed our eyes and endured it.
The whirlwind lasted a long time, but it passed;
And then we looked, and there was Antigone!   330
I have seen
A mother bird come back to a stripped nest, heard
Her crying bitterly a broken note or two
For the young ones stolen. Just so, when this girl
Found the bare corpse, and all her love's work wasted,   335
She wept, and cried on heaven to damn the hands
That had done this thing.
                          And then she brought more dust
And sprinkled wine three times for her brother's ghost.
We ran and took her at once. She was not afraid,
Not even when we charged her with what she had done.   340
She denied nothing.
                    And this was a comfort to me,
And some uneasiness: for it is a good thing
To escape from death, but it is no great pleasure
To bring death to a friend.
                          Yet I always say
There is nothing so comfortable as your own safe skin!   345
CREON: (*Slowly, dangerously*) And you, Antigone,
    You with your head hanging,—do you confess this thing?
ANTIGONE: I do. I deny nothing.
CREON: (*To Sentry*)   You may go.

Exit Sentry.

    (*To Antigone.*) Tell me, tell me briefly:
    Had you heard my proclamation touching this matter?   350
ANTIGONE: It was public. Could I help hearing it?
CREON: And yet you dared defy the law.
ANTIGONE: I dared.
    It was not God's proclamation. That final Justice
    That rules the world below makes no such laws.
    Your edict, King, was strong,   355
    But all your strength is weakness itself against
    The immortal unrecorded laws of God.
    They are not merely now: they were, and shall be,
    Operative for ever, beyond man utterly.

360   I knew I must die, even without your decree:
I am only mortal. And if I must die
Now, before it is my time to die,
Surely this is no hardship: can anyone
Living, as I live, with evil all about me,

365   Think Death less than a friend? This death of mine
Is of no importance; but if I had left my brother
Lying in death unburied, I should have suffered.
Now I do not.
            You smile at me. Ah Creon,
Think me a fool, if you like; but it may well be

370   That a fool convicts me of folly.

CHORAGOS: Like father, like daughter: both headstrong, deaf to reason!
She has never learned to yield:

CREON: She has much to learn.
The inflexible heart breaks first, the toughest iron
Cracks first, and the wildest horses bend their necks
At the pull of the smallest curb.

375   Pride? In a slave?
This girl is guilty of a double insolence,
Breaking the given laws and boasting of it.
Who is the man here,
She or I, if this crime goes unpunished?

380   Sister's child, or more than sister's child,
Or closer yet in blood — she and her sister
Win bitter death for this!
(To Servants)   Go, some of you,
Arrest Ismene. I accuse her equally.
Bring her: you will find her sniffling in the house there.

385   Her mind's a traitor: crimes kept in the dark
Cry for light, and the guardian brain shudders;
But how much worse than this
Is brazen boasting of barefaced anarchy!

ANTIGONE: Creon, what more do you want than my death?

CREON: Nothing.
That gives me everything.

390 ANTIGONE: Then I beg you: kill me.
This talking is a great weariness: your words
Are distasteful to me, and I am sure that mine
Seem so to you. And yet they should not seem so:
I should have praise and honor for what I have done.

395   All these men here would praise me
Were their lips not frozen shut with fear of you.
(Bitterly) Ah the good fortune of kings,
Licensed to say and do whatever they please!

CREON: You are alone here in that opinion.

ANTIGONE: No, they are with me. But they keep their tongues in leash.   400
CREON: Maybe. But you are guilty, and they are not.
ANTIGONE: There is no guilt in reverence for the dead.
CREON: But Eteocles — was he not your brother too?
ANTIGONE: My brother too.
CREON: And you insult his memory?
ANTIGONE: (*Softly*) The dead man would not say that I insult it.   405
CREON: He would: for you honor a traitor as much as him.
ANTIGONE: His own brother, traitor or not, and equal in blood.
CREON: He made war on his country. Eteocles defended it.
ANTIGONE: Nevertheless, there are honors due all the dead.
CREON: But not the same for the wicked as for the just.   410
ANTIGONE: Ah Creon, Creon
    Which of us can say what the gods hold wicked?
CREON: An enemy is an enemy, even dead.
ANTIGONE: It is my nature to join in love, not hate.
CREON: (*Finally losing patience*) Go join them then; if you must have   415
    your love,
    Find it in hell!
CHORAGOS: But see, Ismene comes:

Enter Ismene, guarded.

    Those tears are sisterly, the cloud
    That shadows her eyes rains down gentle sorrow.
CREON: You too, Ismene,   420
    Snake in my ordered house, sucking my blood
    Stealthily — and all the time I never knew
    That these two sisters were aiming at my throne!
                           Ismene,
    Do you confess your share in this crime, or deny it?
    Answer me.   425
ISMENE: Yes, if she will let me say so. I am guilty.
ANTIGONE: (*Coldly*) No, Ismene. You have no right to say so.
    You would not help me, and I will not have you help me.
ISMENE: But now I know what you meant; and I am here
    To join you, to take my share of punishment.   430
ANTIGONE: The dead man and the gods who rule the dead
    Know whose act this was. Words are not friends.
ISMENE: Do you refuse me, Antigone? I want to die with you:
    I too have a duty that I must discharge to the dead.
ANTIGONE: You shall not lessen my death by sharing it.   435
ISMENE: What do I care for life when you are dead?
ANTIGONE: Ask Creon. You're always hanging on his opinions.
ISMENE: You are laughing at me. Why, Antigone?
ANTIGONE: It's a joyless laughter, Ismene.
ISMENE: But can I do nothing?

440   ANTIGONE: Yes. Save yourself. I shall not envy you.
      There are those who will praise you; I shall have honor, too.

ISMENE: But we are equally guilty!

ANTIGONE: No more, Ismene.
      You are alive, but I belong to Death.

CREON: (*to the Chorus*) Gentlemen, I beg you to observe these girls:

445   One has just now lost her mind; the other
      It seems, has never had a mind at all.

ISMENE: Grief teaches the steadiest minds to waver, King.

CREON: Yours certainly did, when you assumed guilt with the guilty!

ISMENE: But how could I go on living without her?

CREON: You are.
      She is already dead.

450   ISMENE: But your own son's bride!

CREON: There are places enough for him to push his plow.
      I want no wicked women for my sons!

ISMENE: O dearest Haimon, how your father wrongs you!

CREON: I've had enough of your childish talk of marriage!

455   CHORAGOS: Do you really intend to steal this girl from your son?

CREON: No; Death will do that for me.

CHORAGOS: Then she must die?

CREON: (*Ironically*) You dazzle me.
                —But enough of this talk!
      (*To Guards*) You, there, take them away and guard them well:
      For they are but women, and even brave men run

460   When they see Death coming.

Exeunt Ismene, Antigone, and Guards.

<u>ODE 2</u>
STROPHE 1

CHORUS: Fortunate is the man who has never tasted God's vengeance!
      Where once the anger of heaven has struck, that house is shaken
      For ever: damnation rises behind each child
      Like a wave cresting out of the black northeast,
465   When the long darkness under sea roars up
      And bursts drumming death upon the windwhipped sand.

ANTISTROPHE 1

I have seen this gathering sorrow from time long past
Loom upon Oedipus' children: generation from generation
Takes the compulsive rage of the enemy god.
470 So lately this last flower of Oedipus' line
Drank the sunlight! but now a passionate word
And a handful of dust have closed up all its beauty.

STROPHE 2

What mortal arrogance
Transcends the wrath of Zeus?
Sleep cannot lull him nor the effortless long months   475
Of the timeless gods: but he is young for ever,
And his house is the shining day of high Olympos.
    All that is and shall be,
    And all the past, is his.
No pride on earth is free of the curse of heaven.   480

ANTISTROPHE 2

The straying dreams of men
    May bring them ghosts of joy:
But as they drowse, the waking embers burn them;
Or they walk with fixed eyes, as blind men walk.
But the ancient wisdom speaks for our own time: 485
    Fate works most for woe
    With Folly's fairest show.
Man's little pleasure is the spring of sorrow.

SCENE 3

CHORAGOS: But here is Haimon, King, the last of all your sons.
Is it grief for Antigone that brings him here,   490
And bitterness at being robbed of his bride?

Enter Haimon.

CREON: We shall soon see, and no need of diviners.
                    —Son,
You have heard my final judgment on that girl:
Have you come here hating me, or have you come
With deference and with love, whatever I do?   495

HAIMON: I am your son, father. You are my guide.
You make things clear for me, and I obey you.
No marriage means more to me than your continuing wisdom.

CREON: Good. That is the way to behave: subordinate
Everything else, my son, to your father's will.   500
This is what a man prays for, that he may get
Sons attentive and dutiful in his house,
Each one hating his father's enemies,
Honoring his father's friends. But if his sons
Fail him, if they turn out unprofitably,   505
What has he fathered but trouble for himself
And amusement for the malicious?
              So you are right

Not to lose your head over this woman.
Your pleasure with her would soon grow cold, Haimon,
510   And then you'd have a hellcat in bed and elsewhere.
Let her find her husband in Hell!
Of all the people in this city, only she
Has had contempt for my law and broken it.
Do you want me to show myself weak before the people?
515   Or to break my sworn word? No, and I will not.
The woman dies.
I suppose she'll plead "family ties." Well, let her.
If I permit my own family to rebel,
How shall I earn the world's obedience?
520   Show me the man who keeps his house in hand,
He's fit for public authority.
                              I'll have no dealings
With lawbreakers, critics of the government:
Whoever is chosen to govern should be obeyed—
Must be obeyed, in all things, great and small,
525   Just and unjust! O Haimon,
The man who knows how to obey, and that man only,
Knows how to give commands when the time comes.
You can depend on him, no matter how fast
The spears come: he's a good soldier, he'll stick it out.
530   Anarchy, anarchy! Show me a greater evil!
This is why cities tumble and the great houses rain down,
This is what scatters armies!
No, no: good lives are made so by discipline.
We keep the laws then, and the lawmakers,
535   And no woman shall seduce us. If we must lose,
Let's lose to a man, at least! Is a woman stronger than we?

Choragos: Unless time has rusted my wits,
What you say, King, is said with point and dignity.

Haimon: (*Boyishly earnest*) Father:
540   Reason is God's crowning gift to man, and you are right
To warn me against losing mine. I cannot say—
I hope that I shall never want to say!—that you
Have reasoned badly. Yet there are other men
Who can reason, too; and their opinions might be helpful.
545   You are not in a position to know everything
That people say or do, or what they feel:
Your temper terrifies—everyone
Will tell you only what you like to hear.
But I, at any rate, can listen; and I have heard them
550   Muttering and whispering in the dark about this girl.
They say no woman has ever, so unreasonably,
Died so shameful a death for a generous act:
"She covered her brother's body. Is this indecent?

She kept him from dogs and vultures. Is this a crime?
Death?— She should have all the honor that we can give her!"

This is the way they talk out there in the city.　　　　　　　555

You must believe me:
Nothing is closer to me than your happiness.
What could be closer? Must not any son
Value his father's fortune as his father does his?　　　　　　560
I beg you, do not be unchangeable:
Do not believe that you alone can be right.
The man who thinks that,
The man who maintains that only he has the power
To reason correctly, the gift to speak, the soul—　　　　　　565
A man like that, when you know him, turns out empty.
It is not reason never to yield to reason!

In flood time you can see how some trees bend,
And because they bend, even their twigs are safe,
While stubborn trees are torn up, roots and all.　　　　　　570
And the same thing happens in sailing:
Make your sheet fast, never slacken,— and over you go,
Head over heels and under: and there's your voyage.
Forget you are angry! Let yourself be moved!
I know I am young; but please let me say this:　　　　　　575
The ideal condition
Would be, I admit, that men should be right by instinct;
But since we are all too likely to go astray,
The reasonable thing is to learn from those who can teach.

CHORAGOS: You will do well to listen to him, King,　　　　580
If what he says is sensible. And you, Haimon,
Must listen to your father.— Both speak well.
CREON: You consider it right for a man of my years and experience
To go to school to a boy?
HAIMON:　　　　　　　　　　It is not right　　　　　　585
If I am wrong. But if I am young, and right,
What does my age matter?
CREON: You think it right to stand up for an anarchist?
HAIMON: Not at all. I pay no respect to criminals.
CREON: Then she is not a criminal?
HAIMON: The City would deny it, to a man.　　　　　　　590
CREON: And the City proposes to teach me how to rule?
HAIMON: Ah. Who is it that's talking like a boy now?
CREON: My voice is the one voice giving orders in this City!
HAIMON: It is no City if it takes orders from one voice.
CREON: The State is the King!
HAIMON:　　　　　　　　　Yes, if the State is a desert.　　　595

Pause.

CREON: This boy, it seems, has sold out to a woman.

HAIMON: If you are a woman: my concern is only for you.

CREON: So? Your "concern"! In a public brawl with your father!

HAIMON: How about you, in a public brawl with justice?

600 CREON: With justice, when all that I do is within my rights?

HAIMON: You have no right to trample on God's right.

CREON: *(Completely out of control)* Fool, adolescent fool! Taken in by a
    woman!

HAIMON: You'll never see me taken in by anything vile.

CREON: Every word you say is for her!

HAIMON: *(Quietly, darkly)*   And for you.

605   And for me. And for the gods under the earth.

CREON: You'll never marry her while she lives.

HAIMON: Then she must die.—But her death will cause another.

CREON: Another?
    Have you lost your senses? Is this an open threat?

610 HAIMON: There is no threat in speaking to emptiness.

CREON: I swear you'll regret this superior tone of yours!
    You are the empty one!

HAIMON: If you were not my father,
    I'd say you were perverse.

CREON: You girl-struck fool, don't play at words with me!

HAIMON: I am sorry. You prefer silence.

615 CREON: Now, by God—
    I swear, by all the gods in heaven above us,
    You'll watch it, I swear you shall!
    (To the Servants)   Bring her out!
    Bring the woman out! Let her die before his eyes!
    Here, this instant, with her bridegroom beside her!

620 HAIMON: Not here, no; she will not die here, King.
    And you will never see my face again.
    Go on raving as long as you've a friend to endure you.

Exit Haimon.

CHORAGOS: Gone, gone.
    Creon, a young man in a rage is dangerous!

625 CREON: Let him do, or dream to do, more than a man can.
    He shall not save these girls from death.

CHORAGOS: These girls?
    You have sentenced them both?

CREON: No, you are right.
    I will not kill the one whose hands are clean.

CHORAGOS: But Antigone?

CREON: *(Somberly)*   I will carry her far away

630   Out there in the wilderness, and lock her
    Living in a vault of stone. She shall have food,

As the custom is, to absolve the State of her death.
And there let her pray to the gods of hell:
They are her only gods:
Perhaps they will show her an escape from death,   635
Or she may learn,
               though late,
That piety shown the dead is pity in vain.

Exit Creon.

ODE 3
STROPHE

CHORUS: Love, unconquerable
    Waster of rich men, keeper
    Of warm lights and all-night vigil   640
    In the soft face of a girl:
    Sea-wanderer, forest-visitor!
    Even the pure Immortals cannot escape you,
    And mortal man, in his one day's dusk,
    Trembles before your glory.   645

ANTISTROPHE

    Surely you swerve upon ruin
    The just man's consenting heart,
    As here you have made bright anger
    Strike between father and son—
    And none has conquered but Love!   650
    A girl's glánce wórking the will of heaven:
    Pleasure to her alone who mocks us,
    Merciless Aphrodite.°

SCENE 4

CHORAGOS: *(As Antigone enters guarded)* But I can no longer stand in awe of this,
    Nor, seeing what I see, keep back my tears.   655
    Here is Antigone, passing to that chamber
    Where all find sleep at last.

STROPHE 1

ANTIGONE: Look upon me, friends, and pity me
    Turning back at the night's edge to say
    Good-by to the sun that shines for me no longer;   660
    Now sleepy Death
    Summons me down to Acheron,° that cold shore:
    There is no bridesong there, nor any music.

°*Aphrodite:* Goddess of love and beauty.   °*Acheron:* A river in Hades, domain of the dead.

CHORUS: Yet not unpraised, not without a kind of honor,
665   You walk at last into the underworld;
           Untouched by sickness, broken by no sword.
           What woman has ever found your way to death?

ANTISTROPHE 1

ANTIGONE: How often I have heard the story of Niobe,°
           Tantalos' wretched daughter, how the stone
670   Clung fast about her, ivy-close: and they say
           The rain falls endlessly
           And sifting soft snow; her tears are never done.
           I feel the loneliness of her death in mine.
CHORUS: But she was born of heaven, and you
675   Are woman, woman-born. If her death is yours,
           A mortal woman's, is this not for you
           Glory in our world and in the world beyond?

STROPHE 2

ANTIGONE: You laugh at me. Ah, friends, friends,
           Can you not wait until I am dead? O Thebes,
680   O men many-charioted, in love with Fortune,
           Dear springs of Dirce, sacred Theban grove,
           Be witnesses for me, denied all pity,
           Unjustly judged! and think a word of love
           For her whose path turns
685   Under dark earth, where there are no more tears.
CHORUS: You have passed beyond human daring and come at last
           Into a place of stone where Justice sits.
           I cannot tell
           What shape of your father's guilt appears in this.

ANTISTROPHE 2

690 ANTIGONE: You have touched it at last: that bridal bed
           Unspeakable, horror of son and mother mingling:
           Their crime, infection of all our family!
           O Oedipus, father and brother!
           Your marriage strikes from the grave to murder mine.
695   I have been a stranger here in my own land:
           All my life
           The blasphemy of my birth has followed me.
CHORUS: Reverence is a virtue, but strength
           Lives in established law: that must prevail.

°*story of Niobe:* When her fourteen children were slain, Niobe wept so copiously that she was transformed into a stone on Mount Sipylus. Her tears became the mountain's streams.

You have made your choice,   700
Your death is the doing of your conscious hand.

EPODE

ANTIGONE: Then let me go, since all your words are bitter,
  And the very light of the sun is cold to me.
  Lead me to my vigil, where I must have
  Neither love nor lamentation; no song, but silence.   705

Creon interrupts impatiently.

CREON: If dirges and planned lamentations could put off death,
  Men would be singing for ever.
  (*To the Servants*)   Take her, go!
  You know your orders: take her to the vault
  And leave her alone there. And if she lives or dies,
  That's her affair, not ours: our hands are clean.   710
ANTIGONE: O tomb, vaulted bride-bed in eternal rock,
  Soon I shall be with my own again
  Where Persephone° welcomes the thin ghosts underground:
  And I shall see my father again, and you, mother,
  And dearest Polyneices —
                              dearest indeed   715
  To me, since it was my hand
  That washed him clean and poured the ritual wine:
  And my reward is death before my time!
  And yet, as men's hearts know, I have done no wrong,
  I have not sinned before God. Or if I have,   720
  I shall know the truth in death. But if the guilt
  Lies upon Creon who judged me, then, I pray,
  May his punishment equal my own.
CHORAGOS: O passionate heart,
  Unyielding, tormented still by the same winds!
CREON: Her guards shall have good cause to regret their delaying.   725
ANTIGONE: Ah! That voice is like the voice of death!
CREON: I can give you no reason to think you are mistaken.
ANTIGONE: Thebes, and you my fathers' gods,
  And rulers of Thebes, you see me now, the last
  Unhappy daughter of a line of kings,   730
  Your kings, led away to death. You will remember
  What things I suffer, and at what men's hands,
  Because I would not transgress the laws of heaven.
  (*To the Guards, simply*) Come: let us wait no longer.

Exit Antigone, left, guarded.

°*Persephone:* Pluto, god of the underworld, abducted her to be his queen.

Johnathan Hyde as Creon in the 1999 Old Vic production of *Antigone*.

<u>ODE 4</u>
STROPHE 1

735 CHORUS: All Danae's beauty was locked away
In a brazen cell where the sunlight could not come:
A small room still as any grave, enclosed her.
Yet she was a princess too,
And Zeus in a rain of gold poured love upon her.°

740 O child, child,
No power in wealth or war
Or tough sea-blackened ships
Can prevail against untiring Destiny!

ANTISTROPHE 1

And Dryas' son° also, that furious king,
745 Bore the god's prisoning anger for his pride:
Sealed up by Dionysos in deaf stone,

°*All Danae's beauty . . . poured love upon her:* In legend, when an oracle told Acrisius, king of Argos, that his daughter Danae would bear a son who would grow up to slay him, he locked the princess into a chamber made of bronze, lest any man impregnate her. But Zeus, father of the gods, entered Danae's prison in a shower of gold. The resultant child, the hero Perseus, was accidentally to fulfill the prophecy by killing Acrisius with an ill-aimed discus throw.
°*Dryas' son:* King Lycurgus of Thrace, whom Dionysos, god of wine, caused to be stricken with madness.

His madness died among echoes.
So at the last he learned what dreadful power
His tongue had mocked:
For he had profaned the revels,   750
And fired the wrath of the nine
Implacable Sisters° that love the sound of the flute.

STROPHE 2

And old men tell a half-remembered tale
Of horror° where a dark ledge splits the sea
And a double surf beats on the gráy shóres: 755
How a king's new woman, sick
With hatred for the queen he had imprisoned,
Ripped out his two sons' eyes with her bloody hands
While grinning Ares watched the shuttle plunge
Four times: four blind wounds crying for revenge,   760

ANTISTROPHE 2

Crying, tears and blood mingled. — Piteously born,
Those sons whose mother was of heavenly birth!
Her father was the god of the North Wind
And she was cradled by gales,
She raced with young colts on the glittering hills   765
And walked untrammeled in the open light:
But in her marriage deathless Fate found means
To build a tomb like yours for all her joy.

SCENE 5

Enter blind Teiresias, led by a boy. The opening speeches of Teiresias should be in sing-song contrast to the realistic lines of Creon.

TEIRESIAS: This is the way the blind man comes, Princes, Princes,
    Lockstep, two heads lit by the eyes of one.   770
CREON: What new thing have you to tell us, old Teiresias?
TEIRESIAS: I have much to tell you: listen to the prophet, Creon.
CREON: I am not aware that I have ever failed to listen.
TEIRESIAS: Then you have done wisely, King, and ruled well.

°*Sisters:* The Muses, nine sister-goddesses who presided over poetry and music, arts and sciences.   °*a half-remembered tale Of horror:* As the Chorus recalls in the rest of this song, the point of this tale is that being nobly born will not save one from disaster. King Phineas cast off his first wife Cleopatra (not the later Egyptian queen but the daughter of Boreas, god of the north wind) and imprisoned her in a cave. Out of hatred for Cleopatra, the cruel Eidothea, second wife of the king, blinded her stepsons. Ares, god of war, was said to gloat over bloodshed.

775   CREON: I admit my debt to you. But what have you to say?

TEIRESIAS: This, Creon: you stand once more on the edge of fate.

CREON: What do you mean? Your words are a kind of dread.

TEIRESIAS: Listen, Creon:

I was sitting in my chair of augury, at the place

780   Where the birds gather about me. They were all a-chatter,

As is their habit, when suddenly I heard

A strange note in their jangling, a scream, a

Whirring fury; I knew that they were fighting,

Tearing each other, dying

785   In a whirlwind of wings clashing. And I was afraid.

I began the rites of burnt-offering at the altar,

But Hephaistos° failed me: instead of bright flame,

There was only the sputtering slime of the fat thigh-flesh

Melting: the entrails dissolved in gray smoke,

790   The bare bone burst from the welter. And no blaze!

This was a sign from heaven. My boy described it,

Seeing for me as I see for others.

I tell you, Creon, you yourself have brought

This new calamity upon us. Our hearths and altars

795   Are stained with the corruption of dogs and carrion birds

That glut themselves on the corpse of Oedipus' son.

The gods are deaf when we pray to them, their fire

Recoils from our offering, their birds of omen

Have no cry of comfort, for they are gorged

With the thick blood of the dead.

800   O my son,

These are no trifles! Think: all men make mistakes,

But a good man yields when he knows his course is wrong,

And repairs the evil. The only crime is pride.

Give in to the dead man, then: do not fight with a corpse—

805   What glory is it to kill a man who is dead?

Think, I beg you:

It is for your own good that I speak as I do.

You should be able to yield for your own good.

CREON: It seems that prophets have made me their especial province.

810   All my life long

I have been a kind of butt for the dull arrows

Of doddering fortune-tellers!

                              No, Teiresias:

If your birds — if the great eagles of God himself

Should carry him stinking bit by bit to heaven,

815   I would not yield. I am not afraid of pollution:

Hephaistos: God of fire.

No man can defile the gods.

              Do what you will,
Go into business, make money, speculate
An India gold or that synthetic gold from Sardis,
Get rich otherwise than by my consent to bury him.
Teiresias, it is a sorry thing when a wise man   820
Sells his wisdom, lets out his words for hire!

TEIRESIAS: Ah Creon! Is there no man left in the world—

CREON: To do what?— Come, let's have the aphorism!

TEIRESIAS: No man who knows that wisdom outweighs any wealth?

CREON: As surely as bribes are baser than any baseness.   825

TEIRESIAS: You are sick, Creon! You are deathly sick!

CREON: As you say: it is not my place to challenge a prophet.

TEIRESIAS: Yet you have said my prophecy is for sale.

CREON: The generation of prophets has always loved gold.

TEIRESIAS: The generation of kings has always loved brass.   830

CREON: You forget yourself! You are speaking to your King.

TEIRESIAS: I know it. You are a king because of me.

CREON: You have a certain skill; but you have sold out.

TEIRESIAS: King, you will drive me to words that—

CREON: Say them, say them!
Only remember: I will not pay you for them.   835

TEIRESIAS: No, you will find them too costly.

CREON: No doubt. Speak:
Whatever you say, you will not change my will.

TEIRESIAS: Then take this, and take it to heart!
The time is not far off when you shall pay back
Corpse for corpse, flesh of your own flesh.   840
You have thrust the child of this world into living night,
You have kept from the gods below the child that is theirs:
The one in a grave before her death, the other,
Dead, denied the grave. This is your crime:
And the Furies and the dark gods of Hell   845
Are swift with terrible punishment for you.
Do you want to buy me now, Creon?

                 Not many days,
And your house will be full of men and women weeping,
And curses will be hurled at you from far
Cities grieving for sons unburied, left to rot   850
Before the walls of Thebes.
There are my arrows, Creon: they are all for you.
(To Boy) But come, child: lead me home.
Let him waste his fine anger upon younger men.
Maybe he will learn at last   855
To control a wiser tongue in a better head.

Exit Teiresias.

CHORAGOS: The old man has gone, King, but his words
    Remain to plague us. I am old, too,
    But I cannot remember that he was ever false.

860 CREON: That is true. . . . It troubles me.
    Oh it is hard to give in! but it is worse
    To risk everything for stubborn pride.

CHORAGOS: Creon: take my advice.

CREON: What shall I do?

CHORAGOS: Go quickly: free Antigone from her vault

865   And build a tomb for the body of Polyneices.

CREON: You would have me do this!

CHORAGOS: Creon, yes!
    And it must be done at once: God moves
    Swiftly to cancel the folly of stubborn men.

CREON: It is hard to deny the heart! But I

870   Will do it: I will not fight with destiny.

CHORAGOS: You must go yourself, you cannot leave it to others.

CREON: I will go.
          —Bring axes, servants:
    Come with me to the tomb. I buried her, I
    Will set her free.
           Oh quickly!

875 My mind misgives—
    The laws of the gods are mighty, and a man must serve them
    To the last day of his life!

Exit Creon.

PAEAN°

STROPHE 1

CHORAGOS: God of many names

CHORUS: O Iacchos
                      son
  of Kadmeian Sémele
              O born of the Thunder!
  Guardian of the West

880   Regent
  Of Eleusis' plain
            O Prince of maenad Thebes
  and the Dragon Field by rippling Ismenós:°

°*Paean:* A song of praise or prayer, here to Dionysos, god of wine.   °*God of many names . . . Dragon Field by rippling Ismenós:* Dionysos was also called Iacchos (or, by the Romans, Bacchus). He was the son of Zeus ("the Thunderer") and of Sémele, daughter of Kadmos (or Cadmus), legendary founder of Thebes. "Regent of Eleusis' plain" is another name for Dionysos, honored in secret rites at Eleusis, a town northwest of Athens. "Prince of maenad Thebes" is yet another: the Maenads were women of Thebes said to worship Dionysos with wild orgiastic rites. Kadmos, so the story goes, sowed dragon's teeth in a field beside the river Ismenós. Up sprang a crop of fierce warriors who fought among themselves until only five remained. These victors became the first Thebans.

ANTISTROPHE 1

CHORAGOS: God of many names
CHORUS: the flame of torches
  flares on our hills
         the nymphs of Iacchos
  dance at the spring of Castalia:°   885
  from the vine-close mountain
             come ah come in ivy:
  Evohé evohé!° sings through the streets of Thebes

STROPHE 2

CHORAGOS: God of many names
CHORUS: Iacchos of Thebes
  heavenly Child
         of Sémele bride of the Thunderer!
  The shadow of plague is upon us:
           come   890
  with clement feet
        oh come from Parnasos
  down the long slopes
         across the lamenting water

ANTISTROPHE 2

CHORAGOS: Io° Fire! Chorister of the throbbing stars!
  O purest among the voices of the night!
  Thou son of God, blaze for us!   895
CHORUS: Come with choric rapture of circling Maenads
  Who cry *Iô Iacche!*
         God of many names!

EXODOS°

Enter Messenger from left.

MESSENGER: Men of the line of Kadmos, you who live
  Near Amphion's citadel,°
         I cannot say
  Of any condition of human life "This is fixed,   900
  This is clearly good, or bad." Fate raises up,

°*Castalia:* A spring on Mount Parnassus, named for a maiden who drowned herself in it to avoid rape by the god Apollo. She became a nymph, or nature spirit, dwelling in its waters. In the temple of Delphi, at the mountain's foot, priestesses of Dionysos (the "nymphs of Iacchos") used the spring's waters in rites of purification.   °*Evohé evohé!:* The cry of the Maenads in supplicating Dionysos: "Come forth, come forth!" °*Io:* "Hail" or "Praise be to. . . ."   °*Exodos:* The final scene, containing the play's resolution.   °*Amphion's citadel:* A name for Thebes. Amphion, son of Zeus, had built a wall around the city by playing so beautifully on his lyre that the charmed stones leaped into their slots.

And Fate casts down the happy and unhappy alike:
No man can foretell his Fate.

         Take the case of Creon:
Creon was happy once, as I count happiness:

905 Victorious in battle, sole governor of the land,
Fortunate father of children nobly born.
And now it has all gone from him! Who can say
That a man is still alive when his life's joy fails?
He is a walking dead man. Grant him rich,

910 Let him live like a king in his great house:
If his pleasure is gone, I would not give
So much as the shadow of smoke for all he owns.

CHORAGOS: Your words hint at sorrow: what is your news for us?

MESSENGER: They are dead. The living are guilty of their death.

CHORAGOS: Who is guilty? Who is dead? Speak!

915 MESSENGER: Haimon.
Haimon is dead; and the hand that killed him
Is his own hand.

CHORAGOS: His father's? or his own?

MESSENGER: His own, driven mad by the murder his father had done.

CHORAGOS: Teiresias, Teiresias, how clearly you saw it all!

920 MESSENGER: This is my news: you must draw what conclusions you can from it.

CHORAGOS: But look: Eurydice, our Queen:
Has she overheard us?

Enter Eurydice from the palace, center.

EURYDICE: I have heard something, friends:

925 As I was unlocking the gate of Pallas'° shrine,
For I needed her help today, I heard a voice
Telling of some new sorrow. And I fainted
There at the temple with all my maidens about me.
But speak again: whatever it is, I can bear it:
Grief and I are no strangers.

930 MESSENGER: Dearest Lady,
I will tell you plainly all that I have seen.
I shall not try to comfort you: what is the use,
Since comfort could lie only in what is not true?
The truth is always best.

          I went with Creon

935 To the outer plain where Polyneices was lying,
No friend to pity him, his body shredded by dogs.
We made our prayers in that place to Hecate

Pallas': Pallas Athene, goddess of wisdom, and hence an excellent source of advice.

And Pluto,° that they would be merciful. And we bathed
The corpse with holy water, and we brought
Fresh-broken branches to burn what was left of it,   940
And upon the urn we heaped up a towering barrow
Of the earth of his own land.
                                        When we were done, we ran
To the vault where Antigone lay on her couch of stone.
One of the servants had gone ahead,
And while he was yet far off he heard a voice   945
Grieving within the chamber, and he came back
And told Creon. And as the King went closer,
The air was full of wailing, the words lost,
And he begged us to make all haste. "Am I a prophet?"
He said, weeping, "And must I walk this road,   950
The saddest of all that I have gone before?
My son's voice calls me on. Oh quickly, quickly!
Look through the crevice there, and tell me
If it is Haimon, or some deception of the gods!"
We obeyed; and in the cavern's farthest corner   955
We saw her lying:
She had made a noose of her fine linen veil
And hanged herself. Haimon lay beside her,
His arms about her waist, lamenting her,
His love lost under ground, crying out   960
That his father had stolen her away from him.
When Creon saw him the tears rushed to his eyes
And he called to him: "What have you done, child? Speak to me.
What are you thinking that makes your eyes so strange?
O my son, my son, I come to you on my knees!"   965
But Haimon spat in his face. He said not a word,
Staring—
                      And suddenly drew his sword
And lunged. Creon shrank back, the blade missed; and the boy,
Desperate against himself, drove it half its length
Into his own side, and fell. And as he died   970
He gathered Antigone close in his arms again,
Choking, his blood bright red on her white cheek.
And now he lies dead with the dead, and she is his
At last, his bride in the house of the dead.

Exit Eurydice into the palace.

Choragos: She has left us without a word. What can this mean?   975

Hecate And Pluto: Two fearful divinities — the goddess of witchcraft and sorcery and the king of Hades, underworld of the dead.

MESSENGER: It troubles me, too; yet she knows what is best,
    Her grief is too great for public lamentation,
    And doubtless she has gone to her chamber to weep
    For her dead son, leading her maidens in his dirge.

Pause.

980 CHORAGOS: It may be so: but I fear this deep silence.
    MESSENGER: I will see what she is doing. I will go in.

Exit Messenger into the palace.

Enter Creon with attendants, bearing Haimon's body.

CHORAGOS: But here is the king himself: oh look at him,
    Bearing his own damnation in his arms.
    CREON: Nothing you say can touch me any more.
985   My own blind heart has brought me
    From darkness to final darkness. Here you see
    The father murdering, the murdered son—
    And all my civic wisdom!

    Haimon my son, so young, so young to die,
990   I was the fool, not you; and you died for me.
    CHORAGOS: That is the truth; but you were late in learning it.
    CREON: This truth is hard to bear. Surely a god
    Has crushed me beneath the hugest weight of heaven,
    And driven me headlong a barbaric way
995   To trample out the thing I held most dear.
    The pains that men will take to come to pain!

Enter Messenger from the palace.

MESSENGER: The burden you carry in your hands is heavy,
    But it is not all: you will find more in your house.
    CREON: What burden worse than this shall I find there?
1000 MESSENGER: The Queen is dead.
    CREON: O port of death, deaf world,
    Is there no pity for me? And you, Angel of evil,
    I was dead, and your words are death again.
    Is it true, boy? Can it be true?
1005   Is my wife dead? Has death bred death?
    MESSENGER: You can see for yourself.

The doors are opened and the body of Eurydice is disclosed within.

CREON: Oh pity!
    All true, all true, and more than I can bear!
    O my wife, my son!
1010 MESSENGER: She stood before the altar, and her heart

Welcomed the knife her own hand guided,
And a great cry burst from her lips for Megareus° dead,
And for Haimon dead, her sons; and her last breath
Was a curse for their father, the murderer of her sons.
And she fell, and the dark flowed in through her closing eyes.   1015
CREON: O God, I am sick with fear.
Are there no swords here? Has no one a blow for me?
MESSENGER: Her curse is upon you for the deaths of both.
CREON: It is right that it should be. I alone am guilty.   1020
I know it, and I say it. Lead me in,
Quickly, friends.
I have neither life nor substance. Lead me in.
CHORAGOS: You are right, if there can be right in so much wrong.
The briefest way is best in a world of sorrow.
CREON: Let it come,   1025
Let death come quickly, and be kind to me.
I would not ever see the sun again.
CHORAGOS: All that will come when it will; but we, meanwhile,
Have much to do. Leave the future to itself.
CREON: All my heart was in that prayer!   1030
CHORAGOS: Then do not pray any more: the sky is deaf.
CREON: Lead me away. I have been rash and foolish.
I have killed my son and my wife.
I look for comfort; my comfort lies here dead.
Whatever my hands have touched has come to nothing.   1035
Fate has brought all my pride to a thought of dust.

As Creon is being led into the house, the Choragos advances and speaks directly to the audience.

CHORAGOS: There is no happiness where there is no wisdom;
No wisdom but in submission to the gods.
Big words are always punished,
And proud men in old age learn to be wise.   1040

Reading and Reacting

1. What ideas does *Antigone* express about duty? About obedience? In what
   ways do these ideas conform (or fail to conform) to your own concepts of duty
   and obedience?
2. The Chorus expresses the values of the community. According to the Chorus, is Antigone a danger to the community? How far do you believe a community should go to protect its values?

Megareus: Son of Creon and brother of Haimon, Megareus was slain in the unsuccessful attack on Thebes.

3. Both Creon and Antigone defend rights that they believe are sacred. What rights are in conflict? Is there any room for compromise?

4. Do you sympathize with Antigone or with Creon? What characteristics of each do you find noble? Do you ever lose patience with either of them? Explain.

5. Aristotle believed that to be effective, tragic heroes must have elements of both good and evil. Does Antigone conform to Aristotle's requirement? Explain.

6. What is Antigone's fatal flaw? How does this flaw lead to the tragic resolution of the play?

7. As the play progresses, do Creon and Antigone change, or do they remain essentially unchanged by events?

8. What lines of dialogue do you believe best express the play's central theme?

9. At the very end of *Antigone*, the Chorus says, "Big words are always punished, / And proud men in old age learn to be wise." Do you think Creon has gained wisdom from his experiences? Why or why not?

10. In what way does Antigone's gender affect her actions? In what way does it determine how she is treated? Are the play's attitudes toward women consistent with those of contemporary American society? Explain.

11. JOURNAL ENTRY If you were Antigone, would you have stuck to your principles, or would you have given in? Explain your reasoning.

12. CRITICAL PERSPECTIVE In *Sophocles the Playwright*, S. M. Adams argues that, to the ancient Greek audience, Antigone and Creon were both tragic heroes. Do you agree? If so, do you see the fact that the play has two tragic heroes as a problem?

Related Works: "A Worn Path" (p. 505), "Bartleby, the Scrivener" (p. 731), "Do not go gentle into that good night" (p. 1065) "On the Notion of Tenderness in Wartime" (p. 1086), "Hamlet" (p. 1656), *Oedipus the King* (p. 1786), *Antigone's Red* (p. 1931)

CHIORI MIYAGAWA was born in Japan and emigrated to the United States when she was sixteen years old. She received her BFA from the New York Institute of Technology and her MFA from Brooklyn College. She is the co-artistic director of the Crossing Jamaica Avenue Theater Company, and she has received numerous awards and fellowships for her plays. She is a professor of theater at Bard College.

Cultural Context In 1941, when Japan bombed Pearl Harbor, approximately 127,000 people of Japanese descent lived in the United States, most of them on the West Coast. After the attack on Pearl Harbor, rumors spread that the Japanese were planning to sabotage American war facilities. As a result, in February of 1942, the federal government forced all Japanese-Americans — even those who were American citizens — to move from the West Coast, which was seen as an area vulnerable to attack. When neighboring states refused to admit the Japanese, the government set up ten internment camps — including Manzanar, the setting for the play *Antigone's Red*. Over 100,000 people were eventually moved to these camps, which, with their barbed wire, wooden barracks, and cramped quarters, resembled prisons. Because of this experience, over 5,000 Japanese-Americans renounced their citizenship. After his reelection in 1944, Franklin Roosevelt rescinded the evacuation order, and by 1945, all the camps had been closed.

Antigone's Red   (2002)

<u>CHARACTERS</u>

Antigone: Japanese-American woman in her early thirties.
Ismene: Antigone's younger sister.
Tadashi: Japanese-American man in his early thirties.
Brian: Caucasian man, Ismene's husband.
Guard: Caucasian man.

TIME: 1942.

<u>PLACE:</u> MANZANAR, CALIFORNIA.

PROLOGUE

ANTIGONE: With my bare hands I dug the dry earth and covered my lover's corpse with dirt and tears. The desert land is cruel to those who want to bury loved ones. My nails ripped from my fingers. I made an offering of my blood. Antigone's lover's grave is red. That was my last red.

Antigone takes a long red ribbon out of her pocket. She holds the ribbon up vertically and with a pair of scissors, cuts the ribbon in half. The bottom half falls to the floor. Lights down.

SCENE 1

Manzanar, California. One of the sites of the relocation camps for Japanese Americans during World War II. 1942.

ANTIGONE: Manzanar, California. The dust storms consume our days. We breathe and eat the sand which fills our lungs, leaving a gritty, bitter taste on our tongue. The air is murky coarse white. Ten thousand Japanese and Japanese Americans are here, imprisoned in the barracks at the foot of the magnificent Sierra Nevada Mountains. In the middle of the ground stands a tall pole with a large American flag violently fluttering in the wind. We were allowed to bring what we could carry of beddings, linens, clothes, and eating utensils. We had forty-eight hours to pack. Forty-eight hours to leave our lives behind. I left my dog with the neighbor who looked at me with blue eyes full of tears and said that she would keep my dog until I return. I said no, he is yours now. I had a piano at home. I made the last payment on it two weeks ago. It took me five years to pay for it. Well. Anyway.

Lights change.

SCENE 2

Antigone *is sitting outside the barracks with* Tadashi.

TADASHI: I'm going to answer no/no to the loyalty oath questions.

ANTIGONE: What will happen?

TADASHI: I don't know. I may get deported.

ANTIGONE: But you were born here. On this land. You've never been anyone other than who you are.

5 **TADASHI:** My father was a Japanese veteran, so he was one of the first people arrested after Pearl Harbor. He had been a gardener for twenty years. He was distraught to leave my mother and sister. I heard he tried to commit suicide by biting off his own tongue while being transported. I received a telegram today that he was shot to death in the Enemy Alien Internment Camp in Oklahoma. I am no longer who I was once. (*Pause.*) I will not go to war to fight for this country from a prison camp. I will not swear allegiance to the country that robbed and humiliated my family. I have to answer no to both questions, even if it means that you and I will not be together.

ANTIGONE: But why allow them to take away your future? If you get stripped of your citizenship for two checkmarks on no and deported to Japan, how will you survive? You don't speak the language. You've never even been to Japan.

TADASHI: They've taken away my past. My life up until the moment of reading the evacuation order was a lie. Thirty years of my life was an illusion. You can't build a future on illusion.

ANTIGONE: They want us to give up. They want to crush us and make us surrender the life we are entitled to. We have to fight them.

TADASHI: I'm not giving up. I'm refusing to compromise the fundamental nature of my being—What I will lose is nothing; it's tarnished forever. Antigone, what we must fight for is the courage to believe in what is right, not what is possible. (*Pause.*) If something happens to me, would you try to find my mother and sister? I think they are in the camp in Heart Mountain.

10 **ANTIGONE:** What shall I say to them?

TADASHI: You'll know then. That part of my history is not written yet. You will tell them either that you are the last person I loved in this country, or the last person I loved in this life.

Pause

ANTIGONE: It's suppertime. I hope to report to the mess hall duty.

TADASHI: Stay for five more minutes.

ANTIGONE: I can't. The tension there is already high because of the rumor that the guards have been stealing meat and sugar from the kitchen. And we found out while we work for eighteen dollars a month, the white commuting workers get paid fifty dollars a week. We're planning a walkout.

15 **TADASHI:** Listen, Antigone, be careful. Stay away from all that. There have been shootings of inmates in different camps. The guards are murdering people claiming that they tried to escape. But all the bodies have been

found inside the fences, shot in the front. They were not running away. They were all facing the guards.

ANTIGONE: You just told me to act on what is right. The only thing I can do is to fight small, insignificant injustice, since I'm unable to fight the big crime, the betrayal of our dreams and violation of our beings.

TADASHI: Stay for five more minutes.

ANTIGONE: Nothing will happen to me. Don't worry. Our time together isn't over yet.

TADASHI: Just stay and hold my hand.

ANTIGONE: Later I'll hold your hand later, my love.   20

Antigone exits. Tadashi is left alone.

SCENE 3

The same evening. Late night. Antigone is asleep. Her sister Ismene comes in quietly and approaches Antigone.

ISMENE: Antigone, wake up.

ANTIGONE: What?

ISMENE: Are you awake?

ANTIGONE: Did something happen to my lover?

ISMENE: Oh my sister. I'm so sorry.   5

ANTIGONE: Stop crying, Ismene. Is he dead?

ISMENE: Yes.

ANTIGONE: (*desperate and angry*) How can I live then? What is life for?

Lights change. Back to the beginning of the moment.

ISMENE: Antigone, wake up.

ANTIGONE: What?   10

ISMENE: Are you awake?

ANTIGONE: Did something happen to my lover?

ISMENE: Oh, my sister. I'm so sorry.

ANTIGONE: Stop crying, Ismene. Is he dead?

ISMENE: Yes.   15

ANTIGONE: (*hysterical*) No, it can't be! Not yet, not yet! I didn't say good-bye to him! I didn't stay and hold his hand!

Lights change. Back to the beginning of the moment.

ISMENE: Antigone, wake up.

ANTIGONE: What?

ISMENE: Are you awake?

ANTIGONE: Did something happen to my lover?   20

ISMENE: Oh, my sister. I'm so sorry.

ANTIGONE: Stop crying, Ismene. Is he dead?

ISMENE: Yes.

ANTIGONE: (*calmly*) Then he is free.

Lights down.

SCENE 4

Lights up immediately on Antigone *and* Ismene *in the exact same positions, but it is two days later.*

ANTIGONE: Tadashi's body has been exposed for forty-eight hours now. An order forbids a burial for him. His corpse is to be left out in the middle of the camp for the dust storm to swirl around until it is rotten to the core of this disappointment.

ISMENE: Oh, my sister, I'm so sorry.

ANTIGONE: Stop crying Ismene. I'm going out there to bury him. Will you help me?

ISMENE: That is insane. We will be killed for it.

5 ANTIGONE: Tadashi exposed the meat and sugar scandal and organized last night's demonstration with twelve men who were willing to die in order to gain justice. He never even told me about his plans. After the tear gas bombs were thrown at the demonstrators, they stormed the guards. The guards opened fire. Tadashi was at the front. (*Pause.*) If not for the sacrifice he made, we still owe him a burial for being a human being and having lived among us.

ISMENE: We will be killed for it.

ANTIGONE: Possibly.

ISMENE: I have a husband. I want to have children.

ANTIGONE: If we don't bury him, then we are allowing them to disgrace a soul, to condemn it to wander eternally. We are allowing them to commit even a greater crime than our imprisonment, our deaths.

10 ISMENE: Antigone, there are certain things that are beyond our power to correct. We had no choice but to give up everything that our parents worked so hard to make possible — our houses, our cars, our jobs, our rights, our dignity. All we can do now is to hold onto the little that is under our power to preserve. Identity. Survival. I want a future.

ANTIGONE: What does your future look like, Ismene? Like an American dream? Like "give me your tired, your poor, your huddled masses yearning to breathe free"?

ISMENE: I will not be victimized anymore. If it means that I'd be accepted, I would cut off my flesh, go along with the system, and lose my name. I want to live.

ANTIGONE: I understand. It's not fair to ask you to give up what's left of your life to allow my lover a noble entrance to the next life. He had no family, so it's my responsibility.

ISMENE: I know you loved Tadashi and that he was brave. But you must it his body disintegrate out there. You cannot fight them. We are too small. Please promise me . . .

15 ANTIGONE: Don't ask me that. I will hate you for it.

ISMENE: Antigone, you are crazy. You will not survive this.

ANTIGONE: And you will?

ISMENE: Don't worry about my soul.

ANTIGONE: Report my crime to the guards. Take the opportunity. Oppress
   someone, Ismene, if you want to move up.
ISMENE: You're my sister.   20
ANTIGONE: I hate you.

SCENE 5

*In Ismene's room. Spare. A bed and a window. Ismene sits with her husband, Brian.
Her back is erect; she is listening intently for sounds outside.*

BRIAN: You have been awfully quiet. What are you thinking?
ISMENE: Do you feel the pressure in the air? It's so heavy. Condensed. I can't
   breathe.
BRIAN: It's a strange night.
ISMENE: There will be a riot.
BRIAN: Just don't go outside. Stay in the room.   5
ISMENE: Antigone is out there.
BRIAN: She'll run straight into her own doom.
ISMENE: She is my sister.
BRIAN: Unfortunately.
ISMENE: What do you know about it?   10
BRIAN: You know she is dangerous. Stay out of her way. Ismene. Your sympa-
   thy for her will harm you in the end.
ISMENE: You don't know what you're talking about. You don't know anything
   about her.
BRIAN: If you go out there tonight and join her, I will leave tomorrow and
   never visit you again.
ISMENE: That's a toss-up.
BRIAN: I know you are upset. These are not normal times. You'll be all right   15
   once the war is over. You can come back and live with me, and no one will
   harm you.
ISMENE: Because you, my husband, my knight, are white.
BRIAN: Do you think I enjoy visiting my wife in a little room that you share
   with two other families separated by hanging sheets? Fair or not, this is not
   my fate. This is yours. I'm willing to share it because I love you.
ISMENE: Thank you.
BRIAN: I'm really sorry this is happening, but I'm not the enemy.
ISMENE: Who is the enemy?   20
BRIAN: The war.
ISMENE: Oh, I thought I was in this predicament because of the Civilian Ex-
   clusion Order 33 that stripped my constitutional rights and made it possible
   to detain me indefinitely against my will, without charge, without represen-
   tation, in a bleak condition in this dump. I guess I was wrong. The war is
   the enemy.
BRIAN: They had to do something.
ISMENE: They?

25 **BRIAN:** There are close to one hundred thousand aliens and non-aliens who could possibly threaten the safety of the country. My heart is torn. I hate my country for what it has done to you. But the second attack must be prevented.

ISMENE: What's a non-alien?

BRIAN: You are, Ismene. You're not an alien. You are my wife.

ISMENE: Brian, who else is non-alien? Citizens! It means citizen if your last name is not Japanese. I am a citizen because I was born in this country. Not because I married you.

BRIAN: Ismene, I'm sorry for all the injustices of the world. I'd fix them for you if I could.

30 **ISMENE:** But you can't, can you?

BRIAN: What do you want me to do?

ISMENE: Be brave.

BRIAN: How can I show you my bravery other than by continuing to love you? Life is about the happiness that you and I will find when this is all over. You'll come home and we'll have children and forget about these difficult times. We'll go back to our life and try to live it the best we can. That's my bravery.

ISMENE: That's not good enough anymore. (*Pause.*) I'm going out there.

35 **BRIAN:** I'm warning you.

ISMENE: What are you warning me? That you will leave and take your white privilege with you?

BRIAN: What have I done to you?

ISMENE: You pampered, arrogant man. You have done exactly nothing, yet you expect everything. You did nothing to prevent my demise, but you expect me to recover and serve your concept of happiness. Nothing will ever be the same. Don't you understand that? I have been disgraced and deprived. We cannot go back to the life we had before I was broken.

BRIAN: Ismene, I can't believe you really think that. That is something Antigone might say. Don't let her poison you. Please. I can't imagine a life without you.

40 **ISMENE:** Brian, try this. When you walk out of here, see if you can take me with you. See if your wife wouldn't be ordered to stop at gunpoint. (*Pause.*) Antigone is out there. Fearless. Stupid. The color of her blood is the same as mine.

Ismene *exits.* Brian *remains motionless.*

EPILOGUE

Lights up on the Guard.

GUARD: These people don't understand the difference between good and evil. It's not in their culture. I had no choice. She was howling over the dead body like a witch, and on her hands and knees, she was throwing dirt over him. She looked like some wild animal with her black hair whirling in the dust storm. It was an ugly sight, this yellow creature spitting and crying, snot hanging from her nose. I have to admit that I was scared. She looked so crazy I thought she could attack me if I tried to stop her illegal act. Anyway, it was my job, so I called out a warning. She turned around and looked at me with red eyes, and stood up with all the threats of murder. I didn't have a choice.

Enormous sound of explosion. Black. A moment of silence and stillness. Lights up on Antigone alone.

ANTIGONE: With my bare hands I dug the dry earth and covered my lover's corpse with dirt and tears. The desert land is cruel to those who want to bury loved ones. My nails ripped from my fingers. I made an offering of my blood. Tadashi's grave is red. That was my last red. Shortly after two enormous explosions over Japan killed 200,000 people who shared my ancestors, Japanese Americans were released from their imprisonment in America — nowhere to go, nothing to return to, their freedom owed to the bloody results of those two bombs. But I was already gone by then. I died without seeing the other red. It belonged to a young girl in Hiroshima. Her skin was hanging from her skinny body in strips of red ribbons. She was trying to hold onto her red.

She takes a long red ribbon out of her pocket. She holds the ribbon up vertically, and with a pair of scissors, cuts the ribbon in half. The bottom half falls to the floor. Lights down.

Reading and Reacting

1. Miyagawa does not assume that her audience knows a lot about Manzanar. How does she communicate information about life at Manzanar? How else could she have conveyed this information?
2. In scene 2, what does Tadashi mean when he says, "My life up until the moment of reading the evacuation order was a lie"? Why does he think that his life was "an illusion"?
3. In scene 3, the same event occurs three times. How is the event different each time it occurs? What is the purpose of this repetition?
4. In Sophocles's *Antigone*, both Creon, who represents the state, and Antigone, who represents the individual, defend rights that they believe are sacred. In *Antigone's Red*, what personal rights is Antigone defending? Who or what represents the state? What rights of the state are being defended?
5. What conflicts occur in the play? Which of these conflicts do you think could have been resolved? Which do you believe could not (or should not) be resolved?
6. In scene 5, Brian, Ismene's husband, blames her predicament on the war; Ismene believes the cause is much more complex. How would she explain why she is confined to Manzanar?
7. Keeping in mind the limitations imposed by the brief length of *Antigone's Red*, do you think the characters are reasonably well developed? Are any characters simply stereotypes? How could they have been developed further in such a short play?

8. In the play's epilogue, a guard delivers a monologue in which he attempts to justify his actions. Is his explanation plausible? What does his monologue reveal about his motives?

9. *Antigone's Red* ends by connecting the incarceration of the Japanese in the United States to the dropping of two atomic bombs on Japan. Do you think this connection is justified? Explain.

10. What is the significance of the play's title? What is the significance of the red ribbon that appears at the beginning and at the end of the play?

11. **Journal Entry** Do you think Antigone is a **tragic hero**? Why or why not? If so, what is her tragic flaw?

12. **Critical Perspective** Playwright and director Caridad Svich was approached by Miyagawa and asked to write a play with Antigone as a central figure. Of her involvement with what would later become known as the Antigone Project, Svich made these comments about the figure of Antigone:

> I suddenly began to think about Antigone as a historical character, as someone we have lived with for centuries and of how indeed we perceive history, time and memory through a character who was once not a mythic figure but simply a woman in a very charged situation. I began to think about archival memory and how the archive lives within us and outside of us, and how women view themselves at one time or another as Antigones.

How do these comments apply to the character of Antigone in Miyagawa's play? Do you see her as representative of all women? What characteristics does Antigone possess that are particular to her time and circumstance? What traits are universal?

Related Works "Seventeen Syllables" (p. 538), "Saboteur" (p. 714), "Suicide Note" (p. 860), "Try to Praise the Mutilated World" (p. 869), "How to Write the Great American Indian Novel" (p. 887), "For the Student Strikers" (p. 910), "Immigrants" (p. 1025), *Antigone* (p. 1899)

AUGUST WILSON (1945–2005) was born in Pittsburgh, Pennsylvania, to a German immigrant father and a black mother and lived in the African-American neighborhood known as the Hill District. After leaving school at fifteen after he was accused of plagiarizing a paper, he participated in the Black Arts movement in Pittsburgh, submitting poems to local African-American publications. In 1969, Wilson and his friend Rob Penny founded the Black Horizons Theatre Company, for which Wilson produced and directed plays. Although Wilson wrote plays while living in Pittsburgh, his work began to gain recognition only after 1978, when he moved to St. Paul, Minnesota. There, in 1982, Lloyd Richards, dean of the Yale School of Drama and artistic director of the Yale Repertory Company, staged a performance of Wilson's *Ma Rainey's Black Bottom*.

Wilson's achievement was epic. Beginning with *Ma Rainey's Black Bottom* in 1984, he wrote a ten-play cycle that chronicled the African-American experience in the United States decade by decade. In addition to *Ma Rainey's Black Bottom,* a Tony Award winner, the plays in this cycle include *Fences* (1985), which won a Pulitzer Prize in 1987; *Joe Turner's Come and Gone* (1986); *Two Trains Running* (1989), which won Wilson his fifth New York Drama Critics Circle Award; *The Piano Lesson* (1987), which won a second Pulitzer Prize for Wilson in 1990; *Seven Guitars* (1996); *Radio Golf*, the last play in the cycle, opened in 2005, the year of wilson's death. To honor his achievements, Broadway's Virginia Theater was renamed the August Wilson Theater.

Fences explores how the long-upheld color barrier in professional baseball affects the main character, Troy, who struggles with the pain of never realizing his dream of becoming a big-league player. Throughout the play, Troy retreats behind literal and figurative barriers that impair his relationships with his family.

Cultural Context The history of African-Americans in baseball began in the period between emancipation and the civil rights movement. Banned from professional baseball by segregationist laws, African-American players formed the Negro Leagues, with stars such as Satchel Paige and Josh Gibson emerging in the 1930s. Then, in 1946, Branch Rickey, the club president and general manager of the Brooklyn Dodgers, changed everything when he set out to sign the Negro Leagues' top players to his team. The first player he chose was Jackie Robinson, who broke the racial barrier and debuted at first base for the Dodgers on April 15, 1947, at the age of 28. Robinson's phenomenal performance earned him the Rookie of the Year award. In 1957, the year in which *Fences* is set, Robinson announced his retirement from baseball after he was traded to the New York Giants. In 1962, he would take his place in the Baseball Hall of Fame.

Fences (1985)

CHARACTERS

Troy Maxson
Jim Bono, *Troy's friend*
Rose, *Troy's wife*
Lyons, *Troy's oldest son by previous marriage*

Gabriel, *Troy's brother*
Cory, *Troy and Rose's son*
Raynell, *Troy's daughter*

SETTING

The setting is the yard which fronts the only entrance to the Maxson household, an ancient two-story brick house set back off a small alley in a big-city neighborhood. The entrance to the house is gained by two or three steps leading to a wooden porch badly in need of paint.

A relatively recent addition to the house and running its full width, the porch lacks congruence. It is a sturdy porch with a flat roof. One or two chairs of dubious value sit at one end where the kitchen window opens onto the porch. An old-fashioned icebox stands silent guard at the opposite end.

The yard is a small dirt yard, partially fenced, except for the last scene, with a wooden sawhorse, a pile of lumber, and other fence-building equipment set off to the side. Opposite is a tree from which hangs a ball made of rags. A baseball bat leans against the tree. Two oil drums serve as garbage receptacles and sit near the house at right to complete the setting.

THE PLAY

Near the turn of the century, the destitute of Europe sprang on the city with tenacious claws and an honest and solid dream. The city devoured them. They swelled its belly until it burst into a thousand furnaces and sewing machines, a thousand butcher shops and bakers' ovens, a thousand churches and hospitals and funeral parlors and money-lenders. The city grew. It nourished itself and offered each man a partnership limited only by his talent, his guile, and his willingness and capacity for hard work. For the immigrants of Europe, a dream dared and won true.

The descendants of African slaves were offered no such welcome or participation. They came from places called the Carolinas and the Virginias, Georgia, Alabama, Mississippi, and Tennessee. They came strong, eager, searching. The city rejected them and they fled and settled along the riverbanks and under bridges in shallow, ramshackle houses made of sticks and tarpaper. They collected rags and wood. They sold the use of their muscles and their bodies. They cleaned houses and washed clothes, they shined shoes, and in quiet desperation and vengeful pride, they stole, and lived in pursuit of their own dream. That they could breathe free, finally, and stand to meet life with the force of dignity and whatever eloquence the heart could call upon.

By 1957, the hard-won victories of the European immigrants had solidified the industrial might of America. War had been confronted and won with new energies that used loyalty and patriotism as its fuel. Life was rich, full, and flourishing. The Milwaukee Braves won the World Series, and the hot winds of change that would make the sixties a turbulent, racing, dangerous, and provocative decade had not yet begun to blow full.

ACT 1

SCENE 1

It is 1957. Troy and Bono enter the yard, engaged in conversation. Troy is fifty-three years old, a large man with thick, heavy hands; it is this largeness that he strives to fill out and make an accommodation with. Together with his blackness, his largeness informs his sensibilities and the choices he has made in his life.

Of the two men, Bono is obviously the follower. His commitment to their friendship of thirty-odd years is rooted in his admiration of Troy's honesty, capacity for hard work, and his strength, which Bono seeks to emulate.

It is Friday night, payday, and the one night of the week the two men engage in a ritual of talk and drink. Troy is usually the most talkative and at times he can be crude and almost vulgar, though he is capable of rising to profound heights of expression. The men carry lunch buckets and wear or carry burlap aprons and are dressed in clothes suitable to their jobs as garbage collectors.

BONO: Troy, you ought to stop that lying!

TROY: I ain't lying! The nigger had a watermelon this big. (*He indicates with his hands.*) Talking about . . . "What watermelon, Mr. Rand?" I liked to fell out! "What watermelon, Mr. Rand?" . . . And it sitting there big as life.

BONO: What did Mr. Rand say?

TROY: Ain't said nothing. Figure if the nigger too dumb to know he carrying a watermelon, he wasn't gonna get much sense out of him. Trying to hide that great big old watermelon under his coat. Afraid to let the white man see him carry it home.

5 **BONO:** I'm like you . . . I ain't got no time for them kind of people.

TROY: Now what he look like getting mad 'cause he see the man from the union talking to Mr. Rand?

BONO: He come to me talking about . . . "Maxson gonna get us fired." I told
him to get away from me with that. He walked away from me calling you a
troublemaker. What Mr. Rand say?

TROY: Ain't said nothing. He told me to go down the Commissioner's office
next Friday. They called me down there to see them.

BONO: Well, as long as you got your complaint filed, they can't fire you. That's
what one of them white fellows tell me.

TROY: I ain't worried about them firing me. They gonna fire me 'cause I asked a   10
question? That's all I did. I went to Mr. Rand and asked him, "Why? Why
you got the white mens driving and the colored lifting?" Told him, "what's
the matter, don't I count? You think only white fellows got sense enough to
drive a truck. That ain't no paper job! Hell, anybody can drive a truck.
How come you got all whites driving and the colored lifting?" He told me
"take it to the union." Well, hell, that's what I done! Now they wanna
come up with this pack of lies.

BONO: I told Brownie if the man come and ask him any questions . . . just tell
the truth! It ain't nothing but something they done trumped up on you
'cause you filed a complaint on them.

TROY: Brownie don't understand nothing. All I want them to do is change the
job description. Give everybody a chance to drive the truck. Brownie can't
see that. He ain't got that much sense.

BONO: How you figure he be making out with that gal be up at Taylors' all the
time . . . that Alberta gal?

TROY: Same as you and me. Getting just as much as we is. Which is to say
nothing.

BONO: It is, huh? I figure you doing a little better than me . . . and I ain't saying   15
what I'm doing.

TROY: Aw, nigger, look here . . . I know you. If you had got anywhere near that
gal, twenty minutes later you be looking to tell somebody. And the first one
you gonna tell . . . that you gonna want to brag to . . . is me.

BONO: I ain't saying that. I see where you be eyeing her.

TROY: I eye all the women. I don't miss nothing. Don't never let nobody tell
you Troy Maxson don't eye the women.

BONO: You been doing more than eyeing her. You done bought her a drink
or two.

TROY: Hell yeah, I bought her a drink! What that mean? I bought you one,   20
too. What that mean 'cause I buy her a drink? I'm just being polite.

BONO: It's all right to buy her one drink. That's what you call being polite.
But when you wanna be buying two or three . . . that's what you call eyeing her.

TROY: Look here, as long as you known me . . . you ever known me to chase
after women?

BONO: Hell yeah! Long as I done known you. You forgetting I knew you when.

TROY: Naw, I'm talking about since I been married to Rose?

BONO: Oh, not since you been married to Rose. Now, that's the truth, there. I   25
can say that.

TROY: All right then! Case closed.

BONO: I see you be walking up around Alberta's house. You supposed to be at
    Taylors' and you be walking up around there.

TROY: What you watching where I'm walking for? I ain't watching after you.

BONO: I seen you walking around there more than once.

30 TROY: Hell, you liable to see me walking anywhere! That don't mean nothing
    cause you see me walking around there.

BONO: Where she come from anyway? She just kinda showed up one day.

TROY: Tallahassee. You can look at her and tell she one of them Florida gals.
    They got some big healthy women down there. Grow them right up out the
    ground. Got a little bit of Indian in her. Most of them niggers down in
    Florida got some Indian in them.

BONO: I don't know about that Indian part. But she damn sure big and healthy.
    Woman wear some big stockings. Got them great big old legs and hips as
    wide as the Mississippi River.

TROY: Legs don't mean nothing. You don't do nothing but push them out of
    the way. But them hips cushion the ride!

35 BONO: Troy, you ain't got no sense.

TROY: It's the truth! Like you riding on Goodyears!

*Rose enters from the house. She is ten years younger than Troy, her devotion to him
stems from her recognition of the possibilities of her life without him: a succession of abusive men and their babies, a life of partying and running the streets, the Church, or
aloneness with its attendant pain and frustration. She recognizes Troy's spirit as a fine
and illuminating one and she either ignores or forgives his faults, only some of which she
recognizes. Though she doesn't drink, her presence is an integral part of the Friday night
rituals. She alternates between the porch and the kitchen, where supper preparations are
under way.*

ROSE: What you all out here getting into?

TROY: What you worried about what we getting into for? This is men talk,
    woman.

ROSE: What I care what you all talking about? Bono, you gonna stay for supper?

40 BONO: No, I thank you, Rose. But Lucille say she cooking up a pot of pigfeet.

TROY: Pigfeet! Hell, I'm going home with you! Might even stay the night if
    you got some pigfeet. You got something in there to top them pigfeet, Rose?

ROSE: I'm cooking up some chicken. I got some chicken and collard greens.°

TROY: Well, go on back in the house and let me and Bono finish what we was
    talking about. This is men talk. I got some talk for you later. You know
    what kind of talk I mean. You go on and powder it up.

ROSE: Troy Maxson, don't you start that now!

45 TROY: *(puts his arm around her)* Aw, woman . . . come here. Look here,
    Bono . . . when I met this woman . . . I got out that place, say, "Hitch up
    my pony, saddle up my mare . . . there's a woman out there for me some-
    where. I looked here. Looked there. Saw Rose and latched on to her." I

---

collard greens: A leafy green vegetable.

latched on to her and told her — I'm gonna tell you the truth — I told her, "Baby, I don't wanna marry, I just wanna be your man." Rose told me . . . tell him what you told me, Rose.

ROSE: I told him if he wasn't the marrying kind, then move out the way so the marrying kind could find me.

TROY: That's what she told me. "Nigger, you in my way. You blocking the view! Move out the way so I can find me a husband." I thought it over two or three days. Come back—

ROSE: Ain't no two or three days nothing. You was back the same night.

TROY: Come back, told her . . . "Okay, baby . . . but I'm gonna buy me a banty rooster and put him out there in the backyard . . . and when he see a stranger come, he'll flap his wings and crow . . ." Look here, Bono, I could watch the front door by myself . . . it was that back door I was worried about.

ROSE: Troy, you ought not talk like that. Troy ain't doing nothing but telling a lie.   50

TROY: Only thing is . . . when we first got married . . . forget the rooster . . . we ain't had no yard!

BONO: I hear you tell it. Me and Lucille was staying down there on Logan Street. Had two rooms with the outhouse in the back. I ain't mind the outhouse none. But when that goddamn wind blow through there in the winter . . . that's what I'm talking about! To this day I wonder why in the hell I ever stayed down there for six long years. But see, I didn't know I could do no better. I thought only white folks had inside toilets and things.

ROSE: There's a lot of people don't know they can do no better than they doing now. That's just something you got to learn. A lot of folks still shop at Bella's.

TROY: Ain't nothing wrong with shopping at Bella's. She got fresh food.

ROSE: I ain't said nothing about if she got fresh food. I'm talking about what   55
she charge. She charge ten cents more than the A&P.

TROY: The A&P ain't never done nothing for me. I spends my money where I'm treated right. I go down to Bella, say, "I need a loaf of bread, I'll pay you Friday." She give it to me. What sense that make when I got money to go and spend it somewhere else and ignore the person who done right by me? That ain't in the Bible.

ROSE: We ain't talking about what's in the Bible. What sense it make to shop there when she overcharge?

TROY: You shop where you want to. I'll do my shopping where the people been good to me.

ROSE: Well, I don't think it's right for her to overcharge. That's all I was saying.

BONO: Look here . . . I got to get on. Lucille going be raising all kind of hell.   60

TROY: Where you going, nigger? We ain't finished this pint. Come here, finish this pint.

BONO: Well, hell, I am . . . if you ever turn the bottle loose.

TROY: *(hands him the bottle)* The only thing I say about the A&P is I'm glad Cory got that job down there. Help him take care of his school clothes and things. Gabe done moved out and things getting tight around here. He got that job . . . He can start to look out for himself.

ROSE: Cory done went and got recruited by a college football team.

65 TROY: I told that boy about that football stuff. The white man ain't gonna let
him get nowhere with that football. I told him when he first come to me
with it. Now you come telling me he done went and got more tied up in it.
He ought to go and get recruited in how to fix cars or something where he
can make a living.

ROSE: He ain't talking about making no living playing football. It's just something the boys in school do. They gonna send a recruiter by to talk to you.
He'll tell you he ain't talking about making no living playing football. It's a
honor to be recruited.

TROY: It ain't gonna get him nowhere. Bono'll tell you that.

BONO: If he be like you in the sports . . . he's gonna be all right. Ain't but two
men ever played baseball as good as you. That's Babe Ruth° and Josh
Gibson.° Them's the only two men ever hit more home runs than you.

TROY: What it ever get me? Ain't got a pot to piss in or a window to throw it out of.

70 ROSE: Times have changed since you was playing baseball, Troy. That was
before the war. Times have changed a lot since then.

TROY: How in hell they done changed?

ROSE: They got lots of colored boys playing ball now. Baseball and football.

BONO: You right about that, Rose. Times have changed, Troy. You just come
along too early.

TROY: There ought not never have been no time called too early! Now you
take that fellow . . . what's that fellow they had playing right field for the
Yankees back then? You know who I'm talking about, Bono. Used to play
right field for the Yankees.

75 ROSE: Selkirk?

TROY: Selkirk! That's it! Man batting .269, understand? .269. What kind of
sense that make? I was hitting .432 with thirty-seven home runs! Man batting .269 and playing right field for the Yankees! I saw Josh Gibson's daughter yesterday. She walking around with raggedy shoes on her feet. Now I bet
you Selkirk's daughter ain't walking around with raggedy shoes on her feet!
I bet you that!

ROSE: They got a lot of colored baseball players now. Jackie Robinson° was the
first. Folks had to wait for Jackie Robinson.

TROY: I done seen a hundred niggers play baseball better than Jackie
Robinson. Hell, I know some teams Jackie Robinson couldn't even make!
What you talking about Jackie Robinson. Jackie Robinson wasn't nobody.
I'm talking about if you could play ball then they ought to have let you

---

°*Babe Ruth:* George Herman Ruth (1895–1948), American baseball player. He played for the New York Yankees
during the 1910s and 1920s and is remembered for his home-run hitting and flamboyant lifestyle.   °*Josh
Gibson:* (1911–1947), American baseball player. He played between the Negro Leagues between 1920s and
1940s and was known as "the Negro Babe Ruth." An unwritten rule against hiring black players kept him out of
the major leagues.   °*Jackie Robinson:* John Roosevelt Robinson (1919–1972). He became the first African
American to play major-league baseball when he was hired by the Brooklyn Dodgers in 1947.

play. Don't care what color you were. Come telling me I come along too early. If you could play . . . then they ought to have let you play.

Troy takes a long drink from the bottle.

ROSE: You gonna drink yourself to death. You don't need to be drinking like that.

TROY: Death ain't nothing. I done seen him. Done wrassled with him. You   80
can't tell me nothing about death. Death ain't nothing but a fastball on the outside corner. And you know what I'll do to that! Lookee here, Bono . . . am I lying? You get one of them fastballs, about waist high, over the outside corner of the plate where you can get the meat of the bat on it . . . and good god! You can kiss it goodbye. Now, am I lying?

BONO: Naw, you telling the truth there. I seen you do it.

TROY: If I'm lying . . . that 450 feet worth of lying! *(Pause.)* That's all death is to me. A fastball on the outside corner.

ROSE: I don't know why you want to get on talking about death.

TROY: Ain't nothing wrong with talking about death. That's part of life. Everybody gonna die. You gonna die, I'm gonna die. Bono's gonna die. Hell, we all gonna die.

ROSE: But you ain't got to talk about it. I don't like to talk about it.   85

TROY: You the one brought it up. Me and Bono was talking about baseball . . . you tell me I'm gonna drink myself to death. Ain't that right, Bono? You know I don't drink this but one night out of the week. That's Friday night. I'm gonna drink just enough to where I can handle it. Then I cuts it loose. I leave it alone. So don't you worry about me drinking myself to death. 'Cause I ain't worried about Death. I done seen him. I done wrestled with him.

   Look here, Bono . . . I looked up one day and Death was marching straight at me. Like Soldiers on Parade! The Army of Death was marching straight at me. The middle of July, 1941. It got real cold just like it be winter. It seem like Death himself reached out and touched me on the shoulder. He touch me just like I touch you. I got cold as ice and Death standing there grinning at me.

ROSE: Troy, why don't you hush that talk.

TROY: I say . . . what you want, Mr. Death? You be wanting me? You done brought your army to be getting me? I looked him dead in the eye. I wasn't fearing nothing. I was ready to tangle. Just like I'm ready to tangle now. The Bible say be ever vigilant. That's why I don't get but so drunk. I got to keep watch.

ROSE: Troy was right down there in Mercy Hospital. You remember he had pneumonia? Laying there with a fever talking plumb out of his head.

TROY: Death standing there staring at me . . . carrying that sickle in his   90
hand. Finally he say, "You want bound over for another year?" See, just like that . . . "You want bound over for another year?" I told him, "Bound over hell! Let's settle this now!"

   It seem like he kinda fell back when I said that, and all the cold went out of me. I reached down and grabbed that sickle and threw it just as far as I could throw it . . . and me and him commenced to wrestling.

We wrestled for three days and three nights. I can't say where I found the strength from. Every time it seemed like he was gonna get the best of me, I'd reach way down deep inside myself and find the strength to do him one better.

ROSE: Every time Troy tell that story he find different ways to tell it. Different things to make up about it.

TROY: I ain't making up nothing. I'm telling you the facts of what happened. I wrestled with Death for three days and three nights and I'm standing here to tell you about it. (*Pause.*) All right. At the end of the third night we done weakened each other to where we can't hardly move. Death stood up, throwed on his robe . . . had him a white robe with a hood on it. He throwed on that robe and went off to look for his sickle. Say, "I'll be back." Just like that. "I'll be back." I told him, say, "Yeah, but . . . you gonna have to find me!" I wasn't no fool. I wan't going looking for him. Death ain't nothing to play with. And I know he's gonna get me. I know I got to join his army . . . his camp followers. But as long as I keep my strength and see him coming . . . as long as I keep up my vigilance . . . he's gonna have to fight to get me. I ain't going easy.

BONO: Well, look here, since you got to keep up your vigilance . . . let me have the bottle.

TROY: Aw hell, I shouldn't have told you that part. I should have left out that part.

95 ROSE: Troy be talking that stuff and half the time don't even know what he be talking about.

TROY: Bono know me better than that.

BONO: That's right. I know you. I know you got some Uncle Remus° in your blood. You got more stories than the devil got sinners.

TROY: Aw hell, I done seen him too! Done talked with the devil.

ROSE: Troy, don't nobody wanna be hearing all that stuff.

Lyons enters the yard from the street. Thirty-four years old, Troy's son by a previous marriage, he sports a neatly trimmed goatee, sport coat, white shirt, tieless and buttoned at the collar. Though he fancies himself a musician, he is more caught up in the rituals and "idea" of being a musician than in the actual practice of the music. He has come to borrow money from Troy, and while he knows he will be successful, he is uncertain as to what extent his lifestyle will be held up to scrutiny and ridicule.

100 LYONS: Hey, Pop.

TROY: What you come "Hey, Popping" me for?

LYONS: How you doing, Rose? (*He kisses her.*) Mr. Bono. How you doing?

BONO: Hey, Lyons . . . how you been?

TROY: He must have been doing all right. I ain't seen him around here last week.

°*Uncle Remus:* The fictional narrator of *Uncle Remus: His Songs and His Sayings* (1880) and a number of sequels by Joel Chandler Harris. Uncle Remus tells tales about characters such as Brer Rabbit and the Tarbaby in exaggerated dialect, now widely considered to be a derogatory representation of African Americans.

ROSE: Troy, leave your boy alone. He come by to see you and you wanna start   105
all that nonsense.

TROY: I ain't bothering Lyons. (*Offers him the bottle.*) Here . . . get you a drink.
We got an understanding. I know why he come by to see me and he know
I know.

LYONS: Come on, Pop . . . I just stopped by to say hi . . . see how you was doing.

TROY: You ain't stopped by yesterday.

ROSE: You gonna stay for supper, Lyons? I got some chicken cooking in the oven.

LYONS: No, Rose . . . thanks. I was just in the neighborhood and thought I'd   110
stop by for a minute.

TROY: You was in the neighborhood all right, nigger. You telling the truth
there. You was in the neighborhood cause it's my payday.

LYONS: Well, hell, since you mentioned it . . . let me have ten dollars.

TROY: I'll be damned! I'll die and go to hell and play blackjack with the devil
before I give you ten dollars.

BONO: That's what I wanna know about . . . that devil you done seen.

LYONS: What . . . Pop done seen the devil? You too much, Pops.   115

TROY: Yeah, I done seen him. Talked to him too!

ROSE: You ain't seen no devil. I done told you that man ain't had nothing to do
with the devil. Anything you can't understand, you want to call it the devil.

TROY: Look here, Bono . . . I went down to see Hertzberger about some furniture. Got three rooms for two-ninety-eight. That what it say on the radio.
"Three rooms . . . two-ninety-eight." Even made up a little song about it.
Go down there . . . man tell me I can't get no credit. I'm working every day
and can't get no credit. What to do? I got an empty house with some
raggedy furniture in it. Cory ain't got no bed. He's sleeping on a pile of rags
on the floor. Working every day and can't get no credit. Come back here —
Rose'll tell you — madder than hell. Sit down . . . try to figure what I'm
gonna do. Come a knock on the door. Ain't been living here but three days.
Who know I'm here? Open the door . . . devil standing there bigger than
life. White fellow . . . white fellow . . . got on good clothes and everything.
Standing there with a clipboard in his hand. I ain't had to say nothing. First
words come out of his mouth was . . . "I understand you need some furniture
and can't get no credit." I liked to fell over. He say, "I'll give you all the
credit you want, but you got to pay the interest on it." I told him, "Give me
three rooms worth and charge whatever you want." Next day a truck pulled
up here and two men unloaded them three rooms. Man what drove the
truck give me a book. Say send ten dollars, first of every month to the address in the book and everything will be all right. Say if I miss a payment
the devil was coming back and it'll be hell to pay. That was fifteen years ago.
To this day . . . the first of the month I send my ten dollars, Rose'll tell you.

ROSE: Troy lying.

TROY: I ain't never seen that man since. Now you tell me who else that could   120
have been but the devil? I ain't sold my soul or nothing like that, you understand. Naw, I wouldn't have truck with the devil about nothing like that. I got
my furniture and pays my ten dollars the first of the month just like clockwork.

James Earl Jones as Troy in a 1986 production of *Fences* at the Goodman Theatre.

BONO: How long you say you been paying this ten dollars a month?

TROY: Fifteen years!

BONO: Hell, ain't you finished paying for it yet? How much the man done charged you?

TROY: Ah hell, I done paid for it. I done paid for it ten times over! The fact is I'm scared to stop paying it.

125 **ROSE:** Troy lying. We got that furniture from Mr. Glickman. He ain't paying no ten dollars a month to nobody.

TROY: Aw hell, woman. Bono know I ain't that big a fool.

LYONS: I was just getting ready to say . . . I know where there's a bridge for sale.

TROY: Look here, I'll tell you this . . . it don't matter to me if he was the devil. It don't matter if the devil give credit. Somebody has got to give it.

ROSE: It ought to matter. You going around talking about having truck with the devil . . . God's the one you gonna have to answer to. He's the one gonna be at the Judgment.

130 **LYONS:** Yeah, well, look here, Pop . . . let me have that ten dollars. I'll give it back to you. Bonnie got a job working at the hospital.

TROY: What I tell you, Bono? The only time I see this nigger is when he wants something. That's the only time I see him.

LYONS: Come on, Pop, Mr. Bono don't want to hear all that. Let me have the ten dollars. I told you Bonnie working.

TROY: What that mean to me? "Bonnie working." I don't care if she working. Go ask her for the ten dollars if she working. Talking about "Bonnie working." Why ain't you working?

LYONS: Aw, Pop, you know I can't find no decent job. Where am I gonna get a job at? You know I can't get no job.

TROY: I told you I know some people down there. I can get you on the rubbish   135
if you want to work. I told you that the last time you came by here asking me for something.

LYONS: Naw, Pop . . . thanks. That ain't for me. I don't wanna be carrying nobody's rubbish. I don't wanna be punching nobody's time clock.

TROY: What's the matter, you too good to carry people's rubbish? Where you think that ten dollars you talking about come from? I'm just supposed to haul people's rubbish and give my money to you 'cause you too lazy to work. You too lazy to work and wanna know why you ain't got what I got.

ROSE: What hospital Bonnie working at? Mercy?

LYONS: She's down at Passavant working in the laundry.

TROY: I ain't got nothing as it is. I give you that ten dollars and I got to   140
eat beans the rest of the week. Naw . . . you ain't getting no ten dollars here.

LYONS: You ain't got to be eating no beans. I don't know why you wanna say that.

TROY: I ain't got no extra money. Gabe done moved over to Miss Pearl's paying her the rent and things done got tight around here. I can't afford to be giving you every payday.

LYONS: I ain't asked you to give me nothing. I asked you to loan me ten dollars. I know you got ten dollars.

TROY: Yeah, I got it. You know why I got it? 'Cause I don't throw my money away out there in the streets. You living the fast life . . . wanna be a musi-cian . . . running around in them clubs and things . . . then, you learn to take care of yourself. You ain't gonna find me going and asking nobody for nothing. I done spent too many years without.

LYONS: You and me is two different people, Pop.   145

TROY: I done learned my mistake and learned to do what's right by it. You still trying to get something for nothing. Life don't owe you nothing. You owe it to yourself. Ask Bono. He'll tell you I'm right.

LYONS: You got your way of dealing with the world . . . I got mine. The only thing that matters to me is the music.

TROY: Yeah, I can see that! It don't matter how you gonna eat . . . . where your next dollar is coming from. You telling the truth there.

LYONS: I know I got to eat. But I got to live too. I need something that gonna help me to get out of the bed in the morning. Make me feel like I belong in the world. I don't bother nobody. I just stay with the music 'cause that's the only way I can find to live in the world. Otherwise there ain't no telling what I might do. Now I don't come criticizing you and how you live. I just come by to ask you for ten dollars. I don't wanna hear all that about how I live.

TROY: Boy, your mama did a hell of a job raising you.   150

LYONS: You can't change me, Pop. I'm thirty-four years old. If you wanted to change me, you should have been there when I was growing up. I come by to see you . . . ask for ten dollars and you want to talk about how I was raised. You don't know nothing about how I was raised.

ROSE: Let the boy have ten dollars, Troy.

TROY: *(to Lyons)* What the hell you looking at me for? I ain't got no ten dollars. You know what I do with my money. *(To Rose.)* Give him ten dollars if you want him to have it.

ROSE: I will. Just as soon as you turn it loose.

155 TROY: *(handing Rose the money)* There it is. Seventy-six dollars and forty-two cents. You see this, Bono? Now, I ain't gonna get but six of that back.

ROSE: You ought to stop telling that lie. Here, Lyons. *(She hands him the money.)*

LYONS: Thanks, Rose. Look . . . I got to run . . . I'll see you later.

TROY: Wait a minute. You gonna say "thanks, Rose" and ain't gonna look to see where she got that ten dollars from? See how they do me, Bono?

LYONS: I know she got it from you, Pop. Thanks. I'll give it back to you.

160 TROY: There he go telling another lie. Time I see that ten dollars . . . he'll be owing me thirty more.

LYONS: See you, Mr. Bono.

BONO: Take care, Lyons!

LYONS: Thanks, Pop. I'll see you again.

Lyons exits the yard.

TROY: I don't know why he don't go and get him a decent job and take care of that woman he got.

165 BONO: He'll be all right, Troy. The boy is still young.

TROY: The *boy* is thirty-four years old.

ROSE: Let's not get off into all that.

BONO: Look here . . . I got to be going. I got to be getting on. Lucille gonna be waiting.

TROY: *(puts his arm around Rose)* See this woman, Bono? I love this woman. I love this woman so much it hurts. I love her so much . . . I done run out of ways of loving her. So I got to go back to basics. Don't you come by my house Monday morning talking about time to go to work . . . 'cause I'm still gonna be stroking!

170 ROSE: Troy! Stop it now!

BONO: I ain't paying him no mind, Rose. That ain't nothing but gin-talk. Go on, Troy. I'll see you Monday.

TROY: Don't you come by my house, nigger! I done told you what I'm gonna be doing.

The lights go down to black.

SCENE 2

The lights come up on Rose hanging up clothes. She hums and sings softly to herself. It is the following morning.

ROSE: *(sings)*

> Jesus, be a fence all around me every day
> Jesus, I want you to protect me as I travel on my way.
> Jesus, be a fence all around me every day.

Troy enters from the house.

> Jesus, I want you to protect me
> As I travel on my way.

(*To Troy.*) 'Morning, You ready for breakfast? I can fix it soon as I finish hanging up these clothes?

TROY: I got the coffee on. That'll be all right. I'll just drink some of that this morning.

ROSE: That 651 hit yesterday. That's the second time this month. Miss Pearl hit for a dollar . . . seem like those that need the least always get lucky. Poor folks can't get nothing.

TROY: Them numbers don't know nobody. I don't know why you fool with them. You and Lyons both.

ROSE: It's something to do.

TROY: You ain't doing nothing but throwing your money away.

ROSE: Troy, you know I don't play foolishly. I just play a nickel here and a nickel there.

TROY: That's two nickels you done thrown away.

ROSE: Now I hit sometimes . . . that makes up for it. It always comes in handy when I do hit. I don't hear you complaining then.

TROY: I ain't complaining now. I just say it's foolish. Trying to guess out of six hundred ways which way the number gonna come. If I had all the money niggers, these Negroes, throw away on numbers for one week — just one week — I'd be a rich man.

ROSE: Well, you wishing and calling it foolish ain't gonna stop folks from playing numbers. That's one thing for sure. Besides . . . some good things come from playing numbers. Look where Pope done bought him that restaurant off of numbers.

TROY: I can't stand niggers like that. Man ain't had two dimes to rub together. He walking around with his shoes all run over bumming money for cigarettes. All right. Got lucky there and hit the numbers . . .

ROSE: Troy, I know all about it.

TROY: Had good sense, I'll say that for him. He ain't throwing his money away. I seen niggers hit the numbers and go through two thousand dollars in four days. Man bought him that restaurant down there . . . fixed it up real nice . . . and then didn't want nobody to come in it! A Negro go in there and can't get no kind of service. I seen a white fellow come in there and order a bowl of stew. Pope picked all the meat out the pot for him. Man ain't had nothing but a bowl of meat! Negro come behind him and ain't got nothing but the potatoes and carrots. Talking about what numbers do for people, you picked a wrong example. Ain't done nothing but make a worser fool out of him than he was before.

ROSE: Troy, you ought to stop worrying about what happened at work yesterday.

TROY: I ain't worried. Just told me to be down there at the Commissioner's office on Friday. Everybody think they gonna fire me. I ain't worried about them firing me. You ain't got to worry about that. *(Pause.)* Where's Cory? Cory in the house? *(Calls.)* Cory?

ROSE: He gone out.

20 TROY: Out, huh? He gone out 'cause he know I want him to help me with this fence. I know how he is. That boy scared of work.

Gabriel enters. He comes halfway down the alley and, hearing Troy's voice, stops.

TROY: *(continues)* He ain't done a lick of work in his life.

ROSE: He had to go to football practice. Coach wanted them to get in a little extra practice before the season start.

TROY: I got his practice . . . running out of here before he get his chores done.

ROSE: Troy, what is wrong with you this morning? Don't nothing set right with you. Go on back in there and go to bed . . . get up on the other side.

25 TROY: Why something got to be wrong with me? I ain't said nothing wrong with me.

ROSE: You got something to say about everything. First it's the numbers . . . then it's the way the man runs his restaurant . . . then you done got on Cory. What's it gonna be next? Take a look up there and see if the weather suits you . . . or is it gonna be how you gonna put up the fence with the clothes hanging in the yard.

TROY: You hit the nail on the head then.

ROSE: I know you like I know the back of my hand. Go on in there and get you some coffee . . . see if that straighten you up. 'Cause you ain't right this morning.

Troy starts into the house and sees Gabriel. Gabriel starts singing. Troy's brother, he is seven years younger than Troy. Injured in World War II, he has a metal plate in his head. He carries an old trumpet tied around his waist and believes with every fiber of his being that he is the Archangel Gabriel.° He carries a chipped basket with an assortment of discarded fruits and vegetables he has picked up in the strip district and which he attempts to sell.

GABRIEL: *(singing)*

Yes, ma'am, I got plums
You ask me how I sell them
Oh ten cents apiece
Three for a quarter
Come and buy now
'Cause I'm here today
And tomorrow I'll be gone

Gabriel enters.

Hey, Rose!

ROSE: How you doing, Gabe?

30 GABRIEL: There's Troy . . . Hey, Troy!

°*Archangel Gabriel:* A messenger of God.

TROY: Hey, Gabe.

Exit into kitchen.

ROSE: *(To Gabriel.)* What you got there?

GABRIEL: You know what I got, Rose. I got fruits and vegetables.

ROSE: *(looking in basket)* Where's all these plums you talking about? 35

GABRIEL: I ain't got no plums today, Rose. I was just singing that. Have some
     tomorrow. Put me in a big order for plums. Have enough plums tomorrow
     for St. Peter and everybody.

Troy reenters from kitchen, crosses to steps.

     (To Rose.) Troy's mad at me.

TROY: I ain't mad at you. What I got to be mad at you about? You ain't done
     nothing to me.

GABRIEL: I just moved over to Miss Pearl's to keep out from in your way. I ain't
     mean no harm by it.

TROY: Who said anything about that? I ain't said anything about that.

GABRIEL: You ain't mad at me, is you? 40

TROY: Naw . . . I ain't mad at you, Gabe. If I was mad at you I'd tell you about it.

GABRIEL: Got me two rooms. In the basement. Got my own door too. Wanna
     see my key? *(He holds up a key.)* That's my own key! Ain't nobody else got a
     key like that. That's my key! My two rooms!

TROY: Well, that's good, Gabe. You got your own key . . . that's good.

ROSE: You hungry, Gabe? I was just fixing to cook Troy his breakfast.

GABRIEL: I'll take some biscuits. You got some biscuits? Did you know when I 45
     was in heaven . . . every morning me and St. Peter° would sit down by the
     gate and eat some big fat biscuits? Oh, yeah! We had us a good time. We'd sit
     there and eat us them biscuits and then St. Peter would go off to sleep and
     tell me to wake him up when it's time to open the gates for the judgment.

ROSE: Well, come on . . . I'll make up a batch of biscuits.

Rose exits into the house.

GABRIEL: Troy . . . St. Peter got your name in the book. I seen it. It say . . .
     Troy Maxson. I say . . . I know him! He got the same name like what I got.
     That's my brother!

TROY: How many times you gonna tell me that, Gabe?

GABRIEL: Ain't got my name in the book. Don't have to have my name. I done
     died and went to heaven. He got your name though. One morning St. Peter
     was looking at his book . . . marking it up for the judgment . . . and he let
     me see your name. Got it in there under M. Got Rose's name . . . I ain't
     seen it like I seen yours . . . but I know it's in there. He got a great big book.
     Got everybody's name what was ever been born. That's what he told me.
     But I seen your name. Seen it with my own eyes.

°*St. Peter:* Disciple of Christ, believed to be the guard at the gates of heaven.

50   TROY: Go on in the house there. Rose going to fix you something to eat.

GABRIEL: Oh, I ain't hungry. I done had breakfast with Aunt Jemima. She come by and cooked me up a whole mess of flapjacks. Remember how we used to eat them flapjacks?

TROY: Go on in the house and get you something to eat now.

GABRIEL: I got to sell my plums. I done sold some tomatoes. Got me two quarters. Wanna see? (*He shows Troy his quarters.*) I'm gonna save them and buy me a new horn so St. Peter can hear me when it's time to open the gates. (*Gabriel stops suddenly. Listens.*) Hear that? That's the hellhounds. I got to chase them out of here. Go on get out of here! Get out!

Gabriel exits singing.

> Better get ready for the Judgment
> Better get ready for the Judgment
> My Lord is coming down

Rose enters from the house.

TROY: He's gone off somewhere.

55   GABRIEL: (*offstage*)

> Better get ready for the Judgment
> Better get ready for the Judgment morning
> Better get ready for the Judgment
> My God is coming down

ROSE: He ain't eating right. Miss Pearl say she can't get him to eat nothing.

TROY: What you want me to do about it, Rose? I done did everything I can for the man. I can't make him get well. Man got half his head blown away . . . what you expect?

ROSE: Seem like something ought to be done to help him.

TROY: Man don't bother nobody. He just mixed up from that metal plate he got in his head. Ain't no sense for him to go back into the hospital.

60   ROSE: Least he be eating right. They can help him take care of himself.

TROY: Don't nobody wanna be locked up, Rose. What you wanna lock him up for? Man go over there and fight the war . . . messin' around with them Japs, get half his head blown off . . . and they give him a lousy three thousand dollars. And I had to swoop down on that.

ROSE: Is you fixing to go into that again?

TROY: That's the only way I got a roof over my head . . . 'cause of that metal plate.

ROSE: Ain't no sense you blaming yourself for nothing. Gabe wasn't in no condition to manage that money. You done what was right by him. Can't nobody say you ain't done what was right by him. Look how long you took care of him . . . till he wanted to have his own place and moved over there with Miss Pearl.

65   TROY: That ain't what I'm saying, woman! I'm just stating the facts. If my brother didn't have that metal plate in his head . . . I wouldn't have a pot to

piss in or a window to throw it out of. And I'm fifty-three years old. Now see if you can understand that!

Troy gets up from the porch and starts to exit the yard.

ROSE: Where you going off to? You been running out of here every Saturday for weeks. I thought you was gonna work on this fence?
TROY: I'm gonna walk down to Taylors'. Listen to the ball game. I'll be back in a bit. I'll work on it when I get back.

He exits the yard. The lights go to black.

SCENE 3

The lights come up on the yard. It is four hours later. Rose is taking down the clothes from the line. Cory enters carrying his football equipment.

ROSE: Your daddy like to had a fit with you running out of here this morning without doing your chores.
CORY: I told you I had to go to practice.
ROSE: He say you were supposed to help him with this fence.   5
CORY: He been saying that the last four or five Saturdays, and then he don't never do nothing, but go down to Taylors'. Did you tell him about the recruiter?
ROSE: Yeah, I told him.
CORY: What he say?
ROSE: He ain't said nothing too much. You get in there and get started on your chores before he gets back. Go on and scrub down them steps before he gets back here hollering and carrying on.
CORY: I'm hungry. What you got to eat, Mama?   10
ROSE: Go on and get started on your chores. I got some meat loaf in there. Go on and make you a sandwich . . . and don't leave no mess in there.

Cory exits into the house. Rose continues to take down the clothes. Troy enters the yard and sneaks up and grabs her from behind.

Troy! Go on, now. You liked to scared me to death. What was the score of the game? Lucille had me on the phone and I couldn't keep up with it.
TROY: What I care about the game? Come here, woman. (*He tries to kiss her.*)
ROSE: I thought you went down Taylors' to listen to the game. Go on, Troy! You supposed to be putting up this fence.
TROY: (*attempting to kiss her again*) I'll put it up when I finish with what is at hand.
ROSE: Go on, Troy. I ain't studying you.   15
TROY: (*chasing after her*) I'm studying you . . . fixing to do my homework!
ROSE: Troy, you better leave me alone.
TROY: Where's Cory? That boy brought his butt home yet?
ROSE: He's in the house doing his chores.
TROY: (*calling*) Cory! Get your butt out here, boy!   20

Rose exits into the house with the laundry. Troy goes over to the pile of wood, picks up a board, and starts sawing. Cory enters from the house.

TROY: You just now coming in here from leaving this morning?

CORY: Yeah, I had to go to football practice.

TROY: Yeah, what?

CORY: Yessir.

25 TROY: I ain't but two seconds off you noway. The garbage sitting in there overflowing . . . you ain't done none of your chores . . . and you come in here talking about "Yeah."

CORY: I was just getting ready to do my chores now, Pop . . .

TROY: Your first chore is to help me with this fence on Saturday. Everything else come after that. Now get that saw and cut them boards.

Cory takes the saw and begins cutting the boards. Troy continues working. There is a long pause.

CORY: Hey, Pop . . . why don't you buy a TV?

TROY: What I want with a TV? What I want one of them for?

30 CORY: Everybody got one. Earl, Ba Bra . . . Jesse!

TROY: I ain't asked you who had one. I say what I want with one?

CORY: So you can watch it. They got lots of things on TV. Baseball games and everything. We could watch the World Series.

TROY: Yeah . . . and how much this TV cost?

CORY: I don't know. They got them on sale for around two hundred dollars.

35 TROY: Two hundred dollars, huh?

CORY: That ain't that much, Pop.

TROY: Naw, it's just two hundred dollars. See that roof you got over your head at night? Let me tell you something about that roof. It's been over ten years since that roof was last tarred. See now . . . the snow comes this winter and sit up there on that roof like it is . . . and it's gonna seep inside. It's just gonna be a little bit . . . ain't gonna hardly notice it. Then the next thing you know, it's gonna be leaking all over the house. Then the wood rot from all that water and you gonna need a whole new roof. Now, how much you think it cost to get that roof tarred?

CORY: I don't know.

TROY: Two hundred and sixty-four dollars . . . cash money. While you thinking about a TV, I got to be thinking about the roof . . . and whatever else go wrong here. Now if you had two hundred dollars, what would you do . . . fix the roof or buy a TV?

40 CORY: I'd buy a TV. Then when the roof started to leak . . . when it needed fixing . . . I'd fix it.

TROY: Where you gonna get the money from? You done spent it for a TV. You gonna sit up and watch the water run all over your brand new TV.

CORY: Aw, Pop. You got money. I know you do.

TROY: Where I got it at, huh?

CORY: You got it in the bank.

TROY: You wanna see my bankbook? You wanna see that seventy-three dollars   45
and twenty-two cents I got sitting up in there.

CORY: You ain't got to pay for it all at one time. You can put a down payment
on it and carry it on home with you.

TROY: Not me. I ain't gonna owe nobody nothing if I can help it. Miss a payment and they come and snatch it right out your house. Then what you
got? Now, soon as I get two hundred dollars clear, then I'll buy a TV. Right
now, as soon as I get two hundred and sixty-four dollars, I'm gonna have
this roof tarred.

CORY: Aw . . . Pop!

TROY: You go on and get you two hundred and buy one if ya want it. I got
better things to do with my money.

CORY: I can't get no two hundred dollars. I ain't never seen two hundred dollars.   50

TROY: I'll tell you what . . . you get you a hundred dollars and I'll put the other
hundred with it.

CORY: All right, I'm gonna show you.

TROY: You gonna show me how you can cut them boards right now.

Cory begins to cut the boards. There is a long pause.

CORY: The Pirates won today. That makes five in a row.

TROY: I ain't thinking about the Pirates. Got an all-white team. Got that   55
boy . . . that Puerto Rican boy . . . Clemente.° Don't even half-play him.
That boy could be something if they give him a chance. Play him one day
and sit him on the bench the next.

CORY: He gets a lot of chances to play.

TROY: I'm talking about playing regular. Playing every day so you can get your
timing. That's what I'm talking about.

CORY: They got some white guys on the team that don't play every day. You
can't play everybody at the same time.

TROY: If they got a white fellow sitting on the bench . . . you can bet your last
dollar he can't play! The colored guy got to be twice as good before he get
on the team. That's why I don't want you to get all tied up in them sports.
Man on the team and what it get him? They got colored on the team and
don't use them. Same as not having them. All them teams the same.

CORY: The Braves got Hank Aaron° and Wes Covington.° Hank Aaron hit   60
two home runs today. That makes forty-three.

°*Roberto Clemente:* (1934–1972), Major League baseball player for the Pittsburg Pirates, known as much for his
humanitarianism as his unique batting style and ability. Clemente received the Most Valuable Player Award in
1966 and died in a plane crash in 1972 while shuttling supplies to Nicaraguan earthquake victims.   °*Hank
Aaron:* Henry Aaron (1934–   ), American baseball player who broke Babe Ruth's career home run record with
a lifetime total of 755 home runs. The holder of 12 other Major League records, Aaron spent his Major League
career with the Braves, first in Milwaukee and later in their hometown of Atlanta.   °*Wes Covington:* John
Wesley Covington (1932–   ), American baseball player known for his ability to frustrate pitchers by wasting
time at the plate. In an eleven year career, Covington played for six Major League teams, beginning with the Milwaukee Braves and retiring with the Los Angeles Dodgers in 1966.

TROY: Hank Aaron ain't nobody. That what you supposed to do. That's how you supposed to play the game. Ain't nothing to it. It's just a matter of timing . . . getting the right follow-through. Hell, I can hit forty-three home runs right now!

CORY: Not off no major-league pitching, you couldn't.

TROY: We had better pitching in the Negro leagues. I hit seven home runs off of Satchel Paige.° You can't get no better than that!

CORY: Sandy Koufax.° He's leading the league in strikeouts.

65 **TROY:** I ain't thinking of no Sandy Koufax.

CORY: You got Warren Spahn° and Lew Burdette.° I bet you couldn't hit no home runs off of Warren Spahn.

TROY: I'm through with it now. You go on and cut them boards. (Pause.) Your mama tell me you done got recruited by a college football team? Is that right?

CORY: Yeah. Coach Zellman say the recruiter gonna be coming by to talk to you. Get you to sign the permission papers.

TROY: I thought you supposed to be working down there at the A&P. Ain't you suppose to be working down there after school?

70 **CORY:** Mr. Stawicki say he gonna hold my job for me until after the football season. Say starting next week I can work weekends.

TROY: I thought we had an understanding about this football stuff? You suppose to keep up with your chores and hold that job down at the A&P. Ain't been around here all day on a Saturday. Ain't none of your chores done . . . and now you telling me you done quit your job.

CORY: I'm going to be working weekends.

TROY: You damn right you are! And ain't no need for nobody coming around here to talk to me about signing nothing.

CORY: Hey, Pop . . . you can't do that. He's coming all the way from North Carolina.

75 **TROY:** I don't care where he coming from. The white man ain't gonna let you get nowhere with that football noway. You go on and get your book-learning so you can work yourself up in that A&P or learn how to fix cars or build houses or something, get you a trade. That way you have something can't nobody take away from you. You go on and learn how to put your hands to some good use. Besides hauling people's garbage.

°*Satchel Page:* Leroy Robert Paige (1906–1982), American baseball player. He played in the Negro Leagues from the 1920s until 1948, when he joined the Cleveland Indians; he reportedly pitched 55 no-hit games during his career. Joe DiMaggio called him "the best pitcher I have ever faced."   °*Sandy Koufax:* Sanford Koufax (1935–   ), left-handed pitcher who won 129 games and lost only 47 for the Los Angeles Dodgers in the six seasons between 1961 and 1966; he won three Cy Young Awards and pitched four no-hit games, the last of which (1965) was a perfect game.   °*Warren Spahn:* (1921–2003), left-handed pitcher who at the time of his retirement in 1966 held the National League record of 363 wins; he won 20 or more games in four consecutive seasons (1947–1950) and in several other seasons during the 1950s.   °*Lew Burdette:* Selva Lewis Burdette (1926–   ), American baseball player who pitched and won three games for the Milwaukee Braves against the New York Yankees in the 1957 World Series; for that Series, his ERA was an amazingly low .067.

CORY: I get good grades, Pop. That's why the recruiter wants to talk with you. You got to keep up your grades to get recruited. This way I'll be going to college. I'll get a chance . . .

TROY: First you gonna get your butt down there to the A&P and get your job back.

CORY: Mr. Stawicki done already hired somebody else 'cause I told him I was playing football.

TROY: You a bigger fool than I thought . . . to let somebody take away your job so you can play some football. Where you gonna get your money to take out your girlfriend and whatnot? What kind of foolishness is that to let somebody take away your job?

CORY: I'm still gonna be working weekends.   80

TROY: Naw . . . naw. You getting your butt out of here and finding you another job.

CORY: Come on, Pop! I got to practice. I can't work after school and play football too. The team needs me. That's what Coach Zellman say . . .

TROY: I don't care what nobody else say. I'm the boss . . . you understand? I'm the boss around here. I do the only saying what counts.

CORY: Come on, Pop!

TROY: I asked you . . . did you understand?   85

CORY: Yeah . . .

TROY: What?!

CORY: Yessir.

TROY: You go on down there to that A&P and see if you can get your job back. If you can't do both . . . then you quit the football team. You've got to take the crookeds with the straights.

CORY: Yessir. (*Pause.*) Can I ask you a question?   90

TROY: What the hell you wanna ask me? Mr. Stawicki the one you got the questions for.

CORY: How come you ain't never liked me?

TROY: Liked you? Who the hell say I got to like you? What law is there say I got to like you? Wanna stand up in my face and ask a damn fool-ass question like that. Talking about liking somebody. Come here, boy, when I talk to you.

Cory comes over to where Troy is working. He stands slouched over and Troy shoves him on his shoulder.

Straighten up, goddammit! I asked you a question . . . what law is there say I got to like you?

CORY: None.

TROY: Well, all right then! Don't you eat every day? (*Pause.*) Answer me when 95 I talk to you! Don't you eat every day?

CORY: Yeah.

TROY: Nigger, as long as you in my house, you put that sir on the end of it when you talk to me!

CORY: Yes . . . sir.

TROY: You eat every day.

100 CORY: Yessir!

TROY: Got a roof over your head.

CORY: Yessir!

TROY: Got clothes on your back.

CORY: Yessir.

105 TROY: Why you think that is?

CORY: 'Cause of you.

TROY: Ah, hell I know it's 'cause of me . . . but why do you think that is?

CORY: *(hesitant)* 'Cause you like me.

TROY: Like you? I go out of here every morning . . . bust my butt . . . putting up with them crackers° every day . . . 'cause I like you? You are the biggest fool I ever saw. *(Pause.)* It's my job. It's my responsibility! You understand that? A man got to take care of his family. You live in my house . . . sleep you behind on my bedclothes . . . fill you belly up with my food . . . 'cause you my son. You my flesh and blood. Not 'cause I like you! 'Cause it's my duty to take care of you. I owe a responsibility to you! Let's get this straight right here . . . before it go along any further . . . I ain't got to like you. Mr. Rand don't give me my money come payday cause he likes me. He give me 'cause he owe me. I done give you everything I had to give you. I gave you your life! Me and your mama worked that out between us. And liking your black ass wasn't part of the bargain. Don't you try and go through life worrying about if somebody like you or not. You best be making sure they doing right by you. You understand what I'm saying, boy?

110 CORY: Yessir.

TROY: Then get the hell out of my face, and get on down to that A&P.

Rose has been standing behind the screen door for much of the scene. She enters as Cory exits.

ROSE: Why don't you let the boy go ahead and play football, Troy? Ain't no harm in that. He's just trying to be like you with the sports.

TROY: I don't want him to be like me! I want him to move as far away from my life as he can get. You the only decent thing that ever happened to me. I wish him that. But I don't wish him a thing else from my life. I decided seventeen years ago that boy wasn't getting involved in no sports. Not after what they did to me in the sports.

ROSE: Troy, why don't you admit you was too old to play in the major leagues? For once . . . why don't you admit that?

115 TROY: What do you mean too old? Don't come telling me I was too old. I just wasn't the right color. Hell, I'm fifty-three years old and can do better than Selkirk's .269 right now!

ROSE: How's was you gonna play ball when you were over forty? Sometimes I can't go no sense out of you.

° *crackers:* Derogatory term for white people, generally poor southern whites.

TROY: I got good sense, woman. I got sense enough not to let my boy get hurt over playing no sports. You been mothering that boy too much. Worried about if people like him.

ROSE: Everything that boy do . . . he do for you. He wants you to say "Good job, son." That's all.

TROY: Rose, I ain't got time for that. He's alive. He's healthy. He's got to make his own way. I made mine. Ain't nobody gonna hold his hand when he get out there in that world.

ROSE: Times have changed from when you was young, Troy. People change. The world's changing around you and you can't even see it. 120

TROY: (slow, methodical) Woman . . . I do the best I can do. I come in here every Friday. I carry a sack of potatoes and a bucket of lard. You all line up at the door with your hands out. I give you the lint from my pockets. I give you my sweat and my blood. I ain't got no tears. I done spent them. We go upstairs in that room at night . . . and I fall down on you and try to blast a hole into forever. I get up Monday morning . . . find my lunch on the table. I go out. Make my way. Find my strength to carry me through to the next Friday. (Pause.) That's all I got, Rose. That's all I got to give. I can't give nothing else.

Troy exits into the house. The lights go down to black.

SCENE 4

It is Friday. Two weeks later. Cory starts out of the house with his football equipment. The phone rings.

CORY: (calling) I got it! (He answers the phone and stands in the screen door talking.) Hello? Hey, Jesse. Naw . . . I was just getting ready to leave now.

ROSE: (calling) Cory! 5

CORY: I told you, man, them spikes° is all tore up. You can use them if you want, but they ain't no good. Earl got some spikes.

ROSE: (calling) Cory!

CORY: (calling to Rose) Mam? I'm talking to Jesse. (Into phone.) When she say that? (Pause.) Aw, you lying, man. I'm gonna tell her you said that.

ROSE: (calling) Cory, don't you go nowhere!

CORY: I got to go to the game, Ma! (Into the phone.) Yeah, hey, look, I'll talk to you later. Yeah, I'll meet you over Earl's house. Later. Bye, Ma.

Cory exits the house and starts out the yard.

ROSE: Cory, where you going off to? You got that stuff all pulled out and thrown all over your room.

CORY: (in the yard) I was looking for my spikes. Jesse wanted to borrow my spikes. 10

ROSE: Get up there and get that cleaned up before your daddy get back in here.

CORY: I got to go to the game! I'll clean it up *when I get back.*

Cory exits.

°*spikes:* Athletic shoes with sharp metal grips set into the soles.

ROSE: That's all he need to do is see that room all messed up.

Rose exits into the house. Troy and Bono enter the yard. Troy is dressed in clothes other than his work clothes.

BONO: He told him the same thing he told you. Take it to the union.

15 **TROY:** Brownie ain't got that much sense. Man wasn't thinking about nothing. He wait until I confront them on it . . . then he wanna come crying seniority. *(Calls.)* Hey, Rose!

BONO: I wish I could have seen Mr. Rand's face when he told you.

TROY: He couldn't get it out of his mouth! Liked to bit his tongue! When they called me down there to the Commissioner's office . . . he thought they was gonna fire me. Like everybody else.

BONO: I didn't think they was gonna fire you. I thought they was gonna put you on the warning paper.

TROY: Hey, Rose! *(To Bono.)* Yeah, Mr. Rand like to bit his tongue.

Troy breaks the seal on the bottle, takes a drink, and hands it to Bono.

20 **BONO:** I see you run right down to Taylors' and told that Alberta gal.

TROY: *(calling)* Hey, Rose! *(To Bono.)* I told everybody. Hey, Rose! I went down there to cash my check.

ROSE: *(entering from the house)* Hush all that hollering, man! I know you out here. What they say down there at the Commissioner's office?

TROY: You supposed to come when I call you, woman. Bono'll tell you that. *(To Bono.)* Don't Lucille come when you call her?

ROSE: Man, hush your mouth, I ain't no dog . . . talk about "come when you call me."

25 **TROY:** *(puts his arm around Rose)* You hear this, Bono? I had me an old dog used to get uppity like that. You say, "C'mere, Blue!" . . . and he just lay there and look at you. End up getting a stick and chasing him away trying to make him come.

ROSE: I ain't studying you and your dog. I remember you used to sing that old song.

TROY: *(he sings)*

> Hear it ring! Hear it ring!
> I had a dog his name was Blue.

ROSE: Don't nobody wanna hear you sing that old song.

TROY: *(sings)*

> You know Blue was mighty true.

30 **ROSE:** Used to have Cory running around here singing that song.

BONO: Hell, I remember that song myself.

TROY: *(sings)*

> You know Blue was a good old dog.
> Blue treed a possum in a hollow log.

That was my daddy's song. My daddy made up that song.

ROSE: I don't care who made it up. Don't nobody wanna hear you sing it.

TROY: (*makes a song like calling a dog*) Come here, woman.

ROSE: You come in here carrying on, I reckon they ain't fired you. What they say down there at the Commissioner's office? 35

TROY: Look here, Rose . . . Mr. Rand called me into his office today when I got back from talking to them people down there . . . it come from up top . . . he called me in and told me they was making me a driver.

ROSE: Troy, you kidding!

TROY: No I ain't. Ask Bono.

ROSE: Well, that's great, Troy. Now you don't have to hassle them people no more.

Lyons enters from the street.

TROY: Aw hell, I wasn't looking to see you today. I thought you was in jail. Got 40 it all over the front page of the *Courier* about them raiding Sefus's place . . . where you be hanging out with all them thugs.

LYONS: Hey, Pop . . . that ain't got nothing to do with me. I don't go down there gambling. I go down there to sit in with the band. I ain't got nothing to do with the gambling part. They got some good music down there.

TROY: They got some rogues . . . is what they got.

LYONS: How you been, Mr. Bono? Hi, Rose.

BONO: I see where you playing down at the Crawford Grill tonight.

ROSE: How come you ain't brought Bonnie like I told you? You should have 45 brought Bonnie with you, she ain't been over in a month of Sundays.

LYONS: I was just in the neighborhood . . . thought I'd stop by.

TROY: Here he come . . .

BONO: Your daddy got a promotion on the rubbish. He's gonna be the first colored driver. Ain't got to do nothing but sit up there and read the paper like them white fellows.

LYONS: Hey, Pop . . . if you knew how to read you'd be all right.

BONO: Naw . . . naw . . . you mean if the nigger knew how to *drive* he'd be all 50 right. Been fighting with them people about driving and ain't even got a license. Mr. Rand know you ain't got no driver's license?

TROY: Driving ain't nothing. All you do is point the truck where you want it to go. Driving ain't nothing.

BONO: Do Mr. Rand know you ain't got no driver's license? That's what I'm talking about. I ain't asked if driving was easy. I asked if Mr. Rand know you ain't got no driver's license.

TROY: He ain't got to know. The man ain't got to know my business. Time he find out, I have two or three driver's licenses.

LYONS: (*going into his pocket*) Say, look here, Pop . . .

TROY: I knew it was coming. Didn't I tell you, Bono? I know what kind of 55 "Look here, Pop" that was. The nigger fixing to ask me for some money. It's Friday night. It's my payday. All them rogues down there on the avenue . . . the ones that ain't in jail . . . and Lyons is hopping in his shoes to get down there with them.

LYONS: See, Pop . . . if you give somebody else a chance to talk sometimes, you'd see that I was fixing to pay you back your ten dollars like I told you. Here . . . I told you I'd pay you when Bonnie got paid.

TROY: Naw . . . you go ahead and keep that ten dollars. Put it in the bank. The next time you feel like you wanna come by here and ask me for something . . . you go on down there and get that.

LYONS: Here's your ten dollars, Pop. I told you I don't want you to give me nothing. I just wanted to borrow ten dollars.

TROY: Naw . . . you go on and keep that for the next time you want to ask me.

60 LYONS: Come on, Pop . . . here go your ten dollars.

ROSE: Why don't you go on and let the boy pay you back, Troy?

LYONS: Here you go, Rose. If you don't take it I'm gonna have to hear about it for the next six months. (*He hands her the money.*)

ROSE: You can hand yours over here too, Troy.

TROY: You see this, Bono. You see how they do me.

65 BONO: Yeah, Lucille do me the same way.

Gabriel is heard singing offstage. He enters.

GABRIEL: Better get ready for the Judgment! Better get ready for . . . Hey! . . . Hey! . . . There's Troy's boy!

LYONS: How are you doing, Uncle Gabe?

GABRIEL: Lyons . . . The King of the Jungle! Rose . . . hey, Rose. Got a flower for you. (*He takes a rose from his pocket.*) Picked it myself. That's the same rose like you is!

70 ROSE: That's right nice of you, Gabe.

LYONS: What you been doing, Uncle Gabe?

GABRIEL: Oh, I been chasing hellhounds and waiting on the time to tell St. Peter to open the gates.

LYONS: You been chasing hellhounds, huh? Well . . . you doing the right thing, Uncle Gabe. Somebody got to chase them.

GABRIEL: Oh, yeah . . . I know it. The devil's strong. The devil ain't no pushover. Hellhounds snipping at everybody's heels. But I got my trumpet waiting on the judgment time.

LYONS: Waiting on the Battle of Armageddon, huh?

75 GABRIEL: Ain't gonna be too much of a battle when God get to waving that Judgment sword. But the people's gonna have a hell of a time trying to get into heaven if them gates ain't open.

LYONS: (*putting his arm around Gabriel*) You hear this, Pop. Uncle Gabe, you all right!

GABRIEL: (*laughing with Lyons*) Lyons! King of the Jungle.

ROSE: You gonna stay for supper, Gabe? Want me to fix you a plate?

GABRIEL: I'll take a sandwich, Rose. Don't want no plate. Just wanna eat with my hands. I'll take a sandwich.

80 ROSE: How about you, Lyons? You staying? Got some short ribs cooking.

LYONS: Naw, I won't eat nothing till after we finished playing. (*Pause.*) You ought to come down and listen to me play, Pop.

TROY: I don't like that Chinese music. All that noise.

ROSE: Go on in the house and wash up, Gabe . . . I'll fix you a sandwich.

GABRIEL: *(to Lyons, as he exits)* Troy's mad at me.

LYONS: What you mad at Uncle Gabe for, Pop?   85

ROSE: He thinks Troy's mad at him cause he moved over to Miss Pearl's.

TROY: I ain't mad at the man. He can live where he want to live at.

LYONS: What he move over there for? Miss Pearl don't like nobody.

ROSE: She don't mind him none. She treats him real nice. She just don't allow all that singing.

TROY: She don't mind that rent he be paying . . . that's what she don't mind.   90

ROSE: Troy, I ain't going through that with you no more. He's over there cause he want to have his own place. He can come and go as he please.

TROY: Hell, he could come and go as he please here. I wasn't stopping him. I ain't put no rules on him.

ROSE: It ain't the same thing, Troy. And you know it.

Gabriel comes to the door.

Now, that's the last I wanna hear about that. I don't wanna hear nothing else about Gabe and Miss Pearl. And next week . . .

GABRIEL: I'm ready for my sandwich, Rose.

ROSE: And next week . . . when that recruiter come from that school . . . I   95
want you to sign that paper and go on and let Cory play football. Then that'll be the last I have to hear about that.

TROY: *(to Rose as she exits into the house)* I ain't thinking about Cory nothing.

LYONS: What . . . Cory got recruited? What school he going to?

TROY: That boy walking around here smelling his piss . . . thinking he's grown. Thinking he's gonna do what he want, irrespective of what I say. Look here, Bono . . . I left the Commissioner's office and went down to the A&P . . . that boy ain't working down there. He lying to me. Telling me he got his job back . . . telling me he working weekends . . . telling me he working after school . . . Mr. Stawicki tell me he ain't working down there at all!

LYONS: Cory just growing up. He's just busting at the seams trying to fill out your shoes.

TROY: I don't care what he's doing. When he get to the point where he wanna   100
disobey me . . . then it's time for him to move on. Bono'll tell you that. I bet he ain't never disobeyed his daddy without paying the consequences.

BONO: I ain't never had a chance. My daddy came on through . . . but I ain't never knew him to see him . . . or what he had on his mind or where he went. Just moving on through. Searching out the New Land. That's what the old folks used to call it. See a fellow moving around from place to place . . . woman to woman . . . called it searching out the New Land. can't say if he ever found it. I come along, didn't want no kids. Didn't know if I was gonna be in one place long enough to fix on them right as their daddy. I figured I was going searching too. As it turned out I been hooked up with Lucille near about as long as your daddy been with Rose. Going on sixteen years.

TROY: Sometimes I wish I hadn't known my daddy. He ain't cared nothing about no kids. A kid to him wasn't nothing. All he wanted was for you to learn how to walk so he could start you to working. When it come time for eating . . . he ate first. If there was anything left over, that's what you got. Man would sit down and eat two chickens and give you the wing.

LYONS: You ought to stop that, Pop. Everybody feed their kids. No matter how hard times is . . . everybody care about their kids. Make sure they have something to eat.

TROY: The only thing my daddy cared about was getting them bales of cotton in to Mr. Lubin. That's the only thing that mattered to him. Sometimes I used to wonder why he was living. Wonder why the devil hadn't come and got him. "Get them bales of cotton in to Mr. Lubin" and find out he owe him money . . .

105 LYONS: He should have just went on and left when he saw he couldn't get nowhere. That's what I would have done.

TROY: How he gonna leave with eleven kids? And where he gonna go? He ain't knew how to do nothing but farm. No, he was trapped and I think he knew it. But I'll say this for him . . . he felt a responsibility toward us. Maybe he ain't treated us the way I felt he should have . . . but without that responsibility he could have walked off and left us . . . made his own way.

BONO: A lot of them did. Back in those days what you talking about . . . they walk out their front door and just take on down one road or another and keep on walking.

LYONS: There you go? That's what I'm talking about.

BONO: Just keep on walking till you come to something else. Ain't you never heard of nobody having the walking blues? Well, that's what you call it when you just take off like that.

110 TROY: My daddy ain't had them walking blues! What you talking about? He stayed right there with his family. But he was just as evil as he could be. My mama couldn't stand him. Couldn't stand that evilness. She run off when I was about eight. She sneaked off one night after he had gone to sleep. Told me she was coming back for me. I ain't never seen her no more. All his women run off and left him. He wasn't good for nobody.

When my turn come to head out, I was fourteen and got to sniffing around Joe Canewell's daughter. Had us an old mule we called Greyboy. My daddy sent me out to do some plowing and tied up Greyboy and went to fooling around with Joe Canewell's daughter. We done found us a nice little spot, got real cozy with each other. She about thirteen and we done figured we was grown anyway . . . so we down there enjoying ourselves . . . ain't thinking about nothing. We didn't know Greyboy had got loose and wandered back to the house and my daddy was looking for me. We down there by the creek enjoying ourselves when my daddy come up on us. Surprised us. He had them leather straps off the mule and commenced to whupping me like there was no tomorrow. I jumped up, mad and embarrassed. I was scared of my daddy. When he commenced to whupping on me . . . quite naturally I run to get out of the way. (*Pause.*) Now I thought he was mad 'cause I ain't done my work. But I see where he was chasing me off so he could have that gal for himself. When I see what the matter of it was, I lost all fear of my daddy. Right there is where I become a man . . . at fourteen years of age. (*Pause.*) Now it was my turn to run him off. I picked up them same reins that he had used on me. I picked up them reins and commenced to whupping on him. The gal jumped up and run off . . . and when my daddy turned to face me, I could see why the devil had never come to get him . . . cause he was the devil himself. I don't know what happened. When I woke up, I was laying right there by the creek, and Blue . . . this old dog we had . . . was licking my face. I thought I was blind. I couldn't see nothing. Both my eyes were swollen shut. I laid there and cried. I didn't know what I was gonna do. The only thing I knew was the time had come for me to leave my daddy's house. And right there the world suddenly got big. And it was a long time before I could cut it down to where I could handle it.

Part of that cutting down was when I got to the place where I could feel him kicking in my blood and knew that the only thing that separated us was the matter of a few years.

Gabriel enters from the house with a sandwich.

LYONS: What you got there, Uncle Gabe?

GABRIEL: Got me a ham sandwich. Rose gave me a ham sandwich.

TROY: I don't know what happened to him. I done lost touch with everybody except Gabriel. But I hope he's dead. I hope he found some peace.

LYONS: That's a heavy story, Pop. I didn't know you left home when you was fourteen.

TROY: And didn't know nothing. The only part of the world I knew was the forty-two acres of Mr. Lubin's land. That's all I knew about life.   115

LYONS: Fourteen's kinda young to be out on your own. (*Phone rings.*) I don't even think I was ready to be out on my own at fourteen. I don't know what I would have done.

TROY: I got up from the creek and walked on down to Mobile.° I was through with farming. Figured I could do better in the city. So I walked the two hundred miles to Mobile.

LYONS: Wait a minute . . . you ain't walked no two hundred miles, Pop. Ain't nobody gonna walk no two hundred miles. You talking about some walking there.

BONO: That's the only way you got anywhere back in them days.

LYONS: Shhh. Damn if I wouldn't have hitched a ride with somebody!   120

TROY: Who you gonna hitch it with? They ain't got no cars and things like they got now. We talking about 1918.

ROSE: (*entering*) What you all out here getting into?

°*Mobile:* City and seaport in southwestern Alabama.

TROY: *(to Rose)* I'm telling Lyons how good he got it. He don't know nothing about this I'm talking.

ROSE: Lyons, that was Bonnie on the phone. She say you supposed to pick her up.

125   **LYONS:** Yeah, okay, Rose.

TROY: I walked on down to Mobile and hitched up with some of them fellows that was heading this way. Got up here and found out . . . not only couldn't you get a job . . . you couldn't find no place to live. I thought I was in freedom. Shhh. Colored folks living down there on the riverbanks in whatever kind of shelter they could find for themselves. Right down there under the Brady Street Bridge. Living in shacks made of sticks and tarpaper. Messed around there and went from bad to worse. Started stealing. First it was food. Then I figured, hell, if I steal money I can buy me some food. Buy me some shoes too! One thing led to another. Met your mama. I was young and anxious to be a man. Met your mama and had you. What I do that for? Now I got to worry about feeding you and her. Got to steal three times as much. Went out one day looking for somebody to rob . . . that's what I was, a robber. I'll tell you the truth. I'm ashamed of it today. But it's the truth. Went to rob this fellow . . . pulled out my knife . . . and he pulled out a gun. Shot me in the chest. I felt just like somebody had taken a hot branding iron and laid it on me. When he shot me I jumped at him with my knife. They told me I killed him and they put me in the penitentiary and locked me up for fifteen years. That's where I met Bono. That's where I learned how to play baseball. Got out that place and your mama had taken you and went on to make life without me. Fifteen years was a long time for her to wait. But that fifteen years cured me of that robbing stuff. Rose'll tell you. She asked me when I met her if I had gotten all that foolishness out of my system. And I told her, "Baby, it's you and baseball all what count with me." You hear me, Bono? I meant it too. She say, "Which one comes first?" I told her, "Baby, ain't no doubt it's baseball . . . but you stick and get old with me and we'll both outlive this baseball." Am I right, Rose? And it's true.

ROSE: Man, hush your mouth. You ain't said no such thing. Talking about "Baby, you know you'll always be number one with me." That's what you was talking.

TROY: You hear that, Bono. That's why I love her.

BONO: Rose'll keep you straight. You get off the track, she'll straighten you up.

130   **ROSE:** Lyons, you better get on up and get Bonnie. She waiting on you.

LYONS: *(gets up to go)* Hey, Pop, why don't you come on down to the Grill and hear me play

TROY: I ain't going down there. I'm too old to be sitting around in them clubs.

BONO: You got to be good to play down at the Grill.

LYONS: Come on, Pop . . .

135   **TROY:** I got to get up in the morning.

LYONS: You ain't got to stay long.

TROY: Naw, I'm gonna get my supper and go on to bed.

LYONS: Well, I got to go. I'll see you again.

TROY: Don't you come around my house on my payday.

ROSE: Pick up the phone and let somebody know you coming. And bring   140
Bonnie with you. You know I'm always glad to see her.

LYONS: Yeah, I'll do that, Rose. You take care now. See you, Pop. See you,
Mr. Bono. See you, Uncle Gabe.

GABRIEL: Lyons! King of the Jungle!

Lyons exits.

TROY: Is supper ready, woman? Me and you got some business to take care of.
I'm gonna tear it up too.

ROSE: Troy, I done told you now!

TROY: (*puts his arm around Bono*) Aw hell, woman . . . this is Bono. Bono like   145
family. I done known this nigger since . . . how long I done know you?

BONO: It's been a long time.

TROY: I done know this nigger since Skippy was a pup. Me and him done been
through some times.

BONO: You sure right about that.

TROY: Hell, I done know him longer than I known you. And we still standing
shoulder to shoulder. Hey, look here, Bono . . . a man can't ask for no more
than that. (*Drinks to him.*) I love you, nigger.

BONO: Hell, I love you too . . . I got to get home see my woman. You got yours   150
in hand. I got to go get mine.

*Bono starts to exit as Cory enters the yard, dressed in his football uniform. He gives Troy
a hard, uncompromising look.*

CORY: What you do that for, Pop?

He throws his helmet down in the direction of Troy.

ROSE: What's the matter? Cory . . . what's the matter?

CORY: Papa done went up to the school and told Coach Zellman I can't play
football no more. Wouldn't even let me play the game. Told him to tell the
recruiter not to come.

ROSE: Troy . . .

TROY: What you Troying me for. Yeah, I did it. And the boy know why I did it.   155

CORY: Why you wanna do that to me? That was the one chance I had.

ROSE: Ain't nothing wrong with Cory playing football, Troy.

TROY: The boy lied to me. I told the nigger if he wanna play football . . . to
keep up his chores and hold down that job at the A&P. That was the
conditions. Stopped down there to see Mr. Stawicki . . .

CORY: I can't work after school during the football season, Pop! I tried to tell
you that Mr. Stawicki's holding my job for me. You don't never want to
listen to nobody. And then you wanna go and do this to me!

TROY: I ain't done nothing to you. You done it to yourself.   160

CORY: Just cause you didn't have a chance! You just scared I'm gonna be better
than you, that's all.

TROY: Come here.

ROSE: Troy . . .

Cory reluctantly crosses over to Troy.

TROY: All right! See. You done made a mistake.

165   CORY: I didn't even do nothing!

TROY: I'm gonna tell you what your mistake was. See . . . you swung at the ball and didn't hit it. That's strike one. See, you in the batter's box now. You swung and you missed. That's strike one. Don't you strike out!

Lights fade to black.

ACT 2
SCENE 1

The following morning. Cory is at the tree hitting the ball with the bat. He tries to mimic Troy, but his swing is awkward, less sure. Rose enters from the house.

ROSE: Cory, I want you to help me with this cupboard.

CORY: I ain't quitting the team. I don't care what Poppa say.

ROSE: I'll talk to him when he gets back. He had to go see about your Uncle Gabe. The police done arrested him. Say he was disturbing the peace. He'll be back directly. Come on in here and help me clean out the top of this cupboard.

Cory exits into the house. Rose sees Troy and Bono coming down the alley.

Troy . . . what they say down there?

TROY: Ain't said nothing. I give them fifty dollars and they let him go. I'll talk to you about it. Where's Cory?

5   ROSE: He's in there helping me clean out these cupboards.

TROY: Tell him to get his butt out here.

Troy and Bono go over to the pile of wood. Bono picks up the saw and begins sawing.

TROY: *(to Bono)* All they want is the money. That makes six or seven times I done went down there and got him. See me coming they stick out their hands.

BONO: Yeah. I know what you mean. That's all they care about . . . that money. They don't care about what's right. *(Pause.)* Nigger, why you got to go and get some hard wood? You ain't doing nothing but building a little old fence. Get you some soft pine wood. That's all you need.

TROY: I know what I'm doing. This is outside wood. You put pine wood inside the house. Pine wood is inside wood. This here is outside wood. Now you tell me where the fence is gonna be?

10   BONO: You don't need this wood. You can put it up with pine wood and it'll stand as long as you gonna be here looking at it.

TROY: How you know how long I'm gonna be here, nigger? Hell, I might just live forever. Live longer than old man Horsely.

BONO: That's what Magee used to say.

TROY: Magee's a damn fool. Now you tell me who you ever heard of gonna
pull their own teeth with a pair of rusty pliers.

BONO: The old folks . . . my granddaddy used to pull his teeth with pliers.
They ain't had no dentists for the colored folks back then.

TROY: Get clean pliers! You understand? Clean pliers! Sterilize them! Besides we   15
ain't living back then. All Magee had to do was walk over to Doc Goldblum's.

BONO: I see where you and that Tallahassee gal . . . that Alberta . . . I see
where you all done got tight.

TROY: What you mean "got tight"?

BONO: I see where you be laughing and joking with her all the time.

TROY: I laughs and jokes with all of them, Bono. You know me.

BONO: That ain't the kind of laughing and joking I'm talking about.   20

Cory enters from the house.

CORY: How you doing, Mr. Bono?

TROY: Cory? Get that saw from Bono and cut some wood. He talking about
the wood's too hard to cut. Stand back there, Jim, and let that young boy
show you how it's done.

BONO: He's sure welcome to it.

Cory takes the saw and begins to cut the wood.

Whew-e-e! Look at that. Big old strong boy. Look like Joe Louis.° Hell,
must be getting old the way I'm watching that boy whip through that wood.

CORY: I don't see why Mama want a fence around the yard noways.

TROY: Damn if I know either. What the hell she keeping out with it? She ain't   25
got nothing nobody want.

BONO: Some people build fences to keep people out . . . and other people build
fences to keep people in. Rose wants to hold on to you all. She loves you.

TROY: Hell, nigger, I don't need nobody to tell me my wife loves me. Cory . . .
go on in the house and see if you can find that other saw.

CORY: Where's it at?

TROY: I said find it! Look for it till you find it!

Cory exits into the house.

What's that supposed to mean? Wanna keep us in?

BONO: Troy . . . I done known you seem like damn near my whole life. You and   30
Rose both. I done know both of you all for a long time. I remember when
you met Rose. When you was hitting them baseballs out the park. A lot of
them gals was after you then. You had the pick of the litter. When you
picked Rose, I was happy for you. That was the first time I knew you had

---

°*Joe Louis:* Joseph Louis Barrow (1914–1981), American boxer known as the "Brown Bomber." In 1937, he became the youngest boxer ever to win the Heavyweight Championship, which he defended twenty-five times; he
retired undefeated in 1949.

any sense. I said . . . My man Troy knows what he's doing . . . I'm gonna follow this nigger . . . he might take me somewhere. I been following you too.
I done learned a whole heap of things about life watching you. I done
learned how to tell where the shit lies. How to tell it from the alfalfa. You
done learned me a lot of things. You showed me how to not make the same
mistakes . . . to take life as it comes along and keep putting one foot in
front of the other. *(Pause.)* Rose a good woman, Troy.

TROY: Hell, nigger, I know she a good woman. I been married to her for
eighteen years. What you got on your mind, Bono?

BONO: I just say she a good woman. Just like I say anything. I ain't got to have
nothing on my mind.

TROY: You just gonna say she a good woman and leave it hanging out there
like that? Why you telling me she a good woman?

BONO: She loves you, Troy. Rose loves you.

35 TROY: You saying I don't measure up. That's what you trying to say. I don't
measure up 'cause I'm seeing this other gal. I know what you trying
to say.

BONO: I know what Rose means to you, Troy. I'm just trying to say I don't want
to see you mess up.

TROY: Yeah, I appreciate that, Bono. If you was messing around on Lucille I'd
be telling you the same thing.

BONO: Well, that's all I got to say. I just say that because I love you both.

TROY: Hell, you know me . . . I wasn't out there looking for nothing. You can't
find a better woman than Rose. I know that. But seems like this woman just
stuck onto me where I can't shake her loose. I done wrestled with it, tried
to throw her off me . . . but she just stuck on tighter. Now she's stuck on for
good.

40 BONO: You's in control . . . that's what you tell me all the time. You responsible
for what you do.

TROY: I ain't ducking the responsibility of it. As long as it sets right in my
heart . . . then I'm okay. 'Cause that's all I listen to. It'll tell me right
from wrong every time. And I ain't talking about doing Rose no bad turn.
I love Rose. She done carried me a long ways and I love and respect her
for that.

BONO: I know you do. That's why I don't want to see you hurt her. But what
you gonna do when she find out? What you got then? If you try and juggle
both of them . . . sooner or later you gonna drop one of them. That's
common sense.

TROY: Yeah, I hear what you saying, Bono. I been trying to figure a way to
work it out.

BONO: Work it out right, Troy. I don't want to be getting all up between you
and Rose's business . . . but work it so it come out right.

45 TROY: Ah hell, I get all up between you and Lucille's business. When you
gonna get that woman that refrigerator she been wanting? Don't tell me you
ain't got no money now. I know who your banker is. Mellon don't need that
money bad as Lucille want that refrigerator. I'll tell you that.

BONO: Tell you what I'll do . . . when you finish building this fence for Rose . . . I'll buy Lucille that refrigerator.

TROY: You done stuck your foot in your mouth now!

Troy grabs up a board and begins to saw. Bono starts to walk out the yard.

Hey, nigger . . . where you going?

BONO: I'm going home. I know you don't expect me to help you now. I'm protecting my money. I wanna see you put that fence up by yourself. That's what I want to see. You'll be here another six months without me.

TROY: Nigger, you ain't right.

BONO: When it comes to my money . . . I'm right as fireworks on the Fourth of July.   50

TROY: All right, we gonna see now. You better get out your bankbook.

Bono exits, and Troy continues to work. Rose enters from the house.

ROSE: What they say down there? What's happening with Gabe?

TROY: I went down there and got him out. Cost me fifty dollars. Say he was   55
disturbing the peace. Judge set up a hearing for him in three weeks. Say to show cause why he shouldn't be recommitted.

ROSE: What was he doing that cause them to arrest him?

TROY: Some kids were teasing him and he run them off home. Say he was howling and carrying on. Some folks seen him and called the police. That's all it was.

ROSE: Well, what's you say? What'd you tell the judge?

TROY: Told him I'd look after him. It didn't make no sense to recommit the man. He stuck out his big greasy palm and told me to give him fifty dollars and take him on home.

ROSE: Where's he at now? Where'd he go off to?

TROY: He's gone about his business. He don't need nobody to hold his hand.

ROSE: Well, I don't know. Seem like that would be the best place for him if   60
they did put him into the hospital. I know what you're gonna say. But that's what I think would be best.

TROY: The man done had his life ruined fighting for what? And they wanna take and lock him up. Let him be free. He don't bother nobody.

ROSE: Well, everybody got their own way of looking at it I guess. Come on and get your lunch. I got a bowl of lima beans and some cornbread in the oven. Come and get something to eat. Ain't no sense you fretting over Gabe.

Rose turns to go into the house.

TROY: Rose . . . got something to tell you.

ROSE: Well, come on . . . wait till I get this food on the table.

TROY: Rose!   65

She stops and turns around.

I don't know how to say this. *(Pause.)* I can't explain it none. It just sort of grows on you till it gets out of hand. It starts out like a little bush . . . and the next thing you know it's a whole forest.

ROSE: Troy . . . what is you talking about?

TROY: I'm talking, woman, let me talk. I'm trying to find a way to tell you . . .
I'm gonna be a daddy. I'm gonna be somebody's daddy.

ROSE: Troy . . . you're not telling me this? You're gonna be . . . what?

TROY: Rose . . . now . . . see . . .

70   ROSE: You telling me you gonna be somebody's daddy? You telling your
wife this?

Gabriel enters from the street. He carries a rose in his hand.

GABRIEL: Hey, Troy! Hey, Rose!

ROSE: I have to wait eighteen years to hear something like this.

GABRIEL: Hey, Rose . . . I got a flower for you. (*He hands it to her.*) That's a
rose. Same rose like you is.

ROSE: Thanks, Gabe.

75   GABRIEL: Troy, you ain't mad at me is you? Them bad mens come and put me
away. You ain't mad at me is you?

TROY: Naw, Gabe, I ain't mad at you.

ROSE: Eighteen years and you wanna come with this.

GABRIEL: (*takes a quarter out of his pocket*) See what I got? Got a brand new
quarter.

TROY: Rose . . . it's just . . .

80   ROSE: Ain't nothing you can say, Troy. Ain't no way of explaining that.

GABRIEL: Fellow that give me this quarter had a whole mess of them. I'm
gonna keep this quarter till it stop shining.

ROSE: Gabe, go on in the house there. I got some watermelon in the
Frigidaire. Go on and get you a piece.

GABRIEL: Say, Rose . . . you know I was chasing hellhounds and them bad
mens come and get me and take me away. Troy helped me. He come down
there and told them they better let me go before he beat them up. Yeah,
he did!

ROSE: You go on and get you a piece of watermelon, Gabe. Them bad mens is
gone now.

85   GABRIEL: Okay, Rose . . . gonna get me some watermelon. The kind with the
stripes on it.

Gabriel exits into the house.

ROSE: Why, Troy? Why? After all these years to come dragging this in to me
now. It don't make no sense at your age. I could have expected this ten or
fifteen years ago, but not now.

TROY: Age ain't got nothing to do with it, Rose.

ROSE: I done tried to be everything a wife should be. Everything a wife could
be. Been married eighteen years and I got to live to see the day you tell me
you been seeing another woman and done fathered a child by her. And you
know I ain't never wanted no half nothing in my family. My whole family
is half. Everybody got different fathers and mothers . . . my two sisters and
my brother. Can't hardly tell who's who. Can't never sit down and talk

about Papa and Mama. It's your papa and your mama and my papa and
my mama . . .

TROY: Rose . . . stop it now.

ROSE: I ain't never wanted that for none of my children. And now you wanna   90
drag your behind in here and tell me something like this.

TROY: You ought to know. It's time for you to know.

ROSE: Well, I don't want to know, goddamn it!

TROY: I can't just make it go away. It's done now. I can't wish the circumstance
of the thing away.

ROSE: And you don't want to either. Maybe you want to wish me and my boy
away. Maybe that's what you want? Well, you can't wish us away. I've got
eighteen years of my life invested in you. You ought to have stayed upstairs
in my bed where you belong.

TROY: Rose . . . now listen to me . . . we can get a handle on this thing. We   95
can talk this out . . . come to an understanding.

ROSE: All of a sudden it's "we." Where was "we" at when you was down
there rolling around with some godforsaken woman? "We" should have
come to an understanding before you started making a damn fool of
yourself. You're a day late and a dollar short when it comes to an
understanding with me.

TROY: It's just . . . She gives me a different idea . . . a different understanding
about myself. I can step out of this house and get away from the pressures
and problems . . . be a different man. I ain't got to wonder how I'm gonna
pay the bills or get the roof fixed. I can just be a part of myself that I ain't
never been.

ROSE: What I want to know . . . is do you plan to continue seeing her. That's
all you can say to me.

TROY: I can sit up in her house and laugh. Do you understand what I'm saying.
I can laugh out loud . . . and it feels good. It reaches all the way down to
the bottom of my shoes. (*Pause.*) Rose, I can't give that up.

ROSE: Maybe you ought to go on and stay down there with her . . . if she's a   100
better woman than me.

TROY: It ain't about nobody being a better woman or nothing. Rose, you ain't
the blame. A man couldn't ask for no woman to be a better wife than
you've been. I'm responsible for it. I done locked myself into a pattern
trying to take care of you all that I forgot about myself.

ROSE: What the hell was I there for? That was my job, not somebody else's.

TROY: Rose, I done tried all my life to live decent . . . to live a clean . . .
hard . . . useful life. I tried to be a good husband to you. In every way I knew
how. Maybe I come into the world backwards, I don't know. But . . . you
born with two strikes on you before you come to the plate. You got to guard
it closely . . . always looking for the curve ball on the inside corner. You
can't afford to let none get past you. You can't afford a call strike. If you going down . . . you going down swinging. Everything lined up against you.
What you gonna do. I fooled them, Rose. I bunted. When I found you and
Cory and a halfway decent job . . . I was safe. Couldn't nothing touch me.

I wasn't gonna strike out no more. I wasn't going back to the penitentiary. I wasn't gonna lay in the streets with a bottle of wine. I was safe. I had me a family. A job. I wasn't gonna get that last strike. I was on first looking for one of them boys to knock me in. To get me home.

ROSE: You should have stayed in my bed, Troy.

105 TROY: Then when I saw that gal . . . she firmed up my backbone. And I got to thinking that if I tried . . . I just might be able to steal second. Do you understand after eighteen years I wanted to steal second.

ROSE: You should have held me tight. You should have grabbed me and held on.

TROY: I stood on first base for eighteen years and I thought . . . well, goddamn it . . . go on for it!

ROSE: We're not talking about baseball! We're talking about you going off to lay in bed with another woman . . . and then bring it home to me. That's what we're talking about. We ain't talking about no baseball.

TROY: Rose, you're not listening to me. I'm trying the best I can to explain it to you. It's not easy for me to admit that I been standing in the same place for eighteen years.

110 ROSE: I been standing with you! I been right here with you, Troy. I got a life too. I gave eighteen years of my life to stand in the same spot with you. Don't you think I ever wanted other things? Don't you think I had dreams and hopes? What about my life? What about me. Don't you think it ever crossed my mind to want to know other men? That I wanted to lay up somewhere and forget about my responsibilities? That I wanted someone to make me laugh so I could feel good? You not the only one who's got wants and needs. But I held on to you, Troy. I took all my feelings, my wants and needs, my dreams . . . and I buried them inside you. I planted a seed and watched and prayed over it. I planted myself inside you and waited to bloom. And it didn't take me no eighteen years to find out the soil was hard and rocky and it wasn't never gonna bloom.

But I held on to you, Troy. I held you tighter. You was my husband. I owed you everything I had. Every part of me I could find to give you. And upstairs in that room . . . with the darkness falling in on me . . . I gave everything I had to try and erase the doubt that you wasn't the finest man in the world. And wherever you was going . . . I wanted to be there with you. 'Cause you was my husband. 'Cause that's the only way I was gonna survive as your wife. You always talking about what you give . . . and what you don't have to give. But you take too. You take . . . and don't even know nobody's giving!

Rose turns to exit into the house; Troy grabs her arm.

TROY: You say I take and don't give!

ROSE: Troy! You're hurting me!

TROY: You say I take and don't give!

ROSE: Troy . . . you're hurting my arm! Let go!

115 TROY: I done give you everything I got. Don't you tell that lie on me.

ROSE: Troy!

TROY: Don't you tell that lie on me!

Cory enters from the house.

CORY: Mama!

ROSE: Troy. You're hurting me.

TROY: Don't you tell me about no taking and giving.   120

Cory comes up behind Troy and grabs him. Troy, surprised, is thrown off balance just as Cory throws a glancing blow that catches him on the chest and knocks him down. Troy is stunned, as is Cory.

ROSE: Troy. Troy. No!

Troy gets to his feet and starts at Cory.

    Troy . . . no. Please! Troy!

Rose pulls on Troy to hold him back. Troy stops himself.

TROY: *(to Cory)* All right. That's strike two. You stay away from around me, boy. Don't you strike out. You living with a full count. Don't you strike out.

Troy exits out the yard as the lights go down.

SCENE 2

It is six months later, early afternoon. Troy enters from the house and starts to exit the yard. Rose enters from the house.

ROSE: Troy, I want to talk to you.

TROY: All of a sudden, after all this time, you want to talk to me, huh? You ain't wanted to talk to me for months. You ain't wanted to talk to me last night. You ain't wanted no part of me then. What you wanna talk to me about now?

ROSE: Tomorrow's Friday.   5

TROY: I know what day tomorrow is. You think I don't know tomorrow's Friday? My whole life I ain't done nothing but look to see Friday coming and you got to tell me it's Friday.

ROSE: I want to know if you're coming home.

TROY: I always come home, Rose. You know that. There ain't never been a night I ain't come home.

ROSE: That ain't what I mean . . . and you know it. I want to know if you're coming straight home after work.

TROY: I figure I'd cash my check . . . hang out at Taylors' with the boys . . .   10
maybe play a game of checkers . . .

ROSE: Troy, I can't live like this. I won't live like this. You livin' on borrowed time with me. It's been going on six months now you ain't been coming home.

TROY: I be here every Friday. Every night of the year. That's 365 days.

ROSE: I want you to come home tomorrow after work.

TROY: Rose . . . I don't mess up my pay. You know that now. I take my pay and
I give it to you. I don't have no money but what you give me back. I just
want to have a little time to myself . . . a little time to enjoy life.

15 ROSE: What about me? When's my time to enjoy life?

TROY: I don't know what to tell you, Rose. I'm doing the best I can.

ROSE: You ain't been home from work but time enough to change your clothes
and run out . . . and you wanna call that the best you can do?

TROY: I'm going over to the hospital to see Alberta. She went into the hospital
this afternoon. Look like she might have the baby early. I won't be gone
long.

ROSE: Well, you ought to know. They went over to Miss Pearl's and got Gabe
today. She said you told them to go ahead and lock him up.

20 TROY: I ain't said no such thing. Whoever told you that is telling a lie. Pearl
ain't doing nothing but telling a big fat lie.

ROSE: She ain't had to tell me. I read it on the papers.

TROY: I ain't told them nothing of the kind.

ROSE: I saw it right there on the papers.

TROY: What it say, huh?

25 ROSE: It said you told them to take him.

TROY: Then they screwed that up, just the way they screw up everything. I
ain't worried about what they got on the paper.

ROSE: Say the government send part of his check to the hospital and the other
part to you.

TROY: I ain't got nothing to do with that if that's the way it works. I ain't made
up the rules about how it work.

ROSE: You did Gabe just like you did Cory. You wouldn't sign the paper for
Cory . . . but you signed for Gabe. You signed that paper.

The telephone is heard ringing inside the house.

30 TROY: I told you I ain't signed nothing, woman! The only thing I signed was
the release form. Hell, I can't read. I don't know what they had on that
paper! I ain't signed nothing about sending Gabe away.

ROSE: I said send him to the hospital . . . you said let him be free . . . now
you done went down there and signed him to the hospital for half his
money. You went back on yourself, Troy. You gonna have to answer
for that.

TROY: See now . . . you been over there talking to Miss Pearl. She done got
mad cause she ain't getting Gabe's rent money. That's all it is. She's liable to
say anything.

ROSE: Troy, I seen where you signed the paper.

TROY: You ain't seen nothing I signed. What she doing got papers on my
brother anyway? Miss Pearl telling a big fat lie. And I'm gonna tell her
about it too! You ain't seen nothing I signed. Say . . . you ain't seen nothing
I signed.

Rose exits into the house to answer the telephone. Presently she returns.

ROSE: Troy . . . that was the hospital. Alberta had the baby. 35

TROY: What she have? What is it?

ROSE: It's a girl.

TROY: I better get on down to the hospital to see her.

ROSE: Troy . . .

TROY: Rose . . . I got to go see her now. That's only right . . . what's the 40
matter . . . the baby's all right, ain't it?

ROSE: Alberta died having the baby.

TROY: Died . . . you say she's dead? Alberta's dead?

ROSE: They said they done all they could. They couldn't do nothing for her.

TROY: The baby? How's the baby?

ROSE: They say it's healthy. I wonder who's gonna bury her. 45

TROY: She had family, Rose. She wasn't living in the world by herself.

ROSE: I know she wasn't living in the world by herself.

TROY: Next thing you gonna want to know if she had any insurance.

ROSE: Troy, you ain't got to talk like that.

TROY: That's the first thing that jumped out your mouth. "Who's gonna bury 50
her?" Like I'm fixing to take on that task for myself.

ROSE: I am your wife. Don't push me away.

TROY: I ain't pushing nobody away. Just give me some space. That's all. Just
give me some room to breathe.

Rose exits into the house. Troy walks about the yard.

TROY: (*with a quiet rage that threatens to consume him*) All right . . . Mr. Death.
See now . . . I'm gonna tell you what I'm gonna do. I'm gonna take and
build me a fence around this yard. See? I'm gonna build me a fence around
what belongs to me. And then I want you to stay on the other side. See?
You stay over there until you're ready for me. Then you come on. Bring your
army. Bring your sickle. Bring your wrestling clothes. I ain't gonna fall down
on my vigilance this time. You ain't gonna sneak up on me no more. When
you ready for me . . . when the top of your list say Troy Maxson . . . that's
when you come around here. You come up and knock on the front door.
Ain't nobody else got nothing to do with this. This is between you and me.
Man to man. You stay on the other side of the fence until you ready for me.
Then you come up and knock on the front door. Anytime you want. I'll be
ready for you.

The lights go down to black.

SCENE 3

*The lights come up on the porch. It is late evening three days later. Rose sits listening to
the ball game waiting for Troy. The final out of the game is made and Rose switches off
the radio. Troy enters the yard carrying an infant wrapped in blankets. He stands back
from the house and calls.*

*Rose enters and stands on the porch. There is a long, awkward silence, the weight of
which grows heavier with each passing second.*

TROY: Rose . . . I'm standing here with my daughter in my arms. She ain't
   but a wee bittie little old thing. She don't know nothing about grownups'
   business. She innocent . . . and she ain't got no mama.

5   ROSE: What you telling me for, Troy?

She turns and exits into the house.

TROY: Well . . . I guess we'll just sit out here on the porch.

*He sits down on the porch. There is an awkward indelicateness about the way he handles
the baby. His largeness engulfs and seems to swallow it. He speaks loud enough for Rose
to hear.*

A man's got to do what's right for him. I ain't sorry for nothing I done. It
felt right in my heart. (*To the baby.*) What you smiling at? Your daddy's a
big man. Got these great big old hands. But sometimes he's scared. And
right now your daddy's scared 'cause we sitting out here and ain't got no
home. Oh, I been homeless before. I ain't had no little baby with me. But I
been homeless. You just be out on the road by your lonesome and you see
one of them trains coming and you just kinda go like this . . .

He sings a lullaby.

> Please, Mr. Engineer let a man ride the line
> Please, Mr. Engineer let a man ride the line
> I ain't got no ticket please let me ride the blinds

Rose enters from the house. Troy, hearing her steps behind him, stands and faces her.

She's my daughter, Rose. My own flesh and blood. I can't deny her no more
than I can deny them boys. (*Pause.*) You and them boys is my family. You
and them and this child is all I got in the world. So I guess what I'm saying
is . . . I'd appreciate it if you'd help me take care of her.

ROSE: Okay, Troy . . . you're right. I'll take care of your baby for you . . .
   'cause . . . like you say . . . she's innocent . . . and you can't visit the sins
   of the father upon the child. A motherless child has got a hard time. (*She
   takes the baby from him.*) From right now . . . this child got a mother. But
   you a womanless man.

Rose turns and exits into the house with the baby. Lights go down to black.

SCENE 4

It is two months later. Lyons enters from the street. He knocks on the door and calls.

LYONS: Hey, Rose! (*Pause.*) Rose!

ROSE: (*from inside the house*) Stop that yelling. You gonna wake up Raynell. I
   just got her to sleep.

5   LYONS: I just stopped by to pay Papa this twenty dollars I owe him. Where's
   Papa at?

ROSE: He should be here in a minute. I'm getting ready to go down to the
   church. Sit down and wait on him.

LYONS: I got to go pick up Bonnie over her mother's house.

ROSE: Well, sit it down there on the table. He'll get it.

LYONS: *(enters the house and sets the money on the table)* Tell Papa I said thanks. I'll see you again.

ROSE: All right, Lyons. We'll see you.   10

Lyons starts to exit as Cory enters.

CORY: Hey, Lyons.

LYONS: What's happening, Cory? Say man, I'm sorry I missed your graduation. You know I had a gig and couldn't get away. Otherwise, I would have been there, man. So what you doing?

CORY: I'm trying to find a job.

LYONS: Yeah I know how that go, man. It's rough out there. Jobs are scarce.

CORY: Yeah, I know.   15

LYONS: Look here, I got to run. Talk to Papa . . . he know some people. He'll be able to help get you a job. Talk to him . . . see what he say.

CORY: Yeah . . . all right, Lyons.

LYONS: You take care. I'll talk to you soon. We'll find some time to talk.

Lyons exits the yard. Cory wanders over to the tree, picks up the bat, and assumes a batting stance. He studies an imaginary pitcher and swings. Dissatisfied with the result, he tries again. Troy enters. They eye each other for a beat. Cory puts the bat down and exits the yard. Troy starts into the house as Rose exits with Raynell. She is carrying a cake.

TROY: I'm coming in and everybody's going out.

ROSE: I'm taking this cake down to the church for the bake sale. Lyons was by   20
to see you. He stopped by to pay you your twenty dollars. It's laying in there on the table.

TROY: *(going into his pocket)* Well . . . here go this money.

ROSE: Put it in there on the table, Troy. I'll get it.

TROY: What time you coming back?

ROSE: Ain't no use in you studying me. It don't matter what time I come back.

TROY: I just asked you a question, woman. What's the matter . . . can't I ask   25
you a question?

ROSE: Troy, I don't want to go into it. Your dinner's in there on the stove. All you got to do is heat it up. And don't you be eating the rest of them cakes in there. I'm coming back for them. We having a bake sale at the church tomorrow.

Rose exits the yard. Troy sits down on the steps, takes a pint bottle from his pocket, opens it, and drinks. He begins to sing.

TROY:

Hear it ring! Hear it ring!
Had an old dog his name was Blue
You know Blue was mighty true
You know Blue was a good old dog
Blue treed a possum in a hollow log
You know from that he was a good old dog

Bono enters the yard.

BONO: Hey, Troy.

TROY: Hey, what's happening, Bono?

30 **BONO:** I just thought I'd stop by to see you.

TROY: What you stop by and see me for? You ain't stopped by in a month of Sundays. Hell, I must owe you money or something.

BONO: Since you got your promotion I can't keep up with you. Used to see you every day. Now I don't even know what route you working.

TROY: They keep switching me around. Got me out in Greentree now . . . hauling white folks' garbage.

BONO: Greentree, huh? You lucky, at least you ain't got to be lifting them barrels. Damn if they ain't getting heavier. I'm gonna put in my two years and call it quits.

35 **TROY:** I'm thinking about retiring myself.

BONO: You got it easy. You can *drive* for another five years.

TROY: It ain't the same, Bono. It ain't like working the back of the truck. Ain't got nobody to talk to . . . feel like you working by yourself. Naw, I'm thinking about retiring. How's Lucille?

BONO: She all right. Her arthritis get to acting up on her sometime. Saw Rose on my way in. She going down to the church, huh?

TROY: Yeah, she took up going down there. All them preachers looking for somebody to fatten their pockets. *(Pause.)* Got some gin here.

40 **BONO:** Naw, thanks. I just stopped by to say hello.

TROY: Hell, nigger . . . you can take a drink. I ain't never known you to say no to a drink. You ain't got to work tomorrow.

BONO: I just stopped by. I'm fixing to go over to Skinner's. We got us a domino game going over his house every Friday.

TROY: Nigger, you can't play no dominoes. I used to whup you four games out of five.

BONO: Well, that learned me. I'm getting better.

45 **TROY:** Yeah? Well, that's all right.

BONO: Look here . . . I got to be getting on. Stop by sometime, huh?

TROY: Yeah, I'll do that, Bono. Lucille told Rose you bought her a new refrigerator.

BONO: Yeah, Rose told Lucille you had finally built your fence . . . so I figured we'd call it even.

TROY: I knew you would.

50 **BONO:** Yeah . . . okay. I'll be talking to you.

TROY: Yeah, take care, Bono. Good to see you. I'm gonna stop over.

BONO: Yeah. Okay, Troy.

Bono exits. Troy drinks from the bottle.

TROY:

> Old Blue died and I dig his grave
> Let him down with a golden chain

Every night when I hear old Blue bark
I know Blue treed a possum in Noah's Ark.
Hear it ring! Hear it ring!

Cory enters the yard. They eye each other for a beat. Troy is sitting in the middle of the steps. Cory walks over.

CORY: I got to get by.

TROY: Say what? What's you say?   55

CORY: You in my way. I got to get by.

TROY: You got to get by where? This is my house. Bought and paid for. In full. Took me fifteen years. And if you wanna go in my house and I'm sitting on the steps . . . you say excuse me. Like your mama taught you.

CORY: Come on, Pop . . . I got to get by.

Cory starts to maneuver his way past Troy. Troy grabs his leg and shoves him back.

TROY: You just gonna walk over top of me?

CORY: I live here too!   60

TROY: (*advancing toward him*) You just gonna walk over top of me in my own house?

CORY: I ain't scared of you.

TROY: I ain't asked if you was scared of me. I asked you if you was fixing to walk over top of me in my own house? That's the question. You ain't gonna say excuse me? You just gonna walk over top of me?

CORY: If you wanna put it like that.

TROY: How else am I gonna put it?   65

CORY: I was walking by you to go into the house 'cause you sitting on the steps drunk, singing to yourself. You can put it like that.

TROY: Without saying excuse me???

Cory doesn't respond.

I asked you a question. Without saying excuse me???

CORY: I ain't got to say excuse me to you. You don't count around here no more.

TROY: Oh, I see . . . I don't count around here no more. You ain't got to say excuse me to your daddy. All of a sudden you done got so grown that your daddy don't count around here no more . . . Around here in his own house and yard that he done paid for with the sweat of his brow. You done got so grown to where you gonna take over. You gonna take over my house. Is that right? You gonna wear my pants. You gonna go in there and stretch out on my bed. You ain't got to say excuse me 'cause I don't count around here no more. Is that right?

CORY: That's right. You always talking this dumb stuff. Now, why don't you just   70
get out my way?

TROY: I guess you got someplace to sleep and something to put in your belly. You got that, huh? You got that? That's what you need. You got that, huh?

CORY: You don't know what I got. You ain't got to worry about what I got.

TROY: You right! You one hundred percent right! I done spent the last seventeen years worrying about what you got. Now it's your turn, see? I'll tell you
what to do. You grown . . . we done established that. You a man. Now, let's
see you act like one. Turn your behind around and walk out this yard. And
when you get out there in the alley . . . you can forget about this house.
See? 'Cause this is my house. You go on and be a man and get your own
house. You can forget about this. 'Cause this is mine. You go on and get
yours 'cause I'm through with doing for you.

CORY: You talking about what you did for me . . . what'd you ever give me?

75 TROY: Them feet and bones! That pumping heart, nigger! I give you more
than anybody else is ever gonna give you.

CORY: You ain't never gave me nothing! You ain't never done nothing but hold
me back. Afraid I was gonna be better than you. All you ever did was try
and make me scared of you. I used to tremble every time you called my
name. Every time I heard your footsteps in the house. Wondering all the
time . . . what's Papa gonna say if I do this? . . . What's he gonna say if I do
that? . . . What's Papa gonna say if I turn on the radio? And Mama, too . . .
she tries . . . but she's scared of you.

TROY: You leave your mama out of this. She ain't got nothing to do with this.

CORY: I don't know how she stand you . . . after what you did to her.

TROY: I told you to leave your mama out of this!

He advances toward Cory.

80 CORY: What you gonna do . . . give me a whupping? You can't whup me no
more. You're too old. You just an old man.

TROY: *(shoves him on his shoulder)* Nigger! That's what you are. You just
another nigger on the street to me!

CORY: You crazy! You know that?

TROY: Go on now! You got the devil in you. Get on away from me!

CORY: You just a crazy old man . . . talking about I got the devil in me.

85 TROY: Yeah, I'm crazy! If you don't get on the other side of that yard . . . I'm
gonna show you how crazy I am! Go on . . . get the hell out of my yard.

CORY: It ain't your yard. You took Uncle Gabe's money he got from the army to
buy this house and then you put him out.

TROY: *(advances on Cory)* Get your black ass out of my yard!

Troy's advance backs Cory up against the tree. Cory grabs up the bat.

CORY: I ain't going nowhere! Come on . . . put me out! I ain't scared of you.

TROY: That's my bat!

90 CORY: Come on!

TROY: Put my bat down!

CORY: Come on, put me out.

Cory swings at Troy, who backs across the yard.

What's the matter? You so bad . . . put me out!

Troy advances toward Cory.

CORY: *(backing up)* Come on! Come on!

TROY: You're gonna have to use it! You wanna draw that bat back on me . . .
you're gonna have to use it.

CORY: Come on! . . . Come on! 95

*Cory swings the bat at Troy a second time. He misses. Troy continues to advance
toward him.*

TROY: You're gonna have to kill me! You wanna draw that bat back on me.
You're gonna have to kill me.

*Cory, backed up against the tree, can go no farther. Troy taunts him. He sticks out his
head and offers him a target.*

    Come on! Come on!

Cory is unable to swing the bat. Troy grabs it.

TROY: Then I'll show you.

*Cory and Troy struggle over the bat. The struggle is fierce and fully engaged. Troy ulti-
mately is the stronger and takes the bat away from Cory and stands over him ready to
swing. He stops himself.*

    Go on and get away from around my house.

*Cory, stung by his defeat, picks himself up, walks slowly out of the yard and up the
alley.*

CORY: Tell Mama I'll be back for my things.

TROY: They'll be on the other side of that fence.

Cory exits.

TROY: I can't taste nothing. Helluljah! I can't taste nothing no more. *(Troy as-* 100
*sumes a batting posture and begins to taunt Death, the fastball on the outside cor-
ner.)* Come on! It's between you and me now! Come on! Anytime you
want! Come on! I be ready for you . . . but I ain't gonna be easy.

The lights go down on the scene.

SCENE 5

*The time is 1965. The lights come up in the yard. It is the morning of Troy's funeral. A
funeral plaque with a light hangs beside the door. There is a small garden plot off to the
side. There is noise and activity in the house as Rose, Gabriel, and Bono have gathered.
The door opens and Raynell, seven years old, enters dressed in a flannel nightgown. She
crosses to the garden and pokes around with a stick. Rose calls from the house.*

ROSE: Raynell!

RAYNELL: Mam?

ROSE: What you doing out there?

RAYNELL: Nothing.

Rose comes to the door.

5   ROSE: Girl, get in here and get dressed. What you doing?

RAYNELL: Seeing if my garden growed.

ROSE: I told you it ain't gonna grow overnight. You got to wait.

RAYNELL: It don't look like it never gonna grow. Dag!

ROSE: I told you a watched pot never boils. Get in here and get dressed.

10   RAYNELL: This ain't even no pot, Mama.

ROSE: You just have to give it a chance. It'll grow. Now you come on and do
what I told you. We got to be getting ready. This ain't no morning to be
playing around. You hear me?

RAYNELL: Yes, mam.

Rose exits into the house. Raynell continues to poke at her garden with a stick. Cory en-
ters. He is dressed in a Marine corporal's uniform, and carries a duffel bag. His posture
is that of a military man, and his speech has a clipped sternness.

CORY: *(to Raynell)* Hi. *(Pause.)* I bet your name is Raynell.

RAYNELL: Uh huh.

15   CORY: Is your mama home?

Raynell runs up on the porch and calls through the screen door.

RAYNELL: Mama . . . there's some man out here. Mama?

Rose comes to the door.

ROSE: Cory? Lord have mercy! Look here, you all!

Rose and Cory embrace in a tearful reunion as Bono and Lyons enter from the house
dressed in funeral clothes.

BONO: Aw, looka here . . .

ROSE: Done got all grown up!

20   CORY: Don't cry, Mama. What you crying about?

ROSE: I'm just so glad you made it.

CORY: Hey Lyons. How you doing, Mr. Bono.

Lyons goes to embrace Cory.

LYONS: Look at you, man. Look at you. Don't he look good, Rose. Got them
Corporal stripes.

ROSE: What took you so long?

25   CORY: You know how the Marines are, Mama. They got to get all their
paperwork straight before they let you do anything.

ROSE: Well, I'm sure glad you made it. They let Lyons come. Your Uncle
Gabe's still in the hospital. They don't know if they gonna let him out or
not. I just talked to them a little while ago.

LYONS: A Corporal in the United States Marines.

BONO: Your daddy knew you had it in you. He used to tell me all the time.

LYONS: Don't he look good, Mr. Bono?

BONO: Yeah, he remind me of Troy when I first met him. (*Pause.*) Say, Rose,   30
   Lucille's down at the church with the choir. I'm gonna go down and get the
   pallbearers lined up. I'll be back to get you all.

ROSE: Thanks, Jim.

CORY: See you, Mr. Bono.

LYONS: (*with his arm around Raynell*) Cory . . . look at Raynell. Ain't she
   precious? She gonna break a whole lot of hearts.

ROSE: Raynell, come and say hello to your brother. This is your brother, Cory.
   You remember Cory.

RAYNELL: No, Mam.   35

CORY: She don't remember me, Mama.

ROSE: Well, we talk about you. She heard us talk about you. (*To Raynell.*) This
   is your brother, Cory. Come on and say hello.

RAYNELL: Hi.

CORY: Hi. So you're Raynell. Mama told me a lot about you.

ROSE: You all come on into the house and let me fix you some breakfast. Keep   40
   up your strength.

CORY: I ain't hungry, Mama.

LYONS: You can fix me something, Rose. I'll be in there in a minute.

ROSE: Cory, you sure you don't want nothing? I know they ain't feeding you right.

CORY: No, Mama . . . thanks. I don't feel like eating. I'll get something later.

ROSE: Raynell . . . get on upstairs and get that dress on like I told you.   45

Rose and Raynell exit into the house.

LYONS: So . . . I hear you thinking about getting married.

CORY: Yeah, I done found the right one, Lyons. It's about time.

LYONS: Me and Bonnie been split up about four years now. About the time
   Papa retired. I guess she just got tired of all them changes I was putting
   her through. (*Pause.*) I always knew you was gonna make something out
   yourself. Your head was always in the right direction. So . . . you gonna stay
   in . . . make it a career . . . put in your twenty years?

CORY: I don't know. I got six already, I think that's enough.

LYONS: Stick with Uncle Sam and retire early. Ain't nothing out here. I guess   50
   Rose told you what happened with me. They got me down the workhouse.
   I thought I was being slick cashing other people's checks.

CORY: How much time you doing?

LYONS: They give me three years. I got that beat now. I ain't got but nine more
   months. It ain't so bad. You learn to deal with it like anything else. You got
   to take the crookeds with the straights. That's what Papa used to say. He
   used to say that when he struck out. I seen him strike out three times in a
   row . . . and the next time up he hit the ball over the grandstand. Right out
   there in Homestead Field. He wasn't satisfied hitting in the seats . . . he
   want to hit it over everything! After the game he had two hundred people
   standing around waiting to shake his hand. You got to take the crookeds
   with the straights. Yeah, Papa was something else.

CORY: You still playing?

LYONS: Cory . . . you know I'm gonna do that. There's some fellows down there we got us a band . . . we gonna try and stay together when we get out . . . but yeah, I'm still playing. It still helps me to get out of bed in the morning. As long as it do that I'm gonna be right there playing and trying to make some sense out of it.

55   ROSE: *(calling)* Lyons, I got these eggs in the pan.

LYONS: Let me go on and get these eggs, man. Get ready to go bury Papa. *(Pause.)* How you doing? You doing all right?

Cory nods. Lyons touches him on the shoulder and they share a moment of silent grief. Lyons exits into the house. Cory wanders about the yard. Raynell enters.

RAYNELL: Hi.

CORY: Hi.

RAYNELL: Did you used to sleep in my room?

60   CORY: Yeah . . . that used to be my room.

RAYNELL: That's what Papa call it. "Cory's room." It got your football in the closet.

Rose comes to the door.

ROSE: Raynell, get in there and get them good shoes on.

RAYNELL: Mama, can't I wear these? Them other ones hurt my feet.

ROSE: Well, they just gonna have to hurt your feet for a while. You ain't said they hurt your feet when you went down to the store and got them.

65   RAYNELL: They didn't hurt then. My feet done got bigger.

ROSE: Don't you give me no backtalk now. You get in there and get them shoes on.

Raynell exits into the house.

Ain't too much changed. He still got that piece of rag tied to that tree. He was out here swinging that bat. I was just ready to go back in the house. He swung that bat and then he just fell over. Seem like he swung it and stood there with this grin on his face . . . and then he just fell over. They carried him on down to the hospital, but I knew there wasn't no need . . . why don't you come on in the house?

CORY: Mama . . . I got something to tell you. I don't know how to tell you this . . . but I've got to tell you . . . I'm not going to Papa's funeral.

ROSE: Boy, hush your mouth. That's your daddy you talking about. I don't want hear that kind of talk this morning. I done raised you to come to this? You standing there all healthy and grown talking about you ain't going to your daddy's funeral?

CORY: Mama . . . listen . . .

70   ROSE: I don't want to hear it, Cory. You just get that thought out of your head.

CORY: I can't drag Papa with me everywhere I go. I've got to say no to him. One time in my life I've got to say no.

ROSE: Don't nobody have to listen to nothing like that. I know you and your daddy ain't seen eye to eye, but I ain't got to listen to that kind of talk this morning. Whatever was between you and your daddy . . . the time has come to put it aside. Just take it and set it over there on the shelf and forget about it. Disrespecting your daddy ain't gonna make you a man, Cory. You got to find a way to come to that on your own. Not going to your daddy's funeral ain't gonna make you a man.

CORY: The whole time I was growing up . . . living in his house . . . Papa was like a shadow that followed you everywhere. It weighed on you and sunk into your flesh. It would wrap around you and lay there until you couldn't tell which one was you anymore. That shadow digging in your flesh. Trying to crawl in. Trying to live through you. Everywhere I looked, Troy Maxson was staring back at me . . . hiding under the bed . . . in the closet. I'm just saying I've got to find a way to get rid of that shadow, Mama.

ROSE: You just like him. You got him in you good.

CORY: Don't tell me that, Mama.

ROSE: You Troy Maxson all over again.

CORY: I don't want to be Troy Maxson. I want to be me.

ROSE: You can't be nobody but who you are, Cory. That shadow wasn't nothing but you growing into yourself. You either got to grow into it or cut it down to fit you. But that's all you got to make life with. That's all you got to measure yourself against that world out there. Your daddy wanted you to be everything he wasn't . . . and at the same time he tried to make you into everything he was. I don't know if he was right or wrong . . . but I do know he meant to do more good than he meant to do harm. He wasn't always right. Sometimes when he touched he bruised. And sometimes when he took me in his arms he cut.

When I first met your daddy I thought . . . Here is a man I can lay down with and make a baby. That's the first thing I thought when I seen him. I was thirty years old and had done seen my share of men. But when he walked up to me and said, "I can dance a waltz that'll make you dizzy." I thought, Rose Lee, here is a man that you can open yourself up to and be filled to bursting. Here is a man that can fill all them empty spaces you been tipping around the edges of. One of them empty spaces was being somebody's mother.

I married your daddy and settled down to cooking his supper and keeping clean sheets on the bed. When your daddy walked through the house he was so big he filled it up. That was my first mistake. Not to make him leave some room for me. For my part in the matter. But at that time I wanted that. I wanted a house that I could sing in. And that's what your daddy gave me. I didn't know to keep up his strength I had to give up little pieces of mine. I did that. I took on his life as mine and mixed up the pieces so that you couldn't hardly tell which was which anymore. It was my choice. It was my life and I didn't have to live it like that. But that's what life offered me in the way of being a woman and I took it. I grabbed hold of it with both hands.

By the time Raynell came into the house, me and your daddy had done lost touch with one another. I didn't want to make my blessing off of nobody's misfortune . . . but I took on to Raynell like she was all them babies I had wanted and never had.

The phone rings.

Like I'd been blessed to relive a part of my life. And if the Lord see fit to keep up my strength . . . I'm gonna do her just like your daddy did you . . . I'm gonna give her the best of what's in me.

RAYNELL: *(entering, still with her old shoes)* Mama . . . Reverend Tollivier on the phone.

Rose exits into the house.

80 RAYNELL: Hi.

CORY: Hi.

RAYNELL: You in the Army or the Marines?

CORY: Marines.

RAYNELL: Papa said it was the Army. Did you know Blue?

85 CORY: Blue? Who's Blue?

RAYNELL: Papa's dog what he sing about all the time.

CORY: *(singing)*

> Hear it ring! Hear it ring!
> I had a dog his name was Blue
> You know Blue was mighty true
> You know Blue was a good old dog
> Blue treed a possum in a hollow log
> You know from that he was a good old dog.
> Hear it ring! Hear it ring!

Raynell joins in singing.

CORY AND RAYNELL:

> Blue treed a possum out on a limb
> Blue looked at me and I looked at him
> Grabbed that possum and put him in a sack
> Blue stayed there till I came back
> Old Blue's feets was big and round
> Never allowed a possum to touch the ground.
> Old Blue died and I dug his grave
> I dug his grave with a silver spade
> Let him down with a golden chain
> And every night I call his name
> Go on Blue, you good dog you
> Go on Blue, you good dog you

RAYNELL:

> Blue laid down and died like a man
> Blue laid down and died . . .

BOTH: 90

> Blue laid down and died like a man
> Now he's treeing possums in the Promised Land
> I'm gonna tell you this to let you know
> Blue's gone where the good dogs go
> When I hear old Blue bark
> When I hear old Blue bark
> Blue treed a possum in Noah's Ark°
> Blue treed a possum in Noah's Ark.

Rose comes to the screen door.

ROSE: Cory, we gonna be ready to go in a minute.
CORY: *(to Raynell)* You go on in the house and change them shoes like Mama
    told you so we can go to Papa's funeral.
RAYNELL: Okay, I'll be back.

Raynell exits into the house. Cory gets up and crosses over to the tree. Rose stands in the screen door watching him. Gabriel enters from the alley.

GABRIEL: *(calling)* Hey, Rose!
ROSE: Gabe?   95
GABRIEL: I'm here, Rose. Hey Rose, I'm here!

Rose enters from the house.

ROSE: Lord . . . Look here, Lyons!
LYONS: See, I told you, Rose . . . I told you they'd let him come.
CORY: How you doing, Uncle Gabe?
LYONS: How you doing, Uncle Gabe?   100
GABRIEL: Hey, Rose. It's time. It's time to tell St. Peter to open the gates. Troy,
    you ready? You ready, Troy. I'm gonna tell St. Peter to open the gates. You
    get ready now.

Gabriel, with great fanfare, braces himself to blow. The trumpet is without a mouthpiece. He puts the end of it into his mouth and blows with great force, like a man who has been waiting some twenty-odd years for this single moment. No sound comes out of the trumpet. He braces himself and blows again with the same result. A third time he blows. There is a weight of impossible description that falls away and leaves him bare and exposed to a frightful realization. It is a trauma that a sane and normal mind would be unable to withstand. He begins to dance. A slow, strange dance, eerie and life-giving. A dance of atavistic signature and ritual. Lyons attempts to embrace him. Gabriel pushes Lyons away. He begins to howl in what is an attempt at song, or perhaps a song-turning back into itself in an attempt at speech. He finishes his dance and the gates of heaven stand open as wide as God's closet.

    That's the way that go!

°*Noah's Ark:* See Genesis 6.14–20.

Reading and Reacting

1. Obviously, fences are a central metaphor of the play. To what different kinds of fences does the play's title refer?

2. How are the fathers and sons in this play alike? How are they different? Does the play imply that sons must inevitably follow in their fathers' footsteps?

3. What purpose does the section of the stage directions entitled "The Play" (p. 1939) serve? How does it prepare readers for the events to follow?

4. What is the significance of the fact that the play is set in 1957? Given the racial climate of the country at that time, how realistic are Cory's ambitions? How reasonable are his father's criticisms?

5. In what ways has Troy's character been shaped by his contact with the white world?

6. Is Troy a tragic hero? If so, what is his flaw?

7. Which of the play's characters, if any, do you consider to be stereotypes? What comment do you think the play makes about stereotypes?

8. In what ways does the conflict between Troy and Cory reflect conflicts within the African-American community? Does the play suggest any possibilities for compromise?

9. Which characters do you like? Which do you dislike? Why?

10. Do you consider the message of this play to be optimistic or pessimistic? Explain.

11. JOURNAL ENTRY How would the play be different if the characters were white? What would remain the same?

12. CRITICAL PERSPECTIVE Robert Brustein, theater critic and artistic director of Harvard's American Repertory Theater, has criticized Wilson on the ground that "his recurrent theme is the familiar American charge of victimization"; in *Fences,* he argues, "Wilson's larger purpose depends on his conviction that Troy's potential was stunted not [by] 'his own behavior' but by centuries of racist oppression."

Do you agree with Brustein's characterization of Wilson's theme? Or do you think there is another theme that Brustein ignores?

Related Works: "Big Black Good Man" (p. 339), "Ex-Basketball Player" (p. 946), "Yet Do I Marvel" (p. 1048), "The *Chicago Defender* Sends a Man to Little Rock" (p. 1148), *Death of a Salesman* (p. 1581)

WRITING SUGGESTIONS: Theme

1. The protagonists of *Antigone* and *Antigone's Red* are strong-willed women whose high principles tend to alienate the people around them. Write an essay in which you compare the two Antigones. In what ways are these characters similar? In what ways are they different? What parallels do you see in the kind of insights they gain before they die?

2. In an interview, writer Lorrie Moore calls *Fences* "an African-American *Death of a Salesman.*" What do you think she means? Do you agree? Write an essay in which you examine the two plays in light of Moore's comment.

3. Write an essay in which you analyze the baseball images in *Fences*. How do the references to baseball help to develop the play's themes?

4. One of the themes of *Fences* is the dream a family has for its children. Compare the development of this theme in *Fences* and in another play in this book — for example, *The Cuban Swimmer* (p. 1772) or *The Glass Menagerie* (p. 1998).

5. *Antigone* explores the theme of obedience to authority: Antigone is executed for denying Creon's orders and thus defying the authority of the state. Write an essay in which you discuss whether Antigone should have compromised her principles. Be specific, and be sure to use examples from the play to support your points.

6. Like *Trying to Find Chinatown*, *Antigone's Red* also explores elements of the characters' Asian heritage. Compare and contrast the characters' attitudes toward their ethnicity in these two plays — or, compare and contrast the development of this theme in Hwang's play and in a short story, such as "Seventeen Syllables" (p. 538) or "Two Kinds" (p. 791).

CHAPTER 43

TENNESSEE WILLIAMS'S
THE GLASS MENAGERIE:
A CASEBOOK FOR READING,
RESEARCH, AND WRITING

This chapter provides all the materials you will need to begin a research project about Tennessee Williams's *The Glass Menagerie*. It includes the 1945 play; questions to stimulate discussion and writing; a collection of source materials;* a paper that shows how one student, Heather Jenkins, used the materials in this chapter in her research; and suggestions for further research on Williams.

Source Materials

- Williams, Tennessee. "Author's Production Notes." *The Glass Menagerie.* New York: Random, 1945. The preface to the published edition of *The Glass Menagerie.* . . . . (p. 2047)
- O'Connor, Jacqueline. From *Dramatizing Dementia: Madness in the Plays of Tennessee Williams.* Bowling Green, OH: Bowling Green State U Popular P, 1997. Excerpt in which the author discusses Laura's loneliness in *The Glass Menagerie.* . . . . (p. 2049)
- Williams, Tennessee. From *Tennessee Williams: Memoirs.* New York: Doubleday, 1975. A memoir written by the playwright. . . . . (p. 2050)
- Evans, Jean. "Interview 1945." *New York PM* (1945). A magazine interview with Tennessee Williams conducted during the initial New York run of *The Glass Menageri.* . . . . (p. 2053)
- King, Thomas L. From "Irony and Distance in *The Glass Menagerie.*" *Educational Theatre Journal* 25.2 (May 1973): 85–94. Excerpts from an article that discusses the importance of Tom's soliloquies. . . . . (p. 2054)

---

* Note that some of the articles included in this Casebook do not use the parenthetical documentation style recommended by the most recent guidelines set by the Modern Language Association and explained in Chapter 7.

- Tischler, Nancy Marie Patterson. From *Student Companion to Tennessee Williams*. Westport, CT: Greenwood, 2000. Excerpt in which the author discusses the use of symbolism and other stylistic approaches in the work of the playwright. . . . . (p. 2057)
- Stein, Roger B. From "*The Glass Menagerie* Revisited: Catastrophe without Violence." *Western Humanities Review* 18 (Spring 1964): 141–53. Excerpt in which the author discusses religious themes in *The Glass Menagerie*. . . . . (p. 2059)
- Scanlan, Tom. From *Family, Drama, and American Dreams*. New York: Greenwood, 1978. A discussion of the portrayal of family life in *The Glass Menagerie*. . . . . (p. 2061)
- Fisher, James. From "'The Angels of Fructification': Tennessee Williams, Tony Kushner, and Images of Homosexuality on the American Stage." *Mississippi Quarterly* 49.1 (Winter 1995):13–20. Excerpts from an article that discusses homosexuality in the work of Williams and other American playwrights. . . . . (p. 2064)
- Williams Tennessee. "Portrait of a Girl in Glass." *Collected Stories*. New York: New Directions, 1985. A 1943 short story that Williams later developed into *The Glass Menagerie*. . . . . (p. 2068)

Each of these sources offers insights that can help you to understand, enjoy, and write about *The Glass Menagerie*. Some offer historical perspectives; some are biographical; others discuss literary devices or offer interpretations. All were selected to help you to understand this classic American play and appreciate its characters and themes. Other kinds of sources can also enrich your understanding of Williams's accomplishments — for example, other plays by Williams, biographical data about the author, or works of imaginative literature by other writers dealing with similar themes. In addition, a number of Web sites devoted to Williams can offer insights into his work.

In preparation for writing an essay on a topic of your choice about *The Glass Menagerie*, read the play and the accompanying source materials carefully. After doing so, explore — in your journal, in group discussions, or in brainstorming notes — the possibilities suggested by the Reading and Reacting questions on pages 2046–47. Think about the ideas expressed in the critical articles, memoirs, and interviews as well as those in the play itself. Your goal is to decide on a topic you can develop in a four- to six-page essay. Remember to document any words or ideas that you borrow from the play or from other sources, enclosing your borrowed words in quotation marks. (For guidelines on evaluating literary criticism, see page 15; for guidelines on using source materials, see Chapter 6, "Writing a Research Paper," and Chapter 7, "Documenting Sources and Avoiding Plagiarism")

A sample student paper, "Laura's Gentleman Caller," based on some of the source materials in this Casebook, begins on page 2076.

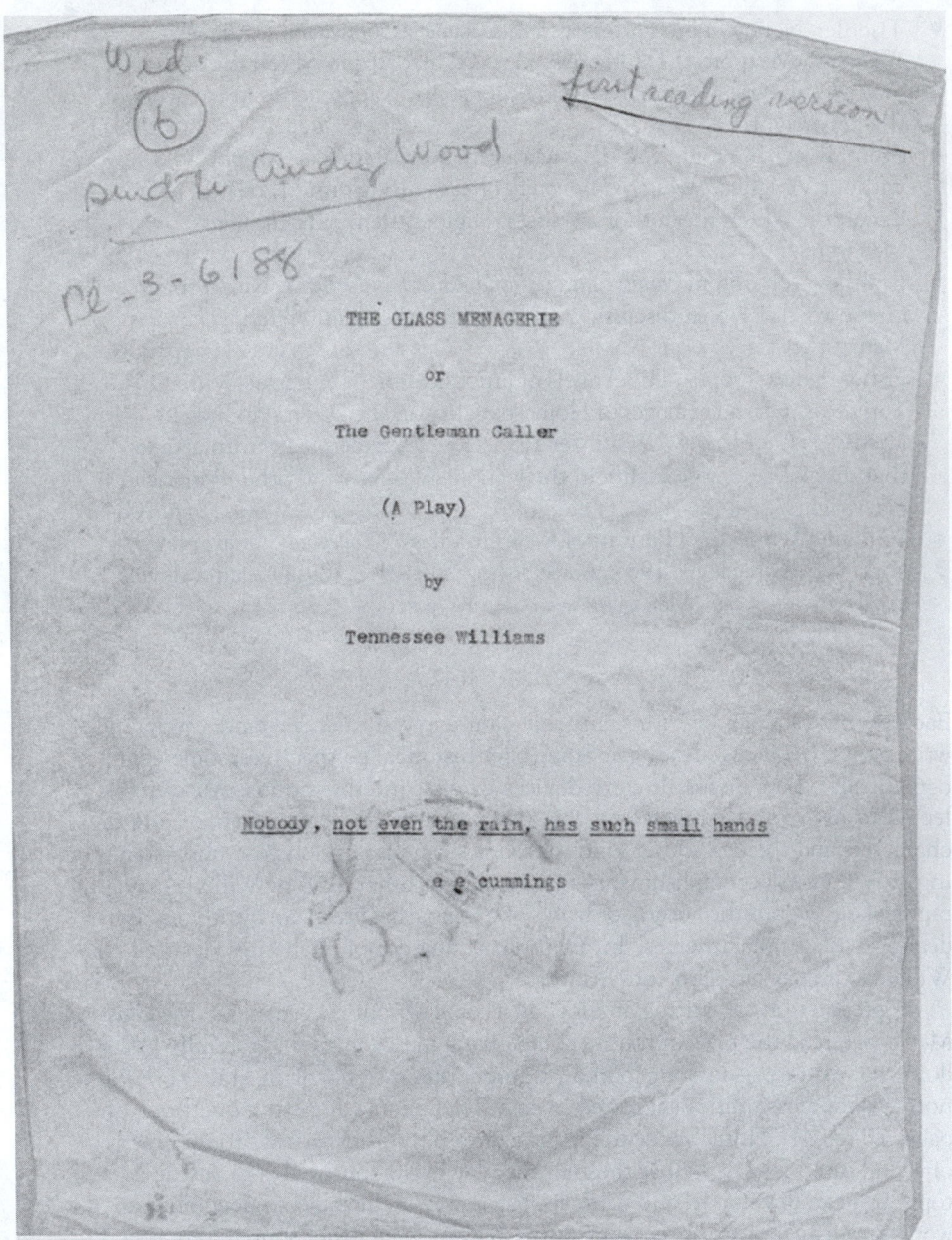

This title page, from a 1944 manuscript, includes as its epigraph the last line from the E. E. Cummings poem "somewhere i have never travelled, gladly beyond."

TENNESSEE WILLIAMS (1911–1983) was born Thomas Lanier Williams in Columbus, Mississippi, on March 26, 1911. His father, who came from a well- to-do and well-connected Tennessee family, was a shoe salesman who was often on the road. His mother was the daughter of a minister, and her genteel ways left her ill-equipped to handle her three rowdy children, who spent more and more time with their maternal grandfather. Williams's grandfather had a stern manner and strong views about right and wrong. His grandson, however, did not always abide by these rules and mocked him playfully whenever he could.

When Williams was eight, his family moved to St. Louis, Missouri, where, only eight years later — at the age of sixteen —Williams made his first mark on the literary world by winning five dollars and placing third in a national essay contest sponsored by *Smart Set* magazine. His essay was entitled "Can a Good Wife Be a Good Sport?" After winning this award, he began to submit his writing widely. He enrolled at the University of Missouri, but he found that college did not give him enough opportunity to write, so he left and worked at his father's shoe company — and as a waiter, an elevator operator, and a theater usher — while he wrote. Hoping to learn playwriting, he eventually went back to college and graduated from the University of Iowa in 1938. A year later, he adopted his college nickname and began to publish as Tennessee Williams.

Williams's earliest staged play, *Cairo, Shanghai, Bombay,* was produced in Memphis in 1937, followed closely by *Candles to the Sun* and *The Fugitive Kind.* Williams's career rocketed, and he went on to write over fifty plays, ten works of fiction, several books of poetry, and other collections of writing, including his letters and memoirs. His most successful plays include *The Glass Menagerie* (1945), A *Streetcar Named Desire* (1947), *Cat on a Hot Tin Roof* (1955), *Night of the Iguana* (1961), and *Sweet Bird of Youth* (1959). A recently rediscovered early play, *Not about Nightingales,* was staged in New York City in 1999.

The Glass Menagerie, Williams's first major success, won the New York Drama Critics Circle Award, freeing Williams to write plays full-time. *The Glass Menagerie* was written partly in Provincetown, Massachusetts, the site of Susan Glaspell's theater company (Glaspell is the author of the play *Trifles,* in Chapter 39), and partly in Hollywood, where Williams was working as a screenwriter. Williams saw the play as somewhat autobiographical: he said his sister Rose had a collection of glass animals in her room in St. Louis, and he gave his own real first name to Tom, Laura's brother in the play. In the first movie version of the play, the story was altered to include a second, more promising Gentleman Caller at its conclusion, giving it a happy ending. To the end of his life, Williams strongly disliked this change.

Tennessee Williams found acclaim wherever he took his plays, from the age of thirty-four and the remarkable success of *The Glass Menagerie* until the end of his life. He received four New York Drama Critics Circle Awards, won a Pulitzer Prize for *Streetcar* in 1948, and saw both *Streetcar* and *The Glass Menagerie* made into successful Hollywood films. *Cat on a Hot Tin Roof* (for which he won his second Pulitzer), *Orpheus Descending*, and *Night of the Iguana* were also filmed.

Like *The Glass Menagerie,* Williams's other work was largely autobiographical, often drawing comparisons between his family and his characters and using the backdrops with which he was most familiar. Williams moved around a good deal — from

New Orleans, to Key West, to New York City, to Provincetown. Each locale had a significant homosexual population, which suited Williams's sexual orientation well. He was a committed partner and suffered greatly when his love of many years, Frank Merlo, died of cancer in 1961.

Tennessee Williams battled alcoholism, drug abuse, and mental illness through much of his life. Along with his older sister Rose, he fought constantly against the fear that he might go insane. Rose, who was diagnosed as schizophrenic, underwent a prefrontal lobotomy in her late twenties and was institutionalized for the remainder of her life; Williams himself suffered a mental breakdown at a young age. In the end, he choked to death on a bottle cap in his room at the Hotel Elysée in New York City.

His life and his work helped make Tennessee Williams one of America's best playwrights and one of the signature writers of the American South. His plays were bold and sometimes considered tawdry while those of his predecessors had been considered genteel and polite. Still, just as he was able to burst onto Broadway, he was able to spring on his readers a new type of drama that would forever change the way they saw the South.

The Glass Menagerie (1945)

Nobody, not even the rain, has such small hands.
E. E. Cummings

CHARACTERS

Amanda Wingfield, *the mother. A little woman of great but confused vitality clinging frantically to another time and place. Her characterization must be carefully created, not copied from type. She is not paranoiac, but her life is paranoia. There is much to admire in Amanda, and as much to love and pity as there is to laugh at. Certainly she has endurance and a kind of heroism, and though her foolishness makes her unwittingly cruel at times, there is tenderness in her slight person.*

Laura Wingfield, *her daughter. Amanda, having failed to establish contact with reality, continues to live vitally in her illusions, but Laura's situation is even graver. A childhood illness has left her crippled, one leg slightly shorter than the other, and held in a brace. This defect need not be more than suggested on the stage. Stemming from this, Laura's separation increases till she is like a piece of her own glass collection, too exquisitely fragile to move from the shelf.*

Tom Wingfield, *her son. And the narrator of the play. A poet with a job in a warehouse. His nature is not remorseless, but to escape from a trap he has to act without pity.*

Jim O'Connor, *the gentleman caller. A nice, ordinary, young man.*

SCENE

An alley in St. Louis.

PART I

Preparation for a Gentleman Caller.

PART II

The Gentleman Calls.

TIME

Now and the Past.

SCENE 1

The Wingfield apartment is in the rear of the building, one of those vast hive-like con-glomerations of cellular living-units that flower as warty growths in overcrowded urban centers of lower middle-class population and are symptomatic of the impulse of this largest and fundamentally enslaved section of American society to avoid fluidity and dif-ferentiation and to exist and function as one interfused mass of automatism.

The apartment faces an alley and is entered by a fire-escape, a structure whose name is a touch of accidental poetic truth, for all of these huge buildings are always burn-ing with the slow and implacable fires of human desperation. The fire-escape is included in the set—that is, the landing of it and steps descending from it.

The scene is memory and is therefore nonrealistic. Memory takes a lot of poetic li-cense. It omits some details; others are exaggerated, according to the emotional value of the articles it touches, for memory is seated predominantly in the heart. The interior is therefore rather dim and poetic.

At the rise of the curtain, the audience is faced with the dark, grim rear wall of the Wingfield tenement. This building, which runs parallel to the footlights, is flanked on both sides by dark, narrow alleys which run into murky canyons of tangled clotheslines, garbage cans and the sinister latticework of neighboring fire-escapes. It is up and down these side alleys that exterior entrances and exits are made, during the play. At the end of Tom's opening commentary, the dark tenement wall slowly reveals (by means of a transparency) the interior of the ground floor Wingfield apartment.

Downstage is the living room, which also serves as a sleeping room for Laura, the sofa unfolding to make her bed. Upstage, center, and divided by a wide arch or second proscenium with transparent faded portieres (or second curtain), is the dining room. In an old-fashioned what-not in the living room are seen scores of transparent glass ani-mals. A blown-up photograph of the father hangs on the wall of the living room, facing the audience, to the left of the archway. It is the face of a very handsome young man in a doughboy's First World War cap. He is gallantly smiling, ineluctably smiling, as if to say, "I will be smiling forever."

The audience hears and sees the opening scene in the dining room through both the transparent fourth wall of the building and the transparent gauze portieres of the dining-room arch. It is during this revealing scene that the fourth wall slowly ascends, out of sight. This transparent exterior wall is not brought down again until the very end of the play, during Tom's final speech.

The narrator is an undisguised convention of the play. He takes whatever license with dramatic convention as is convenient to his purposes.

Tom enters dressed as a merchant sailor from the alley, stage left, and strolls across the front of the stage to the fire-escape. There he stops and lights a cigarette. He addresses the audience.

TOM: Yes, I have tricks in my pocket, I have things up my sleeve. But I am the opposite of a stage magician. He gives you illusion that has the appearance of truth. I give you truth in the pleasant disguise of illusion. To begin with,

I turn back time. I reverse it to that quaint period, the thirties, when the huge middle class of America was matriculating in a school for the blind. Their eyes had failed them, or they had failed their eyes, and so they were having their fingers pressed forcibly down on the fiery Braille alphabet of a dissolving economy. In Spain there was revolution.° Here there was only shouting and confusion. In Spain there was Guernica.° Here there were disturbances of labor, sometimes pretty violent, in otherwise peaceful cities such as Chicago, Cleveland, Saint Louis. . . . This is the social background of the play.

Music.

The play is memory. Being a memory play, it is dimly lighted, it is sentimental, it is not realistic. In memory everything seems to happen to music. That explains the fiddle in the wings. I am the narrator of the play, and also a character in it. The other characters are my mother, Amanda, my sister, Laura, and a gentleman caller who appears in the final scenes. He is the most realistic character in the play, being an emissary from a world of reality that we were somehow set apart from. But since I have a poet's weakness for symbols, I am using this character also as a symbol; he is the long delayed but always expected something that we live for. There is a fifth character in the play who doesn't appear except in this larger-than-life photograph over the mantel. This is our father who left us a long time ago. He was a telephone man who fell in love with long distances; he gave up his job with the telephone company and skipped the light fantastic out of town. . . . The last we heard of him was a picture post-card from Mazatlan, on the Pacific coast of Mexico, containing a message of two words — "Hello — Good-bye!" and an address. I think the rest of the play will explain itself. . . .

Amanda's voice becomes audible through the portieres.

Legend On Screen: "Où Sont Les Neiges."°

He divides the portieres and enters the upstage area.

Amanda and Laura are seated at a drop-leaf table. Eating is indicated by gestures without food or utensils. Amanda faces the audience. Tom and Laura are seated in profile.

The interior has lit up softly and through the scrim we see Amanda and Laura seated at the table in the upstage area.

AMANDA: *(calling)* Tom?

° *revolution:* The Spanish Civil War (1936–1939).   ° *Guernica:* A Basque town in northern Spain, bombed and practically destroyed on April 27, 1937, by German planes aiding fascist General Francisco Franco's Nationalists. The destruction is depicted in one of Pablo Picasso's most famous paintings, *Guernica* (1937).   ° *"Où Sont Les Neiges":* "Where the snows [of yesteryear]." A famous line by French poet François Villon (1431–1463?).

TOM: Yes, Mother.

AMANDA: We can't say grace until you come to the table!

TOM: Coming, Mother. (*He bows slightly and withdraws, reappearing a few moments later in his place at the table.*)

AMANDA: (*to her son*) Honey, don't *push* with your *fingers*. If you have to push with something, the thing to push with is a crust of bread. And chew — chew! Animals have sections in their stomachs which enable them to digest food without mastication, but human beings are supposed to chew their food before they swallow it down. Eat food leisurely, son, and really enjoy it. A well-cooked meal has lots of delicate flavors that have to be held in the mouth for appreciation. So chew your food and give your salivary glands a chance to function!

Tom deliberately lays his imaginary fork down and pushes his chair back from the table.

TOM: I haven't enjoyed one bite of this dinner because of your constant directions on how to eat it. It's you that makes me rush through meals with your hawk-like attention to every bite I take. Sickening — spoils my appetite — all this discussion of animals' secretion — salivary glands — mastication!

AMANDA: (*lightly*) Temperament like a Metropolitan star! (*He rises and crosses downstage.*) You're not excused from the table.

TOM: I am getting a cigarette.

AMANDA: You smoke too much.

Laura rises.

LAURA: I'll bring in the blanc mange.

He remains standing with his cigarette by the portieres during the following.

AMANDA: (*rising*) No, sister, no, sister — you be the lady this time and I'll be the darky.

LAURA: I'm already up.

AMANDA: Resume your seat, little sister — I want you to stay fresh and pretty — for gentlemen callers!

LAURA: I'm not expecting any gentlemen callers.

AMANDA: (*crossing out to kitchenette. Airily*) Sometimes they come when they are least expected! Why, I remember one Sunday afternoon in Blue Mountain — (*Enters kitchenette.*)

TOM: I know what's coming!

LAURA: Yes. But let her tell it.

TOM: Again?

LAURA: She loves to tell it.

Amanda returns with bowl of dessert.

AMANDA: One Sunday afternoon in Blue Mountain — your mother received — *seventeen!* — gentlemen callers! Why, sometimes there weren't chairs enough to accommodate them all. We had to send the nigger over to bring in folding chairs from the parish house.

TOM: *(remaining at portieres)* How did you entertain those gentlemen callers?

AMANDA: I understood the art of conversation!

TOM: I bet you could talk.

25 **AMANDA:** Girls in those days *knew* how to talk, I can tell you.

TOM: Yes?

Image: Amanda As A Girl On A Porch Greeting Callers.

AMANDA: They knew how to entertain their gentlemen callers. It wasn't enough for a girl to be possessed of a pretty face and a graceful figure — although I wasn't slighted in either respect. She also needed to have a nimble wit and a tongue to meet all occasions.

TOM: What did you talk about?

AMANDA: Things of importance going on in the world! Never anything coarse or common or vulgar. *(She addresses Tom as though he were seated in the vacant chair at the table though he remains by portieres. He plays this scene as though he held the book.)* My callers were gentlemen — all! Among my callers were some of the most prominent young planters of the Mississippi Delta — planters and sons of planters!

Tom motions for music and a spot of light on Amanda. Her eyes lift, her face glows, her voice becomes rich and elegiac.

Screen Legend: "Où Sont Les Neiges."

There was young Champ Laughlin who later became vice-president of the Delta Planters Bank. Hadley Stevenson who was drowned in Moon Lake and left his widow one hundred and fifty thousand in Government bonds. There were the Cutrere brothers, Wesley and Bates. Bates was one of my bright particular beaux! He got in a quarrel with that wild Wainright boy. They shot it out on the floor of Moon Lake Casino. Bates was shot through the stomach. Died in the ambulance on his way to Memphis. His widow was also well-provided for, came into eight or ten thousand acres, that's all. She married him on the rebound — never loved her — carried my picture on him the night he died! And there was that boy that every girl in the Delta had set her cap for! That beautiful, brilliant young Fitzhugh boy from Green County!

30 **TOM:** What did he leave his widow?

AMANDA: He never married! Gracious, you talk as though all of my old admirers had turned up their toes to the daisies!

TOM: Isn't this the first you mentioned that still survives?

AMANDA: That Fitzhugh boy went North and made a fortune — came to be known as the Wolf of Wall Street! He had the Midas touch, whatever he touched turned to gold! And I could have been Mrs. Duncan J. Fitzhugh, mind you! But — I picked your *father!*

LAURA: *(rising)* Mother, let me clear the table.

35 **AMANDA:** No dear, you go in front and study your typewriter chart. Or practice your shorthand a little. Stay fresh and pretty! — It's almost time for our

gentlemen callers to start arriving. (*She flounces girlishly toward the kitchenette.*) How many do you suppose we're going to entertain this afternoon?

Tom throws down the paper and jumps up with a groan.

LAURA: (*alone in the dining room*) I don't believe we're going to receive any, Mother.

AMANDA: (*reappearing, airily*) What? No one — not one? You must be joking! (*Laura nervously echoes her laugh. She slips in a fugitive manner through the half-open portieres and draws them gently behind her. A shaft of very clear light is thrown on her face against the faded tapestry of the curtains.*) (*Music: "The Glass Menagerie" under faintly.*) (*Lightly.*) Not one gentleman caller? It can't be true! There must be a flood, there must have been a tornado!

LAURA: It isn't a flood, it's not a tornado, Mother. I'm just not popular like you were in Blue Mountain. . . . (*Tom utters another groan. Laura glances at him with a faint, apologetic smile. Her voice catching a little.*) Mother's afraid I'm going to be an old maid.

The Scene Dims Out With "Glass Menagerie" Music.

SCENE 2

"Laura, Haven't You Ever Liked Some Boy?"

On the dark stage the screen is lighted with the image of blue roses.

Gradually Laura's figure becomes apparent and the screen goes out.

The music subsides.

Laura is seated in the delicate ivory chair at the small clawfoot table.

She wears a dress of soft violet material for a kimono — her hair tied back from her forehead with a ribbon.

She is washing and polishing her collection of glass.

Amanda appears on the fire-escape steps. At the sound of her ascent, Laura catches her breath, thrusts the bowl of ornaments away and seats herself stiffly before the diagram of the typewriter keyboard as though it held her spellbound. Something has happened to Amanda. It is written in her face as she climbs to the landing: a look that is grim and hopeless and a little absurd.

She has on one of those cheap or imitation velvety-looking cloth coats with imitation fur collar. Her hat is five or six years old, one of those dreadful cloche hats that were worn in the late twenties, and she is clasping an enormous black patent-leather pocketbook with nickel clasp and initials. This is her fulldress outfit, the one she usually wears to the D.A.R.°

Before entering she looks through the door.

She purses her lips, opens her eyes wide, rolls them upward and shakes her head.

Then she slowly lets herself in the door. Seeing her mother's expression Laura touches her lips with a nervous gesture.

°*D.A.R.:* Daughters of the American Revolution, an organization for female descendants of participants in the American Revolution, founded in 1890. That Amanda is a member says much about her concern with the past, as well as about her pride and affectations.

LAURA: Hello, Mother, I was — (*She makes a nervous gesture toward the chart on the wall. Amanda leans against the shut door and stares at Laura with a martyred look.*)

AMANDA: Deception? Deception? (*She slowly removes her hat and gloves, continuing the swift suffering stare. She lets the hat and gloves fall on the floor — a bit of acting.*)

LAURA: (*shakily*) How was the D.A.R. meeting? (*Amanda slowly opens her purse and removes a dainty white handkerchief which she shakes out delicately and delicately touches to her lips and nostrils.*) Didn't you go to the D.A.R. meeting, Mother?

AMANDA: (*faintly, almost inaudibly*) — No. — No. (*Then more forcibly.*) I did not have the strength — to go the D.A.R. In fact, I did not have the courage! I wanted to find a hole in the ground and hide myself in it forever! (*She crosses slowly to the wall and removes the diagram of the typewriter keyboard. She holds it in front of her for a second, staring at it sweetly and sorrowfully — then bites her lips and tears it in two pieces.*)

LAURA: (*faintly*) Why did you do that, Mother? (*Amanda repeats the same
5   procedure with the chart of the Gregg Alphabet.*) Why are you—

AMANDA: Why? Why? How old are you, Laura?

LAURA: Mother, you know my age.

AMANDA: I thought that you were an adult; it seems that I was mistaken. (*She crosses slowly to the sofa and sinks down and stares at Laura.*)

LAURA: Please don't stare at me, Mother.

Amanda closes her eyes and lowers her head. Count ten.

10   AMANDA: What are we going to do, what is going to become of us, what is the future?

Count ten.

LAURA: Has something happened, Mother? (*Amanda draws a long breath and takes out the handkerchief again. Dabbing process.*) Mother, has — something happened?

AMANDA: I'll be all right in a minute. I'm just bewildered —(*count five*)—by life. . . .

LAURA: Mother, I wish that you would tell me what's happened.

AMANDA: As you know, I was supposed to be inducted into my office at the D.A.R. this afternoon. (*Image: A Swarm Of Typewriters.*) But I stopped off at Rubicam's Business College to speak to your teachers about your having a cold and ask them what progress they thought you were making down there.

15   LAURA: Oh. . . .

AMANDA: I went to the typing instructor and introduced myself as your mother. She didn't know who you were. Wingfield, she said. We don't have any such student enrolled at the school! I assured her she did, that you had been going to classes since early in January. "I wonder," she said, "if you could be talking about that terribly shy little girl who dropped out of school after only a few days' attendance?" "No," I said, "Laura, my daughter, has been going to school every day for the past six weeks!" "Excuse me," she said. She took the attendance book out and there was your name, unmistakably printed, and all the dates you were absent until they decided that you had dropped out of school. I still said, "No, there must have been some mistake! There must have been some mix-up in the records!" And she said, "No — I remember her perfectly now. Her hand shook so that she couldn't hit the right keys! The first time we gave a speed-test, she broke down completely — was sick at the stomach and almost had to be carried into the wash-room! After that morning she never showed up any more. We phoned the house but never got any answer" — while I was working at Famous and Barr, I suppose, demonstrating those — Oh! I felt so weak I could barely keep on my feet. I had to sit down while they got me a glass of water! Fifty dollars' tuition, all of our plans — my hopes and ambitions for you — just gone up the spout, just gone up the spout like that. (*Laura draws a long breath and gets awkwardly to her feet. She crosses to the Victrola and winds it up.*) What are you doing?

LAURA: Oh! (*She releases the handle and returns to her seat.*)

AMANDA: Laura, where have you been going when you've gone out pretending that you were going to business college?

LAURA: I've just been going out walking.

AMANDA: That's not true.   20

LAURA: It is. I just went walking.

AMANDA: Walking? Walking? In winter? Deliberately courting pneumonia in that light coat? Where did you walk to, Laura?

LAURA: It was the lesser of two evils, Mother. (*Image: Winter Scene In Park.*) I couldn't go back up. I — threw up — on the floor!

AMANDA: From half past seven till after five every day you mean to tell me you walked around in the park, because you wanted to make me think that you were still going to Rubicam's Business College?

LAURA: It wasn't as bad as it sounds. I went inside places to get warmed up.   25

AMANDA: Inside where?

LAURA: I went in the art museum and the bird-houses at the Zoo. I visited the penguins every day! Sometimes I did without lunch and went to the movies. Lately I've been spending most of my afternoons in the Jewel-box, that big glass house where they raise the tropical flowers.

AMANDA: You did all this to deceive me, just for the deception? (*Laura looks down.*) Why?

LAURA: Mother, when you're disappointed, you get that awful suffering look on your face, like the picture of Jesus' mother in the museum!

AMANDA: Hush!   30

LAURA: I couldn't face it.

Pause. A whisper of strings.

Legend: "The Crust Of Humility."

AMANDA: *(hopelessly fingering the huge pocketbook)* So what are we going to do the rest of our lives? Stay home and watch the parades go by? Amuse ourselves with the glass menagerie, darling? Eternally play those worn-out phonograph records your father left as a painful reminder of him? We won't have a business career — we've given that up because it gave us nervous indigestion! *(Laughs wearily.)* What is there left but dependency all our lives? I know so well what becomes of unmarried women who aren't prepared to occupy a position. I've seen such pitiful cases in the South — barely tolerated spinsters living upon the grudging patronage of sister's husband or brother's wife! — stuck away in some little mouse-trap of a room — encouraged by one in-law to visit another — little birdlike women without any nest — eating the crust of humility all their life! Is that the future that we've mapped out for ourselves? I swear it's the only alternative I can think of! It isn't a very pleasant alternative, is it? Of course — some girls *do* marry. *(Laura twists her hands nervously.)* Haven't you ever liked some boy?

LAURA: Yes I liked one once. *(Rises.)* I came across his picture a while ago.

AMANDA: *(with some interest)* He gave you his picture?

35 LAURA: No, it's in the year-book.

AMANDA: *(disappointed)* Oh — a high-school boy.

Screen Image: Jim As A High-School Hero Bearing A Silver Cup.

LAURA: Yes. His name was Jim. *(Laura lifts the heavy annual from the clawfoot table.)* Here he is in *The Pirates of Penzance.*°

AMANDA: *(absently)* The what?

LAURA: The operetta the senior class put on. He had a wonderful voice and we sat across the aisle from each other Mondays, Wednesdays and Fridays in the Aud. Here he is with the silver cup for debating! See his grin?

40 AMANDA: *(absently)* He must have had a jolly disposition.

LAURA: He used to call me — Blue Roses.

Image: Blue Roses.

AMANDA: Why did he call you such a name as that?

LAURA: When I had that attack of pleurosis — he asked me what was the matter when I came back. I said pleurosis — he thought that I said Blue Roses! So that's what he always called me after that. Whenever he saw me, he'd holler, "Hello, Blue Roses!" I didn't care for the girl that he went out with. Emily Meisenbach. Emily was the best-dressed girl at Soldan. She never struck me, though, as being sincere . . . It says in the Personal Section — they're engaged. That's — six years ago! They must be married by now.

AMANDA: Girls that aren't cut out for business careers usually wind up married to some nice man. *(Gets up with a spark of revival.)* Sister, that's what you'll do!

Laura utters a startled, doubtful laugh. She reaches quickly for a piece of glass.

° *The Pirates of Penzance:* A musical by Gilbert and Sullivan.

LAURA: But, Mother—

AMANDA: Yes? (*Crossing to photograph.*)

LAURA: (*in a tone of frightened apology*) I'm — crippled!

Image: Screen.

AMANDA: Nonsense! Laura, I've told you never, never to use that word. Why, you're not crippled, you just have a little defect — hardly noticeable, even! When people have some slight disadvantage like that, they cultivate other things to make up for it — develop charm — and vivacity — and — charm! That's all you have to do! (*She turns again to the photograph.*) One thing your father had *plenty* of — was *charm!*

Tom motions to the fiddle in the wings.

The Scene Fades Out With Music.

SCENE 3

Legend On The Screen: "After The Fiasco —"

Tom speaks from the fire-escape landing.

TOM: After the fiasco at Rubicam's Business College, the idea of getting a gentleman caller for Laura began to play a more important part in Mother's calculations. It became an obsession. Like some archetype of the universal unconscious, the image of the gentleman caller haunted our small apartment. . . . (*Image: Young Man At Door With Flowers.*) An evening at home rarely passed without some allusion to this image, this spectre, this hope. . . . Even when he wasn't mentioned, his presence hung in Mother's preoccupied look and in my sister's frightened, apologetic manner — hung like a sentence passed upon the Wingfields! Mother was a woman of action as well as words. She began to take logical steps in the planned direction. Late that winter and in the early spring — realizing that extra money would be needed to properly feather the nest and plume the bird — she conducted a vigorous campaign on the telephone, roping in subscribers to one of those magazines for matrons called *The Home-maker's Companion,* the type of journal that features the serialized sublimations of ladies of letters who think in terms of delicate cup-like breasts, slim, tapering waists, rich, creamy thighs, eyes like wood-smoke in autumn, fingers that soothe and caress like strains of music, bodies as powerful as Etruscan sculpture.

Screen Image: A Glamour Magazine Cover.

Amanda enters with phone on long extension cord. She is spotted in the dim stage.

AMANDA: Ida Scott? This is Amanda Wingfield! We *missed* you at the D.A.R. last Monday! I said to myself: She's probably suffering with that sinus condition! How is that sinus condition? Horrors! Heaven have mercy!—You're a Christian martyr, yes, that's what you are, a Christian martyr! Well, I just now happened to notice that your subscription to the *Companion's* about to expire! Yes, it expires with the next issue, honey!—just when that wonderful new serial by Bessie Mae Hopper is getting off to such an exciting start. Oh, honey, it's something that you can't miss! You remember how *Gone With the Wind* took everybody by storm? You simply couldn't go out if you hadn't read it. All everybody *talked* was Scarlett O'Hara. Well, this is a book that critics already compare to *Gone With the Wind*. It's the *Gone With the Wind* of the post–World War generation!—What?—Burning?— Oh, honey, don't let them burn, go take a look in the oven and I'll hold the wire! Heavens — I think she's hung up!

Dim Out.

Legend On Screen: "You Think I'm In Love With Continental Shoemakers?"

Before the stage is lighted, the violent voices of Tom and Amanda are heard. They are quarreling behind the portieres. In front of them stands Laura with clenched hands and panicky expression.

A clear pool of light on her figure throughout this scene.

TOM: What in Christ's name am I—
AMANDA: *(shrilly)* Don't you use that—
5 TOM: Supposed to do!
AMANDA: Expression! Not in my—
TOM: Ohhh!
AMANDA: Presence! Have you gone out of your senses?
TOM: I have, that's true, *driven* out!
10 AMANDA: What is the matter with you, you — big — big —IDIOT!
TOM: Look — I've got *no thing*, no single thing—
AMANDA: Lower your voice!
TOM: In my life here that I can call my OWN! Everything is—
AMANDA: Stop that shouting!
15 TOM: Yesterday you confiscated my books! You had the nerve to—
AMANDA: I took that horrible novel back to the library — yes! That hideous book by that insane Mr. Lawrence.° *(Tom laughs wildly.)* I cannot control the output of diseased minds or people who cater to them —*(Tom laughs still more wildly.)* BUT I WON'T ALLOW SUCH FILTH BROUGHT INTO MY HOUSE! No, no, no, no, no!
TOM: House, house! Who pays rent on it, who makes a slave of himself to—
AMANDA: *(fairly screeching)* Don't you DARE to—
TOM: No, no, I mustn't say things! *I've* got to just—
20 AMANDA: Let me tell you—
TOM: I don't want to hear any more! *(He tears the portieres open. The upstage area is lit with a turgid smoky red glow.)*

°*Mr. Lawrence:* English novelist D. H. Lawrence (1885–1930). The reference is to his 1928 novel *Lady Chatterley's Lover,* which was banned in the United States and England because of its frank treatment of sexuality.

Amanda's hair is in metal curlers and she wears a very old bathrobe, much too large for her slight figure, a relic of the faithless Mr. Wingfield.

An upright typewriter and a wild disarray of manuscripts are on the drop-leaf table. The quarrel was probably precipitated by Amanda's interruption of his creative labor. A chair lying overthrown on the floor.

Their gesticulating shadows are cast on the ceiling by the fiery glow.

AMANDA: You *will* hear more, you—

TOM: No, I won't hear more, I'm going out!

AMANDA: You come right back in—

TOM: Out, out out! Because I'm—

AMANDA: Come back here, Tom Wingfield! I'm not through talking to you!   25

TOM: Oh, go—

LAURA: *(desperately)* Tom!

AMANDA: You're going to listen, and no more insolence from you! I'm at the end of my patience! *(He comes back toward her.)*

TOM: What do you think I'm at? Aren't I supposed to have any patience to   30 reach the end of, Mother? I know, I know. It seems unimportant to you, what I'm *doing*— what I *want* to do —having a little *difference* between them! You don't think that—

AMANDA: I think you've been doing things that you're ashamed of. That's why you act like this. I don't believe that you go every night to the movies. Nobody goes to the movies night after night. Nobody in their right mind goes to the movies as often as you pretend to. People don't go to the movies at nearly midnight, and movies don't let out at two A.M. Come in stumbling. Muttering to yourself like a maniac! You get three hours' sleep and then go to work. Oh, I can picture the way you're doing down there. Moping, doping, because you're in no condition.

TOM: *(wildly)* No, I'm in no condition!

AMANDA: What right have you got to jeopardize your job? Jeopardize the security of us all? How do you think we'd manage if you were—

TOM: Listen! You think I'm crazy *about* the *warehouse*? *(He bends fiercely toward her slight figure.)* You think I'm in love with the Continental Shoemakers? You think I want to spend fifty-five *years* down there in that —*celotex interior!* with —*fluorescent* — *tubes!* Look! I'd rather somebody picked up a crowbar and battered out my brains — than go back mornings! I *go!* Every time you come in yelling that God damn *"Rise and Shine!"* *"Rise and Shine!"* I say to myself *"How lucky dead people are!"* But I get up. I *go!* For sixty-five dollars a month I give up all that I dream of doing and being *ever!* And you say self —*self's* all I ever think of. Why, listen, if self is what I thought of, Mother, I'd be where he is —GONE! *(Pointing to father's picture.)* As far as the system of transportation reaches! *(He starts past her. She grabs his arm.)* Don't grab at me, Mother!

AMANDA: Where are you going?   35

TOM: I'm going to the *movies!*

AMANDA: I don't believe that lie!

TOM: *(crouching toward her, overtowering her tiny figure. She backs away, gasping)* I'm going to opium dens! Yes, opium dens, dens of vice and criminals' hang-outs, Mother. I've joined the Hogan gang, I'm a hired assassin, I carry a tommy-gun in a violin case! I run a string of cat-houses in the Valley! They call me Killer, Killer Wingfield, I'm leading a double-life, a simple, honest warehouse worker by day, by night a dynamic *czar of the underworld, Mother.* I go to gambling casinos, I spin away fortunes on the roulette table! I wear a patch over one eye and a false mustache, sometimes I put on green whiskers. On those occasions they call me —*El Diablo!* Oh, I could tell you things to make you sleepless! My enemies plan to dynamite this place. They're going to blow us all sky-high some night! I'll be glad, very happy, and so will you! You'll go up, up on a broomstick, over Blue Mountain with seventeen gentlemen callers! You ugly —babbling old —*witch.* . . . *(He goes through a series of violent, clumsy movements, seizing his overcoat, lunging to the door, pulling it fiercely open. The women watch him, aghast. His arm catches in the sleeve of the coat as he struggles to pull it on. For a moment he is pinioned by the bulky garment. With an outraged groan he tears the coat off again, splitting the shoulders of it, and hurls it across the room. It strikes against the shelf of Laura's glass collection, there is a tinkle of shattering glass. Laura cries out as if wounded.)*

Music Legend: "The Glass Menagerie."

LAURA: My glass! —menagerie. . . . *(She covers her face and turns away.)*

But Amanda is still stunned and stupefied by the "ugly witch" so that she barely notices this occurrence. Now she recovers her speech.

40   **AMANDA:** *(in an awful voice)* I won't speak to you — until you apologize! *(She crosses through portieres and draws them together behind her. Tom is left with Laura. Laura clings weakly to the mantel with her face averted. Tom stares at her stupidly for a moment. Then he crosses to shelf. Drops awkwardly to his knees to collect the fallen glass, glancing at Laura as if he would speak but couldn't.)*

"The Glass Menagerie" steals in as The Scene Dims Out.

SCENE 4

The interior is dark. Faint in the alley.

A deep-voiced bell in a church is tolling the hour of five as the scene commences.

Tom appears at the top of the alley. After each solemn boom of the bell in the tower, he shakes a little noise-maker or rattle as if to express the tiny spasm of man in contrast to the sustained power and dignity of the Almighty. This and the unsteadiness of his advance make it evident that he has been drinking.

As he climbs the few steps to the fire-escape landing light steals up inside. Laura appears in night-dress, observing Tom's empty bed in the front room.

Tom fishes in his pockets for the door-key, removing a motley assortment of articles in the search, including a perfect shower of movie-ticket stubs and an empty bottle. At last he finds the key, but just as he is about to insert it, it slips from his fingers. He strikes a match and crouches below the door.

TOM: *(bitterly)* One crack — and it falls through!

Laura opens the door.

LAURA: Tom! Tom, what are you doing?

TOM: Looking for a door-key.

LAURA: Where have you been all this time?

TOM: I have been to the movies.

LAURA: All this time at the movies?

TOM: There was a very long program. There was a Garbo picture and a Mickey Mouse and a travelogue and a newsreel and a preview of coming attractions. And there was an organ solo and a collection for the milk-fund — simultaneously — which ended up in a terrible fight between a fat lady and an usher!

LAURA: *(innocently)* Did you have to stay through everything?

TOM: Of course! And, oh, I forgot! There was a big stage show! The headliner on this stage show was Malvolio the Magician. He performed wonderful tricks, many of them, such as pouring water back and forth between pitchers. First it turned to wine and then it turned to beer and then it turned to whiskey. I know it was whiskey it finally turned into because he needed somebody to come up out of the audience to help him, and I came up — both shows! It was Kentucky Straight Bourbon. A very generous fellow, he gave souvenirs. *(He pulls from his back pocket a shimmering rainbow-colored scarf.)* He gave me this. This is his magic scarf. You can have it, Laura. You wave it over a canary cage and you get a bowl of gold-fish. You wave it over the gold-fish bowl and they fly away canaries. . . . But the wonderfullest trick of all was the coffin trick. We nailed him into a coffin and he got out of the coffin without removing one nail. *(He has come inside.)* There is a trick that would come in handy for me — get me out of this 2 by 4 situation! *(Flops onto bed and starts removing shoes.)*

LAURA: Tom — Shhh!

TOM: What you shushing me for?

LAURA: You'll wake up Mother.

TOM: Goody, goody! Pay 'er back for all those "Rise an' Shines." *(Lies down, groaning.)* You know it don't take much intelligence to get yourself into a nailed-up coffin, Laura. But who in hell ever got himself out of one without removing one nail?

As if in answer, the father's grinning photograph lights up.

Scene Dims Out.

Immediately following: The church bell is heard striking six. At the sixth stroke the alarm clock goes off in Amanda's room, and after a few moments we hear her calling: "Rise and Shine! Rise and Shine! Laura, go tell your brother to rise and shine!"

TOM: *(sitting up slowly)* I'll rise — but I won't shine.

The light increases.

15 **AMANDA:** Laura, tell your brother his coffee is ready.

Laura slips into front room.

LAURA: Tom! it's nearly seven. Don't make Mother nervous. (*He stares at her stupidly. Beseechingly.*) Tom, speak to Mother this morning. Make up with her, apologize, speak to her!

TOM: She won't to me. It's her that started not speaking.

LAURA: If you just say you're sorry she'll start speaking.

TOM: Her not speaking — is that such a tragedy?

20 **LAURA:** Please — please!

AMANDA: (*calling from kitchenette*) Laura, are you going to do what I asked you to do, or do I have to get dressed and go out myself?

LAURA: Going, going — soon as I get on my coat! (*She pulls on a shapeless felt hat with nervous, jerky movement, pleadingly glancing at Tom. Rushes awkwardly for coat. The coat is one of Amanda's inaccurately made-over, the sleeves too short for Laura.*) Butter and what else?

AMANDA: (*entering upstage*) Just butter. Tell them to charge it.

LAURA: Mother, they make such faces when I do that.

25 **AMANDA:** Sticks and stones may break my bones, but the expression on Mr. Garfinkel's face won't harm us! Tell your brother his coffee is getting cold.

LAURA: (*at door*) Do what I asked you, will you, will you, Tom?

He looks sullenly away.

AMANDA: Laura, go now or just don't go at all!

LAURA: (*rushing out*) Going — going! (*A second later she cries out. Tom springs up and crosses to the door. Amanda rushes anxiously in. Tom opens the door.*)

TOM: Laura?

30 **LAURA:** I'm all right. I slipped, but I'm all right.

AMANDA: (*peering anxiously after her*) If anyone breaks a leg on those fire-escape steps, the landlord ought to be sued for every cent he possesses! (*She shuts door. Remembers she isn't speaking and returns to other room.*)

As Tom enters listlessly for his coffee, she turns her back to him and stands rigidly facing the window on the gloomy gray vault of the areaway. Its light on her face with its aged but childish features is cruelly sharp, satirical as a Daumier print.

Music Under: "Ave Maria."

Tom glances sheepishly but sullenly at her averted figure and slumps at the table. The coffee is scalding hot; he sips it and gasps and spits it back in the cup. At his gasp, Amanda catches her breath and half turns. Then catches herself and turns back to window.

Tom blows on his coffee, glancing sidewise at his mother. She clears her throat. Tom clears his. He starts to rise. Sinks back down again, scratches his head, clears his throat again. Amanda coughs. Tom raises his cup in both hands to blow on it, his eyes staring over the rim of it at his mother for several moments. Then he slowly sets the cup down and awkwardly and hesitantly rises from the chair.

TOM: (*hoarsely*) Mother. I — I apologize. Mother. (*Amanda draws a quick, shuddering breath. Her face works grotesquely. She breaks into childlike tears.*) I'm sorry for what I said, for everything that I said, I didn't mean it.

AMANDA: (*sobbingly*) My devotion has made me a witch and so I make myself hateful to my children!

TOM: No, you *don't*.

AMANDA: I worry so much, don't sleep, it makes me nervous! 35

TOM: (*gently*) I understand that.

AMANDA: I've had to put up a solitary battle all these years. But you're my right-hand bower! Don't fall down, don't fail!

TOM: (*gently*) I try, Mother.

AMANDA: (*with great enthusiasm*) Try and you will SUCCEED! (*The notion makes her breathless.*) Why, you — you're just *full* of natural endowments! Both of my children — they're *unusual* children! Don't you think I know it? I'm so — *proud*! Happy and — feel I've — so much to be thankful for but — Promise me one thing, son!

TOM: What, Mother? 40

AMANDA: Promise, son, you'll — never be a drunkard!

TOM: (*turns to her grinning*) I will never be a drunkard, Mother.

AMANDA: That's what frightened me so, that you'd be drinking! Eat a bowl of Purina!

TOM: Just coffee, Mother.

AMANDA: Shredded wheat biscuit? 45

TOM: No. No, Mother, just coffee.

AMANDA: You can't put in a day's work on an empty stomach. You've got ten minutes — don't gulp! Drinking too-hot liquids makes cancer of the stomach. . . . Put cream in.

TOM: No, thank you.

AMANDA: To cool it.

TOM: No! No, thank you, I want it black. 50

AMANDA: I know, but it's not good for you. We have to do all that we can to build ourselves up. In these trying times we live in, all that we have to cling to is — each other. . . . That's why it's so important to — Tom, I — I sent out your sister so I could discuss something with you. If you hadn't spoken I would have spoken to you. (*Sits down.*)

TOM: (*gently*) What is it, Mother, that you want to discuss?

AMANDA: Laura!

Tom puts his cup down slowly.

Legend On Screen: "Laura."

Music: "The Glass Menagerie."

TOM: — Oh. — Laura . . .

AMANDA: (*touching his sleeve*) You know how Laura is. So quiet but — still water runs deep! She notices things and I think she — broods 55 about them. (*Tom looks up.*) A few days ago I came in and she was crying.

TOM: What about?

AMANDA: You.

TOM: Me?

AMANDA: She has an idea that you're not happy here.

60 TOM: What gave her that idea?

AMANDA: What gives her any idea? However, you do act strangely. I — I'm not criticizing, understand *that!* I know your ambitions do not lie in the warehouse, that like everybody in the whole wide world — you've had to — make sacrifices, but — Tom — Tom — life's not easy, it calls for — Spartan endurance! There's so many things in my heart that I cannot describe to you! I've never told you but I —*loved* your father. . . .

TOM: (gently) I know that, Mother.

AMANDA: And you — when I see you taking after his ways! Staying out late — and — well, you *had* been drinking the night you were in that — terrifying condition! Laura says that you hate the apartment and that you go out nights to get away from it! Is that true, Tom?

TOM: No. You say there's so much in your heart that you can't describe to me. That's true of me, too. There's so much in my heart that I can't describe to *you!* So let's respect each other's —

65 AMANDA: But, why —*why*, Tom — are you always so *restless?* Where do you go to, nights?

TOM: I — go to the movies.

AMANDA: Why do you go to the movies so much, Tom?

TOM: I go to the movies because — I like adventure. Adventure is something I don't have much of at work, so I go to the movies.

AMANDA: But, Tom, you go to the movies *entirely* too *much!*

70 TOM: I like a lot of adventure.

Amanda looks baffled, then hurt. As the familiar inquisition resumes he becomes hard and impatient again. Amanda slips back into her querulous attitude toward him.

Image On Screen: Sailing Vessel With Jolly Roger.

AMANDA: Most young men find adventure in their careers.

TOM: Then most young men are not employed in a warehouse.

AMANDA: The world is full of young men employed in warehouses and offices and factories.

TOM: Do all of them find adventure in their careers?

75 AMANDA: They do or they do without it! Not everybody has a craze for adventure.

TOM: Man is by instinct a lover, a hunter, a fighter, and none of those instincts are given much play at the warehouse!

AMANDA: Man is by instinct! Don't quote instinct to me! Instinct is something that people have got away from! It belongs to animals! Christian adults don't want it!

TOM: What do Christian adults want, then, Mother?

AMANDA: Superior things! Things of the mind and the spirit! Only animals have to satisfy instincts! Surely your aims are somewhat higher than theirs! Than monkeys — pigs —

TOM: I reckon they're not. 80

AMANDA: You're joking. However, that isn't what I wanted to discuss.

TOM: (rising) I haven't much time.

AMANDA: (pushing his shoulders) Sit down.

TOM: You want me to punch in red at the warehouse, Mother?

AMANDA: You have five minutes. I want to talk about Laura. 85

Legend: "Plans And Provisions."

TOM: All right! What about Laura?

AMANDA: We have to be making plans and provisions for her. She's older than you, two years, and nothing has happened. She just drifts along doing nothing. It frightens me terribly how she just drifts along.

TOM: I guess she's the type that people call home-girls.

AMANDA: There's no such type, and if there is, it's a pity! That is unless the home is hers, with a husband!

TOM: What? 90

AMANDA: Oh, I can see the handwriting on the wall as plain as I see the nose in front of my face! It's terrifying! More and more you remind me of your father! He was out all hours without explanation — Then *left! Good-bye!* And me with the bag to hold. I saw that letter you got from the Merchant Marine. I know what you're dreaming of. I'm not standing here blindfolded. Very well, then. Then *do* it! But not till there's somebody to take your place.

TOM: What do you mean?

AMANDA: I mean that as soon as Laura has got somebody to take care of her, married, a home of her own, independent — why, then you'll be free to go wherever you please, on land, on sea, whichever way the wind blows! But until that time you've got to look out for your sister. I don't say me because I'm old and don't matter! I say for your sister because she's young and dependent. I put her in business college — a dismal failure! Frightened her so it made her sick to her stomach. I took her over to the Young People's League at the church. Another fiasco. She spoke to nobody, nobody spoke to her. Now all she does is fool with those pieces of glass and play those worn-out records. What kind of a life is that for a girl to lead!

TOM: What can I do about it?

AMANDA: Overcome selfishness! Self, self, self is all that you ever think of! 95 (*Tom springs up and crosses to get his coat. It is ugly and bulky. He pulls on a cap with earmuffs.*) Where is your muffler? Put your wool muffler on! (*He snatches it angrily from the closet and tosses it around his neck and pulls both ends tight.*) Tom! I haven't said what I had in mind to ask you.

TOM: I'm too late to—

AMANDA: (*catching his arms — very importunately. Then shyly*) Down at the warehouse, aren't there some — nice young men?

TOM: No!

AMANDA: There *must* be —*some* . . .

100 **TOM:** Mother—

Gesture.

AMANDA: Find out one that's clean-living — doesn't drink and — ask him out for sister!

TOM: What?

AMANDA: For *sister!* To *meet!* Get *acquainted!*

TOM: *(stamping to door)* Oh, my go-osh!

105 **AMANDA:** Will you? *(He opens door. Imploringly.)* Will you? *(He starts down.)* Will you? *Will* you, dear?

TOM: *(calling back)* YES!

Amanda closes the door hesitantly and with a troubled but faintly hopeful expression.

(Screen Image: A Glamour Magazine Cover.)

Spot Amanda at phone.

AMANDA: Ella Cartwright? This is Amanda Wingfield! How are you, honey? How is that kidney condition? *(Count five.)* Horrors! *(Count five.)* You're a Christian martyr, yes, honey, that's what you are, a Christian martyr! Well, I just happened to notice in my little red book that your subscription to the *Companion* has just run out! I knew that you wouldn't want to miss out on the wonderful serial starting in this new issue. It's by Bessie Mae Hopper, the first thing she's written since *Honeymoon for Three*. Wasn't that a strange and interesting story? Well, this one is even lovelier, I believe. It has a sophisticated society background. It's all about the horsey set on Long Island!

Fade Out.

SCENE 5

(Legend On Screen: "Annunciation.") Fade with music.

It is early dusk of a spring evening. Supper has just been finished in the Wingfield apartment. Amanda and Laura in light colored dresses are removing dishes from the table, in the upstage area, which is shadowy, their movements formalized almost as a dance or ritual, their moving forms as pale and silent as moths.

Tom, in white shirt and trousers, rises from the table and crosses toward the fire-escape.

AMANDA: *(as he passes her)* Son, will you do me a favor?

TOM: What?

AMANDA: Comb your hair! You look so pretty when your hair is combed!

(Tom slouches on sofa with evening paper. Enormous caption "Franco Triumphs.") There is only one respect in which I would like you to emulate your father.

TOM: What respect is that?

AMANDA: The care he always took of his appearance. He never allowed   5
himself to look untidy. (*He throws down the paper and crosses to fire-escape.*)
Where are you going?

TOM: I'm going out to smoke.

AMANDA: You smoke too much. A pack a day at fifteen cents a pack. How
much would that amount to in a month? Thirty times fifteen is how much,
Tom? Figure it out and you will be astounded at what you could save.
Enough to give you a night-school course in accounting at Washington U!
Just think what a wonderful thing that would be for you, son!

Tom is unmoved by the thought.

TOM: I'd rather smoke. (*He steps out on landing, letting the screen door slam.*)

AMANDA: (*sharply*) I know! That's the tragedy of it. . . . (*Alone, she turns to
look at her husband's picture.*)

Dance Music: "All The World Is Waiting For The Sunrise!"

TOM: (*to the audience*) Across the alley from us was the Paradise Dance Hall.   10
On evenings in spring the windows and doors were open and the music
came outdoors. Sometimes the lights were turned out except for a large
glass sphere that hung from the ceiling. It would turn slowly about and filter
the dusk with delicate rainbow colors. Then the orchestra played a waltz or
a tango, something that had a slow and sensuous rhythm. Couples would
come outside, to the relative privacy of the alley. You could see them kissing behind ash-pits and telephone poles. This was the compensation for
lives that passed like mine, without any change or adventure. Adventure
and change were imminent in this year. They were waiting around the
corner for all these kids. Suspended in the mist over Berchtesgaden,°
caught in the folds of Chamberlain's umbrella°— In Spain there was Guernica! But here there was only hot swing music and liquor, dance halls, bars,
and movies, and sex that hung in the gloom like a chandelier and flooded
the world with brief, deceptive rainbows. . . . All the world was waiting for
bombardments!

Amanda turns from the picture and comes outside.

AMANDA: (*sighing*) A fire-escape landing's a poor excuse for a porch. (*She
spreads a newspaper on a step and sits down, gracefully and demurely as if
she were settling into a swing on a Mississippi veranda.*) What are you
looking at?

TOM: The moon.

°*Berchtesgaden:* A resort in Germany, in the Bavarian Alps; the site of Adolf Hitler's fortified retreat, the Berghof.
°*Chamberlain's umbrella:* (Arthur) Neville Chamberlain (1869–1940)— Conservative Party prime minister of
England (1937–1940) who advocated a policy of appeasement toward Hitler. Political cartoons often showed him
carrying an umbrella.

AMANDA: Is there a moon this evening?

TOM: It's rising over Garfinkel's Delicatessen.

AMANDA: So it is! A little silver slipper of a moon. Have you made a wish on it yet?

15   TOM: Um-hum.

AMANDA: What did you wish for?

TOM: That's a secret.

AMANDA: A secret, huh? Well, I won't tell mine either. I will be just as mysterious as you.

TOM: I bet I can guess what yours is.

20   AMANDA: Is my head so transparent?

TOM: You're not a sphinx.

AMANDA: No, I don't have secrets. I'll tell you what I wished for on the moon. Success and happiness for my precious children! I wish for that whenever there's a moon, and when there isn't a moon, I wish for it, too.

TOM: I thought perhaps you wished for a gentleman caller.

AMANDA: Why do you say that?

25   TOM: Don't you remember asking me to fetch one?

AMANDA: I remember suggesting that it would be nice for your sister if you brought home some nice young man from the warehouse. I think I've made that suggestion more than once.

TOM: Yes, you have made it repeatedly.

AMANDA: Well?

30   TOM: We are going to have one.

AMANDA: What?

TOM: A gentleman caller!

The Annunciation Is Celebrated With Music.

Amanda rises.

Image On Screen: Caller With Bouquet.

AMANDA: You mean you have asked some nice young man to come over?

TOM: Yep. I've asked him to dinner.

35   AMANDA: You really did?

TOM: I did!

AMANDA: You did, and did he —*accept?*

TOM: He did!

AMANDA: Well, well — well, well! That's —lovely!

40   TOM: I thought that you would be pleased.

AMANDA: It's definite, then?

TOM: Very definite.

AMANDA: Soon?

TOM: Very soon.

45   AMANDA: For heaven's sake, stop putting on and tell me some things, will you?

TOM: What things do you want me to tell you?

AMANDA: Naturally I would like to know when he's *coming!*

TOM: He's coming tomorrow.

AMANDA: *Tomorrow?*

TOM: Yep. Tomorrow. 50

AMANDA: But, Tom!

TOM: Yes, Mother?

AMANDA: Tomorrow gives me no time!

TOM: Time for what?

AMANDA: Preparations! Why didn't you phone me at once, as soon as you 55
asked him, the minute that he accepted? Then, don't you see, I could have
been getting ready!

TOM: You don't have to make any fuss.

AMANDA: Oh, Tom, Tom, Tom, of course I have to make a fuss! I want things
nice, not sloppy! Not thrown together. I'll certainly have to do some fast
thinking, won't I?

TOM: I don't see why you have to think at all.

AMANDA: You just don't know. We can't have a gentleman caller in a pig-sty!
All my wedding silver has to be polished, the monogrammed table linen
ought to be laundered! The windows have to be washed and fresh curtains
put up. And how about clothes? We have to *wear* something, don't we?

TOM: Mother, this boy is no one to make a fuss over! 60

AMANDA: Do you realize he's the first young man we've introduced to your sister? It's terrible, dreadful, disgraceful that poor little sister has never received
a single gentleman caller! Tom, come inside! (*She opens the screen door.*)

TOM: What for?

AMANDA: I want to ask you some things.

TOM: If you're going to make such a fuss, I'll call it off, I'll tell him not to come.

AMANDA: You certainly won't do anything of the kind. Nothing offends people 65
worse than broken engagements. It simply means I'll have to work like a
Turk! We won't be brilliant, but we'll pass inspection. Come on inside.
(*Tom follows, groaning.*) Sit down.

TOM: Any particular place you would like me to sit?

AMANDA: Thank heavens I've got that new sofa! I'm also making payments
on a floor lamp I'll have sent out! And put the chintz covers on, they'll
brighten things up! Of course I'd hoped to have these walls re-papered. . . .
What is the young man's name?

TOM: His name is O'Connor.

AMANDA: That, of course, means fish — tomorrow is Friday! I'll have that
salmon loaf — with Durkee's dressing! What does he do? He works at the
warehouse?

TOM: Of course! How else would I— 70

AMANDA: Tom, he — doesn't drink?

TOM: Why do you ask me that?

AMANDA: Your father *did!*

TOM: Don't get started on that!

AMANDA: He *does* drink, then? 75

TOM: Not that I know of!

AMANDA: Make sure, be certain! The last thing I want for my daughter's a boy who drinks!

TOM: Aren't you being a little premature? Mr. O'Connor has not yet appeared on the scene!

AMANDA: But will tomorrow. To meet your sister, and what do I know about his character? Nothing! Old maids are better off than wives of drunkards!

80 TOM: Oh, my God!

AMANDA: Be still!

TOM: (*leaning forward to whisper*) Lots of fellows meet girls whom they don't marry!

AMANDA: Oh, talk sensibly, Tom — and don't be sarcastic! (*She has gotten a hairbrush.*)

TOM: What are you doing?

85 AMANDA: I'm brushing that cow-lick down! What is this young man's position at the warehouse?

TOM: (*submitting grimly to the brush and the interrogation*) This young man's position is that of a shipping clerk, Mother.

AMANDA: Sounds to me like a fairly responsible job, the sort of a job *you* would be in if you just had more *get-up*. What is his salary? Have you got any idea?

TOM: I would judge it to be approximately eighty-five dollars a month.

AMANDA: Well — not princely, but —

90 TOM: Twenty more than I make.

AMANDA: Yes, how well I know! But for a family man, eighty-five dollars a month is not much more than you can just get by on. . . .

TOM: Yes, but Mr. O'Connor is not a family man.

AMANDA: He might be, mightn't he? Some time in the future?

TOM: I see. Plans and provisions.

95 AMANDA: You are the only young man that I know of who ignores the fact that the future becomes the present, the present the past, and the past turns into everlasting regret if you don't plan for it!

TOM: I will think that over and see what I can make of it.

AMANDA: Don't be supercilious with your mother! Tell me some more about this — what do you call him?

TOM: James D. O'Connor. The D. is for Delaney.

AMANDA: Irish on *both* sides! *Gracious!* And doesn't drink?

100 TOM: Shall I call him up and ask him right this minute?

AMANDA: The only way to find out about those things is to make discreet inquiries at the proper moment. When I was a girl in Blue Mountain and it was suspected that a young man drank, the girl whose attentions he had been receiving, if any girl *was*, would sometimes speak to the minister of his church, or rather her father would if her father was living, and sort of feel him out on the young man's character. That is the way such things are discreetly handled to keep a young woman from making a tragic mistake!

TOM: Then how did you happen to make a tragic mistake?

AMANDA: That innocent look of your father's had everyone fooled! He smiled— the world was *enchanted!* No girl can do worse than put herself at the mercy of a handsome appearance! I hope that Mr. O'Connor is not too good-looking.

TOM: No, he's not too good-looking. He's covered with freckles and hasn't too much of a nose.

AMANDA: He's not right-down homely, though? 105

TOM: Not right-down homely. Just medium homely, I'd say.

AMANDA: Character's what to look for in a man.

TOM: That's what I've always said, Mother.

AMANDA: You've never said anything of the kind and I suspect you would never give it a thought.

TOM: Don't be suspicious of me. 110

AMANDA: At least I hope he's the type that's up and coming.

TOM: I think he really goes in for self-improvement.

AMANDA: What reason have you to think so?

TOM: He goes to night school.

AMANDA: (*beaming*) Splendid! What does he do, I mean study? 115

TOM: Radio engineering and public speaking!

AMANDA: Then he has visions of being advanced in the world! Any young man who studies public speaking is aiming to have an executive job some day! And radio engineering? A thing for the future! Both of these facts are very illuminating. Those are the sort of things that a mother should know concerning any young man who comes to call on her daughter. Seriously or — not.

TOM: One little warning. He doesn't know about Laura. I didn't let on that we had dark ulterior motives. I just said, why don't you come have dinner with us? He said okay and that was the whole conversation.

AMANDA: I bet it was! You're eloquent as an oyster. However, he'll know about Laura when he gets here. When he sees how lovely and sweet and pretty she is, he'll thank his lucky stars he was asked to dinner.

TOM: Mother, you mustn't expect too much of Laura. 120

AMANDA: What do you mean?

TOM: Laura seems all those things to you and me because she's ours and we love her. We don't even notice she's crippled any more.

AMANDA: Don't say crippled! You know that I never allow that word to be used!

TOM: But face facts, Mother. She is and — that's not all—

AMANDA: What do you mean "not all"? 125

TOM: Laura is very different from other girls.

AMANDA: I think the difference is all to her advantage.

TOM: Not quite all — in the eyes of others — strangers — she's terribly shy and lives in a world of her own and those things make her seem a little peculiar to people outside the house.

AMANDA: Don't say peculiar.

TOM: Face the facts. She is. 130

The Dance-Hall Music Changes To A Tango That Has A Minor And Somewhat Ominous Tone.

AMANDA: In what way is she peculiar — may I ask?

TOM: *(gently)* She lives in a world of her own — a world of — little glass ornaments, Mother. . . . *(Gets up. Amanda remains holding brush, looking at him, troubled.)* She plays old phonograph records and — that's about all — *(He glances at himself in the mirror and crosses to door.)*

AMANDA: *(sharply)* Where are you going?

TOM: I'm going to the movies. *(Out screen door.)*

135 **AMANDA:** Not to the movies, every night to the movies! *(Follows quickly to screen door.)* I don't believe you always go to the movies! *(He is gone. Amanda looks worriedly after him for a moment. Then vitality and optimism return and she turns from the door. Crossing to portieres.)* Laura! Laura! *(Laura answers from kitchenette.)*

LAURA: Yes, Mother.

AMANDA: Let those dishes go and come in front! *(Laura appears with dish towel. Gaily.)* Laura, come here and make a wish on the moon!

LAURA: *(entering)* Moon — moon?

AMANDA: A little silver slipper of a moon. Look over your left shoulder, Laura, and make a wish! *(Laura looks faintly puzzled as if called out of sleep. Amanda seizes her shoulders and turns her at an angle by the door.)* Now! Now, darling, *wish!*

140 **LAURA:** What shall I wish for, Mother?

AMANDA: *(her voice trembling and her eyes suddenly filling with tears)* Happiness! Good Fortune!

The violin rises and the stage dims out.

SCENE 6

Image: High-School Hero.

TOM: And so the following evening I brought Jim home to dinner. I had known Jim slightly in high school. In high school Jim was a hero. He had tremendous Irish good nature and vitality with the scrubbed and polished look of white chinaware. He seemed to move in a continual spotlight. He was a star in basketball, captain of the debating club, president of the senior class and the glee club and he sang the male lead in the annual light operas. He was always running or bounding, never just walking. He seemed always at the point of defeating the law of gravity. He was shooting with such velocity through his adolescence that you would logically expect him to arrive at nothing short of the White House by the time he was thirty. But Jim apparently ran into more interference after his graduation from Soldan. His speed had definitely slowed. Six years after he left high school he was holding a job that wasn't much better than mine.

Image: Clerk.

He was the only one at the warehouse with whom I was on friendly terms. I was valuable to him as someone who could remember his former glory, who had seen him win basketball games and the silver cup in debating. He knew of my secret practice of retiring to a cabinet of the washroom to work on poems when business was slack in the warehouse. He called me Shakespeare. And while the other boys in the warehouse regarded me with suspicious hostility, Jim took a humorous attitude toward me. Gradually his attitude affected the others, their hostility wore off and they also began to smile at me as people smile at an oddly fashioned dog who trots across their path at some distance.

I knew that Jim and Laura had known each other at Soldan, and I had heard Laura speak admiringly of his voice. I didn't know if Jim remembered her or not. In high school Laura had been as unobtrusive as Jim had been astonishing. If he did remember Laura, it was not as my sister, for when I asked him to dinner, he grinned and said, "You know, Shakespeare, I never thought of you as having folks!" He was about to discover that I did. . . .

Light Up Stage.

Legend On Screen: "The Accent Of A Coming Foot."

Friday evening. It is about five o'clock of a late spring evening which comes "scattering poems in the sky."

A delicate lemony light is in the Wingfield apartment.

Amanda has worked like a Turk in preparation for the gentleman caller. The results are astonishing. The new floor lamp with its rose-silk shade is in place, a colored paper lantern conceals the broken light fixture in the ceiling, new billowing white curtains are at the windows, chintz covers are on chairs and sofa, a pair of new sofa pillows make their initial appearance.

Open boxes and tissue paper are scattered on the floor.

Laura stands in the middle with lifted arms while Amanda crouches before her, adjusting the hem of the new dress, devout and ritualistic. The dress is colored and designed by memory. The arrangement of Laura's hair is changed; it is softer and more becoming. A fragile, unearthly prettiness has come out in Laura: she is like a piece of translucent glass touched by light, given a momentary radiance, not actual, not lasting.

AMANDA: *(impatiently)* Why are you trembling?
LAURA: Mother, you've made me so nervous!
AMANDA: How have I made you nervous?
LAURA: By all this fuss! You make it seem so important!
AMANDA: I don't understand you, Laura. You couldn't be satisfied with just sitting home, and yet whenever I try to arrange something for you, you seem to resist it. *(She gets up.)* Now take a look at yourself. No, wait! Wait just a moment — I have an idea!
LAURA: What is it now?

Amanda produces two powder puffs which she wraps in handkerchiefs and stuffs in Laura's bosom.

LAURA: Mother, what are you doing?

AMANDA: They call them "Gay Deceivers"!

10 LAURA: I won't wear them!

AMANDA: You will!

LAURA: Why should I?

AMANDA: Because, to be painfully honest, your chest is flat.

LAURA: You make it seem like we were setting a trap.

15 AMANDA: All pretty girls are a trap, a pretty trap, and men expect them to be. (*Legend: "A Pretty Trap."*) Now look at yourself, young lady. This is the prettiest you will ever be! I've got to fix myself now! You're going to be surprised by your mother's appearance! (*She crosses through portieres, humming gaily.*)

Laura moves slowly to the long mirror and stares solemnly at herself.

A wind blows the white curtains inward in a slow, graceful motion and with a faint, sorrowful sighing.

AMANDA: (*offstage*) It isn't dark enough yet. (*She turns slowly before the mirror with a troubled look.*)

Legend On Screen: "This Is My Sister: Celebrate Her With Strings!" Music.

AMANDA: (*laughing, off*) I'm going to show you something. I'm going to make a spectacular appearance!

LAURA: What is it, Mother?

AMANDA: Possess your soul in patience — you will see! Something I've resurrected from that old trunk! Styles haven't changed so terribly much after all. . . . (*She parts the portieres.*) Now just look at your mother! (*She wears a girlish frock of yellowed voile with a blue silk sash. She carries a bunch of jonquils — the legend of her youth is nearly revived. Feverishly.*) This is the dress in which I led the cotillion. Won the cakewalk twice at Sunset Hill, wore one spring to the Governor's ball in Jackson! See how I sashayed around the ballroom, Laura? (*She raises her skirt and does a mincing step around the room.*) I wore it on Sundays for my gentlemen callers! I had it on the day I met your father — I had malaria fever all that spring. The change of climate from East Tennessee to the Delta — weakened resistance — I had a little temperature all the time — not enough to be serious — just enough to make me restless and giddy! Invitations poured in — parties all over the Delta! — "Stay in bed," said Mother, "you have fever!" — but I just wouldn't. — I took quinine but kept on going, going! — Evenings, dances! — Afternoons, long, long rides! Picnics — lovely! — So lovely, that country in May. All lacy with dogwood, literally flooded with jonquils! — That was the spring I had the craze for jonquils. Jonquils became an absolute obsession. Mother said, "Honey, there's no more room for jonquils." And still I kept bringing in more jonquils. Whenever, wherever I saw them, I'd say, "Stop! Stop! I see jonquils!" I made the young men help me gather the jonquils! It was a joke, Amanda and her jonquils! Finally there were no more vases to hold them, every available space was filled with jonquils. No vases to hold them? All right, I'll hold them myself! And then I — (*She stops in front of the picture.*) (*Music*) met your father! Malaria fever and jonquils and then — this — boy. . . . (*She switches on the rose-colored lamp.*) I hope they get here before it starts to rain. (*She crosses upstage and places the jonquils in bowl on table.*) I gave your brother a little extra change so he and Mr. O'Connor could take the service car home.

LAURA: (*with altered look*) What did you say his name was?   20
AMANDA: O'Connor.
LAURA: What is his first name?
AMANDA: I don't remember. Oh, yes, I do. It was — Jim!

Laura sways slightly and catches hold of a chair.

Legend On Screen: "Not Jim!"

LAURA: (*faintly*) Not — Jim!
AMANDA: Yes, that was it, it was Jim! I've never known a Jim that wasn't nice!   25

Music: Ominous.

LAURA: Are you sure his name is Jim O'Connor?
AMANDA: Yes. Why?
LAURA: Is he the one that Tom used to know in high school?
AMANDA: He didn't say so. I think he just got to know him at the warehouse.
LAURA: There was a Jim O'Connor we both knew in high school — (*Then,*   30
    with effort.) If that is the one that Tom is bringing to dinner — you'll have
    to excuse me, I won't come to the table.
AMANDA: What sort of nonsense is this?
LAURA: You asked me once if I'd ever liked a boy. Don't you remember I
    showed you this boy's picture?
AMANDA: You mean the boy you showed me in the year book?
LAURA: Yes, that boy.
AMANDA: Laura, Laura, were you in love with that boy?   35
LAURA: I don't know, Mother. All I know is I couldn't sit at the table if it
    was him!
AMANDA: It won't be him! It isn't the least bit likely. But whether it is or not,
    you will come to the table. You will not be excused.
LAURA: I'll have to be, Mother.
AMANDA: I don't intend to humor your silliness, Laura. I've had too much
    from you and your brother, both! So just sit down and compose yourself till
    they come. Tom has forgotten his key so you'll have to let them in, when
    they arrive.
LAURA: (*panicky*) Oh, Mother — *you* answer the door!   40
AMANDA: (*lightly*) I'll be in the kitchen — busy!
LAURA: Oh, Mother, please answer the door, don't make me do it!
AMANDA: (*crossing into kitchenette*) I've got to fix the dressing for the salmon.
    Fuss, fuss — silliness! — over a gentleman caller!

Door swings shut. Laura is left alone.

Legend: "Terror!"

She utters a low moan and turns off the lamp — sits stiffly on the edge of the sofa, knotting her fingers together.

Legend On Screen: "The Opening Of A Door!"

Tom and Jim appear on the fire-escape steps and climb to landing. Hearing their approach, Laura rises with a panicky gesture. She retreats to the portieres.
    The doorbell. Laura catches her breath and touches her throat. Low drums.

AMANDA: *(calling)* Laura, sweetheart! The door!

Laura stares at it without moving.

45   JIM: I think we just beat the rain.
    TOM: Uh-huh. *(He rings again, nervously. Jim whistles and fishes for a cigarette.)*
    AMANDA: *(very, very gaily)* Laura, that is your brother and Mr. O'Connor!
        Will you let them in, darling?

Laura crosses toward kitchenette door.

LAURA: *(breathlessly)* Mother — you go to the door!

Amanda steps out of kitchenette and stares furiously at Laura. She points imperiously at the door.

LAURA: Please, please!
50   AMANDA: *(in a fierce whisper)* What is the matter with you, you silly thing?
    LAURA: *(desperately)* Please, you answer it, *please!*
    AMANDA: I told you I wasn't going to humor you, Laura. Why have you chosen this moment to lose your mind?
    LAURA: Please, please, please, you go!
    AMANDA: You'll have to go to the door because I can't!
55   LAURA: *(despairingly)* I can't either!
    AMANDA: Why?
    LAURA: I'm *sick!*
    AMANDA: I'm sick, too — of your nonsense! Why can't you and your brother be normal people? Fantastic whims and behavior! *(Tom gives a long ring.)* Preposterous goings on! Can you give me one reason — *(Calls out lyrically.)* COMING! JUST ONE SECOND! — why should you be afraid to open a door? Now you answer it, Laura!
    LAURA: Oh, oh, oh . . . *(She returns through the portieres. Darts to the Victrola and winds it frantically and turns it on.)*
60   AMANDA: Laura Wingfield, you march right to that door!
    LAURA: Yes — yes, Mother!

A faraway, scratchy rendition of "Dardanella" softens the air and gives her strength to move through it. She slips to the door and draws it cautiously open. Tom enters with the caller, Jim O'Connor.

TOM: Laura, this is Jim. Jim, this is my sister, Laura.

JIM: *(stepping inside)* I didn't know that Shakespeare had a sister!

LAURA: *(retreating stiff and trembling from the door)* How — how do you do?

JIM: *(heartily extending his hand)* Okay! 65

Laura touches it hesitantly with hers.

JIM: Your hand's *cold*, Laura!

LAURA: Yes, well — I've been playing the Victrola. . . .

JIM: Must have been playing classical music on it! You ought to play a little hot swing music to warm you up!

LAURA: Excuse me — I haven't finished playing the Victrola. . . .

She turns awkwardly and hurries into the front room. She pauses a second by the Victrola. Then catches her breath and darts through the portieres like a frightened deer.

JIM: *(grinning)* What was the matter? 70

TOM: Oh — with Laura? Laura is — terribly shy.

JIM: Shy, huh? It's unusual to meet a shy girl nowadays. I don't believe you ever mentioned you had a sister.

TOM: Well, now you know. I have one. Here is the *Post Dispatch*. You want a piece of it?

JIM: Uh-huh.

TOM: What piece? The comics? 75

JIM: Sports! *(Glances at it.)* Ole Dizzy Dean° is on his bad behavior.

TOM: *(disinterested)* Yeah? *(Lights cigarette and crosses back to fire-escape door.)*

JIM: Where are *you* going?

TOM: I'm going out on the terrace.

JIM: *(goes after him)* You know, Shakespeare — I'm going to sell you a bill of goods! 80

TOM: What goods?

JIM: A course I'm taking.

TOM: Huh?

JIM: In public speaking! You and me, we're not the warehouse type.

TOM: Thanks — that's good news. But what has public speaking got to do with it? 85

JIM: It fits you for — executive positions!

TOM: Awww.

JIM: I tell you it's done a helluva lot for me.

Image: Executive At Desk.

TOM: In what respect?

°*Dizzy Dean:* Jay Hanna Dean (1910–1974), American baseball player who pitched for the St. Louis Cardinals (1930, 1932–1937), winning 30 games in 1934 and averaging 24 wins in his first five full seasons. From 1938 to 1941, he played for the Chicago Cubs.

90 JIM: In every! Ask yourself what is the difference between you an' me and men in the office down front? Brains?— No! — Ability?— No! Then what? Just one little thing—

TOM: What is that one little thing?

JIM: Primarily it amounts to — social poise! Being able to square up to people and hold your own on any social level!

AMANDA: *(offstage)* Tom?

TOM: Yes, Mother?

95 AMANDA: Is that you and Mr. O'Connor?

TOM: Yes, Mother.

AMANDA: Well, you just make yourselves comfortable in there.

TOM: Yes, Mother.

AMANDA: Ask Mr. O'Connor if he would like to wash his hands.

100 JIM: Aw — no — thank you — I took care of that at the warehouse. Tom—

TOM: Yes?

JIM: Mr. Mendoza was speaking to me about you.

TOM: Favorably?

JIM: What do you think?

105 TOM: Well—

JIM: You're going to be out of a job if you don't wake up.

TOM: I am waking up—

JIM: You show no signs.

TOM: The signs are interior.

Image On Screen: The Sailing Vessel With Jolly Roger Again.

110 TOM: I'm planning to change. (*He leans over the rail speaking with quiet exhilaration. The incandescent marquees and signs of the first-run movie houses light his face from across the alley. He looks like a voyager.*) I'm right at the point of committing myself to a future that doesn't include the warehouse and Mr. Mendoza or even a night-school course in public speaking.

JIM: What are you gassing about?

TOM: I'm tired of the movies.

JIM: Movies!

TOM: Yes, movies! Look at them — (*A wave toward the marvels of Grand Avenue.*) All of those glamorous people —having adventures —hogging it all, gobbling the whole thing up! You know what happens? People go to the *movies instead of moving!* Hollywood characters are supposed to have all the adventures for everybody in America, while everybody in America sits in a dark room and watches them have them! Yes, until there's a war. That's when adventure becomes available to the masses! *Everyone's* dish, not only Gable's! Then the people in the dark room come out of the dark room to have some adventures themselves — Goody, goody — It's our turn now, to go to the South Sea Island — to make a safari — to be exotic, far-off — But I'm not patient. I don't want to wait till then. I'm tired of the *movies* and I am *about* to *move!*

115 JIM: (*incredulously*) Move?

TOM: Yes.

JIM: When?

TOM: Soon!

JIM: Where? Where?

Theme three music seems to answer the question, while Tom thinks it over. He searches among his pockets.

TOM: I'm starting to boil inside. I know I seem dreary, but inside — well, I'm   120
boiling! Whenever I pick up a shoe, I shudder a little thinking how short
life is and what I am doing! —Whatever that means. I know it doesn't
mean shoes — except as something to wear on a traveler's feet! *(Finds
paper.)* Look—

JIM: What?

TOM: I'm a member.

JIM: *(reading)* The Union of Merchant Seamen.

TOM: I paid my dues this month, instead of the light bill.

JIM: You will regret it when they turn the lights off.   125

TOM: I won't be here.

JIM: How about your mother?

TOM: I'm like my father. The bastard son of a bastard! See how he grins? And
he's been absent going on sixteen years!

JIM: You're just talking, you drip. How does your mother feel about it?

TOM: Shhh — Here comes Mother! Mother is not acquainted with my plans!   130

AMANDA: *(enters portieres)* Where are you all?

TOM: On the terrace, Mother.

*They start inside. She advances to them. Tom is distinctly shocked at her appearance.
Even Jim blinks a little. He is making his first contact with girlish Southern vivacity and
in spite of the night-school course in public speaking is somewhat thrown off the beam by
the unexpected outlay of social charm.*

*Certain responses are attempted by Jim but are swept aside by Amanda's gay laugh-
ter and chatter. Tom is embarrassed but after the first shock Jim reacts very warmly.
Grins and chuckles, is altogether won over.*

Image: Amanda As A Girl.

AMANDA: *(coyly smiling, shaking her girlish ringlets)* Well, well, well, so this is
Mr. O'Connor. Introductions entirely unnecessary. I've heard so much
about you from my boy. I finally said to him, Tom — good gracious! — why
don't you bring this paragon to supper? I'd like to meet this nice young man
at the warehouse! — Instead of just hearing him sing your praises so much!
I don't know why my son is so stand-offish — that's not Southern behavior!
Let's sit down and — I think we could stand a little more air in here! Tom,
leave the door open. I felt a nice fresh breeze a moment ago. Where has it
gone? Mmm, so warm already! And not quite summer, even. We're going to
burn up when summer really gets started. However, we're having — we're
having a very light supper. I think light things are better fo' this time of
year. The same as light clothes are. Light clothes an' light food are what

warm weather calls fo'. You know our blood gets so thick during th'
winter — it takes a while fo' us to *adjust* ou'selves! — when the season
changes . . . It's come so quick this year. I wasn't prepared. All of a
sudden — heavens! Already summer! — I ran to the trunk an' pulled out
this light dress — Terribly old! Historical almost! But feels so good — so
good an' co-ol, y'know. . . .

TOM: Mother —

135   AMANDA: Yes, honey?

TOM: How about — supper?

AMANDA: Honey, you go ask Sister if supper is ready! You know that Sister is
in full charge of supper! Tell her you hungry boys are waiting for it.
(*To Jim.*) Have you met Laura?

JIM: She —

AMANDA: Let you in? Oh, good, you've met already! It's rare for a girl as sweet
an' pretty as Laura to be domestic! But Laura is, thank heavens, not only
pretty but also very domestic. I'm not at all. I never was a bit. I never could
make a thing but angel-food cake. Well, in the South we had so many servants. Gone, gone, gone. All vestiges of gracious living! Gone completely! I
wasn't prepared for what the future brought me. All of my gentlemen callers
were sons of planters and so of course I assumed that I would be married to one
and raise my family on a large piece of land with plenty of servants. But man
proposes — and woman accepts the proposal! — To vary that old, old saying a
little bit — I married no planter! I married a man who worked for the
telephone company! — that gallantly smiling gentleman over there! (*Points to
the picture.*) A telephone man who — fell in love with long-distance! — Now
he travels and I don't even know where! — But what am I going on for about
my — tribulations? Tell me yours — I hope you don't have any! Tom?

140   TOM: (*returning*) Yes, Mother?

AMANDA: Is supper nearly ready?

TOM: It looks to me like supper is on the table.

AMANDA: Let me look — (*She rises prettily and looks through portieres.*) Oh,
lovely — But where is Sister?

TOM: Laura is not feeling well and says that she thinks she'd better not come
to the table.

145   AMANDA: What? — Nonsense! — Laura? Oh, Laura!

LAURA: (*offstage, faintly*) Yes, Mother.

AMANDA: You really must come to the table. We won't be seated until you
come to the table! Come in, Mr. O'Connor. You sit over there and I'll —
Laura? Laura Wingfield! You're keeping us waiting, honey! We can't say
grace until you come to the table!

*The back door is pushed weakly open and Laura comes in. She is obviously quite faint,
her lips trembling, her eyes wide and staring. She moves unsteadily toward the table.*

Legend: "Terror!"

*Outside a summer storm is coming abruptly. The white curtains billow inward at the
windows and there is a sorrowful murmur and deep blue dusk.*

Laura suddenly stumbles — She catches at a chair with a faint moan.

TOM: Laura!

AMANDA: Laura! *(There is a clap of thunder.) (Legend: "Ah!") (Despairingly.)* Why, Laura, you are sick, darling! Tom, help your sister into the living room, dear! Sit in the living room, Laura — rest on the sofa. Well! *(To the gentleman caller.)* Standing over the hot stove made her ill! — I told her that it was just too warm this evening, but — *(Tom comes back in. Laura is on the sofa.)* Is Laura all right now?

TOM: Yes.

AMANDA: What *is* that? Rain? A nice cool rain has come up! *(She gives the gentleman caller a frightened look.)* I think we may — have grace — now . . . *(Tom looks at her stupidly.)* Tom, honey — you say grace!

TOM: Oh . . . "For these and all thy mercies —" *(They bow their heads, Amanda stealing a nervous glance at Jim. In the living room Laura, stretched on the sofa, clenches her hand to her lips, to hold back a shuddering sob.)* God's Holy Name be praised—

The Scene Dims Out.

150

SCENE 7

A Souvenir.

Half an hour later. Dinner is just being finished in the upstage area which is concealed by the drawn portieres.

As the curtain rises Laura is still huddled upon the sofa, her feet drawn under her, her head resting on a pale blue pillow, her eyes wide and mysteriously watchful. The new floor lamp with its shade of rose-colored silk gives a soft, becoming light to her face, bringing out the fragile, unearthly prettiness which usually escapes attention. There is a steady murmur of rain, but it is slackening and stops soon after the scene begins; the air outside becomes pale and luminous as the moon breaks out.

A moment after the curtain rises, the lights in both rooms flicker and go out.

JIM: Hey, there, Mr. Light Bulb!

Amanda laughs nervously.

Legend: "Suspension Of A Public Service."

AMANDA: Where was Moses when the lights went out? Ha-ha. Do you know the answer to that one, Mr. O'Connor?

JIM: No, Ma'am, what's the answer?

AMANDA: In the dark! *(Jim laughs appreciatively.)* Everybody sit still. I'll light the candles. Isn't it lucky we have them on the table? Where's a match? Which of you gentlemen can provide a match?

JIM: Here.

AMANDA: Thank you, sir.

JIM: Not at all, Ma'am!

5

AMANDA: I guess the fuse has burnt out. Mr. O'Connor, can you tell a burnt-out fuse? I know I can't and Tom is a total loss when it comes to mechanics. (*Sound: Getting Up: Voices Recede A Little To Kitchenette.*) Oh, be careful you don't bump into something. We don't want our gentleman caller to break his neck. Now wouldn't that be a fine howdy-do?

JIM: Ha-ha! Where is the fuse-box?

10 AMANDA: Right here next to the stove. Can you see anything?

JIM: Just a minute.

AMANDA: Isn't electricity a mysterious thing? Wasn't it Benjamin Franklin who tied a key to a kite? We live in such a mysterious universe, don't we? Some people say that science clears up all the mysteries for us. In my opinion it only creates more! Have you found it yet?

JIM: No, Ma'am. All these fuses look okay to me.

AMANDA: Tom!

15 TOM: Yes, Mother?

AMANDA: That light bill I gave you several days ago. The one I told you we got the notices about?

TOM: Oh.—Yeah.

Legend: "Ha!"

AMANDA: You didn't neglect to pay it by any chance?

TOM: Why, I—

20 AMANDA: Didn't! I might have known it!

JIM: Shakespeare probably wrote a poem on that light bill, Mrs. Wingfield.

AMANDA: I might have known better than to trust him with it! There's such a high price for negligence in this world!

JIM: Maybe the poem will win a ten-dollar prize.

AMANDA: We'll just have to spend the remainder of the evening in the nineteenth century, before Mr. Edison made the Mazda lamp!

25 JIM: Candlelight is my favorite kind of light.

AMANDA: That shows you're romantic! But that's no excuse for Tom. Well, we got through dinner. Very considerate of them to let us get through dinner before they plunged us into everlasting darkness, wasn't it, Mr. O'Connor?

JIM: Ha-ha!

AMANDA: Tom, as a penalty for your carelessness you can help me with the dishes.

JIM: Let me give you a hand.

30 AMANDA: Indeed you will not!

JIM: I ought to be good for something.

AMANDA: Good for something? (*Her tone is rhapsodic.*) You? Why, Mr. O'Connor, nobody, *nobody's* given me this much entertainment in years — as you have!

JIM: Aw, now, Mrs. Wingfield!

AMANDA: I'm not exaggerating, not one bit! But Sister is all by her lonesome. You go keep her company in the parlor! I'll give you this lovely old candelabrum that used to be on the altar at the church of the Heavenly Rest. It was melted a little out of shape when the church burnt down. Lightning struck it one spring. Gypsy Jones was holding a revival at the time and he intimated that the church was destroyed because the Episcopalians gave card parties.

JIM: Ha-ha.

AMANDA: And how about coaxing Sister to drink a little wine? I think it would be good for her! Can you carry both at once?

JIM: Sure. I'm Superman!

AMANDA: Now, Thomas, get into this apron!

The door of kitchenette swings closed on Amanda's gay laughter; the flickering light approaches the portieres.

Laura sits up nervously as he enters. Her speech at first is low and breathless from the almost intolerable strain of being alone with a stranger.

The Legend: "I Don't Suppose You Remember Me At All!"

In her first speeches in this scene, before Jim's warmth overcomes her paralyzing shyness, Laura's voice is thin and breathless as though she has run up a steep flight of stairs.

Jim's attitude is gently humorous. In playing this scene it should be stressed that while the incident is apparently unimportant, it is to Laura the climax of her secret life.

JIM: Hello, there, Laura.

LAURA: *(faintly)* Hello. *(She clears her throat.)* 40

JIM: How are you feeling now? Better?

LAURA: Yes. Yes, thank you.

JIM: This is for you. A little dandelion wine. *(He extends it toward her with extravagant gallantry.)*

LAURA: Thank you.

JIM: Drink it — but don't get drunk! *(He laughs heartily. Laura takes the glass 45 uncertainly; laughs shyly.)* Where shall I set the candles?

LAURA: Oh — oh, anywhere . . .

JIM: How about here on the floor? Any objections?

LAURA: No.

JIM: I'll spread a newspaper under to catch the drippings. I like to sit on the floor. Mind if I do?

LAURA: Oh, no. 50

JIM: Give me a pillow?

LAURA: What?

JIM: A pillow!

LAURA: Oh . . . *(Hands him one quickly.)*

JIM: How about you? Don't you like to sit on the floor? 55

LAURA: Oh — yes.

JIM: Why don't you, then?

LAURA: I — will.

JIM: Take a pillow! *(Laura does. Sits on the other side of the candelabrum. Jim crosses his legs and smiles engagingly at her.)* I can't hardly see you sitting way over there.

60   LAURA: I can — see you.

JIM: I know, but that's not fair, I'm in the limelight. (*Laura moves her pillow closer.*) Good! Now I can see you! Comfortable?

LAURA: Yes.

JIM: So am I. Comfortable as a cow. Will you have some gum?

LAURA: No, thank you.

65   JIM: I think that I will indulge, with your permission. (*Musingly unwraps it and holds it up.*) Think of the fortune made by the guy that invented the first piece of chewing gum. Amazing, huh? The Wrigley Building is one of the sights of Chicago. — I saw it summer before last when I went up to the Century of Progress. Did you take in the Century of Progress?

LAURA: No, I didn't.

JIM: Well, it was quite a wonderful exposition. What impressed me most was the Hall of Science. Gives you an idea of what the future will be in America, even more wonderful than the present time is! (*Pause. Smiling at her.*) Your brother tells me you're shy. Is that right, Laura?

LAURA: I — don't know.

JIM: I judge you to be an old-fashioned type of girl. Well, I think that's a pretty good type to be. Hope you don't think I'm being too personal — do you?

70   LAURA: (*hastily, out of embarrassment*) I believe I *will* take a piece of gum, if you — don't mind. (*Clearing her throat.*) Mr. O'Connor, have you — kept up with your singing?

JIM: Singing? Me?

LAURA: Yes. I remember what a beautiful voice you had.

JIM: When did you hear me sing?

Voice Offstage In The Pause.

VOICE (*offstage*):

> O blow, ye winds, heigh-ho,
> A-roving I will go!
> I'm off to my love
> With a boxing glove —
> Ten thousand miles away!

JIM: You say you've heard me sing?

75   LAURA: Oh, yes! Yes, very often . . . I — don't suppose you remember me — at all?

JIM: (*smiling doubtfully*) You know I have an idea I've seen you before. I had that idea soon as you opened the door. It seemed almost like I was about to remember your name. But the name that I started to call you — wasn't a name! And so I stopped myself before I said it.

LAURA: Wasn't it — Blue Roses?

JIM: (*springs up, grinning*) Blue Roses! My gosh, yes — Blue Roses! That's what I had on my tongue when you opened the door! Isn't it funny what tricks your memory plays? I didn't connect you with the high school somehow or other. But that's where it was; it was high school. I didn't even know you were Shakespeare's sister! Gosh, I'm sorry.

LAURA: I didn't expect you to. You — barely knew me!

JIM: But we did have a speaking acquaintance, huh?   80

LAURA: Yes, we — spoke to each other.

JIM: When did you recognize me?

LAURA: Oh, right away!

JIM: Soon as I came in the door?

LAURA: When I heard your name I thought it was probably you. I knew that   85
Tom used to know you a little in high school. So when you came in the
door — Well, then I was — sure.

JIM: Why didn't you *say* something, then?

LAURA: *(breathlessly)* I didn't know what to say, I was — too surprised!

JIM: For goodness' sakes! You know, this sure is funny!

LAURA: Yes! Yes, isn't it, though . . .

JIM: Didn't we have a class in something together?   90

LAURA: Yes, we did.

JIM: What class was that?

LAURA: It was — singing — Chorus!

JIM: Aw!

LAURA: I sat across the aisle from you in the Aud.   95

JIM: Aw.

LAURA: Mondays, Wednesdays and Fridays.

JIM: Now I remember — you always came in late.

LAURA: Yes, it was so hard for me, getting upstairs. I had that brace on my
leg — it clumped so loud!

JIM: I never heard any clumping.   100

LAURA: *(wincing at the recollection)* To me it sounded like — thunder!

JIM: Well, well, well. I never even noticed.

LAURA: And everybody was seated before I came in. I had to walk in front of
all those people. My seat was in the back row. I had to go clumping all the
way up the aisle with everyone watching!

JIM: You shouldn't have been self-conscious.

LAURA: I know, but I was. It was always such a relief when the singing started.   105

JIM: Aw, yes, I've placed you now! I used to call you Blue Roses. How was it
that I got started calling you that?

LAURA: I was out of school a little while with pleurosis. When I came back
you asked me what was the matter. I said I had pleurosis — you thought
I said Blue Roses. That's what you always called me after that!

JIM: I hope you didn't mind.

LAURA: Oh, no — I liked it. You see, I wasn't acquainted with many —
people. . . .

JIM: As I remember you sort of stuck by yourself.   110

LAURA: I — I — never had much luck at — making friends.

JIM: I don't see why you wouldn't.

LAURA: Well, I — started out badly.

JIM: You mean being—

LAURA: Yes, it sort of — stood between me —   115

JIM: You shouldn't have let it!

LAURA: I know, but it did, and —

JIM: You were shy with people!

LAURA: I tried not to be but never could —

120   JIM: Overcome it?

LAURA: No, I — I never could!

JIM: I guess being shy is something you have to work out of kind of gradually.

LAURA: (*sorrowfully*) Yes — I guess it —

JIM: Takes time!

125   LAURA: Yes —

JIM: People are not so dreadful when you know them. That's what you have to remember! And everybody has problems, not just you, but practically everybody has got some problems. You think of yourself as having the only problems, as being the only one who is disappointed. But just look around you and you will see lots of people as disappointed as you are. For instance, I hoped when I was going to high school that I would be further along at this time, six years later, than I am now — You remember that wonderful write-up I had in *The Torch*?

LAURA: Yes! (*She rises and crosses to table.*)

JIM: It said I was bound to succeed in anything I went into! (*Laura returns with the annual.*) Holy Jeez! *The Torch*! (*He accepts it reverently. They smile across it with mutual wonder. Laura crouches beside him and they begin to turn through it. Laura's shyness is dissolving in his warmth.*)

130   LAURA: Here you are in *Pirates of Penzance*!

JIM: (*wistfully*) I sang the baritone lead in that operetta.

LAURA: (*rapidly*) So —*beautifully*!

JIM: (*protesting*) Aw —

135   LAURA: Yes, yes — beautifully — beautifully!

JIM: You heard me?

LAURA: All three times!

JIM: No!

LAURA: Yes!

JIM: All three performances?

LAURA: (*looking down*) Yes.

140   JIM: Why?

LAURA: I — wanted to ask you to — autograph my program.

JIM: Why didn't you ask me to?

LAURA: You were always surrounded by your own friends so much that I never had a chance to.

JIM: You should have just —

145   LAURA: Well, I — thought you might think I was —

JIM: Thought I might think you was — what?

LAURA: Oh —

JIM: (*with reflective relish*) I was beleaguered by females in those days.

LAURA: You were terribly popular!

150   JIM: Yeah —

LAURA: You had such a — friendly way —

JIM: I was spoiled in high school.

LAURA: Everybody — liked you!

JIM: Including you?

LAURA: I — yes, I — I did, too — (*She gently closes the book in her lap.*)   155

JIM: Well, well, well! — Give me that program, Laura. (*She hands it to him. He signs it with a flourish.*) There you are — better late than never!

LAURA: Oh, I — what a — surprise!

JIM: My signature isn't worth very much right now. But some day — maybe — it will increase in value! Being disappointed is one thing and being discouraged is something else. I am disappointed but I'm not discouraged. I'm twenty-three years old. How old are you?

LAURA: I'll be twenty-four in June.

JIM: That's not old age!   160

LAURA: No, but —

JIM: You finished high school?

LAURA: (*with difficulty*) I didn't go back.

JIM: You mean you dropped out?

LAURA: I made bad grades in my final examinations. (*She rises and replaces the   165 book and the program. Her voice strained.*) How is — Emily Meisenbach getting along?

JIM: Oh, that kraut-head!

LAURA: Why do you call her that?

JIM: That's what she was.

LAURA: You're not still — going with her?

JIM: I never see her.   170

LAURA: It said in the Personal Section that you were — engaged!

JIM: I know, but I wasn't impressed by that — propaganda!

LAURA: It wasn't — the truth?

JIM: Only in Emily's optimistic opinion!

LAURA: Oh —   175

Legend: "What Have You Done Since High School?"

Jim lights a cigarette and leans indolently back on his elbows smiling at Laura with a warmth and charm which light her inwardly with altar candles. She remains by the table and turns in her hands a piece of glass to cover her tumult.

JIM: (*after several reflective puffs on a cigarette*) What have you done since high school? (*She seems not to hear him.*) Huh? (*Laura looks up.*) I said what have you done since high school, Laura?

LAURA: Nothing much.

JIM: You must have been doing something these six long years.

LAURA: Yes.

JIM: Well, then, such as what?   180

LAURA: I took a business course at business college —

JIM: How did that work out?

LAURA: Well, not very — well — I had to drop out, it gave me — indigestion —

Jim laughs gently.

JIM: What are you doing now?

185 LAURA: I don't do anything — much. Oh, please don't think I sit around doing nothing! My glass collection takes up a good deal of my time. Glass is something you have to take good care of.

JIM: What did you say — about glass?

LAURA: Collection I said — I have one — (*She clears her throat and turns away again, acutely shy.*)

JIM: (*abruptly*) You know what I judge to be the trouble with you? Inferiority complex! Know what that is? That's what they call it when someone low-rates himself! I understand it because I had it, too. Although my case was not so aggravated as yours seems to be. I had it until I took up public speaking, developed my voice, and learned that I had an aptitude for science. Before that time I never thought of myself as being outstanding in any way whatsoever! Now I've never made a regular study of it, but I have a friend who says I can analyze people better than doctors that make a profession of it. I don't claim that to be necessarily true, but I can sure guess a person's psychology, Laura! (*Takes out his gum.*) Excuse me, Laura. I always take it out when the flavor is gone. I'll use this scrap of paper to wrap it in. I know how it is to get it stuck on a shoe. Yep — that's what I judge to be your principal trouble. A lack of confidence in yourself as a person. You don't have the proper amount of faith in yourself. I'm basing that fact on a number of your remarks and also on certain observations I've made. For instance that clumping you thought was so awful in high school. You say that you even dreaded to walk into class. You see what you did? You dropped out of school, you gave up an education because of a clump, which as far as I know was practically nonexistent! A little physical defect is what you have. Hardly noticeable even! Magnified thousands of times by imagination! You know what my strong advice to you is? Think of yourself as *superior* in some way!

LAURA: In what way would I think?

190 JIM: Why, man alive, Laura! Just look about you a little. What do you see? A world full of common people! All of 'em born and all of 'em going to die! Which of them has one-tenth of your good points! Or mine! Or anyone else's, as far as that goes — Gosh! Everybody excels in some one thing. Some in many! (*Unconsciously glances at himself in the mirror.*) All you've got to do is discover in *what*! Take me, for instance. (*He adjusts his tie at the mirror.*) My interest happens to lie in electro-dynamics. I'm taking a course in radio engineering at night school, Laura, on top of a fairly responsible job at the warehouse. I'm taking that course and studying public speaking.

LAURA: Ohhhh.

JIM: Because I believe in the future of television! (*Turning back to her.*) I wish to be ready to go up right along with it. Therefore I'm planning to get in on the ground floor. In fact, I've already made the right connections and all that remains is for the industry itself to get underway! Full steam — (*His eyes are starry.*) *Knowledge*— Zzzzzp! *Money*— Zzzzzzp!—*Power!* That's the cycle democracy is built on! (*His attitude is convincingly dynamic. Laura stares at him, even her shyness eclipsed in her absolute wonder. He suddenly grins.*) I guess you think I think a lot of myself!

LAURA: No — o-o-o, I—

JIM: Now how about you? Isn't there something you take more interest in than anything else?

LAURA: Well, I do — as I said — have my — glass collection—   195

A peal of girlish laughter from the kitchen.

JIM: I'm not right sure I know what you're talking about. What kind of glass is it?

LAURA: Little articles of it, they're ornaments mostly! Most of them are little animals made out of glass, the tiniest little animals in the world. Mother calls them a glass menagerie! Here's an example of one, if you'd like to see it! This one is one of the oldest. It's nearly thirteen. (*He stretches out his hand.*) (*Music: "The Glass Menagerie."*) Oh, be careful — if you breathe, it breaks!

JIM: I'd better not take it. I'm pretty clumsy with things.

LAURA: Go on, I trust you with him! (*Places it in his palm.*) There now — you're holding him gently! Hold him over the light, he loves the light! You see how the light shines through him?

JIM: It sure does shine!   200

LAURA: I shouldn't be partial, but he is my favorite one.

JIM: What kind of a thing is this one supposed to be?

LAURA: Haven't you noticed the single horn on his forehead?

JIM: A unicorn, huh?

LAURA: Mmm-hmmm!   205

JIM: Unicorns, aren't they extinct in the modern world?

LAURA: I know!

JIM: Poor little fellow, he must feel sort of lonesome.

LAURA: (*smiling*) Well, if he does he doesn't complain about it. He stays on a shelf with some horses that don't have horns and all of them seem to get along nicely together.

JIM: How do you know?   210

LAURA: (*lightly*) I haven't heard any arguments among them!

JIM: (*grinning*) No arguments, huh? Well, that's a pretty good sign! Where shall I set him?

LAURA: Put him on the table. They all like a change of scenery once in a while!

JIM: (*stretching*) Well, well, well, well — Look how big my shadow is when I stretch!

LAURA: Oh, oh, yes — it stretches across the ceiling!   215

JIM: (*crossing to door*) I think it's stopped raining. (*Opens fire-escape door.*) Where does the music come from?

LAURA: From the Paradise Dance Hall across the alley.

JIM: How about cutting the rug a little, Miss Wingfield?

LAURA: Oh, I—

220   JIM: Or is your program filled up? Let me have a look at it. (*Grasps imaginary
      card.*) Why, every dance is taken! I'll just have to scratch some out.
      (*Waltz Music: "La Golondrina."*) Ahhh, a waltz! (*He executes some sweeping
      turns by himself, then holds his arms toward Laura.*)

LAURA: (*breathlessly*) I — can't dance!

JIM: There you go, that inferiority stuff!

225   LAURA: I've never danced in my life!

JIM: Come on, try!

LAURA: Oh, but I'd step on you!

JIM: I'm not made out of glass.

LAURA: How — how — how do we start?

JIM: Just leave it to me. You hold your arms out a little.

LAURA: Like this?

230   JIM: A little bit higher. Right. Now don't tighten up, that's the main thing
      about it — relax.

LAURA: (*laughing breathlessly*) It's hard not to.

JIM: Okay.

LAURA: I'm afraid you can't budge me.

235   JIM: What do you bet I can't? (*He swings her into motion.*)

LAURA: Goodness, yes, you can!

JIM: Let yourself go, now, Laura, just let yourself go.

LAURA: I'm—

JIM: Come on!

240   LAURA: Trying!

JIM: Not so stiff — Easy does it!

LAURA: I know but I'm—

JIM: Loosen th' backbone! There now, that's a lot better.

LAURA: Am I?

JIM: Lots, lots better! (*He moves her about the room in a clumsy waltz.*)

245   LAURA: Oh, my!

JIM: Ha-ha!

LAURA: Goodness, yes you can!

JIM: Ha-ha-ha! (*They suddenly bump into the table, Jim stops.*) What did we hit on?

LAURA: Table.

250   JIM: Did something fall off it? I think—

LAURA: Yes.

JIM: I hope that it wasn't the little glass horse with the horn!

LAURA: Yes.

JIM: Aw, aw, aw. Is it broken?

255   LAURA: Now it is just like all the other horses.

JIM: It's lost its—

LAURA: Horn! It doesn't matter. Maybe it's a blessing in disguise.

JIM: You'll never forgive me. I bet that that was your favorite piece of glass.

LAURA: I don't have favorites much. It's no tragedy, Freckles. Glass breaks so
      easily. No matter how careful you are. The traffic jars the shelves and things
      fall off them.

Laura in the arms of the gentleman caller while Tom and Amanda look on in Tennessee Williams's *The Glass Menagerie* presented in 1956 at the Williamstown Theatre festival.

JIM: Still I'm awfully sorry that I was the cause.   260

LAURA: *(smiling)* I'll just imagine he had an operation. The horn was removed to make him feel less — freakish! *(They both laugh.)* Now he will feel more at home with the other horses, the ones that don't have horns . . .

JIM: Ha-ha, that's very funny! *(Suddenly serious.)* I'm glad to see that you have a sense of humor. You know — you're — well — very different! Surprisingly different from anyone else I know! *(His voice becomes soft and hesitant with a genuine feeling.)* Do you mind me telling you that? *(Laura is abashed beyond speech.)* You make me feel sort of — I don't know how to put it! I'm usually pretty good at expressing things, but — This is something that I don't know how to say! *(Laura touches her throat and clears it — turns the broken unicorn in her hands.) (Even softer.)* Has anyone ever told you that you were pretty? *(Pause: Music.) (Laura looks up slowly, with wonder, and shakes her head.)* Well, you are! In a very different way from anyone else. And all the nicer because of the difference, too. *(His voice becomes low and husky. Laura turns away, nearly faint with the novelty of her emotions.)* I wish you were my sister. I'd teach you to have some confidence in yourself. The different people are not like other people, but being different is nothing to be ashamed of. Because other people are not such wonderful people. They're one hundred times one thousand. You're one times one! They walk all over the earth. You just stay here. They're common as — weeds, but — you — well, you're —*Blue Roses!*

Image On Screen: Blue Roses.

Music Changes.

LAURA: But blue is wrong for — roses . . .

JIM: It's right for you — You're — pretty!

LAURA: In what respect am I pretty?

265 **JIM:** In all respects — believe me! Your eyes — your hair — are pretty! Your hands are pretty! (*He catches hold of her hand.*) You think I'm making this up because I'm invited to dinner and have to be nice. Oh, I could do that! I could put on an act for you, Laura, and say lots of things without being very sincere. But this time I am. I'm talking to you sincerely. I happened to notice you had this inferiority complex that keeps you from feeling comfortable with people. Somebody needs to build your confidence up and make you proud instead of shy and turning away and — blushing — Somebody ought to — ought to — *kiss you, Laura!* (*His hand slips slowly up her arm to her shoulder.*) (*Music Swells Tumultuously.*) (*He suddenly turns her about and kisses her on the lips. When he releases her Laura sinks on the sofa with a bright, dazed look. Jim backs away and fishes in his pocket for a cigarette.*) (*Legend On Screen: "Souvenir."*) Stumble-john! (*He lights the cigarette, avoiding her look. There is a peal of girlish laughter from Amanda in the kitchen. Laura slowly raises and opens her hand. It still contains the little broken glass animal. She looks at it with a tender, bewildered expression.*) Stumble-john! I shouldn't have done that — That was way off the beam. You don't smoke, do you? (*She looks up, smiling, not hearing the question. He sits beside her a little gingerly. She looks at him speechlessly — waiting. He coughs decorously and moves a little farther aside as he considers the situation and senses her feelings, dimly, with perturbation. Gently.*) Would you — care for a — mint? (*She doesn't seem to hear him but her look grows brighter even.*) Peppermint — Life Saver? My pocket's a regular drug store — wherever I go . . . (*He pops a mint in his mouth. Then gulps and decides to make a clean breast of it. He speaks slowly and gingerly.*) Laura, you know, if I had a sister like you, I'd do the same thing as Tom, I'd bring out fellows — introduce her to them. The right type of boys of a type to — appreciate her. Only — well — he made a mistake about me. Maybe I've got no call to be saying this. That may not have been the idea in having me over. But what if it was? There's nothing wrong about that. The only trouble is that in my case — I'm not in a situation to do the right thing. I can't take down your number and say I'll phone. I can't call up next week and — ask for a date. I thought I had better explain the situation in case you misunderstood it and — hurt your feelings. . . . (*Pause. Slowly, very slowly, Laura's look changes, her eyes returning slowly from his to the ornament in her palm.*)

Amanda utters another gay laugh in the kitchen.

LAURA: (*faintly*) You — won't — call again?

JIM: No, Laura. I can't. (*He rises from the sofa.*) As I was just explaining, I've — got strings on me, Laura, I've — been going steady! I go out all the time with a girl named Betty. She's a home-girl like you, and Catholic, and Irish, and in a great many ways we — get along fine. I met her last summer on a moonlight boat trip up the river to Alton, on the *Majestic*. Well — right away from the start it was — love! (*Legend: Love!*) (*Laura sways slightly forward and grips the arm of the sofa. He fails to notice, now enrapt in his own comfortable being.*) Being in love has made a new man of me! (*Leaning stiffly forward, clutching the arm of the sofa, Laura struggles visibly with her storm. But Jim is oblivious, she is a long way off.*) The power of love is really pretty tremendous! Love is something that — changes the whole world, Laura! (*The storm abates a little and Laura leans back. He notices her again.*) It happened that Betty's aunt took sick, she got a wire and had to go to Centralia. So Tom — when he asked me to dinner — I naturally just accepted the invitation, not knowing that you — that he — that I —(*He stops awkwardly.*) Huh — I'm a stumble-john! (*He flops back on the sofa. The holy candles in the altar of Laura's face have been snuffed out! There is a look of almost infinite desolation. Jim glances at her uneasily.*) I wish that you would — say something. (*She bites her lip which was trembling and then bravely smiles. She opens her hand again on the broken glass ornament. Then she gently takes his hand and raises it level with her own. She carefully places the unicorn in the palm of his hand, then pushes his fingers closed upon it.*) What are you — doing that for? You want me to have him?— Laura? (*She nods.*) What for?

LAURA: A — souvenir . . .

She rises unsteadily and crouches beside the Victrola to wind it up.

Legend On Screen: "Things Have A Way Of Turning Out So Badly."

Or Image: "Gentleman Caller Waving Good-bye! — Gaily."

At this moment Amanda rushes brightly back in the front room. She bears a pitcher of fruit punch in an old-fashioned cut-glass pitcher and a plate of macaroons. The plate has a gold border and poppies painted on it.

AMANDA: Well, well, well! Isn't the air delightful after the shower? I've made 270
you children a little liquid refreshment. (*Turns gaily to the gentleman caller.*)
Jim, do you know that song about lemonade?
> "Lemonade, lemonade
> Made in the shade and stirred with a spade —
> Good enough for any old maid!"

JIM: (*uneasily*) Ha-ha! No — I never heard it.
AMANDA: Why, Laura! You look so serious!
JIM: We were having a serious conversation.
AMANDA: Good! Now you're better acquainted!
JIM: (*uncertainly*) Ha-ha! Yes.   275
AMANDA: You modern young people are much more serious-minded than my
generation. I was so gay as a girl!
JIM: You haven't changed, Mrs. Wingfield.
AMANDA: Tonight I'm rejuvenated! The gaiety of the occasion,
Mr. O'Connor! (*She tosses her head with a peal of laughter. Spills lemonade.*)
Oooo! I'm baptizing myself!

JIM: Here — let me —

280 AMANDA: (*setting the pitcher down*) There now. I discovered we had some
maraschino cherries. I dumped them in, juice and all!

JIM: You shouldn't have gone to that trouble. Mrs. Wingfield.

AMANDA: Trouble, trouble? Why it was loads of fun! Didn't you hear me cutting up in the kitchen? I bet your ears were burning! I told Tom how out-
done with him I was for keeping you to himself so long a time! He should
have brought you over much, much sooner! Well, now that you've found
your way, I want you to be a very frequent caller! Not just occasional but all
the time. Oh, we're going to have a lot of gay times together! I see them
coming! Mmm, just breathe that air! So fresh, and the moon's so pretty!
I'll skip back out — I know where my place is when young folks are having
a — serious conversation!

JIM: Oh, don't go out, Mrs. Wingfield. The fact of the matter is I've got to be
going.

AMANDA: Going, now? You're joking! Why, it's only the shank of the evening,
Mr. O'Connor!

285 JIM: Well, you know how it is.

AMANDA: You mean you're a young workingman and have to keep
workingmen's hours. We'll let you off early tonight. But only on the
condition that next time you stay later. What's the best night for you? Isn't
Saturday night the best night for you workingmen?

JIM: I have a couple of time-clocks to punch, Mrs. Wingfield. One at morning,
another one at night!

AMANDA: My, but you are ambitious! You work at night, too?

JIM: No, Ma'am, not work but — Betty! (*He crosses deliberately to pick up his
hat. The band at the Paradise Dance Hall goes into a tender waltz.*)

290 AMANDA: Betty? Betty? Who's Betty! (*There is an ominous cracking sound in
the sky.*)

JIM: Oh, just a girl. The girl I go steady with! (*He smiles charmingly. The sky falls.*)

Legend: "The Sky Falls."

AMANDA: (*a long-drawn exhalation*) Ohhhh . . . Is it a serious romance
Mr. O'Connor?

JIM: We're going to be married the second Sunday in June.

AMANDA: Ohhhh — how nice! Tom didn't mention that you were engaged to
be married.

295 JIM: The cat's not out of the bag at the warehouse yet. You know how they are.
They call you Romeo and stuff like that. (*He stops at the oval mirror to put on
his hat. He carefully shapes the brim and the crown to give a discreetly dashing
effect.*) It's been a wonderful evening, Mrs. Wingfield. I guess this is what
they mean by Southern hospitality.

AMANDA: It really wasn't anything at all.

JIM: I hope it don't seem like I'm rushing off. But I promised Betty I'd pick her
up at the Wabash depot, an' by the time I get my jalopy down there her
train'll be in. Some women are pretty upset if you keep 'em waiting.

AMANDA: Yes, I know — The tyranny of women! (*Extends her hand.*) Good-bye, Mr. O'Connor. I wish you luck — and happiness — and success! All three of them, and so does Laura! — Don't you, Laura?

LAURA: Yes!

JIM: (*taking her hand*) Good-bye, Laura. I'm certainly going to treasure that 300 souvenir. And don't you forget the good advice I gave you. (*Raises his voice to a cheery shout.*) So long, Shakespeare! Thanks again, ladies — Good night!

He grins and ducks jauntily out.

Still bravely grimacing, Amanda closes the door on the gentleman caller. Then she turns back to the room with a puzzled expression. She and Laura don't dare to face each other. Laura crouches beside the Victrola to wind it.

AMANDA: (*faintly*) Things have a way of turning out so badly. I don't believe that I would play the Victrola. Well, well — well — Our gentleman caller was engaged to be married! Tom!

TOM: (*from back*) Yes, Mother?

AMANDA: Come in here a minute. I want to tell you something awfully funny.

TOM: (*enters with macaroon and a glass of the lemonade*) Has the gentleman caller gotten away already?

AMANDA: The gentleman caller has made an early departure. What a wonder- 305 ful joke you played on us!

TOM: How do you mean?

AMANDA: You didn't mention that he was engaged to be married.

TOM: Jim? Engaged?

AMANDA: That's what he just informed us.

TOM: I'll be jiggered! I didn't know about that. 310

AMANDA: That seems very peculiar.

TOM: What's peculiar about it?

AMANDA: Didn't you call him your best friend down at the warehouse?

TOM: He is, but how did I know?

AMANDA: It seems extremely peculiar that you wouldn't know your best friend 315 was going to be married!

TOM: The warehouse is where I work, not where I know things about people!

AMANDA: You don't know things anywhere! You live in a dream; you manufac-ture illusions! (*He crosses to door.*) Where are you going?

TOM: I'm going to the movies.

AMANDA: That's right, now that you've had us make such fools of ourselves. The effort, the preparations, all the expense! The new floor lamp, the rug, the clothes for Laura! All for what? To entertain some other girl's fiancé! Go to the movies, go! Don't think about us, a mother deserted, an unmar-ried sister who's crippled and has no job! Don't let anything interfere with your selfish pleasure! Just go, go, go — to the movies!

TOM: All right, I will! The more you shout about my selfishness to me the 320 quicker I'll go, and I won't go to the movies!

AMANDA: Go, then! Then go to the moon — you selfish dreamer!

Tom smashes his glass on the floor. He plunges out on the fire-escape, slamming the door. Laura screams — cut by door.

Dance-hall music up. Tom goes to the rail and grips it desperately, lifting his face in the chill white moonlight penetrating the narrow abyss of the alley.

Legend On Screen: "And So Good-bye . . ."

Tom's closing speech is timed with the interior pantomime. The interior scene is played as though viewed through sound-proof glass. Amanda appears to be making a comforting speech to Laura who is huddled upon the sofa. Now that we cannot hear the mother's speech, her silliness is gone and she has dignity and tragic beauty. Laura's dark hair hides her face until at the end of the speech she lifts it to smile at her mother. Amanda's gestures are slow and graceful, almost dancelike, as she comforts the daughter. At the end of her speech she glances a moment at the father's picture — then withdraws through the portieres. At close of Tom's speech, Laura blows out the candles, ending the play.

TOM: I didn't go to the moon, I went much further — for time is the longest distance between two places — Not long after that I was fired for writing a poem on the lid of a shoe-box. I left Saint Louis. I descended the steps of this fire-escape for a last time and followed, from then on, in my father's footsteps, attempting to find in motion what was lost in space — I traveled around a great deal. The cities swept about me like dead leaves, leaves that were brightly colored but torn away from the branches. I would have stopped, but was pursued by something. It always came upon me unawares, taking me altogether by surprise. Perhaps it was a familiar bit of music. Perhaps it was only a piece of transparent glass. Perhaps I am walking along a street at night, in some strange city, before I have found companions. I pass the lighted window of a shop where perfume is sold. The window is filled with pieces of colored glass, tiny transparent bottles in delicate colors, like bits of a shattered rainbow. Then all at once my sister touches my shoulder. I turn around and look into her eyes . . . Oh, Laura, Laura, I tried to leave you behind me, but I am more faithful than I intended to be! I reach for a cigarette, I cross the street, I run into the movies or a bar, I buy a drink, I speak to the nearest stranger — anything that can blow your candles out! *(Laura bends over the candles.)* — for nowadays the world is lit by lightning! Blow out your candles, Laura — and so good-bye . . .

She blows the candles out.

The Scene Dissolves.

Reading and Reacting

1. Who is this play really about — Tom, Laura, or Amanda?

2. What is the function of the absent father in the play?

3. Besides serving as a possible suitor for Laura, what other roles does Jim play?

4. Identify references to historical events occurring at the time of the play's action. How are these events related to the play's central theme?

5. Does Tom function primarily as an actor, character, playwright, or narrator? Explain.

6. How do the music, the lighting, and the words and pictures projected on slides — which Tennessee Williams called "extra-literary accents"— contribute to the play's action? Are they essential? (Note that at the urging of the director, Williams eliminated these "accents" when the play opened on Broadway.)

7. In his production notes, Tennessee Williams calls *The Glass Menagerie* a "memory play." What do you think he means?

8. Discuss how props help to develop the play's themes. For example, consider the picture of the father, the Victrola, the fire escape, the telephone, the alarm clock, the high school yearbook, the unicorn, and the candles.

9. What events and dialogue foreshadow Tom's escape? Do you see this escape as inevitable? Do you see it as successful? Explain.

10. Do Amanda and Laura change as the play proceeds? What do you think will happen to them after the play is over? What is the significance of Laura's blowing out the candles at the end of the play?

11. Identify several examples of religious imagery in the play —for example, the Paradise Dance Hall. What is the significance of this imagery? In what way does it relate to the major theme of the play?

12. **JOURNAL ENTRY** Do you think Tom's decision to leave his family is a sign of strength or of weakness?

13. **CRITICAL PERSPECTIVE** Literary critic Roger Boxill contrasts the short story "Portrait of a Girl in Glass" (p. 2068) and *The Glass Menagerie*. According to Boxill, "'Portrait' is a wistful memory, *Menagerie* is a moving elegy."

Do you agree with Boxill's assessment of these two works? What do you see as the major differences between the short story and the play that developed out of it?

Related Works: "A Primer for the Punctuation of Heart Disease" (p. 156), "A&P" (p. 230), "Barn Burning" (p. 356), "Eveline" (p. 722), "The Soul selects her own Society —" (p. 1165), "The Road Not Taken" (p. 1180), *A Raisin in the Sun* (p. 1385).

TENNESSEE WILLIAMS

Author's Production Notes
(Preface to the Published Edition)

Being a "memory play," *The Glass Menagerie* can be presented with unusual freedom of convention. Because of its considerably delicate or tenuous material, atmospheric touches and subtleties of direction play a particularly important part. Expressionism and all other unconventional techniques in drama have only one valid aim, and that is a closer approach to truth. When a play employs unconventional techniques, it is not, or certainly shouldn't be, trying to escape its responsibility of dealing with reality, or interpreting experience, but is actually or should be attempting to find a closer approach, a more penetrating and vivid expression of things as they are. The straight realistic play with its genuine Frigidaire and authentic ice-cubes, its characters that speak exactly as its audience speaks, corresponds to the academic landscape and has the same virtue of a photographic likeness. Everyone should know nowadays the unimportance of the photographic in art: that truth, life, or reality is an organic thing which the poetic imagination can represent or suggest, in essence, only through transformation, through changing into other forms than those which were merely present in appearance.

These remarks are not meant as a preface only to this particular play. They have to do with a conception of a new, plastic theatre which must take the place of the exhausted theater of realistic conventions if the theatre is to resume vitality as a part of our culture.

The Screen Device: There is *only one important difference between the original and acting version of the play* and that is the *omission* in the latter of the device which I tentatively included in my *original* script. This device was the use of a screen on which were projected magic-lantern slides bearing images or titles. I do not regret the omission of this device from the present Broadway production. The extraordinary power of Miss Taylor's performance° made it suitable to have the utmost simplicity in the physical production. But I think it may be interesting to some readers to see how this device was conceived. So I am putting it into the published manuscript. These images and legends, projected from behind, were cast on a section of wall between the front-room and dining-room areas, which should be indistinguishable from the rest when not in use.

The purpose of this will probably be apparent. It is to give accent to certain values in each scene. Each scene contains a particular point (or several) which is structurally the most important. In an episodic play, such as this, the basic structure or narrative line may be obscured from the audience; the effect may seem fragmentary rather than architectural. This may not be the fault of the play so much as a lack of attention in the audience. The legend or image upon the screen will strengthen the effect of what is merely allusion in the writing and allow the primary point to be made more simply and lightly than if the entire responsibility were on the spoken lines. Aside from this structural value, I think the screen will have a definite emotional appeal, less definable but just as important. An imaginative producer or director may invent many other uses for this device than those indicated in the present script. In fact the possibilities of the device seem much larger to me than the instance of this play can possibly utilize.

The Music: Another extra-literary accent in this play is provided by the use of music. A single recurring tune, "The Glass Menagerie," is used to give emotional

---

°*Miss Taylor's performance:* In the original production, the role of Amanda Wingfield was played by the American stage actress Laurette Taylor (1884–1946).

emphasis to suitable passages. This tune is like circus music, not when you are on the grounds or in the immediate vicinity of the parade, but when you are at some distance and very likely thinking of something else. It seems under those circumstances to continue almost interminably and it weaves in and out of the preoccupied consciousness; then it is the lightest, most delicate music in the world and perhaps the saddest. It expresses the surface vivacity of life with the underlying strain of immutable and inexpressible sorrow. When you look at a piece of delicately spun glass you think of two things: how beautiful it is and how easily it can be broken. Both of those ideas should be woven into the recurring tune, which dips in and out of the play as if it were carried on a wind that changes. It serves as a thread of connection and allusion between the narrator with his separate point in time and space and the subject of his story. Between each episode it returns as reference to the emotion, nostalgia, which is the first condition of the play. It is primarily Laura's music and therefore comes out most clearly when the play focuses upon her and the lovely fragility of glass which is her image.

The Lighting: The lighting in the play is not realistic. In keeping with the atmosphere of memory, the stage is dim. Shafts of light are focused on selected areas or actors, sometimes in contradistinction to what is the apparent center. For instance, in the quarrel scene between Tom and Amanda, in which Laura has no active part, the clearest pool of light is on her figure. This is also true of the supper scene, when her silent figure on the sofa should remain the visual center. The light upon Laura should be distinct from the others, having a peculiar pristine clarity such as light used in early religious portraits of female saints or madonnas. A certain correspondence to light in religious paintings, such as El Greco's, where the figures are radiant in atmosphere that is relatively dusky, could be effectively used throughout the play. (It will also permit a more effective use of the screen.) A free, imaginative use of light can be of enormous value in giving a mobile, plastic quality to plays of a more or less static nature.nature.

T.W

JACQUELINE O'CONNOR

from Dramatizing Dementia:
Madness in the Plays of Tennessee Williams

Many of Williams's plays take place in confined space, and the setting often suggests that the characters will face permanent confinement at the play's end. *The Glass Menagerie* is set in "one of those hive-like conglomerations of cellular living-units . . . symptomatic of the impulse of this largest and fundamentally enslaved section of American society to avoid fluidity and differentiation." Confinement figures as a major theme in this drama; Tom speaks frequently about the confinement that keeps him from fulfilling his dreams. In scene three, he berates his mother for the lack of privacy he feels in the apartment, telling her: "I've got nothing, no single thing—in my life that I can call my own!" He feels confined in his job, sarcastically wondering if Amanda thinks he wants to spend "fifty-five *years* down there in that —*celotex interior!* with —*fluorescent*— *tubes!*" When he returns from a night out, he brags to Laura about the magician who performed the coffin trick: "We nailed him into a coffin and he got out of the coffin without removing one nail." This, he claims, constitutes a "trick that would come in handy for me — get me out of this 2 × 4 situation!" Tom escapes from the oppressive apartment and the dead-end job, but does not find the freedom he expects, for he cannot forget his sister or the ties he feels to her, which bind him even in her absence.

Laura is voluntarily confined in the apartment, which, according to her mother, will lead to permanent confinement if she does not pursue a career or marriage. She will end up one of those "barely tolerated spinsters . . . stuck away in some little mouse-trap of a room." To the audience Laura's plight seems as constricted as the future her mother predicts, but if Laura's life proceeds as Lucretia's and Blanche's do, the "mouse-trap of a room" might well be in the state asylum. As Tom realizes, Laura is not just crippled: "In the eyes of others — strangers — she's terribly shy and lives in a world of her own and those things make her seem a little peculiar to people outside the house." Amanda's comment highlights Laura's social shortcomings, while Tom's remark focuses on her psychological ones: both assessments emphasize Laura's isolation.

TENNESSEE WILLIAMS

from Tennessee Williams: Memoirs

Rose was a popular girl in high school but only for a brief while. Her beauty was mainly in her expressive green-gray eyes and in her curly auburn hair. She was too narrow-shouldered and her state of anxiety when in male company inclined her to hunch them so they looked even narrower; this made her strong-featured, very Williams head seem too large for her thin, small-breasted body. She also, when she was on a date, would talk with an almost hysterical animation which few young men knew how to take.

The first real breakdown occurred shortly after I had suffered the heart attack that ended my career as a clerk-errand boy at the shoe company.

My first night back from St. Vincent's, as I mentioned, Rose came walking like a somnambulist into my tiny bedroom and said, "We must all die together."

I can assure you that the idea did not offer to me an irresistible appeal. Being now released at last from my three years as a clerk-typist at Continental, God damn it I was in no mood to consider group suicide with the family, not even at Rose's suggestion —however appropriate the suggestion may have been.

For several days Rose was demented. One afternoon she put a kitchen knife in her purse and started to leave for her psychiatrist's office with apparent intent of murder.

The knife was noticed by Mother and snatched away.

Then a day or so later this first onset of dementia praecox passed off and Rose was, at least on the surface, her usual (now very quiet) self again.

A few days later I departed for Memphis to recuperate at my grandparents' little house on Snowden Avenue near Southwestern University in Memphis.

I think it was about this time that our wise old family doctor told Mother that Rose's physical and mental health depended upon what struck Miss Edwina as a monstrous thing — an arranged, a sort of "therapeutic" marriage. Obviously old Doc Alexander had hit upon the true seat of Rose's afflictions. She was a very normal — but highly sexed — girl who was tearing herself apart mentally and physically by those repressions imposed upon her by Miss Edwina's monolithic Puritanism.

I may have inadvertently omitted a good deal of material about the unusually close relations between Rose and me. Some perceptive critic of the theatre made the observation that the true theme of my work is "incest." My sister and I had a close relationship, quite unsullied by any carnal knowledge. As a matter of fact, we were rather shy of each other, physically, there was no casual physical intimacy of the sort that one observes among the Mediterranean people in their family relations. And yet our love was, and is, the deepest in our lives and was, perhaps, very pertinent to our withdrawal from extra-familial attachments.

There were years when I was in the shoe company and summers when I was a student at the State University of Missouri when my sister and I spent nearly all our evenings together aside from those which I spent with Hazel.

What did we do those evenings, Rose and I? Well, we strolled about the business streets of University City. It was a sort of ritual with a pathos that I assure you was never caught in *Menagerie* nor in my story "Portrait of Girl in Glass," on which *Menagerie* was based.

I think it was Delmar — that long, long street which probably began near the Mississippi River in downtown St. Louis and continued through University City and on out into the country — that Rose and I strolled along in the evenings. There was a root-beer stand at which we always stopped. Rose was inordinately fond of root-beer, especially on warm summer evenings. And before and after our root-beer stop, we would window-shop. Rose's passion, as well as Blanche's, was clothes. And all along that part of Delmar that cut through University City were little shops with lighted windows at night in which were displayed dresses and accessories for women. Rose did not have much of a wardrobe and so her window-shopping on Delmar was like a hungry child's gazing through the window-fronts of restaurants. Her taste in clothes was excellent.

"How about *that* dress, Rose?"

"Oh no, that's tacky. But this one here's very nice."

The evening excursions lasted about an hour and a half, and although, as I've noted, we had a physical shyness of each other, never even touching hands except when dancing together in the Enright apartment, I'd usually follow her into her bedroom when we came home, to continue our warmly desultory chats. I felt most at home in that room, which was furnished with the white ivory bedroom set that had been acquired with the family's "furnished apartment" on Westminster Place when we first moved to St. Louis in 1918.

It was the only attractive room in the apartment — or did it seem so because it was my sister's?

I have mentioned our dancing together.

Rose taught me to dance to the almost aboriginal standing (nonhorned) Victrola that had been acquired in Mississippi and shipped to St. Louis at the time of the disastrous family move there.

As I drifted away from my sister, during this period, she drew close to our little Boston terrier Jiggs. She was constantly holding and hugging him and now and then Miss Edwina would say:

"Miss Florence, I'm afraid that you forget we have neighbors and Mrs. Ebbs upstairs sometimes complains when Cornelius° raises his voice."

Miss Florence would be likely to reply something to the effect that Mrs. Ebbs upstairs could go to hell, for all it mattered to her. . . .

The last time I was in St. Louis, for a visit at Christmas, I had my brother Dakin drive me about all the old places where we had lived in my childhood. It was a melancholy tour. Westminster Place and Forest Park Boulevard had lost all semblance of their charm in the twenties. The big old residences had been converted into sleazy rooming-houses or torn down for nondescript duplexes and small apartment buildings.

The Kramer residence was gone: in fact, all of the family, including dear Hazel, were by then dead.

This can only serve as a preamble, in this "thing," to the story of my great love for Hazel, and not at all an adequate one at that. . . .

In my adolescence in St. Louis, at the age of sixteen, several important events in my life occurred. It was in the sixteenth year that I wrote "The Vengeance of Nitocris" and received my first publication in a magazine and the magazine was *Weird Tales*. The story wasn't published till June of 1928. That same year my grandfather Dakin took me with him on a tour of Europe with a large party of Episcopalian ladies from the Mississippi Delta. . . . And, it was in my sixteenth year that my deep nervous problems approached what might well have been a crisis as shattering as that which broke my sister's mind, lastingly, when she was in her twenties.

I was at sixteen a student at University City High School in St. Louis and the family was living in a cramped apartment at 6254 Enright Avenue.

University City was not a fashionable suburb of St. Louis and our neighborhood, while a cut better than that of the Wingfields in *Menagerie*, was only a little cut better: it was an ugly region of hive-like apartment buildings, for the most part, and fire escapes and pathetic little patches of green among concrete driveways.

My younger brother, Dakin, always an indomitable enthusiast at whatever he got into, had turned our little patch of green behind the apartment on Enright into quite an astonishing little vegetable garden. If there were flowers in it, they were, alas, obscured by the profuse growth of squash, pumpkins, and other edible flora.

I would, of course, have preempted all the space with rosebushes but I doubt they would have borne roses. The impracticalities, let's say the fantastic impracticalities,

---

° *Cornelius:* Cornelius Coffin — father of Tennessee Williams.

of my adolescence were not at all inclined to successful ends: and I can recall no roses in all the years that I spent in St. Louis and its environs except the two living Roses in my life, my grandmother, Rose O. Dakin, and, of course, my sister, Rose Isabel.

My adolescent problems took their most violent form in a shyness of a pathological degree. Few people realize, now, that I have always been and even remain in my years as a crocodile an extremely shy creature — in my crocodile years I compensate for this shyness by the typical Williams heartiness and bluster and sometimes explosive fury of behavior. In my high school days I had no disguise, no facade. And it was at University City High School that I developed the habit of blushing whenever anyone looked me in the eyes, as if I harbored behind them some quite dreadful or abominable secret.

JEAN EVANS

Interview 1945

I'd read four of Mr. Williams's one-act plays. All but one had been about poverty-stricken people whose situations seemed hopeless. I asked Mr. Williams if he always wrote about unhappy, trapped, hopeless people. He'd been half-reclining against a pillow on his bed, but he sat up now.

"I hadn't thought of them as being hopeless," he said. "That's not really what I was writing about. It's human valor that moves me. The one dominant theme in most of my writings, the most magnificent thing in all human nature, is valor — and endurance.

"The mother's valor is the core of *The Glass Menagerie*," he went on. "She's confused, pathetic, even stupid, but everything has *got* to be all right. She fights to make it that way in the only way she knows how."

We talked a little about his other plays and then, a trifle anxiously, he asked if I had found them without humor. I said no. There was a great deal of humor in them if he meant the wry kind that sprang out of incredibly miserable situations, the kind that made an audience want to cry while it was laughing. He nodded.

"George Jean Nathan,° in his review of *Menagerie,* said I was *deficient* in humor," Williams remarked. His manner was casual, but there was an edge of annoyance in his voice. "He said that all the humor had been embroidered into the play by Mr. Dowling." (Dowling is co-producer of the play, plays the narrator, and the son, Tom.) "I'd love for somebody who knows my other work to refute him."

He paused, and then went on defensively, "Not one line of *Glass Menagerie* was changed after the final draft came back from the typist. A scene was inserted, the drunk scene. That was Mr. Dowling's idea, but entirely of my authorship. And one line by Mr. Dowling, was added. The last line, where he says to the

---

°*George Jean Nathan:* American editor and drama critic (1882–1958). His review of the play appeared in the *New York Journal American* on April 9, 1945.

audience, 'Here's where memory stops and your imagination begins.'" He paused. "Mr. Dowling did a great job. A magnificent job. But there was humor *contained* in the play. I had that in mind, along with the rest, when I was writing it."

Mr. Nathan had also written that the play, as originally written, was *freakish*. I wanted to know if Mr. Williams liked writing plays unconventional in form.

"If you mean unconventional in that my plays are light on plot and heavy on characterization, yes. But not in structure. *Glass Menagerie* is not at all freakish in structure.

"Have you read Saroyan's° *Get Away, Old Man?*" Williams gave a peal of gay, sudden laughter that rang through the room. "There's a play that would give Mr. Nathan pause. The curtain goes up and down, up and down, all through the play."

He said he liked Saroyan very much, "his short stories perhaps, more than his plays."

I said I'd like Saroyan better if he were able to admit there was evil under the sun. Mr. Williams smiled. "His point of view — his attitude — I suppose you could say, is childish," he said. "Saroyan's characters are all little Saroyans. He multiplies himself like rabbits. But he is himself so interesting, that he usually gets away with writing only about himself."

How did he think the human situation could be improved? I asked. He looked as though the question had startled him.

"It's a social and economic problem, of course," he said, "not something mystical. I don't think there will be any equity in American life until at least 90 percent of our population are living under different circumstances. The white collar worker, for instance. Most people consider him pretty well off. I think his situation is horrible.

"I'd like to see people getting a lot more for what they invest in the way of effort and time. It's insane for human beings to work their whole lives away at dull, stupid, routine, anesthetizing jobs for just a little more than the necessities of life. There should be time — and money — for development. For living."

THOMAS L. KING

from Irony and Distance in *The Glass Menagerie*

Tennessee Williams's *The Glass Menagerie*, though it has achieved a firmly established position in the canon of American plays, is often distorted, if not misunderstood, by readers, directors, and audiences. The distortion results from an overemphasis on the scenes involving Laura and Amanda and their plight, so that the play becomes a sentimental tract on the trapped misery of two women in St. Louis. This leads to the neglect of Tom's soliloquies — speeches that can be ignored or discounted only at great peril, since they occupy such a prominent position in the play. When not largely ignored, they are in danger of being treated as

---

°*Saroyan's:* William Saroyan (1908–1981), American writer of short stories, plays, novels, and memoirs.

nostalgic yearnings for a former time. But they are not sentimental excursions into the past, paralleling Amanda's, for while they contain sentiment and nostalgia, they also evince a pervasive humor and irony and, indeed, form and contain the entire play. . . .

The play . . . is not Amanda's. Amanda is a striking and a powerful character, but the play is Tom's. Tom opens the play and he closes it; he also opens the second act and two further scenes in the first act — his is the first word and the last. Indeed, Amanda, Laura, and the Gentleman Caller do not appear in the play at all as separate characters. In a sense, as [reviewer], Stark Young noted, Tom is the only character in the play, for we see not the characters but Tom's memory of them — Amanda and the rest are merely aspects of Tom's consciousness. Tom's St. Louis is not an objective one, but a solipsist's created by Tom, the artist-magician, and containing Amanda, Laura, and the Gentleman Caller. Tom is the Prospero of *The Glass Menagerie,* and its world is the world of Tom's mind even more than *Death of a Salesman*'s is the world of Willy Loman's mind. The play is warped and distorted when any influence gives Amanda, Laura, or the glass menagerie any undue prominence. If Amanda looms large, she looms large in Tom's mind, not in her own right: though of course the image that finally dominates Tom's mind is that of Laura and the glass menagerie.

The full meaning of the scenes between the soliloquies lies not in themselves alone but also in the commentary provided by Tom standing outside the scenes and speaking with reasonable candor to the audience and reader. Moreover, the comment that the soliloquies makes is not a sentimental one; that is, they are not only expressions of a wistful nostalgia for the lost, doomed world of Amanda, Laura, and the glass menagerie but also contain a good deal of irony and humor which work in the opposite direction. They reveal Tom as an artist figure whose utterances show how the artist creates, using the raw material of his own life. . . .

Generally, each soliloquy oscillates between a sentimental memory of the past, which draws the narrator into it, and a wry irony which keeps him from being fully engulfed and controlled by it. This tension is found in all the soliloquies, though it is not always handled in the same way: sometimes the fond memory is predominant and sometimes the irony, but both are always present. At times, Tom seems almost deliberately to court disaster by creating for himself and the audience a memory so lovely and poignant that the pain of giving it up to return to reality is too much to bear, but return he does with mockery and a kind of wit that interrupts the witchery of memory just short of a withdrawn madness surrounded by soft music and a mind filled with "delicate rainbow colors." In short, Tom toys with the same madness in which his sister Laura is trapped but saves himself with irony. . . .

The opening soliloquy . . . reveals a number of elements that are to be important in the play: it establishes a tension between sentimental nostalgia and detached irony as well as a narrator who is to function as stage magician. The narrator disavows this, but we cannot take him at his word. He says that he is the opposite of a stage magician, but only because his truth looks like illusion rather than the other way round; he is still the magician who creates the play. He says that the play is sentimental rather than realistic, but that is a half truth, for while it contains large doses of sentiment, for the narrator at least, irony sometimes quenches the sentiment. Indeed, Irving Babbit's° phrase describing romantic irony is appropriate here: "Hot baths of sentiment . . . followed by cold douches of irony." . . .

The culmination of all the soliloquies, and of the tension between irony and nostalgia that is carefully developed in them, is in the final one. Tom's last speech contains just two touches of ironic detachment, but these are critical and are the foci on which this speech and, indeed, for Tom, the whole play turns. The speech begins with a touch of ironic humor. In the preceding scene, Amanda has told Tom to go to the moon. He begins his final speech with "I didn't go to the moon." This is a decidedly humorous line, indicating that Tom still has access to his detachment, but the audience is not laughing anymore, its detachment has been broken down. The speech then quickly moves into a tone of lyric regret:

> I didn't go to the moon, I went much further — for time is the longest distance between two places. Not long after that I was fired for writing a poem on the lid of a shoe-box. I left Saint Louis. I descended the steps of this fire-escape for a last time and followed, from then on, in my father's footsteps, attempting to find in motion what was lost in space. I traveled around a great deal. The cities swept about me like dead leaves, leaves that were brightly colored but torn away from the branches. I would have stopped, but I was pursued by something. It always came upon me unawares, taking me altogether by surprise. Perhaps it was a familiar bit of music. Perhaps it was only a piece of transparent glass. Perhaps I am walking along a street at night, in some strange city, before I have found companions. I pass the lighted window of a shop where perfume is sold. The window is filled with pieces of colored glass, tiny transparent bottles in delicate colors, like bits of a shattered rainbow. Then all at once my sister touches my shoulder. I turn around and look into her eyes. Oh, Laura, Laura, I tried to leave you behind me, but I am more faithful than I intended to be! I reach for a cigarette, I cross the street, I run into the movies or a bar, I buy a drink, I speak to the nearest stranger — anything that can blow your candles out!
>
> For nowadays the world is lit by lightning! Blow out your candles, Laura — and so good-bye.

The irony in this passage is no longer humorous. When Tom says "I didn't go to the moon," no one is laughing, and the final, ironic "and so good-bye" is not even potentially humorous. Tom seems to have been captured by the memory and the audience has almost certainly been captured, but Tom, in the end, still has his detachment. Laura's candles go out and Tom is relieved of his burden, uttering a final, flip farewell, but the audience has been more faithful than it intended to be; they are left behind, tricked by Tom who is free for the moment while they must face their grief, their cruelty, for they are the world that the Wingfields were somehow set apart from, they are the ones who shattered the rainbow.

The soliloquies, then, are of a piece: they all alternate between sentiment and irony, between mockery and nostalgic regret, and they all end with an ironic tag, which, in most cases, is potentially humorous. They show us the artist manipulating

---

°*Babbit's:* Irving Babbit (1865–1933), American scholar-critic and professor of French literature at Harvard.

his audience, seeming to be manipulated himself to draw them in, but in the end resuming once more his detached stance. When Tom departs, the audience is left with Laura and Amanda alone before the dead, smoking candles, and Tom escapes into his artist's detachment having exorcized the pain with the creation of the play. This is the trick that Tom has in his pocket.

NANCY MARIE PATTERSON TISCHLER

from Student Companion to Tennessee Williams

Williams loved symbols. Having started his writing as a lyric poet, he explained that he had a "poet's weakness for symbols." This trait was undoubtedly also a result of his early saturation with the symbolism and thought of the Episcopal Church. He came to see almost every aspect of life as symbolic of some greater truth.

He had originally designed *The Glass Menagerie* as a Christmas story (Letter to Audrey Wood, 12/43), with the opening scene one of gift giving. The change in his point of attack to a family meal, though more secular, is nonetheless introduced by a demand that Tom come to the table so that they can say "grace," which incidentally, they then omit; but it is also to make his failed, secular "communion" a commentary on the painful relationship in this community of believers. Nothing should be more ordinary and comfortable than breaking bread together, yet the Wingfield children can perform no function without scrutiny and advice from the hovering mother. An echo of this scene is a second announcement of the impending blessing, this time a summons for Laura to come to the table when Jim O'Connor is their guest for dinner. Pretending that Laura has prepared the meal for their visitor, Amanda again dominates the event, making it her solo performance rather than a shared experience of hospitality. She turns the ritual of eating into a contest of wills. She has transformed a communion into a celebration of her personal sacrifices and a reinforcement of her children's obligations to her as their appropriately grateful response.

Amanda soon reveals herself as a symbol of the "devouring mother." Though apparently nurturing, she thwarts and hobbles her children, dominating not only their eating habits, but their entire lives, keeping them safely in the nest with her. Portraying herself as a martyr to their needs, she actually requires their submission to feed her own pride, crippling Laura by her outrageous expectations. If she could, she would emasculate Tom as well. As her own beauty fades, her appetite for adulation increases, making her a harpy rather than a saint. In a fit of anger, Tom calls his mother an ugly old "witch." Williams was to continue embellishing his archetypal monster-woman as he met more complex and powerful ogres throughout his career.

The central image in this play, from which the work takes its name, is Laura's glass menagerie. Williams' biographers have traced the origins of this image to a tragic young woman in Clarksdale, Mississippi (Leverich 1995, 55). Within the play, it allows us to see the childlike fixation on a private world of make-believe animals, and delicacy of this isolated girl.

This culture, frozen in time, would limit Tom's reading to proper works by polite writers and Laura's choices. In scene after scene, Williams shows Amanda as a victim of her own assumptions about how women should behave, how they should spend their lives, whom they should marry, what domestic chores they should perform, how they should dress, entertain, and talk. She is not just a peculiar old woman: she is a symbol of a dying civilization.

On an even more universal level, this story is about the effects of the industrial revolution on the American family. Although Williams emphasizes the Depression context of the narrative, we know that the pressures on Tom Wingfield extend beyond the span of the 1930s. The growth of big industries in the nineteenth and twentieth centuries had both forced families from the farms and small towns and lured them to great cities, where the personal needs of fragile folk are easily neglected. The polluted air, boring work, and separation from a caring community proved harmful to the mental and physical health of many displaced people.

The emphasis on the "hivelike" buildings of ugly colors with their fire escapes underscores the separation from nature, beauty, and human values. This is not the proper habitat for the dreamer, the poet, or the fragile cripple. Yet, all too often, it is the setting for the young man or woman in urban America. Williams, in *The Glass Menagerie*, is providing us a microcosm in which we can visualize the larger questions of the entire era.

Taking it as a symbol of Laura herself, fragile and beautiful, the author plays with the more specific figure of the unicorn. Here we see the complete development of a complex idea, hinted at in the dialogue. We know from medieval iconography that this mythical figure is identified with virgins and therefore with sexuality. Although it looks like a horse the unicorn not a horse, but is a unique (if mythical) creature. Thus, when Jim accidentally breaks off its horn, he has not transformed it into a horse: it remains a unicorn, but is now a damaged unicorn that manages to look like an ordinary horse. In some ways, this is what Amanda has done to Laura, distorted her true childish nature to make her seem like all the normal young ladies being courted by nice young gentlemen. (The "gay deceivers" are delightful symbols of Laura's underdeveloped sexuality and Amanda's pressures to appear sexy.) Laura's pained responses to her mother's cruel questions about her plans for the evening expose the anguish that this teasing causes the sensitive girl.

The mock-courtship scene between Laura and Jim contains another cluster of images. Tom, having misused the money for the electric bill, has plunged them into darkness. Amanda, always eager to adopt romantic attitudes, furnishes them with a candelabra, a relic from a church fire, and thereby returns them to the nineteenth century — the family's native habitat. Jim briefly enters into their game of playing at pre-electric life, settles on the floor, and enjoys a childlike moment of shared memories with Laura. But we soon learn that he lives fully in the "Century of Progress," which Laura is blocked from entering. Jim tries, in an act of egocentric kindness, to move her into the adult world of dancing and kissing, but Laura remains a lonely little girl who had a playmate over to visit for the evening. That scene foreshadows the final words, "For nowadays the world is lit by lightning! Blow out your candles, Laura — and so goodbye" . . . .

Other images also populate the play. Williams loved the ocean and frequently used the sea as an escape symbol. His sailors, pirates, and buccaneers are the gallant figures who sail away from the dreary land to have adventures denied to most of mankind. Certainly Americans have known this imagery from their earliest days, America itself being the grand adventure for most of our ancestors. For at least three of Williams' literary heroes°—Melville, O'Neill, and Crane—the sea voyage was also the escape into the life of literature.

Tennessee Williams' delight in earlier poets, novelists, and dramatists gives additional richness to the texture of the phrasing in *The Glass Menagerie*. For example, Tom's final portrayal of cities as leaves blown by the wind, "brightly colored, but torn away from the branches" echoes Shelley's "Ode to the West Wind."° Fortunately, such similes work effectively even if the listener fails to pick up the source of the allusion. We need not picture the famous medieval unicorn tapestry in order to delight in the unicorn reference. Nor do we need to know about D. H. Lawrence's rainbow° of sexuality in order to understand the rainbow colors at the Paradise Dance Hall. Blue Mountain is the right name for a romantic past, and Moon Lake is the ideal name for adventures in love. The words carry the message, regardless of our specific knowledge of Clarksdale's geography. Williams lets his words tell their own stories. The viewer can delight in the surface brilliance or dig deep into allusions, allowing several levels of possible resonance. . . .

ROGER B. STEIN

from The Glass Menagerie Revisited:
Catastrophe without Violence

The religious overtones of *The Glass Menagerie* are even more pervasive. Though they never obscure the literal line of the story or seem self-conscious, as they do in some of the later plays, these overtones add a dimension to the play which reaches beyond individual pathos and social tragedy. Williams's stage directions clearly indicate his intention. As with Hannah in *The Night of the Iguana*, he tells us that the lighting for Laura should resemble that "used in early religious portraits of female saints or madonnas." The scene where Tom tells his mother that a gentleman caller will appear Williams entitles "Annunciation." The dressing of Laura for the caller's appearance should be "devout and ritualistic." During her scene with Jim she is lit "inwardly with altar candles," and when Jim withdraws after kissing her Williams informs us that the "holy candles in the altar of Laura's face have been snuffed out. There is a look of almost infinite desolation."

Those overtones extend beyond Williams's hints to the director and become a crucial part of the fabric of dramatic action. The first scene in both the Acting Version and the Library Edition of the play opens on this note. In the former, Amanda narrates her "funny experience" of being denied a seat in the Episcopal church

---

°*literary heroes:* Herman Melville (1819–1891), Eugene O'Neill (1888–1953), and Stephen Crane (1871–1900).
°*Shelley's "Ode to the West Wind":* See Chapter 34, page 1223.　°*D. H. Lawrence's rainbow:* Lawrence's novel *The Rainbow* was published in 1915.

because she has not rented a pew. The idea of the Wingfields' exclusion from Christian ceremony is established thus at the outset, and it is underlined by the ensuing talk of digesting food, mastication, and salivary glands. In the Wingfield apartment, eating is an animal process only; it lacks ritual significance. The Library Edition opens with Amanda's call to Tom, "We can't say grace until you come to the table," and then moves on to the question of digestion. The lines are different, but their import is the same. When the gentleman caller comes, the scene is repeated, only this time it is Laura whose absence holds up "grace."

Amanda, who condemns instinct and urges Tom to think in terms of the mind and spirit, as "Christian adults" do, is often characterized in Christian terms. Her music, in the Library Edition, is "Ave Maria." As a girl she could only cook angel food cake. She urges Laura, "Possess your soul in patience," and then speaks of her dress for the dinner scene as "resurrected" from a trunk. Her constant refrain to Tom is "Rise an' Shine," and she sells subscriptions to her friends by waking them early in the morning and then sympathizing with them as "Christian martyrs." Laura is afraid to tell her mother she has left the business school because "when you're disappointed, you get that awful suffering look on your face, like the picture of Jesus' mother in the museum!"

The next picture Laura mentions is the one of Jim in the yearbook; though the context seems secular enough at this point — Jim is a high school hero — his religious function emerges later on. In the "Annunciation" scene, when Amanda learns that the gentleman caller's name is O'Connor, she says, "That, of course, means fish — tomorrow is Friday!" The remark functions not only literally, since Jim is Irish Catholic, but also figuratively, for the fish is the traditional symbol of Christ. In a very real sense both Amanda and Laura are searching for a Savior who will come to help them, to save them, to give their drab lives meaning.

Tom is unable to play this role himself. Though he appears as the angel of the Annunciation, he denies the world of belief and in a bitter speech to his mother calls himself "El Diablo." With him Christian terms appear only as imprecations: "what in Christ's name" or "that God damn Rise and Shine." When Tom returns home drunk one night, he tells Laura of a stage show he has seen which is shot through with Christian symbolism, none of which he perceives. Here the magician, Malvolio, whose name suggests bad will, dislike, or even hate, plays the role of the modern Christ. He performs the miracle of turning water into wine and then goes on to blasphemy by turning the wine into beer and then whiskey. He also produces his proper symbol, the fish, but it is goldfish, as if stained by modern materialism. Most important, perhaps, he escapes from a nailed coffin. But Tom reads the symbolism of this trick in personal terms only. When Laura tries to keep him from awakening Amanda, Tom retorts:

> Goody goody! Pay 'er back for all those "Rise an' Shine's." You know it don't take much intelligence to get yourself into a nailed-up coffin, Laura. But who in hell ever got himself out of one without removing one nail?

The illumination of the father's photograph at this point suggests one answer to this question, but the pattern of Christian imagery in the drama, especially when reinforced here by the "Rise an' Shine" refrain, should suggest to us another answer — the resurrection itself — which Tom's rejection of Christian belief prevents him from seeing.

It remains therefore for Jim to come as the Savior to this Friday night supper. The air of expectancy is great, with the ritualistic dressing of Laura, the tension, and the oppressive heat. Jim's arrival is marked by the coming of rain, but the hopes of fertility and renewal which this might suggest are soon dashed. Laura's attempt to come to the dinner table is a failure, signaled by a clap of thunder, and Tom's muttered grace, "For these and all thy mercies, God's Holy Name be praised," is bitterly ironic, mocked by what follows. The only paradise within reach is Paradise Dance Hall, with its "Waste Land" mood of slow and sensuous rhythms and couples kissing behind ashpits and telephone poles, "the compensation for lives that passed . . . without any change or adventure," as Tom remarks. The failure of electric power after dinner — previsioning the blackout of the world — leads to Amanda's joking question, "Where was Moses when the lights went off?" This suggests another savior who would lead his people from the desert into the promised land, but the answer to her question is "In the dark."

Jim's attempt to play the modern savior is an abysmal failure. In the after-dinner scene, he offers Laura the sacrament — wine and "life-savers," in this case — and a Dale Carnegie version of the Sermon on the Mount — self-help rather than divine help — but to no avail. At the end of the play Laura and Amanda are, as the joke bitterly reminds us, "in the dark," and Tom's last lines announce the final failure, the infinite desolation: "For nowadays the world is lit by lightning. Blow out your candles, Laura — and so goodbye."

TOM SCANLAN

from Family, Drama, and American Dreams

The major dilemmas of family life are imbedded in the dramatic action of Williams's plays, and the ideal that haunts his characters is family-related. Moreover, those plays which have been most successful artistically have been those mostly about the family. . . .

In the earlier plays Williams dramatized the family world in a state of collapse; in later ones family collapse is antecedent to the action. These two situations are combined in *The Glass Menagerie*, Williams's first successful play (and probably his most popular one[1]). The play is a perfect fusion of the two subjects and so is a figure for Williams's entire career. In it the family is long lost and, also, we witness its struggle before it is lost. Williams captures the poignancy of family memories in a way all his own, without sacrificing the core of dramatic conflict which makes such memories less static.

The play is a prime example of Williams's artistry in establishing the relation between his own dramatic world and the conventions of realistic domestic drama to which his audience owes great allegiance, as he well knew. The play occurs in the mind of Tom Wingfield, who drifts in and out of the action both as narrator and participant in a peculiarly appropriate way. From the moment at the beginning when the scrim of the tenement wall dissolves and we enter the Wingfields' apartment, we are reminded of the household of so many family plays.

The realistic convention of the fourth wall is evoked as Tom remembers his family.

Tom's evocation is self-conscious, for as "stage manager" he has control over the setting. But Tom is also at the mercy of his memories and irresistibly must relive them. The play keeps us poised between these two styles, these two times, throughout. This is, in fact, its strongest and most subtle conflict. Like Tom, we are continually tempted into the world of a realistic family struggle, but never allowed to enter it completely. The projections and lighting keep the effect slightly stylized during the scenes, the fragmented structure blocks us from too long an absorption in the action, and the re-appearance of Tom as narrator forces us back to the present. It is Tom's final reappearance in this role, when the action of the memory play is completed, which releases the tension created between the two styles and dramatizes, in a final rush of emotion, the irretrievable loss of the family which Tom can never escape.

Tom cannot shake the memory of his family from his mind; the dissolution of time and space in the play — that is, in his consciousness — heightens the importance of what he is remembering to make it the most significant thing about his existence. What he remembers — the bulk of the play — centers around two lines of action. The first is his desire to escape from his family just as his father had done before him: "He was a telephone man who fell in love with long distances."[2] Tom, a would-be writer, is caught between a domineering mother and a stultifying warehouse job. He escapes to the porch, to the movies, to the saloon. And finally, in the end, we learn that he has followed his father out into long distances. The second line of action, the principal one, concerns his mother, Amanda, and her attempts to establish some kind of life for Tom's crippled sister, Laura. Amanda pins her hopes on getting "sister" married, after Laura fails because of painful shyness to continue in business school. A "gentleman caller" is found, Jim O'Connor, "an emissary from the world of reality," but all of Amanda's hopes are crushed as he turns out to be already engaged.

The plot is slight stuff, as Williams himself knew.[3] The effect of the play derives in part from the contrast between its two lines of action. Amanda is given over to memories of her past life of happiness as a young southern debutante in Blue Mountain, Mississippi, where on one incredible Sunday she had seventeen gentlemen callers. She imitates the manners and graciousness of those days, a faintly ludicrous parody of southern gentility, the played-out tradition of the antebellum South and its family of security. But she has spirit, too, and responds to the problems of raising two children in a St. Louis tenement during the Depression. Her practicality is what gives her dignity; as she cares for Laura we realize how much Amanda herself needs to be cared for. Her refusal to give in to her nostalgia, even while she indulges in it, enhances her character and makes us susceptible to her longing.

Tom is smothered by such a woman. He fights with her, in part, because she continually tells him what to do: how to eat; how to sleep; how to get ahead. But he fights, also, because her standards represent the conventionality of family responsibility. . . . The absent father, who still represents the memory of romantic family love to Amanda, is the possibility of romantic escape from family to Tom.[4] He loves his sister Laura, yet he will not accept the responsibility for her which Amanda demands of him. The Wingfields are only a ghost of the family of security, but even this demand to be close-knit repels the restless Tom.

Tom's love for Laura needs to be emphasized, I think, not only because it is one part of the final image of the play — the moment of revelation toward which the action tends — but because it shows Williams's interest in the special qualities of those whom the world has hurt. They are the delicate and fragile people, too sensitive to be able to withstand the crude and harsh necessities by which life drives us along. They have an extraordinary awareness of hidden, almost mystical, qualities of spiritual beauty; and this openness dooms them to be crushed or perverted by the animal vigor of the world.

Laura's specialness is seen largely in contrast with Jim, her gentleman caller. He is, by all odds, the kindest of Williams's emissaries from reality, perhaps because his faith in the American dream of self-improvement and success is so complete as to be itself a touching illusion. . . .

There will be no normal love of marriage and family for Laura nor for any of the Wingfields. Laura is too tender, too special, too fragile like her glass menagerie. It is Tom's painful sensitivity to Laura's predicament which makes him love her and which drives him from her. But he cannot escape Laura. The necessity of leaving her, and the guilt over doing so, haunt him:

> Oh, Laura, Laura, I tried to leave you behind me, but I am more faithful than I intended to be! I reach for a cigarette, I cross the street, I run into the movies or a bar, I buy a drink, I speak to the nearest stranger — anything that can blow your candles out!
>
> (*Laura bends over the candles.*)
>
> For nowadays the world is lit by lightning! Blow out your candles, Laura — and so good-bye. . . .
>
> (*She blows the candles out.*)[5]

Laura's painful encounter with the world's lightning represents all of the Wingfields. Amanda's last glance at her husband's picture reveals as much of her as does Tom's final speech of him. The family is the supreme case of love trying to struggle against the world, and the family fails. Fundamentally romantic, Williams evokes the beauty of failure, the beauty which must fail. . . .

Notes

[1] Jackson, *Broken World*, p. viii, note 1.

[2] Williams, *Menagerie*, p. 145.

[3] "A free, imaginative use of light can be of enormous value in giving a mobile, plastic quality to plays of a more or less static nature." Williams, "Production Notes," *Menagerie*, p. 134.

[4] Tischler, *Williams*, p. 97.

[5] Williams, *Menagerie*, p. 237.

JAMES FISHER

from "The Angels of Fructification°": Tennessee Williams, Tony Kushner, and Images of Homosexuality on the American Stage

Who, if I were to cry out, would hear me among the angelic orders?[1]
—*Rainer Maria Rilke*

*Still obscured by glistening exhaltations, the angels of fructification had now begun to meet the tumescent phallus of the sun. Vastly the wheels of the earth sang Allelulia!
And the seven foaming oceans bellowed Oh!*[2]
—*Tennessee Williams*

Williams was the theatre's angel of sexuality — the dramatist most responsible for forcefully introducing sexual issues, both gay and straight, to the American stage. The fruit of his labor is particularly evident in the subsequent genera- tions of playwrights who present gay characters and situations with increasing frankness, depth, and lyricism. Such works bloom most particularly after the 1960s, and most richly in Tony Kushner's epic *Angels in America*, which has been described by critics as one of the most important American plays of the past fifty years. . . .[3]

In reflecting on the history of homosexuals in American theatre, Kushner be- lieves that "there's a natural proclivity for gay people — who historically have often spent their lives hiding — to feel an affinity for the extended make-believe and donning of roles that is part of theater. It's reverberant with some of the central facts of our lives."[4] It is not surprising that, in a society in which homosex- uals were firmly closeted before the 1960s, the illusions of the stage provided a safe haven. Williams could not be as open about his sexuality in his era as Kushner can be now, and thus had to work with overtly heterosexual situations and characters. Williams's creative achievements grow out of a guarded self-awareness and desire for self-preservation, as well as the constraints of the prevailing values of his day.

Donald Windham believes that Williams "loved being homosexual. I think he loved it more than he loved anybody, more than he loved anything except writing,"[5] and Edward A. Sklepowich seems to agree when he writes that "Williams treats homosexuality with a reverence that at times approaches chauvinism."[6] In fact, Williams was often ambivalent about homosexuality — either his own or anyone else's — in his writings. Although his sexuality was well known in the theatrical community, it is unclear when Williams first "came out" publicly. His 1970 ap- pearance on David Frost's television program seems the earliest public declara- tion. When Frost asked him to comment on his sexuality, Williams replied, "I don't want to be involved in some sort of a scandal, but I've covered the water- front."[7] He also told Frost that "everybody has some elements of homosexuality in him, even the most heterosexual of us" (p. 40), but a few years later he wrote, "I have never found the subject of homosexuality a satisfactory theme for a full- length play, despite the fact that it appears as frequently as it does in my short

---

°*Fructification:* The producing of fruit.

fiction. Yet never even in my short fiction does the sexual activity of a person provide the story with its true inner substance."[8] A couple of years later, in an interview in the *Village Voice*, Williams made the point with bluntness: "I've nothing to conceal. Homosexuality isn't the theme of my plays. They're about all human relationships. I've never faked it,"[9] and in 1975 he stated, "Sexuality is part of my work, of course, because sexuality is a part of my life and everyone's life. I see no essential difference between the love of two men for each other and the love of a man for a woman; no essential difference, and that's why I've examined both. . . ."[10] In his novel, *Moise and the World of Reason* (1975), Williams is franker in his depiction of homosexuality than in any of his plays. However, more important than issues of homosexuality, the characters in the novel feel the absence of love and a need for connection — constant themes in all of Williams's work. There is no question that, as a rule, Williams was writing about love and not gender. He criticized sexual promiscuity as "a distortion of the love impulse,"[11] and for him, this impulse, in whatever form, was sacred. . . .

To understand, in part, why Williams obscured homosexuality in his plays, Gore Vidal explains that Williams "had the most vicious press of almost any American writer I can think of. Fag-baiting was at its peak in the fifties when he was at his peak and it has never given up, actually."[12] Donald Spoto believes that Williams's ambivalence had to do, in part, with the fact that he wanted "to be controversial — the hard-drinking, openly homosexual writer with nothing to hide — and at the same time, a man of his own time, a Southern gentleman from a politer era who would never abandon propriety and privacy."[13] This view might indicate why Williams seemed uncomfortable with public displays of drag or campiness, which, he writes, are

> imposed upon homosexuals by our society. The obnoxious forms of it will rapidly disappear as Gay Lib begins to succeed in its serious crusade to assert, for its genuinely misunderstood and persecuted minority, a free position in society which will permit them to respect themselves, at least to the extent that, individually, they deserve respect — and I think that degree is likely to be much higher than commonly supposed.[14]

And it was in the arena of the arts, Williams believed, that the gay sensibility was most likely to first engender such respect. In his *Memoirs* he states, "There is no doubt in my mind that there is more sensibility — which is equivalent to more talent — among the 'gays' of both sexes than among the 'norms' . . ." (p. 63). At the same time, Williams wished to attract a broader audience than gays for his work and seems to have believed that a so-called gay play would limit his access to universal acceptance.

Williams's concern about acceptance was not without some justice. He did not have to look too far back into the preceding decades of American drama to see that the audience was, at best, uncertain about its willingness to accept homosexual characters and issues. The first American play to deal openly with homosexuality is believed to be Mae West's *The Drag*, which generated so much controversy that it closed before completing a tumultuous pre-Broadway tour in 1927. A few other curiosities appeared in the subsequent decades, most notably Lillian Hellman's *The Children's Hour* (1934), in which the question of a lesbian relationship is at the center. Of course, secondary homosexual characters appear in a few plays of the 1930s and 1940s, but they are rarely identified as such. Simon Stimson, the alcoholic choir master of Thornton Wilder's *Our Town* (1938), is a vivid example of such types, typical in that he is comparatively unimportant to the plot and that he is seen mostly as a tragi-comic victim. With the appearance of Robert Anderson's *Tea and Sympathy* (1953), in which a sensitive young man is viewed by his peers as a homosexual (even though it later becomes clear that he is not), gay issues and characters slowly come out of the shadows.

During the 1950s, other playwrights introduced gay characters and issues, but often not in their most visible work. William Inge, inspired to become a play-wright by Williams's example, did not feature openly homosexual characters in any of his major plays, but in a few lesser-known one-acts he does so vividly. Inge's *The Tiny Closet* (1959), for example, features a man boarding in a rooming house where the nosy landlady has been attempting to break into a padlocked closet in his room. As soon as the man goes out, the landlady and her friend manage to break in and discover an array of elegant women's hats. The landlady's violation — and the presumption that she will cause him public disgrace — leaves the man's ultimate fate in question. Inge's blunt attack on intolerance[15] was written in the aftermath of the McCarthy era and was a forerunner of later gay plays, particularly those written after the late 1960s, which argue for greater acceptance for homosexuals.

Mid-twentieth century dramatists employed various techniques to present gay characters and situations. One device often used is "transference," the act of hid-ing gay viewpoints and situations behind a mask of heterosexuality. Edward Albee, often accused of using transference in the writing of such plays as *Who's Afraid of Virginia Woolf?* (1962), is a gay dramatist who also emerged in the 1950s. With the homosexual triumvirate of Williams, Inge, and Albee dominating the non-musical Broadway stage — and despite the fact that none of them had pub-licly acknowledged their own sexuality — *New York Times* drama critic Stanley Kauffmann "outed" them in 1966. Although he does not give their names, it is clear to whom he is referring in his article "Homosexual Drama and Its Disguises." Kauffmann implies that homosexual writers have no right to write about anything but gay characters — an attitude which would logically imply that men are un-able to write about women and vice versa. Kauffmann's notion, undoubtedly all too prevalent in the mid 1960s, becomes clearer when he writes:

> Conventions and puritanisms in the Western world have forced [homosexuals] to wear masks for generations, to hate themselves, and thus to hate those who make them hate themselves. Now that they have a certain relative freedom, they vent their feelings in camouflaged form. . . . They emphasize manner and style because these elements of art, at which they are often adept, are legal ten-der in their transactions with the world. These elements are, or can be, estheti-cally divorced from such other considerations as character and idea.[16]

Albee firmly refutes the idea that he, or Williams, employs transference in his plays: "Tennessee never did that, and I can't think of any self-respecting worth-while writer who would do that sort of thing. It's beneath contempt to suggest it, and it's beneath contempt to do it.[17] Gore Vidal's explanation of the centrality of women characters in Williams's plays seems a valid alternative to understanding his work and the reasons critics see transference in his plays. Vidal believes that for Williams, a woman was "always more interesting as she was apt to be the victim of a society."[18] Williams understood, as Strindberg did, that there are many aspects of the female in the male and vice-versa. And, also like Strindberg, Williams's pained, driven, poetic, and passionate characters are unquestionably extensions of his own persona regardless of their gender.

Notes

[1] Ranier Maria Rilke, "Duino Elegies. The Ninth Elegy," in *Selected Works. Vol. 11. Poetry*, trans. J. B. Leishman (Norfolk, Connecticut, and New York: A New Directions Book, 1960), pp. 244–245.

[2] Tennessee Williams, "The Angels of Fructification," in *In the Winter of Cities. Selected Poems of Tennessee Williams* (New York: New Directions, 1956, 1964), p. 34.

[3] Kushner's theatrical output thus far includes the plays *Yes, Yes, No, No* (1985; children's play), *Stella* (1987; adapted from a play by Goethe), *A Bright Room Called Day* (1987), *Hydriotaphia* (1987), *The Illusion* (1988; freely adapted from a play by Pierre Corneille), *Angels in America. Part One. Millenium Approaches* (1990), *Angels in America. Part Two. Perestroika* (1991), *Widows* (1991; written with Ariel Dorfman, adapted from Dorfman's novel), *Slavs* (1994), and *The Dybbuk* (1995; adapted from S. Ansky's play).

[4] Bob Blanchard, "Playwright of Pain and Hope," *Progressive Magazine*. October 1994, p. 42.

[5] Donald Windham interviewed in "Tennessee Williams. Orpheus of the American Stage," a film by Merrill Brockway broadcast on "American Masters" (PBS-TV), 1994.

[6] Edward A. Sklepowich, "In Pursuit of the Lyric Quarry: The Image of the Homosexual in Tennessee Williams' Prose Fiction," in *Tennessee Williams: A Tribute*, ed. Jac Tharpe (Jackson: University Press of Mississippi, 1977), p. 541.

[7] David Frost, *The Americans* (New York: Stein and Day, 1970), p. 40.

[8] Tennessee Williams, "Let Me Hang It All Out." *New York Times*, March 4, 1975, Section 11, p. 1.

[9] Tennessee Williams interviewed by Arthur Bell, *Village Voice*, February 24, 1972.

[10] Tennessee Williams interviewed by Robert Berkvist, *New York Times*, December 21, 1975.

[11] Tennessee Williams interviewed on "The Lively Arts" program (BBC-TV), 1976.

[12] Gore Vidal interviewed in "Tennessee Williams. Orpheus of the American Stage," a film by Merrill Brockway for "American Masters" (PBS-TV), 1994.

[13] Donald Spoto, *The Kindness of Strangers, The Life of Tennessee Williams* (Boston / Toronto: Little, Brown and Co., 1985), p. 292.

[14] Tennessee Williams, *Memoirs* (New York: Doubleday, 1975), p. 63.

[15] Inge's one-act *The Boy in the Basement* (1962) makes a similar plea for tolerance.

[16] Stanley Kauffmann, "Homosexual Drama and Its Disguises," *New York Times*, January 23, 1966, Section 2, p. 1.

[17] Edward Albee, cited in *The Playwright's Art. Conversations with Contemporary American Dramatists*, ed. Jackson R. Bryer (New Brunswick, New Jersey: Rutgers University Press, 1995), p. 21.

[18] Gore Vidal interviewed in "Tennessee Williams. Orpheus of the American Stage," a film by Merrill Brockway for "American Masters" (PBS-TV), 1994.

TENNESSEE WILLIAMS

Portrait of a Girl in Glass

We lived in a third floor apartment on Maple Street in Saint Louis, on a block which also contained the Ever-ready Garage, a Chinese laundry, and a bookie shop disguised as a cigar store.

Mine was an anomalous character, one that appeared to be slated for radical change or disaster, for I was a poet who had a job in a warehouse. As for my sister Laura, she could be classified even less readily than I. She made no positive motion toward the world but stood at the edge of the water, so to speak, with feet that anticipated too much cold to move. She'd never have budged an inch, I'm pretty sure, if my mother who was a relatively aggressive sort of woman had not shoved her roughly forward, when Laura was twenty years old, by enrolling her as a student in a nearby business college. Out of her "magazine money" (she sold subscriptions to women's magazines), Mother had paid my sister's tuition for a term of six months. It did not work out. Laura tried to memorize the typewriter keyboard, she had a chart at home, she used to sit silently in front of it for hours, staring at it while she cleaned and polished her infinite number of little glass ornaments. She did this every evening after dinner. Mother would caution me to be very quiet. "Sister is looking at her typewriter chart!" I felt somehow that it would do her no good, and I was right. She would seem to know the positions of the keys until the weekly speed drill got underway, and then they would fly from her mind like a bunch of startled birds.

At last she couldn't bring herself to enter the school any more. She kept this failure a secret for a while. She left the house each morning as before and spent six hours walking around the park. This was in February, and all the walking outdoors regardless of weather brought on influenza. She was in bed for a couple of weeks with a curiously happy little smile on her face. Of course Mother phoned the business college to let them know she was ill. Whoever was talking on the other end of the line had some trouble, it seems, in remembering who Laura was, which annoyed my mother and she spoke up pretty sharply. "Laura has been attending that school of yours for two months, you certainly ought to recognize her name!" Then came the stunning disclosure. The person sharply retorted, after a moment or two, that now she *did* remember the Wingfield girl, and that she had not been at the business college *once* in about a month. Mother's voice became strident. Another person was brought to the phone to verify the statement of the first. Mother hung up and went to Laura's bedroom where she lay with a tense and frightened look in place of the faint little smile. Yes, admitted my sister, what they said was true. "I couldn't go any longer, it scared me too much, it made me sick at the stomach!"

After this fiasco, my sister stayed at home and kept in her bedroom mostly. This was a narrow room that had two windows on a dusky areaway between two wings of the building. We called this areaway Death Valley for a reason that seems worth telling. There were a great many alley cats in the neighborhood and one particularly vicious dirty white Chow who stalked them continually. In the open or on the fire escapes they could usually elude him but now and again he cleverly contrived to run some youngster among them into the cul-de-sac of this narrow areaway at the far end of which, directly beneath my sister's bedroom windows, they made the blinding discovery that what had appeared to be an avenue of escape was really a locked arena, a gloomy vault of concrete and brick with walls too high for any cat to spring, in which they must suddenly turn to spit at their death until it was hurled upon them. Hardly a week went by without a repetition of this violent drama. The areaway had grown to be hateful to Laura because she could not look out on it without recalling the screams and the snarls of killing. She kept the shades drawn down, and as Mother would not permit the use of electric current except when needed, her days were spent almost in perpetual twilight. There were three pieces of dingy ivory furniture in the room, a bed, a bureau, a chair. Over the bed was a remarkably bad religious painting, a very effeminate head of Christ with teardrops visible just below the eyes. The charm of the room was produced by my sister's collection of glass. She loved colored glass and had covered the walls with shelves of little glass articles, all of them light and delicate in color. These she washed and polished with endless care. When you entered the room there was always this soft, transparent radiance in it which came from the glass absorbing whatever faint light came through the shades on Death Valley. I have no idea how many articles there were of this delicate glass. There must have been hundreds of them. But Laura could tell you exactly. She loved each one.

She lived in a world of glass and also a world of music. The music came from a 1920 Victrola and a bunch of records that dated from about the same period, pieces such as "Whispering" or "The Love Nest" or "Dardanella." These records were souvenirs of our father, a man whom we barely remembered, whose name was spoken rarely. Before his sudden and unexplained disappearance from our lives, he had made this gift to the household, the phonograph and the records, whose music remained as a sort of apology for him. Once in a while, on payday at the warehouse, I would bring home a new record. But Laura seldom cared for these new records, maybe because they reminded her too much of the noisy tragedies in Death Valley or the speed drills at the business college. The tunes she loved were the ones she had always heard. Often she sang to herself at night in her bedroom. Her voice was thin, it usually wandered off-key. Yet it had a curious childlike sweetness. At eight o'clock in the evening I sat down to write in my own mousetrap of a room. Through the closed doors, through the walls, I would hear my sister singing to herself, a piece like "Whispering" or "I Love You" or "Sleepy Time Gal," losing the tune now and then but always preserving the minor atmosphere of the music. I think that was why I always wrote such strange and sorrowful poems in those days. Because I had in my ears the wispy sound of my sister serenading her pieces of colored glass, washing them while she sang or merely looking down at them with her vague blue eyes until the points of gem-like radiance in them gently drew the arching particles of reality from her mind and finally produced a state of hypnotic calm in which she even stopped singing or washing the glass and merely sat without motion until my mother knocked at the door and warned her against the waste of electric current.

I don't believe that my sister was actually foolish. I think the petals of her mind had simply closed through fear, and it's no telling how much they had closed upon in the way of secret wisdom. She never talked very much, not even to me, but once in a while she did pop out with something that took you by surprise.

After work at the warehouse or after I'd finished my writing in the evening, I'd drop in her room for a little visit because she had a restful and soothing effect on nerves that were worn rather thin from trying to ride two horses simultaneously in two opposite directions.

I usually found her seated in the straight-back ivory chair with a piece of glass cupped tenderly in her palm.

"What are you doing? Talking to it?" I asked.

"No," she answered gravely, "I was just looking at it."

On the bureau were two pieces of fiction which she had received as Christmas or birthday presents. One was a novel called the *Rose-Garden Husband* by someone whose name escapes me. The other was *Freckles* by Gene Stratton Porter. I never saw her reading the *Rose-Garden Husband*, but the other book was one that she actually lived with. It had probably never occurred to Laura that a book was something you read straight through and then laid aside as finished. The character Freckles, a one-armed orphan youth who worked in a lumber camp, was someone that she invited into her bedroom now and then for a friendly visit just as she did me. When I came in and found this novel open upon her lap, she would gravely remark that Freckles was having some trouble with the foreman of the lumber camp or that he had just received an injury to his spine when a tree fell on him. She frowned with genuine sorrow when she reported these misadventures of her storybook hero, possibly not recalling how successfully he came through them all, that the injury to the spine fortuitously resulted in the discovery of rich parents and that the bad-tempered foreman has a heart of gold at the end of the book. Freckles became involved in romance with a girl he called The Angel, but my sister usually stopped reading when this girl became too prominent in the story. She closed the book or turned back to the lonelier periods in the orphan's story. I only remember her making one reference to this heroine of the novel. "The Angel is nice," she said, "but seems to be kind of conceited about her looks."

Then one time at Christmas, while she was trimming the artificial tree, she picked up the Star of Bethlehem that went on the topmost branch and held it gravely toward the chandelier.

"Do stars have five points really?" she enquired.

This was the sort of thing that you didn't believe and that made you stare at Laura with sorrow and confusion.

"No," I told her, seeing she really meant it, "they're round like the earth and most of them much bigger."

She was gently surprised by this new information. She went to the window to look up at the sky which was, as usual during Saint Louis winters, completely shrouded by smoke.

"It's hard to tell," she said, and returned to the tree.

So time passed on till my sister was twenty-three. Old enough to be married, but the fact of the matter was she had never even had a date with a boy. I don't believe this seemed as awful to her as it did to Mother.

At breakfast one morning Mother said to me, "Why don't you cultivate some nice young friends? How about down at the warehouse? Aren't there some young men down there you could ask to dinner?"

This suggestion surprised me because there was seldom quite enough food on her table to satisfy three people. My mother was a terribly stringent housekeeper, God knows we were poor enough in actuality, but my mother had an almost obsessive dread of becoming even poorer. A not unreasonable fear since the man of the house was a poet who worked in a warehouse, but one which I thought played too important a part in all her calculations.

Almost immediately Mother explained herself.

"I think it might be nice," she said, "for your sister."

I brought Jim home to dinner a few nights later. Jim was a big red-haired Irishman who had the scrubbed and polished look of well-kept chinaware. His big square hands seemed to have a direct and very innocent hunger for touching his friends. He was always clapping them on your arms or shoulders and they burned through the cloth of your shirt like plates taken out of an oven. He was the best-liked man in the warehouse and oddly enough he was the only one that I was on good terms with. He found me agreeably ridiculous I think. He knew of my secret practice of retiring to a cabinet in the lavatory and working on rhyme schemes when work was slack in the warehouse, and of sneaking up on the roof now and then to smoke my cigarette with a view across the river at the undulant open country of Illinois. No doubt I was classified as screwy in Jim's mind as much as in the others', but while their attitude was suspicious and hostile when they first knew me, Jim's was warmly tolerant from the beginning. He called me Slim, and gradually his cordial acceptance drew the others around, and while he remained the only one who actually had anything to do with me, the others had now begun to smile when they saw me as people smile at an oddly fashioned dog who crosses their path at some distance.

Nevertheless it took some courage for me to invite Jim to dinner. I thought about it all week and delayed the action till Friday noon, the last possible moment, as the dinner was set for that evening.

"What are you doing tonight?" I finally asked him.

"Not a God damn thing," said Jim. "I had a date but her Aunt took sick and she's hauled her freight to Centralia!"

"Well," I said, "why don't you come over for dinner?"

"Sure!" said Jim. He grinned with astonishing brightness.

I went outside to phone the news to Mother.

Her voice that was never tired responded with an energy that made the wires crackle.

"I suppose he's Catholic?" she said.

"Yes," I told her, remembering the tiny silver cross on his freckled chest.

"Good!" she said. "I'll bake a salmon loaf!"

And so we rode home together in his jalopy.

I had a curious feeling of guilt and apprehension as I led the lamb-like Irishman up three flights of cracked marble steps to the door of Apartment F, which was not thick enough to hold inside it the odor of baking salmon.

Never having a key, I pressed the bell.

"Laura!" came Mother's voice. "That's Tom and Mr. Delaney! Let them in!"

There was a long, long pause.

"Laura?" she called again. "I'm busy in the kitchen, you answer the door!"

Then at last I heard my sister's footsteps. They went right past the door at which we were standing and into the parlor. I heard the creaking noise of the phonograph crank. Music commenced. One of the oldest records, a march of Sousa's, put on to give her the courage to let in a stranger.

The door came timidly open and there she stood in a dress from Mother's wardrobe, a black chiffon ankle-length and high-heeled slippers on which she balanced uncertainly like a tipsy crane of melancholy plumage. Her eyes stared back at us with a glass brightness and her delicate wing-like shoulders were hunched with nervousness.

"Hello!" said Jim, before I could introduce him.

He stretched out his hand. My sister touched it only for a second.

"Excuse me!" she whispered, and turned with a breathless rustle back to her bedroom door, the sanctuary beyond it briefly revealing itself with the tinkling, muted radiance of glass before the door closed rapidly but gently on her wraithlike figure.

Jim seemed to be incapable of surprise.

"Your sister?" he asked.

"Yes, that was her," I admitted. "She's terribly shy with strangers."

"She looks like you," said Jim, "except she's pretty."

Laura did not reappear till called to dinner. Her place was next to Jim at the drop-leaf table and all through the meal her figure was slightly tilted away from his. Her face was feverishly bright and one eyelid, the one on the side toward Jim, had developed a nervous wink. Three times in the course of the dinner she dropped her fork on her plate with a terrible clatter and she was continually raising the water glass to her lips for hasty little gulps. She went on doing this even after the water was gone from the glass. And her handling of the silver became more awkward and hurried all the time.

I thought of nothing to say.

To Mother belonged the conversational honors, such as they were. She asked the caller about his home and family. She was delighted to learn that his father had a business of his own, a retail shoe store somewhere in Wyoming. The news that he went to night school to study accounting was still more edifying. What was his heart set on beside the warehouse? Radio-engineering? My, my, my! It was easy to see that here was a very up-and-coming young man who was certainly going to make his place in the world!

Then she started to talk about her children. Laura, she said, was not cut out for business. She was domestic, however, and making a home was really a girl's best bet.

Jim agreed with all this and seemed not to sense the ghost of an implication. I suffered through it dumbly, trying not to see Laura trembling more and more beneath the incredible unawareness of Mother.

And bad as it was, excruciating in fact, I thought with dread of the moment when dinner was going to be over, for then the diversion of food would be taken away, we would have to go into the little steam-heated parlor. I fancied the four of us having run out of talk, even Mother's seemingly endless store of questions about Jim's home and his job all used up finally — the four of us, then, just sitting there in the parlor, listening to the hiss of the radiator and nervously clearing our throats in the kind of self-consciousness that gets to be suffocating.

But when the blancmange was finished, a miracle happened.

Mother got up to clear the dishes away. Jim gave me a clap on the shoulders and said, "Hey, Slim, let's go have a look at those old records in there!"

He sauntered carelessly into the front room and flopped down on the floor beside the Victrola. He began sorting through the collection of worn-out records and reading their titles aloud in a voice so hearty that it shot like beams of sunlight through the vapors of self-consciousness engulfing my sister and me.

He was sitting directly under the floor-lamp and all at once my sister jumped up and said to him, "Oh — you have freckles!"

Jim grinned. "Sure that's what my folks call me — Freckles!"

"Freckles?" Laura repeated. She looked toward me as if for the confirmation of some too wonderful hope. I looked away quickly, not knowing whether to feel relieved or alarmed at the turn that things were taking.

Jim had wound the Victrola and put on *Dardanella*.

He grinned at Laura.

"How about you an' me cutting the rug a little?"

"What?" said Laura breathlessly, smiling and smiling.

"Dance!" he said, drawing her into his arms.

As far as I knew she had never danced in her life. But to my everlasting wonder she slipped quite naturally into those huge arms of Jim's, and they danced round and around the small steam-heated parlor, bumping against the sofa and chairs and laughing loudly and happily together. Something opened up in my sister's face. To say it was love is not too hasty a judgment, for after all he had freckles and that was what his folks called him. Yes, he had undoubtedly assumed the identity — for all practical purposes — of the one-armed orphan youth who lived in the Limberlost, that tall and misty region to which she retreated whenever the walls of Apartment F became too close to endure.

Mother came back in with some lemonade. She stopped short as she entered the portieres.

"Good heavens! Laura? Dancing?"

Her look was absurdly grateful as well as startled.

"But isn't she stepping all over you, Mr. Delaney?"

"What if she does?" said Jim, with bearish gallantry. "I'm not made of eggs!"

"Well, well, well!" said Mother, senselessly beaming.

"She's light as a feather!" said Jim. "With a little more practice she'd dance as good as Betty!"

There was a little pause of silence.

"Betty?" said Mother.

"The girl I go out with!" said Jim.

"Oh!" said Mother.

She set the pitcher of lemonade carefully down and with her back to the caller and her eyes on me, she asked him just how often he and the lucky young lady went out together.

"Steady!" said Jim.

Mother's look, remaining on my face, turned into a glare of fury.

"Tom didn't mention that you went out with a girl!"

"Nope," said Jim. "I didn't mean to let the cat out of the bag. The boys at the warehouse'll kid me to death when Slim gives the news away."

He laughed heartily but his laughter dropped heavily and awkwardly away as even his dull senses were gradually penetrated by the unpleasant sensation the news of Betty had made.

"Are you thinking of getting married?" said Mother.

"First of next month!" he told her.

It took her several moments to pull herself together. Then she said in a dismal tone, "How nice! If Tom had only told us we could have asked you *both!*"

Jim had picked up his coat.

"Must you be going?" said Mother.

"I hope it don't seem like I'm rushing off," said Jim, "but Betty's gonna get back on the eight o'clock train an' by the time I get my jalopy down to the Wabash depot —"

"Oh, then, we mustn't keep you."

Soon as he'd left, we all sat down, looking dazed.

Laura was the first to speak.

"Wasn't he nice?" she asked. "And all those freckles!"

"Yes," said Mother. Then she turned to me.

"You didn't mention that he was engaged to be married!"

"Well, how did I know that he was engaged to be married?"

"I thought you called him your best friend down at the warehouse?"

"Yes, but I didn't know he was going to be married!"

"How peculiar!" said Mother. "How very peculiar!"

"No," said Laura gently, getting up from the sofa. "There's nothing peculiar about it."

She picked up one of the records and blew on its surface a little as if it were dusty, then set it softly back down.

"People in love," she said, "take everything for granted."

What did she mean by that? I never knew.

She slipped quietly back to her room and closed the door.

Not very long after that I lost my job at the warehouse. I was fired for writing a poem on the lid of a shoe-box. I left Saint Louis and took to moving around. The cities swept about me like dead leaves, leaves that were brightly colored but torn away from the branches. My nature changed. I grew to be firm and sufficient.

In five years' time I had nearly forgotten home. I had to forget it, I couldn't carry it with me. But once in a while, usually in a strange town before I have found companions, the shell of deliberate hardness is broken through. A door comes softly and irresistibly open. I hear the tired old music my unknown father left in the place he abandoned as faithlessly as I. I see the faint and sorrowful radiance of the glass, hundreds of little transparent pieces of it in very delicate colors. I hold my breath, for if my sister's face appears among them — the night is hers!

June 1943 (Published 1948)

Topics for Further Research

1. In the Jean Evans article "Interview 1945" (p. 2053), Williams responds to the question of his use of "plays unconventional in form." In his response, he states that his plays are "light on plot and heavy on characterization." Does such an emphasis benefit *The Glass Menagerie*, or do you think its plot should be developed further? What other Williams plays share this emphasis on character over plot? Do you see this emphasis as a strength or a weakness?

2. Williams has called himself a "moral symbolist" in the tradition of Nathaniel Hawthorne. Williams, however, has made sexuality's mystery one of his central metaphors. How has he portrayed sexuality in his plays? What is his moral message?

3. Williams writes about his characters' attempt to escape their reality, and most often their reality is a life of loneliness. What methods do his characters use to try to escape their loneliness? Do any of them succeed? When they do not succeed, what causes their failure?

4. Often, writers use biographical information to give their work authenticity or to explore elements of their own lives in fiction. Like the character Tom Wingfield, the young Tennessee Williams fled his family for the refuge of artistic creation, fame, and material success. Research the life of Tennessee Williams. What job did he hold that appears in *The Glass Menagerie*? What characters' names in the play come from his past? How are other elements of Williams's life used in *The Glass Menagerie*, and what do they contribute to the play?

5. One of the criticisms of *The Glass Menagerie* when it was first produced was that its staging was overly complicated. Without the numerous elements of staging used in this play, critics argue, the dialogue and action alone would be quite shallow. Other critics, however, maintain that the complex staging is an integral part of this "memory play," which was intentionally designed to resemble a "magic act" much like the one Tom refers to in Scene 4. Do you see all the staging elements as necessary to the play? How do these devices contribute to the theme Williams establishes of memory versus reality and reality versus illusion?

6. In addition to "Portrait of a Girl in Glass," Williams wrote another short story based on the story of *The Glass Menagerie*: "The Resemblance between a Violin Case and a Coffin." Read this story, and compare it to both the play and "Portrait of a Girl in Glass." What are the similarities and differences? Which version do you prefer? Why?

Jenkins 1

Heather Jenkins

English 202

Professor Spand

17 April 2005

Laura's Gentleman Caller

One of the major points of debate about
Tennessee Williams's play <u>The Glass Menagerie</u> centers
on the character Jim O'Connor, the "gentleman caller."
Jim is an outgoing young man who approaches life
lightheartedly, and his friendliness and charm make
him a good suitor for Laura. But beside being Laura's
suitor, what role does Jim play in the drama? Is Jim
merely another character lost in the play's world
of illusion, or is he something more? The answers

Thesis statement to these questions become clear when we examine
Jim's behavior and his influence on the other
characters.

First possible   One possible interpretation of Jim's role is
interpretation of that as someone who has created his own illusions, he
gentleman caller: encourages other characters to dream and fantasize.
dreamer Jim's vision of the future is a grand (and
unrealistic) one. He dreams of becoming part of the
newly formed television industry, and throughout his
appearance on stage, he rambles on about himself and
his plans for the future:

> Because I believe in the future of
> television! <u>(Turning back to her.)</u> I wish
> to be ready to go up right along with it.
> Therefore I'm planning to get in on the
> ground floor. In fact, I've already made

Jenkins 2

the right connections and all that remains
is for the industry itself to get underway!
Full steam— <u>(His eyes are starry.)</u>
<u>Knowledge</u>—Zzzzzp! <u>Money</u>—Zzzzzp!—<u>Power</u>!
That's the cycle democracy is built on!
<u>(His attitude is convincingly dynamic.</u>
<u>Laura stares at him, even her shyness</u>
<u>eclipsed in her absolute wonder. He</u>
<u>suddenly grins.)</u> I guess you think I think
a lot of myself! (2039)

Jim's fantasies about the future play into
and reinforce Amanda's romantic fantasies. Amanda's
plans to find Laura a husband surface long before Jim
enters the Wingfield apartment, but when Amanda learns
that Jim will attend their dinner, her dream of
entertaining gentlemen callers in the Southern
tradition becomes a reality. As a result, she begins
to have unrealistically high expectations for Jim's
visit. When Jim charms Amanda and attempts to impress
her with his dreams of success, he unknowingly
fulfills her fantasy.

Another possible interpretation of Jim's role is
that he acts as a savior. In his article "<u>The Glass</u>
<u>Menagerie</u> Revisited: Catastrophe without Violence,"
Roger B. Stein, discussing the "religious overtones"
(2059) in the play, sees Jim in exactly this way.
According to Stein, the play's action and language
(as well as Williams's stage directions) make it
clear that Laura's meeting with Jim can be seen in

Second possible
interpretation of
gentleman caller:
savior

Jenkins 3

religious—specifically Christian—terms. It is
obvious that Laura needs a savior, but, as Stein
observes, Tom is not able to play this role, and
it "remains therefore for Jim to come as the
Savior to this Friday night supper" (2061). In the
simplest terms, Jim's role as possible savior for
Laura—and, perhaps, for her family—is suggested by
his ability to reach out to Laura and encourage her
to enjoy the pleasures of the real world, such as
dancing and romance.

Jim's role as Laura's savior can also be seen in
the short story "Portrait of a Girl in Glass," from
which the play developed. In the story, Jim and Laura
begin to dance almost immediately after they are left
alone. Although their encounter in the story is less
intimate than the one in the play, Laura responds to
Jim with joy and hope. In the play, Laura's visit
with Jim evokes a similar response: she enjoys the
feeling of being valued and accepted. Therefore, when
Jim announces his departure (and his engagement),
Laura realizes what she has lost and is overwhelmed
with emotion.

Ironically, however, just as Jim offers Laura
a way to escape her world of illusions, he abandons
her, leaving her trapped in her own world. For this
reason, Jim fails as a savior. One might even argue,
in fact, that he consciously rejects his role as a
savior. Still, we must remember that Jim enters the
play unaware of the family's expectations; he views

*Jim's failure
in role as
savior*

the visit purely as an opportunity to pass the time and to meet his friend's family, not as a prelude to romance. Jim's perception of his visit is made clear in "Portrait of a Girl in Glass," where he agrees to visit the Wingfields only because he has nothing else to do:

> "What are you doing tonight?" I finally asked him.
>
> "Not a God damn thing," said Jim. "I had a date but her Aunt took sick and she's hauled her freight to Centralia!"
>
> "Well," I said, "why don't you come over for dinner?"
>
> "Sure!" said Jim. He grinned with astonishing brightness. (2071)

Although both these interpretations of Jim's role offer insights into the play, neither adequately explains Jim's function. Perhaps the best explanation of Jim's role comes from the play itself, where Jim is called "an emissary from a world of reality" (2000). In this sense, his solid presence in the play emphasizes the fragility of the other characters, who live in a world of illusion and fading memories. As an emissary of reality, Jim lives in the real world and realizes the importance of striving for a better life. He attends public speaking and radio engineering classes so that he can advance beyond his low-level job at the warehouse. He scolds Tom for wanting to be a poet, an impractical goal for anyone

Third possible interpretation of gentleman caller: realist

Jenkins 5

living during the economic depression of the 1930s.
Likewise, Jim challenges Laura to cast off her
feelings of inferiority and difference; he does not
understand why Laura has given up hope and isolated
herself. The contrast between Jim and Laura emphasizes
not only Laura's vulnerability but also her family's
consuming and ultimately debilitating delusions.

Because Jim lives in a world of reality, he is
the only character who escapes the illusions that
engulf the Wingfields. Jim's connection with reality
allows him to continue to search for a better life,
something that none of the Wingfields will ever
attain. Even though Tom escapes the confines of the
apartment, he is unable to leave behind the imaginary
world his mother and his sister have created.
Moreover, like his father, Tom leaves not to seek
reality but to escape from one dream world into
another, a world that is little different from the
movies in which he has lost himself. As the play
ends, Tom delivers a monologue about how he has
been unable to leave the memory of his sister behind.
And we are reminded of Jim, the happy and healthy
gentleman caller, who has moved on.

Although Jim is referred to as the gentleman
caller, his role in the play is much more complex. In
one sense, Jim is a dreamer, detached from reality,
enchanted by his own egotistical vision of how people
should behave. In another sense, he is a kind of
savior who reaches out to Laura, conveying the warmth

and compassion of a saint. But these two images are
overshadowed by Jim's role as an emissary from the
real world who journeys to the seductive world of
fantasy and whose presence there emphasizes the
destructive power of dreams that have become
delusions. In this role, Jim is "the kindest of
Williams's emissaries from reality, perhaps because
his faith in the American dream of self-improvement
and success is so complete as to be itself a touching
illusion" (Scanlan 2063).

Jenkins 7

Works Cited

Kirszner, Laurie G., and Stephen R. Mandell, eds.
Literature: Reading, Reacting, Writing.
6th ed. Boston: Wadsworth, 2007.

Scanlan, Tom. From Family, Drama, and American
Dreams. Kirszner and Mandell 2061-63.

Stein, Roger B. "The Glass Menagerie Revisited:
Catastrophe without Violence." Kirszner and
Mandell 2059-61.

Williams, Tennessee. The Glass Menagerie. Kirszner
and Mandell 1994-2049.

---. "Portrait of a Girl in Glass." Kirszner and
Mandell 2068-75.

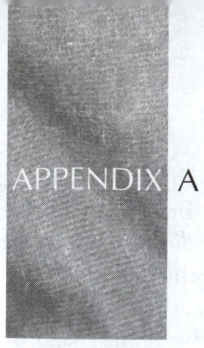

USING LITERARY CRITICISM IN YOUR WRITING

As you become aware of various schools of literary criticism, you see new ways to think — and to write — about fiction, poetry, and drama. Just as you value the opinions of your peers and your instructors, you also will find that the ideas of literary critics can enrich your own reactions to and evaluations of literature. Keep in mind that no single school of literary criticism offers the "right" way of approaching what you read; moreover, no single critic provides the definitive analysis of any short story, poem, or play. As you become aware of the richly varied possibilities of literary criticism, you will begin to ask new questions and discover new insights about the works you read.

Formalism

Formalism stresses the importance of literary form to the meaning of a work. Formalist scholars consider each work of literature in isolation. They consider biographical, historical, and social matters to be irrelevant to the real meaning of a play, short story, novel, or poem. For example, a formalist would see the relationship between Adam and Eve in *Paradise Lost* as entirely unrelated to John Milton's own marital concerns, and they would view theological themes in the same work as entirely separate from Milton's deep involvement with the Puritan religious and political cause in seventeenth-century England. Formalists would also regard Milton's intentions and readers' responses to the epic poem as irrelevant. Instead, formalists would read the text closely, paying attention to organization and structure, to verbal nuances (suggested by word choice and use of figurative language), and to multiple meanings (often created through the writer's use of paradox and irony). The formalist critic tries to reconcile the tensions and oppositions inherent in the text in order to develop a unified reading.

The formalist movement in English-language criticism began in England with I. A. Richard's *Practical Criticism* (1929). To explain and introduce his theory, Richards asked students to interpret famous poems without telling them the poets' names. This strategy encouraged close reading of the text rather than reliance on information about a poet's reputation, the details of a poet's life, or historical context. The American formalist movement, called **New Criticism**, was made popular by college instructors who realized that formalist criticism provided a useful way for students to work along with an instructor in interpreting a literary work rather than passively listening to a lecture on biographical, literary, and historical influences. The New Critical theorists Cleanth Brooks and Robert Penn Warren put together a series of textbooks (*Understanding Poetry, Understanding Fiction,* and *Understanding Drama,* first published in the late 1930s) that were used in colleges for years. After the 1950s, many New Critics began to reevaluate their theories and to broaden their approaches. Although few scholars currently maintain a strictly formalist approach, nearly every critical movement, including feminist, Marxist, psychoanalytic, structuralist, and deconstructionist criticism, owes a debt to the close reading techniques introduced by the formalists.

A Formalist Reading: Kate Chopin's "The Storm" (p. 281)

If you were to apply formalist criticism to Chopin's "The Storm," you might begin by noting the story's three distinctive sections. What relationship do the sections bear to one another? What do we learn from the word choice, the figures of speech, and the symbols in these sections? And, most important, how do these considerations lead readers to a unified view of the story?

In the first section of "The Storm," readers meet Bobinôt and his son Bibi. The description of the approaching clouds as "sombre," "sinister," and "sullen" (281) suggests an atmosphere of foreboding, yet the alliteration of these words also introduces a poetic tone. The conversation between father and son in the final part of this section contrasts, yet does not conflict with, the rather formal language of the introduction. Both Bobinôt and Bibi speak in Cajun dialect, suggesting their humble origins, yet their words have a rhythm that echoes the poetic notes struck in the description of the storm. As the section closes, Bobinôt, thinking of his wife, Calixta, at home, buys a can of the shrimp he knows she likes and holds the treasure "stolidly" (282), ironically suggesting the protection he cannot offer his wife in his separation from her during the coming storm.

The long second section brings readers to the story's central action. Calixta, as she watches the rain, sees her former lover, Alcée, riding up to seek shelter. As in the first section, the language of the narrator is somewhat formal and always poetic, filled with sensuous diction and images. For instance, we see Calixta "unfasten[ing] her white sacque at the throat" (282) and, later, Alcée envisions her lips "as red and moist as pomegranate seed" (283). Again, paralleling the first section, the conversation of the characters is carried on in dialect, suggesting their lack of sophistication and their connection to the powerful natural forces that surround them. The lovemaking that follows, then, seems both natural and poetic. There is nothing sordid about this interlude and, as the final sections of the story suggest through their rather ordinary, matter-of-fact language, nothing has been harmed by Calixta and Alcée's yielding to passion.

In the third section, Bobinôt brings home the shrimp, symbol of his love for Calixta, and, although we recognize the tension between Bobinôt's shy, gentle approach and Alcée's passion, readers can accept the final sentence as literal rather than ironic. The "storms" (both the rain and the storm of passion) have passed, and no one has been hurt. The threat suggested in the opening sentences has been diffused; both the power and the danger evoked by the poetic diction of the first two sections have disappeared, to be replaced entirely by the rhythms of daily life and speech.

For Further Reading: Formalism

Brooks, Cleanth. *The Well Wrought Urn*. 1947.
Empson, William. *Seven Types of Ambiguity*. 1930.
Hartman, Geoffrey H. *Beyond Formalism*. 1970.
Stallman, Robert W. *Critiques and Essays in Criticism. 1920–1948*. 1949.
Wellek, René. *A History of Modern Criticism*. Vol. 6. 1986.
Wimsatt, W. K. *The Verbal Icon*. 1954.

Reader-Response Criticism

Reader-response criticism opposes formalism, seeing the reader's interaction with the text as central to interpretation. Unlike formalists, reader-response critics do not believe that a work of literature exists as a separate, closed entity. Instead, they consider the reader's contribution to the text as essential. A poem, short story, novel, or play is not a solid piece of fabric but rather a series of threads separated by gaps that readers must fill in, drawing on their own experiences and knowledge.

As readers approach a literary text, they contribute their own interpretations. As they read one sentence and then the next, they develop expectations; and, in realistic stories, these expectations are generally met. Nevertheless, nearly every reader supplies personal meanings and observations, making each reader's experience with a work unique and distinctive from every other reader's experience with the same work. For example, imagine Shakespeare's *Romeo and Juliet* as it might be read by a fourteen-year-old high school student and by her father. The young woman, whose age is the same as Juliet's, is almost certain to identify closely with the female protagonist and to "read" Lord Capulet, Juliet's father, as overbearing and rigid. The young reader's father, however, may be drawn to the poignant passage where Capulet talks with a prospective suitor, urging that he wait while Juliet has time to enjoy her youth. Capulet describes the loss of his other children and calls Juliet "the hopeful lady of my earth." Although the young woman reading this line may interpret it as yet another indication of Capulet's possessiveness, her father may see it as a sign of love and even generosity. The twenty-first-century father may "read" Capulet as a man willing to risk offending a friend in order to keep his daughter safe from the rigors of early marriage (and early childbearing). Whose interpretation is correct? Reader-response theorists would say that both readings are entirely possible and therefore equally "right."

The differing interpretations produced by different readers can be seen as simply the effect of the different personalities (and personal histories) involved in constructing meaning from the same series of clues. Not only does the reader "create" the work of literature, in large part, but the literature itself may work on the reader as he or she reads, altering the reader's experience and thus the reader's interpretation. For example, the father reading *Romeo and Juliet* may alter his sympathetic view of Capulet as he continues through the play and observes Capulet's later, angry exchanges with Juliet.

Reader-response theorists believe in the importance of *recursive reading*—that is, reading and rereading with the idea that no interpretation is carved in stone. A second or third interaction with the text may well produce a new interpretation. This changing view is particularly likely when the rereading takes place significantly later than the initial reading. For example, if the young woman just described reread *Romeo and Juliet* when she was middle-aged and herself the mother of teenage children, her reaction to Capulet would quite likely be different from her reaction when she read the work at age fourteen.

In one particular application of reader-response theory, called *reception theory*, the idea of developing readings is applied to the general reading public rather than to individual readers. Reception theory, as proposed by Hans Robert Jauss ("Literary History as a Challenge to Literary Theory," *New Literary History*, Vol. 2 [1970–71]), suggests that each new generation reads the same works of literature differently. Because each generation of readers has experienced different historical events, read different books, and been aware of different critical theories, each generation will view the same works very differently from its predecessors. Certainly a quick look at the summary of literary history in Appendix B will support this idea. (Consider, for example, the changing views toward Shakespeare from the seventeenth century to the present.)

Reader-response criticism has received serious attention since the 1960s, when Norman Holland formulated the theory in *The Dynamics of Literary Response* (1968). The German critic Wolfgang Iser (*The Implied Reader*, 1974) argued that in order to be an effective reader, one must be familiar with the conventions and "codes" of writing. This, then, is one reason for studying literature in a classroom, not to produce approved interpretations but to develop strategies and information that will make sense of a text. Stanley Fish, an American critic, goes even further, arguing that there may not be any "objective" text at all (*Is There a Text in This Class?*, 1980). Fish says that no two readers read the same book, though readers can be trained to have relatively similar responses to a text if they have had relatively similar experiences. For instance, readers who went to college and took an introduction to literature course in which they learned to respond to the various elements of literature, such as character, theme, irony, and figurative language, are likely to have similar responses to a text.

Reader-Response Readings: Kate Chopin's "The Storm" (p. 281)

To demonstrate possible reader-response readings, we can look at the same story previously considered from a formalist perspective. (Of course, if several formalist critics read the story, they too would each write a somewhat different interpretation.)

Written by a twenty-five-year-old man who has studied American literature

In Kate Chopin's "The Storm," attention must be paid to the two adult male characters, Bobinôt and Alcée. Usually, in a love triangle situation, one man is portrayed more sympathetically than the other. But Chopin provides us with a dilemma. Alcée is not a cavalier seducer; he genuinely cares for Calixta. Neither is he a brooding hero. There is nothing gruff or angry about Alcée, and he returns to his family home with no apparent harm done following the passionate interlude. On the other hand, Bobinôt is not a cruel or abusive husband. We can see no clear reason for Calixta's affair except for her desire to fulfill a sexual longing for Alcée.

Written by an eighteen-year-old male student in a first-year literature course

Bibi doesn't seem to be a very important character in the story, but we should pay attention to him as a reflection of his father. At the beginning of the story, Bibi worries about his mother and he expresses his concern to his father. Bobinôt tries to reassure his son, but he gets up and buys a treat for Calixta as much to comfort himself as to get something for her. Then Bibi sits with his father, and it seems as if he has transferred all his worries to Bobinôt. In the third section of the story, after Calixta and Alcée have had their love affair, Bibi and Bobinôt come home. They both seem like children, worried about how Calixta will react. She, of course, is nice to them because she feels so guilty. At the end of the third section, both father and son are happy and enjoying themselves. You can't help but feel great sympathy for them both because they are so loving and simple and because they have been betrayed by Calixta, who has not behaved the way a loving mother and wife should.

Written by a forty-five-year-old woman who has studied Kate Chopin's life and work

A decade after the controversial novel *The Awakening* was published in 1899, one critic protested, "To think of Kate Chopin, who once contented herself with mild yarns about genteel Creole life . . . blowing us a hot blast like that!" (qtd. in Gilbert and Gubar 981). This literary observer was shocked, as one might expect from an early-twentieth-century reader, by Chopin's frank picture of sexual relations, and particularly of the sexual feelings of the novel's heroine. One cannot help but wonder, however, whether the scandalized reader was really widely acquainted with Chopin.

Certainly he could not have read "The Storm." This short story is surprising for many reasons, but primarily because it defies the sexual mores of the late nineteenth century by showing a woman who is neither evil nor doomed enjoying, even glorying in, her sexuality. Calixta is presented as a good wife and loving mother, concerned about her husband and son who are away from home during the storm. Yet her connection to Bobinôt and Bibi does not keep her from passionately enjoying her interlude with Alcée. She goes to his arms unhesitatingly, with no false modesty or guilt (feigned or real) to hold her back. Somehow, this scenario does not seem to fit the definition of "a mild yarn about genteel Creole life."

For Further Reading: Reader-Response Criticism

Bleich, David. *Subjective Criticism*. 1978.
Fish, Stanley. *Is There a Text in This Class?* 1980.
Holland, Norman. *The Dynamics of Literary Response*. 1968.
Iser, Wolfgang. *The Implied Reader*. 1974.
———. *The Act of Reading: A Theory of Aesthetic Response*. 1978.

Rosenblatt, Louise. *The Reader, the Text, the Poem*. 1978.

Sulleiman, Susan, and Inge Crosman, eds. *The Reader in the Text*. 1980.

Tomkins, Jane P., ed. *Reader-Response Criticism*. 1980.

Sociological Criticism

Like reader-response criticism, **sociological criticism** takes issue with formalism. Sociological theorists maintain that the literary work cannot be separated from the social context in which it was created, insisting that literature reflects society and derives its essential existence and significance from the social situations to which it responds. Sociological critics speculate about why a particular work might have been written and explore the ways in which it reacts to a specific situation.

For instance, a sociological literary scholar might note with interest that Shakespeare's history plays about Richard II, Henry IV, and Henry V deal with the consequences of uncertain royal succession and usurpation. These dramas were written during the final years of the reign of Queen Elizabeth I, a monarch who had not produced an heir and refused to designate one. Although the plays cited were set considerably before Elizabeth's time, a sociological critic might conclude that they reflect the English concern about the threat of monarchic chaos should Elizabeth die with no clear line of succession.

In the twentieth century, two strong arms of sociological criticism emerged as dominant: **feminist criticism** and **Marxist criticism.** They remain particularly forceful theories because most of their practitioners have a strong commitment to these ideologies, which they apply as they read literature. Although feminism and Marxism share a concern with segments of society that have been underrepresented and often ignored, scholars working in these fields do not necessarily agree on what constitutes the best response to the issues highlighted by sociological critiques. Both of these views are supported by modern critical theories such as the reader-response idea of gaps in the text that must be filled in through the reader's own experience and knowledge. In addition, the techniques of New Criticism (in particular, close reading of the text), psychoanalysis, and structuralism have allowed sociological critics to focus on what had been overlooked or skewed in traditional readings and to analyze how the experience of marginal and minority groups has been represented in literature. Sociological critics have also employed poststructuralist strategies to reveal and question the assumptions made within their disciplines and to analyze the cultural contexts of their own work.

The late twentieth century has also seen the rise of a third group of theorists, who focus on the relationship between marginalization and ideology. **Postcolonialists, multiculturalists,** and **race theorists** share with other sociological critics a concern with underrepresented and ignored populations, but these schools of criticism focus on representations of ethnic and racial difference. Scholars working from a multicultural perspective seek to develop a more inclusive attitude towards literature, highlighting the contributions of authors working in nonwhite and non-Western traditions. Although both multiculturalist and postcolonialist critics study the social implications of interactions between members of different cultures, postcolonial criticism (like that of the influential critic Edward Said in his landmark text *Orientalism*) analyzes the effects of imperialist discourses on colonized peoples. Race theorists also examine the relationship between literary discourses and racial and ethnic identities in specific political and social contexts, as reflected in the work of bell hooks and Henry Louis Gates Jr. The differences between these branches of criticism are sometimes difficult to articulate, however, as the scholars working in these fields often employ similar strategies of interpretation and analysis.

Feminist Criticism

Throughout the nineteenth century, women such as the Brontë sisters, George Eliot (Mary Ann Evans), Elizabeth Barrett Browning, and Christina Rossetti struggled for the right to be taken as seriously as their male counterparts. In addition, in 1929 Virginia Woolf, an experimental novelist and literary critic, published *A Room of One's Own*, which described the difficulties that women writers faced and defined a tradition of literature written by women.

Feminist criticism emerged as a distinct approach to literature in the late 1960s. Modern feminist criticism began with works such as Mary Ellman's *Thinking about Women* (1968), which focuses on the negative female stereotypes in books authored by men and points out alternative feminine characteristics suggested by women authors. Another pioneering feminist work was Kate Millet's *Sexual Politics* (1969), which analyzes the societal mechanisms that perpetuate male domination of women. Since that time, feminist writings, though not unified in one theory or methodology, have appeared in ever-growing numbers. Some feminist critics have adapted psychoanalytic, Marxist, or other poststructuralist theories, and others have broken new ground. In general, feminist critics take the view that our culture — and by extension our literature — is primarily patriarchal (controlled by males).

According to feminist critics, what is at issue is not anatomical sex but gender. As Simone de Beauvoir explained, a person is not born feminine, as our society defines it, but rather becomes so because of cultural conditioning. According to feminist critics, paternalist Western culture has defined the feminine as "other" to the male, as passive and emotional in opposition to the dominating and rational masculine.

Feminist critics claim that paternalist cultural stereotypes pervade works of literature in the **canon**— those works generally acknowledged to be the best and most significant. Feminists point out that the canon consists of works almost exclusively written by males and about male experiences. Female characters, when they do appear, are often subordinate to male characters. A female reader of these works must either identify with the male protagonist or accept a marginalized role.

One response of feminist critics is to reinterpret works in the traditional canon. As Judith Fetterley explains in *The Resisting Reader* (1978), the reader "revisions" the text, focusing on the covert sexual bias in a literary work. For example, a feminist scholar studying Shakespeare's *Macbeth* might look closely at the role played by Lady Macbeth and argue that she was not simply a cold-hearted villain but a victim of the circumstances of her time: women in her day were not permitted to follow their own ambitions but were relegated to supporting roles, living their lives vicariously through the achievements of their husbands and sons.

A second focus of feminist scholars has been the redefinition of the canon. By seeking out, analyzing, and evaluating little-known works by women, feminist scholars have rediscovered women writers who were ignored or shunned by the reading public and by critics of their own times. Thus, writers such as Kate Chopin and Charlotte Perkins Gilman (see "The Yellow Wallpaper," p. 421), who wrote during the late nineteenth and early twentieth centuries, are now recognized as worthy of study and consideration.

A Feminist Reading: Tillie Olsen's "I Stand Here Ironing" (p. 309)

To approach Tillie Olsen's "I Stand Here Ironing" from a feminist perspective, you might focus on the passages in which the narrator describes her relationships and encounters with men.

> Some readings of Tillie Olsen's "I Stand Here Ironing" suggest that the narrator made choices that doomed her oldest daughter to a life of confusion. If we look at the narrator's relationships with the men in her life, however, we can see that she herself is the story's primary victim.
>
> At nineteen, the narrator was a mother abandoned by her husband, who left her a note saying that he "could no longer endure . . . sharing want" (310) with his wife and infant daughter. This is the first desertion we hear about in the narrator's life, and although she agonizingly describes her painful decisions and the mistakes she made with her daughter Emily, we cannot help but recognize that she was the one who stayed and tried to make things right. Her actions contrast sharply with those of her husband, who ran away, implying that his wife and daughter were burdens too great for him to bear.
>
> The second abandonment is more subtle than the first but no less devastating. After the narrator remarried, she was again left alone to cope with a growing family when her second husband went off to war. True, this desertion was for a "noble" purpose and probably was not voluntary, but the narrator, nevertheless, had to seek one of the low-paying jobs available to women to supplement her allotment checks. She was again forced to leave her children because her husband had to serve the needs of the male-dominated military establishment.
>
> The narrator was alone at crucial points in Emily's life and had to turn away from her daughter in order to survive. Although she has been brought up in a world that teaches women to depend on men, she learns that she is ultimately alone. Although the desertions she endured were not always intentional, she had to bear the brunt of circumstances that were not her choice but were foisted on her by the patriarchal society in which she lives.

For Further Reading: Feminist Criticism

Benstock, Shari, ed. *Feminist Issues in Literary Scholarship.* 1987.

Engleton, Mary, ed. *Feminist Issues in Literary Theory: A Reader.* 1986.

Gilbert, Sandra, and Susan Gubar. *The Madwoman in the Attic*. 1979.

————. *No Man's Land*. 3 vols. 1988, 1989, 1994.

————, eds. *The Norton Anthology of Literature by Women*. 1985.

Heilbrun, Carolyn G. *Hamlet's Mother and Other Women*. 1990.

Jacobus, Mary. *Reading Woman: Essays in Feminist Criticism*. 1986.

Miller, Nancy, K., ed. *The Poetics of Gender*. 1986.

————. *Subject to Change*. 1988.

Showalter, Elaine. *A Literature of Their Own*. 1977.

————. *Sister's Choice: Tradition and Change in American Women's Writing*. 1991.

Marxist Criticism

Marxist criticism bases interpretations of literature on the social and economic theories of Karl Marx (*Das Kapital*, 1867–94) and his colleague and coauthor Friedrich Engels (*The Communist Manifesto*, 1884). Marx and Engels believed that the dominant capitalist middle class would eventually be challenged and overthrown by the working class. In the meantime, however, middle-class capitalists would exploit the working class, who produce excess products and profits yet do not share in the benefits of their labor. Marx and Engels further regarded all parts of the society in which they lived — religious, legal, educational, governmental — as tainted by what they saw as the corrupt values of middle-class capitalists.

Marxist critics apply these views about class struggle to their readings of poetry, fiction, and drama. They tend to analyze the literary works of any historical era as products of the ideology, or network of concepts, that supports the interests of the cultural elite and suppresses those of the working class. Some Marxist critics see all Western literature as distorted by the privileged views of the elite class, but most believe that a few creative writers reject the distorted views of their society and see clearly the wrongs to which working-class people have been subjected. For example, George Lukacs, a Hungarian Marxist critic, proposed that great works of literature create their own worlds and reflect life with clarity. These great works, though not written by Marxists, can be studied for their revealing examples of class conflict and other Marxist concerns. A Marxist critic would look with favor on Charles Dickens, who in nearly every novel pointed out inequities in the political, legal, and educational establishments of his time. Readers who remember Oliver Twist's pitiful plea for "more" workhouse porridge (refused by evil Mr. Bumble, who skims money from funds intended to feed the impoverished inmates) cannot help but see fertile ground for the Marxist critic, who would certainly applaud Dickens's scathing criticism of Victorian social and economic inequality.

Marxist criticism developed in the 1920s and 1930s in Germany and the Soviet Union. Since 1960, British and American Marxism has received greatest attention, with works such as Raymond Williams's *Culture and Society, 1780–1950* (1960) and Terry Eagleton's *Criticism and Ideology* (1976).

A Marxist Reading: Tillie Olsen's "I Stand Here Ironing" (p. 309)

In a Marxist reading of Tillie Olsen's "I Stand Here Ironing," you might concentrate on events that demonstrate how the narrator's and Emily's fates have been directly affected by the capitalist society of the United States.

Tillie Olsen's "I Stand Here Ironing" stands as a powerful indictment of the capitalist system. The narrator and her daughter Emily are repeatedly exploited and defeated by the pressures of the economic system in which they live.

The narrator's first child, Emily, is born into the world of the 1930s depression — an economic disaster brought on by the excesses and greed of Wall Street. When the young mother is deserted by her first husband, there are no government programs in place to help her. She says it was the "pre-relief, pre-WPA world of the depression" that forced her away from her child and into "a job hashing at night" (310). Although she is willing to work, she is paid so poorly that she must finally send Emily to live with her husband's family. Raising the money to bring Emily back takes a long time; and after this separation, Emily's health, both physical and emotional, is precarious.

When Emily gets the measles, we get a hard look at what the few social programs that existed during the Depression were like. The child is sent — at the urging of a government social worker — to a convalescent home. The narrator notes bitterly, "They still send children to that place. I see pictures on the society page of sleek young women planning affairs to raise money for it, or dancing at the affairs, or decorating Easter eggs or filling Christmas stockings for the children" (311). The privileged class basks in the artificial glow of their charity work for the poor, yet the newspapers never show pictures of the hospitalized children who are kept isolated from everyone they loved and forced to eat "runny eggs . . . or mush with lumps" (312). Once again the mother is separated from her daughter by a system that discriminates against the poor. Because the family cannot afford private treatment, Emily is forced to undergo treatment in a public institution that not only denies her any contact with her family but also cruelly forbids her to save the letters she receives from home. Normal family relationships are severely disrupted by an uncaring economic structure that only grudgingly offers aid to the poor.

It is clear that the division between mother and daughter is created and worsened by the social conditions in which they live. Because they are poor, they are separated at crucial times and, therefore, never get to know each other fully. Thus, neither can truly understand the ordeals the other has been forced to endure.

For Further Reading: Marxist Criticism

Agger, Ben. *The Discourse of Domination*. 1992.

Bullock, Chris, and David Peck, eds. *Guide to Marxist Literary Criticism*. 1980.

Eagleton, Terry. *Marxism and Literary Criticism*. 1976.

Frow, John. *Marxism and Literary History*. 1986.

Holub, Renate, and Antonio Gramsci. *Beyond Marxism and Postmodernism*. 1992.

Jameson, Fredric. *Marxism and Form*. 1971.

Lentricchia, Frank. *Criticism and Social Change*. 1983.

Ohmann, Richard M. *Politics of Letters*. 1987.

Strelka, Joseph P., ed. *Literary Criticism and Sociology*. 1973.

Williams, Raymond. *Culture and Society, 1780–1950*. 1960.

———. *Marxism and Literature*. 1977.

New Historicism

New Historicism relates a text to the historical and cultural contexts of the period in which it was created and the periods in which it was critically evaluated. These contexts are not considered simply as "background" but as integral parts of a text. According to the New Historicists, history is not objective facts; rather, like literature, history is subject to interpretation and reinterpretation depending on the power structure of a society. Louis Althusser, for example, suggests that ideology intrudes in the discourse of an era, subjecting readers to the interests of the ruling establishment. Michel Foucault reflects that the discourse of an era defines the nature of "truth" and what behaviors are acceptable, sane, or criminal. "Truth," according to Foucault, is produced by the interaction of power and the systems in which the power flows, and it changes as society changes. Mikhail Bakhtin suggests that all discourse is dialogic, containing within it many independent and sometimes conflicting voices.

Literature, in the opinion of the New Historicist critics, cannot be interpreted without reference to the time and place in which it was written. Criticism likewise cannot be evaluated without reference to the time and place in which it was written. A flaw of much criticism, according to the New Historicists, is the consideration of a literary text as if it were an organic whole. Such an approach ignores the diversity of conflicting voices in a text and in the cultural context in which a text is embedded. Indeed, Stephen Greenblatt prefers the term "cultural poetics" to New Historicism because it acknowledges the integral role that literature and art play in the culture of any era. Works of art and literature, according to Greenblatt, actively foster subversive elements or voices but somehow constrain those forces in ways that defuse challenges to the dominant culture.

New Historicists also point out that readers, like texts, are influenced and shaped by the cultural context of their eras and that a thoroughly objective "reading" of a text is therefore impossible. Acknowledging that all readers to some degree "appropriate" a text, some New Historicists present their criticism of texts as "negotiations" between past and present contexts. Thus, criticism of a particular work of literature would draw from both the cultural context of the era in which the text was written and the critic's present cultural context, and the critic would acknowledge how the latter context influences interpretation of the former.

Since the early 1970s, feminist critics have adopted some New Historicist positions, focusing on male-female power conflicts. And critics interested in multicultural texts have stressed the role of the dominant white culture in suppressing or marginalizing the texts of nonwhites. Marxist critics, including Raymond Williams, have adopted the term "cultural materialism" in discussing their mode of New Historicism, which focuses on the political significance of a literary text.

A New Historicist Reading: Charlotte Perkins Gilman's "The Yellow Wallpaper" (p. 421)

A New Historicist scholar might write an essay about "The Yellow Wallpaper" as an illustration of the destructive effects of the patriarchal culture of the late nineteenth century on women. This reading would be vastly different from that of most nineteenth-century critics, who interpreted the story as a harrowing case study of female mental illness. Even some early-twentieth-century readings posited that the narrator's mental illness is the result of her individual psychological problems. In a New Historicist reading, however, you might focus on the social conventions of the time, which produced conflicting discourses that drove the narrator to madness.

The female narrator of "The Yellow Wallpaper," who is writing in her private journal (which is the text of the short story), explains that her husband, a physician, has diagnosed her as having a "temporary nervous depression — a slight hysterical tendency" (422). She says she should believe such a physician "of high standing" (422) and cooperate with his treatment, which is to confine her to a room in an isolated country estate and compel her to rest and have no visitors and not to write. The "cure" is intended to reduce her nervousness, she further explains. But as the story unfolds, the narrator reveals that she suspects the treatment will not cure her because it leaves her alone with her thoughts without even her writing to occupy her mind. Her husband's "cure" forces her into a passive role and eliminates any possibility of asserting her own personality. However, she guiltily suggests that her own lack of confidence in her husband's diagnosis may be what is preventing her cure.

The text of "The Yellow Wallpaper" can be divided into at least two conflicting discourses: (1) the masculine discourse of the husband, who has the authority both of a highly respected physician and of a husband, two positions reinforced by the patriarchal culture of the time; and (2) the feminine discourse of the narrator, whose hesitant personal voice contradicts the masculine voice but undermines itself because it keeps reminding her that women should obey their husbands and their physicians. A third discourse underlies the two dominant ones — that of the gothic horror tale, a popular genre of the late nineteenth century. The narrator in "The Yellow Wallpaper" is isolated against her will in a room with barred windows in an almost deserted palatial country mansion she describes as "The most beautiful place!" (422). She is at the mercy of her captor, in this case her husband. She is not sure whether she is hallucinating, and she thinks the mansion may be haunted. She does not know whom to trust, not being sure whether her husband really wants to "cure" her or to punish her for expressing her rebellion.

The narrator learns to hide her awareness of the conflicting discourses. She avoids mentioning her thoughts and fears about her illness or her fancies about the house being haunted, and she hides her writing. She speaks reasonably and in "a very quiet voice" (429). But this inability to speak freely to anyone is a kind of torture, and alone in her room with the barred windows, she takes up discourse with the wallpaper. At first she describes it as "One of those sprawling flamboyant patterns committing every artistic sin" (423). But she is fascinated by the pattern, which has been distorted by mildew and by the tearing away of some sections. The narrator begins to strip off the wallpaper to free a woman she

thinks is trapped inside; and, eventually, she visualizes herself as that woman, trapped yet freed by the destruction of the wallpaper. The narrator retreats, or escapes into madness, driven there by the multiple discourses she cannot resolve.

For Further Reading: New Historicist Criticism

Brook, Thomas. *The New Historicism and Other Old Fashioned Topics*. 1991.

Coates, Christopher. "What Was the New Historicism?" *Centennial Review* 32.2 (Spring 1993): 267–80.

Geertz, Clifford. "Thick Description: Toward an Interpretive Theory of Culture." *The Interpretation of Cultures*. By Clifford Geertz. 1973.

Greenblatt, Stephen, ed. *Representing the English Renaissance*. 1988.

Levin, David. "American Historicism: Old and New." *American Literary History* 6.3 (Fall 1994): 527–38.

Rabinov, Paul, ed. *The Foucault Reader*. 1986.

Veeser, H. Aram, ed. *The New Historicism*. 1989.

Psychoanalytic Criticism

Psychoanalytic criticism focuses on a work of literature as an expression in fictional form of the inner workings of the human mind. The premises and procedures used in psychoanalytic criticism were developed by Sigmund Freud (1846–1939), though some critics disagree strongly with his conclusions and their therapeutic and literary applications. Feminists, for example, take issue with Freud's notion that women are inherently masochistic.

Some of the major points of Freud's theories depend on the idea that much of what is most significant to us does not take place in our conscious life. Freud believed that we are forced (mostly by the rigors of having to live in harmony with other people) to repress much of our experience and many of our desires in order to coexist peacefully with others. Some of this repressed experience Freud saw as available to us through dreams and other unconscious structures. He believed that literature could often be interpreted as the reflection of our unconscious life.

Freud was among the first psychoanalytic critics, often using techniques developed for interpreting dreams to interpret literature. Among other analyses, he wrote an insightful study of Dostoevsky's *The Brothers Karamazov* as well as brief commentaries on several of Shakespeare's plays, including *A Midsummer Night's Dream, Macbeth, King Lear,* and *Hamlet*. The study of *Hamlet* may have inspired a classic of psychoanalytic criticism: Ernest Jones's *Hamlet and Oedipus* (1949), in which Jones explains Hamlet's strange reluctance to act against his uncle Claudius as resulting from Hamlet's unresolved longings for his mother and subsequent drive to eliminate his father. Because Hamlet's own father is dead, Jones argues, Claudius becomes, in the young man's subconscious mind, a father substitute. Hamlet, then, cannot make up his mind to kill his uncle because he sees not a simple case of revenge (for Claudius's murder of his father) but rather a complex web that includes incestuous desire for his own mother (now wed to Claudius). Jones extends his analysis to include the suggestion that Shakespeare himself experienced such a conflict and reflected his own Oedipal feelings in *Hamlet*.

A French psychoanalyst, Jacques Lacan (1901–1981), combined Freudian theories with structuralist literary theories to argue that the essential alienating experience of the human psyche is the acquisition of language. Lacan believed that once you can name yourself and distinguish yourself from others, you enter the difficult social world that requires you to repress your instincts. Like Lacan, who modified and adapted psychoanalytic criticism to connect it to structuralism, many twentieth-century literary scholars, including Marxists and feminists, have found useful approaches in psychoanalytic literary theory (for example, see Mary Jacobus's *Reading Woman: Essays in Feminist Criticism*, 1986).

Psychoanalytic Terms

To fully appreciate psychoanalytic criticism, readers need to understand the following terms:

- *id*— The part of the mind that determines sexual drives and other unconscious compulsions that urge individuals to unthinking gratification.
- *ego*— The conscious mind that strives to deal with the demands of the id and to balance its needs with messages from the superego.
- *superego*— The part of the unconscious that seeks to repress the demands of the id and to prevent gratification of basic physical appetites. The superego is a sort of censor that represents the prohibitions of society, religion, family beliefs, and so on.
- *condensation*— A process that takes place in dreams (and in literature) when several elements from the repressed unconscious are linked together to form a new yet disguised whole.
- *symbolism*— The use of representative objects to stand for forbidden (often sexual) objects. This process takes place in dreams and in literature. For instance, a pole, knife, or gun may stand for the penis.
- *displacement*— The substitution of a socially acceptable desire for a desire that is not acceptable. This process takes place in dreams or in literature. For example, a woman who experiences sexual desires for her son may instead dream of being intimate with a neighbor who has the same first name as (or who looks like) her son.
- *Oedipus complex*— The repressed desire of a son to unite sexually with his mother and kill his father. According to Freud, all young boys go through this stage, but most resolve these conflicts before puberty.
- *projection*— A defense mechanism in which people mistakenly see in others antisocial impulses they fail to recognize in themselves.
- *subject*— The term used in Lacanian theory to designate a speaking person, or a person who has assumed a position within language. The Lacanian subject of language is split, or characterized by unresolvable tension between the conscious perception of the self (Freud's ego) and the unconscious desires that motivate behavior.

A Psychoanalytic Reading: Edgar Allan Poe's "The Cask of Amontillado" (p. 350)

Edgar Allan Poe died in 1849, six years before Freud was born, so Poe could not possibly have known Freud's work. Nevertheless, psychoanalytic critics argue that the principles discovered by Freud and those who followed him are inherent in human nature. Therefore, they believe it is perfectly plausible to use modern psychiatric terms when analyzing a work written before their invention. If you approached Poe's "The Cask of Amontillado" from a psychoanalytic perspective, you might write the following interpretation.

> Montresor, the protagonist of Poe's "The Cask of Amontillado," has long fascinated readers who have puzzled over his motives for the story's climactic action when he imprisons his rival, Fortunato, and leaves him to die. Montresor claims that Fortunato insulted him and dealt him a "thousand injuries" (350). Yet when we meet Fortunato, although he appears something of a pompous fool, none of his actions — or even his comments — seems powerful enough to motivate Montresor's thirst for revenge.
>
> If, however, we consider a defense mechanism, first named "projection" and described by Sigmund Freud, we gain a clearer picture of Montresor. Those who employ projection are often people who experience antisocial impulses yet are not conscious of these impulses. It seems highly likely that Fortunato did not persecute Montresor; rather, Montresor himself experienced the impulse to act in a hostile manner toward Fortunato. We know, for instance, that Fortunato belongs to the exclusive Order of Masons because he gives Montresor the secret Masonic sign. Montresor's failure to recognize the sign shows that he is a mason only in the grimmest literal sense. Montresor clearly resents Fortunato's high standing and projects onto Fortunato all of his own hostility toward those who (he thinks) have more or know more than he does. Thus, he imagines that Fortunato's main business in life is to persecute and insult him.
>
> Montresor's obsessive behavior further indicates his pathology. He plans Fortunato's punishment with the cunning one might ordinarily reserve for a major battle, cleverly figuring out a way to keep his servants from the house and to lure the ironically named Fortunato to his death. Each step of the revenge is carefully plotted. This is no sudden crime of passion but rather the diabolically planned act of a deeply disturbed mind.
>
> If we understand Montresor's need to take all of the hatred and anger that is inside himself and to rid himself of those socially unacceptable emotions by projecting them on to someone else, then we can see how he rationalizes a crime that seems otherwise nearly unmotivated. By killing Fortunato, Montresor symbolically kills the evil in himself. It is interesting to note that the final lines of the story support this reading. Montresor observes that "For the half of a century no mortal has disturbed" the bones. In other words, the unacceptable emotions have not again been aroused. His last words, a Latin phrase from the Mass for the Dead meaning "rest in peace," suggest that only through his heinous crime has he found release from the torment of his own hatred.

For Further Reading: Psychoanalytic Criticism

Freud, Sigmund. *The Interpretation of Dreams*. 1900.

Gardner, Shirley N., ed. *The (M)other Tongue: Essays in Feminist Psychoanalytic Interpretation*. 1985.

Hartman, Geoffrey H., ed. *Psychoanalysis and the Question of the Text*. 1979.

Kris, Ernst. *Psychoanalytic Explorations in Art*. 1952.

Kristeva, Julia. *Desire in Language*. 1980.

Nelson, Benjamin, ed. *Sigmund Freud on Creativity and the Unconscious*. 1958.

Wright, Elizabeth. *Psychoanalytic Criticism: Theory in Practice*. 1984.

Structuralism

Structuralism, a literary movement with roots in linguistics and anthropology, concentrates on literature as a system of signs that have no inherent meaning except in their agreed-upon or conventional relation to one another. Structuralism is usually described by its proponents not as a new way to interpret literary works but rather as a way to understand how works of literature come to have meaning. Because structuralism developed from linguistic theory, some structuralists use linguistic approaches to literature. When they talk about literary texts, they use the terms (such as *morpheme* and *phoneme*) that linguists use as they study the nature of language. Many structuralists, however, use the linguistic model as an analogy. To understand the analogy, you need to know a bit of linguistic theory.

The French linguist Ferdinand de Saussure (*Course in General Linguistics*, 1915) suggested that the relationship between an object and the name we use to designate it is purely arbitrary. What, for example, makes "C-A-T" signify a small, furry animal with pointed ears and whiskers? Only our learned expectation makes us associate *cat* with the family feline pet. Had we grown up in France, we would make the same association with *chat*, or in Mexico with *gato*. The words we use to designate objects (linguists call these words *signs*) make sense only within the large context of our entire language system and will not be understood as meaningful by someone who does not know that language system. Further, Saussure pointed out, signs become truly useful only when we use them to designate difference. For instance, the word *cat* becomes useful when we want to differentiate a small furry animal that meows from a small furry animal that barks. Saussure was interested in how language, as a structure of conventions, worked. He asked intriguing questions about the underlying rules that allow this made-up structure of signs to work, and, as a result, his pioneering study caught the interest of scholars in many fields.

Many literary scholars saw linguistic structuralism as analogous to the study of literary works. Literary structuralism leads readers to think of poems, short stories, novels, and plays not as self-contained and individual entities that have some kind of inherent meaning but rather as part of a larger literary system. To fully appreciate and analyze the work, the reader must understand the system within which it operates. Like linguistic structuralism, literary structuralism focuses on the importance of difference. We must, for example, understand the difference between the structure of poetry and the structure of prose before we can make sense of William Carlos Williams's "Red Wheelbarrow" (p. 923):

> so much depends
> upon
> a red wheel
> barrow

Readers unacquainted with the conventions of poetry would find those lines meaningless and confusing, although if they knew the conventions of prose, they would readily understand this sentence:

> So much depends upon a red wheelbarrow.

The way we interpret any group of "signs," then, depends on how they are structured and on the way we understand the system that governs their structure.

Structuralists believe that literature is basically artificial because although it uses the same "signs" as everyday language, whose purpose is to give information, the purpose of literature is *not* primarily to relay data. For example, a poem like Dylan Thomas's "Do not go gentle into that good night" (p. 1065) is written in the linguistic form of a series of commands, yet the poem goes much further than that. Its meaning is created not only by our understanding the lines as a series of commands but also by our recognition of the poetic form, the rhyming conventions, and the figures of speech that Thomas uses. We can only fully discuss the poem within the larger context of our literary knowledge.

Structuralism also provides the foundation for poststructuralism, a theoretical movement that informs the fields of deconstructionist and New Historicist criticism and has influenced the work of many psychoanalytic and sociological critics. Although structuralists claim that language functions by arbitrarily connecting words (signifiers) to ideas (signifieds), poststructuralists develop the implications of this claim, arguing that because the connection of a word to an idea is purely arbitrary, any operation of language is inherently unstable. Poststructuralists believe that to study a literary text is to study a continuously shifting set of meanings.

A Structuralist Reading: William Faulkner's "Barn Burning" (p. 356)

A structuralist reading tries to bring to light some of the assumptions about language and form that we are likely to take for granted. Looking at the opening paragraph of Faulkner's "Barn Burning," from the point of view of structuralist criticism, you might first look at an interpretation that reads the passage as a stream of Sarty's thoughts. The structuralist critic might then consider the assumptions a reader would have to make to see what Faulkner has written as the thoughts of an illiterate child. Next, the structuralist might look at evidence to suggest the language in this section operates outside the system of language that would be available to Sarty and that, therefore, "Barn Burning" opens not with a simple recounting of the main character's thoughts but rather with something far more complex.

The opening paragraph of William Faulkner's "Barn Burning" is often read as an excursion into the mind of Sarty, the story's young protagonist. When we read the passage closely, however, we note that a supposedly simple consciousness is represented in a highly complex way. For Sarty — uneducated and illiterate — the "scarlet devils" and "silver curve of fish" on the labels of food tins serve as direct signs appealing to his hunger. It is unlikely, however, that Sarty could consciously understand what he sees and express it as metaphor. We cannot, then, read this opening passage as a recounting of the thoughts that pass through Sarty's mind. Instead, these complex sentences and images offer possibilities that reach beyond the limits of Sarty's linguistic system.

Because our own knowledge is wider than Sarty's, the visual images the narrator describes take on meanings for us that are unavailable to the young boy. For example, like Sarty, we know that the "scarlet devils" stand for deviled ham. Yet the devils also carry another possible connotation. They may indicate evil and thus serve to emphasize the despair and grief Sarty feels are ever present. So we are given images that flash through the mind of an illiterate young boy, apparently intended to suggest his poverty and ignorance (he cannot read the words on the labels), yet we are led to see a highly complicated set of meanings. When we encounter later in the passage Sarty's articulated thought, *"our enemy . . . ourn! mine and hisn both! . . .,"* his down-to-earth dialect shows clearly the sharp distinction between the system of language the narrator uses to describe Sarty's view of the store shelves and the system of language Sarty uses to describe what he sees and feels.

For Further Reading: Structuralism

Barthes, Roland. *Critical Essays*. 1964.
Culler, Jonathan. *Structuralist Poetics*. 1975.
Greimas, A. J. *Structured Semantics: An Attempt at a Method*. Trans. McDowell, Schleifer, and Velie. 1983.
Hawkes, Terence. *Structuralism and Semiotics*. 1977.
Lentricchia, Frank. *After the New Criticism*. 1980.
Pettit, Philip. *The Concept of Structuralism: A Critical Analysis*. 1975.
Scholes, Robert. *Structuralism in Literature: An Introduction*. 1974.

Deconstruction

Deconstruction is a literary movement that developed from structuralism. Deconstructionists argue that every text contains within it some ingredient undermining its purported system of meaning. In other words, the structure that seems to hold the text together is unstable because it depends on the conclusions of a particular ideology (for instance, the idea that women are inferior to men or that peasants are content with their lowly position in life), conclusions that are not as natural as the text may pretend. The practice of finding the point at which the text falls apart because of these internal inconsistencies is called deconstruction.

Deconstructive theorists share with formalists and structuralists a concern for the work itself rather than for biographical, historical, or ideological influences. Like formalists, deconstructionists focus on possibilities for multiple meanings within texts. However, while formalists seek to explain paradox by discovering tensions and ironies that can lead to a unified reading, deconstructionists insist on the primacy of multiple possibilities. They maintain that any given text is capable of yielding many divergent readings, all of which are equally valid yet may in some way undermine and oppose one another.

Like structuralists, deconstructionists see literary texts as part of larger systems of discourse. A key structuralist technique is identifying opposites in an attempt to show the structure of language used in a work. Having identified the opposites, the structuralist rests the case. Deconstructionists, however, go further. Jacques Derrida, a French philosopher, noticed that these oppositions do not simply reflect linguistic structures but are the linguistic response to the way people deal with their beliefs (their ideologies). For instance, if you believe strongly that democracy is the best possible form of government, you tend to lump other forms of government into the category "nondemocracies." If a government is nondemocratic, that — not its other distinguishing characteristics — would be significant to you. This typical ideological response operates in all kinds of areas of belief, even ones we are not aware of. Deconstructionists contend that texts tend to give away their ideological biases by means of this opposition.

Derrida called this distinction between "A" and "Not-A" (rather than between "A" and "B") *différance*, a word he coined to suggest a concept represented by the French verb *différer*, which has two meanings: "to be different" and "to defer." (Note that in Derrida's new term an "a" is substituted for an "e"— a distinction that can be seen in writing but not heard in speaking.) When a deconstructionist uncovers *différance* through careful examination of a text, he or she also finds an (often unwitting) ideological bias. Deconstructionists argue that the reader must transcend such ideological biases and must instead acknowledge contradictory possibilities as equally worthy of consideration. No one meaning can or should be designated as correct.

Deconstruction, then, is not really a system of criticism (and, in fact, deconstructionists resist being labeled as a school of criticism). Rather, deconstruction offers a way to take apart a literary text and thereby reveal its separate layers. Deconstructionists often focus on the metaphorical nature of language, claiming that all language is basically metaphoric because the sign we use to designate any given object or action stands apart from the object itself. In fact, deconstructionists believe that all writing is essentially literary and metaphorical because language, by its very nature, can only *stand for* what we call reality or truth; it cannot *be* reality or truth.

A major contribution of deconstructive critics lies in their playful approach to language and to literary criticism. They refuse to accept as absolute any one way of reading poetry, fiction, or drama, and they guard against what they see as the fixed conclusions and arbitrary operating assumptions of many schools of criticism.

A Deconstructionist Reading: Flannery O'Connor's "A Good Man Is Hard to Find" (p. 409)

A deconstructionist reading of Flannery O'Connor's "A Good Man Is Hard to Find" might challenge the essentially religious interpretations the author offered of her own stories in essays and letters. If you were applying deconstructionist criticism to the story, you might argue that the author's reading of the story is no more valid than anyone else's, and that the story can just as legitimately be read as an investigation of the functions of irony in language.

> Flannery O'Connor explained that the grotesque and violent aspects of her stories are intended to shock the reader into recognizing the inhospitable nature of the world and thereby the universal human need for divine grace. The last sentence of "A Good Man Is Hard to Find" is spoken by The Misfit, who has just murdered a family of travelers: "It's no real pleasure in life." However, the language of O'Connor's stories is extremely ironic — that is, her narrators and characters often say one thing but mean another. So it is possible that their statements are not empirically true but are representations of a persona or elements of a story they have created using language.
>
> The Grandmother, for example, lives almost entirely in fictions — newspaper clippings, stories for the grandchildren, her belief that The Misfit is a good man. In contrast, The Misfit is more literal than the Grandmother in his perception of reality. He knows, for example, whether the car turned over once or twice. But he too is posing, at first as the tough guy who rejects religious and societal norms by saying, ". . . it's nothing for you to do but enjoy the few minutes you got left the best way you can — by killing somebody or burning down his house or doing some other meanness to him. No pleasure but meanness . . ." (p. 419). Finally, he poses as the pessimist — or, according to O'Connor's reading, the Christian — who claims, "It's no real pleasure in life." The contradictions in The Misfit's language make it impossible to tell which of these facades is "real."

For Further Reading: Deconstruction

Abrams, M. H. "Rationality and the Imagination in Cultural History." *Critical Inquiry* 2 (1976): 447–64. (Abrams claims deconstructionists are parasites who depend on other critics to come up with interpretations that can be deconstructed.)

Arac, Jonathan, Wlad Godzich, and Wallace Martin, eds. *The Yale Critics: Deconstruction in America.* 1983.

Berman, Art. *From the New Criticism to Deconstruction.* 1988.

Culler, Jonathan. *On Deconstruction: Theory and Criticism after Structuralism.* 1982.

Jefferson, Ann. "Structuralism and Post-Structuralism." *Modern Literary Theory: A Comparative Introduction.* 1982.

Johnson, Barbara. *The Critical Difference: Essays in the Contemporary Rhetoric of Reading.* 1980.

Leitsch, Vincent B. *Deconstructive Theory and Practice.* 1982.

Lynn, Steven. "A Passage into Critical Theory." *College English* 52 (1990): 258–71.

Miller, J. Hillis. "The Critic as Host." *Deconstruction and Criticism.* Ed. Harold Bloom et al. 1979. (a response to Abrams's article, listed above)

Norris, Christopher. *Deconstruction: Theory and Practice.* 1982.

LITERARY HISTORY: FROM ARISTOTLE TO THE PRESENT

Beginnings: The Greeks and Romans (c. 450 B.C.–A.D. 400)

The Western critical tradition began in ancient Greece. In the *Republic*, Plato (427–347 B.C.) described the ideal state as well as the role of philosophers and poets. His pupil Aristotle (384–322 B.C.) was by far the most significant classical influence on Europeans of the Middle Ages and the Renaissance. Even today, drama critics and students pay careful attention to the theories presented in Aristotle's *Poetics* about how literature imitates life, how an audience responds with pity and fear to a tragedy, and how a well-written play is constructed.

The Romans contributed works on what would now be called "loftiness of style" (*On the Sublime*, Longinus, first century A.D.) and a treatise on the art of poetry (*Ars Poetica*, Horace, 65–8 B.C.). Roman writers were typically more interested in the craft of poetry — in how to construct a poem that would have a pleasing effect on a reader — than in the power of the poet. In contrast to the Greek philosophical approach, Roman literary criticism brings to mind a practical handbook.

The Middle Ages (c. A.D. 400–1500)

After the fall of the western Roman Empire in the fifth century A.D., Christianity became the unifying force of Western culture. The literature of the European Middle Ages was intended to demonstrate moral virtue in the hopes that people would follow the behavior patterns it praised. Much literature of this period took the form of morality and mystery plays, both of which had religious themes. Worldly art was discouraged because the church believed that the role of literature was to instruct people in the way to lead a virtuous life. Significant departures from moralistic literature appeared in the French romances, which depicted adventures undertaken in the cause of love, and in Chaucer's (c. 1342–1400) *Canterbury Tales*, which drew on English, French, and Italian sources. These served as antidotes to the traditional cautionary plays and tales. It is not surprising, given the strong moral purpose of most literature of the Middle Ages, that literary criticism was not a priority of the intellectual life of the period.

The Renaissance (c. 1500–1660)

During the fourteenth and fifteenth centuries, Europe emerged from the church-centered Middle Ages with a rebirth (*renaissance* is French for "rebirth") of learning. Renewed access to Greek and Roman writers led Renaissance humanists to a broad interest in intellectual considerations. Sir Philip Sidney's (1554–1586) *The Defense of Poesy* (c. 1580) is usually considered the most important work of literary criticism from this period. In the *Defense*, Sidney argues that poetry must not simply give pleasure but also contribute positively to the life of society. Unlike the writers of medieval allegories, Sidney believed that literature could — and should — have a moral impact without being didactic or prescriptive. Despite Sidney's contributions, Aristotle remained the arbiter of critical questions, although his role was complicated by the emergence of William Shakespeare (1564–1616) as a dramatist of exceptional talent.

Shakespeare's work posed a problem because many critics realized that he was a fine playwright despite his frequent disregard for Aristotle's rules governing well-constructed plays. As a result, a major concern of criticism up to the eighteenth century became the reconciling of Aristotle's standards with the practices of contemporary playwrights.

The Enlightenment (1660–1798)

Samuel Johnson (1709–1784), who devoted much of the preface of his edition of Shakespeare's plays to the question of Shakespeare's departures from Aristotle's rules, was a major figure of the Enlightenment, a period of neoclassicism characterized by a revitalized interest in the values and ideas of the classical world, particularly of the Romans. Along with Johnson, poets John Dryden (1631–1700) and Alexander Pope (1688–1744), as well as philosopher Edmund Burke (1729–1797), compared contemporary practice with the ideas of their Roman forebears. Burke, for instance, addressed the subject of Longinus's *On the Sublime* in his own treatise, *The Origin of Our Ideas of the Sublime and the Beautiful* (1757). Eighteenth-century critics stressed the value of reason and what they called "common sense." Their architectural style, familiar to us in the Capitol building in Washington, D.C., and other structures, provides a visual example of what they sought in literature: clarity, symmetry, discipline. They demanded that a play or poem be tightly constructed, and they saw the heroic couplet (two lines of rhymed iambic pentameter) as the perfect building block with which to construct didactic poems such as Pope's *Essay on Criticism* (1711), a scathing statement of neoclassical literary principles.

The literature of the American revolutionary age, when Thomas Paine, Thomas Jefferson, Alexander Hamilton, Philip Freneau, and Joel Barlow were writing, reflected the patriotic concerns of the infant democracy. For example, Paine's *Common Sense: Addressed to the Inhabitants of America* (1776) inspired Americans to revolution, and his *Rights of Man* (1791, 1792) made a stirring case for freedom as the right of every individual.

The Romantic Period (1798–1837)

The Romantics came as perhaps an inevitable counterreaction to the Enlightenment. They believed that poetry was *not* an objective construction like a building with a precise and unchanging meaning but, instead, was a subjective creation whose meaning depends on the poet's emotional state and a reader's personal response. Romantic poet William Blake (1757–1827) illustrated the conflict between romanticism and neoclassicism through his criticism of the opinions of Enlightenment artist Joshua Reynolds. In his notes on Reynolds's views, Blake observed that the Enlightenment emphasis on materialism and on physical evidence (empiricism) impoverishes art. Blake believed that the neoclassicists denied both imagination and subjective experience their preeminent roles in the creative process. He thought that the artist must begin from the most concrete and minute sensory experience in order to reach the truth. Unlike most eighteenth-century writers, Blake and his fellow Romantics believed in the importance of the individual example rather than the general principle.

Like Blake, Samuel Taylor Coleridge (1772–1834) and William Wordsworth (1770–1850) placed value on the mysterious and on the common person's experience. Wordsworth in particular stressed the importance of concrete, simple language and offered, in his preface to the second edition of *Lyrical Ballads* (1800), a definition of poetry that has since become famous. A poem, Wordsworth says, should originate in "the spontaneous overflow of powerful feelings" whose energy comes from "emotion recollected in tranquility." George Gordon, Lord Byron (1788–1824), who himself lived a flamboyant life of publicly expressed powerful emotions, created in his poetry the melancholy Romantic hero, defiant and haunted by secret guilt. Percy Bysshe Shelley (1792–1822) makes perhaps the greatest claims for the poet's power and obligation to society in "A Defense of Poetry" (1821), in which he argues that the "great instrument of moral good is the imagination."

The difference in attitude between neoclassicists and Romantics can also be seen through a comparison of the Shakespearean criticism of Samuel Johnson and Samuel Taylor Coleridge. In his *Preface to Shakespeare* (1765), Johnson argues that Shakespeare's faults include being much more concerned with pleasing an audience than with teaching it morals; he observes that often in Shakespeare's works virtue is not rewarded nor is wickedness suitably punished. In addition, Johnson notes, Shakespeare's diction is too elevated, and he lets the characters in the tragedies talk too much without advancing the action. Coleridge, in contrast, sees in the tragic character of Hamlet the prototype of the Romantic hero and argues in his lecture "Shakespeare's Judgment Equal to his Genius" (1836) that Shakespeare describes how people actually behave rather than how they ought to behave.

John Keats (1795–1821), another Romantic poet, continued Coleridge's defense of Shakespeare. Keats believed that Shakespeare's intensity, particularly evident in the tragedies, moved his work onto another level altogether, where the work itself takes on life through its relationship with "beauty and truth" rather than with teaching proper behavior.

The Romantics in general, both in Britain and in the United States, saw the poet as particularly close to God and nature. The American philosopher Ralph Waldo Emerson (1803–1882) thought nature offered the poet a mystical symbolism, while Henry David Thoreau (1817–1862) extolled the view that man should live close to nature and follow his personal conscience rather than the dictates of society. Mary Shelley (1797–1851) and Edgar Allan Poe (1809–1849) were influential in another strand of romanticism: the macabre, melancholy, and mysterious.

The Victorian Period (1837–1901)

The literary problem facing the post-Romantic generation of critics was how to deal with a world where sublime isolation and communing with nature were less and less possible, even as ideals. During the Victorian era, industrialization, poverty, population growth, and mass transportation contributed to a general sense that the world was changing rapidly, and people had difficulty coping with these changes. In England, critics such as the poet Matthew Arnold (1822–1888) argued that literature could help anchor people to their world and that literary criticism, as an occupation, should be a "disinterested endeavor" whose responsibility was to minister to a modern society that had lost its faith in other things, particularly religion. Arnold differed in many ways from the Romantics; nevertheless, he too believed in the ability of poetry to help people live productive, satisfying lives.

Just before the turn of the nineteenth century, the pendulum swung away from Arnold's view that poetry has moral utility to the view that art should exist for its own sake. The dichotomy seen by the Romantics between intellect and feeling became in the 1890s the split between art and science. Oscar Wilde (1854–1900), Stéphane Mallarmé (1842–1898), and Charles Baudelaire (1821–1867) all dealt with this dichotomy by retreating into the world of art and denying art's connection with anything else. These members of the symbolist movement valued suggestion, private symbols, and evocative references in their poetry. They attempted to connect their writing with a spiritual world that was not accessible by the rational methods of science.

Charles Darwin (1809–1882) presented his theory of natural selection in *Origin of Species* (1859), and his ideas influenced novels and poetry of the latter part of the nineteenth century. Those who believed natural selection contradicted the Bible were outraged, and others interpreted his theories as evidence of humans' latent bestiality. Darwin's ideas undermined the certainty that humankind was the center of the universe and that the universe had been intelligently planned for a good purpose.

American writers of the late nineteenth century, including William Dean Howells and Henry James, were noted for realism. Others, including naturalists Frank Norris and Theodore Dreiser, built on Darwin's views, exploring the idea of individuals being at the mercy of their instinctual drives and of sociological forces.

The Modern Period (Since 1901)

In the next major attempt to establish some objective significance to poetry, T. S. Eliot (1888–1965) argued against the lingering Romantic idea that a poem is the original product of a poet's inspiration. Instead, he proposed in "Tradition and the Individual Talent" (1917) that the poem supersedes the poet, who is merely the agent of its creation. Eliot argues that Wordsworth is wrong to put the poet in the central role of life-experiencer and re-creator. According to Eliot, the poem itself will join the tradition, and it will be up to the *critic* to make sense of that tradition. For example, Eliot's analysis of *Hamlet* focuses neither on the character of Hamlet and his personal agony (as did the Romantics) nor on the moral tone of the play (as did the neoclassicists), but rather on the story of Hamlet as treated by dramatists before Shakespeare. Eliot concludes that the problems with Shakespeare's play come about because Shakespeare cannot successfully balance the early source materials with his own desire to write a play about the effect of Gertrude's guilt on her son. Thus, Eliot judges Shakespeare within a literary and historical tradition rather than within a moral or personal context.

The twentieth century produced many important critics and theoreticians of literature who built on the legacy of the past, though some only to the extent that they attempted to contradict earlier approaches. The dominant critical views (discussed in Appendix A), can be divided into three categories: **formal**, those concerned with the structure or form of texts (formalism, structuralism, deconstruction); **social**, those concerned with texts in relation to social contexts (New Historicism, feminism, Marxism); and **personal**, those concerned with the interaction of the individual (author or reader) and texts (reader-response criticism, psychoanalytic criticism). Each of these theoretical approaches can be traced to the writings of authors in the early part of the twentieth century or before.

Formalism, which acquired prominence in English and American criticism in the middle part of the twentieth century, actually began in the early part of the century in Moscow and Petrograd (St. Petersburg). The word *formalism* was initially a term used in a negative fashion because formalists focused on patterns and devices in a work of literature and ignored the subject matter. Soon, however, formalism's logical appeal took hold, and formalism was advocated by Victor Shklovsky, Boris Eichenbaum, and Roman Jakobson in the 1920s. Though many literary theorists since Aristotle have stressed the importance of structure, the roots of structuralist criticism can be traced more directly to the Russian formalists and to the French anthropologist Claude Levi-Strauss (1908–   ), who posited that all cultural phenomena have an underlying structural system. Deconstruction both reacts against the tenets of structuralism and builds on the theories of German philosophers Friedrich Nietzsche (1844–1900) and Martin Heidegger (1889–1976), who questioned the validity and verifiability of "truth," "knowledge," and other basic philosophical concepts.

Social criticism also had precursors in earlier writing. For example, Mary Wollstonecraft's *A Vindication of the Rights of Woman* (1792) was an early forerunner of feminism. Virginia Woolf's *A Room of One's Own* (1929) anticipated feminist criticism by addressing the effects on women of the patriarchal Western society and identifying deeply entrenched attitudes of male-oriented society that hindered women in the pursuit of their creative possibilities. Similarly, Marxist criticism is based on the writings of Karl Marx and Friedrich Engels; they borrowed their key term *ideology* from French philosophers of the late eighteenth century who used it to label the study of how sense perceptions develop into concepts. The term *Marxism* itself was used in the same period to mean a rigidly held set of political ideas. Marx and Engels adapted and changed the terms, investing them with new meaning that built on meanings already present in the culture. New Historicism — an even more recent mode of literary study (beginning in the 1980s) — reacts to formalism, structuralism, and deconstruction, arguing that the historical context is an integral part of a literary work and that the text cannot be considered in isolation.

Personal criticism too has its origins in earlier writing. For instance, the roots of psychoanalytic criticism can be traced to the psychological criticism of the early nineteenth century. Thomas Carlyle (1795–1881) suggested in 1827 that the best criticism of the day was psychological, deriving meaning from a poem by analyzing the mental state and personality structure of the author. Finally, reader-response criticism, an approach begun in the 1960s, focuses on the reader and the reader's process and experience, rather than on the text or the text and its historical context.

GLOSSARY OF LITERARY TERMS

Action What happens in a drama.

Alexandrine Verse with six iambic feet (iambic hexameter), a common form in French poetry but relatively rare in English poetry.

Allegorical figure or **framework** See **Allegory.**

Allegory Story with two parallel and consistent levels of meaning, one literal and one figurative, in which the figurative level offers a moral or political lesson; John Bunyan's *The Pilgrim's Progress* and Nathaniel Hawthorne's "Young Goodman Brown" are examples of moral allegory. An **allegorical figure** has only one meaning (for instance, it may represent good or evil), as opposed to a **symbol,** which may suggest a complex network of meanings. An **allegorical framework** is the system of ideas that conveys the allegory's message.

Alliteration Repetition of consonant sounds (usually the initial sounds) in a series of words, as in Blake's "The Chimney Sweeper": "So your chimneys I sweep, and in soot I sleep." Alliteration may be reinforced by repeated sounds within and at the ends of words.

Allusion Reference, often to literature, history, mythology, or the Bible, that is unacknowledged in the text but that the author expects a reader to recognize. An example of allusion in a title is Charles Baxter's "Gryphon" (a mythical beast).

Ambiguity Device in which authors intentionally evoke a number of possible meanings of a word or grammatical structure by leaving unclear which meaning they intend.

Anapest See **Meter.**

Antagonist Character who is in conflict with or opposition to the protagonist; the villain. Sometimes the antagonist may be a force or situation (war or poverty) rather than a person.

Antihero Modern character who possesses the opposite attributes of a hero. Rather than being dignified and powerful, the antihero tends to be passive and ineffectual. Willy Loman, the main character in *Death of a Salesman,* is an antihero.

Apostrophe Figure of speech in which an absent character or a personified force or object is addressed directly, as if it were present or could comprehend: "O Rose, thou art sick!"

Archetype Image or symbol that is so common or significant that it seems to have universal significance. The psychologist Carl Jung believed that because archetypes are an inherent part of psyches, we recognize them subconsciously when we encounter them and therefore give them a greater meaning than they would otherwise possess. Many archetypes appear in classical myths (for example, a journey to the underworld).

Arena stage Stage on which the actors are surrounded by the audience; also called **theater in the round.**

Aside Brief comment spoken by an actor to the audience (such as, "Here she comes. I'll play a fine trick on her now!") and assumed not to be heard by the other characters.

Assonance Repetition of the same or similar vowel sounds in a series of words: "creep three feet."

Atmosphere Tone or mood of a literary work, often established by the setting and language. Atmosphere is the emotional aura that determines readers' expectations about a work — for example, the sense of doom established at the beginning of Shakespeare's *Macbeth.*

Aubade Poem about morning, usually celebrating the dawn — for example, Philip Larkin's "Aubade."

Ballad Narrative poem, rooted in an oral tradition, usually arranged in quatrains rhyming *abcb* and containing a refrain.

Ballad stanza See **Stanza.**

Beast fable Short tale, usually including a moral, in which animals assume human characteristics — for example, Aesop's "The Tortoise and the Hare."

Beginning rhyme See **Rhyme.**

Black comedy Comedy that relies on the morbid and absurd. Often black comedies are so satiric that they become ironic and tragic; examples are Joseph Heller's novel *Catch 22* and Edward Albee's play *The Sandbox.*

Blank verse Lines of unrhymed iambic pentameter in no particular stanzaic form. Because iambic pentameter resembles the rhythms of ordinary English speech, blank verse is often unobtrusive; for instance, Shakespeare's noble characters usually use it, though they may seem to us at first reading to be speaking in prose. See **Meter.**

Blocking Decisions about how characters move and where they stand on stage in a dramatic production.

Box set Stage setting that gives the audience the illusion of looking into a room.

Cacophony Harsh or unpleasant spoken sound created by clashing consonants such as "The vorpal blade went snicker-snack!" in Lewis Carroll's "Jabberwocky."

Caesura Strong or long pause in the middle of a poetic line, created by punctuation or by the sense of the poem, as in Yeats's "Leda and the Swan": "And Agamemnon dead. Being so caught up. . . ."

Carpe diem "Seize the day"; the philosophy arguing that one should enjoy life today before it passes by, as seen in Herrick's "To the Virgins, to Make Much of Time."

Catastrophe The moment in a tragedy after the climax, when the rising action has ended and the falling action has begun, when the protagonist begins to understand the implications of events that will lead to his or her downfall.

Catharsis Aristotle's term for the emotional reaction or "purgation" that takes place in an audience watching a tragedy.

Character Fictional representation of a person, usually but not necessarily in a psychologically realistic way. E. M. Forster classified characters as **round** (well developed, closely involved in the action and responsive to it) or **flat** (static, stereotypical, or operating as **foils** for the protagonist). Characters can also be classified as **dynamic** (growing and changing in the course of the action) or **static** (remaining unchanged).

Characterization Way in which writers develop their characters and reveal those characters' traits to readers.

Choragos See **Chorus.**

Chorus Group of actors in classical Greek drama who comment in unison on the action and the hero; they are led by the **Choragos.**

Classicism Attitude toward art that values symmetry, clarity, discipline, and objectivity. **Neoclassicism,** such as that practiced in eighteenth-century Europe, appreciated those qualities as found in Greek and Roman art and culture.

Cliché Overused phrase or expression.

Climax Point of greatest tension or importance, where the decisive action of a play or story takes place.

Closed form Type of poetic structure that has a recognizable rhyme scheme, meter, or stanzaic pattern; also called *fixed form.*

Closet drama Play meant to be read instead of performed — for example, Shelley's *Prometheus Unbound.*

Comedy Any literary work, but especially a play, in which events end happily, a character's fortunes are reversed for the better, and a community is drawn more closely together, often by the marriage of one or more protagonists at the end.

Comedy of humours Comedy that focuses on characters whose behavior is controlled by a single characteristic trait, or humour, such as *Volpone* (1606) by Ben Jonson.

Comedy of manners Satiric comedy that achieved great popularity in the nineteenth century. This form focuses on the manners and customs of society and directs its satire against the characters who violate its social conventions and norms. *The Importance of Being Earnest* by Oscar Wilde is a comedy of manners.

Common measure See **Stanza.**

Conceit See **Metaphor.**

Concrete poem Poem whose typographical appearance on the page reenforces its theme, as with George Herbert's "Easter Wings."

Conflict Struggle between opposing forces (protagonist and antagonist) in a work of literature.

Connotation Meaning that a word suggests beyond its literal, dictionary meaning; its emotional associations, judgments, or opinions. Connotations can be positive, neutral, or negative. For example, *family* has a positive connotation when it describes a group of loving relatives; a neutral connotation when it describes a biological category; and a negative connotation when it describes a criminal organization.

Consonance See **Rhyme.**

Convention See **Literary convention.**

Conventional symbol See **Symbol.**

Cosmic irony See **Irony.**

Couplet See **Stanza.**

Crisis Point at which the decisive action of the plot occurs.

Dactyl See **Meter.**

Denotation Dictionary meaning of a word; its explicit, literal meaning.

Denouement See **Resolution.**

Deus ex machina "The god from the machine": any improbable resolution of plot involving the intervention of some force or agent from outside the story.

Dialect Particular regional variety of language, which may differ from the more widely used standard or written language in its pronunciation, grammar, or vocabulary. Eliza Doolittle's cockney dialect in the George Bernard Shaw play *Pygmalion* is an example.

Dialogue Conversation between two or more characters.

Diction Word choice of an author, which determines the level of language used in a piece of literature. **Formal diction** is lofty and elaborate (typical of Shakespearean nobility); **informal diction** is idiomatic and relaxed (like the dialogue in John Updike's "A&P"). **Jargon** is the specialized diction of a professional or occupational group (such as computer scientists). **Idioms** are the colloquial expressions, including slang, of a particular group or society.

Didactic poetry Poetry whose purpose is to make a point or teach a lesson, particularly common in the eighteenth century.

Double entendre Phrase or word with a deliberate double meaning, one of which is usually sexual.

Double plot See **Plot.**

Drama Literature written to be performed.

Dramatic irony See **Irony.**

Dramatic monologue Type of poem perfected by Robert Browning that consists of a single speaker talking to one or more listeners and often revealing much more about the speaker than he or she seems to intend; Browning's "My Last Duchess" is an example of this form.

Dramatis personae Characters in a play.

Dynamic character See **Character.**

Elegy Poem commemorating someone's death, usually in a reflective or mournful tone, such as A. E. Housman's "To an Athlete Dying Young."

Elision Leaving out an unstressed syllable or vowel, usually in order to keep a regular meter in a line of poetry ("o'er" instead of "over," for example).

End rhyme See **Rhyme.**

End-stopped line Line of poetry that has a full pause at the end, typically indicated by a period or semicolon.

Enjambment See **Run-on line.**

Envoi Three-line conclusion to a sestina that includes all six of the poem's key words, three placed at the ends of lines and three within the lines. See **Sestina.**

Epic Long narrative poem, such as the *Iliad* or the *Aeneid*, recounting the adventures of heroes on whose actions depend the fate of a nation or race. Frequently the gods or other supernatural beings take active interest in the events.

Epigram Short pithy statement — for example, Dorothy Parker's comment on an actress's performance, "She runs the gamut of emotions from A to B."

Epiphany Term first applied to literature by James Joyce to describe a sudden moment of revelation about the deep meaning of something, such as the boy's realization at the end of "Araby."

Euphemism Word consciously chosen for its pleasant **connotations;** often used for subjects like sex and death whose frank discussion is somewhat taboo in our society. For example, a euphemism for "to die" is "to pass away."

Euphony Pleasant spoken sound created by smooth consonants such as "ripple" or "pleasure."

Exposition First stage of a plot, where the author presents the information a reader or viewer will need to understand the characters and subsequent action.

Expressionism Artistic and literary movement that attempts to portray inner experience. It moves away from realistic portrayals of life and is characterized by violent exaggeration of objective reality and extremes of mood and feeling. In drama, expressionistic stage sets mirror the inner states of the character.

Extended metaphor See **Metaphor.**

Extended simile See **Metaphor.** Also see **Conceit.**

Eye rhyme See **Rhyme.**

Fable Short tale, often involving animals or supernatural beings and stressing plot above character development, whose object is to teach a pragmatic or moral lesson. See **Beast fable.**

Fairy tale See **Folktale.**

Falling action Stage in a play's plot during which the intensity of the climax subsides.

Falling meter Trochiac and dactylic meters, so called because they move from stressed to unstressed syllables. See **Rising meter.**

Fantasy Work of literature that takes place in an unreal world or contains unreal or incredible characters. J. R. R. Tolkien's *The Lord of the Rings* is one example.

Farce Comedy in which stereotypical characters engage in boisterous horseplay and slapstick humor, as in Chekhov's *The Brute.*

Feminine rhyme See **Rhyme.**

Fiction Form of narrative that is primarily imaginative, though its form may resemble that of factual writing like history and biography.

Figures of speech Expressions — such as **hyperbole, metaphor, metonymy, personification, simile, synechdoche,** and **understatement**— that use words to achieve effects beyond ordinary language.

Flashback Variation on chronological order that presents an event or situation that occurred before the time in which the story's action takes place.

Flat character See **Character.**

Foil Minor character whose role is to highlight the main character by presenting a contrast with him or her.

Folktale Contemporary version of an old, even ancient, oral tale that can be traced back centuries through many different cultures. Folktales include fairy tales, myths, and fables.

Foot See **Meter.**

Foreshadowing Presentation early in a story of situations, characters, or objects that seem to have no special importance but in fact are later revealed to have great significance. For example, a casual mention of a character's memory for faces becomes significant when his fate hinges on his recognizing a person from his past.

Form Structure or shape of a literary work; the way a work's parts fit together to form a whole. In poetry, form is described in terms of the presence (or absence) in a particular work of elements like rhyme, meter, and stanzaic pattern. See **Open form** and **Closed form.**

Formal diction See **Diction.**

Free verse See **Open form.**

Freytag's pyramid The five parts of classic dramatic plots: *exposition, complication* (the introduction of elements that will lead to conflict and ultimately crisis), *climax, catastrophe,* and *resolution.* In his *Technique of the Drama* (1863) Gustav Freytag suggested that this pattern resembles a pyramid, with rising action leading to the climax and giving way to falling action.

Genre Category of literature. Fiction, drama, and poetry are the three major genres; subgenres include the novel, the farce, and the lyric poem.

Haiku Seventeen-syllable, three-line form of Japanese verse that almost always uses concrete imagery and deals with the natural world.

Hamartia Aristotle's term for the "tragic flaw" in characters that eventually causes their downfall in Greek tragedy.

Hermeneutics Traditionally, the use of the Bible to interpret other historical or current events; in current critical theory, the principles and procedures followed to determine the meaning of a text.

Heroic couplet See **Stanza.**

High comedy Term introduced in 1877 by George Meredith to denote comedy that appeals to the intellect, such as Shakespeare's *As You Like It.* See **Low comedy.**

Hubris Tragic flaw of overwhelming pride that exists in the protagonist of a tragedy.

Hyperbole Figurative language that depends on intentional overstatement; Mark Twain often used it to create humor; Jonathan Swift used it for **satire.**

Iamb See **Meter.**

Image[...]

cr[...]

sig[...]

la[...]

S[...]

th[...] thing visual, smelling something audible, and so on): "He smelled the blue fumes of her scent." **Static imagery** freezes the moment to give it the timeless quality of painting or sculpture. **Kinetic imagery** attempts to show motion or change.

Imagism Movement in modern poetry much influenced by **haiku,** stressing terseness and concrete imagery. **Imagists** were a group of early twentieth-century American poets, such as Ezra Pound, William Carlos Williams, and Amy Lowell, who focused on visual images and created new rhythms and meters.

Imperfect rhyme See **Rhyme.**

In medias res Latin phrase describing works like Homer's *Iliad* that begin in the middle of the action in order to catch a reader's interest.

Informal diction See **Diction.**

Internal rhyme See **Rhyme.**

Irony Literary device or situation that depends on the existence of at least two separate and contrasting levels of meaning or experience. **Dramatic** or **tragic irony,** such as that found in *Oedipus the King,* depends on the audience's knowing something the protagonist has not yet realized. **Situational irony** exists when what happens is at odds with what the story's situation leads readers to expect will happen, as in Browning's "Porphyria's Lover." **Cosmic irony** (or irony of fate) exists when fate frustrates any effort a character might make to control or reverse his or her destiny. **Verbal irony** occurs when what is said is in contrast with what is meant. Verbal irony can be expressed as **understatement, hyperbole,** or **sarcasm.**

Jargon Specialized language associated with a particular trade or profession.

Kinetic imagery Imagery that attempts to show motion or change. See, for example, William Carlos Williams's "The Great Figure."

Literary canon Group of literary works generally acknowledged by critics and teachers to be the best and most significant to have emerged from [...]tory. Many contemporary teachers and [...] have attempted to expand the canon to [...] works by women and by writers of [...]

[...] **onvention** Something whose meaning is [...]ely understood within a society that au[...] can expect their audiences to accept and comprehend it unquestioningly — for example, the division of plays into acts or the fact that stepmothers in fairy tales are likely to be wicked.

Literary criticism Descriptions, analyses, interpretations, or evaluations of works of literature by experts in the field.

Literary symbol See **Symbol.**

Low comedy Introduced by George Meredith, it refers to comedy with little or no intellectual appeal. Low comedy is used as comic relief in *Macbeth.* See **High comedy.**

Lyric Form of poetry, usually brief and intense, that expresses a poet's subjective response to the world. In classical times, lyrics were set to music. The Romantic poets, particularly Keats, often wrote lyrics about love, death, and nature.

Masculine rhyme See **Rhyme.**

Meditation Lyric poem that focuses on a physical object — for example, Keats's "Ode on a Grecian Urn" — using this object as a vehicle for considering larger issues.

Melodrama Sensational play that appeals shamelessly to the emotions, contains elements of tragedy but ends happily, and often relies on set plots and stock characters.

Metaphor Concise form of comparison equating two things that may at first seem completely dissimilar, often an abstraction and a concrete image — for example, "My love's a fortress." Some people consider metaphor to be the essential element of poetry. An **extended metaphor** (or **conceit**) is a comparison used throughout a work; in Tillie Olsen's "I Stand Here Ironing," the mother compares her daughter to a dress waiting to be ironed, thus conveying her daughter's passivity and vulnerability. See **Simile.**

Meter Regular pattern of stressed and unstressed syllables, each repeated unit of which is called a **foot:** an **anapest** has three syllables, two unstressed and the third stressed; a **dactyl** has three syllables, the first stressed and the subsequent ones unstressed. An **iamb** has two syllables, unstressed followed by stressed; a **trochee** has a stressed syllable followed by an unstressed one; a **spondee** has two stressed syllables; and a **pyrrhic** has two unstressed syllables. A poem's meter is described in terms of the kind of foot (anapest, for example) and the number of feet found in each line. The number of feet is designated by the Greek prefix for the number, so one foot per line is called *monometer*, two feet is *dimeter*, followed by *trimeter*, tetrameter, pentameter, hexameter, and so on. The most common meter in English is *iambic pentameter*. See also **Rising meter** and **Falling meter.**

Metonymy Figure of speech in which the term for one thing can be applied to another with which it is closely associated — for example, using "defend the flag" to mean "defend the nation."

Mimesis Aristotle's term for the purpose of literature, which he felt was "imitation" of life.

Monologue Extended speech by one character.

Mood Atmosphere created by the elements of a literary work (setting, characterization, imagery, tone, and so on).

Morality play Medieval Christian allegory, in which personified abstractions, such as Selfishness and Pride, struggle for a person's soul.

Motivation Reasons behind a character's behavior that make us accept or believe that character.

Mystery play Medieval play depicting biblical stories.

Myth Anonymous story reflecting the religious and social values of a culture or explaining natural phenomena, often involving gods and heroes.

Narrative The "storytelling" of a piece of fiction; the forward-moving recounting of episode and description. When an event that occurred earlier is told during a later sequence of events, it is called a **flashback;** suggesting earlier in a narration something that will occur later on is called **foreshadowing.**

Narrator Person who tells the story. See **Point of view.**

Naturalism Nineteenth-century movement whose followers believed that life should not be idealized when depicted in literature. Rather,

literature should show that human experience is a continual (and for the most part losing) struggle against the natural world. Émile Zola, Jack London, and Stephen Crane are important practitioners of naturalism.

New Comedy Greek comedies of the fourth and third centuries B.C. that followed **Old Comedy.** They were comedies of romance with stock characters and conventional settings. They lacked the satire, abusive language, and bawdiness of Old Comedy.

Novel Fictional narrative, traditionally realistic, relating a series of events or following the history of a character or group of characters through a period of time.

Novella Extended short story, usually concentrated in episode and action (like a short story) but involving greater character development (like a novel); Franz Kafka's "The Metamorphosis" is a novella.

Octave See **Sonnet.**

Ode Relatively long lyric poem, common in antiquity and adapted by the Romantic poets, for whom it was a serious poem of formal diction, often addressed to some significant object (such as a nightingale or the west wind) that has stimulated the poet's imagination.

Old Comedy The first comedies, written in Greece in the fifth century B.C., which heavily satirized the religious and social issues of the day. The chief practitioner of Old Comedy was Aristophanes. See **New Comedy.**

Onomatopoeia Word whose sound resembles what it describes: "snap, crackle, pop." Lewis Carroll's "Jabberwocky" uses onomatopoeia.

Open form Form of poetry that makes use of varying line lengths, abandoning stanzaic divisions, breaking lines in unexpected places, and even dispensing with any pretense of formal structure. Sometimes called *free verse* or *vers libre*. See **Form.**

Ottava rima See **Stanza.**

Oxymoron Phrase combining two seemingly incompatible elements: "crashing silence."

Parable Story that teaches a lesson, such as the parable of the prodigal son in the New Testament.

Paradox Seemingly contradictory situation. Adrienne Rich's "A Woman Mourned by Daughters" uses paradox.

Parody Exaggerated imitation of a serious piece of literature for humorous effect. Shakespeare's "My Mistress' Eyes are Nothing Like the Sun" is a parody of traditional Renaissance love poetry.

Pastoral Literary work, such as Christopher Marlowe's lyric poem "The Passionate Shepherd to His Love," that deals nostalgically and usually unrealistically with a simple, preindustrial rural life; the name comes from the fact that traditionally pastorals feature shepherds.

Pastoral romance Prose tale set in an idealized rural world; popular in Renaissance England.

Pathos Suffering that exists simply to satisfy the sentimental or morbid sensibilities of the audience.

Pattern of imagery See **Imagery.**

Perfect rhyme See **Rhyme.**

Persona Narrator or speaker of a poem or story; in Greek tragedy, a persona was a mask worn by an actor.

Personification A figure of speech that endows inanimate objects or abstract ideas with life or human characteristics: "the river wept."

Petrarchan sonnet See **Sonnet.**

Picaresque Episodic, often satirical work, presenting the life story of a rogue or rascal — for example, Cervantes's *Don Quixote.* The form emerged in sixteenth-century Spain.

Picture-frame stage Stage that looks like a room with a missing fourth wall through which the audience views the play. The **proscenium arch** separates the audience from the play.

Plot Way in which the events of the story are arranged. When there are two stories of more or less equal importance, the work has a **double plot;** when there is more than one story but one string of events is clearly the most significant, the other stories are called **subplots.** Plot in fiction often follows the pattern of action in drama, rising to a **climax** and then falling to a resolution.

Poetic rhythm See **Rhythm.**

Point of view Perspective from which a story is told. The storyteller may be a character in the story (*first-person narrator*) or someone who does not figure in the action (*third-person narrator*), in which case he or she may know the actions and internal doings of everyone in the story (*omniscient narrator*) or some part of these (*limited omniscient narrator*). Rarely, there

may be a *second-person narrator* who uses "you" and the imperative mood throughout the story.

The narrator may be an *observer* or a *participant.* If he or she is untrustworthy (stupid or bad, for instance), one has an *unreliable narrator;* narrators who are unreliable because they do not understand what they are reporting (children, for instance) are called *naive narrators.* If the perspective on the events is the same as one would get by simply watching the action unfold on stage, the point of view is *dramatic* or *objective.*

Popular fiction Works aimed at a mass audience.

Prologue First part of a play (originally of a Greek tragedy) in which the actor gives the background or explanations that the audience needs to follow the rest of the drama.

Props (short for **properties**) Pictures, furnishings, and so on that decorate the stage for a play.

Proscenium arch Arch that surrounds the opening in a **picture-frame stage;** through this arch the audience views the performances.

Prose poem Open form poem whose long lines appear to be prose set in paragraphs — for example, Walt Whitman's "Cavalry Crossing a Ford."

Protagonist Principal character of a drama or a work of fiction; the hero. The *tragic hero* is the noble protagonist in classical Greek drama who falls because of a tragic flaw.

Pyrrhic See **Meter.**

Quatrain See **Stanza.**

Realism Writing that stresses life as it really is. Realism relies on careful description of setting and the trappings of daily life, psychological probability, and the lives of ordinary people. Ibsen's *A Doll House* is an example.

Resolution Also called the **denouement,** this is the final stage in the plot of a drama or work of fiction. Here the action comes to an end and remaining loose ends are tied up.

Rhetoric Organization, strategy, and development of literary works, guided by an eye to how such elements will further the writer's intended effect on the reader.

Rhyme Repetition of concluding sounds in different words, often intentionally used at the ends of poetic lines. In **masculine rhyme** (also called *rising rhyme*) single syllables correspond. In **feminine rhyme** (also called *double rhyme* or *falling rhyme*) two syllables correspond, the second of which is stressed. In **triple rhyme,** three syllables correspond. **Eye rhyme** occurs when words look as though they should rhyme but are pronounced differently ("cough/ tough"). In **perfect rhyme** the corresponding vowel and consonant sounds of accented syllables must be preceded by different consonants — for example, the *b* and *h* in "born" and "horn." **Imperfect rhyme,** also called *near rhyme, slant rhyme,* or *consonance* occurs when consonants in two words are the same but intervening vowels are different — for example, "pick/pack," "lads/lids." The most common type of rhyme within a poem is **end rhyme,** where the rhyming syllables are placed at the end of a rhyme. **Internal rhyme** consists of rhyming words found within a line of poetry. **Beginning rhyme** occurs in the first syllable or syllables of the line.

Rhyme royal See **Stanza.**

Rhythm Regular recurrence of sounds in a poem. Ordinarily rhythm is determined by the arrangement of metrical feet in a line, but sometimes an alternate form of *sprung rhythm,* introduced by Gerard Manley Hopkins, is used. In this type of rhythm the number of strong stresses in a line determines the rhythm, regardless of how many weak stresses there might be.

Rising action Stage in a play's plot during which the action builds in intensity. See **Freytag's pyramid.**

Rising meter Iambic and anapestic meters, so called because they move from unstressed to stressed syllables. See **Falling meter.**

Romance Type of narrative that deals with love and adventure in a nonrealistic way, most popular in the Middle Ages but sometimes used by more modern authors, such as Hawthorne.

Romantic comedy Comedy such as Shakespeare's *Much Ado about Nothing* in which love is the main subject and idealized lovers endure great difficulties to get to the inevitable happy ending.

Romanticism Eighteenth- and nineteenth-century literary movement that valued subjectivity, individuality, the imagination, nature, excess, the exotic, and the mysterious.

Round character See **Character.**

Run-on line Line of poetry that ends with no punctuation or natural pause and consequently runs over into the next line; also called *enjambment.*

Sarcasm Form of irony in which apparent praise is used to convey strong, bitter criticism.

Satire Literary attack on folly or vanity by means of humor; usually intended to improve society.

Scansion Process of determining the meter of a poem by analyzing the strong and weak stresses in a line to find the unit of **meter** (each recurring pattern of stresses) and the number of these units (or **feet**) in each line.

Scrim Curtain that when illuminated from the front appears solid but when lit from the back becomes transparent.

Sentimental comedy Reaction against the **comedy of manners.** This type of comedy relies on sentimental emotion rather than on wit or humor and dwells on the virtues of life.

Sestet See **Sonnet.**

Sestina Poem composed of six six-line stanzas and a three-line conclusion called an **envoi.** Each line ends with one of six key words. The alternation of these six words in different positions — but always at the ends of lines — in the poem's six stanzas creates a rhythmic verbal pattern that unifies the poem.

Setting Background against which the action of a piece of literature takes place: the historical time, locale, season, time of day, interior decoration, and so on.

Shakespearean sonnet See **Sonnet.**

Short-short story Short fictional narrative that is generally under five pages or fifteen hundred words in length.

Short story Fictional narrative centered on one climatic event and usually developing only a single character in depth; its scope is narrower than that of the **novel,** and it often uses setting and characterization more directly to make its theme clear.

Simile Comparison of two seemingly unlike things using the words *like* or *as:* "My love is like an arrow through my heart." See **Metaphor.**

Situational irony See **Irony.**

Soliloquy Convention of drama in which a character speaks directly to the audience, revealing thoughts and feelings which other characters present on stage are assumed not to hear.

Sonnet Fourteen-line poem, usually a **lyric** in *iambic pentameter* (see **Meter**). It has a strict rhyme scheme in one of two forms: the *Italian*, or **Petrarchan sonnet** (an eight-line **octave** rhymed *abba/abba* with a six-line **sestet** rhymed *cdc/cdc* or a variation) and the *English*, or **Shakespearean sonnet** (three quatrains rhymed *abab/cdcd/efef* with a concluding couplet rhymed *gg*).

Speaker See **Persona.**

Spenserian stanza See **Stanza.**

Spondee See **Meter.**

Stage directions Words in a play that describe an actor's role apart from the dialogue, dealing with movements, attitudes, and so on.

Stage setting (set) Scenery and props in the production of a play. In *expressionist* stage settings, scenery and props are exaggerated and distorted to reflect the workings of a troubled, even abnormal mind. *Surrealistic* stage settings are designed to mirror the uncontrolled images of dreams or nightmares. See **Staging.**

Staging Overall production of a play in performance: the sets, costumes, lighting, sound, music, and so on.

Stanza Group of lines in a poem that forms a metrical or thematic unit. Each stanza is usually separated from others by a blank space on the page. Some common stanzaic forms are the **couplet** (two lines), **tercet** (three lines), **quatrain** (four lines), **sestet** (six lines), and **octave** (eight lines). The **heroic couplet,** first used by Chaucer and especially popular throughout the eighteenth century, as in Alexander Pope's poetry, consists of two rhymed lines of iambic pentameter, with a weak pause after the first line and a strong pause after the second. **Terza rima,** a form used by Dante, has a rhyme scheme (*aba, bcb, ded*) that creates an interlocking series of stanzas. The **ballad stanza** alternates lines of eight and six syllables. Typically only the second and fourth lines rhyme. **Common measure** is a four-line stanzaic pattern closely related to the ballad stanza. It differs in that its rhyme scheme is *abab* rather than *abcb*. **Rhyme royal** is a seven-line stanza (*ababbcc*) set in iambic pentameter. **Ottava rima** is an eight-line stanza (*abababcc*) set in iambic pentameter. The **Spenserian stanza** is a nine-line form (*ababbcbcc*) with the first eight lines in iambic pentameter and the last line in iambic hexameter.

Static character See **Character.**

Static imagery Imagery that freezes a moment to give it the timeless quality of painting or sculpture. Much visual imagery is static.

Stock character Stereotypical character who behaves consistently and whom the audience of a play can recognize and classify instantly: the town drunk, the nerd, and so on.

Stream of consciousness Form of narration controlled not by external events but by the thoughts and subjective impressions of the narrator, commonly found in modern literature, such as the work of Virginia Woolf and James Joyce.

Stress Accent or emphasis, either strong or weak, given to each syllable in a piece of writing, as determined by conventional pronunciation (cárpĕt, not cărpét) and intended emphasis ("going dówn, dówn, dówn tŏ thĕ bóttŏm ŏf thĕ ócĕan"). Strong stresses are marked with a ´ and weak ones with a ˘.

Structure Formal pattern or arrangement of elements to form a whole in a piece of literature.

Style Way an author selects and arranges words to express ideas and, ultimately, theme.

Subplot See **Plot.**

Surrealism Literary movement that allows unconventional use of syntax; chronology; juxtaposition; and bizarre, dreamlike images in prose and poetry.

Symbol Person, object, action, or idea whose meaning transcends its literal or denotative sense in a complex way. For instance, if someone wears a rose in a lapel to a dance, the rose may simply be a decoration, but in Blake's "The Sick Rose" it becomes a symbol because it takes on a range of paradoxical and complementary meanings. A symbol is invested with significance beyond what it could carry on its own. **Universal symbols,** such as the grim reaper, may be called **archetypes; conventional symbols,** such as national flags, evoke a general and agreed-upon response from most people. There are also *private symbols*, such as the "gyre" created by Yeats, which the poet himself invested with extraordinary significance.

Synecdoche Figure of speech in which a part of something is used to represent the whole — for example, "hired hand" represents a laborer.

Synesthesia See **Imagery.**

Tale Short story often involving mysterious atmosphere and supernatural or inexplicable events, such as "The Tell-Tale Heart" by Edgar Allan Poe.

Ten-minute play Short play written to be performed in ten minutes or less.

Tercet See **Stanza.**

Terza rima See **Stanza.**

Theater in the round See **Arena stage.**

Theater of the absurd Type of drama that discards conventions of plot, character, and motivation in order to depict a world in which nothing makes sense. Albee's *The Sandbox* is an example.

Theme Central or dominant idea of a piece of literature, made concrete by the details and emphasis in the work itself.

Thrust stage Stage that juts out into the audience so the action may be viewed from three sides.

Tone Attitude of the speaker or author of a work toward the subject itself or the audience, as can be determined from the word choice and arrangement of the piece.

Tragedy Literary work, especially a play, that recounts the downfall of an individual. *Greek tragedy* demanded a noble protagonist whose fall could be traced to a *tragic personal flaw*. *Shakespearean tragedy* also treats noble figures, but the reasons for their tragedies may be less clear-cut than in Greek drama. *Domestic* or *modern tragedy* tends to deal with the fates of ordinary people.

Tragic irony See **Irony.**

Tragicomedy Type of Elizabethan and Jacobean drama that uses elements of both tragedy and comedy.

Triple rhyme See **Rhyme.**

Trochee See **Meter.**

Understatement Intentional downplaying of a situation's significance, often for ironic or humorous effect, as in Mark Twain's famous comment on reading his own obituary, "The reports of my death are greatly exaggerated."

Unities Rules that require a dramatic work to be unified in terms of its time, place, and action. *Oedipus the King* illustrates the three unities.

Universal symbol See **Symbol.**

Verbal irony See **Irony.**

Villanelle A nineteen-line poem composed of five tercets and a concluding quatrain; its rhyme scheme is *aba aba aba aba aba abaa*. Two different lines are systematically repeated in the poem: line 1 appears again in lines 6, 12, and 18, and line 3 reappears as lines 9, 15, and 19. Thus each tercet concludes with an exact (or close) duplication of either line 1 or line 3, and the final quatrain concludes by repeating both line 1 and line 3.

Visual poetry Poetry that focuses as much on the words' appearance on the page as on what the words say, using a combination of media that may include video, photography, and even sound as well as text.

Wagons Sets mounted on wheels, which make possible rapid changes of scenery.

CREDITS

William Carlos Williams, "Spring and All, Section I", "The Great Figure" and "The Red Wheelbarrow" by William Carlos Williams from COLLECTED PO-EMS: 1909-1939, VOLUME I, copyright 1938 by New Directions Publishing Corp. Reprinted by permission of New Directions Publishing Corp. "The Dance (In Brueghel's)" by William Carlos Williams, from COLLECTED POEMS 1939-1962, VOLUME II, copyright 1944 by William Carlos Williams. Reprinted by permission of New Directions Publishing Corp.

Greg Williamson, "Group Photo with Winter Trees" by Greg Williamson first appeared in PLEIADES: A JOURNAL OF NEW WRITING, 2002. Reprinted by permission.

August Wilson, From FENCES by August Wilson, copyright © 1986 by August Wilson. Used by permission of Dutton Signet, a division of Penguin Group (USA), Inc.

Tracey Scott Wilson, "Small World"

James Wright, "Autumn Begins in Martins Ferry, Ohio" by James Wright from THE BRANCH WILL NOT BREAK. Copyright © 1963 by James Wright and reprinted by permission of Wesleyan University Press.

Richard Wright, "Big Black Good Man" from EIGHT MEN by Richard Wright. Copyright © 1957 by Esquire, Inc. Reprinted by permission of HarperCollins Publishers Inc. From SIX HAIKU

Hisaye Yamamoto, "Seventeen Syllables" from SEVENTEEN SYLLABLES AND OTHER STORIES by Hisaye Yamamoto. Copyright © 1988 by Hisaye Ya-mamoto-DeSoto. Reprinted by permission of Rutgers University Press.

W.B. Yeats, "The Lake Isle of Innisfree" and "An Irish Airman Foresees His Death" reprinted with the permission of Scribner, an imprint of Simon & Schuster Adult Publishing Group, from THE COLLECTED WORKS OF W.B. YEATS, VOLUME 1: THE POEMS, REVISED, edited by Richard J. Finneran. (New York: Scribner, 1997). "The Second Coming" reprinted with the permission of Scribner, an imprint of Simon & Schuster Adult Publishing Group, from THE COLLECTED WORKS OF W.B. YEATS, VOLUME 1: THE POEMS, RE-VISED, edited by Richard J. Finneran. Copyright 1924 by The Macmillan Company; copyright renewed 1952 by Bertha Georgie Yeats. "Sailing to Byzantium" and "Leda and the Swan" reprinted with the permission of Scribner, an imprint of Simon & Schuster Adult Publishing Group, from THE COLLECTED WORKS OF W.B. YEATS, VOLUME 1: THE POEMS, REVISED, edited by Richard J. Finneran. Copyright 1928 by The Macmillan Company; copyright re-newed © 1956 by Bertha Georgie Yeats. "Crazy Jane Talks With The Bishop" reprinted with the permission of Scribner, an imprint of Simon & Schuster Adult Publishing Group from THE COLLECTED WORKS OF W.B. YEATS, VOL-UME 1: THE POEMS, REVISED, edited by Richard J. Finneran. Copyright 1933 by The Macmillan Company; copyright renewed © 1961 by Georgie Yeats

Adam Zagajewski, "Try To Praise the Mutilated World" from WITHOUT END: NEW AND SELECTED POEMS by Adam Zagajewski, translated by several translators. Copyright © 2002 by Adam Zagajewski. Translation copyright © 2002 by Farrar, Straus and Giroux, LLC. Reprinted by permission of Farrar, Straus and Giroux, LLC. "Poetry Searches for Radiance"

Louis Zukofsky, "I Walk in the Old Street" by Louis Zukofsky from COMPLETE SHORT POETRY, pp. 86. Copyright © 1991 [Copyright Holder]. Reprinted with permission of The Johns Hopkins University Press.

PHOTOS

Thomson has made every effort to trace the ownership of all copyrighted material and to secure permission from the copyright holders. In the event of any question regarding the use of any material, we will be pleased to make the necessary corrections in future printings.

INDEX OF FIRST LINES OF POETRY

INDEX OF AUTHORS AND TITLES

INDEX OF LITERARY TERMS